Proceedings

of the

International Joint Conference on Neural Networks (IJCNN) 2005

July 31 - August 4, 2005

Hilton Montréal Bonaventure Hotel

Montréal, Québec, Canada

Co-organized by:

Volume 1 of 5

IJCNN 2005 Conference Proceedings

Copyright and Reprint Permission: Abstracting is permitted with credit to the source. Libraries are permitted to photocopy beyond the limit of U.S. copyright law for private use of patrons those articles in this volume that carry a code at the bottom of the first page, provided the per-copy fee indicated in the code is paid through Copyright Clearance Center, 222 Rosewood Drive, Danvers, MA 01923. For other copying, reprint or republication permission, write to IEEE Copyrights Manager, IEEE Operations Center, 445 Hoes Lane, P.O. Box 1331, Piscataway, NJ 08855-1331USA. All right reserved. Copyright ©2005 by the Institute of Electrical and Electronics Engineers, Inc.

Papers are printed as received from authors.

All opinions expressed in the Proceedings are those of the authors and are not binding on The Institute of Electrical and Electronics Engineers, Inc.

Additional copies may be ordered from:
IEEE Order Dept.
445 Hoes Lane / PO Box 1331
Piscataway, NJ 08855-1331 USA

Phone: (Toll Free) +1-800-678-4333
Email: customer-service@ieee.org
Web: shop.ieee.org

Bound Edition:
IEEE Catalog No. 05CH37662
ISBN: 0-7803-9048-2
ISSN: 1098-7576

CD Edition:
IEEE Catalog No. 05CH37662C
ISBN: 0-7803-9049-0

IJCNN 2005: SESSION GRID

Sunday, July 31, 2005

Time	Lachine	Hampstead	Mont Royal	Verdun
9:00 a.m.	Evolutionary Robotics		Bioinfomatics and Machine Learning: The Prediction of Protein Structures on a Genomic Scale	
11:00 a.m.	Break			
11:15 a.m.	Neural Networks that Actually Work in Prediction and Decision/Control: Common Misconceptions Versus Real-World Success	Evolving Connectionist Systems for Adaptive Learning and Knowledge Discovery: Principles, Models and Applications	Integrating Language and Cognition: New Results in Computational Intelligence	Feature Extraction in Computational Intelligence
1:15 p.m.	Break			
2:30 p.m.	Neural Networks for Dynamic Systems Feedback	Data Visualization of High Dimensional Scientific Data	New Formulations for Predictive Learning	Unsupervised Learning
4:30 p.m.	Break			
4:45 p.m.	Cognitive Memory	Biologically Plausible Artificial Neural Networks	Support Vector Machines and Kernel Based Learning	Nonlinear Manifolds in Pattern Recognition and Image Analysis
6:45 p.m.	End of the Day			

Monday, August 1, 2005

Time	Westmount	Outremont	Mont Royal/Hampstead	Verdun/Lachine
8:00 a.m.	Plenary: Exploring Chemical Space with Computers: Challenges and Opportunities Professor Pierre Baldi, Director, Institute for Genomics and Bioinformatics, University of California, Irvine			
9:00 a.m.	Break			
9:30 a.m.	Special Session: Neural Networks Applications to Bioinformatics	Information-Theoretic and Bayesian Learning	Special Session: Neurodynamics and Intentional Dynamic Systems	Pattern Recognition
11:30 a.m.	Break			
1:00 p.m.	Bioinformatics	Special Session: Evolvable and Emergent Neural Systems	Models of Neurons, Local Circuits and Systems	Independent Component Analysis and Principal Component Analysis
3:00 p.m.	Break			
3:20 p.m.	Special Session: Computational Neurogenetic Modeling	Control and System Identification	Spiking Neurons	Special Session: Recent Advancements in Adaptive Resonance Theory
5:20 p.m.	Break			
7:00 p.m.	Plenary Poster Session - Fontaine Ballroom			
11:00 p.m.	End of the Day			

Tuesday, August 2, 2005

Time	Westmount	Outremont	Mont Royal/Hampstead	Verdun/Lachine
8:00 a.m.	Functional Organization of the Primate Prefrontal Cortex for Memory Michael Petrides, Professor, Psychology Department/Neurology and Neurosurgery, McGill University and Director, Neuropsychology/Cognitive Neuroscience Unit Montreal, Neurological Institute and Hospital			
9:00 a.m.	Break			
9:30 a.m.	Evolutionary Algorithms and PSO	Special Session: Computational Dynamical Modeling with Echo State Networks	Special Session: Functional Neuroimaging of Cortical and Subcortical Functions	Support Vector Machines I
11:30 a.m.	Break			
1:00 p.m.	Special Session: Applications of Learning and Data-Driven Methods to Earth Sciences and Climate Modeling	Recurrent Neural Networks	Special Session: Transition: Imaging and Cortical Models	Self-Organizing Maps
3:00 p.m.	Break			
3:20 p.m.	Special Session: Applications of Learning and Data-Driven Methods to Earth Sciences and Climate Modeling, Plus Panel Discussion	Diagnostics and Control, Power Systems	Special Session: Models of Cortical and Subcortical Circuits	Visual and Image Processing
5:20 p.m.	Break			
7:00 p.m.	Plenary Poster Session - Fontaine Ballroom			
11:00 p.m.	End of the Day			

Wednesday, August 3, 2005

Time	Westmount	Outremont	Mont Royal/Hampstead	Verdun/Lachine
8:00 a.m.	Plenary: Neural Networks for Feedback Control of Robots and Dynamical Systems Professor Frank L. Lewis, Head, Advanced Controls, Sensors and MEMS Group, Automation and Robotics Research Institute, The University of Texas at Arlington			
9:00 a.m.	Break			
9:30 a.m.	Robotics	Support Vector Machine II	Special Session: Hebb's Legacy	Data Mining
11:30 a.m.	Break			
1:00 p.m.	Hardware	Special Session: Performance of Neuro-Adaptive and Learning Systems: Assessment, Monitoring and Validation	Cognitive Function	Special Session: Constructive/Hierarchical Self-Organizing Maps
3:00 p.m.	Break			
3:20 p.m.	Special Session: Approximate Dynamic Programming	Biomedical Applications	Fuzzy-Neural Systems	Special Session: Biologically Inspired Computational Vision
5:20 p.m.	Break			
7:00 p.m.	Banquet			
9:00 p.m.	End of the Day			

Thursday, August 4, 2005

Time	Westmount	Outremont	Mont Royal/Hampstead	Verdun/Lachine
8:00 a.m.	Plenary: Beyond Correlation – Closing the Loop Between Brain and Theory by Extracting Representations and Altered Feedbacks Professor Mitsuo Kawato, Director, Nara Institute of Science and Technology, ATR Computational Neuroscience Laboratories, Computational Neuroscience Laboratory, Japan			
9:00 a.m.	Break			
9:30 a.m.	Special Session: Neural Prostheses and the Neuron-Silicon Interface	Learning I	Neurodynamics	Applications I
11:30 a.m.	Break			
1:00 p.m.	Neuromorphic Hardware	Learning II	Telecommunications	Applications II
3:00 p.m.	Break			
3:20 p.m.	Plenary: Neuromorphic Engineering: Overview and Potential Professor Carver Mead, Gordon and Betty Moore Professor of Engineering and Applied Science, Emeritus Computation and Neural Systems, Division of Engineering and Applied Science, California Institute of Technology			
4:20 p.m.	End of the Day			

Message from the General Chair

Dear IJCNN 2005 Attendees,

On behalf of the IJCNN 2005 Organizing Committee, I am happy to welcome you to the International Joint Conference on Neural Networks! This year's conference marks another year of fruitful cooperation between the International Neural Network Society (INNS) and the new Computational Intelligence Society (CIS) of the IEEE and continues a legacy of exceptional meetings. For many years the IJCNN has been a "must attend" for all leading neural network researchers, especially those who value interdisciplinary viewpoints. The IJCNN also welcomes other researchers in neuroscience, machine learning, computational intelligence and AI who are undoubtedly attracted by the open-mindedness and the bold spirit of the IJCNN. The IJCNN 2005 is also truly international, with submissions from over 1,500 authors representing 66 countries.

The IJCNN 2005 continues our tradition of quality papers. Our on-line paper collection and review system, expertly created and maintained by Tomasz Cholewo, registered 2,430 reviews from more than 350 reviewers for 752 submitted papers. Moreover, many additional reviews were performed outside of the on-line system. All regular and most of the special session papers received at least three reviews each, which allowed the Program Committee to do a careful job when rejecting 25% of papers. While other conferences may boast higher rejection rates, the high rates do not always guarantee high quality, as those other conferences in the past have accepted papers which could have not made it into the IJCNN Proceedings.

The Organizing Committee worked very hard to create an exciting IJCNN 2005 program. We secured plenary talks from such exceptional speakers as Pierre Baldi, Michael Petrides, Frank Lewis, Mitsuo Kawato and Carver Mead. We scheduled special and regular sessions on the same day to match their plenary talks. Two of our plenary speakers also agreed to give tutorials, complementing an already strong and multidisciplinary tutorial selection. Our 17 special sessions will surely attract your attention.

The IJCNN 2005 landscape is revealed on the next page, with dots representing accepted papers. No differentiation was made in the review and publication processes of papers scheduled for poster or oral presentations. In fact, the majority of the IJCNN 2005 presentations are assembled into two four-hour plenary poster sessions, offering not only plenty of time to present and thoroughly discuss your work with colleagues but also to enjoy the exhibits of our sponsors and the books offered by our invited booksellers. Each poster presentation is much more visible than any of the (just 20-minute!) oral presentations. All poster presenters are in very good company, with several exciting topics appearing only as posters.

We are extremely grateful to the following organizations for their support:

- The INNS (lead society for this year's IJCNN), the IEEE-CIS and their respective leadership.
- Co-sponsors: Florida Institute of Technology, University of Texas at Arlington, Ford Motor Company (the largest donor), ACIL of the University of Missouri-Rolla, Siemens Canada, Cisco Systems and Elsevier.
- Montreal Tourism Bureau.

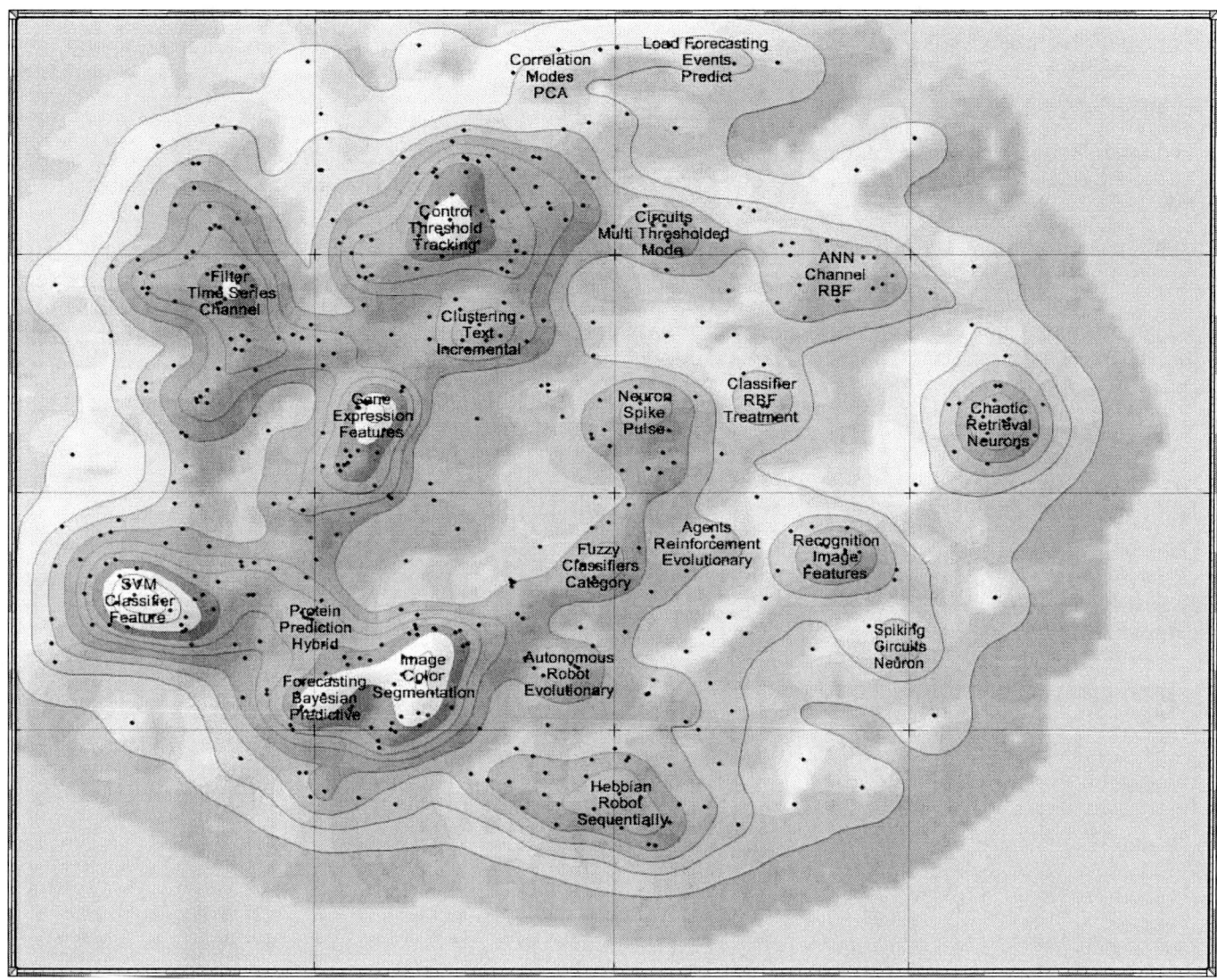

Effective conference organization is impossible without the right people assigned to appropriate positions. In addition to our International Program and Review Committees listed later, I am especially thankful to the following members of the IJCNN 2005 Organizing Committee:

- Dan Levine, Fred Ham and Bill Howell for their outstanding work on both the conference program and the preparations for the IJCNN Special Issue 18(5/6) of Neural Networks. Bill Howell also helped other members of the Organizing Committee on miscellaneous issues including invitation letters for Canadian visas and special sessions.

- Jean-Philippe Thivièrge, Oury Monchi and Mohamed Cheriet for their solid control of all local arrangement issues including the wireless Internet and coordination of volunteers.

- Mike Stiber (conference home page) and Tom Cholewo (on-line paper submission and review system) were invaluable as our web co-chairs. As in the previous years, Tom and his on-line system saved countless hours for our reviewers, the Program and the Organizing Committees.

- Mary Lou Padgett and Carlo Morabito for their expert handling of all tutorial matters.

- David Brown for his timely publicity efforts.

- Daniel Silver and his International Co-Chairs (Emilio del Moral Hernandez, De-Shuang Huang and Radosveta Sokullu) for their extremely critical work on assuring that our international attendees get their Canadian visas on time.

- Vladimir Cherkassky, Dimitri Solomatine, Vladimir Krasnopolsky and Julio Valdes for their exemplary leadership of the special sessions "Application of Adaptive Learning Methods in Earth Sciences and Climate Modeling."
- Slawo Wesolkowski for his handling of student travel support.
- Susan Rees, Jane Shepard, Lisa Horton, Amy Bayer, Stacey Phelps, Lisa Gilbertson and other associates at the Rees Group, Inc., for their expert day-to-day efforts on the conference planning and organization.

I also hope that many of you will stay for our post-conference workshops, which is a new element of the IJCNN program to be held in the evening of August 4 and the full day on August 5. The workshops are supposed to provide a more relaxed forum for development of new concepts and themes and expertise sharing. While several workshops have been scheduled already, there is some flexibility to accommodate small groups of interested participants "self-organized" during the main conference. Please let the Organizing Committee know.

While the program we prepared for you is intense, please do not forget to enjoy the beauty and richness of Montréal, which speaks for itself.

Enjoy the conference!

Danil V. Prokhorov
IJCNN 2005 General Chair
Ford Research and Advanced Engineering
dvprokhorov@gmail.com

Organizing Committee

Danil Prokhorov, General Chair
  Ford Motor Company

Daniel S. Levine, Program Chair
  University of Texas at Arlington

Fredric M. Ham, Program Co-Chair
  Florida Institute of Technology

William Howell, Program Co-Chair
  Natural Resources Canada

David Brown, Publicity Chair, FDA

Michael Stiber, Web Co-Chair
  University of Washington, Bothell

Tomasz Cholewo, Web Co-Chair
  Lexmark International, Inc.

Carlo Morabito, Tutorial Co-Chair
  University of Reggio Calabria, Italy

Mary Lou Padgett, Tutorial Co-Chair, PCI, Inc.

Ivica Kostanic, Workshop Chair
  Florida Institute of Technology

Slawo Wesolkowski, Student Travel Chair
  University of Waterloo, Canada

Dmitry Gorodnichy, Exhibits Chair
  National Research Council, Canada

Mohamed Cheriet, Local Arrangements Co-Chair
  University of Quebec, Montreal, Canada

Jean-Philippe Thivierge, Local Arrangements
  Co-Chair, McGill University, Montreal, Canada

Oury Monchi, Local Volunteer Coordinator
  Universite de Montreal and Centre de Recherche,
  Institut Universitaire de Geriatrie de Montreal,
  Montreal, Canada

Simon Haykin, Canadian Universities Liaison
  McMaster University, Hamilton, Canada

Daniel Silver, International Chair
  Acadia University, Wolfville, Nova Scotia, Canada

Emilio del Moral Hernandez, South America and
  Africa Liaison, Polytechnic University, Sao Paulo,
  Brazil

De-Shuang Huang, Far East Liaison
  Institute of Intelligent Machines, Chinese
  Academy of Science, China

Radosveta Sokullu, Eastern Europe and Middle East
  Liaison, Ege University, Izmir, Turkey

International Program Committee

Adel Alimi, University of Sfax, Tunisia
Georgios Anagnostopoulos
  Florida Institute of Technology, USA
Raju Bapi, University of Hyderabad, India
Yoshua Bengio, University of Montreal, Canada
Gail Carpenter, Boston University, USA
David Casasent, Carnegie-Mellon University, USA
Jordi Cosp, Polytechnic University of Catalonia,
  Spain
Rolf Eckmiller, University of Bonn, Germany
Dario Floreano, Swiss Federal Institute of
  Technology, Switzerland
Kunihiko Fukushima, Tokyo University of Technology,
  Japan
Stan Gielen, University of Nijmegen, Netherlands
Stephen Grossberg, Boston University, USA
Michael Hasselmo, Boston University, USA
Nik Kasabov, University of Otago, New Zealand
Bart Kosko, University of Southern California, USA
Robert Kozma, University of Memphis, USA
George Lendaris, Portland State University, USA

William Levy, University of Virginia, USA
Tony Martinez, Brigham Young University, USA
Risto Miikkulainen, University of Texas, USA
Francesco Morabito, University of Reggio Calabria,
  Italy
Klaus Obermayer, Technical University of Berlin,
  Germany
Erkki Oja, Helsinki University of Technology, Finland
Jose C. Principe, University of Florida, USA
Wang Qiwen, Peking University, China
Tariq Samad, Honeywell, Minneapolis, USA
Edgar Sanchez, CINVESTAV, Mexico
Antony Satyadas, IBM, Cambridge, USA
Johan Suykens, University of Leuven, Belgium
Harold Szu, Office of Naval Research, USA
John Taylor, Kings College, University of London, UK
Deliang Wang, Ohio State University, USA
Lipo Wang, Nanyang University, Singapore
Bernard Widrow, Stanford University, USA
Donald C. Wunsch, University of Missouri at Rolla, USA
Lotfi Zadeh, University of California, Berkeley, USA

2005 Review Committee

We thank the following reviewers for their valuable contributions to IJCNN 2005.

Ashraf M. Abdelbar
Mahmoud Abou-Nasr
Amit Agarwal
Oleg Aksenov
Adel M. Alimi
Cesare Alippi
Alexandre Alves da Silva
Georgios Anagnostopoulos
Razvan Andonie
Peter Andras
Davide Anguita
Sameer Antani
Bruno Apolloni
Paolo Arena
Amir Assadi
Snorre Aunet
Tatyana Baidyk
Leemon Baird
Bram Bakker
David Balya
Raju Bapi
Guilherme Barreto
Gianfranco Basti
Eduardo Bayro-Corrochano
Sophie Beguin
Elizabeth Behrman
Valeriu Beiu
Yoshua Bengio
Brian Blaha
Alexander Bogdanov
Zvi Boger
Abdesselam Bouzerdoum
David Brown
Gavin Brown
John Bullinaria
Mikhail Burtsev
Joan Cabestany
Xindi Cai
Paola Campadelli
Robert Cannon
Dongwei Cao
Jinde Cao
Otavio Carpinteiro
David Casasent
Jose Castro
Gavin Cawley
Michal Cernansky
Nicolo Cesa-Bianchi
Jonathon Chambers
Dimitrios Charalampidis
Apoorv Chaudhri
Antonio Chella
Zhe Chen
Mohamed Cheriet
Vladimir Cherkassky
Yiu Ming Cheung
Chiang-Cheng Chiang
Ratna Babu Chinnam
Jeongho Cho
Seungjin Choi
Tomasz Cholewo
Thomas Cleland
Anna Maria Colla
Fernando Corinto
Andrea Corradini
Jordi Cosp
Marie Cottrell
Sven Crone
Lehel Csato
Ernesto Cuadros-Vargas
Cihan H. Dagli
Tijl De Bie
Oleksiy Dekhtyarenko
Chris Diehl
Michael Dittenbach
Steve Djajasaputra
Simona Doboli
David Dominguez
Jose Dorronsoro
Tim Draelos
Rohit Dua
Witali Dunin-Barkowski
Doug Eck
Rolf Eckmiller
Mehmet Onder Efe
Antonio Eleuteri
Mark Embrechts
David L. Enke
Peter Erdi
Deniz Erdogmus
Marcelo Espinoza
Pablo Estevez
Alexander Ezhov
Lee Feldkamp
Manuel Fernandez-Delgado
Mario Figueiredo
Dario Floreano
Eric Fock
Peter Foldesy
Tyler C. Folsom
Oscar Fontenla-Romero
Jesus Fraile
Roseli Francelin Romero
Damien Francois
Walter J. Freeman
Alexander Frolov
Kunihiko Fukushima
Cesare Furlanello
Prashant Gade
M. Georgiopoulos
Anya Getman
Stan Gielen
Mark van Gils
Nils Goerke
Vladimir Golovko
Eduardo Gomez-Sanchez
Anatoli Gorchetchnikov
Marco Gori
Dmitry Gorodnichy
Alex Graves
Pramod Gupta
Ricardo Gutierrez-Usuna
Fredric Ham
Barbara Hammer
Fei Han
Thomas Hanselmann
Ron Harley
Derek Harter
Michael Hasselmo
Anant Hegde
Malcolm Heywood
Kenneth Hild
Liangwei Ho
James Hornell
Ralf Hornig
Gabor Horvath
Shahram Hosseini
Bill Howell
Guoning Hu
Sanqing Hu
Xiao Hu
De-Shuang Huang
Xiao Huang
Liu Hui
Khan Iftekharuddin
Roman Ilin
Herbert Jaeger
Robert Jenssen
Wei Jiang
Christian Jutten
Szabolcs Kali
Radha Kalyani
Nik Kasabov
Ioannis Kasampalidis
Uzay Kaymak
Vojislav Kecman
Peter Kelly
James Kennedy
Randal Koene
Andreas Koenig
Seong Kong
Ivica Kopriva
Kostadin Korutchev
Bart Kosko
Ivica Kostanic
Robert Kozma
Vladimir Krasnopolsky
Vladik Kreinovich
Stefan C. Kremer
David Krout
Naoyuki Kubota
Anthony Kuh
Suwat Kuntanapreeda
Ernst Kussul
Jing Lan
Marcelino Lazaro
Ian Lee
John Lee
Seok-Beom Lee
Tue Lehn-Schioeler
George G. Lendaris
Daniel Levine
William B. Levy
Shuhui Li
Konstantin Likharev
Chih-Jen Lin
Li-Ju Lin
Bernabe Linares-Barranco
Hailing Liu
Wenxin Liu
Xiuwen Liu
Chris Lowrie
Chuan Lu
Zhao Lu
Joanne Luciano
Teresa Bernarda Ludermir
Yunqian Ma
Jordi Madrenas
Marco Maggini
Dragos Magineantu
Michael Manry
Tony R. Martinez
Weber Martins
Francesco Masulli
Larry Medsker
Marius van der Meer
Phayung Meesad
Martijn Meeter
Karlheinz Meier
Eduardo Mercado
Risto Miikkulainen
Marta Milo
Ali Minai
Sanya Mitaim
Oury Monchi
Carlo Francesco Morabito
Klaus-Robert Mueller
Yi Lu Murphey
Bashan Naidoo
Valentin Nepomnyashchikh
Dagmar Niebur
Nikolay Nikolaev
Yael Niv
Alexander Novokhodko
Andreas Nuernberger
Klaus Obermayer
Bengt Oelmann
Haluk Ogmen
Se-Young Oh
Erkki Oja
Patricia Rufino Oliveira
Mustafa Can Ozturk
Ari Paasio
Alberto Paccanaro
Andrzej Pacut
Federico Palacios
Thomas Parisini
Jung-Wook Park
Sungjin Park
Mary Pastel
Ashok Patel
Arthur Pchelkin
Barak Pearlmutter
W. Pedrycz
Kristiaan Pelckmans
Antonio Luigi Perrone
Nicholas Petrick
Robi Polikar

A. Prieto
Jose Principe
Danil Prokhorov
Wang Qiwen
Jose Quintana
Juan Ramirez
Yadunandana Rao
Larry Reeker
Jose Restrepo
Leon Reznik
Nicoleta Roman
Stefano Rovetta
Stuart Rubin
Imre J. Rudas
Ulrich Rueckert
Joseph Rynkiewicz
Emad Saad
Ralf Salomon
Tariq Samad
Frank Samuelson
Edgar Sanchez
Ignacio Santamaria
Roberto Santiago
Simo Sarkka
Naoyuki Sato
Antony Satyadas
Edward Sazonov
Franco Scarselli
Juergen Schmidhuber
Johann Schumann
Eduardo Serrano
Cosma Shalizi
Tad Shannon
Yang Shao
Dmitry Shaposhnikov
Frederick Sheldon
Bertram Shi
Hyunjung Shin
Sandeep Shukla
Daniel Silver
Geoffroy Simon
Patrick K. Simpson
Olli Simula
Vikas Sindhwani
S. Singh
Leslie Smith
Jordi Sole-Casals
Dimitri Solomatine
Alessandro Sperduti
Soundararajan Srinivasan
Jim Steck
Michael Stiber
Alberto Suarez
Bing-Yu Sun
Ping Sun
Zhan-Li Sun
Johan Suykens
K. Shanti Swarup
Rod Taber
Roberto Tagliaferri
Ranga Tallam
Wendy Tang
John G. Taylor
Geetha Thampi
Jean-Philippe Thivierge
Benjamin Thompson
Georgia Tourassi
Theodore Trafalis
Yuri Tsoy
Kagan Tumer
Ivan Tyukin
Gancho Vachkov
Julio Valdes
Giorgio Valentini
Marc Van Hulle
Joos Vandewalle
Ganesh Kumar
Venayagamoorthy
Dan Ventura
Pablo F. Verdes
Michel Verleysen
Vincent Vigneron
Nikita Visnevski
Frederic Vrins
Eric Wan
DeLiang Wang
Hong-Qiang Wang
Jeen-Shing Wang
Lipo Wang
Xin Wang
Pawel Wawrzynski
Richard Wells
Slawo Wesolkowski
Joerg Wichard
Bernard Widrow
Florentin Woergoetter
Hau San Wong
Don Wunsch
Youshen Xia
Jianwu Xu
Rui Xu
Vladimir Yakhno
Yoko Yamaguchi
Rui Yan
Simon X. Yang
Nadezhda Yarushkina
Syozo Yasui
Gary Yen
Hao Ying
Anthony Zaknich
Gaetano Zanghirati
Zhigang Zeng
Guang-Zheng Zhang
Nian Zhang
Qiang Zhang
Liang Zhao
Xing-Ming Zhao
Daqi Zhu
Mohamed Zohdy

2005 International Neural Network Society Officers

President
Donald C. Wunsch (2006)

President-Elect
Deliang Wang (2007)

Past-President
Jose C. Principe (2005)

Secretary
Fredric M. Ham

Treasurer
David G. Brown

2005 Board of Governors

Gail Carpenter (2007)
Dario Floreano (2007)
Kunihiko Fukushima (2005)
Stephen Grossberg (2007)
Michael Hasselmo (2007)
Nikola Kasabov (2007)
Bart Kosko (2006)
Robert Kozma (2006)
George Lendaris (2005)
Daniel S. Levine (2005)
William Levy (2006)

Francesco Carlo Morabito (2006)
Klaus Obermayer (2006)
Erkki Oja (2007)
Danil Prokhorov (2006)
Ron Sun (2007)
Harold Szu (2006)
John G. Taylor (2005)
Paul Werbos (2005)
Bernard Widrow (2005)
Lotfi A. Zadeh (2007)

The INNS President's Welcome

Dear IJCNN '05 Participants:

Welcome to the International Joint Conference on Neural Networks! IJCNN is the flagship conference of the INNS, as well as the IEEE Neural Networks Society. It has evolved as rapidly as the technology it explores, while maintaining a core emphasis on neural networks. As the number of conferences has grown, much of its competition has lost this core emphasis. IJCNN, on the other hand, has always welcomed neural networks research contributions, while embracing the proliferation of spin-off and related fields. (See the topic list in these Proceedings.) Neural networks continue to be successfully fielded in applications, many of which are featured here. IJCNN is your premier venue to stay current in this increasingly important field.

An event of this magnitude does not occur spontaneously. We owe a tremendous debt of gratitude to the following:

- The General Chair, Danil Prokhorov, who worked indefatigably to ensure IJCNN's success.
- Dan Levine, the Program Chair. His contributions to INNS date back to its inception (including a stint as INNS President).
- Fred Ham and Bill Howell, Program Co-Chairs. Their efforts on behalf of this meeting have been equally heroic.
- Many other volunteers. Danil Prokhorov will mention more of them in his letter, and we should all join him in gratitude to them.
- Last but not least, a heartfelt thanks to YOU – the reader. Whether you attended the meeting in person, or are just reading these proceedings to enhance your knowledge in the field, IJCNN is for you. We encourage you to read and refer to IJCNN papers frequently in your work, and hope to see you at future IJCNN's.

I'd like to particularly mention two other groups: the IEEE Computational Intelligence Society, and the INNS Board. We have, for many years now, enjoyed a mutually beneficial relationship with the IEEE – enhancing value for members of both societies. The INNS Board should also be thanked and recognized, for its valuable volunteer work on behalf of the society. We particularly welcome newly elected Board members Nik Kasabov and Ron Sun. The full Board list is included in this CD. We're truly blessed to benefit from the wisdom of this extraordinary group of scientists.

The INNS exists to support your interests. It has appointed Robert Kosma as Chair of Special Interest Groups, and provided funding to support SIG activities. INNS also produces the INNS Newsletter, and the journal, *Neural Networks*, which consistently enjoys a strong impact factor among the journals in this field. Be sure to visit www.inns.org to learn more, and to join or renew your membership.

Sincerely,

Donald C. Wunsch II
President, International Neural Network Society
University of Missouri-Rolla, Applied Computational Intelligence Lab

Conference Topics

A. PERCEPTUAL AND MOTOR FUNCTION
A1 Vision and image processing
A2 Pattern recognition
A2a Biometric recognition
A2b Handwriting recognition
A2c Other pattern recognition
A3 Auditory and speech processing
A3a Audition
A3b Speech recognition
A3c Speech production
A4 Other perceptual systems
A5 Motor control and response

B. COGNITIVE FUNCTION
B1 Cognitive information processing
B2 Learning and memory
B3 Spatial navigation
B4 Conditioning, reward and behavior
B5 Mental disorders
B6 Attention and consciousness
B7 Language
B8 Emotion and motivation

C. COMPUTATIONAL NEUROSCIENCE
C1 Models of neurons, local circuits and learning rules
C2 Systems neurobiology and neural modeling
C3 Spiking neurons

D. INFORMATICS
D1 Neuroinformatics and brain models
D2 Bioinformatics
D3 Artificial immune systems
D4 Data mining

E. HARDWARE
E1 Neuromorphic hardware and implementations
E2 Embedded neural networks
E3 Reconfigurable systems

F. NEURODYNAMICS
F1 Recurrent networks
F2 Chaotic systems
F3 K sets theory and applications

G. ADAPTATION AND DECISION MAKING
G1 Reinforcement learning
G2 Approximate dynamic programming, adaptive critics and Markov decision processes
G3 Support vector machines
G4 Advanced learning methods and optimization
G5 Mixture models, EM algorithms and ensemble learning
G6 Radial basis functions
G7 Self-organizing maps and associative memory
G8 Adaptive resonance theory
G9 Principal component analysis and independent component analysis
Ga Probabilistic and information-theoretic methods
Gb Neural networks and evolutionary computation
Gc Fuzzy neural systems
Gd Intelligent agents and swarm intelligence
Ge Quantum and molecular computations

H. APPLICATIONS
H1 Signal processing
H2 Control
H3 Diagnostics and quality control
H4 Robotics
H5 Telecommunication applications
H6 Time series analysis
H7 Biomedical applications
H8 Financial engineering
H9 Biomimetic applications
Ha Computer security applications
Hb Power system applications
Hc Aeroinformatics
Hd Military and security applications
He Other applications

IEEE – CIS (EXCOM and ADCOM)

President (2004-05)
Jacek M. Zurada

President-Elect (2005)
Vincenzo Piuri

Vice-President, Finances (2005-06)
Piero P. Bonissone

Vice-President, Conferences (2004-05)
Okyay Kaynak

Vice-President, Members Activities (2005-06)
David B. Fogel

Vice-President, Publications (2005-06)
James M. Keller

Vice-President, Technical Activities (2004-05)
Gary Yen

Secretary (2005)
Glenna Haberzetle

Division X Director (2005-06)
Evangelia Micheli-Tzanakou

Witold Pedrycz (2004-06)
Bernadette Bouchon-Meunier (2004-06)
Bernard Widrow (2004-06)
Gary B. Fogel (2004-06)
Jerry Mendel (2004-06)
Laszlo T. Koczy (2005-07)
George G. Lendaris (2005-07)
Robert J. Marks (2005-07)
Jennie Si (2005-07)
Paul Werbos (2005-07)

IEEE Computational Intelligence Society President's Welcome

I am very pleased to welcome all participants of the 2005 International Joint Conference on Neural Networks (IJCNN). Again as in other odd years, this traditional event in 2005 has been organized and sponsored by the International Neural Network Society (INNS), and organized with technical co-sponsorship of the IEEE Computational Intelligence Society (IEEE CIS).

This address offers me a special opportunity to acknowledge the dedicated efforts of the Organizing and Technical Committees and the IJCNN's General Chair, Dr. Danil Prokhorov, who have all worked hard to put together an exciting technical program. The technical sessions will highlight plenary lectures by leading researchers, and will feature regular and special oral sessions. In addition, poster sessions will provide plenty of opportunities for face-to-face interaction between the authors and small groups of participants.

I believe that a conference such as IJCNN offers a unique opportunity for all of us to become one community of professional colleagues regardless of the native language we speak, and regardless of the academic or professional rank we are holding. At IJCNN, aspiring PhD students can rub shoulders with distinguished neural networks pioneers, and junior researchers can freely interact with senior plenary speakers. IJCNN allows us to truly share our research ideas, and meet partners in our present or future research efforts. It is the democracy of research efforts and information exchange that is at work here.

As many of you know, IEEE CIS has a tradition of supporting student travel to its premier conferences such as IJCNN, FUZZ-IEEE, CEC but also to smaller conferences. Similar to previous years, numerous travel grants have been awarded to students from the USA, Canada, and Regions 8-10. To this aim, IEEE CIS has established a special website where all participants can apply for travel subsidies awarded by the IEEE CIS Education Committee. These new participants have my special welcome to Montreal's IJCNN.

CIS is one of thirty-eight IEEE Societies. Its focus is the theory, design, application, and development of biologically and linguistically motivated computational paradigms emphasizing neural networks, connectionist systems, genetic algorithms, evolutionary programming, fuzzy systems, and hybrid intelligent systems. Created in 2002, the Society is actively seeking new members to join its current membership ranks of over 5,700 and expand its international and North-American presence. To join the IEEE CIS and become an active member of our community, please visit www.ieee.org/join.

Activities in all technical areas are coordinated by one of the Society's eight Technical Committees: Computational Intelligence, Fuzzy Systems, Evolutionary Computation, Emergent Technologies, Bioinformatics and Bioengineering, Intelligent Systems Applications, and Autonomous Mental Development. The Committees serve as forums for the exchange of technical information, the dissemination of ideas and the initiation of new topical trends. It is at this level of involvement where ideas and topics are incubated for special sessions of conferences, new workshops and seminars, and special issues of our journals, and also it is where new conferences are being planned.

IEEE CIS offers its members an amazing range of technical involvement. It publishes three highly-regarded IEEE Transactions as well as the CIS Newsletter (that is destined to emerge as the CIS Magazine in 2006), organizes three major conferences and specialized symposia and workshops. The CIS also supports educational opportunities through its multimedia tutorial program, and summer research programs. Other activities include the Distinguished Lecturers Program available to our Chapters, Technical Field Awards, Best Paper Awards, Pioneer Awards, Meritorious Service Award, and new awards such as Outstanding PhD Dissertation Award, and Best Chapter Award. The Society's other efforts extend special opportunities for women in computational intelligence. All of our members are invited to take full advantage of these exciting chances for their professional growth.

New activities can also be initiated within the local territorial entities of our Society called Chapters. To become involved in a Chapter, a member needs to contact the appropriate regional Chapter Chair. If no Chapter has been established in your area, you may create it by collecting twelve signatures of current CIS members and contacting Dr. David Fogel, VP-Membership Activities, at dfogel@natural-selection.com.

Our members are not only encouraged to get involved in Technical Committees or Chapters. The Society also needs more volunteers to run its daily business. We need people for the Standing Committees, such as Education, Multimedia Tutorials, Standards and other committees. In addition, the Society members cast their votes when electing its governing body called Administrative Committee (ADCOM).

As you have read, the Society offers all its members opportunities to get involved, stay active and participate at the technical level or in its self-governance. We need your support, time and talent, and I am eagerly awaiting your participation in the Society, your contribution to the field, and the further advancement of the society as a whole. For more information, please check our website at www.ieee-cis.org.

One of the special conference activities, the Joint IEEE-INNS Awards Banquet and Awards Ceremony, that will be held on Wednesday, August 3, will be co-hosted by the President of the INNS, Dr. Donald Wunsch, and me. I hope to see you all there. I also wish you a pleasant stay in Montreal. Have a great conference!

Dr. Jacek M. Zurada
President, IEEE Computational Intelligence Society
Chairman and S.T. Fife Professor of Electrical and Computer Engineering
University of Louisville, Louisville, Kentucky
Fellow of IEEE, Foreign Member of the Polish Academy of Sciences
j.zurada@ieee.org

GENERAL INFORMATION

Cooperating Societies and Sponsors:

International Neural Network Society
IEEE Computational Intelligence Society
Florida Institute of Technology
University of Texas at Arlington
Ford Motor Company
Applied Computational Intelligence Laboratory, University of Missouri-Rolla
Siemens Canada
CISCO Systems
Elsevier

Registration

Registration for the conference will be open at the following times at the Inscription 1 Registration Desk at the Hilton Montreal Bonaventure Hotel:

Saturday, July 30 . . . . 5:00 p.m.-8:00 p.m.
Sunday, July 31 . . . . 7:30 a.m.-5:30 p.m.
Monday, August 1 . . . . 7:30 a.m.-6:30 p.m.
Tuesday, August 2 . . . . 8:00 a.m.-5:30 p.m.
Wednesday, August 3 . . . . 8:00 a.m.-5:00 p.m.
Thursday, August 4 . . . . 8:00 a.m.-5:00 p.m.

Internet Café

The Internet Café is located in the Cote St-Luc Room at the Hilton Montreal Bonaventure Hotel. Both wireless and wired connections will be available for your use. The Internet Café will be open during the following hours:

Sunday, July 31 . . . . 7:00 a.m.-9:00 p.m.
Monday, August 1 . . . . 7:00 a.m.-9:00 p.m.
Tuesday, August 2 . . . . 7:00 a.m.-9:00 p.m.
Wednesday, August 3 . . . . 7:00 a.m.-9:00 p.m.
Thursday, August 4 . . . . 7:00 a.m.-4:00 p.m.

Speaker Ready Room

The Speaker Ready Room is located in the St-Laurent Room. Please stop by prior to your presentation to preview your slides and run through your presentation. The Speaker Ready Room will be open during the following times:

Saturday, July 30 . . . . 1:00 p.m.-7:00 p.m.
Sunday, July 31 . . . . 7:00 a.m.-5:00 p.m.
Monday, August 1 . . . . 7:00 a.m.-5:00 p.m.
Tuesday, August 2 . . . . 7:00 a.m.-5:00 p.m.
Wednesday, August 3 . . . . 7:00 a.m.-5:00 p.m.
Thursday, August 4 . . . . 7:00 a.m.-12:00 noon

Conference Badges

Please wear your badge to all IJCNN 2005 functions. It will admit you to the sessions and the exhibit area.

Plenary Poster Session and Discussions

Posters will be available for viewing in the Fontaine Ballroom at the following times:

Monday, August 1, 2005
1:00 p.m.-11:00 p.m.
(Authors present between 7:00 p.m.-11:00 p.m.)

Tuesday, August 2, 2005
1:00 p.m.-11:00 p.m.
(Authors present between 7:00 p.m.-11:00 p.m.)

Plenary Poster Presenter Schedule

If you are presenting a poster at the meeting, please review the schedule carefully and be sure to assemble and teardown your poster when indicated.

Monday, August 1, 2005

Poster Setup . . . . 11:00 a.m.-1:00 p.m.
Poster Viewing . . . . 1:00 p.m.-7:00 p.m.
(Presence of Poster Authors is Optional)

Plenary Poster Session and Discussions
7:00 p.m.-11:00 p.m.
(Presence of Poster Authors is Required)

Poster Teardown . . . . 11:00 p.m.-12:00 midnight

Tuesday, August 2, 2005

Poster Setup . . . . 10:00 a.m.-1:00 p.m.
Poster Viewing . . . . 1:00 p.m.-7:00 p.m.
(Presence of Poster Authors is Optional)

Plenary Poster Session and Discussions
7:00 p.m.-11:00 p.m.
(Presence of Poster Authors is Required)

Poster Teardown . . . . 11:00 p.m.-12:00 midnight

IJCNN 2005 is not responsible for any posters that are not dismantled by 12:00 midnight each evening.

Exhibits

Plan to spend time in the Fontaine Ballroom visiting with the exhibiting companies at IJCNN 2005. Refreshment breaks and poster sessions will be located in the exhibit area. The exposition will be open at the following times:

Monday, August 1, 2005
11:00 a.m.-5:00 p.m. and 7:00 p.m.-11:00 p.m.
(evening Plenary Poster Session)

Tuesday, August 2, 2005
9:00 a.m.-5:00 p.m. and 7:00 p.m.-11:00 p.m.
(evening Plenary Poster Session)

Wednesday, August 3, 2005
9:00 a.m.-4:00 p.m.

Exhibit Directory
(as of May 24, 2005)

Florida Institute of Technology
College of Engineering
150 West University Boulevard
Melbourne, FL 32901-6975
Tel: +321-674-8020
Fax: +321-674-7270
Email: coe@fit.edu
Website: www.coe.fit.edu

The College of Engineering at Florida Tech includes seven departments that administer multiple engineering and applied science programs. The departments are chemical engineering, civil engineering, computer sciences, electrical and computer engineering, marine and environmental systems, and mechanical and aerospace engineering. Engineering management and systems engineering are graduate programs offered in the department of engineering systems. The College of Engineering supports several research institutes, centers and laboratories including the Information Processing Laboratory (IPL). Researchers in the IPL are actively involved in many computational intelligence research projects; these are federally funded as well as funded projects from industry.

Ford Research and Advanced Engineering
2101 Village Road
Dearborn, MI 48124 USA
Tel: +313-478-2614
Fax: +313-337-5581
Contact (Computational Intelligence):
   Danil Prokhorov
Email: dprokhor@ford.com
Website: www.ford.com

Ford Research and Advanced Engineering is one of the world's leading automotive research and engineering organizations engaged in R&D on topics too numerous to list. Ford R & AE will propel Ford Motor Company to world leadership in safe, environmentally responsible and affordable personal mobility through advances in science and technology. Our mission is to ANTICIPATE the technical needs of our customers and the company, INNOVATE solutions to technical challenges, and INCORPORATE developed technology into products and processes. Please come and see some of our exciting new technologies at our IJCNN 2005 booth!

John Wiley & Sons, Ltd.
The Atrium, Southern Gate
Chichester, West Sussex PO1 88Q
United Kingdom
Tel: +44 1243 779 777
Fax: +44 1243 775 878
Email: as-books@wiley.co.uk
Website: www.wiley.com

John Wiley & Sons Ltd. are a leading international publisher of print and electronic products, specializing in scientific and technical books and journals. Visit our stand at IJCNN '05 and view our latest range of electrical engineering publications. All books on display are available at a special conference discount. Alternatively, view our publications online: www.wiley.com/electricalengineering

LMS Medical Systems
5252 de Maison Neuve W, #314
Montreal, Quebec H4A 3S5
Canada
Tel: +514-488-3461
Fax: +514-488-1880
Email: info@lmsmedical.com
Website: www.lmsmedical.com

Developing tools for Obstetrical Decision Support, Risk Management and Clinical Information Systems, LMS Medical is a leader in the application of advanced mathematical modeling and neural networks for medical use.

National Science Foundation
Science of Learning Centers
4201 Wilson Blvd.
Arlington, VA 22230 USA
Tel: +703-292-5111
Website: www.nsf.gov

The Science of Learning Centers program (SLC) offers awards for large-scale, long-term Centers that will extend the frontiers of knowledge on learning of all types.

Palisade Corporation
798 Cascadilla Street
Ithaca, NY 14850
Tel: +607-277-8000
Fax: +607-277-8001
Email: sales@palisades.com
Website: www.palisades.com

Palisade Corporation is a world leader in quantitative analysis add-ins for Microsoft Excel. The company will be demonstrating its new Neural Networks tool at IJCNN.

University of Missouri-Rolla – ACIL
1870 Mines Circle, 131 EECH
Rolla, MO 65409
Tel: +573-341-4521
Fax: +573-341-4532
Website: www.ece.umr.edu/acil

ACIL research includes applications of reinforcement and unsupervised learning: TSP, diagnostics, telecommunications networking, smart sensor networks, the game of Go, and more.

University of Texas at Arlington
Box 19047 (College of Sciences)
Box 19019 (College of Engineering)
Arlington, TX 76019 USA
Tel: +817-272-3491 (College of Sciences)
Fax: +817-272-3511
Tel: +817-272-2571 (College of Engineering)
Fax: +817-272-2548
Tel: +817-272-1021 (Vice President for Research)
Fax: +817-272-2625

The University of Texas at Arlington (UTA) is a growing research university with over 25,000 students, located in the heart of metropolitan Dallas-Fort Worth. UTA's programs include an Automation and Robotics Research Institute, a Technology Incubator, and neural network researchers in the departments of Psychology, Electrical Engineering, and Computer Science.

Browse Table
Book Title:
Bioinformatics: The Machine Learning Approach, Second Edition
Author(s): Pierre Baldi and Søren Brunak
Price: $60.00

ISBN: 0262-02506-X

Contact for Ordering:
  The MIT Press
  55 Hayward Street Cambridge, MA 02142-1315

Telephone (for ordering) 1-800-405-1619
(refer to code MBALB for the 20% discount)
(TriLiteral, the fulfillment center)
Fax: +617-253-1709
Email: orders@triliteral.org
Website: http://mitpress.mit.edu

Florida Institute of Technology

College of Engineering
150 West University Boulevard
Melbourne, FL 32901-6975
Phone: (321) 674-8020
Fax: (321) 674-7270
www.coe.fit.edu

The **College of Engineering** at **Florida Tech** includes seven departments that administer multiple engineering and applied science programs. The departments are chemical engineering, civil engineering, computer sciences, electrical and computer engineering, marine and environmental systems, and mechanical and aerospace engineering. Engineering management and systems engineering are graduate programs offered in the department of engineering systems. The College of Engineering supports several research institutes, centers and laboratories including the Information Processing Laboratory (IPL). Researchers in the IPL are actively involved in many computational intelligence research projects, these are federally funded as well as funded projects from industry.

Hilton Montréal Bonaventure Hotel

Conference Meeting Rooms

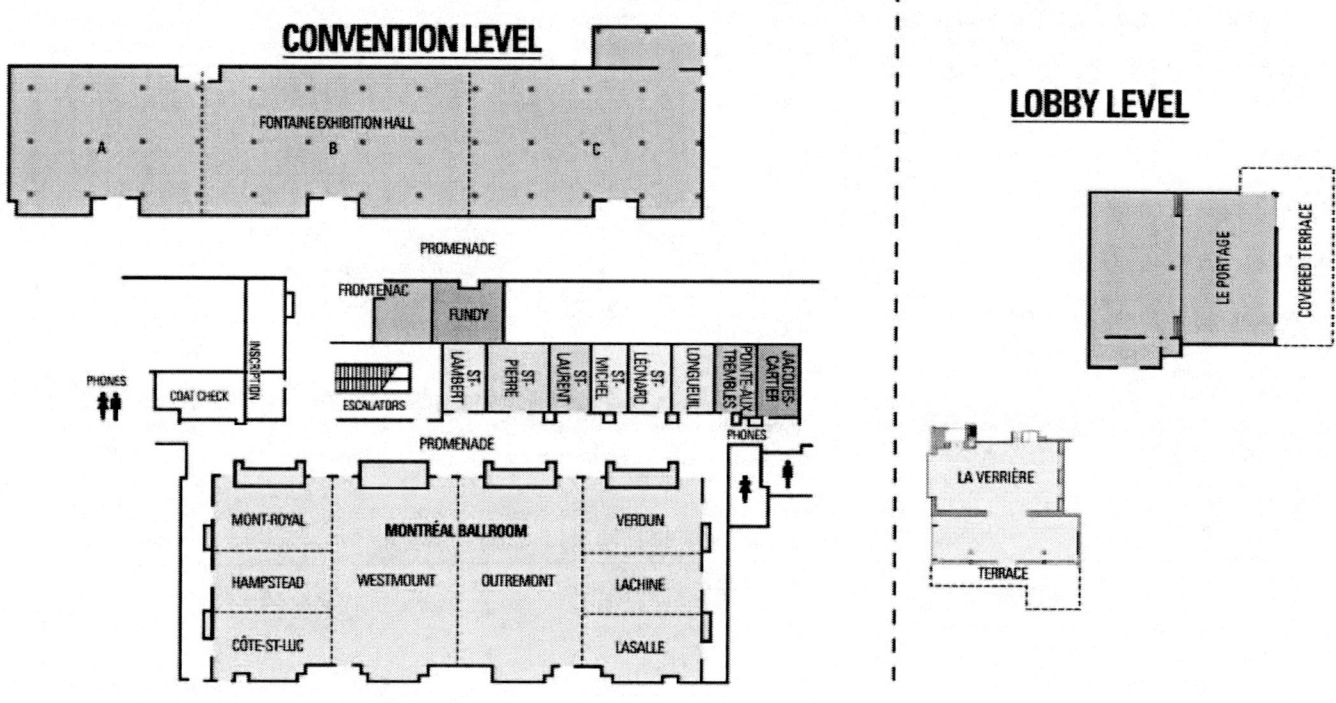

IJCNN 2005 Schedule-At-A-Glance

Saturday, July 30, 2005

1:00 p.m.-7:00 p.m.	Speaker Ready Room	St-Laurent
5:00 p.m.-8:00 p.m.	Registration	Inscription 1

Sunday, July 31, 2005

7:00 a.m.-9:00 p.m.	Internet Café	Cote St-Luc
7:00 a.m.-5:00 p.m.	Speaker Ready Room	St-Laurent
7:30 a.m.-5:30 p.m.	Registration	Inscription 1
9:00 a.m.-11:00 a.m.	Tutorial T01: Evolutionary Robotics	Lachine
9:00 a.m.-11:00 a.m.	Tutorial T03: Bioinfomatics and Machine Learning: the Prediction of Protein Structures on a Genomic Scale	Mont Royal
9:00 a.m.-11:00 a.m.	Tutorial T04: Cyber Security for Intelligent System Specialists	Hampstead
11:15 a.m.-1:15 p.m.	Tutorial T05: Neural Networks That Actually Work In Prediction and Decision/Control: Common Misconceptions Versus Real-World Success	Lachine
11:15 a.m.-1:15 p.m.	Tutorial T06: Feature Extraction in Computational Intelligence	Verdun
11:15 a.m.-1:15 p.m.	Tutorial T07: Integrating Language and Cognition: New Results in Computational Intelligence	Mont Royal
11:15 a.m.-1:15 p.m.	Tutorial T08: Evolving Connectionist Systems for Adaptive Learning and Knowledge Discovery: Principles, Models and Applications	Hampstead
2:30 p.m.-4:30 p.m.	Tutorial T09: Neural Networks for Dynamic Systems Feedback	Lachine
2:30 p.m.-4:30 p.m.	Tutorial T10: Unsupervised Learning	Verdun
2:30 p.m.-4:30 p.m.	Tutorial T11: New Formulations for Predictive Learning	Mont Royal
2:30 p.m.-4:30 p.m.	Tutorial T12: Data Visualization of High Dimensional Scientific Data	Hampstead
4:45 p.m.-6:45 p.m.	Tutorial T13: Cognitive Memory	Lachine
4:45 p.m.-6:45 p.m.	Tutorial T14: Nonlinear Manifolds in Pattern Recognition and Image Analysis	Verdun
4:45 p.m.-6:45 p.m.	Tutorial T15: Support Vector Machines and Kernel Based Learning	Mont Royal
4:45 p.m.-6:45 p.m.	Tutorial T16: Biologically Plausible Artificial Neural Networks	Hampstead

Monday, August 1, 2005

7:00 a.m.-9:00 p.m.	Internet Café	Cote St-Luc
7:00 a.m.-5:00 p.m.	Speaker Ready Room	St-Laurent
7:30 a.m.-6:30 p.m.	Registration	Inscription 1
8:00 a.m.-9:00 a.m.	Plenary Session – Pierre Baldi	Westmount
9:00 a.m.-9:30 a.m.	Refreshment Break	Westmount Foyer
9:30 a.m.-11:30 a.m.	Special Session: Neural Networks Applications to Bioinformatics	Westmount
9:30 a.m.-11:30 a.m.	Information-theoretic and Bayesian Learning	Outremont
9:30 a.m.-11:30 a.m.	Special Session: Neurodynamics and Intentional Dynamic System	Mont Royal
9:30 a.m.-11:30 a.m.	Pattern Recognition	Verdun
11:00 a.m.-5:00 p.m.	Exhibits Open	Fontaine Ballroom
11:30 a.m.-1:00 p.m.	Lunch Break (on your own)	
1:00 p.m.-3:00 p.m.	Bioinformatics	Westmount
1:00 p.m.-3:00 p.m.	Special Session: Evolvable and Emergent Neural System	Outremont
1:00 p.m.-3:00 p.m.	Models of Neurons, Local Circuits and Systems	Mont Royal
1:00 p.m.-3:00 p.m.	ICA and PCA	Verdun
3:00 p.m.-3:20 p.m.	Refreshment Break	Fontaine Ballroom
3:20 p.m.-5:20 p.m.	Special Session: Computational Neurogenetic Modeling	Westmount
3:20 p.m.-5:20 p.m.	Control and System Identification	Outremont
3:20 p.m.-5:20 p.m.	Spiking Neurons	Mont Royal
3:20 p.m.-5:20 p.m.	Special Session: Recent Advancements in Adaptive Resonance Theory	Verdun
6:00 p.m.-8:00 p.m.	Student Reception (students welcome, others by invitation)	Portage
7:00 p.m.-11:00 p.m.	Plenary Poster Session	Fontaine Ballroom
7:00 p.m.-11:00 p.m.	Exhibits Open	Fontaine Ballroom

Tuesday, August 2, 2005

7:00 a.m.-9:00 p.m.	Internet Café	Cote St-Luc
7:00 a.m.-5:00 p.m.	Speaker Ready Room	St-Laurent
8:00 a.m.-5:30 p.m.	Registration	Inscription 1
8:00 a.m.-9:00 a.m.	Plenary Session – Michael Petrides	Westmount

Tuesday, August 2, 2005 - continued

9:00 a.m.-9:30 a.m.	Refreshment Break	Fontaine Ballroom
9:00 a.m.-5:00 p.m.	Exhibits Open	Fontaine Ballroom
9:30 a.m.-11:30 a.m.	Evolutionary Algorithms and PSO	Westmount
9:30 a.m.-11:30 a.m.	Special Session: Computational Dynamical Modeling with Echo State Networks	Outremont
9:30 a.m.-11:30 a.m.	Special Session: Functional Neuroimaging of Cortical and Subcortical Functions	Mont Royal
9:30 a.m.-11:30 a.m.	SVM I	Verdun
11:30 a.m.-1:00 p.m.	Lunch Break (on your own)	
1:00 p.m.-3:00 p.m.	Special Session: Applications of Learning and Data-Driven Methods to Earth Sciences and Climate Modeling	Westmount
1:00 p.m.-3:00 p.m.	Recurrent Neural Networks	Outremont
1:00 p.m.-3:00 p.m.	Special Session: Transition: Imaging and Cortical Models	Mont Royal
1:00 p.m.-3:00 p.m.	Self-Organizing Maps	Verdun
3:00 p.m.-3:20 p.m.	Refreshment Break	Fontaine Ballroom
3:20 p.m.-5:20 p.m.	Special Session Applications of Learning and Data-Driven Methods to Earth Sciences and Climate Modeling, plus Panel Discussion	Westmount
3:20 p.m.-5:20 p.m.	Diagnostics and Control, Power Systems	Outremont
3:20 p.m.-5:20 p.m.	Special Session: Models of Cortical and Subcortical Circuits	Mont Royal
3:20 p.m.-5:20 p.m.	Visual and Image Processing	Verdun
7:00 p.m.-11:00 p.m.	Plenary Poster Session	Fontaine Ballroom
7:00 p.m.-11:00 p.m.	Exhibits Open	Fontaine Ballroom

Wednesday, August 3, 2005

7:00 a.m.-9:00 p.m.	Internet Café	Cote St-Luc
7:00 a.m.-5:00 p.m.	Speaker Ready Room	St-Laurent
8:00 a.m.-5:00 p.m.	Registration	Inscription 1
8:00 a.m.-9:00 a.m.	Plenary Session – Frank Lewis	Westmount
9:00 a.m.-9:30 a.m.	Refreshment Break	Fontaine Ballroom
9:00 a.m.-4:00 p.m.	Exhibits Open	Fontaine Ballroom
9:30 a.m.-11:30 a.m.	Robotics	Westmount
9:30 a.m.-11:30 a.m.	SVM II	Outremont
9:30 a.m.-11:30 a.m.	Special Session: Hebb's Legacy	Mont Royal
9:30 a.m.-11:30 a.m.	Data Mining	Verdun
11:30 a.m.-1:00 p.m.	Lunch Break (on your own)	
1:00 p.m.-3:00 p.m.	Hardware	Westmount
1:00 p.m.-3:00 p.m.	Special Session: Performance of Neuro-Adaptive and Learning Systems: Assessment, Monitoring, and Validation	Outremont
1:00 p.m.-3:00 p.m.	Cognitive Function	Mont Royal
1:00 p.m.-3:00 p.m.	Special Session: Constructive/Hierarchical Self-Organizing Maps	Verdun
3:00 p.m.-3:20 p.m.	Refreshment Break	Fontaine Ballroom
3:20 p.m.-5:20 p.m.	Special Session: Approximate Dynamic Programming	Westmount
3:20 p.m.-5:20 p.m.	Biomedical Applications	Outremont
3:20 p.m.-5:20 p.m.	Fuzzy-Neural Systems	Mont Royal
3:20 p.m.-5:20 p.m.	Special Session: Biologically Inspired Computational Vision	Verdun
7:00 p.m.-9:00 p.m.	Awards Banquet	Westmount

Thursday, August 4, 2005

7:00 a.m.-12:00 noon	Speaker Ready Room	St-Laurent
8:00 a.m.-5:00 p.m.	Registration	Inscription 1
8:00 a.m.-5:00 p.m.	Internet Café	Cote St-Luc
8:00 a.m.-9:00 a.m.	Plenary Session – Mitsuo Kawato	Westmount
9:00 a.m.-9:30 a.m.	Refreshment Break	Westmount Foyer
9:30 a.m.-11:30 a.m.	Special Session: Neural Prostheses and the Neuron-Silicon Interface	Westmount
9:30 a.m.-11:30 a.m.	Learning I	Outremont
9:30 a.m.-11:30 a.m.	Neurodynamics	Mont Royal
9:30 a.m.-11:30 a.m.	Applications I	Verdun
11:30 a.m.-1:00 p.m.	Lunch Break (on your own)	
1:00 p.m.-3:00 p.m.	Neuromorphic Hardware	Westmount
1:00 p.m.-3:00 p.m.	Learning II	Outremont
1:00 p.m.-3:00 p.m.	Telecommunications	Mont Royal
1:00 p.m.-3:00 p.m.	Applications II	Verdun
3:00 p.m.-3:20 p.m.	Refreshment Break	Westmount Foyer
3:20 p.m.-4:20 p.m.	Plenary Session – Carver Mead	Westmount

The IJCNN 2005 Post-Conference Workshops
(as of May 24, 2005)

Workshops are to be held in rooms Fundy, St-Laurent, St-Michel, St-Leonard, Longueuil, Pointe-Aux Trembles and Jacques-Cartier (see near Promenade on the Conference Meeting Rooms page). Individual workshop times may vary. Please consult on-site posters/schedule.

August 4, 7-10PM:

"Artificial Neural Networks, Bioinformatics and Neuroinformatics - A Synergistic Approach"
Organized by: Prof. Nik Kasabov, Knowledge Engineering and Discovery Research Institute, New Zealand, Prof. Amir Assadi, Department of Mathematics, University of Wisconsin, USA.

"Achieving Functional Integration of Diverse Neural Models"
Organized by: Talib S. Hussain, Ph.D., BBN Technologies, Cambridge, MA USA.
Room: St-Leonard.

August 5, 9AM-5PM:

"Verification, Validation and Certification of Neuro-Adaptive Controllers in Safety-Related Areas"
Organized by: Johann Schumann, Ph.D., RIACS/NASA Ames, Pramod Gupta, Ph.D., QSS/NASA Ames, Dragos Margineantu, Ph.D., The Boeing Company, Steven Jacklin, NASA Ames.

"Biologically-Inspired Models and Hardware for Human-like Intelligent Functions"
Organized by: Soo-Young Lee, Director, Brain Science Research Center, KAIST.

"Neurodynamics and Intentional Dynamic Systems"
Organized by: Peter Andras, Newcastle, UK, Ricardo Gutierrez-Osuna, Texas A&M, USA, Walter J Freeman, Berkeley, USA, Robert Kozma, Memphis, USA. Daniel Levine, UTA, USA.

"Computational Intelligence Approaches for the Analysis of Bioinformatics Data: CI-BIO"
Organized by: Francesco Masulli, University of Pisa, Italy, Roberto Tagliaferri, University of Salerno, Italy.

Table of Contents

Schedule Grids iii

Message from the General Chair viii

Organizing, Program and Review Committees xi

INNS Officers and Board of Governors xiv

INNS President's Welcome xv

IEEE EXCOM and ADCOM xvii

IEEE CIS President's Welcome xviii

Cooperating Societies and Sponsors xx

Conference Information xxi

Exhibit Directory xxii

Conference Meeting Rooms xxv

Schedule-at-a-Glance xxvi

Post-Conference Workshops xxviii

Program

Sunday, July 31, 2005

Tutorials

9:00 a.m.-11:00 a.m.
Tutorial T01: Evolutionary Robotics

9:00 a.m.-11:00 a.m.
Tutorial T03: Bioinfomatics and Machine Learning: the Prediction of Protein Structures on a Genomic Scale

11:15 a.m.-1:15 p.m.
Tutorial T05: Neural Networks That Actually Work In Prediction and Decision/Control: Common Misconceptions Versus Real-World Success

11:15 a.m.-1:15 p.m.
Tutorial T06: Feature Extraction in Computational Intelligence

11:15 a.m.-1:15 p.m.
Tutorial T07: Integrating Language and Cognition: New Results in Computational Intelligence

11:15 a.m.-1:15 p.m.
Tutorial T08: Evolving Connectionist Systems for Adaptive Learning and Knowledge Discovery: Principles, Models and Applications

2:30 p.m.-4:30 p.m.
Tutorial T09: Neural Networks for Dynamic Systems Feedback

2:30 p.m.-4:30 p.m.
Tutorial T10: Unsupervised Learning

2:30 p.m.-4:30 p.m.
Tutorial T11: New Formulations for Predictive Learning

2:30 p.m.-4:30 p.m.
Tutorial T12: Data Visualization of High Dimensional Scientific Data

4:45 p.m.-6:45 p.m.
Tutorial T13: Cognitive Memory

4:45 p.m.-6:45 p.m.
Tutorial T14: Nonlinear Manifolds in Pattern Recognition and Image Analysis

4:45 p.m.-6:45 p.m.
Tutorial T15: Support Vector Machines and Kernel Based Learning

4:45 p.m.-6:45 p.m.
Tutorial T16: Biologically Plausible Artificial Neural Networks

Monday, August 1, 2005

8:00 a.m.-9:00 a.m.
Plenary Talk
Exploring Chemical Space with Computers: Challenges and Opportunities 83

9:30 a.m.-11:30 a.m.
Pattern Recognition
- *Automatic Target Recognition Using New Support Vector Machine*......................................84
- *Training with Heterogeneous Data* 90
- *Tracking the States of a Nonlinear System in the Weight-Space of a Feed-Forward Neural Network* 96
- *Data-Dependent Kernels for High-Dimensional Data Classification* 102
- *Generalized 2D Principal Component Analysis* 108
- *Optimal Gradient-Based Learning Using Importance Weights*...114

9:30 a.m.-11:30 a.m.
Special Session: Neurodynamics and Intentional Dynamic Systems
- Cinematographic Construction by Brains of Knowledge from Information 120
- Analysis of Phase Transitions in KIV with Amygdala during Simulated Navigation Control 125
- Mixture Segmentation and Background Suppression in Chemosensor Arrays with a Model of Olfactory Bulb-Cortex interaction 131
- The language of cortical dynamics (no file)
- Evolving Neurodynamic Controllers for Autonomous Robots 137

9:30 a.m.-11:30 a.m.
Special Session: Neural Networks Applications to Bioinformatics
- Data Visualization Methodologies for Data Mining Systems in Bioinformatics 143
- Random projections for assessing gene expression cluster stability 149
- A New Approach to Hierarchical Clustering for the Analysis of Genomic Data 155
- Inferring Protein-Protein Interactions Using Interaction Network Topologies 161
- Predicting sugar regulation in Arabidopsis thaliana using kernel learning methods 167
- Feedback Linearization Using Neural Networks Applied to Advanced Pharmacodynamic and Pharmacogenomic Systems 173

9:30 a.m.-11:30 a.m.
Information-Theoretic and Bayesian Learning
- Improved Spam e-Mail Filtering Based on Committee Machines and Information Theoretic Feature Extraction 179
- A Variational Bayesian Method for Rectified Factor Analysis 185
- An Information Theoretic Approach to Adaptive System Training Using Unlabeled Data 191
- A Study of AdaBoost with SVM Based Weak Learners 196
- Information maximization and cost minimization in information-theoretic competitive learning 202
- Maximally Discriminative Spectral Feature Projections Using Mutual Information 208

1:00 p.m.-3:00 p.m.
ICA and PCA
- Extending Kernel Principal Component Analysis to General Underlying Loss Functions 214
- Nonlinearity and Optimal Component Analysis 220
- Relation between Kernel CCA and Kernel FDA 226
- Extraction of Frame-Difference Features based on PCA and ICA for Lip-Reading 232
- Multinomial PCA for Extracting Major Latent Topics from Document Streams 238
- Post Nonlinear Blind Source Separation by Geometric Linearization 244

1:00 p.m.-3:00 p.m.
Models of Neurons, Local Circuits and Systems
- Which Features Trigger Action Potentials in Cortical Neurons in Vivo 250
- Attention as Sigma-Pi Controlled Ach-Based Feedback 256
- Motivational Modulation of Endogenous Inputs to the Superior Colliculus 262

- Facilitatory Neural Activity Compensating for Neural Delays as a Potential Cause of the Flash-Lag Effect 268
- Fisher Information Quantifies Task-Specific Performance in the Blowfly Photoreceptor 274
- Evolutionary Training of a Biologically Realistic Spino-neuromuscular System 280

1:00 p.m.-3:00 p.m.
Bioinformatics
- Gene Regulatory Networks Inference with Recurrent Neural Network Models 286
- A Self-Organizing Neural Network Approach for the Identification of Motifs with Insertions and Deletions in Protein Sequences 292
- Functional Grouping of Genes Using Spectral Clustering and Gene Ontology 298
- A Simpler Bayesian Network Model for Genetic Regulatory Network Inference 304
- Effect of Non-Target Examples on E.coli Promoters Recognition Using Neural Networks 310
- Predicting Protein-Protein Interactions Based on Protein-Domain Relationships 316

1:00 p.m.-3:00 p.m.
Special Session: Evolvable and Emergent Neural Systems
- Automated Heuristic Growing of Neural Networks for Nonlinear Time Series Models 320
- ECG Signal Classification using Block-based Neural Networks 326
- An Evolved Seeega Player Capable of Strong Novice-Level Play 332
- Evolvable Neural Networks based on Developmental Models for Mobile Robot Navigation 337
- A Recurrent RBF Network Model for Nearest Neighbor Classification 343
- Face Recognition Using Modular Neural Networks and Fuzzy Sugeno Integral for Response Integration 349

3:20 p.m.-5:20 p.m.
Control and System Identification
- Application of a CMAC Neural Network to the Control of a Parallel Hybrid-Electric Propulsion System for a Small Unmanned Aerial Vehicle 355
- Inverse Optimal Nonlinear Recurrent High Order Neural Observer 361
- System and Method for Determining Harmonic Contributions from Non-Linear Loads Using Recurrent Neural Networks 366
- On Output Regulation for SISO Nonlinear Systems with Dynamic Neural Networks 372
- Indirect Field-oriented Linear Induction Motor Drive with Petri Fuzzy-neural-network Control...378
- Wavelet-Neural-Network-Based Backstepping Control for Chaotic Systems.....................384

3:20 p.m.-5:20 p.m.
Spiking Neurons
- Spatially and Temporally Local Spike-Timing-Dependent Plasticity Rule..........................390
- Differences in the subthreshold dynamics of leaky integrate-and-fire and Hodgkin-Huxley neuron models 396
- Rich phenomena of pulse-coupled spiking neurons with triangular waveform input 400
- Synchronized Theta Rhythm Selection in a Dentate Gyrus Network Model 405
- Noise Benefits in Spiking Retinal and Sensory Neuron Models 410
- A Spiking Neuron Representation of Auditory Signals..416

3:20 p.m.-5:20 p.m.
Special Session: Computational Neurogenetic Modeling
- *Comparative genomic study of Parkinson's disease candidate genes* 422
- *NeuroGene: Integrated Simulation of Gene Regulation, Neural Activity and Neurodevelopment* 428
- *A Hierarchical Coevolutionary Method to Support brain-Lesion Modelling* 434
- *Genome Space and Structure Genome Invariants* 440
- *A Computational Neurogenetic Model of a Spiking Neuron* 446

3:20 p.m.-5:20 p.m.
Special Session: Recent Advancements in Adaptive Resonance Theory
- *Self-Organizing Hierarchical Knowledge Discovery by an ARTMAP Information Fusion System* 452
- *Modification of the ART-1 Architecture Based on Category heoretic Design Principles* 457
- *A vigilance-free ART network with general geometry internal classes* 463
- *On the design of an Ellipsoid ARTMAP classifier within the Fuzzy Adaptive System ART Framework* 469
- *Parallelizing the Fuzzy ARTMAP Algorithm on a Beowulf Cluster* 475

7:00 p.m.-11:00 p.m.
Plenary Interactive Session I

Plenary Poster Session: Applications to genomics
- *Using real-valued meta classifiers to integrate binding site predictions* 481
- *Cluster Ensemble for Gene Expression Microarray Data* 487
- *Characterizing Human Gene Splice Sites Using Evolved Regular Expressions* 493
- *Prediction of Contact Map Integrated PNN with Conformational Energy* 499
- *Neural Network-Based Analysis of DNA Microarray Data* 503
- *Neural Networks for Gene Expression Analysis and Gene Selection from DNA Microarray* 509

Plenary Poster Session: Proteomics and neuroinformatics
- *The Molecules Module of the Brain Architecture Management System* 515
- *Protein Flexibility Modeling Using Kernel Based Methods* 521
- *An empirical comparison of individual machine learning techniques and ensemble approaches in protein structural class prediction* 527
- *Prediction of Protein Secondary Structure Using Improved Two-level Neural Network Architecture (no file)*
- *Protein secondary structure prediction using machine learning* 532
- *Protein Secondary Structure Prediction with a Hybrid RNN/HMM System* 538
- *Entropy Based Disease Classification of Proteomic Mass Sepectrometry Data of the Human Serum by a Support Vector Machine* 542

Plenary Poster Session: Data mining, text and pattern recognition

- *A Comparative Study on Term Weighting Schemes for Text Categorization* 546
- *One Class Support Vector Machine based Non-Relevance Feedback Document Retrieval* 552
- *Text Clustering with NTSO* 558
- *A Neuro-SVM Model for Text Classification using Latent Semantic Indexing* 564
- *Fast Text Categorization with Min-Max Modular Support Vector Machines* 570
- *Weight Sharing on Naive Bayes Document Model* 576
- *Optimization of Context Matching Parameters for Web Information Retrieval Using an Evolutionary Algorithm* 582
- *Snap-drift Learning for Phrase Recognition* 588
- *An Adaptive Function Neural Network (ADFUNN) for Phrase Recognition* 593
- *Treatment of Missing Data Using Neural* 598
- *An Iterative Relevance Feedback Learning Algorithm For Image Retrieval Systems* 604

Plenary Poster Session: Hardware

- *Design of an Optical Fixed-Weight Learning Neural Network* 610
- *Forgetful Logic Circuits for Pulse-Mode Neural Networks* 616
- *Artificial Neural Network Computation on Graphic Process Unit* 622
- *Circuit Implementation of Multi-Thresholded Neuron (MTN) Using BiCMOS Technology* 627
- *FPGA Implementation of Pulse Coupled Oscillator* 633
- *Analog Current-Mode Implementation of Central Pattern Generator for Robot Locomotion* 639
- *Toward an Analog VLSI Implementation of a Decision Making Model* 645
- *On Kolmogorov's Superpositions: Novel Gates and Circuits for Nanoelectronics* 651
- *Hardware Implementation of CMAC and B-Spline Neural Networks for Embedded Applications* 657
- *DSP-Based Neural Systems for the Perceptual Assessment of Visual Quality* 663
- *Analog Current-Mode Design for Soft-Max Computation* 669
- *Low-Voltage Pseudo Floating-Gate Reconfigurable Linear* 675
- *The Effects of Quantization on Support Vector Machines with Gaussian Kernel* 681
- *Building a Cheaper Artificial Brain* 685
- *A Digital LSI Architecture of Elastic Graph Matching and Its FPGA Implementation* 689
- *Simulated Control of a Tracking Mobile Robot by Four aVLSI Integrate-and-Fire Neurons Paired into Maps* 695

Plenary Poster Session: Neurodynamics

- *Recurrent Neural Networks Training with Stable Risk-Sensitive Kalman Filter Algorithm* 700
- *A Method of Oscillatory Trajectory Generation Using Recurrent Hybrid Neural Networks* 706
- *A New K-Winners-Take-All Neural Network* 712
- *A Constrained Optimization Algorithm for Training Locally Recurrent Globally Feedforward Neural Networks* 717
- *SCRAM: Statistically Converging Recurrent Associative Memory* 723
- *A New Model for Learning in Graph Domains* 729

- *Empirical Approximation for Lyapunov Functions with Artificial Neural Nets* 735
- *Ability to Skip Steps Emerging from Chaotic Dynamics* 741
- *Nonlinear dynamics on VSF-Network* 747
- *Dynamical Behavior of a Chaotic Neural Network and its Application to Optimization Problems* 753
- *An Analysis of Associative Chaotic Neurodynamics by Using Surrogate Neurons* 758

Plenary Poster Session: Hopfield networks
- *A New Kind of Hopfield Networks for Finding Global Optimum* 764
- *Learning cycles brings chaos in continuous Hopfield networks* 770
- *Phase Diagrams for Locally Hopfield Neural Networks in Presence of Correlated Patterns* 776
- *2 Types of Complex-Valued Hopfield Networks and the Application to a Traffic Signal Control* 782
- *A New N-Parallel Updating Method of the Hopfield-Type Neural Network for N-Queens Problem* 788

Plenary Poster Session: Reinforcement learning
- *On-Line System Identification Using Context Discernment* 792
- *The k-Server Problem: A Reinforcement Learning Approach* 798
- *Task Similarity Measures for Transfer in Reinforcement Learning Task Libraries* 803
- *Neural Network Model for Time Series Prediction by Reinforcement Learning* 809

Plenary Poster Session: Decision making, abductive and transductive reasoning
- *Learning Nonlinear State-Space Models for Control* 815
- *A Neural Network Model for the Decision-Making Process Based on AHP* 821
- *Negative Reinforcement and Backtrack-Points for Recurrent Neural Networks for Cost-Based Abduction* 827
- *Distributed Computation for Neural-Based Abductive Reasoning* 833
- *Transductive Modeling with GA Parameter Optimization* 839
- *Symbolic Rule Extraction with a Scaled Conjugate Gradient Version of CLARION* 845

Plenary Poster Session: Support Vector Machines
- *One-Against-All Multi-Class SVM Classification Using Reliability Measures* 849
- *K-Fold Generalization Capability Assessment for Support Vector Classifiers* 855
- *Weighted Support Vector Machine for Data Classification* 859
- *Algorithms of Fast SVM Evaluation based on Subspace Projection* 865
- *Yet Faster Method to Optimize SVR Hyperparameters based on Minimizing Cross-Validation Error* 871
- *Support Vector Regression Performance Analysis and Systematic Parameter Selection* 877
- *Pre-selection of Working Set for SVM Decomposition Algorithm* 883
- *The Intermediate Matching Kernel for Image Local Features* 889
- *MIMO SVMs for classification and regression using the geometric algebra framework* 895
- *Fuzzy integral for a rapid mixture of support vector machines* 901
- *Feature Subset Selection for Support Vector Machines using Confident Margin* 907
- *Assignment Kernels For Chemical Compounds* 913

- Characterization of Data Complexity for SVM Methods 919
- Optimizing Resources in Model Selection for Support Vectors Machines 925
- A convergence rate estimate for the SVM Decomposition Method 931
- Deriving Kernels from MLP Probability Estimators for Large Categorization Problems 937
- SVM Ensembles for Selecting the Relevant Feature Subsets 943
- Pattern De-Noising Based on Support Vector Data Description 949
- Kernel Relevant Component Analysis for Distance Metric Learning 954

Plenary Poster Session: Learning and optimization

- A new saliency measure for inputs selection and node pruning in neural network 960
- One-Step Neural Network Inversion with PDF Learning and Emulation 966
- Effective neural network pruning using cross-validation..972
- An Efficient Learning Algorithm for Finding Multiple Solutions Based on Fixed-Point Homotopy Method 978
- An Analysis of Overfitting in MLP Networks..984
- Experimental Evaluation of a Hybrid Method for Configuring Ensemble Encoding Receptors 989
- Dynamic construction of fault tolerant multi-layer neural networks 995
- The p-Center Machine 1000
- A Better Scaled Local Tangent Space Alignment Algorithm 1006
- Gaussian Processes of Nonlinear Diffusion Filtering 1012
- Fast Training of Multilayer Perceptrons with a Mixed Norm Algorithm 1018
- Decorrelating Parametrical Neural Network 1023
- Second-order backpropagation algorithms for a stagewise-partitioned separable Hessian matrix..1027
- Prediction of time to event for censored data: ridge regression with linear constraints in kernel space..1033
- A Threshold Varying Bisection Method for Cost Sensitive Learning in Neural Networks 1039
- A Single-Layer Radial Basis Function Network Classifier and Its Applications 1045
- OLS versus SVM approach to learning of RBF network 1051
- Designing RBF classifiers for weighted Boosting..1057
- Iterative Feature Weighting for Identification of Relevant Features with Radial Basis Function Networks 1063
- Sequential Neuron Pruning Algorithm for RBF Network with Guaranteed Stability.........1069
- Factors of Overtraining with Fuzzy ARTMAP Neural Networks 1075
- ART2 Based Classification of Sparse High Dimensional Parameter Sets For A Simulation Parameter Selection Assistant 1081
- Fuzzy PSO: A Generalization of Particle Swarm Optimization 1086
- Simulating A-Life Using Boltzmann Machines 1092
- Artificial Cognitive BP-CT Ant Routing Algorithm..1098
- Basic Property of a Quantum Neural Network Composed of Kane's Qubits...................1104
- Quantum Gauged Neural Networks: Learning and Recalling 1108

Plenary Poster Session: Mixture models and ensemble learning

- Stochastic Complexity of Variational Bayesian Hidden Markov Models 1114
- New Experiments on Ensembles of Multilayer Feedforward
  for Classification Problems 1120
- A Research on Combination Methods for Ensembles of Multilayer Feedforward 1125
- Dynamically Weighted Majority Voting for Incremental Learning and
  Comparison of Three Boosting Based Approaches 1131
- A Comparison of Combination Methods for Ensembles of RBF Networks 1137
- New Boosting Methods of Gaussian Processes for Regression 1142
- Learning Probability Density Functions from Marginal Distributions
  with Applications to Gaussian Mixtures 1148
- Evaluation of Cluster Combination Functions for Mixture of Experts 1154
- Mixture of Heterogeneous Experts Applied to Time Series: A Comparative Study 1160
- Classification and Verification through the Combination of the
  Multi-Layer Perceptron and Auto-Association Neural Networks 1166
- A Classifier Ensemble Model and Its Applications 1172

Plenary Poster Session: Self-organizing maps and associative memory

- Systematic Rewiring in Associative Neural Networks with Small-World Architecture 1178
- Motion Perception with Recurrent Self-Organizing Maps Based Models 1182
- Retrieval Property of Associative Memory with Negative Resistance 1187
- A Weighted Voting Model of Associative Memory: Theoretical Analysis 1193
- New Results on Binary Auto- and Heteroassociative Morphological Memories 1199
- Self-Organizing Neural Grove and Its Applications 1205
- Incremental growing neural gas learns topologies 1211
- Robust Continuous Learning in a WTA Neural Network for
  Clustering Symbol Strings 1217
- An Associative Memory for the Online Recognition and
  Prediction of Temporal Sequences 1223

Plenary Poster Session: Principal and independent component analysis

- Similar-Image Retrieval Systems Using ICA and PCA Bases 1229
- Blind Inversion of Wiener System for Single Source 1235
- Blind Separation of Convolved Sources using the Information
  Maximization Approach 1239
- BSS Toolbox for Delayed and Convolved Mixtures 1245
- Diagonally Weighted and Shifted Criteria for Minor and
  Principal Component Extraction 1251
- Analysis of Signal Separation and Signal Distortion in Feedforward
  and Feedback Blind Source Separation Based on Source Spectra 1257
- Weighted Rayleigh Quotients for Minor and Principal Component Extraction 1263

Plenary Poster Session: Probablistic and information theoretic methods

- Feature Ranking using Supervised Neural Gas and Informational Energy 1269
- An Improved Kernel Fisher Discriminant Classifier and Its Applications 1274
- An Optimal Entropy Estimator for Discrete Random Variables 1280
- Comparing ``Pattern Discovery'' and Back-Propagation Classifiers 1286

- Multivariate Regression Model Selection with KIC for Extrapolation Cases 1292
- Robust Information Clustering 1296
- Learning Nonlinear Constraints with Contrastive Backpropagation 1302
- Sequential Relevance Vector Machine Learning from Time Series 1308

Plenary Poster Session: Neural networks and evolutionary computation
- Performance Optimization of Function Localization Neural Network by Using Reinforcement Learning 1314
- Sparse Bayesian learning and the relevance multi-layer perceptron 1320
- Real-Coded Genetic Algorithm with Average-Bound Crossover and Wavelet Mutation for Network Parameters Learning 1325
- A Directional Multi-resolution Ridgelet Network 1331
- The Emergence of Verbs in an Artificial Life Simulation 1337
- A variable-parameter neural network trained by improved genetic algorithm and its application 1343
- Feature Subset Selection via Multi-Objective Genetic Algorithm 1349
- A Model of Baldwin Effect in Populations of Self-Learning Agents 1355
- Synthesis of Binary Cellular Automata based on Binary Neural Networks 1361
- Genetic Algorithm-Based Variable Translation Wavelet Neural Network and its Application 1365
- Evolution Strategies on Connection Weights into Modified Gradient Function for Multi-layer Neural Network 1371

Plenary Poster Session: Neural network architectures and structures
- Neural Network Initialization with Prototypes - A Case Study in Function Approximation 1377
- A Novel Radial Basis Function Network Classifier with Centers Set by Hierarchical Clustering 1383
- A Simple Hierarchical Approximation RBF Neural Network 1389
- The Evolving Tree, a Hierarchical Tool for Unsupervised Data Analysis 1395
- Optimization of Modular Neural Networks Using Hierarchical Genetic Algorithms Applied to Speech Recognition 1400
- Protein Sequence Classification Using Extreme Learning Machine 1406
- Analyzing the State Space Property of Echo State Networks for Chaotic System Prediction 1412
- Finding a Succinct Multi-layer Perceptron Having Shared Weights 1418

Tuesday, August 2, 2005

8:00 a.m.-9:00 a.m.
General Session
Functional Organization of the Primate Prefrontal Cortex for Memory 1424

9:30 a.m.-11:30 a.m.
SVM I

- A Simple Trick for Constructing Bayesian Formulations of Sparse Kernel Learning Methods 1425
- Efficient Parameter Selection for Support Vector Machines in Classification and Regression via Model-Based Global Optimization 1431
- Sequential Bootstrapped Support Vector Machines - A SVM Accelerator 1437
- Fbeta Support Vector Machines 1443
- Time Series Filtering, Smoothing and Learning using the Kernel Kalman Filter 1449
- A Combined SVM and LDA Approach for Classification 1455

9:30 a.m.-11:30 a.m.
Special Session: Computational Dynamical Modeling with Echo State Networks

- Reservoir Riddles: Suggestions for Echo State Network Research 1460
- Echo State Networks: Appeal and Challenges 1463
- Computing with Transiently Stable States 1467
- The Role of the RKH Space F in the Analysis and Design of Recurrent Neural Networks 1473
- Feed-forward Echo State Networks 1479
- Direct Adaptive Control: An Echo State Network and Genetic Algorithm Approach 1483

9:30 a.m.-11:30 a.m.
Evolutionary Algorithms and PSO

- Non-Linear Mappings Based on Particle Swarm Optimization 1487
- Evolutionary supervision of a dynamical neural network allows learning with on-going weights 1493
- Evolutionary Neural Classification for Evaluation of Retail Stores and Decision Support 1499
- BioAnt - Biologically Plausible Computer Simulation of an Environment with Ants 1505
- Optimizing Class-Related Thresholds with Particle Swarm Optimization 1511
- Lotto-Type Competitive Learning with Particle Swarm Features 1517

9:30 a.m.-11:30 a.m.
Special Session: Functional Neuroimaging of Cortical and Subcortical Functions

- Reorganization and Plasticity in the Adult Brain During Learning of Motor Skills 1523
- Cortico-Basal Ganglia Functional Connectivity Investigated with Transcranial Magnetic Stimulation 1525
- Heading For Data-Driven Measures of Effective Connectivity in Functional MRI 1528
- Connectivity of anatomical and functional MRI data 1534

1:00 p.m.-3:00 p.m.
Recurrent Neural Networks

- Dynamical Consistent Recurrent Neural Networks 1537
- Effectively Using Recurrently-Connected Spiking Neural Networks 1542
- Adaptive Flight Control with Living Neuronal Networks on Microelectrode Arrays 1548
- Introduction of an Hebbian unsupervised learning algorithm 1552

1:00 p.m.-3:00 p.m.
Self-Organizing Maps

- *A visualization technique for Self-Organizing Maps with vector fields to obtain the cluster structure at desired levels of detail* 1558
- *Multi-Topographic Neural Network Communication and Generalization for Multi-Viewpoint Analysis* 1564
- *A Self-Organizing Map for Concept Classification in Information Retrieval* 1570
- *Training the SOFM Efficiently: An Example from Intrusion Detection* 1575
- *Modular Network SOM (mnSOM): From Vector Space to Function Space* 1581
- *Ranked Centroid Projection: A Data Visualization Approach for Self-organizing Maps* 1587

1:00 p.m.-3:00 p.m.
Special Session: Transition: Imaging and Cortical Models

- *fMRI experiments and computational models of the function of the prefrontal cortex and the basal ganglia: a review* 1593
- *Computational Models of Emotion* 1598
- *Neural Networks of the Brain: Their Analysis and Relation to Brain Images* 1603
- *Brain Categorization: Learning, Attention, and Consciousness* 1609

1:00 p.m.-3:00 p.m.
Special Session: Applications of Learning and Data-Driven Methods to Earth Sciences and Climate Modeling

- *Complex Hybrid Models Combining Deterministic and Machine Learning Components as a New Synergetic Paradigm in Numerical Climate Modeling and Weather Prediction* 1615
- *Atmospheric correction and oceanic constituents retrieval with a neuro-variational method* 1621
- *Nonlinear Complex Principal Component Analysis and Its Applications* 1626
- *Nonlinear Principal Predictor Analysis Using Neural Networks* 1630
- *Temporal Neural Networks for Downscaling Climate Variability and Extremes* 1636
- *A Spatiotemporal Approach to Tornado Prediction* 1642

3:20 p.m.-5:20 p.m
Special Session: Models of Cortical and Subcortical Circuits

- *A computational model of reach decisions in the primate cerebral cortex* 1648
- *Modeling Cortico-Subcortical Interactions During Planning, Learning, and Voluntary Control of Actions* 1653
- *Modeling Emotional Influences on Human Decision Making Under Risk* 1657
- *Modelling the Interaction of Attention and Emotion* 1663

3:20 p.m.-5:20 p.m.
Visual and Image Processing
- *Neural Network Model for Analyzing Optic Flow* 1669
- *Face Detection and Identification Using a Hierarchical Feed-forward Recognition Architecture* 1675
- *Lossless High Dynamic Range Image Coding based on Lifting Scheme using Nonlinear Interpolative Effect of Discrete-Time Cellular Neural Networks* 1681
- *Could Early Visual Processes be Sufficient to Label Motions* 1687
- *A Phase-equation Model for a Large Phase Lead in Manual Tracking Caused by Intermittent Visual Information* 1693
- *Investigations into the Analysis of Remote Sensing Images with a Growing Neural Gas* 1698

3:20 p.m.-5:20 p.m.
Special Session: Applications of Learning and Data-Driven Methods to Earth Sciences and Climate Modeling (plus Panel Discussion)
- *Applications of Neural Network Methods to the Processing of Earth Observation Satellite Data* 1704
- *Time Dependent Neural Network Models For Detecting Changes Of State In Earth and Planetary Processes* 1710
- *Local and Hybrid Learning Models in Forecasting Natural Phenomena* 1716
- *Semiblind source separation of climate data detects El Nino as the component with the highest interannual variability* 1722
- *Panel discussion: Applications of Learning and Data-Driven Methods to Earth Sciences and Climate Modeling* 1728

3:20 p.m.-5:20 p.m.
Diagnostics and Control, Power Systems
- *Continuous On-line Identification of Nonlinear Plants in Power Systems with Missing Sensor Measurements* 1729
- *Collective Behavior Implementation in Powerline Surveillance Sensor Network* 1735
- *Neural Networks based Scheme for Fault Diagnosis in Fossil Electric Power Plants* 1740
- *Detection of Actuator Faults Using a Dynamic Neural Network for the Attitude Control Subsystem of a Satellite* 1746
- *Dynamic Bayesian Networks for Machine Diagnostics: Hierarchical Hidden Markov Models vs. Competitive Learning* 1752
- *Fuzzy Multi-Hidden Markov Predictor in Electric Load Forecasting* 1758

7:00 p.m.-11:00 p.m.
Plenary Interactive Session II

Plenary Poster Session: Fuzzy neural systems
- *Flexible Takagi-Sugeno Fuzzy Systems* 1764
- *A New Scene Analysis Using Genetic Algorithm Based Fuzzy ID3 Method* 1770
- *A Comparative Study of the IDS method and Feedforward Neural Networks* 1776

Plenary Poster Session: Vision and image processing

- *Edge Inference for Image Interpolation* 1782
- *Image Recognition Systems with Permutative Coding*..1788
- *A Modified Frequency Domain Cross Correlation Implemented in MATLAB for Fast Sub-Image Detection Using Neural Networks*..1794
- *A Motion Trajectory Based Video Retrieval System Using Parallel Adaptive Self Organizing Maps* 1800
- *Learning Informative Features for Spatial Histogram-Based Object Detection* 1806
- *A Hierarchical Bayesian Model of Invariant Pattern Recognition in the Visual Cortex*......1812
- *Text Extraction from Name Cards Using Neural Network* 1818
- *Visual Deficiency: Cognitive Performance and Adaptive Image Processing* 1824
- *On Using an Associative Memory for Improving Digital Color Images: Color Characterization, Enhancement, and Color Balancing*..................................1830
- *General Design Approach to Unit-linking PCNN for Image Processing*..........................1836
- *Model of Neuron-Like Systems. Examples of Dynamic Processes*.................................1842
- *Temporal Hand Gesture Recognition By Fuzzified TSK-Type Recurrent Fuzzy Network*..1848
- *Using Knowledge of the Region of Interest (ROI) in Automatic Image Retrieval Learning* 1854
- *Using Independent Subspace Analysis to Build Independent Spectral Representations of Images*...1860
- *Natural Image Compression Using An Extended Non-Negative Sparse Coding Neural Network Technique*..1866
- *Object Recognition Using Neurocomputing and Conformal Computing Geometry* 1872

Plenary Poster Session: Biometric, handwriting and other pattern recognition

- *A Robust Deterministic Annealing Algorithm for Data Clustering* 1878
- *Pruning Support Vectors for Imbalanced Data Classification*..1883
- *Normalized Neural Networks for Fast Pattern Detection* 1889
- *Optimal Kernels for Unsupervised Learning*..1895
- *Fast Pattern Detection Using Neural Networks and Cross Correlation in the Frequency Domain* 1900
- *Estimating Accurate Multi-class Probabilities with Support Vector Machines* 1906
- *Modular General Hyperline Segment Neural Network*..1912
- *Fourier Fuzzy Neural Network for Clustering of Objects Based on the Gross Shape and its Application to Handwritten Character Recognition*.......................1918
- *Third-order generalization and a new approach to systematically categorizing higher-order generalization*..1924
- *Low Complexity Iris Recognition Based on Wavelet Probabilistic Neural Networks* 1930
- *Efficient Video Object Classifier using Locality-Enhanced Support Vector Machines* 1936
- *A Comparative Analysis of the Performance of Hybrid and Non-Hybrid Multi-classifier Systems*...1941
- *Pattern Classification by Assembling Small Neural Networks* 1947
- *A Symbolic Approach to the Solution of F-Classification Problems*................................1953
- *Optical Flame Detection Using Large-Scale Artificial Neural Networks*...........................1959

- An Experimental Study of Several Decision Issues for Feature Selection with Multi-Layer Perceptrons 1965
- Spectral Feature Analysis.................1971
- Self-Adaptive Kernel Machine: Online Clustering in RKHS 1977
- An Algorithm for Pruning Redundant Modules in Min-Max Modular Network 1983
- A Novel Fuzzy Clustering Neural Network 1989

Plenary Poster Session: Face and texture recognition
- Performance of Neural Classifiers for Fabric Faults Classification.................1995
- Orientated Texture Segmentation for Detecting Defects 2001
- Modification of Correlation Kernels in SVM, KPCA and KCCA in Texture Classification.................2006
- Neural Network-based Shape Recognition using Generalized Differential Evolution Training Algorithm 2012
- The Effect of Normal Adult Aging on Standard PCA Face Recognition Accuracy Rates 2018
- Face Recognition Method Independent of Rotation and Size Variations 2024
- Combined Subspace Method Using Global and Local Features for Face Recognition 2030

Plenary Poster Session: Audition, speech recognition and production
- Low Order Modeling for Multiple Moving Sound Synthesis using Head-related Transfer Functions' Principal Basis Vectors 2036
- Individualized HRTFs From Few Measurements: a Statistical Learning Approach 2041
- Framewise Phoneme Classification with Bidirectional LSTM Networks.................2047
- Discriminative Training of Hidden Markov Models by Multiobjective Optimization for Visual Speech Recognition 2053
- Harmonic Envelope Prediction for Realistic Speech Synthesis Using Kernel Interpolation 2059
- A Soft Bayes Perceptron 2064
- Chaos and Speech Rhythm 2070
- Exploration of Rank Order Coding with Spiking Neural Networks for Speech Recognition 2076

Plenary Poster Session: Nose, tactile, taste and other senses
- A comparative study of neural network to artificial noses 2081
- Optimization of a learning algorithm for tactile pattern generation 2087
- A Combinative Function Approximation Model and Its Applications to Electronic Noses 2093
- A Novel Hybrid Learning Scheme For Pattern Recognition 2099

Plenary Poster Session: Cognitive function
- Convergence of Coherent Components of Neural Networks by Positive Correlation Learning.................2105
- Learning of an XOR Problem in the Presence of Noise and Redundancy 2111
- A Multiple BAM for Hetero-association and Multisensory Integration Modelling 2117
- Effect of Curriculum on the Consolidation of Neural Network Task Knowledge.................2123

- Creation of Long-term Mental Representations using the
  Dimension of Fractal dendrites 2129
- Neurobiological Data Sustaining Opponent Processing Operations on Self
  Organizing Networks as Tools for the Modeling of Hippocampal Dynamics 2135
- Neural Network Approaches to Personal Change in Psychotherapy 2139

Plenary Poster Session: Computational neuroscience

- Role of Presynaptic Reuptake on Dopamine Modulation of
  Cortico-striatal Activity in TD Learning 2145
- Two state transitions mediated by spontaneous and/or intensive stimulus
  on an integrate-and-fire neural network model 2150
- Learning with Single Integrate-and-Fire Neuron 2156
- Optimizing Neural Model Templates using Covariance Matrix Adaptation
  and Fourier Analysis 2162
- Fast Constructive-Covering Approach for Neural Networks 2167
- Ensembles of membrane proteins as statistical mixed-signal computers 2173
- Towards the Modeling of Dissociated Cortical Tissue in the Liquid State
  Machine Framework 2179
- The Bifurcating Neuron Network 2184
- Spiking Neural Network Training Using Evolutionary Algorithms 2190
- Increased Swimming Control with Evolved Lamprey CPG Controllers 2195

Plenary Poster Session: Signal processing and time series analysis

- Modified Time-Based Multilayer Perceptron for Sensor Networks and
  Image Processing Applications 2201
- On-line Bayesian Change Detection Scheme for Unknown Nonlinear
  Systems via Sequential Monte Carlo 2207
- Independent Component Analysis Applications in Physics 2213
- Embedded FastICA Algorithm Applied to the Sensor Noise Extraction
  Problem of Foundation Fieldbus Network 2217
- Design of Neural Predictors using Tools of Chaos Theory and Bayesian
  Learning 2222
- Harmonic Detection using Wavelet Transforms 2228
- A Recurrent Neural Network for Sound-Source Motion Tracking and Prediction 2232

Plenary Poster Session: Control and robotics

- Artificial neural networks associated to calorimetry to preview polymer
  composition of high solid content emulsion copolymerizations 2237
- Supply Air Temperature Control of AHU with a Cascade Control Strategy
  and a SPSA Based Neural Controller 2243
- Design and stabilization of sampled-data neural-network-based control systems 2249
- Real-time Control of Variable Air Volume System Using a
  SPSA Based Neural Controller 2255
- Discrete-Time Systems Neuro-Riccati Equation Solution 2261
- Predictive Control Based on Feedforward Neural Network
  for Strong Nonlinear System 2266
- Design and Experimental Evaluation of a 3-Mass Speed Control System
  with a Hybrid Structure of Sliding Mode Controller and CMAC 2272

- Total Sliding-mode-based Genetic Algorithm Control for Linear Piezoelectric Ceramic Motor Drive 2278
- Adaptive Tanaka-Sugeno Fuzzy Cerebellar Model Articulation Controller for Output Tracking Control 2284
- Robust Output Tracking CMAC Control: The T-S Fuzzy Model-Based Approach 2290
- Prototype Robotic Arm Assisted by Smart CMOS Vision Chips 2296

Plenary Poster Session: Diagnostics and quality control

- A framework for the verification of air quality forecasting models using self-organizing feature maps 2302
- Bayesian Neural Networks for Nonlinear Multivariate Manufacturing Process Monitoring 2308
- Feature Selection and Condition Monitoring of Gearbox Using SOM 2313
- Engine Data Classification with Simultaneous Recurrent Network Using a Hybrid PSO-EA Algorithm 2319
- An Automatic Method to Detect Missing Components in Manufactured Products 2324
- Cosmetic Defect Classification Found in Ophthalmic Lenses Using Artificial Neural Networks 2330
- A Neuro-Fuzzy Based Sensor and Actuator Fault Estimation Scheme for Unknown Nonlinear Systems 2335
- Aircraft Cabin Noise Minimization via Neural Network Inverse Model 2341
- Dynamic Neural Network-based Estimator for Fault Diagnosis in Reaction Wheel Actuator of Satellite Attitude Control System 2347

Plenary Poster Session: Telecommunication applications

- Modeling of Spiral Inductors Using Artificial Neural Network 2353
- Sparse Channel Estimation With Regularization Method Using Convolution Inequality For Entropy 2359
- A Neural Phase Rotator for PAPR Reduction of PCC-OFDM Signal 2363
- Further Results on the EKF-CRTRL Equalizer for Fast Fading and Frequency Selective Channels 2367
- Hybrid Neural-Phenomenological Sub-Models and its Application to Earth-space Path Signal Attenuation Prediction 2372
- Application of Neural Networks to 3G Power Amplifier Modeling 2378

Plenary Poster Session: Heart applications

- Bayesian ANN Classifier for ECG Arrhythmia Diagnostic System: A Comparison Study 2383
- Input and Data Selection Applied to Heart Disease Diagnosis 2389
- Reliable Determination of Sleep Versus Wake from Heart Rate Variability Using Neural Networks 2394
- Neural Network Based Detection of Fetal Heart Rate Patterns 2400

Plenary Poster Session: Pharmacology and disease diagnosis

- Exploratory Data Analysis of Dynamic Cerebral Contrast—Enhanced Perfusion MRI Time—Series 2406

- A Neural Network-based Prediction Model of AR Inhibitory Activity from a Sparse Set of Compounds 2411
- Multi-class Support Vector Machines for Modeling HIV/AIDS Treatment Adherence using Patient Data 2417
- Neural network-based approach for the classification of wireless-capsule endoscopic images 2423
- The Use of Clustering to Analyze Symptom-Based Case Definitions for Acute Gastrointestinal Illness 2429
- A SVM Approach for Detection of Hemorrhages in Background Diabetic Retinopathy 2435
- QRS Complex Detection Using Backpropagation Neural Network (no files)
- Dynamic Feature Fusion in the Self Organising Tree Map - applied to the segmentation of Biofilm Images 2441

Plenary Poster Session: Brain imaging and brain interfaces

- Independent Component Analysis and High-Order Statistics for Automatic Artifact Rejection 2447
- A Neural Supergraph Matching Architecture 2453
- Comparison of TDNN Training Algorithms in Brain Machine Interfaces 2459
- An Algorithm for Automatic Assignment of Artifact-Related Independent Components in Biomedical SIgnal Analysis 2463

Plenary Poster Session: Application to cancer diagnostics

- Computational Intelligence Techniques for Acute Leukemia Gene Expression Data Classification 2469
- Virtual Reality Visual Data Mining with Nonlinear Discriminant Neural Networks: Application to Leukemia and Alzheimer Gene Expression Data 2475
- SVMs Applied to Objective Aesthetic Evaluation of Conservative Breast Cancer Treatment 2481
- Classification of Breast Abnormalities in Digital Mammograms using Image and BI-RADS Features in Conjunction with Neural Network 2487
- Feasibility of multi-layered perceptron network in discriminating breast magnetic resonance imaging lesions 2493
- Automatic recognition of the blood cells of myelogenous leukemia using SVM 2496

Plenary Poster Session: Electroencephalograms and electromyograms

- Neural Network Classification of EEG Signals using Time-Frequency Representation 2502
- ICA And a Gauge of Filter for the Automatic Filtering of an EEG Signal 2508
- On the Use of Clustering and Local Singular Spectrum Analysis to Remove Ocular Artifacts from Electroencephalograms 2514
- A Fuzzy Approach for Key Variables Identification of EMG Evaluation System 2520
- Extraction of event related potentials from EEG signals using ICA with reference 2526
- PCA and ICA for the Extraction of EEG Dominant Components in Cerebral Death Assessment 2532

Plenary Poster Session: Financial and marketing applications

- Vector Quantized Radial Basis Function Neural Network with Embedded Multiple Local Linear Models for Financial Prediction 2538
- Application of Multi-Branch Neural Networks to Stock Market Prediction 2544
- Data Preprocessing for Stock Market Forecasting using Random Subspace Classifier Network 2549
- Predicting Customer Behavior via Calling Links.................2555

Plenary Poster Session: Computer security, military and biomimetic applications

- A Novel Image Retrieval System Based on BP Neural Network 2561
- Speaker Identification Using Speech and Lip Features 2565
- Comparison of a SOM Based Sequence Analysis System and Naive Bayesian Classifier for Spam Filtering 2571
- Neural Networks Following a Binary Approach Applied to the Integer Prime-Factorization Problem 2577
- Artificial Intelligence for Conflict Management 2583
- Fingerprint Recognition Using Modular Neural Networks and Fuzzy Integrals for Response Integration.................2589
- Chaotic Associative Memory and Private V-mails 2595
- Using Domain Knowledge to Constrain Structure Learning in a Bayesian Bioagent Detector 2601

Plenary Poster Session: Power systems applications

- Power System Reduced Model by Artificial Neural Networks 2607
- FPGA Realization of Power Quality Disturbance Detection: An Approach with Wavelet, ANN and Fuzzy Logic.................2613
- Short Term Load Forecasting for Iran National Power System and Its Regions Using Multi Layer Perceptron and Fuzzy Inference systems.................2619
- Artificial Neural Networks for Temporal Processing Applied to Prediction of Electric Energy Generation in Small Hydroelectric Power Stations 2625
- Streamflow forecasting using neural networks and fuzzy clustering techniques 2631

Plenary Poster Session: Special Session - Earth Sciences & Climate modeling

- Neural Network Modelling of the 20-Year Flood Event for 850 Catchments Across the UK 2637
- Modelling Harbour Sedimentation Using ANN and M5 Model Trees 2643
- Classification of Infrasound Events Using Using Radial Basis Function Neural Networks 2649
- Neural Network River Discharge Forecasters: An Empirical Investigation of Hidden Unit Processing Functions Based on Two Different Catchments.................2655
- Robustness of the NN Approach to Emulating Atmospheric Long Wave Radiation in Complex Climate Models 2661
- A Comparative Study of Artificial Neural Network Techniques for River Stage Forecasting.................2666
- Issues in Designing Automated Minimal Resource Allocation Neural Networks 2671
- Wavelet Networks: An Alternative to Classical Neural Networks 2674
- Streamflow Forecasting with Uncertainty Estimate Using Bayesian Learning for ANN....2680

- *Intelligent systems for meteorological events forecas* 2686
- *A multilayer perceptron approach for the retrieval of vertical temperature profiles from satellite radiation data* 2689
- *Machine Learning in Soil Classification* 2694
- *Estimation of Prediction Intervals for the Model Outputs using Machine Learning* 2700

Plenary Poster Session: Earth Sciences and Climate modelling
- *Determination of optimal batch size in incremental approach for tornado detection* 2706
- *Locally Recurrent Neural Networks Optimal Filtering Algorithms: Application to Wind Speed Prediction Using Spatial Correlation* 2711

Wednesday, August 3, 2005

8:00 a.m.-9;00 a.m.
General Session
Neural Networks for Feedback Control of Robots and Dynamical Systems 2717

9:30 a.m.-11:30 a.m.
Data Mining
- *Automatic Source Attribution: A Neural Networks Approach* 2718
- *Cross-Entropy Approach to Data Visualization Based on the Neural Gas Network* 2724
- *A Model of Document Clustering Using Ant Colony Algorithm and Validity Index* 2730
- *A method to extract Non-Linear Principal Components of Large Datasets - An application in Skill Transfer* 2736
- *Identifying knowledge domain and incremental new class learning in SVM* 2742
- *Real-World Text Clustering with Adaptive Resonance Theory Neural Networks* 2748

9:30 a.m.-11:30 a.m.
Special Session: Hebb's Legacy
- *Hebbian Synaptic Modification in Cortical Circuits and Memory-Guided Behavior in Spatial Alternation and Delayed Non-Match to Position* 1754
- *Faithful Retinotopic Maps with Local Optimum Rules, Axonal Competition, and Hebbian Learning* 2760
- *Modeling Structural Plasticity in the Barn Owl Auditory Localization System with a Spike-Time Dependent Hebbian Learning Rule* 2766
- *Hebbian motor control in a robot-embedded model of habituation* 2772

9:30 a.m.-11;30 a.m.
Robotics
- *Constraints on Body Movement during Visual Development Affect Behavior of Evolutionary Robots* 2778

- Dual Kalman Filters for Autonomous Terrain Aided Navigation
  in Unknown Environments 2784
- New Memory Model for Humanoid Robots -Introduction of
  Co-Associative Memory Using Mutually Coupled Chaotic Neural Networks 2790
- Bi-Criteria Torque Optimization of Redundant Manipulators Based
  on a Simplified Dual Neural Network 2796
- Spatio-Temporal Neural Data Mining Architecture in Learning Robots 2802
- Fault-tolerance by Regeneration: Using Development to Achieve
  Robust Self-Healing Neural Networks 2808

9:30 a.m.-11:30 a.m.
<u>SVM II</u>
- Maximal Variation and Missing Values for Componentwise Support Vector Machines 2814
- Fast Bayesian Support Vector Machine Parameter Tuning with the Nystrom Method 2820
- Maximum Margin Classifiers with Noisy Data: A Robust Optimization 2826
- Data Classification with a Relaxed Model of Variable Kernel Density Estimation 2831
- A Ridgelet Kernel Approach for Regression using
  Particle Swarm Optimization Algorithm 2837

1:00 p.m.-3:00 p.m.
<u>Hardware</u>
- Ultra Low Power Fault Tolerant Neural Inspired CMOS logic.....................................2843
- Noise Performance of Single-Electron Depressing
  Synapses for Neuronal Synchrony Detection..2849
- A New Pulse Mode Self Organizing Map Hardware with
  Digital Phase Locked Loops 2855
- A novel Approach to reduce Interconnect Complexity in
  ANN Hardware Implementation 2861
- A Reconfigurable Parallel Architecture for SVM Classification....................................2867

1:00 p.m.-3:00 p.m.
<u>Cognitive Function</u>
- An Integrate and Fire Model of Prefrontal Cortex provides a
  Biological Implementation of Action Selection in Reinforcement
  Learning Theory that Reuses Known Representations 2873
- Knowing your place: Subfield specific involvement in
  hippocampal spatial processing 2879
- Coherent learning in cortical maps: A generic approach 2885
- Using Neural Dynamics to Switch Attention...2891
- A Continuous Attractor Neural Network Model of Divided Visual Attention 2897
- Bridging the Gap Between Vision and Language:
  A Morphodynamical Model of Spatial Categories 2903

1:00 p.m.-3:00 p.m.
Special Session: Performance of Neuro-Adaptive and Learning Systems: Assessment, Monitoring and Validation
- Challenges in verification and validation of autonomous systems for space exploration 2909
- Rule Extraction as a Formal Method for the Verification and Validation of Neural Networks 2915
- An Approach To Predicting Non-Deterministic Neural Network Behavior 2921
- Testing Decision Systems with Classification Components 2927
- Validity Index in Dynamic Cell Structures 2931
- A Disturbance Rejection based Neural Network Algorithm for Control of Air Pollution Emissions 2937

1:00 p.m.-3:00 p.m.
Special Session: Constructive/Hierarchical Self-Organizing Maps
- A Gradient Descending Solution to the LASSO Criteria 2942
- A Constructive and Hierarchical Self-Organising Model in A Non-Stationary Environment 2948
- Investigation of Alternative Strategies and Quality Measures for Controlling the Growth Process of the Growing Hierarchical Self-Organizing Map 2954
- A hierarchical hybrid neural model with time integrators in long-term peak-load forecasting 2960
- Introduction to the SAM-SOM* and MAM-SOM* Families 2966

3:20 p.m.-5:20 p.m.
Special Session: Approximate Dynamic Programming
- Reinforcement Learning and the Frame Problem 2971
- An Analysis of Gradient-Based Policy Iteration 2977
- An Integrated Fault Tolerant Control Framework Using Adaptive Critic Design 2983
- Approximate Dynamic Programming for High Dimensional Resource Allocation Problems 2989
- Modeling Reward Functions for Incomplete State Representations via Echo State Networks 2995
- Continuous Adaptive Critic Desigs 3001

3:20 p.m.-5:20 p.m.
Biomedical Applications
- Classification of Plantar Pressure and Heel Acceleration Patterns Using Neural Networks 3007
- Feature Selection by Independent Component Analysis and Mutual Information Maximization in EEG Signal Classification 3011
- Neural Network and Principal Component Analyses of Highly Variable Myocardial Mechanical Waveforms Derived from Echocardiographic Ultrasound Images 3017
- A Recurrent Fuzzy-Neural Filter for Real-Time Separation of Lung Sounds 3023
- Stochastic Feature Selection for the Discrimination of Biomedical Spectra 3029
- Ovarian Cancer Diagnosis Using Complementary Learning Fuzzy Neural Network 3034

3:20 p.m.-5:20 p.m.
Fuzzy-Neural Systems
- Fuzzy ROC Curves for Unsupervised Nonparametric Ensemble Techniques 3040
- Neural Network with Fuzzy Dynamic Logic 3046
- Color Image Segmentation Using Fuzzy Min-Max Neural Networks..............................3052
- Skin Color Segmentation by Histogram-Based Neural Fuzzy Network 3058
- Learning a Hierarchical Fuzzy System with Autonomous Navigation as an Example......3063

3:20 p.m.-5:20 p.m.
Special Session: Biologically Inspired Computational Vision
- A Biologically Inspired Computational Vision Front-end based on a
  Self-Organised Pseudo-Randomly Tessellated Artificial Retina......................................3069
- A Chaos Synchronization-Based Dynamic Vision Model for Image Segmentation 3075
- Processing Landsat TM Data Using Complex-Valued NRBF Neural Network..................3081
- Comparison of Linear and Non-linear Data Projection Techniques
  in Recognizing Universal Facial Expressions..3087
- Associative neural networks as means for low-resolution video-based recognition 3093

Thursday, August 4, 2005

8:00 a.m.-9:00 a.m.
General Session
Beyond Correlation – Closing the Loop Between Brain and Theory by Extracting
Representations and Altered Feedbacks 3099

9:30 a.m.-11:30 a.m.
Special Session: Neural Prostheses and the Neuron-Silicon Interface
- Artificial Vision by Electrical Stimulation of the Retina 3100
- Physiological Activation of the Hind Limb Muscles of the
  Anesthetized Cat Using the Utah Slanted Electrode Array 3103
- Replacing Damaged Brain Regions with Biomimetic Microelectronic
  Neural Prostheses to Restore Cognitive Function 3109
- Getting Better Signals Out of the Brain: Decoding Algorithms
  and Autonomous Electrodes 3115
- Application of Polymer Microstructures with Controlled Surface Chemistries
  as a Platform for Creating and Interfacing with Synthetic Neural Networks 3116

9:30 a.m.-11:30 a.m.
Applications I
- An Experimental Comparison of Semi-Supervised ARTMAP
  Architectures, GCS and GNG Classifiers..3121
- Time Series Study of GGAP-RBF Network: Predictions of
  Nasdaq Stock and Nitrate Contamination of Drinking Water 3127
- Environmental Informatics - Long-Lead Flood Forecasting
  Using Bayesian Neural Networks 3133
- Detection of Disease Outbreaks in Pharmaceutical Sales:
  Neural Networks and Threshold Algorithms..3138

- A Fast Neural Network-Based Detection and Tracking of Dim Moving
  Targets in FLIR Imagery 3144
- GETnet: A General Framework for Evolutionary Temporal Neural Networks....................3150

9:30 a.m.-11:30 a.m.
Neurodynamics
- Temporal Discontinuities in Neocortical Dynamics..3156
- Stability Conditions of the full KII Model of Excitatory and Inhibitory
  Neural Populations 3162
- Associative Memory in the Strong Coupling Regime
  of a K-set Oscillator Network (no file)
- Evolving High Capacity Associative Memories with Efficient Wiring 3168

9:30 a.m.-11:30 a.m.
Learning I
- Incremental Learning for Online Face Recognition 3174
- Efficient Online Spherical K-means Clustering 3180
- On Efficient Selection of Binary Classifiers for Min-Max Modular Classifier 3186
- Are ARIMA Neural Network Hybrids Better than Single Models 3192
- Embedding via clustering: Using spectral information to
  guide dimensionality reduction..3198
- On the Evaluation of Relevance Learning by a Multi-layer Perceptron 3204

1:00 p.m.-3:00 p.m.
Telecommunications
- A Hybrid Neural Network for Optimal TDMA Transmission
  Scheduling in Packet Radio Networks 3210
- Nonlinear Channel Equalization with QAM Signal Using
  Chebyshev Artificial Neural Network 3214
- Implementation of an MLP-based DOA System Using a
  Reduced Number of MM-wave Antenna Elements 3220
- Least-Squares Support Vector Machines for DOA Estimation:
  A Step-by-Step Description and Sensitivity Analysis 3226
- Recurrent Neural Equalization for Communication
  Channels in Impulsive Noise Environments 3232

1:00 p.m.-3:00 p.m.
Neuromorphic Hardware
- A New Hybrid Neural System Interfacing Neurons and Silicon
  Hardware for Fast Signal Recognition 3238
- Biologically plausible VLSI neural network implementation with
  asynchronous neuron and spike-based synapse 3244
- Novel Digital Spiking Neuron and its Pulse-Coupled Network:
  Spike Position Coding and Multiplex Communication 3249
- Digital Implementation of a Bio-inspired Neural Model for Motion Estimation 3255
- Emulation Engine for Spiking Neurons and Adaptive Synaptic Weights 3261
- An Orientation-Selective Multi-chip aVLSI Applicable to Texture Analysis......................3267

1:00 p.m.-3:00 p.m.
Applications II
- Information-Theoretic Feature Selection Algorithms for Text Classification 3272
- SOM Based Image Data Structuring in an Augmented Reality Scenario 3278
- Forecasting Energy Product Prices 3284
- Reinforcement Learning Approach to Individualization of Chronic Pharmacotherapy 3290
- "Cognitive" Memory 3296

1:00 p.m.-3:00 p.m.
Learning II
- Hierarchical Fast Learning Artificial Neural Network 3300
- Non-Homogenous Structures in Neural Networks with Chaotic Recursive Nodes: Dealing with Diverse Multi-assemblies Architectures, Connectivity and Arbitrary Bifurcating Nodes 3306
- Improved Chaotic Neuro-Computer with Output-Coding for Quadratic Assignment Problems 3312
- Chaotic Associative Memory using Internal Patterns for Image Retrieval by Color and Shape Information 3318
- Transient Dynamics of Non-Linear Models Describing Multi-Stable Stochastic Systems 3324
- How to Find Different Neural Networks by Negative Correlation Learning 3330

3:20 p.m.-4:20 p.m.
General Session
Neuromophic Engineering: Overview and Potential 3334

DETAILED PROGRAM

Sunday, July 31, 9:00AM-11:00AM

Tutorial: Evolutionary Robotics
Sunday, July 31, 9:00AM-11:00AM, Room: Lachine, Instructor: Dario Floreano

Tutorial: Bioinfomatics and Machine Learning: the Prediction of Protein Structures on a Genomic Scale
Sunday, July 31, 9:00AM-11:00AM, Room: Mt Royal, Instructor: Pierre Baldi

Sunday, July 31, 11:15AM-1:15PM

Tutorial: Neural Networks That Actually Work In Prediction and Decision/Control: Common Misconceptions Versus Real-World Success
Sunday, July 31, 11:15AM-1:15PM, Room: Lachine, Instructor: Paul Werbos

Tutorial: Feature Extraction in Computational Intelligence
Sunday, July 31, 11:15AM-1:15PM, Room: Verdun, Instructor: Evangelia Micheli-Tzanakou

Tutorial: Integrating Language and Cognition: New Results in Computational Intelligence
Sunday, July 31, 11:15AM-1:15PM, Room: Mt Royal, Instructor: Leonid Perlovsky

Tutorial: Evolving Connectionist Systems for Adaptive Learning and Knowledge Discovery: Principles, Models and Applications
Sunday, July 31, 11:15AM-1:15PM, Room: Hampstead, Instructor: Nik Kasabov

Sunday, July 31, 2:30PM-4:30PM

Tutorial: Neural Networks for Dynamic Systems Feedback
Sunday, July 31, 2:30PM-4:30PM, Room: Lachine, Instructor: Frank Lewis

Tutorial: Unsupervised Learning
Sunday, July 31, 2:30PM-4:30PM, Room: Verdun, Instructor: Harold Szu

Tutorial: New Formulations for Predictive Learning
Sunday, July 31, 2:30PM-4:30PM, Room: Mt Royal, Instructor: Vladimir Cherkassky

Tutorial: Data Visualization of High Dimensional Scientific Data
Sunday, July 31, 2:30PM-4:30PM, Room: Hampstead, Instructor: A. Staiano and R. Tagliaferri

Sunday, July 31, 4:45PM-6:45PM

Tutorial: Cognitive Memory
Sunday, July 31, 4:45PM-6:45PM, Room: Lachine, Instructor: Bernard Widrow

Tutorial: Nonlinear Manifolds in Pattern Recognition and Image Analysis
Sunday, July 31, 4:45PM-6:45PM, Room: Verdun, Instructor: A. Srivastava X. Liu and W. Mio

Tutorial: Support Vector Machines and Kernel Based Learning
Sunday, July 31, 4:45PM-6:45PM, Room: Mt Royal, Instructor: Johan A. K. Suykens

Tutorial: Biologically Plausible Artificial Neural Networks
Sunday, July 31, 4:45PM-6:45PM, Room: Hampstead, Instructor: João Luís Garcia Rosa

Monday, August 1, 8:00AM-9:00AM

Plenary Talk: Exploring Chemical Space with Computers: Challenges and Opportunities
Monday, August 1, 8:00AM-9:00AM, Room: Westmount/Outremont, Speaker: Pierre Baldi, University of California, Irvine, United States

Small molecules with at most a few dozen atoms play a fundamental role in organic chemistry and biology. They can be used as combinatorial building blocks for chemical synthesis, as molecular probes for perturbing and analyzing biological systems, and for the screening/design/discovery of new drugs. As datasets of small molecules become increasingly available, it becomes important to develop computational methods for the classification and analysis of small molecules and in particular for the prediction of their physical, chemical, and biological properties. We will describe datasets and machine learning methods, in particular kernel methods, for chemical molecules represented by 1D strings, 2D graphs of bonds, and 3D structures. We will demonstrate state-of-the-art results for the prediction of physical, chemical, or biological properties including the prediction of toxicity and anti-cancer activity. More broadly, we will discuss some of the challenges and opportunities for computer science, AI, and machine learning in chemistry.

Monday, August 1, 9:30AM-11:30AM

Pattern Recognition
Monday, August 1, 9:30AM-11:30AM, Room: Verdun/Lachine, Chair: David Casasent

9:30AM *Automatic Target Recognition Using New Support Vector Machine [#1052]*
David Casasent and Yu-Chiang Wang, Dept ECE, Carnegie Mellon University, United States

A hierarchical classifier using a new SVRDM (support vector representation and discrimination machine) is proposed for automatic target recognition. An accuracy and distance-based method is used to design a hierarchical classifier. Our SVRDM hierarchical classifier has the ability to reject unseen non-object classes and clutter inputs. Uses of both iconic and spatial frequency domain features are considered. Initial recognition and rejection test results on infra-red (IR) data are excellent.

9:50AM *Training with Heterogeneous Data [#1039]*
John Drakopoulos and Ahmad Abdulkader, Microsoft Corporation, United States

Data pruning and ordered training are two methods used to train a learner with heterogeneous data. The former is a typical procedure that attempts to factor out noise from the data; the latter is a novel method that partitions the data into a number of categories and assigns training times to those assuming that data size and training time have a polynomial relation. In its current form, ordered training is an approximate and a priori data-emphasizing method. Both methods have been applied to a time-delay neural network--which is one of the main learners in Microsoft's Tablet PC handwriting recognition system. Their effect on the learner is presented in this paper. The handwriting data and the chosen language are Italian.

10:10AM *Tracking the States of a Nonlinear System in the Weight-Space of a Feed-Forward Neural Network [#1057]*
Takahiro Emoto, Masatake Akutagawa, Udantha Abeyratne, Hirofumi Nagashino and Yohsuke Kinouchi, University of Tokushima, Japan; University of Queensland, Australia

Nonlinear, non-stationary signals are commonly found in a variety of disciplines such as biology, medicine, geology and financial modeling. The complexity (eg. nonlinearity and non-stationarity) of such signals and their low signal to noise ratios often make it a challenging task to use them in critical applications. In this paper we propose a new neural network based technique to address those problems. We show that a feed forward, multi-layered neural network can conveniently capture the states of a nonlinear system in its connection weight-space, after a process of supervised training. The performance of the proposed method is investigated via computer simulations.

10:30AM *Data-Dependent Kernels for High-Dimensional Data Classification [#1184]*
Jingdong Wang, James T. Kwok, Helen C. Shen and Long Quan, The Hong Kong University of Science and Technoly, Hong Kong; Hong Kong University of Science and Technology, Hong Kong

For high-dimensional data classification problems such as face recognition, one of the most efficient classifiers is the Nearest Neighbor (NN) classifier. The kernel method is one of the efficient methods for extracting features. However, the selection of kernel parameters is still difficult. In this paper, we propose a so-called data dependent kernel (DDK) which is defined by generalizing the Gaussian kernel. Also an efficient and practical method is presented to calculate the DDK parameters. Moreover, one DDK based on subspaces is given to improve the recognition performance. Experiments show that the proposed DDK can achieve promising classification performance in face recognition and SPECT heart diagnosis.

10:50AM *Generalized 2D Principal Component Analysis [#1209]*
Hui Kong, Xuchun Li, Lei Wang, Eam Khwang Teoh, Jian Gang Wang and Venkateswarlu Ronda, Nanyang Technological University, Singapore; Institute for Infocomm Research, Singapore

Recently, a Two-Dimensional Principal Component Analysis (2DPCA) \cite{2DPCA} was proposed and the authors have demonstrated its superiority over the conventional Principal Component Analysis (PCA) in face recognition. But the theoretical proof why 2DPCA is better than PCA has not been given until now. In this paper, The essence of 2DPCA is analyzed and a framework of Generalized 2D Principal Component Analysis (G2DPCA) is proposed to extend the original 2DPCA in two perspectives: a Bilateral-projection-based 2DPCA (B2DPCA) and a Kernel-based 2DPCA (K2DPCA) schemes are introduced. Experimental results in face recognition show its excellent performance.

11:10AM *Optimal Gradient-Based Learning Using Importance Weights [#1265]*
Sepp Hochreiter and Klaus Obermayer, Bernstein center and Technical Univ. Berlin, Germany

We introduce a novel "importance weight" method (IW) to speed up gradient based learning. The method is particularly useful for "difficult" data sets like unbalanced data, highly non-linear target relationships, or long-term dependencies in sequences. An importance weight is assigned to every data point of the training set and controls its the contribution to the total training error according to its informativeness. For linear classifiers we show, that the new method is equivalent to standard support vector learning. We apply the IW method to feedforward multi-layer perceptrons and to recurrent neural networks. Results show that the new learning method is usually much faster in terms of epochs as well as in terms of absolute CPU time.

Special Session: Neurodynamics and Intentional Dynamic Systems
Monday, August 1, 9:30AM-11:30AM, Room: Mt Royal/Hampstead, Chair: Robert Kozma

9:30AM *Cinematographic Construction by Brains of Knowledge from Information [#1192]*
Walter Freeman, University of California at Berkeley, United States

Brains create knowledge and express it in information that they post-process into an organized database for exploration by commands that control goal-directed actions. Perception is explained by analyzing the neural activity in human and animal brains as they engage in exploratory behaviors. Measurement is by decomposition and modeling of the neural activity in order to deduce brain operations within and between three levels: microscopic of single neurons, mesoscopic of local networks forming modules, and macroscopic of the global self-organization of the cerebral hemispheres by the organic unity of neocortex. Knowledge is conveyed in fields of dendritic currents in sequences of 'cinematographic' frames.

10:10AM *Analysis of Phase Transitions in KIV with Amygdala during Simulated Navigation Control [#1675]*
Robert Kozma and Mark Myers, University of Memphis, United States

A biologically inspired dynamical neural network model called KIV is used in this work to design autonomous agents. The KIV set models the vertebrate limbic system. Previous studies indicated that KIV is able to provide a control algorithm for navigation and decision-making for autonomous mobile agents. In this work we use Hilbert transform to capture global synchronized spatio-temporal patterns of amplitude modulation in KIV. We identify phase transition in the simulated amygdala and show that it shares several important features of EEG signals.

10:30AM *Mixture Segmentation and Background Suppression in Chemosensor Arrays with a Model of Olfactory Bulb-Cortex interaction [#1631]*
Baranidharan Raman and Ricardo Gutierrez-Osuna, Texas AM University, United States

We present a model of olfactory bulb-cortex interaction for the purpose of mixture processing with gas sensor arrays. The olfactory bulb is modeled with a neurodynamic model whose lateral inhibitory connections are learned through a modified Hebbian-anti-hebbian rule. Bulbar outputs are then projected in a non-topographic fashion onto the olfactory cortex. Associational connections within cortex using Hebbian learning form a content addressable memory. Finally, inhibitory feedback from cortex is used to modulate bulbar activity. Depending on the form of feedback, Hebbian or anti-Hebbian, the model is able to perform background suppression or mixture segmentation. The model is validated on experimental data from a gas sensor array.

10:50AM *The language of cortical dynamics [#1188]*
Peter Andras, University of Newcastle, United Kingdom

Cortical dynamics can be recorded in various ways. Theoretical works suggest that analyzing the dynamics of recorded activities might reveal the workings of the underlying neural system. Here we describe the extraction of an activity pattern language that characterizes the dynamics of high-resolution EEG data recorded. We show that the language can be formulated in terms of probabilistic continuation rules which predict reasonably well the dynamics of activity patterns in the data.

11:10AM *Evolving Neurodynamic Controllers for Autonomous Robots [#1651]*
Derek Harter, Texas AandM University - Commerce, United States

The creation of architectures for controlling the behavior of autonomous systems is a difficult challenge. Evolutionary robotics uses neurally inspired models, rather than explicit symbolic systems, to evolve controllers for robots. Most approaches in evolutionary robotics have used abstract ANN or spiking single neuron models to evolve control architectures. In this paper we apply the evolutionary approach to creating a controller for an autonomous robot based on the aperiodic K-set neural population model. We introduce a discretization of the basic K-set units. We then demonstrate that the evolutionary approach evolves effective controllers for navigation tasks using the basic discrete units.

Special Session: Neural Networks Applications to Bioinformatics
Monday, August 1, 9:30AM-11:30AM, Room: Westmount, Chair: Francesco Masulli and Roberto Tagliaferri

9:30AM *Data Visualization Methodologies for Data Mining Systems in Bioinformatics [#1469]*
Antonino Staiano, Angelo Ciaramella, Giancarlo Raiconi, Roberto Tagliaferri and Giuseppe Longo, DMI, University of Salerno, Italy; DSF, University Federico II of Napoli, Italy

Bioinformatics systems benefit from the use of data mining strategies to locate interesting and pertinent relationships within massive information. Even a cursory glance through the literature in journals reveals the persistent role of data mining in experimental biology. Integrating data mining within the context of experimental investigations is central to bioinformatics software. In this paper we describe the framework of Probabilistic Principal Surfaces which offers a large variety of appealing visualization capabilities and which can be successfully integrated in the context of microarray analysis.

9:50AM *Random projections for assessing gene expression cluster stability [#1554]*
Alberto Bertoni and Giorgio Valentini, Universita' degli Studi di Milano, Italy

One of the main problems in gene expression data clustering is represented by the estimate of the stability of the obtained clusters. Our approach to this problem is based on random projections obeying the Johnson-Lindenstrauss lemma. We experiment with different types of random projections, comparing empirical and theoretical distortions induced by randomized embeddings between euclidean metric spaces, and we present cluster-stability measures that may be used to validate and to quantitatively assess the reliability of the obtained clusters. Experimental results with high dimensional synthetic and DNA microarray data show the effectiveness of the proposed approach.

10:10AM *A New Approach to Hierarchical Clustering for the Analysis of Genomic Data [#1455]*
Francesco Masulli and Stefano Rovetta, University of Pisa, Italy; University of Genova, Italy

Clustering algorithms in biomedical disciplines are usually selected between two main families, k-Means and Agglomerative Hierarchical Clustering. These methods are well studied and well established. However, both categories have some drawbacks related to data dimensionality (for partitional algorithms) and to the bottom-up structure (for hierarchical algorithms). To overcome these limitations, we present a hierarchical clustering algorithm based on a completely different principle, which is the analysis of shared farthest neighbors. The principle of operation and the rationale are illustrated, and experimental results on different data sets are presented.

10:30AM *Inferring Protein-Protein Interactions Using Interaction Network Topologies [#1592]*
Alberto Paccanaro, Valery Trifonov, Haiyuan Yu and Mark Gerstein, Yale University, United States

We describe two novel methods for predicting protein interactions, using only the topology of an observed protein interaction network. The first method searches the protein interaction network for defective cliques (i.e. nearly complete complexes of pairwise interacting proteins), and predicts the interactions that complete them. The second method computes the diffusion distance between each pair of proteins and then infers an interaction when such distance is below a given threshold. We show that both methods have a good predictive performance and compare their results.

10:50AM *Predicting sugar regulation in Arabidopsis thaliana using kernel learning methods [#1472]*
Kamel Saadi, Kee-Khoon Lee, Gavin Cawley and Michael Bevan, University of East Anglia, United Kingdom; John Iness Centre, United Kingdom

Prediction of the transcriptional regulation, based on the composition of the upstream promoter region, would be a useful step in deciphering gene regulatory networks. We perform optimally regularised kernel Fisher discriminant analysis of the promoter sequences to predict whether genes are up or down regulated by glucose in the A. thaliana. Three feature selection strategies are investigated: Use of known promoter motifs drawn from the PLACE database, enumeration of all possible k-mers and the use of the mismatch kernels. The leave-one-out error shows that 68% of regulatory behaviour can be inferred from the presence of motifs. The analysis yielded novel biological insights, since confirmed experimentally in vivo.

11:10AM *Feedback Linearization Using Neural Networks Applied to Advanced Pharmacodynamic and Pharmacogenomic Systems [#1628]*
Alexandru Floares, Oncological Institute Cluj-Napoca, Romania

Advanced pharmacodynamics and pharmacogenomics are dealing with high dimensional,nonlinear, control systems. Our goal is to show that all this systems, being based on a limited array of mechanisms and having some peculiarities, are good candidate for the application of feedback linearization, using neural networks. Unlike Jacobian linearization, this is not only locally valid. Our protocol can be applied even without the aid of a mathematical model. A drug dosage regimen, established in this way, will determine the output of the pharmacological system to track very well the therapeutic objective. This is the first time when a very large class of complex pharmacological problems are formulated and solved in terms of neural network control.

Information-theoretic and Bayesian learning
Monday, August 1, 9:30AM-11:30AM, Room: Outremount, Chair: Jose Principe

9:30AM *Improved Spam e-Mail Filtering Based on Committee Machines and Information Theoretic Feature Extraction [#1749]*
Dimitrios Karras, Chalkis Institute of Tech and Hellenic Open Univ, Greece

A novel approach for spam e-mail filtering is herein considered based on the Committee Machines Neural Network Models and on information theoretic feature extraction. An extensive experimental study is organized, the most extensive so far in the literature, based on widely accepted benchmarking e-mail data sets, comparing the proposed methodology with the Naive Bayes spam filter as well as with the Boosting tree methodology, the linear models based classification (classification via regression) and the nonlinear models based classification using simple neural network models, including Multilayer Perceptrons. Moreover, several feature extraction approaches based on information theory are evaluated.

9:50AM *A Variational Bayesian Method for Rectified Factor Analysis [#1085]*
Markus Harva and Ata Kaban, Helsinki University of Technology, Finland; The University of Birmingham, United Kingdom

Linear factor models with nonnegativity constraints have received a great deal of interest in a number of problem domains. In existing approaches, positivity has often been associated with sparsity. In this paper we argue that sparsity of the factors is not always a desirable option, but certainly a technical limitation of the currently existing solutions. We then reformulate the problem in order to relax the sparsity constraint while retaining positivity. A variational inference procedure is derived and this is contrasted to existing related approaches. Both i.i.d. and first-order AR variants of the proposed model are provided and these are experimentally demonstrated in a real-world astrophysical application.

10:10AM *An Information Theoretic Approach to Adaptive System Training Using Unlabeled Data [#1719]*
Kyu-Hwa Jeong, Jian-Wu Xu and Jose C. Principe, University of florida, United States; University of Florida, United States; CNEL, Department of ECE, University of Florida, United States

Traditionally, supervised learning is performed with pairwise input-output labeled data. After the training procedure, the adaptive system weights are fixed and the system is tested with unlabeled data. Recently, exploiting the unlabeled data to improve classification performance has been proposed in the machine learning community. In this paper, we present an information theoretic approach based on density divergence minimization to obtain an extended training algorithm using unlabeled data during testing. The simulations for classification problems suggest that our method can improve the performance of adaptive system in the application phase.

10:30AM *A Study of AdaBoost with SVM Based Weak Learners [#1253]*
Xuchun Li, Lei Wang and Eric Sung, Nanyang Technological University, Singapore

We proposed an AdaBoostSVM algorithm using SVM as weak learners for AdaBoost by adaptively adjusting the kernel parameter of SVM. Compared with existing AdaBoost methods, AdaBoostSVM has advantages of easier model selection and better generalization performance. An improved version, Diverse AdaBoostSVM, is also developed to deal with the accuracy/diversity dilemma of Boosting methods by balancing the distributions of accuracy and diversity over weak learners. Experimental results demonstrated that proposed algorithms achieve better performance than AdaBoost with other weak learners. The experiments on unbalance databases showed that AdaBoostSVM performs much better than SVM.

10:50AM *Information maximization and cost minimization in information-theoretic competitive learning [#1107]*
Ryotaro Kamimura, Tokai University, Japan

In this paper, we introduce costs in the framework of information maximization and try to maximize the ratio of information to its associated cost. Information maximizing primarily focuses on some parts of input patterns used to distinguish between patterns. Thus, we introduce the cost that represents average distance between input patterns and connection weights. By minimizing the cost, final connection weights by information maximization reflect well input patterns. We applied the method to a political data analysis and a Wisconsin cancer problem. Experimental results confirmed that by introducing the cost, representations faithful to input patterns were obtained. In addition, generalization performance was significantly improved.

11:10AM *Maximally Discriminative Spectral Feature Projections Using Mutual Information [#1125]*
Umut Ozertem and Deniz Erdogmus, OGI, Oregon Health and Science University, United States

Determining the optimal subspace projections, which maintains the best representation of the original data, is an important problem in machine learning and pattern recognition. In this paper, we propose a nonparametric nonlinear subspace projection technique that employs kernel density estimation based information theoretic methods and kernel machines, in order to maintain class separability maximally under the Shannon mutual information criterion.

Monday, August 1, 1:00PM-3:00PM

ICA and PCA
Monday, August 1, 1:00PM-3:00PM, Room: Verdun/Lachine, Chair: Erkki Oja

1:00PM *Extending Kernel Principal Component Analysis to General Underlying Loss Functions [#1419]*
Carlos Alzate and Johan A. K. Suykens, Katholieke Universiteit Leuven, ESAT-SCD-SISTA, Belgium

Kernel Principal Component Analysis can be considered as a natural nonlinear generalization of PCA because it performs linear PCA in a kernel induced feature space. It allows us to extract nonlinear structures in the input data. Starting from the Least Squares Support Vector Machine (LS-SVM) formulation to kernel PCA we extend it to general underlying loss functions. For classical kernel PCA, the underlying loss function is L2. In this approach, one can easily plug in other loss functions and solve a nonlinear optimization problem to achieve desirable properties. Simulations with Huber's loss function for robustness and quadratic epsilon insensitive loss function for sparseness demonstrate the flexibility of our approach.

1:20PM *Nonlinearity and Optimal Component Analysis [#1259]*
Washington Mio, Qiang Zhang and Xiuwen Liu, Florida State University, United States

Optimal Component Analysis is a linear subspace technique for dimensionality reduction designed to optimize object classification and recognition performance in specific applications. The inherently linear nature of OCA often limits recognition performance if the underlying data structure is nonlinear or cluster structures are complex. To address these problems, we investigate kernel OCA (KOCA), which consists of applying OCA techniques to the data after it has been mapped nonlinearly into a new feature space, referred to in the literature as a reproducing kernel Hilbert space. In this paper, we study theoretical and algorithmic aspects of KOCA and report results obtained in several face recognition experiments using the ORL database.

1:40PM *Relation between Kernel CCA and Kernel FDA [#1539]*
Makoto Yamada, Ali Pezeshki and Mahmood Azimi-Sadjadi, Colorado State University, United States

In this paper, relation between multi-class linear and kernel Fisher Discriminant Analysis (FDA) and linear and kernel Canonical Correlation Analysis (CCA) is established. It is shown that in a multi-class classification problem, the CCA between feature vectors (or a nonlinearly mapped version of them) as one-channel and the class label vectors as the second channel is equivalent to multi-class FDA. The multi-class Fisher distance is found to be decomposed into a sum of terms, each of which is determined by a canonical correlation. This result is extended to the kernel formulation without explicit computation of the nonlinear mappings. A simple example is presented to numerically verify the results.

2:00PM *Extraction of Frame-Difference Features based on PCA and ICA for Lip-Reading [#1669]*
Kyungsuk David Lee, Michelle Jeungeun Lee and Soo-Young Lee, University of Wisconsin, United States; Korea Advanced Inst Sscience and Tech, Korea (South)

The features of human lip motion from video clips are extracted by Principle Component Analysis (PCA) and Independent Component Analysis (ICA).

Unlike many other features extracted from single-frame static images or multiframe dynamic images, we extracted the features from the differences of consecutive frames. The PCA results in global features, while local features are extracted by the ICA. The features are extracted from several consecutive multi-frame differences as well as single-frame differences. The dynamic nature of multi-frame differences is more eminent. The resulting features maybe applicable in lip-reading and synthesis of lip motion videos with Text-to-Speech capability.

2:20PM *Multinomial PCA for Extracting Major Latent Topics from Document Streams [#1355]*
Masahiro Kimura, Kazumi Saito and Naonori Ueda, NTT Communication Science Laboratories, Japan

We propose a new unsupervised learning method called Multinomial PCA (MuPCA) for efficiently extracting the major latent topics from a document stream based on the ``bag-of-words" (BOW) representation of a document. Unlike principal component analysis (PCA), MuPCA follows a suitable probabilistic generative model for the document stream represented as time-series of word-frequency vectors. Using real data of document streams on the Web, we experimentally demonstrate the effectiveness of the proposed method.

2:40PM *Post Nonlinear Blind Source Separation by Geometric Linearization [#1320]*
Thang Viet Nguyen, Jagdish Chandra Patra, Amitabha Das and Geok See Ng, Nanyang Technological University, Singapore; Nanyang Technological University (NTU), Singapore

We present a novel geometric approach to the popular Post Nonlinear (PNL) BSS problem. A PNL mixing system includes two stages: a linear mixing followed by a nonlinear transformation. In our method, the process to linearize the nonlinear observed signals, the most critical task in PNL model, is carried out by a geometric transformation. The basic idea is that in a multi-dimensional space, a PNL mixture is represented by a nonlinear surface while a linear mixture is represented by a plane. Thus, by transforming a PNL's representing nonlinear surface to a plane, the PNL mixture can be linearized. The hidden sources are then estimated from linearized signals by a linear BSS algorithm. Experiments show promising performance of our approach.

Models of Neurons, Local Circuits, and Systems
Monday, August 1, 1:00PM-3:00PM, Room: Mt Royal/Hampstead, Chair: Stephen Grossberg

1:00PM *Which Features Trigger Action Potentials in Cortical Neurons in Vivo? [#1185]*
Holger Froehlich, Bjoern Naundorf, Maxim Volgushev and Fred Wolf, Centre for Bioinformatics Tuebingen (ZBIT), Germany; Max-Planck Inst. for Dyn. and Self Organization, Germany; Ruhr-University Bochum, Germany

We study the initiation of action potentials (APs) in in vivo recordings of cortical neurons from cat visual cortex. In this paper we investigate systematically which features of the membrane potential lead to an AP. We use Support Vector Machines (SVMs) to discriminate between trajectories of the membrane potential which lead to an AP and trajectories which do not lead to the initiation of an AP. Based on the results we construct a reduced prediction model. This model suggests that AP occurences can be predicted best by a combination of the 1st temporal derivative of the MP at distance tau to the AP maximum, the MP itself and the mean MP over a longer range.

1:20PM *Attention as Sigma-Pi Controlled Ach-Based Feedback [#1462]*
John Taylor, Matthew Hartley and Neill Taylor, King's College London, United Kingdom

We analyse experimental data on attention to indicate that any attention feedback control signals to lower order cortical sites will lead to a quadratic sigma-pi form of output in its dependence on the lower-order input and the feedback signal. The manner by which this structure works is shown by a brief simulation. We then discuss how such a structure could arise from the action of diffuse acetylcholine signals from the NBM, especially involving nicotinic receptors. We deduce certain structural regularities which should be expected both at local- and at micro-circuit level, mainly in cortical layer V (the output layer).

1:40PM *Motivational Modulation of Endogenous Inputs to the Superior Colliculus [#1510]*
Jason Satel, Thomas Trappenberg and Raymond Klein, Dalhousie University, Canada

Initiation of saccadic eye movements depends on an intricate balance between exogenous and endogenous control mechanisms. The superior colliculus is a major site of signal integration that drives the initiation of saccades. Previous work has shown that a continuous attractor neural network model can explain and reproduce a multitude of behavioural findings, including the gap effect and express saccades. This investigation advances the model in order to account for trial by trial adaptation of saccadic reaction times in a biologically plausible manner. A key hypothesis is that endogenous inputs to the SC can be adapted through motivationally-based feedback from other areas of the brain such as the basal ganglia or higher cortical areas.

2:00PM *Facilitatory Neural Activity Compensating for Neural Delays as a Potential Cause of the Flash-Lag Effect [#1234]*
Heejin Lim and Yoonsuck Choe, Texas AM University (TAMU), United States

In flash-lag effect (FLE), the position of a moving object is perceived to be ahead of a brief flash when they are actually co-localized. This phenomenon may be due to motion extrapolation: The nervous system has internal conduction delay, thus signals received with a delay in central areas have to be extrapolated for the internal state to be temporally aligned with that of the environment. The precise neural mechanism of such a process has not been fully investigated. Here, we propose that facilitating synapses can be a potential candidate. We tested this idea in FLE and showed that our model behavior is consistent with experimental data. In sum, facilitatory neural dynamics may underlie delay compensation, thus giving rise to FLE.

2:20PM *Fisher Information Quantifies Task-Specific Performance in the Blowfly Photoreceptor [#1546]*
Peng Xu and Pamela Abshire, University of Maryland, College Park, United States

We extend information-theoretic investigation of neural systems to task specific information using a detailed biophysical model of the blowfly photoreceptor. We formulate the response of the photoreceptor to incident flashes and determine the optimal detection performance using ideal observer analysis. Furthermore, we derive Fisher information contained in the output of the photoreceptor, and show how Fisher information is related to the detection performance. In addition we use Fisher information to show the connections between detection performance, signal-noise ratio, and discriminability. Our detailed biophysical model of the blowfly photoreceptor provides a rich framework for information-theoretic study of neural systems.

2:40PM *Evolutionary Training of a Biologically Realistic Spino-neuromuscular System [#1283]*
Stanley Gotshall, Canine Christopher, Jennings Benjamin and Soule Terence, University of Idaho, United States; Whitworth College, United States

This paper presents a biologically realistic model of the spino-neuromuscular system (SNMS). The model uses a pulse-coded recurrent neural network to control a simulated human-like arm. We use a genetic algorithm to train the network based on a target behavior for the arm. Our goal is to create a useful model for studying the function and behavior of neural pathways in the SNMS.

Bioinformatics
Monday, August 1, 1:00PM-3:00PM, Room: Westmount, Chair: Lipo Wang

1:00PM *Gene Regulatory Networks Inference with Recurrent Neural Network Models [#1728]*
Rui Xu and Donald C. Wunsch II, ACIL, University of Missouri-Rolla, United States

Large-scale time series gene expression data provide us a new means to reveal fundamental cellular processes, investigate functions of genes, and understand their relations. To infer gene regulatory networks from these data with effective computational tools has attracted intensive efforts from artificial intelligence and machine learning. Here, we use a recurrent neural network (RNN), trained with particle swarm optimization (PSO), to investigate the behaviors of regulatory networks. The experimental results, on a synthetic data set and a real data set, show that the proposed model and algorithm can effectively capture the dynamics of the gene expression time series and are capable of revealing regulatory interactions between genes.

1:20PM *A Self-Organizing Neural Network Approach for the Identification of Motifs with Insertions and Deletions in Protein Sequences [#1513]*
Xiaoxu Xiong, Derong Liu and Huaguang Zhang, University of Illinois at Chicago, United States; Northeastern University, China

Existing algorithms of motif identification in face two difficulties, large computation and insertions/deletions. In this paper, we provide a new strategy that solves this problem. though building a self-organizing neural network with multiple levels of subnetworks to classify subsequences obtained from the protein sequences. We maintain a low computational complexity through the use of this multi-level structure. The definition of pairwise distance between motif patterns provided in this paper can deal with more insertions/deletions allowed in a motif than other algorithms. Simulation results show that our algorithm significantly outperforms existing algorithms in both accuracy and reliability aspects.

1:40PM *Functional Grouping of Genes Using Spectral Clustering and Gene Ontology [#1016]*
Nora Speer, Holger Froehlich, Christian Spieth and Andreas Zell, Centre for Bioinformatics Tuebingen (ZBIT), Germany

With the invention of high throughput methods, researchers are capable of producing large amounts of biological data. During the analysis of such data the need for a functional grouping of genes arises. In this paper, we propose a new method based on spectral clustering for the partitioning of genes according to their biological function. The functional information is based on Gene Ontology annotation, a mechanism to capture functional knowledge in a shareable and computer processable form. Our functional cluster method promises to automatize, speed up and therefore improve biological data analysis.

2:00PM *A Simpler Bayesian Network Model for Genetic Regulatory Network Inference [#1477]*
Gustavo Bastos and Katia Guimaraes, Federal University of Pernambuco, Brazil

We use Bayesian Networks and a nonparametric regression model for inferring genetic regulatory networks. We have used a combination of the Bayesian Information Criterion (BIC) and a 'voting' method to pick out the edges of the output graph. Using BIC makes the model simpler than previous ones, still obtaining, however, good results, as shown in our experiments with synthetic data and Saccharomyces cerevisiae cell cycle microarray gene expression data.

2:20PM *Effect of Non-Target Examples on E.coli Promoters Recognition Using Neural Networks [#1014]*
Paul Conilione and Dianhui Wang, La Trobe University, Australia

This paper aims to evaluate the impact of different types of non- promoters used in training and testing on the classification accuracy. 872 E.coli promoters were used in addition three types of non-promoters, random sequences with the same base frequency as the promoter sequences, genes selected from E.coli and random sequences with the same base frequencies as the gene non-promoters. It was found that the high level features did not perform as well for promoter recognition compared with CODE-4 DNA representation, contrary to expectation. The strongest determining factor in classification accuracy was the type of non-promoter used for training and testing.

2:40PM *Predicting Protein-Protein Interactions Based on Protein-Domain Relationships [#1131]*
Bing Wang, De-Shuang Huang, Peng Chen, Zhu Yunping and Li Yixue, Chinese Academy of Sciences, China; Hefei Institute of Intelligent Machines, CAS, China; Beijing Institute of Radiation Medicine, China

This paper proposes a new method that can predict the interactions between proteins intermediated by the protein-domain relations. We utilize the lazy expectation maximization (LEM) to compute an improved maximization likelihood estimation (MLE) model. The protein-domain relationships are extruded from Pfam database and the combined data set of Uetz and Ito are used as the source of protein-protein interactions. Finally, the efficiency and the effectiveness of our proposed approach can be validated by a better performance such as the sensitivity of 80.1% and the specificity of 43.5%, and the lesser computational cost.

Special Session: Evolvable and Emergent Neural Systems
Monday, August 1, 1:00PM-3:00PM, Room: Outremount, Chair: Seong G. Kong and Jacek M. Zurada

1:00PM *Automated Heuristic Growing of Neural Networks for Nonlinear Time Series Models [#1321]*
Alex Kalos, The Dow Chemical Company, United States

In this paper, we present a method for automatically selecting the optimal architecture of feedforward neural networks to build nonlinear time series models. A heuristic method is used to do an exhaustive search of all possible input/output combinations, while adjusting the lag times and the number of nodes in a fully connected single hidden layer network. Levenberg-Marquardt optimization is performed using the stop-search method of cross-validation. Statistics are maintained for all optimized structures which permits post-processing based on performance criteria for final model selection. The methodology is applied to a case study for developing multi-variate autoregressive models for the day-ahead forecasting of electricity prices.

1:20PM *ECG Signal Classification using Block-based Neural Networks [#1629]*
Wei Jiang, Seong Kong and Gregory Peterson, The University of Tennessee, United States; University of Tennessee, United States

This paper investigates the application of evolvable block-based neural networks (BbNNs) to ECG signal classification. A BbNN consists of a two-dimensional (2-D) array of modular basic blocks that can be easily implemented using reconfigurable digital hardware. BbNNs are evolved for each patient in order to provide personalized health monitoring. A genetic algorithm evolves the internal structure and associated weights of a BbNN using training patterns that consist of morphological and temporal features extracted from the ECG signal of a patient. The remaining part of the ECG record serves as the test signal. The BbNN was tested for ten records collected from different patients provided by the MIT-BIH Arrhythmia database.

1:40PM *An Evolved Seeega Player Capable of Strong Novice-Level Play [#1704]*
Ashraf M. Abdelbar, Ossama Soliman, Sherif Kinawy and Hisham Sayed, American University in Cairo, Egypt

Seega is an ancient Egyptian two-stage board game that, in certain aspects, is more difficult than chess. In the first and more difficult stage of the game, players take turns placing one piece each on the board until the board contains only one empty cell. In the second stage players take turns moving pieces of their color; a piece that becomes surrounded is captured and removed from the board. We present results on the evolution of a Seega player that plays at the level of college students, who have had only a few days' familiarity with the game. The player is based on minimaxing with hand-coded features, and feature weights that are evolved by a co-evolutionary system comprising a particle swarm optimizer and an evolutionary algorithm.

2:00PM *Evolvable Neural Networks based on Developmental Models for Mobile Robot Navigation [#1633]*
Dong-Wook Lee, Seong Kong and Kwee-Bo Sim, The University of Tennessee, United States; University of Tennessee, United States; Chung-Ang University, Korea (South)

This paper presents an evolvable neural network based on a developmental model for navigation control of autonomous mobile robots in dynamic operating environments. Bio-inspired mechanisms have been applied to autonomous design of artificial neural networks for solving practical problems. The proposed neural network architecture is grown from an initial model by a set of production rules of the L-system that are represented by the DNA coding. DNA coding gives an effective method of expressing general production rules. Experiments show that the evolvable neural network designed by the production rules of the L-system develops into a controller for mobile robot navigation to avoid collisions with the obstacles.

2:20PM *A Recurrent RBF Network Model for Nearest Neighbor Classification [#1731]*
Mehmet Muezzinoglu and Jacek Zurada, University of Louisville, United States

Superposition of radial basis functions centered at given prototype patterns constitutes one of the most suitable energy forms for gradient systems that perform nearest neighbor classification with real-valued static prototypes. It is shown in this paper that a continuous-time dynamical neural network model, employing a radial basis function and a sigmoid multi-layer perceptron sub-networks, is capable of maximizing such an energy form locally. The dynamical classification scheme implemented by the network eliminates all comparisons, which are the vital steps of the conventional nearest neighbor classification process. The performance of the proposed network model is demonstrated on image reconstruction applications.

2:40PM *Face Recognition Using Modular Neural Networks and Fuzzy Sugeno Integral for Response Integration [#1762]*
Patricia Melin, Claudia Gonzalez, Felma Gonzalez and Oscar Castillo, Tijuana Institute of Technology, Mexico

We describe in this paper a new approach for pattern recognition using modular neural networks with a fuzzy logic method for response integration. We proposed a new architecture for modular neural networks for achieving pattern recognition in the particular case of human faces. Also, the method for achieving response integration is based on the fuzzy Sugeno integral. Response integration is required to combine the outputs of all the modules in the modular network. We have applied the new approach for face recognition with a real database of faces from students of our institution.

Monday, August 1, 3:20PM-5:20PM

Control and System Identification
Monday, August 1, 3:20PM-5:20PM, Room: Outremount, Chair: Edgar Sanchez

3:20PM *Application of a CMAC Neural Network to the Control of a Parallel Hybrid-Electric Propulsion System for a Small Unmanned Aerial Vehicle [#1141]*
Frederick Harmon, Andrew Frank and Sanjay Joshi, University of California-Davis, United States

Controlling the energy use of a hybrid-electric propulsion system is difficult due to the interaction of nonlinear devices. An optimization routine for the energy use of a parallel hybrid-electric propulsion system for a small unmanned aerial vehicle (UAV), the application of a cerebellar model arithmetic computer (CMAC) neural network to approximate the optimization results and control the hybrid-electric system, and simulation results are presented. The small hybrid-electric UAV is intended for military and homeland security missions involving intelligence, surveillance, or reconnaissance (ISR). The hybrid-electric UAV with the CMAC controller uses 37.8% less energy than a two-stroke gasoline-powered UAV during an ISR mission.

3:40PM *Inverse Optimal Nonlinear Recurrent High Order Neural Observer [#1621]*
Luis J. Ricalde and Edgar N. Sanchez, CINVESTAV, Unidad Guadalajara, Mexico

This paper presents the design of an adaptive recurrent neural observer for nonlinear systems which model is assumed to be unknown. The neural observer is composed of a Recurrent High Order Neural Network which builds an online model of the unknown plant and a learning adaptation law for the neural network weights. This law is obtained by the Lyapunov methodology. The feedback law which guarantees stability of the estimation error is proved to be optimal with respect to a well defined cost functional.

4:00PM *System and Method for Determining Harmonic Contributions from Non-Linear Loads Using Recurrent Neural Networks [#1502]*
Joy Mazumdar, Ronald G. Harley and Frank Lambert, Georgia Institute of Technology, United States; Neetrac, United States

This paper proposes a neural network solution methodology for the problem of measuring the actual amount of harmonic current injected into a power network by a non-linear load. The determination of harmonic currents is complicated by the fact that the supply voltage waveform is distorted by other loads and is rarely a pure sinusoid. A recurrent neural network architecture based method is used to find a way of distinguishing between the load contributed harmonics and supply harmonics, without disconnecting the load from the network. The main advantage of this method is that only waveforms of voltages and currents have to be measured. This method is applicable for both single and three phase loads.

4:20PM *On Output Regulation for SISO Nonlinear Systems with Dynamic Neural Networks [#1611]*
Bernardino Castillo-Toledo and Alberto Hernandez Avalos, Cinvestav-GDL, Mexico

In this work, the output regulation theory is combined with a dynamic neural identifier, in order to improve the robustness properties for trajectory tracking on SISO nonlinear systems. A neural network is used to identify the dynamics of the nonlinear system, by a suitable on-line training, which ensures small identification error. Then, the output regulation technique is applied to the neural network to obtain a controller that, when applied to the original system, guarantee also a bounded output tracking error despite the presence of parameter variations and external perturbations. Simulation results on a model of a chaotic system are presented showing the viability and effectiveness of the proposed technique.

4:40PM *Indirect Field-oriented Linear Induction Motor Drive with Petri Fuzzy-neural-network Control [#1339]*
Rong-Jong Wai and Chia-Chin Chu, Dept. Electrical Engineering, Yuan Ze University, Taiwan

This study focuses on the development of a Petri fuzzy-neural-network (PFNN) control for an indirect field-oriented linear induction motor (LIM) drive. The concept of a Petri net (PN) is incorporated into a traditional fuzzy-neural-network (TFNN) to form a newly-type PFNN framework for alleviating the computation burden. Moreover, the supervised gradient descent method is used to develop the online training algorithm for the PFNN. In order to guarantee the convergence of tracking error, analytical methods based on a discrete-type Lyapunov function are proposed to determine the varied learning rates of the PFNN. In addition, the effectiveness of the proposed control scheme is verified by numerical simulations.

5:00PM *Wavelet-Neural-Network-Based Backstepping Control for Chaotic Systems [#1347]*
Tsu-Tian Lee, Chih-Min Lin and Chun-Fei Hsu, National Taipei University of Technology, Taiwan; Yuan-Ze University, Taiwan; National Chiao-Tung University, Taiwan

This paper proposes a wavelet-neural-network-based backstepping control (WNNBC) for the chaotic systems. The WNNBC is comprised of a neural backstepping controller and an adaptive robust controller. The neural backstepping controller containing a wavelet neural network identifier is the principal controller, and the adaptive robust controller is designed to achieve tracking performance with desired attenuation level. Finally, simulation results verify that the proposed WNNBC can achieve favorable tracking performance.

Spiking Neurons
Monday, August 1, 3:20PM-5:20PM, Room: Mt Royal/Hampstead, Chair: William B. Levy

3:20PM *Spatially and Temporally Local Spike-Timing-Dependent Plasticity Rule [#1568]*
Anatoli Gorchetchnikov, Massimiliano Versace and Michael E. Hasselmo, Dept of CNS, Boston University, United States; Dept. of Psychology, Boston University, United States

Neurophysiological research has focused on the temporal relationships between neuronal firing and plasticity, and has shown the phenomenon of spike-timing-dependent plasticity (STDP). Various models were suggested to implement the STDP learning rule in artificial networks based on spiking neurons. Here we present a simple rule that only depends on the information that is available at the synapse at the time of synaptic modification. This rule is extended by addition of four types of gating derived from conventionally used types of gated decay in learning rules for continuous firing rate neurons. The results show that the advantages of these gatings are transferred to the new rule without sacrificing its dependency on spike-timing.

3:40PM *Differences in the subthreshold dynamics of leaky integrate-and-fire and Hodgkin-Huxley neuron models [#1500]*
Dominic Standage and Thomas Trappenberg, Dalhousie University, Canada

Many spiking neuron models have been proposed over the last decades with varying computational complexity and abstraction from biological neurons. Among the few studies that have compared spiking models, little emphasis has been given to the formal description of calibration methods in tuning model parameters. We give an example of calibrating a leaky integrate-and-fire neuron with the first-spike time of a Hodgkin-Huxley neuron. We further demonstrate how model parameters can be tuned to minimize subthreshold differences in membrane potential. This example emphasizes the dependencies of calibration methods on other experimental parameters, complicating detailed comparisons of spiking models.

4:00PM *Rich phenomena of pulse-coupled spiking neurons with triangular waveform input [#1744]*
Toshimichi Saito, Yoshio Kon'no and Hiroyuki Torikai, Hosei University, Japan

This paper studies a spiking neuron circuit with a periodic triangular base signal. The circuit can output rich pulse-trains and the dynamics can be analyzed exploiting a piecewise linear one-dimensional pulse position map. Using two neurons we construct a pulse-coupled system whose dynamics can be integrated into the composite map of the pulse position maps of two neurons. The composite map is piecewise linear and we can analyze rich phenomena precisely. For example, periodic behavior of each neuron is changed into chaotic behavior and chaotic behavior of each neuron is changed into periodic behavior. These results provide basic information to construct flexible pulse- coupled neural networks.

4:20PM *Synchronized Theta Rhythm Selection in a Dentate Gyrus Network Model [#1365]*
Katsumi Tateno, Hatsuo Hayashi and Satoru Ishizuka, Kyushu Institute of Technology, Japan

The dentate gyrus network model shown here filtered a specific frequency of the periodic synaptic input through the perforant path. The filtering properties were modified by the degree of synchronization of the periodic perforant path input. The random synaptic input through the perforant path also contributed to the modification of the filtering properties. When the random synaptic input of the perforant path was delivered to several granule cells, adequately synchronized periodic perforant path input led to properties of a band-pass filter in the dentate gyrus network model. The bandwidth of the band-pass filter was 2 - 5 Hz. Without the random synaptic input, the dentate gyrus network model showed a property of a low-pass filter.

4:40PM *Noise Benefits in Spiking Retinal and Sensory Neuron Models [#1729]*
Ashok Patel and Bart Kosko, University of Southern California, United States

This paper presents two new theorems that give sufficient conditions (and necessary in the first case) for a noise benefit or stochastic-resonance effect in popular spiking models of retinal neurons and sensory neurons. Small amounts of additive white noise increase the neuron's input-output bit count or Shannon mutual information. This stochastic-resonance (SR) effect applies to standard Poisson spiking models of retinal neurons for all possible types of finite-variance noise and for all impulsive or infinite-variance stable noise. A similar SR result holds for several types of sensory spiking neurons such as the Fitzhugh-Nagumo model and the integrate-and-fire model if the additive noise is Gaussian white noise.

5:00PM *A Spiking Neuron Representation of Auditory Signals [#1697]*
Guoping Wang and Misha Pavel, OGI at Oregon Health and Science University, United States

We describe an auditory model which codes high bandwidth auditory signal using spikes generated by peripheral auditory neurons with slow sampling rates due to the refractory period. Signal is decomposed into multiple narrowbands based on the auditory neuron's narrowband tuning characteristics such that each subband signal can be sampled at frequencies much lower than the center frequency. The computational model consists of a short-term FFT analysis combined with overlap-add and a sampling process where magnitude is digitized but phase is represented by spikes timing. We show that this model can represent arbitrary signals, but redundant signals such as speech are represented with higher accuracy than uncorrelated noise.

Special Session: Computational Neurogenetic Modeling
Monday, August 1, 3:20PM-5:20PM, Room: Westmount, Chair: Nik Kasabov

3:20PM *Comparative genomic study of Parkinson's disease candidate genes [#1151]*
Gavyn Pang and Jagath Rajapakse, Nanyang Technical University, Singapore; Nanyang Technological University, Singapore

Several candidate genes affect Parkinson's disease in a variety ways. A comparative analysis is performed using orthologues of these genes in other vertebrates species, such as chimp, mouse, rat, chicken, fugu, and tetraodon. The analyses reveal the presence of transmembrane regions and signal peptides in several sequences of some species, which provides a better understanding of the variability of structural and functional aspects of these genes in different species.

3:40PM *NeuroGene: Integrated Simulation of Gene Regulation, Neural Activity and Neurodevelopment [#1646]*
Rasmus Storjohann and Gary F. Marcus, School of Comput. Sci., Simon Fraser University, Canada; Dept. of Psychology, New York University, United States

A challenge to understanding the mind and brain is to integrate biochemical, genetic, developmental and neuroscientific information. We present a system for integrated simulation of biochemistry, neurodevelopment and neural activity within a unifying framework of genetic control. Using this system, we have developed a novel model for the formation of topographic projections. We also simulate activity-dependent developmental processes which underlie receptive field refinement and ocular dominance column formation. As an illustration of the overall utility of integrated neurogenetic simulation, we show how axon guidance and learning together may explain the results of a critical study of topographic map development (Brown et al., 2000, Cell).

4:00PM *A Hierarchical Coevolutionary Method to Support brain-Lesion Modelling [#1382]*
Michail Maniadakis and Panos Trahanias, Institute Computer Science, FORTH, Greece

The current work addresses the employment of an evolutionary method for the development of cognitive mechanisms in artificial organisms. Neural network-based agent structures are employed to represent brain areas. We introduce a Hierarchical Collaborative CoEvolutionary approach to design autonomous, yet cooperating agents. Replication of lesion studies is used as a means to increase reliability of brain model. The coevolutionary methos is appropriately designed to support systematic modelling of brain structures, able to reproduce biological lesion data. Thus, the proposed approach designs cooperating agents properly, by considering the desired pre- and post- lesion performance of the model.

4:20PM *Genome Space and Structure Genome Invariants [#1679]*
Germano Resconi, Catholic University, Italy

The traditional approach examines and collects data on a single gene,a single protein or a single reaction at a time. With the advent of the "Age of Genomics" interaction among genes it becomes important to understand the genome functionality. The problem today is that an efficient model to describe the interaction among genes is not yet available. In this paper we suggest a new possible model. Given the states of neural cell as amplitude of fast excitation , fast excitation rise and others,we obtain the gene expression in protein as function of the states. The set of gene expression functions is the genome space. In the genome space is concentrate all the useful information on the genome as correlation, genome network,invariants and so on.

4:40PM *A Computational Neurogenetic Model of a Spiking Neuron [#1768]*
Nikola Kasabov, Lubica Benuskova and Simei Wysoski, Auckland University of Technology, New Zealand; Knowledge Eng. Discovery Res. Inst. AUT, New Zealand

The paper presents a novel, biologically plausible spiking neuronal model that includes a dynamic gene network. Interactions of genes in neurons affect the dynamics of the neurons and the whole network through neuronal parameters that change as a function of gene expression. The proposed model is used to build a spiking neural network (SNN) illustrated on a real EEG data case study problem. The paper also presents a novel computational approach to brain neural network modeling that integrates dynamic gene networks with a neural network model. Interaction of genes in neurons affects the dynamics of the whole neural network through neuronal parameters, which are no longer constant, but change as a function of gene expression.

Special Session: Recent Advancements in Adaptive Resonance Theory
Monday, August 1, 3:20PM-5:20PM, Room: Verdun/Lachine, Chair: Georgios Anagnostopoulos

3:20PM *Self-Organizing Hierarchical Knowledge Discovery by an ARTMAP Information Fusion System [#1049]*
Gail Carpenter and Siegfried Martens, Boston University, United States

Classifying terrain or objects may require the resolution of conflicting information from sensors working at different times, locations, and scales, and from users with different goals and situations. Fusion methods can resolve such inconsistencies, as when evidence suggests that an object is a car, a truck, or an airplane. A complementary approach to the information fusion problem here considers the case where sensors and sources are both nominally inconsistent and reliable, as when evidence suggests that an object is a car, a vehicle, and man-made. Relationships among classes are assumed to be unknown to the automated system or the human user. ARTMAP rule discovery is illustrated with an image example, but is not limited to this domain.

4:00PM *Modification of the ART-1 Architecture Based on Category Theoretic Design Principles [#1529]*
Michael Healy, Richard Olinger, Robert Young, Thomas Caudell and Kurt Larson, Dept of ECE, Univ of New Mexico, United States; Dept of CS, Univ of New Mexico, United States; Dept of ECE and CS, Univ of New Mexico, United States; Sandia National Labs, New Mexico, United States

Many studies have addressed the knowledge representation capability of neural networks. A recently-developed mathematical semantic theory explains the relationship between knowledge and its representation in connectionist systems. The theory yields design principles for neural networks whose behavioral repertoire expresses any desired capability that can be expressed logically. In this paper, we show how the design principle of limit formation can be applied to modify the ART-1 architecture, yielding a discrimination capability that goes beyond vigilance. Simulations of this new design illustrate the increased discrimination ability it provides for multi-spectral image analysis.

4:20PM *A vigilance-free ART network with general geometry internal classes [#1351]*
Dinani Gomes, Manuel Fernandez-Delgado and Senen Barro, University of Santiago de Compostela, Brazil; University of Santiago de Compostela, Spain

Internal categories in ART neural networks have pre-defined geometry. This may limit its ability to fit complex borders among output predictions and may contribute to the category proliferation problem. We propose Polytope ARTMAP (PTAM), which uses internal categories with general geometry (polytopes defined by selected training patterns). Category borders are a piece-wise linear approximation to the prediction borders. Categories do not need to overlap in order to keep their shape during learning, so that category overlapping is avoided. The category choice function does not depend on its size. Class growing is limited by the other categories, and the vigilance parameter can be removed, so that PTAM has no tunning parameter.

4:40PM *On the design of an Ellipsoid ARTMAP classifier within the Fuzzy Adaptive System ART Framework [#1689]*
Ross Peralta, Georgios Anagnostopoulos, Eduardo Gomez-Sanchez and Samuel Richie, Florida Institute of Technology, United States; University of Valladolid, Spain; University of Central Florida, United States

In this paper we present the design of Fuzzy Adaptive System Ellipsoid ARTMAP (FASEAM), a novel neural architecture based on Ellipsoid ARTMAP (EAM) that is equipped with concepts utilized in the Fuzzy Adaptive System ART (FASART) architecture. We derive a new category choice function appropriate for EAM categories that is non-constant in a category's representation region and we augment the EAM category description with a centroid vector, whose learning rate is inversely proportional to the number of training patterns accessing the category. Finally, we demonstrate the merits of our design choices by comparing FASART, EAM and FASEAM in terms of generalization performance and final structural complexity on a set of classification problems.

5:00PM *Parallelizing the Fuzzy ARTMAP Algorithm on a Beowulf Cluster [#1345]*
Jimmy Secretan, Jose Castro, Michael Georgiopoulos, Joe Tapia, Amit Chadha, Brian Huber, Georgios Anagnostopoulos and Samuel Richie, University of Central Florida, United States; Comp. Eng. Instituto Technologico, Costa Rica; Florida Institute of Technology, United States

Fuzzy ARTMAP neural networks have been proven to be good classifiers on a variety of classification problems. However, the time that it takes Fuzzy ARTMAP to converge to a solution increases rapidly as the number of patterns used for training increases. In this paper we propose a coarse grain parallelization technique, based on a pipeline approach, to speed-up Fuzzy ARTMAP's training process. In particular, we first parallelized Fuzzy ARTMAP, without the match-tracking mechanism, and then we parallelized Fuzzy ARTMAP with the match-tracking mechanism. Results run on a Beowulf cluster with a well known large database, show linear speedup with respect to the number of processors used in the pipeline.

Monday, August 1, 7:00PM-11:00PM

Plenary Poster Session: Applications to genomics
Monday, August 1, 7:00PM-11:00PM, Room: Fountaine, Chair: Program Chairs

1001 *Using real-valued meta classifiers to integrate binding site predictions [#1026]*
Yi Sun, Mark Robinson, Rod Adams, Paul Kaye and Alistair Rust, University of Hertfordshire, United Kingdom; Institute of Systems Biology, United States

Currently the best algorithms for transcription factor binding site prediction are severely limited in accuracy. There is good reason to believe that predictions from these different classes of algorithms could be used in conjunction to improve the quality of predictions. In this work, we apply single layer networks, rules sets and support vector machines on predictions from 12 key real valued algorithms. We then use a 'window' of consecutive results in the input vector in order to contextualise the neighbouring results. We improve the classification result with the aid of sampling techniques. We find that support vector machines outperform each of the original individual algorithms and the other classifiers employed in this work.

1002 *Cluster Ensemble for Gene Expression Microarray Data [#1196]*
Marcilio de Souto, Shirlly Silva, Valnaide Bittencourt and Daniel Araujo, Federal University of Rio Grande do Norte, Brazil

Ensemble techniques have been successfully applied in the context of supervised learning to increase the accuracy and stability of classification. Recently, similar techniques have been proposed for clustering algorithms. In this context, we analyze the potential of applying cluster ensemble techniques to gene expression microarray data. Our experimental results show that there is often a significant improvement in the results obtained with the use of ensemble when compared to those based on the clustering techniques used individually.

1003 *Characterizing Human Gene Splice Sites Using Evolved Regular Expressions [#1426]*
Li Jing-Jing, Huang De-Shuang, Robert MacCallum and Wu Xiao-Run, Chinese Academy of Sciences, China; Stockholm University, Sweden

In this paper, an algorithm using evolved regular expressions to characterize and predict human gene splice sites is proposed. The central problem of our method is to discover some potential patterns related to splice sites within a sequence. To achieve our goal, we implement a genetic programming based system to yield and evolve regular expressions which can effectively characterize and predict the splice junctions. The evolved regular expressions may shed some lights on a few subtle underlying rules defining splice sites. Experimental results demonstrate that some widely accepted patterns could indeed be learnt by our method and the prediction accuracy is competitive compared with some other traditional methods.

1004 *Prediction of Contact Map Integrated PNN with Conformational Energy [#1133]*
Peng Chen, De-Shuang Huang, Bing Wang, Yunping Zhu and Yixue Li, Chinese Academy of Sciences, China; Hefei Institute of Intelligent Machines, CAS, China; Beijing Institute of Radiation Medicine, China

This paper presents a novel method to solve the protein's three-dimensional structure prediction problem. It is a machine learning approach by integrating probabilistic neural network (PNN) with conformational energy function and principal component analysis. As a result, it was found that our proposed method is better than the existing methods, such as the hybrid method of HMMSTR and the correlated mutation analysis method. Furthermore, this method can accurately predict 31% of contacts at a distance cutoff of 8 angstrom for proteins of length up to 200.

1005 *Neural Network-Based Analysis of DNA Microarray Data [#1207]*
Jagdish Chandra Patra, Lei Wang, Ee Luang Ang and Narendra S. Chaudhari, Nanyang Technological University (NTU), Singapore; Nanyang Technological University, Singapore; SCE, Nanyang Technological University, Singapore

The analysis of DNA microarray expression data has become an important subject in bioinformatics. Scientists have adopted different approaches to select the informative genes those can distinguish different types of cancers. In this paper, we show the use of a dimension reduction technique such as Singular Value Decomposition (SVD) to capture the genes with similar patterns. We propose a novel method of selection of feature genes based on information loss using SVD. To assign the samples to known classes, we design a Multi-Layer Perceptron- based classifier with reduced dimensional input vectors. We provide performance comparison between different selection methods in terms of classification rate.

1006 *Neural Networks for Gene Expression Analysis and Gene Selection from DNA Microarray [#1157]*
Jagdish Chandra Patra, Qin Zhen, Ee Luang Ang and Amitabha Das, Nanyang Technological University (NTU), Singapore; Nanyang Technological University, Singapore

We propose two approaches for microarray gene expression analysis and gene selection using neural networks. Using these approaches, only those genes which help sample classification are selected from the original set of genes, and the redundant genes expression patterns involved in the huge microarray matrix are eliminated so that dimensionality of the matrix is reduced from a few thousands to a much smaller number. An unsupervised SOM based technique and another supervised single layer perceptron based technique have been utilized for this purpose. Performance of these two approaches is compared in terms of accuracy, implementation and execution time.

Plenary Poster Session: Proteomics and neuroinformatics
Monday, August 1, 7:00PM-11:00PM, Room: Fountaine, Chair: Program Chairs

1007 *The Molecules Module of the Brain Architecture Management System [#1226]*
Mihail Bota and Larry Swanson, NIBS Program in Neurosciences, USC, United States

We present a new module of the Brain Architecture Management System (BAMS; http://brancusi.usc.edu/bkms), which makes this the first online system that handles chemoarchitectonical data of brain regions across species. The module allows insertion of molecules reports as collated from the literature and includes representation of molecule expression in different cell types, coexpression data, and the physiological state of experimental animals. It also allows insertion of time dependent experimental data. The web interface of this module allows users to construct lists of brain regions where a molecule is present depending on the physiological state, retrieve details about inserted records, and compare the time dependent data.

1008 *Protein Flexibility Modeling Using Kernel Based Methods [#1139]*
Xue-wen Chen and Jeremy Chen, The University of Kansas, United States

Proteins play an essential role in nearly all cell functions. The multiplicity of functions that proteins execute is attributed to their 3-D conformational structures. Understanding the conformational changes of a protein molecule is essential in discovering the protein structure and function relationships underlying most biological processes. However, modeling protein flexibility is a very computationally challenging problem with a large number of degrees of freedom involved. In order to address this important challenge, the paper studies protein dynamics and develop a kernel based computational model to characterize protein conformational changes and to reduce the redundancy in protein conformers.

1009 *An empirical comparison of individual machine learning techniques and ensemble approaches in protein structural class prediction [#1266]*
Valnaide Bittencourt, Marjory Abreu, Marcilio de Souto and Anne Canuto, Federal University of Rio Grande do Norte, Brazil

Protein fold recognition is an important approach to structure discovery without relying on sequence similarity. In this context, computer-based tools, mainly the techniques from Machine Learning (ML), have became essential considering the large volume of data. We present an empirical comparison of individual machine learning techniques (k-Nearest Neighbor, Naive Bayes, Decision Trees, Support Vector Machines and Neural Networks) and ensemble approaches (Bagging and Boosting) to the task of protein structural class prediction.

1010 *Prediction of Protein Secondary Structure Using Improved Two-level Neural Network Architecture [#1136]*
Xin Huang, De-Shuang Huang and Guang-Zheng Zhang, Chinese Academy of Sciences, China; Hefei Institute of Intelligent Machines, CAS, China; University of Science and Technology of China, China

In this paper we propose constructing an improved two-level neural network to predict protein secondary structure. Compared with previous networks, there are three innovations with this method. Firstly, we code the whole protein composition information as the inputs to the first-level network besides the evolutionary information. Secondly, we calculate the reliability score for each residue based on the output of the first-level network and then input it into the second-level network. Thirdly, in order to decrease the artificial influences brought by the use of multiple sequence alignment we code single sequence into the second-level network. The experimental results show that our proposed method can efficiently improve the prediction accuracy.

1011 *Protein secondary structure prediction using machine learning [#1290]*
BaiFang Zhang, ZhiHang Chen and Yi Murphey, University of Michigan-Dearborn, United States

This paper presents an intelligent system for protein secondary structure prediction. The system consists of three pairwisely trained neural networks and a Bayesian inference function applied to the neural network outputs for accurate prediction. We tested our system on two well-known protein data set drawn from PDB, our system showed top performances on both data sets.

1012 *Protein Secondary Structure Prediction with a Hybrid RNN/HMM System [#1540]*
Jinmiao Chen and Narendra S. Chaudhari, SCE, Nanyang Technological University, Singapore

In this paper, we propose a hybrid RNN/HMM system for protein secondary structure prediction, where each secondary structure segment is approximated by a second-order recurrent neural network embedded in the state of a segmental hidden Markov model. We evaluate the hybrid system on the RS126 and CB396 sets and obtain promising results.

1013 *Entropy Based Disease Classification of Proteomic Mass Sepectrometry Data of the Human Serum by a Support Vector Machine [#1165]*
Terje Kristensen and Gaurav Kumar, Bergen University College, Norway; Bergen University College, India

Proteomic pattern analysis uses the overall pattern to diagnose disease states without the need to identify the components within the pattern. The patterns are generated from mass spectroscopy (MS) data. A typical sample can have about 15,000 different ions present. A very important question is which ions are the best classifiers? We have used the information-theoretical property, information gain, to measure how well a given attribute separates the training examples according to the target classification. Our algorithm first selects the attributes with highest information gain and then classifies the diseased and healthy data based on these attributes using support vector machines. The method achieves an excellent performance of 100 %.

Plenary Poster Session: Data mining, text and pattern recognition
Monday, August 1, 7:00PM-11:00PM, Room: Fountaine, Chair: Program Chairs

1014 *A Comparative Study on Term Weighting Schemes for Text Categorization [#1688]*
Man Lan, Sam Yuan Sung, Hwee Boon Low and Chew Lim Tan, Institute for Infocomm Research, Singapore; National University of Singapore, Singapore

The term weighting scheme used to convert documents into vectors in the term spaces, is a vital step in text categorization. In this paper, we compared various term weighting schemes with SVM on two widely-used benchmark data sets. We also presented a new term weighting scheme tf.rf for text categorization. The controlled experimental results showed that the newly proposed tf.rf scheme is significantly better than other term weighting schemes. Compared with schemes related with tf factor alone, the idf factor does not improve or even decrease the term's discriminating power for text categorization. The binary and tf.chi representations significantly underperform the other term weighting schemes.

1015 *One Class Support Vector Machine based Non-Relevance Feedback Document Retrieval [#1066]*
Takashi Onoda, Hiroshi Murata and Seiji Yamada, Central Research Inst. of Electric Power Indust., Japan; National Institute of Informatics, Japan

This paper reports a new document retrieval method using non-relevant documents. We applied active learning techniques for the relevance feedback. Our proposed approach has been very usefulfor document retrieval with relevance feedback experimentally. However, the initial retrieved documents sometimes don't include relevant documents. In order to solve this problem, we propose a new feedback method using information of non-relevant documents only. We named this method "non-relevance feedback document retrieval". The non-relevance feedback document retrieval is based on One- class Support Vector Machine.

1016 *Text Clustering with NTSO [#1146]*
Taeho Jo and Nathalie Japkowicz, University of Ottawa, Canada

Text clustering is the process of segmenting a particular collection of texts into subgroups including content-based similar ones. This study proposes a new neural network, called NTSO (Neural Text Self Organizer), which is suitable for text clustering. This neural network uses string vectors instead of numerical vectors as its input vectors and its weight vectors are different from those of other unsupervised neural networks such as Kohonen Networks and ART (Adaptive Resonance Theory), although it is similar to Kohonen Networks at the architecture level and in its learning process.

1017 *A Neuro-SVM Model for Text Classification using Latent Semantic Indexing [#1279]*
Vikramjit Mitra, Chia-Jiu Wang and Satarupa Banerjee, Worcester Polytechnic Institute, United States; University of Colorado at Colorado Springs, United States; Villanova University, United States

This paper presents a new model integrating a recurrent neural network (RNN) and a least squares support vector machine (LS-SVM) for classification of document titles according to different predetermined categories. The new model proposed in this paper is abbreviated as Neuro-SVM. Based on the Neuro-SVM model, a system is implemented, using latent semantic indexing (LSI) to generate probabilistic coefficients from document titles, which are used as the input to the system. The system's performance is demonstrated with a corpus of 96956 words, from University of Denver's Penrose Library catalogue and the accuracy rate of the proposed system is found to be 99.66%.

1018 *Fast Text Categorization with Min-Max Modular Support Vector Machines [#1657]*
Feng-Yao Liu, Ke Wu, Hai Zhao and Bao-Liang Lu, Shanghai Jiao Tong University, China; ShangHai Jiao Tong University, China

The min-max modular support vector machines(M3-SVMs) have been proposed for solving large-scale and complex multiclass classification problems. In this paper, we apply the M3-SVMs to multilabel text categrization and introduce a new task decomposition strategy called hyperplane task decomposition into M3- SVMs. The experimental results on the RCV1-v2 indicate that the new method has better generalization performance than traditional SVMs and previous M3- SVMs using random task decomposition, and is much faster than traditional SVMs.

1019 *Weight Sharing on Naive Bayes Document Model [#1349]*
Kazumi Saito and Ryohei Nakano, NTT Communication Science Laboratories, Japan; Nagoya Institute of Technology, Japan

We study weight sharing on the naive Bayes document model. Firstly we consider splitting words into a relatively small number of groups such that words in each group have the same parameter value. In this task, we formalize the problem in terms of maximum likelihood estimation, and then propose an algorithm for this purpose. Secondly we focus on an adaptive hyperparameter estimation problem based on prior distributions constructed by using such word groups. In this task, we describe a framework and algorithm, which enables to derive the unique optimal solution in the context of leave-one-out cross validation. In our experiments using a benchmark document set, we show a series of simulation results using the proposed algorithms.

1020 *Optimization of Context Matching Parameters for Web Information Retrieval Using an Evolutionary Algorithm [#1399]*
John Zakos, Ping Zhang and Brijesh Verma, Griffith University, Australia; Bond University, Australia; Central Queensland University, Australia

In this paper we present an approach based on the application of an evolutionary algorithm to optimally tune the parameters of a novel technique for effective web information retrieval. Context matching is a context-based technique for the ad-hoc retrieval of web documents that relies on a number of inter-related parameters that define the nature of the context it uses. But the optimal setting of context matching parameters is an important aspect of the technique to ensure effective retrieval. We show how the most effective settings for parameters are obtained efficiently through the evolutionary algorithm and how it achieves effective retrieval results on benchmark data that are a significant improvement on previously published results.

1021 *Snap-drift Learning for Phrase Recognition [#1145]*
Dominic Palmer-Brown and Sin Wee Lee, University of East London, United Kingdom; Leeds Metropolitan University, United Kingdom

A novel snap-drift classifier learning algorithm is applied to the task of recognising phrases from the Lancaster Parsed Corpus. Alongside the fast minimalist snap learning and slow drift towards the input patterns, each node of the network independently swaps between the snap and drift learning modes when declining performance occurs. Adaptation on each node is also reinforced by enabling learning with a probability that decreases with inreasing performance. The simulations demonstrate stability, and the results have shown significant speed and performance advantages over an MLP with back-propagation.

1022 *An Adaptive Function Neural Network (ADFUNN) for Phrase Recognition [#1147]*
Dominic Palmer-Brown and Miao Kang, University of East London, United Kingdom; Leeds Metropolitan University, United Kingdom

We describe an adaptive function neural network (ADFUNN), and apply it to the natural language processing task of phrase recognition. ADFUNN is based on a linear piecewise neuron activation function that is modified by a novel gradient descent supervised learning algorithm. Linearly inseparable problems can be learned with ADFUNN, rapidly and without hidden neurons. We perform phrase recognition on a set of phrases from the Lancaster Parsed Corpus. Generalisation rises to 100% with 150 training patterns (out of a total of 254).

1023 *Treatment of Missing Data Using Neural [#1059]*
Mussa Abdella and Tshilidzi Marwala, University of Witwatersrand, South Africa

Missing data creates various problems in analysing and processing of data in databases. Due to this reason missing data has been an area of research in various disciplines for quite a long time. This paper introduces a new method aimed at approximating missing data in a database using a combination of genetic algorithms and autoassociative neural networks. The research focus also lies on the investigation of using the proposed method to accurately approximate missing data as the number of missing cases within a single record increases. It is observed that approximations obtained using the proposed model to be highly accurate with 95% correlation coefficient between the actual missing values and corresponding approximated values.

1024 *An Iterative Relevance Feedback Learning Algorithm For Image Retrieval Systems [#1198]*
SaravanaKumar Srinivasan and Mahmood Azimi-Sadjadi, Colorado State University, United States

A new feature adaptation mechanism is proposed in this paper that captures the relevance feedback information provided by the expert users. This relevance information is retained for future usage and subsequently made available to other users. The search and retrieval processes are implemented through a two-layer connectionist network structure and the relevance feedback learning is incorporated by appropriately modifying the network structure. The developed algorithm is tested on an electro-optical imagery database collected from different underwater mine-like and non-mine-like objects.

Plenary Poster Session: Hardware
Monday, August 1, 7:00PM-11:00PM, Room: Fountaine, Chair: Program Chairs

1025 *Design of an Optical Fixed-Weight Learning Neural Network [#1559]*
A. Steven Younger and Emmett Redd, Southwest Missouri State University, United States

This paper deals with the design, analysis, and simulation of a prototype Optical Fixed-Weight Learning Neural Network. This type of network could have learning rates five orders of magnitude faster than networks based on Von-Neumann platforms. This network has an embedded learning algorithm and dynamically learns new mappings by changing recurrent neural signal strengths. This will greatly speed up optical neural network learning since the medium containing the synaptic weights does not change during learning. Software simulations suggest that this design is sound. The physical implementation and evaluation of the prototype will be reported elsewhere.

1026 *Forgetful Logic Circuits for Pulse-Mode Neural Networks [#1425]*
Richard B. Wells, Anindya Bhattacharya, Ben Sharon, Priyank Gupta and Sam Young, MRC Institute, University of Idaho, United States; Apex Microtechnology, United States; University of Idaho, United States

We introduce a new class of pulse-mode circuits, called forgetful logic. Forgetful logic circuits can be used to implement more complex waveform signaling modes in pulse-mode artificial neural network circuits. The basic operation of forgetful logic is first explained. Its application is then illustrated by numerous examples.

1027 *Artificial Neural Network Computation on Graphic Process Unit [#1396]*
Zhongwen Luo, Hongzhi Liu and Xincai Wu, China University of Geoscience, China

ANN is widely used in pattern recognition related area. Sometimes the computational load is very heavy and real time process is required. So there is a need to apply a parallel algorithm on it. In this paper, graphic hardware is used to speed up the computation of ANN. In recent years, graphic processing unit (GPU) grows faster than CPU. GPU venders provide programmability on GPU. In this paper, application of commodity available GPU for two kinds of ANN models was explored: self-organizing maps and multi layer perceptron (MLP). The computation result shows that ANN computing on GPU is much faster than on standard CPU when the neural network is large. And some design rules for improve the efficiency on GPU are given.

1028 *Circuit Implementation of Multi-Thresholded Neuron (MTN) Using BiCMOS Technology [#1237]*
Xiaolei Zhu, Jizhong Shen, Baoyong Chi and Zhihua Wang, Zhejiang University, Tsinghua University, China; Zhejiang University, China; Tsinghua University, China; Dept. of EE, Tsinghua University, Beijing, China

By analysing the principle of multi-thresholded neurons (MTNs), a methodology is developed for designing multi-thresholded neuron circuits (MTNCs). First, two n-channel MOS transistors are employed to design the voltage-mode synapse circuit with high simplicity and linearity. Second, a BiCMOS technique based circuit named Judgement-converting switch (JCS) is proposed. Based on this possibility, an approach is put forward to design multi-thresholded judgement function circuits (MTJFCs). Finally, single MTNC is designed for implementing XOR operation at switch level. Simulation results with PSPICE show that the designed circuits not only have the correct logic function but also small propagation delay.

1029 *FPGA Implementation of Pulse Coupled Oscillator [#1737]*
Yutaka Maeda and Makito Nakatsuka, Kansai University, Japan

This paper proposes a learning scheme for pulse coupled oscillators using the simultaneous perturbation optimization method. Moreover, hardware implementation of the pulse coupled oscillator with learning capability using field programmable gate array is described. The simultaneous perturbation optimization method can give a simple solution to this problem. In addition, this scheme is suitable for hardware realization. Some simulation results of the learning method for pulse coupled oscillators are shown. At the same time, we fabricated FPGA pulse coupled oscillator system with learning mechanism. Results by the hardware system are also shown.

1030 *Analog Current-Mode Implementation of Central Pattern Generator for Robot Locomotion [#1709]*
Kazuki Nakada, Tetsuya Asai, Tetsuya Hirose and Yoshihito Amemiya, Hokkaido University, Japan

We propose an analog current-mode subthreshold central pattern generator (CPG). Our circuit is based on the neural oscillator proposed by Matsuoka, well known as a building block for constructing a neuromorphic robot locomotion controller. We modified the Matsuoka's oscillator and implemented it as an analog integrated circuit with current-mode low-pass filters. We constructed a CPG circuit from four oscillator circuits. Through SPICE simulations, we confirmed that the CPG circuit generates stable phase-locked oscillation corresponding to typical locomotion of pattern of animals, and that the amplitude and frequency of the oscillation can be controlled by tuning bias currents over a wide range.

1031 *Toward an Analog VLSI Implementation of a Decision Making Model [#1421]*
Yili Quan and Albert Titus, University at Buffalo, SUNY, United States

This paper describes an analog circuit implementation of on-chip learning for the Lens Model by using Adaptive Linear Neuron networks (ADALINE). The on-chip learning circuit has been designed using MOS transistors operating in the subthreshold regime. The proposed circuit has been developed and simulated using the CMOS 1.5um AMI ABN process. The parameters of the correlation coefficient equation are current signals that can be controlled through the voltages to produce the square root behavior. The circuit is biased at 1.5V to lower the power dissipation. Spice simulations are included to illustrate the circuit performance.

1032 *On Kolmogorov's Superpositions: Novel Gates and Circuits for Nanoelectronics? [#1081]*
Valeriu Beiu and Artur Zawadzki, Washington State University, United States; University of Idaho, United States

Based on Kolmogorov's superpositions (KS) linear size circuits implementing Boolean functions (BFs) are possible. Boolean and threshold logic (TL) implementations require exponential size, so size-optimal solutions should rely on KS gates (KGs). We will examine 3-input BFs and show that the size can be reduced when Boolean gates could be optimally combined with KGs. This shows that there is room for improving on the synthesis of BFs. Finally, the size will be reduced further by allowing TL gates. Such size reductions could help alleviate the challenging power consumption problem, and advocate for the design of KGs and for the development of the theory, algorithms, and CAD tools able to take advantage of different gates and design styles.

1033 *Hardware Implementation of CMAC and B-Spline Neural Networks for Embedded Applications [#1284]*
Qiuye Zhao and Donald Reay, Heriot-Watt University, United Kingdom

The cerebellar model articulation controller (CMAC) is particularly well suited to real-time embedded applications on account of its fast learning, local generalisation, and ease of implementation. Among its drawbacks are a large memory requirement and the inability to model function derivatives. This paper describes a simple modification to the CMAC network that yields characteristics equivalent to an order two B-spline neural network (BSNN), including function derivative modelling, for the same computational complexity as CMAC and is suitable for high speed, low cost, hardware implementation in embedded applications. Two alternative approaches to its realisation using a field programmable gate array (FPGA) are described and compared.

1034 *DSP-Based Neural Systems for the Perceptual Assessment of Visual Quality [#1086]*
Paolo Gastaldo, Giovanni Parodi and Rodolfo Zunino, DIBE University of Genoa, Italy; DIBE, University of Genoa, Italy

The paper presents an efficient hardware realization of Circular Back Propagation (CBP) networks on Digital Signal Processors (DSP). The resulting neural-system is aimed at enhancing "smart" TV displays and supports the estimation of perceptual quality of visual signals. The DSP-based neuro- platform operates on raw digital signals and yields the associate estimate of perceived quality in real time. Experimental results confirm both evaluation accuracy and timing performance.

1035 *Analog Current-Mode Design for Soft-Max Computation [#1217]*
Davide Piombo and Rodolfo Zunino, DIBE - Genoa University, Italy; DIBE, University of Genoa, Italy

A modular design methodology supports CMOS circuits for the analog implementation of the Soft-Max function. An optimization-based strategy allows the designer to fit VLSI-technology requirements to soft max mapping accuracy. Specific circuit solutions to both the approximation of the exp() function and the normalizing ratio enhance overall effectiveness by: 1) reducing VLSI complexity, 2) exploiting inherent parallelism, and 3) limiting power consumption. Simulation results confirm the consistency of the hardware realization with theoretical predictions.

1036 *Low-Voltage Pseudo Floating-Gate Reconfigurable Linear [#1666]*
Oivind Naess, Snorre Aunet and Yngvar Berg, Department of of Informatics, University of Oslo, Norway

We present a reconfigurable linear threshold element which may be used to implement the boolean functions NOR3, CARRY' and NAND3. Several of the blocks may be used to implement any boolean function. Pseudo Floating-Gate transistors are used in order to set the appropriate threshold.

1037 *The Effects of Quantization on Support Vector Machines with Gaussian Kernel [#1329]*
Davide Anguita and Giovanni Bozza, DIBE - University of Genoa, Italy

We apply here a probabilistic method to predict the effect of quantizing the parameters of a Support Vector Machine with Gaussian kernel. Thank to the particular structure of the SVM, the dependency of the output from the quantization noise can be predicted with good accuracy, and a simple closed--form formula can be derived, without imposing any hard--to--verify assumption.

1038 *Building a Cheaper Artificial Brain [#1698]*
Hugo de Garis, Wang Ce and Thayne Batty, Utah State University, United States

This paper presents a methodology for building artificial brains that is much cheaper than the first author's earlier attempt. What initially cost $500,000, now costs about $3000. The much cheaper approach uses a Celoxica programmable board containing a Xilinx Virtex II FPGA chip with 3 million programmable logic gates, to evolve neural networks at electronic speeds. The Genetic Algorithm (GA) and the neural network model are programmed using a high level language called Handel-C. The elite circuit is downloaded from the board into the memory of a PC. This process occurs up to several 10,000s of times, once for each neural net circuit module having a unique function.

1039 *A Digital LSI Architecture of Elastic Graph Matching and Its FPGA Implementation [#1373]*
Teppei Nakano and Takashi Morie, Kyushu Institute of Technology, Japan

The elastic graph matching (EGM) is known as an excellent algorithm in applications of human face recognition. This paper proposes a digital LSI architecture for EGM and a face/object recognition system using its FPGA implementation. In the EGM, the matching evaluation point graph is distorted to find the best trade-off between better matching in the feature space and less distortion of the evaluation point graph. In the proposed architecture, cache memory stores calculation results at the evaluation points and those at their neighboring pixels to reduce the calculation amount. In the FPGA implementation with a system clock of 48 MHz, EGM between the input and one memorized image can be performed in about 1 ms.

1040 *Simulated Control of a Tracking Mobile Robot by Four aVLSI Integrate-and-Fire Neurons Paired into Maps [#1296]*
Jeffrey Dungen and Jean-Jules Brault, Ecole Polytechnique de Montreal, Canada

A simulated four-wheeled robot is controlled exclusively by four aVLSI integrate-and-fire neurons paired into winner-takes-all maps. The neural network takes analog sensor data as input and outputs to stepper motors controlling steering and throttle. The robot follows a randomly moving target in a closed environment 67% better than by chance, based on average distance to target. Simulation results suggest that silicon neural networks based on biological computing principles are effective, efficient, and compact embedded controllers. Test results should be confirmed on a physical implementation of the robot, and research should continue in network and circuit optimisation, as well as in the creation of robot societies.

Plenary Poster Session: Neurodynamics
Monday, August 1, 7:00PM-11:00PM, Room: Fountaine, Chair: Program Chairs

1041 *Recurrent Neural Networks Training with Stable Risk-Sensitive Kalman Filter Algorithm [#1415]*
Wen Yu, Jose de Jesus Rubio and Li Xiaoou, Cinvestav-IPN, Mexico

Compared to normal learning algorithms, for example backpropagation, Kalman filter-based algorithm has some better properties, such as faster convergence. In this paper, Kalman filter is modified with a risk-sensitive cost criterion, we call it as risk-sensitive Kalman filter. This new algorithm is applied to train recurrent neural networks for nonlinear system identification. Input-to- state stability is used to prove that the risk-sensitive Kalman filter training is stable. The contributions of this paper are: 1) the risk-sensitive Kalman filter is used for the state-space recurrent neural networks training, 2) the stability of the risk-sensitive Kalman filter is proved.

1042 *A Method of Oscillatory Trajectory Generation Using Recurrent Hybrid Neural Networks [#1685]*
Yasuaki Kuroe and Kei Miura, Kyoto Institute of Technology, Japan

This paper proposes a method for generating periodic oscillatory trajectories by recurrent neural networks. The problem is formulated as determining the weights of the synaptic connections of neural networks such that, the neural networks generate desired autonomous limit cycles in their state space. We introduce an architecture of neural networks, hybrid recurrent neural networks, in order to enhance the capability of possessing periodic oscillatory trajectories. In order to generate autonomous limit cycles in the neural networks we make use of the bifurcation theory. Efficient learning methods for oscillatory trajectories generation are derived. Experimental examples are presented to demonstrate the performance of the proposed method.

1043 *A New K-Winners-Take-All Neural Network [#1166]*
Shubao Liu and Jun Wang, Chinese University of Hong Kong, Hong Kong

In this paper, the K-Winners-Take-All (KWTA) operation is converted to an equivalent constrained convex quadratic optimization formulation. A simplifified dual neural network, called KWTA network, is further developed for solving the convex quadratic programming problem. The KWTA network is shown to be globablly convergent to the exact optimal solution of the QP problem. Simulation results are presented to show the effectiveness and performance of the KWTA network.

1044 *A Constrained Optimization Algorithm for Training Locally Recurrent Globally Feedforward Neural Networks [#1044]*
Paris Mastorocostas, Technological Educational Institute of Serres, Greece

This paper presents a novel learning algorithm for training locally recurrent globally feedforward neural networks. The training task is formulated as a constrained optimization problem, whose objective is twofold: (i) minimization of an error measure, leading to successful approximation of the input/output mapping and (ii) optimization of an additional functional, which aims at accelerating the learning process. Simulation results on a benchmark identification problem demonstrate that, compared to other learning schemes, the proposed algorithm has enhanced qualities, including improved speed of convergence, accuracy and robustness.

1045 *SCRAM: Statistically Converging Recurrent Associative Memory [#1119]*
Sylvain Chartier, Sebastien Helie, Mounir Boukadoum and Robert Proulx, Universite du Quebec en Outaouais, Canada; Universite du Quebec a Montreal, Canada; University of Quebec in Montreal, Canada

Autoassociative memories are known for their capacity to learn correlated patterns, complete these patterns and filter noisy inputs. However, no autoassociative memory as of yet was able to learn noisy patterns without pre- processing or special procedure. In this paper, we show that a new unsupervised learning rule enables associative memory models to locally learn online noisy correlated patterns. The learning is carried out by a dual Hebbian rule and the convergence is asymptotic. The asymptotic convergence results in an unequal eigenvalues spectrum, which distinguish SCRAM from optimal linear associative memories. Therefore, SCRAM develops less spurious attractors and has better recall performance under noise degradation.

1046 *A New Model for Learning in Graph Domains [#1470]*
Marco Gori, Gabriele Monfardini and Franco Scarselli, Universita' degli Studi di Siena, Italy

In several applications the information is naturally represented by graphs. Traditional approaches cope with graphical data structures using a preprocessing phase which trasforms the graphs into a set of flat vectors. However, in this way, important topological information may be lost and the achieved results may heavily depend on the preprocessing stage. This paper presents a new neural model, called graph neural network (GNN), capable of directly processing graphs. GNN extends recursive neural networks and can be applied on most of the practically useful kinds of graphs, including directed, undirected and labelled graphs. A learning algorithm for GNNs is proposed and some experiments are discussed which assess the properties of the model.

1047 *Empirical Approximation for Lyapunov Functions with Artificial Neural Nets [#1012]*
Gursel Serpen, The University of Toledo, United States

An artificial neural network is proposed as a function approximator for empirical modeling of a Lyapunov function for a nonlinear dynamic system that projects stable behavior as potentially observable in its state space. Theoretical framework for the methodology of designing the so-called Lyapunov neural network, which empirically models a Lyapunov function, is described. Algorithms for training the Lyapunov neural network for a neurodynamics system are presented.

1048 *Ability to Skip Steps Emerging from Chaotic Dynamics [#1223]*
Luciana P. P. Bueno and Aluizio F. R. Araujo, University of Sao Paulo, Brazil; Federal University of Pernambuco, Brazil

A chaotic bidirectional memory model (C-BAM) is constructed through the inclusion of chaotic neurons in the original BAM. Empiric experiments showed the occurrence of a chaotic dynamic capable to generate large diversity of recalled patterns involving complex excursions over all stored memories. This suggested that the retrieval sequence can model the ability of a novice or the ability of an expert to execute a task. Moreover, the paper illustrates a case in which a novice recall can be transformed into an expert recall through parametric variation.

1049 *Nonlinear dynamics on VSF-Network [#1403]*
Yoshitsugu Kakemoto and Shinichi Nakasuka, The Japan Research Institute, Japan; The University of Tokyo, Japan

In this paper, dynamics of VSF-Network (Vibration Synchronize Function Network) is investigated. VSF-network is a model of neural networks that articulates information from external world and fixes the articulated information. VSF-Network is a hybrid-typed neural network, and the chaos neuron is used for the hidden layer. VSF-Network articulates information with the neuron cluster generated by the synchronous vibration which the chaos neuron in hidden layer shows. We analyze the dynamics of generating the neuron cluster. Factors affecting cluster generation are investigated. The stability and the bifurcation of the neuron cluster and factors affecting cluster generation are investigated.

1050 *Dynamical Behavior of a Chaotic Neural Network and its Application to Optimization Problems [#1343]*
Toshijiro Tanaka and Etsumasa Hiura, Hiroshima Prefecture University, Japan; Fukuyama Polytechnic College, Japan

A model of an analog neuron with chaotic dynamics has been considered, and a chaotic neural network composed of this neuron has also been studied. The chaos neuron model has an internal variable which is evolved by a piecewise sine map, and it shows chaotic behavior. The chaotic neural network is applied to well-defined optimization problem in order to investigate computational abilities of the present model.

1051 *An Analysis of Associative Chaotic Neurodynamics by Using Surrogate Neurons [#1387]*
Masaharu Adachi, Tokyo Denki University, Japan

Associative chaotic neurodynamics is analyzed by using a method for nonlinear time series analysis. A method comparing features of the original time series with that of artificially made time series preserving some statistics of the original one is applyed for the analysis as follows. Some of the constituent neurons in the chaotic neural network are replaced by their surrogate data. The retrieval frequencies of the original network and the network with three surrogate methods, that preserve the dynamic range of the original data, are compared. The results show that the cross-spectra among the neurons in the network play certain role for maintaining the associative chaotic neurodynamics.

Plenary Poster Session: Hopfield networks
Monday, August 1, 7:00PM-11:00PM, Room: Fountaine, Chair: Program Chairs

1052 *A New Kind of Hopfield Networks for Finding Global Optimum [#1285]*
Xiaofei Huang, Coding Research, United States

The Hopfield network has been applied to solve optimization problems over decades. However, it still has many limitations in accomplishing this task. Most of them are inherited from the optimization algorithms it implements. The computation of a Hopfield network, defined by a set of difference equations, can easily be trapped into one local optimum or another, sensitive to initial conditions, perturbations, and neuron update orders. It doesn't know how long it will take to converge, as well as if the final solution is a global optimum, or not. In this paper, we present a Hopfield network with a new set of difference equations to fix those problems. The difference equations directly implement a new powerful optimization algorithm.

1053 *Learning cycles brings chaos in continuous Hopfield networks [#1550]*
Colin Molter, Utku Salihoglu and Hugues Bersini, Iridia - ULB, Belgium

This paper studies the impact of an hebbian learning algorithm on the recurrent neural network's inner dynamics. Two different kinds of learning are compared: the storing of static patterns and the storing of cyclic patterns. If the storing of static patterns leads to a reduction of the potential dynamics, the learning of cyclic patterns tends to increase the dimension of the potential attractors. In fact, such learning may be used as a "route to chaos": the more cycles to be learned, the more the network shows as spontaneous dynamics a form of chaotic itinerancy among brief oscillatory periods. It confirms precedent papers in which it was observed that huge encoding capacity in term of cyclic attractors implies strong presence of chaos.

1054 *Phase Diagrams for Locally Hopfield Neural Networks in Presence of Correlated Patterns [#1221]*
Filip Piekniewski and Tomasz Schreiber, Nicolaus Copernicus University, Poland

In this paper we consider non-zero low temperature large-size locally Hopfield neural networks in finite loading regime, learning patterns admitting strong and regular correlation structure. Our aim being to find conditions for pattern stability and successful retrieval as depending on the imposed correlation structure, we propose to apply the so-called Pirogov-Sinai theory from statistical mechanics to describe the geometry of pattern stability regions. We check that this theory does match with the experimental data and we investigate some further interesting phenomena that occur in such systems.

1055 *2 Types of Complex-Valued Hopfield Networks and the Application to a Traffic Signal Control [#1251]*
Ikuko Nishikawa, Kazutoshi Sakakibara, Takeshi Iritani and Yasuaki Kuroe, Ritsumeikan University, Japan; Kyoto Institute of Technology, Japan

Dynamics of 2 types of complex-valued Hopfield networks is analyzed. Both networks are proved to possess an energy function when each neuron is non-rotating. The phase synchronization in the complex plane is used for the signal-offset control. In computer simulations, the offsets obtained by both networks are close to those obtained by a phase oscillator system in simple traffic conditions, while they become different in relatively large and complicated conditions. One type of network includes the dynamics of the oscillator system and always converges to give the offsets, while another type converges to periodic solutions with minute fluctuations. The effectiveness of the both offsets is precisely evaluated under various conditions.

1056 *A New N-Parallel Updating Method of the Hopfield-Type Neural Network for N-Queens Problem [#1721]*
Thanh-Nhat Le and Cong-Kha Pham, Yasukawa Information Systems, Japan; The University of Electro-Communication, Japan

In the previous N-parallel updating methods of the Hopfield-type neural network for N-queens problem, NxN neurons have been grouped into N groups. Each group composed of N neurons which are located in a same horizontal line (column) or in a same diagonal line. However, these method did not give convergence results of 100\% in all size of N. Also, they required a large convergence time steps. In our work, we propose a new N-parallel updating method of the Hopfield-type neural network for N-queens problem, in which, a new grouping method for N neurons composed in the same group has been adopted. As a result, simulation results of the proposed method show a best performance than the previous generally.

Plenary Poster Session: Reinforcement learning
Monday, August 1, 7:00PM-11:00PM, Room: Fountaine, Chair: Program Chairs

1057 *On-Line System Identification Using Context Discernment [#1518]*
Lars Holmstrom, Roberto Santiago and George Lendaris, NWCIL, Portland State University, United States

Mathematical models are often used in system identification applications. The dynamics of most systems, however, change over time and the sources of these changes cannot always be directly determined or measured. To maintain model accuracy, it is desirable to design system identifiers that can adapt to these dynamical shifts. We use reinforcement learning to train an agent to recognize dynamical changes in a modeled system and to estimate new parameter values for the model. The subsequent actions of this agent are characterized as "moving" the parameterized model on an optimal trajectory in model parameter space. It is found that this method is capable of quickly and accurately discerning the correct parameter values.

1058 *The k-Server Problem: A Reinforcement Learning Approach [#1656]*
Manoel Leandro L. Junior, Jorge Dantas de Melo and Adriao Doria Duarte Neto, Universidade Federal do Rio Grande do Norte, Brazil

This work presents an original algorithm, based on reinforcement learning, as a solution for the k-server problem. This problem was modelled as a multi-stage decision-making process, and subsequently the Q-Learning algorithm was used as a means of solution. A series of experiments was conducted with the aim of evaluating the appropriateness and performance of the proposed solution. The results obtained show the efficiency of the suggested algorithm in comparison with other methods of solving the k-server problem frequently cited in the literature, whose rates of competitiveness have already been proven.

1059 *Task Similarity Measures for Transfer in Reinforcement Learning Task Libraries [#1662]*
James Carroll and Kevin Seppi, Brigham Young University, United States

Recent research in task transfer and task clustering has necessitated the need for task similarity measures in reinforcement learning. Determining task similarity is necessary for selective transfer where only information from relevant tasks and portions of a task are transferred. Which task similarity measure to use is not immediately obvious. It can be shown that no single task similarity measure is uniformly superior. The optimal task similarity measure is dependent upon the task transfer method being employed. We define similarity in terms of tasks, propose several possible transfer techniques, evaluate their performance, and propose future work that should be performed in this area.

1060 *Neural Network Model for Time Series Prediction by Reinforcement Learning [#1078]*
Feng Liu, Chai Quek and Geok See Ng, Nanyang Technological University, Singapore

Two important issues when constructing a neural network (NN) for time series prediction: proper selection of (1) the input dimension and (2) the time delay between the inputs. These two parameters determine the structure, computing complexity and accuracy of the NN. This paper is to formulate an autonomous data-driven approach to identify a parsimonious structure for the NN so as to reduce the prediction error and enhance the modeling accuracy. The Reinforcement Learning based Dimension and Delay Estimator (RLDDE) is proposed. It involves a trial-error learning process to formulate a selection policy for designating the above-mentioned two parameters. The proposed method is evaluated by the prediction of the benchmark sunspot time series.

Plenary Poster Session: Decision making, abductive and transductive reasoning
Monday, August 1, 7:00PM-11:00PM, Room: Fountaine, Chair: Program Chairs

1061 *Learning Nonlinear State-Space Models for Control [#1328]*
Tapani Raiko and Matti Tornio, Helsinki University of Technology, Finland

This paper studies the learning of nonlinear state-space models for a control task. This has some advantages over traditional methods. Variational Bayesian learning provides a framework where uncertainty is explicitly taken into account and system identification can be combined with model-predictive control. Three different control schemes are used. One of them, optimistic inference control, is a novel method based directly on the probabilistic modelling. Simulations with a cart-pole swing-up task confirm that the latent state space provides a representation that is easier to predict and control than the original observation space.

1062 *A Neural Network Model for the Decision-Making Process Based on AHP [#1318]*
Satoshi Matsuda, Nihon University, Japan

A neural network model is proposed for the decision-making process based on the Analytic Hierarchy Process (AHP). Although there have been many attempts at developing the neural models of intellectual activities of human beings, to our knowledge there have been few attempts at developing the neural model of decision-making process, which is a typical intellectual activity. By viewing AHP as a model of decision-making, we present a neural network model of the decision-making process. Furthermore, we show that the model also works naturally in more practical situations where we cannot get all the information to make decision. Finally, we apply the proposed neural network to some examples and illustrate its validity through simulations.

1063 *Negative Reinforcement and Backtrack-Points for Recurrent Neural Networks for Cost-Based Abduction [#1220]*
Ashraf M. Abdelbar, Mostafa A. El-Hemaly, Emad A.M. Andrews and Donald C. Wunsch II, American University in Cairo, Egypt; ACIL, University of Missouri-Rolla, United States

Abduction is the process of proceeding from data describing a set of observations or events, to a set of hypotheses which best explains or accounts for the data. Cost-based abduction (CBA) is an AI formalism in which evidence to be explained is treated as a goal to be proven, proofs have costs based on how much needs to be assumed to complete the proof, and the set of assumptions needed to complete the least-cost proof are taken as the best explanation for the given evidence. In this paper, we introduce two techniques for improving the performance of high order recurrent networks (HORN) applied to cost-based abduction: backtrack-points and negative reinforcement.

1064 *Distributed Computation for Neural-Based Abductive Reasoning [#1058]*
Lotfi Ben Romdhane and Mourad Elhadef, Department of Computer Science, FSM, Tunisia; School of Inf. Tech. and Eng., Un. of Ottawa, Canada

This work extends a recent model for neural-based abductive reasoning to account for the monotonic class. A problem is said to be monotonic some causes, together, explain the same effect. For this, we developed a new computational principle, called the softmin, and implemented it within a neural architecture. Simulation results are very satisfactory and should stimulate future research.

1065 *Transductive Modeling with GA Parameter Optimization [#1538]*
Nisha Mohan and Nikola Kasabov, Auckland University of Technology, New Zealand

While inductive modeling is used to develop a model from data of whole problem space and then to recall it on new data, transductive modeling is concerned with creation of single model for every new input vector based on some closest vectors from existing problem space. However, deciding on the appropriate distance measure, on the number of nearest neighbors and on a minimum set of important features is a challenge and is usually based on prior knowledge or exhaustive trial and test experiments. The paper proposes a GA method for optimizing these three factors using a transductive approach. The method is tested on several datasets from UCI repository for classification task and results show that it outperforms conventional approaches.

1066 *Symbolic Rule Extraction with a Scaled Conjugate Gradient Version of CLARION [#1501]*
Tasos Falas and Andreas Stafylopatis, Cyprus College, Cyprus; National Technical University of Athens, Greece

This paper presents a hybrid system where the sub-symbolic module is a neural network trained by a modified Q-learning methodology that employs the scaled conjugate gradient algorithm. The rules in the symbolic module are extracted from the sub-symbolic module during training, similar to CLARION. The two modules augment each other in an effort to obtain a better performance than any of the modules acting alone. The originality lies in the use of the scaled conjugate gradient algorithm. It is expected that it will provide improvements in the performance of the overall system and also make it less dependent on user-selected parameters. This paper emphasises the implementation details, rather that experimental results.

Plenary Poster Session: Support Vector Machines
Monday, August 1, 7:00PM-11:00PM, Room: Fountaine, Chair: Program Chairs

1067 *One-Against-All Multi-Class SVM Classification Using Reliability Measures [#1030]*
Yi Liu and Yuan F. Zheng, The Ohio State University, United States

One drawback of the conventional one-against-all method is the competence of the classifiers is totally neglected when the classification results from the multiple classifiers are combined for the final decision. To overcome this limitation, this paper introduces two reliability measures into the multi-class framework: static reliability measure (SRM) and dynamic reliability measure (DRM). SRM works on a collective basis and yields a constant value regardless of the location of the test sample while DRM accounts for the spatial variation of the classifier's performance. Based on SRM and DRM, a new decision strategy for the one-against-all method is proposed, which is tested on benchmark data sets and demonstrates its effectiveness.

1068 *K-Fold Generalization Capability Assessment for Support Vector Classifiers [#1334]*
Davide Anguita, Sandro Ridella and Fabio Rivieccio, DIBE - University of Genoa, Italy

The problem of how to effectively implement k--fold cross--validation for Support Vector Machines is here considered. Indeed, despite the fact that this selection criterion is widely used due to its reasonable requirements in terms of computational resources and its good ability in identifying a well performing model, it is not clear how one should employ the committee of classifiers coming from the k folds for the task of on- -line classification. Three methods are here described and tested, based respectively on: averaging, random choice and majority voting. Each of these methods is tested on a wide range of data--sets for different fold settings.

1069 *Weighted Support Vector Machine for Data Classification [#1307]*
Xulei Yang, Song Qing and Cao Aize, Nanyang Technological University, Singapore

A weighted support vector machine (WSVM) is presented to improve the outlier sensitivity problem of standard SVM for two-class data classification. The basic idea is to assign different weight to different data point such that the WSVM training algorithm learns the decision surface according to the relative importance of data point in the training data set. The weights used in WSVM are generated by kernel-based possibilistic c-means (KPCM) algorithm, whose partition generates relative high values for important data points but low values for outliers. Experimental results indicate that the proposed method reduces the affect of outliers and yields higher classification rate than standard SVM does when outliers exist in the training data set.

1070 *Algorithms of Fast SVM Evaluation based on Subspace Projection [#1615]*
Jianxiong Dong, Adam Krzyzak and Ching Y. Suen, CENPARMI, Concordia University, Canada; Dept. Computer Science, Concordia University, Canada

A fast iteration algorithm is proposed to approximate the reduced set vectors shared by each binary SVM solution for multi-class classification simultaneously. The iteration algorithm can be applied to the general kernel types such as RBF and polynomial kernels. In addition, we present a fast block algorithm in the test phase to speed up the classification further. Experimental results have shown that the classification speeds on MNIST and Hanwang handwritten digit databases on P4 1.7Ghz were about 16,000 and 10,895 patterns per second without sacrificing the classification accuracy of the original SVM system. The speed-up factor of 110 on MNIST database has been achieved.

1071 *Yet Faster Method to Optimize SVR Hyperparameters based on Minimizing Cross-Validation Error [#1384]*
Kenji Kobayashi, Daisuke Kitakoshi and Ryohei Nakano, Nagoya Institute of Technology, Japan

The performance of Support Vector regression deeply depends on its hyperparameters. A method called MCV-SVR optimizes hyperparams by iterating two steps until convergence; step 1 optimizes params under given hyperparams, while step 2 improves hyperparams under given params. A faster version called MCV-SVR-Light accelerates step 2 by pruning. This paper yet accelerates step 1 of MCV-SVR-Light by pruning. Here the pruning means confining the process to support vectors. Our experiments show that our method converged faster than the existing methods while the generalization performance remained comparable.

1072 *Support Vector Regression Performance Analysis and Systematic Parameter Selection [#1080]*
Pao-Tsun Lin, Shun-Feng Su and Tsu-Tian Lee, National Chiao-Tung University, Taiwan; National Taipei University of Technology, Taiwan

The Support Vector Regression method deals with data in a high dimension space by using linear quadratic programming techniques. As a consequence, the regression result has optimal properties. However, if parameters were not properly selected, overfitting and/or underfitting phenomena might occur in SVR. Two parameters Sigma, the width of Gaussian kernels and Epsilon, the tolerance zone in the cost function are considered in this research. We adopted the concept of the sampling theory into Gaussian Filter to deal with parameter Sigma. For another parameter epslion, it is a tradeoff between the number of Support Vectors and the RMSE. By introducing the confidence interval concept, a suitable selection of Epsilon can be obtained.

1073 *Pre-selection of Working Set for SVM Decomposition Algorithm [#1295]*
Xulei Yang, Song Qing and Liu Sheng, Nanyang Technological University, Singapore

The decomposition algorithm is currently one of the major methods for solving support vector machines (SVM) training problems. The most important issue of this method is the selection of working set, which greatly affects the speed of the decomposition algorithm. In this paper, we propose a novel method for pre-selection of the working set for bound-constrained SVM formulation, which aims to make the training process more efficient. The pre-selection method is implemented based on fuzzy clustering technique in the high dimensional feature space using kernel methods. The effectiveness of the proposed method is supported by experimental results.

1074 *The Intermediate Matching Kernel for Image Local Features [#1541]*
Sabri Boughorbel, Jean-Philippe Tarel and Nozha Boujemaa, Imedia, Inria Rocquencourt, France; ESE Division, LCPC, France

We introduce the Intermediate Matching (IM) kernel for SVM based object recognition. The IM kernel operates on a feature space of vector's sets. Indeed, each image is represented by a set of local features. Matching algorithms have been proved to be efficient for such type of features. Nevertheless, kernelizing the matching for SVM does not lead to positive definite kernels. The introduced IM kernel overcomes this drawback. Indeed, it mimics matching algorithms while being positive definite. The IM kernel introduces an intermediary set of the so-called virtual local features. The latter's select the pairs of local features to be matched. Comparison with Matching kernel shows that the IM kernels leads to similar performances.

1075 *MIMO SVMs for classification and regression using the geometric algebra framework [#1571]*
Eduardo Bayro-Corrochano and Nancy Arana-Daniel, CINVESTAV, Unidad Guadalajara, Computer Science, Mexico

This paper introduces the Clifford Support Vector Machines (CSVM) as a generalization of the real- and complex- valued Support Vector Machines using the Clifford geometric algebra. In this framework we handle the design of kernels involving the Clifford or geometric product for linear and nonlinear classification and regression. The major advantage of our approach is that one requires only one CSVM with one kernel (involving the Clifford product) which can admit multiple multivector inputs and it can carry multi-class classification and regression.In contrast one would need many real valued SVMs for a multi-class problem which is time consuming.

1076 *Fuzzy integral for a rapid mixture of support vector machines [#1214]*
Hassiba Nemmour and Youcef Chibani, Usthb, Algeria; Usthb, Anguilla

In the last years, there was an interest in using mixture of support vector machines for large data bases. This approach aims to reduce the complexity of the training algorithm of SVMs which is at least quadratic to the number of training data. This objective is reached by dividing the data set into small subsets which are much easy to learn. In this paper, we present a new approach for mixture of SVMs based on the notion of fuzzy integral. Experiments were conducted on USPS handwritten digits data base. The results obtained indicate that the proposed scheme improves significantly the training time while keeping accuracy at least as good as the accuracy of a single SVM.

1077 *Feature Subset Selection for Support Vector Machines using Confident Margin [#1309]*
Mauricio Kugler, Anto Satriyo Nugroho, Kazuma Aoki, Susumu Kuroyanagi and Akira Iwata, Nagoya Institute of Technology, Japan; Chukyo University, Japan

The aim of this study is to develop a feature subset selection (FSS) method based on the margin of Support Vector Machines (SVM). The problem of directly using the SVM margin is that it does not always provide clear relationship between its value and the performance of SVM, and the best obtained subset is not guaranteed to be the best possible one. In this paper, a new solution is describe by the introduction of the Confident Margin (CM) in the subset criterion, which permits to get near the best recognition rate by monitoring the peak of CM curve without directly calculating the recognition rate, in order to save computational time. The performance of the proposed method was evaluated in artificial and real-world data experiments.

1078 *Assignment Kernels For Chemical Compounds [#1013]*
Holger Froehlich, Joerg Wegner and Andreas Zell, Centre for Bioinformatics Tuebingen (ZBIT), Germany; University of Tuebingen, Germany

During the last years Kernel Methods like the SVM have gained a growing interest in Machine Learning. One of the strengths of this approach is the ability to deal easily with arbitrarily structured data by means of the kernel function. In this paper we propose a kernel for chemical compounds which is based on the idea of computing optimal assignments between atoms of two different molecules including information about their neighborhood. As a byproduct this leads to a new class of kernel functions. We demonstrate how the necessary computations can be carried out efficiently. We compare our method against the Graph Kernels by Kashima et al. and show its good perfomance on classifying toxicological and human intestinal absorption data.

1079 *Characterization of Data Complexity for SVM Methods [#1103]*
Yunqian Ma and Vladimir Cherkassky, Honeywell International Inc., United States; University of Minnesota, United States

This paper provides new characterization of data complexity for margin-based methods also known as SVMs, kernel methods etc. Under the predictive learning setting, the complexity of a given data set is directly related to model complexity, i.e. the flexibility of a set of admissible models used to describe this data. There are two distinct approaches: traditional model-based where complexity is controlled via parameterization of admissible models, and margin-based where complexity is controlled by the size of margin (in a specially designed empirical loss function). This paper emphasizes the role of margin for complexity control,and proposes a simple index for data complexity suitable for classification and regression problems.

1080 *Optimizing Resources in Model Selection for Support Vectors Machines [#1493]*
Mathias Adankon, Mohamed Cheriet and Ayat Nedjem, LIVIA, Ecole de Technologie Superieure, Canada; LIVIA, Ecole de Technologie Superieure, Montreal, Canada

Tuning SVM kernel parameters is a an important step for achieving a high-performing learning machine. The usual automatic methods used to tune these parameters require an inversion of the Grahm-Schmidt matrix. In the case of a large dataset these methods require the addition of huge amounts of memory and a long CPU time to the already significant ressources used in the SVM training. In this paper, we propose a fast method based on an approximation of the gradient of the empirical error along with incremental learning, which reduces the resources required both in terms of processing time and of storage space.

1081 *A convergence rate estimate for the SVM Decomposition Method [#1029]*
Daniel Lai, Mani Nallasamy, Palaniswami Marimuthu and Shilton Alistair, Monash University, Australia; Melbourne University, Australia

The training of Support Vector Machines using the decomposition method has one drawback; namely the selection of working sets for fast convergence.It has been shown by Lin that the rate is linear in the worse case under certain operating assumptions. However,the rate estimate given is independent of time and hence gives little indication as to how the linear convergence speed varies during the iteration.We provide a treatment of the convergence from a gradient contraction perspective.We propose a necessary and sufficient condition to gurantee strict linear convergence of the algorithm.Based on this condition, a time dependant rate estimate is then further derived. This estimate is shown to monotonically approach unity from below.

1082 *Deriving Kernels from MLP Probability Estimators for Large Categorization Problems [#1526]*
Ivan Titov and James Henderson, University of Geneva, Switzerland; University of Edinburgh, Great Britain

In multi-class categorization problems with a very large number of classes, kernel based methods are often not computationally feasible. One partial solution is to preselect a subset of the classes for reranking with a kernel method. We investigate using trained multi-layer perceptron probability estimators to derive appropriate kernels for such reranking problems. We propose a kernel derivation method which is specifically designed for reranking problems, and a more efficient variant of this method which is designed for neural networks with large numbers of output units. When applied to a neural network model of natural language parsing, these new methods achieve state-of-the-art performance which improves over the original model.

1083 *SVM Ensembles for Selecting the Relevant Feature Subsets [#1312]*
Tao Ban and Shigeo Abe, Kobe University, Japan

In this paper we present a novel feature selection algorithm for SVMs which works by estimating the stability of a feature's contribution to some evaluation criterion. This algorithm is extremely fast as only a small number of SVM classifiers need to be trained for feature selection. Robust results are shown with toy as well as real-life datasets. Furthermore, we combine this method with a backward elimination procedure. The combined algorithm performs stably and shows optimal performance compared with other feature selection methods. Another merit of the combined algorithm is that it can estimate the optimal number of features with the best prediction power. This method is applicable to both linear and nonlinear problems.

1084 *Pattern De-Noising Based on Support Vector Data Description [#1095]*
Jooyoung Park, Daesung Kang, Jongho Kim, James T. Kwok and Ivor W. Tsang, Korea University, South Korea; Hong Kong University of Science and Technology, Hong Kong

The SVDD is one of the most well-known one-class support vector learning methods, in which one tries the strategy of utilizing balls defined on the feature space in order to distinguish a set of normal data from all other possible abnormal objects. The major concern of this paper is to extend the main idea of the SVDD for the problem of pattern de-noising. In the proposed method, we first solve the SVDD for the training data, then for each noisy test pattern, perform de-noising by projecting its feature vector onto the decision boundary on the feature space, and finally find the location of the de-noised pattern by obtaining the pre-image of the projection.

1085 *Kernel Relevant Component Analysis for Distance Metric Learning [#1211]*
Ivor W. Tsang, Pak-Ming Cheung and James T. Kwok, Hong Kong University of Science and Technology, Hong Kong

Defining a good distance measure between patterns is of crucial importance in many classification and clustering algorithms. Recently, relevant component analysis (RCA) is proposed which offers a simple yet powerful method to learn this distance metric. However, it is confined to linear transforms in the input space. In this paper, we show that RCA can also be kernelized, which then results in significant improvements when nonlinearities are needed. Moreover, it becomes applicable to distance metric learning for structured objects that have no natural vectorial representation. Besides, it can be used in an incremental setting. Performance of this kernel method is evaluated on both toy and real-world data sets with encouraging results.

Plenary Poster Session: Learning and optimization
Monday, August 1, 7:00PM-11:00PM, Room: Fountaine, Chair: Program Chairs

1086 *A new saliency measure for inputs selection and node pruning in neural network [#1733]*
Eric Fock, Philippe Lauret and Thierry Mara, University of La Reunion, Reunion

This paper deals with a new saliency measure for ranking and removing the less important inputs and hidden nodes. This new metric is the result of a global sensitivity analysis, EFAST, performed on the neural network. EFAST is model independent, does not interact with the training stage and does not rely on any assumption regards to local minima, contrary to local sensitivity-based saliency. EFAST apportions the output variance among all the units, and allows their quantitative ranking. New input selection and node pruning algorithms have been derived and are presented. Some experimental results are provided and show with a good agreement the efficiency of the approach for input selection, system identification and node pruning applications

1087 *One-Step Neural Network Inversion with PDF Learning and Emulation [#1582]*
Leemon Baird, David Smalenberger and Shawn Ingkiriwang, US Air Force Academy, United States

We present two new types of neural networks and we present a new algorithm for learning a probability density function (pdf) from example vectors. For the new bijective neural network, it is efficient to find an input producing any desired output. Furthermore, it can be used as one component in building a pdf neural network, which is a neural network with a nonnegative output and integral 1. Finally, the new pdf learning algorithm is capable of using those networks to learn a pdf given i.i.d. samples drawn from that pdf, and to then generate new vectors from the learned pdf. This, in turn, allows inversion of a function with non-unique inverses, where each inverse is generated with just a single evaluation of the network.

1088 *Effective neural network pruning using cross-validation [#1627]*
Thuan Huynh and Rudy Setiono, National University of Singapore, Singapore

This paper addresses the problem of finding neural networks with optimal topology such that their generalization capability is maximized. Our approach is to combine the use of a penalty during network training and a subset of the training samples for cross-validation. The penalty function is added to the error function so that the weights of network connections that are not useful have small magnitude. Such network connections can be pruned if the resulting accuracy does not change beyond a preset level. Training samples in the cross-validation set are used to indicate when network pruning is terminated. Our results on 32 data sets show that the method outperforms existing neural network and decision tree methods for classification.

1089 *An Efficient Learning Algorithm for Finding Multiple Solutions Based on Fixed-Point Homotopy Method [#1431]*
Hiroshi Ninomiya, Chikahiro Tomita and Hideki Asai, Shonan Institute of Technology, Japan; Shizuoka University, Japan

This paper describes an efficient learning algorithm based on Fixed-point homotopy method. The proposed algorithm has the ability to train the neural networks with high success rates for the initial guesses compared with other typical second-order training algorithms. Furthermore, the method proposed here not only has the widely convergent property but also find out multiple solutions. The validity of the proposed algorithm for the standard multilayer neural networks is demonstrated through the computer simulations. As a result, it is confirmed that our algorithm is efficient and practical for the learning of the multilayer feedforward neural networks.

1090 *An Analysis of Overfitting in MLP Networks [#1499]*
Sridhar Narayan and Gene A. Tagliarini, University of North Carolina, Wilmington, United States

The generalization ability of an MLP network has been shown to be related to both the number and magnitudes of the network weights. Thus, there exists a tension between employing networks with few weights that have relatively large magnitudes, and networks with a greater number of weights with relatively small magnitudes. The analysis presented in this paper indicates that large magnitudes for network weights potentially increase the propensity of a network to interpolate poorly. Experimental results indicate that when bounds are imposed on network weights, the backpropagation algorithm is capable of discovering networks with small weight magnitudes that retain their expressive power and exhibit good generalization.

1091 *Experimental Evaluation of a Hybrid Method for Configuring Ensemble Encoding Receptors [#1109]*
Ashraf M. Abdelbar, Deena O. Hassan, Gene A. Tagliarini and Sridhar Narayan, American University in Cairo, Egypt; University of North Carolina, Wilmington, United States

Ensemble encoding is a biologically-motivated, distributed data representation scheme for MLP networks. Multiple overlapping receptive fields are used to enhance locality of representation. The number, form, and placement of receptive fields has a great impact on performance. In this paper, we explore a technique in which clustering is used to determine receptive field centers, and a variance-based method is used to determine receptive field widths. The relative performance of this hybrid method to other published methods is evaluated experimentally on three benchmark data sets.

1092 *Dynamic construction of fault tolerant multi-layer neural networks [#1367]*
Haruhiko Takase, Hidehiko Kita and Terumine Hayashi, Mie university, Japan

We propose a new training algorithm for enhance tolerance to physical defects (faults) of multi-layer neural networks (MLNs). We aim to construct such MLNs with the minimal number of hidden units. The proposed method has two characteristics, constructing MLNs dynamically and getting high fault tolerance easily. We proposed dynamic constructive algorithm with weight minimization approach (DCWMA) based on a DCA and WMA. DCA (dynamic constructive algorithm) is a basic dynamic constructive algorithm for MLNs. WMA (weight minimization algorithm) is a training algorithm to enhance the fault tolerance of fixed structure MLNs. The effectiveness of DCWMA is shown by some experiment.

1093 *The p-Center Machine [#1114]*
Michael Brueckner, Chemnitz University of Technology, Germany

We would like to present a new approach to find an optimal large margin classifier based on the p-Center which was proposed by Moretti in 2003. We introduce an algorithm approximating the p-Center of the version space and compare its performance and runtime behavior to the Kernel Perceptron, Support Vector Machine, and the Bayes Point Machine experimentally by using standard benchmark datasets. It turns out that the p-Center is close to the Bayes Point and leads to slightly inferior performance than that of the hard boundary BPM and the hard margin SVM. However, the proposed algorithm is highly parallelizable and thus very efficient in terms of computational effort.

1094 *A Better Scaled Local Tangent Space Alignment Algorithm [#1176]*
Jian Yang, Fuxin Li and Jue Wang, Institute of Automation, Chinese Academy of Sci., China

We present a manifold learning algorithm called partitional local tangent space alignment (PLTSA). In the algorithm, the sample space is divided into overlapped blocks by the X-Means algorithm. Then each point is projected to the local tangent space of the block it belongs, to get its local low-dimensional coordinate. The global low-dimensional embedded manifold is obtained from local coordinates via local affine transformations. PLTSA is a better-scaled algorithm in that it provides a means of mapping newcome data with much smaller time and space requirements than LTSA, and it works on a much smaller optimization matrix. The validity of PLTSA is illustrated by its results on surfaces in 3D Euclidean spaces and MNIST handwritten digit data.

1095 *Gaussian Processes of Nonlinear Diffusion Filtering [#1408]*
Ramunas Girdziusas and Jorma Laaksonen, Helsinki University of Technology, Finland

Nonlinear diffusion filtering can be improved if viewed as Bayesian Gaussian process regression. We relate the covariance functions of the diffusion process outcome to the spatial diffusion operator and show how Bayesian evidence criterion can be utilized to determine the parameters of the nonlinear diffusivity and the optimal diffusion stopping time. Computational example is given where the nonlinear diffusion filtering outperforms typical Gaussian process regression.

1096 *Fast Training of Multilayer Perceptrons with a Mixed Norm Algorithm [#1753]*
Sabeur Abid, Farhat Fnaiech, B. W. Jervis and Mohamed Cheriet, Esstt, Tunisia; Sheffield Hallam University, United Kingdom; LIVIA, Ecole de Technologie Superieure, Montreal, Canada

A new fast training algorithm for the Multilayer Perceptron (MLP) is proposed. This new algorithm is based on the optimization of a mixed Least Square (LS) and a Least Fourth (LF) criterion producing a modified form of the standard back propagation algorithm (SBP). To determine the updating rules in the hidden layers, an analogous back propagation strategy used in the conventional learning algorithms is developed. This permits the application of the learning procedure to all the layers. Experimental results on benchmark applications and a real medical problem are obtained which indicates significant reduction in the total number of iterations, the convergence time, and the generalization capacity when compared to those of the SBP algorithm.

1097 *Decorrelating Parametrical Neural Network [#1244]*
Boris Kryzhanovsky, Vladimir Kryzhanovsky and Anatoly Fonarev, Institute of Optical Neural Technologies RAS, Russian Federation; City University of New York, United States

We developed a new network architecture, allowing us to increase the recognizing characteristics of the Hopfield Model substantively. In addition it is effective when recognizing correlated patterns. It is shown that the storage capacity of the network increases exponentially with increase of the free parameter of the problem. The boundaries restricting the increase of the storage capacity are defined.

1098 *Second-order backpropagation algorithms for a stagewise-partitioned separable Hessian matrix [#1450]*
Eiji Mizutani, Stuart Dreyfus and James Demmel, Tsing Hua University, Taiwan; University of California at Berkeley, United States

We describe two second-order backpropagation (BP) algorithms to evaluate the Hessian matrix of a given objective function for feed-forward neural-network (NN) learning with a special emphasis on how to organize Hessian elements into a so-called stagewise-partitioned block-arrow matrix form: (1) stagewise BP, an extension of the discrete-time optimal-control stagewise Newton of Dreyfus 1966; and (2) nodewise BP, based on direct implementation of the chain rule for differentiation attributable to Bishop 1992. We also show intriguing separable structures of each block in the stagewise-partitioned Hessian, disclosing the rank of blocks.

1099 *Prediction of time to event for censored data: ridge regression with linear constraints in kernel space [#1588]*
Natasha Bagotskaya, Ilia Lossev, Ninel Losseva and Mikhail Parakhin, Parascript LLC, United States

We propose a new method for analyzing time to event in case of partially censored data and compare its performance for the particular task of breast cancer metastasis prediction with the performance of several known methods trained on the same data. In our approach, we use Ridge Regression for uncensored data, treating censored samples as constraints. Instead of initial feature space we use feature space defined by a kernel function. Then we reduce dimensionality by using coefficient of variation for each regression coefficient as a criterion for eliminating corresponding dimension).

1100 *A Threshold Varying Bisection Method for Cost Sensitive Learning in Neural Networks [#1019]*
Parag Pendharkar, Penn State Harrisburg, United States

We propose a bisection method for varying classification threshold value for cost sensitive neural network learning. Using simulated data and different cost asymmetries, we test the proposed threshold varying bisection method and compare it with the traditional fixed-threshold method based neural network learning. The results of our experiments illustrate that the proposed threshold varying bisection method performs better than the traditional fixed-threshold method.

1101 *A Single-Layer Radial Basis Function Network Classifier and Its Applications [#1566]*
Daqi Gao, Mingming Chen and Yongli Li, East China University of Science and Technology, China

This paper focuses on using radial basis function (RBF) network classifiers to solve the large-scale learning problems. Above all, a large-scale dataset is divided into multiple limited- scale subsets, and each subset only includes a small part of samples from the original dataset. Naturally, modular single-layer RBF classifiers come into being, in which each module is made up of multiple RBF kernels. The number, locations, widths of kernels may adaptively be determined, and the module with the max output gives the class label of a certain sample. This paper clarifies that a nonlinearly separable problem may still keep so in the kernel space. Two-spirals and letter recognition results show that the proposed method is quite effective.

1102 *OLS versus SVM approach to learning of RBF network [#1034]*
Stanislaw Osowski and Tomasz Markiewicz, Warsaw University of Technology, Poland

The paper presents the comparative analysis of the learning algorithms of the radial basis function (RBF) neural networks. Two best adaptive algorithms are considered. One is based on the orthogonal least square (OLS) applying Gram-Schmidt orthogonalization and the second is relying on the Support Vector Machine (SVM) approach. Both methods adjust automatically the number of hidden units and the values of all other parameters of the network. They have been compared on two families of problems: the classification and regression tasks. The results show that both methods of learning RBF networks are very reliable and deliver comparable, high quality results.

1103 *Designing RBF classifiers for weighted Boosting [#1495]*
Vanessa Gomez-Verdejo, Jeronimo Arenas-Garcia, Manuel Ortega-Moral and Anibal R. Figueiras-Vidal, Universidad Carlos III de Madrid, Spain

The recent interest in combining Neural Networks has produced a variety of techniques. This paper deals with boosting methods, in particular, with Real AdaBoost schemes built up with Radial Basis Function Networks. Real Adaboost emphasis function can be divided into two different terms: the first only focuses on the quadratic error of each pattern and the second only takes into account its "proximity" to the boundary. Incorporating to this fixed emphasis function an additional degree of freedom, that allows to weight these two terms, and selecting also the Radial Basis Functions centroids according to the emphasized regions, we show performance improvements: an error rate reduction, a faster convergence, and overfitting robustness.

1104 *Iterative Feature Weighting for Identification of Relevant Features with Radial Basis Function Networks [#1583]*
Baofu Duan and Yoh-Han Pao, Case Western Reserve University, United States

This paper reports on advances in identification of relevant features through iterative feature weighting with radial basis function networks. It proceeds with a set of feature weights to scale the data which are used to train a radial basis function network model. Then from the learned model, the feature weights are updated via one-step gradient descent. The updated feature weights are then fed back to build a new model. The procedure continues until we find a satisfactory model and the feature weights converge. Experimental results for some benchmark datasets show that the approach is efficient and effective for selecting relevant features for data modeling and classification tasks.

1105 *Sequential Neuron Pruning Algorithm for RBF Network with Guaranteed Stability [#1129]*
Jie Ni and Qing Song, Nanyang Technologival University, Singapore; Nanyang Technological University, Singapore

A rule of thumb for good generalization in neural systems is that the smallest system should be used to fit the training data. Unfortunately, it is normally difficult to determine the optimal size of networks. In this paper, a novel training and pruning algorithm is proposed for the online tuning and pruning the neural tracking control system. The conic sector theory is introduced in the design of this robust neural control system, which aims at providing guaranteed boundedness for both the input-output signals and the weights of the neural network. The performance improvement of the proposed system over existing systems can be qualified in terms of better generalization ability and preventing weight shifts.

1106 *Factors of Overtraining with Fuzzy ARTMAP Neural Networks [#1635]*
Philippe Henniges, Eric Granger and Robert Sabourin, Ecole de technologie superieure - LIVIA, Canada; LIVIA, Ecole de Technologie Superieure, Montreal, Canada

In this paper, the impact of overtraining on the performance of fuzzy ARTMAP neural networks is assessed for pattern recognition problems consisting of overlapping class distributions, and consisting of complex decision boundaries with no overlap. Computer simulations are performed with fuzzy ARTMAP networks trained with four learning strategies using several data sets. The extent of overtraining due to factors such as data set structure, training strategy, number of training epochs, data normalisation, and training set size, is demonstrated. A significant degradation in fuzzy ARTMAP performance due to overtraining is shown to depend on the training set size for pattern recognition problems with overlapping class distributions.

1107 *ART2 Based Classification of Sparse High Dimensional Parameter Sets For A Simulation Parameter Selection Assistant [#1578]*
Gregory Klotz and Deborah Stacey, University of Guelph, Canada

This paper presents the design and creation of a Simulation Parameter Selection Assistant that helps modeling researchers choose meaningful values for their complex simulations, and encourages collaboration between teams searching through high dimensional parameter spaces. Proposed simulation parameters are compared to past runs using Adaptive Resonance Theory to measure similarity with the goals of preventing repetitive exploitations of parameters and of encouraging the exploration of new regions of the parameter space. The Assistant was designed to be used as part of a high performance animal disease spread simulator but is general and modular enough to be easily adapted to other simulation and search domains.

1108 *Fuzzy PSO: A Generalization of Particle Swarm Optimization [#1517]*
Ashraf M. Abdelbar, Suzan Abdelshahid and Donald C. Wunsch II, American University in Cairo, Egypt; ACIL, University of Missouri-Rolla, United States

In standard particle swarm optimization (PSO), the best particle in each neighborhood exerts its influence over other particles in the neighborhood. In this paper, we propose fuzzy PSO, a generalization which differs from standard PSO in the following respect: charisma is defined to be a fuzzy variable, and more than one particle in each neighborhood can have a non-zero degree of charisma, and, consequently, is allowed to influence others to a degree that depends on its charisma. We evaluate our model on the weighted maximum satisfiability (max-sat) problem, comparing performance to standard PSO and to Walk-Sat.

1109 *Simulating A-Life Using Boltzmann Machines [#1222]*
Leszek Rybicki, Nicolaus Copernicus University, Torun, Poland

This work describes a concept neural architecture and an expandable software library we created to simulate autonomous biologically inspired agents (biots) in a changing environment. The concept and the software developed are based on a set of restrictive rules. First - whenever there is a decision to be taken, the method more alike to biological systems is to be chosen. Second - biots are individual beings capable of learning by their own experiences. Third - the biots are supposed to know as little as possible about methods of reaching the goal or any measurement of progress. Finally, in hope of future hardware implementations, we try to keep the model physically realistic and implementable in hardware.

1110 *Artificial Cognitive BP-CT Ant Routing Algorithm [#1299]*
Xu Jing, Chunyu Liu and Xiaobo Sun, Harbin University of Science and Technology, China

This paper analyses the primary features of computing intelligence in the circumstance of multi-agents modeling, and the artificial cognitive methods with computing intelligent agents, and the artificial cognitive features in reinforcement learning and the Q-routing algorithm which is a kind of reinforcement learning in the domain of intelligent network. At the same time, aiming at the problem in AntNet routing algorithm, this paper introduces BP-CT Ant routing algorithm and simulates the algorithm on OMNeT++ software platform. BP-CT Ant routing algorithm has some potential aspects of intelligent control, and shows good QoS performance.

1111 *Basic Property of a Quantum Neural Network Composed of Kane's Qubits [#1730]*
Yuuki Nakamiya, Mitsunaga Kinjo, Osamu Takahashi, Shigeo Sato and Koji Nakajima, Tohoku University, Japan

It has been known a variety of optimization problems can be solved with a neural network, and a quantum computer executes real parallel computation. A quantum neural network has been proposed in order to incorporate quantum dynamics. In this paper, we test the possibility of real implementation of a quantum neural network with a nuclear spin as a qubit. First, we introduce the relation between spin and neuron, then describe the adiabatic Hamiltonian evolution applied for the state change. Next, we describe a real spin quantum system and show the simulation results. A nuclear spin system proposed by Kane behaves as a neuron with inhibitory interactions as expected in analogy to a Hopfield network.

1112 *Quantum Gauged Neural Networks: Learning and Recalling [#1372]*
Yukari Fujita, Takashi Hiramatsu and Tetsuo Matsui, Kinki University, Japan

We study quantum neural networks on a 3D lattice, which contain neuron variable S_x on each site and synaptic variables $J_{x\mu}$ $(\mu=1,2,3)$ on each link. The networks have a local gauge symmetry, where $J_{x\mu}$ are regarded as gauge variables connecting nearest-neighbor sites. We simulate processes of learning a pattern of S_x and recalling it. The rate of recalling the pattern is calculated and compared for three cases, (I) classical (Hopfield-type) $Z(2)$ model, (II) quantum $U(1)$ Higgs model, (III) quantum $CP1+U(1)$ spin(qubit) model. The quantum effects are found to reduce the performance.

Plenary Poster Session: Mixture models and ensemble learning
Monday, August 1, 7:00PM-11:00PM, Room: Fountaine, Chair: Program Chairs

1113 *Stochastic Complexity of Variational Bayesian Hidden Markov Models [#1317]*
Tikara Hosino, Kazuho Watanabe and Sumio Watanabe, Tokyo Institute of Technology, Nihon Unisys Ltd, Japan; Tokyo Institute of Technology, Japan

Variational Bayesian Learning was proposed as the approximation method of Bayesian learning. In spite of efficiency and experimental good performance, their mathematical property has not yet been clarified. In this paper we analyze variational Bayesian hidden Markov models which include the true one thus the models are non-identifiable. We derive their asymptotic stochastic complexity. It is shown that, in some prior condition, the stochastic complexity is much smaller than those of identifiable models.

1114 *New Experiments on Ensembles of Multilayer Feedforward for Classification Problems [#1570]*
Carlos Hernandez-Espinosa, Joaquin Torres-Sospedra and Mercedes Fernandez-Redondo, Universidad Jaume I, Spain

As shown in the bibliography, training an ensemble of networks is an interesting way to improve the performance. In this paper we present some new results in a comparison of twenty different methods to construct the ensemble. We have trained ensembles of 3, 9, 20 and 40 networks and the results show that the improvement in performance above 9 networks in the ensemble depends on the method but it is usually low. Also, the best method for a ensemble of 3 networks is called "Decorrelated" and uses a penalty term in the usual Backpropagation function to decorrelate the network outputs in the ensemble. For the case of 9 and 20 networks the best method is conservative boosting. And finally for 40 networks the best method is Cels.

1115 *A Research on Combination Methods for Ensembles of Multilayer Feedforward [#1618]*
Joaquin Torres-Sospedra, Mercedes Fernandez-Redondo and Carlos Hernandez-Espinosa, Universidad Jaume I, Spain

As shown in the bibliography, the two key factors to design an ensemble are the training of the networks and how to combine the different outputs of the networks. In this paper, we focus in the combination methods. We study the performance of fourteen different combination methods for ensembles of the type "simple ensemble" and "decorrelated". In the case of the "simple ensemble" and low number of networks in the ensemble, the method Zimmermann gets the best performance. When the number of networks is in the range of 9 and 20 the weighted average is the best alternative. Finally, in the case of the ensemble "decorrelated" the best performing method is averaging over a wide spectrum of the number of networks in the ensemble.

1116 *Dynamically Weighted Majority Voting for Incremental Learning and Comparison of Three Boosting Based Approaches [#1124]*
Aliasgar Gangardiwala and Robi Polikar, Rowan University, United States

We have previously introduced Learn++, an ensemble based incremental learning algorithm for acquiring new knowledge from data that later become available, even when such data introduce new classes. In this paper, we describe a modification to this algorithm, where the voting weights of the classifiers are updated dynamically based on the location of the test input in the feature space. The new algorithm provides improved performance, stronger immunity to catastrophic forgetting and finer balance to the stability-plasticity dilemma then its predecessor, particularly when new classes are introduced. The modified algorithm and its performance, as compared to

Adaboost.M1 and the original Learn++, on real and benchmark datasets are presented.

1117 *A Comparison of Combination Methods for Ensembles of RBF Networks [#1587]*
Joaquin Torres-Sospedra, Carlos Hernandez-Espinosa and Mercedes Fernandez-Redondo, Universidad Jaume I, Spain

Building an ensemble of classifiers is an useful way to improve the performance. In the case of neural networks the bibliography has centered on the use of Multilayer Feedforward (MF). However, there are other interesting networks like Radial Basis Functions (RBF) that can be used as elements of the ensemble. In a previous paper we presented results of different methods to build the ensemble of RBF. The results showed that the best method is in general the Simple Ensemble. The combination methods used in that research was averaging. In this paper we present results of fourteen different combination methods for a simple ensemble of RBF. The best methods are Borda Count, Weighted Average and Majority Voting.

1118 *New Boosting Methods of Gaussian Processes for Regression [#1156]*
Yangqiu Song and Changshui Zhang, Department of Automation, Tsinghua University, China

Neural networks are popular tools for nonlinear regression and classification problems. Gaussian Process(GP) can be viewed as an RBF neural network which have infinite number of hidden neurons. On regression problems, they can predict both the mean value and the variance of the given sample. Boosting is one of the most important recent developments in machine learning. But the application of boosting to regression has received less investigation. In this paper, we develop two boosting methods of GPs for regression according to the characteristic of them. We compare the performance of our ensembles with other boosting algorithms and find that our methods are more stable and essentially have less over-fitting problems than other methods.

1119 *Learning Probability Density Functions from Marginal Distributions with Applications to Gaussian Mixtures [#1167]*
Qutang Cai, Changshui Zhang and Chunyi Peng, Department of Automation, Tsinghua University, China

Probability density function (PDF) estimation is very important in the fields related to artificial intelligence and machine learning. This paper is dedicated to considering problems on estimating a PDF based on its marginal distributions. The possibility of the learning problem is first investigated and a uniqueness proposition involving a large family of distribution functions is proposed. The learning problem is then reformulated into an optimization task which is studied and applied to Gaussian mixture models (GMM). Experimental results show that our approach for GMM, only using partial information of the coordinates of the samples, can obtain satisfactory performance, which in turn verifies the proposed reformulation and proposition.

1120 *Evaluation of Cluster Combination Functions for Mixture of Experts [#1275]*
Robert Redhead and Malcolm Heywood, Dalhousie University, Canada

The Mixtures of Experts (MoE) model provides the basis for building modular neural network solutions. In this work we are interested in methods for decomposing the input before forwarding to the MoE architecture. By doing so we are able to define the number of experts from the data itself. Specific schemes are shown to be appropriate for regression and classification problems, where each appear to have different preferences.

1121 *Mixture of Heterogeneous Experts Applied to Time Series: A Comparative Study [#1759]*
Wilfredo J. Puma-Villanueva, Clodoaldo A. M. Lima, Euripedes P. dos Santos and Fernando J. Von Zuben, LBiC/DCA/FEEC/Unicamp, Brazil

Prediction models for time series generally include preprocessing followed by the synthesis of an input-output mapping. High levels of performance will be achieved if some peculiarities of each time series are properly considered, including trend and seasonality. This paper proposes a novel paradigm based on a mixture of heterogeneous experts (MHE), i.e. a hybrid mixture composed of a set of distinct experts. The purpose is not only to further explore the divide-and-conquer principle, but also to compare the performance of MHE with the standard mixture, using ten distinct time series. The obtained results indicate that MHE generally requires a more elaborate gating device and performs better in the case of more challenging time series.

1122 *Classification and Verification through the Combination of the Multi-Layer Perceptron and Auto-Association Neural Networks [#1178]*
Alexander Iversen, Nicholas K. Taylor and Keith E. Brown, Heriot-Watt University, United Kingdom

The MLP classifier has excellent discriminatory properties but forms open decision boundaries, which makes it inappropriate for pattern rejection. The Auto-association Neural Network (AANN), on the other hand, creates closed decision boundaries and is thus appropriate for detection in the absence of counter-examples. However, we show that AANNs may fall short in discriminating between classes that are overlapping in feature space. To overcome the network types' weaknesses, we propose a combined system consisting of an MLP and AANNs. Experimental results on radio signal recognition show that we maintain good discriminatory properties whilst reliably detecting non-class data.

1123 *A Classifier Ensemble Model and Its Applications [#1671]*
Daqi Gao, Shangming Zhu, Wei Chen and Yongli Li, East China University of Science and Technology, China

In order to use combinative classifiers to effectively solve the large-scale learning problems, this paper focuses on the following aspects. (A) Decomposition of large-scale learning problems. (B) Selection of units of combinative classifiers. (C) Transformation of outputs of single classifiers into the grades of memberships. We select Gaussian kernel, 10-nearest-neighbor, and quadratic polynomial, as the combinative units, only let the most relative part of the original datasets to take part in training a single classifier, and then transform the outputs of each classifier into the same grades of memberships. The experiment for letter recognition shows that the proposed method is effective.

Plenary Poster Session: Self-organizing maps and associative memory
Monday, August 1, 7:00PM-11:00PM, Room: Fountaine, Chair: Program Chairs

1124 *Systematic Rewiring in Associative Neural Networks with Small-World Architecture [#1271]*
Oleksiy Dekhtyarenko, Institute of Mathematical Machines and Systems, Ukraine

It is a known fact that a small amount of randomly rewired connections greatly improves the performance of associative neural network with regular architecture, still preserving its attractive features such as local connectivity and small total connection length. In this paper we propose the systematic way of connection rewiring which further improves the associative properties of the network using the same amount of rewiring.

1125 *Motion Perception with Recurrent Self-Organizing Maps Based Models [#1375]*
Volker Baier, University of Technology, Munich, Germany

Representation and processing of spatio-temporal motion information on different levels of granularity, is one key capability of the visual processing ability of the human brain. We introduce a multi-layered model consisting mainly of Recurrent Self-Organizing Maps and a neural associative memory for motion prediction. This processing structure is psychophysically and biologically inspired and some of the equivalent findings will be discussed. The model is self contained and can be used for motion planning and prediction and also for all kind of context-sensitive information processing with demands on prediction ability.

1126 *Retrieval Property of Associative Memory with Negative Resistance [#1670]*
Yoshihiro Hayakawa, Honnge Li and Koji Nakajima, Tohoku University, Japan

The self-connection can enlarge memory capacity of an associative memory based on the neural network, however, the basin size of the embedded memory state shrinks. The problem of basin size is related to undesirable stable states which are spurious states. If we can destabilize these spurious states, we expect to improve the basin size. The Inverse Function Delayed(ID) model which includes the BVP model has the negative resistance, which can destabilize the equilibrium states on some region, on its dynamics. Hence, the associative memory based on the ID model has possibilities of improving the basin size of the network which has the self-connection in order to enlarge a memory capacity.

1127 *A Weighted Voting Model of Associative Memory: Theoretical Analysis [#1560]*
Xiaoyan Mu, Paul Watta and Mohamad Hassoun, Rose-Hulman Institute of Technology, United States; University of Michigan-Dearborn, United States; Wayne State University, United States

In this paper, we investigate a RAM-based associative memory that uses a weighted voting scheme. We adopt the testing protocols commonly used in the area of face recognition, and propose that the capacity of the system be measured by the results of an identification test (ability to properly recognize known information) and a watch-list test (ability to properly reject inputs that should not be matched with any of the memory set patterns). For the case of binary and random memory sets, we are able to derive theoretical expressions characterizing the performance of the weighted voting memory on both these tests.

1128 *New Results on Binary Auto- and Heteroassociative Morphological Memories [#1111]*
Peter Sussner, University of Campinas, IMECC, Applied Math., Brazil

Morphological neural networks perform operations of mathematical morphology at each node. These operations can also be expressed as matrix operations in minimax algebra. The binary autoassociative morphological memory (AMM) can be viewed as the minimax algebra counterpart of the correlation-recorded discrete Hopfield net. In contrast to the Hopfield net, binary AMM's exhibit attractive properties such as one-step convergence and an optimal absolute storage capacity. Heteroassociative morphological memories (HMM's) have yet to be studied extensively and only a few theorems on HMM's have been proven. This paper proves a number of theorems that yield an exact characterization of the recall phases of binary AMM's as well as binary HMM's.

1129 *Self-Organizing Neural Grove and Its Applications [#1442]*
Hirotaka Inoue and Hiroyuki Narihisa, Kure College of Technology, Japan; Okayama University of Science, Japan

Recently, multiple classifier systems (MCS) have been used for practical applications to improve classification accuracy. Self-generating neural networks (SGNN) are one of the suitable base-classifiers for MCS because of their simple setting and fast learning. However, the computation cost of the MCS increases in proportion to the number of SGNN. In this paper, we propose a novel pruning method for efficient classification. We compare the pruned MCS with two sampling methods. Experiments have been conducted to compare the pruned MCS with an unpruned MCS, the MCS based on C4.5, and k-nearest neighbor method. The results show that the pruned MCS can improve its classification accuracy as well as reducing the computation cost.

1130 *Incremental growing neural gas learns topologies [#1428]*
Yann Prudent and Abdellatif Ennaji, PSI laboratory, France

An incremental and Growing network model is introduced which is able to learn the topological relations in a given set of input vectors by means of a simple Hebb-like learning rule. We propose a new algorithm for a SOM which can learn new input data (plasticity) without degrading the previously trained network and forgetting the old input data (stability). We report the validation of this model on experiments using a synthetic problem, the IRIS database and the handwriting digit recognition problem over a portion of the NIST database. Finally we show how to use this network for clustering and semi-supervised clustering

1131 *Robust Continuous Learning in a WTA Neural Network for Clustering Symbol Strings [#1456]*
John Flanagan, Nokia Research Center, Finland

K-Means and the SOM are two well known algorithms that can be applied to the continuous learning of data. However both implicitly make the assumption that the inputs to the learning are independent and identically distributed (iid) which facilitates the choice of learning parameters. The probability distribution of iid inputs with a cluster structure is modelled by a static mixture model while in the non-iid case a dynamic mixture model is used. The K-SCM (Symbol String Clustering Map) algorithm is described as a robust means of clustering symbol string data requiring no time varying learning rate and hence does not assume the inputs are iid.

1132 *An Associative Memory for the Online Recognition and Prediction of Temporal Sequences [#1480]*
Joy Bose, Steve Furber and Jon Shapiro, University of Manchester, United Kingdom

This paper presents the design of an associative memory with feedback that is capable of on-line temporal sequence learning. A framework for on-line sequence learning has been proposed, and different sequence learning models have been analysed according to this framework. The network model is an associative memory with a separate store for the sequence context of a symbol. A sparse distributed memory is used to gain scalability. The context store combines the functionality of a neural layer with a shift register. The sensitivity of the machine to the sequence context is controllable. The model can store and predict on-line sequences of various types and length.

Plenary Poster Session: Principal and independent component analysis
Monday, August 1, 7:00PM-11:00PM, Room: Fountaine, Chair: Program Chairs

1133 *Similar-Image Retrieval Systems Using ICA and PCA Bases [#1079]*
Naoto Katsumata and Yasuo Matsuyama, Waseda University, Japan

Similar-image retrieval systems are presented and evaluated. The new systems directly use image bases via ICA and PCA. These bases can extract source image's information which is viable to define similarity measures. But, the indeterminacy on amplitude and permutation exists. In this paper, similarity measures which can absorb such indeterminacy are presented. Then, carefully designed opinion tests are carried out to compare the new systems' ability with existing ones. The compatibility of color spaces such as RGB, YIQ, and HSV is also examined. By these massive tests, {ICA, HSV, without filtering} is judged the best. Thus, the resulting system was proved to be highly competent at the similar-image retrieval.

1134 *Blind Inversion of Wiener System for Single Source [#1135]*
Zhan-Li Sun, De-Shuang Huang, Chun-Hou Zheng and Li Shang, Hefei Institute of Intelligent Machines, CAS, China

In this paper, a novel nonlinear blind source separation system with post-nonlinear mixing model, and an unsupervised learning algorithm for the parameters of this separating system are presented for blind inversion of Wiener system for single source. The proposed method firstly changes the deconvolution part of Wiener system into a special case of linear blind source separation (BSS). Then the nonlinear BSS system is applied to derive the source signal. The proposed nonlinear BSS method can dynamically estimate the nonlinearity of mixing model and adapt to the cumulative probability function (CPF) of sources. Finally, experimental results demonstrate that our proposed method is effective and efficient for the problems addressed.

1135 *Blind Separation of Convolved Sources using the Information Maximization Approach [#1264]*
Md. Hasanuzzaman and Khashayar Khorasani, Concordia University, Canada

The problem of independent sources getting distorted by environmental factors, and which can be represented as convolutive mixtures of original signals received at the sensors is considered. The effects of environmental factors and modeling assumptions on the performance capabilities of independent component analysis-based techniques are investigated. Blind source separation feedback network architecture that is capable of coping with convolutive mixtures of sources is derived using information maximization principle. We develop ideal solutions for separation of independent source signals from the convolutive mixtures that is applicable to an arbitrary NxN feedback network architecture. A number of simulation case studies are presented.

1136 *BSS Toolbox for Delayed and Convolved Mixtures [#1467]*
Angelo Ciaramella, Roberto Tagliaferri and Francesco Iorio, DMI, University of Salerno, Italy; University of Salerno, Italy

In this paper a Toolbox to generate and to analyze linear, non-linear, delayed and convolved mixtures of real source signals is presented. From one hand, in fact, a simple interface based on a physical model has been implemented and stereo, dolby, delayed, and convolved mixtures can be generated. On the other hand a Blind Source Separation analysis can be accomplished. In fact, a novel separation algorithm (i.e. APDP) is included in the Toolbox. Several experiments to separate delayed mixtures of real instruments are made. Three musical recordings of different instrumental scores are mixed and analyzed by using the Toolbox. Several comparisons with known methods are made.

1137 *Diagonally Weighted and Shifted Criteria for Minor and Principal Component Extraction [#1391]*
Mohammed Hasan, University of Minnesota Duluth, United States

A framework for a class of minor and principal component learning rules is presented. These rules compute multiple actual eigenvectors and not only a basis for a multi-dimensional eigenspace. constraints using the natural gradient concept. Several MCA/PCA cost functions which are weighted or shifted by a diagonal matrix are optimized subject to orthogonal or symmetric constraints. A number of minor and principal component learning rules for symmetric matrices and matrix pencils, many of which are new, are obtained by exploiting symmetry of constrained criteria. Procedures for converting minor component flows into principal component flows are also discussed.

1138 *Analysis of Signal Separation and Signal Distortion in Feedforward and Feedback Blind Source Separation Based on Source Spectra [#1457]*
Akihide Horita, Kenji Nakayama, Akihide Hirano and Yasuhiro Dejima, Kanazawa Univ, Japan; Kanazawa University, Japan

Source separation and signal distortion in a feedforward (FF-)BSS and a feedback (FB-)BSS are analyzed. An evaluation measure of signal distortion is discussed. Conditions for source separation and distortion free are derived. Based on these conditions, source separation and signal distortion are analyzed. The FF-BSS, trained in the frequency domain can suppress signal distortion. Since, the FF-BSS, trained in the time domain, does not have any constraints on signal distortion free, its output signals can be easily distorted. A new learning algorithm with a distortion free constraint is proposed. The FB-BSS can satisfy both source separation and distortion free conditions simultaneously. Simulation results support the theoretical analysis.

1139 *Weighted Rayleigh Quotients for Minor and Principal Component Extraction [#1401]*
Mohammed Hasan, University of Minnesota Duluth, United States

New criteria are proposed for extracting in parallel multiple minor components associated with the covariance matrix of an input process. The proposed minor component analysis (MCA) algorithms are based on optimizing a weighted inverse Rayleigh quotient so that the optimum equilibrium points are exactly the desired eigenvectors of a covariance matrix instead of an arbitrary orthonormal basis of the minor subspace. Variations of the derived MCA learning rules are obtained by imposing orthogonal and quadratic constraints and change of variables. Similar criteria are proposed for component analysis of the generalized eigenvalue problem.

Plenary Poster Session: Probablistic and information theoretic methods
Monday, August 1, 7:00PM-11:00PM, Room: Fountaine, Chair: Program Chairs

1140 *Feature Ranking using Supervised Neural Gas and Informational Energy [#1708]*
Razvan Andonie and Angel Cataron, Central Washington University, United States; Transylvania University, Romania

In this paper we use the maximization of Onicescu's informational energy as a criteria for computing the relevances of input features. This adaptive relevance determination is used in combination with the neural gas and the generalized relevance LVQ algorithms. The idea of applying the neural gas neighborhood cooperation technique to improve the generalized relevance LVQ is due to Hammer et al. Our approach gives an alternative way for determining the relevances in Hammers's algorithm, and in our experiments it shows at least the same performances. Essentially, the result is an incremental learning algorithm for supervised classification and feature ranking.

1141 *An Improved Kernel Fisher Discriminant Classifier and Its Applications [#1597]*
Daqi Gao, Zhen Wang and Yongli Li, East China University of Science and Technology, China

In order to use kernel Fisher discriminant (KFD) classifiers to solve large-scale learning problems, this paper decomposes an n-class dataset into n two- class subsets, and use a subset only composed of a small part of the original dataset in determining the structure of a single KFD classifier. The large number of samples in a class can be further represented by only a small number of prototypes with changeable widths, which are on behalf of kernels. Training samples are not certainly linearly separable in the kernel space, so additional expansive and contractive transformation is needed. Sigmoid functions can be use to implement such tasks. The results of two-spiral and letter recognition show that the proposed method is quite effective.

1142 *An Optimal Entropy Estimator for Discrete Random Variables [#1261]*
Motoki Shiga and Yasunari Yokota, Gifu University, Japan

This paper presents analytical formulations of averaged squared bias error and mean squared error for the class of entropy estimator expressed as a sum of single variable functions. The class of entropy estimator includes almost all important entropy estimators that have been proposed heretofore. Furthermore, this paper presents an optimal entropy estimator that can minimize mean squared error under the condition that averaged squared bias error is restricted to below an arbitrary value. A numerical experiment demonstrates that the proposed entropy estimator provides a lower mean squared error than conventional estimators when entropy is estimated as an ensemble mean over plural entropy estimates obtained for different independent data.

1143 *Comparing ``Pattern Discovery" and Back-Propagation Classifiers [#1496]*
Andrew Hamilton-Wright and Daniel W. Stashuk, Systems Design Eng., University of Waterloo, Canada

The Pattern Discovery (PD) algorithm was applied as a classifier to several continuous-valued data sets of interesting linearly and non-linearly separable class distributions. Performance of PD and back-propagation (BP) neural network classifiers were compared. Performance of the PD and BP classifiers was found to be similar for all class distributions studied and close to optimal for linearly separable class distributions. Performance of both classifiers was dependent on the configuration. PD performance depended on the number of quantization intervals in a predictable, class-distribution independent way. BP performance depended on the number of hidden nodes in a class-distribution dependent way and was difficult to determine a priori.

1144 *Multivariate Regression Model Selection with KIC for Extrapolation Cases [#1303]*
Abd-Krim Seghouane, National ICT Australia, Australia

In this paper, a new criterion is proposed in order to select a well fitted model for an extrapolation case. The proposed criterion is named, PKIC, where "P" stands for prediction, and is derived as an exact unbiased estimator of an adapted cost function that is based on the Kullback symmetric divergence and the future design matrix. PKIC is an unbiased estimator of its cost function assuming that the true model is correctly specified or overfitted. A simulation study illustrating that model selection with PKIC performs well for some extrapolation cases is presented.

1145 *Robust Information Clustering [#1379]*
Qing Song, Nanyang Technological University, Singapore

We focus on the scenario of robust information clustering (RIC) based on the minimax optimization of mutual information (MI). The minimization of MI leads to the standard mass constrained deterministic annealing clustering which is an empirical risk minimization algorithm. The maximization of MI works out an upper bound of the empirical risk via the identification of outliers. We estimate the real risk VC-bound of the RIC based on the structural risk minimization (SRM) principle and determine an optimal cluster number.

1146 *Learning Nonlinear Constraints with Contrastive Backpropagation [#1292]*
Andriy Mnih and Geoffrey Hinton, University of Toronto, Canada

Certain datasets can be efficiently modelled in terms of constraints that are usually satisfied but sometimes are strongly violated. We propose using energy-based density models (EBMs) implementing products of frequently approximately satisfied nonlinear constraints for modelling such datasets. We demonstrate the feasibility of this approach by training an EBM using contrastive backpropagation on a dataset of idealized trajectories of two balls bouncing in a box and showing that the model learns an accurate and efficient representation of the dataset, taking advantage of the approximate independence between subsets of variables.

1147 *Sequential Relevance Vector Machine Learning from Time Series [#1393]*
Nikolay Nikolaev and Peter Tino, Goldsmiths College, University of London, United Kingdom; The University of Birmingham, United Kingdom

This paper presents an approach to sequential training of the relevance vector machine suitable for Bayesian learning from time series. The key idea is to perform simultaneous incremental optimization of both the weight parameters and their prior hyperparameters using data arriving one at a time. Algorithms for efficient sequential regularized dynamic learning rate training of the weights and gradient-descent training of their priors are derived. It is shown that this fast sequential RVM can outperform similar Bayesian kernel methods, like: batch RVM, fast RVM, variational RVM, and Gaussian Processes on multistep ahead forecasting of time series.

Plenary Poster Session: Neural networks and evolutionary computation
Monday, August 1, 7:00PM-11:00PM, Room: Fountaine, Chair: Program Chairs

1148 *Performance Optimization of Function Localization Neural Network by Using Reinforcement Learning [#1168]*
Takafumi Sasakawa, Jinglu Hu and Kotaro Hirasawa, Waseda University, Japan

According to Hebb's cell assembly theory, the brain has the capability of function localization. On the other hand, it is suggested that the brain has three different learning paradigms: supervised, unsupervised and reinforcement learning. Inspired by the above knowledge of brain, we present a self-organizing function localization neural network (FLNN), that contains supervised, unsupervised and reinforcement learning paradigms. In this paper, we concentrate our discussion mainly on applying a simplified reinforcement learning called evaluative feedback to optimization of the self-organizing FLNN. Numerical simulations show that the self-organizing FLNN has superior performance to an ordinary artificial neural network (ANN).

1149 *Sparse Bayesian learning and the relevance multi-layer perceptron [#1461]*
Gavin Cawley and Nicola Talbot, University of East Anglia, United Kingdom

We introduce a sparse Bayesian learning algortihm for MLP networks, like the RVM, a Bayesian prior is adopted that includes separate hyperparameters for each weight, allowing redundant weights and hidden layer units to be identified and pruned from thenetwork, whilst also providing an effective means to avoid over-fitting. This approach is also more easily implemented, as only the diagonal elements of the Hessian matrix are required by the update formula for the regularisation parameters, rather than the eigenvalues of blocks of the Hessian matrix. The proposed Relevance Multi-Layer Perceptron (RMLP) is evaluated over several publically available benchmark datasets, demonstrating the viability of the approach.

1150 *Real-Coded Genetic Algorithm with Average-Bound Crossover and Wavelet Mutation for Network Parameters Learning [#1726]*
S. H. Ling and F. H. F. Leung, The Hong Kong Polytechnic University, Hong Kong

This paper presents the learning of neural network parameters using a real-coded genetic algorithm (RCGA) with proposed crossover and mutation. They are called the average-bound crossover (AveBXover) and wavelet mutation (WM). By introducing the proposed genetic operations, both solution quality and stability perform better than the RCGA with conventional genetic operations. A suite of benchmark test functions are used to evaluate the performance of the proposed algorithm. An application example on associative memory neural network is used to show the learning performance of the network with the proposed GA.

1151 *A Directional Multi-resolution Ridgelet Network [#1175]*
Shuyuan Yang, Min Wang and Licheng Jiao, Institute of Intelligence Information Processing, China; National Lab of Radar Signal Processing, China; Xidian University, China

In this paper, a directional multi-resolution ridgelet network (DMRN) is proposed based on ridgelet theory. By using ridgelet as the activation function, DMRN has great capabilities in catching essential features of 'direction-rich' data for its multi-resolution property in direction besides scale and position. It proves to be able to approximate any multivariate function in a more stable and efficient way, and is optimal in approximating functions with spatial inhomogeneities. Using binary ridgelet frame for its design, DMRN is characteristic of more flexible structure. Possibilities of applications to regression and recognition are included to demonstrate its superiority.

1152 *The Emergence of Verbs in an Artificial Life Simulation [#1215]*
Vassilios Petridis and Anastasios-Antonios Toulkeridis, Aristotle University of Thessaloniki, Greece

This paper presents an evolutionary communication model that makes use of neural networks and evolutionary computation. It is embedded in a simple two-dimensional artificial world. The work builds on the successful approach of Cangelosi [1] but is designed with considerations of suitability for extensions of more elaborate communication.

1153 *A variable-parameter neural network trained by improved genetic algorithm and its application [#1702]*
S. H. Ling, H.K. Lam and F. H. F. Leung, The Hong Kong Polytechnic University, Hong Kong

This paper presents a neural network with variable parameters. These variable parameters adapt to the changes of the input environment, and tackle different input data sets in a large domain. Each input data set is effectively handled by its corresponding set of network parameters. Thus, the proposed neural network exhibits a better learning and generalization ability than a traditional one. An improved genetic algorithm is proposed to train the network parameters. An application example on hand-written pattern recognition will be presented to verify and illustrate the improvement.

1154 *Feature Subset Selection via Multi-Objective Genetic Algorithm [#1616]*
Hao Lac and Deborah Stacey, University of Guelph, Canada

Real-world datasets tend to be complex, large in size, and may contain many irrelevant features. Eliminating such irrelevant features can significantly improve the performance of a data mining algorithm. In this paper, we propose a multi-objective genetic algorithm that finds a set of Pareto-optimal feature subsets that works as a wrapper around a standard backpropagation algorithm. We also introduce a novel mechanism called the least-crowded selection algorithm that maximizes the diversity of the solutions returned by the algorithm. We justify the proposed method by theoretically and empirically comparing it to the backpropagation neural network and the simple genetic algorithm for feature selection.

1155 *A Model of Baldwin Effect in Populations of Self-Learning Agents [#1247]*
Vladimir Redko, Oleg Mosalov and Danil Prokhorov, Institute of Optical Neural Technologies RAS, Russia; Moscow Institute of Physics and Technologies, Russia; Ford Research and Advanced Engineering, United States

We study an evolution model of adaptive self-learning agents. The control system of agents is based on a neural network adaptive critic design. Each agent is a broker that predicts stock price changes and uses its predictions for action selection. The agent tries to get rich by buying and selling stocks. We demonstrate that the Baldwin effect takes place in our model, viz., originally acquired adaptive policy of an agent-broker becomes inherited in the course of the evolution. In addition, we compare agent behavioral tactics with searching behavior of simple animals.

1156 *Synthesis of Binary Cellular Automata based on Binary Neural Networks [#1750]*
Takashi Yamamichi, Toshimichi Saito, Keisuke Taguchi and Hiroyuki Torikai, Hosei Univ., Japan; Hosei University, Japan

This paper studies a simple synthesis algorithm of desired cellular automata (ab. CAs) based on a binary neural network (ab. BNN). The CAs have binary state variable and the BNN has bipolar connection parameters. In order to realize dynamics of the CA, the bipolar parameters of BNN are determined using the genetic algorithm. Performing basic numerical experiments we show that the BNN can realize desired dynamics with small number of hidden layers for a class of CAs. We also consider the case of noisy teacher signals. These results provide basic information for application to signal processing, analysis of digital nonlinear phenomena, and so on.

1157 *Genetic Algorithm-Based Variable Translation Wavelet Neural Network and its Application [#1219]*
S. H. Ling and F. H. F. Leung, The Hong Kong Polytechnic University, Hong Kong

A variable translation wavelet neural network (VTWNN) trained by genetic algorithm is presented in this paper. In the proposed wavelet neural network, the translation parameters are variables depending on the network inputs. Thanks to the variable translation parameter, the network become an adaptive one. Thus, the proposed network provides better performance and increased learning ability than conventional wavelet neural networks. Genetic algorithm is applied to train the parameters of the proposed wavelet neural network. An application example for short-term daily electric load forecasting in Hong Kong are presented to show the merits of the proposed network.

1158 *Evolution Strategies on Connection Weights into Modified Gradient Function for Multi-layer Neural Network [#1128]*
Sin Chun Ng, Shu Hung Leung and Andrew Luk, Open University of Hong Kong, Hong Kong; City University of Hong Kong, Hong Kong; St. B-P Neural Investments Pty. Ltd., Australia

In this paper, two modifications on the conventional back-propagation algorithm for feedforward multi-layer neural networks are presented. One modification is based on the calculation of the gradient function, while the other one is the use of evolution strategies on connection weights into the gradient search algorithm. From simulation results, the new modified algorithm always converges to the global optimal solution with better performance as compared to other fast learning algorithms and global search methods.

Plenary Poster Session: Neural network architectures and structures
Monday, August 1, 7:00PM-11:00PM, Room: Fountaine, Chair: Program Chairs

1159 *Neural Network Initialization with Prototypes - A Case Study in Function Approximation [#1324]*
Jin-Song Pei, Joseph Wright and Andrew Smyth, University of Oklahoma, United States; Weidlinger Associates Inc., United States; Columbia University, United States

The initialization of neural networks in function approximation has been studied by many researchers yet remains a challenging problem. Another important yet open issue in the neural network community is to incorporate knowledge and hints with regard to training for a meaningful neural network. This study makes an attempt to address these two issues in handling a specific type of engineering problems, namely, modeling nonlinear hysteretic restoring forces of a dynamic system under a specific formulation. The paper showcases a heuristic idea on using a growing technique through a prototype-based initialization where the insight to the governing mathematics/physics are related to the features of the activation functions.

1160 *A Novel Radial Basis Function Network Classifier with Centers Set by Hierarchical Clustering [#1460]*
Yu-Yen Ou, Chien-Yu Chen and Yen-Jen Oyang, CSIE, National Taiwan University, Taiwan; Yuan Ze University, Taiwan

This paper proposes a novel method to construct a radial basis function network (RBFN) classifier. Our contribution consists of two parts. The first one is an incremental hierarchical clustering algorithm for constructing the hidden layer, and the second one is to improve the least mean square error method that calculates the weights between the hidden and the output layers of an RBFN. Experimental results show that the data classifier constructed is capable of delivering comparable classification accuracy as the support vector machine and the kernel density estimation based classifier, while enjoying significant execution efficiency in handling data sets that contains a high percentage of redundant training instances.

1161 *A Simple Hierarchical Approximation RBF Neural Network [#1137]*
Peggy Doerschuk and Sainath Pawaskar, Lamar University, United States; Revtek Consulting Services, United States

The approximation algorithm introduced by Asim Roy et al. generates a hybrid network with RBF neurons and other types of hidden neurons. The network is trained in stages, with RBF neurons at the early stages corresponding to general features in the space and those in later stages corresponding to more specific features. The other types of hidden neurons are added with a view to improving generalization and reducing the number of RBF neurons. The algorithm uses linear programming to design and train the hybrid network. The Simple Hierarchical Approximation RBF Network presented here achieves comparable results in terms of accuracy without the added complexity introduced by the other types of hidden neurons and linear programming.

1162 *The Evolving Tree, a Hierarchical Tool for Unsupervised Data Analysis [#1366]*
Jussi Pakkanen, Jukka Iivarinen and Erkki Oja, Lab. of Comp. and Inform. Science, HUT, Finland; Helsinki University of Technology, Finland

We present and examine a tree-shaped self-organizing neural network called the Evolving Tree. It has been designed to efficiently analyze large databases. We show how the system's architecture makes it efficient for these kinds of tasks. We then analyze the system's behaviour under different circumstances. We find that, despite being simple, the Evolving Tree is a suitable tool for unsupervised data analysis.

1163 *Optimization of Modular Neural Networks Using Hierarchical Genetic Algorithms Applied to Speech Recognition [#1043]*
Gabriela Martinez, Patricia Melin and Oscar Castillo, Tijuana Institute of Technology, Mexico

We describe in this paper the evolution of Modular Neural Networks (MNN) using a Hierarchical Genetic Algorithm (HGA). The HGA is clearly needed due to the fact that topology optimization requires that we are able to manage both the layer and node information for each of the MNN modules. Simulation results for speech recognition show the feasability of the proposed approach.

1164 *Protein Sequence Classification Using Extreme Learning Machine [#1257]*
Dianhui Wang and Guang-Bin Huang, La Trobe University, Australia; Nanyang Technological University, Singapore

In this paper, a recently developed machine learning algorithm referred to as the Extreme Learning Machine (ELM) is used to classify protein sequences with ten classes of super-families downloaded from a public domain database. A comparative study on system performance is conducted between ELM and the main conventional neural network classifier - Backpropagation Neural Networks. Results show that ELM needs up to four orders of magnitude less training time compared to BP Network. The classification accuracy of ELM is also higher than that of BP network. For given network architecture, ELM does not have any control parameters (i.e, stopping criteria, learning rate, learning epoches, etc) to be manually tuned and can be implemented easily.

1165 *Analyzing the State Space Property of Echo State Networks for Chaotic System Prediction [#1227]*
Jianhui Xi, Zhiwei Shi and Min Han, Dalian University of Technology, China

For chaotic system prediction, ESNs (Echo State Networks) are realization of neural state reconstruction, in which the reconstructed state variable is the internal neurons' activation, rather than the delay vector obtained from embedding. In this framework, some quantitative analyses can be made on the issues such as the network configuration and initial state determination. Based on the simulation on chaotic data from Chua's circuit, it is shown that the ESNs is a non-minimum state space realization of the target time series, and the initial state can be freely chosen in the training process, and in prediction, ESNs need to know where the prediction begins by being set a proper initial state through a process of teacher forcing.

1166 *Finding a Succinct Multi-layer Perceptron Having Shared Weights [#1378]*
Yusuke Tanahashi, Xiang-Fang Chin, Kazumi Saito and Ryohei Nakano, Nagoya Institute of Technology, Japan; NTT Communication Science Laboratories, Japan

We present a method to find a succinct neural network having shared weights. We focus on weight sharing. Weight sharing constrains the freedom of weight values and weights are allowed to have one of common weights. Recently, a weight sharing method called BCW has been proposed. The BCW employs merge and split operations and can escape local optima through bidirectional clustering. However, the BCW assumes the number of hidden units J is given. This paper modifies the BCW to make faster so that the selection of J based on cross-validation can be done efficiently. Our experiments showed our method can restore the original model for an artificial dataset and finds a couple of common weights and an interesting tendency for a real dataset.

Tuesday, August 2, 8:00AM-9:00AM

Plenary Talk: Functional Organization of the Primate Prefrontal Cortex for Memory
Tuesday, August 2, 8:00AM-9:00AM, Room: Westmount/Outremount, Speaker: Michael Petrides, McGill University, Montreal, Quebec, Canada

Although it is generally agreed that the lateral prefrontal cortex plays an important role in memory, a precise characterization of the role of the different prefrontal regions in memory has proven elusive. Studies on nonhuman primates show that lesions of the mid-dorsolateral prefrontal cortex give rise to severe impairments on the capacity to monitor information in working memory. Functional neuroimaging studies have provided support to the idea that increased monitoring demands in experimental tasks relative to the control tasks result in increased activity in the mid-dorsolateral prefrontal region regardless of the nature of the stimulus material. By contrast, recent experiments indicate that the mid-ventrolateral prefrontal cortex is selectively involved in the active retrieval of information from posterior cortical association areas. Active retrieval is required when stimuli in memory do not bear stable relations to each other and therefore retrieval cannot be automatically driven by stable and unambiguous context relations.

Tuesday, August 2, 9:30AM-11:30AM

SVM I
Tuesday, August 2, 9:30AM-11:30AM, Room: Verdun/Lachine, Chair: Johan A. K. Suykens

9:30AM *A Simple Trick for Constructing Bayesian Formulations of Sparse Kernel Learning Methods [#1465]*
Gavin Cawley and Nicola Talbot, University of East Anglia, United Kingdom

In this paper, we present a simple mathematical trick that simplifies the derivation of Bayesian treatments of a variety of sparse kernel learning methods. The dual parameter space is transformed, such that Gaussian prior over model parameters becomes spherical. The regularisation term is then the familiar weight-decay regulariser, allowing the Bayesian analysis to proceed straight-forwardly via the methods developed by MacKay. Bayesian treatments of the kernel ridge regression algorithm, with both constant and input dependent variance structures, are given as illustrative examples of the proposed technique, which we hope will be more widely applicable.

9:50AM *Efficient Parameter Selection for Support Vector Machines in Classification and Regression via Model-Based Global Optimization [#1025]*
Holger Froehlich and Andreas Zell, Centre for Bioinformatics Tuebingen (ZBIT), Germany

In SVMs usually the kernel function depends on certain parameters, which, together with other parameters of the SVM, have to be tuned to achieve good results. However, finding good parameters can become a real computational burden as the number of parameters and the size of the dataset increases. In this paper we propose an algorithm to deal with the model selection problem, which is based on the idea of learning an Online Gaussian Process model of the error surface in parameter space and sampling systematically at points for which the so called "expected improvement" is highest. Our experiments show that on this way we can find good parameters very efficiently.

10:10AM *Sequential Bootstrapped Support Vector Machines - A SVM Accelerator [#1354]*
Xuchun Li, Yan Zhu and Eric Sung, Nanyang Technological University, Singapore

An algorithm, named Sequential Bootstrapped SVM, to speed up the training process of SVM, is presented. We proposed to select the so-call convex hull samples that have more probability to be support vectors than other samples and then focus on training SVM classifier based on these samples to decrease the needed number of training samples. The advantage of SeqSVM is experimentally demonstrated for both artificial database and UCI benchmark databases in terms of training time. We claim that the strength of SeqSVM algorithm lies in reducing the needed number of training samples so as to speed up training process. Future work will focus on using extremely large training set to test the SeqSVM.

10:30AM *Fbeta Support Vector Machines [#1376]*
Jerome Callut and Pierre Dupont, Universite catholique de Louvain, Belgium

We introduce in this paper Fbeta SVMs, a new parametrization of support vector machines. It allows to optimize a SVM in terms of Fbeta, a classical information retrieval criterion, instead of the usual classification rate. Experiments illustrate the advantages of this approach with respect to the traditionnal 2-norm soft-margin SVM when precision and recall are of unequal importance. An automatic model selection procedure based on the generalization Fbeta score is introduced. The model is selected by performing a gradient descent of a Fbeta loss function over the set of hyperparameters. Experiments on artificial and real-life data show the benefits of this method when the Fbeta score is considered.

10:50AM *Time Series Filtering, Smoothing and Learning using the Kernel Kalman Filter [#1599]*
Liva Ralaivola and Florence d'Alche-Buc, Lab. d'Informatique Fondamentale de Marseille, France; Lab. des Methodes Informatiques, France

In this paper, we propose a new model, the Kernel Kalman Filter, to perform various nonlinear time series processing. This model is based on the use of Mercer kernel functions in the framework of the Kalman Filter or Linear Dynamical Systems. Thanks to the kernel trick, all the equations involved in our model to perform filtering, smoothing and learning tasks, only require matrix algebra calculus whilst providing the ability to model complex time series. In particular, it is possible to learn dynamics from some nonlinear noisy time series implementing an exact Expectation-Maximization procedure.

11:10AM *A Combined SVM and LDA Approach for Classification [#1294]*
Tao Xiong and Vladimir Cherkassky, University of Minnesota, United States

This paper describes a new large margin classifier, named SVM/LDA. This classifier can be viewed as an extension of support vector machine (SVM) by incorporating some global information about the data. The SVM/LDA classifier can be also seen as a generalization of linear discriminant analysis (LDA) by incorporating the idea of (local) margin maximization into standard LDA formulation. We show that existing SVM software can be used to solve the SVM/LDA formulation. We also present empirical comparisons of the proposed algorithm with SVM and LDA using both synthetic and real world benchmark data.

Special Session: Computational Dynamical Modeling with Echo State Networks
Tuesday, August 2, 9:30AM-11:30AM, Room: Outremount, Chair: Yadunandana Rao and Jose Principe

9:30AM *Reservoir Riddles: Suggestions for Echo State Network Research [#1767]*
Herbert Jaeger, International University Bremen, Germany

Echo state networks (ESNs) offer a simple learning algorithm for dynamical systems. It works by training linear readout neurons that combine the signals from a random, fixed, excitable "dynamical reservoir" network. Often the method works beautifully, sometimes it works poorly - and we do not really understand why. This contribution discusses phenomena related to poor learning performance and suggests research directions. The common theme is to understand the reservoir dynamics in terms of a dynamical representation of the task's input signals.

9:50AM *Echo State Networks: Appeal and Challenges [#1002]*
Danil Prokhorov, Ford Research and Advanced Engineering, United States

The echo state network (ESN) has recently been proposed for modeling complex dynamic systems. The ESN is a sparsely connected recurrent neural network with most of its weights fixed a priori to randomly chosen values. The only trainable weights are those on links connected to the outputs. The ESN can demonstrate remarkable performance after seemingly effortless training. This brief paper discusses ESN in a broader context of applications of recurrent neural networks (RNN) and highlights challenges on the road to practical applications.

10:10AM *Computing with Transiently Stable States [#1720]*
Mustafa C. Ozturk and Jose C. Principe, CNEL, Department of ECE, University of Florida, United States

Stability is an essential constraint in the design of linear dynamical systems. Similar stability restrictions on nonlinear dynamical systems, such as echo state network, have been enforced in order to use them for reliable computation. In this paper we will introduce a novel computational mode for nonlinear systems with sigmoidal nonlinearity, which does not require global stability. In this mode, although the autonomous system is unstable, the input signal forces the system dynamics to become "transiently stable". We demonstrate with a function approximation experiment that the transiently stable system can still do useful computation.

10:30AM *The Role of the RKH Space F in the Analysis and Design of Recurrent Neural Networks [#1765]*
Rui de Figueiredo, EECS Dept., University of California, Irvine, United States

The space F(H), or simply F, is a Reproducing Kernel Hilbert Space (RKHS) of analytic (nonlinear) functionals (Volterra functionals) on a separable Hilbert Space H. It was introduced in the late 1970's by the author, in collaboration with T.A.W. Dwyer, III, and L. Zyla, to represent input-output maps of large-scale nonlinear dynamical systems. In the present paper we show how the properties of F, and, in particular, its reproducing kernel, can be used to model the structure and behavior of Recurrent Neural Networks (RNNs).

10:50AM *Feed-forward Echo State Networks [#1507]*
Michal Cernansky and Matej Makula, FIIT Slovak University of Technology, Slovakia

New method for modeling nonlinear systems called the echo state networks (ESNs) has been proposed recently. ESNs make use of the dynamics created by huge randomly created layer of recurrent units. Dynamical behavior of untrained recurrent networks was already explained in the literature. Knowing how the recurrent part stores the information and understanding the state dynamics of recurrent neural networks we propose modified ESN architecture. The only "true" recurrent connections are backward connection from output to recurrent units and the reservoir is built only by "forwardly" connected recurrent units. We show that this simplified version of the ESNs can also be successful in modeling nonlinear systems.

11:10AM *Direct Adaptive Control: An Echo State Network and Genetic Algorithm Approach [#1718]*
Dongming Xu, Jing Lan and Jose C. Principe, CNEL, Department of ECE, University of Florida, United States

This paper presents a direct adaptive approach to design controllers for nonlinear dynamical systems, where system identification of the unknown dynamical system is not required. The solution is powered by both ESN and genetic algorithm (GA). ESN enables a simple modeling of the controller, with which only a linear readout needs to be trained. GA is used to optimize ESN's linear readout directly so that system identification is not required. Simulation results reveal that the algorithm is capable of achieving very good control performance with computational efficiency.

Evolutionary algorithms and PSO
Tuesday, August 2, 9:30AM-11:30AM, Room: Westmount, Chair: Donald Wunsch

9:30AM *Non-Linear Mappings Based on Particle Swarm Optimization [#1435]*
Cristian J. Figueroa, Pablo A. Estevez and Rodrigo Hernandez, Dept. Electrical Engineering, U. of Chile, Chile

Non-linear mapping methods that minimize the Sammon stress based on Particle Swarm Optimization (PSO) are proposed. The task considered is the mapping of the codebook vectors generated by the Neural Gas (NG) network onto a two-dimensional space. Three methods are explored: the direct application of the traditional PSO, the initialization of PSO with TOPNG, and a dynamically Growing PSO. These methods are compared with the Sammon's mapping and TOPNG in terms of the Sammon stress and the topology preservation measure qm. The best results are obtained when PSO is initialized with TOPNG.

9:50AM *Evolutionary supervision of a dynamical neural network allows learning with on-going weights [#1440]*
David Meunier and Helene Paugam-Moisy, Institute for Cognitive Science, France

Recent electrophysiological data show that synaptic weights are highly influenced by electrical activities displayed by neurons. Weights are not stable as assumed in classical neural network models. What is the nature of engrams, if not stored in synaptic weights? Adopting the theory of dynamical systems, which allows an implicit form of memory, we propose a new framework for learning, where synaptic weights are continuously adapted. Evolutionary computation has been applied to a population of dynamic neural networks evolving in a prey-predator environment. This method allows the emergence of learning capability through generations, as a by-product of evolution.

10:10AM *Evolutionary Neural Classification for Evaluation of Retail Stores and Decision Support [#1506]*
Robert Stahlbock and Sven Crone, University of Hamburg, Germany; Lancaster University, United Kingdom

Classification tasks can be solved with neural networks like learning vector quantization (LVQ). In this paper, a novel approach of evolutionary optimized LVQs is proposed. It is applied to a complex real-world economic task: the evaluation of branch locations of a large trading concern in terms of revenue and profit. Given data reflects external infrastructure and internal aspects of existing branches. Results of computational experiments in a parallelized PC network are compared with results of standard LVQs. They are interpreted as information for support of investment decisions. New branches can be established, or existing branches without prospective profits can be shut down or their style or product lines can be changed.

10:30AM *BioAnt - Biologically Plausible Computer Simulation of an Environment with Ants [#1121]*
Marvin Oliver Schneider and Joao Luis Garcia Rosa, Universitaet Fridericiana zu Karlsruhe, Germany; PUC-Campinas, Brazil

The system BioAnt, presented here, is an artificial life system that simulates an environment with ants. Each ant moves inside the environment on the basis of a Biologically Plausible Artificial Neural Network, which employs the algorithm GeneRec for supervised learning. In order to obtain an initial configuration, a symbolic algorithm (based on a set of production rules) was created. The environment itself is three-dimensional and consists of the anthill, sugar, water, earth elevations, walls, and predators. The ants interact with the environment using the senses of smell, vision, touch, and hearing, always following the commands of the neural controller.

10:50AM *Optimizing Class-Related Thresholds with Particle Swarm Optimization [#1411]*
Luiz S. Oliveira, Alceu Britto Jr. and Robert Sabourin, Pontificia Universidade Catolica do Parana, Brazil; LIVIA, Ecole de Technologie Superieure, Montreal, Canada

This paper addresses the issue of class-related reject thresholds for classification systems. It has been demonstrated that class-related reject thresholds provide an error-reject trade-off better than a single global threshold. In this work we argue that the error-reject trade-off yielded by class-related reject thresholds can be further improved if a proper algorithm is used to find the thresholds. In light of this, we propose using a recently developed optimization algorithm called PSO. It has been proved to be very effective in solving real valued global optimization problems. In order to show the benefits of such an algorithm, we have applied it to optimize the thresholds of a cascading system devoted to recognize handwritten digits.

11:10AM *Lotto-Type Competitive Learning with Particle Swarm Features [#1053]*
Andrew Luk and Sandra Lien, St. B-P Neural Investments Pty. Ltd., Australia; St B-P Neural Investments Pty Limited, Australia

This correspondence describes our attempts of incorporating particle swarm features into competitve learning. We first reinterpret some of the symbols and notations used in particle swarm optimisation (PSO) algorithms in the light of competitive learning. Three versions of modifications to the classical frequency-sensitive competitive learning are presented. Their strengths and weaknesses are highlighted. This then enables us to introduce particle swarm like features into our lotto-type competitive learning. Experimental results indicate that, like the PSO algorithms, a careful selection of the values for the control parameters is necessary for the successful convergence of particles in some of the proposed algorithms.

Special Session: Functional Neuroimaging of Cortical and Subcortical Functions
Tuesday, August 2, 9:30AM-11:30AM, Room: Mt Royal/Hampstead, Chair: Oury Monchi

9:30AM *Reorganization and Plasticity in the Adult Brain During Learning of Motor Skills [#1263]*
Julien Doyon and Habib Benali, Department of Psychology, University of Montreal, Canada; INSERM U678/UPMC, Paris and IFR49, Orsay, France

Motor skill learning refers to the process by which movements either produced alone or in a sequence, come to be performed effortlessly through repeated practice. Doyon et al., have proposed recently that activity within the cortico-striatal and cortico-cerebellar systems is thought to be sufficient, respectively, motor sequence learning and for motor adaptation. In this presentation, the results of a large body of studies in healthy human subjects that examined the functional anatomy and the cerebral plasticity associated with these two forms of memory will be discussed using brain imaging technology and novel models of dynamic functionnal connectivity.

10:00AM *Cortico-Basal Ganglia Functional Connectivity Investigated with Transcranial Magnetic Stimulation [#1048]*
Antonio Strafella, Montreal Neurological Institute, McGill Univ., Canada

Cortico-striatal and cortico-subthalamic pathways,in normal volunteers and parkinsonian patients, were investigated with [11C]raclopride PET following TMS of dorsolateral prefrontal (DLPFC) and motor cortex (MC) and using intra- operative recordings from STN during surgery while stimulating MC with TMS. In normals, TMS of the DLPFC and MC induced focal release of dopamine in ipsilateral caudate nucleus and putamen, respectively. In parkinsonian patients, TMS induced an excitation in 74.9 % of STN neurons investigated followed by a long-lasting inhibition of neuronal activity. These in- vivo studies suggest that cortical projections may promote a powerful modulatory control of their subcortical targets in human brain.

10:30AM *Heading For Data-Driven Measures of Effective Connectivity in Functional MRI [#1595]*
Guillaume Marrelec, Julien Doyon, Melanie Pelegrini-Issac and Habib Benali, Department of Psychology, Universite de Montreal, Canada; Department of Psychology, University of Montreal, Canada; U678 Inserm/UPMC, France

Two standpoints have been considered so far to investigate functional brain interactivity in functional MRI. Effective connectivity (EC), that describes the influence that regions exert on each other, requires the definition of a structural model that is often unknown. Functional connectivity (FC), that measures statistical interdependencies between regions, cannot usually be used to infer patterns of effective connectivity from the data. We here emphasize one major difference that keeps FC away from EC, namely mediation. Using structural equation modeling (SEM), we show how patterns of mediated interaction cannot be differentiated by FC. We then introduce conditional correlation as a way to achieve such a differentiation.

11:00AM *Connectivity of anatomical and functional MRI data [#1693]*
Keith Worsley, Arnaud Charil, Jason Lerch and Alan Evans, McGill University, Canada

We are all familiar with the correlation coefficient between two sets of numbers. Now suppose we replace the numbers by vector-valued images in any number of dimensions. The correlation random field is the 'image' of correlations at all possible pairs of points in the two images. We use random field theory to set a threshold on the correlations so that those above the threshold are statistically significant, corrected for searching over all pairs of points. We apply this idea to resting state networks of fMRI images of brain activity, and networks of connectivity in cortical thickness.

Tuesday, August 2, 1:00PM-3:00PM

Recurrent Neural Networks
Tuesday, August 2, 1:00PM-3:00PM, Room: Outremount, Chair: Danil Prokhorov

1:00PM *Dynamical Consistent Recurrent Neural Networks [#1771]*
Hans-Georg Zimmermann, Ralph Grothmann, Anton Schaefer and Christoph Tietz, Siemens AG, Germany

Recurrent neural networks are typically considered as relatively simple architectures, which come along with complicated learning algorithms. Most researchers focus on the improvement of these algorithms. Our approach is different. Rather than focusing on learning and optimization algorithms, we concentrate on the design of the network architecture. As we will show, many difficulties in the modeling of dynamical systems can be solved with a pre-design of the network architecture. We will focus on large networks with the task of modeling complete high dimensional systems (e.g., financial markets) instead of small sets of time series. Standard neural networks tend to overfit like any other statistical learning system. We will introduce a new recurrent neural network architecture in which overfitting and the associated loss of generalization abilities is not a major problem. We will enhance these networks by dynamical consistency.

1:40PM *Effectively Using Recurrently-Connected Spiking Neural Networks [#1553]*
Eric Goodman and Dan Ventura, Brigham Young University, United States

Recurrently connected spiking neural networks are difficult to use and understand because of the complex nonlinear dynamics of the system. Through empirical studies of spiking networks, we deduce several principles which are critical to success. Network parameters such as synaptic time delays and time constants and the connection probabilities can be adjusted to have a significant impact on accuracy. We show how to adjust these parameters to fit the type of problem.

2:00PM *Adaptive Flight Control with Living Neuronal Networks on Microelectrode Arrays [#1772]*
Thomas DeMarse and Karl Dockendorf, Universirty of Florida, Gainesville, United States

The brain is perhaps one of the most robust and fault tolerant computational devices in existence and yet little is known about its mechanisms. Microelectrode arrays have recently been developed in which the computational properties of networks of living neurons can be studied in detail. In this paper we report work investigating the ability of living neurons to act as a set of neuronal weights which were used to control the flight of a simulated aircraft. These weights were manipulated via a high frequency stimulation inputs to produce a system in which a living neuronal network would "learn" to control an aircraft for straight and level flight.

2:40PM *Introduction of an Hebbian unsupervised learning algorithm [#1555]*
Colin Molter, Utku Salihoglu and Hugues Bersini, Iridia - ULB, Belgium

The learning impact, of an iterative supervised hebbian learning algorithm, on a recurrent neural network's inner dynamics has been discussed in a previous paper. However such supervised learning algorithm seems very unrealistic from a biological point of view. To get closer, this paper introduces an unsupervised version of this algorithm. As a direct result, both the storing capacity and the content addressability are greatly enhanced. Furthermore, stunning dynamical results are observed: chaotic domains are smaller compared to the supervised algorithm. Moreover, chaos obtained looks more structured, made from brief itinerancy among learned cycles.

Self Organizing Maps
Tuesday, August 2, 1:00PM-3:00PM, Room: Verdun/Lachine, Chair: Klaus Obermayer

1:00PM *A visualization technique for Self-Organizing Maps with vector fields to obtain the cluster structure at desired levels of detail [#1751]*
Georg Poelzlbauer, Dittenbach Michael and Rauber Andreas, Vienna University of Technology, Austria; Vienna, eCommerce Competence Center, Austria

Self-Organizing Maps (SOMs) are a prominent tool for exploratory data analysis. One core task within the utilization of SOMs is the identification of the cluster structure on the map for which several visualization methods have been proposed, yet different application domains may require additional representation of the cluster structure. In this paper, we propose such a method based on pairwise distance calculation. It can be plotted on top of the map lattice with arrows that point to the closest cluster center. A parameter is provided that determines the granularity of the clustering. We provide experimental results and discuss the general applicability of our method, along with a comparison to related techniques.

1:20PM *Multi-Topographic Neural Network Communication and Generalization for Multi-Viewpoint Analysis [#1504]*
Shadi Al Shehabi and Jean-Charles Lamirel, Loria-Inria France, France

This paper presents a new generic multi-topographic neural network model whose main area of application is clustering and knowledge extraction tasks on documentary data. The most powefull features of this model are its generalization mechanism and its mechanism of communication between topographies. This paper shows how these mechanisms can be exploited in the framework of the SOM and NG models. An evaluation of the generalization mechanism using original quality and propagation coherency measures is also proposed. A secondary results of this evaluation is to prove that the generalization mechanism could significantly reduce the well-known border effect of the SOM map.

1:40PM *A Self-Organizing Map for Concept Classification in Information Retrieval [#1102]*
Guy Desjardins, Robert Godin and Robert Proulx, University of Quebec in Montreal, Canada

Few connectionist models have been designed for text classification and applied to the information retrieval. We propose a new model in this area. Our model is based on the self-organizing map paradigm to discover the concepts embedded in a collection of documents. The terms are directly classified into concepts, without manual category labelling. The concepts are then used as a new knowledge representation for information retrieval. The model has been tested on a TREC collection. The retrieval using the concepts representation did not outperformed the corresponding full term retrieval. It is a step toward terms classification using self-organizing map and contributes to fully automate the discovery of concepts in text collections.

2:00PM *Training the SOFM Efficiently: An Example from Intrusion Detection [#1150]*
Leigh Wetmore, Nur Zincir-Heywood and Malcolm Heywood, Dalhousie University, Canada

The Dynamic Subset Selection (DSS) Active Learning algorithm is generalized to include the case of unsupervised learning. To do so, training set partitioning, exemplar difficulty and age, and early stopping criteria are introduced into the Self Organizing Feature Map algorithm. The resulting model is able to build a Hierarchical SOFM on a large (500 000 pattern) dataset in 3 hours. In comparison, the same architecture without active learning requires 33 hours to construct. No reduction in accuracy is recorded for the DSS SOFM model.

2:20PM *Modular Network SOM (mnSOM): From Vector Space to Function Space [#1436]*
Tetsuo Furukawa, Kazuhiro Tokunaga, Kenji Morishita and Syozo Yasui, Kyushu Institute of Technology, Japan

The purpose of this study is to develop a novel generalization of SOM called modular network SOM (mnSOM), which enables one to deal with general data classes in a consistent manner. mnSOM has an array structure consisting of function modules which are trainable neural networks, instead of vector units of the conventional SOM family. In the case of MLP-modules, mnSOM learns a group of systems or functions in terms of the input-output relationships, and at the same time mnSOM generates a feature map which tells distances between the learned systems. Thus, mnSOM with MLP modules is a SOM in function space rather than vector space. In this paper, mnSOM with MLP modules is described with some application examples.

2:40PM *Ranked Centroid Projection: A Data Visualization Approach for Self-organizing Maps [#1306]*
Gary Yen and Zheng Wu, Oklahoma State University, United States

The Self-Organizing Map is a tool for visualizing high-dimensional data as it performs a topology-preserving projection of the input space on a low-dimensional grid. To utilize the information provided by the SOM and obtain an approximation of the data structure, a separate data projection method is usually needed. Most of the projection methods are computationally expensive when the size of the data set becomes large. In this paper we present an effective SOM projection method with comparatively low computational complexity. This method maps data vectors on the output space based on their responses to different prototype vectors. The proposed method is demonstrated using both an artificial and a real world data set.

Special Session: Transition: Imaging and Cortical models
Tuesday, August 2, 1:00PM-3:00PM, Room: Mt Royal/Hampstead, Chair: John G. Taylor

1:00PM *fMRI experiments and computational models of the function of the prefrontal cortex and the basal ganglia: a review [#1429]*
Oury Monchi, Geriatric Institute, University of Montreal, Canada

We have previously developed computational neuroscience models of fronto-striatal activity during the performance of the Wisconsin Card Sorting Task, a well-known set-shifting task (Monchi et al., 2000). The simulation of this model helped design a novel event-related functional Magnetic Resonance Imaging protocol that allows for the separation of four temporal stages of the task, that was used in both healthy controls and patients with Parkinson's disease, (Monchi et al., 2001, 2004). Here, the advantages and limitations of our previous computational methods will be discussed with respect to functional neuroimaging data acquisition, and examples of new, on-going studies, using both fMRI and computational neurocscience will be given.

1:30PM *Computational Models of Emotion [#1485]*
Jorge Armony, McGill University, Canada

Emotion is clearly an important aspect of the mind; yet it has been largely ignored by the brain and mind (cognitive) sciences in modern times. However, there are signs that this is beginning to change. Here, we survey some issues about the nature of emotion, describe what is known about the neural basis of emotion, and consider some efforts that have been made to develop computational models of different aspects of emotion.

2:00PM *Neural Networks of the Brain: Their Analysis and Relation to Brain Images [#1410]*
John Taylor, King's College London, United Kingdom

We develop a mathematical framework of continuum neural field theory as the beginning point for an analysis of the multi-modular global brain. Applications to cortical dynamics and learning in somato-sensory cortex, visual cortex and motor control are briefly reviewed. Extensions to a broader range of brain systems, including attention and emotions, are outlined. A deduction of structural equation models for the coupled neural modules is then briefly noted, with all neural variables acting as hidden variables in a well-defined manner.

2:30PM *Brain Categorization: Learning, Attention, and Consciousness [#1287]*
Stephen Grossberg, Gail Carpenter and Bilgin Ersoy, Boston University, United States

How do humans and animals learn to recognize objects and events? Two classical views are that exemplars or prototypes are learned. A hybrid view is that a mixture, called rule-plus-exceptions, is learned. None of these models learn their categories. A distributed ARTMAP neural network with self-supervised learning incrementally learns categories that match human learning data on a class of thirty diagnostic experiments called the 5-4 category structure. Key predictions of ART models have received behavioral, neurophysiological, and anatomical support. The ART prediction about what goes wrong during amnesic learning has also been supported: A lesion in its orienting system causes a low vigilance parameter.

Special Session: Applications of Learning and Data-Driven Methods to Earth Sciences and Climate Modeling
Tuesday, August 2, 1:00PM-3:00PM, Room: Westmount, Chair: Vladimir Krasnopolsky, Dimitri Solomatine, Julio Valdes Vladimir Cherkassky

1:00PM *Complex Hybrid Models Combining Deterministic and Machine Learning Components as a New Synergetic Paradigm in Numerical Climate Modeling and Weather Prediction [#1104]*
Vladimir Krasnopolsky and Michael Fox-Rabinovitz, Saic at Ncep/Noaa and Essic/Umd, United States; Essic/Umd, United States

A new type of numerical models, complex hybrid environmental models (CHEMs) based on a combination of deterministic and machine learning model components, is introduced and developed. Conceptual and practical possibilities of developing CHEM, as an optimal synergetic combination of the traditional deterministic/first principles modeling and machine learning components (like accurate and fast neural network emulations of model physics or chemistry processes), are discussed. An example of developed CHEM (a hybrid climate model) illustrates the feasibility and efficiency of the new approach for modeling extremely complex multidimensional systems.

1:20PM *Atmospheric correction and oceanic constituents retrieval with a neuro-variational method [#1169]*
Julien Brajard, Cedric Jamet, Cyril Moulin and Sylvie Thiria, Locean/ipsl, France; University of British Columbia, Canada; Lsce/cea/ipsl, France

Ocean color sensors on board satellite measure the solar radiation reflected by the ocean and the atmosphere. This information, denoted reflectance, is affected by the atmosphere, the water and the phytoplankton cells in the ocean. Our method focuses on the chlorophyll-a content(chl-a) retrieval. Our algorithm computes relevant atmospheric and oceanic parameters such as chl-a by minimizing the difference between the observed reflectance and the reflectance computed from artificial neural networks that have been learned with a radiative transfer model. Our results are compared to the SeaWiFS algorithm and to in-situ data. It shows a better estimate of the water leaving reflectance and of the low chl-a contents than the standard processing.

1:40PM *Nonlinear Complex Principal Component Analysis and Its Applications [#1278]*
Sanjay Rattan, William Hsieh and Gerben Ruessink, University of British Columbia, Canada; Utrecht University, Netherlands

Complex principal component analysis (CPCA) is a linear multivariate technique commonly applied to complex variables or 2-dimensional vector fields such as winds or currents. A new nonlinear CPCA (NLCPCA) method has been developed via complex-valued multi-layer perceptron neural networks. NLCPCA is applied to the tropical Pacific wind field to study the interannual variability. NLCPCA can also be used to nonlinearly generalize Hilbert PCA (where real data is complexified prior to performing CPCA). An example is provided from the nearshore bathymetry at Egmond, Netherlands, where sand bars propagate offshore, and unlike the CPCA mode 1, the NLCPCA mode 1 detects asymmetry between the bars and the troughs.

2:00PM *Nonlinear Principal Predictor Analysis Using Neural Networks [#1489]*
Alex Cannon, Meteorological Service of Canada, Canada

This study introduces a new neural network approach for performing nonlinear principal predictor analysis. The utility of this approach is demonstrated via two test problems. The first, using synthetic data, gauges the ability of the model to extract known modes of variability from datasets with increasing noise levels. The second, based on the Lorenz system of equations, considers performance in the context of nonlinear prediction. Results suggest that nonlinear principal predictor analysis performs better than nonlinear canonical correlation analysis. In addition, nonlinear principal predictor modes may be extracted in less time than modes from nonlinear canonical correlation analysis.

2:20PM *Temporal Neural Networks for Downscaling Climate Variability and Extremes [#1183]*
Yonas Dibike and Paulin Coulibaly, McMaster University, Canada

This paper presents the issues of 'downscaling' the outputs of global climate models (GCMs) using a temporal neural network (TNN) approach. The method is proposed for downscaling daily precipitation and temperature series for a region in northern Quebec, Canada. The performance of the TNN downscaling model is compared to a regression-based statistical downscaling model. The downscaling results for the base period (1961-2000) suggest that the TNN is an efficient method for downscaling both daily precipitation as well as daily temperature series.

2:40PM *A Spatiotemporal Approach to Tornado Prediction [#1072]*
Valliappa Lakshmanan, Indra Adrianto, Travis Smith and Greg Stumpf, University of Oklahoma and\National Severe Stor, United States; University of Oklahoma, United States

Automated tornado detection or prediction techniques in the literature have all been based on analyzing "signatures" of tornadoes that appear in Doppler radar velocity data. In this paper, we formulate the tornado prediction problem differently. Instead of devising a machine intelligence approach to classify detections, we formulate the problem as a spatio-temporal one: of estimating the probability of a tornado event at a particular spatial location within a given time window. In this paper, we also describe our initial approach to addressing this differently formulated problem.

Tuesday, August 2, 3:20PM-5:20PM

Special Session: Models of Cortical and Subcortical Circuits
Tuesday, August 2, 3:20PM-5:20PM, Room: Mt Royal/Hampstead, Chair: Daniel Levine

3:20PM *A computational model of reach decisions in the primate cerebral cortex [#1694]*
Paul Cisek, University of Montreal, Canada

Neurophysiological evidence suggests that visually-guided reaching movements are produced through "specification" and "selection" processes that overlap both temporally and anatomically. Here, I present a formal computational model which demonstrates how partial specification of several potential movement directions, and the selection of the correct movement, can occur in populations of directionally tuned cells in a distributed cortical network including posterior parietal, premotor, prefrontal, and primary motor cortex. The model reproduces a large set of neurophysiological and psychophysical phenomena, including the behavior of cortical cells during a reach decision task and the spatial and temporal statistics of human reaching choices.

3:50PM *Modeling Cortico-Subcortical Interactions During Planning, Learning, and Voluntary Control of Actions [#1603]*
Daniel Bullock, Boston University, United States

Key for any global brain model is the proposed division of labor among adaptive circuits in frontal cortex, basal ganglia, and the cerebellum, all of which are engaged during most voluntary planning and action. This paper presents an emerging synthesis based on an interlocking set of formal computational hypotheses, which specify how local circuits in the three areas interact, via established pathways, to solve basic learning and performance problems encountered during voluntary planning and action. Results of simulations showing the mutual coherence and explanatory power of the hypotheses, vis-a-vis extensive behavioral and neurophysiological data, are reviewed.

4:20PM *Modeling Emotional Influences on Human Decision Making Under Risk [#1575]*
Daniel Levine, Britain Mills and Steven Estrada, University of Texas at Arlington, United States

We model choices in the Iowa Gambling Task, developed by Bechara and Damasio to diagnose decision making deficits of patients with damage to orbital prefrontal cortex. In this task the subjects choose at each trial between four decks of cards: two decks yield high short-term payoffs but long-term losses, and the other two yield lower short-term payoffs but long-term gains. Normals but not patients learn to choose advantageous decks. We simulate this effect with a model based on connections between prefrontal cortex (orbital, medial, and anterior cingulate), basal ganglia, and thalamus, and emotional signals from amygdala.

4:50PM *Modelling the Interaction of Attention and Emotion [#1273]*
John Taylor and Nickolaos Fragopanagos, King's College London, United Kingdom

We review a recently developed engineering control approach to attention, presenting detailed attention control function assignments to the wealth of brain modules experimentally observed. The control system is extended to include biasing by emotional valence, with qualitative analysis given of a range of emotion paradigms and more detailed simulation described for two further paradigms. The implications of these results for better understanding of the interaction of emotion and attention concludes the paper, and in particular gives a possible resolution of the question as to unaware versus aware processing of emotional material.

Visual and Image Processing
Tuesday, August 2, 3:20PM-5:20PM, Room: Verdun/Lachine, Chair: Kunihiko Fukushima

3:20PM *Neural Network Model for Analyzing Optic Flow [#1619]*
Kazuya Tohyama and Kunihiko Fukushima, Tokyo University of Technology, Japan

When we travel in an environment, we have an optic flow on the retina. Cells in the area MST of macaque monkeys are reported to analyze optic flow. The MST cells respond selectively to rotation, expansion/contraction and spiral motion. We propose a novel neural network model for MST, based on the vector-field hypothesis. Our model consists of hierarchically connected layers: retina, V1, MT and MST. V1 cells measure local velocity. MT cells extract relative velocity with their antagonistic networks. MST cells simply collect the signals from MT cells and respond selectively to various types of optic flows. We show through computer simulation that its simple mechanism can explain a variety of results of neurophysiological experiments.

3:40PM *Face Detection and Identification Using a Hierarchical Feed-forward Recognition Architecture [#1422]*
Ingo Bax, Gunther Heidemann and Helge Ritter, University of Bielefeld, Germany

We apply a hierarchical feed-forward neural architecture to the problem of face recognition. The network is similar to the Neocognitron-approach and a two-layer variation of this architecture, which has previously been successfully applied to patch classification tasks. We extend this architecture to a three-layer one, which allows not only identification of image patches, but also detection in larger images. In the research area of face recognition a lot of expertise has been developed for the problem of either identification or detection, but approaches which deal with both problems simultaneously are rarely to be found. In this work, we apply the hierarchical approach to this problem and evaluate the performance on artificial datasets.

4:00PM *Lossless High Dynamic Range Image Coding based on Lifting Scheme using Nonlinear Interpolative Effect of Discrete-Time Cellular Neural Networks [#1444]*
Hisashi Aomori, Kohei Kawakami, Tsuyoshi Otake, Nobuaki Takahashi, Masayuki Yamauchi and Mamoru Tanaka, Sophia University, Japan; Tamagawa University, Japan; IBM Japan, Ltd., Japan

The lifting scheme is a flexible method for the construction of linear and nonlinear wavelet transforms. In this paper, we propose a novel lossless high dynamic range (HDR) image coding method based on the lifting scheme using discrete-time cellular neural networks (DT-CNNs). In our proposed method, the image is interpolated by using the nonlinear interpolative dynamics of DT-CNN. Because the output function of DT-CNN works as a multi-level quantization function, our method adapts for the prediction of HDR image, and composes the integer lifting scheme for lossless coding. Moreover, our method makes good use of the nonlinear interpolative dynamics by A-template compared with conventional CNN image coding methods using only B-template.

4:20PM *Could Early Visual Processes be Sufficient to Label Motions? [#1051]*
Pierre Kornprobst, Thierry Vieville and Ivan Dimov, Inria, France; Universidad Tecnica Frederico Santa Maria, Chile

Biological motion recognition refers to our ability to recognize a scene based on the evolution of a limited number of points acquired for instance with a motion capture tool. Much work has been done in this direction showing how it is possible to recognize actions based on these points. Following the reference work of Giese and Poggio (2003), we propose an alternative approach to extract such points from a video based on spiking neural networks with rank order coding as described by Thorpe et al. (2001). This allows to select a limited set of relevant points to be used in the motion classification. The result of these simulations is that information from early visual processes appears to be sufficient to classify biological motion.

4:40PM *A Phase-equation Model for a Large Phase Lead in Manual Tracking Caused by Intermittent Visual Information [#1288]*
Yasuhiro Takachi and Yasuji Sawada, Tohoku Institute of Technology, Japan

We propose a phase-equation model for a large phase lead in manual tracking with intermittent visual information. To adapt a general tracking model to the intermittent manual tracking, we suppose that the geometric factor coupling with the target velocity is indispensable as a feedforward control, and the feedback control intermittently contributes to the hand motion. Results of simulations show that the large phase lead is dueto both the decrease in visual information and the synchronicity between the timing of target display and the effect of the rhythmic hand motion caused by the geometric property of the target path.

5:00PM *Investigations into the Analysis of Remote Sensing Images with a Growing Neural Gas [#1497]*
Karl Lalonde, South Dakota School of Mines and Technology, United States

The Growing Neural Gas (GNG) pattern recognition algorithm is an unsupervised algorithm which inserts nodes into the state space of the training data. Observations of the behavior of the algorithm lead to the hypothesis that this method may be an efficient pre-classification clustering algorithm for data in highly discrete state spaces, as in satellite remote sensing images. The GNG algorithm was used to train a net-work using a Landsat image from Wyoming. The initial results of this investigation were extremely positive. The image derived from the trained GNG network is difficult to distinguish from the source image. Preliminary statistical results also indicate a high degree of correlation between the source and resultant images.

Special Session: Applications of Learning and Data-Driven Methods to Earth Sciences and Climate Modeling, plus Panel discussion
Tuesday, August 2, 3:20PM-5:20PM, Room: Westmount, Chair: Vladimir Krasnopolsky, Dimitri Solomatine, Julio Valdes Vladimir Cherkassky

3:20PM *Applications of Neural Network Methods to the Processing of Earth Observation Satellite Data [#1248]*
Diego G. Loyola R., German Aerospace Center (DLR), Germany

The new generation of Earth Observation satellites carry advance sensors that will gather very precise data for studying the Earth system and global climate. This paper shows that neural network methods can be successfully used for solving forward and inverse remote sensing problems, providing both accurate and fast solutions. Two examples of multi-neural network systems for the determination of cloud properties and for the retrieval of total columns of ozone using satellite data are presented. The developed algorithms based on multi-neural network are currently being used for the operational processing of European atmospheric satellite sensors and will play a key role in related satellite missions planed for the near future.

3:40PM *Time Dependent Neural Network Models For Detecting Changes Of State In Earth and Planetary Processes [#1439]*
Julio J. Valdes and Graeme Bonham-Carter, National Research Council Canada, Canada; Geological Survey of Canada, Canada

This paper explores a computational intelligence approach to the detection of internal changes in processes described by heterogeneous, multivariate time series with imprecise and missing values. Time-dependent nonlinear AR models are generated using grid and high throughput computing data-mining procedures. They work with a combination of neuro-fuzzy networks and genetic algorithms. The discovered models are given by sets of time lags, and neuro-fuzzy prediction functions. Their composition and their prediction capabilities, allows the identification of changes in the process, usually associated with steady and transient states, abnormal behavior, instability, etc. This approach is general, and it is applied to paleoclimate and solar data.

4:00PM *Local and Hybrid Learning Models in Forecasting Natural Phenomena [#1362]*
Dimitri P. Solomatine, UNESCO-IHE Institute for Water Education, Delft, Netherlands

Modular models (committee machines, mixtures of experts) are comprised of a set of specialized (local) models each of which is responsible for a particular region of input space, and trained on a subset of the training set. The known algorithms for allocating such regions typically do this in automatic fashion. In forecasting natural processes domain experts, however, want to see more domain knowledge behind such allocation, and to have certain control over such allocation and the choice of models, making thus the overall model hybrid. The paper presents some of the approaches to building modular and hybrid models, new algorithms and reports case studies in the area of river flow forecasting.

4:20PM *Semiblind source separation of climate data detects El Nino as the component with the highest interannual variability [#1459]*
Alexander Ilin, Harri Valpola and Erkki Oja, Helsinki University of Technology, Finland

Denoising source separation (DSS) was applied to extracting components exhibiting slow, interannual temporal behaviour from climate data. Three datasets with daily measurements were used: surface temperature, sea level pressure and precipitation around the globe. For all datasets, the first component captured the well-known El Nino-Southern Oscillation phenomenon and the second component was close to the derivative of the first one. Several other components with slow dynamics were extracted and together the components appear to capture essential features of the slow-dynamics state of the climate system. This paper offers a simple demonstration of exploratory data analysis of climate data by DSS and suggests future lines of research.

4:40PM *Panel discussion: Applications of Learning and Data-Driven Methods to Earth Sciences and Climate Modeling*
Vladimir Cherkassky, Dimitri Solomatine, Vladimir Krasnopolsky and Julio Valdes, University of Minnesota, United States; UNESCO-IHE Institute for Water Education, Netherlands; Environmental Modeling Center, NOAA, United States; National Research Council, Canada

PANEL DISCUSSION: on methodological issues in application of learning methods to Climate Modeling and Earth Sciences. The panel will include informal presentations by the session co-chairs followed by questions-and-answers from the audience. Topics of discussion include the following: - to identify major types of problems encountered in this field; - how to estimate the quality of data-driven models; - what are specific characteristics of data sets in Climate Modeling/ Earth Sciences that make them different from other applications; - try to come to an agreement on possible benchmark data sets in this field.

Diagnostics and Control, Power systems
Tuesday, August 2, 3:20PM-5:20PM, Room: Outremount, Chair: Ronald Harley

3:20PM *Continuous On-line Identification of Nonlinear Plants in Power Systems with Missing Sensor Measurements [#1661]*
Wei Qiao, Zhi Gao and Ronald G. Harley, Georgia Institute of Technology, United States

A novel robust artificial neural network identifier (RANNI) model is proposed in this paper. This RANNI can continuously track the dynamics of the plant model on-line when some sensor measurements are unavailable. A static synchronous series compensator (SSSC) connected to a small power system is used as a test system to examine the validity of the proposed model. In the simulation, one sensor is assumed to be missing; simulation results show that the proposed RANNI tracks the plant dynamics with good precision during the steady state, the small disturbance, and the transient state after a large disturbance. The proposed RANNI is readily applicable to other plant models in power systems.

3:40PM *Collective Behavior Implementation in Powerline Surveillance Sensor Network [#1696]*
Pornchai Chanyagorn, Harold Szu and Hongye Wang, EE Dept., Mahidol University, Thailand; DMLAB, George Washington Univ., United States; National Inst. of Mental Health, Maryland, United States

The paper presents the application of collective swarm intelligence in solving problems of non-multiplexing communication in powerline sensor network. Based on collective intelligence behavior, we design a system that allows local sensors to collect local information acquired from the powerline channel. As the information become available, the sensor can adaptively adjust its parameters in order to achieve a common goal of non-multiplexing sensor communication throughout entire network. The non-multiplexing sensor communications is implemented using uBSS based on the finite alphabet property of the data. The details of hardware implementation are provided as well as the result from the testbed network.

4:00PM *Neural Networks based Scheme for Fault Diagnosis in Fossil Electric Power Plants [#1181]*
Jose A. Ruz-Hernandez, Edgar N. Sanchez and Dionisio A. Suarez, Universidad Autonoma del Carmen, Mexico; CINVESTAV, Unidad Guadalajara, Mexico; Instituto de Investigaciones Electricas, Mexico

This paper presents the development and application of a neural networks-based scheme for fault diagnosis. The scheme is constituted by two components: residuals generation and fault classification. The first component generates residuals via the difference between measurements coming from the plant and a neural network predictor. The neural network predictor is trained with healthy data collected from a full scale simulator reproducing reliably the process behavior. For the second one, thresholds are used to encode the residuals as vectors which represent fault patterns. The fault patterns are stored in an associative memory based on a recurrent neural network.

4:20PM *Detection of Actuator Faults Using a Dynamic Neural Network for the Attitude Control Subsystem of a Satellite [#1118]*
Iz Al-Dein Al-Zyoud and Khashayar Khorasani, Concordia University, Canada

The objective of this paper is to develop a neural network-based residual generator for fault detection in the attitude control subsystem of a satellite. A dynamic multilayer perceptron network where the neuron model consists of a second order linear filter and a nonlinear activation function is considered. The proposed dynamic neural network is utilized for detecting faults in a reaction wheel which is often used as an actuator of a satellite. The performance and capabilities of the proposed dynamic neural network is compared to a model-based observer residual generator design where it is shown that the model-based approach is unable to detect and diagnosis any of the fault scenarios considered.

4:40PM *Dynamic Bayesian Networks for Machine Diagnostics: Hierarchical Hidden Markov Models vs. Competitive Learning [#1589]*
Fatih Camci and Ratna Babu Chinnam, Wayne State University, United States

Tracking the health state of a machine is critical for detecting, identifying, and localizing the failure and estimating the remaining-useful-life for carrying out proper maintenance. Regular and hierarchical HMMs are employed here to estimate the health state of drill-bits as they deteriorate with use on a CNC drilling machine. In the case of regular HMMs, each HMM competes to represent a distinct health state and learns through competitive learning. In the case of hierarchical HMMs, health states are represented as distinct nodes in the top of the hierarchy. Implementation of HMM based models as dynamic Bayesian networks facilitates compact representation as well as additional flexibility with regard to model structure.

5:00PM *Fuzzy Multi-Hidden Markov Predictor in Electric Load Forecasting [#1189]*
Marcelo Teixeira and Gerson Zaverucha, Electric Power Research Center (CEPEL), Brazil; COPPE / Federal University of Rio de Janeiro, Brazil

We present two new systems that approximate probability density functions (pdf's) in order to predict continuous values of time series: the Fuzzy Multi-Hidden Markov Predictor (FMHMP) and the Multi-Hidden Markov Model for Regression (MHMMR). They use fuzzification or discretization of continuous data and Dynamic Bayesian Networks (DBN's) to estimate pdf's and then make continuous predictions. The employed DBN is a generalization of the Hidden Markov Model that allows multiple hidden variables. The new systems are applied to the task of monthly electric load single-step forecasting and successfully compared with other fuzzy and discrete probabilistic predictors, two Kalman Filter Models, and two traditional forecasting methods.

Tuesday, August 2, 7:00PM-11:00PM

Plenary Poster Session: Fuzzy neural systems
Tuesday, August 2, 7:00PM-11:00PM, Room: Fountaine, Chair: Program Chairs

2001 *Flexible Takagi-Sugeno Fuzzy Systems [#1068]*
Krzysztof Cpalka and Leszek Rutkowski, Technical University of Czestochowa, Poland

In the paper a new class of Takagi Sugeno fuzzy systems is derived. Various parameters and weights are incorporated into construction of such systems. The approach presented in the paper introduces more flexibility to the structure and design of neuro fuzzy systems.

2002 *A New Scene Analysis Using Genetic Algorithm Based Fuzzy ID3 Method [#1674]*
Jyh-Yeong Chang and Chien-Wen Cho, National Chiao Tung University, Taiwan

In this paper, we utilize a neural network based machine learning algorithm to segment natural objects in outdoor scene images. We have developed a genetic algorithm based fuzzy ID3 method, which can build a fuzzy decision tree to summarize the regularities existing in the data set. Using this method, we then propose a road scene analysis system, by which natural element segmentation rules can be learned from several road scene images. In the image analysis phase, the natural element regions are obtained through inference on these learned rules. Moreover, we can apply image groundtruthing to further improve the classification accuracy. The testing results have demonstrated that the object segmentation accuracy is quite high.

2003 *A Comparative Study of the IDS method and Feedforward Neural Networks [#1250]*
Masayuki Murakami and Nakaji Honda, University of Electro-Communications, Japan

The ink drop spread (IDS) method is a modeling technique which has been used in the active learning method (ALM). The IDS method is characterized by intuitive pattern-based processing and the architecture comprising heavily parallelized processing units. While being analogous to neural networks in structural characteristics, the IDS method does not require intricate calculations and iteration of the same training data set observed in the learning of neural networks. This paper describes a comparative study of the IDS method and the standard feedforward neural network in terms of their algorithmic and architectural characteristics and shows the effectiveness of the IDS method through regression modeling and classification tasks.

Plenary Poster Session: Vision and image processing
Tuesday, August 2, 7:00PM-11:00PM, Room: Fountaine, Chair: Program Chairs

2004 *Edge Inference for Image Interpolation [#1630]*
Neil Toronto, Dan Ventura and Bryan Morse, Brigham Young University, United States

Image interpolation algorithms try to fit a function to a matrix of samples in a "natural-looking" way. This paper presents edge inference, an algorithm that does this by mixing neural network regression with standard image interpolation techniques. Results on gray level images are presented, and it is demonstrated that edge inference is capable of producing sharp, natural-looking results. A technique for reintroducing noise is given, and it is shown that, with noise added using a bicubic interpolant, edge inference can be regarded as a generalization of bicubic interpolation. Extension into RGB color space and additional applications of the algorithm are discussed, and some tips for optimization are given.

2005 *Image Recognition Systems with Permutative Coding [#1274]*
Ernst Kussul, Tatiana Baidyk and Donald C. Wunsch II, National Autonomous University of Mexico (UNAM), Mexico; ACIL, University of Missouri-Rolla, United States

A feature extractor and neural classifier for image recognition system are proposed. They are based on the Permutative Coding technique which continues our investigations on neural networks. It permits us to obtain sufficiently general description of the image to be recognized. Different types of images were used to test the proposed image recognition system. It was tested on the handwritten digit recognition problem, the face recognition problem and the shape of microobjects recognition problem. The results of testing are very promising. The error rate for the MNIST database is 0.44% and for the ORL database is 0.1%

2006 *A Modified Frequency Domain Cross Correlation Implemented in MATLAB for Fast Sub-Image Detection Using Neural Networks [#1325]*
Hazem EL-Bakry and Qiangfu Zhao, Assistant Lecturer, Egypt; The University of Aizu, Japan

In our previous papers, a fast algorithm for pattern detection using neural nets was presented. For practical implementation using MATLAB, image conversion into symmetric shape was established so that fast neural nets can give the same results as conventional neural nets. Another configuration of symmetry was suggested to improve the speed up ratio. Here, our previous algorithm for fast neural nets is developed. Two new ideas are introduced to modify the cross correlation algorithm. Both methods accelerate the speed of the fast neural nets as there is no need for converting the input image into symmetric one as previous. Theoretical and practical results show that both approaches provide faster speed up ratio than the previous algorithm.

2007 *A Motion Trajectory Based Video Retrieval System Using Parallel Adaptive Self Organizing Maps [#1093]*
Wei Qu, Faisal Bashir, Daniel Graupe, Ashfaq Khokhar and Dan Schonfeld, ECE Dept. University of Illinois at Chicago, United States

We present a motion trajectory based video retrieval system using LAMSTAR-based adaptive self organizing maps (PASOMs) in this paper. The trajectories are extracted from video by a robust tracker. To reduce the high dimension of motion trajectories, we first decompose each trajectory into subtrajectories by using a maximum acceleration based approach. Each subtrajectory is then modeled and coded by two different methods, polynomial curving fitting and independent component analysis. To fuse the different features of subtrajectories for more efficient and flexible retrieval, we use PASOMs as the searching tool. Experimental results show the superior performance of the proposed approach for video retrieval comparing with prior approaches.

2008 *Learning Informative Features for Spatial Histogram-Based Object Detection [#1609]*
Hongming Zhang, Wen Gao, Xilin Chen and Debin Zhao, Harbin Institute of Technology, China; Harbin Institute of Technology and CAS, China

Feature extraction for object representation plays an important role in object detection system. In this paper, we propose methods of learning informative features for spatial histogram based object detection. We employ Fisher criterion to measure the discriminability of each feature and calculate features correlation using mutual information. In order to construct compact feature sets, we propose informative selection algorithm to select uncorrelated and discriminative spatial histogram features. Extensive experiment results on car and text detection show that the proposed approaches are efficient in object detection.

2009 *A Hierarchical Bayesian Model of Invariant Pattern Recognition in the Visual Cortex [#1761]*
Dileep George and Jeff Hawkins, Stanford University, Redwood Neuroscience Inst, United States; Redwood Neuroscience Institute, United States

We describe a hierarchical model of invariant pattern recognition in the visual cortex. In this model, the knowledge of how patterns change when objects move is encapsulated in terms of high probability sequences at each level of the hierarchy and encoded in a Bayesian Network structure. We use a temporal stability criterion to discover object concepts and movement patterns.We show that the architecture and algorithms are biologically plausible and that the micro-circuits derived from the equations for local computations match anatomical data. The system exhibits invariance across a wide variety of transformations and is robust in the presence of noise. The model also offers alternative explanations for various known cortical phenomena.

2010 *Text Extraction from Name Cards Using Neural Network [#1423]*
Lin Lin and Chew Lim Tan, National University of Singapore, Singapore

This paper addresses the problem of text extraction from name card images with fanciful design containing various graphical foreground and reverse contrast regions. The proposed method is to apply a neural network on canny edges with both spatial and relative features like sizes, color attributes and relative alignment features. By making use the alignment information, we can identify the text area from the character level rather than the conventional window block level. This alignment information is based on the human visual perception theory. Some post processing like color identification and binarization will be helpful to get a pure binary text image for OCR.

2011 *Visual Deficiency: Cognitive Performance and Adaptive Image Processing [#1413]*
Anne-Catherine Scherlen and Vincent Gautier, University Jean Monnet LIGIV, France

It is very subtle to define visual needs for central scotoma patients. Some visual aids propose adaptation to handicap subjects with magnifying image but they do not take into account patient behavior to integrate the visual information. Thus, in this study, we have analyzed with a new approach the patient sensory-motor behavior during a reading task. This reader explorative analysis translates a specific visual need. Image magnifying is certainly necessary but dynamic between eye movements and visual integration influence strongly visual identification. The implementation of these results related to our new visual device can increase visual performance and certainly it acceptation.

2012 *On Using an Associative Memory for Improving Digital Color Images: Color Characterization, Enhancement, and Color Balancing [#1622]*
Ming-Jung Seow and Vijayan Asari, Old Dominion University, United States

A color image enhancement procedure based on the concept of color characterization, enhancement, and color balancing is proposed in this paper. The enhancement technique directly operates on pixels using a hyperbolic tangent function to increase the dynamic range of the pixel. The global and local statistics of the image is used to control the curvature of the hyperbolic tangent function. The color characterization and color balancing processes are based on a new nonlinear line attractor network to create a color manifold to restore the relationship of red, green, and blue components of the pixels. The proposed enhancement approach greatly improves the dynamic range compression and color rendition of an image.

2013 *General Design Approach to Unit-linking PCNN for Image Processing [#1069]*
Xiaodong Gu, Liming Zhang and Daoheng Yu, Department of Electronic Engineering, Fudan Univ, China; Department of Electronic Engineering, Fudan Univ, China; Department of Electronics, Peking University, China

PCNN (Pulse Coupled Neural Network) can be used in image processing efficiently by the specified algorithm corresponding to the specified application, but so far there has been no general design approach. This paper describes that the parallel pulse-spreading behavior of Unit-linking PCNN for image processing, based on PCNN, is equal to the operation of mathematic morphology. Hereby we propose the general Unit-linking PCNN design approach for binary image processing. In the meantime, in order to explain how to apply this new general design approach in the specified application, binary image denoising, edge detection, hole-filter based on Unit-linking PCNN are analyzed respectively as examples.

2014 *Model of Neuron-Like Systems. Examples of Dynamic Processes [#1398]*
Vladimir Yakhno, Irina Nuidel and Artem Ivanov, Institute of Applied Physics RAN, Russian Federation

A model system "cortex-thalamus-reticular thalamic neurons", which uses three distributed layers of similar neuron-like elements and describes processing of sensor signals by animals is considered. It is shown that the regime of pulsations and fragmentary persepion of stabilized images, stationarily fixed on the eye retina of a human being corresponds to some dynamic regimes of the considered model system.

2015 *Temporal Hand Gesture Recognition By Fuzzified TSK-Type Recurrent Fuzzy Network [#1117]*
Chia-Feng Juang, Ksuan-Chun Ku and Shin-Kuan Chen, Dept. of Electr. Eng., National ChungHsing Univ., Taiwan; Dept. of Electr. Eng., Chung Chou Inst. of Tech., Taiwan

Temporal hand gesture recognition by Fuzzified Takagi-Sugeno-Kang (TSK)-type Recurrent Fuzzy Network (FTRFN) is proposed in this paper. The temporal hand gesture is captured by CCD and represented by a two-dimensional fuzzy trajectory. To handle fuzzy trajectories, FTRFN is employed. The inputs and outputs of FTRFN are fuzzy patterns represented by Gaussian membership functions, and the recurrent property of FTRFN enables it to deal with fuzzy patterns with temporal context. In recognition scheme, the FTRFN performs trajectory recognition by prediction instead of classification. Experiments on ten categories of gestures are performed to verify the proposed approach.

2016 *Using Knowledge of the Region of Interest (ROI) in Automatic Image Retrieval Learning [#1232]*
Paisarn Muneesawang and Ling Guan, United Arab Emirates University, United Arab Emirates; Ryerson University, Canada

We propose an automatic relevance feedback retrieval system using perceptually important features extracted from regions of interest. The system is implemented via self-learning using a self-organizing tree map (SOTM) neural network. Our proposed method involves the construction of regions of interest from retrieved images using Edge Flow model, and the grouping of the regions into a single perceptually significant entity. This knowledge is fed into a set of unsupervised relevance feedback learning modules based on the SOTM to guide the adaptation of relevance feedback parameters through a machine learning approach without user interaction.

2017 *Using Independent Subspace Analysis to Build Independent Spectral Representations of Images [#1414]*
Carlos Silva Santos, Joao Eduardo Kogler, Jr. and Emilio del Moral Hernandez, Polytechnic School - University of Sao Paulo, Brazil

In this work we propose using Independent Subspace Analysis (ISA) to select filters used to build image representations. ISA is an extension of Independent Component Analysis which does not require complete independence of features. Features that possess mutual dependence are associated in feature subspaces. The ISA subspaces enclose features of similar frequency and orientation. This helps in determining a reduced set of filters to be employed in image classification. Here we address the task of classifying patches of textured images. Preliminary results here presented show that our proposed ISA criterion can attain performance comparable to other filter based classification schemes while resulting in a considerably smaller filter bank.

2018 *Natural Image Compression Using An Extended Non-Negative Sparse Coding Neural Network Technique [#1163]*
Li Shang, De-Shuang Huang, Chun-Hou Zheng and Zhan-Li Sun, Hefei Institute of Intelligent Machines, CAS, China

This paper proposes an extended non-negative sparse coding (NNSC) neural network method for image compression. This method can exploit the NNSC to obtain transform-based compression schemes adapted to standard natural image classes, which results from the statistics property of natural image data. In particular, several methods of image compression such as linear principal component analysis (PCA), wavelet-based analysis, independent component analysis (ICA), etc., are evaluated and compared based on both the standard signal to noise ratio (SNR) and picture quality scale (PQS) criteria. The simulation results show that our NNSC algorithm indeed outperforms other algorithms mentioned above in the application of image compression.

2019 *Object Recognition Using Neurocomputing and Conformal Computing Geometry [#1634]*
Carlos Lopez-Franco and Eduardo Bayro-Corrochano, CINVESTAV, Unidad Guadalajara, Computer Science, Mexico

In this paper we present an object recognition technique based on neural computing and projective invariants but now using an omnidirectional vision system and conformal geometric algebra. We also show how to recover the projective invariants from a catadioptric image, where the projective invariants do not hold. With this invariants we train a multilayer perceptron (MLP) neural network to recognize objects.

Plenary Poster Session: Biometric, handwriting and other pattern recognition
Tuesday, August 2, 7:00PM-11:00PM, Room: Fountaine, Chair: Program Chairs

2020 *A Robust Deterministic Annealing Algorithm for Data Clustering [#1297]*
Xulei Yang, Song Qing and Liu Sheng, Nanyang Technological University, Singapore

In this paper, a new robust deterministic annealing (RDA) clustering algorithm is proposed. This method takes advantages of conventional noise clustering (NC) and deterministic annealing (DA) algorithms in terms of independence of data initialization, ability to avoid poor local optima, better performance for unbalanced data, and robustness against noise. The superiority of the proposed RDA clustering algorithm is supported by simulation results.

2021 *Pruning Support Vectors for Imbalanced Data Classification [#1138]*
Xue-wen Chen, Byron Gerlach and David Casasent, The University of Kansas, United States; Dept ECE, Carnegie Mellon University, United States

In many practical applications, learning from imbalanced data poses a significant challenge that is increasingly faced by the machine learning community. The class imbalance problem raises issues that are either nonexistent or less severe compared to balanced class cases. This paper presents a new method for imbalanced data classification. The proposed method is based on support vector machine classifiers and backward pruning technique. The experimental results obtained on two data sets demonstrate the effectiveness of the new algorithm.

2022 *Normalized Neural Networks for Fast Pattern Detection [#1690]*
Hazem EL-Bakry and Zhao Qiangfu, Assistant Lecturer, Egypt; Prof., Japan

Neural nets have shown good results for detecting a certain pattern in a given image. In our previous papers, a fast algorithm for face detection was presented. Such algorithm was designed based on cross correlation in the frequency domain between the input image and the input weights. Our previous work solved the problem of local subimage normalization in the frequency domain. In this paper, the effect of image normalization on the speed up ratio of pattern detection is presented. Simulation results show that local subimage normalization through weight normalization is faster than subimage normalization in the spatial domain. The overall speed up ratio of the detection process is increased as the normalization of weights is done off line.

2023 *Optimal Kernels for Unsupervised Learning [#1262]*
Sepp Hochreiter and Klaus Obermayer, Bernstein center and Technical Univ. Berlin, Germany

We investigate the optimal kernel for sample-based model selection in unsupervised learning if maximum likelihood approaches are intractable. Given training and model data, two kernel density estimators are constructed. A model is selected through gradient descent w.r.t. the model parameters on the integrated squared difference between the density estimators. We prove that convergence is optimal, i.e. that the cost function has only one global minimum w.r.t. the locations of the model samples, if and only if the kernel in the reparametrized cost function is a Coulomb kernel. We show that the absolute value of the difference between model and reference density convergences at least with 1/t. Finally, we apply the new methods to ICA problems.

2024 *Fast Pattern Detection Using Neural Networks and Cross Correlation in the Frequency Domain [#1101]*
Hazem EL-Bakry and Qiangfu Zhao, Assistant Lecturer, Egypt; The University of Aizu, Japan

Recently, fast neural networks for object/face detection were presented in [1-3]. The speed up factor of these networks based on cross correlation in the frequency domain between the input image and the weights of the hidden layer. The equations given in [1-3] for conventional and fast neural networks are not valid for many reasons presented here. In this paper, correct equations for cross correlation in the spatial and frequency domains are presented. A new formula for the speed up ratio is established. Furthermore, corrections for the equations of fast multi scale object/face detection are given. Moreover, commutative cross correlation is achieved. Simulation results show that the new algorithm is faster than classical neural networks.

2025 *Estimating Accurate Multi-class Probabilities with Support Vector Machines [#1734]*
Jonathan Milgram, Mohamed Cheriet and Robert Sabourin, LIVIA, Ecole de Technologie Superieure, Montreal, Canada

In this paper, we propose a comparison of several post-processing methods for estimating multi-class probabilities with standard Support Vector Machines. The different approaches have been tested on a real pattern recognition problem with a large number of training samples. The best results have been obtained by using a "one against all" coupling strategy along with a softmax function optimized by minimizing the negative log-likelihood of the training data. Finally, the analysis of the error-reject tradeoff have shown that SVM allows to estimate probabilities more accurate than a classical MLP, which is indeed promising in the view of incorporated within pattern recognition system using probabilistic framework.

2026 *Modular General Hyperline Segment Neural Network [#1389]*
Pradeep Patil and Manish Deshmukh, Vishwakarma Institute of Technology, Pune, India; SSBT's COET, Jalgaon, India

This paper describes modular General fuzzy Hyperline segment Neural Network which is an extension of GFHLSNN proposed by Patil et al that combines supervised and unsupervised learning. MGFHLSNN offers high degree of parallism since each module is exposed to the patterns of only one class and trained without overlap and removal leading to reduction in training time. The generalization performance is found superior with equivalent testing time. thus it can be used for voluminious realistic database where new patterns can be added on fly.

2027 *Fourier Fuzzy Neural Network for Clustering of Objects Based on the Gross Shape and its Application to Handwritten Character Recognition [#1386]*
Pradeep Patil and Manish Deshmukh, Vishwakarma Institute of Technology, Pune, India; SSBT's COET, Jalgaon, India

In this paper an unsupervised feedforward fourier fuzzy neural network is proposed which is suitable for clustering of object images based on their gross shapes. It is a three layer feedforward neural network. its performance is tested for synthetic images and realastic database of handwritten devnagari digits. The performance of FFNN is found superior than FMN clustering and takes less recall time per pattern than FMN.

2028 *Third-order generalization and a new approach to systematically categorizing higher-order generalization [#1004]*
Richard Neville, School of Informatics, University of Manchester, United Kingdom

Higher-order generalization is a means of categorizing different types of generalization. The paper presents a framework within which higher-order generalization can be evaluated in a detailed and systematic way. Previous research divided generalization into three categories. However, these categories were fuzzy and imprecise. This paper further refines existing definitions by first assigning each category a logical predicate that it must fulfil in order to achieve a specific order (type) of generalization. Then, it breaks the orders down into four different categories in a detailed and systematic way. The paper focuses on early (initial) results; some of the aims have been demonstrated and amplified through the experimental work.

2029 *Low Complexity Iris Recognition Based on Wavelet Probabilistic Neural Networks [#1448]*
Ching-Han Chen and Chia-Te Chu, I-Shou University, Taiwan

In this paper, a new technique is proposed for high efficiency iris recognition, which adopts Sobel transform and vertical projection to extract iris texture feature and wavelet probabilistic neural network (WPNN) as iris biometric classifier. The WPNN combines wavelet neural network and probabilistic neural network for a new classifier model which will be able to improve the biometrics recognition accuracy as well as the global system performance. A simple and fast training algorithm, particle swarm optimization (PSO), is also introduced for training the wavelet probabilistic neural network. In iris matching, the CASIA iris database is used and the experimental results show that the feasibility and performance of the proposed method.

2030 *Efficient Video Object Classifier using Locality-Enhanced Support Vector Machines [#1280]*
Seun T. Jan, University of Technology Sydney, Australia

In multimedia applications such as MPEG-4, an efficient model is required to encode and classify video objects. Recently, Support Vector Machine (SVM) has been shown to be a good classifier; however, their use is prohibited in video processing due to large computational requirement. In this paper, a model is proposed to merge multi-scale based selective encoding/classification technique and locality-enhanced SVM. The proposed model allows only the selected image scales (of interest) to be encoded and classified more accurately by SVM. Experiment with MPEG-4 video object encoding and classification shows that the performance of the proposed model is comparable with other models, under significantly reduced computations.

2031 *A Comparative Analysis of the Performance of Hybrid and Non-Hybrid Multi-classifier Systems [#1405]*
Anne Canuto, Marcilio de Souto, Araken Santos, Valeria Bezerra and Sussany Mirelli, Federal University of Rio Grande do Norte, Brazil

This paper investigates the performance of some multi-classifier systems, focusing on the benefits that can be gained when integrating different types of classifiers (hybrid multi-classifier systems). An empirical evaluation shows that the integration of different types of classifiers can lead to an improvement in performance in some practical classification tasks.

2032 *Pattern Classification by Assembling Small Neural Networks [#1161]*
Liang Chen, University of N. British Columbia, Canada

For pattern classification applications, where the objects are represented by 2-dimensional (or 1-dimensional) arrays, a districted neural network can be used to reduce the complexity. A districted NN consists of two levels of sub-neural networks, where each of the lower level sub-neural networks takes the elements in a region of the array as its inputs and outputs a temperate class label, while the higher level sub-neural network uses the outputs of lower level networks as inputs and derives the final decision. We show, by using a simple model, that a districted NN is more stable than a general (undistracted) NN. The conclusion is verified by an experiment of using neural networks for nucleotide sequences promoter predication.

2033 *A Symbolic Approach to the Solution of F-Classification Problems [#1342]*
Antonello Rizzi and Guido Del Vescovo, INFOCOM Dpt. University of Rome "La Sapienza", Italy

We propose a symbolic classification system able to solve automatically a great number of different image classification problems, without any need to adapt the preprocessing procedure to the specific problem instance at hand. By means of a segmentation procedure, each image is represented by a set of semantically defined objects that can be recognized on images. The inductive inference is performed directly in this symbolic domain through a parametric dissimilarity measure. The system is able to adapt the dissimilarity measure to the specific problem, by finding the optimal values of the dissimilarity function parameters. A compact model can be obtained by representing each cluster with the corresponding set median point.

2034 *Optical Flame Detection Using Large-Scale Artificial Neural Networks [#1353]*
Javid Huseynov, Zvi Boger, Gary Shubinsky and Shankar Baliga, University of California Irvine, United States; OPTIMAL - Industrial Neural Systems, Ltd., Israel; General Monitors, Inc., United States

A model for intelligent hydrocarbon flame detection using artificial neural networks (ANN) with a large number of inputs is presented. Joint time-frequency analysis in the form of Short-Time Fourier Transform was used for extracting the relevant features from infrared sensor signals. After appropriate scaling, this information was provided as an input for the ANN training algorithm based on principal component analysis (PCA) and conjugate- gradient (CG) descent method. A classification scheme with trained ANN connection weights was implemented on a digital signal processor for an industrial hydrocarbon flame detector.

2035 *An Experimental Study of Several Decision Issues for Feature Selection with Multi-Layer Perceptrons [#1338]*
Enrique Romero and Josep Maria Sopena, Universitat Politecnica de Catalunya, Spain; Universitat de Barcelona, Spain

An experimental study of several decision issues for wrapper Feature Selection with Multi-Layer Perceptrons is presented. Experimental results with the Sequential Backward Selection procedure indicate that the increase in the computational cost associated with retraining the network with every feature temporarily removed before computing the saliency is rewarded with a significant performance improvement. Despite being quite intuitive, this idea has been hardly used in practice. The procedure profits from measuring the saliency in a validation set, as reasonably expected. A somehow non-intuitive conclusion can be drawn by looking at the stopping criterion, where it is suggested that forcing overtraining may be as useful as early stopping.

2036 *Spectral Feature Analysis [#1170]*
Wang Fei, Wang Jingdong and Zhang Changshui, Department of Automation, Tsinghua University, China; Hong Kong University of Science and Technology, Hong Kong

In this paper, we give theoretically an explicit relation between spectral clustering and weighted kernel principal component analysis (WKPCA). We show that spectral clustering is not only a method for data clustering, but also for feature extraction. We are then able to re-interpret the spectral clustering algorithm in terms of WKPCA and propose our spectral feature analysis

(SFA) method. The spectral features extracted by SFA can capture the distinguishing information of data from different classes effectively. Finally some experimental results are presented to show the effectiveness of our method.

2037 *Self-Adaptive Kernel Machine: Online Clustering in RKHS [#1418]*
Habiboulaye Amadou Boubacar, Stephane Lecoeuche and Salah Maouche, LAGIS USTL Lille and GIP Ecole de Mines Douai, France; LAGIS USTL Lille, France

This paper presents a new online clustering algorithm (called SAKM) that is developed to learn continuously evolving clusters from non-stationeries data. The SAKM algorithm is based on SVM and kernel methods, and utilises a fast incremental learning procedure. Dedicated to online clustering in multi-class environment, the algorithm is based on an unsupervised learning process with self-adaptive abilities. The SAKM learning process uses a specific kernel- induced similarity measure and is designed in four stages: Creation, Adaptation, Fusion and Elimination. In addition to its new properties, the algorithm is attractive to be very computationally efficient. After a comparison with NORMA and ALMA algorithms, some experiments are presented.

2038 *An Algorithm for Pruning Redundant Modules in Min-Max Modular Network [#1368]*
Hui-Cheng Lian and Bao-Liang Lu, ShangHai Jiao Tong University, China

The min-max modular (M3) network is a framework that is capable of solving large-scale pattern classification problems in a parallel way. The M3 network has been successfully applied to several large-scale real-world prblems. When a complex problem is decomposed into a number of separable problems, however, the M3 network suffers from its high redundancy of individual modules. This paper proposes an algorithm, called back-searching (BS) algorithm, to prune these redundant modules.

2039 *A Novel Fuzzy Clustering Neural Network [#1725]*
Pradeep Patil, Manish Deshmukh and Punamchand Mahajan, Vishwakarma Institute of Technology, Pune, India; SSBT's COET, Jalgaon, India; JTM COE, Faizpur, India

In this paper Fuzzy clustering Neural network (FCNN) is proposed with its learning algorithm, which utilizes fuzzy sets as cluster of patterns. The performance of FCNN is found better than FMN, FMPCNN, FHLSCNN and MBCNN clustering algorithms when compared with moderate number of clusters created. The cluster prototypes calculated reduces the confusion by giving fair treatment to the dense populated patterns. The performance is found equiporable when total number of clusters created are less. The total number of clusters created can be controlled by grouping factor The recall time per pattern of FCNN is smaller than the FMN, FMPCNN, FHLSCNN and MBCNN. Hence it can be used for real time applications.

Plenary Poster Session: Face and texture recognition
Tuesday, August 2, 7:00PM-11:00PM, Room: Fountaine, Chair: Program Chairs

2040 *Performance of Neural Classifiers for Fabric Faults Classification [#1115]*
Mohamed Abdulhady, Hazem M. Abbas, Yaser H. Dakrowry and Salwa Nassar, Electronics Research Institute (ERI), Egypt; Mentor Graphics Egypt, Egypt; Ain Shams University, Egypt

The fabric faults classification using competitive neural tree [1] is studied. The basic objectives are to improve the features selection used in CNeT [1] classifier and compare the results with other neural network classifier. A set of features are calculated for each defect using the Haralick [2] spatial features. The feature selection is done by calculating the classification factor [6] for each feature vector to improve the classification process. The selected features are then used to train (CNeT) [1] in a supervised manner. The approach is experimented with a set of images of fault free and faulty textiles and output results are compared with Radial Basis Function classifiers

2041 *Orientated Texture Segmentation for Detecting Defects [#1397]*
Pradeep Patil, Maheshwari Biradar and Snehal Jadhav, Vishwakarma Institute of Technology, Pune, India; DYPatil Institute of Engg and Tech, Pune, India; All India Shri Shivaji Memorial Society's WCOE,, India

Visual inspection is an important part of quality control in industries. In order to increase accuracy AVI is used, where texture based segmentation plays a vital role. In segmentation all the feature vectures are calculated using various transforms like Gabor, Wavelet,etc. There is no necessity of calculating all the feature vectors for defect detection. This is an approach to concentrate on orientation as a feature vector. It is found that this increases the computational speed, reliability as well as reduces the memory requirement, hence feasible for real time factory implimentation. The number of clusters used for classification plays a vital role in final segmentation results.

2042 *Modification of Correlation Kernels in SVM, KPCA and KCCA in Texture Classification [#1308]*
Yo Horikawa, Faculty of Engineering, Kagawa University, Japan

Modified versions of the correlation kernels in the kernel methods, e.g., SVMs, kPCA and kCCA are presented, which are based on the Lp norm and max norm as well as the blindness of the odd-order autocorrelations to sinusoidal or symmetrically distributed signals. The poor generalization of the higher-order correlation kernels and the inferior performance of the correlation kernels of odd-orders to even-orders are improved with the modifications. The performance of the modified correlation kernels is evaluated and compared in texture classification experiments.

2043 *Neural Network-based Shape Recognition using Generalized Differential Evolution Training Algorithm [#1216]*
Ji-Xiang Du, De-Shuang Huang, Xiao-Feng Wang and Xiao Gu, Hefei Institute of Intelligent Machines, CAS, China

In this paper a new method for recognition of 2D occluded shapes based on neural network using generalized differential evolution training algorithm is proposed. Firstly, a generalized differential evolution (GDE) algorithm is introduced. And this GDE algorithm is applied to train multilayer perceptron neural networks. Then a new shape feature, refer to as multiscale Fourier descriptors (MFDs) is proposed. Finally, the superiority of GDE training method over traditional approaches to train networks is demonstrated by experiment. The experimental results show that our proposed GDE training method is much efficient and effective. And they also showed that the MFDs method is suitable for the shape recognition.

2044 *The Effect of Normal Adult Aging on Standard PCA Face Recognition Accuracy Rates [#1512]*
Karl Ricanek, Jr. and Edward Boone, Univerisity of North Carolina, Wilmington, United States

The issue of face aging has not been focused upon in the research on Face Recognition (FR) systems. What has been introduced by a few researchers is the impact of a probe against a match of different acquisition dates; the time span between probe and match image has not been sufficiently large enough to fully explore the impacts of age-progression on performance rates. In this work, we will address the impacts of age-progression, which includes both structural and texture changes, on the standard PCA FR algorithm. A face database designed specifically to address the issues of age-progression is used with FERET database. This work examines why the PCA FR system, and other appearance based systems, will have diminished performance.

2045 *Face Recognition Method Independent of Rotation and Size Variations [#1370]*
Kiyomi Nakamura, Hironobu Takano and Tsukasa Sakamoto, Toyama Prefectural University, Japan

Emulating the parietal cortex, a "rotation and size spreading associative neural network" (RS-SAN net) was developed. We extended the original system to make a human face recognition system independent of rotation and size variations. In the present study, we investigated the recognition characteristics for learned and unlearned faces. We introduced an inner product and a minimum distance as shape recognition criteria. By setting the threshold ranges of the inner product and the minimum distance as 0.999 - 0.998 and 0.04 - 0.06, respectively, the false rejection and the false acceptance rate became 0 % in both criteria.

2046 *Combined Subspace Method Using Global and Local Features for Face Recognition [#1350]*
Chunghoon Kim, Jiyong Oh and Chong-Ho Choi, Seoul National University, Korea, Republic of

This paper proposes the combined subspace method using both global and local features for face recognition. The global and local features are obtained by applying the LDA-based method to either the whole or part of a face image, respectively. The combined subspace is constructed with the projection vectors corresponding to large eigenvalues of the between-class scatter matrix in each subspace. The combined subspace is evaluated in view of the Bayes error, and it gives small Bayes error than other subspaces. Comparative experiments using the Color FERET database show that the combined subspace method gives better recognition rate than other subspace methods.

Plenary Poster Session: Audition, speech recognition and production
Tuesday, August 2, 7:00PM-11:00PM, Room: Fountaine, Chair: Program Chairs

2047 *Low Order Modeling for Multiple Moving Sound Synthesis using Head-related Transfer Functions' Principal Basis Vectors [#1305]*
Pinaki Chanda and Sungjin Park, LG Soft India, India; LG Mobile Handset Research Center, Korea (South)

An algorithm for simulating multiple moving-sound sources in a virtual auditory space is developed. Sound sources are localized with balanced model approximation of principal basis vectors extracted from the head-related transfer functions (HRTFs) dataset. This approach enables a low complexity implementation and real-time rendering of multiple sound sources in motion.

2048 *Individualized HRTFs From Few Measurements: a Statistical Learning Approach [#1061]*
Vincent Lemaire, Fabrice Clerot, Sylvain Busson, Rozenn Nicol and Vincent Choqueuse, France Telecom Research and Development, France; Univeristy of Troyes, France

Virtual Auditory Space requires the use of individualized head-related transfer functions (HRTFs) which describe the acoustic filtering properties of the listener's external auditory periphery. HRTFs serve the increasingly dominant role of implementation 3-D audio systems. However, the cost of a 3-D audio system cannot be brought down because the efficiency of computation, the size of memory, and the synthesis of unmeasured HRTFs remain to be made better. Because HRTFs are unique for each user, the economically realist synthesis of individualized HRTFs has to rely on some measurements. This paper presents a way to reduce the cost of a 3-D audio system using a statistical modeling which allows to use only few measurements for each user.

2049 *Framewise Phoneme Classification with Bidirectional LSTM Networks [#1614]*
Alex Graves and Juergen Schmidhuber, Istituto Dalle Molle, Switzerland

In this paper, we apply bidirectional training to a Long Short Term Memory (LSTM) network for the first time. We also present a modified, full gradient version of the LSTM learning algorithm. We discuss the significance of framewise phoneme classification to continuous speech recognition, and the validity of using bidirectional networks for online causal tasks. On the TIMIT speech database, we measure the framewise phoneme classification scores of bidirectional and unidirectional variants of both LSTM and conventional Recurrent Neural Networks (RNNs). We find that bidirectional LSTM outperforms both RNNs and unidirectional LSTM.

2050 *Discriminative Training of Hidden Markov Models by Multiobjective Optimization for Visual Speech Recognition [#1315]*
Jong-Seok Lee and Cheol Hoon Park, Kaist, Korea, Republic of

This paper proposes a novel discriminative training algorithm of hidden Markov models (HMMs) based on the multiobjective optimization for visual speech recognition.We develop a new criterion composed of two minimization objectives for training HMMs discriminatively and a global multiobjective optimization algorithm based on the simulated annealing algorithm to find the Pareto solutions of the optimization problem. We demonstrate the effectiveness of the proposed method via an isolated digit recognition experiment. The results show that the proposed method is superior to the conventional maximum likelihood estimation and the popular discriminative training algorithms.

2051 *Harmonic Envelope Prediction for Realistic Speech Synthesis Using Kernel Interpolation [#1644]*
Pierre-Alexandre Fournier and Jean-Jules Brault, Ecole Polytechnique de Montreal, Canada

Harmonic and noise diphone concatenation is a proven method to obtain high-quality speech synthesis, but cannot be used when the basis corpus does not contain all the diphones needed. We propose a method to complete an individual's corpus using examples from other corpuses. Parametrisation of five vowels from different speakers is done with an harmonic and noise model (HNM). We use multi-frame analysis (MFA) and smoothing kernels to estimate the harmonic power spectrum envelopes. Different kernels are compared to predict the harmonic envelopes of vowels using training data. Our results show Gaussian kernels can achieve a 1.8 dB (34.4%) reduction of harmonic distorsion compared to the mean harmonic envelope estimator.

2052 *A Soft Bayes Perceptron [#1116]*
Michael Brueckner and Werner Dilger, Chemnitz University of Technology, Germany

The Kernel Perceptron is one of the simplest and fastest Kernel Machines, its performance, however, is inferior to other well known Kernel Machines. We introduce an algorithm that combines several approaches, mainly Herbrich's large-scale Bayes Point Machine and the Soft Perceptron in order to improve the Kernel Perceptron. Our experiments, which were based on standard benchmark datasets, show that the performance of the Perceptron can be improved significantly with similar computational effort.

2053 *Chaos and Speech Rhythm [#1009]*
Oleg Skljarov and Tatjana Bortnik, Research Institute of Ear, Throat, Nose and Spee, Russia

The new definition of speech rhythm is given. This definition is based on the principle of segmentation: Voiced segment - Unvoiced segment. Owing to established in paper fact that the rhythm evolution is described as the logistic mapping on this set, the dynamic regimes of the rhythm in both normal speech and stuttering speech are described. It turned out that the nets offered by van der Maas have exactly same route to chaos in dependence on the changing control parameter. Within the framework of the offered mathematical model the causes which change these rhythm regimes are established. It allowed to apply in clinic optimal course of treatment for each stutterer individually.

2054 *Exploration of Rank Order Coding with Spiking Neural Networks for Speech Recognition [#1542]*
Stephane Loiselle, Jean Rouat, Daniel Pressnitzer and Simon Thorpe, Universite de Sherbrooke, Canada; Ecole normale superieure, France; Centre de Recherche Cerveau et Cognition, France

Speech recognition is very difficult in the context of noisy and corrupted speech. Most conventional techniques need huge databases to estimate speech (or noise) density probabilities to perform recognition. We discuss the potential of perceptive speech analysis and processing in combination with biologically plausible neural network processors. We illustrate the potential of such non-linear processing of speech by means of a preliminary test with recognition of French spoken digits from a small speech database.

Plenary Poster Session: Nose, tactile, taste and other senses
Tuesday, August 2, 7:00PM-11:00PM, Room: Fountaine, Chair: Program Chairs

2055 *A comparative study of neural network to artificial noses [#1471]*
Aida Ferreira, Teresa Ludermir and Ronaldo Aquino, Center of Informatics - Federal University of Pe, Brazil; Federal University of Pernambuco, Brazil; Departments of Electrical Engineering, Brazil

Artificial neural networks have been used to classify odor patterns and are showing promising results. In this paper we present four different models of neural networks to implement pattern recognition system in artificial noses. The models investigated are the multi-layer perceptrons, two different implementations of the radial basis function networks and the probabilistic neural network. All the models were tested with and without temporal processing. A complex data base with nine different classes was used in this paper.

2056 *Optimization of a learning algorithm for tactile pattern generation [#1381]*
Carsten Wilks and Rolf Eckmiller, University of Bonn, Germany

In this paper we present an optimization method for a learning algorithm for tactile stimuli generation which are adapted by means of the tactile perception of a human. Because of special requirements for a learning algorithm for tactile perception tuning the optimization cannot be performed based on gradient-descent or likelihood estimation methods. Therefore an Automatic Tactile Classification (ATC) is introduced for the optimization process. The results show that the ATC equals the tactile comparison of humans and that the learning algorithm is successfully optimized by means of the ATC.

2057 *A Combinative Function Approximation Model and Its Applications to Electronic Noses [#1701]*
Daqi Gao, Tong Tong and Yongli Li, East China University of Science and Technology, China

This paper focuses on combinative and modular approximation models to simultaneously estimate odor classes and strengths. We first decompose a many-to-many approximation task into multiple many-to-one tasks, and then realize them using multiple many-to-one approximation models. A single model is regarded as an expert, and a panel or ensemble is made up of multiple such experts. Each expert is either a multivariate logarithmic regression model, or a multilayer perceptron (MLP), or a support vector machine (SVM). A panel is on behalf of a kind of odor. The most similar panel gives the class label and strength of an odor. The experiment for estimating 4 kinds of fragrant materials shows that the proposed model is effective.

2058 *A Novel Hybrid Learning Scheme For Pattern Recognition [#1330]*
Lai Ping Wong, Leng Phuan Alex Tay and Jian Xu, Nanyang Technological University, Singapore

This paper presents a novel hybrid learning scheme to serve pattern classification task. The proposed self-supervised learning method is a combination of unsupervised clustering K-Means Fast Learning Artificial Neural Network (KFLANN) and supervised a typical Backpropagation learning algorithm (BP Network). Complementary benefits of both algorithms motivated the development of the hybrid model. KFLANN clustering output is used as the target value for BP training, resulting in an efficient self-supervised learning model. Experimental results are comparable with non-hybrid individual algorithm.

Plenary Poster Session: Cognitive function
Tuesday, August 2, 7:00PM-11:00PM, Room: Fountaine, Chair: Program Chairs

2059 *Convergence of Coherent Components of Neural Networks by Positive Correlation Learning [#1291]*
Md. Shahjahan, Md. Monirul Kabir and K. Murase, University of Fukui, Japan; Dhaka University of Engineering and Technology, Bangladesh

This paper presents a learning approach, positive correlation learning (PCL), that discovers coherent components of a multilayer neural network. A correlation function is added to the standard error function of the back propagation learning and the error function is minimized by a steepest-descend method, while correlation function is maximized. In this multi-objective training, all the units in the hidden layer are not only correlated in a positive sense, but also exhibits coherent components of the input patterns. In addition, we show that the PCL can reduce the information about the input patterns. The generalization ability can be formulated in terms of correlation of coherent components.

2060 *Learning of an XOR Problem in the Presence of Noise and Redundancy [#1023]*
Denis Cousineau, Universite de Montreal, Canada

Time-based networks represent an alternative to the usual strength-based networks. In this paper, we compare two instances of each family of networks that are of comparable complexity, the Perceptron and the race network when faced with uncertain input. Uncertainty was manipulated in two different ways, within channel by adding noise and between channels by adding redundant inputs. For the Perceptron, results indicate that if noise is high, redundancy must be low, otherwise learning does not occur. For the race network, the opposite is true: If both noise and redundancy increase, learning remains both fast and reliable. Asymptotic statistic theories suggest that these results may be true of all the networks belonging to these two families.

2061 *A Multiple BAM for Hetero-association and Multisensory Integration Modelling [#1424]*
Emanuelle Reynaud and Helene Paugam-Moisy, Institut des Sciences Cognitives CNRS UMR 5015, France; Institute for Cognitive Science, France

We present in this article a dynamic neural network that works as a memory for multiple associations. Heterogeneous pairs of patterns can be tied together through learning within this memory, and recalled easily. Starting from Kosko's Bidirectional Associative Memory, we modify some fundamental features of the network (topology and learning algorithm). We show empirically that this network has a high storage capacity and is only weakly dependent upon learning hyperparameters. We demonstrate its robustness to corrupted or missing data. We finally present results from experiments where this network is used as a multisensory associative memory.

2062 *Effect of Curriculum on the Consolidation of Neural Network Task Knowledge [#1658]*
Ryan Poirier and Daniel L. Silver, Acadia University, Canada

We investigate the effect of curriculum, i.e., a selection of tasks and the order in which they are are learned, on the consolidation of neural network task knowledge. Relevant background material on knowledge transfer and consolidation using multiple task learning (MTL) neural networks is reviewed. A large MTL network is used as the long-term memory structure and task rehearsal overcomes the stability-plasticity problem and the loss of prior knowledge. Experimental results demonstrate that curriculum has an important effect on the accuracy of consolidated knowledge during early learning.

2063 *Creation of Long-term Mental Representations using the Dimension of Fractal dendrites [#1596]*
Richard Gagne and Simon Gagne, Laval Universite, Canada

This work explores the possibility of using a neuron's dendrite spatial dimension as primitives for creating representations of mental activity. Recent {\it in-vivo} experimental results show that spines are structurally unstable suggesting that using the synapse alone to create mental representations isinsufficient. The voltage fluctuations at the cable equation with fractal boundary conditions due to massive synaptic activity was compared to those of the Ornstein-Uhlenbeck and Tuckwell-Walsh random processes and the fluctuations remained unchanged in spite of drastic regression of its branches. These results hint at a remarkably stable possible form of ``information" storage.

2064 *Neurobiological Data Sustaining Opponent Processing Operations on Self Organizing Networks as Tools for the Modeling of Hippocampal Dynamics [#1608]*
Renan Vitral, Glaucio Araujo, Fabrizzio Oliveira, Daves Martins, Eliane Christo, Anderson Moreira, Cristiani Vitral and Dimitri Abramov, Federal University of Juiz de Fora, Brazil

This paper intends to show how the advancement on neurobiological knowledge sustains the use of opponent processing for the modeling of hippocampal dynamics. Two distinct functional classes of afferents, i.e., excitatory afferents to principal cells and both interneurons and glia acting as either inhibitory or secondarily excitatory afferents to these principal cells form very distinct functional states that sustain a double system for the balanced activity into the hippocampus. We did represent principal cells as dipoles of opponent processing on self organizing networks. Our results reproduce the pattern of place cells firing that are dependent on the hippocampal oscillations.

2065 *Neural Network Approaches to Personal Change in Psychotherapy [#1522]*
Ana Maria Aleksandrowicz and Daniel Levine, ENSP-Fiocruz, Brazil; University of Texas at Arlington, United States

A neural network theory is proposed for how psychotherapy can move the mind's dynamical system from a less optimal to a more optimal steady state. Parts of the proposed network are analogous to pathways connecting prefrontal cortex and subcortical brain regions.

Plenary Poster Session: Computational neuroscience
Tuesday, August 2, 7:00PM-11:00PM, Room: Fountaine, Chair: Program Chairs

2066 *Role of Presynaptic Reuptake on Dopamine Modulation of Cortico-striatal Activity in TD Learning [#1672]*
Shesharao Wanjerkhede and Bapi Raju, University of Hyderabad, India

It has been shown that midbrain dopamine neurons and the dopamine neuronal activity in the striatum mimic reward prediction error signal of the temporal difference learning (TDL) paradigm. James Houk proposed a theoretical model to explain the cellular basis of this dopamine activity. Our goal is to verify this model with simulations in GENESIS and CHEMESIS. This paper reports preliminary results from the simulations of this intracellular signaling scheme. The main result reported here is the influence of presynaptic reuptake on dopamine activity at the cortico-striatal synapse. It appears that the reuptake affects the rate of formation of D1_DA receptor complex that in turn would have a bearing on the timing mechanisms operating in TDL.

2067 *Two state transitions mediated by spontaneous and/or intensive stimulus on an integrate-and-fire neural network model [#1333]*
Kazuki Tsutsumi and Osamu Araki, Tokyo University of Science, Japan

Recent studies reported that there are two states in the internal potential of a neuron: one of which is called "UP state", another is called "DOWN state". These states transit each other by spontaneous and/or intensive stimulus. We performed the computer simulations using a neural network model to exemplify those states. We assume that the synaptic weights between cells are clustered such as an associative memory model. The simulations show three results: 1) the "UP/DOWN states" are switched by spontaneous and/or intensive stimulus, 2) the "UP/DOWN states" are also synchronized within the clustered cells, and 3) the transitions are invoked more easily when the network state is out of the attractor than it is in an attractor.

2068 *Learning with Single Integrate-and-Fire Neuron [#1479]*
Abhishek Yadav, Deepak Mishra, R. N. Yadav, Sudipta Ray and Prem K. Kalra, IIT Kanpur, India

In this paper, a learning algorithm for a single Integrate-and-Fire Neuron (IFN) is proposed and tested for various applications in which a multilayer perceptron based neural network is conventionally used. It is found that a single IFN is sufficient for the applications that require a number of neurons in different hidden layers of a conventional neural network. Several benchmark and real-life problems of classification and function-approximation have been illustrated. It is observed that the inclusion of some more biological phenomenon in an artificial neural network can make it more powerful.

2069 *Optimizing Neural Model Templates using Covariance Matrix Adaptation and Fourier Analysis [#1519]*
Keith Bush, James Knight and Charles Anderson, Colorado State University, United States

Advancement in neural modeling requires the development of methods for deriving computational models from observed biological data. We propose general analysis techniques to construct distance measures that are applicable across a broad range of cell types. We investigate the use of multiple stimuli to evoke model behaviors characteristic of the underlying channel densities. We examine the use of frequency analysis on multiple membrane recordings to improve channel density optimization for two simple compartment models. Applying Covariance Matrix Adaptation (CMA-ES) to this problem yielded near optimal results. Solutions given by CMA-ES are equivalent to parameter distributions and serve as templates for neural model generation.

2070 *Fast Constructive-Covering Approach for Neural Networks [#1091]*
Di Wang, Narendra S. Chaudhari and Jagdish Chandra Patra, Nanyang Technological University (NTU), Singapore; SCE, Nanyang Technological University, Singapore

We propose a fast training algorithm called Fast Constructive-Covering Approach (FCCA) for neural network construction based on geometrical expansion. Parameters are updated according to the geometrical location of the training samples in the input space, and each sample in the training set is learned only once. By doing this, FCCA is able to avoid iterations and is much faster than traditional training algorithms. Given an input sequence in an arbitrary order, FCCA learns 'easy' samples first and the 'confusing' samples are easily learned after these 'easy' samples. This sample reordering process is done on the fly based on geometrical concept. A comparison of this method with a few other methods on the well-known Iris data set is given.

2071 *Ensembles of membrane proteins as statistical mixed-signal computers [#1203]*
Victor Eliashberg, Stanford University, United States

The paper presents a formalism that connects functional properties of neurons with the properties of membrane proteins treated as abstract probabilistic machines. The machines are referred to as Probabilistic Molecular Machines (PMM). It is shown that ensembles of PMMs (EPMM) provide robust statistical implementation of mixed-signal computers combining the dynamical capabilities of analog computers with the sequencing capabilities of state machines. The classical Hodgkin and Huxley model is reformulated in terms of two EPMMs and is used as a detailed example illustrating the structure and the representational possibilities of the PMM/EPMM formalism.

2072 *Towards the Modeling of Dissociated Cortical Tissue in the Liquid State Machine Framework [#1716]*
Dilip Goswami, Klaus Schuch, Yi Zheng, Thomas DeMarse and Jose C. Principe, University of Florida, United States; Technische Universitat Graz, Austria; Universirty of Florida, Gainesville, United States; CNEL, Department of ECE, University of Florida, United States

The advent of the liquid state machine (LSM) as a computational model for cortical processing, taken with the ability to experiment with dissociated cortical tissue (DCT) cultures provides new opportunities in advancing our understanding of biological information processing systems. We attempt to model the behavior of the DCT cultures in the LSM framework. We show that the LSM framework can model the spontaneous activity and burstiness of the DCT cultures. Fractal measures are used to compare the long range dependencies (LRD) of the data. Though the detrended fluctuation analysis (DFA) used to estimate the LRD does not completely match, the endogenously active neurons that drive the networks are found to have similar fractal structure.

2073 *The Bifurcating Neuron Network 3 [#1641]*
Jinhyuk Choi and Geehyuk Lee, Information and Communications University, Korea (South)

The Bifurcating Neuron (BN) is an integrate-and-fire model neuron that exhibits bistability and attractor-merging crisis. The Bifurcating Neuron Network 1, a network of such neurons, was shown to make a robust associative memory against spurious minima problems. It was noted that the BN could be naturally generalized to have multi-stability, which will make the BN a chaotic, multi-state, integrate-and-fire model neuron. This paper is a report of our preliminary study on the tri-stability of the BN, the behaviors of interacting such BNs, and a design of a network of BNs that interact via "mutually-exclusive" coupling, thereby solving a 3-coloring problem.

2074 *Spiking Neural Network Training Using Evolutionary Algorithms [#1443]*
Nicos Pavlidis, Dimitris Tasoulis, Vassilis Plagianakos, Giorgos Nikiforidis and Michael Vrahatis, Department of Mathematics, University of Patras, Greece; School of Medicine, University of Patras, Greece

Networks of spiking neurons can perform complex non--linear computations in fast temporal coding just as well as rate coded networks. These networks differ from previous models in that spiking neurons communicate information by the timing, rather than the rate, of spikes. To apply spiking neural networks on particular tasks, a learning process is required. Most existing training algorithms are based on unsupervised Hebbian learning. In this paper, we investigate the performance of the Parallel Differential Evolution algorithm, as a supervised training algorithm for spiking neural networks. The approach was successfully tested on well--known and widely used classification problems.

2075 *Increased Swimming Control with Evolved Lamprey CPG Controllers [#1171]*
Leena Patel, Alan Murray and John Hallam, The University of Edinburgh, United Kingdom; University of Southern Denmark, Denmark

This paper shows that the lamprey's neural swimming controller (central pattern generator (CPG)) is not a unique solution and that improved performance can be obtained by evolving the CPG's neural parameters and connection weights. Propulsion in the lamprey, an eel-like fish, is governed by activity in its spinal neural network. This CPG is simulated, in accordance with Ekeberg's model, and then evolved using genetic algorithm techniques to explore the domain of alternative configurations. The best controller produces a controllable frequency range of 1.42 - 12.16 Hz, a substantial increase on the biological network frequency range (1.74 - 5.56 Hz). Connectivity is lower, with 16 instead of 26 connections of Ekeberg's model.

Plenary Poster Session: Signal processing and time series analysis
Tuesday, August 2, 7:00PM-11:00PM, Room: Fountaine, Chair: Program Chairs

2076 *Modified Time-Based Multilayer Perceptron for Sensor Networks and Image Processing Applications [#1567]*
Gregory Von Pless, Tayeb Al Karim and Leonid Reznik, Rochester Institute Of Technology, United States; Rochester Institute of Technology, United States

The modified time-based multilayer perceptron (MTBMLP), which is a complex structure composed by a few time based multilayer perceptrons is introduced. This neural network is applied for change detection in sensor network signals and edge detection in images. In both applications a MTBMLP is utilized for function predictions and, after a further structure development is implemented, for an error prediction also. A number of experiments with Crossbow sensor kits and Lena image have been conducted and analyzed. The results demonstrate that MTBMLP is more efficient and reliable than other methodologies in sensor network change detection and that its application in change detection is more effective than in edge detection.

2077 *On-line Bayesian Change Detection Scheme for Unknown Nonlinear Systems via Sequential Monte Carlo [#1239]*
Yohei Nakada and Takashi Matsumoto, Waseda University, Japan; Waseda University and CREST, Japan

An attempt is made to performe on-line change detection given sequential data from an unknown nonlinear system. The algorithm sequentially estimates the probability of occurrence of a change within a Bayesian framework. The implementation is done via Sequential Monte Carlo (SMC). The proposed scheme is tested against two specific examples.

2078 *Independent Component Analysis Applications in Physics [#1149]*
Christy Fernandez, Soudabeh Nayeri and Larry Medsker, Duke University, United States; American University, United States; Siena College, United States

Although several applications of Independent Component Analysis (ICA) reported in the literature are related to physics, none have focused on the analysis of data typical of energy spectrum measurements. The present work has identified promising opportunities for future exploration in this area. Preliminary results are reported for some particular applications including one that improves the analysis of angular distribution spectra from nuclear reactions and one that is effective for the analysis of resonance data.

2079 *Embedded FastICA Algorithm Applied to the Sensor Noise Extraction Problem of Foundation Fieldbus Network [#1687]*
Isabele Costa, Adriao Doria Duarte Neto, Jorge Melo and Jose Oliveira, Universidade Federal do Rio Grande do Norte, Brazil

This paper presents the description and the operation of a system composed of an intelligent algorithm, that separates information and noise coming from different sources, implemented with embedded technology in a DSP (Digital Sign Processor), that interacts with fieldbus devices connected through a Foundation Fieldbus network. The technique used in this Blind Source Separation (BSS) process was the Independent Component Analysis (ICA), that explores the possibility of separating mixed signals based on the fact that they are statistically independent. The algorithm and its implementation are presented, as well as the test results.

2080 *Design of Neural Predictors using Tools of Chaos Theory and Bayesian Learning [#1144]*
Salvatore Marra, Francesco Carlo Morabito and Mario Versaci, University Mediterranea of Reggio Calabria, Italy; DIMET, University Mediterranea of Reggio Calabria, Italy

In this paper a new approach to design neural networks based predictors of chaotic time series is proposed. Using tools of chaos theory, we can provide helpful indications to correctly design the architectures of TDNNs in a very rapid fashion. By combining an efficient data pre-processing with Bayesian learning, we train neural models able to fully capture the dynamics of the underlying systems creating powerful predictors of chaotic time series. We test on several benchmarks the new approach achieving results comparable or even better than those of many Recurrent Neural Networks. We prove that the existing Local Models lose their well-known advantage when compared to our method, with the benefit of using a much smaller number of parameters

2081 *Harmonic Detection using Wavelet TRansforms [#1739]*
Sangeetha Priya and Prabhakar Mahalingam, Anna University, India

Power quality is increasingly becoming a major concern due to excessive use of sensitive equipments. Determining the cause of power quality disturbances using various approaches such as neural network and expert system becomes essential in order to take suitable corrective action. In this paper, wavelet transform is proposed to identify the predominant harmonic content, the instant of occurrence and take suitable corrective action. Comparison between mean absolute deviation (MAD) levels for a pure sinusoidal and polluted waveform is used to detect the predominant harmonic content. The system has been simulated in MATLAB and Simulink environment.

2082 *A Recurrent Neural Network for Sound-Source Motion Tracking and Prediction [#1606]*
John Murray, Harry Erwin and Stefan Wermter, University of Sunderland, United Kingdom

Recurrent neural networks (RNN) have been used in many applications for both pattern detection and prediction. This paper shows the use of RNN's as a speed classifier and predictor for a robotic sound-source tracking system. The system requires extensive training to classify all possible speeds enabling dynamic tracking.

Plenary Poster Session: Control and robotics
Tuesday, August 2, 7:00PM-11:00PM, Room: Fountaine, Chair: Program Chairs

2083 *Artificial neural networks associated to calorimetry to preview polymer composition of high solid content emulsion copolymerizations [#1064]*
Domingos Savio Giordani, Amilton Martins dos Santos, Maria Alvina Krahenbuhl and Liliane M. F. Lona, Faenquil, Brazil; Unicamp, Brazil

Artificial Neural Networks have demonstrated to be powerful tools to model non linear systems, such as high solid content latexes produced by emulsion polymerisation. This system has a great importance in the polymeric industry since they usually have water as continuous phase. In order to propose technical feasible alternatives to control polymeric structure, this work is aimed to develop a new methodology based on artificial neural networks associated with calorimetry to preview polymeric structure. It was possible to conclude that artificial neural networks, associated to calorimetry, lead to an efficient method to preview the polymer composition in emulsion copolymerizations.

2084 *Supply Air Temperature Control of AHU with a Cascade Control Strategy and a SPSA Based Neural Controller [#1612]*
Chengyi Guo, Qing Song and Wenjian Cai, Nanyang Technological University, Singapore

A cascade control strategy for temperature control of AHU is proposed. Instead of a fixed PID controller, a neural network controller is used in the outer control loop. This approach not only avoids the tedious tuning procedure for the PID parameters of a conventional cascade control system, but also it can make the whole control system more adaptive and robust. The multilayer neural network is trained online by a special SPSA based training algorithm. The novel cascade control system has been implemented to improve supply air temperature control performance of AHU in a pilot HVAC system. The experimental results demonstrate the effectiveness of proposed control scheme over single loop PID control and conventional cascade control.

2085 *Design and stabilization of sampled-data neural-network-based control systems [#1327]*
H.K. Lam and F. H. F. Leung, The Hong Kong Polytechnic University, Hong Kong

This paper presents the design and stability analysis of sampled-data neural-network-based control systems. A continuous-time nonlinear plant and a sampled-data three-layer fully-connected feed-forward neural-network-based controller will be connected in closed-loop to perform a control task. Stability conditions will be derived to guarantee the closed-loop system stability. Linear-matrix-inequality- and genetic-algorithm-based approaches will be employed to obtain the maximum sampling period and connection weights of the neural network subject to the considerations of the system stability and performance. An application example will be given to illustrate the design procedure and effectiveness of the proposed approach.

2086 *Real-time Control of Variable Air Volume System Using a SPSA Based Neural Controller [#1564]*
Chengyi Guo, Qing Song and Wenjian Cai, Nanyang Technological University, Singapore

A neural control scheme for variable air volume (VAV) air-conditioning system is proposed. The neural network is trained online by the simultaneous perturbation stochastic approximation (SPSA) method instead of the standard back-propagation algorithm. The closed-loop stability of the proposed control scheme is guaranteed based on the conic sector theory. The new control scheme provides the desired functionality as well as the adaptation of the VAV control system for a wide range of disturbances and parameter changes. To demonstrate the applicability of the proposed method, real-time experiments were carried out on a pilot VAV air-conditioning system and good testing results are obtained.

2087 *Discrete-Time Systems Neuro-Riccati Equation Solution [#1684]*
Annabell Tamariz and Celso Bottura, University Candido Mendes/Unicamp, Brazil; Unicamp, Brazil

In this article proposal for solving the Discrete-Time Algebraic Riccati Equation (DARE) using a multilayer Recurrent Neural Network (RNN) approach is presented. Systems of coupled matricial nonlinear differential equations are derived describing the neural dynamics of the Neuro-Riccati equation. By solving these coupled matrix equations using recurrent neural networks a symmetric and positive definite solution is obtained. Several examples demonstrate the effectiveness of this proposal and respective implementation.

2088 *Predictive Control Based on Feedforward Neural Network for Strong Nonlinear System [#1228]*
Min Han, Wei Guo and Jincheng Wang, Dalian University of Technology, China

The paper presents a generalized predictive control (GPC) algorithm based on feedforward neural network (FNN) to control nonlinear system. In recent years, approximate linearization theory is used to control nonlinear system, but robustness can not be guaranteed. Considering neural network can accomplish nonlinear mapping from input to output, FNN is chosen as a nonlinear model of process. Based on such model, GPC is applied to control a second-order nonlinear system. Simulation results demonstrate that the performance of the system controlled by the algorithm is good, and that system essentially responds in the desired manner. It is also demonstrated that the GPC based on FNN is provided with good adaptation and robustness.

2089 *Design and Experimental Evaluation of a 3-Mass Speed Control System with a Hybrid Structure of Sliding Mode Controller and CMAC [#1748]*
Masanobu Obika, Kazuo Kawada, Toru Yamamoto and Shoichiro Fujisawa, ADAPTEX Inc./ Hiroshima University, Japan; Hiroshima University, Japan; University of Tokushima, Japan

This paper deals with a design scheme of the speed control for a 3-mass system, which has a hybrid structure of a sliding mode controller and a cerebellar model articulation controller(CMAC). The nonlinear part in the sliding mode controller is firstly designed, and then a real-coded genetic algorithm is utilized to optimize the output from the sliding mode controller. The CMAC compensates the sliding mode controller so that the control performance is improved well. In this scheme, the divergent property of the CMAC caused by a disturbance is fairly suppressed by effects of the nonlinear control part. The behavior of the newly proposed control scheme is experimentally examined.

2090 *Total Sliding-mode-based Genetic Algorithm Control for Linear Piezoelectric Ceramic Motor Drive [#1340]*
Rong-Jong Wai and Ching-Hsiang Tu, Dept. Electrical Engineering, Yuan Ze University, Taiwan

This study presents a total sliding-mode-based genetic algorithm control (TSGAC) system for a linear piezoelectric ceramic motor (LPCM) driven by a newly designed hybrid resonant inverter. In the hybrid resonant drive system, it has the merits of the high voltage gain from a parallel-resonant current source, and the invariant output characteristic from a LLCC resonant driving circuit. Since the dynamic characteristics and motor parameters of the LPCM are highly nonlinear and time varying, a TSGAC system is therefore investigated based on direction-based genetic algorithm with the spirit of total sliding-mode control (TSC) and fuzzy evolutionary procedure to achieve high-precision position control.

2091 *Adaptive Tanaka-Sugeno Fuzzy Cerebellar Model Articulation Controller for Output Tracking Control [#1268]*
Tung-Sheng Chiang and Chian-Song Chiu, Ching-Yun University, Taiwan; Chien-Kuo Technology University, Taiwan

This study introduces an adaptive Tanaka-Sugeno fuzzy CMAC (TS-FCMAC) for output tracking control of nonlinear systems. This structure has two advantages in two aspects. First, to deal with highly nonlinear and time varying plant, we modified traditional CMAC into a simple structure. This will significantly increase the learning speed and performance. Second, if the controlled plants are well known, TS_FCMAC is constructed as similar as the TS fuzzy system such that PDC can be directly applied for the output tracking. Two examples, linear piezoelectric ceramic motors and Lorenz's equation, are given to illustrate output tracking performances.

2092 *Robust Output Tracking CMAC Control: The T-S Fuzzy Model-Based Approach [#1267]*
Chian-Song Chiu and Tung-Sheng Chiang, Chien-Kuo Technology University, Taiwan; Ching-Yun University, Taiwan

This paper proposes a robust T-S FCMAC controller for general uncertain T-S fuzzy systems. Combining the T-S fuzzy PDC concept and the FCMAC compensation, the overall control scheme guarantees the asymptotic output tracking and all bounded internal states. Moreover, the proposed T-S FCMAC control scheme has an easy implementation structure, i.e., the smaller number of nodes of the CMAC network is used. Finally, the simulations show the expected performances.

2093 *Prototype Robotic Arm Assisted by Smart CMOS Vision Chips [#1558]*
Victor Ponce-Ponce, Felipe Gomez-Castaneda and Jose Moreno-Cadenas, Cinvestav, Mexico

This work presents the computational modules that control a robotic arm system. These modules are: 1) an early self-organizing algorithm, which is in charge of coordinating the movement in three dimensions of this mechanical arm and, 2) a center-of-mass algorithm implemented by two vision CMOS silicon chips that estimate the position of a target object relative to the tip of the arm. To probe and to validate the functionality of the above modules working together an emulation program was created.

Plenary Poster Session: Diagnostics and quality control
Tuesday, August 2, 7:00PM-11:00PM, Room: Fountaine, Chair: Program Chairs

2094 *A framework for the verification of air quality forecasting models using self-organizing feature maps [#1577]*
Xavier Guilbeault, Stephane Gaudreault, Louis-Philippe Crevier, Hugo Landry and Joel Martin, Sherbrooke University, Canada; Meteorological Service of Canada, Canada

A fundamental problem in the development of an air quality forecast system is the implementation of an evaluation protocol. Traditionally, statistics are computed to compare the model output to the observations. These methods are limited in that they are generally insensitive to location and timing error. In this paper we describe a framework that attempts to address such limitations. It makes use of self-organizing feature maps to compute the classification of feature vectors from the regions of interest. It encompasses both formalism and a software tool that is under active development. More specifically, the framework permits the specification and manipulation of invariants associated with topological elements of an air quality forecast.

2095 *Bayesian Neural Networks for Nonlinear Multivariate Manufacturing Process Monitoring [#1077]*
Feng Zhang, Fairchild Semiconductor, United States

As a linear method, PCA is not accurate for complicated processes control when nonlinear correlations are involved in the multivariate measurement variables. As one appealing nonlinear PCA method, principal curves generalized PCA to nonlinear domain and provide a better way to nonlinear feature extraction and dimension reduction. A multivariate process monitoring method based on Bayesian neural networks is proposed in this paper, which involves a projection network and reconstruction network to describe the nonlinearities and helps avoid the overfitting problem in the weight parameter learning. Experimental study has illustrated the potential applicability of this method for nonlinear feature extraction and multivariate process monitoring.

2096 *Feature Selection and Condition Monitoring of Gearbox Using SOM [#1249]*
Guanglan Liao, Tielin Shi and Jianping Xuan, Huazhong University of Science and Technology, China

Feature selection is a key issue to pattern recognition and condition monitoring. This paper presents an investigation that uses self-organizing maps (SOM) network to realize feature selection for gearbox condition monitoring. With the use of the responses of every dimensional feature in SOM network neurons weights to the input data evaluated according to the Euclidean distances between them, the feature sets being sensitive to pattern recognition are selected. Gearbox vibration signals measured under different operating conditions are analyzed with the proposed method. The experimental results demonstrate that the method selects sensitive feature sets effectively and has a good potential for gearbox condition monitoring in practice.

2097 *Engine Data Classification with Simultaneous Recurrent Network Using a Hybrid PSO-EA Algorithm [#1740]*
Xindi Cai and Donald C. Wunsch II, ACIL, Dept. of ECE, Univ. of Missouri - Rolla, United States; ACIL, University of Missouri-Rolla, United States

We applied an architecture which automates the design of simultaneous recurrent network (SRN) using a new evolutionary learning algorithm. This new evolutionary learning algorithm is based on a hybrid of particle swarm optimization (PSO) and evolutionary algorithm (EA). By combining the searching abilities of these two global optimization methods, the evolution of individuals is no longer restricted to be in the same generation, and winning individuals may produce offspring to replace the losing ones. The novel algorithm is then applied to the simultaneous recurrent network for the engine data classification. The experimental results show that our approach gives solid performance in categorizing the non-linear car engine data.

2098 *An Automatic Method to Detect Missing Components in Manufactured Products [#1743]*
Giuseppe Acciani, Ernesto Chiarantoni, Girolamo Fornarelli and Gioacchino Brunetti, Politecnico di Bari, Italy

In this paper we describe a method to recognize missing components on manufactured products. The proposed approach exploits the wavelet transform to extract features from the acquired data, while the diagnosis is performed by means of a neural network. The results show that this method achieves an high recognition rate. At the same time the method allows to use a very cheap diagnostic system.

2099 *Cosmetic Defect Classification Found in Ophthalmic Lenses Using Artificial Neural Networks [#1018]*
Mario Chacon, Dora Rodriguez, Jose Rivera and Adiel Astudillo, Chihuahua Institute of Technology, Mexico; Chihuahua Institute of Technology, Moldova, Republic of

In an industrial inspection process cosmetic defect classification involves a lot of subjectivity because the test depends on the appreciation of the defect by a human inspector, HI. Therefore, a machine classifier is of great help in order to reduce the effect of the subjectivity. The paper demonstrates the applicability of ANN classifiers to solve real world problems. The paper shows the performance of several ANN classifiers designed. The final classifier discovers a bias criteria during the inspection performed by HIs. The best ANN turned out to be a MLP trained with the BP. This classifier has 94% of correct classification and solves the controversies between the production and quality departments due to subjectivity of the inspection.

2100 *A Neuro-Fuzzy Based Sensor and Actuator Fault Estimation Scheme for Unknown Nonlinear Systems [#1563]*
Abbas Khosravi, Heidar Ali Talebi and Mehdi Karrari, Amirkabir University of Technology, Iran; University of Western Ontario, Canada

In this paper, a new approach for sensor and actuator fault detection and estimation in unknown nonlinear systems is proposed. Model-free structure and no a priori knowledge about the faults are two main properties of the proposed method that make it a viable candidate for real-time applications. First, a neuro-fuzzy technique is used to obtain a nominal model based on input-output data of normal system operation. Actuator and sensor faults are then estimated such that the error between the output of the model and the actual output is minimized. The gradient decent method is used to update the fault estimated values. The estimated values are subsequently used for fault accommodation.

2101 *Aircraft Cabin Noise Minimization via Neural Network Inverse Model [#1714]*
Xiao Hu, Gregory Clark, Matt Travis, John Vian and Donald C. Wunsch II, ACIL, University of Missouri-Rolla, United States; Boeing Phantom Works, United States

This paper describes research to investigate an artificial neural network (ANN) approach to minimize aircraft cabin noise in flight. The ANN approach is shown to be able to accurately model the non-linear relationships between engine unbalance, airframe vibration, and cabin noise to overcome limitations associated with traditional linear influence coefficient methods. ANN system inverse models are developed using engine test-stand vibration data and on-airplane vibration and noise data supplemented with Influence Coefficient empirical data. The inverse models are able to determine balance solutions that satisfy cabin noise specifications.

2102 *Dynamic Neural Network-based Estimator for Fault Diagnosis in Reaction Wheel Actuator of Satellite Attitude Control System [#1557]*
Ehsan Sobhani Tehrani, Khashayar Khorasani and S. Tafazoli, Concordia University, Canada; Canadian Space Agency, Canada

An approach to simultaneous fault detection and isolation in the reaction wheel actuator of the satellite attitude control system is considered. A model-based adaptive nonlinear parameter estimation technique is used. The estimation is based on the nonlinear finite-memory filtering strategy that is solved for optimal estimation functions. To make the optimization feasible for on-line application, the optimal estimation functions are approximated by MLP neural networks. The standard back-propagation and back-propagation through-time were employed for the neural adaptation algorithms for obtaining the required gradients. Simulation results show the effectiveness of the methodology for the proposed application.

Plenary Poster Session: Telecommunication applications
Tuesday, August 2, 7:00PM-11:00PM, Room: Fountaine, Chair: Program Chairs

2103 *Modeling of Spiral Inductors Using Artificial Neural Network [#1335]*
Tao Liu, Wenjun Zhang and Zhiping Yu, Tsinghua University, China

A new model for spiral inductors, which covers wide operation frequency range and full design parameters, is proposed by using artificial neural network (ANN). It is pointed out that a four-layered neural network is superior to a three-layered neural network both on the mapping and generalization abilities in spiral inductor modeling. For the first time, a novel physics-based sampling technique is adopted in modeling procedure. Equipped with this new sampling method, ANN model achieves better speed and accuracy performances though the training data are substantially reduced. The new sampling method can be easily applied to other passive components and be embedded in various modeling frameworks.

2104 *Sparse Channel Estimation With Regularization Method Using Convolution Inequality For Entropy [#1437]*
Dongho Han, Sung-Phil Kim and Jose C. Principe, CNEL, Dept. of ECE, University of Florida, United States; CNEL, Department of ECE, University of Florida, United States

In this paper, we show that the sparse channel estimation problem can be formulated as a regularization problem between mean squared error(MSE) and the L1-norm constraint of the channel impulse response. A simple adaptive method to solve regularization problem using the convolution inequality for entropy is proposed. Performance of this proposed regularization method will be compared to the Wiener filter, the matching pursuit (MP) algorithm and the information criterion based method. The results show that the estimate of the sparse channel using the MSE criterion with the L1-norm constraint outperforms the Wiener filter and the conventional sparse solution methods in terms of MSE of the estimates and the generalization performance.

2105 *A Neural Phase Rotator for PAPR Reduction of PCC-OFDM Signal [#1346]*
Masaya Ohta, Hideyuki Yamada and Katsumi Yamashita, Osaka Prefecture University, Japan

This article proposes a novel OFDM system that is based on PCC-OFDM and can reduce ICI and PAPR at the same time by using neural phase rotator. The proposed system does not have use side information to transmitting phase rotation factors. It is clarified from numerical experiments that the system can reduce PAPR of PCC-OFDM, and BER performance is improved drastically.

2106 *Further Results on the EKF-CRTRL Equalizer for Fast Fading and Frequency Selective Channels [#1094]*
Pedro Coelho and Luiz Biondi, State University of Rio de Janeiro, Brazil

This paper shows further results on the EKF-RTRL (Extended Kalman Filter - Real Time Recurrent Learning) Equalizer comparing its performance with the PSP-LMS (Per Survivor Processing - Least Mean Squares) Equalizer for fast fading selective frequency channels using the WSS_US (Wide Sense Stationary - Uncorrelated Scattering) model. The EKF-RTRL is a symbol by symbol neural equalizer and the PSP-LMS equalizer uses the maximum likelihood criterion for symbol sequence estimation and the per survivor processing principle. The performance here presented depicts several scenarios regarding the channel variation speed. The performance considered in this paper is the symbol error rate (SER).

2107 *Hybrid Neural-Phenomenological Sub-Models and its Application to Earth-space Path Signal Attenuation Prediction [#1475]*
Luiz Caloba, Gilson Alencar and Mauro Assis, Universidade Federal do Rio de Janeiro, Brazil; Universidade Gama Filho, Brazil; Instituto Militar de Engenharia, Brazil

The problem of radiowave attenuation by rain is critical for the design of reliable earth-satellite communication links operating above 10 GHz. The phenomenological models presented in the literature are complex and includes a large number of sub-models, but show only poor accuracy. In this paper we discuss the use of neural techniques to evaluate and to provide information on each sub-model that composes a phenomenological model of a process. Then, we show how hybrid neural-phenomenological sub-models may be used to maximally preserve the phenomenological information of the model while improving its numerical precision. The use this technique in the UIT-R propagation model significantly improved its precision.

2108 *Application of Neural Networks to 3G Power Amplifier Modeling [#1530]*
Taijun Liu, Slim Boumaiza and Fadhel M. Ghannouchi, Ecole Polytechnique de Montreal, Canada

In this paper a Real-Valued Time-Delayed Neural Network (RVTDNN) is utilized to build a baseband behavioral model of a 3G power amplifier. The RVTDNN is firstly trained in Matlab and then implements in Agilent Design System software. In order to speed up the training process, a second-order learning algorithm namely Scaled Conjugate Gradient Method (SCGM) is employed to extract the RVTDNN model parameters (weights and biases). The comparison of the simulation based results to the measured ones reveals the ability of the identified RVTDNN to accurately predict the dynamic nonlinear behavior of a 90- Watt LDMOS power amplifier under a two-carrier 3GPP-FDD excitation signal.

Plenary Poster Session: Heart applications
Tuesday, August 2, 7:00PM-11:00PM, Room: Fountaine, Chair: Program Chairs

2109 *Bayesian ANN Classifier for ECG Arrhythmia Diagnostic System: A Comparison Study [#1521]*
Dayong Gao, Michael Madden, Des Chambers and Gerard Lyons, National University of Ireland, Ireland

This paper outlines a system for detection of cardiac arrhythmias within ECG signals, based on a Bayesian Artificial Neural Network (ANN) classifier. The Bayesian (or Probabilistic) ANN Classifier is built by the use of a logistic regression model and the back propagation algorithm based on a Bayesian framework. Its performance for this task is evaluated by comparison with other classifiers including Naive Bayes, Decision Trees, Logistic Regression, and RBF Networks. A paired t-test is employed in comparing classifiers to select the optimum model. The system is evaluated using noisy ECG data, to simulate a real-world environment. It is hoped that the system can be further developed and fine-tuned for practical application.

2110 *Input and Data Selection Applied to Heart Disease Diagnosis [#1468]*
Carlos Pedreira, Leonardo Macrini and Elaine Costa, Catholic University of Rio de Janeiro - PUC-RIO, Brazil; Federal University of Rio de Janeiro - UFRJ, Brazil

In this paper we present an application of data and input selection to a heart disease diagnosis problem. We approach the problem by using a modified LVQ scheme that selects a subset of the training data points to update the prototypes. The main model goal is to identify patients with relevant coronary vessels obstruction. The selected subset provides an interesting interpretation. We associate this methodology with a weighted norm, instead of the Euclidean, in order to establish different levels of importance for the input attributes. Again, interesting interpretation arises concerning the relevance of the input attributes.

2111 *Reliable Determination of Sleep Versus Wake from Heart Rate Variability Using Neural Networks [#1406]*
Aaron Lewicke, Edward Sazonov, Michael Corwin and Stephanie Schuckers, Clarkson Univeristy, United States; Clarkson University, United States; Boston Medical Center, Boston University, United States

Heart rate, heart rate variability (HRV), and sleep state are some of the common physiologic parameters used in studies of infants. HRV is easily derived from infant electrocardiograms (ECG), but sleep state scoring is a time consuming task using many physiological signals. We propose a technique to reliably determine sleep and wake using only the ECG. The method will be tested with simultaneous ECG and polysomnograph (PSG) determined sleep scores from the Collaborative Home Infant Monitoring Evaluation (CHIME) study. Learning vector quantization and multi-layer perceptron (MLP) neural networks are tested as the predictors.

2112 *Neural Network Based Detection of Fetal Heart Rate Patterns [#1770]*
Philip Warrick, Emily Hamilton and Maciejszczak Maciej, McGill University, Canada; LMS Medical Systems, Canada

Automated detection of Fetal Heart Rate (FHR) patterns can potentially improve intra-partum care by providing consistent and reliable measures that assist health-care professionals in their assessment of the state of the fetus. We use the combined tools of signal processing and neural networks to detect the FHR patterns of baseline, acceleration and deceleration. Comparison to previous results reported in the literature are provided.

Plenary Poster Session: Pharmacology and disease diagnosis
Tuesday, August 2, 7:00PM-11:00PM, Room: Fountaine, Chair: Program Chairs

2113 *Exploratory Data Analysis of Dynamic Cerebral Contrast--Enhanced Perfusion MRI Time--Series [#1056]*
Anke Meyer-Baese, Florida State University, United States

We compare experimentally four different unsupervised clustering techniques as a tool for the analysis of dynamic cerebral contrast-enhanced perfusion MRI time-series in patients with and without stroke. The goal of the paper is to determine the robustness and reliability of clustering methods in providing a self-organized segmentation of perfusion MRI data sharing common properties of signal dynamics. By using the whole information provided by the dynamic time-series, we introduce an extension to the conventional method of analyzing perfusion MRI studies based on the evaluation of a few parameters such as MTT, rCBV, and rCBF.

2114 *A Neural Network-based Prediction Model of AR Inhibitory Activity from a Sparse Set of Compounds [#1277]*
Rafael Parra-Hernandez, Erik M. Laxdal, Nikitas J. Dimopoulos and Polyxeni Alexiou, University of Victoria, Canada; Aristotle University of Thessaloniki, Greece

In this paper, we present a mechanism to obtain a Neural Network-based model that predicts an enzyme inhibitory activity of a group of compounds. The mechanism selects the compounds, among a sparse set of, that should be used to obtain models of the inhibitory activity of interest. That is, the mechanism is aimed at the selection of a training set of compounds which will ensure that the training of a Neural Network-based model will result in a system capable of generalization.

2115 *Multi-class Support Vector Machines for Modeling HIV/AIDS Treatment Adherence using Patient Data [#1561]*
Zhao Lu, Hao Ying, Feng Lin, Stewart Neufeld, Mark Luborsky, David Brawn and Andrea Sankar, Wayne State University, United States

As the only effective treatment strategy against HIV/AIDS, highly active antiretroviral therapy (HAART) is an extremely promising development in the treatment of HIV/AIDS. However, recent studies found that poor adherence was a major cause of treatment failure and emerging drug resistance. For this reason, we apply the Support Vector Machine (SVM) to relate nine patient factors to adherence level. The results show that the SVM significantly outperformed the neural networks and SVM techniques can be effective in quantitatively modeling complex relationships in medicine even when the data set size is very small by industrial standard.

2116 *Neural network-based approach for the classification of wireless-capsule endoscopic images [#1054]*
Vassilis Kodogiannis and Maria Boulougoura, University of Westminster, United Kingdom

The importance of computer-assisted diagnosis in endoscopy is to assist physicians in detecting the status of tissues by characterising the features from images. In this paper schemes have been developed to extract new features from the texture spectra in the chromatic and achromatic domains for a selected region of interest from each colour component histogram of images acquired by the new M2A Swallowable Imaging Capsule. The concept of fusion of multiple classifiers and the implementation of an intelligent scheme has been also adopted in this study. The high accuracy of the proposed system provides thus an indication that such intelligent scheme could be used as a supplementary diagnostic tool in capsule endoscopy.

2117 *The Use of Clustering to Analyze Symptom-Based Case Definitions for Acute Gastrointestinal Illness [#1584]*
Shannon Majowicz and Deborah Stacey, Public Health Agency of Canada, Canada; University of Guelph, Canada

Gastrointestinal illness (GI) is an important public health issue. To better estimate the true level of morbidity associated with GI illness in the community, several countries have conducted population-based studies. Unfortunately, comparing the results is complicated because the symptom-based case definitions used varies. This potential problem, although widely noted in the literature, has not been formally explored. The research presented here demonstrates the impact of using different symptom-based case definitions on the observed epidemiology of acute GI by applying previously published case definitions to a common, population-based data set and then using clustering (k-means and SOM) to create a data-driven view of the cases.

2118 *A SVM Approach for Detection of Hemorrhages in Background Diabetic Retinopathy [#1246]*
Xiaohui Zhang and Opas Chutatape, School of EEE, Nanyang Technological University, Singapore

Hemorrhages are main symptoms in background diabetic retinopathy and early detection is essential for an effective treatment. In this paper, a top-down strategy is applied to detect hemorrhages. After color normalization preprocessing stage, an evidence value for every pixel is calculated by SVM. The SVM classifier uses features extracted by Combined 2DPCA instead of explicit image features as the input vector. After locating the hemorrhages in the ROI, the boundaries of the hemorrhages can be accurately segmented by the post-processing stage. The paper demonstrates a new implementation of various techniques on the problem and shows the improvement it offers over the others.

2119 *QRS Complex Detection Using Backpropagation Neural Network [#1015]*
Mamun Bin Ibne Reaz, Multimedia University, Malaysia

In this research, Backpropagation Neural Network is used to learn the characteristics of R peak to detect QRS complex. This allows R peak to be differentiated from large peaked T and P waves with higher accuracy and minimizes the problem associated with the noises in the ECG signal includes power line interference, motion artifacts, baseline drift, ECG amplitude modulation and other composite noises. The features that trains the network includes amplitude, differentiation value, duration exceed threshold, RR interval and crossing-zero. The performance was tested using 10 ECG signals data from MIT-BIH Database. The correct positive peak detection gave an accuracy of 91.16% with 8.84% of missing peak count and 6.51% of false positive peak.

2120 *Dynamic Feature Fusion in the Self Organising Tree Map - applied to the segmentation of Biofilm Images [#1673]*
Matthew Kyan, Ling Guan and Steven Liss, University of Sydney, Australia; Ryerson University, Canada

The Self Organising Tree Map is investigated for segmenting microorganisms from microscope image data. Significance of individual feature sets are explored and established, in terms of their impact on SOTM topology, and it is proposed that better object delineation can be achieved if certain features dominate early stages of learning, deferring others until later, as knowledge builds. The flexibility of the SOTM in adaptively preserving the topology of input space makes it an appropriate candidate for segmentation. We find that by favouring signal features in early stages of learning and relaxing proximity constraints in later stages, a general mechanism is offered, through which we can improve the segmentation of microbial constituents.

Plenary Poster Session: Brain imaging and brain interfaces
Tuesday, August 2, 7:00PM-11:00PM, Room: Fountaine, Chair: Program Chairs

2121 *Independent Component Analysis and High-Order Statistics for Automatic Artifact Rejection [#1087]*
Nadia Mammone and Francesco Carlo Morabito, DIMET University Mediterranea of Reggio Calabria, Italy; DIMET, University Mediterranea of Reggio Calabria, Italy

One of the aims of biomedical signal processing is to extract some features from the data in order to make diagnosis and to understand the biological phenomena but, often, a preprocessing step is essential because some unwelcome signals, the artifacts, are superimposed to the useful signals we want to analyse. In literature, Independent Component Analysis (ICA) has been exploited for artifact isolation and the joint use of some high order statistics, kurtosis and Shannon's entropy has been exploited to automatically detect the artifacts. In this paper we propose the joint use of kurtosis and Renyi's entropy as a new tool for automatic detection and we show that it outperforms the other tool thanks to the features of the Renyi's entropy

2122 *A Neural Supergraph Matching Architecture [#1412]*
Stefan Klinger and Jim Austin, University of York, United Kingdom

A neural supergraph matching architecture is introduced based on relaxation labeling and the minimum common supergraph of pairs of graphs. The system is implemented on correlation matrix memories and is efficient in constructing this supergraph. We test the effectiveness of this graphical cluster representation on two different sets of graphs.

2123 *Comparison of TDNN Training Algorithms in Brain Machine Interfaces [#1711]*
Yiwen Wang, Sung-Phil Kim and Jose C. Principe, CNEL, Dept. of ECE, University of Florida, United States; CNEL, Department of ECE, University of Florida, United States

Linear or non-linear models are used in Brain Machine Interfaces (BMIs) to map the neural activity to the associated behavior, typically the primate's hand position. Linear models assume a linear relationship between neural activity and hand position that may not be the case. A solution would be time-delay neural network (TDNN) that provides effectively a nonlinear combination of linear models. However, this model results in a drastic increase of free parameters and slow convergence when trained by an error backpropagation learning rule. We propose to train the TDNN by scaled conjugate gradient, which avoids timeconsuming linear search, coupled with weight decay to reduce the free parameters number and produce generally faster convergence.

2124 *An Algorithm for Automatic Assignment of Artifact-Related Independent Components in Biomedical SIgnal Analysis [#1055]*
Matthias Boehm, Kurt Stadlthanner, Elmar W. Lang, Ana Maria Tome, Ana Rita Teixeira, Carlos Puntonet, Peter Gruber and Fabian Theis, Institute of Biophysics, University of Regensbur, Germany; DETUA/IEETA, University of Aveiro, Portugal; Dep. Computer Architecture, University of Grana, Spain; Institute of Biophysics, University of Regensburg, Germany

In this work an automatic assignment tool for estimated independent components within an independent component analysis is presented. The tool is applied to the problem of removing the water artifact from multi-dimensional proton NMR spectra. The algorithm uses local PCA to approximate the water artifact and defines a suitable cost function which is optimized using simulated annealing. The blind extraction of artifact-related source signals is effected by a recently developed algorithm called dAMUSE.

Plenary Poster Session: Application to cancer diagnostics
Tuesday, August 2, 7:00PM-11:00PM, Room: Fountaine, Chair: Program Chairs

2125 *Computational Intelligence Techniques for Acute Leukemia Gene Expression Data Classification [#1466]*
Vassilis Plagianakos, Dimitris Tasoulis and Michael Vrahatis, Department of Mathematics, University of Patras, Greece

Recent advances in microarray technologies have allowed scientists to discover and monitor the mRNA transcript levels of thousands of genes in a single experiment. The data obtained from microarray studies present a challenge to data analysis. In this paper, we design an expression--based classification method for acute leukemia. Different dimension reduction techniques are considered to tackle the very high dimensionality of this kind of data. Subsequently, the classification system employs Artificial Neural Networks. The comparative results reported, indicate that high classification rates are possible and moreover that subsets of features that contribute significantly to the success of the neural classifiers can be identified.

2126 *Virtual Reality Visual Data Mining with Nonlinear Discriminant Neural Networks: Application to Leukemia and Alzheimer Gene Expression Data [#1623]*
Julio J. Valdes and Alan J. Barton, National Research Council Canada, Canada

A hybrid stochastic-deterministic approach for solving NDA problems on very high dimensional biological data is investigated. It is based on networks trained with a combination of simulated annealing and conjugate gradient within a broad scale, high throughput computing data mining environment. High quality networks from the point of view of both discrimination and generalization capabilities are discovered. The NDA mappings generated by these networks, together with unsupervised representations of the data, lead to a deeper understanding of complex high dimensional data like Leukemia and Alzheimer gene expression microarray experiments.

2127 *SVMs Applied to Objective Aesthetic Evaluation of Conservative Breast Cancer Treatment [#1193]*
Jaime Cardoso, Joaquim Pinto da Costa and Maria Joao Cardoso, Faculdade de Engenharia da Universidade do Porto, Portugal; Faculdade de Ciencias da Universidade do Porto, Portugal; Faculdade de Medicina da Universidade do Porto, Portugal

Cosmetic assessment of conservative breast cancer treatment plays a major role in the study of breast cancer techniques. Objective assessment methods are being preferred to overcome the drawbacks of subjective evaluation. In this paper a methodology for the objective assessment of conservative breast cancer treatment is proposed. The quantitative measures used in this research provide an objective way to calculate the overall cosmetic result. We report experiments using support vector machines to derive an optimal assessment rule. The results seem to indicate that it is possible to construct an algorithm for a complete objective classification of the aesthetic result of breast conservative treatment.

2128 *Classification of Breast Abnormalities in Digital Mammograms using Image and BI-RADS Features in Conjunction with Neural Network [#1551]*
Rinku Panchal and Brijesh Verma, Central Queensland University, Australia

This paper investigates the significance of combining grey-level based image features and BI-RADS lesion descriptors along with patient age and a subtlety value (radiologists' interpretation) for the reliable classification of calcification and mass type breast abnormalities into malignant and benign classes. Three sets of experiments using grey-level based image features, BI- RADS features and combined features were conducted on DDSM benchmark database. The classification rate 91% on mass dataset and 74% on calcification dataset was obtained when both types of features combined together.

2129 *Feasibility of multi-layered perceptron network in discriminating breast magnetic resonance imaging lesions [#1678]*
Sreenivas Muthyala, Peter Gibbs and Lindsay Turnbull, Centre for MR Investigations, University of Hull, United Kingdom

The feasibility of MLP networks in reliably discriminating between benign and malignant lesions is demonstrated in this pilot study. MLP networks can be trained on similar information that a radiologist would use to interpret lesions on DCE-MRI study of breast and perform as well as a trained radiologist.. In the future, this work will be extended to a larger data set and the feasibility of other neural networks such as radial basis function will be tested.

2130 *Automatic recognition of the blood cells of myelogenous leukemia using SVM [#1032]*
Stanislaw Osowski, Tomasz Markiewicz, Bozena Marianska and Leszek Moszczynski, Warsaw University of Technology, Poland; Institute of Haematology, Poland

The paper presents the system for automatic recognition of the leukemia blast cells on the basis of the image of the bone marrow aspirate. The recognizing system uses Support Vector Machine (SVM) as the classifier and exploits the features of the image of the blood cells related to the texture, geometry and histograms. The results presented in the paper are concerned with the features generation and selection in order to get the best results of recognition. The results of numerical experiments of recognition of 17 classes of blood cells of myelogenous leukemia are presented and discussed.

Plenary Poster Session: Electroencephalograms and electromyograms
Tuesday, August 2, 7:00PM-11:00PM, Room: Fountaine, Chair: Program Chairs

2131 *Neural Network Classification of EEG Signals using Time-Frequency Representation [#1120]*
Chandan Gope, Nasser Kehtarnavaz and Dinesh Nair, University of Texas at Dallas, Texas, United States; National Instruments, Austin, Texas, United States

This paper addresses the problem of classification of EEG signals obtained from human subjects performing two mental tasks, namely, "baseline" and "multiplication". First, the EEG signals are pre-processed using Independent Component Analysis for removal of artifacts. Then, a time- frequency representation of the signals is generated, from which wavelet-based texture features are extracted for classification. The texture features are fed into a three-layer neural network classifier trained by the backpropagation algorithm. A classification rate of 96% is obtained for the dataset used. The entire classification system has been implemented in the LabVIEW graphical programming environment.

2132 *ICA And a Gauge of Filter for the Automatic Filtering of an EEG Signal [#1113]*
Nabila Bouzida, Laurent Peyrodie and Christian Vasseur, HEI, University of Lille1, France; University of Lille1, France

The EEG signal, a recording of the brain activity using multiple electrodes placed on the scalp, can be hardly contaminated by lot of noises called artifacts. They are generated by the action of the skeletal muscles such as: eye movements, jaw clenching, etc. Indeed, the signals recorded are mixture of phenomenon issuing from multiple generators. Therefore it is important to search for a method which can separate the muscular activity from the neuronal one. The ICA is a statistical analysis method largely used for the study of biomedical data. Using the data recorded from several subjects (epileptic and healthy) we are going to prove the effectiveness of our approach based on the ICA and on a characterization of a filter model.

2133 *On the Use of Clustering and Local Singular Spectrum Analysis to Remove Ocular Artifacts from Electroencephalograms [#1096]*
Ana Rita Teixeira, Ana Maria Tome, Elmar Lang, Peter Gruber and Antonio Martins da Silva, DETUA/IEETA, University of Aveiro, Portugal; University of Regensburg, Germany; Institute of Biophysics, University of Regensburg, Germany; Instituto de Ciencias Biomedicas Abel Salazar, Portugal

We present a method based on singular spectrum analysis to remove ocular artifacts (EOG) from an Electroencephalogram (EEG). After embedding the EEG signals in a feature space of time-delayed coordinates, feature vectors are clustered and the principal components (PCs) are computed locally within each cluster. Then, we assume that the EOG artifact is associated with the PCs belonging to largest eigenvalues. We incorporate a Minimum Description Length (MDL) criterion to estimate the number of eigenvectors needed to represent the EOG artifact faithfully. The extracted EOG signal is subtracted from the original EEG signal to obtain the corrected EEG signal we are interested in.

2134 *A Fuzzy Approach for Key Variables Identification of EMG Evaluation System [#1695]*
Yanfeng Hou, Jacek Zurada, Waldemar Karwowski and William Marras, University of Louisville, United States; The Ohio State University, United States

Identification of influence of input variables is very important for complex nonlinear systems with high dimensional input space. In this paper we propose a method using fuzzy average with fuzzy cluster distribution (FAFCD). To avoid the interference of different distribution of the sampling data, we deal with the distribution of fuzzy clusters in the sampling data, instead of the original data set. We first use fuzzy methods to partition the sampling data set into fuzzy clusters and produce a new data set. Then the fuzzy average method is applied to the new data set. This method is straightforward and computationally easy. The performance is tested on both benchmark data and the electromyographic (EMG) signal Evaluation System.

2135 *Extraction of event related potentials from EEG signals using ICA with reference [#1153]*
Joshua Lau and Jagath Rajapakse, Nanyang Technological University, Singapore

This paper delves into the application of a new technique, Independent Component Analysis with Reference (ICA-R), in order to obtain the components of ERPs from the EEG data. The technique is tested on available EEG data on a picture matching task performed by alcoholic and non-alcoholic subjects. The accuracy, efficiency, and usefulness of ICA-R is demonstrated in extracting the relevant components of single-trial ERPs.

2136 *PCA and ICA for the Extraction of EEG Dominant Components in Cerebral Death Assessment [#1427]*
Fabio La Foresta, Francesco Carlo Morabito, Bruno Azzerboni and Maurizio Ipsale, DIMET University Mediterranea of Reggio Calabri, Italy; DIMET, University Mediterranea of Reggio Calabria, Italy; DFMTFA - University of Messina, Italy

The electroencephalogram (EEG) analysis provides a functional tool to verify a qualitative clinical check. In this paper some techniques, i.e. Principal Component Analysis (PCA) and Independent Component Analysis (ICA), are implemented in order to extrapolate in EEG signals very few dominant components that contain almost all the information necessary to have an adequate knowledge of the brain activity. To obtain that, the compression ability of PCA is mixed with the statistical independence property of the ICA. The achieved results show that in most cases of cerebral death diagnosis, in which the EEG analysis is performed when the brain activity is very reduced, even few components are enough to depict the complete brain activity.

Plenary Poster Session: Financial and marketing applications
Tuesday, August 2, 7:00PM-11:00PM, Room: Fountaine, Chair: Program Chairs

2137 *Vector Quantized Radial Basis Function Neural Network with Embedded Multiple Local Linear Models for Financial Prediction [#1182]*
Tony Jan and Maria Kim, University of Technology Sydney, Australia

In this paper, a model is proposed which combines multiple local linear models with a novel modified probabilistic neural network (MPNN). The proposed model is developed to approximate multiple nonlinear model with reduced computational requirement. The proposed model shows to provide both low bias and variance with reduced computations by utilizing semiparametric local linear approximation and efficient vector quantization of data space. The proposed model is shown to provide comparable performance to other state-of-the-art models in terms of bias, variance and computational requirement in short-term financial prediction.

2138 *Application of Multi-Branch Neural Networks to Stock Market Prediction [#1337]*
Takashi Yamashita, Kotaro Hirasawa and Jinglu Hu, Waseda University, Japan

Recently, artificial neural networks (ANNs) have been utilized for financial market applications. On the other hand, we have so far shown that multi-branch neural networks (MBNNs) could have higher representation and generalization ability than conventional NNs. In this paper, we investigate the accuracy of prediction of TOPIX (Tokyo Stock Exchange Prices Indexes) using MBNNs. Using the TOPIX related values in time series and other information, MBNNs can learn the characteristics of time series and predict the future TOPIX. Several simulations were carried out in order to compare the proposed predictor using MBNNs with that using conventional NNs. The results show that the proposed method can have higher accuracy of the prediction.

2139 *Data Preprocessing for Stock Market Forecasting using Random Subspace Classifier Network [#1509]*
Dmitry Zhora, Institute of Software Systems, Ukraine

Financial forecasting is a challenging problem which attracts researchers from different fields. In order to predict the future with some degree of confidence it's better to make sure the forecasting method provides expected results for different time frames. This article analyses the application of random subspace classifier for predicting the next day stock price return. Different data preprocessing approaches, particularly for stock price normalization, are suggested. Forecasting performance is tested for different time periods. Besides, the ability of the network to predict the price change is considered within the test set.

2140 *Predicting Customer Behavior via Calling Links [#1040]*
Lian Yan, Michael Fassino and Patrick Baldasare, atRISK, Inc., United States

Typically several data sources can be used to predict customer behavior in telecommunications industry. However, in some cases, e.g., for prepaid customers, there is often little data available except for the Call Detail Record (CDR) data. We tackle this challenging problem, using significantly delayed CDR data as the primary data source to predict customer behavior. We extract calling links, i.e., who called whom, from the CDR data, and propose several distance measures based on calling links. We demonstrate that using information derived from calling links alone can achieve an acceptable accuracy for predicting churn. Calling links can also be used to identify calling communities, which may be used for targeted marketing campaigns.

Plenary Poster Session: Computer security, military and biomimetic applications
Tuesday, August 2, 7:00PM-11:00PM, Room: Fountaine, Chair: Program Chairs

2141 *A Novel Image Retrieval System Based on BP Neural Network [#1154]*
Jun-Hua Han, De-Shuang Huang, Tat-Ming Lok and R. Lyu Michael, Institute of Intelligent Machines, CAS, China; Hefei Institute of Intelligent Machines, CAS, China; The Chinese University of Hong Kong Shatin, Hong Kong

This paper presents a novel BP-based image retrieval (BPBIR) system, which is based on the observation that the images users need are often similar to a set of images with the same conception instead of one query image and the assumption that there is a nonlinear relationship between different features. If users aren't satisfied with the retrieved result, relevance feedback method is used to enhance the performance of the proposed system by changing the weights of the BP neural networks. In addition, we discuss some divisional methods to give rough information on the spatial color composition. Finally, we compare the performance of the proposed system with other systems. Experimental results show the efficacy of the proposed system.

2142 *Speaker Identification Using Speech and Lip Features [#1494]*
Guobin Ou, Xin Li, Xiaochao Yao, HongBin Jia and Yi Murphey, University of Michigan-Dearborn, United States

We present a speaker identification system that uses synchronized speech signals and lip features. We developed an algorithm that automatically extracts lip areas from speaker images, and a neural network system that integrates the two different types of signals to give accurate identification of speakers. We show that the proposed system gives better performances than the systems that use only speech or lip features in both text dependant and text independent speaker identification applications.

2143 *Comparison of a SOM Based Sequence Analysis System and Naive Bayesian Classifier for Spam Filtering [#1523]*
Xiao Luo and Nur Zincir-Heywood, Dalhousie University, Canada

The problem introduced by the unsolicited bulk emails, also known as "spam" generates a need for reliable anti-spam filters. In this paper, we design and compare the performance of a newly designed SOM based sequence analysis(SBSA) system for the spam filtering task. The system is based on a SOM based sequential data representation combined with a kNN classifier designed to make use of word sequence information. We compare this system with the traditional baseline method Naive Bayesian filter. Three different cost scenarios and suitable cost-sensitive measurements are employed. The results show that the SBSA system is superior to the Naive Bayesian filter, particularly when the misclassification cost for non-spam message is high.

2144 *Neural Networks Following a Binary Approach Applied to the Integer Prime-Factorization Problem [#1336]*
Boris Jansen and Kenji Nakayama, Kanazawa University, Japan

Nowadays, the integer factorization problem finds its application often in modern cryptography. Artificial Neural Networks (ANNs) have been applied to this problem. A composite is applied to the ANNs, and one of its prime factors is obtained as the output. Previously, ANNs dealing with the input and output data in a decimal form have been proposed. However, accuracy is not sufficient. Here, ANNs following a binary approach are proposed. The proposed neural networks are expected to be more stable, i.e. less sensitive to small errors in the network outputs. Simulations have been performed and the results are compared with the results reported in the previous study. The number of required searches for the true prime number can be well reduced.

2145 *Artificial Intelligence for Conflict Management [#1067]*
Eyasu Habtemariam, Tshilidzi Marwala and Monica Lagazio, University of the Witwatersrand, South Africa; University of Witwatersrand, South Africa; University of Kent, South Africa

One of the risks that have a great impact on society is militarized conflict. Militarized Interstate Dispute (MID) is defined as an outcome of interstate interactions which result on either peace or conflict. Effective prediction of the possibility of conflict between states is a good decision support tool for policy makers. In a previous research, neural networks have been implemented to predict the MID. Support Vector Machines (SVMs) have proven themselves to be very good prediction techniques in many other real world problems. In this research we introduce SVMs to predict MIDs. The results found show that SVM predicts MID better than NN.

2146 *Fingerprint Recognition Using Modular Neural Networks and Fuzzy Integrals for Response Integration [#1624]*
Patricia Melin, Diana Bravo and Oscar Castillo, Tijuana Institute of Technology, Mexico

We describe in this paper a new approach for pattern recognition using modular neural networks with a fuzzy logic method for response integration. We proposed a new architecture for modular neural networks for achieving pattern recognition in the particular case of human fingerprints. Also, the method for achieving response integration is based on the fuzzy Sugeno integral. Response integration is required to combine the outputs of all the modules in the modular network. We have applied the new approach for fingerprint recognition with a real database of fingerprints from students of our institution

2147 *Chaotic Associative Memory and Private V-mails [#1637]*
Harold Szu and Ming-Kai Hsu, DMLAB, George Washington Univ., United States; Digital Media RF Lab, Dept ECE, GWU, United States

To support the 3rd generation cellular phone with broad band wireless video emails (V-mails), we developed a Chaotic Neural Network (CNN) Associative Memory whose tying and initial value were sent by a private and free version of RSA security algorithm (patent expired). Receiver devices with the embedded system chip regenerate the specific CNN image series, so called the spatial-temporal keys (STK), which allow the RSA and the V-mail data to be correctly decrypted. Due to the fading and fatal noise in wireless communication channel, the STK must be robust and fault-tolerant proved by a field theory of Associative Memory and demonstrated by a collective fixed point of cycles of the whole bifurcated images.

2148 *Using Domain Knowledge to Constrain Structure Learning in a Bayesian Bioagent Detector [#1533]*
Anshu Saksena, Dennis Lucarelli and I-Jeng Wang, Johns Hopkins University Applied Physics Lab, United States

A novel procedure for learning a probabilistic model from mass spectrometry data that accounts for domain specific noise and mitigates the complexity of Bayesian structure learning is presented. We evaluate the algorithm by applying the learned probabilistic model to microorganism detection from mass spectrometry data.

Plenary Poster Session: Power systems applications
Tuesday, August 2, 7:00PM-11:00PM, Room: Fountaine, Chair: Program Chairs

2149 *Power System Reduced Model by Artificial Neural Networks [#1100]*
Juan M. Ramirez, Cinvestav, Mexico

This paper is aimed to the application of artificial neural networks (ANN) for constructing a power system reduced model, also termed dynamic equivalent. ANN are trained to help in constructing dynamic equivalents, which is considered a hard task in the context of electrical power systems. The main objective is to reproduce the complex voltage at some relevant nodes. The simulation results prove the applicability and robustness of this innovative approach.

2150 *FPGA Realization of Power Quality Disturbance Detection: An Approach with Wavelet, ANN and Fuzzy Logic [#1007]*
Florence Choong, Mamun Ibne Reaz, Faisal Mohd Yasin and Mohd Shahiman Sulaiman, Multimedia University, Malaysia

New intelligent system technologies using wavelet transform, expert systems and artificial neural networks provide some unique advantages regarding fault analysis. This paper presents new approach aimed at automating the analysis of power quality disturbances including sag, swell, transient, fluctuation, interruption and normal waveform. The approach focuses on the application of discrete wavelet transform technique to extract features from disturbance waveforms and their classification using a powerful combination of neural network and fuzzy logic. Comparisons, verification and analysis made from the results obtained from the application of this system validate the utility of this approach and achieved a classification accuracy of 98.17%.

2151 *Short Term Load Forecasting for Iran National Power System and Its Regions Using Multi Layer Perceptron and Fuzzy Inference systems [#1047]*
Roohollah Barzamini, Mohammad Bagher Menhaj, Abbas Khosravi and Shadi Kamalvand, Amirkabir University of Technology, Iran; Professor, Iran; Student, Iran

In this paper a Multi Layers Perceptron (MLP) Neural Network (NN) is designed for load forecasting in normal weather condition and ordinary days. The architecture of the proposed network is a three-layer feedforward neural network whose parameters are tuned by Levenberg-Marquardt Bock Propagation (LMBP). For abrupt weather changes and special holidays, we have added a Fuzzy Inference Systems (FIS) to modify the forecasted load appropriately. We show that this method satisfy the Iran electricity market rule. Simulation examples for Iran National Power System (INPS) and any of its regions, Bakhtar Region Electric Co (BREC) demonstrate capabilities of proposed method for load forecasting.

2152 *Artificial Neural Networks for Temporal Processing Applied to Prediction of Electric Energy Generation in Small Hydroelectric Power Stations [#1186]*
Paulo Cesar Endo Joaquim and Joao Luis Rosa, PUC-Campinas, Brazil

The purpose of this work is to present a computational prediction of temporal series through Artificial Neural Networks (ANN) with temporal features based on short-term memory structures and episodic long-term memory. The connectionist prediction is applied to a Brazilian small hydroelectric power station, because conventional prediction statistical techniques show inadequacy in relation to noise, acquisition fails, and need for generalization, when applied to this model. Departing from the proposed system, it is intended also to develop, in the future, a non-linear complex system, employing ANNs, with the inclusion of new variables in the decision process.

2153 *Streamflow forecasting using neural networks and fuzzy clustering techniques [#1394]*
Ivette Luna, Secundino Soares, Marina Magalhaes and Rosangela Ballini, State University of Campinas, Brazil

Planning of hydroelectric systems is a complex and difficult task once it involves non-linear production characteristics. Streamflow values covering the entire planning period must be accurately forecasted because they strongly influence energy production. This paper suggests an application of a FIR neural network and a fuzzy clustering-based model to evaluate one-step and multi-step ahead predictions. Results are compared with a periodic autoregressive model (PAR). It is interesting to apply a recurrent neural network for prediction task due to its ability for temporal processing and efficiency to solve nonlinear problems. The results show a generally better performance of the FIR neural network for the case studied.

Plenary Poster Session: Special Session - Earth Sciences & Climate modeling
Tuesday, August 2, 7:00PM-11:00PM, Room: Fountaine, Chair: Vladimir Krasnopolsky, Dimitri Solomatine, Julio Valdes Vladimir Cherkassky

2154 *Neural Network Modelling of the 20-Year Flood Event for 850 Catchments Across the UK [#1177]*
Christian Dawson, Robert Abrahart, Asaad Shamseldin, Robert Wilby and Linda See, Loughborough University, United Kingdom; University of Nottingham, United Kingdom; University of Auckland, New Zealand; Environment Agency, United Kingdom; University of Leeds, United Kingdom

Limited use has been made of artificial neural networks for regionalisation purposes or for flood event estimation in ungauged catchments. This paper uses data from the Centre for Ecology and Hydrology's Flood Estimation Handbook to predict the 20-year flood event for 850 catchments across the UK. Neural network solutions and stepwise multiple linear regressions are compared. The neural network solutions provided superior flood event predictions and their use for subsequent hydrological modelling and flood engineering applications is recommended.

2155 *Modelling Harbour Sedimentation Using ANN and M5 Model Trees [#1357]*
Biswa Bhattacharya and Dimitri P. Solomatine, UNESCO-IHE Institute for Water Education, Delft, Netherlands

The paper presents machine learning (ML) models that predict sedimentation in the harbour basin of the Port of Rotterdam. The important factors affecting the sedimentation process such as waves, wind, tides, surge, river discharge, etc. are studied, and the most important variables behind the process are chosen as the inputs. Two ML methods are used: MLP ANN and M5 model tree, the latter is a collection of piece-wise linear regression models, each being an expert for a particular region of the input space. The models are trained on the data collected during 1992-1998 and tested by the data of 1999-2000. The predictive accuracy of the models is found to be adequate for the potential use in the operational decision making.

2156 *Classification of Infrasound Events Using Using Radial Basis Function Neural Networks [#1071]*
Fredric Ham, Kamel Rekab, Sungjin Park, Ranjan Acharyya and Young-Chan Lee, Florida Institute of Technology, United States; LG Mobile Handset Research Center, Korea (South)

In this paper we present results for a bank of Radial Basis Function (RBF) neural networks, to discriminate between six different man-made infrasound events. Each module in the bank of RBF networks is responsible for classifying one of the six events, and thus, is trained to identify only this particular event.Output thresholds of each module are set according to specific ROC curves. Moreover, the spread parameter for the RBFs of each neural network module has been optimized. For six man-made events, the classifier accuracy achieved is 96%. A confusion matrix of the complete network is shown along with confidence intervals for each class and the overall accuracy.

2157 *Neural Network River Discharge Forecasters: An Empirical Investigation of Hidden Unit Processing Functions Based on Two Different Catchments [#1515]*
Asaad Shamseldin, Robert Abrahart and Linda See, University of Auckland, New Zealand; University of Nottingham, United Kingdom; University of Leeds, United Kingdom

This paper extends previous attempts at detecting physical process representation inside a neural network. The hidden units inside two neural networks are examined for two river catchments. The residual plots, from regression analysis, were used to explore the role of the different processing units. One hidden unit was discovered to have captured most of the input-output relationship. The other hidden units exhibited much weaker relationships with respect to observed discharge. Their main influence on model outputs was instead found to be a complex and integrated non-linear correction factor that had differential impacts on linear unit approximations at low-to-intermediate and upper magnitude flood events.

2158 *Robustness of the NN Approach to Emulating Atmospheric Long Wave Radiation in Complex Climate Models [#1105]*
Vladimir Krasnopolsky, Michael Fox-Rabinovitz and Ming-Dah Chou, Saic at Ncep/Noaa and Essic/Umd, United States; Essic/Umd, United States; National Taiwan University, Taiwan

In this paper we present comparisons of NN emulations developed for two different complex climate models: NCAR CAM model and NASA NSIPP. These models have different dynamics, different horizontal and vertical resolutions and different physics (including different long wave radiation schemes). Comparison of two (NCAR and NASA) NN emulations shows their profound similarity in terms of the accuracy of emulation vs. the original parameterizations and complexity of emulating NNs, i.e. the methodological robustness and portability of our NN emulation approach.

2159 *A Comparative Study of Artificial Neural Network Techniques for River Stage Forecasting [#1179]*
Christian Dawson, Linda See, Robert Abrahart, Robert Wilby and Asaad Shamseldin, Loughborough University, United Kingdom; University of Leeds, United Kingdom; University of Nottingham, United Kingdom; Environment Agency, United Kingdom; University of Auckland, New Zealand

In order to explore the different approaches neural network modellers use to forecasting river stage, an international comparison study was undertaken during 2004. This research was based on a set of rainfall and river stage data covering three winter periods for an unidentified river basin in England sampled at 15 minute intervals. Several neural network enthusiasts took part in the study from a number of different countries. The preferred methodologies and forecasting outputs from a number of 'blind' models of river stage developed by the participants have been collated and are presented in this paper.

2160 *Issues in Designing Automated Minimal Resource Allocation Neural Networks [#1769]*
Momcilo Markus, Illinois State Water Survey, Champaign, Illinois, United States

Neural Networks have a long record of promising results in hydrology. The earlier applications were mainly based on the back-propagation feed-forward method, which often used a lengthy trial-and-error method to determine the final network parameters. An attempt to overcome this shortcoming of the traditional applications is the Minimal Resource Allocation Network (MRAN). MRAN is on-line adaptive method which automatically configures the number of hidden nodes based on the input-output patterns presented to the network. This research addresses determining the user-defined parameters prior to the model run. The research also compares MRAN results from two applications, and discusses a pathway towards designing a fully automated MRAN.

2161 *Wavelet Networks: An Alternative to Classical Neural Networks [#1727]*
Kamban Parasuraman and Amin Elshorbagy, University of Saskatchewan, Canada

Artificial Neural Networks (ANNs) are being widely used to predict and forecast highly nonlinear systems. Recently, Wavelet Networks (WNs) have been shown to be a promising alternative to traditional neural networks. In this study, the robustness of WNs and ANNs in modeling two distinct time series is investigated. The first series represents a chaotic system (Henon map) and the second series represents a stochastic geophysical time-series (streamflows). Results from the study indicate that, WNs are more suitable for modeling short- time high-frequency time series like Henon map. However, performance of WNs is comparable with that of ANNs in modeling low-frequency time series like streamflows.

2162 *Streamflow Forecasting with Uncertainty Estimate Using Bayesian Learning for ANN [#1433]*
Mohammad Khan and Paulin Coulibaly, McMaster University, Canada

Bayesian learning approach is introduced for artificial neural network (ANN) modeling of daily streamflows. In the Bayesian approach, an optimum distribution of the parameters of a network is obtained, and a predictive distribution of the network outputs is created integrating over that parameter space. The Bayesian learning is implemented with a multilayer perceptron (MLP). The proposed model results are compared with those obtained from a MLP trained with a standard method. Overall, the model validation statistics and hydrograph analysis indicate that the Bayesian approach outperforms the standard ANN learing approach. Moreover, the Bayesian approach provides uncertainty estimates of the predicted flows in the form of confidence interval.

2163 *Intelligent systems for meteorological events forecast [#1420]*
Eros Pasero, Walter Moniaci and Tassilo Meindl, Polytechnic of Turin, Italy

In this paper a committee of "intelligent systems" evaluates the occurrence of meteorological phenomena. Rain and fog are the events which are considered. The forecast system is based on a multi-network approach which evaluates data coming from electronic sensors and from satellite observations. More data and more engines are used to increase the reliability of the event prediction. The increased complexity of the global system requires more data coming from different sources but gives a good reliability. This artcle is for special session:"Application of adaptive learning methods in Earth Sciences and Climate Modeling"

2164 *A multilayer perceptron approach for the retrieval of vertical temperature profiles from satellite radiation data [#1692]*
Elcio Hideiti Shiguemori, Jose Demisio Simoes da Silva, Haroldo Fraga Campos Velho and Joao Carlos Carvalho, National Institute for Space Research - INPE, Brazil

In this paper a multilayer perceptron neural network is used to retrieve vertical atmospheric temperature profiles from satellite radiation data. The training set consists of data provided by the direct model characterized by the Radiative Transfer Equation (RTE) and by real radiation data from the NOAA - HIRS/2 (High Resolution Infrared Radiation) Sounder. The retrieved vertical temperature profiles are compared to radiosonde measured data. The neural network performance is compared to the results of [1] and [2] who used regularization techniques. Neural network approaches are especially advantageous due to the embed parallelism that may imply in faster vertical temperature profiles retrieving systems.

2165 *Machine Learning in Soil Classification [#1358]*
Biswa Bhattacharya and Dimitri P. Solomatine, UNESCO-IHE Institute for Water Education, Delft, Netherlands

In geotechnics, petroleum engineering, etc., intervals of measured series data (signals) are to be attributed a class maintaining the constraint of contiguity. Classification in this case needs an expert. The paper presents an approach to automate this classification procedure. Firstly, a segmentation algorithm is applied to segment the measured signals. Secondly, the salient features of these segments are extracted using boundary energy method. Based on the measured data and extracted features classifiers using Decision Trees, ANNs and Support Vector Machines are built. The methodology was tested for classifying sub-surface soil using measured data from Cone Penetration Testing and satisfactory results were obtained.

2166 *Estimation of Prediction Intervals for the Model Outputs using Machine Learning [#1390]*
D. L. Shrestha and Dimitri P. Solomatine, UNESCO-IHE Institute for Water Education, Netherlands; UNESCO-IHE Institute for Water Education, Delft, Netherlands

A new method for estimating prediction intervals for a model output using machine learning is presented. In it, first the prediction intervals for in-sample data using clustering techniques to identify the distinguishable regions in input space with similar distributions of model errors are constructed. Then regression model is built for in-sample data using computed prediction intervals as targets, and, finally, this model is applied to estimate the prediction intervals for out-of-sample data. The method was tested on artificial and real hydrologic data sets using various machine learning techniques. Preliminary results show that the method is superior to other methods estimating the prediction intervals.

Plenary Poster Session: Earth Sciences and Climate modelling
Tuesday, August 2, 7:00PM-11:00PM, Room: Fountaine, Chair: Program Chairs

2167 *Determination of optimal batch size in incremental approach for tornado detection [#1576]*
Hyung-Jin Son, Theodore B. Trafalis and Michael B. Richman, IE, The University of Oklahoma, United States; University of Oklahoma, United States; Meteorology, The University of Oklahoma, United States

Computing time and memory space limitations in applying support vector machines (SVMs) for large-scale problems are recognized as critical limiting factors. Incremental approaches have serve as a remedy for large-scale problems. However, determination of the appropriate batch size for incremental approaches has been explored rarely. In this study, the optimal batch size is defined as tradeoff between computing time and generalization error rate. Experiments for the determination of the optimal batch size, based on the mixture ratio of tornado and non-tornado data and a comparison between fixed batch size and knowledge-based batch size, are performed.

2168 *Locally Recurrent Neural Networks Optimal Filtering Algorithms: Application to Wind Speed Prediction Using Spatial Correlation [#1132]*
Thanasis Barbounis and John Theocharis, Aristotle University of Thessaloniki, Greece

This paper focuses on a locally recurrent multilayer network with internal feedback paths, the IIR-MLP. The computation of the partial derivatives of the network's output with respect to its trainable weights is achieved using backpropagation through adjoints and a second order global recursive prediction error (GRPE) training algorithm is developed. Also, a local version of the GRPE is presented in order to cope with the increased computational burden of the global version. The efficiency of the proposed learning schemes, as compared to conventional gradient-based methods, is tested on the wind prediction problem from 15 min to 3 h ahead on a site, using spatial correlation and facilitating measurements from nearby sites up to 40 km away.

Wednesday, August 3, 8:00AM-9:00AM

Plenary Talk: Neural Networks for Feedback Control of Robots and Dynamical Systems
Wednesday, August 3, 8:00AM-9:00AM, Room: Westmount/Outremount, Speaker: Frank Lewis, The University of Texas at Arlington, United States

Practical industrial, robotic, and aerospace systems have unknown disturbances, unmodeled dynamics, actuator constraints, friction, and restricted availability of measurements. Such systems cannot easily be dealt with using standard adaptive or robust feedback control techniques. Over the past years we have developed a family of feedback controllers that can confront these systems using neural networks as the basic control block structure. The learning abilities of neural networks considered as Intelligent Systems allow these controllers to learn on-line and improve their performance through tuning of the weights. We will present a catalog of neural network controllers designed based on feedback linearization, backstepping, singular perturbations, and dynamic inversion techniques. These neural network controllers are all tuned on-line in real time based on the system errors. Then, we will present some recent results on H-infinity feedback control for constrained input nonlinear systems. The constraints on the input to the system are encoded via a quasi-norm that allows non-quadratic supply rates along with dissipativity theory to formulate the robust output feedback control problem using Hamilton-Jacobi-Isaac (HJI) equations. An iterative solution technique based on a game theoretic interpretation is presented. To provide a computationally tractable controller design method, the solution is approximated at each iteration with a neural network. The result is a closed-loop control based on a neural net that has been tuned a priori off-line.

Wednesday, August 3, 9:30AM-11:30AM

Data Mining
Wednesday, August 3, 9:30AM-11:30AM, Room: Verdun/Lachine, Chair: Antony Satyadas

9:30AM *Automatic Source Attribution: A Neural Networks Approach [#1208]*
Foaad Khosmood and Franz Kurfess, California Polytechnic State University, United States

Much of the work in the area of authorship attribution does remain in the realm of statistics best suited for human assistance rather than autonomous attribution. While there have been attempts at using neural networks in the area in the past, they have been extremely limited and problem-specific. This paper addresses the latter points by demonstrating a practical and truly autonomous attribution process using neural networks. Furthermore, we use a common-word-frequency classification technique to demonstrate the feasibility of this process in particular and the applications of neural networks to text analysis in general.

9:50AM *Cross-Entropy Approach to Data Visualization Based on the Neural Gas Network [#1585]*
Pablo A. Estevez, Cristian J. Figueroa and Kazumi Saito, Dept. Electrical Engineering, U. of Chile, Chile; NTT Communication Science Laboratories, Japan

A new approach to mapping high-dimensional data into a low-dimensional space embedding is presented. The aim of this approach is to project simultaneously the input data and the codebook vectors into a low-dimensional output space, preserving the local neighborhood. The Neural Gas algorithm is used to obtain codebook vectors. A cost function based on the cross-entropy (CE) between input and output probabilities is minimized by using a Newton-Raphson method. The new approach is compared with multidimensional scaling (MDS) using benchmark and real-world data sets. In comparison with MDS, our method delivers a clear visualization of both data points and codebooks, and better CE and topology preservation measurements.

10:10AM *A Model of Document Clustering Using Ant Colony Algorithm and Validity Index [#1732]*
Yan Yang, Mohamed Kamel and Fan Jin, Southwest Jiaotong University, China; University of Waterloo, Canada

This paper discusses document clustering using ant colony algorithm and validity index. Clusterings are formed on the plane by ants walking, picking up or dropping down projected document vectors with different probability. The proposed model uses a clustering validity index not only to evaluate the performance of the algorithm, but also to find the optimal number of clusters and reduce outliers. Experiments on data from the Reuters-21578 collection show that the proposed model has better performance than that of LF algorithm and ART neural networks.

10:30AM *A method to extract Non-Linear Principal Components of Large Datasets - An application in Skill Transfer [#1508]*
Silvia Botelho, Rodrigo de Bem, Mateus Figueiredo, Willian Lautenschlager and Centeno Tania, Furg, Brazil; Cefetpr, Brazil

This article presents a methodology to extract principal components of large datasets, called C-NLPCA (Cascaded nonlinear principal component analysis), and evaluates its use in the extraction of main human movements in image series, aiming for the development of methodologies and techniques for skill transfer from humans to robotic/virtual agents. Aiming for the validation of the method a human moving hand test is presented, where C-NLPCA is applied and the patterns of the obtained movements are confronted with traditional linear techniques.

10:50AM *Identifying knowledge domain and incremental new class learning in SVM [#1447]*
HongBin Jia, Yi Murphey, Daniel Gutchess and Tzyy-Shuh Chang, University of Michigan-Dearborn, United States; OG Technologies, Inc, United States

An incremental class learning system for support vector machine (SVM) is presented for learning new knowledge from newly available data without forgetting the existing knowledge. We present algorithms for knowledge domain description, new knowledge detection, and incremental learning of new class knowledge. We have applied the incremental learning system to a data set provided by the UCI machine learning website, and the results show that the proposed SVM incremental class learning system is quite effective.

11:10AM *Real-World Text Clustering with Adaptive Resonance Theory Neural Networks [#1028]*
Louis Massey, Royal Military College, Canada

Most work on document clustering has focused on batch processing in a static environment. For real-world applications, on-line and incremental processing of highly dynamic data is required. Adaptive Resonance Theory (ART) neural networks possess several interesting properties that make them appealing as a potential solution to this problem. In this paper, we present experimental results that examine ART text clustering under several situations characteristic of real-life applications. We also compare our present results with work we have conducted previously on the batch static case, hence determining how clustering quality is affected by incremental processing.

Special Session: Hebb's Legacy
Wednesday, August 3, 9:30AM-11:30AM, Room: Mt Royal/Hampstead, Chair: Jean-Philippe Thivierge

9:30AM *Hebbian Synaptic Modification in Cortical Circuits and Memory-Guided Behavior in Spatial Alternation and Delayed Non-Match to Position [#1713]*
Michael E. Hasselmo and Eric Zilli, Dept. of Psychology, Boston University, United States; Boston University, United States

Physiological data demonstrates Hebbian synaptic plasticity within the hippocampus. This paper presents a model demonstrating how Hebbian synaptic modification could mediate encoding to allow context- dependent retrieval of episodes necessary for memory guided behavior in specific tasks. The model links the behavioral function of Hebbian synaptic modification to physiological data on theta rhythm oscillations and neuronal spike firing in the hippocampus, including 1.) context-sensitivity of neuronal firing ("splitter cells") during spatial alternation, 2.) theta phase precession of place cells, and 3.) changes in theta phase precession across different trials on the same day.

10:00AM *Faithful Retinotopic Maps with Local Optimum Rules, Axonal Competition, and Hebbian Learning [#1491]*
Jean-Philippe Thivierge and Evan Balaban, McGill University, Canada

Innervation of the visual midbrain by axons from the retina can be described as a stochastic mapping process that maintains topography and polarity between the two regions. Previous work has identified a number of mechanisms that insure proper guidance of the axons. In the current report, we combine three of these mechanisms, servomechanical guidance with local optimum rules, axonal competition, and Hebbian plasticity. Although each of these separate processes are stochastic and therefore subject to imprecision, their combination guides growth cones to precise termination points.

10:30AM *Modeling Structural Plasticity in the Barn Owl Auditory Localization System with a Spike-Time Dependent Hebbian Learning Rule [#1484]*
Shreesh Mysore and Steven Quartz, California Institute of Technology, United States

Auditory localization behavior in barn owls is mediated by the integration of topographically encoded visual and auditory space maps. In juvenile owls, disruption of this alignment between auditory and spatial representations by exposure to spectacles that laterally shift the visual field of view results in behavioral adaptation over the course of several weeks. It has been reported in literature that this adaptation is produced by structural plasticity in the neural circuits encoding the space maps. In this work, we demonstrate that a Hebbian spike-time dependent learning rule, coupled with an activity-dependent mechanism that induces growth, can account for the essentials of circuit-level plasticity associated with prism experience.

11:00AM *Hebbian motor control in a robot-embedded model of habituation [#1514]*
Sylvain Sirois, The University of Manchester, United Kingdom

Experiments using a mobile robot examine the performance of a neural network model of habituation. Input to the network is the video feed from the robot's camera, processed to model the visual system. Images, after retinal processing, are translated in the frequency domain and Gabor-filtered. Output of the network controls the robot's motors, thus where it looks. In a condition, network output directly controls motors. In a second condition, network outputs are connected to control units via weights modified with simple hebbian learning. In both cases, robot behavior reproduces the important familiarity-to-novelty shift observed in human infants. Hebbian learning, however, helps to increase and stabilize novelty preference.

Robotics
Wednesday, August 3, 9:30AM-11:30AM, Room: Westmount, Chair: Dario Floreano

9:30AM *Constraints on Body Movement during Visual Development Affect Behavior of Evolutionary Robots [#1722]*
Mototaka Suzuki, Dario Floreano and Ezequiel Di Paolo, Swiss Federal Institute of Technology (EPFL), Switzerland; University of Sussex, England

We explore the role of active body movement in the developmental process of the visual system. Receptive fields of an evolved mobile robot are developed during active or passive movement with the generalized Hebbian algorithm (Sanger, 1989). In accordance to experimental observations of kitten, we show that the receptive fields and behavior of the robot developed under active condition significantly differ from those developed under passive condition. A possible explanation of this difference is derived by correlating receptive field formation and behavioral performance in the two conditions.

9:50AM *Dual Kalman Filters for Autonomous Terrain Aided Navigation in Unknown Environments [#1579]*
Anindya Paul and Eric Wan, OGI school of Science and Engineering, OHSU, United States

We address a method for terrain aided navigation of unmanned vehicles in unknown environments. The task is to simultaneously estimate the state of the vehicle (position and attitude) and a map of the surrounding environment. Possible available sensors include an inertial measurement unit and other simple "terrain sensors". This problem is widely known as Simultaneous Localization and Mapping (SLAM). A dual Kalman filter framework is proposed that works by alternating between using one filter to localize the vehicle and a second filter to update the estimate of the map. Results are generated for a simulated environment comparing the Extended Kalman filter (EKF) and Sigma Point Kalman filter (SPKF) based implementations.

10:10AM *New Memory Model for Humanoid Robots - Introduction of Co-Associative Memory Using Mutually Coupled Chaotic Neural Networks- [#1474]*
Kazuko Itoh, Hiroyasu Miwa, Yuko Nukariya, Massimiliano Zecca, Hideaki Takanobu, Paolo Dario and Atsuo Takanishi, Waseda University, Japan; Scuola Superiore Sant'Anna, RoboCasa, Italy; Kogakuin University, HRI, Japan; Scuola Superiore Sant'Anna, Italy; Waseda University, HRI, RoboCasa, Japan

We have been developing new mechanisms and functions for a humanoid robot that has the ability to express emotions and to communicate with humans in a human- like manner. In 2004, we introduced the "Behavior Model" and "Consciousness Model" to the robot mental model. However, the robot could generate one behavior to a stimulus. In this paper, we proposed an associative memory model using mutually coupled chaotic neural networks for generating an optimum behavior to a stimulus. We implemented this model in the Emotional Expression Humanoid Robot WE-4RII (Waseda Eye No.4 Refined II).

10:30AM *Bi-Criteria Torque Optimization of Redundant Manipulators Based on a Simplified Dual Neural Network [#1164]*
Shubao Liu and Jun Wang, Chinese University of Hong Kong, Hong Kong

The bi-criteria joint torque optimization of kinematically redundant manipulators balances between the energy consumption and the torque distribution among the joints. In this paper, a simplified dual neural network is proposed to solve this problem. Joint torque limits are incorporated simultaneously into the proposed optimization scheme. The simplified dual network has a simple architecture compared with other recurrent neural networks and is proved to be globally convergent to optimal solutions. The control scheme based on the recurrent neural network is simulated with the PUMA 560 robot manipulator to demonstrate effectiveness.

10:50AM *Spatio-Temporal Neural Data Mining Architecture in Learning Robots [#1441]*
James Malone, Mark Elshaw, Ken McGarry, Chris Bowerman and Stefan Wermter, University of Sunderland, United Kingdom

There has been little research into the use of hybrid neural data mining to improve robot performance or enhance their capability. This paper presents a novel neural data mining technique that analyses robot sensor data for imitation learning. Learning by imitation allows a robot to learn from observing either another robot or a human to gain skills, understand the behaviour of others and create solutions to problems. We demonstrate a hybrid approach of differential ratio data mining to perform analysis on spatio-temporal robot behavioural data. The technique offers classification performance gains for recognition of robot actions by highlighting points of variance and hence interest within the data.

11:10AM *Fault-tolerance by Regeneration: Using Development to Achieve Robust Self-Healing Neural Networks [#1213]*
Diego Federici, NTNU - norwegian university of technology and sc, Norway

Opposed to the standard paradigm of fault-tolerance by redundancy, ontogeny offers the possibility to engineer artificial organisms which can re-grow faulty components. In this paper we present a system which evolves developing spiking neural networks capable of controlling Khepera robots in a wall avoidance task. To test the system's self-healing capability, networks are subjected to random faults during development and mutilated during operation. Results demonstrate how development can rapidly produce proper neuro-controllers and re-grow neurons to recover normal operation. These results show that development, originally proposed to increase the evolvability of large phenotypes, also allows the achievement of sustained fault-tolerance.

SVM II
Wednesday, August 3, 9:30AM-11:30AM, Room: Outremount, Chair: Theodore Trafalis

9:30AM *Maximal Variation and Missing Values for Componentwise Support Vector Machines [#1487]*
Kristiaan Pelckmans, Jos De Brabanter, Johan A. K. Suykens and Bart De Moor, KULeuven - ESAT - SCD/SISTA, Belgium; KaHo Sint Lieven, Belgium; Katholieke Universiteit Leuven, ESAT-SCD-SISTA, Belgium

This paper proposes primal-dual kernel machine classifiers based on worst-case analysis of a finite set of observations including missing values of the inputs. Key ingredients are the use of a componentwise Support Vector Machine (cSVM) and an empirical measure of maximal variation of the components to bound the influence of the component which can not be evaluated due to missing values. A regularization term based on the L_1 norm of the maximal variation is used to obtain a mechanism for structure detection in that context. An efficient implemtation using the hierarchical kernel machines framework is elaborated.

9:50AM *Fast Bayesian Support Vector Machine Parameter Tuning with the Nystrom Method [#1537]*
Carl Gold and Peter Sollich, California Institute of Technology, United States; King's College London, United Kingdom

We experiment with speeding up a Bayesian method for tuning the hyperparameters of a Support Vector Machine (SVM) classifier. The Bayesian approach gives the gradients of the evidence as averages over the posterior, which can be approximated using Hybrid Monte Carlo simulation (HMC). By using the Nystrom approximation to the SVM kernel, our method reduces the dimensionality of the space to be simulated in the HMC. This speeds up the running time of the HMC simulation from $O(n^2)$ to effectively $O(n)$. The Nystrom approximation has an almost insignificant effect on the performance of the algorithm when compared to the full Bayesian method, and gives excellent performance in comparison with other approaches to hyperparameter tuning.

10:10AM *Maximum Margin Classifiers with Noisy Data: A Robust Optimization [#1202]*
Theodore B. Trafalis and Robin Gilbert, University of Oklahoma, United States

In this paper, we investigate the theoretical aspects of robust classification using support vector machines. Given training data (x_1,y_1), ..., (x_l,y_l), where l represents the number of samples, $x\_i\in\mathbb{R}^n$ and $y\_i\in\{-1,1\}$, we investigate the training of a support vector machine in the case where bounded perturbation is added to the value of the input $\ve{x}\_i\in\mathbb{R}^n$. We consider both cases where our training data are either linearly separable and non linearly separable respectively. We show that we can perform robust classification by using linear or second order cone programming.

10:30AM *Data Classification with a Relaxed Model of Variable Kernel Density Estimation [#1451]*
Yen-Jen Oyang, Yu-Yen Ou, Shien-Ching Hwang, Chien-Yu Chen and Darby Tien-Hau Chang, CSIE, National Taiwan University, Taiwan; Yuan Ze University, Taiwan

This paper proposes a relaxed model of the variable ker-nel density estimation and analyzes its performance in data classification applications. It is proved in this pa-per that, in terms of pointwise MSE, the convergence rate of the relaxed variable kernel density estimator can approach O(1/n) regardless of the dimension of the data set, where n is the number of samples. Experiments with the data classification applications have shown that the data classifier constructed based on the relaxed vari-able kernel density estimator is capable of delivering the same level of prediction accuracy as the SVM with the Gaussian kernel.

10:50AM *A Ridgelet Kernel Approach for Regression using Particle Swarm Optimization Algorithm [#1238]*
Shuyuan Yang, Min Wang and Licheng Jiao, Institute of Intelligence Information Processing, China; National Lab of Radar Signal Processing, China; Xidian University, China

In this paper, a ridgelet kernel approach is proposed for approximation of multivariate functions, especially those with certain kinds of spatial inhomogeneities. It is based on ridgelet theory, kernel and regularization technology from which we can deduce a regularized kernel regression form. Taking the objective function solved by quadratic programming to define a fitness function, we use particle swarm optimization algorithm to optimize the directions of ridgelets. Experiments in the tasks of regression prove its efficiency.

Wednesday, August 3, 1:00PM-3:00PM

Hardware
Wednesday, August 3, 1:00PM-3:00PM, Room: Westmount, Chair: Valeriu Beiu

1:00PM *Ultra Low Power Fault Tolerant Neural Inspired CMOS logic [#1636]*
Snorre Aunet and Valeriu Beiu, Department of of Informatics, University of Oslo, Norway; Washington State University, United States

We present a new defect/fault tolerant ultra low power CMOS circuit solution exploiting low level redundancy. We show that wiring and transistors may be damaged while the functionality is still kept. We also demonstrate a new full adder based on the basic building block, capable of sub fJ PDP for supply voltages below 100 mV, in a 120 nm process. Transistors are exploited as four terminal devices operating in subthreshold and a threshold element (perceptron) is demonstrated by chip measurements.

1:20PM *Noise Performance of Single-Electron Depressing Synapses for Neuronal Synchrony Detection [#1361]*
Takahide Oya, Tetsuya Asai, Ryo Kagaya and Yoshihito Amemiya, Hokkaido University, Japan

Synchrony detection between burst and non-burst spikes is known to be one functional example of depressing synapses. Kanazawa et al. demonstrated synchrony detection with MOS depressing synapse circuits. They found that the performance of a network with depressing synapses that discriminates between burst and random input spikes increases nonmonotonically as the static device mismatch is increased. We designed a single-electron depressing synapse and constructed the same network as in Kanazawa's study to develop noisetolerant single-electron circuits. We examined the temperature characteristics and explored possible architecture that enables single electron circuits to operate at T > 0 K.

1:40PM *A New Pulse Mode Self Organizing Map Hardware with Digital Phase Locked Loops [#1356]*
Hiroomi Hikawa, Oita University, Japan

The self-organizing map (SOM) has found applicability in a wide range of application areas. This paper proposes a new SOM hardware with phase modulated pulse signal and digital phase-locked loops (DPLLs). The system uses the DPLL as a computing element because the operation of the DPLL is very similar to that of SOM's computation. The system also uses square waveform phase to hold the value of the each input vector element. The proposed SOM architecture is described in VHDL and its feasibility is verified by simulation. Results show that the proposed SOM has good quantization capability.

2:00PM *A novel Approach to reduce Interconnect Complexity in ANN Hardware Implementation [#1073]*
Luiz Brunelli, Elmar U. K. Melcher, Alisson V. de Brito and Raimundo C. S. Freire, Universidade Federal de Campina Grande, Brazil; Universidade Federal de Campina Grande, Brazil

Hardware implementation of large digital artificial neural networks is limited by several constraints, such as the complexity of neural interconnections.This paper presents a novel approach to solve the interconnection problem for artificial neural networks, using reconfigurable computing and dynamically reconfigured FPGAs in a new computational way: the Execution Patterns (EPs). The EPs allow to reduce the influence of interconnections through the removal of data transport via busses.Thus data transport is not necessary to perform the computation and interconnection complexity between neurons is reduced.

2:20PM *A Reconfigurable Parallel Architecture for SVM Classification [#1212]*
Ivan Biasi, Andrea Boni and Alessandro Zorat, DIT - University of Trento, Italy; DIT - University of Trento, Italy

The availability of powerful Field Programmable Gate Arrays (FPGA) has been exploited for their ability to provide hardware solutions for many application areas, resulting in high-performance systems that can operate in real time by operating in parallel. The Support Vector Machine computational paradigm can be cast as a collection of multiple streams operating in parallel on one such FPGA. This paper presents a parallel architecture that implements an SVM on a Xilinx FPGA. The results obtained by using this architecture for a complex pattern classification from high-energy physics involving thousands of patterns are also reported and discussed.

Cognitive Function
Wednesday, August 3, 1:00PM-3:00PM, Room: Mt Royal/Hampstead, Chair: Michael E. Hasselmo

1:00PM *An Integrate and Fire Model of Prefrontal Cortex provides a Biological Implementation of Action Selection in Reinforcement Learning Theory that Reuses Known Representations [#1143]*
Randal Koene and Michael E. Hasselmo, Boston University, United States; Dept. of Psychology, Boston University, United States

Task specific spiking activity that is selective for specific perceptions and actions is observed in the prefrontal cortex (PFC) of primates and rats during goal-directed behavior. A spiking neuron model of minicolumn circuits in PFC has been shown to successfully replicate the performance and categories of selective neuronal responses recorded in a primate visual discrimination task. The model provides a biological implementation of the action selection process used in reinforcement learning theory. Using this model, we propose a mechanistic explanation based on the reuse of previous encoding in PFC minicolumns for the ability to find short-cuts during the learning of some novel goal-directed tasks, but not others.

1:20PM *Knowing your place: Subfield specific involvement in hippocampal spatial processing [#1269]*
Matthew Hartley, Neill Taylor and John Taylor, King's College London, United Kingdom

Spatial navagation is a critical part of animal behaviour. Experimental data show that some cells in the hippocampus of animals engaged in exploration respond preferentially to particular physical locations. These place cells give us an important indication of hippocampal participation in spatial processing. Recent work has examined differences in place field representations between hippocampal subfields. We discuss these findings and show, using a computational model, how known aspects of hippocampal physiology can explain these differences.

1:40PM *Coherent learning in cortical maps: A generic approach [#1486]*
Olivier Menard and Herve Frezza-Buet, Loria, Supelec, France; Supelec, France

This paper presents a computational model inspired from the cortex organization that defines coherent learning in multiple cortical maps, in order to perform multi-modal coordination. The joint self-organization of the maps is described as a process allowing to deal with multi-modal information within cooperative distributed modules. The very purpose of this approach is the design of a generic distributed architecture for robotic servo-control from a functional view of the cortical information processing.

2:00PM *Using Neural Dynamics to Switch Attention [#1438]*
Julien Vitay and Nicolas Rougier, Loria, France

We present a distributed and dynamic model of visual attention based on the Continuum Neural Field Theory that allows to sequentially focus salient locations in an image. A working memory system ensures that the corresponding objects are only focused once, even if they are moving around, such that the visual search is efficient. The model has been implemented on a robotic platform in order to search for natural objects such as fruits.

2:20PM *A Continuous Attractor Neural Network Model of Divided Visual Attention [#1505]*
Dominic Standage, Thomas Trappenberg and Raymond Klein, Dalhousie University, Canada

The biologically realistic model of selective visual attention by Deco et al uses a continuous attractor neural network to simulate a saliency map in posterior parietal cortex. We test the ability of the model to explain experimental evidence on the distribution of spatial attention. The majority of evidence supports the view that attention is a unitary construct, but recent experiments provide evidence for split attentional foci. We simulate two such experiments. Our results suggest that the ability to divide attention depends on sustained endogenous signals from short term memory to the saliency map, stressing the interplay between working memory mechanisms and attention.

2:40PM *Bridging the Gap Between Vision and Language: A Morphodynamical Model of Spatial Categories [#1276]*
Rene Doursat and Jean Petitot, University of Nevada, Reno, United States; Ecole Polytechnique, France

We propose a spiking neural network for mapping the infinity of schematic visual scenes to a small set of semantic symbols. According to cognitive linguistics, spatial prepositions such as 'in' or 'above' are neutral toward the shape and size of objects. We suggest that they correspond to morphodynamical transforms erasing details and creating virtual structures (boundaries, skeleton). These singularities arise from a large-scale lattice of coupled excitable units exhibiting pattern formation through spatiotemporal order, especially traveling waves. Our model addresses the fundamental cognitive mechanisms of spatial schematization and categorization, which mediate vision and language and are crucial in designing intelligent systems.

Special Session: Performance of Neuro-Adaptive and Learning Systems: Assessment, Monitoring, and Validation
Wednesday, August 3, 1:00PM-3:00PM, Room: Outremount, Chair: Pramod Gupta

1:00PM *Challenges in verification and validation of autonomous systems for space exploration [#1591]*
Guillaume Brat and Ari Jonsson, Riacs/Usra, United States

Space exploration applications offer a unique opportunity for the development and deployment of autonomous systems, due to limited communications and large distances. However, the risk and cost of space missions leads to reluctance to taking on new and complex technology. A key issue in addressing these concerns is the validation of autonomous systems. Recently, higher-level autonomous systems have been applied in space applications. In this presentation, we will highlight those autonomous systems, and discuss issues in validating these systems. We will then look to future demands on validating autonomous systems for space, identify promising technologies and open issues.

1:20PM *Rule Extraction as a Formal Method for the Verification and Validation of Neural Networks [#1464]*
Brian Taylor and Marjorie Darrah, Institute for Scientific Research, Inc., United States

The term formal method refers to the use of techniques from formal logic and discrete math in the specification, design, and construction of computer systems and software. These techniques enable the formalization of software for development and testing so that it may be verified and validated in a more thorough way. Although not specifically identified in the literature as a verification and validation (V and V) formal method technique, neural network rule extraction fits the basic definition by using techniques from formal logic to formalize neural network software so that it may be examined more completely. This paper identifies several areas where rule extraction can be an effective tool for the V and V of neural networks.

1:40PM *An Approach To Predicting Non-Deterministic Neural Network Behavior [#1527]*
Edgar Fuller, Sampath Yerramalla, Bojan Cukic and Srikanth Gururajan, Department of Mathematics, WVU, United States; West Virginia University, United States

This paper describes a methodology for generating indicators of performance for the Dynamic Cell Structures neural network, a type of growing self-organizing map. The performance indicators are based on the learning architecture of the neural network and are validated using correlation measures of Murphy's rule. Time estimates for neural network convergence are generated based on the current data conditions and the confidence in the neural network, which is provided by the performance indicators. Analytical and experimental results are presented for the Dynamic Cell Structures neural network during its training from the Carnegie Mellon University two-spirals benchmark data.

2:00PM *Testing Decision Systems with Classification Components [#1642]*
Dragos Margineantu, Michael Drumheller and Roman Fresnedo, The Boeing Company, United States

Many decision tools employ learning to improve the quality of their output. In order to employ these tools and systems in high- or medium-risk applications the design, implementation, and deployment process needs to follow principled verification, validation, and testing procedures that assure a reliable operation. This task is far from being trivial because of the very nature of learning. Only little research efforts have been dedicated so far to validating and testing learning-based systems. This paper describes a laboratory for the testing and the validation of learning systems and a set of statistical tests that are employed by this tool for the assessment of learned classification decisions.

2:20PM *Validity Index in Dynamic Cell Structures [#1625]*
Yan Liu, Bojan Cukic, Sampath Yerramalla and Srikanth Gururajan, West Virginia University, United States

The appeal of including adaptive components in flight control applications is in their ability to cope with a changing environment. The Dynamic Cell Structure (DCS) network is a dynamically growing structure designed to achieve better adaptability. It is employed for online learning of the Intelligent Flight Control System (IFCS). The predictions of DCS networks are hard to validate due to the locally poor fitting during a relatively short period of learning. We present the validity index, an estimated confidence interval associated with each DCS output, as a reliability-like measure of the network's prediction performance. Experimental results of validity index on the IFCS demonstrate an effective validation scheme for DCS networks.

2:40PM *A Disturbance Rejection based Neural Network Algorithm for Control of Air Pollution Emissions [#1199]*
Steve Piche and Paul Sabiston, Pegasus Technologies, United States; Pavilion Technologies, United States

A novel neural network algorithm for training a model of a nonlinear systems that is significantly affected by unmeasured disturbances is presented. In this paper, the algorithm is used to develop a model of nitrogen oxides (NOx) emitted from a coal-fired, power plant. The NOx emissions are affected by unmeasured disturbances such as those caused by changes in fuel characteristics and ambient conditions. The resulting NOx model is subsequently used in a control system for reduction of NOx emissions, therefore, increased accuracy of the model leads to improved verification and validation of the control system. Two examples illustrate that the resulting model provides a better prediction of NOx emitted from coal fired, power plants.

Special Session: Constructive/Hierarchical Self-Organizing Maps
Wednesday, August 3, 1:00PM-3:00PM, Room: Verdun/Lachine, Chair: Ernesto Cuadros-Vargas and Roseli A. Francelin Romero

1:00PM *A Gradient Descending Solution to the LASSO Criteria [#1649]*
Nan Zhang and Shuqing Zeng, Michigan State University, United States

In this paper, we propose a new perspective to achieve sparseness via the winner-take-all principle for the linear kernel regression and classification task. We form the duality of the LASSO criteria, and transfer an L1 norm minimization to an L_inf norm maximization problem. We introduce a novel winner-take-all neural network solution derived from gradient descending, which links the sparse representation and the competitive learning scheme. This scheme is a form of unsupervised learning in which each input pattern comes through learning, to be associated with the activity of one or at most a few neurons. However, the lateral interaction between neurons in the same layer is strictly preemptive in this model.

1:20PM *A Constructive and Hierarchical Self-Organising Model in A Non-Stationary Environment [#1204]*
Chihli Hung and Stefan Wermter, De Lin Institute of Technology, Taiwan; University of Sunderland, United Kingdom

Several neural models have been proposed to enhance the flexibility of self-organising maps in a non-stationary environment. These models predefine several thresholds which are used as guidance of neural behaviours for specific data sets. However, when a proper threshold has been determined, this threshold may not be suitable for the future. We compare the dynamic adaptive self-organising hybrid (DASH) model with the growing neural gas model by introducing several different initial thresholds to test their feasibility. Our experiments show that the DASH model is more stable and practicable in a non-stationary environment since DASH adjusts its behaviour not only by modifying its parameters but also by an adaptive structure.

1:40PM *Investigation of Alternative Strategies and Quality Measures for Controlling the Growth Process of the Growing Hierarchical Self-Organizing Map [#1545]*
Michael Dittenbach, Andreas Rauber and Georg Poelzlbauer, eCommerce Competence Center - ec3, Austria; Vienna University of Technology, Austria

The Growing Hierarchical Self-Organizing Map (GHSOM) is a neural network architecture combining the advantages of two principal extension of the Self-Organizing Map, dynamic growth and hierarchical structure. So far, the quantization error has been used as a measure to automatically guide the growth process of the architecture, both in terms of map and hierarchical growth. In this paper we investigate alternative SOM quality measures as well as en enhanced growth strategy for their suitability to be used for controlling the growth process of the GHSOM. We report on their effects on the structure of the architecture by comparing the characteristics of trained GHSOMs using an artificial data set.

2:00PM *A hierarchical hybrid neural model with time integrators in long-term peak-load forecasting [#1172]*
Otavio Carpinteiro, Rafael Leme, Antonio Zambroni de Souza and Paulo Quintanilha Filho, Federal University of Itajuba, Brazil

A novel hierarchical hybrid neural model to the problem of long-term peak-load forecasting is proposed in this paper. The neural model is made up of two self-organizing map nets --- one on top of the other ---, and a single-layer perceptron. It has application into domains in which the context information given by former events plays a primary role. The model is compared to a multilayer perceptron. Both the hierarchical and the multilayer perceptron models are trained and assessed on load data extracted from a North-American electric utility. They are required to predict either once every week or once every month the electric peak-load during the next two years. The results are presented and evaluated in the paper.

2:20PM *Introduction to the SAM-SOM* and MAM-SOM* Families [#1282]*
Ernesto Cuadros-Vargas and Roseli Francelin, Peruvian Computer Society, Peru; University of Sao Paulo, Brazil

In this paper, two new families of constructive \ac{SOM} \SAMSOMStar and \MAMSOMStar are proposed. These families are generated by incorporating \ac{SAM} and \ac{MAM} into \ac{SOM} with the maximum insertion rate, i.e. the case when a new unit is created for each pattern presented. It creates networks with quite different properties when compared with traditional SOMs.

Wednesday, August 3, 3:20PM-5:20PM

Special Session: Approximate Dynamic Programming
Wednesday, August 3, 3:20PM-5:20PM, Room: Westmount, Chair: George Lendaris

3:20PM *Reinforcement Learning and the Frame Problem [#1659]*
Roberto Santiago and George Lendaris, NWCIL, Portland State University, United States

The Frame Problem, originally proposed within AI, has grown to be a fundamental stumbling block for building intelligent agents and modeling the mind. The source of the frame problem stems from the nature of symbolic processing. Unfortunately, connectionist approaches have long been criticized as having weaker representational capabilities than symbolic systems so have not been considered by many. The equivalence between the representational power of symbolic systems and connectionist architectures is redressed through neural manifolds, and reveals an associated frame problem. Working within the construct of neural manifolds, the frame problem is solved through the use of contextual reinforcement learning, a new paradigm recently proposed.

3:40PM *An Analysis of Gradient-Based Policy Iteration [#1525]*
James Dankert, Lei Yang and Jennie Si, Arizona State University, United States

Recently, a system theoretic framework for learning and optimization has been developed that shows how many approximate dynamic programming paradigms such as perturbation analysis, Markov decision processes, and reinforcement learning are very closely related. Using this system theoretic framework a new optimization technique called gradient-based policy iteration (GBPI) has been developed. In this paper we will show how GBPI iteration can be extended to partially observable Markov decision processes (POMDPs). We will also develop the value iteration analogue of GBPI and show that this new version of value iteration, extended to POMDPs, not only theoretically acts like value iteration but also does so numerically.

4:00PM *An Integrated Fault Tolerant Control Framework Using Adaptive Critic Design [#1302]*
Gary Yen and deLima Pedro, Oklahoma State University, United States

An integrated Fault Tolerant Control solution calls for a nonlinear adaptive controller with universal approximation capability and guaranteed stability. To fulfill this requirement we propose the use of Neural Networks trained online under a Globalized Dual Heuristic Programming architecture supervised by a decision logic capable of identifying controller malfunctions in early stages and providing new avenues with greater probability of convergence using information from a Dynamic Model Bank. The classification and distinction of controller malfunctions and of the faults in the system is achieved through three independent quality indexes. Proof-of-the-concept simulations of nonlinear plants demonstrate the approach legitimacy.

4:20PM *Approximate Dynamic Programming for High Dimensional Resource Allocation Problems [#1070]*
Warren Powell, Abraham George, Belgacem Bouzaiene-Ayari and Hugo Simao, Princeton University, United States

There are a wide array of discrete resource allocation problems (buffers in manufacturing, complex equipment in electric power, aircraft and locomotives in transportation) which need to be solved over time, under uncertainty. These can be formulated as dynamic programs, but typically exhibit high dimensional state, action and outcome variables (the three curses of dimensionality). For example, we have worked on problems where the dimensionality of these variables is in the ten thousand to one million range. We describe an approximation methodology for this problem class, and summarize the problem classes where the approach seems to be working well, and research challenges that we continue to face.

4:40PM *Modeling Reward Functions for Incomplete State Representations via Echo State Networks [#1620]*
Keith Bush and Charles Anderson, Colorado State University, United States

The Echo State Network (ESN) architecture is used as a recurrent network strategy for approximating the Q-function of the mass-spring-damper linear dynamical system when only partial state is observable. The ESN architecture's approximation performance is compared against feed forward neural networks given perfect state information (FNN) and a finite window of time-delayed partial state (TDNN), respectively. Both feed forward representations are known to perform well in approximating the Q-function in this problem domain. We demonstrate that the ESN, given partial state, well-represents temporally dependent rewards and exhibits similar performance to FNN and TDNN architectures in approximating the Q-function during on-line learning.

5:00PM *Continuous Adaptive Critic Desigs [#1310]*
Thomas Hanselmann, Lyle Noakes and Anthony Zaknich, University of Melbourne, Australia; University of Western Australia, Australia; Murdoch University, Australia

A continuous formulation of an adaptive critic design (ACD) is investigated. Connections to the discrete case are made, where backpropagation through time (BPTT) and real-time recurrent learning (RTRL) are prevalent. A second order actor adaptation, based on Newton's method, is established for fast actor convergence. Also a fast critic update for concurrent actor-critic training is outlined that keeps the Bellman optimality correct to first order approximation after actor changes. Note: An extended version where all necessary equations are fully expanded, so that the method can be implemented, is in preparation for later publication.

Biomedical Applications
Wednesday, August 3, 3:20PM-5:20PM, Room: Outremount, Chair: David Brown

3:20PM *Classification of Plantar Pressure and Heel Acceleration Patterns Using Neural Networks [#1106]*
Edward Sazonov, Timothy Bumpus, Stacey Zeigler and Samantha Marocco, Clarkson University, United States

Postural control in humans relies on information from receptors in the proprioceptive, visual, and vestibular systems of the body. Excessive weight bearing on the heels during standing or forefoot dominated walking create risk factors for falls and injury within this population. Identification of these abnormal patterns by a computerized technique can help in early detection of gait changes and prevention of falls. We conducted a case study to see if plantar pressure and heel acceleration patterns attributed to different motion activities can be accurately identified by a neural network classifier. The results show good sensitivity and specificity of the classifier, confirming the feasibility of further research.

3:40PM *Feature Selection by Independent Component Analysis and Mutual Information Maximization in EEG Signal Classification [#1122]*
Tian Lan, Deniz Erdogmus, Andre Adami and Michael Pavel, OGI, Oregon Health and Science University, United States; OGI at Oregon Health and Science University, United States

Feature selection and dimensionality reduction are important steps in pattern recognition. In this paper, we propose a scheme for feature selection using linear independent component analysis and mutual information maximization method. The method is theoretically motivated by the fact that the classification error rate is related to the mutual information between the feature vectors and the class labels. The feasibility of the principle is illustrated on a synthetic dataset and its performance is demonstrated using EEG signal classification. Experimental results show that this method works well for feature selection.

4:00PM *Neural Network and Principal Component Analyses of Highly Variable Myocardial Mechanical Waveforms Derived from Echocardiographic Ultrasound Images [#1664]*
Eileen McMahon, Josef Korinek, Honghai Zhang, Milan Sonka, Armando Manduca and Marek Belohlavek, Mayo Clinic College of Medicine, United States; The University of Iowa, United States

We introduce a new type of data for classification of regional segments of myocardium. We have analyzed strain measurements taken throughout the cardiac cycle from the echocardiograms of pigs. Classification by both Principal Component Analysis (PCA) and by Neural Network (NN) are combined for a data mining operation. Differences in strain waveforms between normal and diseased myocardium may further elucidate the corresponding changes in physiology. Altered functioning of the heart muscle is reflected by strain, and objective computer analysis should aid in the diagnosis of ischemia. We hypothesize that the entire strain waveform over one heart cycle can be classified to functionally determine whether or not a myocardial region is perfused.

4:20PM *A Recurrent Fuzzy-Neural Filter for Real-Time Separation of Lung Sounds [#1005]*
Paris Mastorocostas and John Theocharis, Technological Educational Institute of Serres, Greece; Aristotle University of Thessaloniki, Greece

This paper presents a recurrent filter that performs real-time separation of discontinuous adventitious sounds from vesicular sounds. The filter uses two Dynamic Fuzzy Neural Networks, operating in parallel, to perform the task of separation of the lung sounds, obtained from patients with pulmonary pathology. Extensive experimental results, including fine/coarse crackles and squawks, are given, and a performance comparison with a series of other models is conducted, underlining the separation capabilities of the proposed filter and its improved performance with respect to its competing rivals.

4:40PM *Stochastic Feature Selection for the Discrimination of Biomedical Spectra [#1123]*
Nick Pizzi, Mark Alexiuk and Witold Pedrycz, National Research Council, Canada; University of Manitoba, Canada; University of Alberta, Canada

When dealing with the curse of dimensionality (small sample size with many dimensions), feature subset selection is an important preprocessing strategy. This issue is particularly germane to the discrimination of class-labeled high-dimensional biomedical spectra as is often acquired from magnetic resonance and infrared spectrometers. A technique is presented that stochastically selects feature subsets with varying cardinality for discrimination by probabilistic neural networks. The results are benchmarked against two classifiers using the entire feature set both with and without feature averaging. The new technique had significantly fewer misclassifications than either of the benchmarks.

5:00PM *Ovarian Cancer Diagnosis Using Complementary Learning Fuzzy Neural Network [#1011]*
Tuan Zea Tan, Chai Quek and Geok See Ng, Nanyang Technological University, Singapore

DNA microarray is an emerging technique in ovarian cancer diagnosis. However microarray data is ultra-huge and difficult to analyze. Thus, it is desirable to utilize Fuzzy Neural Network (FNn) approach for assisting the diagnosis and analysis process. Amongst FNN, complementary learning is able to rapidly derive fuzzy sets and formulate fuzzy rules. Complementary learning uses positive and negative learning, and hence it escapes from the curse of dimension. Furthermore, FALCON-AART has human-like reasoning that eases and allows physician to examine its computation in a familiar way. Hence, FALCON-AART is applied in ovarian cancer diagnosis as a clinical decision support system in this work. Its experimental results are encouraging.

Fuzzy-Neural Systems
Wednesday, August 3, 3:20PM-5:20PM, Room: Mt Royal/Hampstead, Chair: Bart Kosko

3:20PM *Fuzzy ROC Curves for Unsupervised Nonparametric Ensemble Techniques [#1488]*
Paul Evangelista, Piero Bonissone, Mark Embrechts and Boleslaw Szymanski, Rensselaer Polytechnic Institute, United States; GE Global Research, United States

This paper explores a novel ensemble technique for unsupervised classification using nonparametric statistics. Successful performance of an unsupervised ensemble can be measured with improvement of the receiver operating characteristic curve (ROC), and the performance of different aggregation techniques for the combination of the multiple classification system decision values, or rankings in this paper, is illustrated. The area under the curve (AUC) and relationship with the Wilcoxon Rank Sum or Mann-Whitney U statistics are discussed. Aggregation techniques of the multiple classifiers are based upon fuzzy logic theory, creating the fuzzy ROC curve. The one-class SVM is utilized for the unsupervised classification.

3:40PM *Neural Network with Fuzzy Dynamic Logic [#1536]*
Leonid Perlovsky, Air Force Researcj Lab, United States

The paper describes a neural network utilizing models and extending Fuzzy Logic. The motivation is to explain the process of learning as joint model improvement and fuzziness reduction. An initial state of this neural network is highly fuzzy with uncertain knowledge; it dynamically evolves into a low-fuzzy state of certain knowledge. This neural system resembles several known mechanisms of the mind and overcomes certain long-standing difficulties in several application fields. We present an example and briefly discuss mechanisms of concepts, emotions, including aesthetic emotions, instincts, conscious, unconscious, imagination, perception, cognition and relate them to the introduced neural network and dynamic logic

4:00PM *Color Image Segmentation Using Fuzzy Min-Max Neural Networks [#1638]*
Pablo A. Estevez, Rodrigo J. Flores and Claudio A. Perez, Dept. Electrical Engineering, U. of Chile, Chile

In this work a new color image segmentation method, based on fuzzy min-max neural networks is presented. The proposed method is called FMMIS (Fuzzy Min-Max neural network for Image Segmentation). The FMMIS method grows boxes from a set of seed pixels, to find the minimum bounded rectangle (MBR) for each object present in the images. The algorithm was tested on wood images of 10 defect categories and with images of frontal faces taken from the FERET database. The FMMIS algorithm outperformed alternative methods in terms of object detection rate, false positive detection rate, average execution time and the RUMA index. The proposed method is very fast and it may be applied to real-time image segmentation tasks.

4:20PM *Skin Color Segmentation by Histogram-Based Neural Fuzzy Network [#1173]*
Chia-Feng Juang, Hwai-Sheng Perng and Shin-Kuan Chen, Dept. of Electr. Eng., National ChungHsing Univ., Taiwan; Dept. of Electr. Eng., Chung Chou Inst. of Tech., Taiwan

Skin color image segmentation by a histogram-based Self-cOnstructing Neural Fuzzy Inference Network (SONFIN) is proposed in this paper. Each color pixel is represented by a Hue-Saturation (HS) space. To represent a block color by histogram as accurately as possible, a non-uniform quantization approach of HS space is considered. Histogram information of HS from images under different environments is used to train SONFIN to make the method as robust as possible. To verify performance of the proposed method, experiment on human-hand segmentation is performed. For comparison, other segmentation methods are applied to the same problem.

4:40PM *Learning a Hierarchical Fuzzy System with Autonomous Navigation as an Example [#1573]*
Shuqing Zeng, Yongbao He and Jie Jiang, Michigan State University, United States; Fudan University, China

In this paper, a hierarchical fuzzy system for high-dimensional dataset is proposed. The sequential least-squares method is introduced to estimate Takagi-Sugeno rules. A hierarchical clustering takes place in the product space of input and output, and each path from the root to a leaf corresponds to a fuzzy IF-THEN rule. Only a subset of the rules is considered, based on the location of the input query data. At each level of the hierarchy, a discriminating subspace is generated automatically from the high-dimensional input space for a good generalization capability. Both a synthetic data set and a real robot autonomous navigation experiment are considered to illustrate how effective the system is.

Special Session: Biologically Inspired Computational Vision
Wednesday, August 3, 3:20PM-5:20PM, Room: Verdun/Lachine, Chair: Khan M. Iftekharuddin

3:20PM *A Biologically Inspired Computational Vision Front-end based on a Self-Organised Pseudo-Randomly Tessellated Artificial Retina [#1653]*
Sumitha Balasuriya and Paul Siebert, University of Glasgow, Scotland

A biologically inspired front-end for computer vision based on an artificial retina pyramid with a self-organized pseudo-randomly tessellated receptive field tessellation is described. The tessellation locally resembles a hexagonal mosaic, whereas globally is organized with a very densely tessellated central foveal region which seamlessly merges into an increasingly sparsely tessellated periphery. Scale-space interest points which are suitable for many higher level attention and reasoning tasks are efficiently extracted. All operations were conducted on a geometrically irregular foveated representation (data structure for visual information) which is radically different to the uniform rectilinear arrays used in conventional computer vision.

3:40PM *A Chaos Synchronization-Based Dynamic Vision Model for Image Segmentation [#1434]*
Hanif Azhar, Khan Iftekharuddin and Robert Kozma, Univ. of Memphis, United States; University of Memphis, United States

There have been intense research in feature binding to understand the parallel processing of features in visual information processing. The synchronization of spiking neurons is important for successful feature binding. In this work, we propose a novel approach to feature binding in spiking neurons using chaotic synchronization. We exploit each image pixel intensity value as individual neuron to generate chaotic time series. We produce the Coupled Map Lattice series for neighborhood interaction and synchronization in spatio-temporal space. The largest cluster in the time series with similar chaotic synchronization parameter is used to generate segmented image. We compare our results with the existing Otsu adaptive segmentation technique.

4:00PM *Processing Landsat TM Data Using Complex-Valued NRBF Neural Network [#1383]*
Xiaoli Tao and Howard Michel, University of Massachusetts Dartmouth, United States

This paper describes a novel classification technique -- a Complex-Valued Normalized Radial Basis Function (NRBF) neural network classifier. Complex-valued weights are used in the supervised learning part of NRBF neural networks. Different from the original NRBF neural network, another activation function for the output is added in NRBF neural network. This new neural network model improves the classification ability of NRBF neural networks regardless of the learning method in the unsupervised part. This classifier was tested with satellite multi-spectral image data. Classification results show that this new neural network model is more accurate and powerful than the conventional NRBF mod

4:20PM *Comparison of Linear and Non-linear Data Projection Techniques in Recognizing Universal Facial Expressions [#1197]*
Mohammed Yeasin and Baptiste Bullot, Dept. of ECE, University of Memphis, United States; Software Engineer, Amadeus Inc., France

This paper compares the performances of data projection techniques in classifying facial expressions. The classification approach relies on a two-step strategy on the top of projected facial motion information obtained from sequence of facial expression images. First, a bank of linear classifier was applied on projected data and decision made is coalesced to produce a characteristic signature for each facial expressions. The signatures thus computed from the training data set were used to learn the model for each facial expressions using discrete HMMs. The performances of each data representations, namely the PCA, NMF and LLE, in classifying facial expressions were compared on a database of 488 video sequences that include 97 subjects.

4:40PM *Associative neural networks as means for low-resolution video-based recognition [#1572]*
Dmitry Gorodnichy, NRC-CNRC Institute for Information Technology, Canada

The paper introduces a neuro-associative approach to recognition which is shown to be able to both learn and identify an object from low-resolution low-quality video sequences. The approach is derived from a mathematical model of biological visual memory, in which correlation-based projection learning is used to memorize a face from a video sequence and attractor-based association is performed to recognize a face over several video frames. The approach is demonstrated using a video-based facial database and real-time video annotation of TV shows.

Wednesday, August 3, 7:00PM-9:00PM

Banquet
Wednesday, August 3, 7:00PM-9:00PM, Room: Westmount, Chair: ALL

Thursday, August 4, 8:00AM-9:00AM

Plenary Talk: Beyond Correlation - closing the loop between brain and theory by extracting representations and altered feedbacks
Thursday, August 4, 8:00AM-9:00AM, Room: Westmount/Outremount, Speaker: Mitsuo Kawato, Computational Neuroscience Laboratory, Japan

Computational neuroscience research, or more in general, system neuroscience research, is much more difficult than molecular research although it is essential to understand brain mechanisms. One of the reasons for this difficulty is that experimental link between the theory and experiment is largely only temporal correlation while many manipulative experimental techniques are available for molecular cell biology. Even successful computational-model based neurophysiology (e.g. Shidara et al., Nature 1993; Kobayashi et al., JNP, 1998) and neuroimaging studies (e.g. Imamizu et al., Nature 2000; Haruno et al., JNS, 2004) relied only on temporal correlation between neural activities or BOLD signal with theory predictions. Causality between neural or brain activity and computational representations cannot be guaranteed by correlation study only and different approaches based on lesion, stimulation or circuit analysis are essential. Because our ATR CNS labs are unique in integrating computational theories, human, animal and robot experiments and developing new research tools, we have been exploring an "all mighty" methodology that can ensure causality from the beginning. Recent efforts in our labs including computational-model based imaging, the hierarchical variational Bayesian method, noninvasive decoding of neural representations, and robotics experiments could be the bases of the new methodology. The abstract description of the new paradigm is as follows. Suppose one has a computational theory, which postulates that some brain networks solve some computational problems and a specific brain locus contains a specific computational representation. Then one needs to extract this information either by some noninvasive method or unit recording, and manipulate this by altered computational algorithms derived from the theory. The altered or processed information is fed back to the brain by appropriate methods (e.g. visual or tactile feedbacks, TMS, electrical stimulation). Observed brain activity and behavior are now guaranteed causally linked. I will explain backgrounds of this new paradigm and several possible applications.

Thursday, August 4, 9:30AM-11:30AM

Special Session: Neural Prostheses and the Neuron-Silicon Interface
Thursday, August 4, 9:30AM-11:30AM, Room: Westmount, Chair: Thedore W. Berger

9:30AM *Artificial Vision by Electrical Stimulation of the Retina [#1758]*
James Weiland and Mark Humayun, University of Southern California, United States

Retinitis pigmentosa (RP) and age-related macula degeneration (AMD) lead to the degeneration of the light sensitive cells of the eye (photoreceptors), resulting in a significant visual deficit for the afflicted individual. Simulations of prosthetic vision predict that 1000 electrodes will be needed to restore visual function such as face recognition, reading, and mobility. The proposed retinal prosthesis system would include an external video camera to capture an image and electronics to code the image and transmit the coded data to an implanted system. The implanted electronics will receive the data, decode the signal and generate the desired current pulse pattern for the stimulating array.

9:50AM *Physiological Activation of the Hind Limb Muscles of the Anesthetized Cat Using the Utah Slanted Electrode Array [#1724]*
Richard Normann, Daniel McDonnall, Gregory Clark, Richard Stein and Almut Branner, University of Utah, United States; University of Utah, United States; University of Alberta, Canada; Cyberkinetics Neurotechnology, United States

We have implanted a 10 x 10 grid of graded-length microelectrodes in cat sciatic nerve, and selectively stimulated small, independent ensembles of motoneurons that innervate the calf muscles in order to address problems of muscle force recruitment and fatigue. We have shown that motoneuron stimulation via specific electrodes can evoke a maximal force in each of these muscles without producing substantive forces in the others. Further, because different electrodes excite different motoneurons innervating a particular muscle, we have been able to interleave low-frequency stimulation through these electrodes to produce ripple-free, fatigue-resistant forces over a large range of forces.

10:10AM *Replacing Damaged Brain Regions with Biomimetic Microelectronic Neural Prostheses to Restore Cognitive Function [#1745]*
Theodore Berger, John Granacki, Vasilis Marmarelis, Armand Tanguay, Jr., Sam Deadwyler and Greg Gerhardt, University of Southern California, United States; Information Sciences Institute, United States; Wake Forest School of Medicine, United States; University of Kentucky Medical Center, United States

We are developing a microchip-based neural prosthesis for the hippocampus, a region of the brain responsible for long-term memories, and that frequently is damaged in epilepsy, stroke, and Alzheimer's disease. The goals of this effort include: (1) experimental characterization of hippocampal neuron and network function, (2) biologically realistic mathematical models of neural system dynamics, (3) microchip implementation of hippocampal system models, and (4) hybrid neuron-silicon interfaces for bi-directional communication with the brain. A proof-of-concept is presented in the context of an application to the hippocampal slice. How the current work in brain slices is being extended to behaving rats and primates also is described.

10:30AM *Getting Better Signals Out of the Brain: Decoding Algorithms and Autonomous Electrodes*
Joel Burdick, California Institute of Technology, United States

This talk will summarize our efforts to develop new technologies whose aim is to improve the quality and quantity of the information derived from extracellular recordings. This work is motivated by ongoing activities at Caltech to develop neural prostheses based on the brain's Parietal Reach Region (PRR). The talk will first review our progress towards developing a functioning neural prosthesis in order to motivate the need to develop long-lasting chronic interfaces between electrodes and neurons. The second half of the talk will focus on our efforts to develop a new class of "movable" electrodes that autonomously isolate a neural cell so as to optimize the recorded signal quality, and then maintain optimal signal quality using feedback. Such devices are likely to improve the reliability and robustness of future chronic neural prosthetic systems. We will also summarize current research in neural decoding algorithms, whose aim is to extract the maximum information content from the recorded signals.

10:50AM *Application of Polymer Microstructures with Controlled Surface Chemistries as a Platform for Creating and Interfacing with Synthetic Neural Networks [#1195]*
Geoffrey Mealing, Mahmud Bani-Yaghoub, Roger Tremblay, Robert Monette, John Mielke, Raluca Voicu, Christophe Py, Raluca Barjovanu and Karim Faid, IBS, National Research Council of Canada, Canada; IMS, National Research Council of Canada, Canada

Hybrid silicon-polymer chips with microscale topography and contrasting surface chemistries were created using soft lithography techniques, and evaluated for their suitability to guide cell attachment, growth and differentiation. Neurons developed on these chips exhibit patterned growth and functional communication, as evidenced by spontaneous and stimulated action potentials and intracellular calcium oscillations. Preliminary work to integrate planar patch-clamp technology into this platform and create a long-term interface will be presented. This platform is being developed to investigate mechanisms underlying neurogenesis, synaptic transmission and neurodegeneration.

Applications I
Thursday, August 4, 9:30AM-11:30AM, Room: Verdun/Lachine, Chair: Michael Georgiopoulos

9:30AM *An Experimental Comparison of Semi-Supervised ARTMAP Architectures, GCS and GNG Classifiers [#1652]*
Quang Le, Georgios Anagnostopoulos, Michael Georgiopoulos and Ken Ports, Florida Institute of Technology, United States; University of Central Florida, United States

In this paper we present an experimental comparison of Growing Cell Structures (GCS), Growing Neural Gas (GNG), Semi-Supervised Fuzzy ARTMAP (ssFAM) and Semi- Supervised Ellipsoid ARTMAP (ssEAM) classifiers. Earlier studies that had appeared in the literature showed that Fuzzy ARTMAP, which utilizes fully- supervised learning, may suffer from poor generalization performance, when compared to GCS and GNG classifiers. We present new results indicating that ARTMAP classifiers equipped with semi-supervised learning capabilities can improve their performance with respect to GCS and GNG classifiers, while maintaining lower structural complexity.

9:50AM *Time Series Study of GGAP-RBF Network: Predictions of Nasdaq Stock and Nitrate Contamination of Drinking Water [#1240]*
Ying Wang, Guang-Bin Huang, P. Saratchandran and N. Sundararajan, Nanyang Technological University, Singapore

This paper investigates the performance of the latest developed GGAP-RBF network in time series applications. The growing and pruning strategy of GGAP-RBF are based on linking the required accuracy with the significance of the nearest added new neuron. Significance of a neuron is a measure of the average information content of that neuron. GGAP-RBF algorithm may be attractive in time-series applications due to its good efficiency and simple topology. This paper investigate its performance in two important real time-series applications: predictions of Nasdaq stock and weekly nitrate contamination of drinking water. The simulation results demonstrate that GGAP-RBF network can achieve good prediction accuracy in an efficient way.

10:10AM *Environmental Informatics - Long-Lead Flood Forecasting Using Bayesian Neural Networks [#1715]*
Ana Barros, Duke University, United States

Previously, our applications of neural networks in hydrometeorology focused on the development of complex architectures of neural networks built to embody clearly defined hypothesis of functional relationships among relevant physical processes using multisensor, multiresolution mixes of ground observations and satellite data One challenge we have not addressed previously is how to quantify the uncertainty in NN-based forecasts or estimates. We begin to address this question through the use of Bayesian Neural Networks (BNNs) for long-lead flood forecasting.

10:30AM *Detection of Disease Outbreaks in Pharmaceutical Sales: Neural Networks and Threshold Algorithms [#1574]*
Glenn Guthrie, Deborah Stacey, David Calvert and Victoria Edge, University of Guelph, Canada; Public Health Agency of Canada, Canada

Syndromic surveillance involves monitoring data that could indicate disease trends a population, such as gastrointestinal illness and respiratory illness. Different types of data can be used to detect potential outbreaks of disease or biological contaminant based on deviations from historical norms. The system discussed in this paper is intended to detect aberration by identifying changes in sequence data that do not match the norms for a given time and location. Artificial neural networks (ANNs) were used to detect changes in the sales trends for over-the-counter (OTC) pharmaceuticals. Early detection of an outbreak will allow public health officials to respond faster to potential outbreak situations.

10:50AM *A Fast Neural Network-Based Detection and Tracking of Dim Moving Targets in FLIR Imagery [#1210]*
Jagdish Chandra Patra, Ferdinan Widjaja, Amitabha Das and Ee Luang Ang, Nanyang Technological University (NTU), Singapore; Nanyang Technological University, Singapore

Usually the targets in forward looking infra-red imagery are dim, slowly moving, and buried under clutter and noise. Detecting and tracking of such targets is a challenging task. Although Artificial Neural Networks (ANNs) have been used to solve this problem, they need a lot of training time. In order to reduce the training time, we propose Principal Component Analysis as a dimension reduction technique. We used an MLP with LM learning algorithm and a RBF Neural Network (RBFNN) with K-means algorithm to cluster the data. Both the ANNs are used in a Neural Adaptive Line Enhancer (NALE) configuration. Extensive computer simulations showed the combination of PCA and ANNs gives satisfactory results with significant reduction in training time.

11:10AM *GETnet: A General Framework for Evolutionary Temporal Neural Networks [#1742]*
Reza Derakhshani, University of Missouri, Kansas City, United States

This paper introduces a new general evolutionary temporal neural network framework (GETnet) for the automated design of neural nets with distributed memories. GETnet utilizes nonlinear moving average and autoregressive nodes that are trained by enhanced gradient descent and evolutionary search in architecture, delay, and weight spaces. The ability to evolve arbitrary time-delay connections enables GETnet to find novel answers to classification and system identification tasks. A new temporal minimum description length policy ensures the creation of fast and compact networks with improved generalization capabilities. Results of simulations using Mackey-Glass data are presented to demonstrate the above stated capabilities of GETnet.

Neurodynamics
Thursday, August 4, 9:30AM-11:30AM, Room: Mt Royal/Hampstead, Chair: Walter Freeman

9:30AM *Temporal Discontinuities in Neocortical Dynamics [#1194]*
Walter Freeman and Mark Holmes, University of California at Berkeley, United States; University of Washington, Seattle, United States

Our aim is to define and measure parameters of intracranial EEG that characterize stable states of neocortex and its capacity for rapid state transitions. Our experimental data consist of recordings of "spontaneous" EEG from intracranial arrays in animals and a human subject. We pre-process the data to extract large-scale "global" patterns in contrast to "localizing" neural signals. We define a set of novel parameters and measure them over numerous trials. We use the values and ranges of variation of these new parameters in the EEG to define quantitatively the differences in EEGs in four states: awake, asleep, and before and during partial complex seizure.

9:50AM *Stability Conditions of the full KII Model of Excitatory and Inhibitory Neural Populations [#1544]*
Roman Ilin and Robert Kozma, The University of Memphis, United States; University of Memphis, United States

We consider the model of interacting neural populations to be the main building block of K-sets, as suggested by W.J. Freeman. The full KII set's dynamics is understood through building the system up from the reduced KII. Theoretical condition for stability of the intermediate KII model is derived and the regions of structural stability of the full KII model are identified based on numeric data.

10:10AM *Associative Memory in the Strong Coupling Regime of a K-set Oscillator Network [#1593]*
Mark D. Skowronski, John G. Harris and Jose C. Principe, University of Florida, United States; CNEL, Department of ECE, University of Florida, United States

Many oscillator networks that implement associative memories assume weak coupling among oscillators. Weak coupling ensures that only the oscillator phases are affected while the amplitudes remain unperturbed. However, amplitude modulation in brain activity, the computational system modeled by such networks, is pervasive, creating spatio-temporal patterns in response to external stimuli. In this work we demonstrate an associative memory using a network of strongly coupled K-set oscillators. The parameter estimation procedure is provided that focuses on synchronization among oscillators belonging to the same learned patterns. Two examples of the associative memory are presented showing qualitative and quantitative performance.

10:30AM *Evolving High Capacity Associative Memories with Efficient Wiring [#1532]*
Rod Adams, Lee Calcraft and Neil Davey, University of Hertfordshire, United Kingdom

We investigate sparse networks of threshold units, trained with the perceptron learning rule to act as associative memories. The units are placed in a ring so that the wiring cost is a meaningful measure. A Genetic Algorithm is used to evolve networks that have efficient wiring, but also good functionality. It is shown that this is possible and that the connection strategy used by the networks is to maintain connectivity at all distances but with the probability of a connection decreasing linearly with distance.

Learning I
Thursday, August 4, 9:30AM-11:30AM, Room: Outremount, Chair: Rolf Eckmiller

9:30AM *Incremental Learning for Online Face Recognition [#1543]*
Seiichi Ozawa, Soon Toh, Shigeo Abe, Shaoning Pang and Nikola Kasabov, Kobe University, Japan; Auckland University of Technology, New Zealand

A new approach to face recognition tasks is presented in which not only a classifier but also a feature space of input variables is trained incrementally to adapt to incoming unknown samples. The benefit of this type of incremental learning is that the search for useful features and the learning of an optimal decision boundary are carried out online. To implement this idea, an extended Incremental Principal Component (IPCA) and Resource Allocating Network with Long-Term Memory (RAN-LTM) are effectively combined. To adapt the classifier to the evolution of the feature space due to the rotation of eigen-axes and the dimensional augmentation by IPCA, we propose an efficient way to retrain RAN-LTM.

9:50AM *Efficient Online Spherical K-means Clustering [#1089]*
Shi Zhong, Florida Atlantic University, United States

The spherical k-means algorithm, i.e., the k-means algorithm with cosine similarity, is a popular method for clustering high-dimensional text data. However, it has been mainly used in batch mode. This paper investigates an online version of the spherical k-means algorithm based on the well-known

Winner-Take-All competitive learning. We demonstrate that the online spherical k-means algorithm can achieve significantly better clustering results than the batch version, especially when an annealing-type learning rate schedule is used. We also present heuristics to improve the speed, yet almost without loss of clustering quality.

10:10AM *On Efficient Selection of Binary Classifiers for Min-Max Modular Classifier [#1404]*
Hai Zhao and Bao-Liang Lu, Shanghai Jiao Tong University, China; ShangHai Jiao Tong University, China

Binary classifiers are fundamental components of multiclass pattern classifiers. How to construct a solution to a multiclass problem by efficiently combining the outputs of binary classifiers is a very important issue in neural network and machine learning research. In this paper, we present three different algorithms for selecting binary classifiers for min-max modular classifier to improve its response performance. We also give a theoretical performance estimation of the proposed algorithms. We prove that quadratic complexity of original min-max combination can be reduced to the level of linear complexity in the number of binary classifiers. The experimental results indicate that our proposed algorithms are efficient and effective.

10:30AM *Are ARIMA Neural Network Hybrids Better than Single Models? [#1581]*
Tugba Taskaya-Temizel and Khurshid Ahmad, University of Surrey, United Kingdom

Hybrid methods comprising autoregressive integrated moving average (ARIMA) and neural network models are generally favored against single neural network and single ARIMA models in the literature. The benefits of such methods appear to be substantial especially when dealing with non-stationary series: nonstationary linear component can be modeled using ARIMA and nonlinear component using neural networks. Our studies suggest that the use of a nonlinear component may degenerate the performance of such hybrids and that a simpler hybrid comprising linear AR model with a TDNN outperforms the more complex hybrid in tests on benchmark economic and financial time series.

10:50AM *Embedding via clustering: Using spectral information to guide dimensionality reduction [#1224]*
Roland Memisevic and Geoffrey Hinton, University of Toronto, Canada

We describe an approach to improve iterative dimensionality reduction methods by using information contained in the leading eigenvectors of a data affinity matrix. Using an insight from the area of spectral clustering, we suggest modifying the gradient of an iterative method, so that latent space elements belonging to the same cluster are encouraged to move in similar directions during optimization. We also describe way to achieve this without actually having to explicitly perform an eigendecomposition. Preliminary experiments show that our approach makes it possible to speed up iterative methods and helps them to find better local minima of their objective function.

11:10AM *On the Evaluation of Relevance Learning by a Multi-layer Perceptron [#1360]*
Kenji Suzuki and Shuji Hashimoto, University of Tsukuba, Japan; Waseda University, Japan

We propose a novel method of Relevance Learning by a MLP, which is regarded as learning from the relationship among two or more outputs of the network. Unlike the traditional MLP that learns from a set of an input feature vector and the target output, the proposed network learns from a set of two or more vector inputs and the target relevance. In this paper, the theoretical background underlying the relevance learning is discussed. We show the performance with some experiments with artificially generated data set in comparison with the result of PCA and MDS. Some results on the low-dimensional representation of color hue data set and emotional facial images will be then presented as an example of multidimensional perceptual scaling.

Thursday, August 4, 1:00PM-3:00PM

Telecommunications
Thursday, August 4, 1:00PM-3:00PM, Room: Mt Royal/Hampstead, Chair: Carlo Morabito

1:00PM *A Hybrid Neural Network for Optimal TDMA Transmission Scheduling in Packet Radio Networks [#1126]*
Shi Haixiang and Wang Lipo, Nanyang Technological University, Singapore

In this paper we propose a hybrid method to solve the broadcast scheduling problem in packet radio networks. In the first stage, we use a backtracking sequential coloring algorithm to obtain a minimal TDMA frame length and the corresponding transmission assignments. In the second stage, we employ the noisy chaotic neural network to find the maximum node transmission based on the results obtained in the previous stage. Simulation results show that this hybrid method outperforms previous approaches, such as mean field annealing, a hybrid of the Hopfield neural network and genetic algorithms, the sequential vertex coloring algorithm, and the gradual neural network.

1:20PM *Nonlinear Channel Equalization with QAM Signal Using Chebyshev Artificial Neural Network [#1235]*
Jagdish Chandra Patra, Wei Beng Poh, Narendra S. Chaudhari and Amitabha Das, Nanyang Technological University (NTU), Singapore; Nanyang Technological University, Singapore; SCE, Nanyang Technological University, Singapore

A computational efficient artificial neural network for adaptive channel equalization in a digital communication system with 4-QAM signal constellation is purposed. We proposed a single layer Chebyshev neural network (ChNN) by expanding the input pattern by Chebyshev polynomials. Performance comparison was carried out through extensive computer simulations with two other neural networks: an MLP and a functional link ANN together with a linear LMS-based equalizer. It is shown that the ChNN provides satisfactory results in terms of convergence rate, MSE floor and BER over a wide range of EVR, SNR and nonlinear conditions with substantial reduction in the computational complexity.

1:40PM *Implementation of an MLP-based DOA System Using a Reduced Number of MM-wave Antenna Elements [#1639]*
Eric Danneville, Jean-Jules Brault and Jean-Jacques Laurin, Ecole Polytechnique de Montreal, Canada

In car tracking and many other applications, it is required to know the direct direction of arrival (DOA) of a signal. In practice, presence of a coherent and unknown ground reflection greatly affects the computation. A network of 3 MLP is proposed to estimate the true angle of the source. Only six antennas are used but several power signals are generated by a combiner to increase the dimension of the input space. An original NN training strategy has been implemented based on a smart choice of training points and on an unusual validation technique to find out optimized NN's structure. Tests have been successfully carried out with datasets provided by real antennas outputs obtained by using an asphalt reflector in an anechoic room.

2:00PM *Least-Squares Support Vector Machines for DOA Estimation: A Step-by-Step Description and Sensitivity Analysis [#1764]*
Clodoaldo A. M. Lima, Cynthia Junqueira, Ricardo Suyama, Fernando J. Von Zuben and Joao Marcos T. Romano, LBiC/DCA/FEEC/Unicamp, Brazil; CTA/Institute of Aeronautics and Space, Brazil; DSPCOM/FEEC/Unicamp, Brazil

Adaptive beamforming in antenna arrays aims at proposing weighted linear combinations for detecting the received signal. The weights can be directly obtained if the direction of arrival (DOA) of the signals has already been estimated. The DOA estimation involves the prediction of the angle of arrival by means of monitoring the output of the antennas. Even though signal subspace techniques have made a good job in DOA estimation, they present some drawbacks that will be alleviated here using a multiclass LS-SVM classifier. The main contribution are: a complete description of the set of algebraic manipulation for the synthesis of the classification device, and an analysis of the effect in performance when relevant parameters vary.

2:20PM *Recurrent Neural Equalization for Communication Channels in Impulsive Noise Environments [#1498]*
Jongsoo Choi, Martin Bouchard and Tet Hin Yeap, University of Ottawa, Canada

Non-Gaussian noise causes significant performance degradation to communication receivers. In this paper we apply a recurrent neural equalizer to impulsive noise channels, for which the performance of neural network equalizers has never been evaluated. This new application is motivated from the fact that the unscented Kalman filter (UKF), which is suited for training of the recurrent neural equalizer, provides a higher accuracy than the extended Kalman filter (EKF) in capturing the statistical characteristics for non-Gaussian random variables. The performance of the recurrent neural equalizer is evaluated for impulsive noise channels through Monte Carlo simulations.

Neuromorphic Hardware
Thursday, August 4, 1:00PM-3:00PM, Room: Westmount, Chair: Bernard Girau

1:00PM *A New Hybrid Neural System Interfacing Neurons and Silicon Hardware for Fast Signal Recognition [#1683]*
Zihong Liu and Zhihua Wang, Dept. of EE, Tsinghua University, Beijing, China

......In our this paper, a novel mixed neural system interfacing biological neurons and semiconductor chip on a shared silicon wafer substrate for fast signal recognition is proposed, where three blocks are designed and interconnected. Recorded simulations with a 5*5 microelectrode-array covered by a 100*100 BNN show that combining the individual advantages of large-scale integrated circuits and BNN, this system will have faster and more intelligent capabilities for fuzzy control, speech or pattern recognition as compared with common ways. At the same time, it can resolve the problems of huge memory space in ANN chips and the high complexity for algorithms, with an average 90.3% degree reduced efficiently between 5 trials.

1:20PM *Biologically plausible VLSI neural network implementation with asynchronous neuron and spike-based synapse [#1613]*
Il Song Han, University of Sheffield, United Kingdom

This paper describes a new asynchronous spike based neuromorphic VLSI implementation, inspired by the biological plausibility and low power requirement. The voltage-controlled conductance produces the synaptic function of multiplication, and spike currents for the neuron. The overall power consumption can be less in real applications, as a synapse only consumes the power when there is a neural input. The neuron is based on multiple combination of synapses and the HSPICE simulation demonstrates the asynchronous spike neural behavior of integration-and- firing with a refractory period. The asynchronous spike based neural networks in 0.18um CMOS VLSI technology is proposed to small power consumption and no need for a synchronous operation.

1:40PM *Novel Digital Spiking Neuron and its Pulse-Coupled Network: Spike Position Coding and Multiplex Communication [#1686]*
Hiroyuki Torikai, Hiroshi Hamanaka and Toshimichi Saito, Hosei University, Japan

We present a novel digital spiking neuron that can generate various spike-trains. Based on a spike position modulation, the neuron can code multiple digital informations into a single spike-train. We also present a pulse-coupled network of the neurons to which the coded spike- train is input. The network can retrieve the digital informations from the input spike-train, based on a synchronization phenomenon. Applications of the network to multiplex communications are discussed, and typical phenomena are confirmed by an HDL simulation.

2:00PM *Digital Implementation of a Bio-inspired Neural Model for Motion Estimation [#1463]*
Cesar Torres-Huitzil, Bernard Girau and Claudio Castellanos-Sanchez, LORIA-INRIA Lorraine, France

In this paper, the design of a digital hardware architecture for a bio-inspired neural model for motion estimation is presented. The motion estimation is based on a strongly localized bio-inspired connectionist model. The architecture is constituted by three main modules that perform three different kinds of processing: spatial, temporal, and excitatory-inhibitory connectionist processing. The architecture is modeled, simulated and validated in VHDL. Synthesis results of the spatial and temporal processing modules of the bio-inspired model on a Field Programmable Gate Array (FPGA) device are presented to validate the architecture. The results show the potential achievement of real-time performance at an affordable silicon area.

2:20PM *Emulation Engine for Spiking Neurons and Adaptive Synaptic Weights [#1363]*
Heik Heinrich Hellmich, Martin Geike, Patrick Griep, Philipp Mahr, Marco Rafanelli and Heinrich Klar, Technical University Berlin, Germany

The simulation of pulse-coded neural networks (PCNNs) for the evaluation of a biology-oriented image processing is still very time-consuming. The main bottle-neck during the simulation is the sequential access to the weight memory for the calculation of the neuron states. A field-programmable gate array (FPGA) based emulation engine, called Spiking Neural Network Emulation Engine (SEE), for spiking neurons and adaptive synaptic weights is presented, that tackles this bottle-neck problem. It is evaluated that the current implementation of SEE achieves an acceleration factor of 30 for sparsely connected networks compared to a software implementation running on a stand-alone PC (2.4 GHz CPU and 1 GB RAM main memory).

2:40PM *An Orientation-Selective Multi-chip aVLSI Applicable to Texture Analysis [#1617]*
Kazuhiro Shimonomura and Tetsuya Yagi, Osaka University, Japan

A high resolution neuromorphic aVLSI was fabricated to emulate the orientation selective response of the simple cell in the primary visual cortex. The aVLSI circuits consist of a silicon retina and an orientation chip. Both chips have 100 x 100 pixles. Using the multi-chip system, a texture segregation was conducted based on a similar algorithm of the energy computation. The texture image was filtered by the two orthgonally oriented receptive fields and were combined to segregate the area of different texture orientaion with the aid of a PC. The study demonstrated that the orientation-selective multi-chip system developed is useful and applicable to robotic vision.

Applications II
Thursday, August 4, 1:00PM-3:00PM, Room: Verdun/Lachine, Chair: Bernard Widrow

1:00PM *Information-Theoretic Feature Selection Algorithms for Text Classification [#1483]*
Jana Novovicova and Antonin Malik, Institute of Information Theory and Automation, Czech Republic

The new feature selection algorithms for the purpose of text classification are presented. Sequential forward selection methods based on improved mutual information criterion functions are investigated. The performance of the proposed criteria are compared to the information gain which evaluate features individually is discussed. Experimental results using naive Bayes classifier based on multinomial model, linear Support Vector Machine and k-nearest neighbor classifiers on the Reuters data set are presented. Results are analysed from various perspectives, including F1-measure, precision and recall. Preliminary results indicate the effectiveness of the proposed feature selection algorithms in a text classification.

1:20PM *SOM Based Image Data Structuring in an Augmented Reality Scenario [#1492]*
Holger Bekel, Gunther Heidemann and Helge Ritter, University of Bielefeld, Germany

Our research focuses on the development of a mobile Augmented Reality System which is capable of acquiring image data in an unrestricted environment and which provides a comfortable facility to label this data. To structure the image data modified MPEG-7 features are computed and by means of Self organizing maps (SOM) the imagery can be labeled stepwise. First the complete data set is projected onto the SOM using a combination of color and edge features. In a second step selected parts of the imagery are retrained weighting the feature blocks depending on characteristics of the acquired image data. Within few steps the partitioning leads to SOM nodes on which the projected imagery can be labeled as objects or rejected.

1:40PM *Forecasting Energy Product Prices [#1528]*
Mary Malliaris and Steven Malliaris, Loyola University Chicago, United States; Massachusetts Institute of Technology, United States

Five inter-related energy products are forecasted one month into the future using both linear and non-linear techniques. Both spot prices and data derived from those prices are used as input data in the models. The models are tested by running data from the following year through them. Results show that, even though all products are highly correlated, the prediction results are asymmetric. In forecasts for crude oil, heating oil, gasoline and natural gas, the nonlinear forecasts were best while for propane, the nonlinear model had the largest average absolute error.

2:00PM *Reinforcement Learning Approach to Individualization of Chronic Pharmacotherapy [#1650]*
Adam Gaweda, Mehmet Muezzinoglu, George Aronoff, Alfred Jacobs, Jacek Zurada and Michael Brier, University of Louisville, United States

Effective pharmacological therapy in chronic treatments poses many challenges to physicians. Individual response to treatment varies across patient populations. Furthermore, due to the prolonged character of the therapy, the response may change over time. A Reinforcement Learning-based framework is proposed for treatment individualization in the management of renal anemia. The approach is based on numerical simulation of the patient performed by Takagi-Sugeno fuzzy model and a Radial Basis Function network implementation of an on-policy Q-learning critic. Simulation results demonstrate the potential of the proposed method to yield policies that achieve the therapeutic goal in individuals with different response characteristics.

2:20PM *"Cognitive" Memory [#1773]*
Bernard Widrow and Juan Carlos Aragon, Stanford University, United States

Regarding the workings of the human mind, memory and pattern recognition seem to be intertwined. You generally do not have one without the other. Taking inspiration from life experience, a new form of computer memory has been devised. It has been used successfully in diverse applications such as visual aircraft identification, aircraft navigation, and human facial recognition. Other uses are being explored. The basic idea will have many new areas of application.

Learning II
Thursday, August 4, 1:00PM-3:00PM, Room: Outremount, Chair: Deliang Wang

1:00PM *Hierarchical Fast Learning Artificial Neural Network [#1332]*
Lai Ping Wong, Leng Phuan Alex Tay and Jian Xu, Nanyang Technological University, Singapore

The Hierarchical Fast Learning Artificial Neural Network (HieFLANN) is proposed as an unsupervised learning model that incorporates a hierarchical approach to address pattern classification for high dimensional data. It utilizes K-Means Fast Learning Artificial Neural Network (KFLANN) subnets and a Canonical Covariance Feature Compression (C2FeCom) process. The embedded individual KFLANN subnet autonomously derives the essential localized network parameters from the input data and in the process, builds a hierarchical network. The C2FeCom feature compression process extracts the independent parameters in compact representations from subnets. The proposed algorithm is experimentally evaluated using benchmark datasets.

1:20PM *Non-Homogenous Structures in Neural Networks with Chaotic Recursive Nodes: Dealing with Diverse Multi-assemblies Architectures, Connectivity and Arbitrary Bifurcating Nodes [#1752]*
Emilio Del-Moral-Hernandez, Polytechnic School of University of Sao Paulo, Brazil

The paper addresses neural architectures based on nodes with chaotic dynamics. These nodes interact through parametric coupling, and the network evolves to spatio-temporal attractors that encode stored patterns. This strategy is used to implement associative memories. The impact of the synaptic connections magnitude on architecture performance is analyzed, and a strategy for minimizing degradation when the number of stored patterns grows is developed. Experiments show the success of such strategy. Mechanisms for allowing asynchronous changes in input patterns and tools for the interconnection between associative assemblies are developed. Finally, the coupling and information coding in heterogeneous assemblies with diverse nodes are analyzed

1:40PM *Improved Chaotic Neuro-Computer with Output-Coding for Quadratic Assignment Problems [#1326]*
Koji Mori, Yoshihiko Horio and Kazuyuki Aihara, Tokyo Denki University, Japan; University of Tokyo, Japan

We improve performance of a chaotic neuro-computer in solving quadratic assignment problems (QAPs) by adopting an output-coding which constructs a feasible solution from analog internal-states of neurons at each iteration. Through measurements from the chaotic neuro-computer hardware, we show that we constantly obtain the optimum solution for size-10 QAPs. Furthermore, chaotic search dynamics through chaotic itinerancy is confirmed from time evolutions of a cost function and an energy function. Moreover, we observe internal states of three neurons in a network to extract useful information on network dynamics that is effective in solving the QAPs.

2:00PM *Chaotic Associative Memory using Internal Patterns for Image Retrieval by Color and Shape Information [#1322]*
Satoshi Kosuge and Yuko Osana, Tokyo University of Technology, Japan

In this paper, we propose a Chaotic Associative Memory using Internal Patterns for Image Retrieval (CAMIP-IR) by color and shape information. This model is based on the Chaotic Associative Memory which can realize dynamic associations and the Self-Organizing Map. In the proposed model, the similarity-based image retrieval can be realized using color and shape information.

2:20PM *Transient Dynamics of Non-Linear Models Describing Multi-Stable Stochastic Systems [#1323]*
Miika Rajala and Risto Ritala, Tampere University of Technology, Finland

Multi-stable stochastic systems are inherently nonlinear and typically have long transient times before stationary state is reached. Black-box dynamic models always assume the data to be from a stationary system. In this paper we discuss a method to assess whether data is long enough to justify non-linear time series model. Our method discretizes state space and studies the corresponding Markov chain. The eigenvalues of the Markov transition operator provide leading transient time constants. The method is illustrated by generating data with a known multi-stable model and then analyzing the data with NNAR(1) and polynomial lag-1 time series model.

2:40PM *How to Find Different Neural Networks by Negative Correlation Learning [#1344]*
Yong Liu, The University of Aizu, Japan

Two penalty functions are introduced in the negative correlation learning for finding different neural networks in an ensemble. One is based on the average output of the ensemble. The other is based on the classification. The idea of penalty function based on the average output is to make each individual network has the different output value to that of the ensemble on the same input. In comparison, the penalty function based on the classification is to lead each individual network to have different class to that of the ensemble on the same input. Experiments on a classification task show how the negative correlation learning generates different neural networks with two different penalty functions.

Thursday, August 4, 3:20PM-4:20PM

Plenary Talk: Neuromorphic Engineering: Overview and Potential
Thursday, August 4, 3:20PM-4:20PM, Room: Westmount/Outremount, Speaker: Carver Mead, California Institute of Technology, United States

It is evident to even the most casual observer that the nervous systems of animals are able to accomplish feats that cannot be approached by our most powerful computing systems. Given the exponential increase in computing power over the last 45 years, our inability to rival the common housefly has become downright embarrassing. What is going on?

Exploring Chemical Space with Computers: Challenges and Opportunities

Professor Pierre Baldi
School of Information and Computer Science
Department of Biological Chemistry
Director Institute for Genomics and Bioinformatics
University of California, Irvine
Irvine, CA 92697-3425
http://www.ics.uci.edu/~pfbaldi

Small molecules with at most a few dozen atoms play a fundamental role in organic chemistry and biology. They can be used as combinatorial building blocks for chemical synthesis, as molecular probes for perturbing and analyzing biological systems, and for the screening/design/discovery of new drugs. As datasets of small molecules become increasingly available, it becomes important to develop computational methods for the classification and analysis of small molecules and in particular for the prediction of their physical, chemical, and biological properties.

We will describe datasets and machine learning methods, in particular kernel methods, for chemical molecules represented by 1D strings, 2D graphs of bonds, and 3D structures. We will demonstrate state-of-the-art results for the prediction of physical, chemical, or biological properties including the prediction of toxicity and anti-cancer activity. More broadly, we will discuss some of the challenges and opportunities for computer science, AI, and machine learning in chemistry.

Automatic Target Recognition Using New Support Vector Machine

David Casasent and Yu-Chiang Wang
Dept. of Electrical and Computer Engineering, Carnegie Mellon University
Pittsburgh, PA 15213, USA
casasent@ece.cmu.edu, ycwang@cmu.edu

Abstract - A hierarchical classifier using a new SVRDM (support vector representation and discrimination machine) is proposed for automatic target recognition. An accuracy and distance-based method is used to design a hierarchical classifier. Our SVRDM hierarchical classifier has the ability to reject unseen non-object classes and clutter inputs. Uses of both iconic and spatial frequency domain features are considered. Initial recognition and rejection test results on infra-red (IR) data are excellent.

I. INTRODUCTION

In this automatic target recognition case, we assume regions containing possible targets (ROIs, regions of interest) are provided. We address an enhancement stage which performs background removal and noise reduction, a feature extraction stage which selects the input features to the last classification stage. We emphasize the classifier. We address reducing the number of features and providing shift and scale-invariant features, since the test object may not always be centered in the ROI.

A standard approach to a C-class classification problem is to consider a collection of C binary classifiers. Each is a separate classifier that distinguishes one class from all of the rest *(one-vs-rest)* [1]. Their results are then combined by winner-take-all etc methods [2]. Alternatively, $C(C-1)/2 \approx C^2/2$ classifiers or hyperplanes can be used (the *one-vs-one* method). These hyperplanes separate each class from every other class and a decision function is constructed using some voting system. However, there is no guarantee that one class and the remaining classes can be separated well in the one-vs-rest classifier case; for the one-vs-one method, the number of classifiers and computations required is prohibitive [3]. We consider a hierarchical classifier approach with a top-down design, which is a modular learning problem inspired by the divide-and-conquer strategy. The modular learning has been found to learn concepts more effectively (performs better) and more efficiently (learns faster), since learning a large number of simple local concepts is both easier and more useful than learning a single complex global concept [4]. The use of a hierarchical classifier has been shown to give better classification results than use of a single complex classifier, such as a neural network or a k-nearest neighbors (kNN) [3, 6].

The top-down hierarchical classifier we propose involves a tree structure of C-1 classifiers rather than a single layer set of C (as in the one-vs-rest approach) or $C^2/2$ classifiers (as in the one-vs-one approach). At each node in the hierarchy, we divide the classes to be recognized into two smaller macro-classes; this procedure continues at subsequent levels and nodes. Only $\log_2 C$ classifiers are used in traversing a path from the top to a bottom decision node in the hierarchy. Thus, the number of required calculations is reduced in this approach and P_C (percentage of correct classification) results are generally better, because the classifier at each node is simpler [3].

We need to estimate the separation between the two macro-classes at each node to decide which two macro-classes to use there. Cost-based, distance-based, and accuracy-based methods are generally used to solve this problem [5]. We use a combination of the accuracy and distance-based methods to select the macro-classes, as we detail in Sect. 4.3. A new support vector representation and discrimination machine (SVRDM) classifier (Sect. 2) is used at each node in the hierarchy. Sect. 3 describes the IR (infra-red) database we used. In Sect. 4, the image preprocessing, feature spaces used, and the design procedure for the hierarchical classifier are detailed. In Sect. 5, the design result and the performance of our hierarchical classifiers using different feature spaces are discussed.

II. SUPPORT VECTOR REPRESENTATION AND DISCRIMINATION MACHINE (SVRDM)

A. SVRDM Algorithm

The SVRDM [7] is an extension of the SVM that provides better rejection performance, which is vital for many applications. To produce more general decision surfaces (better separation between the two classes), SVMs use various kernel functions for nonlinearly mapping the inputs x to a higher-order decision domain [8]. Here we consider only Gaussian kernel functions [9], $\exp[-\|x_i - x_j\|^2/2\sigma^2]$, since this allows the distance between two vectors to be represented by their inner product. To classify an input

x into one of two classes, we thus compute the VIP (vector inner product) evaluation function output of the transformed test input $\Phi(x)$ and our nonlinear filter function h as $f(x) = h^T\Phi(x)$. The filter h is computed from the training set and solving the following quadratic programming problem

$$\text{Min}\|h\|^2/2$$
$$h^T\Phi(x_i) \geq T, i=1,2,...,N_1 \quad (1)$$
$$h^T\Phi(x_j) \leq -T, j=1,2,...,N_2,$$

where N_1 and N_2 are the number of training set samples in each class and the threshold T is ideally chosen to be 1 for an SVM, i.e. the VIP outputs are ≥ 1 for one class and ≤ -1 for the other class. When an SVM is used at each node in the hierarchical classifier, at each node, the classifier separates one macro-class from another. The VIP determines to which macro-class the input belongs.

Since the standard SVM cannot reject non-object inputs well, we extended [7] the SVM to the new SVRDM with its better rejection performance in the multiple-object-class case. In our new hierarchical classifier, each node handles classification of two macro-classes. The two solution vectors h_1 and h_2 for macro-classes 1 and 2 in our SVRDM for a given node must satisfy

$$\begin{array}{ll}\text{Min}\|h_1\|^2/2 & \text{Min}\|h_2\|^2/2 \\ h_1^T\Phi(x_{1i}) \geq T, i=1,2,...,N_1 & h_2^T\Phi(x_{2j}) \geq T, j=1,2,...,N_2 \\ h_1^T\Phi(x_{2j}) \leq p, j=1,2,...,N_2, & h_2^T\Phi(x_{1i}) \leq p, i=1,2,...,N_1.\end{array} \quad (2)$$

In (2), there are N_1 and N_2 samples in each macro-class. Note that the second class output is specified to be $\leq p$ (and not $-T$ or -1, as in the standard SVM). This improves rejection. Typically, we choose p in the range [-1, 0.6]. If $p = -1$, then (2) describes the standard SVM. In the presence of outliers (training class errors), slack variables ξ are used in both h_1 and h_2. Thus, the final h_1 in (2) satisfies

$$\text{Min}\left\{\|h_1\|^2/2 + C\left(\sum \xi_{1i} + \sum \xi_{2j}\right)\right\} \xi_{1i} \geq 0, \xi_{2j} \geq 0$$
$$h_1^T\Phi(x_{1i}) \geq T - \xi_{1i}, i=1,2,...,N_1 \quad (3)$$
$$h_1^T\Phi(x_{2j}) \leq p + \xi_{2j}, j=1,2,...,N_2.$$

In (3), C is the weight of the penalty term for the slack variables. The final version of h_2 is similar.

At each node in our hierarchical classifier, we evaluate the associated two VIPs of the transformed input $\Phi(x)$ and the h_1 and h_2 (at that node). The VIP with the largest output ($\geq T$) denotes the macro-class decision made at that node. If neither VIP gives an output $\geq T$, the test input is rejected as a non-object (clutter in our ATR case).

A. SVRDM Parameter Selection

For each SVRDM in the hierarchy, we must choose values for several parameters. If we choose too small of a value for σ in the Gaussian kernel function, the bounded region for the class samples will be tight, more samples will be viewed as support vectors. This causes an over-fitted problem, and the generalization will be poor. We developed a new automated method to select σ [7].

The selection of the threshold T decides the acceptable range of the input x in (3). Lower T values result in worse rejection but better classification. From initial tests, we chose T = 0.9, reducing T until P_C on the validation set is good. *Note that no test set images are present in the training or validation sets and that **no non-object data be rejected are used** in training or validation tests.* Others also make this assumption that no non-objects to be rejected are used in training or validation data [9].

The value of p in (2) and (3) mainly affects P_C (it has little affect on the rejection rate). It is also affected by the distribution of non-object class data. If the non-object class samples (to be rejected) are distributed in the entire input space, a higher p is preferred and it will reject samples not close to training set data (this also reduces P_C for true samples), as it provides a smaller decision region. We detailed this recently [10]. For the TRIM-2 database we use here, the non-object class samples are different aircraft and background clutter images; thus, a larger $p = 0.6$ is preferable. The last parameter to choose is the factor C in (3). We set $C = 20$. This choice is not critical in our initial tests, since our scores are nearly perfect, i.e. there were no slack variables to be weighted in (3) during training our SVRDM classifiers.

II. DATABASE DESCRIPTION (TRIM-2)

The TRIM-2 database used contained 21 aspect views of each of twelve military objects (eight vehicles and four aircraft) in several different thermal states at a range of 1.5 km. Each image was 150 x 50 pixels. The eight vehicles were chosen as our targets; all four aircraft in all thermal states and backgrounds and thirty clutter regions in different backgrounds were chosen as false alarms to be rejected.

The 21 aspect view images for each object-class were divided into: a *training set* of 9 aspect views used for synthesis of the SVRDM classifiers, a *validation set* of 5 other aspect views used to select the SVRDM classifier parameters p and T and the macro-classes used at each node in our hierarchy, and a *test set* of 7 aspect views used to obtain final P_C scores. Test set data differed from other data by up to 15° in aspect. To test the rejection ability of our classifier (P_{FA} or percent false alarms not rejected), we used 21 aspect x 4 aircraft x 4 thermal states plus 30 clutter chips (ten each from the three backgrounds) = 366 *non-object chips* at the same 1.5 km range. *No non-object data are used in training or validation.* The chip for each image includes many non-zero background pixels (See Fig. 1). The false alarm database used only the central 150 x 50 pixel region of each aircraft and of each clutter chip.

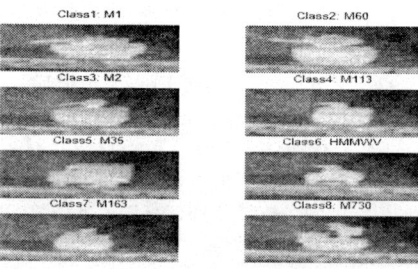

Fig. 1 IR Images of eight vehicles in TRIM-2 database (only +90° aspect view shown)

III. Hierarchical SVRDM Classifier Design

A. Image Preprocessing

We now note the preprocessing we used to provide input data with better quality and hence better classification results. We linearly normalize the minimum and maximum pixel values in each grayscale image to the [0, 255] range. This enhances the contrast of the original image. This is preferable to histogram equalization, which maps different input gray levels to the same output gray level; this can cause problems when object and background pixel levels are similar and spatially close. Next we estimate the background and reduce it by morphological processing. We open the image by an erosion followed by a dilation. This removes any bright region whose size is less than the structuring element, while preserving the shape and size of larger objects in the image. The structuring element used in dilation and erosion is slightly larger than the size of the largest object and is much less than the size of the full image. We used a binary 2D 30 x 80 pixel rectangular structuring element. This provides an estimate of the background. We then subtract this estimated background image from the contrast-enhanced image to obtain the final preprocessed result. Since salt-and-pepper noise is usually seen in many IR images and since the background reduction procedure does not remove this type of noise, we applied a 3 x 3 median filter to produce the final image.

B. Feature Spaces Used

We considered three different types of feature spaces of the data as input to our classifiers. The first were iconic (pixel-based) features; specifically, the 150 x 50 pixel target images are lexicographically ordered into a 7500 x 1 element feature column vector input. However, these features are not shift-invariant. The P_C performance will significantly decrease if the test inputs are not centered within a few pixels of the center of the object, as we will show. To solve the problem of shift-invariance, we considered magnitude Fourier Transform (|FT|) features. This is also a feature space in which compression is possible. Analysis of the |FT| of the images showed negligible energy in higher spatial frequencies. Thus, only the lowest 50 x 50 spatial frequencies were retained to reduce the number of |FT| features to 2500 compared to 7500 iconic features. Since the |FT| is symmetric, we can use half of the |FT| plane with no loss of information. We further retained only one quadrant of this |FT| feature space for greater compression. We thus retained only the lowest 25 x 25 spatial frequencies in the first |FT| quadrant and thus only 625 |FT| features. We refer to these as *reduced |FT| features*.

To handle different thermal states of the vehicles, we normalize each ROI (training, validation, test, and false alarm data) chip image so that the energy of each is the same. This is done by dividing each pixel value by the average value of all pixels in the image. This is needed to reduce the effects of thermal variations of targets in ROIs (i.e. hot and cold targets and target parts). This normalization makes images of objects in different thermal states more similar (this is its purpose), but it makes different objects more similar (all have the same energy) and thus complicates classification (but this is necessary for IR data).

C. Hierarchical Top-Down Classifier Design

The structure of a multi-class hierarchical classifier system requires selection of the macro-classes to be separated at each node and in each level in the hierarchy. For the *C*-class problem, at node 1, we determine to which of two *macro-classes* (sets of *C*/2 etc. classes) the input belongs. At subsequent nodes of the tree, the input class is further restricted to a smaller set of macro-classes until, at the bottom nodes (final leafs), the class of the input is determined. We could design the hierarchical classifier by a bottom-up or a top-down method [3]. We chose a top-down design so that the classifiers with the most difficult decisions (the most similar macro-classes) are present later in the hierarchy and that the macro-classes that are best separated are present at higher levels in the hierarchy. Others [11] also note that this is the preferable method.

At the top level in our top-down design, we separate the eight object classes in the training data into two macro-groups, each with four classes. There are now $0.5 \times C_4^8 = 35$ choices for dividing the eight classes into two such macro-groups. There are thus 35 possible classifier designs for the classifier in level one of the hierarchy. We form 35 SVRDMs, one for each of the possible choices of macro-classes. The macro-sets we chose to separate at node1 are those that can be best separated. We design the remaining lower level classifiers similarly. At each node, we select the pair of macro-classes which minimize the number of classification errors on the validation set (if several sets give the same performance, we consider the macro-class sets with the largest margin (separation between classes)).

In the design of the SVRDM classifier for each node we use training set data; to select the macro-classes to be separated at each node, performance on the validation set is used. We must also *design the SVRDM classifier* for each level and node, i.e. we must select its T and p parameters (using the validation set data). To achieve the design without an exhaustive search of all combinations of macro-classes and all p and T choices, we perform initial tests to determine a tentative range of p values (0.4-0.6) and of T values (0.7-0.9), with incremental step size of 0.1 to be considered. This range can later be modified, if needed. We note that p and T must satisfy $p \leq T$ and realistically $p < T$ to allow different outputs for the two class case. We note that, for each SVRDM or pair of macro-classes, there is a pair of discriminant vectors $\mathbf{h}_1$ and $\mathbf{h}_2$ as in Sect. 2.1, one (e.g. $\mathbf{h}_1$) gives an output ≥ 1 for macro-class 1 inputs (e.g. one subset of 4 classes for node 1 for the eight class TRIM-2 database) and for the other set of four classes in macro-class 2 (at node 1) it gives an output $\leq p$. The other discriminant vector $\mathbf{h}_2$ gives outputs ≥ 1 for macro-class 2 and outputs $\leq p$ for macro-class 1. The vector $\mathbf{h}$ ($\mathbf{h}_1$ or $\mathbf{h}_2$) with the largest output $\geq T$ (for validation or test set data) determines the class of the input. Inputs with outputs $< T$ for both $\mathbf{h}_1$ and $\mathbf{h}_2$ are rejected as non-objects.

To select the pair of macro-classes to be separated, we fixed $p = 0.6$ (since higher p gives better rejection, theoretically). We start at node 1 (the top of the hierarchy). For each choice of a pair of macro-classes, we form an SVRDM using only training set data. We test each SVRDM with T = 0.9, then T = 0.8 and 0.7 (if needed) on the validation set until we achieve $P_C = 100\%$ (or the highest P_C). We select the pair of macro-classes that gives the highest P_C on the validation set. This selects the design of the pair of macro-classes at node 1. Thus, the accuracy-based separation between two classes (macro-classes) is first considered. However, there are often several macro-class pairs with the same $P_C = 100\%$ or the same highest P_C. To select the best macro-class pair, we vary T (in increments of 0.1) for each pair of macro-classes with the highest P_C score. We select the solution that gives the largest separation margin M between the two macro-classes. Therefore, the distance-based separation between two classes (macro-classes) is also considered. The margin M we use is the sum of the amounts by which the different evaluation function outputs exceed T averaged over all samples. This *accuracy and distance-based parameter selection procedure* is repeated at each subsequent levels and nodes, with a reduced number of classes used at each node.

In general, use of a low T provides better P_C (this is more necessary as the test set becomes more different from the training set) but poorer rejection; thus, we prefer not to use T < 0.7. Similarly, use of a larger p will give better rejection, due to the lower decision volume or envelope it provides. An initial upper limit of $p = 0.6$ was chosen. Sect. 5.1 provides example results. For each node, we consider only the same number of classes in each macro-class; this is done for simplicity. This finalizes the hierarchical and the SVRDM design at each node.

IV. Hierarchical SVRDM Classifier Results

This section presents TRIM-2 results for hierarchical designs and test results using different feature spaces. The choices of targets and false alarms (aircraft and clutter) of the TRIM-2 database are detailed in Sect. 3. We detail our hierarchical classifier design (Sect. 5.1) using reduced |FT| features; the design approach for other feature spaces is similar. The test results are presented in Sect. 5.2.

A. Hierarchical SVRDM Classifier Design (Reduced |FT| Features with preprocessing)

At the first (top) node 1, we separated the eight classes into different pairs of macro-classes, each with four classes. There are $0.5 \times C_4^8 = 35$ different combinations of macro-class pairs. For each, we formed an SVRDM, using different training set images of the different combinations of two macro-classes. Each of the 35 SVRDM choices (of macro-class pairs) for node 1 was evaluated on the validation set and the P_C (percentage of correct recognition) score was noted at T = 0.9 (for an SVRDM with $p = 0.6$). We found that seven different macro-class combinations gave P_C (validation) = 100% (see Table 1). If we decreased T, more macro-class pairs gave P_C (validation) = 100%; thus, we stopped at T = 0.9, since P_C (validation) = 100% was obtained. For each macro-class pair with the same best P_C score, we formed SVRDMs for all p and T choices in the ranges noted ($p = 0.4$ to 0.6 and T = 0.7 to 0.9, with an increment step size of 0.1). For each choice, we evaluated P_C and the margin M for the validation set. In practice, M improves (increases) as we decrease T. For the TRIM-2 database, as we increase p, the volume of acceptance decreases and thus the class separation M increases. Thus, for the TRIM-2 database, the best M is achieved for an SVRDM with the largest p (=0.6) and the lowest T (=0.7) in the ranges chosen. To understand results, note that classes 1 and 2 are tanks, class 3 is a Bradley, class 4 is an APC, class 5 is a truck, class 6 is a jeep, and classes 7 and 8 are ADUs. For node 1, the pair of macro-classes that gave $P_C = 100\%$ on the validation set with the largest separation margin M was macro-class 1, 2, 3, 5 vs macro-class 4, 6, 7, 8; i.e. separating classes 1, 2, 3, and 5 from classes 4, 6, 7, and 8 is best at node 1. The SVRDM chosen for this pair of macro-classes used $p = 0.6$ and T = 0.7.

TABLE 1
NUMBER OF VALIDATION SET SAMPLES CORRECTLY CLASSIFIED (OUT OF 40) AND MARGIN M SCORES FOR THE SEVEN SETS OF MACRO-CLASSES AT NODE 1 WITH PERFECT $P_C = 100\%$ ON THE VALIDATION SET AT T = 0.9 AND $P = 0.6$ USING REDUCED |FT| FEATURES. THE MACRO-CLASS PAIR WITH $P_C = 100\%$ AND THE LARGEST MARGIN IS SELECTED.

	T	1235 vs 4678	1238 vs 4567	1378 vs 2456
0.6	0.9	32	34	34
	0.8	40	40	40
	0.7	40	40	40
p	T	margin	margin	margin
0.6	0.9	0.2477	0.1934	0.1805
	0.8	0.374	0.3552	0.3425
	0.7	0.574	0.5552	0.5425

Table 1 notes the P_C (validation) and margin M scores (as we vary T) for the three macro-class pairs at node 1 that gave P_C = 100% on the validation set at $p = 0.6$ and at $T \leq 0.8$. We note that many margin values are very close and that no one macro-class pair choice is much better than another. Thus, for this database, the specific macro-class pair chosen (at node 1) is not critical, and several pairs are expected to give similar test set performance.

This general design procedure is repeated at subsequent levels and nodes with different macro-classes. In level 2 of the hierarchy, we now subdivide each of the two macro-classes into two smaller macro-classes. At node 2 in level 2 of our hierarchy, we separated classes 1, 2, 3, 5 into two smaller macro-classes (we chose an equal number of classes (two) per new macro-class). There are $0.5 \times C_2^4 = 3$ pairs of two macro-classes to consider (each macro-class now contains only 2 classes), where we found that only the macro-class (1, 3) vs macro-class (2, 5) gave P_C = (validation) 100% at $p = 0.6$ and $T = 0.7$ and 0.8, respectively. See Fig. 2. This thus defines the macro-class decision to be made at this level 2 node 2 in our hierarchical classifier (class 1, 3, vs 2, 5). By a similar procedure, we chose to separate macro-class (4, 7) and (6, 8) at node 3, since it gave the best margin M and P_C = (validation) 100%.

At the last layer of the hierarchical classifier, the classes to be separated are the four pairs chosen in level 2: class 1 vs 3, 2 vs 5, 4 vs 7, 6 vs 8. All SVRDMs again used $p = 0.6$ and $T = 0.7$, determined to be the best choices in the range given with the largest M. Fig. 2 shows the class divisions chosen at the different nodes and levels in the hierarchical classifier using reduced |FT| features. The hierarchy design (macro-classes separated) using other features differed from Fig. 2 by different class (macro-class) combinations. We note that the macro-class pairs are selected automatically and the tanks (classes 1 and 2) are not necessary in the same macro-classes; our method is thus preferred.

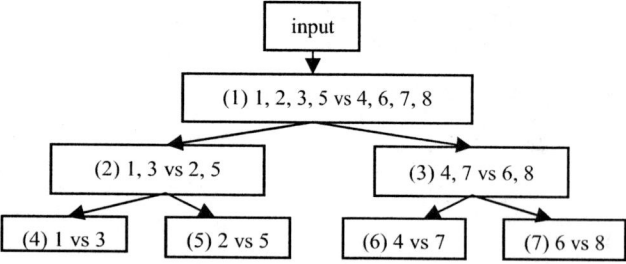

Fig. 2 Hierarchical Classifier Structure (reduced |FT| features with preprocessing)

B. Hierarchical SVRDM Classifier Results

Table 2 lists the performance of the hierarchical SVRDM classifiers using different features. The recognition rate is P_C = 98.2% using iconic features (55 of 56 test inputs correct) and false alarm rejection P_{FA} is perfect; however, this feature space is not shift-invariant and the dimension of each input is very high (7500 x 1 pixels). In tests, we determined that if the chip images of true inputs are shifted by three pixels, then many true class inputs will be rejected as non-objects. This is why we consider |FT| features for our further designs. The next two entries in the top row of Table 2 show the good performance obtained with the |FT| feature spaces with shift-invariance. Rejection P_{FA} is perfect. This is because of our SVRDM used. A standard SVM performs worse [7]. Classification is perfect (all 56 test objects correctly identified) using fewer 2500 |FT| vs 7500 iconic features. Normalized features are needed to handle thermal variations in the state of the vehicles. Reduced |FT| normalized features gave comparable results (P_C = 96.4% and P_{FA} = 0%) to the use of unnormalized data. This is encouraging because with energy normalized images, all aspect views of all objects have the same energy and thus all vehicles are more similar. All non-object chips to be rejected have the same energy as targets and thus rejection is more difficult. They were very encouraging (P_C = 97.3% and P_{FA} = 1.9%) indicating that normalized data aids in handling thermal variations. Only the reduce |FT| features used our image preprocessing. They gave an excellent classification result with P_C = 98.22% and P_{FA} = 0%; these results were better in P_C by 2% from prior results without preprocessing.

TABLE 2
TEST RESULTS OF HIERARCHICAL SVRDM CLASSIFIERS USING DIFFERENT FEATURES

Feature	Iconic	50x50 pixel |FT|	Reduced 25x25 pixel |FT|
P_C	98.22 %(55/56)	100 % (56/56)	94.6 % (53/56)
P_{FA}	0%	0%	0%
Feature	Normalized Reduced |FT| (1 thermal state)	Reduced |FT| with image preprocessing (1 thermal state)	Normalized Reduced |FT| (2 thermal states)
P_C	96.4 % (54/56)	98.22 % (55/56)	97.3 %(109/112)
P_{FA}	0%	0 %	1.9% (7/366)

We also calculated the average time to classify an input (after its feature vector has been formed). This includes traversing the SVRDMs in the tree structure. The average calculation time was 0.13 sec for the 7500 (150 x 50) iconic features, 0.04 sec for the 2500 (50 x 50) |FT| feature, and 0.01 sec for the reduced 625 (25 x 25) |FT| features. These computations were made in Matlab on a P4 1.8GHz PC with 256MB RAM.

V. CONCLUSION

A new SVRDM hierarchical classifier was described for shift-invariant classification with excellent rejection ability. To select the best set of macro-classes at each node in the hierarchy, a new SVRDM algorithm is used. We use reduced |FT| features to provide shift-invariance and achieved excellent performance (for both classification and rejection).

ACKNOWLEDGMENT

The support of this work by ARO STTR Phase-2 contract W911NF-04-C-0099 is gratefully acknowledged. We also sincerely thank Clare Walters and Anita Burrell from NVESD for providing us the TRIM-2 database.

REFERENCES

[1] R. Duda, P. Hart, and D. Stork, *Pattern Classification*, Wiley-interscience, New York, 2000.
[2] R. Anand, K. Mehrotra, C.K. Mohan, and S. Ranka, "Efficient classification for multiclass problems using modular neural networks," *IEEE Trans on Neural Networks*, Vol. 6, Jan 1995, pp. 117-124.
[3] S. Kumar, J. Ghosh, M. Crawford, "Hierarchical Fusion of Multiple Classifiers for Hyperspectral Data Analysis," *Pattern Analysis and Applications*, 5, 2002, pp. 210 – 220.
[4] S. Kumar and J. Ghosh, "GAMLS: A generalized framework for associative modular learning systems," *SPIE Conf. on Applications and Science of Computer Intelligence* II, *Proc. of SPIE*, Vol. 3722, Orlando, FL, 1999, pp. 24-35.
[5] H. Blockeel, M. Bruynooghe, S. Dzeroski, J. Ramon, and J. Struyf. Hierarchical multi-classification. In *Proc. First International Workshop on Multi-Relational Data Mining*, Edmonton, Canada, 2002, pp.21-35.
[6] F. Schwenker, "Hierarchical support vector machines for multi-class pattern recognition," *4th Int'l Conf. on Knowledge-based Intelligent Engeneering Systems & Allied Technologies, Proc. 4th KES*, Vol. 2, Brighton, UK, Aug. 2000, 561-565.
[7] C. Yuan and D. Casasent, "Support Vector Machines for Class Representation and Discrimination," *Int'l Joint Conf. on Neural Networks*, Portland, July 2003.
[8] C. J. C. Burges, "A Tutorial on Support Vector Machines for Pattern Recognition," *Data Mining and Knowledge Discovery*, Vol.2, No.2, 1998, 121-167.
[9] Y. Q. Chen, X. S. Zhou, and T. S. Huang, "One-Class SVM for Learning in Image Retrieval," *IEEE Conf. on Image Processing*, 2001, pp. 34-37.
[10] C. Yuan and D. Casasent, "Face recognition and imposter rejection using a new SVRDM modified support vector machine," *Proc. of SPIE*, Vol. 5779 (29), Orlando, FL, March 2005.
[11] S. Kumar, J. Ghosh, and M. M. Crawford, "Classification of Hyperspectral Data Using Best-bases Feature Extraction Algorithms," *Proc. of SPIE*, Vol. 4055, Orlando, FL, March 2000, pp. 362-373.

Training with Heterogeneous Data

John A. Drakopoulos
Tablet PC Handwriting Recognition Group
Microsoft Corporation
One Microsoft Way
Redmond, WA 98052-6399
E-mail: johndra@microsoft.com

Ahmad Abdulkader
Tablet PC Handwriting Recognition Group
Microsoft Corporation
One Microsoft Way
Redmond, WA 98052-6399
E-mail: ahmadab@microsoft.com

Abstract--**Data pruning and ordered training are two methods used to train a learner with heterogeneous data. The former is a typical procedure that attempts to factor out noise from the data; the latter is a novel method that partitions the data into a number of categories and assigns training times to those assuming that data size and training time have a polynomial relation. In its current form, ordered training is an approximate and a priori data-emphasizing method. Both methods have been applied to a time-delay neural network--which is one of the main learners in Microsoft's Tablet PC handwriting recognition system. Their effect on the learner is presented in this paper. The handwriting data and the chosen language are Italian.**

Keywords: heterogeneous data, neural networks, training schedule, data emphasizing, boosting.

I. INTRODUCTION

In handwriting recognition, we usually have to train our learners with heterogeneous data, or, more precisely, with handwriting samples of varying types and sizes. For example, the Tablet PC handwriting data are a collection of natural data, telephone numbers, dates, times, people names, geographical names, web and e-mail addresses, postal addresses, numbers, formulas, single character data etc. Such a multitude of types and subsequently distinct and differing statistical properties raises an obvious question: should training methods take data heterogeneity into account and how?

In this paper, we attempt to answer the above question. The overall problem, which applies not only to handwriting recognition but also to every training problem with prevalent heterogeneity, does admit such general solution.

The first step in our approach is to factor out low quality data e.g. data that have a high level of noise. Our ink data are stored in a number of *ink files*; each file contains a number of *panels*; each panel is a sequence of *words;* and words can be dictionary words, e-mail addresses, numbers, dates, single characters etc. Using a combination of machine and human labeling, we label words as good or bad, and our pruning method merely discards the files with a high percentage of bad words.

The second step is to train using the o*rdered training* method: we initially partition the data into a number of categories that share some common properties and then we specify training times for those categories based on the ordered training model. The model itself derives from a single premise that training time and data size have a polynomial relation. (One can dispute this premise, of course, but we believe that whenever training time grows exponentially with data size the underlying problem should be truly hopeless.)

Furthermore, in order to define good or optimal data categories for our methods we resort to co-operational game theory [4]. We treat our problem as an n-player game and we apply a standard hill-climbing method ([6] section 3.2) .

Finally, to avoid catastrophic interference [1], [5], we combine all data categories and train our learner using a single training stream that has the recommended distribution.

There are other approaches to the data heterogeneity problem such as the mixture of experts [3], which attempts to train different learners for distinct data collections or categories and posteriori methods like data-emphasizing and boosting [2]. Although posteriori methods have their advantages--and indeed, we are currently extending our system into a hybrid that would take error rates into account during re-train--we believe that an a priori method, which trains with no prior knowledge of learner's accuracy level, is necessary in order to get the most accurate initial solution. Our results indicate that our a priori methods can improve accuracy significantly for a single learner.

The rest of this paper is organized as follows. The next section describes our pruning procedure. Section 3 contains a formal definition of the ordered training model for single and multi-category data. Section 4 contains the hill-climbing algorithm for partitioning the data into categories while section 5 contains the experimental results (derived from our Italian data and learner). Finally, section 6 addresses current and future extensions of our work.

II. DATA PRUNING

A fundamental entity in our ink collection process is the ink file. Users of our collection system copy a certain script that is presented to them and their ink is stored into a separate ink file. The script, and thus the stored ink, consists of a sequence of panels, each containing a sequence of words--whereby words we mean dictionary words, e-mail addresses, numbers, dates etc.

Subsequently, the ink words are being labeled as bad or good depending on whether they are legible rendering of the intended text (as it appears in the script). The labeling process is a combination of machine and human classification.

A brief study revealed that a fraction of the ink was entirely bogus: straight lines, random curves or drawings, which, of course, had nothing to do with the text in the script. Furthermore, the distribution of such bogus ink was not uniform but rather showed clear concentrations in certain files. The ink in those files was very often of low quality. Thus, we decided to use the percentage of bad words in a file as an index of ink quality and discard the training files with the highest percentage (thus the term 'pruning'). We did not, or course, prune our test sets. Instead, after we trained our system, we computed three word error rates based on all panels, good panels (i.e. panels that contain only good words), and good words (across all panels).

Furthermore, in order to account for the higher accuracy of human labeling, we used two distinct pruning thresholds, one for machine-labeled files and one for human-labeled files.

After we pruned our training data, we used them to train one of our learners using the ordered training model, while we trained the rest of the system treating the pruned data in a uniform manner. The results are presented in section 5.

III. ORDERED TRAINING

Assume a training data set of size S, where S is in terms of fixed units (e.g. bytes) or units that do not vary significantly (e.g. ink segments). Furthermore, assume that the set contains m samples and that we train for time T (which corresponds to E epochs, or N iterations, one sample used per iteration). It would then be $E = N / m$. If we define the training (or data processing) speed u to be the amount of data processed in a time unit i.e. $u = SE / T$ then it would also be $N = muT / S$ and $E = uT / S$.

Assuming that S and m are known and that u can be estimated, we only need a formula for T in order to compute N and E. The *ordered training hypothesis* specifies that the relationship between training time and data size is polynomial:

$$T = aS^o$$

where o is the *order* of training. Apparently, low order means an easier problem or, as we shall see later, a benign data distribution; high order means a more difficult problem or adverse data distribution. a is merely a coefficient that represents 'importance' of our data. (This should be clearer after we study the multi-category case.)

Applying the ordered training hypothesis to the formula of the epochs, we get

$$E = bS^{o-1}$$

where $b = au$. Thus, b is a coefficient that encodes both processing speed and importance of data.

In the following, we shall work mainly with iterations and epochs, and therefore we shall use the second form of the ordered training hypothesis. To simplify the rest of our formulas, we also define the volume, volume per sample, and density of a training set:

$$V = bmS^{o-1} \quad \text{(volume of data)}$$
$$\beta = V / m = bS^{o-1} \quad \text{(volume per sample)}$$
$$d = m / V = (bS^{o-1})^{-1} \quad \text{(density of data)}$$

Intuitively, we can imagine each sample as occupying unit volume in some imaginary space and ordered training as a process that expands each sample to volume β. (At this point, this is merely a scaling operation. However, in the multi-category case, the scaling would be different for each category resulting in a non-linear transformation of the data.)

Using the above definitions, we can rewrite the formulas for time, iterations and epochs:

$$T = \beta S / u$$
$$N = V$$
$$E = \beta$$

It is now clear that higher volume corresponds to more iterations while higher volume per sample (or, equivalently, lower density) corresponds to more epochs.

In order to apply the ordered training hypothesis to the multi-category case, we assume that the data have been partitioned into c categories. For each category $i=0,1, \ldots ,c-1$, we define S_i to be its size, m_i to be its number of samples, T_i to be its allocated training time, N_i to be the corresponding number of training iterations, and E_i to be the corresponding number of training epochs. The coefficient b_i represents the relative importance and processing speed of category i. The volume (V_i), density (d_i), and volume per sample (β_i) are defined as before for each category separately. Apparently it would be $N_i = V_i$. And if we constrain the total number of iterations to be N, by introducing a normalizing constant λ,

$$N_i = \lambda V_i$$
$$N = \sum_{i=0}^{c-1} N_i$$

then we get the following formula

$$N_i = \frac{V_i}{\sum_j V_j} N = \frac{b_i m_i S_i^{o-1}}{\sum_j b_j m_j S_j^{o-1}} N$$

Alternatively, we may require the total number of epochs E or the total time T to be fixed. Yet, all those constraints result in identical models. We have chosen the fixed-iteration model only because it is more suitable to our training software.

At this point, one may be tempted to start training on each category separately using the above model of training iterations. However, such sequential training suffers from catastrophic interference [1], [5]. Very briefly, training on category i interferes catastrophically with the training on the previous categories and disrupts the knowledge that has already been stored in the learner. As a result, one must combine their data into a single training stream and in such a way that the data distribution will be compatible with the ordered training model--that is N_i iterations would eventually be allocated to category i.

The latter requirement can be easily achieved through data sampling and replication. More specifically, assume that we replicate data r_i times for each category i. If r_i is an integer, then we merely copy the data r_i times; if it is not, then we use sampling (random selection) to achieve the proper fraction. Eventually, we shall end up with $m_i r_i$ samples; and, in order to be compatible with the ordered training hypothesis, it must be that

$$\frac{r_i m_i}{r_j m_j} = \frac{N_i}{N_j}$$

for all categories i, j.

The above condition can be satisfied by choosing $r_i = N_i / m_i$. However, such a choice will result in a data collection of N samples--a number that can be prohibitively large for applications such as handwriting recognition. Furthermore, normalizing the replication ratios (by dividing with the smallest one) is not guarantee to decrease them enough. Indeed, if we had used this approach in our experiments, we would have created training files much larger than 100 GB; and if we had scaled the replication rations arbitrarily so that the files were small enough, some of the ratios would have been much smaller than one, resulting in data loss.

Given the above problem and the fact that the iteration estimates of ordered training are assumptive and approximate, we created an input component that provided the training samples to our learner choosing each sample with probability $P_i = N_i/N$ from category i and scanning the training set of each category sequentially. We trained and tested the combined system and we present the results in section 5.

IV. TURNING DATA PARTITIONING INTO A GAME

Having defined ordered training, we still have to determine how to split the data into categories. In our approach, we treat the problem as an *n*-player game. Each category is represented as a player who attempts to maximize their training iterations. The initial system configuration is determined by *compatibility*: data sets with similar S/m distributions are assumed to be compatible. System evolution is based on unions and partitions:

- Uniting players A and B benefits the united entity at the expense of their competitors.
- Union benefit increases monotonically with density (which is the inverse of player competitiveness).
    - Uniting compatible players benefits them all (almost equally).
    - When uniting incompatible players, the better (sparser/larger) player may pay some penalty.
- Partition is the inverse operation of union and has the opposite effects.

The following two theorems prove the above claims. To simplify our formulas we use the following shorthand notation:

$$X_{q...r} = \sum_{j=q}^{r} X_j$$

Theorem 1. The union of categories 0, 1, ..., g into category g with a new assigned coefficient b is equivalent to replacing each coefficient b_i (for i = 0, 1, ... , g) with

$$b \left(\frac{S_{0...g}}{S_i} \right)^{o-1}$$

Proof.

The union of the first $g+1$ categories results in a new category with $m = m_{0...g}$ samples and volume $V = b m_{0...g} S_{0...g}^{o-1}$. If we define $\overline{N}_i$ to be the new iteration numbers after the union operation (for $i = g, g+1, ..., c-1$; we assume g to be the resulting category after the union) then we can easily prove that

$$\overline{N}_i = \begin{cases} \dfrac{V_i}{V+V_{g+1...c-1}} N & \text{if } i > g \\ \dfrac{m_i V}{m_{0...g}(V+V_{g+1...c-1})} N & \text{if } i \le g \end{cases}$$

Using a new set of coefficients on the original set of categories

$$c_i = \begin{cases} b_i & \text{if } i > g \\ b(S_{0...g}/S_i)^{o-1} & \text{if } i \le g \end{cases}$$

we derive new volumes

$$U_i = \begin{cases} V_i & \text{if } i > g \\ m_i V/m_{0...g} & \text{if } i \le g \end{cases}$$

and new iterations

$$M_i = \dfrac{U_i}{U_{0...c-1}} N$$

It is now easy to show that $M_i = \overline{N}_i$, for all i, (since $V + V_{g+1...c-1} = U_{0...c-1}$). Q.E.D.

Theorem 2. The union of categories $0, 1, ... g$ into category g with a new assigned coefficient b changes the number of epochs for category $i = 0, ..., g$ by ΔE_i so that

$$\Delta E_i - \Delta E_j = \dfrac{\beta_j - \beta_i}{V_{0...c-1}} N$$

Proof.

Defining V and $\overline{N}_i$ as in the proof of the previous theorem we can easily find that, for $i = 0, ..., g$, it is:

$$\Delta E_i = \dfrac{\overline{N}_i}{m_i} - \dfrac{N_i}{m_i} = \dfrac{bS_{0..g}^{o-1} N}{V+V_{g+1...c-1}} - \dfrac{\beta_i N}{V_{0...c-1}}$$

A mere subtraction now completes our proof. Q.E.D.

From theorem 2, we can easily derive the following corollary.

Corollary. If $\beta_0 \le \beta_1 \le ... \le \beta_g$ then the union of categories $0, 1, ..., g$ would change epochs so that $\Delta E_0 \ge \Delta E_1 \ge ... \ge \Delta E_g$.

Having established the dynamics of our n-player game, we can describe a hill-climbing algorithm to solve the data-partitioning problem (albeit, of course, there is no guarantee of an optimal solution):

```
Start with an initial configuration of categories
Repeat until no more progress
    Train
    Test and identify strong and weak categories
    Unite and partition accordingly
```

(We use the term *strong* for categories that have relatively low error rates, and *weak* for categories that have relatively high error rates.)

In the following section, we show some experimental results using the best data partitioning and the best configuration of pruning and ordered training parameters that we found.

V. EXPERIMENTAL RESULTS

In order to measure the effect of our methods on accuracy, we trained one of our main learners (which is a time delay neural network consisting of 150 hidden units) with three different settings:

1. plain: we used all the data uniformly
2. pruned: we pruned and then used all the data uniformly
3. ordered: we pruned and trained according to the ordered training model.

For pruning, we pruned single-character data by 90% (because we have a specific learner for single character data and because the effect single-character training on a general learner can be quite harmful) while we pruned everything else by 16%.

For the ordered training method, order was set to 2.0 (determined with an iterative gradient descent procedure) and the data were eventually partitioned into five categories as shown in the following table:

TABLE I

DATA CATEGORIES

Data Category	Coefficient
Single character	0.25
Postal addresses	1.00
Filenames, names, currency amounts, dates, numbers, telephone numbers, times, single word natural data	
E-mail addresses, URL addresses	1.00
Natural data	4.00

For each version (plain, pruned, ordered), we used the same test set and we estimated three word error rates taken over (a) all panels in the test set (b) good panels, which are panels with only good words in them, and (c) good words of all panels. Then we used the error rates for the plain version as reference points and we estimated the relative improvement for the pruning and ordered version. The following table and charts show our results.

TABLE II
ERROR RATE REDUCTION

	Version	Relative Error Reduction (%)		
		AP	GP	GW
Natural Data	pruned	6.90	13.98	14.54
	ordered	13.48	24.74	21.29
All Data	pruned	4.87	11.56	12.96
	ordered	7.38	12.52	15.92

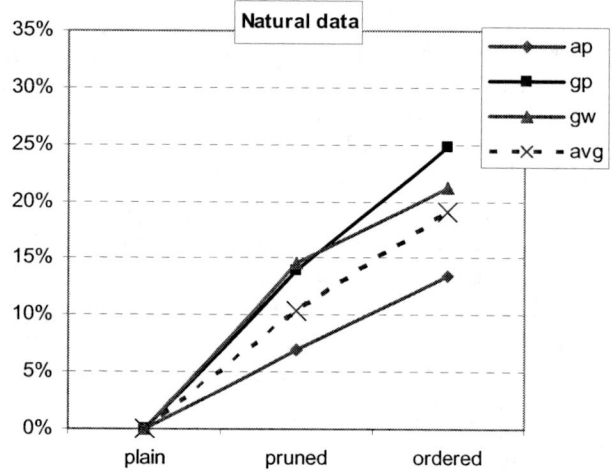

Fig. 1 Relative error reduction on natural data. Dotted line is the average of all-panel and good-panel error reduction.

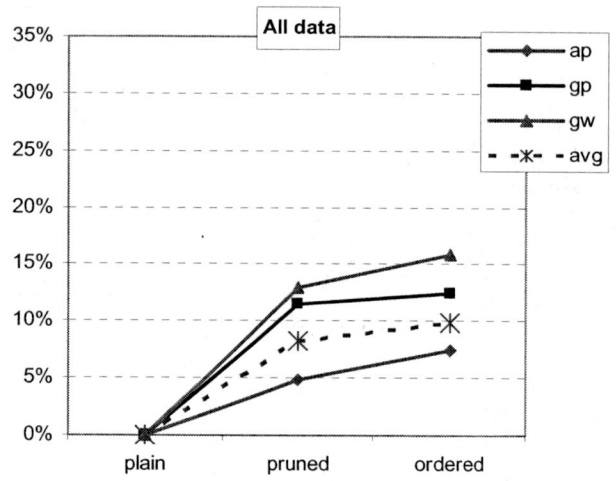

Fig. 2 Relative error reduction on all data. Dotted line is the average of all-panel and good-panel error reduction.

As expected, the effect on natural data is greater. However, given that our learner performs rather poorly on e-mail and URL addresses (due to internal limitations) and those are included in the overall test set, the difference between all data and natural data error reduction is somewhat exaggerated.

Furthermore, our data contain a considerable amount of noise--including bogus ink that has nothing to do with the intended text. Those have a translation effect to the all-panel error rate, which increases the measured error while it decreases the measured error reduction.

For the same reason, good panel and good word error rates, which, by definition, are estimated over relatively clean and neat ink, are somewhat optimistic.

Thus, we believe that the actual improvements affected by our methods on our TDNN learner are somewhere between the all-panel and good-panel numbers and perhaps their average is a better estimate (19.11% for natural data, 9.95% for all data).

VI. CONCLUSION AND FUTURE WORK

As shown in the previous section, data pruning and ordered training is a powerful combination that can increase accuracy significantly. The methods apply to any number of learners. They allow emphasizing different training categories across learners, and thus they provide a method for dividing and distributing the overall recognition task. In addition, ordered training provides a method for splitting the data into 'compatible' categories before distributing them. At this point, we have not yet precisely measured the effect of our methods on our multi-learner system but we expect it to be greater than the effect on any single learner.

The overall functionality can be extended, too. Given that ordered training is an a priori method, one might consider posteriori extensions that could improve accuracy further. We are currently working on such a method, which we call the *Replication Error Model*, and which incorporates character error rates from previous training or testing sessions into the ordered training model. The idea is to use the error rates--which reflect learning difficulty--when estimating training times.

In conclusion, we believe that treating heterogeneous data in a uniform way is not optimal in any way. A priori methods such as pruning and ordered training (especially when combined with posteriori models) are almost guarantee to outperform any uniform approach and result in better systems. The amount of the improvement may of course vary across systems but our experience with our handwriting recognition system provides clear evidence and support for such approaches. Evolution and increased sophistication of such methods would only improve accuracy further. To understand why, one might make an analogy with the human education system. In that regard, a non-uniform method corresponds to a teacher who allocates different time to different concepts based on some assumed metric while a uniform training model corresponds to a teacher who spends the same time and same effort on all concepts irrespectively of how difficult or trivial they are.

ACKNOWLEDGEMENT

The authors would like to thank Henry Rowley for his comments and suggestions in the early, formative days of the ordered training model.

REFERENCES

[1] M. McCloskey and N. J. Cohen, Catastrophic interference in connectionist networks: The sequential learning problem. In G.H. Bower (Ed.), The psychology of learning and motivation: Volume 23. New York: Academic Press, 1989.

[2] Y. Freund and R.E. Schapire, Experiments with a new boosting algorithm, International Conference on Machine Learning, pp. 148–156, 1996.

[3] R. A. Jacobs, M. I. Jordan, S. J. Nowlan and G. E. Hinton. Adaptive mixtures of local experts. Neural Computation, 3, 79-87, 1991.

[4] E. Rasmusen, *Games and Information: An Introduction to Game Theory*, 3rd ed. Blackwell, Oxford, 2001.

[5] R. Ratcliff, Connectionist models and recognition memory: Constraints imposed by learning and forgetting functions. Psychological Review, 97, No. 2, pp. 285-308, 1990.

[6] E. Rich and K. Knight, *Artificial Intelligence*. McGraw-Hill, 1992.

Tracking the States of a Nonlinear System in the Weight-Space of a Feed-Forward Neural Network

Takahiro Emoto* Masatake Akutagawa* Udantha R Abeyratne[†] Hirofumi Nagashino** Yohsuke Kinouchi *

* Faculty of Engineering, The University of Tokushima, Japan
E-mail: doraemoy@ee.tokushima-u.ac.jp
** School of Health Sciences, The University of Tokushima, Japan
E-mail: nagasino@medsci.tokushima-u.ac.jp
[†] School of Info. Tech. and Electrical Engineering, The University of Queensland, Australia
E-mail: udantha@itee.uq.edu.au

Abstract— Nonlinear, non-stationary signals are commonly found in a variety of disciplines such as biology, medicine, geology and financial modeling. The complexity (eg. nonlinearity and non-stationarity) of such signals and their low signal to noise ratios often make it a challenging task to use them in critical applications. In this paper we propose a new neural network based technique to address those problems. We show that a feed forward, multi-layered neural network can conveniently capture the states of a nonlinear system in its connection weight-space, after a process of supervised training. The performance of the proposed method is investigated via computer simulations.

I. INTRODUCTION

Nonlinear, non-stationary signals are found in a range of disciplines such as biology, medicine, geology and financial modeling. Such signals arise as a result of the complex dynamics of an underlying system, which is often not directly accessible to an observer. It is usually possible to characterize the states of the system by characterizing the externally accessible signals. For instance, in medical diagnosis, physiological signals are routinely used to probe the state of the underlying system, i.e. the human, or a particular organ system.

The complexity and low signal to noise ratios (SNR) of real-world nonlinear signals often make it a challenging task to use them in critical applications.

Neural networks (NN) have recently been proposed as a robust tool in non-linear signal classification. They have also been extensively studied in their ability to capture the dynamics of a complex system via self-learned input-output mappings. *The target of this paper is to harness both of these capabilities and provide a novel solution to the problem of characterization of nonlinear time-series data.*

The existing literature proposes several NN-based solutions to the problem. In the most ubiquitous approach, a multi-layer perceptron-like NN is trained using the error back-propagation (BP) algorithm [1]. The NN is expected to discover the mapping between the input and output via supervised training, such that it can accurately classify even previously unseen data. The state of the system generating the observed time-series (non-linear signal) is captured by the activation levels of the output neurons. This approach has had many successes, but requires a-priori knowledge of possible classes and a carefully constructed training data set.

A rare few researchers have analyzed the activation/weight patterns of hidden-layer neurons in a NN as a means of studying a non-linear signal [2]-[4]. Hidden layer neuron activations were considered to be a low-dimensional representation of the information available in the higher-dimensional space of the input data. This approach, however, did not reduce the computation burden associated with the method, because the size of the input/output spaces did not decrease.

NN have been used to predict/characterize non-linear time series [5],[6] in the past. In [5], an example for the state estimation of a biological system via time series prediction is given. The issue of time-variant time series prediction has been investigated in [6].

Concepts used in NN-based time series prediction [5],[6] provide a solid starting point for the novel work presented in this paper. The fundamental premise of the paper is that once a *low-capacity* NN is trained to accurately predict the given non-linear time series at *all points*, the trained NN include the information of the model order in linear process, and the connection-weight-space (CWS) of the NN has captured sufficient information on the state of the underlying system generating the time-series. The theoretical foundation for this is provided by the traditional study [7], [8].

The CWS of the NN can be used as an excellent space to characterize and dynamically track state changes of the system. Note that the capacity of the NN should be much smaller than the training data presented to the network, so that pure memorization can be ruled out.

In this paper, we propose a new method to conveniently track the state of a non-linear system through NN-based time-series prediction followed by CWS-analysis. Via extensive Monte Carlo simulations, we illustrate the robustness of the proposed technique and its plausibility in actual practical use.

II. METHODS

The type of NN used in this study is a fully connected, feed forward, Perceptron-like one with three layers of neurons. The output layer always had only one neuron, which used a linear activation function. The hidden layer consisted of H neurons, all using hyperbolic tangent activation functions. All output and hidden layer neurons had been assigned unity bias terms.

The number of input layer neurons, D, depends on the number of input data samples used in the prediction and thus treated as a variable parameter of the method. In this paper, we denote such a NN by the symbol $N_T(D,H)$.

The connection weight space CWS of the NN is defined as the vector space spanned by *all* the connection weights within $N_T(D,H)$. Thus, a general point in the CWS is represented by a *Weight-Vector* (*WV*) given by $W = [W_{ih} | W_{ho} | W_{bh} | W_{bo}]^T$, where the row vector W_{ih} has connection weights between input and hidden layers as its entries. Similarly, vector W_{ho} contain connection weights between hidden and output layers. The terms W_{bh} and W_{bo} respectively represent bias weight connections of hidden and output layer neurons.

The method proposed in this paper involves two steps: (i) NN-based time series prediction followed by (ii) an analysis of the CWS. In Section II*A*, the time-series prediction technique proposed in the paper is discussed; Section II*B* introduces the concept of CWS analysis.

A. The NN-Based Time Series Prediction

Consider a time series $\{x(n), n = 1,2,..., N\}$ of length N satisfying the condition $N \gg D$. The *k-step*, D^{th}-*order* prediction of the time series can then be defined as obtaining the estimate $x(n+k)$ of the sample $x(n+k)$ based on the set $\mathbf{S} = \{x(n), x(n-1),..., x(n-D+1)\}$ over the domain $n = D, D+1,..., N-k$.

In the first step of our technique, we train a set of NNs to achieve the *k-step*, D^{th}-*order* prediction of the time series $x(n)$ using the following procedure:

(P1) Divide the total data length N into segments of length M, with the segment overlap length given by L samples. Let the time series data in the jth segment be represented by $x_j(n)$, $n=1,2,...,M$ and $j=1,2,...,J$, where J is the total number of segments contained within the data of length N.

(P2) perform steps **(P3)-(P5)** for all segments $j=1,2,...,J$.

(P3) Consider the segment $x_j(n)$ of the time series. Define a NN of the type $N_T(D,H)$ which is restricted to be used only for the jth segment, and label it $N_T^{(j)}(D,H)$; initialize the *WV* of $N_T^{(j)}(D,H)$ according to a uniform probability density function in $[-1, 1]$ and let the initialized *WV* be denoted by W_{jb}.

(P4) Use the data in segment j to train the network $N_T^{(j)}(D,H)$. The training data at the input side is given by the set $\mathbf{S}_j = (x_j(n), x_j(n-1) ,..., x_j(n-D+1)))$, and the corresponding data at the output side is given by the sample $x_j(n+k)$. Note that the training is carried out in sequence for all the training input/output pairs, ie. $\{\mathbf{S}_j, x_j(n+k)\}$, in the domain $n=D, D+1,..., M-k$. Let the learning rate be given by η.

(P5) The training is deemed to have completed for $N_T^{(j)}(D,H)$ when *all* the training input/output pairs $\{(\mathbf{S}_j, x_j(n+k)) | n = D, D+1,...,M-k\}$ have been used in a predetermined number, q, of training epochs. Once the training is over, obtain the trained *WV* and denote it by W_{jf}.

As the main outcome of steps **(P1)-(P5)**, we get a set of trained NN $\{N_T^{(j)}(D,H) | j = 1, 2,...,M\}$, represented by the corresponding *end-of-training WV* set given by $\{W_{jf} | j=1,2,...,M\}$. Similarly, the initial *WV* set is given by $\{W_{jb} | j=1,2,...,M\}$. However, for the work of this paper, we force all *initial WV*s to have the same random values, i.e., $W_{1b} = W_{2b} =...= W_{jb}$ by computing them just one time for $j=1$ and then fixing it at that value for all other j.

Due to the facts that (a) W_{jf} are the results obtained by minimizing the *k-step estimation error* in the sense of BP learning, and, (b) the number of training samples far exceed the number of free parameters within $N_T^{(j)}(D,H)$, the estimated W_{jf} should indeed capture the important information on the underlying system.

It is not efficient or feasible to visualize the temporal changes in individual weights as a means of monitoring the CWS. In Section II*B*, we propose two measures which describe the relative positions of W_{jf} in the CWS and thus help us track the states of the system.

B. The Connection Weight Analysis

The concept of CWS proposed in this paper allows us to represent each $N_T^{(j)}(D,H)$ as a point in the CWS given by the *WV* symbolized by W_{jf}. The implication is that two different states "u" and "v" of a system should occupy two separate positions in the CWS. This separation of the two *WV*s can be captured in their angular separation in CWS as defined by:

$$\lambda_{uv} = \text{cosine}(\theta_{uv}) = <W_{uf}, W_{vf}> / |W_{uf}||W_{vf}|, \quad (1)$$

where "< , >" denotes the inner product of the two *WV*s given by W_{uf} and W_{vf}. The measure λ_{uv} has the advantage that it inherently evaluates the amount of correlation between the two states. However, it has the disadvantage that it only evaluates the *angular separation* of the two vectors in CWS and thus is blind to pure radial separations. Furthermore, because cosine (θ) has a very low gradient near $\theta=0$, changes accompanied by a smaller angular separation tend to get discounted.

Attempting to address some of these issues, we defined a novel measure, γ_{uv}, as given by:

$$\gamma_{uv} = |W_{uf} - W_{vf}| / \{|W_{uf}||W_{vf}|\}^{1/2} \quad (2)$$

Note that the measure γ_{uv} is dimensionless, and is sensitive to both angular and radial separation of *WV*s.

In the work of this paper, we consider both nonlinear and linear models for the time series $x(n)$, and track changes in the states of the systems by observing the evolution of the measures λ_{uv} and γ_{uv} over time.

In Section III, we briefly describe the mathematical models of the systems used in our work.

III. SYSTEM MODELS

We are interested in investigating the efficacy of the proposed method in detecting changes in a system. For this purpose, we consider two parametric system models, one linear and the other nonlinear, for the work of this paper. In both cases, changes in the system were simulated by introducing changes to system parameters.

A. Linear System Model

For the linear system we chose an autoregressive model of order 'p', i.e, AR(p) as defined in (3) below.

$$x(n) = -\sum_{i=1}^{p} a_i x(n-i) + \varepsilon(n) \quad (3)$$

The quantity $\varepsilon(n)$ is the generating noise, or the *innovation sequence*, for the system and a_i are model parameters. The AR(p) model is well known in the research community and its behavior has been extensively documented. We can conveniently change AR parameters and investigate whether the methods proposed in this paper can capture changes in the CWS.

B. Nonlinear System Model

While the AR(p) model considered in Section III*B* provides an excellent medium to test our methods, we are also interested in investigating their performance on nonlinear systems. This interest stems form the facts that nonlinear signals abound in nature. In addition, NNs are ideally suited to analyze nonlinear systems, where ubiquitous linear techniques fail.

In this paper, we chose the "Mackey and Glass model" (MG) describing Cheyne-Stockes respiration and other biological fluctuations [9], [10] (see (4)). The MG model has found wide usage in time series analysis and practical signal modeling due to its versatility. It is known that the model can generate limit-cycle oscillations and even chaotic behavior.

The MG model is a nonlinear first-order different-delay equation given by,

$$\frac{dx}{dt} = -ax(t) + \frac{bx(t-\tau)\theta^c}{\theta^c + x(t-\tau)^c}, \quad (4)$$

where a, b and c are parameters of the model and θ is a constant.

IV. RESULTS

All the results reported in this paper were generated by considering systems as described by the AR(p) and MG models described in Section III. For each system, two states S1 and S2 were obtained by changing system parameters. The target was to find out if the method proposed in this paper could indeed detect the changes of the states from S1→S2 and vice versa. In Figs. 1 and 2, we illustrate the systems used in the study. For the ease of explanation, we list our collection of system changes into different cases.

CASE I: *(Linear AR(2) System)* Fig.1(c) shows the values of parameters defining the two states S1≡{a_1=0.1, a_2=0.6}, S2≡{a_1=0.1, a_2=-0.6} for an AR(2) system. Note that the state changes three times, from S1→S2, S2→S1 and then S1→S2 within the time frame considered. In Fig.1(a) we show the time series obtained from the AR(2) model, corresponding to the parameters shown in Fig.1(c). For the innovation sequence $\varepsilon(n)$ in (3), we used a white, Gaussian random process of zero mean and variance equal to 0.001. Fig.1(e) shows the Fourier magnitude spectrum of the time series shown in Fig.1(a). Note that in this case the two states S1 and S2 are well separated in the frequency domain, even though it is difficult to visualize the difference in time series (Fig.1 (a)).

CASE II: *(Linear AR(2) System)*

Fig.1(b), (d) and (f) show results similar to the ones shown in Fig.1(a), (c) and (e) under CASE I, but with S1 and S2 now given by S1≡{a_1=0.8, a_2=0.8}, S2≡{a_1=0.4, a_2=0.4}. In this case, the two states S1 and S2 are overlapped in the frequency domain.

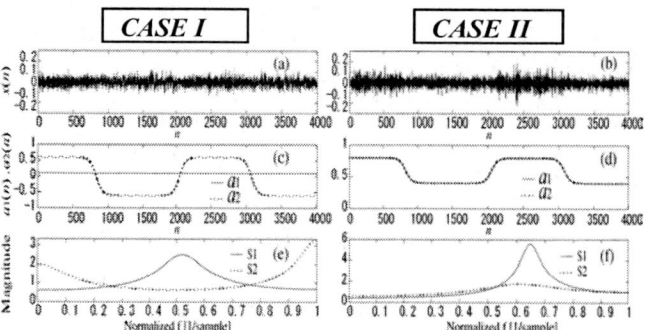

Fig.1 (top): $x(n)$ for the AR(2) model; (middle): solid line shows parameter a_1 and the broken line shows a_2; (bottom): frequency characteristic of $x(n)$.

CASE III: *(Nonlinear MG System)*

In CASE *III*, we used the nonlinear MG system and defined the two states as S1≡{a=0.3, b=0.8}, S2≡{a=0.1, b=0.2}. Other parameters in the model were held common to both states at: τ = 25, c = 10, θ=1. Fig.2(b) shows how we changed the parameters to move the system between states S1 and S2. The corresponding time series data were generated by solving (4) based on a 4th order Runge-Kutta technique. The MG model is highly sensitive to parameter changes, and small change can cause a big difference in the properties of the time series. This is illustrated in Fig.2(a), where the time series corresponding to parameters shown in Fig.2(b) are shown.

In the rest of this paper, we investigate the performance of our methods in detecting the system state changes introduced under *CASE I- CASE III*.

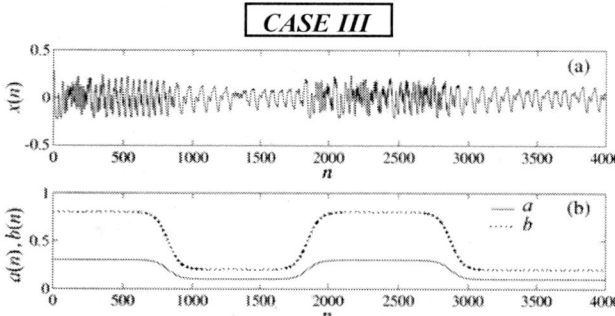

Fig.2 (top): x(n) for the MG Model; (bottom): solid line indicates parameter a, and the broken line shows parameter b.

A. Monte Carlo Experiments

In order to make our analysis as close as possible to a real-world scenario, we ran Monte Carlo Experiments (MCE). *Each experiment consisted of 20 Monte Carlo runs*. In **each** Monte Carlo **run**, we:

(i) generated a fresh time series sequence $x(n)$ via (3) or (4), depending on the system under study. In the case of the AR(2) system, different innovation sequences were used in each Monte Carlo run. In the case of the MG system, a similar effect was obtained by slightly changing the initial condition used to solve the differential equation (4),

(ii) added white Gaussian observation noise $v(n)$ to the generated time series $x(n)$ to get the observation $y(n) = x(n)+v(n)$. The amount of noise added was specified by the *SNR*, which was defined to be the ratio of signal power to noise power,

(iii) followed the procedures **(P1)-(P5)** defined in Section IIA. In each Monte Carlo run, the initial *WV*s given by $\{W_{jb} \mid j=1,2,..M\}$, where $W_{1b} = W_{2b} =....= W_{Mb}$, was freshly set with random weights uniformly distributed between -1 and 1. After the 20 Monte Carlo runs are completed, the mean $\pm$ standard deviation of any desired quantity is calculated. All the results shown in the rest of this paper are based on such MCE.

B. Network Structure and the Time Series Prediction

In Section II, we mentioned that the first step of our method was to train the NN $N_T(D,H)$ such that it gains the capability of time series prediction. In this Section, we show results of our investigation in to how the parameters D and H affect the accuracy of time series prediction. We ran a series of MCE with the following parameters: $k = 1$; $M = 98$; $q=200$ (AR(2) system), 1000 (MG system); $\eta = 0.05$; $H = 1$, 3 and 5; $D = 1, 2, .., 20$; $SNR = 3.5$dB, 10dB and ∞dB.

In the present series of experiments, the target quantity is the learning and generalization capability of the networks. Thus, as the performance measure we can use e, which is the root mean square (RMS) error between the actual and estimated values of the time series at the output of the NN. RMS error is defined as follows.

$$e = \sqrt{\frac{\sum_{n=D}^{M-k}(\hat{x}(n+k) - x(n+k))^2}{M-k-D+1}} \quad (5)$$

which is the RMS error between the actual and estimated values of the time series at the output of the NN. This is routinely calculated in the BP learning algorithm, and can be conveniently acquired.

The results of our investigation are summarized in Fig.3, where the solid lines indicate the average value of e estimated over the 20 Monte Carlo runs during the network learning phase; the shaded area represents the standard deviation. Fig. 3(a)-3(c) shows the result for the *CASE-I* of the AR(2) system, and Fig. 3(d)-3(f) shows those for the *CASE-III* of the MG system.

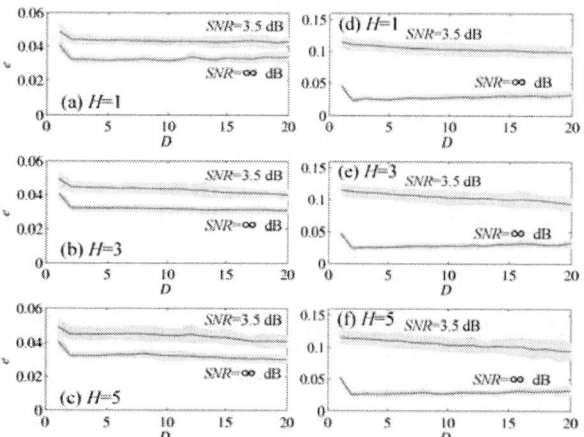

Fig.3 The prediction error (e) for AR(2) model (a)-(c), and, MG model (d)-(f) at different SNR and D during learning.

As expected, the case $SNR=\infty$ leads to better learning performance than $SNR=3.5$dB under all the combination of parameters considered. Also, the performance generally improves with increasing number of hidden neurons at smaller D. It is interesting to observe that for the AR(2) system, 2nd order prediction, i.e. $D=2$, provides the best solution. However, the accuracy of the solution does not deteriorate much even for Ds higher than 2, making it quite unnecessary to know, in advance, the model order of the AR process. This is a remarkable advantage of our method over conventional linear techniques, which require the actual model order, or a very close estimate of it. At very large Ds, the performance appears to have dropped; our investigation revealed that it is due to the bigger networks needing more learning iterations than $q=200$, 1000 used here. Using $q=3000$ immediately solved that apparent anomaly.

However, our actual interest here is not learning but the generalization capability of the NNs. Better learning accuracy or larger NNs do not necessarily mean that generalization accuracy will be higher. In the next series of MCE we investigated the generalization capability, as revealed by the network performance measure, e, computed over previously unseen data inputs. Other than that, all parameters remained at the values used with the previous series of experiments.

The generalization results are shown in Fig.4. Comparing Figs. 3 and 4, we conclude that both learning and generalization has proceeded well. Furthermore, an increase in the size of D led to a significant deterioration of the generalization ability. This behavior was observed even at q=3000. The generalization performances at q=3000, 200 (AR(2) system) and 1000 (MG system) were similar for our signals, and thus we adopted q=200, 1000 for further studies, respectively.

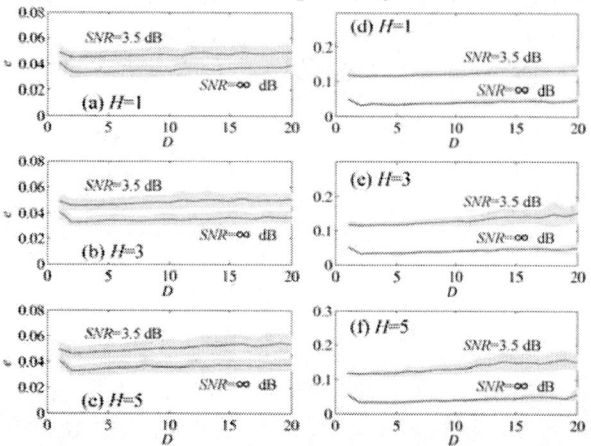

Fig.4 The prediction error (e) for AR(2) model (a)-(c), and, MG model (d)-(f) at different SNR and D during generalization(testing).

C. Connection Weight-Space Analysis

In Section IVC, we illustrated the feasibility of the first step of our method, i.e., the Dth-order, k-step prediction of linear and nonlinear time series as the activation at the output of the NN. This capability, however, does not lend by itself the ability to detect changes in the system producing the signal. It is our hypothesis that the system changes are encoded in the CWS of the NN.

To investigate the relationship between system changes and the CWS, we ran a series of MCE.

Simulation parameters: k=1; N=4000; M=98; L=97; q=200(AR(2) system), 1000 (MG system); η =0.05; H = 1, 3 and 5; D = 2; SNR = 3.5dB, 10dB and ∞dB.

System: AR(2) Model, *CASE-I* (Experiment Series *ES-1*)
AR(2) Model, *CASE-II*(Experiment Series *ES-2*)
MG Model, *CASE-III*(Experiment Series *ES-3*)

In all Experiments, steps (i)-(iv) proposed in Section IVA under MCE were followed. After that, we evaluated WV set $\mathbf{S}_w \equiv \{W_{jf} | j=1,2,...,J\}$ as defined in Section IIA. For all WVs in $\mathbf{S}_w$ we calculated λ_{1j} and γ_{1j} according to (3) and (4). Note that we have fixed u at 1 in all cases; thus λ_{1j} and γ_{1j} measure the changes of the system (in weight space) with respect to the state at the segment number 1. This enables us to track the state changes of the system as it evolves in time. Results of Experiment Series *ES-1* to *ES-3* are respectively shown in Figs.5-7. In all figures, the solid lines indicate the average value of λ_{1j} or γ_{1j} estimated over the 20 Monte Carlo runs; the shaded area represents the standard deviation. Note that the results shown in Figs.5-7 represent a pessimistic estimate, because, in our MCE, we have allowed innovation sequence, additive noise, as well as initial weights of the NN to change at the same time.

In Fig.5(a)-(c) both λ_{1j} (top curve) and γ_{1j} (bottom curve) are shown for the AR(2) system *CASE-I*.

Comparing these with Fig. 1(a), where the original time series x(n) is displayed, we conclude that both measures succeed in capturing the system changes in the CWS of the NN. Both states S1 and S2 are clearly seen in λ_{1j} and γ_{1j} even at such low SNR as 3.5dB. *It is clearly evident that the states of the system are mapped to CWS after a process of supervised training.*

According to Fig.5(a)-(c), the measure γ_{1j} clearly outperforms λ_{1j}. All our simulations indicated this trend. This result is not surprising because, as mentioned in the introduction, λ_{1j} is only sensitive to angular changes in the *WV*. Furthermore, at smaller θ, the rate of change of cos θ is low. Due to the higher performance of λ_{1j}, we adopted it as the preferred measure for this study.

Comparing the frames in Fig. 5 in a row-wise fashion, we note that the number of neurons (H) in the hidden layer has a distinct effect on the results. The higher the H, the lower is the estimation variance. However, when the size of the network increases, the measures λ_{1j} and γ_{1j} become less sensitive.

All the NNs used in the Experiments are rather small in size, with the largest and smallest network respectively given by $N_T(2,5)$ and $N_T(2,1)$. These translate to 21 and 5 connection weights, including bias connections. Training such small networks is rather simple and straightforward. This is indeed one of *the remarkable features* of the method proposed in this paper.

Fig.6 corroborates results illustrated and discussed for Fig.5. Furthermore, it provides support to the assertion that even when the parameter changes associated with the states S1 and S2 are small, and the corresponding signals are overlapped in the frequency domain, the system change can still be detected in the CWS.

Fig.7 for the MG system high lights the performance of the proposed method when the system is highly nonlinear. The states S1 and S2 can be conveniently tracked in the CWS of the NN even at SNR=3.5dB.

Note that the estimation variation of Experiment *ES-3* is slightly larger than those for the linear system (*ES-1* and *ES-2*). One of the reasons for this is the extra complexity added in the case of the nonlinear model. The MG system is sensitive to slight changes in parameters, and also the system can be chaotic. When it becomes chaotic, a slight change in the initial conditions used to solve (4) may result in a large change in the signal being generated.

According to Figs. 3-7, the estimation variance can be traded with the NN network complexity, as seen from the lowering of the variance with increasing number of hidden layer neurons. Furthermore, to reduce variance, we can average λ_{1j} and γ_{1j} values over multiple results obtained by changing the initial weights of the NN.

V. CONCLUSIONS

We showed that a feed forward, multi-layered neural network can conveniently capture the states of a linear or highly nonlinear system in its connection weight-space after a process of supervised training. The method is robust to observation noise and proven to work down to SNR=3.5dB.

Based on extensive Monte Carlo experiments, we conclude that the initial weight selection of the NN does not pose any remarkable threat to network convergence. The relatively small size of the networks needed to be trained, irrespective of the complexity of the time series, makes the proposed method an attractive alternative to existing techniques.

ACKONWLEDGEMENTS. This work was partly supported by Grants-in-Aid for Scientific Research #16560353 and #16700440 from Japan Society of Promotion of Science. The authors would also like to thank The University of Queensland, Australia for access to research facilities and hosting the first author as a Visiting Researcher during the work.

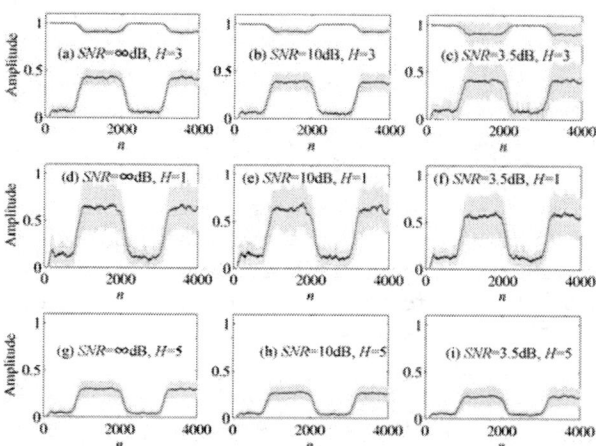

Fig.5 Measure γ_{1j} for AR(2) System (Experiment Series *ES-1*): solid lines indicate average values; shaded area indicates standard deviation over 20 Monte Carlo runs. In (a)-(c), top line shows λ_{1j}.

REFERENCES

[1] D.E. Rumelhart, G.E. Hinton and R.J. Williams,"Learning internal representation by error propagation." In: D.E. Rumelhart, J.L. McClelland and thePDP Research Group(Eds.), *Parallel Distributed Processing,MIT press*, Cambridge, pp.318–362, 1986..
[2] G. E. Hinton, "How neural networks learn from experience." *Sci. Amer.*,pp. 105–109, Sept. 1992.
[3] R. P. Gorman and T. J. Sejnowski, "Analysis of hidden units in a layered network trained to classify sonar targets." *Neural Networks*, vol. 1, pp.75–89, 1988.
[4] Oud, M, "Internal-State Analysis in a Layered Artificial Neural Network Trained to Categorize Lung Sounds." Systems, Man and Cybernetics, Part A, *IEEE Transactions on System*, Volume: 32 , pp.757-760, 2002
[5] Y. Cisse, Y. Kinouchi, H. Nagashino and M. Akutagawa,"BP neural networks approach for identifying biological signal source in circadian data fluctuations."*IEICE Transactions on Information and Systems*, vol.E85-D, no.3, pp.568–576, 2002.
[6] E. Watanabe, N. Nakasako, and Y. Mitani. "A prediction method of non-stationary time series data by using a modular structured neural network." *IEICE Transactions on Fundamentals*, E80-A(6):971-976, 1997.
[7] Funahashi, K. "On the approximate realization of continuous mappings by neural networks." *Neural Networks*, 2, 183-192, 1989.
[8] Takens, F. "Detecting strange attractors in turbulence." In D. A.Rand and L. S. Young (eds), *Lecture notes in Math.*, Vol. 898. Berlin: Springer-Verlag, 1981.
[9] J.D. Murray, "Mathematical Biology", *Springer*, Berlin, 2nd edition, 1993.
[10] .C.Mackey & L.Glass, "Oscillation and chaos in physiological control systems." *Science*, vol. 197, pp.287-289, 1977.

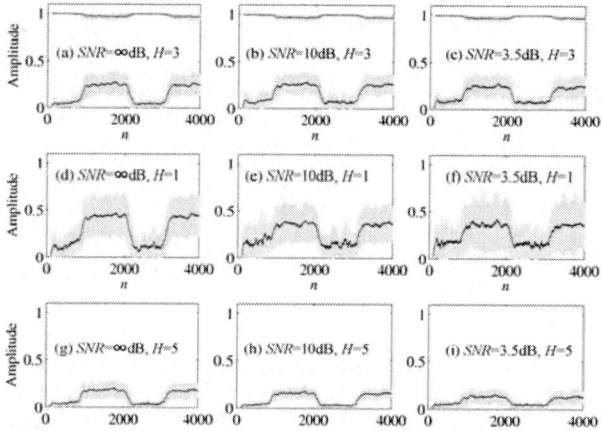

Fig.6 Measure γ_{1j} for AR System (Experiment Series *ES-2*): solid lines indicate average values; shaded area indicates standard deviation over 20 Monte Carlo runs. In (a)-(c), top line shows λ_{1j}.

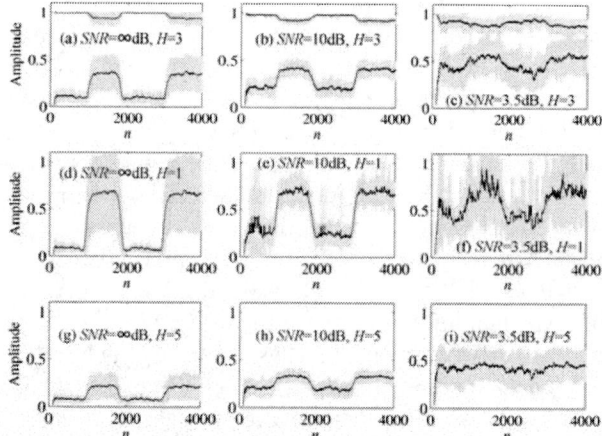

Fig.7 Measure γ_{1j} for MG System (Experiment Series *ES-3*): solid lines indicate average values; shaded area indicates standard deviation over 20 Monte Carlo runs. In (a)-(c), top line shows λ_{1j}.

Data-Dependent Kernels for High-Dimensional Data Classification

Jingdong Wang James T. Kwok Helen C. Shen Long Quan

Department of Computer Science
The Hong Kong University of Science and Technology
Clear Water Bay
Hong Kong
Email: {welleast,jamesk,helens,quan}@cs.ust.hk

Abstract— For high-dimensional data classification problems such as face recognition, one of the most efficient classifiers is the Nearest Neighbor (NN) classifier. What mostly affects the NN classification performance is the feature extracted by some methods. And the kernel method is one of the efficient methods for extracting features. However, the selection of kernel parameters is still difficult. In this paper, we propose a so-called data dependent kernel (DDK) which is defined by generalizing the Gaussian kernel. Also an efficient and practical method is presented to calculate the DDK parameters. Moreover, one DDK based on subspaces is given to improve the recognition performance. Experiments show that the proposed DDK can achieve promising classification performance in face recognition and SPECT heart diagnosis.

I. Introduction

In pattern classification, one of the most difficult problems is high-dimensional data classification problem with a small number of training samples, such as face recognition in which there are only several instances of high dimension for each subject. Some powerful classifiers, which usually require a large number of training samples compared with the dimension, may not obtain satisfactory performance. In practice, the Nearest Neighbor classifier can achieve promising performance. Recently, extracting and selecting features for NN classifiers have become a hot topic in high-dimensional data classification problems.

One classical algorithm is the Principal Component Analysis (PCA) [1]. PCA is to extract the features as the projections on the principal subspace whose basis vectors correspond to the maximum variance directions in the original space, while discard the complementary subspace as a noise subspace. In some cases, PCA can obtain satisfactory performance. However, no theory can prove the complementary subspace is useless for recognition, and, on the contrary, experiments show that using the complementary subspace properly may improve recognition performance.

There are other component analysis methods, such as Linear Discriminant Analysis (LDA) [2], and Independent Component Analysis (ICA) [3]. However, both methods usually use PCA dimension reduction as the preprocessing step. Therefore, the two methods still discard the so-called noise subspace. To efficiently utilize the entire space, Wang and Tang [4] proposed the technique of random sampling the two base vectors on the principal and complementary subspaces for face recognition, which, however, in some sense, causes over-selecting features.

Recently, kernel methods, such as kernel PCA [5], kernel LDA [6] and kernel ICA [7], have been introduced to extract features for recognition. However, kernel parameter selection is difficult. One method is by trial-and-error heuristics, which is easy to implement but not efficient and also causes overfitting problem. The second is using boosting method [8] to learn the combination of kernel functions with different kernel types or different kernel parameters. In [9] one transformed kernel function is discussed, which is good in theory but can not give an easy and efficient way to obtain the transformation matrix.

The goal of this paper is to give an efficient and convenient approach to extract features for high-dimensional data classification problems by generalizing the Gaussian kernel function. We analyze the NN classifier for high-dimensional data classification problems. To obtain better performance, we generalize the Gaussian Kernel to the so-called Data Dependent kernel, which can be easier to calculate compared with the invariant kernel in [9] and obtain better performance than conventional Gaussian kernel and Bayesian Face Matching method [10]. Moreover, we explain why the specified DDK based on subspaces works well.

The paper is organized as follows. Section II analyzes the NN classifier for the high dimensional data classification problem and reviews the data dependent kernel in unsupervised problems. In section III, the proposed data dependent kernel is presented. Section IV presents the comparisons with other related methods. Experiment results are given in section V. Final section is about the conclusion.

II. Background

A. Nearest Neighbor Classifier in High-Dimensional Classification Problems

In pattern recognition, low-dimensional problems with large scale seem easy to process except sometimes the large computation cost. However, few algorithms can well deal with high-dimensional classification problems with small scale, especially when the samples in the different classes are much similar. For example, in face recognition, the faces of different subjects seems also very similar, but the between-class difference is much different from the within-class difference.

How do we use the property? One method is LDA, which usually suffers from the singularity problem. Another method is based on kernels, which selects a proper kernel parameter according to the property. Both methods usually use the NN classifier. Consider the NN classifier with Euclidean distance measure, and we can get at least two observations: (1) NN actually considers the differences rather than the original samples; (2) To improve the recognition performance, it is important to choose some features to discriminate the with- and between-class differences so as to reduce the within-class distance and increase the between-class distance. One straightforward method is to discover two complementary subspaces: one (called the principal subspace) only for within-class differences and the other (called the complementary) only for between-class differences. Then, by assigning less weight on the principal subspace while more weight on the complementary subspace, we can obtain a better distance measure. In this paper, we will incorporate this idea into kernel design to obtain an efficient data-dependent kernel based on subspace.

B. Data-Dependent Kernels in Unsupervised Learning

Kernel methods have been successfully applied in many problems. Its basic idea is to implicitly map the data from the input space $\mathcal{X}$ to a high-dimensional feature space $\mathcal{H}$ via a nonlinear function $\phi : \mathcal{X} \to \mathcal{H}$, and then a similarity measure in $\mathcal{H}$ is defined as the dot product:

$$\mathbf{k}(\mathbf{x}, \mathbf{x}') \equiv \langle \phi(\mathbf{x}) \cdot \phi(\mathbf{x}') \rangle.$$

Here, the kernel function $\mathbf{k}$ should satisfy *Mercer condition* [11].

However, one major question is how to choose $\mathbf{k}(\cdot, \cdot)$ and its associated kernel parameters. One approach to alleviate this problem is using the data-dependent kernel. The concept of data-dependent kernels is first introduced in [12], as shown in Table I. In that paper, the data-dependent kernel is used in unsupervised problems, such as nonlinear dimension reduction and clustering. In spectral clustering [13], one divisive-normalized kernel is proposed, where the divisive coefficient is determined by all the data. The divisive-normalized kernel is proved to help clustering the data. In Isometric Feature Mapping (Isomap) [14], they used so-called geodesic distance kernel to keep the geodesic distance of the data manifold to reduce the dimension. In Local Linearly Embedding (LLE) [15], they use the kernel to keep the local linear reconstruction. All the methods are applied in unsupervised problems.

TABLE I
DATA-DEPENDENT KERNELS IN UNSUPERVISED LEARNING.

Method	Data-dependent Kernel
KPCA	Centralization Normalization
Isomap	Isomap Kernel
LLE	LLE Kernel
Spectral Clustering	Division Normalization

Actually, the data-dependent kernel can also be used in supervised problems. For example, spectral clustering has been used in recognition. In this paper, we want to design special data dependent kernel for high-dimensional classification problems based on the Gaussian Kernel.

III. DATA DEPENDENT KERNELS FOR CLASSIFICATION

In this section, we start with the generalized Gaussian kernel:

$$\mathbf{k}(\mathbf{x}, \mathbf{y}) = \exp\{-\frac{1}{2}(\mathbf{x} - \mathbf{y})'\mathbf{H}^{-1}(\mathbf{x} - \mathbf{y})\}, \quad (1)$$

where $\mathbf{H}$ is a transformation matrix and $'$ denotes the transpose operation. In cases where certain input transformations are known to leave function values unchanged, the use of $\mathbf{H}$ can also allow such invariance to be incorporated into the kernel function [9]. In the following, we propose several methods for obtaining $\mathbf{H}$ from the training data, and the corresponding kernels are called data dependent kernels $\mathbf{k}_d(\mathbf{x}, \mathbf{y})$.

A. Using the Covariance Matrix

An obvious choice for $\mathbf{H}$ is the $d \times d$ covariance matrix:

$$\mathbf{H} = E[(\mathbf{x} - \bar{\mathbf{x}})(\mathbf{x} - \bar{\mathbf{x}})'], \quad (2)$$

where $\mathbf{x} \in \mathbb{R}^d$ is the data vector and $\bar{\mathbf{x}}$ the corresponding mean vector. By assuming that the entries of the sample vector are independent, (2) can be simplified by dropping the off-diagonal elements as:

$$\mathbf{H} = \mathrm{Diag}[\mathrm{diag}[E[(\mathbf{x} - \bar{\mathbf{x}})(\mathbf{x} - \bar{\mathbf{x}})']]].$$

Here, $\mathrm{diag}(\cdot)$ extracts the diagonal elements of (2), which are then used to construct a diagonal matrix by $\mathrm{Diag}(\cdot)$, and the obtained kernel by this matrix $\mathbf{H}$ is called Independent DDK.

For high-dimensional training sets with small scale, such an $\mathbf{H} = \mathrm{Diag}(\mathbf{h}_1, \cdots, \mathbf{h}_d)$ obtained[1] from the empirical data is often singular, as the data dimensionality is larger than the sample size. To avoid this problem, we replace the $d - p$ smallest diagonal elements in $\mathbf{H}$ by their average, i.e.,

$$\hat{\mathbf{H}} = \begin{bmatrix} \mathbf{H}_p & \\ & \rho \mathbf{I}_{d-p} \end{bmatrix}. \quad (3)$$

Here, $p \in \{0, 1, \ldots, d\}$ is a user-defined parameter,

$$\rho = \frac{1}{d-p} \sum_{i=p+1}^{d} \mathbf{h}_i, \quad (4)$$

$\mathbf{H}_p = \mathrm{Diag}(\mathbf{h}_1, \cdots, \mathbf{h}_p)$ and $\mathbf{I}_{d-p}$ is the $(d-p) \times (d-p)$ identity matrix. (4) can be justified from an information-theoretic point of view. Details can be found in [10].

Notice that when p is set to zero, $\mathbf{H}$ is of the form $\mathbf{H} = \sigma^2 \mathbf{I}$ (where σ is a measure of the data spread) and (1) reduces to the conventional Gaussian kernel:

$$\mathbf{k}(\mathbf{x}, \mathbf{y}) = \exp\{-\frac{\|\mathbf{x} - \mathbf{y}\|^2}{2\sigma^2}\} \quad (5)$$

[1]Here, we assume that the entries of the sample vector have been permutated such that $\mathbf{h}_1 \geq \mathbf{h}_2 \geq \cdots \geq \mathbf{h}_d$.

While (5) implicitly assumes the same variance for each entry of the sample vector (i.e., the data is isotropic, and accordingly the kernel is called Isotropic DDK when σ^2 is calculated as in (4)), this is not necessary for the generalized Gaussian kernel.

In a classification problem, a major deficiency of the $\mathbf{H}$'s defined in (2) and (3) is that they do not utilize the class labels. Thus, they are not discriminative in nature. As will be demonstrated in Section V, experimental results obtained with the corresponding kernels are not satisfactory in practice.

B. Subspace-Based Data Dependent Kernel

As discussed in Section II, it is desirable to have a kernel such that the corresponding intra-class (within-class) difference is reduced while the inter-class (between-class) difference is increased. In this paper, we adopt the subspace method, and use one subspace for the intra-class difference and another for the inter-class difference. Different distance measures are then defined on these two complementary subspaces. Here, the two subspaces are obtained as follows:

1) For each class, obtain all the intra-class differences $\{\mathbf{x}_i^c - \mathbf{x}_j^c\}_{i,j}$, where $\mathbf{x}_i^c, \mathbf{x}_j^c$ are samples from the same class c.
2) Pool the intra-class differences from all classes together, and then perform PCA.
3) The principal subspace is used to represent the intra-class difference, while the remaining subspace for the inter-class difference.

Note that as class information is used, the resulting kernel, called Intra-DDK, is discriminative.

PCA in Step 2 involves eigendecomposition on the $d \times d$ matrix

$$\mathbf{H} = \sum_{c=1}^{C} \mathbf{H}_c \qquad (6)$$

where $\mathbf{H}_c = \sum_{i,j=1}^{N_c}(\mathbf{x}_i^c - \mathbf{x}_j^c)(\mathbf{x}_i^c - \mathbf{x}_j^c)'$, $\mathbf{x}_i^c, \mathbf{x}_l^c$'s are samples from class c, N_c is the number of patterns belonging to class c, and C is the total number of classes. As d is assumed to be large here, so, instead of eigendecomposing (6), a common trick is to perform eigendecomposition on the $\frac{1}{2}\sum_{c=1}^{C} N_c(N_c-1) \times \frac{1}{2}\sum_{c=1}^{C} N_c(N_c-1)$ matrix

$$\begin{bmatrix} \vdots \\ (\mathbf{x}_i^c - \mathbf{x}_j^c)' \\ \vdots \end{bmatrix} \begin{bmatrix} \cdots (\mathbf{x}_k^c - \mathbf{x}_l^c) \cdots \end{bmatrix}.$$

However, this is still more computationally expensive than performing standard PCA on the whole data set, which only involves a matrix of size $\sum_{c=1}^{C} N_c \times \sum_{c=1}^{C} N_c$.

To improve efficiency, instead of (6), we will use

$$\mathbf{H} = \sum_{c=1}^{C} \mathbf{S}_c, \qquad (7)$$

where $\mathbf{S}_c = \sum_{i=1}^{N_c}(\mathbf{x}_i^c - \boldsymbol{\mu}_c)(\mathbf{x}_i^c - \boldsymbol{\mu}_c)'$ is the covariance matrix for class c (with $\boldsymbol{\mu}_c$ being the mean of class c). Now,

it can be easily proved that

$$\mathbf{S}_c = \frac{1}{2N_c}\mathbf{H}_c.$$

and so (6) and (7) only differ by the term $\frac{1}{2N_c}$. Let $\mathbf{X}_c = \{\frac{1}{\sqrt{2N_c}}(\mathbf{x}_1^c - \boldsymbol{\mu}_c), \cdots, \frac{1}{\sqrt{2N_c}}(\mathbf{x}_{N_c}^c - \boldsymbol{\mu}_c)\}$. Therefore, we can perform PCA on $\mathbf{X} = \{\mathbf{X}_1, \cdots, \mathbf{X}_C\}$ instead of Step 2, which will only require eigendecomposing a matrix of size $\sum_{c=1}^{C} N_c \times \sum_{c=1}^{C} N_c$.

As mentioned earlier, the leading p-dimensional subspace is used to encode the intra-class difference, while the remaining subspace is for the inter-class difference. To avoid the problem of having a singular matrix, we use the same technique as in Section III-A. Suppose that the eigendecomposition of $\mathbf{H}$ is $\mathbf{H} = \mathbf{U}\boldsymbol{\Lambda}\mathbf{U}'$, where $\boldsymbol{\Lambda} = \text{Diag}(\lambda_1, \ldots, \lambda_d)$ is the diagonal matrix containing the eigenvalues of $\mathbf{H}$ and $\mathbf{U}$ is the matrix containing the corresponding eigenvectors. The data dependent kernel matrix $\hat{\mathbf{H}}$ is then defined as

$$\hat{\mathbf{H}} = \mathbf{U}\begin{bmatrix} \boldsymbol{\Lambda}_p & \\ & \rho\mathbf{I}_{d-p} \end{bmatrix}\mathbf{U}', \qquad (8)$$

where $p \in \{0, 1, \ldots, d\}$, $\boldsymbol{\Lambda}_p = \text{Diag}(\lambda_1, \cdots, \lambda_p)$, and

$$\rho = \frac{1}{d-p}\sum_{i=p+1}^{d}\lambda_i.$$

IV. DISCUSSION

A. Relationship to Bayesian Face Matching and Relevant Component Analysis

Matrix $\mathbf{H}$ in the subspace-based data dependent kernel is obtained in a similar way as the Bayesian face matching (BFM) algorithm [10] and relevant component analysis (RCA) [16]. In some sense, this paper can be viewed as combining BFM or RCA into kernel PCA. In this paper, (1) the matrix $\mathbf{H}$ in Section III-B is derived from the insight that there exist two subspaces to represent the intra-class and inter-class differences, while the authors in [17] gives the intuitive interpretation. (2) In Section III-B, the principal and complementary subspaces from $\mathbf{H}$ are assigned different weights, while the complementary subspace in RCA is discarded. (3) We give an effective method to calculate the matrix $\mathbf{H}$ and eigendecompose $\mathbf{H}$. (4) We combine the matrix $\mathbf{H}$ into the generalized Gaussian kernel to obtain better recognition performance.

B. Comparison with Invariant Kernels

The invariant kernels in [9] is also closely related to the proposed data-dependent kernels. In [9], PCA is performed on the tangent vector set as a pre-processing step. Let the tangent covariance matrix be $\mathbf{C}$ and $\mathbf{B} = \mathbf{C}^{-\frac{1}{2}}$. Then, the invariant kernel is:

$$\mathbf{k}(\mathbf{x},\mathbf{y}) = \langle \mathbf{Bx}, \mathbf{By} \rangle.$$

In essence, our data-dependent kernel also finds the matrix $\mathbf{B}$, though there are some important differences. On the one hand, our data-dependent kernel provides an easy and feasible way to calculate $\mathbf{B}$, while the work in [9] requires prior knowledge on the tangent vectors. On the other hand, the subspace based data-dependent kernel, which is derived from the insight that there exist two subspaces to represent the intra-class and inter-class differences, is designed specially for high-dimensional classification problems and in some sense can also be viewed as a discriminative kernel.

V. EXPERIMENTS

Section V-A demonstrates the difference between the data-dependent kernel based on subspaces and the conventional Gaussian kernel (i.e., Isotropic DDK). In the later subsections, the performance of the proposed data-dependent kernels is then evaluated on two face recognition problems and non-image data sets. All the proposed data-dependent kernels are used in kernel PCA to extract low-dimensional features. Then the low-dimensional features are used in the Nearest Neighbor classifier to classify the test samples. The detailed algorithm is in Table II. The corresponding data dependent kernel PCAs are called Isotropic-KPCA, Independent-KPCA and Intra-KPCA.

TABLE II
CLASSIFICATION USING THE DATA DEPENDENT KERNEL.

Step 1. Compute the matrix $\mathbf{H}$ of the data dependent kernel.

Step 2. Compute the kernel matrix $\mathbf{K}_{ij} = \mathbf{k}_d(\mathbf{x}_i, \mathbf{x}_j)$ using the data dependent kernel

Step 3. Solve
$$M\lambda\alpha = \mathbf{K}\alpha,$$
where M is the number of training samples, then normalize the eigenvector expansion coefficients. Let $\lambda_1 \geq \lambda_2 \geq \cdots \geq \lambda_M$ denote the eigenvalues of $\mathbf{K}$ and $\alpha^1, \cdots, \alpha^M$ the corresponding eigenvectors. Normalize the coefficients by requiring $\lambda_i \langle \alpha^i \cdot \alpha^i \rangle = 1$.

Step 4. Extract d principal components $\mathbf{f}_{\mathbf{x}}$ (corresponding to the data dependent kernel) of the training point $\mathbf{x}$ by computing the projections onto the first p eigenvectors as
$$\langle w^n \cdot \phi(\mathbf{x}) \rangle = \sum_{i=1}^{M} \alpha_i^n \mathbf{k}_d(\mathbf{x}_i, \mathbf{x}).$$

Step 5. Extract the features $\mathbf{f}_{\mathbf{t}}$ of the test point $\mathbf{t}$ as in step 4.

Step 6. Obtain the same classification label with the training sample whose feature $\mathbf{f}_{\mathbf{x}}$ has the shortest distance to $\mathbf{f}_{\mathbf{t}}$.

A. Demonstration

Figures 1 and 2 show the training kernel matrix $\mathbf{K}_{tr}$ and the similarity matrix $\mathbf{K}_s$ between the training and testing patterns on AR[2] [18] and ORL[3] face databases. We observe that the within-class similarity is larger than the between-class similarity in both the two matrices (The gray of the pixel represents the similarity of the associated two samples.). If we observe carefully the images, the within-class samples using Intra-DDK are more similar than using Isotropic-DDK, while the between-class samples using Intra-DDK are less similar

[2]http://rvl1.ecn.purdue.edu/~aleix/ar.html.
[3]http://www.uk.research.att.com/facedatabase.html.

than using Isotropic-DDK. From this sense, the Intra-DDK is more discriminative than Isotropic-DDK.

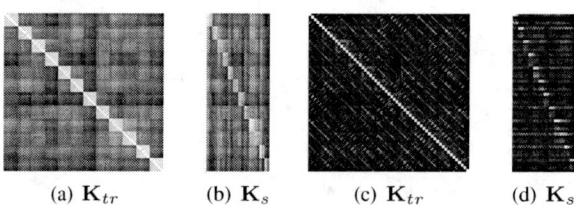

(a) $\mathbf{K}_{tr}$ (b) $\mathbf{K}_s$ (c) $\mathbf{K}_{tr}$ (d) $\mathbf{K}_s$

Fig. 1. The training kernel and similarity matrices on the AR database using Intra-DDK ((a), (b)) and Isotropic-DDK ((c), (d)).

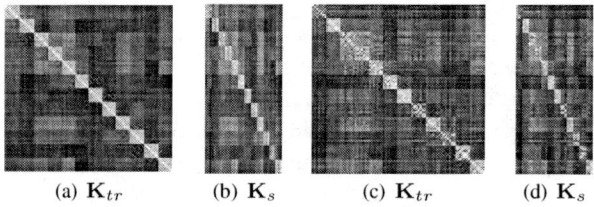

(a) $\mathbf{K}_{tr}$ (b) $\mathbf{K}_s$ (c) $\mathbf{K}_{tr}$ (d) $\mathbf{K}_s$

Fig. 2. The training kernel and similarity matrices on the ORL database using Intra-DDK ((a), (b)) and Isotropic-DDK ((c), (d)).

B. SPECT Heart Diagnosis

In this section, experiments are performed on the SPECT/SPECTF heart diagnosis data sets[4] from the UCI Machine Learning Repository. Both are on diagnosing of cardiac Single Proton Emission Computed Tomography (SPECT) images. Each contains 267 samples, which are represented by attributes summarizing the original SPECT images. The SPECT data has 22 binary attributes, whereas the SPECTF data has 44 continuous attributes. The task is to diagnose whether the heart in each patient or image is normal or not. The training set contains 80 samples (40 samples in each category), and the test set contains 187 samples.

For comparison with the proposed data-dependent kernel, we also run the following methods:

1) 1-nearest-neighbor (1-NN) classifier;
2) PCA; and
3) SVM.

For PCA, the dimensionality of the principal subspace is set to 10. The kernel parameter in SVM is well-tuned. Table III shows the accuracy. The known best result on this task, which is achieved by CLIP4 (Cover Learning using Integer Programming) and the ensemble of CLIP4 [19], is shown in the table for comparison.

As can be seen, the proposed data-dependent kernels (Isotropic, Independent, Intra-KPCA) obtain promising results, though not the best, on the SPECT data set. They get the best result on the SPECTF data set.

[4]http://www.ics.uci.edu/~mlearn/MLSummary.html.

TABLE III
CLASSIFICATION ACCURACY ON THE SPECT TASK.

METHOD	SPECT	SPECTF
1-NN	80.2	72.1
PCA	73.3	75.1
SVM	89.9	93.7
^{5}CLIP4	**90.4**	77.0
ISOTROPIC-KPCA	88.7	**94.4**
INDEPENDENT-KPCA	89.9	**94.4**
INTRA-KPCA	89.9	**94.4**

C. AR Database

In this subsection, experiments are performed on the AR-face database, which consists of over 3200 color images of the frontal faces of 126 subjects. There are 26 different images for each subject. For each subject, these images were recorded in two different sessions separated by two weeks, each session consisting of 13 images. Each image is of size 768×576.

We choose the first 7 face images of the first session by eliminating occluded face images for each subject. Then, we have 126×7 face images. We manually locate the centers of the eyes and then perform geometric normalization with the eye locations fixed to get geometric normalized face image with size 24×18. Examples of the normalized faces are shown in Figure 3.

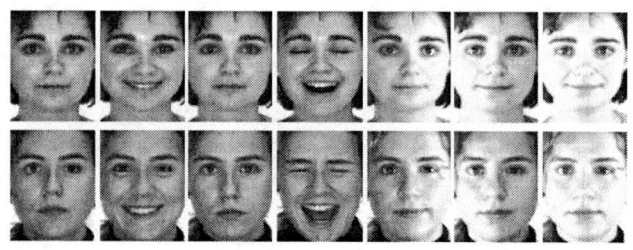

Fig. 3. Example face images from the AR database.

In the experiment, we perform ten trials by randomly selecting five faces for training and two for testing (for each subject) in each trial. Results are then averaged over 10 trials. For comparison, we also show the results of 1-NN, PCA and Bayesian face recognition method. As can be seen in Table IV with the accuracy and the standard deviation, Intra-KPCA obtains the best recognition result.

TABLE IV
CLASSIFICATION ACCURACIES ON THE AR DATABASE.

METHOD	ACCURACY
1-NN	85.54 ± 3.4
PCA	87.88 ± 3.1
BAYESIAN	94.08 ± 2.4
ISOTROPIC-KPCA	83.96 ± 3.5
INDEPENDENT-KPCA	83.12 ± 3.8
INTRA-KPCA	$\mathbf{94.67 \pm 2.3}$

TABLE V
CLASSIFICATION ACCURACIES ON THE ORL DATABASE.

METHOD	ACCURACY
1-NN	97.50 ± 1.0
PCA	94.16 ± 1.4
BAYESIAN	96.92 ± 1.5
ISOTROPIC-KPCA	97.17 ± 1.0
INDEPENDENT-KPCA	97.08 ± 1.2
INTRA-KPCA	$\mathbf{97.92 \pm 1.3}$

D. ORL Database

The ORL (Olivetti Research Laboratory) face database contains a set of face images taken between April 1992 and April 1994 at the Olivetti Research Laboratory. There are ten different images of each of 40 distinct subjects (Figure 4). For some subjects, the images were taken at different times, varying the lighting, facial expressions (open/closed eyes, smiling/not smiling) and facial details (glasses/no glasses). All the images were taken against a dark homogeneous background with the subjects in an upright, frontal position (with tolerance for some side movement). The original image size is 112×92. For convenience, they are downsampled to 28×23.

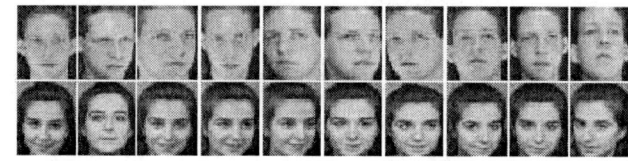

Fig. 4. Example face images from the ORL database.

We perform ten trials by randomly selecting seven faces for training and three for testing (for each subject) in each trial. Results are then averaged over 10 trials. For comparison, we also show the results on 1-NN, PCA, Bayesian face recognition method's results. As can be seen in Table V, Intra-KPCA again obtains the best recognition result.

VI. CONCLUSION

This paper addressed the data-dependent kernels for high-dimension classification problems, which can be efficient to calculate and would improve the recognition performance. We give and analyze the different candidates for the matrix **H** in data dependent kernels. The experiments show that the proposed data dependent kernels especially subspace based DDK can get better recognition performance.

REFERENCES

[1] I. Jolliffe, *Principle Component Analysis*. New York: Springer-Verlag, 1986.
[2] W. Zhao, R. Chellappa, and P. Phillips, "Subspace linear discriminant analysis for face recognition," Tech. Rep. CAR-TR-914, Center for Automation Research, University of Maryland, College Park, 1999.
[3] A. Hyvärinen, "Survey on independent component analysis," *Neural Computing Surveys*, vol. 2, pp. 94–128, 1999.

[4] X. Wang and X. Tang, "Random sampling LDA for face recognition.," in *Proceedings of the IEEE Conference on Computer Vision and Pattern Recognition*, vol. 2, pp. 259–265, 2004.

[5] B. Schölkopf, A. Smola, and K. Müller, "Nonlinear component analysis as a kernel eigenvalue problem," *Neural Computation*, vol. 10, pp. 1299–1319, 1998.

[6] S. Mika, G. Rätsch, J. Weston, B. Schölkopf, and K.-R. Müller, "Fisher discriminant analysis with kernels," in *Neural Networks for Signal Processing IX* (Y.-H. Hu, J. Larsen, E. Wilson, and S. Douglas, eds.), pp. 41–48, IEEE, 1999.

[7] F. Bach and M. Jordan, "Kernel independent component analysis," *Journal of Machine Learning Research*, vol. 3, pp. 1–48, 2002.

[8] K. Crammer, J. Keshet, and Y. Singer, "Kernel design using boosting," in *Advances in Neural Information Processing Systems 15* (S. T. S. Becker and K. Obermayer, eds.), pp. 537–544, Cambridge, MA: MIT Press, 2003.

[9] B. Schölkopf, P. Simard, A. J. Smola, and V. Vapnik, "Prior knowledge in support vector kernels.," in *NIPS*, 1997.

[10] B. Moghaddam and A. Pentland, "Probabilistic visual learning for object representation," *IEEE Transactions on Pattern Analysis and Machine Intelligence*, vol. 19, no. 7, pp. 696–710, 1997.

[11] V. Vapnik, *The nature of statistical learning theory*. Statistics for Engineering and Information Science, Berlin: Springer Verlag, 2000.

[12] Y. Bengio, O. Delalleau, N. L. Roux, J.-F. Paiement, P. Vincent, and M. Ouimet, "Learning eigenfunctions links spectral embedding and kernel pca.," *Neural Computation*, vol. 16, no. 10, pp. 2197–2219, 2004.

[13] A. Ng, M. Jordan, and Y. Weiss, "On spectral clustering: Analysis and an algorithm," 2001.

[14] J. B. Tenenbaum, V. d. Silva, and J. C. Langford, "A Global Geometric Framework for Nonlinear Dimensionality Reduction," *Science*, vol. 290, no. 5500, pp. 2319–2323, 2000.

[15] S. T. Roweis and L. K. Saul, "Nonlinear Dimensionality Reduction by Locally Linear Embedding," *Science*, vol. 290, no. 5500, pp. 2323–2326, 2000.

[16] N. Shental, T. Hertz, D. Weinshall, and M. Pavel, "Adjustment learning and relevant component analysis," in *Proceedings of the Seventh European Conference on Computer Vision*, vol. 4, (Copenhagen, Denmark), pp. 776–792, 2002.

[17] X. Wang and X. Tang, "Unified subspace analysis for face recognition.," in *ICCV*, pp. 679–686, 2003.

[18] A. Martinez and R. Benavente, "The AR face database," Tech. Rep. CVC 24, 1998.

[19] L. A. Kurgan, K. J. Cios, R. Tadeusiewicz, M. R. Ogiela, and L. S. Goodenday, "Knowledge discovery approach to automated cardiac spect diagnosis.," *Artificial Intelligence in Medicine*, vol. 23, no. 2, pp. 149–169, 2001.

Generalized 2D Principal Component Analysis

Hui Kong, Xuchun Li, Lei Wang, Eam Khwang Teoh
School of Electrical and Electronic Enineering
Nanyang Technological University
Singapore 639798
E-mail: {pg03802060, pg03454644, elwang, eekteoh}@ntu.edu.sg

Jian-Gang Wang, Ronda Venkateswarlu
Division of Media
Institute for Infocomm Research
Singapore 119613
E-mail: {jgwang,vronda}@i2r.a-star.edu.sg

Abstract— Recently, a Two-Dimensional Principal Component Analysis (2DPCA) [1] was proposed and the authors have demonstrated its superiority over the conventional Principal Component Analysis (PCA) in face recognition. But the theoretical proof why 2DPCA is better than PCA has not been given until now. In this paper, The essence of 2DPCA is analyzed and a framework of Generalized 2D Principal Component Analysis (G2DPCA) is proposed to extend the original 2DPCA in two perspectives: a Bilateral-projection-based 2DPCA (B2DPCA) and a Kernel-based 2DPCA (K2DPCA) schemes are introduced. Experimental results in face recognition show its excellent performance.

I. INTRODUCTION

Principal Component Analysis (PCA) is a classical dimension-reduction method for feature extraction, which has been widely used in signal processing, pattern recognition and data mining. The application of PCA in face recognition is particularly of our interest in this paper. Sirovich and Kirby first used PCA to represent the human face images [2], [3]. Turk and Pentland proposed the well-known Eigenface for face recognition [4]. Since then, PCA-based face recognition schemes have been extensively investigated. To deal with pose variation problem, Pentland et al. proposed the view-based and modular eigenspaces [5]. Murase and Naya introduced the appearance manifolds [6]. In investigating the illumination variation problem in PCA-based face recognition, Shashua [7], Hallinan [8], Epstein [9], Zhao [10] analyzed the ways of modelling the arbitrary illumination condition for PCA-based recognition methods.

Linear/Fisher Discriminant Analysis (LDA/FDA) [11], [12], [13] and [14] is another important analysis tool for face recognition, LDA/FDA can generally achieve better performance than PCA when there exist noticeable illumination and pose variations. However, LDA/FDA will be inferior to PCA if there are very limited training samples due to the *Small Sample Size* (SSS) problem [15].

Currently, there is also an increasing trend of exploring the kernel subspace representations, where Kernel PCA (KPCA) [16], Kernel FDA (KFDA) [17] and Kernel Direct LDA [18] etc have been proposed. By performing the mapping implicitly using a property of reproducing kernel Hilbert space, which is a high- or infinite-dimensional space, the kernel methods are able to capture higher order statistical dependencies among the input data.

One common property of the face recognition techniques mentioned above is that the 2D face image matrix is typically transformed into a long vector by concatenating the row vectors. However, this will introduce several problems: Firstly, the integral 2D structure of image matrix is disintegrated, therefore, the spatial information could be lost. Secondly, the feature vector lies in a very high-dimensional space, which will bring *the Curse of Dimensionality* dilemma. Thirdly, only sparse data are available in many application areas such as face recognition, image retrieval and text classification, consequently, the SSS problem is inevitable there.

Recently, an image projection technique, Two-Dimensional Principal Component Analysis (2DPCA) [1], is developed for face recognition. Different from PCA, 2DPCA is based on 2D image matrices rather than 1D image vectors. That is, the image matrix does not need to be transformed into a vector beforehand. Instead, the covariance matrix is constructed directly using the 2D image matrices. Although it achieves better performance than PCA, there remain several shortcomings in 2DPCA. Firstly, the authors did not clarify explicitly why 2DPCA is better than PCA. Secondly, a unilateral projection (right multiplication) scheme is adopted in the original 2DPCA. However, the disadvantage arising in this way is that more coefficients are needed to represent an image in 2DPCA than PCA. Thirdly, 2DPCA is a linear method, which neglects the higher-order statistics among the row/column vectors of the images. However, it is well known that the object/face appearances lie on a nonlinear low-dimensional manifold when there exist pose or/and illumination variations [6]. 2DPCA cannot effectively model such a nonlinearity, and this prevents it from higher recognition rate.

In this paper, a framework of Generalized Two-Dimensional Principal Component Analysis is proposed to extend the original 2DPCA in the following three ways: firstly, the essence of 2DPCA and the relationship between 2DPCA and PCA are revealed to explicitly explain the reason why 2DPCA can achieve better performance than PCA in face recognition. Secondly, a bilateral projection scheme, called B2DPCA, is introduced to simultaneously construct two subspaces to encode the row and column vectors of the image matrices respectively. In this way, B2DPCA can achieve higher compression rate and efficiency than 2DPCA and PCA. Thirdly, a Kernel-based 2DPCA (K2DPCA) is investigated to remedy the shortcoming of 2DPCA in modelling the nonlinear manifold of face images.

The remainder of this paper is organized as follows: The 2DPCA algorithm is reviewed in section 2. The essence of

2DPCA and the relationship between 2DPCA and PCA are revealed in section 3. The B2DPCA algorithm is given in section 4. The Kernel based 2DPCA is introduced in section 5. Experimental results in face recognition and discussions are presented in section 6. We draw the conclusions in the last section.

II. 2D PRINCIPAL COMPONENT ANALYSIS

Let $\mathbf{x}$ be an n-dimensional unitary column vector. The idea is to project image $\mathbf{A}$, an $m \times n$ matrix, onto $\mathbf{x}$ by $\mathbf{y} = \mathbf{A}\mathbf{x}$. To determine the optimal projection vector $\mathbf{x}$, the total scatter of the projected samples, $\mathbf{S}_x$, is used to measure the goodness of $\mathbf{x}$. $\mathbf{S}_x = \mathbf{x}^T E\{[\mathbf{A} - E(\mathbf{A})]^T[\mathbf{A} - E(\mathbf{A})]\}\mathbf{x} = \mathbf{x}^T \mathbf{S}_A \mathbf{x}$, where $\mathbf{S}_A = E\{[\mathbf{A} - E(\mathbf{A})]^T[\mathbf{A} - E(\mathbf{A})]\}$, called the image covariance matrix. Suppose that there are totally M training samples $\{\mathbf{A}_i\}, i = 1, 2, ..., M$, and the average image is denoted by $\overline{\mathbf{A}}$, then $\mathbf{S}_A = \frac{1}{M}\sum_{i=1}^{M}[\mathbf{A}_i - \overline{\mathbf{A}}]^T[\mathbf{A}_i - \overline{\mathbf{A}}]$. The optimal projection direction, $\mathbf{x}_{opt}$, is the eigenvector of $\mathbf{S}_A$ corresponding to the largest eigenvalue. Usually a set of orthonormal projection directions, $\mathbf{x}_1, \mathbf{x}_2, ..., \mathbf{x}_d$, are selected and these projection directions are the orthonormal eigenvectors of $\mathbf{S}_A$ corresponding to the first d largest eigenvalues. For a given image $\mathbf{A}$, let $\mathbf{y}_k = \mathbf{A}\mathbf{x}_k, k = 1, 2, ..., d$. A set of projected feature vectors $\mathbf{y}_k$, the *principal components (vectors)* of $\mathbf{A}$, are obtained. Then the *feature matrix* of $\mathbf{A}$ is formed as $\mathbf{B} = [\mathbf{y}_1, \mathbf{y}_2, ..., \mathbf{y}_d]$. The nearest-neighborhood classifier is adopted for classification. The distance between two arbitrary *feature matrices*, $\mathbf{B}_i$ and $\mathbf{B}_j$, is defined as $d(\mathbf{B}_i, \mathbf{B}_j) = \sum_{k=1}^{d} \|y_k^i - y_k^j\|_2$, where $\|y_k^i - y_k^j\|_2$ is the Euclidean distance between y_k^i and y_k^j.

III. THE ESSENCE OF 2DPCA

The essence of the 2DPCA is not discussed in [1]. However, it is important to investigate the essence for understanding the advantages of the 2DPCA. Apparently, the newly defined covariance matrix in 2DPCA should have more physical meaning in the matrix space than in the vector space. However, Theorem 1 will give another perspective to make the 2DPCA more physically meaningful even in vector space.

Theorem 1: The 2DPCA performed on the 2D images is essentially the PCA performed on the rows of the images if each row is viewed as a computational unit.

Proof: Let $\mathbf{A}_i$ be the i-th training sample, $\mathbf{A}_i^j$ be the j-th row of the i-th training sample. Let $E(\mathbf{A})$ be the mean of all the training samples, $E(\mathbf{A})^j$ be the j-th row of $E(\mathbf{A})$. Let $\hat{\mathbf{A}}_i$ be the centered $\mathbf{A}_i$ and $\hat{\mathbf{A}}_i^j$ be the centered $\mathbf{A}_i^j$, where $\hat{\mathbf{A}}_i = \mathbf{A}_i - E(\mathbf{A})$ and $\hat{\mathbf{A}}_i^j = \mathbf{A}_i^j - E(\mathbf{A})^j$.

Because of the limited number of available samples in specific applications, $\mathbf{S}_A$ is often estimated by: $\mathbf{S}_A = \frac{1}{M}\sum_{i=1}^{M}[\mathbf{A}_i - E(\mathbf{A})]^T[\mathbf{A}_i - E(\mathbf{A})] = \frac{1}{M}[[\mathbf{A}_1 - E(\mathbf{A})]^T, ..., [\mathbf{A}_M - E(\mathbf{A})]^T][[\mathbf{A}_1 - E(\mathbf{A})]^T, ..., [\mathbf{A}_M - E(\mathbf{A})]^T]^T = \frac{1}{M}[\hat{\mathbf{A}}_1^T, ..., \hat{\mathbf{A}}_M^T][\hat{\mathbf{A}}_1^T, ..., \hat{\mathbf{A}}_M^T]^T = \frac{1}{M}[[(\hat{\mathbf{A}}_1^1)^T, ..., (\hat{\mathbf{A}}_1^m)^T], ..., [(\hat{\mathbf{A}}_M^1)^T, ..., (\hat{\mathbf{A}}_M^m)^T]][[(\hat{\mathbf{A}}_1^1)^T, ..., (\hat{\mathbf{A}}_1^m)^T], ..., [(\hat{\mathbf{A}}_M^1)^T, ..., (\hat{\mathbf{A}}_M^m)^T]]^T = \frac{1}{M}\sum_{i=1}^{M}\sum_{j=1}^{m}(\hat{\mathbf{A}}_i^j)^T(\hat{\mathbf{A}}_i^j) = \frac{1}{M}\Psi^T\Psi$.

where $\Psi = [[(\hat{\mathbf{A}}_1^1)^T, ..., (\hat{\mathbf{A}}_1^m)^T], ..., [(\hat{\mathbf{A}}_M^1)^T, ..., (\hat{\mathbf{A}}_M^m)^T]]^T$. Therefore, $\mathbf{S}_A$ can be viewed as the covariance matrix evaluated using the rows of all the centered training samples. In 2DPCA, the maximization of $\mathbf{S}_x$ is equal to maximize $\mathbf{x}^T \Psi^T \Psi \mathbf{x}$. This translates into the eigen-analysis of $\Psi^T\Psi$:

$$\lambda_i \mathbf{x}_i = \Psi^T \Psi \mathbf{x}_i \quad (1)$$

Hence, the 2DPCA performed on the image matrices is essentially the PCA performed on the rows of all the images. □

As a result, 2DPCA has the following advantages over PCA. Firstly, as the dimension of the row of each image is much smaller than that of the entire image vector, the dilemma of *Curse of Dimensionality* diminishes. Secondly, as the input feature vectors to be analyzed are factually the rows of all the training images, the feature set is significantly enlarged. Therefore, SSS problem does not exist in 2DPCA. Thirdly, the 2D spatial information is kept integrally by reserving the 2D image matrix rather than disintegrate it. Fourthly, the distance function adopted in the classification criterion in 2DPCA is a global combination of all the local Eigen-feature distances. In terms of the first two advantages, it can be concluded that the covariance matrix in 2DPCA can be estimated more robustly and accurately than that in PCA. Although [1] also drew this conclusion, it did not give the intrinsic reason mentioned above.

IV. BILATERAL 2D PRINCIPAL COMPONENT ANALYSIS

As mentioned in section I, 2DPCA is a unilateral-projection-based scheme. However, as we have described, 2DPCA is actually PCA performed on the rows of all the images. Therefore, the unilateral scheme will lose those spatial information embedded in the columns of the images. In addition, a disadvantage (compared to PCA) resulting from the unilateral-projection scheme is that more coefficients are needed to represent an image. Consider this, a bilateral-projection-based 2DPCA (B2DPCA) is proposed in this section. Compared with the standard 2DPCA, it can remove the redundancies among both rows and columns of the images, and be consequently able to reduce the number of coefficients for representing an image. Additionally, it encodes completely the spatial information that is beneficial for classification.

Let $\mathbf{U} \in \mathcal{R}^m \times \mathcal{R}^l$ and $\mathbf{V} \in \mathcal{R}^n \times \mathcal{R}^r$ be the left- and right-multiplying projection matrix respectively. It is assumed that all the samples are all centered in the later sections. For an $m \times n$ image $\mathbf{A}_i$ and an $l \times r$ projected image $\mathbf{B}_i$, the bilateral projection is formulated as follows:

$$\mathbf{B}_i = \mathbf{U}^T \mathbf{A}_i \mathbf{V} \quad (2)$$

where $\mathbf{B}_i$ is the extracted feature matrix for image $\mathbf{A}_i$.

The optimal projection matrices, $\mathbf{U}_{Opt}$ and $\mathbf{V}_{Opt}$ in Eq.2 can be computed by solving the following minimization problem such that $\mathbf{U}_{Opt}\mathbf{B}_i\mathbf{V}_{Opt}^T$ gives the best approximation of $\mathbf{A}_i$:

$$[\mathbf{U}_{Opt}, \mathbf{V}_{Opt}] = \arg\min \sum_{i=1}^{M} \|\mathbf{A}_i - \mathbf{U}\mathbf{B}_i\mathbf{V}^T\|_F^2 \quad (3)$$

where M is the number of data samples and $\|\bullet\|_F$ is the Frobenius norm of a matrix.

Theorem 2: The minimization equation (3) equals to the maximization of $\sum_{i=1}^{M} \|\mathbf{U}^T\mathbf{A}_i\mathbf{V}\|_F^2$.

Proof: Let $\nabla = \sum_{i=1}^{M} \|\mathbf{A}_i - \mathbf{U}\mathbf{B}_i\mathbf{V}^T\|_F^2$. According to the property of *trace* of matrix, we have

$\nabla = \sum_{i=1}^{M} tr((\mathbf{A}_i - \mathbf{U}\mathbf{B}_i\mathbf{V}^T)(\mathbf{A}_i - \mathbf{U}\mathbf{B}_i\mathbf{V}^T)^T)$
$= \sum_{i=1}^{M} tr(\mathbf{A}_i\mathbf{A}_i^T) + tr(\mathbf{U}\mathbf{B}_i\mathbf{V}^T\mathbf{V}\mathbf{B}_i^T\mathbf{U}^T) - 2tr(\mathbf{U}\mathbf{B}_i\mathbf{V}^T\mathbf{A}_i^T)$
$= \sum_{i=1}^{M} tr(\mathbf{A}_i\mathbf{A}_i^T) + tr(\mathbf{U}\mathbf{B}_i\mathbf{B}_i^T\mathbf{U}^T) - 2\sum_{i=1}^{M} tr(\mathbf{U}\mathbf{B}_i\mathbf{V}^T\mathbf{A}_i^T)$
$= \sum_{i=1}^{M} tr(\mathbf{A}_i\mathbf{A}_i^T) + \sum_{i=1}^{M} tr(\mathbf{B}_i^T\mathbf{U}^T\mathbf{U}\mathbf{B}_i) - 2tr(\mathbf{U}\mathbf{B}_i\mathbf{V}^T\mathbf{A}_i^T)$
$= \sum_{i=1}^{M} \{tr(\mathbf{A}_i\mathbf{A}_i^T) + tr(\mathbf{B}_i^T\mathbf{B}_i) - 2tr(\mathbf{U}\mathbf{B}_i\mathbf{V}^T\mathbf{A}_i^T)\}$
$= \sum_{i=1}^{M} \{tr(\mathbf{A}_i\mathbf{A}_i^T) + tr(\mathbf{B}_i\mathbf{B}_i^T) - 2tr(\mathbf{U}\mathbf{B}_i\mathbf{V}^T\mathbf{A}_i^T)\}$

where the second term derives from the facts that (1) both $\mathbf{U}$ and $\mathbf{V}$ have orthonormal columns, and (2) $tr(\mathbf{AB}) = tr(\mathbf{BA})$ for any two matrices.

Since the first term is a constant, the minimization of Eq.(3) is equivalent to minimizing:

$$\mathbf{J} = \sum_{i=1}^{M}\{tr(\mathbf{B}_i\mathbf{B}_i^T) - 2tr(\mathbf{U}\mathbf{B}_i\mathbf{V}^T\mathbf{A}_i^T)\} \quad (4)$$

Let,

$$\frac{\partial \mathbf{J}}{\partial \mathbf{B}_i} = 2\sum_{i=1}^{M}\{\mathbf{B}_i - \mathbf{U}^T\mathbf{A}_i\mathbf{V}\} = 0 \quad (5)$$

Therefore, only if $\mathbf{B}_i = \mathbf{U}^T\mathbf{A}_i\mathbf{V}$, the minimum value of $\mathbf{J}$ can be achieved. We substitute $\mathbf{B}_i$ in Eq.(3) by $\mathbf{U}^T\mathbf{A}_i\mathbf{V}$:

$\nabla = \sum_{i=1}^{M} tr((\mathbf{A}_i - \mathbf{U}\mathbf{B}_i\mathbf{V}^T)(\mathbf{A}_i - \mathbf{U}\mathbf{B}_i\mathbf{V}^T)^T)$
$= \sum_{i=1}^{M}\{tr(\mathbf{A}_i\mathbf{A}_i^T) + tr(\mathbf{B}_i\mathbf{B}_i^T) - 2tr(\mathbf{U}\mathbf{B}_i\mathbf{V}^T\mathbf{A}_i^T)\}$
$= \sum_{i=1}^{M}\{tr(\mathbf{A}_i\mathbf{A}_i^T) + tr(\mathbf{B}_i\mathbf{B}_i^T) - 2tr(\mathbf{B}_i\mathbf{B}_i^T)\}$
$= \sum_{i=1}^{M}\{tr(\mathbf{A}_i\mathbf{A}_i^T) - tr(\mathbf{B}_i\mathbf{B}_i^T)\}$
$= \sum_{i=1}^{M}\|\mathbf{A}_i\|_F^2 - \sum_{i=1}^{M}\|\mathbf{B}_i\|_F^2$
$= \sum_{i=1}^{M}\|\mathbf{A}_i\|_F^2 - \sum_{i=1}^{M}\|\mathbf{U}^T\mathbf{A}_i\mathbf{V}\|_F^2$

where the first term is a constant, therefore, the minimization of Eq.(3) is equivalent to the maximization of the following Eq.(6) and the solutions that maximize Eq.(6) are the optimal ones.

$$\delta = \sum_{i=1}^{M}\|\mathbf{U}^T\mathbf{A}_i\mathbf{V}\|_F^2 \quad (6)$$

□

Given the data set $\mathbf{A}_i \in \mathcal{R}^m \times \mathcal{R}^n, i = 1,...,M$ and finally reserved dimension l and r, the covariance matrix of the projected samples is defined as:

$$\mathbf{C} = \frac{1}{M}\sum_{i=1}^{M}\mathbf{B}_i^T\mathbf{B}_i \quad (7)$$

where $\mathbf{B}_i$ is defined in Eq.(2). By replacing $\mathbf{B}_i$ with $\mathbf{U}^T\mathbf{A}_i\mathbf{V}$, it translates into: $\mathbf{C} = \frac{1}{M}\sum_{i=1}^{M}(\mathbf{U}^T\mathbf{A}_i\mathbf{V})^T(\mathbf{U}^T\mathbf{A}_i\mathbf{V})$ and $tr(\mathbf{C}) = tr(\frac{1}{M}\sum_{i=1}^{M}(\mathbf{U}^T\mathbf{A}_i\mathbf{V})^T(\mathbf{U}^T\mathbf{A}_i\mathbf{V})) = \frac{1}{M}\sum_{i=1}^{M}\|\mathbf{U}^T\mathbf{A}_i\mathbf{V}\|_F^2$.

In this regard, maximizing the trace of the covariance matrix of the projected samples is equivalent to maximizing $\sum_{i=1}^{M}\|\mathbf{U}^T\mathbf{A}_i\mathbf{V}\|_F^2$, while maximizing $\sum_{i=1}^{M}\|\mathbf{U}^T\mathbf{A}_i\mathbf{V}\|_F^2$ has been shown to be equivalent to minimizing $\sum_{i=1}^{M}\|\mathbf{A}_i - \mathbf{U}\mathbf{B}_i\mathbf{V}^T\|_F^2$ and optimally reconstructing (approximating) the images. Therefore, the proposed bilateral-projection scheme can be viewed as a generalized 2DPCA, i.e., the standard 2DPCA is a special form of the bilateral 2DPCA.

To our knowledge, there is no close-form solution for the maximization of Eq.(6) because $\mathbf{C} = \frac{1}{M}\sum_{i=1}^{M}\mathbf{V}^T\mathbf{A}_i^T\mathbf{U}\mathbf{U}^T\mathbf{A}_i\mathbf{V}$ and there is no direct method for the eigen decomposition of such a coupled covariance matrix. Considering this, an iterative algorithm is proposed to compute the $\mathbf{U}_{Opt}$ and $\mathbf{V}_{Opt}$.

Lemma 1: Given the $\mathbf{U}_{Opt}$, $\mathbf{V}_{Opt}$ can be obtained as the matrix formed by the first r eigenvectors corresponding to the first r largest eigenvalues of $\mathbf{C}_v = \frac{1}{M}\sum_{i=1}^{M}\mathbf{A}_i^T\mathbf{U}_{Opt}\mathbf{U}_{Opt}^T\mathbf{A}_i$.

Proof: Since $\mathbf{U}_{Opt}$ and $\mathbf{V}_{Opt}$ maximize $tr(\mathbf{C})$, which equals $tr(\frac{1}{M}\sum_{i=1}^{M}\mathbf{V}^T\mathbf{A}_i^T\mathbf{U}\mathbf{U}^T\mathbf{A}_i\mathbf{V})$. If $\mathbf{U}_{Opt}$ is known, $tr(\mathbf{C}) = tr(\frac{1}{M}\sum_{i=1}^{M}\mathbf{V}^T\mathbf{A}_i^T\mathbf{U}_{Opt}\mathbf{U}_{Opt}^T\mathbf{A}_i\mathbf{V}) = tr(\mathbf{V}^T\mathbf{C}_v\mathbf{V})$.

Therefore, the maximization of $tr(\mathbf{C})$ equals to solve the first r eigenvectors of $\frac{1}{M}\sum_{i=1}^{M}\mathbf{A}_i^T\mathbf{U}_{Opt}\mathbf{U}_{Opt}^T\mathbf{A}_i$ corresponding to the first r largest eigenvalues. □

Lemma 2: Given the $\mathbf{V}_{Opt}$, $\mathbf{U}_{Opt}$ can be obtained as the matrix formed by the first l eigenvectors corresponding to the first l largest eigenvalues of $\mathbf{C}_u = \frac{1}{M}\sum_{i=1}^{M}\mathbf{A}_i\mathbf{V}_{Opt}\mathbf{V}_{Opt}^T\mathbf{A}_i^T$.

The proof of Lemma 2 is similar to that of Lemma 1. □

By Lemma 1 and 2, the detailed iterative scheme designed to compute the $\mathbf{U}_{Opt}$ and $\mathbf{V}_{Opt}$ is listed in Table 1:

The obtained solutions are locally optimal because the solutions are dependent on the initialized $\mathbf{U}_0$. By extensive experiments, $\mathbf{U}_0 = \mathbf{I}_m$, a setting we adopted, will produce excellent results. Another issue deserving attention is that this algorithm is convergency because of the timely update of $\mathbf{V}_i$ and $\mathbf{U}_i$ ensures that Eq.(3) can be minimized.

TABLE I
THE ALGORITHM FOR COMPUTING $\mathbf{U}_{Opt}$ AND $\mathbf{V}_{Opt}$

S_1.	Initialize $\mathbf{U}$, $\mathbf{U} = \mathbf{U}_0$ and $i = 0$
S_2.	While not convergent
S_3.	Compute $\mathbf{C}_v$ and the eigenvectors $\{e_j^V\}_{j=1}^r$ corresponding to its r top eigenvalues, then $\mathbf{V}_i \leftarrow [e_1^V,...,e_r^V]$
S_4.	Compute $\mathbf{C}_u$ and the eigenvectors $\{e_j^U\}_{j=1}^l$ corresponding to its l top eigenvalues, then $\mathbf{U}_i \leftarrow [e_1^U,...,e_l^U]$
S_5.	$i \leftarrow i + 1$
S_6.	End While
S_7.	$\mathbf{V}_{Opt} \leftarrow \mathbf{V}_{i-1}$ and $\mathbf{U}_{Opt} \leftarrow \mathbf{U}_{i-1}$
S_8.	Feature extraction: $\mathbf{B}_i = \mathbf{U}_{Opt}^T\mathbf{A}_i\mathbf{V}_{Opt}$

V. KERNEL BASED 2D PRINCIPAL COMPONENT ANALYSIS

Let $\Phi : \mathbf{R}^t \to \mathbf{R}^f, f > t$, be a nonlinearly mapping, where t is the length of the rows of an image and f can be arbitrarily large. The dot product in the feature space of $\mathbf{R}^f$ can be conveniently calculated via a pre-defined kernel function, such as the commonly used Gaussian RBF kernel function.

For the sake of simplicity, it is assumed that all the mapped data are centered by the method in [16]. Let $\widehat{\Phi}(\mathbf{A}_i)$ be the i-th mapped image in which $\widehat{\Phi}(\mathbf{A}_i^j)$ be the j-th centered row vector of it. The covariance matrix $\mathbf{C}^\Phi$ in $\mathbf{R}^f$:

$$\mathbf{C}^\Phi = \frac{1}{M}\sum_{i=1}^{M}\widehat{\Phi}(\mathbf{A}_i)^T\widehat{\Phi}(\mathbf{A}_i) \quad (8)$$

where $\widehat{\Phi}(\mathbf{A}_i) = [\widehat{\Phi}(\mathbf{A}_i^1)^T, \widehat{\Phi}(\mathbf{A}_i^2)^T, ..., \widehat{\Phi}(\mathbf{A}_i^m)^T]^T$ and m is the number of row vectors. Therefore, if $\mathbf{R}^f$ is infinite-dimensional, $\mathbf{C}^\Phi$ is $inf \times inf$ in size. It is intractable to directly calculate the eigenvalues, λ_i, and the eigenvectors, $\mathbf{v}_i$, that satisfy

$$\lambda_i \mathbf{v}_i = \mathbf{C}^\Phi \mathbf{v}_i \quad (9)$$

However, K2DPCA can be implemented using KPCA according to the following theorem.

Theorem 3: The above defined kernelized 2DPCA on the images is essentially the KPCA performed locally on the rows of all the training image matrices.

Proof: Since, $\mathbf{v}_i = \frac{1}{\lambda_i} \mathbf{C}^\Phi \mathbf{v}_i$
$= \frac{1}{\lambda_i} [\frac{1}{M} \sum_{k=1}^M \widehat{\Phi}(\mathbf{A}_k)^T \widehat{\Phi}(\mathbf{A}_k)] \mathbf{v}_i$
$= \frac{1}{\lambda_i M} [\widehat{\Phi}(\mathbf{A}_1)^T, ..., \widehat{\Phi}(\mathbf{A}_M)^T][\widehat{\Phi}(\mathbf{A}_1)^T, ..., \widehat{\Phi}(\mathbf{A}_M)^T]^T \mathbf{v}_i$
$= \frac{1}{\lambda_i M} [[\widehat{\Phi}(\mathbf{A}_1^1)^T, ..., \widehat{\Phi}(\mathbf{A}_1^m)^T], [\widehat{\Phi}(\mathbf{A}_2^1)^T, ..., \widehat{\Phi}(\mathbf{A}_2^m)^T],$
$..., [\widehat{\Phi}(\mathbf{A}_M^1)^T, ..., \widehat{\Phi}(\mathbf{A}_M^m)^T]] \vec{\alpha}_i,$

and,
$\vec{\alpha}_i = [\alpha_i^{1,1}, \alpha_i^{1,2}, ..., \alpha_i^{M,m}]^T$
$= [[\widehat{\Phi}(\mathbf{A}_1^1)^T, ..., \widehat{\Phi}(\mathbf{A}_1^m)^T], [\widehat{\Phi}(\mathbf{A}_2^1)^T, ..., \widehat{\Phi}(\mathbf{A}_2^m)^T],$
$..., [\widehat{\Phi}(\mathbf{A}_M^1)^T, ..., \widehat{\Phi}(\mathbf{A}_M^m)^T]]^T \mathbf{v}_i.$

Thus, the solutions $\mathbf{v}_i$ lie in the span of $\widehat{\Phi}(\mathbf{A}_k^l)^T, k = 1, ..., M; l = 1, ..., m$. In other words,

$$\mathbf{v}_i = \sum_{k=1}^M \sum_{l=1}^m \alpha_i^{k,l} \widehat{\Phi}(\mathbf{A}_k^l)^T.$$

Since,
$$\lambda_i \mathbf{v}_i = \mathbf{C}^\Phi \mathbf{v}_i,$$
we have,
$$\lambda_i (\widehat{\Phi}(\mathbf{A}_g^h)^T \bullet \mathbf{v}_i) = (\widehat{\Phi}(\mathbf{A}_g^h)^T \bullet \mathbf{C}^\Phi \mathbf{v}_i),$$
That is,
$\lambda_i \sum_{k=1}^M \sum_{l=1}^m \alpha_i^{k,l} (\widehat{\Phi}(\mathbf{A}_g^h)^T \bullet \widehat{\Phi}(\mathbf{A}_k^l)^T)$
$= (\widehat{\Phi}(\mathbf{A}_g^h)^T \bullet [\frac{1}{M} \sum_{t=1}^M \widehat{\Phi}(\mathbf{A}_t)^T \widehat{\Phi}(\mathbf{A}_t) \sum_{k=1}^M \sum_{l=1}^m \alpha_i^{k,l} \widehat{\Phi}(\mathbf{A}_k^l)^T])$
$= (\widehat{\Phi}(\mathbf{A}_g^h)^T \bullet [\frac{1}{M} \sum_{p=1}^M \sum_{q=1}^m \widehat{\Phi}(\mathbf{A}_p^q)^T \widehat{\Phi}(\mathbf{A}_p^q)$
$\sum_{k=1}^M \sum_{l=1}^m \alpha_i^{k,l} \widehat{\Phi}(\mathbf{A}_k^l)^T])$
$= \frac{1}{M} \sum_{k=1}^M \sum_{l=1}^m \alpha_i^{k,l} (\widehat{\Phi}(\mathbf{A}_g^h)^T \bullet \sum_{p=1}^M \sum_{q=1}^m \widehat{\Phi}(\mathbf{A}_p^q)^T)$
$(\widehat{\Phi}(\mathbf{A}_p^q)^T \bullet \widehat{\Phi}(\mathbf{A}_k^l)^T).$

Defining an $(M \times m) \times (M \times m)$ matrix $\mathbf{K}$ by
$$\mathbf{K}_{(k \times l, p \times q)} = (\widehat{\Phi}(\mathbf{A}_k^l)^T \bullet \widehat{\Phi}(\mathbf{A}_p^q)^T)$$
The above equation can be converted into:

$$M \lambda_i \mathbf{K} \vec{\alpha}_i = \mathbf{K}^2 \vec{\alpha}_i \quad (10)$$

or

$$M \lambda_i \vec{\alpha}_i = \mathbf{K} \vec{\alpha}_i \quad (11)$$

Since $\mathbf{K}$ is positive semidefinite, $\mathbf{K}$'s eigenvalues will be nonnegative, the eigenvalues $\lambda_1 \leq \lambda_2 \leq, ..., \leq \lambda_{M \times m}$ and the corresponding eigenvectors $\vec{\alpha}_1, \vec{\alpha}_2, ..., \vec{\alpha}_{M \times m}$ can be solved by diagonalize $\mathbf{K}$, with λ_p being the first nonzero eigenvalue. We normalize $\vec{\alpha}_p, \vec{\alpha}_2, ..., \vec{\alpha}_{M \times m}$ by enforcing the unitilization of the corresponding $\mathbf{v}$ in $\mathbf{F}$, i.e., $(\mathbf{v}_d \bullet \mathbf{v}_d) = 1$ for all $d = p, ..., M \times m$. In terms of $\mathbf{v}_i = \sum_{k=1}^M \sum_{l=1}^m \alpha_i^{k,l} \widehat{\Phi}(\mathbf{A}_k^l)^T$, this turns into: $1 = ((\sum_{k=1}^M \sum_{l=1}^m \alpha_d^{k,l} \widehat{\Phi}(\mathbf{A}_k^l)^T)$
$\bullet (\sum_{p=1}^M \sum_{q=1}^m \alpha_d^{p,q} \widehat{\Phi}(\mathbf{A}_p^q)^T) = (\vec{\alpha}_d \bullet \mathbf{K} \vec{\alpha}_d) = \lambda_d (\vec{\alpha}_d \bullet \vec{\alpha}_d).$

To extract the principal component of each row, we need to project each mapped image row vector $\widehat{\Phi}(\mathbf{A}_i^j)$ onto the eigenvectors $\mathbf{v}_k$ in $\mathbf{F}$, i.e., $(\mathbf{v}_k \bullet \widehat{\Phi}(\mathbf{A}_i^j)) = \sum_{p=1}^M \sum_{q=1}^m \alpha_k^{p,q} (\widehat{\Phi}(\mathbf{A}_p^q)^T \bullet \widehat{\Phi}(\mathbf{A}_i^j)).$

Hence, the K2DPCA performed on 2D images can be regarded as the KPCA performed on 1D rows of all the training images. □

After projecting each mapped row vector of all the training and test images onto the first d reserved eigenvectors in the feature space, a $m \times d$ feature matrix is obtained for each image. The nearest-neighborhood classifier is then adopted for classification which is similar to 2DPCA [1].

VI. EXPERIMENTAL RESULTS AND DISCUSSIONS

A. Face Recognition on ORL and UMIST

The proposed B2DPCA and K2DPCA methods are applied to the face recognition and are evaluated on two well-known face image databases: *ORL* and *UMIST* face databases. The *ORL* face database contains images from 40 individuals, each providing 10 different images. The pose, expression and facial details (e.g., with glasses or without glasses) variations are also included. The images are taken with a tolerance for some tilting and rotation of the face of up to 20 degrees. Moreover, there are also some variations in the scale of up to about 10 percent. Ten sample images of two persons from the *ORL* database are shown in Fig.1. The *UMIST* face database consists of 564 images of 20 people with large pose variations. In our experiment, 360 images with 18 samples for each subject are used to ensure that face appearance changes from profile to frontal orientation with a step of 5° separation (labelled from 1 to 18). The sample images for subject 1 are shown in Fig.2.

Fig. 1. Ten sample images of two subjects in *ORL* database

Fig. 2. Eighteen sample images of subject 1a from *UMIST* face database labelled by #1, #2,..., #18 from left to right

All images in *ORL* and *UMIST* databases are grayscale and normalized to a resolution of 56×46 pixels. The *ORL* database is employed to check whether the proposed methods have good generalization ability under the circumstances that the pose, expression, and face scale variations exist concurrently. The *UMIST* face database is used to examine the performance when face orientation varies significantly.

To test the recognition performance with different training numbers on *ORL*, k ($1 \leq k \leq 5$) images of each subject are randomly selected for training and the remaining ($10-k$) images of each subject for testing. when $2 \leq k \leq 5$, 50 times of random selections are performed. When k equals 1, there are 10 possible selections for training. The final recognition

TABLE II
EXPERIMENTS ON ORL DATABASE

	1	2	3	4	5
PCA [4]	69.5	82.5	88.8	92.1	94.1
KPCA [16]	69.5	82.5	88.8	92.1	94.2
LDA [12]		75.8	87.0	90.1	91.7
KLDA [17]		85.5	92.2	95.6	97.5
2DPCA [1]	72.5	84.5	89.9	93.1	95
KDDA [18]		85.0	88.6	92.8	96.0
DCV [14]		74.3	82.9	87.1	88.7
B2DPCA	72.8	85.1	90.3	93.5	95.4
K2DPCA	74.5	86.9	92.0	94.6	96.2

TABLE III
EXPERIMENTS ON $UMIST$ DATABASE

	#5, #14	#1, #7, #13	#2, #8, #14	#3, #9, #15	#4, #10, #16	#5, #11, #17	#6, #12, #18
PCA [4]	80.3	82.7	89.7	90.7	90.7	88.0	86.0
KPCA [16]	80.9	86.0	87.0	91.0	92.0	89.3	87.3
LDA [12]	77.5	90.0	91.3	95.0	96.3	94.3	91.7
KLDA [17]	92.5	94.7	96.7	98.3	99.0	98.0	97.3
2DPCA [1]	90.3	91.0	93.0	95.0	95.0	93.7	92.3
KDDA [18]	87.8	94.0	96.0	95.7	97.3	95.7	95.7
DCV [14]	84.1	89.7	93.7	97.7	94.7	92.7	88.0
B2DPCA	90.7	91.7	93.4	95.3	95.8	94.0	92.8
K2DPCA	92.7	94.0	94.3	95.7	97.0	95.7	94.0

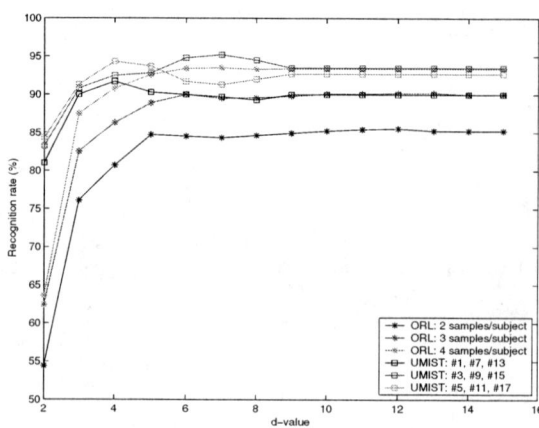

Fig. 3. The effect of different d-value on recognition rate of B2DPCA

rate is the average of all. The performance of the B2DPCA and K2DPCA compared with that of the state-of-the-art methods is listed in the Table 2.

The experiments, with small number of training samples (2 and 3), are conducted on $UMIST$ database. When the number of training samples for each individual is 2, we select {#5,#14} face images of each subject for training, the remaining for test. When the number of training samples is 3 for each subject, six groups are selected for training, i.e., 1{#1,#7,#13}, 2{#2,#8,#14}, 3{#3,#9,#15}, 4{#4,#10,#16}, 5{#5,#11,#17} and 6{#6,#12,#18}, the remaining images corresponding to each group are used to test. The performance of the B2DPCA and K2DPCA is compared with that of the state-of-the-art methods in the Table 3.

The Gaussian RBF kernel is adopted in the K2DPCA in all the experiments, the optimal results are achieved when the width, δ, of the kernel is around 2.718. The optimal dimensions of $\mathbf{U}_{opt}$ and $\mathbf{V}_{opt}$ of B2DPCA in both experiments are around 56×5 and 56×5, therefore, the size of the extracted feature matrix for each image is 5×5. For both experiments, the nearest-neighborhood classification criterion is adopted and the distance function between any two feature matrices is the same as the one used in 2DPCA. Through experiments, we find that B2DPCA is better than 2DPCA, K2DPCA does outperform 2DPCA and KPCA as explained in the previous part. We also find that K2DPCA is superior to LDA and DCV. Additionally, K2DPCA is comparable to KDDA in all the experiments we have done. K2DPCA is even better than KLDA, which is the best of all the subspace methods, when the number of training sample is 2. The K2DPCA is better than B2DPCA in generalization ability.

B. the Effect of d-value on Recognition Performance

We set a common d for both l and r in B2DPCA, therefore, the final feature image obtained from B2DPCA for each image is a $d \times d$ square matrix. A large d will result in a small compression rate while a small d will lose some important information for classification. To illustrate this situation, lots of experiments are conducted on the two databases. The results are shown in Fig.3, where the x-axis denotes the d-value and the y-axis denotes the recognition rate. Three experiments with different number of training samples (2, 3 and 4 respectively) for each subject are done on ORL database. Three experiments with different training set (1{#1,#7,#13}, 3{#3,#9,#15}, 5{#5,#11,#17}) are conducted on $UMIST$. From Fig.3, when the d-value is about 5, the B2DPCA will achieve the highest recognition rate. When d is larger, the recognition rate is nearly constant. Meantime, to ensure an efficient classification and high compression rate, d is therefore set to be 5.

C. Face Image Reconstruction and Compression

2DPCA is an excellent dimension-reduction tool for image processing, compression, storage and transmission. In this part, we compare the compression rate and reconstruction effect of B2DPCA with that of 2DPCA. Fig.4 shows the reconstruction effect of them, where the raw images lie on the first row and the reconstructed image by 2DPCA using 2 and 8 *principal component (vectors)* are shown in the second and fourth rows respectively. The reconstructed images by B2DPCA with $d = 10$ and $d = 20$ are shown in the third and fifth rows. Therefore, the second and third rows have almost the same compression rate since $\frac{56\times 46}{56\times 2} \approx \frac{56\times 46}{10\times 10}$, while the fourth and fifth rows have almost the same compression rate since $\frac{56\times 46}{56\times 8} \approx \frac{56\times 46}{20\times 20}$. But the effect of reconstruction by B2DPCA on the third and fifth rows are much better than that by 2DPCA on the second and fourth rows respectively.

D. Convergence

The image reconstruction error can be used as a measure to check the convergency of the B2DPCA algorithm. In this experiment, the reconstruction error is shown as the

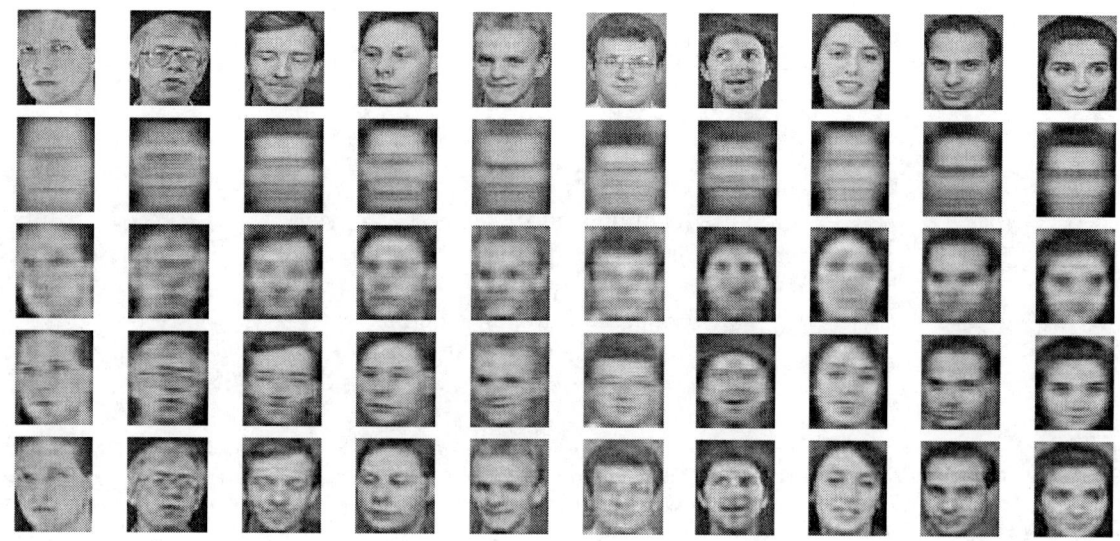

Fig. 4. First row: raw images. Second row and fourth row: image reconstructed and compressed by 2DPCA using 2 and 8 *principal component (vectors)* respectively. Third row and fifth row: image reconstructed and compressed by B2DPCA with $d=10$ and $d=20$ respectively.

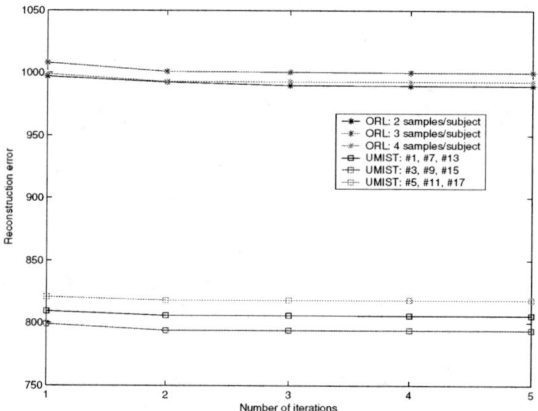

Fig. 5. Convergency of B2DPCA

iteration proceeds. The reconstruction error is defined as $\frac{1}{M}\sum_{i=1}^{M}\|\mathbf{A}_i - \mathbf{U}\mathbf{B}_i\mathbf{V}^T\|_F$. For simplicity, we set d=10 for all cases. Six experiments same as those of section VI.B are conducted and the results are reported in Fig.5, where the x-axis denotes the iteration number and the y-axis denotes the error. Obviously, after two iterations, the error converges.

VII. Conclusions

A framework of Generalized 2D Principal Component Analysis is proposed to extend the original 2DPCA in three ways: firstly, the essence of 2DPCA is clarified. Secondly, a bilateral 2DPCA scheme is introduced to remove the necessity of more coefficients in representing an image in 2DPCA than in PCA. Thirdly, a kernel-based 2DPCA scheme is introduced to remedy the shortage of 2DPCA in exploring the higher-order statistics among the rows/columns of the input data.

References

[1] J. Yang, D. Zhang, A. F. Frangi and J. Yang, "Two-Dimensional PCA: A New Approach to Appearance-Based Face Representation and Recognition," *IEEE Transactions on Pattern Analysis and Machine Intelligence*, 2004.
[2] L. Sirovich and M. Kirby, "Low-Dimensional Procedure for the Characterization of Human Faces," *Journal of Optical Society of America, A*, 1987
[3] M. Kirby and L. Sirovich, "Application of the KL Procedure for the Characterization of Human Faces," *IEEE Transactions on Pattern Analysis and Machine Intelligence*, 1990
[4] M. Turk and A. Pentland, "Eigenfaces for Recognition," *Journal of Cognitive Neuroscience*, 1991
[5] A. Pentland, B. Moghaddam and Thad Starner, "View-based and Modular Eigenspaces for Face Recognition," *IEEE Conference on Computer Vision and Pattern Recognition*, 1994
[6] H. Murase and S. Nayar, "Visual Learning and Recognition of 3D Objects from Appearance," *International Journal on Computer Vision*, 1995
[7] A. Shashua, "Geometry and Photometry in 3D Visual Recognition," Ph.D Thesis, MIT, 1992
[8] P. Hallinan, "A Low-Dimensional Representation of Human Faces for Arbitrary Lighting Conditions," *IEEE Conference on Computer Vision and Pattern Recognition*, 1994
[9] R. Epstein, P. Hallinan and A. L. Yuille, "5 ± 2 Eigenimages Suffice: An Empirical Investigation of Low-Dimensional Lighting Models," *IEEE Workshop on Physics-Based Modeling in Computer Vision*, 1995
[10] L. Zhao and Y. Yang, "Theoretical Analysis of Illumination in PCA-Based Vision Systems," *Pattern Recognition*, 1999
[11] Daniel L. Swets and Juyang Weng, "Using Discriminant Eigenfeatures for Image Retrieval," *IEEE Transactions on PAMI*, 1996
[12] P. N. Belhumeur and J. Hespanha and D. J. Kriegman, "Eigenfaces vs. Fisherfaces: Recognition Using Class Specific Linear Projection," *IEEE Transactions on PAMI*, 1997
[13] W. Zhao, "Discriminant Component Analysis for Face Recognition," *Int. Conf. on Pattern Recognition*, 2000
[14] H. Cevikalp, M. Neamtu, M. Wilkes and A. Barkana, "Discriminative Common Vectors for Face Recognition," *IEEE Trans. on PAMI*, Jan 2005.
[15] K. Fukunnaga, "Introduction to Statistical Pattern Recognition," Academic Press, second edition, 1991.
[16] B. Scholkopf, A. Smola and K. R. Muller, "Nonlinear Component Analysis as a Kernel Eigenvalue Problem," *Neural Computation*, 1998
[17] M. H. Yang, "Kernel Eigenface vs. Kernel Fisherface: Face Recognition Using Kernel Methods," *IEEE Int. Conf. on FGR* 2002
[18] J. Lu, K.N. Plataniotis, and A.N. Venetsanopoulos, "Face Recognition Using Kernel Direct Discriminant Analysis Algorithms", *IEEE Trans. on NN*, January 2003.

Optimal Gradient-Based Learning Using Importance Weights

Sepp Hochreiter and Klaus Obermayer
Bernstein Center for Computational Neuroscience
and
Technische Universität Berlin
10587 Berlin, Germany
{hochreit,oby}@cs.tu-berlin.de

Abstract— We introduce a novel "importance weight" method (IW) to speed up learning of "difficult" data sets including unbalanced data, highly non-linear data, or long-term dependencies in sequences. An importance weight is assigned to every training data point and controls its contribution to the total weight update. The importance weights are obtained by solving a quadratic optimization problem and determines the learning informativeness of a data point. For linear classifiers we show, that IW is equivalent to standard support vector learning. We apply IW to feedforward multi-layer perceptrons and to recurrent neural networks (LSTM). Benchmarks with QuickProp and standard gradient descent methods show that IW is usually much faster in terms of epochs as well as in terms of absolute CPU time, and that it provides equal or better prediction results. IW improved gradient descent results on "real world" protein datasets. In the "latching benchmark" for sequence prediction, IW was able to extract dependencies between sites which are 1,000,000 sequence elements apart – a new record.

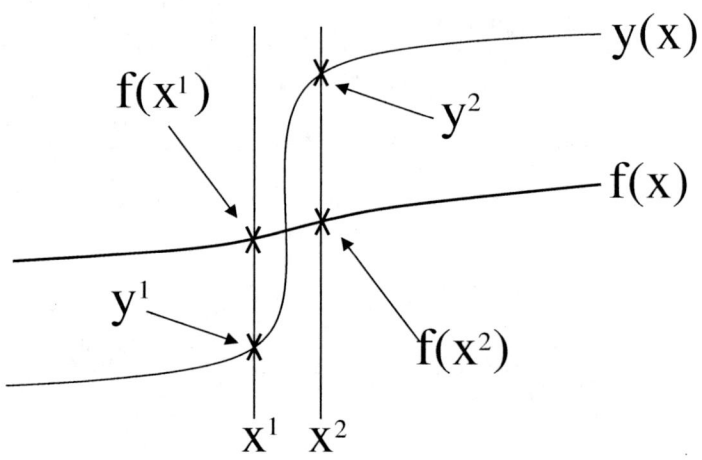

Fig. 1. Gradient contributions at x^1 and x^2 cancel each other.

I. INTRODUCTION

Various methods have been proposed to improve or speed up gradient-based methods for supervised learning. Prominent methods include the natural gradient [1], step-size optimization [17], (pseudo) Newton methods [27], [3], [4], or momentum term methods [14], [20], and usually adapt the direction and/or the step-size of the gradient of the error function - given the local properties of the error surface. For certain data sets, however, gradient-based learning becomes unreliable and slow. This is due to the fact, that the gradient of the total training error becomes either very small or very large leading to a very small or a very large cumulative update.

Fig. 1 illustrates the problem of the vanishing gradient. Consider two points x^1 and x^2 close to one another in input space at a location, where the target function $y(x)$ changes rapidly in a nonlinear way. Gradient-based learning of a model function $f(x)$ using, for example, the squared error $E_{sqr}(x^i) = \frac{1}{2}(y^i - f(x^i))^2$ may then lead to $\nabla_w f(x^1) \approx \nabla_w f(x^2)$ for the current choice of the function's parameters. Since the targets y^1 and y^2 differ and $f(x^1) \approx f(x^2) \approx \frac{1}{2}(y^1 + y^2)$, we obtain $\nabla_w E(x^1) \approx -\nabla_w E(x^2)$. The cumulative effect of the individual gradients at x^1 and x^2 almost vanish and f hardly changes where it is required to change most. The situation depicted in Fig. 1 is often observed in sequence analysis, when sequences (for example proteins) which differ only at few positions may belong to different classes. If standard recurrent networks are used, the situation may become even worse, because recurrent networks face the vanishing gradient problem for long-term correlations [13], hence may not exploit this information.

Very large cumulative updates - on the other hand - usually occur for unbalanced data sets, i.e. for data sets with unbalanced target values, e.g. if class cardinalities are strongly different or certain output values are dominant. In this case cumulative updates introduce an undesired bias towards the dominant target values. A similar effect appears for unbalanced input data, where the input data distribution has high density regions from which many training points are chosen. For unbalanced input data the cumulative update over-weights the error in high density regions, i.e. it does not take into account that a small weight update can improved the error of many data points. Using our IW method the data is still unbalanced but the bias towards overrepresented regions is corrected. Prominent tasks, for which unbalanced data sets are common, are 3D-protein prediction [2] and text classification [31], because the number of training examples of the positive class is usually small (and costly to obtain). The lack of balance usually leads to a poor performance on either precision or recall (false positives or negatives) [30] and to a small area under the receiver operating curve. A common strategy to tackle this problem is to under-sample the larger class (cf. [2]), but how should one select the examples? Another aspect is that unbalanced data sets often slow down learning because the output is attracted to the dominant value.

In order to overcome the abovementioned problems, we propose a novel strategy for improving gradient-based learning. Each data point is weighted by an "importance value", which determines its influence on the total gradient and which can be interpreted as an individual learning step. These factors depend on the location in input space and on the interaction between different data points. They are calculated at every iteration by solving a convex optimization problem as described in the next section. These weighting factors then lead - for example - to an amplification of differences between similar gradients (cf. Fig. 1 or a selection of only a few important locations in an unbalanced situation.

II. THE IMPORTANCE WEIGHT METHOD

Consider N training examples $x^i \in \mathbb{R}^M$, $1 \leq i \leq N$ together with their corresponding target values y^i. The relationship between the x^i and the y^i should be described by a model function $f(x; w)$ with parameter vector w, for example a feedforward multilayer perceptron or a recurrent neural network. For every training data we define an individual error measure $E(x^i)$ and use it to construct the total error $E = \sum_i E(x^i)$ for the training set. Typically, $E(x^i) = E_{sqr}(x^i) = \frac{1}{2}(y^i - f(x^i))^2$ or $E(x^i) = E_{abs}(x^i) = |y^i - f(x^i)|$.

We now construct an optimal learning step for the parameter vector w in order to achieve the following two goals: (a) The learning step should be such, that the individual error for every data point decreases by at least a value of p (if possible), and (b) the associated weight change Δw should be as small as possible. Consider the Taylor expansion

$$E(x^i; w + \Delta w) = E(x^i; w) + \langle \nabla_w E(x^i; w), \Delta w \rangle + O(\|\Delta w\|^2). \quad (1)$$

up to the first order. We then obtain the optimization problem

$$\min_{\Delta w} \frac{1}{2} \|\Delta w\|^2$$
$$s.t. \quad \langle -\nabla_w E(x^i; w), \Delta w \rangle \geq p,$$

where the constraints ensure goal (a) and the minimization ensures goal (b) in order to be consistent with the linear approximation, eq. 1. p is a free parameter which corresponds to a learning rate. Note, that this optimization does not lead to $\Delta w \propto -\nabla_w E$, but the constraints ensure a positive dot product: $\langle -\nabla_w E, \Delta w \rangle \geq N p$.

In general, one cannot guarantee that the error can be improved by a value of p at every training data position x^i at every iteration. Therefore, slack variables ξ_i are introduced which allow for a violation of the constraints but where large values are penalized by regularization parameter C. We then obtain the convex optimization problem

$$\min_{\Delta w} \frac{1}{2}\|\Delta w\|^2 + C \sum_i \xi_i \quad (2)$$
$$s.t. \quad \langle -\nabla_w E(x^i), \Delta w \rangle \geq p - \xi_i, \quad 0 \leq \xi_i.$$

and its dual formulation

$$\min_\alpha \frac{1}{2} \sum_{i,j} \alpha_i \alpha_j \langle \nabla_w E(x^i), \nabla_w E(x^j) \rangle - p \sum_i \alpha_i$$
$$s.t. \quad 0 \leq \alpha_i \leq C. \quad (3)$$

for the change of the model parameters, where α_i are the Lagrange multipliers corresponding to the constraints. The dual problem can then be solved using the sequential minimal optimization (SMO) procedure [19]. A fast and efficient implementation can be obtained, if one takes into account that there are no equality constraints and if the SMO is always initialized with the values of the α_i from the previous learning step [12]. The new learning step can then be calculated using the Karush-Kuhn-Tucker conditions

$$\Delta w = -\sum_i \alpha_i \nabla_w E(x^i) \quad \text{and} \quad (4)$$
$$\|\Delta w\|^2 = p \sum_i \alpha_i + C \sum_{i: \alpha_i = C} \xi_i.$$

Given eq. (4) we can now interpret the Lagrange multipliers α_i as the importance weights for training vectors and as the individual step sizes for the standard gradient update rule. The importance weights are determined by minimizing the contributions of the coupling strengths $\langle \nabla_w E(x^i), \nabla_w E(x^j) \rangle$, eq. (3), which relate the gradients of the error function for every pair of data points. A good solution is obtained, if at least one $\alpha_i = 0$ for as many pairs of data points with similar gradient information and if the values of the α_i are large for pairs whose gradients tend to be antiparallel. The number of non-zero importance weights is controlled by the values of the hyperparameters p and C, and we will show in the next section that their number can be very small. Data points which are never used during learning allow to construct a new bound on the generalization error using leave-one-out estimators in analogy to the construction of bounds for support vector machines [26].

For perceptrons, $f(x^i; w) = \langle x^i, w \rangle$, and binary classification tasks using the classification error $E(x^i) = \max\{0, -y_i f(x^i)\}$, we obtain the error gradient is $\nabla_w E(x^i; w) = -y_i x^i$, if $y^i \langle x^i, w \rangle \leq 0$, and 0, otherwise. Since the constraints of the optimization problem (2) can be written in the form $y^i \langle x^i, \Delta w \rangle \geq p$ we obtain the standard support vector machine (SVM) learning rule [26]. In this case, gradient-based learning reduces to one iteration of the update rule eq. (4) for the initial values $w = 0$. Also nonlinear SVMs are covered by applying the kernel trick. The advantage of the IW method and of the neural networks over SVMs is that the nonlinearities are learned and must not be chosen a priori. SVMs are sensitive to the choice of the kernel, i.e. the choice of the similarity measure.

III. NUMERICAL EXPERIMENTS

A. Application to Feedforward Networks (MLP)

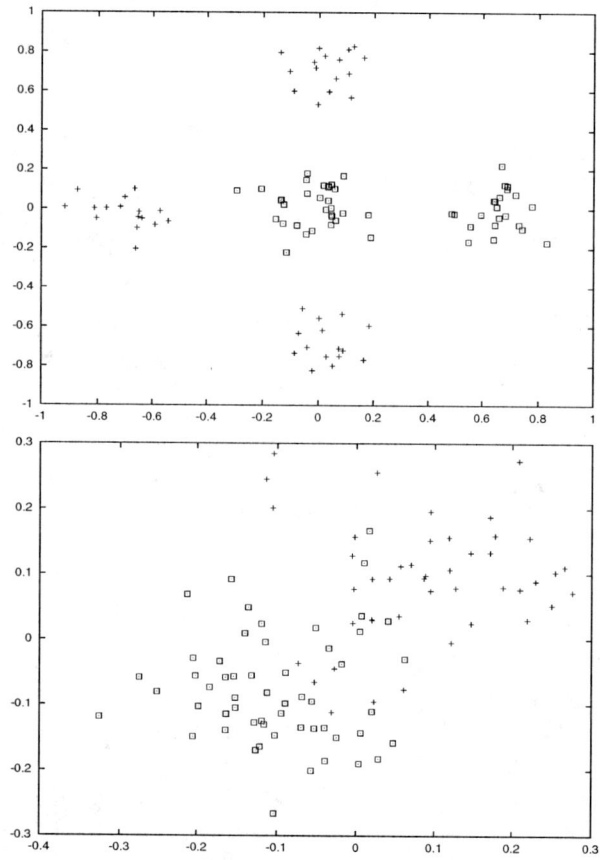

Fig. 2. Toy data sets for the binary classification task. Top: 4-Gaussian linear separable (L, data points from the central cluster are deleted and drawn again from the Gaussian which forms the right cluster) and "simple" 5-Gaussian nonlinear (NL1) dataset. Bottom: "difficult" nonlinear (NL2) dataset. Crosses (class +1) and squares (class -1) denote the location of the data points in a two-dimensional feature space.

1) Toy Data – Binary Classification Problem: We applied the new learning method to the three artificial data sets shown in Fig. 2: a linear separable data set L (Fig. 2, top, without the central cluster), a "simple" nonlinear data set NL1 (Fig. 2, top), and a "difficult" nonlinear data set NL2 (Fig. 2, bottom). A multi-layer perceptron (4 layers, 10 units per hidden layer, one output unit, sigmoid transfer functions $\frac{1}{1+\exp(-x)}$ for the hidden units and $\frac{2}{1+\exp(-x)}-1$ for the output unit) was trained to predict the binary class labels $y^i \in \{-1, +1\}$ by minimizing the standard quadratic error function E_{sqr} on the training set. The IW method was compared with the "QuickProp" [10]. We chose "QuickProp" because in [23] and [24] the authors compared

- "Backprop" [6],
- "Backprop (batch mode)" [6],
- "Backprop (batch mode) + Eaton and Oliver" [9],
- "Backprop + Darken and Moody" [8],
- "J. Schmidhuber" [25],
- "R. Salomon" [22],
- "Chan and Fallside " [7],
- "Polak-Ribiere + line search" [15],
- "Conjugate gradient + line search" [18],
- "Silva and Almeida" [28],
- "SuperSAB" [29],
- "Delta-Bar-Delta" [14],
- "QuickProp" [10],
- "RPROP" [21], and
- "Cascade correlation" [11]

and concluded in [24]:

> "In terms of learning speed RPROP and Quickprop seems to be superior to all other training algorithms using fixed topologies."

TABLE I

QUICKPROP (QP) VS. IMPORTANCE WEIGHT (IW) METHOD APPLIED TO THE TOY DATA SETS L, NL1, AND NL2 (CF. FIG. 2). THE COLUMNS SHOW (LEFT TO RIGHT): (1) LEARNING METHOD, (2) TRAINING EXAMPLES (N), (3) IW PARAMETERS, (4) TRAINING EPOCHS NEEDED FOR ZERO TRAINING ERROR – MAX. 10^6 EPOCHS ("EP."), (5) TRAINING POINTS USED (k), (6) TRAINING MISCLASSIFICATIONS ("M").

Method	N	parameters	EP.	k	M
IW (L)	100	$C = 10^{-1}, p = 10^{-2}$	4	3	0
IW (L)	100	$C = 10^{-1}, p = 10^{0}$	1	7	0
IW (NL1)	100	$C = 10^{1}, p = 10^{-1}$	5	63	0
IW (NL1)	100	$C = 10^{1}, p = 10^{-2}$	37	47	0
IW (NL1)	100	$C = 10^{2}, p = 10^{-2}$	46	29	0
IW (NL1)	100	$C = 10^{3}, p = 10^{-2}$	75	18	0
IW (NL1)	300	$C = 10^{3}, p = 10^{-2}$	86	34	0
QP (NL1)	100		95	100	0
IW (NL2)	100	$C = 10^{3}, p = 10^{-3}$	91	100	0
IW (NL2)	100	$C = 10^{4}, p = 10^{-3}$	63	100	0
QP (NL2)	100		10^6	100	11

The results are summarized in Table I. The model was a MLP (2-10-10-1) with sigmoid units. All weights were initialized with values drawn randomly and uniformly from $[-0.1, 0.1]$. A data point was correctly classified if the difference between the output value of the MLP and the target values ± 1 was less than 0.2.

The 300 training examples for NL1 are obtained by drawing additional 200 data points from the corresponding input distribution (5 Gaussians). For data set L only 3 to 7 examples were selected by IW during training, all other data points were not considered ($\alpha_i = 0$) for learning the network's weights. For data set NL1 there is a trade-off between speed of convergence and the number of selected data points, depending on the values of the hyperparameters of IW. If only few examples are considered (18 out of 100) learning is slow (75 epochs), while learning becomes faster (5 epochs) if more data points are selected (63 out of 100). QuickProp needs more epochs than IW for convergence on NL1. For data set NL2 the importance weight method converged within the first 100 epochs whereas QuickProp did not find a solution with zero misclassification error within 10^6 epochs.

2) Prediction of Protein Interactions: In this section IW is applied to unbalanced data sets and compared to standard gradient methods. We report benchmark results for five data sets describing protein-protein interactions for yeast proteins taken from the PepSPOT experiments of [16]. Each data set consists of the binding affinities between one out of five SH3 domains (Boi1, Boi2, Rvs167, Yfr024, Yhr016c). 672 peptides are selected by scanning with PatMatch the yeast proteome for the relaxed, 7 amino acids (AAs) long consensus pattern (R/K)xxPxxP (standard notation, "x" denotes "arbitrary amino acid"). The selected peptides of length 14 AAs were synthesized at high density on cellulose membranes by the SPOT technology. Then the membranes were probed by the corresponding SH3 domain fused to glutathion S-transferase (GST). Bound domains were detected by an anti-GST antibody and a secondary anti-immunoglobulin G (IgG) coupled to horseradish peroxidase (POD). Finally, spot intensity are given as real valued, positive Boehringer light units (BLU). For details of experiments and data sets see [16].

The BLU values were mapped to the interval $[-1, 1]$ by $\frac{2\,(a/a_0)^2}{1+(a/a_0)^2} - 1$ (see table II, 3rd column). However, the data sets are highly unbalanced with most of the transformed BLU values (tBLU) being close to zero and only approx. 7% being of order one (see Table II, 2nd column).

The machine learning task is to predict - for each SH3 domain - the tBLU values from the amino acid sequence of the 14 amino acid long peptides. The sequence was coded using a 1-out-of-20 binary code for every of the 11 variable amino acids of the peptide and a indicator variable for the presence of R vs. K at position 4. We used a multi-layer perceptron with 221 units in the input layer, one unit in the hidden, and one unit in the output layer - more complex networks led to inferior performance. Hidden and output units had sigmoid transfer functions as in previous experiment. The hidden unit effect is equivalent to a slope parameter of the output sigmoid in an architecture without a hidden layer. The MLP was trained with IW and with batch backpropagation (BP) using a regularized (weight decay for the input weights with Laplacian prior) squared error cost-function:

$$E_{sqr-reg}\left(x^i\right) = \frac{1}{2}\left(y^i - f\left(x^i; w\right)\right)^2 + \kappa \sum_l |w_l| \,. \quad (5)$$

Note, that IW only uses gradients, therefore it can be applied to regularized cost functions. Additionally, early stopping was used. The first 400 peptides were used for training, the following 100 peptides served as a validation set to select both the regularization parameter κ and the stopping time, and the remaining 172 peptides were used as a final test set. All weights were initialized with values drawn randomly and uniformly from $[-0.1, 0.1]$. The BP learning rate was 0.001, higher values led to instabilities. The IW parameters were $p = 0.01$ and $C = 0.1$.

The benchmark results are summarized in Table II. The IW method does not only require much less epochs for learning,

TABLE II

BENCHMARK RESULTS FOR THE FIVE PROTEIN INTERACTION DATA SETS. THE COLUMNS SHOW (LEFT TO RIGHT): SH3 DOMAIN, PEPTIDES (TARGET ≥ -0.8), a_0, USED TRAINING AND VALIDATION DATA POINTS (u), REGULARIZATION PARAMETER (κ), TRAINING MSE, TEST MSE, EPOCHS (EP.), AND CPU TIME IN MINUTES.

SH3	$\geq$	a_0 10^3	u	κ 10^{-5}	train 10^{-2}	test 10^{-2}	EP. 10^3	CPU time
batch backpropagation method							
Boi1	73	5	500	0.1	5.2	16.3	46	422
Rvs167	39	5	500	0.1	3.2	12.1	64	595
Boi2	21	1	500	0.1	2.6	5.3	67	622
Yfr024	32	20	500	0.1	2.6	6.5	100	920
Yhr016c	34	5	500	0.1	2.6	8.6	100	944
importance weight method							
Boi1	73	5	363	50	4.2	14.3	0.14	56
Rvs167	39	5	394	50	2.2	11.6	0.15	62
Boi2	21	1	401	100	1.4	5.1	0.14	57
Yfr024	32	20	500	1	0.8	5.7	0.28	128
Yhr016c	34	5	500	1	1.1	7.9	0.43	202

but it is also faster in terms of CPU time. The increased computational costs for every learning step due to the solution of the optimization problem eq. (3) is over compensated by the much lower number of epochs. The error on the test set achieved by the IW method is always less than the error achieved by the BP procedure.

TABLE III

BINDING AFFINITIES PREDICTED BY THE IW METHOD FOR THE FIVE PROTEIN-PROTEIN INTERACTION DATA SETS. THE COLUMNS SHOW (LEFT TO RIGHT): SH3 DOMAIN, THRESHOLD "BINDING" VS. "NON-BINDING", POSITIVES: PREDICTED BINDING PEPTIDES (P), TRUE POSITIVES (TP), FALSE NEGATIVES (FN), FALSE POSITIVES (FP).

SH3	threshold	P	TP	FN	FP
Boi1	-0.96	4	4	0	43
	-0.85	4	3	1	18
Rvs167	-0.97	7	7	0	36
	-0.85	7	4	3	5
Boi2	-0.98	2	2	0	16
	-0.85	2	1	1	3
Yfr024	-0.995	8	8	0	125
	-0.99	8	7	1	34
	-0.98	8	6	2	11
	-0.96	8	5	3	6
Yhr016c	-0.99	4	4	0	16
	-0.85	4	2	2	1

Table III shows an analysis of the binding affinities predicted by the multilayer perceptron which was trained using the IW method. Peptides with a high predicted binding affinity (higher than a given threshold) were selected from the test set, and their total number, the number of true and false positives, and the number of true negatives are given for different threshold values and for the five different data sets.

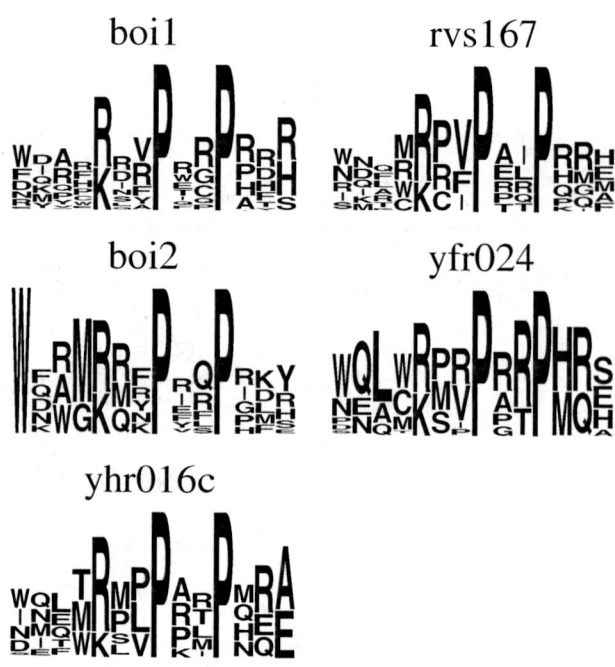

Fig. 3. Sequence logos of 14 amino acid peptide binding pattern for the five experiments.

Fig. 3 shows the sequence logos for the five different data sets. Every column corresponds to one position within the peptide of 14 amino acid length. The size of each letter (the abbreviation for the amino acid) corresponds to the strength of positive input weights of the trained MLP to the corresponding component of the 20 dimensional input vector at every location (except for positions 8 and 11, which were not part of the input, see description of MLP architecture). These results are in agreement with the findings in [16], e.g. with the strict consensus binding motif RxFPxPP of the Rvs167 SH3 domain and with the class 2 binding motif PxxPxR for Yfr024c and Ysc84 SH3 domains.

B. Application to Recurrent Networks (LSTM)

1) Sequence Analysis – The Latching Benchmark: The latching experiment [5] is one of the best known benchmark for the ability of a new method to recognize long-term dependencies in sequences. The data set consists of sequences of real numbers which are drawn randomly and uniformly from the interval $[-0.1, 0.1]$, except for the first and the last element, which are either both 1 or -1. The task is to learn a predictor for the last element of the sequence, based on the other elements.

In [13] it was shown, that a "Long Short-Term Memory" (LSTM) recurrent network was able to successfully solve this problem for sequences up to a length of 1000. Here we generated 200 sequences – 100 for training and 100 for test – of length 1,000,002, i.e. the first element of the sequence must be stored over one million (!) steps in order to predict the value of the last element. We used an LSTM network with two memory cells of size 1, no hidden units, one input unit and one output unit (activation function $\frac{2}{1+\exp(-x)} - 1$). The LSTM network has standard memory cells as described in [13] and all non-input units have a bias weight which leads to 51 weights. The network was trained by the IW methods ($p = 0.01$, $C = 10000$) using the squared error cost function (E_{sqr}), where the first and second input gate had an initial bias of -10 and -15. We stopped learning if the all training sequences were processed correctly, i.e. the absolute prediction error of the final element was below 0.2. In 10 trials IW stopped on average after 83 epochs whereafter all test examples were processed correctly. This is a new record for recurrent neural networks in the detection of long term dependencies.

2) Sequence Analysis – Protein Classification: In this section we report benchmark results for three data sets of labeled sequences of proteins. Protein sequences from the three classes IG_MHC (360 sequences), UPF (25 sequences), and MYELIN (18) were chosen from the Prosite database and complemented by a large number of randomly selected "negative" examples from unrelated families (IG_MHC-dataset: 1959 "negative" sequences, UPF-dataset: 1836 "negative" sequences, MYELIN-dataset: 1930 "negative" sequences). For each of the three data sets, the machine learning task was to correctly predict class membership based on the sequence of amino acids. By construction, the data sets were highly unbalanced and had an average sequence length of about 200. Long-term dependencies result from the fact that class relevant information may be located at the beginning of a sequence but prediction must be performed at sequence end. Further, long-term dependencies between groups of amino acids at distant location may be important features for a given class.

The classification task was solved using a recurrent LSTM network. The idea is to learn pattern recognizers for amino acid patterns indicative for a given class and use those at the input of a memory cell in order to store the occurrence of a pattern until the end of the sequence. The LSTM input gates, which serve as the pattern recognizers, receive their (only) input from a window of 20 adjacent amino acids (1-out-of-20 binary coding for every amino acid). The window is shifted over the sequence, and the network's prediction is evaluated after one full sweep. The initial bias of the input gates is set to -8.0. The LSTM architecture consisted of only one memory cell and no hidden units. The LSTM network was trained using gradient descent method (LSTM learning) from [13] as well as with the new IW method ($p = 0.01$). The size of the training and validation sets were ("positives/all"): 338/2072 and 43/268 for IG_MHC, 22/1638 and 3/223 for UPF, and 15/1625 and 3/323 for MYELIN.

Table IV summarizes the results. The IW method was always faster than gradient descent learning, in terms of epochs as well as in terms of CPU time. The test mean squared error was comparable for both methods. However, the average balanced classification error (mean of false positive and false negative rates) of the IW method was always better or equal to error achieved by standard BP.

TABLE IV
BENCHMARK RESULTS FOR THE PROTEIN CLASSIFICATION WITH LSTM USING GRADIENT DESCENT (CF. [13]) AND IW. COLUMNS SHOW (LEFT TO RIGHT): DATA SET, LEARNING RATE OR C, TRAINING MSE, TRAINING BALANCED ERROR, TEST MSE, TEST BALANCED ERROR, EPOCHS, CPU-TIME.

Prot. class	par.	train MSE	train BE	test MSE	test BE	ep.	CPU min
gradient descent							
IG_MHC	0.1	0.050	33.8	0.047	4.3	3177	150
IG_MHC	0.2	0.050	33.8	0.048	4.3	3188	150
IG_MHC	0.5	0.051	33.8	0.048	4.3	3183	150
UPF	0.2	10e-6	0	10e-6	0	1360	32
MYELIN	0.2	10e-6	0	10e-6	0	440	10.1
importance weight method							
IG_MHC	10	0.001	6.9	0.006	2.6	64	74
UPF	1	6x10e-4	0	2x10e-4	0	61	3.4
MYELIN	10	10e-6	0	10e-6	0	100	7.5

IV. CONCLUSION

We have introduced a new learning technique, the IW method, which assigns importance weights to training data points for learning. IW is suited to speed up learning for highly non-linear data and long-term dependencies in sequences. IW reduces to standard support vector machine (SVM) with a linear model and with the kernel trick also to nonlinear SVMs. Advantage of IW over SVMs is that the kernel is learned and must not be chosen a priori and – more important – that sequences can be processed. In experiments we have shown that IW is faster than QuickProp for MLPs and that IW applied to sequence data allowed to speed up learning and to obtain a new latching record.

ACKNOWLEDGMENTS

We thank Martin Heusel and Rene Pfeifer for their help with the experiments. This work was funded in part by BMBF project no. 10025304. and by the DFG (SFB 618).

REFERENCES

[1] S.-I. Amari. Natural gradient works efficiently in learning. *Neural Computation*, 10(2):251–276, 1998.
[2] P. Baldi, G. Pollastri, C. A. Andersen, and S. Brunak. Matching protein beta-sheet partners by feedforward and recurrent neural networks. In *Proc. Int. Conf. Int. Systems for Molecular Biology 8*, pages 25–36, 2000.
[3] R. Battiti. First- and second-order methods for learning: between steepest descent and Newton's method. *Neural Computation*, 4:141–166, 1992.
[4] H. S. M. Beigi and C. J. Li. Learning algorithms for neural networks based on quasi-Newton with self-scaling. *Intelligent Control Systems*, 23:23–28, 1990.
[5] Y. Bengio, P. Simard, and P. Frasconi. Learning long-term dependencies with gradient descent is difficult. *IEEE Trans. on Neur. Net.*, 5(2):157–166, 1994.
[6] C. M. Bishop. *Neural Networks for Pattern Recognition*. Clarendon Press, Oxford, 1995.
[7] L. W. Chan and F. Fallside. An adaptive training algorithm for backpropagation networks. *Computer Speech and Language*, 2:205–218, 1987.
[8] C. Darken and J. Moody. Note on learning rate schedules for stochastic optimization. In J. E. Moody, S. J. Hanson, and R. P. Lippmann, editors, *Advances in Neural Information Processing Systems 4*, pages 832–838. Morgan Kauffmann, 1992.
[9] H. A. C. Eaton and T. L. Oliver. Learning coefficient dependence on training set size. *Neural Networks*, 5:283–288, 1992.
[10] S. E. Fahlman. Faster-learning variations on back-propagation: an empirical study. In *Proc. of the 1988 Conn. Models Summer School*, pages 38–51, 1989.
[11] S. E. Fahlman and C. Lebiere. The cascade-correlation learning algorithm. In D. S. Touretzky, editor, *Advances in Neural Information Processing Systems 2*, pages 525–532. San Mateo, CA: Morgan Kaufmann, 1990.
[12] S. Hochreiter and K. Obermayer. Classification, regression, and feature selection on matrix data. Technical Report 2004/2, Technische Universität Berlin, Fakultät für Elektrotechnik und Informatik, 2004.
[13] S. Hochreiter and J. Schmidhuber. Long short-term memory. *Neural Computation*, 9(8):1735–1780, 1997.
[14] R. A. Jacobs. Increased rates of convergence through learning rate adaptation. *Neural Networks*, 1:295–307, 1988.
[15] A. H. Kramer and A. Sangiovanni-Vincentelli. Efficient parallel learning algorithms for neural networks. In D. S. Touretzky, editor, *Advances in Neural Information Processing Systems 1*, pages 40–48. San Mateo, CA: Morgan Kaufmann, 1989.
[16] C. Landgraf, S. Panni, L. Montecchi-Palazzi, L. Castagnoli, J. Schneider-Mergener, R. Volkmer-Engert, and G. Cesareni. Protein interaction networks by proteome peptide scanning. *PLoS Biol.*, 2(1):94–103, 2004.
[17] Y. LeCun, P. Simard, and B. Pearlmutter. Automatic learning rate maximization by on-line estimation of the Hessian's eigenvectors". In *Advances in Neural Information Processing Systems 5*, pages 156–163, 1993.
[18] J. Leonard and M. A. Kramer. Improvement of the backpropagation algorithm for training neural networks. *Computers Chemical Engineering*, 14(3):337–341, 1990.
[19] J. Platt. Fast training of support vector machines using sequential minimal optimization. In B. Schölkopf, C. J. C. Burges, and A. J. Smola, editors, *Advances in Kernel Methods — Support Vector Learning*, pages 185–208, 1999.
[20] N. Qian. On the momentum term in gradient descent learning algorithms. *Neural Networks*, 12(1):145–151, 1999.
[21] M. Riedmiller and H. Braun. A direct adaptive method for faster backpropagation learning: The RPROP algorithm. In *Proc. of the IEEE International Conference on Neural Networks*, pages 586–591, San Francisco, CA, 1993.
[22] R. Salomon. Improved convergence rate of back-propagation with dynamic adaption of the learning rate. In *Parallel Problem Solving From Nature (Dortmund, 1990)*, volume 496 of *Lecture Notes in Computer Science*, pages 269–273, 1991.
[23] W. Schiffmann, M. Joost, and R. Werner. Comparison of optimized backpropagation algorithms. In *Proc. of the European Symposium on Artificial Neural Networks, ESANN 93*, pages 97–104, 1993.
[24] W. Schiffmann, M. Joost, and R. Werner. Optimization of the backpropagation algorithm for training multilayer perceptrons. Technical report, Institute of Physics, University of Koblenz, Koblenz, Germany, 1994.
[25] J. Schmidhuber. Accelerated learning in back-propagation nets. In R. Pfeifer, Z. Schreter, Z. Fogelman, and L. Steels, editors, *Connectionism in Perspective*, pages 429–438. Amsterdam: Elsevier, North-Holland, 1989.
[26] B. Schölkopf and A. J. Smola. *Learning with Kernels — Support Vector Machines, Regularization, Optimization, and Beyond*. MIT Press, 2002.
[27] R. Setiono and L. Hui. Use of a quasi-Newton method in a feedforward neural network construction algorithm. *IEEE Trans. Neural Net.*, 6(1):273–277, 1995.
[28] F. M. Silva and L. B. Almeida. Speeding up back-propagation. In R. Eckmiller, editor, *Advanced Neural Computers*, pages 151–158, Amsterdam, 1990. Elsevier.
[29] T. Tollenaere. SuperSAB: fast adaptive back propagation with good scaling properties. *Neural Networks*, 3:561–573, 1990.
[30] G. M. Weiss and F. Provost. Learning when training data are costly: The effect of class distribution on tree induction. *J. Artifi. Int. Res.*, 19:315–354, 2003.
[31] T. Zhang and V. S. Iyengar. Recommender systems using linear classifiers. *Journal of Machine Learning Research*, 2:313–334, 2002.

Cinematographic Construction by Brains of Knowledge from Information

Walter J Freeman

Department of Molecular and Cell Biology
University of California
Berkeley CA 94720-3206 USA
http://sulcus.berkeley.edu

Abstract - **Brains create knowledge and express it in information that they post-process into an organized database for exploration by commands that control goal-directed actions. Perception is explained by analyzing the neural activity in human and animal brains as they engage in exploratory behaviors. Measurement is by decomposition and modeling of the neural activity in order to deduce brain operations within and between three levels: microscopic of single neurons, mesoscopic of local networks forming modules, and macroscopic of the global self-organization of the cerebral hemispheres by the organic unity of neocortex. Knowledge is conveyed in fields of dendritic currents in sequences of 'cinematographic' frames.**

1. Introduction

Brains create knowledge and express it in information. They select and pre-process the information carried by sensory stimuli as sense data, from which they construct patterns that constitute hypotheses about the sense data. They post-process the patterns into an organized database that serves to support exploration of the environment through informative commands that control goal-directed actions. The process of perception by which brains construct knowledge from information can be explained by analyzing the neural activity in human and animal brains as subjects engage in exploratory behaviors.

Measurement is followed by decomposition and modeling of the neural activity in order to deduce brain operations. Brains function hierarchically with neuronal interactions within and between three levels: microscopic of single neurons, mesoscopic of local networks forming modules, and macroscopic of the global self-organization of the cerebral hemispheres by the organic unity of neocortex. Information is carried in continuous streams of microscopic axonal pulses. Knowledge is conveyed in mesoscopic local mean fields of dendritic currents in discontinuous frames resembling cinemas, each frame having spatial patterns of amplitude (AM) and phase (PM) modulation of an aperiodic carrier wave.

James Barham [1] laid a foundation in physics for a theory of meaning in terms of nonequilibrium thermodynamics and the nonlinear dynamics of coupled oscillators. He described these oscillators as self-governed by attractors in phase space. He proposed that a biological system should be characterized as a generalized nonlinear oscillator that is stabilized far from thermodynamic equilibrium by means of successive phase transitions. The stability is achieved by effective interaction of the high-energy system with other high-energy oscillators sharing the environment that serve as constraints. Effective interactions are by thermodynamic engagement of the inner and outer high-energy oscillators (for example, attack and consumption by a predator or evasion and escape by its prey). Both predator in search of food and its prey in search of shelter are high-energy oscillators. The predator is stabilized when it captures and consumes its prey. The prey is stabilized when it escapes and finds shelter (Fig. 1).

Information exists in low-energy environmental energy fluxes that are correlated with the high-energy fluxes so as to serve as signals of distant events. Examples are the sights, sounds and odors of both predator and prey. He called the brain counterpart of an environmental low-energy flux an "epistemon" and identified it with a chaotic attractor in the attractor landscape of a sensory system.

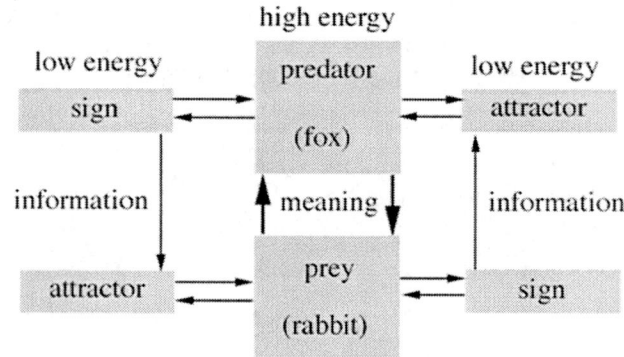

Fig. 1. The dynamic relation between meaning and information is sketched. Knowledge exists within each brain; meaning exists in relationships.

Barham interpreted the meaning of the information in the low-energy flux as the "prediction of successful functional action" [1, p. 235], so that information could be either correct or wrong. In biological terms, the meaning of a stimulus for an organism is demonstrated by the use to which it is put, which was described by J. J. Gibson [2] as its 'affordance'; that is, he defined objects in terms of their utilities for the observers, what could be done with them.

The meaning is valid when it leads to successful adaptation to environmental constraints through the action-perception cycle [3-4]. The problem to be solved in order to apply this theory is to translate Barham's "epistemon" (sign) and the attractor and its basin of attraction into terms of neurodynamics. In order to test and validate the theory, it must also be recast in engineering terms. For example, the meaning for robots of low-energy environmental constraints would be observed in the successful adaptation of autonomous intentional robots to cope successfully with environmental challenges without the intervention of observers or controllers [5]. However, the meaning exists in the relationship of the device or animal to its environment, not in the brain. The object of exploration in the brain is the knowledge about the world from the information provided by the senses, which predicts and guides actions that are taken in search of meaning. Hence the question: What are the characteristics of the neural activity patterns that might reasonably be construed as constituting the active knowledge of an animal subject, so that these patterns might be simulated in the brains of robots engaged in intentional behaviors?

2. EXPERIMENTAL FOUNDATION

A major constraint in devising a neurobiological theory of knowledge is that no physical or chemical measurement of brain activity is a direct measure. Knowledge can be experienced subjectively in oneself, and one can infer it in other subjects from the behavioral context in which measurements are made, but one cannot measure it to express it in numbers. An equally important constraint is that no measurement of brain activity makes sense unless the investigator has sufficient control over the behavior of a subject to be able to infer the teleology of the subject, whether animal or human, at the time of measurement. The teleology includes the history, intention, expectation, motivation, and attentiveness of the subject. For this reason, all of the data on brain function must be accumulated from studies in which the subjects are carefully trained or coached to enter and maintain overt states of normal behavior that can be reproduced and measured along with the measurements of brain activity.

Yet another requirement is stability. Bak, Tang and Wiesenfeld [6] proposed that a complex system such as a brain evolves by self-organization to a critical state at the edge of chaos, by which it maintains a readiness to adapt rapidly to unpredictable changes in its environment and thereby maintain its integrity. Adaptation is by repetitive phase transitions; the space-time patterns of its state variables re-organize themselves abruptly and repeatedly. Their prime example was the performance of a sand pile, in which a steady drip of grains of sand onto the central peak gave the pile the shape of a cone. The slope of the cone increased to a maximal critical angle that was maintained by repeated avalanches as sand continued to pour onto the apex. The avalanches had fractal distributions in size and time intervals. Bak [7] called this a state of "self-organized criticality" (SOC), and he characterized it by the fractal distributions and the $1/f^\alpha$ form of the temporal spectra of the avalanches with α as the critical exponent. He concluded that the $1/f^\alpha$ spectra were explained by the self-similarity of the recurrent events over broad scales of time and space. The $1/f^\alpha$ form of the EEG PSD has been repeatedly demonstrated in both temporal [8-10] and spatial spectra of EEG recorded intracranially in animals [8,11] and surgical patients [12].

Recent advances in technology have made it possible to for neurobiologists to observe the electrochemical oscillations of energy that enable brains to maintain their states far from equilibrium at the edge of stability [13]. Interactive populations of neurons are nonlinear oscillators that create and maintain landscapes of chaotic attractors. Their oscillatory activity in primary sensory cortices can be observed, measured and analyzed by simultaneously recording the EEG [14] of multiple populations with high-density arrays of electrodes placed epidurally over the cortex. This technique is feasible, because the main source of EEG potentials is the sum of the dendritic currents of the neurons in local neighborhoods that control the firing rates of the action potentials. That sum is accompanied by extracellular potential differences giving access to spatiotemporal patterns of the local mean fields [15, 16].

These spatial patterns reveal "itinerant trajectories" through successions of chaotic attractors, which begin to dissolve into "attractor ruins" as soon as they are accessed [17]. The patterns are recorded with high-density electrode arrays, intracranially on or in the brains of cats, rabbits, and neurosurgical patients, and from the scalps of normal volunteers. Each attractor forms during training of the subjects by reinforcement to discriminate sensory stimuli. An attractor that is selected by the information in sensory input is realized in the spatial pattern of amplitude modulation (AM) of a chaotic carrier wave. Spatial AM patterns form repeatedly with exposure to the conditioned stimulus that is paired with an unconditional stimulus (Fig. 2). Each pattern is measured with an array of 64 electrodes on the cortical surface. Signal identification and pattern classification have been done with high temporal resolution using Fourier decomposition [8, 18], wavelets [19] and the Hilbert transform [14, 20]. The differences among the 64 EEGs across the array for each AM pattern are expressed by the 64 amplitudes that specify a 64x1 column vector and a point in 64-space [8, 21].

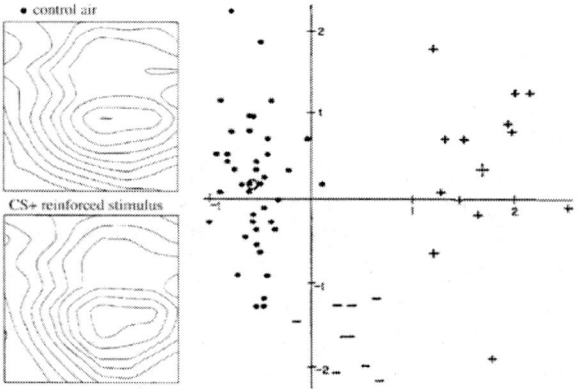

Fig. 2. Left frames: Examples of RMS patterns of amplitude modulation of gamma bursts. Right frame: Classification by stepwise discriminant analysis of bursts from trials with CS+ or CS- or control air.

The AM patterns are never twice identical; however, because of their similarity within the class, they form a cluster in 64-space, in which the center of gravity specifies an average AM pattern. A cluster forms for each stimulus that a subject learns to discriminate. Statistical classification of EEG patterns is done by assigning membership to clusters on the basis of minimizing Euclidian distances in 64-space. The basin of attraction provides for abstraction and generalization that is needed to define the class of each stimulus. The site of the cluster in 64-space changes whenever the meaning of the stimulus changes, revealing the adaptability of the mechanism for classification, and the unique dependence on the cumulative experience of each subject.

3. PHASE TRANSITIONS CONSTITUTING 'CINEMATOGRAPHIC' CORTICAL DYNAMICS

A unique 2-D phase gradient in the form of a cone has been found to accompany each AM pattern in the olfactory bulb and also in the visual, auditory and somatic primary sensory cortices. The phase velocities were commensurate with the distribution of conduction velocities of intrabulbar and intracortical axons running parallel to the surfaces [8, 11]. As a result, the modal half-power diameter (15 mm) and the 95% upper inclusion range (28 mm) of neocortical AM patterns were substantially larger than the bulbar surface (10 mm). Unlike the bulbar EEG in which the phase velocity was invariant with gamma frequency [11], in the neocortical EEG the phase velocity co-varied with gamma frequency, but the half-power diameter did not vary with carrier frequency [18}.

The conclusion was drawn that visual, auditory, somatosensory, and olfactory receiving areas had the capacity for input-dependent gain increase [22] leading to destabilization. Emergence of self-organized mesoscopic patterns was by a 1st order phase transition that was completed within 3-7 ms depending on the center carrier frequency, independently of the radius of the conic section

that accompanied the AM pattern. The location, time of onset, size and duration of each wave packet were demarcated by the phase, whereas its perceptual content was expressed in an AM pattern, which appeared within 25-35 ms of the wave packet onset [23, 24]. The content, as defined by classification with respect to CSs, was context-dependent, unique to each subject, and it was distributed with long-range correlations over delimited domains of both the cortical surface and the gamma spectrum. Clearly the content did not come directly from the stimulus, nor was it imported from other parts of the brain. It was realized in the landscape by the selection of an appropriate attractor by the stimulus. It was the phase transition that released the cortex from its existing state, giving it the degree of freedom necessary to advance to a new state along the chaotic itinerant trajectory.

Evidence for global phase transitions has now been accrued from scalp EEG recording in normal human volunteers at recurrence rates in the alpha range. They were clearly seen in the time derivative of the instantaneous phase of the EEG calculated from the Hilbert transform [14, 13, 25] (Fig. 3). The scalp EEG was recorded with a 1x64 electrode array spaced 3 mm from the forehead to the occiput. The derivative of the analytic phase from Hilbert transform of the beta EEG was approximated by time differences [25]. This function revealed an abrupt change in phase that took place over the frontal lobe and the parietal lobe but not at the same times. The time differences of the jump were under the 5 ms resolution of the digitizing. At other times in other subjects the phase locking was over the parietal or occipital area, or over all areas.

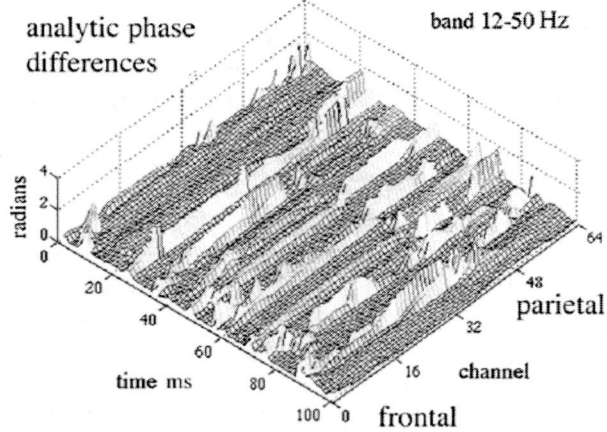

Fig. 3. Coordinated analytic phase differences (CAPD) were calculated for the beta pass band of the scalp EEG.

The statistical relations between the unfiltered EEG averaged across the 64 channels and the standard deviation (SD) of the coordinated analytic phase differences were investigated by cross-correlating the two time series from the array over a time period of 5 sec (1000 time points at 5 ms sample interval) and calculating its power spectral density using the

FFT. In subjects with eyes closed and at rest a prominent peak appeared in the autospectrum of the EEG and also in the cospectrum of the EEG and the CAPD cross-correlation (Fig. 4). When the subjects opened their eyes or engaged in the intentional action of tensing their scalp muscles to produce controlled amounts of muscle noise (EMG), the alpha peak (8-12 Hz) disappeared from the autospectrum and cospectrum, and a theta peak (3-7 Hz) often appeared. The results indicate that the CAPD are manifestations of the cinematographic dynamics of neocortex, which is constituted by successive frames formed by phase transitions, and that the theta and alpha rhythms are the macroscopic manifestations of this on-going process. The disappearance of alpha waves ('alpha blocking') appears not to be 'desynchronization' but 'deperiodicization' owing to an increase in the mean wave length of the oscillation and an increase in its variance; hence the appearance of alpha blocking is the result of applying linear analysis to the output of a nonlinear system.

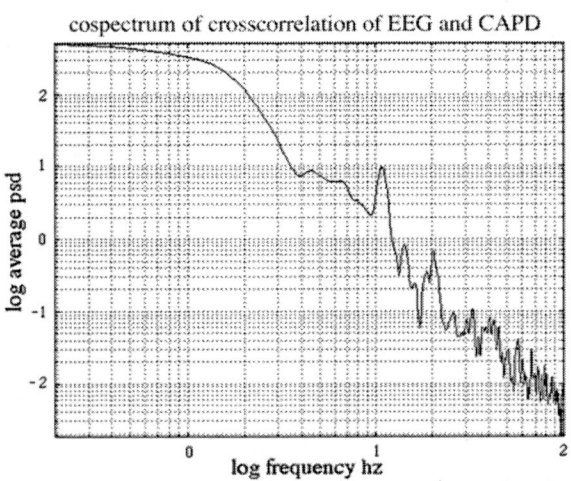

Fig. 4. The cospectrum of the crosscorrelation between the EEG and the coordinated analytic phase differences revealed a peak in the alpha range (8-12 Hz) or in the theta range (3-7 Hz).

This finding indicated that the recurrence rate of the global state transitions was most prominent in the alpha band (as shown in Fig. 5 in a subject with eyes closed), and in the theta band in a subject with eyes open (Fig. 2). The close relationship documented in [26] implies that the theta and alpha rhythms may manifest the frame rates at which AM patterns succeed one another at rest and during the course of thought.

A starting point is to visualize the receptor input from the retinas that enables a person to recognize a familiar face breaking into a smile [16, 24]. Sensory receptors are selective for types of environmental energy, not for information. The cortex must constantly receive an enormous barrage of action potentials that induces in the visual cortex explosions of action potentials from all of the motion, edge, and color detectors in the visual field. Experimental evidence summarized here indicates that any heightening of activity as during saccades can destabilize the cortex and induce the formation of sequences of brief spatial patterns of neural activity. The phenomenon of coalescence or condensation may resemble the formation by fish, birds and insects of schools, flocks and swarms [27] or by water molecules into raindrops and snowflakes. Individuals synchronize their activities to conform to the whole, yet they retain their autonomy. In the sensory cortices the patterns bind only a small fraction of the total variance of "neural swarms", so the patterns may not be observable in recording from one or a few neurons. They can be observed by multichannel EEG recording with high-density arrays of electrodes placed epidurally over the cortex. This is because the main source of EEG potentials is the sum of the dendritic currents of the neurons in local neighborhoods that control the firing rates of the action potentials. That sum is accompanied by extracellular potential differences that give access to the local mean fields of activity governing the collective behavior [15, 28].

By these techniques meaning is seen to exist in the relations between each animal and human individual and its environment that is shared with others. Thus meaning is ontological; it is understood epistemologically in three ways: by introspection and phenomenological experience, by observing others' goal-directed actions, and now for the first time by measuring the patterns of neural activity that form within brains in the normal course of the creation and exercise of the knowledge base, by which the search for meaning is directed.

ACKNOWLEDGEMENTS

This work was funded in part by research grants from NIMH (MH06686), ONR (N63373 N00014-93-1-0938), NASA (NCC 2-1244), and NSF (EIA-0130352).

REFERENCES

[1] Barham, J. (1996) A dynamical model of the meaning of information. *Biosystems* **38**: 235-241.
[2] Gibson, J.J. (1979) The Ecological Approach to Visual Perception. Boston: Haughton Mifflin.
[3] Piaget, J. (1930) *The Child's Conception of Physical Causality.* (Harcourt, Brace, New York).
[4] Merleau-Ponty M. (1945/1962) *Phenomenology of Perception.* (C Smith, Trans.). (Humanities Press, New York).
[5] Kozma, R., Freeman, W.J. and Erdí, P. (2003) The KIV model - Nonlinear spatiotemporal dynamics of the primordial vertebrate forebrain. Neurocomputing **52**: 819-826.

[6] Bak, P., Tang, C. and Wiesenfeld, K. (1987) Self-organized criticality: an explanation of 1/f noise. *Phys. Rev. Lett.* **59**: 364-374.

[7] Bak, P. (1996) How Nature Works: The Science of Self-organized Criticality. New York: Copernicus.

[8] Barrie, J.M., Freeman, W.J. and Lenhart, M.D. (1996) Spatiotemporal analysis of prepyriform, visual, auditory and somesthetic surface EEG in trained rabbits. *J. Neurophysiol.* **76**: 520 539.

[9] Hwa, R.C. and Ferree, T. (2002) Scaling properties of fluctuations in the human electroencephalogram. *Physical Rev. E* **66**: 021901.

[10] Srinivasan, R., Nunez, P. L. and Silberstein, R. B. (1998) Spatial filtering and neocortical dynamics: estimates of EEG coherence. *IEEE Trans. Biomed Engin.* **45**: 814-826.

[11] Freeman, W.J. and Baird, B. (1987) Relation of olfactory EEG to behavior: Spatial analysis. *Behav. Neurosci.* **101**: 393-408.

[12] Freeman, W.J., Rogers, L.J., Holmes, M.D. and Silbergeld, D.L. (2000) Spatial spectral analysis of human electrocorticograms including the alpha and gamma bands. *J. Neurosci. Meth.* **95**: 111-121.

[13] Freeman W.J. [2004] Origin, structure, and role of background EEG activity. Part 2. Amplitude. Clin. Neurophysiol. 115: 2089-2107.

[14] Barlow, J.S. (1993) The Electroencephalogram: Its Patterns and Origins. (MIT Press, Cambridge MA).

[15] Freeman, WJ (1992) Tutorial in Neurobiology: From Single Neurons to Brain Chaos. *Int. J. Bifurc. Chaos* **2:** 451-482.

[16] Freeman, WJ. (2003a) A neurobiological theory of meaning in perception. Part 1. Information and meaning in nonconvergent and nonlocal brain dynamics. Int. J. Bifurc. Chaos**13**: 2493-2511.

[17] Tsuda, I. (2001) Toward an interpretation of dynamics neural activity in terms of chaotic dynamical systems. Behav. Brain Sci. 24: 793-847.

[18] Freeman, W.J. and Barrie, J.M. (2000) Analysis of spatial patterns of phase in neocortical gamma EEG in rabbit. *J. Neurophysiol.* **84**: 1266-1278.

[19] Freeman, W.J. and Grajski, K.A. (1987) Relation of olfactory EEG to behavior: Factor analysis. *Behav. Neurosci.* **101**: 766-777.

[20] Freeman, W.J. and Rogers, L.J. (2002) Fine temporal resolution of analytic phase reveals episodic synchronization by state transitions in gamma EEG. *J. Neurophysiol.* **87**, 937-945.

[21] Freeman, W.J. (2004b) Origin, structure and role of background EEG activity. Part 2. Analytic phase. Clin. Neurophysiol. 115: 2089-2107.

[22] Freeman, W.J. (1975) *Mass Action in the Nervous System.* (Academic Press, New York).

[23] Freeman, W.J. (2003b) A neurobiological theory of meaning in perception. Part 2. Spatial patterns of phase in gamma EEG from primary sensory cortices measured by nonlinear wavelets. Intern J Bifurc. Chaos**13**: 2513-2535.

[24] Freeman WJ. (2004a) Origin, structure and role of background EEG activity. Part 1. Analytic amplitude. Clin. Neurophysiol. 115: 2077-2088.

[25] Freeman, W.J., Burke, BC and Holmes, M.D. (2003) Application of Hilbert transform to scalp EEG. Human Brain Mapping **19**(4):248-272.

[26] Freeman, W.J., Burke, B.C., Holmes, M.D. and Vanhatalo, S. (2003) Spatial spectra of scalp EEG and EMG from awake humans. Clin. Neurophysiol. **114**: 1055-1060.

[27] Edelstein-Keshet, L., Watmough, J. and Grunbaum, D. (1998) Do traveling band solutions describe cohesive swarms? An investigation for migratory locusts. *J. Math. Biol.* **171**: 515-549.

[28] Freeman, W.J. (1975/2004) Mass Action in the Nervous System. New York: Academic Press. Now available in electronic version: http://sulcus.berkeley.edu/MANSWWW/MANSWWW

Analysis of Phase Transitions in KIV with Amygdala During Simulated Navigation Control

Robert Kozma
Division of Computer Science, 373 Dunn Hall
University of Memphis, Memphis, TN 38152
rkozma@memphis.edu

Mark Myers
Division of Computer Science, 373 Dunn Hall
University of Memphis, Memphis, TN 38152
http://cnd.memphis.edu

Abstract-- **A biologically inspired dynamical neural network model called KIV is used in this work to design autonomous agents. The KIV set models the vertebrate limbic system. Previous studies indicated that KIV is able to provide a control algorithm for navigation and decision-making for autonomous mobile agents. In this work we use Hilbert transform to capture global synchronized spatio-temporal patterns of amplitude modulation in KIV. We identify phase transition in the simulated amygdala and show that it shares several important features of EEG signals.**

I. INTRODUCTION

Large-scale organization of dynamical neural activity has been studied intensively in the past years (Arnhem et al., 2000; Bressler & Kelso, 2001, Bressler, 2002; Liang et al, 2002). Synchronization of neural electical activity while completing cognitive tasks is studied in various animals, e.g., in cats, rabbits, gerbils, and macaque monkeys (Barrie et al, 1996; Ohl, et al, 2002, 2003; Freeman et al, 2003a; Bressler, 2003). These studies have demonstrated that using an animal model of category learning, the sorting of stimuli into categories emerges as a sudden change in the animal's learning strategy.

EEG and ECG recordings show that the transition is accompanied by a change in the dynamics of cortical stimulus representation. Synchrony of firing of widely distributed neurons in large numbers is necessary for emergence of spatial structure in cortical activity by reorganization of unpatterned background activity. Characteristic oscillations in the beta and gamma ranges, i.e., 12-30 Hz and 20-80Hz, respectively, arise due to the negative feedback among excitatory and inhibitory neurons (Traub et al., 1996; Whittington et al., 2000; Kopell et al., 2000). The synchrony between pairs of EEG records can be measured by any of a variety of methods (Lachaux et al., 1999; Le Van Quyen et al., 2001; Quiroga et al., 2002), including the phase difference of oscillations in which they share the same frequency.

An increasing volume of research work aims at the interpretation of dynamic brain activity in terms of aperiodic, chaotic processes (Skarda & Freeman, 1987; Schiff et al, 1994; Steyn-Ross et al, 1999; Arhem et al., 2000; Dafilis et al., 2001; Korn & Faure, 2003; Kozma et al., 2003). A chaotic system has the capacity to create novel and unexpected patterns of activity. It can jump instantly from one mode of behavior to another.

Phase transitions between chaotic states constitute the dynamics that explains how brains perform such remarkable feats as abstraction of the essentials of figures from complex, unknown and unpredictable backgrounds, generalization over examples of recurring objects, reliable assignment to classes that lead to appropriate actions, and constant updating by way of the learning process (Freeman, 1999).

The present work aims at benefiting from recent progress on detecting and characterizing phase transitions in brains using advanced, high-resolution spatio-temporal EEG measurements (Freeman, 2003, 2004). We study a special class of dynamical neural network models, called the K sets, and its most advanced form the KIV set. Simulated EEG signals generated by the KIV model are analyzed and show striking similarity to animal EEG signals, in particular concerning sudden transitions in spatio-temporal oscillation patterns. This result indicates that KIV may provide a tool for the interpretation and simulating experimental EEG results.

II. OUTLINE OF K SETS

The hierarchy of K sets describes various components of the central nervous system. K sets produce dynamic behavior that approximates measured EEG signals (Chang et al., 1996; Freeman, 2000). K sets have been used successfully for pattern recognition and classification of various input data (Kozma & Freeman, 2001). The highest level in the hierarchy of K sets is the KIV model (Kozma et al., 2003). In this work, we study the chaotic dynamics of the KIV model.

by analyzing global phase transitions in the simulated Amygdala.

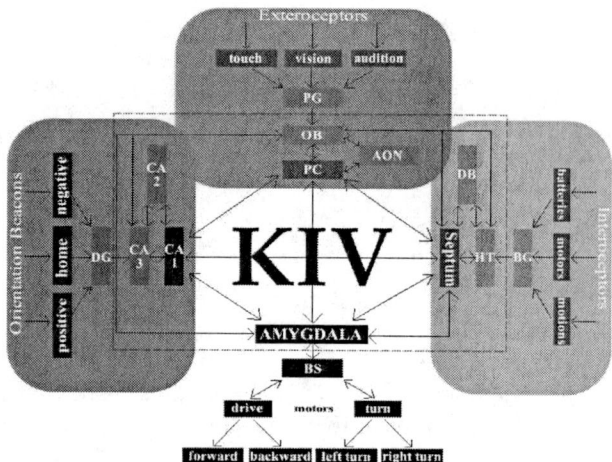

Figure 1. Structure of the KIV model. Abbreviations: DG, dentate gyrus; CA1–CA3, Cornu Ammonis (hippocampal sections); PG, periglomerular; OB, olfactorybulb; AON, anterior olfactorynucleus; PC, prepyriform cortex; Spt, septum; DB, diagonal band; HT, hypothalamus; BC, basal ganglia, corpus striatum including thalamus; BS, brain stem (see, Kozma et al. 2003).

The complete structure of the KIV model is shown in Fig. 1. In the current implementation, we employ a simplified version of the KIV model. We consider the cortex and the hippocampal formation as KIII units comprising KIV, without incorporating the septum, hippothalamus, and the basal ganglia. Cortex is used for local sensing and obstacle avoidance, while hippocampus processes global information for goal-oriented navigation. Positive reinforcement learning is applied in the hippocampus when the robot correctly moves towards the specified goal location. On the other hand, learning in cortical KIII is based on a negative reinforcement signal. Accordingly, we use negative reinforcement e.g., when the robot approaches an obstacle or if it gets trapped.

The developed model is implemented in a 2D Martian-like environment (Tunstel, 2001), see Fig. 2. In the environment, the simulated robot moves along the grid and uses global landmark detector and local distance sensor to collect sensory information as an input to the KIV model. Details of the simulation environment and KIV implementations are given in (Wong et al., 2004).

By using Hilbert transform for EEG analysis (Freeman, 2002, 2003, 2004), we are able to capture fast global synchronized spatial patterns of amplitude modulation. The ultimate goal of identifying phase transition in the Amygdala is to support the system's control algorithm for intentional navigation in a challenging environment.

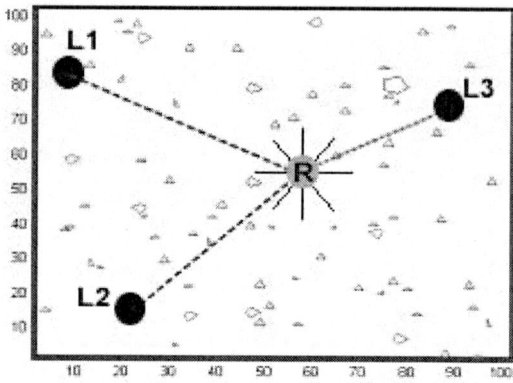

Figure 2: The simulated Martian environment; note the global landmark detectors and local distance sensor of the robot (Tunstel, 2001).

III. DESCRIPTION OF KIV SIMULATIONS

Based on biological evidence, the amygdala, together with the orbitofrontal cortex, is involved in decision-making (Bechara et al., 2000; Le Doux, 2000; Zhou & Coggins, 2002). We model the decision-making by integrating all the signals from the cortical and hippocampal KIII units into the amygdala. We then analyze the activation of the amygdala and try finding sudden changes in its spatio-temporal dynamics. Such changes will be identified as phase transitions. Cognitive processing utilizes global phase jumps to cortico-cortical communication across the hemisphere at high speed.

In this section we introduce results of the analysis of the simulated amygdala. The amygdala is described as an array of excitatory and inhibitory nodes, which is called the KII set (Kozma et al., 2003). K sets are described by a set of ordinary differential equations and solved using Runge-Kutta numerical method. Our model solves the differential equations using a fixed time step of 0.5 ms.

We conduct simulations with the KIV model as it continuously interacts with the simulated 2D environment and receives sensory information through the sensory cortex (local obstacles) and hippocampus (global orientation). The sensory signals modify the oscillatory spatio-temporal patters across KIV layers. It can be shown that the perturbation patterns of the oscillations contain useful information on the input signals. In the language of dynamical systems theory we say that sensory inputs destabilize the high-dimensional chaotic/aperiodic basal oscillations and constrain them to a lower-dimensional manifold, called an attractor wing. As long as the input is maintained, the oscillation remains in this wing. This is called recall of a previously learnt memory pattern. As the input stream is stopped, the oscillation returns to the high-dimensional oscillatory mode of the complex attractor with multiple wings.

In this work, we concentrate on the signals of the amygdala. The size of the amygdale is a free parameter of the model. We have selected an array of 80 amygdala nodes, which is comparable to the size of the simulated cortex (120 nodes) and hippocampus (60 nodes); for details see (Wong et al., 2004).

During the experiments the simulated robot moves into the 2D environment. After each step it stops and collects sensory information for a given time interval, then makes the next step. In the actual experiments a 154 ms temporal window is applied, which included a 104 ms active sensory period and 50 ms relaxation time (no sensing) while moving to the next position. We have recorded the signals from the 80 channels of the amygdala, for 12 seconds, which corresponds to 24,000 time samples. Results obtained by analyzing these time series are given below.

IV. IDENTIFICATION OF PHASE TRANSITION IN THE AMYGDALA

In order to test our models performance, we use the Hilbert transformation-based signal processing method proposed by (Freeman & Rogers, 2002; Freeman, 2004). He we briefly summarize the main steps of the signal processing method. We apply the Hilbert transform to the 80 channel data, and get the analytic phase and amplitude $A_j(t)$, $j = 1, …, N$, where N is the number of channels, $N = 80$. The following quantities are defined (Freeman, 2004):

$A_j^2(t)$ – squared analytic amplitude,
$P_j(t)$ -- analytic phase,
SDt -- standard deviation of $A_j^2(t)$ across channels,
D_e -- Euclidian dist. between consecutive amplitude modulation (AM) patterns,
H_e -- = $A_j^2(t) / D_e$, pragmatic information.

Details of the methodology are given in (Freeman, 2004). Here we point it out that pragmatic information H_e can be interpreted as the measure of the time varying information incorporated in the sequence of activity patterns of EEG signals. Pragmatic information is an extension of the Shannonian information (Atmanspacher et al, 1990) and it is an order parameter (Haken, 1983).

The bottom part of Fig. 3 shows the activation of an amygdala channel for the duration of 4 s; the top section represents SDt during the same interval. The regular oscillations on the bottom panel correspond to the theta gating induced in our system. The standard deviation has a low value most of the time, but exhibits sudden spikes at irregular intervals. Please note that spikes in SDt appear at irregular intervals and they are clearly distinct from activation spikes caused by the sensory temporal gating.

Figure 4 shows temporal variation of H_e, where spikes can be seen at irregular intervals. In order to quantify the amplitude distribution of H_e, we calculate its histogram as shown in Fig. 5. The observed distribution looks meaningful from the point of view of neurobiology, as quantitatively similar distribution has been observed in actual EEG measurements (Freeman, 2003). EEG studies indicate the incidence of high H_e values shortly after conditioned stimuli. Potential implications of this observation will be studied in the future in our model.

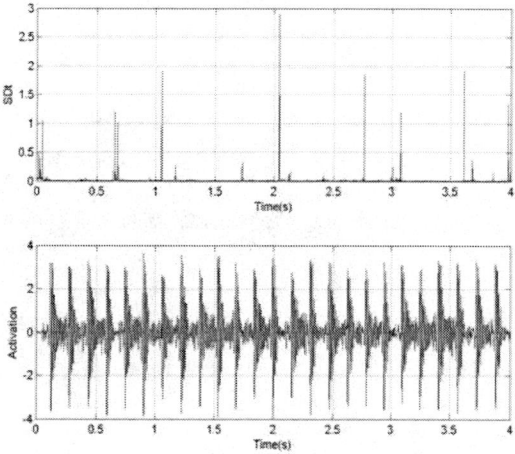

Figure 3. Temporal evolution of the amygdala activation in the KIV model; bottom panel: raw activation of channel #1; top panel: SDt of the squared analytic amplitude. The irregular spikes of SDt are clearly visible.

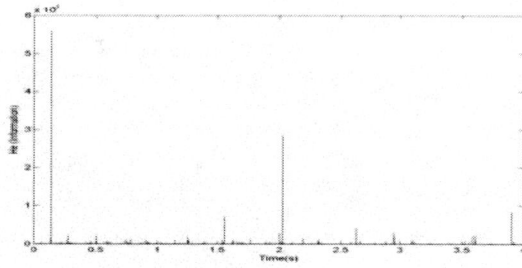

Figure 4. Pragmatic information H_e evaluated during a 4s simulation interval by KIV.

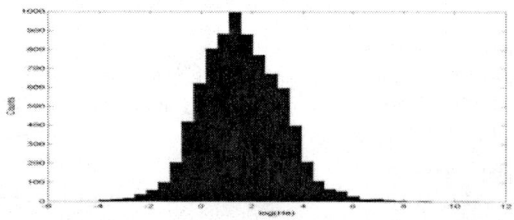

Figure 5. Distribution of log(H_e) over a 4 s interval.

Finally, we show the spatio-temporal distribution of the analytic phase differences; see Fig. 6. In the gray scale image darker shades represent near zero values, and light shades show increased phase differences. It is remarkable that our KIV model shows relatively long periods of highly coherent state with low phase differences, which are interrupted from time to time by brief periods of high phase differences.

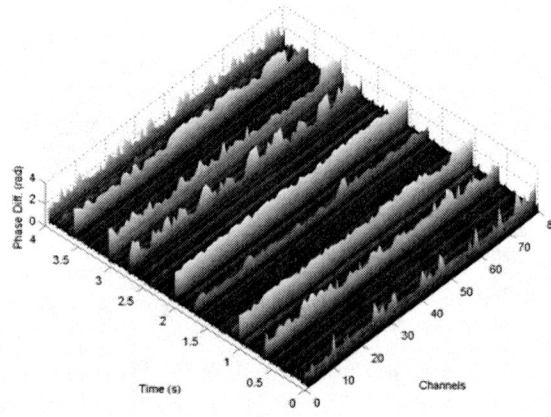

Figure 6: Successive differences of the analytic phase in the amygdala with 80 channels, during an experimental period of 4 s using KIV model.

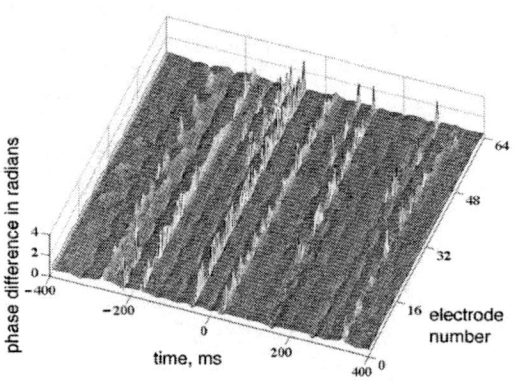

Figure 7. Successive differences of the analytic phase changing with time across the 64 EEG channels; from Freeman (2004).

This behavior is similar to the one observed in EEG data, see Fig. 7. and it indicates that, using Hilbert transform, we are able to capture synchronized patterns of neural activity. At some instances the synchronization breaks down leading to global phase transitions.

V. CONCLUSIONS

In this work, we have studied the chaotic dynamics of the KIV model. In particular we analyzed global phase transitions in the simulated amygdala. By using Hilbert transform methodology we were able to capture fast global synchronized spatial patterns of amplitude modulation. Our results indicate various phase transitions in the amygdala while the simulated robot is navigating the environment.

The ultimate goal of future research is to establish a link between cortical phase transitions and behavioral patterns. We also aim at benefiting from phase transition to develop robust control algorithms for intentional robot navigation in a challenging, remote, and potentially hostile environment. We can analyze the relationship between the robot's behavior and the observed phase jumps. Future research will clarify the behavioral correlates of observed dynamical behavior in the KIV model.

Acknowledgments: This work was supported in part by grants NASA NCC2-1244, and NSF EIA-0130352. The help of Dr Murat Demirer in signal processing developments, and of Derek Wong in conducting KIV simulations is appreciated.

REFERENCES

Arhem, P., C. Blomberg, H. Liljenstrom, Disorder versus order in brain function, *Progr. Neural Processing*, Vol. 12, ISBN 981-02-4008-2, World Scientific, 2000.

Atmanspacher, H., Scheingraber, H. (1990) Pragmatic information instabilities in a multi-mode continuous-wave dye laser, Can. J. Phys. 68: 728-737.

Barrie JM. Freeman WJ, Lenhart M. Modulation by discriminative training of spatial patterns of gamma EEG amplitude and phase in neocortex of rabbits. *J. Neurophysiol.* 1996, 76: 520-539.

Bechara, A., Damasio, H., Damasio, A.R. (2000) Emotion, decision making and the orbitofrontal cortex. *Cerebral Cortex*. 10, 295-307.

Bressler SL, Kelso JAS. (2001) Cortical coordination dynamics and cognition. *Trends in Cognitive Sciences*, 2001, 5:26-36.

Bressler SL. (2002) Understanding cognition through large-scale cortical networks. *Current Directions in Psychological Science*, 2002, 11:58-61.

Bressler SL. (2003) Cortical coordination dynamics and the disorganization syndrome in schizophrenia. *Neuropsychopharmacology, 28: S35-S39*.

Chang H.J. & Freeman W.J. (1996) Parameter optimization in models of the olfactory system, *Neural Networks*, 9, 1-14.

Dafilis, M.P., D. T. J. Liley and P. J. Cadusch, (2001) Robust chaos in a model of the electro-encephalogram: Implications for brain dynamics." *Chaos* 11, 474-478.

Freeman, W.J. (2000) *Neurodynamics – An exploration of mesoscopic brain dynamics.* Springer Verlag, London, U.K.

Freeman WJ, Rogers LJ. (2002) Fine temporal resolution of analytic phase reveals episodic synchronization by state transitions in gamma EEGs. *J. Neurophysiol.* 87: 937-945.

Freeman WJ, Burke BC, Holmes MD. (2003) Aperiodic phase re-setting in scalp EEG of beta-gamma oscillations by state transitions at alpha-theta rates. *Hum. Brain Mapp.* 19: 248-272.

Freeman WJ. (2004): Origin, structure, and role of background EEG activity. Part 1. *Phase. Clin. Neurophysiol.* 115: 2077-2088.

Haken, H. (1983) *Synenergetics – An Introduction.* Springer-Verlag, Berlin.

Kopell N, Ermentrout GB, Whittington MA, Traub RD. Gamma rhythms and beta rhythms have different synchronization properties. *Proc. Natl. Acad. Sci. U.S.A.* 2000, 97:1867-1872.

Korn, H., P. Faure, Is there chaos in the brain? II. Experimental evidence and related models, *Comptes Rendus Biologies* 326 (2003) 787–840

Kozma, R. & W.J., Freeman (2001) Chaotic resonance: Methods and applications for robust classification of noisy and variable patterns. *Int. J. Bifurcation & Chaos*, 11(6): 2307-2322.

Kozma, R., W.J. Freeman, (2003). Basic principles of the KIV model and its application to the navigation problem, *Journal of Integrative Neuroscience*, 2, 125-145.

Kozma, R., W.J. Freeman, P. Erdi (2003) "The KIV Model – Nonlinear spatio-temporal dynamics of the primordial vertebrate forebrain," *Neurocomputing*, 55-56, 819-826.

Lachaux J-P, Rodriguez E, Martinerie J, Varela FA. Measuring phase synchrony in brain signals. *Hum. Brain Mapp.* 1999, 8: 194-208.

LeDoux, J.E. (2000) Orbitofrontal cortex and basolateral amygdala encode expected outcomes during learning. *Annu. Rev. Neurosci.* 23, 155–184.

Le Van Quyen M, Foucher J, Lachaux J-P, Rodriguez E, Lutz A, Martinerie J, Varela F. Comparison of Hilbert transform and wavelet methods for the analysis of neuronal synchrony. *J. Neurosci. Meth.* 2001, 111: 83-98.

Liang H, Bressler SL, Ding M, Truccolo WA, Nakamura R. Synchronized activity in prefrontal cortex during anticipation of visuomotor processing. *NeuroReport*, 2002, 13:2011-2016.

Ohl, FW, Scheich, H and Freeman, WJ (2001) Change in pattern of ongoing cortical activity with auditory category learning *Nature* 412: 733-736.

Ohl FW, Deliano M, Scheich H, Freeman WJ (2003) Early and late patterns of stimulus-related activity in auditory cortex of trained animals. *Biol. Cybernetics* online: DOI 10.1007/s00422-002-0389-z.

Quiroga RQ, Kraskov A, Kreuz T, Grassberger P. Performance of different synchronization measures in real data: A case study on electroencephalographic signals. *Physical Rev E* 2002, 6504:U645-U6 58 - art. no. 041903.

Schiff, S.J. et al. (1994). Controling chaos in the brain, *Nature*, 370, 615-620.

Skarda, C.A. and Freeman W.J., (1987). How brains make chaos in order to make sense of the world, *Behavioral & Brain Sci.*, 10, 161-195.

Steyn-Ross, M.L., D. A. Steyn-Ross, J. W. Sleigh, and D.T.J. Liley, Theoretical electro-encephalogram stationary spectrum for a white-noise-driven cortex: Evidence for a general anesthetic-induced phase transition, Physical Review E (1999) 60, 7299-7311

Traub RD, Whittington MA, Stanford IM, Jefferys JGR. A mechanism for generation of long-range synchronous fast oscillations in the cortex. *Nature* 1996, 383: 421-424.

Tunstel, E., (2001). "Ethology as an Inspiration for Adaptive Behavior Synthesis in Autonomous Planetary Rovers," *Autonomous Robots*, 11, 333–339.

Whittington MA, Faulkner HJ, Doheny HC, Traub RD Neuronal fast oscillations as a target site for psychoactive drugs. *Pharmacol. Therap.* 2000, 86: 171-190.

Wong, D., Kozma, R., E. Tunstel, Freeman, W.J. (2004) Navigation in a Challenging Martian Environment Using Multi-Sensory Fusion in KIV Model," *International*

Conference on Robotics and Automation ICRA'04, April 26-May 1, 2004, New Orleans (accepted).

Zhou, W., Coggins, R. (2002) Computational Models of the Amygdala and the orbitofrontal cortex: A hierarchical reinforcement learning system for robotic control, R.I. McKay and J. Slaney (eds), *Lecture Notes AI: LNAI 2557*, 419–430.

Mixture segmentation and background suppression in chemosensor arrays with a model of olfactory bulb-cortex interaction

B. Raman and R. Gutierrez-Osuna
Department of Computer Science, Texas A&M University, College Station, Texas, USA
{barani, rgutier}@cs.tamu.edu

Abstract

We present a model of olfactory bulb-cortex interaction for the purpose of mixture processing with gas sensor arrays. The olfactory bulb is modeled with a neurodynamic model whose lateral inhibitory connections are learned through a modified Hebbian-anti-hebbian rule. Bulbar outputs are then projected in a non-topographic fashion onto the olfactory cortex. Associational connections within cortex using Hebbian learning form a content addressable memory. Finally, inhibitory feedback from cortex is used to modulate bulbar activity. Depending on the form of feedback, Hebbian or anti-Hebbian, the model is able to perform background suppression or mixture segmentation. The model is validated on experimental data from a gas sensor array.

I. INTRODUCTION

Recognizing odorants against complex backgrounds and identifying the components of a mixture are common olfactory discrimination tasks encountered in daily life situations. Several computational models have put forth the hypothesis that cortical feedback to the bulb may play a role in achieving these computational functions. Ambrose-Ingerson et al. [1] have modeled these feedback connections to account for hierarchical recognition of odors by humans. In this model, cues common to a subset of odorants are recognized before those that are odorant-specific. Li and Hertz [2] have shown that centrifugal connections may cause odor-specific adaptation, leading to segmentation of odor mixtures. Grossberg [3] has proposed that cortical connections to the bulb may selectively filter the bulb input and cause resonance between the two regions. Yao and Freeman [4] have implicated these feedback connections with chaotic dynamics in the bulb.

In this paper, we will present a model of olfactory bulb–cortex interaction, and show that two different computational functions can be achieved (mixture segmentation, weaker odor/background suppression) depending upon the learning rule that is used to establish the cortical feedback connections to the bulb: anti-Hebbian or Hebbian, respectively. We validate the use of these computational models to handle odor mixture signals from an array of gas sensors.

II. NEURODYNAMICS MODEL

The olfactory bulb is the first relay station in the olfactory pathway, and the site where the bulk of the signal processing takes place. We model the OB using the classical additive model from neurodynamics [5, p. 676], as follows:

$$\frac{dv_j^O(t)}{dt} = -\frac{v_j^O(t)}{\tau_j} + \sum_{k=1}^{M} L_{kj} \varphi(v_k^O(t)) + I_j^O + \sum_{i=1}^{P} FB_{ij} \varphi(y_i^O(t)) \quad (1)$$

where v_j is the activity of bulb neuron j, τ_j is the time constant that captures the dynamics of the neuron, L_{kj} is the synaptic weight between neurons k and j, M is the number of neurons, I_j is the external input from the olfactory epithelium, FB is the feedback connectivity matrix, y_i is the activity of cortical neuron i, and $\varphi(\cdot)$ is a non-linear activation function (logistic function) given by:

$$\varphi(v_j) = \frac{1}{1 + \exp(-a_1 \cdot (v_j - a_2))} \quad (2)$$

where the constants a_1 and a_2 are set to 5.8889 and 0.5 respectively to match the dynamic range of input signals from the chemosensor array ([0, 1]).

The lateral connections L in the bulb are established through a Hebbian update rule proposed in [6] as follows:

$$L = \alpha \cdot \sum_{O_1=1}^{N} I^{O_1} \cdot (I^{O_1})^T - \beta \cdot \sum_{O_1=1}^{N} \sum_{\substack{O_2=1 \\ O_2 \neq O_1}}^{N} I^{O_1} \cdot (I^{O_2})^T \quad (3)$$

where I^{O_1} is the input olfactory bulb pattern for odor O_1, α and β are scaling parameters, which provide a necessary tradeoff between the first correlation term and the second decorrelation term. This form of update has been shown to enhance the contrast between input patterns [6].

The olfactory bulb sends non-topographic and many-to-many projections to the olfactory cortex. These convergent and divergent (many-to-many) projections suggest that cortical neurons detect combinations of co-occurring molecular features of the odorant, and therefore function as "coincidence detectors" [7]. Apart from these forward connections, the cortex is characterized by excitatory and inhibitory lateral connections that are known to play an important role in the storage odors with minimum interference and pattern completion of degraded stimuli [8]. Together, these two architectural features of the PC (many-to-many connection from OB, and lateral association connections between cortical cells) form the basis for the synthetic processing of odors [7].

We model these olfactory circuits using an additive model, similar to the olfactory bulb in equation (1), as follows:

$$\frac{dy_i^O(t)}{dt} = -\frac{y_i^O(t)}{\lambda_i} + \sum_{\substack{k=1\\k\neq i}}^{P} AC_{ki}\varphi\left(y_k^O(t)\right) + \sum_{j=1}^{M} FF_{ji}\varphi\left(v_j^O(t)\right) \quad (4)$$

where y_j is the activity of cortical pyramidal neuron i, λ_i is the time constant of the neuron, AC_{ki} is the synaptic weight between neurons k and i obtained through Hebbian learning, P is the number of neurons, FF is the feedforward connectivity matrix established through Hebbian learning, and v_j is the activity of bulb neuron j.

The associational connections AC within cortex are established through Hebbian learning, such that neurons that code for *at least* one common odor have purely excitatory connections between them, and neurons that encode for different odors (no common odor) have purely inhibitory connections between them. The excitatory lateral connections perform pattern-completion of degraded inputs from the bulb [8], whereas the inhibitory connections introduce winner-take-all competition among cortical neurons [9].

The last component of the model involves feedback connections from the cortex to the bulb. To model these feedback connections (*FB*) in equation (1), we use either anti-Hebbian or Hebbian rule as follows:

$$\begin{aligned} FB &= \gamma(-YV^T) \quad (anti-Hebbian)\\ FB &= \gamma(YV^T) \quad (Hebbian) \end{aligned} \quad (5)$$

where Y is the matrix of cortical neuron outputs to different pure odors (organized as row vectors), V is the matrix of bulb neuron outputs to pure odors (row vectors), and γ is a scaling parameter.

In the case of anti-Hebbian learning, all connections are initialized to *0*. The anti-Hebbian update forms feedback connections between the cortical and the bulb neurons that respond to *at least* one common odor. The resulting feedback from cortex inhibits bulb neurons responsible for the cortical response, in a manner akin to the model proposed in [1], resulting in the temporal segmentation of binary mixtures.

In the case of Hebbian learning, all connections are initialized to *–1*. The Hebbian update retains only those connections between cortical neurons and bulb neurons that respond to different odors (no common odor). The resulting feedback from cortex inhibits bulb neurons other than those responsible for the cortical response, causing cortical activity to resonate with OB activity as suggested in [3]. This type of resonance allows the model to lock onto a particular odor and suppress the background/weaker odor.

Proof of concept for this model is best illustrated with an example. Let the encoding of two simulated odors at the bulb be $OB_A=[1,0,0,1,1,0]^T$ and $OB_B=[0,1,1,1,0,0]^T$, and the encoding at the cortex be $OC_A=[1,1,0,0,0,0]^T$ and $OC_B=[0,0,1,1,0,0]^T$, respectively. Using these patterns, lateral connections in the OB (not shown in Fig 1) and associational connections within cortex (shown in Fig 1 (a)) were established through Hebbian learning as described above. Time constants were set to 10ms and 5ms for bulb and cortical neurons, respectively. Model parameters were set as follows: $\alpha=0.1$, $\beta=0.075$, and $\gamma=1$.

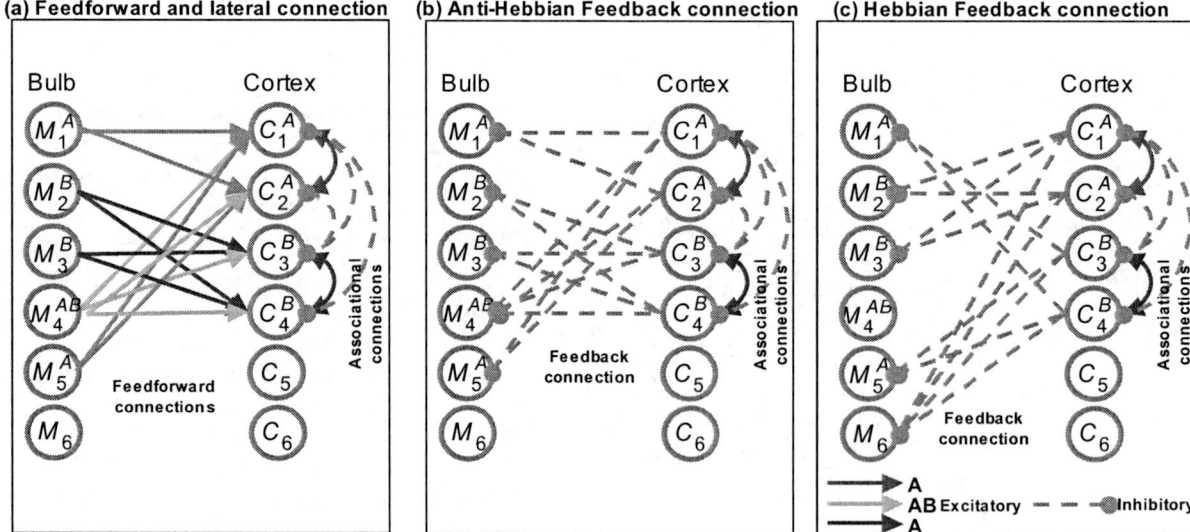

Fig 1. Bulb-cortex interaction. (a) Lateral connections in OC are learned through Hebbian updates (single analytes used for training). (b) Feedback connections established through anti-Hebbian updates. (c) Feedback connections established through Hebbian updates.

A. Case 1: Anti-Hebbian learning for temporal segmentation

Anti-Hebbian feedback connections are shown in Fig 1(b). Note that these connections are the reverse of the forward connections in Fig 1(a). Following learning with pure odors, the model is exposed to a mixture of odor A and B $[0.8, 0.5, 0.5, 0.6, 0.8, 0.0]^T$. As a result of lateral inhibition, OB activity for the stronger odor A suppresses the weaker activity of odor B. Hence odor A is first recognized by the cortex. Subsequently, feedback from cortex suppresses odor A activity in the bulb, allowing odor B to win the competition. To illustrate this effect, Fig 2 shows the activity in the OB and the OC over the course of several periods. The activity of B1 and B5, which code for odor A, become out of phase with B2 and B3, which code for odor B. The common mode B4 is removed. Further, the activity of C1 and C2, which code for odor A, becomes out of phase with C3 and C4, which code for odor B. Hence anti-Hebbian learning of centrifugal projections realizes temporal segmentation of odor mixtures in both bulb and cortex.

B. Case 2: Hebbian learning for background suppression and resonance

Hebbian feedback connections are shown in Fig 1(c). Following learning with pure odors, the model is exposed to a mixture of odors A and B $[0.8, 0.5, 0.5, 0.6, 0.8, 0.0]^T$. In this case, cortical feedback suppresses the weaker background odor (B) immediately and resonates with odor A, as shown in Fig 2.

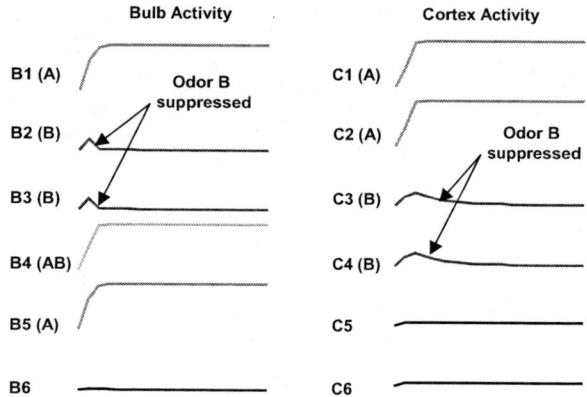

Fig 3. Suppression of background/weaker odor through Hebbian feedback connections.

III. EXPERIMENTAL RESULTS

To validate the model, we have used experimental data from an array of gas sensors exposed to acetone (A), isopropyl alcohol (I), ammonia (M), as well as their binary mixtures. Two Figaro MOS sensors (TGS 2600, TGS 2620) [10] were temperature modulated using a sinusoidal heater voltage (0-7 V; 2.5min period; 10Hz sampling frequency). The L1-normalized response of a single MOS sensor (TGS 2620) to each of these analytes is shown in Fig 4. Since the selectivity of MOS materials is dependent on the operating temperature [11], the response of the sensors at each point in the temperature cycle can be considered as a separate pseudo-sensor, and used to generate a high-dimensional odor signal.

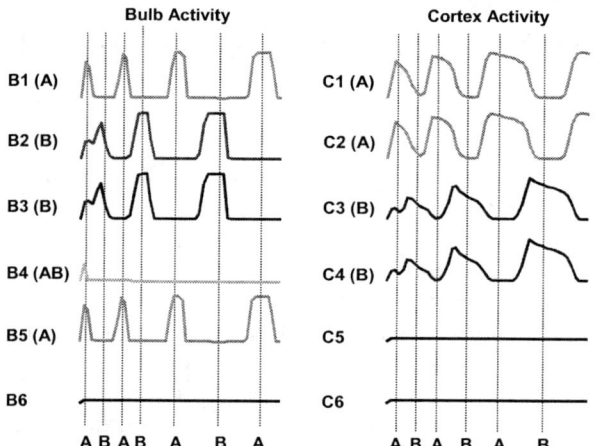

Fig 2. (a) Temporal segmentation of binary mixtures through anti-Hebbian feedback connections.

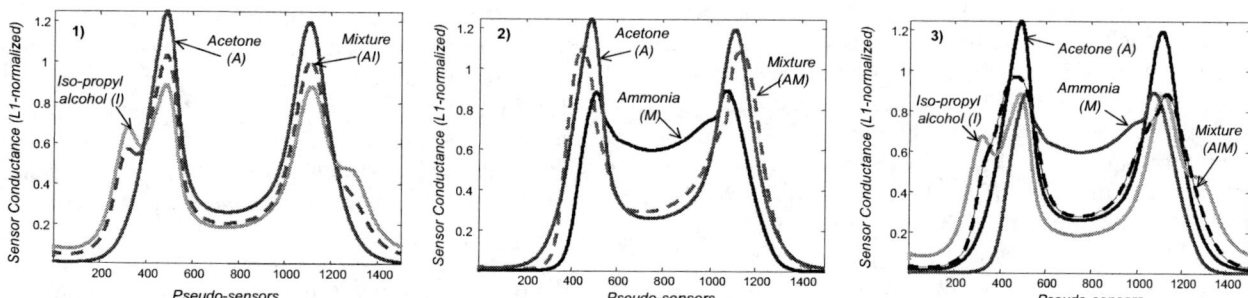

Fig 4. Temperature-modulated response of a MOS sensor to three pure analytes and their binary mixtures: (1) acetone (A), isopropyl alcohol (I) and their binary mixture (AI); (2) acetone (A), ammonia (M) and their binary mixture (AM); (3) acetone (A), isopropyl alcohol (I), ammonia (M) and their ternary mixture (AIM). Only the pure analytes were used to train the model.

A. Forming olfactory bulb patterns

In the biological olfactory system, the projection of olfactory receptor neurons (ORNs) in the epithelium onto the OB is organized such that ORNs expressing the same receptor gene converge onto one or a few OB neurons [12]. To mimic this convergence, we cluster the pseudo-sensors based on their selectivity, which we defined as the vector of responses across the three pure odors. Fig 5 shows the clustering of the pseudo-sensors based on their response to each of three pure odors. All the pseudo-sensors belonging to a particular cluster then project to a single olfactory bulb neuron. The input to each bulb neuron is given by:

$$I_j^O = \frac{\sum_{i=1}^{N} W_{ij} R_i^O}{\sum_{i=1}^{N} W_{ij}} \quad (6)$$

where R_i^O is the response of pseudo-sensor i to odorant O, N is the number of pseudo-sensors, and $W_{ij}=1$ if pseudo-sensor i converges to bulb neuron B_j and zero otherwise.

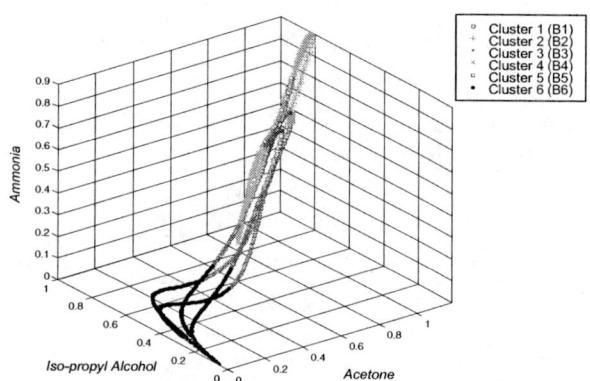

Fig 5. k-means clustering of pseudo-sensors based on their selectivity.

B. Mixture Segmentation

In order to perform binary mixture segmentation on the experimental datasets, we used a model with six bulbar neurons in the olfactory bulb, and six cortical neurons. The OB-OC network was initially trained using the three pure odors. The activity of the trained network with anti-Hebbian feedback connections when exposed to the each of two binary mixtures and the ternary mixture is shown in Fig 6 (a-c). As mentioned in section II, anti-Hebbian feedback results in the removal of bulb activity that is responsible for activity in the cortex. In case a), isopropyl alcohol is first recognized in the cortex since is the stronger odor in the mixture. Subsequently, feedback from cortex inhibits bulb neurons (B1, B6) responsible for this cortical activity, allowing acetone to be detected. Fig 7(a) shows the relationship between the activity of cortical neuron C3 and bulb neuron B6, both of which encode for isopropyl alcohol. Input from the bulb neuron B6 increases the activity in cortical neuron C3. The cortical feedback from C3 then suppresses the activity of B6 and thereby itself, allowing the next odor to be recognized. The removal of feedback again increases activity in B6 and this cycle is repeated. Fig 7 (b) shows the negative correlation between cells C2 and C3, which represent acetone and isopropyl alcohol, respectively.

Similar behavior can be observed in case b), where acetone (the stronger odor) is detected prior to ammonia, and the activity of cortical and bulb neurons for these two odors become out of phase. In the case of iso-propyl alcohol and ammonia (results not shown), the mixture response resembles that of iso-propyl alcohol alone. As a result, the model is unable to segment the mixture into its constituents. Hence, the proposed anti-Hebbian feedback mechanism appears to be limited to the segmentation of binary odor mixtures that are relatively additive. Finally, the response of the model to the ternary mixture of acetone, isopropyl alcohol, and ammonia is shown in Fig 6 (c). The two strong components in the ternary mixture (isopropyl alcohol and acetone) are clearly detected and segmented. However, cortical neurons encoding ammonia show feeble activity, and only during the period of transition of cortical response from acetone to isopropyl alcohol.

C. Background suppression

In order to perform background suppression, the same model with six bulbar neurons and six cortical neurons was used. The OB-OC network was initially trained using the three pure odors. The activity of the trained network with Hebbian feedback connections when exposed to the each of three binary mixtures is shown in Fig 8 (a-c). In case a) and c), cortical feedback from the stronger odor (isopropyl alcohol) suppresses the weaker odor (acetone and ammonia, respectively). In case b), cortical activity for acetone suppresses the weaker odor, in this case ammonia. Hence, Hebbian feedback leads to suppression of the weaker odor in a binary mixture.

IV. CONCLUSIONS

We have presented a neurodynamic model of the bulb-cortex interaction. Depending on the type of update rule used to learn these feedback connections, Hebbian or anti-Hebbian, the model realizes background suppression or mixture segmentation functions, respectively. Anti-Hebbian feedback connections result in the identification of binary mixture components as a time series. Hebbian feedback connections allow the olfactory cortex to selectively filter the background or weaker odor input from the bulb, in analogy with the selective attention mechanism proposed by Grossberg [3]. The next stage in this research is to extend the model to the segmentation of higher mixtures, and suppression of strong background odor.

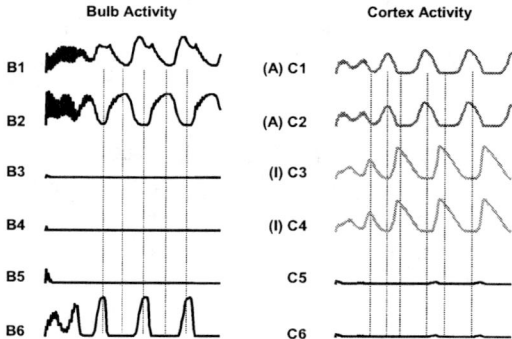

a) Segmenting mixture of Acetone & Iso-propyl alcohol (AI)

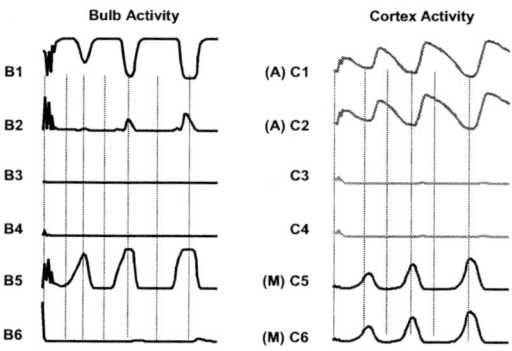

b) Segmenting mixture of Acetone & Ammonia (AM)

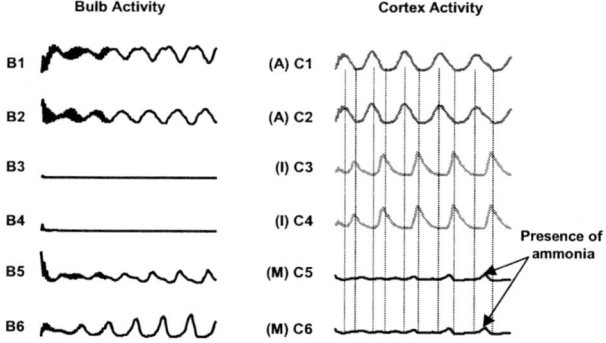

a) Segmenting ternary mixture of Acetone, Iso-propyl Alcohol & Ammonia (AIM)

Fig 6. Segmentation of binary mixtures by anti-Hebbian cortical feedback. The parameter were set as follows: $\tau=$ 10ms, $\lambda=$5ms, $\alpha = 0.8$, $\beta=0.6$, and $\gamma=0.4$.

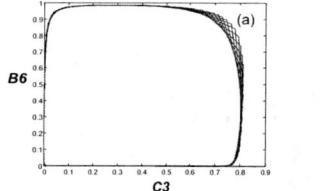 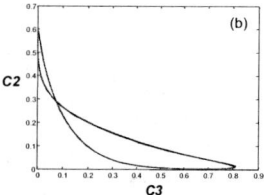

Fig 7. Evolution of activity a) C3 (coding Iso-propyl alcohol) vs. B6 (coding Iso-propyl alcohol) b) C3 (coding Iso-propyl alcohol) vs. C2 (coding Acetone).

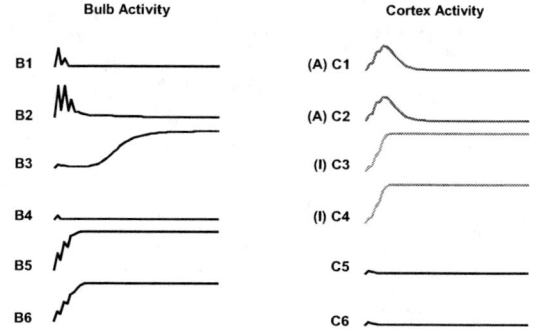

a) Suppressing weaker odor in a of Acetone & Iso-propyl alcohol (AI)

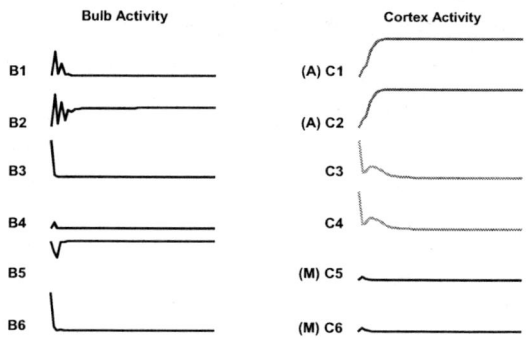

b) Suppressing weaker odor in a mixture of Acetone & Ammonia (AM)

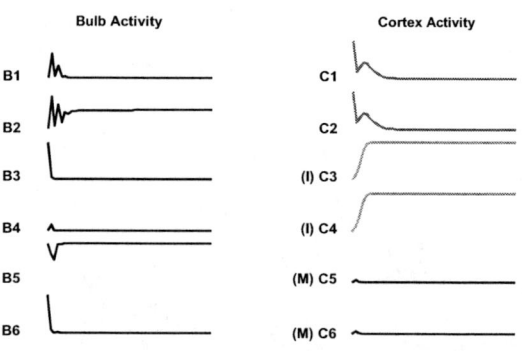

c) Suppressing weaker odor in a mixture of Acetone & Iso-propyl alcohol (IM)

Fig 8. Suppression of weaker/background odor by Hebbian cortical feedback. The parameter were set as follows: $\tau=$ 10ms, $\lambda=$5ms, $\alpha = 0.8$, $\beta=0.6$, and $\gamma=0.1$.

ACKNOWLEDGEMENTS

This material is based upon work supported by the National Science Foundation under CAREER award 9984426/0229598. Takao Yamanaka and Agustin Gutierrez-Galvez are gratefully acknowledged for valuable suggestions during the preparation of this manuscript.

REFERENCES

[1] J. Ambros-Ingerson, R. Granger and G. Lynch, "Simulation of paleocortex performs hierarchical clustering," Science, Vol. 247, pp. 1344-1348, 1990.

[2] Z. Li and J. Hertz, "Odor recognition and segmentation by a model olfactory bulb and cortex," Network: Computation in Neural Systems 11 (2000) 83-102.

[3] S. Grossberg, "Adaptive Pattern Classification and Universal Recording: II. Feedback, Expectation, Olfaction and Ilusion", Biological Cybernetics, Vol. 23, pp. 187-02, 1976.

[4] Y. Yao and W.J. Freeman, "Model of Biological Pattern Recognition with Spatially Chaotic Dynamics", Neural Networks, Vol.3, pp.153-170, Pergamon Press, 1990.

[5] S. Haykin, Neural Networks, A Comprehensive Foundation, 2nd ed., Upper Saddle River, NJ: Prentice Hall, 1999.

[6] A. Gutierrez-Galvez and R. Gutierrez-Osuna, "Contrast enhancement and background suppression of chemosensor array patterns with the KIII model," to appear in International Journal of Intelligent Systems.

[7] D. A. Wilson and R. J. Stevenson, "The Fundamental Role of Memory in Olfactory Perception," Trends in Neurosciences, Vol. 26, No. 5, pp. 243-247, 2003.

[8] M. A. Wilson, and J.M. Bower, "A computer simulation of olfactory cortex with functional implications for storage and retrieval of olfactory information", In D. Z. Anderson, D.Z. (ed), Neural Information Processing Systems, pp. 114-126, American Institute of Physics. 1988.

[9] X. H. Xie, R. Hahnloser and H. S. Seung, "Learning winner-take-all competition between groups of neurons in lateral inhibitory networks," Adv. Neural Info. Proc. Syst. 13, pp. 350-356, 2001.

[10] Figaro 1996, Figaro Engineering, Inc., Osaka, Japan.

[11] A. P. Lee and B. J. Reedy, "Temperature modulation in semiconductor gas sensing," Sensors and Actuators, Vol. B60, pp. 35-42, 1999.

[12] R. Vassar et al., "Topographic Organization of Sensory Projections to the Olfactory Bulb," Cell, Vol. 79, pp. 981-991, 1994.

Evolving Neurodynamic Controllers for Autonomous Robots

Derek Harter
Department of Computer Science
Texas A&M University
Commerce, TX 75422
E-mail: Derek_Harter@tamu-commerce.edu

Abstract—The creation of architectures for controlling the behavior of autonomous systems is a difficult challenge. Evolutionary robotics uses neurally inspired models, rather than explicit symbolic systems, to evolve controllers for robots. Most approaches in evolutionary robotics have used abstract ANN or spiking single neuron models to evolve control architectures. In this paper we apply the evolutionary approach to creating a controller for an autonomous robot based on the aperiodic K-set neural population model. We introduce a discretization of the basic K-set units. We then demonstrate that the evolutionary approach evolves effective controllers for navigation tasks using the basic discrete units.

I. INTRODUCTION

The concept of evolutionary robotics (ER) is based on the use of artificial evolutionary techniques, such as genetic algorithms (GA), to develop control architectures for autonomous robotic systems [1, pg. 19]. Most work in ER have been based on artificial neural network (ANN) models, and the evolution of small controllers for performing navigation, object avoidance and path planning. More recent work in the ER community has focused on single neuron spiking models, such as [2], that use Gerstner's spike response model [3], or other similar single-neuron spiking models. Spiking models are more biologically realistic than abstract ANN's, and rely on the timing of individual spikes as a way of communicating meanings between units in the evolved controllers.

Much is known about details of microscopic neuronal processes that regulate single cell spiking and firing dynamics, and how simple abstract networks may be formed into pattern recognizers/classifiers. At the macroscopic level, there is some understanding of human behavior in terms of symbolic or statistical models, among psychology and cognitive science disciplines. A full mechanist account of how the micro-level dynamics give rise to macro-scale behavior is very much an open question. In particular, single neuron models give no real explanation for the types of collective dynamics that are observed over larger populations. These middle, or mesoscopic-level, population dynamics display rich patterns that are not easily explained or captured in single-neuron micro-level models. In particular, the formation of aperiodic attractors at the population level, and the propagation of waves of activation through populations appear to play important roles in the construction of memories and meanings in biological brains [4], [5].

Neural populations generate aperiodic patterns of activity that have many properties in common with mathematical chaos [6], [5], [7], [8]. The stochastic firings of individual neurons give rise to cycles of activity at the population level. However, these cycles are not perfectly periodic, nor are they simply random noise from the firings of the individual neurons. Investigations into the olfactory system of mammals [6], [9] has raised much interest in the possibility that aperiodic patterns of activity are useful in the formation of perceptual categories. In effect, different aperiodic attractors become associated with different categories of input stimuli, but in a non-obvious and complex way that also has a lot of feedback and dependence on the intentional state of the animal. The formation of such attractor landscapes in biological neural material has some properties in common with the similar formation of point attractors in associative memory models such as the Hopfield model [10]. However, it is clear that in biological neural material, the formation of point attractors would be impossible as it would require the neural matter to settle down into a relatively static pattern, a situation that would cause many neurons to simply die as they must continually be active in order to keep functioning properly. Therefore the formation of some type of periodic attractor would seem to be necessary for biological populations to form associative memories. At the other extreme, completely random activity at the mesoscopic level is not observed. We do instead see somewhat periodic behavior that is observable as the well know alpha, gamma and theta waves from EEG recordings of active brains. However, more detailed spatial/temporal EEG recordings have revealed the complexity of such mesoscopic dynamics and some of their dependence on the intentional states of the organism.

Another process believe to be important at the mesoscopic population level is the propagation waves of activation through populations, known as wave packets [4], [11]. Microscopic activity, expressed by action potentials and neuron firing rates, is directly affected by sensory neurons. Changes in the energy received by sensory neurons (light, chemical, pressure, temperature, sound waves, etc.) directly induce changes in the firing rates of those neurons tuned to be sensitive to various energy levels or ranges. Macroscopic activity involves the whole forebrain and is most closely tied with behavior and conscious experience. Mesoscopic activity bridges the gap between the micro and macro levels, by the formation and transmission of such waves of activity. The waves form when sensory input destabilizes the primary receiving areas by local state transitions. The sensory-driven action potentials condense into mesoscopic wave packets like molecules forming raindrops from vapor. The condensation of these waves can be detected in the spatial patterns of phase and amplitude of the carrier waves in EEG recordings. The patterns correlate not with features but with the context and value of sensory stimuli for the subjects, in a word, their meaning.

K-sets are neural population models that are capable of reproducing the aperiodic dynamics observed in mammalian perceptual systems. K-sets have been used to demonstrate how aperiodic attractors might be formed and associated with perceptual categories using Hebbian mechanisms to shape the attractor space [12], [13]. K-set models have also been used to demonstrate the formation of cognitive maps in autonomous agents [14], [15]. In the next section we introduce briefly a discretized version of the original K-set model. We then demonstrate the evolution of a robotic controller for object-avoidance using the K-model population dynamics.

II. MESOSCOPIC POPULATION MODEL

A. K-Sets: Continuous Differential Equation Model

The K-set dynamics are designed to model the dynamics of the mean field (e.g. average) amplitude of a neural population. A nonlinear, second order, ordinary differential equation was developed to model the dynamics of such a population. The parameters for this equation were derived by experimentation and observation of isolated neural populations of animals prepared through brain slicing techniques and chemical inhibition. The isolated populations were subjected to various levels of stimulation, and the resulting impulse response curves were replicated by the K-set equations.

The basic ODE equation of a neural population of the K-model is:

$$\alpha\beta\frac{d^2 a_i(t)}{dt^2} + (\alpha + \beta)\frac{da_i(t)}{dt} + a_i(t) = net_i(t) \quad (1)$$

In this equation $a_i(t)$ is the activity level (mean field amplitude) of the ith neural population. α and β are time constants (derived from observing biological population dynamics to various amounts of stimulation). The left side of the equation expresses the intrinsic dynamics of the K unit (which captures a neural populations characteristic responses).

On the right side of the equation are factors that allow for external network input to the population $net_i(t)$ Stimulation between populations is governed by a nonlinear transfer function. The nonlinear transfer function used in the K-models is an asymmetric sigmoid that was again derived through measurements of the stimulation between biological neural populations:

$$net_i(t) = \sum_j w_{ij} o_j(t) \quad (2)$$

$$o_j(t) = \epsilon\{1 - exp[\frac{-(e^{a_j(t)} - 1)}{\epsilon}]\} \quad (3)$$

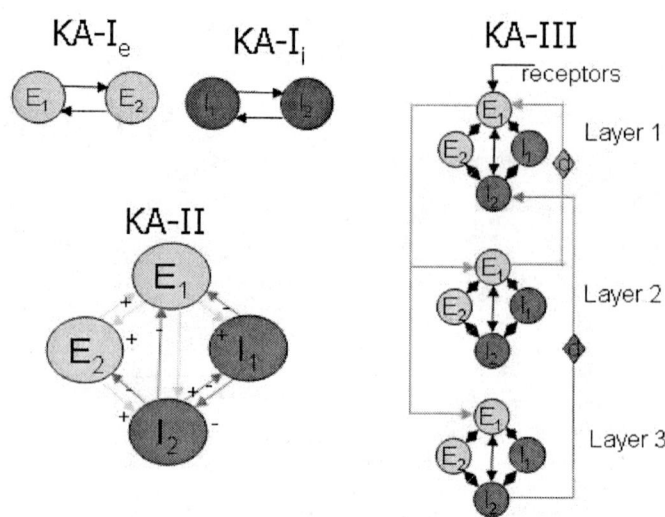

Fig. 1. The KA hierarchy. The KA-I are a combination of two excitatory or two inhibitory units connected with mutual feedback. The KA-II is a combination of a KA-I_e and a KA-I_i, connected with various weights between them. The KA-II level allows for both positive and negative feedback which can create oscillatory behavior. The KA-III level is a collection of three (or more) KA-II connected with various feedforward and feedback connections. When the three layers of the KA-III are nonhomogeneous, the resulting dynamics of the KA-III system is chaotic.

where ϵ is a parameter that indicates the level of arousal in the population (high values indicated a more aroused, motivated state), and $a_j(t)$ is the activation of the jth population connected to the target unit. The asymmetry is an important property in the transfer function as it means that excitatory input causes a destabilization of the dynamics of networks. This destabilization is essential in the collapse of aperiodic attractors observed in biological perceptual systems. See [16], [6], [17] for a more complete description of the basic K-Set model.

These equations model the dynamic behavior of the activity of isolated neural populations. In Freeman's K-model, these are the basic units that are connected together to form larger cooperating components. Two excitatory or inhibitory units together form a K-I set. A K-I excitatory with a K-I inhibitory pair form a K-II set of four units (see Figure 1). Freeman and associates used these neural population units to construct a model of the olfactory system that replicate the dynamics observed from EEG recordings. Three or more groups of K-II units connected together form a K-III unit. The K-III forms a multi-layer, highly-recurrent neural population model of biological perceptual systems. The K-III model was originally used to replicate the chaotic dynamics observed in the olfactory bulb of rabbits and rats.

According to this view, the dynamics of the brain, as modeled by the K-III, is characterized by a high-dimensional chaotic attractor with multiple wings. The wings can be considered as memory traces formed by learning through the animal's life history. In the absence of sensory stimuli, the system is in a high-dimensional itinerant search mode, visiting various wings. In response to a given stimulus, the dynamics of the system is constrained to oscillations in one of the wings, which is identified with the stimulus. Once the input is removed, the system switches back to the high-dimensional, itinerant basal model [8]. These results from the study and development of the K-models have led to the establishment of a dynamical theory of perception [18].

B. KA-Sets: Discretization of Continuous K-Sets

The motivation behind discretization is to develop a simplification of the original K-sets that is still capable of performing the essential dynamics, but is simpler and faster and therefore more suitable for use in large-scale simulations of autonomous robotic agent architectures. In particular, a discretized model is more suitable to evolutionary robotics approaches where evolving controllers can be overly time consuming with a continuous ODE. The discretization is to be used in developing autonomous agents that take advantage of aperiodic dynamics for perception, memory and action. There have been other approaches to discretizing the continuous K-set model [19]. The approach used here was previously described in [15]. However, in this paper we present an alternative and cleaner formulation of the discretization process. The discretized model have been named KA sets, K-Sets for autonomous agents.

We use a method for determining a discrete approximation of a sampled continuous time signal [20], [21]. We will use the dynamics produced by the K-0 set (equation 1) as the signal that is to be approximated. The signal will be approximated using a second-order difference equation, where we look back 2 discrete time steps to develop the approximation. Equation 4 is the difference equation to be used.

$$y(t) = a_1 y(t-1) + a_2 y(t-2) + b_1 u(t-1) + b_2 u(t-2) \quad (4)$$

Here y is the signal at some discrete time step and u is an external input being fed into the system. The signal y at time t will be computed based on the signal at $y(t-1)$ and $y(t-2)$. We also use the input into the system in two previous time steps $u(t-1)$ and $u(t-2)$. Our task is to find values for the parameters a_1, a_2, b_1 and b_2 so that the difference equation approximates the dynamics of a sampled signal.

At any given time step t, the approximation in Equation 4 plus some ε error value will equal the actual signal. We can write this as a summation:

$$y = \sum_{j=1}^{P} \beta_j X_j + \varepsilon \quad (5)$$

$$\beta_1 = a_1 \; \beta_2 = a_2 \; \beta_3 = b_1 \; \beta_4 = b_2$$
$$X_1 = y(t-1) \; X_2 = y(t-2)$$
$$X_3 = u(t-1) \; X_4 = u(t-2)$$

where P is 4 approximating using a second-order difference equation (since we have 4 parameters). X_j are the signal and input to the system in the previous two time steps, and β_J are the parameters we are to determine.

From Equation 5 we can see that the error for a single particular time step is $\varepsilon = y - \sum \beta X$. Our task, however, is to develop an approximation for all of the sampled time steps, not simply a single time step. We can write an equation for the sum squared error as:

$$S = \sum_{i=1}^{N}(y_i - \sum_{j=1}^{P} \beta_j X_{ij})^2. \quad (6)$$

Here we have N discrete sampled time steps, and S, the sum squared error, is the sum of the errors squared. Equation 6 can be rewritten in matrix form as:

$$S = (Y - XB)^T (Y - XB) \quad (7)$$

$$Y = \begin{vmatrix} y_1 \\ \vdots \\ y_N \end{vmatrix} \; B = \begin{vmatrix} \beta_1 \\ \vdots \\ \beta_P \end{vmatrix}$$

Equation 7 gives the error of a discrete approximation, given the β parameters. We are attempting to find the best discrete approximation, therefore we are trying to minimize the error S. Taking S to be 0 in Equation 7, we can solve the matrix equation for the B parameters:

$$\hat{B} = (X^T X)^{-1} X^T Y \quad (8)$$

Equation 8 states that, in order to get the error S as close to 0 as possible, B needs to equal $(X^T X)^{-1} X^T Y$. Y is the signal we are trying to approximate, and X can be found if we know the previous values of Y at sampled time steps, and also previous inputs to the system in sampled time steps.

With Equation 8 we only need a sampled signal, and recordings of external stimulation, to create an approximation. Using the K-0 Equation 1 we generate a sample time series. We can create a sample time series using a K-0 by giving it varying intensities and durations of external stimulation. For example, we simulate 100ms of activity of a K-0 using the basic K-set equation. After 25ms of time we feed in external input with an intensity of 0.25 (arbitrary units), for 13 ms. Figure 2 shows the typical response of a K-0 unit to such a stimulation.

We create a representative signal of the K-0 dynamics by varying duration of stimulation from 1 to 50ms in 1ms increments, and intensity of stimulation from -0.5 (inhibition) to 0.5 (excitation) in 0.01 increments. We simulate all combinations of intensity and duration of the external stimulation to the K-0. The external stimulation represents the external input to the system (u in Equation 4), and the activation of the K-0 unit represents the signal we are approximating (y in Equation 4). The sample K-0 signal and inputs was recorded and used to solve for $\hat{B}$ in Equation 8. The values of the parameters that were determined to give he least square error for the KA discrete approximation are shown in Table I.

As another demonstration of the KA discrete approximation, we simulate a K-II and compare the signal with a KA-II system configured with the same values. Figure 3 shows the results this comparison. For both the K and KA systems, we created

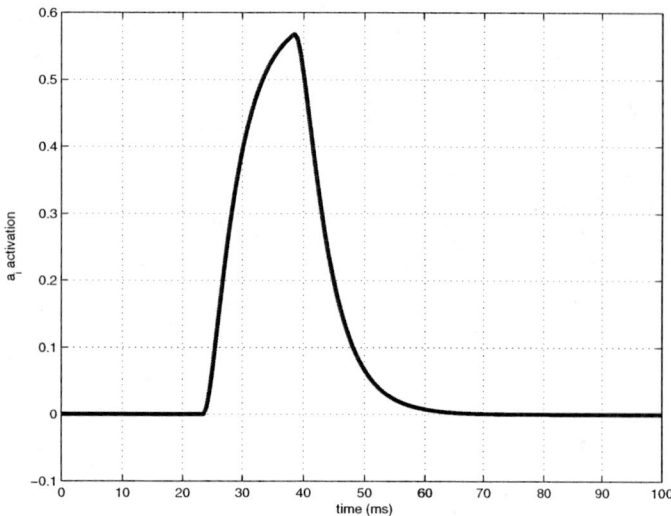

Fig. 2. Response of a K-0 unit to 13ms of stimulation with intensity of 0.25. Stimulation of the unit begins at t=25ms.

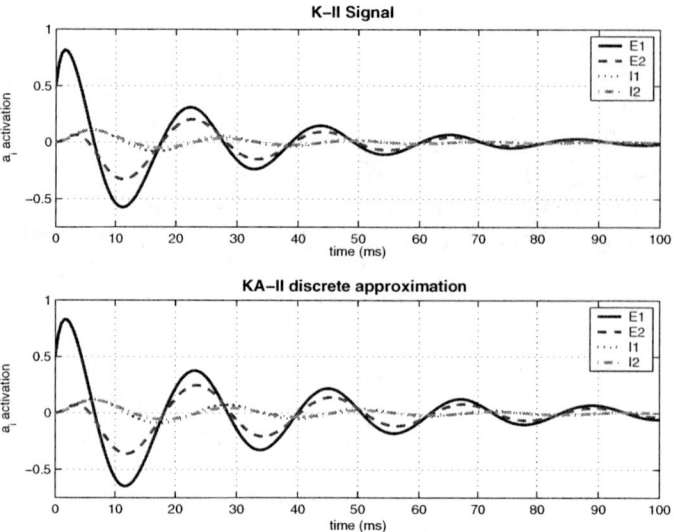

Fig. 3. Comparison of continuous K-II signal (top) with the KA-II discrete approximation (bottom).

TABLE I
KA DISCRETE APPROXIMATION PARAMETER RESULTS

a_1	1.6198
a_2	-0.6497
b_1	0.0234
b_2	0.0059

level II system of 4 units, connected as shown in Figure 1, bottom left. In both systems $w_{ee} = 0.3$, $w_{ei} = 5.0$, $w_{ie} = 0.2$ and $w_{ii} = 0.25$. Also both systems were started at the same initial conditions. The K-II, simulated in Matlab on a Pentium III 2.0Ghz using Matlab's ode45 function (an implementation of the Runge-Kutta integration method), takes 191.57 seconds of CPU time to simulate 12 seconds. The KA-II approximation on the same system takes 52 seconds to simulate the same 12 seconds of activity. A targeted discretization of the continuous K-sets yields much faster performance than general integration approximation methods. This is due to the nature of such general approximation methods, that can be very inefficient as they must be useful in the general case for many types of ODE equations. The targeted discretization approximates the continuous K-sets very well and is much faster to simulate than Runge-Kutta or Euler approximation methods.

As shown in Figure 3, the KA discretization approximates the K-set model fairly well. This good approximation occurs even though we are simulating a more complex network of 4 neural populations connected with various levels of positive and negative feedback among the units. The dynamics produced by the discretization remain relatively close to the desired system even in a system of units, even though it was only created using a sampled signal from the dynamics of a single unit. In the next section, we demonstrate using Evolutionary Robotics (ER) techniques to evolve a neural controller, using the KA discretization described above, to control a simulated robot.

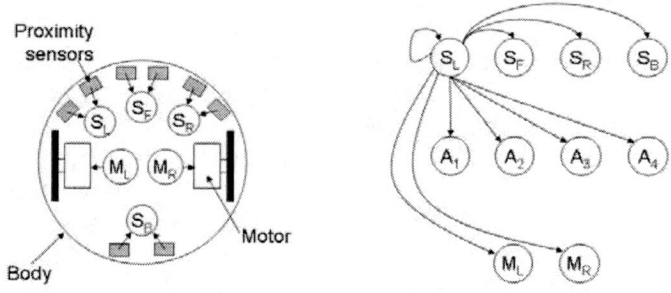

Fig. 4. Architecture used in evolution of neural controller. (Left) The Khepera robot. Each S_i is a KA unit and receives external stimulation from two proximity sensors. The two KA motor unit (M_i) activation levels control the speed of the two wheels of the robot. (Right) Each KA unit is fully connected to all other units (including itself), total of 10 connections per unit, 100 connections total.

III. EVOLUTION OF KA CONTROLLER FOR OBJECT AVOIDANCE

For this simulation we use a Khepera robot in a simulated environment using the Webots robot simulation software. Figure 4 gives the setup of the simulation. The Khepera robot has 8 proximity sensors spread around the perimeter of its body, and two individually controlled motors. We use four KA units to receive sensory input. Each KA unit receives external stimulation from two proximity sensors. Stimulation is scaled to an appropriate value and is linearly proportional to the activation of the external sensor. Two KA units will act as the output controllers for the motors. The activation of the two units will be translated into values for the two motors.

In addition to the 4 sensory and 2 motor KA units the simulation has 4 more KA associative units (labeled A_1 through A_4, Figure 4, right), for a total of 10 KA units all together. The 10 units are fully connected. That is, each unit may be potentially connected to each of the 9 other units, as well as to itself. Even motor units can be connected back to associative or even sensory units. This gives a potential of 100 connections in the simulation. Connections between units are real-valued numbers that can range from -1.0 to 1.0. Negative weights indicate inhibitory connections, and positive weights are excitatory connections.

Therefore the genome of the simulation consists of 100 real-valued numbers that can range from -1.0 to 1.0. We use a standard generational genetic algorithm with a fixed population size. A population of 50 individuals is evolved using rank-based truncated selection (10 best individuals, each generating 5 offspring), one-point crossover (p=0.1 per pair), bit mutation (p=0.05 of +/- 5% change in weight), and elitism (size=1) so that the best individual is always copied into the next generation.

Each individual of the population is decoded and tested on the simulated Khepera robot two times for 30 seconds each. Our KA model use 0.5ms discretization steps, so a 30 second simulation consists of 60,000 discrete time steps. Sensory input and motor output are only sampled once every 100ms. This means that the value of the proximity sensors will be used for 200 simulated time steps before being sampled again, and likewise motor output values are only updated every 100ms (200 time steps). We use a standard fitness function [1] that rewards the robots for going as straight and as fast as possible. The fitness function ϕ is the sum of the speeds of the two wheels v_{left} and v_{right}, measured by the simulated optical encoder, at every 100ms sampling time step, averaged over T time steps available (here T = 300 + 300)

$$\phi = \frac{1}{T} \sum_{t}^{T} (v_{left}^{t} + v_{right}^{t}) \qquad (9)$$

This fitness function selects individuals for the ability to go as straight and as fast forward as possible. But, if the robot gets stuck against a wall, the wheels will rotate considerably less. Therefore the fitness function also implicitly selects for individuals that can avoid walls.

In Figure 5 we show an example of the behavior of an evolved individual. In this figure we have plotted the path taken by the best individual evolved after 40 generations in the simulated environment. The figure shows the path of the individual for a 30 second trial. The individual does well in the environment, moving fast and avoiding the obstacles.

IV. CONCLUSIONS

In this paper we have developed a simplified version of a discrete approximation of the K-set neurodynamical population model. The discretization provides good approximation of the original continuous K-set equations, even when we start simulating networks of interacting K units. It is also much faster and simpler and provides simple enough units that we can perform ER techniques to evolve neurocontrollers using such population models for autonomous robots.

The KA discrete approximation was then used to demonstrate the evolution of such a controller for a simple robot. This

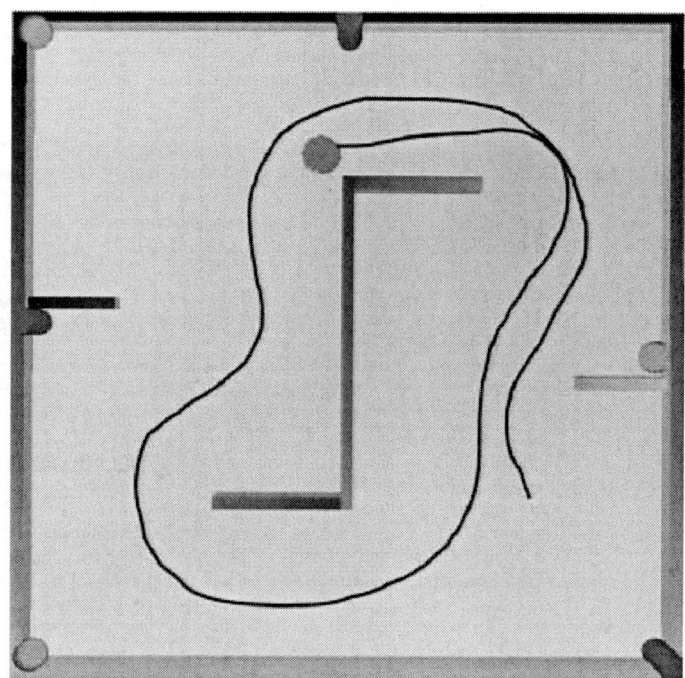

Fig. 5. Path of best performing robot after 40 generations.

demonstration shows that KA units can be evolved to control a robot for simple navigation tasks, much as previous work using single neuron models has shown. The evolved controller works with only 10 units to provide simple but effective movement in the environment.

The KA discretization is also capable of replicating the aperiodic dynamics of the K-III set, when 3 or more KA-II units are connected with one another. The evolved controller presented in this paper does not produce chaotic dynamics in solving the navigation task, thus it is similar in scope to previous neurodynamic models that rely on fixed point and oscillatory dynamics [22]. Future work will concentrate on evolving controllers using KA-II oscillatory units as basic pieces of the evolving architecture. Combining KA-II units should allow a neurocontroller that produces chaotic dynamics, and will let us determine if an evolutionary approach can find robust controllers that take advantage of such dynamics in the perceive/think/act cycle of a simple autonomous robot.

ACKNOWLEDGMENT

This work was supported in part by NASA Intelligent Systems Research Grant NCC-2-1244.

REFERENCES

[1] S. Nolfi and D. Floreano, *Evolutionary Robotics: The Biology, Intelligence, and Technology of Self-Organizing Machines*. Cambridge, MA: The MIT Press, 2000.
[2] D. Floreano and C. Mattiussi, "Evolution of spiking neural controllers for autonomous vision-based robots," in *Evolutionary Robotics IV*, T. Gomi, Ed. Berlin: Springer-Verlag, 2001, pp. 38–61.
[3] W. Gerstner, "Associative memory in a network of biological neurons," in *Advances in Neural Information Processing Systems 3*, R. P. Lippmann, J. E. Moody, and D. S. Touretzky, Eds. San Mateo, CA: Morgan Kaufmann, 1991, pp. 85–90.

[4] W. J. Freeman, "The wave packet: An action potential for the 21st century," *Journal of Integrative Neuroscience*, 2003, in press.

[5] C. A. Skarda and W. J. Freeman, "How brains make chaos in order to make sense of the world," *Behavioral and Brain Sciences*, vol. 10, pp. 161–195, 1987.

[6] W. J. Freeman, "Simulation of chaotic EEG patterns with a dynamic model of the olfactory system," *Biological Cybernetics*, vol. 56, pp. 139–150, 1987.

[7] I. Aradi, G. Barna, and P. Erdi, "Chaos and learning in the olfactory bulb," *International Journal Intelligent Systems*, vol. 1091, pp. 89–117, 1995.

[8] I. Tsuda, "Towards an interpretation of dynamic neural activity in terms of chaotic dynamical systems," *Behavioral and Brain Sciences*, vol. 24, no. 4, pp. 793–847, 2001.

[9] L. Kay, K. Shimoide, and W. J. Freeman, "Comparison of EEG time series from rat olfactory system with model composed of nonlinear coupled oscillators," *International Journal of Bifurcation and Chaos*, vol. 5, no. 3, pp. 849–858, 1995.

[10] J. J. Hopfield, "Neuronal networks and physical systems with emergent collective computational abilities," *Proceedings of the National Academy of Science*, vol. 81, pp. 3058–3092, 1982.

[11] W. J. Freeman, B. C. Burke, and M. D. Holmes, "Aperiodic phase resetting in scalp EEG of beta-gamma oscillations by state transitions at alpha-theta rates," *Human Brain Mapping*, vol. 19, pp. 248–272, 2003.

[12] R. Kozma and W. J. Freeman, "Chaotic resonance - methods and applications for robust classification of noisy and variable patterns," *International Journal of Bifurcation and Chaos*, vol. 11, no. 6, pp. 1607–1629, 2001.

[13] ——, "Basic principles of the KIV model and its application to the navigation problem," *Journal of Integrative Neuroscience*, vol. 2, no. 1, pp. 125–145, 2003.

[14] R. Kozma and P. Ankaraju, "Learning spatial navigation using chaotic neural network model," in *Proceedings of the IJCNN 2003 International Joint Conference on Neural Networks*, Portland, OR, July 2003, pp. 1476–1479.

[15] D. Harter and R. Kozma, "Chaotic neurodynamics for autonomous agents," *IEEE Transactions on Neural Networks*, 2005, in press.

[16] W. J. Freeman, *Mass Action in the Nervous System*. New York, NY: Academic Press, 1975.

[17] ——, *How Brains Make Up Their Minds*. London: Weidenfeld & Nicolson, 1999.

[18] ——, "The physiology of perception," *Scientific American*, vol. 264, no. 2, pp. 78–85, 1991.

[19] J. C. Principe, V. G. Tavares, and J. G. Harris, "Design and implementation of a biologically realistic olfactory cortex in analog VLSI," *Proceedings of the IEEE*, vol. 89, pp. 1030–1051, 2001.

[20] A. J. Jerri, *Linear Difference Equations with Discrete Transform Methods*. Kluwer Academic, 1996.

[21] Z. Kowalczuk, "Discrete approximation of continuous-time systems: a survey," *IEEE Proceedings-G*, vol. 140, no. 4, pp. 264–278, 1993.

[22] R. D. Beer, "The dynamics of active categorical perception in an evolved model agent," *Adaptive Behavior*, vol. 11, pp. 209–243, 2003.

Data Visualization Methodologies for Data Mining Systems in Bioinformatics

A. Staiano, A. Ciaramella, G. Raiconi, R. Tagliaferri
Department of Mathematics and Informatics
University of Salerno
Fisciano, Italy
E-mail: {astaiano,ciaram,gianni,robtag}@unisa.it

R. Amato, G. Longo, G. Miele, C. Donalek
Department of Physics
University Federico II
Napoli, Italy
E-mail: {roamato,longo,miele,donalek}@na.infn.it

Abstract— Bioinformatics systems benefit from the use of data mining strategies to locate interesting and pertinent relationships within massive information. For example, data mining methods can ascertain and summarize the set of genes responding to a certain level of stress in an organism. Even a cursory glance through the literature in journals, reveals the persistent role of data mining in experimental biology. Integrating data mining within the context of experimental investigations is central to bioinformatics software. In this paper we describe the framework of Probabilistic Principal Surfaces, a latent variable model which offers a large variety of appealing visualization capabilities and which can be successfully integrated in the context of microarray analysis. A preprocessing phase consisting of a nonlinear PCA neural network which seems to be very useful to deal with noisy and time dependent nature of microarray data has been added to this framework.

I. INTRODUCTION

Many results in experimental biology first appear in image form: a photo of an organism, cells, gels, or microarray scans. As the quantity of these results accelerates, automatic extraction of features and meaning from experimental images becomes crucial. At the other end of the data pipeline, naïve 2D or 3D visualizations alone are inadequate for exploring bioinformatics data. Biologists need a visual environment that facilitates exploring high-dimensional data dependent on many parameters. Hybrid approaches that combine powerful algorithms with interactive visualization tools will join the strengths of fast processors with detailed understanding of domain experts. In this context research needs further work into bioinformatics visualization to develop tools that will meet the upcoming genomic and proteomic challenges. At this aim we provide an integrated environment for a $3D$ visualization of high dimensional biomedical data enabling the user to:

- project and visualize data on a spherical surface (which provide a useful continuous manifold which can be rotated and manipulated in several ways) ;
- find out a number of natural cluster present in the data by means of a wide variety of clustering approaches;
- visualize the clusters and the data therein;
- perform deeper studies on the data by localizing region of interests and interacting with the data themselves;
- interact with data, choose the points of montest, visualize their neighbors and similar points, print of all related information etc.;
- evaluate the relevance of each feature in the resulting trained model and visualize it by means of pie or bar charts.

The system is a latent variable model, namely the Probabilistic Principal Surfaces (PPS)[3], whose goal is to model a probability density function of the input data samples. Generally speaking, a latent variable model is defined by associating a latent variable space (usually two or three dimensional) to a D-dimensional input data space in which latent variables lie in a uniform distributed way. The two spaces are linked together through a nonlinear function (usually in the form of a RBF Neural Network [1] or a Generalized linear regression model) which maps every latent variable into a corresponding point of the input space. These points represent the centres of a set of Gaussian density functions. Therefore, it is possible to define a constrained mixture model which can be trained by the Expectation Maximization algorithm. Expressed in a more formal way (see [4] and [16] for more details), PPS defines a non-linear, parametric mapping $\mathbf{y}(\mathbf{x}; \mathbf{W})$ from a Q-dimensional latent space ($\mathbf{x} \in \mathbb{R}^Q$) to a D-dimensional data space ($\mathbf{t} \in \mathbb{R}^D$), where normally $Q < D$. The mapping $\mathbf{y}(\mathbf{x}; \mathbf{W})$ (defined continuous and differentiable) maps every point in the latent space to a point into the data space. PPS builds a constrained mixture of Gaussians (where the priors are all fixed to $\frac{1}{M}$)

$$p(\mathbf{t}|\mathbf{W}, \mathbf{\Sigma}_m) = \frac{1}{M} \sum_{m=1}^{M} p(\mathbf{t}|\mathbf{x}_m, \mathbf{W}, \mathbf{\Sigma}_m), \quad (1)$$

and each component has the form:

$$\frac{|\mathbf{\Sigma}_m|^{-\frac{1}{2}}}{2\pi^{\frac{D}{2}}} e^{\left\{-\frac{1}{2}(\mathbf{y}(\mathbf{x}_m;\mathbf{W})-\mathbf{t})\mathbf{\Sigma}_m^{-1}(\mathbf{y}(\mathbf{x}_m;\mathbf{W})-\mathbf{t})^T\right\}}, \quad (2)$$

where $\mathbf{t}$ is a point in the data space and $\mathbf{\Sigma}_m^{-1}$ denotes the noise variance. The covariance is defined as

$$\mathbf{\Sigma}_m = \frac{\alpha}{\beta} \sum_{q=1}^{Q} \mathbf{e}_q(\mathbf{x})\mathbf{e}_q^T(\mathbf{x}) + \frac{(D - \alpha Q)}{\beta(D - Q)} \sum_{d=Q+1}^{D} \mathbf{e}_d(\mathbf{x})\mathbf{e}_\mathbf{d}^T(\mathbf{x}), \quad (3)$$

$$0 < \alpha < \frac{D}{Q}$$

where α is a clamping factor and
- $\{e_q(x)\}_{q=1}^Q$ is the set of orthonormal vectors tangential to the manifold at $y(x;w)$,
- $\{e_d(x)\}_{d=Q+1}^D$ is the set of orthonormal vectors orthogonal to the manifold in $y(x;w)$.

The complete set of orthonormal vectors $\{e_d(x)\}_{d=1}^D$ spans $\mathcal{R}^D$. The EM algorithm[6] can be used to estimate the PPS parameters W and β, while the clamping factor is fixed by the user and is assumed to be constant during the EM iterations. The peculiarity of PPS is the form of the covariance structure of the mixture: it is parameterized by a so called clamping factor which determines the shape and the orientation of the covariance. The form of the mapping $y(x;w)$ is defined as a generalized linear regression model

$$y(x;w) = W\phi(x) \quad (4)$$

where the elements of $\phi(x)$ consist of L fixed basis functions $\{\phi_l(x)\}_{l=1}^L$, and W is a $D \times L$ matrix.

If $Q = 3$ is chosen, a spherical manifold [3] can be constructed using a PPS with nodes $\{x_m\}_{m=1}^M$ arranged regularly on the surface of a sphere in $\mathbb{R}^3$ latent space, with the latent basis functions evenly distributed on the sphere at a lower density. The sphere provides a continuous manifold onto which project the data and is particularly well suited for the visualization of high-D data since it is able to better characterize the sparsity and periphery of the data samples when their dimension increases (curse of dimensionality). Since the latent space is three dimensional, it is possible to visualize the input data points, in fact, after a spherical PPS model is fitted to the data, the data themselves are projected into the latent space as points onto a sphere (see Fig. 2). The latent manifold coordinates $\hat{x}_n$ of each data point t_n are computed as

$$\hat{x}_n \equiv \langle x|t_n \rangle = \int x p(x|t) dx = \sum_{m=1}^M r_{mn} x_m$$

where r_{mn} are the latent variable responsibilities, defined as

$$r_{mn} = p(x_m|t_n) = \frac{p(t_n|x_m)P(x_m)}{\sum_{m'=1}^M p(t_n|x_{m'})P(x_{m'})} =$$

$$= \frac{p(t_n|x_m)}{\sum_{m'=1}^M p(t_n|x_{m'})}.$$

The responsibility r_{mn} corresponds to the posterior probability that that the nth data point was generated by the mth component. Since $\|x_m\| = 1$ and $\sum_m r_{mn} = 1$, for $n = 1,\ldots,N$, these coordinates lie within a unit sphere, i.e. $\|\hat{x}_n\| \leq 1$.
The basic PPS model, while showing powerful abilities, only permits the possibility to project the data into the latent space thus providing no way to properly exploit the resulting trained density model and to interact with data. Therefore all the system features of the integrated environment described before have been added by us [14], [16] thus providing an effective visualization and clustering tool through which interact with data for complex scientific data mining activities. The remainder of this paper is organized as follows: section II describe the visualization possibilities offered by our framework, while section III gives a detailed description of the preprocessing based on nonlinear PCA. Section IV shows results obtained on a yeast gene microarray data set. Finally, in section V, conclusions close the paper.

II. SPHERICAL PPS FOR VISUALIZATION

Spherical PPS can be used to produce different kinds of plots in a much more effective way than the simple projections of data onto the latent manifold. For instance, some significant information is gained by plotting the probability density of the input data onto the latent sphere. This plot gives a first idea about the number of clusters inherently present in the data. The simultaneous plot of the clusters and of the points therein is another useful plot for a data miner. All the plots onto the spherical manifold can be easily looked at by interactively rotating the sphere. In the following we shall describe these plots and a further plot concerning with the relevance of the input data components on each latent variable.

A. Visualizing the latent variable responsibilities on the sphere

A first insight on the number of agglomerates localized into the spherical latent manifold is provided by mean of the responsibilities for each latent variable [14], [15]. If we build a spherical manifold which is composed by a set of faces each one delimited by four vertices (each one corresponding to a latent variable), then we can color each face with colors varying in intensity on the basis of the value of the responsibility associate to that given vertex (and hence, to each latent variable). The overall result is that the sphere will contain regions denser than others and this information is easily visible and understandable (see Fig. 3 as an example); obviously, denser areas of the spherical manifold might contain more than one cluster, and this calls for further investigations.

B. A method to visualize clusters on the sphere

Once the user has an overall idea of the number of clusters on the sphere, he can exploit this information through the use of agglomerative hierarchical clustering techniques [7], [8] to find out the clusters. This task is accomplished by running the clustering algorithm on the Gaussian centers in the data space. Once the centers have been agglomerated, the points for which the centers are falling in the same agglomerate, are assigned to the same cluster. The projections of the points into the latent space are then used to visualize the clusters onto the latent sphere [15] (see Fig. 4).

C. Parameter incidence of latent variable computation

An interesting issue is the assessment of the incidence of each input data feature on the latent variables (see Fig. 5) which helps to understand the relation between the features and the clusters found. The feature incidences are computed by evaluating the probability density of the input vector components with respect to each latent variable.

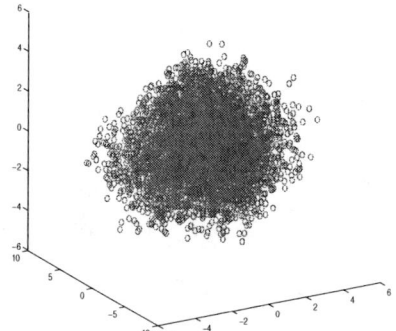

Fig. 1. Yeast Gene Data Set: $3D$ PCA projection.

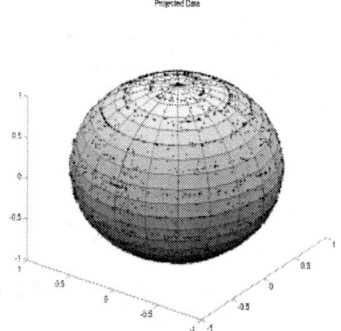

Fig. 2. Yeast Gene Data Set: Data point projections in the latent space.

Specifically, let $\{\mathbf{t}_n\}_{n=1}^N$ be the set of the D-dimensional input data, i.e $\mathbf{t}_n = (t_{n1}, \ldots, t_{nD}) \in \mathbb{R}^D$ and $\{\mathbf{x}_m\}_{m=1}^M$ be the set of latent variables with $\mathbf{x}_m \in \mathbb{R}^3$. For each data point $\mathbf{t}_n = (t_{n1}, \ldots, t_{nD})$ we want to evaluate $p(t_{ni}/t_{n1}, \ldots, t_{ni-1}, t_{ni+1}, \ldots, t_{nD}, \mathbf{x}_m)$, for $m = 1, \ldots, M$ and $i = 1, \ldots, D$. In detail

$$p(t_{ni}/t_{n1}, \ldots, t_{ni-1}, t_{ni+1}, \ldots, t_{nD}, \mathbf{x}_m) = \quad (5)$$
$$\frac{p(t_{n1}, t_{n2}, \ldots, t_{nD}, \mathbf{x}_m)}{p(t_{n1}, \ldots, t_{ni-1}, t_{ni+1}, \ldots, t_{nD}, \mathbf{x}_m)} =$$
$$= \frac{p(t_{n1}, \ldots, t_{nD}/\mathbf{x}_m) P(\mathbf{x}_m)}{p(t_{n1}, \ldots, t_{ni-1}, t_{ni+1}, \ldots, t_{nD}/\mathbf{x}_m) P(\mathbf{x}_m)} =$$
$$\frac{p(t_{n1}, \ldots, t_{nD}/\mathbf{x}_m)}{p(t_{n1}, \ldots, t_{ni-1}, y_{ni+1}, \ldots, t_{nD}/\mathbf{x}_m)}.$$

The last term is easily obtained since the numerator is simply the m-th Gaussian component of the mixture computed by the PPS model with mean $y(\mathbf{x}_m; \mathbf{W})$ and oriented variance Σ_m, while the denominator is the same Gaussian component in which the i-th component is missing. Finally the mean of (5) over the N input data points, for each $\mathbf{x}_m$, is computed.

III. NON-LINEAR PCA BASED FEATURE EXTRACTION MODEL FOR PREPROCESSING

Genetic data, particularly microarray data, have a strongly noisy nature, and in all the papers concerning with such a kind

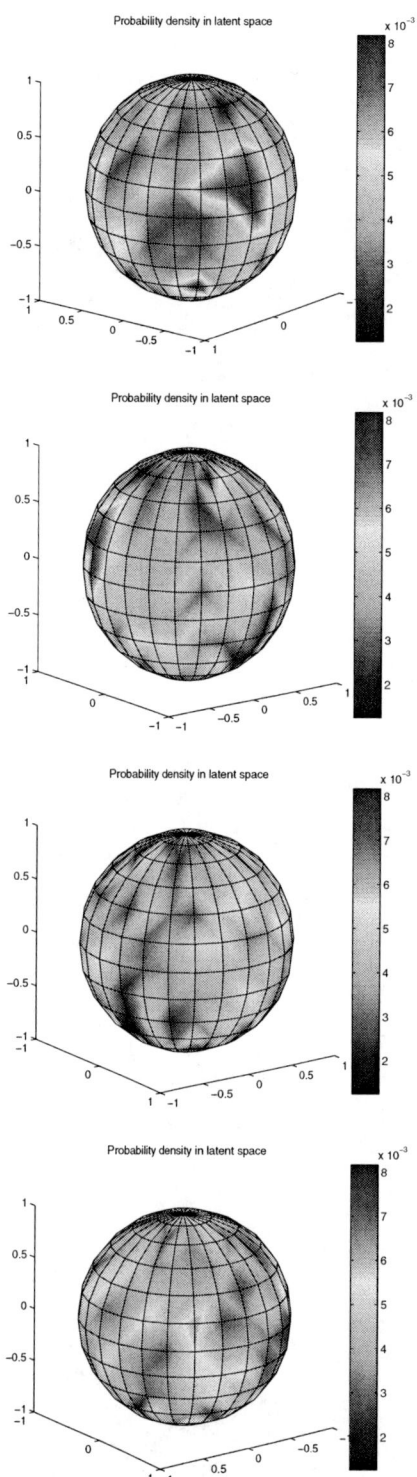

Fig. 3. Data probability density function in the latent space. The figure displays four points of view obtained by rotating the sphere. Looking at this density function we could discover about 30 clusters. This value can be used to fix the number of clusters of k-means or an agglomerative hierarchical clustering procedure.

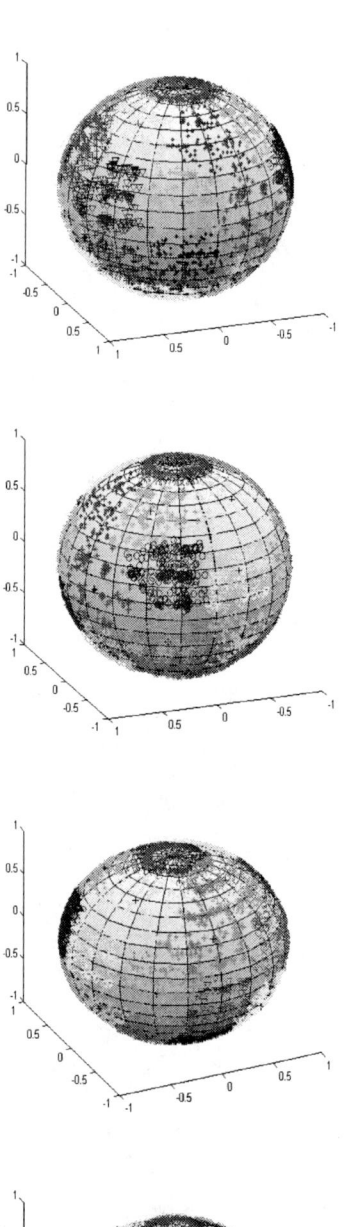

Fig. 4. The 30 computed clusters by the agglomerative hierarchical clustering. The figure displays four points of view obtained by rotating the sphere. It is worth noting how most of the computed clusters do not overlap each other. The point falling in common region of the clusters need further understanding.

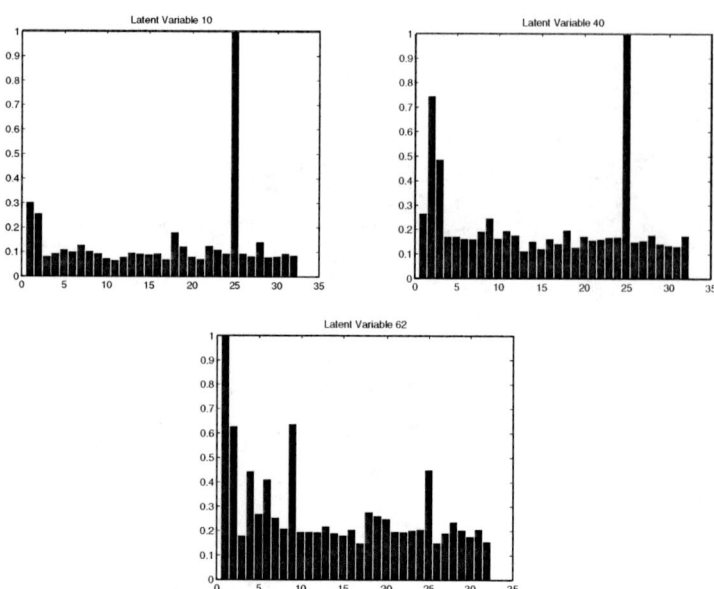

Fig. 5. From left to right: feature (32 in this example) incidences on latent variables 10,40,62

of experiments researchers focus on the preprocessing phase before applying whatever machine learning model for the analysis process. Preprocessing, therefore, assumes a crucial role in this context. Microarrays produce (often, unevenly sampled) time series data which can be preprocessed in several ways [13]. In our approach we extract the features by using an approach based on a non-linear PCA method that permit to extract the eigenvectors directly from the unevenly sampled data. The approach is based on a novel periodicity estimator, STIMA algorithm, described in [5], [17], [18].

A. PCA Neural Nets

Principal Component analysis (PCA) is a widely used technique in data analysis. Mathematically, it is defined as follows: let $\mathbf{C} = E(\mathbf{xx}^T)$ be the covariance matrix of L-dimensional zero mean input data vectors $\mathbf{x}$. The i-th principal component of $\mathbf{x}$ is defined as $\mathbf{x}^T\mathbf{c}(i)$, where $\mathbf{c}(i)$ is the normalized eigenvector of $\mathbf{C}$ corresponding to the i-th largest eigenvalue $\lambda(i)$. The subspace spanned by the principal eigenvectors $\mathbf{c}(1), \ldots, \mathbf{c}(M), (M < L)$ is called the PCA subspace (of dimensionality M) [11], [12]. PCA's can be neurally realized in various ways [9], [10], [11]. The PCA neural network used by us is a one layer feedforward neural network which is able to extract the principal components of the stream of input vectors. Typically, Hebbian type learning rules are used, based on the one unit learning algorithm originally proposed by [11]. Many different versions and extensions of this basic algorithm have been proposed during the recent years; see [9], [10], [11].

B. Non-Linear PCA Based Feature Extractor

This extractor is based on a nonlinear PCA Neural Network that is used to extract the principal components of the autocorrelation matrix of the input sources.

The features extraction process can be divided in the following two steps:
- Preprocessing: we first calculate and subtract the average pattern to obtain zero mean process;
- Neural computing: the fundamental learning parameters are: i) the initial $\mathbf{W}$ weight matrix; ii) the number of neurons, which is the number p of principal eigenvectors that we need; iii) γ, the nonlinear learning function parameter; iv) the learning rate μ; v) early stopping parmeter ε (see [5], [17], [18] for a different early stopping);

We then initialize the weight matrix $\mathbf{W}$ assigning the classical small random values. Otherwise we can use the first patterns of the signal as the columns of the matrix.

We then have the following general algorithm:
- STEP 1: initialize the weight vectors $\mathbf{w}_0(i)$, $\forall i = 1, ..., p$ with small random values, or with orthonormalized signal patterns. Then initialize the learning threshold ϵ and the learning rate μ. Then reset pattern counter $k = 0$.
- STEP 2: input the $k-th$ pattern

$$\mathbf{x}_k = [x(k), ..., x(k+N+1)]$$

where N is the number of input components.
- STEP 3: calculate the output for each neuron $y(j) = \mathbf{w}^T(j)\mathbf{x}_i$, $\forall i = 1, ..., p$.
- STEP 4: $\forall i = 1, ..., p$ modify the weights

$$\mathbf{w}_{k+1}(i) = \mathbf{w}_k(i) + \mu_k g(y_k(i))\mathbf{e}_k(i)$$

where $\mathbf{w}_{k+1}(i) = [w_{k+1}(i,1), ..., w_{k+1}(i,N)]$ and $g(y)$ is the $\tanh(y)$ function that derives from the $\log\cosh(y)$ of the nonlinear PCA objective function.
- STEP 5: convergence test. If

$$\sum_{i=1}^{p}\sum_{j=1}^{N}(w_{k+1}(i,j) - w_k(i,j)) < \varepsilon$$

, then GO TO STEP 7.
- STEP 6: $k = k + 1$. GO TO STEP 2.
- STEP 7. End.s

IV. EXPERIMENTS

In [13] a comprehensive catalog of yeast genes whose transcript levels vary periodically within the cell cycle is provided. In order to produce the catalog, samples from yeast cultures synchronized with different experiments were used. The data set consist of a set of 6125 genes subject to four different experiments. Each experiment consists of a series of measurements at different time points. The overall data set consist, therefore, of 6125 genes and 73 parameters (see Fig. 1 for its $3D$ PCA projection). In [13] a type of agglomerative hierarchical clustering [8] was used in order to identify clusters of genes behaving similarly in each experiment and which represent groups of apparently co-regulated genes. These clusters provide a solid basis for understanding the transcriptional mechanism of cell cycle regulation. In order to make the data set more apt to be processed with PPS, we first eliminated the

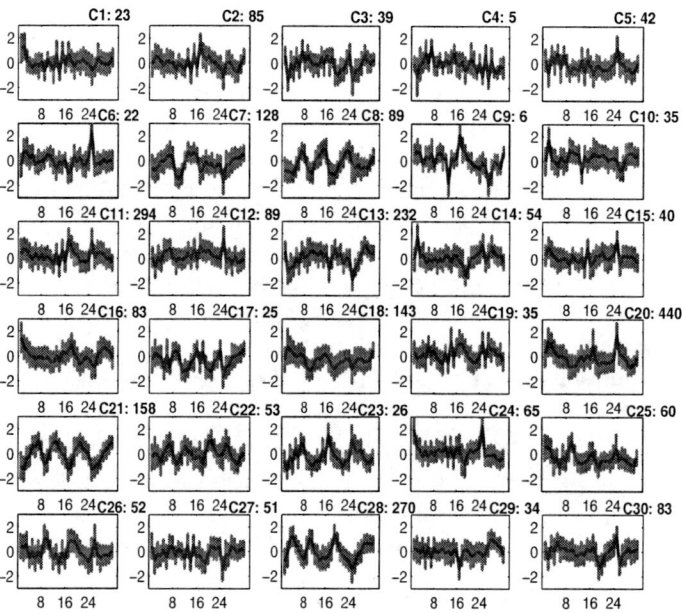

Fig. 6. PPS cluster prototype periodic behaviors and error bars (3σ) showing the standard deviation of genes from the prototypes for a fixed cluster. On the top of each subplot are the cluster number and the number of genes within each cluster.

genes, for each experiment, having too many missing features, and then applied the nonlinear PCA described in section III. So doing each experiment, for each gene, was reduced to 8 measurements. Hence, the adopted data set consisted of 5425 genes and 32 features. We then used a PPS with 266 latent variables and 40 latent basis functions and a clamping factor α set to 0.5. All these parameters were set empirically. After the completion of the training phase we projected the data into the latent space and computed the responsibility for each latent variable as shown in Fig. 2 and 3. The result of our analysis led us to identify 30 clusters whose prototype behaviors are depicted in Figure 6. It is interesting to note how the parameter relevances distinguish between latent variables belonging to different clusters. For example, as illustrated in figure 5 latent variables 10, 40 and 62 belong to three different clusters computed by our system. While latent variable 10 seems to be mostly dominated by feature 25, latent variable 40 has an higher average relevance dominated by features 25, 1, 2 and 3. Latent variable 62, instead, has an higher relevance for features from 1 to 9 and feature 25. The biological meaning of this analysis is currently under study.

V. CONCLUSIONS

We discussed a machine learning data mining framework based on Probabilistic Principal Surfaces for a bioinformatics system. Our aim was to highlight the power of the proposed method rather than showing a specific application or problem solved by the model. By the way, the next step of this work will show the complete meaning of all the preliminary results just illustrated. PPS is a very powerful and efficient model in several data mining activities, and in particular for high-D data visualization and clustering. Above all, the spherical

PPS, which consists of a spherical latent manifold lying in a three dimensional latent space, is better suitable to high-D data since the sphere is able to capture the sparsity and periphery of data in large input spaces which are due to the curse of dimensionality. Even though the results are in the preliminary phase from a biological point of view, PPS seem to offer a promising approach for aiding the biologist work.

It is worth noting that fundamental, in our analysis, is the nonlinear PCA preprocessing phase, since this extractor is robust with respect to the noise and permits to obtain evenly sampled features from unevenly sampled data.

Currently we are pursuing two directions to further enhance the capabilities of our system:

1) to develop a clustering algorithm able to directly exploit the PPS mixture Gaussian density in order to compute the optimal number of clusters.
2) to build a hierarchical PPS for constructing localized nonlinear projection manifold as it was already done for GTM [19], and previously for a linear latent variable model [2].

REFERENCES

[1] C.M. Bishop: Neural Networks for Pattern Recognition, Oxford University Press (1995)

[2] C.M. Bishop and M.E. Tipping, *A hierarchical latent variable model for data visualization*, IEEE Transactions on Pattern Analysis and Machine Intelligence 20(3), 281293,1998

[3] K. Chang: *Nonlinear Dimensionality Reduction Using Probabilistic Principal Surfaces*, PhD Thesis, Department of Electrical and Computer Engineering, The University of Texas at Austin, USA, (2000)

[4] K. Chang, J. Ghosh: *A unified Model for Probabilistic Principal Surfaces*, IEEE Transactions on Pattern Analysis and Machine Intelligence, Vol. 23, NO. 1, (2001)

[5] A. Ciaramella, C. Bongardo, H. D. Aller, M. F. Aller, G. De Zotti, A. Lähteenmaki, G. Longo, L. Milano, R. Tagliaferri, H. Teräsranta, M. Tornikoski, S. Urpo, A Multifrequency Analysis of Radio Variability of Blazars, Astronomy & Astrophysics Journal, vol. 419, Page(s): 485-500, 2004

[6] A.P. Dempster, N.M. Laird, D.B. Rubin, *Maximum-Likelihood from Incomplete Data Via the EM Algorithm*, J. Royal Statistical Soc., Vol. 39, NO. 1, 1977

[7] R.O. Duda, P.E. Hart, D.G. Stork, *Pattern Classification*, John Wiley and Sons, 2001

[8] M.B. Eisen, P.T. Spellman, P.O. Brown, D. Botstein: *Cluster analysis and display of genome-wide expressionpatterns*, PNAS, 95:14863–14868 (1998)

[9] J. Karhunen , J. Joutsensalo , Representation and Separation of Signals Using non-linear PCA type Learing, Neural Networks, vol. 7, pp. 113-127, 1994

[10] J. Karhunen , J. Joutsensalo , Generalizations of Principal Component Analysys, Optimization Problems and Neural Networks, Neural Networks, vol. 8, pp. 549-563, 1995

[11] E. Oja , H. Ogawa , J. Wangviwattana , 1991, Learning in nonlinear constrained Hebbian network. In T. Kohonen et al. (Eds.), Artificial neural networks, North-Holland, Amsterdam, p. 385

[12] E. Oja , J. Karhunen , L. Wang , R. Vigario , 1996, Principal and independent components in neural networks - recent developments. In Marinaro M., Tagliaferri R. (eds), WIRN Vietri '95,World Scientific Pu., Singapore, p. 16-35

[13] P.T. Spellman, G. Sherlock, M.Q. Zhang, V.R. Iyer, K. Anders, M.B. Eisen, P.O. Brown, D. Botstein, B. Futcher, Comprehensive identification of cell cycle-regulated genes of the yeast saccharomyces cerevisiae by microarray hybridization, Molecular Biology of the Cell, 9:3273–3297 (1998)

[14] A. Staiano: *Unsupervised Neural Networks for the Extraction of Scientific Information from Astronomical Data*, PhD thesis, University of Salerno, ITALY (2003).

[15] A. Staiano, L. De Vinco, R. Tagliaferri, G. Longo, *Advanced Data Mining and Visualizations with Probabilistic Principal Surfaces*, in MML'04 - Mathematical Methodsfor Learning Proceedings, Como, Italy, (2004)

[16] A. Staiano, R. Tagliaferri, G. Longo et al., Probabilistic Principal Surfaces for Yeast Gene Microarray Data Mining, R.Rastogi, K.Morik, M.Bramer and X.Wu (eds.) (2004) Proceedings of the Fourth IEEE International Conference on Data Mining: ICDM 2004, Brighton (UK), pp. 202-208.

[17] R. Tagliaferri, N. Pelosi, A. Ciaramella, G. Longo, M. Milano, F. Barone, Soft Computing Methodologies for Spectral Analysis in Cyclostratigraphy, Computer and Geosciences, vol. 27, issue 5, Page(s): 535-548, June 2001;

[18] R. Tagliaferri, A. Ciaramella, L. Milano, F. Barone, G. Longo, Spectral Analysis of Stellar Light Curves by Means of Neural Networks, Astronomy and Astrophysics Supplement Series vol. 137, Page(s): 391-405, 1999.

[19] P. Tino, I. Nabney,*Hierarchical GTM: constructing localized non-linear projection manifolds in a principled way*, IEEE Transactions on Pattern Analysis and Machine Intelligence, in print

Random projections for assessing gene expression cluster stability

Alberto Bertoni
DSI, Dipartimento di Scienze dell' Informazione,
Università degli Studi di Milano,
Via Comelico 39, Milano, Italy
E-mail: bertoni@dsi.unimi.it

Giorgio Valentini
DSI, Dipartimento di Scienze dell' Informazione,
Università degli Studi di Milano,
Via Comelico 39, Milano, Italy
E-mail: valentini@dsi.unimi.it

Abstract— Clustering analysis of gene expression is characterized by the very high dimensionality and low cardinality of the data, and two important related topics are the validation and the estimate of the number of the obtained clusters. In this paper we focus on the estimate of the stability of the clusters. Our approach to this problem is based on random projections obeying the Johnson-Lindenstrauss lemma, by which gene expression data may be projected into randomly selected low dimensional subspaces, approximately preserving pairwise distances between examples. We experiment with different types of random projections, comparing empirical and theoretical distortions induced by randomized embeddings between euclidean metric spaces, and we present cluster-stability measures that may be used to validate and to quantitatively assess the reliability of the clusters obtained by a large class of clustering algorithms. Experimental results with high dimensional synthetic and DNA microarray data show the effectiveness of the proposed approach.

I. INTRODUCTION

Clustering methods may discover gene expression signatures related to specific biological processes or to specific diseases. Moreover unsupervised learning methods, exploiting the overall gene expression profile of a patient, may research and discover subclasses of pathologies that cannot be detected with traditional biochemical, histopathological and clinical criteria [4].

Two of the main concerns with gene expression clustering analysis are the estimate of the number of clusters in a dataset, and the stability of the obtained clusters [3]. Indeed in many cases we have no sufficient biological knowledge to "a priori" evaluate both the number of clusters (e.g. the number of biologically distinct tumor classes), as well as the validity of the discovered clusters (e.g. the reliability of new discovered tumor classes).

Several approaches for assessing the reproducibility and stability of clustering patterns in gene expression data have been recently proposed [8], [9], [13].

In this paper we present an approach that exploits the very high dimensionality and relatively low cardinality of gene expression data, using multiple random projections of the original data, to assess the reliability of the discovered clusters. The main idea behind our approach consists in evaluating the stability of the clusters discovered in the original high dimensional space comparing them with the clusters discovered in randomly projected lower dimensional subspaces. To this end we use the concept of random projections with bounded metric distortions, according to the Johnson-Lindenstrauss (*JL*) theory [7].

The proposed method is related to the Smolkin and Gosh [12] approach based on an unsupervised version of the random subspace method [5]. We extend the unsupervised random subspace approach to more general random projections, in the framework of random embeddings between euclidean spaces, and we propose a new cluster stability measure based on similarity between randomly projected data.

In the next section we present a brief introduction to randomized embeddings of metric spaces, focusing on random projections obeying the *JL* lemma. In Sect. III we compare the theoretical and empirical distortion induced by randomized embeddings using two high-dimensional synthetic data. Then in Sect. IV we present our approach to the estimate of cluster stability based on random projections, and we apply the proposed stability measures to both synthetic and "real" gene expression data.

For all the experiments presented in this paper we developed *R* functions and programs to implement both the random projections described in Sect.III and the stability measures described in Sect. IV.

II. DIMENSIONALITY REDUCTION AND RANDOMIZED EMBEDDINGS

Dimensionality reduction may be obtained by mapping points from a high to a low-dimensional space, approximately preserving some characteristics, i.e. the distances between points. In this context randomized embeddings with low distortion represent a key concept. Randomized embeddings have been successfully applied both to combinatorial optimization and data compression [6].

A *randomized embedding* between L_2 normed metric spaces with distortion $1 + \epsilon$, with $\epsilon > 0$ and failure probability P is a distribution probability over mappings $\mu : \mathbb{R}^d \to \mathbb{R}^{d'}$, such that for every pair $p, q \in \mathbb{R}^d$, the following property holds with probability $1 - P$:

$$\frac{1}{1+\epsilon} \leq \frac{||\mu(p) - \mu(q)||_2}{||p - q||_2} \leq 1 + \epsilon \qquad (1)$$

The main result on randomized embedding is due to Johnson and Lindenstrauss [7], who proved the existence of a randomized embedding $\mu : \mathbb{R}^d \to \mathbb{R}^{d'}$ with distortion $1+\epsilon$ and failure probability $e^{\Omega(-d'\epsilon^2)}$, for every $0 < \epsilon < 1/2$. As a consequence, for a fixed data set $S \subset \mathbb{R}^d$, with $|S| = n$, by union bound, for all $p, q \in S$, it holds:

$$Prob\left(\frac{1}{1+\epsilon} \leq \frac{||\mu(p) - \mu(q)||_2}{||p-q||_2} \leq 1+\epsilon\right) \geq 1 - n^2 e^{\Omega(-d'\epsilon^2)} \quad (2)$$

Hence, by choosing d' such that $n^2 e^{\Omega(-d'\epsilon^2)} < 1/2$, it is proved the following:

Johnson-Lindenstrauss (JL) lemma: Given a set S with $|S| = n$ there exists a $1+\epsilon$-distortion embedding into $\mathbb{R}^{d'}$ with $d' = c \log n / \epsilon^2$, where c is a suitable constant.

The embedding exhibited in [7] consists in random projections from $\mathbb{R}^d$ into $\mathbb{R}^{d'}$, represented by matrices $d' \times d$ with random orthonormal vectors. Similar results may be obtained by using simpler embeddings, represented through random $d' \times d$ matrices $P = 1/\sqrt{d'}(r_{ij})$, where r_{ij} are random variables such that:

$$E[r_{ij}] = 0, \qquad Var[r_{ij}] = 1$$

For sake of simplicity, we call random projections even this kind of embeddings. In particular in [1] matrices are proposed such that their entries are uniformly chosen in $\{-1, 1\}$, or in $\{-\sqrt{3}, 0, \sqrt{3}\}$, by choosing 0 with probability $2/3$ and $-\sqrt{3}$ or $\sqrt{3}$ with probability $1/6$. In this case the *JL lemma* holds with $c \simeq 4$.

Consider now a data set represented by a $d \times n$ matrix X whose columns represent n d-dimensional observations. Suppose that $d' = 4 \log n / \epsilon^2 << d$; the *JL lemma* guarantees the existence of a $d' \times d$ matrix P such that the columns of the "compressed" data set $X^P = PX$ have approximately the same distance (up to a distortion $1 + \epsilon$) of the corresponding columns in X. Moreover there is a randomized algorithm that, having in input X, outputs X^P in time $\mathcal{O}(dd'n)$ with high confidence.

This fact suggests that we can speed-up algorithms for solving *proximity problems*. Instances of a *proximity problem* are sets $I \subset \mathbb{R}^d$ (described by a data set X), and the goal consists in computing some properties defined in terms of distances between points in I: clustering is an example. In particular consider an algorithm $\mathcal{A}$ that, having as input a $d \times n$ data set X, outputs the solution of a *proximity problem* in time $T(n, d)$. An approximate solution of the problem can be obtained by computing firstly the projection P and the "compressed" data set $X^P = PX$, and finally by applying $\mathcal{A}$ to X^P. In this way the time complexity may be reduced from $T(n,d)$ to $\mathcal{O}(nd \log n) + T(n, \mathcal{O}(\log n))$.

III. DISTORTION INDUCED BY RANDOM PROJECTIONS

In this section we consider two random embeddings, proposed respectively in [1] and [5]. We estimate the distortions induced by the random embeddings with respect to high dimensional synthetic data, comparing them with the theoretical bounds predicted by the *JL lemma*.

A. Distortion measures

Given a data set $X \subset \mathbb{R}^d$ and a map $\mu : \mathbb{R}^d \to \mathbb{R}^{d'}$, for $x, y \in X$ the *distortion* $dist_\mu(x, y)$ is defined:

$$dist_\mu(x, y) = \frac{||\mu(x) - \mu(y)||_2}{||x - y||_2} \quad (3)$$

Of course, $dist_\mu(x,y) = 1$ means that no distortion is introduced. The *maximum, minimum* and *average distortion* of μ on X respectively are:

$$\begin{aligned}
max.dist_\mu(X) &= \max_{x,y \in X} dist_\mu(x, y) \quad (4)\\
min.dist_\mu(X) &= \min_{x,y \in X} dist_\mu(x, y) \\
ave.dist_\mu(X) &= \frac{1}{|X|(|X|-1)} \sum_{x,y \in X, x \neq y} dist_\mu(x, y)
\end{aligned}$$

B. Empirical estimation of distortions induced by randomized maps

In this section we estimate, given a data set X and a randomized map μ, the expectation of the random variables $max.dist_\mu(X), min.dist_\mu(X)$ and $ave.dist_\mu(X)$ (eq.4)

1) Randomized maps: We considered two randomized maps:

- *Random Projection (RP)*: represented by $d' \times d$ matrices $P = 1/\sqrt{d'}(r_{ij})$, where r_{ij} are uniformly chosen in $\{-1, 1\}$. As observed in Sect.II RP satisfies the *JL lemma*.
- *Random Subspace (RS)* [5]: represented by $d' \times d$ matrices $P = \sqrt{d/d'}(r_{ij})$, where r_{ij} are uniformly chosen with entries in $\{0, 1\}$, and with exactly one "1" per row and at most one "1" per column. It is worth noting that for a $d \times n$ data set X and a projection matrix P, the "compressed" data set $X^P = PX$ can be computed in time $\mathcal{O}(nd')$, independently from d. Unfortunately, RS does not satisfy the *JL lemma*.

2) Synthetic data generation: We developed two generators for synthetic data sets (*sample1* and *sample2*):

- *Sample1* is a generator for 6000-dimensional data sets composed by 3 clusters of data normally distributed. The elements of each cluster are distributed according to a spherical gaussian with unitary standard deviation. The first cluster is centered in the middle of a 6000-dimensional hypercube with an edge of length equal to 20 conventional units. The other two clusters are centered at the opposite vertices of the hypercube. Hence the tree clusters are completely separated with no overlapping between them.
- *Sample2* is a a generator for 6000-dimensional data sets composed by 5 clusters of data normally distributed. All the examples have 1000 no-noisy and 5000 noisy variables; for all the examples the noisy variables are distributed according to a spherical gaussian centered in 0 and with standard deviation equal to 2. Considering only the 1000 no-noisy variables there is substantial overlapping between classes 1 and 2 and 1 and 3, while class 4 and 5 are quite well separated.

Using the generators we drew two data set (respectively X_1 and X_2), each one composed by 50 examples.

3) Results: Setting a distortion value $1 + \epsilon$, $(0 < \epsilon < 0.5)$, a dimension $d' = 4 \log 50/\epsilon^2$ is computed according to the *JL lemma*. For every data set X_1 and X_2 we performed 50 *RP* and 50 *RS* projections, computing the empirical average of $max.dist_\mu, min.dist_\mu$ and $ave.dist_\mu$, according to eq.4.

The results for *RP* and *RS* on *sample2* are summarized in Fig.1. As expected, for *RP* the empirical average of $max.dist_\mu$ and $min.dist_\mu$ are significantly better than the theoretical bound. Quite surprisingly, similar results have been also obtained with *RS* projections, where *JL* bounds are not guaranteed. A similar behaviour of *RP* and *RS* projections has been also observed with *sample1* (data not shown).

of the pairwise distances are quite well preserved, at least if we project data with low distortion. With the well separated clusters of the *sample1* data set the distribution of the distances are better preserved (data not shown).

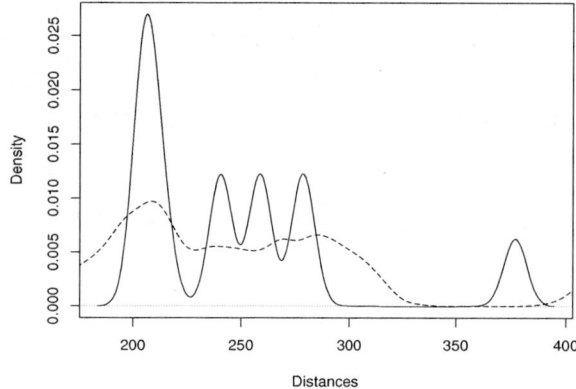

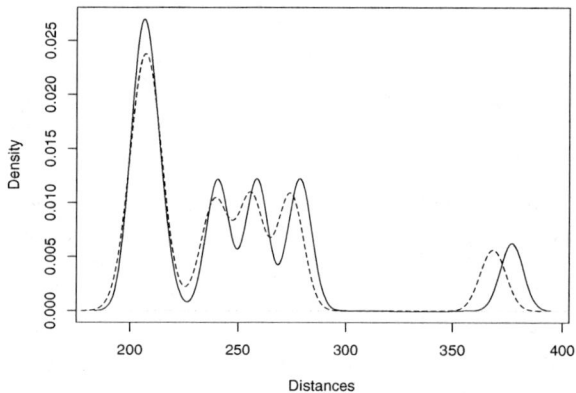

Fig. 2. Distribution of the pairwise distances between examples in original and randomly projected data (*sample2*). The continuous line represents the distribution in the original 6000-dimensional space, the dashed line the distribution in the projected space. Above: Projection into a 63-dimensional space (corresponding to a 1.50 upper-bound distortion according to JL lemma). Below: Projection into a 1565-dimensional space (corresponding to a 1.10 upper-bound distortion according to JL lemma).

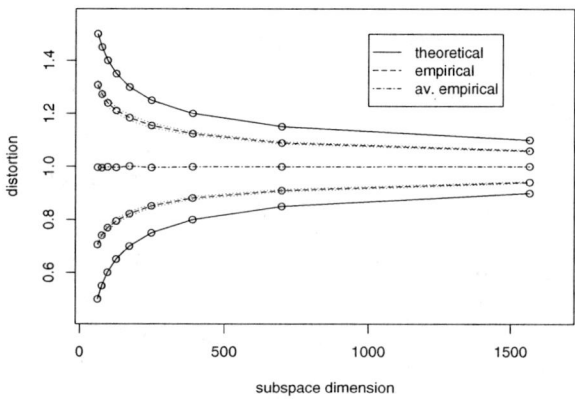

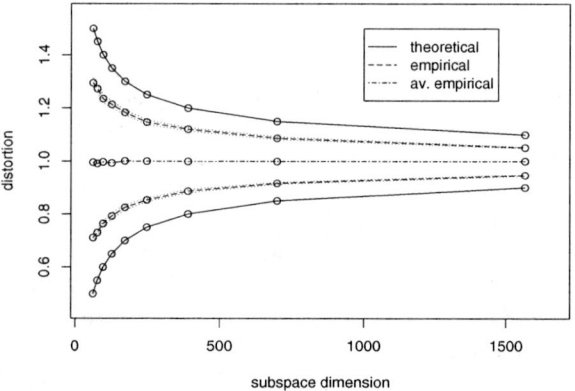

Fig. 1. Comparing theoretical and empirical distortion with *sample2* using *RP* and *RS* projections. Continuous lines represent the bounds of the maximum and minimum distortion according to the *JL* lemma. Dashed lines represent the average maximum and minimum distortion empirically computed and averaged over 50 random projections. The pairs of dotted lines just above and below the the dashed lines represent the confidence interval at 99 % confidence level. The dash-dotted line represents the expected average distortion. Above: *RP* projection. Below: *RS* projection.

Fig. 2 shows the distribution of the pairwise distances between examples in original and randomly projected data (*sample2* data set). We may see that the also the distributions

IV. RANDOM PROJECTIONS AND CLUSTER STABILITY

The *JL* lemma shows that we may generate relatively low-distorted random projected data, and our experimental results show that we may also obtain empirical estimate of the expectation of the random variables $max.dist_\mu$ and $min.dist_\mu$ that are better than the theoretical bounds.

Our aim is to exploit random projections to estimate stability of clusters, because random projections do not induce relevant distortions (as long as we provide a projection into a sufficiently high-dimensional subspace).

A. Cluster stability measures

Given a finite set $X \subset \mathbb{R}^d$, we denote (with abuse of notation) with X the metric space $< X, f >$, where $f(x,y) = ||x - y||_2$, $x, y \in \mathbb{R}^d$. In the following of this section we consider a fixed random projection $\mu : \mathbb{R}^d \to \mathbb{R}^{d'}$ that verifies the *JL* lemma (i.e. *RP*, Sect. III-B.1), and we propose a stability index for clustering by using a pairwise similarity matrix between the projected examples.

Let $\mathcal{C}$ be a clustering algorithm, that, having in input X, outputs a set of k clusters:

$$\mathcal{C}(X) = < A_1, A_2, \ldots, A_k >, \; A_j \subset X, 1 \leq j \leq k \quad (5)$$

Then we compute a "similarity" matrix M, with indices in X, using the following algorithm:

1) Generate t independent projections $\mu_i : \mathbb{R}^d \to \mathbb{R}^{d'}$, $1 \leq i \leq t$, such that $d' = 4 \frac{\log |X| + \log t}{\epsilon^2}$
2) Apply $\mathcal{C}$ to the new projected data $\mu_i(X)$, obtaining a set of clusterings, for $1 \leq i \leq t$:

$$\mathcal{C}(\mu_i(X)) = < B_1^i, \ldots, B_k^i >, \; B_j^i \subset X_i, 1 \leq j \leq k \quad (6)$$

where B_j^i is the jth cluster of the ith clustering.

3) Set the elements M_{xy} of the similarity matrix:

$$M_{xy} = \frac{1}{t} \sum_{j=1}^{k} \sum_{i=1}^{t} \chi_{B_j^i}(\mu_i(x)) \cdot \chi_{B_j^i}(\mu_i(y)) \quad (7)$$

where $\chi_{B_j^i}$ is the characteristic function for the cluster B_j^i.

Since the elements M_{xy} measure the occurrences of the examples $\mu_i(x), \mu_i(y) \in \mu_i(X)$ in the same clusters B_j^i for $1 \leq i \leq t$, then M represents the "tendency" of the projections to belong to the same cluster. It is easy to see that $0 \leq M_{xy} \leq 1$, for each $x, y \in X$.

With respect to the algorithm above we may observe:

Remark 1. Since the failure probability is $e^{\Omega(-d' \epsilon^2)}$, similarly to eq.2 in Sect. II, by union bound we have, for all $x, y \in X$, $1 \leq i \leq t$:

$$P\left(\frac{1}{1+\epsilon} \leq \frac{||\mu_i(y) - \mu_i(x)||_2}{||x-y||_2} \leq 1+\epsilon\right) \geq 1 - t|X|^2 e^{\Omega(-d' \epsilon^2)}$$

Therefore for $d' \simeq \mathcal{O}\left(\frac{\log |X| + \log t}{\epsilon^2}\right)$, we obtain with high probability that all the projections preserve the distances between the elements in X up to a distortion $1 + \epsilon$.

Remark 2. A fuzzy similarity matrix may be obtained simply substituting in eq. 7 the characteristic function with a membership function and the algebraic product with a suitable *t-norm*. In this way fuzzy or possibilistic clustering approaches may also be applied.

Using the similarity matrix M (eq. 7) we propose the following *stability index s* for a cluster A_i:

$$s(A_i) = \frac{1}{|A_i|(|A_i| - 1)} \sum_{(x,y) \in A_i \times A_i, x \neq y} M_{xy} \quad (8)$$

The index $s(A_i)$ estimates the stability of a cluster A_i in the original non projected space, by measuring how much the projections of the pairs $(x, y) \in A_i \times A_i$ occur together in the same cluster in the projected subspaces. The stability index has values between 0 and 1: values near 1 denote stable clusters, while lower values indicate less reliable clusters. The above stability index is very similar to that proposed by [10]. The main difference of our approach consists in the way the similarity matrix is computed: we applied randomized projections into lower dimensional subspaces, while [10] applied bootstrap techniques.

An overall measure of the stability of the clustering in the original space may be obtained averaging between the stability indices:

$$S(k) = \frac{1}{k} \sum_{i=1}^{k} s(A_i) \quad (9)$$

In this case also we have that $0 \leq S(k) \leq 1$, where k is the number of clusters.

B. Assessing cluster stability in synthetic and gene expression data

We applied the stability measures proposed in the previous section to high dimensional synthetic and gene expression data, using the Ward's hierarchical agglomerative clustering algorithm [14], and using as dissimilarity function the euclidean distance.

For each data set we computed the average stability index $S(k)$ (eq. 9) for different number k of clusters, and the stability index s (eq. 8) for each corresponding cluster, considering different $1 + \epsilon$ distortions induced by *RS* and *RP* projections (Sect. III-B.1) into subspaces whose dimension was computed according to the *JL lemma*.

1) Results with synthetic data: Tab.I summarizes the results with *sample1*. The maximum of the average stability index $S(k)$ is reached when the dendrogram is cut at 3 clusters level, and the corresponding stability indices s are equal to 1 for each of the 3 clusters. Both the average and the individual stability indices are lower when different number of clusters are selected, showing that the proposed stability measures correctly detect 3 clusters, identifying them as highly reliable.

With *sample2* the stability indices correctly predict largely separated as well as less reliable clusters. Indeed the stability indices are high for the 2 well separated clusters, while for the other overlapped clusters the stability indices are significantly lower (data not shown).

2) Results with gene expression data data: We applied the proposed stability indices to a set of gene expression tumor specimens from 58 Diffuse large B-cell lymphoma (DLBCL) and 19 Follicular lymphoma (FL) patients [11].

Tab. II shows the estimate of cluster stability for the *DLBCL-FL* data set. Note that in the first column of Tab. II the clusters are labeled with numbers, and these number assignments correspond to left-to-right clusters in the dendrogram of Fig. 3. The average S index is slightly larger when the hierarchical clustering dendrogram is cut at 2 clusters level (Fig. 3), but comparable (even if lower) values are also registered with $3, 4$ and 5 clusters. In this case indeed the

TABLE I

Sample1: ESTIMATE OF CLUSTER STABILITY.

Clusters	Members of Clusters	Stability index s				
		$\epsilon = 0.5$	$\epsilon = 0.4$	$\epsilon = 0.3$	$\epsilon = 0.2$	$\epsilon = 0.1$
2 clusters		$S = 0.8631$	$S = 0.8684$	$S = 0.8684$	$S = 0.9157$	$S = 0.9421$
1	11-20	1.0000	1.0000	1.0000	1.0000	1.0000
2	1-10,21-30	0.7263	0.7368	0.7368	0.8314	0.8842
3 clusters		$S = 1.0000$	$S = 1.0000$	$S = 1.0000$	$S = 1.0000$	$S = 1.0000$
1	11-20	1.0000	1.0000	1.0000	1.0000	1.0000
2	21-30	1.0000	1.0000	1.0000	1.0000	1.0000
3	1-10	1.0000	1.0000	1.0000	1.0000	1.0000
5 clusters		$S = 0.7059$	$S = 0.6843$	$S = 0.7044$	$S = 0.7004$	$S = 0.7472$
1	11,13,16,17,19,20	0.6973	0.7346	0.7293	0.6506	0.7560
2	12,14,15,18	0.6666	0.7066	0.6866	0.6466	0.7133
3	21-30	0.7155	0.7582	0.7448	0.7591	0.8364
4	5,7	0.7600	0.5600	0.6800	0.7400	0.7800
5	1-4,6,8-10	0.6900	0.6621	0.6814	0.7057	0.6507
10 clusters		$S = 0.3093$	$S = 0.3043$	$S = 0.2651$	$S = 0.3286$	$S = 0.3936$
1	19	0.0600	0.1200	0.0600	0.2000	0.2400
2	11,13,16,17,20	0.4260	0.3520	0.2900	0.3360	0.4560
3	12	0.1400	0.1600	0.1600	0.2000	0.1400
4	14,15,18	0.4066	0.3533	0.3200	0.3800	0.4200
5	23,28,29	0.3733	0.3000	0.2866	0.3600	0.4200
6	21,22,24-27,30	0.3276	0.3419	0.3285	0.3866	0.3933
7	5,7	0.3600	0.2800	0.3000	0.3600	0.3800
8	2,3,8,10	0.3000	0.3366	0.3066	0.3433	0.3866
9	4,9	0.3400	0.4000	0.2600	0.4200	0.5000
10	1,6	0.3600	0.4000	0.3400	0.3000	0.6000

clusters are not clearly delineated. For instance, considering a cut at 4 clusters level, the first cluster (with a relatively high s stability index equal to 0.8748) is composed by homogeneous FL patients (Fig. 3), the second (less reliable $s = 0.6004$) is composed by both DLBCL and FL patients, while the third (more reliable $s = 0.8123$) is composed only by DLBCL patients, as well as the less reliable ($s = 0.6005$) fourth cluster. Splitting the fourth cluster, we obtain two DLBCL subclusters, more reliable than the previous one (Tab. II, 5 clusters). If we split the data in 10 or more clusters we note a significant decrement of both the s indices and the average S index: this fact suggests that no significant structure can be observed in small-sized clusters (data not shown).

These results are congruent with the bio-medical characteristics of the data. Indeed even if nodal tumor specimens are subdivided into 2 groups (DLBCL and FL), Alizadeh et al. [2] discovered subclasses among DLBCL patients, and Shipp et al. [11] highlighted that FL patients frequently evolve over time and acquire the morphologic and clinical features of DLBCLs.

V. CONCLUSIONS

Our experiments with synthetic and gene expression data show that the proposed stability indices based on random projections with bounded metric distortion may be used to identify stable clusters directly from the data, without "a priori" knowledge and without assumptions about the distribution of the data (apart of the choice of the clustering algorithm). Moreover our experiments show that the average stability index may also be useful to identify the most likely number of clusters.

We experimented with agglomerative hierarchical clustering, but the proposed approach may be used with any clustering algorithm, comprising also fuzzy and possibilistic clustering methods.

Our experimental results show also that, according to the *JL* lemma, if the dimension of the subspace induced by a random projection is sufficiently high, no significant distortion is introduced into the embedding, and clustering may be performed on random subspaces approximately preserving pairwise distances between examples. From this standpoint, our random projection-based stability measures may help biomedical researchers to identify stable and reliable clusters (e.g. new pathological classes), exploiting the high dimension of gene expression data.

ACKNOWLEDGMENT

This work has been developed in the context of *CIMAINA* Center of Excellence and it has been partially funded by the italian COFIN project *Linguaggi formali ed automi: metodi, modelli ed applicazioni*.

REFERENCES

[1] D. Achlioptas. Database-friendly random projections. In *Proc. ACM Symp. on the Principles of Database Systems*, Contemporary Mathematics, pages 274–281, 2001.
[2] Alizadeh, A. et al. Distinct types of diffuse large B-cell lymphoma identified by gene expression profiling. *Nature*, 403:503–511, 2000.
[3] S. Dudoit and J. Fridlyand. Bagging to improve the accuracy of a clustering procedure. *Bioinformatics*, 19(9):1090–1099, 2003.
[4] M.B. Eisen, P.T. Spellman, P.O. Brown, and D. Botstein. Cluster analysis and display of genome-wide expression patterns. *PNAS*, 95(25):14863–14868, 1998.
[5] T.K. Ho. The random subspace method for constructing decision forests. *IEEE Transactions on Pattern Analysis and Machine Intelligence*, 20(8):832–844, 1998.
[6] P. Indyk. Algorithmic Applications of Low-Distortion Geometric Embeddings. *Proceedings of the 42nd IEEE symposium on Foundations of Computer Science*, pp. 10-33, IEEE Computer Society, Washington DC, USA, 2001.

TABLE II

DLBCL-FL: Estimate of cluster stability.

Clusters	Stability index s				
	$\epsilon = 0.5$	$\epsilon = 0.4$	$\epsilon = 0.3$	$\epsilon = 0.2$	$\epsilon = 0.1$
2 clusters	$S = 0.6620$	$S = 0.6433$	$S = 0.6624$	$S = 0.7140$	$S = 0.7826$
1	0.6998	0.6864	0.6893	0.7620	0.8936
2	0.6242	0.6002	0.6355	0.6660	0.6716
3 clusters	$S = 0.5369$	$S = 0.5303$	$S = 0.5720$	$S = 0.6655$	$S = 0.7536$
1	0.5258	0.5038	0.5222	0.5115	0.6474
2	0.6081	0.6197	0.6749	0.8419	0.9149
3	0.4767	0.4675	0.5190	0.6432	0.6986
4 clusters	$S = 0.4822$	$S = 0.4829$	$S = 0.5167$	$S = 0.6025$	$S = 0.7220$
1	0.5443	0.5392	0.6351	0.6828	0.8748
2	0.4949	0.4760	0.4496	0.4909	0.6004
3	0.5265	0.5327	0.5725	0.7340	0.8123
4	0.3633	0.3839	0.4094	0.5024	0.6005
5 clusters	$S = 0.4164$	$S = 0.4378$	$S = 0.4608$	$S = 0.5660$	$S = 0.6946$
1	0.4825	0.4979	0.5646	0.6335	0.8492
2	0.4281	0.4329	0.3995	0.4362	0.5257
3	0.4437	0.4621	0.5087	0.6417	0.7241
4	0.3443	0.3921	0.4165	0.5418	0.6275
5	0.3836	0.4038	0.4146	0.5769	0.7467

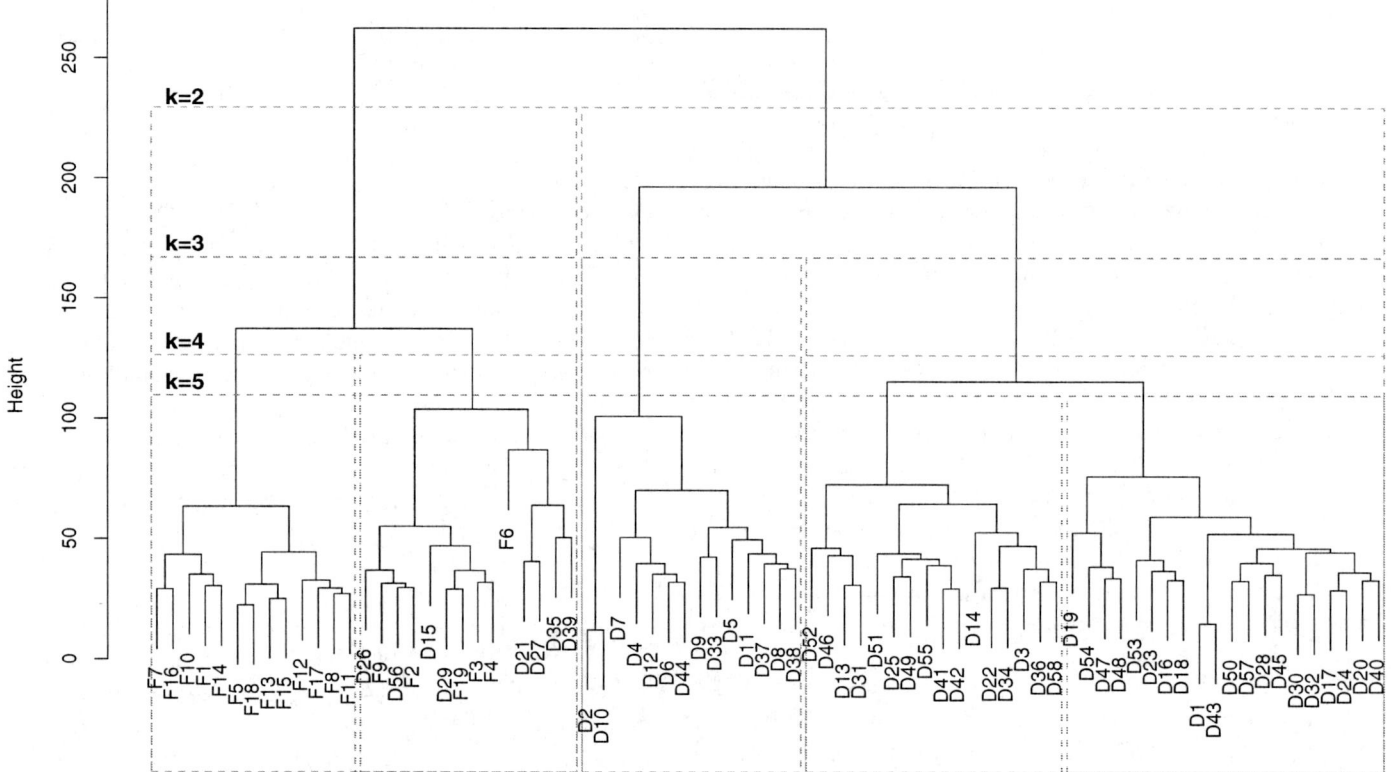

Fig. 3. Hierarchical clustering of *DLBCL-FL* examples (Ward method). Leaves labeled with "D" refer to DLBCL patients, while "F" to FL patients. Gray dotted lines cut the dendrogram such that exactly k clusters are produced, for $k = 2, 3, 4, 5$.

[7] W.B. Johnson and J. Lindenstrauss. Extensions of Lipshitz mapping into Hilbert space. In *Conference in modern analysis and probability*, volume 26 of *Contemporary Mathematics*, pages 189–206. Amer. Math. Soc., 1984.

[8] M.K. Kerr and G.A. Curchill. Bootstrapping cluster analysis: assessing the reliability of conclusions from microarray experiments. *PNAS*, 98:8961–8965, 2001.

[9] L.M. McShane, D. Radmacher, B. Freidlin, R. Yu, M.C. Li, and R. Simon. Method for assessing reproducibility of clustering patterns observed in analyses of microarray data. *Bioinformatics*, 18(11):1462–1469, 2002.

[10] S. Monti et al. Consensus Clustering: A Resampling-based Method for Class Discovery and Visualization of Gene Expression Microarray Data. *Machine Learning*, 52:91–118, 2003.

[11] M. Shipp et al. Diffuse large B-cell lymphoma outcome prediction by gene-expression profiling and supervised machine learning. *Nature Medicine*, 8(1):68–74, 2002.

[12] M. Smolkin and D. Gosh. Cluster stability scores for microarray data in cancer studies. *BMC Bioinformatics*, 4(36), 2003.

[13] R. Tibshirani, T. Hastie, B. Narasimham, M. Eisen, G. Sherlock, P. Brown, and D. Botstein. Exploratory screening of genes and clusters from microarray experiments. *Statist. Sinica*, 12:47–60, 2002.

[14] J.H. Ward. Hierarchical grouping to optimize an objective function. *J. Am. Stat. Assoc.*, 58:236–244, 1963.

A New Approach to Hierarchical Clustering for the Analysis of Genomic Data

Francesco Masulli
Dept of Computer Science
University of Pisa
Largo B. Pontecorvo, 3 I-56125 Pisa, Italy
masulli@di.unipi.it

Stefano Rovetta
Department of Computer and Information Sciences
University of Genova
Via Dodecaneso 35 I-16146 Genova, Italy
rovetta@disi.unige.it

Abstract— Clustering algorithms in biomedical disciplines are usually selected between two main families, k-Means and Agglomerative Hierarchical Clustering. These methods are well studied and well established. However, both categories have some drawbacks related to data dimensionality (for partitional algorithms) and to the bottom-up structure (for hierarchical algorithms). To overcome these limitations, we present a hierarchical clustering algorithm based on a completely different principle, which is the analysis of shared *farthest neighbors*. The principle of operation and the rationale are illustrated, and experimental results on different data sets are presented.

I. INTRODUCTION

Clustering algorithms in biomedical disciplines are usually selected between two main families. When the number of experimental observations (cardinality) is high and the number of observed variables (dimensionality) is not very large, it is possible to use iterative, partitional algorithms such as k-Means [1]. When data dimensionality is very large, or the number observations is small, then hierarchical agglomerative algorithms [2] are normally used. Popular examples include average linkage [3] methods and Ward's method [4].

All of these methods are well studied and established. In the hierarchical cases, the resulting tree structure can be easily represented in visual form as a dendrogram [5] or color diagram [2]. However, both categories have some drawbacks related to data dimensionality (for partitional algorithms) and to the bottom-up structure (for hierarchical algorithms).

To overcome these limitations, we present a hierarchical clustering algorithm based on a completely different principle, which is the analysis of shared *farthest neighbors*. This approach share some similarities with Jarvis-Patrick clustering [6], which however is based on the analysis of shared *nearest neighbors* and is not a hierarchical method.

II. LIMITATIONS OF CURRENT METHODS

The clustering methods usually adopted have their own weaknesses, which we are going to point out in this section. In the following section we will propose countermeasures.

The k-Means clustering method is one of the most popular. It is well known that it is prone to local minima; however, when data are sampled in sufficient quantity and the number k of centroids is small, this may not be a problem.

However, with biomedical data, the typical situation is that a single experimental observation is very expensive, therefore many variable are observed at any experiment. This is exactly the situation we have with genomic data, and even more so with microarray experiments. This raises the issue of the curse of dimensionality [7][8], that is, the need for exponentially many data points as a function of space dimensionality.

The k-Means algorithm (as well as any one of its many variants) searches for regions where data are especially dense. However we expect that, when clustering experiments, the cardinality of the data sets available is not only small with respect to the size of the data space (dimension equal to the number of variables), which would lead to insufficient sampling of the space: it is usually even less than the number of variables. This means that the data span only a subspace within the data space. In these conditions, it is not even easy to define the concept of (hyper)volumetric density, let alone estimating it. Therefore k-Means is typically adequate for clustering variables across experiments, rather than clustering experiments.

There have been many efforts in solving the dimensionality problem. We refer the reader for instance to [9], in which the problem is tackled by seeking clusters on subspaces of the data space (projection clustering), and to the literature cited therein for other examples.

Another drawback, shared by both types of techniques, is related to the number of clusters. The "k" in k-Means, number of expected clusters, should be known in advance, or estimated either by prior knowledge or by a-posteriori validation. These approaches are implemented in many variants, such as ISO-DATA [10].

The standard hierarchical approach, on the other hand, makes no attempt at defining proper clusters, leaving up to subsequent analysis to split the hierarchy into clusters (at appropriate levels). The problem is related to the binary procedure of agglomeration, whereby at each stage only two objects (clusters or data objects) are merged. In this sense, we could even say that this it is not a true clustering technique, since it does provide an organization of data, but with no attempt at identifying clusters. The method retains its usefulness in its ability to visualize a structure in the form of a taxonomy, which makes it interesting in a number of applications.

A derivative problem, which is produced by clusters being obtained only a-posteriori in hierarchical techniques, is that the taxonomy obtained is not very robust with respect to noise. In the presence of perturbations, different taxonomic trees can be obtained even if the perturbations are small. Usually this problem is tackled with resampling approaches (bootstrap), but this is again an a-posteriori remedy.

A further problem is again related to space dimensionality. Defining clusters on the basis of distance requires that distances can be estimated. However there are results [11] stating that, when space dimensionality is high or even moderate (as low as 10-15), the distance of a point to its farthest neighbor and to its nearest neighbor tend to become equal. This causes the actual evaluation of distances, and the concept of "nearest neighbor" itself, to become less and less meaningful with growing dimensionality.

We can also add to the list the minor inconvenience, for agglomerative methods, of not being able to produce a partial (rough) result, to be refined only if needed. In the data mining jargon, algorithms with this property are called "anytime" algorithms. In our case this may not be a significant factor from the computational point of view, but it depends on the application.

III. ADDRESSING THE LIMITATIONS

We outline now the remedies which we propose to overcome the limitations above. To avoid the problems with the number of clusters, an algorithm should be hierarchical, but at the same time it should allow for more than two objects at any level in the hierarchy. The procedure should be divisive rather than agglomerative, which produces an algorithm that we can use up to a desired level of detail without being constrained to proceed to the level of single data objects. In this way, the criterion used to divide each cluster into (possibly more than two) subclusters provides an indication of the "appropriate" number of clusters for that level in the hierarchy, although assessing that this number is the true number of natural clusters would typically require further analysis. For instance, our choice is an indirect approach whereby class labels in supervised problems are used to validate clustering results (see Section VI).

To tackle the dimensionality problem, a typical countermeasure found in traditional statistics is moving from the analysis of values (in our case, distances) to the analysis of their *ranks*. Rank is the position of a given value in the ordered list of all values. This technique is adopted when using actual values is either difficult or inadequate. The approach is followed for instance by Spearman with his rank-correlation index r_s [12] or by Kendall with his correlation index τ and coefficient of concordance W [13].

Regarding noise robustness, it is certainly possible to apply some technique to filter out noisy samples and outliers. This however requires prior knowledge on the statistics of data, so that the definition of noise and outliers allows labeling as such those points which do not reflect this statistics. This approach is not very attractive from the viewpoint of the

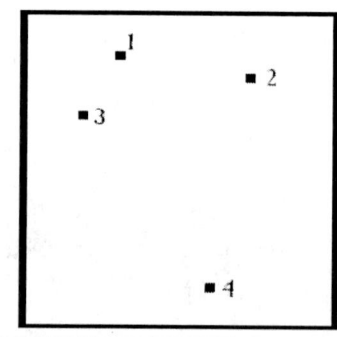

Fig. 1. An example data set to illustrate the "Points in perspective" principle. For each point the table lists the distance ranks of all other points.

Data points	1	2	3	4
I Neighbor	3	1	1	3
II Neighbor	2	3	2	2
III Neighbor	4	4	4	1

present paper. We try to avoid the assumption of a given distribution or cluster shape, both because this would limit the generality of the approach we are proposing, and because very small samples are not statistically significant. Besides, filtering out what we have labeled as noise may throw away relevant information which might be important in an exploratory data analysis step, and reducing an already scarce data set is not advisable anyway.

The following section will present a principle of operation based on these considerations and the resulting clustering algorithm.

IV. THE "POINTS IN PERSPECTIVE" PRINCIPLE

We propose to adopt the following principle of operation: *Two points should be considered similar if they share the same farthest point among all remaining data.* We term this the "Points in Perspective" Principle, since the points are examined not with reference to their neighborhood (locally), but with reference to far-away points in the data set, therefore in perspective.

Note that usually similarity is assessed on the basis of the nearest neighbor. For instance, k-Means clustering is done by associating each data point to the closest cluster centroid or prototype. However, we do not want to resort to centroids to define clusters, since this would limit the procedure to metric data only, and since this would require estimation of centroids (which we have seen to be an ill-posed problem when the data set is of lower cardinality than dimensionality). This leaves open the option of the Jarvis-Patrick [6] approach, termed "shared nearest neighbors" (SNN). Points are considered similar if they share the nearest neighbor, or a list of a given number of nearest neighbors.

However, the SNN produces the following odd result. The higher the rank of neighbors, the larger their "agglomerative" significance. Two points which are very close to each other and distant to other data points should be considered as a good cluster. But since the (first) nearest neighbor of either

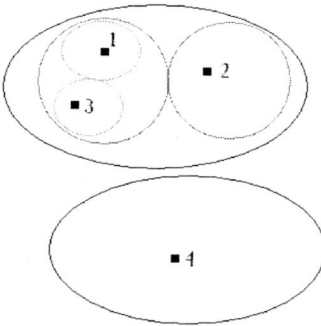

Fig. 2. The example data set clustered according to the proposed method.

point is the other point, the first nearest neighbor is *always different*. This of course is not a major drawback (SNN simply counts k neighbors and groups objects with at least k_t shared neighbors), but it offers some evidence that the principle itself may be only partially justified.

Moreover, the SNN approach can be unreliable with very sparse data, where clusters may be sampled by only one or two objects. This poses the issue of selecting the clustering threshold k_t.

As a last remark, we recall that we are seeking a hierarchical method, and SNN provides only partitional clustering, although in the original presentation the authors suggest repeated applications of the method to obtain tree-structured clusters.

The example shown in Figure 1 clarifies these remarks.

Clustering according to the proposed "Points in Perspective" principle of operation is done according to the following very simple procedure: First, all points are labeled. We compute the distance of each point to all others, and for each point we identify the farthest neighbor. We define clusters at the first level by aggregating all points sharing a common farthest neighbor label.

We should point out that, although we are discussing the method in terms of distance, it is applicable to more general dissimilarity definitions than proper distance.

Then, within each cluster, the second farthest neighbor can be considered exactly in the same way. This produces a second level clustering within each cluster of the first level.

The procedure is recursively repeated until no further differentiation is found (all points within a level $l-1$ cluster share the same l-th farthest neighbor), or until a predefined maximum level is reached.

We term this algorithm *Shared Farthest Neighbor* clustering (SFN). The example shown in Figure 2 illustrated the result of applying the SFN procedure to the data of Figure 1.

Here a proposed implementation of the SFN algorithm is sketched. The algorithm starts computing the distance matrix D (the matrix of distance between each point i and each point j). This is not a symmetric matrix in the case of more general dissimilarity measures, but the method does not require symmetry and remains applicable in more general cases. Note also that, if we have a *similarity* measure instead of dissimilarity, we only need to change the direction of the comparison used in the sorting phase. Finally, this is the phase where, if required, we can take care of missing data by adequately defining the measure (imputation seems a less appropriate technique, given the small cardinality which we have set as our starting hypothesis).

Once we have D, which may also be given as the input to the algorithm, we proceed as follows. For each point in the data set (a row of D) the distances to other data points are ordered and the corresponding rank is written in place of the actual distance, obtaining a rank matrix R.

Now each row of this matrix should be "inverted", that is, cell contents should be swapped with the corresponding cell indexes. We obtain an index matrix X listing, for each data point, all point labels in order of distance. This can be done simply looking up ranks in R and writing point labels in the corresponding position of X (that is, $x_{i,r_{ij}} = j$).

Clustering is now performed simply by sorting the rows of matrix X. Conceptually, this is done according to each column, starting from the first (nearest neighbors) up to the last. However, we can decrease the algorithm complexity as a function of data cardinality, and at the same time allow for a partial clustering, i.e. stopping at a given level of the hierarchy. This can be obtained if we start sorting from the farthest neighbor, then partially sort the rows within each individual cluster, and so on.

The following algorithm summarizes the procedure. The method can be implemented in many ways, but this pseudocode reflects the structure of the implementation which is available at the web address http://mlsc.disi.unige.it/C/sfn/.

```
Algorithm SFN
Data structures:
   matrix D (n x n)
   matrix X (n x n)
   matrix R (n x n)
Input:
   training set T (cardinality n)
Compute D = distance matrix for T
Compute R = ranks of distances in D
|  (within each row)
Compute X = index matrix
|  (by swapping cell contents with indexes in R)
for i = n to 1 {
   Sort rows of Y using column i as key
}
Output:
   clusters
|  clusters at hierarchical depth i share the
|  same value in column i of matrix Y
end algorithm
```

V. PROPERTIES OF THE PROPOSED APPROACH

In this section we highlight some features of the approach presented and of the resulting algorithm.

The algorithm implemented according to the above sketch is of the "anytime" type, because it is a *divisive* technique, not an agglomerative one. We can decide to stop it when the hierarchy is partially built, and obtain a usable clustering result. Usually it is advisable to make use of this property, so that the result is more understandable (fewer larger clusters). It also makes little sense to split clusters into extremely small partitions when the data set is already scarce.

With respect to the position of points and to its perturbations, the hierarchy of dichotomies is more stable than in hierarchical agglomerative clustering algorithms. This is because clustering is based on the largest distances, over which the effect of small perturbations is usually negligible, rather than on the smallest.

A cluster is not constrained to be separated in exactly two sub-clusters, and the clustering structure is therefore allowed to fit the natural structure of data (that can be non-dichotomic).

After the distance matrix D has been obtained, the algorithm operation (and computational complexity) is independent on data dimensionality. On the other hand, the dependence on the data cardinality (number of points) is not important, since by design we are in the case of small cardinality. Moreover, distances in the data space are used only for computing ranks and not for estimating densities or approximating region geometries. Therefore the algorithm is especially appropriate in those situations where cardinality is low and dimensionality is high. This makes it well suited to the analysis of genomic data, for instance with DNA microarrays. In general, many bio-medical data analysis problems fall within this category, and the algorithm can be successfully applied.

VI. EXPERIMENTAL VALIDATION

We have validated the SFN algorithm on medical diagnosis and genomic data analysis problems, some of which are publicly available. The data sets include:

1) Lung cancer. Five patients with lung cancer have been analyzed with a DNA microarray technique. These are preliminary results from an on-going study and are not publicly available. Given the very small cardinality, these data have been used to validate the method against the results obtained with hierarchical agglomerative clustering.
2) Pima Indians diabetes [14]. Pima Indians are affected by an endemic form of diabetes, which is found with much higher frequency than in other populations, and have agreed to be the subject of a study. The data collected have been put in the public access on the UCI repository of machine learning databases [15].
3) Wisconsin diagnostic breast cancer [16]. Samples of breast mass are microscopically analyzed. The data are obtained by digitizing an image from each sample. Features describe the cell nuclei present in the image. These data are from the UCI repository as above.
4) Lyme disease [17][18]. A disease discovered in the relatively recent past. It has initial effects on skin, then it can reach the nervous system, heart, connective tissue

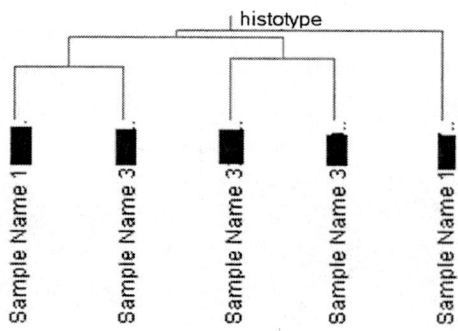

Fig. 3. Dendrogram obtained on Problem 1 by the SFN algorithm and by hierarchical agglomerative clustering.

(Lyme arthritis). In regions where it is not endemic, the diversity of signs can be confusing even to medical professionals trying to diagnose it, if they are not specifically trained. One of the authors has worked on this data set, which is currently not publicly available.
5) Molecular classification of leukemia [19]. DNA microarray are used to characterize two forms of leukemia at the molecular level, and within one of the two forms to separate two further sub-classes which are not distinguishable at the morphologic or serologic level, but have dramatically different prognoses. There are a training set and a test set, both available from the web address http://www.broad.mit.edu/cgi-bin/cancer/datasets.cgi.
6) Splice junction sequences [20]. Splice junction sites are point in the genome where introns (non-coding sequences) and exons (coding sequences) are joined together. The task is to identify splicing sites. These data have been obtained from the UCI repository as above.

Please note that full documentation and credits for the publicly accessible databases, as well as references to the relevant literature, should be obtained from the cited sources. The Lung cancer data are **not** the same as the data set with the same name available from the UCI repository.

The first experiment consists in validating the clustering result on problem 1. This is to achieve a first indication that the clusters we get are reasonable. This problem has a very small data cardinality, so the number of possible clusterings is limited and, arguably, there is only one "correct" result.

Figure 3 show the dendrogram obtained with the SFN algorithm and with hierarchical agglomerative clustering. Similarity is defined as the correlation between data points. We obtain the same result in both cases, which is therefore shown only once. The picture is a screenshot from the commercial data analysis package which produced the hierarchical agglomerative dendrogram.

The experimental results reported on Table 1 are obtained on Problems 2–5, all with Euclidean distance.

To evaluate the quality of clustering, we adopt the following approach. The result of clustering is usually assessed on the basis of some external knowledge about how clusters should

TABLE I
EXPERIMENTAL RESULTS

Problem	n	Preprocessing	Error %
2	768	Normalized with respect to average/stdev	12.40%
3	569	Normalized with respect to average/2*stdev	5.60%
4	684	Normalized with respect to average/2*stdev	6.00%
5 (training set)	38	none	0.00%
5 (training+test sets)	72	none	6.90%

be structured. This may imply evaluating separation, density, connectedness, diameter, and so on. However, these are all evaluations of results against a given expectation, which may not translate into good performance when the method is applied to a problem.

The only way to assess the usefulness of a clustering result is indirect validation, whereby clusters are applied to the solution of a problem and the correctness is evaluated against objective external knowledge. For this reason we need labeled data sets, where the external knowledge is the class information provided by labels. The experiments are therefore all performed on supervised problems.

We expect that, if the algorithm finds significant structures in the data, these will be reflected by the distribution of classes. Therefore we operate a "calibration" step for clusters (assigning to each cluster the class label which is most represented among its data points) and compare them to the behavior of *supervised* methods from the literature.

In this way we cannot obtain a direct assessment of the goodness of clusters per se; in exchange, we obtain valuable information about how these clusters map on the natural structure of the problem.

Regarding the evaluation method, we choose not to perform cross-validation or similar procedures, considering that the algorithm is "trained" in a completely unsupervised manner, and calibration already occurs (in a sense) on an external validation data set, which is the set of class labels. Cross-validation or resampling methods, however, can be very useful to assess the stability of the proposed method, by comparing clustering structures in repeated experiments.

The results we achieve are comparable with those obtained by supervised approaches proposed in the literature. This should be a confirmation of the validity of the method. Since clustering is done in a completely unsupervised manner, finding that the cluster structure is reasonably mapped onto the true classes supports the hypothesis that the algorithm is capable of discovering the "true" structure, the one which is inherent in data.

In particular, the results on the Leukemia dataset show that the method compares favorably with the approach by Golub et al. [19]. For instance, performance on the training set of 38 samples is errorless in our case, whereas the original self-organizing map (SOM) approach yielded 4 misclassified samples.

It is not easy to compare the deeper trees obtained by standard agglomerative hierarchical clustering to those obtained with the proposed method, which may be much less deep and still convey significant structure, since they have no constraint on the number of subclusters. In the case of Leukemia data, the tree depth for standard hierarchical clustering is at least 6 (for instance, with the average linkage method we obtain a tree depth of 9). For SFN, splitting stopped at level 4, although only 1 cluster was split up to the fourth level, whereas 12 clusters with no further sub-structure were present at level 1. Calibration itself is not a well-defined process for a binary tree, since the structure of clusters is not related to the depth of the tree, but rather to the linkage value. The tree should therefore be trimmed to a given (arbitrary) linkage value.

We can comment further on the clusters obtained by taking also into account the class labels, which are "ALL" for 27 Acute Lymphoblastic Leukemia patients and "AML" for 11 Acute Myeloid Leukemia. The distribution of cardinality among the clusters at level 1 is as follows:

Cardinality	Clusters	Class
10	1	AML
5	1	ALL
4	1	ALL
2	5	ALL
1	4	ALL

The cluster with further structure had cardinality 5 and contained one data object of class AML. All other AML were in the largest level 1 cluster. All leaf clusters (those which are not further split) are homogeneous with respect to the diagnosis.

This suggests a structure in data whereby AML profiles are better characterized than ALL profiles. This is clearly true when we notice that there are two sub-classes of ALL, which are T-cell ALL and B-cell ALL.

The distribution in general is well represented by a partitional clustering (this is a confirmation of the already good result obtained by Golub et al. with the SOM approach), However there is a subset of the data which needs a deeper structure for adequate representation. After the calibration step, we see that this subset contains a sample diagnosed as AML which is correctly separated from the other samples. Cluster structure is again confirmed by the class labels.

Problem 6 is different in that it involves data objects which are not metric vectors, but strings of DNA sequences, 60 bases long and centered around the candidate splicing site. Distance here is defined as the number of mismatches between bases in corresponding positions (only the 40 central bases have been considered). Here the result is very good: Figure 4 illustrates the hierarchy obtained (graphics from a program by the authors). Fixing the maximum level at 2, the structure is very simple, with a cluster further split into two sub-clusters and another cluster without sub-clusters. Yet the resulting

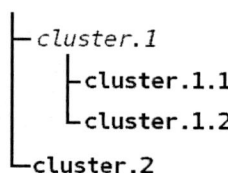

count	pos	neg	class	perc
2495	1593	902	1	63.8%
902	0	902	-1	100.0%
1593	1593	0	1	100.0%
695	0	695	-1	100.0%

Fig. 4. Performance on Problem 6. In the diagram: clusters in slanted font are further split into sub-clusters. In the table: *count* is number of objects in each cluster; *pos* and *neg* indicate splicing and non-splicing sites, resp.; *class* is the majority class; *perc* is the percentage of objects in the majority class.

classification, after performing the calibration step, is errorless, as indicated in the figure.

These data should be compared to results of other methods. Among the results reported in the accompanying documentation to the data set, no supervised method is capable of errorless performance. Comparison with centroid-based clustering methods (k-Means) is not possible, since a proper centroid (barycenter) is not obtainable from non-metric data. It is also difficult to compare the obtained tree to that given by the standard agglomerative hierarchical methods, since, in contrast to Problem 1, here the cardinality is high as an absolute value (although still very low when related to the dimensionality). Trees obtained with these methods may or may not be comparable to the one presented.

VII. Conclusion

The clustering algorithm presented here is based on a novel principle of operation, and as such has properties not found in other more commonly used methods. It is especially designed for the analysis of data sets with high dimensionality and low cardinality, and is therefore well suited to DNA microarray data analysis, as demonstrated by the experiments. However it is more generally applicable in the field of biomedical data analysis, where these conditions are often met.

We have observed that, similarly to the Jarvis-Patrick algorithm, the method presented may suffer from many small or singleton clusters. This happens especially when data cardinality grows. Future developments include criteria for controlling the proliferation of singletons (cluster validity) and applications to outlier detection.

Acknowledgment

Work funded by the Italian National Institute for the Physics of Matter (INFM), the Italian Ministry of Education, University and Research (2004 "Research Projects of Major National Interest", code 2004062740), and the Biopattern EU Network of Excellence.

References

[1] A. K. Jain, M. N. Murty, and P. J. Flynn, "Data clustering: a review", *ACM Computing Surveys*, vol. 31, no. 3, pp. 264–323, 1999.

[2] M. B. Eisen, P. T. Spellman, P. O. Brown, and D. Botstein, "Cluster analysis and display of genome-wide expression patterns", *Proceedings of the National Academy of Sciences*, vol. 95, no. 25, pp. 14863–14868, 1998.

[3] R. R. Sokal and C. D. Michener, "A statistical method for evaluating systematic relationships", *University of Kansas Science Bulletin*, vol. 38, pp. 1409–1438, 1958.

[4] J. H. Ward, "Hierarchical grouping to optimize an objective function", *Journal of American Statistical Association*, vol. 58, no. 301, pp. 236–244, 1963.

[5] R. R. Sokal and P. H. Sneath, *Principles of Numerical Taxonomy*, Freeman, San Francisco, USA, 1963.

[6] R. A. Jarvis and E. A. Patrick, "Clustering using a similarity measure based on shared near neighbors", *IEEE Transactions on Computers*, vol. C22, pp. 1025–1034, 1973.

[7] R. Bellman, *Adaptive Control Processes: A Guided Tour*, Princeton University Press, 1961.

[8] R. O. Duda and P. E. Hart, *Pattern Classification and Scene Analysis*, John Wiley and Sons, New York (USA), 1973.

[9] C. C. Aggarwal and P. S. Yu, "Redefining clustering for high-dimensional applications", *IEEE Transactions on Knowledge and Data Engineering*, vol. 14, no. 2, pp. 210–225, March/April 2002.

[10] G. H. Ball and D. J. Hall, "ISODATA, an iterative method of multivariate analysis and pattern classification", *Behavioral Science*, vol. 12, pp. 153–155, 1967.

[11] K. Beyer, J. Goldstein, R. Ramakrishnan, and U. Shaft, "When is nearest neighbor meaningful?", in *7th International Conference on Database Theory Proceedings (ICDT'99)*. 1999, pp. 217–235, Springer-Verlag.

[12] C. Spearman, "'General intelligence,' objectively determined and measured", *American Journal of Psychology*, vol. 15, pp. 201–293, 1904.

[13] M. Kendall and J. D. Gibbons, *Rank Correlation Methods*, Oxford University Press, Oxford (UK), fifth edition, 1990.

[14] J. W. Smith, J. E. Everhart, W. C. Dickson, W. C. Knowler, and R. S. Johannes, "Using the adap learning algorithm to forecast the onset of diabetes mellitus", in *Proceedings of the Symposium on Computer Applications and Medical Care*. 1988, pp. 261–265, Computer Society Press.

[15] C. L. Blake and C. J. Merz, "UCI repository of machine learning databases", 1998. http://www.ics.uci.edu/~mlearn/MLRepository.html.

[16] W. N. Street, W. H. Wolberg, and O. L. Mangasarian, "Nuclear feature extraction for breast tumor diagnosis", in *IS&T/SPIE 1993 International Symposium on Electronic Imaging: Science and Technology*, 1993, vol. 1905, pp. 861–870.

[17] C. Moneta, G. Parodi, S. Rovetta, and R. Zunino, "Automated diagnosis and disease characterization using neural network analysis", in *Proceedings of the 1992 IEEE International Conference on Systems, Man and Cybernetics - Chicago, IL, USA*, October 1992, pp. 123–128.

[18] G. Bianchi, L. Buffrini, P. Monteforte, G. Rovetta, S. Rovetta, and R. Zunino, "Neural approaches to the diagnosis and characterization of lyme disease", in *Proceedings of the 7th IEEE Symposium on Computer-Based Medical Systems, Winston-Salem, NC*, 1994, pp. 194–199.

[19] T. R. Golub, D. K. Slonim, P. Tamayo, C. Huard, M. Gaasenbeek, J. P. Mesirov, H. Coller, M. L. Loh, J. R. Downing, M. A. Caligiuri, C. D. Bloomfield, and E. S. Lander, "Molecular classification of cancer: Class discovery and class prediction by gene expression monitoring", *Science*, vol. 286, no. 5439, pp. 531–537, October 1999.

[20] M. O. Noordewier, G. G. Towell, and J. W. Shavlik, "Training knowledge-based neural networks to recognize genes in dna sequences", in *Advances in Neural Information Processing Systems III*. 1991, vol. 3, Morgan Kaufmann.

Inferring Protein-Protein Interactions Using Interaction Network Topologies

Alberto Paccanaro[†*], Valery Trifonov[‡*], Haiyuan Yu[†], Mark Gerstein[†]
[†]Department of Molecular Biophysics and Biochemistry
[‡]Department of Computer Science
Yale University, New Haven, CT 06520, USA
E-mail: {alberto.paccanaro, valery.trifonov, haiyuan.yu, mark.gerstein}@yale.edu
[*these authors contributed equally to this work]

Abstract— We describe two novel methods for predicting protein interactions, using only the topology of an observed protein interaction network. The first method searches the protein interaction network for defective cliques (*i.e.* nearly complete complexes of pairwise interacting proteins), and predicts the interactions that complete them. The second method computes the diffusion distance between each pair of proteins and then infers an interaction when such distance is below a given threshold. We show that both methods have a good predictive performance and compare their results.

I. Introduction

A fundamental problem in modern biology is the identification of the complete set of interactions among the proteins in a cell [12], [10], [7]. Different experimental methods are available to identify such interactions, and they can be roughly divided into two main categories: small-scale (low throughput) and large-scale (high throughput) techniques. Given a set of proteins, small-scale techniques such as co-IP determine the interaction between one pair of proteins at a time [18], [11], [17], [1]. On the other hand, large-scale techniques, *e.g.* yeast two-hybrid and TAP-tagging, allow identifying a large number of interacting pairs in a single experiment [3], [4], [5], [15].

With the advent of genome-wide analysis, we are interested in the identification of the interaction among a great number of proteins (even of all the proteins in a genome). When the number of proteins is in the thousands, the number of possible interacting pairs is in the millions [8]. To discover all these interactions using small-scale experiments becomes very labor-intensive and time-consuming, and in this situation large-scale experiments are preferred.

However, low throughput experiments allow much more precise identification of the interacting pairs than high throughput experiments — the latter are known to be more error-prone [6], [16].

Two types of errors are possible: the large-scale experiment can wrongly indicate that an interaction exists, *i.e.* yield a false positive (FP); or it can fail to detect an interaction that actually exists, thus producing a false negative (FN). However, experimentalists would agree that the these two types of errors occur with different frequency in large-scale experiments. While false positives have "higher visibility" due to the relatively small number of true interactions, it is generally observed that experiments allow a higher absolute degree of confidence when an interaction is observed, but a much lower degree when no interaction is detected. In other words, most of the errors (as an absolute count, not relative to the numbers of actual interacting or noninteracting protein pairs) are false negatives: it is believed that when no interaction is detected, it is not unlikely that the interaction actually exists, but the experiment has failed to detect it. In support of this observation, Figure 1 shows the differences between the low-throughput and high-throughput experimental data on protein-protein interactions in a subset of 56 proteins of *S. cerevisiae*, for which we were able to obtain complete matrices of experimental results. Of the 1596 pairs of proteins (including possible self-interactions), the results of the two types of experiments were the same for 1033; in the 563 cases when the results were different, 521 (92.5%) were false negatives and 42 (7.5%) were false positives.

Ideally, we would like to have a computational method which would be able to correct many of the errors made by large-scale interaction experiments.

In this paper we propose two new methods, based purely on topological properties of graphs representing protein interaction networks, that attempt to infer those interactions that have been missed by large-scale experiments.

II. The Defective Clique Completion algorithm

The basic idea of the defective clique completion algorithm derives from the way in which pull down experiments, a particular type of large scale experiments, are carried out, and particularly from the matrix model interpretation of their results [3], [4], [13], [2]. In these experiments one protein—the bait—is used to pull out the set of proteins interacting with it, *i.e.* its protein complex, in the form of a list. When such lists differ only in a few elements, it is reasonable to assume that this is due to experimental errors, and such elements should therefore be added (thus making the lists equal). Each list can be represented as a fully connected graph in which proteins occupy the nodes. Then the problem of identifying lists that differ in only a few elements is equivalent to finding a clique

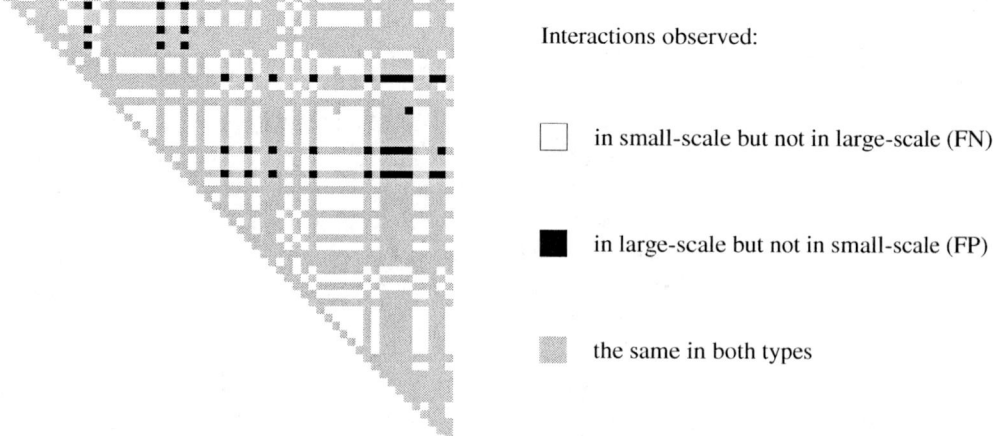

Fig. 1. A graphical representation of the symmetric matrix of the differences between complete protein-protein interaction data obtained in small-scale and large-scale experiments on 56 proteins of *S. cerevisiae*. Only the upper triangular part is shown, and element (i, j) of the matrix represents the interaction between protein i and protein j. White squares indicate interactions observed in small-scale but not in large-scale experiments (false negatives); black squares stand for interactions observed in large-scale but not in small-scale experiments (false positives); gray squares show protein pairs for which both the small- and the large-scale experiments produced the same result. The number of false negatives exceeds the number of false positives by an order of magnitude.

with a few missing edges, which we shall call a *defective clique*.

We shall represent a protein interaction network with a graph G, whose vertices V are proteins, and whose edges E are the pairs of interacting proteins. A *clique* in a graph is a set K of vertices such that $K \times K \subseteq E$, *i.e.* each pair of vertices in K is connected by an edge in E. The *size* of this clique is the number of vertices in it.

As we just discussed, under the matrix model interpretation of the results of large-scale experiments, two proteins interacting with the same protein clusters are likely to interact with each other. Thus in graph-theoretic terms our approach is based on the following observation about protein interaction networks:

(∗) If vertices P and Q are both adjacent to each vertex in a clique K, then it is likely that P and Q are adjacent to each other, if they are not adjacent already.

This observation can be depicted as shown in Figure 2; in this example the size of the clique K is 5. The dashed edge between P and Q corresponds to an interaction which is missing from the experimental data, but which (according to observation (∗)) is very likely to occur. We say that P, Q, and K form a *defective clique* KPQ with a missing edge PQ.

Clearly the size of K plays an important role in determining how likely it is that P and Q interact. For example, if the size of K is 1 (*i.e.* P and Q both interact with one or more proteins, but those proteins do not interact among themselves), the likelihood of an interaction between P and Q is much smaller than it is in the case when the size of K is, say, 42. Thus a natural parameter of a prediction algorithm based on observation (∗) is the minimal size k of K for which the interaction PQ is predicted.

Another parameter with which we can extend observation (∗) is the number of edges missing from the clique when its size is sufficiently large. We will discuss the effects of this parameter in subsection B, when we describe our algorithm in detail.

A. An algorithm for finding defective cliques

Our definition of a defective clique does not suggest immediately a method for finding such patterns in a protein interaction network. For this purpose it is useful to find an alternative characterization of a defective clique in standard graph-theoretic terms, which will allow us to use some off-the-shelf algorithms.

The main idea of our algorithm is based on the realization that a defective clique KPQ of size n with one missing edge is the union of two (complete) cliques of size $n-1$, namely $K \cup \{P\}$ and $K \cup \{Q\}$, as shown in Figure 3. Thus we can reduce the algorithm for finding defective cliques to repeating the following steps until reaching a fixed point:

1) Step 1: Find all cliques in the network.
2) Step 2:
   - Find pairs of cliques overlapping on all but one node each.
   - In each of these pairs predict the edges between the non-overlapping nodes.
   - Add the new edges to the network.

The algorithm terminates when no new edges were added in Step 2.

However, directly applying this naïve recipe to typical protein interaction networks is unrealistic, for the following reason: Since every subset of nodes in a given clique is itself a clique, the number of all cliques in a graph is at least 2^m, where m is the size of the largest clique in the graph. For example, the experimental data for the protein interaction

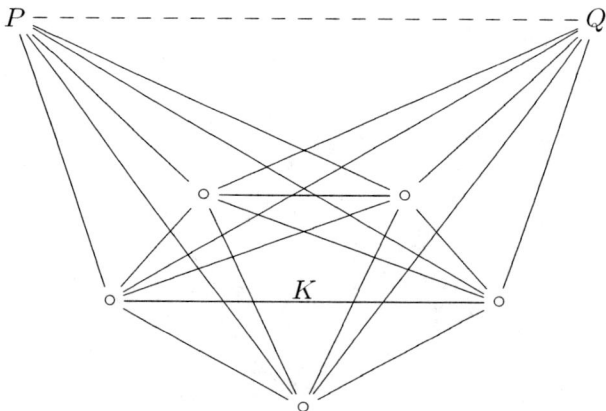

Fig. 2. A defective clique in a protein interaction network; the dashed edge between proteins P and Q corresponds to a predicted interaction.

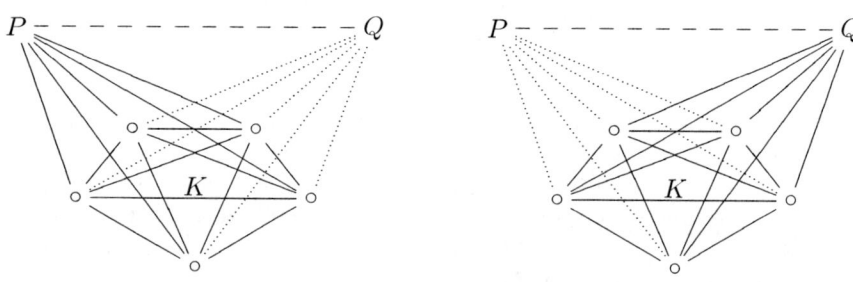

Fig. 3. The decomposition of a defective clique into the union of two overlapping cliques.

network of *S. cerevisiae* we used to test our algorithm (see Section IV) contains four cliques of size 38; this yields more than 10^{12} cliques (even if we do not consider cliques of size less than 5, whose number is negligible), hence more than 10^{23} pairs of cliques to check in Step 2 of the algorithm. Since this number is prohibitively large, we need a more effective formulation of the algorithm. For this purpose in the next section we design an equivalent algorithm which only considers the *maximal* cliques in the graph.

B. Improving Efficiency Using Maximal Cliques

A *maximal* clique in a graph G is one which is not contained in any other clique in G. In the worst case the problem of finding all maximal cliques still takes time exponential in the size of the graph[1]; however, if Step 1 is modified to only produce the maximal cliques in the graph, as discussed in the previous section its output would be exponentially smaller than with the naïve approach. This would reduce by an exponent the running time of Step 2 of the algorithm.

In practice, the protein interaction networks are rather sparse (*e.g.* less than 15,000 interactions are observed with high confidence in the network of *S. cerevisiae*, out of over 18 million possible pairs of about 6,000 proteins [16]). Our results show that existing algorithms for finding maximal cliques [14] are very efficient on graphs with this structure.

However, if we only compare maximal cliques for overlap on all but one node each, as we did with all cliques in the naïve version, the output of this algorithm will not be the same as that of the naïve version. The reason is that if a defective clique KPQ consists of a core clique K and two nodes P and Q, we know that $K \cup \{P\}$ and $K \cup \{Q\}$ are cliques, but in general they are not maximal cliques. Suppose K_P and K_Q are cliques containing P and Q respectively, and such that $K \cup K_P$ and $K \cup K_Q$ are maximal cliques. (If $K \cup \{P\}$ and $K \cup \{Q\}$ are cliques, then K_P and K_Q always exist, but are not necessarily unique.) Then Step 2 of the algorithm will compare $K \cup K_P$ and $K \cup K_Q$; however, K_P in general may contain other nodes in addition to P, and these nodes will not necessarily all be in K_Q. As a result, the nonoverlapping parts of the maximal cliques will consist of more than one node each, and the naïve algorithm will ignore the pair and thus fail to predict the edge PQ.

Hence, to obtain the same results as with our original algorithm, we have to modify Step 2 of the algorithm to look for partial overlaps of maximal cliques which differ in more than one node. This leads us to generalize the notion of a

---

[1]More precisely, the problem is NP-complete, *i.e.* only exponential-time algorithms are known for it.

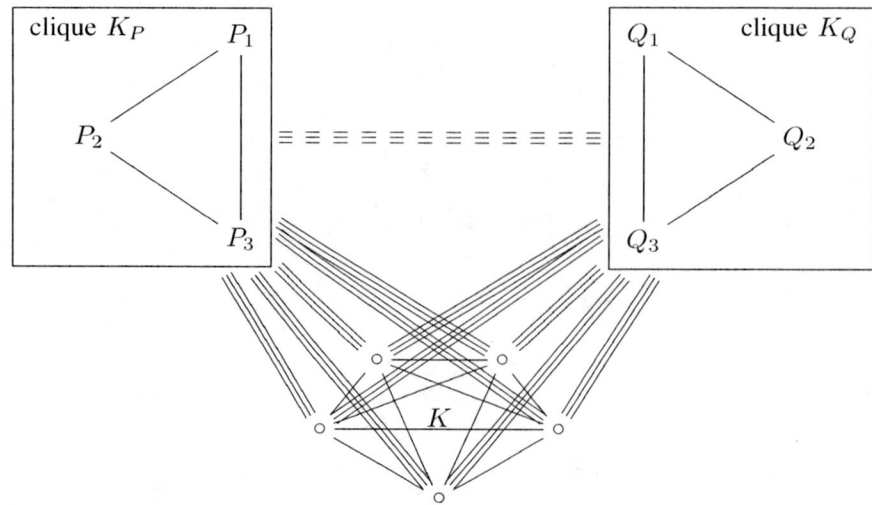

Fig. 4. Generalized defective cliques.

defective clique as shown in Figure 4. To obtain the same result as in the original approach, any pair of nodes P_i and Q_j, belonging to the two non-overlapping components K_P and K_Q respectively, must be predicted as interacting, because the original algorithm would have predicted it (since it completes the defective non-maximal clique KP_iQ_j). The maximal size n of non-overlapping sub-cliques K_P and K_Q is a parameter of the algorithm.

Since even the number of maximal cliques can be significant (in the hundreds of thousands for some of our experimental datasets), and their sizes can be in the hundreds of nodes, the number of comparisons between nodes in pairs of cliques in Step 2 can still be formidable in practice. We further reduce the time complexity of Step 2 by organizing the cliques (represented as strings sorted by node index) into a prefix tree. This structure allows us to reuse some comparison results among cliques sharing a common prefix of nodes.

III. THE DIFFUSION DISTANCE ALGORITHM

As we stated earlier, two proteins interacting with the same protein cluster are likely to interact with each other. This principle is derived from the way in which pull down experiments are carried out, and the clique completion algorithm that we have just described is the literal implementation of this idea. One possible shortcoming of this method is that edges are inferred only when they are found within specific defective cliques which comply with a particular setting of the parameters of the algorithm. However, we may want to think about our principle in a softer way, and realize that ideally what we would really like is to infer an edge between two proteins whenever they are connected by *many short* paths in the graph. A possible way of implementing this idea is by considering diffusion distances.

Let us again think about our protein-protein interaction prediction problem in terms of graphs, but this time we think of a graph as a system with some dynamics. We can imagine that at any given time there are some particles on the vertices of the graph, and at each time step these particles jump from one vertex to another with certain probabilities. Since our links are binary (either an edge exists between two proteins or it is missing) we shall assign equal probability $p_{i,j}$ to each existing link going from node i to node j: $p_{i,j} = 1/d_i$ where d_i is the degree of node i. We can collect these probabilities into a matrix: $M = A \cdot D^{-1}$ where A is the adjacency matrix of the graph and D is the diagonal matrix of the degree of the nodes. This matrix is called Markov transition matrix and a path that a particle travels is called a random walk.

Given a graph with n vertices, we can describe the initial position of a particle as a discrete probability distribution over the n vertices, that can be written out as a vector $v_0 \in R^n$ whose components are all positive and sum to one. Then the probability distribution of the particle at the next time step is given by: $v_1 = M \cdot v_0$ and the probability after k iterations is given by: $v_k = M^k \cdot v_0$. Therefore, for any initial configuration, we can compute the probability of ending up in any final configuration after a given number of steps.

We can now think of this probability as defining some kind of distance: starting from a given initial node, the higher the probability of ending up at a certain node, the smaller the distance between the two nodes. Clearly, such distance between two nodes will depend on two factors: how many different paths connect the two nodes, and how long these paths are.

This type of distance is called Diffusion Distance, and our idea is to use it in order to measure the connectivity between two nodes: when two proteins are connected by many short paths in the graph such distance would be small, and we could infer an edge between them.

It is possible to show [9] that such distance between nodes x and y has a simple form:

$$D_m(x,y) = \sum_{i=1}^{n} \lambda_i^m \cdot [u_i(x) - u_i(y)]^2$$

where u_i and λ_i, $i = 1 \ldots n$ are respectively the eigenvectors and eigenvalues of a symmetric matrix similar to M, and m is a parameter denoting the maximum length of the Markov random walks between x and y which are taken into account by the measure. The algorithm for inferring protein-protein interaction then consists of two steps:

1) For each pair of proteins compute the diffusion distance between them
2) Infer that two proteins interact if their diffusion distance is lower than a certain threshold τ.

Therefore, as for the clique completion algorithm, this method requires the setting of two parameters: m, the maximum length of the Markov random walks; and τ, the threshold for the distance, below which we should infer the interaction.

IV. RESULTS

Here we shall present the results obtained using our two methods for inferring protein-protein interactions which had been missed by large scale experiments.

A. Performance of the Clique Completion Algorithm

We applied the clique completion method to a large scale experimental dataset of the protein interaction network of *S. cerevisiae* obtained combining the results of different separate experiments by [3], [4], [5], [15]. For this organism we also had available a gold standard set of protein pairs known with high degree of confidence to be "positive" (interacting) or "negative" (noninteracting), published in [7]. The gold standard set for these tests contained 8250 positive and 2708622 negative pairs. Our idea was to use the gold standard set in order to check the performance of our algorithm at predicting protein-protein interactions from a large scale experiment.

Given their experimental and heterogeneous origin, these datasets present some complications. Firstly, the adjacency matrix for the gold standard is incomplete, in the sense that for many pairs of proteins no experiment was performed in order to verify their interaction. Secondly, the large scale dataset is also incomplete, in the sense that its adjacency matrix does not overlap perfectly with the gold standard dataset — some proteins present in the gold standard were not included in any of the large scale experiments. So we had to decide how to treat such missing datapoints and how to evaluate the performance of the algorithm.

As regards the missing values in the large scale experimental data, we assumed that in these cases the input data showed no interaction between the proteins (therefore notice that the performance of the algorithm should improve if all possible experiments were performed).

For evaluating the performance of the algorithm we used the likelihood ratio of the predicted interactions, defined in [7] as

$$L = \frac{\frac{P_+}{G_+}}{\frac{P_-}{G_-}}$$

where

P_+ is the number of true positives – predicted interactions which are positive in the gold standard;
P_- is the number of false positives – predicted interactions which are negative in the gold standard;
G_+ is the total number of positive pairs in the gold standard; and
G_- is the total number of negative pairs in the gold standard.

Higher values of L correspond to sets of predictions having higher overlap with the positive and/or lower overlap with the negative gold standard, and generally indicate better predictors.

The initial large scale experiment graph contains 7047 edges between 2283 nodes. In this graph the Maximal Cliques algorithm found 543 maximal cliques of size at least 4. Step 2 of the algorithm, configured to search for partial overlaps of size at least $k = 5$ and non-overlapping parts of size at most $n = 3$, predicted 270 new interactions. Of these, 49 were in the gold standard set; of them 38 were positive and 11 negative, which yields a likelihood ratio of 1134.19, significantly higher than the likelihood ratios of other single features reported in [7] (essentiality, expression correlation, MIPS function, and GO biological process), which are below 400.

The chosen values of the parameters are in a "plateau" of relative stability of the results. The likelihood ratio of the predicted set was between 59.13 and 3720.94 when varying the parameters of the algorithm as follows: k (the minimal overlap size) between 4 and 7, and n (the maximal size of the non-overlapping parts) between 1 and 20; the number of predicted interactions was between 12 and 8993. The average running time was below 4 seconds on a desktop machine.

Taking into account the size of the predicted set, we believe its high likelihood ratio with respect to the gold standard is a strong argument for the usefulness of this method as a predictor of new interactions.

B. Performance of the Diffusion Distance Algorithm

Here we show a preliminary result of the performance of the diffusion distance algorithm. We took a sub-graph of the protein interaction network of S. cerevisiae for a set of 43 proteins for which we had information about the interactions of each pair of proteins in the gold standard set. In other words, this is a subset of the gold standard set for which there were no missing values. Then we simulated the experimental noise present in the large scale experiments by randomly creating false negatives (FN) in this dataset; that is we randomly turned a certain percentage of the 1s into 0s. We then tried to see how many of these FN were fixed by running our diffusion distance algorithm. Figure 5 shows the results obtained for different level of noise, for $m = 3$, and $\tau = 0.1$.

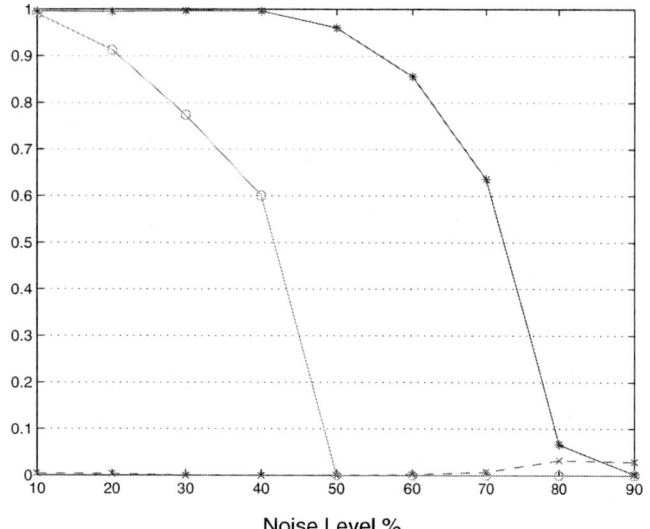

Fig. 5. Performance of the two algorithms on the 43x43 subset of the gold standard, for different values of the noise level. The continuous lines represent the ratio of the number of errors which were recovered over the total number of errors — the (red) '*' line represents the result for the diffusion distance algorithm, the (green) 'o' line represents the result for the clique completion algorithm. The (magenta) 'x' dashed line represents the ratio of the number of errors which were introduced over total size of the matrix for the diffusion distance algorithm. The clique completion algorithm never introduced any error.

We can see that the diffusion distance algorithm is able to recover a very high percentage of FN, even for very high level of noise: when 40% of all 1s are turned into 0s, the algorithm can correctly recover 99% of them; with 40% noise the algorithm still recovers about 96% of them. At the same time, almost no errors are introduced even for high level of noise.

These results are possible because in this dataset things are as anticipated by our biological hypothesis: proteins interact in complexes. Clearly when the noise level is too high, the complex structure is disrupted and therefore interactions cannot be recovered and many errors are introduced.

C. Comparison of the two methods

We performed the same experiment using the clique completion algorithm, with parameters $k = 6$, $n = 17$, and results are also shown in fig.5. We can see that this algorithm also performs quite well, although it seems to be more sensitive to noise than the diffusion distance algorithm. For this experiment, the clique completion algorithm never introduced a false positive, *i.e.* when it inferred an interaction between two proteins it was always correct.

V. CONCLUSION

We presented two methods for predicting new protein-protein interactions, based purely on topological properties of networks of observed interactions. Each of the two methods discussed in this paper has its advantages. The main advantage of the clique completion algorithm over the diffusion distance one, is that it can always provide an explanation of why a certain interaction has been inferred, in terms of the cliques that are completed. Also, it will never introduce a false negative. On the other hand, the diffusion distance algorithm seem to provide a better performance due to the extra flexibility afforded by such distance.

We believe that these methods, although computationally expensive, have the advantage of being more robust than other protein-protein interaction prediction methods by virtue of their independence of non-topological features such as functional classification.

ACKNOWLEDGMENT

We are grateful to Ronald Jansen, David Lu, Jason Lu, and Yu Xia for many discussions and insightful suggestions.

REFERENCES

[1] G D Bader, D Betel, and C W Hogue. BIND: the Biomolecular Interaction Network Database. *Nucleic Acids Res*, 31(1):248–50, 2003.
[2] G D Bader and C W Hogue. Analyzing yeast protein-protein interaction data obtained from different sources. *Nat Biotechnol*, 20(10):991–7, 2002.
[3] A C Gavin et al. Functional organization of the yeast proteome by systematic analysis of protein complexes. *Nature*, 415(6868):141–7, 2002.
[4] Y Ho et al. Systematic identification of protein complexes in Saccharomyces cerevisiae by mass spectrometry. *Nature*, 415(6868):180–3, 2002.
[5] T Ito et al. Toward a protein-protein interaction map of the budding yeast: A comprehensive system to examine two-hybrid interactions in all possible combinations between the yeast proteins. *Proc Natl Acad Sci USA*, 97(3):1143–7, 2000.
[6] R Jansen et al. Integration of genomic datasets to predict protein complexes in yeast. *J Struct Funct Genomics*, 2:71–81, 2002.
[7] R Jansen et al. A Bayesian networks approach for predicting protein-protein interactions from genomic data. *Science*, 302(5644):449–53, 2003.
[8] A Kumar and M Snyder. Protein complexes take the bait. *Nature*, 415(6868):123–4, 2002.
[9] S Lafon. *Diffusion maps and geometric harmonics.* PhD thesis, Yale University, 2004.
[10] E M Marcotte et al. Detecting protein function and protein-protein interactions from genome sequences. *Science*, 285(5428):751–3, 1999.
[11] H W Mewes et al. MIPS: a database for genomes and protein sequences. *Nucleic Acids Res*, 30(1):31–4, 2002.
[12] M Pellegrini et al. Assigning protein functions by comparative genome analysis: protein phylogenetic profiles. *Proc Natl Acad Sci USA*, 96(8):4285–8, 1999.
[13] G Rigaut et al. A generic protein purification method for protein complex characterization and proteome exploration. *Nat Biotechnol*, 17(10):1030–2, 1999.
[14] S Tsukiyama, M Ide, H Ariyoshi, and I Shirakawa. A new algorithm for generating all the maximal independent sets. *SIAM J. Comput.*, 6(3):505–17, September 1977.
[15] P Uetz et al. A comprehensive analysis of protein-protein interactions in Saccharomyces cerevisiae. *Nature*, 403(6770):623–7, 2000.
[16] C von Mering et al. Comparative assessment of large-scale data sets of protein-protein interactions. *Nature*, 417(6887):399–403, 2002.
[17] I Xenarios et al. DIP, the Database of Interacting Proteins: a research tool for studying cellular networks of protein interactions. *Nucleic Acids Res*, 30(1):303–5, 2002.
[18] Y Xia et al. Analyzing cellular biochemistry in terms of molecular networks. *Annu Rev Biochem*, 73:1051–87, 2004.

Predicting Sugar Regulation in *Arabidopsis thaliana* using Kernel Learning Methods

Kamel Saadi, Kee-Khoon Lee, Gavin C. Cawley
School of Computing Sciences
University of East Anglia
Norwich NR4 7TJ U.K.
E-mail: {ks,kkl,gcc}@cmp.uea.ac.uk

Michael W. Bevan
John Innes Centre
Norwich Research Park
Norwich NR4 7UA U.K.
E-mail: mike.bevan@bbsrc.ac.uk

Abstract—The ability to predict the transcriptional regulation of genes, based on the composition of the upstream promoter region, would be a useful step in deciphering gene regulatory networks in eukaryotic organisms. In this paper we perform optimally regularised kernel Fisher discriminant (ORKFD) analysis of the upstream promoter sequences of genes to predict whether they are up- or down-regulated in response to glucose in the model plant *Arabidopsis thaliana*. Three feature selection strategies are investigated, namely use of known promoter motifs drawn from the PLACE database, explicit enumeration of all possible k-mers and the use of the mismatch kernels (which effectively permits the construction of a linear model in the space of all possible k-mers with up to m mismatches). The leave-one-out cross-validation (LOOCV) error rate indicates that approximately two-thirds of of the observed regulatory behaviour can be inferred by the presence of particular motifs in the upstream promoter sequence. The analysis has yielded novel biological insight, which has since been confirmed experimentally *in vivo*.

I. INTRODUCTION

The genomes of animals, plants and micro-organisms are comprised of thousands of genes whose expression is regulated to co-ordinate growth and development. One of the most exciting and complex challenges in biological research is to understand the mechanisms regulating gene expression, and to understand how gene expression is integrated in space and time. Multicellular organisms have a relatively complex gene structure comprising the coding regions or exons that encode protein sequence, introns that separate the individual exons comprising a gene, and conserved regulatory sequences flanking the gene that confer specific patterns of expression and direct the start and stop points for messenger RNA synthesis. Strategies to identify DNA sequence motifs implicated in regulating gene expression are less clear and effective, because these motifs are poorly defined, are relatively short, and are not generally strongly conserved within and between species. In this paper, we aim to estimate the degree to which up- or down-regulation can be inferred from the presence or absence of these conserved regulatory motifs, using glucose regulation in *A. thaliana* as a test-case. For this study we adopt kernel learning methods (see e.g. [1–3]), which facilitate the construction of classifiers acting directly on biological sequence data.

A. A Brief Overview Gene Regulation in Eukaryotes

The DNA of eukaryotic organisms is arranged in a number of chromosomes, each of which is a single molecule consisting of a linear polymer comprised of four different basic building blocks, known as "nucleotides" (adenine, cytosine, guanine and thyamine, usually represented by the letters A, C, G and T respectively). Each chromosome is divided into *genes*, each of which contains the genetic information specifying the sequence of amino acids forming a particular protein. Figure 1 shows a schematic representation of the structure of a gene in a eukaryotic organism. The DNA sequence of a gene is comprised of two sections, the transcribed region and the promoter region. For the synthesis of a protein to occur, a copy of the transcribed region must first be made in messenger RNA (mRNA). The transcribed region consists of *exons*, which specify the sequence of amino acids comprising the protein, separated by *introns*. Before leaving the cell nucleus, the mRNA is *spliced* to remove the sections corresponding to the introns. Some genes may be spliced in a number of alternative configurations, allowing a number of related proteins to be synthesised from a given gene. The exons consist of a sequence of *codons*, groups of three contiguous nucleotides, each of which specifies one of the twenty amino acids concatenated to form a protein.

The concentration of a protein within the cell body then depends on the rate at which the protein is synthesised and degraded by the biochemical machinery of the organism. The primary control on the rate of synthesis of a protein is provided by *transcriptional regulation*, which governs the rate at which mRNA copies of the coding region of the gene are transcribed. The *promoter* is a region of the DNA sequence that occurs "upstream" of the transcribed region of the gene. The transcription of the majority of eukaryotic genes is performed by an enzyme called RNA polymerase II, which moves downstream along the DNA sequence transcribing the mRNA copy one nucleotide at a time. In order for RNA polymerase II to bind to the appropriate starting position, a number of proteins known as *transcription factors* must first bind onto transcription factor binding sites within the promoter region. Transcription factors can act to encourage or inhibit transcription, in which case they are called *enhancers* or *silencers* respectively. Combinations

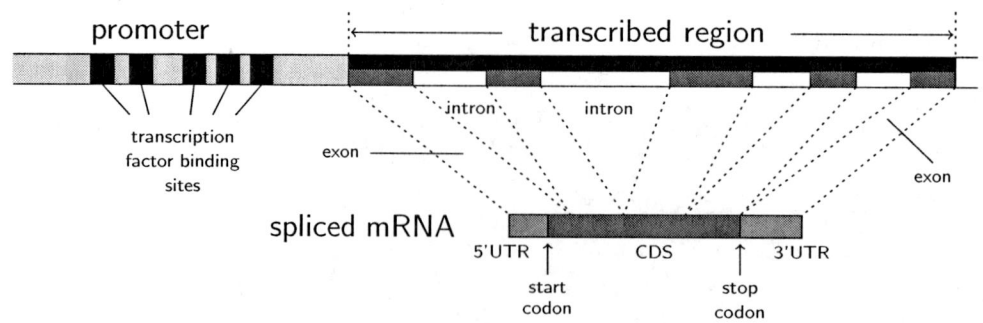

Fig. 1. Schematic representation of the structure of the eukaryotic gene, after Zien [4].

of different transcription factors binding to regulatory regions provide the high specificity of gene expression. Note that the sequence of bases forming a transcription factor binding site results in a specific conformation of (usually) the major groove of the double-helix structure, which matches the shape of part of the transcription factor. The complementary sequence (formed by reversing the order of bases and exchanging As and Ts and Cs and Gs) results in an identical conformation, but with the opposite orientation with respect to the transcribed region. The orientation of a transcription factor is not thought to be significant, and so the sequence corresponding a binding site and its complement are considered to be equivalent representations. The transcription of genes is then *regulated* by the nuclear concentrations of these transcription factors. For a more detailed, but accessible introduction to gene regulation in both prokaryotes and eukaryotes, see Alberts *et al.* [5].

B. Promoter-based Gene Classification

By identifying transcription factor binding sites and their relative positions in promoter region of genes it will be possible to establish the complex regulatory circuitry coordinating the expression of thousands of genes necessary to execute a given biological process. The transcription of all genes can now be accurately measured using microarray technology in many species. By establishing relationships and dependencies between transcript abundance and regulatory sequences it may be possible to identify specific combinations of transcription factor binding sites that confer transcript levels. We propose the use of kernel learning methods (e.g. [1–3]) to classify co-regulated genes, whose transcriptional abundance increases or decreases in response to a given environmental stimulus, as a means of identifying putative transcription factor binding sites. As an experimental system we use microarray and genome data from the plant *Arabidopsis*, which is completely sequenced and has a well characterised and compact genome. Classification of gene expression in response to the simple nutrient glucose identified a large number of putative transcriptional regulatory circuits that were verified by subsequent experiments.

The use of kernel learning methods provides a flexible means to efficiently investigate ways in which to select discriminative features for classification. Here we investigate features selected from a database of known transcription factor binding sites, selection from the set of all possible k-mers and through the use of the spectrum and mismatch kernels, linear combinations of all possible k-mers (perhaps allowing mismatches). An efficient kernel learning algorithm, namely optimally regularised kernel Fisher discriminant (ORKFD) analysis, which provides a computationally efficient means of constructing a kernel machine with the regularisation tuned so as to minimise the leave-one-out cross-validation error. This ensures that the complexity of the model is well-matched to the complexity of the learning task.

II. OPTIMALLY REGULARISED KERNEL FISHER DISCRIMINANT ANALYSIS

In this section, we give a brief review of the optimally regularised kernel Fisher discriminant analysis algorithm introduced by Saadi *et al.* [6]. Assume we are given training data $\mathcal{X} = \{x_1, x_2, \ldots, x_\ell\} = \{\mathcal{X}_1, \mathcal{X}_2\} \subset \mathbb{R}^d$, where $\mathcal{X}_1 = \{x_1^1, x_2^1, \ldots, x_{\ell_1}^1\}$ is a set of patterns belonging to class $\mathcal{C}_1$ and similarly $\mathcal{X}_2 = \{x_1^2, x_2^2, \ldots, x_{\ell_2}^2\}$ is a set of patterns belonging to class $\mathcal{C}_2$; Fisher's linear discriminant (e.g. [7, 8]) attempts to find a linear combination of input variables, $w \cdot x$, that maximises the average separation of the projections of points belonging to $\mathcal{C}_1$ and $\mathcal{C}_2$, whilst minimising the within class variance of the projections of those points. The innovation introduced by Mika *et al.* [9] is to construct Fisher's linear discriminant in a fixed feature space $\mathcal{F}$ ($\phi : \mathcal{X} \to \mathcal{F}$) induced by a positive definite *Mercer* kernel $\mathcal{K} : \mathcal{X} \times \mathcal{X} \to \mathbb{R}$ defining the inner product $\mathcal{K}(x, x') = \phi(x) \cdot \phi(x')$. The kernel Fisher discriminant (KFD) is then given by the kernel expansion,

$$f(x) = \sum_{i=1}^{\ell} \alpha_i \mathcal{K}(x_i, x) + b. \qquad (1)$$

It is well known that Fisher discriminant analysis is equivalent to linear least-squares regression on the class labels (e.g. [8]), and so the optimal parameters α and b are given by the solution of the following system of linear equations (Xu *et al.* [10]):

$$\begin{bmatrix} KK + \mu I & K\mathbf{1} \\ (K\mathbf{1})^T & \ell \end{bmatrix} \begin{bmatrix} \alpha \\ b \end{bmatrix} = \begin{bmatrix} K \\ \mathbf{1} \end{bmatrix} y, \qquad (2)$$

where $\mathbf{1}$ is a column vector of ℓ ones and $\mathbf{y}$ is a column vector with elements $y_i = \ell/\ell_j \; \forall i : \mathbf{x}_i \in \mathcal{X}_j$, $\mathbf{K} = [k_{ij} = \mathcal{K}(\mathbf{x}_i, \mathbf{x}_j)]_{i,j=1}^{\ell}$ is the kernel or Gram matrix and μ is a regularisation parameter [11] controlling the bias-variance trade-off [12]. The KFD classifier has been shown experimentally to demonstrate near state-of-the-art performance on a range of artificial and real world benchmark datasets [9] and so is worthy of consideration for small to medium scale applications, such as that considered here. The key step in maximising generalisation performance is model selection, i.e. the choice of good values for kernel and regularisation parameters. The leave-one-out cross-validation error rate gives an almost unbiased estimate of the probability of test error [13], and so provides an attractive model selection criterion. In the remainder of this section, we show that the regularisation parameter of a KFD classifier can be efficiently tuned so as to minimise the leave-one-out error with a computational cost of only $\mathcal{O}(\ell^2)$ operations, giving rise to the optimally regularised kernel Fisher discriminant (ORKFD) classifier.

A. Kernel Fisher Discriminant Analysis in Canonical Form

In this paper we present an efficient algorithm for approximate cross-validation of kernel Fisher discriminant models, providing a practical criterion for model selection. The system of linear equations (2) can be written more concisely in the form

$$\boldsymbol{\beta} = \left[\mathbf{Z}^T\mathbf{Z} + \mathbf{R}\right]^{-1} \mathbf{Z}^T\mathbf{y}, \quad (3)$$

where $\mathbf{Z} = [\mathbf{K} \; \mathbf{1}]$ and $\mathbf{R}$ is a diagonal matrix with elements given by the vector of regularisation parameters $\boldsymbol{\mu}$. Let $\mathbf{V}$ be an orthogonal matrix, the columns of which are the eigenvectors of $\mathbf{Z}^T\mathbf{Z}$, and $\boldsymbol{\Lambda}$ be a diagonal matrix containing the corresponding eigenvalues $\lambda_0 \geq \lambda_1 \geq \cdots \geq \lambda_\ell \geq 0$, such that $\mathbf{Z}^T\mathbf{Z} = \mathbf{V}\boldsymbol{\Lambda}\mathbf{V}^T$ and $\mathbf{V}\mathbf{V}^T = \mathbf{V}^T\mathbf{V} = \mathbf{I}$. The principal components of $\mathbf{Z}$ are then given by the columns of $\mathbf{U} = \mathbf{Z}\mathbf{V}$; note that $\mathbf{U}^T\mathbf{U} = \boldsymbol{\Lambda}$. The system of linear equations (3) can then be expressed in *canonical form* [14] as

$$\boldsymbol{\alpha} = \mathbf{C}^{-1}\mathbf{U}^T\mathbf{y} = [\boldsymbol{\Lambda} + \mathbf{R}]^{-1}\mathbf{U}^T\mathbf{y}, \quad (4)$$

where $\boldsymbol{\alpha} = \mathbf{V}^T\boldsymbol{\beta}$. The principal advantage of expressing the system of linear equations (3) in this form is that the matrix $\mathbf{C}$ is diagonal, and so can be inverted in linear time, i.e. $\mathcal{O}(\ell)$ operations, and the parameters of the KFD can be updated following a change in the vector of regularisation parameters with a computational complexity of only $\mathcal{O}(\ell)$ operations.

B. Efficient Leave-One-Out Cross-Validation

At each step of the leave-one-out cross-validation procedure, a kernel Fisher discriminant classifier is constructed excluding a single example from the training data. The vector of canonical model parameters, $\boldsymbol{\alpha}_{(i)}$ at the ith step, in which pattern i is excluded, is then given by the solution of a modified system of linear equations,

$$\boldsymbol{\alpha}_{(i)} = \left[\mathbf{R} + \mathbf{U}_{(i)}^T\mathbf{U}_{(i)}\right]^{-1} \mathbf{U}_{(i)}^T\mathbf{y}$$

where $\mathbf{U}_{(i)}$ is the sub-matrix formed by omitting the ith row of $\mathbf{U}$. Note that $\mathbf{U}_{(i)}^T\mathbf{U}_{(i)}$ is in general no longer diagonal, and so the most computationally expensive step is again the inversion of the matrix $\mathbf{C}_{(i)} = \left[\mathbf{R} + \mathbf{U}_{(i)}^T\mathbf{U}_{(i)}\right]$, with a complexity of $\mathcal{O}(\ell^3)$ operations. Fortunately $\mathbf{C}_{(i)}$ can be written as a rank one modification of $\mathbf{C}$,

$$\mathbf{C}_{(i)} = \left[\mathbf{R}_{(i)} + \mathbf{U}^T\mathbf{U} - \mathbf{u}_i\mathbf{u}_i^T\right] = \left[\mathbf{C} - \mathbf{u}_i\mathbf{u}_i^T\right], \quad (5)$$

where $\mathbf{u}_i$ is the ith row of $\mathbf{U}$. This allows $\mathbf{C}_{(i)}^{-1}$ to be found in only $\mathcal{O}(\ell^2)$ operations [15], given that $\mathbf{C}^{-1}$ is already known, via the following matrix inversion formula : Given an invertible matrix $\mathbf{A}$ and column vectors $\mathbf{u}$ and $\mathbf{v}$, then assuming $\mathbf{v}^T\mathbf{A}^{-1}\mathbf{u} \neq -1$, we have that

$$\left(\mathbf{A} + \mathbf{u}\mathbf{v}^T\right)^{-1} = \mathbf{A}^{-1} - \frac{\mathbf{A}^{-1}\mathbf{u}\mathbf{v}^T\mathbf{A}^{-1}}{1 + \mathbf{v}^T\mathbf{A}^{-1}\mathbf{u}}.$$

The computational complexity of the matrix inversion at each step is thus reduced from $\mathcal{O}(\ell^3)$ to $\mathcal{O}(\ell^2)$. The computational complexity of the leave-one-out cross-validation process is then only $\mathcal{O}(\ell^3)$ operations, which is the same as that of the basic training algorithm for the kernel Fisher discriminant classifier. However, a further refinement is possible, it can be shown [16] that the leave-one-out error $E_{loo} = E_{loo}(\{\mathbf{r}_{(i)}\}_{i=1,\ell}, \mathbf{y})$, can be computed analytically in closed form using

$$\{\mathbf{r}_{(i)}\}_i = \frac{1}{1 - h_{ii}}r_i.$$

where $\{\mathbf{r}_{(i)}\}_i = y_i - \mathbf{w}_{(i)} \cdot \boldsymbol{\phi}(\mathbf{x}_i) - b_{(i)}$ is the residual error for the ith training pattern during the ith iteration of the leave-one-out cross-validation procedure, $r_i = y_i - \mathbf{w} \cdot \boldsymbol{\phi}(\mathbf{x}_i) - b$ is the residual error for the ith training pattern for a kernel Fisher discriminant classifier trained on the entire dataset, and $\mathbf{H} = \mathbf{U}\mathbf{C}^{-1}\mathbf{U}^T$ is the *hat* matrix of which h_{ii} is the ith element of the leading diagonal [14]. In this case, $\mathbf{C}$ is diagonal and can be inverted in linear time, and therefore

$$h_{ii} = \sum_{j=1}^{\ell} u_{ij}^2 c_{jj}^{-1} = \sum_{j=1}^{\ell} \frac{u_{ij}^2}{(\lambda_j + \mu_j)}.$$

The leave-one-out error rate can thus be evaluated in closed form without explicit inversion of $\mathbf{C}_{(i)} \; \forall i \in \{1, 2, \ldots, \ell\}$, with a computational complexity of only $\mathcal{O}(\ell^2)$ operations. To find the optimal regularisation parameters we will assume, as is normally the case, a single regularisation parameter μ, the optimal value, minimising the leave-one-out error, is then found using a simple line search.

III. IDENTIFICATION OF PUTATIVE REGULATORY MOTIFS

Three different feature extraction methods were used to extract motifs corresponding to putative transcription factor binding sites (regulatory motifs). The first approach simply took sequences from the PLACE database [17] representing experimentally determined plant cis-acting regulatory elements. These are sequences that are known to influence regulation in a variety of plants under a variety of stimuli (i.e. not necessarily implicated in glucose response). The second approach generated a small number of motifs using a partially automated "heuristic" approach, involving some intervention from the investigator. Lastly, the spectrum and mismatch kernels were used to implicitly create classifiers in a kernel-induced feature space comprised of all possible k-mers with up to m mismatched symbols. These approaches employ varying degrees of expert knowledge, from PLACE (high) to mismatch kernel (low), varying numbers of features, from mismatch kernel (high) to heuristic (low), and provide varying degrees of interpretability, from PLACE (high) to mismatch kernel (low).

A. Features Extracted from the PLACE Database

PLACE[1] is a database of motifs representing plant cis-acting regulatory DNA elements that have been obtained through experiments described in previously published reports on genes (principally) in vascular plants [17]. These sequences represent regulatory elements from a variety of plants, controlling regulatory response to a variety of stimuli, some of which relate to specific parts of the plant. No attempt was made to account for genetic divergence between *Arabidopsis thaliana* and the other plants targeted by entries in the PLACE database, which include rice (*Oryza sativa*), maize (*Zea mays*), tomato (*Lycopersicon esculentum*) and wheat (*Triticum aestivum*). Note also that many of the elements described in the PLACE database have not previously been implicated in glucose-response in any plant. A matrix was constructed, each column of which gives the number of occurrences of the sequence representing a PLACE element, or its complement, in the promoter of every gene co-regulated in response to glucose. Of the 381 PLACE elements, only 253 were found to occur in the promoters of the genes included in this study.

B. Features Extracted via Heuristic Search

A heuristic search, guided by the investigator, was used to test whether the use of a highly compact feature set substantially improved or degraded performance. The search began with the set of 4^5 distinct 5−mers drawn from the alphabet $\{A,C,G,T\}$. As we count a each 5-mer and its complement as being the same feature (as we do not distinguish between conformations of the double-helix that differ only in their orientation with respect to the transcribed region), and so we discard any sequence that is lexically greater than its complement. The remaining sequences were then scored according to a commonly used correlation coefficient (e.g. [18]),

$$f(x_j) = \frac{\mu^+ - \mu^-}{\sigma^+ + \sigma^-} \qquad (6)$$

where x_j is the jth motif, μ^+ and μ^- represent the mean number of occurrences of the jth in the promoters of genes in the positive (e.g. up-regulated) and negative (e.g. down-regulated) classes, and and σ^+ and σ^- are the corresponding standard deviations. This formula is related to the criterion

[1]Available from http://www.dna.affrc.go.jp/htdos/PLACE.

used in Fisher's linear discriminant analysis [7, 8] and a high positive or negative value indicates a highly discriminant feature. A three-way comparison was performed, investigating up-versus-down, up-versus-unregulated and down-verses-unregulated sets of genes. The features with high scores on up-versus-down, up-versus-unregulated *and* down-versus-unregulated were rejected as being equivocal. Next any motif with low coverage (below 30%) in either the up- or down-regulated sets were discarded, before selecting the motifs achieving correlation scores in the top 10% in the comparison of up-versus-down and up-versus-unregulated genes. At this point, five 5-mers associated with enhanced glucose response (AAACC, AACCC, ACCCT, CCCTA and CTACT) and eighteen 5-mers associated with glucose suppression (AAGAT, AATAT, ACGTG, AGATA, ATCAT, ATCCA, ATTAT, CACAT, CCACT, CTATC, GATAA, GATAT, TAAAG, TACGT, TATCC, TATCT, TATTA and TATAC) had been identified).

TABLE I

IUPAC WILDCARD SYMBOLS USED IN ADDITION TO A, C, G AND T.

Symbol	Bases	Symbol	Bases
B	C, G or T	D	A, G or T
H	A, C or T	K	G or T
M	A or C	N	A, C, G or T
R	A or G	S	C or G
V	A, C or G	W	A or T
Y	C or T		

Motifs were then grouped, such that any two 5-mers that share at least four consecutive bases were combined to form a 4-mer, e.g. AAACC and AACCC were combined to form AACC. Many transcription factor binding sites are assumed to be composed of a "core" sequence providing the bulk of its specificity, surrounded on both sides by less specific "flanking" sequences. The remaining features were then augmented by 3 base pairs of up-stream and down-stream flanking sequences. These were formed by an analysis of the regions immediate up- and down-stream of matches between the promoters of the co-regulated genes and the "core" sequence. IUPAC wildcard symbols (Table I) were added to the core motifs to accommodate any over-represented nucleotide in any of the six flanking positions. This resulted in the final set of 11 motifs : AAACCCTAA and CTACT associated with up-regulated genes and AAGATAW, YACGTG, YTATCYA, TATTAT, AATAT, ATCAT, CACAT, CCACT, TAAAG associated with down-regulated genes. It is interesting to note that two of these motifs are also found in the PLACE database, namely AAACCCTAA, known as the "TELOBOX" element and YACGTG forming a substantial part of the "ABREATCONSENSUS" element.

C. Features "Extracted" from Sequence Kernels

Kernel learning methods have been found to be particularly well suited to many problems arising in computational biology [19] as it is relatively straight-forward to construct kernel functions operating directly on structured data, for instance variable length sequences of symbols drawn from a fixed alphabet, such as DNA sequence data. In this study, we use two such kernel functions, the k-spectrum kernel the k-spectrum kernel [20] and the closely related $(k$-$m)$-mismatch kernel [21, 22]. The feature space of the k-spectrum kernel records the number of occurrences of all possible substrings of length k from an alphabet $\mathcal{A}$ found in string, $\boldsymbol{x}$, i.e.

$$\boldsymbol{\Phi}_k(\boldsymbol{x}) = (\phi_a(\boldsymbol{x}))_{a \in \mathcal{A}^k}$$

where $\phi_a(\boldsymbol{x})$ gives the number of times the substring a occurs in $\boldsymbol{x}$. The k-spectrum kernel, which computes the inner product between vectors in the space of all possible k-mers,

$$\mathcal{K}_k(\boldsymbol{x}, \boldsymbol{x}') = \boldsymbol{\Phi}_k(\boldsymbol{x}) \cdot \boldsymbol{\Phi}_k(\boldsymbol{x}')$$

then measures the similarity of a pair of strings in terms of the "density" of shared substrings of length k. The (k, m)-mismatch kernel,

$$\mathcal{K}_{(k,m)}(\boldsymbol{x}, \boldsymbol{x}'),$$

extends the k-spectrum kernel, by allowing up to m mismatches in the determination of the set of shared substrings [20]. The feature space is then defined as follows : Let α, β represent k-mers in $\mathcal{A}$, then

$$\boldsymbol{\Phi}_{(k,m)}(\alpha) = (\phi_\beta(\boldsymbol{x}))_{\beta \in \mathcal{A}^k}.$$

where $\phi_\beta(\alpha)$ is 1 if the k-mers α and β differ in at most m locations and 0 otherwise. The feature vector for the entire string $\boldsymbol{x}$ is then found by summing over all substrings of length k occurring in $\boldsymbol{x}$,

$$\boldsymbol{\Phi}_{(k,m)}(\boldsymbol{x}) = \sum_{\alpha \in \boldsymbol{x}} (\boldsymbol{\Phi}_{(k,m)}(\alpha)).$$

The k-spectrum and $(k$-$m)$-mismatch kernels allow us to implicitly construct classifiers in the space of all possible substrings of length k, possibly allowing up to m mismatches to account for variation in transcription factor binding sites in genes with different evolutionary paths. Importantly, these kernels place no limitations on the initial set of putative regulatory motifs, but also incorporate very little expert knowledge.

A third kernel used in this study is the inhomogeneous polynomial kernel

$$\mathcal{K}(\boldsymbol{x}, \boldsymbol{x}') = (\boldsymbol{x} \cdot \boldsymbol{x}' + 1)^p,$$

which induces a feature space comprised of products of all combinations of p or less of the input variables. The use of this kernel allows us to implicitly include features representing *combinations* of regulatory motifs, without incurring the computational expense in evaluating these product features explicitly.

IV. Results

A database was assembled comprising approximately 1000 b.p. of 5' flanking sequences of 1051 genes with greater than 2.5 fold increase in response to glucose at 2, 4 and 6 hrs (the "Up" set), 793 promoters of genes with reduced expression in response to glucose at 2, 4 and 6 hrs (the "Down" set) and 964 un-regulated genes (the "Neutral" set) for this work. The

TABLE II

LEAVE-ONE-OUT CROSS-VALIDATION ERROR RATES OBTAINED FOR ORKFD CLASSIFIERS, BASED ON A POLYNOMIAL KERNEL, USING FEATURES DERIVED FROM THE PLACE DATABASE AND FEATURES EXTRACTED VIA HEURISTIC SEARCH.

p	PLACE	Heuristic
1	**0.33**	**0.34**
2	0.47	0.36
3	0.48	0.39
4	0.49	0.43
5	0.49	0.47
6	0.48	0.48
7	0.47	0.47
8	0.47	0.49
9	0.48	0.48
10	0.46	0.48

experimental results presented in this section are concerned with distinguishing between up- and down-regulated sets of genes. Table II shows the leave-one-out cross-validation error rates for ORKFD classifiers, based on a polynomial kernel, for feature sets derived from PLACE elements and extracted via the heuristic search procedure. Two features are immediately apparent: Firstly the feature set derived from the set of PLACE elements out-performed the feature set extracted via heuristic search, suggesting that the heuristic search procedure did not extract all of the useful discriminatory motifs from the promoters. Secondly, in both cases, the performance deteriorated as the order, p, of the polynomial kernel increased. This suggests that the discriminatory a combination of motifs is not greater than the sum of their parts, providing a useful insight into the co-ordination of gene regulation. Experiments using both the PLACE and heuristic feature sets demonstrated the "TELOBOX" motif to be discriminative in distinguishing up- from down-regulated genes. This is interesting as this regulatory element has not previously been implicated in sugar-regulation. We have since verified this result experimentally *in vivo*, demonstrating that our approach can be used to extract novel biological knowledge from microarray data.

Table III shows the leave-one-out cross-validation error for ORKFD classifiers based on the $(k$-$m)$-mismatch kernel, for various values of k and m. The best classifier is obtained for $(k=4, m=1)$ suggesting that over-fitting becomes more difficult to prevent for very precise feature sets (i.e. as k becomes large). However, the best classifier out-performs classifiers based on PLACE and heuristic search feature sets, suggesting that there are regulatory elements not well represented by the latter. Note also that for small k, longer regulatory motifs may be represented by $(k$-$m)$-mismatch features may be encoded by a pattern of activation over a number of length k features.

V. Conclusion

In this paper, we have applied a new kernel learning method, namely the optimally regularised kernel Fisher discriminant

TABLE III
LEAVE-ONE-OUT CROSS-VALIDATION ERROR (LOOCVE) RATES
OBTAINED FOR ORKFD CLASSIFIERS, BASED ON THE (k-m)-MISMATCH
KERNEL.

k	m	LOOCVE
4	1	**0.32**
5	1	0.34
5	2	0.34
6	1	0.38
6	2	0.38
6	3	0.38
7	1	0.37
7	2	0.37
7	3	0.37
8	2	0.38

(ORKFD) classifier, for promoter-based gene classification. The ORKFD provides an efficient means to set the regularisation parameter so as to minimise the leave-one-out cross-validation error. This makes the ORKFD an attractive tool for applications in computational biology as it not only avoids over-fitting, but also greatly simplifies the model selection procedure, where only the values of a small number of typically discrete kernel parameters remain to be found. The analysis of glucose response in *Arabidopsis thaliana* has revealed a novel role for the "TELOBOX" regulatory element, that had not previously been implicated in glucose response - a finding that has since been verified *in vivo*. The study has also suggested that, although regulatory elements act in combination to co-ordinate gene expression, the discriminatory power of a combination of motifs is not greater than the sum of the individual elements, so a linear learning method should suffice.

VI. Acknowledgements

This work was supported by a grant from the Biotechnology and Biological Sciences Research council (BBSRC), grant number 83/EGM16128.

References

[1] N. Cristianini and J. Shawe-Taylor. *An Introduction to Support Vector Machines (and other kernel-based learning methods)*. Cambridge University Press, Cambridge, U.K., 2000.
[2] B. Schölkopf and A. J. Smola. *Learning with kernels - support vector machines, regularization, optimization and beyond*. MIT Press, Cambridge, MA, 2002.
[3] J. Shawe-Taylor and N. Cristianini. *Kernel methods for pattern analysis*. Cambridge University Press, 2004.
[4] A. Zien. A primer on molecular biology. In B. Schölkopf, K. Tsuda, and J.-P. Vert, editors, *Kernel methods in computational biology*, chapter 1, pages 3–34. MIT Press, 2004.
[5] B. Alberts, D. Bray, A. Johnson, J. Lewis, M. Raff, K. Roberts, and P. Walter. *Essential cell biology : An introduction to the molecular biology of the cell*. Garland Science, 1997.
[6] K. Saadi, N. L. C. Talbot, and G. C. Cawley. Optimally regularised kernel Fisher discriminant analysis. In *Proceedings of the 17th International Conference on Pattern Recognition (ICPR-2004)*, volume 2, pages 427–430, Cambridge, United Kingdom, August 23–26 2004.
[7] C Bishop. *Neural Networks for Pattern Recognition*. Oxford university Press, Oxford, UK, 1995.
[8] A. Webb. *Statistical pattern recognition*. Wiley, second edition, 2002.
[9] S. Mika, G. Rätsch, J. Weston, B. Schölkopf, and K.-R. Müller. Fisher discriminant analysis with kernels. In *Neural Networks for Signal Processing*, volume IX, pages 41–48. IEEE Press, New York, 1999.
[10] J. Xu, X. Zhang, and Y. Li. Kernel MSE algorithm: A unified framework for KFD, LS-SVM and KRR. In *Proc. IJCNN*, pages 1486–1491, Washington, DC, July 2001.
[11] A. N. Tikhonov and V. Y. Arsenin. *Solutions of ill-posed problems*. John Wiley, New York, 1977.
[12] S. Geman, E. Bienenstock, and R. Doursat. Neural networks and the bias/variance dilema. *Neural Computation*, 4(1):1–58, 1992.
[13] A. Luntz and V. Brailovsky. On estimation of characters obtained in statistical procedure of recognition (in russian). *Techicheskaya Kibernetica*, 3, 1969.
[14] S. Weisberg. *Applied linear regression*. John Wiley and Sons, New York, second edition, 1985.
[15] M. Woodbury. Inverting modified matrices. Memorandum report 42, Princeton University, Princeton, U.S.A., 1950.
[16] G. C. Cawley and N. L. C. Talbot. Efficient leave-one-out cross-validation of kernel Fisher discriminant classifiers. *Pattern Recognition*, 36(11):2585–2592, November 2003.
[17] K. Higo, Y. Ugawa, M. Iwamoto, and T. Korenaga. Plant cis-acting regulatory dna elements (PLACE) database. *Nucleic Acids Research*, 27:297–300, 1999.
[18] T. Golub and *etal*. Molecular classification of cancer: Class discovery and class prediction by gene expression monitoring. *Science*, 286:531–537, 1999.
[19] B. Schölkopf, K. Tsuda, and J.-P. Vert. *Kernel methods in computational biology*. MIT Press, Cambridge, MA, 2004.
[20] C. Leslie, E. Eskin, and W. Stafford Noble. The spectrum kernel : A string kernel for SVM protein classification. In *Proceedings of the Pacific Symposium on Biocomputing*, pages 564–575, January 2–7 2002.
[21] C. Leslie, E. Eskin, J. Weston, and W. Stafford Noble. Mismatch string kernels for SVM protein classification. In S. Becker, S. Thrun, and K. Obermayer, editors, *Advances in Neural Information Processing Systems 15*, pages 1417–1424. MIT Press, Cambridge, MA, 2003.
[22] C. Leslie, E. Eskin, A. Cohen, J. Weston, and W. Stafford Noble. Mismatch string kernels for discriminative protein classification. *Bioinformatics*, 20(4):467–476, 2004.

Feedback Linearization Using Neural Networks Applied to Advanced Pharmacodynamic and Pharmacogenomic Systems

(Invited Paper)

Alexandru Floares
Oncological Institute Cluj-Napoca
Str. Republicii, Nr. 34-36, Cluj-Napoca, 400015, Romania
Email: alexandru.floares@iocn.ro

Abstract— At present, pharmacological modeling is developing from an empirical discipline into a mechanistic science. Also, new and important fields like pharmacogenomics appeared. As a consequence, pharmacology is dealing with high dimensional, nonlinear, control systems. The intent of this paper is to show that all this systems, being based on a limited array of mechanisms and having some structural peculiarities, are good candidate for the application of feedback linearization techniques, using neural networks. Unlike Jacobian linearization, feedback linearization is not only locally valid. The proposed protocol can be applied even without the aid of a mathematical model. A drug dosage regimen, established in this way, will determine the output of the pharmacological system to track very well the therapeutic objective. To the best of author's knowledge, this is the first time when a very large class of complex pharmacological problems are formulated and solved in terms of neural network control.

I. INTRODUCTION

In the last years, the reductionist paradigm, which dominated the last century life sciences, becomes gradually balanced with the systemic view of living organisms. In clinical pharmacology, detailed data about the complex molecular mechanisms of the interactions between drug(s) and organism become available. Most notably, the target genes of many drugs are being discovered, and the differential genes expression, induced by drugs, can be investigated by microarray techniques [1]. This data allow conceptual and mathematical models building. Unfortunately, this is a very difficult task because of the inherent complexity of the *nonlinear* physiological control mechanisms interacting with an external control, represented by the drug and it's dosage regimen. Also, the dimensions of this nonlinear control system is very high; drugs usually alter the expression of thousands genes.

Building mathematical models is important for understanding this pharmacological systems. At least as important is to be able to adequately control them, even with a limited understanding - a gray or black box approach. In the end, both approaches have the same very important goal: optimizing and individualizing medical therapy in the presence of variate degrees of knowledge and uncertainty. Mathematical modeling requires detailed knowledge of the mechanism involved and the estimation of numerous parameters; it is a tedious and time consuming process. This probably explains the law impact of this approach on clinical practice, even for simple models.

Neural networks (NN), despite their recent rapid growth in the implementation in various fields of applications, have their potential in clinical pharmacology largely unexplored. The essential features of NN, nonlinearity, adaptivity, independence of statistical and other modeling assumptions, fault tolerance, universality, and real time operation, make them suitable for clinical pharmacology applications.

Feedback linearization (FBL) is one of the most important nonlinear control design strategy developed during the last few decades [2]. This approach may results in linearization which are valid for larger practical operating regions of the system, as opposed to a local Jacobian linearization about an operating point. Neural adaptive control of feedback linearizable nonlinear systems was first proposed in [3] and extensively analyzed in [4]. In a previous work, we obtained the best published result in a cancer chemotherapy problem using neural network feedback linearization (NN FBL) [5]. This motivates this study and the use of multilayer perceptrons, instead of other possible NN like radial basis functions or dynamical neural networks [6]. As will be shown, the proposed protocol can be applied to complex pharmacological systems, with or without the aid of a conceptual or mathematical model. A drug dosage regimen, established in this way, will determine the output of the pharmacological system to track very well the therapeutic objective - formulated as a reference signal. To the best of author's knowledge, this is the first time when a very large class of complex pharmacological problems are formulated and solved in terms of neural network control.

II. PHARMACOLOGICAL SYSTEMS

A. Pharmacogenomics Data

For illustrating the proposed methods, the synthetic corticoid (CS) methylprednisolone (MPL) pharmacogenomic (PG) data, studied using gene microarray in rat liver (see [7]), were investigated. The dataset is available online at http://microarray.cnmcresearch.org/ (link *Programs* in *Genomic Applications*. Methylprednisolone (MPL), with different dosage regimens, is indicated in various conditions: endocrine disorders, rheumatic disorders, collagen diseases, dermatologic diseases, allergic states and inflammatory processes, hematologic disorders, neoplastic diseases, edematous states, and nervous system diseases. Therefore, optimization and individualization of clinical therapy with corticoids is very important. In the pharmacological experiment, forty-three male rats weighing 225 to 250 g received a single intravenous bolus dose of 50 mg/kg MPL. Rats were sacrificed and liver, an important action site for corticoids, excised at 17 time points over 72 hours. Four untreated rats were sacrificed at 0 hours as controls. RNAs from individual livers were used to investigate 8000 genes with Affymetrix GeneChips. Cluster analysis revealed six temporal pattern consisting of 197 CS-responsive probes representing 143 genes.

B. Pharmacological Mathematical Models

Pharmacokinetics (PK), the relationship between time and plasma concentration, can be simply described as "what the body does to the drug". The clinical interpretation of pharmacokinetic results requires another set of information, the relationship between plasma concentrations (or dose) and effect, or pharmacodynamics (PD). This can be described as "what the drug does to the body"

1) Preliminaries and Definitions: A multivariate nonlinear dynamic system with m inputs $\{u_1, ..., u_m\}$ and p outputs $\{y_1, ..., y_p\}$ is described in a state space form by the following equations:

$$\dot{x} = f(x) + \sum_{j=1}^{m} g_j(x) u_j \quad (1)$$
$$y_i = h_i(x), i = 1, ..., p$$

where $x = [x_1, ..., x_n]^T \in \Re^n$ is the state vector, $f(x), g_1(x), ..., g_m(x)$ are differentiable vector fields, and $h_1(x), ..., h_p(x)$ are smooth functions, all defined on an open set of $\Re^n$. This class of systems is known as control *affine*, because the control input u appears linearly in the state equation. The theory of nonlinear control systems is a still developing area when compared to the vast amount of knowledge and tools that can be invoked in the analysis and control of linear systems. That is why is often desired to convert a nonlinear system into an equivalent linear system through some sort of co-ordinate transformation. Feedback linearization (FBL) is one of the recent methods employed to achieve this goal [6]. It is distinguished from approximate (Jacobian) linearization of a nonlinear system at a particular operating point in that FBL often offers linearizations valid for a larger operating space. By eliminating nonlinearities in the closed loop system, conventional linear control techniques can be applied [6]. A key concepts of the feedback linearization theory for nonlinear control affine systems is the relative degree. The relative degree r_i is the number of times the output $y(t)$ has to be differentiated in order to have at least one component of the input vector u explicitly appearing. Pharmacological mathematical models are continuous systems. The use of NN requires sampling the input-output data, and the systems become discrete. For reasons that will become clear later we will investigate single input-single output (SISO) discrete systems. A SISO discrete time system [8] has the form:

$$x(k+1) = f(x(k), u(k))$$
$$y(k) = h(x(k)) \quad (2)$$

where $x(\cdot) \in \Re^n$, $u(\cdot) \in \Re$, $y(\cdot) \in \Re$, f and h are analytic functions on their domains. Let f_0 denote the autonomous (undriven) state dynamics $f(\cdot, 0)$ and f_0^j its j-time iterated compositions. The system (2) is said to have relative degree d if

$$\frac{\partial h \circ f_0^k \circ f(x, u)}{\partial u} \equiv 0 \quad 0 \leq k < d$$
$$\frac{\partial h \circ f_0^k \circ f(x, u)}{\partial u} \neq 0 \quad k = d$$

Since f and h are analytic, it follows that either $d < n$ or $d = \infty$ and the output is not affected by the input (control) u. Let $v \in \Re$ be an external control input and $\gamma : \Re^{n+1} \to \Re$ be a nonlinear static feedback of the form $u = \gamma(x, v)$. If $\partial \gamma / \partial v \neq 0$, there exists a local change of coordinate $z = T(x)$ such that the closed loop system can be described by

$$\begin{aligned} z_1(k+1) &= Az_1(k) + Br(k) \\ z_2(k+1) &= F(z_1(k), z_2, r(k)) \\ y(k) &= Cz_1(k) \end{aligned} \quad (3)$$

with $dim(z_1) = d+1$ and (A, B, C) a controllable-observable triple. If the system (3) were initially at $z_1 \equiv 0$, and $r \equiv 0$, then $z_1 \equiv 0$ and the system output stays at zero, and the motion of the system will be determined solely by the dynamics of z_2. This leads to the concept of zero dynamics for discrete-time systems: the zero dynamics of the system (3) are defined by $z_2(k+1) = F(0, z_2(k), 0)$. The discrete-time system is said to be *minimum phase* if the zero dynamics have an asymptotically stable equilibrium at the origin.

A pharmacokinetic model of a drug attempts to relate the input - drug dosage regimens - to the output. Usually the output is the drug and/or metabolite concentration in blood, or the drug and/or metabolite excretion in urine. PK models describe the rates of drug movement into, within and exit from the body. Conceptually the body is represented by one, two, or three interconnected theoretical compartments. Rate processes in the field of pharmacokinetics are usually first order, zero order or nonlinear - Michaelis-Menten kinetics (see below). These rate processes can be described mathematically by the following PK blocks:

1) Zero order kinetics: $dX/dt = -k$; rate processes are described by the rate constant alone.
2) First order kinetics: $dX/dt = -kX$, where k is a rate constant and X is the amount or concentration of the drug remaining to be transferred.
3) Michaelis-Menten (nonlinear) kinetics: $dX/dt = -(V_m X)/(K_m + X)$, where V_m is a maximum rate and K_m is the Michaelis constant.

A PK model is the algebraic sum of the corresponding PK blocks resulting in one ore more differential equations. Whatever route of drug administration is used - intravenous or extravascular - the equation term containing the input in (1), $g(x)u(t)$ has the form of a zero or first order kinetics. This implies that the input $u(t)$ appears linearly in the state space description of *all* pharmacokinetics systems, and that they are *affine* systems. This is a key aspect of the approach to pharmacological systems proposed in this study, as will become clear in the next sections.

A pharmacodynamic model attempts to relate drug concentration, ideally at the site of action of the drug, but more usually in blood, to some pharmacological effect. The pharmacological effects of the drug can be described mathematically by the following, most used, PD blocks [9]:

1) Linear model: $E = SCe + E_0$
2) Log-linear model: $E = S\log(Ce) + E0$
3) Ordinary E_{max} model: $E = E_0 + E_{max}C_e/(C_e + EC_{50})$
4) Ordinary inhibition E_{max} model: $E = E_0 - E_{max}C_e/(C_e + EC_{50})$
5) Sigmoid E_{max} model (Hill): $E = E_0 + E_{max}C_e^n/(C_e^n + EC_{50}^n)$
6) Sigmoid inhibition E_{max} model (Hill): $E = E_0 - E_{max}C_e^n/(C_e^n + EC_{50}^n)$

where E is the effect variable, E_0 is the baseline effect, E_{max} is the maximum drug induced effect, EC_{50} is the plasma concentration at 50% of maximal effect, S is the slope of the line relating the effect to the concentration, C_e is the concentration to which the effect is related, and n is the sigmoidicity factor (Hill exponent).

2) MPL Pharmacokinetics and Pharmacodynamics: The PK of MPL is described [7] by the following biexponential equation:

$$C_p = C_1 \cdot \exp(-\lambda_1 \cdot t) + C_2 \cdot \exp(-\lambda_2 \cdot t) \quad (4)$$

where C_p is the plasma concentration of MPL, C_i and λ_i (see Table I) are the coefficients for intercepts and slopes.

The cellular mechanisms of the corticosteroids pharmacogenomics [7] are briefly described. Unbounded MPL in blood freely diffuse into the cytoplasm of liver cells and quickly binds to the cytosolic receptor and activate it. The activated drug-receptor complex rapidly translocates in the nucleus were it binds to the glucocorticoid responsive element (GRE) in the target DNA and alter rates of transcription of target genes. Binding of the activated drug-receptor complex to the GRE results in decreased transcription and reduced levels of receptor mRNA. The mRNA translocates to the cytoplasm were is translated to protein. This further decreases the free receptor cytosolic density. The drug-receptor complex in nucleus may dissociate from the GRE and return to the cytosol. Part of the receptors may be degraded, whereas the rest may be recycled. A PD model, describing the receptor dynamics in rat liver after MPL administration, being at its fifth-generation, was proposed in [7]:

$$\frac{dmRNA_R}{dt} = k_{s\_Rm} \cdot \left(1 - \frac{DR\_N}{IC_{50\_Rm} + DR\_N}\right) \quad (5)$$
$$- k_{d\_Rm} \cdot mRNA_R$$

$$\frac{dR}{dt} = k_{s\_R} \cdot mRNA_R + R_f \cdot k_{re} \cdot DR\_N \quad (6)$$
$$- k_{on} \cdot D \cdot R - k_{d\_R} \cdot R$$

$$\frac{dDR}{dt} = k_{on} \cdot D \cdot R - k_T \cdot DR \quad (7)$$

$$\frac{dDR\_N}{dt} = k_T \cdot DR - k_{re} \cdot DR\_N \quad (8)$$

where symbols represent the plasma concentration of the drug (D), the receptor mRNA ($mRNA_R$), the free cytosolic receptor density (R), cytosolic drug-receptor complex (DR), and drug-receptor complex in nucleus (DR_N); the rate constants include zero-order rates of receptor mRNA synthesis (k_{s_Rm}), the first-order rates of receptor mRNA degradation (k_{d_Rm}), receptor synthesis (k_{s_R}) and degradation (k_{d_R}), translocation of the drug-receptor complex into the nucleus (k_T), the second-order rate constant of drug-receptor association (k_{on}), the concentration of DR_N at which the synthesis rate of receptor mRNA drops to 50% of its baseline value (IC_{50_Rm}), and R_f is the fraction of free receptor being recycled. The baseline were defined in [7] using the following equations: $k_{d\_Rm} = (k_{s\_Rm})/(mRNA_R^0)$ and $k_{s_R} = (R^0/mRNA_R^0) \cdot k_{d_R}$, where $mRNA_R^0$ and R_0 are the baseline values of receptor mRNA and free cytosolic receptor density.

3) MPL Pharmacogenomics: Binding of the activated steroid (drug)-receptor complex to the GRE or negative GRE in target DNA induces or represses several genes. This study investigates two of the six mathematical models proposed in [7] to describe different patterns of gene expression, after MLP treatment, in rat liver. The first model was selected because is typical, and the second because it is the most complex. In the first model the synthesis and degradation of target RNA (normalized as ratio to control), without drug administration, was assumed as follows:

$$\frac{dmRNA}{dt} = k_{s\_m} - k_{d\_m} \cdot mRNA \quad (9)$$

The $mRNA$ level was assumed to be at steady-state at time 0 in control animals, yielding the following baseline equation: $k_{s\_m} = k_{d\_m} \cdot mRNA^0$. Baseline level of $mRNA^0$ was fixed to 1 for the most genes.

Model I. The induced production of $mRNA$ was described as follows:

$$\frac{dmRNA}{dt} = k_{s\_m} \cdot (1 + S \cdot DR\_N) - k_{d\_m} \cdot mRNA \quad (10)$$

where the increase of transcription rate k_{s_m} is proportional with DR_N with the constant of proportionality S.

Model II. mRNA with induced degradation in cytosol and secondarily induced transcription by biosignals (BS) was described as follows:

$$\frac{dmRNA_{BS}}{dt} = k_{s\_m} \cdot (1 + S_{BSm} \cdot DR\_N) \quad (11)$$
$$- k_{d\_BSm} \cdot mRNA_{BS}$$

$$\frac{dBS_r}{dt} = k_{s\_BS} \cdot mRNA_{BS} - k_{d\_BS} \cdot BS_r \quad (12)$$

$$\frac{dmRNA}{dt} = k_{s\_m} \cdot (1 + S_{m\_s} \cdot BS_r) \quad (13)$$
$$- k_{d\_m} \cdot (1 + S_{m\_d} \cdot DR) \cdot mRNA$$

where $mRNA_{BS}$ is the mRNA of the regulatory biosignals and BS represents their levels, both normalized as ratio to control; k_{s_BSm} is the rate of BS mRNA synthesis, k_{d_BSm} is the rate of BS mRNA degradation, k_{s_BS} is the rate of mRNA translation to BS, and k_{d_BS} is the rate of BS protein degradation. The stimulation of BS transcription is proportional with DR_N with a proportionality constant S_{BSm}. The stimulation of $mRNA$ synthesis is proportional with BS with a proportionality constant S_{m_s}; this stimulation is also present at baseline condition. The cytosolic $mRNA$ degradation is regulated by DR and S_{m_d} is the corresponding stimulation factor. At time 0 (11), (12), and (13) yield the following baseline equations: $k_{s\_BSm} = k_{d\_BSm} \cdot mRNA^0_{BS}$, $k_{s\_BS} = (BS^0_r/mRNA^0_{BS}) \cdot k_{d\_BS}$, and $k_{s\_m} = (k_{d\_m} \cdot mRNA^0)/(1 + S_{m\_s} \cdot BS^0_r)$, were $mRNA^0_{BS}$ and BS^0_r are the baseline values of normalized BS mRNA and protein levels, which were fixed as 1.

TABLE I
PHARMACOKINETIC AND PHARMACODYNAMIC PARAMETERS

Parameter	Value
Pharmacokinetics (fixed)	
C_1 (ng/ml)	39,130
C_2 (ng/ml)	12,670
λ_1 (h^{-1})	7.54
λ_2 (h^{-1})	1.20
Pharmacodynamics (fixed)	
k_{s_Rm} (fmol/g liver/h)	2.90
IC_{50_Rm} (fmol/mg of protein)	26.2
k_{on} (l/nmol/h)	0.00329
k_T (h^{-1})	0.63
k_{re} (h^{-1})	0.57
R_f	0.49
k_{d_R} (h^{-1})	0.0572
$mRNA^0_R$ (fmol/g liver)	25.8
R^0 (fmol/mg protein)	540.7

C. Neural Networks Approach

Multilayer perceptrons (MLP) have been successfully applied in optimizing therapeutical strategies - cancer chemotherapy [5]. The universal approximation capabilities of the multilayer perceptron (MLP) make it a particular choice for modeling nonlinear systems and for implementing general-propose nonlinear controllers [10]. There are typically two steps involved when using neural networks for control:

1) system identification, and
2) control design.

Feedback linearization, using neural networks, can be applied to complex pharmacological control systems, in order to find adequate drug(s) dosage regimens, in two main ways. We distinguish between two different situations:

1) A pharmacological mathematical model exists, or the available information is sufficient to infer one by fitting elementary PK and PD blocks to a conceptual model and the data.
2) Neither a mathematical model nor a well developed conceptual model exists but good experimental data are available.

In the first situation, neural networks are applied to the input-output data resulting from model simulations. In the second case, a NN model of the pharmacological system must be first obtained from data - neuro-identification. In both situations there are two alternatives [6]. The *input-state* feedback linearization approach: the system state becomes a linear function of a new control input and a new state, while the output is still a nonlinear function. The nonlinearities in the output map make it very difficult to achieve good tracking of the therapeutic objectives formulated as reference signals. In the alternative approach, *input-output* feedback linearization, which is used in this study, the output becomes a linear function of a new control input.

III. SYSTEM IDENTIFICATION

A. Neural Networks Systems Identification of Pharmacological Systems

The purpose of system identification is to infer a NN model of the pharmacokinetic, pharmacodynamic, and pharmacogenomic system (PK-PD-PG) to be controlled, from a set of input-output data pairs collected in an experiment. The procedure consists of four basic steps:

1) Experiment: In this study, the proposed methods are applied to laboratory pharmacogenomics experimental data and to simulation data. In simulations the input has to be persistently exciting and its values should be such that the output does not saturate. This condition is necessary to preserve uniqueness of the mapping from input to output. It should span the entire operating range of the system, and contains enough dynamics to adequately characterize the response of the system.

The input is the plasma concentration of MPL (D), and the output is the mRNA of the target genes ($mRNA$). We simulate the PK-PD-PG models composed by the PK component (4), the PD component represented by the equations (5), (6), (7), and (8), and the equation(s) of one of the PG models (see section II-B.3). To illustrate the methods, neuro-identification is applied to simulation data using the two PK-PD-PG models. The sampling time must be chosen in accord with the fastest dynamic of the system. Practically, a random input, with the maximal value close to the initial plasma concentration of MPL and a minimal value of zero, is injected into the system at random intervals of time.

2) Select Model Structure: The next step is to select a model structure. One standard model that has been used to represent general discrete-time nonlinear systems is the Nonlinear Autoregressive-Moving Average (NARMA) model (see [12] for a detailed discussion of system identification, and [13] for NN based system identification). This model, adapted to the feedback linearization of affine systems, has the following form:

$$\begin{aligned} y(k+d) = &f[y(k), y(k-1), \ldots, y(k-n_a+1), \\ &u(k-1), \ldots, u(k-n_b+1)] \\ &+ g[y(k), y(k-1), \ldots, y(k-n_a+1), \\ &u(k-1), \ldots, u(k-n_b+1)] \cdot u(k) \end{aligned} \quad (14)$$

where y is the system output ($mRNA$), u is the system input (D), n_a is the number of past outputs, n_b is the number of past inputs, d is the system delay, k is the sampling instant number; f and g are two nonlinear functions, and the controller input $u(k)$ is *not* contained in the nonlinearity. We want the system output to follow a reference trajectory which is a mathematical formulation of a *therapeutic objective*. This has to be establish in accord with the clinical situation. Due to the very large variety of clinical situations in which MPL is indicated, and for more generality, we prefer a somewhat arbitrary reference signal.

After the model structure has been selected, the next choice, which has to be made, is the number of past signals used as model regressors, i.e., the model order. Lag-space method, which identifies the model order as the coordinates of the minima of the order index, can be used (see [11], and [12] for details). This indicates the same model order, equal with two, for the PK-PD-PG models with mechanisms I and II, and for the experimental data of an arbitrary selected genes (PROBESTEID interleukin 4 in the table from http://microarray.cnmcresearch.org). However, it is always better to have enough physical insight into the system to be modeled to choose the model order properly. Because the order of the ODE systems, corresponding to the above PK-PD-PG models, are bigger, different order are investigated, the final choice depending on the quality of identification.

3) Estimate Model: The purpose of this step is to generate NN models from the specified model structure. We try different NN architectures and training parameters for the two MLP approximating the functions f and g in (14). We use regularization and early stopping to avoid over-training, and we start with different random initial conditions to avoid ending in "bad" local minima. The experimental data, consisting only in 17 time points (see section II-A), are interpolated and resampled to obtain more data points. The data were partitioned in a training set (60%), a cross-validation set (15%), and a test set (25%). The number of hidden layers is one for all neural networks. The number of neurons in the hidden layer is 5 for f and 3 for g, for simulated data. For both mathematical models, f and g have 7 neurons. The activation functions are tangent hyperbolic for the neurons in the hidden layer and linear in the output layer for all NN. The training algorithm is Levenberg-Marquardt, with Bayesian regularization and early stopping, for all trainings. The model orders are: number of past output, $na = 2$, number of past input, $nb = 2$, and the time lag, $d = 1$, for simulated data; $n_a = 5$, $nb = 3$, and $d = 1$ for the first mathematical model; $n_a = 7$, $nb = 3$, and $d = 1$ for the second mathematical model. The sampling time is $Ts = 0.1$ for all estimations. The total number of samples is about 10,000 for all estimations, and the number of training epochs is between 100 and 300.

4) Validate Model: When a NN has been trained, the next step is to evaluate it. The most common method of validation is to investigate the prediction errors by cross-validation on a test set. Control performances depend crucially on the quality of identification and this was very good. For illustration purpose,
the output - measured mRNA for the arbitrary selected gene, scaled to zero mean and variance one - versus one-step-ahead prediction of the NN identified model is depicted in Fig. 1.

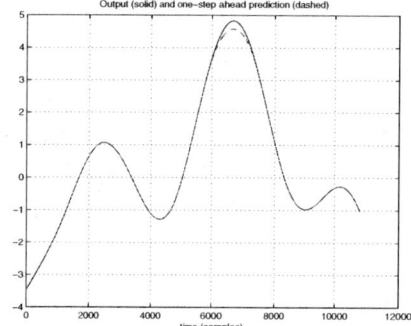

Fig. 1. System identification from experimental data

B. Adaptive Neural Networks Control. Drug Dosage Regimens

Based on the identified model the next step is to develop a neural controller. Due to the rigorous and elegant theoretical foundations of *feedback linearization*, a version of this type of controller has been used - NARMA-L2 [14]. The general idea of the input-output linearization technique is to linearize the input-output characteristics of a nonlinear system, via an appropriate nonlinear feedback control law, by canceling the nonlinearities. To apply the exact input-output feedback linearization theory, affine models are necessary - input must appear linearly in the state-space description of the model. The choice of this neurocontroller is also motivated by the fact that *all* important pharmacologic models are affine. In practice, exact cancelation of the nonlinearities proved to be less efficient than NARMA-L2 approximation controller. Using the NARMA-L2 model, the following controller, which is the base for rationally establishing drug dosage regimens, is obtained:

$$u(k+1) = \{y_r(k+d) - f[y(k),...,y(k-n+1), \\ u(k),...,u(k-n+1)]\} \times \\ \times g[y(k),...,y(k-n+1), \\ u(k),...,u(k-n+1)]\}^{-1}. \quad (15)$$

where y_r is the reference signal, and $d \geq 2$. The fact that g (the denominator) is never equal to zero induces a globally valid feedback linearizing control law, i.e., which is valid everywhere in the space of admissible inputs and outputs. This is not the same as the Jacobian linearization around an equilibrium point. The latter one is only a linear approximation of the process at a particular operation point. Tracking results, of the proposed NN FBL methods, applied to the two PK-PD-PG models (see III-A.1), are shown in Fig. 2 and Fig. 3.

IV. CONCLUSIONS

Feedback linearization using neural networks is applied to the most complex category of nonlinear pharmacological

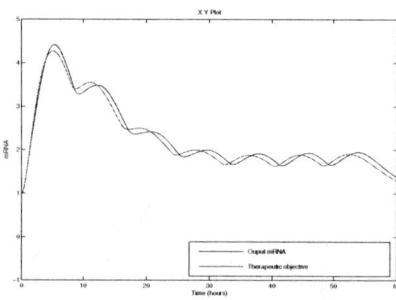

Fig. 2. Tracking results PK-PD-PG model I

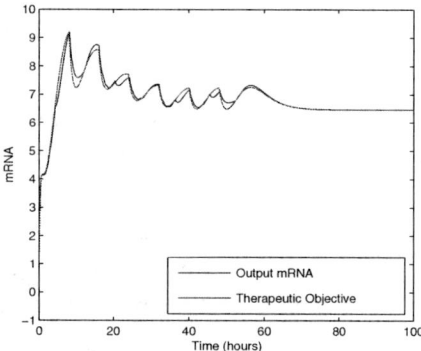

Fig. 3. Tracking results PK-PD-PG model II

systems, combining pharmacokinetic, pharmacodynamic and pharmacogenomic processes. The goal is to develop powerful but easy to use methods for optimizing and individualizing medical therapy in the presence of variate degrees of knowledge and uncertainty. The proposed methods can be applied to experimental data, when neither a mathematical nor a conceptual model exist. When a mathematical model exists, or the available information is sufficient to infer one by fitting elementary PK and PD blocks to a conceptual model and the data, the methods can be applied to simulated data. For both kind of input-output data the protocol is the same, consisting in identifying a neural network model of the system and designing a neuro-controller.

Feedback linearization is a proper choice having a strong theoretical foundation, being simple, and giving a linear control low valid (unlike Jacobian linearization) everywhere in the space of admissible inputs and outputs. An other important reason is the fact that, as we show, the most representative advanced pharmacological systems are affine, and for affine systems feedback linearization is particulary simple to apply and very powerful.

The investigation of differential gene expressions induced by different drugs represents a strong foundation for optimizing and individualizing medical therapies. Probably, the most important application, of the proposed protocol, is the possibility to elaborate drug dosage regimens, which determine the pharmacological systems to follow the desired therapeutic objectives, without the aid of mathematical models, which are difficult to build for such complex data.

REFERENCES

[1] D. P. Berrar, W. Dubitzky, M. Granzow,eds, *A Practical Approach to Microarray Data Analysis*, Ed: Kluwer Academic Publisher, New York, 2003.
[2] A. Isidori, *Nonlinear Control Systems: an introduction*, Springer, Berlin, New York, 3rd edition, 1995.
[3] F. C. Chen, "Back-propagation neural networks for nonlinear self-tuning adaptive control," *IEEE Control Systems Magazine*, Special Issue on Neural Networks for Control Systems, April 1990, pp. 44-48.
[4] F. C. Chen and H. K. Khalil, "Adaptive control of a class of nonlinear discrete-time systems using neural networks," *IEEE Trans. Automatic Control*, vol. 40, no. 5, pp. 791-801, May 1995.
[5] A. Floares, C. Floares, M. Cucu, L. Lazar, Adaptive Neural Networks Control of Drug Dosage Regimens in Cancer Chemotherapy, *Proceedings of the IJCNN 2003*, Portland OR, Jully 20-24, pp 154–159, 2003.
[6] F. Garces, V.M. Becerra, C. Kambhampati, and K. Warwick, *Strategies for feedback linearisation: a dynamic neural network approach*, Springer series *Advances in Industrial Control*, London, 2003.
[7] J. J. Jin, R. R. Almon, D. C. Dubois and W. J. Jusko, "Modeling of Corticoids Pharmacogenomics in Rat Liver Using Gene Microarrays", *J Pharmacol Exp Ther*, 307, pp. 93–109, 2003.
[8] K. O. C. Fregene, Neural adaptive Feedback Linearizing Control of a High-Order Power System, Master Thesis, University of Waterloo, Ontario, Canada, p. 56, 1999.
[9] D. E. Mager, E. Wyska, and W. J. Jusko, Diversity of mecanism-based pharmacodynamic models, *Drug Metabolism and Disposition*, Vol. 31, No. 5, 2003.
[10] M. T. Hagan, and H. B. Demuth, "Neural Networks for Control", *Proceedings of the 1999 American Control Conference*, San Diego, CA, pp. 1642-1656, 1999.
[11] M. Nrgaard, *Neural Network Based System Identification toolbox*, Version 2 Technical Report 00-E-891,Department of Automation, Technical University of Denmark, January 23, 2000
[12] X. He and H. Asada: "A New Method for Identifying Orders of Input-Output Models for Nonlinear Dynamic Systems" *Proc. of the American Control Conf.*, S.F., California, 1993
[13] L. S. Goodman, A. Gilman *The pharmacological basis of therapeutics*, London: Macmillan, pp. 21, 1996.
[14] K. S Narendra, and S. Mukhopadhyay, "Adaptive Control Using Neural Networks and Approximate Models", *IEEE Transactions on Neural Networks*, Vol. 8, 1997, pp. 475-485.

Improved Spam e-Mail Filtering Based on Committee Machines and Information Theoretic Feature Extraction

V. Zorkadis[1], M. Panayotou[2], D. A. Karras[3]

[1] Data Protection Authority and Hellenic Open University, Greece,
Email: zorkadis@dpa.gr
[2] Hellenic Open University, Greece.
[3] Chalkis Institute of Technology, Dept. Automation and Hellenic Open University.,
Rodu 2, Ano Iliupolis, Athens 16342, Greece,
Email: dakarras@teihal.gr, dakarras@usa.net, dakarras@ieee.org

Abstract--- A novel approach for spam e-mail filtering is herein considered based on the Committee Machines Neural Network Models and on information theoretic feature extraction. An extensive experimental study is organized, the most extensive so far in the literature, based on widely accepted benchmarking e-mail data sets, comparing the proposed methodology with the Naive Bayes spam filter as well as with the Boosting tree methodology, the linear models based classification (classification via regression) and the nonlinear models based classification using simple neural network models, including Multilayer Perceptrons. Moreover, several feature extraction approaches based on information theory are evaluated. It is shown that the Committee Machines mail categorization performance is compared very favorably to the other rival methods performance, including the Bayes spam filter which is the most widely used approach in the e-mail services market. It is, also, found that the proposed information theoretic Boolean features present a remarkably high spam categorization performance compared to their analog counterparts performance.

Keywords Spam filtering, Naïve Bayes, Committee machines, Multilayer Perceptrons, Linear models for classification

I. INTRODUCTION

E-mail is a very efficient communication media with large impact to society. The increasing e-mail popularity in combination with the low cost of message sending drove to the creation of a new product marketing strategy which is based on the massive e-mail sending to thousands of recipients no matter if they have given authority to the e-mail senders or not. These messages are called unsolicited electronic messages and are known as spam messages. Recipients e-mail addresses are gathered from web pages or newsgroups. The common characteristic of all these messages is that they are of low importance for the recipient. In some cases they could be even harmful e.g. spam messages containing pornographic material that can be read by children. Apart from wasting time and bandwidth spam e-mail also costs money to users with dial-up connections. Spam messages constitute approximately 15% of the incoming messages to a corporate network. The situation gets worst and without appropriate counter measures spam messages could eventually undermine the usability of e-mail due to serious impacts on users productivity, corporate functional cost, individual users payment per time of internet use, workload and security of networks and systems, as well as, companies legal issues.

From a legal point of view, EU's directive 58/2002 for 'protection of the private life in electronic communication', as well as the US CAN-SPAM Act/2003 for 'Controlling the Assault of Non-Solicited Pornography and Marketing' determine the existing legal framework against spamming. Attempts to introduce legal measures against spam mailing have had a limited effect. A more effective solution is to develop tools to help recipients identify or remove automatically spam messages. Such tools vary in functionality from black list of frequent spammers to content based filters. Content based filters are generally more powerful as spammers often use face addresses. Existing content based filters search for particular keyword patterns in the messages. These patterns need to be crafted by hand and to achieve better results they need to be tuned to each user and to be constantly maintained, a task requiring expertise that a user may not have [1,2].

In this work we confront the spam messages problem with the aid of machine learning [3-9]. More specifically, we examine supervised machine learning methods which are trained to identify spam messages through well defined learning algorithms, based on a specific message corpus included manually classified spam and non spam messages [3,4,8].

In technical level the two basic anti spam approaches are message filtering and blocking. The technique of filtering is based on a list of words and phrases that characterize spam messages. So each incoming message is analyzed and examined against this list and finally, gets a degree corresponding to the possibility of being spam mail. The messages are categorized as spam or non spam according to the specific program threshold. The technique of blocking identifies suspicious mail servers and blocks mail delivery during the transfer process and includes black and white lists. Creators of black lists try to stop spam by determining the domain names or IP addresses of known spammers and ISPs that tolerate spammers. E-mail administrators and filtering software flag or even delete e-mail from those sources by using the lists to create rules at the mail server or router level. White lists, instead of trying to turn away spammer's domain names or IP addresses, require from unknown senders to perform some task in order to get registered. This paper follows the message filtering approach in the anti-spam line of research.

The prevailing machine learning method for spam message filtering is the Bayesian approach [1,3,7]. On the other hand, boosting trees [4] and Support Vector Machines [8] have already been used with good results. However, there is lack of extensive experimental studies comparing different classification approaches on clearly defined training and validation (testing) sets so as to have reproducible results. In addition, there are no studies on feature extraction methods for spam mail categorization. The herein presented approach aims, first, at illustrating that Random Committee Machine [12] as well as ADTree [6] are better machine learning methods than the usually employed Bayesian spam filtering as well as the Boosting filtering approach through conducting an extensive experimental study based on Ling-Spam collection of legitimate and spam messages [3], so as that the results could be compared with that of other studies. Although Ling-Spam collection is smaller than other ones is balanced in terms of ham and spam message frequencies and is well known in the literature since many papers on the issue use it as basis for experimentation. The herein experimental study is the most extensive in the literature regarding spam mails filtering, not in terms of involving the largest data set but in terms of extensively crossvalidating filtering approaches over a well defined and known message collection of medium size. It is shown that the proposed machine learning classification approaches deserve the attention of the anti-spam filtering research community. Moreover, an investigation of information theoretic measures for efficient feature extraction is, also, presented in this paper.

II. THE PROPOSED INFORMATION THEORETIC FEATURE EXTRACTION AND COMMITTEE MACHINES SPAM CATEGORIZATION METHODOLOGY

Most of the existing anti-spam filters are based on pattern matching that must be tuned for the specific type of messages that every user receives. In addition the content characteristics are changing through time which results to demand for retune the pattern matching rules. The classification of e-mail messages is a classic case of text classification problem in two classes and it could be handled by a series of feature detection algorithms and machine learning methods. The most appropriate feature selection includes cognitive areas of text classification such as the use of mutual information gain for the selection of the best features specification, the optimal number of features and the vector type representation. As soon as the feature selection is decided, a variety of machine learning algorithms can be used for the messages classification. The solution is the development of a system that could learn to classify the incoming messages to spam and non spam automatically. In our work, message features are the words of the message.

Feature Selection: Several methods exist for optimal feature selection of text documents. Among those analyzed in this work are word stemming, stop terms, mutual information feature selection, selecting the optimal number of features.

Word Stemming: Text classification accuracy can often be improved by using a word stemming algorithm. Words stemming is the act of removing suffixes by automatic means and is a method with close ties to linguistics. When classifying a document by features, it is often useful to analyse only the root of any given word. In our work we implement a variant of M.F. Porter's algorithm [10].

Stop Terms: Another method used in simplifying the task of text classification is stop terms. A stop list is a collection of words that are not used in feature selection. A stop list may include words such as "a", "as", "the", "for", etc. that are not useful in classification because of their high appearance frequency in all documents, regardless of class. Although mildly helpful from a computational aspect, some researchers argue against the usefulness of this method.

Mutual information based feature selection: Once all the data from an example set is read and stemming and stop terms have been applied to all words, feature selection begins. The purpose of feature selection is to choose the most valuable features from all documents where a feature's value is based on its usefulness in classifying a document in the example set. The impetus behind finding the best features for classification is that using all features requires a great deal of computational time and space. A feature's value can be measured in several ways. The most common methods involve computing, its entropy or information gain. In our work, the mutual information (MI) was calculated for each feature and the features with the highest MI were selected for use in the feature vector which in turn is later used for classification.

The algorithm of calculating the MI of each feature is :

1. Read all the messages from example set
2. Word Stemming
3. Use stop terms
4. For every message store each feature (word) f_m in a vector such as, $F=\{f_1,f_2,f_3,\ldots f_N\}$.
5. For each message i create a Boolean feature vector $V_i=\{v_1,v_2,\ldots,v_N\}$ where v_j is true implies message i contains feature f_j.

6. For each feature f_m compute the I with the following formula [11]:

$$I_{f_m}(X;Y) = \sum_{i=1}^{2}\sum_{j=1}^{2} p(x_i, y_j) \log \frac{p(x_i, y_j)}{p(x_i)p(y_j)}.$$

Where X and Y are two random variables with a joint probability mass function p(x,y) and marginal probability mass functions p(x) and p(y), correspondingly. The random variables X and Y are defined as follows:

$$X = \begin{cases} x_1 \text{ denoting that a message is spam with probability } p(x_1) \\ x_2 \text{ denoting that a message is ham with probability } p(x_2) \end{cases}$$

$$Y = \begin{cases} y_1 \text{ denoting that a feature is contained in a message with probability } p(y_1) \\ y_2 \text{ denoting that a feature is not contained in a message with probability } p(y_2) \end{cases}$$

With respect to the joint probabilities mentioned above, $p(x_1, y_1)$ denotes the probability that a message is spam and that it contains the feature under consideration, $p(x_1, y_2)$ denotes the probability that a message is spam and that it doesn't contain the feature under consideration, $p(x_2, y_1)$ denotes the probability that a message is ham and that it contains the feature under consideration, and $p(x_2, y_2)$ denotes the probability that a message is ham and that it doesn't contain the feature under consideration.

For every feature the probabilities defined above are calclulated as follows:

$$p(x_1) = \frac{SpamMessages}{TotalMessages}, \quad p(x_2) = \frac{HamMessages}{TotalMessages}$$

$$p(y_1) = \frac{FeatureFrequency}{TotalMessages}, \quad p(y_2) = 1 - p(y_1)$$

$$p(x_1, y_1) = \frac{SpamFeatureFrequency}{TotalMessages}$$

$$p(x_1, y_2) = \frac{SpamMessages - SpamFeatureFrequency}{TotalMessages}$$

$$p(x_2, y_1) = \frac{HamFeatureFrequency}{TotalMessages}$$

$$p(x_2, y_2) = \frac{HamMessages - HamFeatureFrequency}{TotalMessages}$$

where, *FeatureFrequency, SpamFeatureFrequency,* and *HamFeatureFrequency* for feature, for instance, y_1 are: the number of times feature y_1 is $y_1>0$ in the total number of messages, the number of times feature y_1 is $y_1>0$ in the total number of spam messages and the number of times feature y_1 is $y_1>0$ in the total number of ham messages respectively.

Feature Vector Size: Once the MI for each feature has been calculated it is possible to take the top X features (X in the naturals) to create the format for the feature vectors. A feature vector F has the form $\{f_1, f_2, ..., f_X\}$ where f_1 corresponds to the feature with the greatest MI, and f_X corresponds to the feature with the Xth greatest MI. The values that any f_i can take are described in the proceeding section. Choosing the optimal number of features to use in the feature vector is another problem that must be considered. This research tests these results by analysing performance of classifiers using fewer than the total number of features available.

Feature vector type: Another variant in constructing the feature vector is the type of feature vector used. In our work three types of feature vectors can be used: Boolean, Term Frequency (TF), and Term Frequency – Inverse Document Frequency (TFIDF) feature vectors. Using Boolean feature vectors, f_1 = true implies that the message to which this feature vector corresponds contains at least one instance of the feature f_1. TF feature vectors use $f_i \in N$ (set of Natural numbers) to denote the number of times feature f_i appears in that message. TF-IDF feature vectors use $f_i \in R$ (set of Real numbers) where f_i is the inverse document frequency of the feature with the ith greatest MI:

$$f_i = \log(|D| / TF(f_i))$$

where |D| is the total number of documents and $TF(f_i)$ is the number of time feature f_i appears in all documents.

In our work the vector's type selection is parametric. The feature selection process and the feature vectors creation in our application is based on the mutual information gain of words that are contained in e-mails. The optimal message features selection criteria is the word appearance frequency in spam and ham messages.

This method has been chosen because it is easily adapted to possible message content changes from spammers and to user's preferences. Finally, this procedure must be automated and must handle various training example sets and different vector types since machine learning methods don't support the same vector type.

In our work we used the Ling-Spam example set [3] which contains 2.893 messages from which 2.412 (83.37%) are legitimate messages and 481 (16.63%) are spam. We used this example set since it is the most widely used from other researchers in order to compare our results with theirs.

Classification Algorithms: The classification algorithms chosen in our comparisons are the following: Naïve-Bayes [7], AdaBoostM1 [12], Classification Via Regression [12], MultiBoostAB [12], Random Committee [12], ADTree (Alternate Decision Tree) [6], ID3 [5], RandomTree [12] and Multilayer Perceptron (MLP) [9]. All these machine learning algorithms are sufficiently described in their respective references. Some words should be added, however, for the random committee machine case. It is known that such a meta-learning technique [12] involves several randomized instances of the same type of classifier. In our experiments we have used the Support Vector Machine (SVM) classifier. We have involved 10 randomized instances of SVM. However, many different learning algorithms apart from SVM, including decision trees as well as many randomization schemes, including architectural changes of the respective neural networks, could be involved in the random committee meta-learner. Even bagging schemes [12] or other hybrid/ heuristic methods could enhance its performance. However, the goal of our investigations was to illustrate that such a meta-learning approach presents several advantages. Apart from boosting schemes [4] meta-learners have not been studied in the spam-filtering problem.

III. EXPERIMENTAL STUDY AND DISCUSSION OF THE RESULTS

There are several collections of ham and spam messages that are known, well defined and many researchers use them as a basis in their comparisons. The most important of them are the following:

- SpamAssassin Public Corpus, included in the Apache SpamAssassin Project (spam and legitimate email) (http://spamassassin.apache.org/publiccorpus/)
- Enron Email Dataset, basically a giant & realistic source of legitimate email. (http://www-2.cs.cmu.edu/~enron/)
- Ling-spam, with legitimate (linguist-list) email and spam. (http://www.iit.demokritos.gr/skel/i-config/downloads/)
- Spambase, hosted at the UCI Knowledge Discovery in Databases Archive, with preprocessed spam and legitimate email. (ftp://ftp.ics.uci.edu/pub/machine-learning-databases/spambase/)

The experimental study herein conducted is based on the Ling-Spam example set of legitimate/ spam messages [3] as previously mentioned, which is of medium size but well balanced in terms of ham and spam message numbers. We have extensively crossvalidated all spam filtering approaches herein presented over this well defined data set and in terms of this crossvalidation aspect over a widely used data set our study is the most extensive so far, although there are many other studies using very large but rather ad hoc and not widely accepted data sets [13].

The way that we decided to validate our system was to perform 50 tests with 100 and 500 features by accordingly using boolean and TF vector types as discussed in section II. Actually, using the feature extraction and selection methodology of section II we compare all classification methods involving different vector types having dimensions of 100 or 500. The decision for these specific dimensions has come from experimentation on Ling-Spam example set in order to achieve the best classification performance for all the algorithms involved and, on the other hand to deal with the curse of dimensionality problem [9].

In order to have statistically valid results regarding classification methods performance and comparisons we have employed the cross-validation approach [9]. Thus, we have divided the Ling-Spam example set into training and validation (testing) sets keeping, in each such set, the same proportions of ham (legitimate) and spam messages as in the original example set. Each training set produced contained 60% of the original example set, while each test set contained the 40% respectively. 50 such random divisions have been performed for the Ling-Spam example set in order to apply the cross-validation approach. Therefore, we will be able to compare in a statistically valid manner the performance of each algorithm in the same example set as well as the performance of each algorithm regarding different type of vectors.

Results analysis: The following tables show how many times (out of the fifty runs) each algorithm has achieved the best overall percentage on correct classification of spam and legitimate messages during training and validation stages. Also, a classification threshold of 99.5% for the training stage and a classification threshold of 99.0% for the validation stage has been considered in these tables. That is, each table entrance means that the classification accuracy achieved by involving the corresponding method is over these two defined thresholds.

Studying tables 1, 2, 3, 4 we could remark several issues:

- The selected number of features influences the performance of all algorithms. More specifically while the NaiveBayes algorithm has succeeded 20 / 50 times the best results in classification of legitimate messages with vectors of 100 features the same algorithm could not accomplish the same results with vectors of 500 features.

- In addition the selected number of features influences the performance of the algorithms in the area of false positives against false negatives. So, while the number of features increases, the number of false positives decreases while the number of false negatives increases.

- The vector type influences the performance of specific algorithms. Particularly, while the NaiveBayes algorithm has succeeded 20 / 50 times the best results with vectors of boolean features, did not accomplish to succeed more than 5 / 50 times with vectors of TF Features.

- The algorithm which succeeded the best classification results for legitimate messages is the Random Committee with vectors of Boolean 500 features, with 100% in half of the tests, while on the other half was over 99.79%, but it didn't achieve the same results in classification of spam messages. We should note, therefore, that the Random

Committee algorithm has achieved the best overall performance regarding the false positives. Such a performance is remarkable and very important since a major problem in spam filters is the large number of false positives, that is, legitimate mails categorized as spam mails.

- On the other hand, ADTree had quite a successful performance regarding spam mail categorization. That is, it constantly achieved good performance regarding false negatives.

It should be noted that, although each column should had a sum of 100% it happens that several times this percentage is exceeded. The reason is simply that several classifiers in such a column achieve the same performance (up to the first decimal)

Table 1: Performance for feature vectors with 100 boolean features (number of times each algorithm achieved best overall performance out of the 50 cross-validation runs)

	Training Stage		Validation Stage	
Algorithm	Legitimate Messages	Spam Messages	Legitimate Messages	Spam Messages
Naive Bayes			20 (40%)	
AdaBoostM1				10 (20%)
ClassificationVia Regression				
MultiBoostAB				10 (20%)
Random Committee	50 (100%)	50 (100%)	35 (70%)	
ADTree				25 (50%)
trees.ID3	50 (100%)	50 (100%)		20 (40%)
RandomTree	50 (100%)	50 (100%)		
MLP	16 (32%)	16 (32%)		

Table 2: Performance for feature vectors with 100 TF features. (number of times each algorithm achieved best overall performance out of the 50 cross-validation runs)

	Training Stage		Validation Stage	
Algorithm	Legitimate Messages	Spam Messages	Legitimate Messages	Spam Messages
NaiveBayes			5 (10%)	
AdaBoostM1				
ClassificationVia Regression				10 (20%)
MultiBoostAB				
Random Committee	50 (100%)	50 (100%)	45 (90%)	5 (10%)
ADTree				40 (80%)
RandomTree	50 (100%)	50 (100%)		
MLP	21 (42%)	19 (38%)	6 (12%)	6 (12%)

Table 3: Performance for feature vectors with 500 boolean features (number of times each algorithm achieved best overall performance out of the 50 cross-validation runs)

	Training Stage		Validation Stage	
Algorithm	Legitimate Messages	Spam Messages	Legitimate Messages	Spam Messages
NaiveBayes				
AdaBoostM1				
ClassificationViaRegression				
MultiBoostAB				
Random Committee	50 (100%)	50 (100%)	50 (100%)	
ADTree				5 (10%)
trees.ID3	50 (100%)	50 (100%)		45 (90%)
RandomTree	50 (100%)	50 (100%)		
MLP	7 (14%)	7 (14%)		

Table 4: Performance for feature vectors with 500 TF features. (number of times each algorithm achieved best overall performance out of the 50 cross-validation runs)

	Training Stage		Validation Stage	
Algorithm	Legitimate Messages	Spam Messages	Legitimate Messages	Spam Messages
Naive Bayes				
AdaBoostM1				5 (10%)
Classification ViaRegression				35 (70%)
MultiBoostAB				5 (10%)
Random Committee	50 (100%)	50 (100%)	50 (100%)	
ADTree				15 (30%)
RandomTree	50 (100%)	50 (100%)		
MLP	4 (8%)			7 (14%)

IV. CONCLUSIONS AND FUTURE TRENDS

A spam mail filtering approach is presented based on information thoretic feature extraction for efficient feature selection, and machine learning based classification. Namely, Random Committee machine achieves the best performance regarding false positives and the ADTree approach achieves the best performance regarding false negatives. These results are the outcome of an extensive experimental study, the most extensive in the literature so far, and show that the widely used Bayesian spam filter approach could be largely improved by using the above mentioned machine learning methods. Previous research in the literature has not employed and compared so far these algorithms. There are many things left to investigate for spam mails filtering. The most important is to design a machine learning system capable of handling both false positives and false negatives.

REFERENCES

[1]. S.J. Vaughan-Nichols, "Saving Private E-mail", IEEE Spectrum magazine, August 2003, pp. 40-44

[2]. S. Kaplan, "How antispam software works", Wired Magazine, April 2003, pp. 43

[3]. Ion Androutsopoulos, John Koutsias, Konstantinos V. Chandrinos, George Paliouras, and Constantine D. Spyropoulos, 'An evaluation of naïve Bayesian anti-spam filtering' 11th European Conference on Machine Learning, 2000, Barcelona, Spain, p.p. 9-17.

[4]. X. Carreras, L. Marquez, "Boosting Trees for Anti-Spam Email Filtering" in Proceedings of RANLP-01, 4th International Conference on Recent Advances in Natural Language Processing.

[5]. E. Frank, Y. Wang, S. Inglis, G. Holmes, and I.H. Witten 'Using model trees for classification', Machine Learning, (1998), Vol.32, No.1, pp. 63-76.

[6]. Y. Freund, L. Mason, 'The alternating decision tree learning algorithm', Proceeding of the Sixteenth International Conference on Machine Learning, 1999, Bled, Slovenia, p.p. 124-133.

[7]. C. Elkan, 'Naïve Bayesian Learning', Adapted from Technical Report No. CS97-557, Department of Computer Science and Engineering, University of California, San Diego, September 1997.

[8]. H. Drucker, D. Wu, V. Vapnik, 'Support Vector Machines for Spam Categorization', IEEE Transactions On Neural Networks, Vol. 10, No. 5, September 1999.

[9]. S. Haykin, "Neural Networks, A comprehensive foundation", Prentice Hall, 1999

[10]. M.F.Porter, 'An algorithm for suffix stripping', http://telemat.det.unifi.it/book/2001/wchange/download/stem_porter.html, 20/10/2003

[11]. T. M. Cover, J. A. Thomas, 'Elements of Information Theory', John Wiley & Sons, Inc., 1991

[12]. Volker Tresp, 'Committee Machines', book chapter in: *Handbook for Neural Network Signal Processing*, Yu Hen Hu and Jenq-Neng Hwang (eds.), CRC Press, 2001.

[13]. K. Tretyakov, "Machine Learning Techniques in Spam Filtering," *Institute of Computer Science,* University of Tartu Data Mining Problem-oriented Seminar, MTAT, vol. 3, pp. 60-79, 2004.

A Variational Bayesian Method for Rectified Factor Analysis

Markus Harva
Neural Networks Research Centre
Helsinki University of Technology
P.O. Box 5400, FI-02015 HUT, Espoo, Finland

Ata Kabán
School of Computer Science
The University of Birmingham
Birmingham B15 2TT, UK

Abstract— Linear factor models with nonnegativity constraints have received a great deal of interest in a number of problem domains. In existing approaches, positivity has often been associated with sparsity. In this paper we argue that sparsity of the factors is not always a desirable option, but certainly a technical limitation of the currently existing solutions. We then reformulate the problem in order to relax the sparsity constraint while retaining positivity. A variational inference procedure is derived and this is contrasted to existing related approaches. Both i.i.d. and first-order AR variants of the proposed model are provided and these are experimentally demonstrated in a real-world astrophysical application.

I. INTRODUCTION

Factor analysis is a widespread statistical technique, which seeks to relate multivariate observations to typically smaller dimensional vectors of unobserved variables. These unobserved (latent) variables, termed as factors, are hoped to explain the systematic structure inherent in the data. In standard factor analysis [1], the factors may contain both positive and negative elements. However, in many applications negative values are difficult to interpret. Hence, nonnegativity often is a desirable constraint, that has received considerable interest in recent years.

Positive matrix factorisation [2], nonnegative matrix factorisation [3] and nonnegative independent component analysis [4] are methods that perform a factorisation into positively constrained components. These methods are relatively fast and stable under reasonably mild assumptions, however, they lack a clear probabilistic generative semantics. Bayesian formulations of similar ideas have also been studied [5], [6], [7] in order to enable a series of advantages such as a principled model comparison and inference from previously unseen observations. In these works, positivity of the factors is achieved by formulating a prior that has zero probability mass on the negative axis, such as the exponential, the rectified Gaussian, or mixtures of these. The rectified Gaussian distribution is particularly convenient, as it is conjugate to the Gaussian likelihood and hence it yields a rectified Gaussian posterior distribution.

Unfortunately, all these existing solutions have a serious technical limitation: they hard-wire the assumption that the latent factors are sparse. This is because the likelihood for the location parameter of the latent prior is very awkward and makes it technically impossible to handle a hierarchical prior over it [5]. However, while in some applications both sparsity and positivity are desirable, in others sparsity is inappropriate.

In this paper we provide a different formulation of the positivity constraint in linear factor analysis, which gets round of the mentioned problems. This is achieved by employing a rectification nonlinearity as part of the model. An ordinary Gaussian prior is then employed for the argument of the rectification function, which can further have hierarchical priors for both its location and scale parameter. In this setup, the posterior is no longer of any convenient form, consequently the inference procedure is not as simple as with conjugate priors. However, we show that the free-form variational approximation for the factors is still tractable.

The remainder of the paper is organised as follows: Section II reviews existing solutions to the problem of Bayesian positively constrained factor analysis. Section III presents the proposed formulation and provides the associated inference procedure. Section IV demonstrates a real-world application of the proposed method to astrophysical data analysis. Finally we conclude and discuss further directions.

II. POSITIVELY CONSTRAINED GENERATIVE FACTOR ANALYSIS

Consider a set of N observed variables, each measured across T different instances. We denote by $\boldsymbol{x}_t \in \mathbb{R}^N$ the t-th instance. The $N \times T$ matrix formed by these vectors is referred to as $\boldsymbol{X}$ and single elements of this matrix will be denoted by x_{nt}. Similar notational convention will also apply to other variables.

As in linear factor analysis, the modelling hypothesis made is that the N observations can be explained as a superposition of $K < N$ underlying latent components $\boldsymbol{s}_t \in \mathbb{R}^K$ (factors or hidden causes) through a linear mapping $\boldsymbol{A} \in \mathbb{R}^{N \times K}$

$$\boldsymbol{x}_t = \boldsymbol{A}\boldsymbol{s}_t + \boldsymbol{n}_t. \tag{1}$$

The noise term $\boldsymbol{n}_t$ is assumed to be zero-mean i.i.d. Gaussian, to account for the notion that all dependencies that exist in $\boldsymbol{x}_t$ should be explained by the underlying hidden components.

A. Imposing Positivity as a Distributional Assumption

A straightforward approach to constraining the factors to be nonnegative is to formulate a nonnegatively supported prior distribution. In doing so, the computationally most convenient alternative is to employ a rectified Gaussian distribution as considered by several authors [5], [6], [7]. It is defined as

$$\mathcal{N}^R(s_k|\bar{s}_k,\tilde{s}_k) = \frac{2}{\text{erfc}(\bar{s}_k/\sqrt{2\tilde{s}_k})} u(s_k)\mathcal{N}(s_k|\bar{s}_k,\tilde{s}_k),$$

where $u(\cdot)$ is the standard step function. It is easy to see that the rectified Gaussian prior is conjugate to a Gaussian likelihood and the posterior can be computed in exactly same manner as with an ordinary Gaussian distribution.

However, as also noted in these works, the computations with the rectified Gaussian prior are only possible if the location parameter $\bar{s}_k$ is fixed to zero, effectively making the erfc term vanish. In all other cases, computations needed to solve the variational problem are intractable.

Consequently, due to the use of a zero-location rectified Gaussian prior on the latent variable, sparse positive factors are induced. While this may be desirable in some applications, it is clearly inappropriate in others as will be shown in Section IV.

B. Imposing Positivity Through a Rectification Nonlinearity

Let us make the following substitution in (1),

$$s_t := f(r_t), \qquad (2)$$

where $f : \mathbb{R}^K \to \mathbb{R}^K$ is the component-wise rectification function such that $f_k(r_t) = \max(r_{kt}, 0)$. This guarantees that the factors s_{kt} are positive, no matter what the distribution of r_{kt} is. We employ a Gaussian prior: $r_{kt} \sim \mathcal{N}(m_{rk}, \exp(-v_{rk}))$.

This rectification nonlinearity has previously been used within nonlinear belief networks in [8]. A variational solution is developed in the mentioned work by employing a fixed form Gaussian approximation to the true posterior. By doing so, the cost function can be written analytically [8]. However, the stable points cannot be analytically solved, but require numerical optimisation. Note that finding the global optimum is not trivial due to the existence of multiple stable points. These issues will be illustrated in the next section, where we develop a free-form variational posterior approximation for positively constrained factor analysis.

III. VARIATIONAL BAYESIAN RECTIFIED FACTOR ANALYSIS

In this section we propose a linear factor model that satisfies the positivity constraint by employing the rectification nonlinearity. We refer to this model as Rectified Factor Analysis (RFA).

Once the substitution (2) has been made in (1), a Gaussian prior is then employed over r. The resulting model is still linear w.r.t. s_t, it satisfies the required positivity constraint due to $f(\cdot)$ and also offers flexibility regarding the location of the probability mass in the latent space. The model can be summarised by the following set of equations:

$$x_t \sim \mathcal{N}(Af(r_t), \text{diag}(\exp(-v_x)))$$
$$r_{kt} \sim \mathcal{N}(m_{rk}, \exp(-v_{rk}))$$
$$a_{nk} \sim \mathcal{N}(0, 1).$$

To obtain a truly nonnegative model, the weights of the linear mapping need to be constrained to be positive too. This can be achieved by putting a rectified Gaussian prior on them. Vague hierarchical priors are formulated for the rest of the variables.

To make the notation concise, we will refer to the latent variables by θ and to the data by X. Handling the posterior distribution $p(\theta|X)$ is intractable and hence we resort to a variational scheme [9], [10], [11], where an approximative distribution $q(\theta)$ is fitted to the true posterior. This is done by constructing a lower bound of the log evidence, based on Jensen's inequality:

$$\log p(X) = \log \int p(X,\theta)\,d\theta$$
$$\geq \langle \log p(X,\theta) \rangle_{q(\theta)} - \langle \log q(\theta) \rangle_{q(\theta)}, \quad (3)$$

where $\langle . \rangle_q$ denotes expectation w.r.t. q.

The variational approach to be tractable, the distribution q needs to have suitably factorial form. Here a fully-factorial posterior [12], [10], [11], [13], [14], [6] will be employed.

The model estimation algorithm consists of iteratively updating each variable's posterior approximation in turn, while keeping all other posterior approximations fixed. It can be shown that due to the fully-factorial posterior approximation, all updates are local, i.e. requiring posterior statistics of the so called Markov blanket only. That is, for updating any of the variable nodes, the posterior statistics of its children, parents and co-parents are needed only. This has been exploited in the Bayes Blocks framework [13], [15], [16] which is also used in this work. The scaling of the resulting variational Bayesian algorithm is thus multi-linear in N, T and K, giving the theoretical computational complexity of $O(NTK)$ per iteration.

A. Free-form Posterior Approximation

The fixed form approximation employed in [8] essentially fixes $q(r_{kt})$ to a Gaussian. In this subsection we show that although the free-form approximation of the posterior has a non-standard form, it can be handled analytically, it is more accurate compared to the fixed form approximation and it is also computationally more convenient.

The relevant term of the cost function when updating any given factor r_{kt} is

$$\left\langle \log \frac{q(r_{kt})}{\mathcal{N}(a|f(r_{kt}),b)\mathcal{N}(r_{kt}|c,d)} \right\rangle, \quad (4)$$

where a, b, c and d are constants w.r.t. $q(r_{kt})$ and can be computed from the Markov blanket of r_{kt}. Because of the rectification f, the likelihood part in the denominator of (4) is no longer Gaussian, and hence no easy conjugate update rule for $q(r_{kt})$ exists.

Before proceeding to derive the update rule for $q(r_{kt})$, it is worth noticing that once this is completed, the same methodology will apply if a first order AR prior

$$r_t \sim \mathcal{N}(Br_{t-1}, \text{diag}[\exp(-v_r)])$$

is considered. Indeed, since the likelihood term at index $t+1$ can be combined with the prior at index $t-1$ (due to the Gaussianity of the prior on r_t), an expression that has exactly the same form as (4) is obtained.

We now proceed to deriving the required inference procedure for our model. Tractability of the variational posterior means that analytical expressions can be derived for the following: (i) the cost function:[1]

$$\mathcal{C} = \mathcal{C}_q + \mathcal{C}_p = \langle \log q(r) \rangle - \langle \log p(r|m_r, v_r) \rangle ,$$

(ii) the posterior mean $\langle r \rangle$ and the variance $\text{Var}\{r\}$ and (iii) the mean $\langle f(r) \rangle$ and the variance $\text{Var}\{f(r)\}$. Here and throughout, $\langle \cdot \rangle$ denote expectations over $q(r)$.

1) The Form of the Posterior: From (4), an invocation of Gibbs' inequality immediately gives us the free form solution:

$$q(r) = \frac{1}{Z} \mathcal{N}(a|f(r), b) \mathcal{N}(r|c, d) , \quad (5)$$

where Z is the scaling constant, that will be computed shortly. After some manipulations, (5) can be written as

$$q(r) = q_p(r) + q_n(r) = \frac{w_p}{Z} \mathcal{N}(r|m_p, v_p) u(r) + \frac{w_n}{Z} \mathcal{N}(r|m_n, v_n) u(-r),$$

where

$$w_p = \mathcal{N}(a|c, b+d), \quad w_n = \mathcal{N}(a|0, b),$$
$$v_p = (b^{-1} + d^{-1})^{-1}, \quad m_p = v_p(a/b + c/d),$$
$$v_n = d \quad \text{and} \quad m_n = c.$$

Thus, it turns out that the free form posterior approximation is a mixture of two rectified Gaussians. One of these has all its probability mass on the positive real axis whereas the other on the negative axis. The normalisation constant Z of the posterior is then the following:

$$Z = \int \mathcal{N}(a|f(r), b) \mathcal{N}(r|c, d) \, dr$$
$$= \frac{w_n}{2} \text{erfc}[m_n/\sqrt{2v_n}] + \frac{w_p}{2} \text{erfc}[-m_p/\sqrt{2v_p}].$$

2) Relating the Free-Form Approximation to the Fixed-Form Gaussian Approximation: Now, consider fitting the fixed form Gaussian posterior to the true one, e.g. when the quantities in (4) are $a = 1.1$, $b = 0.17$, $c = -1.5$ and $d = 1.2$. The free-form posterior is shown in Figure 1. Looking at its form it should not be surprising that the cost function (which essentially measures the misfit between the approximate and the true posterior) has two stable points. These are shown in Figure 1 in dashed and dot-dashed lines. The dot-dashed line represents the global minimum whereas the dashed line is just a local minimum. The cost function is shown in Figure 2, where the crosses mark the stable points. It is thus clear, that an inference procedure that is able to handle the free-form posterior is preferable to an inference based on the fixed-form Gaussian approximation.

[1]The sub-indexes of r are dropped at this point for convenience.

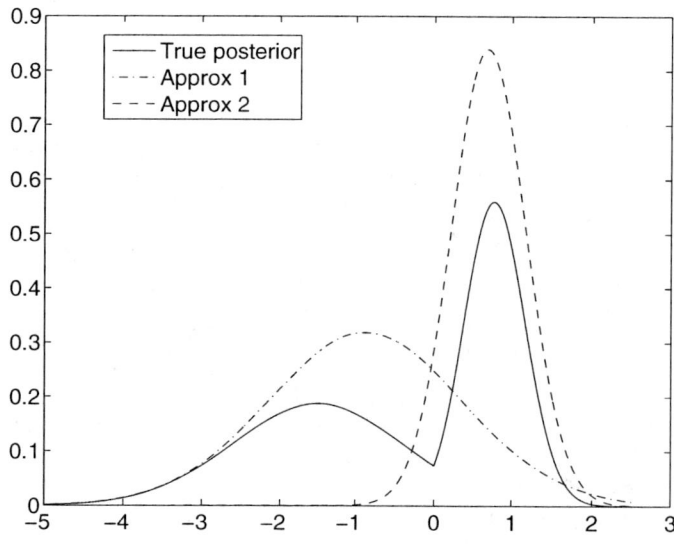

Fig. 1. The true posterior and two Gaussian approximations that are locally optimal.

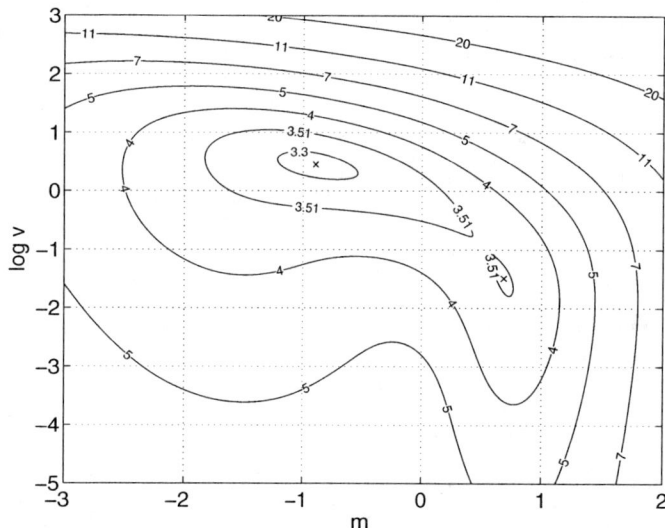

Fig. 2. The cost as a function of the mean m and the log-variance $\log v$ of the Gaussian approximation.

3) Posterior Statistics: Before proceeding to derive the required variational posterior statistics and the cost function, a set of moments are computed. Using these, the expectations as well as the $\mathcal{C}_q$ term of the cost function can be easily expressed.

We define the positive and negative ith order moments as

$$M_p^i = \int r^i q_p(r) \, dr \quad \text{and} \quad M_n^i = \int r^i q_n(r) \, dr . \quad (6)$$

It turns out, that we can express the required expectations and the cost function using the moments of order 0, 1, and 2. The evaluation of these can be cast back to evaluation of the equivalent moments of the rectified Gaussian distribution. The derivations are lengthy and are omitted.

The required posterior statistics are now easily obtained

using these moments

$$\langle r \rangle = \int r\, q(r)\, dr = \int r\, q_p(r)\, dr + \int r\, q_n(r)\, dr$$
$$= M_p^1 + M_n^1$$
$$\langle r^2 \rangle = \int r^2\, q(r)\, dr = \int r^2\, q_p(r)\, dr + \int r^2\, q_n(r)\, dr$$
$$= M_p^2 + M_n^2$$
$$\langle f(r) \rangle = \int f(r) q(r)\, dr = \int r\, q_p(r)\, dr = M_p^1$$
$$\langle f^2(r) \rangle = \int f^2(r) q(r)\, dr = \int r^2\, q_p(r)\, dr = M_p^2.$$

The variances are computed using the familiar formula $\mathrm{Var}\{x\} = \langle x^2 \rangle - \langle x \rangle^2$.

4) Cost Function: The cost function, which is the negative of the log evidence bound (3), can be used both for monitoring the convergence of the algorithm and more importantly, for comparing different solutions and models.

The term $\mathcal{C}_p$ of the cost function is computed as in the case of ordinary Gaussian variable, see [16] for details. The $\mathcal{C}_q$ term in turn is completely different due to the complex form of the posterior:

$$\mathcal{C}_q = \langle \log q(r) \rangle_{q(r)} = \int q(r) \log q(r)\, dr$$
$$= \int q_p(r) \log q(r)\, dr + \int q_n(r) \log q(r)\, dr$$
$$= \int q_p(r) \log q_p(r)\, dr + \int q_n(r) \log q_n(r)\, dr. \quad (7)$$

The two terms in (7) can be expressed using the moments derived above. The first term yields

$$\int q_p(r) \log q_p(r)\, dr$$
$$= \int q_p(r) \log \left\{ \frac{w_p}{Z} \frac{1}{\sqrt{2\pi v_p}} \exp\left[-\frac{1}{2v_p} (r - m_p)^2 \right] \right\} dr$$
$$= \int q_p(r) \left\{ \log \frac{w_p}{Z\sqrt{2\pi v_p}} - \frac{m_p^2}{2v_p} + \frac{m_p}{v_p} r - \frac{1}{2v_p} r^2 \right\} dr$$
$$= \left(\log \frac{w_p}{Z\sqrt{2\pi v_p}} - \frac{m_p^2}{2v_p} \right) M_p^0 + \frac{m_p}{v_p} M_p^1 - \frac{1}{2v_p} M_p^2.$$

Similarly

$$\int q_n(r) \log q_n(r)\, dr$$
$$= \left(\log \frac{w_n}{Z\sqrt{2\pi v_n}} - \frac{m_n^2}{2v_n} \right) M_n^0 + \frac{m_n}{v_n} M_n^1 - \frac{1}{2v_n} M_n^2.$$

IV. Experiments

In this section we present an application of the proposed model to astrophysical data analysis. Experiments have been conducted on both real and synthetic stellar population spectra of elliptical galaxies, addressing both the physical interpretability of the representations created and the predictive capabilities of the models. Ellipticals are the oldest galactic systems in the local Universe and are relatively well understood in physics. The hypothesis that some of these old galactic systems may actually contain young components is relatively new [17]. It is therefore interesting to investigate whether a set of stellar population spectra can be decomposed and explained in terms of a small set of unobserved spectral prototypes in a data driven manner. The positivity constraint is important here, as negative values of flux would not be physically interpretable. The mixing proportions also need to be positive, hence standard rectified Gaussians are employed for the weights s.t. $a_{nk} \sim \mathcal{N}^R(a_{nk}|0,1)$.

A. Missing Values and Measurements Errors

Classical non-probabilistic approaches do not offer the flexibility for taking known measurement errors into account. It is an important practical advantage of the probabilistic framework adopted, that it allows us to handle them in a principled manner. This is achieved simply by making the 'clean' vectors $\boldsymbol{x}_t$ become hidden variables of the additional error model below

$$y_{nt} = x_{nt} + e_{nt}.$$

Here e_{nt} is a zero-mean Gaussian noise term with variance v_{ynt} fixed to values that are known from the properties of the physical instrument, for each individual measurement $n = 1:N, t = 1:T$. Missing values can also be handled in this framework by setting v_{ynt} to a very large value.

B. Results on Real Data

A number of $N = 21$ real stellar population spectra will be analysed in this subsection. The data [18] was collected from real elliptical galaxies, along with known measurement uncertainties, given as individual standard deviations on each spectrum & wavelength pair. The data also contains missing entries.

Each of these 21 spectra is characterised by flux values (measured in arbitrary units [18]) given at a number of $T = 339$ different wavelength bins, ranging between 2005-8000 Angstroms. A part of this data set is shown in Figure 3.

In this section we demonstrate three models in terms of the interpretability of their factor representation created. Positive Factor Analysis (PFA) will refer to the method reviewed in Section II-A. Rectified Factor Analysis (RFA) and Dynamic Rectified Factor Analysis (DRFA) refer to the model proposed in this paper and its AR variant respectively. We have fixed the number of factors to two, as inferring subsequent components turns out to have no physical interpretation. We repeated each run ten times with random initialisations drawn from $\mathcal{N}^R(0,1)$. The model with smallest cost function value was then selected. The two components[2] for each of the models are shown in Figure 4. The shape of the first component is very similar for all three methods considered. This component can visually be recognised to correspond to an old and high

---
[2]The order of the components is of course arbitrary, we have manually grouped them for the ease of visual inspection.

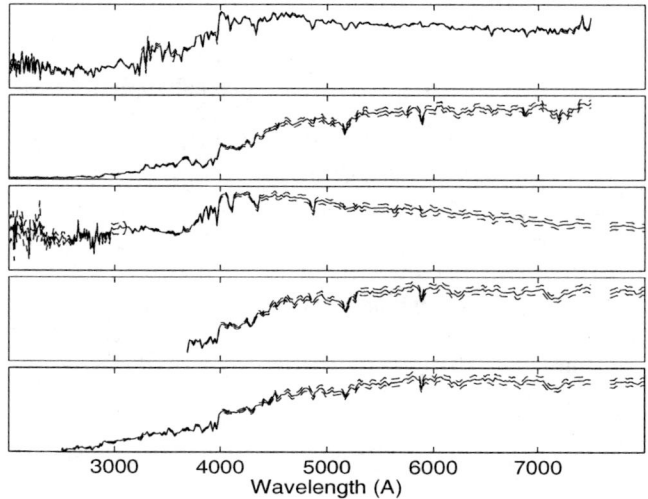

Fig. 3. A sample from the real data of spectral measurements. The dashed lines show the standard deviations of the errors in the data. The blank entries denote missing values.

metallicity stellar population. This kind of component in elliptical stellar populations has been known to physicists for a long time. In turn, the existence of a second component is a relatively recent finding in astrophysics [18].

Interestingly, the second component inferred from the data differs more across the models considered. However, the RFA second component turned out to be physically interpretable, as it exhibits many of the characteristic features of a young and low metallicity stellar population spectrum. The second component from DRFA is similar in its main shape, providing an indication for the age of this stellar population component, however it lacks some of the wiggles that encode metallicity characteristics of the stellar population.

From astrophysical point of view, the second component of PFA has no clear physical interpretation, as its distribution is biased toward zero. This is most likely due the fact that the location parameter for the rectified Gaussian distribution is required to be zero and hence small values are favoured. This results in a poor match with any known physical model. The sparsity constraint of PFA is clearly inappropriate in this application.

The values of the cost function at $K = 2$ are detailed in Figure 5. The contributions of the various individual terms of the overall cost associated to these methods are also shown in this figure. DRFA provides the lowest overall cost, since it is able to code the factors most compactly [19]. However, as we can also read from the figure, the error term corresponding to the data reconstruction accuracy is a little larger (compared to the other two methods considered here). RFA has the smallest cost for the data reconstruction term as well, implying an accurate reconstruction of the data details.

C. Prediction Results on Synthetic Data

Here we employ synthetic spectra in order to assess the predictive performance of the proposed methods in an ob-

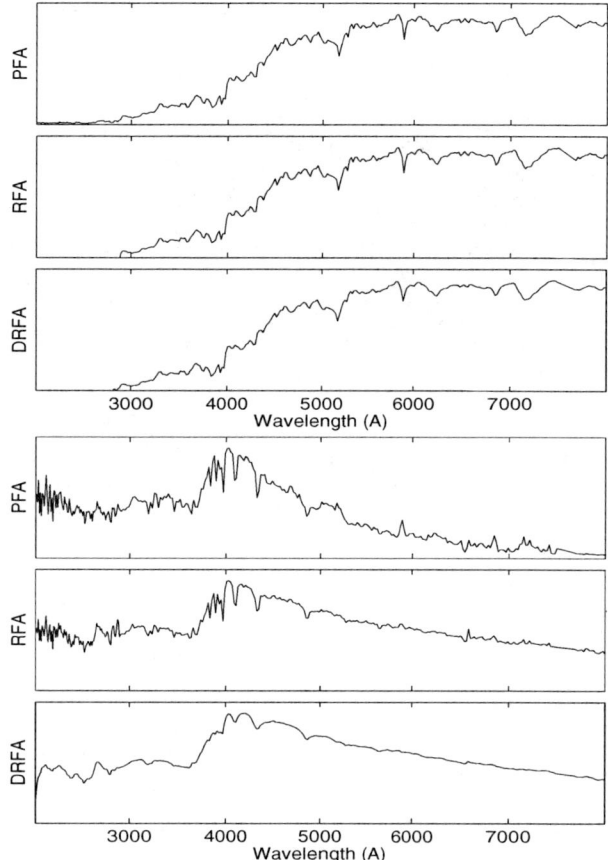

Fig. 4. The first (above) and second (below) components for the different models.

jective and controlled manner. A random selection of 100 synthetic composite spectra produced from the stellar population evolutionary synthesis model of Jimenez [18] is utilised. Each of the these may contain the superposition of two stellar population spectra with varying parameters (age, metallicity and proportion). The wavelength coverage as well as the binning of these spectra is identical to those described for the real data. The mixing proportions depend on the masses of the component stellar populations in a physically realistic manner. There are no missing entries or measurement errors in this data set, making it suitable for an controlled assessment.

We consider an inference task where half of the flux values at a random selection of wavelength bins are held out as a test set and used for evaluation purpose only. Missing values are artificially created at random in the test set. The RFA and DRFA models are trained on the same training set and asked to predict the artificially created missing entries in the previously unseen test set. The prediction can be obtained simply from the posterior mean of $q(x_{nt})$. The number of factors has been $K = 3$, determined from the evidence bound, for both models in this experiment. The SNR between the predictions and the true values, when varying the percentage of missing values in the test set, are shown in Figure 6. Clearly, as expected, DRFA outperforms RFA in this prediction task, especially

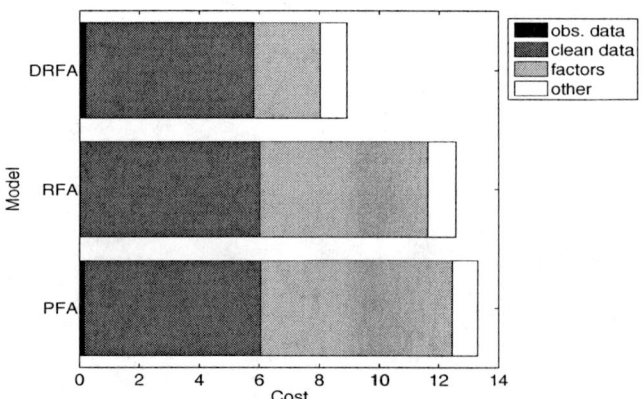

Fig. 5. The cost (divided by the number of samples) of the various models considered. Individual terms of the overall cost are highlighted for each model. Obs. data stands for y_t, clean data for x_t, factors for r_t (or s_t in case of PFA) and other for other variables in the models such as the noise variances v_{xn}.

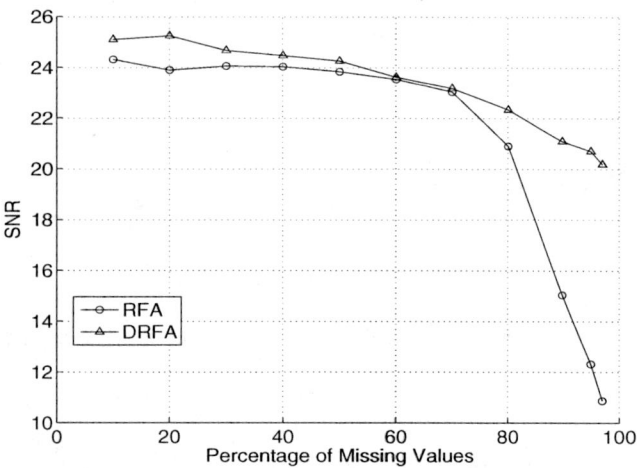

Fig. 6. Prediction of missing entries in out-of-sample wavelength bins.

when the amount of missing values gets large. The reason for this is that DRFA includes the modelling of the correlations between fluxes at neighbouring wavelength bins. Evidently this information turns out to be useful in the prediction task considered.

V. Discussion

We presented a method for nonnegative factor analysis, based on variational Bayesian learning. The proposed solution gets round of the shortcomings of approaches that impose a positively supported prior directly on the latent space. We derived analytical expressions for performing inference in this model, using a factorial free-form approximation for the factors. We demonstrated the proposed model in an astrophysical data analysis application, where approaches that induce sparse representations are inappropriate. The presented approach is applicable in any situation where flexible latent densities over the positive domain are required.

We note that the methodology developed and employed here can straightforwardly be extended e.g. to include multiple rectification. Also, Gaussian mixture priors for the argument of this function could be employed in place of the single Gaussian utilised here, in order to further enhance flexibility.

Acknowledgements

This research has been funded by the Finnish Centre of Excellence Programme (2000-2005) under the project New Information Processing Principles and a Paul & Yuanbi Ramsay research award at the School of Computer Science of The University of Birmingham. Many thanks to Louisa Nolan and Somak Raychaudhury for sharing their astrophysical expertise and supplying the data.

References

[1] R. L. Gorsuch, *Factor Analysis*, 2nd ed. Hillsdale, NJ: Lawrence Erlbaum Associates, 1983.

[2] P. Paatero and U. Tapper, "Positive matrix factorization: A nonnegative factor model with optimal utilization of error estimates of data values," *Environmetr.*, vol. 5, pp. 111–126, 1994.

[3] D. D. Lee and H. S. Seung, "Learning the parts of objects by nonnegative matrix factorization," *Nature*, vol. 401, pp. 788–791, 1999.

[4] M. Plumbley and E. Oja, "A "nonnegative PCA" algorithm for independent component analysis," *IEEE Transactions on Neural Networks*, vol. 15, no. 1, pp. 66–76, 2004.

[5] J. Miskin, "Ensemble learning for independent component analysis," Ph.D. dissertation, University of Cambridge, UK, 2000.

[6] J. Winn and C. M. Bishop, "Variational message passing," *Journal of Machine Learning Research*, 2004, submitted.

[7] M. Harva, "Hierarchical variance models of image sequences," Master's thesis, Helsinki University of Technology, Espoo, 2004.

[8] B. J. Frey and G. E. Hinton, "Variational learning in nonlinear Gaussian belief networks," *Neural Computation*, vol. 11, no. 1, pp. 193–214, 1999.

[9] M. Jordan, Z. Ghahramani, T. Jaakkola, and L. Saul, "An introduction to variational methods for graphical models," in *Learning in Graphical Models*, M. Jordan, Ed. Cambridge, MA, USA: The MIT Press, 1999, pp. 105–161.

[10] H. Lappalainen, "Ensemble learning for independent component analysis," in *Proc. Int. Workshop on Independent Component Analysis and Signal Separation (ICA'99)*, Aussois, France, 1999, pp. 7–12.

[11] H. Attias, "A variational Bayesian framework for graphical models," in *Advances in Neural Information Processing Systems*, S. Solla, T. Leen, and K.-R. Müller, Eds., vol. 12. MIT Press, 2000, pp. 209–215.

[12] D. J. C. MacKay, *Information Theory, Inference and Learning Algorithms*. Cambridge University Press, 2003.

[13] H. Valpola, T. Raiko, and J. Karhunen, "Building blocks for hierarchical latent variable models," in *Proc. 3rd Int. Conf. on Independent Component Analysis and Signal Separation (ICA2001)*, San Diego, USA, 2001, pp. 710–715.

[14] C. M. Bishop, D. Spiegelhalter, and J. Winn, "VIBES: A variational inference engine for Bayesian networks," in *Advances in Neural Information Processing Systems*, S. Becker, S. Thrun, and K. Obermayer, Eds., vol. 15. MIT Press, 2003, pp. 793–800.

[15] H. Valpola, A. Honkela, M. Harva, A. Ilin, T. Raiko, and T. Östman, "Bayes blocks software library," http://www.cis.hut.fi/projects/bayes/software/, 2003.

[16] T. Raiko, H. Valpola, M. Harva, and J. Karhunen, "Building blocks for variational Bayesian learning of latent variable models," *Journal of Machine Learning Research*, 2004, submitted.

[17] D. S. Madgwick, A. L. Coil, C. J. Conselice, M. C. Cooper, M. Davis, R. S. Ellis, S. M. Faber, D. P. Finkbeiner, B. Gerke, P. Guhathakurta, N. Kaiser, D. C. Koo, J. A. Newman, A. C. Phillips, C. C. Steidel, B. J. Weiner, C. N. A. Willmer, and R. Yan, "The DEEP2 galaxy redshift survey: Spectral classification of galaxies at $z \sim 1$," *The Astrophysical Journal*, vol. 599, no. 2, pp. 997–1005, 2003.

[18] L. Nolan, "The star formation history of elliptical galaxies," Ph.D. dissertation, The University of Edinburgh, UK, 2002.

[19] A. Honkela and H. Valpola, "Variational learning and bits-back coding: an information-theoretic view to Bayesian learning," *IEEE Transactions on Neural Networks*, vol. 15, no. 4, pp. 800–810, 2004.

An Information Theoretic Approach to Adaptive System Training Using Unlabeled Data

Kyu-Hwa Jeong, Jian-Wu Xu, Jose C. Principe
Computational NeuroEngineering Laboratory
Department of Electrical and Computer Engineering, University of Florida
Gainesville, FL 32611 U.S.A.
E-mail: {khjeong, jianwu, principe}@cnel.ufl.edu

Abstract— Traditionally, supervised learning is performed with pairwise input-output labeled data. After the training procedure, the adaptive system weights are fixed and the system is tested with unlabeled data. Recently, exploiting the unlabeled data to improve classification performance has been proposed in the machine learning community. In this paper, we present an information theoretic approach based on density divergence minimization to obtain an extended training algorithm using unlabeled data during testing. The simulations for classification problems suggest that our method can improve the performance of adaptive system in the application phase.

I. INTRODUCTION

Supervised learning, including system identification and regression, is performed with input-output labeled data using linear and nonlinear system topologies and optimal criteria based on statistics of the error between the desired samples and system output. The purpose of learning is to extract as much information as possible from the labeled training data to obtain optimal system weights so that they generalize in unlabeled data (typically by splitting the data set into training and testing sets). Once the system is trained, there is no further optimization carried out over the unlabeled data during the actual application (testing) phase [1], [2]. This approach is considered natural to all since we do not have the labels for the testing data to further train the adaptive system.

Due to the fact that labeled samples are much more expensive to collect when compared with unlabeled samples, researchers in machine learning are proposing ideas of *learning from unlabeled data*. The goal is to design classifiers that can utilize the information present in both the labeled as well as in unlabeled data. One method is *transductive inference* using support vector machines proposed by Vapnik et al. [3], [4]. Transduction goes from particular (past) samples to particular (future) samples without any attempt to generalize. Another prominent approach is *active learning* where the learner can 'ask' the expert for a label of a sample in contrast to normal (passive) machine learning where the learner is presented with a static set of examples used to construct a model [5]. There are also some other methods in the literature such as the EM algorithm in a maximum likelihood framework [6], [7]; Smoother function approximation of unlabeled data using the representer theorem in the context of regularization [8]. Recently, Erdogmus et al. introduced an information theoretic framework based on Kullback-Leibler divergence minimization for training adaptive systems in supervised learning settings using both labeled and unlabeled data [9].

In this paper, we propose the Euclidean distance based probability density function (pdf) matching algorithm to extend adaptive system training even after supervised learning is completed. We use the information of the desired signal from the training data and the unlabeled novel testing data to adjust the classifier weights. One big advantage of this new information theoretic approach is the simplicity of computation. We also elucidate the circumstances under which our method can improve the performance of classification by using the unlabeled data in the proposed information theoretic framework.

The paper is organized as follows. First, we give the description of the problem. Then the Euclidean distance based probability density function matching algorithm is presented in section 3. Next, we discuss the conditions under which our method might improve the performance of classification. In order to test our algorithm, we apply our method to an artificial data set and a real biomedical data set in section 5.

II. PROBLEM DESCRIPTION

Consider a general function approximation problem. Suppose we have input-output data $\{(u_1, y_1), \ldots, (u_N, y_N)\}$ available from an unknown nonlinear function as follow:

$$d = f(\mathbf{u}) + n \qquad (1)$$

The observed output (desired response) d is called the label of the input signal $\mathbf{u}$ and n is corrupted noise. In function approximation, the labels are continuous-valued while in classification problem, the labels are discrete. The goal of supervised learning is to construct an adaptive system with input signal $\mathbf{u}$, output y, and weights $\mathbf{w}$ to approximate the function f or classify the output into different categories.

$$y = g(\mathbf{u}, \mathbf{w}) \qquad (2)$$

The adaptive system could be a linear filter ($y = \mathbf{w}^T \mathbf{u}$), a neural network, or any other topology. The process of supervised learning seeks to optimize the weights to extract relevant information from input-output sample pairs for a specific task. The optimization is carried out by minimization or maximization of an optimality criterion. Typically the mean square error (MSE) [1], [2] is used, however there are also alternative selections such as minimum error entropy [10] or the ϵ-insensitive loss function [11]. The error signal is defined as the difference between the available desired output and the output produced by the adaptive system for a particular input ($e = d - y$).

In the training phase, the adaptive system weights are adjusted to obtain an approximation to f or classify the input data into different categories by minimizing the error. In the application (testing) phase, the weights are fixed and the trained system is tested on novel unlabeled input data $\{u_{N+1}, \ldots, u_K\}$. The probability distributions of the input signal for training $\{u_1, \ldots, u_N\}$ and for testing $\{u_{N+1}, \ldots, u_K\}$ can be the same or different. The following question is to be answered in this paper: *How can we continue updating the weights of the adaptive system in the application phase and under what conditions can we improve performance?*

III. EUCLIDEAN DISTANCE PDF MATCHING ALGORITHM

Our idea is to combine the unlabeled input data in the testing set and the information of the desired output for training in order to continue adjusting the system weights. We assume here that the *a priori* probability of each class during testing is the same as for training. We will discuss more details about this hypothesis in the next section. Based on this assumption, the Euclidean distance pdf matching algorithm is proposed to adapt the system weights in application phase as

$$\min_{\mathbf{w}} \int (f_{dtrn}(x) - f_{ytst}(x))^2 \, dx \qquad (3)$$

where $f_{dtrn}(x)$ is the pdf of desired signal during training phase, $f_{ytst}(x)$ is the pdf of system output signal during testing phase and $\mathbf{w}$ is the weight vector of the adaptive system. The Euclidean distance pdf matching cost function minimizes the pdf divergence between the training desired signal and the testing output signal based on the Euclidean distance between the pdfs. In other words, we create a desired signal for the input data during testing by utilizing the pdf information of the desired signal encountered during training. This is also the reason why we must require the same *a priori* probability among training and testing. Instead of setting the problem in the input data space directly, the Euclidean distance pdf matching criterion utilizes the information at the system output, which avoids the curse of dimensionality. Next we derive a gradient descent algorithm for the cost function in (3).

We propose to compute the Euclidean distance pdf matching cost function directly from data samples, i.e. nonparametrically. This requires a smooth (i.e., continuous and differentiable) estimator for the two probability density functions $f_{dtrn}(x)$ and $f_{ytst}(x)$. Parzen windowing is a suitable method, which is an asymptotically unbiased and consistent pdf estimator [12]. Given N independent and identically distributed (iid) samples $\{x_1, \ldots, x_N\}$, the pdf can be approximated by

$$\hat{f}_x(\xi) = \frac{1}{N} \sum_{i=1}^{N} \kappa(\xi - x_i, \sigma^2) \qquad (4)$$

where $\kappa(\cdot, \sigma^2)$ is typically a zero-mean Gaussian kernel with standard deviation σ. One of the advantages of Parzen window with Gaussian kernel is that we can avoid the integral computation directly, since the integral of two Gaussian kernels generates another Gaussian kernel with different double standard deviation. For convenience, we derive the algorithm in one dimension, but this can be easily extended to multidimensional cases.

$$\begin{aligned}
J(\mathbf{w}) &= \int (\hat{f}_{dtrn}(x, d) - \hat{f}_{ytst}(x, y))^2 \, dx \\
&= \int \hat{f}_{dtrn}^2(x, d) \, dx - 2 \int \hat{f}_{dtrn}(x, d) \hat{f}_{ytst}(x, y) \, dx \\
&\quad + \int \hat{f}_{ytst}^2(x, y) \, dx \\
&= J_0 + J_1(\mathbf{w}) + J_2(\mathbf{w})
\end{aligned} \qquad (5)$$

where

$$\begin{aligned}
J_0 &= \frac{1}{N^2} \sum_{i=1}^{N} \sum_{j=1}^{N} \kappa(d_i - d_j, 2\sigma^2) \\
J_1(\mathbf{w}) &= -\frac{2}{NM} \sum_{i=1}^{N} \sum_{j=1}^{M} \kappa(d_i - y_j(\mathbf{w}), 2\sigma^2) \\
J_2(\mathbf{w}) &= \frac{1}{M^2} \sum_{i=1}^{M} \sum_{j=1}^{M} \kappa(y_i(\mathbf{w}) - y_j(\mathbf{w}), 2\sigma^2)
\end{aligned} \qquad (6)$$

J_0 is not a function of $\mathbf{w}$, d is the desired training phase signal, N is the number of training samples and y is the system output during testing phase with M samples. Only J_1 and J_2 are functions of $\mathbf{w}$ through $y = g(\mathbf{u}, \mathbf{w})$. In order to adjust the weights in the testing phase, we take the derivative of J with respect to $\mathbf{w}$ to obtain the gradient descent update

$$\mathbf{w}_{new} = \mathbf{w}_{old} - \eta \nabla J(\mathbf{w}) \qquad (7)$$

where the gradient is evaluated from

$$\begin{aligned}
\nabla J(\mathbf{w}) &= \nabla J_1(\mathbf{w}) + \nabla J_2(\mathbf{w}) \\
\nabla J_1(\mathbf{w}) &= \frac{2}{NM} \sum_{i=1}^{N} \sum_{j=1}^{M} \kappa'(d_i - y_j, 2\sigma^2) \frac{dy_j}{d\mathbf{w}} \\
\nabla J_2(\mathbf{w}) &= \frac{1}{M^2} \sum_{i=1}^{M} \sum_{j=1}^{M} \kappa'(y_i - y_j, 2\sigma^2) \frac{d(y_i - y_j)}{d\mathbf{w}}
\end{aligned} \qquad (8)$$

A batch method is used here to compute the weights update. An online approach is also possible with the introduction of stochastic information gradient [13].

IV. Discussion

Our methodology requires that the *a priori* probability of each class remains the same during the training and application phase, but it allows for slight differences between the pdf of training and testing. To examine further, we employ the Bayesian method to find out under what conditions performance can be improved.

Consider a classification problem with two classes, C_1 and C_2 with the *a priori* probability $P(C_1)$ and $P(C_1)$ respectively. The optimal discriminant function separating the two classes is given by

$$P(y = C_i \mid \mathbf{u}) = \frac{P(\mathbf{u} \mid y = C_i) P(y = C_i)}{P(\mathbf{u})}, i = 1, 2 \quad (9)$$

Since we use the probability of output data for training as a pseudo desired signal in testing phase in order to continue updating the classifier weights, we have to assume that priors do not change from the training to the testing set, i.e. $P(C_i; training) = P(C_i; testing)$ for $i = 1, 2$. In the case that the likelihood functions $P(\mathbf{u} \mid y = C_i)$ change from training to the testing set, obviously the optimal decision boundary obtained from training set will not be the optimal for testing set. Under this condition, our algorithm will adjust the decision boundary to a better position such that the correct classification probability increases. In the case that the likelihood functions do not change from the training to the testing set, then according to the Bayesian equation (9) the optimal decision boundary obtained from training phase will remain optimal, since the value of the *a posterior* probability remains the same. Then there is no need to apply our algorithm. We will illustrate these two cases in the next simulation section.

V. Simulation Results

In this section, we will give the simulation results of Euclidean distance pdf matching algorithm applied to adaptive systems in a simple pattern classification problem as well as a real biomedical classification problem. In the simulation, we used the same neural network topology for training and testing. The objective of the experiment is to distinguish (classify) two classes of overlapping two-dimensional patterns labeled class 1 and class 2. Let $C1$ and $C2$ denote the set of events for which a random vector $\mathbf{u}$ belong to Class 1 and 2, respectively.

In the first simulation, we artificially generated two classes with conditional pdf for class 1, $P(\mathbf{u} \mid C_1)$, being a Gaussian distributed with zero mean and unit variance; the conditional pdf for class 2, $P(\mathbf{u} \mid C_2)$, has mean vector $[2, 2]$ and unit variance respectively. The two classes have equal *a priori* probabilities.

In order to illustrate the effectiveness of our algorithm, we simulated two cases. In the first case, the conditional distributions of the testing pattern 1 and 2 are the same as those of the training patterns. Ideally, the decision boundary will not change after we apply our algorithm since the decision boundary is optimal both for training and testing data sets. But due to the finite sample data effects, the likelihood functions

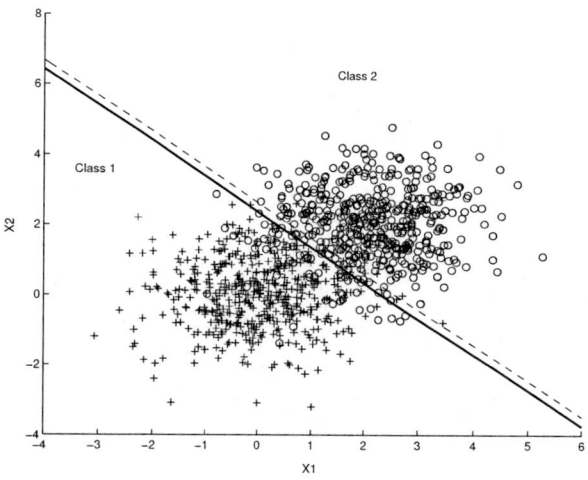

Fig. 1. Two decision boundaries with and without continuous training in testing data set in the case $P(\mathbf{u} \mid C_i; training) = P(\mathbf{u} \mid C_i; testing)$ for simulation 1

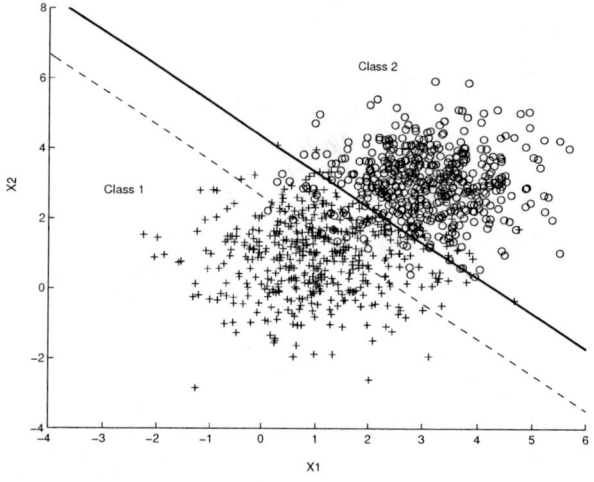

Fig. 2. Two decision boundaries with and without continuous training in testing data set in the case $P(\mathbf{u} \mid C_i; training) \neq P(\mathbf{u} \mid C_i; testing)$ for simulation 1

will differ slightly for both simulations and the decision boundary will not be optimal during testing. In Fig. 1, the dashed line is the decision boundary for training data set and the solid line is the one after we applied the algorithm for the unlabeled data set (this assignment will be kept for all other figures). The figure shows that the decision boundary resulted from training data moves slightly in the testing data after we applied our algorithm. The correct classification probability increases from 0.905 to 0.919 by using our algorithm. In this situation, our algorithm is able to improve generalization by counteracting overfitting.

In the second case, we generated another testing data set of slightly different likelihood functions compared with training data to mimic the normal variability between experimental conditions. For the testing data class 1 is a gaussian with

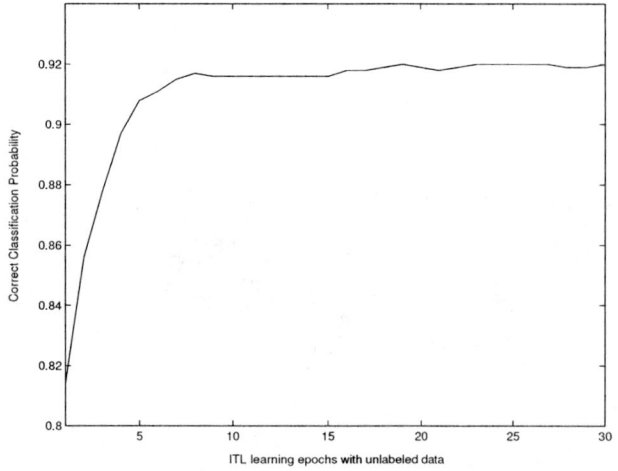

Fig. 3. Correct classification probability curve in the case $P(\mathbf{u} \mid C_i; training) \neq P(\mathbf{u} \mid C_i; testing)$ for simulation 1

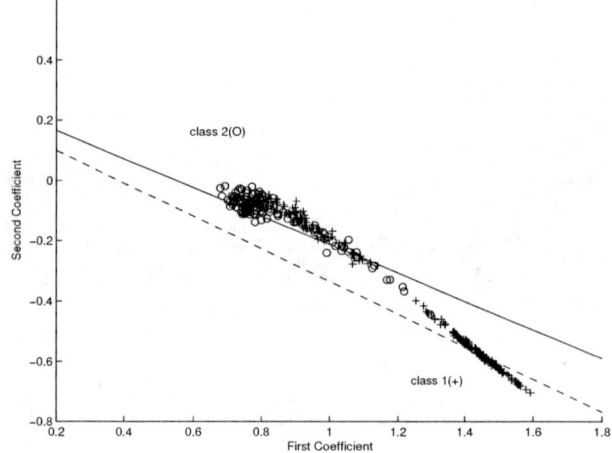

Fig. 5. Two decision boundary with and without continuous training in testing data set for patient 1 in simulation 2

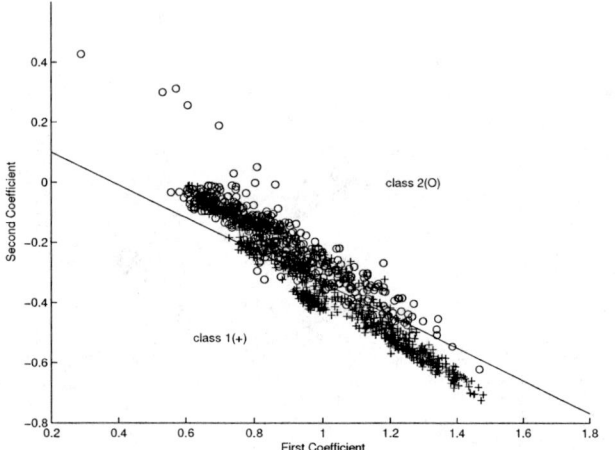

Fig. 4. Training data set and decision boundary in simulation 2

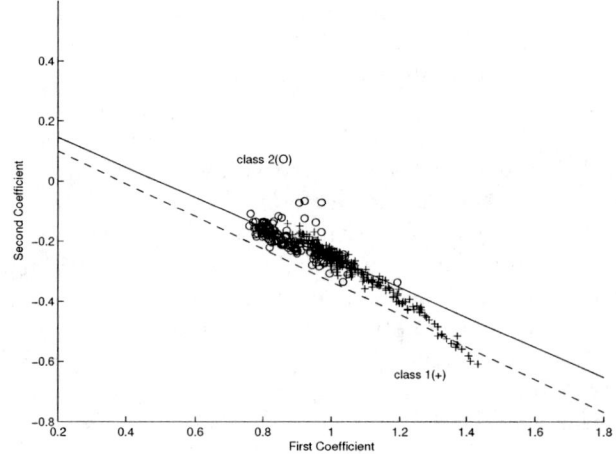

Fig. 6. Two decision boundary with and without continuous training in testing data set for patient 2 in simulation 2

mean vector $[0.2, 0.2]$ and variance vector $[1.2, 1.2]$, while class 2 is a gaussian with mean vector $[2.1, 2.1]$ and variance vector $[0.8, 0.8]$. The results are given in fig. 2 and 3. Fig. 2 plots the two decision boundaries with and without continuous training presented in the testing data set. We can see that the decision boundary shifts to a new position where the correct classification probability increases. Fig. 3 gives the correct classification probability curve as a function of iterations. The correct classification probability increases from 0.8 to 0.92 by applying our algorithm.

In the second simulation, we apply the Euclidean distance pdf matching algorithm to the classification of a biomedical data set. This data set was obtained from neural recordings in the surgical treatment of Parkinson's disease. Spike trains are collected from thalamic (Thal) and subthalamic nucleus (STN) cellular activity using deep brain stimulation. The objective of classification is to distinguish the two classes Thal and STN. As a preprocessor, a second order autoregressive (AR) model is applied to segments of the neural activity, where the details

are fully given in [14]. We created the testing data to comply with the hypothesis of equal *a priori* probabilities of each class as required by our method.

The classifier uses the weights of the AR model. Since Thal and STN signals are different across patients, the conditional probability functions for training and testing will differ. The simulation results are presented in fig. 4 to 7 with class 1 for STN and class 2 for Thal. Fig.4 shows the scatter plot of the two classes and the decision boundary obtained from a perceptron in the training set comprising the three patients. The total number of training set is 12198 samples and the correct classification probability after the conventional training is 0.7537. Then we tested our algorithm in each of the different patients and the results are given in fig. 5,6 and 7 respectively. The number of testing set in each test patients are 1976, 2148 and 4086 samples respectively. Since the distributions of each test patients are different from that of the training set, the classification performance in the testing phase is not good as much as training result. It is worth mentioning

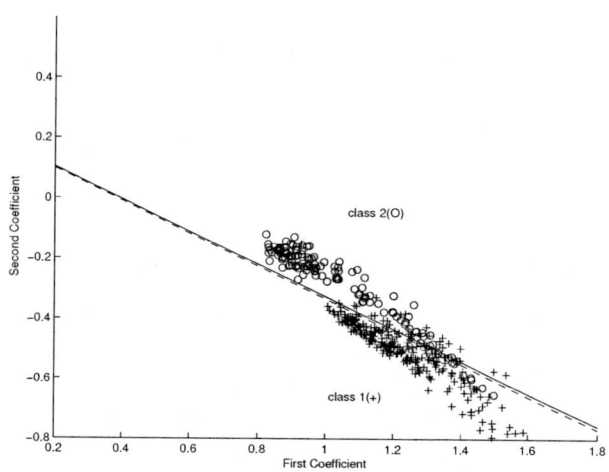

Fig. 7. Two decision boundary with and without continuous training in testing data set for patient 3 in simulation 2

TABLE I
CORRECT CLASSIFICATION PROBABILITY WITH AND WITHOUT CONTINUOUS TRAINING

overall correct probability	without continuous training	after applying our algorithm
Test patient 1	0.583	0.7844
Test patient 2	0.3073	0.5601
Test patient 3	0.8823	0.8921

that the hyperplanes in testing also rotate with respect to the training set position by our algorithm. We compare the correct classification probability with and without continuous training in Table 1. The simulation in the real biomedical data suggests that the decision boundaries shift so that the overall correct classification probabilities increase after applying the Euclidean distance pdf matching algorithm.

VI. Conclusion

This paper proposed a new information theoretic approach for training adaptive system using unlabeled data even after supervised learning is completed. This so called the Euclidean distance pdf matching algorithm utilizes the information of desired signal and unlabeled input signal during the testing phase, which provides a straightforward method to adjust system weights for a better performance. The method requires constant *a prior* probability for each class during both training and testing, which may be unrealistic in many applications. The simulations on an artificial data set and on real biomedical data suggest that the Euclidean distance pdf matching algorithm can improve classification performance when the *a priori* hypothesis is met.

Acknowledgment

This work was supported in part by the National Science Foundation under grant ECS-0300340. We thank Dr. Michael Okun for letting us use the data set collected in the University of Florida Movement Clinic.

References

[1] S. Haykin, *Neural Networks: A Comprehensive Foundation*, 2nd edition, New Jersey, Prentice Hall, 1999.
[2] B. Widrow, S.D. Stearns, *Adaptive Signal Processing*, New Jersey, Prentice Hall, 1985.
[3] A. Gammerman, V. Vapnik and V. Vowk, "Learning by Transduction," Proceedings of the Conference on Uncertainty in Artificial Intelligence, pp. 148–155, 1998.
[4] C. Saunders, A. Gammerman and V. Vowk, "Transduction with Confidence and Credibility," Proceedings of the Conference on Uncertainty in Artificial Intelligence, pp. 722–726, 1999.
[5] B. Novak, "Use of Unlabeled Data in Supervised Machine Learning," Proceedings of the Conference on Data Mining and Warehourses, pp. 834–846, Sept./Oct. 2004.
[6] A. Blum and T. Mitchell, "Combining Labeled and Unlabeled Data with Co-Training," Proceedings of the Conference on Compuational Learning Theory, pp. 92–100, 1998.
[7] K. Nigram, A. McCallum, S. Thrum and T. Mitchell, "Text Classification from Labeled and Unlabeled Documents using EM," Machine Learning Theory, vol. 39, no. 2, pp. 103–134, 2000.
[8] M. Belkin, P. Niyogi and V. Sindhwani, "Manifold Regularization: A Geometric Framework for Learning from Examples," Technical Report TR-2004-06, Department of Computer Science, University of Chicago, Chicago, Illinois.
[9] D. Erdogmus, Y. Rao and J. C. Principe "Supervised Training of Adaptive Systems with Partially Labeled Data," Proceedings of the International Conference on Accoustic, Speech and Signal Processing, Philadelphia, Pennsylvania, 2005.
[10] J. C. Principe, J. W. Fisher and D. Xu "Information Theoretic Learning," in *Unsupervised Adaptive Filtering*, S. Haykin Editor, New York, Wiley, pp. 265–319, 2000.
[11] N. Cristianini and J. Shawe-Taylor *An Introduction to Support Vector Machines*, Cambridge University Press, 2000.
[12] E. Parzen "On Estimation of a Probability Density Function and Mode," in *Time Series Analysis Papers*, San Diego, Holden-Day, 1967.
[13] D. Erdogmus, J. C. Principe and K. E. Hild, "On-Line Entropy Manipulation: Stochastic Information Gradient," Signal Processing Letters, vol. 10, no. 8, pp. 242–245, Aug. 2003.
[14] J. Sanchez, J. Pukala, J. C. Principe, F. Bova and M. Okun, "Linear Predictive Analysis for Targeting the Basal Ganglia in Deep Brain Stimulation Surgeries," Proceedings of the Conference on 2nd Int IEEE Workshop on Neural Engineering, Washington 2005.

A Study of AdaBoost with SVM Based Weak Learners

Xuchun Li, Lei Wang, Eric Sung
School of Electrical and Electronic Engineering
Nanyang Technological University, Singapore, 639798
E-mail: xuchunli@pmail.ntu.edu.sg, elwang@ntu.edu.sg, eericsung@ntu.edu.sg

Abstract—In this article, we focus on designing an algorithm, named *AdaBoostSVM*, using SVM as weak learners for AdaBoost. To obtain a set of effective SVM weak learners, this algorithm adaptively adjusts the kernel parameter in SVM instead of using a fixed one. Compared with the existing AdaBoost methods, the *AdaBoostSVM* has advantages of easier model selection and better generalization performance. It also provides a possible way to handle the over-fitting problem in AdaBoost. An improved version called *Diverse AdaBoostSVM* is further developed to deal with the accuracy/diveristy dilemma in Boosting methods. By implementing some parameter adjusting strategies, the distributions of accuracy and diversity over these SVM weak learners are tuned to achieve a good balance. To the best of our knowledge, such a mechanism that can conveniently and explicitly balances this dilemma has not been seen in the literature. Experimental results demonstrated that both proposed algorithms achieve better generalization performance than AdaBoost using other kinds of weak learners. Benefiting from the balance between accuracy and diversity, the *Diverse AdaBoostSVM* achieves the best performance. In addition, the experiments on unbalanced data sets showed that the *AdaBoostSVM* performed much better than SVM.

I. INTRODUCTION

One of the major developments in machine learning in the past decade is the ensemble method, which finds a highly accurate classifier by combining many moderately accurate component classifiers. Two of the commonly used techniques for constructing ensemble classifiers are Boosting [1] and Bagging [2]. Comparing with Bagging, Boosting performs better in most situations [3]. As the most popular Boosting method, AdaBoost [4] creates a collection of weak learners by maintaining a set of weights over training samples and adjusting these weights after each weak learning cycle adaptively: the weights of the samples which are misclassified by current weak learner will be increased while the weights of the samples which are correctly classified will be decreased.

The success of AdaBoost can be explained as enlarging the margin [5], which could enhance AdaBoost's generalization capability. Many studies that use decision trees [6] or neural networks [7] [8] as weak learners for AdaBoost have been reported. These studies showed the good generalization performance of AdaBoost. However, when decision trees are used as weak learners, what is the suitable tree size? When RBF neural networks are used as weak learners, how to control their complexity to avoid overfitting? How to decide the number of centers and how to set the width values of the RBFs? All of these have to be carefully tuned in practical use of AdaBoost. Furthermore, *diversity* is known as an important factor which affects the generalization accuracy of ensemble classifiers [9][10]. It is also known that AdaBoost exists an accuracy/diversity dilemma [6], which means that the more accurate two weak learners become, the less they can disagree with each other. However, the existing AdaBoost algorithms have not yet explicitly taken sufficient measurement to deal with this dilemma. Finally, It is reported that AdaBoost may overfit the training samples [11] and result in poor generalization performance. Therefore, it is necessary to stop AdaBoost's learning cycles at a suitable moment. But how to truncate the AdaBoost learning process to avoid overfitting is still an open problem [11].

Support Vector Machine [12] was developed from the theory of Structural Risk Minimization. By using a kernel trick to map the training samples from an input space to a high dimensional feature space, SVM finds an optimal separating hyperplane in the feature space and uses a regularization parameter, C, to balance its model complexity and training error. One of the popular kernels used by SVM is the RBF kernel, which has a parameter known as Gaussian width, σ. Comparing with RBF networks, SVM with RBF kernel (RBFSVM) can automatically calculate the number and location of the centers and the weights [13]. Also, it can effectively avoid overfitting by selecting proper parameters C and σ. From the performance analysis of RBFSVM [14], we know that σ is a more important parameter: although RBFSVM cannot learn well when a very low value of C is used, its performance largely depends on the σ value if a roughly suitable C is given. This means that, for a given roughly suitable C, the performance of RBFSVM can be conveniently changed by simply adjusting the value of σ.

Therefore, in this paper, we try to answer the following questions: Can SVM be used as a weak learner of AdaBoost? If yes, how about the generalization performance of this AdaBoost? Does this AdaBoost have some advantages over the existing ones, especially about the aforementioned problems? Also, compared with using a single SVM, what is the benefit of using this AdaBoost which is a combination of multiple SVMs? In this work, the RBFSVM is adopted as a weak learner for AdaBoost. As mentioned above, the RBFSVM has a parameter of σ which has to be set beforehand. An intuitive way is to simply apply a single σ to all SVM weak learners. However, we observed that this way cannot lead to successful AdaBoost due to over-weak or over-strong SVM weak learners. Although there may exist a single best σ, searching for it will largely increase the computational load of Boosting process and therefore should be avoided if possible.

The following fact opens a door for us to avoid searching for the single best σ. It is known that the classification performance of RBFSVM can be conveniently changed by adjusting the value of σ. Based on this, the algorithm, *AdaBoostSVM*, is developed, where a set of moderately accurate RBFSVM is trained for AdaBoost by adaptively adjusting the σ values instead of using a fixed one. This gives rise to a successful SVM based AdaBoost. Compared with the existing AdaBoost methods, proposed *AdaBoostSVM* has the following advantages: It needs not perform accurate parameter tuning. Instead, giving a rough range of σ is often enough. By setting the lower end of this range, proposed algorithm also provides a possible way to truncate the Boosting process to handle the over-fitting problem when other kinds of weak learners are used. Besides these, proposed algorithm achieves better classification performance than AdaBoost with other weak learners such as neural networks.

Furthermore, since proposed *AdaBoostSVM* invents a convenient way to control the classification accuracy of each weak learner, it also provides an opportunity to deal with the well-known accuracy/diveristy dilemma in Boosting methods. This is a happy accident from the investigation of AdaBoost based on SVM weak learners. Through some parameter adjusting strategies, we can tune the distributions of accuracy and diversity over these weak learners to achieve a good balance. To the best of our knowledge, there is no such a mechanism which can conveniently and explicitly balance this dilemma in the literature. The improved version of *AdaBoostSVM* is called *Diverse AdaBoostSVM* in this work. It is observed that, benefiting from the balance between accuracy and diversity, it gives better performance than *AdaBoostSVM*.

Finally, compared with a single SVM, proposed algorithms, which are the combination of multiple SVMs, can achieve much better performance on unbalanced data sets. This also justifies, from another perspective, that AdaBoost with SVM weak learners is worth of investigation.

II. BACKGROUND

A. AdaBoost

Given a set of training samples, AdaBoost [15] maintains a probability distribution, W, over these samples. This distribution is initially uniform. Then, AdaBoost algorithm calls WeakLearn algorithm repeatedly in a series of cycles. At cycle t, AdaBoost provides training samples with a distribution W_t to the WeakLearn algorithm. In response, the WeakLearn trains a classifier h_t. The distribution W_t is updated after each cycle according to the prediction results on the training samples. "Easy" samples that are correctly classified by the weak learner, h_t, get low weights, and "hard" samples that are misclassified get higher weights. Thus, AdaBoost focuses on the samples with more weights, which seem to be harder for WeakLearn. This process continues for T cycles, and at last, AdaBoost uses weighted vote to combine all the obtained weak learners into a single final hypothesis f. Greater weights are given to weak learners with lower errors. The important theoretical property of AdaBoost is that if the weak learners consistently have accuracy only slightly better than half, then the error of the final hypothesis drops to zero exponentially fast. This means that the weak learners need be only slightly better than random.

TABLE I

Algorithm: AdaBoost [15]
1. **Input:** a set of training samples with labels $\{(\mathbf{x}_1, y_1), ..., (\mathbf{x}_N, y_N)\}$, WeakLearn algorithm, the number of cycles T.
2. **Initialize:** the weight of samples: $w_i^1 = 1/N$, for all $i = 1, ..., N$.
3. **Do for** $t = 1, ..., T$
   (1) Use WeakLearn algorithm to train the weak learner h_t on the weighted training sample set.
   (2) Calculate the training error of h_t: $\epsilon_t = \sum_{i=1}^{N} w_i^t$, $y_i \neq h_t(\mathbf{x}_i)$.
   (3) Set weight of weak learner h_t: $\alpha_t = \frac{1}{2} \ln(\frac{1-\epsilon_t}{\epsilon_t})$.
   (4) Update training samples' weights: $w_i^{t+1} = \frac{w_i^t \exp\{-\alpha_t y_i h_t(\mathbf{x}_i)\}}{C_t}$
   where C_t is a normalization constant, and $\sum_{i=1}^{N} w_i^{t+1} = 1$.
4. **Output**: $f(\mathbf{x}) = sign(\sum_{t=1}^{T} \alpha_t h_t(\mathbf{x}))$.

B. Support Vector Machine

Support Vector Machine (SVM) [12] was developed from the theory of Structural Risk Minimization. In a binary classification problem, SVM's decision function is

$$f(\mathbf{x}) = \langle \mathbf{w}, \phi(\mathbf{x}) \rangle + b \quad (1)$$

where $\phi(\mathbf{x})$ is a mapping of sample $\mathbf{x}$ from the input space to a high-dimensional feature space. $\langle \cdot, \cdot \rangle$ denotes the dot product in the feature space. The optimal values of $\mathbf{w}$ and b can be obtained by solving the following optimization problem,

$$\text{minimize:} \quad g(\mathbf{w}, \xi) = \frac{1}{2} \|\mathbf{w}\|^2 + C \sum_{i=1}^{N} \xi_i \quad (2)$$

$$\text{subject to:} \quad y_i(\langle \mathbf{w}, \phi(\mathbf{x}_i) \rangle + b) \geq 1 - \xi_i, \xi_i \geq 0 \quad (3)$$

Here, ξ_i is the i-th slack variable and C is the regularization parameter. According to the Wolfe dual form, the above minimization problem can be written as

$$\text{minimize:} \quad W(\alpha) = -\sum_{i=1}^{N} \alpha_i + \frac{1}{2} \sum_{i=1}^{N} \sum_{j=1}^{N} y_i y_j \alpha_i \alpha_j k(\mathbf{x}_i, \mathbf{x}_j) \quad (4)$$

$$\text{subject to:} \quad \sum_{i=1}^{N} y_i \alpha_i = 0, \quad \forall i : 0 \leq \alpha_i \leq C \quad (5)$$

where α_i is a Lagrange multiplier which corresponds to the sample $\mathbf{x}_i$, $k(\cdot, \cdot)$ is a kernel function that implicitly maps the input vectors into a suitable feature space

$$k(\mathbf{x}_i, \mathbf{x}_j) = \langle \phi(\mathbf{x}_i), \phi(\mathbf{x}_j) \rangle \quad (6)$$

Compared with the RBF networks [13], SVM algorithm automatically computes the number and location of the centers, the weights, and the threshold in the following way: by the use of a suitable kernel function(in this paper, the RBF kernel is used), the samples are mapped nonlinearly into a high dimensional feature space. In this space, an optimal separating hyperplane is constructed by the support vectors which are closest to the decision boundary. Support vectors correspond to the centers of RBF kernels in the input space.

III. PROPOSED ALGORITHM: ADABOOSTSVM

This work uses the RBFSVM as weak learner for AdaBoost. But how to set the σ value for these weak learners? Problems are encountered when applying a single σ to all weak learners. In detail, an over-large σ often results in too weak RBFSVM. Its classification accuracy is often less than 50% and cannot meet the requirement on a weak learner given in AdaBoost. On the other hand, a smaller σ often makes the RBFSVM stronger and boosting them may become inefficient because the errors of these weak learners are highly correlated. Furthermore, too small σ can even make RBFSVM overfit the training samples and they also cannot be used as weak learners. Hence, finding a suitable σ for AdaBoost with SVM weak learners becomes a problem. By using model selection techniques such as cross-validation or leave-one-out, a single best σ may be found, with which the AdaBoost may achieve good classification performance. However, the process of model selection is time-consuming and should be avoided if possible.

The classification performance of SVM is affected by its parameters. For RBFSVM, they are the Gaussian width, σ, and the regularization parameter, C. The variation of either of them leads to the change of classification performance. However, as reported in [14], although RBFSVM cannot learn well when a very low value of C is used, its performance largely depends on the σ value if a roughly suitable C is given. This means that, for a given C, the performance of RBFSVM can be changed by simply adjusting the value of σ. Increasing this value often reduces the learning model complexity and then lowers down the classification performance, whereas decreasing it can lead to more complex learning model and higher performance. Therefore, this gives a chance to get around the problem resulting from using a fixed σ for all RBFSVM weak learners. In the following proposed algorithm, we generate a set of moderately accurate RBFSVM classifiers for AdaBoost by adaptively adjusting the σ values.

When applying Boosting method to strong component classifiers, these classifiers must be appropriately weakened in order to benefit from Boosting [6]. Hence, if RBFSVM is used as weak learner for AdaBoost, a relatively large σ value, which corresponds to a RBFSVM with relatively weak learning ability, is preferred. Both re-sampling and re-weighting can be used to train AdaBoost. In the proposed algorithm, without loss of generality, re-weighting technique is used. We proposed an *AdaBoostSVM* algorithm as follows (Table. II): Firstly, a large value is set to σ, which corresponds to a RBFSVM classifier with very weak learning ability.

Then, RBFSVM with this σ is used in as many cycles as possible as long as more than half accuracy on weighted training samples can be obtained. Otherwise, this σ value is decreased slightly to make the RBFSVM with the new σ value obtain more than half accuracy. This process continues until the σ is decreased to the given minimal σ value. By doing so, the proposed AdaBoostSVM algorithm can often generate a set of moderately accurate SVM classifiers with possibly uncorrelated errors.

TABLE II

Algorithm: AdaBoostSVM
1. Input: a set of training samples with labels $\{(\mathbf{x}_1, y_1), ..., (\mathbf{x}_N, y_N)\}$; the initial σ, σ_{ini}; the minimal σ, σ_{min}; the step of σ, σ_{step}.
2. Initialize: the weight of samples: $w_i^1 = 1/N$, for all $i = 1, ..., N$.
3. Do While ($\sigma > \sigma_{min}$)
 (1) Use RBFSVM algorithm to train the weak learner h_t on the weighted training sample set.
 (2) Calculate training error of h_t : $\epsilon_t = \sum_{i=1}^N w_i^t, y_i \neq h_t(\mathbf{x}_i)$.
 (3) If $\epsilon_t > 0.5$, decrease σ value by σ_{step} and goto (1).
 (4) Set weight of weak learner h_t : $\alpha_t = \frac{1}{2} \ln(\frac{1-\epsilon_t}{\epsilon_t})$.
 (5) Update training samples' weights: $w_i^{t+1} = \frac{w_i^t \exp\{-\alpha_t y_i h_t(\mathbf{x}_i)\}}{C_t}$
 where C_t is a normalization constant, and $\sum_{i=1}^N w_i^{t+1} = 1$.
4. Output: $f(\mathbf{x}) = sign(\sum_{t=1}^T \alpha_t h_t(\mathbf{x}))$.

IV. IMPROVEMENT: DIVERSE ADABOOSTSVM

A. Accuracy/Diversity Dilemma of AdaBoost

Diversity is known to be an important factor affecting the generalization performance of ensemble methods [9][10], which means that the errors made by different component classifiers are uncorrelated. If each component classifier is moderately accurate and these component classifiers disagree with each other, the uncorrelated errors of these component classifiers will be removed by the voting process so as to achieve good ensemble results [16]. This also applies to AdaBoost. For AdaBoost, it is known that there exists a dilemma between weak learner's accuracy and diversity [6], which means that the more accurate two weak learners become, the less they can disagree with each other. Hence, how to select SVM weak learners for AdaBoost? Select accurate but not diverse weak learners? Or select diverse but not too accurate ones? In the proposed AdaBoostSVM, the obtained SVM weak learners are mostly moderately accurate, which give chances to obtain more un-correlated weak learners. As aforementioned, through adjusting the σ value, a set of SVM weak learners with different learning abilities is obtained. This provides an opportunity of selecting more diverse weak learners from this set to deal with the accuracy/diversity dilemma. Hence, we proposed a *Diverse AdaBoostSVM algorithm* (Table. III), and it is hoped to achieve higher generalization performance than AdaBoostSVM.

B. Diverse AdaBoostSVM

Although how to measure and use diversity for ensemble methods is still an open problem [10], recently some promising results have been reported. By focusing on increasing diversity, these methods [9][17] achieved higher generalization accuracy. In the proposed Diverse AdaBoostSVM algorithm, we will use the definition of diversity in [9], which measures the disagreement between one weak learner and all the existing weak learners. In the Diverse AdaBoostSVM, the diversity is calculated as follows: If $h_t(\mathbf{x}_i)$ is the prediction label of t-th weak learner on sample $\mathbf{x}_i$, and $f(\mathbf{x}_i)$ is the combined prediction label of all the existing weak learners, the diversity of the t-th weak learner on sample $\mathbf{x}_i$ is defined as:

$$d_t(\mathbf{x}_i) = \begin{cases} 0: & \text{if } h_t(\mathbf{x}_i) = f(\mathbf{x}_i) \\ 1: & \text{if } h_t(\mathbf{x}_i) \neq f(\mathbf{x}_i) \end{cases} \quad (7)$$

and the diversity of AdaBoostSVM with T weak learners on N samples is defined as:

$$D = \frac{1}{TN} \sum_{t=1}^{T} \sum_{i=1}^{N} d_t(\mathbf{x}_i) \quad (8)$$

In each cycle of Diverse AdaBoostSVM, this diversity value is calculated first. If this value is larger than the predefined threshold, DIV, this new RBFSVM weak learner will be selected. Otherwise, this weak learner will be thrown away. Through this mechanism, a set of moderately accurate and yet diverse SVM weak learners can be generated. This is different from the AdaBoostSVM which simply takes all the available SVM weak learners. As seen from the following experimental results, the Diverse AdaBoostSVM algorithm gives the best performance. We think that the improvement is due to its explicitly dealing with the accuracy/diversity dilemma.

TABLE III

Algorithm: Diverse AdaBoostSVM
1. **Input:** a set of training samples with labels $\{(\mathbf{x}_1, y_1), ..., (\mathbf{x}_N, y_N)\}$; the initial σ, σ_{ini}; the minimal σ, σ_{min}; the step of σ, σ_{step}; the threshold on diversity DIV.
2. **Initialize:** the weight of samples: $w_i^1 = 1/N$, for all $i = 1,...,N$.
3. **Do While** ($\sigma > \sigma_{min}$)
   (1) Use RBFSVM algorithm to train the weak learner h_t on the weighted training sample set.
   (2) Calculate training error of h_t: $\epsilon_t = \sum_{i=1}^{N} w_i^t$, $y_i \neq h_t(\mathbf{x}_i)$.
   (3) Calculate diversity of h_t: $D_t = \sum_{i=1}^{N} d_t(\mathbf{x}_i)$.
   (4) If $\epsilon_t > 0.5$ or $D_t < DIV$, decrease σ by σ_{step} and goto (1).
   (5) Set weight of weak learner h_t: $\alpha_t = \frac{1}{2} \ln(\frac{1-\epsilon_t}{\epsilon_t})$.
   (6) Update training samples' weights: $w_i^{t+1} = \frac{w_i^t \exp\{-\alpha_t y_i h_t(\mathbf{x}_i)\}}{C_t}$
   where C_t is a normalization constant, and $\sum_{i=1}^{N} w_i^{t+1} = 1$.
4. **Output:** $f(\mathbf{x}) = sign(\sum_{t=1}^{T} \alpha_t h_t(\mathbf{x}))$.

V. EXPERIMENTAL RESULT

Since AdaBoost with neural networks weak learners performs better than those with decision trees weak learners [7], we compare proposed AdaBoostSVM and Diverse AdaBoost-SVM algorithms with AdaBoost with neural networks weak learners. A large scale of experiments are generated on 13 benchmark data sets and an unbalanced data sets.

A. Benchmark Data Sets

1) Data set information and parameter setting: The 13 benchmark data sets come from UCI Repository, DELVE, and STATLOG. The dimensions of these data sets range from 2 to 60, the numbers of training samples range from 140 to 1300, the numbers of test samples range from 75 to 7000. Detailed information of these data sets can be found at [18] and all of these data sets can be downloaded there. For each data set, 100 partitions are generated into training and test sets. On each partition, for each algorithm, a classifier is trained and then test error is calculated. The final performance of each algorithm on a data set is its average performance over these 100 partitions of this data set.

It is known that σ mainly affects the performance of RBFSVM classifier compared with C. Hence, C is set as a value within 10 to 100 in proposed algorithms. The σ_{min} is set as the average minimal distance between any two training samples and the σ_{ini} is set as about 10 to 15 times of the σ_{min} value or the scatter radius of the training samples in the input space. Although the value of σ_{step} can affect the number of AdaBoostSVM's learning cycles, it has less effect on the final generalization performance, as shown later. Therefore, σ_{step} is set as a value within 1 to 3. The 'DIV' value in the Diverse AdaBoostSVM algorithm is set as 0.7 to 1 times of the maximal diversity value obtained in previous cycles. "0.7" is used as the tolerance of the possible variation of diversity.

2) General performance: In Table IV, the average generalization performance (with standard deviation) for the four algorithms is shown. The test errors of AdaBoost with Neural Networks weak learners (AdaBoost$_{NN}$) and SVM are directly obtained from [8]. From these results, it can be found that proposed AdaBoostSVM algorithm (AdaBoost$_{SVM}$) performs better than AdaBoost$_{NN}$ algorithm, and is comparable to SVM algorithm. Proposed Diverse AdaBoostSVM (Diverse AdaBoost$_{NN}$) performs a little better than SVM algorithm.

TABLE IV

Data set	AB$_{NN}$	AB$_{SVM}$	Diverse AB$_{SVM}$	SVM
Banana	12.3±0.7	12.1±1.7	**11.3±1.4**	11.5±0.7
B. Cancer	30.4±4.7	25.5±5.0	**24.8±4.4**	26.0±4.7
Diabetes	26.5±2.3	24.8±2.3	24.3±2.1	**23.5±1.7**
German	27.5±2.5	23.4±2.1	**22.3±2.1**	23.6±2.1
Heart	20.3±3.4	15.5±3.4	**14.9±3.0**	16.0±3.3
Image	2.7±0.7	2.7±0.7	**2.4±0.5**	3.0±0.6
Ringnorm	1.9±0.3	2.1±1.1	2.0±0.7	**1.7±0.1**
F. Solar	35.7±1.8	33.8±1.5	33.7±1.4	**32.4±1.8**
Splice	**10.1±0.5**	11.1±1.2	11.0±1.0	10.9±0.7
Thyroid	4.4±2.2	4.4±2.1	**3.7±2.1**	4.8±2.2
Titanic	22.6±1.2	22.1±1.9	**21.8±1.5**	22.4±1.0
Twonorm	3.0±0.3	2.6±0.6	**2.5±0.5**	3.0±0.2
Waveform	10.8±0.6	10.3±1.7	10.2±1.2	**9.9±0.4**
Average	16.0±1.6	14.6±1.9	**14.2±1.7**	14.5±1.5

Comparison among four algorithms: AdaBoost with neural networks weak learners (AB$_{NN}$), proposed AdaBoostSVM (AB$_{SVM}$), proposed Diverse AdaBoostSVM (Diverse AB$_{SVM}$) and SVM

3) Influence of C and σ_{ini}: In order to investigate the influence of parameter C on the proposed algorithms, we vary the value of C from 1 to 100, and perform experiments on

100 partitions of the "Titanic" data set of UCI benchmark to obtain their average performances. Figure. 1 shows the comparison result. It can be found that in a considerable scale (in this case, it is from 1 to 100), the variation of C has little effect (less than 1%) on the final generalization performance of proposed algorithm. This is also consistent with the analysis of RBFSVM that C value has less effect on the performance of RBFSVM. Note that the σ value decreases from σ_{ini} to σ_{min} as the number of SVM weak learners increases (See the label of horizontal axis). The small platform at the left top corner of this figure means that the test error does not decrease until the σ decreases to a certain value. Then, the test error decreases quickly to the lowest value and keeps this value with a little variation. This shows that the σ_{ini} value does not have much impact on the final performance of AdaBoostSVM. Furthermore, the learning cycle will be truncated when σ reaches the given σ_{min} value. This makes it possible to truncate the learning cycle to handle the overfitting problem by setting a suitable σ_{min}. This will be investigated in our future work. This property is more valuable because when to stop AdaBoost's learning cycle is still an open problem for AdaBoost.

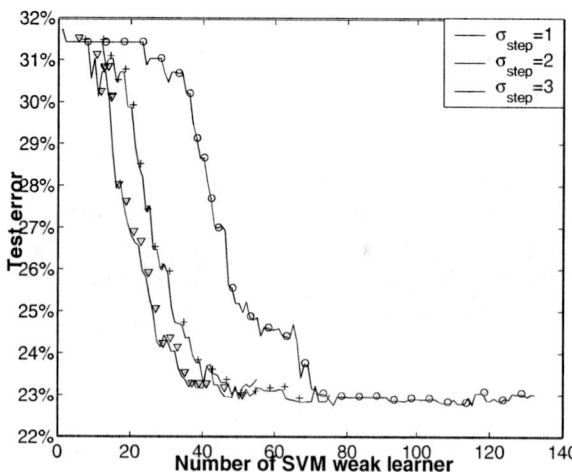

Fig. 2. Compare the performance of AdaBoostSVM with different σ_{step}

5) Accuracy-Diversity diagram: In order to see the effect of Diverse AdaBoostSVM, we used an Accuracy-Diversity diagram to visualize the distribution of accuracy and the diversity over the SVM weak learners. The Accuracy-Diversity diagram is a scatterplot where each point corresponds to a weak learner. In this diagram, a point's x coordinate value is the diversity value after the corresponding weak learner is trained while y coordinate value of this point is the accuracy rate of the corresponding weak learner. Similar diagram was also used in [6]. Due to the lack of space, we report only the Accuracy-Diversity diagrams of Diverse AdaBoostSVM and AdaBoost with neural networks weak learner algorithms on the 'Splice' data set of the UCI benchmark. From Figure. 3, we can observe that proposed Diverse AdaBoostSVM algorithm can obtain more high-diversity and moderately accurate weak learners, which may produce the uncorrelated error among different weak learners more efficiently.

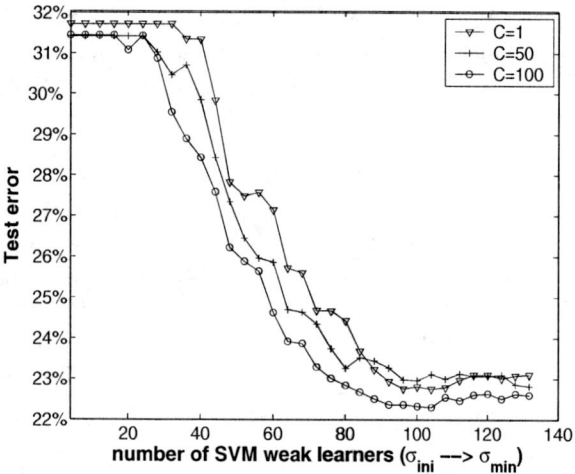

Fig. 1. Compare the performance of AdaBoostSVM with different C values

4) Influence of σ_{step}: In order to see the influence of σ_{step} on the proposed AdaBoostSVM algorithm, we did a set of experiments with different σ_{step} values for AdaBoostSVM on the "Titanic" data set of UCI benchmark. Figure. 2 gives the result. From this figure, we can find that although the number of learning cycles in AdaBoost changes with the value of σ_{step}, the final generalization accuracy is relatively stable. Similar conclusions can also be drawn from other benchmark data sets that the value of σ_{step} has less effect on the final generalization performance of AdaBoostSVM.

From the above discussion of parameters C, σ_{ini}, σ_{step}, it can be concluded that, compared with AdaBoost with neural networks weak learners, proposed AdaBoostSVM algorithm is easier to do parameter tuning.

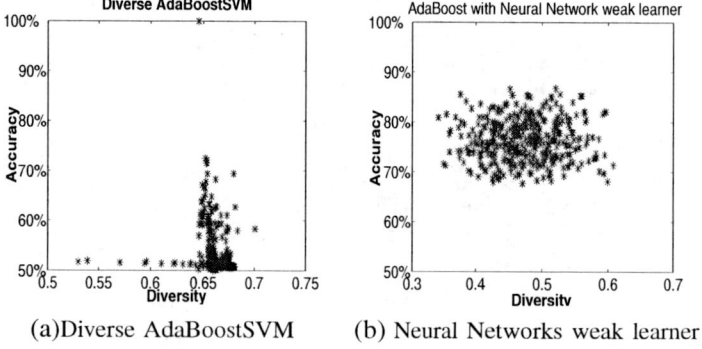

Fig. 3. Compare the accuracy and the diversity's distributions between Diverse AdaBoostSVM and AdaBoost with Neural Networks weak learners

B. Unbalanced Data Sets

We also find that the proposed AdaBoostSVM algorithm performs much better than a single SVM when facing unbalanced classification problems. In the case of binary classification, unbalanced problem means that the number of positive samples is much larger than that of negative samples, or vice versa. It is known that standard SVM algorithm cannot handle such kind of problems well. Proposed AdaBoostSVM algorithm includes many moderately accurate SVM weak learners, some of which can focus on the misclassified samples of the non-dominant class. By combining these moderately accurate SVM classifiers, AdaBoostSVM performs better than standard SVM on unbalanced problems. In the following experiments, we compare the performance of proposed AdaBoostSVM and standard SVM on unbalanced data sets. We used the 'Splice' data set of the UCI benchmark. Splice data set has 483 positive training samples, 517 negative training samples and 2175 test samples. In the following experiments, the number of negative samples is fixed as 500 and the number of positive samples is reduced from 150 to 30. From Figure. 4, it can be found that along with the decreasing ratio of the number positive samples to that of negtive samples, the improvement of AdaBoostSVM over SVM becomes more and more. When the ratio reaches 30:500, SVM almost cannot work and performs like random guess, while proposed AdaBoostSVM can still work with a relatively good performance. The good performance of ensemble methods to handle unbalanced problems was also observed in [19] [20].

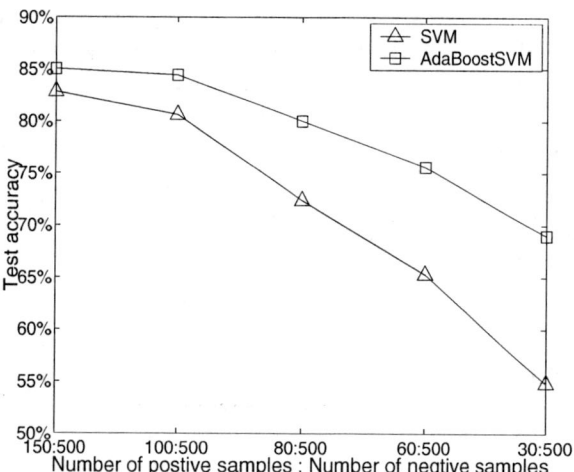

Fig. 4. Compare SVM and AdaBoostSVM on unbalanced problem

VI. CONCLUSION AND DISCUSSION

AdaBoost with SVM weak learners is proposed in this paper, which is achieved by adaptively adjusting the kernel parameter to get a set of effective weak learners. Experiments on benchmark data sets demonstrated that proposed AdaBoostSVM performs better than AdaBoost with neural networks weak learners. In addition, it needs not accurate model selection and thus saves computational cost. Based on AdaBoostSVM, an improved version is further developed to deal with the accuracy/diversity dilemma, and promising result is obtained. Besides these, it is found that proposed AdaBoostSVM algorithm has much better performance than SVM on unbalanced problems. The reported in this paper is a general framework of AdaBoost with SVM weak learners, which can be tailored for different purposes through changing the parameter scales or selection criterion. In the future work, more theoretical analysis and comparison with AdaBoost with all kinds of weak learners will be conducted.

REFERENCES

[1] Robert E. schapire, "The boosting approach to machine learning: An overview," *In MSRI Workshop on Nonlinear Estimation and Classification*, 2002.
[2] Leo Breiman, "Bagging predictors," *Machine Learning*, vol. 24, pp. 123–140, 1996.
[3] Eric Bauer and Ron Kohavi, "An empirical comparison of voting classification algorithms: Bagging, boosting, and variants," *Machine Learning*, vol. 36, no. 1, pp. 105–139, Jul 1999.
[4] Yoav Freund and Robert E. Schapire, "A decision-theoretic generalization of on-line learning and an application to boosting," *Journal of Computer and System Sciences*, vol. 55(1), pp. 119–139, August 1997.
[5] R. E. Schapire, Y. Singer, P. Bartlett, and W. Lee, "Boosting the margin: A new explanation for the effectiveness of voting methods," *The Annals of Statistics*, vol. 26, no. 5, pp. 1651–1686, 1998.
[6] Thomas G. Dietterich, "An experimental comparison of three methods for constructing ensembles of decision trees: Bagging, boosting, and randomization," *Machine Learning*, vol. 40, no. 2, pp. 139–157, Aug 2000.
[7] Holger Schwenk and Yoshua Bengio, "Boosting neural networks," *Nueral Computation*, vol. 12, pp. 1869–1887, 2000.
[8] Gunnar Ratsch, "Soft margins for adaboost," *Machine Learning*, vol. 42, no. 3, pp. 287–320, Mar 2001.
[9] Prem Melville and Raymond J. Mooney, "Creating diversity in ensembles using artificial data," *Information Fusion*, vol. 6, no. 1, pp. 99–111, Mar 2005.
[10] Ludmila I. Kuncheva and Christopher J. Whitaker, "Measures of diversity in classifier ensembles and their relationship with the ensemble accuracy," *Machine Learning*, vol. 51, no. 2, pp. 181–207, May 2003.
[11] Wenxin Jiang, "Process consistency for adaboost," *Annals of Statistics*, vol. 32, no. 1, pp. 13–29, 2004.
[12] Vladimir Vapnik, *Statistical Learning Theory*, John Wiley and Sons Inc., New York, 1998.
[13] Bernhard Scholkopf, Kah-Kay Sung, Chris Burges, Federico Girosi, Partha Niyogi, Tomaso Poggio, and Vladimir Vapnik, "Comparing support vector machines with gaussian kernels to radial basis function classifiers," *IEEE Transactions on Signal Processing*, vol. 45, no. 11, pp. 2758–2765, 1997.
[14] Giorgio Valentini and Thomas G. Dietterich, "Bias-variance analysis of support vector machines for the development of svm-based ensemble methods," *Journal of Machine Learning Research*, vol. 5, pp. 725–775, Jul 2004.
[15] Robert E. Schapire and Yoram Singer, "Improved boosting algorithms using confidence-rated predictions," *Machine Learning*, vol. 37, no. 3, pp. 297–336, Dec 1999.
[16] H.W.Shin and S.Y.Sohn, "Selected tree classifier combination based on both accuracy and error diversity," *Pattern Recognition*, vol. 38, pp. 191–197, 2005.
[17] Sanjoy Dasgupta and Philip M. Long, "Boosting with diverse base classifiers," in *Proceeding of the 16th Annual Conference on Learning Theory*, Aug 2003, pp. 273–287.
[18] http://mlg.anu.edu.au/~raetsch/data.
[19] Rong Yan, Yan Liu, Rong Jin, and Alex Hauptmann, "On predicting rare class with svm ensemble in scene classification," in *Proceeding of the IEEE International Conference on Acoustics, Speech, and Signal 2003*, Apr 2003, pp. III – 21–4.
[20] Hyun-Chul Kim, Shaoning Pang, Hong-Mo Je, Daijin Kim, and Sung Yang Bang, "Constructing support vector machine ensemble," *Pattern Recognition*, vol. 36, no. 12, pp. 2757–2767, Dec 2003.

Information Maximization and Cost Minimization in Information-Theoretic Competitive Learning

Ryotaro Kamimura
Information Science Laboratory, Tokai University,
1117 Kitakaname Hiratsuka Kanagawa 259-1292, Japan
ryo@cc.u-tokai.ac.jp

Abstract—In this paper, we introduce costs in the framework of information maximization and try to maximize the ratio of information to its associated cost. We have shown that competitive learning is realized by maximizing mutual information between input patterns and competitive units. One shortcoming of the method is that maximizing information does not necessarily produce representations faithful to input patterns. Information maximizing primarily focuses on some parts of input patterns that are used to distinguish between patterns. Thus, we introduce the cost that represents average distance between input patterns and connection weights. By minimizing the cost, final connection weights by information maximization reflect well input patterns. We applied the method to a political data analysis and a Wisconsin cancer problem. Experimental results confirmed that by introducing the cost, representations faithful to input patterns were obtained. In addition, generalization performance was significantly improved.

I. INTRODUCTION

In this paper, we introduce a cost in the framework of information maximization. The new method can increase information content while minimizing the corresponding cost. The new method can contribute to neural computing from two perspectives: (1) this is a new type of information-theoretic competitive learning in which competition is realized by maximizing mutual information between input patterns and competitive units; (2) the ratio of information to the cost is maximized to produce faithful representations.

First, this is a new type of information-theoretic method to realize competition. Information-theoretic methods have been applied to competitive learning and self-organizing maps. For example, van Hulle [1] attempted to use entropy maximization for realizing equiprobabilistic outputs and to solve the fundamental problems of competitive learning such as dead neurons and dependency on initial conditions [2], [3], [4], [5], [6], [7], [8], [9], [10]. On the other hand, Linsker tried to use a more direct method to maximize mutual information. He assumed that living systems should preserve as much information as possible in every stage of processing. However, it seems to us that his method could not give clear rules to maximize mutual information, and their validity may be confined to simple artificial data [11], [12], [13]. We have used information-theoretic methods to realize competitive processes and applied them to feature extraction and improved generalization [14], [15], [16]. Our method proposed here is based upon these methods in which mutual information between input patterns and connection weights is directly maximized. Contrary to Linsker's formulation, our method is simple and powerful enough to be applied to practical problems. In our method, competitive unit outputs are computed directly by using a Gaussian function of distance between input patterns and connection weights. Then, information is directly maximized by using the ordinary update rules.

Second, we introduce the ratio of information to the cost. A cost function is introduced in our framework of information maximization to produce representations more faithful to input patterns. We have observed that connection weights by conventional competitive learning and our information-theoretic method are sometimes different from each other. By examining carefully a mechanism of information maximization, we find that information maximization focuses upon some parts of input patterns that are necessary to distinguish between patterns. On the other hand, conventional competitive learning imitates input patterns as much as possible. Information maximization focuses on some parts of input patterns at the expense of imitating input patterns. At this stage, to incorporate the property of conventional competitive learning in the framework of information maximization, we introduce a cost function that measures how much connection weights are similar to input patterns. The cost is actually average distance between input patterns and connection weights. By minimizing the cost, connection weights become similar to input patterns. In the previous model [17], we maximize information and at the same time minimize the cost with two learning parameters. In the present model, for minimizing the cost and maximizing information, we introduce the ratio of information to the cost, and we try to maximize this ratio. Thus, the number of learning parameters to be tuned is decreased from two to one, which makes us to tune model more easily. By maximizing the ratio, it is possible to maximize information, while keeping representations faithful to input patterns.

II. COST MINIMIZATION AND INFORMATION MAXIMIZATION

We consider information content stored in competitive unit activation patterns. For this purpose, let us define information to be stored in neural systems. Information stored in systems is represented by decrease in uncertainty [18]. Uncertainty

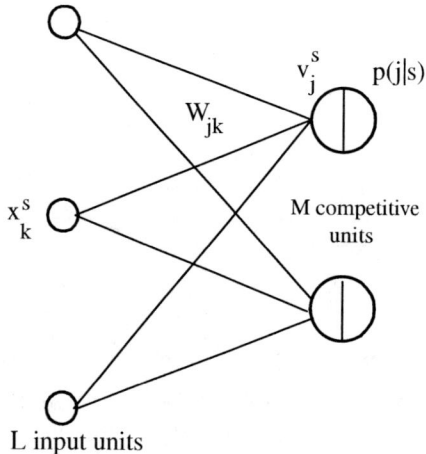

Fig. 1. A network architecture for information maximization.

decrease, that is, information I, is defined by

$$I = -\sum_{\forall j} p(j)\log p(j) + \sum_{\forall s}\sum_{\forall j} p(s)p(j\mid s)\log p(j\mid s), \quad (1)$$

where $p(j)$, $p(s)$ and $p(j|s)$ denote the probability of firing of the jth unit, the probability of the sth input pattern and the conditional probability of firing of the jth unit, given the sth input pattern, respectively. Let us define a cost function

$$C = \sum_{\forall s} p(s)\sum_{\forall j} p(j\mid s)C_j^s, \quad (2)$$

where C_j^s is a cost of the jth unit for the sth input pattern. Thus, we must maximize the ratio R of information to the cost

$$R = \left(-\sum_{\forall j} p(j)\log p(j) + \sum_{\forall s}\sum_{\forall j} p(s)p(j\mid s)\log p(j\mid s)\right) \times \left(\sum_{\forall s} p(s)\sum_{\forall j} p(j\mid s)C_j^s\right)^{-1}. \quad (3)$$

Let us present update rules to maximize the ratio in neural networks. As shown in Figure 1, a network is composed of input units x_k^s and competitive units v_j^s. The jth competitive unit receives a net input from input units, and an output from the jth competitive unit can be computed by

$$v_j^s = \exp\left(-\frac{\sum_{k=1}^{L}(x_k^s - w_{jk})^2}{2\sigma^2}\right), \quad (4)$$

where L is the number of input units, w_{jk} denote connections from the kth input unit to the jth competitive unit and σ controls the width of the Gaussian function. The output is increased as connection weights are closer to input patterns.

The conditional probability $p(j\mid s)$ is computed by

$$p(j\mid s) = \frac{v_j^s}{\sum_{m=1}^{M} v_m^s}, \quad (5)$$

where M denotes the number of competitive units. Since input patterns are supposed to be given uniformly to networks, the probability of firing of the jth competitive unit is computed by

$$p(j) = \frac{1}{S}\sum_{s=1}^{S} p(j\mid s). \quad (6)$$

Information I is computed by

$$I = -\sum_{j=1}^{M} p(j)\log p(j) + \frac{1}{S}\sum_{s=1}^{S}\sum_{j=1}^{M} p(j\mid s)\log p(j\mid s). \quad (7)$$

A cost function is computed by

$$C = \frac{1}{S}\sum_{s=1}^{S}\sum_{j=1}^{M} p(j\mid s)\sum_{k=1}^{L}(x_k^s - w_{jk})^2. \quad (8)$$

Thus, we must maximize the following function:

$$R = \left(-\sum_{j=1}^{M} p(j)\log p(j) + S^{-1}\sum_{s=1}^{S}\sum_{j=1}^{M} p(j\mid s)\log p(j\mid s)\right) \times \left(S^{-1}\sum_{s=1}^{S}\sum_{j=1}^{M} p(j\mid s)\sum_{k=1}^{L}(x_k^s - w_{jk})^2\right)^{-1}. \quad (9)$$

Differentiating information with respect to input-competitive connections w_{jk}, we have

$$\Delta w_{jk} = -\frac{\beta}{SC\sigma^2}\sum_{s=1}^{S}\left(\log p(j) - \sum_{m=1}^{M} p(m\mid s)\log p(m)\right)Q_{jk}^s + \frac{\beta}{SC\sigma^2}\sum_{s=1}^{S}\left(\log p(j\mid s) - \sum_{m=1}^{M} p(m\mid s)\log p(m\mid s)\right)Q_{jk}^s - \frac{\beta I}{SC^2}\sum_{s=1}^{S}\left(\sum_{k=1}^{L}(x_k^s - w_{jk})^2 - \sum_{m=1}^{M} p(m\mid s)\sum_{k=1}^{L}(x_k^s - w_{jk})^2\right)Q_{jk}^s + \frac{2\beta I}{SC^2}\sum_{s=1}^{S} Q_{jk}^s, \quad (10)$$

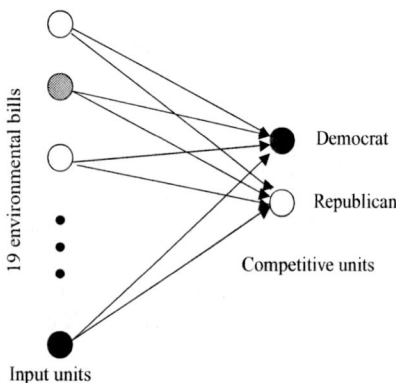

Fig. 2. A network architecture for the Senate problem.

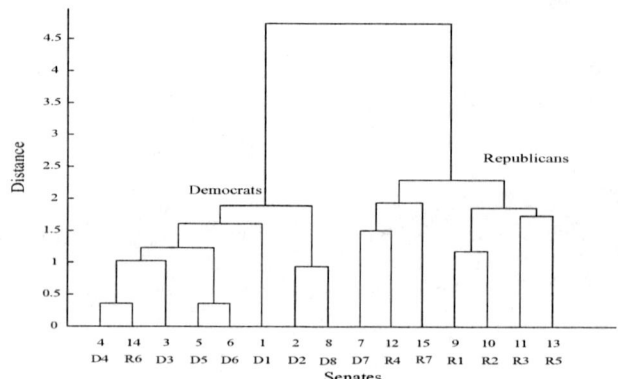

Fig. 3. A dendrogram for the Senate data by the cluster analysis.

where β is the learning parameter, and

$$Q_{jk}^s = p(j \mid s)(x_k^s - w_{jk}). \qquad (11)$$

III. POLITICAL DATA ANALYSIS

We attempted to classify congressmen in terms of their voting attitudes. The data was represented as a qualitative matrix of U.S. congressmen with their voting attitudes toward 19 environmental bills [19]. The first eight congressmen are Democrats, while the latter seven are Republicans. In the data, 1, 0 and 0.5 represent *yes*, *no* and *undecided*, respectively. The learning rate β is 0.1, and the Guassian width is 0.5[1]. Initial weight values were set to the midpoints of input patterns with small random values[2]. Figure 2 shows a network architecture for this problem. Because the number of environmental bills is 19, the number of input units is 19. The number of competitive units is two, corresponding to *Democrats* and *Republicans*. By cluster analyses [19], it was confirmed that these data could be classified into two groups in several ways except for Republican No.6, who responds to the bills according to the line of Democrats. For example, Figure 3 shows a final dendrogram by a cluster analysis[3]. As can be seen in the figure, the Republican No.6 and the Democrat No.7 are misclassified.

Figure 4 shows information, cost, competitive unit activations and connection weights by three methods. Information is normalized so as to range between zero and one. Figure 4(a1) shows information as a function of the number of epochs by maximizing information without costs. As can be seen in the figure, information is rapidly increased to a maximum point with less than twenty epochs. However, as shown in Figure 4(a2), the associated cost is first decreased, and then increased significantly. This means that information is forced to be maximized at the expense of the associated cost. Figure 4(a3) shows competitive unit activations $p(j \mid s)$, showing that only the fourteenth input pattern is misclassified. Figure 4(a4) shows connection weights. We can see that negative connection weights represented by white squares are seen. Since negative values do not exist in actual data, information maximization does not necessarily represent input patterns faithfully. Figure 4(b1) shows information as a function of the number of epochs by introducing the cost. Information is increased more slowly than by maximizing only information. However, we can see from Figure 4(b2) that the cost is gradually decreased as information is increased. Figure 4(b3) shows competitive unit activations $p(j \mid s)$. We can see that only the fourteenth pattern is misclassified. Figure 4(b4) shows connection weights. Compared with connection weights by information maximization shown in Figure 4(a4), negative connection weights disappear significantly. Finally, we show experimental results by standard competitive learning[4] for comparison. Figure 4(c1) shows competitive unit activations (winners) by standard competitive learning. As can be seen in the figure, the seventh and the fourteenth input pattern are misclassified. Figure 4(c2) shows connection weights by the standard competitive learning. We can see that weights seem to be quite similar to those by information maximization with costs. Because this is unsupervised learning, it is difficult to evaluate final results. However, at least we can say that information maximization with costs can produce representations similar to those by competitive learning, and that information maximization with costs classifies input patterns more naturally than competitive learning.

IV. CANCER PROBLEM

The second example is the Wisconsin Diagnostic Breast Cancer data that is borrowed from the machine learning database[5]. The number of input patterns was 569, and the number of attributes was 32. Thus, as shown in Figure 5, the number of input units and competitive units were 32 and two, respectively. Figure 6(a) shows information as a function of the number of epochs by information maximization with

---

[1] We chose the parameter σ so as to increase information with a reasonably short time. If the parameter σ is too small, information is too rapidly increased with some troubles in learning. If the parameter is too large, information is very slowly increased. By many experiments, we chose the parameter value 0.5 for the first approximation. With this parameter value, information is increased to a maximum point with a reasonably short time without any troubles in learning for many problems. In all experiments presented in this paper we used the same parameter values.

[2] In all experiments in this paper, the same type of initial conditions were used.

[3] We used a Matlab program with the Ward method.

[4] We used Matlab programs with default parameter values except the number of epochs was fifty.

[5] http://www1.ics.uci.edu/ mlearn/MLRepository.html

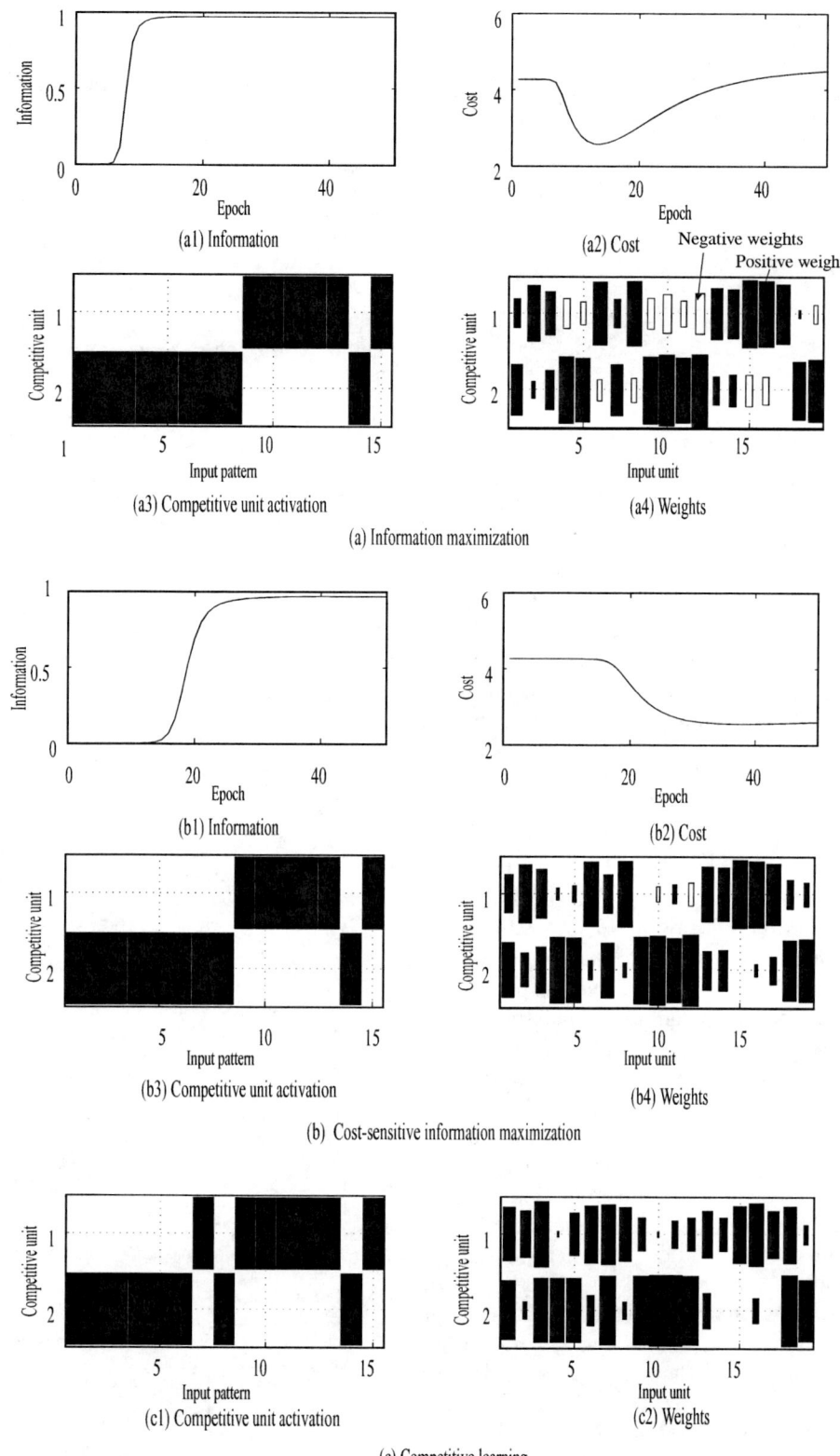

Fig. 4. Experimental results for the Senate problem. Figure (a), (b) and (c) show results by information maximization, information maximization with costs and competitive learning, respectively. In connection weights, black and white squares mean positive and negative weights. Information is normalized information ranging between zero and one.

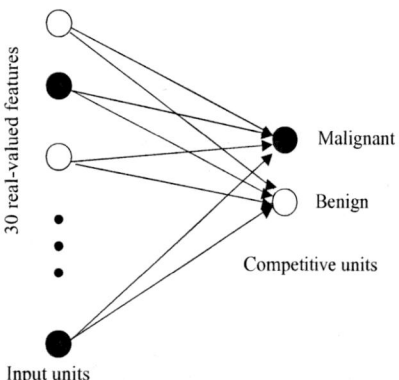

Fig. 5. A network architecture for the cancer problem.

costs. Information is gradually increased, while the associated cost in Figure 6(b) is gradually decreased. Figure 6(c) and (d) show training and generalization errors[6]. As shown in the figures, errors reaches their lowest points in the early stage of learning, and errors are inversely increased as the number of training epochs is increased. Figure 6(e) show training and generalization errors by three methods. As can be seen in the figure, by using the standard competitive learning, the generalization error is the highest, that is, 0.077. By maximizing information, the generalization error is decreased to 0.061. Finally, by using information maximization with costs, we have the lowest error, that is, 0.054. These results show that information can be maximized and simultaneously the cost can be decreased significantly and that generalization performance could be improved by introducing the cost.

V. CONCLUSION

In this paper, we have introduced costs in the framework of information maximization. One of the main problems in information theoretic methods is that information maximization does not necessarily produce representations faithful to input patterns. Information is forced to be maximized by focusing upon some parts of input patterns that are useful in distinguishing between input patterns. To obtain more faithful representations, we have introduced costs in the framework of information maximization. The costs measure how much connection weights are similar to input patterns. By minimizing the cost and maximizing information, information maximization can produce more faithful representations. We have applied the method to a political data analysis and a Wisconsin Cancer problem. Experimental results have shown that cost minimization can produce representations faithful to input patterns. We have also found that generalization performance is better than a method that only maximize information and competitive learning. In addition, we have shown that we need a relatively short learning time to have better results.

Though our method has shown fairly good experimental results, we can point out several problems for the present method to be more practically applicable. First, we maximize the ratio of information to its cost to reduce the number of learning parameters. However, it is better to evaluate more exactly relations between information and its cost. Second, we have shown that generalization errors are significantly improved by our method. However, relations between information and generalization remain obscure at the present stage of research. We need to examine the relations more explicitly. Third, as mentioned in the main text, the parameter δ controls the Gaussian width, and is directly related to a process of information maximization. Thus, more subtle analysis of the relations should be needed. Though some improvement must be needed for practical applications, it is certain that our new method can open up a new perspective in neural networks.

REFERENCES

[1] M. Marc and M. V. Hulle, *Faithful representations and topographic maps*. New York: John Wiley and Sons, Inc, 2000.
[2] S. Grossberg, "Competitive learning: From interactive activation to adaptive resonance," *Cognitive Science*, vol. 11, pp. 23–63, 1987.
[3] D. E. Rumelhart and D. Zipser, "Feature discovery by competitive learning," in *Parallel Distributed Processing* (D. E. Rumelhart and G. E. H. et al., eds.), vol. 1, pp. 151–193, Cambridge: MIT Press, 1986.
[4] D. E. Rumelhart and J. L. McClelland, "On learning the past tenses of English verbs," in *Parallel Distributed Processing* (D. E. Rumelhart, G. E. Hinton, and R. J. Williams, eds.), vol. 2, pp. 216–271, Cambridge: MIT Press, 1986.
[5] S. Grossberg, "Competitive learning: from interactive activation to adaptive resonance," *Cognitive Science*, vol. 11, pp. 23–63, 1987.
[6] D. DeSieno, "Adding a conscience to competitive learning," in *Proceedings of IEEE International Conference on Neural Networks*, (San Diego), pp. 117–124, IEEE, 1988.
[7] S. C. Ahalt, A. K. Krishnamurthy, P. Chen, and D. E. Melton, "Competitive learning algorithms for vector quantization," *Neural Networks*, vol. 3, pp. 277–290, 1990.
[8] L. Xu, "Rival penalized competitive learning for clustering analysis, RBF net, and curve detection," *IEEE Transaction on Neural Networks*, vol. 4, no. 4, pp. 636–649, 1993.
[9] A. Luk and S. Lien, "Properties of the generalized lotto-type competitive learning," in *Proceedings of International conference on neural information processing*, (San Mateo: CA), pp. 1180–1185, Morgan Kaufmann Publishers, 2000.
[10] M. M. V. Hulle, "The formation of topographic maps that maximize the average mutual information of the output responses to noiseless input signals," *Neural Computation*, vol. 9, no. 3, pp. 595–606, 1997.
[11] R. Linsker, "Self-organization in a perceptual network," *Computer*, vol. 21, pp. 105–117, 1988.
[12] R. Linsker, "How to generate ordered maps by maximizing the mutual information between input and output," *Neural Computation*, vol. 1, pp. 402–411, 1989.
[13] R. Linsker, "Local synaptic rules suffice to maximize mutual information in a linear network," *Neural Computation*, vol. 4, pp. 691–702, 1992.
[14] R. Kamimura, T. Kamimura, and O. Uchida, "Flexible feature discovery and structural information," *Connection Science*, vol. 13, no. 4, pp. 323–347, 2001.
[15] R. Kamimura, T. Kamimura, and H. Takeuchi, "Greedy information acquisition algorithm: A new information theoretic approach to dynamic information acquisition in neural networks," *Connection Science*, vol. 14, no. 2, pp. 137–162, 2002.
[16] R. Kamimura, "Information theoretic competitive learning in self-adaptive multi-layered networks," *Connection Science*, vol. 13, no. 4, pp. 323–347, 2003.
[17] R. Kamimura, "Cost-sensitive information maximization," in *Proceedings of IASTED International Conference on Artificial Intelligence*, 2003.
[18] L. L. Gatlin, *Information Theory and Living Systems*. Columbia University Press, 1972.
[19] H. C. Romesburg, *Cluster Analysis for Researchrers*. Florida: Krieger Publishing Company, 1984.

---

[6]We took training and generalization errors when the generalization errors show the lowest levels.

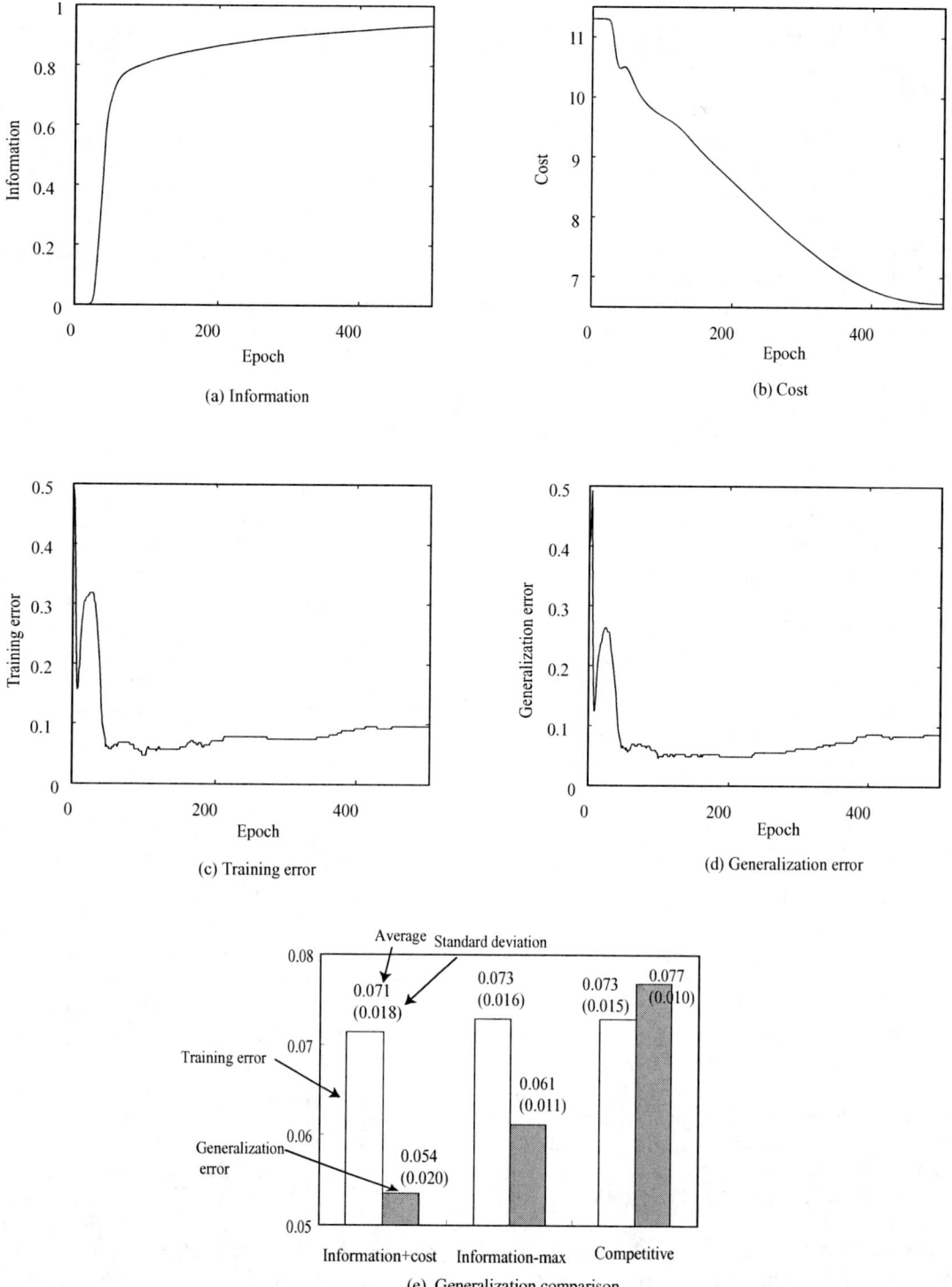

Fig. 6. Experimental results for the cancer problem: Figure (a), (b), (c), (d) and (e) show information as a function of the number of epochs, the cost as a function of the number of epochs, training errors as a function of the number of epochs, generalization errors as a function of the number of epochs and error comparison by three methods, respectively.

Maximally Discriminative Spectral Feature Projections Using Mutual Information

Umut Ozertem
CSEE Department, OGI
Oregon Health & Science University
Portland, OR 97006, USA

Deniz Erdogmus
CSEE Department, OGI
Oregon Health & Science University
Portland, OR 97006, USA

Abstract—Determining the optimal subspace projections, which maintains the best representation of the original data, is an important problem in machine learning and pattern recognition. In this paper, we propose a nonparametric nonlinear subspace projection technique that employs kernel density estimation based information theoretic methods and kernel machines, in order to maintain class separability maximally under the Shannon mutual information criterion.

I. INTRODUCTION

Dimensionality reduction is an important step in a variety of applications including pattern recognition, data compression, and exploratory data analysis. This results from the fact that the relevant information of the data can be represented in lower dimensions, which not only reduces the computational complexity but also provides a generalization of the data, leading to a robust solution.

Projection can be achieved either by a feature transformation or a feature selection. Optimal feature selection coupled with a specific classifier topology, namely the wrapper approach, results in a combinatorial computational requirement, thus, is unsuitable for adaptive learning of feature projections. Besides, since feature selection is a special case of feature transformations, we are mainly interested in feature transformations.

Adaptive learning of nonlinear feature transformations, namely the filter approach, is achieved by optimizing a suitable criterion. The possibility of learning the optimal feature projections sequentially, decreases the computational requirements making the filter approach especially attractive.

Principle components analysis (PCA) is historically the first dimensionality reduction technique [1]. PCA and its nonlinear extension to nonlinear projections, Kernel PCA [2,3], exhibit the same shortcoming, namely, the projected features are not necessarily useful for classification.

Linear Discriminant Analysis (LDA) attempts to tackle this shortcoming of PCA by searching for linear projections that maximizes class separability under Gaussianity assumption. LDA projections are optimized based on the means and covariance matrices of classes, which are not descriptive for an arbitrary probability density function. Its nonlinear extension Kernel LDA [4], generalizes this assumption by first projecting the data to a hypothetical high dimensional space where the Gaussianity condition is assumed to be satisfied. However, the kernel functions used in practice do not necessarily validate this assumption.

Second-order statistical measures have found widespread application in many areas of machine learning and pattern recognition. However, the insufficiency of only second-order statistics in many application areas have been discovered and more advanced concepts including higher-order statistics, especially those stemming from information theory are now being studied and applied in many contexts, and proven to be superior to the traditional second-order measures. In the filter approach, it is important to optimize a criterion that is relevant to Bayes risk, which is typically measured by the probability of error. A suitable criterion is mutual information (MI) between the projected features and the class labels, which is motivated by lower and upper bounds in information theory that relate this MI to probability of error. In principle, MI measures nonlinear dependencies between a set of random variables taking the higher order statistical structures existing in the data into account, as opposed to linear and second-order statistical measures such as correlation and covariance [7].

Mutual information can be estimated nonparametrically from the training samples [8]. Since the class label vector is discrete-valued, the problem reduces to just estimating entropies of continuous random vectors. The multi-dimensional entropy can be estimated nonparametrically using a number of techniques. However, techniques based on sample spacing are not differentiable, hence not suitable for adaptive learning of feature projections [9]. On the other hand, entropy estimators based on kernel density estimation (KDE) provide a differentiable alternative [8,10].

In this paper, we propose a method for determining optimal nonlinear feature projections that maximize the Shannon mutual information between the projections and the class labels. Nonparametric entropy estimation using KDE results in $O(N^2)$ complexity, where N is the number of training samples. Therefore, gradient-based methods are computationally prohibitive for large training sets. We propose to avoid this complication by exploiting the kernel induced feature (KIF) transformation to obtain an algorithm that has $O(N)$ complexity. Further computational savings are achieved by employing the deflation procedure in the KIF space to determine each projection sequentially rather than simultaneously.

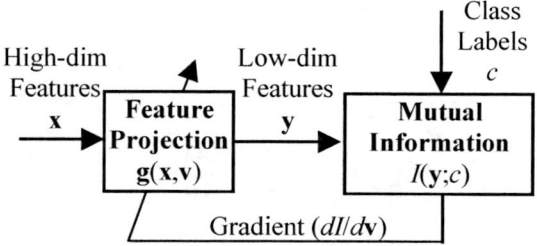

Figure 1. Determining optimal feature subspace projections using mutual information.

II. THEORETICAL BACKGROUND

The aim of the feature subspace projections is to establish a generalization of the data in order to improve the classifier robustness as well as reducing the computational complexity of the classifiers. On the other hand, the classifier performance must not be compromised during the projections by losing information about the data by throwing away some useful components. Theoretically, the optimal subspace projections should minimize the Bayesian risk, and since it is a widely used and accepted risk function, we will use the probability of error as Bayesian risk function.

The average probability of error has been shown to be related to MI between the feature vectors and the class labels. Specifically, Fano's and Hellman & Raviv's bounds demonstrate that probability of error is bounded from below and above by quantities that depend on the Shannon MI between these variables [11,12]. Maximizing this MI reduces both bounds, therefore, forces the probability of error to decrease, leading to an improved classifier performance [6].

In feature extraction, we are interested in the MI between the continuous-valued feature vector $\mathbf{y}$ and the discrete-valued class labels c. We formulate the problem using Renyi's generalized definition of MI between $\mathbf{y}$ and c with respect to α is defined in terms of the overall data and the individual class distributions as [7]

$$I_\alpha(\mathbf{y};c) = \frac{1}{\alpha-1}\log \sum_c \int p_{\mathbf{y}c}^\alpha(\mathbf{y},c) p_\mathbf{y}^{1-\alpha}(\mathbf{y}) p_c^{1-\alpha}\, d\mathbf{y} \quad (1)$$
$$= \frac{1}{\alpha-1}\log \sum_c p_c \int p_{\mathbf{y}|c}^\alpha(\mathbf{y}|c) p_\mathbf{y}^{1-\alpha}(\mathbf{y})\, d\mathbf{y}$$

where p_c are the prior class probabilities, The overall data distribution in terms of class conditional distributions $p(\mathbf{y}|c)$ is given as,

$$p(\mathbf{y}) = \sum_c p_c p(\mathbf{y}|c) \quad (2)$$

As seen in (1), in order to estimate MI we need to estimate the conditional class probability distributions as well as the overall data distribution. Density estimators based on sample spacing are not suitable for gradient-based adaptation, and a feasible alternative is the KDE-based plug-in estimator [8]. Clearly, optimizing a nonlinear topology to maximize (1) using the KDE-based estimators will be computationally expensive as N increases. In the next section we propose a nonparametric nonlinear topology that stems from the theory of reproducing kernels in Hilbert spaces.

Under the framework of *optimal feature subspace projections that maximize mutual information with class labels*, the adaptive learning procedure to find these optimal projections follows the block diagram shown in Fig. 1. A high dimensional feature vector is projected to a lower dimensional vector by a nonlinear topology (such as a neural network), whose weights (denoted by $\mathbf{v}$) are optimized to maximize the MI criterion [5,6].

III. SPECTRAL TRANSFORMATIONS AND MAXIMALLY SEPARABLE PROJECTIONS

We are given a set of features $\{\mathbf{x}_1,\mathbf{x}_2,...,\mathbf{x}_N\}$ and their corresponding class labels $\{c_1,c_2,...,c_N\}$, where the number of samples in each class is denoted by N_c and the total number of classes is C. We are interested in finding a nonlinear subspace projection such that the MI between the projection and the class labels, namely $I_S(\mathbf{y},c)$, is maximized.

According to the theory of reproducing kernels for Hilbert spaces (RKHS), the eigenfunctions $\{\overline{\varphi}_1(\mathbf{x}), \overline{\varphi}_2(\mathbf{x}),...\}$ collected in vector notation as $\overline{\boldsymbol{\varphi}}(\mathbf{x})$, of a kernel function K that satisfy the Mercer conditions [13] form a basis for the Hilbert space of finite power nonlinear functions, where the bar denotes true eigenfunctions and eigenvalues of the kernel [14]. Therefore, every finite-L_2-norm nonlinear transformation $g_d(\mathbf{x})$ can be expressed as a linear combination of these bases:

$$y_d = g_d(\mathbf{x}) = \mathbf{v}_d^T \overline{\boldsymbol{\varphi}}(\mathbf{x}) \quad (3)$$

where y_d is the dth component of the projection vector $\mathbf{y}$. As we will show next, such linear combinations of nonlinear basis functions arise naturally from the KDE-based nonparametric estimates of mutual information in the context of feature subspace projections.

A. Estimating the MI Nonparametrically Using KDE

Consider the Renyi's MI between the high-dimensional original feature vectors and the class labels.

$$I_\alpha(\mathbf{x};c) = \frac{1}{\alpha-1}\log \sum_c p_c E_{\mathbf{x}|c}\left[\left(\frac{p_{\mathbf{x}|c}(\mathbf{x}|c)}{p_\mathbf{x}(\mathbf{x})}\right)^{\alpha-1}\right] \quad (4)$$

Estimating the pdf's using a KDE estimator with kernel $K(.)$ and approximating the conditional expectation by a sample mean we obtain

$$I_\alpha(\mathbf{x};c) \approx \frac{1}{\alpha-1}\log \sum_c \frac{p_c}{N_c}\sum_{j=1}^{N_c}\left(\frac{(1/N_c)\sum_{i=1}^{N_c} K(\mathbf{x}_j^c-\mathbf{x}_i^c)}{(1/N)\sum_{i=1}^{N} K(\mathbf{x}_j^c-\mathbf{x}_i)}\right)^{\alpha-1} \quad (5)$$

Assuming that K is a Mercer kernel we can write, $K(\mathbf{x}-\mathbf{x}') = \overline{\boldsymbol{\varphi}}^T(\mathbf{x})\overline{\boldsymbol{\Lambda}}\overline{\boldsymbol{\varphi}}(\mathbf{x}')$. Hence, the MI estimate becomes

$$I_\alpha(\mathbf{x};c) \approx \frac{1}{\alpha-1}\log \sum_c \frac{p_c}{N_c}\sum_{j=1}^{N_c}\left(\frac{N\overline{\boldsymbol{\varphi}}^T(\mathbf{x}_j^c)\overline{\boldsymbol{\Lambda}}\boldsymbol{\Phi}_\mathbf{x}\mathbf{m}_c}{N_c\overline{\boldsymbol{\varphi}}^T(\mathbf{x}_j^c)\overline{\boldsymbol{\Lambda}}\boldsymbol{\Phi}_\mathbf{x}\mathbf{1}}\right)^{\alpha-1} \quad (6)$$

where we define the membership vector $\mathbf{m}_c$ for each class c, such that $\mathbf{m}_{ci}=1$ if $c_i=c$, 0 otherwise, as well as a vector of ones, denoted by **1**. Besides, we introduced the matrix $\overline{\Phi}_x = [\overline{\varphi}(x_1) \cdots \overline{\varphi}(x_N)]$, where $N=N_1+\ldots+N_C$. Defining the mean vectors in the transformed domain as $\overline{\mu}_c = (1/N_c)\overline{\Phi}_x m_c$ and $\overline{\mu} = (1/N)\overline{\Phi}_x \mathbf{1}$ for class c and whole data set respectively, we obtain

$$I_\alpha(\mathbf{x};c) \approx \frac{1}{\alpha-1} \log \sum_c \frac{p_c}{N_c} \sum_{j=1}^{N_c} \left(\frac{\overline{\varphi}^T(\mathbf{x}_j)\overline{\Lambda}\overline{\mu}_c}{\overline{\varphi}^T(\mathbf{x}_j)\overline{\Lambda}\overline{\mu}} \right)^{\alpha-1} \quad (7)$$

As also seen from (7), we can obtain different cost functions for different values of α. The robustness and the performance of the projection results strictly depend on the choice of α. As an example, one can easily see that for increasing values of α the MI estimator is becoming to be less dependent to the outliers in the data. For the limiting case as α approaches to 1, Renyi's MI converges to Shannon's MI definition, which is widely used and merits special attention. At this point, we will use the Shannon's MI by taking the limit as $\alpha \to 1$, leaving the dependency on α to be studied later.

$$I_S(\mathbf{x};c) = \lim_{\alpha \to 1} I_R(\mathbf{x};c) \approx \sum_c \frac{p_c}{N_c} \sum_{j=1}^{N_c} \log \left| \frac{\overline{\varphi}^T(\mathbf{x}_j)\overline{\Lambda}\overline{\mu}_c}{\overline{\varphi}^T(\mathbf{x}_j)\overline{\Lambda}\overline{\mu}} \right| \quad (7)$$

Note that so far we have only utilized the true eigenfunctions and the eigenvectors of the kernel function.

B. Spectral Transformations that Maximize Shannon Mutual Information in the Kernel-Induced Feature Space

According to our projection model in (3), effectively, the projection is accomplished in the kernel-induced φ-space. If the target reduced dimensionality is D, we have $\mathbf{y} = \mathbf{V}^T \overline{\varphi}(\mathbf{x})$, where $\mathbf{V}=[\mathbf{v}_1 \ldots \mathbf{v}_D]$ consists of orthonormal columns $\mathbf{v}_d$. Therefore, the best L_2-orthogonal approximation for $\overline{\varphi}(\mathbf{x})$ is

$$\overline{\varphi}(\mathbf{y}) = \mathbf{V}\mathbf{V}^T \overline{\varphi}(\mathbf{x}) \quad (8)$$

This leads to the following cost function that needs to be maximized by optimizing $\mathbf{V}$:

$$J(\mathbf{V}) = \sum_c \frac{p_c}{N_c} \sum_{j=1}^{N_c} \log \left| \frac{\overline{\varphi}^T(\mathbf{x}_j)\mathbf{V}\mathbf{V}^T \overline{\Lambda} \mathbf{V}\mathbf{V}^T \overline{\mu}_c}{\overline{\varphi}^T(\mathbf{x}_j)\mathbf{V}\mathbf{V}^T \overline{\Lambda} \mathbf{V}\mathbf{V}^T \overline{\mu}} \right| \quad (9)$$

Analytical expressions for the eigenfunctions of the kernel $\overline{\varphi}(\mathbf{x})$ are not available. However, spectral methods provide necessary tools to approximate these from the training samples. Following the common procedure in spectral methods, using all training samples in pairs as $K_{ij} = K(\mathbf{x}_i - \mathbf{x}_j)$, we define the symmetric kernel matrix $\mathbf{K}$ (also called the affinity matrix). The matrix $\mathbf{K}$ can be decomposed into its eigenvalues and eigenvectors as $\mathbf{K} = \Phi_x^T \Lambda \Phi_x$, which are essentially approximations of the sought eigenfunctions and eigenvalues of the kernel function. Hence the eigenfunctions can be approximated using the eigendecomposition of the affinity matrix $\mathbf{K}$ as follows:

$$\varphi(\mathbf{x}) = \sqrt{N} \Lambda^{-1} \Phi_x \mathbf{k}(\mathbf{x}) \quad (10)$$

where $\mathbf{k}(\mathbf{x})=[K(\mathbf{x}-\mathbf{x}_1),\ldots, K(\mathbf{x}-\mathbf{x}_N)]^T$. Substituting this, the transformations become $\mathbf{y} = \mathbf{V}^T \varphi(\mathbf{x})$ and (9) becomes,

$$J(\mathbf{V}) = \sum_c \frac{p_c}{N_c} \sum_{j=1}^{N_c} \log \left| \frac{\varphi^T(\mathbf{x}_j)\mathbf{V}\mathbf{V}^T \Lambda \mathbf{V}\mathbf{V}^T \mu_c}{\varphi^T(\mathbf{x}_j)\mathbf{V}\mathbf{V}^T \Lambda \mathbf{V}\mathbf{V}^T \mu} \right| \quad (11)$$

where $\mu_c = (1/N_c)\Phi_x m_c$ and $\mu = (1/N)\Phi_x \mathbf{1}$ are the class and overall mean vectors of the data in the φ-space. It is important to note that the class priors p_c are estimated from the training data by N_c/N and $\mu=p_1\mu_1+\ldots+p_C\mu_C$.

A critical issue affecting the performance of the subspace projections is the suitable selection of the kernel function. A practical consideration in selecting the kernel function is the selection of the functional form of the kernel as well as the width of the kernel. Typically, this problem is tackled by trying to optimize the parameters for a family of kernels of some specific type. The connection to kernel density estimation, presented in (5), clearly indicates that the kernel function should be selected to match the distribution of the data as much as possible. For simplicity, in the following experiments, a circular Gaussian kernel is assumed and its width parameter (variance) is determined utilizing the rule of thumb by Silverman that gives the *optimal* kernel size for the data set assuming that a Gaussian distribution underlies [16]:

$$\sigma^2 = \frac{1}{n} tr(\Sigma_x) \left(\frac{4}{(2n+1)N} \right)^{2/(n+4)} \quad (12)$$

where n is the dimensionality of the data $\mathbf{x}$, N is the number of samples, and Σ_x is the sample covariance of the training set. Clearly, certain obvious improvements include utilizing a different kernel, however, such modifications will be studied in future publications, since the goal of this paper is to demonstrate the concept, rather than optimizing every little implementation detail.

C. Projections to a Single Dimension

For illustration, first we focus on finding a one-dimensional nonlinear projection that maximizes MI with the class labels. For multi-dimensional projections the deflation procedure can be employed after optimizing each projection vector, yielding the optimal projection directions sequentially, which results in lower computational load as compared to searching for all the projections simultaneously.

Imposing the constraint $\mathbf{v}^T\mathbf{v}=1$, we need to maximize

$$J(\mathbf{v}) = \sum_c p_c \log \left| \frac{\mathbf{v}^T \mu_c}{\mathbf{v}^T \mu} \right| \quad (13)$$

A very important observation is that these mean vectors are orthogonal to each other with their individual norms equal to $p_c^{-1/2}$, p_c being the class prior probability. This is due to the fact that the data transformations are calculated using (10) for both training and testing data. This leads to the following:

$$\boldsymbol{\mu}_c = \frac{1}{N_c}\sum_{j=1}^{N_c}\sqrt{N}\boldsymbol{\Lambda}^{-1}\boldsymbol{\Phi}_{\mathbf{x}}k(x_j^c) \approx \frac{\sqrt{N}}{N_c}\boldsymbol{\Phi}_{\mathbf{x}}\mathbf{m}_c \quad (14)$$

Now consider the inner product between two mean vectors:

$$\boldsymbol{\mu}_c^T\boldsymbol{\mu}_d = \frac{N}{N_c N_d}\mathbf{m}_c^T\mathbf{m}_d = \begin{cases} N/N_c & \text{if } c=d \\ 0 & \text{if } c\neq d \end{cases} \quad (15)$$

Thus, the mean vectors of each class in the φ-space create an orthogonal (but not normal) basis for the space in which our optimization variable $\mathbf{v}$ lies in. Defining a basis matrix $\mathbf{M}=[\boldsymbol{\mu}_1...\boldsymbol{\mu}_C]$ —which satisfies $\mathbf{M}^T\mathbf{M}=\mathbf{P}^{-1}$, where is $\mathbf{P}=diag(p_1,...,p_C)$— we can express $\mathbf{v}$ as

$$\mathbf{v} = \mathbf{M}\mathbf{P}^{1/2}\boldsymbol{\alpha} \quad (16)$$

where $\boldsymbol{\alpha}^T\boldsymbol{\alpha}=1$. Using (16), and the identities $\boldsymbol{\mu}=\mathbf{M}\mathbf{p}$ and $\mathbf{M}^T\boldsymbol{\mu}_c = p_c^{-1}\mathbf{e}_c$, where $\mathbf{p}$ is the vector of class priors and $\mathbf{e}_c$ is the canonical unit vector in direction, the maximization problem in (13) can be converted to a problem in terms $\boldsymbol{\alpha}$ subject to $\boldsymbol{\alpha}^T\boldsymbol{\alpha}=1$ as:

$$\max_{\boldsymbol{\alpha}} J(\boldsymbol{\alpha}) = \sum_{c=1}^{C} p_c \log \frac{\left|\boldsymbol{\alpha}^T \mathbf{P}^{1/2}\mathbf{e}_c / p_c\right|}{\sum_{d=1}^{C} p_d \boldsymbol{\alpha}^T \mathbf{P}^{1/2}\mathbf{e}_d / p_d}$$

$$= \sum_{c=1}^{C} p_c \log \frac{|\alpha_c| p_c^{1/2}}{\sum_{d=1}^{C} \alpha_d p_d^{1/2}} - \sum_{c=1}^{C} p_c \log p_c \quad (17)$$

Notice that, due to the constraint $\boldsymbol{\alpha}^T\boldsymbol{\alpha}=1$, we can express all feasible solutions of $\boldsymbol{\alpha}$ in terms of rotations of a unit norm vector. For convenience, consider rotations of the form $\boldsymbol{\alpha}=\mathbf{R}\mathbf{q}$, where $\mathbf{q}$ is a vector consisting of entries $q_c=p_c^{1/2}$. With this substitution, we can rewrite (17) as shown in (18), where D_{KL} denotes the Kullback-Leibler divergence measure. Clearly, the first term is an inconsequential constant in the optimization problem, and a rotation matrix that achieves $\mathbf{q}^T\mathbf{R}\mathbf{q}=0$ maximizes the criterion. Note that this is equivalent to selecting $\mathbf{R}\mathbf{q}$ orthogonal to $\mathbf{q}$. Since the coordinates of the mean vector $\boldsymbol{\mu}$ in terms of the bases given by the normalized class means $\boldsymbol{\mu}_c p_c^{1/2}$ is also $p_c^{1/2}=q_c$, this solution coincides with the observation that the optimal projection should be orthogonal to the overall data mean vector in the φ-space.

$$\max_{\mathbf{R}} J(\mathbf{R}) = \sum_{c=1}^{C} p_c \log \frac{|\mathbf{R}_{c:}\mathbf{q}|q_c}{|\mathbf{q}^T\mathbf{R}\mathbf{q}|} - \sum_{c=1}^{C} p_c \log p_c$$

$$= -D_{KL}(\mathbf{p}\|\mathbf{q}) + E_{\mathbf{p}}\left[\log \frac{|\mathbf{R}_{c:}\mathbf{q}|}{|\mathbf{q}^T\mathbf{R}\mathbf{q}|}\right] \quad (18)$$

In general, rotation matrices corresponding to orthogonal transformations of the vector consist of 0's and ±1's (the cosine and sine of ±π/2). Therefore, the projections of a data to one dimension under this methodology can be completely determined by the entries of $\mathbf{q}$, i.e., $\{p_1^{1/2},...,p_C^{1/2}\}$, by shuffling them and modifying their signs as necessary (and perhaps replacing some with as determined by the appropriate rotation matrix). For example, in the case of 2 classes (C=2), the two solutions are $\boldsymbol{\alpha}=[-p_2^{1/2},p_1^{1/2}]^T$ and its negative, which is an equivalent solution. In the case of C=3, the three distinct solutions are given by $\boldsymbol{\alpha}=[-p_2^{1/2},p_1^{1/2},0]^T$, $\boldsymbol{\alpha}=[-p_3^{1/2},0,p_1^{1/2}]^T$, $\boldsymbol{\alpha}=[0,-p_3^{1/2},p_2^{1/2}]^T$. These solutions differ in their ordering of the projected classes on the projection axis and in general, the solution that also maximizes the numerator of the first term in (17) is preferable. The reason for this will become apparent in the next section.

Similar analytical expressions could be derived for candidate projections in the case of more than 3 classes, but the general iterative procedure proposed in the next section already considers these issues and constructs the solution without having to go through all possible rotations that result in orthogonal vectors in the C dimensional space. Nevertheless, for cases with few classes, these analytical solutions are very practical, since it only takes evaluating a portion of (17) for all candidate solutions and selecting the one that yields the maximum value. The function to be evaluated is specifically

$$\sum_{c=1}^{C} p_c \log|\alpha_c| p_c^{1/2} \quad (19)$$

D. Algorithm for Determining Optimal Projections to C or Fewer Dimensions

In this section, we generalize the intuition developed in the previous section about determining the optimal projections by finding orthogonal directions to the mean vector $\boldsymbol{\mu}$. To this end, a procedure based on Gram-Schmidt orthogonalization will be employed. Note that the deflation will be implemented through the class mean vectors $\boldsymbol{\mu}_c$, therefore, the complexity of this algorithm is relatively low.

We start by constructing the matrix $\mathbf{M}=[\boldsymbol{\mu}_1...\boldsymbol{\mu}_C]$, where the mean vector norms satisfy (15). Consequently, all columns lie in one half of the vector space. This matrix is renamed as $\mathbf{M}^C$ to denote that its column rank is C. We introduce the sign vector $\mathbf{s}^C=[1,...,1]^T$ (for reasons that will become clear shortly). Using the elementwise multiplication operator •, we calculate $\mathbf{r}^C=\mathbf{s}^C\bullet\mathbf{p}$. The overall mean vector $\boldsymbol{\mu}^C$ is then given by $\boldsymbol{\mu}^C=\mathbf{M}^C\mathbf{r}^C$. The optimal projection of the data to C-1 dimensions is determined by the C-1 dimensional subspace orthogonal to $\boldsymbol{\mu}^C$; therefore, $\mathbf{M}^C$ is deflated as:

$$\mathbf{M}^{C-1} = \left(\mathbf{I}_N - \boldsymbol{\mu}^C\boldsymbol{\mu}^{CT}/\|\boldsymbol{\mu}^C\|^2\right)\mathbf{M}^C \quad (20)$$

Any orthonormal bases that span the same space as the columns of the deflated matrix $\mathbf{M}^{C-1}$ is a valid candidate for the projection matrix $\mathbf{V}$ with C-1 orthonormal columns. Possible methods to obtain these bases is to employ Gram-Schmidt orthonormalization to the columns of $\mathbf{M}^{C-1}$ and determining the eigenvectors of $\mathbf{M}^{C-1}\mathbf{M}^{C-1,T}$ that correspond to the C-1 nonzero eigenvalues (which could be achieved sequentially). In the latter case, for example, the determined eigenvectors can be immediately assigned as $\mathbf{V}$.

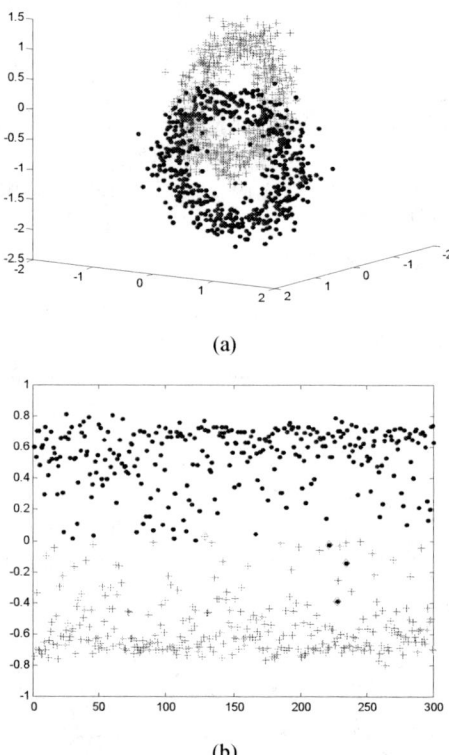

(a)

(b)

Figure 2. The original samples for both classes indicated by + and • signs are shown in (a). In (b), the values of the one-dimensional projection are shown for both classes with the same signs. The ◊ symbols indicate the classification errors made using a threshold on the projections values.

The procedure continues similarly for reducing dimensionality further: Construct s^{C-1}, Calculate the mean vector in the deflated space using $\mu^{C-1}=M^{C-1}r^{C-1}$, deflate the class means matrix using

$$M^{C-2} = \left(I_N - \mu^{C-1}\mu^{C-1,T} / \|\mu^{C-1}\|^2\right)M^{C-1} \quad (21)$$

As before, the orthonormal projection matrix V to C-2 dimensions is determined by finding the nonzero eigenvectors of $M^{C-2}M^{C-2,T}$. The procedure is carried out in this manner until deflation down to the desired number of dimensions is achieved.

Once the column-orthonormal projection matrix V, which is $N \times D$, is obtained previously unseen test samples can be transformed using

$$\varphi(y) = \sqrt{N} V^T \Lambda^{-1} \Phi_x k(x) \quad (22)$$

Note that the procedure described here requires determining the larger eigenvectors of an $N \times N$ symmetric matrix at every step of the deflation process. Unless certain simplifications are introduced, this process can potentially become $O(N^3)$. It is possible to avoid this level of complexity by determining the required eigenvectors sequentially using a suitable algorithm. Nevertheless, such algorithms still require $O(N^2)$ calculations per eigenvector per iteration. Due to the iterative nature, the overall complexity might easily exceed analytical methods, such as those based on factorization techniques [17]. Alternatively, the eigendecomposition of the kernel matrix could be performed on smaller data matrices using representative subsets and the Lanczos method or the Nystrom routine could be employed [15,17]. In fact, in practice, such an approach using a balanced number of samples from each class to determine the eigenfunctions could become preferable, as the prior class probabilities become more unbalanced, the eigenfunction estimates will become more biased towards emphasizing the stronger classes, thus yielding high-variance projection solutions.

Outline of the algorithm:

- Given a set of training data $\{x_1, x_2, ..., x_N\}$ and their corresponding class labels $\{c_1, c_2, ..., c_N\}$, determine the kernel size (for Gaussian kernels according to Silverman's rule of thumb):

$$\sigma^2 = \frac{1}{n} tr(\Sigma_x)\left(4/((2n+1)N)\right)^{2/(n+4)}$$

- Construct the kernel matrix K, where $K_{ij} = K(x_i - x_j)$.
- Decompose K into its eigenvectors and eigenvalues such that $K = \Phi_x^T \Lambda \Phi_x$.
- For the training data, calculate the kernel induced feature transformations as follows: $\varphi(x_j) = \sqrt{N}\Lambda^{-1}\Phi_x k(x_j)$
- Determine the class means and the overall mean using $\mu_c = (1/N_c)\Phi_x m_c$ and $\mu = (1/N)\Phi_x 1$.
- Perform the following deflation procedure until the desired projection dimensionality is reached:
  1. Set $s^{C-d}=[1,...,1]^T$ in the first step, $s'^{C-d}_j=\text{sign}(\mu_j^T u^{C-d})$ in the following steps.
  2. Calculate $r^{C-d}=s^{C-d}\bullet p$ and determine the *new* overall mean vector μ^{C-d} by $\mu^{C-d}=M^{C-d}r^{C-d}$. (The symbol • denotes elementwise vector product.)
  3. Construct the matrix $M^{C-d} = [\mu_1^{C-d}...\mu_C^{C-d}]$. If C-d is the desired projection dimension, determine the eigenvectors of $M^{C-d}M^{C-d,T}$ that correspond to the C-d nonzero eigenvalues. Assign these eigenvectors to V.
  4. Otherwise, perform the following deflation operation and go back to the first step:

$$M^{C-1} = \left(I_N - \mu^C \mu^{CT} / \|\mu^C\|^2\right) M^C$$

IV. EXPERIMENTS

In order to illustrate how the proposed nonparametric nonlinear projection scheme works, simulations using two datasets will be presented. The chain dataset is selected to demonstrate the effectiveness of the nonlinear projections obtained through this methodology in determining nonparametric projections to separate classes with nonlinear discriminant boundaries, and the matched filter example is chosen to motivate the use of these techniques as nonlinear filters.

Chain Dataset: Chain dataset consists of two interlocked and circular shaped classes with 300 three-dimensional samples for each class, uniformly distributed around the circle and perturbed around the circle with Gaussian distributed random values. This dataset is generated such that there is a nonlinear decision boundary between the classes, in order to eliminate the possibility of having a linear projection direction on which the classes become easily separable; hence, nonlinear projections are required here.

Sample simulation results using the chain dataset are presented in Fig. 2. The original data set is shown in Fig. 2a, and the values of the one-dimensional projection are presented in Fig. 2b. The errors based on the optimal threshold are indicated by diamonds.

Nonlinear matched filter: Interpreting the matched filter problem as a two-class clustering problem, we can use the given algorithm in order to use a projection to one dimension and distinguish between two possible cases, namely $r=n$ or $r=s+n$, where r is the received signal, n is the channel noise, and s is the signal to be detected. Since the linear matched filter is optimal under quite restrictive conditions such as linearity and Gaussianity, the nonlinear matched filter is strongly superior to the linear matched filter in the absence of these restrictions. In order to simulate the case that the optimal threshold is unknown, ROC curves can be used in order to evaluate the system performance. Under the assumption that the signal suffers a nonlinear distortion in the channel, ROC curves for the nonlinear matched filter are depicted in Fig. 4 along with the traditional linear matched filter for a comparison. In consistency with the literature on digital communications, the channel nonlinearity in this example is taken to be a third order polynomial [18]. As expected, an increase in the overlap, hence a decrease in SNR, results in *worse* ROC curves. Given the ROC, the optimal threshold for a given data set can be easily determined using a line passing from (0,1), and whose slope is determined by the ratio of a priori class probabilities.

V. CONCLUSIONS

In this paper, we have proposed a nonparametric nonlinear subspace projection methodology based on maximizing the Shannon mutual information between the projections and the class labels. Interpreting the nonparametric kernel estimator for mutual information as a nonparametric kernel-machine, we are able to determine nonlinear projections that maintain class separability nonparametrically. The proposed method lays out an interesting framework under which nonparametric kernel-density estimates of information theoretic optimality criteria can be linked to nonparametric nonlinear kernel-machines.

The most important feature of the proposed approach is that the kernel calculations are done only once for the training data in order to determine the optimal nonlinear projection, in contrast with the traditional parametric projection algorithms based on optimizing the same nonparametric MI estimate that have to rely on gradient updates of the weights, which requires the $O(N^2)$ kernel matrix calculations at every iteration of the gradient algorithm.

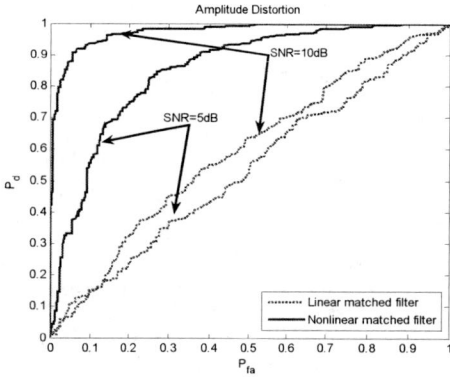

Figure 3. Performance comparison for signal detection in AWGN with nonlinear amplitude distortion. p_d and p_{fa} stand for probability of detection and probability of false alarm respectively.

REFERENCES

[1] E. Oja, *Subspace Methods of Pattern Recognition*, Wiley, New York, 1983.

[2] B. Scholkopf, A. Smola, K.R. Muller, "Nonlinear Component Analysis as a Kernel Eigenvalue Problem," Neural Computation, vol. 10, pp. 1299-1319, 1998.

[3] K. Fukunaga, *Introduction to Statistical Pattern Recognition*, Academic Press, New York, 1990.

[4] G. Baudat, F. Anouar, "Generalized Discriminant Analysis Using a Kernel Approach," Neural Computation, vol. 12, pp. 2385-2404, 2000.

[5] J.C. Principe, J.W. Fisher, D. Xu, "Information Theoretic Learning," in *Unsupervised Adaptive Filtering*, S. Haykin Editor, John Wiley & Sons, New York, 2000, pp.265-319.

[6] K. Torkkola, "Feature Extraction by Non-Parametric Mutual Information Maximization," Journal of Machine Learning Research, vol. 3, pp. 1415-1438, 2003.

[7] T. Cover, J. Thomas, *Elements of Information Theory*, Wiley, New York, 1991.

[8] D. Erdogmus, *Information Theoretic Learning: Renyi's Entropy and its Applications to Adaptive System Training*, PhD Dissertation, University of Florida, Gainesville, Florida, 2002.

[9] E.G. Learned-Miller, J.W. Fisher III, "ICA Using Spacings Estimates of Entropy," Journal of Machine Learning Research, vol. 4, pp. 1271-1295, 2003.

[10] D. Erdogmus, J.C. Principe, "An Error-Entropy Minimization Algorithm for Supervised Training of Nonlinear Adaptive Systems," IEEE Transactions on Signal Processing, vol. 50, no. 7, pp. 1780-1786, 2002.

[11] R.M. Fano, *Transmission of Information: A Statistical Theory of Communications*, MIT Press, New York, 1961.

[12] M.E. Hellman, J. Raviv, "Probability of Error, Equivocation and the Chernoff Bound," IEEE Transactions on Information Theory, vol. 16, pp. 368-372, 1970.

[13] J. Mercer, "Functions of Positive and Negative Type, and Their Connection with the Theory of Integral Equations," Transactions of the London Philosophical Society A, vol. 209, pp. 415-446, 1909.

[14] H. Weinert (ed.), *Reproducing Kernel Hilbert Spaces: Applications in Statistical Signal Processing*, Hutchinson Ross Pub. Co., Stroudsburg, Pennsylvania, 1982.

[15] C. Fowlkes, S. Belongie, F. Chung, J. Malik, Spectral Grouping Using the Nystrom Method," IEEE Transactions on Pattern Analysis and Machine Intelligence, vol. 23, pp. 298-305, 2004.

[16] B.W. Silverman, *Density Estimation for Statistics and Data Analysis*, Chapman and Hall, London, 1986.

[17] G.H. Golub, C.F. van Loan, *Matrix Computations*, 3rd ed., Johns Hopkins University Press, Baltimore, Maryland, 1996.

[18] X.N. Fernando, A.B. Sesay, "Nonlinear Channel Estimation Using Correlation Properties of PN Sequences," *Proc. IEEE Canadian Conference on Electrical and Computer Engineering*, pp. 469-474, 2001.

Extending Kernel Principal Component Analysis to General Underlying Loss Functions

Carlos Alzate, Johan A. K. Suykens
Katholieke Universiteit Leuven, ESAT-SCD-SISTA
Kasteelpark Arenberg 10
B-3001 Leuven (Heverlee), Belgium
E-mail: {carlos.alzate, johan.suykens}@esat.kuleuven.ac.be

Abstract—Kernel Principal Component Analysis can be considered as a natural nonlinear generalization of PCA because it performs linear PCA in a kernel induced feature space. It allows us to extract nonlinear structures in the input data. The classical kernel PCA formulation leads to an eigendecomposition of the kernel matrix: eigenvectors with large eigenvalue correspond to the principal components in the feature space. Starting from the Least Squares Support Vector Machine (LS-SVM) formulation to kernel PCA we extend it to general underlying loss functions. For classical kernel PCA, the underlying loss function is L_2. In this approach, one can easily plug in other loss functions and solve a nonlinear optimization problem to achieve desirable properties. Simulations with Huber's loss function for robustness and quadratic epsilon insensitive loss function for sparseness demonstrate the flexibility of our approach.

I. INTRODUCTION

Principal Components Analysis (PCA) is a powerful unsupervised learning technique widely used for feature extraction, denoising and compression [1]. It is a linear orthogonal basis transformation where the new basis is found by an eigendecomposition of the centered covariance matrix C of a dataset. One is interested in finding the directions in which the variance is maximal and each eigenvalue λ of C equals the amount of variance in the direction of the associated eigenvector. In this way, one can achieve de-noising by dropping directions with small variance or feature extraction by projecting onto the most informative directions (largest eigenvalue). Although PCA is a powerful technique, it cannot detect nonlinear structures in the input data [2]. Kernel PCA as a natural nonlinear generalization of PCA first maps the input data into some feature space F via a nonlinear feature map φ induced by a kernel and then performs linear PCA on the mapped data. The projections onto the subspace spanned by the eigenvectors now lie in F but we need the corresponding patterns in the input space. In order to recover the extracted features or the denoised patterns we have to map from F back to the input space (also called the pre-image problem [3]). This is a nontrivial problem because the pre-image may not exist, so we can only approximate it [3]. Several approaches have been developed for the pre-image problem [4], [3], [5]. In [6] it was shown that kernel PCA can be derived as the dual problem to a primal optimization problem formulated in a kernel induced feature space. In this paper we consider this formulation for general nonlinear loss functions. Within this formulation other loss functions can be applied to achieve desirable properties such as robustness or sparseness.

This paper is organized as follows: In Section II we describe the links between LS-SVM and kernel PCA. In Section III we extend the kernel PCA formulation to other loss functions. In Section IV we briefly describe two pre-image algorithms. In Section V we propose an algorithm to find the principal components with general loss function. In Section VI we report the empirical results for two loss functions and in Section VII we give conclusions.

II. LS-SVMs AND KERNEL PCA

LS-SVM formulations to different problems were discussed by Suykens *et al.* in [7]. It emphasizes primal-dual interpretations for a class of kernel machines in the context of constrained optimization problems. LS-SVMs have natural links with kernel Fisher discriminant analysis, kernel ridge regression, kernel canonical correlation analysis, kernel partial least-squares, recurrent networks, control and kernel PCA [7], [6].

A. Classical PCA formulation

In the classical PCA formulation, one considers a given set of zero mean data $\{x_k\}_{k=1}^{N}$. The objective is to find projected variables $w^T x$ with maximal variance:

$$\max_{w} Var(w^T x) \simeq \frac{1}{N} \sum_{k=1}^{N} (w^T x_k)^2 = w^T C w \quad (1)$$

such that $w^T w = 1$, where C is the covariance matrix. The Lagrangian for this constrained optimization problem is given by:

$$\mathcal{L}(w; \lambda) = \frac{1}{2} w^T C w - \lambda(w^T w - 1) \quad (2)$$

where λ is a Lagrange multiplier. Using the conditions for optimality: $\partial \mathcal{L}/\partial w = 0$, $\partial \mathcal{L}/\partial \lambda = 0$ one obtains the eigenvalue problem:

$$Cw = \lambda w. \quad (3)$$

The eigenvector w corresponding to the largest eigenvalue defines the direction in which the projected variables have maximal variance.

B. LS-SVM Approach to Kernel PCA

Extending the LS-SVM interpretation of linear PCA to a high dimensional feature space, we have (See [6]):

$$\max_{w,e} J_p(w,e) = \gamma \frac{1}{2}\sum_{k=1}^{N} e_k^2 - \frac{1}{2}w^T w \quad (4)$$

$$\text{such that} \quad e_k = w^T(\varphi(x_k) - \hat{\mu}_\varphi), \ k=1,...,N$$

where $\hat{\mu}_\varphi = (1/N)\sum_{k=1}^{N} \varphi(x_k)$ and $\varphi(.) : \mathbb{R}^n \to \mathbb{R}^{n_h}$ is the mapping to a high dimensional feature space. In this representation the role of the loss function is made explicit. The Lagrangian becomes:

$$\mathcal{L}(w,e;\alpha)$$
$$= \gamma \frac{1}{2}\sum_{k=1}^{N} e_k^2 - \frac{1}{2}w^T w - \sum_{k=1}^{N} \alpha_k(e_k - w^T(\varphi(x_k) - \hat{\mu}_\varphi)) \quad (5)$$

with conditions for optimality

$$\frac{\partial \mathcal{L}}{\partial w} = 0 \ \to \ w = \sum_{k=1}^{N} \alpha_k(\varphi(x_k) - \hat{\mu}_\varphi)$$
$$\frac{\partial \mathcal{L}}{\partial e_k} = 0 \ \to \ \alpha_k = \gamma e_k, \ k=1,...N \quad (6)$$
$$\frac{\partial \mathcal{L}}{\partial \alpha_k} = 0 \ \to \ e_k - w^T(\varphi(x_k) - \hat{\mu}_\varphi) = 0, \ k=1,...N.$$

By elimination of e and w one obtains

$$\frac{1}{\gamma}\alpha_k - \sum_{l=1}^{N} \alpha_l(\varphi(x_l) - \hat{\mu}_\varphi)^T(\varphi(x_k) - \hat{\mu}_\varphi) = 0, \ k=1,...,N. \quad (7)$$

Defining $\lambda = 1/\gamma$ we have the following dual problem

$$\Omega_c \alpha = \lambda \alpha \quad (8)$$

with centered kernel matrix given by Ω_c:

$$\Omega_{c,kl} = (\varphi(x_k) - \hat{\mu}_\varphi)^T(\varphi(x_l) - \hat{\mu}_\varphi), \ k,l=1,...,N. \quad (9)$$

Applying the kernel trick one obtains:

$$(\varphi(x_k) - \hat{\mu}_\varphi)^T(\varphi(x_l) - \hat{\mu}_\varphi) =$$
$$K(x_k, x_l) - \frac{1}{N}\sum_{r=1}^{N} K(x_k, x_r) - \frac{1}{N}\sum_{r=1}^{N} K(x_l, x_r) \quad (10)$$
$$+ \frac{1}{N^2}\sum_{r=1}^{N}\sum_{s=1}^{N} K(x_r, x_s)$$

where K is a Mercer kernel.

Hence (8) corresponds to kernel PCA as proposed by Schölkopf *et al.* in [2], where [6] showed that L_2 is the underlying loss function associated to it. It is also remarkable that Ω_c in (8) does not contain a regularization term while is present on the other hand in the primal problem in (4). The score variables become:

$$z(x) = w^T(\varphi(x) - \hat{\mu}_\varphi)$$
$$= \sum_{l=1}^{N} \alpha_l \Bigg(K(x_l, x) - \frac{1}{N}\sum_{r=1}^{N} K(x_r, x) \quad (11)$$
$$- \frac{1}{N}\sum_{r=1}^{N} K(x_r, x_l) + \frac{1}{N^2}\sum_{r=1}^{N}\sum_{s=1}^{N} K(x_r, x_s) \Bigg).$$

III. EXTENSION TO OTHER LOSS FUNCTIONS

As discussed before, classical kernel PCA uses the L_2 loss function. Let us now extend the formulation to other loss functions:

$$\max_{w,e} J_p(w,e) = \gamma \frac{1}{2}\sum_{k=1}^{N} L(e_k) - \frac{1}{2}w^T w \quad (12)$$
$$\text{such that} \quad e_k = w^T(\varphi(x_k) - \hat{\mu}_\varphi), \ k=1,...,N$$

where $L(\cdot)$ is any differentiable loss function. The Lagrangian becomes:

$$\mathcal{L}(w,e;\alpha)$$
$$= \gamma \frac{1}{2}\sum_{k=1}^{N} L(e_k) - \frac{1}{2}w^T w - \sum_{k=1}^{N} \alpha_k(e_k - w^T(\varphi(x_k) - \hat{\mu}_\varphi)) \quad (13)$$

with conditions for optimality:

$$\frac{\partial \mathcal{L}}{\partial w} = 0 \ \to \ w = \sum_{k=1}^{N} \alpha_k(\varphi(x_k) - \hat{\mu}_\varphi)$$
$$\frac{\partial \mathcal{L}}{\partial e_k} = 0 \ \to \ \alpha_k = \gamma L'(e_k), \ k=1,...N \quad (14)$$
$$\frac{\partial \mathcal{L}}{\partial \alpha_k} = 0 \ \to \ e_k - w^T(\varphi(x_k) - \hat{\mu}_\varphi) = 0, \ k=1,...N.$$

Eliminating w, e leads to:

$$\alpha_k = \gamma L'\Bigg(\sum_{l=1}^{N} \alpha_l \Omega_c(x_l, x_k)\Bigg), \ k=1,...,N \quad (15)$$

which is a set of nonlinear equations to be solved in α_k.

Rewriting (15) as:

$$f_k(\alpha) = \alpha_k - \gamma \ L'\Bigg(\sum_{l=1}^{N} \alpha_l \Omega_c(x_l, x_k)\Bigg) = 0, \ k=1,...,N \quad (16)$$

and defining $f(\alpha) = [f_1(\alpha); \ldots ; f_N(\alpha)]$ leads to:

$$f(\alpha) = \begin{bmatrix} \alpha_1 \\ \vdots \\ \alpha_N \end{bmatrix} - \gamma L'\Bigg(\begin{bmatrix} \Omega_c(x_1, x_1) & \ldots & \Omega_c(x_1, x_N) \\ \vdots & \ddots & \vdots \\ \Omega_c(x_N, x_1) & \ldots & \Omega_c(x_N, x_N) \end{bmatrix} \begin{bmatrix} \alpha_1 \\ \vdots \\ \alpha_N \end{bmatrix} \Bigg) = 0. \quad (17)$$

The roots of (17) are the principal components and (11) still holds.

IV. THE PRE-IMAGE PROBLEM

The projections onto the subspace spanned by the principal components lie in some feature space F but in most applications of kernel PCA we are interested in a reconstruction in the input space rather than in F. This mapping from the feature space back to the input space is called the pre-image problem and is nontrivial because typically the exact pre-image does not exist and one can only approximate it [3]. An iterative nonlinear optimization method is proposed in [4] for Gaussian kernels, but it can suffer from numerical instabilities and local minima. Given a test point x we want to recover $\hat{x}$ for which $\varphi(\hat{x}) \approx P_{N_c}\varphi(x)$, where $P_{N_c}\varphi(x)$ is the projection of $\varphi(x)$ onto the subspace spanned by the first N_c principal components. For Gaussian kernels, the approximate pre-image $\hat{x}$ can be computed using the following iteration [4]:

$$\hat{x}_{t+1} = \frac{\sum_{k=1}^{N} \eta_k \exp(-\|\hat{x}_t - x_k\|^2/\sigma^2) x_k}{\sum_{k=1}^{N} \eta_k \exp(-\|\hat{x}_t - x_k\|^2/\sigma^2)} \quad (18)$$

where $\eta_k = \sum_{i=1}^{N_c} \beta_i u_k^i$ and β_i is the projection of $\varphi(x)$ onto the i-th component u^i. This approach will be referred to as "pre-image algorithm 1" in the sequel.

A newer approach is proposed in [5]. This method is non-iterative, involves only linear algebra and uses the distances between the projection $P_{N_c}\varphi(x)$ and its nearest neighbors. The method can be summarized as follows: given the N_n neighbors $\{x_1, \ldots, x_{N_n}\}$ and the input space distances between $P_{N_c}\varphi(x)$ and its N_n nearest neighbors $d^2 = [d_1^2, \ldots d_{N_n}^2]^T$ first construct the matrix $X = [x_1, x_2, \ldots, x_{N_n}]$ and compute its singular value decomposition (SVD):

$$XH = U\Lambda V^T = UZ \quad (19)$$

where H is the centering matrix, and $Z = [z_1, \ldots, z_{N_n}]$ with columns z_i being the projections of x_i onto U. The approximate pre-image can be obtained as:

$$\hat{z} = -\frac{1}{2}\Lambda^{-1}V^T(d^2 - d_0^2) \quad (20)$$

where $d_0^2 = [\|z_1\|^2, \ldots, \|z_{N_n}\|^2]^T$. Transforming back to the original coordinate system in the input space leads to:

$$\hat{x} = U\hat{z} + \bar{x} \quad (21)$$

where $\bar{x} = \frac{1}{N_n}\sum_{i=1}^{N_n} x_i$. This method will be referred to as "pre-image algorithm 2" in the sequel.

V. ALGORITHM

It is required that the principal components are mutually orthogonal. Therefore we can solve (17) using constrained nonlinear optimization to impose orthogonality constraints:

$$\min_{\alpha \in \mathbb{R}^N} f(\alpha)^T f(\alpha) \quad (22)$$

$$\text{such that } \begin{cases} A\alpha = 0 \\ \alpha^T \alpha = 1. \end{cases}$$

where A is the constraint matrix containing all previously found principal components in the rows. We need to provide the algorithm with initial values for α and also set γ. Kernel PCA eigenvectors are good starting points for the α vectors and γ is inversely related to the eigenvalues. Given a set of N d-dimensional data points $\mathcal{X} = \{x^1, \ldots, x^N\}$, the algorithm gives as output a set of N_c N-dimensional principal components: $\mathcal{A} = \{\alpha^1, \ldots, \alpha^{N_c}\}$ as follows:

1) Set the kernel parameters and the number of principal components N_c to be extracted.
2) Find the eigenvectors $\mathcal{U} = \{u^1, \ldots, u^{N_c}\}$ and eigenvalues $\mathcal{W} = \{\lambda_1, \ldots, \lambda_{N_c}\}$ of the centered kernel matrix Ω_c using singular value decomposition (SVD).
3) Calculate the first principal component α^1 by minimizing $f(\alpha)^T f(\alpha)$ with starting points $\alpha_{ini} = u^1$ and $\gamma_1 = 1/\lambda_1$ such that $(\alpha^1)^T \alpha^1 = 1$.
4) **for** $i = 2, \ldots, N_c$ **do**
   a) Add the previously found principal component to the constraint matrix $A \to A(i-1, :) = \alpha_{i-1}^T$.
   b) Compute the i-th principal component α^i by minimizing $f(\alpha)^T f(\alpha)$ with starting points $\alpha_{ini} = u^i$ and $\gamma_i = 1/\lambda_i$ such that α^i is orthogonal to all the previously found components$\to A\alpha^i = 0$ and $(\alpha^i)^T \alpha^i = 1$.

   end for
5) Normalize each component:

$$\alpha^i := \frac{\alpha^i}{\sqrt{\lambda_i}}, \; i = 1, \ldots, N_c.$$

VI. EMPIRICAL RESULTS

In this section, some experimental results using two different loss functions are presented. We used the MATLAB function *fmincon* to solve the constrained nonlinear optimization problem. First, Huber's loss function (Fig. 1) was chosen to include robustness into kernel PCA. In the context of robust statistics [8], [9], it is known that the L_2 loss function is not robust against outliers (data points that do not follow the distribution of the bulk of the data) because an arbitrary outlier can have a large influence on the solution. This is due to the fact that the influence function of L_2 is not bounded and increases linearly with the error. Huber's loss function has a bounded influence function so a single outlying data point cannot cause a large influence.

The second experiment consisted in using a quadratic epsilon-insensitive loss function [10] (Fig. 2) to achieve sparseness. With this loss function only a fraction of the principal component vectors will be non-zero which can be controlled with the epsilon parameter which controls the width of the zero region around the origin. In that case in (11) one only has to take the sum over the data points corresponding to the non-zero α_k (the support vectors), which is also a computational advantage.

A. Experiment 1 - Robustness

In this experiment we report denoising results on 15 x 16 handwritten digits. The training set consisted of 200 images

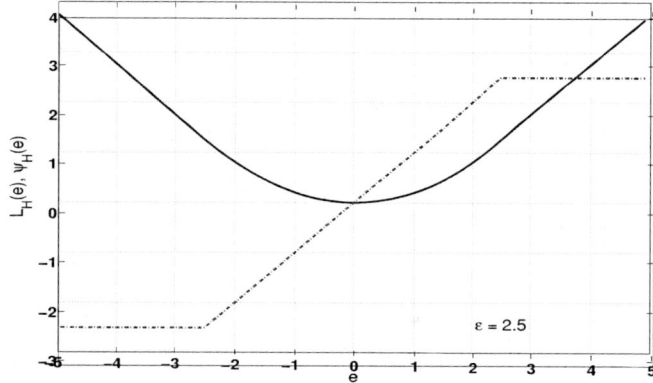

Fig. 1. Huber's loss function (solid line) with epsilon = 2.5 and its influence function (dashed line).

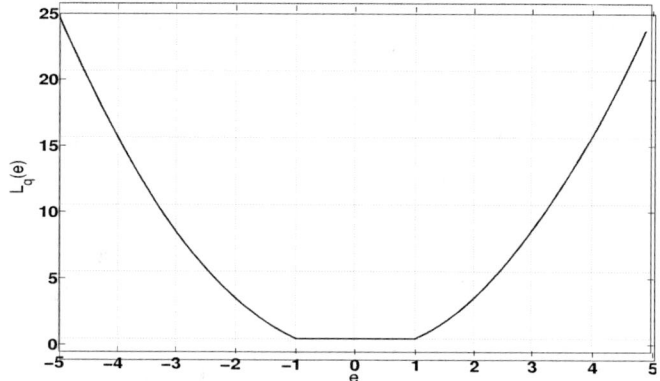

Fig. 2. Quadratic epsilon insensitive loss function with epsilon = 1.0.

(20 for each digit) with 22 outliers (from the Columbia image dataset [11]) (Fig. 3(a)). The denoised test digits using kernel PCA with robust Huber's loss function and two pre-image algorithms can be seen in (Fig. 3). From (Fig. 3(c)) one can see that the results from kernel PCA are not very accurate, nevertheless using the robust approach the denoised digits are visually more appealing. In Fig. (3(d)) kernel PCA with Huber's loss function outperforms the classical one. Table I shows the mean squared error (MSE) between the denoised test digits and the original test set. Table II shows the computation time in seconds.

TABLE I
EXPERIMENT 1 MSE OF THE DENOISED TEST DIGITS

	Pre-image algorithm	
	Algorithm 1	Algorithm 2
Kernel PCA	0.29	0.17
Kernel PCA with Huber's loss function	0.21	0.07

B. Experiment 2 - Sparseness

Here we considered two datasets: a simple curve of 500 data points and a square-like dataset of 600 data points. For the curve dataset we trained with 200 data points and kernel

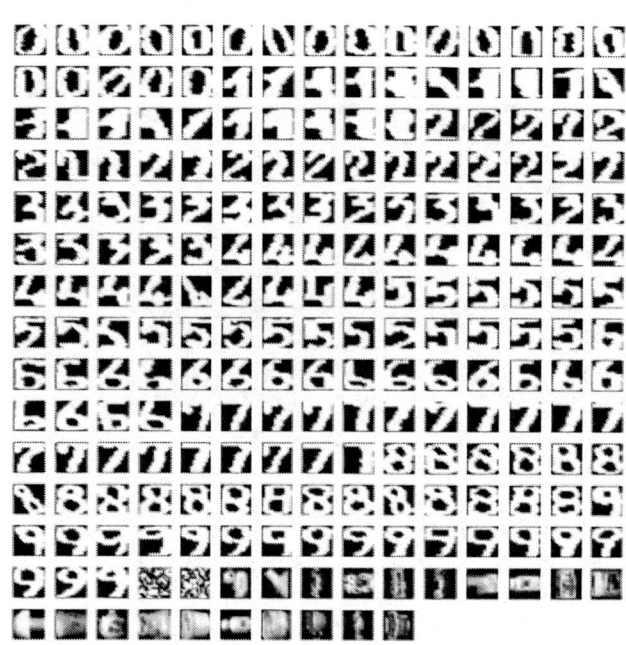

(a) Handwritten digit training set with outliers

(b) Test set corrupted with Gaussian noise and outliers imposed on each digit. *Top:* Original test set. *Bottom:* Corrupted test set.

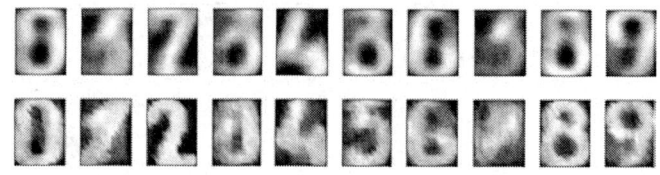

(c) Denoised digits using pre-image algorithm 1.

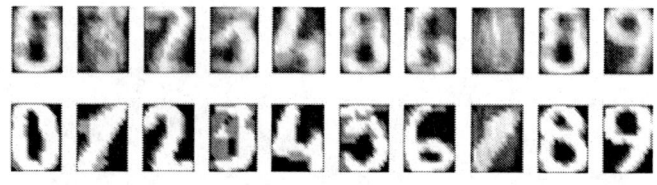

(d) Denoised digits using pre-image algorithm 2. The number of nearest neighbors (N_n) was set to 5.

Fig. 3. Handwritten digits denoising. All simulations were done with RBF kernel $\sigma^2 = 50$, $N_c = 190$, $\epsilon = 15$. The top part of (c) and (d) corresponds to classical kernel PCA and the bottom part to kernel PCA with Huber's loss function.

TABLE II
EXPERIMENT 1 COMPUTATION TIME IN SECONDS FOR PRINCIPAL COMPONENTS EXTRACTION + DENOISING

	Pre-image algorithm	
	Algorithm 1	Algorithm 2
Kernel PCA	1.3	6.1
Kernel PCA with Huber's loss function	46.2	50.0

PCA with quadratic epsilon insensitive loss function with epsilon value of 0.8 and RBF kernel with $\sigma^2 = 0.2$. The denoising results using all 500 data points and the first 5 principal components can be seen in (Fig. 4). Table III shows the number of non-zero α_k for each principal component. The support vectors in the first three principal components are shown in (Figs. 5, 6, 7).

For the square dataset we trained with 200 data points and used an epsilon value of 1.8 and RBF kernel with $\sigma^2 = 0.1$. The denoising results using all 600 data points and 8 components are shown in (Fig. 8). The support vectors in the first principal component are shown in (Fig. 9). Table IV shows the number of non-zero α_k for each principal component.

TABLE III
EXPERIMENT 2 - CURVE - NUMBER OF NON-ZERO α_k FOR EACH PRINCIPAL COMPONENT

Principal Component	Number of non-zero α_k
First	92 out of 200
Second	86 out of 200
Third	34 out of 200
Fourth	49 out of 200
Fifth	87 out of 200

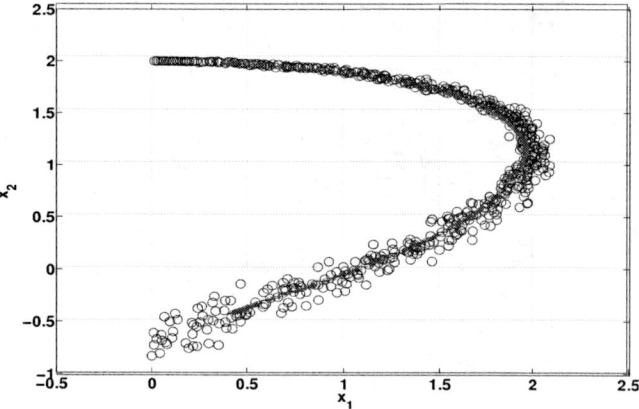

Fig. 4. Denoising results using kernel PCA with quadratic epsilon insensitive loss function and pre-image algorithm 1. Original variables are depicted as 'o' and reconstructed data points as '+'.

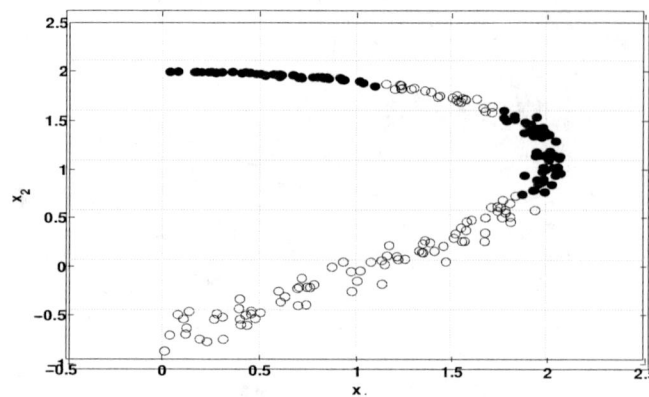

Fig. 5. Support vectors (filled circles) corresponding to the non-zero α_k in the first principal component.

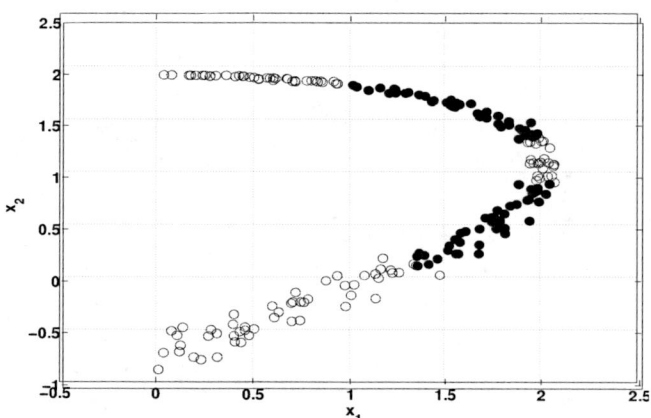

Fig. 6. Support vectors (filled circles) corresponding to the non-zero α_k in the second principal component.

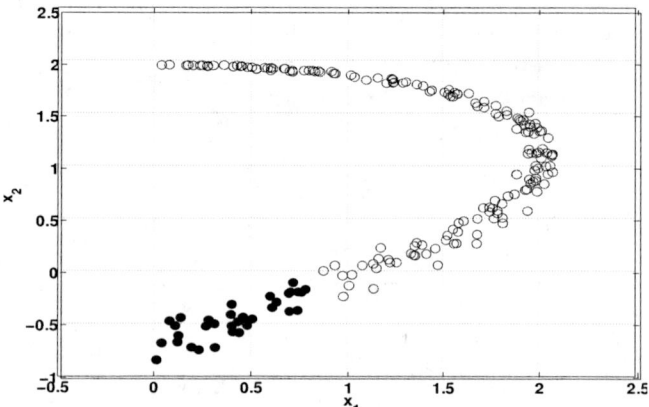

Fig. 7. Support vectors (filled circles) corresponding to the non-zero α_k in the third principal component.

TABLE IV
EXPERIMENT 2 - SQUARE - NUMBER OF NON-ZERO α_k FOR EACH PRINCIPAL COMPONENT

Principal Component	Number of non-zero α_k
First	110 out of 200
Second	84 out of 200
Third	58 out of 200
4th	65 out of 200
5th	78 out of 200
6th	108 out of 200
7th	62 out of 200
8th	131 out of 200

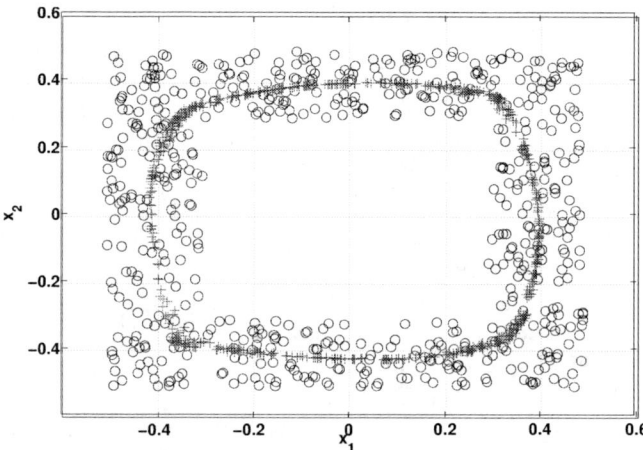

Fig. 8. Denoising results using kernel PCA with quadratic epsilon insensitive loss function and pre-image algorithm 1.

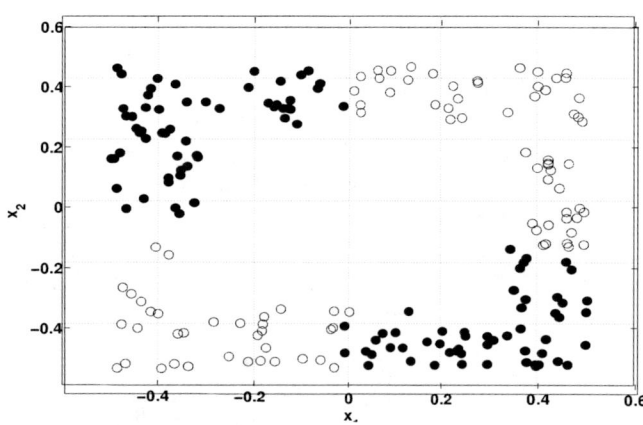

Fig. 9. Support vectors (filled circles) corresponding to the non-zero α_k in the first principal component.

at the origin. When extracting few components, both kernel PCA and our approach take approximately the same time but when the number of components is large the difference in time will be noticeable.

ACKNOWLEDGMENTS

This work was supported by grants and projects for the Research Council K.U.Leuven (GOA-Mefisto 666, GOA-Ambiorics, several PhD/Postdocs & fellow grants), the Flemish Government FWO: PhD/Postdocs grants, projects G.0240.99, G.0407.02, G.0197.02, G.0080.01, G.0141.03, G.0211.05, G.0491.03, G.0120.03, G.0452.04, G.0499.04, ICCoS, ANMMM; AWI; IWT: PhD grants, GBOU (Mc-Know) Soft4s, the Belgian Federal Government (Belgian Federal Science Policy Office: IUAP V-22; PODO-II (CP/01/40), the EU(FP5-Quprodis;ERNSI, Eureka 2063-Impact; Eureka 2419-FLiTE) and Contracts Research/Agreements (ISMC/IPCOS, Data4s, TML, Elia, LMS, IPCOS, Mastercard). Johan Suykens is an associate professor at the K.U.Leuven, Belgium. The scientific responsibility is assumed by its authors.

VII. CONCLUSION AND DISCUSSION

Starting from the LS-SVM context, a generalized form of kernel PCA is derived in order to include other loss functions. In this representation, the kernel PCA loss function is made explicit so we can easily plug in other loss functions and solve a nonlinear optimization problem. From simulation results, our approach with Huber's loss function performed better than classical kernel PCA in the sense of robustness demonstrating some insensitivity to the outliers. In the case of quadratic epsilon insensitive loss function, the epsilon value controls the number of non-zero α_k in the principal components introducing sparseness into the formulation. With this sparse representation, the score variables can be calculated using only the support vectors, which is a computational advantage. Even though our approach produced good results and converged for most of the parameter values, its convergence is not guaranteed. However, we noticed that using kernel PCA eigenvectors/eigenvalues as initial values for the nonlinear optimization problem leads to quick convergence. For very small epsilon values in the first experiment, the algorithm tends to get stuck, because we are using a gradient-based optimization algorithm and for very small epsilon values Huber's loss function behaves as L_1 and is non-differentiable

REFERENCES

[1] I. T. Jolliffe, *Principal Component Analysis*. Springer Verlag, 1986.
[2] B. Schölkopf, A. Smola, and K. R. Muller, "Nonlinear component analysis as a kernel eigenvalue problem," *Neural Computation*, vol. 10, pp. 1299–1319.
[3] B. Schölkopf, S. Mika, C. J. C. Burges, P. Knirsch, K.-R. Müller, M. Scholz, G. Rätsch, and A. J. Smola, "Input space versus feature space in kernel-based methods," *IEEE Trans. Neural Networks*, vol. 10, no. 5, pp. 1000–1017, Sept. 1999.
[4] S. Mika, B. Schölkopf, A. J. Smola, K.-R. Müller, M. Scholz, and G. Rätsch, "Kernel PCA and de–noising in feature spaces," in *Advances in Neural Information Processing Systems 11*, M. S. Kearns, S. A. Solla, and D. A. Cohn, Eds. MIT Press, 1999.
[5] J. Kwok and I. Tsang, "The pre-image problem in kernel methods," *IEEE Trans. Neural Networks*, vol. 15, no. 6, pp. 1517–1525, Nov. 2004.
[6] J. A. K. Suykens, T. Van Gestel, J. Vandewalle, and B. De Moor, "A support vector machine formulation to PCA analysis and its kernel version," *IEEE Trans. Neural Networks*, vol. 14, no. 2, pp. 447–450, Mar. 2003.
[7] J. A. K. Suykens, T. Van Gestel, J. De Brabanter, B. De Moor, and J. Vandewalle, *Least Squares Support Vector Machines*. World Scientific, Singapore, 2002.
[8] P. Huber, *Robust Statistics*. John Wiley & Sons, 1981.
[9] P. J. Rousseeuw and A. M. Leroy, *Robust Regression and Outlier Detection*. Wiley New York (N. Y.), 1987.
[10] V. Vapnik, *Statistical Learning Theory*. Wiley, New York, 1998.
[11] S. Nene, S. Nayar, and H. Murase, "Columbia object image library: Coil," Columbia University," Technical Report CUCS-006-96, 1996.

Nonlinearity and Optimal Component Analysis

Washington Mio
Department of Mathematics
Florida State University
Tallahassee, FL 32306-4510
E-mail: mio@math.fsu.edu

Qiang Zhang
Department of Computer Science
Florida State University
Tallahassee, FL 32306-4530
E-mail: zhang@cs.fsu.edu

Xiuwen Liu
Department of Computer Science
Florida State University
Tallahassee, FL 32306-4530
E-mail: liux@cs.fsu.edu

Abstract— Optimal Component Analysis (OCA) is a linear subspace technique for dimensionality reduction designed to optimize object classification and recognition performance in specific applications. The inherently linear nature of OCA often limits recognition performance, if the underlying data structure is nonlinear or cluster structures are complex. To address these problems, following a modern trend, we investigate kernel OCA (KOCA), which consists of applying OCA techniques to the data after it has been mapped nonlinearly into a new feature space, referred to in the literature as a reproducing kernel Hilbert space. In this paper, we study theoretical and algorithmic aspects of KOCA and report results obtained in several face recognition experiments using the ORL database.

I. INTRODUCTION

The general problem of dimensionality reduction in data representation for the execution of tasks such as classification and detection of objects and patterns arises in many different contexts. The recognition of objects from images is an example where computational feasibility typically relies heavily on dimension reduction techniques. For data represented in finite-dimensional inner product spaces such as n-dimensional Euclidean space $\mathbb{R}^n$, one of the most commonly used techniques is to project the data orthogonally onto "optimal" low-dimensional subspaces. Principal Component Analysis (PCA) [6] and Independent Component Analysis (ICA) [5] are classical linear subspace methods designed to optimize data reconstruction and statistical independence, respectively, but they are not directly related to recognition performance. Fisher Discriminant Analysis (FDA) optimizes recognition performance, but only under some quite restrictive assumptions; see [10] and [3] for PCA and FDA, respectively, applied to face recognition. In [7], Liu et al. introduced Optimal Component Analysis (OCA), a technique for finding optimal linear subspaces for specific classification or recognition tasks; improvements in recognition performance with OCA are documented in [7].

Complex decision boundaries needed for the separation of classes of objects represented in a dataset and nonlinear relations between data points are some of the factors that often limit the performance of classification and recognition algorithms. To cope with this type of problems, one often maps a given collection of points $x_1, \ldots, x_M \in \mathbb{R}^n$ non-linearly into a higher (possibly infinite) dimensional Hilbert space $\mathbb{H}$ to reshape the geometry of the clusters, and then apply linear subspace techniques in this new environment. Since the dimension of $\mathbb{H}$ is usually very high, the typical assumption is that the nonlinear map $\Phi \colon \mathbb{R}^n \to \mathbb{H}$ is not known explicitly, only the relative positions of the points $\Phi(x)$, $x \in \mathbb{R}^n$, given by the inner products $k(x,y) = \Phi(x) \cdot \Phi(y)$, $x, y \in \mathbb{R}^n$. The function $k(x,y)$ is referred to as a *kernel function*. Thus, dimension reduction techniques and classifiers should only require knowledge of k, not the function Φ. In machine learning, these ideas were initially explored in the context of support vector machines [4]. Kernel PCA (KPCA) was introduced subsequently by Schölkopf et al. in [9]. FDA and ICA have been investigated in this setting in [2] and [1], respectively. In this paper, we develop a kernel analogue of Optimal Component Analysis, which we refer to as KOCA; a preliminary study of KOCA that only applies to a special class of kernel functions appeared in [12]. We study KOCA for general kernels, devise and implement a computational strategy, and test the proposed algorithmic approach in several face recognition experiments. The results indicate that significantly higher recognition rates can be achieved with KOCA using very low dimensional data representations as compared to several other methods. Issues related to computational efficiency will be further investigated in future work using the differential geometry of Grassmann manifolds.

A word about the organization of the paper. In Sec. II, we briefly review OCA, as developed in [7]. Sec. III is devoted to the investigation of theoretical aspects of KOCA. Some geometric aspects of the problem related to the computational methods utilized are discussed in Sec. IV. An implementation of KOCA is discussed in Sec. V, which is followed by a report of experimental results in Sec. VI.

II. OPTIMAL COMPONENT ANALYSIS

In this section, we briefly review OCA in Euclidean space $\mathbb{R}^m$. We assume that a set of *training* data is given, as well as a *validation set* used to evaluate recognition performance, each consisting of representatives of P different classes of objects. For $1 \leq c \leq P$, we denote by $x_{c,1}, \ldots, x_{c,t_c}$ and $y_{c,1}, \ldots, y_{c,v_c}$ the elements in the training and validation sets, resp., that belong to class c. Given an r-dimensional subspace U of $\mathbb{R}^m$ and $x, y \in \mathbb{R}^m$, we let $d(x, y; U)$ denote the distance between the orthogonal projections of x and y onto U. The quantity

$$\ell(y_{c,i}; U) = \frac{\min_{d \neq c, j} d(y_{c,i}, x_{d,j}; U)}{\min_j d(y_{c,i}, x_{c,j}; U) + \epsilon}$$

measures how well the *nearest-neighbor classifier* applied to the data projected onto U identifies the element $y_{c,i}$ as belonging to class c. Here, $\epsilon > 0$ is a small number used to prevent vanishing denominators. Let

$$F(U) = \frac{1}{P} \sum_{c=1}^{P} \frac{1}{v_c} \sum_{i=1}^{v_c} h(\ell(y_{c,i}; U) - 1),$$

where h is a monotonically increasing bounded function. A common choice is $h(x) = \frac{1}{1+e^{-2\beta x}}$, for which the limit value of $F(U)$, as $\beta \to \infty$, is precisely the recognition performance of the nearest-neighbor classifier after projection to the subspace U.

Let $\mathcal{G}_{m,r}$ be the Grassmann manifold, whose elements are the r-dimensional vector subspaces of $\mathbb{R}^m$. An optimal r-dimensional subspace for the given classification problem from the viewpoint of the available data is given by $\hat{U} = \arg\max_{U \in \mathcal{G}_{m,r}} F(U)$. An algorithmic procedure for estimating $\hat{U}$ using a stochastic gradient search on $\mathcal{G}_{m,r}$ is described in [7].

III. SUBSPACE REPRESENTATION FOR KOCA

In data analysis with kernel methods, one maps a given set of points $x_1, \ldots, x_M$ in $\mathbb{R}^n$ into a Hilbert space $\mathbb{H}$ using a nonlinear map $\Phi: \mathbb{R}^n \to \mathbb{H}$, and then applies linear subspace techniques to the collection $\Phi(x_1), \ldots, \Phi(x_M)$. We shall assume that $\mathbb{H} = \mathbb{R}^m$, but all arguments are general. As pointed out in the Introduction, the typical assumption is that Φ is not known explicitly, only the kernel function $k(x, y) = \Phi(x) \cdot \Phi(y)$. The problem of determining what functions $k(x, y)$ are kernels associated with a mapping Φ has been studied in [4], [11], [9]. Some of the most commonly used kernel functions are $k(x, y) = (x \cdot y)^d$, which corresponds to mapping $\mathbb{R}^n$ into a higher dimensional space using all monomials of order d in the input variables [8], and the *Gaussian kernels* $k(x, y) = \exp\left(-\frac{\|x-y\|^2}{2\sigma^2}\right)$.

We are interested in reducing dimension by projecting $\mathbb{R}^m$ orthogonally onto r-dimensional subspaces of

$$V = \text{span}\{\Phi(x_1), \ldots, \Phi(x_M)\} \subseteq \mathbb{R}^m.$$

Thus, we first seek to develop appropriate subspace representations. Each $a = (a_1, \ldots, a_M)^T \in \mathbb{R}^{M \times 1}$ defines a vector $v \in V$ given by $v = \sum_{i=1}^{M} a_i \Phi(x_i)$. Form the symmetric $M \times M$ Gram matrix K, whose (i, j) entry is

$$K_{ij} = \Phi(x_i) \cdot \Phi(x_j). \tag{1}$$

If $a, b \in \mathbb{R}^{M \times 1}$ represent vectors $v, w \in V$, then their inner product can be calculated as

$$v \cdot w = a^T K b. \tag{2}$$

For $1 \leq r \leq \dim V$, subspaces of V of dimension r will be represented by orthonormal r-frames in V. For each $1 \leq j \leq r$, let $\alpha_j = (\alpha_{1j}, \ldots, \alpha_{Mj})^T$ represent a vector $v_j \in V$, and let α be the $(M \times r)$-matrix whose entries are α_{ij}; that is, the columns of α are α_j. From Eqn. 2, it follows that $\{v_j, 1 \leq j \leq r\}$ is orthonormal if and only if

$$\alpha^T K \alpha = I_r, \tag{3}$$

where I_r is the $r \times r$ identity matrix. Thus, the collection $\mathcal{A}$ of $M \times r$ matrices α representing orthonormal r-frames in V can be described as

$$\mathcal{A} = \{\alpha \in \mathbb{R}^{M \times r} : \alpha^T K \alpha = I_r\}.$$

By symmetry, (3) consists of $r(r+1)/2$ independent conditions on α.

It should be noted that a given r-dimensional subspace of V has multiple representatives in $\mathcal{A}$, for two reasons: (i) the choice of spanning orthonormal frames; (ii) for any $M \times r$ matrix β such that $K\beta = 0$, the matrices α and $\alpha + \beta$ represent the same orthonormal r-frame in V.

A. The Subspace W_α

Given $\alpha \in \mathcal{A}$, let W_α be the r-dimensional subspace of V spanned by the orthonormal frame determined by α; i.e.,

$$W_\alpha = \text{span}\{v_j, 1 \leq j \leq r\},$$

with $v_j = \sum_{i=1}^{M} \alpha_{ij} \Phi(x_i)$. Let $\pi_\alpha : \mathbb{R}^m \to W_\alpha$ be the orthogonal projection of $\mathbb{R}^m$ onto W_α. For $x \in \mathbb{R}^n$, we wish to derive an expression for $\Phi^\alpha(x) = \pi_\alpha(\Phi(x))$. Think of x as a test (or validation) vector to be compared with the training vectors x_i, $1 \leq i \leq M$, after orthogonal projection of $\Phi(x)$ and $\Phi(x_i)$ to W_α.

The product $\Phi^\alpha(x) \cdot v_j = \pi_\alpha(\Phi(x)) \cdot v_j = \Phi(x) \cdot v_j$, for $1 \leq j \leq r$, can be calculated as

$$\Phi(x) \cdot v_j = \sum_{i=1}^{M} \alpha_{ij} \Phi(x) \cdot \Phi(x_i) = \sum_{i=1}^{M} \alpha_{ij} k(x, x_i),$$

which implies that

$$\Phi^\alpha(x) = \sum_{j=1}^{r} \left(\sum_{i=1}^{M} \alpha_{ij} k(x, x_i) \right) v_j. \tag{4}$$

B. Distance in W_α

In applications using nearest-neighbor classifiers, we will be primarily interested in the distance between $\Phi^\alpha(x)$ and $\Phi^\alpha(y)$, for $x, y \in \mathbb{R}^n$. Since

$$\|\Phi^\alpha(x) - \Phi^\alpha(y)\|^2 = \Phi^\alpha(x) \cdot \Phi^\alpha(x) - 2\Phi^\alpha(x) \cdot \Phi^\alpha(y) + \Phi^\alpha(y) \cdot \Phi^\alpha(y), \tag{5}$$

it suffices to derive expressions for inner products of the form $\Phi^\alpha(w) \cdot \Phi^\alpha(z)$, $w, z \in \mathbb{R}^n$. From Eqn. 4, we obtain

$$\Phi^\alpha(w) \cdot \Phi^\alpha(z) = \sum_{\ell=1}^{r} \left(\sum_{i=1}^{M} \alpha_{i\ell} k(w, x_i) \right) \left(\sum_{j=1}^{M} \alpha_{j\ell} k(z, x_j) \right)$$
$$= \alpha^T h(w) \cdot \alpha^T h(z),$$

where $h(w)$ denotes the vector $(k(w, x_1), \ldots, k(w, x_M))^T \in \mathbb{R}^{M \times 1}$ and $h(z)$ is defined similarly. In (5), we obtain

$$\|\Phi^\alpha(x) - \Phi^\alpha(y)\|^2 = \|\alpha^T h(x)\|^2 - 2\alpha^T h(x) \cdot \alpha^T h(y) + \|\alpha^T h(y)\|^2. \tag{6}$$

This expresses the distance solely in terms of α and the kernel function k, as desired.

IV. THE MANIFOLD $\mathcal{A}$

We inspect condition (3), which defines the manifold $\mathcal{A}$, more closely. First, we introduce some notation. For $1 \leq k \leq r$, let E_k be the $r \times r$ matrix whose only nonzero entry is at position (k, k) and equals 1. For each $1 \leq i, j \leq r$, define S_{ij} to be the $r \times r$ matrix obtained from I_r by interchanging the ith and jth columns. Right multiplication of a matrix by E_k has the effect of preserving the kth column and setting all other columns to zero. Right multiplication by S_{ij} simply swaps the ith and jth columns leaving the remaining ones unchanged.

Let
$$\langle A, B \rangle = \text{tr}(A^T B) = \text{tr}(AB^T) \tag{7}$$

be the usual inner product on the vector space of all real $M \times r$ matrices. The (i, j)-entry of (3) can be written as

$$\langle \alpha E_i S_{ij}, K\alpha E_j \rangle = \delta_{ij},$$

for $1 \leq i \leq j \leq r$. Define $F_{ij} : \mathbb{R}^{M \times r} \to \mathbb{R}$ by

$$F_{ij}(\alpha) = \langle \alpha E_i S_{ij}, K\alpha E_j \rangle. \tag{8}$$

For $1 \leq j < i \leq r$, to make the collection symmetric in (i, j), define $F_{ij}(\alpha) = F_{ji}(\alpha)$. These functions can be assembled into a map $F : \mathbb{R}^{M \times r} \to S_r$, where S_r is the space of all $r \times r$ real symmetric matrices, which is isomorphic to $\mathbb{R}^{r(r+1)/2}$. The space $\mathcal{A}$ can now be described as the level set

$$\mathcal{A} = F^{-1}(I_r). \tag{9}$$

A. Projection onto $\mathcal{A}$

To implement gradient searches on $\mathcal{A}$, as proposed below, we need a projection mechanism that maps matrices in $\mathbb{R}^{M \times r}$ near $\mathcal{A}$ back onto $\mathcal{A}$. This is the case because given a cost function $H : \mathcal{A} \to \mathbb{R}$, if we update $\alpha \in \mathcal{A}$ in the direction of the negative gradient of H according to

$$\alpha_{\text{new}} = \alpha - \epsilon \nabla H(\alpha),$$

$\epsilon > 0$ small, the new point usually falls off of the manifold $\mathcal{A}$. A back projection allows us to iterate the procedure.

For this purpose, we first calculate the gradient of F_{ij} at α. Differentiating (8), we get

$$\nabla F_{ij}(\alpha) = K\alpha E_j S_{ij} + K\alpha E_i S_{ij}$$
$$= K(\alpha E_j S_{ij} + \alpha E_i S_{ij}). \tag{10}$$

It can be shown that $\{\nabla F_{ij}(\alpha), 1 \leq i \leq j \leq r\}$ is a linearly independent set for α on or near $\mathcal{A}$.

Remark. For computational purposes, note that the term $(\alpha E_j S_{ij} + \alpha E_i S_{ij})$ on the right-hand side of (10) can be calculated as follows: (i) if $i \neq j$, swap the ith and jth columns of α and set all others to be zero; (ii) if $i = j$, it equals $2\alpha E_i$.

Given an $M \times r$ matrix α, the $r \times r$ symmetric residual matrix

$$R(\alpha) = I_r - F(\alpha) \tag{11}$$

quantifies how far off α is from $\mathcal{A}$. Pulling α toward $\mathcal{A}$ is equivalent to shrinking $\|R(\alpha)\|^2$ to zero. This can be done by moving α, iteratively, along the direction of the negative gradient of the function $\|R(\alpha)\|^2$ according to the update equation

$$\alpha_{\text{new}} = \alpha + \delta \sum_{1 \leq i \leq j \leq r} R_{ij}(\alpha) \nabla F_{ij}(\alpha), \tag{12}$$

with a small $\delta > 0$. The projected point is denoted $\Pi(\alpha)$.

B. The Tangent Space at α

Since $\mathcal{A}$ is defined as a level set of F, the tangent space $T_\alpha \mathcal{A}$ consists of all matrices in $\mathbb{R}^{M \times r}$ that are orthogonal to $\nabla F_{ij}(\alpha)$, for $1 \leq i \leq j \leq r$. Thus, if $Q^\alpha : \mathbb{R}^{M \times r} \to \mathbb{R}^{r(r+1)/2} \cong S_r$ is the linear map whose (i, j) component is

$$Q_{ij}^\alpha(z) = z \cdot \nabla F_{ij}(\alpha),$$

it follows that $T_\alpha \mathcal{A} = \ker Q^\alpha$. The tangent space $T_\alpha \mathcal{A}$ is a vector space of dimension $p = Mr - r(r+1)/2$. An orthonormal basis $\{\eta_1, \ldots, \eta_p\}$ of $T_\alpha \mathcal{A}$ can be obtained using a singular value decomposition of Q^α.

V. GRADIENT FLOWS AND KOCA

Let $H : \mathcal{A} \to \mathbb{R}$ be an objective function defined on the manifold $\mathcal{A}$. A deterministic gradient search for (local) maxima of H can be carried out as follows:

1) Initialize the search with $\alpha = \alpha_0 \in \mathcal{A}$.
2) Construct an orthonormal basis $\eta_1, \ldots, \eta_p$ of $T_\alpha \mathcal{A}$, as discussed in Sec. IV-B.
3) For $1 \leq i \leq p$, estimate the partial derivatives $\partial_i H$ at α using

$$\partial_i H(\alpha) \approx \frac{H(\Pi(\alpha + \epsilon \eta_i)) - H(\Pi(\alpha))}{\epsilon},$$

where Π is the projection onto $\mathcal{A}$ described earlier.

4) For a small $\delta > 0$, update α according to
$$\alpha_{\text{new}} = \Pi\left(\alpha + \delta \sum_{i=1}^{p} \partial_i H \, \eta_i\right),$$
where Π is the projection onto $\mathcal{A}$ described in Sec. IV-A.

5) Iterate until the norm of the gradient becomes smaller than a set threshold value.

In general, one encounters many local maxima during a gradient search. To escape such local peaks, a stochastic variant of the procedure just described can be used, which normally produces better estimations of global maxima. Although we do not present the details here, as in [7], a stochastic version is utilized in our implementation.

A. Application to KOCA

We apply the search strategy just described to KOCA. Suppose training data $x_1, \ldots, x_M \in \mathbb{R}^n$ and validation elements $y_1, \ldots, y_T \in \mathbb{R}^n$, both representing various classes of objects, are given. For each α in $\mathcal{A}$, recall that W_α is the subspace of $V = \text{span}\{\Phi(x_1), \ldots, \Phi(x_M)\}$ of $\mathbb{R}^m$ spanned by the orthonormal frame determined by α. Let $F(W_\alpha)$ be the recognition performance associated with W_α defined in Sec. II, and let $H: \mathcal{A} \to \mathbb{R}$ be given by
$$H(\alpha) = F(W_\alpha).$$
A stochastic gradient search for global maxima of H yields an estimation of
$$\hat{\alpha} = \underset{\alpha \in \mathcal{A}}{\arg\max}\, H(\alpha),$$
which represents the best linear subspace in the reproducing kernel Hilbert space for recognition based on the available data and the nearest-neighbor classifier.

As noted in Sec. III, a subspace of V can be represented by many different matrices α due to the possible choices of spanning orthonormal frame and the fact that $\ker(K)$ might be nonzero; K is the Gram matrix defined in (1). This implies that the partial derivatives of the cost function H vanish along the corresponding directions. Thus, in the calculation of the gradient of H, it suffices to calculate partial derivatives in directions orthogonal to these. Although it is possible to determine these directions explicitly, in practice, the computational gains are not significant. For most common choices of k, the Gram matrix K tends to be a nearly full rank matrix. In addition, the number of independent directions that correspond to choices of orthonormal frames is $r(r+1)/2$, which is rather small as compared to the dimension of $\mathcal{A}$ since $r \ll M$.

VI. Experimental Results

To illustrate the effect of kernels, we first present the results of a simple experiment using synthetic data. We considered data consisting of 63 points on each of three

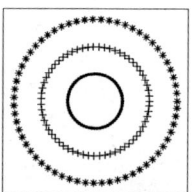

Fig. 1. Data points representing three concentric circles.

concentric circles in $\mathbb{R}^2$, as shown in Fig. 1. For each circle, we chose 8 points as training points, 47 as cross-validation points, and 8 as test points. Applying OCA with $r = 1$ (i.e., projecting the data over an optimal 1-dimensional subspace of $\mathbb{R}^2$), the best recognition performance obtained was 66%. As expected, for $r = 1$, OCA does not perform well. On the other hand, KPCA with a Gaussian kernel gives 100% recognition performance. Since the KPCA performance is already maximal, initializing a KOCA search with a 1-dimensional subspace associated with KPCA keeps the performance at 100%.

Using part of the ORL face database, we have applied the proposed algorithm to the search for optimal linear basis in the context of face recognition. The dataset used consists of faces of 10 different subjects with 10 images each. The subjects are shown in Fig. 2(a), and the images of two particular subjects are shown in Fig. 2(b) to illustrate the variation of facial expression and lighting condition.

As in other gradient-based methods, the choice of free parameters may affect results significantly. Instead of pursuing asymptotic convergence results, we have conducted numerical simulations to demonstrate the effectiveness of the proposed algorithm. We varied the subspace dimension, as well as the kernel functions.

Figure 3 shows a set of results using the polynomial kernel $k(x, y) = (x \; y)^3$ of degree 3, with subspaces of dimensions $r = 2, 3$, respectively. In each case, the search is initialized randomly, and the performance function as well as the corresponding recognition rate on test images improve significantly. In Fig. 3(a), the performance reaches 93% from the initial 40% recognition rate; in Fig. 3(b), the performance grows to 100% from the initial 53%. In both cases, the recognition rates achieved with KOCA are significantly higher than the KPCA performances, which are 53.3% and 63.3%, respectively. Three images were used for training, four as cross-validation images, and three as test images.

Similar experiments were carried out with a Gaussian kernel for several different values of r; that is, for subspaces of different dimensions. Since an important problem in object recognition is to learn representations and classifiers that generalize well to new test sets, in addition to the evolution of the performance function during the KOCA gradient search, we show the evolution of the recognition rate on

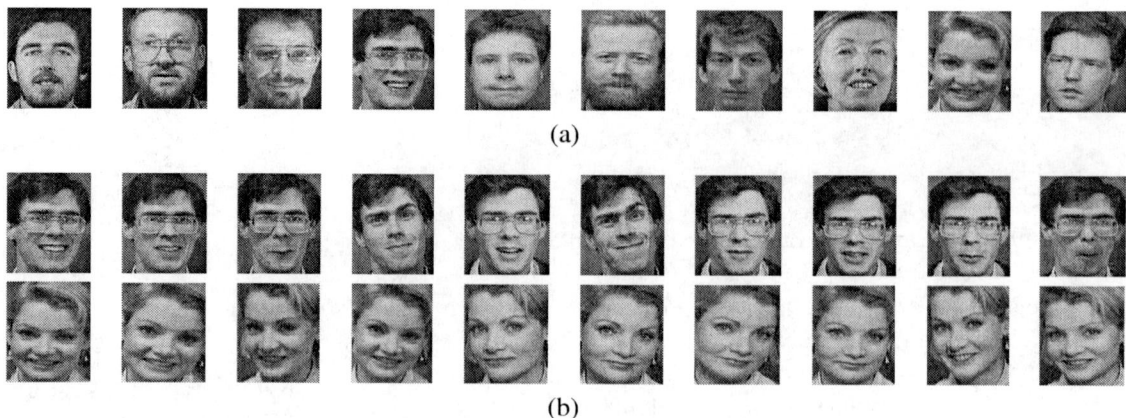

Fig. 2. Part of the ORL dataset: (a) 10 subjects used in the experiments; (b) images of three selected subjects taken at different facial expression and illumination conditions.

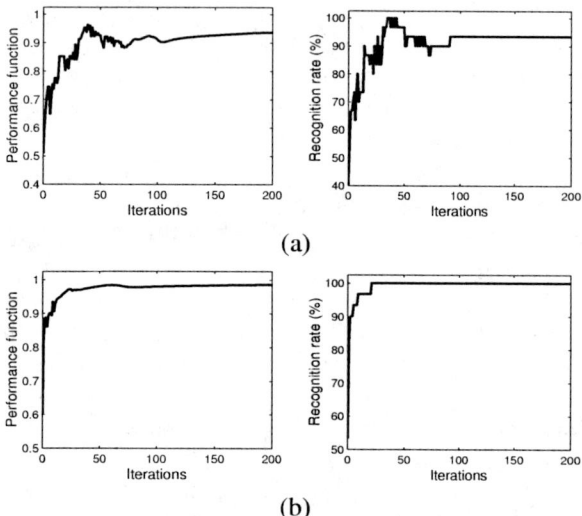

Fig. 3. Plots of the performance function H (left) and the corresponding recognition rate (right) versus the number t of iterations using projections onto r-dimensional subspaces. (a) $r = 2$ with 53.3% recognition rate from KPCA. (b) $r = 3$ with 63.3% recognition rate from KPCA.

both cross-validation and test sets. For comparison purposes, the KOCA search is always initialized with the subspace associated with KPCA. Results obtained are also compared with those for OCA, which is initialized with the subspace obtained from PCA. The results for a Gaussian kernel with $= 1.2$, as well as the corresponding results for OCA, are shown in Table I. The evolution of the performance function and recognition rate on test images during the KOCA and OCA searches are depicted in Fig. VI. Each row displays the results for a fixed value of r. In each plot, solid and dashed lines represent results for test and cross-validation images, respectively. In each row, the first two panels display the performance function and the recognition rate on test images versus the number of iterations for KOCA with a Gaussian kernel. The plots on the right show the corresponding results for OCA.

VII. SUMMARY AND DISCUSSION

In this paper, we presented a kernel analogue of Optimal Component Analysis, termed KOCA, in the framework of reproducing kernel Hilbert spaces. The basic principle is to map data in a space into a new high-dimensional feature space using a nonlinear map Φ in order to capture nonlinearities underlying the original data set using methods of linear data analysis in the new environment. We investigated both the theoretical and algorithmic aspects of KOCA and developed a computational strategy for the estimation optimal (low-dimensional) subspaces for dimension reduction and recognition performance. We applied the algorithms developed to various face recognition experiments to demonstrate the feasibility of the proposed computational approach and compared results obtained from KOCA to those derived from methods such as PCA, KPCA, and OCA. Alternative algorithmic approaches exploiting the differential geometry of Grassmann manifolds will be investigated in future work in order to enhance the computational efficiency of KOCA.

ACKNOWLEDGMENT

This work was supported in part by ARO grant W911NF-04-01-0268 and NSF grant IIS-0307998.

REFERENCES

[1] F. Bach and M. I. Jordan. Kernel independent component analysis. Technical Report CSD-01-1166, University of California, Berkeley, 2001.
[2] G. Baudat and F. Anouar. Generalized discriminant analysis using a kernel approach. *Neural Computation*, 12:2385–2404, 2000.
[3] P. N. Belhumeur, J. P. Hespanha, and D. J. Kriegman. Eigenfaces vs. fisherfaces. *IEEE Trans. Pattern Analysis and Machine Intelligence*, 19:711–720, 1997.
[4] B. Boser, I. Guyon, and V. Vapnik. A training algorithm for optimal margin classifiers. In *Proc. of the 5th Annual Workshop on Computational Learning Theory*, pages 144–152, 1992.
[5] A. Hyvarinen, J. Karhunen, and E. Oja. *Independent Component Analysis*. John Wiley and Sons, 2001.
[6] I. T. Jolliffe. *Principal component analysis*. Springer series in statistics. Springer-Verlag, 1986.

Method	r	Performance Function			Recognition Rate (test)			Recognition Rate (validation)		
		Initial	Final	Best	Initial	Final	Best	Initial	Final	Best
KOCA	1	9%	54%	57%	37%	40%	53%	20%	53%	57%
OCA	1	48%	60%	60%	37%	47%	47%	45%	28%	58%
KOCA	2	75%	84%	85%	90%	83%	97%	73%	95%	95%
OCA	2	72%	88%	88%	77%	87%	87%	75%	92%	95%
KOCA	4	83%	99%	91%	97%	97%	97%	88%	100%	100%
OCA	4	81%	94%	94%	90%	100%	100%	90%	100%	100%

TABLE I

Results of KOCA and KPCA with a Gaussian kernel, OCA and PCA applied to a collection of 10 subjects from the ORL database. KOCA and OCA are initialized with the subspaces associated with KPCA and PCA, respectively.

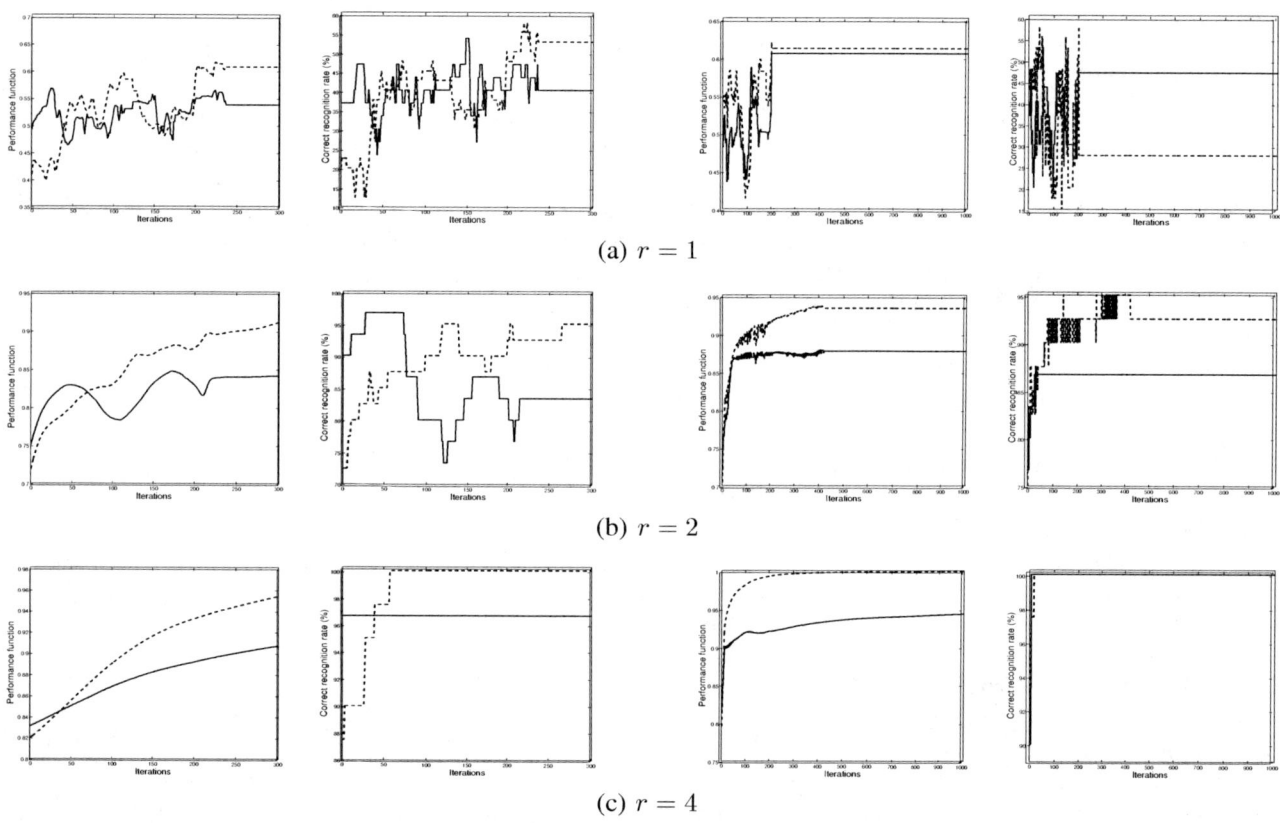

(a) $r = 1$

(b) $r = 2$

(c) $r = 4$

Fig. 4. A face recognition experiment with part of the ORL dataset. In each row, the first two panels display the evolution of the performance function and the recognition rate on test (solid lines) and cross-validation (dashed lines) images versus the number of iterations during a KOCA search with a Gaussian kernel with $\sigma = 1.2$. The KOCA search is initialized with the subspace obtained from KPCA. The corresponding results for OCA initialized with the PCA subspace is shown on the right panels.

[7] X. Liu, A. Srivastava, and K. Gallivan. Optimal linear representations of images for object recognition. *IEEE Trans. Pattern Analysis and Machine Intelligence*, 26:662–666, 2004.

[8] T. Poggio. On optimal nonlinear associative recall. *Biological Cybernetics*, 19:201–209, 1975.

[9] B. Schölkopf, A. Smola, and K. R. Müller. Nonlinear component analysis as a kernel eigenvalue problem. *Neural Computation*, 10:1299–1319, 1998.

[10] M. Turk and A. Pentland. Eigenfaces for recognition. *Journal of Cognitive Neuroscience*, 3:72–86, 1991.

[11] V. Vapnik. *The Nature of Statistical Learning Theory*. Springer-Verlag, New York, 1995.

[12] Q. Zhang and X. Liu. Kernel optimal component analysis. In *Proc. of the IEEE Workshop on Learning in Computer Vision and Pattern Recognition*, Washington, DC, 2004.

Relation between Kernel CCA and Kernel FDA

Makoto Yamada, Ali Pezeshki, and Mahmood R. Azimi-Sadjadi
Department of Electrical and Computer Engineering
Colorado State University
Fort Collins, CO 80523-1373
Tel:(970) 491-7956
E-mail: azimi@engr.colostate.edu

Abstract—In this paper, relation between multi-class linear and kernel Fisher Discriminant Analysis (FDA) and linear and kernel Canonical Correlation Analysis (CCA) is established. It is shown that in a multi-class classification problem, the CCA between feature vectors (or a nonlinearly mapped version of them) as one-channel and the class label vectors as the second channel is equivalent to multi-class FDA. The multi-class Fisher distance is found to be decomposed into a sum of terms, each of which is determined by a canonical correlation. This result is extended to the kernel formulation without explicit computation of the nonlinear mappings. A simple example is presented to numerically verify the results.

I. INTRODUCTION

Fisher Discriminant Analysis (FDA) is widely used in feature analysis and pattern classification applications, e.g. see [1]. FDA maps the original feature space into a feature subspace in order to maximize the separability between feature vectors in different classes. FDA works efficiently if the original data set is linearly separable. However, if the data is nonlinearly separable, FDA does not necessarily provide the best coordinate system for separating different classes. To address the deficiencies of the inherently linear FDA, kernel FDA has been proposed [2], [3], in which the feature vectors are implicitly mapped to a higher dimensional space, using some nonlinear mapping. Kernel FDA has been found useful in many applications such as face recognition and detection e.g. see [4] and [5].

Canonical Correlation Analysis (CCA) was proposed by Hotelling [6] and further developed by Anderson [7] for the analysis of linear dependence between two data channels. CCA decomposes the linear dependence between the original channels into the linear dependence between the canonical coordinates of the channels, where this linear dependence is easily determined by the corresponding canonical correlations [8]. CCA is also linear in nature like the original FDA. Consequently, the original CCA is not appropriate to analyze nonlinear dependence in two-channel problems. Recently, kernel-based formulations of CCA for decomposing nonlinear maps of two data channels into their canonical coordinates have been developed, e.g. see [9] -[14].

Owing to the fact that CCA maximizes the correlations between pairs of linear combinations of the two data channels, when one of the channels is the class label vector, it should lead to maximal class separability similar to FDA. This has been established in [15] in the context of Partial Least Squares (PLS). In this paper, we derive the relation between CCA and FDA for a multi-class problem in a more systematic and rigorous way. Further, we extend our results to the kernel formulations of CCA and multi-class FDA. We note that in the two-class case, the relationship between kernel FDA and kernel CCA has been shown in [12].

In [8], it has been shown that canonical correlations are fundamental for filtering and communications, as the performance measures of interest in these problems, such as information rate, linear dependence and determinant of error covariance matrix, are determined by the canonical correlations. Our results in this paper show that canonical correlations are also fundamental for pattern classification as they determine the multi-class Fisher distance.

II. A REVIEW OF CANONICAL CORRELATION ANALYSIS

Let $\mathbf{x} \in \mathbb{R}^m$ and $\mathbf{y} \in \mathbb{R}^l$ $(l \leq m)$ be two random vectors with mean vectors $\boldsymbol{\mu}_x$ and $\boldsymbol{\mu}_y$ and composite covariance matrix

$$E\left[\begin{pmatrix}\mathbf{x}-\boldsymbol{\mu}_x\\\mathbf{y}-\boldsymbol{\mu}_y\end{pmatrix}\begin{pmatrix}\mathbf{x}-\boldsymbol{\mu}_x\\\mathbf{y}-\boldsymbol{\mu}_y\end{pmatrix}^T\right]=\begin{bmatrix}R_{xx}&R_{xy}\\R_{yx}&R_{yy}\end{bmatrix} \quad (1)$$

where R_{xx} and R_{yy} are covariance matrices of $\mathbf{x}$ and $\mathbf{y}$ and $R_{xy}=R_{yx}^T$ is the cross-covariance matrix between them. The *canonical coordinates* of $\mathbf{x}$ and $\mathbf{y}$ are then defined as [8]

$$\begin{bmatrix}\mathbf{u}\\\mathbf{v}\end{bmatrix}=\begin{bmatrix}F^T&0\\0&G^T\end{bmatrix}\begin{bmatrix}R_{xx}^{-1/2}&0\\0&R_{yy}^{-1/2}\end{bmatrix}\begin{bmatrix}\mathbf{x}-\boldsymbol{\mu}_x\\\mathbf{y}-\boldsymbol{\mu}_y\end{bmatrix}, \quad (2)$$

where $R_{xx}^{1/2}$ is a square-root of $R_{xx}=R_{xx}^{1/2}R_{xx}^{T/2}$, and $F \in \mathbb{R}^{m \times m}$ and $G \in \mathbb{R}^{l \times l}$ carry the left and right singular vectors of the coherence matrix $C=R_{xx}^{-1/2}R_{xy}R_{yy}^{-T/2}$:

$$C = F\Lambda G^T \quad \text{and} \quad F^T C G = \Lambda,$$
$$F^T F = FF^T = I, \quad G^T G = GG^T = I, \quad (3)$$

$$\Lambda = \begin{bmatrix}\Lambda_l\\\mathbf{0}\end{bmatrix}; \quad \Lambda_l = diag[\lambda_1,\ldots,\lambda_l] \quad (4)$$

The diagonal singular value matrix Λ is the *canonical correlation matrix* of canonical correlations $\lambda_i = E[u_i v_i]$. Thus, the canonical correlations λ_i's are the singular values of the coherence matrix C. It is easy to verify that the squared canonical correlations λ_i^2 are the eigenvalues of the squared coherence matrix $C^2 = R_{xx}^{-1/2}R_{xy}R_{yy}^{-1}R_{yx}R_{xx}^{-T/2} = F\Lambda^2 F^T$. Clearly, $D_x^T = F^T R_{xx}^{-1/2}$ and $D_y^T = G^T R_{yy}^{-1/2}$ are the canonical coordinate maps as $\mathbf{u} = D_x^T(\mathbf{x} - \boldsymbol{\mu}_x)$ and $\mathbf{v} = D_y^T(\mathbf{y} - \boldsymbol{\mu}_y)$, and $E[\mathbf{u}\mathbf{v}^T] = D_x^T R_{xy} D_y = \Lambda$.

III. Relation between CCA and Multi-Class FDA

In this section, we establish the relationship between CCA and FDA for a multi-class problem for both linear and kernel formulations.

A. Multi-Class FDA

1) Linear Case: Let $X = [X_1, \ldots, X_l] \in \mathbb{R}^{m \times n}$ denote the original data matrix, in which $X_k = [\mathbf{x}_{k,1}, \ldots, \mathbf{x}_{k,n_k}] \in \mathbb{R}^{m \times n_k}$ contains the n_k sample vectors (patterns $\mathbf{x}_{k,i}$) that belong to class k, $n = \sum_{k=1}^{l} n_k$ is the total number of samples, and l is the number of classes. The multi-class Fisher distance is defined as [1] - [3],

$$J(W) = tr\{(W^T S_w W)^{-1}(W^T S_b W)\} \quad (5)$$

where $tr\{\cdot\}$ represents the trace operator, and

$$\begin{aligned}
S_b &= \frac{1}{n} M_x Q M_x^T \\
M_x &= [\boldsymbol{\mu}_{x_1}, \ldots, \boldsymbol{\mu}_{x_l}] \\
Q &= \left(\Omega - \frac{1}{n}\boldsymbol{\nu}\boldsymbol{\nu}^T\right) \\
\Omega &= diag[n_1, \ldots, n_l] \\
\boldsymbol{\nu} &= [n_1, \ldots, n_l]^T
\end{aligned} \quad (6)$$

and

$$\begin{aligned}
S_w &= \sum_{k=1}^{l} \frac{n_k}{n} R_{x_k x_k} \\
R_{x_k x_k} &= \frac{1}{n_k} X_k X_k^T - \boldsymbol{\mu}_{x_k} \boldsymbol{\mu}_{x_k}^T
\end{aligned} \quad (7)$$

where the matrices $S_b \in \mathbb{R}^{m \times m}$ and $S_w \in \mathbb{R}^{m \times m}$ denote the between-class and within-class scatter matrices, respectively, $\boldsymbol{\mu}_{x_k}$ is the sample mean vector of the data vectors in class k, $R_{x_k x_k}$ is the sample covariance matrix of data vectors in class k, and $W \in \mathbb{R}^{m \times r}$ ($r \leq l-1$) is the mapping matrix that maximizes $J(W)$. Here r is the number of desired FDA coordinates. The solution to W is found by solving the generalized eigenvalue problem [1] - [3]

$$S_b W = S_w W \Sigma \quad (8)$$

with $\Sigma = diag[\sigma_1, \ldots, \sigma_r]$ being the generalized eigenvalue matrix, $\sigma_1 \geq \ldots \geq \sigma_r \geq 0$. Finally, the FDA coordinates are given by $\mathbf{z} = W^T(\mathbf{x} - \boldsymbol{\mu}_x)$. Since $rank\{S_b\} = l - 1$, there are only *l-1* nonzero eigenvalues, and hence only *l-1* FDA coordinates are useful for classification.

Now, let us define the class label matrix $Y = [Y_1, \ldots, Y_l] \in \mathbb{R}^{l \times n}$, where $Y_k = [\mathbf{0}, \ldots, \mathbf{1}, \ldots, \mathbf{0}]^T \in \mathbb{R}^{l \times n_k}$ is the class label matrix for the data samples in class k, and $\mathbf{1} = [1, \ldots, 1]^T \in \mathbb{R}^{n_k}$ is a one vector. The between-class scatter matrix can be rewritten in terms of X and Y matrices as

$$S_b = \frac{1}{n} M_x Q M_x^T = \frac{1}{n} X \Theta X^T \quad (9)$$

where $\Theta = Y^T \Omega^{-1} Q \Omega^{-T} Y$. As a result, the sample data covariance matrix R_{xx} can be expressed as

$$\begin{aligned}
R_{xx} &= \frac{1}{n} X X^T - \boldsymbol{\mu}_x \boldsymbol{\mu}_x^T \\
&= \frac{1}{n} \sum_{k=1}^{l} X_k X_k^T + \frac{1}{n^2} M_x \boldsymbol{\nu} \boldsymbol{\nu}^T M_x^T \\
&= \sum_{k=1}^{l} \frac{n_k}{n} R_{x_k x_k} + \frac{1}{n} M_x Q M_x^T \\
&= S_w + S_b
\end{aligned} \quad (10)$$

Alternatively, R_{xx} can be expressed as

$$R_{xx} = \frac{1}{n} X X^T - \frac{1}{n^2} X \mathbf{1} \mathbf{1}^T X^T = \frac{1}{n} X P_{\mathbf{1}}^{\perp} X^T \quad (11)$$

where $P_{\mathbf{1}}^{\perp} = I - \frac{1}{n} \mathbf{1}\mathbf{1}^T$ is a centering matrix. Combining (10) and (11) gives

$$S_w = R_{xx} - S_b = \frac{1}{n} X \Xi X^T \quad (12)$$

where $\Xi = P_{\mathbf{1}}^{\perp} - \Theta$. From (9) and (12), the generalized eigenvalue problem in (8) can be written, in terms of the data matrix X,

$$X \Theta X^T W = X \Xi X^T W \Sigma \quad (13)$$

2) Kernel Case: In this case, the data vectors $\mathbf{x}$ are mapped using a nonlinear mapping, say $\phi : \mathbb{R}^m \longrightarrow \mathbb{R}^{m'}$ into $\phi(\mathbf{x}) \in \mathbb{R}^{m'}$, with $m' \geq m$, prior to FDA. Let us define the mapped data matrix, $\Phi = [\Phi_{\mathbf{x}_1}, \ldots, \Phi_{\mathbf{x}_l}] \in \mathbb{R}^{m' \times n}$, where $\Phi_{\mathbf{x}_k} = [\phi(\mathbf{x}_{k,1}), \ldots, \phi(\mathbf{x}_{k,n_k})] \in \mathbb{R}^{m' \times n_k}$ is the data matrix containing all the mapped data samples in class k. Also, $\boldsymbol{\mu}_\phi$ is the mean vector of Φ. Now, if we replace X by Φ in (13), we will get the following generalized eigenvalue problem for the nonlinear FDA mapping matrix $W_\phi \in \mathbb{R}^{m' \times r}$:

$$\Phi \Theta \Phi^T W_\phi = \Phi \Xi \Phi^T W_\phi \Sigma_\phi \quad (14)$$

where $\Sigma_\phi = diag[\sigma_{\phi,1}, \ldots, \sigma_{\phi,r}]$ with $\sigma_{\phi,1} \geq \ldots \geq \sigma_{\phi,r} \geq 0$. In [3], it has been shown that the solution to $W_\phi \in \mathbb{R}^{m' \times r}$ lies in the column-span of $\Phi \in \mathbb{R}^{m' \times n}$. Therefore, we can write $W_\phi = \Phi \hat{W}_\phi$, where $\hat{W}_\phi \in \mathbb{R}^{n \times r}$. Pre-multiplying (14) by Φ^T and defining the kernel Gram matrix K as $K = \Phi^T \Phi$ yields the following generalized eigenvalue problem for the kernel FDA,

$$\Gamma \hat{W}_\phi = \Upsilon \hat{W}_\phi \Sigma_\phi \quad (15)$$

where $\Gamma = K \Theta K$, $\Upsilon = K \Xi K^T$. We note this generalized eigenvalue problem has also been derived in [2]. Finally, the FDA coordinates of the nonlinearly mapped data are given by $\mathbf{z}_\phi = W_\phi^T(\phi(x) - \boldsymbol{\mu}_\phi) = \hat{W}_\phi^T(k_\phi(X, \mathbf{x}) - k_\phi(X, \boldsymbol{\mu}_x))$, where $k_\phi(X, \mathbf{x}) = \Phi^T \phi(\mathbf{x})$ and $k_\phi(X, \boldsymbol{\mu}_x) = \Phi^T \boldsymbol{\mu}_\phi$.

B. Relation to CCA

1) Linear Case: Let, the ensemble set for the **x**-channel be formed by the sample vectors in the data matrix X, then the sample covariance matrix for **x** is given by (11). Similarly, let the ensemble set of the **y**-channel be formed by the class label matrix Y. Thus, the sample covariance matrix for **y** is

$$R_{yy} = \frac{1}{n}YY^T - \boldsymbol{\mu}_y \boldsymbol{\mu}_y^T \quad (16)$$

where $\boldsymbol{\mu}_y = \frac{1}{n}Y\mathbf{1} = \frac{1}{n}\boldsymbol{\nu}$. Using the definitions of Ω, $\boldsymbol{\nu}$, and Q, the matrix R_{yy} may be rewritten as

$$R_{yy} = \frac{1}{n}\left(\Omega - \frac{1}{n}\boldsymbol{\nu}\boldsymbol{\nu}^T\right) = \frac{1}{n}Q \quad (17)$$

In a similar fashion, the sample cross-covariance matrix R_{xy} between the mapped data and their corresponding labels is given by

$$\begin{aligned} R_{xy} &= \frac{1}{n}XY^T - \boldsymbol{\mu}_x \boldsymbol{\mu}_y^T \\ &= \frac{1}{n}M_x\left(\Omega - \frac{1}{n}\boldsymbol{\nu}\boldsymbol{\nu}^T\right) = \frac{1}{n}M_x Q \end{aligned} \quad (18)$$

Using the expression for the squared coherence matrix C^2 in Section II, and $R_{xx} = S_w + S_b$, we can write

$$\begin{aligned} C^2 = F\Lambda^2 F^T &= R_{xx}^{-1/2} R_{xy} R_{yy}^{-1} R_{yx} R_{xx}^{-T/2} \\ &= (S_w + S_b)^{-1/2} (\frac{1}{n}M_x Q)(\frac{1}{n}Q)^{-1} \\ &\quad \times (\frac{1}{n}M_x Q)^T (S_w + S_b)^{-T/2} \\ &= (S_w + S_b)^{-1/2} S_b (S_w + S_b)^{-T/2} \end{aligned} \quad (19)$$

Pre-multiplying the last line in (19) by $(S_w + S_b)^{-T/2}$ and post-multiplying it by $(S_w + S_b)^{T/2}$, and rearranging the equation yields

$$(S_w + S_b)^{-1} S_b = (S_w + S_b)^{-T/2} F\Lambda^2 F^T (S_w + S_b)^{T/2} \quad (20)$$

Using $S_b = (S_w + S_b) - S_w$, (20) can alternatively be written as

$$\begin{aligned} (S_w + S_b)^{-1} S_w &= (S_w + S_b)^{-T/2} F(I - \Lambda^2) \\ &\quad \times F^T (S_w + S_b)^{T/2} \end{aligned} \quad (21)$$

Taking the inverse of both sides of (21), assuming S_w is nonsingular matrix and noting that F is an orthogonal matrix, gives

$$\begin{aligned} S_w^{-1} S_b &= (S_w + S_b)^{-T/2} F((I - \Lambda^2)^{-1} - I) \\ &\quad \times F^T (S_w + S_b)^{T/2} \end{aligned} \quad (22)$$

Now, pre-multiplying (22) by S_w, and post-multiplying it by $(S_w + S_b)^{-T/2} F$ gives,

$$S_b D_x = S_w D_x (\Lambda^{-2} - I)^{-1} \quad (23)$$

where $D_x = (S_w + S_b)^{-T/2} F = R_{xx}^{-T/2} F$ was defined in Section II. Equation (23) is the same as the generalized eigenvalue problem of FDA in (8) with $W = D_{x,r}$ and $\Sigma = [(\Lambda^{-2} - I)^{-1}]_{r \times r}$ where $D_{x,r} \in \mathbb{R}^{m \times r}$ and $[(\Lambda^{-2} - I)^{-1}]_{r \times r} \in \mathbb{R}^{r \times r}$ carry the first r canonical coordinate mapping vectors (the first r columns of $D_x \in \mathbb{R}^{m \times m}$) and the upper $r \times r$ block of $\Sigma = (\Lambda^{-2} - I)^{-1}$. Applying the trace operator to both sides of (23) and using the properties of trace, the Fisher Distance d can be written in terms of the canonical correlations as

$$d = \sum_{k=1}^{l-1} \frac{\lambda_k^2}{1 - \lambda_k^2} \quad (24)$$

i.e. Fisher distance is decomposed into sum of terms each of which is determined by a canonical correlation. This shows that the contribution of each canonical coordinate pair to the Fisher distance is determined by its corresponding canonical correlation. This property can be used to find a subset of canonical coordinates that contribute the most towards the Fisher distance.

Remark 1: We note that the generalized eigenvalue problem of (23) for D_x must be solved while enforcing the orthogonality condition $D_x^T S_w D_x = I$. With this $D_{x,r}$ and $[(\Lambda^{-2} - I)^{-1}]_{r \times r}$ will be equal to W and Σ, if in solving (8) $W^T S_w W = I$ is enforced. Although in the original formulation of multi-class FDA in (5) $W^T S_w W = I$ is not enforced, it can easily be verified that maximizing $J(W)$ is equivalent to maximizing $tr\{W^T S_b W\}$ under the constraint that $tr\{W^T S_w W\} = I$. The reason is that in (5), $J(W)$ is invariant to nonsingular transformations of W.

2) Kernel Case: In this case, the **x**-channel data vectors **x** are mapped using the nonlinear mapping $\phi : \mathbb{R}^m \longrightarrow \mathbb{R}^{m'}$ into $\phi(\mathbf{x}) \in \mathbb{R}^{m'}$, with $m' \geq m$, prior to CCA, while the **y**-channel vectors, i.e. class labels, are not mapped. Now, if we replace X by the mapped data matrix Φ in (19), we can rewrite C^2

$$S_b^\phi D_\phi = R_{\phi\phi} D_\phi \Lambda_\phi^2 \quad (25)$$

where

$$\begin{aligned} D_\phi &= R_{\phi\phi}^{-T/2} F_\phi \\ R_{\phi\phi} &= \frac{1}{n} \Phi P_1^\perp \Phi^T \\ S_b^\phi &= \frac{1}{n} \Phi \Theta \Phi^T \end{aligned} \quad (26)$$

The matrices $P_1^\perp$ and Θ are defined as before. Using (26) for $R_{\phi\phi}$ and S_b^ϕ in (25) gives

$$\Phi \Theta \Phi^T D_\phi = \Phi P_1^\perp \Phi^T D_\phi \Lambda_\phi^2 \quad (27)$$

In [10] and [11], it has been shown that $D_\phi = \Phi \hat{D}_\phi$ with $\hat{D}_\phi \in \mathbb{R}^{n \times n}$. Inserting this expression in (27), pre-multiplying it by Φ^T, and using $K = \Phi^T \Phi$ yields the following generalized eigenvalue problem for kernel CCA,

$$\Gamma \hat{D}_\phi = \Psi \hat{D}_\phi \Lambda_\phi^2 \quad (28)$$

where $\Gamma = K\Theta K$ and $\Psi = KP_1^\perp K$. The canonical coordinate mapping matrix D_ϕ^T resolves $\phi(\mathbf{x})$ into its corresponding canonical coordinates, $\mathbf{u}_\phi = D_\phi^T(\phi(x) - \boldsymbol{\mu}_\phi) = \hat{D}_\phi^T(k_\phi(X, \mathbf{x}) - k_\phi(X, \boldsymbol{\mu}_x))$, where $k_\phi(X, \mathbf{x}) = \Phi^T \phi(\mathbf{x})$ and $k_\phi(X, \boldsymbol{\mu}_x) = \Phi^T \boldsymbol{\mu}_\phi$.

Using (9)-(12), the kernel version of (10) is $\Psi = \Gamma + \Upsilon$ where Ψ, Γ, and Υ are defined as before. Using this property, (28) may be rewritten as,

$$\begin{aligned} \Gamma \hat{D}_\phi &= (\Gamma + \Upsilon)\hat{D}_\phi \Lambda_\phi{}^2 \\ &= \Upsilon \hat{D}_\phi (\Lambda_\phi^{-2} - I)^{-1} \end{aligned} \quad (29)$$

Comparing (29) with (15), it is evident that $D_{\phi,r}$ is the same as kernel FDA mapping matrix W_ϕ, when proper orthogonality conditions (like those in *Remark 1*) are enforced in solving (15) and (29). Moreover, the eigenvalues $\frac{\lambda_{\phi,k}^2}{1-\lambda_{\phi,k}^2}$ are equal to the eigenvalues in the kernel FDA $\sigma_{\phi,i}$.

Consequently, the multi-class Fisher distance for the non-linear mapped data is

$$d_\phi = \sum_{k=1}^{l-1} \frac{\lambda_{\phi,k}^2}{1-\lambda_{\phi,k}^2} \quad (30)$$

The same observation made about the connection between canonical correlations and Fisher distance in the linear case may also be made here.

IV. SIMULATION RESULTS

In this section, the simple 3-class IRIS data set is used to validate the relationship between kernel CCA and kernel FDA developed in this paper. The main objective is to show the multi-class FDA (or kernel FDA) is equivalent to CCA (or kernel CCA) between feature vectors and the corresponding class label vectors. Thus, it is not our intention to compare the class separability of the linear FDA or CCA versus their kernel version.

The IRIS data is two dimensional (2-D) and the three classes correspond to three Iris flower types, namely Setosa, Versicolour, and Virginica. The 2-D feature vector consists of petal and sepal length. For each class, there are 50 samples. Thus, for kernel CCA, the data matrix for all 3 classes $X \in \mathbb{R}^{2 \times 150}$ and class label matrix is $Y \in \mathbb{R}^{3 \times 150}$. The kernel function is chosen to be a Gaussian kernel with variance of 0.3.

The mapping matrices D_ϕ and W_ϕ and eigenvalues of kernel CCA and kernel FDA are calculated using the corresponding expressions in (28) and (15). Figure 1 shows the plot of the first canonical coordinate of the mapped data versus the second one. The three classes are shown by 'o' for the Iris Setosa, '▷' for the Iris Versicolour, and '+' for the Iris Virginica classes. As can be seen, the first canonical coordinate with the canonical correlation 0.9997 can separate the combined Setosa and Versicolour classes from Virginica class. The second canonical coordinate with the canonical correlation 0.8861 can then be used to separate the Setosa and Virginica classes from Versicolour. Figure 2 shows the same plot for kernel FDA. As can be seen, the results are the same ignoring the sign change of the mapped Versicolour and Virginica classes.

We note that flipping the signs of canonical coordinates of x- and y-channels does not change the canonical correlations, and hence the Fisher distance. The differences between the

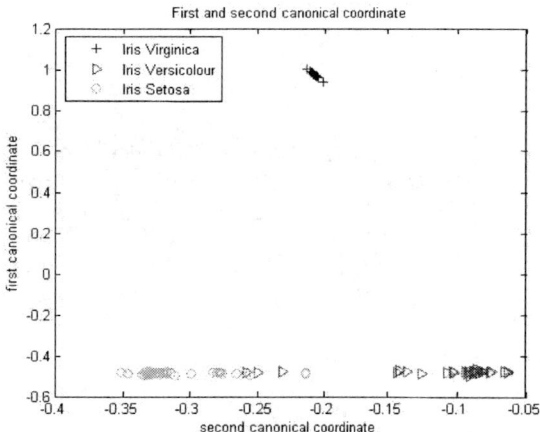

Fig. 1. First and second kernel CCA coordinates.

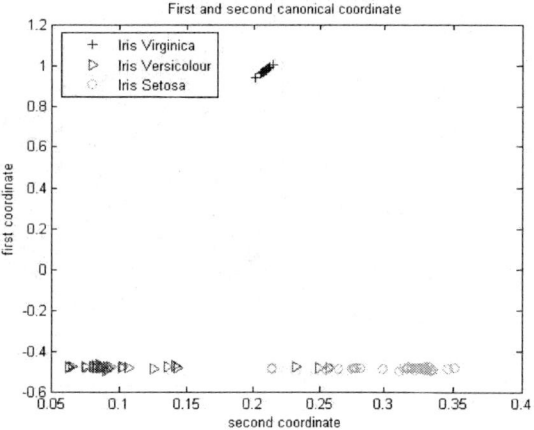

Fig. 2. First and second kernel FDA coordinates.

ith canonical coordinates, $||u_{\phi_i}| - |z_{\phi_i}||, \forall i$, were found to be very small (on the order of 10^{-11}) suggesting that they are almost identical. Figures 3 and 4 show the contour plots of the first mapped coordinate by kernel CCA and kernel FDA, respectively, while Figures 5 and 6 show the plots of the second mapped coordinate for each. The white regions represent high values while dark regions correspond to lower values. Although, the intensities in Figure 5 are negative of those in Figure 6, visual evaluation of these results reveal the fact that the mapped coordinates of kernel CCA are the same as those of kernel FDA. Moreover, from the results in Table I, the corresponding Fisher distances are found to be exactly the same, as expected.

When the classes are separable, their canonical correlations approach 1.0, because CCA maximizes the correlation between class features and distinct class labels. As mentioned before, the first canonical coordinate separates Setosa and Versicolour classes from Virginica class and the second canonical coordinate separates Setosa and Virginica classes from Versicolour class. This result implies that a coordinate may be

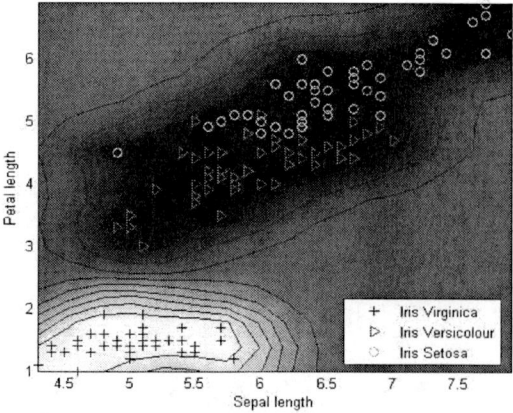

Fig. 3. First kernel CCA coordinate.

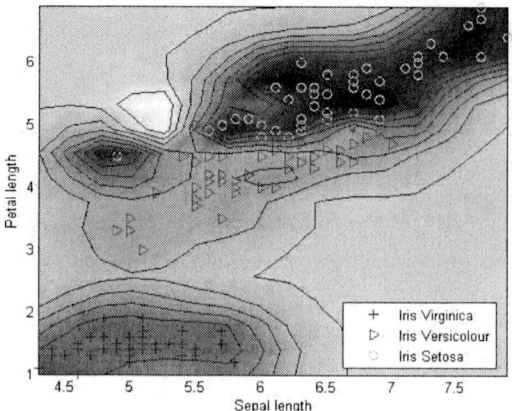

Fig. 5. Second kernel CCA coordinate.

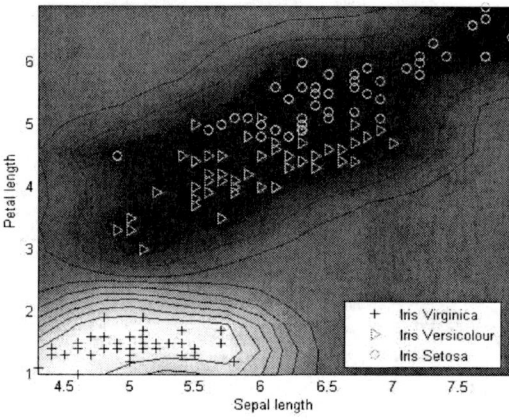

Fig. 4. First kernel FDA coordinate.

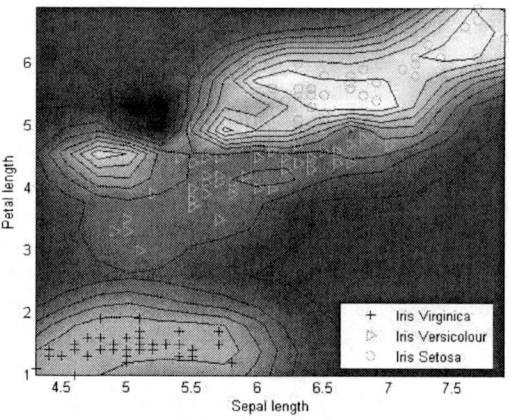

Fig. 6. Second kernel FDA coordinate.

able to separate one class from the others, and the corresponding canonical correlation is a measure of the separability of these classes. Therefore, from (24), Fisher distance, which is a measure of total class separability, represents the contributions from each important coordinate.

The ith Fisher Distance	kernel FDA	kernel CCA
$i = 1$	3588.4	3588.4
$i = 2$	7.7796	7.7796
$i = 3 \ldots 150$	0.0	0.0

TABLE I
MULTI-CLASS FISHER DISTANCE USING KERNEL FDA AND KERNEL CCA.

Table II shows the two canonical correlations of the original channels $\mathbf{x}$- and $\mathbf{y}$-channels and the canonical correlations of $\phi(\mathbf{x})$ and $\mathbf{y}$ obtained from the kernel-based CCA. For the linear CCA, since only the first canonical correlation has high value, the class separability depends almost exclusively on the first canonical coordinate.

Figure 7 shows the first and second canonical coordinates of the linear CCA (or linear FDA), and as can be seen only the first coordinate is useful for classification. On the other hand, kernel CCA leads to high values for both the first and second canonical correlations (see Table II), and thus both of the canonical coordinates have significant contributions to class separation. As a result, using kernel CCA (or kernel FDA) all three classes are better separated than the linear CCA (or linear FDA).

The ith Canonical Correlation	Linear	Kernel
$i = 1$	0.9507	0.9997
$i = 2$	0.0328	0.8861
$i = 3 \ldots 150$	0.0	0.0

TABLE II
CANONICAL CORRELATIONS OF ORIGINAL $\mathbf{x}$ AND $\mathbf{y}$, AND MAPPED $\phi(\mathbf{x})$ AND $\mathbf{y}$.

As a final note, it is obvious that any other data set could have been used to numerically verify the fact that CCA (or

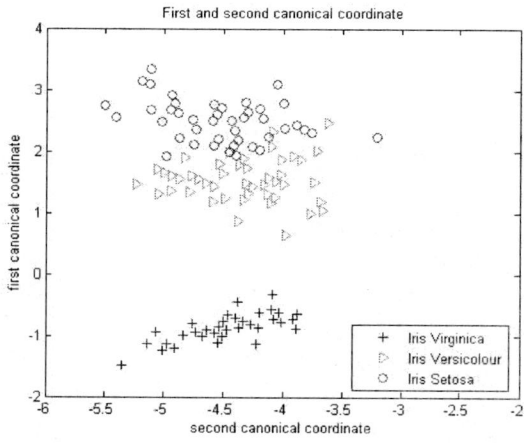

Fig. 7. First and second linear CCA coordinates.

kernel CCA) with one channel being class label vectors is equivalent to FDA (or kernel FDA). Nonetheless, the IRIS data set is used here for providing better insight on the properties of CCA (or kernel CCA) for this application.

V. Conclusion

The relation between the multi-class Fisher Discriminant Analysis (FDA) and Canonical Correlation Analysis (CCA) has been established. In a multi-class classification problem CCA between the feature vectors and class label vectors is equivalent to FDA. The multi-class Fisher distance is decomposed into the sum of terms, each of which is determined by a canonical correlation. The relation between CCA and FDA for both linear and kernel-nonlinear formulations has been established. Simulation results on the three class IRIS data set verified that the mapped coordinates in kernel CCA indeed correspond to those of the kernel FDA. The relations between canonical correlations and the multi-class Fisher distance were also numerically verified.

Finally, in [3] and [16], a kernel formulation for Principal Component Analysis (PCA) has been derived. Although, there is no direct connection between PCA and CCA, the way the kernel formulations are derived are more or less similar, in the sense that both PCA and CCA involve kernelizing an eigenvalue problem. To be more specific, in PCA a standard eigenvalue problem and in CCA a generalized eigenvalue problem is kernelized. Nonetheless, PCA is inherently a one-channel problem while CCA is a two-channel problem. Thus, canonical coordinates are as fundamentals for a two-channel problem as principal components are for a one-channel problems.

VI. Acknowledgement

This study was funded by the Office of Naval Research (ONR) under contracts N00014-02-1-0006 and N00014-02-C-0185.

References

[1] R. O. Duda, P. E. Hart, and D. G. Stork, *Pattern Classification* (2nd ed), New York: Wiley, 2001.

[2] J. Ma, J. L. Sancho-Gómez, and S. C. Ahalt, "Nonlinear multiclass discriminant analysis," *IEEE Signal Process. Lett.*, vol. 10, pp. 196-199, July 2003.

[3] B. Schölkopf and A. J. Smola, *Learning with Kernels, Support Vector Machines, Regularization, Optimization, and Beyond.* Cambridge, MA: MIT Press, 2002.

[4] O. Hasegawa and T. Kurita, "A kernel logit approach for face and non-face classification," *Sixth IEEE Workshop on Applications of Computer Vision*, pp. 100-104, Dec 2002.

[5] L. Qingshan, L. Hanqing, and M. Songde, "Improving kernel Fisher discriminant analysis for face recognition," *IEEE Trans. Circuits Systems Video Technol.*, vol. 14, pp. 42-49, Jan 2004

[6] H. Hotelling, "Relation between two sets of variates," *Biometrika*, vol. 28 pp. 321-377, 1936.

[7] T. W. Anderson, *An Introduction to Multivariate Statistical Analysis*, New York: Wiley, 2003.

[8] L. L. Scharf and C. T. Mullis, "Canonical coordinates and the geometry of inference, rate and capacity," *IEEE Trans. Signal Processing*, vol. 48, pp. 824-831, March 2000.

[9] A. Pezeshki, M. R. Azimi-Sadjadi, and L. L. Scharf, "Kernel-based canonical coordinate decomposition of two-channel nonlinear maps," *Proc. 2004 Int. Joint Conf. Neural Networks (IJCNN2004)*, pp. 3019-3024, July 2004.

[10] A. Pezeshki, L. L. Scharf, M. R. Azimi-Sadjadi, "Empirical canonical coordinate decompositions in subspaces for two-channel linear and nonlinear maps," *IEEE Trans. Signal Processing*, submitted sept. 2004, under revision.

[11] A. Pezeshki, L. L. Scharf, M. R. Azimi-Sadjadi, "Empirical canonical correlation analysis in subspaces," *Thirty-Eighth Asilomar Conference on Signals, Systems, and Computers*, pp. 994-997, Pacific Grove, CA, Nov. 2004.

[12] T. Van Gestel, J. A. K. Suykens, J. De Brabanter, B. De Moor, and J. Vandewalle, "Kernel canonical correlation analysis and least-squares support vector machines," *Proc. 2001 Int. conf. Artificial Neural Networks (ICANN2001)*, pp. 384-389, 2001.

[13] S. Akaho, "A kernel method for canonical correlation analysis," *International Meeting on Psychometric Society (IMPS2001)*, 2001.

[14] M. Kuss and T. Graepel, "The geometry of kernel canonical correlation analysis," *Technical Report TR-108*, Max Planck Institute for Biological Cybernetics, Tbingen, Germany, May 2003.

[15] M. Barker and W. S. Rayens, "Partial least squares for discrimination," *Journal of Chemometrics*, vol. 17, pp. 166-173, 2003.

[16] B. Schölkopf, A. Smola, and K. R. Müller, "Nonlinear component analysis as a kernel eigenvalue problem," *Neural Computation*, 10:1299-1319, 1998.

[17] G. H. Golub and C. F. Van Loan, *Matrix Computations* (3rd ed), Baltimore, MD: John Hopkins Univ. Press, 1996.

Extraction of Frame-Difference Features based on PCA and ICA for Lip-Reading

Kyungsuk David Lee[1], Michelle Jeungeun Lee[2], and Soo-Young Lee[2]
[1] Department of Computer Science, University of Wisconsin, Madison, WI, USA
[2] Department of BioSystems, Korea Advanced Institute of Science and Technology
373-1 Guseong-dong, Yuseong-gu, Daejeon 305-701, Korea (South)
E-mail: ksdavidlee@gmail.com, michelle_lee@kaist.ac.kr, sylee@kaist.ac.kr

Abstract - **The features of human lip motion from video clips are extracted by Principal Component Analysis (PCA) and Independent Component Analysis (ICA). Unlike many other features extracted from single-frame static images or multi-frame dynamic images, we extracted the features from the differences of consecutive frames. The PCA results in global features, while local features are extracted by the ICA. The features are extracted from several consecutive multi-frame differences as well as single-frame differences. The dynamic nature of multi-frame differences is more eminent. The resulting features maybe applicable in lip-reading and synthesis of lip motion videos with Text-to-Speech capability.**

Keywords- **Principal Component Analysis (PCA), Independent Component Analysis (ICA), lip-reading, feature extraction**

I. INTRODUCTION

Recently the extraction of basis features from motion video has attracted a lot of attention. Especially extracted features from lip motion may be utilized to recognize noisy speeches in cooperation with lip-reading as well as to graphically synthesize the lip motion for Text-To-Speech applications [1]. Different decomposition techniques are applied for extracting basis elements of video images.

Principal Component Analysis (PCA) had been widely used for feature extraction from images [2], while Non-negative Matrix Factorization (NMF) [3] and Independent Component Analysis (ICA) [4] have been applied recently. The PCA-basis features are non-local, and ICA results in localized basis features [5].

In previous studies the features are extracted from single-frame images and the sequential nature of the motion video is not utilized. However, it is commonly understood that the human perception of facial motion goes through two different pathways, i.e., the lateral fusifom gyrus for the invariant aspects of faces and the superior temporal sulcus for the changeable aspects of faces such as lip movement. [6] Therefore, the features of lip motion may be different from the features for the face recognition, and require more representation from consecutive multiple frames. In this context we recently had reported features extracted from multi-frame images of video clips. [7] The PCA, NMF, and ICA algorithms were applied with efficient information representation.

On the other hand the differences between consecutive frame images are the popular choice of efficient video coding. In this paper, we further extended the feature extraction into the difference of consecutive video frames with PCA and ICA algorithms. It corresponds to the difference coding in the video compression. Although the NMF algorithm had also been applied to the extraction of multi-frame features [7], the non-negative characteristics are not appropriate for the frame differences and only PCA and ICA algorithms are studied here.

Both the results from the single-differences and multiple consecutive differences are reported here. The effects of the time frames and statistical characteristics are investigated for both the extracted features and corresponding representation coefficients.

II. FEATURE EXTRACTION ALGORITHMS

Let $\mathbf{s} = [s_1 \ldots s_N]^T$ be the unknown basis image (features), and $\mathbf{x} = [x_1 \ldots x_N]^T$ be the observed image which are considered as the linear mixture of basis images. Here, N is the number of pixels in the images, and $\mathbf{s}$ and $\mathbf{x}$ are 1-dimensional re-shaped versions of 2-dimensional images by concatenating all columns. As shown in Fig.1, the mixing model can be written as the combination of s and unknown mixing matrix **A**, i.e.,

$$\mathbf{x} = \mathbf{A}\mathbf{s} \text{ or } \mathbf{X}=\mathbf{A}\mathbf{S}, \qquad (1)$$

where $\mathbf{X} = [\mathbf{x}_1 \ldots \mathbf{x}_M]$ and $\mathbf{S} = [\mathbf{s}_1 \ldots \mathbf{s}_M]$ are matrices consisting of all the observed and basis images as the columns, respectively, and *M* is the number of images. The feature extraction algorithms find the unknown basis images (features) **S** and the mixing matrix **A** from the observed images **X** only.

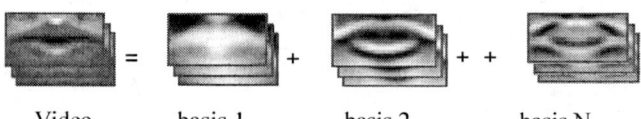

Video   basis 1   basis 2   basis N

Fig.1. The video clip consists of linear combination of basis features with multiple frames. For the difference coding in this paper the video is divided into the initial image and the differences of consecutive frames.

This is an underdetermined problem, and additional constraints are usually required. The popular choices are orthogonal basis images for PCA, linear independence for ICA, and non-negative characteristics of NMF. Since the non-negative characteristics are not guaranteed for the frame differences, only PCA and ICA are adopted here.

Principal Component Analysis (PCA) is probably the most commonly used technique for image processing tasks. PCA is an unsupervised learning that produces global feature vectors. PCA computes a set of subspace basis vectors for an image database, and project the images into the compressed subspace. PCA generates compressed data with minimum mean-squared reprojection error.

Data samples are arrayed in a matrix $\mathbf{X}$, with one column per sample image. The basis images are the eigenvectors of the covariance matrix, $(\mathbf{X} - \mathbf{\mu})(\mathbf{X} - \mathbf{\mu})^T$, and are ordered according to the eigenvalues of the covariance matrix. Here, $\mathbf{\mu}$ is a matrix, of which each column is the mean vector of $\mathbf{X}$.

Only the eigenvectors associated with large eigenvalues may be used to define the subspace for efficient representation. This compression makes the computation more efficient to compare images in subspaces with significantly reduced dimensions [5]. Since the axes of larger variance are more likely contribute to the significant part of images and axes of small variance are probably less important, this compression is reasonable.

The ICA decomposes observed data images into linear combinations of statistically independent sources. While PCA is based on the second-order statistics of the images set, ICA decorrelates the high-order moments of the input in addition to the second-order moments [8][9]. Also, with the super-Gaussian probability density functions for the spare coding, this algorithm results in local features.

By maximizing the log-likelihood of $\mathbf{x}$ with a given $\mathbf{A}$, the learning rule can be derived as

$$\Delta \mathbf{A} \propto \mathbf{A}\mathbf{A}^T \frac{\partial}{\partial \mathbf{A}} \log P(\mathbf{x}|\mathbf{A}) = -\mathbf{A}(\mathbf{I} - \varphi(\hat{\mathbf{s}}) \cdot \hat{\mathbf{s}}^T), \quad (2)$$

where $\varphi(\hat{s}_i) = -\partial \log P(\hat{s}_i)/\partial s_i$ is the score function, $\mathbf{I}$ is the identity matrix. The $\mathbf{A}\mathbf{A}^T$ is multiplied for the faster convergence with natural gradients [9]. $\hat{\mathbf{s}} = [\hat{s}_1 \, \hat{s}_2 \, \cdots \, \hat{s}_N]^T$ is the inferred hidden variables, which can be obtained by finding the maximum a *posteriori* value of $\mathbf{s}$:

$$\hat{\mathbf{s}} = \max_{\mathbf{s}} P(\mathbf{s}|\mathbf{x},\mathbf{A}) = \max_{\mathbf{s}} P(\mathbf{x}|\mathbf{A},\mathbf{s}) P(\mathbf{s}). \quad (3)$$

When the mixing matrix is square nonsingular and the additive noise does not exist, the solution for $\mathbf{s}$ can be found as $\hat{\mathbf{s}} = \mathbf{A}^{-1}\mathbf{x}$.

III. LIP MOTION DATA

The lip motion videos employed for this research are the video part of the Tulips database [11], which consists of both video and audio data. The data set contains 96 digitized videos of 12 individuals (9 males and 3 females) saying the first four digits in English ("one", "two", "three" and "four") twice. The images are made for every 1/30 second, and the number of image frames for each video clip is between 6 and 16. The original dataset consists of 934 images, with 65 x 87 pixels each with 8-bit gray levels. Ten corners of the lips are marked by human hands for each of the images.

The images were first corrected for the rotation based on the manually-specified critical points (corners) on the lip boundary. Then, the lip images are segmented and normalized in fixed size, i.e., 32 x 18 pixels. To reduce the computational complexity, each image was vertically cut into the left-half and the right-half, and considered to be two different images. The dataset now consists of 1868 images of which each one is re-sampled into 16 x 18 (288 in total) pixels.

All the feature extractions were done on these half-images. However, in all the subsequent lip figures, the full images were restored with left-to-right symmetry for easy visual understanding.

The iterative ICA algorithm requires extensive computation for the large number of images. For the efficient computation of the ICA-based features it is commonly adopted to get the essence of the original images using the PCA. It this paper the dominant 60 principal components, which approximate the frame-difference images with about 95% accuracy, are used for the extraction of ICA-based features.

Before applying the PCA and ICA for the feature extraction, we first made a new database for the frame differences. A frame-difference image was obtained by subtracting the current frame image from the next-frame image, i.e., $\mathbf{x}^d(t)=\mathbf{x}(t+1)-\mathbf{x}(t)$, within one video clip. Since the video clips in the original Tulips database have 6 to 16 frames, each element in this new database had 5 to 15 frames. By considering these difference images as independent, we obtained the single-frame-difference database. The sample original image frames and their frame differences in the reduced images are shown in Figs.2(a) and 2(b), respectively.

IV. EXTRACTED FEATURES

The *n*-frame-difference database was obtained by considering the *n* consecutive difference-frame images as an element of the database. Therefore, the *n*-frame-difference images consist of $288n$ pixels. Both the PCA and ICA are applied to these databases with the *n* from 1 to 4.

In Table I the numbers of principal components are shown with given representation accuracy for the frame-difference images. The results for the framed images are shown in Table II for comparison. Here, the principal components of the *L*-highest covariance are used for the representation. Also, the compression ratio, i.e., *C = (Number of PCAs) / (Number of Pixels)*, is shown.

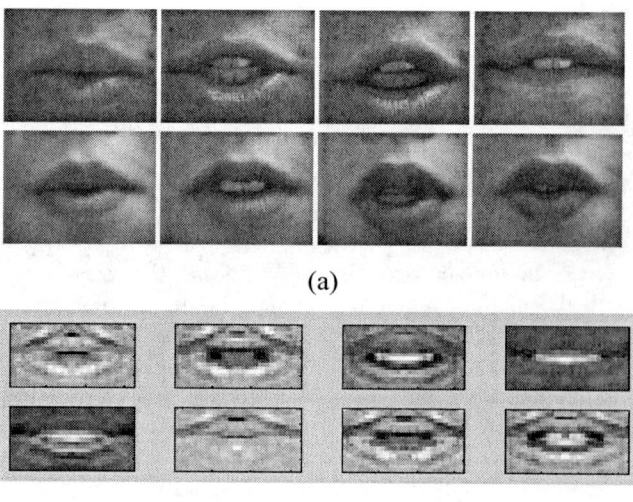

(a)

(b)

Fig.2. (a) Example original images from the Tulips database. Each image consists of 65 x 87 pixels with 8-bit gray levels. (b) Differences of consecutive frame images. The lip images were corrected for the rotation and segmented by the manually-marked corners, and the segmented images were resized to 32 x 18 pixels.

Table I. Numbers of Principal Components and Compression Ratios for Given Representation Accuracy with PCAs from Frame-Difference Images

Accuracy	Single Frame	2 Frames	3 Frames	4 Frames
90%	36 (0.13)	62 (0.11)	84 (0.10)	102 (0.09)
95%	62 (0.22)	108 (0.19)	144 (0.17)	173 (0.15)
99%	139 (0.48)	246 (0.43)	327 (0.38)	382 (0.33)

Table II. Numbers of Principal Components and Compression Ratios for Given Representation Accuracy with PCAs from Frame Images

Accuracy	Single Frame	2 Frames	3 Frames	4 Frames
90%	11 (0.038)	12 (0.021)	14 (0.016)	15 (0.013)
95%	19 (0.066)	23 (0.040)	27 (0.031)	30 (0.026)
99%	56 (0.194)	78 (0.135)	95 (0.110)	109 (0.095)

It turned out that for the single-frame-difference images the L becomes 36, 62, and 139 for the 90%, 95%, and 99% accuracy, respectively. For the original frame images it is 11, 19, and 56, respectively. Although the frame-difference images require more numbers of principal components than the original images for the same representation accuracy, the frame-differences have usually much smaller covariance than the images themselves and the absolute values of the representation errors may be comparable with the same number of principal components.

The more consecutive frames are used, i.e., the larger values of L, the more principal component features needed to perform the same representation accuracy. It is shown that single-frame approaches are more efficient compare to the multi-frame approaches. However, for videos with the same number of frames, much smaller numbers of multi-frame features are required, and the multi-frame features have much higher compression ratios for the video representation.

In Figures 3 and 4 the extracted difference features of the lip motion videos are shown for the PCA and ICA, respectively. In the figures (a), (b), (c), and (d) represent features with single, 2, 3 and 4 consecutive frames, respectively. Only top features, sorted by the variance of the corresponding coefficients and their accumulated values are shown for simplicity. Unlike the features from multi-frame images with strong static characters [6], i.e., small differences between consecutive frames in the multi-frame features, the multi-frame effects on the extracted features are much more eminent for the frame-difference features. The large changes of difference features between consecutive frames denote the dynamic nature of the extracted features, and the multiple-frame approaches may be advantageous over the popular single-frame approach.

It is interesting to compare the results between the PCA and ICA-based features. As expected from the single-frame cases [7], the PCA results in global features, while the ICA results in local features. Also, the dynamic characteristics of multi-frame differences are more eminent with the ICA-based features. It may be understood that the sparse representation of the ICA-based features contributes to the high dynamic characteristics, which may be useful to the classification.

The efficiency of data representation may be related to the sparseness of the features and corresponding coefficient values. With only a few non-zero values, the sparse representation results in efficient data coding, transmission, and storage.

In Fig.5, the distribution of extracted features and corresponding representation coefficients are shown as histograms for the single-frame-difference images. For the PCA, while the features have sub-Gaussian distributions, the representation coefficients are very sparse with super-Gaussian distribution functions. The reverse is true for the ICA-based features. Therefore, the distributions of the features and representing coefficients are complimentary. For the proper comparison the number of feature are set to 60 for both PCA and ICA cases. The cases with multiple-frame-differences show similar characteristics.

A qualitative measure of the sparseness is the kurtosis, which is related to the 4th order moments. Positive kurtosis denotes super-Gaussian distribution functions, and the higher value of kurtosis means only a few values is enough to represent the data with less error. In Tables III and IV, the kurtosis values are summarized for the features and their representation coefficients, respectively.

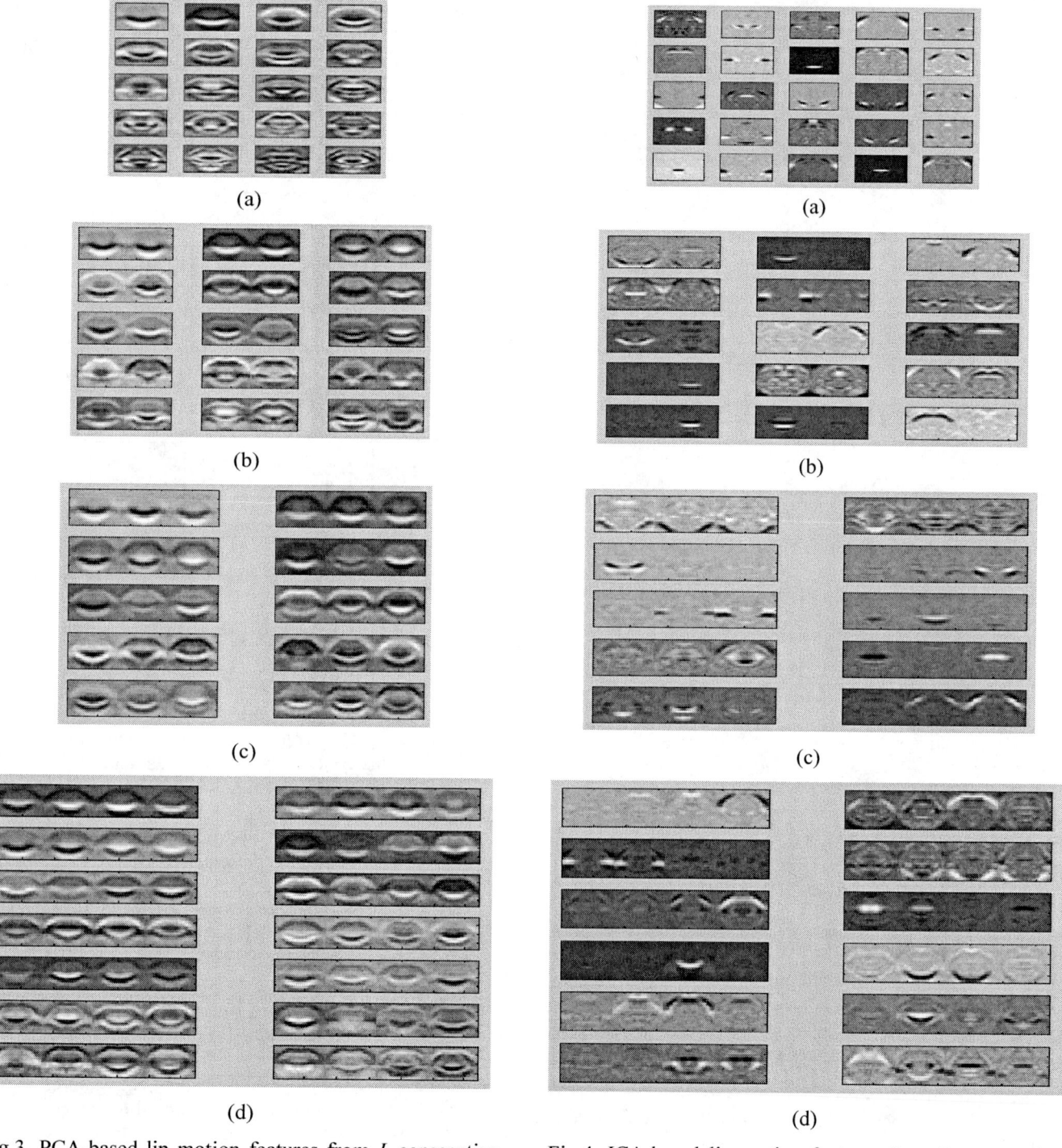

Fig.3. PCA-based lip motion features from L consecutive frame-difference images. (a) single (L=1), (b) 2, (c) 3, and (d) 4 consecutive-frame-differences. Only several top principal components are shown for simplicity.

Fig.4. ICA-based lip motion features from L consecutive frame-difference images. (a) single (L=1), (b) 2, (c) 3, and (d) 4 consecutive-frame-differences. Only several top principal components are shown for simplicity.

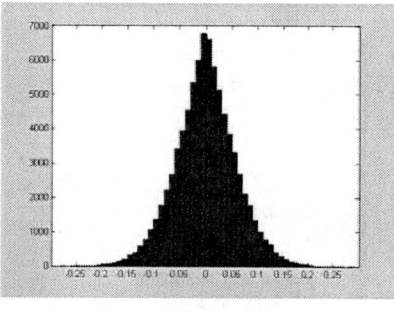

(a)

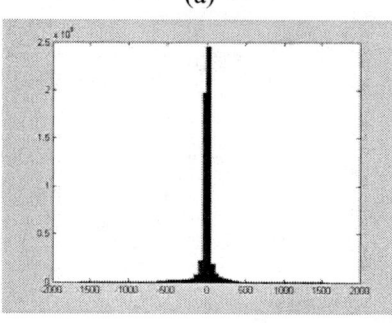

(b)

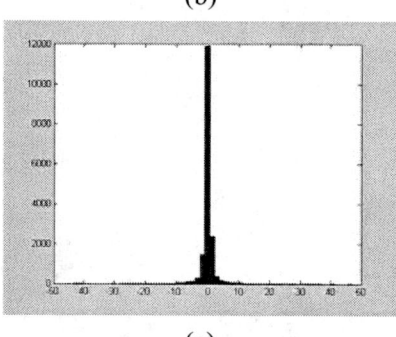

(c)

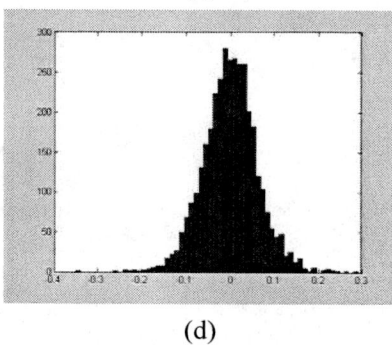

(d)

Fig. 5. Histograms of feature values for single-frame-difference images. (a) PCA-based features; (b) Coefficients for PCA-based features; (c) ICA-based features; (d) Coefficients for ICA-based features.

Using different number of frames to find the basis components, we found that the kurtosis values decrease as the number of frames increases for the ICA features and PCA coefficients. In our previous results for the multi-frame images [7] the kurtosis values do not change much among the same decomposition method. The ICA results in the greatest kurtosis for feature values, and the PCA results in the lowest value. On the other hand, the kurtosis of coefficients is the other way around. The high kurtosis values for the ICA features and PCA coefficients are actually almost twice of those from the multi-frame images without frame differences [7]. Higher kurtosis value means that there are more data concentrated near the zero. Therefore, it may demonstrate the efficiency of the proposed frame-difference approach.

Table III. Kurtosis of features extracted using different methods and different number of frames.

	Single Frame	2 Frames	3 Frames	4 Frames
PCA	0.47	0.66	1.00	0.93
ICA	60.2	50.9	35.4	32.4

Table IV. Kurtosis of coefficient extracted using different methods and different number of frames.

	Single Frame	2 Frames	3 Frames	4 Frames
PCA	71.9	35.1	24.3	17.4
ICA	1.18	0.68	0.56	0.42

V. DISCUSSION

Comparison the feature extraction methods based on PCA and ICA is not straight-forward. Since the efficiency of the data representation depends not only on the coefficient matrix but also the features matrix, it is difficult to predict the best technique based on the value of its kurtosis.

While ICA results in much sparse features, PCA results in much sparse representation coefficients. Also the number of frames affects on the sparseness. Since only a small number of features are needed for the videos of the same frame length, the multiple-frame features have higher compression ratio and becomes more advantageous in efficiency.

The frame-difference images may be applicable for the speech recognition and lip movement synthesis. Each difference image shows how much the component has been changed throughout one time frame. The features are also extracted from L-consecutive frame-differences to show much more dynamic nature of the lip motion.

The lip motion synthesis can be done by adding and subtracting the frame-difference components to the one's static lip image respect to time sequence. Combining these images will create a video clip of lip motion. Also, the lip-motion features and phonetic speech features will be combined for the audio-visual speech recognition. Provided the lip-motion features were associated to the phonetic features, it will also be applied to the lip motion synthesis in close correlation to the human speeches.

In the future the coding efficiency and statistical characteristics of the time sequences with the basis elements will be further investigated for the bigger data sets. Then, the extracted features of the lip movement will be utilized to classify for speech recognition in noisy environment and to synthesize the lip motion for artificial agents with Text-To-Speech (TTS) ability.

Acknowledgment: S.Y. Lee was supported by the Brain Neuroinformatics Research Program sponsored by Korean Ministry of Science and Technology and Korean Ministry of Commerce and Industries.

REFERENCES

[1] F. Berthommier, "Direct Synthesis of Video from Speech Sounds for New Telecommunication Applications," Smart Object Conference, 2003

[2] M. Turk and A. Pentland, "Eigenfaces for recognition," Journal of Cognitive Neruoscience, Vol. 3, pp.71-86, 1991

[3] D.D. Lee, H.S. Seung, "Learning the parts of objects by non-negative matrix factorization," Nature, Vol. 401(6775). pp.788-791, 1999

[4] S. Choi, A. Cichocki, H.M. Park, and S.Y. Lee, "Blind signal separation and independent component analysis: a review," Neural Information Processing – Letters and Reviews, Vol.6(1), pp. 1-57, 2005.

[5] B.A. Draper, K. Baek, M.S. Bartlett, and J. Ross Beveridge. "Recognizing faces with PCA and ICA," Computer Vision and Image Understanding, Vol.91, pp.115-137, 2003.

[6] J.V. Haxby, E.A. Hoffman, and M.I. Gobbini, "The distributed human neural system for face perception," Trens in Cognitive Sciences, Vol.4, No.6, pp. 223-233, 2000.

[7] M.J. Lee, K.D. Lee, and S.Y. Lee, "Unsupervised feature extraction from multi-frame images for lip-reading," Computational Neuroscience Annual Meeting, Madison, 2005.

[8] M.S. Barlett, H.M. Lades, T.J. Sejnowski, "Independent component representations for face recognition," SPIE Symposium on Electronic Imaging: Science and Technology, 1998

[9] M.S. Gray, Javier R.Movellan, Terrence J. Sejnowski. "A comparison of local versus global image decompositions for visual speechreading," Fourth Symposium Neural Computation, pp.92-98, 1997

[10] S. Amari, A. Cichocki, and H.H. Yang, "A new learning algorithm for blind source separation," in Proc. Neural Information Processing Systems, 1996.

[11] J.R. Movellan. "Visual speech recognition with stochastic networks," Advances in Neural Information Processing Systems, Vol. 7. pp. 851-858, 1995.

Multinomial PCA for Extracting Major Latent Topics from Document Streams

Masahiro KIMURA[†]
NTT Communication Science Labs
Seika-cho, Kyoto 619-0237, Japan
kimura@cslab.kecl.ntt.co.jp

Kazumi SAITO
NTT Communication Science Labs
Seika-cho, Kyoto 619-0237, Japan
saito@cslab.kecl.ntt.co.jp

Naonori UEDA
NTT Communication Science Labs
Seika-cho, Kyoto 619-0237, Japan
ueda@cslab.kecl.ntt.co.jp

Abstract— We propose a new unsupervised learning method called *Multinomial PCA (MuPCA)* for efficiently extracting the major latent topics from a document stream based on the "bag-of-words" (BOW) representation of a document. Unlike PCA, MuPCA follows a suitable probabilistic generative model for the document stream represented as time-series of word-frequency vectors. Using real data of document streams on the Web, we experimentally demonstrate the effectiveness of the proposed method.

I. INTRODUCTION

Recently, much attention has been devoted to modeling and mining the World Wide Web, and investigating the Web is becoming a new research field for computational intelligence, since various problems for learning can be posed [8], [10], [1], [5], [6]. Since the Web continues to grow as an important medium of communication and can now be considered to be the epitome of human society, it is interesting to understand the dynamics of social phenomena based on Web information. In this paper, we deal with the problem of extracting the major latent topics from a document stream on the Web such as news articles, research paper archives, and blogs.

Swan and Allan [9] developed a method for both extracting the major events from a stream of news articles and identifying the intervals of dates when they were active, and Kleinberg [7] extended the work to construct a temporal hierarchical structure for an event. However, these studies addressed the issue of finding specific events represented by key phrases, whereas we would like to consider extracting latent topics. Moreover, these methods required finding in advance named entities and noun phrases from the corpus as the features to explore, and hence heavily depended on natural language processing (NLP) technologies. Alternatively, we explore a simple statistical approach that does not depend on NLP technologies, but is based on the "bag-of-words" (BOW) representation [1] of a document, that is, the high-dimensional vector-space representation by the word-frequency vector that ignores the order of word occurrence in the document.

On the other hand, to extract latent topics from a corpus, one might consider applying principal component analysis (PCA) [3] or latent semantic analysis (LSA) [2]. However, these approaches do not follow a suitable probabilistic generative model for documents. For example, when applying PCA to the BOW data of documents, the underlying assumption is that the data can be modeled by a Gaussian distribution. This model is not, however, suitable as a probabilistic model for documents since the BOW data of documents are frequency information. Hofmann proposed probabilistic LSA (PLSA) as LSA based on a probabilistic model for documents, and experimentally showed the effectiveness of the PLSA approach for the LSA approach [4]. However, for very large-scale datasets, the PLSA approach can become unstable and in that case could not work efficiently.

In order to efficiently extract the major latent topics from a document stream represented as time-series of word-frequency vectors, we propose a new unsupervised learning method called *multinomial PCA (MuPCA)*, which follows a suitable probabilistic generative model with latent variables for the document stream. Using real data of document streams on the Web, we experimentally demonstrate the effectiveness of the proposed method.

II. MODEL

Aiming to extract the major latent topics in a document stream, we introduce a probabilistic generative model with latent variables for the document stream.

A. Document Streams

We consider a document stream $\mathcal{D}$, a time-series data of documents that belongs to one category,

$$\mathcal{D} = \bigcup_{t=1}^{T} D(t); \; D(t) = \{d(t,n); \; n = 1, \cdots, N(t)\}, \; \forall t,$$

where T denotes the number of time-steps in the document stream, $D(t)$ is the set of documents at time-step t, $d(t,n)$ represents the nth document at time-step t, and $N(t)$ denotes the number of documents at time-step t. According to the BOW representation, $d(t,n)$ can be represented by a word-frequency vector $\boldsymbol{x}(t,n) = (x_1(t,n), \cdots, x_V(t,n))$, where each $x_i(t,n)$ is the number of word w_i occurrence in $d(t,n)$ among the vocabulary $\{w_1, \cdots, w_V\}$.

B. Probabilistic Generative Model

In order to model the appearance and disappearance of latent topics in document stream $\mathcal{D}$, we consider modeling the generative process of the time-series $\{D(t); t = 1, \cdots T\}$ of sets of documents.

We first identify the set $D(t)$ with a long document constructed by simply combining the documents in $D(t)$. Then, according to the BOW representation, $D(t)$ can be represented by a word-frequency vector $\boldsymbol{X}(t) = (X_1(t), \cdots, X_V(t))$, where

$$X_i(t) = \sum_{n=1}^{N(t)} x_i(t,n), \ (i=1,\cdots,V).$$

Thus, by assuming the naive Bayes model [1], the generative process of $D(t)$ can be modeled in the following way: The feature vector $\boldsymbol{X}(t)$ is generated from a multinomial distribution

$$P(\boldsymbol{X}(t)) \propto \prod_{i=1}^{V} \psi_i(t)^{X_i(t)}$$

where each $\psi_i(t)$ denotes the probability that word w_i appears in the document $D(t)$ at time-step t, and $\psi_i(t) \geq 0$, $(i = 1, \cdots, V)$; $\sum_{i=1}^{V} \psi_i(t) = 1$. We define the multinomial parameter vector $\boldsymbol{\psi}(t)$ at time-step t by $\boldsymbol{\psi}(t) = (\psi_1(t), \cdots, \psi_V(t))$.

Since $D(t)$ can be regarded as a document with multiple topics, we consider modeling the generative process of $D(t)$ based on a *parametric mixture model (PMM)* [11], [12]. PMMs assume that words in a document with multiple topics are a mixture of characteristic words related to each of the topics. Namely, in PMMs, the distribution of word-frequency vectors of multi-topic text is modeled by a multinomial distribution with a parameter vector generated by a mixture of basis parameter vectors, where each basis parameter vector corrresponds to a multinomial distribution for a single topic. Hence, according to PMMs, we assume that the multinomial parameter vector $\boldsymbol{\psi}(t)$ at time-step t is obtained by

$$\boldsymbol{\psi}(t) = \left(1 - \sum_{\ell=1}^{L} h_\ell(t)\right) \bar{\boldsymbol{\psi}} + \sum_{\ell=1}^{L} h_\ell(t) \boldsymbol{\phi}_\ell. \quad (1)$$

Here, we assume that in document stream $\mathcal{D}$, there exist not only L major latent topics but also one ordinary topic. Each $\boldsymbol{\phi}_\ell$ denotes the multinomial parameter vector of the ℓth major-latent-topic in $\mathcal{D}$, and $\bar{\boldsymbol{\psi}}$ denotes the multinomial parameter vector of the ordinary topic in $\mathcal{D}$. Each $h_\ell(t)$ represents the relative weight of the ℓth topic at time-step t, where $0 \leq h_\ell(t) \leq 1$, $(\ell = 1, \cdots, L)$; $\sum_{\ell=1}^{L} h_\ell(t) \leq 1$.

We assume that there exists the interval of main activity for each major-latent-topic. Let $[t_{\ell,0}, t_{\ell,1}]$ denote the interval of the main activity for the ℓth major-latent-topic. In particular, we assume that for each ℓ,

$$h_\ell(t) = \begin{cases} c_\ell, & t \in [t_{\ell,0}, t_{\ell,1}], \\ 0, & \text{otherwise}, \end{cases} \quad (2)$$

where c_ℓ is a constant such that $0 \leq c_\ell \leq 1$ and $\sum_{\ell=1}^{L} c_\ell \leq 1$. Let $\mathcal{M}$ denote this probabilistic generative model for $\mathcal{D}$.

In contrast with the model $\mathcal{M}$, we also consider the following probabilistic generative model $\overline{\mathcal{M}}$ without major latent topics: The feature vector $\boldsymbol{X}(t)$ is generated from a multinomial distribution

$$P(\boldsymbol{X}(t)) \propto \prod_{i=1}^{V} \{\bar{\theta}_i\}^{X_i(t)},$$

where each $\bar{\theta}_i$ denotes the probability that word w_i appears in $D(t)$ for any time-step t, and $\bar{\theta}_i \geq 0$, $(i = 1, \cdots, V)$; $\sum_{i=1}^{V} \bar{\theta}_i = 1$.

We consider the *time-independent* model $\overline{\mathcal{M}}$ as averaging the L major-latent-topics of the *time-dependent* model $\mathcal{M}$ to only one ordinary topic. We define the multinomial parameter vector $\bar{\boldsymbol{\theta}}$ of $\overline{\mathcal{M}}$ by $\bar{\boldsymbol{\theta}} = (\bar{\theta}_1, \cdots, \bar{\theta}_V)$.

III. MULTINOMIAL PCA

In general, it is difficult to infer the model parameters of the proposed generative model $\mathcal{M}$ from the observed data $\mathcal{D}$, since there are too many parameters. Therefore, as an alternative approach we could consider applying an projection approach such as PCA. Unlike PCA, our proposed method follows a suitable probabilistic generative model for $\mathcal{D}$.

Let Δ^{V-1} be the $(V-1)$-dimensional canonical simplex in the V-dimensional Euclidean space $\mathbf{R}^V$ defined by

$$\Delta^{V-1} = \left\{ (y_1, \cdots, y_V) \in \mathbf{R}^V; 0 \leq y_1, \cdots, y_V \leq 1, \sum_{i=1}^{V} y_i = 1 \right\}.$$

For each t and n, let $M(t,n)$ and $M(t)$ denote the numbers of words in $d(t,n)$ and $D(t)$, respectively;

$$M(t,n) = \sum_{i=1}^{V} x_i(t,n), \ M(t) = \sum_{i=1}^{V} X_i(t).$$

Note that $\bar{\boldsymbol{\psi}}, \boldsymbol{\phi}_\ell, \bar{\boldsymbol{\theta}}, \boldsymbol{x}(t,n)/M(t,n), \boldsymbol{X}(t)/M(t) \in \Delta^{V-1}$ for each ℓ, t and n.

A. Projection Approach

The goal is to efficiently find the documents $d(t,n)$'s that represent a major latent topic in $\mathcal{D}$. For this goal, we propose a projection approach called MuPCA.

We hypothesize that each major-latent-topic $\boldsymbol{\phi}_\ell$ is far from the ordinary topic $\bar{\boldsymbol{\psi}}$ in Δ^{V-1}, and also hypothesize that $\boldsymbol{\phi}_1, \cdots, \boldsymbol{\phi}_L$ are independent of each other based on $\bar{\boldsymbol{\psi}}$. In particular, taking into account the high-dimensionality of Δ^{V-1}, we assume that if $k \neq \ell$, $\boldsymbol{\phi}_k - \bar{\boldsymbol{\psi}}$ and $\boldsymbol{\phi}_\ell - \bar{\boldsymbol{\psi}}$ are orthogonal in Δ^{V-1},

$$(\boldsymbol{\phi}_k - \bar{\boldsymbol{\psi}}) \cdot (\boldsymbol{\phi}_\ell - \bar{\boldsymbol{\psi}}) = 0, \quad (3)$$

where "$\cdot$" denotes the inner product in $\mathbf{R}^V$ (see Fig. 1).

In MuPCA, $\bar{\boldsymbol{\psi}}$ is estimated to be the multinomial parameter vector $\bar{\boldsymbol{\theta}}$ for the model $\overline{\mathcal{M}}$. By performing the maximum likelihood estimation from the data $\{\boldsymbol{X}(t); t = 1, \cdots, T\}$ based on $\overline{\mathcal{M}}$, $\bar{\boldsymbol{\theta}}$ is estimated as

$$\bar{\theta}_i = \frac{\sum_{t=1}^{T} X_i(t)}{\sum_{t=1}^{T} M(t)}, \ (i = 1, \cdots, V). \quad (4)$$

A straight line through $\bar{\boldsymbol{\theta}}$ in Δ^{V-1} is referred to as an *axis*. When an axis passes through $\boldsymbol{\phi}_\ell$, it is called the ℓ*th topic axis*. In MuPCA, for the sample data $\{\boldsymbol{X}(t)/M(t); t = 1, \cdots, T\}$ in Δ^{V-1}, the first topic axis is estimated to be the axis such that the projection of the sample data to the axis maximizes the variance, the second topic axis is estimated to

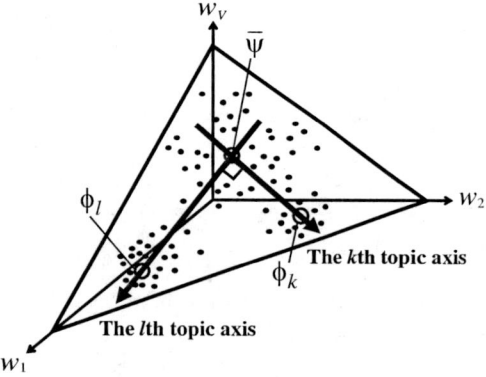

Fig. 1. A conceptual illustration of the relationship between the topic axes and the sample data $\{X(t)/M(t); t = 1, \cdots, T\}$. The big triangle represents the simplex Δ^{V-1}, and the filled circles indicate samples $X(t)/M(t)$'s. ϕ_k, ϕ_ℓ and $\bar{\psi}$ are indicated by the unfilled circles. The thick arrows indicate the topic axes.

be the axis such that the projection of the sample data to the axis maximizes the variance in the set of axes orthogonal to the first topic axis, and so forth (see, Fig.1). Next, for each ℓ, by projecting the data $\{x(t,n)/M(t,n); t = 1, \cdots, T, n = 1, \cdots, N(t)\}$ of original documents to the ℓth topic axis and ranking them, the documents $d(t,n)$'s that represent the ℓth major latent topic in $\mathcal{D}$ are extracted. Note here that maximizing the variance for projected data is defined below through a Gaussian approximation of the generative model via the central limit theorem.

B. Topic Axes

Now, we explicitly describe how to estimate the ℓth topic axis for each ℓ. Let us represent document $D(t)$ as an ordered set of word occurrence:

$$D(t) = \langle w_{\lambda_1(t)}, \cdots, w_{\lambda_{M(t)}(t)} \rangle,$$

where each $w_{\lambda_m(t)}$ denotes the mth word of document $D(t)$. Then, for any time-step t and any real V-dimensional vector $\boldsymbol{u} = (u_1, \cdots, u_V)$, we consider the quantity

$$A(t; \boldsymbol{u}) = \frac{1}{M(t)} \sum_{m=1}^{M(t)} u_{\lambda_m(t)}.$$

Note that in our generative models for $\mathcal{D}$, $\{u_{\lambda_m(t)}; m = 1, \cdots, M(t)\}$ becomes a set of statistically independent and identically distributed random variables.

First, let us assume the model $\overline{\mathcal{M}}$ for the generative process of $\mathcal{D}$. Then, each $u_{\lambda_m(t)}$ follows the probability distribution $\bar{\boldsymbol{\theta}}$. We also assume that $M(t)$ is sufficiently large. Then, by the central limit theorem, we can consider that $A(t; \boldsymbol{u})$ is generated from the Gaussian distribution $\mathcal{N}(\mu(\boldsymbol{u}), \sigma(t; \boldsymbol{u})^2)$ with mean $\mu(\boldsymbol{u})$ and variance $\sigma(t; \boldsymbol{u})^2$, where

$$\mu(\boldsymbol{u}) = \bar{\boldsymbol{\theta}} \cdot \boldsymbol{u} = \sum_{i=1}^{V} \bar{\theta}_i u_i \quad (5)$$

$$\sigma(t; \boldsymbol{u})^2 = \frac{1}{M(t)} \left\{ \sum_{i=1}^{V} \bar{\theta}_i u_i^2 - \mu(\boldsymbol{u})^2 \right\}. \quad (6)$$

On the other hand, it is easily seen that

$$A(t; \boldsymbol{u}) = \frac{1}{M(t)} \boldsymbol{X}(t) \cdot \boldsymbol{u}.$$

Thus, the quantity

$$A_0(t; \boldsymbol{u}) = A(t; \boldsymbol{u}) - \bar{\boldsymbol{\theta}} \cdot \boldsymbol{u} \quad (7)$$

represents the projection value of $\boldsymbol{X}(t)/M(t)$ to the axis determined by vector $\boldsymbol{u}$. Also, by Eqs. (5), (6), and (7), the distribution $p(A_0(t; \boldsymbol{u}))$ of random variable $A_0(t; \boldsymbol{u})$ can be modeled as

$$p(A_0(t; \boldsymbol{u})) = \frac{1}{\sqrt{2\pi \bar{\sigma}(\boldsymbol{u})^2 / M(t)}} \exp\left(-\frac{A_0(t; \boldsymbol{u})^2}{2\bar{\sigma}(\boldsymbol{u})^2 / M(t)}\right),$$

where $\bar{\sigma}(\boldsymbol{u}) \, (> 0)$ is a parameter that depends on $\boldsymbol{u}$. Therefore, maximizing the variance for the projection of sample data $\{X(t)/M(t); t = 1, \cdots, T\}$ to the axis determined by $\boldsymbol{u}$ can be defined as maximizing the estimator of $\bar{\sigma}(\boldsymbol{u})^2$. By performing the maximum likelihood estimation, $\bar{\sigma}(\boldsymbol{u})$ is estimated as

$$\bar{\sigma}(\boldsymbol{u})^2 = \frac{1}{T} \sum_{t=1}^{T} M(t) A_0(t; \boldsymbol{u})^2. \quad (8)$$

Thus, by Eq. (8), the problem of finding topic axes essentially results in the problem of maximizing the function

$$E(\boldsymbol{u}) = \sum_{t=1}^{T} M(t) \left\{ \left(\frac{1}{M(t)} \boldsymbol{X}(t) - \bar{\boldsymbol{\theta}}\right) \cdot \boldsymbol{u} \right\}^2 \quad (9)$$

with respect to $\boldsymbol{u}$ under $\|\boldsymbol{u}\| = 1$. Hence, for each ℓ, the ℓth topic axis can be dentermined by an ℓth unit eigen vector $\boldsymbol{u}_\ell$ of the $V \times V$ real matrix $B = (b_{i,j})$,

$$b_{i,j} = \sum_{t=1}^{T} M(t) \left(\frac{X_i(t)}{M(t)} - \bar{\theta}_i\right) \left(\frac{X_j(t)}{M(t)} - \bar{\theta}_j\right).$$

By employing *the power method*, we can efficiently estimate $\{\boldsymbol{u}_\ell; \ell = 1, \cdots, L\}$ up to signs.

C. Intervals of Main Activity

Next, let us assume the model $\mathcal{M}$ for the generative process of $\mathcal{D}$. Let $\boldsymbol{u}_\ell = (u_{\ell,1}, \cdots, u_{\ell,V})$ be an ℓth eigen unit vector of B for each ℓ. Then, by the central limit theorem, we can consider that $A(t; \boldsymbol{u}_\ell)$ is generated from the Gaussian distribution $\mathcal{N}(\mu(t; \boldsymbol{u}_\ell), \sigma(t; \boldsymbol{u}_\ell)^2)$ such that

$$\mu(t; \boldsymbol{u}_\ell) = \boldsymbol{\psi}(t) \cdot \boldsymbol{u}_\ell = \sum_{i=1}^{V} \psi_i(t) u_{\ell,i}$$

$$\sigma(t; \boldsymbol{u}_\ell)^2 = \frac{1}{M(t)} \left\{ \sum_{i=1}^{V} \psi_i(t) u_{\ell,i}^2 - \mu(t; \boldsymbol{u}_\ell)^2 \right\}.$$

Since $\boldsymbol{u}_\ell$ is parallel to $\boldsymbol{\phi}_\ell - \bar{\boldsymbol{\theta}}$ and $\bar{\boldsymbol{\psi}}$ is estimated as $\bar{\boldsymbol{\theta}}$, we have

$$\mu(t; \boldsymbol{u}_\ell) = \boldsymbol{\theta} \cdot \boldsymbol{u}_\ell + h_\ell(t)(\boldsymbol{\phi}_\ell - \bar{\boldsymbol{\theta}}) \cdot \boldsymbol{u}_\ell$$

by Eqs. (1),(3). Hence, by Eq. (2), we have

$$\mu(t; \boldsymbol{u}_\ell) = \begin{cases} \bar{\boldsymbol{\theta}} \cdot \boldsymbol{u}_\ell + c_\ell(\boldsymbol{\phi}_\ell - \bar{\boldsymbol{\theta}}) \cdot \boldsymbol{u}_\ell, & t \in [t_{\ell,0}, t_{\ell,1}], \\ \bar{\boldsymbol{\theta}} \cdot \boldsymbol{u}_\ell, & \text{otherwise.} \end{cases} \quad (10)$$

Based on the above facts, we assume that $A(t; \boldsymbol{u}_\ell)$ is generated from a Gaussian distribution $\mathcal{N}(\mu_\ell, \sigma_\ell^2/M(t))$ for any $t \in [t_{\ell,0}, t_{\ell,1}]$ and a Gaussian distribution $\mathcal{N}(f_\ell, \sigma_\ell^2/M(t))$ for any $t \notin [t_{\ell,0}, t_{\ell,1}]$, where μ_ℓ, f_ℓ, σ_ℓ, $t_{\ell,0}$ and $t_{\ell,1}$ are parameters. By performing the maximum likelihood estimation, we can analytically estimate the parameters μ_ℓ, f_ℓ, σ_ℓ, $t_{\ell,0}$ and $t_{\ell,1}$. In particluar, we can estimate the interval $[t_{\ell,0}, t_{\ell,1}]$ of main activity for the ℓth major-latent-topic in document stream $\mathcal{D}$.

D. Document Ranking Method

For each ℓ, we extract the documents $d(t, n)$'s that represent the ℓth major-latent-topic in $\mathcal{D}$ by ranking $\{d(t, n); t = 1, \cdots, T, n = 1, \cdots, N(t)\}$ based on the ℓth topic degree of a document, which is defined below through projecting $\boldsymbol{x}(t, n)/M(t, n)$ to the ℓth topic axis.

Let us define the V-dimensional unit vector $\boldsymbol{v}_\ell$ in the following way: If $\mu_\ell > f_\ell$, then $\boldsymbol{v}_\ell = \boldsymbol{u}_\ell$, and if $\mu_\ell < f_\ell$, then $\boldsymbol{v}_\ell = -\boldsymbol{u}_\ell$. By Eq. (10), $\boldsymbol{v}_\ell$ can be regarded as the unit vector directed from $\bar{\boldsymbol{\theta}}$ to $\boldsymbol{\phi}_\ell$ in Δ^{V-1}. Now, we consider the projection of $\boldsymbol{x}(t, n)/M(t, n)$ to the ℓth topic axis oriented by $\boldsymbol{v}$,

$$A_1(t, n; \boldsymbol{v}_\ell) = \left\{ \frac{1}{M(t, n)} \boldsymbol{x}(t, n) - \bar{\boldsymbol{\theta}} \right\} \cdot \boldsymbol{v}_\ell.$$

By applying the discussion similar to Sec. III-B, we can consider that $A_1(t, n; \boldsymbol{v}_\ell)$ follows the Gaussian distribution $\mathcal{N}(0, \bar{\sigma}_\ell^2/M(t, n))$, where $\bar{\sigma}_\ell (> 0)$ is estimated as

$$\bar{\sigma}_\ell^2 = \frac{1}{\sum_{t=1}^T N(t)} \sum_{t=1}^T \sum_{n=1}^{N(t)} M(t, n) A_1(t, n; \boldsymbol{v}_\ell)^2,$$

(see Eq. (8)). Thus, we define the ℓth topic degree $r_\ell(t, n)$ of document $d(t, n)$ by

$$r_\ell(t, n) = A_1(t, n; \boldsymbol{v}_\ell) / \left\{ \bar{\sigma}_\ell / \sqrt{M(t, n)} \right\}$$

Note that $r_\ell(t, n)$ can be considered as measuring how close $\boldsymbol{x}(t, n)/M(t, n)$ is to $\boldsymbol{\phi}_\ell$ in Δ^{V-1} by taking into account the number $M(t, n)$ of words in the document as well.

E. The Difference between MuPCA and PCA

In the sense of a projection approach, MuPCA is similar to PCA. However, MuPCA is based on the assumption that the sample data follow a multinomial distribution, while PCA is based on the asumption that they follow a Gaussian distribution. Thus, MuPCA finds the topic axes based on the problem of maximizing the function $E(\boldsymbol{u})$ under $\|u\| = 1$, while PCA finds them based on the problem of maximizing the function $E_0(\boldsymbol{u})$ under $\|u\| = 1$,

$$E_0(\boldsymbol{u}) = \sum_{t=1}^T \left\{ \left(\boldsymbol{X}(t) - \frac{1}{T} \sum_{t=1}^T \boldsymbol{X}(t) \right) \cdot \boldsymbol{u} \right\}^2. \quad (11)$$

By Eqs. (4), (9), and (11), it is easily shown that if $M(t) = M$ (a positive constant) for any t, then $E(\boldsymbol{u}) = E_0(\boldsymbol{u})$; namely, if the number $M(t)$ of words in $D(t)$ does not depend on t, MuPCA coincides with PCA. Hence, MuPCA can be regarded as an extension of PCA. We believe that incorporating $M(t)$ and $M(t, n)$, that is, taking into account the length of a document, is an important extension, since long documents must be more reliable information than short documents in order to infer latent topics.

IV. EXPERIMENTAL EVALUATION

A. NSF Data

First, we descirbe the results of the experiment using the data of "the National Science Foundation (NSF) Research Awards Abstracts" from August 1989 to September 2003 [1]. In the experiment, we used only the portion of the field "Computer and Information Science and Engineering." The total number of documents in this dataset was $10,595$, and $V = 21,036$. Figure 2 displays the time-series $M(t)$, ($t = 1, \cdots, 170$). Here, one time-step was one month, and $T = 170$. From Fig. 2 we observe that $M(t)$ depends heavily on time-step t, and hence we apply MuPCA.

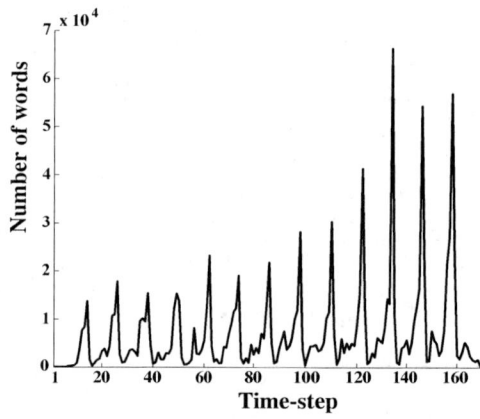

Fig. 2. Fluctuation in the number $M(t)$ of words for the NSF dataset.

Figure 3 shows the normalized projection values to the estimated first topic axis, $A_0(t; \boldsymbol{u}_1) / \{\bar{\sigma}(\boldsymbol{u}_1) / \sqrt{M(t)}\}$, ($t = 1, \cdots, 170$), and Fig. 4 illustrates the normalized projection values to the estimated second topic axis. In Figs. 3 and 4, the line with circles indicates the estimated interval $[t_{\ell,0}, t_{\ell,1}]$ of main activity for $\ell = 1, 2$. Here, $[t_{1,0}, t_{1,1}]$ was $[110, 170]$, that is, from September 1998 to September 2003, and $[t_{2,0}, t_{2,1}]$ was $[39, 68]$, that is, from October 1992 to March 1995. Table I and Table II respectively present the titles of the ten most highly ranked documents for the extracted first and second major-latent-topics. The extracted first and second major-latent-topics could be respectively regarded as the one related to "networking research," such as investigation of network architecture, and the one related to "network infrastucture," such as connections to high-performance networks. Moreover,

---
[1] One can download from the following Web site:
"http://kdd.ics.uci.edu/databases/nsfabs/nsfawards.data.html".

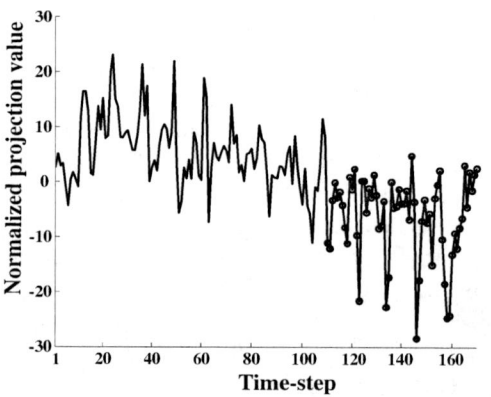

Fig. 3. Fluctuation in the normalized projection value $A_0(t; \boldsymbol{u}_1) / \{\bar{\sigma}(\boldsymbol{u}_1)/\sqrt{M(t)}\}$ to the first topic axis for the NSF dataset.

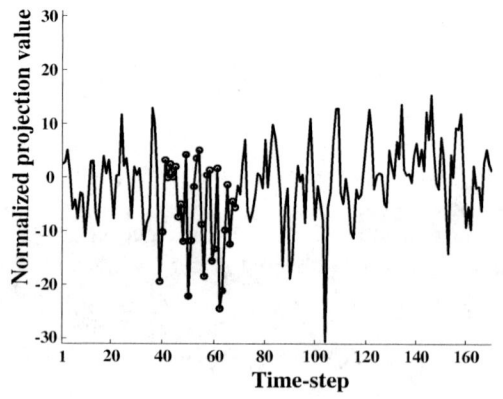

Fig. 4. Fluctuation in the normalized projection value $A_0(t; \boldsymbol{u}_2) / \{\bar{\sigma}(\boldsymbol{u}_2)/\sqrt{M(t)}\}$ to the second topic axis for the NSF dataset.

TABLE I
TOP 10 DOCUMENTS FOR THE FIRST MAJOR-LATENT-TOPIC EXTRACTED FROM THE NSF DATASET.

Title of document	Month
An Event-driven Programmable Network Architecture for the NextGeneration Internet	October 1998
Secure Communications for Ad Hoc Networking	June 2000
CAREER: Towards an Efficient Ubiquitous Computing Infrastructure	June 2001
Collaborative Research: Design and Restoration Techniques for Fault-Tolerant Wireless Access Networks	October 2000
CAREER: Flexible, Large-Scale Best-Effort Quality of Service in the Internet	July 2002
ITR: Protocol Coordination for Multistream Applications	October 2002
ITR/SI - A Networking Protocol for Underwater Acoustic Networks	September 2001
SGER: Exploratory Research on A New Survivable, Scalable, and Self-Adapting Network Architecture Based on Biological Concepts	September 1999
ITR: The Bio-Networking Architecture: A Biologically Inspired Approach to the Design of Scalable, Adaptive, and Survivable/Available Network Applications	September 2000
CAREER: Programmable Mobile Networking	May 1999

TABLE II
TOP 10 DOCUMENTS FOR THE SECOND MAJOR-LATENT-TOPIC EXTRACTED FROM THE NSF DATASET.

Title of document	Month
High Performance Connection to the Internet	March 1998
Connections to netILLINOIS	July 1993
HPNC: HPNC for Science Research at Loyola University Chicago	October 2002
Connections to NetIllinois — Phase V	June 1994
Connections to netILLINOIS — Phase IV	June 1994
High-Performance Network Connectivity for the University of Nebraska-Lincoln	March 1998
Connections to netILLINOIS — Phase III	September 1993
Connections to NSFNET for North Carolina Institutions	September 1993
Proposal to Create an Academic / Research Network for the State of Kentucky	September 1993
Connection of School to OARnet and NSFNET — Washington State Community College	July 1995

we confirmed that MuPCA extracted significant topics for other major-latent-topics.

B. TDT Data

Next, we describe the results of the experiment using the Topic Detection and Tracking (TDT) study's corpus [2]. In this experiment we used only the English language portion of the TDT-2 corpus, consisting of articles from ABC News, CNN, Public Radio International, Voice of America, the New York Times, and the Associated Press newswire from January 4, 1998 to June 30, 1998. In this dataset, the total number of documents was $54,040$, and $V = 113,898$. Figure 5 displays the time-series $M(t)$, $(t = 1, \cdots, 178)$. Here, one time-step was one day, and $T = 178$. From Fig. 5, we also observe that $M(t)$ depends heavily on time-step t, and hence we apply MuPCA.

In Fig. 6, the normalized projetion values to the estimated first topic axis, $A_0(t; \boldsymbol{u}_1) / \{\bar{\sigma}(\boldsymbol{u}_1)/\sqrt{M(t)}\}$, $(t = 1, \cdots, 178)$ are shown, where the line with circles indicates the estimated interval $[t_{1,0}, t_{1,1}]$ of main activity. Here, $[t_{1,0}, t_{1,1}]$ was $[21, 52]$, that is, from January 24 to February 24. In Table III, the titles of the ten most highly ranked documents are presented for the extracted first major-latent-topic. The extracted first major-latent-topic could be regarded as the one related to "the problem of weapons inspection for Iraq by the United Nations." We also confirmed that the extracted second major-latent-topic could be regarded as the one related to "the

[2] See the Web site "http://www.ldc.upenn.edu/TDT/".

Monica Lewinsky case," and the proposed method extracted significant topics for other major-latent-topics.

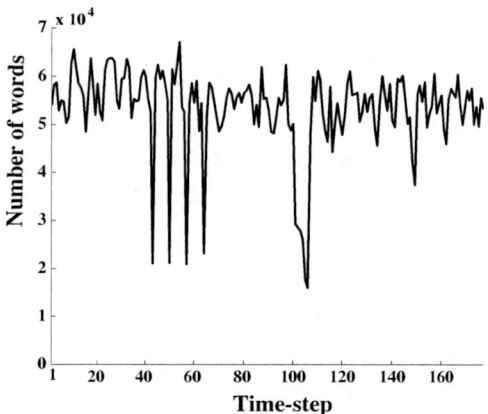

Fig. 5. Fluctuation in the number $M(t)$ of words for the TDT dataset.

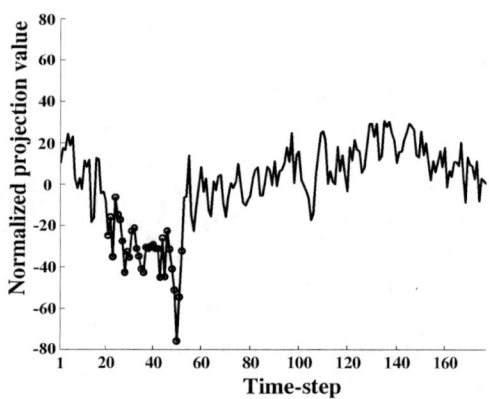

Fig. 6. Fluctuation in the normalized projection value $A_0(t; \boldsymbol{u}_1) / \{\bar{\sigma}(\boldsymbol{u}_1)/\sqrt{M(t)}\}$ to the first topic axis for the TDT dataset.

V. Concluding Remarks

In order to efficiently extract the major-latent-topics from a document stream, we proposed a new unsupervised learning method called MuPCA. Unlike PCA, MuPCA is based on a suitable probabilistic generative model with latent variables for a time-series data of word-frequency vectors. MuPCA can be considered as a natural generalization of PCA for frequency data, since MuPCA and PCA output the same result if the total number of words is equal for every time-step. Using the stream of NSF research award abstracts and the stream of news articles (the TDT-2 corpus), we experimentally demonstrated that the proposed method works well.

On the other hand, qualitative and quantiative verifications of the proposed method for various naive methods, including PCA combined with a feature transformation such as TF-IDF [1], remain important tasks. Also, developing the technique to automatically annotate extracted topics is an important future work. However, we have already made substantial progress, and we are encouraged by the initial results of our efforts to efficiently extract the major latent topics from a document stream.

TABLE III
Top 10 documents for the first major-latent-topic extracted from the TDT dataset.

Title of document	Date
American U.N. expert starts his first day of weapons inspections	March 6
How U.S. got Iraq deal and resolved its own internal debate	Feburuary 24
Defense Ministry acts on Saddam's call to mobilize Iraqis	January 18
Diplomatic flurry to try to avert military action	Feburuary 5
Clinton warns of air strikes to 'seriously diminish' threats	Feburuary 17
The State Department said today it has been reassured by the United Nations that U.N. weapons inspectors will remain in control of the U.N. weapons inspection program for Iraq	Feburuary 25
Analysis: Modest goals point to a modest victory	Feburuary 17
Amid tension, Iraqi paper says Butler 'must be tied down'	January 31
Butler says Iraq wants freeze on inspecting Saddam's palaces	January 21
Iraqis told to prepare for 'holy war' on U.N. sanctions	January 18

References

[1] P. Baldi, P. Fransconi, and P. Smyth, *Modeling the Internet and the Web: Probabilistic Methods and Algorithms*, Wiley, 2003.
[2] S. Deerwester, S. T. Dumais, G. W. Furnas, T. K. Landauer, and R. Harshman, "Indexing by latent semantic analysis," *Journal of the American Society for Information Science*, vol. 41, pp391-407, 1990.
[3] R. O. Duda, P. E. Hart, and D. G. Stork, *Pattern Classification*, Wiley, 2000.
[4] T. Hofmann, "Unsupervised learning by probabilistic latent semantic analysis," *Machine Learning*, vol. 42, pp. 177–196, 2001.
[5] M. Kimura, K. Saito, and N. Ueda, "Modeling of growing networks with directional attachment and communities," *Neural Networks*, vol. 17, pp. 975–988, 2004.
[6] M. Kimura, K. Saito, and N. Ueda, "Modeling share dynamics by extracting competition structure," *Physica D*, vol. 198, pp. 51–73, 2004.
[7] J. Kleinberg, "Bursty and hierarchical structure in streams," *Proceedings of the Eighth ACM SIGKDD International Conference on Knowledge and Data Mining*, Edmonton, Alberta, Canada, 2002, pp. 91–101.
[8] J. Kleinberg and S. Lawrence, "The structure of the web." *Science*, vol. 294, pp. 1849–1850, 2001.
[9] R. Swan and J. Allan, "Automatic generation of overview timelines," *Proceedings of the 23rd Annual International ACM SIGIR Conference on Research and Development in Information Retrieval*, Athens, Greece, 2000, pp. 49–56.
[10] S. K. Pal, V. Talwar, and P. Mitra, "Web mining in soft computing framework: relevance, state of the art and future directions," *IEEE Transactions on Neural Networks*, vol. 13, pp. 1163–1177, 2002.
[11] N. Ueda and K. Saito, "Single-shot detection of multiple topics using parametric mixture models," *Proceedings of the Eighth ACM SIGKDD International Conference on Knowledge and Data Mining*, Edmonton, Alberta, Canada, 2002, pp. 626–631.
[12] N. Ueda and K. Saito, "Parametric mixture models for mult-labeled text," *Advances in Neural Information Processing Systems 15*, MIT Press, 2002, pp. 737–744.

†Current address: Department of Electronics and Informatics, Ryukoku University, Otsu, Shiga 520-2194, Japan.

Post Nonlinear Blind Source Separation by Geometric Linearization

Thang Viet Nguyen, Jagdish Chandra Patra, Amitabha Das and Geok See Ng
School of Computer Engineering, Nanyang Technological University, Singapore 639798
E-mail: thangnguyen@pmail.ntu.edu.sg, aspatra@ntu.edu.sg, asadas@ntu.edu.sg, asgsng@ntu.edu.sg

Abstract—We present a novel geometric approach to the popular Post Nonlinear (PNL) BSS problem. A PNL mixing system includes two stages: a linear mixing followed by a nonlinear transformation. In our method, the process to linearize the nonlinear observed signals, the most critical task in PNL model, is carried out by a geometric transformation. The basic idea is that in a multi-dimensional space, a PNL mixture is represented by a nonlinear surface while a linear mixture is represented by a plane. Thus, by transforming a PNL's representing nonlinear surface to a plane, the PNL mixture can be linearized. The hidden sources are then estimated from linearized signals by a linear BSS algorithm. Experiments show promising performance of our approach.

I. INTRODUCTION

In recent years, Blind Source Separation (BSS) emerged as an important topic and attracts many researchers because of its potential use many fields such as signal processing, image processing, speech enhancement and biomedicine [1]. Generally, from the observed signals only, the goal of BSS is to estimate the hidden original sources which are mixed by an unknown mixing process. Let $\mathbf{s} = [s_1(t), s_2(t), ..., s_m(t)]^T$ denote the vector representing m unknown source signals at time t. The unknown BSS mixing system can be formulated as

$$\mathbf{x} = \mathcal{F}(\mathbf{s}) \tag{1}$$

where $\mathbf{x} = [x_1(t), x_2(t), ..., x_n(t)]^T$ is a vector representing n observed signals at time t. And $\mathcal{F}$ is a real-valued n-component mixing function representing the unknown mixing system. To estimate the original source signals $\mathbf{s}$, an inverse system, termed separating system, needs to be built. That is, find a mapping $\mathcal{G}: \mathcal{R}^n \rightarrow \mathcal{R}^m$ such as

$$\mathbf{y} = \mathcal{G}(\mathbf{x}) \tag{2}$$

where $\mathbf{y} = [y_1(t), y_2(t), ..., y_m(t)]^T$ is an estimate of $\mathbf{s}$.

The very first approach to BSS problem is the linear model. Because of its simplicity, linear BSS has been thoroughly studied in the last two decades and many effective algorithms were proposed. In linear model, the mixing system, i.e., function $\mathcal{F}$ in (1), is simply a matrix. The observed signals are then the linear mixtures of the unknown sources. That is, the model in (1) is reformulated as

$$\mathbf{x} = \mathbf{A}\mathbf{s} \tag{3}$$

where $\mathbf{A}$ is a full rank matrix of size $n \times m$, called mixing matrix. The objective is to find an inverse matrix $\mathbf{W}$ of $\mathbf{A}$, i.e., $\mathbf{W} \approx \mathbf{A}^{-1}$, such that

$$\mathbf{y} = \mathbf{W}\mathbf{x} = \mathbf{W}\mathbf{A}\mathbf{s} \approx \mathbf{s} \tag{4}$$

where $\mathbf{y}$ is the estimate of $\mathbf{s}$, and $\mathbf{W}$ is a matrix of size $m \times n$, termed as demixing matrix. The separating process used to find $\mathbf{W}$ and $\mathbf{y}$ is usually carried out by maximizing the statistical independence among the outputs $y_1, y_2, ..., y_m$. For more detail on linear BSS methods, see [1].

However, in many situations, the basic linear model can not describe the real system adequately. It challenges researchers to look for a more general model: the nonlinear model. The early approaches to nonlinear BSS were proposed in [2], [3]. The authors tried to apply Self Organizing Maps (SOM) [2] and later the Generative Topographic Mapping (GTM) [3] to the model in (1). These algorithms, however, suffer from computational complexity when the number of sources is increased [1]. Moreover, another fundamental problem of the general nonlinear BSS is that the solutions are highly non-unique [1], [4]. Without any constrain to the general nonlinear BSS model, there always exists an infinite number of solutions [5]. Hence, nonlinear BSS approaches are focussed on the sub-classes of the general model by setting restrictions on the nonlinear transformations [4].

The Post Nonlinear (PNL) model, introduced by Taleb et al. [6], is an important sub-class that constrains the transformations to one-dimensional invertible nonlinear functions. The PNL mixing model includes two stages: the first stage is a linear mixing process and the second stage is a one-dimensional nonlinear transformation. Mathematically, the PNL model can be represented as

$$\mathbf{v}(t) = \mathbf{A}\mathbf{s}(t), \tag{5}$$
$$x_i(t) = f_i(v_i(t)) \quad i = 1, 2, .., n \tag{6}$$

where $\mathbf{v} = [v_1(t), v_2(t), ..., v_n(t)]^T$ is a vector of the linear mixtures, and f_i is the one-dimensional invertible function. Because of its simplicity and practicability, many studies have been focused on this model [6]–[8]. The PNL applications can be seen in sensor array processing, digital satellite and microwave communications, and biological systems [6].

In this work, we propose a geometric method for the PNL BSS problem. In the first stage, the observed signals are converted back to the linear mixtures by using the difference in geometric properties between linear and nonlinear presentations. These linear mixtures are the inputs for the second stage in which any normal linear BSS algorithm can be used to extract back the unknown source signals. With the geometric approach, our method has some advantages over the other PNL algorithms: (i) since the first stage and second stage in our method are independent from each other, we can apply any linear BSS algorithm in the second stage. It is very useful since each of the linear algorithms is suitable only in some specific applications [1]; (ii) the proposed method does not need a prior knowledge about the number of sources, thus, can be applied to both underdetermined and overdetermined BSS models; and (iii) unlike some of the other algorithms, it does not require any assumption on the distribution of the input signals, hence, it can be applied to various types of input signal. For example, it can be used on both Gaussian and non-Gaussian distributed input signals.

II. GEOMETRIC APPROACH TO PNL BSS

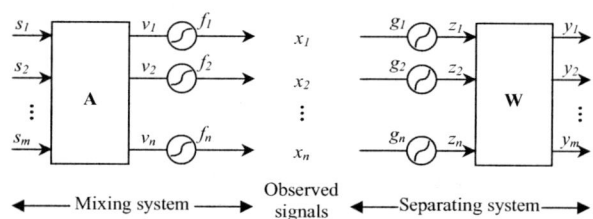

Fig. 1. The Post Nonlinear (PNL) mixing and separating system.

The PNL mixing model (shown in Fig. 1) is a two stage system: a linear mixing process followed by an one-dimensional (1-D) nonlinear transformation. Hence, the PNL separating model also has two stages, the linearizing stage tries to linearize the observed signals, i.e., to transform them into linear mixtures before applying a BSS separation method in the demixing stage. As we can see, the most important task of all the PNL-tailored methods is to linearize the nonlinear observations. The early approach introduced by Taleb et al. [6], using independent criteria may not work well with hard nonlinear distortions. The Yang's approach [8] needs an assumption that the model can be approximated by an artificial neural network (ANN) and requires a lot of computation. Recently, Ziehe et al. [7] proposed simple and effective PNL nonlinear blind separation methods but required the mixtures to be Gaussian-like distributions.

In this paper, we propose a novel approach to the linearizing problem by exploiting the geometric properties between a linear mixture's representation and a nonlinear one. A preliminary version of this approach has been reported in [9], [10] in which only midpoint transformation was used. Whereas in this work, it is extended to any arbitrary point transformation. The proposed method will be detailed for the case of two hidden sources and two observed signals. Thereafter it will be generalized to more number of sources and observed signals.

A. Nonlinear and Linear Mixture in Multi-Dimensional Space

Let v be a linear mixture of two signals, s_1 and, s_2 and is expressed as

$$v(t) = as_1(t) + bs_2(t). \quad (7)$$

This mixture undergoes a transformation by a nonlinear function to which generates the post nonlinear mixture given by

$$x(t) = f(v(t)). \quad (8)$$

Now let us illustrate the linear mixture, v, and PNL mixture, x, in a 3-D space with α, β and γ as the coordinates. A set of points having coordinate $(s_1(t), s_2(t), v(t))$ forms a presentation for the linear mixture v. Similarly, a set of points having coordinate $(s_1(t), s_2(t), x(t))$ forms a presentation for the nonlinear mixture x. The difference between linear mixture v and nonlinear mixture x can be seen from their presentations. For example, 5000 points ($t = 1, 2, ..., 5000$) each for v and x are plotted in Fig. 2. The linear mixture v is represented by a plane V while the nonlinear mixture x is represented by a nonlinear surface X. This difference leads to the following idea: the task to change a nonlinear mixture to a linear one (called linearization) can be done by transforming its surface representation to a plane. In the case when s_1 and s_2 are available, changing the surface X to a plane V is not a problem, for example, we can simply replace the right side of (8) to that of (7). In BSS problem, however, both s_1 and s_2 are unknown and only x is available. Thus, the above simple change is not applicable to transform the nonlinear surface X to the linear plane V. Instead, we developed a heuristic method that iteratively transforms the surface X point-by-point by applying the property of the straight lines and the points lying on a line.

B. Plane and Straight Lines

Let x_1 and x_2 be the two nonlinear mixtures given by

$$x_1(t) = f_1(a_{11}s_1(t) + a_{12}s_2(t)), \quad (9)$$
$$x_2(t) = f_2(a_{21}s_1(t) + a_{22}s_2(t)) \quad (10)$$

where f_i are the nonlinear functions, s_i are the unknown source signals, and a_{ij} are the arbitrary constants ($i, j = 1, 2$). Let X_1 and X_2 be two surfaces in a 3-D space those represent x_1 and x_2, respectively. Since the values of s_1 and s_2 (i.e., α and β coordinates) are unknown, we can not identify the absolute position of a point p_i $(s_1(t), s_2(t), x_i(t))$ in the space. However, we know the value on the third dimension (the γ coordinate) and the time index t. With the same time t, the two points p_1 and p_2, which represent for $x_1(t)$ and $x_2(t)$, will have the same values on α and β coordinates. We define these two points as a companion pair

Definition 1: *Let p_1 and p_2 be the two points that represent for $x_1(t)$ and $x_2(t)$ (i.e., the γ coordinate), respectively. Then p_1 is called the companion point of p_2, and the pair $(p_1, p_2)_t$ is called a companion pair.*

From the nature of plane and surface in a 3-D space, we have the following Proposition

Proposition 1: *Let (p_1, p_2) be a pair of two arbitrary points on a surface X in 3-D space. Let $\overline{p_1p_2}$ be a straight line joining p_1 and p_2. And let p_m be an arbitrary point lying on $\overline{p_1p_2}$. Then the surface X is a plane if and only if for every pairs (p_1, p_2), the point p_m also lies on X.*

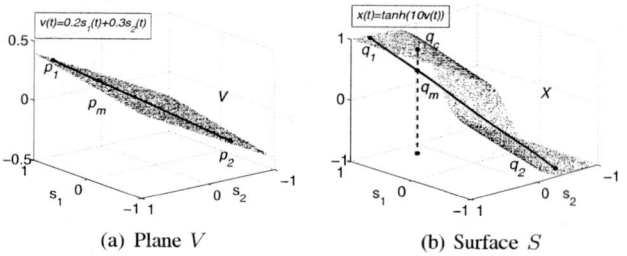

(a) Plane V (b) Surface S

Fig. 2. Using two random signals, s_1 and s_2, 5000 points are plotted. (a) The points are for linear mixture V, giving rise to a plane. The arbitrary point p_m of $\overline{p_1p_2}$ is on V. (b) The points are for nonlinear mixture X, giving rise to a nonlinear surface. The point q_m of $\overline{q_1q_2}$ is not on X.

An illustration of the Proposition 1 is shown in Fig. 2. Since p_1 and p_2 are on the plane V, the point p_m of $\overline{p_1p_2}$ lies on V. Whereas, as X is a nonlinear surface, the point q_m of $\overline{q_1q_2}$ falls out of X with $q_1, q_2 \in X$. From Fig. 2, it is suggested that if we want the surface X to be a plane, the point q_m must $\in X$. In other words, the point $q_c \in X$, which is the companion point of q_m, should be changed to the position of q_m. Thus, by repeating this changing process until for any arbitrary pair $(q_1, q_2) \in X$, all the points $q_m \in \overline{q_1q_2}$ are on X, we can transform the nonlinear surface X into an arbitrary plane.

C. Geometric Linearization of a Mixture

In this section, we propose a method that utilizes the above idea of changing point to point. However, we have to overcome another problem before this idea can be realized into an algorithm. Since the values of s_1 and s_2 are unknown, we can not calculate the value of the companion point $q_m \in X$ directly. To solve this problem, we come up with a solution of using an additional plane (defined as 'reference plane') for identifying q_m. We observed the following property

Proposition 2: *Given four points p_1, p_2, q_1, q_2 such that $(p_1, q_1)_{t_1}$ and $(p_2, q_2)_{t_2}$ are the companion pairs. Let $z_p(t_1)$, $z_p(t_2)$, $z_q(t_1)$ and $z_q(t_2)$ be the values of γ coordinate of the four points p_1, p_2, q_1 and q_2, respectively. And let p_m and q_m be the points lying on $\overline{p_1p_2}$ and $\overline{q_1q_2}$, respectively. If p_m and q_m are the companion points, i.e., $(p_m, q_m)_{t_m}$ is a companion pair, then the following expression holds true*

$$\frac{z_p(t_m) - z_p(t_1)}{z_p(t_2) - z_p(t_1)} = \frac{z_q(t_m) - z_q(t_1)}{z_q(t_2) - z_q(t_1)} \quad (11)$$

where $z_p(t_m)$ and $z_q(t_m)$ are the values of γ coordinate of p_m and q_m, respectively.

Now assume that V is a 'reference plane' representing the linear mixture in (7) and X is a nonlinear surface representing the nonlinear mixture in (8) that needs to be transformed to a plane. Firstly, we pick up any two arbitrary points p_1, p_2 on V and locate their companion points q_1, q_2 on X by using the time index t_1, t_2, respectively. Secondly, we select a random point $p_m \in \overline{p_1p_2}$ and then locate its companion q_c on X by using the time index t_m. Thirdly, by using (11), we find the point $q_m \in \overline{q_1q_2}$ such that $(p_m, q_m)_{t_m}$ is a companion pair. Finally, we move the point q_c to the position of q_m. In Fig. 3 we can see an illustration of the above points before and after the move. The process is repeated until certain conditions are attained, for example, the change is smaller than a preset threshold.

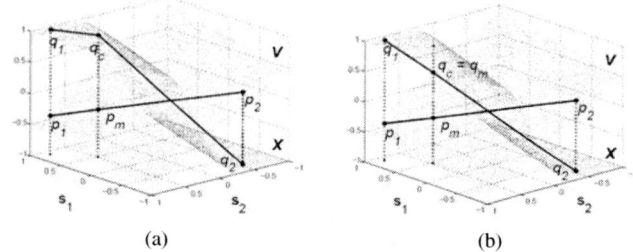

(a)   (b)

Fig. 3. An iteration of the linearizing process. (a) The point q_c before and (b) after transformation. $V = 0.2s_1 - 0.7s_2$ and $X = tanh(10(0.1s_1 + 0.3s_2))$.

D. Application of Geometric Linearization to PNL BSS

The first issue when we apply the above geometric approach to a real PNL BSS problem is: there is no 'reference plane' to use. The available observations are only the two nonlinear input signals, i.e. two surfaces. Thus, a possible solution to use a surface as a 'reference plane' to update the other surface. The surface used as 'reference plane', therefore, is called 'fake plane'. The role of 'fake plane' is alternatively changed from one input (surface) to the other during the updating process.

Another issue is the ambiguity of the point $q_m \in \overline{q_1q_2}$. Proposition 2 implies that if $(p_m, q_m)_{t_m}$ is a companion pair then only (11) holds true, but the reverse is not always held. There may have more than one points q_m that satisfy (11) but are not the companion point of p_m. An incorrect selection of q_m will make q_c, the point that needs to be changed, move to an incorrect position. Thus, we apply a local transformation, i.e. the surface is divided into small areas and the updating process is done within these areas. And instead of moving q_c right to the position of q_m, we apply a learning rate μ. The transformation will take longer time to accomplish but converge steadily to a plane. Figure 4 illustrates an iteration of the method. The selected point is shown in Fig. 4(a) and its new position after the update is shown in Fig. 4(b).

After the transformation, we receive the planes that represent for the linearized signals z_i. However, to ensure the smoothness of the output signals (the linearized z_i), a smoothing function is utilized. In this work, we use a simple averaging function which is formulated as

$$z_i(t) = \frac{1}{2L+1} \sum_{j=-L}^{L} z(t+j) \quad (12)$$

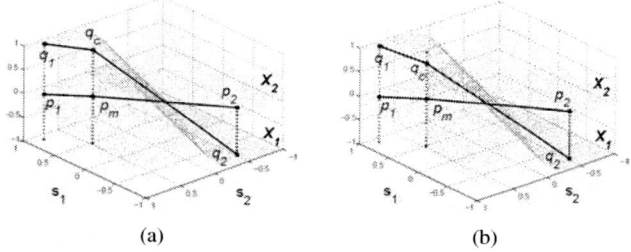

Fig. 4. An example of the algorithm. X_1 is linearized by using X_2 as the reference plane. (a) Position of q_c before the updating process. (b) q_c after updating with learning rate $\mu = 0.5$. $X_1 = tanh(10(0.1s_1 + 0.3s_2))$ and $X_2 = (0.2s_1 - 0.7s_2)^3$.

where L is the window length. The function replaces the value at time t by the average of the values inside a window sized $2L + 1$, centered at t.

Finally, our proposed algorithm is extended for the PNL model of n observations, $x_1, ..., x_n$. Each input signal x_i is presented by a surface X_i, $i = 1, 2, ..., n$. In a single iteration, one surface is randomly chosen among the n surfaces, and is used as the 'fake plane' to update the other surfaces. A framework of the geometric method can be described by the following pseudo-code

===
The geometric PNL method
Input
  n /* number of observed signals */
  T /* number of samples */
  $\mathbf{x} = [x_1(t), x_2(t), ..., x_n(t)]^T$ /* observed signals */
  ϵ_T /* threshold to stop the transformation */
  μ /* learning rate */
  L /* smoothing window length */
Output
  $\mathbf{z} = [z_1(t), z_2(t), ..., z_n(t)]^T$ /* linearized signals */
  $\mathbf{y} = [y_1(t), y_2(t), ..., y_m(t)]^T$ /* estimated signals */

procedure main()
{
  Load data and parameters;
  $\mathbf{z}$ = g_linearize($\mathbf{x}$); /* invoke the geometric method */
  $\mathbf{y}$ = BSS_linear($\mathbf{z}$); /* invoke a linear BSS method */
} /* end of main() procedure*/

function $\mathbf{z}$ = g_linearize($\mathbf{x}$)
{
  $\mathbf{z} = \mathbf{x}$;
  Repeat {
    Randomly select fake plane ID, k in range $[1..n]$;
    Randomly generate T_k in range $[1..T]$;

    For $i = 0$ to T_k **do** {
    /* update the other surfaces */
      Randomly generate t_1, t_2, t_m in range $[1..T]$;
      Compute r by (11). $r = \frac{z_k(t_m) - z_k(t_1)}{z_k(t_2) - z_k(t_1)}$;

      For $j = 1$ to n **do** {
        Compute $z_c = r(z_j(t_2) - z_j(t_1)) + z_j(t_1)$;
        Update $z_j(t_m)^{new} = (1 - \mu)z_j(t_m)^{old} + \mu z_c$;
      } /* end of the inner For loop */
    } /* end of the outer For loop */

    For $j = 1$ to n **do**
      Smoothen z_j using (12);

    Compute $\epsilon = \frac{1}{nT} \sum_{j=1}^{n} \sum_{t=1}^{T} (z_j(t)^{new} - z_j(t)^{old})$;
  Until ($\epsilon < \epsilon_T$);
} /* end of g_linearize() function */
===

To verify the performance of the proposed method, simulations have been carried out on different data sets and the results are provided in the next section.

III. SIMULATIONS

Several simulations are provided in this section. Framework for a simulation includes the following steps:

- Load the source signals, generate a mixing matrix $\mathbf{A}$ randomly, and set the nonlinear function f_i.
- Create the linear mixtures $\mathbf{v}$ and PNL mixtures $\mathbf{x}$.
- Select parameters for the algorithm.
- Run the proposed algorithm to get the estimates $\mathbf{z}$ and $\mathbf{y}$.
- Run other competitive algorithms on the same inputs and compare their results with those of our method.

In the linear demixing process, we have applied several typical linear BSS methods such as SOBI (Second Order Blind Identification) [11], JADETD (Joint Approximate Diagonalization of Eigen matrices with time delays) [12], and FPICA (Fixed-Point ICA) [13]. As their results were almost identical, we show only the results obtained by applying SOBI in the demixing process.

To give a perspective comparison of the algorithm's performance, we compare our method with a linear BSS and a competitive PNL method. For linear one, we choose SOBI, and for the PNL one, we choose Gauss-TD [7], one of the effective reported PNL methods. The performance were measured by the correlation coefficient index r between an original source s and an output signal y.

A. Simulation 1: Mixture of Two Sinusoidal Signals

The simulation was carried out on two sinusoidal signals. The formulas of the sources, the mixing matrix and nonlinear functions are given by

$$\begin{aligned} s_1(t) &= sin(0.33t) \\ s_2(t) &= sin(2\pi(0.3t) + 6cos(2\pi(0.06t))), \end{aligned} \quad (13)$$

$$\mathbf{A} = \begin{pmatrix} 0.3553 & -0.0172 \\ -0.6693 & 0.2001 \end{pmatrix}, \quad (14)$$

$$\begin{aligned} f_1(v) &= 3v^3 \\ f_2(v) &= tanh(10v). \end{aligned} \quad (15)$$

Our method was run with 2000 samples ($T = 2000$), smoothing function window size $L = 300$, learning rate $\mu = 0.4$ and stopping threshold $\epsilon_T = 0.4$. The outputs z_i are plotted in Fig. 5(d) in comparing with the linear mixtures v_i (Fig. 5(a)), $i = 1, 2$. Clearly, the two 3-D plots are almost identical to each other, showing a very good performance of our method in linearizing the signals. The nonlinearity in x_i has been eliminated in z_i.

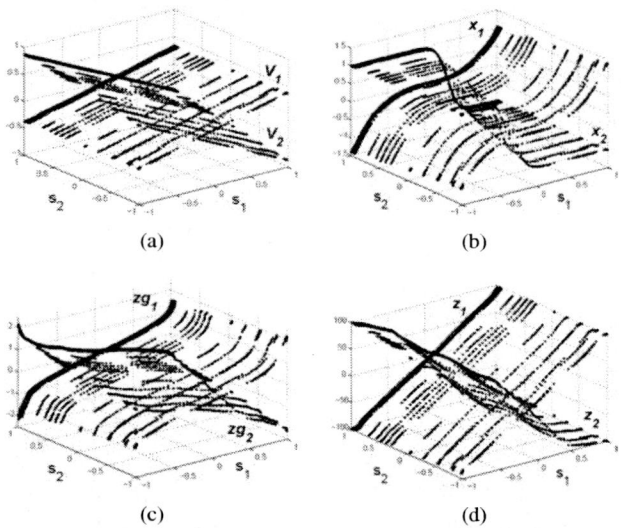

Fig. 5. 3-D Plots of (a) the linear mixtures v_i, (b) the PNL mixtures x_i, (c) the Gauss-TD's linearized signals zg_i and (d) the proposed method's linearized signals z_i, ($i = 1, 2$).

Next, we applied SOBI on z_i to estimate the original sources. The plots of the results y_i are compared with the plots of the original signals s_i in Fig. 6. As it is shown, the unknown original sources have been successfully estimated. In addition, the outputs of the comparing PNL method, the Gauss-TD, and linear BSS method, the SOBI are also plotted in Fig. 6 to complete the comparison.

A quantitative comparison between our method with SOBI and Gauss-TD is reported Table I. Comparing to the result obtained by SOBI, our result is much better with very high correlation coefficient values. In the comparison with Gauss-TD, our method is also obtained a better result.

TABLE I

EXPERIMENT 1: MIXTURE OF TWO SINUSOIDAL SIGNALS - CORRELATION COEFFICIENT r BETWEEN THE ORIGINAL SOURCES AND THEIR ESTIMATES.

	$\hat{s}_1$	$\hat{s}_2$
SOBI	-0.98	0.09
Gauss-TD	-0.96	-0.85
Our method	-0.99	-0.92

B. Simulation 2: Mixture of Four Speech Signals

In this subsection, we carried out the simulation on a typical data set including 5000 samples of four speeches [14]. The

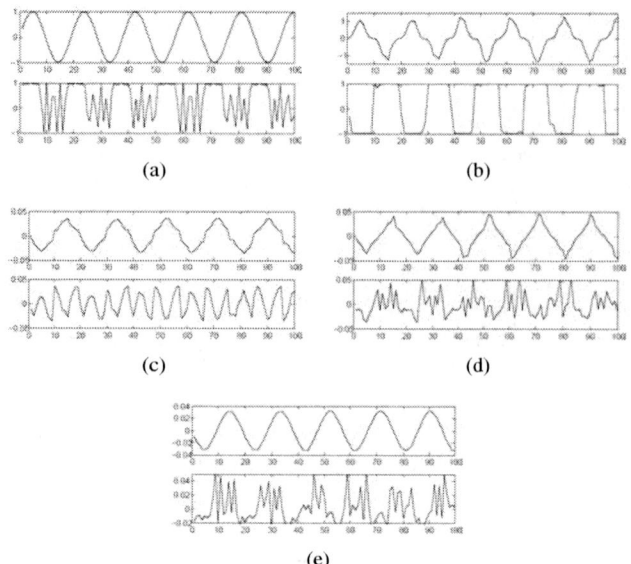

Fig. 6. Plots of (a) the unknown original sources s_i, (b) the PNL mixtures x_i, (c) the SOBI result, (d) the Gauss-TD result and (e) the proposed method result, ($i = 1, 2$).

original speech signals were linearly mixed and nonlinearly transformed by a matrix $\mathbf{A}$ and functions f_i given by

$$\mathbf{A} = \begin{pmatrix} -0.7056 & -0.2723 & -0.8562 & -0.4275 \\ 0.3966 & 0.1866 & -0.2596 & 0.0014 \\ -0.7758 & 0.7012 & 0.1318 & -0.4642 \\ 0.8582 & -0.229 & 0.3806 & -0.8994 \end{pmatrix} \quad (16)$$

$$\begin{aligned} f_1(v) &= tanh(10v) \\ f_2(v) &= 0.1v + v^3 \\ f_3(v) &= tanh(2v) + v^3 \\ f_4(v) &= v + tanh(7v). \end{aligned} \quad (17)$$

The parameters were set at $L = 300$, $\mu = 0.4$ and $\epsilon_T = 0.4$. The results are shown in Fig. 7, together with the original speeches, the PNL mixtures (the observed signals), the SOBI's results and Gauss-TD's results. The correlation coefficients between the estimates $\hat{s}_i$ and their original signals s_i of our method, SOBI and Gauss-TD are provided in Table II.

TABLE II

EXPERIMENT 2: MIXTURE OF FOUR SPEECH SIGNALS - CORRELATION COEFFICIENT r BETWEEN THE ORIGINAL SOURCES AND THEIR ESTIMATES.

	$\hat{s}_1$	$\hat{s}_2$	$\hat{s}_3$	$\hat{s}_4$
SOBI	-0.59	0.55	0.47	-0.65
Gauss-TD	0.97	0.91	0.93	-0.95
Our method	0.98	0.92	0.95	0.98

In this simulation, the proposed method continues to provide a very good performance, it was capable of estimating all the four speech signals effectively. Whereas, SOBI could not estimate any speech with adequate quality. In term of the performance index r, i.e., the correlation coefficient, our method obtained a very high value ($r > 0.92$) for all the estimated signals. It means the hidden source speeches were

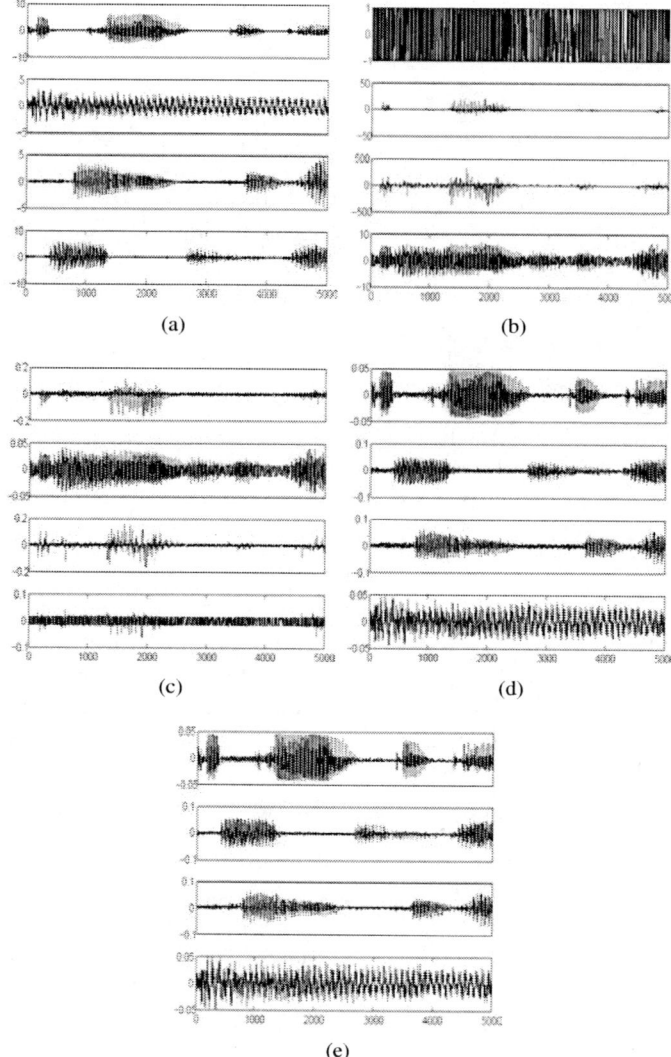

Fig. 7. Plots of (a) the unknown original sources s_i, (b) the PNL mixtures x_i, (c) the SOBI result, (d) the Gauss-TD result and (e) the proposed method result, ($i = 1, 2, ..., 4$).

clearly separated from mixtures. Moreover, comparing with the Gauss-TD algorithm, which uses additional assumption of the Gaussianity of the mixtures, our method performance is slightly better.

IV. CONCLUSIONS

A geometric approach for the Post Nonlinear Blind Source Separation has been presented in this paper. By considering the characteristics of a plane and a surface, a simple linearizing process has been developed to transform the PNL mixtures to the linear ones without any additional assumption. From the linearized signals, the hidden sources can be estimated by any basic linear BSS algorithm. Extensive simulations have been carried out to analyze the algorithm's performance. The advantages of our algorithm can be summarized as follow:

- Besides the PNL mixture assumption, it does not use any assumption about the original sources and the nonlinear mixtures. The algorithm can work on both Gaussian and non-Gaussian mixtures.
- In the proposed method, the linearization and demixing process are independent. The users can choose any suitable linear BSS algorithm for demixing. Thus, it increases the performance of the method in each specific environment.
- Through out extensive experiments, our algorithm turns out to be a very effective solution for PNL BSS problem.

However, several issues still exist and we need further work to improve the algorithm. The first issue is the ambiguity of the point q_m caused by the heuristic criterion in (11). A possible solution could be another version with multiple updating points or multiple 'fake planes'. The convergence conditions and the best configuration are also other issues that need more study in the future. Finally, geometric approach to nonlinear BSS is not constrained to PNL model only, studies of an extended method for a broader nonlinear BSS model are being carried on.

REFERENCES

[1] A. Cichocki and S. Amari, *Adaptive blind signal and image processing*. John Wiley & Sons Ltd, 2002.
[2] P. Pajunen, A. Hyvärinen, and J. Karhunen, "Nonlinear blind source separation by self-organizing maps," in *Proc. Int. Conf. on Neural Information Processing (ICONIP'96)*, vol. 2, Hong Kong, China, 1996, pp. 1207–1210.
[3] P. Pajunen and J. Karhunen, "A maximum likelihood approach to nonlinear blind source separation," in *Proc. Int. Conf. on Artificial Neural Networks (ICANN'97)*, Lausanne, Switzerland, 1997, pp. 541–546.
[4] C. Jutten and J. Karhunen, "Advances in nonlinear blind source separation," in *Proc. Int. Symposium on Independent Component Analysis and Blind Signal Separation (ICA'03)*, Nara, Japan, Apr. 2003, pp. 245–256.
[5] A. Hyvärinen and P. Pajunen, "Nonlinear independent component analysis: Existence and uniqueness results," *Neural Networks*, vol. 12, no. 3, pp. 429–439, 1999.
[6] A. Taleb and C. Jutten, "Source separation in post-nonlinear mixtures," *IEEE Trans. Signal Processing*, vol. 47, no. 10, pp. 2807–2820, Oct. 1999.
[7] A. Ziehe, M. Kawanabe, S. Harmeling, and K. R. Müller, "Blind separation of post-nonlinear mixtures using linearizing transformations and temporal decorrelation," *Journal of Machine Learning Research*, vol. 4, pp. 1319–1338, Dec. 2003.
[8] H. Yang, S. Amari, and A. Cichocki, "Information-theoretic approach to blind separation of sources in nonlinear mixture," *Signal Processing*, vol. 64, pp. 291–300, 1998.
[9] T. V. Nguyen, J. C. Patra, and A. Das, "A geometric approach to post nonlinear mixture in blind source separation," in *Proc. IEEE International Conference on Communications Systems (ICCS'04)*, vol. 1, Singapore, Sept. 2004, pp. 260–264.
[10] T. V. Nguyen and J. C. Patra, "A post nonlinear geometric algorithm for independent component analysis," *Digital Signal Processing*, 2005 (in press).
[11] A. Belouchrani, K. Abed-Meraim, J. F. Cardoso, and E. Moulines, "A blind source separation technique using second-order statistics," *IEEE Trans. Signal Processing*, vol. 45, no. 2, pp. 434–444, Feb. 1997.
[12] P. G. Georgiev and A. Cichocki, "Robust independent component analysis via time-delayed cumulant functions," *IEICE Transactions on Fundamentals*, vol. E86-A, no. 3, pp. 573–579, 2003.
[13] A. Hyvärinen, "Fast and robust fixed-point algorithms for independent component analysis," *IEEE Trans. Neural Networks*, vol. 10, no. 3, pp. 626–634, 1999.
[14] A. Cichocki and S. Amari and K. Siwek and T. Tanaka et al. (2003) Icalab toolboxes. [Online]. Available: {http://www.bsp.brain.riken.jp/ICALAB/}

Which Features Trigger Action Potentials in Cortical Neurons *in Vivo*?

Holger Fröhlich
Center for Bioinformatics Tübingen (ZBIT)
Sand 1, 72076 Tübingen, Germany
Email: froehlic@informatik.uni-tuebingen.de

Björn Naundorf
Dept. Nonlinear Dynamics
Max-Planck Institute for Dynamics and Self Organization
Göttingen, Germany
Email: bjoern@chaos.gwdg.de

Maxim Volgushev
Dept. Neurophysiology MA 4/149
Ruhr-Universität Bochum, Germany
Email: maxim@neurop.ruhr-uni-bochum.de

Fred Wolf
Dept. Nonlinear Dynamics
Max-Planck Institute for Dynamics and Self Organization
Göttingen, Germany
Email: fred@chaos.gwdg.de

Abstract—We study the initiation of action potentials (APs) in *in vivo* recordings of cortical neurons from cat visual cortex. Recently, it was shown that cortical neurons are not simple threshold devices, emitting an AP each time a fixed voltage threshold is reached, but that the emission of an AP partly depends on the rate of change of the membrane potential preceeding an AP. In this paper we investigate systematically which features of the membrane potential lead to an AP by means of Machine Learning methods. We use Support Vector Machines (SVMs) to discriminate between trajectories of the membrane potential which lead to an AP within the next ms and trajectories which do not lead to the initiation of an AP. For every point in a trajectory of the membrane potential (MP) we compute a set of 11 features and use a forward selection algorithm to find out the relevant features for the occurence of an AP. Based on the results we construct a reduced prediction model. This model suggests that AP occurences can be predicted best by a combination of the 1st temporal derivative of the MP at distance to the AP maximum, the MP itself and the mean MP over a longer range.

I. INTRODUCTION

The human brain is the most complex information processing device known to date. Its basic computational units are neural cells which dynamically transform synaptic inputs into action potentials (APs) by an intrinsically nonlinear process. This process enables networks of neurons to perform complex computations [10], [11], [7]. Classically, neurons are viewed as integrators, summing synaptic inputs and emitting an AP once the neurons' membrane potential (MP) reaches a threshold voltage. This reductionistic view was extended by Hodgkin and Huxley [6] who developed a biophysical theory, which could explain the generation of APs. They showed that the emission of an AP is a non-linear high-dimensional process involving the detailed dynamics of voltage-dependent channels in the membrane of a neuron. Although major advances were achieved in describing the dynamics of the underlying voltage-gated channels individually in great detail, emergent mechanisms which result from their dynamical interplay were investigated only recently [8], [1]. In these studies it was predicted that the voltage at which an AP initiates partially depends on the velocity with which the membrane potential depolarates. This prediction was confirmed in recent experiments, which investigated the generation of APs in cortical neurons. They demonstrated that APs initiate at a low voltage when the membrane potential depolarized quickly and at a high voltage when the membrane potential depolarizes slowly [2].

From a functional point of view the mechanism of AP initiation has a strong qualitative impact on the information processing in the brain. In simplified models it was demonstrated that seemingly minor details of the AP generating mechanism can fundamentally alter the nature of the encoding of synaptic inputs into sequences of APs, as shown in [5], [12].

The goal of this paper is to clarify, which features of the MP lead to the occurence of an AP in cortical neurons *in-vivo*. For this purpose we investigated 9 *in-vivo* recordings of neurons from cat visual cortex. Neurons *in-vivo* are subject to an immense synaptic bombardment, leading to large fluctuations of their MP. Although the functional role of these fluctuations is still unclear, it significantly alters the neurons' dynamical properties [4], [16]. We analyzed the AP generation in this "natural environment" and examined which patterns in the subthreshold fluctuations of the MP could predict best the occurrence of an AP. To do this, we defined a set of 11 features, which we computed for every MP point in a recording.

To discriminate MP trajectories leading to APs from those which did not lead to the generation of an AP, we employed Support Vector Machines (SVMs). SVMs belong to the family of "Kernel Methods" [13], [15], [14] and are one of the most popular Machine Learning methods today. Without making any a-priori assumptions about the relevance of certain features, we used a forward selection algorithm [9] to find out the features which contributed most to the classification in each dataset. From all feature subsets that were selected for a single recording we infered a reduced model, which incorporated only those three features that were top ranked for all traces. These were the 1st temporal derivative and the height of the MP at AP onset, as well as the mean AP 5ms prior AP onset. We evaluated the reduced model on all datasets and showed that indeed the classification performance was at least as good as when using all 11 features. Our results thus suggest that the occurence of an AP is mostly determined by the mean potential over a longer range, the height of the potential shortly before the AP and the 1st temporal derivative of the membrane potential shortly before the AP. Thereby the feature with the largest impact was the first temporal derivative whereas the influence of the two other features was significantly lower. In conclusion our results imply that the AP generation mechanism in cortical neurons *in vivo* acts rather as a coincidence detector than as an integrator.

In the next section we will first give a brief review on SVMs and highlight the relevant features for our study. Afterwards we will describe our method in detail. In section III we present the results of the application of our method on *in-vivo* recordings from cat visual cortex. In section IV we summarize our results and conclude.

II. METHODS

A. Support Vector Machines - a Brief Review

Support Vector Machines (SVMs) were introduced in 1995 by V. Vapnik and C. Cortes [3], [15], [14] and are one of the most popular Machine Learning methods today: Given some empirical dataset $\mathcal{D} = \{(x_i, y_i) \in \mathcal{X} \times \{\pm 1\} | i = 1, ..., N\}$ with $x_i \in \mathcal{X}$ being observations in some arbitrary input domain and $y_i \in \{\pm 1\}$ the class labels we want to construct a decision hyperplane $f(x) = \text{sign}(\langle \mathbf{w}, \phi(x) \rangle + b)$ in some Hilbert space $\mathcal{H}$. Thereby $\phi : \mathcal{X} \rightarrow \mathcal{H}$ is a (possibly nonlinear) map of the original data into *feature space* $\mathcal{H}$. The hyperplane is constructed such that *margin size* (that is the distance of the hyperplane to points closest to it in feature space) is maximal. This is achieved by solving the quadratic program

$$\min_{\mathbf{w},\xi,b} \frac{1}{2}\|\mathbf{w}\|^2 + \frac{C}{N}\sum_{i=1}^{N}\xi_i \quad (1)$$
$$\text{subject to } y_i(\langle \mathbf{w}, \phi(x_i)\rangle + b) \geq 1 - \xi_i$$
$$\xi_i \geq 0$$

where $C > 0$ is a constant that regularizes the trade-off between minimizing the training error $\frac{1}{N}\sum \xi_i$ and maximizing the size of the margin $1/\|\mathbf{w}\|$ in feature space. Equivalently one can solve the dual of (1):

$$\max_{\alpha} \sum_i \alpha_i - \frac{1}{2}\sum_{i,j} \alpha_i \alpha_j y_i y_j \langle \phi(x_i), \phi(x_j)\rangle \quad (2)$$
$$\text{subject to } \sum_i \alpha_i y_i = 0$$
$$\alpha_i \in (0, C]$$

Thereby the apearing dot products $\langle \phi(x_i), \phi(x_j)\rangle$ in (2) can be implicitly computed via a so called *kernel function* $k : \mathcal{X} \times \mathcal{X} \rightarrow \mathbb{R}$. Popular examples of kernel functions are e.g. the radial basis function, which allows nonlinear class separation, but also the ordinary dot product $\langle \cdot, \cdot \rangle$ can be viewed as a special kernel (the linear kernel) with the property $\mathcal{X} = \mathcal{H}$ and $\phi = id$.

A special property of SVMs is, that only points for which $\alpha_i \neq 0$ contribute to the decision function. They are called *support vectors* (SVs). Geometrically they correspond to points lying on or within the margin. They are the extreme examples within each class, i.e. examples which are most similar to those of the opposite class. In fact by removing all training examples except the support vectors one recovers the same solution as when using all data. This property is called *sparseness* of the solution.

An alternative formulation to the so called C-SVM Eq. (1), introduced by Schölkopf [13] is the ν-SVM:

$$\min_{\mathbf{w},\xi,\rho,b} \frac{1}{2}\|\mathbf{w}\|^2 - \nu\rho + \frac{1}{N}\sum_{i=1}^{N}\xi_i \quad (3)$$
$$\text{subject to } y_i(\langle \mathbf{w}, \phi(x_i)\rangle + b) \geq \rho - \xi_i$$
$$\xi_i \geq 0, \rho \geq 0$$

Here $\rho/\|\mathbf{w}\|$ is the size of the margin in feature space and $\nu \in (0, 1]$ the regularization constant. Schölkopf et al. proved that ν is both, an upper bound on the fraction of training errors and a lower bound on the fraction of support vectors. Furthermore, for $N \rightarrow \infty$ ν equals both, the fraction of training errors and the fraction of support vectors [13]. Like for the C-SVM a dual formulation for (3) can be found which allows the usage of arbitrary kernel functions.

We now turn to the description of our method, which employs SVMs as an essential tool for classification, in detail.

B. Our Approach

1) In-vivo Recordings: We analyzed 9 *in-vivo* recordings from cat visual cortex, where each recording contained at least 100 APs. The recordings exhibited only spontaneous activity, generated from the surrounding network, leading to low firing rates < 2Hz. The experimental details and the data acquisition are published in [17]. Each recording consists of a discrete time trajectory $T_V = \{(t_i, V(t_i)) | i = 1, ..., N\}$ of length N with membrane potentials $V(t_i)$ at times points t_i. All datasets except the last 3 were recorded at a time resolution of 0.1ms while the last three had a resolution of 0.05ms. The times of the AP maxima in the following are denoted by $\hat{t}_1, ..., \hat{t}_\ell$.

2) Preprocessing and Feature Construction: We first low-pass filtered all recordings using a 5-point sliding window average. The MP at every point t_i was embedded in a 11-dimensional feature space, resulting in a vector $\mathbf{x}(t_i)$. The single coordinates of the feature space were defined as:

- the MP $V(t_i)$
- the 1st to 5th derivatives $\frac{d^k V}{dt^k}(t_i)$ of the MP
- the mean MP potentials $\bar{V}_r(t_i), r = 0.5, 1, 2.5, 10$ms before t_i.

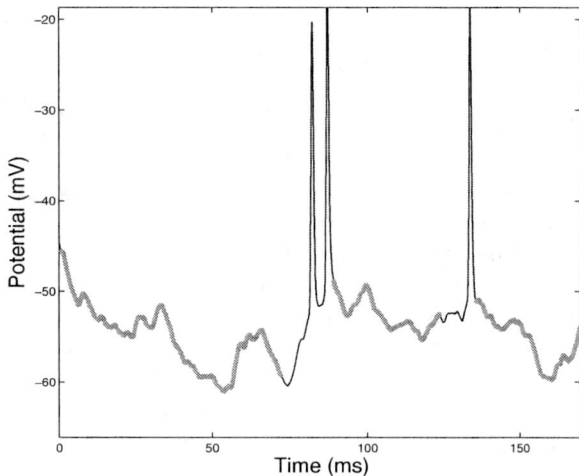

Fig. 1. Small piece of an example trajectory with negative examples marked thicker.

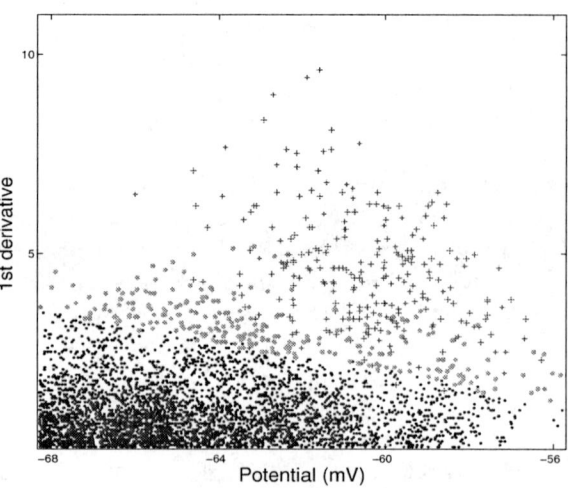

Fig. 2. Example of the first two features of positive ('+') and negative examples (dots) plotted against each other ($\tau = 0.7$ms). The subsampled negative support vectors are marked thicker. Positive and negative examples overlap with regard to all features individually (see text).

3) Negative Examples: We next constructed the set of those examples $\{x_i^{(n)}\}$, which do not lead to the generation of an AP. They will be called *negative examples* in the following. They were chosen such that their distance was more than 10ms to the following AP and more than 2ms from the preceeding AP (Fig. 1). This safety distance excluded the small trajectories between two burst APs and ensured that negative examples were not close to the AP initiation where active conductances play an important role.

4) Positive Examples: As the set of *positive examples* $\{x_i^{(p)}\}$ we chose all trajectories ending at time points $\tilde{t}_j - \tau$. Thereby the time points $\tilde{t}_j$ are all those times of AP maxima $\hat{t}_j$ which have a time distance of at least 10ms to the preceeding AP. This procedure reliably removed all burst APs.

Obviously, for small distances τ, the set of positive and negative examples can be trivially distinguished by the height of the MP. To ensure that the classification is not trivial we increased the value of τ in steps of 0.1ms until the two sets could not be separated by a threshold with regard to any feature. The distance was then further increased until the number of points which overlapped in any feature was at least as large as the number of APs in the whole recording. Figure 2 illustrates this construction by showing the first feature plotted against the second feature. Both classes overlap and a simple threshold separation in the first or second feature individually is not possible. The positions $\tilde{t}_j - \tau$ are in the following also called the onset positions of APs.

5) Subsampling of Negative Examples: Compared to the length of the whole trajectory T_V, a AP is a quite rare event. This implies that in a recording we have only few positive examples compared to a huge number of negative examples (approx. 10^5 as many as positive examples). To achieve a high accuracy of our classifier and to reduce the computational cost we thus selected a subset of negative examples, which were most similar to the set positive examples, i.e. which

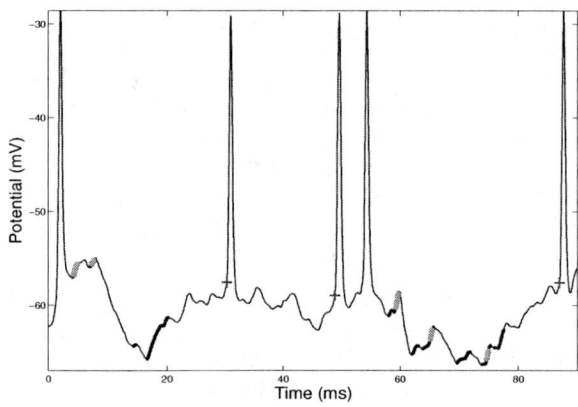

Fig. 3. Positive and negative examples in an example trajectory ($\tau = 0.7$ms). End points of positive examples are marked with red crosses, end points of negative examples are marked a little bit thicker than the rest of the trajectory. Selected support vectors are marked with big green dots. Negative examples are all those which overlap with the positive ones with regard to all features plus or minus one standard deviation (see text). Note that the third AP is neglected, because it follows the previous AP too closely.

were hardest to classify. Obvious candidates for this are those negative examples which overlap with the positive ones. To have a sufficient coverage of the whole space we extended this set of overlapping negatives by all those negatives which lay within one standard deviation of the features of the positive examples.

Figure 2 shows a scatter plot, graphing the first two features of positive and negative examples. The number of negative examples m' (dots) exceeds the number of positive examples m (crosses) by several orders of magnitude. Training a SVM with this data would lead to an unnecessary computational burden. On the other hand, a uniform random subsampling of the negative examples would produce many examples which are quite far away from our decision line and hence do not contribute to the classification, i.e. they are not support vectors. This would lead to a suboptimal performance of the classifier. Thus our goal should be to select our negative training data among those which will likely become support vectors later. As we know from subsection II-A, for ν-SVMs the parameter ν is a lower bound on the fraction of support vectors. Hence, by setting $\nu = 2m/(m' + m)$ and training a SVM on the whole data, we get approximately $2m$ support vectors of which around m should be negative examples. This firstly leads to a nicely balanced dataset and secondly it automatically produces those examples, we should concentrate on during training. Note that we are not interested in the decision hyperplane itself here, but just in the selected support vectors. In Fig. 2 the selected negative examples are marked by thick green dots. The SVM training was performed using a linear kernel, and the data was normalized to mean 0 and standard deviation 1 before training. To get a better impression, Fig. 3 displays an example trajectory with overlapping negative examples and selected support vectors. Alltogether we now have a set of positive examples (crosses) and a set of negative examples (big dots) which can be used to design a model. Only these two sets were considered in the following in order to find out the relevant features.

6) Finding Out The Relevant Features in a Recording: To find out the relevant features in a recording we employed a forward selection algorithm [9]. Starting with an empty set of features, we successively added those feature which, if added to the existing ones, lead to the lowest 5-fold cross-validation error. This procedure was continued until all features had been included. The order of inclusion into the feature set induces a ranking of the features. In the end the feature set with the lowest cross-validation error was returned.

During the feature selection we used a linear $C-$SVM, because in general training is a little bit faster compared to the ν-SVM. We chose the parameter C via a 5-fold cross-validation from the grid $2^{-4}, ..., 2^5$ at each stage of the feature selection algorithm. Like above, before training each feature for the whole data was normalized to mean 0 and standard deviation 1.

7) Construction of a Generalized Reduced Model: As a result of the forward selection algorithm we obtained a ranked feature subset for each recording which could classify best the positive and negative examples in the training set. It is, however, not a-priori clear that a feature set, which performs well on one recording will also perform as good on another recording, i.e. if the prediction model generalizes well across different recordings. We thus constructed a reduced model in which we included only those features, which were ranked most frequently among the 5 best features for each single recording.

8) Evaluation of the Reduced Model: This reduced model was evaluated subsequently for every recording using 5-fold cross-validation. Thereby each training set consisted of 4/5 of the examples obtained by the procedure described in II-B.5

TABLE I
OVERVIEW OF THE DIFFERENT DATASETS USED IN OUR EXPERIMENTS.

Dataset	#AP	#Test Instances	#Negative SVs	τ(ms)
1	121	216661	121	1.1
2	188	1376364	188	0.6
3	177	38241	178	0.9
4	258	22400	259	0.7
5	252	27028	253	0.7
6	183	41674	183	0.7
7	128	1463434	128	0.6
8	1098	2909598	1097	0.6
9	385	3867932	385	0.6

and the testing set of *all* examples in the recording that were not used for training. As before, a linear C-SVM was used. To prevent overfitting the parameter C was adapted via an extra level of 5-fold cross-validation within each cross-validation procedure. To determine the relative impact of each feature on the classification, we computed the weight vector $\mathbf{w}$ of the decision hyperplane:

$$\mathbf{w} = \sum_i \alpha_i y_i \mathbf{x}_i$$

were α_i are the Lagrangian multipliers obtained by solving the quadratic program Eq. (2). This was possible, because we used a linear kernel. The absolute value $|w_j|$ can be viewed as a measure for the relative influence (weight) of feature j on the decision hyperplane $f(\mathbf{x}) = \text{sign}(\langle \mathbf{w}, \mathbf{x} \rangle + b)$. During the evaluation we computed the mean of the weight vectors over all cross-validation folds for each recording, and normalized each compound of the mean weight vector by its standard deviation.

III. RESULTS

We applied our method to 9 *in-vivo* recordings of spontaneous activity from cat visual cortex. Table I shows an overview of the different datasets with respect to the number of APs, the selected distance τ from AP maxima, the number of subsampled negative examples (negative SVs) selected by the ν-SVM and the number of overall test examples.

Table II shows which features were selected for each dataset in the order of their inclusion together with the 5-fold cross-validation error on the reduced set of examples obtained by the procedure described in section II-B.5.

We then evaluated how frequent each feature was ranked among the first 5 (table III). Including only those features which were ranked among the first 5 in at least 50% of all cases we constructed a reduced model, which incorporated the following features:

- the mean potential over a longer range (i.e. $\bar{V}_5$)
- the membrane potential at AP onset (i.e. at $\tilde{t}_i - \tau$)
- the 1st derivative of the membrane potential at AP onset

We tested the generalized model on all recordings as described in the previous section. The number of false negatives (FN) and the number of false positives (FP) are listed together with the relative false negative (fnr) and false positive rates (fpr) in table IV. The relative false negative rate is defined

TABLE II
SELECTED FEATURES FOR 9 REAL LIFE DATASETS IN THE ORDER THEY WERE INCLUDED AND 5-FOLD CROSS-VALIDATION ERROR (%) ± STANDARD DEVIATION (%).

Recording	Features	CV error (%)
1	$\frac{dV}{dt}$, V, $\bar{V}_5$, $\bar{V}_1$, $\bar{V}_{0.5}$	5.33 ± 3.12
2	$\frac{d^2V}{dt^2}$, V, $\frac{dV}{dt}$, $\frac{d^4V}{dt^4}$, $\bar{V}_{0.5}$, $\bar{V}_{2.5}$, $\bar{V}_{10}$, $\frac{d^3V}{dt^3}$, $\frac{d^5V}{dt^5}$, $\bar{V}_1$	0.79 ± 0.72
3	$\frac{dV}{dt}$, $\bar{V}_1$, $\bar{V}_{10}$, $\frac{d^2V}{dt^2}$, $\frac{d^4V}{dt^4}$, $\bar{V}_5$, $\bar{V}_{2.5}$, $\frac{d^5V}{dt^5}$, V	15.07 ± 2.39
4	$\frac{dV}{dt}$, $\bar{V}_{0.5}$, $\bar{V}_5$, $\frac{d^5V}{dt^5}$, V	4.25 ± 2.86
5	$\frac{dV}{dt}$, V, $\bar{V}_{10}$, $\frac{d^2V}{dt^2}$, $\bar{V}_{0.5}$, $\bar{V}_{2.5}$, $\bar{V}_{0.5}$, $\frac{d^4V}{dt^4}$, $\frac{d^3V}{dt^3}$, $\frac{d^5V}{dt^5}$, $\bar{V}_1$	3.96 ± 1.86
6	$\frac{dV}{dt}$, $\bar{V}_1$, $\bar{V}_5$, $\frac{d^3V}{dt^3}$, $\frac{d^4V}{dt^4}$, $\frac{d^5V}{dt^5}$, $\bar{V}_{10}$, $\bar{V}_{0.5}$, $\bar{V}_{2.5}$, V, $\frac{d^2V}{dt^2}$	7.89 ± 5.75
7	$\frac{dV}{dt}$, V, $\bar{V}_5$, $\frac{d^2V}{dt^2}$, $\frac{d^3V}{dt^3}$, $\frac{d^5V}{dt^5}$, $\bar{V}_{2.5}$, $\bar{V}_1$, $\bar{V}_{0.5}$, $\bar{V}_{10}$, $\frac{d^4V}{dt^4}$	5.05 ± 1.74
8	$\frac{dV}{dt}$, V, $\bar{V}_{10}$, $\frac{d^2V}{dt^2}$, $\frac{d^5V}{dt^5}$, $\bar{V}_5$, $\frac{d^4V}{dt^4}$, $\bar{V}_{0.5}$, $\frac{d^3V}{dt^3}$, $\bar{V}_1$	5.33 ± 1.12
9	$\frac{dV}{dt}$, V, $\bar{V}_{2.5}$, $\frac{d^3V}{dt^3}$, $\bar{V}_{10}$, $\frac{d^4V}{dt^4}$, $\frac{d^2V}{dt^2}$, $\bar{V}_1$, $\frac{d^5V}{dt^5}$, $\bar{V}_5$	9.22 ± 2.26

TABLE III
ANALYSIS OF THE FREQUENCY OF THE RANKING OF THE FEATURES AMONG THE FIRST BEST ONES IN ALL DATASETS.

Feature	#Selected	%	Among First 5	%
V	9	100	7	77
$\bar{V}_{10}$	7	77	4	44
$\bar{V}_5$	7	77	5	55
$\bar{V}_{2.5}$	6	66	1	11
$\bar{V}_1$	8	89	3	33
$\bar{V}_{0.5}$	7	77	3	33
$\frac{dV}{dt}$	9	100	9	100
$\frac{d^2V}{dt^2}$	7	77	4	44
$\frac{d^3V}{dt^3}$	6	66	3	33
$\frac{d^4V}{dt^4}$	7	77	2	22
$\frac{d^5V}{dt^5}$	8	89	1	11

TABLE IV
RESULTS ON THE EVALUATION EXPERIMENT USING OUR REDUCED MODEL: NUMBER OF FALSE NEGATIVES (FN), OF FALSE POSITIVES (FP), AND RELATIVE FALSE NEGATIVE (FNR) AND FALSE POSITIVE RATE (FPR) ± STANDARD DEVIATION. SIGNIFICANT IMPROVEMENTS IN COMPARISON TO THE USAGE OF ALL FEATURES ARE MARKED BY "*", DETORIATIONS BY "-".

dataset	FN	FP	fnr (%)	fpr (%)
1	2.2 ± 1.3	$63 \pm 8.2^-$	9.13 ± 5.47	0.02 ± 0.01
2	0.8 ± 0.8	0.8 ± 1.3	2.12 ± 2.21	0 ± 0
3	$3.2 \pm 1.5^*$	$2 \pm 1.2^*$	9 ± 4.16	0.01 ± 0
4	3.6 ± 1.3	1.6 ± 1.1	6.97 ± 2.56	0.01 ± 0.01
5	$4 \pm 1.4^-$	$2.2 \pm 1.5^*$	7.95 ± 2.82	0.01 ± 0.01
6	$0.2 \pm 0.4^*$	$0.4 \pm 0.5^*$	0.54 ± 1.21	0 ± 0
7	2.6 ± 3.1	1.6 ± 1.1	10.25 ± 12.57	0 ± 0
8	25.6 ± 6.5	$10 \pm 1.6^*$	11.65 ± 2.97	0 ± 0
9	11 ± 2.2	$52 \pm 4.2^*$	14.29 ± 2.9	0.01 ± 0

TABLE V
RESULTS ON THE EVALUATION EXPERIMENT USING ALL FEATURES: NUMBER OF FALSE NEGATIVES (FN), OF FALSE POSITIVES (FP), AND RELATIVE FALSE NEGATIVE (FNR) AND FALSE POSITIVE (FPR) RATE ± STANDARD DEVIATION.

dataset	FN	FP	fnr (%)	fpr (%)
1	2.6 ± 1.1	26 ± 8.3	10.8 ± 4.81	0.01 ± 0.01
2	0.6 ± 1.3	0.4 ± 0.5	1.57 ± 3.53	0 ± 0
3	6 ± 1.2	27.8 ± 15.3	16.8 ± 3.33	0.07 ± 0.04
4	3 ± 1.2	3.2 ± 2.1	5.81 ± 2.34	0.01 ± 0.01
5	1.8 ± 0.8	10.4 ± 2.9	3.58 ± 1.69	0.04 ± 0.01
6	4 ± 2.6	9.6 ± 3.85	10.89 ± 6.87	0.02 ± 0.01
7	2.2 ± 2.3	1 ± 1	8.65 ± 9.16	0 ± 0
8	13.8 ± 4	142.2 ± 71.5	6.28 ± 1.8	0.01 ± 0
9	8.6 ± 1.8	87.6 ± 7.5	11.17 ± 2.36	0.02 ± 0

as $fnr = FN/NEG$, and the relative false positive rate as $fpr = FP/POS$ with POS being the number of positive examples and NEG the number of negative examples in the test set. Additionally, we tested against the usage of all features. The results of this experiment are shown in table V. Compared to the usage of all features, our reduced model in 7 cases leads to a significant improvement and to a significant detoriation in only 2 cases. The significance was tested separately for the number of false negatives and false positives by means of a paired t-test at significance level 5%. This shows that in general the reduced model, which incorporated only features that we assumed to be most relevant for the occurence of an AP, has a better generalization capability than the full model using all features. This nicely corroborates our generalized model.

We finally investigated the relative influence of each of the three most relevant features on the decision hyperplane by means of the mean weight vector obtained on each recording. Figure 4 shows a histogram of the mean weight vector components divided by the 1-norm of the vector and averaged over all recordings. The influence of the mean potential over the last 5ms is comparable to the potential at AP onset, while the 1st derivative on average has a much higher impact. This result is consistent with the ranking obtained in table II.

IV. CONCLUSION

We investigated the AP generation in *in-vivo* recordings from cat visual cortex. We introduced an empirical method to work out which features of the trajectory of the membrane potential are most relevant for the occurence of an AP. Based on statistical tools, namely Support Vector Machines, we developed a technique to infer a model automatically from empirical data. Without making any a-priori assumptions about the relevance of certain features, we used a forward selection algorithm to find features which discriminated well between trajectories leading to an AP and others which do not. Based on the results for each of our recordings we constructed a reduced model, which only included the MP, the rate of change of the MP and the MP averaged over 5ms. Using this reduced model, APs could be predicted with a very high accuracy on all

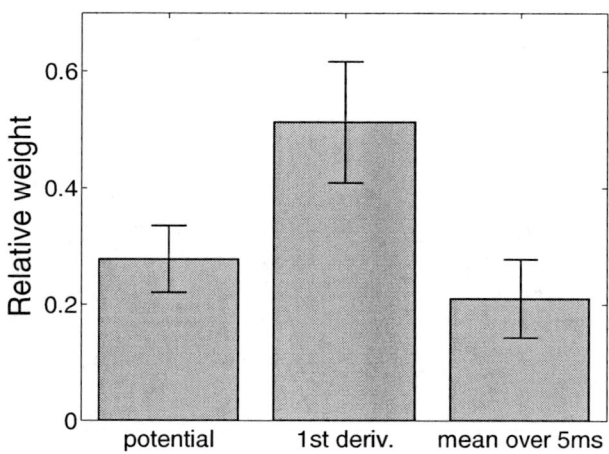

Fig. 4. Relative influence of the three most relevant features on the decision hyperplane averaged over all datasets.

our recordings, which reveals the high statistical consistency and generalization capability of our reduced model. Our results suggest that qualitatively the occurence of an AP is mostly determined by the mean potential over a longer range before AP, the height of the membrane potential shortly before the AP and the 1st temporal derivative of the membrane potential shortly before the AP. Surprisingly, the 1st temporal derivative of the MP had a much larger impact on the classification than the mean MP over a long range. This suggests that cortical neurons act as coincidence detectors, which are most sensitive to fast changes of the MP. Models of cortical neurons which assume a voltage threshold for AP initiation might not reflect the dynamics of AP generation of cortical neurons.

Several previous theoretical studies assessed the computation performed in single neurons (e.g. [8], [1]). These studies were almost exclusively based on the Hodgkin-Huxley model [6], which describes the dynamical interplay of voltage-gated sodium and potassium channels in the generation of an AP. It is, however, not a-priori clear that this dynamics is equivalent with the AP generation in cortical neurons. Experimentally, the AP generation in cortical neurons *in vivo* was recently addressed in [2] *in vivo*. In this study, a correlation between the potential and the first derivative at AP onset was proposed to explain the large variability of AP onset potentials found *in vivo*. Our approach generalizes these results by using a set of 11 features without any a-priori weighting. It therefore allowed for the systematic construction of a simple phenomenological models, which reproduces the AP generation with very high accuracy and serves as a starting point for the development for simplified phenomenological neuron models, which reproduce the dynamical AP initiation of cortical neurons *in vivo*.

References

[1] B. Aguera y Arcas, A.L. Fairhall, W. Bialek. Computation in a single neuron: Hodgkin and Huxley revisited. *Neural Comp.*, 15, 1715-1749, 2003

[2] R. Azouz and C.M. Gray. Dynamic spike threshold reveals a mechanism for synaptic coincidence detection in cortical neurons in vivo. *PNAS*, 97, 8110-5, 2000.

[3] C. Cortes and V. Vapnik. Support vector networks. *Machine Learning*, 20:273–297, 1995.

[4] Destexhe A, Pare D. Impact of network activity on the integrative properties of neocortical pyramidal neurons in vivo. *J Neurophysiol.*, 81, 1531-47, 1999.

[5] Fourcaud-Trocmé N, Hansel D, van Vreeswijk C, Brunel N. How spike generation mechanisms determine the neuronal response to fluctuating inputs. *J Neurosci.*, 23, 11628-40, 2000.

[6] A.L. Hodgkin and A.F. Huxley. A quantitative description of ion currents and its applications to conduction and excitation in nerve membranes. *Journal of Physiology (London)*, 117:500–544, 1952.

[7] J.J. Hopfield. Neural networks and physical systems with emergent collective computational abilities. *PNAS*, 79, 2554–2558, 1982.

[8] C. Koch, O. Bernander, R.J. Douglas. Do neurons have a voltage or a current threshold for action potential initiation?, Comp. Neuroscience, 2, 63-82, 1995.

[9] R. Kohavi and G. John. Wrappers for Feature Subset Selection. *Artificial Intelligence*, 97(12):273 – 324, 1997.

[10] W. McCulloch and W. Pitts. A logical calculus of ideas immanent in nervous activity. *Bulletin of Mathematical Biophysics*, 5:115–133, 1943.

[11] M. Minsky and S. A. Papert. *Perceptron*. MIT Press, Cambridge, 1988.

[12] Naundorf B, Geisel T, Wolf F. (2004). Dynamical Response Properties of a Canonical Model for Type-I Membranes. *Neural Comp.*, In Press

[13] B. Schölkopf and A. J. Smola. *Learning with Kernels*. MIT Press, Cambridge, MA, 2002.

[14] V. Vapnik. *The Nature of Statistical Learning Theory*. Springer, New York, NY, 1995.

[15] V. Vapnik. *Statistical Learning Theory*. John Wiley and Sons, New York, 1998

[16] M. Volgushev, U.T. Eysel. Noise makes sense in neuronal computing. *Science*, 290, 1908-9, 2000.

[17] M. Volgushev, J. Pernberg, U.T. Eysel. Gamma-frequency fluctuations of the membrane potential and response selectivity in visual cortical neurons, *Eur. J. Neurosci.*, 17, 1768-1776, 2003.

Attention as Sigma-Pi Controlled ACh-Based Feedback

John Taylor
Department of Mathematics
King's College London
The Strand, London, WC2R 2LS
United Kingdom
E-mail: john.g.taylor@kcl.ac.uk

Matthew Hartley
Department of Mathematics
King's College London
The Strand, London, WC2R 2LS
United Kingdom
E-mail: mhartley@mth.kcl.ac.uk

Neill Taylor
Department of Mathematics
King's College London
The Strand, London, WC2R 2LS
United Kingdom
E-mail: ntaylor@mth.kcl.ac.uk

Abstract— We analyse experimental data on attention to indicate that any attention feedback control signals to lower order cortical sites will lead to a quadratic sigma-pi form of output in its dependence on the lower-order input and the feedback signal. The manner by which this structure works is shown by a brief simulation. We then discuss how such a structure could arise from the action of diffuse acetylcholine signals from the NBM, especially involving nicotinic receptors. We deduce certain structural regularities which should be expected both at local- and at micro-circuit level, mainly in cortical layer V (the output layer).

I. INTRODUCTION

Attention has been studied extensively in the mammalian brain. Both brain imaging techniques and multi-unit and single cell recordings have been used to advance this knowledge. At the same time, the effect on attention of deficits has led to further insights. More recently elucidation has begun of the manner in which acetylcholine, noradrenaline and possibly dopamine function as essential neuro-modulators in attention. On this broad base of results a general picture has emerged of the attention circuits and microcircuits in the brain.

This picture is not yet clear enough to set up detailed simulations of the various processes and to relate these to the data obtained by neuroscience. In other words the general picture is still only that, a qualitative one, and not yet of quantitative form. The reasons for this are unclear, but may depend on more experiments aimed especially at the critical questions:

1) Is the feedback attention control signal (to lower sensory cortices from the parietal control centres) of additive or multiplicative form with respect to input stimuli and feedback signal?
2) How is the feedback control specificity with respect to input stimuli obtained from what appears to be a diffuse ACh signal from the NBM (Nucleus Basalis of Meynert)?

It is these two critical questions (chosen for the relevance to our own work out of many possible questions about attention) which we address here.

II. SIGMA-PI ATTENTION FEEDBACK

There are now several experimental results showing that attention functions so as to increase the contrast gain of the psychological response function. The critical results here are results of attention on single cell responses [1], [2]. These were, in particular, modelled in the original paper of Reynolds et al, as well as somewhat more fully in [3]. The basic result is that the response of a neuron, say in V4, to an attended stimulus was shown to be (in terms of mean firing rate neurons):

$$OUT = f(\text{attention amplification} \times \text{input activation}) \quad (1)$$

where f is some sigmoidal response function. Moreover the attention amplification factor in (1) is dependent on some prefrontal goal, as the preferred stimulus. Thus the attention amplification signal has to arise from some top-down signal specifying the goal. Then (1) has the form of a sigma-pi neuron, with the membrane potential depending quadratically on the product of the feedback signal and the input signal. A more complete expression for (1), in standard sigma-pi form, is

$$OUT(i) = f(\Sigma w_{ijk} x_j x_k) \quad (2)$$

where i denotes the label of lower sensory cortical neuron under consideration, j denotes the label of the attention feedback source, and k denotes the label of the stimulus input being attentionally amplified. This attention amplification has value $w_{ijk}x_j$, so increasing with the strength of the attention feedback.

It is not the case that present single cell data support (1) if the feedback signal is taken to be graded. No experimental data as to how the strength of the attention feedback signal modulates the stimulus strength in (1) is known to us. This is part of the critical data mentioned earlier needed to move the picture of attention towards a quantitative form.

It has been alternately supposed, and used in simulations [4] that attention feedback acts in an additive manner, so that what replaces (1) is:

$$OUT = f(\text{stimulus input} + \text{attention feedback}). \quad (3)$$

It has been claimed that (3) can lead to similar contrast gain attention results as does (1), but it is clear that in the Reynolds et al paradigm [1] that is not possible. Indeed the attention feedback in (3) functions only in a general manner to boost the total activity of a given neuron and not to amplify a given (attended) input against un-amplified distracters.

To see this in more detail, we reconsider the analysis of the Reynolds et al data given in Appendix B of [3], to take account of the possibility that attention has a linear feedback form as in (3). The data were taken from single cells in monkeys who were attending, or not, either to a probe P or a reference stimulus R, shone so as to be in the receptive field of the cell. The important indices SE and SI were defined as

$$SE = P - R \quad (4)$$
$$SI = (P + R) - R$$

where $(P + R)$ denotes the activation of the neuron when both P and R are present. Therefore SE is the difference in response between the probe and reference stimuli and SI is the diference between the response generated by the probe and reference stimuli together and the reference stimulus alone. Data on an ensemble of cells lead to the linear regression formula:

$$SI = \text{constant} \times SE + \text{constant}. \quad (5)$$

This formula was derived analytically in Appendix B of [3], with the value of the regression constant in 5 shown to be $\frac{1}{1+(1/u)}$, where u is the amount of relative attention paid to the reference stimulus, as compared to the probe stimulus.

The data of [1] was shown in [3] to be well fitted by choice of u = 1 when no attention is paid to either the reference of probe, u = 5 when attention is paid to the reference and u = 1/5 when attention is paid to the probe.

When the same analysis is performed with only an additive attention effect as in (3), this can be absorbed by redefinition of the positive reference input, so leading to the result (5), but with no dependence of the regression constant on whether or not attention is being paid to either the reference or probe or to neither of them. This is clearly in contradiction with the data of [1]. The slopes in the attend reference, attend probe and no attend cases were found to be about 0.5, 0.83 and 0,2, values that clearly are very different.

We conclude that this data is in contradiction with the assumption that attention acts purely by a feedback additive bias, as in (3).

Our result can be extended to spiking neurons, in which various models of contrast gain, driven by modulatory inputs, have been suggested [5], [6], [7]. All of these would still give, for an additive attention feedback signal (in which the feedback is independent of what is attended to), that the attend P and attend R slopes of the curve of SI against SE would be the same; as noted above these slopes are experimentally very different.

III. SIGMA-PI SIMULATION

The use of sigma-pi attention feedback is investigated in a simple model of spatial attention. The model is based upon the dorsal route of visual cortex, parietal areas and the frontal eye field (FEF), regions known to be involved in spatial attention. The structure is shown in Figure 1, each region modelled is composed of an excitatory layer (e) and an inhibitory layer (i), with each layer composed of 14*14 leaky integrate and fire neurons (the numbers of neurons are chosen to be equal rather than 4:1, excitatories to inhibitories, for simplicity in connectivity).

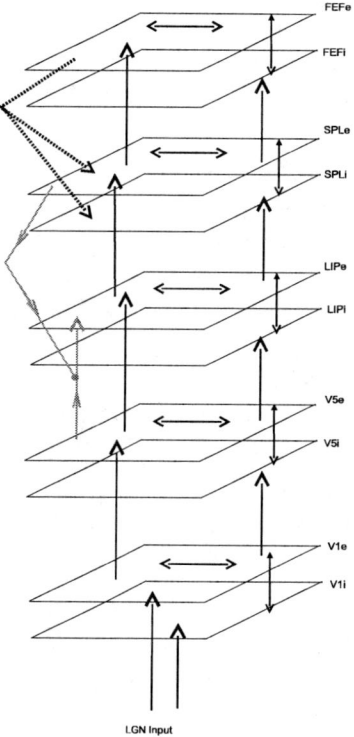

Fig. 1. Structure of the model. Excitatory connections are indicated by open arrow-heads, inhibitory connections by close arrow-heads, sigma-pi connections by grey arrows.

There are lateral excitatory connections within each excitatory group of neurons, with excitatory projections to the related inhibitory nodes. Inhibition then flows back to the excitatory component of the region, to refine the pattern of activation. The flow of activity is, generally, upwards from lateral geniculate nucleus to primary visual cortex (V1), then to V5, up to lateral intra-parietal cortex (LIP), then superior parietal lobe (SPL) and finally FEF. As a spatial input is processed at each subsequent level its representation becomes more focused as it moves up the network. FEF acts as a working memory, holding its processed spatial representation for up to 500ms.

Feedback weights from FEF to SPLe (1:1 connections) and SPLi (1:all) leads to priming of SPL nodes (some sporadic firing may occur).

The sigma-pi weights link SPLe (as feedback controller) and V5e (as input to LIPe) to LIPe, with connectivities being 1:1, and for the sigma-pi weights to exhibit their multiplicative effects SPLe and V5e spikes to LIPe must occur within some time-window (here chosen to be 20ms). With a memory held in FEF of the desired spatial location to attend an input composed of the preferred location and a distracter is presented to the network. These two inputs are processed in the lower levels up to LIP as normal, when activity is now input to SPL the priming from FEF preferentially activates the representation in SPL of the location to be attended rather than the distracter. This speed up in activation of SPL allows the sigma-pi connections to LIPe nodes from SPL and V5 to start working causing a higher firing rate at LIPe nodes representing the location to be attended, the spread of inhibition in LIP over time leads to the destruction in LIPe of most of the representation of the distracter location (Figure 2) and subsequently at higher levels.

IV. THE NEUROCHEMISTRY OF ATTENTION

If we are to understand how attention operates in the brain, we need to know what the underlying neurochemical processes that facilitate attention are. The brain has a number of neuromodulatory chemicals, all of which are possible candidates for use in attention, we will look at these and explain which are the most important.

A. Neuromodulators – which are important?

Of the brain's four primary neuromodulators - acetylcholine (ACh), norepinephrine/noradrenaline, serotonin and dopamine, the most important seem to be ACh and noradrenaline. Serotonin's role in visual attention seems to be limited, while dopamine affects attention [8], but in a manner that is not yet entirely clear.

Noradenaline's role in attentional processing seems to be that of alerting to a new stimulus, rather than focussing of attention – see [9], for example. The locus coeruleus (the source of cortical noradrenaline) appears to participate in generating a general state of alertness in the brain, rather than allowing concentration on a single stimulus.

From these results, it appears that ACh is the most important neuromodulator for specific attentional focus, a conclusion that is supported by numerous studies of the effects of cholinergic deficits on attention [10], [11]. We will next look at the types of ACh receptor that might be involved.

B. Nicotinic and Muscarinic ACh receptors

There are two types of ACh receptor, muscarinic and nicotinic. Muscarinic receptors have been shown to be capable of modulating glutamatergic response [12], [13]. In the hippocampus, these modulatory effects have shown to be a potential mechanism for sleep state switching [14].

They also have some role in attention – in [15], it is shown that scopolamine (a muscarinic antagonist) adversely affects attentional processing. Muscarinic receptors do, however, seem to be responsible more for alerting [11], orienting [15] and modulation of visual attribute processing [16]. However, we believe that nicotinic acetylcholine receptors (nAChRs) are the more important for visual attention (based on [11] among others). We will therefore focus on the mechanisms by which nAChRs might direct attention.

C. Mechanisms of nAChR function – a problem with varicosities?

The second question raised in the introduction was as to the mechanism allowing the acetylcholine to achieve the attended stimulus specificity as show in (1) (or (2)). This is clearly a problem in view of the general diffuse spread of axons from the NBM (the source of cortical ACh) [17], [18], [19]. There have been numerous studies of the distribution of ACh varicosities in the cortex [20], [21]. In general they conclude that, in the rat, only about 15% of such varicosities are synaptic. In the macaque, this number is closer to 45%. This leads to the acceptance of the idea that ACh acts in cortex in a diffuse manner, undergoing volume distribution. However that leads to a clear inability that ACh could thereby support any stimulus or goal specific effects. It would only be able to amplify (or reduce) all input stimuli.

In humans there appears to be a glimmer of hope, in that the proportion of synaptic ACh varicosities is higher, at 67% [22]. These let us consider how such ACh varicosities could function so as to lead to a quadratic sigma-pi form of attention feedback control.

There are several steps we need to take to get to our final point:

1) Assume a suitably high proportion of the ACh varicosities are synaptic,
2) Nicotinic receptors on cortical neurons, associated with the synaptic varicosities, act in an amplificatory manner on nearby synaptic weights [19].
3) Attention feedback control signals axon boutons arrive close to the nicotinic receptors on the cortical neurons, so as to amplify the level of ACh release.

The sigma-pi structure is seen to arise on the basis of the above steps.

Thus we make several predictions about the architecture needed to carry out this construction:

1) There should be local apposition of axon boutons from higher areas and ACh varicosities associated with nicotinic receptor units.
2) Given that higher-level feedback can go to layer V, the output layer (where there are known to be a relatively high density of ACh varicosities) and that lower area feedforward will go to layer IV then II/III before output layers, we expect to see correlation of activities arriving from LII/IV and from higher areas onto, or nearby to, the ACh synaptic varicosities for a given LV pyramidal cell.

We note that there is support for the effect of nAChRs on several nearby synaptic sites, as reported in [23] in the case

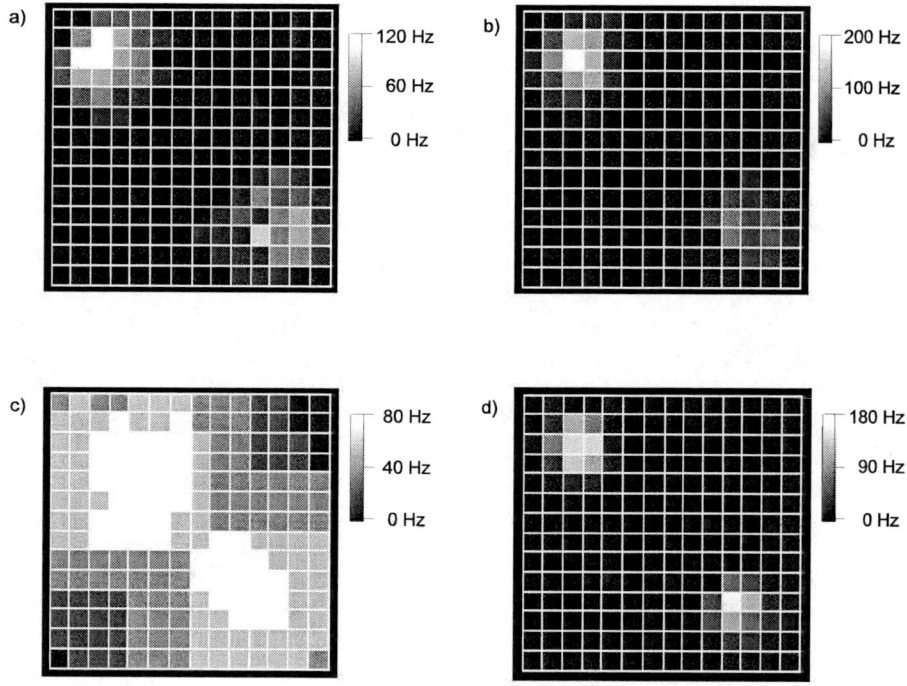

Fig. 2. Development of activity in LIPe neurons a) and b) have sigma-pi weights, c) and d) show the response of the system without sigma-pi weights. Picture a) shows average firing rates of neurons in the first 50ms of 2 location presentation, where the location top-left has been held in FEF working memory. Picture b) indicates the firing rates for the same 2 inputs 100ms later (50 ms time-window). Pictures c) and d) show the development of the firing rates in LIPe nodes without sigma-pi connections, same time periods as a) and b), respectively. There is a greater spread of activity in c) as against a), though the maximum firing rate is lower in c) than a), these effects are a result of the sigma-pi weights causing a higher firing rate (a) which leads to a stronger inhibition reducing the initial representation of locations.

of interneurons in cortex. Generation of GABA currents was shown to occur in interneurons in slices of human cortex, due to the presence of nAChRs. It was suggested there that there is important control of inhibition, say by use of disinhibitory circuits, as in fig 8 of [23]. Such disinhibition may be a crucial component of the overall attention control circuitry. Moreover the amplification of transmitter release by nearby nAChRs is well documented in [24], in [19] and in [25].

The resulting model is expected to have a sigma pi structure of a product form:

$$w_{i,j,k} = w_j w'_k \quad (6)$$

where w'_k is the strength of the connection of the feedback from the kth higher-order attention control neuron to the ith neuron, and w_j that for the input from the jth lower level neuron. This is a specific form which can, we assume, ultimately be tested.

Finally learning of the product form (6) can be expected to be through separate learning of the separate factors in the product term on the right. Thus the total learning rule will have the form:

$$\Delta w_{i,j,k} = OUT_i[OUT_j w'_k + OUT_k w_j] \quad (7)$$

Thus whilst we have made more specific the sigma-pi weights structure, as in (7) and (6), this is still very conjectural, and needs strong experimental support

D. Modulation of glutamatergic input

For ACh to act by contrast gain on excitatory input, it must affect synaptic transmission. Glutamate is the brain's primary excitatory neurotransmitter. Its action at a synapse involves binding to NMDA (N-methyl-D-aspartate) or AMPA (α-amino-3-hydroxy-5-methylisoxazolepropionate) receptors. These receptors cause opening of ion channels through which ions can flow to alter the neuron's membrane potential.

A possible mechanism by which ACh could act at synapses would be by increase of the proportion of ion channels opened by each quantity of glutamate. This would have the effect of amplifying the effects of glutamatergic stimulation.

We can simulate this process, to demonstrate its effects. We use a leaky integrate-and-fire neuron, the membrane potential of which obeys the equation:

$$C\frac{dV}{dt} = g_{leak}(V - V_{leak}) + I_{NMDA} \quad (8)$$

where C is the neuron's capacitance, g_{leak} the leak conductance of the membrane, V_{leak} the neuron's resting potential and I_{NMDA} is a current arising from glutamate activated NMDA receptors. This model is a simplified version of that used in [26].

The NMDA current depends on two kinetic variables, x and s which we calculate as:

$$\frac{dx}{dy} = \phi(\alpha_x \sum_j \delta(t - t_j) - x/\tau_x) \quad (9)$$

where the sum, j, is over pre-synaptic spike times (representing glutamate arriving from a pre-synaptic neuron). s is then described by:

$$\frac{ds}{dt} = \phi(\alpha_s x(1-s) - s/\tau_s) \quad (10)$$

such that s, which represents the fraction of open NMDA channels, varies between 0 and 1 (all channels closed and all channels open, respectively). α_s, τ_s and ϕ are constants. The NMDA current is then calculated as:

$$I_{NMDA} = g_{NMDA} s \frac{(V_m - V_E)}{1 + [Mg^{2+}]e^{\frac{-0.062V_m}{3.57}}} \quad (11)$$

where g_{NMDA} is the conductance of ions flowing through these channels. The exponential term represents the effect of a magnesium block on the calcium channels. $[Mg^{2+}]$ is the concentration of magnesium ions around the extracellular end of the ion channel (and assumed to be constant).

We model the effects of ACh, by including a dependency of the constant α_s on the ACh concentration:

$$\alpha_s = \alpha_{s,base}(1 + k|ACh|) \quad (12)$$

where k and $\alpha_{s,base}$ are constants and $|ACh|$ is the local ACh concentration. This models a process by which ACh causes a greater proportion of ion channels to be opened by NMDAR (NMDA receptor) activation.

Simulating the effects of this dependency, we arrive at Figure 3. In 3**A**, the neuron responds to a periodic glutamatergic input by producing spikes at a rate of 10Hz. When the neuron is also subject to a cholinergic input, in 3**B**, its activity increases, raising its firing rate to 20Hz. The cholinergic input has no effect on the neuron without glutamatergic stimulation, however. In 3**C** where the neuron is subject to a purely cholinergic input, it is not activated at all.

This demonstrates a potential neurophysiological mechanism by which ACh can cause gain of glutamatergic input. The model is simple, and would benefit from further expansion and development in accordance with existing technical data on cholinergic modulation of glutamateric synaptic transmission.

V. CONCLUSIONS

To summarise we have:

1) Shown the need for attention feedback control as having a sigma-pi structure.
2) Shown how such a feedback, guided by working memory in FEF, is efficient in removing distracters for SPL sigma-pi feedback to LIP related to VR input.

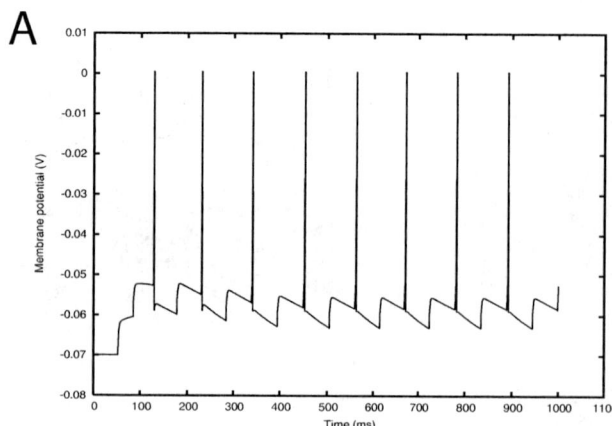
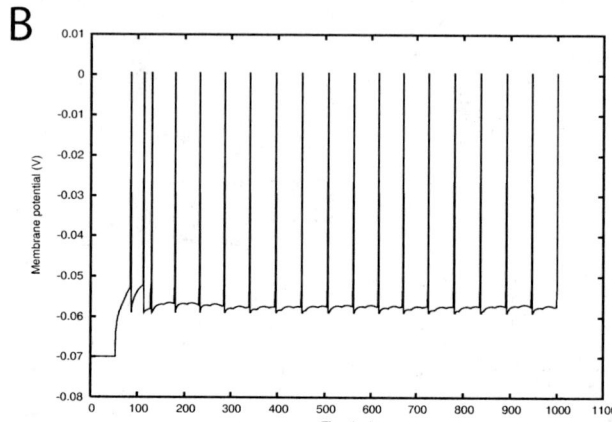
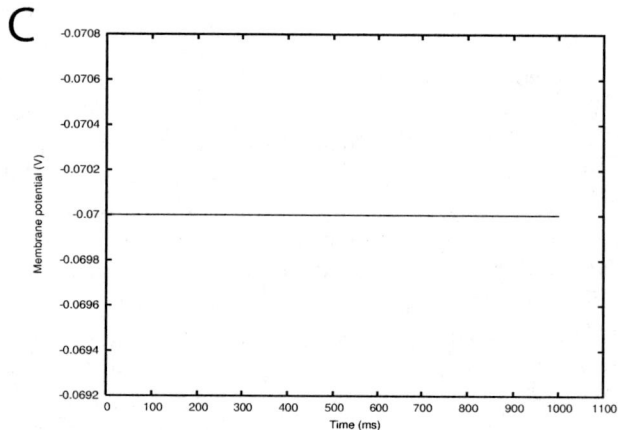

Fig. 3. Effects of ACh on neuron membrane potential and firing rate. In **A**, the neuron is driven by a periodic glutamatergic input which produces a resultant firing rate of approximately 10Hz. In **B**, the neuron also receives cholinergic input which increases the net firing rate (via modulation of the neuron's NMDA channels) to 20Hz. Without glutamate, however, the ACh has no direct affect - **C** shows the neuron's response to a purely cholinergic input.

3) Suggested a possible microstructure to obtain such a sigma-pi feedback from an otherwise diffuse ACh flow into cortex, in terms of synaptic nAChRs on cortical neurons, with conjoint feedback axon endings form

higher areas.

4) Proposed a simple mechanism as to how there can be amplification of transmitters by nAChR activation and subsequent Ca ion inflow.

The above mechanisms are still very conjectural. What is needed is primate studies on the ultrastructure of synaptic nAChR varicosities in cortex, as well as detailed in vitro or in vivo single cell studies, extending that of [23] to pyramidal cells.

VI. APPENDIX

A. Glossary of abbreviations used in the paper

- ACh Acetylcholine
- NBM Nucleus Basalis of Meynert
- FEF Frontal Eye Field
- LIP Lateral Interparietal Cortex
- SPLi/e Superior Partietal Lobe interior/exterior
- nAChR Nicotinic Acetylcholine Receptor
- SE Difference in cell response between total response to probe and reference and reference alone
- SI Difference in cell response between probe and reference stimuli

REFERENCES

[1] J. H. Reynolds, I. Chelazzi, and R. Desimone, "Competitive mechanisms subserve attention in macaque areas V2 and V4," *J. Neurosci.*, vol. 19, pp. 1736–1753, 1999.

[2] T. Ogawa and H. Komatsu, "Target selection in area V4 during a multidimensional visual search task," *J. Neurosci.*, vol. 24, pp. 6371–6382, 2004.

[3] J. G. Taylor and M. Rogers, "A control model of the movement of attention," *Neural Netw.*, vol. 15, pp. 309–326, 2002.

[4] G. Deco and E. T. Rolls, "A neurodynamical cortical model of visual attention and invariant object recognition," *Vision Res.*, vol. 44, pp. 621–642, 2004.

[5] B. K. Murphy and K. D. Miller, "Multiplicative gain changes are induced by excitation or inhibition alone," *J. Neurosci.*, vol. 23, pp. 10 040–51, 2003.

[6] S. J. Mitchell and R. A. Silver, "Shunting inhibition modulates neuronal gain during synaptic excitation," *Neuron*, vol. 38, pp. 433–445, 2003.

[7] F. S. Chance, L. F. Abbott, and A. D. Reyes, "Gain modulation from background synaptic input," *Neuron*, vol. 35, pp. 773–782, 2002.

[8] Y. Ye, W. Xi, Y. Peng, Y. Wang, and A. Guo, "Long-term but not short-term blockade of dopamine release in drosophila impairs orientation during flight in a visual attention paradigm," *Eur J Neurosci*, vol. 20, pp. 1001–1007, 2004.

[9] S. L. Foote, C. W. Berridge, L. M. Adams, and J. A. Pineda, "Electrophysiological evidence for the involvement of the locus coeruleus in alerting, orienting, and attending," *Prog. Brain. Res*, vol. 88, pp. 531–532, 1991.

[10] J. W. Dalley, D. E. Theobald, P. Bouger, Y. Chudasama, R. N. Cardinal, and T. W. Robbins, "Cortical cholinergic function and deficits in visual attentional performance in rats following 192 igg-saporin-induced lesions of the medial prefrontal cortex," *Cereb. Cortex.*, vol. 14, pp. 922–932, 2004.

[11] E. A. Witte, M. C. Davidson, and R. T. Marrocco, "Effects of altering brain cholinergic activity on covert orienting of attention: comparison of monkey and human performance," *Psychopharmacology*, vol. 132, pp. 324–334, 1997.

[12] H. Markram and M. Segal, "Acetylcholine potentiates responses to n-methyl-d-aspartate in the rat hippocampus," *Neurosci. Lett.*, vol. 18, pp. 62–65, 1990.

[13] ——, "Long-lasting facilitation of excitatory postsynaptic potentials in the rat hippocampus by acetylcholine." *J. Physiol.*, vol. 427, pp. 381–393, 1990.

[14] M. E. Hasselmo, "Neuromodulation: acetylcholine and memory consolidation," *Trends in Cog. Sci.*, vol. 3, pp. 351–359, 1999.

[15] M. C. Davidson and R. T. Marrocco, "Local infusion of scopolamine into intraparietal cortex slows covert orienting in rhesus monkeys," *J. Neurophysiol*, vol. 83, pp. 1536–1549, 200.

[16] M. J. M. et al, "Muscarinic versus nicotinic modulation of a visual task: A PET study using drug probes," *Neuropsychopharmacology*, vol. 25, pp. 555–563, 2001.

[17] B. J. Everitt and T. W. Robbins, "Central cholinergic systems and cognition," *Annu. Rev. Psychol.*, vol. 48, pp. 649–684, 1997.

[18] E. Lucas-Meunier, P. Fossier, G. Baux, and M. Amar, "Cholinergic modulation of the cortical neuronal network," *Pflugers Arch. 2003*, vol. 446, pp. 17–29, 2003.

[19] F. Kimura, "Cholinergic modulation of cortical function: a hypothetical role in shifting the dynamics in cortical network," *Neurosci. Res.*, vol. 38, pp. 19–26, 2000.

[20] P. T. et al, "Cholinergic nerve terminals establish classical synapses in the rat cerebral cortex: synaptic pattern and age-related atrophy," *Neuroscience*, vol. 105, pp. 277–285, 2001.

[21] D. Umbriaco, K. C. Watkins, L. Descarries, C. Cozzari, and B. K. Hartman, "Ultrastructural and morphometric features of the acetylcholine innervation in adult rat parietal cortex: an electron microscopic study in serial sections," *J. Comp. Neurol.*, vol. 348, pp. 351–373, 1994.

[22] J. F. Smiley, F. Morrell, and M. M. Mesulam, "Cholinergic synapses in human cerebral cortex: an ultrastructural study in serial sections," *Exp. Neurol.*, vol. 144, pp. 361–368, 1997.

[23] M. Alkondon, E. F. Pereira, H. M. Eisenberg, and E. X. Albuquerque, "Nicotinic receptor activation in human cerebral cortical interneurons: a mechanism for inhibition and disinhibition of neuronal networks," *J. Neurosci.*, vol. 20, pp. 66–75, 2000.

[24] J. A. Dani, "Overview of nicotinic receptors and their roles in the central nervous system," *Biol. Psychiatry*, vol. 49, pp. 166–174, 2001.

[25] D. Paterson and A. Nordberg, "Neuronal nicotinic receptors in the human brain," *Prog. Neurobiol.*, vol. 61, pp. 75–111, 2000.

[26] X.-J. Wang, "Synaptic basis of cortical persistent activity: the importance of NMDA receptors to working memory," *J. Neurosci.*, vol. 19, pp. 9587–9603, 1999.

Motivational modulation of endogenous inputs to the superior colliculus

Jason Satel
Faculty of Computer Science
Dalhousie University
Halifax, NS B3H 1W5
E-mail: satel@cs.dal.ca

Thomas Trappenberg
Faculty of Computer Science
Dalhousie University
Halifax, NS B3H 1W5
E-mail: tt@cs.dal.ca

Raymond Klein
Department of Psychology
Dalhousie University
Halifax, NS B3H 4J1
E-mail: klein@dal.ca

Abstract—Proper initiation of saccadic eye movements depends on an intricate balance between exogenous and endogenous control mechanisms. The superior colliculus (SC) is a major site of signal integration that has been shown to drive the initiation of saccades in the brainstem. Previous work has shown that a winner-take-all mechanism implemented with a continuous attractor neural network (CANN) can explain and reproduce a multitude of behavioural findings, including the gap effect and the production of express saccades [1], [2]. This investigation advances the CANN model of saccade initiation in several important ways in order to account for trial by trial adaptation of saccadic reaction times in a biologically plausible manner. A key hypothesis is that endogenous inputs to the intermediate layer of the SC can be adapted through motivationally-based feedback from other areas of the brain such as the basal ganglia or higher cortical areas.

I. Introduction

Rapidly directing gaze to targets in response to external cues such as unexpected noise is crucial for responding to potentially dangerous situations. However, reflexive behaviour under exogenous control can sometimes be undesirable so there must be a mechanism to balance this with voluntary, goal directed behaviour under endogenous control. The superior colliculus (SC) is a major site of signal integration [3], [4], [5] that drives the initiation of saccades in the brainstem [6], [7]. Kopecz and colleagues have shown how the dynamics of this integration, based on a continuous attractor neural network (CANN) model which implements a winner-take-all mechanism, can explain several behavioural findings, such as the gap effect [1], [8]. Our group has advanced this research by integrating the model with physiological findings of the SC and extending it to additional behavioural findings [2], [9]. In this paper we advance the model with a reward-based, adaptive control mechanism. This mechanism performs the necessary empirical tuning of parameters in the model and is consistent with experimental findings of trial-by-trial modulations of saccade reaction times [10], [11].

In the previous study we were able to adjust some parameters such as the interaction profile from physiological studies, while other parameters, such as the strength of input signals, had to be chosen empirically to account for the different behavioural findings. Here, we argue that the effective strength of information converging on the SC can be modulated to accomplish a better situation-based response of the oculomotor system. We demonstrate that a simple adaptation mechanism based on reward signals can account for some behavioural findings, in particular the motivationally-dependent balance between exogenously driven express saccades and endogenously driven regular saccades. In particular, we give a mechanistic explanation of findings similar to the ones by Juttner and Wolf [11] that, following a catch trial, saccade reaction times (SRTs) are increased and the probability of an exogenously driven saccade is reduced. We also extend the simulations to an antisaccade task [12], [13] that can demonstrate related effects more clearly.

II. Biological background

The SC receives convergent input from a variety of sub-cortical and cortical areas. While the SC is a multimodal integration area [14], here we concentrate entirely on visual processing. There is a direct pathway from the retina to the intermediate layer of the SC, as well as two main cortico-collicular pathways along which saccade related activity can be recorded [15]. The first cortico-collicular pathway proceeds through the frontal eye field (FEF) [16], [17], supplementary eye field (SEF) [18], dorsolateral prefrontal cortex (DLPF) [19], and the lateral intraparietal area (LIP) [20], while the more indirect, second pathway proceeds through the FEF, SEF and DLPF to the caudate nucleus (CD) [21], [22] and then the substantia nigra pars reticulata (SNr) [23], [24] before converging on the SC [15]. Furthermore, inputs to the intermediate layer of the SC from other areas such as the oculomotor thalamus (OcTh) [25], posterior cingulate cortex (CGp) [26], orbitofrontal cortex (OFC) [27], and the cerebellum [28] all contribute to the initiation of saccadic eye movements. The SC itself projects to the brainstem saccade generator which in turn directly drives the eye muscles [6], [7].

In behavioural terms it is useful to divide input to the SC into two categories, namely exogenous signals that are mainly driven by direct, only marginally processed visual signals and endogenous signals that are highly processed cortical inputs that might include instructional processing leading to more voluntary control of eye movements [29]. Based on physiological findings, we assume that the exogenous input is mainly driven by the direct pathway with a time delay of about 70 ms after target presentation. This delay can be approximately broken down into 20 ms for transduction in the retinal ganglion cells, 10 ms for transmission up to the striate cortex, an additional 20 ms to arrive at the SC, with only 20 ms left for processing [30]. A longer time delay of 120 ms is associated with endogenous input, which presumably is due to an additional 50 ms of transmission and processing time in higher cortical areas. We further assume that the time course of exogenous signals are mainly transient, while endogenous input could be maintained longer if necessary [1], presumably based on working memory. The spatial distribution of signals on the SC map is presumed to be location specific with input to the rostral pole effecting fixation related activity and peripheral input effecting saccades to specific eye directions [31].

The strengths of the various input signals were empirically adjusted in our previous work to account for a variety of behavioural findings [2]. In this paper, we study the situation-based alterations of the signal strength in a systematic way. Exogenous signal strength is thereby kept constant as the form of reward-based adaptation discussed in this paper is likely not effected in the direct pathway. However, the endogenous signal strength to the SC is altered in a systematic way. It is possible that this signal strength alteration is supported cortically, for example through attentional, intentional, and working memory mechanisms. However, we specifically discuss the strength modulation in terms of reward mechanisms, in which the basal ganglia has been implicated [32], [33]. For example, Hikosaka's group has elegantly demonstrated the rapid changes of caudate responses after changing rewards to different saccade targets [34], [15]. Houk and colleagues [33] have described an intriguing possibility for the role of the basal ganglia in the reward-based learning of motor actions, and it has been demonstrated [35] that this scheme is consistent with the findings of Kawagoe et al. [34]. Direct output from the substantia nigra to the SC does indicate that such reward-based mechanisms can influence saccade programming. In the model studied in this paper we use a simplified generic reward adaptation scheme to illustrate the basic consequences of reward-based modulations of endogenous inputs to the SC.

III. THE MODEL

A. Dynamics of the superior colliculus

The basic model of the intermediate layer of the superior colliculus is based on the neural-field model with lateral inhibition studied by Amari [36] which can function as a winner-take-all network (see [37] for a review). The implementation in this paper is unchanged from our previous implementation [2]. Namely, it consists of a recurrent network in which the firing rate $r_i(t)$ of a node i is given by

$$\tau \frac{du_i}{dt} = -u_i(t) + \sum_j w_{ij} A_j(t) \Delta x + I_i^{in}(t) - u_0 + \eta \quad (1)$$

$$r_i(t) = \frac{1}{1 + \exp(-\beta u_i(t) + \theta)}, \quad (2)$$

where τ is a time constant, w_{ij} represents the synaptic efficiency (weight) from node i to node j, Δx is a scaling factor, $I_i^{in}(t)$ describes the external input to the system, η is a noise term introduced to represent stochastic processing in the system, u_0 is a global constant set to zero except for burst nodes during active fixation, when it is set to 100, and β and θ are parameters of the sigmoidal gain function. If a node's firing rate reaches 80% of maximum, then a signal is sent to the brainstem, initiating a saccade. The parameters used in the following simulations are summarized in Table 1.

Category	Parameters
Architecture	N = 501; $\Delta t = 1$ ms
SC dynamics	$\tau = 10$ ms; $u_0 = 0$ (buildup)
	$u_0 = 100$ (burst during fixation)
Transfer function	$\beta = 0.07$; $\theta = 0$
Weight matrix	$a = 180$; $b = 60$; $\sigma_a = 0.6$ mm; $\sigma_b = 3\sigma_a$
Noise η	Normal distributed random variable $N(1, x)$

TABLE I
PARAMETERS OF THE MODEL

The weight matrix w_{ij} describes the lateral interaction in the collicular map, and their center-surround form is parameterized as a difference of two Gaussians

$$w_{ij} = a * exp(\frac{-(j-i)^2}{2\sigma_a^2}) + b * exp(\frac{-(j-i)^2}{2\sigma_b^2}) - c \quad (3)$$

The parameters of this profile have been adjusted to fit physiological data from a distracter experiment in monkeys [2]. A similar interaction profile was used by Kopecz [1] and was also found by Arai et al. [38] when training a network based on electrical recordings of movement fields in monkeys. A graphical illustration of the interaction profile is shown in Figure 2.

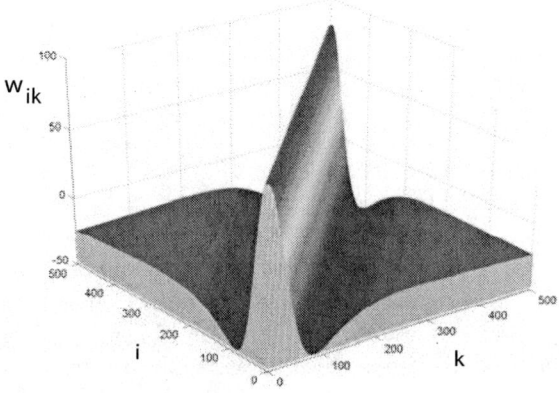

Fig. 1. Graphical illustration of the Mexican Hat-type lateral interaction profile in the collicular map. The center-surround form of this weight profile is parameterized as a difference of two Gaussians.

The input signals are modeled using a Gaussian spatial shape, that is, the external input to a node i in the network is given by

$$I_i = a * exp(\frac{(k-i)^2}{2\sigma^2}) \quad (4)$$

when a visual cue is centered around location k. The parameter a corresponds to the strength of the input signal. The strength of exogenous inputs were kept constant in all simulations, reflecting the relatively direct pathway from the retinal ganglion cells to the SC. Target appearance was modeled as an exogenous input at the target location with a strength value of 60, presented 70 ms after target onset. Removal of the fixation point and the corresponding off-set effect was modeled as an exogenous input to the center node with a strength value of -10, presented 70 ms after fixation point removal.

Endogenous inputs include location specific anticipation (a_s), presented to the anticipated target node, global fixation disengagement (a_g), presented to the center node, and the move signal. The move signal was kept constant in all simulations, with a strength of 10, and was presented 120 ms after target presentation. Location specific anticipation and fixation disengagement were independently modulated in the different simulations as described below, and were presented to the system 120 ms after fixation point removal.

B. Reward adaptation of endogenous signals

In typical saccade experiments with monkeys, the animals are rewarded with a small amount of liquid after each correct trial. Kawagoe et al. [34] found that saccades to rewarded targets are faster than saccades to non-rewarded targets even though the task requires saccades to all targets. They also found that cell activity in the basal ganglia reflected a change in reward contingencies soon after the change occurred (within one or two trials). We captured these findings by a small increase of anticipation after a correct trial, either by an increase of endogenous input at the target location (local effect) or an increase in the endogenous fixation disengagement (global effect), which is equivalent to a reduction of fixation activity after fixation offset.

$$a_{\{s,g\}} = a_{\{s,g\}(previous-trial)} + 0.1. \quad (5)$$

Juttner and Wolf [11] found that the probability of express saccades following a incorrect saccade is highly reduced. We capture this finding by a large decrease of endogenous anticipation (either local or global) after an incorrect saccade

$$a_{\{s,g\}} = a_{\{s,g\}(previous-trial)} - 2. \quad (6)$$

An analogy of this algorithm is the following: Some people (not including the authors) tend to increase their driving speed on highways over time until they are caught by police. The fine is typically sufficient to slow down the drivers for a while, though the average speed is typically increasing again over time.

It is possible to model the reward machinery in much more detail. For example, the involvement of the basal ganglia in reward-based learning of motor responses has been widely discussed in recent years [32], [39] and some detailed models have been developed [33], [35], [40], [41], [42]. While the involvement of the basal ganglia in modulating saccade activities is likely given that the substantia nigra is projecting to the SC, it is also possible that anticipatory signals are modulated in other brain areas. We are here more interested in exploring the consequences of the alterations of endogenous anticipation, and the simple algorithm specified above is sufficient to outline some experiments that could help investigate the important question of global versus local anticipation effects.

IV. SIMULATIONS

A number of simulations were performed in order to test the idea that the strength of endogenous input signals to the SC can be modulated based on local reward optimization after each trial.

A. Simulations of pro-saccades

A basic saccade experiment is the gap paradigm in which saccades are made to one of two possible targets that appear randomly with equal probability following fixation point removal. A saccade reaction time (SRT) distribution of a simulation of this paradigm is shown in Figure 2A. In this simulation we used a global fixation strength of $a_g = 7$ and allowed the location specific anticipation to change up to a maximum value of $a_s = 3$. This maximum was reached after only a few trials because no catch trials are included that would penalize express saccades. SRT distributions from a monkey performing an equivalent gap experiment are shown in Figure 2B (data courtesy of Stefan Everling; see also Tinsley and Everling [43]).

This simulation illustrates the idea that express saccades are driven by exogenous input, whereas regular saccades are under endogenous control. The cap on the strength of endogenous anticipation input has been chosen in this simulation so that fluctuations produced SRT distributions comparable to the monkey data. Thus, the strength used in this simulation can be interpreted as a maximal possible strength although this value is different for different values of a_g.

B. Simulations of pro-saccades with no-go trials

To study the effects of penalizing express saccades we propose a slightly modified experiment that includes no-go trials in a go/no-go paradigm. For example, two different targets such as different symbols or cues with different colors could indicate if a saccade should be made or not. Our adaptation scheme does predict that the presence of such no-go trials will suppress express saccades in direct proportion to the percentage of no-go trials. The SRT distribution of such a simulation with 20% no-go trials using a global adaptation algorithm is shown in Figure 2C. Note that using a location specific adaptation algorithm results in a nearly identical distribution, motivating our analysis of the differences between using these two different algorithms in the following section.

Similar findings of reduced express saccades and increased SRTs with catch trials and a reduced probability of express saccades after a catch trial was reported by Juttner and Wolf [11]. However, the catch trials in their experiment were an absence of any stimulus so that a saccade was triggered even without exogenous input. Our model does not include such purely anticipatory saccades, which is why we used a modified go/no-go paradigm rather a typical catch trial paradigm.

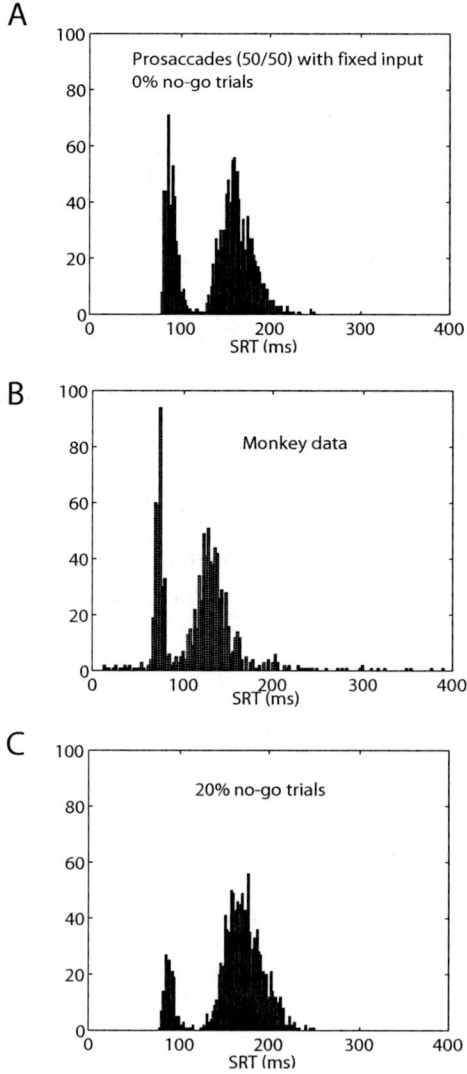

Fig. 2. SRT distribution in 200 ms gap paradigm. (A) Monkey data from pro-saccade experiments. (B) Model without no-go trials but with a cap on the maximal endogenous anticipation. (C) Model with 20% no-go trials.

C. Global versus location specific adaptation

To illustrate more generally the effect of specific modulations of the global (a_g) or location specific (a_s) endogenous signal strength we show in Figure 3 SRTs in a simulation without noise in which we vary only one specific input strength while keeping all others fixed. The solid lines in this figure represent SRTs to a high probability target, while the dashed lines represent SRTs to a low probability target on the opposite side of the visual field. In Figure 3A we set the location specific anticipation to a high probability target to $a_s = 7$ (solid line) and the location specific anticipation to an alternative low probability target to $a_s = 1$ (dashed line) while altering the global fixation disengagement (a_g). The SRTs of both targets are affected by altering a_g with larger values for the fixation disengagement resulting in lower SRTs. However, the effect in the high probability site is larger as the SRTs to this site are shorter and an increase of the fixation disengagement leads to a transition to the regime of express saccades. The adaptation mechanism is designed to find the transition point when express saccades are punished sufficiently.

In Figure 3B we set the global fixation disengagement to $a_g = -3$ and the location specific anticipation to one target $a_s = 1$ (dashed line) while varying systematically a_s to the other target. The SRTs agree for equal a_s to both targets, but the SRTs will decrease for increasing the anticipation of the target corresponding to the solid line and also transition to the express saccade domain. As expected, SRTs to the other target are not much affected. However, for large values of a_s there is a slight increase in SRTs as this strong anticipation level will produce some inhibition of the target corresponding to the dashed line.

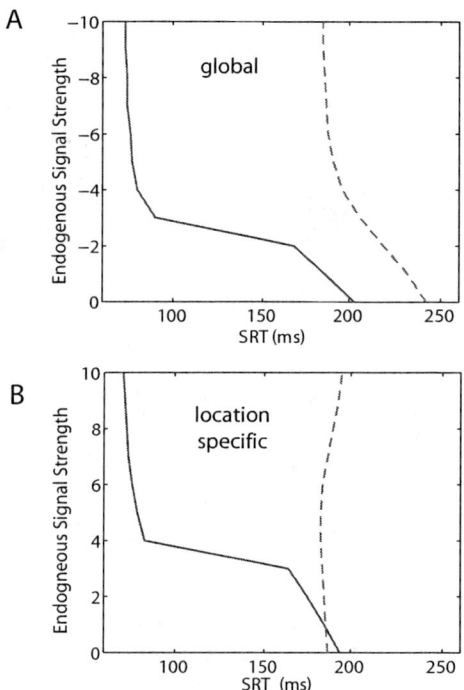

Fig. 3. SRT as a function of altering an endogenous input while keeping the other fixed. (A) Exogenous input to the high probability side (solid line) is set to $a_s = 7$ and to the low probability side (dashed line) to $a_s = 1$, while the endogenous fixation disengagement a_g is varied from $a_g = 0$ to -10. (B) Endogenous fixation disengagement input is fixed to $a_g = -3$ and the endogenous anticipation is fixed to $a_s = 1$ on one side (dashed line) while the other side (solid) was varied from $a_s = 0$ to 10.

D. Simulations of anti-saccades

A useful paradigm to explore the integration of exogenous and endogenous processing is an anti-saccade paradigm where a saccade is to be made to the opposite location of target presentation. Thus, correct saccades are completely under endogenous control so any express saccades to the target location would be deemed an incorrect response resulting in no reward being given. There is therefore no need to include catch or no-go trials in this paradigm.

We performed several simulations with an anti-saccade task. In these experiments we altered the target probabilities of the two possible target locations which was either 50/50 or 30/70. These experiments were run with the two distinct adaptation protocols, either a global protocol or a location specific protocol as outlined above. Both algorithms were able to produce SRTs as found in experimental studies [12], [13].

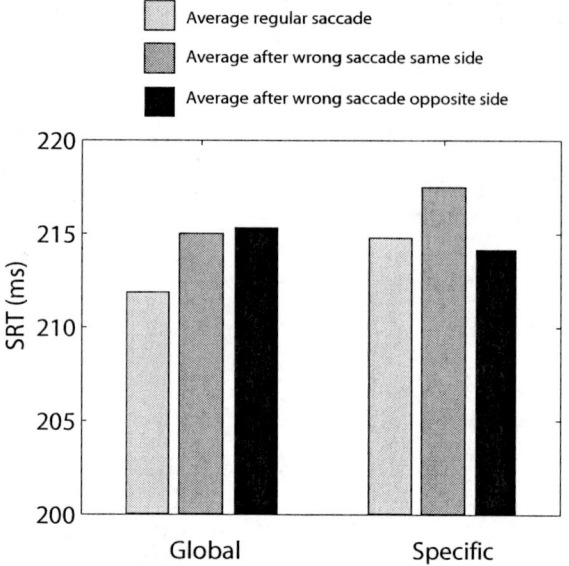

Fig. 4. Mean SRTs in an anti-saccade paradigm to illustrate global versus location specific modulation of endogenous inputs. In the global protocol SRTs are increased to both sides after an incorrectly performed express saccade. With location specific anticipation, however, SRTs are only increased to the same side as the error was performed. Saccades to the opposite side are actually decreased after an incorrect saccade.

To further illustrate the differences between a global protocol or a location specific protocol, the mean SRTs found in each protocol are compared in Figure 4. In the location specific protocol, we fix $a_g = -3$ while allowing a_s to be independently modulated according to the previously stated adaptation algorithm. In the global protocol, we fix $a_s = 3.5$ on each side, while allowing a_g to be modulated according to the previously stated adaptation algorithm. Global modulation results in a similar increase to mean SRT on the trials immediately after an error has been produced to both the same and opposite side on which the error occurred. Location specific modulation, however, results in a slight decrease to mean SRT on the opposite side as the error occurred, but an increase to mean SRT on the same side as the error occurred, as illustrated in Figure 4. Note that these effects are very small and so are very difficult to see when noise is added to the simulation. Thus, the stochastic nature of neural systems would make it very difficult to reproduce the effect experimentally.

V. CONCLUSIONS

We have previously suggested that express saccades are fast saccades that are elicited by exogenous input to the SC. In this investigation we explored further consequences of this suggestion. That is, an increase in saccade anticipation, either through a global fixation disengagement or a location specific anticipation should increase the probability of express saccades. We demonstrated this consequence in various simulations. In particular, we find that the fraction of express saccades should depend on the percentage of no-go trials in a go/no-go paradigm, a behavioural experiment that can be easily implemented.

These findings parallel the findings of Juttner and Wolf [11]. However, the catch trials in their experiments are an absence of targets that nevertheless trigger saccades to the anticipated targets. Such purely anticipatory saccades have not been studied here. It is possible to get these results with larger levels of location specific anticipation, but this would drive the model into a regime where no regular saccades are made with exogenous inputs. While buildup neurons in the SC do show a systematic activation proportional to anticipations, this activation would have to be considerably larger than has been seen in cell recordings. Future work should analyze cell activity in the SC under such conditions to further investigate such purely anticipatory saccades.

We also highlighted the behavioural consequences of modulating global versus location specific endogenous signals. Location specific anticipation could readily simulate well studied effects such as inhibition of return (IOR) and is thus worth examining further since the mechanisms of IOR are still to a large extent unknown. Behavioural experiments corresponding to the simulations in this paper should be very straight forward.

Finally, the precise mechanisms of motivational effects on the SC should be explored further. We hypothesize that motivational modulation of endogenous inputs occurs after every trial. This is a form of extremely short-term neural plasticity leading to a local optimization of reward [10]. The possible involvement of the basal ganglia can be explored with more specific simulations and contrasted with other possible sources of such modulations of endogenous inputs to the SC.

ACKNOWLEDGMENT

TT would like to thank Stefan Everling for useful discussions and for providing behavioural monkey data. This work was supported in part by the NSERC grant RGPIN 249885-03.

REFERENCES

[1] K. Kopecz, "Saccadic reaction times in gap/overlap paradigms: A model based on integration of intentional and visual information on neural, dynamic fields," *Vision Research*, vol. 35, no. 20, pp. 2911–2925, 1995.
[2] T. P. Trappenberg, M. C. Dorris, D. P. Munoz, and R. M. Klein, "A model of saccade initiation based on the competitive integration of exogenous and endogenous signals in the superior colliculus," *Journal of Cognitive Neuroscience*, vol. 13, no. 2, pp. 256–271, 2001.
[3] M. C. Dorris, M. Pare, and D. P. Munoz, "Neuronal activity in monkey superior colliculus related to the initiation of saccadic eye movements," *Journal of Neuroscience*, vol. 17, no. 21, pp. 8566–8579, 1997.
[4] J. A. Edelman and E. L. Keller, "Activity of visuomotor burst neurons in the superior colliculus accompanying express saccades," *Journal of Neurophysiology*, vol. 76, no. 2, pp. 908–926, 1996.
[5] P. H. Schiller, J. H. Sandell, and J. H. Maunsell, "The effect of frontal eye and superior colliculus lesions on saccadic latencies in the rhesus monkey," *Journal of Neurophysiology*, vol. 57, no. 4, pp. 1033–1050, 1987.

[6] C. A. Scudder, C. R. Kaneko, and A. F. Fuchs, "The brainstem burst generator for saccadic eye movements: A modern synthesis," *Experimental Brain Research*, vol. 142, pp. 439–462, 2002.

[7] G. Gancarz and S. Grossberg, "A neural model of the saccade generator in the reticular formation," *Neural Networks*, vol. 11, pp. 1159–1174, 1998.

[8] K. Kopecz and G. Schoner, "Saccadic motor planning by integrating visual information and pre-information on neural dynamic fields," *Biological Cybernetics*, vol. 73, pp. 49–60, 1995.

[9] T. P. Trappenberg, S. Simpson, R. M. Klein, D. Munoz, M. C. Dorris, and P. McMullen, "Neural field model of oculomotor preparation and disengagement," in *Proceedings of the 1997 IEEE International Conference on Neural Networks (ICNN'97)*, vol. 1, 1997, pp. 591–595.

[10] M. C. Dorris, M. Pare, and D. P. Munoz, "Immediate neural plasticity shapes motor performance," *Journal of Neuroscience*, vol. 20, pp. 1–5, 2000.

[11] M. Juttner and W. Wolf, "Occurence of human express saccades depends on stimulus uncertainty and stimulus sequence," *Experimental Brain Research*, vol. 89, pp. 678–681, 1992.

[12] S. Everling, M. C. Dorris, R. M. Klein, and D. P. Munoz, "Role of primate superior colliculus in preparation and execution of anti-saccades and pro-saccades," *Journal of Neuroscience*, vol. 19, no. 7, pp. 2740–2754, 1999.

[13] B. Fischer, S. Gezeck, and K. Hartnegg, "On the production and correction of involuntary prosaccades in a gap antisaccade task," *Vision Research*, vol. 40, pp. 2211–2217, 2000.

[14] M. Wallace and B. Stein, "Onset of cross-modal synthesis in the neonatal superior colliculus is gated by the development of cortical influences," *Journal of Neurophysiology*, vol. 83, no. 6, pp. 3578–3582, 2000.

[15] K. Watanabe, J. Lauwereyns, and O. Hikosaka, "Effects of motivational conflicts on visually elicited saccades in monkeys," *Experimental Brain Research*, vol. 152, pp. 361–367, 2003.

[16] S. Everling and D. P. Munoz, "Neuronal correlates for preparatory set associated with pro-saccades and anti-saccades in the primate frontal eye field," *Journal of Neuroscience*, vol. 20, no. 1, pp. 387–400, 2000.

[17] D. P. Hanes and R. H. Wurtz, "Interaction of the frontal eye field and superior colliculus for saccade generation," *Journal of Neurophysiology*, vol. 85, pp. 804–815, 2001.

[18] N. Amador, M. Schlag-Rey, and J. Schlag, "Reward-predicting and reward-detecting neuronal activity in the primate supplementary eye field," *Journal of Neurophysiology*, vol. 84, pp. 2166–2170, 2000.

[19] J. D. Wallis and E. K. Miller, "Neuronal activity in primate dorsolateral and orbital prefrontal cortex during performance of a reward preference task," *European Journal of Neuroscience*, vol. 18, pp. 2069–2081, 2003.

[20] M. Pare and R. H. Wurtz, "Progression in neuronal processing for saccadic eye movements from parietal cortex area lip to superior colliculus," *Journal of Neurophysiology*, vol. 85, no. 6, pp. 2545–2562, 2001.

[21] O. Hikosaka, M. Sakamoto, and S. Usui, "Functional properties of monkey caudate neurons iii. activities related to expectation of target and reward," *Journal of Neurophysiology*, vol. 61, no. 4, pp. 814–832, 1989.

[22] R. Kawagoe, Y. Takikawa, and O. Hikosaka, "Reward-predicting activity of dopamine and caudate neurons - a possible mechanism of motivational control of saccadic eye movement," *Journal of Neurophysiology*, vol. 91, pp. 1013–1024, 2004.

[23] A. Handel and P. W. Glimcher, "Quantitative analysis of substantia nigra pars reticulata activity during a visually guided saccade task," *Journal of Neurophysiology*, vol. 82, pp. 3458–3475, 1999.

[24] M. Sato and O. Hikosaka, "Role of primate substantia nigra pars reticulata in reward-oriented saccadic eye movement," *Journal of Neuroscience*, vol. 22, no. 6, pp. 2363–2373, 2002.

[25] M. T. Wyder, D. P. Massoglia, and T. R. Stanford, "Quantitative assessment of the timing and tuning of visual-related, saccade-related, and delay period activity in primate central thalamus," *Journal of Neurophysiology*, vol. 90, pp. 2029–2052, 2003.

[26] A. N. McCoy, J. C. Crowley, G. Haghighian, H. L. Dean, and M. L. Platt, "Saccade reward signals in the posterior cingulate cortex," *Neuron*, vol. 40, pp. 1031–1040, 2003.

[27] L. Tremblay and W. Schultz, "Reward-related neuronal activity during go-nogo task performance in primate orbitofrontal cortex," *Journal of Neurophysiology*, vol. 83, pp. 1864–1876, 2000.

[28] P. Lefevre, C. Quaia, and L. M. Optican, "Distributed model of control of saccades by superior colliculus and cerebellum," *Neural Networks*, vol. 11, pp. 1175–1190, 1998.

[29] R. M. Klein and D. I. Shore, "Relationships among modes of visual orienting," in *Attention and Performance: XVIII. Control of Cognitive Processes*, S. Monsell and J. Driver, Eds. MIT Press, 1997, pp. 195–208.

[30] B. Fischer and H. Weber, "Express saccades and visual attention," *Behavioral and Brain Sciences*, vol. 16, pp. 553–610, 1993.

[31] J. A. M. Van Gisbergen, A. J. Van Opstal, and A. A. M. Tax, "Collicular ensemble coding of saccades based on vector summation," *Neuroscience*, vol. 21, pp. 541–555, 1987.

[32] W. Schultz, "Responses of midbrain dopamine neurons to behavioral trigger stimuli in the monkey," *Journal of Neurophysiology*, vol. 56, pp. 1439–1462, 1986.

[33] J. C. Houk, J. L. Adams, and A. G. Barto, "A model of how the basal ganglia generate and use neural signals that predict reinforcement," in *Models of information processing in the basal ganglia*, J. C. Houk, J. L. Davis, and D. G. Beiser, Eds. MIT Press, 1995, pp. 249–270.

[34] R. Kawagoe, Y. Takikawa, and O. Hikosaka, "Expectation of reward modulates cognitive signals in the basal ganglia," *Nature Neuroscience*, vol. 1, no. 5, pp. 411–416, 1998.

[35] T. P. Trappenberg, H. Nakahara, and O. Hikosaka, "Modeling reward dependent activity pattern of caudate neurons," in *Proceedings of the International Conference on Artificial Neural Networks (ICANN'98)*, 1998.

[36] S. Amari, "Dynamics of pattern formation in lateral-inhibition type neural fields," *Biological Cybernetics*, vol. 27, pp. 77–87, 1977.

[37] T. P. Trappenberg, "Continuous attractor neural networks," in *Recent Developments in Biologically Inspired Computing*, L. N. de Castro and F. J. V. Zuben, Eds. ., 2003.

[38] K. Arai, E. L. Keller, and J. A. Edelman, "A spatio-temporal neural network model of saccade generation," in *Proceedings of the IEEE International Conference on Neural Networks*, 1993, pp. 70–74.

[39] J. O'Doherty, P. Dayan, K. Friston, H. Critchley, and R. Dolan, "Temporal difference learning model accounts for responses in human ventral striatum and orbitofrontal cortex during pavlovian appetitive learning," *Neuron*, vol. 38, pp. 329–337, 2003.

[40] P. Dayan and B. W. Balleine, "Reward, motivation and reinforcement learning," *Neuron*, vol. 36, pp. 285–298, 2002.

[41] F. Worgotter and B. Porr, "Temporal sequence learning, prediction and control - a review of different models and their relation to biological mechanisms," *Neural Computation*, vol. 17, pp. 1–75, 2004.

[42] P. R. Montague, S. E. Hyman, and J. D. Cohen, "Computational roles for dopamine in behavioural control," *Nature*, vol. 431, pp. 760–767, 2004.

[43] C. Tinsley and S. Everling, "Contribution of the primate prefrontal cortex to the gap effect," *Progressive Brain Research*, vol. 140, pp. 61–72, 2002.

Facilitatory Neural Activity Compensating for Neural Delays as a Potential Cause of the Flash-Lag Effect

Heejin Lim and Yoonsuck Choe
Department of Computer Science
Texas A&M University
3112 TAMU, College Station, TX 77843-3112
Email: hjlim@cs.tamu.edu, choe@tamu.edu

Abstract—In flash-lag effect (FLE), the position of a moving object is perceived to be ahead of a brief flash when they are actually co-localized. This phenomenon may be due to motion extrapolation: The nervous system has internal conduction delay, thus signals received with a delay in central areas have to be extrapolated for the internal state to be temporally aligned with that of the environment. The precise neural mechanism of such a process has not been fully investigated. Here, we propose that facilitating synapses can be a potential candidate. We tested this idea in FLE and showed that our model behavior is consistent with experimental data. In sum, facilitatory neural dynamics may underlie delay compensation, thus giving rise to FLE.

I. INTRODUCTION

Flash-lag effect refers to a visual phenomenon in which the position of a moving object is perceived to be ahead of a briefly flashed object when they are actually co-localized [1], [2]. Interestingly, flash-lag effect has been found in various sensorimotor modalities such as motor performance [3], auditory perception [4]; and in various visual modalities such as color, pattern entropy, and luminance [5].

A potential explanation for flash-lag effect (FLE) is motion extrapolation: Flash-lag effect may be caused by a delay compensation mechanism embedded in our nervous system (see, e.g., [2], [6]). Fig. 1 illustrates visual motion flash-lag effect in view of the motion extrapolation hypothesis. In Fig. 1a, the state $S(t)$ of a moving object (black rectangle) which is physically aligned with a flashed object (white solid rectangle) in the environment is received at a peripheral sensor (such as the retina) at time t. The state information $S(t)$ takes time ($= \Delta t$) to travel from the sensor to the central nervous system in the organism. If the delay is not taken into consideration, the perceived location of the moving object based on state $S(t)$ will be outdated by time $t + \Delta t$ (Fig. 1b). In that case, there will be no flash-lag effect because the location information of moving stimulus and flashing stimulus are the same, albeit delayed (Fig. 1b). On the other hand, if the received object location is corrected based on a predicted (or extrapolated) state of the moving object for $t + \Delta t$, i.e., $S(t + \Delta t)$, then the extrapolated object location will be closer to the actual environmental state at the time of the perception (Fig. 1c). The flashed object, on the contrary, is perceived without extrapolation because the abrupt flashing has no previous history to be extrapolated from. Thus, visual displacement occurs between the moving bar and the flashed bar due to such a discrepancy in extrapolation.

However, the motion extrapolation model has some limitations. For example, humans do not perceive displacement between a flashed object and a moving object when the moving object stops or reverses its direction of motion at the time of the flash [7] (see Fig. 2a for an illustration of motion reversal). In other words, to make human subjects perceive a moving bar and a flashed bar to be aligned at the instant of flash, the flashed bar should be presented ahead of the moving bar. However, as the position of the moving bar approaches the motion reversal point, the gap between the perceived location of the two objects decreases (i.e., diminished flash-lag effect) and increases again after motion reversal. As illustrated in Fig. 2a, the perceived location of the moving bar leads (solid line), while that of the flashed object lags behind (points marked ∗).

As an alternative hypothesis, differential latency model [7], [8] suggests that flash-lag effect occurs simply because the visual system responds with shorter latency to moving stimuli than to flashed stimuli. However, recent work on auditory and cross modal flash-lag effect indicates that differential latency model may be inaccurate: The size of auditory FLE was much larger than visual FLE, whereas neural latency in the auditory system are known to be much shorter than those in the visual system (see [4], [9]).

"Postdiction" [10] has been also suggested as an alternative, which explains that the visual system uses motion information occurring *after* time t to compute the perceived location at time t. It successfully explains the lack of flash-lag effect in the flash-terminated cycle or motion reversal condition (more detail will be described in Sec. II-A). However, with this scheme, the nervous system would face perceptual processing delay (over 80 ms; see [10]) in addition to neural transmission delay (hundreds of milliseconds), which can become a serious problem for real-time computation.

Despite its limitation in explaining motion reversal (or termination) condition, the extrapolation model has many

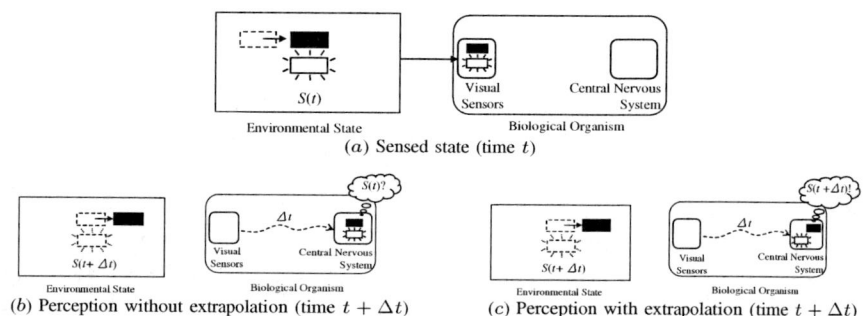

Fig. 1. Flash-lag effect in the view of compensation mechanism for neural delay.

desirable properties [11], [12], [13], [14]. In this paper, we suggest that the limitation can be overcome by an extended extrapolation model. An interesting question arises at this point: "What is the neural mechanism embedded in central nervous system to implement such an extrapolation process?" This is an important question that has not been fully investigated. One potential mechanism is the facilitatory dynamics found in neurons. Previously, facilitating (or depressing) synapses have been studied in the context of memory (e.g., sensitization and habituation, [15], [16]) or temporal information processing [17], [18], [19], [20]. Here, we suggest that facilitating synapses may also play an important role in compensating for neural delays. Facilitatory neural activity may effectively compensate for neural delays, and as a result it may cause extrapolation in perception (e.g., as expressed in the visual flash-lag effect).

To test our idea, we formalized the extrapolation mechanism as facilitatory neural activity (we call it the *facilitation model*) and revisited the motion reversal FLE previously modeled by postdiction [21]. The results indicate that our facilitation model can successfully account for the data from human subjects for both FLE in continuous motion and abolished FLE in motion reversal point, while minimizing the effect of neural conduction delay.

Our initial facilitation model is based on a firing-rate model, where continuous-valued neural activity was represented as a single real number. However, biological neurons communicate via spikes, thus the biological plausibility of the facilitation model may be questioned. To address this issue, we derived a spike-based model based on known neurophysiological mechanisms that can express facilitatory behavior. We extended an existing facilitating synapse model [17], [18] to account for both increasing and decreasing firing rates, thus firmly grounding the facilitation model on a biological foundation.

In the following, first, the model and experiment with motion reversal FLE will be presented to test whether the facilitation model can explain the FLE in terms of delay compensation (Sec. II). Next, a spike-based single-neuron model for facilitating activity will be proposed, followed by tests with luminance FLE (Sec. III). Finally, we will conclude, with a brief discussion of possible extensions of the model presented in this paper (Sec. IV–V).

II. FACILITATION MODEL FOR DELAY COMPENSATION

To test our facilitation model as a delay compensation method, we conducted experiments in the motion reversal FLE and compared the results to that of postdictive optimal smoothing model. First, we will briefly review the postdiction model by Rao et al. [21] (Sec. II-A) and then present our facilitation model (Sec. II-B).

A. Optimal Smoothing: Postdictive Perception

Rao et al. [21] formalized postdiction using *optimal smoothing*, a commonly used method in engineering applications [22]. They tested the model in motion reversal FLE and showed that optimal smoothing can successfully account for the curve around the reversal point which is observed in human experiments (Fig. 2a, $t = t_1$). Using Kalman filtering [23], the best estimate of the location $\hat{X}(t)$ of a moving object at time t is derived from its predicted location $\bar{X}(t)$ with error correction $G(t)(X(t)-\bar{X}(t))$ after observing the current value $X(t)$ [21]:

$$\hat{X}(t) = \bar{X}(t) + G(t)(X(t) - \bar{X}(t)), \quad (1)$$
$$\bar{X}(t) = \hat{X}(t-1) + c(t-1)\hat{Y}(t-1), \quad (2)$$

where $G(t)$ is a gain term, $c(t-1)$ denotes motion direction at time $t-1$ (1 for forward and -1 for reverse trajectory), and $\hat{Y}(t-1) = \bar{Y}(0) = a$, which indicates the velocity of the object ($a = 1$). To estimate the final perceived location, the best estimate $\hat{X}$ is recursively smoothed using the estimation from future time steps:

$$X_{sm}(t) = \hat{X}(t) + h(t)(X_{sm}(t+1) - \bar{X}(t+1)), \quad (3)$$

where $h(t)$ is a gain term and $X_{sm}(t)$ the final perceived location of the moving object at time t.

Fig. 2b shows results from motion reversal experiments modeled by Eq. 2 through 3 (with $G(t) = 0.7$, $h(t) = 0.5$). The x axis represents time (second) and the y axis the location of the object. The velocity of the moving bar was 1 m/sec and the neural delay 500 ms. The actual trajectory of the two objects (solid line for the moving bar and * for the flashed bar) resulted in delayed neural activity X. Based on the input X, the optimal smoothing method generates a predicted, filtered, and smoothed estimation for the perceived object location. Notice that even though the smoothed trajectory (solid dark line) faithfully reproduced the curve around reversal point (Fig. 2a, $t = t_1$), the estimated location undershot the actual

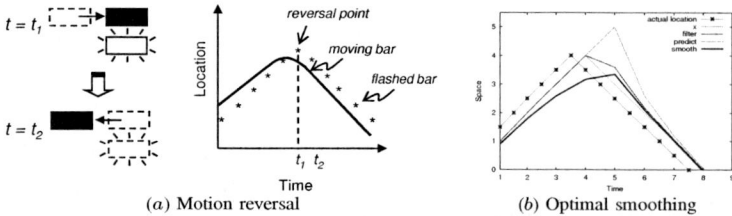
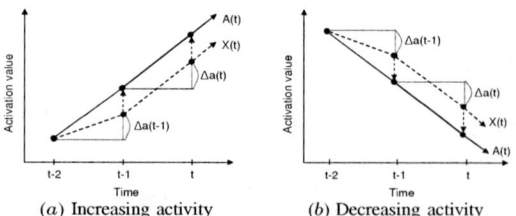

Fig. 2. Motion reversal experiment and optimal smoothing.

Fig. 3. Facilitatory neural activity.

locations unlike in the standard flash-lag effect for continuous motion without reversal. Another point to note here is that for the standard FLE, the smoothed trajectory should be shifted to the left based on the temporal integration of position signals (see [10], [21] for details). Certain problems arise here since the final perceptual location is determined by recursive smoothing (which is possible only *after* observing all the input data), and the temporal window needs visual integration mark (i.e., flash) to be set on, which contradicts with the finding that localization error exists when there is no accompanying flash [11], [13]. Also, the window size is hard to determined for a varying stimulus configuration. In sum, the smoothing model may be difficult to be applied within the nervous system, which has to work in almost real time.

B. Facilitation Model: Extrapolative Perception

Besides its limitation in explaining motion reversal in FLE, the extrapolation model has many desirable properties [11], [12], [13], [14]. In this section, we will derive a simple facilitation (extrapolation) model and its extension to overcome limitations regarding motion reversal or termination.

How can the motion extrapolation model be implemented in the nervous system? Our hypothesis is that for fast extrapolation, single neurons should be able to extrapolate. Let us assume that the activation value $X_i(t)$ of a neuron i at time t represent the the perceived location of a moving object at time t. In a network of neurons, the activation level can be defined as follows:

$$X_i(t) = g(\sum_{j \in N_i} w_{ij} X_j(t)), \quad (4)$$

where $g(\cdot)$ is a nonlinear activation function (such as a sigmoid function), N_i the set of neurons sending activation to neuron i (the connectivity graph should be free of cycles), and w_{ij} the connection weight from neuron j to neuron i. Based on Eq. 4, the activity of a neuron with facilitating mechanism can be defined as follows (we will drop the neuron index i for notational simplicity):

$$A(t) = X(t) + (X(t) - A(t-1))r, \quad (5)$$

where $A(t)$ is the facilitated activation level at time t, $X(t)$ the instantaneous activation solely based on the present input at time t, and r the facilitation rate ($0 \leq r \leq 1$). The basic idea is that the current instantaneous activation $X(t)$ is augmented with the rate of change $X(t) - A(t-1)$ modulated by the facilitation rate r. We will refer to the rate of change as $\Delta a(t)$ ($= X(t) - A(t-1)$).

Note that Eq. 5 is similar to extrapolation using forward Euler's method where the continuous derivative $A'(\cdot)$ is replaced with its discrete approximation $\Delta a(\cdot)$ [24] (p. 710). Fig. 3 shows how facilitatory activity is derived from the current and past neural activity (for both increasing and decreasing activation levels). Basically, the activation level $A(t)$ at time t (where t coincides with the environmental time) is estimated using the input $X(t)$ that arrived with a delay of Δt. If the facilitatory rate r is close to 0.0, $A(t)$ reduces to $X(t)$, thus it will lag behind in comparison to the environment. If r is close to 1.0, maximum extrapolation will be achieved.

We will now apply our model to the motion reversal experiment under the same conditions as in Sec. II-A. Fig. 4a shows the results where $X(t)$ corresponds to the delayed neural activity arrived in the visual cortex and $A(t)$ the facilitated perception for the location of the moving bar ($r = 0.5$). If there is no facilitating neural activity, the perceived location will be significantly behind the real positions (refer to Fig. 1b for better understanding of this point). With facilitatory neural activity, however, the delayed neural signal is facilitated so that the perceived locations (solid line) become closer to the actual location (solid line with ∗) of the moving bar in the environment at the same instant. Notice that the visual FLE occurs due to the spatial gap between the facilitated activity for the moving bar (solid line) and the non-facilitated activity for the flashed bar (dotted line). However, as mentioned above as a shortcoming of the extrapolation model, the facilitated perception generates an overshoot around the reversal point, which is not found in human experiments.

What happens at the instant of the motion termination or reversal? A potential answer is that the misperception (i.e., overshoot at reversal) is corrected by backward masking with an immediate motion offset signal (see [25] for details). The motion offset signal which arrives at the time of extrapolation can cancel out the extrapolatory neural activity so that there is no overshooting perceived at the terminating (or reversal) point. This is consistent with the postdiction model to some extent such that information occurring after time t can affect the judgment about the perceived location at time t. However, differentiating from optimal smoothing, our model uses extrapolated activity $A(t)$ instead of the filtered estimate $\hat{X}(t)$ for smoothing, and considers only one step future event to modify the estimate. (We assume that the time step is much smaller than the transmission delay, i.e., $1 \ll \Delta t$.) Thus, the perceived location can be redefined as follows:

$$A_{sm}(t) = A(t) + h(t)(X(t+1) - A(t)), \quad (6)$$

where A_{sm} (facilitated-smoothing value) represents the perceived location of the moving object. Compared to Eq. 3,

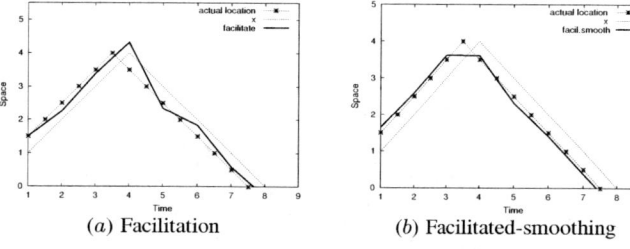

(a) Facilitation (b) Facilitated-smoothing

Fig. 4. Perceived trajectory in the facilitation model.

Eq. 6 is much simpler and suitable for real-time perception. Fig. 4b shows the result using Eq. 6 (with $h(t)$ set to 0.4). Compared to Fig. 4a, facilitated smoothing (A_{sm}; dark solid line) successfully produces no-overshoot at the time of reversal as well as closely approximating the overshoot events for continuous visual motion.

This computational result strongly suggests that our nervous system may use extrapolatory neural mechanisms for delay compensation as well as a small delay in perception to increase perceptual accuracy.

III. SPIKE-BASED MODEL FOR FACILITATING ACTIVITY

The model in the previous section treated neural activity as a single real number. How could the facilitatory dynamics as described in Eq.5 and Eq.6 be implemented in a more biologically plausible manners? In this section, we will propose a spike-based model based on known neurophysiological mechanisms that can potentially express facilitatory behavior.

A. Single Neuron Model with Facilitating Synapses

Dynamic synapses generate short-term plasticity which shows activity-dependent decrease (depression) or increase (facilitation) in synaptic transmission occurring within several hundred milliseconds from the onset of the activity (for reviews see [26], [19], [27]). Especially, facilitating synapses cause growth of postsynaptic response through increasing synaptic efficacy with successive presynaptic spikes. (Synaptic efficacy is the fraction of neural transmitter released when presynaptic action potentials arrive at the axon terminal.) Unlike depressing synapses, the rate of neural transmitter release is not constant but is a dynamic variable in facilitating synapses.

According to the dynamic synapse model by Markram and colleagues, based on neurophysiological data [18], [17], synaptic efficacy U evolves over time as described in the following differential equation:

$$\frac{dU}{dt} = -\frac{U}{\tau_f} + C(1-U)\delta(t-t_s), \qquad (7)$$

where τ_f is the time constant for the decay of U; C a constant determining the increase in U when a successive action potential (AP) arrives at time t_s at the synaptic terminal; and $\delta(\cdot)$ the Dirac delta function. This equation is already suitable enough to replicate the facilitating dynamics in Eq. 5 when the activation level is increasing (as in Fig. 3a). However, it is not capable of handling cases where the activation level is decreasing (as in Fig. 3b). Ideally, extrapolation should work for both increasing and decreasing trends.

Here we modify the equation by redefining C as a dynamic variable which is varied in proportion to the change of input firing rate:

$$C = Sgn(I(n-1) - I(n))\left(\frac{I(n-1)}{I(n)}\right)r, \qquad (8)$$

where $Sgn(\cdot)$ is the sign function, $I(n)$ is the interspike interval between the n-th spike and the $(n-1)$-th spike which reflects whether a spike train consists of high-frequency APs or low-frequency APs. The first term in Eq. 8 determines the sign of C: "+" for increase or "−" for decrease in firing rate. The second term represents the ratio of the change in frequency, and r is a gain parameter. As the input firing rate increases, C becomes positive and increases proportional to the rate of change in frequency. On the contrary, as the firing rate decreases, $I(n)$ becomes larger which results in a negative C and thus leads to the decrease in the synaptic efficacy U.

With this, we can now fully describe our membrane potential model, (cf. [18], [17]). The time course of postsynaptic current $P(t)$ at time t triggered by incoming spikes is defined as follows:

$$P(t) = Ee^{-\frac{t}{\tau_p}}, \qquad (9)$$
$$E = AU, \qquad (10)$$

where E is the excitatory postsynaptic potential (EPSP) amplitude; τ_p the time constant of decay in $P(t)$; A a constant for maximum postsynaptic response amplitude; and U the synaptic efficacy as defined above. Finally, the membrane potential $V_m(t)$ at time t evolves as follows:

$$V_m(t) = V_m(t-1)e^{-\frac{t}{\tau_m}} + P(t)(1 - e^{-\frac{t}{\tau_m}}). \qquad (11)$$

The membrane potential is determined by the membrane current $P(t)$ at that moment and the previous membrane potential $V_m(t-1)$, both of which are regulated by a membrane time constant τ_m. The last part of the spiking neuron model is the spike generation mechanism. Once V_m exceeds the spike threshold θ, a spike is generated, followed by an absolute refractory period of τ_{refrac} during which spikes cannot be generated. With the model above, we simulated a single neuron under increasing or decreasing input firing rate.

B. Experiment with Visual Luminance Flash-lag Effect

When a stationary disk continuously becomes brighter in luminance, it appears brighter than a neighboring flashed object of equal luminance (and analogously, darker for a disk becoming darker) [5]. Such perceptual phenomena expressing extrapolation (brighter than bright, and darker than dark) can be modeled at a single-neuron level using facilitating synapses as described in the previous section.

Through sensory transduction, sensory signals such as photons hitting the retina are converted into spikes (or action potentials). These spikes cause a chain reaction through the sensory pathway to reach the primary sensory area (the primary visual cortex, in case of vision). Our interest mostly lies in the last part of the journey of these spikes, where the input spike train releases neurotransmitters from presynaptic neurons to a postsynaptic neuron through facilitating synapses. Further simplifying this, we assumed that there is only one synapse. By varying the spike firing rate in the presynaptic neuron, we are able to model the extrapolatory phenomenon described above.

We tested two types of input: (1) increasing firing rate (analogous to the visual stimulus becoming brighter) and (2) decreasing firing rate (modeling the visual stimulus becoming darker). The parameters used for the simulation below were as follows: Initial value for synaptic efficacy $U = 0.2$; U-recovery time constant $\tau_f = 150$ ms; postsynaptic potential time constant $\tau_p = 30$ ms; membrane current time constant $\tau_m = 200$ ms; spike threshold $\theta = 160$ mV; duration of absolute refractory period $\tau_{\text{refrac}} = 4$ ms; maximum postsynaptic response amplitude $A = 300$; and C-gain $r = 0.175$. The results are shown in Fig. 5. As the results show, the facilitating synapse model generated extrapolatory neural activity for both increasing and decreasing firing rate conditions. Dynamic change in the synaptic efficacy U caused the postsynaptic neuron to generate more spikes than the input when the input firing rate was increasing (Fig. 5a). On the other hand, the postsynaptic neuron generated less spikes than what it received when the input firing rate was decreasing (Fig. 5b).

This kind of behavior is quite reasonable if we consider the following. Suppose the spikes in the presynaptic neuron (the top rows in Fig. 5) were originated earlier (about 100 ms) in peripheral sensors. Here is an example sequence of events: (1) Peripheral spiking at 300 ms would be replicated at 400 ms in the presynaptic neuron in the top row, due to the delay. (2) The postsynaptic neuron (bottom row) receiving input from the presynaptic neuron (top row) at 300 ms fires from information from 200 ms in the periphery. (3) However, the postsynaptic neuron's firing rate at 300 ms (bottom row) is nearly the same as that of the presynaptic neuron's rate at 400 ms (top row). This means that the postsynaptic neuron, at time 300 ms, is exactly firing at the same frequency as the peripheral neuron at time 300 ms (refer to (1) above), precisely reflecting the present environmental state. Note that the presynaptic (top row) and the postsynaptic (bottom row) neuron in Fig. 5 are both located in the central nervous system as shown in Fig. 1.

In contrast with the previously defined facilitating synapse equation (Eq. 7, [18], [17]), our modified equation (Eq. 7 with Eq. 8) was able to generate extrapolated neural activity under both increasing and decreasing firing rate. These experiments suggest that dynamic facilitating synapses can trigger a general extrapolatory neural activity, thus providing a neurophysiological basis for the model in Sec. II. In sum, the time-varying stimuli (brighter or darker in luminance) were extrapolated to be perceived close to the present intensity of light, while the firing rate of abrupt stimulus was the same as the presynaptic neuron (not shown). The different firing rates between two stimuli might cause FLE in visual luminance change.

The last question to be resolved is what neural mechanisms can implement backward masking so that it can cancel out potential overshooting occurring at a motion-reversal point. We suggest that inhibitory synaptic transmission conveying motion offset signal may prevent the postsynaptic neuron from generating surplus spikes. Fig. 6 shows the pre-postsynaptic neural activity where motion offset signal follows the input spike train (top row) consisting of increasing firing rate.

The second row in Fig. 6 shows that spikes of motion offset stimulus are delivered by an inhibitory synapse immediately following the input spike train. The motion offset signal was generated immediately after the last signal of continuously changing stimuli (around 400 ms at the periphery), and delivered with neural delay (100 ms) at presynaptic neuron. Influenced by inhibitory postsynaptic potential (IPSP) the increased postsynaptic membrane current is pulled down (the third row), which makes the postsynaptic neuron to fire the same number of APs as that of the presynaptic neuron (cf. Fig. 5a) so that extrapolation of firing rate did not occur at the moment of stimulus termination.

IV. DISCUSSION

The main contribution of this paper is that it proposed a biologically plausible neural mechanism on which motion extrapolation model can be grounded. We proposed and tested a neurophysiologically based facilitating synapse model, demonstrating that extrapolatory dynamics can compensate for neural transmission delay and various FLE may arise due to such a mechanism. We also showed that the lack of such an effect at motion reversal (or termination) can be interpreted as due to inhibitory synaptic dynamics. In fact, the motion reversal of moving bar and the visual luminance experiments showed that facilitatory neural activity helped align the internal state of the nervous system with the present rather than with the past environmental state.

We expect that our approach can be extended to explain other extrapolatory phenomena in perceptual experiments such as flash-lag effects in color, pattern entropy, localization, or orientation. However, to do this, our single-neuron approach has to be extended. For example, unlike luminance, neurons sensitive to orientation only respond to a narrow range of orientations. This means that a whole range of orientation cannot be represented with a single neuron, thus increase or decrease in firing rate in these neurons cannot indicate the presence of varying orientations in the input. For this case, facilitation has to go across different orientation-selective neurons. Moreover, we expect that the extended crossneuronal facilitation structure might be able to explain other visual illusions such as Hess effect [28](a high-contrast moving object is perceived to lead a low-contrast one where they actually move in alignment) or Fröhlich effect (when a moving object appears abruptly, the initial segment of the object's trajectory is perceived to be invisible) by combining the spatial mechanisms and temporal mechanisms of facilitating synapses.

Another interesting future direction would be to verify whether neurons with facilitating synapses are more often found in places where delay compensation is needed more, for example, at the end of long, slow axons, or where precise real-time information is needed.

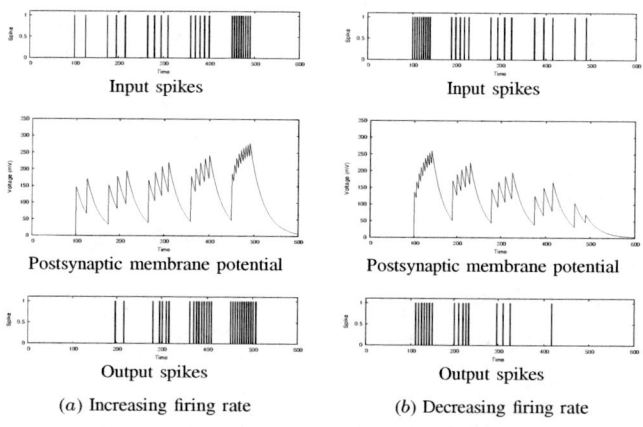

(a) Increasing firing rate (b) Decreasing firing rate

Fig. 5. Extrapolation with facilitating synapses.

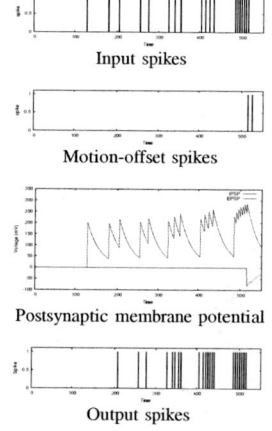

Fig. 6. Facilitating synapse with motion-off signal.

V. CONCLUSION

In this paper, we have shown that facilitatory (extrapolatory) dynamics found in facilitating synapses can be the basic neural mechanism for motion extrapolation. Experiments with a moving object trajectory showed that facilitatory activation can successfully reproduce the visual motion flash-lag effect (i.e., overshooting in continuous motion as well as the lack of such an effect at motion reversal). Also, an extended facilitating synapse model allowed the facilitation model to be firmly grounded on neurophysiology. Experiments with FLE with change in visual luminance turned out that facilitating postsynaptic activity can generate extrapolated neural activity under both increasing and decreasing firing rate conditions. In sum, we showed that facilitating synaptic dynamics can serve as a delay compensation mechanism, which may give rise to the various flash-lag effects, and help biological organisms to perceive the present environmental state in real time.

ACKNOWLEDGMENTS

We would like to thank R. P. N. Rao et al. [21] for publicly making available the optimal smoothing code; B. Sheth and R. Nijhawan for helping us interpret their FLE results more clearly; and anonymous reviewers for helpful references.

REFERENCES

[1] D. M. Mackay, "Perceptual stability of a stroboscopically lit visual field coontaining self-luminous objects," *Nature*, vol. 181, pp. 507–508, 1958.
[2] R. Nijhawan, "Motion extrapolation in catching," *Nature*, vol. 370, pp. 256–257, 1994.
[3] R. Nijhawan and K. Kirschfeld, "Analogous mechanisms compensate for neural delays in the sensory and motor pathways: Evidence from motor flash-lag," *Current Biology*, vol. 13, pp. 749–753, 2003.
[4] D. Alais and D. Burr, "The flash-lag effect occurs in audition and cross-modally," *Current Biology*, vol. 13, pp. 59–63, 2003.
[5] B. Sheth, R. Nijhawan, and S. Shimojo, "Changing objects lead breifly flashed ones," *Nature Neuroscience*, vol. 3, pp. 489–495, 2000.
[6] R. Nijhawan, "Visual decomposition of colour through motion extrapolation," *Nature*, vol. 386, pp. 66–69, 1997.
[7] D. Whitney and I. Murakami, "Latency difference, not spatial extrapolation," *Nature Neuroscience*, vol. 1, pp. 656–657, 1998.
[8] D. H. Arnold, S. Durant, and A. Johnston, "Latency differences and the flash-lag effect," *Vision Research*, vol. 43, pp. 1829–1835, 2003.
[9] B. Krekelberg, "Sound and vision," *Trends in Cognitive Sciences*, vol. 7, pp. 277–279, 2003.

[10] D. Eagleman and T. J. Sejnowski, "Motion integration and postdiction in visual awareness," *Science*, vol. 287, pp. 2036–2038, 2000.
[11] J. Müsseler, S. Storck, and D. Kerzel, "Comparing mislocalizations with moving stimuli: the fröhlich effect, the flash-lag, and representational momentum," *Visual Cognition*, vol. 9(1/2), pp. 120–138, 2002.
[12] Y.-X. Fu, Y. Shen, and Y. Dan, "Motion-induced perceptual extrapolation of blurred visual targets," *The Journal of Neuroscience*, vol. 21, 2001.
[13] D. Kerzel and K. R. Gegenfurtner, "Neuronal processing delays are compensated in the sensorimotor branch of the visual system," *Current Biology*, vol. 13, pp. 1975–1978, 2003.
[14] R. Nijhawan, K. Watanabe, B. Khurana, and S. Shimojo, "Compensation of neural delays in visual-motor behaviour: No evidence for shorter afferent delays for visual motion," *Visual Cognition*, vol. 11, pp. 275–298, 2004.
[15] R. S. Zucker, "Short-term synaptic plasticity," *Annual Review of Neuroscience*, vol. 12, pp. 13–31, 1989.
[16] S. A. Fisher, T. M. Fisher, and T. J. Carew, "Multiple overlapping processes underlying short-term synaptic enhancement," *Trends in Neurosciences*, vol. 20, pp. 170–177, 1997.
[17] G. Fuhrmann, I. Segev, H. Markram, and M. Tsodyks, "Coding of temporal information by activity-dependent synapses," *Journal of Neurophysiology*, vol. 87, pp. 140–148, 2002.
[18] H. Markram, Y. Wang, and M. Tsodyks, "Differential signaling via the same axon of neocortical pyramidal neurons," *Proceedings of the National Academy of Sciences, USA*, vol. 95, 1998.
[19] E. S. Fortune and G. J. Rose, "Short-term synaptic plasticity as a temporal filter," *Trends in Neurosciences*, vol. 24, pp. 381–385, 2001.
[20] T. Natschläger, W. Maass, and A. Zador, "Efficient temporal processing with biologically realistic dynamic synapses," *Network: Computation in Neural Systems*, vol. 12, pp. 75–87, 2001.
[21] R. P. Rao, D. M. Eagleman, and T. J. Sejnowski, "Optimal smoothing in visual motion perception," *Neural Computation*, vol. 13, pp. 1243–1253, 2001.
[22] A. E. Bryson and Y. Ho, *Applied Optimal Control*. Waltham, MA: Blaisdell Publishing Company, 1975.
[23] R. E. Kalman, "A new approach to linear filtering and prediction theory," *Journal of Basic Engineering*, vol. 82, pp. 35–45, 1960.
[24] W. H. Press, B. P. Flannery, S. A. Teukolsky, and W. T. Vetterling, *Numerical Recipes in FORTRAN: The Art of Scientific Computing*, 2nd ed. Cambridge, UK: Cambridge University Press, 1992.
[25] R. Nijhawan, "Neural delays, visual motion and the flash-lag effect," *Trends in Cognitive Sciences*, vol. 6, pp. 387–393, 2002.
[26] J. Liaw and T. W. Berger, "Dynamic synapse: Harnessing the computing power of synaptic dynamics," *Neurocomputing*, vol. 26-27, pp. 199–206, 1999.
[27] H. Markram, "Elementary principles of nonlinear synaptic transmission," in *Computational Models for Neuroscience: Human Cortical Information Processing*, R. Hecht-Nielsen and T. McKenna, Eds. London, UK: Springer, 2002, ch. 5, pp. 125–169.
[28] C. V. Hess, "Untersuchungen über den erregungsvorgang in sehorgan bei kurz und bei länger dauernder reizung," *Pflügers Arch. Gesamte Physiol.*, vol. 101, pp. 226–262, 1904.

Fisher Information Quantifies Task-Specific Performance in the Blowfly Photoreceptor

Peng Xu and Pamela Abshire
Department of Electrical and Computer Engineering and the Institute for Systems Research
University of Maryland
College Park, MD 20742
E-mail: pxu,pabshire@glue.umd.edu

Abstract—Performance on specific tasks in an organism's everyday activities is essential to survival. In this paper, we extend information-theoretic investigation of neural systems to task specific information using a detailed biophysical model of the blowfly photoreceptor. We formulate the response of the photoreceptor to incident flashes and determine the optimal detection performance using ideal observer analysis. Furthermore, we derive Fisher information contained in the output of the photoreceptor, and show how Fisher information is related to the detection performance. In addition we use Fisher information to show the connections between detection performance, signal-noise ratio, and discriminability. Our detailed biophysical model of the blowfly photoreceptor provides a rich framework for information-theoretic study of neural systems.

I. INTRODUCTION

Biological sensory organs operate under severe constraints of size, weight, structural composition, and energy resources. In many cases, the performance levels are near fundamental physical limits [1]. Nowhere is evolutionary pressure on information processing stronger than in visual systems, where speed and sensitivity can mean the difference between life and death. Consider fly photoreceptors, capable of responding to single photons, while successfully adapting to light up to $\sim 10^6$ effectively absorbed photons per second [2]. Relying on their visual input, flies can chase mates at turning velocities of more than $3000°\ s^{-1}$ with delay time of less than $30\ ms$ [3].

The marvelous efficiency and effectiveness of neural systems motivate both scientific research to elucidate the underlying principles of biological information processing and engineering efforts to synthesize microsystems that abstract their organization from biology. It is crucial to quantify information processing in neural systems for both purposes. Developed in the 1940s [4], information theory is the study of information transmission in communication systems. It has been successful in estimating the maximal information transmission rate of communication channels, *information channel capacity*, and in designing codes that take advantage of it. The usefulness of information theory in neural information processing was recognized early [5], [6], [7]. Information transmission rate has been measured in many neural systems [8], and information channel capacity has been estimated in fly photoreceptors [7]. However, in most previous work, the system was treated as a black-box and the analysis was performed from input-output measurements. This approach provides little insight into the internal factors of the system that limit information transmission. To address this issue, we decomposed the black-box of one extensively studied system, the blowfly photoreceptor, into its elementary biophysical components, and derived a communication model. Since information channel capacity is a fundamental measurement of communication channel, we quantified the effect of individual components on information capacity in the blowfly photoreceptor [9].

Although information capacity gives an upper bound on information transmission rate, it is unclear how it extrapolates to performance on specific tasks that are directly related to survival of the organism. In this work we extend the information-theoretic investigation of neural systems to task specific information using our blowfly photoreceptor model. We focus on the behaviorally relevant task of photoreceptors detecting changes in light intensity. Performance in such visual detection tasks is limited by noise intrinsic to the photon stream as well as noise contributed by transduction components within the photoreceptor, which are determined using the detailed biophysical model of blowfly phototransduction. We formulate the response of the photoreceptor to incident flashes and compute the optimal detection performance using ideal observer analysis. Furthermore, we derive Fisher information contained in the output of the photoreceptor, and show that Fisher information is directly related to the detection performance. Therefore it quantifies task specific information.

The remainder of the paper is organized as follows, in Section II we briefly describe our blowfly photoreceptor model; in Section III we compute the information capacity using the model; in Section IV, we analyze flash detection using ideal observer analysis; in Section V we relate Fisher information to the optimal detection performance; in Section VI we discuss and summarize our work.

II. PHOTORECEPTOR MODEL

Vision in the blowfly begins with two compound eyes that cover most of the head. Each of the two compound eyes is composed of a hexagonal array of ommatidia. Each ommatidium contains eight photoreceptors which receive light through a facet lens and respond in graded fashion to the incident light. Each photoreceptor has an associated waveguide, or rhabdomere, which consists of thousands of microvilli

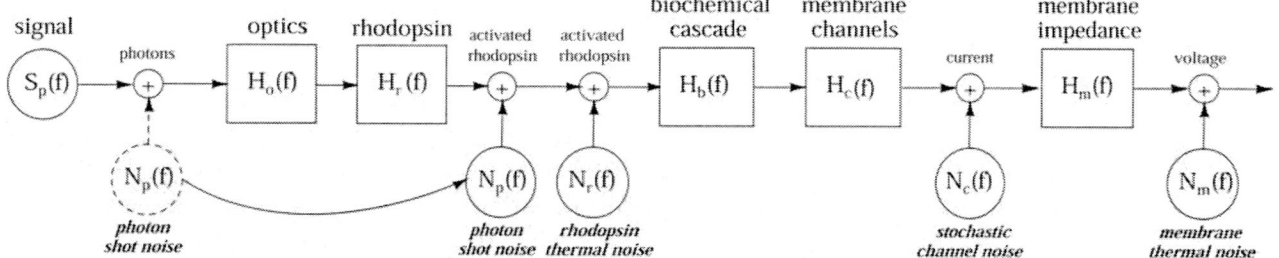

Fig. 1. Communication channel model of the blowfly photoreceptor.

contiguous with the membrane of the photoreceptor. The rhabdomeres of photoreceptors R1-R6 form an asymmetric ring in the periphery of the ommatidium, while the rhabdomeres of photoreceptors R7 and R8 lie end to end in the center. Electrical signals from the non-spiking photoreceptor cells R1-R6 project to the large monopolar cells (LMCs) in the lamina, while R7 and R8 project to cells in the medulla [10]. In this investigation, we focus on the photoreceptors R1-R6, which play the major role in optical sensing.

The photoreceptors communicate information about visual stimuli to LMCs through a series of signal transformations. Behaviorally relevant visual input is received by flies as incident light on their eyes. Photons are guided through the optics of the compound eyes, attenuated by an intracellular pupil mechanism, and absorbed by the photosensitive pigment, rhodopsin, in the rhabdomere. The activated pigment triggers a cascade of biochemical reactions that open light-gated ion channels in the membrane. The open channels provide a membrane conductance that allows an ionic current to flow, changing the membrane voltage. The voltage changes propagate down a short axon to the synaptic terminal in the lamina. The synaptic terminal voltage is the output of the system. Each of these transformations is associated with changes in the signal itself and inevitable introduction of noise. Sources of noise include photon shot noise, thermal activation of rhodopsin, stochastic channel transitions, and membrane thermal noise.

We model these transformations which comprise phototransduction in the blowfly photoreceptor as a cascade of signal transformations and noise sources as shown in Fig. 1. While the photoreceptors exhibit nonlinearity at very low light levels or for large signals, their linear properties are well documented [11]. We linearize these nonlinear transformations about an operating point, given by the average light intensity, and consider them as linear systems. Such analysis is expected to be accurate only when the operating point remains fixed, i.e. for small signals about a background intensity, a reasonable assumption for many visual tasks. We assume that each noise source contributes independent, additive noise at the location where it appears in Fig. 1. Photon shot noise arises in the original photon stream, as indicated by the dashed noise source; however, it remains a Poisson source until the photons are absorbed. So it appears as an additive noise at the location indicated by the arrow and solid noise source. The magnitude transfer functions and noise components of this model were described in [9]. Parameters of the model were estimated using experimental data as described in [9]. The extension of the model into the time domain was described in [12]. The entire model allows us to compute the response of the system to stimuli in the linear operating range.

III. MUTUAL INFORMATION AND INFORMATION CAPACITY

The use of entropy as a measure of information was first developed by Shannon [4]. Entropy is a measure of uncertainty of a random variable defined as $H(X) = E_{P(x)}[\log_2 1/P(X)]$, where $E[\ ]$ is the expectation operator, and $P(x)$ is the probability mass function for a discrete random variable X or probability density function for a continuous random variable X. For each value x that X takes, it provides $\log_2 1/P(x)$ information in bits. The average uncertainty $H(X)$ specifies the required bits to perfectly encode the variable. Whereas entropy quantifies the uncertainty associated with one random variable, in many cases we are interested in how two or more random variables are related. Mutual information $I(X,Y)$ measures the amount of information one variable contains about the other, $I(X,Y) = E_{P(x,y)}\left[\log_2 \frac{P(X,Y)}{P(X)P(Y)}\right]$. $I(X,Y)$ can be written as

$$I(X,Y) = H(X) - H(X|Y) = H(Y) - H(Y|X), \quad (1)$$

thus the mutual information is the reduction in the uncertainty of one variable provided the other is known.

A discrete channel is defined as a system consisting of an input random variable X, an output random variable Y, and a probability function $P(y|x)$ that expresses the probability of observing the output y given the input x. The channel is said to be memoryless if the probability distribution of the output depends only on the current input and is conditionally independent of previous channel inputs or outputs given the current input. The information channel capacity of a discrete memoryless channel is defined as the maximum of the mutual information between the input and output over all possible input distributions.

$$C = \max_{P(x)} I(X,Y). \quad (2)$$

For an additive Gaussian noise channel, if there is no constraint on the input, the capacity of the channel is infinite. However, unconstrained inputs are physically implausible. The most common limitation on the input is an energy or power constraint. We assume an average power constraint $E[X^2] \leq P$. The information capacity is therefore defined as

$$C = \max_{P(x):E[X^2]\leq P} I(X,Y). \quad (3)$$

The capacity of an additive Gaussian noise channel with a noise power spectrum $N(f)$ and a power constraint P can be determined according to the water-filling procedure [13]:

$$C = \int \frac{1}{2} \log_2 \left[1 + \frac{(\nu - N(f))^+}{N(f)}\right] df, \quad (4)$$

where ν is the total power spectrum of signal and noise. ν satisfies

$$\int (\nu - N(f))^+ df = P, \quad (5)$$

where $(x)^+ = x$ if $x \geq 0$, otherwise, $(x)^+ = 0$.

The biophysical model of phototransduction of Fig. 1 can be viewed as an additive Gaussian communication channel. We compute input-referred noise using the transfer function and noise sources introduced at each stage. We then apply (4) to compute the information capacity of the blowfly photoreceptor. This computation was performed at various incident light intensities, and the capacity is plotted as a function of incident light intensity in Fig. 2. In Fig. 2, the estimate of the information capacity computed directly from physiological measurements of transfer characteristics and noise is also shown as '*'s [7]. The dash line shows the capacity for the case where the photoreceptor does not contribute noise, i.e., for photon shot noise only. The capacity predicted by the model corresponds closely to the capacity computed from the physiological measurements.

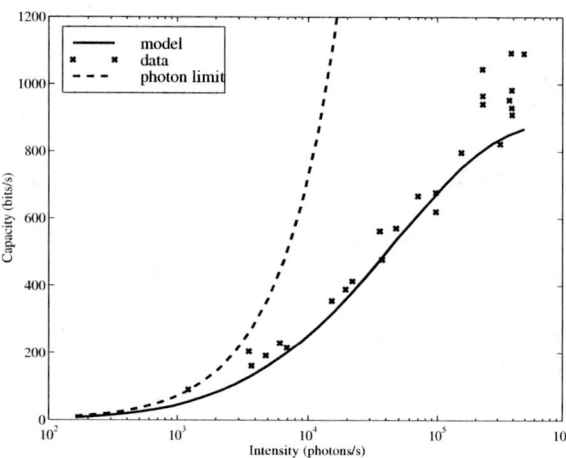

Fig. 2. Information capacity computed from our model and estimated from experimental data.

IV. FLASH DETECTION

The channel capacity given by (4) is an upper bound on the rate of information transmission, assuming that the signal is limited only in average power and the noise is normally distributed. It does not inform us about how information is actually transmitted and used in specific tasks involved in the organism's everyday activity. In order to further investigate the role of information and signal integrity in specific tasks, we study performance in the context of a simple but important visual detection task, discrimination of the presence or absence of brief flashes of light. We assume that flashes are detected under a forced choice between two alternatives, presence and absence (i.e. the task is a two-alternative forced choice (2-AFC) task). We apply ideal observer analysis to quantify the optimal performance from the output of the system and later relate Fisher information to the detection performance.

A. Mean system response to a flash stimulus

Phototransduction is a stochastic process because of the randomness of photon arrival and the noise introduced by the physical components of the system. Responses to the same flash stimulus are different for each trial. In order to perform ideal observer analysis, we compute the mean system response to the flash stimulus. Photon arrival rate defines the background light intensity Λ which determines the operating point of the system. For a flash of duration T and incremental intensity λ, the average number of photons comprising the flash is given by $n = \lambda T$. If we assume that the system responds linearly to each photon, for n arrivals at times t_i, $i = 1, \ldots, n$, the system response will be:

$$f(t) = \sum_{i=1}^{n} B(t - t_i), \quad (6)$$

where $B(t)$ is the single photon response to a photon arrival at time 0. $B(t)$ varies according to the operating point of the system determined by the background light level [14]. We compute the mean system response as the expected system response to photons arriving during a flash:

$$E[f(t)] = E\left[\sum_{i=1}^{n} B(t - t_i)\right] = \sum_{i=1}^{n} E[B(t - t_i)]. \quad (7)$$

Photon arrival is a Poisson process. For this 2-AFC visual detection task the order of photon arrivals is irrelevant, so for a uniform flash with n photons in an interval, each arrival time is uniformly distributed in that period. Therefore each arrival time t_i, $i = 1, \ldots, n$, satisfies:

$$P(t_i) = 1/T, \quad t_i \in [0, T]. \quad (8)$$

We compute the mean response to a single photon arrival as:

$$E[B(t - t_i)] = \int_0^t B(t - t_i) P(t_i) dt_i \quad (9)$$

$$= \int_0^t B(t - t_i) \cdot 1/T dt_i. \quad (10)$$

Then we compute the mean response to the photon stream as:

$$m(\lambda, t) = E[f(t)] = \lambda T \int_0^t B(t - t_i) \cdot 1/T dt_i \quad (11)$$

$$= \lambda m'(t, T) \quad (12)$$

where

$$m'(t,T) = \begin{cases} 0 & \text{if } t \leq 0 \\ \int_0^t B(t-t_i)dt_i & \text{if } 0 < t \leq T \\ \int_0^T B(t-t_i)dt_i & \text{if } t > T \end{cases} \quad (13)$$

Thus we see that the mean response is a linear function of the flash intensity λ because $m'(t,T)$ is determined by the background light level and flash duration. This agrees with our linear model.

B. Ideal observer analysis on flash detection

An ideal observer is a theoretical idealization that performs a specific task in an optimal fashion, given available observations and constraints. The performance of an ideal observer on a task can be used to quantify the best possible performance of the system as it relates to that task. Therefore, ideal observer analysis applied to different stages of a system can reveal how the system transforms signals and transmits task specific information. Furthermore, it can be used as a benchmark to evaluate the performance of a system in comparison with other systems, biological or manmade [15], [16].

We apply ideal observer analysis to the photoreceptor model described above in the 2-AFC detection of flashes. A 2-AFC task presents one of two stimuli in an interval and requires the subject, in this case an ideal observer, to select one of the two choices based on the observation during the interval. In the present work the two stimuli consist of background light alone and a light flash superimposed on the background light; the observation is a vector $\vec{v} \in \Re^k$, $\vec{v} = [v_0, v_1, \ldots, v_{k-1}]$, from the uniformly sampled membrane voltage at the synaptic terminal of the photoreceptor over the interval. The ideal observer determines the presence or absence of the flash stimulus in the test interval optimally by minimizing detection error given the observation vector.

A test statistic d is computed according to [17]:

$$d^2 = \vec{m}(\lambda)^T \Sigma^{-1} \vec{m}(\lambda) \quad (14)$$

where $\vec{m}(\lambda)$ is the mean observation vector for a flash stimulus with duration T and intensity λ and Σ is the covariance matrix of the observation. $\vec{m}(\lambda)$ is obtained by uniformly sampling the mean response $m(\lambda, t)$ over the interval $[0, T]$. From (12) we compute

$$\vec{m}(\lambda) = \lambda \vec{m}' \quad (15)$$

where $\vec{m}'$ is a vector from the sampled function of $m'(t,T)$ in $[0, T]$ with $m'_i = m'(i\tau, T)$, $i = 0, 1, \ldots, k-1$. τ is the sampling period. $m'(t,T)$ does not vary with flash intensity for a given background level and flash duration. Therefore $\vec{m}(\lambda)$ is a function only of the flash intensity λ for a given background level and flash duration. Σ is the covariance matrix of the observation, and is a symmetric matrix. Under the assumptions that the operating point for the system remains fixed, i.e. the noise is a wide sense stationary (WSS) signal, and that noise covariance is equal for background alone and background with flashes, Σ is also the covariance matrix of the noise. Furthermore, under the same assumptions, the probability of detection error can be computed according to [17]:

$$\Pr(\text{error}) = 1 - \Phi(d/2) \quad (16)$$

where Φ denotes the cumulative distribution function (cdf) of a standard normal variable.

We vary the intensity of the flash stimulus to find the threshold intensity, defined as the lowest light intensity with detection error less than or equal to 25%. Fig. 3 shows how the flash detection threshold varies as a function of background light level and stimulus duration [12].

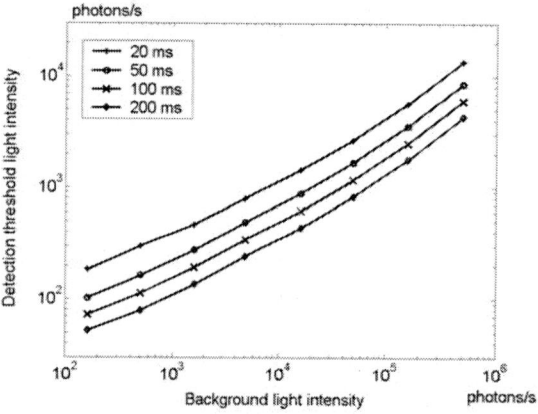

Fig. 3. Performance of the ideal observer on the 2-AFC flash detection task under different background light intensities and for different flash durations in the photoreceptor system.

The optimal performance is specified by the test statistic d, which directly quantifies the detection threshold and provides a comparison for the detection performance of different systems or a system at different operating points.

V. FISHER INFORMATION

In statistics, Fisher information $I_F(\theta)$ is used as a measure of the amount of information that an observable random variable X carries about an unobservable parameter θ upon which the probability distribution of X depends. It has been shown that Fisher information limits the accuracy of signal estimation according to Cramér-Rao bound [17],

$$\text{Var}_\theta[\hat{\theta}(X)] \geq \frac{\{\frac{\partial}{\partial \theta} E[\hat{\theta}(X)]\}^2}{I_F(\theta)}, \quad (17)$$

where

$$I_F(\theta) \triangleq E\left[\left(\frac{\partial}{\partial \theta} \log P_\theta(X)\right)^2\right]. \quad (18)$$

$\hat{\theta}(X)$ is the estimate of parameter θ from observations of the random variable X. $P_\theta(X)$ is the probability density function of X conditioned on θ.

At a given background light level Λ, the photoreceptor system can be modeled as a linear system with responses varying around the operating point set by the background light level. The background light level determines the single photon response $B(t)$, and together the background level and flash duration T determine the shape of the mean response. Flash intensity Λ determines the magnitude of the mean response. We sample the synaptic terminal voltage during the observation interval to obtain the sampled voltage vector $\vec{v}$ of length k. Considering the noise sources in the model as described in section II, the observation vector follows the multidimensional Gaussian distribution:

$$P(\vec{v}|\Lambda) = \frac{1}{(2\pi)^{\frac{k}{2}}|\Sigma|^{\frac{1}{2}}} \exp\left[-\frac{1}{2}(\vec{v}-\vec{m}(\Lambda))^T \Sigma^{-1}(\vec{v}-\vec{m}(\Lambda))\right] \quad (19)$$

where $\vec{m}(\Lambda)$ is the mean vector of $\vec{v}$. $\vec{m}(\Lambda)$ is a function of Λ for a given background light and flash duration, therefore $P(\vec{v}|\Lambda)$ is solely determined by Λ for a given background light and flash duration. This allow us to compute the Fisher information at the synaptic terminal using the distribution of the membrane voltage vector.

$$\frac{\partial \ln P(\vec{v}|\Lambda)}{\partial \Lambda} = \frac{\partial}{\partial \Lambda}\left[-\frac{1}{2}(\vec{v}-\vec{m}')^T \Sigma^{-1}(\vec{v}-\vec{m}')\right] \quad (20)$$

$$= -\frac{1}{2}\left[-\vec{v}^T \Sigma^{-1}\vec{m}' - \vec{m}'^T \Sigma^{-1}\vec{v}\right]$$
$$+ \vec{m}'^T \Sigma^{-1}\vec{m}' \quad (21)$$

$$= \vec{v}^T \Sigma^{-1}\vec{m}' - \vec{m}'^T \Sigma^{-1}\vec{m}' \quad (22)$$

$$= (\vec{v}-\vec{m}')^T \Sigma^{-1}\vec{m}' \quad (23)$$

$$= (\vec{v}-\vec{m}(\Lambda))^T \Sigma^{-1}\vec{m}' \quad (24)$$

$$I_F(\Lambda) = \int_{\Re^k} P(\vec{v}|\Lambda)\left(\frac{\partial \ln P(\vec{v}|\Lambda)}{\partial \Lambda}\right)^2 d\vec{v} \quad (25)$$

$$= \vec{m}'^T (\Sigma^{-1})^T \left[\int_{\Re^k} P(\vec{v}|\Lambda)(\vec{v}-\vec{m}(\Lambda))(\vec{v}-\vec{m}(\Lambda))^T dt\right]$$
$$\Sigma^{-1}\vec{m}' \quad (26)$$

$$= \vec{m}'^T (\Sigma^{-1})^T \Sigma \Sigma^{-1}\vec{m}' \quad (27)$$

$$= \vec{m}'^T \Sigma^{-1}\vec{m}' \quad (28)$$

$$= \frac{1}{\Lambda^2}\vec{m}(\Lambda)^T \Sigma^{-1}\vec{m}(\Lambda) \quad (29)$$

$$= \frac{d^2}{\Lambda^2} \quad (30)$$

Consequently we can express the detection performance in terms of Fisher information as

$$\Pr(\text{error}) = 1 - \Phi\left(\frac{1}{2}\Lambda\sqrt{I_F(\Lambda)}\right). \quad (31)$$

The optimal detection performance is directly related to the Fisher information available from the observation for a given stimulus. Therefore Fisher information is a measurement of the information relevant to performance in the detection task.

From (28) we see that Fisher information can be computed by $\vec{m}'$ and Σ which are functions of background light level and flash duration T. $\vec{m}'$ is determined by the single photon response at the background light level of interest, and Σ is determined by the noise characteristics of the channel at the same background light level. Therefore the Fisher information in this system is a function only of the background light level Λ, and remains the same for different flash intensities Λ; we will write it as $I_F(\Lambda)$ instead of $I_F(\Lambda)$ from now on.

Once we define detection threshold as the flash intensity corresponding to a specific detection error, i.e. 25%, Fisher information also determines the threshold intensity, or minimum detectable flash intensity. The threshold is a function of background light level according to

$$\Lambda_{min} = \frac{d_{25\%}}{\sqrt{I_F(\Lambda)}}, \quad (32)$$

where $d_{25\%}$ is the value of the test statistic that satisfies $1 - \Phi(d_{25\%}/2) = 0.25$. The larger the Fisher information is, the smaller the minimum detectable flash of light.

VI. Discussion

In the preceding section we have shown that Fisher information relates directly to detection performance. It is also related to basic characteristics of signal and noise. One fundamental property of Fisher information can be elucidated by considering the simple case where the noise at each sampling point is independent and identically distributed (i.i.d.) Gaussian $N(0, \sigma^2)$ of zero mean and variance σ^2. Here the covariance matrix Σ of noise is $\sigma^2 I$ where I denotes the $k \times k$ identity matrix. In this case,

$$\sigma^2 I_F(\Lambda) = \vec{m}(\Lambda)^T \Sigma^{-1}\vec{m}(\Lambda) = \frac{\vec{m}(\Lambda)^T \vec{m}(\Lambda)}{\sigma^2} = k\frac{\overline{m^2}}{\sigma^2}, \quad (33)$$

where $\overline{m^2}$ is the average signal power defined as $\frac{1}{k}\sum_{i=0}^{k-1} m_i^2$. Note that σ^2 is the average noise power, so that $\sigma^2 I_F(\Lambda)$ is equivalent to the signal-noise ratio (SNR) times the number of samples. For a given Λ, the higher the SNR is, the higher the Fisher information.

Fisher information also serves as a link between optimal detection and optimal parameter estimation. The ideal observer performs optimal parameter estimation of Λ in the sense that it minimizes the expected estimation error. Given the conditional distribution of the observation vector $P(\vec{v}|\Lambda)$, the minimum estimation variance is obtained from the Cramér-Rao bound,

$$\sigma^2(\hat{\Lambda}) = \frac{1}{I_F(\Lambda)}. \quad (34)$$

The discriminability of a signal depends on the separation between the signal and its absence and the spread of the signal. The bigger the separation is, the easier the discrimination; the smaller the spread is, the easier the discrimination. A common measure of discriminability is defined by the ratio of the separation to the spread. In the case of flash discrimination, it is written as:

$$d' = \frac{\Lambda}{\sigma(\hat{\Lambda})}. \quad (35)$$

Replacing $\sigma(\hat{\Lambda})$ from (34) we see that d' is equal to the detection statistic d obtained for the optimal detection. Thus the detection performance and the signal characteristics are also connected through Fisher information.

In this paper, we have extended the information-theoretic investigation of neural systems using the framework provided by a detailed biophysical model of blowfly photoreceptors. Specifically, we perform ideal observer analysis of flash detection in the photoreceptor model. We demonstrate that Fisher information is an information measure that quantifies performance in a specific task. We also show how the detection performance is connected to signal characteristics such as SNR and discriminability through Fisher information. In our future work, we will investigate in further detail how the individual components in the photoreceptor model and their biophysical parameters contribute to the Fisher information.

REFERENCES

[1] W. Bialek, "Physical limits to senstation and perception," *Ann. Rev. Biophys. Biophys. Chem.*, vol. 16, pp. 455–478, 1987.

[2] R. C. Hardie and P. Raghu, "Visual transduction in Drosophila," *Nature*, vol. 413, pp. 186–193, Sept. 2001.

[3] A. Borst and J. Haag, "Neural networks in the cockpit of the fly," *J. Comp. Physiol. A*, vol. 188, pp. 419–437, 2002.

[4] C. E. Shannon, "A mathematical theory of communication," *Bell Syst. Tech. J.*, vol. 27, pp. 379–423, Oct. 1948.

[5] H. Barlow, "Possible principles underlying the transformation of sensory messages," in *Sensory Communication*, W. A. Rosenblith, Ed. Cambridge, MA: MIT Press, 1961.

[6] J. J. Atick, "Could information theory provide an ecological theory of sensory processing?" *Network*, vol. 3, pp. 213–251, 1992.

[7] R. de Ruyter van Steveninck and S. Laughlin, "The rate of information transfer at graded-potential synapses," *Nature*, vol. 379, pp. 642–645, Feb. 1996.

[8] A. Borst and F. Theunissen, "Information theory and neural coding," *Nature Neurosci.*, vol. 2, no. 11, pp. 947–957, Nov. 1999.

[9] P. Abshire and A. G. Andreou, "A communication channel model for information transmission in the blowfly photoreceptor," *Biosystems*, vol. 62, no. 1-3, pp. 113–133, 2001.

[10] A. Roberts and B. M. H. Bush, Eds., *Neurons without impulses*. Cambridge, UK: Cambridge University Press, 1981.

[11] M. Juusola, E. Kouvalainen, M. Järvilehto, and M. Weckström, "Contrast gain, signal-to-noise ratio, and linearity in light-adapted blowfly photoreceptors," *J. Gen. Physiol.*, vol. 104, pp. 593–621, 1994.

[12] P. Xu and P. Abshire, "Threshold detection of intensity flashes in the blowfly photoreceptor by an ideal observer," *Neurocomputing*, 2005, to appear.

[13] T. M. Cover and J. A. Thomas, *Elements of information theory*. New York: John Wiley and Sons, Inc., 1991.

[14] F. Wong, "Adapting-bump model for eccentric cells of Limulus," *J. Gen. Physiol.*, vol. 76, pp. 539–557, 1980.

[15] W. Geisler, "Ideal observer analysis," in *The visual neurosciences*, L. Chalupa and J. Werner, Eds. Cambridge, MA: MIT Press, 2003, pp. 825–837.

[16] P. N. Steinmetz and R. L. Winslow, "Detection of flash intensity differences using rod photocurrent observations," *Neural Comput.*, vol. 11, no. 5, 1999.

[17] H. Poor, *An introduction to signal detection and estimation*. New York: Springer, 1994.

Evolutionary Training of a Biologically Realistic Spino-neuromuscular System

Stanley Gotshall
Department of
Computer Science
University of Idaho
Moscow, ID
gots9018@uidaho.edu

Christopher Canine
Department of Electrical and
Computer Engineering
University of Idaho
Moscow, ID
cani6203@uidaho.edu

Benjamin Jennings
Department of
Physics
Whitworth College
Spokane, WA
bjennings07@whitworth.edu

Terence Soule
Department of
Computer Science
University of Idaho
Moscow, ID
tsoule@cs.uidaho.edu

Abstract— This paper presents a biologically realistic model of the spino-neuromuscular system (SNMS). The model uses a pulse-coded recurrent neural network to control a simulated human-like arm. We use a genetic algorithm to train the network based on a target behavior for the arm. Our goal is to create a useful model for studying the function and behavior of neural pathways in the SNMS. The genetic algorithm is able to train the network to actuate the arm to achieve controlled motion. Our experimental results demonstrate that certain types of feedback pathways are important for controlling certian movements.

I. INTRODUCTION

Despite considerable advances in knowledge about the structure and function of the Spino-neuromuscular system (SNMS), there is still a need to expand the understanding of the role of neural pathway diversity in motor control and in compensating for injury and disease [3], [8], [15], [18]. If a movement is disrupted, it is not known which neural pathways are most significant in correcting the movement [27], [11], [20], [28]. If a limb is injured, it is generally unknown how the selection of neural pathways change to compensate for the injury. Advances in the field of artificial neural networks has made it plausible to simulate portions of the human nervous system at the level of individual neurons. The goal of this paper is to show that this is possible for the SNMS with automated training and that this can be a useful tool for modelling complex neural pathways.

In this paper we use a biologically realistic neural network to control a joint with a Hill muscle system [7], [12]. The Hill muscle is used as the bicep in a model of a human-like arm with a single degree of freedom. The control network is modelled after the neural connections in the spinal cord's ventral horn. The synaptic connections in the network are trained with an evolutionary algorithm, specifically a genetic algorithm (GA), which is easily generalized to any topology. GAs automatically sample a wide range of possible solutions and select, by analogy to biological evolution, the most fit ones [6]. The SNMS model simulates the function of key spinal neurons and links to the Hill muscle simulation. The experiments presented here investigate the significance of Renshaw cells and their synaptic links in controlling movement [21], [10].

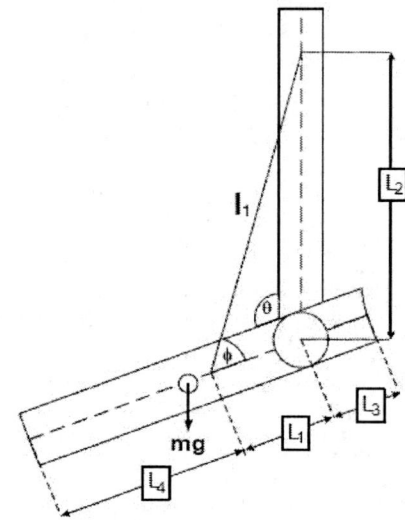

Fig. 1. The joint has a movable lower limb with center of mass indicated by mg. Gravitational torque on the joint changes as the angle Θ changes. This figure is adapted from [25]. The parameters of the joint model are listed in Table I.

II. BACKGROUND

Numerous researchers have used models of the muscular and skeletal system to resolve redundancy questions by assuming that selected movements are optimal with respect to some unknown criterion [4], [13], [17], [19]. However, this research usually does not include neural circuitry connected to the muscle systems. In contrast, research focused on modelling the neural circuitry of the SNMS has generally been used to demonstrate that a particular model, with a limited number of specific neural pathways, can generate biologically realistic neural activity or biologically realistic movements [4], [1], [2], [9], [14], [23]. Such research is useful in showing that the particular neural pathway(s) encoded in the model can account for any particular behavior. However, showing that a particular neural pathway *can* generate a biologically realistic movement in a model is not the same as showing that the pathway *does* generate the movement in an actual organism. Thus, our goal is to use a GA to find the most natural neural pathways for specific motions.

Boothe and Cohen model a neural circuit after a central pattern generator (CPG) to study inhibitory interactions between agonist and antagonist muscle pairs [2]. Their experiments support the idea that motor control is strongly influenced by a neural CPG. However, their model does not include quantitative simulations of the muscles themselves. Thus, the next step is to include a biologically realistic muscle for the neural model to control.

Ivashko et al. also use a CPG based model and include Hill-type muscles [9]. They successfully use their neural model to control a simulated cat hind limb. However, in their experiments, they configure the synaptic links manually to achieve stable motion. This makes generalizing the neural model to different topologies difficult because one change to the network could require manual re-tuning of the entire network and incorporates user bias. Therefore, our goal is to make a generalizable SNMS model to answer questions about the importance of certain spinal neural pathways in motor control. This requires a rapid and bias-free training mechanism, thus a GA is a logical choice.

III. MODELS

A. Joint Model

The joint model used here (Fig. 1) has a single degree of freedom. The vertical segment of the arm is fixed and tension due to the bicep and force due to gravity move the forearm. To better simulate a human arm, springs are placed at π-2.4 and π-0.4 radians to reflect the arms innate resistance to extreme angles. The spring at π-2.4 radians models the natural resistance while fully contracting the arm. The spring at π-0.4 is meant to model the behavior of the arm while muscles are relaxed. At rest there is a small amount of bicep tension resulting in a slight inclined angle. The connections and placement of the bicep is shown as I_1 in Fig. 1.

The movable limb is a uniform cylinder with parameters shown in Table I.

TABLE I
JOINT MODEL PARAMETERS

Movable Limb Radius	0.2 meters
Movable Limb Mass	0.75 kg
Timestep	0.02 seconds
L1	0.24 meters
L2	1.0 meter
L3	0.2 meters
L4	0.96 meters
Spring Constant	150

The mass and dimensions of the arm model are somewhat greater than that of an actual human arm because lighter limbs are more sensitive to the simulated muscle contractions. In this model, slightly heavier limbs are easier to actuate.

B. Hill Muscle

The Hill model is commonly used to simulate muscle systems and their nonlinearities. The muscle has three independently triggerable contractile elements connected to a common tendon. Each contractile element receives a binary neural signal from its alpha-motoneuron (α-MN) and contracts according to the Hill equations. A contractile element contracts if its α-MN is active and relaxes otherwise. The tendon component also stretches depending on the activity of each of the three contractile elements. The muscle connects to the upper portion of the arm and to the forearm near the joint as indicated in Fig. 1. The total contractile force of the muscle is calculated with Equation 1

$$T = \sum_{all\ \gamma} (T_{sec}^{\gamma}) + T_{pec} \qquad (1)$$

where γ is a given contractile element, T_{sec}^{γ} is the force due to a given contractile element (serial elastic component), and T_{pec} is the force due to the common tendon (parallel elastic component). To match the joint simulation (Table 1), the Hill muscle timestep is also 0.02 seconds.

C. Integrate-and-Fire Neuron

Each neuron in the network uses the pulse-coded integrate-and-fire (IF) model. This is a logical choice for biologically realistic neural networks because IF neurons integrate potential over time just as biological neurons. It is important to note that all of the IF neurons are either excitatory or inhibitory. That is, a given IF neuron can only have positive outgoing synaptic weights or negative outgoing synaptic weights. Classical artificial neurons do not have time-dependant behavior and do not retain phase information which is present in biological networks. However, IF neurons, when modelled individually, do have time dependant behavior and retain phase information.

With the exception of the α-MNs and Renshaw cells, each IF neuron outputs a single pulse when firing. The α-MNs and Renshaw cells fire two consecutive pulses when activated. This is to better simulate these neuron types. Renshaw cells are known to have burst firing patterns [16] and certain classes of α-MNs are easily excited leading to burst-like behavior [22]. Each neuron is modelled with Equation 2

$$f(t + \Delta t) = f(t) + \Delta t (\frac{1}{\tau}(g(t) - s(t))) \qquad (2)$$

where $g(t)$ is the current input sum to the neuron and $s(t)$ is the current level of stored potential. The constant τ, 0.6, determines the decay rate of the neuron. This decay is electronically similar to that of a leaky integrator [24]. To match the joint and muscle simulations, Δt is 0.02 seconds. This timestep allows for the α-MN to have a maximum firing frequency of $(\frac{2}{3})50$ hertz which is reasonably close to biological firing rates [22].

After a neuron fires it enters a refractory period of a single timestep during which it cannot build up any potential. After the refractory period, the neuron can build potential and fire again.

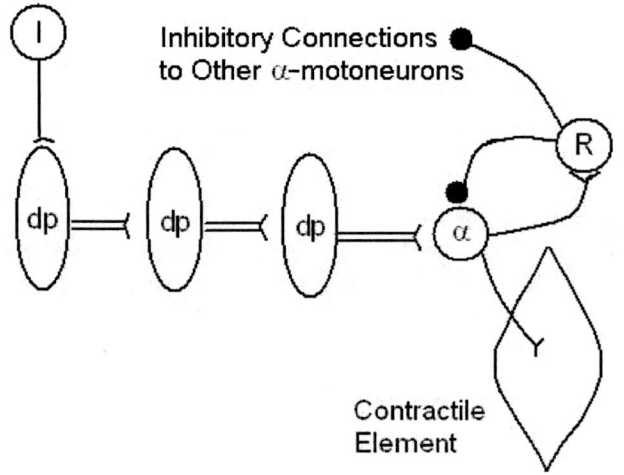

Fig. 2. This figure illustrates the descending neural pathways to the α-MN and Renshaw cell. The nodes labelled dp represent synfire nodes and the input to the subnet is the node labelled I. The Renshaw cell interconnections are also indicated.

D. Neural Network

The neural network is composed of three subnets, one for each of the three contractile elements in the Hill muscle. Each subnet is identical and can receive independent inputs (Fig. 2). The individual subnets contain neural chains which model individual descending pathways to the spinal cord neurons.

Each *dp* node in Fig. 2 is implemented as a synfire node [26]. Each synfire node is a collection of five neurons which are fully connected to the preceding and following node. It is difficult for a simple chain of IF neurons to propagate a signal, however a chain of synfire nodes models the robustness of neural connections in the SNMS. The use of synfire nodes also allows for complex variations in descending signal patterns.

The node labelled *I* represents the input to the subnet and is implemented as five synchronous binary inputs. Placement of the α-MN and Renshaw cell are also indicated in the figure. Each Renshaw cell has inhibitory links to all three α-MNs in the network and each α-MN signals to its respective contractile element. Despite the simplicity of this model, training the network requires adjusting 261 real-valued weights. We use the genetic algorithm for training because adjusting this number of weights by hand would be prohibitive.

In biology, it is generally accepted that Renshaw cells are important for controlled muscle movement. Inhibitory signals from Renshaw cells appear to modulate and control α-MNs to avoid sudden muscle contractions and possible injury [16]. Our goal is to train the neural model to control specific movements in light of the interconnections between the Renshaw cells and α-MNs.

E. Genetic Algorithm

We used a steady state Genetic Algorithm (GA) to train the synaptic links of the network. The GA maintains a population of individuals (chromosomes) where each individual encodes a string of synaptic weight values which corresponds to a given network. In the GA, these real values range from 0 to 30 and are interpreted as negative numbers if they correspond to inhibitory links as defined by the known biology incorporated into the network model. During each iteration, the GA selects two parents and generates two offspring. The two offspring then replace the two least fit individuals in the population.

Our goal is to produce a particular movement measured in response to the input from the simulated descending pathways. Fitness, or error, is calculated by summing the difference between the desired behavior and the actual behavior at each timestep t. The smaller the error associated with a given network, the higher the fitness. Specifically, fitness is calculated with Equation 3.

$$F = -\sum_{all\ t}(\Theta(t) - target(t))^2 \qquad (3)$$

At the end of execution, the most fit individual is taken as the best solution. Specific parameters for the GA are listed in Table II.

TABLE II
GA PARAMETERS

Number of Trials Per Network	50
Population Size	500
Iterations	75000
Parent Selection	2-way Tournament
Representation	String of 64-bit IEEE Doubles
Weight Range	[0,30] ([-30,0] Inhibitory Links)
Crossover Type	Arithmetic ([5])
Crossover Probability	1.0
Mutation Type	N(0,0.75)
Mutation Probability per Gene	$\frac{1}{n}$ (n = Number of Weights)

IV. EXPERIMENTS

In these experiments our goal is to train a biologically realistic neural network to control a simulated neuromuscular system. The general research methodology is to make changes to the network and observe how these changes affect the network's ability to control movement.

The training is based on a target behavior for the arm which involves the arm raising itself from a resting position, holding at a fixed angle, and returning to the resting position. The target velocity for the upward and downward motion is -0.5 and 0.5 radians per second, respectively, which is much less than the maximum possible. The target holding period is 4.5 seconds.

The descending neural signals are modelled with the three binary inputs to the neural network. The input signals are single timestep bursts and are evenly distributed over the three subnets over a given number of timesteps. The training input to raise the arm is three spiking inputs rotating over the subnets. For example, the pattern for upward motion is

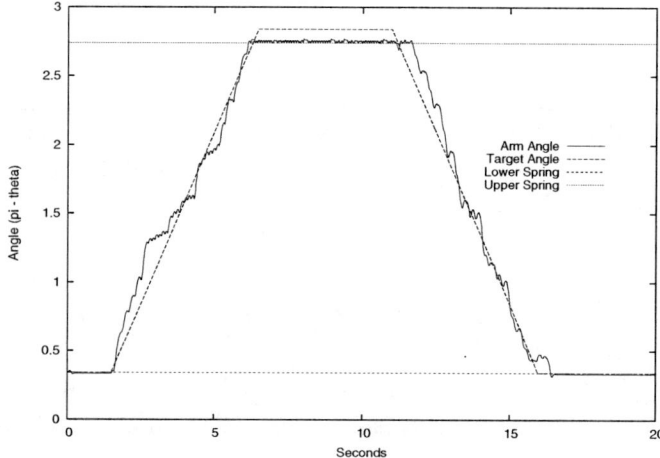

Fig. 3. This behavior is the result of training the network with each Renshaw cell sending inhibitory signals to every α-MN. The arm's behavior binds closely to the target behavior during nearly the entire training. This sample is shown because it is representative of the average best fitness at the end of the GA training (Fig. 8). This behavior's fitness (error) is -10.08.

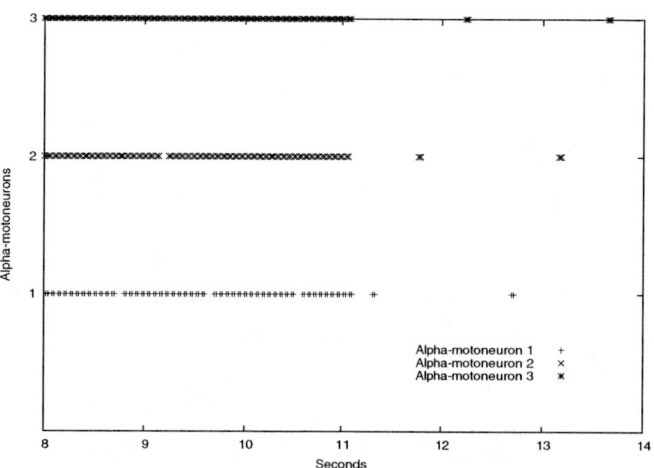

Fig. 4. This figure shows the α-MN firing patterns of the sample taken in the experiment with interconnecting Renshaw cells. This data shows the transition from the up input signal to the down input signal. Each α-MN, with the exception of α-MN 3, is periodically inhibited by its own Renshaw cell and neighboring Renshaw cells.

as follows: at timestep 0 subnet 1 receives an input signal, at the next timestep the subnet 1 signal deactivates and the subnet 2 signal activates, and so on for the third subnet. The input signals continue to cycle for the duration of the upward motion. The input pattern to lower the arm are pulses evenly distributed over 70 timesteps (1.4 seconds). Thus, during every 70 timesteps each subnet receives a single input pulse in intervals of about 23 timesteps. These input periods for training are arbitrary. Other similar values are equally successful.

In general, rapidly pulsed inputs (1 pulse per 3 timesteps) are signals to raise the arm and slower pulses (1 pulse per 70 timesteps) are signals to lower the arm. Gravity provides most of the force needed to lower the arm, however a low frequency input is required to control the downward motion. The input patterns are timed with when the target angle increases and decreases. The full duration of each training run is 20 seconds (1000 timesteps).

The experiments involve training three network configurations.

A. Renshaw Cells with Neighboring α-MN Connections

B. Renshaw Cells with Single α-MN Connection

C. No Renshaw Cells

Experiment A involves training the neural model with connections from each Renshaw cell to each α-MN. Therefore, it is possible for a single α-MN to inhibit the other two indirectly through its own Renshaw cell. In experiment B, the network is trained with no Renshaw cell links between subnets. Thus, the α-MNs are only inhibited as a function of their own firing patterns. Experiment C removes all the Renshaw cells so the α-MN firing patterns are only a function of their own subnet input patterns and the descending synaptic links.

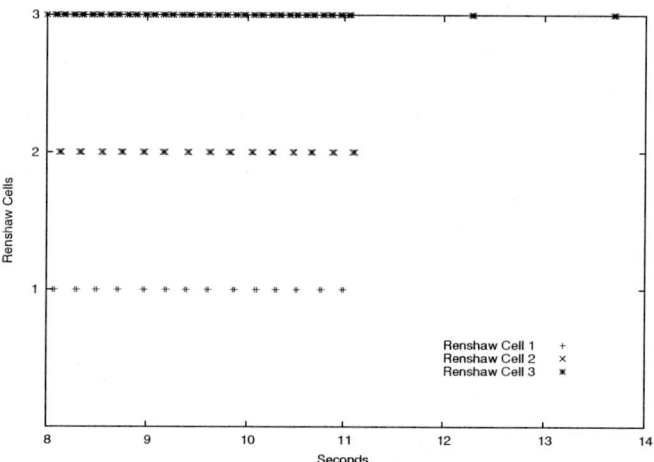

Fig. 5. This figure shows the Renshaw cell firing patterns of the sample taken in the experiment with interconnecting Renshaw cells. This data shows the transition from the up input signal to the down input signal. Each time a Renshaw cell fires, it sends an inhibitory pulse to each α-MN. Note that when the signal to lower the arm begins, two of the Renshaw cells cease firing.

V. RESULTS

On average, removing Renshaw cell interconnections increases training error by approximately 70% and removing them altogether increases error by a much larger amount (Fig. 8 and 9). Removing all Renshaw cells results in a statistically significant difference in fitness (Student's t-test, $p < 0.0005$) at every GA iteration.

A. Renshaw Cells with Neighboring α-MN Connections

Fig. 3 shows that the GA can successfully train the network to move the arm upward and downward at a controlled rate. The arm's behavior closely matches the target behavior during

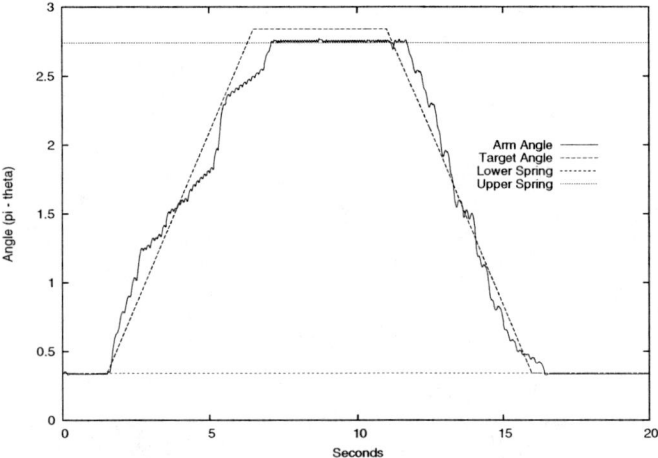

Fig. 6. This behavior is the result of removing Renshaw cell connections to other subnets' α-MN. On average this network yields lower fitness values due to the difficulty in matching the target behavior during the upward motion. This sample is shown because it is representative of the average best fitness at the end of the GA training (Fig. 8). This behavior's fitness (error) is -16.09.

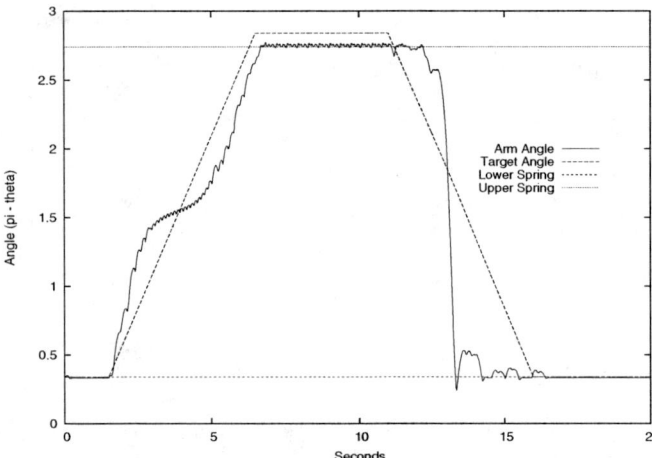

Fig. 7. This behavior is the result of removing all Renshaw cells in the network. The arm moves upward in a way roughly consistent with constant force applied by the bicep. The arm drops rapidly as the input pattern for downward motion begins. This behavior's fitness (error) is -114.51 and is representative of the average best fit found by the GA (Fig. 8).

most of the upward and downward motions. Fig. 4 shows the individual firing patterns of the α-MNs. Note that each α-MN has its own unique firing pattern. Each Renshaw cell periodically inhibits the three α-MNs (Fig. 5) which causes gaps in the α-MN firing patterns. Note that the frequency of gaps varies among the three α-MNs. This variance is possible because the IF neurons in the network retain phase and time-dependant information.

B. Renshaw Cells with Single α-MN Connections

Fig. 6 shows the result of removing interconnecting Renshaw cell links. In the sample, upward movement becomes more irregular and it takes longer to reach the uppermost angle.

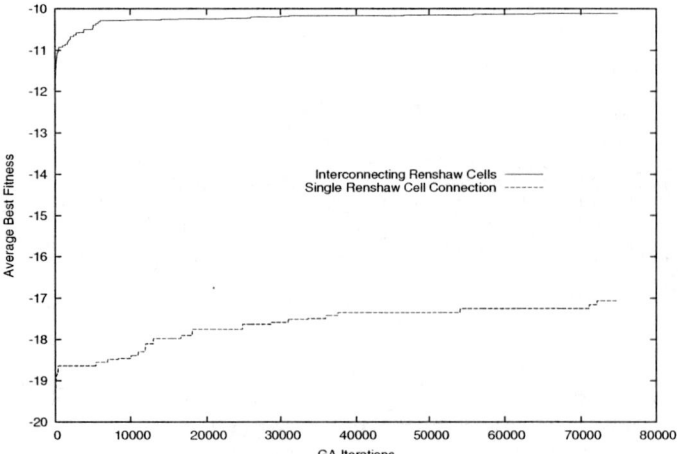

Fig. 8. This figure shows the average best fit individual of 50 trials over 75,000 GA iterations. In training the network with interconnecting Renshaw cells, the GA continues to find better individuals until approximately 60,000 iterations reaching an average fitness of -10.2 ($\pm$ 0.9). The GA also continues to find better individuals in training the network single Renshaw connections, though on average it only reaches fitness values of -17 ($\pm$ 5.5). The average best fit of networks with no Renshaw cells only reaches -114 ($\pm$ 8.9) (not shown).

The upward motion has distinct shifts in velocity resulting in large deviations from the target behavior. The holding motion is stable and the downward motion appears unchanged from experiment A.

C. No Renshaw Cells

The trained networks with no Renshaw cells nearly always moves the joint in an s-shaped path upward and rapidly drops while moving down (Fig. 7). It appears that with no Renshaw cells, the GA selects a weight set which makes the descending pathways behave like a central pattern generator (CPG). That is, the α-MNs produce a regular pattern of signals that is constant despite the changes in gravitational torque as the arm moves. This produces the s-shaped path during the upward motion because movement slows when the gravitational torque is greatest. The arm suddenly drops down because without feedback the network can not effectively compensate for the changing velocity.

VI. CONCLUSIONS

These results show that it is possible to use a GA to train a biologically realistic pulse-coded neural network to control a complex muscle system. Of the three tested network variations, the data shows that the GA takes advantage of the more effective and the more biologically natural neural pathways to achieve the target motion. The Renshaw cell connections appear to be important during upward motion when the α-MNs fire at a high frequency as well as downward motion to avoid uncontrolled descent (Fig 7). When compared with the networks with interconnections, networks trained without them results in significantly higher deviations from the target behavior. These results support the claim that Renshaw

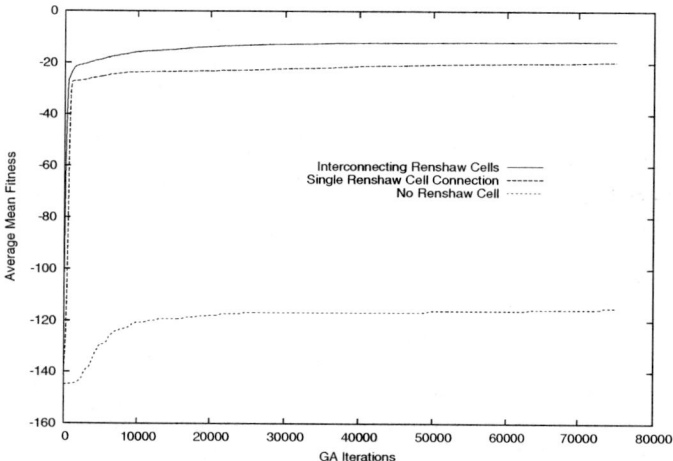

Fig. 9. This figure shows the average mean fit individual of 50 trials over 75,000 GA iterations. The GA progressively improves its average individual in all cases. However, the fitness of the trained networks with no Renshaw cells are significantly lower than the other two. The average mean fitness at the end of the GA training for the first, second, and third experiments are -11.6 ($\pm$ 1.4), -19.4 ($\pm$ 5.5), and -115 ($\pm$ 9.3), respectively.

cells and their interconnections to other α-MNs contribute to controlled motion of skeletal muscle systems.

VII. FUTURE WORK

We have shown that our SNMS model is trainable with an evolutionary algorithm, thus future work would include expanding on this network model. In biological muscle systems afferent feedback mechanisms in the muscle fibers stimulate afferent neurons. These neurons feed key information back to the α-MN and other spinal neurons. Thus, future work includes training a single network with afferent neurons and testing that network with forearms of various weights. Ideally, the network would compensate for the change in weight. Our training method and SNMS model generalizes to accommodate this addition.

ACKNOWLEDGMENTS

This work is supported by NSF EPSCoR EPS-0132626. These experiments were performed on a Beowulf cluster built with funds from NSF grant EPS-80935 and a generous hardware donation from Micron Technologies.

REFERENCES

[1] David P. Bashor. A large-scale model of some spinal reflex circuits. *Biological Cybernetics*, 78(2):147–157, 1998.
[2] D.L. Boothe and A.H. Cohen. A model of limbed locomotion for a four muscle system. *Neurocomputing*, 44-46:743–752, 2002.
[3] A.G. Brown. *Oranization in the Spinal Cord*. Springer-Verlag, New York, 1981.
[4] T.S. Buchanan, D.G. Lloyd, and T.F. Besier. Neuromusculoskeletal modeling: Estimation of muscle forces and joint movements and moments from measurements of neural command. *Journal of Applied Biomechanics*, 20:367–395, 2004.
[5] S. Carlson. A general method for handling constraints in genetic algorithms. In *Second Annual Joint Conference on Information Science*, pages 663–667, 1995.
[6] D.E. Goldberg. *Genetic Algorithms in Search, Optimization, and Machine Learning*. Addison-Wesley, 1989.
[7] A.V. Hill. The abrupt transition from rest to activity in muscles. *Proc. Roy. Soc. London B*, 136(884):399–420, 1949.
[8] H. Hillman. *The Cellular Structure of the Mammalian Nervous System*. MTP Press Limited, The Hague, 1986.
[9] D.G. Ivashko, B.I. Prilutsky, S.N. Markin, J.K. Chapin, and I.A. Rybak. Modeling the spinal cord neural circuitry controlling cat hindlimb movement. *Neurocomputing*, 52(54):621–629, 2003.
[10] E. Janskoska and S. Lindstrom. Morphological identification of renshaw cells. *Acta Physiol Scand.*, 81(3):428–430, 1971.
[11] F. Kaneko, K. Onari, K. Kawaguchi, K. Tsukisaka, and S.H. Roy. Electromechanical delay after acl reconstruction: An innovative method for investigating central and peripheral contributions. *Journal of Orthopaedic and Sports Physical Therapy*, 32:158–165, 2002.
[12] Glenn Klute, Joseph M. Czerniecki, and Blake Hannaford. Mckibbeb artificial muscles: Pneumatic actuators with biomechanical intelligence. In *IEEE/ASME International Conference on Advanced Intelligent Mechatronics*, Atlanta, GA, 1999.
[13] M.L. Latash, J.P. Scholz, and G. Schoner. Motor control strategies revealed in the structure of motor variability. *Exercise Sports Science Reviews*, 30(1):26–31, 2002.
[14] E.P. Leob, S.F. Giszter, P. Saltiel, E. Bizzi, and Mussa-Ivaldi. Output units of motor behavior: An experimental study. *Journal of Cognitive Neuroscience*, 12(1):78–97, 2000.
[15] C.T. Leonard. *The Neuroscience of Human Movement*. Mosby, St. Louis, 1998.
[16] M.G. Maltenfort, C.J Heckman, and W.Z Rymer. Decorrelating actions of renshaw interneurons on the firing of spinal motoneurons within a motor nucleus: A simulation study. *Journal of Neurophysiology*, 30(1):309–323, 1998.
[17] K.M. Newell and D.M. (Eds) Corcos. *Variability and Motor Control*. Human Kinetics, Champaign, 1993.
[18] J. Nolte. *The Human Brain. An Introduction to its Functional Anatomy*. St. Louis, 5 edition, 2002.
[19] B.I. Prilutsky and V.M. Zatsiorsky. Optimization-based models of muscle coordination. *Exercise Sports Science Reviews*, 30(2):32–38, 2002.
[20] B. Reider, M.A. Arcand, and L.H. Diehl. Proprioception of the knee before and after anterior cruciate ligament reconstruction. *Arthroscopy*, 19:20–12, 2003.
[21] B. Renshaw. Central effects of centripetal impulses in axons of spinal ventral roots. *Journal of Neurophysiology*, 9(191):204, 1946.
[22] G. Shepherd. *Neurobiology*. Oxford University Press, New York, 3 edition, 1994.
[23] D.G. Thelen, F.C. Anderson, and S.L. Delp. Generating dynamic simulations of movement using computed muscle control. *Journal of Applied Biomechanics*, 36:321–328, 2003.
[24] Rick Wells. The integrate-and-fire neuron model as a sensory neuron model. Technical report, University of Idaho, 2003.
[25] Rick Wells. Kinetics and muscle modeling of a single degree of freedom joint part i: Mechanics. Technical report, University of Idaho, 2003.
[26] T. Wennekers and G Palm. Controlling the speed of synfire chains. In *International Conference on Artificial Neural Networks (ICANN)*, pages 451–456, Berlin, 1996. Springer.
[27] G.N. Williams, P.J. Barrance, L. Snyder-Mackler, and T.S. Buchanan. Altered quadriceps control in people with anterior cruciate ligament deficiency. *Medicine and Science in Sports and Exercise*, 36:1089–1097, 2004.
[28] G.N. Williams, T. Chmielewski, K. Rudolph, T.S. Buchanan, and L. Snyder-Mackler. Current theory and implications for clinicians and scientists. *Journal of Orthopaedic and Sports Physical Therapy*, 31:546–566, 2001.

Gene Regulatory Networks Inference with Recurrent Neural Network Models

Rui Xu and Donald C. Wunsch II
Applied Computational Intelligence Laboratory
Dept. of Electrical and Computer Engineering
University of Missouri - Rolla
Rolla, MO 65409-0249 USA
rxu@umr.edu, dwunsch@umr.edu

Abstract – Large-scale time series gene expression data generated from DNA microarray experiments provide us a new means to reveal fundamental cellular processes, investigate functions of genes, and understand their relations and interactions. To infer gene regulatory networks from these data with effective computational tools has attracted intensive efforts from artificial intelligence and machine learning. Here, we use a recurrent neural network (RNN), trained with particle swarm optimization (PSO), to investigate the behaviors of regulatory networks. The experimental results, on a synthetic data set and a real data set, show that the proposed model and algorithm can effectively capture the dynamics of the gene expression time series and are capable of revealing regulatory interactions between genes.

I INTRODUCTION

With the rapid advancement of DNA microarray technologies [1, 2], inferring genetic regulatory networks from time series gene expression data has become increasingly important, in order to reveal fundamental cellular processes, investigate functions of genes, and understand complex relations and interactions among genes [3, 4]. A genetic regulatory network consists of a set of DNA, RNA, proteins, and other molecules, and describes regulatory mechanisms among these components. Genetic information that determines structures, functions, and properties of living cells is stored in DNA, whose coding regions, known as genes, encode proteins. According to the central dogma of molecular biology, genes are transcribed into mRNA molecules, which are then translated to proteins. Since all cells for a specific organism include the same genetic material, it is important to know which proteins are synthesized, or which genes are expressed, under certain conditions. This is achieved through the actions of some proteins, which can activate or inhibit the transcription rate of certain genes by binding to their regulatory regions. Therefore, the transcription of a specific gene, or the control of its gene expression, can be regarded as a combinatorial effect of a set of other genes.

Conventional methods can only investigate activities between a pair of genes, or among several genes, which is far from sufficient, for exploring the complicated regulatory mechanisms. DNA microarray technologies provide an effective and efficient way to measure gene expression levels of thousands of genes simultaneously under different conditions, which makes it possible to investigate gene activities from the angle of the whole genome [3]. Several computational models, rooted in artificial intelligence and machine learning, have been proposed to unveil the behaviors of regulatory networks from time series gene expression data [4].

Boolean networks are binary models, which consider that a gene has only two states: 1 for active and 0 for inactive [5-7]. The effect of other genes on the state change of a given gene is described through a Boolean function. Although Boolean networks make it possible to explore the dynamics of a genetic regulatory system, they ignore the effect of genes at intermediate levels. Loss of information is inevitable with the discretizaiton process. Furthermore, Boolean networks assume the transitions between activation states of the genes are synchronous, which usually is not true. Bayesian networks are graph models that estimate complicated multivariate joint probability distributions through local probabilities [8]. Under this framework, a genetic regulatory network is described as a directed acyclic graph, including a set of vertices and edges. The vertices are related to random variables and represent genes or other components while the edges capture the conditional dependence relation and represent the interactions among genes. Bayesian networks are effective in dealing with noise, incompleteness, and stochastic aspects of gene expression data. Graph representation makes it convenient to investigate interactions between the genes. However, Bayesian networks do not consider dynamical aspects of gene regulation and leave temporal information unhandled. Recently, dynamic Bayesian networks (DBN) attract more attention [9-11], DBN can model behaviors emerging temporally, and effectively handle problems like hidden variables, prior knowledge, and missing data. The disadvantage of DBN is that they cannot scale well to large-scale data sets. For the linear additive regulation models [12-14], the expression level of a gene at a certain time point can be calculated by the weighted sum of the expression levels of all genes in the network at a previous time point. Although linear additive regulation can reveal certain linear relations in the regulatory systems, it lacks the capability to capture the nonlinear dynamics between gene regulations.

Considering the limitations of these methods, here, we use recurrent neural network (RNN) models to infer gene regulatory networks from time series gene expression data. In using RNNs for gene network inference, we are mainly concerned with the ability of RNNs to interpret complex temporal behavior. Generalized recurrent neural network models can be considered as signal processing units forming a global regulatory network. The similarity between RNNs and gene networks makes RNNs an important method in unraveling the mystery of gene regulation relationships. In order to estimate the networks parameters, we use particle swarm optimization (PSO) as the training algorithm, which is an evolutionary computational algorithm for global optimization, based on the simulation of complex social behavior [15-16]. The effectiveness of the model is demonstrated by the simulation on a synthetic data set and a real data set.

The paper is organized as follows. Section II describes the model and training algorithm of recurrent neural networks used for regulatory network inference. Experimental results on the synthetic and real data sets are summarized in Section III and section IV concludes the paper.

II. RECURRENT NEURAL NETWORKS

A. Model

For a continuous time system, the genetic regulation model can be represented through a recurrent neural network formulation [17-20],

$$\tau_i \frac{de_i}{dt} = f(\sum_{j=1}^{N} w_{ij} e_j + \sum_{k=1}^{K} v_{ik} u_k + \beta_i) - \lambda_i e_i \quad (1),$$

where e_i is the gene expression level for the ith gene ($1 \leq i \leq N$, N is the number of genes in the model), $f()$ is a nonlinear function (usually, sigmoid function is used $f(z) = 1/(1+e^{-z})$), w_{ij} represents the effect of the jth gene on the ith gene ($1 \leq i, j \leq N$), u_k is the kth ($1 \leq k \leq K$, K is the number of external variables) external variable, v_{ik} represents the effect of the kth external variable on the ith gene, τ is the time constant, β is the bias term, and λ is the decay rate parameter. A negative value of w_{ij} represents the inhibition of the jth gene on the ith gene, while a positive value indicates the activation controls. When w_{ij} is zero, there is no influence of the jth gene on the expression change of the ith gene.

Correspondingly, its discrete form is

$$e_i(t+\Delta t) = \frac{\Delta t}{\tau_i} f(\sum_{j=1}^{N} w_{ij} e_j(t) + \sum_{k=1}^{K} v_{ik} u_k(t) + \beta_i) + \left(1 - \frac{\lambda_i \Delta t}{\tau_i}\right) e_i(t) \quad (2).$$

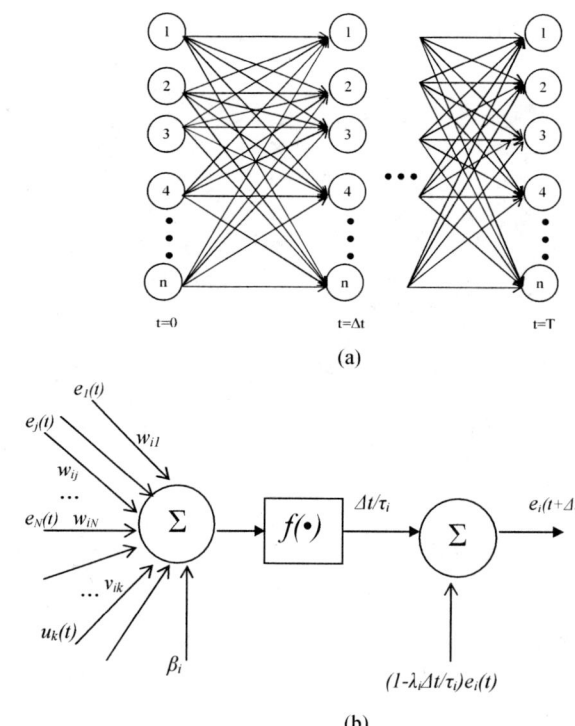

Fig. 1. (a) The description of a genetic network through a recurrent neural network model. This network is unrolled in time from $t=0$ to T with an interval Δt. Here, the regulatory network is shown in a fully connected form, although, in practice, the network is usually sparsely connected. (b) A node (neuron) in the recurrent neural network model

Fig. 1 (a) depicts a recurrent neural network, which is unrolled in time from $t=0$ to T with an interval Δt, for modeling genetic network, Here, each node corresponds to a gene and a connection between two nodes defines their interaction. The weight values can be either positive, negative, or zero, as mentioned above. Fig. 1 (b) illustrates a node in the recurrent neural network, which realizes the equation in (2).

Since it is usually difficult to have the measurements of the external variables, it is a common practice to ignore the term $\sum_{k=1}^{K} v_{ik} u_k(t)$. From the following section, we can see that its addition does not affect the derivation of the learning algorithm. In our work, we also assume that the decay rate parameter λ is 1. The final model we process in the paper is represented as

$$e_i(t+\Delta t) = \frac{\Delta t}{\tau_i} \times f(\sum_{j=1}^{N} w_{ij} e_j(t) + \beta_i) + \left(1 - \frac{\Delta t}{\tau_i}\right) e_i(t) \quad (3).$$

B. Training algorithm

There exist ample algorithms for RNN training in the literature, e.g., back-propagation through time (BPTT) and genetic algorithm (GA). BPTT was first proposed by Paul Werbos [21], as an extension of the standard back-propagation algorithm. By using BPTT, we find the derivatives of the cost function with respect to the individual weights of the network. These derivatives can be used to do gradient descent on the weights, updating them in the direction that minimizes the error [22]. However, the use of gradient descent required the error function to be differentiable, and also makes the procedure easy to get stuck in some local minima. We used BPTT to train the RNN models for genetic networks inference, and the results are reported in [23] and [24]. Inspired by the natural evolution process, GA tends to optimize a population of structure, evaluated according to a fitness function, by using a set of evolutionary operators [25].

Here, we use particle swarm optimization (PSO) [16] for network parameters learning. Similar to GA, PSO is based on a swarm of particles, each of which represents a candidate solution in the multidimensional problem space. The difference lies that a random velocity is associated with each particle, which is considered to "be flown through the problem space" [16]. The basic idea of PSO is to accelerate each particle towards its previous best solution, called *pbest*, and the overall best locations in the swarm, called *gbest*, at each time step. These best locations are determined based on the calculated values of the defined fitness function. This concept is depicted in Fig. 2, in which L^t and L^{t+1} represent the locations at current and next time point, V^t and V^{t+1} represent the velocities at current and next time point, V_{pbest} is the velocity according to *pbest*, and V_{gbest} is the velocity according to *gbest*. It has been shown that PSO require less computational cost and can achieve faster convergence than conventional back-propagation in training feedforward neural networks for approximating a nonlinear function [26]. Meanwhile, compared with GA, PSO has many desirable characteristics, e.g., the flexibility in balancing global and local search, computational efficiency on both time and memory, and the ease to implement. Particularly, PSO is equipped with the memory mechanism for keeping previous best solutions, therefore, avoids the possible loss of learned knowledge. PSO proves to be a powerful tool to explore sophisticated space [15], and this makes it suitable for regulatory networks inference.

Given a set of particles $\mathbf{X} = (\mathbf{x}_1, \mathbf{x}_2, ..., \mathbf{x}_M)$, where M is the number of particles in the swarm, the ith particle (candidate solution) can be represented as a D-dimensional vector $\mathbf{x}_i = (w_{i,11}, ..., w_{i,N1}, w_{i,12}, ..., w_{i,1N}, ..., w_{i,NN}, \beta_{i,1}, ..., \beta_{i,N}, \tau_{i,1}, ..., \tau_{i,N})$, $1 \leq i \leq M$, where $D = N(N+2)$. Its velocity is described as $\mathbf{v}_i = (v_{i,1}, v_{i,2}, ..., v_{i,D})$. A fitness function is used to measure the deviation of network output $e(t)$ from the real measurement (target) $d(t)$, defined as

$$Fitness(x_i) = \frac{1}{TN} \sum_{t=0}^{T} \sum_{i=1}^{N} (e_i(t) - d_i(t))^2 \quad (4)$$

More elaborate error terms can be easily added based on the specific requirement of the problem at hand. Note here,

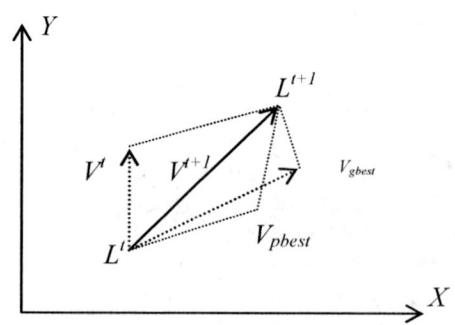

Fig.2. Basic concept of the position change of a particle in PSO [27].

we use a batch mode for training, which means the parameters updating is performed after all input data points are presented to the model [22, 26]. The basic procedure of implementing PSO for learning network parameters in the RNN model can be summarized as follows.

i). Initialize a population of particles with random positions and velocities of D dimensions. Specifically, the connection weights, biases, and time constants are randomly generated with uniform probabilities over the range $[w_{min}, w_{max}]$, $[\beta_{min}, \beta_{max}]$, and $[\tau_{min}, \tau_{max}]$, respectively. Similarly, the velocities are randomly generated with uniform probabilities in the range $[-V_{max}, V_{max}]$, where V_{max} is the maximum value of the velocity allowed.

ii). Calculate the estimated gene expression time series based on the RNN model and evaluate the optimization fitness function for each particle.

iii). Compare the fitness value of each particle with its *pbest*. If current value is better than *pbest*, reset both *pbest* value and location to the current value and location.

iv). Compare the fitness value of each particle with *gbest*. If current value is better than *gbest*, reset *gbest* to the current particle's array index and value.

v). Update the velocity and position of the particles with the following equations

$$\mathbf{v}_i = W_I \times \mathbf{v}_i + c_1 \times rand_1 \times (\mathbf{pbest}_i - \mathbf{x}_i) + c_2 \times rand_2 \times (\mathbf{gbest}_i - \mathbf{x}_i) \quad (5)$$

$$\mathbf{x}_i = \mathbf{x}_i + \mathbf{v}_i \quad (1 \leq i \leq M) \quad (6)$$

where W_I is the inertia weight, c_1 and c_2 are the acceleration constants, and $rand_1$ and $rand_2$ are uniform random functions.

vi). Return to step ii until a stop criterion is satisfied. Usually the learning stops when a maximum number of iterations or high-quality solutions are met.

PSO has only four major parameters needed to be determined in advance. The inertial weight W_I is designed as a tradeoff between the global and local search. Larger values of W_I facilitate global exploration while lower values encourage local search. Usually, the inertial weight is set to decrease linearly. Here, we utilize a strategy that generates a random value varying between 0 and W_{max}, represented as $W_I = W_{max} - (rand/2)$, where *rand* is a uniform random function. In our study, this strategy usually achieves better result than any other methods. c_1 and c_2 are known as the cognition and social components, respectively, and are used to control the effects of a particle itself and its surrounding environment, which is achieved through adjusting the velocity towards *pbest* and *gbest*. Commonly, both parameters are set to 2.0 based on the past experience [15]. During the evolutionary procedure, the velocity for each particle is restricted to a limit V_{max}, like the way in velocity initialization. When the velocity exceeds V_{max}, it is re-assigned to V_{max}. If V_{max} is too small, particles may become trapped into local optima, while if V_{max} is too large, particles may miss some good solutions. V_{max} is usually set around 10-20% of the dynamic range of the variable on each dimension [15].

III. RESULTS

We applied the recurrent neural network model, along with the PSO training algorithm, to a synthetic data set and a real data set. The goal is to recover the basic genetic regulatory networks from the generated time series gene expression data.

The interaction weight matrix W, the bias β, and the time constant τ for the simplified genetic network, which has 4 genes and was used in [28], are set as in Table I. The total number of weights that are non-zero is 8, which is half of the total number of weights. The network was simulated from a random initial state for each gene. We generated 300 time points based on Equation (3), at a time resolution of $\Delta t=0.1$. The expression levels for these genes generally get saturated very fast, since we do not consider the stimulus from the external environment. We performed analysis for both single time series and multiple (including three series) time series, in which 100 time points are used for each time series and most of them were taken from the early stage of the process.

We ran the algorithm 300 times with different random initial values for the weights, biases, and time constants. The performance is based on the averages across these experiments, unless otherwise indicated. This is achieved by checking the *gbest* solution for each run. The network weights were evolved for 10,000 generations. The parameters for PSO are set as follows: $W_{max}=0.7$, $c_1 = c_2 = 2$, and $V_{max} = 2$. The initial values for the weights (including biases) and time constants lie between -1 and 1 and 0 and 10, respectively.

One of the major obstacles for current exploration is "curse of dimensionality", which indicates the exponential growth in computational complexity and the demand for more samples as a result of high dimensionality in the feature space [14, 22,

TABLE I
THE SYNTHETIC GENETIC NETWORK USED FOR THE GENERATION OF THE DATA

w_{IJ}				β_I	τ_I
20.0	-20.0	0.0	0.0	0.0	10.0
15.0	-10.0	0.0	0.0	-5.0	5.0
0.0	-8.0	12.0	0.0	0.0	5.0
0.0	0.0	8.0	-12.0	0.0	5.0

29]. Typically, gene expression data contain measurements of thousands of genes, but only have a limited number of time points. This situation limits the application of many data-driven computational models and makes it very difficult to infer a fully determined large-scale regulatory network. Fortunately, in genetics, it is assumed that a gene is only regulated by a limited number of genes. In other words, the regulatory networks are sparsely connected rather than fully connected. In this sense, it is reasonable to identify the weights whose values are non-zeroes from expression data, which indicate the potential interactions between genes, and furthermore, whether the interaction is activation or inhibition, based on the sign of the weights, although it may not be possible to accurately recover the values of the weights, due to the limitation of the available time points. Based on the results of the 300 runs, we discretize the weights into three classes according to the criterion similar to what are used in [9]:

- class + representing activation: $\mu_{ij} > \mu + \sigma$ and $\sigma_{ij} < |\mu_{ij}|$;
- class − representing inhibition: $\mu_{ij} < \mu - \sigma$ and $\sigma_{ij} < |\mu_{ij}|$;
- class 0 representing absence of regulation: otherwise.

where μ_{ij} and σ_{ij}^2 are the mean and variance for the element w_{ij} in the weight connection matrix and μ and σ^2 are the mean and variance of the means of all the 16 elements. The original and the identified weight connection matrix with the single series and multiple series are summarized in Table II. Compared with the original weight matrix, both ways can find some important relations existing in the network. For the single time series, 4 out of 8 non-zero weights are correctly identified in the inferred genetic network, while for three time series, 5 out of 8 non-zero weights are identified with only one false positive, which is wrongly identified as activation between genes. By using more time series, more information is provided to the model, therefore, we can usually achieve better result, which agrees with the conclusion in [20].

We also employed the proposed method to analyze the SOS DNA Repair network in bacterium *Escherichia coli*

TABLE II
THE GENERATED CONNECTION MATIRX (UPPER PANEL) AND THE LEARNED CONNECTION MATRIX WITH THE SINGLE SERIES (SECOND PANEL) AND MULTIPLE SERIES (LOWER PANEL). EACH ELEMENT w_{ij} IN THE MATRIX REPRESNETS THE RELATION BETWEEN THE ith AND j^{th} GENE, AS ACTIVATION (+), INHIBITION (-), AND ABSENCE OF REGULATION (0).

w_{ij}			
+	-	0	0
+	-	0	0
0	-	+	0
0	0	+	-
+	-	+	0
0	0	0	0
+	-	0	0
0	0	0	-
+	-	0	0
0	0	0	0
+	-	+	0
0	0	0	-

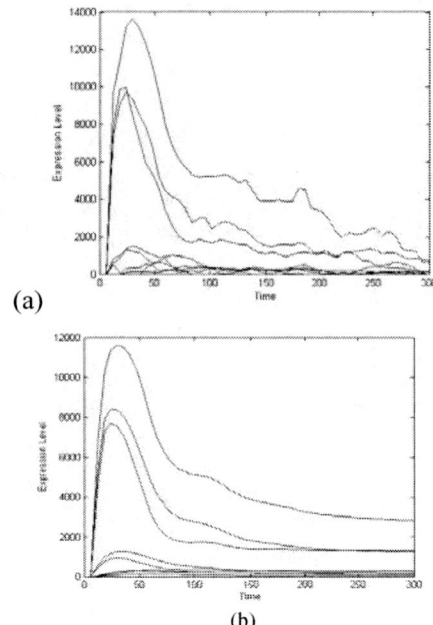

Fig. 4. (a) The measured gene expression profiles for Exp. 2; (b) The learned mean expression profiles with PSO (300 runs).

depicted in Fig. 3 [31]. When damage occurs, protein RecA, which functions as a sensor of DNA damage in the SOS system, becomes activated and mediates LexA autocleavage by binding to single-stranded DNA molecule. Protein LexA is a master repressor that represses all genes when no damage occurs. The drop in LexA expression levels causes the activation of the SOS genes. After the damage is repaired or bypassed, the expression level of RecA drops, which causes the accumulation of LexA. Then, LexA binds sites in the promoter regions of these SOS genes and represses their expression. The cells return to their original states. Four experiments have been conducted by Uri Alon with different light intensities and each experiment includes the expression measurements for 8 major genes (uvrD, lexA, umuD, recA, uvrA, uvrY, ruvA, and polB) through 50 time points, sampled every 6 minutes. In our study, we only used the data from experiment 2 for further analysis.

We set the major parameters for PSO as before. Fig. 4 shows the real gene expression profiles and the learned mean expression profiles with PSO. The average mean square error between the real profiles and learned profiles is 0.0313. We can see the proposed model can effectively capture the dynamics of most genes (lexA, recA, uvrA, uvrD, and umuD) in the network, and the major change trends of the gene expression levels are reflected in the learning curves. The expression profiles for gene uvrY, ruvA, and polB oscillate dramatically between the maximum value and zero, and the obtained models generally use their means to represent the profiles because of the definition of the fitness function. However, when we tried to infer the potential interactions among genes by using the criterion aforementioned, we find that we can only correctly identify 2 out of 9 potential connections between genes. These connections we find include the inhibition of lexA on uvrD, and the activation of recA on lexA. The variance is quite large for most of the weights, which causes most of the weights are regarded as zeros. Also, three false positives are included, which do not exist in the network. The result may suggest that, although we can find some meaningful insight between the genes by using this simple criterion, it is still too rough to be used to deal with more complicated genetic networks satisfactorily. We propose an iterative procedure with PSO to select important non-zero weights [30] and the information about motif can also be used to examine the validity of the unveiled relations in the genes [10]. This method can achieve better results in analyzing larger genetic networks; however, it is still work-in-progress. [30].

IV. CONCLUSIONS

To understand the genetic regulatory mechanisms is one of the central tasks in molecular genetics. Inference of genetic regulatory networks based on the time series gene expression

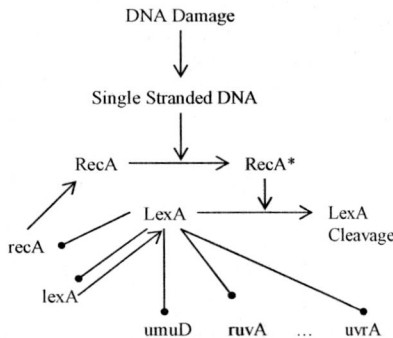

Fig. 3. The SOS DNA Repair network [31]. Inhibitions are represented by - •, while activations are represented by →.

data from microarray experiments becomes an important and effective way to achieve this goal. Here, we utilize recurrent neural network models to model regulatory systems and unveil potential gene interactions. Initial experiments have shown some promising results and demonstrate the potential of this model in gene regulatory network inference. However, with the limited data, current research only focuses on the modeling of network from synthetic data, or simulation of small-scale network including only several genes or gene clusters. Several strategies, such as clustering and interpolation, have been proposed to deal with this still-open problem. No attempt has been seen to infer large-scale genetic regulatory networks. High quality time series gene expression data with sufficient number of time points is particularly important. In the meantime, further improvement for the current computational models is also required in order to explore gene regulation more effectively. Another factor that needs further investigation is the time delay, which is ubiquitous in gene regulatory activities and has already been widely reported in the literature. To incorporate time delay into the current model may reflect the system dynamics more effectively. Furthermore, genetic networks are known to be robust to noise. Gene expression levels in the networks will not be affected greatly due to the small changes, caused by noise, in expression levels of some genes. Many genes have same functions and express themselves in a similar way under certain pathways. Proposed computational models should be capable of interpreting these phenomena.

Acknowledgment

Partial support for this research from the National Science Foundation, and from the M.K. Finley Missouri endowment, is gratefully acknowledged.

References

[1] M. Eisen and P. Brown, "DNA Arrays for Analysis of Gene Expression," *Methods Enzymol*, vol. 303, pp. 179-205, 1999.
[2] R. Lipshutz, S. Fodor, T. Gingeras, and D. Lockhart, "High Density Synthetic Oligonucleotide Arrays," *Nature Genetics*, vol. 21, pp. 20-24, 1999.
[3] P. D'haeseleer, S. Liang, and R. Somogyi, "Genetic Network Inference: From Co-expression Clustering to Reverse Engineering," *Bioinformatics*, vol. 16, no. 8, pp. 707--726, 2000.
[4] H. De Jong, "Modeling and Simulation of Genetic Regulatory Systems: A Literature Review", *Journal of Computational Biology*, vol. 9, pp. 67-103, 2002.
[5] S. Kauffman, "The Origins of Order: Self-Organization and Selection in Evolution", Oxford University Press, New York, 1993.
[6] S. Liang, S. Fuhrman, and R. Somogyi, "REVEAL: A General Reverse Engineering Algorithm for Inference of Genetic Network Architectures", *Proceedings of the Pacific Symposium Biocomputing (PSB'98)*, vol. 3, pp. 18-29, 1998.
[7] I. Shmulevich, E. Dougherty, and W. Zhang, "From Boolean to Probabilistic Boolean Networks as Models of Genetic Regulatory Networks", *Proceedings of IEEE*, vol. 90, no. 11, pp. 1778-1792.
[8] N. Friedman, M. Linial, I. Nachman, and D. Pe'er, "Using Bayesian Networks to Analyze Expression data", *Journal of Computational Biology*, vol. 7, pp. 601-620, 2000.
[9] B. Perrin, L. Ralaivola, A. Mazurie, S. Battani, J. Mallet, and F. d'Alché-Buc, "Gene Networks Inference Using Dynamic Bayesian Networks", *Bioinformatics*, vol. 19, Suppl.2, pp. ii138- ii148, 2003.
[10] Y. Tamada, S. Kim, H.Bannai, S. Imoto, K. Tashiro, S. Kuhara, and S. Miyano, "Estimating Gene Networks from Gene Expression Data by Combing Bayesian Network Model with Promoter Element Detection", *Bioinformatics*, vol. 19, Suppl.2, pp. ii227- ii236, 2003.
[11] D. Husmeier, "Sensitivity and Specificity of Inferring Genetic Regulatory Interactions from Microarray Experiments with Dynamic Bayesian Networks", *Bioinformatics*, vol. 19, no. 17, pp. 2271- 2282, 2003.
[12] P. D'haeseleer, X. Wen, S. Fuhrman, and R. Somogyi, "Linear Modeling of mRNA Expression Levels during CNS Development and Injury", In R.B. Altman, K. Lauderdale, A.K. Dunker, L. Hunter, and T.E. Klein, editors, *Proceedings of the Pacific Symposium Biocomputing (PSB'99)*, pp. 41-52., 1999.
[13] E. van Someren, L. Wessels, M. Reinders, "Linear Modeling of Genetic Networks from Experimental Data", *Proceedings of the 8th International Conference on Intelligent Systems for Molecular Biology (ISMB00)*, pp. 355-366, 2000.
[14] P. D'haeseleer, "Reconstructing Gene Network from Large Scale Gene Expression Data", Dissertation, University of New Mexico, 2000.
[15] R. Eberhart and Y. Shi, "Particle swarm optimization: Developments, applications and recourses," *Proc. of the 2001 Congress on Evolutionary Computation*, vol. 1, pp. 81-86, 2001.
[16] J. Kennedy, R. Eberhart, Y. Shi, "Swarm Intelligence", Morgan Kaufmann Publishers, 2001.
[17] E. Mjolsness, T. Mann, R. Castaño, and B. Wold, "From Co-expression to Co-regulation: An Approach to Inferring Transcriptional Regulation among Gene Classes from Large-scale Expression Data", in *Advances in neural Information Processing Systems 12*, pp. 928-934, MIT Press, 2000.
[18] D. Weaver, C. Workman, and G. Stormo, "Modeling Regulatory Networks with Weight Matrices", *Proceedings of the Pacific Symposium on Biocomputing*, pp. 112-123, 1999.
[19] J. Vohradsky, "Neural Network Model of Gene Expression", *the FASEB Journal*, vol. 15, pp. 846-854, 2001.
[20] M. Wahde and J. Hertz, "Modeling Genetic Regulatory Dynamics in Neural Development", *Journal of Computational Biology*, 8, 429-442, 2001.
[21] P.J. Werbos, "Backpropagation Through Time: What It Does And How to Do It", *Proceedings of IEEE*, 78(10), pp. 1550-1560, 1990.
[22] S. Haykin, "Neural Networks: A Comprehensive Foundation", 2nd Ed., Prentice Hall, New Jersey, 1999.
[23] Rui Xu, Xiao Hu, and Donald C. Wunsch II, "Inference of Genetic Regulatory Networks with Recurrent Neural Network Models," *Proceedings of the 26th International Conference of IEEE EMBS*, September, 2004.
[24] X. Hu, A. Maglia, and D. Wunsch II, "A General Recurrent Network Approach to Model Decay Constants in A Genetic Network", submitted for publication 2004.
[25] D. Fogel, "An Introduction to Simulated Evolutionary Optimization," *IEEE Transactions on Neural Networks*, vol. 5, no. 1, pp. 3-14, 1994.
[26] V. Gudise and G. Venayagamoorthy, "Comparison of Particle Swarm Optimization and Backpropagation as Training Algorithms for Neural Networks", *Proceedings of the 2003 IEEE Swarm Intelligence Symposium*, pp. 110-117, 2003.
[27] H. Yoshida, K. Kawata, Y. Fukuyama, S. Takayama, and Y. Nakanishi, "A particle swarm optimization for reactive power and voltage control considering voltage security assessment," *IEEE Transactions on Power Systems*, vol. 15, no. 4, pp. 1232-1239, 2000.
[28] M. Wahde and J. Hertz, "Coarse-grained Reverse Engineering of Genetic Regulatory Networks", *Biosystems*, 55, 129–136, 2000.
[29] E. van Someren, L. Wessels, and M. Reinders, "Genetic Network Models: A Comparative Study", In *Proc. of SPIE, Micro-arrays: Optical Technologies and Informatics (BIOS01)*, vol. 4266, pp. 236--247, 2001.
[30] R. Xu and D. Wunsch, "Genetic Regulatory Networks Inference with Particle Swarm Optimization," in preparation, 2005.
[31] M. Ronen, R. Rosenberg, B. Shraiman, and U. Alon, "Assigning Numbers to the Arrows: Parameterizing A Gene Regulation Network by Using Accurate Expression Kinetics", *Proc. Natl. Acad. Sci.*, vol. 99, no. 16, pp.10555-10560, 2002.

A Self-Organizing Neural Network Approach for the Identification of Motifs with Insertions and Deletions in Protein Sequences

Xiaoxu Xiong and Derong Liu
Department of Electrical and Computer Engineering
University of Illinois at Chicago
Chicago, IL 60607, USA
Tel: (312) 355-4475, Fax: (312) 996-6465
E-mails: xxiong@cil.ece.uic.edu, dliu@ece.uic.edu

Huaguang Zhang
School of Information Science and Engineering
Northeastern University
Shenyang, Liaoning 110004, P. R. China
Tel: (86) 24-83687762, Fax: (86) 24-83671498
Emails: hg_zhang@21cn.com

Abstract— Current popular algorithms of motif identification in protein sequences face two difficulties, large computation and insertions and deletions of letters. In this paper, we provide a new strategy that solves this problem in a more efficient and effective way. We build a self-organizing neural network with multiple levels of subnetworks to classify subsequences obtained from the protein sequences. We maintain a low computational complexity through the use of this multi-level structure so that the classification of each subsequence is performed with respect to a small subspace of the whole input space. The new definition of pairwise distance between motif patterns provided in this paper can deal with more insertions/deletions allowed in a motif than other algorithms. In the simulation result, our algorithm significantly outperforms existing algorithms in both accuracy and reliability aspects.

Keywords: DNA, MSA, protein sequences, self-organizing neural networks.

I. INTRODUCTION

Multiple sequence alignment (MSA) and motif discovery are two important problems in molecular biology. Recent development in biological data analysis has led to tremendous improvements in these two areas. Protein sequences are made of 20 different letters, and they can be thought of as being composed of motifs interspersed in relatively unconstrained sequence. A motif is a short stretch of a molecule that forms a highly constrained sequence, usually 8 to 20 letters long. Motif discovery is a basic problem in molecular biology, as sequence similarity usually implies homology and functional similarity of the proteins or genes encoded by such sequences.

One of the potential applications of motif discovery is sequence alignment in which identified motifs are used as marks for alignments. The alignment of a set of sequences is basically a matrix where the rows correspond to the sequences in the set, possibly with some spaces inserted, or some gaps in between. Figure 1 shows an example of alignment of pieces of protein sequences gathered from rice, mosquito, human and monkey. The protein pieces are obtained from the Swiss-Prot protein library. The goal of MSA is to generate a concise, information-rich summary of sequence data, sometimes used to illustrate the dissimilarity between a group of sequences. After all, by aligning protein sequences, we can discover similarities and changes in the sequence group, which may help to make further decision including gene classification as well as finding cause of disease. Popular MSA algorithms are progressive alignment [6], [17], iterative alignment [15], Markov model [7] and other stochastic algorithms [1], [8], [10], [19]. Based on these algorithms, several MSA tools have been developed, such as ClustalW [6], [17] and Gibbs sampling [11]. Among existing algorithms and tools, algorithms based on progressive alignment are the most widely used. However, the computational cost of these algorithms is up to $O(L^2)$, where L is the sum of the length of all sequences. The reason that these algorithms have high computational cost is that the pairwise alignment algorithm is applied on every column of each sequence. Such a table is huge and not necessary. As shown in Figure 1, after identifying motifs in the given sequences, we can align the same motif in each sequence, then align the rest in between the motifs. In the motif discovery problem, we have to deal with motifs with mutations, insertions and deletions. Current motif finding algorithm such as MEME [1], Gibbs sampling [11] and WINNOWER [14], perform well in finding motifs with only mutations. When dealing with insertions and deletions, these algorithms have trouble in identifying them. The Bayesian algorithm [19] can deal with cases with insertions and deletions, but not with two consecutive insertions or deletions. The motif discovery problem in protein sequences can be described as finding similar fields with certain length,

```
Rice:     CNGTTDQVDKIVKILNEGQIASTDVVEVVV... KGVSA
Mosquito: MNGDKASIADLCKVLTTGPLNADTEVVVGC... ISP
Human:    MNGRKQSLGELIGTLNAAKVPADTEVVCAP... ISP
Monkey:   MNGRKQNLGELIGTLNAAKVPADTEVVCAP... ISP
```

After alignment, we get

```
1   CNGTTDQVDKIVKI LNEGQIASTDVVEVVV ... VSA
2   MNGDKASIADLCKV LTTGPLNAD__TEVVV ... ISP
3   MNGRKQSLGELIGT LNAAKVPAD__TEVVC ... ISP
4   MNGRKQNLGELIGT LNAAKVPAD__TEVVC ... ISP
```
↑ motif patterns with insertions

Fig. 1. The MSA of protein pieces from rice, mosquito, human and monkey

with certain maximum number of columns mutated and with certain number of insertions or deletions tolerance. In this paper, we consider the case with at most two insertions or deletions or their combinations in a single motif pattern.

II. SELF-ORGANIZING NEURAL NETWORK FOR MOTIF IDENTIFICATION

A. Encoding of the Input Patterns

Under the assumption that there are at most two consecutive letter insertions or deletions in a motif pattern, we analyze a group of motif patterns from protein sequences, e.g., patterns in Figure 2. We observe that in these patterns, column i of a pattern can be aligned to one of the columns in the range from $i-4$ to $i+4$ of other patterns. The two aligned columns can have a maximum index difference of 4. The extreme case happens when one of the pattern has two insertions and the other pattern has two deletions, e.g., pattern #1 and pattern #2 in Figure 2. Before we align the patterns, pattern #1 has 2 insertions at column 4 and column 14, while pattern #2 has 2 deletions at column 2 and column 4. We notice that columns 15 to 17 of pattern #1 should be aligned to column 11 to 13 of pattern #2. The column index difference in this case is 4. In the illustration of Figure 2, we assume the length of motif to be 15. Since we allow each appearance of motif to have a maximum of 2 letter insertions, we can choose test subsequences of length 17.

Test subsequences are obtained from the given protein sequences. We call these test subsequences input patterns to the self-organizing neural network. We use a sliding window to get input patterns. Let L be the length of protein sequence, and let m be the length of the motif to be found. The length of the sliding window will be $m' = m + 2$. Placing the sliding window at

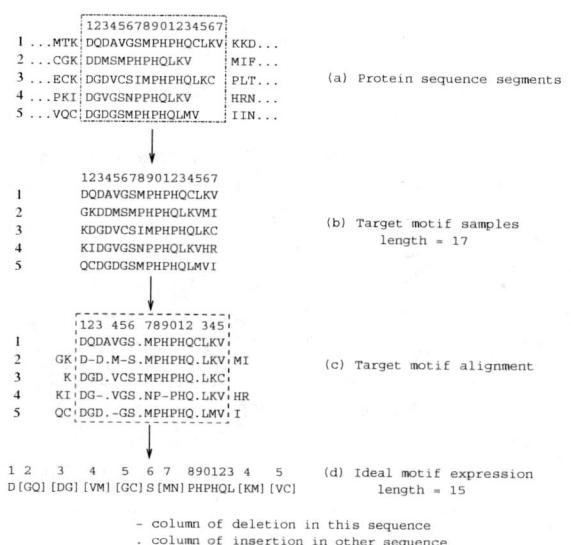

Fig. 2. The aligned motif patterns example with at most 2 insertions/deletions

the beginning of the sequence, we get the first input pattern with length of $m + 2$. Shift the window one column at a time to get all the input patterns. The total number of input patterns we get from the sequence will be $L - m - 1$. In order to define the pairwise similarity value (distance) between a pair of input patterns that may have column index difference up to 2 due to insertions and deletions, we put every 3 consecutive letters in a group. We will now consider the distance between groups of letters. Comparing between two appearances of a motif, every group of three consecutive letters in one appearance will have at least one letter in common with the corresponding group in the other appearance, assuming a maximum of 2 letter insertions or deletions when there is no mutations. The groups can be obtained by applying sliding window of length 3 to each input pattern. For each input pattern with length of m', we will get m groups of letters, each with length of 3. For example, for input pattern #2 of Figure 2 (b), we get the following groups of 3 letters:

$\{GKD, KDD, DDM, DMS, MSM, SMP, MPH, PHP,$

$HPH, PHQ, HQL, QLK, LKV, KVM, VMI\}.$

Next, we will encode all the input patterns using binary digits for our network training algorithm. Each protein letter will be encoded using a 20-digit binary vector, with one digit flipped from $\{1, 1, ..., 1, 0, 0, ..., 0\}$ (ten 1's followed by ten 0's). This coding strategy guarantees that the coded vectors of any two different protein letters have exactly two digits that are different.

B. Pairwise Distance Between Input Patterns

First we study the 3-letter groups from corresponding positions of two input patterns. We consider two possibilities. The first one is that there is one insertion or one deletion in either of the groups. If this is the case, a sub-group of 2 letters from one of the groups may match a 2-letter sub-group from the other group. All these 2-letter sub-groups should follow the same order as they appear in the 3-letter groups. For example, 2-letter sub-groups are AB, BC or AC from ABC. Such 2-letter sub-groups from a 3-letter group will always have 3 possibilities. Second, there are two insertions or two deletions in either one of the 3-letter groups. In this case, as long as there is a common letter appearing in both groups, we would grant a relatively smaller pairwise distance value between these 3-letter groups. The above strategy can be expressed by the following mathematical description. Each input pattern is converted into a test pattern with m 3-letter groups. After encoding, each input pattern will be in the form of binary vectors $P = \{p_1, p_2, ..., p_m\}$, where the length of each binary vector p_i is 60. Each binary vector p_i has 3 pieces. Each piece has 20 binary digits corresponding to a letter in a protein sequence. These vectors can be expressed as $p_{i,1-20}$, $p_{i,21-40}$ and $p_{i,41-60}$. Now we form groups using two of the three vectors following the same order as they have in the 60-digit 3-letter group vector. We will get 3 groups and we denote them as

$$p'_i = (p'_{i[1]}, p'_{i[2]}, p'_{i[3]})$$
$$= (\{p_{i,1-20}p_{i,21-40}\}, \{p_{i,1-20}p_{i,41-60}\},$$
$$\{p_{i,21-40}p_{i,41-60}\}).$$

The pairwise distance of any two given vectors p_i and q_i will be defined as,

$$d_i = \min_{j,k,l \in \{1,2,3\}, j \neq k \neq l} \left(\sum_{r=1}^{40} |p'_{i[1],r} - q'_{i[j],r]}| \right.$$
$$+ \sum_{r=1}^{40} |p'_{i[2],r} - q'_{i[k],r}|$$
$$+ \sum_{r=1}^{40} |p'_{i[3],r} - q'_{i[l],r}| \bigg)$$
$$+ \sum_{m=1}^{20} |(p_{i,m} + p_{i,m+20} + p_{i,m+40})$$
$$- (q_{i,m} + q_{i,m+20} + q_{i,m+40})|.$$

Let $\mathcal{D}(P,Q)$ denotes the pairwise distance of any two input patterns P and Q. We get

$$\mathcal{D}(P,Q) = \sum_{i=1}^{m} d_i. \quad (1)$$

C. Network Structure

This subsection describes the structure of our self-organizing neural networks for motif discovery. The basic structure of the networks is hierarchical subnetworks and each subnetwork contains two layers, i.e., an input layer and an output layer. The number of output neurons of a subnetwork is the same as the number of categories classified by this subnetwork. The number of input neurons equals the projected length of motifs after encoding, e.g., $m' \times 20$. The input patterns are obtained from the given protein sequences by taking all subsequences with the same length as the length of projected motifs. Each output neuron represents a category that has been classified by a subnetwork and each output category is represented by the connection weights from all input neurons to the corresponding output neuron. Subnetworks perform function of classification in a hierarchical manner. The last subnetwork in our self-organizing neural network will be placed at the lowest level and it classifies all the input patterns into either a motif or a non-motif category with one or a few patterns. Typically, the number of output neurons will be very large for the last subnetwork and gradually reduced to a small number for the first subnetwork. Figure 3 shows the structure of our self-organizing neural network with three subnetworks. In the structure shown in the figure, there are four input neurons and three subnetworks. The first subnetwork has 2 output neurons, the second subnetwork has 3 output neurons, and the third subnetwork has 4 output neurons. Each of the output neurons represents a category that has been created and it is represented by the connection weights to the output neuron. The output category α of the first subnetwork contains two patterns (a and b) and the other contains one pattern (c). The output category a of the second subnetwork contains two patterns (1 and 2) and the other two categories each contains just one pattern. The output categories 1 and 2 of the third subnetwork represent two motifs while categories 3 and 4 are not motifs (if we desire to have at least three patterns for each motif identified).

D. Rules for Weight Update and Output Node Creation

When an input pattern is introduced to our self-organizing neural network, it will be either classified to an existing output category or be put into a new category by every subnetwork. An output category of a lower level subnetwork is said to belong to an output category of a higher level subnetwork if one or more input patterns are classified to both of these two output categories. The connection weights for each category of the last subnetwork (at the lowest level) are calculated as the center of the category, i.e., the geometric center

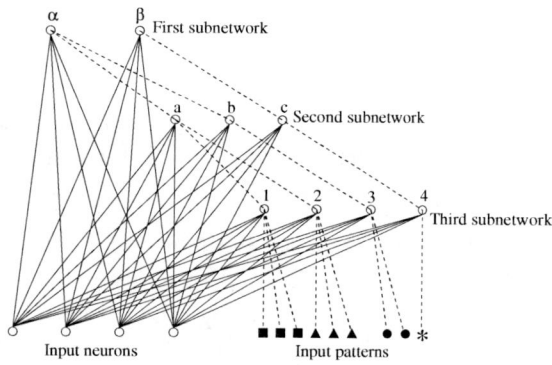

Fig. 3. Structure of the self-organizing neural networks

of all input patterns that are currently classified into the category associated with the corresponding output neuron. The connection weights for an output category of all other subnetworks (except the last subnetwork) are calculated as the geometric center of all categories from the lower level of subnetwork that belong to this category.

When a new input pattern is introduced to a subnetwork, its classification to an output neurons of every subnetwork involves the following three steps.

1) We do match test on the new input pattern with the output neurons of the network at each level. At the top level, all the output categories will be tested. At the next level, only those neurons classified to the winner of the top level will be tested, so on and so forth. By this means only a small number of categories need to be tested. That will save much computation time. These groups of neurons form the tree of classification as shown in Figure 3. For the network example shown in Figure 3, an input pattern will be first compared to the two categories at the top level. At the next level, it will be either compared to $\{a, b\}$ or $\{c\}$ depending on which of the two output categories at the first level becomes the winning category. The pairwise distances between the input pattern and patterns in each category are calculated by (1). The largest pairwise distance within each category is determined and compared to a threshold value. If the largest pairwise distance of a category is smaller than the threshold value, we will regard this category as a winning category.

2) There can be more than one category won in the first step, but only one of them will be the final winner in each level. In this step we make a distance test between the input pattern and the center of each winning category in step one. This test is calculated by comparing the input pattern with the connection weights to each neuron in the winning group. The minimum of these distances is determined and thus a winning category is also determined. This step works similarly to the winner-take-all networks [9].

3) If in the preceding step, there are still more than one winning category (categories have the same minimum pattern to center distance). If this happens, within the winning categories we pick the one that has the most number of members.

Assume that there are a total of L subnetworks for $l = 1, 2, \cdots, L$. Assume that there are M input neurons and the lth subnetwork has N_l output neurons. The patterns obtained form the given protein sequences are used as input sequences to each subnetwork of our self-organizing neural network. The outputs of the last subnetwork correspond to classifications of all subsequences into motifs and non-motif categories. The projected length of motif patterns possibly existing in the input sequences is m'.

We denote the input patterns as x^i, $i = 1, 2, \cdots$. Suppose that t input patterns have been presented to the network and have been classified. When a new input pattern, i.e., the $(t+1)$st pattern x^{t+1}, is introduced to the network, we do the matching test in the three steps we described above. In the lth subnetwork, if output neuron q is one of the categories that have been classified into the winning neuron in the $(l-1)$st subnetwork, the pairwise distance calculations in category q of the lth subnetwork are described as

$$d_j^l = \mathcal{D}(x_m^{t+1}, e_j^{l+1}), \quad j = 1, 2, \cdots, p_q,$$

where

$$e_j^{l+1} = \begin{cases} x^j, & \text{if } l = L \text{ and } x^j \text{ belongs to the category } q \text{ of the lowest level} \\ w_j^{l+1}, & \text{if } 1 \leq l < L \text{ and } w_j^{l+1} \text{ belongs to the category } q \text{ of the } l\text{th level,} \end{cases} \quad (2)$$

and $\mathcal{D}$ is defined in (1). We then perform the following threshold tests. If

$$\max_{1 \leq j \leq p_q} \{d_j^l\} < \rho_l, \quad (3)$$

this new input pattern will be considered to match the category q of the lth subnetwork. The threshold value ρ_l in (3) takes different values for different level of subnetwork. We note that all pairwise distances in this category will be less than the threshold ρ_l if (3) is satisfied for the new input pattern since all other patterns are previously classified into this category using the same threshold value.

If there is only one category wins the match, this new input pattern will be classified into the category q of the lth subnetwork. Otherwise we need to do further similarity test described in step 2. If the set of winning category is Q, we calculate the distance from the new input pattern to the center of each category in Q. For example if $n \in Q$,

$$y_n^l = \mathcal{D}(x^{t+1}, w_n^l), n \in Q,$$

where w_n^l is the connection weight vector from the input neurons to the nth output neuron after the presentation of the tth input pattern. Denote

$$y_q^l = \min_{1 \leq n \leq N_l} \{y_n^l\}, \quad (4)$$

if the qth output category is the winning category that has the smallest distance to the new input pattern. If there are more than one category having the same smallest value, we pick the category that has the most number of patterns in it.

If there is a category q wins in both (3) and (4), this new input pattern will be classified into this winning category of the lth subnetwork. Otherwise, the new input pattern cannot be classified into any existing category at this level.

We describe the updates of our network in the following details.

a) We start from the top level, i.e., the first subnetwork, and work down level by level, when classifying a new input pattern. After a winning category is determined at the lth level, the input pattern will only be compared to those patterns at the $(l+1)$st level that are classified to belong to the winning category at the lth level and are denoted by W_q^l.

b) If the threshold tests in (3) and (4) are successful for $l = 1, 2, \cdots, L$, we perform the following updates for the Lth subnetwork:

$$w_{mq}^L := \frac{1}{p_q^L + 1} \sum_{j=1}^{p_q^L+1} x_m^j = \frac{1}{p_q^L + 1} \left[p_q^L \times w_{mq}^L + x_m^{t+1}\right]$$

$$m = 1, 2, \cdots, M,$$

$$p_q^L := p_q^L + 1,$$

where the $(p_q^L + 1)$st item in $\sum_{j=1}^{p_q^L+1} x_m^j$ indicates the mth component of the new input pattern x^{t+1}. We perform the following updates for the rest of subnetworks:

$$w_{mq}^l := \frac{1}{p_q^L} \sum_{j=1}^{p_q^L} w_{mj}^{l+1},$$

$$m = 1, 2, \cdots, M, l = L-1, L-2, \cdots, 2, 1.$$

c) If the threshold tests in (3) and (4) are successful for $l = 1, 2, \cdots, L_1$, where $L_1 < L$, we will add an output neuron to subnetworks $L_1 + 1, L_1 + 2, \cdots, L$. Each of these newly added categories will contain only one pattern and the weights of the new categories are chosen as

$$w_{mn}^l = x_m^{t+1}, \; m = 1, 2, \cdots, M,$$

$$n = N_l + 1, \; l = L_1 + 1, L_1 + 2, \cdots, L.$$

We also update the number of output neurons for these subnetworks as

$$N_l := N_l + 1, \; p_{N_l} = 1, \; l = L_1 + 1, L_1 + 2, \cdots, L.$$

In this case, it is not necessary to perform threshold tests for subnetworks $L_1 + 1, L_1 + 2, \cdots, L$ anymore. For subnetworks $1, 2, \cdots, L_1$, we will perform the following updates:

$$p_q^{L_1} := p_q^{L_1} + 1$$

$$w_{mq}^l := \frac{1}{p_q^l} \sum_{j=1}^{p_q^l} w_{mj}^{l+1},$$

$$m = 1, 2, \cdots, M, \; l = L_1, L_1 - 1, \cdots, 2, 1.$$

III. SIMULATION RESULT

We first test our algorithm for motif finding in randomly generated protein sequences. We randomly generate 20 protein sequences with average length of 300 letters in each sequence. We generate a 20-pattern motif set with insertions, deletions and mutations at random columns in each pattern. We insert these patterns into random locations of the protein sequences. It is not necessary that each sequence has exactly one motif pattern. Some sequences may have more than one pattern and others may have none. The length of the motif is fixed. The number of mutations in the pattern are not fixed. Let R denote the motif set we generated and T denote the motif set identified by the self-organizing neural network. Then the performance of the motif discovery algorithm is defined as

$$\text{PER} = \frac{R \cap T}{R \cup T}. \quad (5)$$

Figure 4 shows the performance of the system on finding motif with length of 15. The horizontal axis represents the percentage of mismatch of the motifs (i.e., ϵ/M, where ϵ is the number of letters that is tolerable in the representation of a motif), and the vertical axis indicates the average of the performances in 8 such simulations defined above. In this simulation, we fix the distribution of the number of insertions and deletions. 30 percent of the motif patterns we generated have two insertions or deletions or their combination. 40 percent of them

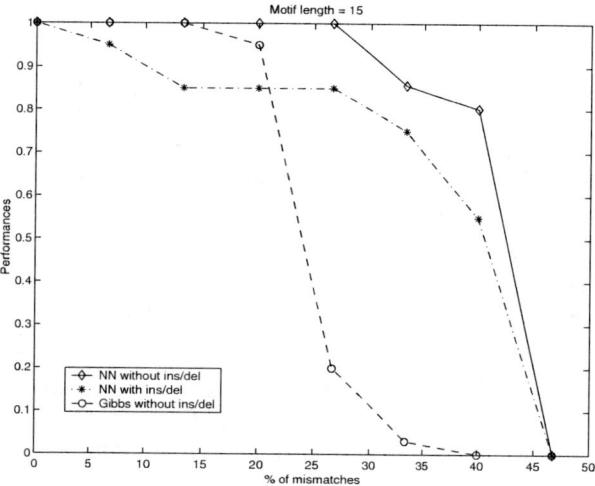

Fig. 4. Comparison result for motif length = 15

have only one insertion or deletion. The rest patterns do not have insertion or deletion. Besides these insertions and deletions, all the patterns have a certain number of columns mutated according to the horizontal axis of the figure. In Figure 4, we compare our result to the performance of Gibbs algorithm.

From the figure we find out that compared with the Gibbs algorithm, our algorithm have a much better performance. Let (15, 4) denote the case of setting motif length to 15 and number of mismatch columns to 4. Our neural network system performs well and finds nearly all the patterns generated in the case of (15, 4). In the case of having insertions and deletions, our algorithm works well until mismatch number reaches 6, i.e., (15, 6).

IV. CONCLUSION

We studied the problem of motif discovery in protein sequences with insertions and deletions. We developed a self-organizing neural network with multiple levels of subnetworks to make an intelligent classification on the subsequences obtained from the protein sequences. We maintain a low computational complexity through the use of this multi-level structure so that each subsequence's classification is performed with respect to a small subspace of the whole input space. Our algorithm can find motifs with two letters of insertions, deletions or their combinations. We solve the problem of finding motifs with 2 consecutive insertions or deletions, and our algorithm outperforms other existing algorithms. The simulation result shows that the performance of our algorithm is more accurate and costs less computation.

REFERENCES

[1] T. L. Bailey and C. Elkan, "Unsupervised learning of multiple motifs in biopolymers using expectation maximization," *Machine Learning*, vol. 21, no. 1–2, pp. 51–80, Oct.-Nov. 1995.

[2] E. Birney, J. D. Thompson, and T. J. Gibson, "Pairwise and searchwise: finding the optimal alignment in a simultaneous comparison of a protein profile against all DNA translation frames," *Nucleic Acids Research*, vol. 24, no. 14, pp. 2730–2739, July 1996.

[3] J. Buhler and M. Tompa, "Finding motifs using random projections," *Journal of computational biology*, vol. 9, no. 2, pp. 225–242, Apr. 2002.

[4] G. A. Carpenter and S. Grossberg, "A self-organizing neural network for supervised learning, recognition, and prediction," *IEEE Communications Magazine*, vol. 30, no. 9, pp. 38–49, Sept. 1992.

[5] M. S. S. Chang and S. A. Benner, "Empirical analysis of protein insertions and deletions determining parameters for the correct placement of gaps in protein sequence alignments," *Journal of Molecular Biology*, vol. 341, no. 2, pp. 617–631, Aug. 2004.

[6] R. Chenna, H. Sugawara, T. Koike, R. Lopez, T. J. Gibson, D. G. Higgins, and J. D. Thompson, "Multiple sequence alignment with the Clustal series of programs," *Nucleic Acids Research*, vol. 31, no. 13, pp. 3497–3500, July 2003.

[7] W. N. Grundy, T. L. Bailey, C. P. Elkan, and M. E. Baker, "Hidden Markov model analysis of motifs in steroid dehydrogenases and their homologs," *Biochemical & Biophysical Research Communications*, vol. 231, no. 3, pp. 760–766, Feb. 1997.

[8] M. Gupta and J. S. Liu, "Discovery of conserved sequence patterns using a stochastic dictionary model," *Journal of the American Statistical Association*, vol. 98, no. 461, pp. 55–66, Mar. 2003.

[9] S. Haykin, *Neural Networks: A Comprehensive Foundation*, Upper Saddle River, NJ: Prentice Hall, 1999.

[10] G. Z. Hertz and G. D. Stormo, "Identifying DNA and protein patterns with statistically significant alignments of multiple sequences," *Bioinformatics*, vol. 15, no. 7–8, pp. 563–577, July 1999.

[11] C. E. Lawrence, S. F. Altschul, M. S. Boguski, J. S. Liu, A. F. Neuwald, and J. C. Wootton, "Detecting subtle sequence signals: a Gibbs sampling strategy for multiple alignment," *Science*, vol. 262, no. 5131, pp. 208–214, Oct. 1993.

[12] J. J. Miret, B. O. Parker, and R. S. Lahue, "Recognition of DNA insertion/deletion mismatches by an activity in Saccharomyces cerevisiae," *Nucleic Acids Research*, vol. 24, no. 4, pp. 721–729, Feb. 1996.

[13] A. F. Neuwald and A. Poleksic, "PSI-BLAST searches using hidden Markov models of structural repeats: prediction of an unusual sliding DNA clamp and of β-propellers in UV-damaged DNA-binding protein," *Nucleic Acids Research*, vol. 28, no. 18, pp. 3570–3580, Sept. 2000.

[14] P. A. Pevzner and S. H. Sze, "Combinatorial approaches to finding subtle signals in DNA sequences," *Proceedings of the 8th International Conference on Intelligent Systems for Molecular Biology*, pp. 269–278, San Diego, CA, Aug. 2000.

[15] K. Reinert, J. Stoye, and T. Will, "An iterative method for faster sum-of-pairs multiple sequence alignment," *Bioinformatics*, vol. 16, no. 9, pp. 808–814, Sept. 2000.

[16] J. B. Spalding and P. J. Lammers, "BLAST filter and graphalign: rule-based formation and analysis of sets of related DNA and protein sequences," *Nucleic Acids Research*, vol. 32, Web Server issue, pp. W26–W32, July 2004.

[17] J. D. Thompson, D. G. Higgins, and T. J. Gibson, "CLUSTAL W: improving the sensitivity of progressive multiple sequence alignment through sequence weighting, position-specific gap penalties and weight matrix choice," *Nucleic Acids Research*, vol. 22, no. 22, pp. 4673–4680, Nov. 1994.

[18] B.-J. M. Webb, J. S. Liu, and C. E. Lawrence, "BALSA: Bayesian algorithm for local sequence alignment," *Nucleic Acids Research*, vol. 30, no. 5, pp. 1268–1277, Mar. 2002.

[19] J. Xie, K. C. Li, and M. Bina, "A Bayesian insertion/deletion algorithm for distant protein motif searching via entropy filtering," *Journal of the American Statistical Association*, vol. 99, no. 466, pp. 409–420, June 2004.

Functional Grouping of Genes Using Spectral Clustering and Gene Ontology

Nora Speer, Holger Fröhlich, Christian Spieth and Andreas Zell
University of Tübingen
Centre for Bioinformatics Tübingen (ZBIT)
Sand 1, D-72076 Tübingen, Germany
Email: {nspeer,froehlic,spieth,zell}@informatik.uni-tuebingen.de

Abstract—With the invention of high throughput methods, researchers are capable of producing large amounts of biological data. During the analysis of such data the need for a functional grouping of genes arises. In this paper, we propose a new method based on spectral clustering for the partitioning of genes according to their biological function. The functional information is based on Gene Ontology annotation, a mechanism to capture functional knowledge in a shareable and computer processable form. Our functional cluster method promises to automatize, speed up and therefore improve biological data analysis.

I. INTRODUCTION

In the past few years, DNA microarrays have become major tools in the field of functional genomics. In contrast to traditional methods, these technologies enable researchers to collect tremendous amounts of data, whose analysis itself constitutes a challenge. On the other side, these high-throughput methods provide a global view on the cellular processes as well as on their underlying regulatory mechanisms and are therefore quite popular among biologists.

During the analysis of such data, researchers use different approaches in order to deal with the huge amounts of data they gathered. Some use statistics to find significantly regulated genes that may be involved in the underlying process due to their change in expression. Others apply pattern recognition methods to cluster the genes according to their expression profiles. The hypothesis is, that genes with expression pattern similar to those of known genes involved in the examined biological process, may play a role in the process, too. In both cases, researchers often end up with long lists of interesting candidate genes that need further examination. At this point, a second step is almost always applied: biologists categorize these genes by known biological functions and thus try to combine a pure numerical analysis with biological information.

So far, many approaches are known that address the problem of combining new experimental data with existing biological knowledge. Some methods score whole clusterings or each single cluster due to their biological relevance [5], [12], [7], [15]. Others evaluate all annotations in a group of genes and score each single annotation using sophisticated methods [2], [17], [20]. In order to receive more meaningful clustering results, some methods use the Gene Ontology as a filter to find genes that belong to a special functional category. These genes are then clustered according to their expression pattern [1]. Approaches intending to find clusters of co-expressed genes that share a common function directly incorporate the biological knowledge into the clustering process [8], [23], [21].

In this paper we address the problem of finding functional gene clusters only based on Gene Ontology terms. The advantage of such a method is that no *a priori* knowledge about relevant pathways is necessary except a mapping from genes to their ontological information. The latter is often available in public databases. Given the GO terms we are able to compute a functional similarity between genes [13]. This information is fed into a clustering algorithm. To our best knowledge, so far there exists no automatic method that produces a biologically plausible functional clustering of genes just based on the GO apart from our earlier publication [22]. In contrast to this earlier publication, in this paper we represent each gene by its functional similarity to all other genes. This encoding allows us to construct a valid mathematical distance measure between genes. There is also a deeper connection to "Kernel Methods" [19], which will be discussed later on in this paper. The final grouping of the genes is performed by a spectral clustering method [14].

The organization of this paper is as follows: a brief introduction to the Gene Ontology is given in section II. Section III explains our method in detail. The performance of our functional clustering algorithm on real world datasets is shown in section IV. Finally, in section V, we conclude.

II. THE GENE ONTOLOGY

The Gene Ontology (GO) is one of the most important ontologies within the bioinformatics community and is developed by the GO Consortium [24]. It is specifically intended for annotating gene products with a consistent, controlled and structured vocabulary. Gene products are for instance sequences in databases as well as measured expression profiles. The GO independent from any biological species and additionally new ontologies covering other biological or medical aspects are being developed.

The GO represents terms in a directed acyclic graph (DAG) covering three orthogonal taxonomies or "aspects": *molecular*

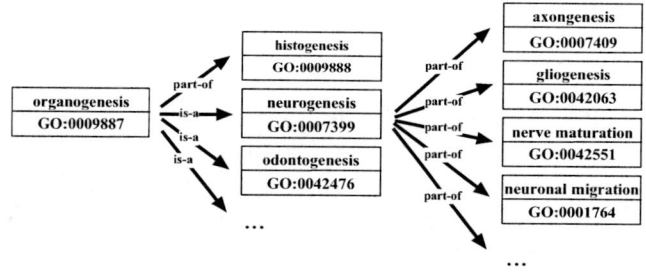

Fig. 1. Relations in the Gene Ontology. Each node is annotated with a unique accession number.

function, *biological process*, and *cellular component*. The GO graph consists of over 18.000 terms represented as nodes, which are connected by relationships represented as edges. Terms are allowed to have multiple parents as well as multiple children. Two different kinds of relationship exist: the "is-a" relationship (*neurogenesis* and *odontogenesis* are for example children of *organogenesis*) and the "part-of" relationship, which describes e.g. that *histogenesis* is part of *organogenesis* or *axongenesis* is part of *neurogenesis*. Providing a standard vocabulary across any biological resources, the GO enables researchers to use this information for automated data analysis.

III. METHODS

A. Distances within the Gene Ontology

There are a couple of semantic similarity and distance measures of different complexity [3], most of them were originally developed for taxonomies like WordNet. In this paper we use a distance measure based on the information content of each GO term developed by Jiang and Conrath in [11]. The information content of a term is defined as the probability of occurrence of this term or any child term in a dataset [16]. Following the notation in information theory, the information content (IC) of a term c can be quantified as follows:

$$IC(c) = -\ln P(c)$$

where $P(c)$ is the probability of encountering an instance of term c.

In the case of a hierarchical structure, such as the GO, where a term in the hierarchy subsumes those lower in the hierarchy, this implies that $P(c)$ is monotonic as one moves towards the root node. As the node's probability increases, its information content or its informativeness decreases. The root node has a probability of 1, hence its information content is 0. As the three aspects of the GO are disconnected subgraphs, this is still true if we ignore the root node (*Gene Ontology*, GO:0003673) and take, e.g., *cellular component* (GO:0005575) as our root node instead. $P(c)$ is simply computed using maximum likelihood estimation: $P(c) = \text{freq}(c)/N$, where N is the total number of terms occurring in the dataset and freq(c) is the number of times term c or any child term of c occurs in the dataset.

The similarity of two terms c_i, c_j can then be defined as followed:

$$\text{sim}(c_i, c_j) = -\ln \min_{c \in S(c_i, c_j)} P(c) = -\ln P_{ms}(c_i, c_j) \quad (1)$$

where $S(c_i, c_j)$ is the set of parental terms shared by both c_i and c_j. As the GO allows multiple parents for each term, two terms can share parents by multiple paths. We take the minimum $P(c)$, if there is more than one parent. This is called P_{ms}, for *probability of the minimum subsumer* [13]:

$$P_{ms}(c_i, c_j) = \min_{c \in S(c_i, c_j)} P(c)$$

Given the similarity score (Eqn. 1), Jiang and Conrath [11] developed a distance measure, which is the inverse of similarity. They defined the semantic distance of two classes c_i, c_j as follows:

$$d(c_i, c_j) = 2\ln P_{ms}(c_i, c_j) - (\ln P(c_i) + \ln P(c_j)) \quad (2)$$

Since genes are often annotated with more than one GO term, multiple functional distances can be computed between two genes. Therefore, we need to combine all or choose one of the calculated distances. We decided to use the smallest distance found. Obviously, this causes a loss of information (from multiple known gene functions, only one is used). Additionally, the problem with using the smallest GO-distance (Eqn. 2) between two genes x and y is that it can be 0, even if two genes are not identical, because they belong to the same functional class. This prevents us from using (Eqn. 2) directly as a metric for clustering. We solve both problems, by using a feature vector representation for each gene.

B. Distances between Genes Using Feature Vectors

For each gene x we construct a feature vector $\phi_p(x)$ relative to prototypes $\mathbf{p} = (p_1, ..., p_N)^T$

$$\phi_p(x) = (d(x, p_1), ..., d(x, p_N))^T$$

This construction is known as an *empirical feature map* [19]. In our case prototypes are just all genes from our data set. That means each gene x is represented by its smallest functional distance to all other genes. Now, the distance between two genes x and y is simply given by $\hat{d}(x, y) = \|\phi(x) - \phi(y)\|$.

There exists a deep connection to the construction of so called "kernel functions", which can be viewed as a general similarity measure $k: \mathcal{X} \times \mathcal{X} \to \mathbb{R}$ with the property of being symmetric and positive definite: More specifically, we have the equality (c.f. [19])

$$\begin{aligned}\hat{d}^2(x, y) &= \|\phi(x) - \phi(y)\|^2 \\ &= \langle \phi(x), \phi(x) \rangle - 2\langle \phi(x), \phi(y) \rangle + \langle \phi(y), \phi(y) \rangle \\ &= k(x, x) - 2k(x, y) + k(y, y)\end{aligned}$$

That means by defining $\phi: \mathcal{X} \to \mathcal{H}$ we map our data into some Hilbert space $\mathcal{H}$. The scalar product in this space defines a kernel $k: \mathcal{X} \times \mathcal{X} \to \mathbb{R}$ and hence a similarity measure between two genes x and y in our original input space $\mathcal{X}$. If we take the normalization $\phi_{norm}(x) = \frac{\phi(x)}{\|\phi(x)\|}$, we recover the normalized kernel [19]

$$k_{norm}(x,y) = \langle \phi_{norm}(x), \phi_{norm}(y) \rangle = \frac{k(x,y)}{\sqrt{k(x,x)k(y,y)}}$$

C. Spectral Clustering using Feature Vector Representation

Given our representation of each gene as a feature vector, we can choose any clustering algorithm to group our data. In this paper we took the spectral clustering algorithm by Ng et al. [14]: given the distance measure $\hat{d}$ on data $x_1, ..., x_n$ one computes the k largest eigenvalues and corresponding Eigenvectors of the graph Laplacian $L = D^{-1/2} K D^{-1/2}$ where $K = (\exp(\hat{d}^2(x_i, x_j)/2\sigma^2))_{ij}$ and D is a diagonal matrix with $D_{jj} = \sum_i K_{ij}$. After renormalization to unit length the Eigenvectors are then clustered e.g. by k-means. Here we choose the k-means algorithm by Zha et al. [25], which leads to a unique and global optimal solution. This has the advantage that no restarts are necessary. The parameter σ can be tuned automatically such that the average distortion of the points in eigenvector space becomes minimal (c.f. [14]).

D. Cluster Validity

We selected the number of clusters k in our data according to the maximal mean Silhouette index [18]. The Silhouette value for each point is a measure of how similar that point is to points in its own cluster vs. points in other clusters, and ranges from -1 to +1. It is defined as:

$$S(i) = \frac{\min(\bar{d}_B(i,j)) - \bar{d}_W(i)}{\max(\bar{d}_W(i), \min(\bar{d}_B(i,j)))} \quad (3)$$

where $\bar{d}_W(i)$ is the average distance from the j-th point to the other points in its own cluster, and $\bar{d}_B(i,j)$ is the average distance from the i-th point to points in another cluster j.

IV. EXPERIMENTS

A. Datasets

One possible scenario where researchers would like to group a list of genes according to their function is when they examine gene expression with DNA microarray technology, afterwards apply some filtering or statistical analysis and end up with a list of genes that show a significant change in their expression according to a control experiment. Thus, we chose two publicly available microarray datasets, annotated the genes with GO information and used them for functional clustering.

The authors of the first dataset examined the response of human fibroblasts to serum on cDNA microarrays in order to study growth control and cell cycle progression. They found 517 genes whose expression levels varied significantly, for details see [10]. We used these 517 genes for which the authors provide NCBI accession numbers. The GO mapping was done via GeneLynx Ids [6]. Since we are interested in gene function, we only use the taxonomy *biological process* of the GO. Out of the 517 genes, 238 genes showed one or more GO mappings to *biological process* or a child term of *biological process*. These 238 genes were used for the functional clustering.

In order to study gene regulation during eukaryotic mitosis, the authors of the second dataset examined the transcriptional profiling of human fibroblasts during cell cycle using microarrays [4]. Duplicate experiments were carried out at 13 different time points ranging from 0 to 24 hours. Cho et al. found 388 genes whose expression levels varied significantly. Hvidsten et al. [9] provide a mapping of the dataset to GO. 233 of the 388 genes showed at least one mapping to the GO *biological process* taxonomy and were thus used for clustering.

B. Results

In the experiments, we compared our method to k-means and Single Linkage clustering which are also based on the proposed feature vector representation, and evaluated them by means of the Silhouette clustering index (Eqn. 3). Beside that, we show the actual GO annotations of some selected clusters. Due to space limitations, we cannot show all clusters.

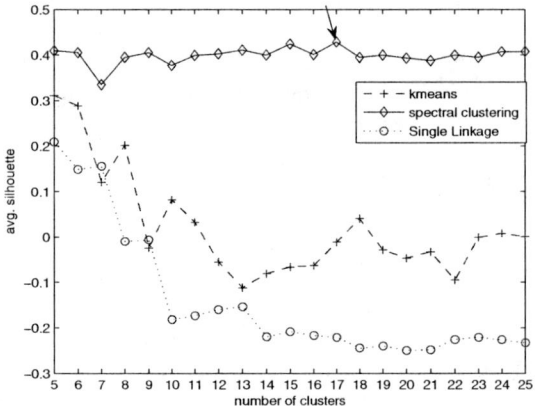

Fig. 2. Average Silhouette index of dataset I. The arrow indicates the solution with the best Silhouette index that was examined in more detail.

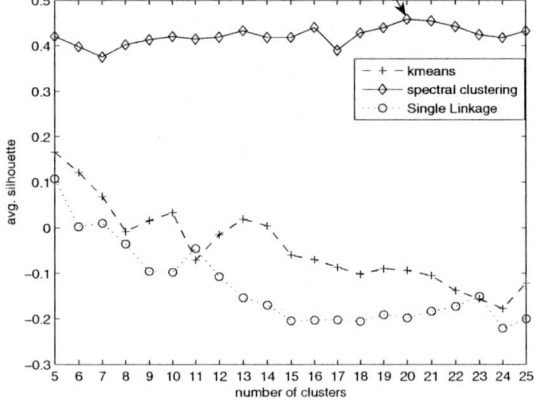

Fig. 3. Average Silhouette index of dataset II. The arrow indicates the solution with the best Silhouette index that was examined in more detail.

Figures 2 and 3 show the average Silhouette index for

cluster numbers $k = 5, ..., 25$ for all three clusterings (spectral, k-means and Single Linkage). Both figures show that the spectral clustering method gives significant better results than the other two approaches.

TABLE I
CLUSTER 7 FROM DATASET I: APOPTOSIS RELATED GENES

Acc. number	Gene Ontology terms
AA029909	**apoptosis** RNA splicing response to stress
AA012996	**anti-apoptosis**
N67978	**anti-apoptosis**
N79013	**apoptosis** **induction of apoptosis**
R62600	**apoptosis** axon guidance embryogenesis and morphogenesis neurogenesis proteolysis and peptidolysis
AA025275	**apoptosis** **induction of apoptosis by extracellular signals** protein amino acid phosphorylation
R51770	**apoptosis**
AA053239	**apoptosis**
AA037369	electron transport **induction of apoptosis**

TABLE II
CLUSTER 12 FROM DATASET I: PROTEIN METABOLISM AND MODIFICATION RELATED GENES

Acc. number	Gene Ontology terms
AA044619	**proteolysis and peptidolysis**
AA027277	**protein biosynthesis**
AA043103	**protein modification**
AA044425	**amino acid activation** **protein biosynthesis**
W73157	**protein amino acid dephosphorylation**
AA045480	**protein biosynthesis**
AA039663	response to oxidative stress **protein amino acid phosphorylation**
AA004517	**protein modification**
H94471	**protein complex assembly**
AA024572	**protein biosynthesis**
AA057638	**protein biosynthesis**
AA056621	**protein folding**
AA043969	**proteolysis and peptidolysis** vision
N49296	**protein folding**
AA045437	**protein modification**
N98463	**protein modification**
AA057826	**protein biosynthesis**
AA057359	**protein amino acid phosphorylation** sodium ion transport response to stress

According to these plots, we picked 17 clusters for dataset I and 20 clusters for dataset II. These solutions were then used for further examination. For dataset I, we show three selected clusters: cluster 7, 12, and 13. Each gene in cluster 7 is beside other functions related to apoptosis (Tab. I).

All genes of cluster 12 have at least one, but in most of the cases more than one GO annotation that is related to

TABLE III
CLUSTER 13 FROM DATASET I: REGULATION OF TRANSCRIPTION RELATED GENES

Acc. number	Gene Ontology terms
W90080	cellular morphogenesis embryogenesis and morphogenesis microtubule cytoskeleton organization and biogenesis pattern specification **regulation of transcription, DNA-dependent**
AA034054	cellular defense response **regulation of transcription, DNA-dependent** **regulation of transcription from Pol II promoter**
AA029205	**transcription from Pol II promoter**
W70150	**regulation of transcription, DNA-dependent**
N39221	response to heat **transcription from Pol II promoter** **regulation of transcription, DNA-dependent**
H14569	**regulation of transcription, DNA-dependent** **regulation of transcription from Pol II promoter**
AA040156	**transcription from Pol II promoter** **regulation of transcription, DNA-dependent**
AA035360	**regulation of transcription, DNA-dependent**
N98485	**transcription from Pol II promoter** **regulation of transcription, DNA-dependent**
T91871	anterior compartment specification oncogenesis posterior compartment specification **regulation of transcription, DNA-dependent**
H27557	**regulation of transcription, DNA-dependent**
T50056	**regulation of transcription, DNA-dependent**
R39209	**regulation of transcription, DNA-dependent**
W44416	drug resistance glutamine metabolism nucleobase, nucleoside, nucleotide and nucleic acid metabolism 'de novo' pyrimidine base biosynthesis
R49309	**regulation of transcription, DNA-dependent**
AA026120	protein modification **regulation of transcription, DNA-dependent**
N99070	**regulation of transcription, DNA-dependent** **regulation of transcription from Pol II promoter**
AA055585	**regulation of transcription, DNA-dependent**

TABLE IV
CLUSTER 12 FROM DATASET II: DNA REPLICATION, REPAIR AND RECOMBINATION RELATED GENES

Acc. number	Gene Ontology terms
D26018_at	**DNA dependent DNA replication**
D38073_at	**DNA replication initiation**
D38551_at	**double-strand break repair** **DNA recombination** meiotic recombination
D50370_at	nucleosome assembly
J04611_at	**DNA ligation** **double-strand break repair** **double-strand break repair via nonhomologous end-joining** **DNA recombination**
L07541_at	**DNA strand elongation**
M87339_at	**DNA strand elongation**
U27516_at	**double-strand break repair** mitotic recombination meiotic recombination
X62153_at	**DNA replication initiation**
X74331_at	**DNA replication, priming**

TABLE VI
CLUSTER 19 FROM DATASET II: CELL CYCLE, CELL PROLIFERATION RELATED GENES.

Acc. number	Gene Ontology terms
L11353_at	**negative regulation of cell proliferation**
L22005_at	**cell cycle checkpoint** DNA replication checkpoint **G1/S transition of mitotic cell cycle**
M60974_at	**regulation of cell cycle** **regulation of CDK activity** DNA repair apoptosis response to stress **cell cycle arrest**
M81933_at	**regulation of cell cycle** **regulation of CDK activity**
M90657_at	N-linked glycosylation **cell proliferation** pathogenesis
S81914_at	apoptosis anti-apoptosis embryogenesis and morphogenesis **cell growth and/or maintenance**
U05340_at	**regulation of cell cycle** ubiquitin-dependent protein catabolism **cell cycle**
U33286_at	nucleocytoplasmic transport apoptosis **cell proliferation**
U37426_at	**mitotic spindle assembly** **mitosis**
U40343_at	**regulation of CDK activity** **cell cycle arrest** **negative regulation of cell proliferation**
U47414_at	**cell cycle checkpoint**
U53446_at	**cell proliferation**
U56816_at	**regulation of CDK activity** **mitosis** **regulation of mitosis**
Z36714_at	**regulation of cell cycle**

Acc. number	Gene Ontology terms
U63743_at	**centromere binding** **mitosis** **cell proliferation**
X00588_at	cellular morphogenesis EGF receptor signaling pathway **cell proliferation**
X05360_at	**regulation of cell cycle** **start control point of mitotic cell cycle**
X54941_at	**regulation of cell cycle** **regulation of CDK activity** **cell proliferation**
X54942_at	**regulation of CDK activity** **cell proliferation**
X58377_at	**cell-cell signaling cell proliferation** **positive regulation of cell proliferation**
X62048_at	**regulation of cell cycle**
X65550_at	**regulation of cell cycle** **cell proliferation**
X66364_at	**cell proliferation**
X80230_at	**regulation of cell cycle** transcription initiation from Pol II promoter RNA elongation from Pol II promoter **cell proliferation**
X81851_at	chemotaxis immune response cellular defense response **cell proliferation**
X85137_at	**mitotic spindle assembly** **mitosis**
Z24725_at	**regulation of cell cycle** **cell proliferation**
Z29066_at	**regulation of cell cycle** **mitosis** **regulation of mitosis**
Z29067_at	**cell cycle**

protein modification, either by (de-)phosphorylation, protein folding, protein complex assembly or protein biosynthesis in general (Tab. II). The genes of cluster 13 are mainly involved in transcription and regulation of transcription (Tab. III). Other clusters (the data is not shown due to space limitations) contain genes that share the three functions cell growth, cell-cell-signalling and transcription regulation (cluster 6). Others are related to development (cluster 8), DNA repair and replication (cluster 9), cell adhesion in combination with cell-cell-signalling (cluster 10), immune and stress response (cluster 11), electron transport, gycolysis and small molecule transport (cluster 14), signal transduction (cluster 15), fatty acid, amino acid and cholesterol biosynthesis and metabolism (cluster 16) and cell cycle (cluster 17).

For dataset II we show 3 clusters: cluster 10 (Tab. V), 12 (Tab. IV) and 19 (Tab. VI). The genes of cluster 10 are completely annotated with GO terms related to DNA replication, repair and recombination whereas those of cluster 12 are related to cell cycle (mitosis) in combination with oncogenesis. Oncogenes are cancer inducing genes and cancer is often known to occur due to defects in cell cycle regulation. Cluster 19 genes are also related to cell cycle (mitosis), but are not related to oncogenesis. Beside these three, similar clusters are found in dataset II as in dataset I (data not shown), e.g. protein modification and catabolism (cluster 13), energy pathways and metabolism (cluster 16), signal transduction (cluster 17), cell-cell signalling (cluster 18) and transcription and RNA processing (cluster 20). Beside that, four smaller clusters are present containing genes with identical GO annotations of two or three completely independent biological functions.

V. CONCLUSION

In this paper we presented a new functional clustering method for genes based on the GO that is available in most public databases. The fact that we use the smallest distance to combine different GO term distances to one functional distance between on the gene level previously caused the two problems: first too much information is discarded and second one does not operate in a proper metric space. With the feature vector representation of each gene used in this method, we are now able to overcome this problem. We showed that our method is able to detect functional clusters of genes. Additionally, we are able to distinguish between clusters of genes that share one, but differ in a second function, e.g. cell cycle genes related to

TABLE V
CLUSTER 10 FROM DATASET II: CELL CYCLE, CELL PROLIFERATION AND ONCOGENESIS RELATED GENES

Acc. number	Gene Ontology terms
M13150_at	oncogenesis G-protein coupled receptor protein signaling pathway embryogenesis and morphogenesis **cell proliferation**
M31423_at	oncogenesis cell growth and/or maintenance
M86699_at	regulation of cell cycle oncogenesis spindle assembly mitotic spindle assembly mitotic spindle checkpoint positive regulation of cell proliferation
U01038_at	regulation of cell cycle oncogenesis mitosis cell proliferation
U09579_at	regulation of cell cycle regulation of CDK activity oncogenesis cell cycle arrest negative regulation of cell proliferation induction of apoptosis by intracellular signals
U33203_at	oncogenesis negative regulation of cell proliferation
U33761_at	regulation of cell cycle G1/S transition of mitotic cell cycle oncogenesis cell proliferation
U43916_at	oncogenesis development cell death cell proliferation epidermal differentiation
U58090_at	G1/S transition of mitotic cell cycle oncogenesis cell cycle arrest negative regulation of cell proliferation induction of apoptosis by intracellular signals
X51688_at	regulation of CDK activity oncogenesis mitotic G2 checkpoint

oncogenesis and cell cycle genes not related to oncogenesis. Our experiments revealed that the spectral clustering algorithm using our feature vector representation lead to significantly better results than k-means and Single Linkage clustering. The clusters found by our method contain genes annotated with the same or very similar functions. Thus, our method enormously facilitates the analysis of high throughput data.

ACKNOWLEDGMENT

This work was supported by the National Genome Research Network (NGFN) of the Federal Ministry of Education and Research in Germany under contract number 0313323.

REFERENCES

[1] B. Adryan and R. Schuh. Gene Ontology-based clustering of gene expression data. *Bioinformatics*, 20(16):2851–2852, 2004.
[2] T. Beißbarth and T. Speed. GOstat: find statistically overexpressed Gene Ontologies within groups of genes. *Bioinformatics*, 20(9):1464–1465, 2004.
[3] A. Budanitsky and G. Hirst. Semantic distance in WordNet: An experimental, application-oriented evaluation of five measures. In *Workshop on WordNet and other Lexical Resources, Second meeting of the Nord American Chapter of the Association for Computational Linguistics*. Pittsburgh, 2001.
[4] R.J. Cho, M. Huang, M.J. Campbell, H. Dong, L. Steinmetz, L. Sapinoso, G. Hampton, S.J. Elledge, R.W. Davis, and D.J. Lockhart. Transcriptional regulation and function during the human cell cycle. *Nature Genetics*, 27(1):48–54, 2001.
[5] I. Gat-Viks, R. Sharan, and R. Shamir. Scoring clustering solutions by their biological relevance. *Bioinformatics*, 19(18):2381–2389, 2003.
[6] Gene Lynx. http://www.genelynx.org, 2004.
[7] J.J. Goeman, S.A. van de Geer, F. de Kort, and H.C. van Houwelingen. A global test for groups of genes: testing association with a clinical outcome. *Bioinformatics*, 20(1):93–99, 2004.
[8] D. Hanisch, A. Zien, R. Zimmer, and T. Lengauer. Co-clustering of biological networks and gene expression data. *Bioinformatics*, 18 (Supplement):S145–S154, 2002.
[9] T.R. Hvidsten, A. Laegreid, and J. Komorowski. Learning rule-based models of biological process from gene expression time profiles using Gene Ontology. *Bioinformatics*, 19(9):1116–1123, 2003.
[10] V.R. Iyer, M.B. Eisen, D.T. Ross, G. Schuler, T. Moore, J.C.F. Lee, J.M. Trent, L.M. Staudt, J. Hudson Jr, M.S. Boguski, D. Lashkari, D. Shalon, D. Botstein, and P.O. Brown. The transcriptional program in response of human fibroblasts to serum. *Science*, 283:83–87, 1999.
[11] J.J. Jiang and D.W. Conrath. Semantic similarity based on corpus statistics and lexical taxonomy. In *Proceedings of the International Conference on Research in Computational Linguistics*, Taiwan, 1998. ROCLING X.
[12] S.G. Lee, J.U. Hur, and Kim Y.S. A graph-theoretic modeling on go space for biological interpretation on gene clusters. *Bioinformatics*, 20(3):381–388, 2004.
[13] P.W. Lord, R.D. Stevens, A. Brass, and C.A. Goble. Semantic similarity measures across the gene ontology: the relationship between sequence and annotation. *Bioinformatics*, 19:1275–1283, 2002.
[14] A. Ng, M. Jordan, and Y. Weiss. On spectral clustering: Analysis and an algorithm. In *Adv. in Neural Inf. Proc. Syst. 14*, 2002.
[15] S. Raychaudhuri and R.B. Altman. A literature-based method for assessing the functional coherence of a gene group. *Bioinformatics*, 19(3):396–401, 2003.
[16] P. Resnik. Using information content to evaluate semantic similarity in a taxonomy. In *Proceedings of the 14th International Joint Conference on Artificial Intelligence*, volume 1, pages 448–453, Montreal, 1995.
[17] P.N Robinson, A. Wollstein, U. Böhme, and B. Beattie. Ontologizing gene-expression microarray data: characterizing clusters with gene ontology. *Bioinformatics*, 20(6):979–981, 2003.
[18] P.J. Rousseeuw. Silhouettes: a graphical aid to the interpretation and validation of cluster analysis. *Journal of Computational Applications in Math*, 20:53–65, 1987.
[19] B. Schölkopf and A. J. Smola. *Learning with Kernels*. MIT Press, Cambridge, MA, 2002.
[20] N.H. Shah and N.V. Fedoroff. CLENCH: a program for calculating Cluster ENriCHment using Gene Ontology. *Bioinformatics*, 20(7):1196–1197, 2004.
[21] F. Sohler, D. Hanisch, and R. Zimmer. New methods for joint analysis of biological networks and expression data. *Bioinformatics*, 20(10):1517–1521, 2004.
[22] N. Speer, C. Spieth, and A. Zell. A memetic clustering algorithm for the functional partition of genes based on the Gene Ontology. In *Proceedings of the 2004 IEEE Symposium on Computational Intelligence in Bioinformatics and Computational Biology (CIBCB 2004)*, pages 252–259. IEEE Press, 2004.
[23] N. Speer, C. Spieth, and A. Zell. A memetic co-clustering algorithm for gene exression profiles and biological annotation. In *Proceedings of the IEEE 2004 Congress on Evolutionary Computation, CEC 2004*, volume 2, pages 1631–1638. IEEE Press, 2004.
[24] The Gene Ontology Consortium. The gene ontology (GO) database and informatics resource. *Nucleic Acids Research*, 32:D258–D261, 2004.
[25] H. Zha, C. Ding, X. He M. Gu, and H. Simon. Spectral relaxation for k-means clustering. In *Proc. Neural Inf. Proc. Syst. 14*, pages 1057–1064, 2001.

A Simpler Bayesian Network Model for Genetic Regulatory Network Inference

Gustavo Bastos
Center of Informatics
Federal University of Pernambuco
Recife, PE 50740-540 Brazil
E-mail: gbs@cin.ufpe.br

Katia S. Guimarães
Center of Informatics
Federal University of Pernambuco
Recife, PE 50740-540 Brazil
E-mail: katia@cin.ufpe.br

Abstract— We use Bayesian Networks and a nonparametric regression model for inferring genetic regulatory networks. We have used a combination of the Bayesian Information Criterion (BIC) and a 'voting' method to pick out the edges of the output graph. Using BIC makes the model simpler than previous ones, still obtaining, however, good results, as shown in our experiments with synthetic data and *Saccharomyces cerevisiae* cell cycle microarray gene expression data.

I. INTRODUCTION

With the development of functional genomics, data on a great number of species are being obtained in huge volumes. That is leading to a great change from the traditional Molecular Biology approach, which explores complex interaction networks of cell components focusing only on simple molecules and reactions [1]. Technologies to measure the differences of the gene expression, through mRNA concentration, have become extremely popular [2], [3], and costs are decreasing.

The reconstruction of genetic networks from gene expression data to study the organism dynamics is an important process and raises the challenge of connecting genes and their products in metabolic pathways, circuits and functional networks.

A genetic regulatory network is a model that represents the regulations between genes using a directed graph where the nodes indicate genes, and an edge (Gene_1, Gene_2) indicates that Gene_1 regulates Gene_2 (with activation and/or repression) (Figure 1). Several methods have been proposed during the last years to infer a genetic network from microarray data using mathematical models, such as differential equations [4], Boolean networks [5], and Bayesian networks [6], [7], [8], [9].

The first approach tries to create a gene expression model through differential equations, based on the mechanisms of translation and transcription. The main disadvantages of this method are: not considering time delays in translation and transcription, not using regulators other than mRNA and protein concentrations, and not being a graphical representation of a gene network, which makes visualization hard.

The second approach defines a Boolean network $G(V, F)$ as a set $V = \{v_1, \ldots, v_n\}$ of nodes and a list $F = (f_1, \ldots, f_n)$ of boolean functions. A boolean function $f_i(v_{i_1}, \ldots, v_{i_k})$, with inputs from the specified nodes $v_{i_1}, \ldots, v_{i_k}$ is defined for each node v_i, producing corresponding outputs. The drawback with this approach is the execution time, which depends on the number of parents of each gene. If the maximum number of parents is set to 2, execution time is $O(n^3 m)$, where n is the number of nodes and m is the quantity of samples.

There are several works which use Bayesian networks to infer gene networks. Friedman *et al.* [6] used Bayesian networks with score function *Bayesian score* and turned microarray information into discrete data. Imoto *et al.* [7] proposed a different criterion called Bayesian Nonparametric Regression Criterion (BNRC), based on Laplace approximation, to choose the best network. Kim *et al.* [8] and Tamada *et al.* [9] expanded Imoto's work, the former used a dynamic Bayesian network while the latter added biological information to a Bayesian network model. All these methods present satisfactory results in building genetic networks in certain conditions. However, they also present problems, such as computing time and accuracy of results.

A recent approach [10] treats regulators' activity levels as unobserved variables, thus handling important cellular biochemical events not directly measured in the data, and explains the process that generated the data through a dynamic Bayesian network model. Even though the approach is interesting, it requires learning the kinetic parameters and the hidden activity levels of regulators from observations, which implies even more computation.

In the present paper we show the use of a Bayesian Network model for inferring genetic networks from microarray data. We use Bayesian Information Criterion (BIC) [11], a simpler but still effective approach, to calculate the network score. Among other reasons, BIC makes the score calculation easier for not taking into consideration prior probabilities of the graph parameters.

The goal of our work is to investigate the method which is the most suitable to solve the problem, while spending as little computational time as possible. We compare our results to previous works by Imoto *et al.* [7], on artificial data, and by Kim *et al.* [8] using *Saccharomyces cerevisiae* cell cycle microarray data [12] to infer the TCA cycle (*tricarboxylic acid*).

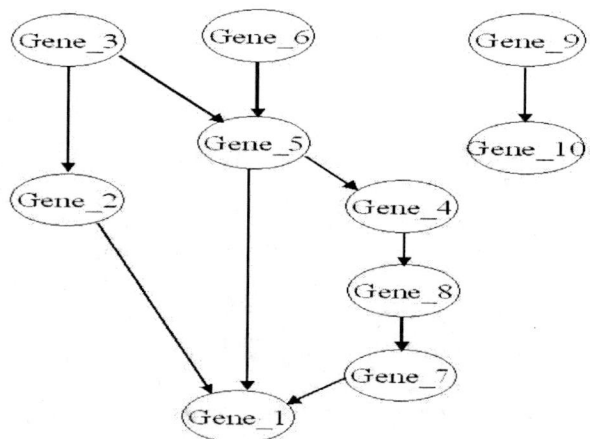

Fig. 1. Example of a genetic regulatory network

II. BAYESIAN NETWORK AND NONPARAMETRIC REGRESSION

Let $\mathbf{X} = (X_1, X_2, \ldots, X_n)^T$ be a random n-dimensional vector containing the genes to be analyzed, and assume that G is a directed graph. Under Bayesian Network theory, genes are random variables and it is possible to decompose their joint probability into the product of conditional probabilities:

$$P(X_1, X_2, \ldots, X_n) = P(X_1|\mathbf{P}_1) \times P(X_2|\mathbf{P}_2) \times \ldots \times P(X_n|\mathbf{P}_n), \quad (1)$$

where $\mathbf{P}_i = (P_1^{(i)}, P_2^{(i)}, \ldots, P_{q_i}^{(i)})^T$ is a q_i-dimensional vector of parent variables of X_i in graph G.

Suppose that s observations $x_1, x_2, \ldots, x_s$ of random vector X are performed and the observations of $\mathbf{P}_i$ are denoted $\mathbf{p}_{1i}, \mathbf{p}_{2i}, \ldots, \mathbf{p}_{si}$, where $\mathbf{p}_{ji} = (p_{j1}^{(i)}, \ldots, p_{jq_i}^{(i)})^T$ is a q_i-dimensional observation vector of parent genes. For example, assume $\mathbf{X}_{ns}$ as an $n \times s$ matrix, given that each one of its components $\mathbf{x}_i$ ($i = 1, \ldots, n$) is a vector of length s. Therefore, $\mathbf{X}_{ns} = (x_1, \ldots, x_n)^T = (x_{(1)}, \ldots, x_{(s)}) = (x_{ij})_{i=1,\ldots,n; j=1,\ldots,s}$, $\mathbf{x}_i = (x_{i1}, \ldots, x_{is})$, $\mathbf{x}_{(j)} = (x_{1j}, \ldots, x_{nj})^T$, and $\mathbf{x}_i^T$ is the transposed vector of $\mathbf{x}_i$. If X_1, for instance, has a parent vector $\mathbf{P}_1 = (X_4, X_5)^T$, we can obtain $\mathbf{p}_{11} = (x_{14}, x_{15})^T, \ldots, \mathbf{p}_{s1} = (x_{s4}, x_{s5})^T$.

Formula (1) still holds if we replace the P probabilities by density functions:

$$f(x_{1j}, x_{2j}, \ldots, x_{nj}) = f_1(x_{1j}|\mathbf{p}_{j1}) \times f_2(x_{2j}|\mathbf{p}_{j2}) \times \ldots \times f_n(x_{nj}|\mathbf{p}_{jn}).$$

To build conditional densities $f_i(x_{ij}|\mathbf{p}_{ji})$, with $i = 1, \ldots, n$ and $j = 1, \ldots, s$, we use nonparametric regression models to try and capture the relations between x_{ij} and $\mathbf{p}_{ji} = (p_{j1}^{(i)}, \ldots, p_{jq_i}^{(i)})^T$ through the following equation:

$$x_{ij} = m_1(p_{j1}^{(i)}) + m_2(p_{j2}^{(i)}) + \cdots + m_{q_i}(p_{jq_i}^{(i)}) + \varepsilon_{ij},$$
$$i = 1, \ldots, n; j = 1, \ldots, s,$$

where $m_k (k = 1, \ldots, q_i)$ are smoothing functions from $\Re$ (the set of real numbers) to $\Re$, and ε_{ij} follows a normal distribution with mean 0 and variance σ_i^2. For each function m_k, we assume that:

$$m_k(p_{jk}^{(i)}) = \sum_{m=1}^{M_{ik}} \gamma_{mk}^{(i)} b_{mk}^{(i)}(p_{jk}^{(i)}), \quad (2)$$
$$j = 1, \ldots, s, \ k = 1, \ldots, q_i,$$

where $\{b_{1k}^{(i)}, b_{2k}^{(i)}, \ldots, b_{M_{ik}k}^{(i)}\}$ is a preconceived set of "basis functions" (such as Fourier series, polynomial bases, β-splines and others), the coefficients $\gamma_{1k}^{(i)}, \ldots, \gamma_{M_{ik}k}^{(i)}$ are unknown parameters, and M_{ik} is the number of basis functions.

If we choose the basis function as a β-spline, we can build a β-spline nonparametric regression model with Gaussian noise [13]. We define the probability density function of the model when the ith gene has q_i parents as:

$$f_i(x_{ij}|\mathbf{p}_{ji}; \gamma_i; \sigma_i^2) = \frac{1}{\sqrt{2\pi\sigma_i^2}} \exp\left[-\frac{\left\{x_{ij} - \sum_{k=1}^{q_i} m_k(p_{jk}^{(i)})\right\}^2}{2\sigma_i^2}\right]. \quad (3)$$

If the ith gene has no parents, the portion of the model corresponding to its node is based on normal distribution with mean μ_i and variance σ_i^2.

Therefore, the Bayesian network model based on a nonparametric regression model with Gaussian noise cited above can be defined as:

$$f(x_{(j)}|\theta_G) = \prod_{i=1}^{n} \prod_{j=1}^{s} f_i(x_{ij}|\mathbf{p}_{ij}; \theta_i),$$

where $\theta_G = (\theta_1^T, \ldots, \theta_n^T)^T$ is a parameter vector in graph G, and θ_i is a parameter vector in the model of f_i, that is, $\theta_i = (\gamma_i^T, \sigma_i^2)^T$ or $\theta_i = (\mu_i, \sigma_i^2)^T$.

III. GRAPH CHOICE CRITERION

One of the goals of Bayesian networks is to find the network which best suits the observed data. In our context, we want to find the network that best reproduces the gene expression relations. An easy way to perform this is to use scoring functions, also called evaluation criteria, which assign scores to each network according to its adherence to the observed data. Most of the evaluation criteria used to analyze the best network use maximization (or minimization) of the posterior probability,

$$p(G|\mathbf{X}) = \frac{p(G)p(\mathbf{X}|G)}{p(\mathbf{X})}, \quad (4)$$

where $p(G)$ is the prior probability of the graph G, and $p(\mathbf{X}|G)$ is the probability of the observations given the graph. The term $p(\mathbf{X})$ (prior probability of the data) is constant and not related to $p(G)$, and therefore will not be taken into account in the model's evaluation. Under specific conditions [14], we can rewrite the term $p(\mathbf{X}|G)$ as:

$$p(\mathbf{X}|G) = \int \prod_{i=1}^{n} \prod_{j=1}^{s} f(\mathbf{X}_{(j)}|\theta_G, G) f(\theta_G|G) d\theta_G,$$

where $f(\theta_G|G)$ is the probability of the parameters given the graph and $\prod_{j=1}^{s}$ is an integration over all observed data. Hence, (4) may be rewritten as:

$$p(G|\mathbf{X}) = p(G) \int \prod_{i=1}^{n}\prod_{j=1}^{s} f(\mathbf{X_{(j)}}|\theta_G, G)f(\theta_G|G)d\theta_G. \quad (5)$$

The main problem with (5) is to solve the integral. There are some methods to compute it, the most used of which is Laplace approximation, used by Imoto *et al.* [7] to create his BNRC (Bayesian Nonparametric Regression Criterion). Laplace approximation, under some regularity conditions, presents low error rates, being therefore extremely accurate [14]. However, this is a complex and computationally difficult method to implement. For this reason, we adopt BIC, which keeps the terms from Laplace approximation that increase with n and uses the log of posterior probability, in order to obtain:

$$\log p(G|\mathbf{X}) = -\log p(G) - \log \sum_{i=1}^{n}\sum_{j=1}^{s} f(\mathbf{X_{(j)}}|\theta_G, G) + \frac{d}{2}\log n, \quad (6)$$

where d is the dimension of θ_G. The chosen optimum graph is the one with minimum score.

BIC has two convenient aspects: First, it is not dependent of the prior probabilities of the graph parameters, given the graph ($f(\theta_G|G)d\theta_G$), which lowers the complexity and avoids the assessment of these probabilities; secondly, BIC is a rather intuitive approximation, having a term to measure the accuracy of the model in predicting data ($f(\mathbf{X_{(j)}}|\theta_G, G)$) and another term to penalize the complexity of the model ($\frac{d}{2}\log n$).

Based on some properties of Bayesian networks [14], such as conditional dependence (one node's probability only depends on its parents probability) and independence of parameters (the parameters related to each node of the network are independent), we can obtain the criterion of (6) using local graph scores, through the definition of a local BIC for each ith variable X_i as follows:

$$node\_score_{(i)} = -\log p(L_i) + \sum_{j=1}^{s}\left\{-\log f_i(x_{ij}|\mathbf{p}_{ji}, \theta_i) + \frac{d_i}{2}\log n\right\}, \quad (7)$$

where $p(L_i)$ is the prior probability of the local structure associated with X_i, and d_i is the dimension of θ_i. We assume that those probabilities are independent of each other, so that $\sum_{i=1}^{n} -\log p(L_i) = -\log p(G)$. The value of $p(L_i)$ is defined as $p(L_i) = \exp[NPi + 1]$, where NPi is the number of parents of the ith gene.

Applying BIC to (5) we obtain:

$$\log p(G|\mathbf{X}) = -\log p(G) + \sum_{i=1}^{n}\{node\_score_{(i)} + \log p(L_i)\}. \quad (8)$$

The chosen final graph is the one which minimizes (8), minimizing each node individually.

IV. SCORE CALCULATION AND GRAPH CHOICE USING BIC

To implement the nonparametric regression mentioned in Section II, we choose a type of β-spline [15] called *P-spline* to be the basis function used in (2). These functions were defined by Eilers and Marx [16] and share many properties of the β-splines, having however different penalties on the estimated coefficients. The knots of the β-splines are placed dividing the domain $[min(p_{jk}^{(i)}), max(p_{jk}^{(i)})]$ (with $i = 1, \ldots, n$; $j = 1, \ldots, s$; $k = 1, \ldots, q_i$) into M_{ik} - 3 equidistance intervals, forming therefore M_{ik} β-splines of degree 3. With that, for each gene i, we determine a domain for the nonparametric regression ranging from the smallest obtained value among all its parent variables ($min(p_{jk}^{(i)})$) to the greatest value ($max(p_{jk}^{(i)})$).

In this work, we set M_{ik}, the number of β-splines, to 20. Although that number might be a parameter as well, it was not changed during the experiments.

Given the parents of the ith gene, we can determine the $s \times M_{ik}$ matrix $B_i^{(k)}$, which contains the values of the β-splines of the kth parent of the ith gene. We will then have k matrices B_i, with $k = 0, \ldots, q_i$.

Each matrix $B_i^{(k)}$ is created in the following manner:

$$B_i^{(k)} = (\mathbf{b}_{ik}(p_{1k}^{(i)}), \ldots, \mathbf{b}_{ik}(p_{pk}^{(i)}))^T, \text{ with}$$
$$\mathbf{b}_{ik}(p_{jk}^{(i)}) = (b_{1k}^{(i)}(p_{jk}^{(i)}), \ldots, b_{M_{ik}k}^{(i)}(p_{jk}^{(i)})), \text{ that is,}$$
$b_{mk}^{(i)}(p_{jk}^{(i)})$ is the value of the mth β-spline being applied to the jth value observed for the kth parent of the ith gene.

The values of the β-splines in each matrix $B_i^{(k)}$ are calculated through Equations (9a) and (9b).

$$B_{i,0}(x) = \begin{cases} 1 & \text{if } x_i \leq x < x_{i+1} \\ 0 & \text{otherwise} \end{cases} \quad (9a)$$

$$B_{i,p}(x) = \frac{x - x_i}{x_{i+p} - x_i}B_{i,p-1}(x) + \frac{x_{i+p+1} - x}{x_{i+p+1} - x_i}B_{i+1,p-1}(x), \quad (9b)$$

We use BIC approximation for each network node (7) to calculate the local score for each gene. After that, the local scores are added to obtain the network score (8).

It is possible to calculate the $\gamma_{mk}^{(i)}$ values of (2) [16], which minimize the BIC scores, through the Parameters Optimization Algorithm (see Algorithm 1).

The λ_w values are real numbers previously chosen. W is also a predefined parameter. After some experiments, we chose the values $W = 3$ and $\lambda = (-0.5, 0.0001, 0.5)$. In Algorithm 1, B_{ik} is a $s \times M_{ik}$ matrix with β-spline values of X_i for all parents, *i.e.*, $B_{ik} = (\mathbf{b}_{ik}(p_{1k}^{(i)}), \ldots, \mathbf{b}_{ik}(p_{pk}^{(i)}))^T$ with $\mathbf{b}_{ik}(p_{jk}^{(i)}) = (b_{1k}^{(i)}(p_{jk}^{(i)}), \ldots, b_{M_{ik}k}^{(i)}(p_{jk}^{(i)}))$; B_{ik}^T is the transposed matrix of B_{ik}; D_{ik} is the difference matrix; D_{ik}^T is the transposed matrix of D_{ik}. The algorithm stops when it reaches a fixed number of iterations (*maxIteration*) or when the new

Algorithm *Parameters Optimization*
1 **for** k from 1 to q_i **do**
2      $\gamma_{ik} \leftarrow 0$, where $\gamma_{ik} = \gamma_{1k}^{(i)}, \ldots, \gamma_{M_{ik}k}^{(i)}$
3 **end for**
4 **while** $newScore < oldScore$ **and** $g < maxIteration$ **do**
5   **for** k from 1 to q_i and w from 1 to W **do**
6   **for** w from 1 to W **do**
7              $\gamma_{ik} \leftarrow \left[(B_i^{(k)})^T B_i^{(k)} + \lambda_w (D_i^{(k)})^T D_i^{(k)}\right]^{-1}$
8              $\gamma_{ik} \leftarrow \gamma_{ik}(B_i^{(k)})^T (\mathbf{x}_i - \sum_{k' \neq k} B_i^{(k')} \gamma_{ik'})$
9              $newScore_k \leftarrow node\_score_{(i)}$
10   **if** $newScore_k < oldScore_k$ **then**
11                 $oldScore_k \leftarrow newScore_k$
12   **end if**
13   **end for**
14   **end for**
15     $newScore \leftarrow oldScore_k$
16     $g \leftarrow g + 1$
17 **end while**
end

Algorithm 1: Parameters Optimization

Algorithm *Best Network Choice*
1 **for** i from 1 to n **do**
2   **for** j from 1 to n **do**
3          $arrayParentScore(i,j) \leftarrow node\_score_{(i)}$
4          $sortIncreaseOrder(arrayParentScore(i))$
5   **end for**
6      $parentNumber_i \leftarrow rand()$
7   pick $parentNumber_i$ **from** $arrayParentScore(i)$
8 **end for**
9 **while not** Stop condition **do**
10   run Parameters Optimization Algorithm
11   **for** i from 1 to n **do**
12   choose one of three proceedings: add, remove or replace a parent
13   **if** $newScore < oldScore$ **then**
14   keep the new local network
15   **else**
16   keep the old local network
17   **end if**
18   **end for**
19   compute the network score
20 **end while**
end

Algorithm 2: Best Network Choice

score is higher than the previous node score. The first condition acts as a threshold for the number of times that the γ_{ik} values may be changed. After some tests, we chose value 50 for *maxIteration*.

It is clear from (7) and (8) that the network structure optimization is similar to choosing the parent genes which regulate the gene being observed at that moment. However, considering all possible combinations of genes is an exhaustive task; that is why in the present work we use a reduction of the initial search space, through a selection of parent genes. After that, a hill-climbing algorithm is used to find the best network. The final algorithm is called *Best Network Choice* (see Algorithm 2).

We use two stop conditions in Algorithm 2: First, a maximal number of iterations; second, a maximal number of iterations without score improvement.

V. Experiments

Two experiments were carried out: **Experiment 1** replicated Imoto's experiments [7] using a Monte Carlo simulation with artificial data obtained through an artificial network, and **Experiment 2** used biological data of *Saccharomyces cerevisiae* [12] to try and infer its respiration cycle presented in [8].

The number of possible network structures is exponential, therefore we used a 'voting' criterion: the program is executed a certain number of times, and, after that, the edges which had a score above a threshold a minimum number of times are selected. This score corresponds to the sum of the two possible directions of a relation between the two genes considered. The direction of the edge is chosen as the one which occurred the most. As an example, consider the relation between Gene_1 and Gene_2. Suppose we run the program 10 times and in 4 of them (Gene_1, Gene_2) (meaning that Gene_1 is the parent of Gene_2), in 2 other executions (Gene_2, Gene_1), and no direct relation between Gene_1 and Gene_2 appeared in the left 4 runs. If the threshold to pick an edge is 5, this edge is chosen and its direction is (Gene_1, Gene_2).

Experiment 1 used artificial data which were created to try to reproduce Imoto's experiments [7]. The formulas used to generate the data are shown in Table I and the graphical illustration of the artificial gene network that they represent is shown in Figure 1.

TABLE I

Formulas that generate the artificial network

$$x_1 = x_2^2 + 2\sin(x_5) - 2x_7 + \varepsilon_1$$
$$x_2 = [1 + \exp(-4x_3)]^{-1} + \varepsilon_2$$
$$x_3 = \varepsilon_3$$
$$x_4 = \frac{x_5^2}{3} + \varepsilon_4$$
$$x_5 = x_3 - x_6^2 + \varepsilon_5$$
$$x_6 = \varepsilon_6$$
$$x_7 = \begin{cases} -1 + \varepsilon_7, & x_8 \leq -0.5 \\ x_8 + \varepsilon_7, & -0.5 < x_8 \leq 0.5 \\ 1 + \varepsilon_7, & 0.5 < x_8 \end{cases}$$
$$x_8 = \frac{\exp(-x_4 - 1)}{2} + \varepsilon_8$$
$$x_9 = \varepsilon_9$$
$$x_{10} = \cos x_9 + \varepsilon_{10}$$

In our experiment, **Gene_3**, **Gene_6** and **Gene_9** followed a normal probability distribution with mean 0 and variance 0.5 [$\varepsilon_3 = \varepsilon_6 = \varepsilon_9 = N(0, 0.5)$]; **Gene_2**, **Gene_7**, **Gene_8** and **Gene_10** followed a normal probability distribution with mean 0 and variance 0.1 [$\varepsilon_2 = \varepsilon_7 = \varepsilon_8 = \varepsilon_{10} = N(0, 0.1)$]; and **Gene_1**, **Gene_4** and **Gene_5** followed a normal probability distribution with mean 0 and variance 0.4 [$\varepsilon_1 = \varepsilon_4 = \varepsilon_5 = N(0, 0.4)$]. We set the number of iterations to 1000 and the threshold to select edges to 88% of the total number of iterations. In addition to this, we entered some prior information that indicated which genes had no parents (**Gene_3**, **Gene_6** and **Gene_9**).

Figure 2 shows the results obtained through the application of the model proposed in this work (on the left). For comparison of those results with previous works, we present Imoto's model [7] (on the right). In Figure 2 a circle represents a correct edge, while a triangle indicates inverted direction or gene bypassing and a square represents an extra edge (not in the original graph).

The method shows good results, finding 7 correct out of 10 proposed edges. Two of the other three edges are inverted, which means that the relation between the genes was correctly established but its direction was wrong. It is certain that the use of prior biological information was extremely important to obtain this result.

In comparison, Imoto found 9 correct out of 11 proposed edges, with one inverted and one nonexistent edges. When comparing the two resulting networks, it is important to remark that our method used a simpler criterion and the data set was not identical (as we generated our own data and used different normal distributions).

In order to demonstrate how the proposed method behaves when applied to biological data, we ran **Experiment 2** to try to infer the aerobic respiration cycle (TCA cycle) of *Saccharomyces cerevisiae*, using the microarray data in the *alpha* time series generated by Spellman *et al.* [12]. Based on our experiments with artificial data, including **Experiment 1**, in **Experiment 2** we set the number of iterations to 600 and the threshold to select edges to 50% of the total number of iterations.

The results were compared to Kim's [8], who used a superset of the data, comprised of all of the four series in Spellman's data: *alpha, cdc15, cdc28* and *elu*, which have 18, 24, 17 and 14 time points, respectively.

Figure 3 shows the TCA cycle genetic network. The target network is presented on the left side whilst our result is shown in the middle, and Kim's network is presented on the right side. Circles, triangles and squares in this figure have the same meaning as in Figure 2. As we can see, the method adopted in this work presents good results, showing 46% of correct edges in spite of the small input data set.

Our model selected 13 edges (6 correct, 2 incorrect and 5 inverted or bypassing), while Kim's model selected 11 edges (6 correct, 2 incorrect and 3 inverted or bypassing). Differently from Kim's network, our result is comprised of one unique connected component, which involves all the genes in the target metabolic pathway.

We can notice some problems with inverted edges and indirect relations are present in five of the edges with problems. That is the most common problem, which has already been mentioned in the literature as being difficult to solve [17].

Another important remark is that the use of the 'voting' method prevented graph overgrowth (adding many extra edges), mentioned by Imoto *et al.* [7].

VI. Discussion and Future Work

In this paper we presented a Bayesian network and nonparametric regression model to infer a genetic regulatory network. The model uses BIC for assigning the network score according to the observed data. Despite using a simpler criterion to compute scores and not taking into account prior densities on the graph's parameters, our model proved to be effective. The quantity of correct edges found in the final graph is believed to be due to the 'voting' criterion adopted. Comparing to existent models, mainly when dealing with biological data, we obtained good results. We ran several experiments consisting of hundreds of iterations. The results of the experiments yielded similar results which shows the consistency of the method.

Two problems already mentioned in other works as difficult-solving problems, such as edges direction and genes bypassing, were also faced by our model.

Inferring genetic regulatory networks from microarray gene expression data is a hard task, but the solution may be in adding prior biological information to the models. The Bayesian network model is fairly suitable for this purpose. As future work, the authors intend to add prior probabilities based on biological data, which will certainly improve the model.

VII. Acknowledgements

The authors would like to thank Taciana Falcão and the anonymous referees, whose comments helped improve the presentation and general quality of the paper. The first author would also like to thank sponsoring agency CNPq.

References

[1] P. Brazhnik, A. de la Fuente, and P. Mendes, "Gene networks: how to put the function in genomics," *TRENDS in Biotechnology*, vol. 20, no. 11, pp. 467–472, November 2002.

[2] M. Chee, R. Yang, E. Hubbell, A. Berno, X. C. Huang, D. Stern, J. Winkler, D. J. Lockhart, M. S. Morris, and S. P. A. Fodor, "Accessing Genetic Information with High-Density DNA Arrays," *Science*, vol. 274, no. 5287, pp. 610–614, 1996. [Online]. Available: http://www.sciencemag.org/cgi/content/abstract/274/5287/610

[3] M. Schena, R. A. Heller, T. P. Theriault, K. Konrad, E. Lachenmeier, and R. W. Davis, "Microarrays: biotechnology's discovery platform for functional genomics," *TRENDS in Biotechnology*, vol. 16, no. 7, pp. 301–306, July 1998.

[4] T. Chen, H. L. He, and S. Kuhara, "Modeling gene expression with differential equations," in *Proc. of the Pacific Symp. on Biocomputing*, no. 4, 1999, pp. 29–40.

[5] T. Akutsu, S. Miyano, and S. Kuhara, "Identification of Genetic Networks from a Small Number of Gene Expression Patterns under the Boolean Network Model," in *Proc. of the Pacific Symp. on Biocomputing*, no. 4, 1999, pp. 17–28.

[6] N. Friedman, M. Linial, I. Nachman, and D. Pe'er, "Using Bayesian Networks to Analyze Expression Data," in *Proc. of the fourth Annual Intern. Conf. on Computational Molecular Biology*, ACM. Tokyo, Japan: ACM Press, 2000, pp. 127–135.

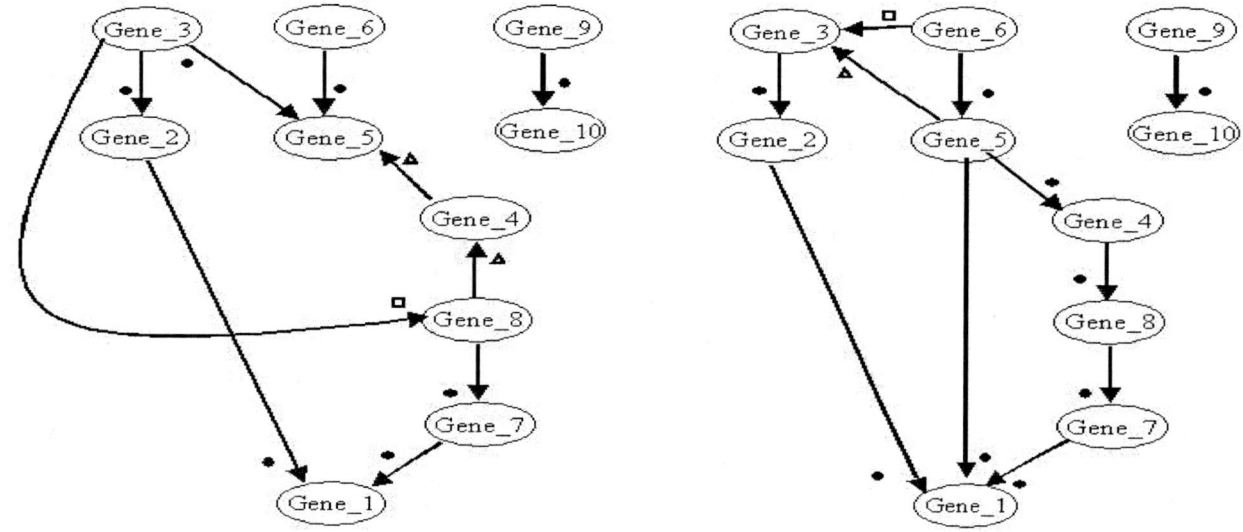

Fig. 2. Artificial gene networks inferred by Bayesian Network models. On the left, our result. On the right, Imoto's result [7].

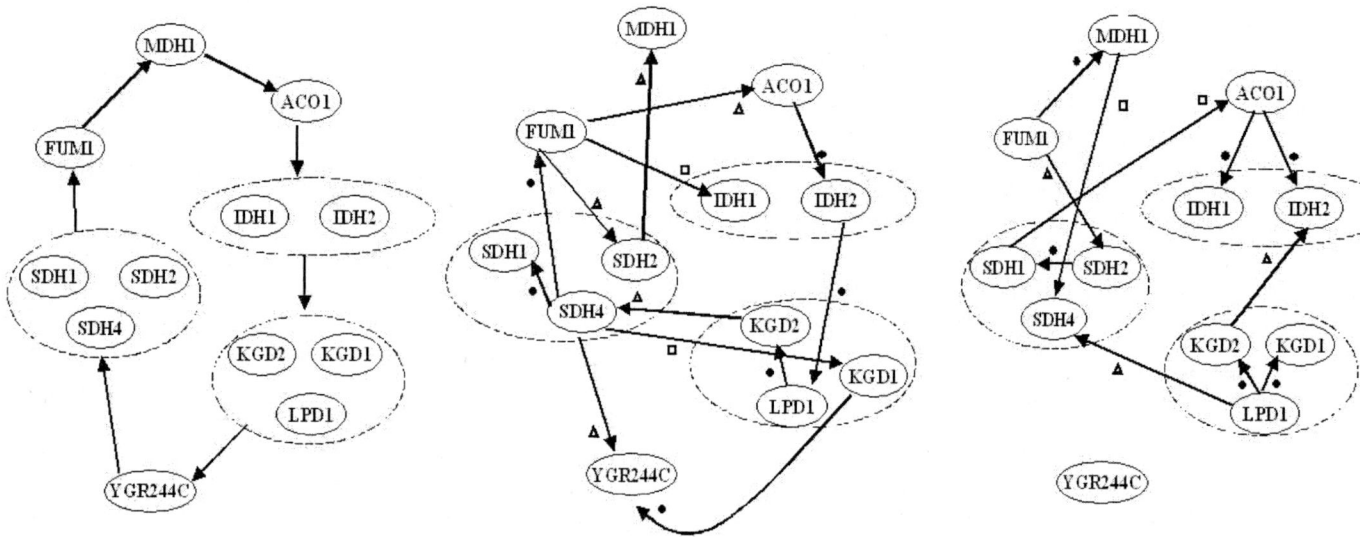

Fig. 3. Respiration metabolic pathway in [8]. On the left, real network. In the middle, our result. On the right, network inferred by Kim et al.

[7] S. Imoto, T. Goto, and S. Miyano, "Estimation of genetic networks and functional structures between genes by using bayesian networks and nonparametric regression," in *Proc. of the Pacific Symp. on Biocomputing*, no. 7, 2002, pp. 175–186.

[8] S. Kim, S. Imoto, and S. Miyano, "Dynamic bayesian network and nonparametric regression for nonlinear modeling of gene networks from time series gene expression data," in *Proc. of First Computational Methods in Systems Biology (CMSB)*, ser. LNCS, C. Priami, Ed., no. 2602. Springer, February 24-26 2003, pp. 104–113.

[9] Y. Tamada, S. Kim, H. Bannai, S. Imoto, K. Tashiro, S. Kuhara, and S. Miyano, "Estimating gene networks from gene expression data by combining Bayesian network model with promoter element detection," *BioInformatics*, vol. 19, no. 2, pp. 227–236, 2003.

[10] I. Nachman, A. Regev, and N. Friedman, "Inferring quantitative models of regulatory networks from expression data," in *Eleventh Inter. Conf. on Intelligent Systems for Molecular Biology*, 2004, appeared in Bioinformatics. 20 Suppl. 1:I248-I256, 2004.

[11] G. Schwarz, "Estimating the dimension of a model," in *Annals of Statistics*, no. 6, 1978, pp. 461–464.

[12] P. Spellman, G. Sherlock, M. Zhang, V. Iyer, K. Anders, M. Eisen, P. Brown, D. Botstein, and B. Futcher, "Comprehensive identification of cell cycle-regulated genes of yeats *Saccharomyces cerevisiae* by microarray hybridization," *Molecular Biology of the Cell*, vol. 9, pp. 3273–3297, 1998.

[13] S. Imoto and S. Konishi, "β-spline nonparametric regression models and information criteria," in *Proc. 2nd. Intern. Symp. on Frontiers of Time Series Modeling*, 2000, pp. 240–241.

[14] D. Heckerman, "A tutorial on learning bayesian networks," Microsoft Corporation, Advanced Technology Division, Redmond, Tech. Rep., November 1996.

[15] G. Farin, *Curves and surfaces for computer-aided geometric design a pratical guide*, 4th ed. San Diego CA: Academic Press, 1988.

[16] P. H. C. Eilers and B. D. Marx, "Flexible smoothing with *B*-splines and penalties," *Statistical Science*, vol. 11, no. 2, pp. 89–121, 1996.

[17] S. Imoto, S. Kim, T. Goto, S. Aburatani, K. Tashiro, S. Kuhara, and S. Miyano, "Bayesian network and nonparametric heteroscedastic regression for nonlinear modeling of genetic network," *Journal of Bioinformatics and Computational Biology*, vol. 1, no. 2, pp. 231–252, 2003, this paper is invited and an extended version of CSB2002 paper.

Effect of Non-Target Examples on E.coli Promoters Recognition Using Neural Networks

Paul C. Conilione and Dianhui Wang
Department of Computer Science and Computer Engineering
La Trobe University, Melbourne, VIC 3086, Australia
E-mail: csdhwang@ieee.org

Abstract— Previous research into the recognition of E.coli promoters has focused on the use of raw DNA sequences and alignment methods to find interesting features in the promoter regions. In this paper we aim to compare the classification accuracy of a neural network trained on DNA sequences encoded using orthogonal representation of the nucleotides, and a set of high level features from the DNA. In addition to this, we evaluate the impact of different types of non-promoters used in training and testing on the classification accuracy. 872 E.coli promoters were used and three types of non-promoters, which included random sequences with the same base frequency as the promoter sequences, genes sequences selected from E.coli and random sequences with the same base frequencies as the gene non-promoters. Raw DNA sequences were encoded using CODE-4 and high level features, which were outlined by previous researchers and subsequently formally defined in this paper. We found that the high level features did not perform as well for promoter recognition compared with CODE-4 DNA representation, contrary to expectation. The strongest determining factor in classification accuracy was the type of non-promoter used for training and testing. Overall non-promoters from coding regions and random sequences with the same base frequency as the gene non-promoter resulted in the best classification accuracy.

I. INTRODUCTION

A promoter is a region of DNA, recognized by and a binding target for RNA (ribonucleic acid) polymerase, which then starts transcription of the coding region. The RNA polymerase consists of two components, the core enzyme and σ-factor. The core enzyme can weakly bind to any part of the DNA strand. It is the σ-factor that recognises the promoter region and binds strongly to it. The core enzyme then binds to the σ-factor, forming the complete RNA polymerase, which then starts transcription from the Transcription Start Site (TSS).

Within the promoter region, there are sequences of nucleotides that are more conserved than other regions, i.e. the sequences do not change significantly from promoter to promoter of the same species, due to their function as a binding site for the RNA polymerase. These conserved regions can be characterised by a *consensus* sequence, which is the sequence of most commonly occurring nucleotides found in that region.

Using biochemical or genetic means to identify the promoter regions and pinpointing the binding site(s) at which the RNA polymerase comes into contact with the DNA is difficult and the information for individual genes is generally unavailable [1]. For this reason, analytical techniques to identify the promoter regions from the DNA sequences are used. Traditionally, techniques for identification of the promoter regions are based on statistical and alignment techniques. Research by [1], [2] and [3] compiled increasingly larger number of promoter regions of E.coli. Using statistical methods, they identified two major consensus sequences, which consist of two hexamers (6 base pairs (bps)) long. The first consensus sequence is TATAAT and is approximately 35 bps upstream from the TSS, (labelled -35 hexamer). The second consensus sequence is TTGACA and is approximately 10 bps upstream from the TSS (labelled -10 hexamer).

There are two reasons why identifying the -10 and -35 consensus sequences is non-trivial. The first is that both hexamers' composition vary from one promoter to another, but are identified by the σ-factor. The second is that the hexamers position relative to the TSS is not fixed. It is this variability that makes the task of recognising promoter regions in unknown sequences difficult for traditional statistical and sequence alignment methods. One approach to recognising promoters is the use of Artificial Neural Networks (ANN's), which have the flexibility to accurately recognise difficult to define patterns [4].

Previous researchers have applied ANN's to the problem of promoter recognition, [4], [5], [6], [7], achieving promoter recognition in the 90% range and false positive rates of around 5-10%. In general, these researchers first identified the -35, -10 hexamers by various means, such as statistical methods or by applying the Expectation Maximisation algorithm [7]. They then aligned the identified hexamers, either by inserting gaps into the promoter sequence, or aligning the whole sequences around one of the hexamers. The ANNs were then trained and tested on the aligned promoter and non-target DNA sequences. For non-target DNA sequences, previous efforts used either randomly generated sequences, or sequences from the coding regions of E.coli.

Hirsh and Noordewier [8] employed an alternative technique for promoter identification. Rather than using the raw DNA sequences and applying an alignment procedure, they used various biologically significant *high level* features that are derived from the raw DNA sequences. Using both an ANN and C4.5 decision tree, they recorded a statistically significant improvement in E.coli promoter recognition accuracy for both classifiers. With the ANN, the accuracy of promoter recognition using raw DNA was 74.7%, whilst when using the extracted features, the accuracy was 89.8%.

In this paper we explore the effect of using CODE-4 and high level features on the classification accuracy by ANNs. Previous researchers have used, random sequences [5] [4] [9], sequences from the gene regions of E.coli [6], and sequences that have been shown not to bind with RNA polymerase [6]. To our knowledge, no one has done a comparison of the effect of the type of non-promoter on classification accuracy. We investigate the effect of using different types of non-promoter DNA sequences on classification accuracy.

Section II-A details the promoter and non-promoter data used for training and testing. Sections II-B and II-C define the CODE-4 encoding scheme and the definitions of the 19 high level features as first outlined by [8]. The specifics of the ANNs training and testing methodology are discussed in sections II-D and II-F respectively. Section III presents the results, discussion of these results is given in section IV and the research conclusions are in section V.

II. METHODS

A. Data

We used a pool of 872 promoter sequences of E.coli (K12 strain), from the compilation of E.coli promoters in the *RegulonDB* database [10]. Table I summarises the different sets of promoter and non-promoter sequences that comprised the data sets used for classification in this paper.

TABLE I
DETAILS OF THE DATA SETS USED IN THIS PAPER.

Label	Region	N(bps)	Size	Non-prom	Size	Total
A	-60 to +21	81	872	rand-prom[1]	872	1774
B	-60 to +21	81	872	gene	872	1774
C	-60 to +21	81	872	rand-gene[2]	872	1774

The promoter sequences were taken from 60 bases upstream of the TSS, to 21 bases downstream of the TSS. Three different types of non-target DNA sequences were used. The first type was randomly generated DNA sequences with the same base frequency as the target DNA. The second type was taken from the gene coding regions of the E.coli K12 strain [10]. The appropriate number and length of DNA sequences were selected from the pool of approximately 4400 known genes, starting 100 bps downstream of the TSS. The third type used were randomly generated sequences, but using the same base frequencies of occurrences as the coding DNA sequences.

For both the random and gene sequences, no attempt was made to remove sequences that match or were similar to the -35 and -10 consensus as done by other researchers [9] and [6]. The reason for this was that a σ-factors is able to distinguish promoter from coding regions, even when the coding regions

[1]Randomly generated sequences with the promoter base frequency.
[2]Randomly generated sequences with the gene base frequency.

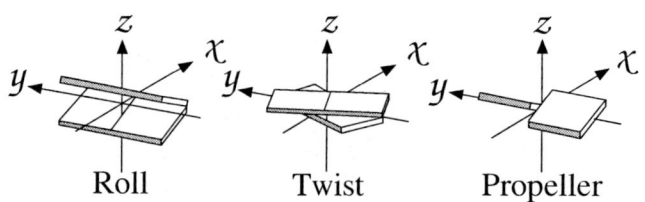

Fig. 1. Illustration of roll, helix twist and propeller twist.

contain nucleotide sequences that match or are similar to the -35 and -10 consensus sequences. Hence we require the ANN be able to recognise and learn this behaviour.

B. DNA Encoding

The nucleotides of DNA are represented by four symbols, {A, T, C, G}, and are encoded using four binary bits, where $A \rightarrow 0001$, $T \rightarrow 0010$, $G \rightarrow 0100$ and $C \rightarrow 1000$. This scheme is commonly referred to as CODE-4 encoding. As each base is represented by four binary bits, to represent a sequence of length N, requires $4N$ input nodes of the ANN.

C. High Level Features

The following are the definitions of the higher level features of a DNA sequence as outlined in [8].

1) Features 1 to 12 - Helical Parameters: The three dimensional structure of the DNA double helix can be described by the angles and displacements between complementary and adjacent nucleotides. The most common of these parameters are roll, helix twist and propeller twist angles, which are illustrated in figure 1.

The local shape of the DNA double helix is determined by the differences in angle between base pair steps. Nussinov and Lennon [11] found that there were particular purine (G and A) and pyrimidine (C and T) patterns along the DNA helix that shared the same amount of helical twist or roll over a local region of DNA. Knowing this, and if such patterns are present in a given sequence, an approximation of the local structure can then be created.

Formally, given a sequence S, the number of times a non-overlapping pattern occurs in the sequence is counted. Table II lists the 12 different patterns as defined in [12], where R and Y denotes purine (A or G) and pyrimidine (T or C) respectively.

2) Features 13 and 14 - Site Specific Information: There are particular sequence patterns, called motifs, that play an important role in DNA-protein interaction. Unfortunately most of these motifs are function or protein specific. However, it has been found that the GTG/CAC motifs and their repeats are found near the sites of protein-DNA interaction for both eukaryotes and prokaryotes. The GTG/CAC motifs had a higher frequency of occurring every single helical turn (10.5bps in B form DNA), implying that the interacting protein came into contact with GTG/CAC pair on the same side of the double

TABLE II
FEATURES 1 TO 12.

Feature	Label	Pattern
1	twist1a	RRRRY
2	twist1b	YRYYY
3	twist3a	RRRYR
4	twist3b	RYYYY
5	roll4a	RRRYY
6	roll4b	RYYYR
7	roll5a	RRYYY
8	roll5b	YRRRY
9	twist7a	RYRRR
10	twist7b	YYRYR
11	twist8a	YRYRR
12	twist8b	YYYRY

helix [13], [14]. In this context, the definitions of features 13 and 14 as used by [8] are shown in table III. Feature 13 is the number of times the gtg_motif occurs in a DNA sequence S, where it does not overlap. For the gtg_pair motif, the *spacer* is a multiple of 10 ± 1 bases from the beginning of each motif. For example, if a GTG is followed by a CAC 21 bases apart from the left side of each motif, then this would be counted as one occurrence of feature 14.

TABLE III
FEATURES 13 TO 14

Feature	Label	Pattern
13	gtg_motif	GTG or CAC
14	gtg_pair	gtg_motif *spacer* gtg_motif

3) Features 15 to 16 - Local Secondary Structure: The *local secondary structures* are characterised by the presences of *tandem* and *invert* repeats. Let S be a sequence of N bases, drawn from an alphabet of $\{A, T, C, G\}$. $S = s_1, s_2, ..., s_m$, where s_i is a base at position i in S. The reverse of S is denoted S^{-1}. The complement of a base is the nucleotide that binds to it on the opposite strand of the DNA sequence and is denoted as $\overline{s_i}$, e.g. if $s_i = A$, then its complement is $\overline{s_i} = T$. The complement of a sequence is denoted $\overline{S}$.

a) Feature 15 - Tandem repeats: Direct repeats are repeating sequences of nucleotides that occur two or more times on the same DNA strand. Where there are only two repeating sequences, it is called a tandem repeat. Due to substitution errors, the presence of mismatches in the repeat structure must be accommodated in the definition. We define an imperfect tandem repeat with no gaps between repeating sequences as $T = UV$, where the subsequences U and V are expressed as $U = u_1, u_2, ..., u_m$ and $V = v_1, v_2, ..., v_m$. The period p of T is the minimum integer such that $u_i = v_{i+p}$ for some i [15]. The mismatch between subsequences U and V is given by the hamming distance, $d(U, V) = c$, where c is the number of mismatches. The no-gap condition is met iff $u_1 = v_1$ and $u_m = v_m$.

For sequence S, all tandem repeats are found and the size of the repeat n and number of matches $b = n - c$ are recorded.

For each tandem repeat, the probability of one or more of the repeats being found in a random sequence S of size N is calculated using the process detailed in section II-C.3.c. The smallest probability of finding a tandem repeat is used for feature 15 of the sequence.

b) Feature 16 - Inverted repeats: An inverted repeat is a sequence of nucleotides that is found to be repeated in the reverse order on the opposite strands of the DNA double helix. We define an imperfect inverted repeat as $I = UV$, where the subsequences $U = u_1, u_2, ..., u_m$ and $V = v_1, v_2, ..., v_m$, and the number of mismatches is given by the hamming distance $d(U, \overline{V}^{-1}) = c$. For a sequence S of size N all inverted repeats are found and the size of the repeat fold, n, and number of matches $b = n - c$ are recorded. For each invert repeat, the probability of one or more of the repeats being found in the sequence S of size N is calculated using the process detailed in section II-C.3.c. The minimum probability is used as feature 16 of the sequence.

c) Probability of Repeat structure: To calculate the probability of a 2-fold repeat structure, there are two steps involved as described in [16]. First we calculate the probability of a repeat with b or more matches in a fold size of m occurring. Let m be the number of bases in a single fold, b is the number of matches, $p = Pr(match)$ and B is a random variable equal to the number of matches.

The probability of B matches in m bases of one fold is given by (1).

$$Pr(B = b) = \binom{m}{b} p^b (1-p)^{m-b} \quad (1)$$

The probability of a match between two bases in an inverted repeat or tandem repeat structure is given in (2) and (3) respectively.

$$Pr(match)_{inv} = 2Pr(T)Pr(A) + 2Pr(C)Pr(G) \quad (2)$$
$$Pr(match)_{tan} = Pr(T)^2 + Pr(A)^2 + Pr(C)^2 + Pr(G)^2 \quad (3)$$

The probability of B or more matches in m bases is given by (4).

$$Pr(b \leq B \leq m) = \sum_{j=b}^{m} Pr(B = j) \quad (4)$$

The second step is to calculate the probability that a repeat with B or more matches in a fold size of n is found in a sequence of length N, (5).

$$Pr(L, Q, \alpha) = \binom{L}{Q} \alpha^Q (1-\alpha)^{L-Q} \quad (5)$$

Where $L = 2(N - 2n) + 1$ is the number of axis's of symmetry a fold can take, Q is the number of occurrences of the repeat and $\alpha = Pr(b \leq B \leq m)$ (4). The probability of one or more 2-fold symmetric repeats occurring in a nucleotide sequence of size N is given by (6).

$$1 - Pr(L, Q, \alpha)|_{Q=0} \quad (6)$$

4) Features 17 to 19 - DNA compositions: The proportion of the different nucleotides are known to determine the structural and chemical properties of DNA. Consequently, several measures of composition are used.

  a) Feature 17 - AT content: AT-rich regions have lower stacking energy, and hence a lower melting temperature T_m. They also have a higher intrinsic curvature, and are less flexible [17].

$$AT\_content = \frac{A+T}{N} \quad (7)$$

where A and T are the number of adenosine's and thymindine's respectively, and N is the total number of nucleotides in the sequence window.

  b) Feature 18 - AG/TC ratio:

$$AG\_TC\_ratio = \begin{cases} \frac{A+G}{T+C} & T+C \neq 0 \\ 0 & T+C = 0 \end{cases} \quad (8)$$

  c) Feature 19 - AC/GT ratio:

$$AC\_TG\_ratio = \begin{cases} \frac{A+C}{T+G} & T+G \neq 0 \\ 0 & T+G = 0 \end{cases} \quad (9)$$

D. Neural Network

The ANN architecture used for classification of the promoter DNA sequences was a fully connected three layer feed forward network with a single neuron to represent the two classes. The activation function of all neurons was the logarithmic sigmoid function. The training algorithm used depended on the size of the network being trained, which in turn depended on the size of the feature vector of the input data.

For the networks trained on DNA encoded using the high level features, the network size is comparatively small and so were trained using the Levenberg-Marquardt (LM) algorithm. The Matlab implementation of the the LM algorithm adjusts λ, where λ is increased by a factor of λ_inc each epoch, until there is a reduction in performance, then once the network is updated, λ is decreased by a factor of λ_dec. We used $\lambda = 10^{-3}$, $\lambda\_inc = 10$ and $\lambda\_dec = 0.1$

For 81bps sequences encoded in CODE-4, there are 324 features. Consequently, the ANNs were trained using the resilient back-propagation algorithm, which is fast compared to other training algorithms for large networks. For the resilient back-propagation algorithm, we initially set $\triangle x = 0.07$ and allowed it to be increased and decreased by $\triangle x\_inc = 1.20$ and $\triangle x\_dec = 0.50$ respectively.

The performance function used was the *mean square error*. When training the ANN, the target value was taken as 1 for a promoter and 0 for a non-promoter. All data were normalised to the range of $[-1, 1]$.

E. Performance Evaluation

The performance of the ANN classifier was measured using a confusion matrix and derived F-measure, (10), and accuracy (11) metrics. From table IV, a promoter that is correctly classified is called a *true positive* (TP), whilst a promoter classified as a non-promoter is called a *false positive* (FP). A non-promoter that is correctly classified is called a *true negative* (TN) and an incorrectly classified non-promoter is called a *false negative* (FN).

TABLE IV
CONFUSION MATRIX

Actual Class	Predicted Class	
	Promoter	Non-Promoter
Promoter	TP	FP
Non-promoter	FN	TN

$$F = \frac{2 \times precision \times recall}{precision + recall} = \frac{TP}{TP+FP+FN} \quad (10)$$

$$acc = \frac{TP+TN}{TP+FP+TN+FN} \quad (11)$$

Where recall and precision are defined in equations (12) and (13) respectively.

$$recall = \frac{TP}{TP+FP} \quad (12)$$

$$precision = \frac{TP}{TP+FN} \quad (13)$$

The accuracy of classifying each class is given by the promoter and non-promoter sensitivity in (14) and (15).

$$S_P = \frac{TP}{TP+FP} \quad (14)$$

$$S_{NP} = \frac{TN}{TN+FN} \quad (15)$$

F. Training and Testing Process

To train and test the ANN based promoter classifiers, K-fold cross validation was used. K-fold cross validation segments a data set D it into K folds $F_1, .., F_K$ of approximately the same size. As our data sets are composed of two classes, promoters and non-promoters, care was taken to ensure each fold contained an equal number of instances from each class. For each step, i, we trained the ANN on folds $F_j, 1 \leq j \leq K, j \neq i$, and tested the ANN using F_i. To find the best generalisation of a data set D, at step i, the network was trained over a number of epochs. At regular periods, training was paused, and the classification performance of the training data and test data were recorded in separate confusion matrices. During training, the highest F-measure for the test data were recorded for fold F_i. If the networks test data F-measure did not improve after a set number of epochs, training was halted. This process was repeated for each fold, and the overall classification accuracy of the network was the summation of the test classification confusion matrices of each fold. The F-measure was used as it favours TP results, which hopefully will lead to a higher promoter recognition rate.

If the network output was above 0.5, the instance was classified as a promoter. Whilst if the output was below 0.5, then the instances was classified as a non-promoter.

To explore the effect of the number of neurons in the hidden layer for each data set on classification accuracy, the number of neurons were varied. For a particular number of neurons in the hidden layer, 3-fold cross validation was performed. The number of neurons that produced the highest F-measure were recored and taken as the optimal network topology for the data set and coding scheme.

Once the approximate number of neurons that produced the best F-measure for a given data set was found, 10-fold cross validation, repeated 10 times, with a different random seed each time, was performed to determine the mean and standard deviation of the classification accuracy of the ANN.

G. Implementation

The high level feature definitions was implemented in PERL (v5.8.4). We used Matlab (v7.0.0) with the Neural Network Toolbox (v4.0.3) for network training and testing.

III. RESULTS

A. Number of Neurons in Hidden Layer.

Using CODE-4 to encode all DNA sequences it was observed that for data set A, the best classification accuracy was found to occur with 325 neurons in the hidden layer, with an F-measure of 0.6863. The best F-measure for data set B was 0.8888 with 175 neurons, and the best F-measure for data set C was 0.8444 with 75 neurons.

The use of high level features for the encoding of the DNA resulted in the best F-measure for data set A of 0.6361 with 16 neurons, the best F-measure for data set B was 0.7964 with 13 neurons, and the best F-measure for data set C was 0.8305 with 0 neurons (no hidden layer).

B. Classification Accuracy.

The results of classification using 10-fold cross validation, repeated 10 times is given in tables V and VI. The mean and standard deviations are given for the accuracy, f-measure, promoter and non-promoter sensitivity over the 10 iterations.

TABLE V
TEST CLASSIFICATION RESULTS FOR CODE-4.

Data set	A		B		C	
# neurons	325		150		75	
	mean	std	mean	std	mean	std
Acc	0.6749	0.0168	0.8951	0.0051	0.8513	0.0061
F-m	0.6715	0.0191	0.8951	0.0051	0.8508	0.0061
S_P	0.6516	0.0554	0.8963	0.0070	0.8289	0.0082
S_{NP}	0.6982	0.0604	0.8939	0.0066	0.8737	0.0092

TABLE VI
TEST CLASSIFICATION RESULTS FOR HIGH LEVEL FEATURES.

Data set	A		B		C	
# neurons	16		13		0	
	mean	std	mean	std	mean	std
Acc	0.6479	0.0061	0.7999	0.0034	0.8303	0.0018
F-m	0.6474	0.0063	0.7998	0.0034	0.8299	0.0017
S_P	0.6640	0.0163	0.7986	0.0098	0.8099	0.0023
S_{NP}	0.6318	0.0192	0.8012	0.0067	0.8507	0.0026

IV. DISCUSSION

Generally, it was found that varying the number of neurons in the hidden layer does not produce a clear winner for classification accuracy, something that was also observed by other researches [4].

We have found that there was a statistically significant reduction in classification accuracy of DNA sequences represented as high level features compared with CODE-4 for all three data sets A, B and C, which is contrary to the findings of [8] where a statistically significant improvements were observed.

However, a direct comparison between the results and those in [8] is not necessarily valid, as our definitions of high level features may differ from the methodology they used. Furthermore, our data set is significantly larger with 872 promoters, compared to 300 promoters used by [8].

The intersting results from our research was the observed effect the types of non-promoter DNA sequences have on the overall classification accuracy and the promoter sensitivity. For CODE-4 representation of DNA, the use of E.coli gene non-promoters (data set B), provided the highest classification accuracy with an overall accuracy of 89.51%, and promoter error rate of 10.37%. This was closely followed by random DNA having the same base frequency as the gene non-promoters (data set C), with an overall accuracy of 85.13% and promoter error rate of 17.11%. Using randomly generated DNA with the same base frequency as the promoters produced poor results, with an overall accuracy of 67.15% and promoter error rate of 34.84%. The significant improvement of accuracy with data sets B and C compared to A indicate that an important feature that the ANN seems to learn to differentiate between promoter and non-promoter is the frequency of bases within the sequences. However, even though the gene (data set B) and rand-gene (data set C) have the same base frequencies, using gene non-promotes produced a higher level of promoter recognition. This would further suggest that the ANN also found a possible interdependence in bases in the gene sequences (that differentiate it more from the promoter sequences), than the random-genes sequences.

Using high level feature representation of the DNA sequences yielded similar trends as the CODE-4 representation. Overall, the classification accuracy was lower compared to CODE-4 representation. Again, it was found that using data sets B and C resulted in a higher classification accuracy compared to data set A. The gene non-promoters resulting in a classification accuracy of 79.99%, and promoter error rate of 20.14%. With random non-promoters the classification accuracy was 83.03% and promoter error rate of 19.02%. Comparing these results with CODE-4 encoding suggest that the high level features do not capture important base interdependences that maybe present in the DNA sequences, possibly preserved by CODE-4 encoded.

Using random DNA sequences with the same base frequency as the promoter for either encoding scheme produced poor results, indicating that the nucleotide frequency plays a pivotal role in distinguishing promoter from non-promoter.

V. Conclusion

The results presented in section III have not replicated the conclusions drawn by [8]. It is observed that using high level feature encoding resulted in lower classification accuracy compared to that when CODE-4 encoding was employed. The opposite to what was stated in [8]. However, since Hirsh et al did not provide clear definitions of their high level features, meaningful comparisons can not be made between their results and ours.

The most significant result coming from this research is that the overall classification accuracy and promoter error rate is largely determined by the type of non-target DNA sequence selected. This was the case whether CODE-4 or high level representation of the DNA sequences was used. The classification accuracy was highest and promoter error rate was lowest when using non-promoters from gene regions of E.coli and random DNA sequences with the same base frequency as the gene non-promoters. When using CODE-4 the gene non-promoter resulted in higher classification accuracy compared to using random-gene non-promoters. However, with the high level features, the reverse was found to be true, with gene non-promoters producing lower classification accuracies compared to random-gene non-promoters.

In addition to a study of optimal network topologies, research questions flowing from this current study include testing the ANN classifiers developed in this paper to identify promoters within a genome or phage by using a sliding window to scan the DNA sequence. This would be a more meaningful measure of the performance of a promoter classifier as the ANN would be presented with fragments of DNA sequences of unknown classification in the laboratory situation. Further work needs to be conducted on different sets of high level features, such as adding additional features and refining the existing features used. Another area of interest is the use of ANNs to differentiate between promoters of different σ-factors: which is of greater use to molecular biologists as it would not only indicate the possibility that a given unclassified DNA sequence is a promoter, but also what type of σ-factor binds to it. Also, a recently developed fast learning technique, namely Extreme Learning Machine (ELM) [18], will be examined in our further study.

VI. Acknowledgements

The authors would like to thank Heladia Salgado for supplying the RegulonDB data set files.

References

[1] C. B. Harley and R. P. Reynolds, "Analysis of E. coli promoter sequences," *Nucl. Acids. Res.*, vol. 15, no. 5, pp. 2334–2361, 1987.

[2] D. K. Hawley and W. R. McClure, "Compilation and analysis of Escherichia coli promoter DNA sequences," *Nucl. Acids. Res.*, vol. 11, no. 8, pp. 2237–2255, 1983.

[3] S. Lisser and H. Margalit, "Compilation of E.coli mRNA promoter sequences," *Nucl. Acids. Res.*, vol. 21, no. 7, pp. 1507–1516, April 1993.

[4] B. Demeler and G. Zhou, "Neural Network optimization for E.coli promoter prediction," *Nucl. Acids. Res.*, vol. 19, no. 7, pp. 1593–1599, April 1991.

[5] A. Lukashin, V. Anshelevich, B. Amirikyan, A. Gragerov, and M. FrankKamenetskii, "Neural network models for promoter recognition," *Journal of Biomolecular Structure and Dynamics*, vol. 6, pp. 1123–1133, 1989.

[6] I. Mahadevan and I. Ghosh, "Analysis of E.coli Promoter Structures using Neural Networks," *Nucl. Acids. Res.*, vol. 22, no. 11, pp. 2158–2165, June 1994.

[7] Q. Ma, J. T. L. Wang, D. Shasha, and C. H. Wu, "DNA Sequence Classification via an Expectation Maximization Algorithm and Neural Networks: A Case Study," *IEEE Transactions on Systems, Man and Cybernetics, part c*, vol. 31, no. 4, pp. 468–475, November 2001.

[8] H. Hirsh and M. Noordewier, "Using background knowledge to improve inductive learning of DNA sequences," in *Artificial Intelligence for Applications, 1994., Proceedings of the Tenth Conference on*, March 1994, pp. 351–357.

[9] M. C. O'Neil, "Escherichia coli promoters: neural networks develop distinct descriptions in learning to search for promoters of different spacing classes," *Nucl. Acids. Res.*, vol. 20, no. 13, pp. 3471–3477, 1992. [Online]. Available: http://nar.oupjournals.org/cgi/content/abstract/20/13/3471

[10] H. Salgado, A. Santos-Zavaleta, S. Gama-Castro, D. Milln-Zrate, E. Daz-Peredo, F. Snchez-Solano, E. Prez-Rueda, C. Bonavides-Martinez, and J. Collado-Vides, "RegulonDB (version 3.2): Transcriptional Regulation and Operon Organization in Escherichia coli K-12," *Nucl. Acids. Res.*, vol. 29, no. 1, pp. 72–74, 2001.

[11] R. Nussinov and G. G. Lennon, "Periodic structurally similar ogligomers are found on one side of the axes of symmetry in the lac, trp, and gal operators," *Journal of Biomolecular Structure and Dynamics*, vol. 2, pp. 237–395, 1984.

[12] G. G. Lennon and R. Nussinov, "Homonyms, synonyms and mutations of the sequence/structure vocabulary." *J Mol Biol.*, vol. 175, no. 3, pp. 425–430, May 1984.

[13] S. Cheung, K. Arndt, and P. Lu, "Correlation of lac operator DNA imino proton exchange kinetics with its function." *Proc Natl Acad Sci U S A.*, vol. 81, no. 12, pp. 3665–3669, June 1984.

[14] P. Lu, S. Cheung, and K. Arndt, "Possible molecular detent in the DNA structure at regulatory sequences." *J Biomol Struct Dyn.*, vol. 1, no. 2, pp. 509–521, Oct 1983.

[15] R. M. Kolpakov and G. Kucherov, "Finding Approximate Repetitions under Hamming Distance," in *ESA*, ser. Lecture Notes in Computer Science, F. M. auf der Heide, Ed., vol. 2161. Springer, 2001, pp. 170–181.

[16] G. Dykes, R. Bambara, K. Marians, and R. Wu, "On the statistical significance of primary structural features found in DNA-protein interaction sites," *Nucl. Acids. Res.*, vol. 2, no. 3, pp. 327–345, 1975. [Online]. Available: http://nar.oupjournals.org/cgi/content/abstract/2/3/327

[17] L. J. Jensen, C. Friis, and D. W. Ussery, "Three views of microbial genomes," *Res Microbiol*, vol. 150, no. 9–10, pp. 773–777, Nov–Dec 1999.

[18] G.-B. Huang, Q.-Y. Zhu, and C.-K. Siew, "Extreme Learning Machine: A New Learning Scheme of Feedforward Neural Networks," in *2004 International Joint Conference on Neural Networks (IJCNN'2004)*. IEEE, July 2004.

Predicting Protein-Protein Interactions Based on Protein-Domain Relationships

Bing Wang[1,2], De-Shuang Huang[1], Peng Chen[1,2], Yunping Zhu[3], and Yixue Li[4]

[1] Intelligent Computing Lab, Hefei Institute of Intelligent Machines, Chinese Academy of Sciences,
Hefei, Anhui, 230031, China
[2] Dept. of Automation, Univ. of Science and Technology of China, Hefei, Anhui, 230026, China
[3] Beijing Institute of Radiation Medicine, Taiping Road 27, Beijing 100850, China
[4] Bioinformatics Center, Shanghai Institutes for Biological Sciences, Chinese Academy of Sciences
320 Yue Yang Road, Shanghai, 200031, China
E-mail: dshuang@iim.ac.cn

Abstract— This paper proposes a new method that can predict the interactions between proteins intermediated by the protein-domain relations. We utilize the lazy expectation maximization (LEM) to compute an improved maximization likelihood estimation (MLE) model. The protein-domain relationships are extruded from Pfam database and the combined data set of Uetz and Ito are used as the source of protein-protein interactions. Finally, the efficiency and the effectiveness of our proposed approach can be validated by a better performance such as the sensitivity of 80.1%, the specificity of 43.5%, and the lesser computational cost.

I. INTRODUCTION

The interactions between proteins play a critical role in the live biologic cells by controlling proteins to perform corresponding functions. Recently, some experimental techniques and computational methods have been developed to study protein-protein interactions [1]-[5]. As the experimental techniques are tedious, time-consuming and labor-intensive, computational approaches are becoming more and more important for researchers to predict whether some proteins interact each other or not. These approaches attempt to deal with the prediction problem of protein-protein interactions based on different biological background knowledge, including genomic information, evolutionary relationships, three-dimensional features, protein sequence properties, and so on. In addition, the prediction method drawn from the relationships between proteins and domains is another way to investigate protein-protein interactions. Domains are modules of protein sequences, which are evolutionarily conserved. Domain can be regarded as a structural or/and functional unit of protein, and each protein can also be characterized by a distinct domain or combination of domains. This is the fundament on which ones can decompose protein-protein interactions into domain-domain interactions. Recently, several new methods have been developed in literatures [6][7]. Deng et al. [8] applied the Maximum Likelihood Estimation (MLE) method to infer the domain-domain interactions from protein-protein interactions, which had been shown to be of robustness in dealing with various experimental errors. But, to the larger scale datasets like interactions between proteins, the computational cost is high and the convergent speed is insufferable.

In this paper, we present a new MLE model and use the lazy expectation maximization (LEM) algorithm to tackle the prediction problem of the protein-protein interactions based on domain-domain interactions. We share the assumptions adopted by most previous researchers that two proteins interact if and only if at least one pair of domains from the two proteins interact and domain-domain interactions are independent with each other. There are, however, many instances that some domain-domain interactions may occur in some protein pairs, but reversely in other protein pairs. So, we utilize an occurring-coefficient, which indicates the probability of the interaction between a pair of domains occurring in a certain proteins pairs, to revise the computational models presented by previous researchers [8]. In our study, we applied an accelerated EM algorithm by selecting only a subset of data cases, which is thought as significant cases for problem solving, to compute in some successive partial E-step iterations. The results demonstrated that this approach is more effective and efficient than other related methods by achieving the sensitivity of 80.1% and the specificity of 43.5%.

This paper is organized as follows. Section II describes our proposed approach in details and its application to the prediction problem of protein-protein interactions. Experimental results are reported in section III. Finally, some conclusive remarks are included in section IV.

II. METHODS

In order to describe our method accurately, we need to make some notations. Let $d_1, d_2, ...d_M$ denote M domains, and $p_1, p_2, ...p_N$ denote N proteins. We say $d_m \in p_i$ if d_m is one of the domains contained in the protein p_i. Let $IP(p_i, p_j)$ and $IP(d_m, d_n)$ denote the probability of protein p_i interacting with protein p_j, and the probability of domain d_m interacting with domain d_n, respectively.

It has been known that protein-protein interactions not only depend on the space structures of the involved proteins, but also depend on the environmental conditions. When we decompose protein-protein interactions into the interactions between domains which form protein pairs, we can detect that some protein pairs containing potentially interacting domains may not interact with each other because they may be expressed at different times during the cell cycle, or may be located at different cell compartments. This exists widely in the database of protein-protein interactions that can be obtained currently. So we must take account of this problem when we apply computational method to resolve the puzzle of predicting the protein-protein interactions. Considering this point, we present a new MLE model as follows:

$$IP(p_i, p_j) = 1.0 - \prod_{d_m \in p_i, d_n \in p_j} (1.0 - \gamma_{mn} IP(d_m, d_n)) \quad (1)$$

where γ_{mn} is an occurring-coefficient that indicates the probability of the interaction between domain pair (d_m, d_n) occurring in a certain protein pairs.

Recently, some researchers claimed that each protein approximately has 5 interacting partners [9]. In this study, we apply the protein interactions data from the result of Uetz and Ito's experimental data. There are only 5719 observed interaction pairs among 6359 proteins in *Saccharomyces cerevisiae*, which possibly exist some errors. So, we denote fp as false positive rate and fn as the false negative rate, in which fp shows that two proteins do not interact in reality but were observed to be interacting in the experiments, and fn shows that two proteins interact in reality but were not observed to be interacting in the experiments. Then, the probability for the observed protein-protein interaction between protein pair (p_i, p_j) can be computed by:

$$P(O_{ij}) = IP(p_i, p_j)(1 - fn) + (1 - IP(p_i, p_j))fp \quad (2)$$

where O_{ij} denotes the interaction between protein pair (p_i, p_j) that can be observed. Thus, the log-likelihood function of the probability of the observed whole proteome interaction data can be written as:

$$\begin{aligned}
\ell &= g(\prod (P(O_{ij}))^{e_{ij}} (1 - P(O_{ij}))^{1-e_{ij}}) \\
&= \sum (e_{ij} g(P(O_{ij})) + (1 - e_{ij}) g(1 - P(O_{ij}))) \quad (3)
\end{aligned}$$

where $e_{ij} = 1$ if the interaction of p_i and p_j is observed, and $e_{ij} = 0$ otherwise. In practice, we adopt the log-likelihood function ℓ, which is the function of parameter $\theta = (IP(d_m, d_n), \gamma_{mn}, fp, fn)$.

We estimate the parameter θ by the lazy expectation maximization (LEM) method, an extension of the EM algorithm [10]. The EM algorithm estimates the unknown parameters of a model iteratively under some initializations. In its general form, the EM algorithm repeats estimation (E) step and maximization (M) step until convergence, where E-step finds the distribution for the unobserved variables given the known values for the observed variables and the current estimate of the parameters, and M-step re-estimates the parameters with maximum likelihood under the assumption that the distribution found in the E-step is correct.

The EM algorithm is a popular method for parameter estimation in a variety of problems involving missing data. However, the EM algorithm often requires significant computational resources and has been dismissed as impractical for larger databases. The LEM algorithm, which was studied by Thiesson et al. [11], applies a partial E-step to speed up the convergence of the standard EM. It is very suitable for a larger scale database of protein-protein interactions because the time spent in the E-step depends linearly on the number of data cases.

The feasibility of the LEM algorithm is based on the assumption that not all data are of equal significance at each iteration. Given completed data cases Y, the LEM algorithm attempts to periodically identify significant cases in a full E-step, and focus on this subset of data to execute the EM algorithm for some successive steps until the next full E-step as schedule. In a word, between big circulations from a full E-step to a M-step, there are several small circulations from a partial E-step to a M-step in the LEM algorithm. In particular, the LEM algorithm has been shown to be able to guarantee to converge to a local or global maximum as the EM algorithm [12].

Let X denote the observed data that are the experimentally observed interactions. Let $Y = X \bigcup Z$ be the complete data including Z, which denotes all the domain-domain interactions for each protein-protein pair. Let A_m be the set of proteins containing domain d_m. Let N_{mn} be the total number of protein pairs between A_m and A_n. Define $Z = \{d_{mn}^{(ij)} | p_i \in A_m, p_j \in A_n, \forall m, n\}$, where $d_{mn}^{(ij)} = 1$ if domain d_m and domain d_n interact in the protein pair (p_i, p_j), and $d_{mn}^{(ij)} = 0$ otherwise. Before we perform the LEM algorithm, we need to initialize the parameters θ, successive partial E-steps times (PT) and a predefined significance threshold (ST). Then, according to a predetermined schedule, we iterate either the full E-step or the lazy E-step before the M-step, as illustrated below.

Initialization: Set θ^0, ST and PT as schedule;

Full E-step: Take the complete data Y;

Step 1: Compute $IP(p_i, p_j)$, $P(O_{ij})$ and the expected log-likelihood ℓ by Eqns. (1), (2) and (3), respectively;

Step 2: Calculate the expectation of interaction probability of each domain-domain pair on the condition of each protein pair based on the current hypothesis θ^t;

$$\begin{aligned}
E(d_{mn}^{(ij)} | Y, \theta^t) &= E(d_{mn}^{(ij)} | O_{ij} = e_{ij}, \theta^t) \\
&= \frac{P(d_{mn}^{(ij)} = 1, O_{ij} = e_{ij} | \theta^t)}{P(O_{ij} = e_{ij} | \theta^t)} \\
&= \frac{IP^{(t)}(d_m, d_n)(1 - fn)^{e_{ij}} fn^{1-e_{ij}}}{P(O_{ij} = e_{ij} | \theta^t)} \\
&= \frac{IP^{(t)}(d_m, d_n)(1 - fn)^{e_{ij}} fn^{1-e_{ij}}}{P^{(t)}(O_{ij})} \quad (4)
\end{aligned}$$

step 3: Identify the significant domain pair using ST, and divide the complete data Y into two subsets: Y_{l_zy} and Y_{l_zy}, where Y_{l_zy} is deemed as significant cases, and Y_{l_zy} otherwise;

Step 4: Aimed to Y_{l_zy}, we obtain $IP_{l\_zy}(p_i, p_j)$, $P_{l\_zy}(O_{ij})$ and log-likelihood ℓ_{l_zy}.

Lazy E-step: Focus on the significance data Y_{l_zy}
  Step 1: Calculate $IP_{l\_zy}(p_i, p_j)$, $P_{l\_zy}(O_{ij})$ and $\_{l\_zy}$;
  Step 2: Compute $E(d_{mn}^{(ij)}|Y_{l\_zy}, \theta^t)$;
  Step 3: Construct $= \_{l\_zy} + \_{l\_zy}$;

M-step: Update the parameter as follows:

$$IP^{(t+1)}(d_m, d_n) = \frac{1}{N_{mn}} \sum_{i \in\ m,j \in\ n} E(d_{mn}^{(ij)}|Y, \theta^t)$$

$$= \frac{IP^{(t)}(d_m, d_n)}{N_{mn}} \sum_{i \in\ m, j \in\ n} \frac{(1-fn)^{e_{ij}} fn^{1-e_{ij}}}{P^{(t)}(O_{ij})} \quad (5)$$

If the pervious step is the partial E-step, Y is replaced by Y_{l_zy}.

$$\gamma_{mn} = \frac{N_{mn}^+}{N_{mn}} \quad (6)$$

where N_{mn}^+ is the number of interacting proteins pairs containing the domain pair $(d_m.d_n)$ whose interacting probability is over a certain threshold.

Circulation: If the recurrent times less than PT, go to the lazy E-step, else to the full E-step. Repeat the circulations until the value of the likelihood function is almost unchanged.

III. METHODS

A. Source of Data and Parameter Selection

We focus on the yeast *Saccharomyces cerevisiae* organism. The protein-protein interactions data are obtained from the combined data set of Uetz and Ito (as shown in Table I). Domain information can be obtained from Pfam database [13]. Pfam contains a large collection of multiple sequence alignments and profile hidden Markov models (HMM) covering the majority of protein domains. Proteins for which no domain information is available are classified as superdomains, and those domains that always coexist in proteins are merged as one domain as well.

TABLE I
SOURCE OF PROTEIN-PROTEIN INTERACTIONS DATA

	Uetz	Ito	Combined	Overlap
Number of PPI	1445	4475	5719	201

False positive and false negative cases, first of all, must be considered since there are many errors in the existing protein-protein interactions data. The previous work has discovered that different values of fp and fn affect little the specificity and the sensitivity of the prediction of protein-protein interactions by MLE model. We therefore fix fp=2.5E-4 and fn=0.80 through the whole computing process as Deng et al. did [8]. In order to derive the LEM algorithm, it is critical to set the significance threshold (ST) and successive partial E-steps times (PT) as schedule. If ST is chosen as a lower value, only a few cases will be considered in the lazy E-step and the convergence time will be longer. On the other hand, a too large ST will lead to overfull cases being used for the lazy E-step and the advantage of the LEM will become not clear. It is known that the pace of convergence will be smaller with the running of the algorithm. The setting of PT is important because it is unreasonable if the effectiveness of convergence cannot offset the runtime of the additional lazy steps. In order to select the two parameters reasonably, we import an index, denoting as speedup (SU), which can weight the effect of the method by the quotient of the runtime divided by that of the standard EM algorithm. By comparing the speedup, we can set the ST value to 85% and 3 successive partial E-steps after each full E-step for schedule (as shown in Fig.1).

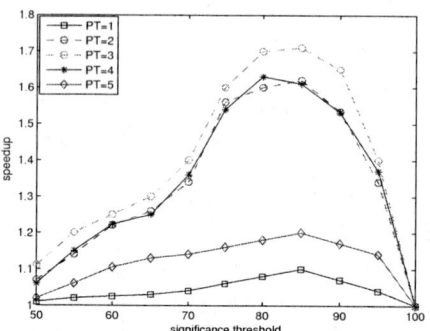

Fig. 1. The Comparison of Speedups Based on Different STs and PTs

B. Results

We obtain many novel protein-protein interactions not detected by Utez and Ito, some of which cannot be predicted by the previous predicting approaches. For example, ADE2 protein (Phosphoribosylaminoimidazole carboxylase) has 24 pieces of interaction information in the experimental data, and a same number in two databases of protein physical interaction of MIPS [14] and DIP [15]. We consider the interactions between ADE2 and other proteins to have higher reliability because the overlap of the three data is very high (23/24). Deng et al. calculated the probability of ADE2 interacting with other proteins, and there are about 35 pairs more likely interacting each other. Using the method proposed in this paper, we can predict out other interactions existing in protein ADE2 (as shown in Table II).

Since there are very few domain-domain interactions known currently, it is difficult to estimate the accuracies of the methods predicting the protein-protein interactions based on protein-domain relationships. However, we can evaluate the accuracy using two indexes, i.e., specificity (SP) and sensitivity (SN), where SP is defined as the ratio of the number of matched interactions between the predicted set and the observed set over the total number of predicted interactions, and SN is the ratio of the number of matched interactions over the total number of observed interactions. We compare the prediction ability of our approach to predict protein-protein interactions against AM [5] and MLE [8]. By fixing the threshold at 0.80, we can achieve 80.1% for the SN and 43.5%

TABLE II
SOURCE OF PROTEIN-PROTEIN INTERACTIONS DATA$

Partner	Description of the interacting proteins+
LSC2	Beta subunit of succinyl-CoA ligase
FUI1*	High affinity uridine permease
ENO2*	Enolase II
ERR2*	Protein of unknown function, has similarity to enolases
ENO1*	Enolase I
GCD7*	Beta subunit of the translation initiation factor eIF2B, the guanine-nucleotide exchange factor for eIF2
GCD2*	Delta subunit of the translation initiation factor eIF2B, the guanine-nucleotide exchange factor for eIF2
THO1	Suppressor of the Transcriptional (T) defect of Hpr1 (H) by Overexpression (O); (putative) involved in transcription
YMR003W	Hypothetical ORF
SMK1#	Mitogen-activated protein kinase required for spore morphogenesis that is expressed as a middle sporulation-specific gene
DBF2*	Ser/Thr kinase involved in transcription and stress response
SEC12*	Guanine nucleotide exchange factor (GEF);
YLR427W	Protein of unknown function
YPR118W*	Methylthioribose-1-phosphate isomerase

$ Table II only contains the partial predicted interacting partners;
+The description of protein partners is quoted from GSD database;
*The partners were also predicted by Deng et al.;
The partner can be observed by experiments.

for the SP. Fig. 2 shows that the LEM method outscores in both the SP and the SN than the two related approaches of the MLE and the AM.

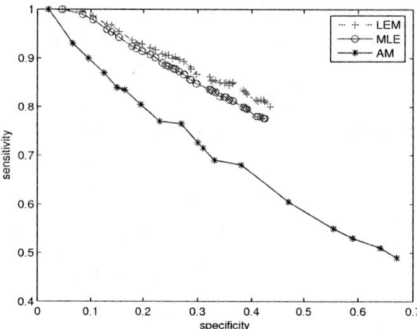

Fig. 2. The Comparison of Specificity (SP) and Sensitivity (SN) for Our Approach and the MLE as well as the AM

IV. CONCLUSIONS

In this paper, we adopted an occurring-coefficient, which indicated whether the interaction between domain pair occurs or not, to reconstruct the MLE model. The results we got suggest that it is a feasible way. Considering a large scale of protein-protein interaction database, we chose a fast convergent algorithm to deal with the task of predicting the interacting proteins. The LEM method assumes that the interacting probability of all domains is not so significant at each iteration of the EM method. In the partial E-step, only a subset of data is updated. The speedup depends on the schedule for lazy iterations and the significance threshold. Consequently, we obtained a better performance by carefully choosing these parameters. Here, we could only predict the direct interactions between proteins, but this method might extend to study indirect interactions if the biologic significations of domains have been mined much more. Furthermore, as more and more protein-protein interactions are drawn, it can be inferred that the effectiveness and the efficiency of our proposed method will be improved steadily and greatly.

ACKNOWLEDGMENT

This work was supported by the National Science Foundation of China (Nos.60472111 and 60405002) and Chinese Human Liver Proteome Project (No.2004BA711A21).

REFERENCES

[1] Ito, T., Tashiro, K. and Muta, S. et al. "Toward a protein-protein interaction map of the budding yeast: A comprehensive system to examine two-hybrid interactions in all possible combinations between the yeast proteins". Proc. Natl. Acad. Sci. 97: 1143-1147. 2000.
[2] Ito, T., Chiba, T., and Ozawa, R. et al. "A Comprehensive two-hybrid analysis to explore the yeast protein interactome". Proc. Natl. Acad. Sci. 98: 4569-4574. 2001.
[3] Ito, T., Chiba, T., and Yoshida, M. "Exploring the protein interactome using comprehensive two hybrid projects". Trends Biotechnol. 19: S23-S27. 2001.
[4] Uetz, P., Giot, L. and Cagney, G. et al. "A Comprehensive analysis of protein-protein interactions in Saccharomyces cerevisiae". Nature 403: 623-627. 2000.
[5] Sprinzak, E. and Margalit, H. "Correlated sequence-signatures as markers of protein-protein interaction". J. Mol. Biol. 311: 681-692. 2001.
[6] Ng SK, Zhang Z, Tan SH "Integrative approach for computationally inferring protein domain interactions". Bioinformatics. 19(8):923-9.2003.
[7] Han.,D., Kim, HS. And Seo,J. et al. "A Domain Combination Based Probabilistic Framework for Protein-Protein Interaction Prediction". Genome Informatics. 14: 250-259.2003.
[8] Deng, M., Mehta, S. and Sun, F. et al. "Inferring domain-domain interactions from protein-protein interactions". Genome Research, 12:1540-1548. 2002.
[9] Sprinzak E, Sattath S, Margalit H. "How reliable are experimental protein-protein interaction data?" J Mol Biol. 327(5):919-23. 2003
[10] Dempster, A.P., Laid, N.M., and Rubin, D.B. "Maximum likelihood from incomplete data via the EM algorithm (with discussion)". J. Roy. Statist. Soc. Ser. B. 39: 1-38. 1977.
[11] Thiesson, B., Meek, C. and Heckerman, D. "Accelerating EM for Large Databases". Machine Learning, 45: 279-299, 2001.
[12] Neal,R., Hinton,G. "A view of the EM algorithm that justifies incremental,sparse, and other variants". In M.Jordan (Ed.), Learning in Graphical Models. pp.355-371. The Netherlands, Kluwer Academic Publishers.
[13] Bateman,A., Coin,L., and Durbin,R. et al. "The Pfam protein families database". Nucleic Acids Res., 32:D138-D141. 2004.
[14] Mewes H.W. , Amid C. and Arnold R. et al. "MIPS: analysis and annotation of proteins from whole genomes". Nucleic Acids Res.,32 Database issue:D41-4, 2004.
[15] Salwinski L., Miller C.S. and Smith A.J. et al. "The Database of Interacting Proteins: 2004 update". . Nucleic Acids Res.,32 Database issue:D449-51. 2004

Automated Heuristic Growing of Neural Networks for Nonlinear Time Series Models

Alex Kalos

Physical Sciences, Corporate Research & Development
The Dow Chemical Company
Freeport, Texas, 77541, USA
E-mail: akalos@dow.com

Abstract— In this paper, we present a method for automatically selecting the optimal architecture of feedforward neural networks to build nonlinear time series models. A heuristic method is used to do an exhaustive search of all possible input/output combinations, while adjusting the lag times and the number of nodes in a fully connected single hidden layer network. Levenberg-Marquardt optimization is performed using the stop-search method of cross-validation. Statistics are maintained for all optimized structures which permits post-processing based on performance criteria for final model selection. The methodology is applied to a case study for developing multi-variate autoregressive models for the day-ahead forecasting of electricity prices.

Index Terms— automated neural networks growing

I. INTRODUCTION

Classical feedforward neural networks are known to be universal approximators [1]. As a result they have enjoyed wide spread use in many areas from research, to banking and financing and industrial applications. However, to a large extent they are considered by many as highly specialized and their design still largely remains in the domain of highly skilled experts. This in turn provides a barrier to their acceptance in mainstream data mining applications.

Several reasons contribute to this, paramount of which are: (a) the difficulty in interpreting the results (i.e., why is the network making this prediction?), and (b) the trial-and-error nature of the process required to design the architecture (i.e., setup a neural network). This work focuses on the latter problem. Recently, researchers have worked at addressing various aspects of this problem. Efforts have gone into self-tuning or adapting some of the parameters; such as a method to auto-tune the saturation function of neural networks [2], and the use of genetic algorithms to determine the number of inputs and the order of the polynomial for building fuzzy polynomial neural networks [3] as an extension to the group method of data handling (GMDH) [4]. Other efforts have gone into enhancing the optimization algorithms, such as robust and adaptive training algorithms for improving capabilities of self-organizing maps and radial basis functions (RBF) networks [5], or using entirely different approaches to minimization, such as the use of genetic programming to vary the weights and bias terms essentially as an alternative to standard back propagation [6]. Further efforts focus on the direct manipulation of network structural elements, such as automatic basis function selection in RBF networks [7], the use of second-order derivatives of the error surface to guide in pruning nodes from a network in order to determine optimal network structure [8], and the use of evolutionary computing for co-operative co-evolution of sub-components to evolve neural network structures [9]. There is also a lot of literature that addresses self-organizing maps (SOM), or self-learning networks and most of this is in regards to Kohonen type networks [10], [11], [12].

Here, we deal with classical neural networks, i.e., fully populated, feedforward networks, the type found in most commercially available packages. The application area is for nonlinear time series forecasting models for energy price indices (natural gas and electrical price indices). In this case, the networks are set up as auto-regressive models with additional inputs. However, the methodology is applicable to static feed-forward structures as well.

II. METHODOLOGY

Our aim is to find a network that can make a step-ahead prediction for an energy index (e.g., the natural gas opening price on the New York Mercantile Exchange (NYMEX)), based on historical data of that index as well as other energy price indices and related data. We would like to (a) find and include in the model (1) only the relevant inputs (i.e., those that improve the predictive power of the model), and (b) determine the optimal structure of the model (i.e., the model that has the appropriate lag steps and the appropriate number of nodes in the hidden layer:

$$\hat{y}(t) = f(y(t-1)...y(t-l), x_k(t-1)..x_k(t-L_k)) \quad (1)$$

where, $k=1...p$, p is the number of x (input) variables, y is the output variable, t is time, l and L_k are the lag steps for the y and each of the x variables respectively, and $\hat{y}$ is the predicted output. Essentially, we develop nonlinear multi-variate time series models of energy prices, and the modeling and prediction is performed from the moving window on some selected variates.

The basic approach is to put the construction of the network and its training in a loop. At each step of the loop, we build, test and optimize a network, by adding a different element to the network structure. An element is defined as either a step into the lag matrix for a particular input, or a hidden node. Once each structure is optimized with respect to this element, the performance statistics for this structure are recorded, and a new element is added. The process is repeated, until all possible combinations have been tried. At the end we have a collection of different networks. Then it is a simple matter to sort the collection according to performance criteria and pick the best network structure. In practice, we find that several networks lead the pack and usually there is a small collection that is clearly superior to the rest. If desired, this collection can then be used as a model ensemble, to provide a collective output (e.g., the mean of the ensemble) instead of a value from just a single model.

A. Data Pre-processing and Parameter Initialization

We separate the data into three sets: the *training* set (which consists of the *estimation* and *validation* subsets), and the *test* set. Since we are building time series models, we partition the data into sets that are consecutive in time: the estimation subset precedes the validation subset, which in turn precedes the test set. This kind of partitioning allows to objectively evaluate our models' performance in the future. The only question is what percent of the available data we place into each of the sets. To guide us in this task, we run a standard Box-Jenkins [13] univariate linear time series analysis in an attempt to build autoregressive (AR) type models on the target output variable. By examining the spectral density plot we can get an estimate of the periodicity in the data, and thus select subsets such that each spans at least one complete cycle. In any case, we try to adhere as much as possible to the 80/20 split [14] between the training and test sets, as well between the training subsets, i.e., 60:20:20 for estimation, validation, and test sets respectively. In addition, inspection of the autocorrelation function plot can provide a good estimate on the upper bound of the lag steps (Lmax) that we will consider for our nonlinear models. The default value of Lmax is set to 12, which we found empirically is generally adequate for the class of problems in this study. Visual inspection of the time series plot reveals obvious outliers or errors in the data and such erroneous data is deleted from the data set. Finally, if needed, the data is smoothed using moving averages. Difference plots of various orders are made to determine whether models of the difference time series should be attempted instead of the original time series. The final data series of target output variable as well as all potential input variables are standardized to avoid instabilities in the resulting neural network models [1].

B. Network Growing Algorithm

1) Parameter Estimation

The Levenberg-Marquardt (LM) [15] optimization method is used for parameter estimation [16]. This method is a hybrid of the Gauss-Newton (NG) conjugate-gradient method and of the steepest descent (SD) method, as a result it works well for ill-defined minimization problems (i.e., where the Hessian is ill-defined [1]). Equation (2) shows the learning law for the LM method:

$$\Delta_w = -(J^T J + \lambda I)^{-1} J^T \varepsilon \qquad (2)$$

where ε is the error vector, J is the Jacobian of the error vector with respect to the weights, J^T is the transpose of the Jacobian, I is the identity matrix and λ is the control parameter. As λ approaches zero, LM behaves more like GN which assumes that the error function is linear. This is not a bad assumption when the error is close to a minimum. If a change in the weight matrix (Δ_w) results in lower error, λ is divided by 10, which results in larger leaps toward the minimum. On the other hand, if a change in the weights results in greater error, which inevitably happens when the linearity assumption breaks down, λ is multiplied by 10 and as it increases, the second term in (2) dominates, making LM behave more a like the SD method, resulting in smaller step changes down the error gradient. The robustness of LM is due to this switching between the two modes, which ensures escaping from being trapped in local minima, with quick search at near minimum conditions. The LM is preferred over standard back propagation [17], which is strictly a steepest descent method, and thus more prone to getting stuck in local minima, particularly if the momentum parameter is not set or varied properly. Also, in LM λ is manipulated automatically, so LM requires less manual tuning of its parameters and so it is preferred especially in this type of application which requires a large number of unattended runs.

The early stopping (or stop-search) method of cross-validation is used for determining the optimal set of weights for a given structure [1],[18],[19]. With this method (see Figure 1), the weights are adjusted during training on the basis of the root mean-squared error (RMSE) shown in (3), of the *estimation* data set, but the accepted set of weights is that which corresponds to the minimum RMSE for the *validation* data set.

$$RMSE = \sqrt{\frac{1}{N}\sum_{i=1}^{N}(y_i - f(w_i, x_{ki}))^2} \qquad (3)$$

for $k=1...p$, where p is the number of x (input) variables, y is the measured output variable, N is the number of (x_{ki}, y_i) observations, w is the weight vector determined during optimization, and f is the neural network model. This method of partitioning the data sets and training has stood the test of time – models continue to work well for over two years after initial deployment without re-training. At the end of the training for a particular structure, we maintain the RMSE as well as the correlation-coefficient from regressing the actual vs. the calculated values for all three data sets (estimation, validation, and test). Performance against the test set is from data never before seen by the training algorithm and which is also considerably later in the future with respect to the estimation data set.

For each run, in addition to the performance statistics, we also maintain information about the structure (the actual combination of input/output variables, and number of nodes in the hidden layer), the training record, which includes the set of weights at each iteration, and the iteration number that corresponds to the returned set of weights. If this number is less than the maximum number of iterations (Imax), then it is considered that the minimization converged. If convergence is not reached, a flag is set for the run, but no attempt is made to extend the iterations. Later, during the post-processing step, the convergence flags are examined. If none of the selected "best" models have their non-convergence flag set, there is no need to do anything. On the other hand, if any of the chosen models have not converged, this means that they can do even better, and thus they can be trained further. Since we maintain the training records, we could resume optimization from the point where training stopped. In practice however, we find that non-converged models are not among the top performers and so there is no need to re-train further. The default value of Imax=20 was determined empirically as adequate for the current study.

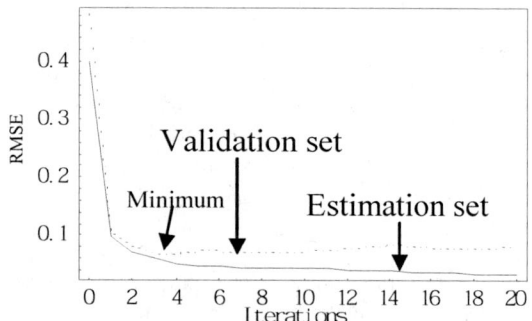

Fig. 1. Illustration of the Stop-Search Method of Cross-Validation.

2) Determining the Lag Structure

For a given input/output variable combination the lag structure is kept fixed during the training and during the search for the optimal number of nodes. The number of lag steps that is used for each combination is determined as follows: We start by the setting the number of lag steps to the maximum number, Lmax. For autoregressive models (i.e., where we have just the output (y), and no input (x) variables), this means that there will be Lmax number of network inputs (the Lmax lag steps of the y variable, y(t-1), y(t-2), ... y(t-Lmax)). In the case of autoregressive models with extra inputs (ARX), we start with Lmax lag steps for each of the x variables, in addition to the y variable, e.g., y(t-1), y(t-2), ... y(t-Lmax), x1(t-1), x2(t-2), ... x2(t-Lmax), etc. We do not include any data from time t=0 even for the x variables, because for our purpose of forecasting future values, these data will not be available during runtime.

We begin by setting the number of hidden nodes to zero and we estimate the weights. This amounts to running standard linear regression and the weights correspond to the linear regression coefficients. Since our data is normalized, the magnitude of the coefficients can be compared on a relative basis. We essentially throw out a lagged input whose coefficient's absolute value is below a certain threshold (0.15 by default, or 15%). This results in a flexible lag structure which is not necessarily sequential (e.g., x(t-1) and x(t-3) may be selected instead of x(t-1) and x(t-2)), although in general, the correlation strength drops monotonically as you go back in time. This also allows for different variables to have different number of lags. Using linear methodology for pre-selecting the lag structure may not be strictly valid, but in practice we have found this to be a reasonable approach. Our aim is to pre-select the minimal number of lagged nodes that will have the best chance of contributing to the nonlinear model, while preventing over-determination of the system. Although there is no guarantee that such rejected lag nodes may not prove to be good predictors in a nonlinear model, in our experiments we did not encounter a situation where this was the case. The end result is a pruned set of lags, which at least for the data under study here, is generally at most 6 or 7 lag steps. This then forms the basis for the nonlinear models.

3) Determining the Number of Nodes

The aim here is to build a fully populated single-layer feedforward neural network. After the lag structure has been determined for a particular combination of variables, we begin by adding one hidden node at a time. The procedure is the same for AR and ARX models. We optimize the weights as described in the *Parameter Estimation* section, store the performance statistics, add another node and repeat. At each step of this process we compare the RMSE of the validation data set with that of the previous step. If there is improvement, i.e., the new RMSE value is lower than the previous one, we add yet another node, up until a maximum number of nodes (Nmax), or until there is no improvement. We retain the number of nodes that gives the lowest RMSE for the validation data set. A value of Nmax=10 was determined empirically as suitable for the current study. As the network grows either through the addition of nodes or lags, it is possible to run into an over-determination, where the model has more capacity that can be justified by the data. In this case, as error is returned and we stop growing further in that direction. In some cases, it might be possible to add more nodes if we were to cut back on the lag steps, but at the moment, the lag structure is fixed as explained earlier for each input/output set combination. This is a potential area for improvement in the current algorithm.

4) Selecting Inputs

Because we are interested in an exhaustive search, by default the algorithm sets up a list that consists of all possible combinations of the x variables; all single variables, e.g., (x1, x2, x3), all pairs (x1,x2), (x2,x3), (x1,x3), all triplets, all quartets, etc. This can result in a very large number of runs. There is an option to specify a smaller subset and thus restrict the search space. However, if during our pre-processing we find that some variables are highly inter-correlated, it is easier to simply eliminate redundant variables at that stage, and then let the algorithm take over, rather than manually creating candidate variable sets at this point.

C. Model Selection

At the end of the network growth phase, we have a report which consists of the statistics maintained throughout the run for each of the structures. We can sort the selection in various ways. Doing single sorts by RMSE of estimation, validation, and test sets allows to examine the top *n*% of best performers in each category, and by generating an intersection of the winners in each of the three categories, we can identify the models that stood up well to estimation, validation, and testing. Alternatively, we may limit our sorting to just the best performers in the test set. After all, this is the best measure of performance against completely unseen data and this sets our expectation for future forecasts.

Often we find that more than one model has acceptable performance for our purposes, so we may choose one over the other based on domain-specific knowledge. For example, the data for one of the input variables may not be available as a frequently as another at runtime, so in this case we would choose the model that has the more readily accessible inputs. Alternatively, we may choose to use all of the models, and for our runtime application, return the mean of the ensemble, rather than a point prediction. This has the further advantage that, provided we have a sufficient number of models in the ensemble, we can also generate consensus statistics which give a kind of "confidence" measure of the forecasts. Finally, we can use the statistics generated during the growth phase as a way of assessing the modeling power of the input variables, by examining histograms of the frequency of occurrence of each variable in the top performing models. For example, if we make such a histogram for say the top *n*=50% of the models, we find that most of the variables have similar frequency of occurrence. As *n* decreases, we see that some variables start to drop off and eventually only those inputs that have the greatest modeling power survive in the best of the best.

D. Implementation

We perform our initial data exploration and classic Box-Jenkins linear time series analysis using JMP [20]. The setup and training of the neural networks is done using the *Mathematica* Neural Network add-on package [21]. The heuristics for the growth algorithm are also implemented in *Mathematica*, as a wrapper around functions defined in the commercial package. The advantage of this approach is that the package itself is robust and includes a variety of pre-coded optimization methods, but it is also possible to incorporate custom methods. Since the package is setup essentially as a set of callable functions, it presents and ideal environment for algorithm development and experimentation.

Furthermore, there are facilities to build up a regressor which can then be passed to the neural network optimization functions. The regressor is what is used to specify the lag structure, i.e., how many and which lag steps each variable has. This is a big time saver since the data can be kept in the raw flat column/row format without the need to explicitly unfold each column to accommodate various lags.

III. CASE STUDY

The data set consists of daily values of on-peak and off-peak electricity prices from various regions in the United States from the Electric Reliability Council of Texas (ERCOT) database [22], as well as natural gas prices from the New York Mercantile Exchange (NYMEX) database [23]. The input/output variables used are shown in Table I. The goal is to develop a model to forecast the day-ahead on-peak electricity price in the southern region of the United States.

TABLE I
Variables used in Case Study

Variable	Description
x1	Seller on-peak electricity price
x2	North USA on-peak electricity price
x3	Houston USA on-peak electricity price
x4	West USA on-peak electricity price
x5	North USA off-peak electricity price
x6	Houston USA off-peak electricity price
x7	West USA off-peak electricity price
x8	South USA off-peak electricity price
x9	NYMEX natural gas opening price
x10	NYMEX natural gas high price
x11	NYMEX natural gas low price
x12	NYMEX natural closing price
y	South USA on-peak electricity price

The data spans from 8-March-2002 to 24-Feb-2004, a total of 493 data points with a 64%:18%:18% split between the estimation, validation and test sets respectively.

A total of 4095 models were automatically evaluated. The calculation took approximately 12 hours of wall clock time on a 1500MHz Intel(R) Pentium(R) M processor with 1GB RAM. The root mean-squared error of the top 40 models based on performance on the validation data set is plotted in Figure 2. A summary of the top 10 models based on the validation data set is shown in Table II.

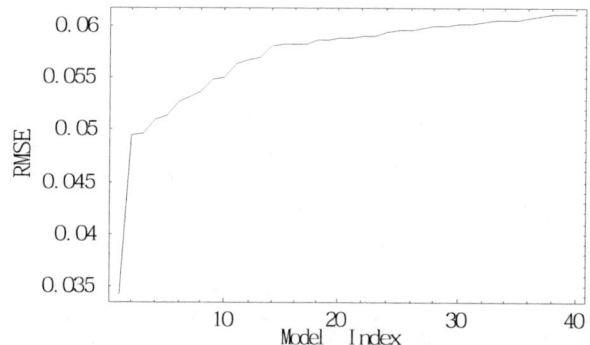

Fig. 2. Performance of the top 40 models against the validation data set.

The model that performs best against the validation data has an RMSE of 0.034, it has 5 inputs variables (x2, x4, x5, x7, x12) each with 4 lag steps in addition to the 4 lag steps in the output variable which are also used as inputs. The neural network has 3 nodes in the hidden layer. This model is clearly differentiated from the rest. The next two best models each have error of approximately 0.05 and use inputs (x3, x4, x5, x8, x11, x12) and (x1, x3, x4, x5, x8. x10). The next seven models have error less than 0.055. The error of the subsequent 30 models gradually increases leveling off around 0.06.

Evaluating the models based on performance on the test data set, i.e., on data not seen during training, allows us to assess how the models will perform in the future, revealing a different picture. The single best model based on performance from each of the data sets (estimation, validation, and test sets) is shown in Table III and in Figure 3. The data plotted in the figure span the entire time, including the estimation, validation, and test sets.

TABLE II
Summary of Top 10 Models According to the Validation Data Set

#	RMSE	Num. Inputs	Input Number
1	0.0342	5	2, 4, 5, 7, 12
2	0.0495	6	3, 4, 5, 8, 11, 12
3	0.0496	6	1, 3, 4, 5, 8, 10
4	0.0510	6	1, 4, 5, 6, 8, 9
5	0.0514	6	1, 2, 4, 7, 9, 10
6	0.0527	5	1, 4, 8, 10, 12
7	0.0530	7	1, 2, 3, 4, 5, 6, 9
8	0.0536	5	4, 6, 8, 11, 12
9	0.0548	3	1, 4, 12
10	0.0550	7	1, 4, 5, 6, 7, 10, 12

In the following discussion a model is considered "best" in a category, if it has the least error (lowest RMSE value). The table lists each model's RMSE (and the R-squared value in parenthesis), as well as the number of inputs, p, and the input indices.

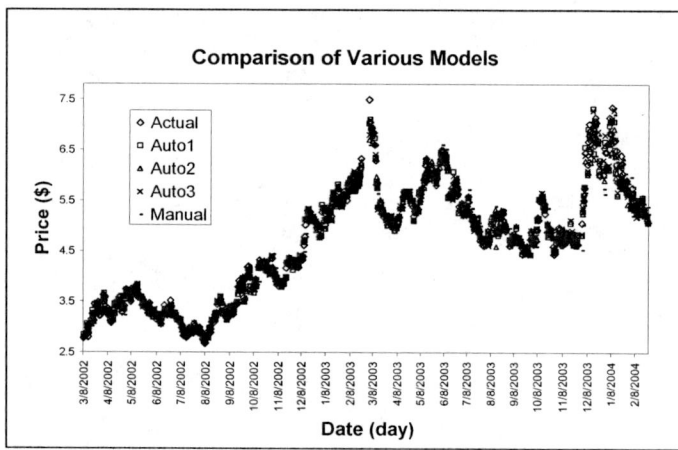

Fig. 3. Comparison of model predictions to the actual data.

Model *auto1* has the least error and better correlation based on the test data set. Model *auto1* uses 6 input variables and is the best based on test data, whereas model *auto2* ranks best according to the estimation data. Model *auto2* uses all 12 input variables and has the lowest RMSE value in the table, however it is second in rank among the three models with respect to the test data set. And while model *auto3* which uses 5 input variables has the lowest error against validation data, it's the worst among the three against test data. In fact, as compared to all other models on the basis of their performance against test data, model *auto3*'s rank is 3857.

TABLE III
Comparison of Best Models According to Various Data Sets

Model	p	RMSE (R-squared)			Inputs
		Est.	Val.	Test	
Auto1	6	0.0307 (0.92)	0.0691 (0.72)	0.0469 (0.72)	1, 3, 4, 8, 11, 12
Auto2	12	0.0197 (0.89)	0.0675 (0.74)	0.0597 (0.61)	1, 2, 3, 4, 5, 6, 7, 8, 9, 10, 11, 12
Auto3	5	0.0308 (0.97)	0.0342 (0.93)	0.0754 (0.66)	2, 4, 5, 7, 12
Manual	4	0.0438 (0.93)	0.0691 (0.71)	0.0549 (0.65)	1, 2, 7, 8

In addition to the models discovered by the automated approach, Table III also shows a model which was discovered previously via manual efforts by trial and error. It uses 4 inputs with 6 lags for each input and 3 hidden nodes. As compared to the other models in the table, the *manual* model is not a bad performer; it is second only to our best model, *auto1*, on the basis of test data. Still, its rank among the best test performers is 524 (in the top 13%).

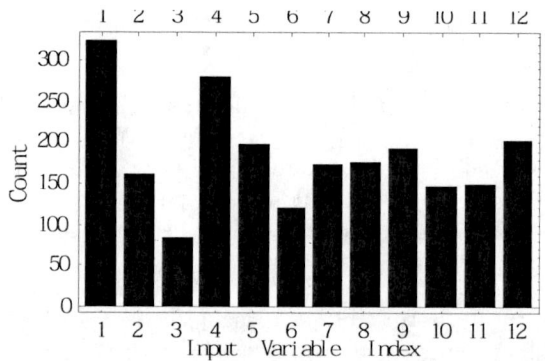

Fig. 4. Bar chart of the number of times each input variable appears in the top 400 models based on the validation data set.

Initially, we had also discovered manually a variant of model *auto2* (with 6 lag steps), since our first attempt was to use all 12 inputs. We eventually abandoned it however, after a lot of trial-and-error, in favor of the 4-input model whose performance based on the test set is slightly better than that of *auto2*, and it is a less complex model. Another use of the statistics collected during training is to plot bar charts of the frequency of occurrence of each input variable in subsets of the models. For example, if we examine the top 400 models based on the least RMSE with validation data (Figure 4), we see that inputs 1, 4, 12, 5, and 9 are most prevalent followed by inputs 8 and 7 and then 2, 11, 10, 6, 3. If we examine the top 40 models again with respect to validation data performance (Figure 5), we see most of the input variables that are prevalent among the top 400 models are prevalent here also, although their order is different. The order of prevalence now is: 4, 1, 12, 5, 8, 7, 2, 11, 9, 6, 3, 10. These bar charts can be useful when trying to decide which models to use from the many available with comparable performance. We would choose models whose variables are more prevalent during the growth phase than others.

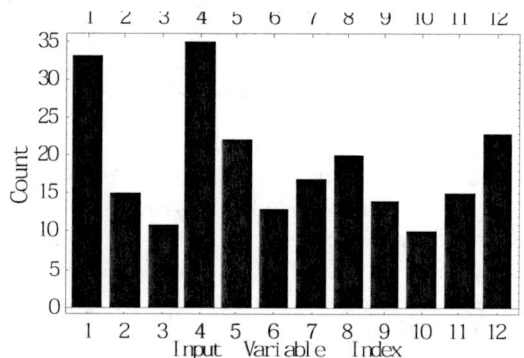

Fig. 5. Bar chart of the number of times each input variable appears in the top 40 models based on the validation data set.

IV. CONCLUSION

It is often said that developing neural networks is as much an art as it is a science. This stems from the fact that even though they can be used to solve many different kinds of problems, including classification and function approximation, for certain applications a fair amount of tweaking of the parameters is necessary. The evaluation of the outcome of these modifications is discovered generally via a lot of trial and error; changing this or that and seeing if it improves the results or not. After working on many different types of problems, one acquires experience so the setup of subsequent problems becomes easier and faster. Still, this manual approach is quite time consuming.

The approach described here essentially automates this trial-and-error process by encapsulating some of the heuristics that have been acquired over time as well as reported by many in the field. Tweaking and testing various options is done by the computer, reporting back the results to the researcher who may then pick the best solution. Furthermore, since usually several models prove to have comparable modeling power, one can choose the best model (or set of models) meeting other domain-dependent criteria. The reality is that via a strictly manual mode we often find a model that is good enough and move on. The automated heuristic growing method affords us the "patience" to keep looking for even better solutions, or at the very least, provide us with options that may be suitable alternatives for our application. There are a lot of opportunities for improvements in the method, particularly in the dynamic adjustment of lag steps as nodes are added. Yes, this method is computationally intensive because it is an exhaustive search of all possible models for a given set of inputs and outputs. However, today's improvements in hardware and software make this possible within a timeframe that is reasonable for many off-line (non real-time) problems. It's a gain in personal time at the expense of computing time. Finally, the methodology can be easily implemented as a short code module in commercially available mathematical/numerical packages.

ACKNOWLEDGMENT

The author would like to thank Dr. Arthur Kordon for his insightful discussions.

REFERENCES

[1] S. Haykin, *Neural Networks: A Comprehensive Foundation*, Second Edition, Prentice Hall, New Jersey, 1999
[2] C-T. Chen and W-D. Chang, "A Feedforward Neural Network with Function Shape Auto-tuning", *Neural Networks*, Vol. 9, No. 4, pp.627-641, 1996.
[3] S-K. Oh and W. Pedrycz, "A new approach to self-organizing multi-layer fuzzy polynomial neural networks based on genetic optimization", *Advanced engineering Infomatics*, 18, pp. 29-39, 2004.
[4] A.G. Ivahnenko, "Polynomial Theory of Complex Systems", *IEEE Trans Systems Man. Cybernet.*, 12, pp 364-378, 1971.
[5] I. Pitas, C. Kotropoulos, N. Nikolaidis, and A. Bors, "Robust and Adaptive Techniques in Self-Organizing Neural Networks", *Nonlinear Analysis, Theory & Applications*, Vol. 30, No. 7, pp 4517-4528, 1997.
[6] D. B. Fogel, L. J. Fogel, and V. W. Porto, "Evolving Neural Networks", *Biol. Cybern.*, 66, pp. 487-493, 1990.
[7] A. Ghodi and D. Schuurmans, "Automatic basis selection techniques for RBF networks", *Neural Networks*, 16, pp. 809-816, 2003.
[8] R. J. Poppi and D. L. Massart, "The optimal brain surgeon for pruning neural network architecture applied to multivariate calibration", *Analytica Chimica Acta*, 375, pp. 187-195, 1998.
[9] N. Garcia-Pedrajas, C. Hervas-Martinez, and J. Munoz-Perz, "Multi-objective cooperative coevolution of artificial neural networks (multi-objective cooperative networks)", *Neural Networks*, 15, pp. 1259-1278 (2004).
[10] T. Kohonen, *Self-Organizing Maps*, Springer, Berlin, 1997.
[11] G. Leng, G. Prasad, and T.M. McGinnity, "An on-line algorithm for creating self-organizing neural networks", *Neural Networks*, 17, pp.487-493, 2004.
[12] B. Hammer, A. Micheli, A. Sperduti, and M. Strickert, "Recursive self-organizing network models" *Neural Networks*, 17, pp. 1061-1085, 2004.
[13] G. Box, G. Jenkins, and G. Reinsel, *Time Series Analysis - Forecasting and Control*, Third Edition., Pearson Education, Inc, 1994.
[14] M. Kearns, "A bound on error of cross validation using the approximation and estimation rates, with consequences for the training-test split", *Advances in Neural Information Processing Systems*, Vol. 8, pp. 183-189, Cambridge, MA, 1996.
[15] D.W. Marquardt, *Journal of the Society for Industrial and Applied Mathematics*, vol. 11, pp. 431-441, 1963.
[16] R. Fletcher, *Practical Methods of Optimization*, John Wiley & Sons, Chippenham, Great Britain, 1987.
[17] P. J. Werbos, *Beyond regression: New tools for prediction and analysis in the behavioral sciences*, Ph.D. Thesis, Harvard University, Cambridge, MA, 1974.
[18] J. Sjoberg and L. Ljung, "Overtraining, Regularization, and Searching for Minimum with Application to Neural Nets", *Int. J. Control*, vol. 62, no. 6, pp. 1391–1407, 1995.
[19] J. Sjoberg and M. Viberg, "Separable Non-linear Least-squares minimization—Possible Improvements for Neural Net Fitting", *IEEE Workshop in Neural Networks for Signal Processing*, Amelia Island Plantation, Florida, Sep. 24–26, pp. 345–354, 1997.
[20] JMP by SAS Corporation, JMP Release 5.0.1a, a business unit of SAS Institute Inc., http://www.jmp.com.
[21] *Mathematica* 5.0 by Wolfram Research, http://www.wolfram.com. The Neural Networks package is an add-on component to the standard *Mathematica* software and must be purchased separately.
[22] Electric Reliability Council of Texas (ERCOT), http://www.ercot.com/.
[23] New York Mercantile Exchange (NYMEX), http://www.nymex.com/.

ECG Signal Classification using Block-based Neural Networks

Wei Jiang, Seong G. Kong, and Gregory D. Peterson

Department of Electrical and Computer Engineering
The University of Tennessee
Knoxville, TN 37996-2100, U.S.A.
E-mail: skong@utk.edu

Abstract – This paper investigates the application of evolvable block-based neural networks (BbNNs) to ECG signal classification. A BbNN consists of a two-dimensional (2-D) array of modular basic blocks that can be easily implemented using reconfigurable digital hardware. BbNNs are evolved for each patient in order to provide personalized health monitoring. A genetic algorithm evolves the internal structure and associated weights of a BbNN using training patterns that consist of morphological and temporal features extracted from the ECG signal of a patient. The remaining part of the ECG record serves as the test signal. The BbNN was tested for ten records collected from different patients provided by the MIT-BIH Arrhythmia database. The evolved BbNNs produced higher than 90% classification accuracies.

I. Introduction

The electrocardiogram (ECG) makes a useful diagnostic technique for monitoring heart activities. Analysis of heartbeat patterns extracted from the ECG signal may reflect the symptoms indicating that the heart needs immediate attention. Several methods have been proposed to classify ECG heartbeat patterns. Various features are obtained from the ECG signal such as morphological features [1], heartbeat temporal intervals [2], frequency domain features [3], and wavelet transform coefficients [4]. Classification techniques of ECG patterns include linear discriminant analysis [1], support vector machines [5], and artificial neural network [6]. Unsupervised clustering of ECG complexes using self-organizing maps has been studied [7].

ECG signal patterns vary greatly for different individuals. Even for the same individual, heartbeat patterns significantly change with the time of day and under different situations. Abnormal patterns result from a wide variety of heart problems. As a consequence, a certain classification method that works well for a given dataset may produce inconsistent results on different datasets. A fixed-structure classifier trained with a limited number of data may not be able to track the time-varying nature of ECG signals.

Evolvable classifiers change the structure and configurations as well as internal parameters to cope with dynamic environments. Block-based neural network (BbNN) [8] models incorporate modular neural networks and evolutionary algorithms. BbNNs offer simultaneous optimization of structure and weight with a genetic algorithm (GA). The modular structure of BbNNs enables easy expansion in size by adding more blocks. BbNNs can be implemented by use of reconfigurable digital electronic hardware such as FPGAs that allow on-line partial reorganization of internal structures. BbNNs have been applied to the problems such as mobile robot navigation [8], pattern recognition [9], and time series prediction [10].

This paper presents evolvable BbNNs for the classification of abnormal heartbeat patterns from the ECG signal. The internal structure and associated weights of a BbNN are evolved to classify heartbeat patterns of each individual for personalized health monitoring. The BbNNs use both morphological and temporal features extracted from the ECG signal. The evolved BbNN produced an average of 98% classification accuracy of the ECG signals from the MIT-BIH Arrhythmia database [15].

II. Block-based Neural Networks

A. Network Structures

A BbNN can be represented by a two-dimensional (2-D) array of blocks. Each block is a basic processing element that corresponds to a feedforward neural network with four variable input/output nodes. A block is connected to its four neighboring blocks with signal flow represented by an arrow between the blocks. Leftmost and rightmost blocks are laterally interconnected. Signal flow uniquely specifies the internal configurations of a block as well as the overall network structure. Figure 1 illustrates the network structure of an $m \times n$ BbNN of m rows and n columns of blocks labeled as B_{ij}. The first row of blocks $B_{11}, B_{12}, \ldots, B_{1n}$ is an input stage and the blocks $B_{m1}, B_{m2}, \ldots, B_{mn}$ form an output stage. BbNNs with n columns can have up to n inputs and n outputs.

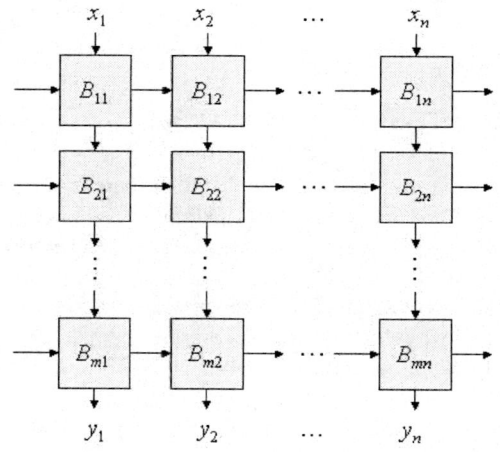

Figure 1: Structure of block-based neural networks

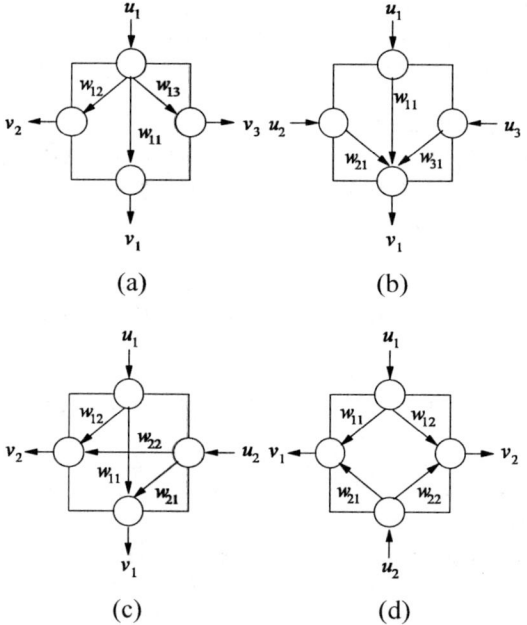

Figure 2: Four possible internal configuration types of a block. (a) One input and three outputs (1/3), (b) Three inputs and one output (3/1), (c) Two inputs and two outputs (2/2), (d) A different arrangement of 2/2

Internal configuration is characterized by the input-output connections of the nodes. A node can be either an input or an output according to the internal configuration determined by the signal flow. An incoming arrow to a block specifies the node as an input, and output nodes are associated with outgoing arrows. Generalization capability emerges through various internal configurations of a block. A block can be represented by one of the four different types of internal configurations. Figure 2(a) shows a block with one input and three outputs (1/3). A block in (b) has three inputs and an output (3/1). Both Figure 2(c) and (d) correspond to the type of two inputs and two outputs (2/2), but with different placement of the nodes. The cases of all input nodes (4/0) or all output nodes (0/4) are considered as invalid configurations and therefore are not allowed.

The four nodes inside a block are connected with each other with the weights. The signal u_j denotes the input and v_k indicates the output of the block. A weight w_{jk} denotes a connection between the jth input node u_j and the kth output node v_k. A block can have up to six connection weights including the bias. For the case of two inputs and two outputs (2/2), there are four weights and two biases. The 1/3 case has three weights and three biases, and the 3/1 configuration has three weights and one bias. An output node produces an output v_k with an activation function $g(\cdot)$:

$$v_k = g\left(w_{0k} + \sum_{j=1}^{J} w_{jk} u_j\right), \quad k = 1, 2, \cdots, K \quad (1)$$

where J and K denote the number of input and output nodes of the block. For the type 1/3 basic block, $J = 1$ and $K = 3$. For blocks of the type 3/1, $J = 3$ and $K = 1$. Type 2/2 blocks have $J = 2$ and $K = 2$. The term w_{0k} is called a bias, or the weight corresponding to a constant input $u_0 = 1$. A bipolar logistic sigmoid function in the range [-1,1] is chosen as an activation function:

$$g(u) = \frac{2}{1 + e^{-u}} - 1 \quad (2)$$

Other popular choices of the activation function include saturated linear or logistic sigmoid functions.

B. Evolutionary Optimization of BbNN

Network structure and connection weights of an individual BbNN are encoded to form a chromosome for optimization using the GA. The overall structure of a BbNN can be effectively encoded with binary directions of signal flow. Signal flow provides an integrated representation of BbNN structure and internal configurations. The signal flow determines the structure and the internal configuration of a BbNN using a sequence of binary numbers. Any connection between the blocks is represented with either 0 or 1. Bit 0 denotes down (↓) and left (←), and bit 1 indicates up (↑) and right (→) signal flows. The signal flow bits associated with the blocks in the input and output stages are all zeros and therefore are not included in structure encoding.

Each generation of the GA process involves the three stages: fitness evaluation, selection, and genetic operation. The current population of BbNNs are evaluated and ranked in terms of fitness value. The population goes through the selection and the genetic operation until the maximum fitness reaches the desired value.

The selection schemes used in this paper are elitist method, binary tournament with disruptive pressure. Popular selection methods such as roulette-wheel often show premature convergence in early phases of evolution or genetic drift in later phases. Elitist methods ensure that the best individuals pass their traits to the next generation in order to reduce a genetic drift. The individual with the highest fitness value in the previous generation is preserved in the next generation. The elitist method increases selection pressure by preventing the loss of important genes. Elitist methods can also speed up the convergence. In the elitist method, individuals with the lowest and the highest fitness values are exchanged only when the individual with the highest fitness value in the previous generation does not exist in the current generation. Tournament selection [11][12] has the same effects as both fitness proportional sampling and selection probability adjustment [13][14]. The binary tournament scheme finds one of the two individuals selected by a fitness comparison. The tournament size can adjust the selection pressure to reduce disruptive effect of uniform crossover. A larger tournament size usually increases the selection pressure.

Crossover and mutation serve as basic genetic operators used to evolve the structure and weights of the BbNN. Connection weights and biases are represented with real-valued numbers. For a crossover operation of a pair of BbNNs, a group of signal flow bits are selected with a crossover probability. The selected signal flow bits are exchanged. After the exchange, the internal structure of a block is reconfigured according to the new signal flow bits. Corresponding weights will be updated by a weighted combination of the two weights.

$$w_j^* = \alpha w_j + (1-\alpha) w_k \\ w_k^* = (1-\alpha) w_j + \alpha w_k \quad (3)$$

where α denotes a uniform random number in [0, 1]. New connection weights generated accordingly are initialized with random numbers, and unconnected weights are removed.

Mutation operator randomly adds a perturbation in an individual according to the mutation probability. A BbNN can have different probabilities for the mutation of structure and weight bit strings. When signal flow is reversed after mutation, all the irrelevant weights are removed and created with a random value on a proper direction. A weight selected for mutation will be updated with:

$$w_k^* = w_k + r \quad (4)$$

where r denotes a zero mean, unit variance Gaussian random variable. Mutation probabilities for weight and structure were 0.005 and 0.001 in the experiments.

III. ECG Signal Classification

A. Dataset

The MIT-BIH Arrhythmia Database [15] provides the ECG signals used in the experiment. The database contains 48 records obtained from 47 different individuals (Two records came from the same patient). Each record contains 2-channel ECG signals measured for 30 minutes. Twenty-three records serve as representative samples of routine clinical recordings. The remaining 25 records include heartbeat waveforms such as complex ventricular, junctional, and supra-ventricular arrhythmias. Continuous ECG signals were filtered using a bandpass filter with a passband from 0.1 to 100 Hz. Filtered signals were then digitized at 360 Hz. The beat locations are automatically labeled at first and verified later by independent experts to reach consensus. The whole database contains more than 109,000 annotations of normal and 14 different types of abnormal heartbeats. Four records containing paced heartbeats were excluded in this study according to Association for the Advancement of Medical Instrumentation recommended practices [16]. Several noisy records were also excluded. Channel 1 signals of the 10 records (100, 106, 119, 202, 205, 209, 210, 212, 213, and 215) were chosen from the dataset for experiment.

B. Feature Extraction

A heartbeat template defines a partial waveform of an ECG signal that includes an R-peak [6]. Figure 3 shows heartbeat templates H_{k-1}, H_k, and H_{k+1}. Let T_k and T_{k+1} denote the time intervals between the neighboring R-peaks of the current heartbeat template H_k. The template H_k includes all the samples in the interval $[t-T_k/2, t+T_{k+1}/2]$. The intervals range from 132 to 819 ms in the selected MIT-BIH database. Heartbeat templates are then normalized to have an equal number of samples. In each heartbeat template, the R peak is shifted to the center and then linearly interpolated to have a uniform number of samples among all the heartbeat templates of a record.

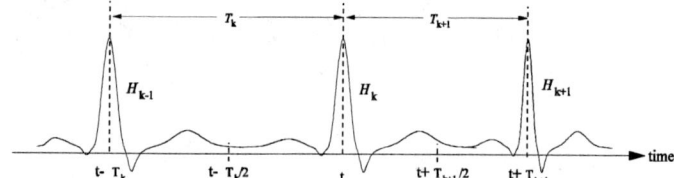

Figure 3: Definition of an ECG heartbeat template

Heartbeat templates are processed by a dimensionality reduction technique to reduce the amount of data to be processed each time. Principal components analysis (PCA) finds a projection that best represents the data in a least mean-squared error sense for feature dimensionality reduction [17]. The PCA reduces the original dimensions of heartbeat templates (greater than 150) to three principal components as the morphological features of the heartbeat template. The time interval T_k between neighboring R peaks gives useful information for the classification of abnormal heartbeat patterns. A feature vector is composed of three principal components (x_1, x_2, x_3) as morphological features and the time interval T_k (x_4) between the R peaks as a temporal feature. The 4-dimensional features serve as the input to the BbNN for the classification of ECG heartbeat patterns after proper normalization.

C. Evolution of BbNN

For the BbNN training patterns we use the heartbeat templates corresponding to the first five minutes of a record. The remaining templates of the record are used for test patterns.

A 2×4 BbNN was chosen for classification of ECG heartbeat patterns. The GA optimizes network structure and connection weights by maximizing the fitness function given by:

$$\text{Fitness} = \frac{p_1 p_2}{1 + \frac{1}{N}\sum_{j=1}^{N}\sum_{k=1}^{n_0}(d_{jk} - y_{jk})^2} \quad (5)$$

where N denotes the number of training data, n_0 is the number of actual output nodes. d_{jk} and y_{jk} are desired and actual outputs of the kth output block referred to jth pattern. The term p_1 prevents an invalid internal block configuration with all input nodes (4/0) or all output nodes (0/4), while p_2 excludes invalid structures that all the outputs of a middle stage are composed of only upward signal flow. Both terms are initially set to 1. An invalid configuration results in a smaller value of 0.9. Table 1 lists detailed parameter settings used in the GA evolution.

TABLE 1: PARAMETERS FOR GA EVOLUTION

Parameter	Value
Population	100
Crossover Probability	0.30
Mutation for Weight	0.005
Mutation for Structure	0.001
Max. Fitness Value	0.999
Max. Generations	50

IV. EXPERIMENT RESULTS

Six different types of abnormalities are considered: atrial premature, premature ventricular contraction, aberrated atrial premature, ventricular escape, right bundle branch block, and the fusion of ventricular and normal beats. Figure 4 shows example waveforms of normal and two abnormal heartbeats (atrial premature and premature ventricular contraction). There exists a morphological similarity between the normal and atrial premature pattern. The temporal feature gives higher discrimination of atrial premature pattern since the time interval (652.8 ms) is smaller than that of normal pattern (813.9 ms). For a premature ventricular contraction pattern, the time intervals of both patterns are similar (644.4 ms), while the shapes are quite different. A combined use of morphological and temporal features provides successful classification of abnormal heartbeat patterns.

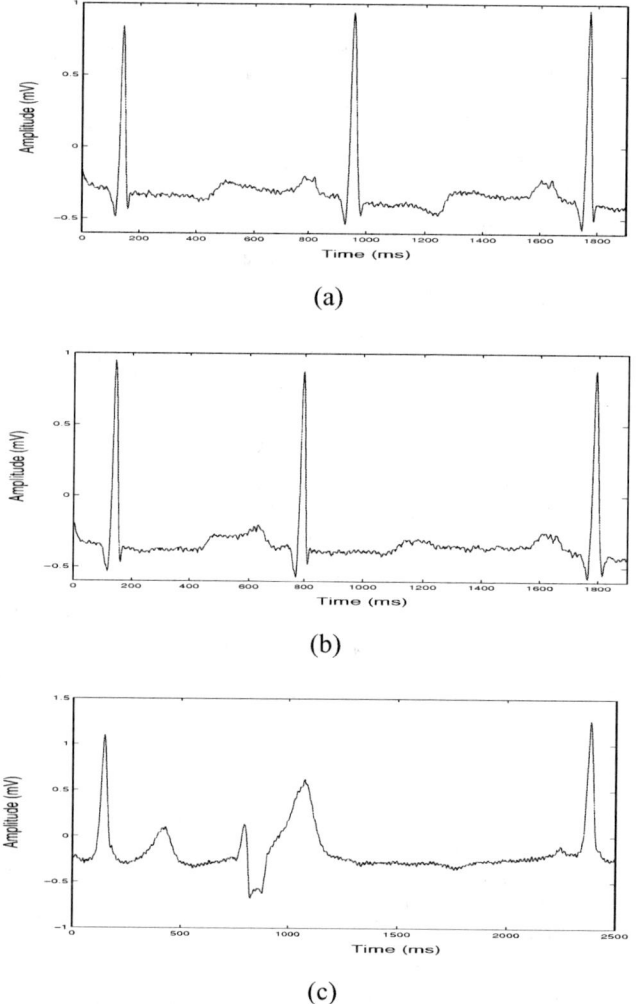

Figure 4: Sample ECG heartbeats, (a) Normal, (b) Atrial premature, and (c) Premature ventricular contraction

Figure 5 shows a scatter plot of normal and abnormal heartbeats in terms of the first principal component (x_1) and the time interval (x_4). The temporal feature increases the separability of normal and abnormal patterns.

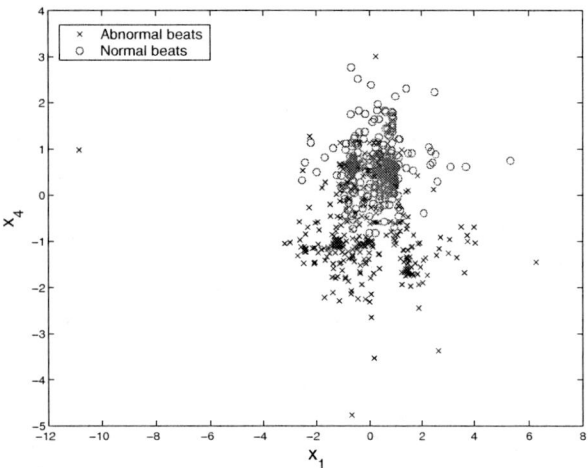

Figure 5: Scatter plot of normal and abnormal heartbeats in terms of the first principal component (x_1) and the time interval (x_4)

Figure 6 displays a typical evolution trend of BbNNs for ECG heartbeat classification. The solid line indicates the maximum fitness trend and dotted line shows the average fitness values. Evolution stops if the maximum fitness value does not reach the limit of 0.999 in 50 generations.

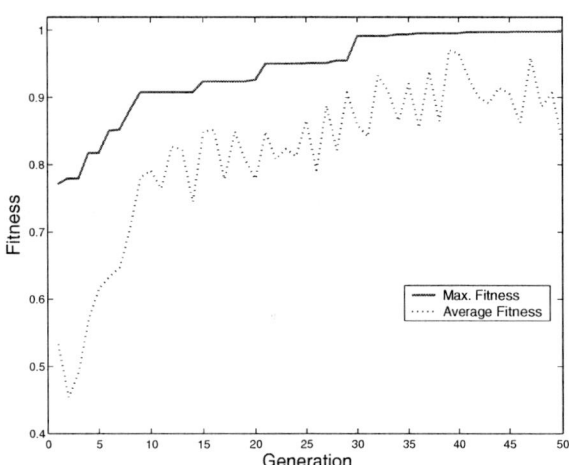

Figure 6: Evolution trend of BbNNs

A near-optimal BbNN structure is found during the evolution process. In Figure 7, a BbNN with near-optimal structure survives the competition. The number of BbNNs with a near-optimal structure increases, while the number of all the other structures gradually decreases during the evolution. The solid line indicates the near-optimal structure and the dotted lines represent five non-optimal structures. Finally all the BbNN individuals are evolved to the near-optimal structure.

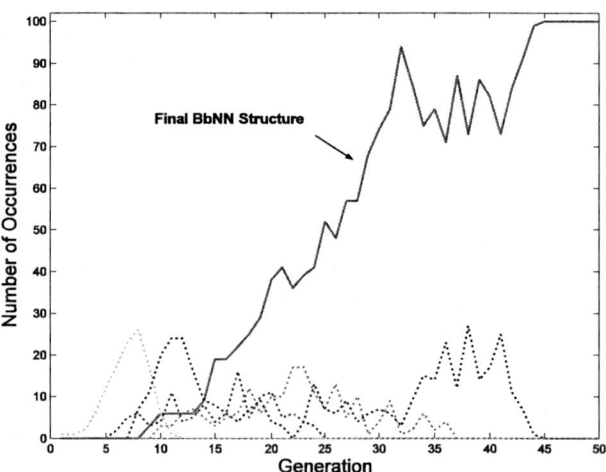

Figure 7: A structure evolution trend

Figure 8 shows the structure and weights of the evolved BbNN for classification of ECG heartbeat classification. The last output block was chosen as the output y. All the other redundant output nodes marked as * are ignored. Inputs $x_1, \ldots, x_4$ to the BbNN correspond to the three morphological features and the temporal feature. The output indicates either a normal or an abnormal heartbeat class.

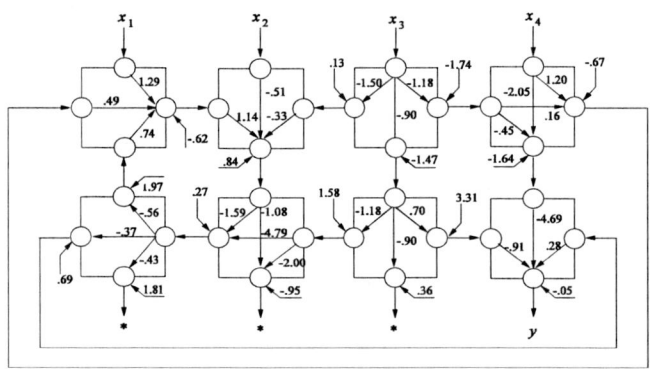

Figure 8: Evolved BbNN for ECG signal classification after 50 generations

Classification of ECG heartbeat patterns using the BbNN is summarized in Table 2. True positive (TP) and true negative (TN) indicate the correct classification of normal and abnormal patterns. False negative (FN) refers to misclassification of normal patterns as abnormality and false positive (FP) defines misclassification of abnormal patterns into normality. Classification accuracy is then defined as the ratio of the number of correctly classified patterns (TP and TN) and the total number of patterns. Each experiment was averaged over five repeated trials. An average classification rate obtained by the evolved BbNNs was approximately 98%. A two-layer multiplayer neural network of the size 51-25-2 reported an average accuracy of 90% [6]. Although a direct comparison of the results is not possible because of the difference in the datasets selected, the evolved BbNN demonstrates its potential for ECG signal classification.

TABLE 2: SUMMARY OF CLASSIFICATION ACCURACIES

Record	TP	TN	FP	FN	Accuracy (%)
100	1799	30	0	72	96.21
106	1234	460	0	1	99.94
119	1296	364	0	0	100.00
202	1789	25	46	10	97.01
205	2120	54	24	2	98.82
209	2100	348	25	45	97.22
210	2001	174	20	8	98.73
212	787	1482	9	6	99.34
213	2135	405	86	73	94.11
215	2661	131	2	0	99.93
Total	17922	3473	212	217	98.03

V. CONCLUSION

This paper presents ECG signal classification with evolvable block-based neural network. Heartbeat signals vary significantly depending on many factors such as individual differences and time. A variety of heart problems are responsible for abnormal heartbeat signals. Block-based neural networks offer an evolvable ECG signal classifier that can change structure and internal parameters for personalized health monitoring system. The internal structure and associated weights are optimized simultaneously with the GA. A 2×4 BbNN evolved with a subset of ECG signals produced an average of 98% classification accuracy for the ECG signals from the MIT-BIH database.

ACKNOWLEDGEMENT

This work was supported in part by the National Science Foundation under grant No. ECS-0319002.

REFERENCES

[1] P. de Chazal, M. O'Dwyer, and R. B. Reilly, "Automatic Classification of Heartbeats Using ECG Morphology and Heartbeat Interval Features," *IEEE Trans. on Biomedical Engineering*, Vol. 51, No. 7, pp.1196-1206, July 2004.
[2] C. Alexakis, H. O. Nyongesa, R. Saatchi, N. D. Harris, C. Davis, C. Emery, R. H. Ireland, and S. R. Heller, "Feature Extraction and Classification of Electrocardiogram (ECG) Signals Related to Hypoglycaemia," *Computers in Cardiology*, Vol. 30, pp.537-540, 2003.
[3] I. Romero and L. Serrano, "ECG Frequency Domain Features Extraction: A New Characteristic for Arrhythmias Classification," *Proc. Int'l. Conf. on Engineering in Medicine and Biology Society (EMBS'2001)*, pp.2006-2008, October 2001.
[4] P. de Chazal and R. B. Reilly, "A Comparison of the ECG Classification Performance of Different Feature Sets," *Computers in Cardiology*, Vol. 27, pp.327-330, 2000.
[5] S. Osowski, L. T. Hoai, and T. Markiewicz, "Support Vector Machine-based Expert System for Reliable Heartbeat Recognition," *IEEE Trans. on Biomedical Engineering*, Vol. 51, No. 4, pp.582-589, April 2004.
[6] Y. H. Hu, W. J. Tompkins, J. L. Urrusti, and V. X. Afonso, "Applications of Artificial Neural Networks for ECG Signal Detection and Classification," *Journal of Electrocardiology*, Vol. 26. (Suppl.), pp.66-73, 1994.
[7] M. Lagerholm, C. Peterson, G. Braccini, L. Edenbrandt, and L. Sörnmo, "Clustering ECG Complexes Using Hermite Functions and Self-organizing Maps," *IEEE Trans. on Biomedical Engineering*, Vol. 47, No. 7, pp.838-848, July 2000.
[8] S. W. Moon and S. G. Kong, "Block-based Neural Networks," *IEEE Trans. on Neural Networks*, Vol. 12, No. 2, pp.307-317, March 2001.
[9] S. W. Moon and S. G. Kong, "Pattern Recognition with Block-based Neural Networks," *Proc. Int'l J. Conf. on Neural Networks (IJCNN-2002)*, pp.992-996, May 2002.
[10] S. G. Kong, "Time Series Prediction with Evolvable Block-based Neural Networks," *Proc. Int'l J. Conf. on Neural Networks (IJCNN-2004)*, July 2004.
[11] T. Bäck, "Generalized Convergence Models for Tournament- and (μ, λ)-Selection," *Proc. Int'l Conf. on Genetic Algorithms (ICGA-95)*, pp.2-8, 1995.
[12] T. Blickle and L. Thiele, "A Mathematical Analysis of Tournament Selection," *Proc. Int'l Conf. on Genetic Algorithms (ICGA-95)*, pp.9-16, 1995.
[13] B. A, Julstrom, "It's All the Same to Me: Revisiting Rank-based Probabilities and Tournaments," *Proc. Congress on Evolutionary Computation (CEC-99)*, Vol. 2, pp.1501-1505, 1999.
[14] J. Sarma and K. De Jong, "An Analysis of Local Selection Algorithms in a Spatially Structured Evolutionary Algorithm," *Proc. Int'l Conf. on Genetic Algorithms (ICGA-97)*, pp.181-186, 1997.
[15] R. Mark and G. Moody, MIT-BIH Arrhythmia Database Directory (http://ecg.mit.edu/dbinfo.html).
[16] Association for the Advancement of Medical Instrumentation, *Recommended Practice for Testing and Reporting Performance Results of Ventricular Arrhythmia Detection Algorithms*, 1987.
[17] R. O. Duda, P. E. Hart, and D. G. Stork, *Pattern Recognition*, 2nd Edition, New York: Wiley-Interscience, 2000.

An Evolved Seega Player Capable of Strong Novice-Level Play

Ashraf M. Abdelbar, Ossama Soliman, Sherif Kinawy, Hisham Sayed
Department of Computer Science,
American University in Cairo

Abstract—Seega is an ancient Egyptian two-stage board game that, in certain aspects, is more difficult than chess. The two-player game is most commonly played on a 7×7 board, but is also sometimes played on a 5×5 or 9×9 board. In the first and more difficult stage of the game, players take turns placing one piece each on the board until the board contains only one empty cell. In the second stage players take turns moving pieces of their color; a piece that becomes surrounded by pieces of the opposite color is captured and removed from the board. A player wins when he has captured all, or all except one, of his opponent's pieces. We present results on the evolution of a Seega player that plays at the level of college students, who have had only a few days' familiarity with the game. The player is based on minimaxing with 12 hand-coded features, and feature weights that are evolved by a co-evolutionary system comprising a particle swarm optimizer (PSO) and an evolutionary algorithm (EA). Separate White and Black populations of feature weight vectors are maintained; each population is evaluated based on play against players from the top-, middle-, and bottom-third of the other population.

I. INTRODUCTION

Games such as chess [5], backgammon [21], checkers [19], Othello [3], [14], and Go [4], [17] have been of considerable interest to the AI research community [22]. Evolutionary computation techniques have been applied to many games including poker [12], checkers [6], [8], [10], chess [9], Pac-Man [11], and others. The ancient Egyptian board game of Seega is a challenging two-stage game that, in some ways, is more difficult than chess. Seega is a two-player game that is most frequently played on a 7×7 board. White and Black players each have 24 pieces, traditionally called *dogs*.

The first game stage is considered the heart of the game and the one where the bulk of the skill is needed; the second game stage is considered easier and requires less skill than the first stage. In the first stage the board is filled with pieces that the players place in turn. In the second stage, players capture each other's pieces to determine the winner of the game. The rules of the game are explained in detail in the following section.

The game is difficult for a minimax-based lookahead strategy because in the first stage, when the important decisions must be made, it is not feasible for the lookahead to reach into the second stage where the actual captures are made. The evaluation function therefore has to capture much more game knowledge than a chess, checkers, or Othello evaluation function.

In this paper we use a minimax search that looks ahead a number of ply and then applies an evaluation function.

The evaluation function uses 12 features in the first stage, one feature (material) in the second stage, and two features in the end-game of the second stage. A weighted linear combination is used to aggregate the features into a single position evaluation. The vector of coefficients for the feature combiner is determined by a co-evolutionary [18] system.

In previous work [1], [2], the co-evolutionary system was based on particle swarm optimization (PSO) and used two swarms of 32 particles each, one swarm for each color. Here, we use four populations: two White populations, one evolved by an evolutionary algorithm (EA) and one by PSO, and two Black populations, one evolved by an EA and one by PSO. The fitnesses of individuals in the two Black populations is determined by play against individuals drawn from the White EA's population; similarly, both White populations are evaluated against the black EA's population. In each iteration, each EA's population is ranked and two individuals are drawn randomly from each of the top-, middle-, and bottom-thirds of the population. These individuals are fixed and used to evaluate the populations of the opposing color in the following iteration.

In the following section, we present a fuller description of Seega and its rules. Section III describes the features that are extracted by the feature evaluators. In Section IV, we present the evolution process in greater detail. Sections V and VI discuss the performance of the evolved player and its evaluation against human players. Concluding remarks are presented in Section VII.

II. GAME OF SEEGA

Seega is a two-player ancient Egyptian capture board game, developed while Egypt was under Roman rule, and is still played in rural areas of Egypt. The game is most often played on a 7×7 board, with 24 White and 24 Black pieces. The game consists of two stages. White starts the first stage, during which pieces are placed on the board by each player in turn until all the squares, except the central one (square **d4** in Figure 1) are occupied. Players may place pieces on any unoccupied square except the central square.

Black starts the second stage, the aim of which is to capture as many of the opponent's pieces as possible. Figure 1 shows an example of a board at the start of stage two. In this example, Black has only one legal move at the beginning of stage two. It must move the piece in cell **c4** to **d4**; this will result in the capture of the two White pieces in **e4**, and **d3**. The game continues until one player loses because all, or all but one, of

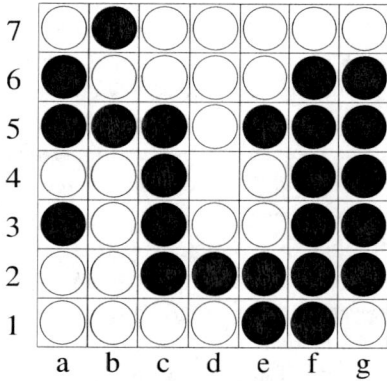

Fig. 1. An example of a Seega board position at the end of stage one. Black has only one move at the start of stage two: it must move **c4** to **d4**, capturing the two White pieces in **e4**, and **d3**.

his pieces have been captured or there is a draw because 40 moves have been made without any captures.

A player is allowed to move any of his pieces into a horizontally or vertically adjacent unoccupied square on a turn. For the first move of the second stage, there is no choice but to move a piece into the central square. A player that makes a capture plays again.

A player captures one of the opponent's pieces by enclosing it from two opposite sides (horizontal or vertical), but only when this is the result of a move. If a player has no legal moves available, the opponent plays again until a path is cleared for the other player.

Seega is difficult because during the first stage, a player needs to plan ahead to the second stage, even though looking ahead to the second stage is not feasible except at the very end of the first stage. The difficulty and skill of the game therefore lies in placing the pieces during the first stage in preparation for the second stage.

III. Feature Evaluators

Our approach uses minimax search with a small lookahead. At the leaves of the minimax tree, an evaluation function is applied to board positions measuring how good the board position is for Black. The evaluation function returns a weighted linear combination of several feature evaluations, each of which quantitatively describes a particular aspect of the board. This section describes the feature evaluator functions. Figure 2 shows a sample mid-stage-one board position we will use to illustrate the features.

- **blackstart.** This function returns 1 if Black currently occupies one of the four squares that are horizontally or vertically adjacent to the central square, and returns 0 otherwise. The significance of these four squares is that if Black does not occupy one of these squares then it will be forced to pass at the beginning of stage 2. In Figure 2, the black piece in **c4** can move into the center square and, therefore, this function would return 1.
- **starttwo.** This function evaluates who will have the advantage at the beginning of stage 2. Specifically, it measures whether Black has a chance to capture a White piece in all four directions; it gives a score of 0.25 for each potentially capturable White piece. In Figure 2, if the black piece in **c4** moves to **d4**, it can capture the White piece in **d3**. Therefore, the value returned is 0.25.
- **vmassdist.** This function obtains the sum of the vertical coordinates of the Black pieces divided by the number of Black pieces, i.e., it obtains the average vertical coordinate. It then obtains the average White vertical coordinate and subtracts it from the average Black. In Figure 2, the Black vertical average is 48/16 and the White is 58/16.
- **hmassdist.** This function proceeds similarly to **vmassdist** but for the horizontal coordinates. In Figure 2, the Black horizontal average is 82/16 and the White is 57/16.
- **vencapsulation.** This function measures the degree to which one color surrounds the other vertically. Specifically, it gives four points for every piece in each border row (rows **1** and **7**), three points for every piece in each next row (rows **2** and **6**), two points for the next (rows **3** and **5**), and one point for every piece in the center row (row **4**). It then subtracts the total points for Black from the total points for White. In Figure 2, the Black total is 38 and the White total is 50.
- **hencapsulation.** This function is similar to **vencapsulation** but proceeds horizontally: four points are given for the border columns (columns **a** and **g**), three for the next columns (columns **b** and **f**), two for the next (columns **c** and **e**), and one for the center column (column **d**). In Figure 2, the Black total is 42 and the White total is 39.
- **corners.** This function awards 0.25 for every corner occupied by Black and -0.25 for every corner occupied by White. In Figure 2, Black has no corners and White has four corners.
- **borders.** This function measures how many of the 24 border squares have been occupied by each color. Specifically, it awards 0.25 for every Black-occupied border square and -0.25 for every White-occupied border square. In Figure 2, Black has 5 border cells and White has 8.

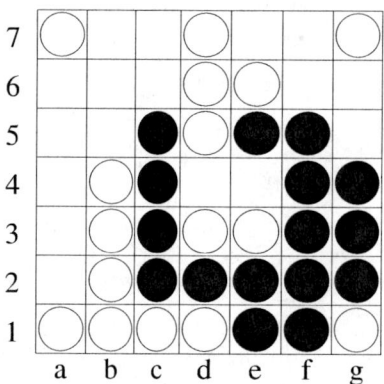

Fig. 2. An example mid-stage-one board position, used in the text to illustrate the feature evaluations.

- **connectivity.** This function returns the number of pieces in the largest mass of connected pieces for the current player, where diagonal adjacencies are included in the determination of adjacency. In Figure 2, all the Black pieces are connected in one 16-piece mass; on the other hand, the largest White mass is the 7-piece mass spanning from **a1** to **d1** and **b4**.
- **subspace.** This function returns the ratio of Black pieces to White pieces in a specific 3×3 portion of the board. For example, in Figure 2, in the subspace (**b2:d4**), Black has 4 pieces and White has 4 pieces.
- **material.** This function simply returns the ratio of Black pieces to White pieces on the entire board. This function is meaningless in stage 1.

These functions are used to form the following 12 stage-one features:

1) Feature1 = **blackstart** ;
2) Feature2 = **starttwo** $\times \alpha_1$;
3) Feature3 = ((**vmassdist** $\times$ **vencapsulation**) + (**hmassdist** $\times$ **hencapsulation**)) $\times \alpha_2$;
4) Feature4 = (**vmassdist** + **hmassdist**) $\times 0.5 \times \alpha_3$;
5) Feature5 = **corners** $\times 0.5 \times \alpha_4$;
6) Feature6 = **borders** $\times 0.5 \times \alpha_5$;
7) Feature7 = **connectivity** $\times \alpha_6$;
8) Feature8 = **subspace (b2:d4)** $\times \alpha_7$;
9) Feature9 = **subspace (b4:d6)** $\times \alpha_8$;
10) Feature10 = **subspace (d2:f4)** $\times \alpha_9$;
11) Feature11 = **subspace (d4:f6)** $\times \alpha_{10}$;
12) Feature12 = **subspace (c3:e5)** $\times \alpha_{11}$.

At the start of stage 2, only a single feature is used: **material**; when there are fewer than 16 pieces left on the board, the status is considered to be end-game and two features are used:

1) Feature13 = **material**;
2) Feature14 = **material** $\times$ (**vmassdist** + **hmassdist**) $\times \alpha_{12}$.

Often, several different board positions will have the same score. To prevent the minimax algorithm from always selecting the same one, a very small random variation is added to the score before it is returned by the evaluation function. In this way, a different game is played every time, even if the weights are the same.

IV. Architecture of the Evolutionary System

The objective of the co-evolutionary system is to evolve the feature weight vector $(\alpha_1, \alpha_2, \ldots, \alpha_{12})^T$. For each color, two populations are maintained:

1) A 25-element population that is evolved by an incremental EA (see Sect. IV-A).
2) A 32-element population that is evolved by hierarchical PSO (see Sect. IV-B).

The fitness of both the EA population and the PSO population of each color is obtained by playing against the EA population of the opposite color. The PSO populations are not used to evaluate other populations: initial experiments indicated the EA populations to have greater diversity than the PSO populations. In each iteration, a test suite of six individuals is obtained from each EA population: two individuals chosen randomly from the top-, middle-, and bottom-third, respectively, of the ranked population. These six individuals are then used to evaluate the opposing color's populations in the following iteration.

Each individual is evaluated by playing one game against each member of the test suite. A score of 100 is given for a win, -100 for a loss, and 0 for a draw. In addition, a bonus of between 15 and 104 is computed for each game based heuristically on the number of moves and the number of pieces left on the board; the bonus is added to the score of the winner and subtracted from the score of loser.

Each game is played using the minimax algorithm, with alpha-beta pruning, and with search depth varying heuristically between 2 and 8. In earlier work [2], we used eight features in the second game stage. Here, interestingly, we found that better performance is obtained by using only a single feature (material) in the early part of the second stage, and a second feature in the end-game of the second stage (as described in an earlier section).

The product of the evolutionary system is two feature weight vectors for each color: the best feature weight vector in the EA population and the best in the PSO population.

A. Details of Evolutionary Algorithm

We used an incremental EA with a population size of 25. In each generation, a total of 30 offspring are obtained, half by recombination and half by mutation. For recombination, a single offspring is obtained from two randomly selected (with uniform distribution) parents; each feature weight for the offspring element is chosen from one of the parents with equal probability (i.e., uniform crossover). For mutation, a single parent is randomly selected and a feature weight on that parent is identified randomly, and, then, with 0.5 probability, the feature weight is perturbed with $\pm 20\%$ random noise; with the opposite probability, the weight is replaced with a random weight. After generating the 30 offspring, the 55 population elements are sorted by fitness, and only the best 25 elements are retained.

B. Details of Hierarchical PSO

Particle swarm optimization (PSO) [7], [15], [16] is a population-oriented general-purpose optimization method based on the behavior of populations (swarms) of simple individuals, for example, swarms of insects, or flocks of birds. Introduced in 2003, hierarchical PSO (HPSO) [13] is a variation on the original technique; in HPSO, particles are arranged in a tree-based topology (as in, e.g., Figure 3), in which the better-performing particles float towards the top of the tree. In each iteration, starting from the root of the tree, and moving downwards in breadth-first fashion, each particle i is compared to its immediate children. If at least one of the children is better than i, then the best of the children is swapped with i. The breadth-first movement means that, in a

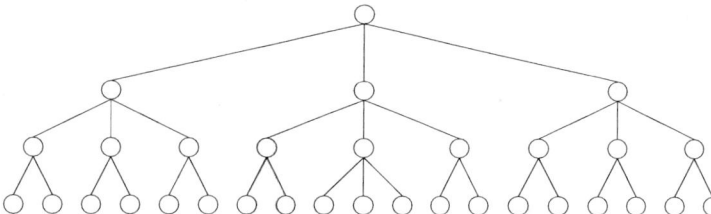

Fig. 3. An example of a hierarchical PSO topology, with height $h = 4$, maximum degree $d = 3$, and number of nodes $m = 32$. In this example, nodes in the level above the leaves have a degree of either 2 or 3.

TABLE I

THE BEST FEATURE WEIGHT VECTOR EVOLVED IN EACH OF THE FOUR POPULATIONS: PSO-BLACK, EA-BLACK, PSO-WHITE, AND EA-WHITE.

Weight	PSO-Black	EA-Black	PSO-White	EA-White
α_1	0.988021	0.930099	0.542265	0.795618
α_2	-0.228469	0.084069	0.055377	-0.146864
α_3	0.331516	0.193723	0.088739	0.184188
α_4	0.291941	0.336607	-0.157061	0.28233
α_5	0.184507	0.347457	-0.324747	0.275687
α_6	-0.167745	-0.165667	-0.211657	0.080616
α_7	-0.037574	0.343597	0.075385	-0.338474
α_8	-0.133232	-0.109202	0.246862	-0.040846
α_9	0.041575	0.22805	0.122303	-0.21524
α_{10}	0.106109	0.349485	0.095553	0.339723
α_{11}	-0.363315	0.342831	-0.106383	0.238417
α_{12}	0.704393	0.956548	0.923068	0.759679

single iteration, a particle can move upwards only one level in the tree but can move downwards many levels.

In standard PSO, each particle i is influenced by its own best-ever position p_i and the best-ever position of the best particle in its neighborhood p_g:

$$v_i = \alpha v_i^{old} + \phi_1 r(\cdot)(p_i - x_i) + \phi_2 r(\cdot)(p_g - x_i), \quad (1)$$

where α denotes inertia, $r(\cdot)$ denotes a uniform random number generator, x_i and v_i denote particle i's state and velocity vectors respectively, and g denotes the best particle in i's neighborhood.

In HPSO, Equation (1) continues to apply, except that g now represents particle i's immediate parent in the tree.

The topology of the tree used in HPSO is defined by three parameters: the height h, the node degree d, and the total number of nodes m. All nodes in the tree have the same degree except for the level immediately above the leaf nodes in which nodes might have a degree less than d; for that level, the leaves are distributed so that the maximum difference in degree in the nodes at that level is at most 1.

We used a height $h = 4$, degree $d = 3$, and number of particles $m = 32$ (this topology is shown in Figure 3). The number of particles was chosen initially for compatibility with a previous version [1], [2] of our work in which the PSO used a hypercube topology with number of nodes equal to $2^5 = 32$.

V. EXPERIMENTAL RESULTS

Five hundred generations of evolution were executed, using the evolutionary system described in the previous section.

TABLE II

RESULTS OF PLAYING BEST EVOLVED PLAYERS AGAINST EACH OTHER

Match (10 games)	# Black wins	# White wins	# Draws
EA-Black vs. EA-White	4	0	6
PSO-Black vs. EA-White	4	0	6
PSO-Black vs. PSO-White	0	0	10
EA-Black vs. PSO-White	1	2	7

Table I shows the weights of the resulting best players in the EA and PSO populations, respectively. It is interesting to note that the four evolved weight vectors are quite different from each other. Although, for example, the difference in performance between EA-Black and PSO-Black is fairly small, the two vectors are quite different (e.g., the magnitude of the difference vector is 0.975).

The final evolved players were evaluated by playing them against each other and against human players (results of human-play are described in Section VI). Four matches of 10 games each were played between the following:

- EA-Black vs. EA-White,
- PSO-Black vs. PSO-White,
- EA-Black vs. PSO-White,
- PSO-Black vs. EA-White.

The results are shown in Table II; several observations can be made:

- Both EA-Black and PSO-Black won 4 games and tied 6 games when playing against EA-White. However, when playing against PSO-White, EA-Black won 1 game and lost 2 games while PSO-Black tied all 10 games.
- There is a clear difference in performance between PSO-White and EA-White. PSO-White won 2 games and lost 1 game against EA-Black; the same EA-Black won 4 games against EA-White. Also, PSO-White did not lose a single game to PSO-Black (tying all 10 games) while EA-White lost 4 games to PSO-Black.
- The two PSO-evolved players are evenly matched (tying all 10 games), but there is a difference in performance between the two EA-evolved players, with EA-Black winning 4 games against EA-White.

In general, it is true, for both colors, that the performance of the PSO-evolved player is better than the EA-evolved players. Therefore, when evaluating the performance of the system against human players, we use the PSO-Black weights when the system plays as Black and the PSO-White weights when the system plays as White. This player is available at www.aucegypt.edu/faculty/abdelbar/SeegaRev.tar.Z

VI. PERFORMANCE AGAINST HUMAN PLAYERS

Eight human volunteers with no previous exposure to Seega were obtained from the student population of the American University in Cairo. Students were given the rules of Seega and given several days in which they were encouraged to play against each other and to familiarize themselves with the game. A tournament was then played between the human players;

TABLE III
SOME INFORMATION ABOUT THE WINNER OF THE TOURNAMENT OF HUMAN PLAYERS.

Name	Mohamed Noweir
Age	21 years
Email	noweir@gmail.com
Measured IQ	131
University GPA	3.5

TABLE IV
RESULTS OF PLAYING AGAINST THE HUMAN PLAYER DESCRIBED IN TABLE III.

Match (3 games)	Black wins	White wins	draws
PSO-Black vs. Human-White	1	0	2
Human-Black vs. PSO-White	1	1	1

Table III provides some information about the tournament winner, Mohamed Noweir. The tournament winner then played two 3-game matches against the computer: one match as Black and one match as White.

The results are shown in Table IV; we observe the following:
- Of the six games, three ended in a tie.
- The computer lost only one game, while the human player lost two games.

In general, the results suggest that the performance of the evolved player is similar to that of the winner of the human tournament.

VII. Concluding Remarks

In this paper, we have described the evolution, using particle swarm optimization and an evolutionary algorithm, of a Seega player that plays at the level of smart college students, with limited prior exposure to the game.

The most urgent future work direction is the development of a specialized end-game engine. This would be a hand-coded system that takes over when a small number of pieces are left on the board at the end of stage 2. At present, even with the use of Feature14 (see Sect. III), it still occasionally occurs that the computer has the advantage at the end of stage 1, but then the human player is able to produce a draw by forcing 40 capture-less moves. This does not commonly occur in human versus human play, and it is likely that it can be avoided with the use of a well-designed end-game engine.

Acknowledgements

We would like to express our gratitude to David Fogel who graciously gave of his time to read this paper and provide many useful comments which significantly improved the work. Any errors or omissions that remain are the responsibility of the authors.

We would like to express our gratitude to Sherif Ragab and Sara Mitri. The work described here is based on their game engine, and roughly half of our board features are inherited from [1].

References

[1] A.M. Abdelbar, S. Ragab and S. Mitri, "Applying co-evolutionary particle swarm optimization to the Egyptian board game Seega" *Proceedings* **CEC-03** *Workshop on Genetic Programming*, pp. 9–15, 2003.

[2] A.M. Abdelbar, S. Ragab and S. Mitri. "Co-evolutionary particle swarm optimization applied to the 7×7 Seega game," *Proceedings* **IJCNN-04** *IEEE/INNS International Joint Conference on Neural Networks*, 2004.

[3] A.M. Abdelbar, and G. Tagliarini, "Using neural network learning in an Othello evaluation function," *Journal of Experimental and Theoretical Artificial Intelligence*, Vol. 10, pp. 217–229, 1998.

[4] M. Burmeister, and J. Wiles, "AI techniques used in computer Go," In *Proceedings Fourth Conference of the Australasian Cognitive Science Society*, 1997.

[5] M. Campbell, A. J. Hoane, Jr., and F. Hsu, "Deep Blue," *Artificial Intelligence*, Vol. 134, pp. 57–83, 2002.

[6] K. Chellapilla, and D.B. Fogel, "Anaconda defeats Hoyle 6-0: a case study competing an evolved checkers program against commercially available software," *Proceeding* **CEC-03** *IEEE Congress on Evolutionary Computation*, 2000, Vol. 2, pp. 857-863.

[7] R.C. Eberhart, and J. Kennedy, "A new optimizer using particle swarm theory," In *Proceedings International Symposium on Micro Machine and Human Science*, pp. 39-43, 1995.

[8] D.B. Fogel, *Blondie24: Playing at the Edge of AI*, Morgan Kauffman, 2001.

[9] D.B. Fogel, T.J. Hays, S.L. Hahn, and J. Quon, "A self-learning evolutionary chess program," *Proceedings of the IEEE*, Vol. 92, No. 12, 2004, pp. 1947-1954.

[10] N. Franken, and A.P. Engelbrecht, "Comparing PSO structures to learn the game of checkers from zero knowledge," *Proceedings* **CEC-03** *IEEE Congress on Evolutionary Computation*, 2003.

[11] M. Gallagher, and A. Ryan, "Learning to play Pac-Man: an evolutionary, rule-based approach," *Proceedings IEEE Congress on Evolutionary Computation*, 2003, pp. 2462-2469.

[12] E.J. Hughes, "The evolution of blackjack strategies," *Proceedings IEEE Congress on Evolutionary Computation*, 2003, pp. 2474-2481.

[13] S. Janson, and M. Middendorf, "A hierarchical particle swarm optimizer," *Proceedings IEEE Congress on Evolutionary Computation*, 2003.

[14] K.-F. Lee, and S. Mahajan, "The development of a world-class Othello program," *Artificial Intelligence*, Vol. 43, pp. 21–36, 1990.

[15] J. Kennedy, and R.C. Eberhart, "Particle swarm optimization," In *Proceedings IEEE International Conference on Neural Networks*, Vol. IV, pp. 1942–1948, 1995.

[16] J. Kennedy, and R. C. Eberhart, *Swarm Intelligence*, Morgan Kaufmann, San Francisco, 2001.

[17] M. Müller, "Computer Go," *Artificial Intelligence*, Vol. 134, pp. 145–179, 2002.

[18] M. A. Potter, and K. A. De Jong, "A cooperative coevolutionary approach to function optimization," In *Proceedings Third Conference on Parallel Problem Solving from Nature*, pp 249–257, 1994.

[19] A. L. Samuel, "Some studies in machine learning using the game of checkers," *IBM Journal of Research and Development*, Vol. 3, pp. 211–229, 1959. Reprinted in E.A. Feigenbaum, and J. Feldman, eds., *Computers and Thought*, McGraw-Hill, New York, 1963.

[20] Y. Shi, and R.A. Krohling, "Co-evolutionary particle swarm optimization to solve min-max problems," In *Proceedings IEEE Congress on Evolutionary Computation*, 2002.

[21] G. Tesauro, "TD-Gammon, a self-teaching backgammon program, achieves master-level play," *Neural Computation*, Vol. 6, pp. 215–219, 1994.

[22] H. J. van den Herik, J. W. H. M. Uiterwijk, and J. van Rijswijck, "Games solved: now and in the future," *Artificial Intelligence*, Vol. 134, pp. 277–311, 2002.

Evolvable Neural Networks based on Developmental Models for Mobile Robot Navigation

Dong-Wook Lee and Seong G. Kong

Department of Electrical and Computer Engineering
The University of Tennessee
Knoxville, TN 37996-2100, U.S.A.
E-mail: {dlee27, skong}@utk.edu

Kwee-Bo Sim

School of Electrical and Electronic Engineering
Chung-Ang University
Seoul, 156-756 Korea
kbsim@cau.ac.kr

Abstract – This paper presents evolvable neural networks based on a developmental model for navigation control of autonomous mobile robots in dynamic operating environments. Bio-inspired mechanisms have been applied to autonomous design of artificial neural networks for solving practical problems. The proposed neural network architecture is grown from an initial developmental model by a set of production rules of the *L*-system that are represented by the DNA coding. The *L*-system is based on parallel rewriting mechanism motivated by the growth models of plants. DNA coding gives an effective method of expressing general production rules. Experiments show that the evolvable neural network designed by the production rules of the *L*-system develops into a controller for mobile robot navigation to avoid collisions with the obstacles.

I. INTRODUCTION

Evolutionary neural networks (ENNs) adopt the concept of biological evolution as an adaptation mechanism [1][2]. ENNs with direct coding of architecture [3]-[5] use one-to-one mapping of genotype and phenotype. ENNs with direct encoding may not be practical except for small size neural networks due to high computational cost. The networks lack scalability as the size of the genetic description of a neural network grows as the network size increases [5]. Indirect encoding [6]-[11] can construct ENNs with complex network structures having repeated substructures in compact genotypes by recursive application of developmental rules. Development refers to an organization process in biological organisms, an indirect genotype-to-phenotype mapping.

Lindenmayer-system (*L*-system) [12][13] provides a mathematical model of a biological development process in multi-cellular organisms as a special class of fractal. A development begins with an initial string (axiom) that consists of symbols (modules) with associated numerical parameters. Rewriting (production) rules replace all modules in the predecessor string by successor modules. This feature makes *L*-system especially suitable for describing fractal structures, such as cell divisions in biological organisms and modeling the growth of plants in computer graphics. Boers *et al.* [8] and Gruau [9] propose neural network design methods based on *L*-systems and the GAs. Kodjabachian *et al.* [6] develops a neuro-controller based on the Gruau model.

Developmental models require an appropriate encoding scheme. Encoding methods based on tree structure may not be suitable to represent production rules in developmental models. A coding scheme inspired by biological DNA offers advantages over conventional coding methods [14][15]. DNA coding is suitable for representing the developmental rules, and shows good performance when longer chromosomes are required. DNA coding shows floating representations that do not have a fixed location for interpretation. DNA coding can arbitrarily represent developmental rules without the limitations of the length and the number of rules.

This paper presents an evolvable neural network model that grows from a simple structure to a network with higher connection complexity according to the developmental rules. The network consists of a set of homogeneous neurons and associated connection weights with lateral connections. The network model is developed using the production rules represented by a DNA coding. A chromosome in DNA coding represented an individual network. The chromosomes are mapped the set of production rules of the *L*-system. Evolutionary algorithms update the chromosome represented by the DNA coding using evaluation. The evolved neural network demonstrates the potential of evolutionary neural networks for navigation control of autonomous mobile robots.

II. EVOLVABLE NEURAL NETWORK REPRESENTATION

A. DNA Coding

Motivated by biological DNA, DNA coding uses four symbols *A* (Adenine), *G* (Guanine), *T* (Tymine), and *C* (Cytocine) that denote nucleotide bases [15], not a binary representation as in the GA. A chromosome is represented by three successive symbols called a codon. A DNA code that begins from a START codon (*ATA* or *ATG*) and ends at a STOP codon (*TAA, TAG, TGA,* or *TGG*) is translated into a meaningful code. This representation of chromosome can have multiple interpretations since the interpretations of START and STOP codons allow overlaps as shown in Figure 1. The length of chromosomes varies. DNA coding has floating representations without fixed crossover points. Wu and Lindsay [16] proved that floating representation is effective for the representation of long chromosomes by schema analysis in GAs. The diversity of population is high since the DNA coding has a good parallel search and recombination ability. The DNA coding method can encode developmental rules without limitation of the number and the length of rule. DNA coding requires a translation table to decode codons. A codon is translated into an amino acid according to a translation table in TABLE I. For example, a codon AGG is translated into an amio acid $AA15$. START codons ATA and ATG are translated into AA3 within the chromosome.

TABLE I   DNA CODE TRANSLATION TABLE

Codon	Amino acid	Codon	Amino acid	Codon	Amino acid	Codon	Amino acid
TTT	AA1	TCT	AA5	TAT	AA9	TGT	AA13
TTC		TCC		TAC		TGC	
TTA		TCA		TAA	STOP	TGA	STOP
TTG		TCG		TAG		TGG	
CTT	AA2	CCT	AA6	CAT	AA10	CGT	AA14
CTC		CCC		CAC		CGC	
CTA		CCA		CAA		CGA	
CTG		CCG		CAG		CGG	
ATT	AA3	ACT	AA7	AAT	AA11	AGT	AA15
ATC		ACC		AAC		AGC	
ATA	AA3	ACA		AAA		AGA	
ATG	/ START	ACG		AAG		AGG	
GTT	AA4	GCT	AA8	GAT	AA12	GGT	AA16
GTC		GCC		GAC		GGC	
GTA		GCA		GAA		GGA	
GTG		GCG		GAG		GGG	

Figure 1 shows an example of how to translate a DNA sequence. Two different translations are possible since any three symbols are grouped to a codon starting from different positions. Gene 1 is obtained from a START codon (ATG) to a STOP codon (TGA). Gene 2 appears from ATG to another STOP codon (TAA). The two genes overlap. Gene 1 results in a sequence of amio acids (protein) AA15-AA13-AA14-AA15-AA6, while Gene 2 gives AA6-AA8-AA2-AA7.

Gene 1 |START|AA15|AA13|AA14|AA15|AA6|STOP|
CG<u>ATG</u>CGGGA<u>ATG</u>CCGGCCC<u>TGA</u>CA<u>TAA</u>CT...
Gene 2 |START|AA6|AA8|AA2|AA7|STOP|

Figure 1: Gene translation of a DNA sequence

Figure 2 illustrates how the crossover and mutation operations work in DNA coding. In Figure 2(a), two parent chromosomes containing genes 1, 2 and 3, 4, 5 produce two offspring chromosomes with genes 1, 6 and 2, 3, 7, and 8 using a one-point crossover operation. The crossover point is not at the same location of two chromosomes. The lengths of the chromosomes become different before and after crossover. Figure 2(b) shows a mutation operation. Selected base will be changed to one of the other three bases. For example, base C in gene 1 becomes to base G.

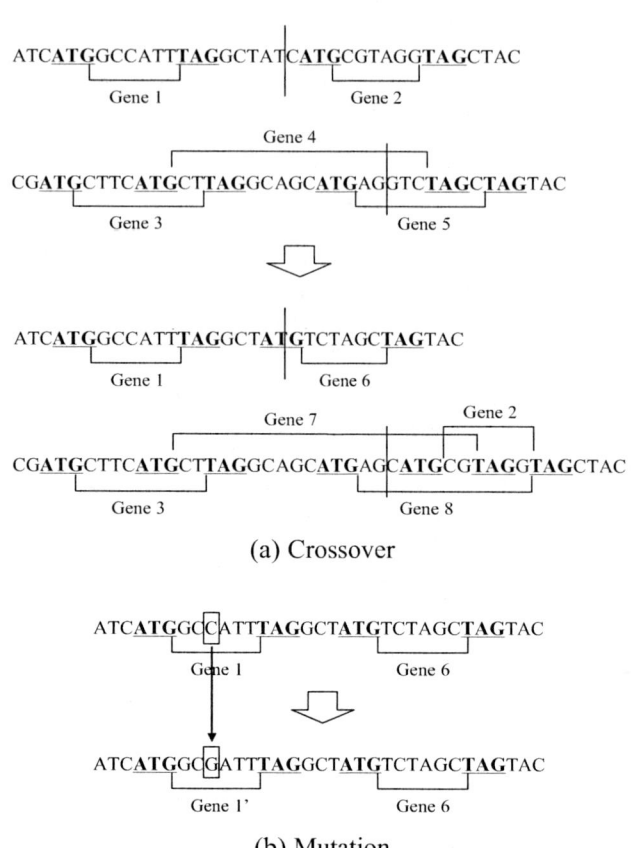

(a) Crossover

(b) Mutation

Figure 2: Evolutionary operations

B. L-systems

A simple L-system can be defined as a grammar of string writing in the form $G = \{V, P, \omega\}$, where $V = \{A_1, A_2, ..., A_n\}$ is a finite set of alphabets A_i. $P = \{p_1, p_2, ..., p_n\}$ denotes a set of production rules $p_i = p(A_i)$. ω is an initial string (combination of alphabets), commonly referred to as an axiom. A production rule $p: V \rightarrow V^*$ maps alphabets to a set V^* of finite strings. Let S_k denote a string in the k-th rewriting step. The rewriting procedure can be described as

$$S_k = p^k(S_0) = \overbrace{p \circ p \circ \cdots \circ p}^{k}(S_0) \quad (1)$$

where $\circ$ denotes a composite operator of the rewriting operation p. The first rewriting step gives $S_1 = p(S_0)$ with $S_0 = \omega$, and $S_2 = p(S_1) = p(p(S_0)) = (p \circ p)(S_0) = p^2(S_0)$. For example, consider a simple L-system with three alphabets V

= {*A*, *B*, *C*}. Suppose the growth model $G = \{V, P, \omega\}$ have a set of developmental rules $P = \{p(A), p(B), p(C)\}$ with $p(A) = BA$, $p(B) = CB$, and $p(C) = AC$. Applying the production rules to the axiom $\omega = ABC$ result in the strings:

$$S_1 = p(S_0) = p(ABC) = p(A)p(B)p(C) = BACBAC \quad (2)$$

$$S_2 = p(S_1) = p(BACBAC) \\ = p(B)p(A)p(C)p(B)p(A)p(C) = CBBAACCBBAAC \quad (3)$$

III. DESIGN OF EVOLVABLE NEURAL NETWORKS BASED ON DEVELOPMENTAL MODELS

A. Structure of Evolvable Neural Networks

The proposed evolvable neural network model consists of an array of neurons whose structure grows according to the developmental rules. A string of N symbols $n_1 n_2 n_3 \cdots n_N$, generated from a set of production rules, finds a neural network with N nodes, n_i, $i = 1, 2, ..., N$. Figure 3 shows the structure of the evolvable neural network based on a developmental model. There are L input nodes and M output nodes.

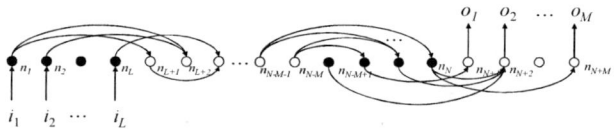

Figure 3: Structure of the evolvable neural network with developmental models.

Nodes are connected with the connection range of the form (x, y). A pair of integers x and y ($1 \leq x \leq y$) configures the connection between the neighboring nodes. The parameter x denotes the index of the first node to be connected from a base node. The parameter y indicates the last node to be connected. Figure 4 illustrates the connection of the neurons. A node at l-th location is connected to all the neurons between $(l+x)$-th and $(l+y)$-th locations. Input nodes are not connected with each other. Therefore, the indices of the first and last nodes become $(l+m+x)$ and $(l+m+y)$ since connection begins after skipping input neurons.

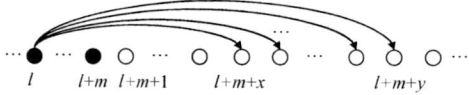

Figure 4: Connection of nodes with a connection range (x, y).

An evolutionary neural network is constructed from a string according to the following procedures.

1. Determine the numbers of input (L) and output (M).
2. Set the first L and the last M characters in a string to input and output neurons. All the others are set to hidden neurons. If the total characters in a string are fewer than $L+M$, then stop the construction.
3. Add M neurons as output nodes next to output neurons.
4. Connect all neurons according to connection range and the weights.

Input and output neurons are not conncected with the neurons of the same type. Input neurons use linear activation functions while hidden and output neurons use bipolar sigmoid functions.

B. DNA Coding of Production Rules

A DNA chromosome is translated into an amino acid and then into a production rule of *L*-system. The *L*-system for a mobile robot control uses four alphabets $V = \{A, B, C, D\}$. The maximum connection range is set to 5. TABLE II converts an amino acid to a node name and connection range. Each node name (alphabet) is assigned to four types of amino acid. In this case, the second base of amino acid determines the node name. The first and the third bases are don't care nodes. Connection range is assigned to one amino acid since the conncetion range between nodes has 15 types ((1,1) (1,2), ..., (5,5)). The third base of the connection range is redundant. Coding redundancy using don't care bases enables to increase the effciency of overlapping genes. If the two useful genes are combined, these two genes will spread easily in the population.

TABLE II TRANSLATION TABLE OF AMINO ACIDS

Amino acid	Node name	Connection range	Amino acid	Node name	Connection range
AA1	A	(1,4)	AA9	C	(1,5)
AA2	A	(1,1)	AA10	C	(3,3)
AA3	A	(1,3)	AA11	C	(3,5)
AA4	A	(1,2)	AA12	C	(3,4)
AA5	B	(2,5)	AA13	D	(1,5)
AA6	B	(2,2)	AA14	D	(4,4)
AA7	B	(2,4)	AA15	D	(5,5)
AA8	B	(2,3)	AA16	D	(4,5)

A production rule of *L*-system consists of alphabets, which are interpreted as nodes. The predecessor has only node but the alphabet of the successor has node name with conncetion range, bias, and weights. Figure 5 shows a production rule of the form $p(A) = B$ with connection range (x,y). A production rule is composed of nine codons corresponding a predecessor node, a successor node, a connection range, a bias, five connection weights. Five weights are needed since the maximum connection range is set to 5. A single predecessor node can have multiple successor nodes as in the rule $p(A) = BC$.

Node(P)	Node(S)	Connection Range	Bias	Weights
A	B	(x,y)	w_0	w_1, w_2, w_3, w_4, w_5

Figure 5: DNA coding of a production rule

Bias and weights are real values calculated by Eq. (4). The bias and weights have values of bound from -3.2 to 3.1 at 0.1 intervals.

$$w = \frac{(b_2 \cdot 4^2 + b_1 \cdot 4^1 + b_0 \cdot 4^0) - 32}{10} \quad (4)$$

where b_0, b_1, and b_2 are the three DNA symbols of the codon (e.g. ACG). The values of each DNA symbol are $T = 0$, $C = 1$, $A = 2$, and $G = 3$.

Figure 6 shows an example of translating a DNA code into a production rule. Two production rules can be created since two START codons (ATG) exist in the chromosome. The codon TAC followed by ATG is translated to AA9 (Node C) according to TABLE II. The next codon CGG is translated to AA14 (Node D). The next codon (CGT) is also translated to AA14, which corresponds to the connection range (4,4). The following codon (GAA) denotes a bias of the value 2.6 (=[3×4²+2×4¹+2×4⁰-32]/10). The next five codons determine weight values. This procedure is repeated for the next production rule until the STOP codon is met. The first rule is represented by $p(C) = D(4,4)A(4,5)$. The second rule $p(B) = D(1,5)$ is obtained from the different reading frame. Not-used codons are denoted by 'NU.' If multiple rules have the same predecessor but different successors as in $p(A) = B$ and $p(A) = CB$, only the first rule $p(A) = B$ is used, and the others are eliminated. If no rule is found for a predecessor A_i, a rule $p(A_i) = A_i$ is used.

	predecessor	successor	
Rule 1	(AA9)	(AA14) (AA14) GAA TGC CGG GGT CCA CGG	(AA2) (AA16) ACA ACC ACC GTT AGC GTT
	C	D (4,4) 2.6 -1.9 -0.1 2.8 -1.0 -0.1	A (4,5) 0.6 0.5 0.5 1.6 1.3 1.6
Rule 2	(AA6)	(AA16) (AA13) ACG GCT CGG GAC AAC CAC	
	B	D (1,5) 0.7 2.0 -0.1 2.5 0.9 -0.7	

Figure 6: Interpretation of production rules from a DNA code.

IV. EXPERIMENT RESULTS

The evolvable neural network developed in the previous section is applied to the mobile robot navigation control problem. The goal is to make a mobile robot find the target as fast as possible and to avoid collisions with the obstacles. Autonomous mobile robots decide an action at each time step by sensing the environment. A Khepera mobile robot is used to test how to develop an evolvable neural network controller. Figure 7(a) shows a Khepera robot with a linear vision turret. The mobile robot detects near objects using eight (six front and two rear) IR proximity sensors. The sensing range is approximately 50 mm. A linear vision sensor finds the target by 64×1 pixels in 256 gray levels.

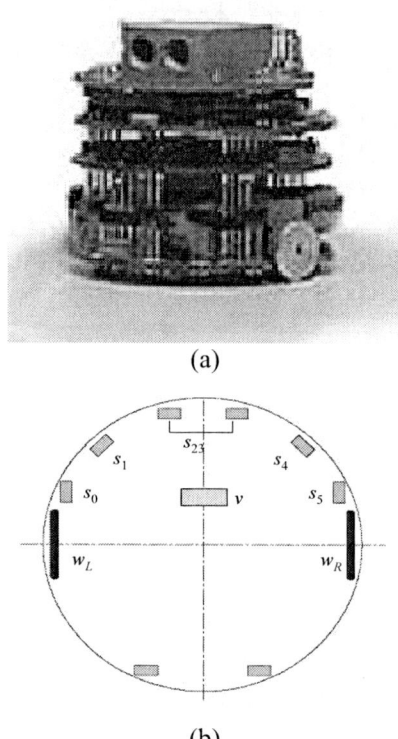

Figure 7: (a) A Khepera robot with vision turret, (b) Sensors

A neural network controller has 6 inputs (5 IR sensors and a vision sensor) and 2 outputs. The sensors s_2 and s_3 are connected together to produce a single input s_{23}. Two rear IR sensors are not used. IR sensors are scaled as the value in the range [0, 1] but the vision sensor has a binary value {-1,1}. If the target is on the left then the vision sensor gives -1, otherwise 1. The output from neural network is the values beteen 0 and 1. To evolve the neural network controller, the fitness function is chosen as:

$$\text{Fitness} = \frac{1}{2}\left(\frac{d_{max} - d_R}{d_{max}} + \frac{c_{max} - c_R}{c_{max}}\right) \quad (5)$$

where d_{max} denotes the maximum distance from start point to the target, d_R is the distance from the robot to the target, c_{max} is predefined value of maximum number of collisions, and c_R is the number of collisions. If c_R is greater than c_{max} then $c_R = c_{max}$. The parameters of experiment are set as follows; The size of work space is 700×700 mm. d_{max} is $600\sqrt{2}$, and c_{max} was set to 100. The number of populations is 200, the probability of crossover is 0.8, the probability of mutation is 0.05, and the initial length of chromosome is 1,000. Figure 8 displays the fitness change through the evolution. The mobile robot with the evolved neural network controller finds the target without collision in 95 generations and therefore reached the maximum fitness value.

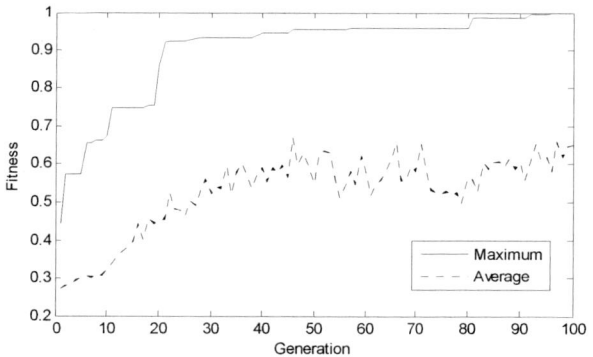

Figure 8: Transition of fitness for mobile robot navigation

To construct a neural network, the L-system with grammar $G = \{V, P, \omega\}$ is used, where $V = \{A, B, C, D\}$, $P = \{p_1, p_2, p_3, p_4\}$, and $\omega = A$. The production rules are as follows:

$p_1 = p(A) = A(5,5)C(1,2)D(2,3)B(2,4)$
$p_2 = p(B) = D(1,5)B(2,4)C(1,4)$
$p_3 = p(C) = A(3,3)D(1,4)C(2,4)$
$p_4 = p(D) = B(4,5)$

The neural network is created from three rewriting steps using evolved rules. A node of $N(x,y)$, N is an alphabet that represents a node, x and y are the parameters that show the connection range. Using these rule and ω, we can obtain the following strings, S_1, S_2, and S_3 after three rewriting steps:

$S_1 : A(5,5)C(1,2)D(2,3)B(2,4)$
$S_2 : A(5,5)C(1,2)D(2,3)B(2,4)A(3,3)D(1,2)C(2,4)B(4,5)$
$\quad\quad D(1,5)B(2,4)C(1,4)$
$S_3 : ACDBADCBDBCACDBBADCDBCBDBCADC$.

Figure 9 shows the evolved network architecture obtained from the string S_2. The string obtained from S_3 is discarded since the network shows low performance.

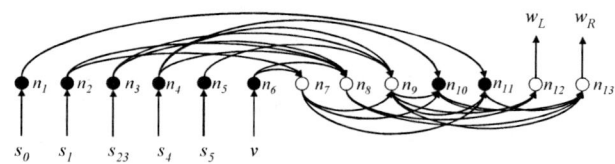

Figure 9: An evolved neural network from the string S_2.

The maximum rewriting step should be determined. As rewriting steps increase, a neural network tends to grow. If the network is bigger than the best individual in the previous generation, then the rewriting process will be stopped.

Figure 10 shows a simulation environment, with a starting point on the bottom left and the target point on the top right corner. A mobile robot is controlled to navigate from the starting point to reach the target without collisions with the obstacles. The neural network controller developed in the maze in Figure 10(a) shows good navigation performances in testing maze given in Figure 10(b).

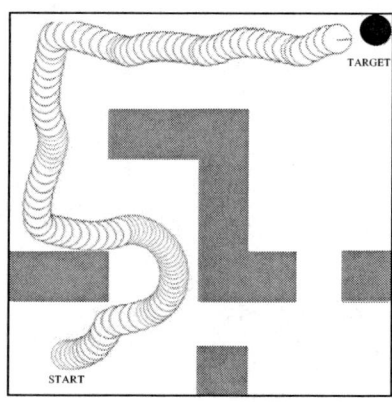

(a) Evolution

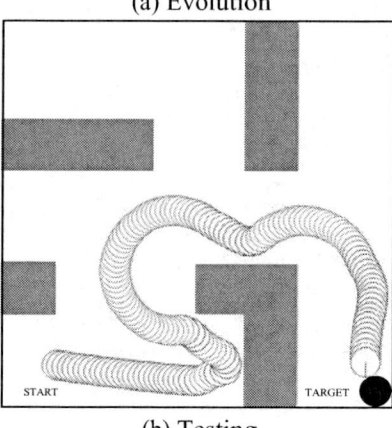

(b) Testing

Figure 10: Simulation environments and navigation result of using evolved neural network.

V. CONCLUSION

This paper proposes a combined method of *L*-systems and DNA coding for developing evolutionary neural networks. The goal is to design a self-organizing modular neural network based on development and evolution. *L*-system, developmental model is used to design the architecture of neural network and DNA coding is used to encode the production rule of *L*-system. To evaluate the effectiveness of our scheme, we applied proposed evolvable neural network to designing the controller of autonomous mobile robot for navigation. Autonomous mobile robot that has evolved neural network controller could go to the target without collision. A mobile robot with the controller obtained from the proposed developmental model navigates and avoids the collisions with obstacles in a new operating environment.

VI. REFERENCES

[1] X. Yao, "Evolving artificial neural networks," *Proceedings of the IEEE*, Vol. 87, No. 9, pp.1423-1447, 1999.
[2] S. W. Moon and S. G. Kong, "Block-based Neural Networks," *IEEE Transactions on Neural Networks*, Vol. 12, No. 2, pp.307-317, March 2001.
[3] P. J. Angeline, G. M. Sauders, and J. B. Pollack, "An evolutionary algorithm that constructs recurrent neural networks," *IEEE Trans. on Neural Networks*, Vol. 5, No. 1, pp.54-65, 1994.
[4] X. Yao and Y. Lie, "A new evolutionary system for evolving artificial neural networks," *IEEE Trans. on Neural Networks*, Vol. 8, No. 3, pp.54-65, 1994.
[5] F. H. F. Leung, H. K. Lam, S. H. Ling, and P. K. S. Tam, "Tuning of the structure and parameters of neural network using an improved genetic algorithm," *IEEE Trans. on Neural Networks*, Vol. 14, No. 1, pp.79-88, 2003.
[6] J. Kodjabachian and J. A. Meyer, "Evolution and development of neural controllers for locomotion, gradient-following, and obstacle-avoidance in artificial insects," *IEEE Trans. on Neural Networks*, Vol. 9, No. 5, pp.796-812, 1998.
[7] B. L. M Happel and J. M. J. Murre, "The design and evolution of modular neural network architecture," *Neural Networks*, Vol. 7, pp.985-1004, 1994.
[8] E. J. W. Boers and I. G. Sprinkhuizen-Kuyper, "Combined biological metaphors," *Advances in the Evolutionary Synthesis of Intelligent Agents*, M. J. Patel, V. Honavar, and K. Balakrishnan, Eds., MIT Press, Ch. 6, pp.153-183, 2001.
[9] F. Gruau, "Automatic definition of modular neural networks," *Adaptive Behavior*, Vol. 3, No. 2, pp.151-183, 1995.
[10] A. Cangelosi, S. Nolfi, and D. Parisi, "Artificial life models of neural development," *On Growth, Form and Computers*, S. Kumar and P. J. Bently, Eds., Elsevier Academic Press, pp.339-352, 2003.
[11] D. W. Lee and K. B. Sim, "Evolving chaotic neural systems for time series prediction," *Proc. of Congress on Evolutionary Computation*, Vol. 1, pp.310-316, 1999.
[12] A. Lindenmayer, "Mathematical models for cellular interaction in development, Part I, II," *Journal of Theoretical Biology*, Vol. 18, No. 3, pp.280-315, 1968.
[13] A. Lindenmayer, "Developmental models of multicellular organisms: A computer graphics perspective," *Artificial Life*, Addison-Wesley, pp.221-249, 1987.
[14] S. Kumar and P. Bently, "Biologically inspired evolutionary development," *Proc. of International Conference on Evolvable Systems: From Biology to Hardware*, A. Tyrrell, P. Haddow, and J. Torresen Eds., LNCS-2606, Springer, pp.57-68, 2003.
[15] Y. Yoshikawa, T. Furuhashi, and Y. Uchikawa, "Knowledge acquisition of fuzzy control rules using DNA coding method and pseudo-bacterial GA," *Lecture Notes in Artificial Intelligence*, Springer, Vol. 1285, pp.126-135, 1997.
[16] A. S. Wu and R. K. Lindsay, "A computation of the fixed and floating building block representation in genetic algorithms," *Evolutionary Computation*, Vol. 4, No. 2, pp.169-193, 1996.

A Recurrent RBF Network Model for Nearest Neighbor Classification

Mehmet K. Muezzinoglu
Computational Intelligence Lab.
University of Louisville
Louisville, KY 40292, U.S.A.
E-mail: mkerem@ieee.org

Jacek M. Zurada
Department of Electrical and
Computer Engineering
University of Louisville
Louisville, KY 40292, U.S.A.
E-mail: j.zurada@ieee.org

Abstract—Superposition of radial basis functions centered at given prototype patterns constitutes one of the most suitable energy forms for gradient systems that perform nearest neighbor classification with real-valued static prototypes. It is shown in this paper that a continuous-time dynamical neural network model, employing a radial basis function and a sigmoid multi-layer perceptron sub-networks, is capable of maximizing such an energy form locally, thus performing almost perfectly nearest neighbor classification, when initiated by a distorted pattern. The dynamical classification scheme implemented by the network eliminates all comparisons, which are the vital steps of the conventional nearest neighbor classification process. The performance of the proposed network model is demonstrated on image reconstruction applications.

I. INTRODUCTION

Nearest neighbor pattern classification is the problem of evaluating the association map

$$f(\mathbf{z}) = \arg \min_{\mathbf{y} \in M} d(\mathbf{z}, \mathbf{y}), \qquad (1)$$

defined on a pattern space $\mathbb{P}$, where $M \subseteq \mathbb{P}$ is a finite set of prototype patterns and $d(\,,\,)$ is a metric on $\mathbb{P}$. A system that calculates (1) for given M and $\mathbf{z}$, called the Nearest Neighbor Classifier (NNC), is the focus of the design problem in this paper.

A straightforward way of evaluating exactly (1) for any given instance $(\mathbf{z} \in \mathbb{P}, M \subseteq \mathbb{P})$ requires computation of an array of $m = |M|$ distances from $\mathbf{z}$ to each $\mathbf{y} \in M$, then obtaining the index of the minimum element through comparisons, and finally extracting the pattern $\mathbf{y}^* \in M$ associated with the resulting index. This three-stage procedure can be implemented easily on digital computers and it necessitates m evaluations of the metric $d(\,,\,)$ together with $m-1$ pairwise comparisons among the distance array. In addition to its high computational requirements, the method also requires the prototype patterns stored explicitly in the physical memory of the system to be extracted after the comparison phase. A particular case of the problem for $\mathbb{P} = \{0, 1\}^n$, named the nearest codeword problem, has been reported in [1] as NP-complete. This result may be extended to an arbitrary $\mathbb{P}$.

In the development years of neural network theory, a single layer of n discrete neurons within a feedback loop was facilitated to retrieve binary patterns from their distorted versions in [2]. This concept has triggered an enormous interest in analysis and design of finite-state recurrent neural networks, since these neurodynamical systems exploit the memory storage and recovery property, providing a motivation towards explaining the biological associative memory by collective operation of basic computational units. It is possibly for this reason that, artificial neural systems that demonstrate the pattern reconstruction property, even partially for some $\mathbf{z} \in \mathbb{P}$, have been accepted conceptually as associative memories in the related literature. However, there is still a significant gap from engineering viewpoint between NNC, i.e. the ideal associative memory, and the conventional neural associative systems, as detailed below. Based on this fact, we view the iterative map realized by a recurrent network model from its initial state vector to the steady state as an approximation of (1), setting formally the NNC as the objective in auto-associative memory design.

The way Hopfield Associative Memory (HAM) [2] operates has indeed three major advantages over the conventional implementation described above:

1) The computation of the associative map is left to the autonomous dynamics of the network, so no comparison is performed explicitly throughout the process.
2) The network structure is independent of the number m of prototypes to be stored.[1]
3) Convergence to a fixed point is guaranteed in at most n^2 steps, when the network has symmetric weight parameters and is operated in asynchronous mode [3].

On the other hand, HAM performs so poor by evaluating (1) that it hardy qualifies as a binary NNC.

Most of the limitations of conventional HAM in approximating (1) apply in general for any recurrent network with a fixed structure independent of the cardinality of M. They can be explained by an energy function approach to the network dynamics: A *fixed network model* may be associated only to a *fixed form of energy function* defined over its state space, which is minimized locally along trajectories generated by the network dynamics. In particular, as proven in [3], the energy function associated to the HAM model has a quadratic form,

---
[1]This would have been a really valuable property from information theoretic point of view, if there would have existed a design method capable of mapping an arbitrary M as the fixed point set of the network, which utilizes $n^2 + n$ parameters.

and hence the network is able to recall a point only if it is designated as a local minimum to this energy form by a design method. In other words, a given set M of n-dimensional prototype vectors cannot be stored altogether as fixed points of HAM, unless there exists a pair $(\mathbf{Q}, \mathbf{c})$ such that the quadratic $Q(\mathbf{x}) = \mathbf{x}^T \mathbf{Q} \mathbf{x} + \mathbf{c}^T \mathbf{x}$ has a local minimum at each element of M. Similar restrictions apply for energy forms associated with other recurrent models with a fixed structure. Therefore, no fixed network model is capable of handling all possible (unrestricted) prototype combinations $M \subseteq \mathbb{P}$ in general.

In this paper, we propose a continuous-time gradient neural network model with adaptive structure that qualifies as an NNC. The dynamics of the model is defined in the bounded state space $[0, 1]^n$ such that it maximizes an associated scalar energy function, which is in the form of a sum of Gaussian functions. Since the maxima of such a form can be allocated at any point of the unit-hypercube $[0, 1]^n$ (not necessarily at the vertices), our approach relaxes the conventional restriction of binary prototypes in neural associative memory towards real-valued ones.

The proposed dynamic model employs a hybrid of two algebraic networks, namely a Radial Basis Function (RBF) network and a Multi-Layer Perceptron (MLP) network. Each RBF node in the model inserts into the state space an open basin of attraction around its center, thus introducing a stable fixed point, whereas MLP is utilized merely as a multiplier.

Recurrent RBF networks have been applied successfully to such areas that require rapid and accurate data interpolation, such as adaptive control [4], noise cancellation [5]. Their performance as finite-state automata has also been demonstrated in [6]. To our knowledge, this paper constitutes the first application of the RBF network structure in a feedback loop working as a nearest neighbor classifier.

The outline of the paper is as follows. The design constraints, energy function-based design procedure, and network model are derived in the following section. In Section III, we demonstrate performance of the resulting network as an NNC is demonstrated on binary and gray-scale image restoration applications. The concluding remarks are given in Section IV.

II. METHODOLOGY

A. Design Problem and Constraints

The objective is to design a continuous-time autonomous neurodynamical system operating on the continuous state space $\mathbb{R}^n$ to evaluate (1) as a map from the initial state vector to the steady state response. This setting assumes initially $\mathbb{P} = \mathbb{R}^n$ with a metric induced by the Euclidean norm: $d(\mathbf{u}, \mathbf{v}) = \|\mathbf{u} - \mathbf{v}\|_2$.

We limit the search for the dynamical system within the gradient networks in order to utilize the one-to-one correspondence between the stable equilibria of a gradient network and the local extrema of its energy function. In fact, this allows to pose the design problem of the classifier solely in the function space: Assign each prototype to a local maximum of an energy form $E(\cdot)$ in a bijective way, rendering every $\mathbf{p} \in M$ a local maximum of $E(\cdot)$ without creating any extraneous one.

The design problem cast in this way reduces the feasible energy functions to the ones that assume multiple and easily-adjustable local maxima. The energy function must also allow the designer to tune the basins of attraction of such fixed points that they share the state-space of the system in the way the ideal classifier (1) quantizes $\mathbb{P}$. Finally, the gradient of $E(\cdot)$ must be well defined and assume a valid neural implementation. Fortunately, these design constraints are not contradicting as they are satisfied simultaneously by at least one particular class of functions as shown below.

B. Radial Basis Functions

Radial basis functions are extensively used to implement algebraic mappings that interpolate and/or generalize a finite set of samples [7], [8]. The nonlinearities possess the localization property [9], which makes the network sensitive only to particular regions of the input space. The centers and widths of high-sensitivity regions are expressed explicitly as network parameters. Hence, the RBF network design problem can be cast directly in the input space by shaping the regions according to data distribution. Encoding the sample features as network-specific quantities, which is often tackled in MLP design, is not needed. We make use of this property of RBF networks to represent the prototypes in the design of our neurodynamical NNC. However, instead of the regression capability of RBF networks, carefully studied in statistical learning literature, we are interested here in evaluating their input-output function as an energy form for dynamical NNCs.

An admissible RBF $\phi(\cdot) : \mathbb{R}^n \to \mathbb{R}^+$ possesses the following three attributes:

1) $\phi(\cdot)$ is continuous and bounded.
2) $\phi(\cdot)$ attains its unique maximum at a point $\mathbf{c} \in \mathbb{R}^n$, called center.
3) $\lim_{\|\mathbf{x} - \mathbf{c}\| \to \infty} \phi(\mathbf{x}) = 0$.

Note that, such a $\phi(\cdot)$ discriminates the points within a vicinity $\mathcal{D}$ of $\mathbf{c}$ from others by returning a higher value. The width of $\mathcal{D}$ is usually parameterized in the expression of $\phi(\cdot)$ as in the case of the most popular RBF, the Gauss function

$$\phi(\mathbf{x}) = \exp\left(-\frac{\|\mathbf{x} - \mathbf{c}\|_2^2}{\gamma}\right), \qquad (2)$$

where $\gamma \geq 0$ is the width parameter[2]. Hereinafter we will assume this form for $\phi(\cdot)$ and maintain the design based on Gaussian RBF, though the arguments in the sequel could be derived in a similar way for any other admissible RBF as well.

A single RBF $\phi(\cdot)$ centered at $\mathbf{c}$ is viewed here as a continuous function to be maximized by the gradient system

$$\begin{aligned} \dot{\mathbf{x}}(t) &= \nabla_\mathbf{x} \phi(\mathbf{x})|_{\mathbf{x}=\mathbf{x}(t)} \\ &= -\frac{2}{\gamma}(\mathbf{x}(t) - \mathbf{c})\phi(\mathbf{x}(t)) \end{aligned} \qquad (3)$$

---

[2] The width of a Gauss curve has been traditionally denoted by the standard deviation, equal to $\sqrt{\gamma}$ in (2). For conciseness of the notation, we prefer parameterizing it merely by γ.

along all trajectories. Such a convergence to the unique fixed point $\mathbf{c}$ from all initial conditions $\mathbf{x}(0) \in \mathbb{R}^n$ is interpreted as a trivial instance of nearest neighbor classification for $M = \{\mathbf{c}\}$. Among infinitely many state equation forms on the same state space, all bearing a unique stable fixed point at $\mathbf{c}$,[3] we specifically adopt (3) as the basic building block of our design, since this setting allows proper concurrence of systems with a single fixed point to form a single dynamics with multiple fixed points.

C. Dynamical Classifier

Given m prototypes $M = \{\mathbf{p}_i\}_{i=1}^m \subset \mathbb{R}^n$, let us set first m distinct energy functions $\{\phi_i(\cdot)\}_{i=1}^m$ each centered at $\mathbf{c}_i = \mathbf{p}_i$ with the width parameter $\gamma_i > 0$. These energy forms yield m separate dynamical classifiers in the form of (3). Note that each classifier is perfect in the sense that it evaluates (1) exactly for the (unique) prototype $\mathbf{c}_i = \mathbf{p}_i$. In order to obtain a single state equation with stable fixed points at the prototypes, we propose summing up merely the right-hand sides of the individual equations:

$$\dot{\mathbf{x}}(t) = \sum_{i=1}^m \frac{2}{\gamma_i} (\mathbf{x}(t) - \mathbf{c}_i) \phi_i(\mathbf{x}(t)). \quad (4)$$

The resulting state equation (4) defines a gradient system which now maximizes the continuous and bounded energy function

$$E(\mathbf{x}) = \sum_{i=1}^m \phi_i(\mathbf{x}). \quad (5)$$

This relation guarantees that the continuous-time system (4) is globally convergent, due to Lyapunov's indirect method [10], and its fixed points are the extremum points of (5).

In light of the discussion of Section II-A, the qualitative performance of (4) as an NNC is dependent upon the degree to which (5) fits the design constraints.

In [11], we account for the impact of the width parameters $\gamma_1, \ldots, \gamma_\ell$, the only adjustable parameters of the proposed model, on the qualitative properties of the dynamical system (4). It is shown in [11] that the width parameters must be chosen all equal ($\gamma_1 = \cdots = \gamma_m \triangleq \gamma$) and sufficiently small due to three particular reasons: (1) The basins of attractions of the prototypes in (4) share the state space optimally only when $\gamma_1 = \cdots = \gamma_m$; (2) The dynamical system defined by (4) has exactly m stable fixed points only if $\max_i \gamma_i$ is sufficiently small; (3) The distance between the stable fixed points of the state equation (4) and the original prototypes $\{\mathbf{c}_1, \ldots, \mathbf{c}_m\}$ diminish exponentially as $\gamma_i \to 0$ for all $i \in \{1, \ldots, m\}$.

D. Transform to Bounded State Space

The nearest neighbor classification problem considered initially on $\mathbb{P} = \mathbb{R}^n$ is equivalent to the one posed within the unit hypercube $\mathbb{P} = [0, 1]^n$ through a bijective transform, which maps the prototypes and the distorted pattern to $[0, 1]^n$ in a distance-preserving way. If the given prototypes $M = \{\mathbf{p}_i\}_{i=1}^m$

---

[3]The simplest form of such systems is $\dot{\mathbf{x}}(t) = -\mathbf{x}(t) + \mathbf{c}$, which maximizes the energy function $E(\mathbf{x}) = -\|\mathbf{x} - \mathbf{c}\|_2^2 / 2$.

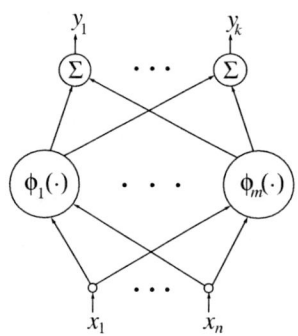

Fig. 1. RBF network model with n inputs, m RBF nodes, and k outputs.

are not contained already within the unit-hypercube, then a linear contraction that scales them by the maximum entry $\max_{i,j}(\mathbf{p}_i)_j$ among all prototypes transforms the problem to $[0, 1]^n$. The contracted prototypes reduce the state space of (4) to $[0, 1]^n$ due to the following corollary:

Corollary 1: If $\mathbf{c}_1, \ldots, \mathbf{c}_m \in [0, 1]^n$, then, for all initial conditions $\mathbf{x}(0) \in [0, 1]^n$, the solution of (4) is bounded by the unit hypercube.

Proof: Let $\mathbf{x}$ be an arbitrary point on a face of the unit hypercube, i.e. $x_j = 0$ or $x_j = 1$ for some $j \in \{1, \ldots, n\}$. For $x_j = 0$, the right-hand side of the j-th differential equation in (4) is nonnegative due to the assumption that all prototypes lie within the hypercube. Similarly, $\dot{x}_j \leq 0$ for $x_j = 1$. Hence, the vector field defined by (4) never points toward the exterior of $[0, 1]^n$ along the faces, constraining all solutions starting within the hypercube into $[0, 1]^n$. ∎

The unit-hypercube as a state-space has nice features, among them it offers a clearer analysis and a canonical implementation. Therefore, without loss of generality, we focus on the transformed classification problem by assuming that $M \in [0, 1]^n$.

E. Gradient Network Model

In this subsection, we outline the neural network model of the proposed system (4). Its key component is the RBF network model, shown in Figure 1.

We begin by rearranging the state representation (4) as

$$\dot{\mathbf{x}}(t) = \frac{2}{\gamma} \left[\mathbf{x}(t) \sum_{i=1}^m \exp\left(-\frac{\|\mathbf{x}(t) - \mathbf{c}_i\|_2^2}{\gamma}\right) - \sum_{i=1}^m \mathbf{c}_i \exp\left(-\frac{\|\mathbf{x}(t) - \mathbf{c}_i\|_2^2}{\gamma}\right) \right], \quad (6)$$

and focus on realizing the right-hand side by an algebraic neural network. In the direct realization scheme adopted here, the network has the feedforward path and the feedback provided via n integrators.

Note that the form (6) requires one straight and n weighted summations of the RBFs, which could be achieved by an RBF

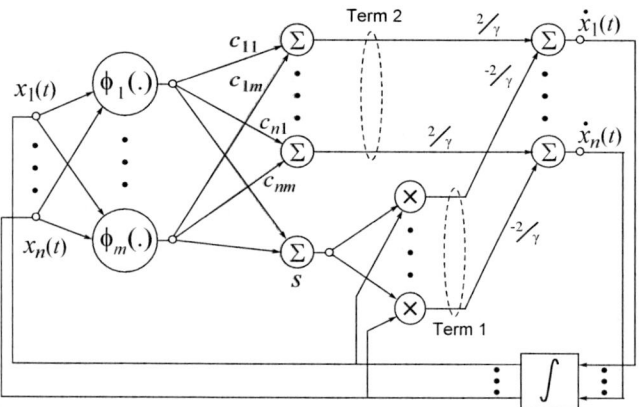

Fig. 2. Block diagram of the proposed neurodynamical NNC. The variables labelled by Term 1 and Term 2 denote the first and the second term in brackets of (6), respectively.

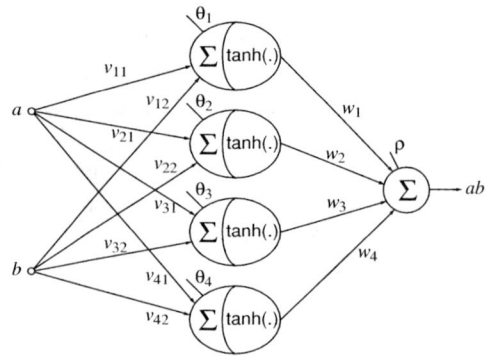

Fig. 3. MLP network model to multiply two bounded variables a and b.

TABLE I
PARAMETERS OF THE MLP NETWORK OF FIGURE 3 TO REALIZE $a \times b$ FOR $a \in [0, 1]$ AND $b \in [0, m]$.

v_{11}	0.02418	θ_2	6.77450
v_{21}	16.34820	θ_3	-0.78514
v_{31}	0.12108	θ_4	-0.68511
v_{41}	0.09868	w_1	$82.46650m$
v_{12}	$-0.10386/m$	w_2	$0.00004m$
v_{22}	$-58.58570/m$	w_3	$59.61670m$
v_{32}	$0.12528/m$	w_4	$-84.57270m$
v_{42}	$-0.02288/m$	ρ	$-60.5247m$
θ_1	0.68984		

network with $n + 1$ output nodes. This network employs m RBF nodes, to compute the vector

$$\mathbf{r} = \begin{bmatrix} \exp\left(-\frac{\|\mathbf{x} - \mathbf{c}_1\|_2^2}{\gamma}\right) & \cdots & \exp\left(-\frac{\|\mathbf{x} - \mathbf{c}_m\|_2^2}{\gamma}\right) \end{bmatrix}^T,$$

where $\mathbf{x}$ is the input vector. The output node computing the straight sum is a single summing unit labelled by s, whereas the remaining n output nodes perform the matrix multiplication $\mathbf{Cr}$, where

$$\mathbf{C} = \begin{bmatrix} \mathbf{c}_1 & \cdots & \mathbf{c}_m \end{bmatrix}.$$

To realize the first term within the parenthesis in (6), n additional blocks are required in order to multiply the state vector $\mathbf{x}(t)$ by the output of node s. Finally, a single linear layer subtracts the second term from the first one and scales the outcome by the constant $-2/\gamma$. The block diagram of the gradient model is shown in Figure 2.

Multiplication of variables is in general an expensive task in neural-like architectures within the conventional and widely-accepted McCullogh-Pitts model [12], which assumes a neuron to be a computational unit capable of summing its weighted inputs, and then passing the result through a simple nonlinearity. It is not possible in general to fit the fundamental arithmetic operation of multiplication within this scheme. Fortunately, the bounded state-space of the classifier, as shown by Corollary 1, together with the upper bound m on the sum of RBFs, constitute a particular case that allows a simple and efficient neural network realization of the multiplier blocks in Figure 2.

To achieve multiplication of two arbitrary scalar variables $a, b \in [0, 1]$, we consider the two-layer perceptron network shown in Figure 3, which utilizes four sigmoidal nodes and a linear one. The activation functions of the first layer nodes are all $\tanh(\cdot)$. To determine the parameters of this subnetwork to perform multiplication, we generated the training set

$$\mathcal{S} = \left\{ \left(\begin{bmatrix} x_1 & x_2 \end{bmatrix}^T, x_1 \cdot x_2 \right) : \right.$$

$$\left. x_1 = 10^{-2}k, x_2 = 10^{-2}\ell, k, \ell = 0, 1, \ldots, 100 \right\},$$

then performed the classical backpropagation training algorithm with adaptive step-size and random initial conditions. The training results after 2000 epochs are shown in Table 1 (to be evaluated for $m = 1$ for now), yielding a mean-square error of less than 10^{-8} on $\mathcal{S}$. Since $\mathcal{S}$ represents the input space $[0, 1]^2$ effectively enough, having obtained such a small training error, we conclude that the proposed MLP network realizes successfully $a \cdot b$.

Due to Corollary 1, each state variable is constrained within $[0, 1]$ along the classification, so can be applied directly as an input to the resulting MLP network to be multiplied with the other operand. However, the sum of m Gaussians (the node labelled by s in Figure 2) is in general not within this bound, but definitely in $[0, m]$. Thus, it can be applied as the second input to the MLP subnetwork only after being scaled by $1/m$. The output of the multiplier should then be scaled by m in order to realize the first term in the parenthesis. These two modifications on the second operand can be achieved by scaling the input layer weights v_{i2}, $i = 1, \ldots, 4$ and the output layer parameters $w_1, \ldots, w_4, b$ by $1/m$ and m, respectively, as given in Table 1. With these parameters, the resulting MLP could replace the multiplier blocks in Figure 2.

As a result, the overall model proposed to realize (4) employs a hybrid of one RBF and n MLP networks on the feedforward path to implement the right-hand side of (4), plus n integrator blocks on the feedback path to provide dynamics. The number of RBF nodes in the first layer equals

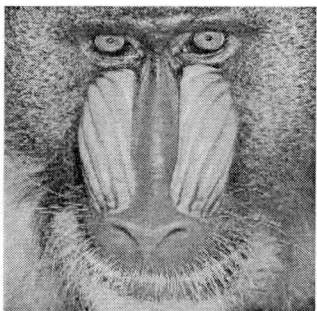

Fig. 4. Four 64-level 512 × 512 gray-scale images used in image reconstruction experiment.

the cardinality of M. This provides the key feature of the model, namely a structure adaptive to the given prototypes, as discussed in the introduction. Also note that the centers and the columns of the weight matrix $\mathbf{C}$ are set directly to the given prototypes. This reduces the burden of adding a new prototype to the existing fixed points (i.e. memorizing) to incorporating merely a new RBF node and augmenting $\mathbf{C}$ by the new prototype, without requiring any computations. Similarly, removing (or forgetting) an existing prototype can be directly achieved by removing the associated RBF node and its connections. The only tunable parameter of the n identical MLP subnetworks is m, the number of prototypes. Then the sole scalar parameter to be adjusted by the designer is γ to improve the classification performance, as explained in [11] and summarized above.

Since the considered state equation (6) implements a gradient system, the convergence speed of the proposed model is dependent on the magnitude of $\nabla E(\ )$ along the trajectory followed. The convergence time of the system is expected to worsen in general as the width parameter γ decreases, because the energy landscape turns out to be almost flat on the entire state space, but in the vicinity of the prototypes. This problem could be circumvented by scaling the right hand side of (6) by a large positive constant. We omit this extension here, under which the reasoning above about the qualitative features of the model would still be valid.

We finally note that the proposed neurodynamic model does compute the distances from the current state vector to the prototypes,[4] but still performs no comparisons to evaluate (1), differing itself from the straightforward NNC.

III. Experimental Results

In this section, we present the application of the neurodynamical NNC on gray-scale image reconstruction.

To simulate the continuous-time system (4) on a digital computer, we used the MATLAB® ODE Toolbox function ode23s [14]. This numerical solver implements a modified version of Rosenbrock method, a generalization of Runge-Kutta discretization, and is specialized in ordinary stiff differential equations, such as (4) with a small γ.

In this experiment, we used the four 64-level 512 × 512 gray-scale images shown in Figure 4. To process these images by our dynamical NNC, which operates within the unit-hypercube, we represented them with 4 matrices by mapping linearly each pixel intensity to the interval $[0, 1]$, where 0 denotes the black level and 1 denotes the white one.

Using these matrices, we generated the prototype sets $\{\mathbf{p}_1^i, \mathbf{p}_2^i, \mathbf{p}_3^i, \mathbf{p}_4^i\}_{i=1}^{512}$, where $\mathbf{p}_j^i$ is the i-th column of j-th matrix. Then, we constructed the 512 dynamical NNCs for each prototype set. The width parameter of each NNC was set equal to $\min_{j,k \in \{1,2,3,4\}, j \neq k} \|\mathbf{p}_j^i - \mathbf{p}_k^i\|_2^2/4$ calculated using the i-th prototype set. It has been shown [11] that such a width parameter ensures the effective representation of all prototypes as stable fixed points in the associated dynamical NNC.

We then obtained the corrupted versions of the original images with 40% salt-and-pepper noise by choosing 40% of the 262144 pixels of each image randomly and assigning randomly their new values as 0 or 1 with equal probabilities.[5] The corrupted images are shown on the first row of Figure 5. Each corrupted image was segmented into their columns and each column was applied to the corresponding NNC as the initial condition. The entries of resulting vectors were then quantized to 64 gray levels between 0 and 1, and combined finally in a matrix for interpretation. The results shown on the second row of Figure 5 were obtained. This experiment shows that the proposed model was successful in the classification task on non-binary patterns.

IV. Conclusions

We have presented a novel continuous-time neurodynamical model that performs nearest neighbor classification on the continuous pattern space $[0, 1]^n$. The design procedure proposed for the model imposes no restriction on prototypes due to the adaptive structure of RBF network to the cardinality of M. The prototypes are represented explicitly as network parameters (weights and thresholds), so the given information needs not be encoded in the system. Moreover, this representation ensures localized parameters in the dynamical model associated to each fixed point so that a prototype can be added, removed, or modified independently, i.e. without affecting the

---

[4] Such explicit distance calculations are avoided really in conventional neural associative memory models [13].

[5] The salt-and-pepper noise is known as one of the most challenging corruption types for image processing systems.

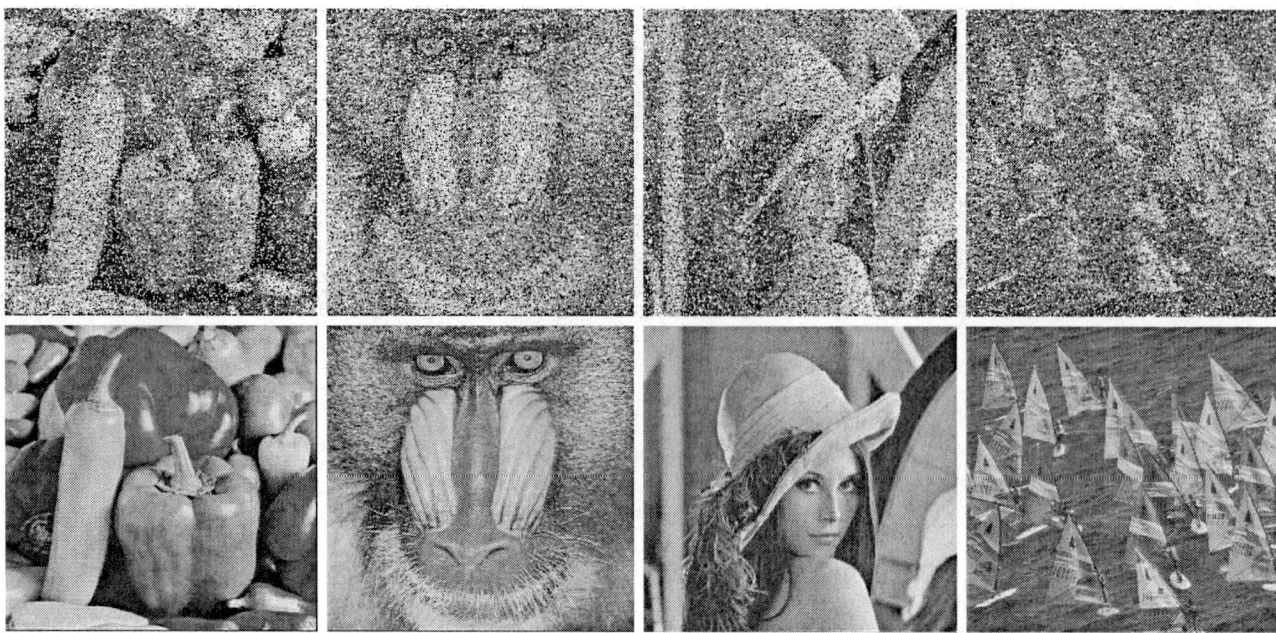

Fig. 5. Images corrupted by 40% salt-and-pepper noise (above) and their reconstructions by the dynamical NNCs (below).

parameters associated to rest of the fixed points. Although the network calculates all distances from the current state vector to prototypes, the convergence to the nearest one is guaranteed for each initial state vector without comparisons along the autonomous process. The only network parameter influencing the classification accuracy of the proposed NNC is the width parameter γ of the Gaussian RBFs used in the design. We have also demonstrated the classification performance of the model on a gray-scale image processing application. The results show that the model implements the association map (1) almost perfectly, so it qualifies as a neurodynamic NNC.

ACKNOWLEDGMENT

The work of J.M. Zurada has been sponsored in part by the Systems Research Institute (IBS) of the Polish Academy of Science (PAN) 01-447 Warsaw, ul. Newelska 6.

REFERENCES

[1] M. R. Garey and D. S. Johnson, *Computers and Intractability*. New York: W.H. Freeman, 1979.
[2] J. J. Hopfield, "Neural networks and physical systems with emergent collective computational abilities", *Proc. National Acad. Sci.*, vol. 79, pp. 2554-2558, 1982.
[3] J. Bruck and J. W. Goodman, "A generalized convergence theorem for neural networks", *IEEE Trans. Information Theory*, vol. 34, pp. 1089-1092, 1988.
[4] R. M. Sanner and J. J. M. Slotine, "Gaussian networks for direct adaptive control", *IEEE Trans. Neural Networks*, vol. 3, pp. 837-863, 1992.
[5] S. A. Billings and C. F. Fung, "Recurrent radial basis function networks for adaptive noise cancellation", *Neural Networks*, vol. 8, pp. 273-290, 1995.
[6] P. Frasconi, M. Gori, M. Maggini, and G. Soda, "Representation of finite state automata in recurrent radial basis function networks", *Machine Learning*, vol. 23, pp. 5-32, 1996.
[7] T. Poggio and F. Girosi, "Networks for approximation and learning", *Proceedings of the IEEE*, vol. 78, pp. 1481-1497, 1990.
[8] J. Park and I. W. Sandberg, "Universal approximation using radial-basis-function networks", *Neural Computation*, vol. 3, pp. 246-257, 1991.
[9] N. B. Karayiannis, "Reformulated radial basis neural networks trained by gradient descent", *IEEE Trans. Neural Networks*, vol. 10, pp. 657-671, 1999.
[10] H. K. Khalil, *Nonlinear Systems*. 3rd Edition, Prentice-Hall, 2001.
[11] M. K. Muezzinoglu and J. M. Zurada, "RBF-based neurodynamic nearest neighbor classification in real pattern space", submitted to *Pattern Recognition* in 2005.
[12] J. M. Zurada, *Introduction to Artificial Neural Systems*. St. Paul, MN: West, 1992.
[13] A. N. Michel and D. Liu, *Qualitative Analysis and Sythesis of Recurrent Neural Networks*. New York: Marcel Dekker, 2002.
[14] L. F. Shampine and M. W. Reichelt, "The MATLAB ODE Suite", *SIAM Journal on Scientific Computing*, vol. 18, pp 1-22, 1997.

Face Recognition Using Modular Neural Networks and Fuzzy Sugeno Integral for Response Integration

Patricia Melin, Claudia Gonzalez, Felma Gonzalez and Oscar Castillo
Dept. of Computer Science, Tijuana Institute of Technology
Tijuana, Mexico
pmelin@tectijuana.mx

Abstract-We describe in this paper a new approach for pattern recognition using modular neural networks with a fuzzy logic method for response integration. We proposed a new architecture for modular neural networks for achieving pattern recognition in the particular case of human faces. Also, the method for achieving response integration is based on the fuzzy Sugeno integral. Response integration is required to combine the outputs of all the modules in the modular network. We have applied the new approach for face recognition with a real database of faces from students of our institution.

I. INTRODUCTION

Response integration methods for modular neural networks that have been studied, to the moment, do not solve well real recognition problems with large sets of data or in other cases reduce the final output to the result of only one module. Also, in the particular case of face recognition, methods of weighted statistical average do not work well due to the nature of the face recognition problem. For these reasons, a new approach for face recognition using modular neural networks and fuzzy integration of responses was proposed in this paper.

The basic idea of the new approach is to divide a human face in to three different regions: the eyes, the nose and the mouth. Each of these regions is assigned to one module of the neural network. In this way, the modular neural network has three different modules, one for each of the regions of the human face. At the end, the final decision of face recognition is done by an integration module, which has to take into account the results of each of the modules. In our approach, the integration module uses the fuzzy Sugeno integral to combine the outputs of the three modules. The fuzzy Sugeno integral allows the integration of responses from the three modules of the eyes, nose and mouth of a human specific face. Other approaches in the literature use other types of integration modules, like voting methods, majority methods, and neural networks.

The new approach for face recognition was tested with a database of students and professors from our institution. This database was collected at our institution using a digital camera. The results with our new approach for face recognition on this database were excellent.

II. MODULAR NEURAL NETWORKS

There exists a lot of neural network architectures in the literature that work well when the number of inputs is relatively small, but when the complexity of the problem grows or the number of inputs increases, their performance decreases very quickly. For this reason, there has also been research work in compensating in some way the problems in learning of a single neural network over high dimensional spaces.

In the work of Sharkey [1], the use of multiple neural systems (Multi-Nets) is described. It is claimed that multi-nets have better performance or even solve problems that monolithic neural networks are not able to solve. It is also claimed that multi-nets or modular systems have also the advantage of being easier to understand or modify, if necessary.

In the literature there is also mention of the terms "ensemble" and "modular" for this type of neural network. The term "ensemble" is used when a redundant set of neural networks is utilized, as described in Hansen and Salomon [2]. In this case, each of the neural networks is redundant because it is providing a solution for the same task, as it is shown in Fig. 1.

On the other hand, in the modular approach, one task or problem is decompose in subtasks, and the complete solution requires the contribution of all the modules, as it is shown in Fig. 2.

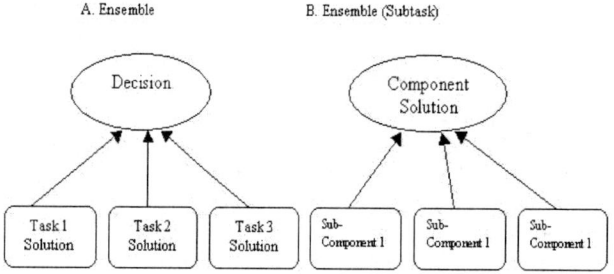

Fig. 1. Ensembles for one task and subtask.

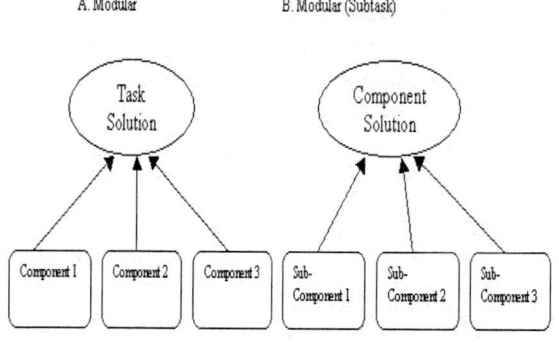

Fig. 2 Modular approach for task and subtask.

A. Multiple Neural Networks

In this approach we can find networks that use strongly separated architectures. Each neural network works independently in its own domain. Each of the neural networks is build and trained for a specific task. The final decision is based on the results of the individual networks, called agents or experts.

One example of this is shown by Schmidt [3], in Fig. 3, where a multiple architecture is used, one module consists of a neural network trained for recognizing a person by the voice, while the other module is a neural network trained for recognizing a person by the image.

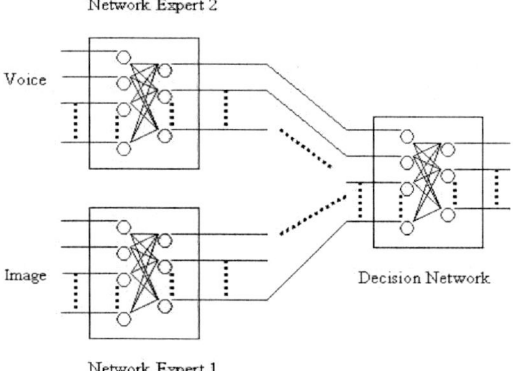

Fig. 3 Multiple networks for voice and image.

The outputs by the experts are the inputs to the decision network, which is the one making the decision based on the outputs of the expert networks.

B. Main Architectures With Multiple Networks

Within multiple neural networks we can find three main classes of this type of networks [4]:

- Mixture of Experts (ME): The mixture of experts can be viewed as a modular version of the multi-layer networks with supervised training or the associative version of competitive learning. In this design, the local experts are trained with the data sets to mitigate weight interference from one expert to the other.
- Gate of Experts: In this case, an optimization algorithm is used for the gating network, to combine the outputs from the experts.
- Hierarchical Mixture of Experts: In this architecture, the individual outputs from the experts are combined with several gating networks in a hierarchical way.

C. "Modular" Neural Networks

The term "Modular Neural Networks" is very fuzzy. It is used in a lot of ways and with different structures. Everything that is not monolithic is said to be modular. In the research work by Egbert [5], the concept of a modular architecture is introduced as the development of a large network using modules.

One of the main ideas of this approach is presented in [3], where all the modules are neural networks. The architecture of a single module is simpler and smaller than the one of a monolithic network. The tasks are modified in such a way that training a subtask is easier than training the complete task. Once all modules are trained, they are connected in a network of modules, instead of using a network of neurons. The modules are independent to some extent, which allows working in parallel. Another idea about modular networks is presented by Boers and Kuiper [5], where they used an approach of networks not totally connected. In this model, the structure is more difficult to analyze, as shown in Fig. 4. A clear separation between modules can't be made. Each module is viewed as a part of the network totally connected.

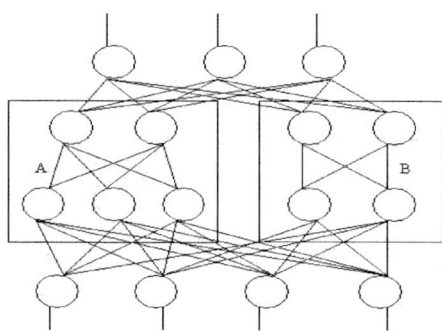

Fig. 4 One type of modular network.

In this figure, we can appreciate two different sections from the monolithic neural network, namely A and B. Since there are no connections between both parts of the network, the dimensionality (number of weights) is reduced. As a consequence the required computations are decreased and speed of convergence is increased.

D. Advantages of Modular Neural Networks

A list of advantages of modular networks is given below:

- They give a significant improvement in the learning capabilities, over monolithic neural networks, due to the constraints imposed on the modular topology.
- They allow complex behavior modeling, by using different types of knowledge, which is not possible without using modularity.
- Modularity may imply reduction of number of parameters, which will allow and increase in computing speed and better generalization capabilities.
- They avoid the interference that affects "global" neural networks.
- They help determine the activity that is being done in each part of the system, helping to understand the role that each network plays within the complete system.

- If there are changes in the environment, modular networks enable changes in an easier way, since there is no need to modify the whole system, only the modules that are affected by this change.

E. Elements of Modular Neural Networks

When considering modular networks to solve a problem, one has to take into account the following points [6]:
- Decompose the main problem into subtasks.
- Organizing the modular architecture, taking into account the nature of each subtask.
- Communication between modules is important, not only in the input of the system but also in the response integration.

In the particular case of this paper, we will concentrate in more detail in the third point, the communication between modules, more specifically information fusion at the integrating module to generate the output of the complete modular system.

F. Main Task Decomposition into Subtasks

Task Decomposition can be performed in three different ways, as mentioned by Lu and Ito [7]:
- *Explicit Decomposition*: In this case, decomposition is made before learning and requires that the designer has deep knowledge about the problem. Of course, this maybe a limitation if there isn't sufficient knowledge about the problem.
- *Automatic Decomposition*: In this case, decomposition is made as learning is progressing.
- *Decomposition into Classes*: This type of decomposition is made before learning, a problem is divided into a set of sub-problems according to the intrinsic relations between the training data. This method only requires knowledge about the relations between classes.

G. Communication Between Modules

In the research studies made by Ronco and Gawthrop [6], several ways of achieving communication between modules are proposed. We can summarize their work by mentioning the following critical points:
1. How to divide information, during the training phase, between the different modules of the system.
2. How to integrate the different outputs given by the different modules of the system to generate the final output of the complete system.

H. Response Integration

Response integration has been considered in several ways, as described by Smith and Johansen [8] and we can give the following list:
- Using Kohonen's self organizing maps, Gaussian mixtures, etc.
- The method of "Winner Takes All", for problems that require similar tasks.
- Models in series, the output of one module is the input to the following one.
- Voting methods, for example the use of the "Softmax" function.
- Linear combination of output results.
- Using discrete logic.
- Using finite state automata.
- Using statistical methods.
- Using fuzzy logic.

III. METHODS FOR RESPONSE INTEGRATION

The importance of this part of the architecture for pattern recognition is due to the high dimensionality of this type of problems. As a consequence in pattern recognition is good alternative to consider a modular approach. This has the advantage of reducing the time required of learning and it also increases accuracy. In our case, we consider dividing the images of a human face in three different regions, and applying a modular structure for achieving pattern recognition.

In the literature we can find several methods for response integration, that have been researched extensively, which in many cases are based on statistical decision methods. We will mention briefly some of these methods of response integration, in particular de ones based on fuzzy logic. The idea of using this type of methods is that the final decision takes into account all of the different kind of information available about the human face. In particular, we consider aggregation operators, and the fuzzy Sugeno integral [9].

Yager [10] mentions in his work, that fuzzy measures for the aggregation criteria of two important classes of problems. In the first type of problems, we have a set $Z=\{z_1,z_2,...,z_n\}$ of objects, and it is desired to select one or more of these objects based on the satisfaction of certain criteria. In this case, for each $z_i \in Z$, it is evaluated $D(z_i)=G(A_i(z_i),...,A_j(z_i))$, and then an object or objects are selected based on the value of G. The problems that fall within this structure are the multi-criteria decision problems, search in databases and retrieving of documents.

In the second type of problems, we have a set $G=\{G_1,G_2,...,G_q\}$ of aggregation functions and object z. Here, each G_k corresponds to different possible identifications of object z, and our goal is to find out the correct identification of z. For achieving this, for each aggregation function G, we obtain a result for each z, $Dk(z)=Gk(A1(z), A2(z), ... ,An(z))$. Then we associate to z the identification corresponding to the larger value of the aggregation function.

A typical example of this type of problems is pattern recognition. Where A_j corresponds to the attributes and $A_j(z)$ measures the compatibility of z with the attribute. Medical applications and fault diagnosis fall into this type of problems. In diagnostic problems, the A_j corresponds to symptoms associated with a particular fault, and G_k captures the relations between these faults.

A. Fuzzy Integral and Sugeno Measures

Fuzzy integrals can be viewed as non-linear functions defined with respect to fuzzy measures. In particular, the "gλ-fuzzy measure" introduced by Sugeno [9] can be used to define fuzzy integrals. The ability of fuzzy integrals to combine the results of multiple information sources has been mentioned in previous works.

Definition 1. A function of sets $g:2^x \rightarrow (0.1)$ is called a fuzzy measure if:
1) $g(0)=0$ $g(x)=1$
2) $g(A) \leq g(B)$ if $A \subset B$
3) if $\{A_i\}i^\alpha =1$ is a sequence of increments of the measurable set then

$$\lim_{i \to \infty} g(A_i) = g(\lim_{i \to \infty} A_i) \quad (1)$$

From the above it can be deduced that g is not necessarily additive, this property is replaced by the additive property of the conventional measure.

From the general definition of the fuzzy measure, Sugeno introduced what is called "gλ-fuzzy measure", which satisfies the following additive property: For every $A, B \subset X$ and $A \cap B = \theta$,

$$g(A \cup B) = g(A) + g(B) + \lambda\, g(A)g(B), \quad (2)$$

for some value of $\lambda > -1$.

This property says that the measure of the union of two disjunct sets can be obtained directly from the individual measures. Using the concept of fuzzy measures, Sugeno [9] developed the concept of fuzzy integrals, which are non-linear functions defined with respect to fuzzy measures like the gλ-fuzzy measure.

Definition 2 let X be a finite set and $h:X \rightarrow [0,1]$ be a fuzzy subset of X, the fuzzy integral over X of function h with respect to the fuzzy measure g is defined in the following way,

$$h(x) \circ g(x) = \max [\min (\min h(x), g(E))] \quad (3)$$

$$E \subseteq X \quad x \in E$$

$$= \sup [\min(\alpha, g(h_\alpha))]$$

$$\alpha \in [0, 1]$$

where h_α is the level set α of h,

$$h_\alpha = \{ x \mid h(x) \geq \alpha \}. \quad (4)$$

We will explain in more detail the above definition: h(x) measures the degree to which concept h is satisfied by x. The term min(h_x) measures the degree to which concept h is satisfied by all the elements in E. The value g(E) is the degree to which the subset of objects E satifies the concept measure by g. As a consequence, the obtained value of comparing these two quantities in terms of operator min indicates the degree to which E satifies both criteria g and min(h_x). Finally, operator max takes the greatest of these terms. One can interpret fuzzy integrals as finding the maximum degree of similarity between the objective and expected value.

IV. PROPOSED ARCHITECTURE AND RESULTS

In the experiments performed in this research work, we used 20 photographs that were taken with a digital camera from students and professors of our Institution. The photographs were taken in such a way that they had 148 pixels wide and 90 pixels high, with a resolution of 300x300 ppi, and with a color representation of a gray scale, some of these photographs are shown in Fig. 5. In addition to the training data (20 photos) we did use 10 photographs that were obtained by applying noise in a random fashion, which was increased from 10 to 100%.

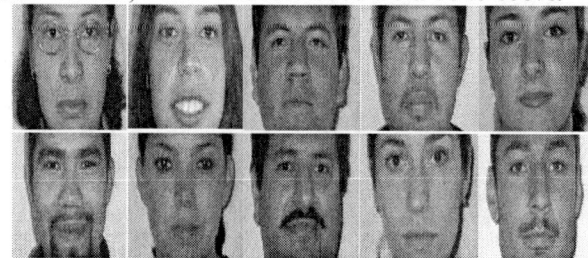

Fig. 5 Sample Images Used for Training.

A. Proposed Architecture

The architecture proposed in this work consist of three main modules, in which each of them in turn consists of a set of neural networks trained with the same data, which provides the modular architecture shown in Fig. 6.

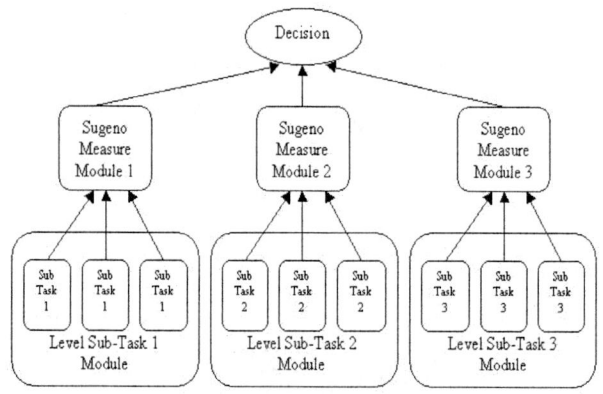

Fig. 6 Final Proposed Architecture.

The input to the modular system is a complete photograph. For performing the neural network training, the images of the human faces were divided in three different regions. The first region consists of the area around the eyes, which corresponds to Sub Task 1. The second region consists of the area around the nose, which corresponds to Sub Task 2. The third region consists of the area around the mouth, which corresponds to Sub Task 3. An example of this image division is shown in Fig. 7.

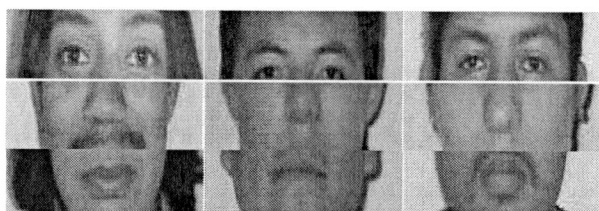

Figure 7 Example of Image Division.

As output to the system we have an image that corresponds to the complete image that was originally given as input to the modular system, we show in Figure 8 an example of this.

B. Description of the Integration Module

The integration modules performs its task in two phases. In the first phase, it obtains two matrices. The first matrix, called h, of dimension 3x3, stores the larger index values resulting from the competition for each of the members of the modules. The second matrix, called I, also of dimension 3x3, stores the photograph number corresponding to the particular index.

Once the first phase is finished, the second phase is initiated, in which the decision is obtained. Before making a decision, if there is consensus in the three modules, we can proceed to give the final decision, if there isn't consensus then we have search in matrix g to find the larger index values and then calculate the Sugeno fuzzy measures for each of the modules, using the following formula,

$$g(M_i) = h(A) + h(B) + \lambda\, h(A)\, h(B) \qquad (5)$$

Where λ is equal to 1. Once we have these measures, we select the largest one to show the corresponding photograph.

C. Summary of Results

We describe in this section the experimental results obtained with the proposed approach using the 20 photographs as training data. We show in Table 1 the relation between accuracy (measured as the percentage of correct results) and the percentage of noise in the figures.

TABLE I Relation between the1 % of noise and the % of correct results

% of noise	% accuracy
0	100
10	100
20	100
30	100
40	95
50	100
60	100
70	95
80	100
90	75
100	80

In Table I we show the relation that exists between the % of noise that was added in a random fashion to the testing data set, that consisted of the 20 original photographs, plus 200 additional images. We show in Fig. 9 sample images with noise.

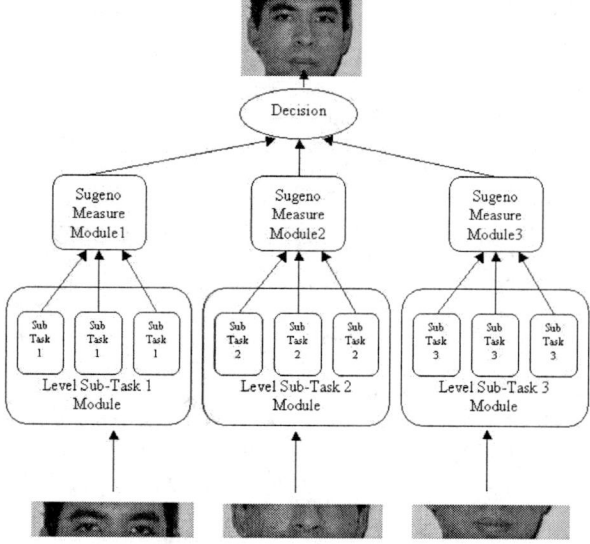

Figure 8 Final architecture showing inputs and outputs.

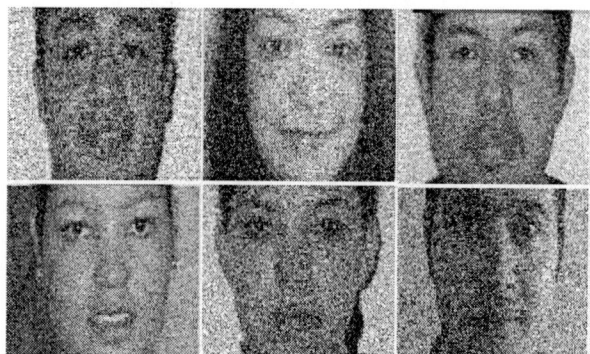

Fig. 9 Sample images with noise.

In Table II we show the reliability results for the system. Reliability was calculated as shown in the following equation.

$$\text{Reliability} = \frac{\text{correct results} - \text{error}}{\text{correct results}} \qquad (6)$$

TABLE II Relation between reliability and accuracy.

% errors	%reliability	%correct results
0	100	100.00
0	100	100.00
0	100	100.00
0	100	100.00
5	94.74	95.00
0	100	100.00
0	100	100.00
5	94.74	95.00
0	100	100.00
25	66.67	75.00
20	75	80.00

We show in Fig. 10 a plot relating the percentage of recognition against the number of examples used.

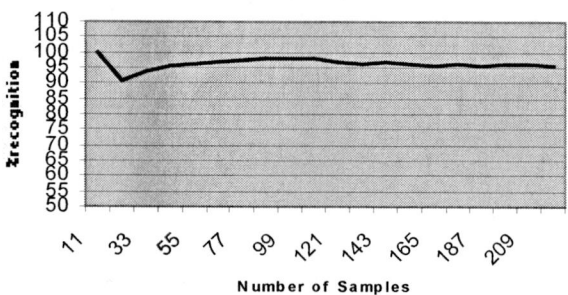

Fig. 10 Relation between recognition and number examples

In addition to the results presented before, we also compared the performance of the modular approach, against the performance of a monolithic neural network approach. The conclusion of this comparison was that for this type of input data, the monolithic approach is not feasible, since not only training time is larger, also the recognition is too small for real-world use. We show in Fig. 11 a plot showing this comparison but now in a graphical fashion.

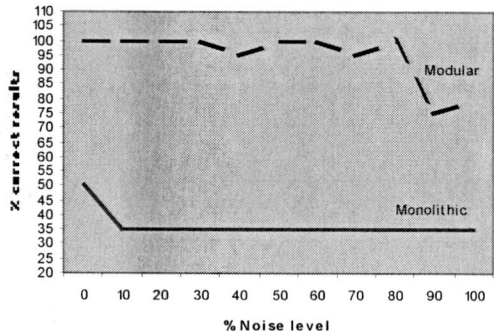

Fig. 11 Comparison between the modular and monolithic approach.

V. CONCLUSIONS

We showed in this paper the experimental results obtained with the proposed modular approach. In fact, we did achieve a 98.9% recognition rate on the testing data, even with an 80% level of applied noise. For the case of 100% level of applied noise, we did achieve a 96.4 % recognition rate on the testing data. The testing data included 10 photographs for each image in the training data. These 10 photographs were obtained by applying noise in a random fashion, increasing the level of noise from 10 to 100 %, to the training data. We also have to notice that it was achieved a 96.7 % of average reliability with our modular approach. This percentage values was obtained by averaging. In light of the results of our proposed modular approach, we have to notice that using the modular approach for human face pattern recognition is a good alternative with respect to existing methods, in particular, monolithic, gating or voting methods. As future research work, we propose the study of methods for pre-processing the data, like principal components analysis, eigenfaces, or any other method that may improve the performance of the system. Other future work include considering different methods of fuzzy response integration, or considering evolving the number of layers and nodes of the neural network modules.

VI. REFERENCES

[1] A.J.C. Sharkey, Combining Artificial Neural Nets: Ensemble and Modular Multi-Nets Systems, Ed. Springer-Verlag, New York, 1998.
[2] L. K. Hansen Y P. Salomon. Neural Network Ensembles, IEEE Transactions on Pattern Analysis and Machine Intelligence, 1990.
[3] Schdmit Albrecht, A Modular Neural Network Architecture with Additional Generalization Abilities for High Dimensional Input Vectors, 1996.
[4] Hsin-Chia Fu, Yen-Po Lee, Cheng-Chin Chiang Y Hsiao-Tien Pao. Divide-and-Conquer Learning and Modular Perceptron Networks in IEEE Transaction on Neural Networks, vol. 12.
[5] Egbert J.W. Boers Y Herman Kuiper. Biological Metaphors and the Design of Modular Artificial Neural Networks. Departments of Computer Science and Experimental and Theoretical Psychology at Leid University, the Netherlands. 1992.
[6] Eric Ronco Y Peter Gawthrop. Modular neural networks: A State of the Art. Technical Report, Center for System and Control. University of Glasgow, Glasgow, UK, 1995.
[7] B. Lu Y M. Ito. Task Decomposition and module combination based on class relations: modular neural network for pattern classification. Technical Report, Nagoya Japan, 1998.
[8] R. Murray-Smith Y T. A. Johansen. Multiple Model Approaches to Modeling and Control. Taylor and Francis, 1997.
[9] M Sugeno. Theory of fuzzy integrals and its application, Doctoral Thesis, Tokyo Institute of Technology, 1974.
[10] Ronald R. Yager. Criteria Aggregations Functions Using Fuzzy Measures and the Choquet Integral, International Journal of Fuzzy Systems, Vol. 1, No. 2, December 1999.

Application of a CMAC Neural Network to the Control of a Parallel Hybrid-Electric Propulsion System for a Small Unmanned Aerial Vehicle

Frederick G. Harmon, Andrew A. Frank, and Sanjay S. Joshi
Dept. of Mechanical and Aeronautical Engineering
University of California-Davis, Davis, CA 95616
E-mail: fgharmon@ucdavis.edu, aafrank@ucdavis.edu, and maejoshi@ucdavis.edu

Abstract—Optimizing and controlling the energy use of a hybrid-electric propulsion system is difficult due to the interaction of nonlinear mechanical, thermodynamic, and electromechanical devices. An optimization routine for the energy use of a parallel hybrid-electric propulsion system for a small unmanned aerial vehicle (UAV), the application of a cerebellar model arithmetic computer (CMAC) neural network to approximate the optimization results and control the hybrid-electric system, and simulation results are presented. The small hybrid-electric UAV is intended for military and homeland security missions involving intelligence, surveillance, or reconnaissance (ISR). The flexible optimization routine allows relative importance to be assigned between the use of gasoline, electricity, and recharging. The CMAC controller saves on the required memory compared to a look-up table by two orders of magnitude. The hybrid-electric UAV with the CMAC controller uses 37.8% less energy than a two-stroke gasoline-powered UAV during a three-hour ISR mission.

I. INTRODUCTION

A hybrid-electric vehicle (HEV) is "a vehicle in which propulsion energy is available from two or more kinds or types of energy stores, sources, or converters, and at least one of them can deliver electrical energy" [1]. HEV technology leads to automobiles with increased fuel economy and reduced emissions. The same technology would have similar benefits if applied to unmanned aerial vehicles (UAVs) used for military and homeland security missions. A parallel hybrid-electric propulsion system for a small UAV provides increased time-on-station and longer range as compared to an electric-powered UAV such as the Dragon Eye or Desert Hawk [2]. The internal combustion engine (ICE) is down-sized and operated near a constant torque output. The electric motor (EM) provides additional power for acceleration or climbing and serves as a generator during charge-sustaining operation or regeneration. Electric-only operation provides stealth operation not available with gasoline-powered UAVs by reducing the acoustic, smoke, and thermal signatures. Also, electric-only operation eliminates exhaust emissions that could interfere with chemical-detecting sensors. The battery pack/generator provides power for the avionics, payload, and propulsion system. The electric system provides redundancy for the ICE while the UAV is operating in hazardous conditions to minimize the risk to expensive avionics and surveillance sensors. Various agencies have begun to realize these benefits and are considering hybrid-electric systems for UAVs such as DARPA's Micro Air Vehicle project, DARPA/Boeing's Ultra Leap project, and Aerovironment/NASA's Helios UAV.

The parallel hybrid-electric propulsion system and the neural network controller for a small UAV have several objectives: 1) increase the range 2) provide adequate time for the UAV to operate in stealth (electric-only) mode while conducting intelligence, surveillance, or reconnaissance (ISR) and 3) provide adequate battery power for the payload. A small UAV with a parallel hybrid-electric propulsion system could meet the capability metrics of a "30% increase in time-on-station requirement with the same fuel load" and "a UAV inaudible from a 500-1000 ft slant range" [2].

An optimization routine for the energy use of the propulsion system, the application of a cerebellar model arithmetic computer (CMAC) neural network to approximate the optimization results, and simulation results are provided. The control of the hybrid-electric propulsion system is based on an instantaneous optimization routine that produces a hyper-plane generated from the nonlinear efficiency maps for the ICE, EM, and battery pack. The CMAC neural network is applied to the control of the parallel hybrid-electric propulsion system by approximating the nonlinear hyper-plane. A Simulink model was developed to compare energy use results between different configurations and controllers during a typical ISR mission.

II. HEV CONFIGURATIONS & OPERATING STRATEGIES

The mechanical configuration of a HEV is either series or parallel (see Fig. 1) [3]. The ICE in a series configuration drives a generator for the battery pack or the EM. Only the EM is connected to the mechanical drive train. The ICE is not connected to the mechanical drive path so it can operate in an optimum torque and speed range. However, large energy conversion losses exist between the mechanical and electrical systems diminishing the overall system efficiency. Also, the EM has to be sized for the maximum power required [3]. In a parallel configuration, the ICE and EM can both provide propulsion energy since both are mechanically linked to the drive train. The torque of the EM can supplement the torque of the ICE or additional ICE torque can operate the EM as a generator to recharge the battery pack. The speed of the drive train is not always the optimum speed for the engine, but the energy conversion losses are minimized. The ICE and EM can be sized smaller than in a series configuration and the EM is used as the generator so a separate generator is not required. The parallel configuration is used in most FutureTruck competition vehicles [4] and in the Honda Insight and Civic. The parallel and series hybrid configurations are the traditional configurations, but others have been used such as the series-parallel configuration used in the Toyota Prius.

An estimate was completed between a parallel and series configuration for a small UAV (≤50 lbs) [5]. The parallel configuration is lighter by ≈2.5 lbs (≈8%) of the proposed UAV's gross weight of 30 lbs. The extra weight for the series configuration is primarily due to the required generator and the larger EM. Harmats also concluded that the parallel configuration was more effective than the series configuration for a hybrid-electric propulsion system (solar power/EM/ICE) for a UAV [6]. During flight, the parallel hybrid-electric propulsion system allows the vehicle to be propelled directly with the ICE, EM, or both.

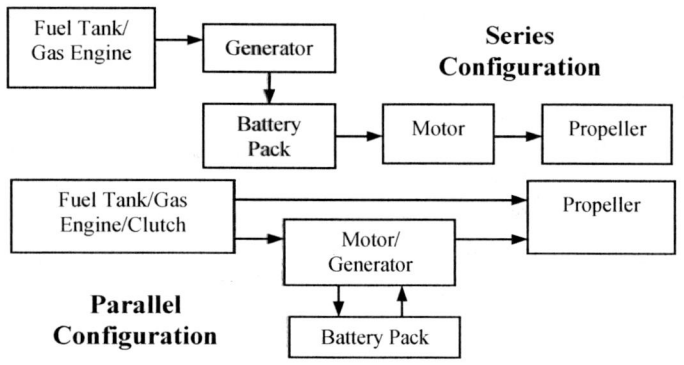

Fig. 1. Series and Parallel Hybrid-Electric Configurations

In addition to the HEV configurations, three overarching operating strategies are used for the energy management of a HEV: electric-only, charge-sustaining (CS), and charge-depleting (CD) [7]. The electric-only strategy depends on the ICE turn-on speed, the battery pack size, and the amount of low-speed operation. The other two strategies are the hybrid approaches. The CS strategy often uses a "thermostat" approach with an attempt to maintain the battery state-of-charge (SOC) at a certain level. In contrast to the CS strategy, the CD strategy allows the battery SOC to decrease maximizing the use of electricity from off-board charging.

The hybrid-electric UAV (HEUAV) uses a mix of the operating strategies depending on the mission. Due to the weight limitations, a relatively large battery pack and a purely CD strategy cannot be used. A purely CS strategy will limit the time-on-station. Sufficient SOC is required for the enemy area or whenever the stealth mode is required. Because of this rationale, a combination of the charging strategies is used during an ISR mission.

III. Control Algorithms For Hybrid-Electric Systems

The hybrid-electric vehicle operating strategies (i.e. electric-only, CS, and CD) are overarching approaches. For each operating strategy, control algorithms are used to optimize the energy use or power consumption. In addition to rule-based or logic-based strategies, several advanced control approaches have been reported in the literature: 1) optimal control 2) fuzzy logic 3) adaptive control 4) nonlinear control and 5) genetic algorithms. A brief overview of each and their application to the control of HEV power trains is given by Harmon [5].

The goal of an advanced control system is to use a minimal amount of energy by finding the best combination of motor and engine torque as a function of rotational speed, torque demand, or other parameters. Of the potential hybrid-electric power train advanced control schemes, those based on artificial neural networks (ANN) or fuzzy logic appear to be the most promising due to the relatively low computational resources needed and because an accurate power train model is not required (an accurate model is required for simulations).

ANNs can approximate nonlinear functions so an ANN has tremendous potential if applied to the control of the nonlinear HEUAV propulsion system. A specific type of neural network, the Cerebellar Model Arithmetic Computer (CMAC), was chosen for this application due to its rapid training time, practical hardware implementation, and low computational cost [8]. The CMAC is an alternative to the more common back-propagation multilayer network [9]. The CMAC ANN has been successfully applied to robotic control, fuel processors, and fuel-injection systems [10-12].

IV. Overview Of The CMAC Neural Network

The CMAC neural network was originated by James Albus in 1975 [13, 14]. The CMAC is modeled after the method that the cerebellum uses to learn and store information and control reflexive movement which is in contrast to a traditional ANN that attempts to mimic the interactions between the brain's neurons. The CMAC attempts to duplicate the functional properties of the brain instead of the structure of it [14]. The CMAC can be thought of as an adaptive look-up table (LUT). The CMAC is better suited to real-time control as compared to a LUT for two reasons: the CMAC can generalize whereas a LUT cannot and the CMAC requires much less memory than a LUT [15].

The CMAC is a feed-forward, supervised, lattice-based, associative memory network that nonlinearly maps the inputs to a hidden associative memory. The hidden memory is linearly mapped to an adaptive weight vector that generates the output. The output is the sum of the activated weights. For each input, only a small subset of the network influences the instantaneous output which minimizes the computational time. The number of training iterations is orders of magnitude smaller than that of other ANNs [9]. The CMAC ANN is applied to the control of the propulsion system to produce torque commands for the ICE and EM.

There are several disadvantages of the back-propagated multilayer perceptron ANN for a real-time controls application. First, the back-propagated ANN is usually not feasible for on-line learning since numerous iterations are needed for the ANN to converge during training. On-line learning is not used for the HEUAV application but could be an area of future research. Second, many calculations are needed per training iteration for the back-propagated ANN. Third, the commonly used training algorithms for back-propagation are based on gradient techniques where the ANN can get "stuck" in a relative minimum during training vs. converging to a global minimum as for the CMAC ANN. Fourth, it has been shown that the local learning approaches used in the CMAC ANN and other associative memory networks are superior for control applications [16]. For these reasons, the CMAC was selected for the HEUAV application instead of the back-propagated multilayer ANN.

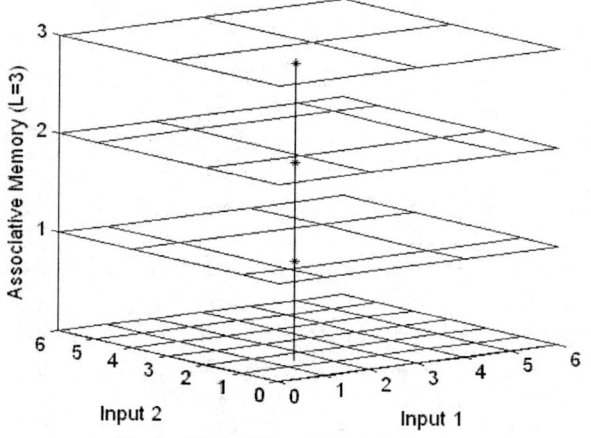

Fig. 2. CMAC Neural Network Structure

A typical CMAC neural network structure is shown in Fig. 2. Continuous vectors are first transformed into quantized input vectors. The maximum and minimum values of the inputs (range) are needed along with the quantization width (resolution) of the inputs to determine the size of the input space [11]. Second, the input space is nonlinearly mapped into exactly L locations (generalization factor) in the associative memory. Please note that the nonlinear mapping in a CMAC structure occurs in the initial mapping and not in the sigmoid/threshold function of a neuron as in other types of ANNs. Each of the association cells (also referred to as basis functions with support or receptive fields) within each parallel layer of the memory has a corresponding weight. Each association cell has a support area of L^n where n is the dimension of the input space. Third, for each possible input, the weights corresponding to the L activated memory locations are then summed to form the output. The weights mapped to each memory location determine the output and are adaptively updated [15].

The CMAC structure parameters typically have the following relationship for a controls application:
$$n \leq L < b < N \quad (1)$$
where b is the total number of basis functions, and N is the total number of possible inputs (number of LUT entries). The example in Fig. 2 has n=2, L=3, b=22, and N=36. The CMAC is considered well defined if $1 \leq L \leq \max(v_i)$ for $1 \leq i \leq n$ where v_i is the number of intervals in an input dimension [15]. If the CMAC is not well defined, a basis function will cover a relatively large area of the input space.

The distribution of the association layers is determined by a displacement vector. The original Albus scheme offset the layers by one from each other. The displacement vector is (1,1,1), (2,2,2), and (3,3,3) for the example in Fig. 2. Parks and Militzer produced tables of displacement vectors that optimized the structure by relating the Hamming distance between the association vectors to the Euclidian distance between the input values [9, 17]. The improved displacement vectors generally produce a smoother approximation.

The CMAC's weights are updated using an instantaneous gradient descent method to minimize the mean square error (MSE). For the CMAC ANN, the error surface has a global minimum. The instantaneous estimate of the MSE is [11]:
$$E = \frac{1}{2} \cdot (y_{Desired} - y_{CMAC})^2 \quad (2)$$
Taking a partial derivative w.r.t. an activated weight, w_j:
$$\frac{\partial E}{\partial w_j} = -(y_{Desired} - \sum_{i=1}^{L} w_{i,Activated}) \quad (3)$$
Only local learning occurs since only the activated weights are updated. The resulting first-order update training rule using the instantaneous gradient descent method is [15]:
$$w_{j,updated} = w_{j,previous} + \frac{\delta}{L} \cdot (y_{Desired} - y_{CMAC}) \quad (4)$$
where δ is the training rate. The learning algorithm requires minimal computational cost.

The CMAC generalizes due to the width and overlap of the association cells in the hidden layers [14]. The generalization is determined by the initial nonlinear mapping since each basis function has a pre-determined corresponding support or receptive field. The supports each have a volume of L^n or less if on the edge of the input space. Therefore, the generalization parameter, L, determines the number of association layers, the number of weights contributing to each output, and the size of support for each basis function [15]. If two inputs are relatively close to each other in the input space, then approximately the same association cells will be activated to produce an output. For two inputs that are spaced far apart, different association cells are activated. The CMAC generalizes over a small area which minimizes the computations required for each training iteration. If L is large, the generalization is less local but the memory requirement decreases.

The CMAC neural network approximations will include modeling errors. The initial nonlinear mapping, generalization parameter, and the displacement vector influence the modeling capabilities. As L increases, the generalization is less local and the modeling error typically increases. The flexibility of the CMAC decreases as L increases due to the decreased generalization. The advantage is the decreased memory requirement. For most applications, including the HEUAV, the modeling error is low even if the CMAC cannot model the function exactly.

In addition to comparing performance and energy use between the rule-based and CMAC controllers, the microprocessor memory requirements are considered for the CMAC ANN controller. A typical processor has ≈512 KB of flash memory and if each CMAC weight is assumed to be a float value requiring 4 bytes (32 bits), the allowable size of the associative memory in the CMAC can be determined.

V. OPTIMIZATION ALGORITHM & CMAC APPROXIMATIONS

The energy available in the small HEUAV is either from the gasoline or the electrical energy stored in the battery pack. To provide power to the propeller, the energy can take one of three paths. For the first path, energy stored within the gasoline is used by the ICE to deliver power directly to the propeller (see Fig. 1). Electrical energy can be delivered directly to the propeller from the batteries and EM via the second path. The third path uses the ICE and EM to recharge the battery pack. The stored electrical energy is delivered to the propeller at a later time (i.e. electric-only (stealth) mode).

The simple rule-based controller used for a baseline comparison has two inputs: demanded torque and rotational speed. The engine is operated on a line of maximum efficiency, the ideal operating line (IOL) [18, 19], unless the demanded torque is less than the IOL torque or if the demanded torque is greater than the combined IOL torque and maximum EM torque. Only the ICE generates torque if the demanded torque is less than the IOL torque. If the demanded torque is greater than the combined IOL torque and the maximum EM torque, then additional torque from the ICE is provided. The rule-based controller logic does not include any recharging so it is a CD strategy. If the mission requirements cannot be met with CD, then a CS algorithm is used. A proportional-derivative (PD) controller, with the SOC as the input, determines the amount of recharging.

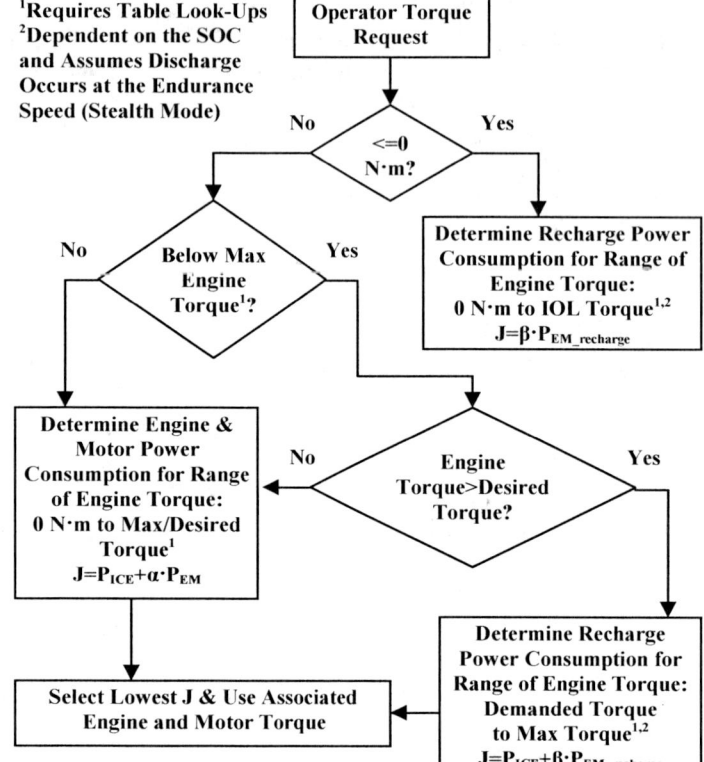

Fig. 3. CMAC Controller Optimization Algorithm

The CMAC controller is used to approximate a nonlinear control surface generated from a separate off-line optimization routine (see flowchart in Fig. 3). The optimization of the energy use is achieved by minimizing the instantaneous rate of energy consumption. The nonlinear efficiency maps for the two-stroke gasoline ICE, EM, and lithium-ion battery pack are used in the off-line optimization routine to minimize the power consumption by determining the torque split between the ICE and EM during hybrid-electric operation. The optimization results are used to generate a nonlinear control surface for the engine and motor torque commands.

The optimization algorithm uses the battery SOC (e.g. determined by integrating the current) as an input in addition to the demanded torque and rotational speed. The algorithm minimizes the total power consumption:

$$J = P_{ICE} + \alpha \cdot P_{EM} + \beta \cdot P_{EM\_recharge} \quad (5)$$

P_{ICE} is the power consumption equivalent (33.44 kWh/gal of gasoline) of the ICE to rotate the propeller. P_{EM} is the electrical power consumption of the EM whereas $P_{EM\_recharge}$ is the power consumption equivalent for the ICE to operate the EM as a generator to recharge the batteries. The weighting factors, α and β, penalize the amount of electricity use and the amount of recharging, respectively, and are mission dependent. If the mission is relatively short, CD values are used but if a longer mission is required, different values are used to produce a CS control surface.

The efficiency maps are stored in tables and interpolation is used to calculate the efficiency at specific points in the input space during the off-line optimization calculations. The two-stroke ICE, EM, and lithium-ion battery pack efficiency maps are derived from estimates and manufacturer data. Simulation results for a more efficient four-stroke engine have been submitted to an AIAA journal publication.

The flowchart for the optimization routine requires numerous calculations. The calculations require numerous table look-ups and interpolations that would be excessive for an embedded microcontroller. For branches of the flowchart, the objective function is calculated in the off-line optimization routine by stepping the engine torque by 0.02 N·m increments to determine which torque split will minimize the power consumption.

Table 1. CMAC Controller Parameters

Parameter	Value
Output	Commanded Engine Torque
Inputs	Rotational Speed, Demanded Torque, SOC
Input Ranges	Speed: 190-880 rad/s, Torque: 0-2.5 N·m, SOC: 2-100%
Input Resolution	Speed: 10 rad/s, Torque: 0.05 N·m, SOC: 2%
Number of Input Cells, N	70·51·50=178,500
Generalization Factors, L[1]	3, 7, 9, 14, 19, 25
Learning Rate, δ	0.05
Training Iterations	150-200

[1]The generalization factors correspond to displacement vectors that provide a CMAC structure of good quality.

To implement the CMAC controller, various parameters were chosen such as the inputs, generalization parameter, and learning rate (see Table 1). Brown and Harris state "that most reasonable choices give acceptable results" [15]. Simulations using the original configuration (ICE only) were useful for designing the input space for the CMAC controller by determining the range of the input parameters.

Table 2. CMAC Approximation Results, Two-Stroke Engine, Charge-Sustaining Strategy

Generalization Parameter	RMS Error	Displacement Vector	Weights in Memory	Memory Savings[1]
3	$1.31 \cdot 10^{-2}$	(1,1,1)	21,767	8.20
7	$2.41 \cdot 10^{-2}$	(1,2,3)	4,888	36.5
9	$2.90 \cdot 10^{-2}$	(1,2,4)	3,266	54.7
14	$4.37 \cdot 10^{-2}$	(1,3,5)	1,696	105.2
19	$5.82 \cdot 10^{-2}$	(1,3,7)	1,137	157.0

[1]Number of entries in a LUT/number of weights for the CMAC memory

A summary of the CMAC approximation results for the CMAC controller using the two-stroke engine is shown in Table 2. CS weighting factors of α=10+10·(1-SOC) and β=0.05·SOC permit the HEUAV to complete a three-hour ISR mission. The runs for L=3, 7, and 9 used 200 training iterations and the other two runs used 150 iterations. The CMAC approximations for L=14 and 19 save on at least two orders of magnitude as compared to a LUT. The CMAC approximation (L=14) for a SOC=25% is shown in Fig. 4. The approximation to the original control surface gets worse (RMS increases) as the generalization factor increases because a cell in the associative memory covers more of the input space. The CS surfaces for L=3, 7, 9, and 14 produced acceptable results. A generalization factor of L=19 did not produce acceptable results since the approximation causes too much recharging due to larger modeling errors.

VI. Flight Profile Simulation Results

A conceptual design of the HEUAV and propulsion system components is presented in [20]. The simulation results presented here use the two-point conceptual design results that include an ICE sized for cruise speed (50 kts) and an EM and battery pack sized for the endurance speed (25 kts). A typical ISR flight profile (see Fig. 5) includes a take-off, climb, cruise, endurance speed, high speed dash, descent, and landing. The ISR segment is split into two different segments to simulate the observation of two different ground locations. At endurance speed, the hybrid-electric UAV operates in electric-only (stealth) mode.

The rule-based controller provides a baseline. CS is allowed during the mission to provide sufficient electrical energy for the two half-hour ISR mission segments. The rule-based controller manages the electrical energy sufficiently for the hybrid-electric system but the CMAC controller improves on the rule-based controller.

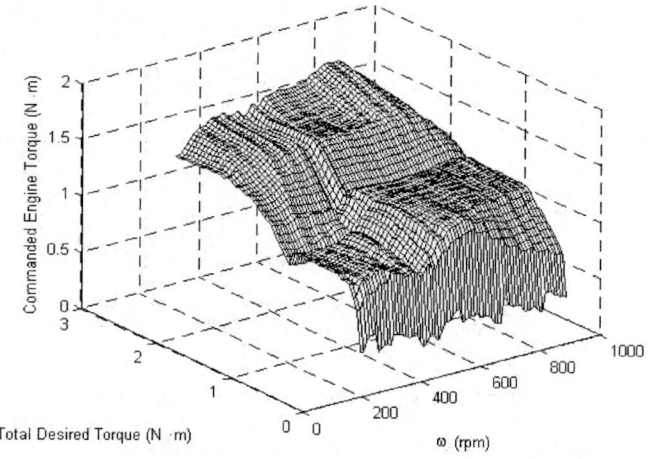

Fig. 4. CMAC Approximation (L=14) for Engine Torque Control Surface, Two-Stroke Engine, Charge-Sustaining Strategy, SOC=25%

The battery SOC for the controllers is shown in Fig. 6. During cruise, an error in the approximation will cause a difference in the amount of recharging. For L=3, 7, 9 and 14, the battery SOC follows a similar path. For L=19, too much recharging was commanded and the hybrid-electric system used more energy than necessary. All of the simulations end with a SOC of approximately 20%.

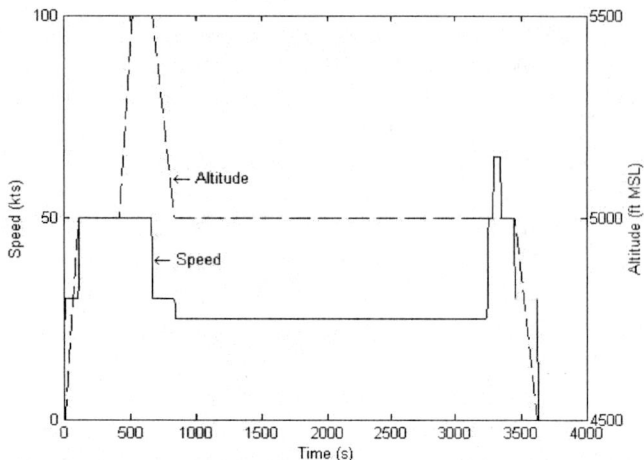

Fig. 5. Three-Hour Flight Profile, ISR Mission

For the CMAC controller, the recharging is completed at a relatively constant rate throughout the SOC range as compared to the rule-based controller. Since the rule-based controller uses a PD algorithm, the rate increases as the SOC decreases. The CMAC controller keeps the engine running at a continuous power level. Since the CMAC controllers keep the SOC near a constant SOC, most of the recharging is used to provide power to the avionics and payload.

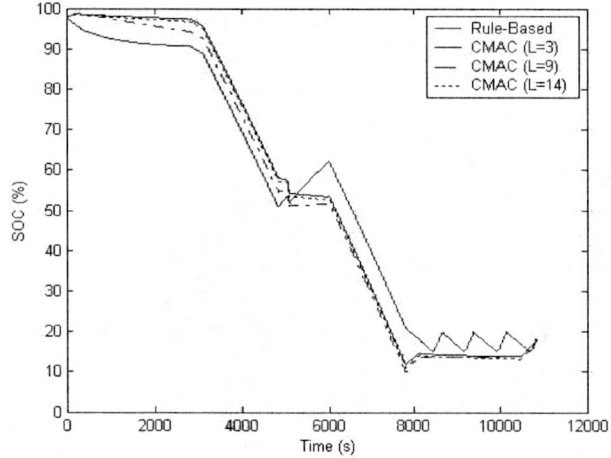

Fig. 6. Battery SOC During Three-Hour ISR Mission

Table 3. Energy Use Summary for Three-Hour ISR Mission

Energy Type	Engine Only	Rule-Based	CMAC Controller, CS			
			L=3	L=7	L=9	L=14
Fuel (kg)	2.025	1.318	1.224	1.216	1.223	1.234
Fuel (kWh)	24.1	15.8	14.7	14.6	14.7	14.8
Electricity (kWh)	N/A	0.241	0.250	0.257	0.253	0.256
Total (kWh)	24.1	16.0	14.9	14.8	14.9	15.0

The energy use for the three-hour ISR mission using the different controllers is summarized in Table 3. The energy use for the HEUAV with the CMAC controller (L=14) is 37.8% less than the original configuration and 6.3% less than the HEUAV with the baseline rule-based controller.

References

[1] C. C. Chan and K. T. Chau, *Modern Electric Vehicle Technology*. Oxford, New York: Oxford University Press, 2001.
[2] E. C. Aldridge and J. P. Stenbit, "Unmanned Aerial Vehicles Roadmap: 2002-2027," Office of the Secretary of Defense, 2003.
[3] I. Husain, *Electric and Hybrid Vehicles Design Fundamentals*. Boca Rotan, FL: CRC Press, 2003.
[4] N. Meyr, et al., "Design and Development of the 2002 UC Davis FutureTruck," *SAE Paper 2003-01-1263*, 2003.
[5] F. G. Harmon, "PhD Dissertation: Neural Network Control of a Parallel Hybrid-Electric Propulsion System for a Small Unmanned Aerial Vehicle," in *Dept. of Mechanical and Aeronautical Engineering*. Davis, CA: University of California-Davis, 2005.
[6] M. Harmats and D. Weihs, "Hybrid-Propulsion High-Altitude Long-Endurance Remotely Piloted Vehicle," *Journal of Aircraft*, vol. 36, pp. 321-331, 1999.
[7] R. W. Schurhoff, "M.S. Thesis: The Development and Evaluation of an Optimal Powertrain Control Strategy for a Hybrid Electric Vehicle," in *Dept. of Mechanical and Aeronautical Engineering*. Davis, CA: University of California-Davis, 2002.
[8] F. H. Glanz, T. W. Miller, and L. G. Kraft, "An Overview of the CMAC Neural Network," presented at IEEE Conference on Neural Networks for Ocean Engineering, 1991.
[9] W. T. Miller, F. H. Glanz, and L. G. Kraft, "CMAC: An Associative Neural Network Alternative to Backpropagation," *Proceedings of the IEEE*, vol. 78, pp. 1561-1567, 1990.
[10] W. T. Miller, "Real-Time Neural Network Control of a Biped Walking Robot," *IEEE Control Systems Magazine*, vol. 14, pp. 41-48, 1994.
[11] L. C. Iwan and R. F. Stengel, "The Application of Neural Networks to Fuel Processors for Fuel-Cell Vehicles," *IEEE Transactions on Vehicular Technology*, vol. 50, pp. 125-143, 2001.
[12] H. Shiraishi, S. L. Ipri, and D. D. Cho, "CMAC Neural Network Controller for Fuel-Injection Systems," *IEEE Transactions on Control Systems Technology*, vol. 3, pp. 32-38, 1995.
[13] J. S. Albus, "Data Storage in the Cerebellar Model Articulation Controller (CMAC)," *Journal of Dynamic Systems, Measurement, and Control*, vol. 63, pp. 228-233, 1975.
[14] J. S. Albus, "A New Approach to Manipulator Control: The Cerebellar Model Articulation Controller (CMAC)," *Journal of Dynamic Systems, Measurement, and Control*, vol. 63, pp. 220-227, 1975.
[15] M. Brown and C. Harris, *Neurofuzzy Adaptive Modelling and Control*. New York: Prentice Hall, 1994.
[16] D. A. White and D. A. Sofge, *Handbook of Intelligent Control: Neural, Fuzzy, and Adaptive Approaches*. New York: Van Nostrand Reinhold, 1992.
[17] P. C. Parks and J. Militzer, "Improved Allocation of Weights for Associative Memory Storage in Learning Control Systems," *IFAC Design Methods of Control Systems*, pp. 507-512, 1991.
[18] A. B. Francisco, "M.S. Thesis: Implementation of an Ideal Operating Line Control Strategy for Hybrid Electric Vehicles," in *Dept. of Mechanical and Aeronautical Engineering*. Davis, CA: University of California-Davis, 2002.
[19] A. A. Frank, "Control Method and Apparatus for Internal Combustion Engine Electric Hybrid Vehicles," in *USPTO Patent Database*. USA: The Regents of the University of California, 2000.
[20] F. G. Harmon, A. A. Frank, and J. J. Chattot, "Parallel Hybrid-Electric Propulsion System for an Unmanned Aerial Vehicle," presented at AUVSI's Unmanned Systems North America 2004 Symposium, Anaheim, CA, 2004.

Inverse Optimal Nonlinear Recurrent High Order Neural Observer

Luis J. Ricalde and Edgar N. Sanchez

CINVESTAV, Unidad Guadalajara, Apartado Postal 31-430, Plaza La Luna, Guadalajara, Jalisco C.P. 45091, Mexico, e-mail: [lricalde,sanchez]@gdl.cinvestav.mx

Abstract— This paper presents the design of an adaptive recurrent neural observer for nonlinear systems which model is assumed to be unknown. The neural observer is composed of a Recurrent High Order Neural Network which builds an online model of the unknown plant and a learning adaptation law for the neural network weights. This law is obtained by the Lyapunov methodology. The feedback law which guarantees stability of the estimation error is proved to be optimal with respect to a well defined cost functional.

I. INTRODUCTION

The state estimation problem for nonlinear systems, with uncertainties and unmodeled dynamics, is a topic of recent interest. Most of the control algorithms for nonlinear systems use the assumption that all the states are available for measurement, which is a constraint seldom satisfied. The nonlinear observers arise as a solution, and have received much attention lately.

For linear unknown systems, the observer design has been widely investigated. For nonlinear systems, the results are too restrictive according to the nonlinearity and system structure. In [8], an adaptive observer for nonlinear systems is proposed, where the uncertainties are assumed to be linear and the nonlinearities are functions of the output.

Over the past decade, adaptive neural control schemes have received an increasing attention for applications on nonlinear systems control. Mainly due to the seminal paper [10], there has been continuously increasing interest in applying neural networks to identification and control of nonlinear systems. Lately, the use of recurrent neural networks is being developed, which allows more efficient modeling of the underlying dynamical systems [11]. In [7], an nonlinear observer based on neural networks is developed. The nonlinearities are not required to depend only on the system output, but the system structure presents some restrictions.

In this paper, a nonlinear observer based on recurrent high order neural networks is discussed. This observer requires fewer restrictions on the system structure than the ones on previous works [8],[7]. A learning law for the on-line adapted weights of the neural network is developed based on the Lyapunov analysis. The stability of the state estimation error is ensured via control Lyapunov functions. The obtained control law is proven to be optimal with respect to a well defined cost functional, which puts penalty on the estimation error.

II. MATHEMATICAL PRELIMINARIES

A. Recurrent Higher-Order Neural Networks

Artificial Recurrent Neural Networks are mostly based on the Hopfield model [2]. These networks are considered as good candidates for nonlinear systems applications, which deal with uncertainties, and are attractive due to their easy implementation, relatively simple structure, robustness and the capacity to adjust their parameters on-line.

In [5], Recurrent Higher-Order Neural Networks (RHONN) are defined as

$$\dot{\chi}_i = -a_i \chi_i + \sum_{k=1}^{L} w_{ik} \prod_{j \in I_k} y_j^{d_j(k)}, \qquad i = 1, ..., n \quad (1)$$

where χ_i is the ith neuron state, L is the number of higher-order connections, $\{I_1, I_2, ..., I_L\}$ is a collection of non-ordered subsets of $\{1, 2, ..., m+n\}$, $a_i > 0$, w_{ik} are the adjustable weights of the neural network, $d_j(k)$ are nonnegative integers, and y is a vector defined by

$$y = [y_1, ..., y_n, y_{n+1}, ..., y_{n+m}]^\top = [S(\chi_1), ..., S(\chi_n), S(u_1), ..., S(u_m)]^\top,$$

with $u = [u_1, u_2, ..., u_m]^\top$ being the input to the neural network, and $S(\cdot)$ a smooth sigmoid function formulated by $S(\chi) = \frac{1}{1+\exp(-\beta\chi)} + \varepsilon$. For the sigmoid function, β is a positive constant and ε is a small positive real number. Hence, $S(\chi) \in [\varepsilon, \varepsilon + 1]$. It is well known that this function is globally Lipschitz [14].

As can be seen, (1) allows the inclusion of higher-order terms.

By defining the vector

$$\begin{aligned} z(\chi, u) &= [z_1(\chi, u), ..., z_L(\chi, u)]^\top \\ &= \left[\prod_{j \in I_1} y_j^{d_j(1)}, ..., \prod_{j \in I_L} y_j^{d_j(L)} \right]^\top \end{aligned} \quad (2)$$

(1) can be rewritten as

$$\begin{aligned} \dot{\chi}_i &= -a_i \chi_i + \sum_{k=1}^{L} w_{ik} z_k(\chi, u), \qquad i = 1, ..., n \\ \dot{\chi}_i &= -a_i \chi_i + w_i z(\chi, u) \qquad i = 1, ..., n \end{aligned} \quad (3)$$

where $w_i = [w_{i,1} ... w_{i,L}]$. We assume that the RHONN is

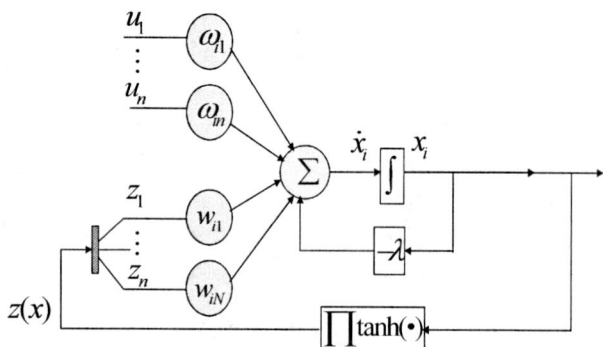

Fig. 1. Recurrent High Order Neural Network

affine in the control; hence, (3) can be rewritten as

$$\dot{\chi}_i = -a_i \chi_i + w_i^T z(\chi) + w_{gi} u_i, \quad i = 1, ..., n \quad (4)$$

Reformulating (3) in the matrix form yields

$$\dot{\chi} = A\chi + Wz(\chi) + W_g u \quad (5)$$

where $\chi \in \Re^n, W \in \Re^{n \times L}, W_g \in \Re^{n \times n}, z(\chi) \in \Re^L, u \in \Re^n$, and $A = -\lambda I, \lambda > 0$.

For nonlinear identification applications, the term y_j in (2) can be either an external input or the state of a neuron passed through the sigmoid function. Depending on the sigmoid function input, the RHONN can be classified as a Series-Parallel structure if $z(\cdot) = z(\nu)$, where ν is an external input, or a Parallel one if $z(\cdot) = z(\chi)$, where χ is the neural network state [13]. This terminology is standard in adaptive identification and control [9].

B. Observability results

The single input-single output linear system

$$\dot{x} = Ax + bu$$
$$y = cx$$

where $x \in \Re^n, A \in \Re^{n \times n}, b \in \Re^n, y \in \Re$ is said to be in observer canonical form if A and C are given by

$$A = \begin{bmatrix} 0 & 1 & 0 & \cdots & 0 \\ 0 & 0 & 1 & \cdots & 0 \\ & & \vdots & & \\ 0 & 0 & \cdots & 1 & 0 \\ 0 & 0 & 0 & \cdots & 0 \end{bmatrix}, c = \begin{bmatrix} 0 & 0 & \cdots & 0 & 1 \end{bmatrix}$$

III. RECURRENT HIGH ORDER NEURAL OBSERVER (RHONO) DESIGN

Consider the single input-single output nonlinear system

$$\dot{x} = f(x) + g(x)u(t) \quad (6)$$
$$y = Cx$$

which is assumed to be observable. We assume that only $y(t)$ is measurable.

Let us consider that the system (6) can be modeled by the RHONN

$$\dot{\chi} = A\chi + W^* z(y) + w_{per} \quad (7)$$
$$y_{NN} = Cx$$

where the pair (A, c) is in observer canonical form and there exist unknown but constant weights W^* such that the modelling error w_{per} is minimized.

Consider the recurrent high order neural observer (RHONO),

$$\dot{\hat{\chi}} = A\hat{\chi} + Wz(\hat{y}) - bv(t) \quad (8)$$
$$\hat{y} = c\hat{\chi}$$

where the pair (A, c) is in observer canonical form.

Assuming no modelling error for the RHONN, we define the state estimation error

$$\tilde{\chi} = \chi - \hat{\chi}$$

whose dynamics is given by

$$\dot{\tilde{\chi}} = A\tilde{\chi} + W^* z(y) - Wz(\hat{y}) - bv(t)$$
$$\tilde{y} = y - c\hat{\chi}$$

Adding and substracting the term $Wz(y)$, we obtain

$$\dot{\tilde{\chi}} = A\tilde{\chi} + (W^* - W)z(y) + W(z(y) - z(\hat{y}))$$
$$\quad + bv(t)$$
$$\dot{\tilde{\chi}} = A\tilde{\chi} + \tilde{W}z(y) + W\phi_z(y) + bv(t) \quad (9)$$
$$\tilde{W} = W^* - W$$
$$\phi_z(y) = z(y) - z(\hat{y})$$
$$\leq L_\phi \|\tilde{y}\|$$
$$\leq \|\tilde{y}\|$$

The signal $v(t)$, which stabilizes (9), is developed via the Lyapunov methodology.

IV. STABILITY ANALYSIS.

Consider the Lyapunov function candidate

$$V = \frac{1}{2}\tilde{\chi}^T P \tilde{\chi} + \frac{1}{2\gamma} tr\{\tilde{W}^T \tilde{W}\} \quad (10)$$

where P is a positive definite symmetric matrix, which solves the Ricatti equation,

$$A^T P + P^T A = -Q$$
$$Pb = c^T \quad (11)$$
$$\tilde{\chi}^T P = \frac{b^T}{\|b\|^2}\tilde{y}$$

with Q a positive definite symmetric matrix, i.e. $\tilde{\chi}^T Q \tilde{\chi} > 0$.

The time derivative of (10) is given by

$$\dot{V} = \frac{1}{2}\tilde{\chi}^T P \left(A\tilde{\chi} + \bar{f} + bv(t)\right) + \frac{1}{\gamma}tr\left\{\dot{\tilde{W}}^T \tilde{W}\right\} \quad (12)$$
$$+ \frac{1}{2}\left(A\tilde{\chi} + \bar{f} + bv(t)\right)^T P \tilde{\chi}$$
$$\bar{f} = \tilde{W}z(y) + W\phi_z(y)$$

which can be simplified as

$$\dot{V} = \frac{1}{2}\tilde{\chi}^T PA\tilde{\chi} + \frac{1}{2}\tilde{\chi}^T P\bar{f} + \frac{1}{2}\tilde{\chi}^T Pbv(t)$$
$$+ \frac{1}{2}\tilde{\chi}^T A^T P\tilde{\chi} + \frac{1}{2}\bar{f}^T P\tilde{\chi} + \frac{1}{2}v(t)^T b^T P\tilde{\chi} \quad (13)$$
$$+ \frac{1}{\gamma}tr\left\{\dot{\tilde{W}}^T \tilde{W}\right\}$$

Taking into account (11), we rewrite (13) as

$$\dot{V} = -\frac{1}{2}\tilde{\chi}^T Q\tilde{\chi} + \tilde{\chi}^T P\bar{f} + \tilde{y}v(t) + \frac{1}{\gamma}tr\left\{\dot{\tilde{W}}^T \tilde{W}\right\} \quad (14)$$

Replacing the term $\bar{f}$, we obtain

$$\dot{V} = -\frac{1}{2}\tilde{\chi}^T Q\tilde{\chi} + \tilde{\chi}^T P\tilde{W}z(y) + \tilde{\chi}^T PW\phi_z(y)$$
$$+ \tilde{y}v(t) + \frac{1}{\gamma}tr\left\{\dot{\tilde{W}}^T \tilde{W}\right\} \quad (15)$$

To this end, we now define the learning adaptation law

$$\frac{1}{\gamma}tr\left\{\dot{\tilde{W}}^T \tilde{W}\right\} = -\tilde{\chi}^T P\tilde{W}z(y) \quad (16)$$
$$tr\left\{\dot{\tilde{W}}^T \tilde{W}\right\} = -\gamma \frac{b^T}{\|b\|^2}\tilde{y}\tilde{W}z(y)$$

which can be written term by term as

$$\dot{\hat{w}}_{ij} = -\frac{\gamma}{\|b\|^2}b_i^T \tilde{y} z_j(y) \quad (17)$$

Replacing the learning law, we obtain

$$\dot{V} = -\frac{1}{2}\tilde{\chi}^T Q\tilde{\chi} + \frac{b^T}{\|b\|^2}W\phi_z(y)\tilde{y} + \tilde{y}v(t) \quad (18)$$
$$\dot{V} = \Lambda_f V + \Lambda_g V v(t)$$
$$\Lambda_f V = -\frac{1}{2}\tilde{\chi}^T Q\tilde{\chi} + \frac{b^T}{\|b\|^2}W\phi_z(y)\tilde{y}$$
$$\Lambda_g V = \tilde{y}$$

Next, we consider the following inequality [11],

$$X^T Y + Y^T X \leq X^T \Lambda X + Y^T \Lambda^{-1} Y \quad (19)$$

which holds for all matrices $X, Y \in \Re^{n \times k}$ and $\Lambda \in \Re^{n \times n}$ with $\Lambda = \Lambda^T > 0$.

Applying (19) to $W\phi_z(y)\tilde{y}$ with $\Lambda = I$, we obtain

$$\dot{V} \leq -\frac{1}{2}\tilde{\chi}^T Q\tilde{\chi} + \frac{b^T}{\|b\|^2}\left(\|\tilde{y}\|^2 + \|W\|^2 \|\phi_z(y)\|^2\right)$$
$$+ \tilde{y}v(t)$$
$$\leq -\frac{1}{2}\tilde{\chi}^T Q\tilde{\chi} + \frac{b^T}{\|b\|^2}\left(1 + \|W\|^2\right)\|\tilde{y}\|^2$$
$$+ \tilde{y}v(t) \quad (20)$$

The asymptotic stability of the estimation error is achieved if we select the control law

$$v(t) = -\mu \frac{b^T}{\|b\|^2}\left(1 + \|W\|^2\right)\tilde{y} - K\tilde{y} \quad (21)$$
$$\triangleq -\beta R^{-1}(\tilde{y}, W)\Lambda_g V$$

where $\beta \in \Re^+$, $\mu > 1$ and K is selected such that $\left(A - KC^T\right)$ is a Hurwitz matrix.

Then, the RHONO structure is given by

$$\dot{\hat{\chi}} = A\hat{\chi} + Wz(\hat{y}) + bK(y - C\hat{\chi}) + \mu\left(1 + \|W\|^2\right)\tilde{y} \quad (22)$$

However, the assumption of no modelling error is seldom satisfied. Hence, the adjusted weight parameters could drift to infinity. In order to avoid the parameter drift, the following robust learning law for the neural network weights is proposed as in [13]:

$$\dot{W} = \begin{cases} -\gamma e_i z(x_{p_j}) & \text{if } |w_i| < w_m \\ -\gamma e_i z(x_{p_j}) - \sigma\gamma w_i & \text{if } |w_i| \geq w_m \end{cases}$$

where σ is a positive constant and w_m is the upper bound for the neural network weights. It can be shown that the robust learning law does not affect the stability of the estimation error but improves it, making the Lyapunov function time derivative more negative. For a detailed demonstration, see [13].

A. Optimization with respect to a cost functional

Once the feedback (21) is obtained, we proceed to analyze its optimality with respect to a cost functional which considers the estimation error and the magnitude of the applied input $v(t)$.

Next, we prove that the control law (21), minimizes the cost functional given by

$$J(v) = \lim_{t\to\infty}\left\{2\beta V + \int_0^t \left(l(\tilde{\chi}, W) + v(t)^T R(\tilde{\chi}, W)v(t)\right)d\tau\right\} \quad (23)$$

where the Lyapunov function solves the following Hamilton-Jacobi-Bellman family of partial derivative equations parametrized with $\beta > 0$

$$l(\tilde{\chi}, W) + 2\beta\Lambda_f V - \beta^2 \Lambda_g V R(\tilde{\chi}, W)^{-1}\Lambda_g V^T = 0 \quad (24)$$

Note that $2\beta V$ in (23) is bounded when $t \to \infty$, since by (20) and (21), V is decreasing and bounded from below by $V(0)$. Therefore, $\lim_{t \to \infty} V(t)$ exists and is finite.

In [6], $l(\tilde{\chi}, W)$ is required to be positive definite and radially unbounded with respect to $\tilde{\chi}$. Here, from (24) we have

$$l(\tilde{\chi}, W) = -2\beta \Lambda_f V + \beta^2 \Lambda_g V R(\tilde{\chi}, W)^{-1} \Lambda_g V^\top \quad (25)$$

Substituting (21) into (25), the learning adaptation law (16) and then applying (19) to the second term on the right side of $\Lambda_f V$, we have

$$l(\tilde{\chi}, W) \geq \tilde{\chi}^T Q \tilde{\chi} + K \|\tilde{y}\|^2 \quad (26)$$
$$+ \frac{b^T}{\|b\|^2} (\mu - 1) \left(1 + \|W\|^2\right) \|\tilde{y}\|^2$$

Selecting $\mu > 1$, we ensure that $l(\tilde{\chi}, W)$ satisfies the condition of being positive definite and radially unbounded. Hence, (23) is a suitable cost function.

The integral term in (23) can be written as

$$l(\tilde{\chi}, W) + v(t)^T R(e, \hat{W}) v(t) \quad (27)$$
$$= -2\beta (\Lambda_f V) + 2\beta^2 (\Lambda_g V) [R(\tilde{\chi}, W)]^{-1} (\Lambda_g V)^T$$

The Lyapunov time derivative is defined as

$$\dot{V} = \Lambda_f V + \Lambda_g V v(t) \quad (28)$$

and substituting (27) in (23), we obtain

$$\dot{V} = \Lambda_f V + \Lambda_g V \left[-\beta (R(\tilde{\chi}, W))^{-1} \right] (\Lambda_g V)^\top$$

Then, multiplying $\dot{V}$ by -2β, we have

$$l(\tilde{\chi}, W) + v(t)^\top R(\tilde{\chi}, W) v(t) = -2\beta \dot{V} \quad (29)$$

Replacing (29) in the cost functional (23), we obtain

$$\begin{aligned} J(u_2) &= \lim_{t \to \infty} 2\beta V - 2\beta \int_0^t \dot{V} d\tau \\ &= \lim_{t \to \infty} \{2\beta V(t) - 2\beta V(t) + 2\beta V(0)\} \\ &= 2\beta V(0) \end{aligned}$$

The cost function optimal value is given by $J^* = 2\beta V(0)$. This is achieved by the control law (21).

V. SIMULATION RESULTS

In this section, the neural observer is applied to the Van der Pol dynamical system.

$$\begin{aligned} \dot{x}_{p_1} &= x_{p_2} \\ \dot{x}_{p_2} &= \left(0.5 - x_{p_1}^2\right) x_{p_2} - x_{p_1} + 0.5 \cos(1.1t) \quad (30) \\ y &= x_{p_1} \\ x_p(0) &= \begin{bmatrix} 0 & 0.25 \end{bmatrix} \end{aligned}$$

We use the RHONO (22) with the following parameters

$$\begin{aligned} z(y)_i &= \tanh^i(y) \quad i = 1, \ldots 10 \quad (31) \\ \gamma &= 470, \ k = 0.65 \\ K &= \begin{bmatrix} 400 & 2600 \end{bmatrix} \\ \hat{\chi}(0) &= \begin{bmatrix} 0.5 & 0.5 \end{bmatrix} \end{aligned}$$

In order to show the influence of introducing high order terms

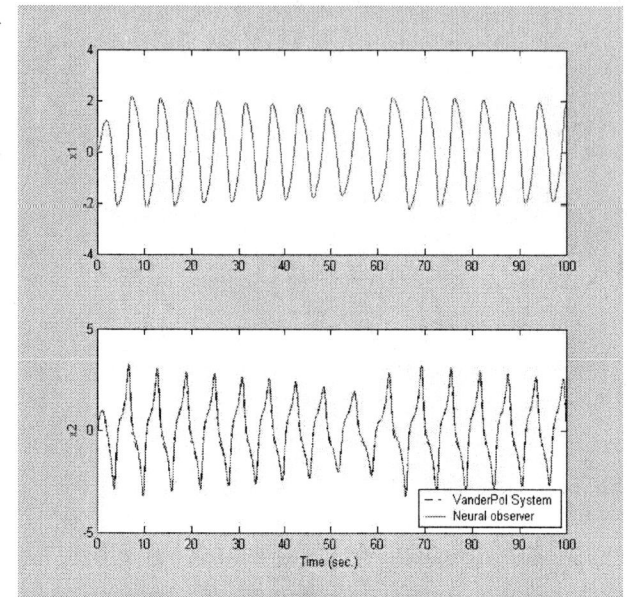

Fig. 2. Time evolution of the estimated states for the RHONO without high order terms

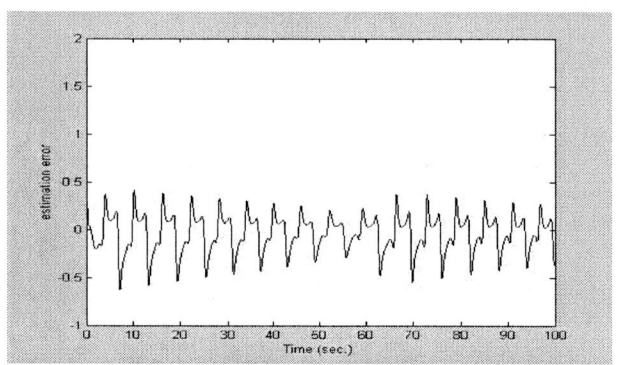

Fig. 3. State estimation error for the RHONO without high order terms

in the neural network, in Fig. 2 and 3 we display the performance of the neural observer without including the high order terms ($i = 1$ in (31)). As can be seen, a good performance of the Recurrent Neural Observer is obtained, achieving a bounded error which can be reduced by including more high order terms. Fig. 4 to Fig. 6 illustrate that a better estimation performance is obtained for ten high order terms. The estimation error can be made arbitrarily small by the inclusion of more high order terms in the RHONO.

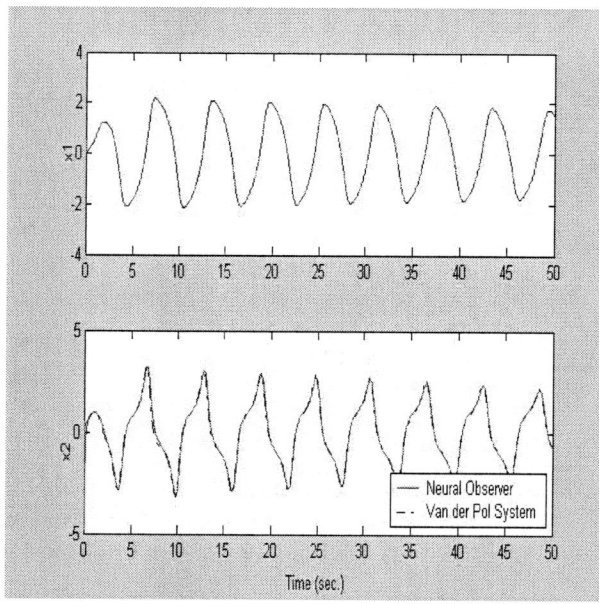

Fig. 4. Time evolution of the estimated states.

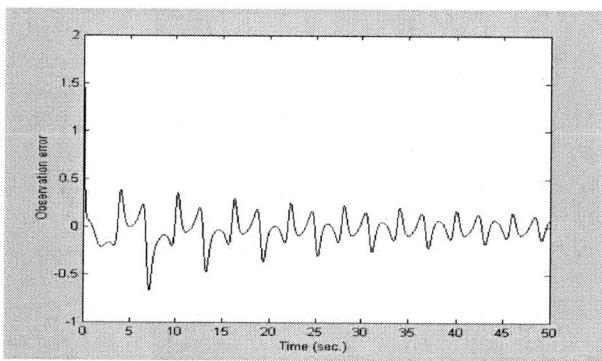

Fig. 5. State estimation error for the RHONO with high order terms

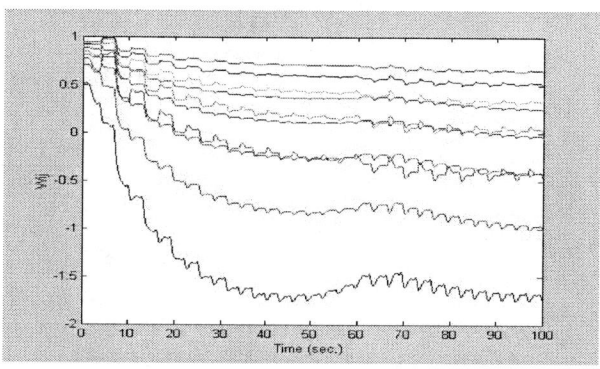

Fig. 6. Time evolution of the neural network weights for the RHONO with high order terms

VI. Conclusions

We have developed an adaptive recurrent neural observer for nonlinear systems with uncertainties and unmodeled dynamics. The neural observer is composed of a Recurrent High Order Neural Network which builds and on-line model of the unknown plant and a learning adaptation law for the neural network weights obtained via the Lyapunov methodology. Stability of the state estimation error is ensured via the inverse optimal control approach. The results are validated via simulations for estimation of the states for the Van der Pol forced oscillator. The results are encouraging; research along this line will introduce the observer in a neural control scheme.

Acknowledgements. The authors thank CONACyT, Mexico, Project 39866Y, for supporting this research.

References

[1] T. Basar and P. Bernhard, *H-Infinity Optimal Control and Related Minimax Design Problems*, Birkhauser, Boston, USA, 1995.

[2] J. Hopfield, "Neurons with graded responses have collective computational properties like those of two state neurons" *Proc. Nat. Acad. Sci.*, USA, 1984, 81, pp. 3088-3092.

[3] K. Hunt, G. Irwin and K. Warwick (Eds.), *Neural Networks Engineering in Dynamic Control Systems*, Springer Verlag, New York, USA, 1995.

[4] H. Khalil, *Nonlinear Systems*, 2nd Ed., Prentice Hall, Upper Saddle River, NJ, USA, 1996.

[5] E. B. Kosmatopoulos, M. A. Christodoulou and P. A. Ioannou, "Dynamical neural networks that ensure exponential identification error convergence", *Neural Networks*, vol. 1, no. 2, pp 299-314, 1997.

[6] M. Krstic and H. Deng, *Stabilization of Nonlinear Uncertain Systems*, Springer Verlag, New York, USA, 1998.

[7] Y. H. Kim, F. L. Lewis and C. T. Abdallah, "Nonlinear observer design using dynamic recurrent neural networks", *Proceedings of the 35th Conference on Decision and Control*, Kobe, Japan, December, 1996.

[8] R. Marino, "Observers for single output nonlinear systems", *IEEE Trans. Automat. Contr.*, vol. 35, pp. 1054-1058, Sept. 1990.

[9] K. S. Narendra and A. M. Annaswamy, *Stable Adaptive Systems*, Prentice Hall, Englewood Cliffs, NJ, USA, 1989.

[10] K. S. Narendra and K. Parthasarathy, "Identification and control of dynamical systems using neural networks", *IEEE Trans. on Neural Networks*, vol. 1, no. 1, pp 4-27, 1990.

[11] A. S. Poznyak, W. Yu, E. N. Sanchez, and J. P. Perez, "Nonlinear adaptive trajectory tracking using dynamic neural networks", *IEEE Trans. on Neural Networks*, vol. 10, no 6, pp 1402-1411, Nov. 1999.

[12] A. S. Poznyak , E. N. Sanchez and W. Yu, *Differential Neural Networks for Robust Nonlinear Control*, Worl Scientific, USA, 2000.

[13] G. A. Rovitahkis and M. A. Christodoulou, *Adaptive Control with Recurrent High-Order Neural Networks*, Springer Verlag, New York, USA, 2000.

[14] E. N. Sanchez and J. P. Perez, "Input-to-state stability analysis for dynamic neural networks", *IEEE Trans. Circuits Syst. I*, vol. 46, pp 1395-1398, 1999.

[15] K. Suykens, L. Vandewalle and R. de Moor, *Artificial Neural Networks for Modelling and Control of Nonlinear Systems*, Kluwer Academic Publishers, Boston, USA,1996.

System and Method for Determining Harmonic Contributions from Non-Linear Loads Using Recurrent Neural Networks

Joy Mazumdar and Ronald G. Harley
School of Electrical and Computer Engineering
Georgia Institute of Technology
Atlanta, GA 30332-0250 USA
ron.harley@ece.gatech.edu

Frank Lambert
National Electric Energy Testing Research and
Applications Center (NEETRAC)
Forest Park, GA 30297 USA
frank.lambert@neetrac.gatech.edu

Abstract - This paper proposes a neural network solution methodology for the problem of measuring the actual amount of harmonic current injected into a power network by a non-linear load. The determination of harmonic currents is complicated by the fact that the supply voltage waveform is distorted by other loads and is rarely a pure sinusoid. Harmonics may therefore be classified as *contributions from the load* on the one hand and *contributions from the power system* or *supply harmonics* on the other hand. A recurrent neural network architecture based method is used to find a way of distinguishing between the load contributed harmonics and supply harmonics, without disconnecting the load from the network. The main advantage of this method is that only waveforms of voltages and currents have to be measured. This method is applicable for both single and three phase loads. This could be fabricated into a commercial instrument that could be installed in substations of large customer loads, or used as a hand-held clip on instrument.

I. INTRODUCTION

The objective of the electric utility is to deliver a sinusoidal voltage at fairly constant magnitude and frequency throughout its network. However, with the widespread proliferation of power electronic and other non-linear loads, significant amounts of harmonic currents are being injected into the network by these loads. When such loads are supplied from a sinusoidal voltage source, their injected harmonic currents are referred to as *contributions from the load*. Figure 1 shows a simple network structure.

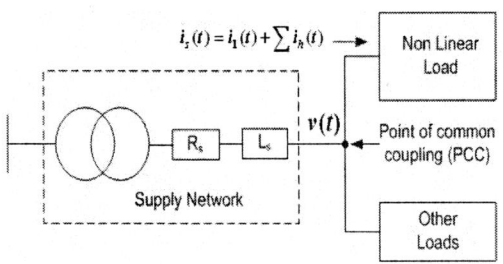

Fig. 1. Simple power system network

The harmonic currents cause harmonic volt drops in the supply network. Any other loads, even linear loads, connected to the PCC, will have harmonic currents injected into them by the distorted PCC voltage. Such currents are referred to as *contributions from the power system*, or supply harmonics.

If the sum of the harmonic currents in the network exceeds a certain limit, it creates problems. Limits of the levels of harmonic currents injected into the system are specified in various IEEE as well as IEC standards, guidelines and recommended practices [1, 2].

If several loads are connected to a PCC, it is not possible to accurately determine the amount of harmonic current injected by each load, in order to tell which load(s) is injecting the excessively high harmonic currents. If individual harmonic current injections were known, then a utility could penalize the offending consumer in some appropriate way, including say a special tariff or insist on corrective action by the consumer. Simply measuring the harmonic currents at each individual load is not sufficiently accurate since these harmonic currents may be caused by not only the non-linear load, but also by a non-sinusoidal PCC voltage.

This paper proposes a novel method based on Artificial Neural Networks (ANN) to distinguish between the two components of harmonic sources (i.e. load or power system). This will enable standards of harmonic pollution to be enforced by utilities and most importantly improve the power quality. Several methods like DFT/FFT [3], stochastic method [4] and in recent years artificial neural networks (ANN) [5, 6, 7, 8, 9] have been proposed to measure the harmonic content in the load current, or to predict it, but most of them assume a radial feeder supplying a single load through a known feeder impedance, or multiple loads connected to a PCC which has a sinusoidal voltage and with zero impedance in the supply feeder.

II. RECURRENT NEURAL NETWORK

Recurrent neural networks (RNN) are feedback networks in which the present activation state is a function of the previous activation state as well as the present inputs. Adding feedback from the prior activation step introduces a kind of memory to the process. Thus adding recurrent connections to a back propagation network enhances its ability to learn temporal sequences without fundamentally changing the training process. Recurrent networks will, in general, perform better than regular feed forward networks on systems with transients. They may be trained to identify or approximate any desired continuous vector mapping function $f(.)$ over a specified range.

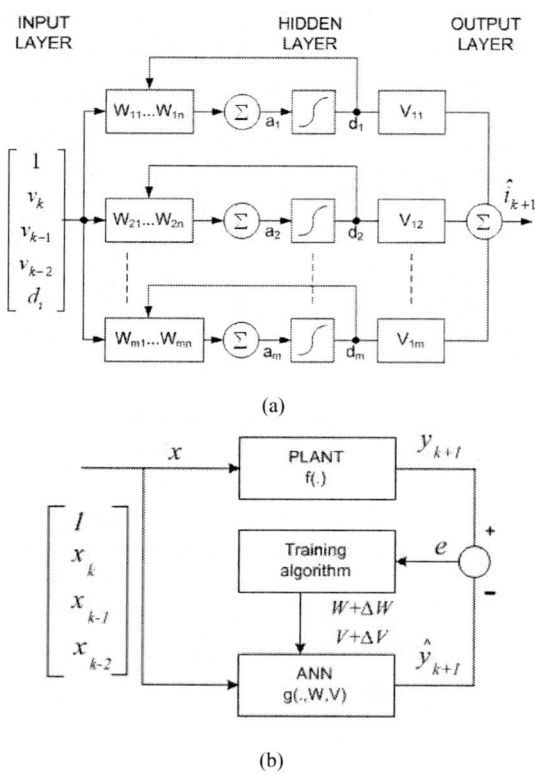

Fig. 2. (a) RNN Architecture (b) Training Scheme of ANN

Figure 2 shows the block diagram of a three layer RNN interconnected by weight matrices W and V. The objective of the training is to modify W and V such that the ANN function $g(.,W,V)$ approximates the desired function $f(.)$, so that the error e between the desired function output y and the ANN output $\hat{y}$ is minimal.

Continual online training (COT) is required whenever $f(.)$ is a time varying signal and $g(.,W,V)$ has to track $f(.)$. The online training cycle has two distinct paths: forward propagation and error back-propagation. Forward propagation is the passing of inputs through the ANN structure to its output. Error back-propagation is the passing of the output error to the input in order to estimate the individual contribution of each weight in the network to the final output error. The weights are then modified so as to reduce the output error. The generalized equations are shown below [10].

A. Forward Propagation

Every input in the input column vector $\underline{x}$ is fed via the corresponding weight in the input weight matrix W to every node in the hidden layer. The activation vector $\underline{a}$ is determined as the sum of its weighted inputs. In vector notation

$$\underline{a} = W\underline{x} \qquad (1)$$

where the input column vector $\underline{x} \in R^{n+m}$, hidden layer activation column vector $\underline{a} \in R^m$ and input weight matrix $W \in R^{m \times n}$, n is the number of ANN inputs and m is the number of neurons in the hidden layer. Each of the hidden node activations in $\underline{a}$ is then passed through a sigmoid function to determine the hidden-layer decision vector $\underline{d}$.

$$d_i = \frac{1}{1+e^{(-a_i)}}, \quad i \in \{1,2,....,m\} \qquad (2)$$

where the decision column vector $\underline{d} \in R^m$.

The decision vector $\underline{d}$ is then fed back to the input layer (this introduces the recurrence) as well as fed to the corresponding weight in the output weight matrix V. The ANN output $\hat{y}$ is computed as

$$\hat{y} = (V\underline{d})^T \qquad (3)$$

For a single output system the output weight matrix $V \in R^{1 \times m}$ and $\hat{y}$ is a scalar.

B. Error back-propagation

The output error e is calculated as

$$e = y - \hat{y} \qquad (4)$$

The output error is back propagated through the ANN to determine the errors $\underline{e}_d$ and $\underline{e}_a$ in the decision vector $\underline{d}$ and activation vector $\underline{a}$ respectively, such that

$$\underline{e}_d = V^T e \qquad (5)$$

The activation errors e_{ai} are given as a product of the decision errors e_{di} and the derivative of the decisions d_i with respect to the activations a_i, where

$$e_{ai} = \left(\frac{d}{da_i}d_i\right)e_{di}$$
$$= d_i(1-d_i)e_{di}, \quad i \in \{1,2,....,m\} \qquad (6)$$

The change in input weights ΔW and output weights ΔV are calculated as

$$\Delta W = \gamma_m \Delta W + \gamma_g \underline{e}_a \underline{x}^T$$
$$\Delta V = \gamma_m \Delta V + \gamma_g \underline{e}_y \underline{d}^T \qquad (7)$$

where $\gamma_m, \gamma_g \in [0,1]$ are the momentum and learning gain constants respectively. The last step in the training process is the actual updating of the weights.

$$W = W + \Delta W$$
$$V = V + \Delta V \qquad (8)$$

III. ESTIMATION OF HARMONIC CURRENT

Figure 3 is a one-line diagram of a three-phase supply network having a sinusoidal voltage source v_s, network impedance L_s, R_s and several loads (one of which is non-linear) connected to a PCC.

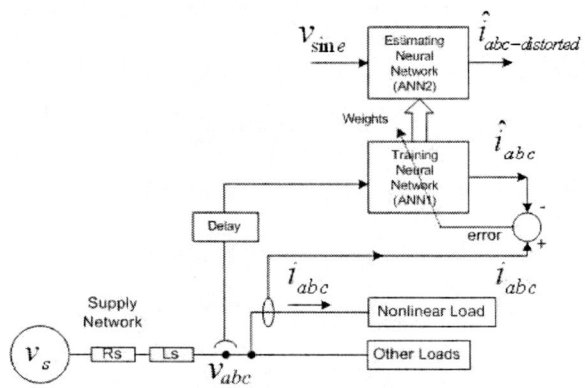

Fig. 3. Proposed scheme (V_{abc} is the voltage at the PCC)

The nonlinear load injects distorted line current i_{abc} into the network. A neural network is trained to identify the non-linear characteristics of the load. This neural network is called the Training neural network (ANN1). A second neural network exists and is called the Estimating neural network (ANN2). ANN2 is an exact replica of the trained ANN1. Existence of ANN2 enables the simulation action of isolating the load from the network and testing it without physically disconnecting the load from the network. The function of ANN2 can very well be carried out by ANN1, however that would disrupt the continual online training of ANN1 during the brief moments of testing.

A. ANN1 Training

The proposed method measures the instantaneous values of the three voltages v_{abc} at the PCC, as well as the three line currents i_{abc} at the kth moment in time. The voltages v_{abc} could be line-to-line or line-to-neutral measurements. The neural network ANN1 is designed to predict one step ahead the line current $\hat{i}_{abc}$ as a function of the present and delayed voltage vector values $v_{abc}(k)$, $v_{abc}(k-1)$ and $v_{abc}(k-2)$. When the $k+1$ moment arrives (at the next sampling instant), the actual instantaneous values of i_{abc} are compared with the previously predicted values of $\hat{i}_{abc}$, and the difference (or error e) is used to train the ANN1 weights. Initially the weights have random values, but after several sampling steps, the training soon converges and the value of the error e diminishes to an acceptably small value. Proof of this is illustrated by the fact that the waveforms for i_{abc} and $\hat{i}_{abc}$ should practically lie on top of each other. At this point the ANN1 therefore represents the admittance of the nonlinear load. This process is called *identifying* the load admittance. Since continual online training is used, it will correctly represent the load admittance from moment to moment. At any moment in time after the ANN1 training has converged, its weights are transferred to ANN2. The training cycle of ANN1 continues and in this way ANN2 always has updated weights available when needed.

B. ANN2 Estimating

ANN2 uses the load admittance identified by ANN1, applies a mathematically generated sine wave voltage to it, and calculates an estimated current $\hat{i}_{abc-distorted}$. The $\hat{i}_{abc-distorted}$ therefore represents the current that the nonlinear load would have drawn had it been supplied by a sinusoidal voltage source. In other words, this gives the same information that could have been obtained by quickly removing the distorted PCC voltage (if this were possible) and connecting a pure sinusoidal voltage to supply the nonlinear load, except that it is now not necessary to actually do this interruption. Any distortion present in the $\hat{i}_{abc-distorted}$ waveform can now be attributed to the non-linearity of the load admittance.

IV. EXPERIMENTAL RESULTS

In most non-linear circuits, some sort of switching power devices are used as the interface between the supply network and the actual load. Experiments with different circuits have been carried out.

A. Light Dimmer Test

The experimental setup is shown in Fig.4.

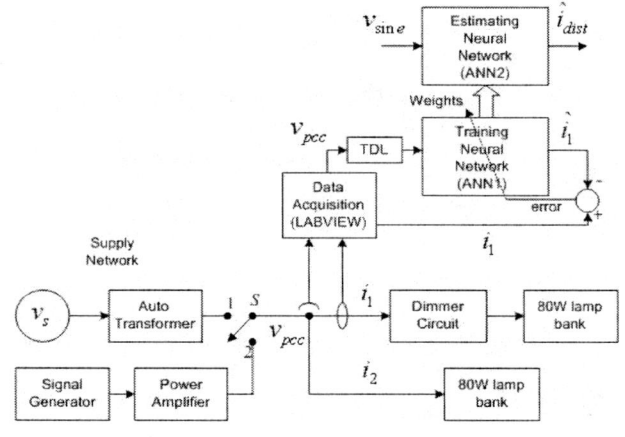

Fig. 4. Experimental setup with dimmer circuit

The proposed scheme is implemented with a single phase dimmer feeding a lamp bank (Load-1) and another lamp bank (Load-2), both connected to the PCC. The voltage at the PCC is fixed at 50 Vrms, 60 Hz. Two different cases are evaluated with switch S either in position 1 or 2. Total Harmonic Distortion is measured by a dedicated spectrum analyzer which measures up to the 20th harmonic as well as by MATLAB software.

Data acquisition for cases 1 and 2 is carried out with a system from National Instruments and LABVIEW software which stores the data on a personal computer. This data is then imported to MATLAB and using the *powergui* block of SIMULINK, the THD's are recomputed. These recomputed THD's are then compared with measurements taken directly by a spectrum analyzer, in order to verify that the LABVIEW and MATLAB computer code are working correctly. The sampling frequency for data acquisition is 4 kHz which ensures that harmonics up to the 30th can be measured.

Case 1 : Switch S in position 1
The circuit is supplied from the 120V utility wall socket and stepped down by the auto-transformer to 50V.
THD of voltage at PCC without any loads = 4.25%. (MATLAB computation yielded 3.37%)
THD of voltage at PCC with both loads connected = 4.24%
THD of current i_1 = 14.5%. (MATLAB computation yielded 13.27%)

Case 2 : Switch S in position 2
A sine wave voltage generated by a function generator is the closest approximation to a pure sine wave. The current signal from the function generator is amplified by a power amplifier and that is used as the power source.
THD of voltage at the PCC without any loads is 1.9%. (MATLAB computation yielded 1.89%)
THD of voltage at PCC with both loads connected = 1.9%
THD of current i_1 = 16.7%. (MATLAB computation yielded 15.68%)

A small discrepancy is seen between the readings of the spectrum analyzer and that obtained from MATLAB. This could probably be attributed to the way the data is acquired. The input channels of the data acquisition system are equipped with elliptic filters and that smoothens out the waveforms to some extent. However an important result is that the current THD of the dimmer circuit is higher when it is being supplied by the function generator (less THD in v_{pcc}) as compared to when it is supplied by the utility (more THD in v_{pcc}). When several loads are supplied from the PCC, with its own background THD, the individual currents are due to the combined effects of the distorted v_{pcc} and the non-linearities of the loads. This results in some amount of phase cancellation which may reduce the overall harmonic current in the network [11] and thus benefit some of the non-linear loads. Linear loads do not introduce harmonics into the network, but do get affected by the distorted PCC voltage. Hence, it is essential that the method should be able to analyze each and every load on its own merit [12].

The data obtained from case 1 is used to train the neural network ANN1 until the training error converges to near zero, and the current i_1 of Load-1 correctly tracks the output of ANN1. Figure 5 indicates how well ANN1 has converged since its output $\hat{i}_1$ lies on top of the actual i_1 waveform.

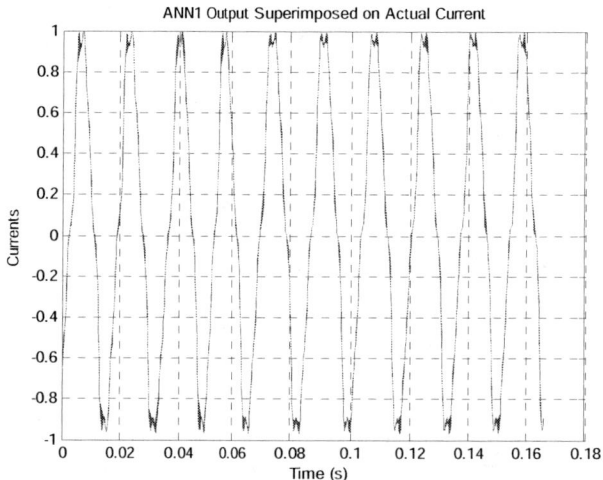

Fig. 5. i_1 and $\hat{i}_1$ superimposed

The convergence of the training can also be verified by looking at the tracking error ($i_1 - \hat{i}_1$). Once the tracking error is below a pre-defined level, it can be concluded that ANN1 has learned the admittance of Load-1 to an acceptable level of accuracy. The weights of ANN1 are now passed to ANN2 which ideally should be supplied by a sine wave voltage with zero distortion. However such a sine wave source is difficult to obtain in reality. Hence ANN2 is tested with the voltage data captured from case 2.

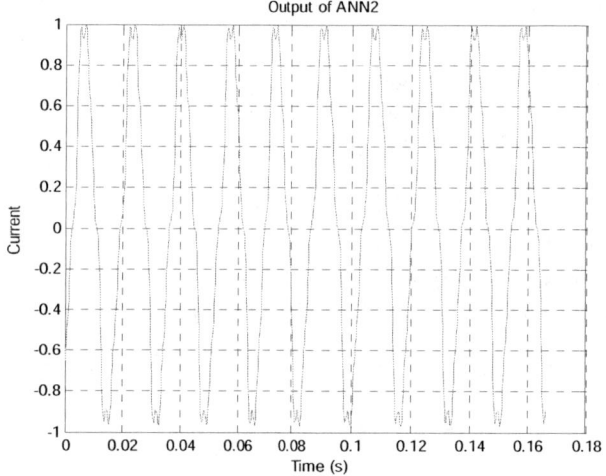

Fig. 6. $\hat{i}_{1-dist}$ waveform (THD=15.23%)

The output of ANN2 is $\hat{i}_{1-dist}$ and it appears in Fig. 6 which shows what Fig. 5 would have looked like if the voltage at the PCC had a THD of 1.9% of case 2. The THD of $\hat{i}_{1-dist}$ in Fig. 6 is 15.23% which is very close to the THD of the actual current (15.68%) measured in case 2.

ANN2 is now tested with a mathematically generated sine wave. Figure 7 shows the output of ANN2. This is the current waveform we would expect to see from the dimmer circuit if it were supplied by a pure sine wave voltage.

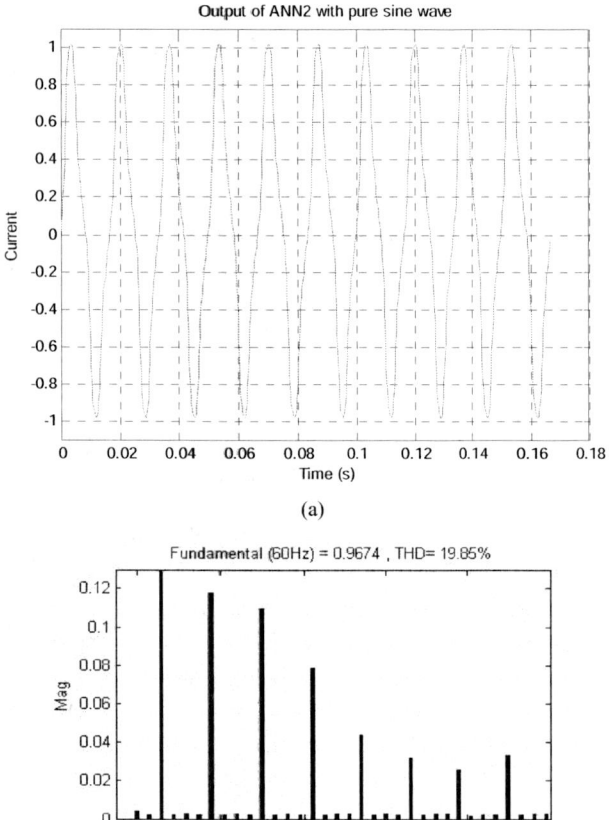

Fig. 7. (a) $\hat{i}_{1-dist}$ waveform when supplied by mathematically generated sine wave. (b) FFT Spectrum (THD=19.85%)

The true current THD of $\hat{i}_{1-dist}$ in Fig. 7 turns out to be 19.85% instead of 14.5%.

B. Diode Bridge Rectifier Load

A second experiment has been performed with diode bridge rectifiers. The experimental setup is shown in Fig. 8.

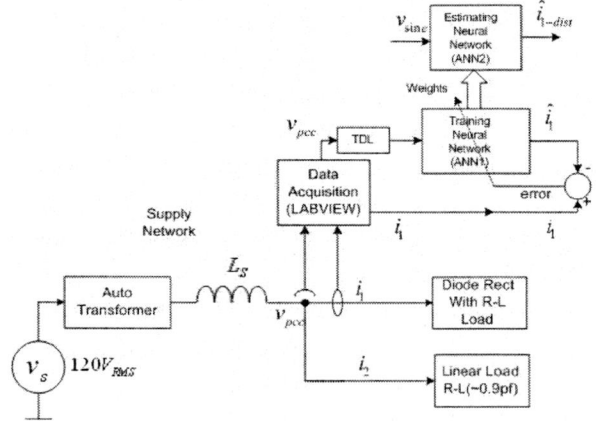

Fig. 8. Single-phase diode bridge rectifier setup

The proposed scheme is implemented with a single phase diode bridge rectifier feeding an R-L load (Load-1) and a linear R-L load (Load-2), both connected to the PCC. The operating voltage at the PCC is $5V_{RMS}$, 60Hz which is obtained by using an auto transformer. This reduced voltage allows low voltage diodes to be used. Each individual load is rated at 1amp, and the THD of i_1 is 7.8% (measured by spectrum analyzer), but some of this is due to the non-linearity of Load-1 and some is due to the distortion in the PCC voltage. Without any load connected, the background THD at v_{pcc} is 3.4%. With both loads connected, this THD rises to 6.2%. As before, v_{pcc} and i_1 are acquired into MATLAB. The online training result of ANN1 in MATLAB is shown in Fig. 9.

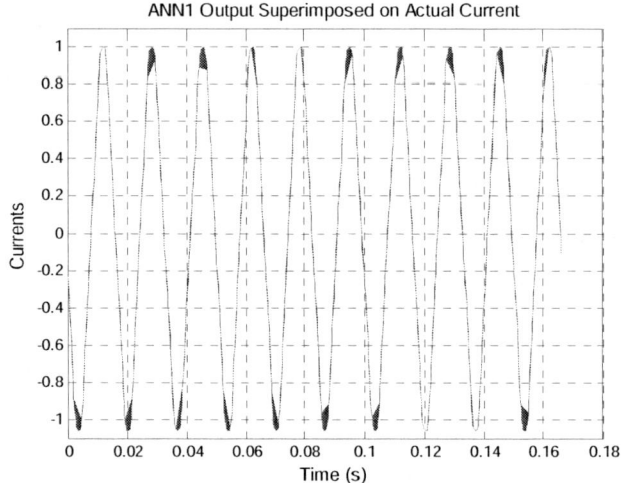

Fig. 9. i_1 and $\hat{i}_1$ superimposed

The weights of ANN1 are now transferred to ANN2 (still in MATLAB), and ANN2 is tested with a mathematically generated sine wave voltage with zero distortion. The Fourier spectrum of the output $\hat{i}_{1-dist}$ from ANN2 is plotted in Fig.10 and shows what the Fourier spectrum of $\hat{i}_1$ in Fig. 9 would have looked like if the voltage v_{pcc} had no distortion.

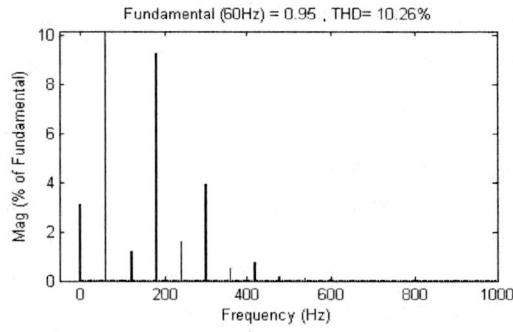

Fig. 10. FFT spectrum of $\hat{i}_{1-dist}$ .THD=10.26%

The THD of $\hat{i}_{1-dist}$ is now 10.26% instead of 7.8%. This means that the true current THD of Load-1 is higher than what was measured when it was a part of the power network and supplied by a distorted v_{pcc}.

C. DC motor-converter load

A final experiment was conducted with a controlled thyristor rectifier driving a DC motor on no-load. The operating voltage at the PCC is $120 V_{RMS}$, 60 Hz, taken directly from the laboratory supply network. The speed reference of the motor is set at about 70%. v_{pcc} and i_1 are recorded with both the loads operating. Without any load connected, the background THD at v_{pcc} is 3.76%. The input current i_1 of the drive has a current THD of 36.01% and the THD of v_{pcc} is 3.97%. As before once convergence in training of ANN1 is obtained, the next step is to transfer the weights to ANN2 and test it with a mathematically generated sine wave (in MATLAB). The output of ANN2 is $\hat{i}_{1-dist}$ and has a THD of 26.79% as shown in Fig. 11.

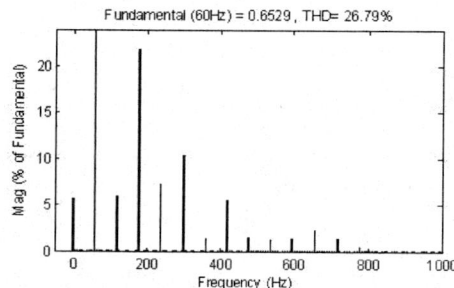

Fig. 11. FFT spectrum of $\hat{i}_{1-dist}$ waveform. THD=26.79%

A. Summary of results

The salient results from the three tests above are summarized in Table I.

TABLE I: TABULATION OF RESULTS

Load	THD_d	THD_s	$\left(\frac{THD_s - THD_d}{THD_s}\right)\%$
Dimmer	14.5%	19.85%	26.95%
Rectifier	7.68%	10.26%	25.15%
DC motor	36.01%	26.79%	-34.42%

where THD_d is i_{THD} from distorted v_{pcc} and THD_s is i_{THD} from pure sine wave.

For the light dimmer and diode bridge rectifiers, the THD in the nonlinear load's current increased when calculated for a sine wave v_{pcc}. However for the dc motor-converter, it decreased. This important finding means that it is erroneous to think intuitively that the current THD, when supplied from a distorted v_{pcc} should always be higher than if the v_{pcc} had no distortion. The neural network is implemented with 20 neurons in the hidden layer and the learning gain of 0.05.

V. CONCLUSIONS

Non-linear loads exhibit customer contributed harmonics. Linear loads draw distorted currents because of a distorted v_{pcc} caused by non-linear loads. However in an actual network, loads cannot be isolated. Therefore it is impossible to say which load is causing the pollution and which load is getting penalized. The novel method described in this paper avoids disconnecting any loads from the system and estimates the actual harmonic current injected by each load. This information could be used to penalize the offending load.

The biggest advantage of this method is that only waveforms of voltages and currents have to be measured. On a practical system the neural network computations can be carried out on a DSP, together with a suitable A-D interface. Such a system could be installed permanently or be portable from one customer to another in order to simply monitor pollution levels at a particular PCC in the network.

ACKNOWLEDGEMENT

Financial support by the National Electric Energy Testing Research and Applications Center (NEETRAC), USA for this research is greatly acknowledged.

REFERENCE

[1] IEEE Power System Harmonic Working Group, "Bibliography of Power System Harmonics, Part I and II", *IEEE PES Winter Power Meeting*, Paper 84 WM 214-3, Jan. 29-Feb. 3, 1984.
[2] IEEE Standard 519-1992, IEEE Recommended Practices and Requirements for Harmonic Control in Electric Power Systems.
[3] T. A. George, and D. Bones, "Harmonic power flow determination using the fast Fourier transform", *IEEE Transactions on Power Delivery*, Volume: 6 Issue: 2, April 1991, pp. 530 –535.
[4] Y. Baghzouz, and O. T. Tan, "Probabilistic Modeling of Power System Harmonics", *IEEE Transactions on Industry Applications*, Vol, IA-23, No. 1, January/February 1987, pp. 173-180.
[5] H. Mori, and S. Suga, "Power system harmonics prediction with an artificial neural network", *IEEE International Symposium on Circuits and Systems*, 11-14 June 1991, Vol. 2, pp. 1129 –1132.
[6] M. Rukonuzzaman, A.A.M Zin, H. Shaibon, and K. L. Lo, "An application of neural network in power system harmonic detection",. *IEEE World Congress on Computational Intelligence. The 1998 IEEE International Joint Conference on Neural Networks*, Vol. 1, 4-9 May 1998, pp. 74 –78.
[7] S. Osowski, "Neural network for estimation of harmonic components in a power system", *IEE Proceedings on Generation, Transmission and Distribution*, Vol. 139, Issue 2, March 1992, pp. 129 – 135.
[8] W.W.L Keerthipala, Low Tah Chong and Tham Chong Leong, "Artificial neural network model for analysis of power system harmonics", *IEEE International Conference on Neural Networks, 1995*, 27 Nov.-1 Dec. 1995, Vol.2, pp. 905 – 910.
[9] N. Pecharanin, H. Mitsui, and M. Sone, "Harmonic detection by using neural network", *IEEE International Conference on Neural Networks, 1995*, 27 Nov.-1 Dec. 1995, Vol.2, pp. 923 – 926.
[10] B. Burton and R.G. Harley, "Reducing the computational demands of continually online-trained artificial neural networks for system identification and control of fast processes", *IEEE Transactions on Industry Applications*, Vol. 34, Issue: 3, May-June 1998 pp. 589 – 596.
[11] W.M. Grady, A. Mansoor, E.F. Fuchs, P. Verde and M. Doyle, "Estimating the net harmonic currents produced by selected distributed single-phase loads: computers, televisions, and incandescent light dimmers", *IEEE Power Engineering Society Winter Meeting, 2002*, Vol. 2 , 27-31 Jan. 2002, pp. 1090 – 1094.
[12] C.R. van Niekerk, A.P.J. Rens and A.J. Hoffman, "Identification of types of distortion sources in power systems by applying neural networks", 6th IEEE AFRICON, Oct. 2002, Vol. 2, pp. 829 – 834.

On Output Regulation for SISO Nolinear Systems with Dynamic Neural Networks

B. Castillo-Toledo and A. Hernández Avalos
CINVESTAV-IPN Unidad Guadalajara
A.P. 31-438. Pza. La Luna Col Verde Valle, 44550,Guadalajara México
{toledo,aavalos}@gdl.cinvestav.mx

Abstract— In this work, the output regulation theory is combined with a dynamic neural identifier, in order to improve the robustness properties for trajectory tracking on SISO nonlinear system's.

A neural network is used to identify the dynamic's of the nonlinear system, by a suitable on-line training, which ensures small identification error. Then, the output regulation technique is applied to the neural network to obtain a controller that, when applied to the original system, guarantee also a bounded output tracking error despite the presence of parameter variations and external perturbations..

Simulation results on a model of a chaotic system are presented showing the viability and effectiveness of the proposed technique.

I. INTRODUCTION

Recently the popularity of neural networks has grown due its effectiveness in areas such as pattern recognition and control issues like identification, input-output linearization, stabilization, tracking etc. In particular, stabilization and tracking are of two of the most studied problems, due to the wide application possibilities. In general, the particular techniques used to guarantee the tracking requirements provide in each case, advantages and disadvantages that the designer has to consider for its application. One of these techniques is the Output Regulation Theory, which consist in the problem of designing a feedback controller making the system to move along a prescribed steady state behavior for which the tracking error is identically zero, rejecting, at the same time, any undesired disturbance belonging to an allowable family of disturbances. The conditions for the solution of the output regulation problem have been presented, among other works, in [2] for continuous time and [3] for discrete time.

The structurally stable regulation problem, namely the problem of finding a neighborhood of the nominal values of the parameters of the system on which, for all the parameter values, the regulation properties are maintained, has also studied intensively. It has been shown that this problem can be solved by means of a dynamic controller containing an internal model, i.e., a model which generates all the possible steady state input for any admissible parameter variations [13],[14]. In the case of unknown dynamics or unmeasured disturbances sophisticated techniques may be necessary [4],[5].

Due the success of neural networks in control problems, their use for overcoming the drawbacks of the output regulation theory, especially those related to the necessity of having a precise modelling of the nonlinear systems, is a very interesting alternative to the classical solution. Thanks to the learning capability of the neural networks with on-line training we are able to model parametric variations, unknown dynamics, including disturbances; giving a way to design robust controllers.

The adaptive neural tracking problem has been dealt in the literature ([11], [12]) by minimizing by any performance index the state tracking error between the vector state of the neural network and a vector reference, yet not guaranteing a zero tracking error because many times the final state tracking error depends on the chosen vector reference. In this sense, the the output regulation theory may provide a prescribed steady state and a steady state input for which the state tracking error is zero.

The main motivation in this work is to investigate a technique that combines the output regulation theory with the robustness properties of a neural identifier. For the identification step, some tools developed in [6] and [7] which works with dynamic neural networks, specifically a Hopfield network [8] are adapted in the proposed scheme.

The main idea is to solve the output regulation problem for the neural network which approximate the nonlinear system, and apply to the original nonlinear system the controller obtained.

II. IDENTIFICATION

A. Neuro-observer

The problem of the identification consists of choosing an appropriate identification model and adjusting its parameters such that the response of the model to an input signal approximates the response of the plant under the same input. The most of the publications assume complete accessibility of the state of the systems to be controlled, in order to do zero the *identification error*, that is, the difference between the vector state of the system and the vector state of the model. But in the realty this is not always true, so we will work with a neuro-observer with time delay term developed in [7]. Now we going to consider the class of nonlinear system given by

$$\dot{x}_t = f(x_t, u_t, t) + \xi_{1,t} \quad (1)$$
$$y_t = Cx + \xi_{2,t}$$

where ξ_1 and ξ_2 are vector functions representing external perturbations and satisfies the assumption of the "*bounded power*" given by

$$\limsup_{T\to\infty} \frac{1}{T}\int_0^T \|\xi_{i,t}\|^2_{\Lambda_{\xi i}} dt = \Upsilon_i < \infty \quad (2)$$
$$0 < \Lambda_{\xi i} = \Lambda_{\xi i}^T, \quad i = 1, 2$$

We will consider the luneburger-like second order neuro-observer with the additional time delay term [9] and it has the following structure:

$$\dot{\hat{x}}_t = A\hat{x}_t + W_{1,t}\sigma(V_{1,t}\hat{x}_t) + W_{2,t}\phi(V_{2,t}\hat{x}_t)u_t \quad (3)$$
$$+ L_1[y_t - \hat{y}_t] + L_2/h[(y_t - y_{t-h}) - (\hat{y}_t - \hat{y}_{t-h})]$$
$$\hat{y} = C\hat{x}$$

The vector $\hat{x}_t \in \Re^n$ is the state of the neural network, $u_t \in \Re^m$ is its input. The matrix $A \in \Re^{n\times n}$ is a Hurwitz matrix. $W_1 \in \Re^{n\times q}$, $V_1 \in \Re^{q\times n}$, $W_2 \in \Re^{n\times m}$, $V_2 \in \Re^{m\times n}$. W_1, W_2, and V_1, V_2 are the weight matrices describing output and hidden layers connections, respectively. $L_1 \in \Re^{n\times q}$ and $L_2 \in \Re^{n\times q}$ are first and second-order gain, matrices. The scalar $h > 0$ and $\phi(\cdot)$ is $\Re^{m\times m}$ the diagonal matrix, that is,

$$\phi(\cdot) = diag[\phi_1(V_{2,t}\hat{x}_t)_1 .... \phi_m(V_{2,t}\hat{x}_t)_m]$$

$\sigma(\cdot) \in \Re^q$ and ϕ_i are sigmoid functions.

The nonlinear system satisfies the following assumption.

A1: For a bounded nonlinear feedback control $(\|u_t(x_t)\|^2 \leq \overline{u})$, the nominal closed-loop nonlinear system is *quadratically stable*, that is, there exist a Lyapunov (may be, unknown) function $\overline{V}_t \geq 0$ satisfying

$$\frac{\partial \overline{V}_t}{\partial x} f(x_t, u_t) \leq -\lambda_1 \|x_t\|^2, \quad \left\|\frac{\partial \overline{V}_t}{\partial x}\right\| \leq \lambda_2 \|x_t\|$$
$$\lambda_1, \lambda_2 > 0$$

Let us define the *estimation error* and the *output error* at time t

$$\Delta_t = \hat{x}_t - x_t, \quad e_t = \hat{y} - y = C\Delta_t - \xi_{2,t}$$

that implies

$$C^T e_t = C^T(C\Delta_t - \xi_{2,t})$$
$$= (C^T C + \delta I)\Delta_t - \delta I \Delta_t - C^T \xi_{2,t} \quad (4)$$
$$\Delta_t = C_\delta^+ e_t + \delta N_\delta \Delta_t + C_\delta^+ \xi_{2,t}$$

where

$$C_\delta^+ = (C^T C + \delta I)^{-1} C^T$$
$$N_\delta = (C^T C + \delta I)^{-1}$$

and δ is a small positive scalar.

It is clear that all sigmoidal functions, commonly used in neural networks, satisfy the Lipschitz condition, and is natural assume that

$$\tilde{\sigma}_t^T \Lambda_1 \tilde{\sigma}_t \leq \Delta_t^T \Lambda_\sigma \Delta_t, \quad (\tilde{\phi}u_t)^T \Lambda_2(\tilde{\phi}u_t) \leq u^2 \Delta_t^T \Lambda_\phi \Delta_t$$
$$\tilde{\sigma}_t' = D_\sigma \tilde{V}_{1,t}\hat{x}_t + v_\sigma, \quad \phi_t' u_t = D_\phi \tilde{V}_{2,t}\hat{x}_t + v_\phi$$

In the general case, when the neural network

$$\dot{\hat{x}}_t = A\hat{x}_t + W_{1,t}\sigma(V_{1,t}\hat{x}_t) + W_{2,t}\phi(V_2\hat{x}_t)u_t$$

cannot follow the nonlinear system (1) exactly and this case may be written as

$$\dot{x}_t = Ax_t + W_1^*\sigma(V_1^* x_t) + W_2^*\phi(V_2^* x_t)u_t + \tilde{f}_t$$
$$\tilde{f}_t = f(x_t, u_t, t) - Ax_t - W_1^*\sigma(V_1^* x_t) - W_2^*\phi(V_2^* x_t)u_t$$
$$+ \xi_{1,t} \quad (5)$$

where $\tilde{f}_t$ is unmodelled dynamic term and W_1^*, W_2^*, V_1^* and V_2^* are any known matrices which are selected below as initial for the designed differential learning law.

To guarantee the global existence of the solution for (1), the following condition should be satisfied

$$\|f(x_t, u_t, t)\|^2 \leq C_1 + C_2 \|x_t\|^2$$

Due that σ and ϕ are sigmoid functions uniformly bounded, the following assumption, concerning the unmodelled dynamics $\tilde{f}_t$:

A2: There exist the known positive constants $\overline{\eta}$ and $\overline{\eta}_1$ such that

$$\left\|\tilde{f}_t\right\|^2_{\Lambda_f} \leq \overline{\eta} + \overline{\eta}_1 \|x_t\|^2_{\Lambda_f}, \quad \Lambda_f = \Lambda_f^T > 0$$

Now taking into account that if the matrix A is stable, the pair $(A, R^{1/2})$ is controllable and the pair $(Q^{1/2}, A)$ is observable and the *local frequency condition* satisfies

$$A^T R^{-1} A - Q \geq \frac{1}{4}\left[A^T R^{-1} - R^{-1} A\right] R \left[A^T R^{-1} - R^{-1} A\right]^T \quad (6)$$

then the algebraic matrix Riccati equation

$$A^T P + PA + PRP + Q = 0 \quad (7)$$

has a positive solution. Now the following assumption is demanded.

A3: There exist a stable matrix A and a positive parameter δ such that the matrix Riccati equation (7) with

$$R = 2\overline{W}_1 + 2\overline{W}_2 + \Lambda_f^{-1} + \Lambda_{\xi_1}^{-1} + \delta R_1 \quad (8)$$
$$Q = \Lambda_\sigma + \overline{u}^2 \Lambda_\phi + P_1 + Q_0 - 2C^T \Lambda_\xi C$$

has positive solution P, where Q_0 is a positive definite matrix and

$$R_1 = 2N_\delta K_1^T \Lambda_\sigma^{-1} K_1 N_\delta^T + 2N_\delta K_1^T \Lambda_\phi^{-1} K_1 N_\delta^T$$
$$+ N_\delta K_3^T \Lambda_\sigma^{-1} K_3 N_\delta^T + N_\delta K_4^T \Lambda_\phi^{-1} K_4 N_\delta^T$$

This condition can be easily verified if we select A as stable diagonal matrix. Denote by $\mathcal{H}$ the class of unknown nonlinear systems satisfying A1-A3.

Consider the new differential learning law given by the following system of **matrix differential equations**:

$$\begin{aligned}
\dot{W}_{1,t} &= -K_1 P C_\delta^+ e_t \sigma^T - (1+\delta)W_{\delta 1} + \\
&\quad K_1 P C_\delta^+ e \widehat{x}_t^T \widetilde{V}_{1,t}^T D_\sigma \\
\dot{W}_{2,t} &= -K_2 P C_\delta^+ e_t (\phi u_t)^T - (1+\delta)W_{\delta 2} + \\
&\quad K_2 P C_\delta^+ e \widehat{x}_t^T \widetilde{V}_{2,t}^T \sum_{i=1}^q (u_{i,t} D_{i\phi}^T) \qquad (9)\\
\dot{V}_{1,t} &= -K_3 P W_{1,t} D_\sigma C_\delta^+ e \widehat{x}_t^T - (1+\delta)V_{\delta 1} - \\
&\quad \frac{l_1}{2} K_3 \Lambda_1 \widetilde{V}_{1,t} \widehat{x}_t \widehat{x}_t^T \\
\dot{V}_{2,t} &= -K_4 P W_{2,t} D_\phi C_\delta^+ e \widehat{x}_t^T - (1+\delta)V_{\delta 2} - \\
&\quad \frac{q l_2 \overline{u}}{2} K_4 \Lambda_2 \widetilde{V}_{2,t} \widehat{x}_t \widehat{x}_t^T
\end{aligned}$$

where

$$\begin{aligned}
W_{\delta 1} &= \sigma^T \Lambda_\sigma^{-1} \widetilde{W}_{1,t} \sigma + \widehat{x}_t^T \widetilde{V}_{1,t}^T D_\sigma \Lambda_\sigma^{-1} D_\sigma \widetilde{V}_{1,t} \widehat{x}_t \\
W_{\delta 2} &= (\phi u_t)^T \Lambda_\phi^{-1} \widetilde{W}_{2,t}(\phi u_t) + \widehat{x}_t^T \widetilde{V}_{2,t}^T D_\phi \Lambda_\phi^{-1} D_\phi \widetilde{V}_{2,t} \widehat{x}_t \\
V_{\delta 1} &= \widehat{x}_t^T \widetilde{W}_{1,t}^T D_\sigma \Lambda_\sigma^{-1} D_\sigma \widetilde{W}_{1,t} \widehat{x}_t \qquad (10)\\
V_{\delta 2} &= \widehat{x}_t^T \widetilde{W}_{2,t}^T D_\phi \Lambda_\phi^{-1} D_\phi \widetilde{W}_{2,t} \widehat{x}_t
\end{aligned}$$

$K_i \in \Re^{n \times n}$ ($i = 1, 2, 3, 4$) are positive defined matrices, P is the solution of the matrix Riccati equation given by (7). The initial weight are

$$W_{1,0} = W_1^*, W_{2,0} = W_2^*, V_{1,0} = V_1^*, V_{2,0} = V_2^*$$

The global asymptotic error stability is guaranteed by the learning law because of the fact that it is derived based on the Lyapunov approach, for this take account the theorem [7].

Theorem 1 ([7]): If the gain matrices are selected as

$$L_1 = P^{-1} C^T \Lambda_{\xi 2}, \qquad L_2 = h P^{-1} C^T \Lambda_\xi \qquad (11)$$

and the weights are adjusted as in (9), for a given class $\mathcal{H}$ of nonlinear systems (1), the following properties hold:

(a) the weight matrices remain bounded during period, that is

$$W_{1,t} \in L_\infty, W_{2,t} \in L_\infty, V_{1,t} \in L_\infty, V_{2,t} \in L_\infty$$

(b) the identification error Δ_t satisfies the following tracking performance

$$\limsup_{T \to \infty} \int_0^T \Delta_t^T Q_1 \Delta_t dt \leq \overline{d} \qquad (12)$$

where

$$\overline{d} = \overline{\eta} + \Upsilon_1 + 10 \Upsilon_2 \qquad (13)$$

III. OUTPUT REGULATION PROBLEM

The Output regulation problem has been dealt in [10] for linear systems and [2] for nonlinear systems.

In this work we shall consider SISO nonlinear systems described by

$$\begin{aligned}
\dot{x}_t &= f(x_t, \omega_t) + g(x_t) u_t \qquad (14)\\
\dot{\omega}_t &= s(\omega_t) \qquad (15)\\
e_t &= h(x_t) - r(\omega_t)
\end{aligned}$$

where $x \in \Re^n$, $u, e \in \Re$, $\omega \in \Re^n$. The first equation describes the dynamics of the plant, the second equation is known as the *exosystem* which generates all the possible reference and/or perturbation signals. The third equation defines the output tracking error between the output of the plant and a reference signal. For this system, the *State Feedback Regulator Problem* (SFRP) consists on finding, if possible, a controller $\alpha(x_t, \omega_t)$ with $\alpha(0,0) = 0$ such that:

S1: The equilibrium $x = 0$ of

$$\dot{x}_t = f(x_t, 0, \alpha(x_t, 0))$$

is asymptotically stable.

R1: There exists a neighborhood $U \subset X \times W$ of $(0,0)$ such that, for each initial condition on U, the solution of the closed loop system:

$$\begin{aligned}
\dot{x}_t &= f(x_t, \omega_t, \gamma(x_t, \omega_t)) \\
\dot{\omega}_t &= s(\omega_t)
\end{aligned}$$

satisfies

$$\lim_{t \to \infty} h(x_t) - r(\omega_t) = 0$$

Sufficient conditions for the existence of a solution is given in the following theorem ([2]):

Theorem 2 ([2]): Assume the following conditions hold:

H1: The equilibrium $\omega = 0$ of the exosytem is Lyapunov stable, and the Jacobian matrix $S = \frac{\partial s(\omega_t)}{\partial \omega}$ at the equilibrium $\omega = 0$, has all its eigenvalues on the imaginary axis.

H2: There exists a function $k(x_t)$ such the Jacobian matrix

$$\overline{A} = \left[\frac{\partial [f(x_t, 0) + g(x_t) k(x_t)]}{\partial x} \right]_{x=0}$$

has all eigenvalues on the open left-halft side of the complex plane.

Then, the State Feedback Regulator Problem is solvable if there exist C^r ($r \geq 2$) mappings $x_t = \pi(\omega_t)$ and $u_t = c(\omega_t)$ with $\pi(0) = 0$ and $c(0) = 0$, both defined in a neighborhood $W^0 \subset W$ of 0, satisfying the conditions

$$\begin{aligned}
\frac{\partial \pi(\omega_t)}{\partial \omega} s(\omega_t) &= f(\pi(\omega_t), \omega_t) + g(\pi(\omega_t)) c(\omega_t) \qquad (16)\\
0 &= h(\pi(\omega_t)) - r(\omega_t) \qquad (17)
\end{aligned}$$

Remark 3: It is straightforward to check that the choice of $\alpha(x_t, \omega_t) = c(\omega_t) + k(x_t - \pi(\omega_t))$ satisfies (S1), since

$\alpha(x_t, 0) = k(x_t)$ stabilizes the linear approximation of $f(x_t, 0) + g(x_t)k(x_t)$. Moreover, in [2] it is also shown that such a choice also satisfies (*R1*).

IV. PROPOSED ADAPTIVE CONTROL SCHEME

The classical output regulator is not robust with respect to plant uncertainties because an exact knowledge is assumed and this is not viable in practice. A way to overcome parametric variations is work with the *immersion* of $c(\omega_t)$ (see [11]) and get a robust controller but this implies to have a higher dimensional controller and many times the inmersion is difficult or even impossible to found, except in very particular cases, when $c(\omega_t)$ is given in polynomial form.

Taking this into account, we will assume that the *dynamic neural network* can replace the unknown system and model it including parametric variations and the plant uncertainties. In this work we propose the following scheme:

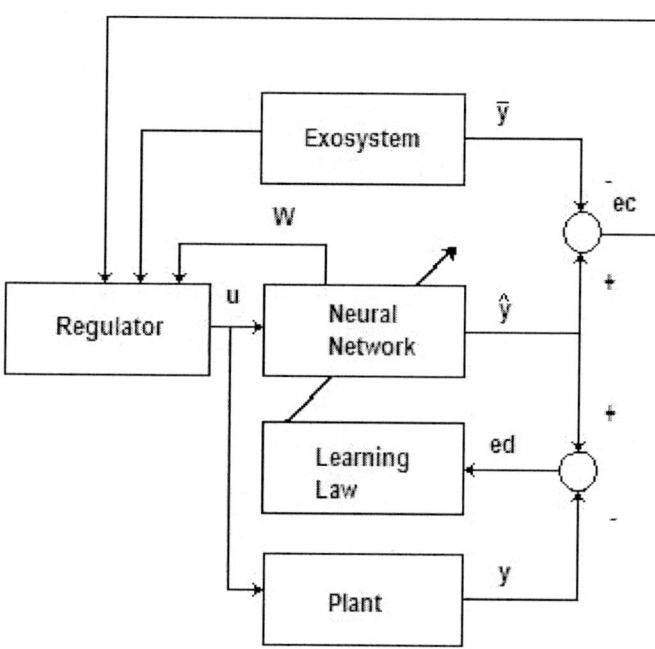

Fig. 1. the identification-control scheme

Under perfect identification, the neuro-observer is described by

$$\widehat{x}_t = A\widehat{x}_t + BW_{1,t}\sigma(\widehat{x}_t) + BW_{1,t}\phi(\widehat{x}_t)u_t$$

From the figure 1, the identification error e_d is used by the learning law presented in the section I which allows to adapt the parameters involved in W_1 and W_2 to minimize e_d. Due that the regulator equation is solved for the DNN this ensures the asymptotic convergence of the tracking error between the reference signal and the output of the DNN to zero.

The parameters of the DNN are adapted on-line including parametric variations of the plant, the output tracking error $e = y_t - r(\omega_t)$ is such that

$$\begin{aligned} e_t &= h(x_t) - r(\omega_t) = [h(\widehat{x}_t) - r(\omega_t)] - [h(\widehat{x}_t) - h(x_t)] \\ e_t &= e_c - e_d \end{aligned}$$

where

$$e_{c,t} = [h(\widehat{x}_t) - \overline{y}_t], \qquad e_{d,t} = [h(\widehat{x}_t) - h(x_t)]$$

The identification error e_d is minimized by the learning law shown in the section I and the tracking error e_c between the reference signal and the output of the DNN. This is stead in the following result:

Theorem 4: Assume that H1 holds and the and the solution of the exosystem is such that the conditions for the construction of a neuro-observer (13) are fulfilled such that a bounded identification error is bounded by the condition

$$\limsup_{T \to \infty} \int_0^T \Delta_t^T Q_1 \Delta_t dt \leq \overline{d}$$

Assume also that there exist a matrix K that stabilizes the linear approximation of the DNN $(\overline{A} + BW_2K)$. If there exist mappings $\widehat{x}_{ss,t} = \widehat{\pi}(\omega_t)$ and $u_{ss,t} = \widehat{c}(\omega_t)$ solving the equations

$$\begin{aligned} \frac{\partial \widehat{\pi}(\omega_t)}{\partial \omega}s(\omega_t) &= A\widehat{\pi}(\omega_t) + BW_1\sigma(\widehat{\pi}(\omega_t)) \\ &\quad + BW_2\phi(\widehat{\pi}(\omega_t))\widehat{c}(\omega_t) \\ 0 &= h(\widehat{\pi}(\omega_t)) - r(\omega_t) \end{aligned}$$

then the output tracking error between the output of the nonlinear system (14)-(15) and the reference signal is bounded moreover the controller that minimizes the output tracking error is then given by

$$\alpha(\widehat{x}_t, \omega_t) = \widehat{c}(\omega_t) + K(\widehat{x}_t - \widehat{\pi}(\omega_t))$$

Remark 5: When we find the output regulator solution, the mapping $x_{ss,t} = \pi(\omega_t)$ represents a surface where the system keep a state stable and $c(\omega_t)$ represents the steady state input that keep the dynamic of the system constrained on the steady state surface.

Proof: The result is an immediate consequence of the properties of the neuro-observer, which guarantees a bounded identification error. Also, the regulator solution guarantee that the tracking error between output the neural identifier and the reference signal, namely $[h(\widehat{x}_t) - r(\omega_t)]$, tends asymptotically to zero, no matter the values of the weighting matrices are given by the identification process and thus, when the dynamics of the system is in the steady state surface $\widehat{x}_{ss,t} = \widehat{\pi}(\omega_t)$, the tracking error e_t is bounded by the identification error $\widehat{x}_t - x_t$ through the term $[h(\widehat{x}_t) - h(x_t)]$ ∎

V. An Illustrative Example

We apply the previous scheme to a model of a Duffing Oscillator described by

$$\dot{x}_1 = x_2$$
$$\dot{x}_1 = x_1 - x_1^3 - dx_2 + g\cos(\varpi t) + u_t$$

The neuro-observer corresponds to (3) with $V_1 = I$ and $V_2 = I$ and has the structure

$$\dot{\widehat{x}}_t = A\widehat{x}_t + W_{1,t}\sigma(\widehat{x}_t) + BW_{2,t}\phi(\widehat{x}_t)u_t$$
$$+ L_1[y_t - \widehat{y}_t] + L_2/h[(y_t - y_{t-h}) - (\widehat{y}_t - \widehat{y}_{t-h})]$$
$$\widehat{y}_t = \widehat{x}_1$$

were we have chosen

$$A = \begin{bmatrix} -7 & 0 \\ 0 & -8 \end{bmatrix}; \quad B = \begin{bmatrix} 0 & 0 \\ 0 & 1 \end{bmatrix}$$
$$\phi(\widehat{x}_t) = \begin{bmatrix} \phi(\widehat{x}_{1,t}) & 0 \\ 0 & \phi(\widehat{x}_{2,t}) \end{bmatrix}; \quad \sigma(\widehat{x}_t) = \begin{bmatrix} \sigma(\widehat{x}_{1,t}) \\ \sigma(\widehat{x}_{2,t}) \end{bmatrix}$$
$$W_{1,0} = \begin{bmatrix} 2 & .25 \\ -.5 & 2 \end{bmatrix}; \quad BW_{2,0} = \begin{bmatrix} 0 & 0 \\ 0 & 1 \end{bmatrix}$$

and $\Lambda_1 = I$, $\Lambda_2 = I$, $P_1 = I$, $Q_0 = I$, $\delta = 0.001$, $\Lambda_\xi = 1$, $\Lambda_{\xi_2} = 0.3$ $h = 0.1$ The solution of the Riccati equation (7) with R and Q like in (8) in this case is found to be

$$P = \begin{bmatrix} 0.2562 & 0.0892 \\ 0.0892 & 0.2222 \end{bmatrix}$$
$$L_1 = \begin{bmatrix} 1.3612 \\ -0.5464 \end{bmatrix}; \quad L_2 = \begin{bmatrix} 0.4537 \\ -0.1821 \end{bmatrix}$$

The following figures gives the simulation results for this case.

The figures 1 and 2 shows the identification results for the DNN. To adapt on line the neuro-observer weights, we use the learning law (9) and the control law is $\alpha(\widehat{x}_t, \omega_t) = \widehat{c}(\omega_t) + K(\widehat{x}_t - \widehat{\pi}(\omega_t))$

The output reference is chosen like $\overline{y}_t = \beta\sin(\alpha t)$ with $\alpha = 1$ and $\beta = 1$, and is supposed to be generated by the exosystem

$$\dot{\omega}_{1,t} = \omega_{2,t}$$
$$\dot{\omega}_{1,t} = -\omega_{1,t}$$

with the initial conditions $\omega_{1,0} = 0$ and $\omega_{2,0} = 1$. The following figures gives the results of the output tracking scheme:

We may observe that the output tracking error is bounded.

VI. Conclusions

We have investigated the output regulator control theory combined with a dynamic neural network guaranteeing a bounded output tracking error. The on-line learning law give us an adaptive strategy to model parametric variations, dynamic changes or external disturbances. The regulator controller designed on the basis of the neuro-observer scheme

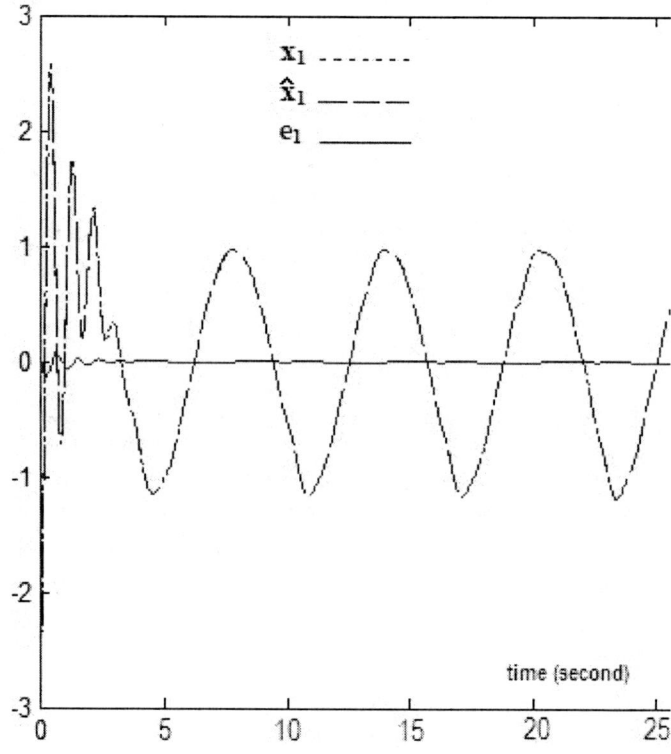

Fig. 2. Identification results for x_1

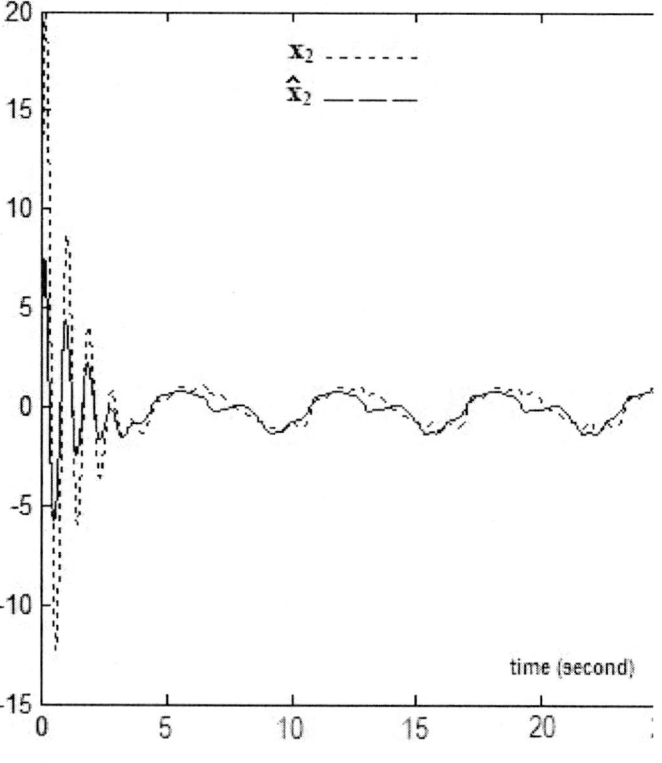

Fig. 3. Neuro-observer results for x_2

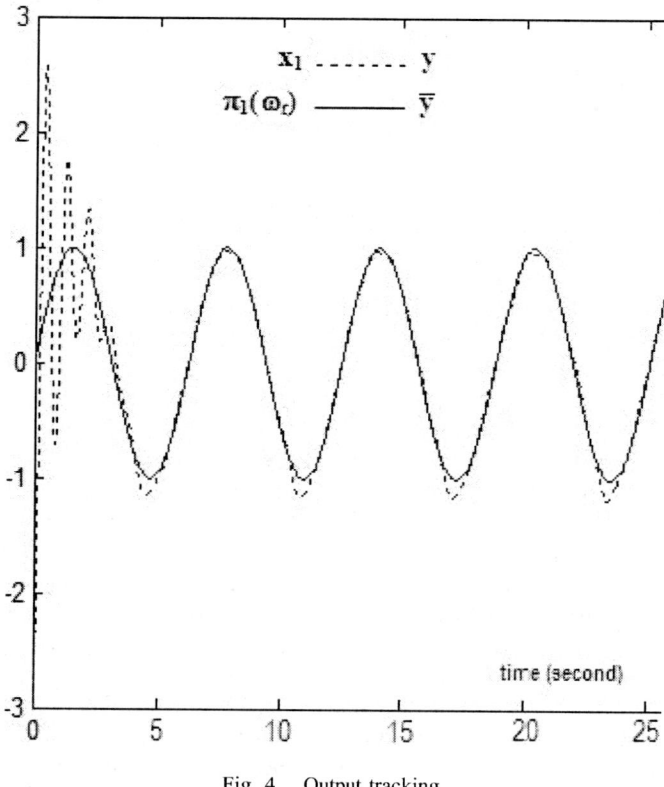

Fig. 4. Output tracking

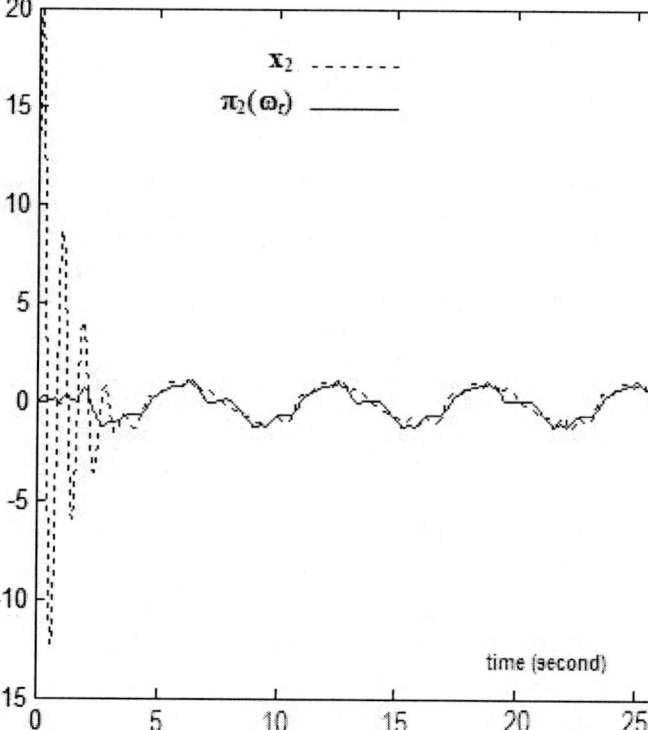

Fig. 5. Approximation of x_2 to $\pi_2(\omega_t)$

adjust the feedback control action to force the trajectory tracking error into some bounded values. The application to a model os a chaotic system shows the potentiality of this scheme. Future research are directed to show the stability of the closed loop scheme when considering the effect of the bounded inputs in the regulator solutions.

REFERENCES

[1] M. Agarwal, "A systematic classification of neural networks based control", *IEEE Control Systems,* vol 17, No. 2,66-74, 1997
[2] Isidori, A. and Byrnes, C. "Output regulation for nonlinear systems", *IEEE Trans. Automat. Control*, 26, 131-140, 1990
[3] Castillo, B., Di Gennaro, S. and Normand –Cyrot, D. " Nonlinear regulation for a class of discrete time systems" *Systems & Cont Letters*, 20, 57-65,1993
[4] V. Utkin, A. Loukianov, Castillo-Toledo B.,and J. Rivera,"Sliding mode regulator design in variable structure systems: from principles to implementation", *The institution of Electrical Engineers, IEE Control Engineering Series,* vol 6, Sabanovi A., Fridman L and Spurgeon S. Eds.- 2004 pp 19-44
[5] B. Castillo-Toledo and J. Jalomo Cuevas,"Fuzzy Robust tracking for a class of nonlinear systems. Aplication to the Chen's attractor", *Intelligent Automation and Soft Computing,* vol. 10 No 1, 2004, pp 37-50
[6] W.Yu , X Li, "Some new results on system identification with dynamic neural networks", *IEEE Trans Neural Networks* vol 12, No 2 2001
[7] Alexander S. Poznyak, W. Yu," Robust asymptotic neuro-observer with time delay term", *Int. J. Robust Nonlinear Control* 2000 10:535-559
[8] J. j: Hopfield "Neurons with grade response have collective computational properties like those a two state neurons" *in Proc. Nat Academy Sci. USA*, vol 81 pp3088-3092, 1984
[9] A. S. Poznyak and E. N. Sanchez, "Nonlinear system approximation by neural networks: error stability analysis", *Intelligent Automation and Soft Computing*, vol. 1, 247-258, 1995
[10] Francis, B. "The linear multivairiable regulator problem", *SIAM J. Control Optim.*, 15, 484-505, 1997
[11] Alexander S.Poznyak, Wen Yu, Edgar N. Sanchez, Jose P. Perez, Nonlinear "Nonlinear adaptive trajectory tracking using neural networks", *IEEE Trans Neural Networks* vol 10, No 6 1999
[12] Yeong-Chan Chang and Bor-Sen Chen"A Nonlinear adaptive H^∞ tracking control design in robotic systems via neural networks", *IEEE Trans Control Systems Technology* vol 5, No 1 1997
[13] Francis, B.A. , The internal model principle of control theory, *Automatica.*, 1976, Vol. 12, pp. 457-465.
[14] Isidori A., *Nonlinear Control Systems*, 3rd Ed., Springer, London, 1995.

Indirect Field-oriented Linear Induction Motor Drive with Petri Fuzzy-neural-network Control

Rong-Jong Wai[1], Member, IEEE, and Chia-Chin Chu[2]

[1,2] Department of Electrical Engineering, Yuan Ze University, Chung Li 32026, Taiwan, R.O.C.

Abstract—This study focuses on the development of a Petri fuzzy-neural-network (PFNN) control for an indirect field-oriented linear induction motor (LIM) drive. The concept of a Petri net (PN) is incorporated into a traditional fuzzy-neural-network (TFNN) to form a newly-type PFNN framework for alleviating the computation burden. Moreover, the supervised gradient descent method is used to develop the online training algorithm for the PFNN. In order to guarantee the convergence of tracking error, analytical methods based on a discrete-type Lyapunov function are proposed to determine the varied learning rates of the PFNN. With the proposed PFNN control system, the mover position of the controlled LIM drive possesses the advantages of good transient control performance and robustness to uncertainties for the tracking of periodic reference trajectories. In addition, the effectiveness of the proposed control scheme is verified by numerical simulations.

I. INTRODUCTION

Linear induction motors have many excellent performance features such as high-starting thrust force, alleviation of gear between motor and the motion devices, reduction of mechanical losses and the size of motion devices, high-speed operation, silence, and so on [1], [2]. Due to these advantages, the LIM has been used widely in the field of industrial processes and transportation applications [3], [4]. The driving principles of the LIM are similar to a traditional rotary induction motor (RIM), but its control characteristics are more complicated than the RIM, and the motor parameters are time-varying due to the change of operating conditions, such as speed of mover, temperature and configuration of rail. Though much research has modelled the dynamic performance of the LIM and taken some significant variations into consideration [1]–[5], there still exist uncertainties, usually composed of unpredictable plant parameter variations, external force disturbance, unmodelled and nonlinear dynamics, in practical applications of the LIM. In addition, complicated dynamic model of the LIM increases the complexity of the analyses and the design of servo controllers. On the other hand, the dynamic model of the LIM can be modified from the dynamic model of the RIM at certain low speed since the LIM can be visualized as an unrolled RIM. Thus, field-orientated control [6], [7] commonly used in the RIM also can be adopted to decouple the dynamics of the thrust force and the flux amplitude of the LIM. The motivation of this study is to simplify the dynamic model of the LIM and to design a suitable control scheme to confront the uncertainties existing in the field-oriented LIM drive.

In recent years, the concept of incorporating fuzzy logic into a neural network has been grown into a popular research topic [8], [9]. In contrast to the pure neural network or fuzzy system, the fuzzy neural network (FNN) possesses both their advantages; it combines the capability of fuzzy reasoning in handling uncertain information [10] and the capability of artificial neural networks in learning from process [11]. For the last decades, Petri net (PN) has been developed into a powerful tool for modeling, analysis, control, optimization, and implementation of various engineering systems [12]–[15]. In this study, the basic concept of a PN incorporated into a TFNN is used to organize a PFNN control system for the position control of an indirect field-oriented LIM drive. This newly-design PFNN framework has less computation amount than a TFNN. Moreover, supervised gradient descent method is used to develop the online training algorithm for the PFNN, and varied learning-rate parameters are derived in the sense of Lyapunov stability theorem such that the stability of the control system can be guaranteed under the occurrence of system uncertainties.

II. INDIRECT FIELD-ORIENTED LINEAR INDUCTION MOTOR

The structure of a LIM is depicted in Fig. 1, which comprises a primary mover, a secondary stator, a linear slider, and a linear encoder. In primary side, it is composed of three-phase windings and laminated steel cores. Moreover, the combination of aluminum sheets (nonmagnetic conductors) and back irons (magnetic conductors) is used to form the secondary side. In addition, the dynamic model of the LIM modified from the traditional model of a three-phase, Y-connected induction motor in a synchronous rotating reference frame can be described by the following differential equations [6], [7]:

$$\dot{i}_{qs} = -\frac{\pi}{h} v_e i_{ds} - \left(\frac{R_s}{\sigma L_s} + \frac{1-\sigma}{\sigma T_r}\right) i_{qs} - \frac{n_p L_m \pi}{\sigma L_s L_r h} v \lambda_{dr} + \frac{L_m}{\sigma L_s L_r T_r} \lambda_{qr} + \frac{1}{\sigma L_s} V_{qs} \quad (1)$$

$$\dot{i}_{ds} = -\left(\frac{R_s}{\sigma L_s} + \frac{1-\sigma}{\sigma T_r}\right) i_{ds} + \frac{\pi}{h} v_e i_{qs} + \frac{L_m}{\sigma L_s L_r T_r} \lambda_{dr} + \frac{n_p L_m \pi}{\sigma L_s L_r h} v \lambda_{qr} + \frac{1}{\sigma L_s} V_{ds} \quad (2)$$

$$\dot{\lambda}_{qr} = \frac{L_m}{T_r} i_{qs} - (\frac{\pi}{h} v_e - n_p \frac{\pi}{h} v) \lambda_{dr} - \frac{1}{T_r} \lambda_{qr} \quad (3)$$

$$\dot{\lambda}_{dr} = \frac{L_m}{T_r} i_{ds} - \frac{1}{T_r} \lambda_{dr} + (\frac{\pi}{h} v_e - n_p \frac{\pi}{h} v) \lambda_{qr} \qquad (4)$$

$$F_e = K_f (\lambda_{dr} i_{qs} - \lambda_{qr} i_{ds}) = M\dot{v} + Dv + F_L \qquad (5)$$

where R_s is the winding resistance per phase; R_r is the secondary resistance per phase referred primary; L_m is the magnetizing inductance per phase; L_r is the secondary inductance per phase; L_s is the primary inductance per phase; v_e is the synchronous linear velocity; v is the mover linear velocity; h is the pole pitch; n_p is the number of pole pairs; λ_{dr} and λ_{qr} are d-axis and q-axis secondary flux; i_{ds} and i_{qs} are d-axis and q-axis primary current; V_{ds} and V_{qs} are d-axis and q-axis primary voltage; $T_r = L_r/R_r$ is the secondary time-constant; $\sigma = 1 - (L_m^2/L_s L_r)$ is the leakage coefficient; $K_f = 3n_p \pi L_m/(2hL_r)$ is the force constant; F_e is the electromagnetic force; F_L is the external force; M is the total mass of moving element; D is the viscous friction and iron-loss coefficient.

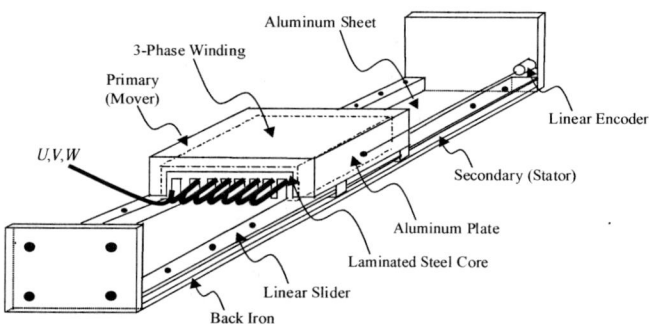

Fig. 1. Structure of LIM.

In an ideally decoupled LIM, the secondary flux linkage axis is forced to align with the d-axis. It follows that

$$\lambda_{qr} = 0, \qquad \dot{\lambda}_{qr} = 0 \qquad (6)$$

Using (6), the desired secondary flux linkage in terms of i_{ds} can be found from (4) as

$$\lambda_{dr} = \frac{L_m / T_r}{s + 1/T_r} i_{ds} \qquad (7)$$

where s is the Laplace operator. According to (3), the feedforward slip velocity signal ($v_{sl} = v_e - n_p v$) can be estimated via λ_{dr} shown in (7) and i_{qs} as follows:

$$v_{sl} = \frac{hL_m}{\pi T_r \lambda_{dr}} i_{qs} \qquad (8)$$

In the steady state, the desired secondary flux linkage shown in (7) can be represented as $\lambda_{dr} = L_m i_{ds}^*$, in which i_{ds}^* is the flux current command. Moreover, the synchronous linear velocity (v_e) in the indirect field-oriented mechanism is generated by using the measured mover linear velocity (v) and the following estimated slip linear velocity:

$$v_{sl} = \frac{h i_{qs}^*}{\pi T_r i_{ds}^*} \qquad (9)$$

where i_{qs}^* is the force current command. Consequently, the electromagnetic force (5) can be simplified as

$$F_e = K_F i_{qs}^* \qquad (10)$$

with the force coefficient K_F defined as

$$K_F = \frac{3}{2} n_p \frac{\pi L_m^2}{h L_r} i_{ds}^* \qquad (11)$$

According to the above derivation, the most important factor in the indirect field-oriented mechanism is the precision of the estimated slip linear velocity. Since the secondary time-constant T_r is sensitive to different operating conditions, a sliding-mode parameter estimation in Wai et al. [16] is adopted in this study to guarantee a correct estimation of the slip linear velocity, and to preserve the decoupling control characteristic.

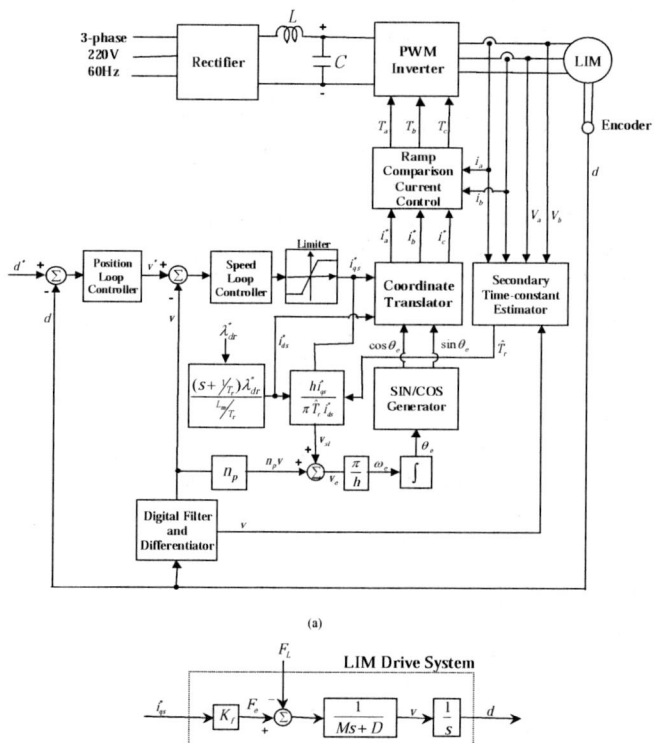

Fig. 2. (a) Indirect field-oriented LIM drive. (b) Simplified LIM drive.

The block diagram of an indirect field-oriented LIM drive system is depicted in Fig. 2(a), which consists of a LIM, a ramp comparison current-controlled pulse-width-modulation (PWM) voltage source inverter (VSI), an indirect field-oriented mechanism, a coordinate translator, a unit vector ($\cos\theta_e + j\sin\theta_e$, where θ_e is the position of the secondary flux) generator, a speed control loop, and a position control loop. In Fig. 2(a), d^* and v^* denote the commands of mover position and linear velocity; d is the actual mover position of the LIM. The LIM used in this drive system is a three-phase Y-connected two-pole 3kW 60Hz 180V/14.2A type. The detailed parameters of the LIM are

$$i_{ds}^* = 2.35\text{A} \quad R_s = 5.3685\Omega \quad R_r = 3.5315\Omega \quad h = 0.027\text{m}$$
$$L_m = 24.19\text{mH} \quad L_s = 28.46\text{mH} \quad L_r = 28.46\text{mH} \quad (12)$$

By use of the indirect field-oriented control technique and with the fact that the electrical time-constant is much smaller than the mechanical time-constant, the LIM drive system shown in Fig. 2(a) can be reasonably simplified as Fig. 2(b). The curve fitting technique based on step response is applied to find the drive model off line at the nominal case ($F_L = 0$). The results are (on a scale of 1.5915 (m/s)/V)

$$\overline{K_F} = 33.73\text{N/A} \quad (13)$$
$$\overline{M} = 2.78\text{Kg} = 4.4245\text{Ns/V} \quad (14)$$
$$\overline{D} = 36.0455\text{Kg/s} = 57.3664\text{ N/V} \quad (15)$$

The "—" symbol represents the system parameters in the nominal condition. With the indirect field-oriented mechanism, the dynamic behavior of the LIM is rather similar to that of a separately excited dc motor. However, the control performance of the LIM drive is easily influenced by the system uncertainties such as mechanical parameter variations, external force disturbance, unstructured uncertainty due to nonideal field orientation in transient state, and unmodelled dynamics in practical applications. For this reason, a suitable position control system is necessary to handle the dynamic motion of the LIM.

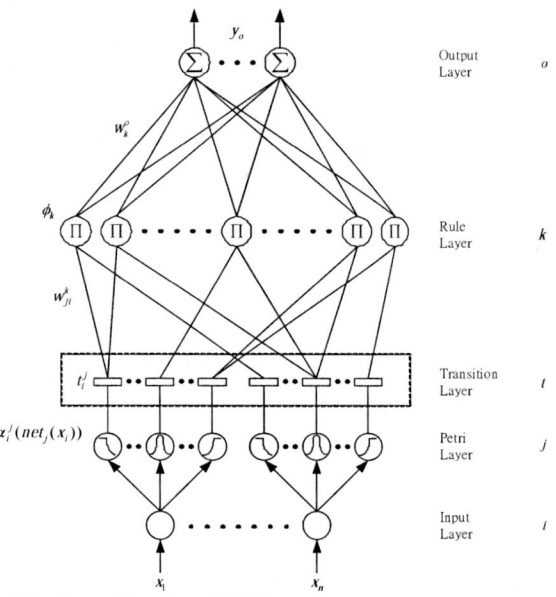

Fig. 3. Structure of five-layer PFNN.

III. Petri Fuzzy-neural-network Control

Recently, the TFNN has been proven to be a powerful technique in the discipline of system control, especially in model-free control design. However, real-time implementation may be difficult or impossible due to heavy computation burden if the network parameters to be tuned or inference strategies are complicated. In order to overcome this problem, the concept of a PN is incorporated into a TFNN to reduce redundant or inefficient computation for improving online learning abilities.

A. Petri Fuzzy-neural-network Structure

The newly-design PFNN framework is depicted in Fig. 3, where the major difference between the TFNN and PFNN is the transition layer. The signal propagation and the basic function in each layer of the PFNN are introduced in the following paragraph.

For every node i in the input layer transmits the input linguistic variables x_i ($i = 1, \cdots, n$) to the next layer directly. Moreover, the output of each node in the Petri layer is used to represent tokens with the following Gaussian function:

$$net_j(x_i) = -\frac{(x_i - m_i^j)^2}{(s_i^j)^2}, \quad \alpha_i^j(net_j(x_i)) = \exp(net_j(x_i)) \quad (16)$$

where m_i^j and s_i^j ($i = 1, \cdots, n; j = 1, \cdots, N_{p_i}$) are, respectively, the mean and the standard deviation of the Gaussian function in the jth term of the ith input variable x_i to the node of this layer, and N_{p_i} is the total number of the linguistic variables with respect to the input nodes. Unlike the traditional PN, the transition layer of the PFNN in this study to produce tokens makes use of competition learning laws as follows to select suitable fired nodes.

$$g_{i,l}^j = \max\_l \{ \underset{j=1,\cdots,N_{p_i}}{\text{sort}} [\alpha_i^j(net_j(x_i))]\}$$
$$\underset{l=1,\cdots,(N_d \le N_{p_i})}{i=1,\cdots,n}$$

$$t_i^j = \begin{cases} 1, & g_{i,l}^j = \alpha_i^j(net_j(x_i)) \\ 0, & otherwise \end{cases} \quad (17)$$

where $\max\_l(\cdot)$ is the lth maximum operator, and N_d is the predetermined fired number. In addition, each node k in the rule layer is denoted by $\prod$, which multiplies the input signals and outputs the result of the product. The output of this layer is given as

$$\phi_k = \begin{cases} \prod_{i=1}^n w_{ji}^k \alpha_i^j(net_j(x_i)) , & t_i^j = 1 \\ 0 , & t_i^j = 0 \end{cases} \quad (18)$$

where ϕ_k ($k = 1, \cdots, N_y$) represents the kth output of the rule layer; w_{ji}^k, the weights between the membership layer and the rule layer, are assumed to be unity; N_y is the total number of rules. Furthermore, the single node o in the output layer is labeled with $\sum$, each node y_o ($o = 1, \cdots, N_o$) which computes the overall output as the summation of all input signals.

$$y_o = \sum_{k=1}^{N_r} w_k^o \phi_k \quad (19)$$

where the connecting weight w_k^o is the output action strength of the oth output associated with the kth rule.

B. Online Learning Algorithm

The central part of the learning algorithm for a PFNN concerns how to recursively obtain a gradient vector in which each element in the learning algorithm is defined as the derivative of an energy function with respect to a parameter of the network using the chain rule. Since the gradient vector is calculated in the direction opposite to the flow of the output of each node [17], the method is generally referred to as the backpropagation learning rule. To describe the online learning algorithm of the PFNN using the supervised gradient descent method, first the energy function E is defined as

$$E = \frac{1}{2}(y_d - y)^2 = \frac{1}{2}e^2 \quad (20)$$

where y_d is the desired response; y is the actual system output; e is the output error between the desired response and the actual output. Then, the learning algorithm based on the backpropagation method is described below.

In the output layer, the error term to be propagated is given by

$$\delta_o = -\frac{\partial E}{\partial y_o} = -\frac{\partial E}{\partial e}\frac{\partial e}{\partial y_o} = -\frac{\partial E}{\partial e}\frac{\partial e}{\partial y}\frac{\partial y}{\partial y_o} \quad (21)$$

and the weight is updated by the amount

$$\Delta w_k^o = -\eta_w \frac{\partial E}{\partial w_k^o} = \eta_w \left[-\frac{\partial E}{\partial y_o}\right]\left(\frac{\partial y_o}{\partial w_k^o}\right) = \eta_w \delta_o \phi_k \quad (22)$$

where η_w is the learning-rate parameter of the connecting weights. The weights of the output layer are updated according to the following equation:

$$w_k^o(N+1) = w_k^o(N) + \Delta w_k^o \quad (23)$$

where N denotes the number of iterations. Since the weights in the rule layer are unified, only the error term to be calculated and propagated.

$$\varsigma_k = -\frac{\partial E}{\partial \phi_k} = \left[-\frac{\partial E}{\partial y_o}\right]\left(\frac{\partial y_o}{\partial \phi_k}\right) = \begin{cases} \delta_o w_k^o, & \phi_k \neq 0 \\ 0, & \phi_k = 0 \end{cases} \quad (24)$$

In the Petri layer, the error term is computed as follows:

$$\rho_j(x_i) = -\frac{\partial E}{\partial net_j(x_i)} = \begin{cases} \sum_k \varsigma_k \phi_k, & t_i^j = 1 \\ 0, & t_i^j = 0 \end{cases} \quad (25)$$

The update laws of m_i^j and s_i^j can be denoted as

$$\Delta m_i^j = -\eta_m \frac{\partial E}{\partial m_i^j} = \eta_m \rho_j(x_i)\frac{2(x_i - m_i^j)}{(s_i^j)^2} \quad (26)$$

$$\Delta s_i^j = -\eta_s \frac{\partial E}{\partial s_i^j} = \eta_s \rho_j(x_i)\frac{2(x_i - m_i^j)^2}{(s_i^j)^3} \quad (27)$$

where η_m and η_s are the learning-rate parameters of the mean and the standard deviation of the Gaussian function. The mean and standard deviation of the Petri layer are updated as follows:

$$m_i^j(N+1) = m_i^j(N) + \Delta m_i^j \quad (28)$$

$$s_i^j(N+1) = s_i^j(N) + \Delta s_i^j \quad (29)$$

The exact calculation of the Jacobian of the actual plant, $\partial y/\partial y_o$ in (21), cannot be determined due to the uncertainties of the plant dynamics. Similar to [18], the following delta adaptation law is adopted in this study.

$$\delta_o \cong e + e_s \quad (30)$$

where e_s is the derivative of the output error, e.

C. Convergence Analyses

Selection of the values for the learning-rate parameters has a significant effect on the network performance. In order to train the PFNN effectively, varied learning rates, which guarantee convergence of the output error based on the analyses of a discrete-type Lyapunov function, are derived in this section. The convergence analyses in this study are to derive specific learning-rate parameters for specific types of network parameters to assure convergence of the output error [18].

Theorem 1: Let η_w, η_m and η_s be the learning-rate parameters of the weights in the output layer, the means and the standard deviations of the Gaussian functions for the PFNN, respectively. Then, $P_{w\max}$ is defined as $P_{w\max} \equiv \max_N \|P_w(N)\|$, where $P_w(N) = \partial y_o / \partial w_k^o$; $P_{m\max}$ is defined as $P_{m\max} \equiv \max_N \|P_m(N)\|$, where $P_m(N) = \partial y_o / \partial m_i^j$; $P_{s\max}$ is defined as $P_{s\max} \equiv \max_N \|P_s(N)\|$, where $P_s(N) = \partial y_o / \partial s_i^j$; $\|\cdot\|$ is the Euclidean norm in $\Re^n$. Thus, the convergence of output error can be guaranteed if η_w is chosen as $\eta_w^* = \lambda/(3R_d)$ and $0 < \lambda \leq \frac{e^2(N)}{(\delta_o^2 + \varepsilon_o)}$, in which ε_o is a small positive constant and R_d is the number of fired rules in the PFNN; η_m and η_s are chosen as $\eta_m^* = \eta_s^* = \eta_w^*[|w_{k\max}^o|(2/s_{i\min}^j)]^{-2}$, in which $w_{k\max}^o = \max_N[w_k^o(N)]$, $s_{i\min}^j = \min_N[s_i^j(N)]$ and $|\cdot|$ is the absolute value.

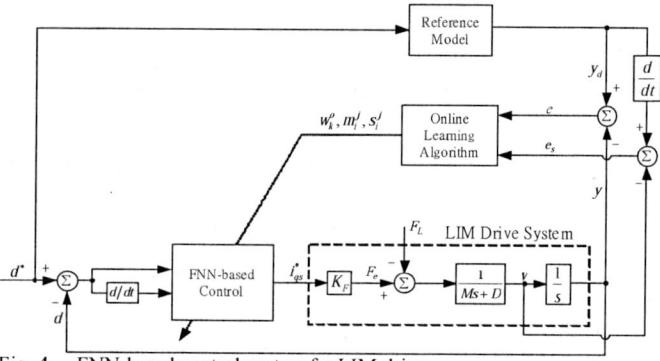

Fig. 4. FNN-based control system for LIM drive.

IV. NUMERICAL SIMULATIONS

In order to exhibit the superiority of the proposed PFNN control system, a TFNN control scheme investigated in [18] is also implemented for the position control of a LIM drive system in this study. The detailed theoretical derivations of network parameters training and varied learning rates can be found in [18] and are omitted here. The block diagram of FNN-based control systems for a LIM drive is depicted in Fig. 4, where the FNN-based control part could be the TFNN controller in [18] or the proposed PFNN controller in this study. Anyway, the inputs of the FNN-based control are the tracking error ($x_1 = d^* - d$) and its derivative ($x_2 = v^* - v$). The initial weights in the output layer are set at zero, and the initial values of the means and the standard deviations of the Gaussian functions can be determined roughly by dividing equally as follows:

$$m_1^j = e_{max} - (j-1)\frac{e_{max} - e_{min}}{N_{p_1} - 1}, \quad s_1^j = 2\frac{e_{max} - e_{min}}{N_{p_1} - 1} \quad (31)$$

$$m_2^j = e_{smax} - (j-1)\frac{e_{smax} - e_{smin}}{N_{p_2} - 1}, \quad s_2^j = 2\frac{e_{smax} - e_{smin}}{N_{p_2} - 1} \quad (32)$$

where e_{max}, e_{min}, e_{smax} and e_{smin} are the predetermined maximal and minimal bounds of e and e_s. In this study, it is assumed that each input node has the same linguistic variables, i.e., $N_{p1} = N_{p2}$. For a given input variable, the exciting number of Gaussian functions with partial overlap is generally equal to three, therefore, the conservative selection of the predetermined fire number at each input node is $N_d = 5$ and the corresponding number of fired rules is $R_d = N_d \times N_d = 25$. The effect due to the inaccurate selection of the initialized parameters can be retrieved by online parameter training methodologies. Moreover, the single output of the FNN-based control is the control effort for the LIM drive system, i.e., $y_1 = i_{qs}^*$. The reference model in Fig. 4 is used to specify the reference trajectories for the mover position of the LIM. When the position demand is a step command, the reference model could be a first-order or second-order low-pass filter to prevent the sudden command change. If the position command is a sinusoidal reference trajectory, the reference model is set to be one. The control objective is to control the mover to move 0.1m to –0.1m periodically.

All numerical simulations are carried out using Windows Matlab. To investigate the effectiveness of the proposed PFNN control system, the followings three cases with parameter variations and time-varying external force disturbance are addressed:

Case 1: $M = \overline{M}$, $D = \overline{D}$, $F_L = 0N$

Case 2: $M = 2.4 \times \overline{M}$, $D = 1.05 \times \overline{D}$, $F_L = 0N$

Case 3: $M = 2.4 \times \overline{M}$, $D = 1.05 \times \overline{D}$, $F_L = 10\sin(t-5.5)N$

In the simulation, the effect of the FNN-based control systems due to different rule numbers (network sizes) is examined firstly. The performance comparison of the TFNN and PFNN control systems due to periodic sinusoidal commands at Case 1, Case 2 and Case 3 via the measure criteria of mean square error (MSE) is depicted in Fig. 5, where the total running time is 10s. It can be seen that the reported MSE values of the PFNN control system labeled with circles are smaller than the ones of the TFNN control system labeled with stars. Among these data, one can obtain the best tracking performance produced by the rule numbers $N_y = 121$. In other words, the network with $n = 2$, $N_{p_1} = 11$, $N_{p_2} = 11$, $N_y = 121$ and $o = 1$ is more suitable for the position control of the LIM drive system than others, and this structure is fixed for the following simulation. In this structure, the total number of network parameters required to be tuned in the TFNN control system is $2(N_{p_1} + N_{p_2}) + N_{p_1} N_{p_2} = 165$, however, the one of the proposed PFNN control system is $2(N_d + N_d) + N_d N_d = 45$. Thus, the memory requirement and computational amount of the PFNN control system is less than the TFNN control system. Though more rule number may be helpful to improve the tracking response, it will result in heavy computation burden, even in computer or microprocessor crashed.

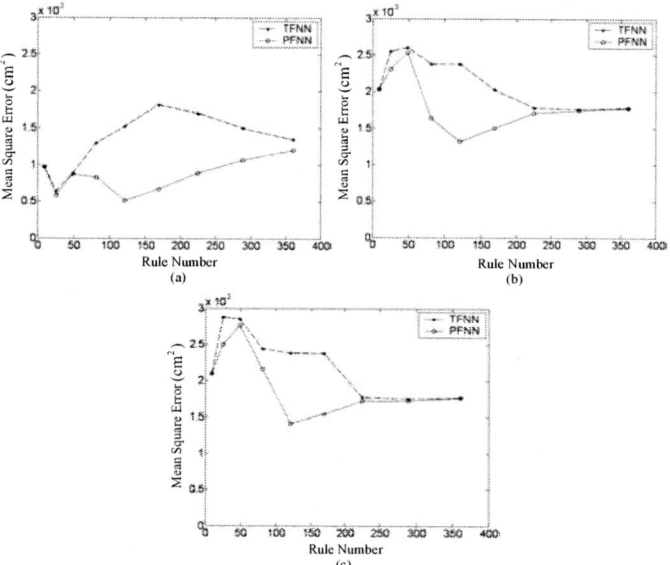

Fig. 5. Performance comparison of TFNN and PFNN control systems. (a) Case 1. (b) Case 2. (c) Case 3.

The position response, control effort and tracking error of the TFNN control system due to periodic sinusoidal commands at Case 1, Case 2 and Case 3 are illustrated in Fig. 6, moreover, the ones of the PFNN control system are depicted in Fig. 7. From the simulated results, favorable tracking response and robust control performance can be obtained both at the TFNN and PFNN control systems due to their powerful learning ability. However, the serious chattering phenomena in transient state are caused by the TFNN control system due to the tuning of entire network parameters. In the PFNN control system, the fact that meaningful rules with high grades are fired and the network parameters in the corresponding path are tuned will result in less computation burden and transient chattering. Consequently, the proposed PFNN system is more suitable to control the mover position of the LIM than the TFNN control system. Due to the page limit, the real data collected from a LIM in operation are not provided in this content.

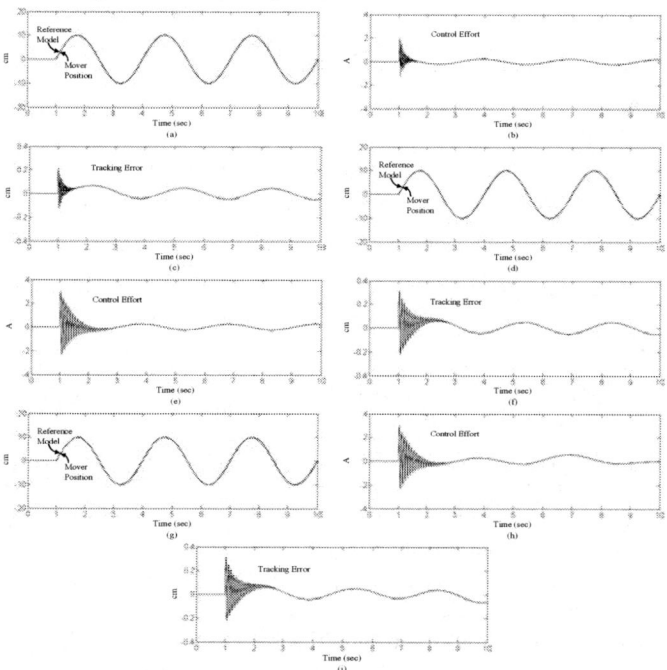

Fig. 6. Simulated results of TFNN control system. (a)–(c) Case 1. (d)–(f) Case 2. (g)–(i) Case 3.

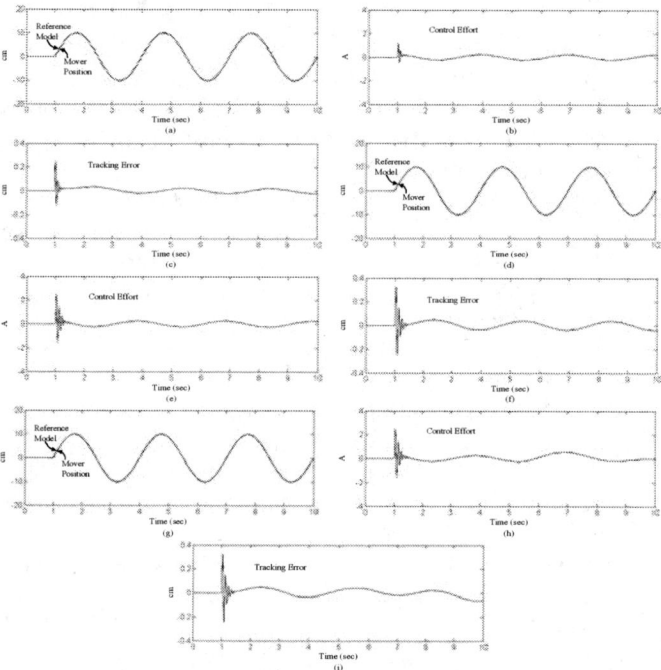

Fig. 7. Simulated results of PFNN control system. (a)–(c) Case 1. (d)–(f) Case 2. (g)–(i) Case 3.

V. CONCLUSIONS

This study has successfully incorporated the concept of a PN into a TFNN and implemented the formed PFNN control system to manipulate the mover position of an indirect field-oriented LIM drive. Numerical simulations of FNN-based control systems were provided to verify the superiority of the proposed PFNN framework. As a result of simplified rule firing mechanism with less computation burden, the proposed PFNN control system can provide more than fifty-percentage improvement about the control performance in comparison with the TFNN control system. The idea of the PN operation can be easily applied for pure fuzzy or neural network systems.

ACKNOWLEDGMENT

The authors would like to acknowledge the financial support of the National Science Council in Taiwan, R.O.C. through grant numbers NSC 90-2213-E-155-003 and NSC 93-2213-E-155-014.

REFERENCES

[1] I. Takahashi and Y. Ide, "Decoupling control of thrust and attractive force of a LIM using a space vector control inverter," *IEEE Trans. Ind. Applicat.*, vol. 29, no. 1, pp. 161–167, 1993.

[2] I. Boldea and S. A. Nasar, "Linear electric actuators and generators," *IEEE Trans. Energy Conversion*, vol. 14, no. 3, pp. 712–717, 1999.

[3] Z. Zhang, T. R. Eastham, and G. E. Dawson, "Peak thrust operation of linear induction machines from parameter identification," in *IEEE IAS Conf. Rec.*, 1995, pp. 375–379.

[4] G. Bucci, S. Meo, A. Ometto, and M. Scarano, "The control of LIM by a generalization of standard vector techniques," in *IEEE IAS Conf. Rec.*, 1994, pp. 623–626.

[5] Z. Zhang, G. E. Dawson, and T. R. Eastham, "Microcontroller based on-line identification of variable parameters in induction motors," *Electr. Machine Power Syst.*, vol. 23, pp. 353–360, 1995.

[6] W. Leonhard, *Control of Electrical Drives*. Berlin: Springer–Verlag, 1996.

[7] R. Krishnan, *Electric Motor Drives: Modeling, Analysis, and Control*. New Jersey: Prentice–Hall, 2001.

[8] J. Nie and D. Linkens, *Fuzzy–Neural Control: Principles, Algorithms and Applications*. New Jersey: Prentice–Hall, 1995.

[9] C. T. Lin and C. S. George Lee, *Neural Fuzzy Systems*. New Jersey: Prentice–Hall, 1996.

[10] L. X. Wang, *A Course in Fuzzy Systems and Control*. New Jersey: Prentice–Hall, 1997.

[11] O. Omidvar and D. L. Elliott, *Neural Systems for Control*. Academic Press, 1997.

[12] R. David and H. Alla, "Petri nets for modeling of dynamic systems–A survey," *Automatica*, vol. 30, no. 2, pp. 175–202, 1994.

[13] V. R. L. Shen, "Reinforcement learning for high-level fuzzy petri nets," *IEEE Trans. Syst., Man, Cybern. B*, vol. 33, no. 2, pp. 351–362, 2003.

[14] K. Hirasawa, M. Ohbayashi, S. Sakai, and J. Hu, "Learning petri network and its application to nonlinear system control," *IEEE Trans. Syst., Man, Cybern. B*, vol. 28, no. 6, pp. 781–789, 1998.

[15] M. Hanna, A. Buck, and R. Smith, "Fuzzy petri nets with neural networks to model products quality from a CNC-Milling machining centre," *IEEE Trans. Syst., Man, Cybern. A*, vol. 26, no. 5, pp. 638–645, 1996.

[16] R. J. Wai, D. C. Liu, and F. J. Lin, "Rotor time-constant estimation approaches based on energy function and sliding mode for induction motor drive," *Elect. Power Syst. Res.*, vol. 52, pp. 229–239, 1999.

[17] C. T. Chao and C. C. Teng, "Implementation of fuzzy inference systems using a normalized fuzzy neural network," *Fuzzy Sets Syst.*, vol. 75, pp. 17–31, 1995.

[18] F. J. Lin, R. J. Wai, and C. C. Lee, "Fuzzy neural network position controller for ultrasonic motor drive using push-pull DC-DC converter," *IEE Proc. Control Theory Appl.*, vol. 146, no. 1, pp. 99–107, 1999.

Wavelet-Neural-Network-Based Backstepping Control for Chaotic Systems

Tsu-Tian Lee[#]
Department of Electrical Engineering, National Taipei University of Technology, Taipei 106, Taiwan, Republic of China
E-mail: president@ntut.edu.tw

Chih-Min Lin*
Department of Electrical Engineering, Yuan-Ze University, Chung-Li 320, Taiwan, Republic of China
E-mail: ml@saturn.yzu.edu.tw

Chun-Fei Hsu[#]
Department of Electrical and Control Engineering, National Chiao-Tung University, Hsinchu 300, Taiwan, Republic of China
E-mail: fei@cn.nctu.edu.tw

Abstract - This paper proposes a wavelet-neural-network-based backstepping control (WNNBC) for the chaotic systems. The WNNBC is comprised of a neural backstepping controller and an adaptive robust controller. The neural backstepping controller containing a wavelet neural network identifier is the principal controller, and the adaptive robust controller is designed to achieve L_2 tracking performance with desired attenuation level. Finally, simulation results verify that the proposed WNNBC can achieve favorable tracking performance.

Index Terms - Backstepping control, chaotic system, wavelet neural network.

1 INTRODUCTION

Recently, neural-network-based control technique has represented an alternative method to solve the control problems [1]-[4]. The most useful property of neural networks is their ability to approximate arbitrary linear or nonlinear mapping through learning. Based on their approximation ability, the neural networks have been used for approximation of control system dynamics or controllers. Recently, some researchers have developed the structure of neural network based on the wavelet functions to construct the wavelet neural network (WNN) [5]-[7]. Unlike the sigmoidal functions used in neural networks, wavelet functions are spatially localized. Thus, the training algorithms for WNN typically converge in a smaller number of iterations than for the neural networks [5]. There has been considerable interest in exploring the applications of WNN to deal with nonlinearity and uncertainties of real-time control system [8]-[10]. These WNN controllers combine the capability of artificial neural networks for learning ability and the capability of wavelet decomposition for identification ability.

In the past decade, backstepping design procedures have been intensively introduced [11], [12]. The backstepping control is a systematic and recursive design methodology for nonlinear systems. The essence of backstepping is the identification of a virtual control state and forces it to become a stabilizing function. The backstepping approach offers a choice to accommodate the unmodelled nonlinear effects and parameter uncertainties. The idea of backstepping design is to select recursively some appropriate functions of state variables as pseudo-control inputs for lower dimension subsystems of the overall system. Each backstepping stage results in a new pseudo-control design, expressed in terms of the pseudo-control design from preceding design stages.

Recently, the issue of chaotic control system design has become a significant research topic in the physics, mathematics and engineering communities. This paper proposes a wavelet-neural-network-based backstepping control (WNNBC) for a chaotic system, this control system combines the advantages of WNN identification, adaptive backstepping control and L_2 control techniques. The proposed WABC is comprised of a neural backstepping controller and an adaptive robust controller. The adaptive laws of the WNNBC system are derived in the sense of Lyapunov function and Barbalat's lemma; thus the system can be guaranteed to be asymptotically stable. Finally, some simulations of chaotic system control are provided to verify that the proposed WNNBC scheme can achieve favorable tracking performance with regard to parameter variations and unknown dynamic function.

II DESCRIPTION OF CHAOTIC SYSTEMS

Chaotic systems have been known to exhibit complex dynamical behavior. The interest in chaotic systems lies mostly upon their complex, unpredictable behavior, and extreme sensitivity to initial conditions as well as parameter variations. Consider a second-order chaotic system such as well known Duffing's equation describing a special nonlinear circuit or a pendulum moving in a viscous medium under control [13]

$$\ddot{x} = -p\dot{x} - p_1 x - p_2 x^3 + q\cos(wt) + u$$
$$= f(x, \dot{x}) + u \qquad (1)$$

where p, p_1, p_2 and q are real constants; t is the time variable; w is the frequency; $f(x, \dot{x})$ is the system dynamic function; and u is the control effort. Depending on the choice of these constants, it is known that the solutions of system (1) may exhibit periodic, almost periodic and chaotic behavior. For observing the chaotic unpredictable behavior, the open-loop system behavior with $u=0$ was simulated with $p=0.4$, $p_1=-1.1$, $p_2=1.0$ and $w=1.8$. The phase plane plots from an initial condition point (1,1) are shown in Figs. 1(a) and 1(b) for $q=0.62$ nd $q=7.00$, respectively. It is shown that the uncontrolled chaotic system has different trajectories for different q values.

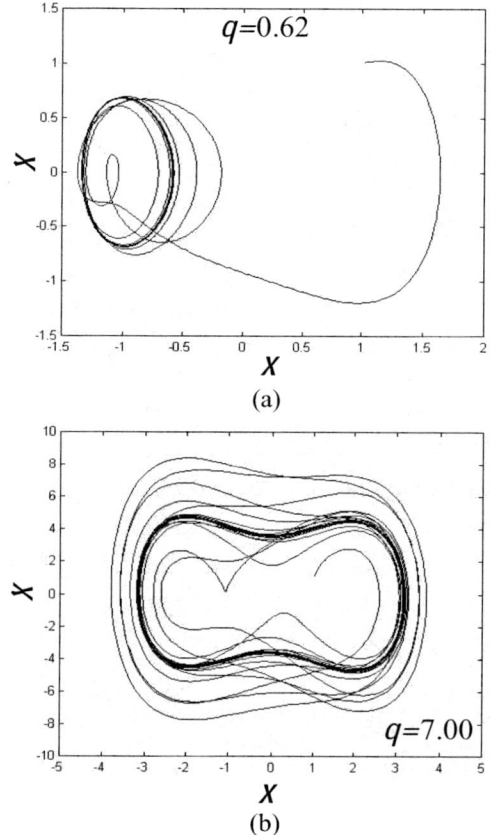

Fig. 1. Phase plane of uncontrolled chaotic system

III WAVELET NEURAL NETWORK IDENTIFIER

The network structure of the WNN identifier is shown in Fig. 2, which can be considered as "1"-layer feedforward neural network with input preprocessing element. The WNN output with m wavelet basis functions can perform the mapping according to

$$f(z) = \sum_{j=1}^{m} \alpha_j \Theta_j(\omega_j,(z-c_j)) \qquad (2)$$

where $z = [z_1\ z_2\ ...\ z_n]^T \in R^n$ is the input vector, $\Theta_j(\omega_j,(z-c_j)) \in R$, $j=1,2,...,m$ are the wavelet functions, $\omega_j = [\omega_{1j}\ \omega_{2j}\ ...\ \omega_{nj}]^T \in R^n$ and $c_j = [c_{1j}\ c_{2j}\ ...\ c_{nj}]^T \in R^n$ are the dilation and translation parameters, respectively, $\alpha_j \in R$ is the output layer weight, and m is the number of units (also called nodes and neurons) in the translation layer. Each wavelet network's neuron in the translation layer can be represented by

$$\Theta_j = h_j(z)\exp(-\sum_{k=1}^{n}\omega_{kj}^2(z_k - c_{kj})^2/2) \qquad (3)$$

where the "Mexican hat" mother wavelet function is defined as $h_j(z) = \prod_{k=1}^{n}(1 - w_k^2 z_k^2)$. For ease of notation, (2) can be expressed in a compact vector form as

$$f(z,\alpha,\omega,c) = \alpha^T \Theta(z,\omega,c) \qquad (4)$$

where $\alpha = [\alpha_1\ \alpha_2\ ...\ \alpha_m]^T \in R^m$, $\Theta = [\Theta_1\ \Theta_2\ ...\ \Theta_m]^T \in R^m$, $\omega = [\omega_1\ \omega_2\ ...\ \omega_m]^T \in R^{n\times m}$ and $c = [c_1\ c_2\ ...\ c_m]^T \in R^{n\times m}$.

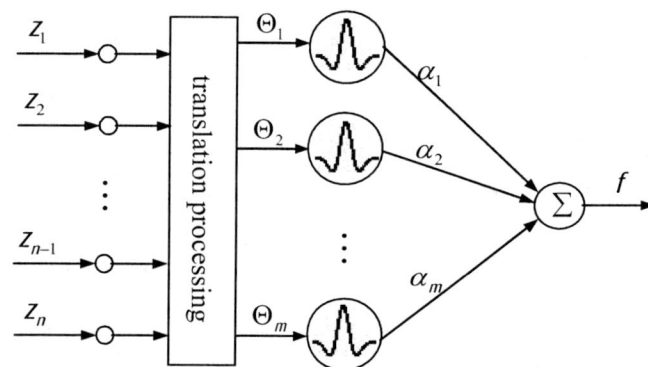

Fig. 2. Network structure of a wavelet neural network

By the universal approximation theorem, there exists an ideal WNN identifier f^* such that

$$f = f^*(z) + \Delta = \alpha^{*T}\Theta(z,\omega^*,c^*) + \Delta \qquad (5)$$

where Δ denotes the approximation error and ω^*, c^* and α^* are the optimal parameter matrices and vector of ω, c and α, respectively. In fact, the optimal parameter vectors that are needed to best approximate a given nonlinear function are difficult to determine. Thus, an estimate function is defined as

$$\hat{f}(z,\hat{\alpha},\hat{\omega},\hat{c}) = \hat{\alpha}^T\Theta(z,\hat{\omega},\hat{c}) \qquad (6)$$

where $\hat{\omega}$, $\hat{c}$ and $\hat{\alpha}$ are the estimation of ω^*, c^* and α^*, respectively. For notational convenience, denote $\Theta^* = \Theta(z,\omega^*,c^*)$ and $\hat{\Theta} = \Theta(z,\hat{\omega},\hat{c})$. Define the estimated error as

$$\tilde{f} = f - \hat{f} = f^* - \hat{f} + \Delta$$

$$= \tilde{\boldsymbol{\alpha}}^T \tilde{\boldsymbol{\Theta}} + \hat{\boldsymbol{\alpha}}^T \tilde{\boldsymbol{\Theta}} + \tilde{\boldsymbol{\alpha}}^T \hat{\boldsymbol{\Theta}} + \Delta \quad (7)$$

where $\tilde{\boldsymbol{\alpha}} = \boldsymbol{\alpha}^* - \hat{\boldsymbol{\alpha}}$ and $\tilde{\boldsymbol{\Theta}} = \boldsymbol{\Theta}^* - \hat{\boldsymbol{\Theta}}$. In the following, some tuning laws will be derived to on-line tune the parameters of the WNN identifier to achieve favorable estimation of the system dynamic function. To achieve this goal, the Taylor expansion linearization technique is employed to transform the nonlinear function into a partially linear form, i.e.

$$\tilde{\boldsymbol{\Theta}} = \begin{bmatrix} \tilde{\Theta}_1 \\ \tilde{\Theta}_2 \\ \vdots \\ \tilde{\Theta}_m \end{bmatrix} = \begin{bmatrix} \frac{\partial \Theta_1}{\partial \boldsymbol{\omega}} \\ \frac{\partial \Theta_2}{\partial \boldsymbol{\omega}} \\ \vdots \\ \frac{\partial \Theta_m}{\partial \boldsymbol{\omega}} \end{bmatrix}\bigg|_{\boldsymbol{\omega} = \hat{\boldsymbol{\omega}}} \tilde{\boldsymbol{\omega}} + \begin{bmatrix} \frac{\partial \Theta_1}{\partial \mathbf{c}} \\ \frac{\partial \Theta_2}{\partial \mathbf{c}} \\ \vdots \\ \frac{\partial \Theta_m}{\partial \mathbf{c}} \end{bmatrix}\bigg|_{\mathbf{c} = \hat{\mathbf{c}}} \tilde{\mathbf{c}} + \mathbf{h} \quad (8)$$

or

$$\tilde{\boldsymbol{\Theta}} = \mathbf{A}^T \tilde{\boldsymbol{\omega}} + \mathbf{B}^T \tilde{\mathbf{c}} + \mathbf{h} \quad (9)$$

where $\tilde{\boldsymbol{\omega}} = \boldsymbol{\omega}^* - \hat{\boldsymbol{\omega}}$; $\tilde{\mathbf{c}} = \mathbf{c}^* - \hat{\mathbf{c}}$; $\mathbf{h}$ is a vector of higher-order terms; $\mathbf{A} = \begin{bmatrix} \frac{\partial \Theta_1}{\partial \boldsymbol{\omega}} & \frac{\partial \Theta_2}{\partial \boldsymbol{\omega}} & \cdots & \frac{\partial \Theta_m}{\partial \boldsymbol{\omega}} \end{bmatrix}\big|_{\boldsymbol{\omega}=\hat{\boldsymbol{\omega}}}$;

$\mathbf{B} = \begin{bmatrix} \frac{\partial \Theta_1}{\partial \mathbf{c}} & \frac{\partial \Theta_2}{\partial \mathbf{c}} & \cdots & \frac{\partial \Theta_m}{\partial \mathbf{c}} \end{bmatrix}\big|_{\mathbf{c}=\hat{\mathbf{c}}}$; and $\frac{\partial \Theta_l}{\partial \boldsymbol{\omega}}$ and $\frac{\partial \Theta_l}{\partial \mathbf{c}}$ are defined as

$$\left[\frac{\partial \Theta_l}{\partial \boldsymbol{\omega}}\right]^T = \begin{bmatrix} 0 \cdots 0 & \frac{\partial \Theta_l}{\partial \omega_{1l}} \cdots \frac{\partial \Theta_l}{\partial \omega_{nl}} & 0 \cdots 0 \\ {}_{(l-1)\times n} & & {}_{(m-l)\times n} \end{bmatrix} \quad (10)$$

$$\left[\frac{\partial \Theta_l}{\partial \mathbf{c}}\right]^T = \begin{bmatrix} 0 \cdots 0 & \frac{\partial \Theta_l}{\partial c_{1l}} \cdots \frac{\partial \Theta_l}{\partial c_{nl}} & 0 \cdots 0 \\ {}_{(l-1)\times n} & & {}_{(m-l)\times n} \end{bmatrix} \quad (11)$$

Substituting (9) into (7), gives

$$\tilde{f} = \tilde{\boldsymbol{\alpha}}^T (\hat{\boldsymbol{\Theta}} - \mathbf{A}^T \hat{\boldsymbol{\omega}} - \mathbf{B}^T \hat{\mathbf{c}}) + \tilde{\boldsymbol{\omega}}^T \mathbf{A} \hat{\boldsymbol{\alpha}} + \tilde{\mathbf{c}}^T \mathbf{B} \hat{\boldsymbol{\alpha}} + \varepsilon \quad (12)$$

where $\tilde{\boldsymbol{\omega}}^T \mathbf{A} \hat{\boldsymbol{\alpha}} = \hat{\boldsymbol{\alpha}}^T \mathbf{A}^T \tilde{\boldsymbol{\omega}}$ and $\tilde{\mathbf{c}}^T \mathbf{B} \hat{\boldsymbol{\alpha}} = \hat{\boldsymbol{\alpha}}^T \mathbf{B}^T \tilde{\mathbf{c}}$ are used since they are scales; and the sum of matching error $\varepsilon = \tilde{\boldsymbol{\alpha}}^T \mathbf{A}^T \boldsymbol{\omega}^* + \tilde{\boldsymbol{\alpha}}^T \mathbf{B}^T \mathbf{c}^* + \boldsymbol{\alpha}^* \mathbf{h} + \Delta$.

IV Design of WNNBC

The proposed wavelet-neural-network-based backstepping control (WNNBC) system is shown in Fig. 3, which is comprised of a neural backstepping controller u_{nb} and an adaptive robust controller u_{ar}.

Step 1. Define the tracking error

$$e_1 = x - x_c \quad (13)$$

and the derivative of tracking error is defined as

$$\dot{e}_1 = \dot{x} - \dot{x}_c. \quad (14)$$

The $\dot{x}$ can be viewed as a virtual control in the equation. Define the following stabilizing function

$$\delta = -c_1 e_1 + \dot{x}_c \quad (15)$$

where c_1 is a positive constant.

Step 2. Define

$$e_2 = \dot{x} - \delta \quad (16)$$

then the derivative of e_2 is expressed as

$$\dot{e}_2 = \ddot{x} - \dot{\delta} = \ddot{x} - (-c_1 \dot{e}_1 + \ddot{x}_c)$$
$$= \ddot{e}_1 + c_1 \dot{e}_1. \quad (17)$$

Step 3. The control law of the WABC is developed as follow

$$u_{wc} = u_{nb} + u_{ar}. \quad (18)$$

The neural backstepping controller is chosen as

$$u_{nb} = \ddot{x}_c - \hat{f} - c_1 \dot{e}_1 - c_2 e_2 - e_1 \quad (19)$$

where the WNN identifier $\hat{f}$ is designed to on-line estimate the system dynamic function f.

Step 4. Substituting (18) into (1), it can be obtained that

$$\dot{e}_2 = f - \hat{f} - c_2 e_2 - e_1 + u_{ar}. \quad (20)$$

By substituting (12) into (20), equation (20) can be obtained as follows:

$$\dot{e}_2 = \tilde{\boldsymbol{\alpha}}^T (\hat{\boldsymbol{\Theta}} - \mathbf{A}^T \hat{\boldsymbol{\omega}} - \mathbf{B}^T \hat{\mathbf{c}}) + \tilde{\boldsymbol{\omega}}^T \mathbf{A} \hat{\boldsymbol{\alpha}} + \tilde{\mathbf{c}}^T \mathbf{B} \hat{\boldsymbol{\alpha}} + \varepsilon$$
$$- c_2 e_2 - e_1 + u_{ar}. \quad (21)$$

Step 5. The adaptation laws of the wavelet neural network identifier are designed as

$$\dot{\hat{\boldsymbol{\alpha}}} = -\dot{\tilde{\boldsymbol{\alpha}}} = \eta_1 e_2 (\hat{\boldsymbol{\Theta}} - \mathbf{A}^T \hat{\boldsymbol{\omega}} - \mathbf{B}^T \hat{\mathbf{c}}) \quad (22)$$

$$\dot{\hat{\boldsymbol{\omega}}} = -\dot{\tilde{\boldsymbol{\omega}}} = \eta_2 e_2 \mathbf{A} \hat{\boldsymbol{\alpha}} \quad (23)$$

$$\dot{\hat{\mathbf{c}}} = -\dot{\tilde{\mathbf{c}}} = \eta_3 e_2 \mathbf{B} \hat{\boldsymbol{\alpha}} \quad (24)$$

where η_1, η_2 and η_3 are the learning rates with positive constants, and the adaptive robust controller is designed as

$$u_{ar} = -\frac{(\rho^2 + 1)e_2}{2\rho^2} \quad (25)$$

where ρ is a prescribed attenuation constant.

Proof:

Define a Lyapunov function as

$$V = \frac{e_1^2}{2} + \frac{e_2^2}{2} + \frac{\tilde{\boldsymbol{\alpha}}^T \tilde{\boldsymbol{\alpha}}}{2\eta_1} + \frac{\tilde{\boldsymbol{\omega}}^T \tilde{\boldsymbol{\omega}}}{2\eta_2} + \frac{\tilde{\mathbf{c}}^T \tilde{\mathbf{c}}}{2\eta_3} \quad (26)$$

Differentiating (26) with respect to time and using (22)-(25), it is obtained that

$$\dot{V} = e_1 \dot{e}_1 + e_2 \dot{e}_2 + \frac{\tilde{\boldsymbol{\alpha}}^T \dot{\tilde{\boldsymbol{\alpha}}}}{\eta_1} + \frac{\tilde{\boldsymbol{\omega}}^T \dot{\tilde{\boldsymbol{\omega}}}}{\eta_2} + \frac{\tilde{\mathbf{c}}^T \dot{\tilde{\mathbf{c}}}}{\eta_3}$$

$$= -c_1 e_1^2 - c_2 e_2^2 - \frac{e_2^2}{2} - \frac{1}{2}(\frac{e_2}{\rho} - \rho\varepsilon)^2 + \frac{\rho^2 \varepsilon^2}{2}$$

$$\leq -c_1 e_1^2 + \frac{\rho^2 \varepsilon^2}{2} \qquad (27)$$

Integrating the above equation from $t=0$ to $t=T$, yields

$$V(T) - V(0) \leq -c_1 \int_0^T e_1^2(\tau) d\tau + \frac{\rho^2}{2} \int_0^T \varepsilon^2(\tau) d\tau \qquad (28)$$

Since $V(T) \geq 0$, the above inequality implies the following inequality

$$c_1 \int_0^T e_1^2(\tau) d\tau \leq V_2(0) + \frac{\rho^2}{2} \int_0^T \varepsilon^2(\tau) d\tau \qquad (29)$$

Since $V(0)$ is finite, if the approximation error $\varepsilon \in L_2$, that is $\int_0^T \varepsilon^2(\tau) d\tau < \infty$, using the Barbalat's lemma, it implies that $\lim_{t \to \infty} |e_1| = 0$.

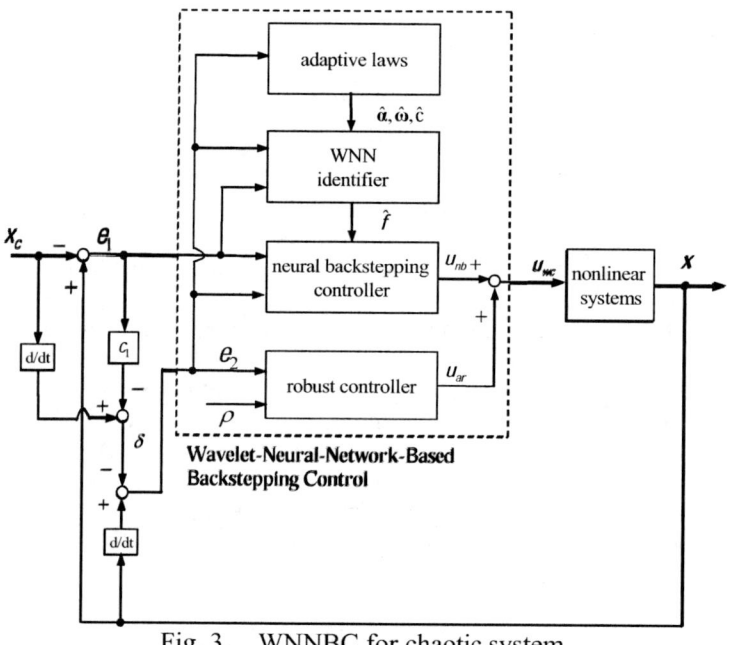

Fig. 3. WNNBC for chaotic system.

V SIMULATION RESULTS

The simulation results of the chaotic control system are presented here to verify the effectiveness of the proposed WNNBC scheme. It should be emphasized that the derivation of WNNBC do not need to know the system dynamic function. The system dynamic function would be on-line estimated by the WNN identifier. A WNN identifier with 5 hidden nodes is utilized to approach the system dynamic function of the chaotic system. In addition, the control parameters are selected as $c_1 = c_2 = 1$, $\eta_1 = \eta_2 = \eta_3 = 10$ and $w_k = 0.8$ for $k = 1,2,...,5$. These parameters are chosen to achieve favorable transient control performance considering the requirement of asymptotic stability and the possible operating conditions. The trajectory command is set as $x_c = \cos(t)$. The simulation results of the WABC for $q = 0.62$ and $q = 7.00$ are shown in Figs. 4 and 5, respectively. For the attenuation level $\rho = 0.5$, the tracking responses of state x are shown in Figs. 4(a) and 5(a); the tracking responses of state $\dot{x}$ are shown in Figs. 4(b) and 5(b); and the associated control efforts are shown Figs. 4(c) and 5(c), respectively. Moreover, to achieve smaller attenuation level, the case for $\rho = 0.2$ is reconsidered. In this case, the tracking responses of state x are shown in Figs. 4(d) and 5(d); the tracking responses of state $\dot{x}$ are shown in Figs. 4(e) and 5(e); and the associated control efforts are shown Figs. 4(f) and 5(f), respectively. It is shown that the proposed WNNBC can achieve favorable tracking performance; moreover, the better tracking performance can be achieved as specified attenuation level ρ is chosen smaller.

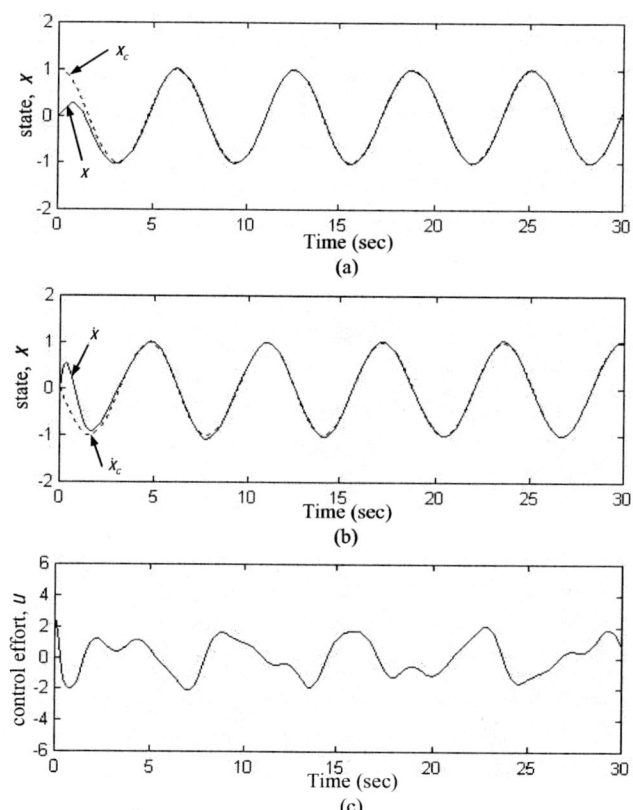

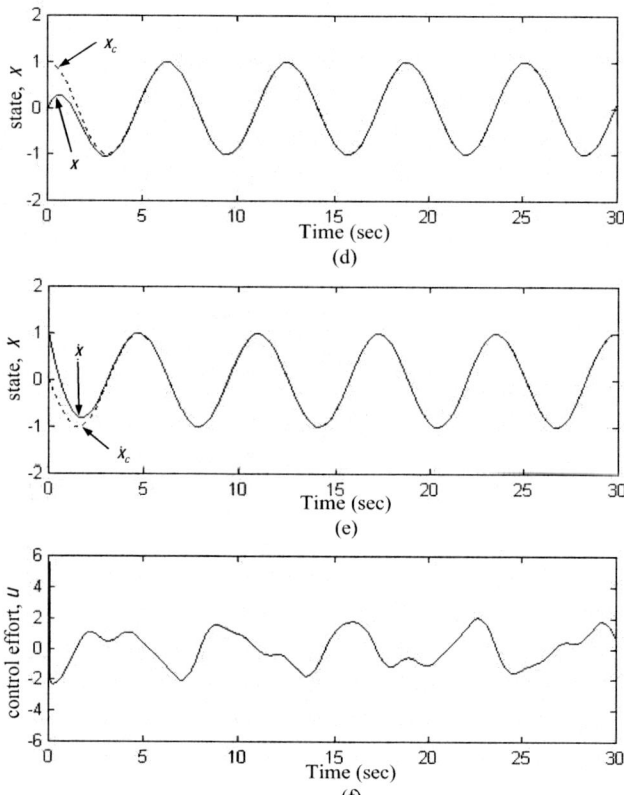

Fig. 4. Simulation results of chaotic system for $q = 0.62$.

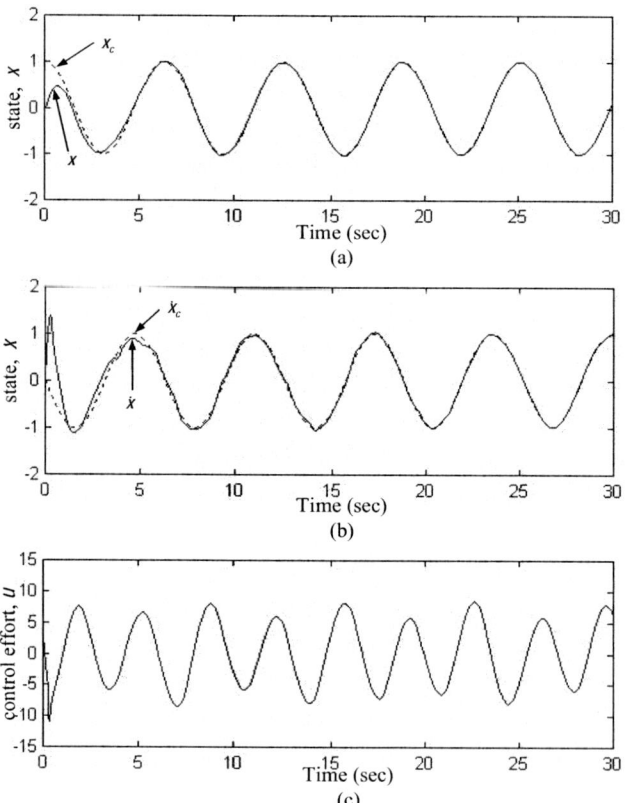

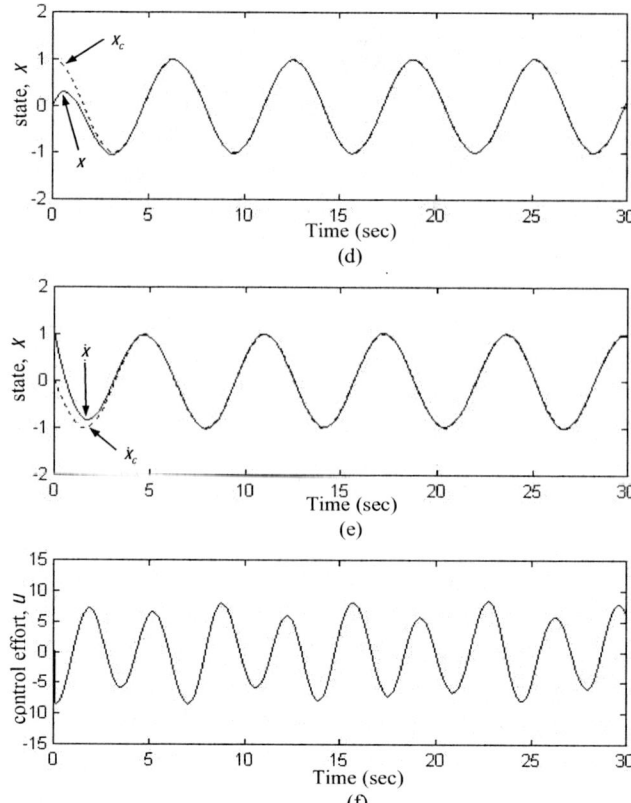

Fig. 5. Simulation results of chaotic system for $q = 7.00$.

VI CONCLUSIONS

For some systems, since the dynamic characteristics of the control system are nonlinear and the precise models are difficult to obtain, the model-based control approaches are difficult to be implemented for these systems. To overcome this drawback, a WNNBC system has been proposed. The developed WNNBC system is comprised of a neural backstepping controller with a wavelet neural network (WNN) identifier and an adaptive robust controller. The WNN identifier is utilized to on-line estimate the system dynamic function. The adaptive laws of the WNNBC system are synthesized using the Lyapunov function and Barbalat's lemma so that the asymptotic stability of the control system can be guaranteed. Finally, simulation results verified that the proposed WNNBC system can achieve favorable tracking performance of the nonlinear chaotic systems.

ACKNOWLEDGMENTS

The authors appreciate the partial financial support from the National Science Council of Republic of China under grant NSC 92-2213-E-009-009.

REFERENCES

[1] F. L. Lewis, A. Yesildirek, and K. Liu, "Multilayer neural-net robot controller with guaranteed tracking performance," *IEEE Trans. Neural Networks*, vol. 7, pp. 388-399, March 1996.

[2] F. J. Lin, R. J. Wai, and H. P. Chen, "A PM synchronous servo motor drive with an on-line trained fuzzy neural network controller,"

[3] H. Wang and Y. Wang, "Neural-network-based fault-tolerant control of unknown nonlinear systems," *IEE Proc., Contr. Theory Appl.*, vol. 146, pp. 389-398, Sept. 1999.

[4] J. T. Spooner and K. M. Passino, "Decentralized adaptive control of nonlinear systems using radial basis neural networks," *IEEE Trans. Automat. Contr.*, vol. 44, pp. 2050-2057, Nov. 1999.

[5] Q. Zhang and A. Benveniste, "Wavelet networks," *IEEE Trans. Neural Networks*, vol. 3, pp. 889-898, Nov. 1992.

[6] B. Delyon, A. Juditsky, and A. Benveniste, "Accuracy analysis for wavelet approximations," *IEEE Trans. Neural Networks*, vol. 6, pp. 332-348, March 1995.

[7] Q. Zhang, "Using wavelet network in nonparametric estimation," *IEEE Trans. Neural Networks*, vol. 8, pp. 227-236, March 1997.

[8] C. K. Lin, "Adaptive tracking controller design for robotic systems using Gaussian wavelet networks," *IEE Proc., Contr. Theory Appl.*, vol. 149, pp. 316-322, July 2002.

[9] C. D. Sousa, E. M. Hemerly, and R. K. H. Galvao, "Adaptive control for mobile robot using wavelet networks," *IEEE Trans. Syst., Man and Cybern. pt B*, vol. 32, pp. 493-504, Aug. 2002.

[10] R. J. Wai and J. M. Chang, "Implementation of robust wavelet-neural-network sliding-mode control for induction servo motor drive," *IEEE Trans. Ind. Electron.*, vol. 50, pp. 1317-1334, Dec. 2003.

[11] J. Y. Choi and J. A. Farrell, "Adaptive observer backstepping control using neural networks," *IEEE Trans. Neural Networks*, vol. 12, pp. 1103-1112, Sept. 2001.

[12] R. J. Wai, F. J. Lin and S. P. Hsu, "Intelligent backstepping control for linear induction motor drive," *IEE Proc., Contr. Theory Appl.*, vol. 148, pp. 193-202, May 2001.

[13] G. Chen, and X. Dong, "On feedback control of chaotic continuous-time systems," *IEEE Trans. Circuits Syst., Pt I*, vol. 40, pp. 591-601, Sept. 1993.

Spatially and Temporally Local Spike-Timing-Dependent Plasticity Rule

Anatoli Gorchetchnikov and Massimiliano Versace
Dept of Cognitive and Neural Systems,
Boston University,
677 Beacon St, Boston, MA 02215, USA
Emails: (anatoli, versace)@cns.bu.edu

Michael E. Hasselmo
Dept of Psychology,
Boston University,
64 Cummington St, Boston, MA 02215, USA
Email: hasselmo@bu.edu

Abstract— Recent neurophysiological research has focused on the temporal relationships between neuronal firing and plasticity, and has shown the phenomenon of spike-timing-dependent plasticity (STDP). Various models were suggested to implement the STDP-like learning rule in artificial networks based on spiking neuronal representations. Here we present and analyze a simple rule that only depends on the information that is available at the synapse at the time of synaptic modification. This rule is further extended by addition of four different types of gating derived from conventionally used types of gated decay in learning rules for continuous firing rate neural networks. The results show that the advantages of using these gatings are transferred to the new rule without sacrificing its dependency on spike-timing.

Most neural models have focused on the Hebb rule for synaptic plasticity, which is usually written as:

$$\frac{dw}{dt} = \lambda X_{pre} X_{post} \qquad (1)$$

where λ is the learning rate and X are pre- and postsynaptic signals. This formula is based on correlation and does not include precise information about firing times of neurons, unless X_{pre} and X_{post} are specifically designed to include this information. Hebb [1], on the other hand, emphasized causality and, therefore, a temporal order of neuronal firing.

Moreover, neurophysiological studies explored the phenomenon of spike-timing-dependent plasticity (STDP) [2]–[4]. STDP more closely reflects the idea of the Hebbian postulate than the equation (1). Various implementations of learning rules that can model this type of plasticity were proposed in recent years [5]–[8].

The model presented here also assumes that the adaptation is based on temporally asymmetric adjustment of projection weights, and develops the mechanism to implement STDP on the basis of information available in the synapse at the moment of learning. The resulting learning rule can be integrated over time to achieve results similar to these produced by a well studied rule suggested by Gerstner et al [5], which is discussed in the next section.

I. Previous Analysis and Notation

Gerstner et al [5] suggested and analyzed the following STDP rule:

$$\Delta w_{ij} = \int_0^T \int_0^T W(t - t') S_i(t) S_j(t') \, dt \, dt' \qquad (2)$$

where w_{ij} is the synaptic weight of a connection from j to i, T is the duration of a learning experiment, $S_i(t)$ is the postsynaptic spike train, $S_j(t)$ is the presynaptic spike train, and $W(t - t')$ is the learning window that depends on the time difference between the postsynaptic t and presynaptic t' spikes.

Equation (2) contains the information about timing of the *presynaptic* spike arrival, timing of the *postsynaptic* spike generation, and *efficiency* of learning for a specific time difference between the two. These are the three critical components that have to be present in any STDP rule. The rule (2) has several advantages. First, it is spatially local in the sense that it does not require any information that is not available at the synapse the rule is applied to. Second, the number of parameters in the learning window provides enough flexibility to fit any experimental data. Finally, it reduces to Hebbian learning for the continuous firing rate coding [5].

The downside of this rule is its requirement for the timing information over the interval $[0, T]$, so it is temporally global. Efficient simulation software will prefer a temporally local rule based only on the information available here and now over the one that requires keeping track of recent events.

II. Components of a Temporally and Spatially Local STDP Rule

To create a temporally and spatially local STDP rule one should identify three components of the plasticity, namely presynaptic timing, postsynaptic timing, and the efficiency of learning for a certain time difference, so that all of them are available at the synapse at every moment of time.

Levy and Steward [2] suggested that the accumulation of specific ions in the spine can indicate recent presynaptic spiking. A related indicator of presynaptic spike timing at the site of the synapse is the synaptic conductance. It has a temporal profile, which is triggered by a presynaptic spike and approximated here by a dual-exponential equation.

Retrograde electrical invasion was suggested by Levy and Steward [2] to subserve the indication of postsynaptic spike timing. The model presented here uses the membrane potential directly. Moreover, since the model assumes that 0 is the resting potential, and the time of the spike is the moment when potential crosses 0 between the depolarization part of the spike and the afterhyperpolarization (AHP), membrane potential is positive before the spike and negative after the spike. This can be used to determine the efficiency of learning.

The efficiency of learning at every moment of time is the slice of the learning window W in equation (2). The Gerstner et al [5] description of the formation of such a window is based on two factors. The first (a) is triggered by the presynaptic spike. The second (b) is triggered by the postsynaptic spike and can have potentiation and depression components (b_+ and b_-, respectively). This discussion applies here if one considers synaptic conductance as an a factor (which is always positive), and membrane potential as a sum of positive (depolarization) b_+ and and negative (AHP) b_- components.

Substituting synaptic conductance as a presynaptic signal ($X_{pre} = g_s$) and membrane potential as a postsynaptic signal ($X_{post} = V_{soma}$) in equation (1) can produce STDP due to the mechanism discussed in [9]. A similar idea was used in [8], but the authors use the derivative of back-propagating action potential as X_{post}. Numerical simulations [9] generally confirmed the approach to the STDP rule presented here, but the formal analysis of a simplified version can provide additional insights on the dynamics of this rule.

III. ANALYSIS OF THE SIMPLIFIED RULE

The following simplifications were made for the analysis:

Simplification 1: Assume that synaptic time constants $\tau_r = \tau_f = \tau$, so that g_s is an alpha function $\frac{t}{\tau} e^{(1-\frac{t}{\tau})}$. Also assume that it starts at $t = 0$ (and therefore $s = t_{post}$) and completely decays at $t = 10\tau$.

Simplification 2: Approximate the postsynaptic action potential with a piecewise linear function

$$X_{post} = \begin{cases} A(t-s) + B & \text{if } s - \frac{B}{A} < t \leq s \\ C(t-s) + D & \text{if } s < t < s - \frac{D}{C} \\ 0 & \text{otherwise} \end{cases} \quad (3)$$

as shown in Figure 1: $X_{post} = A(t-s) + B$ models the depolarization part, where $A > 0$ is the slope of a spike and $B > 0$ is a peak amplitude, and $X_{post} = C(t-s) + D$ models the hyperpolarization part, where $C > 0$ is the slope and $D < 0$ is the trough amplitude.

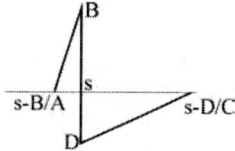

Fig. 1. Approximation of the action potential with a piecewise linear function.

Then the rule (1) becomes

$$\frac{dw}{dt} = \begin{cases} (A(t-s) + B) \frac{t}{\tau} e^{(1-\frac{t}{\tau})} & \text{if } s - \frac{B}{A} < t \leq s \\ (C(t-s) + D) \frac{t}{\tau} e^{(1-\frac{t}{\tau})} & \text{if } s < t < s - \frac{D}{C} \end{cases} \quad (4)$$

With the above simplifications learning only happens if $\frac{D}{C} < s < 10\tau + \frac{B}{A}$ as illustrated in Figure 2.

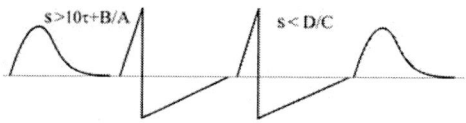

Fig. 2. Cases with no learning after simplifications.

To estimate the total weight change during one learning window, equation (4) has to be integrated over the length of the learning window. This integral has an analytic solution

$$-e^{(1-\frac{t}{\tau})} \left((\nu - \mu s)(t + \tau) + \mu(t+\tau)^2 + \mu\tau^2 \right) + X \quad (5)$$

where $\mu = A$, $\nu = B$ for $s - \frac{B}{A} < t \leq s$, and $\mu = C$, $\nu = D$ for $s < t < s - \frac{D}{C}$. Separating these two cases, one can denote part of this solution for potentiation while $s - \frac{B}{A} < t \leq s$ as Φ_P, and for depression while $s < t < s - \frac{D}{C}$ as Φ_D. The total weight change is

$$\Delta w = \Phi_P \Big|_{t_1}^{t_2} + \Phi_D \Big|_{t_2}^{t_3} \quad (6)$$

The limits of integration are determined as follows.

Case 1: if $\frac{D}{C} < s < 0$, then $\Phi_P = 0$, Φ_D starts at $t = 0$ and lasts till either $t = s - \frac{D}{C}$ or $t = 10\tau$, whichever comes first.

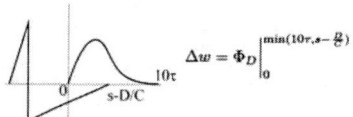

Case 2: if $0 < s < 10\tau$, then Φ_P starts at either $t = s - \frac{B}{A}$ or $t = 0$, whichever comes last, and lasts till $t = s$. Φ_D starts at $t = s$ and lasts till either $t = s - \frac{D}{C}$ or $t = 10\tau$, whichever comes first.

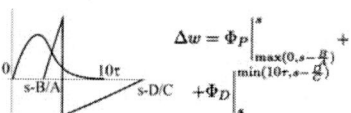

Case 3: if $10\tau < s < 10\tau + \frac{B}{A}$, then $\Phi_D = 0$, Φ_P starts at either $t = s - \frac{B}{A}$ or $t = 0$, whichever comes last and lasts till $t = 10\tau$.

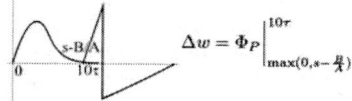

Combining all cases yields:

$$\Delta w = \Phi_P \Big|_{\max(0, s - \frac{B}{A})}^{\max(0, \min(s, 10\tau))} + \Phi_D \Big|_{\max(s, 0)}^{\max(s, \min(10\tau, s - \frac{D}{C}))} \quad (7)$$

IV. LIMITING THE WEIGHTS

There are several approaches to prevent unbounded weight growth in the Hebbian rule:
- Renormalizing the weights to keep the total weight constant;
- Imposing a limit on the weight value;

- Adding to equation (1) the decay term proportional to the current weight value. Grossberg introduced the postsynaptic and presynaptic gated decay laws and called them the Instar and Outstar learning rules [10]–[12].

Here we consider the last approach. This leads to the rule

$$\frac{dw}{dt} = \lambda X_{pre} X_{post} - f(X_{pre}, X_{post}) w \qquad (8)$$

where $f(X_{pre}, X_{post})$ is a scaling function. Some scaling functions that are widely used with continuous firing rate neuronal representations are listed in Table I.

TABLE I
GATED DECAY FOR CONTINUOUS FIRING RATE REPRESENTATIONS

Common name	$f(X_{pre}, X_{post})$	$\lim_{t\to\infty} w$
Grossberg outstar [11], [12] (Postsynaptically Gated Decay)	X_{post}	X_{pre}
Grossberg instar [11], [12] (Presynaptically Gated Decay)	X_{pre}	X_{post}
Oja rule [13]	X_{post}^2	$\frac{X_{pre}}{X_{post}}$

All functions listed in Table I only make sense when one considers pre- and postsynaptic signals as firing rates. In this case the firing patterns of cells have only a spatial component, the temporal component is coded as the level of activity. In the case of spiking neurons, the temporal component of the pattern is the specific time difference between the presynaptic and postsynaptic spike. The next section starts the design of a scaling function f applicable for spiking networks.

V. COMBINING GATED DECAY AND THE STDP RULE

Rule (4) provides the measure of the time difference between the presynaptic and postsynaptic spike based on the product of X_{pre} and X_{post}. The successful learning rule for spiking neurons can sample some function q of this product in order to encode both spatial and temporal components of the pattern. To achieve this, the rule should lead to

$$\lim_{t\to\infty} w = q(X_{pre} X_{post}) \qquad (9)$$

From a biophysical point of view, the synaptic weight can not be negative if it is defined as a density of the ion channels in the synapse. To satisfy this constraint $q(X_{pre} X_{post})$ should be non-negative in equation (9). While $X_{pre} = g_s \in [0,1]$, $X_{post} = V_{soma}$ can be both positive and negative. Moreover, the bounds of X_{post} can be only approximated from the data on membrane potential.

To overcome the problem of loosely defined bounds, X_{post} can be replaced by a variable triggered by membrane potential but bounded within a certain interval. This is done by setting the parameters A, B, C, and D of equation (3) to normalize the values of X_{post} over the interval $|D,B|$ of the length 1. Figure 3 plots equation (7).

The piecewise linear X_{post} used in Figure 3 changes between $D < 0$ and $B > 0$. Hence, the product $X_{pre} X_{post} \in |D,B|$, and since $B - D = 1$

$$q(X_{pre} X_{post}) = X_{pre} X_{post} - D \in |0,1| \qquad (10)$$

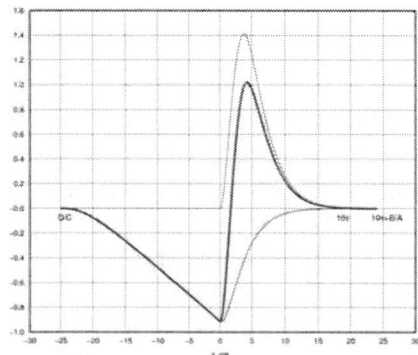

Fig. 3. Example plot of STDP curve for a simplified rule with normalized parameters. Φ_P is shown in blue, Φ_D in red, and their sum (equation 7) in bold green. $A = 0.2$, $B = 0.8$, $C = 0.008$, $D = -0.2$, and $\tau = 2$ms.

This function q leads to following:

- $\lim_{t\to\infty} w = 1$ when $X_{pre} X_{post} = B$ (positive correlation),
- $\lim_{t\to\infty} w = 0$ when $X_{pre} X_{post} = D$ (negative correlation), and
- $\lim_{t\to\infty} w = -D$ when $X_{pre} X_{post} = 0$ (no correlated activity between pre- and postsynaptic cells).

There are three issues with the equation (3) and the resulting STDP curve in Figure 3. First, in general case the shape of the action potential during simulation will not follow the linear approximation used here. To keep the learning rule simple yet applicable with any spike shape the approximated X_{post} still can be used, but instead of precisely following the shape of the spike it should be triggered by action potential generation.

Second, for the case of spike-generating mechanisms that have internal dynamics (e.g. the classic Hodgkin-Huxley model [14]), the length of the spike is not constant. To accommodate this, the positive part of X_{post} should be triggered by an instantaneous event that signals the generation of an action potential in the near future, and should last for the duration of the spike. The simplest function that satisfies these requirements and does not depend on the length of the spike is $X_{post} = constant$ starting when V_{soma} crosses the spiking threshold and ending when V_{soma} drops below the resting potential after the spike.

The third problem is the shift of zero-crossing towards positive s in Figure 3. It is due to the instantaneous effect of the emitted spike on the synapse in the model. In real cells there is a delay before the chemical and electrical influence of the action potential can reach the synapse. A delay in the transition from a positive to a negative component of X_{post} can correct the shift in zero-crossing. Moreover, from a biophysical standpoint this transition should be gradual and not instantaneous as was used in equation (3). Linear decay is sufficient as the first approximation. The resulting X_{post} is

$$X_{post} = \begin{cases} B & \text{if } V_{soma} > V\theta \\ A(t-s) + B & \text{if } s < t < s - \frac{1}{A} \\ C(t-s+\frac{1}{A}) + D & \text{if } s - \frac{1}{A} < t < s - \frac{D}{C} - \frac{1}{A} \\ 0 & \text{otherwise} \end{cases} \quad (11)$$

where $A < 0$ (note the change of the sign from equation 3) is the slope of a transition from a positive to a negative component, $B > 0$ is the peak amplitude of a positive component, $C > 0$ is the slope of recovery and $D = B - 1 < 0$ is the trough amplitude of a negative component. Figure 4 shows the resulting X_{post}.

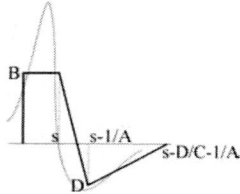

Fig. 4. X_{post} as piecewise linear function (equation 11). The action potential represented by this X_{post} is outlined in gray in the background.

The new X_{post} adds an extra term to equation (6)

$$\Delta w = \Phi_P \Big|_{t_1}^{t_2} + \Phi_T \Big|_{t_2}^{t_3} + \Phi_D \Big|_{t_3}^{t_4} \quad (12)$$

where Φ_D is a depression component similar to the one discussed for equation (6) and calculated using equation (5), Φ_T is a transition component also calculated using equation (5), and Φ_P is a potentiation component calculated as

$$\Phi_P \Big|_{t_1}^{t_2} = \int_{t_1}^{t_2} B \frac{t}{\tau} e^{(1-\frac{t}{\tau})} dt = -e^{(1-\frac{t}{\tau})} B(t+\tau) \Big|_{\min(\max(0,t^*),s)}^{\max(t^*,\min(s,10\tau))} \quad (13)$$

where t^* is the time when V_{soma} crosses the threshold. The result of equation (12) is presented in Figure 5.

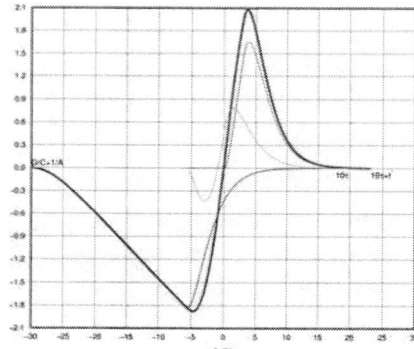

Fig. 5. Example plot of STDP curve for an extended rule. Φ_P is shown in blue, Φ_D in red, Φ_T in yellow, and their sum (equation 12) in bold green. $A = -0.175$, $B = 0.6$, $C = 0.016$, $D = B - 1 = -0.4$, $t^* = s - 3$ms, and $\tau = 2$ms.

As a result of these adjustments, the target of the learning rule becomes

$$\lim_{t \to \infty} w = q(X_{pre}X_{post}) = X_{pre}X_{post} + 1 - B \quad (14)$$

with three free parameters: $A < 0$, $0 < B < 1$, and $C > 0$. Equation (14) keeps the resulting weights in the interval $[0, 1]$.

VI. EXTENDING THE INTERVAL FOR SYNAPTIC WEIGHTS

The regular procedure to extend the range of $q(X_{pre}X_{post})$ over $|\breve{w}, \hat{w}|$ is to multiply it by the length of the interval and add $\breve{w}$

$$q(X_{pre}X_{post}) = (X_{pre}X_{post} + 1 - B)(\hat{w} - \breve{w}) + \breve{w} \quad (15)$$

Similar to equation (10) it can be shown that $\lim_{t \to \infty} w = \hat{w}$ when $X_{pre}X_{post} = B$, and $\lim_{t \to \infty} w = \breve{w}$ when $X_{pre}X_{post} = 1 - B$.

In the case where $X_{pre}X_{post} = 0$

$$\lim_{t \to \infty} w = \hat{w} - B(\hat{w} - \breve{w}) = w_0 \quad (16)$$

where w_0 stands for the baseline weight achieved when there is no correlation between presynaptic and postsynaptic firing. Rewriting the parameter B in terms of maximal, minimal and baseline weights and substituting it in the equation (15) yields

$$\lim_{t \to \infty} w = q(X_{pre}X_{post}) = X_{pre}X_{post}(\hat{w} - \breve{w}) + w_0 \quad (17)$$

To achieve this limit, the differential equation for the weight should be

$$\frac{dw}{dt} = \lambda(X_{pre}X_{post}(\hat{w} - \breve{w}) + w_0 - w) \quad (18)$$

which suggests in comparison with equation (8) that for spiking neurons a reasonable scaling function is $f(X_{pre}, X_{post}) = \lambda$. Unfortunately, this scaling function was shown to force the weights towards the baseline since the events of pre- and postsynaptic coactivity are quite rare and the drive towards the baseline is constant [10].

The solution for continuous firing rate neurons was to gate the decay by either pre- or postsynaptic activity. But gating the decay term alone would change the limit in equation (9) and, therefore, invalidate the reasoning of the previous two sections. The solution suggested here is to gate not the decay term but the whole learning process of equation (18) by either presynaptic, or postsynaptic, or both activities (for an example of such a dual gating during visual perceptual learning see [15]). The resulting rule becomes

$$\frac{dw}{dt} = \lambda(X_{pre}X_{post}(\hat{w} - \breve{w}) + w_0 - w) f_G(X_{pre}, X_{post}) \quad (19)$$

and the next section discusses the results for five different gating functions f_G.

VII. COMPARISON OF FIVE GATING FUNCTIONS

The simulations presented in this section used the network of three fully interconnected cells named A, B, and C. Cells A and B were spiking so that cell B was lagging behind cell A by 10ms, and cell C was always silent. The pair of spikes in cells A and B constitutes a learning trial. These trials were repeated every 200ms, and over the total length of the simulation (1s) there were 5 trials. This was sufficient for the weights to get within 1% of their asymptotes under all but the last gating function described below. For the last gating function the total length of the simulation was 5s and included 25 learning trials. Parameters in these simulation were: $\breve{w} = 0$, $\hat{w} = 5$, $w_0 = 0.5$, and $\lambda = 1$. All simulations started with random weights between cells presented in Table II that were drawn from a uniform distribution between $\breve{w}$ and $\hat{w}$.

TABLE II
INITIAL WEIGHTS IN THE STUDY OF GATING FUNCTIONS

Postsynaptic cell	Presynaptic cell		
	A	B	C
A	1.278943	3.706319	1.975214
B	3.632909	4.055134	3.862882
C	0.659782	4.121144	3.365119

In the simplest case there is no gating

$$f_G(X_{pre}, X_{post}) = const \qquad (20)$$

and the weight decays exponentially all the time. Since spikes are relatively rare events, $X_{pre}X_{post} = 0$ most of the time, and the weight decays to w_0 so fast, that the timing of pre- and postsynaptic spikes has a very small effect on the resulting weights as shown in the respective rows of Table III. The constant in equation (20) was set as $const = 0.04$.

TABLE III
RESULTING WEIGHTS IN THE STUDY OF GATING FUNCTIONS

Postsynaptic cell	Gating	Presynaptic cell		
		A	B	C
A	No Gating	0.499858	0.499484	0.5
	Dual OR	0.424987	0.455724	0.5
	Presynaptic	0.419419	0.455241	*1.975214*
	Postsynaptic	0.568417	0.489494	0.5
	Dual AND	0.763313**	0.301894	*1.975214*
B	No Gating	0.505287	0.499787	0.5
	Dual OR	0.750113	0.423737	0.5
	Presynaptic	1.201898	0.418226	*3.862882*
	Postsynaptic	1.026381	0.569432	0.5
	Dual AND	1.191229*	0.761404**	*3.862882*
C	No Gating	0.5	0.5	0.5
	Dual OR	0.5	0.5	*3.365119*
	Presynaptic	0.5	0.5	*3.365119*
	Postsynaptic	*0.659782*	*4.121144*	*3.365119*
	Dual AND	*0.659782*	*4.121144*	*3.365119*

While the magnitude of the deviation of resulting weights from w_0 is too small to be usable, the sign of this deviation is correct. For the cases when the presynaptic spike follows the postsynaptic spike (A to A, B to B, and B to A) the weights settle to the value below w_0, while for the case A to B when the presynaptic spike precedes the postsynaptic spike, the weight settles to a value greater than w_0.

Assuming that in an attempt to learn the correlation of activities of two cells one can safely ignore intervals when both of the activities are zero, the first gating function studied here is

$$f_G(X_{pre}, X_{post}) = aX_{pre} + bX_{post}^2 \qquad (21)$$

where a and b are positive coefficients, and the square is used to make the second term nonnegative. In this case the decay only happens during the nonzero signal in either the presynaptic or postsynaptic cell. This type of gating is termed *dual OR gating* henceforth. The results for this function with $a = b = 2$ are presented in the respective rows of Table III. Since cell C is silent, there is no change in the strength of its projection to itself ($f_G = 0$ throughout the simulation; weights italicized in the table). A comparison of these results with the results for no gating shows that the deviations of the resulting weights were amplified by more than an order of magnitude, while the pattern of these weights was preserved for active cells.

Presynaptic gating is defined as

$$f_G(X_{pre}, X_{post}) = aX_{pre} \qquad (22)$$

where a is a positive coefficient. The results for this function with $a = 2$ are presented in the respective rows of Table III. Presynaptic gating leads to even better separation of learned weights than dual OR gating. In addition to this, it leaves all projections from a silent cell intact (italicized).

Postsynaptic gating is defined as

$$f_G(X_{pre}, X_{post}) = bX_{post}^2 \qquad (23)$$

where b is a positive coefficient, and the square is used to make the gating nonnegative. The results for this function with $b = 2$ are presented in the respective rows of Table III.

While presynaptic gating prevents modification of the outgoing projections from a silent cell, postsynaptic gating leaves incoming projections to a silent cell intact (italicized). The increase of A to B weight is less prominent than with presynaptic gating, but better than with dual OR gating. Unlike the previous three cases, A to A and B to B projection weights do not decrease below w_0 with the postsynaptic gating, and the B to A weight decreases only slightly below w_0. The reason for these results is investigated in the next section.

Finally, one can restrict the decay even further, and require that it only happens during the learning window, when $X_{pre}X_{post} \neq 0$. This leads to *dual AND gating*:

$$f_G(X_{pre}, X_{post}) = cX_{pre}X_{post}^2 \qquad (24)$$

where c is a positive coefficient, and the square is used to make the gating nonnegative. The results for this function with $c = 10$ are presented in the respective rows of Table III.

This approach is the least intrusive, it only reshapes the pattern of weights when cells on both ends of projection are active. Projections to and from a silent cell don't change (italicized). The only role of decay here is to enforce equation (17). Since the learning is so restricted, it takes longer for the weights to reach their asymptotes than in the previous four cases. One value of the weight (marked with asterisk) reached the asymptote after 1s of the simulation. Values marked with double asterisk reached the asymptote at 5s. Dual AND gating showed the best separation between A to B and B to A weights, but it also inherited from postsynaptic gating and amplified the problem with A to A and B to B projections. Since this problem can stem from the different shapes of STDP curves for these gating functions, the next section compares these curves for all five functions.

VIII. STDP CURVES FOR FIVE GATING FUNCTIONS

STDP curves in this section were built using simulations. In these simulations the time interval between the presynaptic and the postsynaptic spike varied on the interval [-30, 30]ms. Trial setup was the same as in the previous section. Parameters for the X_{post} approximation were: $A = -0.175$ and $C = 0.02$. $B = 0.5$ and $D = -0.5$ were calculated through $\breve{w} = 0$, $\hat{w} = 2$, and $w_0 = 1$. Learning rate was set to $\lambda = 1$; all coefficients in equations (21)-(24) were set to 1. All simulations started with initial weights equal to $w_0 = 1$. Cells in these simulations had axons with 3ms delay, and the timing of the presynaptic spike was recorded at the soma. Since the effects of these spikes only manifested themselves 3ms later, all plots appear shifted to the right. The actual arrival of the presynaptic spike to the axonal terminal is marked in Figure 6 with a vertical pink line.

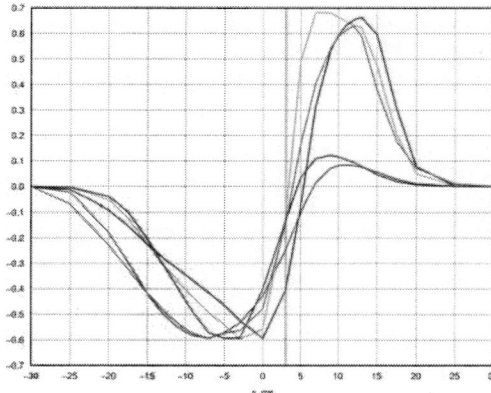

Fig. 6. Comparison of STDP curves for five gating functions. Grey: no gating; blue: dual OR gating; red: presynaptic gating; green: postsynaptic gating; yellow: dual AND gating.

The results are plotted in Figure 6. All STDP curves follow a general trend for the amplitude of weight change shown in the previous section. To compare the relative shapes of these curves on a single plot they were rescaled to an identical peak depression amplitude. It shows that on the depression part of the curve the dual OR gating (blue curve) is the closest in shape to the non-gated learning (gray curve). The postsynaptic, dual AND, and presynaptic gatings are respectively shifting the peak depression further and further towards 0.

On the potentiation part of the curve in Figure 6, postsynaptic gating is the closest resembling the non-gated learning. Dual OR, postsynaptic, and dual AND gatings progressively shift the peak potentiation towards 0. Postsynaptic and dual AND gatings have the two leftmost zero-crossings, which can account for the weights from a cell to itself settling to the values above w_0 as was shown in the previous section.

Additionally, these plots show that postsynaptic gating introduces asymmetry in the learning, where the depression is favored over the potentiation. This asymmetry is also present with dual OR gating, but not with dual AND gating, which suggests that it is caused by the enhanced depression during the time when the postsynaptic signal is present, while the presynaptic signal is absent. Note that relative magnitudes of potentiation and depression can be manipulated through the parameter settings. In the simulations presented here $w_0 - \breve{w} = \hat{w} - w_0$. Setting $7(w_0 - \breve{w}) = \hat{w} - w_0$ will lead to equal magnitudes of potentiation and depression for postsynaptic and dual OR gating, but will favor potentiation over depression for other types of gating.

IX. CONCLUSION

The rule (19) suggested here follows the general requirements for STDP and easily accommodates gating functions used in learning rules for continuous firing rate neuronal representations. We suggest it as a mechanism for instantaneous synaptic weight change, which is simple, reliable and computationally cheap to calculate in spiking neural networks.

ACKNOWLEDGMENTS

AG and MH were supported in part by NIH grants MH60013, MH61492, MH60450, and DA16454. MV was supported in part by AFOSR F49620-01-1-0397 and ONR N00014-01-1-0624.

REFERENCES

[1] D. Hebb, *The Organization of Behavior*. New York, NY: Wiley, 1949.
[2] W. B. Levy and O. Steward, "Temporal contiguity requirements for long-term associative potentiation/depression in the hippocampus," *Neuroscience*, vol. 8, no. 4, pp. 791–797, 1983.
[3] H. Markram, J. Lubke, M. Frotscher, and B. Sakmann, "Regulation of synaptic efficacy by coincidence of postsynaptic APs and EPSPs," *Science*, vol. 275, pp. 213–215, 1997.
[4] G.-q. Bi and M.-m. Poo, "Synaptic modification by correlated activity: Hebb's postulate revisited," *Annu Rev Neurosci*, vol. 24, pp. 139–166, 2001.
[5] W. Gerstner, R. Kempter, J. L. van Hemmen, and H. Wagner, "Hebbian learning of pulse timing in the Barn Owl auditory system," in *Pulsed Neural Networks*, W. Maass and C. M. Bishop, Eds. Cambridge, MA: MIT Press, 1999, ch. 14, pp. 353–377.
[6] S. Song, K. D. Miller, and L. F. Abbott, "Competitive Hebbian learning through spike-timing-dependent synaptic plasticity," *Nature Neurosci*, vol. 3, pp. 919–926, 2000.
[7] A. Kepecs, M. C. W. van Rossum, S. Song, and J. Tegner, "Spike-timing-dependent plasticity: Common themes and divergent vistas," *Biol Cybern*, vol. 87, pp. 446–458, 2002.
[8] B. Porr, A. Saudargiene, and F. Wörgötter, "Analytical solution of spike-timing dependent plasticity based on synaptic biophysics," in *Advances in Neural Information Processing Systems 16*, S. Thrun, L. Saul, and B. Schölkopf, Eds. Cambridge, MA: MIT Press, 2004.
[9] A. Gorchetchnikov and M. E. Hasselmo, "A simple rule for spike-timing-dependent plasticity: Local influence of AHP current," *Neurocomputing*, 2005, (in press).
[10] S. Grossberg, "Classical and instrumental conditioning by neural networks," *Prog Theor Biol*, vol. 3, pp. 51–141, 1974.
[11] ——, "Adaptive pattern classification and universal recoding i: Parallel development and coding of neural feature detectors," *Biol Cybern*, vol. 23, pp. 121–134, 1976.
[12] ——, "Adaptive pattern classification and universal recoding ii: Feedback, expectation, olfaction, and illusions," *Biol Cybern*, vol. 23, pp. 187–202, 1976.
[13] E. Oja, "A simplified neuron model as a principal component analyzer," *J Math Biol*, vol. 15, pp. 267–273, 1982.
[14] A. L. Hodgkin and A. F. Huxley, "Quantitative description of membrane current and its application to conduction and excitation in nerve," *J Physiol*, vol. 117, pp. 500–544, 1952.
[15] S. Grossberg, S. Hwang, and E. Mingolla, "Thalamocortical dynamics of the McCollough effect: Boundary-surface alignment through perceptual learning," *Vision Research*, vol. 42, pp. 1259–1286, 2002.

Differences in the subthreshold dynamics of leaky integrate-and-fire and Hodgkin-Huxley neuron models

Dominic I. Standage and Thomas P. Trappenberg
Faculty of Computer Science
Dalhousie University
Halifax, NS, B3H 1W5, Canada
E-mail: {standage, tt}@cs.dal.ca

Abstract—Many spiking neuron models have been proposed over the last decades with varying computational complexity and abstraction from biological neurons. Among the few studies that have compared spiking models, little emphasis has been given to the formal description of calibration methods in tuning model parameters. We give an example of calibrating a leaky integrate-and-fire neuron with the first-spike time of a Hodgkin-Huxley neuron. We further demonstrate how model parameters can be tuned to minimize subthreshold differences in membrane potential. This example emphasizes the dependencies of calibration methods on other experimental parameters, complicating detailed comparisons of spiking models.

I. INTRODUCTION

Models of spiking neurons are increasingly important to the investigation of spike-time dependent brain mechanisms and the dynamics of cell assemblies. Many spiking models have been proposed, and Izhikevich [1] has recently provided a summary and discussion of a number of these model neurons. Most network investigations use leaky integrate-and-fire (LIF) neurons [2], [3], but little emphasis has been given to their relation to conductance-based models. While many investigations are not crucially dependent on the choice of neuron model, the response of LIF and Hodgkin-Huxley (HH) nodes to stochastic input has been shown to differ [4], and divergent network behaviour has also been mentioned [5].

We investigate sub-threshold differences between standard HH and LIF models. These models are fundamentally different, but there are good reasons why LIF nodes provide a functional approximation of HH nodes and a good description of spike-time dependent information processing in the brain. Prior to the opening of ion channels leading to spike generation, neurons are essentially leaky integrators, and the rapid opening of these channels lends further support to the use of LIF neurons. Additionally, the spike form is stereotypical, so it doesn't contribute to information transmission. The principle task in using LIF nodes, then, is choosing parameters that facilitate particular features of corresponding conductance-based neurons.

One approach to making LIF nodes better approximate conductance-based models is to allow for a dynamic time-scale parameter in the LIF model [6]. Another is to replace their constant threshold with a variable threshold [7]. Here, we keep this scale parameter constant for each trial, adjusting its magnitude for different input signals. We thus tune the time constant of an LIF neuron such that LIF and HH models spike at the same time in response to the same input. We show that this time constant and the time course of the subthreshold dynamic depend on the specific amplitude and waveform of the input stimulus, and that an adjustment to the form of the input stimulus can be used to reduce sub-threshold differences between LIF and HH nodes.

The focus of this paper is to demonstrate that adjustments to model parameters are necessary if spiking models are to be compared. Our simple input types (step and alpha functions) serve to demonstrate the susceptibility of these nodes to changes in input, stressing the need for calibrating conditions in comparative studies.

II. THE MODELS

The baseline model to which we compare the LIF model is the standard Hodgkin-Huxley model given by the four coupled differential equations [8]

$$C\frac{dV}{dt} = -g_K n^4 (V - E_K) - g_{Na} m^3 h (V - E_{Na})$$
$$- g_L (V - E_L) + C I_{\text{ext}}^{\text{HH}}(t) \quad (1)$$
$$\tau_n \frac{dn}{dt} = -[n - n_0(V)] \quad (2)$$
$$\tau_m \frac{dm}{dt} = -[m - m_0(V)] \quad (3)$$
$$\tau_h \frac{dh}{dt} = -[h - h_0(V)], \quad (4)$$

where C is the capacitance of the membrane, $g_i, i \in \{K, Na, L\}$ are conductance parameters for the different ion channels, and E_i are the corresponding equilibrium potentials. The variables n, m, and h describe the opening and closing of the voltage dependent channels. We use the standard parameters derived by Hodgkin and Huxley to simulate the action potential of the giant axon of a squid [8], $g_K = 36, g_{Na} = 120, g_L = 0.3, E_K = -12, E_{Na} = 115, E_L = 10.613$. Note that normalization sets the resting potential of the membrane to 0 ($u_{\text{res}} \approx 0$).

We choose the HH model as an example of a conductance-based model, treating it as the baseline for neuronal behavior. We recognise that the model is an approximation of real neuronal behavior, and that more advanced models have been proposed that include the effects of additional ion channels [9]. Furthermore, the HH model can be simplified, as the voltage dependence of the variables n_0 and m_0 show similar characteristics and can be combined [10], [11], [9].

The HH model is compared to the LIF model, described in three steps

1) Subthreshold leaky integrator:
$$\tau_m \frac{du(t)}{dt} = -u(t) + I_{ext}^{IF}(t). \quad (5)$$

2) Firing Threshold: the firing time t^f is given by a constant delay (t^c) after the potential crosses the firing threshold ϑ:
$$u(t^f - t^c) = \vartheta. \quad (6)$$

3) Refractory time and reset: the membrane potential is reset to a value u_{res} after a fixed absolute refractory time t^R
$$u(t^f - t^c + t^R) = u_{res}. \quad (7)$$

Due to its apparent simplicity, the LIF model is common in computational studies of spiking neurons. Unfortunately, steps 2 and 3 must be coded with conditional statements unless their effect is altered so they may be described with continuous functions in the form of a differential equations. Solving differential eqn. (5) with conditional eqns. (6) and (7) can only be integrated piecewise due to non-differentiable points in the model at $t^f - t^c$ and $t^f - t^c + t^R$. In contrast, ODE solvers can be applied directly to the HH equations. We use numerical solutions for the HH equations and analytical solutions for the subthreshold dynamics eqn. (5) of LIF nodes. Another advantage of the HH model is that parameters may be given physical meaning and assigned measurable values.

III. CALIBRATING CONDITIONS: INPUT SIGNALS AND FIRING TIME

While it is clear that the HH and LIF models are inherently different, we ask how they may be compared. The models have thus to be calibrated so their features are equivalent under equivalent conditions. In this study, we choose parameters in the LIF model such that the time of its first spike matches that of the HH model following sufficient external stimulus. We calibrate the models on their first spikes to provide a simple example of possible calibration methods. Matching the firing times in a spike train provides a more challenging problem.

There is no firing threshold in HH nodes. Their sub-threshold dynamic models that of biological neurons [12] and any perceived threshold is variable. The HH 'firing threshold' then, is not a constant, and depends on sub-threshold dynamics consistent with biological neurons [12]. To match the firing times of HH and LIF nodes, we first approximate a firing threshold for the HH model for step and alpha input (from an initial membrane potential of 0). We apply a series of inputs of decreasing amplitude a_{ext} to the HH node. The maximum value of V elicited by the maximum amplitude of input *in*sufficient to cause a spike is considered the threshold (ϑ^{HH}). For each input type, this approximate threshold is used as the firing threshold of the LIF node in subsequent experiments ($\vartheta^{IF} = \vartheta^{HH}$).

The membrane time constant τ_m must be determined such that in response to the same input, the LIF node crosses the firing threshold at the same time as the HH node. The differential equation for the LIF subthreshold dynamic (eqn. (5)) can be solved analytically for specific input functions. For a step input function with amplitude a_{ext},
$$I_{ext}^{\Theta} = a_{ext}\Theta(t_{on}), \quad (8)$$

this is given by
$$u(t) = u_{res} + a_{ext} * (1 - e^{\frac{-t+t_{on}}{\tau}}). \quad (9)$$

For an alpha function input
$$I_{ext}^{\alpha} = a_{ext}(t - t_{on})e^{\frac{-t}{\tau_\alpha}} \quad (10)$$

this is given by
$$u(t) = u_{res} + \frac{a_{ext}}{\tau}\left((\frac{t^2}{a} - \frac{2t}{a^2} + \frac{2}{a^3})e^{-\frac{t}{\tau_\alpha}} - \frac{2}{a^3}e^{-\frac{t}{\tau}}\right), \quad (11)$$

where
$$a = \frac{1}{\tau} - \frac{1}{\tau_\alpha}. \quad (12)$$

An example of the time course of the membrane potentials of the HH and LIF neurons with these adjustments is shown in Figure 1 for a step function input. The LIF node responds with a stronger initial increase in membrane potential, which is then compensated by a lower rate close to the firing threshold.

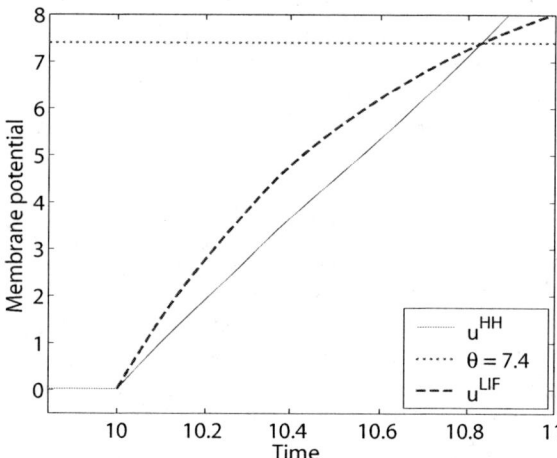

Fig. 1. The evolution of membrane potential in HH (solid line) and LIF (dashed line) model neurons in response to a constant external input $I_{ext} = 10$ applied at $t = 10$ms. The firing threshold is indicated as dotted line.

The difference between the HH and LIF curves depends on details of the models and experimental settings. For step and alpha inputs, Figure 2 shows the maximum difference between these curves for different amplitudes a_{ext}. Increasing a_{ext} reduces the difference between these curves for both input types. Because the shape of the sub-threshold curve is fundamentally different in these models (the LIF curve is convex, shown in Figure 1) reducing this difference becomes increasingly relevant as the potential approaches threshold, where the LIF node is more susceptible to noise due to its convex sub-threshold curve.

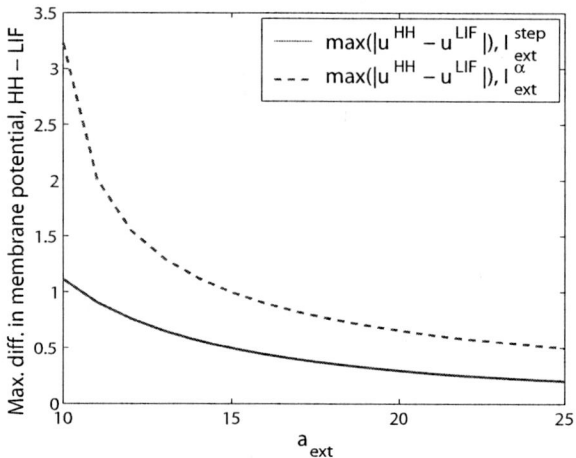

Fig. 2. Maximal difference between the subthreshold membrane potential between the HH and LIF model neurons in response to increasing amplitude of step input (solid line) and alpha function input (dashed line).

IV. REDUCING SUB-THRESHOLD DIFFERENCES BY ADJUSTMENTS TO INPUT

We have so far assumed that the form and amplitude of the input signals driving the different models should be the same for each model, but this need not be the case. One approach to finding a better correspondence between LIF and HH nodes is to modify the input each model receives. The difference curve for the membrane potential of the HH and LIF models when driven by a step function is shown in Figure 3a with a solid line. The dashed line shows the difference between the HH and LIF models if the amplitude of the LIF input is increased,

$$a_{\text{ext}}^{\text{IF}} = 10 * a_{\text{ext}}^{\text{HH}}, \qquad (13)$$

followed by recalculation of τ. This simple adjustment reduces the difference between models. Similar results can be achieved by adjusting the amplitude of the alpha function (Figure 3b.).

The difference between the models' subthreshold dynamics may be further adjusted by a time-dependent alteration to the input signal to the LIF node, or a transformation $I_{\text{ext}}^{\text{IF}} = F(I_{\text{ext}}^{\text{HH}})$ may exist to further minimize differences. This adjusted input function mimics the slower response of the HH nodes (due to the opening dynamics of the channels) by a time-delayed LIF input stimulus. Such an approach is similar to that of Stevens and Zador [6].

We adjust the membrane time constant as necessary to match the spike time of the HH neuron, therefore changing

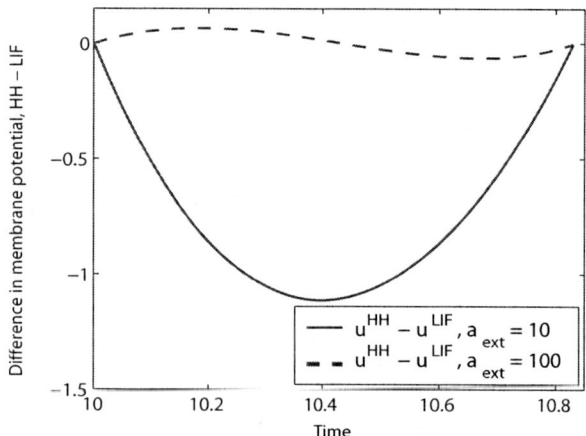
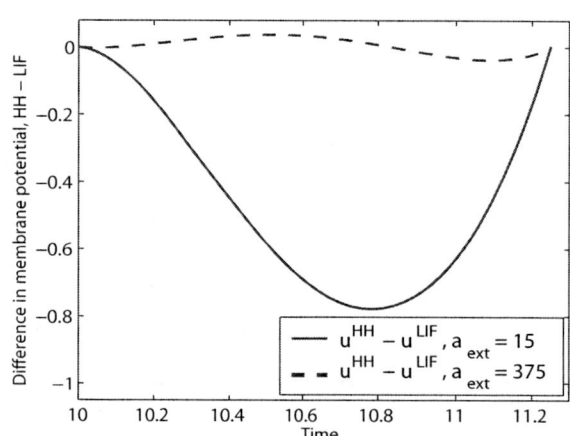

Fig. 3. Difference between the subthreshold membrane potential of HH and LIF models in response to (a) step-function input and (b) alpha function input. Solid lines are under the condition $a_{\text{ext}}^{\text{IF}} = a_{\text{ext}}^{\text{HH}}$. Dashed lines correspond to (a) $a_{\text{ext}}^{\text{IF}} = 10 * a_{\text{ext}}^{\text{HH}}$ and (b) $a_{\text{ext}}^{\text{IF}} = 25 * a_{\text{ext}}^{\text{HH}}$.

this constant for the different curves shown in Figure 3. For example, the time constant for the solid line in Figure 3a is $\tau = 0.62$, whereas $\tau = 10.84$ in the adjusted case (dashed line in Figure 3a). Similarly, in the case of the unadjusted alpha function in Figure 3b, $\tau = 0.6$, whereas $\tau = 28.32$ in the adjusted case (dashed line in Figure 3b). These adjustments serve to further demonstrate that the time constant of the LIF neuron should not be treated as the membrane time scale parameter of a biophysical neuron. Note that we still keep the time parameter constant within each trial and do not consider varying time scale parameters such as in [6].

V. Discussion and Conclusions

When comparing different models, care must be given to the specification of calibrating conditions such as the adjustment of spike times. Here we discuss only a noise-free case, but the curves in Figure 1 demonstrate that noise may influence LIF nodes more than HH nodes due to a larger buildup of potential for longer periods close to threshold. Adjustments to noise models must therefor be considered with the use of these nodes.

Differences between HH and LIF models can be minimized by transformations in their driving signals. Unfortunately, such transformations are dependent on the signals themselves. It is unknown whether a general methodology for the specification of such transformations can be found.

We have only discussed the subthreshold response for the first spike in the HH and LIF models. Further issues need consideration when comparing spike trains in different models, such as differences in refractory periods. The LIF model discussed here has an absolute refractory time, while the HH model includes a more precise approximation of the hyperpolarization dynamics. This difference further highlights the necessity of carefully chosen parameters in comparison-based studies.

Comparative studies of neuron models are important to verify that perceived discrepancies between models do not depend on un-tuned parameters, where tuning depends on the specific simulations or network behaviour under study. Comparative studies must therefor specify the methods of calibration used to create an adequate baseline for comparison. If the use of different neuron models leads to divergent experimental results following careful tuning of model parameters, further study should focus on appropriate use of models at various levels of abstraction, and on the calibration of neuron simulations under relevant experimental conditions. In this study, we compare a relatively simple conductance-based model with the LIF neuron. If LIF nodes are insufficient to reproduce network effects found with conductance models, then a mechanistic account of the phenomena under study may be found in the detail of the conductance model.

Acknowledgment

This work was supported by the NSERC grant RGPIN 249885-03.

References

[1] I. E.M., "Which model to use for cortical spiking neurons?" *IEEE Transactions on Neural Networks*, vol. 15, pp. 1063–1070, 2004.

[2] R. B. Stein, "The information capacity of nerve cells using a frequency code," *Biophysics Journal*, vol. 7, pp. 797–826, 1967.

[3] H. C. Tuckwell, *Introduction to theoretical neurobiology*. Cambridge University Press, 1988.

[4] J. Feng and G. Li, "Integrate-and-fire and hodgkin-huxley models with current inputs," *Journal of Physics A: Mathematical and General*, vol. 34, no. 8, pp. 1649–1664, 2001.

[5] X. Wang, "Personal correspondence," 2004.

[6] C. F. Stevens and A. M. Zador, "Novel integrate-and-fire-like model of repetitive firing in cortical neurons," in *Proceedings of 5th Joint Symposium of Neural Computation*, 1998. [Online]. Available: citeseer.ist.psu.edu/256574.html

[7] W. M. Kistler, W. Gerstner, and J. L. van Hemmen, "Reduction of hodgkin-huxley equations to a single-variable threshold model," *Neural Computation*, vol. 9, pp. 1015–1045, 1997.

[8] A. L. Hodgkin and A. F. Huxley, "A quantitative description of membrane current and its application to conduction and excitation in nerve." *Journal of Physiology*, vol. 117, pp. 500–544, 1952.

[9] H. R. Wilson, "Simplified dynamics of human and mammalian neocortical neurons," *J. theor. Biol.*, vol. 200, pp. 375–388, 1999.

[10] R. FitzHugh, "Impulses and physiological states in theoretical models of nerve membranes," *Biophysics Journal*, vol. 1, pp. 445–466, 1961.

[11] J. S. Nagumo, S. Arimoto, and S. Yoshizawa, "An active pulse transmission line simulating nerve axon," in *Proceedings IRE*, vol. 50, 1962, pp. 2061–2070.

[12] R. Azouz and C. M. Gray, "Dynamic spike threshold reveals a mechanism for synaptic coincidence detection in cortical neurons in vivo," in *Proc. Natl. Acad. Sci*, vol. 97, 2000, pp. 8110–8115.

Rich phenomena of pulse-coupled spiking neurons with triangular waveform input

Toshimichi Saito
Department of EECS
Hosei University
Tokyo, 184-8584 Japan
E-mail: tsaito@k.hosei.ac.jp

Yoshio Kon'no
Department of EECS
Hosei University
Tokyo, 184-8584 Japan
E-mail: conno@nonlinear.k.hosei.ac.jp

Hiroyuki Torikai
Department of EECS
Hosei University
Tokyo, 184-8584 Japan
E-mail: torikai@k.hosei.ac.jo

Abstract— This paper studies a spiking neuron circuit with a periodic triangular base signal. The circuit can output rich pulse-trains and the dynamics can be analyzed exploiting a piecewise linear one-dimensional pulse position map. Using two neurons we construct a pulse-coupled system whose dynamics can be integrated into the composite map of the pulse position maps of two neurons. The composite map is piecewise linear and we can analyze rich phenomena precisely. For example, periodic behavior of each neuron is changed into chaotic behavior and chaotic behavior of each neuron is changed into periodic behavior. These results provide basic information to construct flexible pulse-coupled neural networks.

I. INTRODUCTION

The spiking neuron circuit (ab. SNC) is known as a simple artificial neuron model having interesting dynamics [1] - [6]. The SNC has a periodic base signal and the state variable repeats integrate-and-fire behaviors between the threshold and base levels. Depending on the shape of the base the SNC can output rich periodic/nonperiodic pulse-trains. Using plural SNCs we can construct pulse-coupled networks (ab. PCNNs). The networks can exhibit rich synchronous/asynchronous phenomena that have been utilized for applications including dynamic associative memory, image segmentation and pulse-based communications [3] [5] [7] - [9]. However in the study of such spiking systems analysis of nonlinear phenomena is not sufficient.

This paper presents a SNC with a triangular base signal. The dynamics of SNC can be analyzed using one-dimensional pulse position map. Since the base signal is piecewise linear the map is also piecewise linear and precise analysis of rich pulse-trains is possible. We then construct a pulse-coupled system of two SNCs (ab. PCSNC). The pulse-coupling is realized by interaction of firings and the dynamics can be integrated into the composite map of the pulse position maps of the two SNCs. The composite map is also piecewise linear. For example, we can confirm interesting phenomena such that periodic behavior of each SNC is changed into chaotic behavior and chaotic behavior of each SNC is changed into periodic behavior. It should be noted that Ref. [6] presents such pulse-coupled method, however, the base is sinusoidal, the map is not piecewise linear and chaotic behavior has not been analyzed.

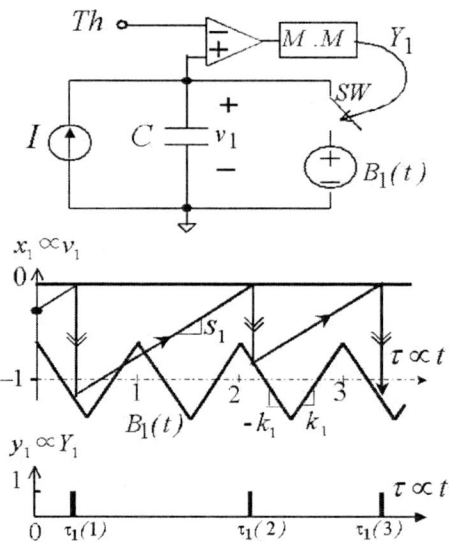

Fig. 1. Single spiking circuit with triangular inputs and basic dynamics

The motivations for studying the PCSNC include the following two points. First, the analysis of rich pulse-trains is important as a fundamental study. It is an interesting problems to explore how rich pulse-trains can be generated by interactions of firings of each SNC. Although there exist many interesting results on pulse-coupled systems, we can not find analysis based on composite pulse-position maps except for our works. Second, our simple pulse-coupling method is fundamental to construct PCNNs. It should be noted that our pulse-coupling method is different from usual smooth coupling method [10] but can generate rich pulse-train dynamics. Our results may be developed into a novel PCNN with flexible functions.

II. SINGLE SPIKING NEURON

As preparations we introduce dynamics of the spiking neuron circuit (ab. SNC [1] - [5]). As shown in Fig.1 the SNC has a base signal $B_1(t)$ that is a triangular shape with period T. The capacitor voltage v_1 is increased to Th by integrating positive current I. If v_1 reaches threshold Th, the SNC outputs the firing-pulse Y_1 that closes the switch SW_1 and v_1 is rest to the base $B_1(t)$. Referring to Ref. [5], the circuit operation is assumed to be ideal for simplicity: we omit inner resistors of the sources and the reset of v_1 is instantaneous without delay. Repeating in this manners, the SNC generates a pulse-train. The SNC dynamics is described by Equation(1).

$$\begin{cases} C\frac{dv_1(t)}{dt} = I & \text{and} \quad Y_1(t) = -E \quad \text{for} \quad v_1(t) < Th \\ v_1(t^+) = B_1(t^+) & \text{and} \quad Y_1(t^+) = E \quad \text{if} \quad v_1(t) \geq Th \end{cases}$$

$$B_1(t) = \begin{cases} -K_1(t - \frac{1}{4}T) - V_D & 0 \leq t < \frac{1}{2}T \\ K_1(t - \frac{3}{4}T) - V_D & \frac{1}{2}T \leq t < 1T \end{cases}$$

$$B_1(t + T) = B_1(t) \tag{1}$$

Using dimensionless variables and parameters

$$\tau = \frac{t}{T}, \quad x_1 = \frac{v_1 - Th}{Th + V_D}, \quad \dot{x}_1 = \frac{d}{d\tau}x_1, \quad y_1 = \frac{Y_1 + E}{2E}$$
$$k_1 = \frac{K_1 T}{Th + V_D}, \quad |k_1| < 4, \quad s_1 = \frac{IT}{C(Th + V_D)} > 0 \tag{2}$$

Equation (1) is transformed into Equation (3).

$$\begin{cases} \dot{x}_1 = s_1 & \text{and} \quad y_1(\tau) = 0 \quad \text{for} \quad x_1 < 0 \\ x_1(\tau^+) = b_1(\tau^+) & \text{and} \quad y_1(\tau^+) = 1 \quad \text{if} \quad x_1 \geq 0 \end{cases}$$

$$b_1(\tau) = \begin{cases} -k_1(\tau - \frac{1}{4}) - 1 & 0 \leq \tau < \frac{1}{2} \\ k_1(\tau - \frac{3}{4}) - 1 & \frac{1}{2} \leq t < 1 \end{cases}$$

$$b_1(\tau + 1) = b_1(\tau) \tag{3}$$

This normalized equation is characterized by two positive parameters s_1 and k_1 correspond to slope of integrating waveform of v_1 and amplitude of base signal $B_1(t)$, respectively.

As shown in Fig.1 let $\tau_1(n)$ denote the n-th pulse-position. The pulse-train is governed by the pulse-position map f_1 from positive reals to itself (see Fig.2).

$$\tau_1(n+1) = f_1(\tau_1(n)) \equiv \tau_1(n) - \frac{1}{s_1}b_1(\tau_1(n)). \tag{4}$$

Since $f_1(\tau + 1) = f_1(\tau) + 1$ we can define a return map F_1 from $I \equiv [0, 1)$ to itself.

$$\theta_1(n+1) = F_1(\theta_1(n)) \equiv f_1(\theta_1(n)) \pmod 1$$
$$= \begin{cases} (1 + \frac{k_1}{s_1})\theta_1(n) + \frac{1}{s_1}(1 - \frac{k_1}{4}) & 0 \leq \theta_1(n) < \frac{1}{2} \\ (1 - \frac{k_1}{s_1})\theta_1(n) + \frac{1}{s_1}(1 + \frac{3k_1}{4}) & \frac{1}{2} \leq \theta_1(n) < 1 \end{cases} \tag{5}$$

where $\theta_1(n)$ is the decimal part of the n-th pulse position: $\theta_1(n) \equiv \tau_1(n)$ modulus 1. The dynamics of the SNC is integrated into the pulse-position map and the return map. It should be noted that varying the shape of the base signal can realize various shapes of the maps [2]. Since the maps are piecewise linear we can analyze the dynamics precisely. Fig.3 shows typical return maps and bifurcating diagram. Because of triangular shape of the base signal the map has two kinds of slopes: $(1 + \frac{k_1}{s_1})$ for $0 \leq \theta_1(n) < \frac{1}{2}$ and $(1 - \frac{k_1}{s_1})$ for $\frac{1}{2} \leq \theta_1(n) < 1$. We then notice the following characteristics of the maps.

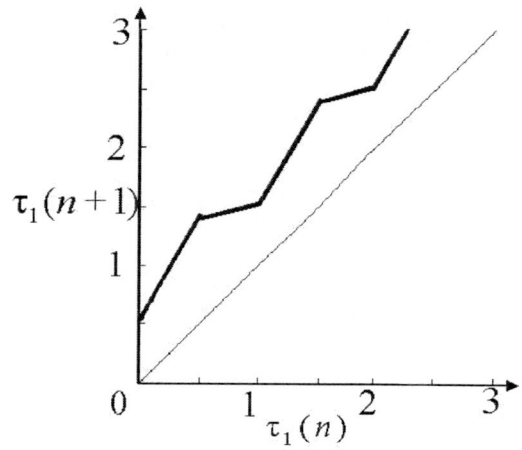

Fig. 2. Pulse position map of SNC ($s_1 = 1.4$, $k_1 = 1.1$)

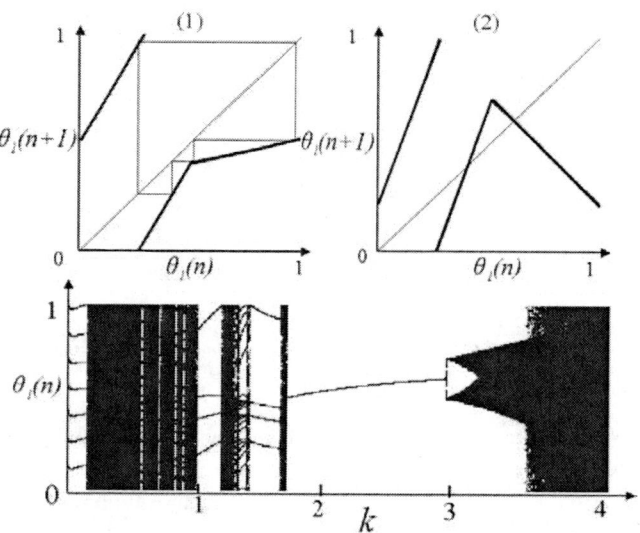

Fig. 3. Typical return maps and bifurcating phenomena ($s_1 = 1.4$). (1) $k_1 = 1.1$, (2) $k_1 = 2.75$.

- If $k_1 < s_1$, the pulse-position map f_1 is monotone increasing and the return map F_1 is onto and one-to-one. The return map is equivalent to the circle map having rich periodic and quai-periodic behavior [11].
- If $s_1 = k_1$, f_1 (and F_1) have segments with slope zero. It can cause superstable behavior.
- $s_1 > k_1$, f_1 (and F_1) can have negative slopes and extrema.

III. PULSE-COUPLED SPIKING NEURONS

In this section we present the pulse-coupled spiking neuron circuits (ab. PCSNC) and derive the composite pulse-position map. As shown in Fig.4 we prepare the first and second spiking neurons (ab. SNC1 and SNC2). If the pulse-coupling is not present SNC1 and SNC2 are described by Equation (3) with subscripts 1 and 2, respectively. In the PCSNC, the self-switching of each neuron is changed into the cross-switching for the pulse-coupling: if v_1 reaches the threshold Th then

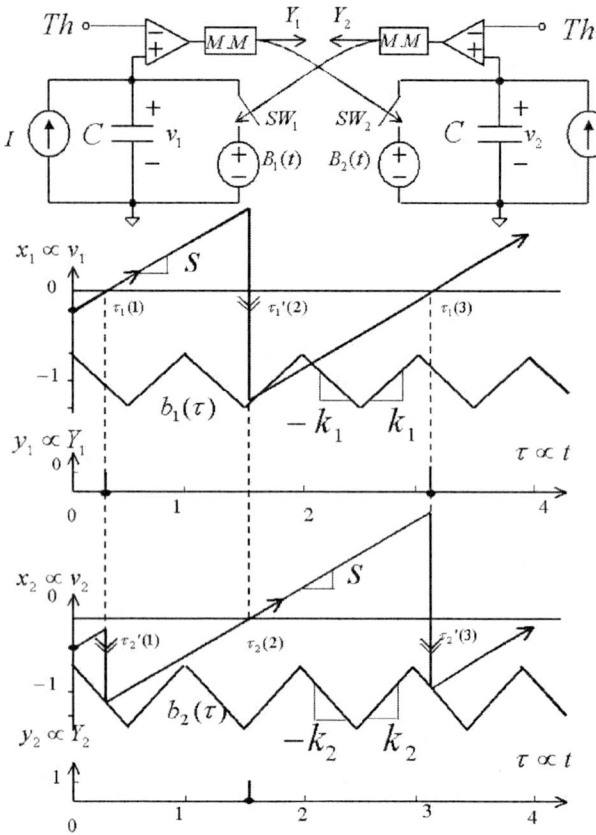

Fig. 4. Pulse-coupled spiking neuron circuits and basic dynamics

SNC1 outputs a firing pulse Y_1 that resets v_2 to the base $B_2(t)$ and vice versa. Using dimensionless parameters and variables in Equation (2) with subscripts 1 and 2, the dynamics of the PCSNC is described by

$$\begin{aligned}
&\dot{x}_1 = s_1 \text{ and } y_1(\tau) = 0 && \text{for } x_2 < 0 \\
&x_1(\tau^+) = b_1(\tau^+) \text{ and } y_2(\tau^+) = 1 && \text{if } x_2(\tau) = 0 \\
&\dot{x}_2 = s_2 \text{ and } y_2(\tau) = 0 && \text{for } x_1 < 0 \\
&x_2(\tau^+) = b_2(\tau^+) \text{ and } y_1(\tau^+) = 1 && \text{if } x_1(\tau) = 0
\end{aligned}$$

$$b_1(\tau) = \begin{cases} -k_1(\tau - \frac{1}{4}) - 1 & \text{for } 0 \leq \tau < \frac{1}{2} \\ k_1(\tau - \frac{3}{4}) - 1 & \text{for } \frac{1}{2} \leq \tau < 1 \end{cases}$$
$$b_2(\tau) = \begin{cases} -k_2(\tau - \frac{1}{4}) - 1 & \text{for } 0 \leq \tau < \frac{1}{2} \\ k_2(\tau - \frac{3}{4}) - 1 & \text{for } \frac{1}{2} \leq \tau < 1 \end{cases} \quad (6)$$

It should be noted that Equation(6) has four parameters (s_1, s_2, k_1, k_2). For simplicity let $s_1 = s_2 \equiv s$ in this paper: the PCSNC is characterized by three parameters s, k_1 and k_2. Fig. 4 illustrates switching dynamics for $x_1(0) > x_2(0)$. Exchanging subscripts gives the case $x_1(0) < x_2(0)$. At time $\tau_1(1) = \tau_2'(1) = -x_1(0)$, x_1 reaches the threshold 0 and SNC1 outputs a pulse $y_1 = 1$ that resets x_2 to the base $b_2(\tau)$. Next x_2 increases from $b_2(\tau)$ and x_1 increases from 0. At time $\tau_1'(2) = \tau_2(2)$, x_2 reaches 0 and SNC2 outputs a pulse $y_2 = 1$ that resets x_1 to the base $b_1(\tau)$. $\tau_2(2)$ is given by the pulse position map of SNC2: $\tau_2(2) = f_2(\tau_1(1))$. Next x_1 increases from $b_1(\tau)$ and x_2 increases from 0. At time $\tau_1(3) = \tau_2'(3)$, x_1 reaches 0 and SNC1 outputs a pulse $y_1 = 1$ that resets x_2 to the base $b_2(\tau)$. $\tau_1(3)$ is given by the pulse position map of SNC1: $\tau_1(3) = f_1(\tau_2(2))$. We refer to the time $\tau_1(n) = \tau_2'(n)$ as n-th pulse position (or zero-crossing moment) for SNC1 and n-th firing moment for SNC2. Similar definition is possible for $\tau_2(m) = \tau_1'(m)$. That is, each neuron repeats zero-crossing and firing alternatively and the pulse-trains are determined by the following iterations.

$$\begin{cases} \tau_2(n+1) = f_2(\tau_2'(n)) \\ \tau_2'(n) = \tau_1(n) \end{cases} \text{for odd } n$$
$$\begin{cases} \tau_1(n+1) = f_1(\tau_1'(n)) \\ \tau_1'(n) = \tau_2(n) \end{cases} \text{for even } n \quad (7)$$

where the discrete time n represents the n-th zero-crossing of either SNC1 or SNC2. Noting Equation (7), we obtain the following description.

$$\begin{aligned}
\tau_1(n+2) &= f_1 \circ f_2(\tau_1(n)), \quad \text{for odd } n \\
\tau_2(n+2) &= f_2 \circ f_1(\tau_2(n)), \quad \text{for even } n.
\end{aligned} \quad (8)$$

where $f_1 \circ f_2$ denotes the composite map of f_2 and f_1. We can also define the return map:

$$\begin{aligned}
\theta_1(n+2) &= F_1 \circ F_2(\theta_1(n)) \quad \text{for positive odd } n \\
\theta_2(n+2) &= F_2 \circ F_1(\theta_2(n)) \quad \text{for positive even } n \quad (9) \\
F_1(\theta) &= f_1(\theta) \mod 1 \qquad F_2(\theta) = f_2(\theta) \mod 1
\end{aligned}$$

That is, pulse-trains of PCSNC are governed by composition of pulse-position maps (and return maps) of the two SNCs. Hereafter we focus on $f_1 \circ f_2$ ($F_1 \circ F_2$) because $f_2 \circ f_1$ ($F_2 \circ F_1$) gives equivalent dynamics. Using the composite maps, we can analyze bifurcation phenomena of PCSNC as well as SNC. We emphasize again that the composite maps are piecewise linear and precise analysis is possible. The composite return map has at most four kinds of slopes.

Fig. 5 shows typical composite return maps with original return maps of each SNC1 and SNC2 where we can see interesting phenomena caused by the pulse-coupling.

Fig.5 (a) shows that two periodic behavior in return maps (the same as Fig.3(1) and (2)) are changed into chaotic behavior in composite return map: periodic pulse-train of each neuron is changed into chaotic pulse-train by the pulse-coupling.

Fig.5 (b) shows that periodic and chaotic pulse-trains are changed into another periodic pulse-trains by the pulse-coupling.

Fig.5 (c) shows that periodic and chaotic pulse-trains are changed into superstable periodic pulse-trains caused by zero-slope of the composite return map. Such zero-slope is possible for $s = k_1$ and/or $s = k_2$ and is impossible in the case of sinusoidal base signal in [6].

Fig.5 (d) shows that chaotic pulse-train of each neuron is changed into periodic pulse-train by the pulse-coupling.

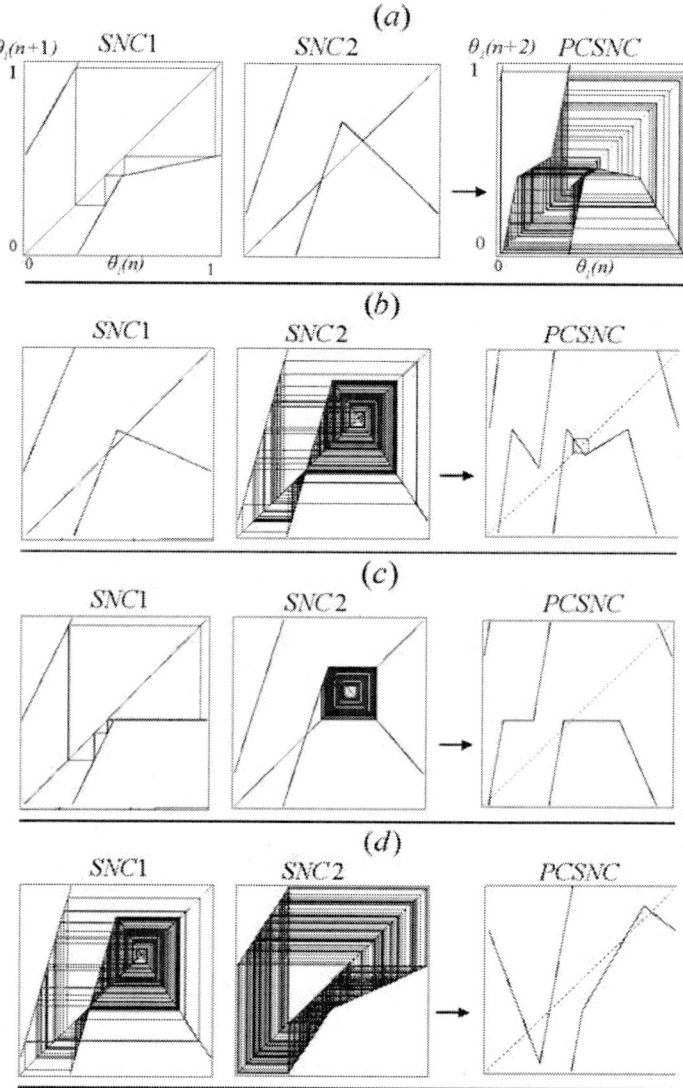

Fig. 5. Typical composite return maps and return maps of neurons ($s = 1.4$). (a)$k_1 = 1.1, k_2 = 2.75$, (b)$k_1 = 2.0, k_2 = 3.5$, (c)$k_1 = 1.4, k_2 = 3.0$, (d)$k_1 = 3.8, k_2 = 0.75$.

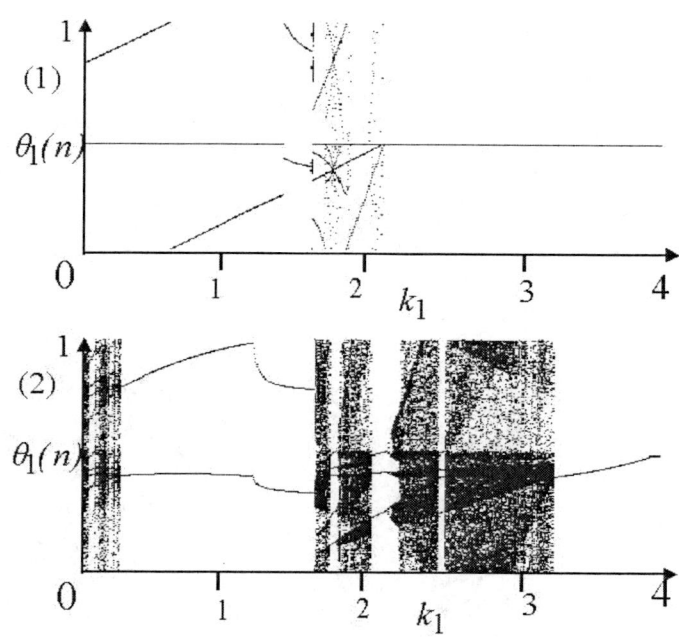

Fig. 6. Typical bifurcating phenomena for $s = 1.4$. (1) $k_2 = 1.4 = s$, (2) $k_2 = 1.1$)

Represented by these phenomena, the PCSNC can generate rich periodic/chaotic pulse-trains. Fig. 6 (1) shows bifurcation diagram of superstable periodic pulse-trains including Fig.5 (c) right: the return map has zero-slope for $s = k_2$ and all the pulse-trains are superstable. Fig. 6 (2) shows bifurcation diagram relating to chaotic pulse-train in Fig.5 (a) right. It should be noted that we have confirmed only local stability for the phenomena and there may be co-existing periodic/chaotic phenomena depending on initial condition.

Fig. 7 shows the distribution diagram of periods on k_1-k_2 plane. The period is defined by the return map $F \equiv F_1 \circ F_2$: a point θ_p is said to be a periodic point with period p if $\theta_p = F^p(\theta_p)$ and $\theta_p \neq F^k(\theta_p)$ for $0 < k < p$ where F_p denotes the p-fold composition of F. In the figure the tone is to be dark as the period increases: complicated pulse-trains are generated in the black region. The line $k_1 = k_2$ in this diagram corresponds to bifurcating phenomena of single SNC: difference from this line means difference between single SNC and PCSNC. Although this diagram is calculated by brute force, the results suggest rich and interesting behavior caused by the pulse-coupling.

IV. CONCLUSIONS

We have studied rich dynamics of a spiking neuron and its pulse-coupled system. Using the pulse-position map and its composite map, rich pulse-train dynamics has been analyzed. Especially, interesting change between chaotic and periodic pulse-trains has been confirmed. Future problems include analysis of rich bifurcation phenomena and development of an efficient PCNN with practical applications.

REFERENCES

[1] L. Glass and M. C. Mackey, A simple model for phase locking of biological-oscillators, J. Math. Biology, vol. 7, pp.339-352, 1979.
[2] H. Torikai and T. Saito, Return map quantization from an Integrate-and-Fire Model with two periodic inputs, IEICE Trans. Fund. E82-A, no. 7, pp.1336-1343, 1999.
[3] G. Lee and N. H. Farhat, The bifurcating neuron network 2, Neural networks, vol. 15, pp.69-84, 2002.
[4] H. Torikai, M. Shimazaki and T. Saito, Master-slave synchronization of pulse-coupled bifurcating neurons, IEICE Trans. Fundamentals, E86-A, no. 3, pp. 740-747, 2004.
[5] H. Torikai and T. Saito, Synchronization phenomena in pulse-coupled networks driven by spike-train inputs, IEEE Trans. Neural Networks, vol. 15, no. 2, pp. 337-347, 2004.
[6] H. Hamanaka, H. Torikai and T. Saito, Analysis of composite dynamics of two bifurcating neurons, IEICE Trans. Fundamentals, E88-A, no. 2, pp. 561-567, 2005
[7] S. R. Campbell, D.L.Wang and C.Jayaprakash, Synchrony and desynchrony in integrate-and-fire oscillators, Neural computation, vol.11, pp.1595-1619, 1999.

[8] E.M. Izhikevich, Weakly Pulse-coupled oscillators, FM Interactions, Synchronization, and oscillatory associative memory, IEEE Trans. Neural Networks, vol.10, no.3, 508-526, 1999.

[9] G.M.Maggio, N.Rulkov and L.Reggiani, Pseudo-chaotic time hopping for UWB impulse radio, IEEE Trans. Circuits Syst. I, vol.48, no.12, pp.1424-1435, 2001.

[10] L. O. Chua and L. Yang, Cellular neural networks: Theory, IEEE Trans.Circuits Syst., vol. 35, no. 10, pp. 1257-1272, 1988.

[11] H.Torikai and T.Saito, Resonance phenomena of interspike intervals from a spiking oscillator with two periodic inputs, IEEE Trans. Circuit Syst. I, vol. 48, no. 10, pp.1198-1204, 2001.

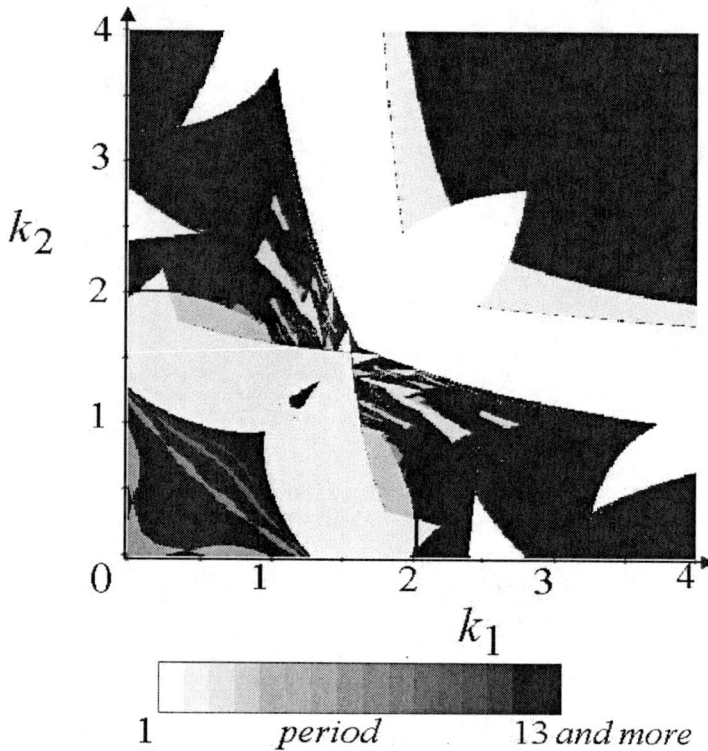

Fig. 7. The distribution diagram of period of pulse-trains on $k_1 - k_2$ plane ($s = 1.4$)

Synchronized Theta Rhythm Selection in a Dentate Gyrus Network Model

Katsumi Tateno, Hatsuo Hayashi and Satoru Ishizuka
Department of Brain Science and Engineering
Graduate School of Life Science and Systems Engineering
Kyushu Institute of Technology
Kitakyushu, Japan 808-0196
E-mail: {tateno, hayashi, ishizuka}@brain.kyutech.ac.jp

Abstract—The dentate gyrus network model shown here filtered a specific frequency of the periodic synaptic input through the perforant path. The filtering properties were modified by the degree of synchronization of the periodic perforant path input. The random synaptic input through the perforant path also contributed to the modification of the filtering properties. When the random synaptic input of the perforant path was delivered to several granule cells, adequately synchronized periodic perforant path input led to properties of a band-pass filter in the dentate gyrus network model. The bandwidth of the band-pass filter was 2 - 5 Hz. Without the random synaptic input, the dentate gyrus network model showed a property of a low-pass filter.

I. INTRODUCTION

The dentate gyrus has been found to work as a filter for theta rhythm in *in vivo* experiments [1]. We have also reported a property of a band-pass filter for theta rhythm in the dentate gyrus using *in vitro* hippocampal slice preparations [2]. The periodic perforant path stimulation induces high amplitude of population spikes in the frequency range between 5 Hz and 10 Hz. This frequency range corresponds to the frequency range of the theta rhythm.

In our previous paper [2], we proposed a fundamental dentate gyrus network model including mossy cells in a hilar region. A random synaptic input to mossy cells contributes to determine filtering properties of the dentate gyrus network model. The fundamental network model of the dentate gyrus accounts for mechanisms of the theta rhythm selection.

The dentate gyrus receives synaptic input from the entorhinal cortex. The layer II of the entorhinal cortex potentially works as an independent pacemaker [3]. Rhythmic neurons are found in the layer II [4]. Firing of the rhythmic neurons is locked on a certain phase of theta rhythm. Non-rhythmic neurons are also found during theta rhythm in the entorhinal cortex [4]. The non-rhythmic neurons have a Poisson-like interval histogram. Those regular and irregular activities are sent to mossy cells through granule cells. We hypothesize that a change in the balance between rhythmic and non-rhythmic neural activities in the entorhinal cortex may modify responses of the dentate gyrus. In the present study, we assumed that the dentate gyrus network model received synchronized periodic input and random synaptic input from outside of the network, such as the entorhinal cortex. As a result, the present dentate gyrus network model exhibited the theta rhythm selection. The theta rhythm selection depended on the degree of synchronization of the periodic synaptic input through the perforant path.

II. METHODS

1) Dentate Gyrus Network Model: The dentate gyrus network model consisted of 9 granule cells, 9 basket cells, and 3 mossy cells (Fig.1). Each granule cell received the inhibitory synaptic input from a basket cell and the excitatory synaptic input from two mossy cells. Each basket cell received the excitatory synaptic input from a granule cell and two mossy cells. Each mossy cell received the excitatory synaptic input from two granule cells. The granule cells and the basket cells received the excitatory synaptic input from the perforant path.

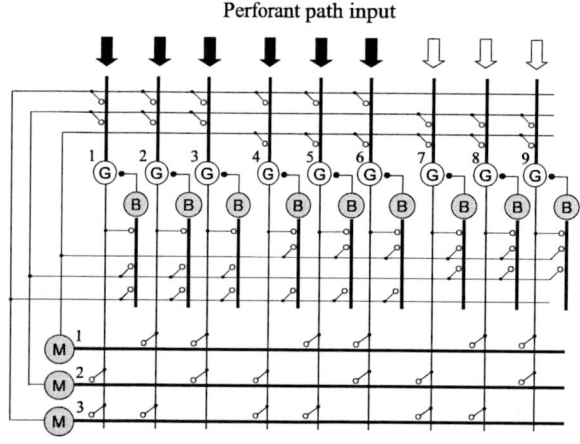

Fig. 1. The dentate gyrus network model. G: granule cell, B: basket cell, M: mossy cell. Several granule cells and basket cells received the synchronized periodic input through the perforant path (black arrows). Several other granule cells received the random synaptic input (white arrows).

The granule cell model introduced here has been proposed by Yuen and Durand [5]. Minor modifications have been done in our previous paper [2]. The granule cell model consisted of one soma compartment and 12 dendritic compartments. The voltage-gated ionic channels were concentrated at the soma compartment. The dendritic compartments had a leak channel.

The soma compartment is given below:

$$C_m \frac{dV}{dt} = \bar{g}_{Na}m^3h(E_{Na} - V) + \bar{g}_K n^4(E_K - V)$$
$$+ \bar{g}_{Ca}e^2(E_{Ca} - V) + \bar{g}_{K-AHP}q^2(E_K - V)$$
$$+ g_l(E_l - V) \quad (1)$$

$$\frac{d[Ca^{2+}]}{dt} = -\frac{[Ca^{2+}]_i - [Ca^{2+}]_{i0}}{\tau} - \frac{I_{Ca}}{w \cdot z \cdot F} \quad (2)$$

where w is the shell thickness (w=0.2 μm), z is the valence of Ca^{2+}, F is the Faraday constant. The Ca^{2+} removal rate τ was 9 ms. The variable q depends on $[Ca^{2+}]_i$. $\bar{g}_{Na}$ = 250 mS/cm^2, $\bar{g}_K$ = 40 mS/cm^2, $\bar{g}_{Ca}$ = 1 mS/cm^2, $\bar{g}_{K-AHP}$ = 4.7 mS/cm^2, $\bar{g}_l$ = 0.025 mS/cm^2. E_{Na} = 45 mV. E_K = -85 mV. E_{Ca} = 70 mV. E_l = -67.46 mV. C_m = 3.4 μF/cm^2. For the dendritic compartment, g_l = 0.04 mS/cm^2.

We used Traub's basket cell model [6] as an inhibitory interneuron. The ion channels g_{Na} and g_K were concentrated at the soma compartment. The dendritic compartments consisted of a leak channel. The soma compartment is given below:

$$C_m \frac{dV}{dt} = \bar{g}_{Na}m^3h(E_{Na} - V) + \bar{g}_K n^4(E_K - V)$$
$$+ g_l(E_l - V) \quad (3)$$

where $\bar{g}_{Na}$ = 500 mS/cm^2, $\bar{g}_K$ = 250 mS/cm^2, $\bar{g}_l$ = 0.1 mS/cm^2. E_{Na} = 45 mV, E_K = -95 mV, E_l = -70 mV. C_m = 1 μF/cm^2. The leak conductance $\bar{g}_l$ of the dendritic compartment was 0.1 mS/cm^2.

The mossy cell model consisted of one soma compartment and one dendritic compartment. The soma compartment had g_{Na}, g_K, and g_h. The dendritic compartment had g_{Ca}, g_{K-C}, and g_{K-AHP}. The equations of the mossy cell model are given below:

$$C_m \frac{dV}{dt} = \bar{g}_{Na}m^2h(E_{Na} - V_s) + \bar{g}_K n(E_K - V_s)$$
$$+ \bar{g}_h a(E_h - V_s) + g_{ls}(E_l - V_s) \quad (4)$$

$$C_m \frac{dV}{dt} = \bar{g}_{Ca}s^2(E_{Ca} - V_d)$$
$$+ \bar{g}_{K-C} \cdot c \cdot \min(\frac{[Ca^{2+}]_i}{250}, 1) \cdot (E_K - V_d)$$
$$+ \bar{g}_{K-AHP}q(E_K - V_d) + g_{ld}(E_l - V_d) \quad (5)$$

$$\frac{d[Ca^{2+}]_i}{dt} = -\beta \cdot [Ca^{2+}]_i - \phi \cdot I_{Ca} \quad (6)$$

where β = 0.075 ms^{-1} and ϕ = 130. $\bar{g}_{Na}$ = 30 mS/cm^2, $\bar{g}_K$ = 15 mS/cm^2, $\bar{g}_h$ = 0.22 mS/cm^2, $\bar{g}_{Ca}$ = 7 mS/cm^2, $\bar{g}_{K-C}$ = 15 mS/cm^2, $\bar{g}_{K-AHP}$ = 1 mS/cm^2, $\bar{g}_{ls}$ = 0.1 mS/cm^2, $\bar{g}_{ld}$ = 0.1 mS/cm^2. E_{Na} = 60 mV, E_K = -75 mV, E_{Ca} = 80 mV, E_h = -38 mV, E_l = -60 mV. C_m = 3 μF/cm^2.

Excitatory synaptic current is given below:

$$i = C \cdot k \cdot \{\exp(-\frac{t}{\tau_2}) - \exp(-\frac{t}{\tau_1})\}(V - E_{ep}) \quad (7)$$

where

$$k = \frac{1}{-\exp(-\frac{\tau_2}{\tau_2-\tau_1} \cdot \ln(\frac{\tau_2}{\tau_1})) + \exp(-\frac{\tau_1}{\tau_2-\tau_1} \cdot \ln(\frac{\tau_2}{\tau_1}))} \quad (8)$$

The time constants of the excitatory synaptic connections were summarized in Table I.

Inhibitory synaptic current is given below:

$$i = \frac{C}{2} \cdot \{\exp(-\frac{t}{\tau_1}) + \exp(-\frac{t}{\tau_2})\}(V - E_{GABAA}) \quad (9)$$

where C = 0.006 μS, τ_1 = 2 ms, τ_2 = 54.4 ms, E_{GABAA} = -80 mV. We assumed that the synaptic delay was 1 ms from/to the granule cell to/from the basket cells. The synaptic delay from/to the mossy cell was 2 ms.

TABLE I
TIME CONSTANTS OF THE SYNAPTIC CONNECTIONS

	$C(\mu S)$	τ_1(ms)	τ_2(ms)	E_{ep}(mV)
Granule $\rightarrow$ Basket	0.04	0.5	1	-10
Granule $\rightarrow$ Mossy	0.005	2	3	-10
Mossy $\rightarrow$ Granule	0.001	0.3	3.2	-6
Mossy $\rightarrow$ Basket	0.07	0.5	1	-10
Perforant path $\rightarrow$ Granule	0.06	0.3	3.2	-6
Perforant path $\rightarrow$ Basket	0.04	0.5	1	-10

The computations were performed by the simulator NEURON. The time step was 25 μs.

2) Frequency Characteristics of the Dentate Gyrus Network Model: In the first part of the results, we delivered 100 pulses of the periodic excitatory synaptic input to N_{sync} of the granule cells and the basket cells through the perforant path (black arrows in Fig.1). The rest of the granule cells received the random synaptic input through the perforant path (white arrows in Fig.1). In the second part of the results, the number of the granule cells received the random synaptic input, N_{rand}, was fixed at 3 (granule cells #7 - #9 in Fig.1). The number of the granule cells (and the basket cells) received the periodic input, N_{sync}, was varied.

The random synaptic input through the perforant path was drawn from an exponential distribution with a negative exponent. The mean interval of the exponential distribution was 30 ms. The standard deviation was 15 ms. The random synaptic input was not delivered to the basket cells.

We counted the number of spikes of the granule cell #1. The firing probability was defined as the number of spikes of the granule cell #1 divided by the number of pulses of the periodic input through the perforant path. This trial was repeated 5 times. The mean firing probability was plotted as a function of the frequency of the periodic perforant path input. The frequency of the periodic input was varied from 0.3 Hz to 100 Hz.

III. RESULTS

Figure 2 shows the firing probability of the granule cell #1 as a function of the perforant path input frequency in the dentate gyrus network model. When the granule cells received only periodic input through the perforant path (N_{sync} = 9), the firing probability showed a property of a low-pass filter ($\triangle$ in Fig.2). The firing probability was 100 % in the frequency range of the perforant path input below 5 Hz. The firing probability decreased with an increase in the input frequency above 6 Hz.

At $N_{\text{sync}} = 6$, 3 granule cells (#7 - #9) received a random synaptic input through the perforant path. The firing probability was reduced to about 70 % in the frequency range of the perforant path input below 1 Hz (■ in Fig2). In the input frequency range from 2 Hz to 5 Hz, the firing probability was higher than 93 %. In the frequency range above 6 Hz, the firing probabilities were suppressed.

The firing probability was suppressed in the entire frequency range of the periodic perforant path input at $N_{\text{sync}} = 3$ (× in Fig.2). In this situation, 6 of 9 granule cells (#4 - #9) randomly fired by the random synaptic input of the perforant path. Those random firing of the granule cells caused frequent firing of mossy cells. Consequently, the mossy cells elicited firing of the basket cells. Therefore, firing of the granule cells was prevented by frequent inhibitory input from the basket cells.

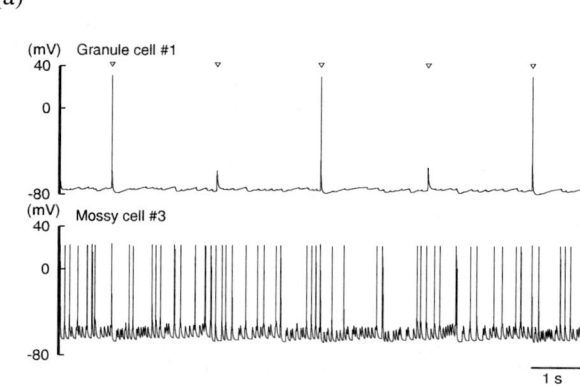

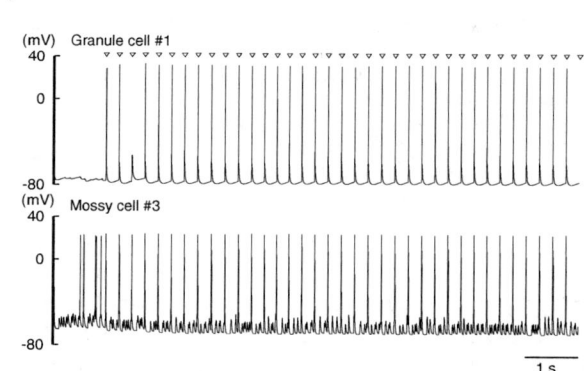

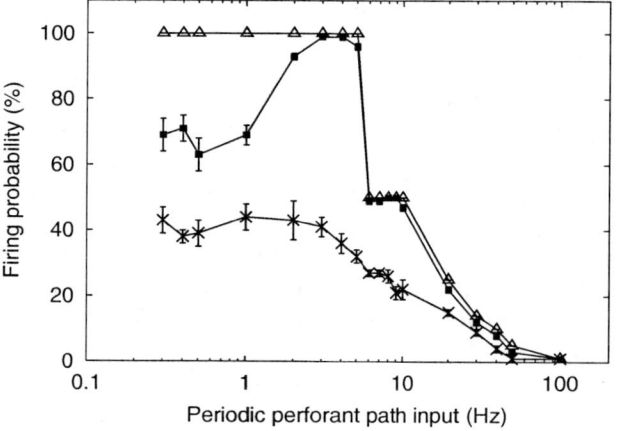

Fig. 2. Firing probability of the granule cell #1 in the dentate gyrus network model. Without the random synaptic input ($N_{\text{sync}} = 9$), the dentate gyrus showed a property of a low-pass filter (△). When 6 granule cells received periodic input and the rest of the granule cells received random synaptic input, a property of a band-pass filter emerged (■). At $N_{\text{sync}} = 3$, the firing probability were relatively low in the entire input frequency range(×). Bars represent the standard deviation.

Fig. 3. Membrane potentials of the granule cell #1 and the mossy cell #3. $N_{\text{sync}} = 6$, $N_{\text{rand}} = 3$. (a) The input frequency was 0.5 Hz. The mossy cell frequently fired prior to the granule cell. Spikes of the granule cells were suppressed by the mossy cells via basket cells. (b) The input frequency was 4 Hz. The mossy cell was phase-locked with the granule cell. The mossy cell was elicited by the periodic input from the granule cell, but not the random synaptic input. Triangles at the top trace of each figure represent the periodic perforant path input.

Firing patterns of mossy cells help to understand mechanisms of the theta rhythm selection. At 0.5 Hz of the perforant path input, mossy cells frequently fired by the random excitatory synaptic input from granule cells #7 - #9 (Fig.3(a)). Frequent firing of the mossy cells continuously inhibited the granule cells. This inhibition prevented firing of the granule cells. At 4 Hz of the perforant path input, mossy cells did not prevent firing of granule cells (Fig.3(b)). Spikes of the mossy cells were phase-locked with spikes of the granule cells. This is because firing of the mossy cells were elicited by the periodic input from the granule cells #1 - #6. The random synaptic input did not disturb firing of the mossy cells. Because the granule cells fired prior to the mossy cells, the mossy cells did not inhibit firing of the granule cells.

In the following results, the number of the granule cells received the random synaptic input, N_{rand}, was fixed at 3 (granule cells #7 - #9). We varied N_{sync} from 6 to 3 (Fig.4). At $N_{\text{sync}} = 4$, the granule cells #5 and #6 did not receive synaptic input through the perforant path. The granule cells had relatively high firing probability in the frequency range between 2 Hz and 5 Hz (□ in Fig.4). The firing probability in the frequency range below 1 Hz was about 70 %. This value of the firing probability did not significantly different from the firing probability at $N_{\text{sync}} = 6$.

A further decrease in the number of the granule cells received the periodic input suppressed the firing probability in the frequency range between 2 Hz and 5 Hz (× in Fig.4). At $N_{\text{sync}} = 3$, the firing probability was 61 % at 5 Hz of the perforant path input. The firing probability in the frequency ranges below 1 Hz and above 6 Hz were not affected by the number of the granule cells received the periodic input. Synchronization of the periodic synaptic input increased the firing probability in the frequency range between 2 Hz and 5 Hz, while a moderate amount of the random synaptic input limited the firing probability in the frequency range below 1 Hz.

Figure 5 shows that histograms of spike timing of the

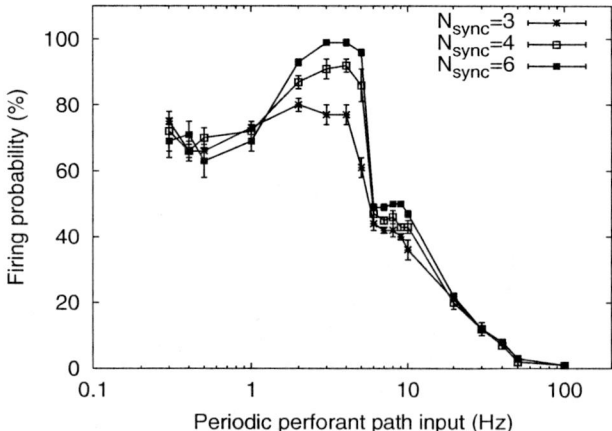

Fig. 4. Suppression of the firing probability in the frequency range between 2 Hz and 5 Hz by a small number of the perforant path conducting the periodic input. $N_{\text{rand}} = 3$. ■: The granule cells #1 to #6 received the periodic perforant path input. □: The granule cells #1 to #4 received the periodic input. The granule cells #5 and #6 did not receive the perforant path input. ×: The granule cells #1 to #3 received the periodic input. No perforant path input to the granule cells #4 to #6. Bars represent the standard deviation.

mossy cell #3 to 4 Hz of the periodic perforant path input. At $N_{\text{sync}} = 6$, the mossy cells mostly fired about 10 ms after the periodic input through the perforant path. The mossy cells were highly synchronized with the periodic input. At $N_{\text{sync}} = 3$, the number of spikes after the perforant path decreased. Several spikes of the mossy cells were found before the periodic input through the perforant path. Spikes of the mossy cells prior to the perforant path input could prevent firing of the granule cells through the basket cells.

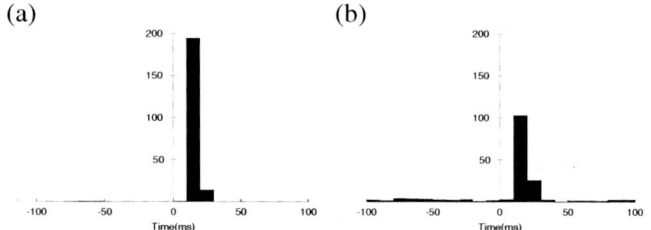

Fig. 5. Histograms of spikes timing of the mossy cell #3 to the periodic perforant path input. The number of spikes was an average of 5 trials. The frequency of the periodic perforant path input was 4 Hz. The mean interval of random synaptic input was 30 ms. SD was 15 ms. $N_{\text{rand}} = 3$. (a) $N_{\text{sync}} = 6$. (b) $N_{\text{sync}} = 3$. Bin size was 10 ms.

IV. DISCUSSION

In the previous study, we proposed a possible mechanism of the theta rhythm selection in the dentate gyrus [2]. The random synaptic input to mossy cells contributes to the theta rhythm selection. In the present study, the random synaptic input to mossy cells was delivered from the perforant path via granule cells. Without the random synaptic input, the periodic perforant path input led to a property of a low-pass filter. The random synaptic input through a moderate number of the perforant path decreased the firing probability in the frequency range below 1 Hz; but in the frequency range between 2 Hz and 5 Hz the firing probability was higher than 93 %. The dentate gyrus network model showed a property of a band-pass filter. When a large number of the perforant path conducted the random synaptic input, a low firing probability emerged in the entire frequency range of the periodic input.

When the number of the granule cells received the random synaptic input through the perforant path was fixed, the firing probability in the frequency range between 2 Hz and 5 Hz depended on the number of the granule cells received the periodic synaptic input through the perforant path. Enough degree of synchronization of the periodic input led to a high firing probability in that frequency range. A decrease in the number of the granule cells received the periodic input caused the suppression of the firing probability. A small number of the granule cells received the periodic input did not entrain the mossy cells though the granule cells, but the mossy cells were frequently elicited by the random synaptic input. This frequent firing of the mossy cells inhibited firing of the granule cells through basket cells. On the one hand, the number of the granule cells received the periodic input did not affect the firing probability in the frequency range below 1 Hz.

The cholinergic and GABAergic medial septum cells send axons to the dentate gyrus [7]. Those synaptic projections potentially modulate the filtering property of the dentate gyrus. However, the elimination of the projections from the medial septum does not prevent the theta rhythm selection of the dentate gyrus in hippocampal slice preparations [2]. This indicates that the synaptic projections from the medial septum are not necessary to the theta rhythm selection.

In summary, a moderate amount of the random synaptic input through the perforant path causes the suppression of the firing probability in the frequency range below 1 Hz in the dentate gyrus network model. Synchronization of the periodic input through the perforant path pulls up the firing probability in the frequency range between 2 Hz and 5 Hz. The balance between the synchronized periodic input and the random input determines the filtering property of in the dentate gyrus network model.

ACKNOWLEDGMENT

This work was supported in part by the Ministry of Education, Culture, Sports, Science and Technology (the 21st Century Center of Excellence Program in Kyushu Institute of Technology, entitled "World of brain computing interwoven out of animals and robots", and Grant-in-Aid for Scientific Research No.16015289).

REFERENCES

[1] M. D. Muñoz, A. Núñez, and E. García-Austt, "Frequency potentiation in granule cells *in vivo* at θ frequency perforant path stimulation," *Experimental Neurology*, vol. 113, pp. 74-78, 1991.
[2] K. Tateno, T. Hashimoto, S. Ishizuka, K. Nakashima, and H. Hayashi, "Theta rhythm selection of a dentate gyrus network model," *Proceedings of the International Joint Conference on Neural Networks*, vol. 2, pp. 1529-1532, 2004
[3] C. T. Dickson, J. Magistretti, M. Shalinsky, B. Hamam, A. Alonso, "Oscillatory activity in entorhinal neurons and circuits," *The Parahippocampal Region*, vol. 911, pp. 127-150, 2000.

[4] A. Alonso, E. García-Austt, "Neuronal sources of theta rhythm in the entorhinal cortex of the rat. II. Phase relations between unit discharges and theta field potentials," *Experimental Brain Research*, vol. 67, pp. 502-509, 1987.

[5] G. L. F. Yuen and D. Durand, "Reconstruction of hippocampal granule cell electrophysiology by computer simulation," *Neuroscience*, vol. 41, pp. 411-423, 1991.

[6] R. D. Traub, R. Miles, G. Buzsáki, "Computer simulation of carbachol-driven rhythmic population oscillations in the CA3 region of the *in vitro* rat hippocampus," *Journal of Physiology*, vol. 451, pp. 653-672, 1992.

[7] P. E. Patton and B. McNaughton, "Connection matrix of the hippocampal formation: I. the dentate gyrus," *Hippocampus*, vol. 5, pp. 245-286, 1995.

Noise Benefits in Spiking Retinal and Sensory Neuron Models

Ashok Patel and Bart Kosko
Department of Electrical Engineering, Signal and Image Processing Institute
University of Southern California, Los Angeles, California 90089-2564

Abstract—This paper presents two new theorems that give sufficient conditions (and necessary in the first case) for a noise benefit or stochastic-resonance effect in popular spiking models of retinal neurons and sensory neurons. Small amounts of additive white noise increase the neuron's input-output bit count or Shannon mutual information. This stochastic-resonance (SR) effect applies to standard Poisson spiking models of retinal neurons for all possible types of finite-variance noise and for all impulsive or infinite-variance stable noise. A similar SR result holds for several types of sensory spiking neurons such as the Fitzhugh-Nagumo model and the integrate-and-fire model if the additive noise is Gaussian white noise.

I. Introduction

Stochastic resonance (SR) occurs when noise benefits a nonlinear system [3], [10], [12], [14], [16], [17], [20], [19]. Figure 1 shows that adding Gaussian white noise to a spiking retinal neuron model helps the neuron discriminate between two levels of brightness contrast. The neuron should emit more spikes when the brightness contrast level is low rather than high. The right amount of Gaussian noise helps the neuron discriminate between two levels of brightness contrast. The retinal neuron emits too few spikes if no noise corrupts the Bernoulli sequence of contrast levels. The neuron also emits too many spikes and emits many of them at the wrong time if too much noise corrupts the sequence.

The next section presents a new theorem that gives necessary and sufficient conditions for an SR effect in standard models of spiking retinal neurons. The final section presents a sufficient SR condition for standard models of spiking sensory neurons.

Our earlier work proved that SR always occurs in a threshold system such as a simple threshold neuron if the signal is subthreshold and if a technical condition holds for the noise mean or location parameter. Shannon mutual information measures the system performance. The result is a logical characterization for simple memoryless threshold neurons in the face of noisy Bernoulli input sequences: *SR occurs if and only if the noise mean $E(n)$ does not lie in the "forbidden interval"* $(\theta - A, \theta + A)$ where $-A < A < \theta$ for threshold θ and signal amplitude $A > 0$. The sufficient or if-part of the theorem first appeared in [21] while the converse only-if part first appeared in [22]. The result holds for all noise types that have finite variance and for all infinite-variance noise types from the broad family of stable distributions [32]. The proof technique assumes that the nonnegative mutual information is positive and then shows that it goes to zero as the noise variance or dispersion goes to zero—so the mutual information must increase as the noise dispersion increases from zero.

This paper extends the above memoryless SR theorem to the more complex models of retinal and sensory neurons that produce spike trains. We specifically prove that a general retinal model with two noise sources exhibits SR if and only if the sum of the two noise means does not lie in the forbidden interval $(\theta_1 - V_1, \theta_2 - V_2)$ that depends on the threshold values θ_1 and θ_2 and on the subthreshold signal values V_1 and V_2. We then show that the SR effect holds for a general family of nonlinear sensory neural models if the additive noise is Gaussian white noise. These models include the popular FitzHugh-Nagumo (FHN) model [5], [7], [8] and the integrate-and-fire model [8], [13], [28].

II. Stochastic Resonance in Spiking Retinal Models

We first present a general theorem that shows that standard spiking retinal models benefit from additive white noise if and only if a joint noise mean or location parameter does not fall in a forbidden interval of threshold-based values. Theorem 1 holds for all finite-variance noise and for all impulsive or infinite-variance stable noise [15], [20], [32]. The performance measure is the input-output Shannon mutual-information bit count $I(S, R) = H(R) - H(R|S)$ for input signal random variable S and output response random variable R. So $I(S, R) \geq 0$ because conditioning reduces entropy [9]: $H(R|S) \leq H(R)$. Figure 1 shows a simulation instance of Theorem 1 for Gaussian white noise that corrupts a random Bernoulli sequence of brightness contrast levels in a Poisson-spiking retinal neuron.

The retina model of Theorem 1 is a noisy version of a common Wiener-type cascade model [6], [18], [23], [29], [30]:

$$r(t) = r_0 h\left[\int_{-\infty}^{\infty} f(z)\{S(t-z) + n_1(t)\}dz + n_2(t)\right] \quad (1)$$

where S is the input stimulus defined below, r is the instantaneous Poisson spike rate that gives the exponential interspike-interval density function as $p(t) = r(t)\exp[-\int_0^t r(\tau)d\tau]$, f is a band-pass linear filter function, and h is a memoryless monotone–increasing function. Here n_1 denotes the combined stimulus and photoreceptor noise

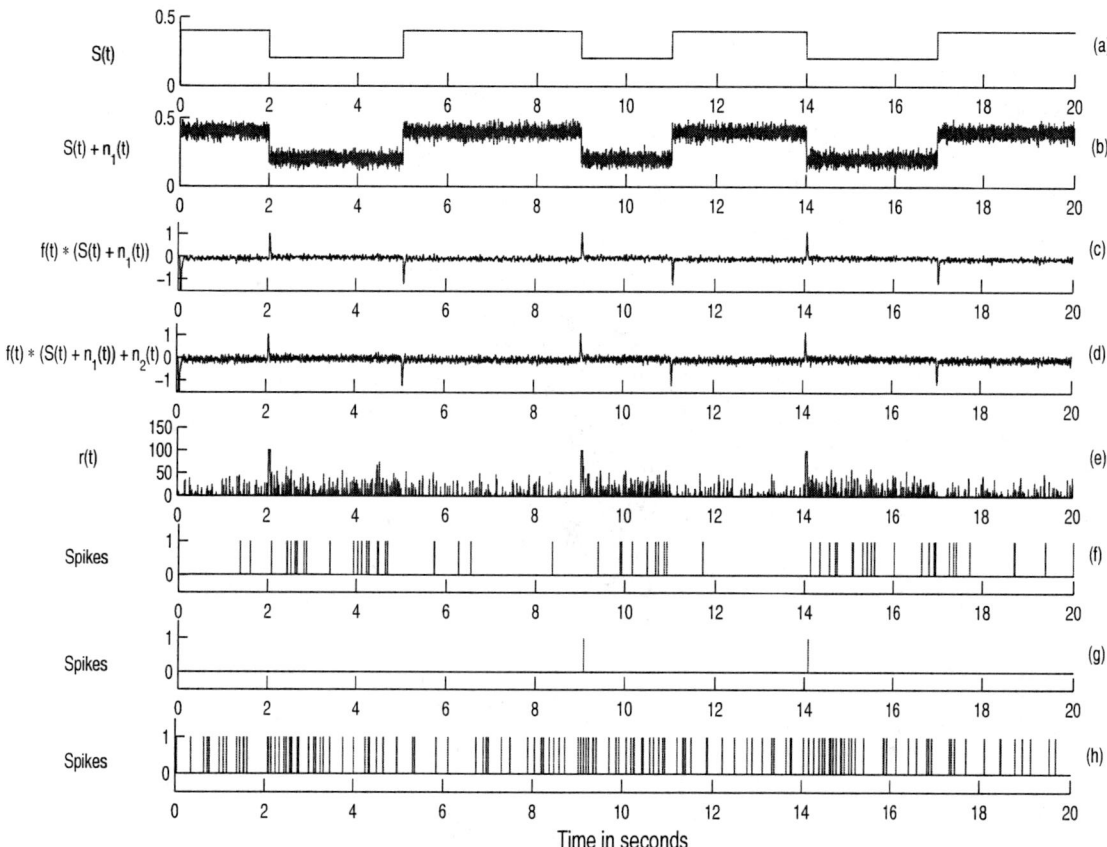

Fig. 1. Noise improves the discrimination of subthreshold contrast stimuli in the retina model (1)-(3). The neuron should emit more spikes when the brightness contrast level is low rather than high. (a) Bernoulli contrast signal S as a function of time t. (b) Contrast signal S plus Gaussian white noise n_1 with variance $\sigma_1 = 0.03$. (c) Signal in plot (b) filtered with f in (1). (d) Filtered noisy signal in (c) plus noise n_2 (synaptic and ion-channel noise) with variance $\sigma_2 = 0.06$. (e) Noisy spike rate $r(t)$. (f) SR effect: Output Poisson spikes that result from the noisy spike rate $r(t)$. (g) Output spikes in the absence of noise. (h) Output spikes in the presence of too much noise.

[1], [25], [29] and n_2 denotes the combined ion-channel noise [31], [33] and the synaptic noise [11], [26], [27].

The input stimulus S is Michelson's visual contrast signal [4]: $S = (L_c - L_s)/(L_c + L_s)$. L_c is the amount of light that falls on the center of the ganglion cell's receptive field. L_s is the light that falls on its surround region.

The sigmoid-shaped memoryless function h approximates the spike threshold and saturation level. We define h as a piecewise linear function for simplicity as

$$h(x) = \begin{cases} \theta_2 - \theta_1 & \text{if } x > \theta_2 \\ x - \theta_1 & \text{if } \theta_1 \leq x \leq \theta_2 \\ 0 & \text{if } x < \theta_1 \end{cases} \quad (2)$$

and so

$$r(g(t)) = \begin{cases} r_0(\theta_2 - \theta_1) & \text{if } g(t) > \theta_2 \\ r_0(g(t) - \theta_1) & \text{if } \theta_1 \leq g(t) \leq \theta_2 \\ 0 & \text{if } g(t) < \theta_1 \end{cases} \quad (3)$$

The Shannon mutual information $I(S, R)$ between the input contrast signal S and the output average spiking rate R measures the neuron's bit count and allows us to detect the noise enhancement or SR effect.

The subthreshold contrast signal $S(t) \in \{A, B\}$ is a random Bernoulli sequence with $P[S(t) = A] = p$ and $P[S(t) = B] = 1 - p$. The time duration of each signal value A and B in $S(t)$ is much larger than the time constant of the linear filter $f(t)$. We define $v(t)$ as the filtered output of the contrast signal $S(t)$ without noise $n_1(t)$ and such that $v(t)$ reaches its steady-state value of V_1 when $S(t) = A$ and such that it reaches its steady-state value of V_2 for $S(t) = B$ where $V_1 > V_2$ and $\max(V_1, V_2) < \theta_1 < \theta_2$. So the input signal $S(t)$ is subthreshold. We measure the average spike rate for each symbol only when the corresponding value of $v(t)$ is in steady-state. Then the filtered noise z is $z(t) = f(t) * n_1(t)$ where '$*$' denotes convolution.

Theorem 1 below gives necessary and sufficient conditions for an SR noise effect in the retina neuron model (1)-(3) for either noise source n_1 or n_2. The theorem shows that some increase in such noise *must* increase the neuron's mutual

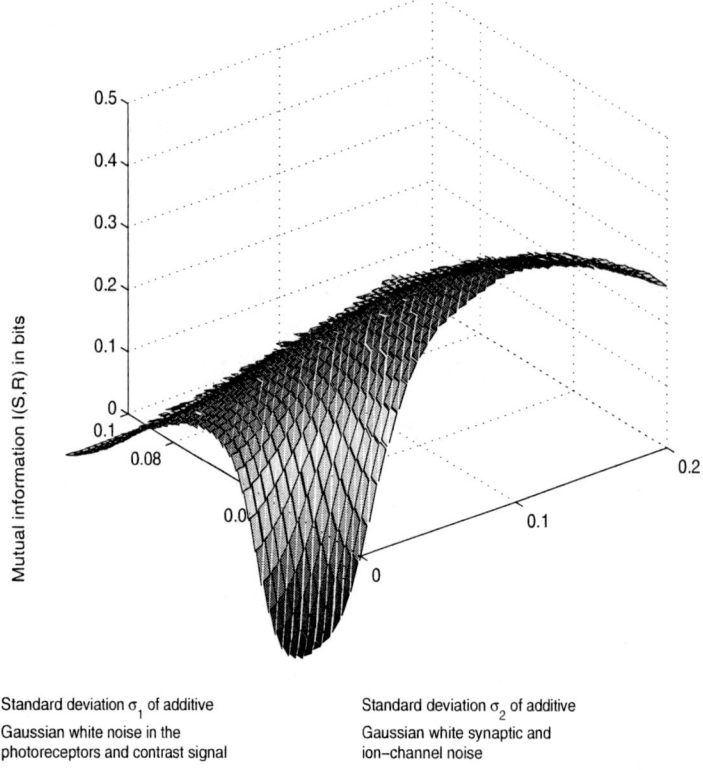

Fig. 2. SR in the retina model with additive Gaussian white noise. The noisy retina model has the spiking Poisson form (1)-(3) with thresholds $\theta_1 = 0$ and $\theta_2 = 0.3$. The maximum firing rate is 100 spikes/sec. The Bernoulli contrast signal takes the value of 0.2 with success probability $p = 1/2$ and takes the value of 0.4 otherwise. The graph shows the retina model's smoothed input-output mutual information surface as a function of the noise standard deviations σ_1 and σ_2.

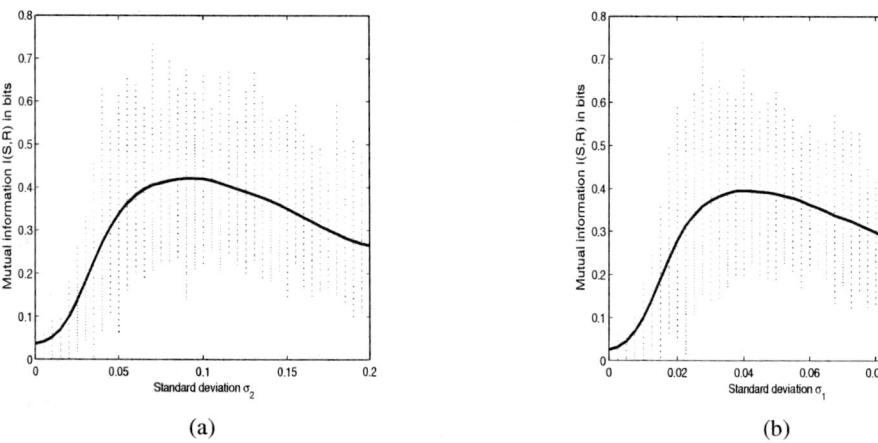

Fig. 3. SR in the retina model with additive Gaussian white noise. The noisy retina model has the spiking Poisson form (1)-(3) with thresholds $\theta_1 = 0$ and $\theta_2 = 0.3$. The maximum firing rate is 100 spikes/sec. The Bernoulli contrast signal takes the value of 0.2 with success probability $p = 1/2$ and takes the value of 0.4 otherwise. Plots (a) and (b) show the respective cross-sections of the mutual-information surface of Figure 2 for $\sigma_1 = 0.01$ and $\sigma_2 = 0.02$. Thick lines show the average mutual information. Vertical lines show the total min-max deviations of the mutual information in 100 simulation trials.

information $I(S, R)$—and thus must increase the neuron's ability to discriminate subthreshold contrast signals—if the noise mean or location parameter obeys a simple interval constraint. This SR effect holds for *all* finite-variance probability density functions. The result is robust because it further holds for all infinite-variance stable noise densities such as impulsive Cauchy or Levy noise [15], [20], [21], [22] and the uncountably many other stable densities that obey a generalized central limit theorem [32]. The proof follows the technique of [21], [22].

Theorem 1. Suppose that the noise sources n_1 and n_2 in the retina model (1)-(3) are white and have finite-variance (or finite-dispersion in the stable case) probability density functions $p_1(n)$ and $p_2(n)$ with corresponding variances (dispersions) σ_1^2 and σ_2^2 (γ_1 and γ_2). Suppose that the input signal S is subthreshold ($V_2 < V_1 < \theta_1 < \theta_2$) and that there is some statistical dependence between the input contrast random variable S and the output random variable R so that $I(S,R) > 0$. Then the retina model (1)-(3) exhibits the nonmonotone SR effect in the sense that $I(S,R) \to 0$ as σ_1^2 and σ_2^2 (or γ_1 and γ_2) decrease to zero if and only if the mean sum $E(n_1)\int f(\tau)d\tau + E(n_2)$ (or the location parameter sum in the stable case) does not lie in the interval $(\theta_1 - V_1, \theta_2 - V_2)$.

Simulation results confirm this mathematical result that noise in retinal signal processing can help retinal neurons detect subthreshold contrast signals. Figures 2-3 show detailed simulation instances of the predicted SR effect in Theorem 1. Figure 2 shows a 3-D plot of the Shannon mutual information versus the standard deviations of Gaussian white noise sources n_1 and n_2 in (1). Figure 3 shows their respective cross-section plots for the values $\sigma_1 = 0.01$ and $\sigma_2 = 0.02$. We computed the bit count $I(S,R)$ using a discrete density of R based on the number of spikes in 1-second intervals for each input symbol. Each plot shows the nonmonotonic signature of SR.

III. STOCHASTIC RESONANCE IN SPIKING SENSORY NEURON MODELS

We next present a new theorem that characterizes the SR effect in a wide range of spiking sensory neuron models in the special but ubiquitous case of additive white Gaussian noise. Theorem 2 shows that these sensory neuron models enjoy an SR noise benefit if the noise mean $E(n)$ falls to the left of a bound and if the average firing rate depends on the Kramers's rate solution [24] of the Fokker-Planck diffusion equation. Theorem 2 applies to popular spiking sensory neuron models such as the FitzHugh-Nagumo (FHN) model [5], [7], [8] and the leaky integrate-and-fire model [8], [13], [28].

The FHN neuron model has the form

$$\epsilon \dot{v} = -v(v^2 - \frac{1}{4}) - w + A_T - d + n, \quad (4)$$
$$\dot{w} = v - w \quad (5)$$

where v is the membrane voltage (fast) variable, w is a recovery (slow) variable, $A_T = -5/(12\sqrt{3})$ is a threshold voltage, S is the input signal, $d = B - S$, B is the constant signal-to-threshold distance, and n is independent Gaussian white noise. The input signal is subthreshold when $d > 0$ and so $S < B$.

Kramers rate formula gives the average firing-rate of the FHN neuron model with subthreshold input signals ($S(t) << B$) [8]

$$E(r(t)) = \frac{B}{2\pi\sqrt{3}\epsilon} \exp\left[\frac{-2\sqrt{3}\epsilon[B^3 - 3B^2 S(t)]}{3\sigma^2}\right]. \quad (6)$$

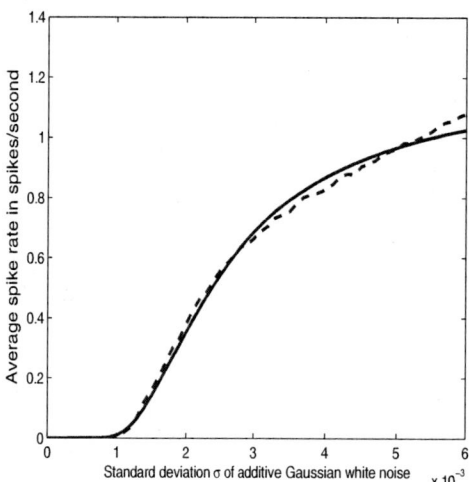

Fig. 4. Comparison of the average firing rate (dashed line) and its estimate (solid line) for the FHN neuron model (4)-(5) using (7). Model parameters: A_T = -5/12($\sqrt{3}$), B = 0.07, S = 0.01. Nonlinear least-squares fitted the parameters in (7) as a = 1.1718, b = 0.0187, and c = 0.0680 with coefficient of determination r^2 = .9976.

The average spike rate model poorly estimated the averge firing rates of the FHN model in simulations. So we instead fitted the equation

$$E(r(t)) = a \exp\left[\frac{-bB^3 + cB^2 S(t)}{\sigma^2}\right] \quad (7)$$

to the simulation data. Nonlinear least-squares gave the parameters a, b, and c in (7). Figure 4 shows that (7) with the proper choice of parameters a, b, and c closely estimate the average spike rates of the FHN neuron model because the coefficient of determination was r^2 = .9976.

The leaky integrate-and-fire neuron model has the form

$$\dot{v} = -av + a - \delta + S + n \quad (8)$$

where v is the membrane voltage, a and δ are constants, δ/a is the barrier height of the potential, S is an input signal, and n is independent Gaussian white noise. The input signal S is subthreshold when $S < \delta$. The neuron emits a spike when the membrane voltage v crosses the threshold value of 1 from below to above. The membrane voltage v resets to $1 - \delta/a$ just after the neuron emits a spike. Then the ensemble-averaged spike rate $E(r(t))$ for subthreshold inputs ($S^2 << \delta$) has the form [8]

$$E(r(t)) = \frac{\delta}{\sqrt{\sigma^2 \pi}} \exp\left[\frac{-\delta^2 + 2\delta S(t)}{\sigma^2 a}\right] \quad (9)$$

where σ^2 is the variance of n.

We can combine (6)-(7) and (9) into the general form

$$E(r(t)) = g(B, S(t), \sigma) \exp\left[\frac{h(B, S(t))}{k\sigma^2}\right] \quad (10)$$

where $E(r(t))$ is the average escape rate and k is a constant. The functions $g(B, S, \sigma)$ and $h(B, S)$ depend on the potential barrier B, the subthreshold input signal S, and on the variance σ^2 of the additive Gaussian white noise n so that $E(r(t)) \to 0$ as $\sigma \to 0$. We note that the formula for the average Poisson spike rate in excitable cells due to the voltage-gated ion channels dynamics has a form similar to (10) [2].

We can now state Theorem 2. This theorem gives a sufficient condition for SR to occur in spiking sensory neuron models if their average output spike rates have the general form of (10). The proof again follows the proof in [21], [22].

Theorem 2. Suppose that the average spike rate of a sensory neuron model has the form (10) and that $E(n)$ is the mean of the model's additive Gaussian white noise n. Suppose that input signal $S(t) \in \{s_1, s_2\}$ is subthreshold: $S(t) < B$. Suppose that there is some statistical dependence between the input signal random variable S and the output average spike-rate random variable R so that $I(S,R) > 0$. Then the spiking sensory neuron exhibits the nonmonotone SR effect in the sense that $I(S,R) \to 0$ as the noise intensity $\sigma \to 0$ if $E[n] < B - s_2$.

Figure 5 shows a simulation instance of the SR effect in The-

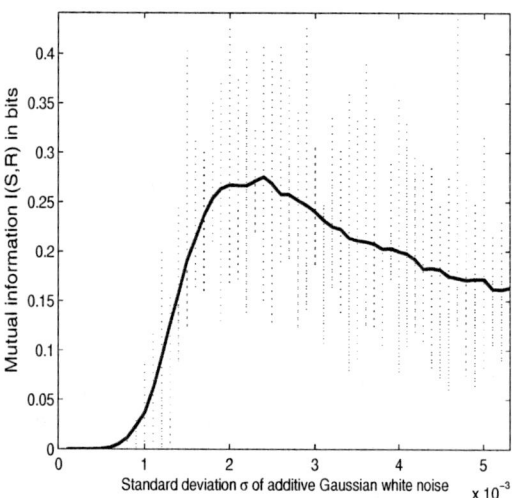

Fig. 5. Stochastic resonance in the FHN spiking neuron model in accord with Theorem 2. The model parameters are $A_T = -5/12(\sqrt{3})$, $B = 0.07$, and $S = \pm 0.0025$. The solid curve shows the average mutual information. The dashed vertical lines show the total min-max deviations of mutual information in 100 simulation trials.

orem 2 for the special but important case of the FHN neuron model. The mutual-information plot shows the predicted nonmonotonic signature of SR. The leaky integrate-and-fire neuron model produces similar nonmonotonic SR plots. Figure 6 goes beyond the scope of Theorem 2 and shows a simulation instance of the SR effect in the leaky integrate-and-fire neuron model with implusive infinite-variance α-stable white noise.

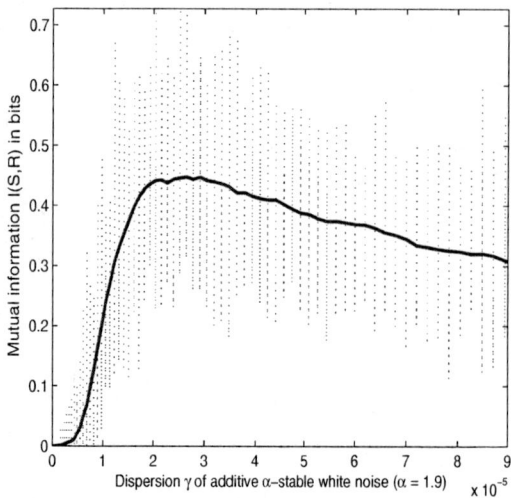

Fig. 6. Stochastic resonance in the leaky integrate-and-fire spiking neuron model with subthreshold input signals and infinite-variance α-stable white noise ($\alpha = 1.9$). The model parameters are $a = 0.5$, $\delta = 0.01$, $s_1 = 0.0025$, and $s_2 = 0.005$. The solid curve shows the smoothed average mutual information. The dashed vertical lines show the total min-max deviations of mutual information in 100 simulation trials.

IV. CONCLUSION

Several of the most popular models of biological neurons provably benefit from appropriate amounts of additive white noise. Spiking retinal models benefit from almost all types of noise because Theorem 1 holds both for all finite-variance noise and for the large class of infinite-variance stable noise. Theorem 2 applies only to additive Gaussian white noise although simulations confirm a comparable noise benefit for infinite-variance stable noise (see Figure 6) and other types of finite-variance noise. An open research question is whether other noise types produce a noise benefit in sensory neurons or in the more complex cortical neurons that take spikes as input as well as emit spikes as output.

ACKNOWLEDGEMENT

National Science Foundation Grant ECS-0070284 supported this research.

REFERENCES

[1] P. Ala-Laurila, K. Donner, and A. Koskelainen, "Thermal Activation and Photoactivation of Visual Pigments," *Biophysical Journal*, Vol. 86, pp. 3653-3662, 2004.

[2] S.M. Berzukov and I. Vodyanoy, "Stochastic Resonance in Thermally Activated Reactions: Applications to Biological Ion Channel," *Chaos*, Vol. 8, No. 3, pp. 557-566, 1998.

[3] A.R. Bulsara and A. Zador, "Threshold Detection of Wideband Signals: A Noise Induced Maximum in the Mutual Information," *Physical Review E*, Vol. 54, No. 3, R2185-R2188, 1996.

[4] D.A. Burkhardt, J. Gottesman, D. Kersten, and G.E. Legge, "Symmetry and Constancy in the Perception of Negative and Positive Luminance Contrast," *Jornal of the Optical Society of America A*, Vol. 1, pp. 309-316, 1984.

[5] D.R. Chialvo, A. Longtin, and J. Muller-Gerkin, "Stochastic Resonance in Models of Neuronal Ensembles Revisited," *Physical Review E*, Vol. 55, No. 2, pp. 1798-1808, 1997.

[6] D. Chander and E.J. Chichilnisky, "Adaptation to Temporal Contrast in Primate and Salamander Retina," *Journal of Neuroscience*, Vol. 21, No. 24, pp. 9904-9916, 2001.

[7] J.J. Collins, C.C. Chow, A.C. Capela, and T.T. Imhoff, "Aperiodic Stochastic Resonance in Excitable Systems," *Physical Review E*, Vol. 52, No. 4, pp. R3321-R3324, 1995.

[8] J.J. Collins, C.C. Chow, A.C. Capela, and T.T. Imhoff, "Aperiodic Stochastic Resonance," *Physical Review E*, Vol. 54, No. 5, pp. 5575-5584, 1996.

[9] T.M. Cover and J.A. Thomas, *Elements of Information Theory*. New York: Wiley, 1991.

[10] G. Deco and B. Schurmann, "Stochastic Resonance in the Mutual information Between Input and Output Spike Trains of Noisy Central Neurons", *Physica D*, Vol. 117, pp. 276-282, 1998.

[11] M.A. Freed, "Rate of Quantal Excitation to a Retinal Ganglion Cell Evoked by Sensory Input," *Journal of Neurophysiology*, Vol. 83, pp. 2956-2966, 2000.

[12] L. Gammaitoni, "Stochastic Resonance and the Dithering Effect in Threshold Physical Systems," *Physical Review E*, Vol. 52, No. 5, pp. 4691-4698, 1995.

[13] W. Gerstner and W.M. Kistler, *Spiking Neuron Models: Single Neurons, Populations, Plasticity*, Cambridge University Press, 2002.

[14] X. Godivier and F. Chapeau-Blondeau, "Stochastic Resonance in the Information Capacity of a Nonlinear Dynamic System," *International Journal of Bifurcation and Chaos*, Vol. 8, No. 3, pp. 581-589, 1998.

[15] M. Grigoriu, *Applied Non-Gaussian Processes*, Englewood Cliffs, NJ:Prentice Hall, 1995.

[16] M.E. Inchiosa, J.W.C. Robinson, and A.R. Bulsara, "Information-theoretic Stochastic Resonance in Noise-floor Limited Systems: The Case for Adding Noise," *Physical Review Letters*, Vol. 85, pp. 3369-3372, 2000.

[17] P. Jung, "Stochastic Resonance and Optimal Design of Threshold Detectors," *Physics Letters A*, Vol. 207, pp. 93-104, 1995.

[18] K.J. Kim and F. Rieke, "Temporal Contrast Adaptation in the Input and Output Signals of Salamander Retinal Ganglion Cell," *Journal of Neuroscience*, Vol. 21, pp. 287-299, 2001.

[19] S. Mitaim and B. Kosko, "Adaptive Stochastic Resonance," *Proceedings of the IEEE: Special Issue on Intelligent Signal Processing*, Vol. 86, No. 11, pp. 2152-2183, 1998.

[20] B. Kosko and S. Mitaim, "Robust Stochastic Resonance: Signal Detection and Adaptation in Impulsive Noise," *Physical Review E*, Vol. 64, No. 5, 051110-1 – 051110-11, 2001.

[21] B. Kosko and S. Mitaim, "Stochastic Resonance in Noisy Threshold Neurons," *Neural Networks*, Vol. 14, No. 6-7, pp. 755-761, 2003.

[22] B. Kosko and S. Mitaim, "Robust Stochastic Resonance for Simple Threshold Neurons," *Physical Review E*, Vol. 70, 031911-1 – 031911-10, 2004.

[23] M.J. Korenberg and I.W. Hunter, "The Identification of Nonlinear Biological Systems: LNL Cascade Models," *Biological Cybernetics*, Vol. 55, pp. 125-134, 1986.

[24] H.A. Kramers, "Brownian Motion in a Field of Force and the Diffusion Model of Chemical Reaction," *Physica*, Vol. 7, pp. 284-304, 1940.

[25] T.D. Lamb, "Sources of Noise in Photoreceptor Transduction," *Jornal of the Optical Society of America A*, Vol. 4, pp. 2295-2300, 1987.

[26] W.B. Levy and R.A. Baxter, "Energy-Efficient Neural Computation via Quantal Synaptic Failures," *Journal of Neuroscience*, Vol. 22, No. 11, pp. 4746-4755, 2002.

[27] A. Manwani and C. Koch, "Detecting and Estimating Signals in Noisy Cable Structures, I: Neuronal Noise Sources." *Neural Computation*, Vol. 11, pp. 1797-1829, 1999.

[28] K. Pakdaman, "Periodically Forced Leaky Integrate-and-fire Model," *Physical Review E*, Vol. 63, 041907-1 – 041907-5, 2001.

[29] F. Rieke, D. Warland, R. de Ruyter van Steveninck, and W. Bialek, *Spikes: Exploring the Neural Code*, Cambridge, MA: MIT Press, 1996.

[30] H.M. Sakai, J.-L. Wang, and K.-I. Naka, "Contrast Gain Control in the Lower Vertebrate Retinas," *Journal of General Physiology*, vol. 105, pp. 815-835, 1995.

[31] E. Schneidman, B. Freedman, and I. Segev, "Ion Channel Stochasticity may be Critical in Determining the Reliability and Precision of Spike Timing," *Neural Computation*, vol. 10, pp. 1679-1703, 1998.

[32] M. Shao and C.L. Nikias, "Signal Processing with Fractional Lower Order Moments: Stable Processes and Their Applications," *Proceedings of the IEEE*, Vol. 81, pp. 984-1010, 1993.

[33] M.C.W. Van Rossum, B.J. O'Brien, and R.G. Smith, "Effects of Noise on the Spike Timing Precision of Retinal Ganglion Cells," *Journal of Neurophysiology.*, vol. 89, pp. 2406-2419, 2003.

A Spiking Neuron Representation of Auditory Signals

Guoping Wang and Misha Pavel
OGI School of Science & Engineering
Oregon Health & Science University
20000 NW Walker Road
Beaverton, OR 97006
{gpwang, pavel}@bme.ogi.edu

Abstract—We describe a model of the auditory system in which a population of spiking neurons with limited sampling rates represents the magnitude and phase of high bandwidth auditory signals. The basic premise of this model is based on the fact that each peripheral auditory neuron appears to have a very narrow band tuning characteristics. The signal in each narrow-band channel can, therefore, be sampled at frequencies that are much lower than the center frequency of the band, e.g., < 50 Hz and consistent with the capabilities of neurons. The new idea here is that the system can use non-uniform sampling, consistent with the refractory periods of the neurons, to capture both the amplitude of the modulation and the phase of the carrier signal. The computational model described in this paper consists of a short-term FFT analysis combined with overlap-add and a sampling process where magnitude is digitized but phase is represented using a temporal code of spiking neurons. The coding/decoding mechanism is using knowledge of the properties of the refractory period. We show that this model can represent arbitrary signals, but redundant signals such as speech are represented with higher accuracy than uncorrelated noise. We note that this basic coding approach may be useful for representation of signals in situation where binary representation is not feasible.

I. INTRODUCTION

Understanding the auditory code of natural peripheral auditory systems is a critical aspect in the research of biological systems as well as important information for the development of robust pattern-recognition systems such as automatic speech recognition systems. In particular, it is likely that the peripheral representation plays an important role in the ability of natural systems to adapt to dynamic and unpredictable conditions. Unlike the biological system that is quite robust when confronted with complex and unpredictable world [1], most engineering systems are sensitive to the contextual and environmental changes. For example, typical automatic speech recognition systems are designed to perform well in well-defined situations and contexts, but exhibit undue sensitivity to irrelevant changes. Similarly, image recognition that work well in numerous specific domains, cannot solve the general problem of object recognition plagued by its dependency on the specific representation, pose and lighting condition. Another example, although a number of DARPA-sponsored competitions over the years have led to decreasing error rates on increasingly difficult problems, the ability of a machine to recognize speech is still so inferior to the ability of a human [2,3]. Lippman (1997) gives us some comparisons between the error rate of machines and humans on a range of tasks [4]. Roughly, his results indicate that human error rates are an order of magnitude smaller than those obtained by ASR algorithms for clean speech, and two orders of magnitude smaller for typical noise conditions.

It is possible that the robustness of biological systems relies on their ability to combine the representation of sensory signals with prior knowledge. Biological perceptual systems seem to deploy redundant, multi-feature approaches that are highly adaptive and do not rely on neither single most important cue, nor invariant cue. Instead, these recognizers seem to be able to select the most appropriate cues for any given situation. Biological representations are typically redundant and not statistically efficient, but, in turn, they provide mechanisms to achieve robustness. In contrast, the traditional approach to statistically optimal pattern recognition uses a fixed and limited feature approach and strive to exploit as much as possible the information in the training data by removing all detectable redundancy. It is not surprising that the statistically efficient representation will perform poorly whenever the test conditions compromise information that was reliable in the training set [5].

In most biological systems sensory information is represented reliably and with sufficient completeness with action potentials – spikes – carried by massively parallel neural subsystems. This representation may be the result of the biological constraints of the processes and structures making up the neural system. At the same time this type of distributed, stochastic representation of the signals may in part be responsible for the superior resilience of these systems to the transformations of the physical signals and the changing environmental conditions.

It is not surprising, therefore, that, many recent research efforts have been focused on spike-based representation of signals [11, 12, 14]. In this paper, we discuss a way that the natural auditory system represents high-bandwidth acoustic information with relatively slow sampling rates of the individual neurons. This notion provides a reason for the well-known narrow tuning of the peripheral auditory system. We explore the ability of the temporal code generated by spiking neurons to represent and communicate acoustic signals in narrow frequency bands. This type of representation is consistent with the findings that temporal envelope plays an important role in human speech recognition [6], and therefore, this type of representation may be useful for automatic speech recognition systems.

II. Signal Processing and Representation

It is well known that the acoustic signal processing in mammal peripheral auditory systems can be characterized by three processing stages [7]:
- Narrow band filtering by the mechanical vibrations of the basilar membrane in the inner ear and transduction by the hair cells.
- The information in the narrow-band filter is coded in spike trains generated by cochlea neurons.
- Pattern recognition performed on the neural representation. Since the focus of this paper is the signal representation rather than pattern recognition, we use signal reconstruction instead of pattern recognition.

These three processing stages are represented in the present model by the following three algorithms:
- Short time Fourier analysis that generate narrow band signals.
- Model individual neurons and the processes that generate spikes.
- Reconstruction of the input signal from the spike train.

The last algorithm is included in the present model in order to enable an evaluation of the representation in terms of the reconstruction of the original signal.

A. Narrow Band Signal Representation Using Short-Time Fourier Analysis

The first component of the model uses Fourier analysis to simulate the narrow band signal that serves as the input to the individual auditory neurons. The Short Time Fourier Transform (STFT) is applied to the signal and then obtain the subband signal by inverse STFT analysis of each frequency component (other components are set to zero). With an appropriate type of window (Hanning) combined with an overlap-add process we can perfectly reconstruct the original signal. Therefore, this narrow-band representation preserves all the original signal information.

More specifically, given a digital signal $x(n)$, we first calculate the short time Fourier transform $X(l,k)$ of the lth frame Hanning windowed signal as follows:

$$X(l,k) = \sum_{n=0}^{N-1} w(n) x(n+lH) e^{-jw_k n}, \ l = 0,1,\cdots \quad , \text{ where}$$

$w(n) = 0.5 \left(1 + \cos\left(\frac{2\pi n}{N_{FFT}}\right)\right)$ is the real Hanning window with length equal to the number of FFT point N_{FFT}, l is the frame number and H indicates the offset by each successive frame. The kth subband real time signal for the lth frame can be obtained by inverse Fourier transform of the kth component (others are set to zero), written as:

$$x_l(k,n) = real\big(IFFT(X(l,k))\big)$$
$$= real\big(X(l,k) e^{jw_k n}\big), \ l = 0,1,\cdots$$

The whole range subband signal can be obtained by overlap adding $x_l(k,n)$, resulting:

$$x(k,n) = \sum_{\substack{\forall l \text{ which covers} \\ \text{sample } n}} x_l(k, n \bmod H), \ l = 0,1,\cdots \quad .$$ Note

that the resulting narrow-band signal can be represented in terms of a carrier signal with frequency at the center of the band amplitude-modulated by band-limited signal with frequency determined by the narrow band

B. Sampling – Spike Train Generation

A complete model of a spiking neuron would include integrate and fire model [8, 9, 13] in combination with a process that represent the refractory period of the neuron. For the purpose of simplicity of this presentation, we focus on the effect of the refractory period. In fact, we assume that after firing, a neuron will slowly recover its sensitivity and we represent this process by a monotonically decreasing refractory function $g(t-t_{i-1})$ where t_{i-1} is the time of the previous firing – for the purpose of this presentation we ignore the short absolute refractory period. This function can be interpreted as a threshold which, when exceeded by the input signal, is responsible for a generation of a spike. The actual shape of the threshold function is not critical and for the purpose of this paper, we assumed that it is well approximated by an exponential, namely

$$g(t) = A\exp\left(-\tfrac{1}{\tau}(t-t_{i-1})\right), \text{ where } t_{i-1} \text{ is the previous}$$

firing time and τ controls the decay of the threshold over time. We assume that the membrane potential is generated proportional to the amplitude of the input stimuli, so that we generate a spike whenever the instantaneous amplitude of the input signal exceeds the value of the threshold function as shown as in Fig.1 (a) and (b).

Because of the non-linearity of this system, we examine its properties using simulation. The input is white Gaussian noise and the states of the subband neurons is randomized, so that the first firing time t_1 is in the range of 0 – 12.5msec (τ) after the signal onset. Each subsequent firing occurs at the peak of the carrier nearest to the point at which the threshold function was exceeded. After a spike is generated, the refractory function is initialized and the process is repeated. The resulting signal representation is a sample sequence with sample times $t_k^{samp} = [t_1^k \ t_2^k \ \cdots \ t_{N(k)}^k]$. Because of the nature

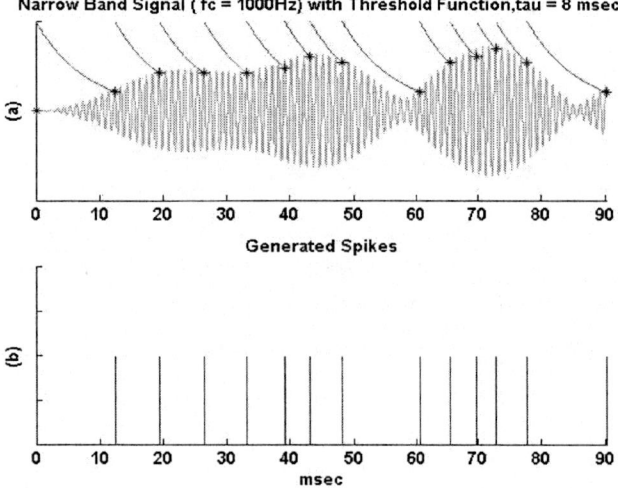

Fig.1. Illustration of spike generation

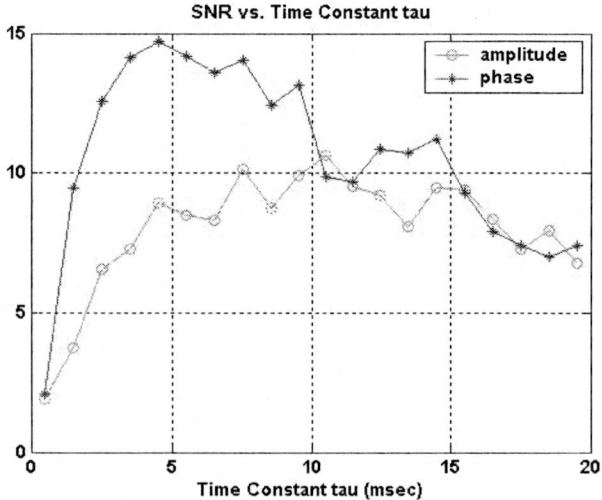

Fig.2. Comparison of phase-based coding and amplitude-based coding

of the sampling process, $N(k)$ and the spike train may be different for different bands. Since the function g and the time of the spikes are known, both the phase and the amplitude modulation of the narrow-band signal can be reconstructed – see Section II (C). The critical aspect of this sampling process is that the carrier phase is preserved by triggering the spikes at the peaks of the carrier signal. This sampling process preserves the phase of the carrier, but introduces amplitude errors in the modulating signal. The sampling process can be modified by trading off between the phase and amplitude errors. An illustration of the tradeoff is shown in figure (Fig.2) where we compare phase-based and amplitude-based coding. This result illustrates the fact that the signal-to-noise ratios (SNR) are much higher when spikes are generated at the peaks of the signal, thereby preserving the phase of the carrier.

In order to represent the biological systems more accurately, we introduced additive noise that randomized the sampling times [9].

C. Reconstruction of the Signal

To assess the amount of information encoded in the spike train $t_k^{samp} = [t_1^k \; t_2^k \; \cdots \; t_{N(k)}^k]$, we compared the original signal to its estimate obtained by signal reconstruction from the samples. We note that the spike train provides amplitude information about the original signal because $\hat{a}_k^{samp} = [g(t_1^k) \; g(t_2^k) \; g(t_3^k) \; \cdots \; g(t_{N(k)}^k)]$ provides an approximation to the amplitude samples:

$a_k^{samp} = [x(t_1^k) \; x(t_2^k) \; x(t_3^k) \; \cdots \; x(t_{N(k)}^k)]$.

The first step of the reconstruction process involves interpolation of the amplitudes $\hat{a}_k^{samp}$ providing amplitude estimates at each point t $\tilde{a}_k(t)$, for $t = 1 \ldots N$. The phase is calculated using the assumption that the signal was sampled at the peaks of the subband signal. Theoretically, each subband signal can be approximated as $x_k(t) = a_k(t)\cos(2\pi kt + \phi(t))$, at the spikes (peaks) $\cos(2\pi kt_k^{samp} + \phi(t_k^{samp})) = 1$, $2\pi kt_k^{samp} + \phi(t_k^{samp}) = 0$, $\phi(t_k^{samp}) = -2\pi kt_k^{samp}$ so the phase at the sampled point $\phi(t_k^{samp})$ is also known. We interpolate and smooth (unwrap) the phase to obtain the phase estimates at each sample point $\tilde{\phi}_k(t)$, for $t = 1 \ldots N$. The kth subband signal is reconstructed using:

$$\tilde{x}_k(t) = \tilde{a}_k(t)\cos(2\pi kt + \tilde{\phi}_k(t)).$$

The temporal encoding of the amplitude is transparent in the analytic expression for the spike signal, given by the expression:

$$a_k(t_i) = g(t_i) = A\exp\left(-\tfrac{1}{\tau}(t_i - t_{i-1})\right)$$
$$\approx A\left(1 - \tfrac{1}{\tau}(t_i - t_{i-1})\right) = \tfrac{A}{\tau}\left(\tau - (t_i - t_{i-1})\right).$$

III. EVALUATION

A. Evaluation by White Gaussian Noise

As noted in Section II we first evaluated the proposed signal representation using white Gaussian noise with zero mean and unity standard deviation, i.e. $x \sim N(0,1)$ as the input to the model. This type signal is characterized by high degree of uncertainty (low autocorrelation) and therefore is not predictable. This evaluation was performed using segments of the signal with 4096 samples, at the sampling frequency of 16 kHz. These segments were filtered using a 512-point short time Fourier transform described in section II. To simulate the spontaneous and random spikes of the neuron, we added random Gaussian noise to the subband signal and also controlled the probability of neuron firing at each cross point of $g(t)$ and $x_f(t)$. Fig.3 (a) shows subband signal centered at $f_c = 1000\ Hz$ after the inverse transform and overlap adding. It is very clear that although only a few spikes are generated (53 spikes) for the signal which consists of 4096 samples (Fig.3 (b)); the signal is still represented very well (Fig.3(c)). We note that in this representation only one bit is allocated for each spike and the total number of bytes required for the spike train is approximately 53*256/8 = 1696, and the bit rate is reduced to 1696/4096 = 41.41% of the original bit rate, assuming each sample of the signal being represented only by one byte.

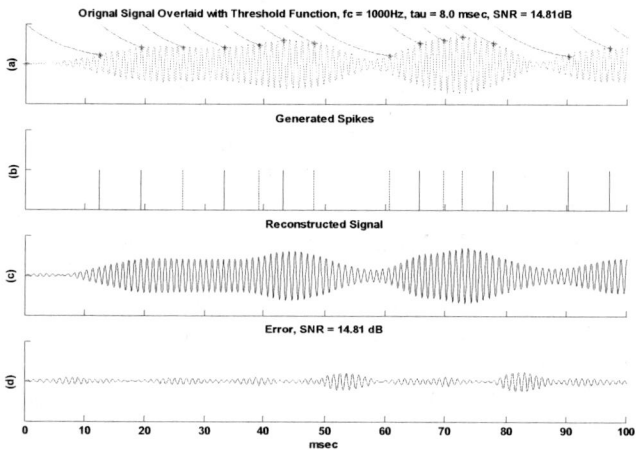

Fig.3. (a) Subband signal $f_c = 1000\ Hz$ (b) spike train (c) reconstructed signal (d) Error

The full band signal was obtained by summing up all the individual subbands, as shown in Fig. 4.

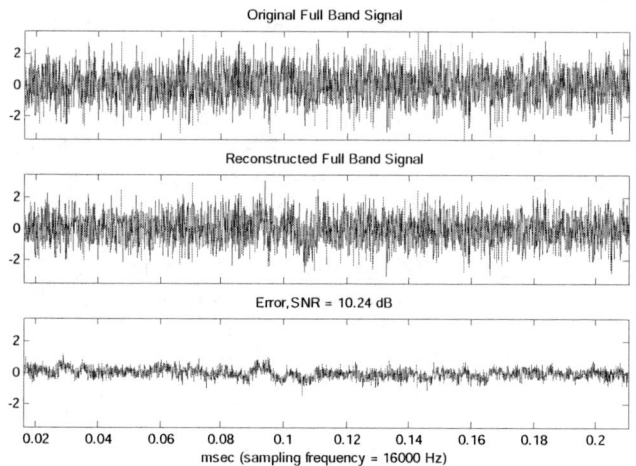

Fig.4. (a) original noise input (b) reconstructed (c) error

The histogram of interspike interval (Fig. 5) from 20 neurons shows that the time intervals between nerve firings are approximately integral multiples of the period (1 millisecond for $f_c = 1000\ Hz$) of the stimulating waveform, which is consistent with the prior experimental results of Rose et al. in [7,10].

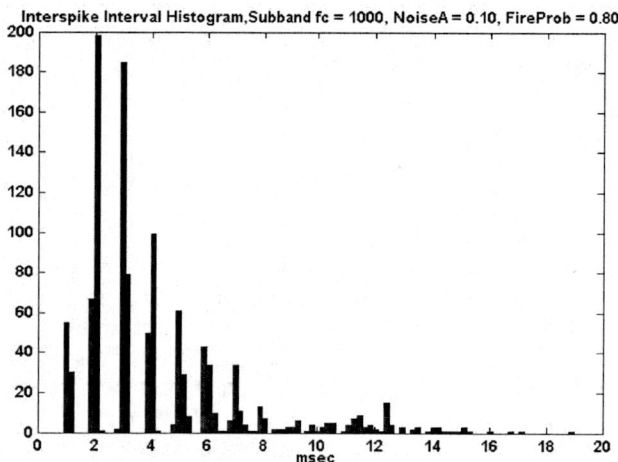

Fig.5. Histogram of interspike interval for subband signal ($f_c = 1000\ Hz$) extracted from 20 neurons

B. Evaluation by Speech

In the second part of the evaluation we used speech signal from TIMIT database. The length of the signal was 8192 samples at the sampling frequency of 16 kHz. The signal to noise ratio for the reconstructed speech was 12.95dB (see Fig. 6). This value is to be compared with the signal to noise ratio for the reconstructed noise, namely 10.24dB (Fig.4.). This result is consistent with the observation that human auditory system is more accurate in representing speech than random noise.

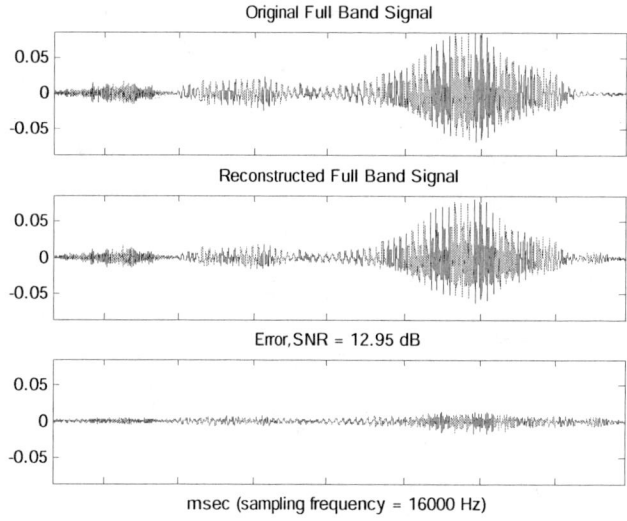

Fig.6. (a) original speech input (b) reconstructed (c) error
This figure shows the initial section of the speech signal in file \TIMIT\TEST\DR1\FAKS0\SA.WAV- "she had"

In addition to the evaluation of the coding scheme with deterministic neurons, we thought it useful to add a stochastic element to the responses of each neuron. In particular, to simulate the spontaneous and random nature of the neuronal spikes, we added random Gaussian noise to the subband signal at around 13dB. We then compared the reconstructed signal to both the original speech signal and to that contaminated by noise. In particular, if we denote the original clean speech $s(n)$, the reconstructed speech $r(n)$, the original signal contaminated by noise $x(n)$, it turns out that $\|r-s\|/\|s\| < \|r-x\|/\|x\|$.

To investigate this signal enhancement effect with respect to the individual channel bandwidths, we used different lengths of FFT points to evaluate how narrow the subband should be for better reconstruction and the results are shown in Fig.7. The results suggest that 512 – point Fourier transform is sufficiently long for accurate signal representation. For shorter windows, i.e., NFFT<256, the bandwidth of the subband signal wasn't narrow enough and the subband signal could no longer be approximated by amplitude modulated sinusoidal. The resulting increase in the reconstruction error is shown in Fig. 7. The results in Fig. 7 also demonstrate that the reconstructed signal is consistently closer to the original clean speech signal than to the noisy speech signal for different length of FFT. The signal to noise ratio of the noisy speech presented to the model was 13dB for all cases of NFFT.

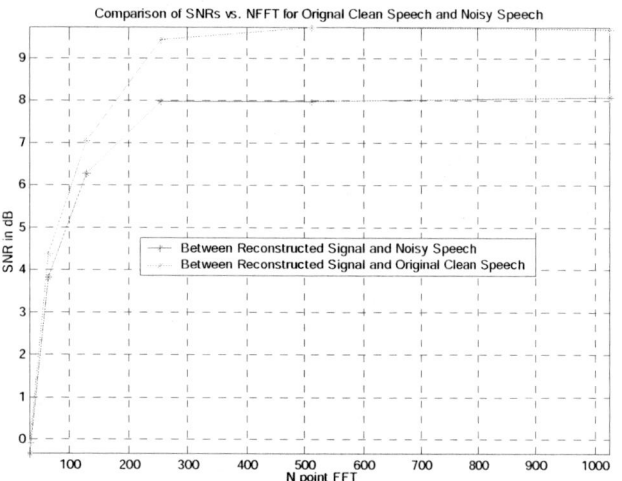

Fig.7. Comparison of SNR for original clean speech and noisy speech as a function of the length of the FFT window.

IV. Conclusions

In this paper, we have examined a possible neural model that underlies the mechanisms of the auditory neurons used to encode the acoustic input stimuli. The model based on the fact that the refractory period of each neuron represents a natural mechanism that can convert amplitude to temporal code while maintaining phase information of the carrier. We found that the narrow band envelope information could be encoded simply in the temporal inter-spike intervals. Using this model, auditory neurons can encode the narrow band signal in the neuron spiking trains and we demonstrated the utility of this model by comparing the reconstructed signal to the original input signal. The preliminary results suggest that the mechanisms in this model can represent natural signals such as speech with higher signal to noise ratio than signals such as white noise. This result is consistent with the notion that signal representation in biological systems is resilient to noise.

Acknowledgments

This research was supported by a NASA Grant NCC2-1218 to Oregon Health & Science University. We are grateful to Hynek Hermansky for fruitful discussions.

References

[1] M. Pavel and H. Hermansky, "Information Fusion by Human and Machine," First European Conference on Signal Analysis and Prediction, Strahov Monastery, Prague, Czech Republic, June 24~27, 1997.

[2] DARPA's EARS Conference (Boston, MA, May 21-22,2003)

[3] DARPA's EARS Kickoff Meeting (Vienna, VA, May 9-10,2002)

[4] R.P.Lippman, "Speech recognition by machines and humans", Speech Communication 22(1997) 1-15.

[5] Guoping Wang, Misha Pavel and Xubo Song, Robust recognition based on adaptive combination of weak classifiers, Proceedings of the International Joint Conference on Neural Networks, 20-24 July 2003.

[6] Robet V. Shannon, Fan-Gang Zeng;,Vivek Kamath; John Wygonski; Michael Ekelid, Speech Recognition with Primarily Temporal Cues, Science, New Series, Vol.270, No.5234 (Oct.13,1995), 303-304.

[7] Moore, Brian C. J., An introduction to the psychology of hearing, Imprint London : Academic Press, c1989.

[8] Wulfram Gerstner, Werner Kistler, Spiking Neuron Models – single neurons, populations, plasticity, Cambridge University Press, 2002

[9] Rieke F., Warland D., van Steveninck R., Bialek W (1997) Spikes: Exploring the Neural Code MIT Press

[10] Rose, J.E., Brugger, J.F., Anderson, D.J. and Hind, J.E. (1968). Patterns of activity in single auditory nerve fibers of the squirrel monkey. In Hearing Mechanism in Vertebrates (ed. A.V.S. de Reuck and J. Knight), Churchill, London.

[11] M.S. Lewicki, Efficient coding of natural sounds, Nature Neuroscience 5(4) 354-363, 2002.

[12] Lewicki, M.S. and Sejnowski, T.J. (1999), Coding time-varying signals using sparse, shift-invariant representations. Advances in Neural Information Processing Systems 11, 730-736. MIT Press

[13] L./S. Smith, D. S. Fraser, Robust sound onset detection using leaky integrate and fire neurons with depressing synapses, IEEE Transactions on Neural Networks, 15, 5, (Sept 2004), pp 1125-1134.

[14] DeLiang Wang and Guy. J Brown, "Separation of speech from. interfering sounds based on oscillatory correlation," IEEE. Transactions on Neural Networks, vol.10, No.3, May 1999.

Comparative Genomic Study of Parkinson's Disease Candidate Genes

Gavyn W.L Pang
BioInformatics Research Centre
Nanyang Technological University
Singapore 639798
E-mail: gavyn@pmail.ntu.edu.sg

Jagath C. Rajapakse
School of Computer Engineering
Nanyang Technological Univerisity
Singapore 639798
E-mail: asjagath@ntu.edu.sg

Abstract—Several candidate genes affect Parkinson's Disease in a variety of ways. A comparative analysis is performed using orthologues of these genes in other vertebrates species, such as chimp, mouse, rat, chicken, fugu, and tetraodon. The analysis reveals the presence of transmembrane regions and signal peptides in several sequences of some species, which provides a better understanding of the variability of structural and functional aspects of these genes in different species.

I. INTRODUCTION

Over the few decades, the advances in the field of molecular biology and bio-instrumentalism have allowed rapid sequencing of complete genomes of several species. The recent advancements in the field of bioinformatics have enabled the efficient use of tools on similar analysis of various genomes, allowing the application of comparative analysis on biological sequences from different genomes. This provides the chance to view cross species synteny using whole genomes.

Research has almost convinced us that many diseases have genetic mechanisms and many of the disease traits pass down from one generation to another. Evolutionary studies of the genes that affect these diseases may answer some questions and provide evidences from the past of the present status of these diseases. Looking for similar genes in other species like chimp, chicken, mouse, rat, fugu, and tetraodon allows us to cross examine the disease candidate genes in human, using computational methods [4]; thus disease, virus genes, and their orthologues can be compared between hosts and other species [22]. While the use of homology modelling and heuristics allow better analysis and prediction of the structures of genes, comparison of disease genes in different species provides insights as to how they affect their hosts under different functional constraints [2][12].

In this study, we are interested in finding out some of the biological functions of the genes which affect Parkinson's disease (PD). Genes recognized as candidate genes for PD are TGFA, SPR, UCH-L1, DRD2, Parkin and α-synuclein. All of these genes have been extensively researched and identified to affect PD in various ways. Orthologous genes can be found in other species and are well-conserved [8]. By subjecting PD candidate genes and their orthologues in other species to a comparative analysis, signals that control gene function maybe identified, which enables innovative approaches for treating the disease possible [19].

PD is a disorder of the brain cells, in which parts of the brain progressively stop working and cause disintegration and malfunctions to the sufferer. The disease particularly affect people aged 65 and above [14]. Diagnosing PD can be difficult and inefficient, primarily due to its slow progressive impacts and symptoms. One of the more obvious symptoms includes problems with movement and dementia [10]. Genetics has greatly improved the research on PD, with better drugs being discovered and treatments improved, but research is still being handicapped by the inability to obtain accurate data involving human linkage of patients [1].

There are currently eight loci of human linked to PD. The more conclusive genes, which had been found to hold disease causing mutations include α-synuclein (PARK1) on 4q21-22 [16], parkin (PARK2) on 6q25.2-q27 [5] and ubiquitin C-terminal hydrolase gene (PARK5) on 4p16. The other five loci include PARK3 on 2p13, PARK4 on 4p14-15 [6], PARK6 on 1p35-36, PARK7 on 1p35-36 and PARK8 on 12p11.2-q13.1 [14][7]. These loci contain candidate genes which are suspects for PD causing mutations [11]. These genes might have various biological and functional inferences [17]. By looking for conservation of these genes in other species, we may get an idea of how homologous genes function in different species [21].

One biological inference we can obtain is to investigate if the sequence translate to transmembrane proteins. Membrane proteins can be viewed as important members in a cell to cell signalling mechanism and other related signalling features. They often serve as a medium for transport for ions and solutes through the membrane [23]. Many other gene functions are known to relate themselves with the membrane. These information is of great interest to pharmaceutical companies since membrane-bound receptors and channels have repeatedly proven to be fruitful therapeutic targets. Another valuable information relates to whether membrane proteins can mediate acquired resistance to drugs. All these allow practical research to be carried out with the support of the pharmaceutical industry.

Another study we perform, in this paper, is to find peptide binding sites from the genes. Many different secretory signals can be found in genes, they are usually used to indicate to the endoplasmatic reticulum for passage to the secretory pathway. Some of the proteins might subsequently go through translational modifications. Our results will show that there is an obvious correlation between prediction of transmembrane regions and signal peptides. Many of the genes involved in PD have evoked pharmaceutical interest as they indicate roles in the regulation of peptide hormones in some species.

II. METHODS

A. Candidate genes

Parkin is one of the well-researched genes and the evaluation of transmembrane regions and signal peptides will allow us to know its reaction to certain drug types and some of its functions. There is little, if any, evidence that indicates the presence of any transmembrane regions and signal peptides. This is the same for all its orthologues in other species.

The α-synuclein (PARK1) gene was found using Mediterranean kindred, affecting a number of families from Italy and Greece [15]. This was the first candidate gene discovered for PD and had been defined as a rare cause of early-onset PD. The disease has an autosomal dominant pattern of inheritance [18]. The gene was shown to be much conserved in various species, which could in turn relate to a conservation of functional importance.

Autosomal Recessive Juvenile (ARJP) Parkinson's disease, a form of PD, has been attributed to a number of point mutations and deletions of the parkin (PARK2) gene [9]. ARJP is specifically characterized by a very early onset, mostly before forty years of age; typically the symptoms can appear from age seven to 58. Variants of parkin (PARK2) are frequently found in families where PD is inherited in an autosomal recessive pattern. Many families with PD history reported occurrence of this gene. In humans, the parkin gene encodes a 465 amino acid protein that functions as one of a number of E3 ubiquitin protein ligases, components of the ubiquitin/proteasome degradation pathway. Ubiquitin protein ligases act to identify damaged, misfolded, and short-lived proteins to mediate the ubiquitination of these proteins, which are targeted to the proteasome. The loss of parkin may lead to an accumulation of one or a number of proteins in sufficient quantities to cause neuronal cell death [24].

SPR (PARK3) is located to the region of chromosome 2p13 in a subset of families with autosomal dominant inheritance. The authors described a genetic locus that appeared to be involved in the development of parkinsonism closely resembling typical PD. This locus was detected in a group of six families of European origin and in two of these families from a relatively small area in Northern Germany and Southern Denmark. The penetrance of the disease at this locus was estimated to be 40% because of the relatively frequent occurrence of the affected haplotype in clinically asymptomatic members in the two families. Although the sequencing of 14 candidate genes within the region did not reveal any potentially pathogenic mutations segregating the disease, the gene SPR, together with TGFA, are very much suspected candidates, therefore the need for further research.

The gene DRD2 is at the PARK4 locus. The disease segregated as an apparent autosomal dominant trait. The family involved had other atypical features such as dysautonomia and dementia. The locus was found on chromosome 4p12-15. For the individuals involved, some who do not suffer from the disease suffer from a postural and kinetic tremor, often linked with essential tremor. The gene is close to the location of UCH-L1 but later found to have different linkages.

The UCH-L1 (PARK5) gene which maps to 4p16, was sequenced using a sibling pair of German orgin with typical PD. The brother experienced resting tremors at age 51 while the sister at age 49. Other symptoms include rigidity, bradykinesia and postural instability with a beneficial response to levodopa. Isoleucine 93 is conserved across species in UCH-L1 and UCH-L3 in human, rat and mouse. UCH-L1 is an abundant brain protein accounting for 1-2% of total soluble brain proteins present in all neurons and is also present in Lewy bodies. UCH-L1 is a thiol protease belonging to a family of deubiquitinating enzymes. An association study using a polymorphism within this gene demonstrated that it may confer a protective affect adding to the possibility that this protein may play a role in the pathogenesis [20].

B. Orthologues

The dataset for our experiments was obtained from the Ensembl database (www.ensembl.org). We obtained the peptide sequences, corresponding to candidate genes of PD, from the human database. The genes we will be focusing on are the PD causing genes which are located at the various human loci. We are interested in comparing these genes with similar genes in other species or, more specifically, in vertebrates, taking a purely comparative analysis approach, to make inferences about their structure and function.

The nucleotide sequence of each gene was compared across the whole genome using BLAST to search for orthologous genes in rat, mouse, chimp, chicken, fugu, and tetraodon. Orthologues refer to genes which have evolved directly from the same ancestral locus whereas paralogues more commonly refer to genes which were originated by duplication and then diverged from the parent copy by mutation and selection or drift. The results showed us a combination of reciprocal best matches and syntenic evidence across the genomes. It is not easy to separate true orthologues from paralogues by using similarity searches alone. BLAST was used to identify the largest aligned segment and those with good scores, high sequence identity and expectation value of less than 0.001 were considered as orthologous.

Sequences of orthologous ambiguity, for example those with bad scores and badly aligned sequences, were not used. After we obtained sets of orthologues from various species, we need to align them in order to proceed to other analysis, looking for transmembrane regions and signal peptides. ClustalW (version 1.83) was used as the alignment tool and the default parameters were used. Alignments were manually examined and those poorly aligned were removed or added different parameters to improve the alignment. Frequently, alignments produced many gaps and extending the overall length of the sequence significantly, which were considered statistical outliers and were removed.

C. Protein transmembrane structure

Very few studies have been carried out on transmembraneous properties of the PD candidate genes; therefore it is interesting to compare these properties across species. All the gene sequences including their respective orthologues, were analyzed with TMHMM program [13] to decide whether they correspond to transmembrane proteins. The TMHMM program is very efficient in detecting transmembraneous regions in the sequences and shown to be the best transmembrane protein structure prediction program among the currently available, and is the most widely used transmembrane prediction tool.

Due to the presence of distinctive patterns of hydrophobic and polar regions in the sequences, we are able to give an accurate prediction of the presence of transmembrane regions. Research shows that different species have roughly the same percentage of transmembrane proteins. A quarter of all the proteins in public domain databases like SWISS-PROT and TrEMBL are transmembrane sequences. This shows that these proteins are very commonly found and therefore contain distinctive biological and functional roles. By finding transmembrane regions in the genes that affect PD, we are able to see how the genes do signalling and whether there are specific functions involved.

Proteins can also be membrane bound even if they do not possess a transmembrane sequence but if they contain a lipid anchor. In that case the protein is post-translationally modified with a glycosylphosphatidylinositol (GPI) moiety and anchored on the extracellular side of the plasma membrane.

D. Signal peptides cleavage sites

The presence of signal sequences in the genes and their possible cleavage sites were predicted with the SignalP V2.0 program. SignalP is one the more commonly used methods to predict presence of signal peptidase cleavage sites [3]. The program consists of two different predictors based on (1) neural networks and (2) a hidden Markov model. The basic idea behind SignalP is that cleavage site position and the amino acid composition of the signal peptide are correlated. In the latest version of the program, signal peptide discrimination has improved mainly due to the elimination of false-positive predictions.

The SignalP program gives a score Y combining two scores: C-score and S-score. The C-score refers to the cleavage site positional score. The score will be significantly high at predicted cleavage sites. The position range of the predicted cleavage site refers to the start and end of the site. The S-score is a determinant for differentiating secretory and non-secretory protein. The Y-score is the derivative of the C-score combined with the S-score to obtain a better prediction.

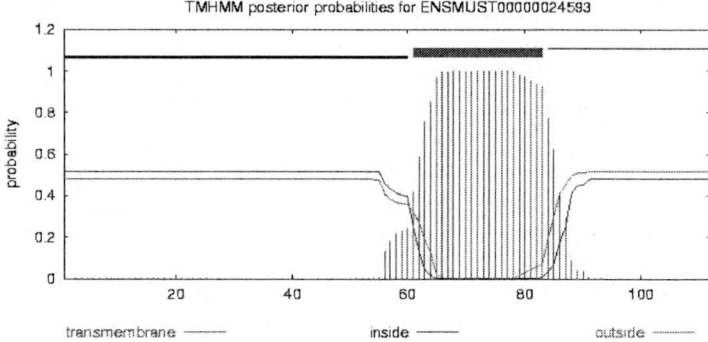

Fig. 1. The TMHMM results of Parkin in mouse

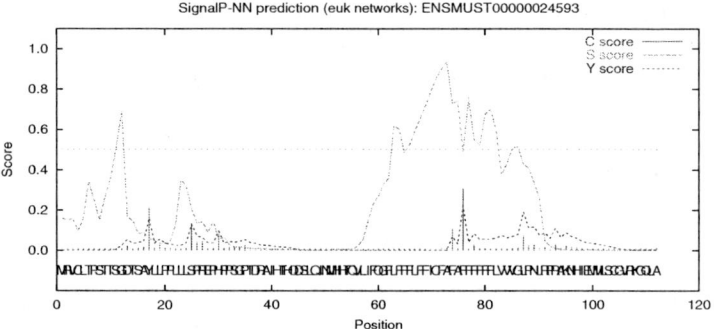

Fig. 2. The SignalP results of Parkin in mouse

III. RESULTS

The two programs, TMHMM and SignalP, were used to reveal prediction of the presence of the transmembrane regions and the signal peptides of the candidate PD genes sequences, respectively.

A. α-synuclein

α-synuclein is one of the most conserved gene among the PD candidate genes. TMHMM failed to find any trace of transmembrane region in human, chicken, mouse, chimp, rat, or fugu. SignalP also did not predict any signal peptide in the various sequences.

B. Parkin

There is no evidence of any transmembrane region or any similar features in the 386 amino acid sequence of the human gene. TMHMM gave a probability of less than 1% chance of finding a transmembrane region, but a transmembrane region was predicted in mouse at the 60 to 80 position (Figure 1) . Other orthologues which did not show significance include chimp, rat, and fugu. Figure 2 shows the presence of signal peptides, predicted in the mouse orthologue as well. Neural networks predicted the likely cleavage site to be at 75 and 76 position. This is very consistent with TMHMM which revealed the only significant result belonged to the mouse orthologue.

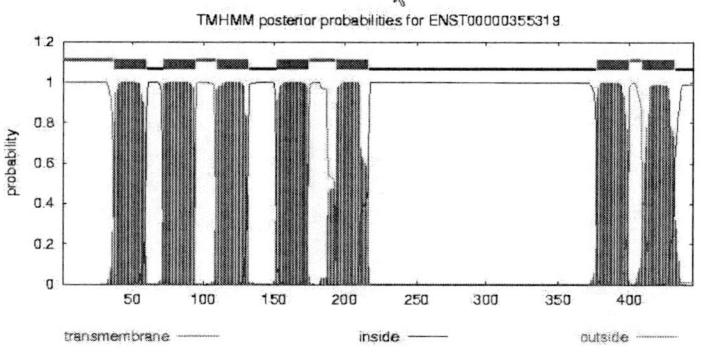

Fig. 3. The TMHMM results of DRD2 in human

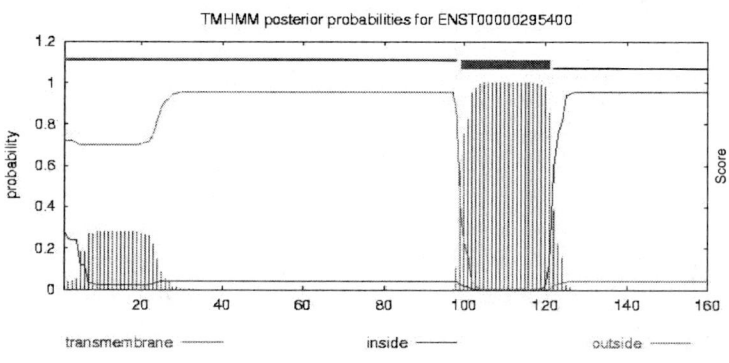

Fig. 4. The TMHMM results of TGFA in human

Fig. 5. The SignalP results of TGFA in human

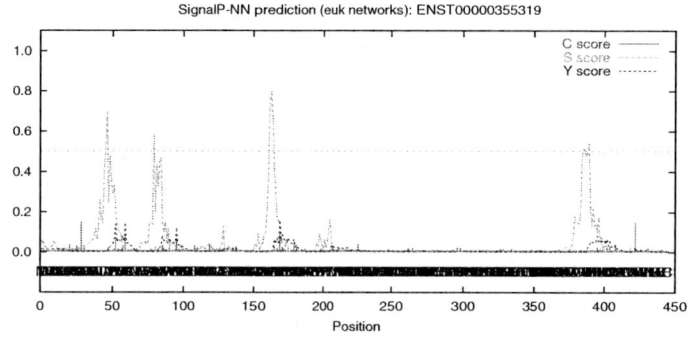

Fig. 6. The SignalP results of DRD2 in human

C. SPR

Results from TMHMM predicted no evidence of transmembrane regions in SPR. All the orthologues revealed low probability scores, except for tetraodon, which revealed a suspected region at 20 to 40 position. While TMHMM revealed little for SPR, the SignalP program predicted specific sites for signal peptides residues in the human sequence with a high probability of 0.813 and a cleavage site, probably at the 40 and 41 position in the sequence. Chicken orthologues showed the same prediction of signal peptide and cleavage position while using mouse orthologue, predicted the cleavage position to be at around 19 and 20 position in the sequence. Naturally, the rat orthologue showed a prediction much closer to mouse than to human or chimp. Fugu was not predicted to contain signal peptide and the probability that it may contain one is 0.290.

D. TGFA

The TMHMM predicted a similar region for human, mouse, chimp, and rat. This region is located at the 100 to 120 position (Figures 3-4). Tetraodon has a predicted region at 60 to 80 position, slightly dissimilar to the rest, while there is no indication of transmembrane regions in fugu. The SignalP predicted at similar cleavage site at the 20 to 23 position, and all orthologues are interpreted as signal peptides.

E. DRD2

Orthologous sequences for DRD2 were only found in rat, mouse, chimp, chicken, fugu, and tetraodon. The TMHMM predicted seven tranmembrane regions in a sequence length of the gene in human is 445. The seven regions were evenly spaced in the range of 37-445 (Figures 5 and 6). The results from the SignalP predicted the tranmembrane regions in human corresponding to high S-score in the neural networks prediction. There is no signal peptide predicted in human and the sequence is found to be non-secretory protein. There is a prediction of a signal peptide at the location of 49-50 with the rat orthologue. This is very similar to the prediction from the mouse orthologue due to the close similarity of the rat and mouse genome. Signal peptides are clearly predicted in the tetraodon orthologue with a probability of 0.864. the cleavage site is probably between 30 and 31. Fugu showed very similar evidences to tetraodon, with clear indication of the presence of signal peptides and likely cleavage position. The likely cleavage position between 26-27 is not far from that of tetraodon's.

F. UCH-L1

UCH-L1 was clearly predicted as having no transmembrane regions. SignalP's prediction showed very weak signals at 0-50 regions for all the sequences. TMHMM predicted no transmembrane regions in the human, rat, mouse, chimp, tetraodon, and fugu genes. A significant finding is the presence of an ambiguous transmembrane region located at the 100-150 position (Figures 7 and 8). Generally, weak signals were predicted by SignalP for all genes. Signal peptide was predicted using the chicken orthologue, with cleavage site around the 44

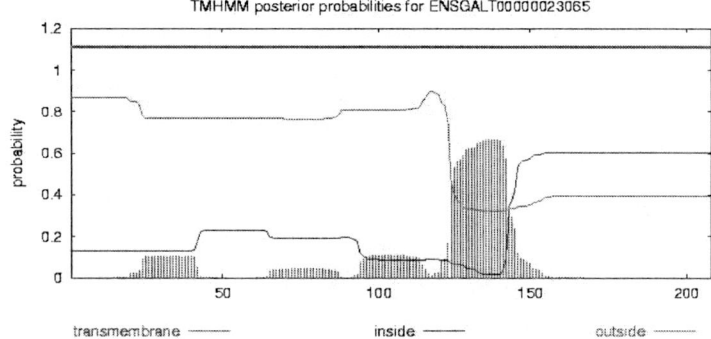

Fig. 7. The TMHMM results of UCH-L1 in human

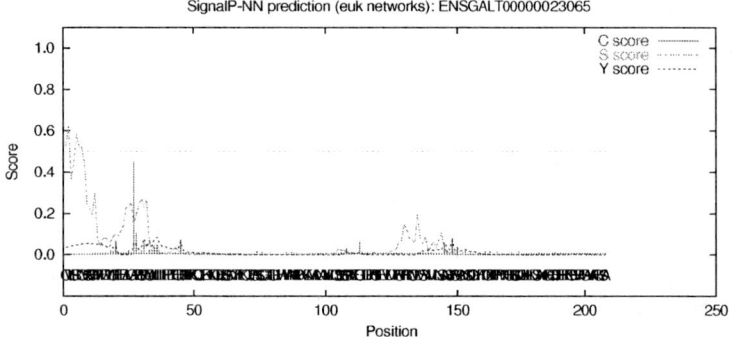

Fig. 8. The SignalP results of UCH-L1 in chicken

and 45 position. Very similar signals and scores were predicted using the mouse, chimp and tetraodon orthologues.

IV. Discussion and Conclusion

According to our analysis conducted using the TMHMM program, some of the genes were predicted to contain transmembrane regions. The genes like TGFA and DRD2 were predicted to have significant evidences of containing several transmembrane regions.

α-synuclein is a presynaptic nerve terminal protein and is an important candidate gene in PD. Our analysis showed there are no evidences of transmembrane region and signal peptide presence. Membrane proteins have different susceptibility as compared to non-membrane proteins and the lack of signal peptide provides a clue that should lead to the underlying pathways leading to PD. It is also very possible that neighboring genes of α-synuclein are also responsible for the disease pathology and structural mutation. If signal peptides are responsible for various signaling functions of the protein, then α-synuclein would seem to be an isolated protein and therefore the cause of the disease due to the mutation of this protein, may seem even more probable.

TGFA is discovered as a transforming growth factor alpha precursor protein and there are predicted transmembrane regions for human and all the orthologues we have chosen. SignalP also made strong prediction of signal peptides and anchors in human and other orthologues. It is interesting to note that, TGFA and DRD2, two of the lesser known PD candidate genes, contain transmembrane regions and signal peptides while very conserved genes like α-synuclein, parkin and UCH-L1 do not.

Sequence analysis with the SignalP program resulted in the identification of signal peptide sequences in the genes. This can mean that enzymes are secreted through the cell membrane. Genes like TGFA and DRD2 contained high probability values in both tests. In relation to the two tests, those corresponding to high probability values in the transmembrane test show similar result in signal peptide detection as well. There is a correlation between transmembrane regions and the signal peptides. When the presence of transmembrane region is detected, there is usually a prediction of signal peptides and vice versa.

PD is a complicated disease and inheriting candidate genes and mutations only convey susceptibility. There is still much information to be learnt regarding interactions between the genes and how they relate to PD. In this paper, we have found out there is a correlation between transmembrane regions and signal peptides; and in the case of these PD candidate genes, the more conserved and functionally significant genes like α-synuclein, parkin and UCH-L1 do not contain these features. However, there is some variability of the functional aspects investigated in different species, which are worthwhile for further investigation.

TABLE I
Summary Result of Transmembrane Region and Signal Peptide Prediction

Genes	Transmembrane Segments (TMS)	Signal Peptides (SP)
α-synuclein	No TMS in all species	No SP in all species
Parkin	TMS present in mouse, (60-80) chimp, rat, and fugu;	SPs found in mouse, no signs in human
SPR	TMS in tetraodon at (20-40)	SPs in human, chicken, mouse, and rat
TGFA	TMS found for human mouse, chimp, rat and tetraodon	SPs found in all species
DRD2	Multiple TMS in all species	SPs present except IN human and chicken
UCH-L1	No TMS in all species	Weak SP in chicken

References

[1] O. Bandmann, J. Vaughan, P. Holmans, C. D. Marsden, and N. W. Wood, "Association of slow acetylator genotype for N-acetyltransferase 2 with familial parkinson's disease," *Lancet*, vol. 350, pp. 1136–1139, 1997.
[2] A. K. Bansal and T. E. Meyer, "Evolutionary analysis by whole-genome comparisons," *Journal of Bacteriology*, vol. 184, no. 8, pp. 2260–2272, 2002.
[3] J. D. Bendtsen, H. Nielsen, G. V. Heijne, and S. Brunak, "Improved prediction of signal peptides - SignalP 3.0," *J. Mol. Biol*, 2004.
[4] A. Bernot and J. Weissenbach, "Estimation of the extent of synteny between Tetraodon nigroviridis and Homo sapiens genomes," *J Mol Evol*, vol. 59, pp. 556–569, 2004.

[5] R. Cesari, E. Martin, G. Calin, F. Pentimalli, R. Bichi, H. McAdams, F. Trapasso, A. Drusco, M. Shimizu, V. Masciullo, G. d'Andrilli, G. Scambia, M. Picchio, H. Alder, A. Godwin, and C. Croce, "Parkin, a gene implicated in autosomal recessive juvenile parkinsonism, is a candidate tumor suppressor gene on chromosome 6q25-27," *Proc.Natl.Acad.Sci*, vol. 100, no. 10, pp. 5956–5961, 2003.

[6] M. Farrer, K. Gwinn-Hardy, M. Muenter, F. DeVrieze, R. Crook, J. Perez-Tur, S. Lincoln, D. Maraganore, C. Adler, S. Newman, K. MacElwee, P. McCarthy, C. Miller, C. Waters, and J. Hardy, "A chromosome 4p haplotype segregating with Parkinson's disease and postural tremor," *Human Molecular Genetics*, vol. 8, no. 1, pp. 81–85, 1999.

[7] M. Funayama, K. Hesegawa, H. Kowa, M. Saito, S. Tsuji, and F. Obata, "A new locus for Parkinson's disease (park8) maps to chromosome 12p11.2-q13.1," *Ann Neurol*, vol. 51, pp. 296–301, 2002.

[8] G. N. Goulielmos, E. Eliopoulos, M. Loukas, and S. Tsakas, "Functional constraints of 6-Phosphogluconate Dehydrogenase (6-PGD) based on sequence and structural information," *J Mol Evol*, vol. 59, pp. 358–371, 2004.

[9] D. Grimes and D. Bulman, "Parkinson's genetics-creating exciting new insights," *Parkinsonism and Related Disorders*, vol. 8, pp. 459–464, 2002.

[10] A. Guttmacher and F. Collins, "Alzheimer's disease and Parkinson's disease," *N Engl J Med*, vol. 348, pp. 1356–1364, 2003.

[11] B. U. Halbach, "Synucleins and their relationship to Parkinson's disease," *Cell Tissue Res*, vol. 318, pp. 163–174, 2004.

[12] I. K. Jordan, F. A. Kondrashov, I. B. Rogozin, R. L. Tatsusov, Y. I. Wolf, and E. V. Koonin, "Constant relative rate of protein evolution and detection of functional diversification among bacterial, archeal and eukaryotic proteins," *Genome Biology*, vol. 2, no. 12, pp. 0053.1–0053.9, 2001.

[13] A. Krogh and B. Larsson, "Predicting transmembrane protein topology with a hidden markov model: application to compete genomes," *J.Mol.Biol*, 2001.

[14] J. Lambert, L. Goumidi, F. Vrieze, B. Frigard, J. Harris, A. Cummings, J. Coates, F. Pasquier, D. Cottel, M. Gaillac, D. Clair, D. Mann, J. Hardy, C. Lendon, P. Amouyel, and M. Chartier-Harlin, "The transcriptional factor LBP-1c/CP2/LSF gene on chromosome 12 is a genetic determinant of Alzheimer's disease," *Human Molecular Genetics*, vol. 9, no. 15, pp. 2275–2280, 2000.

[15] C. Lavedan, "The Synuclein family," *Genome Res*, vol. 8, pp. 871–880, 1998.

[16] D. Lee, S. R. Paik, and K. Y. Choi, "Beta-synuclein exhibits chaperone activity more efficiently than alpha-synuclein," *FEBS*, vol. 574, pp. 256–260, 2004.

[17] A. F. G. Leentjens, R. Lousberg, and F. R. J. Verhey, "Markers for depression in Parkinson's disease," *Acta Psychiatr Scand*, vol. 106, pp. 196–201, 2002.

[18] J. Y. Li, J. P. Henning, and A. Dahlstrom, "Differential localization of alpha-, beta- and gamma-synuclein in the rat cns," *Neuroscience*, vol. 113, pp. 463–478, 2002.

[19] W. H. Li, Z. L. Gu, H. D. Wang, and A. Nekrutenko, "Evolutionary analyses of the human genome," *Nature*, vol. 409, pp. 847–849, 2001.

[20] D. M. Maraganore, M. J. Ferrer, and J. A. Hardy, "Case-control study of the ubiquitin carboxy-terminal hydrolase l1 gene in parkinson's disease," *Neurology*, vol. 53, no. 8, pp. 1858–1860, 1999.

[21] F. Nikitin, B. Rance, and M. Itoh, "Using protein motis combinations to update kegg pathway maps and orthologue tables," *Genome Informatics*, vol. 15, no. 2, pp. 266–275, 2004.

[22] N. Stojanovic, "Computational methods for the analysis of differential conservation in groups of similar DNA sequences," *Genome Informatics*, vol. 15, no. 2, pp. 21–30, 2004.

[23] J. I. Venalainen, R. O. Juvonen, and P. T. Mannisto, "Evolutionary relationships of the prolyl oligopeptidase family enzymes," *Eur. J. Biochem*, vol. 271, pp. 2705–2715, 2004.

[24] A. West, M. Farrer, L. Petrucelli, M. Cookson, P. Lockhart, and J. Hardy, "Identification and characterization of the human parkin gene promoter," *Journal of Neurochemistry*, vol. 78, pp. 1146–1152, 201.

NeuroGene: Integrated simulation of gene regulation, neural activity and neurodevelopment

Rasmus Storjohann
School of Computing Science
Simon Fraser University
Burnaby, B.C. V5A 1S6
E-mail: rstorjoh@sfu.ca

Gary F. Marcus
Department of Psychology
University of New York
New York, N.Y. 10012
E-mail: gary.marcus@nyu.edu

Abstract— A challenge to understanding the mind and brain is to integrate biochemical, genetic, developmental and neuroscientific information. We present a system for integrated simulation of biochemistry, neurodevelopment and neural activity within a unifying framework of genetic control. Using this system, we have developed a novel model for the formation of topographic projections. We also simulate activity-dependent developmental processes which underlie receptive field refinement and ocular dominance column formation. As an illustration of the overall utility of integrated neurogenetic simulation, we show how axon guidance and learning together may explain the results of a critical study of topographic map development (Brown et al., 2000, Cell).

I. Introduction

Gaining an understanding of the human brain, one of the most complex systems in the known universe, will require ways of integrating a wealth of genetic, biochemical, neurological and developmental information. Towards this end, we present a novel simulation framework called NeuroGene. It is designed to simulate a wide range of neurodevelopmental processes, including gene regulation, protein expression, chemical signalling, neural activity and neuronal growth. Central is a computational model of genes, which allows protein concentrations, neural activity and cell morphology to affect, and be affected by, gene expression.

To illustrate the value of NeuroGene, we consider the development of topographic projections, such as the set of connections from retina to thalamus. Long a touchstone in neural development, topographic maps are now increasingly well understood at the genetic level. They are characterized by axons originating in adjacent locations in some afferent tissue projecting to adjacent locations in the target area, maintaining the spatial relationships in the transmitted information. Involved in a variety of sensory systems, topographic maps transmit visual, auditory, and somatosensory information, and play a role in connecting the thalamus to the cortex and the cortical halves to each other [1]. Further evidence suggests that topographic organization is maintained also in neural structures where learning occurs [2].

As is often the case in development, the formation of mature topographic projections depends on both activity-independent and activity-dependent processes [3, 4]. The former seem to lay down a "rough draft", while the latter tune the strength of synapses, leading to more focused connections where each afferent neuron connects to one or a few target cells while maintaining topographic order. Using NeuroGene, we have developed a novel model of topographic map formation that integrates both types of processes and yields results which are strikingly similar to those of a pivotal experimental study [5].

A. NeuroGene design

1) Genes and genetic control: The central role played by simulated genes within NeuroGene mimics the role of genes in coordinating developmental processes in nature. The NeuroGene gene model integrates intracellular signalling, gene transcription, translation, protein distribution across complex neurons as well as the effects of gene expression on cellular structure and function. Direct and indirect mechanisms of gene regulation by, and genetic control of, all aspects of cellular function may be represented. The genes are encoded in a simple programming language, as shown in fig. 1. Genes are common to all cells in a simulation.

NeuroGene can represent complex neuronal shapes and neural networks consisting of thousands of neurons. Complex neurons are represented by collections of *cell components* representing somas, linear segments of axons and dendrites and

```
gene Xyz {
    decay     = 0.3;
    diffusible = true;
    diffusion = 0.01;
    regulation {
        variable c = externalConcentrationOf(Xyz);
        if (insidePreSynapse() && c>0) {
            expressExternally(2.5 * log(c));
        }
    }
    effects {
        setSynapticWeight(1.1 * synapticWeight());
    }
}
```

Fig. 1. Example of a gene definition. Lines 2–4 specify the properties of the protein produced by the expression of the gene. The *regulation* portion determines the gene's expression rate, while the *effects* section contains actions triggered by the expression of the gene, carried out only if the expression rate is greater than zero. This gene causes extracellular production of a protein Xyz in presynaptic termini in response to extracellular Xyz, and at the same time also adjusts the synaptic weight.

presynaptic and postsynaptic terminals. Neurons are controlled by the genes, which are evaluated in all cell components.

Regulation of gene transcription and translation is simulated through the use of *queries*; see fig. 2. During the evaluation

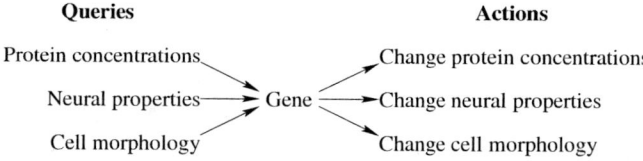

Fig. 2. NeuroGene uses queries and actions to represent the input and output of modelled genes.

of a gene within a given cell component, the gene queries the cell component, retrieving information about the biochemical, neural or morphological state of a cell component or its immediate environment. This information is used to determine the expression rate of the gene in that cell component, according to the gene's *regulation* section (fig. 1). It is the state of the individual cell component (not the cell as a whole) which determines the expression rate of the gene. Effects of the gene, including protein production, apply to the cell component.

In nature, many proteins are found primarily in particular sub-cellular structures, such as dendrites or postsynaptic termini. The expression of a gene can be limited to certain cell component types by using queries such as "`inside-PreSynapse()`" (fig. 1). This query is *true* when evaluated within presynaptic termini and *false* otherwise. Used in the regulation section of a gene, such queries can limit the expression of the gene to particular cellular substructures.

Genes' influence on cellular behaviour, morphology and neural properties in nature is mediated through molecular interactions involving proteins and other molecules. In NeuroGene, this relationship is modelled by *actions* (fig. 2). The actions in a gene's *effects* section (fig. 1) are only invoked when and where the gene is expressed (i.e., the expression rate is greater than zero), reflecting the causal relationship between gene expression and cellular changes. NeuroGene can thus represent genetic control over cellular biochemistry, morphology and neural activity.

2) Growth cones: Neural growth cones control axon growth, guidance and synapse formation. A growth cone consists of a number of short fibres, known as *filopodia*, which extend from the axon tip. These perceive their environment, primarily through chemical signalling. Axon growth occurs though the selective enlargement of one filopodium. The enlarged filopodium is converted into axon trunk while the remaining filopodia are retracted.

In our model, growth cones consist of N filopodia, each extending a distance R from the axon tip in a randomly chosen direction. The behaviour of the growth cone is determined by the *growth cone function* (GCF), which is encoded in the genetic programming language (fig. 3). The competitive interaction among filopodia is modelled using an *auction* mechanism. The evaluation of the GCF for each filopodium gives a real number (the *bid*) and an action; fig. 4. The filopodium with the highest bid wins the auction and the corresponding action is carried out, while the other filopodia and their computed actions are discarded.

Filopodia interact directly with individual cell components in their vicinity, and perceive their individual surface protein concentrations, whereas other cell component types only perceive concentrations averaged over all neighbours. This can be used to simulate specific synapse formation.

3) Proteins: Key components in development, both in nature and in NeuroGene, are proteins. Proteins play a vital role in chemical communication both within and between cells, and in coordinating developmental processes. The properties of simulated proteins are defined as part of the corresponding gene definition (fig. 1). We distinguish between soluble and membrane bound proteins which may exist inside cell components, bound to their surface membranes, and dissolved in the extracellular space. All proteins are subject to first-order decay with rate constants specific to each protein. In the extracellular space, soluble proteins are also subject to simulated diffusion. Simulation of receptor-ligand binding assuming chemical equilibrium permits simple implementation of some competitive processes.

Modelling chemical signalling is central to NeuroGene simulations. Gene expression within a particular cell component may depend on extracellular protein concentrations, concentration gradients and/or the average concentrations of membrane bound proteins bound to neighbouring cell components. Intra-

```
growthconefunction findSourceOfXyz {
    filopodiumCount  = 9;
    filopodiumLength = 0.2;
    if (neighbourConcentrationOf(Robo) > 0) {
        presynapse(1.0/neighbourRange());
    } else {
        migrate(externalConcentrationOf(Xyz));
    }
}
```

Fig. 3. An example NeuroGene growth cone function with $N = 9$ and $R = 0.2$. The actions `presynapse()` and `migrate()` specify the corresponding actions as shown in figure 4. The query `neighbourConcentrationOf()` returns zero for all proteins if the filopodium does not interact with any neighbouring cell component.

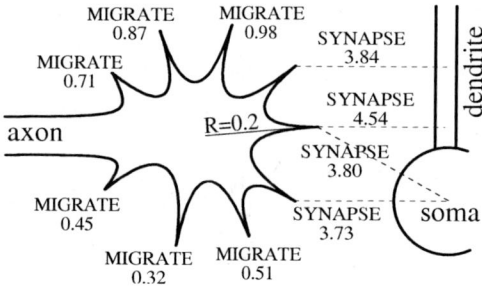

Fig. 4. Growth cone mechanism using the growth cone function from fig. 3, assuming a vertical gradient of Xyz. Here the winning bid is 4.54, and causes the axon to form a synapse with the neighbouring dendrite. A filopodium may interact with more than one neighbouring cell component, in which case a bid value and action is computed for each neighbour as shown.

```
growthconefunction TopographicMap {
   variable TectumGrad = 50*(externalConcentrationOf(Tectum) - growthconeConcentrationOf(Tectum));
   variable ephrinGrad = externalConcentrationOf(ephrinA) - growthconeConcentrationOf(ephrinA);
   variable PeckingOrder = surfaceConcentrationOf(EphA) - neighbourConcentrationOf(EphA);
   if (neighbourConcentrationOf(EphA)==0) {
      migrate (TectumGrad);
   } else if (PeckingOrder > 0) {
      migrate (TectumGrad - ephrinGrad);
   } else if (PeckingOrder < 0) {
      migrate (TectumGrad + ephrinGrad);
   }
}
```

Fig. 5. Growth cone function encoding a 1D version of the topographic map formation mechanism. The contribution from the protein Tectum, which also guides RGC axons to the tectum, ensures that the growth cones remain within the tectal target area. Tectum is not involved in the map formation itself. The model of topographic ordering in the vertical dimension is based on the same map formation mechanism, while making the ephrinB–EphB interaction attractive rather than repellent. In the 2D version, the contributions to the bid from each dimension are additive.

cellular and membrane bound protein concentrations may also affect gene expression through the use of appropriate queries.

4) Neural activity: The simulation of neural activity is based on a traditional connectionist approach. Neurons sum the neural activity they receive via synaptic inputs, and provide output to other neurons which is either a linear or non-linear function of the input. Neural parameters and activity may affect gene expression through queries. This can be used to model genes which are expressed in response to neural activity [6]. Gene expression may in turn affect neural activity through actions which alter parameters such as synaptic weights.

B. Topographic maps

Topographic maps are central to the processing of sensory information [1], and have also been implicated in learning [2]. Although topographic maps have been studied for decades and much is known about the roles of chemical signalling, axon guidance [4] and neural activity [3] in their formation, most of the existing literature is punctate. We use NeuroGene to bring much of this information together into a single simulation. Our model of map formation is based on the simulation of growth cones, and speaks directly to signal transduction processes at retinal ganglion cell (RGC) growth cones. All aspects of the model are based on the properties of several classes of proteins known to be involved in map formation [7].

The topographic projection from the retina to the mid-brain is formed when RGCs extend axons to the mid-brain and form connections with tectal neurons. Retinal and tectal chemical markers are central to this process. RGCs express EphA and B receptors in perpendicular concentration gradients, with EphA levels varying from high at the temporal edge of the retina to low at the nasal edge, and EphB levels varying from high at the ventral to low at the dorsal edge [7]. Tectal neurons express ephrinA and B, ligands to EphA and B respectively, in similar perpendicular gradients. EphrinA increases from the anterior towards the posterior tectum and ephrinB increases from the lateral to the medial tectum. The projection forms such that RGCs with increasing levels of EphA project their axons to tectal points with decreasing levels of ephrinA, while along the other dimension, RGCs with increasing levels of EphB project to tectal locations with increasing levels of ephrinB.

In an important experiment, Brown and coworkers [5] induced a random subset of RGC axons, representing approximately half the RGC population, to express an increased level of EphA receptors. The increase was the same for all these cells. They found that RGCs expressing their normal level of EphA formed one topographic projection filling the posterior tectum, while RGCs with increased EphA levels formed a second map with the same orientation in the anterior tectum. There was no significant gap or overlap between the two projections, which together filled the normal target area of the projection. This experiment (which we will refer to as the "knockin" experiments, since it relies on genetically knocking in a new set of EphA receptors) suggests that relative, rather than absolute levels of EphA on RGC axons determine their termination zones in the tectum [5]. It also shows that RGC axons with abnormally high EphA levels can induce other axons with normal EphA levels to project further posteriorly than normal, suggesting that direct axon-axon interactions are involved in map formation.

II. METHODS

A. A new model for topographic map formation

Using NeuroGene, we have developed a model of topographic map formation in which axon-axon interactions play an important role. Below, we characterize the performance of this model with respect to map formation both under natural conditions and under those of the EphA knockin study [5].

According to our model, RGC axons detect both ephrinA/B carried by the tectal target tissue and EphA/B receptors carried by other RGC axons. The EphA/B receptor concentrations establish "pecking-orders" among RGC axons. All axons have an inherent tendency to move towards the attractive end of the ephrin gradient [7]. In our model, high Eph axons are able to induce nearby axons with relatively lower Eph concentrations to move towards the nominally repellent end of the ephrin gradient. On the other hand, low-Eph axons do not affect the behaviour of high-Eph axons. This asymmetry in the axon–axon interaction based on relative Eph-receptor concentrations [5] gives rise to the concept of the pecking order. The growth cone function in fig. 5 captures this mechanism.

We assume that RGC growth cones can perceive not only tectal ephrinA/B [7], but also the EphA/B receptors carried by other RGC axons. Both ephrinA [8] and B [9] are known to act as receptors as well as ligands, responding to EphA/B of other cells. RGC axons express ephrin A/B as well as Eph receptors [10]. RGC ephrin may be involved in the axon-axon interaction entailed by our model, allowing RGC axons to detect the presence of other RGC axons carrying Eph. The expression pattern of RGC ephrin in counter-gradients to retinal Eph receptors [10] may also explain the asymmetry of the axon pecking order: temporal axons (high-EphA, low-ephrinA) are insensitive to the EphA carried by other axons, while nasal axons (low-EphA, high-ephrinA) are sensitive to temporal axons with higher levels of EphA. We also assume that an RGC growth cone can compare its own Eph receptor concentration with those of other RGC axons. This may involve cis-interactions which occur between Eph receptors and ephrin bound to the same cell membrane [10].

In our model, individual growth cones switch between being attracted and repelled by ephrin gradients. Such switching between different behaviour patterns has been observed in growth cones, and has been induced by altering the intracellular concentration of signalling molecules such as cAMP [11]. Both the ephrinA/EphA and ephrinB/EphB interactions may be attractive or repellent depending on the circumstances [12]. Our model is implemented using genes encoding the properties and expression profiles of known proteins (ephrins and Eph receptors), genes encoding postulated proteins such as retinal and tectal cell markers, and genes causing morphological change, including growth cone formation. All aspects of the model can thus be related to genetic processes which regulate protein expression and morphological change in nature.

B. Implementation of Hebbian learning

We implemented a biologically inspired learning rule developed by Elliott and Shadbolt [13]. Waves of neural activity generated by simulated retinal star-burst cells drive the refinement process, which tune the synaptic weights between RGCs and tectal cells. The learning rule is encoded entirely in simulated genes. RGC presynaptic terminals express receptors on their surface in response to action potentials. Similarly, tectal postsynaptic cells secrete a soluble protein into the extracellular environment in response to received neural activity. This protein binds to the RGC presynaptic receptors. Simulated ligand-receptor binding, assuming chemical equilibrium with $K_d = 10^{-12} M$, is used to model the competition among presynaptic terminals for the postsynaptic protein. The binding of ligand molecules to receptors indicates synchronous firing of both cells, and forms basis of a Hebbian learning rule [13].

III. RESULTS

A. Developmental simulations

Figure 6 shows the formation of a topographic projection as simulated in NeuroGene. The map formation process is tolerant to changes in the shapes of gradients; both the slope and absolute magnitude of retinal Eph and tectal ephrin gradients can be varied without disrupting the map formation (data not shown). The simplicity of the model, consisting of inter-axon comparisons of Eph levels, followed by either simple attraction or repulsion by the tectal ephrin gradients, explains the model's resilience to changes in conditions.

We have simulated Brown et al.'s [5] EphA knockin experiments by increasing the EphA level of half the RGCs by a constant amount equal to the maximum "natural" EphA concentration as expressed by extreme temporal RGCs. As in their experiments, we observed two separate well-ordered projections which together fill the entire target area (fig. 7).

As a further test of the model, we simulated a variation of the EphA knockin experiment in which the retinal EphA level in the knockin RGC cells was increased by a smaller amount, equivalent to about 50% of the maximal normal EphA level [5]. In Brown et al.'s experiment, two projections formed in the posterior tectum, but these coalesced into a single map in a region near the anterior edge of the tectum. When we run the simulation with reduced levels of EphA knockin, we also find that the split projections coalesce at the anterior edge of the tectum (fig. 8). At high levels of EphA knockin (fig. 8, left), the two projections have very little overlap in the central tectum, and both are of uniform density. At the lower level of EphA knockin (fig. 8, right), the knockin (KI, expressing elevated EphA levels) projection covers more than half the tectal area with uniform density. The "wild-type" (WT, expressing their "natural" EphA levels) projection is of high density in the posterior reaches of the tectum, but also extends with lower density to the anterior edge. There, WT axons project to tectal points which receive KI axons with similar EphA concentrations. The topographic sorting based on RGC EphA levels is therefore maintained, while giving rise to a

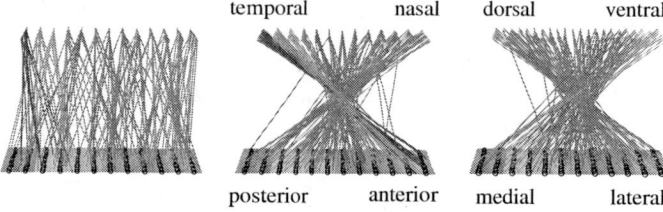

Fig. 6. Simulated topographic map formation, with the retina at the top and the tectum at the bottom. On the left is the simulation after 1,000 iterations, centre and right after 25,000 iterations. Left and centre images show the EphA receptor concentration gradient in the RGC axons (red is high concentration and blue is low), while the ephrin gradient in the tectal target area is displayed at the bottom using a similar colour scale. On the right is shown the same situation rotated 90° about the vertical axis, showing the topographic ordering due to the EphB–ephrinB interaction. Here the colours represent the ephrinB and EphB concentrations.

Fig. 7. EphA knockin experiment after 130,000 iterations. The left and right images show the same view, with RGC axons coloured according to EphA levels on the left. In the right image, the RGCs are coloured according to whether they express the normal (blue) or elevated (red) level of EphA, showing that the two populations segregate into the two distinct maps.

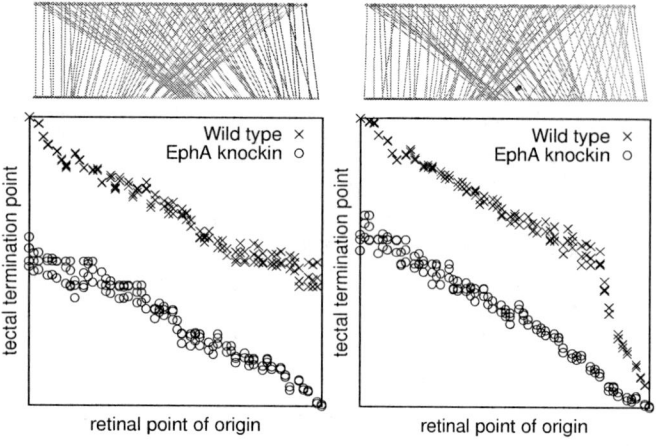

Fig. 8. Results from 1D simulations with varying levels of EphA knockin. The EphA level in knockin (KI) neurons was increased by an amount equal to 100% (left) and 30% (right) of the maximum "natural" EphA level.

projection split in the posterior tectum, but in which the WT and KI projections coalesce at the anterior tectal edge.

These simulations show that the map formation model we have developed is consistent with important experimental observations of the retino-tectal topographic projection. They also show that the NeuroGene growth cone mechanism is capable of modelling complex axon guidance behaviour that can be directly related to the receptors and ligand carried by these growth cones and the target tissue in nature.

B. Activity-dependent refinement

Activity dependent development processes play a central role in the formation of many neural systems, including topographic maps [3]. During such development, neuronal shapes, synapse distribution and synaptic conductances (or *weights*) change in response to neural activity. The simplest form of activity dependent change follows the Hebbian learning rule, which strengthens the synaptic connections between neurons which fire in synchrony.

Activity-dependent remodelling of synapses in topographic projections have two results [14]: First, retino-tectal arbors, which initially form connections to many tectal cells over a large area, become focused so that each RGC connects to only one or a few tectal cells. This improves the topographic ordering of the projection. Secondly, the tectum, which receives overlapping topographic projections from both eyes, becomes subdivided into domains (known as ocular dominance columns, ODCs) which receive neural input exclusively from one or the other eye. We have successfully simulated these processes (data not shown).

Here we report the simulated activity-dependent tuning of retino-tectal synapses in the EphA knockin experiment. Brown et al. [5] showed map coalescence in the low-EphA knockin experiment: While in most of the tectum, each tectal location received neural input from WT cells KI cells in a different retinal locations, in the anterior ~20%, the projections coalesced so that each tectal point received input from WT and KI cells with the same retinal locations. However, the maps formed by our topographic map model at low EphA knockin levels coalesce only at the anterior edge of the map (fig. 8, right). We hypothesize that the extended coalescence of the two projections seen by Brown et al. [5] is due to activity-dependent refinement processes taking place after an initial topographic projection (similar to that in fig. 8) has formed.

The waves of retinal neural activity which drive the developmental change have the property that the correlation of neural activity in different RGCs decreases with increasing inter-RGC distance. We suggest that the WT and KI maps coalesce only where WT and KI cells with similar retinal locations (and correlated neural activity) have significant overlap between their initial arbors connecting to the tectum. Where the tectum receives input from widely separated WT and KI cells with dissimilar neural activity patterns, the maps remain distinct.

We hand-crafted a network topology representing a 2D projection with a geometry similar to that shown in fig. 8, right. RGCs initially have arbors forming synapses with all tectal cells within a given radius of the axon tip, see fig. 9, top. Each dot in fig. 9 represents a tectal cell, and their shade indicates the relative activation received from WT and KI retinal cells. A light dot represents a tectal cell which receives most of its neural activity from WT RGCs, while a dark dot indicates a cell receiving input primarily from KI RGCs. The initial WT projection is dense in the posterior (left) region of the tectum, and more sparse in the anterior (right), just as shown in fig.

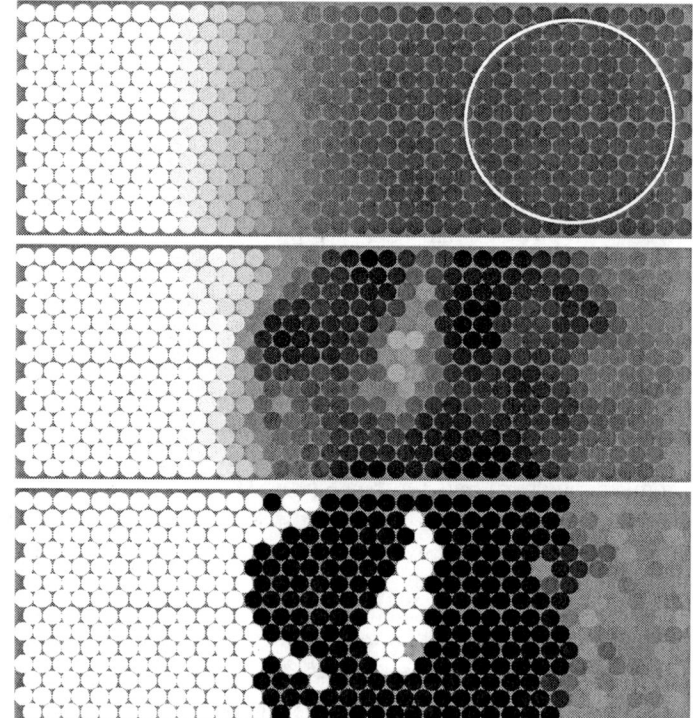

Fig. 9. Activity dependent refinement of the network topology similar to that formed by the topographic map model at low levels of EphA knockin. Images show the relative WT versus KI dominance of tectal cells at the simulation outset and after 3,000 and 15,000 iteration time steps. The large, white circle shows the size of the initial retinotectal arbors. The background shade is that which represents equal activity received from both cell populations.

8, right. The KI projection covers only the anterior region of the tectum with uniform density. This gives rise to complete WT dominance in the posterior and slight KI dominance in the central and anterior tectum at the outset (fig. 9, top).

The second and third panels in fig. 9 show the evolution of the WT versus KI dominance over tectal cells as simulated activity-dependent development proceeds. The tectum becomes subdivided into three clearly delineated domains. In the posterior tectum (left), the dominance of WT cells remains unchallenged, since KI cells do not project to this area. In the central tectum, the two RGC populations have a similar competitive relationship to that which causes the formation of ocular dominance columns (ODCs) [3]. We observe a pattern akin to ODCs in this region, with smaller WT patches due to the lower density of the WT projection. This area of the tectum receives neural input from WT and KI cells from different retinal locations with uncorrelated neural activity. This causes competition between WT and KI cells for tectal connectivity, similarly to how axons from the two eyes compete, giving rise to ODCs proper. In the anterior tectum (right), the projections from the WT and KI populations originate in retinal locations that are closer together, carrying more correlated neural activity, and competition does not occur. Here, all tectal cells receive similar activation patterns from cells within both RGC populations, and consequently form connections of comparable synaptic strengths to both.

In short, when the pre-organized network is submitted to activity-driven development, the unusual topographic projection observed by Brown et al. [5] emerges, with a close fit between the real and modelled data. The ability of our model, which involves both activity-independent and activity-dependent processes, to reproduce experimental data over a wide range of conditions and at this level of detail provides further support for the accuracy of the model. More generally, taken together our results show how an integrated simulation strategy can be used to develop a new understanding of a neurodevelopmental process, where isolated simulation of neither axon guidance nor activity-dependent development alone would be sufficient.

IV. Conclusion

Furthering our understanding of the interactions between genetic, biochemical, developmental and neural processes in the development and function of nervous systems is essential to our progress toward understanding the brain. NeuroGene has been designed for the concurrent and integrated simulation of all these aspects of neural function. The system is implemented in Java for portability, and is computationally efficient, as the simulations presented here were all carried out on a commodity PC in days or less. Within NeuroGene, biochemical processes, neural activity and development can be simulated concurrently within a unifying genetic framework. NeuroGene is ideally suited to the study of neurodevelopment because it allows such different but interacting processes to be studied concurrently. The genetic programming language makes NeuroGene a flexible and versatile system for the study of a wide array of developmental processes. A range of biological mechanisms can be accessed from the genome through queries and actions. Genomes are encoded in such a way that they relate directly to the biological processes they represent, using biologists' terminology.

We have shown how NeuroGene can be applied to the study of topographic projections, yielding a novel explanation for the EphA knock-in experiments. In this instance, activity-independent and activity-dependent processes work together in development — a scenario that we expect will represent the rule, rather then the exception, in the future of neurodevelopmental research. We hope to apply NeuroGene to the study of more speculative scenarios, where the biological accuracy of this system will allow us to determine whether hypothesized neural structures could potentially be formed through neurodevelopmental processes.

References

[1] J. H. Kaas, "Topographic maps are fundamental to sensory processing," *Brain Res. Bull.*, vol. 44, no. 2, pp. 107–112, 1997.

[2] M. E. Diamond, R. S. Petersen, J. A. Harris, and S. Panzeri, "Investigations into the organization of information in sensory cortex," *J. Physiol. Paris*, vol. 97, no. 4-6, pp. 529–536, 2003.

[3] L. C. Katz and J. C. Crowley, "Development of cortical circuits: Lessons from ocular dominance columns," *Nature Rev. Neurosci.*, vol. 3, no. 1, pp. 34–42, Jan 2002.

[4] G. J. Goodhill and L. J. Richards, "Retinotectal maps: molecules, models and misplaced data," *Trends in Neurosci.*, vol. 22, no. 12, pp. 529–534, 1999.

[5] A. Brown, P. A. Yates, P. Burrola, D. Ortuno, V. Ashish, T. M. Jessell, S. L. Pfaff, D. D. M. O'Leary, and G. Lemke, "Topographic mapping from the retina to the midbrain is controlled by relative but not absolute levels of EphA receptor signaling," *Cell*, vol. 102, pp. 77–88, July 2000.

[6] A. E. West, E. C. Griffith, and M. E. Greenberg, "Regulation of transcription factors by neuronal activity," *Nature Rev. Neurosci.*, vol. 3, no. 12, pp. 921–31, 2002.

[7] J. G. Flanagan and P. Vanderhaegen, "The ephrins and Eph receptors in neural development," *Annu. Rev. Neurosci.*, vol. 21, pp. 309–345, 1998.

[8] A. Davy, N. W. Gale, E. W. Murray, R. A. Klinghoffer, P. Soriano, C. Feuerstein, and S. M. Robbins, "Compartmentalized signaling by GPI-anchored ephrin-A5 requires the Fyn tyrosine kinase to regulate cellular adhesion," *Genes devel.*, vol. 13, pp. 3125–35, 1999.

[9] F. Mann, S. Ray, W. A. Harris, and C. E. Holt, "Topographic mapping in dorsoventral axis of the *Xenopus* retinotectal system depends on signaling through ephrin-B ligands," *Neuron*, vol. 35, no. 3, pp. 461–473, Aug 2002.

[10] M. R. Hornberger, D. Dütting, T. Ciossek, T. Yamada, C. Handwerker, S. Lang, F. Weth, J. Huf, R. Weßel, C. Logan, H. Tanaka, and U. Drescher, "Modulation of EphA receptor function by coexpressed ephrinA ligands on retinal ganglion cell axons," *Neuron*, vol. 22, pp. 731–742, 1999.

[11] H.-j. Song, G.-l. Ming, and M.-m. Poo, "cAMP-induced switching in turning direction of nerve growth cones," *Nature*, vol. 388, no. 17, pp. 275–279, July 1997.

[12] B. Knöll, H. Schmidt, W. Andrews, S. Guthrie, A. Pini, V. Sundaresan, and U. Drescher, "On the topographic targeting of basal vomeronasal axons through Slit-mediated chemorepulsion," *Development*, vol. 130, pp. 5073–82, 2003.

[13] T. Elliott and N. R. Shadbolt, "A neurotrophic model of the development of the retinogeniculocortical pathway induced by spontaneous retinal waves," *J. Neurosci.*, vol. 19, no. 18, pp. 7951–7970, 1999.

[14] E. S. Ruthazer and H. T. Cline, "Insights into activity-dependent map formation from the retinotectal system: a middle-of-the-brain perspective," *J. Neurobiol.*, vol. 59, no. 1, pp. 134–146, Apr 2004.

A Hierarchical Coevolutionary Method to Support Brain-Lesion Modelling

Michail Maniadakis and Panos Trahanias

Institute of Computer Science, Foundation for Research and Technology-Hellas (FORTH), 71110 Heraklion, Crete, Greece
and
Department of Computer Science, University of Crete, 71409 Heraklion, Crete, Greece
E-mail: {mmaniada, trahania}@ics.forth.gr

Abstract— The current work addresses the development of cognitive abilities in artificial organisms, a topic that has attracted many research efforts recently. In our approach, neural network-based agent structures are employed to represent distinct brain areas. We introduce a Hierarchical Collaborative CoEvolutionary (HCCE) approach to design autonomous, yet cooperating agents. Thus, partial brain models consisting of many substructures can be designed. Replication of lesion studies is used as a means to increase reliability of brain model, highlighting the distinct roles of agents. The HCCE is appropriately designed to support systematic modelling of brain structures, able to reproduce biological lesion data. The proposed approach designs cooperating agents properly, by considering the desired pre- and post- lesion performance of the model. The effectiveness of the proposed approach is illustrated on the design of a computational model of Primary Motor cortex and Premotor cortex interactions in the mammalian brain. The model is successfully tested in driving a simulated robot, with different pre- and post- lesion performance.

I. INTRODUCTION

Cognitive abilities of animals are supported by the performance of their Central Nervous System (CNS). The latter consists of several interconnected modules with different functionalities [1]. A lot of research is recently oriented towards determining how these modules cooperate to accomplish real world tasks [2]. Even if the detailed, exact properties of each brain area are not clear yet, many computational models have been proposed capturing their basic characteristics [3], [4], [5], [6]. Recently, computational studies investigate the performance of the models in lesion conditions as a means to increase their reliability [7], [8], [9].

We have recently introduced a systematic method to design biologically plausible computational models of partial CNS structures [10], [11]. In accordance to the distributed organization of the mammalian CNS, an agent-based modelling approach is followed. Specifically, the model consists of a collection of neural agents, each one representing a CNS area. The agent-based approach enforces the autonomy of brain areas, supporting also problem decomposition in small tractable tasks.

The performance of agents is specified by means of environmental interaction similar to an epigenetic[1] learning process. The dynamics of epigenetic learning are designed by an evolutionary process which simulates phylogenesis, similar to [12], [13]. Consequently, both genetically encoded features and subjective experience have a significant role in the formation of model's performance. Following the phylogenetic/epigenetic approach, the objective adopted during the evolution of agents, is to furnish them with abilities to develop similar performance to the respective brain areas, after a certain amount of environmental interaction.

Instead of using a unimodal evolutionary process we employ a cooperative coevolutionary approach which is able to highlight the specialties of brain areas represented by distinct agents [10]. Additionally, the coevolutionary approach facilitates the integrated performance of substructures in the composite model. The combination of these two particular features (partial autonomy and collaborative performance) in a single design method seems particularly appropriate for brain modelling.

In the present work, we propose a hierarchical extension of this approach, which exploits the inherent ability of coevolutionary methods to integrate partial structures. We introduce a Hierarchical Colaborative CoEvolutionary (HCCE) scheme which supports the coevolution of a large number of species (populations). Specifically, evolutionary processes at lower levels are driven by their own dynamics to fulfill the special objectives of each brain area. The evolutionary process at the higher levels, tunes lower level coevolutionary process to achieve the integrated performance of partial structures. The architecture of multiple coevolutionary processes tuned by a higher level evolution can be repeated for as many levels as necessary, forming a tree hierarchy.

It should be noted that the composite model does not have to perform in a hierarchical mode. The performance of partial CNS structures can be either hierarchical or completely parallel, depending on the biological prototype. Hence, the hierarchical coevolutionary approach does not imply any further constraints. It is introduced only to support the design process of brain modelling.

Furthermore, following recent trends aiming at the study of computational models in lesion conditions [7], [8], [9], we adapt our method to accomplish systematic modelling of biological lesion experiments. The agent-based representation of brain areas facilitates lesion simulation by simply deactivating appropriate agent structures. Thus, the performance of

---
[1]Epigenesis here, includes all learning processes during lifetime.

the model in pre- and post- lesion conditions can be tested. Furthermore, appropriate fitness functions can be specified for the evolution of partial structures, to indicate the performance of the model when all substructures are present, and also indicate the performance when some partial structures are eliminated. Following this approach, biological lesion data can be considered during the coevolutionary design process and computational structures are properly formulated to replicate pre- and post- lesion performance. Consequently, increased reliability is offered to the final model.

The rest of the paper is organized as follows. In the next section, we present the basic characteristics of the neural agent structures employed for the representation of CNS areas, and the hierarchical collaborative coevolutionary scheme which supports agents' design. The results of the proposed approach on a brain modelling task are presented in section III. Specifically we demonstrate the design of a computational model of primary motor cortex - premotor cortex interactions in the mammalian brain. The model is embedded in a robotic platform, which supports environmental interaction. When both cortical agents are active the robot is able to achieve goal oriented purposeful motion, while when the agent of premotor cortex is eliminated it can only achieve a wall avoidance behavior. Finally, conclusions and suggestions for future work are drawn in the last section.

II. METHOD

Modern theories for the explanation of mammalian cognition argue that the observed behavior of animals is a result of phylogenetic development, and epigenetic environmental experience [14]. Evidently, this argument may also form a basis to accomplish brain modelling tasks [12], [13]. An evolutionary method can be employed to specify the dynamics of real-time learning process.

A. Computational Model

We have implemented two different neural network based agents, to supply general computational structures for brain modelling: (a) a computational cortical agent to represent brain areas, and (b) a link agent to support information flow across brain areas. Thus, an appropriately complex connectivity can be defined, to simulate connectivity of CNS modules.

We note that the proposed computational model is not restrictive for the coevolutionary method, but rather serve as a guide on how coevolutionary approaches can be employed to support brain modelling tasks. Additional constraints can be integrated to increase its biological reliability. The computational details of cortical and link agents have been presented elsewhere [6], [10], [11]. In the present document, due to space limitations, we will summarize only their basic characteristics.

1) Cortical Agent: Each cortical agent consists of a population of excitatory and inhibitory neurons, following the Wilson-Cowan model similar to [15]. A rectangular plane simulates cortical area. Both sets of neurons are uniformly distributed in the cortical plane. Four sets of intra-cortical

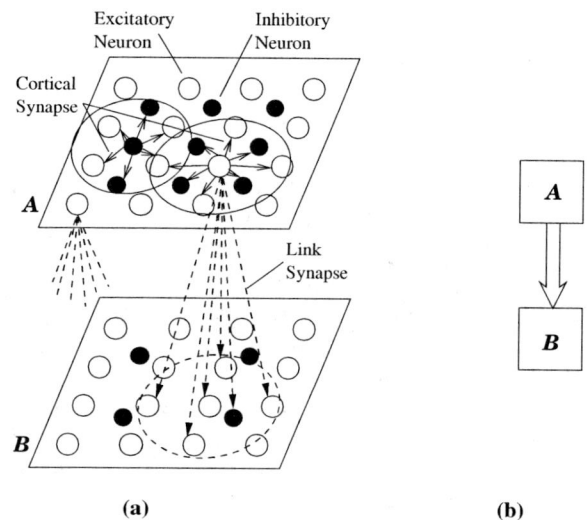

Fig. 1. A schematic representation of the agents employed to represent brain areas. Part (a) illustrates the artificial neural structure of cortical and link agents. Intra-cortical synapses and neighborhoods are illustrated with solid lines. Inter-cortical synapses and neighborhoods are illustrated with dashed lines. Part (b) illustrates the compact representation of agents connectivity which is followed throughout the paper. Cortical agents are illustrated with blocks, while link agents are illustrated with double arrows.

synapses are defined depending on the nature of presynaptic and postsynaptic neurons (excitatory-excitatory, excitatory-inhibitory, inhibitory-excitatory, inhibitory-inhibitory). The connectivity of neurons follows the general rule of locality. Synapse formation in cortical agents is based on circular neighborhoods. This is demonstrated graphically in Fig 1.

2) Link Agent: An appropriate link agent is specified to allow information flow across cortical agents. Inter-cortical synapses of link agents are specified based on the spatial properties inherited by the planar model of cortical agents. Synapse definition follows the principle that neighboring cells project to neighboring areas. Thus, a circular neighborhood measure is also employed to specify locality across cortical agents. Inter-cortical locality is approximated by the circular neighborhoods defined after projecting the neurons of the linked cortical agents on a common virtual plane (Fig 1). Only excitatory neurons are used as outputs of the efferent cortical module, while both excitatory and inhibitory neurons receive input in the afferent module. Thus, two sets of synapses are specified for each link agent (excitatory-excitatory, excitatory-inhibitory). Using the link structure any two cortical agents can be connected. As a result, the connectivity of CNS modules can be easily simulated.

3) Epigenetic Learning: Experience based subjective learning has an important contribution to the final performance of brain models. To enforce epigenetic learning, each set of synapses (for both link and cortical agents) is assigned a Hebbian-like learning rule to enforce agents' self-organization, similar to [16]. The assignment of the proper learning rule in each synapse set allows the emergence of the desired performance in agent structures, after a certain amount of environmental interaction. We have implemented a pool of

Hebbian-like rules that can be appropriately combined to produce a wide range of functionalities during lifetime adjustment.

B. Hierarchical Collaborative CoEvolution (HCCE)

Similar to a phylogenetic process the specification of parameter values for all agents is approached in a systematic way by using an evolutionary mechanism, as it has been suggested in [12], [13]. Furthermore, coevolutionary algorithms have been recently proposed that facilitate exploration, in problems consisting of many decomposable subcomponents [17]. They involve two or more coevolved species (populations) with interactive performance. The brain modelling problem fits very well to collaborative coevolutionary approaches, because separate coevolved species can be used to perform design decisions for each partial model of a brain area, enforcing both a performance similar to reality and the cooperation within computational brain modules.

We have presented a new evolutionary scheme to improve the performance of collaborative coevolutionary algorithms, by explicitly addressing the collaborator selection issue [10], [11]. The present work extents this scheme to a hierarchical multi-level architecture. Our method combines the hierarchical evolutionary approach [18], with the maintenance of successful collaborator assemblies [19], to develop a powerful coevolutionary scheme.

We employ two different kinds of species (populations) to support the coevolutionary process encoding the configurations of either a Primitive agent Structure (PS) or a Coevolved agent Group (CG). PS species specify partial elements of the model, encoding the exact structure of either cortical or link agents. A CG consists of groups of PSs with common objectives. Thus, CGs specify configurations of partial solutions by encoding individual assemblies of cortical and link agents. The evolution of CG modulates partly the evolutionary process of its lower level PS species to enforce their cooperative performance. A CG can also be a member of another CG. Consequently several CGs can be organized hierarchically in a tree-like architecture, with the higher levels enforcing the cooperation of the lower ones.

The HCCE-based design method for brain modelling is demonstrated by means of an example (Fig 2). We assume the existence of two cortical agents connected by three link agents representing their afferent and efferent projections (Fig 2(a)). One hypothetical HCCE process employed to specify agent structure is illustrated in (Fig 2(b)).

Similar to [18], [10] all individuals in all species are assigned an identification number which is preserved during the coevolutionary process. The identification number is employed to form individual assemblies within different species. Each assembly specifies a complete problem solution which is further tested on the desired task.

Each variable in the genome of a CG is joined with one lower level CG or PS species. The value of that variable can be any identification number of the individuals from the species it is joined with. PSs encode the structure of either cortical or

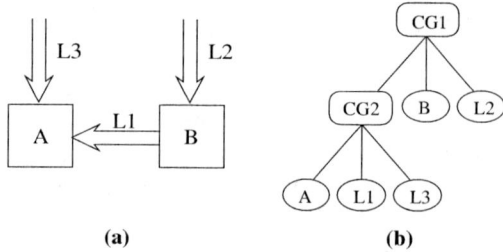

Fig. 2. Hierarchical collaborative coevolutionary design of agents. Part (a) represents schematically a hypothetical connectivity of agents. Part (b) represents the hierarchical coevolutionary scheme utilized to evolve partial structures. CGs are illustrated with oval boxes, while PSs are represented by ovals.

link agents. The details of the encoding have been presented in [10], [11], and thus they are omitted here due to space limitations. CGs enforce cooperation of PS structures by selecting the appropriate cooperable individuals among species. Additionally, a new genetic operator, termed Replication [10], exploits the most able to cooperate individuals in each partial species. A snapshot of the exemplar HCCE process described above is illustrated in (Fig 3).

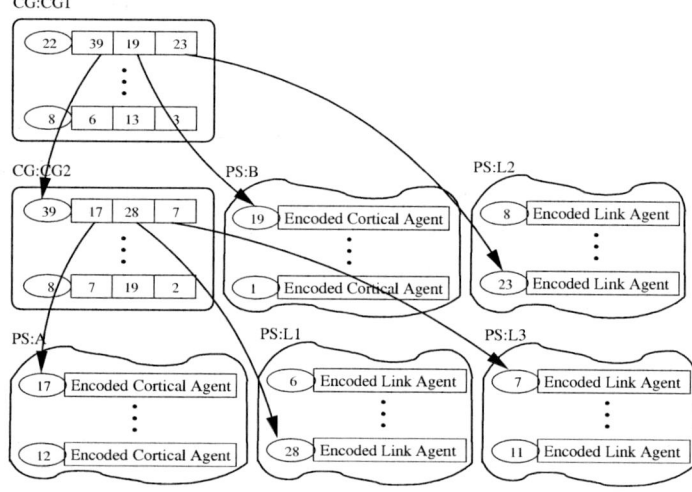

Fig. 3. An overview of the hierarchical coevolutionary scheme, with CG species tuning the evolutionary processes of PS species. Identification numbers are represented with an oval.

In order to test the performance of a complete problem solution, populations are sequentially accessed starting by the higher level. The values of CG individuals at various levels are used as guides to select collaborators among PS species. Then, PS individuals are decoded to specify the structure of cortical and link agents, and the performance of the proposed overall solution is tested on the desired task.

The hierarchical organization is able to simulate lesion studies by deactivating appropriate nodes of the tree hierarchy. Deactivated nodes correspond to lesioned structures of the composite model. Consequently, all lesion conditions can be considered. Furthermore, the coevolutionary process can utilize appropriately formulated fitness functions to specify the desired pre- and post- lesion performance of the model. As a result, the proposed architecture is able to reproduce data obtained by biological lesion studies.

Evolutionary processes at both CG and PS species are driven by their own fitness functions. This is particularly important for agents' coevolution since different objectives can be defined for each agent, thus preserving their autonomy. Especially for a brain modelling application, separate fitnesses are able to highlight the special features of partial agents representing distinct brain areas.

An evaluation index represents how good is the solution formed by an individual assembly in a given task. In the case of lesion experiments, individuals are assigned a combination of evaluation indexes (for the accomplishment of tasks where the composite model is performing, and the accomplishment of tasks with performance of the eliminated model). For each task, individuals are assigned the maximum of the evaluation indexes achieved by all solutions formed with their membership. Evaluation indexes are further combined to form the fitness value of the individual under discussion.

Just after the testing of collaborator assemblies and the assignment of their fitness values, an evolutionary step is performed on each species to formulate the new generation of its individuals. This process is repeated for a predefined number of evolutionary epochs.

III. RESULTS

The effectiveness of the proposed approach is illustrated on the design of a partial brain computational model, which simulates primary motor cortex (M1) - premotor cortex (PMC) interactions. The relevant experiments are indicative of the proposed coevolutionary CNS modelling approach.

PMC (including all non-primary motor areas) is referred as the higher level of motor programming [20], while M1 is considered as the place where the final commands of movement are generated by encoding movement parameters [21]. Thus, PMC activation modulates M1 performance to accomplish goal-driven movements [22]. This organization has been mostly concluded from lesion studies regarding upper limb movement, but similar conclusions are drawn from recent studies aiming at the movement of lower limbs [23], [24].

Computational models of both PMC and M1 have been proposed in the literature eg. [3], [5], [4], which however do not emphasize on their interactions. Recently a simple model of PMC modulating M1 performance is presented in [20], but it is not tested on a real application.

The present work employs the hierarchical collaborative coevolutionary approach to design a model of PMC-M1 real-time performance. In this endeavor, environmental interaction is of utmost importance, since it is difficult to investigate CNS areas performance without embedding the models into a body to interact with its environment. A mobile robot is utilized to support environmental interaction, in order to prove the validity of the result. Specifically, we employ a two wheeled robotic platform equipped with 8 uniformly distributed distance and light sensors.

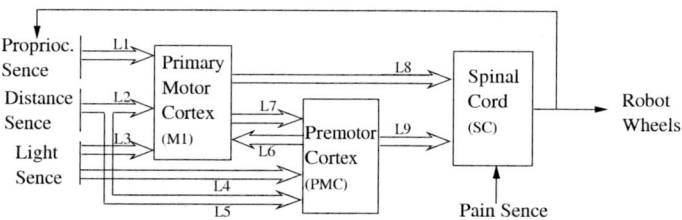

Fig. 4. A schematic overview of the PMC-M1 model. Computational cortical agents are illustrated with blocks, while link agents are illustrated with double arrows.

The experiment aims at reproducing a lesion scenario which is in agreement to the biological data presented above. In accordance to the long-term goal of facilitating artificial organisms with intelligent performance, we emphasize on the accomplishment of behavioral tasks by the robot. The scenario assumes that the performance of the composite PMC-M1 model is able to achieve goal-oriented light following robot movement, but when PMC lesion is performed, the goal oriented behavior is affected, and the robot is only able to achieve wall avoidance navigation. By means of the above scenario, the role of each agent in the composite model can be highlighted.

The composite computational model follows the biological prototype [25]. Sensory information is projected to the reciprocally connected neocortical structures via link agents, and from there to the spinal cord with appropriate additional link structures (Fig 4). Pain sense is activated when robot bumps in a wall, and is directly projecting to spinal cord motor neurons to produce a reflexive movement.

The model consists of 12 subcomponents (3 cortical and 9 links agents) which have to cooperate to accomplish the desired performance. A hierarchical coevolutionary process is utilized to specify the dynamics of real-time learning in each agent structure. The partial computational structures of the composite model are mapped in a hierarchical coevolutionary tree, as it is illustrated in (Fig 5). Comparing figures 4 and 5, it can be easily realized that hierarchical coevolutionary design does not imply hierarchical performance of the computational model.

One PS species is employed for each partial component of the computational model. Three CG structures are used to drive the hierarchical coevolutionary process. CG1 coordinates coevolution of structures relevant to M1 functionality, CG2 coordinates coevolution of structures relevant to PMC functionality, while CG3 coordinates coevolution of groups CG1 and CG2 and also SC structure which is common for both M1 and PMC performance.

PMC lesion is simulated, by deactivating CG2 node, together with all lower level substructures. PMC lesion assumes also the deactivation of all link agent structures under CG2, since their performance has no computational meaning without PMC functioning.

The performance of the PMC-M1 computational model is tested on two different tasks. The composite model is tested

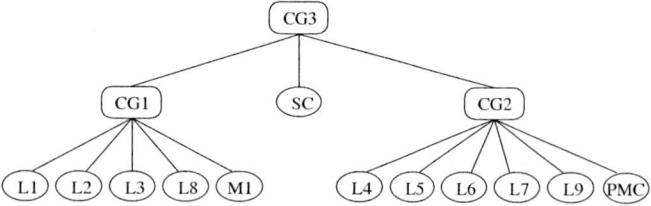

Fig. 5. A schematic overview of the hierarchical coevolutionary process, illustrating the hierarchical mapping of PMC-M1 model.

on the accomplishment of light following behavior, while the eliminated model (after PMC lesion) is tested on wall avoidance navigation. Both behaviors emerge after real-time adjustment of agent structures by means of robot-environment interaction. Separate criteria are designed to evaluate the accomplishment of each task.

The goal-oriented task is simulated by a moving light source that the robot should follow. The success of the task is evaluated by the function:

$$F_F = \left(1 - \frac{2B}{M}\right)^3 \sum_M \ell^2$$

where we assume that the robot is tested for M steps, ℓ is the maximum instant value of all light sensors, and B is the total number of robot bumps. The first term minimizes the number of robot bumps on the walls, while the second supports robot following of the light source.

The success of wall avoidance task is evaluated by the function:

$$F_W = \left(\sum_M (s_l + s_r - 1) * (1.0 - p^2)\right)$$
$$* \left(1 - \frac{3}{M} \sum_M \sqrt{|s_l - s_r|}\right)^3$$
$$* \left(1 - \frac{(s_l + s_r)B}{M}\right)^3$$

where we assume that the robot is again tested for M steps, s_l, s_r are the instant speeds of the left and right wheel, p is the maximum instant activation of distance sensors, and B is the total number of robot bumps. The first term seeks for forward movement far from the walls, the second supports straight movement without unreasonable spinning, and the last term minimizes the number of robot bumps on the walls.

These evaluation criteria are used to design fitness functions which guide the coevolutionary process. Specifically, a separate fitness function is designed for each CG:

$$F_{C_1} = F_W \sqrt{F_F}$$
$$F_{C_2} = \sqrt{F_W} F_F$$
$$F_{C_3} = F_W F_F$$

where F_{C_i} represent the fitness function of the $i-th$ CG. All PS species share a common fitness function with the owner CG. It is clear that F_{C_1} emphasize more the accomplishment of wall avoidance navigation, F_{C_2} pays more attention on the accomplishment of light following, while F_{C_3} aims to coordinate lower level coevolutionary processes by equally enforcing the accomplishment of both tasks.

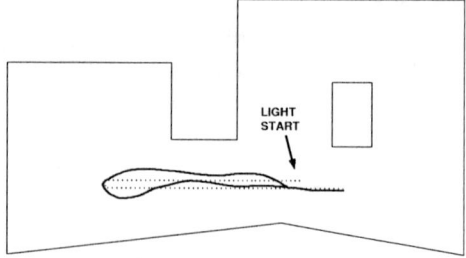

Fig. 6. A sample result of model performance in the light following task by the composite PMC-M1 model. Robot path is illustrated by a solid line, while the dashed line, illustrates the path of light source.

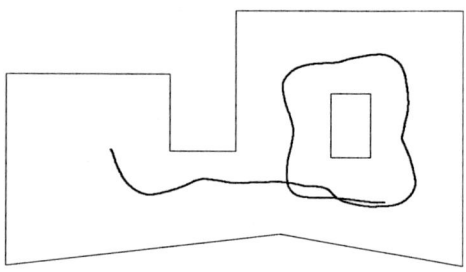

Fig. 7. A sample result of model performance after PMC lesion in the wall avoidance navigation task.

The employment of the above fitness functions enforces the coevolutionary process to consider the hypothetical lesion scenario during the design process. Consequently, partial computational structures are properly designed to develop the desired pre- and post- lesion performance. We mention that even if CG2 structures are not participating in the wall avoidance task, they are also affected by its success in order to avoid exploiting the subset of M1 structures that are unable to accomplish wall avoidance navigation.

Following the above fitness functions different agent structures are designed emphasizing in different criteria of the composite model performance. This fact, together with the successful accomplishment of the lesion scenario highlights the different roles of partial structures in the composite model.

Specifically, M1 is able to move the robot, but without the ability to achieve purposeful motion. The latter is achieved by means of PMC which successfully modulates M1 performance to develop light-following behavior. A sample result of light following behavior from the PMC-M1 model is illustrated in Fig. 6. Wall avoidance behavior from the eliminated model is illustrated in Fig. 7.

All PS species evolved by populations of 100 individuals. CG1, CG2, and CG3 species are evolved by populations of 200, 200, 300 individuals respectively. Evolution was performed for 70 epochs in synchronous steps for all populations.

IV. CONCLUSIONS

In the present work, we introduced a computational framework for the design and implementation of brain models able to replicate biological lesion data. The proposed method is based on the employment of neural agent modules to represent brain areas, which are connected using appropriate link agent structures. The agent-based approach is in accordance to the distributed nature of mammalian CNS. Furthermore, it supports the autonomy of brain areas, and consequently allows the investigation of model performance in lesion conditions.

Agent structures are adjusted in real-time by following a self-organized process which simulates epigenetic learning of biological organisms. The dynamics of epigenetic learning are designed following an evolutionary approach which simulates phylogenesis. As a result, both genetically encoded features and environmental experience specify the performance of the model.

We employ a hierarchical collaborative coevolutionary (HCCE) approach to support design specification of agent structures. The collaborative coevolutionary process is suitable for agents' design because it offers increased search abilities of partial components, and is able to emphasize both the specialty of brain areas and their cooperative performance.

The hierarchical organization of the coevolutionary process supports the elimination of agent structures to simulate lesion experiments. Thus, the role of each partial structure in the composite model can be examined. Additionally, HCCE supplies a mechanism to specify the performance of the model in pre- and post- lesion conditions, by forming appropriate fitness functions. Consequently, the proposed method seems particularly appropriate for implementing reliable models of brain areas, with the ability to replicate lesion data.

Following this approach, the distinct role of each agent structure in the composite model is highlighted. This has been confirmed with the results shown in the previous section, as well as other results obtained in our experiments (not presented here due to space limitations). Evidently, further work is needed to fully ascertain the general applicability and validity of our approach.

We also note that by adopting the coevolutionary method for design specification, our approach is inherently furnished with the ability to integrate partial brain models. The proposed hierarchical collaborative coevolutionary scheme can be also utilized to integrate the performance of partial brain models, by introducing an appropriate number of additional higher level evolutionary process. Thus, the incremental integration of gradually more partial brain models on top of existing ones constitutes the main direction of our future work. We believe that by exploiting the proposed approach, a powerful method to design large scale reliable brain models can emerge.

REFERENCES

[1] E. R. Kandel, J. Schwartz, and T. M. Jessell, *Principles of Neural Science*. Mc Graw Hill, 2000.

[2] R. Cotterill, "Cooperation of the basal ganglia, cerebellum, sensory cerebrum and hippocampus: possible implications for cognition, consciousness, intelligence and creativity," *Progress in Neurobiology*, vol. 64, no. 1, pp. 1 – 33, 2001.

[3] R. Ajemian, D. Bullock, and S. Grossberg, "A model of movement coordinates in motor cortex: posture-dependent changes in the gain and direction of single cell tuning curves." *Dep. Cognitive and Neural Systems, Boston University*, 2000.

[4] A. Fagg and M. Arbib, "Modeling parietal-premotor interactions in primate control of grasping." *Neural Networks*, vol. 11, pp. 1277–1303, 1998.

[5] E. Todorov, "Direct cortical control of muscle activation in voluntary arm movements: a model." *Nature Neuroscience*, vol. 3, pp. 391–398, 2000.

[6] M. Maniadakis and P. Trahanias, "A computational model of neocortical-hippocampal cooperation and its application to self-localization," in *Proceedings of 7th European Conference on Artificial Life (ECAL 2003)*. Springer-Verlag Heidelberg, 2003, pp. 183–190.

[7] R. Aharonov, L. Segev, I. Meilijson, and E. Ruppin, "Localization of function via lesion analysis," *Neural Computation*, vol. 15, no. 4, pp. 885–913, 2003.

[8] V. Goel, S. Pullara, and J. Grafman, "A computational model of frontal lobe dysfunction: working memory and the tower of hanoi task." *Cognitive Science*, vol. 25, pp. 287–313, 2001.

[9] T. Polk, P. Simen, R. Lewis, and E. Freedman, "A computational approach to control in complex cognition." *Brain Research Interactive*, vol. 15, pp. 71–83, 2002.

[10] M. Maniadakis and P. Trahanias, "Modelling brain emergent behaviors through coevolution of neural agents," *accepted for publication, Neural Networks*, 2005.

[11] ——, "Evolution tunes coevolution: modelling robot cognition mechanisms." in *Proc. of Genetic and Evolut. Comput. Conference, (GECCO-2004)*, 2004.

[12] E. Rolls and S. Stringer, "On the design of neural networks in the brain by genetic evolution." *Progress in Neurobiology*, vol. 61, pp. 557–579, 2000.

[13] N. Kasabov and L. Benuskova, "Computational neurogenetics." *Journal of Computational and Theoretical Nanoscience*, vol. 1, no. 1, pp. 1–15, 2004.

[14] D. Geary and K. Huffman, "Brain and cognitive evolution: Forms of modularity and functions of mind," *Psych. Bulletin*, vol. 128, pp. 667–698, 2002.

[15] E. Tkaczyk, "Pressure hallucinations and patterns in the brain." *Morehead El. Journal of Applicable Mathematics*, vol. 1, pp. 1–26, 2001.

[16] D. Floreano and J. Urzelai, "Evolutionary robots with on-line self-organization and behavioral fitness." *Neural Networks*, vol. 13, pp. 431–443, 2000.

[17] M. Poter and K. De Jong, "Cooperative coevolution: An architecture for evolving coadapted subcomponents." *Evol. Computation*, vol. 8, pp. 1–29, 2000.

[18] M. Delgado, V. F. Zuben, and F. Gomide, "Coevolutionary genetic fuzzy systems: a hierarchical collaborative approach," *Fuzzy Sets and Systems*, vol. 141, no. 1, pp. 89–106, 2004.

[19] D. Moriarty and R. Miikkulainen, "Forming neural networks through efficient and adaptive coevolution." *Evolutionary Computation*, vol. 5, no. 4, pp. 373–399, 1997.

[20] S. Kakei, D. Hoffman, and P. Strick, "Sensorimotor transformations in cortical motor areas." *Neuroscience Research*, vol. 46, pp. 1–10, 2003.

[21] J. Fuster, "Executive frontal functions," *Experimental Brain Research*, vol. 133, pp. 66–70, 2000.

[22] J. Kalaska, S. Scott, P. Cisek, and L. Sergio, "Cortical control of reaching movements." *Current Opinion in Neurobiology*, vol. 7, pp. 849–859, 1997.

[23] I. Miyai, H. Tanabe, I. Sase, H. Eda, I. Oda, I. Konishi, Y. Tsunazawa, T. Suzuki, T. Yanagida, and K. Kubota, "Cortical mapping of gait in humans: a near-infrared spectroscopic topography study." *Neuroimage*, vol. 14, no. 5, pp. 1186–1192, 2001.

[24] C. Sahyoun, A. Floyer-Lea, H. Johansen-Berg, and P. Matthews, "Towards an understanding of gait control: brain activation during the anticipation, preparation, and execution of foot movements." *NeuroImage*, vol. 21, no. 2, pp. 568–575, 2004.

[25] R. Dum and P. Strick, "Motor areas in the frontal lobe of the primate." *Physiology & Behavior*, vol. 77, pp. 677–682, 2002.

Genome Space and Structure Genome Invariants

Germano Resconi

Catholic University, via Trieste 17
resconi@numerica.it

Abstract- The traditional approach examines and collects data on a single gene, a single protein or a single reaction at a time. Given the state space of the cell, any gene can be represented by a point (vector) in this space and its components are the protein expressions of the same gene for any state. When the same process is repeated for all the genes, we obtain a set of points (vectors) which is a new space or genome space. Inside the genome space we can define invariants that give us the structure of the genome space. With the genome space and state space we can give a model for any cell and in particular for the neurons in the brain.

I INTRODUCTION

We know that the activity of the cell is connected with the type of individual gene inside the genome. A mutation of a gene can justify abnormality in the states of the cell. But in many cases mutations of the genes are not so important for the activity of the cell. Interactions among genes reduce the expression of the abnormal genes. A typical interaction among genes is the source of the cell difficulties. To model the structure of the interaction we define the genome space GS.: Every coordinate in GS is a point (vector) in the state space. The components of the point are the gene protein expression for any state. When in the genome space the coordinates are orthogonal every gene is independent on the others. The variation of one gene expression does not affect the variation of the other gene expression. When one gene depends on another in the genome space the coordinates are not orthogonal. . In the genome network A is a regulator of B if the GN predicts a casual relation between the expression of A and the change of the level expression of the gene B. When every gene is independent on the others the expression of the gene B at the time $t + \Delta t$ is the superposition of the individual expression of the genes that regulate B at the time t. When A is a regulator of B only when C is present the gene A depends on the gene C. In general the regulation of A on B is function of the pattern of expression of all the other genes. The aim of this paper is to describe the properties of the genome space both in the simple case of the independence and in a more complex situation of the pattern dependence among agents.

With the properties of the genome space we can compensate the dependence and generate virtual gene expressions that are independent. In the same time we give a global genome measure that is a structural invariant for every change of the coordinates in the genome space. This invariant is analogous to the energy in physics so it gives us the possibility to check the dynamic of the gene expression in a global way We denote this invariant as the structural genome invariant. We remark that the genome space is embedded in the space of the cell states (state space). For example in [6] the state of the cell neuron in the brain is given by a set of parameters as Amplitude of fast excitation, Fast excitation rise , Amplitude of slow excitation and so on. The data that give us the genome space are obtained by the data of the gene expression inside the state space.

II GENE NETWORK AND GENOME SPACE

In the paper [6] is defined the gene network GN where the change of the gene expression $\psi_j(t + \Delta t)$ is the superposition of the gene expression $\psi_k(t)$ at the time t.

$$\psi_j(t + \Delta t) = \sum_{k=1}^{n} w_{j,k} \psi_k(t)$$

(1)

In expression (1) the set of the gene expressions $\psi_j(t)$ is associated with different proteins that have different functionalities.

The first point is to define the genome space the coordinates of which are the gene expression in different states of the cell. In figure 1 we show an image of the genome space for three genes.

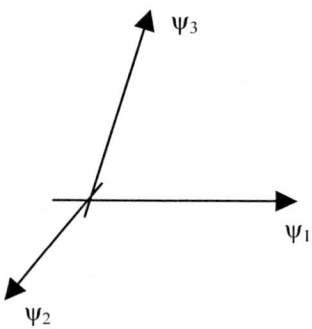

Fig. 1 The genome space the coordinates of which are the genome expression of the proteins. In this case we have three genes and their expressions are ψ_1, ψ_2, ψ_3.

We remark that the gene expressions are represented by coordinates that are not orthogonal. This means that one gene depends on the others So in figure 1 no correlation exists between gene 1 and gene 2 because the two coordinates are orthogonal. But between gene 1 and gene 3 there is a correlation because the two coordinates are not orthogonal and so are dependent.

The genome space in a more explicit way is given by the set of gene expressions or coordinates the values of which are given in different states q_1, q_2, ..., q_n of the cell. In table I we show the gene expressions for different states of the cell.

TABLE 1.
Table of gene protein expressions $\psi_k(x)$ for different values q_k of the cell states

	Gene 1 $\psi_1(q)$	Gene 2 $\psi_2(q)$	...	Gene n $\psi_n(q)$
State 1 q_1	$\psi_1(q_1)$	$\psi_2(q_1)$	...	$\psi_n(q_1)$
State 2 q_2	$\psi_1(q_2)$	$\psi_2(q_2)$	...	$\psi_n(q_2)$
...	...	...	...	...
State m1 q_{m-1}	$\psi_1(q_{m-1})$	$\psi_2(q_{m-1})$	...	$\psi_n(q_{m-1})$
State m q_m	$\psi_1(q_m)$	$\psi_2(q_m)$	...	$\psi_n(q_m)$

Table I can be shown in this synthetic way

$$X = \begin{bmatrix} \psi_1(q_1) & \psi_2(q_1) & ... & \psi_n(q_1) \\ \psi_1(q_2) & \psi_2(q_2) & ... & \psi_n(q_2) \\ ... & ... & ... & ... \\ \psi_1(q_m) & \psi_2(q_m) & ... & \psi_n(q_m) \end{bmatrix} \quad (2)$$

For the (2), the (1) is written as follows

$$\begin{bmatrix} \psi_j(q_1, t+\Delta t) \\ \psi_j(q_2, t+\Delta t) \\ ... \\ \psi_j(q_m, t+\Delta t) \end{bmatrix} = w_{j,1} \begin{bmatrix} \psi_1(q_1, t) \\ \psi_1(q_2, t) \\ ... \\ \psi_1(q_m, t) \end{bmatrix} +$$

$$w_{j,2} \begin{bmatrix} \psi_2(q_1, t) \\ \psi_2(q_2, t) \\ ... \\ \psi_2(q_m, t) \end{bmatrix} + ... + w_{j,n} \begin{bmatrix} \psi_n(q_1, t) \\ \psi_n(q_2, t) \\ ... \\ \psi_n(q_m, t) \end{bmatrix} = X W_j \quad (3)$$

Where $W_j = w_{j,k}$.

Table I for every gene expression ψ_k associates a coordinate of the genome space. This coordinate is a vector in the state space the components of which for the gene k are $\psi_k(q_1)$, $\psi_k(q_2)$, ..., $\psi_k(q_m)$. We remark that the coordinates of the genome space are not only symbolic entities but are vectors in the state space obtained by the measure of the gene expressions in different states of the cell. For the expression (1) we can see that for the gene j the gene expression at the time t + Δt or $\psi_j(t+\Delta t)$ is a vector in the genome space as shown in figure 2

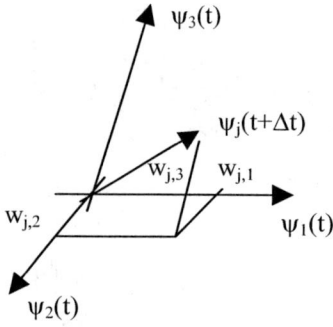

Fig. 2 The genome space for three genes and vector $\psi_j(t+\Delta t)$ with its components in a non orthogonal coordinate.

In a more formal way every vector V inside the state space will be represented by the matrix

$$V = \begin{bmatrix} \psi(q_1) \\ \psi(q_2) \\ ... \\ \psi(q_m) \end{bmatrix} \quad (4)$$

where $\psi(q)$ is the function that gives the component of V on the space of the states. In figure 3 we show the same vector V in the genome space with its components in the space.

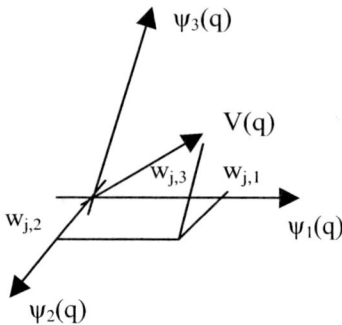

Fig. 3   Representation of the vector V in the coordinates of the cell states inside the space of the gene expressions which are again vectors in the state space q.

When two genes A and B are independent it means that

$$\sum_j \psi_A(q_j) \psi_B(q_j) = 0 \quad (5)$$

where $\sum_j \psi_A(q_j)^2 = 1$ and $\sum_j \psi_B(q_j)^2 = 1$ (6)

in a graphic way we have

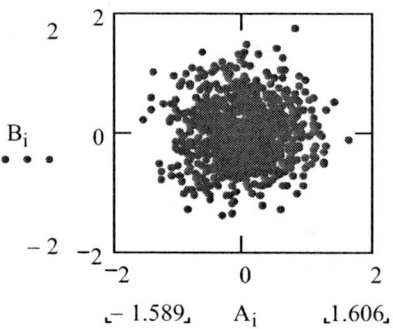

Fig. 4   The two genes A and B are independent. The values A_i and B_i are the gene expressions for different states q of the cell. In this case the gene expressions satisfy the properties (5) and (6)

In general when the genes are independent we have

$$\sum_j \psi_k(q_j) \psi_h(q_j) = X^T X =$$

$$G = G_{h,k} = \begin{bmatrix} 1 & 0 & ... & 0 \\ 0 & 1 & ... & 0 \\ ... & ... & ... & ... \\ 0 & 0 & 0 & 1 \end{bmatrix} = I \quad (7)$$

The (7) is the formal representation of the relation (5). In (7) we remember that X^T is the transpose matrix of X. We show the transpose matrix in (8)

When $X = \begin{bmatrix} \psi_1(q_1) & \psi_2(q_1) & \psi_3(q_1) \\ \psi_1(q_2) & \psi_2(q_2) & \psi_3(q_2) \\ \psi_1(q_3) & \psi_2(q_3) & \psi_3(q_3) \\ \psi_1(q_4) & \psi_2(q_4) & \psi_3(q_4) \end{bmatrix}$ we have

$$X^T = \begin{bmatrix} \psi_1(q_1) & \psi_1(q_2) & \psi_1(q_3) & \psi_1(q_4) \\ \psi_2(q_1) & \psi_2(q_2) & \psi_2(q_3) & \psi_2(q_4) \\ \psi_3(q_1) & \psi_3(q_2) & \psi_3(q_3) & \psi_3(q_4) \end{bmatrix} \quad (8)$$

For the (7) and the (8) the colon vectors in X are the coordinates of the genome space and one is orthogonal to the others. The scalar product of different colon vectors in X is equal to zero.

for $V_j = \psi_j(t + \Delta t)$, we have that

$$V_j = \psi_j(t + \Delta t) = \sum_{k=1}^n w_{j,k} \psi_k(t) = X W_j \quad (9)$$

where $X_k = \psi_k(t)$ and $W_j = w_{j,k}$ with $k = 1, 2, ..., n$

For $m = n$ we have $X^T X = X X^T = I$ so $V_j = X X^T V_j$

For (9) we have $W_j = X^T V_j$ (10)

When $m > n$, we can use again the (10) but in this case we have

$$V_j^* = \psi_j(t + \Delta t) = \sum_k w_{j,k} X_k = X W_j = X X^T V_j \quad (11)$$

where $V_j^* \neq V_j$ and V_j^* is the orthogonal projection of the vector V_j. The distance $D = |V_j^* - V_j|$ is the minimum distance between V_j and all possible vectors inside the genome space.. The operator $Q = X X^T$ is the projection operator. We remark that

$$Q^2 = X X^T X X^T = X G X^T = X X^T = Q \quad (12)$$

When the genes are one dependent on the others the (5) is not true and we have

$$\sum_j \psi_k(x_j)\psi_h(x_j) = X^T X = G = $$

$$G_{h,k} = \begin{bmatrix} g_{1,1} & g_{1,2} & \cdots & g_{1,n} \\ g_{2,1} & g_{2,2} & \cdots & g_{1,1} \\ \cdots & \cdots & \cdots & \cdots \\ g_{n,1} & g_{n,2} & \cdots & g_{n,n} \end{bmatrix} \quad (13)$$

In this case the coordinates in the genome space are not orthogonal one to the other as in the figures 2 and 3. The activity of one gene must take care of the activities of the others. In this case we cannot separate the genome in individual genes but for the interdependence of the genes we must consider all the genes as an indivisible unity.
The network that represents the correlation among the genes is given in figure 6

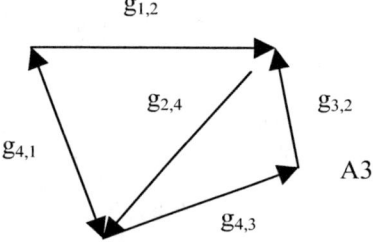

Fig.6 Correlation network or CN for four genes A1, A2, A3, A4. The elements $G = g_{j,k}$ are the elements that give the pattern of the correlation among the genes

When we fix the values of $V_j = \psi_j(t + \Delta t)$ and we put m = n we have

$$V_j = \psi_j(t + \Delta t) = \sum_{k=1}^{n} w_{j,k} \psi_k(t) = X W_j = $$
$$X X^{-1}(X^T)^{-1} X^T V_j = X (X^T X)^{-1} X^T V_j =$$
$$X G^{-1} X^T V_j = X (G^{-1} X^T V_j) = (X G^{-1} X^T) V_j \quad (14)$$

and $W_j = (G^{-1} X^T V_j)$

When m > n as in (10) we have that

$$V_j^* = X W_j = X(G^{-1} X^T V_j) = (X G^{-1} X^T) V_j \quad (15)$$

The operator $Q = X G^{-1} X^T$ is the projection operator

The distance $D = |V_j^* - V_j|$ is the minimum distance between V_j and all possible vectors inside the genome space.. We remark that by the components W_j we build the genome network or GN

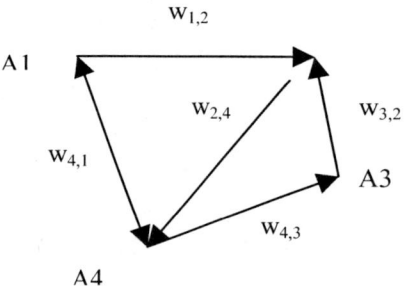

Fig.7 Genome network for four genes A1, A2, A3, A4 or GN. The components $W_j = w_{j,k}$ are the elements that connect the genes and determine the interaction and the dynamic in time.

Now we compute the structure genome invariant.
Given the vector V, the square module of the vector V in the space of the inputs $x_1, x_2, \ldots, x_m$ is given by the product

$$M = V^T V = \begin{bmatrix} \psi(x_1) & \psi(x_2) & \cdots & \psi(x_m) \end{bmatrix} \begin{bmatrix} \psi(x_1) \\ \psi(x_2) \\ \cdots \\ \psi(x_m) \end{bmatrix} = \quad (16)$$

$$\psi(x_1)^2 + \psi(x_2)^2 + \cdots + \psi(x_m)^2$$

For m = n and for (14) we can write M as follows

$$M = V^T V = (XW)^T (XW) = W^T X^T X W = W^T G W \quad (17)$$

For the formula (1) we have a set of invariants the expression of which is

$$M_j = W_j^T G W_j = \sum_{k,h} g_{k,h} w_{j,k} w_{j,h} \quad (18)$$

We remark that given the vector V the (17) is true for every value of the matrix X and so for every type of correlations among the genes. The (17) is the *invariant term* that always assumes the same value given V independently on the genome space X that we use. We remark that when the genes are independent one on the others G = I as in (7), the structure genome invariants M_j in (18) become

$$M_j = w_{j,1}^2 + w_{j,2}^2 + \ldots + w_{j,n}^2 \quad (19)$$

where $W_j = w_{j,k}$ are the parameters by which we define the GN. When the genes are one dependent on the others the expression of the invariants changes as follows

$$M_j = g_{1,1} w_{j,1}^2 + g_{2,2} w_{j,2}^2 + \ldots + g_{n,n} w_{j,n}^2$$
$$+ g_{1,2} w_{j,1} w_{j,2} + g_{1,3} w_{j,1} w_{j,3} +$$
$$+ \ldots + g_{2,3} w_{j,2} w_{j,3} + \ldots + g_{n-1,n} w_{j,n-1} w_{j,n} = \quad (20)$$
$$\sum_{k,h} g_{k,h} w_{j,k} w_{j,h}$$

At this point it is important to consider not only the genome space but also the possible transformations. Given the transformation U, we ask if the transformation U can change the pattern of mutual correlations among the genes.
So given the transformation X' = U X, we have that

$$G' = (X')^T (X') = (UX)^T (UX) = X^T U^T U X \quad (21)$$

So for the family of transformation for which $U^T U = I$, we have that G' = G and the pattern of interactions among the genes is the same. In conclusion the pattern of interaction among the genes is the same for many different genome spaces when one is obtained from the other by the transformation U with the property $U^T U = I$. For example different types of rotations of the genome space always give the same pattern of interactions.
Another important transformation C gives us the possibility to compensate the interaction among the genes in such a way as to compute virtual activities of the genes where the correlation is eliminated. In fact given the matrix C for which

$$G = C^T C \quad (22)$$

We have

$$I = (C^{-1})^T G C^{-1} = (C^{-1})^T X^T X C^{-1} = (XC^{-1})^T (XC^{-1})$$

So for the transformation $X' = X C^{-1}$ we have that

$$X^T X = G_{h,k} = \begin{bmatrix} g_{1,1} & g_{1,2} & \cdots & g_{1,n} \\ g_{2,1} & g_{2,2} & \cdots & g_{2,n} \\ \cdots & \cdots & \cdots & \cdots \\ g_{n,1} & g_{n,2} & \cdots & g_{n,n} \end{bmatrix} \text{ with}$$

$$(XC^{-1})^T (XC^{-1}) = \begin{bmatrix} 1 & 0 & \cdots & 0 \\ 0 & 1 & \cdots & 0 \\ \cdots & \cdots & \cdots & \cdots \\ 0 & 0 & \cdots & 1 \end{bmatrix} \quad (23)$$

In the new reference X' we have virtual activities where the interconnections among agents is completely compensate. In this way it is possible to simplify the study of the gene action. With the transformation $X' = X C^{-1}$ it is possible to come back to the situation when every gene can be considered independent on the others.
Given G when we compute the matrix F (eigenvectors of G) and the diagonal matrix λ (eigenvalues of G) we have equation (24)

$$\begin{bmatrix} g_{1,1} & g_{1,2} & \cdots & g_{1,n} \\ g_{2,1} & g_{2,2} & \cdots & g_{1,1} \\ \cdots & \cdots & \cdots & \cdots \\ g_{n,1} & g_{n,2} & \cdots & g_{n,n} \end{bmatrix} \begin{bmatrix} F_{1,1} & F_{1,2} & \cdots & F_{1,n} \\ F_{2,1} & F_{2,2} & \cdots & F_{2,n} \\ \cdots & \cdots & \cdots & \cdots \\ F_{n,1} & F_{n,2} & \cdots & F_{n,n} \end{bmatrix} =$$

$$\lambda_1 \begin{bmatrix} F_{1,1} \\ F_{2,1} \\ \cdots \\ F_{n,1} \end{bmatrix} + \lambda_2 \begin{bmatrix} F_{1,2} \\ F_{2,2} \\ \cdots \\ F_{n,2} \end{bmatrix} + \cdots + \lambda_n \begin{bmatrix} F_{1,n} \\ F_{2,n} \\ \cdots \\ F_{n,n} \end{bmatrix} = \quad (24)$$

$$\begin{bmatrix} F_{1,1} & F_{1,2} & \cdots & F_{1,n} \\ F_{2,1} & F_{2,2} & \cdots & F_{2,n} \\ \cdots & \cdots & \cdots & \cdots \\ F_{n,1} & F_{n,2} & \cdots & F_{n,n} \end{bmatrix} \begin{bmatrix} \lambda_1 & 0 & \cdots & 0 \\ 0 & \lambda_2 & \cdots & 0 \\ \cdots & \cdots & \cdots & \cdots \\ 0 & 0 & \cdots & \lambda_n \end{bmatrix}$$

)

or $G F = F \lambda$ that can be written in this way $G = F \lambda F^{-1}$

Because $F^{-1} = F^T$ we can write the generic invariant M as follows

$$M = W^T G W = W^T F \lambda F^T W =$$
$$(F^T W)^T \lambda (F^T W) \quad (25)$$

For $Z = F^T W$, we have $M = Z^T \lambda Z$

that can be written in this way

$$M_j = \lambda_1 z_{j,1}^2 + \lambda_2 z_{j,2}^2 + \cdots + \lambda_n z_{j,n}^2 \quad (26)$$

where we give different weights λ_k to the genes.

III CONCLUSION

In this paper we define the genome space and its invariants. The components in the genome space are the elements that define the genome network. Beside the genome network we have the network of the correlation among the genes. The forms of the genome structure invariants as we show in (19) and (20) are determined by the elements in G. The genome space, the matrix G and the invariants have a geometric image. In fact G is the metric tensor, the invariants are the distance inside the genome space. When we change the genome space we change the reference.

REFERENCES

[1] Germano Resconi, " The morphogenetic Neuron" in Computational Intelligence : Soft Computing and Fuzzy.-Neuro Integration with Application, Springer NATO ASI Series F Computer and System Science vol 162, pp. 304-331, 1998. editors Okyay Kaynak, Lotfi Zadeh , Burhan Turksen , Imre J.Rudas

[2] E. Salinas and L.F. Abbott, "A model of multiplicative neural responses in parietal cortex", Proc. Natl. Acad. Sci. USA Vol.93, 11956-11961, 1996.

[3] Alexandre Pouger and Lawrence H.Snyder, Computational approaches to sensorimotor transformations ,nature neuroscience –supplement – volume 3 – November 2000 pag 1192-1198

[4] Germano.Resconi, A.J. van der Wall , Morphogenetic neural networks encode abstract rules by data, Information Sciences 142 (2002) 249-273

[5] Germano Resconi , lakhmi Jain , Intelligent Agents , Springer 2004

[6] Nikola Kasabov , Lubica Benuskova and Simei Gomes Wysoski, Computational Neurogenetic Modelling : Gene Networks within Neural Networks, 2004 IEEE , Budapest Hungary 25-29.2004

[7] G.Resconi and van der Wall A.J. Morphogenetic neural networks encode abstract rules by data , Information Sciences vol.142 pp.249-273 , 2002

[8] Purushothman G. & Bradely D.C. Neural population code for fine perceptual decision in Area MT , NatureNeuroscience 8,pp.99-106 (2005)

A Computational Neurogenetic Model of a Spiking Neuron

Nikola Kasabov, Lubica Benuskova and Simei Gomes Wysoski
Knowledge Engineering & Discovery Research Institute
Auckland University of Technology
Auckland, New Zealand
E-mail: {nkasabov, lbenusko, swysoski} @aut.ac.nz

Abstract— The paper presents a novel, biologically plausible spiking neuronal model that includes a dynamic gene network. Interactions of genes in neurons affect the dynamics of the neurons and the whole network through neuronal parameters that change as a function of gene expression. The proposed model is used to build a spiking neural network (SNN) illustrated on a real EEG data case study problem. The paper also presents a novel computational approach to brain neural network modeling that integrates dynamic gene networks with a neural network model. Interaction of genes in neurons affects the dynamics of the whole neural network through neuronal parameters, which are no longer constant, but change as a function of gene expression. Through optimization of the gene interaction network, initial gene/protein expression values and ANN parameters, particular target states of the neural network operation can be achieved, and statistics about gene intercation matrix can be extracted. It is illustrated by means of a simple neurogenetic model of a spiking neural network (SNN). The behavior of SNN is evaluated by means of the local field potential, thus making it possible to attempt modeling the role of genes in different brain states, where EEG data is available to test the model. We use standard signal processing techniques like FFT to evaluate the SNN output to compare it with real human EEG data.

I. INTRODUCTION

With the advancement of molecular research technologies more and more data and information is being made available about the genetic basis of neuronal functions and diseases [1, 2]. This information can be utilized to create models of brain functions and diseases that include models of gene interaction. This area integrates knowledge from computer and information science, brain science, molecular genetics and we call it *computational neurogenetic modeling* (CNGM) [3, 4].

CNGM is a new area of research that has many open questions, some of them listed below:

(1) Which real neuronal parameters are to be included in an ANN model and how to link them to activities of genes/proteins?
(2) Which genes/proteins are to be included in the model and how to represent the gene interaction over time within each neuron?
(3) How to integrate in time the activity of genes and neurons in an ANN model as it is known that neurons spike in millisecond intervals and the process of gene transcription and translation into proteins takes minutes or even hours?
(4) How to integrate internal and external variables in a CNGM (e.g., genes and neuronal parameters with external signals acting on the brain) and how to treat various perturbations?
(5) How to create and validate a CNG model in the presence of scarce data?
(6) How to measure brain activity and the CNGM activity in order to validate the model?
(7) What kind of useful information can be derived from CNGM?

Our approach is illustrated by means of a simple neurogenetic model of SNN. The behavior of SNN is evaluated by means of the local field potential (LFP), thus making it possible to attempt modeling the role of genes in different brain states, where EEG data is available to test the model. Support for this approach comes from recent studies that have shown that brain electrical oscillations are genetically determined and differ between individuals and families [5].

II. A BIOLOGICALLY PLAUSIBLE COMPUTATIONAL NEUROGENETIC MODEL OF A SPIKING NEURON

Here we propose a biologically plausible model of a spiking neuron that includes genes and proteins that interact between each other and affect the spiking characteristics of the neuron.

In general, we consider two sets of genes – a set G_{gen} that relates to general cell functions and a set G_{spec} that defines specific neuronal information-processing functions (e.g. receptors, ion channels, etc.). The two sets form together a set $\mathbf{G}=\{G_1, G_2, ..., G_n\}$. We assume that the expression level of each gene $g_j(t+\Delta t_j)$ is a nonlinear function of expression levels of all the genes in $\mathbf{G}(t)$, inspired by discrete models from [6, 7]:

$$g_j(t+\Delta t_j) = \sigma\left(\sum_{k=1}^{n} w_{jk} g_k(t)\right) \quad (1)$$

We work with normalized gene expression values in the interval $g_j(t) \in (0, 1)$. Each gene has its own delay Δt_j that represents the delay along the axis: $\{genes\}_{k=1}^{n} \to$ proteins $\to$ transcription factors (TFs) $\to$ gene j [8]. The coefficients $w_{ij} \in (-5, 5)$ are elements of the square matrix $\mathbf{W}$ of gene interaction weights. These borders have been chosen experimentally to lead to various types of nonlinear dynamics, i.e. constant, periodic, quasi-periodic and chaotic. Initial values of gene expressions are small random values, i.e. $g_j(0) \in (0, 0.1)$.

In the current model we assume a simple scenario where: (1) one protein is coded by one gene; (2) relationship between the protein level and the gene expression level is linear; (3) protein levels lie between the minimal and maximal values (not necessarily being equal to 0 and 1, respectively). Thus, the protein level $p_j(t+\Delta t)$ is expressed by

$$p_j(t+\Delta t) = (p_j^{max} - p_j^{min})\sigma\left(\sum_{k=1}^{n} w_{jk} g_k(t)\right) + p_j^{min} \quad (2)$$

The delay Δt corresponds to the delay caused by the gene j transcription and its initiation, mRNA translation into protein and posttranslational protein modifications [8]. In our model, some protein levels will be directly related to neuronal parameters P_j such that

$$P_j(t) = P_j(0) p_j(t) \quad (3)$$

where $P_j(0)$ is the initial value of the neuronal parameter at time $t = 0$. In such a way the gene/protein dynamics is linked to the dynamics of ANN. Some neuronal parameters and their correspondence to particular proteins are summarized in Table I. The choice of neural parameters depends on a task, which we want to simulate. In our case, let it be for instance a normal resting EEG signal.

Moreover, besides the genes coding for the proteins listed in Table I, we include in our gene network nine more genes that are not directly linked to neuronal information-processing parameters. These genes are: c-jun, mGLuR3, Jerky, BDNF, FGF-2, IGF-I, GALR1, NOS, S100beta. These other proteins and genes are known to have a regulatory effect upon genes and proteins that are directly linked to neural information-processing parameters. An example of a particular gene regulatory network (GRN) is given in figure 1.

TABLE I
NEURON'S PARAMETERS AND THEIR RELATED PROTEINS

Neuron's parameter	PROTEIN*
Amplitude and time constants of:	
Fast excitation	AMPAR
Slow excitation	NMDAR
Fast inhibition	GABRA
Slow inhibition	GABRB
Firing threshold	SCN, KCN, CLC

*Abbreviations: AMPAR = (amino-methylisoxazole- propionic acid) AMPA receptor, NMDAR = (*N*-methyl-D-aspartate acid) NMDA receptor, GABRA = (gamma-aminobutyric acid) GABA receptor A, GABRB = GABA receptor B, SCN = Sodium voltage-gated channel, KCN = kalium (potassium) voltage-gated channel, CLC = chloride channel.

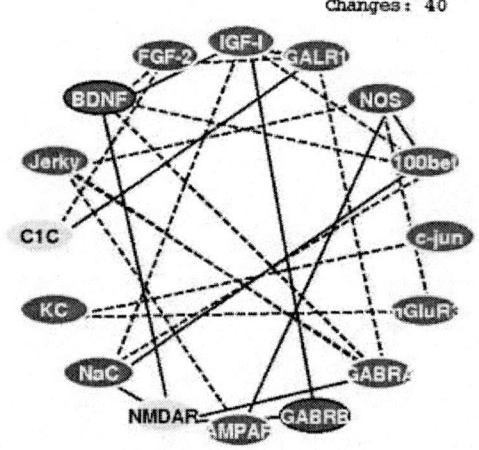

Fig. 1. Illustration of GRN. Solid (dashed) lines denote positive (negative) interactions between genes, respectively. For clarity of illustration, only the stronger of two-way connections are shown. Intensity of grey reflects the level of gene expression after 40 updates.

The CNGM model from formulas (1)–(3) is a general one and can be integrated with an SNN or any other neural network model. Unfortunately the model requires many parameters to be either known in advance or optimized during a model simulation. In the presented experiments we have made several

simplifying assumptions:
1. Each neuron has the same gene regulatory network (GRN), i.e. the same genes and the same interaction gene matrix **W**.
2. Each GRN starts from the same initial values of gene expressions.
3. Feedbacks from neuronal activity or any other external factors to gene expression levels or protein levels are not explicitly considered.
4. Delays Δt are the same for all proteins. This is based on the fact that protein expression data are being gathered for all proteins of interest at the same time instant.

III. AN EXAMPLE OF USING THE CNG MODEL OF A NEURON FOR BUILDING SPIKING NEURAL NETWORK MODELS

The SNN used in our CNGM has been described elsewhere [3, 4]. Each postsynaptic potential has a fast and slow component, otherwise the model is based upon a classical Spike Response Model (SRM) [9].

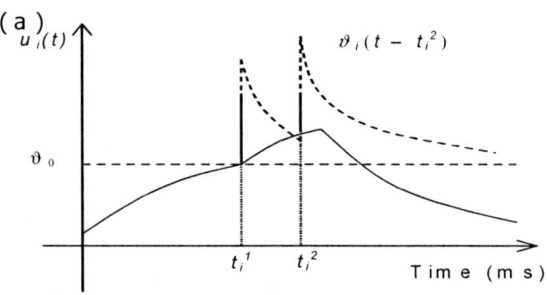

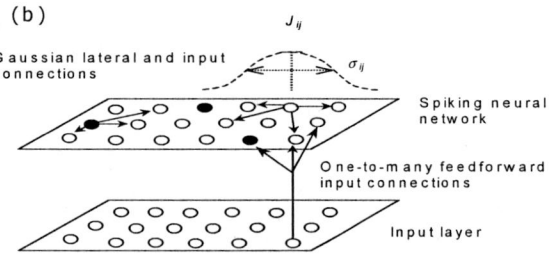

Fig. 2. (a) Spiking neuron model. When the membrane potential $u_i(t)$ of the ith spiking neuron reaches the firing threshold $\vartheta_i(t)$ at time t^k_i, the neuron fires an output spike. $\vartheta_i(t)$ rises after each output spike and decays back to the resting value ϑ_0. (b) The SNN architecture. About 10–20% of n = 120 neurons are inhibitory neurons that are randomly positioned on the grid (filled circles). External input is a randomly Poisson with average frequency between 10–20 Hz.

Figure 2 illustrates the set up of the SNN. We keep the record of spiking activities of all neurons as well as record of the local field potential (LFP), the sum of many of which is in the brain proportional to EEG [10]. We define LFP as an average of all instantaneous membrane potentials, i.e. $\Phi(t) = (1/N) \Sigma\, u_i(t)$. For its analysis we use the fast Fourier method [11].

Frequency spectrum of LFP is divided into five frequency sub-bands, i.e. delta (0.1–3.5 Hz), theta (3.5–7.5 Hz), alpha (7.5–12.5 Hz), gamma 1 (12.5–18.0 Hz), gamma 2 (18.0–30.0 Hz), beta (30.0–50.0 Hz). For these frequency sub-bands we calculate the relative intensity ratios (RIR) over the relevant period of measurement. An example of a human resting interictal EEG is in figure 3 (obtained with permission from [12]). Temporal changes of RIRs for frequency sub-bands over the measurement time period are shown in figure 4.

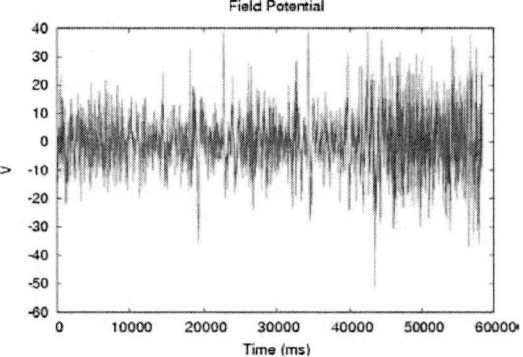

Fig. 3. Human interictal resting EEG signal.

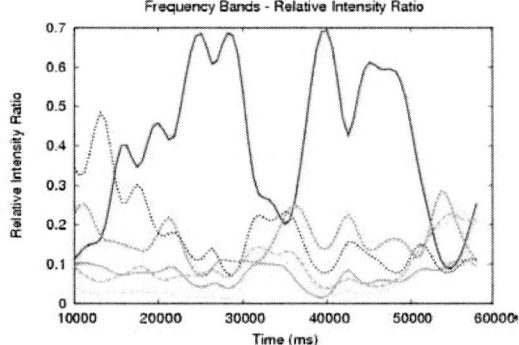

Fig. 4. Temporal course of RIRs for clinically relevant frequency sub-bands of the EEG signal from figure 3. Most of the time, the dominant sub-band is delta (0.5–3.5 Hz).

Thus, any EEG or LFP signal can be characterized by vector of five numbers expressing the average RIRs of particular frequency sub-bands over some time interval. For the EEG signal from figure 2, the average vector RIR (delta, theta, alpha, gamma 1, gamma 2, beta) = (0.56, 21, 0.16, 0.04, 0.007, 0.002). During our simulations we will try to find such gene networks that will lead to the SNN LFP with average RIR vector as closest as possible to the average RIR vector of the resting human EEG in terms of Euclidean distance.

Just for computational reasons, we will employ the delays Δt in equation (2) being equal to just 1s of the SNN time instead of minutes or tens of minutes of the real time [8]. Justification for this time compression in our simulations is illustrated in figures 5 and 6, where we show that the spectral characteristics of the SNN LFP do not change in time when neural parameters are constant (i.e. during the time interval Δt). Thus, with respect to spectral characteristics of the LFP signal, 1 s of SNN simulation with constant parameters can represent an arbitrarily long time interval of real time. This match allows us to update protein levels and the corresponding parameters values every 1s of SNN simulation instead of let us say every fifteen or even more minutes.

IV. OPTMIZATION OF CNGM AND KNOWLEDGE DISCOVERY METHODS

We want to achieve a desired SNN output through optimization of the model 294 parameters. We are optimizing the interaction matrix **W** between 16 genes, initial values of neural parameters, architectural parameters of SNN (except the total number of neurons, spike delays and probability of establishing a synaptic connection) and input frequency to the SNN. All model parameters and their value ranges to choose from during optimization are listed in Table II. These parameter ranges reflect considerable variations of values in real neurons and are taken from neurobiological data [13, 14]. We evaluate the LFP of the SNN by means of FFT in order to compare the SNN output with the EEG signal analyzed in the same way. It has been shown that LFPs in principle have the same spectral characteristics as EEG [15].

TABLE II
MODEL PARAMETERS AND THEIR VALUE RANGES

MODEL PARAMETERS	VALUE RANGE
Fast excitation: Amplitude	0.5 – 3.0
rise / decay time constants	1 – 5 / 5 – 10
Slow excitation: Amplitude	0.5 – 4.0
rise / decay time constants	10 – 20 / 30 – 50
Fast inhibition: Amplitude	4 – 8
rise / decay time constants	5 – 10 / 20 – 30
Slow inhibition: Amplitude	5 – 10
rise / decay time constants	20 – 80 / 50 – 150
Resting firing threshold,	19 – 25
decay time constant / rise	5 – 50 / 2 – 5
Proportion of inhibitory neurons	0.15 – 0.2
Probability of external input firing	0.011 – 0.019
Peak/sigma of external input weight	5 – 10 / 0.1 – 2
Peak/sigma of lateral exc weights	5 – 14 / 2 – 8
Peak/sigma of lateral inh weights	10 – 60 / 4 – 10
Unit delay in e/i spike propagation	1 ms / 2 ms
Probability of connection	0.5
Number of neurons	120
Gene interaction weight	(– 5 , +5)
Gene initial expression	(0.0, 0.1)
Gene normalized expression	(0.0, 1.0)

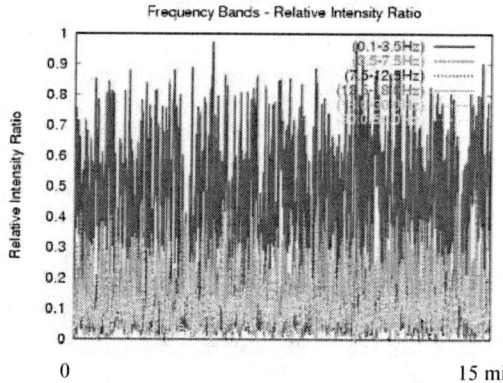

Fig. 5. 15 min of SNN spontaneous activity with constant parameters. The dominant frequency sub-band is delta.

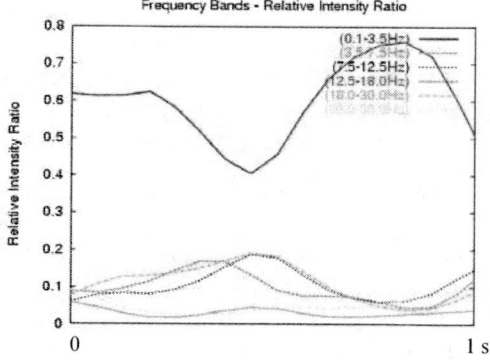

Fig. 6. The first second of the simulation from figure 5. The dominant frequency sub-band is still delta.

In order to find an optimal GRN within the SNN model so that the frequency characteristics of the LFP of the SNN model are similar to the brain EEG characteristics, we use the following simple optimization procedure:

1. Generate a population of N CNGMs, each with randomly generated values of coefficients for the GRN matrix **W**, initial gene expression values **g**(0), initial values of SNN parameters **P**(0), and different connectivity (all these

parameters can have some predefined borders, see Table II);
2. Run each SNN over a period of time T = 1 min and record the LFP, $\Phi(t)$;
3. Calculate the spectral characteristics of the LFP using FFT;
4. Compare the spectral characteristics of SNN LFP to the characteristics of the target EEG signal. Evaluate the closeness of the LFP signal for each SNN to the target EEG signal characteristics. Find SNN models that match the EEG spectral characteristics better than other solutions. Let us say, the Euclidean distance between the RIR vectors be smaller than 0.1;
5. Analyze the GRN and the SNN parameters for significant gene patterns that cause the SNN model behavior.

Alternatively, we can use a genetic algorithm to find an optimal solution or solutions, but for illustration of our knowledge discovery method, the above simple optimization procedure will be sufficient.

N = 400 random gene interaction matrices **W**s show almost a uniform distribution of interaction strengths between genes as can be seen in figure 7.

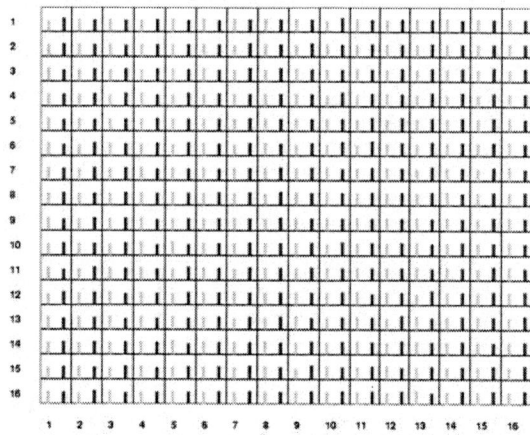

Fig. 7. Black and grey histograms show the percentage of positive and negative gene interactions, respectively, in 400 randomly generated interaction matrices **W**.

Among these 400 random solutions, 15 **W**s matrices led to an SNN LFP with spectral characteristics very close to the target EEG signal in terms of Euclidean distance between the RIR vectors belonging to the SNN LFP and human EEG being smaller than 0.1. Visual inspection of these 15 solutions also confirmed that the LFP signal and its spectral characteristics are similar to the target EEG signal. Distribution of gene interactions in these 15 **W** matrices that led to the desired SNN output is no longer uniform (see figure 8).

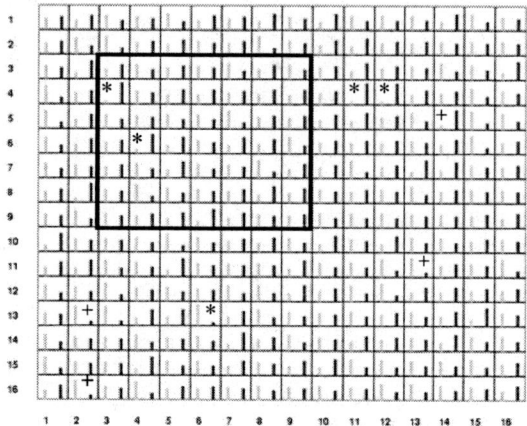

Fig. 8. Black and grey histograms show the percentage of positive and negative gene interactions, respectively, in 15 winner interaction matrices **W** after experimental running of CNGM. * means $\alpha = 0.005$, and + means $\alpha = 0.025$ in the X^2 test.

To discover the knowledge, e.g. to find out what these solutions have in common, we have calculated how many times the interactions between genes become positive and how many times they become negative. We can use a basic frequency statistical analysis, for instance the X^2-statistic, to make predictions about interactions between real genes in neurons. Let us consider the genes, which are directly related to information-processing parameters of neurons. In figure 8, they are outlined by a black rectangle. We have found that a statistically significant difference at greater than the 0.005 level of probability holds for interactions $w_{43} > 0$ and $w_{64} > 0$ (denoted by asterisks in black rectangle in figure 8 matrix). What that means is that the gene No. 3 (coding for the $GABA_A$ receptor) when elevated in expression is accompanied by elevated expression of gene No. 4 (coding for $GABA_B$ receptor), and that the gene No. 4 (coding for the $GABA_B$ receptor) when elevated in expression is accompanied by elevated expression of gene No. 6 (coding for NMDA receptor). These interactions are intuitively reasonable since one can assume that when the inhibition is somehow enhanced, the system tries to keep balance by enhancing excitation as well, and vice versa. Table III summarizes all statistically significant deviations from uniformity among all the gene interactions in our sample of 15 **W**s leading to LFP with frequency spectrum similar to a normal resting EEG. The meaning of these other interactions with genes that do not have any assigned functions is not relevant for now, except as an illustration of expansion of our approach to genes that can have an indirect yet important effect.

TABLE III
STATISTICALLY SIGNIFICANT GENE INTERACTIONS

Significance α	Gene interaction $w(j, k)$
0.005 (*)	$w(4,3) > 0$, $w(6, 4) > 0$, $w(4, 11) > 0$, $w(4, 12) > 0$, $w(13, 6) < 0$
0.025 (+)	$w(5, 14) > 0$, $w(11, 13) < 0$, $w(13, 2) < 0$, $w(16, 2) < 0$

V. DISCUSSION

In real neural networks neuronal parameters that define the functioning of a neural network depend on genes and proteins in a complex way. Gene and protein expression values change due to internal dynamics of the gene/protein regulatory (interaction) network, initial conditions of the genes and external conditions. All this may affect gradually or quickly the functioning of the neural network as a whole. In our computer experiments, we have observed for example that different initial gene conditions can lead to the same outcome in terms of neuronal activity. Moreover, different types of gene interaction dynamics, i.e. be it constant, periodic, quasi-periodic or even chaotic, can lead to a similar LFP of an associated SNN model, provided some statistical distribution of gene interactions is maintained. Different statistics can be linked to different values in Table II. Thus, in the diseased brain, either altered initial conditions, mutated genes and/or altered interactions within GRN can lead to abnormalities in network activity. Realistic models of gene networks within neural networks should account for these processes.

In order to investigate these phenomena, we have set up a novel model of a CNGM that is simple and biologically plausible. Associated SNN uses principles from the simple spiking neuron models [9]. More detailed models of SNN can include for instance detailed ion receptor and channel kinetics and also multiple neuron compartments. It is possible to include also more than one brain areas in our CNG model. Particular neural network model should be chosen based on a problem, which we want to account for. On the example of a resting human EEG signal we have demonstrated our CNGM approach with the introduction of generic CNGM equations, optimization and knowledge discovery techniques.

ACKNOWLEDGMENT

The work has been supported by the NERF grant X0201 funded by FRST and by KEDRI funds (www.kedri.info).

REFERENCES

[1] G. Marcus, *The Birth of the Mind: How a Tiny Number of Genes Creates the Complexity of the Human Mind*, Basic Books, New York, 2004.

[2] "The Nervous System," in *Genes and Disease*, National Centre for Biotechnology Information (NCBI), http://www.ncbi.nlm.nih.gov/books/bv.fcgi?call=bv.View..ShowSection&rid=gnd.chapter.75, 2003.

[3] N. Kasabov and L. Benuskova, "Computational neurogenetics," *Journal of Computational and Theoretical Nanoscience*, 1, 1, pp. 47-61, 2004.

[4] N. Kasabov, L. Benuskova and S. G. Wysoski, "Computational neurogenetic modelling: gene networks within neural networks," *Proc. IJCNN'2004: IEEE Press*, Budapest, 2004, vol. 2, pp. 1203-1208.

[5] C. E. M. vanBeijsterveldt and G. C. M. vanBaal, "Twin and family studies of the human electroencephalogram: a review and meta-analysis," *Biological Psychology*, 61, pp. 111-138, 2002.

[6] D. C. Weaver, C. T. Workman and G. D. Stormo, "Modeling regulatory networks with weight matrices," *Proc. Pacific Symp. Biocomputing*, 1999, vol. 4, pp. 112-123.

[7] L. F. A. Wessels, E. P. vanSomeren and M. J. T. Reinders, "A comparison of genetic network models," *Proc. Pacific Symp. Biocomputing*, 2001, vol. 6, pp. 508-519.

[8] H. Lodish, A. Berk, S. L. Zipursky, P. Matsudaira, D. Baltimore and J. Darnell, "Nucleic acids, the genetic code, and the synthesis of macromolecules," in *Molecular Cell Biology*, W. H. Freeman & Co., New York, 2000, pp. 100-137.

[9] W. Gerstner and W. M. Kistler, *Spiking Neuron Models*, Cambridge Univ. Press, Cambridge, MA, 2002.

[10] J. W. Freeman, *Mass action in the nervous system*, Academic Press, New York, 1975.

[11] R. Q. Quiroga, *Quantitative Analysis of EEG Signals: Time-Frequency Methods and Chaos Theory.*, Institute of Physiology and Institute of Signal Processing. Medical University Lübeck: Lübeck, 1998.

[12] R. Q. Quiroga, *Dataset # 3: Tonic-clonic (Grand Mal) seizures. http://www.vis.caltech.edu/~rodri/data.htm*, 1998.

[13] A. Destexhe, "Spike-and-wave oscillations based on the properties of $GABA_B$ receptors," *J. Neurosci.*, 18, pp. 9099-9111, 1998.

[14] F. Wendling, F. Bartolomei, J. J. Bellanger and P. Chauvel, "Epileptic fast activity can be explained by a model of impaired GABAergic dendritic inhibition," *Eur. J. Neurosci.*, 15, pp. 1499-1508, 2002.

[15] A. Destexhe, D. Contreras and M. Steriade, "Spatiotemporal analysis of local field potentials and unit discharges in cat cerebral cortex during natural wake and sleep states," *J. Neuroscience*, 19, 11, pp. 4595-4608, 1999.

Self-Organizing Hierarchical Knowledge Discovery by an ARTMAP Information Fusion System

Gail A. Carpenter, Siegfried Martens
Boston University, Department of Cognitive and Neural System
677 Beacon Street, Boston, MA 02215 USA.
[gail, sig] @cns.bu.edu   http://cns.bu.edu/techlab/

Abstract – Classifying terrain or objects may require the resolution of conflicting information from sensors working at different times, locations, and scales, and from users with different goals and situations. Current fusion methods can help resolve such inconsistencies, as when evidence variously suggests that an object is a car, a truck, or an airplane. The methods described here define a complementary approach to the information fusion problem, considering the case where sensors and sources are both nominally inconsistent and reliable, as when evidence suggests that an object is a car, a vehicle, and man-made. Underlying relationships among classes are assumed to be unknown to the automated system or the human user. The ARTMAP self-organizing rule discovery procedure is illustrated with an image example, but is not limited to the image domain.

I. INTRODUCTION

Image fusion has been defined as "the acquisition, processing and synergistic combination of information provided by various sensors or by the same sensor in many measuring contexts." [1, p. 3] When multiple sources provide inconsistent data, such methods are called upon to select the accurate information components. As quoted by the International Society of Information Fusion (http://www.inforfusion.org/terminology.htm):
"Evaluating the reliability of different information sources is crucial when the received data reveal some inconsistencies and we have to choose among various options." For example, independent sources might label an identified vehicle *car* or *truck* or *airplane*. A fusion method could address this problem by weighing the confidence and reliability of each source, merging complementary information, or gathering more data. In any case, at most one of these answers is correct.

The methods described here address a complementary and previously unexamined aspect of the information fusion problem, seeking to derive consistent knowledge from sources that are inconsistent – yet accurate. This is a problem that the human brain solves naturally. A young child who hears the family pet variously called *Spot*, *puppy*, *dog*, *dalmatian*, *mammal*, and *animal* is not only not alarmed by these conflicting labels but readily uses them to infer functional relationships. An analogous problem for information fusion methods seeks to classify the terrain and objects in an unfamiliar territory based on intelligence supplied by several reliable sources. Each source labels a portion of the region based on sensor data and observations collected at specific times and based on individual goals and interests. Across sources, a given pixel might be correctly but inconsistently labeled *car*, *vehicle*, and *man-made*. A human mapping analyst would, in this case, be able to apply a lifetime of experience to resolve the paradox by placing objects in a knowledge hierarchy, and a rule-based expert system could be constructed to codify this knowledge. Alternatively, an analyst could be faced with complex or unfamiliar labels, or the structure of object relationships may vary from one region to the next.

The current study shows how an ARTMAP neural network can act as a self-organizing expert system to derive hierarchical knowledge structures from nominally inconsistent training data. This ability is implicit in the network's learning strategy, which creates one-to-many, as well as many-to-one, maps of the input space. During training, the system can learn that disparate pixels map to the output class *car*; but, if similar or identical pixels are later labeled *vehicle* or *man-made*, the system can associate multiple classes with a given input. During testing, distributed code activations predict multiple output class labels. A rule production algorithm uses the pattern of distributed network predictions to derive a knowledge hierarchy for the output classes. The resulting diagram of the relationships among classes can then guide the construction of consistent layered maps.

II. MULTI-CLASS PREDICTIONS BY ARTMAP NEURAL NETWORKS

While the earliest unsupervised ART [2] and supervised ARTMAP networks [3] feature winner-take-all code representations, many of the networks developed since the mid-1990s incorporate distributed code representations. Comparative analyses of these systems have led to the specification of a *default ARTMAP* network, which features simplicity of design and robust performance in many application domains [4]. Selection of one particular

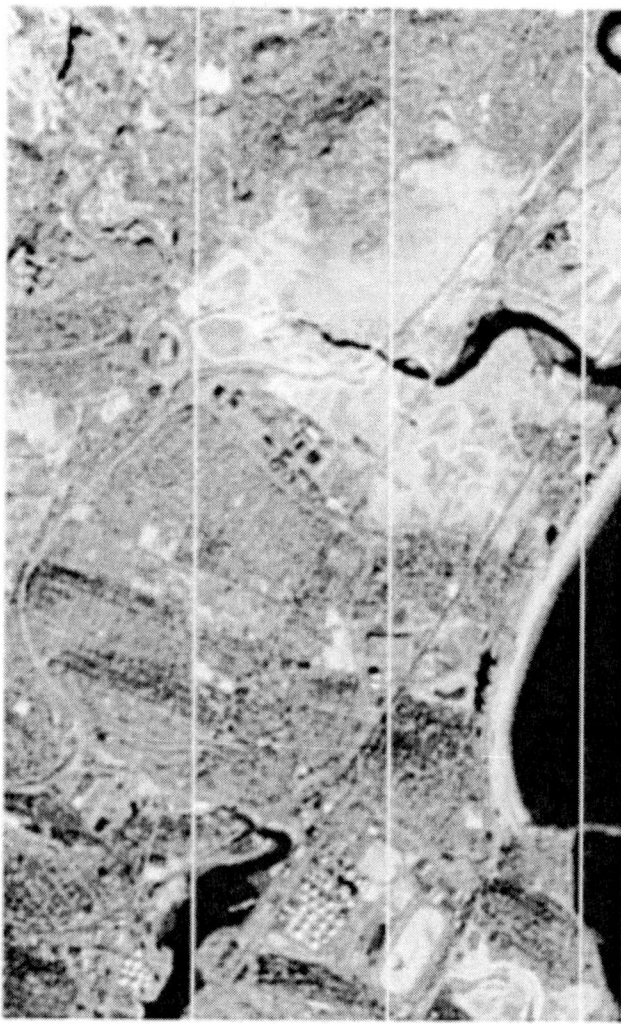

Fig. 1. Testbed Boston image for ARTMAP information fusion methods, in grey scale representation of preprocessed inputs. The city of Revere is at the center, surrounded by (clockwise from lower right) portions of Winthrop, East Boston, Chelsea, Everett, Malden, Melrose, Saugus, and Lynn. Logan Airport runways and Boston Harbor are at the lower center, with Revere Beach and the Atlantic Ocean at the right. The Saugus and Pines Rivers meet in the upper right, and the Chelsea River is in the lower left of the image. Dimensions: 360 x 600 pixels (15*m* resolution) $\cong$ 5.4 *km* x 9 *km*. The image is divided into four vertical strips: two for training, one for validation (if needed), and one for testing. This protocol produces geographically distinct training and testing areas, to assess regional generalization. Typically, class label distributions vary substantially across strips.

a priori algorithm is intended to facilitate technology transfer. This network, which here serves as the recognition engine of the information fusion system, uses winner-take-all coding during training and distributed coding during testing. Distributed test outputs have helped improve various methods for categorical decision-making. One such method, in a map production application, compares a baseline mapping procedure, which selects the class with the largest total output, with a procedure that enforces *a priori* output class probabilities and another one that selects class-specific output thresholds via validation [5]. Distributed coding supports each method, but the ultimate prediction is one output class per test input. This procedure also specifies a canonical training/testing method which partitions the area in question into four vertical or horizontal strips. A given simulation takes training pixels from two of these strips; uses the validation strip to choose parameters, if necessary; and tests on the fourth strip. Methods are thus compared with training and test sets that are not only disjoint but drawn from geographically separate locations. This separation tests for generalization to new regions, where output class distributions could typically be far from those of the training and validation sets.

The information fusion techniques developed in the current study modify the baseline mapping procedure by allowing the system to predict more than one output class during testing. A given test pixel either predicts the N classes receiving the largest net system outputs or predicts all classes whose net output exceeds a designated threshold Γ. A preliminary version of the ARTMAP information fusion system [6] chose a global selection parameter N or Γ based on analysis of the validation strip. This method succeeds when most validation and test items share a common number of correct output classes. The preferable procedure used here allows each test exemplar to choose its own number N of output class predictions. This per-pixel filtering method thus does not rely on the strong assumption that the correct number of output classes per item is approximately uniform across the test set.

An image testbed demonstrates the robustness of the ARTMAP information fusion procedure. This example was derived from a Landsat 7 Thematic Mapper (TM) data acquired on the morning of January 1, 2001 by the Earth Resources Observation System (EROS) Data Center, U.S. Geological Survey, Sioux Falls, SD (http://edc.usgs.gov). The area includes portions of northeast Boston and suburbs (Fig. 1), and encompasses mixed urban, suburban, industrial, water, and park spaces. Ground truth pixels are labeled *ocean, ice, river, beach, park, road, residential, industrial, water, open space, built-up, natural, man-made*. During training, ARTMAP is given no information about relationships among the target classes.

III. DERIVING A KNOWLEDGE HIERARCHY FROM A TRAINED NETWORK: PREDICTIONS, RULES, AND GRAPHS

The *ARTMAP fusion system* provides a canonical procedure for assigning to each input an arbitrary number of output classes in a supervised learning setting. Information implicit in the distributed predictions of a trained ARTMAP network, trained with prescribed protocols [7], can be used to generate a hierarchy of output class relationships. To accomplish this, each test pixel first produces a set of output class predictions. The resulting list of test predictions determines a list of rules $x \Rightarrow y$ which define relationships between pairs of output classes, with each rule carrying a confidence value. The rules are then used to assign classes to levels, with rule antecedents x at lower levels and consequents y at higher levels. Classes connected by arrows that codify the list of rules and confidence values form a graphical representation of the knowledge hierarchy, as follows.

A. Predictions

A critical aspect of the **default ARTMAP network** (Fig. 2) is the distributed nature of its internal code representation, which produces continuous-valued predictions across output classes during testing. In response to a test input, distributed activations in the default ARTMAP coding field send a net signal σ_k to each output class k. A winner-take-all method predicts the single output class $k=K$ receiving the largest signal σ_k. Alternatively, a single test input can predict multiple output classes. The *per-pixel filtering* method employed here allows the output activation pattern produced by each test pixel to determine the number of predicted classes. Namely, if the net signals σ_k projecting to the output classes k are arranged from largest to smallest, the system predicts all the classes up to the point of maximum decrease in the signal size from one class to the next. This strategy is motivated by the behavior of a hypothetical system that accurately represents all the output classes. In such a system, if a pixel should predict three classes (e.g., road, pavement, man-made), then the output signals σ_k to each of these classes would typically be large compared to those of the remaining classes. The maximum decrease in size would then occur between the third and fourth largest signal, and the per-pixel filtering method would predict three classes.

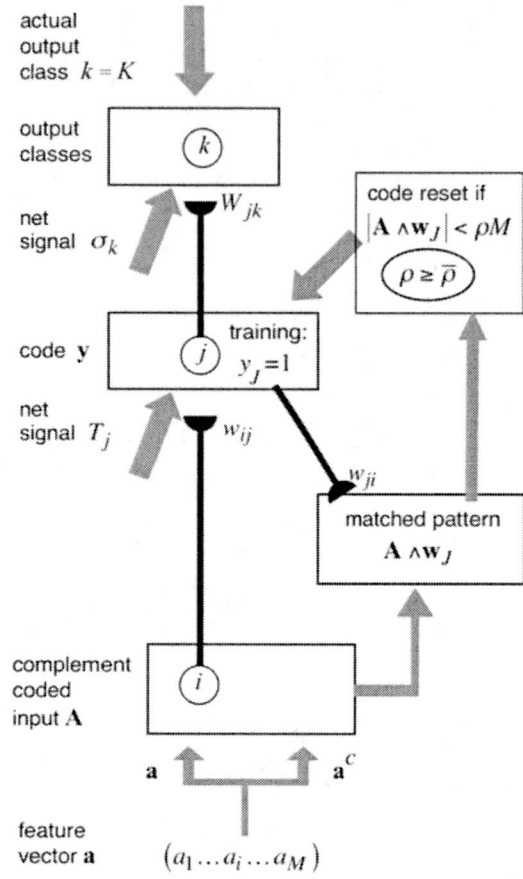

Fig. 2. Default ARTMAP notation: An M-dimensional feature vector **a** is complement coded to form the $2M$-D ARTMAP input **A**. Vector **y** represents a winner-take-all code during training, when a single category node ($j=J$) is active; and a distributed code during testing. With fast learning, bottom-up weights w_{ij} equal top-down weights w_{ji}, and the weight vector $\mathbf{w}_j$ represents their common values. When a coding node j is first selected during training, it is connected to the output class k of the current input ($W_{jk} = 1$). During testing, a distributed code **y** produces predictions σ_k distributed across output classes. In all simulations reported here, the baseline vigilance matching parameter $\overline{\rho} = 0$. [4]

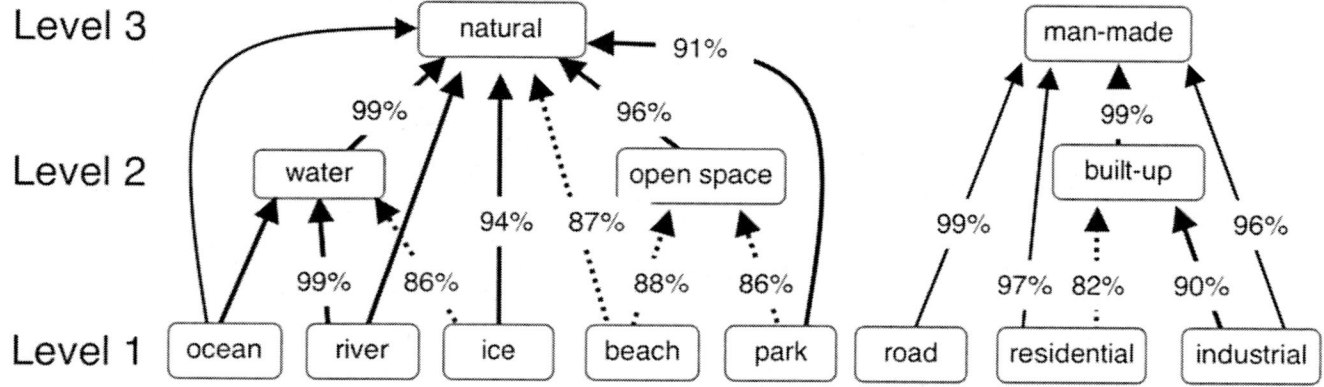

Fig. 3. For the Boston example, the ARTMAP fusion system correctly produces all class rules and levels. Each rule's confidence, if less than 100%, is printed on its arrow. Dashed arrows indicate rules with confidence below 90%.

B. Rules

Once each test pixel has produced a set of output class predictions $\{x,y,...\}$ from its distributed signals σ_k, according to the per-pixel selection method, the list of multi-valued test set predictions is then used to deduce a list of output class implications of the form $x \Rightarrow y$, each carrying a confidence value $C\%$. This rule creation method is related to the Apriori algorithm in the association rule literature [8, 9].

The five steps listed below produce the list of rules that label class relationships. The algorithm employs an *equivalence parameter* $e\%$ and a *minimum confidence parameter* $c\%$. Rules with low confidence ($C<c$) are ignored, with one exception: if all rules that include a given class have confidence below c, then the list retains the rule derived from the pair predicted by the largest number of pixels. Although this "no extinction" clause may produce low-confidence rules, these may occasionally correspond to cases that are rare but important. The user can easily take these exceptions under advisement, since the summary graph displays each confidence value. Two classes x and y are treated as *equivalent* ($x \equiv y$) if both rules $x \Rightarrow y$ and $y \Rightarrow x$ hold with confidence greater than e. In this case, the class predicted by fewer pixels is ignored in subsequent computations, but equivalent classes are displayed as a single node on the final rule summary graph.

Reasonable default values set the equivalence parameter e in the range 90-95% and the minimum confidence parameter c in the range 50-70%. In all simulations reported here, parameter values were set *a priori* to e=90% and c=50%. Alternatively, e and c may be chosen by validation.

Step 1 : List the number of test set pixels predicting each output class x. Order this list from the classes with the fewest predictions to the classes with the most.

Step 2 : List the number of test set pixels $\#(x \& y)$ simultaneously predicting each pair of distinct output classes. Omit pairs with no such pixels. Order the list so that $\#(x) \leq \#(y)$: classes x observe the order established in Step 1; and for each such class x, classes y observe the same order.

Step 3 : Identify equivalent classes, where $x \equiv y$ if $[\#(x \& y) / \#(y)] \geq e\%$. Remove from the list all class pairs that include x (where $\#(x) \leq \#(y)$, as in Step 2).

Step 4 : Each pair remaining on the list produces a rule $x \Rightarrow y$ with confidence $C\% = [\#(x \& y) / \#(x)]$. If Step 3 determined that $x \equiv y$, record the confidence $C \geq e$ of each rule in the pair $\{ x \Rightarrow y, y \Rightarrow x \}$.

Step 5 : Remove from the list all rules with confidence $C < c$. Exception (*no extinction*): If all rules that include a given class have confidence below the minimum confidence c, then retain the rule $x \Rightarrow y$ with maximal $\#(x \& y)$ pixels.

C. Graphs

A directed graph summarizes the list of implication rules. These rules suggest a natural hierarchy among output classes, with antecedents sitting below consequents. For each rule $x \Rightarrow y$, class x is located at a lower level of the hierarchy than class y, according to the iterative algorithm below. Once each class is situated on its level, a listed rule $x \Rightarrow y$ produces an arrow from x to y. Each rule's confidence is indicated on the arrow, with lower-confidence rules (say $C<90\%$) having dashed arrows. For arrows with no displayed confidence values, $C=100\%$.

The following procedure assigns each output class to a level.

Top Level: Items that appear only as consequents y.

Level 1: Classes that do not appear as consequents in any rule. Remove from the list all rules $x \Rightarrow y$ where x is in Level 1.

Next Level: Classes that do not appear as consequents in any remaining rule. Remove from the list all rules $x \Rightarrow y$ where x is in this level.

Iterate: Repeat until all rules have been removed from the list.

Note that Level 1 includes classes that do not appear in any rule as well as those that appear only as antecedents.

The graph in Fig. 3 depicts the implication rules, hierarchy levels, and confidence values derived for the Boston example. ARTMAP information fusion has placed each class in its correct level and discovers all the correct rules.

IV. CONCLUSION

The ARTMAP neural network produces one-to-many mappings from input vectors to output classes, as well as the more traditional many-to-one mappings, as the normal product of its supervised learning laws. During training, a given input may learn associations to more than one output class. Some of these associations could be erroneous: when different observers label an image *dog*, *coyote*, or *wolf*, at most one of these classes is correct. Inconsistent data may, however, be completely correct, as when observers variously label the image *wolf*, *mammal*, and *carnivore*. By resolving such paradoxes during everyday knowledge acquisition, humans naturally infer complex, hierarchical relationships among classes without explicit specification of the rules underlying these relationships. One-to-many learning allows the ARTMAP information fusion system to associate any number of output classes with each input. Although inter-class information is not given with the training inputs, the system readily derives knowledge of the rules, confidence estimates, and multi-class hierarchical relationships from patterns of distributed test predictions.

The Boston image testbed example demonstrates how ARTMAP information fusion resolves apparent contradictions in input pixel labels by assigning output classes to levels in a knowledge hierarchy. This methodology is not, however, limited to the image domain illustrated here, and could be applied, for example, to infer patterns of drug resistance or to improve marketing suggestions to individual consumers. One such pilot study has created a hypothetical set of relationships among protease inhibitors, based on resistance patterns from genome sequences of HIV patients.

ACKNOWLEDGMENTS

This work was supported by research grants from the Air Force Office of Scientific Research (AFOSR F49620-01-1-0423), the National Geospatial-Intelligence Agency (NMA 201-01-1-2016), the National Science Foundation (NSF SBE-0354378), and the Office of Naval Research (ONR N00014-01-1-0624); and by postdoctoral fellowships from the National Geospatial-Intelligence Agency and the National Science Foundation for Siegfried Martens (NMA 501-03-1-2030 and NSF DGE-0221680).

REFERENCES

[1] Simone, G., Farina, A., Morabito, F.C., Serpico, S.B., & Bruzzone, L. (2002). Image fusion techniques for remote sensing applications. *Information Fusion*, **3**, 3-15.

[2] Carpenter, G.A. & Grossberg, S. (1987). A massively parallel architecture for a self-organizing neural pattern recognition machine. *Computer Vision, Graphics, and Image Processing*, **37**, 54-115.

[3] Carpenter, G.A. Grossberg, S., & Reynolds, J.H. (1991). ARTMAP: Supervised real-time learning and classification of nonstationary data by a self-organizing neural network. *Neural Networks*, **4**(5), 565-588.

[4] Carpenter, G.A. (2003). Default ARTMAP. In *Proceedings of the international joint conference on neural networks (IJCNN'03)*, Portland, Oregon (pp. 1396-1401).

[5] Parsons, O. & Carpenter, G.A. (2003). ARTMAP neural networks for information fusion and data mining: map production and target recognition methodologies. *Neural Networks*, **16**(7), 1075-1089.

[6] Carpenter, G.A., Martens, S., & Ogas, O.J. (2004). Self-organizing hierarchical knowledge discovery by an ARTMAP image fusion system. In *Proceedings of the 7th international conference on information fusion*, Stockholm, Sweden (pp. 235-242).

[7] Carpenter, G.A., Martens, S., & Ogas, O.J. (2005). Self-organizing information fusion and hierarchical knowledge discovery: a new framework using ARTMAP neural networks. *Neural Networks*, **18**.

[8] Agrawal, R., Imielinski, T., & Swami, A. (1993). Mining association rules between sets of items in large databases. In *Proceedings of the international conference on management of data (ACM SIGMOD)*, Washington, DC (pp. 207-216).

[9] Agrawal, R. & Srikant, R. (1994). Fast algorithms for mining association rules. In *Proceedings of the 20th international conference on very large data bases (VLDB)*, Santiago, Chile (pp. 487-499).

Modification of the ART-1 Architecture Based on Category Theoretic Design Principles

Michael J. Healy†, Richard D. Olinger†
†Department of Electrical and
Computer Engineering
University of New Mexico
Albuquerque, New Mexico 87131
E-mails: mjhealy@ece.unm.edu,
rolinger@ece.unm.edu

Robert J. Young‡, Thomas P. Caudell†‡
‡Department of Computer Science
University of New Mexico
Albuquerque, New Mexico 87131
E-mails: ryoung@cs.unm.edu,
tpc@ece.unm.edu

Kurt W. Larson§
§Sandia National Laboratory
Albuquerque, New Mexico
E-mail: kwlarso@sandia.gov

Abstract—Many studies have addressed the knowledge representation capability of neural networks. A recently-developed mathematical semantic theory explains the relationship between knowledge and its representation in connectionist systems. The theory yields design principles for neural networks whose behavioral repertoire expresses any desired capability that can be expressed logically. In this paper, we show how the design principle of limit formation can be applied to modify the ART-1 architecture, yielding a discrimination capability that goes beyond vigilance. Simulations of this new design illustrate the increased discrimination ability it provides for multi-spectral image analysis.

I. INTRODUCTION

Many studies (see for example [2], [5], [10], [9], [16], and the review [1]) have addressed the knowledge representation capability of neural networks. We present an example to illustrate the improved performance achievable by applying neural network design principles derived from a recently-developed theory for knowledge representation. The example is a small but significant modification to an ART-1 network[3], applied to multi-spectral image analysis. The knowledge representation theory is based upon the mathematical rigor of category theory applied to neural network semantic modeling. Because category theory is as yet unfamiliar to many (until recently being regarded as the ultimate in pure mathematics), we begin with a brief overview of the topics necessary for understanding the work described here. Our semantic theory in its current state of development is described in full in [14], which contains a more comprehensive overview of category theory. Our previous work in applying the semantic theory to neural network analysis and design is described in [11], [12], [13]. Many applications of category theory exist, both to physical and computational theory ([7], [8], [19], [21], [22]) and to practice ([15], [23]).

The semantic theory addresses the question of where and how knowledge is acquired, organized, and stored in connectionist systems. The knowledge has the structure of a hierarchical system of concepts, directed from the abstract to the specific. The theory explains knowledge acquisition and representation in a neural network as an incremental re-use of existing concept representations combined with data to form new representations of both more abstract (or general) concepts and more specific (or specialized) ones. Applied to a neural network with many sensors and other functional sub-networks, the semantic model provides a mathematically rigorous yet natural explanation of the combining of network-region-specific hierarchy representations so that the overall network, if well-designed, acts as if there were a single knowledge structure guiding its behavior. Here, we focus upon the incremental knowledge representation in an ART-1 network, which has only a single region, associated with a single input layer. What we show is that the theory can be applied to improve the performance of even a single-region network in processing multi-modal information derived from a single sensor.

The paper is organized as follows. Section II provides a very brief grounding in the category theory used. In Section III we show how our categorically-based semantic theory is applied to neural networks. In Section IV we describe the use of the theory in obtaining the ART-1 modification for our example. Section V describes our experimental method, Section VI the results, and Section VII is the Conclusion.

II. CATEGORY THEORY: A BRIEF INTRODUCTION

Category theory (see [20], [6], [17], [18], or the tutorial in [14]) is based upon the notion of an arrow, or *morphism*—a relationship between two *objects* in a *category*. A morphism $f: a \longrightarrow b$ has a *domain* object a and a *codomain* object b, and serves as a sort of directed relationship between a and b. In a category C, each pair of arrows $f: a \longrightarrow b$ and $g: b \longrightarrow c$ (where the codomain b of f is also the domain of g as indicated) has a *composition* arrow $g \circ f: a \longrightarrow c$ whose domain a is the domain of f and whose codomain c is the codomain of g. Composition is associative, that is, for three arrows of the form $f: a \longrightarrow b$, $g: b \longrightarrow c$ and $h: c \longrightarrow d$, the result of composing them is order-independent, with $h \circ (g \circ f) = (h \circ g) \circ f$. For each object a, there is an *identity morphism* $\text{id}_a: a \longrightarrow a$ such that for any arrows $f: a \longrightarrow b$ and $g: b \longrightarrow a$, $\text{id}_a \circ g = g$ and $f \circ \text{id}_a = f$. A familiar example of a category is one called **Set**, which has sets as its

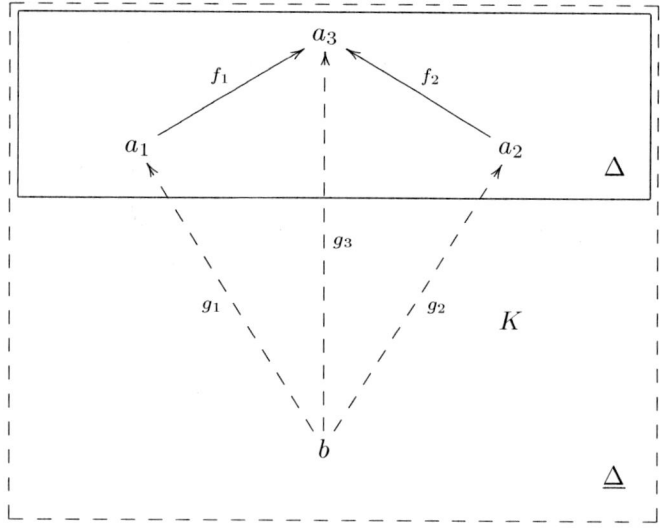

Fig. 1. **A limit for a diagram** Δ.

objects, functions as its morphisms, and whose composition is just the composition of functions, $(g \circ f)(x) = g(f(x))$.

Key notions for the theoretical background of this paper are *commutative diagrams* and *initial and terminal objects*. A diagram is a collection of objects and morphisms of C. In a commutative diagram, any two morphisms with the same domain and codomain, where at least one of the morphisms is the composition of two or more diagram morphisms, are equal. An initial object, where one exists in C, is an object i for which every object a of C is the codomain of a unique morphism $f: i \longrightarrow a$. A terminal object t has every object a of C as the domain of a unique morphism $f: a \longrightarrow t$.

An important use of these key notions is in the definition of *limits* and *colimits*. In [11] and [14] we have shown how colimits model the learning of more complex concepts through re-use of simpler concepts already represented in the connection-weight memory of a neural network. In [14] we show how limits model the learning of simpler, more abstract concepts through re-use of existing representations. Let Δ be a diagram in a category C as shown in Fig. 1, with objects a_1, a_2, a_3 and morphisms $f_1: a_1 \longrightarrow a_3$ and $f_2: a_2 \longrightarrow a_3$. The diagram $\underline{\Delta}$ extends Δ to a commutative diagram with an *apical object* b and morphisms $g_i: b \longrightarrow a_i$ ($i = 1, \ldots, 3$), with $f_1 \circ g_1 = g_3 = f_2 \circ g_2$, provided additional objects and morphisms with the requisite properties exist in C. The conical structure K is called a *cone*. Cones for Δ are the objects of a category **cone**$_\Delta$ (whose morphisms are described in [14]). A *limit for the diagram* Δ is a terminal object K in **cone**$_\Delta$.

The importance of category theory lies in its ability to formalize the notion that things that differ in substance can have an underlying similarity of "structural" form. A mapping between categories that preserves compositional structure, called a *functor*, formalizes this notion. A functor $F: C \longrightarrow D$ associates to each object a of C a unique image object $F(a)$ of D and to each morphism $f: a \longrightarrow b$ of C a unique morphism $F(f): F(a) \longrightarrow F(b)$ of D, and is such that (1) For each composition $g \circ_C f$ in C, $F(g \circ_C f) = F(g) \circ_D F(f)$, where $\circ_C$ and $\circ_D$ denote the respective compositions in C and D; (2) for each object a of C, $F(\text{id}_a) = \text{id}_{F(a)}$. It follows that F maps commutative diagrams of C to commutative diagrams in D. This means that any structural constraints expressed in C are translated into D.

III. APPLYING CATEGORY THEORY TO NEURAL NETWORK SEMANTIC ANALYSIS

Knowledge can be seen as a system of symbolic concepts - descriptions of objects, events, and anything else one can imagine, at any arbitrary level of generality or specificity. The system is organized as a hierarchy ordered from the abstract to the specific. Learning, the acquisition of a knowledge representation in a neural network, begins at the sensor level of processing. Concepts associated with sensor elements describe the sensor primitives. These are far from being the most complex, yet are not the simplest, concepts possible. Indeed, the neural network's learning algorithm effectively re-uses the sensor concepts in many ways in combination with the input data to form concepts not yet represented by the connection-weight array of the network. The more complex concept representations are formed via colimit generation in the network structure. (Obviously, this implies that a category can be used to represent the diagrams and colimits; neural categories will be discussed briefly here.) An abstraction process proceeds in the other direction via limit generation. The abstract concepts describe items that are shared by the more complex concepts in the diagrams over which limits are formed. Thus, the knowledge-representation process proceeds in both directions — specialization and abstraction — beginning at the sensor-percept level.

A category **Concept** provides the required mathematical model for the hierarchical structure of knowledge. In actuality, this is a category whose objects are formal logic theories T and whose morphisms are theory morphisms $s: T \longrightarrow T'$. Briefly, s is a mapping of the quantities and axioms expressed in T into the theory T' such that the images of the axioms of T are either axioms or theorems of T' (see [14] or any of [6], [8], [19]). Categories $\mathbf{N}_{A,w}$, where A is a neural network architecture (such as a specific ART-1 network) and w is an array of connection weight values for it, provide the required mathematical model for neural networks in specified states of learning. The objects of $\mathbf{N}_{A,w}$ are the sets of inputs that "activate" pairs (p_i, η) given the weights in w, where p_i is a node of A and η is a set of output values for p_i. The set η is often modeled as an interval of real values where p_i has a real-valued signal function. A member of the activating set for (p_i, η) is an input pattern that causes p_i to generate an output signal in the set η. A morphism $m: (p_i, \eta) \longrightarrow$

(p_j, η') is the set of inputs that cause all the nodes lying along the paths of connections forming a bundle Γ to generate outputs within specified intervals. The paths in Γ share the common source and target objects (p_i, η) and (p_j, η'). If A is properly designed and w is an array of weight values acquired at some stage of learning from input patterns, it will be possible to define a functor $M: \textbf{Concept} \longrightarrow \textbf{N}_{A,w}$. This is a mathematical description of the representation of concepts and their morphisms in A at the stage of learning represented by w.

Each concept morphism $s: T \longrightarrow T'$ has an associated *model-space morphism*, a functor $\text{Mod}(s): \text{Mod}(T') \longrightarrow \text{Mod}(T)$. Here, $\text{Mod}(T)$ and $\text{Mod}(T')$ are categories of models, possible worlds or instances within which T and T' hold, respectively. Since $\text{Mod}(s)$ reverses the direction of s, each instance of T' has a corresponding instance of T. *This fact has great significance for neural networks.* To see this, suppose that (p_i, η) and (p_j, η') are the images of objects T and T' under the functor M, $(p_i, \eta) = M(T)$ and $(p_j, \eta') = M(T')$, and that $m: (p_i, \eta) \longrightarrow (p_j, \eta')$ is the image of $s: T \longrightarrow T'$, $m = M(s)$. We associate the activating inputs for the objects $(p_i, \eta) = M(T)$ and $(p_j, \eta') = M(T')$ with objects in the model categories $\text{Mod}(T)$ and $\text{Mod}(T')$, respectively. Given this association, *every input that activates (p_j, η') must also activate (p_i, η)*, a consequence of the existence of the model-space morphism $\text{Mod}(s): \text{Mod}(T') \longrightarrow \text{Mod}(T)$. Let T be the apical concept of a limit cone for a diagram Δ in **Concept** and let $s: T \longrightarrow T'$ be one of the leg morphisms for the limit cone. Then, (p_i, η) must be activated whenever (p_j, η') is, where (p_j, η') can be any object in the diagram image $M(\Delta)$.

IV. AN ART-1 NETWORK MODIFIED WITH LIMITS AT F_1

In the following, we apply limits to supplement the ART-1 vigilance mechanism. This enhances the resolving power of ART-1, allowing it to control information loss in specific regions of the templates as they form. Use of the vigilance mechanism alone allows control only over information loss in a whole template. Applying limits requires that we discuss ART-1 as an architecture that can be extended to have a categorical representation capable of containing the image of a functor from the **Concept** category. This is not a trivial task with any existing artificial neural architecture, but this need not prevent us from testing a partial categorically-based extension. Accordingly, we have modified an ART-1 network by applying limits to discrete diagrams (i.e., having objects only) comprising disjoint subsets of nodes whose union is the entire F_1 layer. Each node is associated with an object whose output set η includes all positive outputs. This allows the apical objects of the limit cones to be shown simply as nodes (see Fig. 2, where the apical objects are labelled "SM_i limit", SM standing for "sub-modality"). These form a new layer which we call F_{-1}. The limit cone leg morphisms are represented by bundles consisting of a single connection each, projecting from a limit node SM_i to each of the F_1 nodes representing an object in its diagram. Each feedforward

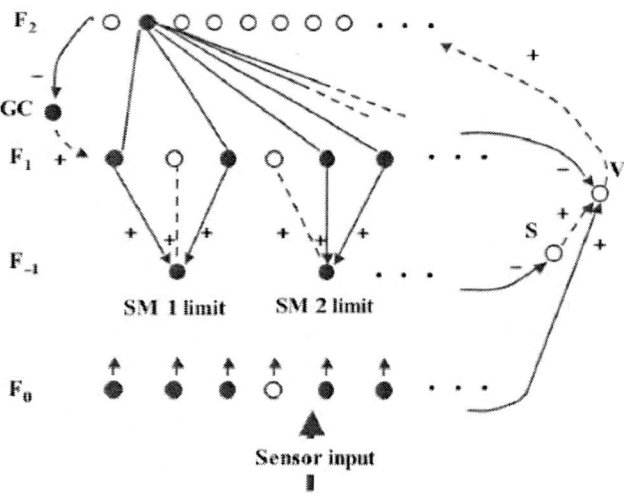

Fig. 2. **A resonating template in an ART-1 network modified to extract abstract concepts corresponding to sub-modalities in each input pattern. The F_1 nodes represent input concepts and the SM nodes represent the extracted sub-modality concepts.**

connection is paired with a feedback connection. If the neural cones are the functor images of limit cones in the category **Concept**, the reciprocal feedback connections represent the model-space morphisms corresponding to each of the limit cone leg morphisms. The feedforward connections have small positive weights and their reciprocal connections have unit positive weight, so that activity in SM_i has a minimal impact upon its F_1 nodes while they, in contrast, provide excitatory input to it proportional to the number of them that are active. Letting the set of all nonzero outputs from each F_{-1} node represent the limit object of that node ensures the enforcement of the property that a concept morphism is accompanied by model-space morphisms: That is, if any one of its F_1 nodes is active, a node SM_i will be active. Thus, the F_1 nodes represent neural category objects which in turn represent concepts specifying sensor input properties, while the subset constituting the diagram for an SM_i limit node represents a property comprising a group of input properties. Each SM_i node in F_{-1} represents an aspect of the group property shared by the F_1 nodes in its diagram.

The basic idea in making use of the F_{-1} nodes was to have them supplement the vigilance node's F_2 reset capability. This is the purpose of the connections from the F_{-1} nodes to node V via node S as shown in Fig. 2. If resonance between the current input and a template pattern is about to occur, but one of the F_{-1} nodes is inactive because none of its F_1 correspondents is active, the resulting lack of an inhibitory signal to S can allow its (tonic) activity to activate V, thereby effectively vetoing the resonance. In this way, each sub-modality is required to maintain at least one binary 1 in each template. A further idea is to require an arbitrary number of binary 1s for each sub-modality in each template by having an adjustable but uniform threshold value t for the F_{-1} nodes. Here, all of the m sub-modality regions $F_{1,i}$ of F_1 ($i = 1, \ldots, m$) have the same number of nodes s, so that $n = ms$ where n is the number of nodes in F_1 (hence, also in F_0). The bit-wise "AND" $I \wedge T^k$ of the current input pattern I and choice template T^k consists of sub-patterns $I_i \wedge T_i^k$. Let $\|X\|$ be the number of 1-bits in a binary pattern X. To avoid activating V, then, each sub-modality i must satisfy the inequality $\|I_i \wedge T_i^k\| \geq ts/2$ (the factor $1/2$ is based upon our use of complement-coded input patterns [10]). This requirement allows the user of the network to exercise a more specific control over template information loss during re-coding than is allowed by having a vigilance parameter alone, which requires only that $\|I \wedge T^k\| \geq \rho \|I\|$, where ρ is the usual vigilance parameter. Just as ρ can be applied to control the amount of specialization versus generalization allowed in the templates (a higher value means fewer input exemplars per template, hence, greater specialization), t can be applied to control the specialization versus generalization allowed in each sub-modality region of the templates (a higher value means greater specialization within the sub-modality).

Given that an F_1 activity pattern $I \wedge T^k$ is made up of the activity patterns $I_i \wedge T_i^k$, and any F_{-1} node can activate V if its activity falls below its threshold t, it is natural to ask if t can be used to eliminate ρ altogether. It can be shown that the usual test involving ρ is indeed redundant if $t \geq \rho$. However, this is not the case when $t < \rho$, and therefore the parameter ρ cannot be eliminated.

V. THE EXPERIMENTAL METHOD

A multi-spectral image was given as a set of 10 optical band amplitudes for each pixel ($m = 10$). This was to be used to produce a false color image. Our method for this was as follows. First, the 10-dimensional vector of analog values for each pixel was converted to a binary input pattern for an ART-1 network by converting the values to complement-coded stack numerals; each stack code consists of a 0-1 binary array which is activated in contiguous fashion, with the number of binary 1s representing an amplitude (this is known widely as "thermometer code"), together with an array with the same number of binary values representing the complement of the first array (see [10], where ART-1 with this representation was proven equivalent to fuzzy ART.). If there are N bits for the "positive" stack representing the amplitude, then there are $s = 2N$ bits in the complement-coded stack numeral and, hence, $ms = 10 \times 2N = 20N$ bits in the resulting input pattern for ART-1 (hence, 20N input F_0 nodes and 20N F_1 nodes). An ART-1 network sorts the input patterns so formed into clusters so that the templates can be decoded into hyperbox regions in 10-dimensional space. The hyperboxes all lie within the 10-cube defined by lower and upper bounds on the variation in band values. The color code for a pixel was then selected by first assigning a color code to the template with which it was associated following training on all pixels, and then using that color for the pixel. The color codes for the templates were

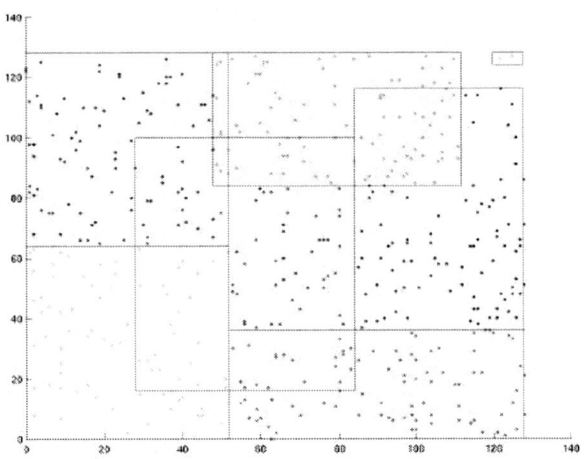

Fig. 3. **Two-dimensional hyperboxes generated by ART-1 with sub-modality limits: vigilance $= 0.47$, F_{-1} threshold $= 0.32$.**

assigned by first sorting the templates in decreasing order of the number of pixels with which they were associated, and then assigning colors starting with blue and proceeding through the visible spectrum to red and, for templates associated with fewer than 10 pixels, white (therefore, the color white can be associated with more than one template).

Two versions of ART-1 were used in the experiment, the modified ART-1 network with an F_{-1} layer as described and an unmodified ART-1 network. For the modified network, the spectral bands were the sub-modalities, with each F_{-1} node serving as a limit node for the set of 2N F_1 nodes representing its complement-coded band value. An activation threshold was used for the F_{-1} nodes, allowing control over information loss in all bands at an arbitrary, uniform level by the user. All ART-1 simulations for this experiment were performed with our recently-developed network specification and simulation package eLoom[4].

VI. RESULTS

To illustrate the formation of hyperbox templates with the modified ART-1 network, a simpler, two-dimensional example was processed first at several combinations of vigilance and F_{-1} threshold values (see Figs. 3 and 4). A data file of 500 random 2D points was created in Matlab using the rand function with lower and upper bounds on x and y component variation of 0.0 and 128.0. These points were then preprocessed in Matlab to generate complement-coded binary input vectors based upon an N = 32-bit "positive" stack for each dimension, resulting in 2 x 2N = 4N = 128 bits per input pattern to ART-1. The resulting hyperboxes are shown along with the points in each in Figs. 3 and 4 for a vigilance level of 0.47 and thresholds of 0.32 and 0.40, respectively.

A single multi-spectral image was used in the 10-band image experiment. Each "positive" binary stack had N = 8

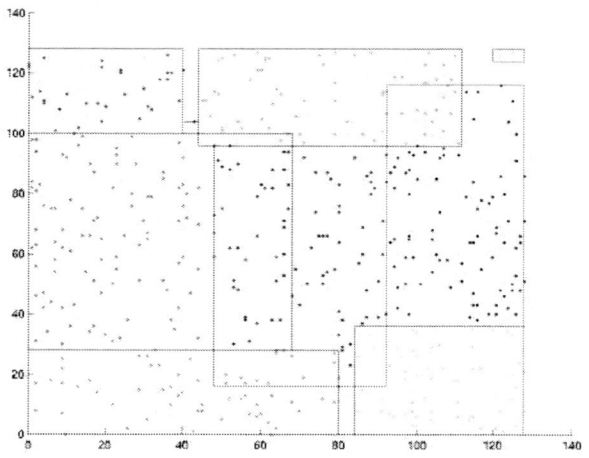

Fig. 4. Two-dimensional hyperboxes generated by ART-1 with submodality limits: vigilance = 0.47, F_{-1} threshold = 0.40.

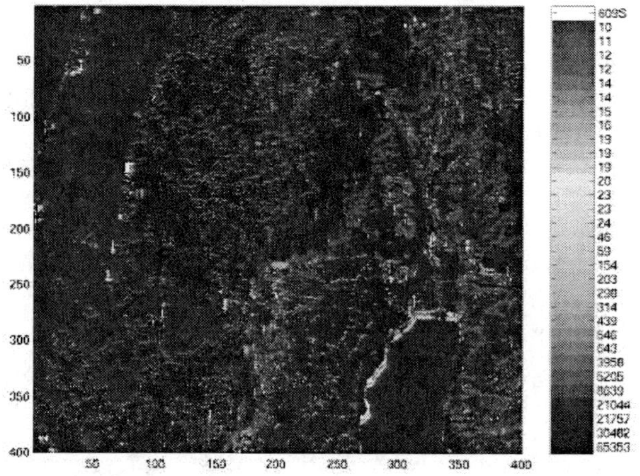

Fig. 6. False color image generated by ART-1 modified with band limits at F_{-1}, vigilance = 0.55, F_{-1} threshold = 0.55.

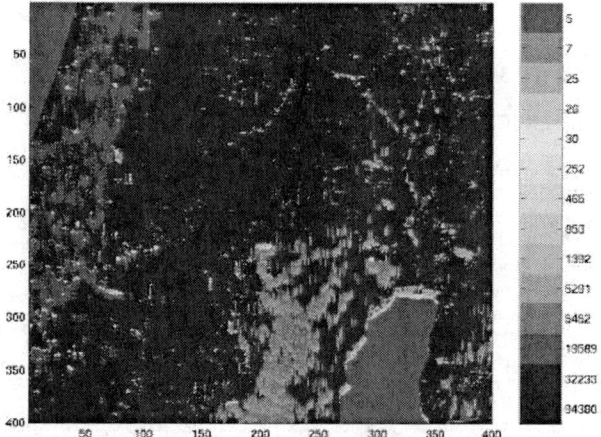

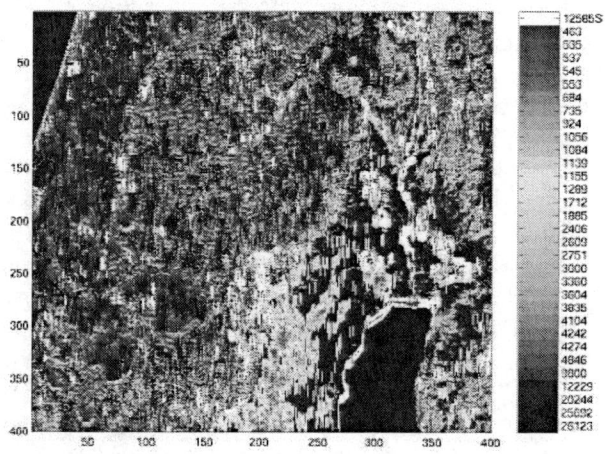

Fig. 5. False color image generated by unmodified ART-1, vigilance = 0.55.

Fig. 7. False color image generated by unmodified ART-1, vigilance = 0.795, same number of template colors as in Fig. 6.

bits, yielding a binary input pattern for ART-1 for each pixel having 20N = 160 bits. The modified ART-1 network was trained several times and the resulting template color codes were used to form false color images. Several combinations of values for vigilance and F_{-1} threshold were used, to produce a variety of false color images from which the best could be selected by human visualization. The same process but without threshold values was used with the unmodified ART-1 network for comparison. A "best" false color image (having greatest discernible resolution) occurred for the modified network at vigilance values of zero to 0.55 and an F_{-1} threshold of 0.55. It was based upon 452 templates, essentially produced by F_{-1}-threshold resets. For comparison, the image generated with the unmodified ART-1 network at a vigilance value of 0.55 is shown in Fig. 5 and the image generated with the modified ART-1 network is shown in Fig. 6. The latter is clearly superior in resolution; the former was produced with far fewer templates. To obtain an even-handed comparison between modified and unmodified networks, successively higher vigilance values were tried with the unmodified network to approximate the number of templates yielded by the modified network as shown in Fig. 6. A "best" image generated with the unmodified ART-1 network, which generated 399 templates at a vigilance value of 0.795, is shown in Fig. 7. This and higher vigilance values, generating even more templates, produced roughly the same false color image quality. The ART-1 network modified with the thresholded band limit nodes at F_{-1} yielded a superior image over the unmodified ART-1 network.

Finally, notice the color bar legend, labelled with positive integers, at the far right of each image in figs. 5 - 7. With the exception of white, each color is associated with a single template and the number of pixel input patterns associated with it is shown. All templates associated with 10 or fewer pixels are colored white in Fig. 6. To achieve a fair comparison, a higher breaking point for templates associated with fewer pixels was used in Fig. 7; again, all such templates are colored white. This has the effect of producing a color bar equivalent to that for Fig. 6, with both having 32 colors and therefore an equivalent color code. Colors for each figure are assigned to the templates in the order of decreasing number of associated pixels, going from blue to red and then white, where the total number of pixels for all templates with fewer pixels (i.e., white templates) is shown.

VII. Discussion and Conclusion

The objective of this paper was to illustrate the potential in designing neural networks or improving upon existing designs by applying a mathematical semantic model for neural networks based upon category theory. The categorical constructs of the semantic model determine neural representations of knowledge structures involving concepts and their relationships, or morphisms. This puts constraints on architectural design and operational properties.

The result of the experiment discussed here illustrates the potential in applying these constraints. Through a relatively simple modification, the vigilance capability of an ART-1 network has been supplemented to provide increased discrimination in clustering. Limits were provided for discrete diagrams in the F_1 layer, producing the layer we refer to as F_{-1}. In the context of concept representation, this layer performs an abstraction process by representing subconcepts shared by the concepts represented in the diagrams at F_1. In the experiment, the concepts are aspects of multispectral image data. We have shown, by visual inspection of the results, that modifying an ART-1 network to include limits can yield increased performance. At the cost of an increase in the number of templates generated, the modified network, applying a threshold value uniformly over the limit-representing nodes at F_{-1}, yields a false color image with superior resolution compared with the resolution achievable with an unmodified ART-1 network. This example shows that the mathematical semantic model can be a useful guide for improving the ART-1 design.

Acknowledgement

This work was supported in part by Sandia National Laboratories, Albuquerque, New Mexico, under contract no. 238984. Sandia is a multiprogram laboratory operated by Sandia Corporation, a Lockheed Martin Company, for the United States Department of Energy's National Nuclear Security Administration under Contract DE-AC04-94AL85000.

References

[1] R. Andrews, J. Diederich, and A. B. Tickle. Survey and critique of techniques for extracting rules from trained artificial neural networks. *Knowledge-Based Systems*, 8(6):373–389, 1995.

[2] G. Bartfai. Hierarchical clustering with ART neural networks. In *Proceedings of the IEEE International Conference on Neural Networks, June 28–July 2, 1994*, volume II, pages 940–944. IEEE, 1994.

[3] G. A. Carpenter and S. Grossberg. A massively parallel architecture for a self-organizing neural pattern recognition machine. *Computer Vision, Graphics, and Image Processing*, 37:54–115, 1987.

[4] Thomas Preston Caudell, Yunhai Xiao, and Michael John Healy. eloom and flatland: Specification, simulation and vizualization engines for the study of arbitrary hierarchical neural architectures. *Neural Networks*, 16:617–624, 2003.

[5] M. W. Craven and J. W. Shavlik. Learning symbolic rules using artificial neural networks. In *Proceedings of the 10th International Machine Learning Conference, Amherst, MA*, pages 73–80, San Mateo, CA, 1993. Morgan Kaufmann.

[6] R L Crole. *Categories for Types*. Cambridge University Press, 1993.

[7] A. C. Ehresmann and J.-P. Vanbremeersch. Information Processing and Symmetry-Breaking in Memory Evolutive Systems. *BioSystems*, 43:25–40, 1997.

[8] J. A. Goguen and R. M. Burstall. Institutions: Abstract model theory for specification and programming. *Journal of the Association for Computing Machinery*, 39(1):95–146, 1992.

[9] Michael J. Healy. A topological semantics for rule extraction with neural networks. *Connection Science*, 11(1):91–113, 1999.

[10] Michael J. Healy and Thomas P. Caudell. Acquiring rule sets as a product of learning in a logical neural architecture. *IEEE Transactions on Neural Networks*, 8(3):461–474, 1997.

[11] Michael J. Healy and Thomas P. Caudell. A categorical semantic analysis of ART architectures. In *IJCNN'01:International Joint Conference on Neural Networks, Washington, DC*, volume 1, pages 38–43. IEEE,INNS, IEEE Press, 2001.

[12] Michael J. Healy and Thomas P. Caudell. Aphasic compressed representations: A functorial semantic design principle for coupled ART networks. In *The 2002 International Joint Conference on Neural Networks (IJCNN'02). Honolulu. (CD-ROM Proceedings)*, page 2656. IEEE,INNS, IEEE Press, 2002.

[13] Michael J. Healy and Thomas P. Caudell. From categorical semantics to neural network design. In *The Proceedings of the IJCNN 2003 International Joint Conference on Neural Networks. Portland, OR, USA. (CD-ROM Proceedings)*, pages 1981–1986. IEEE,INNS, IEEE Press, 2003.

[14] Michael John Healy and Thomas Preston Caudell. Neural networks, knowledge, and cognition: A mathematical semantic model based upon category theory. Technical Report EECE-TR-04-020, Department of Electrical and Computer Engineering, University of New Mexico, June 2004.

[15] R. Jullig and Y. V. Srinivas. Diagrams for software synthesis. In *Proceedings of KBSE '93: The Eighth Knowledge-Based Software Engineering Conference*, pages 10–19. IEEE Computer Society Press, 1993.

[16] N. K. Kasabov. Adaptable neuro production systems. *Neurocomputing*, 13:95–117, 1996.

[17] F. W. Lawvere and S. H. Schanuel. *Conceptual Mathematics: A First Introduction to Categories*. Cambridge University Press, 1995.

[18] S. Mac Lane. *Categories for the Working Mathematician*. Springer, 1971. This is the standard reference for mathematicians, written by one of the two co-discoverors of category theory. The other was S. Eilenberg.

[19] J. Meseguer. General logics. In *Logic Colloquium '87*, pages 275–329. Science Publishers B. V. (North-Holland), 1987.

[20] B. C. Pierce. *Basic Category Theory for Computer Scientists*. MIT Press, 1991.

[21] Viggo Stoltenberg-Hansen, Ingrid Lindstroem, and Edward R. Griffor. *Mathematical Theory of Domains*. Cambridge University Press, 1994.

[22] Stephen Vickers. *Topology via Logic*. Cambridge University Press, 1993.

[23] Keith Williamson, Michael Healy, and Richard Barker. Industrial applications of software synthesis via category theory-case studies using specware. *Automated Software Engineering*, 8(1):7–30, 2001.

A vigilance-free ART network with general geometry internal categories

D. Gomes, M. Fernández-Delgado and S. Barro
Department of Electronics and Computer Science
University of Santiago de Compostela
Santiago de Compostela, 15782, A Coruña, Spain
E-mail: delga@dec.usc.es

Abstract—ART neural networks are important tools for on-line supervised pattern recognition. They use internal categories with pre-defined geometry, given by the category choice function. Pre-defined geometry limits the ability of the categories to fit complex borders among output predictions for a given data set, and may contribute to the category proliferation problem. This work proposes Polytope ARTMAP (PTAM), whose category representation regions have general geometry– polytopes in $\mathbb{R}^n$ whose vertices are selected training patterns–. The category borders compose a piece-wise linear approximation to the borders among predictions. Overlapping among categories is avoided in PTAM because they do not need to overlap in order to keep their geometry during learning. The choice function does not depend on the category size. Category growing is only limited by the other categories, and the vigilance parameter can be removed, so that PTAM learns a training data set without any parameter tunning.

I. INTRODUCTION

ART neural networks are popular models for on-line learning which inherit this ability from the studies of Grossberg and Carpenter [1] about the human learning processes. The ART framework addresses the stability-plasticity dilemma [2], and it features localized, incremental learning. Several ART models have been proposed, with unsupervised (ART1, ART2, Fuzzy ART) and supervised learning (ARTMAP [3], Fuzzy ARTMAP (FAM) [4], Gaussian ARTMAP (GAM) [5], Distributed ARTMAP (DAM) [6], Ellipsoid ARTMAP (EAM) [7] and FasArt [8], among others), and they have been applied to many fields, including robotics [9], data mining [10], multi-channel pattern recognition [11], etc.

Internal categories in classical ART networks (FAM, DAM) have hyperbox geometry, although several models with non-rectangular category representation regions (CRRs) have been proposed: hyperspherical CRRs in HAM [12], ellipsoidal CRRs in EAM and ellipsoidal category choice functions in GAM. The performance and the number of internal categories created by FAM and DAM depend on the correspondence between the geometries of the data set and the internal categories [13]. These facts suggest that pre-defined CRR geometries may limit the performance of ART networks and may lead to category proliferation. In order to remove this limitation, we propose to use general geometry CRRs defined by the input patterns assigned to the category, in order to adapt the CRR to the geometry of the data set. This approach requires several vectors, as opposite to ART networks, to define the CRR, because there is no pre-defined CRR geometry. In a previous work (Simplex ARTMAP [14]) we propose to use non-overlapping internal categories with simplex CRRs, defined by a sum of Gaussian functions. This approach does not need the vigilance parameter, but it is replaced by the Gaussian width, and the number of Gaussian functions grows exponentially with the dimension of the input space. In the present work, we propose to use CRRs with general geometry– specifically, polytope CRRs– whose borders are sets of hyperplanes defined by selected training patterns.

This paper is organized as follows. Section 2 explains the basics of our proposal, called Polytope ARTMAP (PTAM), and section 3 describes the whole algorithm. Section 4 compares the results of PTAM and the other ART networks. Section 5 discusses the results and, finally, section 6 summarizes the main conclusions and future research lines.

II. OUTLINE OF POLYTOPE ARTMAP

A weight vector and a category choice function (CCF) are not enough to define a CRR with general geometry. Categories in PTAM are polytopes whose borders give a piece-wise linear approximation to the borders among output predictions in the training set. The polytope vertices are training patterns which define these borders. Each prediction can be associated to one or several polytopes. Each polytope category is managed as a set of simplexes– the closed volume in $\mathbb{R}^n$ with less vertices $(n+1)$–, and its CCF is a combination of the simplexes choice functions. A category learns an input pattern by growing only towards it, either by creating a new simplex between them or by expanding one or several simplexes towards the input pattern. In the ART networks, each category can grow in directions different from the input pattern in order to keep its pre-defined geometry. Each category usually has one associated prediction, but it can cover regions not belonging to this prediction, although other categories with the right prediction can also cover these regions. Thus, categories need overlap among them to keep its geometry during learning (figure 1). If an input pattern falls inside an overlapping region, then it is assigned to the most specific category– the smallest one–. The category size is introduced to solve this ambiguity, but this criterion is not directly defined by the classification process. Also, category size is upper bounded depending on

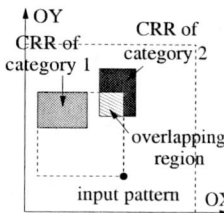

Fig. 1. Learning in FAM. When category 1 learns the input pattern, while keeping its hyperbox shape, it overlaps with category 2, which has a different associated prediction.

the initial template weights and on the vigilance parameter, which becomes very important for the classification results. Since the internal categories are different depending on the algorithm used to create them, the calculation of an upper bound for their size is not easy, so that the vigilance value must be determined by a trial-and-error procedure.

Thus, category overlapping and vigilance test are somehow required by using CRRs with pre-defined geometry. Geometry of CRRs in PTAM is not pre-defined, so that they can expand only towards the input pattern, and they do not need to cover wrong regions only to keep its shape, as in ART networks. Learning in PTAM avoids category overlapping. The category size is not necessary as a criterion to select one among several overlapping categories. Category growing is naturally limited by the other categories, because they can not overlap. The vigilance parameter is removed, so that PTAM does not have any tunning parameters– appart from the presentation order of the training patterns, as the other ART networks–. The vigilance test is replaced by the overlapping test, which determines if a category can grow towards an input pattern without overlapping with the other categories– otherwise, it is reset–. This test does not need any parameter. However, it is not enough to avoid overlapping among categories, because the patterns with the wrong prediction may be presented to the network after the category expansion, and then it would cover the wrong region. In these cases, internal categories in PTAM are corrected. Specifically, if an input pattern falls inside a CRR with a different prediction, then the CRR is corrected by removing the simplex which contains the input pattern. The simplex vertices which do not belong to any other simplex are classified again as new input patterns.

III. POLYTOPE ARTMAP ALGORITHM

Let $\mathbf{I}$ the n-dimensional input pattern $\mathbf{I} \in [0,1]^n$ with desired prediction P_d. Each category C_i has an associated output prediction $P(C_i)$ and a polytope-shaped CRR defined by several simplexes $\{S_{\xi(i,j)}\}_j$, each one defined by $n+1$ vectors (simplex vertices) $\mathbf{w}_l$, which are training patterns previously presented to the network. The following subsections describe the training and test stages of PTAM.

A. Category Choice Function

The CCF $T_i(\mathbf{I})$ of category C_i is the maximum of the choice functions $T_{ij}(\mathbf{I})$ of its N_i^s simplexes $S_{\xi(i,j)}$:

$$T_i(\mathbf{I}) = \max_{j=1,\ldots,N_i^s} \{T_{ij}(\mathbf{I})\} \qquad i = 1,\ldots,N_c \quad (1)$$

If $\mathbf{I}$ falls inside the simplex $S_{\xi(i,J)}$, then $T_{iJ}(\mathbf{I}) = 1$ and $T_i(\mathbf{I}) = T_{iJ}(\mathbf{I}) = 1$. Otherwise, $T_{iJ}(\mathbf{I}) < 1$ and it is decreasing with the Euclidean distance $d(\mathbf{I}, S_{\xi(i,J)})$. In this case, $T_i(\mathbf{I}) = T_{iJ}(\mathbf{I})$, where $S_{\xi(i,J)}$ is the nearest simplex to $\mathbf{I}$. We describe separately both cases.

1) Input pattern inside a simplex: The border of simplex $S_{\xi(i,j)}$ in category C_i is defined by $n+1$ hyperplanes $\{h_{\zeta(i,j,1)}, \ldots, h_{\zeta(i,j,n+1)}\}$, where hyperplane $h_{\zeta(i,j,k)}$ is defined by n vectors $\{\mathbf{w}_{\pi(i,j,k,1)}, \ldots \mathbf{w}_{\pi(i,j,k,n)}\}$. The equation of hyperplane $h_{\zeta(i,j,k)}$ can be written as:

$$g_{ijk}(\mathbf{I}) \equiv \pm \begin{vmatrix} \alpha_1 & \ldots & \alpha_n \\ \beta_{21} & \ldots & \beta_{2n} \\ \ldots & & \\ \beta_{n1} & \ldots & \beta_{nn} \end{vmatrix} = 0 \quad (2)$$

where $\alpha_l = I_l - w_{\pi(i,j,k,1),l}$; $\beta_{ml} = w_{\pi(i,j,k,m),l} - w_{\pi(i,j,k,1),l}$, $m = 2, \ldots, n; l = 1, \ldots, n$; and $w_{\pi(i,j,k,l),m}$ is the m-th component of $\mathbf{w}_{\pi(i,j,k,l)}$. The sign in eq. 2 is taken in such a way that $g_{ijk}(\mathbf{x}) > 0$ if $\mathbf{x}$ is in the side of $h_{\zeta(i,j,k)}$ inside $S_{\xi(i,j)}$. If $g_{ijk}(\mathbf{I}) > 0$ for the $n+1$ hyperplanes $h_{\zeta(i,j,1)}, \ldots, h_{\zeta(i,j,n+1)}$ of simplex $S_{\xi(i,j)}$, then $\mathbf{I}$ falls inside the simplex and $T_{ij}(\mathbf{I}) = 1$.

2) Input pattern outside the simplex: The choice function of simplex $S_{\xi(i,j)}$ outside its support must be $T_{ij}(\mathbf{I}) < 1$ and decreasing with the distance pattern-simplex: we have used $T_{ij}(\mathbf{I}) = e^{-d(\mathbf{I}, S_{\xi(i,j)})/\gamma}$. Calculation of distance $d(\mathbf{I}, S_{\xi(i,j)})$ is complex, specially for $n > 2$, and we have approximated its value by using the minimum distance between $\mathbf{I}$ and a vertex of $S_{\xi(i,j)}$: $d(\mathbf{I}, S_{\xi(i,j)}) \simeq \min_{\mathbf{w}_l \in S_{\xi(i,j)}} \{\|\mathbf{I} - \mathbf{w}_l\|\}$. The scale parameter $\gamma = \sqrt{n}/10$ defines a range $e^{-10} < T_{ij}(\mathbf{I}) < 1$ for the simplex choice function.

Finally, the complete choice function of simplex $S_{\xi(i,j)}$ is given by the following equation ($k = 1, \ldots, n+1$):

$$T_{ij}(\mathbf{I}) = \begin{cases} 1 & g_{ijk}(\mathbf{I}) > 0 \quad \forall k \\ exp\left[-\frac{1}{\gamma} \min_{\mathbf{w}_l \in S_{\xi(i,j)}} \|\mathbf{I} - \mathbf{w}_l\|\right] & \text{otherwise} \end{cases} \quad (3)$$

B. Overlapping Test

The competition process selects the non-reset category C_I with the highest CCF. If all the categories are reset, then a new category or vector is created with $\mathbf{I}$ (subsection III-E). Otherwise, overlapping test (OT) checks if C_I can be expanded towards $\mathbf{I}$ without overlap with the other categories. If C_I passes OT, then the next step (section III-C) is executed. Otherwise, C_I is reset ($r_I = 1$) and a new non-reset category is selected in the competition process.

If $T_I(\mathbf{I}) = 1$, then $\mathbf{I}$ falls inside the CRR of C_I, which does not need to grow in order to cover $\mathbf{I}$. Overlapping is not possible and C_I passes the OT. If $T_I(\mathbf{I}) < 1$, then $\mathbf{I}$ falls outside C_I, and the set $\mathcal{A}$ of vectors in category C_I

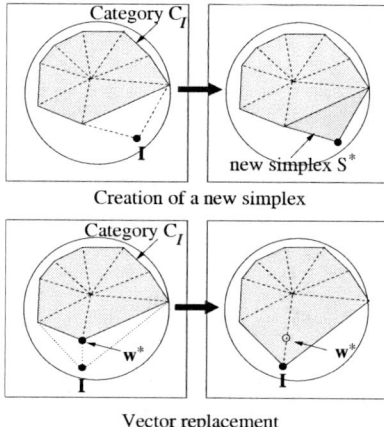

Fig. 2. Learning examples using polytope categories for the "Circle-In-the-Square" (CIS) problem in $\mathbb{R}^2$. Upper panels: $n = 2$ vectors are connectable from $\mathbf{I}$, and a new simplex S^* can be created. Lower panel: the number of connectable vectors from $\mathbf{I}$ is 3 ($> n = 2$): vector $\mathbf{w}^*$ can be replaced by $\mathbf{I}$ without volume loss for category C_I.

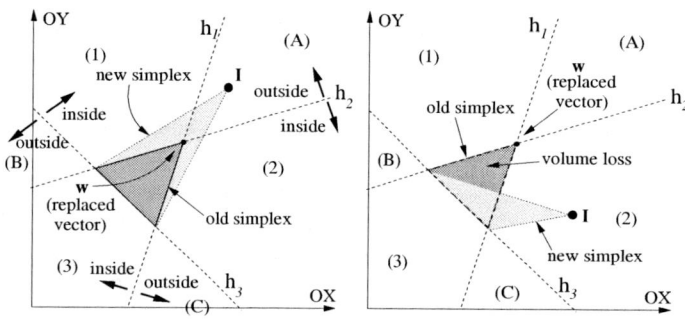

Fig. 3. Example of vector replacement condition in $\mathbb{R}^2$. Patterns in regions A, B and C can replace vectors of the old simplex (left panel), but patterns in regions 1, 2 and 3 can not, because the replacement reduces the simplex volume (right panel).

which are connectable from $\mathbf{I}$ without overlapping is created. Vectors $\mathbf{w} \in \mathcal{A}$ verify that $\not\exists S_{\xi(i,j)}$ with $O_{ls}(\mathbf{I}, \mathbf{w}, S_{\xi(i,j)}) = 1$. Function $O_{ls}(\mathbf{I}, \mathbf{w}, S_{\xi(i,j)}) = 1$ if segment line $\{\mathbf{w}, \mathbf{I}\}$ and simplex $S_{\xi(i,j)}$ overlap, i.e., if the former intersects with some hyperplane of the latter. This intersection is tested by solving the system of linear equations composed by the parametric equations of line segment and hyperplane. Depending on $|\mathcal{A}|$ (cardinal of $\mathcal{A}$), three cases are possible:

1) If $0 \le |\mathcal{A}| < n$, then C_I can not expand towards $\mathbf{I}$ without overlapping, so that C_I does not pass OT.
2) If $|\mathcal{A}| = n$ (figure 2, upper panel), then a new simplex S^*, composed by $\mathbf{I}$ and the vectors of $\mathcal{A}$, is tested. If S^* does not overlap with any simplex, then C_I passes OT. Otherwise, $\exists S_{\xi(i,j)}$ with $O_{ss}(S_{\xi(i,j)}, S^*) = 1$, and category C_I does not pass OT. Overlapping function $O_{ss}(S_{\xi(i,j)}, S_{\xi(k,l)}) = 1$ if simplexes $S_{\xi(i,j)}$ and $S_{\xi(k,l)}$ overlap. This happens if some vertex $\mathbf{w}$ of $S_{\xi(i,j)}$ falls inside $S_{\xi(k,l)}$ (then, $T_{kl}(\mathbf{w}) = 1$) or vice-versa, and also if some line segment of simplex $S_{\xi(i,j)}$ intersects with simplex $S_{\xi(k,l)}$, which can be tested by using function O_{ls} previously defined. On the other hand, if S^* is extremely sharp– i.e., some angle of S^* is less than 10 degree–, then C_I does not pass OT. In this case, S^* has negligible volume and input patterns can not fall inside it, so that it can never be removed in the Category Correction stage (subsection III-C).
3) If $|\mathcal{A}| > n$ (lower panel in figure 2), then some of the vectors in $\mathcal{A}$ may be replaced by $\mathbf{I}$ without volume loss for the CRR. A vector $\mathbf{w} \in \mathcal{A}$ can be replaced only if $\mathbf{I}$ falls in the outer side of the n hyperplanes which cross at $\mathbf{w}$ (figure 3). This happens if $R_{ij}(\mathbf{I}, \mathbf{w}) = 1$, where:

$$R_{ij}(\mathbf{I}, \mathbf{w}) = \prod_{k \in H_{ij}(\mathbf{w})} \Phi[g_{ijk}(\mathbf{I})] \quad (4)$$

$$\Phi(x) = \begin{cases} 0 & x > 0 \\ 1 & x \le 0 \end{cases} \quad (5)$$

$g_{ijk}(\mathbf{I})$ is defined in eq. 2 and $H_{ij}(\mathbf{w})$ is the set of hyperplanes in $S_{\xi(i,j)}$ which contain $\mathbf{w}$. The replacement of the nearest vector $\mathbf{w}^*$ from $\mathbf{I}$ in $\mathcal{A}$ which verifies $R_{ij}(\mathbf{I}, \mathbf{w}^*) = 1$ by $\mathbf{I}$ is tested. Category C_I passes OT only if the simplexes which contain $\mathbf{w}^*$ do not overlap with the other simplexes after replacement. This means that $O_{ss}(S_{\xi(I,j)} \setminus \{\mathbf{w}^*\} \cup \{\mathbf{I}\}, S_{\xi(k,l)}) = 0$, $\forall S_{\xi(I,j)} : \mathbf{w} \in S_{\xi(I,j)}, \forall S_{\xi(k,l)} : \mathbf{w}^* \notin S_{\xi(k,l)}$.

C. Prediction Test and Category Correction

If $P(C_I) = P_d$ (Prediction Test) then the active category C_I has the right prediction and there is resonance between pattern and category (subsection III-D). Otherwise, C_I is reset ($r_I = 1$) and the overlapping test (subsection III-B) is repeated. Also, if $T_I(\mathbf{I}) = 1$, then the input pattern falls inside the CRR of C_I, and the simplex $S_{\xi(i,j)}$ for which $T_{Ij}(\mathbf{I}) = 1$ is removed (Category Correction). The vertices of simplex $S_{\xi(I,j)}$ which do not belong to any other simplex in C_I are classified again as new input patterns.

D. Resonance

If $\mathbf{I}$ falls inside the CRR of C_I ($T_I(\mathbf{I}) = 1$), then C_I does not change, because it already covers $\mathbf{I}$. If $T_I(\mathbf{I}) < 1$, since C_I passed OT, it can be expanded towards $\mathbf{I}$ without overlapping, either by creating a new simplex or by replacing an existing vector. In the former case, the new simplex S^* tested during OT is created only if C_I is not the most active category ($T_I(\mathbf{I}) < max_i\{T_i(\mathbf{I})\}$). Otherwise, C_I does not expand towards $\mathbf{I}$ because it is already its nearest category and it has the right prediction. In the latter case, the vector $\mathbf{w}^*$ tested during OT is replaced by $\mathbf{I}$.

E. Creation of new categories or vectors

If resonance is not achieved with any category, PTAM tests the creation of a new simplex S^*, and a new category C^*, with **I** and its n nearest connectable vectors– selected by using function O_{ls} (section III-B)– with prediction P_d. If there are less than n connectable vectors with prediction P_d, or if S^* overlaps with other categories, or if S^* is sharp (section III-B-2), then it does not pass the test and **I** is learnt as an insolated vector $\mathbf{v} = \mathbf{I}$, not belonging to any category, with prediction $P(\mathbf{v}) = P_d$. Otherwise, a new category C^* with simplex S^* is created.

F. Polytope ARTMAP Training

The training stage in PTAM can be summarized in the following steps:

1. Presentation of a new input pattern **I**. Let $r_i = 0, i = 1, \ldots, N_c$.

2. Category Choice Function: Calculate the CCF $T_i(\mathbf{I}), i = 1, \ldots, N_c$ (eqs. 1, 3) for all the categories.

3. Competition: Select the category C_I with $r_I = 0$ and highest CCF: $T_I(\mathbf{I}) = max_i\{T_i(\mathbf{I})\}$. If all the categories are reset, then go to step 8 (*Creation of a new category or vector*).

4. Overlapping Test: Test if C_I can grow towards **I** by creating a new simplex S^* between C_I and **I**, or by replacing a vector in C_I by **I**. If the new simplex S^* or the modified ones overlap with other categories, or if S^* is sharp (section III-B-2), then reset category C_I ($r_I = 1$) and go to step 3 (*Competition*).

5. Prediction Test: If $P(C_i) \neq P_d$, then reset category C_I ($r_I = 1$). Otherwise, go to step 7 (*Resonance*).

6. Category Correction: If $T_I(\mathbf{I}) = 1$, then **I** falls inside CRR of C_I, and the simplex $S_{\xi(I,j)}$ for which $T_{Ij}(\mathbf{I}) = 1$ is removed. The simplex vertices which do not belong to any other simplex are classified again. Go to step 3 (*Competition*).

7. Resonance: The input pattern is assigned to C_I, which is expanded towards **I**. Step 4 determined if a new simplex must be created, only if C_I is not the most active category, or if a vector belonging to C_I must be replaced by **I**. Go to step 1 (*Presentation of a new input pattern*).

8. Creation of a new category or vector: Select the n nearest connectable vectors to **I** with the desired prediction, and test the creation of a new simplex S^* with these n vectors and **I**. If there are less than n vectors, or if S^* overlaps with some existing category, or if S^* is sharp (section III-B-2), then create a new insolated vector $\mathbf{v} = \mathbf{I}$. Otherwise, create a new category C^* with simplex S^* and prediction P_d. Go to step 1 (*Presentation of a new input pattern*).

G. Polytope ARTMAP Testing

The processing stage has the following steps:

1. Presentation of a new input pattern **I**.

2. Choice Function: Calculate the choice functions $T_i(\mathbf{I}), i = 1, \ldots, N_c + N_{iv}$ for all the N_c categories (eqs. 1, 3) and for all the N_{iv} insolated vectors: $T_{N_c+j}(\mathbf{I}) = e^{-\|\mathbf{I}-\mathbf{v}_j\|/\gamma}, j = 1, \ldots, N_{iv}$.

3. Competition: Select the category C_I or the insolated vector $\mathbf{v}_I$ with highest choice function: $T_I(\mathbf{I}) = max_i\{T_i(\mathbf{I})\}$.

4. Output prediction: Give as output prediction the associated to the active category $P(C_I)$ or to the active vector $P(\mathbf{v}_I)$.

IV. RESULTS

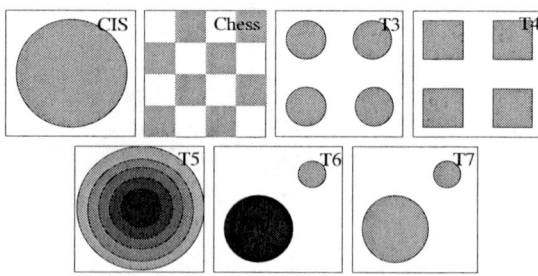

Fig. 4. Datasets CIS [15], Chess [16], T3, T4, T5, T6 and T7 [13] used in the experimental work. In T6 the number of patterns of each category is proportional to its size. In T7 there are 50% patterns outside the circles, 30% in the big circle and 20% in the small circle.

Polytope ARTMAP algorithm has been compared with several ART networks (Fuzzy ARTMAP [4], Gaussian ARTMAP [5], Distributed ARTMAP [6], Ellipsoid ARTMAP [7] and FasArt [8]) and with Support Vector Machines (SVM) [17] on a set of benchmark data sets (figure 4), which include CIS (Circle-In-the-Square) [15], Chess [16] and datasets T3, T4, T5, T6 and T7, used in [13]. For each data set, 20 pairs of training-test sets, with 10,000 patterns each one, were randomly generated, and results were averaged over them. In the CIS dataset, circles with sizes ranging from 10%-70% of the square area were used. The Torch library [18] was used to implement the SVM, which obtained the best results using Gaussian kernels with deviation 0.1. Vigilance values from 0.02 to 0.98 step 0.02 were tried for FAM, GAM, DAM, EAM and FasArt. Weber Law and Choice-by-difference functions, with 1 and 5 training epochs, were tried with FAM– PTAM uses one epoch–, and the best results were selected.

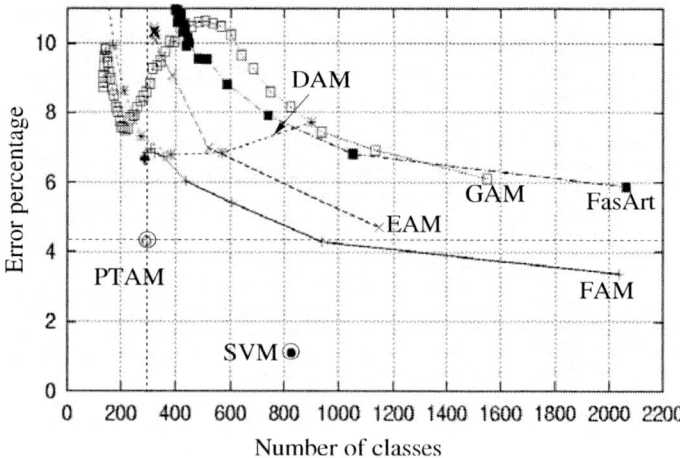

Fig. 5. Error rate against number of categories (vectors for PTAM, support vector for SVM) varying vigilance of the ART networks for the T5 data set.

In the ART networks there is a trade-off between error and number of categories (less error usually means more categories, and vice-versa), which is controlled by the vigilance

TABLE I
COMPARISON OF PTAM WITH FAM, GAM, DAM, EAM, FASART (WITH THE SAME ERROR ϵ THAN PTAM) AND SVM.

	PTAM			FAM		GAM		DAM		EAM		FasArt		SVM	
	%	#C	#V		#C		#C		#C		#C		#C		#SV
CIS	1.0	16.4	75.3	0.9	871	2.6	208	1.6	428	1.6	380	1.5	685	0.2	578.0
Chess	2.0	33.3	197.9	1.9	233	3.9	67	6.5	446	2.8	1102	6.0	735	0.8	475.8
T3	2.2	21.5	123.3	2.3	275	1.8	50	2.0	34	1.9	249	2.7	584	0.3	180.6
T4	1.9	22.4	113.6	0.5	35	2.5	52	0.4	48	1.8	337	2.6	561	0.6	271.8
T5	4.3	61.9	294.7	4.3	921	7.5	216	6.8	383	4.7	1146	6.8	1052	1.1	827.3
T6	1.0	21.1	109.0	0.9	879	1.7	1056	1.6	532	2.0	278	1.7	688	0.2	163.8
T7	1.7	16.8	91.1	1.5	89	2.0	43	1.8	402	1.7	365	1.5	657	0.3	163.4
Avg.	2.0	27.6	**144**	1.8	**472**	3.1	**242**	3.0	**325**	2.2	**551**	3.3	**709**	0.5	**380**

parameter. Figure 5 shows this trade-off for the T5 data set– the most complex one– by representing the error rate against the number of categories. PTAM and SVM have no vigilance parameter, so that they are single points in the figure. Tables I and II show the error (ϵ) and the number of categories (#C) for each algorithm. The former also reports the number of support vectors (#SV) for the SVM and the number of vectors (#V) created by PTAM, which is the equivalent to #C for the ART networks, whose categories have only one vector. The comparison between PTAM and the ART networks is two-sided. On the one hand, table I reports the results obtained by the ART networks for the same error than PTAM (horizontal dashed line in figure 5). This table measures the number of categories created by the ART networks to achieve the same error as PTAM. Table II shows the results obtained for the same number of categories than vectors in PTAM (vertical dashed line in figure 5). These results determine if ART networks get more or less error than PTAM with the same number of categories.

V. DISCUSSION

SVM obtains less error than ART networks (table I), although its number of support vectors is higher than the number of categories used by PTAM. However, SVM does not allow on-line learning, as ART networks do, and it has tunning parameters– type and parameters of the kernel–, as opposite to PTAM.

The behavior of number of categories for the same error is reported in columns #C of table I. PTAM creates less vectors than categories in FAM, except for data set T4– due to its rectangular geometry (figure 4)– and T7. GAM creates less categories than vectors in PTAM, except for data sets CIS and T6, but its average error is higher (3.1% against 2.0%). DAM also creates more categories than vectors in PTAM, except for T4, which has rectangular geometry, and T3. EAM and FasArt create more categories than PTAM in all the data sets, usually with a higher error. The average #C (in bold) at the bottom line shows that the number of vectors created by PTAM is lower than the number of categories created by the ART networks for the same error, and some ART networks (DAM/GAM-Chess, GAM-T5) do not achieve this error. It is interesting the high number of categories created by EAM for data sets Chess, due to its square geometry, not suited to ellipsoid categories, and T5, due to its complexity. Also, FasArt and GAM create many categories for data sets T5 and T6 respectively. Simplex ARTMAP [14] obtained similar error than PTAM (1.2% and 4.1% for data sets CIS and T5 respectively) but much more categories (579 and 1141 for CIS and T5 respectively) than PTAM. PTAM creates less polytope categories than the other ART networks (column PTAM-#C in table I), although each category needs several vectors.

Columns ϵ in table II compare errors obtained by PTAM and the ART networks with the same number of categories. For the majority of the data sets, ART networks obtain higher error than PTAM, except for FAM-Chess, FAM-T7 and DAM-T4. The other ART networks, specially EAM and FasArt, are not able to get the same performance as PTAM with the same number of categories. The average ϵ (in bold) is also higher than PTAM for all the ART networks.

Figure 5 compares graphically the algorithms for the T5 data set (graphics for the other data sets are similar). PTAM is under the curves for the ART networks (lower ϵ), and in their left (lower #C), except for GAM and DAM, which obtain less categories but more error. These results show that categories with general geometry– polytopes defined by training patterns– are able to learn the borders among predictions better than categories with pre-defined geometry, without the creation of more categories. Finally, we must emphasize that these results are obtained without any vigilance parameter tunning.

VI. CONCLUSIONS

The learning abilities of the ART networks are somehow limited by the pre-defined geometry of their category representation regions (rectangular, ellipsoidal, ...). This work proposes Polytope ARTMAP, which uses polytope-shaped category representation regions whose geometry is built during the training stage by the patterns assigned to them. Each category can learn an input pattern by expanding towards it without

TABLE II
COMPARISON OF PTAM WITH FAM, GAM, DAM, EAM AND FASART (WITH THE SAME NUMBER OF CATEGORIES #C THAN PTAM).

	PTAM		FAM		GAM		DAM		EAM		FasArt	
	%	#V		#C		#C		#C		#C		#C
CIS	1.0	75.3	2.9	72	2.6	208	3.4	74	3.1	96	2.9	99
Chess	2.0	197.9	2.1	186	6.6	194	7.3	204	7.1	221	11.5	201
T3	2.2	123.3	3.3	198	3.4	124	2.2	107	2.5	121	4.5	121
T4	1.9	113.6	2.6	111	3.4	110	1.0	107	3.2	109	5.5	112
T5	4.3	294.7	6.8	297	8.6	294	7.3	274	10.3	323	11.3	398
T6	1.0	109.0	2.0	107	2.8	107	2.9	99	2.9	109	3.4	114
T7	1.7	91.1	1.5	89	2.5	88	2.4	71	3.1	91	3.8	101
Avg.	**2.0**	144	**3.0**	151	**4.3**	161	**3.8**	134	**4.6**	153	**6.1**	164

category overlapping. Category growing is limited by the other categories, and the vigilance test is not necessary. Polytope ARTMAP has been tested on several data sets and it provides a better trade-off between error and number of categories than classical ART networks. We would like to emphasize that these results are obtained without any parameter tunning. This is very important because the performance of ART networks strongly depends on the vigilance parameter, whose tunning may be difficult. PTAM is computationally more complex than ART networks, specially for higher dimensions, but it is easier to use, because no tunning is necessary.

We think that the performance of PTAM may be raised by allowing to expand the categories even if less than n vectors are connectable from the input pattern. Replacement of simplexes by hyperplanes in the management of convex polytopes may also remove some limitations in the category expansion. The category correction stage can also be modified in order to reduce the sensitivity to noise. Finally, an efficient implementation of the overlapping test is necessary to apply PTAM to high-dimensional data sets.

ACKNOWLEDGMENT

The authors would like to thank Dr. Anagnostopoulos for allowing the use of demonstration code for GAM and EAM and the anonymous referees for their constructive comments. This work was supported by the Spanish CICyT and the Xunta de Galicia under projects TIC2003-09400-C04-03 and PGIDIT04SIN206003PR respectively.

REFERENCES

[1] G. Carpenter and S. Grossberg, "The ART of adaptive pattern recognition by a self-organizing neural network," *Computer*, vol. 21, no. 3, pp. 77–87, 1988.
[2] S. Grossberg, *Studies of mind and brain*. Reidel, 1982.
[3] G. A. Carpenter, S. Grossberg, and J. H. Reynolds, "ARTMAP: supervised real-time learning and classification of nonstationary data by a self-organizing neural network," *Neural Networks*, vol. 4, pp. 565–588, 1991.
[4] G. Carpenter, S. Grossberg, N. Markuzon, J. Reynolds, and D. Rosen, "Fuzzy ARTMAP: A neural network architecture for incremental supervised learning of analog multidimensional maps," *IEEE Transactions on Neural Networks*, vol. 3, no. 5, pp. 698–712, 1992.
[5] J. Williamson, "Gaussian ARTMAP: A neural network for fast incremental learning of noisy multidimensional maps," *Neural Networks*, vol. 9, no. 5, pp. 881–897, 1996.
[6] G. Carpenter, B. Milenova, and B. Noeske, "Distributed ARTMAP: a neural network for fast distributed supervised learning," *Neural Networks*, vol. 11, no. 5, pp. 793–813, 1998.
[7] G. Anagnostopoulos and M. Georgiopoulos., "Ellipsoid ART and Ellipsoid ARTMAP for incremental clustering and classification," in *Proceedings of 2001 IEEE Int. Joint Conf. on Neural Networks*, vol. 2, 2001, pp. 1221–1226.
[8] J. Cano-Izquierdo, Y. Dimitriadis, E. Gómez-Sánchez, and J. López-Coronado, "Learning from noisy information in FasArt and FasBack neuro-fuzzy systems," *Neural Networks*, vol. 14, no. 4/5, pp. 407–425, 2001.
[9] W. Fung and Y. Liu, "Adaptive categorization of ART networks in robot behavior learning using game-theoretic formulation," *Neural Networks*, vol. 16, pp. 1403–1420, 2003.
[10] O. Parsons and G. Carpenter, "ARTMAP neural networks for information fusion and data mining: map production and target recognition methodologies," *Neural Networks*, vol. 16, pp. 1075–1089, 2003.
[11] M. Fernández-Delgado and S. Barro, "A multi-channel ART-based neural network," *IEEE Transactions on Neural Networks*, vol. 9, pp. 139–150, 1998.
[12] G. Anagnostopoulos and M. Georgiopoulos, "Hypersphere ART and ARTMAP for unsupervised and supervised incremental learning," in *Proceedings of 2000 IEEE Int. Joint Conf. on Neural Networks*, vol. 6, 2000, pp. 59–64.
[13] E. Parrado-Hernández, E. Gómez-Sánchez, and Y. Dimitriadis, "Study of distributed learning as a solution to category proliferation in Fuzzy ARTMAP based neural systems," *Neural Networks*, vol. 16, no. 7, pp. 1039–1057, 2003.
[14] D. Gomes, M. Fernández-Delgado, and S. Barro, "Simplex ARTMAP: building general geometry borders among predictions with simplex-shaped classes," in *Proceedings of 2004 IASTED Artificial Intelligence and Soft Computing*, vol. 1, 2004, pp. 232–237.
[15] G. Wilensky, "Analysis of neural network issues: scaling, enhanced nodal processing, comparison with standard classification," DARPA Neural Network Program Review, pp. 29–30, 1990.
[16] E. G. Sánchez, Y. A. Dimitriadis, J. Cano-Izquierdo, and J. Coronado, "Safe-μARTMAP: A new solution for reducing category proliferation in Fuzzy ARTMAP," in *Proceedings of 2000 IEEE Int. Joint Conf. on Neural Networks*, vol. 6, 2000, pp. 1221–1226.
[17] C. Cortes and V. Vapnik, "Support-Vector Networks," *Machine Learning*, vol. 20, no. 3, pp. 273–297, 1995.
[18] R. Collobert, S. Bengio, and J. Mariéthoz, "Torch: a modular machine learning software library," IDIAP, Tech. Rep., 2003, http://www.idiap.ch/~bengio/publications/pdf/rr02-46.pdf.

On the Design of an Ellipsoid ARTMAP Classifier within the Fuzzy Adaptive System ART Framework

Ross Peralta
Electrical & Computer Eng.[1]
rperalta@fit.edu

Georgios C. Anagnostopoulos
Electrical & Computer Eng.[1]
georgio@fit.edu

Eduardo Gomez-Sanchez
Comm. & Telematics[2]
edugom@tel.uva.es

Samuel Richie
Electrical Eng.[3]
richie@mail.ucf.edu

[1]Florida Institute of Technology, Melbourne, FL 32901
[2]University of Valladolid, Valladolid, Spain 47011
[3]University of Central Florida, Orlando, FL 32816

Abstract – In this paper we present the design of Fuzzy Adaptive System Ellipsoid ARTMAP (FASEAM), a novel neural architecture based on Ellipsoid ARTMAP (EAM) that is equipped with concepts utilized in the Fuzzy Adaptive System ART (FASART) architecture. More specifically, we derive a new category choice function appropriate for EAM categories that is non-constant in a category's representation region. Additionally, we augment the EAM category description with a centroid vector, whose learning rate is inversely proportional to the number of training patterns accessing the category. Finally, we demonstrate the merits of our design choices by comparing FASART, EAM and FASEAM in terms of generalization performance and final structural complexity on a set of classification problems.

I. INTRODUCTION

Adaptive resonance theory (ART) based neural networks constitute a large family of neural architectures that have been used in a plethora of applications ranging from data clustering, classification and function approximation tasks. They are all based on the ART paradigm first introduced in [1] and feature a variety of highly desirable properties, like the ability of incremental (online) learning, network response transparency and fast training phase. A characteristic of these networks is that they summarize the input data into clusters via the use of prototypes called categories, whose geometrical representation may vary (depending on the particular architecture) from being hyper-rectangles, hyper-spheres or hyper-ellipsoids embedded in the input space.

A member of the ART-based family is the Fuzzy Adaptive System ART (FASART) architecture, which was first presented in [2] as an enhancement to the standard Fuzzy ARTMAP (FAM) network [3]. FASART networks have also been successfully used for function approximation, data clustering, as well as classification tasks; see for example [4] and [5]. Both FAM and FASART employ categories, whose geometric representations are hyper-rectangles. However, FASART extends FAM by equipping categories with an additional centroid element and by introducing a new, parameterized category choice function (CCF). In FAM, the CCF value is constant within a category's representation region (see [6] for related definitions), while in FASART it monotonically decreases from 1 (at the centroid) to 0 beyond the boundaries of the category's representation region. Furthermore, while FAM's CCF depends on the category's size and the distance of the pattern from the category's representation region, in FASART the CCF depends on the distance of the pattern from the centroid and, implicitly, on the size of the category in a component-wise fashion. In this manner, FASART categories are appropriately defined as fuzzy sets and the CCF's value with respect to a pattern can be interpreted as its normalized, fuzzy membership in that fuzzy set. This permits the dual interpretation of FASART as a neural model as well as a formal fuzzy logic inference system, which is not the case for FAM according to [7].

Yet another ART-based architecture is Ellipsoid ARTMAP (EAM) [8]. The network shares almost all structural and behavioral features, as well as properties of learning with FAM. While FAM and FASART categories are represented as hyper-rectangles, EAM categories are of hyper-ellipsoid shape, which may be more suitable for certain learning problems. Like in the case of FAM, in EAM the CCF is of constant value within a category's representation region. In certain classification problem domains this CCF constancy may lead to unsatisfactory classification performance. More specifically, it is a known fact that patterns located inside the representation regions of two or more categories will access the category of the smallest size. This effect may potentially lead to poor approximation of the decision boundaries and could be avoided by using a CCF that is not constant within the representation region.

This paper focuses on the design of a variant of EAM, which we named FASEAM classifier. The relationship of FASEAM to EAM is the same as the one of FASART to FAM. We equip EAM categories with a centroid vector that is adjusted according to patterns accessing the categories. Furthermore, we derive a new CCF that is reminiscent (with respect to some properties) of the one used in FASART. Finally, we replace EAM's match tracking mechanism with an alternative secondary search procedure, since we discovered via experimentation that FASART's match tracking does not preserve the principle of incremental, instantaneous learning. In order to assess our design of FASEAM we performed experiments on four artificial databases, where we compared FASEAM to EAM in terms of structural complexity and generalization performance.

The rest of the paper is organized as follows. In Section II we highlight some of the main characteristics of FASART and EAM networks in terms of category descriptions. Section III talks about FASEAM's design with accompanying justifications. Section IV describes the data sets that were used in order to compare the original EAM classifier to FASEAM, our experimental settings and the results we obtained. Finally, Section V provides a brief summary of our contributions and observations.

II. FASART AND EAM CATEGORIES

A FASART category j is described by the min- and max-vectors u_j and v_j respectively as well as by their centroid vector c_j, as depicted in Figure 1. The collection of the aforementioned vectors is called category description of j or template elements of category j. The region RR_j defined by the min- and max-vectors is called the representation region of category j (also shown in Figure 1) and represents all input patterns that are considered summarized/learned by the category. In order for a training pattern to be learned, categories compete in terms of their category choice function (CCF) values; the category featuring the highest CCF value is the winner of the competition, in which case we say that the training pattern accesses the category. Upon access (and under certain special circumstances that are not mentioned here) the category may learn the training pattern.

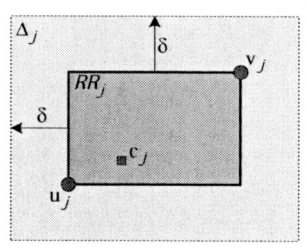 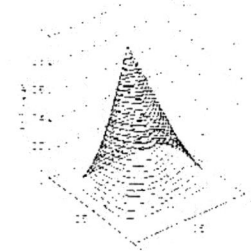

Fig. 1. Right: Geometrical depiction of a FASART category for a 2-dimensional input space. Left: Plot of the CCF values of a typical FASART category, again, for a 2-dimensional input space.

In FASART the CCF value is highest at the centroid (equal to 1) and decreases monotonically with increasing distance from the centroid c_j towards 0 at the boundary of the category's delta region Δ_j (also depicted in Figure 1). Note that outside Δ_j the CCF remains 0 and that the region's size is controlled by a network parameter δ (in [2] the equivalent of $\gamma=1/\delta$ is used instead).

On the other hand, EAM categories are characterized by a center m_j, a unit-length direction vector d_j and a Mahalanobis radius R_j, as depicted in Figure 2. The representation region RR_j of an EAM category j is of hyper-ellipsoidal form; the hyper-ellipsoid's eccentricity is determined by a network parameter μ called axes ratio. A value of $\mu = 1$ results in hyper-spherical representation regions.

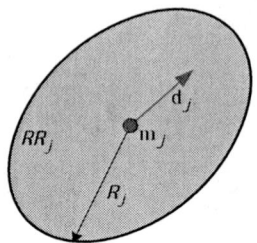

Fig. 2. Geometrical depiction of an EAM category for a 2-dimensional input space.

While in FASART distances are measured primarily using the L_1 vector norm, in EAM they are measured using a weighted Euclidian (Mahalanobis) vector norm (see Eq. 1), whose weight (shape) matrix C_j depends on a category's direction vector:

$$\|x-y\|_{C_j} = \sqrt{(x-y)^T C_j (x-y)} \quad (1)$$

$$C_j = \frac{1}{\mu^2}\left[I - (1-\mu^2) d_j d_j^T\right] \quad (2)$$

Both network families accomplish their learning task via creation of new categories and by expanding representation regions of already existing categories. We refer the interested reader to references [2], [9] and [8] for more detailed descriptions of FASART and EAM respectively.

An advantage of FASART over FAM is that the decision boundaries created by FASART are additionally influenced by the specific location of centroid vectors, while in FAM they are influenced only by the relative shape and position of representation regions. As an example, Figure 3 compares the decision boundaries between two FAM and two FASART categories predicting different class labels.

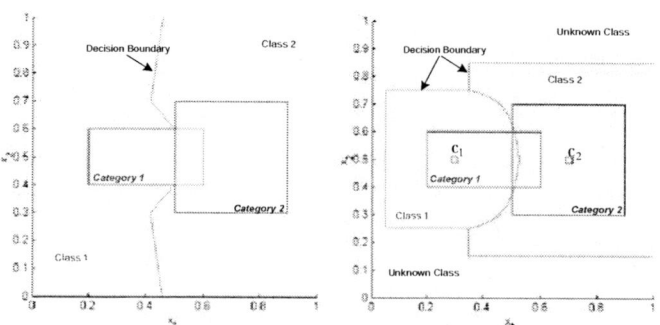

Fig. 3. Decision boundaries for two competing FAM (on the left) and two competing FASART categories (on the right).

In FAM, when two categories compete for a pattern that is inside both representation regions, the winning category is the one of the smallest size, regardless of where most of the already encoded patterns are located within the corresponding representation regions (Figure 3, right). In such a case, FASART categories, via their centroid, provide a more reasonable approach in forming smoother decision boundaries, as depicted on the right of Figure 3. As in FAM, EAM exhibits similar characteristics in decision boundary formation. This last fact has been our main motivation to derive FASEAM as an EAM variant with FASART characteristics.

III. DESIGN OF THE FASEAM CLASSIFER

Our goal is to design a variant of EAM, which we will refer to as FASEAM that resembles the original FASART architecture. As a first step, we augment the standard EAM category description with a centroid vector c_j and allow it to be updated by training patterns that access the category. However, instead of the standard instar learning rule for the centroid update in FASART, we update the centroid as in Gaussian ARTMAP [10]:

$$c_j^{(k+1)} = (1-\beta_c^{(k)})c_j^{(k)} + \beta_c^{(k)} x^{(k+1)}$$
$$\beta_c^{(k)} \triangleq \frac{1}{k+1}, \quad c_j^{(1)} = x^{(1)} \quad (3)$$

where $c_j^{(k)}$ is the updated centroid vector after the presentation of the kth training pattern accessing category j. In other words, in FASEAM centroids are updated with a variable learning rate, unlike FASART centroids that are updated via a constant learning rate. The update rule in Eq. 3 forces the centroid to be the sample average of the training patterns that have accessed the category rather than a moving sample average with emphasis on the last pattern accessing the category. We chose this particular update rule to primarily enhance the stability of FASEAM during learning, since $\beta_c^{(k)} \leq 0.5$ $\forall k \geq 2$. Let us note here that in order for the centroid to remain within the representation region of a FASEAM category after an update via Eq. 3, the learning rate β used for updating the category's center and Mahalanobis radius must be larger than 0.5.

Secondly, we have to derive a new CCF $T(j|x)$ that has similar properties to the one utilized in FASART while being compatible to the geometry of EAM categories. More specifically, these properties are

(i) The CCF takes values in [0,1], that is, $T(j|x) \in [0,1]$
(ii) The CCF is maximum at the centroid vector and equal to 1, viz. $T(j|x)=1 \Leftrightarrow x = c_j$.
(iii) The CCF value is zero for any pattern outside or on the boundary of the category's delta region, i.e. $T(j|x)=0 \quad \forall x \notin \text{int}(\Delta_j)$
(iv) The CCF value monotonically decreases inside the delta region with increasing distance of a training pattern from the category's centroid, viz. $\frac{dT(j|x)}{d\|x-c_j\|} < 0 \quad \forall x \in \Delta_j$, where $\|\ \|$ denotes any vector norm. Here, it is also implicitly assumed that $T(j|x)$ is continuous.

Although conditions (i)-(iv) reflect the behavior of FASART's CCF, they are not sufficient to uniquely determine the CCF to be used for FASEAM. Nevertheless, we start with the assumption that the constant T (CCF value) locus for a FASEAM category j should be a hyper-ellipsoid of a given center z and a Mahalanobis radius r, both of which depend on the specific value of T. In particular, we assume that the points x of the input space, that would feature a specific value $T \in [0,1]$, satisfy the equation

$$\|z(T) - x\|_{C_j} = r(T) \quad (4)$$

where

$$z(T) \triangleq Tc_j + (1-T)m_j$$
$$r(T) \triangleq (1-T)R'_j \quad (5)$$

In the above equations m_j, c_j, R_j and C_j are the center vector, centroid vector, Mahalanobis radius and shape matrix of category j. It can be shown with relative ease that Eq. 5 in conjunction with Eq. 4 satisfy properties (ii) and (iv), while property (i) is automatically satisfied by the assumed range of T. From these two equations we readily obtain

$$T(j|x) = \begin{cases} 1 - \dfrac{q_j(x) + \sqrt{q_j^2(x) - (R'^2_j - d^2_{mc})d^2_{cx}}}{R'^2_j - d^2_{mc}} & R'_j > d_{mx} \\ 0 & d_{mx} \geq R'_j \end{cases} \quad (6)$$

where we have defined the following quantities:

$$q_j(x) \triangleq (m_j - c_j)^T C_j (c_j - x) \quad (7)$$
$$R'_j \triangleq R_j + \delta \quad (8)$$
$$d_{mc} \triangleq \|m_j - c_j\|_{C_j} \quad (9)$$
$$d_{cx} \triangleq \|c_j - x\|_{C_j} \quad (10)$$
$$d_{mx} \triangleq \|m_j - x\|_{C_j} \quad (11)$$

Moreover, it is straightforward to observe that the CCF in Eq. 6 also satisfies condition (iii). The derived CCF for FASEAM depends on the relative distances between the training pattern, the center, and centroid, as measured in the category's metric (expressed by its shape matrix), as well as on the category's Mahalanobis radius. Figure 4 shows a contour plot of the derived CCF for a typical FASEAM category in a 2-

dimensional setting, which verifies that the CCF given in Eq. 6 indeed satisfies conditions (i) through (iv).

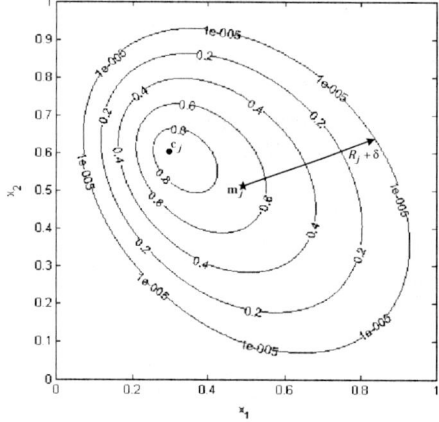

Fig. 4. Contour plot of the FASEAM CCF for an arbitrary category assuming a 2-dimensional input space.

Additionally, we had to replace the match tracking mechanism with an alternative secondary search process, since match tracking in FASART is mostly ineffective: during fast learning, when a winning category learns a pattern after match tracking has been invoked, if we were to immediately present again the same training pattern, the pattern may access a completely different category. In other words, FASART with match tracking does not preserve the principle of instantaneous, incremental learning of FAM, a fact that was first pointed out in [11]. To that effect, when a winning category fails the prediction test for a specific pattern, instead of invoking match tracking, FASEAM was designed to leave the vigilance parameter value unchanged and search for a suitable category that passes the prediction test and, if updated, to preserve the aforementioned principle.

IV. EXPERIMENTAL RESULTS

In order to assess the effectiveness of our design choices regarding FASEAM, we conducted a series of experiments using four artificially-generated, classification data sets. Based on these sets we compared FASART, EAM and FASEAM classifiers in terms of generalization performance and post-training structural complexity. In the next subsection we provide a short description for each data set.

A. Description of data sets

1) 4-Gaussian Datasets: Three datasets were generated by sampling from a bi-variate mixture of isotropic Gaussian distributions with equal priors consisting of 4 components; each component corresponded to a separate class distribution. The means of the class conditional distributions are placed symmetrically with respect to the coordinate axes, so that by changing their relative separation the Bayes error can be analytically calculated. We generated 3 datasets named G4LO, G4ME and G4HI with predetermined Bayes errors 0.05, 0.15 and 0.4 respectively. Each data set consisted of a training set, a cross-validation set and a test set of 500, 5,000 and 5,000 patterns respectively. The training set was kept small to facilitate speedier training phases, while the cross-validation and test set were chosen to be large, so that the statistical tests comparing the models' generalization performance would have good resolution in determining superiority among similarly performing networks.

2) Noisy Circle in the Square: The data set (abbreviated as NCINS) consists of 2-dimensional input data sampled from within the unit square $[0,1]^2$. In the noiseless version of the related classification problem, uniformly sampled data points, that are located within a specified radius r from $[0.5\ 0.5]^T$, are labeled as '1' and the rest as '0'. The radius r is chosen so that both classes have equal prior probabilities. In the noisy version of the problem, the label of the noiseless patterns is flipped with probability $p \leq 0.5$ resulting in a classification problem with Bayes probability of error equal to p. We chose a value of $p=0.1$. The classifier's task is to learn the decision boundary of the 2-class problem (the circle or radius r centered at $[0.5\ 0.5]^T$) despite the presence of the noisy patterns. Training, cross-validation and test sets were generated with cardinalities 500, 4000 and 4000 respectively.

B. Experimental Setup

For each dataset we trained a large number of FASART, EAM and FASEAM classifiers using several thousands combinations of training parameter values. Let us mention here that the same combinations of parameter values for each classifier type were used for all 4 data sets. Next, for a given data set we identified via cross-validation the 100 best-performing classifiers from each model family, whose generalization performance we subsequently assessed on the test set. With respect to training parameter values, for EAM we used the Weber Law CCF with a constant value for the choice parameter $a=0.001$ and a CCF value of 0 for uncommitted, F_2 layer nodes. For both EAM and FASEAM the axes ratio μ took values in $[0.2:0.1:1.0]$. Additionally, for both FASART and FASEAM the δ parameter took values in $[0.05:0.05:0.5]$. Finally, for FASART the learning rate β_c used for updating the centroid was held at constant value of 0.05.

Settings common to all three architectures were (i) a baseline vigilance $\bar{\rho}$ in $[0.0:0.05:0.95]$ for the training phase, (ii) a baseline vigilance $\bar{\rho}$ of 0 during performance phase to force the classification of all cross-validation and test patterns and (iii) a learning rate β of 1 for min- and max-vector updates (fast learning mode). Also, all three classifier types were trained with 50 different orders of training pattern presentations. The above training parameter values in conjunction with the 50 different presentation orders resulted in 9,000 EAM, 10,000 FASART and 90,000 FASEAM trained networks for each dataset; 436,000 models were trained in total.

C. Observations

In the following presentation and discussion of the results PIC will stand for percent incorrect classification, that is, the error rate of a classifier, while PCC will stand for percent correct classification (equals 100%-PIC). Additionally, we measure the size (structural complexity) of an architecture by the number of categories created during training. Ideally, a classifier should have the lowest possible PIC (equal to the Bayes error) and have the smallest possible size (equal to the number of classes) for a given classification problem. All inter-model comparisons drawn are based on test set performance.

Table I depicts the maximum, median, minimum and standard deviation for the PCC as measured on the test set for each classifier type and each data set considered. Furthermore, in this table, best values for each row are depicted in bold. On the other hand, Figures 5(a), 5(b), 5(c) and 5(d) depict the generalization performance (PIC on test set) versus structural complexity (size) of the 10 best models from each network family; each plot corresponds to one of the four data sets. In the sequel, statements about a difference in PIC (or PCC) being statistically significant are based on a test of hypothesis with significance level (Type I error probability) of 0.01. The test's null hypothesis amounts to the two classifiers compared being equally good (0 difference in PIC/PCC), while the alternative hypothesis is that the classifier featuring the highest PCC (lowest PIC) point estimate indeed performs better than the other one.

TABLE I

	PCC Test for 100 best networks		
	FASART	EAM	FASEAM
G4LO			
Max	87.4200	88.0000	**88.4600**
Median	85.9000	87.1000	**87.8000**
Min	85.7000	86.8600	**87.6800**
Std.	0.5219	**0.2422**	0.2451
G4ME			
Max	67.1400	69.6200	**73.7400**
Median	65.3300	68.2600	**72.8000**
Min	64.8000	67.8400	**72.6000**
Std.	0.6017	0.3848	**0.3612**
G4HI			
Max	49.2800	52.3800	**56.9800**
Median	48.5400	51.4100	**56.2400**
Min	47.9000	51.0200	**55.7800**
Std.	0.4232	**0.2801**	0.3656
NCINS			
Max	81.2250	**84.4250**	83.4250
Median	80.4875	**83.2375**	82.1625
Min	80.0750	**82.6250**	81.9250
Std.	**0.2811**	0.4084	0.2863

For the G4LO and NCINS datasets (Bayes errors of 0.05 and 0.1 respectively) Table I reflects that the 100 best networks from each family are comparable in classification performance. On the other hand, for harder problems like G4ME the results show that FASEAM performs better by approximately 5% and 7% than EAM and FASART respectively. Similarly, for the G4HI data set, the homologous differences are about 5% and 8% respectively. These last differences in PCC turn out to be statistically significant. In summa, it seems that FASEAM outperforms the standard EAM classifier in hard classification domains by a noticeable difference. This effect may be attributed to the fact that FASEAM uses a CCF that is not constant within category representation regions and allows for better, maybe smoother, approximation of the decision boundaries than in the case of EAM's CCF.

Turning to Figures 5(a) through 5(d) we may have expected an increased size of the FASART models in comparison to FASEAM and EAM due to FASART's match tracking ineffectiveness. However, this doesn't seem to be the case, maybe because FASART uses a different type of category than FASEAM and EAM (hyper-rectangular versus hyper-ellipsoidal representation regions) and, therefore, the model sizes of these families cannot be compared. However, FASART's training took up to three times more list presentations than EAM and FASEAM models (not shown here), which definitely can be attributed to the ineffectiveness of its match tracking process. Yet another observation pertaining to the 4-Gaussians problems is the high variability in network size of the 10 best EAM classifiers, when compared to the 10 best FASEAM and FASART classifiers, a fact that again could be attributed to the special nature of the CCFs the latter ones employ. For the NCINS dataset all three types of models exhibited noticeable variation in network size, which could be due to the problem's uniform class overlap. Nevertheless, FASEAM's performance is statistically indistinguishable from EAM's, while it employs less categories.

V. Summary

In this paper we presented Fuzzy Adaptive System Ellipsoid ARTMAP (FASEAM), a novel neural architecture based on Ellipsoid ARTMAP (EAM) that is designed around the framework utilized in the Fuzzy Adaptive System ART (FASART) architecture. The design was made by augmenting EAM categories with an adjustable centroid vector and utilizing an appropriate category choice function (CCF) that shares the major properties of FASART's CCF. After performing a series of experiments using four artificially-generated data sets, we obtained preliminary indications that FASEAM may perform (in terms of classification) significantly better than the standard EAM architecture, especially when the classification problem features highly overlapping class distributions. This fact could be attributed to FASEAM's CCF that is not constant within category representation regions and allows for better, maybe smoother, approximation of the decision boundaries involved.

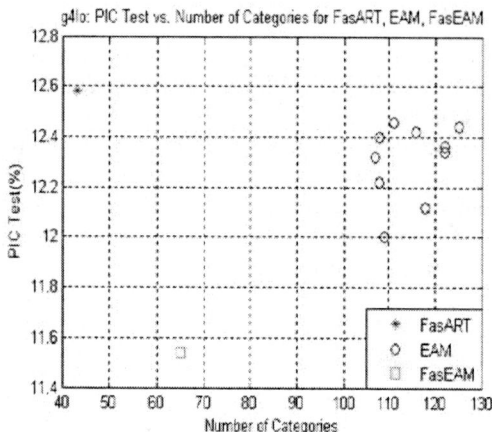

Fig. 5(a). PIC on test set versus network size; 4-G dataset; 5% overlap.

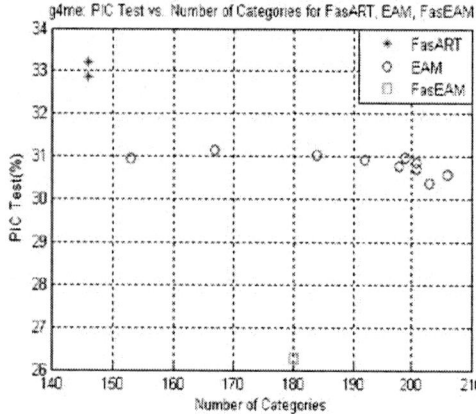

Fig. 5(b). PIC on test set versus network size; 4-G dataset; 15% overlap.

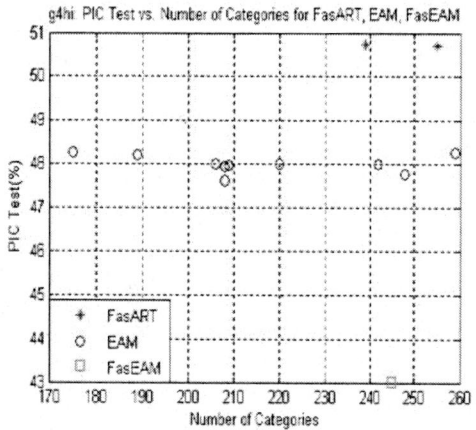

Fig. 5(c). PIC on test set versus network size; 4-G dataset; 40% overlap.

Acknoledgement

The authors would like to thank Manuel Fernández Delgado for helpful comments and suggestions on the manuscript. Also, the authors' research was partially supported by the National Science Foundation under CCLI-EMD grant No. 0341601.

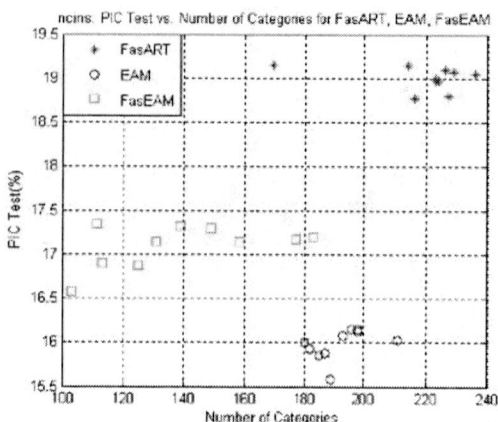

Fig. 5(d). PIC on test set versus network size; NCINS dataset; 10% overlap.

References

[1] S. Grossberg, "Adaptive Pattern Recognition and Universal Encoding II: Feedback, Expectation, Olfaction, and Illusions," Biological Cybernetics, 23, pp. 187-202, 1976.

[2] Cano, J. M., Dimitriadis, Y. A., Arau¬zo, M. J., & Coronado, J. "FasArt: A new neuro-fuzzy architecture for incremental learning in systems identification," *Proceedings of 13th World Congress of IFAC*, San Francisco, 1996, vol. F, pp. 133-138.

[3] G.A. Carpenter, S. Grossberg, N. Markuzon, J.H. Reynolds and D.B. Rosen, "Fuzzy ARTMAP: A Neural Network Architecture for Incremental Supervised Learning of Analog Multidimensional Maps," IEEE Transaction on Neural Networks, Vol. 3:5, pp. 698-713, 1992.

[4] Gomez, E., Gago, J. A., Dimitriadis, Y. A., Cano, J. M., & Coronado, J., "Experimental study of a novel neuro-fuzzy system for on-line handwritten UNIPEN digit recognition," Pattern Recognition Letters, 19 (3), pp. 357-364, 1998.

[5] Sainz, G. I., Dimitriadis, Y. A., Cano, J. M., Go¬mez, E., & Parrado, E. *ART based model set for pattern recognition: FasArt family*. In H. Bunke, & A. Kandel (Eds.), Neuro-fuzzy pattern recognition. World Scientific Publ. Co., 2000.

[6] Anagnostopoulos, G.C., & Georgiopoulos, M. "Category Regions as New Geometrical Concepts in Fuzzy ART and Fuzzy ARTMAP," Neural Networks, 15(10), 1205-1221, 2002.

[7] Cano-Izquierdo, J.M., Dimitriadis, Y.A., Gomez-Sanchez, E. And Coronado, J.L., "Learning from noisy information in FasArt and FasBack neuro-fuzzy systems," Neural Networks, 14(4,5), pp. 407-425, 2001.

[8] Anagnostopoulos, G.C., & Georgiopoulos, M. "Ellipsoid ART and ARTMAP for Incremental Unsupervised and Supervised Learning," *Proceedings of the IEEE-INNS-ENNS International Joint Conference on Neural Networks (IJCNN '01)*, Washington, Washington D.C, 2001, Vol. 2, (pp. 1221-1226).

[9] Gomez-Sanchez, E., "ART neural architectures for pattern recognition and function approximation", Ph.D. Dissertation, University of Valladolid, Spain, 2001.

[10] Williamson, J.R., "Gaussian ARTMAP: A Neural Network for Fast Incremental Learning of Noisy Multidimensional Maps", Neural Networks, 16(1), pp. 881-897, 1996.

[11] Parrado-Hernandez, E., Gomez-Sanchez, E. and Dimitriadis, Y.A., "Study of distributed learning as a solution to category proliferation in Fuzzy ARTMAP based neural systems", Neural Networks, 16(7), pp. 1039-1057, 2003.

Parallelizing the Fuzzy ARTMAP Algorithm on a Beowulf Cluster

Jimmy Secretan(*), José Castro(**), Michael Georgiopoulos(*),
Joe Tapia(*), Amit Chadha(*), Brian Huber(*), Georgios Anagnostopoulos(***), Samuel Richie(*)

(*) Dep. of Electrical and Computer Engineering, University of Central Florida, Orlando, FL 32816
(**) Comp. Eng., Instituto Technologico de Costa Rica, Cartago, Costa Rica
(***) Dept of Electrical and Computer Engineering, Florida Institute of Technology, Melbourne, FL, 32901

Abstract— Fuzzy ARTMAP neural networks have been proven to be good classifiers on a variety of classification problems. However, the time that it takes Fuzzy ARTMAP to converge to a solution increases rapidly as the number of patterns used for training increases. In this paper we propose a coarse grain parallelization technique, based on a pipeline approach, to speed-up Fuzzy ARTMAP's training process. In particular, we first parallelized Fuzzy ARTMAP, without the match-tracking mechanism, and then we parallelized Fuzzy ARTMAP with the match-tracking mechanism. Results run on a Beowulf cluster with a well known large database (Forrest Covertype database from the UCI repository) show linear speedup with respect to the number of processors used in the pipeline.

I. INTRODUCTION

Neural Networks have been used extensively and successfully to tackle a wide variety of problems. As computing capacity and electronic databases grow, there is an increasing need to process considerably larger databases. Neural network algorithms can have a prohibitively slow convergence to a solution, especially when they are trained on large databases. Even one of the fastest (in terms of training speed) neural network algorithms, the Fuzzy ARTMAP algorithm [3], and its faster variations ([6], [9]) tend to converge slowly to a solution as the size of the network increases.

One obvious way to address the problem of slow convergence to a solution is by the use of parallelization. This paper focuses on parallelization strategies for FAM on a Beowulf cluster. A Beowulf cluster is a collection of standard PC workstations formed into a single, cohesive supercomputer by a fast network and open source software. For many applications, especially those of interest to the data mining community, the Beowulf architecture offers unparalleled performance for the price.

Regarding the parallelization of ART neural networks it is worth mentioning the work by Manolakos [8] who has implemented the ART1 neural network [4] on a ring of processors, and the work of Malkani and Vassiliadis [7], who have implemented Fuzzy-ARTMAP on a hypercube architecture. In the latter paper, a hypercube topology is utilized for transferring data to all of the nodes involved in the computations. Each of the processors maintains a subset of the architecture's templates, and finds the template with the maximum match in its local collection. Finally, in its d-dimensional hypercube, it finds the global maximum through d different synchronization operations. This can limit the scalability of this approach.

The Fuzzy ARTMAP neural network has many desirable characteristics, such as the ability to solve any classification problem, the capability to learn from data in an on-line mode, the advantage of providing interpretations for the answers that it produces, the capacity to expand its size as the problem requires it and the ability to recognize novel inputs, among others. Due to all of its above properties it is worth investigating Fuzzy ARTMAP's parallelization in an effort to improve its convergence speed to a solution when it is trained with large datasets. In this paper, our focus is to improve the convergence speed of ART-like neural networks through a parallelization strategy applicable for a pipeline structure (Beowulf cluster). We chose to demonstrate the effectiveness of our proposed parallelization strategy on Fuzzy ARTMAP since, if we demonstrate its effectiveness for Fuzzy ARTMAP, its extension to other ART structures can be accomplished without much additional effort. This is due to the fact that the other ART structures share a lot of similarities with Fuzzy ARTMAP, and as a result, the proposed parallelization approach can be readily extended to other ART variants.

II. FUZZY ARTMAP ALGORITHM

The Fuzzy ARTMAP neural network and its associated architecture was introduced by Carpenter and Grossberg in their seminal paper [3]. Kasuba [6] and Taghi, Baghmisheh, and Pavesic [9] presented a simplified version of the original Fuzzy ARTMAP architecture that was equivalent to Fuzzy ARTMAP for classification problems. In our paper, we have implemented the simplified Fuzzy ARTMAP version from Taghi, called SFAM2.0, that we refer to as FS-FAM or alternately as Fuzzy ARTMAP. We assume that the reader is familiar with the simplified Fuzzy ARTMAP architecture consisting of an input layer, a category representation layer (where compressed representations of the inputs are formed) and an output layer.

FS-FAM can operate in two distinct phases: the *training phase* and the *performance phase*. In the training phase of FS-FAM a collection of input/output (such as $\{(\mathbf{I}^1, ab\ (\mathbf{I}^1)), \ldots, (\mathbf{I}^r, ab\ (\mathbf{I}^r)), \ldots, (\mathbf{I}^{PT}, ab\ (\mathbf{I}^{PT}))\}$) are repeatedly presented to FS-FAM until FS-FAM learns the desired mappings from inputs to outputs (referred to as labels of inputs). The training process in FS-FAM is succinctly described in Taghi's et al., paper [9]. We repeat it here to give the reader a good, well-explained overview of the operations involved in its training phase.

1) Find the nearest category in the category representation layer of FS-FAM that "resonates" with the input pattern.
2) If the labels of the chosen category and the input pattern match, update the chosen category to be closer to the input pattern.
3) Otherwise, reset the winner, temporarily increase the resonance threshold (called *vigilance parameter*), and try the next winner. This process is referred to as match-tracking.
4) If the winner is uncommitted, create a new category (assign the representative of the category to be equal to the input pattern, and designate the label of the new category to be equal to the label of the input pattern).

The nearest category to an input pattern $\mathbf{I}^r$ presented to FS-FAM is determined by finding the category that maximizes the function:

$$T_j(\mathbf{I}^r, \mathbf{w}_j, \alpha) = \frac{|\mathbf{I}^r \wedge \mathbf{w}_j|}{\alpha + |\mathbf{w}_j|} \quad (1)$$

The resonance of a category is determined by examining if the function, called *vigilance ratio*, and defined below

$$(\mathbf{I}^r, \mathbf{w}_j) = \frac{|\mathbf{I}^r \wedge \mathbf{w}_j|}{|\mathbf{I}^r|} \quad (2)$$

satisfies the following condition:

$$(\mathbf{I}^r, \mathbf{w}_j) \geq \quad (3)$$

If the label of the input pattern ($\mathbf{I}^r$) is the same as the label of the resonating category, then the category's template ($\mathbf{w}_j$) is updated as follows:

$$\mathbf{w}_j = \mathbf{w}_j \wedge \mathbf{I}^r \quad (4)$$

If the category j is chosen as the winner and it resonates, but the label of this category $\mathbf{w}_j$ is different than the label of the input pattern $\mathbf{I}^r$, then this category is reset and the vigilance parameter is increased to the level:

$$\frac{|\mathbf{I}^r \wedge \mathbf{w}_j|}{|\mathbf{I}^r|} + \epsilon \quad (5)$$

In the above equations the quantities α, , and ϵ are FS-FAM network parameters; α usually takes small positive values, is chosen as a value in the interval $[0, 1]$, and ϵ is a very small positive parameter.

In all of the above equations (equations (1)-(5)) there is a specific operator involved, called *fuzzy min operator*, and designated by the symbol $\wedge$. Actually, the fuzzy min operation of two vectors $\mathbf{x}$, and $\mathbf{y}$, designated as $\mathbf{x} \wedge \mathbf{y}$, is a vector whose components are equal to the minimum of components of $\mathbf{x}$ and $\mathbf{y}$. Another specific operator involved in these equations is designated by the symbol $|\ |$. In particular, $|\mathbf{x}|$ is the size of a vector $\mathbf{x}$ and is defined to be the sum of its components.

In the performance phase of FS-FAM, a test input is presented to FS-FAM and the category node in FS-FAM that has the maximum bottom-up input is chosen. The label of the chosen category is the label that FS-FAM predicts for this test input. By knowing the correct labels of test inputs, belonging to a test set, we can calculate the classification error of FS-FAM for this test set.

A simplification that can be applied to the FS-FAM algorithm is the elimination of the match-tracking process. This modification was originally proposed by Anagnostopoulos [1] and turned out to yield improved classification performance on some databases. Our interest in using this FS-FAM variant lies in the fact that it simplifies the FS-FAM algorithm and allows one to concentrate on the parallelization of the competition loop in Fuzzy ARTMAP.

III. PARALLEL FS-FAM ARCHITECTURES

The design of the parallel FS-FAM implementation used in this paper was somewhat inspired by the architecture in [8]. In this paper, we present two variations of the parallel FS-FAM, the parallel no match-tracking FS-FAM, and the parallel FS-FAM (which includes match-tracking). While these parallel implementations could be adapted to a physical pipeline/ring network topology, the run environment was emulated by nodes of the Beowulf cluster connected by a standard switch (star topology). The different nodes of the Beowulf were logically arranged in a pipeline, with the capability of bidirectional communication with their neighbors. The input patterns to be learned are read into the first node of the pipeline. Each node in the pipeline has its own collection of templates, against which the input patterns are compared. The input patterns are sent in batches, whose size is an adjustable parameter of the program. As a batch of inputs enters a node, it is processed sequentially. That is, the processing always starts with the first input pattern in the batch. The incoming patterns search through the node's collection of available templates. The maximum template that meets the vigilance is then coupled with the incoming input pattern. This coupling removes the pattern from the available pool of templates for the node. In all subsequent comparisons, if a better template is found, it is switched out with the one currently coupled to the input. The template comparisons proceed until the input pattern reaches the end of the pipeline. At this point, if the chosen template is mapped to the correct output, then learning of the pattern by the template ensues. If on the other hand the chosen template is mapped to the wrong output two different strategies are implemented. In the no match-tracking FS-FAM case a new template is added to the last node's template list which learns the designated input pattern. In the FS-FAM case the match-tracking mechanism is enforced and the input pattern is re-presented to the first node in the pipeline with an increased vigilance value and the search for the right template starts all over again. In addition to processing inputs the system is also performing load balancing. New templates are created only at the end stage of the pipeline. To achieve load balancing the last node's pool of excess templates, must be re-distributed to other nodes, further upstream in the pipeline. At the time that each node sends its input patterns and winning templates forward through the pipeline, it also sends its excess templates backward through the pipeline. An illustration of the flow of input patterns and templates through the system can be seen in figure 1. In this figure, the focus is on processor k and the exchange of information (patterns and templates) between processor k and its neighboring processors (i.e., processors $k-1$ and $k+1$).

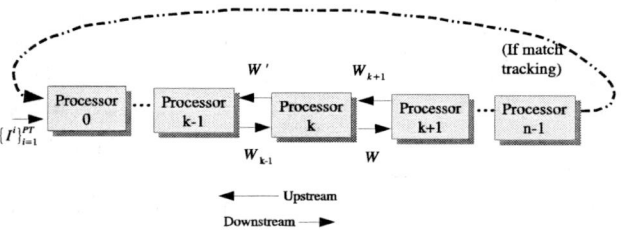

Fig. 1. Diagram to illustrate the exchange of input patterns and templates in the Beowulf processor pipeline.

A. No Match-Tracking Parallel FS-FAM

As part of our previous research, we presented a parallel pipelined version of the no match-tracking FS-FAM [5]. When inputs reach the end of the pipeline in the no match-tracking FS-FAM, they either update their associated templates or create new templates. This is the final point for all inputs. And as templates accumulate in the last processor in the pipeline, they are load balanced in the way explained earlier. Because of the lack of space in this paper, we refer the reader to our previous work for more a thorough explanation of the parallelization of the no match-tracking FS-FAM [5]. Note that in [5], we presented proofs of the parallel no match-tracking FS-FAM's equivalence to its serial counterpart, as well as description of some of its favorable load balancing properties. Throughout the rest of this paper, we concentrate on the generalization of the parallel no match-tracking FS-FAM design for the case of the match-tracking FS-FAM. However, we present scaling results for the no match-tracking FS-FAM for comparison purposes.

B. Parallel FS-FAM with Match-Tracking

The parallel implementation of FS-FAM is shown in figure 2. The variables involved are as follows:

- n: number of processors in the pipeline.
- k: index of the current processor in the pipeline, $k \in \{0, 1, \ldots, n-1\}$.
- p: packet size, number of patterns sent downstream; $2p$ = number of templates sent upstream.
- $(\mathbf{I}, \mathbf{w}, T, \cdot)$: 4-tuple corresponding to the format of the elements that are packed downstream in the pipeline. $\mathbf{I}$ is the input pattern, $\mathbf{w}$ is the current best candidate template for input pattern $\mathbf{I}$. T is the activation of the pattern with the given template. And is the current value of the vigilance parameter for this input pattern.
- *myTemplates*: set of templates that belong to the current processor.
- *nodes*: variable local to the current processor that holds the total number of templates the process is aware of (its own plus the templates of the other processors).
- *myShare*: amount of templates that the current processor should not exceed.
- $\mathbf{W}_{k-1}$: *Ordered* set of 4-tuples coming from the previous processor in the pipeline.
- $\mathbf{W}_{k+1}$: Set of templates (*not* 4-tuples) coming from the next processor in the pipeline.
- $\mathbf{W}$: *Ordered* set of 4-tuples going to the next processor in the pipeline.
- $\mathbf{W}'$: Set of templates (*not* 4-tuples) going to previous processor in the pipeline.
- $class(\mathbf{I})$: class label associated with a given input pattern.
- $class(\mathbf{w})$: class label associated with a given template.
- $index(\mathbf{w})$: sequential index assigned to a template.
- $newNodes_{k+1}$: number of new nodes (templates) that were created and that processor $k+1$ communicates upstream in the pipeline.
- *newNodes*: number of new nodes (templates) that were created and that processor k communicates upstream in the pipeline.

For the sake of brevity, we omit the pseudocode for the utility functions used here, but provide their high level descriptions. For a more thorough explanation of these functions, the reader is referred to [5]. To begin with, there are the network communications functions. They behave exactly as their names would indicate. The SENDNEXT functions, sends data to the next processor in the pipeline, and so fourth. The INIT function serves to initialize the variables and data structures for the algorithm. The function FINDWINNER is vital to the algorithm. This function searches through a set of templates $\mathcal{S}$ to find if there exists a template $\mathbf{w}^i$ that is a better choice for representing $\mathbf{I}$ than the current best representative $\mathbf{w}$. If it finds one it swaps it with $\mathbf{w}$, leaving $\mathbf{w}$ in $\mathcal{S}$ and extracting $\mathbf{w}^i$ from it.

Each processor in the pipeline will execute the algorithm of figure 2 for as long as there are input patterns to be processed. The input parameter k tells the process which stage of the pipeline it is, where the value k varies from 0 to $n-1$. After initializing most of the values as empty we enter the loop of lines 2 through 43. This loop continues execution until there are no more input patterns to process. As before, the first activity of each process is to create a packet of excess templates to send back (line 3 to 5). Lines 6 to 9 correspond to the information exchange between contiguous nodes in the pipeline. The function RECVNEXT on line 7, does not do anything if the process is the last in the pipeline ($k = n-1$). The same is true for the function SENDPREV when the process is the first in the pipeline ($k = 0$). On the other hand, function SENDNEXT sends packets to the *first* processor in the pipeline, when a given input pattern is forced to engage the match-tracking mechanism. In this case, the input pattern will increment its vigilance in its 4-tuple and start afresh at the beginning of the pipeline (process 0). The function RECVPREV does the normal procedure if it is not the first process in the pipeline. If it is the first process though, it will receive the pattern 4-tuples that come from the last process in the pipeline (the ones that are engaged in match-tracking), and read input patterns from the input stream if the amount of match-tracking packets is less than p. The fresh patterns from the input stream will be paired with a dummy template called the *uncommitted* node with index ∞ as their best representative so far. On all other cases these functions do the obvious information exchange between contiguous processes in the pipeline.

By sending the input patterns downstream in the pipeline coupled with their current best representative template we guarantee that the templates are not duplicated among different processors and that we do not have multiple–instance consistency issues. Also when exchanging templates between nodes in the pipeline we have to be careful that patterns that are sent downstream do not miss the comparison with templates that are being sent upstream. This is the purpose of lines 11 to 13 (communication with the next one in the pipeline) and lines 18-20 of PROCESS (communication with the previous process in the pipeline). We loop through each 4-tuple (lines 11–13) to see if one of the templates, sent upstream, has a higher activation (bottom-up input) than the ones that were sent downstream; if this is true then the template will be extracted from $\mathbf{W}_{k+1}$. The net result of this is that $\mathbf{W}_{k+1}$ ends up containing the templates that lost the competition, and therefore the ones that process k should keep (line 13). The converse process is done on lines 18 to 20. Here we compare the pattern, template pairs 4-tuples that $k-1$ sent upstream in the pipeline with the templates in W' that process k sent downstream in the pipeline. On line 20 we set our current 4-tuple to the winners of this competition. The set W' is discarded since it contains the losing templates and therefore the templates that process $k-1$ keeps.

The primary competition loop is in lines 21 to 39. On line 22, we start by comparing the pertinent 4-tuples to the processor's main collection of templates with the FINDWINNER function as described earlier. If it is on the last processor ($n-1$), there are additional steps that must be taken. If the final associated template is uncommitted, we add a new template to the system (lines 25-27). We also remove the 4-tuple from $\mathbf{W}$ (line 28), as we are done processing it. If a regular (committed) template has been associated with the input in question, and it maps to the correct class, then we update the template as per the Fuzzy ARTMAP algorithm (lines 31 to 34). Again, as before, the 4-tuple in question is removed from $\mathbf{W}$ (line 34). If the labels of the input and template do not match, we must use our match tracking mechanism (lines 35-38). We first increase its associated vigilance (line 36). We then remove the template that was associated with the input back into the processor's general pool and reset the template in the 4-tuple to be the uncommitted node. Since this 4-tuple is not removed from $\mathbf{W}$ as in the other cases, it remains to be sent back to processor 0, and start its competition loop all over again.

A processor continues until it receives nothing in $\mathbf{W}_{k-1}$. Finally, lines 45 and 46 of PROCESS make sure that the templates that are sent upstream in the pipeline are not lost after the pool of training input patterns that are processed is exhausted.

IV. EXPERIMENTS

The database used for the testing the performance of both the parallel no match-tracking FS-FAM and parallel FS-FAM was the Forest CoverType database provided by Blackard and donated to the UCI Machine Learning Repository. The database consists of a total of 581,012 patterns, with each one associated with 1 of 7 different forest tree cover types. The number of attributes of each pattern is 54, but this number is misleading since attributes 11 to 14 are actually a binary tabulation of the attribute Wilderness-Area, and attributes 15 to 54 (40 of them) are a binary tabulation of the attribute Soil-Type. The original database values are not normalized to fit in the unit hypercube. Thus, we transformed the data to achieve this. There are no omitted values in the data. Patterns 1 through 512,000 were used for training. The test set consisted of patterns 561,001 to 581,000. Although lack of space does not allow a comprehensive comparison of how different classification algorithms performed on this database, Blackard cites performance of 70% for backpropagation neural networks and 58% for Linear Discriminant Analysis [2]. Training set sizes of $1000 \cdot 2^i$, where $i \in \{5, 6, 7, 8, 9\}$ were used, that is 32,000 to 512,000 patterns were used for the training of parallel no match-tracking FS-FAM and FAM. The test set size, as mentioned above, was fixed at 20,000 patterns. The number of processors in the pipeline varied from $p = 1$ to $p = 32$, in powers of 2 (obviously the case of $p = 1$ corresponds to the sequential no match-tracking FS-FAM, and FS-FAM). To avoid additional computational complexities in the experiments the values of the ART network parameters and α were fixed (i.e., the values chosen were ones that gave reasonable results). For every combination of (p, PT) = (pipeline size, training set size) values, we conducted 12 independent experiments (training and performance phases), corresponding to different orders of pattern presentations within the training set. All results reported are averages over the 12 runs. All the tests where conducted on the OPCODE Beowulf cluster at the Institute for Simulation and Training, an institute affiliated with the University of Central Florida. This cluster consists of 96 nodes, with dual Athlon 1500+ processors and 512MB of RAM. The implementation of the algorithm was done in C++ with the MPI (Message Passing Interface) libraries. MPI provides a simple interface for communication among processes running on either one node or several different nodes. The runs were done in such as way as to utilize half as many nodes as p. Thus, there were two MPI processes per node, one per processor.

The metrics used to measure the performance of the pipelined approach were:

Fig. 2: Pseudocode for the parallel FS-FAM.

Procedure: Process($k, n, , \alpha, \varepsilon, p$)
1 Init(p);
2 **while** continue **do**
3     $W' = \{\}$;
4   **while** |myTemplates| > myShare **do**
5   ExtractTemplate(myTemplates, W');
6   SendNext(k, n, W);
7   RecvNext($k, n, \mathbf{W}_{k+1}, n\ wN\ d\ s_{k+1}$);
8   SendPrev($k, W', n\ wN\ d\ s$);
9   RecvPrev($k, n, p, , \alpha, \mathbf{W}_{k-1}$);
10   newNodes= $n\ wN\ d\ s_{k+1}$;
11   **foreach** (**I**, **w**, T,) $\in W$ **do**
12   FindWinner(**I, w**, T, , α, $\mathbf{W}_{k+1}$);
13   *myTemplates*= *myTemplates* $\cup\ \mathbf{W}_{k+1}$;
14    $\mathbf{W} = \{\}$;
15   **if** $|\mathbf{W}_{k-1}| == 0$ **then**
16   *continue*= FALSE;
17   **else**
18   **foreach** (**I, w**, T,) $\in \mathbf{W}_{k-1}$ **do**
19   FindWinner(**I, w**, T, , α, W');
20         $\mathbf{W} = \mathbf{W} \cup \{$ **I, w**, T, $\}$;
21   **foreach** (**I, w**, T,) $\in \mathbf{W}$ **do**
22   FindWinner(**I, w**, T, , α, myTemplates);
23   **if** $k == n-1$ **then**
24   **if w** == uncommitted **then**
25   *newTemplate*= **I**;
26   *index*(*newTemplate*) = newNodes+ nodes;
27   *myTemplates*= *myTemplates*$\cup$ {*newTemplate*};
28             $\mathbf{W} = \mathbf{W} - \{$ **I, w**, T, $\}$;
29   newNodes= newNodes+ 1;
30   **else**
31   **if** class(**I**) == class(**w**) **then**
32   **w** = **I** $\wedge$ **w**;
33   *myTemplates*= *myTemplates*$\cup$ {**w**};
34               $\mathbf{W} = \mathbf{W} - \{$ **I, w**, T, $\}$;
35   **else**
36   = (**I,w**) + ε;
37   *myTemplates*= *myTemplates*$\cup$ {**w**};
38   **w** = *uncommitted*;
39
40   **if** newNodes> 0 **then**
41   nodes= nodes+newNodes;
42   myShare= $\lceil \frac{nodes}{n} \rceil$;
43
44 SendNext($k, n, \mathbf{W}$);
45 RecvNext($k, n, \mathbf{W}_{k+1}$, newNode$_{k+1}$);
46 *myTemplates*= *myTemplates*$\cup\ \mathbf{W}_{k+1}$;

1) Classification performance of pipelined no match-tracking FS-FAM and pipelined FS-FAM.
2) Size of the trained, pipelined, no match-tracking FS-FAM and pipelined FS-FAM.
3) Speedup of pipelined no match-tracking FS-FAM and FS-FAM compared to their sequential counterparts.

To calculate the speedup, we simply measured the CPU time for each run.

V. RESULTS

The Forrest Covertype results are depicted in Tables I and II (parallel no match-tracking FS-FAM and parallel FS-FAM average classification performance and average number of templates created), and in Figures 3 and 4 (speed-up of the parallel FS-FAM versions compared to their sequential counterparts). As seen in [1], the no match-tracking version of the algorithm can yield increased classification performance at the expense of creating more templates in the system. The speed-up curves for the parallel no match-tracking FS-FAM and, to a lesser degree, the ones for the FS-FAM exhibit a linear behavior with respect to the number of processors in the pipeline. The speed-up curves though level off after we reach a certain number of processors in the pipeline for lower values of training patterns in our training collection; this is due to the fact that for smaller number of training patterns the number of templates created is not large enough to justify the usage of processors beyond a certain number. It is also worth emphasizing that the speed-ups achieved by the no match-tracking parallel FS-FAM are more impressive, compared to the corresponding speed-ups attained by the parallel FS-FAM. This result is also expected, since the number of templates that the no match-tracking parallel FS-FAM creates is significantly larger than the corresponding number of templates that the parallel FS-FAM creates (at times 10 times as many). In essence, the benefits of the proposed parallelization strategy are more pronounced for larger datasets and/or larger ART architectures.

The speedup curve for the FS-FAM has a spike toward the beginning of the curve. The spike occurs as the scaling goes up relatively well for $p = 2$ and then drops down to a more moderate scaling trend for $p \geq 4$. This is most likely related to the cluster design itself. As mentioned earlier, the cluster consists of dual processor nodes, with each processor running a copy of the program. In the case with $p=2$, this means both copies of the program were communicating on the same motherboard, which is much faster than the fast Ethernet network. This suggests that the parallel FS-FAM architecture's performance will improve by utilizing faster networking technologies. For 32k inputs, the graph is superlinear for the 2 processor case. It is very likely that this is because of caching. For the dimensionality of the templates (108, 4-bytes floats), and the average number of templates generated in this case (1263.09), split up between two processors is equal to about 256k bytes. This means that in this case, the templates fit much better into the cache than they did in the single processor case.

TABLE I
PARALLEL NO MATCH-TRACKING FS-FAM AVERAGE CLASSIFICATION PERFORMANCE AND AVERAGE NUMBER OF TEMPLATES CREATED WITH THE FORREST COVERTYPE DATA

Examples (1000s)	Avg. Classification	Avg. Templates
32	70.29	5148.83
64	74.62	11096.66
128	75.05	22831
256	77.28	49359.33
512	79.28	100720.75

TABLE II
PARALLEL FS-FAM AVERAGE CLASSIFICATION PERFORMANCE AND AVERAGE NUMBER OF TEMPLATES CREATED WITH FORREST COVERTYPE DATA.

Examples (1000s)	Avg. Classification	Avg. Templates
32	69.84	1263.09
64	73.26	2147.36
128	73.30	3346.64
256	73.93	5178.27
512	75.13	8013.82

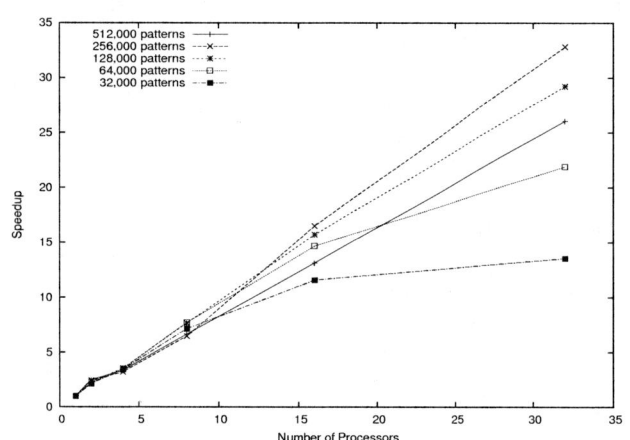

Fig. 3. Speedup of the parallel NMT-FS-FAM algorithm for differing numbers of processors and input patterns.

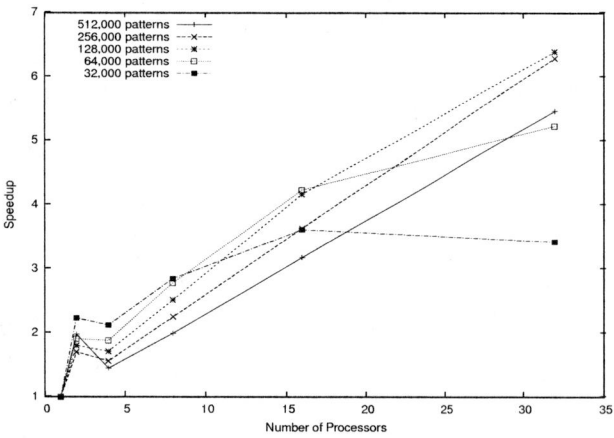

Fig. 4. Speedup of the parallel version of the FS-FAM algorithm for differing numbers of processors and input patterns.

VI. SUMMARY/CONCLUSIONS

We have produced a pipelined implementation of the no match-tracking FS-FAM and FS-FAM algorithms. This implementation can be extended to other ART architectures that have similar competitive structure as FS-FAM. It can also be extended to other neural network architectures that are designated as "competitive" neural networks, such as PNNs, RBFs, as well as other "competitive" classifiers. We have introduced and proven a number of theorems (see [5]) that show that the pipeline implementations of FS-FAM are efficient and correct. These theorems were omitted due to lack of space, but the interested reader can consult [5] for more details. We believe that our objective of appropriately implementing FS-FAM on the Beowulf cluster has been accomplished, as evidenced by Figures 3 and 4.

ACKNOWLEDGMENT

José Castro would like to thank the Computer Research Center of the Technological Institute of Costa Rica, the Institute of Simulation and Training (IST) and the Link Foundation Fellowship program for partially funding this project. This work was also supported in part by the National Science Foundation under grants # CRCD:0203446 and # CCLI:0341601.

REFERENCES

[1] G. C. Anagnostopoulos, "Putting the utility of match tracking in fuzzy ARTMAP to the test," in *Proceedings of the Seventh International Conference on Knowledge–Based Intelligent Information Engineering*, vol. 2, University of Oxford, UK. KES'03, 2003, pp. 1–6.

[2] J. A. Blackard, "Comparison of neural networks and discriminant analysis in predicting forest cover types," Ph.D. dissertation, Department of Forest Sciences, Colorado State University, 1999.

[3] G. A. Carpenter, S. Grossberg, N. Markuzon, J. H. Reynolds, and D. B. Rosen, "Fuzzy ARTMAP: A neural network architecture for incremental learning of analog multidimensional maps," *IEEE Transactions on Neural Networks*, vol. 3, no. 5, pp. 698–713, September 1992.

[4] G. A. Carpenter, S. Grossberg, and J. H. Reynolds, "Fuzzy ART: An adaptive resonance algorithm for rapid, stable classification of analog patterns," in *International Joint Conference on Neural Networks, IJCNN'91*, vol. II, IEEE/INNS Inc. Seattle, Washington: IEEE–INNS–ENNS, 1991, pp. 411–416.

[5] J. Castro, J. Secretan, M. Georgiopoulos, R. Demara, G. Anagnostopoulos, and A. Gonzalez, "Pipelining of fuzzy ARTMAP without matchtracking: Correctness, performance bound, and Beowulf evaluation," *Neural Networks (under review)*.

[6] T. Kasuba, "Simplified Fuzzy ARTMAP," *AI Expert*, pp. 18–25, November 1993.

[7] A. Malkani and C. A. Vassiliadis, "Parallel implementation of the Fuzzy ARTMAP neural network paradigm on a hypercube," *Expert Systems*, vol. 12, no. 1, pp. 39–53, 1995.

[8] E. S. Manolakos, *Parallel Architectures for Neural Networks: Paradigms and Implementations*. IEEE Computer Society Press and John Wiley & Sons, 1998, ch. Parallel Implementation of ART1 Neural Networks on Processor Ring Architectures.

[9] M. Taghi, V. Baghmisheh, and N. Pavesic, "A fast simplified Fuzzy ARTMAP network," *Neural Processing Letters*, vol. 17, pp. 273–316, 2003.

Using Real-Valued Meta Classifiers To Integrate Binding Site Predictions

Yi Sun, Mark Robinson, Rod Adams, Paul Kaye, Alistair G. Rust, Neil Davey
University of Hertfordshire, College Lane, Hatfield, Hertfordshire AL10 9AB
comrys, m.robinson, r.g.adams, p.h.kaye, n.davey@herts.ac.uk, arust@systemsbiology.org

Abstract— Currently the best algorithms for transcription factor binding site prediction are severely limited in accuracy. There is good reason to believe that predictions from these different classes of algorithms could be used in conjunction to improve the quality of predictions. In this paper, we apply single layer networks, rules sets and support vector machines on predictions from 12 key real valued algorithms. Furthermore, we use a 'window' of consecutive results in the input vector in order to contextualise the neighbouring results. We improve the classification result with the aid of under- and over- sampling techniques. We find that support vector machines outperform each of the original individual algorithms and the other classifiers employed in this work. In particular they have a better tradeoff between recall and precision.

I. INTRODUCTION

In this paper, we address the problem of identifying transcription factor binding sites on sequences of DNA. There are many different algorithms in current use to search for binding sites [22], [3], [23], [5]. However, most of them produce a high rate of false positive predictions. The problem addressed here is to reduce these false positive predictions by means of classification techniques taken from the field of machine learning.

To do this we first integrate the results from 12 different base algorithms for identifying binding sites, using non-linear classification techniques. To further improve classification results, we employ windowed inputs, where a fixed number of consecutive results are used as an input vector, so as to contextualise the neighbouring results. The data has two classes labeled as either binding sites or non-binding sites, with about 93% used being non-binding sites. We make use of sampling techniques, working with a traditional neural network: single layer networks (SLN), rules sets (C4.5-Rules) and a contemporary classification algorithm: support vector machines (SVM).

In previous work we have used binary valued base algorithms [19], here we extend this to use as much information as possible as provided by the real valued base algorithms.

We expound the problem domain in the next section. In Section III, we introduce the datasets used in this paper. We explain how we apply under- and over- sampling techniques in Section IV. A set of common metrics and receiver operating characteristics graphs for assessing classifier performance are covered in Section V. Section VI briefly introduces our experiments and Section VII gives all the experimental results. The paper ends in Section VIII with conclusions.

II. PROBLEM DOMAIN

One of the most exciting and active areas of research in biology currently, is understanding how the exquisitely fine resolution of gene expression is achieved at the molecular level. It is clear that this is a highly nontrivial problem. While the mapping between the coding region of a gene and its protein product is straightforward and relatively well understood, the mapping between a gene's expression profile and the information contained in its non-coding region is neither so simple, nor well understood at present. It is estimated that as much as 50% of the human genome is cis-regulatory DNA [15], undeciphered for the most part and tantalisingly full of regulatory instructions. A cis-regulatory component consists of DNA that encodes a site for protein-DNA interaction in a gene regulatory system, conversely, a trans-regulatory component consists of a protein that binds to a cis-regulatory DNA sequence. Cis-regulatory elements form the nodes connecting the genes in the regulatory networks, controlling many important biological phenomena, and as such are an essential focus of research in this field [2]. Lines of research likely to directly benefit from more effective means of elucidating the cis-regulatory logic of genes include embryology, cancer and the pharmaceutical industry.

It is known that many of the mechanisms of gene regulation act directly at the transcriptional or sequence level, for example in those genes known to play integral roles during embryogenesis [2]. One set of regulatory interactions are those between a class of DNA-binding proteins known as transcription factors and short sequences of DNA which are bound by the proteins by virtue of their three dimensional conformation. Transcription factors will bind to a number of different but related sequences. A base substitution in a cis-regulatory element will commonly, simply modify the intensity of the protein-DNA interaction rather than abolish it. This flexibility ensures that cis-regulatory elements, and the networks in which they form the connecting nodes, are fairly robust to various mutations. Unfortunately, it complicates the problem of predicting the cis-regulatory elements from out of the random background of the non-coding DNA sequences.

The current state of the art algorithms for transcription factor binding site prediction are, in spite of recent advances, still severely limited in accuracy. We show that in a large sample of annotated yeast promoter sequences, a selection of 12 key algorithms were unable to reduce the false positive predictions below 80%, with between 20% and 65% of annotated binding sites recovered. These algorithms represent a wide variety of approaches to the problem of transcription factor binding site prediction, such as the use of regular expression searches, PWM scanning, statistical analysis, co-regulation and evolutionary comparisons. There is however good reason to believe that the predictions from these different classes of algorithms are complementary and could be integrated to improve the quality of predictions.

In the work described here we take the results from the 12 aforemention algorithms and combine them into 2 different feature vectors, as shown in next section. We then investigate whether the integrated classification results of the algorithms can produce better classifications than any one algorithm alone.

III. DESCRIPTION OF THE DATA

The data has 68910 possible binding positions and a prediction result for each of the 12 algorithms. The 12 algorithms can be categorised into higher order groups as Single sequence algorithms (7) [22], [1], [17], [20]; Coregulatory algorithms (3) [3], [11]; A Comparative algorithm (1) [23]; An Evolutionary algorithm (1) [5].

The label information contains the best information we have been able to gather for the location of known binding sites in the sequences. We use -1 to denote the prediction that there is no binding site at this location and $+1$ to denote the predictions that there is a binding site at this location. For each of the base 12 algorithms, a prediction result can be either binary or real valued, see Figure 1. The data therefore consists of 68910 12-ary real vectors each with an associated binary value.

In this work, we divide our dataset into a training set and a test set: the first $2/3$ is the training set and the last $1/3$ is the test set. Amongst the data there are repeated vectors, some with the same label (repeated items) and some with different labels (inconsistent items). It is obviously unhelpful to have these repeated or inconsistent items in the training set, so they are removed. We call the resulting data the consistent training set. However in the case of the test set we consider both the full set of

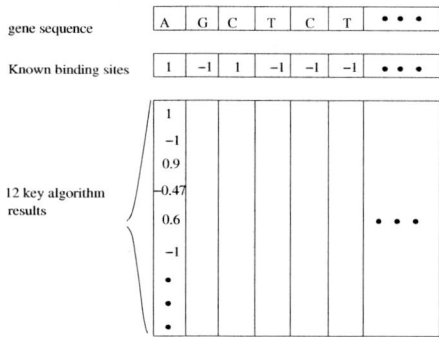

Fig. 1. The dataset has 68910 columns, each with a possible binding prediction (binary or real value). The 12 algorithms give their own prediction for each sequence position and one such column is shown.

data and the subset consisting of only the consistent test items. As can be seen in Table 1, the removal of repeated and inconsistent data dramatically reduces the number of data items: roughly 70% of data is lost.

As the data is drawn from a sequence of DNA nucleotides the label of other near locations is relevant to the label of a particular location. We therefore contextualise the training and test data by windowing the vectors as shown in Figure 2. We use the locations up to three either side, giving a window size of 7, and a consequent input vector size of 84. This has the considerable additional benefit of eliminating most of the repeated and inconsistent data: as can be seen in Table 1 now less than 5% of the data is lost.

Table 1 gives the sizes of all the different data sets used in this paper. The training set consists of either single vectors or windowed vectors. In both cases only consistent, non-repeating data is used. The test data consists of either single vectors or windowed vectors as appropriate. Either the full test set or the relevant consistent subset is used. There is however, a special case, namely when we want to compare the windowed model with the single input version. Here we want to evaluate the windowed model on the locations represented in the consistent test set of the single vector model. We therefore construct a test set for the windowed model consisting of only those vectors corresponding to the 7 locations around each of the data points in the single consistent test set.

IV. SAMPLING TECHNIQUES FOR IMBALANCED DATASET LEARNING

In our dataset, there are less than 10% binding positions amongst all the vectors, so this is an *imbalanced* dataset [13]. Since the dataset is imbalanced, the supervised classification algorithms will be expected to over predict the majority class, namely the non-binding site category. There are various methods of dealing with

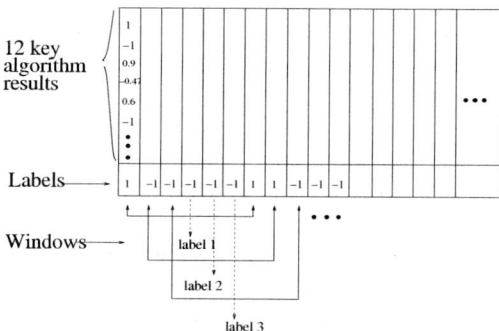

Fig. 2. The window size is set to 7 in this study. The middle label of 7 continuous prediction sites is the label for a new windowed inputs. The length of each windowed input now is 12×7.

TABLE I
DESCRIPTION OF THE DATASETS USED IN THIS WORK.

	type		size
training	consistent	single	12790
		windowed	42919
test	consistent	single	5966
		restricted windowed	5966
	full	single	22967
		windowed	22967

imbalanced data [12]. In this work, we concentrate on the data-based method [7]: using under-sampling of the majority class (negative examples) and over-sampling of the minority class (positive examples). We combine both over-sampling and under-sampling methods in our experiments.

For under-sampling, we randomly selected a subset of data points from the majority class. The over-sampling case is more complex. In [13], the author addresses an important issue that the class imbalance problem is only a problem when the minority class contains very small subclusters. This indicates that simply over sampling with replacements may not significantly improve minority class recognition. To overcome this problem, we apply a synthetic minority over-sampling technique as proposed in [7]. For each pattern in the minority class, we search for its K−nearest neighbours in the minority class using Euclidean distance. Since the dataset is a mixed one of continuous and binary features, we follow the suggestion in [7]: when the binary features differ between a pattern and its nearest neighbours, then the median of standard deviations of all continuous features for the minority class is included in the Euclidean distance. A new pattern belonging to the minority class can then be generated as follows: for continuous features, the difference of each feature between the pattern and its nearest neighbour is taken, and then multiplied by a random number between 0 and 1, and added to the corresponding feature of the pattern; for binary features, the majority voting principle to each element of the K−nearest neighbours in the feature vector space is employed. We take 5 nearest neighbours, and double the number of items in the minority class. The actual ratio of minority to majority class is determined by the under-sampling rate of the majority class. According to our previous experience, we set the final ratio to a half, which works well in this work.

V. CLASSIFIER PERFORMANCE

It is apparent that for a problem domain with an imbalanced dataset, classification accuracy rate is not sufficient as a standard performance measure. To evaluate classifiers used in this work, we apply Receiver Operating Characteristics (ROC) analysis [8], and several common performance metrics, such as recall, precision and F-score [6], [14], which are calculated to understand the performance of the classification algorithm on the minority class. Prior to introducing ROC curves, we give definitions of several common performance metrics.

A. Performance metrics

Based on the confusion matrix computed from the test results, several common performance metrics can be defined as in Table II, where TN is the number of true negative samples; FP is false positive samples; FN is false negative samples; FP is true positive samples.

TABLE II
PERFORMANCE METRICS

$$\text{Recall} = \text{TP} / (\text{TP} + \text{FN}), \quad \text{Precision} = \text{TP} / (\text{TP} + \text{FP}),$$
$$\text{F-score} = \frac{2 \cdot \text{Recall} \cdot \text{Precision}}{\text{Recall} + \text{Precision}}, \quad \text{Accuracy} = \frac{\text{TP}+\text{TN}}{\text{TP}+\text{FN}+\text{TN}+\text{FP}},$$
$$\text{fp\_rate} = \frac{\text{FP}}{\text{FP}+\text{TN}}.$$

B. ROC curves

ROC analysis has been used in the field of signal detection for a long time. Recently, it has also been employed in the machine learning and data mining domains. Here we follow [8] to give a basic idea of ROC curves.

1) ROC curves: In a ROC diagram, the *true positive rate* (also called recall) is plotted on the Y axis and the *false positive rate* (fp_rate) is plotted on the X axis. Points in the top left of the diagram therefore have a high TP rate and a low FP rate, and so represent good classifiers. The classifiers used here all produce a real valued output, that can be considered as a class membership probability. It is normal when using a ROC diagram to compare classifiers, to generate a set of points in ROC space by varying the threshold used to determine class membership. In this way a ROC curve corresponding to the performance of a single classifier, but with a varying threshold, is produced. One classifier is clearly better only when it dominates another over the entire performance space [8]. One attractive property of ROC curves is that they are insensitive to changes in class distribution, which makes them useful for analysing performance of classifiers using imbalanced datasets.

As noted for a ROC curve to be generated a real valued classifier is needed. The original SVM is a binary classifier. As described in [21] it is possible for the SVM to generate probabilistic outputs. For majority voting and weighted majority voting, we adopt methods proposed in [9]. The score assigned to each pattern is the fraction of votes won by the majority in majority voting; while in weighted majority voting, each base algorithm votes with its *confidence*, which is measured by the probability that the given pattern ($\mathbf{I}$) is positive ($\mathbf{P}$), i.e., $p(\mathbf{P}|\mathbf{I}) \approx$ TP / (TP + FP). The class with the highest summed confidence wins, and the score is the average confidence. For the neural network classifiers a real valued output is automatically generated.

Often to measure a classifier performance, it is convenient to use a single metric and the area under a ROC curve (AUC) can be used for this purpose. Its value ranges from 0 to 1. An effective classifier should have an AUC more than 0.5.

VI. EXPERIMENTS

The classification techniques used in this work are single layer network (SLN) [4], support vector machine (SVM) [18], rule sets (C4.5-Rules) [16], majority voting (MV), and weighted majority voting (WMV).

The SVM experiments were completed using LIBSVM, which is available from the URL
http://www.csie.ntu.edu.tw/~cjlin/libsvm.
The C4.5-Rules experiments were done using C4.5 software from [16]. C4.5-Rules is a companion program to C4.5. It creates rules sets by post-processing decision trees generated using C4.5 algorithm first. The others were implemented using the NETLAB toolbox, which is available from the URL
http://www.ncrg.aston.ac.uk/netlab/.

A. Parameter Settings

Since we do not have enough data to build up an independent validation set to evaluate the model, all the user-chosen parameters are obtained using cross-validation. There are two training sets (single or windowed), and for each of these sets, and each classifier, the following cross validation procedure is carried out. The training set is divided into 5 equal subsets, one of which is to be a validation set, and there are therefore 5 possible such sets. For each classifier a range of reasonable parameter settings are selected. Each parameter setting is validated on each the five validation sets, having previously been trained on the other 4/5 of the training data. The mean performance, as measured by the AUC metric over these 5 validations, is taken as the overall performance of the classifier with this parameter setting. The parameter setting with best performance is then used with this classifier and the corresponding data set (single or windowed) in the subsequent experiments. For example the SVM has two parameters and six different combinations were evaluated.

There are several approaches to generate an averaging ROC curve from different test sets [8]. In this paper, average ROC curves of the cross-validation results are obtained by first generating a ROC curve for each of the validation sets, and then by calculating the average scores from them.

The standard deviation of the AUC can therefore be attained either using the cross-validation method, or when only a single curve is available, approximated as follows [10], $se = \sqrt{\frac{A(1-A)+(N_p-1)(Q_1-A^2)+(N_n-1)(Q_2-A^2)}{N_n N_p}}$, where A denotes AUC, N_n and N_p are the number of negative and positive examples respectively, and $Q_1 = \frac{A}{2-A}$, $Q_2 = \frac{2A^2}{1+A}$.

VII. RESULTS

A. Cross validation

In this experiment, we trained and tested the classifiers using 5-fold cross-validation as described above. The best set of parameters for each classifier were selected and the resulting AUC value (averaged over the 5-fold validation) is shown in Table III. Table III also shows standard deviations computed using cross-validation. For both single and windowed inputs, the C4.5-Rules have the best performance. In addition, due to the different size of the training sets (see Table I), almost all classifiers have smaller standard deviations with windowed inputs than single inputs.

TABLE III
CROSS VALIDATION WITH DIFFERENT CLASSIFIERS.

input	classifier	Mean of AUC	std
single	SLN	74.41	2.04
	SVM	78.36	1.8
	C4.5-Rules	86.55	1.21
windowed	SLN	75.94	0.59
	SVM	75.14	0.31
	C4.5-Rules	87.01	1.24

B. Classification results on the fixed consistent test set with single and windowed inputs

This test set has 5966 data points (see section III) in both the single and windowed versions.

TABLE IV
COMMON PERFORMANCE METRICS (%) TESTED ON THE SAME CONSISTENT POSSIBLE BINDING SITES WITH SINGLE AND WINDOWED INPUTS SEPARATELY.

input	Classifier	recall	precision	F-score	Accuracy	fp_rate	AUC±se
single	best Alg.	40.95	17.46	24.48	82.22	14.66	-
	MV	43.10	13.14	20.14	75.95	21.57	58.54±1.50
	WMV	41.19	17.35	24.42	82.05	14.86	61.28±1.51
	SLN	28.81	22.16	25.05	87.86	7.66	69.27±1.47
	SVM	32.14	24.46	**27.78**	88.23	7.52	69.49±1.47
	C4.5-Rules	29.29	23.08	25.81	88.15	7.39	64.59±1.50
windowed	SLN	34.29	18.87	24.34	85.00	11.16	69.21±1.47
	SVM	38.81	20/25	26.61	84.93	11.58	**72.58±1.44**
	C4.5-Rules	23.57	18.64	20.82	87.38	7.79	58.94±1.50

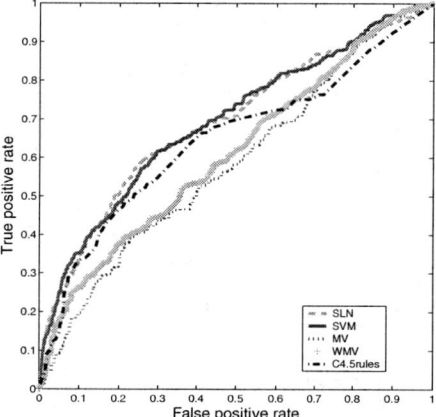

Fig. 3. ROC graph: five classifiers applied to the consistent test set with single inputs.

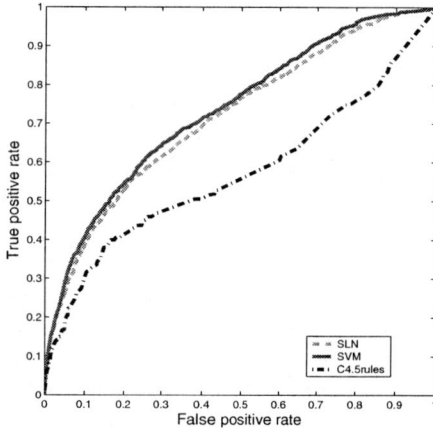

Fig. 4. ROC graph: three classifiers applied to the full test set using windowed inputs.

The results are shown in Table IV, together with the best base algorithm (the one with the highest F-score). Compared with the best base algorithm, all classifiers, except MV and WMV decrease the fp_rate. It can be seen that with both single and windowed inputs, the SVM is clearly the best classifier - it outperforms the others in terms of the F-score and AUC performance metrics. However this is at a cost: in comparison to the best base algorithm the recall has been decreased, especially with single inputs. The classifier has become more conservative, predicting binding sites less often but with greater accuracy. When comparing the single and windowed results the only major difference is that C4.5-Rules does a lot better with single input data.

Figure 3 shows ROC curves obtained using the consistent test set and single inputs. The curves show that the SVM and SLN have similar performance, outperforming the others. MV and WMV are the weakest.

C. Classification results on the full test set with single and windowed inputs

In this experiment, we use the full contiguous test set. All the results are presented in Table V, with one of the corresponding ROC curves shown in Figures 4.

Looking at the results for the single inputs, the SLN performs well in the AUC, while the SVM in F-score. Although their recalls are lower than the best base algorithm, this is explained by their far lower fp_rate. With windowed inputs the story is very much the same. In fact the windowed SVM is the overall best performer across single and windowed classifiers. The C4.5-Rules perform particularly poorly, as is shown in Figure 4, where over some of the range it is predicting below random.

VIII. CONCLUSIONS

The significant result presented here is that by integrating the 12 algorithms we can considerably improve binding site prediction. In fact when considering the

TABLE V
COMMON PERFORMANCE METRICS (%) TESTED ON THE FULL TEST SET WITH SINGLE AND WINDOWED INPUTS.

input	Classifier	recall	precision	F-score	Accuracy	fp_rate	AUC±se
single	best Alg.	36.36	18.40	24.44	85.97	10.73	-
	MV	35.73	15.12	21.25	83.48	13.35	61.66±0.81
	WMV	34.75	20.04	25.42	87.28	9.23	63.75±0.81
	SLN	25.19	25.09	25.14	90.64	5.01	70.54±0.79
	SVM	27.91	26.97	27.43	90.79	5.03	69.30±0.79
	C4.5-Rules	23.03	23.14	23.08	90.43	5.09	60.45±0.81
windowed	SLN	31.82	22.66	26.47	88.97	7.23	71.93±0.78
	SVM	36.78	23.50	**28.67**	88.58	7.97	**73.65±0.77**
	C4.5-Rules	22.26	19.70	20.90	89.49	6.04	57.21±0.81

full contiguous test set, we are able to reduce the false positive predictions of the best base algorithm by 26%, whilst maintaining about the same number of true positive predictions. As expected the SVM gave a better classification result than the SLN and the decision trees. Majority voting was actually worse than the best individual algorithm. However, weighted majority voting was a little better. C4.5 has a tendency to badly overfit the training data and produce very poor predictions, sometimes worse than random.

Future work will investigate i) searching for a method to find out a suitable ratio of minority to majority classes, which could give better results; ii) using algorithm based technologies to cope with the imbalanced dataset; iii) considering a wider range of supervised meta-classifiers or ensemble learning algorithms. Another important avenue to explore will be to examine the biological significance of the results and we are currently working on using a visualisation tool.

REFERENCES

[1] A. Apostolico, M. E, Bock, S. Lonardi and X. Xu, "Efficient Detection of Unusual Words," *Journal of Computational Biology*, Vol.7, No.1/2, 2000.
[2] M. I. Arnone and E. H. Davidson, "The hardwiring of development: Organization and function of genomic regulatory systems", Development 124, 1851-1864, 1997.
[3] T. L. Bailey and C. Elkan, "Fitting a mixture model by expectation maximization to discover motifs in biopolymers," *Proceedings of the Second International Conference on Intelligent Systems for Molecular Biology*, 28-36, AAAI Press, 1994.
[4] C. M.Bishop. (1995) *Neural Networks for Pattern Recognition*. Oxford University Press, New York.
[5] M. Blanchette and M. Tompa, "FootPrinter: a program designed for phylogenetic footprinting," *Nucleic Acids Research*, Vol. 31, No. 13, 3840-3842, 2003.
[6] M. Buckland and F. Gey, "The relationship between Recall and Precision," *Journal of the American Society for Information Science*, Vol. 45, No. 1, pp. 12–19, 1994.
[7] N. V. Chawla, K. W. Bowyer, L. O. Hall and W. P. Kegelmeyer, "SMOTE: Synthetic minority over-sampling Technique," *Journal of Artificial Intelligence Research*. Vol. 16, pp. 321-357, 2002.
[8] R. Fawcett, "ROC graphs: notes and practical considerations for researchers," Kluwer Academic publishers, 2004.
[9] T. Fawcett, "Using rule sets to maximize ROC performance," *Proceedings of the IEEE International Conference on Data Mining (ICDM-2001)*, Los Alamitos, CA, pp 131-138, IEEE Computer Society, 2001.
[10] J. A. Hanley and B. J. McNeil, "The meaning and use of the area under a receiver operating characteristic (ROC) curve," *Radiology*, 143, 29-36, 1982.
[11] J. D. Hughes, P. W. Estep, S. Tavazoie and G. M. Church, "Computational identification of cis-regulatory elements associated with groups of functionally related genes in Saccharomyces cerevisiae," *Journal of Molecular Biology*, Mar 10;**296**(5):1205-1214, 2000.
[12] Wu, G and Chang, E. Y.: Class-boundary alignment for imbalanced dataset learning. *Workshop on learning from imbalanced datasets, II, ICML*, Washington DC, 2003.
[13] N. Japkowicz, "Class imbalances: Are we focusing on the right issue?" *Workshop on learning from imbalanced datasets, II, ICML*, Washington DC, 2003.
[14] M. Joshi, V. Kumar and R. Agarwal, "Evaluating Boosting algorithms to classify rare classes: Comparison and improvements," *First IEEE International Conference on Data Mining*, San Jose, CA, 2001.
[15] M. Markstein, A. Stathopoulos, V. Markstein, P. Markstein, N. Harafuji, D. Keys, B. Lee, P. Richardson, D. Rokshar and M. Levine, "Decoding Noncoding Regulatory DNAs in Metazoan Genomes", *proceeding of 1st IEEE Computer Society Bioinformatics Conference (CSB 2002)*, Stanford, CA, USA, 14-16, August, 2002.
[16] J. R. Quinlan, *C4.5: Programs for Machine Learning*, Morgan Kauffman, 1993.
[17] N. Rajewsky, M. Vergassola, U. Gaul and E. D. Siggia, "Computational detection of genomic cis regulatory modules, applied to body patterning in the early Drosophila embryo," BMC *Bioinformatics*, 3:30, 2002.
[18] B. Scholköpf and A. J. Smola, *Learning with Kernels: Support Vector Machines, Regularization, Optimization, and Beyond*, The MIT Press, 2002.
[19] Y. Sun, M. Robinson, R. Adams, P. Kayes, A. G. Rust and N.Davey, "Integrating binding site predictions using meta classification methods", *Proceedings ICANNGA05*, 2005.
[20] G. Thijs, K. Marchal, M. Lescot, S. Rombauts, B. De Moor, RouzP and Y. Moreau, "A Gibbs Sampling method to detect over-represented motifs in upstream regions of coexpressed genes," *Proceedings Recomb'2001*, 305-312, 2001.
[21] T. F. Wu, C. J. Lin and R. C. Weng, "Probability Estimates for multi-class classification by pairwise coupling," *Journal of Machine Learning Research*, 5 pp. 975-1005, 2004.
[22] http://www.hgmp.mrc.ac.uk/Software/EMBOSS/.
[23] http://family.caltech.edu/SeqComp/index.html.

Cluster Ensemble for Gene Expression Microarray Data

Marcilio C. P. de Souto*, Shirlly C. M. Silva*, Valnaide G. Bittencourt†, and Daniel S. A. de Araujo*
*Department of Informatics and
Applied Mathematics
Federal University of Rio Grande do Norte
Natal, RN, Brazil, 59072-970
E-mail: marcilio@dimap.ufrn.br, shirlly@ppgsc.ufrn.br, danielsa@lcc.ufrn.br
†Department of Computing and Automation
Federal University of Rio Grande do Norte
Natal, RN, Brazil, 59072-970
E-mail: valnaide@dca.ufrn.br

Abstract—Ensemble techniques have been successfully applied in the context of supervised learning to increase the accuracy and stability of classification. Recently, similar techniques have been proposed for clustering algorithms. In this context, we analyze the potential of applying cluster ensemble techniques to gene expression microarray data. Our experimental results show that there is often a significant improvement in the results obtained with the use of ensemble when compared to those based on the clustering techniques used individually.

I. INTRODUCTION

Data mining methods have been widely applied to discover patterns and relations in complex datasets [1]. In this paper, we are particularly concerned with a type of taxonomy discovery called cluster analysis: the discovery of distinct and non-overlapping sub-population within a large population, the member items of each sub-population sharing some common features considered relevant in the problem domain of study [2], [3].

As pointed out by [3], this type of unsupervised analysis is of increasing interest in the field of functional genomics and gene expression data analysis. One of the reasons for this is the need for molecular-based refinement of broadly defined biological classes, with implications in cancer diagnosis, prognosis and treatment [3], [4], [5].

Cluster analysis frequently involves repeated runs of different clustering algorithms with random restart, followed by a selection of an individual solution that maximizes a user-defined criterion [2]. However, rather merely selecting the "best" partition as a solution, recent work has shown that combining the strengths of an ensemble of clusterings can often produce better results.

Ensemble techniques have been successfully applied in supervised learning to improve the accuracy and stability of classification algorithms [6], [7]. However, only recently have attempts been made to apply this type of combination to unsupervised algorithms, such as clustering techniques [8], [9], [10], [11], [12], [13], [14].

Thus, in this paper, we analyze the potential of applying cluster ensemble techniques to gene expression microarray data. More specifically, we develop experiments with the cluster ensemble method described in [13]. In order to so, the results of three clustering algorithms, representative of different clustering paradigms, are selected as input for building the ensembles: the k-means, the Expectation-Maximization (EM) algorithm, and the average linkage hierarchical method [2], [1]. All these algorithms have been widely used in the gene expression literature [3], [4], [5].

In our experiments, we also consider three broadly used datasets for which multi-class distinction (a phenotype) is available: Leukemia, Novartis multi-tissue, and St. Jude leukemia [15], [3], [16]. These datasets allow us, among other things, analyze the ability of the clustering method finding refinement of broadly defined biological classes.

II. ENSEMBLE GENERATION

According to [17], the problem of ensemble generation (consensus clustering) can be formally defined as follows. Let X be a set of N data points (objects) in d-dimensional space. Suppose that we are given a set of partitions $\Pi = \{\pi_1, \pi_2, ..., \pi_H\}$ of objects. Each component partition in Π is a set of disjoint, exhaustive and nonempty clusters $\pi_i = \{L_1^i, L_2^i, ..., L_{K(i)}^i\}$, $X = L_1^i \cup ... \cup L_{K(i)}^i$, $\forall \pi_i$, and $K(i)$ is the number of clusters in the i-partition. The problem of consensus clustering is to find a new partition $\sigma = \{C_1, ..., C_2\}$ of X given the partition in Π, such that the objects in cluster of σ are more similar to each other than to objects in different clusters of σ.

The previous definition leads to the following questions: how to generate different partitions? how to combine multiple partitions? With respect to the first question, several approaches comparable to those used in supervised learning have been proposed to introduce artificial instabilities in clustering algorithms. Doing so, different clusterings of the same data can be produced, what can lead to the improvement of the quality and robustness of the ensemble output [8], [9], [10], [11], [12], [3], [13], [14].

For example, in [9], [10], [3] multi-clustering fusion algorithms are presented based on combining several runs of a clustering algorithm, resulting in a common partition. Another approach is to generate ensembles from the combination of different clustering methods such as the work in [8], [12], [13], [14].

The combination of multi-partitions, the second question, is often accomplished via the definition of a consensus function. A consensus function maps a given set of partitions $\Pi = \{\pi_1, \pi_2, ..., \pi_H\}$ to a target partition σ [17]. Some examples of consensus functions found in the literature are the following:

- Co-association matrix [18]: the similarity between two objects are estimated by counting the number of shared clusters. Then, the single-linkage clustering algorithm is used for finding the consensus partition.
- Hyper-graph methods [13]: clusters in different partitions are represented by hyper-edges. The consensus partition is found by a k-way min-cut of the hyper-graph.
- Re-labeling and voting [9]: if the label correspondence problem[1] is solved for the given partitions, a simple voting procedure can be used to assign objects in clusters.
- Mutual Information [17]: the procedures maximizes the mutual information between the individual partitions and the target consensus partition.

In this paper, we choose to analyze the successful cluster ensemble method presented in [13]. In such a framework, all the clusters in the ensemble partitions can be represented as hyperedges on a graph with N vertices. Each hyperedge describes a set of objects belonging to the same clusters. A consensus function is formulated as a solution to k-way min-cut hypergraph partitioning problem. Each connected component after the cut corresponds to a cluster in the consensus partition.

Hypergraph partitioning problem is NP-hard, but very efficient heuristics are developed for its solution with complexity proportional to the number of hyperedges $O(|E|)$. In fact, in their work, [13] use three consensus functions based on hypergraph models: CSPA (*Cluster-based Similarity Partitioning Algorithm*), HGPA (*HiperGraph-Partitioning Algorithm*), and MCLA (*Meta-CLustering Algorithm*). The output of this method is a consensus partition, found by the consensus functions, with the maximum average normalized mutual information, as defined by the authors.

Intuitively, in their strategy a set of different crisp partitions of a dataset is combined to a new partition which optimally represents these partitions. In this context, an input partition is represented by a row vector with the cluster labels for each pattern in training dataset - no other information is needed. As mentioned before, in this case, it is not important whether these different partitions are the results of the application of different clustering algorithms or the results of the repeated application of one clustering algorithm with different random initialization.

In this paper, we compare the results obtained by using individually three clustering algorithms, representative of different clustering paradigms (the k-means, the Expectation-Maximization (EM) algorithm, and the average linkage hierarchical method [2], [1]) to two different ways of forming ensembles: (1) by combining partitions produced by these three clustering algorithms; and (2) by combining several runs of each of these clustering algorithm, with exception of the hierarchical method (it has no random restart).

III. EVALUATION METHODOLOGY

The evaluation we use is aimed at assessing how good the clustering methods investigated is at recovering known clusters from gene expression microarray data. In order to do so, we consider three datasets for which multi-class distinction (a phenotype) is available. As in other works, each of this datasets constitutes the *gold standard* against which we evaluate the clustering results [2], [3]. Following the conversion in [3], we refer to the gold standard partition as *class*, while we reserve the world *clusters* for the partition returned by the clustering algorithm.

A. External Indices

The cluster composition can be evaluated by measuring the degree of agreement between two partitions (U and V), where partition U is the result of a clustering method and partition V (the gold standard) is formed by an a priori information independent of partition U, such as a class label. There are a number of indices, external indices, defined in the literature, such as Hubbert, Jacard, Rand and corrected Rand (or adjusted Rand) [2] that can be used for this measurement.

One characteristic of most of these indices is that they can be sensitive to the number of classes in the partitions or to the distributions of elements in the clusters. For example, some indices have a tendency to present higher values for partitions with more classes (Hubbert and Rand), others for partitions with a smaller number of classes (Jaccard) [19].

The corrected Rand index, which has its values corrected for chance agreement, does not have any of these undesirable characteristics [20]. Thus, the corrected Rand index - CR, for short - is the external index used in the evaluation methodology used in this work. The corrected Rand index can take values from -1 to 1, with 1 indicating a perfect agreement between the partitions, and the values near 0 or negatives corresponding to cluster agreement found by chance.

Formally, let $U = \{u_1, ..., u_r, ..., u_R\}$ be the partition given by the clustering solution, and $V = \{v_1, ..., v_c, ..., v_C\}$ be the partition formed by an a priori information independent of partition U (the gold standard). The corrected Rand is defined as

$$\frac{\sum_i^R \sum_j^C \binom{n_{ij}}{2} - \binom{n}{2}^{-1} \sum_i^R \binom{n_i}{2} \sum_j^C \binom{n_{\cdot j}}{2}}{\frac{1}{2}[\sum_i^R \binom{n_i}{2} + \sum_j^C \binom{n_{\cdot j}}{2}] - \binom{n}{2}^{-1} \sum_i^R \binom{n_i}{2} \sum_j^C \binom{n_{\cdot j}}{2}},$$

---

[1]In the absence of labeled training data, we face the correspondence problem between cluster labels in different partitions of an ensemble.

where (1) n_{ij} represents the number of objects in clusters u_i and v_j; (2) $n_{i.}$ indicates the number of objects in cluster u_i; (3) $n_{.j}$ indicates the number of objects in cluster v_j; (4) n is the total number of objects; and (5) $\binom{a}{b}$ is the binomial coefficient $\frac{a!}{b!(a-b)!}$.

B. Cross-validation

The comparison of two supervised learning methods is, often, accomplished by analyzing the statistical significance of the difference between the mean of the classification error rate, on independent test sets, of the methods evaluated. In order to evaluate the mean of the error rate, several (distinct) data sets are needed. However, the number of data sets available is often limited. One way to overcome this problem is to divide the data sets into training and test sets by the use of a k-fold cross validation procedure [21].

In unsupervised learning (or cluster analysis), when there is an a priori classification of the data set available, the comparison between two methods can also be done by detecting the statistical significance of the difference between the mean values of a certain external index. But again, the number of training sets available is also limited. In [22], a method to overcome this problem was presented. Such a method, which will be used in this work, is an adaptation of the k-fold cross-validation procedure for unsupervised methods, as described below.

The data set is, in the unsupervised k-fold cross-validation procedure proposed in [22], also divided in k folds. At each iteration of the procedure, one fold is used as the test set, and the remaining folds as the training set. The training set is presented to a clustering method, giving a partition as result (training partition). Then, the nearest centroid technique is used to build a classifier from the training partition. The centroid technique calculates the proximity between the elements in the test set and the centroids of each cluster in the training partition (the proximity must be measured with the same proximity index used by the clustering method evaluated).

A new partition (test partition) is then obtained by assigning each object in the test set to the cluster with nearest centroid. Next, the test partition is compared with the a priori partition (gold standard) by using an external index (this a priori partition contains only the objects of the test partition). At the end of the procedure, a sample with size k of the values for the external index is available.

The general idea of the k-fold cross-validation procedure is to observe how well data from an independent set is clustered, given the training results. If the results of a training set have a low agreement with the a priori classification, so should have the results of the respective test set. In conclusion, the objective of the procedure is to obtain k observations of the accuracy of the unsupervised methods with respect to the gold standard, all this with the use of independent test folds.

IV. Datasets

The three gene expression datasets used in this work are the Leukemia, Novartis multi-tissue, and St. Jude Leukemia datasets exactly as presented in [3]. For example, to make sure that the known phenotype for a given data set is the dominant signature in the data, the authors [3] projected the dataset on the space of gene makers for that phenotype. This is needed, since the given phenotype's information (i.e., its number of classes and its label assignments) is used as the gold standard against which to test the clustering.

- Leukemia [15]: bone marrow samples obtained from acute leukemia patients at the time of diagnosis - 11 acute myeloid leukemia (AML) samples; 8 T-lineage acute lymphoblastic leukemia (ALL) samples; and 19 B-lineage ALL samples.
- Novartis multi-tissue [3]: tissue samples from four distinct cancer types - 16 breast, 26 prostate, 28 lung, and 23 colon samples.
- St. Jude leukemia [16]: diagnostic bone marrow samples from pediatric acute leukemia patients corresponding to 6 prognostically important leukemia subtypes - 43 T-lineage ALL; 27 E2A-PBX1; 15 BCR-ABL; 79 TEL-AML1 and 20 MLL rearrangements; and 64 "hyperdiploid > 50" chromosomes.

In the work in [3], a simple signal-to-noise ration was used to rank the genes of each dataset. Final gene pool is obtained by selecting the most up-regulated genes for each class, where the exact number depends on the data set (Table I).

TABLE I
Description of the dataset.

Dataset	Classes	Samples	Features
Leukemia	3	38	999
Novartis multi-tissues	4	103	1000
St. Jude leukemia	6	248	985

Additionally to the pre-processing steps applied by [3], we scaled the expression levels to the interval between 0 and 1 (in terms of clustering techniques, [23] found that this type of standardization more effective than z-score transformations).

V. Experiments

The experiments were accomplished by presenting the three datasets (Leukemia, Norvatis multi-tissue, and St. Jude Leukemia) to the individual clustering methods: k-means, EM algorithm, and the average linkage hierarchical method (all of them implemented with the Euclidian distance). Initially, a five replication of the 2-fold cross-validation of each dataset was applied such that 10 samples of each dataset was formed.

In terms parameters settings, the number of cluster for the k-means and the EM algorithm was set to the number of class in dataset being considered. Furthermore, as these algorithms are dependent on the choice of the initial conditions (e.g., initial centers and means), for them we repeated each run 10 times, each one with a distinct random initialization. For example, for each one of the 10 cross-validation samples of each dataset, the experiment with k-means (or the EM algorithm) yielded 10 partitions.

Since the average linkage hierarchical method is deterministic, only 10 runs of this algorithm was executed, that is, one run for each cross-validation sample of the dataset. Furthermore, as the external index used in this work is suitable only for partition comparison, in order to build the partition from the hierarchical methods, the trees were run from root to the leaves, then the n first sub-trees were taken as the clusters (with n equal to the number of class in the dataset being considered).

The Cluster Ensemble Toolbox for Matlab was used to run the experiments with the ensemble technique in [13] (Cluster Ensemble Toolbox available at: http://www.lans.ece.utexas.edu/~strehl/soft.html). The ensembles were formed as follows. First, for the k-means (EM algorithm) we created 10 ensemble, where each ensemble was formed by combining the 10 runs of the k-means (EM algorithm) for a given cross-validation partition (10 samples in total - 2x5 cross-validation). That is, we formed homogeneous ensembles in that the partitions used to form the consensus come from the same type of algorithm.

Then, in order to investigate the diversity in forming the ensembles we combine partitions produced by the clustering algorithms. But before doing so, for the k-means experiment (EM algorithm experiment), from the 10 partitions generated by the repeated random restarts, we choose only one for further analysis: the one with the lowest Davies-Boldin (DB) index.

The DB index is a function of the ratio of the distance within clusters (internal dispersion) and the distance between clusters [2]. A good partition of the dataset is indicated by low values of the DB index. In summary, at the end of an experiment with the k-means (or EM algorithm), for a given dataset, we have only one partition for each cross-validation sample (that is, 10 partitions in total).

In these context, the ensemble were formed according to the cross-validation samples for each dataset, that is, we built 10 different ensembles. More specifically, the inputs for building a given ensemble (e.g., for a given cross-validation sample for a certain dataset) were the multiple clustering label vectors, where each vector represented the resulting partition of given individual technique.

Finally, for all the experiments, the mean values of the corrected Rand index (CR) for the test folds were measured. Next, the mean of CR obtained with the individual methods were compared two by two to those obtained with the ensembles. This was accomplished by means of a paired t-test, as described in [24].

VI. Results

Before starting the investigation of the performance of the cluster ensemble systems, we analyze the performance of the individual clustering methods. Tables II, III and IV illustrate the mean of the CR for the test sets (and the standard deviation) for, respectively, the Leukemia, Novartis multi-tissues and St. Jude leukemia datasets.

According to Table II, although the k-means obtained the highest accuracy (0.40), there is no statistical evidence to state that the accuracy obtained by this method and the one achieved by the EM algorithm (0.36) are significantly different at $\alpha = 0.05$, where α stands for the significance level of the equal means hypothesis test. Nevertheless, such methods achieved a significant higher accuracy than the average linkage hierarchical method ($\alpha = 0.05$).

TABLE II
INDIVIDUAL METHODS - LEUKEMIA

Algorithm	Mean of CR	St. Dev.
k-means	0.40	0.29
EM	0.36	0.28
Hier.	0.14	0.11

For the Novartis multi-tissues dataset (Table III), the EM algorithm obtained the highest accuracy (0.81), however there is no statistical evidence to state that the accuracy obtained by such a method and the one by the average linkage hierarchical method (0.78) are significantly different at $\alpha = 0.05$. Nevertheless, such methods achieved a significant higher accuracy than the k-means ($\alpha = 0.05$).

TABLE III
INDIVIDUAL METHODS - NOVARTIS

Algorithm	Mean of CR	St. Dev.
k-means	0.75	0.18
EM	0.81	0.18
Hier.	0.78	0.14

Table IV illustrates the results for the St. Jude dataset. Here, as in the case for the Leukemia dataset, although the k-means obtained the highest accuracy (0.81), there is no statistical evidence to state that the accuracy obtained by such a method and the one by the EM algorithm (0.79) are significantly different at $\alpha = 0.05$. Nevertheless, such methods achieved a significant higher accuracy than the average linkage hierarchical method ($\alpha = 0.05$).

TABLE IV
INDIVIDUAL METHODS - ST. JUDE

Algorithm	Mean of CR	St. Dev.
k-means	0.81	0.12
EM	0.79	0.10
Hier.	0.50	0.03

Now, we turn our attention to the evaluate the performance of cluster ensemble methods against the individual methods. Tables V, VI and VII illustrate the mean of the CR for the test sets (and the standard deviation) for, respectively, the Leukemia, Novartis multi-tissue and St. Jude leukemia datasets.

According to Table V, the ensemble generated only from k-means partitions (homogeneous ensemble) obtained the highest accuracy (0.60) when compared to the results achieved with the individual methods shown in Table II ($\alpha = 0.05$). For example, the individual k-means obtained a mean CR of only 0.40 (Table II). The other homogeneous ensemble, that is, one formed by partitions from the EM algorithm presented a significant higher accuracy only when compared to the individual average linkage hierarchical method (Table II), which had a poor performance for this dataset ($\alpha = 0.05$). With respect to the heterogeneous ensemble (generated from partitions of the k-means, EM algorithm and average linkage hierarchical method), it had a significant higher accuracy when compared to the EM algorithm and the average linkage hierarchical method ($\alpha = 0.05$). However, at $\alpha = 0.05$, there is no statistical evidence to state that its performance is different from that of the k-means.

TABLE V

CLUSTER ENSEMBLE - LEUKEMIA

Algorithm	Mean of CR	St. Dev.
Ensemble k-means	0.60	0.25
Ensemble EM	0.48	0.31
Ensemble Het.	0.54	0.41

As Table VI illustrates all the ensemble generated for this dataset, either homogeneous or heterogeneous ensembles, obtained the same accuracy (0.96). When compared to the results achieved with the individual methods shown in Table III, all the ensembles had a significant higher accuracy ($\alpha = 0.05$). In the case of this dataset, the ensemble obtained mean CR on average 0.18 larger than ones obtained for the individual methods.

TABLE VI

CLUSTER ENSEMBLE - NOVARTIS

Algorithm	Mean of CR	St. Dev.
Ensemble k-means	0.96	0.02
Ensemble EM	0.96	0.02
Ensemble Het.	0.96	0.02

Results presented in Table VII below show that the homogeneous ensembles, either with k-means or with EM algorithm, obtained higher accuracy results than those obtained by the average linkage hierarchical method ($\alpha = 0.05$). However, at $\alpha = 0.05$, there is no statistical evidence to state that its performance is different from that of the k-means and EM algorithm. The heterogeneous ensemble performed poorly for this data set - its accuracy was equal to the average linkage hierarchical method (0.50), which obtained the worst performance for this dataset. As a whole, for this dataset the use of ensemble techniques did not represent a significant improvement, as compared to the two other datasets.

TABLE VII

CLUSTER ENSEMBLE - ST. JUDE

Algorithm	Mean of CR	St. Dev.
Ensemble k-means	0.82	0.06
Ensemble EM	0.83	0.08
Ensemble Het.	0.5	0.03

VII. CONCLUSIONS

In this paper, we discussed cluster ensemble and conducted a series of experiments on real-world datasets, analyzing some strategies for generating and integrating the ensembles. We have shown that the ensemble techniques used often offered considerable potential to improve the accuracy, when compared to those achieved by the individual clustering methods. Our results have also shown, at least for the methods and the datasets used, that there was no significant performance gain by combining partitions produced by different clustering algorithms, compared to the strategy of combining several runs of each of clustering algorithm. However, this issue should be further investigated.

ACKNOWLEDGMENT

The authors would like to thank the financial support of CNPq/FAPERN via grant 350200/2004-1.

REFERENCES

[1] I. H. Witten and E. Frank, *Data mining: practical machine learning tools and techniques with Java implementation.* USA: Morgan Kaufman Publishers, 2000.
[2] A. K. Jain and R. C. Dubes, *Algorithms for clustering data.* Prentice Hall, 1988.
[3] S. Monti, P. Tamayo, J. Mesirov, and T. Golub, "Consensus clustering: a resampling-based method for class discovery and visualization of gene expression microarray data," *Machine Learning*, vol. 52, pp. 91–118, 2003.
[4] J. Quackenbush, "Computational analysis of cDNA microarray data," *Nature Reviews*, vol. 6, no. 2, pp. 418–428, 2001.
[5] D. Slonim, "From patterns to pathways: gene expression data analysis comes of age," *Nature Genetics*, vol. 32, pp. 502–508, 2002.
[6] L. Breiman, "Bagging predictors," *Machine Learning*, vol. 24, no. 2, pp. 123–140, 1996.
[7] T. G. Dietterich, "Ensemble methods in machine learning." in *Multiple Classifier Systems*, ser. Lecture Notes in Computer Science, vol. 1857, 2000, pp. 1–15.
[8] E. Dimitriadou, A. Weingessel, and K. Hornik, "A cluster ensembles framework." in *Third International Conference on Hybrid Intelligent Systems (HIS)*, 2003, pp. 528–534.
[9] S. Dudoit and J. Fridlyand, "Bagging to improve the accuracy of a clustering procedure," *Bioinformatics*, vol. 19, no. 9, pp. 1090–1099, 2003.
[10] D. S. Frossyniotis, M. Pertselakis, and A. Stafylopatis, "A multi-clustering fusion algorithm." in *Second Hellenic Conference on AI, SETN 2002*, ser. Lecture Notes in Computer Science, 2002, pp. 225–236.
[11] D. Greene, A. Tsymbal, N. Bolshakova, and P. Cunningham, "Ensemble clustering in medical diagnostics." in *17th IEEE Symposium on Computer-Based Medical Systems (CBMS2004)*, 2004, pp. 576–581.
[12] X. Hu and I. Yoo, "Cluster ensemble and its applications in gene expression analysis," in *Second Asia-Pacific Bioinformatics Conference (APBC 2004)*, 2004, pp. 297–302.
[13] A. Strehl and J. Ghosh, "Cluster ensembles – a knowledge reuse framework for combining multiple partitions," *Journal on Machine Learning Research (JMLR)*, vol. 3, pp. 583–617, 2002.

[14] Y. Zeng, J. Tang, J. Garcia-Frias, and G. R. Gao, "An adaptive meta-clustering approach: Combining the information from different clustering results." in *1st IEEE Computer Society Bioinformatics Conference (CSB 2002)*, 2002, pp. 276–287.

[15] T. Golub, D. Slonim, P. Tamayo, C. Huard, M. Gaasenbeek, J. Mesirov, H. Coller, M. Loh, J. Downing, M. Caliguiri, C. Bloomfield, and E. Lander, "Molecular classification of cancer: class discovery and class prediction by gene expression monitoring," *Science*, vol. 5439, no. 286, pp. 531–537, 1999.

[16] E. J. Y. et al., "Classification, subtype discovery, and prediction of outcome in pediatric acute lymphoblastic leukemia by gene expression profiling," *Cancer Cell.*, vol. 1, no. 2, pp. 133–143, 2002.

[17] A. P. Topchy, A. K. Jain, and W. F. Punch, "Combining multiple weak clusterings." in *Proceedings of the 3rd IEEE International Conference on Data Mining (ICDM 2003)*, 2003, pp. 331–338.

[18] A. L. N. Fred and A. K. Jain, "Data clustering using evidence accumulation." in *16th International Conference on Pattern Recognition*, 2002, pp. 276–280.

[19] R. Dubes, "How many clusters are best? An experiment," *Pattern Recognition*, vol. 20, no. 6, pp. 645–663, 1987.

[20] G. W. Milligan and M. C. Cooper, "A study of the comparability of external criteria for hierarchical cluster analysis," *Multivariate Behavorial Research*, vol. 21, pp. 441–458, 1986.

[21] T. Mitchell, *Machine Learning*. New York: McGraw Hill, 1997.

[22] I. G. Costa, F. A. T. de Carvalho, and M. C. P. de Souto, "Comparative study on proximity indices for cluster analysis of gene expression time series," *Journal of Inteligent and Fuzzy Systems*, pp. 133–142, 2003.

[23] G. W. Milligan and M. C. Cooper, "A study of standardization of variables in cluster analysis," *Journal of Classification*, vol. 5, pp. 181–204, 1988.

[24] T. G. Dietterich, "Approximate statistical test for comparing supervised classification learning algorithms," *Neural Computation*, vol. 10, no. 7, pp. 1895–1923, 1998.

Characterizing Human Gene Splice Sites Using Evolved Regular Expressions[+]

Jing-Jing Li[1], De-Shuang Huang[2*], Robert M. MacCallum[3] and Xiao-Run Wu[4]

[1,2,4]Intelligent Computation Lab, Institute of Intelligent Machines, Chinese Academy of Sciences, P.O.Box 1130, 230031 Hefei, Anhui, China; [3]Stockholm Bioinformatics Center, Stockholm University, 106 91 Stockholm, Sweden

Email: [1]jjli@iim.ac.cn; [2]dshuang@iim.ac.cn; [3]maccallr@sbc.su.se; [4]xrwu@iim.ac.cn

Abstract - In this paper, an algorithm using evolved regular expressions to characterize and predict human gene splice sites without any prior knowledge is described. In contrast to previous pattern-based approaches to the splice site detection problem, the patterns to be matched are unknown in advance and are discovered using a supervised learning approach. We have used a genetic programming based system, PerlGP, to evolve regular expressions and proper length windows for a long sequence in which the evolved regular expressions can effectively characterize and predict the splice junctions. Since the gene splicing process is too complex to be fully understood currently, and the widely accepted consensus sequences only reflect some partial statistical information around splice sites, not to mention defining a splice site. However, our evolved regular expressions may shed new light on the underlying rules that define splice sites. Experimental results demonstrate that using the evolved regular expressions, splice junctions could be accurately characterized, furthermore, these evolved regular expressions could also be employed as a predictor to detect whether a GT/AG containing sequence is a splice site or not. Our experimental results also exhibit that the performance of this approach for predicting human gene splice junctions is competitive compared with some other traditional methods.

I. INTRODUCTION

Modern molecular biology is being revolutionized by the development of new technology. With the complete sequencing of several model organisms, a pressing problem is how to describe and understand the huge amount of the biological data which is accumulating. Fortunately, the marriage of biology and computer science makes the analysis of genomic data much more tractable. To annotate genomes automatically, splice site identification is of vital importance, because it is an essential step for gene prediction. As the central dogma [1] says: "DNA makes RNA makes Protein", when most genes of eukaryotic organisms are translated into proteins, intervening sequences known as introns are removed from the pre-mRNA in the nucleus before the matured mRNA is transported into the cytoplasm and translated. The regions of genes that are ultimately translated into proteins are often referred to as exons, and a splice site is just the boundary of an intron and an exon. Fig.1 presents a visual description of splice junctions in the gene structure. Hence, if we could identify splice sites accurately, a specific gene structure will become much clearer. In this sense, a good method for characterizing and predicting splice junctions would surely improve automatic genome annotation.

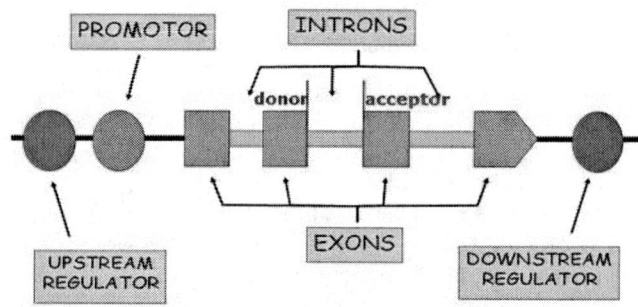

Fig. 1. A visual description of splice junctions in the gene structure

The problem of splice site identification can be stated as follows. When given a set of sequences, which contain GT (for the donor sites) or AG (for the acceptor sites) dinucleotides in these sequences, how can one distinguish authentic sites from the non-sites (where GT or AG occur for some other reasons) both accurately and efficiently? Here, we shall limit our discussion to the canonical sites as we mentioned above because the non-canonical sites, such as AC/AT pair and GC/AG pair in human genes, only account for about 3.45% of all in GenBank [2]. In particular, since the mechanism of pre-mRNA splicing is a complex procedure involving numerous protein and RNA components, the detailed characterization of splice sites and the splicing mechanism by "wet" experiments is major undertaking, which may not produce results for some years. Considering the neighborhood adjacent to the GT/AG dinucleotide to be a highly conserved region in a splice site, a number of methods have been proposed to

---

[+] This work was supported by the National Natural Science Foundation of China (Nos.60472111 and 60405002) and Chinese Human Liver Proteome Project (No.2004BA711A21).
* To whom correspondence should be addressed.

describe and predict splice sites.

A widely accepted method to represent the highly conserved regions both in DNA and protein sequences is the concept of the consensus sequence. The so-called consensus sequence is a symbolic sequence representing the most common features of a specific region, such as TATA box for promoter regions [1], AGGTRAGT for 5'-splice site (donor sites) and YYTTYYYYYYNCAGG for 3'-splice site (acceptor sites) in vertebrates [2]. A consensus sequence is usually derived from a positional weight matrix (PWM) [3], which stores the frequencies of A, T, C, G occurring at every position along a sequence. Using the PWM, a base with the highest frequency appearing at an individual position is selected as a representative at this position. Although consensus sequences can characterize some properties of interested sequences, for example, from the consensus sequence of the 3'-splice site (acceptor sites), a conserved polypyrimidine tract before the AG dinucleotide could be easily identified, this description is not precise enough and cannot reflect some subtle changes in the sequences; moreover, an underlying assumption of consensus sequence is that every base in a sequence is statistically independent, which is not necessarily true at most cases, so a consensus sequence can just be used to show some partial information about a splice site and it cannot be employed as a predictor immediately.

When it comes to splice site prediction, typically, a prediction process is a two-pass procedure: firstly features of a splice sites should be extracted and then predictions are made using those features. Although splice sites prediction approaches [4][5][6][7][8][9] have achieved success at a certain level, there still exists a big gap between the mathematical and biological explanation of splice junctions. Genesplicer [10], a newly developed technique, which incorporates Markov modeling techniques and maximal dependence decomposition method (MDD) [9] into a single systematic prediction procedure, was reported to achieve better accuracy compared to other predictors. However, does this algorithm essentially reveal the true, or nearly true, mechanism of splicing procedure in eukaryotic organisms? Undoubtedly, the statistical differences indeed exist around splice junctions and using these features will surely lead to a surge in prediction accuracy, however it cannot, to the best of our knowledge, give a graceful biological explanation with respect to the splicing procedure. Contrarily, we strongly believe that there should be one or more subtle patterns around a splice site so that proteins (or protein complexes) could easily identify them, bind them, and then trigger the splicing procedure.

This paper presents our first attempt to address this problem, diminish the gap between computational approaches and biological explanations and discover the subtle patterns defining splice sites. Our experiments also show that the proposed method is both flexible to design and simple to implement. Generally speaking, the key idea of discovering such underlying patterns in a long sequence is to use string matching approaches, however, our problem is just opposite to the traditional ones [7] because the patterns to be matched are not known in advance. To represent various sequence patterns, regular expressions (*aka*, *REs*,or *regexes*) are exploited which are used by many Unix programs, such as *grep*, *sed* and *awk*. A regular expression is a way of describing a set of strings without having to list all the possible strings in one's set. All of our experiments are based on Perl programming language [11] since regular expressions are much more flexible and powerful in Perl than, in most, other programming languages. To generate and evolve the regular expressions automatically, the genetic programming [12] approach is used. The combination of genetic programming and regular expressions was successfully applied to predict protein nuclear localization [13]. However, in our problem, the regular expressions and the window size of a sequence are evolved simultaneously so that some novel patterns could be easily discovered. Just based on those patterns, prediction can also be made with a relatively high accuracy.

This remainder of this paper is organized as follows. Section 2 gives an overall introduction of our algorithm. In Section 3, the experimental results are demonstrated to evaluate our approach. Finally, some conclusive remarks and future research works are included in Section 4.

II. METHODS

2.1 Data collection

The accuracy of splice site identification often suffers from relatively insufficient data for both training and testing. Although quite a few databases have been constructed to provide standard data for further research, some passive factors such as typos, annotation errors tend to influence the performance of a predictor.

The data we used were taken from HS3D [14] (Homo Sapiens Splice Sites Dataset), which contains sequence data of *Homo Sapiens* introns, exons, and splice regions and was collected from GenBank *Rel.*123, aiming at offering standardized material to train and assess the prediction accuracy for computational approaches. Originally, 3799 authentic donor sites and 3799 acceptor sites were extracted; after filtering sequences that including non-canonical sites, redundant data, and other abnormal data, there were totally 2,769 donor sites and 2,858 acceptor sites we finally made use of. Apart from true sites, 271,937 pseudo donor sites and 329,374 false acceptor sites are also available in this dataset. For each site, true or false, a window of 140 nucleotides around GT/AG dinucleotide was extracted. The reasons why we chose this dataset are that HS3D provides us high quality data and sufficient information we can exploit, and the window of 140 bases is appropriate for different algorithms, and is long enough to cover most local information defining a splice site. Considering the number of negative samples is roughly as 100 times as that of positive samples, it seems unwise to use all these false ones. In our experiment, for donor sites, we randomly extracted 1973 positive samples, 1999 negative samples to form a training set and the rest 796 true sites and 1000 negative pseudo sites were also arbitrarily selected for testing. Similarly, for acceptor sites, totally 3978 samples (containing 1978 positive and 2000 negative samples) were collected for training and 1880 samples (including the rest 880 positive samples and other 1000 negative samples) were used for testing according to the randomized procedure we mentioned above.

2.2 An overview of our approach

Essentially, the problem of characterizing gene splice junctions is just an inverse problem of the standard string matching. Assuming we already know what the patterns look like that ultimately define splice sites, to distinguish the authentic sites from the pseudo ones, a simple string matching method could be used. In other words, the true sites should contain these patterns while the false sites should not. In our problem, however, we want to discover the patterns which the true sites always contain but which are lacking in the false sites. This will be done with the reference only to sequence data labeled by HS3D as containing true or false sites, in a standard supervised approach.

Another problem in most splice site prediction algorithms is the dilemma of selecting a proper window size containing GT/AG dinucleotide in a long sequence. If long windows are used, much noise would be introduced so that some interested patterns might be inundated while if short windows are selected, useful information outside the windows would probably be lost.

To address those problems, considering the search space is too large if direct search approaches are actually employed, we herein adopt the genetic programming approach to produce numerous individual Perl programs in each population mainly composed of string matching instructions using automatically generated regular expressions. Meanwhile, windows with different sizes are produced simultaneously.

The aim of our approach is to let those regular expressions and the length of different windows be evolved under a pre-specified fitness function so that the evolved regular expressions within an optimal window of a long sequence could best characterize splice sites and yield a decision rule for the splice site prediction.

2.3 Implementation

2.3.1 Fitness function

The fitness function plays a central role in genetic programming as in other evolutionary algorithms. In our experiment, Matthews Correlation Coefficient (MCC) [15] is used as a fitness, because it is the measure taking into account a possible difference in the sizes of the positive and negative datasets.

MCC can be written as follows:

$$MCC = \frac{tp \cdot tn - fp \cdot fn}{\sqrt{(tp+fp)(tn+fn)(tp+fn)(tn+fp)}} \quad (1)$$

where tp, tn, fp and fn denote true positives, true negatives, false positives and false negatives respectively.

Based on this fitness, it is obvious that the higher the MCC is, the better performance of our algorithm could achieve.

2.3.2 Parameter selection

We have modified PerlGP [16] which is purely developed in Perl to implement our genetic programming because the regular expressions we actually used are also based on Perl language. PerlGP is a strongly typed, grammar driven and tree-based system [17], which is suitable for producing mixed expressions (regular expressions combined with arithmetic) of any size and shape.

In our experiment, a population of each generation is composed of 2000 individuals which may migrate occasionally from one population to another. The maximum depth of a program tree is limited to 20 in the initial random population; A tournament strategy is used, and the system is kept running until satisfying results are obtained. For each tournament, 50 individuals are selected, and the fittest 20 individuals are permitted to reproduce with each other, and replace the least fit 20 individuals. Individuals that have taken part in more than 4 tournaments are assigned zero fitness. During a run, two genetic operators, crossover and mutation, are used with some variable probabilities. In the training phase, because of the limitation of our training samples, a resampling technique is employed, and we set the fraction of resampling equal to 0.25, which means only 1/4 of the training samples is randomly selected at each time. The resampling is performed once every 1000 tournaments. Other parameters follow the default settings of PerlGP.

2.3.3 Implementation of genetic programming

Our goal is to evolve programs which are mainly composed of functions used to extract substrings of a long sequence and to perform string matching operations on them using regular expressions in order to characterize splice sites. We let the system automatically generate a number of regular expressions within different stretches of a sequence according to a pre-designed *grammar* which specifies the structure of all evolved code belonging to the individuals of population. Then after some simple arithmetic computations, each individual is expected to yield an output, which is set to be 1 if the output is greater than 0, and 0 if less than 0.

Since PerlGP is a tree-based system the terminal set and the function set of the trees should be pre-defined. In our experiment, the terminal set includes each sequence in our data set, integers from 0 to 9 and real numbers from 0 to 1; as for the function set, some algebraic operators: +, -, ×, ÷, abs, log, substring extracting and string matching functions are included. Note here that, we use the traditional division and logarithm operators instead of the protected division and logarithm computations following the suggestions of Keijzer [18] so that any illegal computation would make the individual be reinitialized. The string matching functions are mainly composed of evolved regular expressions; they first match a stretch of a DNA sequence from our dataset then return the number of matches which is finally fed into evolved arithmetic expressions. The evolved program code belonging to each individual is simply generated from the tree-like genotype and then executed with Perl's `eval()` function. In the use of Perl's regular expression, nesting, quantifiers, and character classes are included.

To clarify the approach, an example of an individual from a population is presented as follows:

```
sub sequence_classifier {
  my @s = @_;
  push @s, safesubstr($s[(3) % @s],74,67);
  push @s, safesubstr($s[(5+5+0+5+1)
%@s],91.7,270.3);
  my @t;

  return((abs(scalar(@t=$s[(3+4)%@s]=~/([T]){2,4}/
go))/6*(scalar(@t=$s[(0+4)%@s]=~/[TA]/go)*0.4715)
)-scalar(@t=$$s[(1+3)%@s]=~/[C](((([A][^G]){1,1}|
([T]|[T])[T])|[C]((([A][^T]){1,1}|([T]|(([T]|[TA]
)){4,}([CC]){5,}[T]))|[T][G])[C])|[C])/go))
}
```

This individual (Perl code) first extracts substrings from a 140bp long sequence into the array `@s`, and then use regular expressions to match patterns in those substrings. Here, `@s` is an array storing our initial 140bp long sequences and its substrings; `safesubstr( )` is a predefined subroutine extracting a substring from an element of `@s`, the expression "scalar(@t=$s[(0+4)%@s]=~/[TA]/go)" actually returns the number of times [TA] matches in substring $s[1] (the (0+4)%@s provides safe indexing of the substring array). If the final return value of an individual is greater than 0, we set it to be 1 and the corresponding sequence is regarded as a true splice site.

III. EXPERIMENTAL RESULTS

To reduce the possibility that genetic programming would be trapped in some local minima, 20 parallel runs both for donor sites and acceptor sites training were performed on our data with the same algorithm in 48 hours.

The following figure shows the dynamic change of the mean training fitness, testing fitness, and the standard errors in the 20 parallel runs for donor sites (the corresponding figure for acceptor sites is not shown here because of the space limitation).

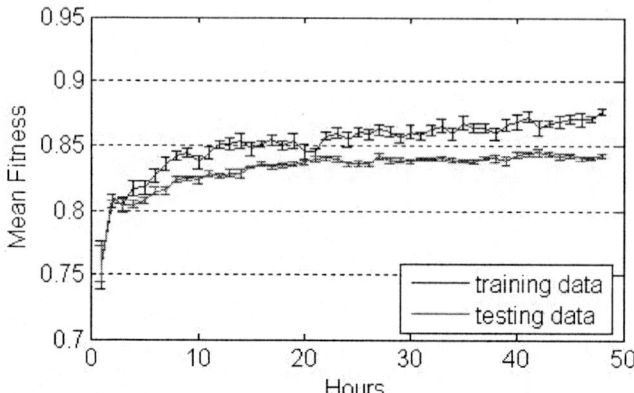

Fig.2. The mean fitness on donor sites in each training hour is calculated over the 20 independent runs and the standard errors are also shown in this figure.

Based on all the 20 parallel runs, the individual with the best performance was selected as the final representation approach for human gene splice sites. Fig.3 presents the dynamic change of the fitness of the individual we finally selected for donor sites (The figure for acceptor sites is not shown here).

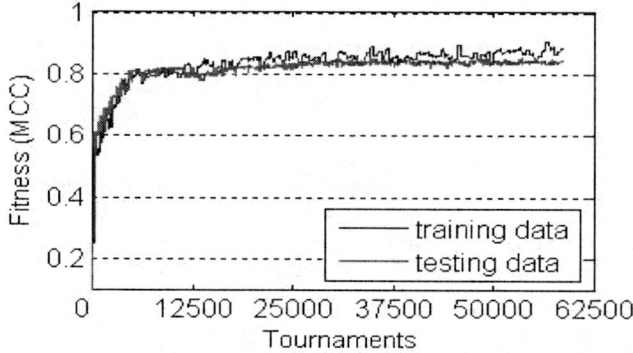

Fig.3 the dynamic change of fitness of the population containing the individual we finally selected on training and testing samples for donor sites.

To evaluate the effectiveness of this method, the individual (actually it is just several lines of Perl code with simple algebraic operators, substring extracting functions and string match instructions) we mentioned above is used as a predictor to predict whether a sequence in testing set is a splice site or not. And several measures (accuracy, sensitivity, specificity and MCC) are calculated. To compare with other traditional splice site predictors, we trained the PWM (positional weight matrices) scoring algorithm [3] and the NN (neural networks) based algorithm [8] on our training data, and the same measures are also calculated on our testing data. All the results are listed in the following table.

	Accuracy		Sensitivity		Specificity		MCC	
	EI	IE	EI	IE	EI	IE	EI	IE
PWM	0.88	0.85	0.79	0.83	0.92	0.85	0.80	0.70
NN	0.93	0.88	0.92	0.88	0.92	0.86	0.86	0.75
ERE	0.92	0.86	0.89	0.81	0.94	0.92	0.85	0.73

Table 1. Comparisons for three approaches. In this table we denote donor sites as EI (Exon-Intron boundary), acceptor sites as IE (Intron-Exon boundary) and our algorithm, the evolved regular expression, as ERE. The neural networks we implemented both for donor and acceptor sites were composed of 140*4=560 nodes in input layer (because of the binary encoding scheme), 32 nodes in hidden layer and one node in output layer (1 for true and 0 for false), and the training strategy is the conjugate gradient back propagation.

From the above table, generally speaking, although the performance of our approach may be slightly worse than NN-based algorithm, specificity for both donor and acceptor sites of our approach is higher, so it is difficult to say which is better; further more, in the neural networks based system, every alphabetical sequence is encoded as a binary string, so with neural networks, the position of every nucleotide could be identified, therefore a shift of even one base in 5' or 3' direction would produce a completely new input. However, within our approach, small sequence shifts would not make an obvious difference, since just motif frequencies are actually measured, which are independent of nucleotide position. When compared with PWM-scoring method, obviously, the performance of our approach is much better, and the reason for this fact is partially because unlike the PWM-scoring method, whose underlying assumption is that every base in a sequence is statistically independent, our approach however might evolve expressions like "TT ([AC]..[TG] | [GT]..[AC])AC" so that the relationship between two positions in theory could be learnt.

Except for predicting splice sites, some patterns (both subtle and significant ones) could also be identified by our algorithm. Here, we only demonstrate the pattern discovering for donor sites as an example because of the space limitation. Obviously, some information could be obtained by just looking at the regular expressions in the finally selected individual if the regular expressions are simple enough. To highlight such patterns, the following trick is used: for every sequence in the training set, from 5' end to 3' end, each time a base (totally there are 140 bases in each sequence in our training and testing set) at the same position in all sequences is masked with a character which cannot be matched by the evolved regular expressions, then all the masked sequences are fed into the predictor. The fraction of positively classified sequences is determined for each masking position. The positive fraction should be affected most strongly at the positions where biological signals are located.

Similarly, we also analyzed the relationship between the weights and positions for the aforementioned NN-based algorithm in order to make a comparison using the following procedure: for each position in a sequence, the absolute values of corresponding weights are added after training the neural network; the summations of weights are negated and then normalized to [0, 1] so that, like the positive fraction defined above, small values indicate important sequence positions. Fig.5 shows the results of these analyses.

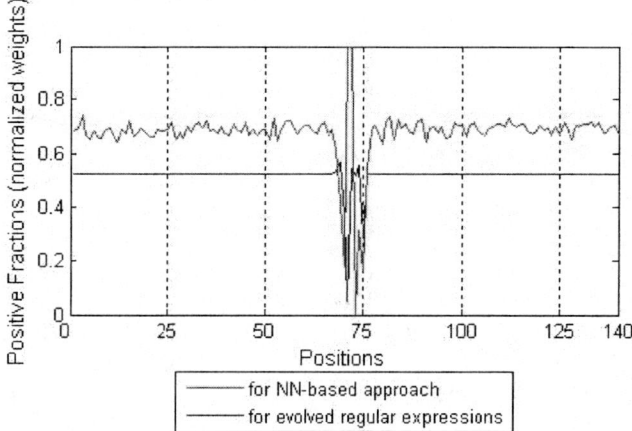

Fig.4 Positive fractions versus base positions for our algorithm (in blue lines) and the weights versus positions for NN-based approach (in red lines).

Interestingly, the positive fraction dramatically changes between the 68th and 75th position (for NN-based algorithm, the weighs fluctuate greatly in the region from 68th position to the 76th position), which means the bases in this region are strongly related to splice site definition. More interestingly, the region between the 68th and 75th position is exactly the one traditional consensus sequence describes: AGGTRAGT for donor sites [2]; hence, at this point, our approach can really reveal something interesting and the result of our method is completely consistent with our common sense. The lowest positive fractions occur at the 70th, 71st, and 75th position; obviously the two bases appearing at the 70th and 71st position are just the strongly conserved GT dinucleotide, and as for the 75th position (note that there is also a valley at the 75th position in the figure derived from the NN-based approach), a hypothesis could be proposed that the base occurring at the 75th position is crucial for defining a splice site. Also in this sensitive region (from the 68th to the 75th position), the positive fraction fluctuates slightly indicating some bases in this region might be related to splice site definition to some extent, which is worthy of being investigated in the future.

IV. CONCLUSIVE REMARKS

In this paper, we have presented a method for characterizing and predicting human gene splice junctions using evolved regular expressions. However, this approach is not confined to splice sites prediction, since no prior knowledge is required in our approach, it could also be extended to characterizing and predicting other functional regions both in genomic and proteomic data. The patterns our approach finally discovered may shed some light on the natural mechanism of gene splicing procedure. Generally speaking, the advantage of our algorithm could be summarized as follow: firstly unlike other algorithms[7] in which the significant statistical differences between true sites and false sites should be known in advance, within our method, no prior knowledge is required; secondly, unlike traditional pattern recognition methods which are typically a two pass procedure explicitly composed of feature extraction and classification process, in our approach however features are automatically extracted during training procedure, so a pattern recognition problem is just reduced to a string matching problem with some simple arithmetic computations; thirdly, using the evolved regular expressions, splice sites might be directly defined and some novel patterns near splice sites could also be discovered which remain to be further verified by biological experiments.

With evolved regular expressions, although some global information of a sequence containing splice sites could be employed, our algorithm actually only made use of the local information because we tend to believe that local information can be directly applied to recognize possible potential alternative splice sites in a particular gene while global information not.

For future study of gene splice site identification, more attention would be paid on seeking for biological explanation to the novel patterns currently discovered, so that we may understand gene splicing in more detail.

REFERENCES

[1] Robert H. Tamarin, *Principles of Genetics: From Genes to Genomes*, 7th Edition, McGraw-Hill Companies, Inc.,2002.
[2] Tao Jiang, Ying Xu, and Michael Q. Zhang, *Current Topics in Computational Molecular Biology*, Tsinghua University Press and The MIT Press, 2002.
[3] Staden,R, "The current status and portability of our sequence handling software.", *Nucleic Acids Research*,14, pp.217-231, 1986.
[4] Zhang,M.Q. and Marr,T.G, "A weight array method for splicing signal analysis.", *Computer applications in the biosciences*, 9, pp. 499-509, 1993.
[5] Guigo,R., Knudsen,S., Drake,N. and Smith,T, "Prediction of gene structure." *Journal of Molecular Biology*, 226, pp. 141-157, 1992
[6] Brendel,V., Kleffe,J., Carle-Urioste,J.C. and Walbot,V, "Prediction of splice sites in plant pre-mRNA from sequence properties.", *Journal of Molecular Biology*, 276, pp. 85-04, 1998.
[7] Solovyev, V. V., salamov, A. A., and Lawrence, C. B, "predicting intrenal exonsby olidonucleotide composition and discriminant analysis of splicable open reading frames.", *Nucleic Acids Research*, 22, pp.6156-5153, 1994.
[8] Brunak, S., Engelbrecht, J., and Knudsen, S. "prediction of human mRNA donor and acceptor sites from the DNA sequence", *Journal of Molecular Biology*, 220, pp. 49–65, 1991.
[9] Burge,C. and Karlin,S, "Prediction of complete gene structures in human genomic DNA.", *Journal of Molecular Biology*, 268, pp.78-94, 1997.
[10] Pertea,M.,Lin,X.Y. and Salzberg,S.L., "Genesplicer: a new computational method for splice site prediction.", *Nucleic Acids Research*,29,pp. 1185-1190, 2001.
[11] Larry Wall, Tom Christiansen and Randal L. Schwartz, *Programming Perl*, O'Reilly Press, 1996.
[12] John R. Koza, *on the programming of computers by means of natural selection*, Cambridge, MA: MIT Press, 1992.
[13] Amine Heddad, Markus Brameier and Robert M. MacCallum, "Evolving Regular Expression-based Sequence Classifiers for Protein Nuclear Localisation", *In Proceedings of the Second European Workshop on Evolutionary Bioinformatics (EvoBIO2004)*, LNCS 3005, pp 31--40, Springer, Berlin, 2004.
[14] P.Pollastro, S.Rampone, "HS3D: Homo Sapiens Splice Site Data Set." *Nucleic Acids Research*, 2003 Annual Database Issue, 2003.
[15] B.W. Mattews, "Comparison of the predicted and observed secondary structure of T4 phase lysozyme.",*Biochem. Biophys.Acta*, 405, pp.441-451, 1975.
[16] R. M. MacCallum, "Introducing a Perl Genetic Programming System: and Can Meta-evolution Solve the Bloat Problem?" *In Genetic Programming, Proceedings of Eurogp'2003*, vol. 2610 of LNCS, pp. 369-378, 2003.
[17] http://www.perlgp.org.
[18] Maarten Keijzer, "Improving Symbolic Regression with Interval Arithmetic and Linear Scaling", *Genetic Programming, Proceedings of EuroGP'2003*, vol.2610, pp. 71-83, 2003.

Prediction of Contact Map Integrated PNN with Conformational Energy

Peng Chen [1,2], De-Shuang Huang [1,†], Bing Wang [1,2], Yunping Zhu [3], and Yixue Li [4]

[1] Intelligent Computing Lab, Hefei Institute of Intelligent Machines, Chinese Academy of Sciences,
Hefei, Anhui, 230031, China
[2] Dept. of Automation, Univ. of Science and Technology of China, Hefei, Anhui, 230026, China
[3] Beijing Institute of Radiation Medicine, Taiping Road 27, Beijing 100850, China
[4] Bioinformatics Center, Shanghai Institutes for Biological Sciences, Chinese Academy of Sciences
320 Yue Yang Road, Shanghai, 200031, China
[†]The corresponding author; Email: dshuang@iim.ac.cn

Abstract— This paper presents a novel method to solve the protein's three-dimensional structure prediction problem. It is a machine learning approach by integrating probabilistic neural network (PNN) with conformational energy function (CEF) based on chemico-physical knowledge of amino acids. In this method, firstly, the principal components are extracted from selected protein structures with lower sequence identity, and an initial matrix of contact map is constructed by K-L expansion. Secondly, PNN is used for predicting the long-range interaction of amino acids in protein. In particular, this method uses the CEF and chemico-physical characteristics of amino acids to run the PNN predictor. Consequently, it was found that our proposed method is better than the existed methods, such as the hybrid method of HMMSTR and the correlated mutation analysis method. As a result, this method can accurately predict 31% of contacts at a distance cutoff of 8Å for proteins whose sequence length is up to 200.

I. INTRODUCTION

As bioinformatics has been achieving tremendous development since the end of last century, more and more primary sequences of proteins and peptides were being sequenced, but there always existed a colossal gap between primary sequences and three-dimensional (3D) structures for proteins. Generally, current approaches to solve this problem could be divided roughly into three categories, i.e., comparative modeling method [1], inverse folding or threading method [2] and *ab initio* folding method [3]. More or less, these methods had their own restriction on some aspects [4].

Because of the absence of efficient measure technologies and the slow development on exploring protein's spatial structures, there really need to find another efficient route to simulate and predict the 3D structures of proteins by computer.

It is well known that the contact map is the intermediate state from primary structure to tertiary structure, which may be advanced to the protein's tertiary structure prediction and protein folding. Usually, the non-local interactions are crucial for proteins to attain their native state [5]. Specifically, identifying pairs of non-sequential amino acid residues that interact in 3D space can provide a set of topological constraints that can be utilized in protein folding recognition.

In this method, firstly, the principal components are extracted from known protein structures with lower sequence identity, and an initial matrix of contact map is constructed by the principal component analysis (PCA) method. Secondly, the information about contact map is encoded and then applied to PNN. In particular, this method uses the conformational energy function combined with chemico-physical characteristics of amino acids to trim the output of PNN predictor.

The rest of this paper is organized as follows. Section II provides the background. Section III describes our approach for predicting contact maps. Section IV provides the detailed experimental results based on the PNN predictor integrated with conformational energy. Section V discusses some important observations based on the experiment results.

II. BACKGROUND

A. The Definition of Contact Map

In this paper a widely used definition on contact is defined. Assumed that the coordinates of C atom are chosen to represent the spatial position of each residue in protein. A contact matrix A for a protein with *num* residues is a *num*× *num* binary matrix whose element $A(i,j)=1$ if residue pairs are in contact, and $A(i,j)=0$ otherwise. Then we will have the following equation:

$$\begin{array}{ll} A(i,j) = 1, & if \quad d(i,j) < d \\ A(i,j) = 0, & if \quad d(i,j) >= d \end{array} \quad (1)$$

where $d(i,j)$ denotes the distance between the ith and jth residues, d denotes a threshold value (always $d=4$-$8Å$).

B. Principal Component Analysis (PCA) [6]

It has been showed that a matrix B, which is expanded by the parameters including several larger eigenvalues and their corresponding eigenvectors of a contact matrix A, can approximate A perfectly. The PCA can be used for reducing the dimensions of contact matrix and extracts the useful information from known proteins.

C. The Input-Encoding Schema for Probabilistic Neural Network (PNN) [6, 8]

In this paper, probabilistic neural networks are used to predict the contact map, which is guaranteed to converge to a Bayesian classifier providing it is given enough training data.

However, the input-encoding schema of PNN is thought to be a simplified, accelerated, and feasible means for the PNN predictor model. For predicting the contact map, a series of parameters are defined for performing this task that includes inter-residues, distances in protein sequence, and the spatial distances of inter-residues. Afterward, these useful parameters were integrated as the input vectors for PNN.

D. Conformational Energy Function (CEF)

The conformational energy [9] based on statistical estimation can be used to estimate the interaction energies of all residue pairs from the observed structures in Protein Database Bank.

Our efficient conformational energy ($\varepsilon_{i,j}$) can be defined as:

$$\varepsilon_{i,j} = -\ln\left(\sum_m \frac{1}{N_m} \frac{N_m N_{i,j}}{N_i N_j} + \frac{h_i + h_j}{2} p_{i,j}\right) \quad (2)$$

where N_m is the total number of residues in protein m, $N_{i,j}$ is the number of inter-residue contacts that can be gotten from the diagonal values of A^2, N_i and N_j are the numbers of residues of each type in each separate protein, h_i, h_j denote the values of hydrophobic measurements of amino acids, and the weight value $p_{i,j}$ is changed with different proteins.

III. Method

To predict the contact map, we use an integrated algorithm including PNN predictor and conformational energy function. Simultaneously, some chemico-physical characteristics are also included. Afterward, the detailed method is introduced below.

A. The Initial Contact Matrix

Our work starts from the initial matrix, and then the inclination of the contact distribution can be obtained. Efficient results are obtained by applying the helpful information to the PNN predictor. Firstly, the contact matrix A making use of PCA rule is defined to calculate the eigenvalue $\lambda_i, i = 0, 1, \cdots, n \ m-1$ and its corresponding eigenvector. From these eigenvalues, we can choose four largest ones and discard the remaining ones in general, as it can obtain clear separation area. The selected eigenvalues are shown in Table I.

TABLE I
THE SELECTED EIGENVALUES

λ_1	λ_2	λ_3	λ_4
11.404	10.406	9.786	9.211

where λ_m is the eigenvalue, v_i^m is the corresponding eigenvector, σ_m denotes the coefficient of eigenvalue λ_m that can be changed with the length of protein sequence, where σ_m is assigned to 1.

Now $p_{i,j}$ is defined as the contact probability of residues i and j:

$$p_{i,j} = \frac{1}{N} \sum_m \sigma_m \lambda_m (v_i^m (v_j^m)') \cos((i-j)/(i+j)) \quad (3)$$

B. Transfer Function of PNN Optimized by CEF

Integrating conformational energy with the entropy of the inter-residue contact probability, the PNN transfer function can be optimized. The likelihood goal function can be defined as follows:

$$Q(i,j) = -\sum_{n=1}^{num} p_{i,j} \log p_{i,j} + \lambda_{i,j}(\varepsilon_{i,j} - s_{i,j}) \quad (4)$$

where $p_{i,j}$ is derived from equation (3), $\lambda_{i,j}$ is the parameter of Lagrange, and $s_{i,j}$ is the constraint condition from equation (2). Minimizing this function with respect to $p_{i,j}$, the optimized contact probability can be achieved with running the PNN predictor over the all residues of training protein. The PNN predictor may stop for a given protein until the PNN obtain a satisfactory result. The conformational energy can also be integrated into the input-encoding schema of PNN to adjust the weight values of probabilistic neural networks.

IV. Experimental Results

Based on the methods described above, experimental results will be described in this section. A protein 1AX8 is selected for the tested sample from the Protein Database Bank.

A. Data Source

The data files used in this paper are chosen from PDB [7] bank. Table II shows the composition of the data files.

TABLE II
THE PROTEIN SELECTED FROM PDB

	Length of protein sequence				
	n<100	100<n<200	200<n<300	300<n<400	n>400
number	378	221	210	117	74

B. Initial Matrix and Contact Map

Using equation (3) with the training proteins based on the PCA rule, the initial contact map can be achieved for unknown structure protein 1AX8, where we choose 8Å as the threshold value of inter-residue contacts.

Aimed to an unknown protein 1AX8, the useful information about the length $N_{unknown}$ and the amino acids in this protein sequence is extracted for comparing with other training proteins. As described above, a contact matrix A may represent the contact map for a training protein. Based on the matrix A, a coordinate mapping can link the training proteins with unknown protein 1AX8. For a training protein has the sequence with length $N_{tr\ ining}$, a fitting method can be applied to map the $N_{tr\ ining} \times N_{tr\ ining}$ data to $N_{unknown} \times N_{unknown}$ data. As a simplified denotation, v_i^m is postulated as the eigenvector according to eigenvalue λ_i^m in training protein A^m. As a result, the vector v_i^m is fitted to a vector with length $N_{unknown}$ based on some fitting method. Moreover, the method of least squares is chosen to perform the task with fitting data between two proteins. Subsequently, a new matrix B can be constructed by vectors v_i^m and the corresponding fitting eigenvalues λ_i^m, $i = 1 \ldots N_{unknown}$, to represent the protein 1AX8.

$$B = \sum_{m=1}^{N} \sum_{i=1}^{N_{raining}} {}^m \lambda_i^m v_i^m \quad (5)$$

where N is the number of training proteins, ^{m} is the coefficient of eigenvalue λ_i^m.

In this paper, a least square fitting method is used to perform the task for the fitting data between two proteins satisfactorily. In this case, the goal is to compute the corresponding weight vector under a suitable optimality criterion. The fitting process requires a model that relates the response data to the predictor data with one or more coefficients. The result of the fitting process is an estimate of the "true" but unknown coefficients of the model. To obtain the coefficient estimates, the least squares method is used to minimize the summed square of residuals. The residual r^i for the ith data point of the eigenvectors, which is defined as the error associated with the *data* and its corresponding fitting value *fit*, denotes the difference between the observed response value y_i and the fitted response value $\widehat{y_i}$ as,

$$\begin{aligned} r^i &= y_i - \widehat{y_i} \\ r\ sid\ a\ &= data - fit \end{aligned} \quad (6)$$

Consequently, the summed square of residuals is given by

$$S = \sum_{i=1}^{n} r_i^2 = \sum_{i=1}^{n} (y_i - \widehat{y_i})^2 \quad (7)$$

where n is the number of data points, i.e., the length $N_{unknown}$ of amino acids of protein included in the fit, and S is the sum of squares error estimate.

Integrating equations (3) ~ (6), the predicted contact map based on the PCA and the least square fitting can be achieved, and the results are displayed in Fig. 1. There we postulate $a_{i,j} = 1$, where $a_{i,j}$ is the element of contact matrix for protein 1AX8, if $p_{i,j} >= 0.012$ by calculating equation (3), and $a_{i,j} = 0$ otherwise.

In fact, Fig. 1 describes the two contrasting sub-maps, one of which is the actual contact map (blue, lower triangle) and the other is the predicted contact map (red, upper triangle). The figure are also showed the changing tendencies of inter-residue contacts distinctly. In addition, this result also describes the contact area including main chain and non-local contact area where the inter-residue contact probability can be optimized to a maximum. So, it can be inferred that this PCA method is very useful for predicting the contact map with respect to a random predictor that produced initial contact map.

C. The Application of Hydrophobicity of Amino Acids to Inter-residue Contact

For a given protein 1AX8, the visualized result of Eisenberg hydrophobic profiles in protein sequence is shown in Fig. 2.

From equation (2), the effective conformational energy ${}_{i,j}$ can be calculated and then applied to predict the contact

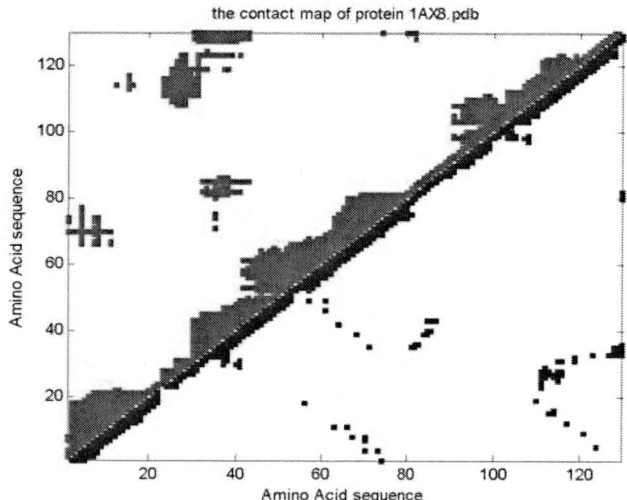

Fig. 1. The Initial Contact Map of Protein 1AX8 Based on PCA Method

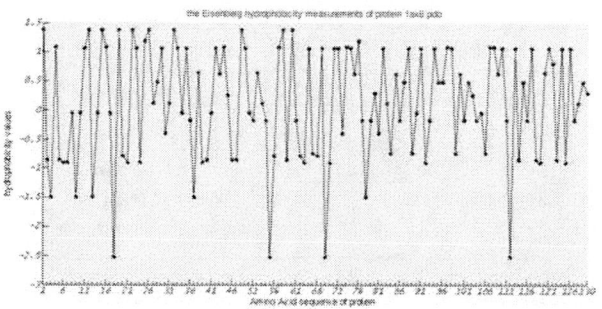

Fig. 2. The Eisenberg Hydrophobicity of Protein 1AX8

map. Making use of the conformational energy, the optimal prediction on contact map may be achieved more quickly.

In this work, the PNN predictor can adopt the complex association between the sequence and the structure of protein to get the connection weights of neural network. The outputs from PNN predictor are classified into two classes, i.e., contact or non-contact. Using a general transfer function for PNN predictor with the likelihood goal function equation (3), the contact map of unknown protein can be achieved conveniently. The experimental results are achieved in Fig. 3 as below.

As a result, Fig.3 describes the two contrasting sub-maps, one of which is the actual contact map (blue, lower triangle), and the other is the predicted contact map (red, upper triangle). The experimental results are obtained on the condition of the threshold value of contact inter-residue selected here is 8 Å.

V. DISCUSSIONS

Based on the above experiments, the accuracy and coverage in predicting contact map at several distance cutoff are shown in Table III and Table IV, respectively.

Note that the numbers of the parenthesis in Table III are the numbers of amino acids for the contact maps in the local or non-local area.

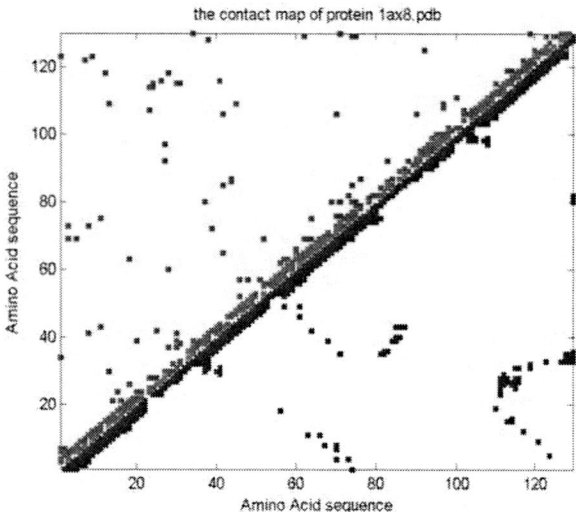

Fig. 3. The Prediction of Contact Map Based on PNN for Protein 1AX8

TABLE III
THE ACCURACY OF CONTACT PREDICTION FOR PROTEIN 1AX8

	5Å	8Å	10Å	12Å
Local	103(312)	350(1130)	651(2046)	1182(3350)
Non-local	50(153)	106(391)	598(1865)	933(2867)
Average	31.05%			
HMMSTR	26% (N<100)			

TABLE IV
THE COVERAGE OF CONTACT PREDICTION FOR PROTEIN 1AX8

	5Å	8Å	10Å	12Å
Local	124(312)	442(1130)	769(2046)	1476(3350)
Non-local	65(153)	134(391)	602(1865)	960(2867)
Average	36.2%			
HMMSTR	63% (N<100)			

From Table IV, it can be seen that the coverage contact maps of proteins only starting from the amino acids sequence with great extent. Moreover, the numbers of the parenthesis in Table IV are the numbers of amino acids for the contact maps in the local or non-local area.

From the above experimental results, the generalization capability of the PNN integrated with CEF predictor was compared with other methods [11]. The best performances described so far were obtained with a comparable hybrid method [10] of HMMSTR, which achieved the accuracy of 26% and the coverage of 63% for the protein length of $N < 100$, and the accuracy of 21.5% and the coverage of 10% for the protein length of $100 < N < 170$. Our proposed approach has gotten the accuracy of 31% and the coverage of 36.2% for the protein length of $100 < N < 200$. Obviously, our approach has achieved better accuracy performance based on primary sequence of unknown protein only.

However, the obtained results also depended on the input-encoding schema. In fact, there had a lot of efforts devoted to determine the most appropriate input-encoding schema. Generally, the long range interaction information of inter-residue is always associated with the parameter of distance in sequence and therefore the parameter of the distance in sequence is indispensable since the unknown protein has a number of amino acids in protein sequence. In addition, it is well known that the protein folding is performed based on the remote interaction. Afterwards, considering the environmental hydrophobicity, the conformational energy is used to reconstruct the input-encoding schema, and then the weights of neural networks are readjusted correspondingly. As a result, our approach proposed in this paper is a promising method for predicting the contact map.

ACKNOWLEDGMENT

This work was supported by the National Science Foundation of China (Nos.60472111 and 60405002) and Chinese Human Liver Proteome Project (No.2004BA711A21).

REFERENCES

[1] Sánchez, R. & Sali, A. Evaluation of comparative protein structure modeling by MODELLER -3. *Proteins* Suppl. 1, 50-58 (1997).
[2] Panchenko, A. R., Marchler-Bauer, A. & Bryant S. H. Combination of threading potentials and sequence profiles improves fold recognition. *J. Mol. Biol.* 2000; 296: 1319–1331.
[3] Simons, K. T., Strauss, C. & Baker, D. Prospects for *ab initio* protein structural genomics. *J. Mol. Biol.* 2001; 306: 1191–1199.
[4] Kihara, D., Lu, H., Kolinski, A. & Skolnick, J. An ab initio protein structure prediction method that uses threading-based tertiary restraints *Proc. Natl. Acad. Sci. USA* 98(18), 10125–10130.
[5] M. Niggemann and B. Steipe. Exploring local and non-local interactions for protein stability by structural motif engineering. *J. Mol. Biol.*, 296:181–195, 2000.
[6] D.S.Huang, Systematic Theory of Neural Networks for Pattern Recognition. Beijing: Publishing House of Electronic Industry of China, 1996.
[7] H.M. Berman, J. Westbrook, Z. Feng, G. Gilliland, T.N. Bhat, H. Weissig, I.N. Shindyalov, P.E. Bourne: The Protein Data Bank. Nucleic Acids Research, 28 pp. 235-242 (2000).
[8] Donald F.Specht. Probabilistic neural networks. Neural Nerworks 1990,Vol 3, Issue 1. p.109-118.
[9] Miyazawa S, Jernigan RL: An empirical energy potential with a reference state for protein folding and sequence recognition. Proteins 1999, 36:357-369.
[10] Zaki MJ, Shan J, Bystroff C. Mining residue contacts in proteins using local structure predictions. *IEEE Transactions on Systems, Man and Cybernetics* 2003; **33**: 789-801.
[11] Simons KT, Kooperberg C, Huang E, Baker D: Assembly of protein tertiary structures from fragments with similar local sequences using simulated annealing and Bayesian scoring functions, J. Mol. Biol, 1997, vol. 268,pp. 209–225.

Neural Network-Based Analysis of DNA Microarray Data

Jagdish Chandra Patra, Lei Wang, Ee Luang Ang, and Narendra S. Chaudhari
School of Computer Engineering, Nanyang Technological University, Singapore 639798
Email: {aspatra, 150353908, aselang, and asnarendra}@ntu.edu.sg

Abstract— The analysis of DNA microarray expression data has become an important subject in bioinformatics. Scientists have adopted different approaches to select the informative genes those can distinguish different types of cancers. In this paper, we show the use of a dimension reduction technique such as Singular Value Decomposition (SVD) to capture the genes with similar patterns. We propose a novel method of selection of feature genes based on information loss using SVD. To assign the samples to known classes, we design a Multi-Layer Perceptron- based classifier with reduced dimensional input vectors. We provide performance comparison between different selection methods in terms of classification rate.

I. INTRODUCTION

DNA microarray technology provides a wealth of large scale gene expression data. The first major computational task is to cluster genes into biologically meaningful clusters according to their expression patterns [1]. Clustering analysis plays an important role in analysis of gene expression profiles. Different methods have been proposed to analyse the expression data in many literatures. Generally, they can be divided into supervised learning scenarios and unsupervised class-discovery scenarios [2]. Many neural network approaches such as Self-Organizing map and Fuzzy ARTMAP have been used in the unsupervised class-discovery manner [3], [4].

A critical step in clustering analysis is the determination of a suitable distance or similarity measure. In this paper, we compare different distance and similarity measure approaches for effective gene clustering, and introduce a novel method that utilizes Singular Value Decomposition (SVD) technique.

A. Singular Value Decomposition (SVD)

SVD is a mathematical method to identify the pattern relationship in data, and expresses data in such a way to highlight their similarities and differences. Also, it is widely adopted to compress data by reducing the number of dimensions without much loss of information. It is also known as Principal Component Analysis in statistics. SVD provides a useful mathematical framework for processing and modeling genome-wide expression data, in which both the mathematical variables and operations may be assigned some biological meaning [5].

The main procedure of SVD is to work out the eigenvalues and eigenvectors of the covariance matrix of the entire sample-gene matrix. The eigenvalues, i.e. singular values, provide us with the variability of their respective eigenvectors; the larger the singular value is, the higher variability the respective eigenvector contains. Usually the first few eigenvectors with higher variability are selected as significant Principal Components (PCs) to compress the data into less number of dimensions [6]. Due to the discarding of the rest feature elements, we will lose some information when recovering the original data. Our proposed method exploits this information loss to extract the feature genes.

B. Data Set

Data set that we have used is from the report on molecular classification of cancer by Golub *et al*. [7]. The gene expression data set consists of 72 leukemia samples in total. These 72 patients have either acute lymphoblastic leukemia (ALL) or acute myeloid leukemia (AML), and each sample is composed of 7129 gene expressions.

From Golub *et al*. data set, we know that 38 samples were used for gene selection purpose. We define it as "training set", and it includes 27 ALL and 11 AML samples. The rest 34 samples which include 20 ALL and 14 AML samples are used for testing purpose. Thus, we have one 7129×38 training matrix and another 7129×34 testing matrix.

II. GENE SELECTION

For efficient classification of the samples, we need to find out the informative genes which can distinguish the two types of leukemia tumors. This can be done by distance measures, statistical methods, signal-to-noise ratio approach and our proposed information loss technique. These methods rank each of the genes, and we simply select the top 50 ranked genes as informative genes [8].

We consider each of the 7129 genes in the data set as a row vector which is expressed in a 38-dimensional sample space. Let us use g_i to represent the ith gene vector, where i=1, 2, …, 7129. We may express the gene vector g_i as

$$g_i = (e_{i1} \cdots e_{i27} \; e_{i28} \cdots e_{i38}), \qquad (1)$$

where e_{ij} is the expression level of ith gene for sample j (j = 1, 2, …, 38). Here, $\{e_{i1}, e_{i2}, \ldots, e_{i27}\}$ are the gene expression data belong to ALL group and $\{e_{i28}, e_{i29}, \ldots, e_{i38}\}$ belong to AML group.

A. Euclidean Distance

Since the Golub *et al.* data set contains integers varying from tens to thousands, the Euclidean Distance (ED) is calculated based on the normalized dispersion in expression level of each gene across the samples. The normalized expression level is obtained by subtracting the mean across the samples from expression levels of each gene, and dividing the result by corresponding standard deviation (SD) [9].

We need an ideal gene expression as a reference, so that we can calculate the distances between each of the 7129 gene vectors and this ideal gene vector. From equation (1) we know that the ideal gene should have different expression values on the samples in different groups and have the similar values on the samples in the same group. Based on this feature, we define the following ideal gene vectors

$$\text{Sample Number}$$
$$1\ 2\ \ldots\ 27\ 28\ \ldots\ 38$$
$$\mathbf{g}_{ideal\_ALL} = (1\ 1\ \ldots\ 1\ 0\ \ldots\ 0), \quad (2)$$
$$\mathbf{g}_{ideal\_AML} = (0\ 0\ \ldots\ 0\ 1\ \ldots\ 1). \quad (3)$$

The following formula calculates the ED values between each normalized $\mathbf{g}_i$ and the ideal genes as

$$ED(\mathbf{g}_i, \mathbf{g}_{ideal}) = \sqrt{\sum_{k=1}^{38}(e_{ik} - e_{ideal\,k})^2}, \quad (4)$$

where $\mathbf{g}_{ideal}$ indicates either $\mathbf{g}_{ideal\_ALL}$ or $\mathbf{g}_{ideal\_AML}$, e_{ik} and $e_{ideal\,k}$ represent the elements of vector $\mathbf{g}_i$ and $\mathbf{g}_{ideal}$, respectively.

The genes are ranked based on their ED values with respect to the ideal genes, the topmost rank being the least ED. The top 25 ranked genes from each group are selected as the informative genes.

B. Spearman Correlation Coefficient

Correlation is a technique for investigating the relationship between two quantitative, continuous variables. The correlation coefficient can take on the values from -1.0 to 1.0. Where -1.0 is a perfect negative (inverse) correlation, 0.0 means no correlation, and 1.0 is a perfect positive correlation. The Spearman Correlation Coefficient (SP) is given by

$$SP(\mathbf{g}_i, \mathbf{g}_{ideal}) = 1 - \frac{6\sum_{k=1}^{N}(d_{ik} - d_{ideal\,k})^2}{N(N^2 - 1)}, \quad (5)$$

where d_{ik} and $d_{ideal\,k}$ represent the elements of the rank matrices of $\mathbf{g}_i$ and $\mathbf{g}_{ideal}$, respectively, and $N = 38$.

C. Signal-to-Noise Ratio

We look for two characteristics of the informative genes. Firstly, their typical expressions in one class should be quite different from the other class. Secondly, they have similar expressions in the corresponding class, and there should be as little variation as possible [10]. The Signal-to-Noise Ratio (SNR) method exploits the above two characteristics, and defined as:

$$SNR(\mathbf{g}_i) = \frac{\mu_{ALL} - \mu_{AML}}{\sigma_{ALL} + \sigma_{AML}}. \quad (6)$$

For each gene vector, $\mathbf{g}_i$, μ_{ALL} and σ_{ALL} are the mean and SD of the 27 ALL samples, and μ_{AML} and σ_{AML} are for the 11 AML samples. Large absolute values are meant to indicate a strong correlation between the gene expression and the class distinction [11]. The genes with negative SNR values can highly express AML samples; similarly, genes with positive SNR can highly express the ALL samples. After ranking the genes in each group by sorting their absolute SNR values in descending order, we choose the top 25 ranked genes from each group as informative genes.

D. Information Loss Technique

As we have stated in the introduction section, our proposed Information Loss Technique (ILT) exploits the properties of principal components analysis which implemented by Singular Value Decomposition (SVD).

Figure 1 shows the flow chart of this algorithm. There are three main steps to implement ILT.

1) T-test filter: Since only tens or hundreds of genes among the more than 7000 genes contain discriminatory information, we may consider the others as "noise genes". The SVD attempts to maximize the variations that it captures in the data. However, in this case, the discriminatory information is not the most important type of variation due to the presence of a large number of "noise genes" [12]. We apply a T-test to each gene vector and set the significance at 0.05. The T-test is used to determine whether two groups of data could have the same mean. We assume that our two groups of data are independent and randomly selected from the population with a normal distributions with the same SD. In our case, for each gene vector, $\mathbf{g}_i$ we consider the expression data on the 27 samples as one group and the data on the 11 AML samples as another group. By T-test we have

$$T = \frac{\mu_{ALL} - \mu_{AML} - \delta}{s\sqrt{\frac{1}{n_{ALL}} + \frac{1}{n_{AML}}}}, \quad (7)$$

where μ_{ALL} and n_{ALL} are mean and number of data of the ALL group; μ_{AML} and n_{AML} are for AML group. The parameter, δ is termed as level of significance. The pooled standard deviation (SD) s is an estimated deviation which had been assumed the same in the two populations. The SD can be calculated as

$$s = \sqrt{\frac{\sigma_{ALL}^2(n_{ALL}-1) + \sigma_{AML}^2(n_{AML}-1)}{n_{ALL} + n_{AML} - 2}}, \quad (8)$$

where σ_{ALL} and σ_{AML} are the standard deviations of the two classes, respectively.

We test the null hypothesis: "no difference on the means", i.e. $\mu_{ALL} - \mu_{AML} = \delta = 0$ [13]. We use the 0.05 level of significance to test whether the difference between the two means is significant. In another words, the gene will reject the null hypothesis if there exists a significant different between the two means. A total of 1651 genes are rejected by the T-test and then they are selected for the next steps.

2) Disjoint Principal Component Models: Biccoato et al. [14] studied the soft independent modeling of class analogy technique which implemented by Principal Component Analysis, and provided us an idea of disjoint principal component scheme. In our technique, we combine this disjoint scheme and the SNR method stated in Section II together. We divide the 38 training samples into two classes: 27 ALL and 11 AML. Thus, let the matices $\mathbf{Q_1}$ and $\mathbf{Q_2}$ consist 27 ALL samples and 11 AML samples, respectively, described by 1651 gene expressions as row vectors. Each column vector represents a gene vector described by samples. Let j indicates the class number, and it is either 1 or 2 here. Before applying SVD, we zero-mean matrix $\mathbf{Q_j}$ to get normalized matrix $\mathbf{X_j}$. We apply SVD to $\mathbf{X_j}$ as [6]:

$$\mathbf{X_j} = \mathbf{U_j S_j V_j^T}, \quad (9)$$

where $\mathbf{U_j}$ and $\mathbf{V_j}$ contain the left singular and right singular vectors, respectively, and $\mathbf{S_j}$ is a matrix whose leading diagonal contains singular values with the other elements set to zeros.

Each column vector in $\mathbf{V_j}$ is considered as a Principal Component (PC). Let a matrix $\mathbf{L_j}$ contains the first n_j PCs in $\mathbf{V_j}$. The number n_j of significant principal components can be obtained by setting a threshold on the minimum variance contained by these n_j PCs.

The information loss in each class $\mathbf{E_j}$ is defined as

$$\mathbf{E_j} = \left| \mathbf{X_j} - \mathbf{X_j L_j L_j^T} \right|, \quad (10)$$

where "$|\;|$" converts each element in the matrix into its absolute value.

3) Applying Signal-to-Noise Ratio: For each of the 1651 genes, we apply SNR method based on how much information they lost during the data recovering process. The Information Loss Ratio (ILR) is computed as

$$ILR(\mathbf{g_i}) = \frac{\mu_i^{(1)} - \mu_i^{(2)}}{\sigma_i^{(1)} + \sigma_i^{(2)}}, \quad (11)$$

where $\mu_i^{(j)}$ and $\sigma_i^{(j)}$ indicate the mean value and standard derivation of column i in $\mathbf{E_j}$. Negative ILR value signifies the gene loses less information in class 1 than class 2, and the gene can be considered belonging to ALL group; otherwise, the gene belongs to AML group. Top ranked 25 genes from each class are selected as informative genes.

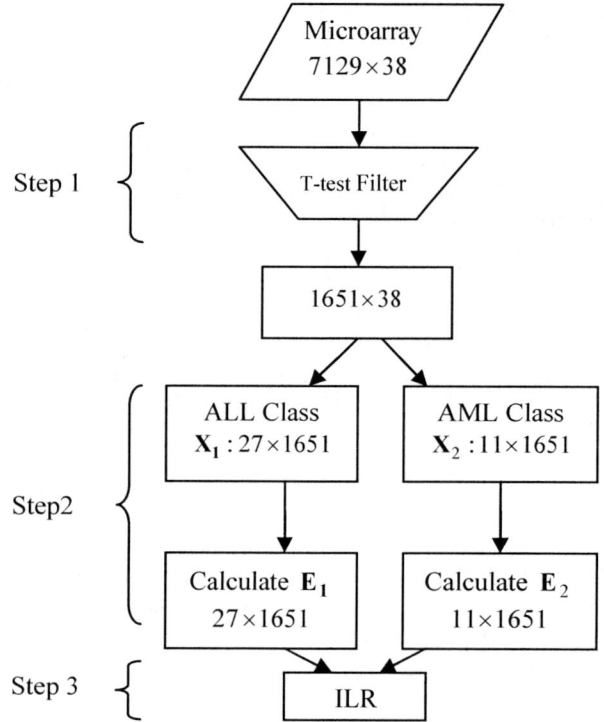

Fig. 1. Flow chart of the proposed Information Loss Technique.

III. MLP-BASED CLASS PREDICTION

Many promising machine learning algorithms have been adopted in class prediction problems, such as support vector machine (SVM) and k-nearest neighbor [8]. Other researchers have used Artificial Neural Network for analysis of gene expression data of cancer cells [15], [16]. These algorithms are trained with the informative genes selected by different techniques.

Multi-Layer Perceptron (MLP) is a feedforward neural network trained with the standard error backpropagation algorithm. It has been applied successfully to solve some difficult and diverse problems by training them in a supervised manner [17]. One disadvantage of MLP is that it requires a long time to train the network, especially when the input vector has large dimensions.

In order to reduce the training time, we design a MLP-based classifier that adopts SVD as a data compression tool.

Using each group of 50 informative genes selected by its corresponding method in Section II, we construct a new training matrix contains 27 ALL and 11 AML sample, and each sample is described as a row vector in 50 dimensional gene space. A new testing matrix is constructed in the same way. Let's define this 38×50 training matrix as $\mathbf{Q}_T$. We zero-mean $\mathbf{Q}_T$ by subtracting the mean value vector $\mathbf{\mu}_T$ from each row of $\mathbf{Q}_T$, so that input matrix $\mathbf{X}_T$ is obtained.

After obtaining $\mathbf{X}_T$, we apply SVD to compress $\mathbf{X}_T$ into lower dimensional space. Matrix $\mathbf{L}_T$ contains the first m significant PCs. We can obtain the new 38 sample vectors in reduced dimensional space by

$$\mathbf{Y}_T = \mathbf{X}_T \mathbf{L}_T. \quad (12)$$

In order to train the MLP network properly, normalization is necessary for all the sample vectors. We may easily normalize each vector by dividing its magnitude so that all of the 38 sample vectors in $\mathbf{Y}_T$ become unit vectors. Figure 2 shows the MLP-based classifier with three dimensional normalized inputs and any proper training algorithms.

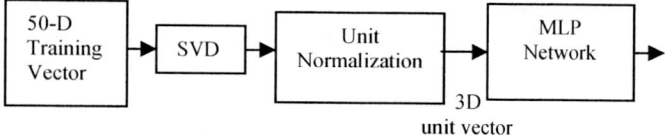

Fig. 2. MLP-based classifier structure.

After completion of training, classification of the testing samples or unknown samples is carried out. We apply the same procedure and use the same parameters to translate each testing sample vector $\mathbf{t}_k (1 \leq k \leq 34)$ in the new 34×50 testing matrix to the reduced dimensional space by

$$\mathbf{p}_k = (\mathbf{t}_k - \mathbf{\mu}_T)\mathbf{L}_T. \quad (13)$$

To predict testing sample k, we simply pass the normalized $\mathbf{p}_k$ into the trained MLP network and check its output.

IV. RESULTS AND DISCUSSION

The first three gene selection methods in Section II can easily be implemented. For Information Loss Technique, we set the threshold on the minimum variance provided by n_j PCs as 70%. As a result, a total of 7 and 4 most significant principal components accounting for 71.49% and 75.66% of the overall variance have been chosen for ALL and AML classes, respectively. After computing the ILR values for the 1651 genes by using equation (11), we choose the first 25 ranked genes from each of ALL and AML classes.

To have a visualization of the scatter plot of the samples, we may translate both the 38 training samples and 34 testing samples into a 2D space according their respective algorithms in Section III without normalization. Figure 3 shows the visualization of the scatter plot of all of the leukemia samples.

Figure 3 (a), (b), (c) and (d) correspond to the plot of the samples based on feature selection by ED, SP, SNR and ILT techniques, respectively. There are at most 2 of the 72 samples those cannot be classified properly in Fig. 3 (a) and (b) by the piece-wise linear decision boundary. From Fig. 3 (c) and (d), it can be seen that there is only one AML sample that is assigned to the ALL class.

Next, we train a two-layer MLP classifier as described in Section III with m input nodes, one output neuron and varying the number of hidden layer neurons. After experimenting with 1, 5, 10, 15 and 20 hidden layer neurons, we observed that even a single node is capable of providing good classification rates. The input layer contains m nodes which indicate the sample vectors have been reduced into m dimensional space. The targets values of ALL and AML samples were set to 1 and -1, respectively. The initial weights were randomly generated and varied from -1.0 to 1.0. The learning rate ranging from 0.02 to 0.6 was adopted in each of the combinations. In order to obtain a perfect output such as -1.0 or 1.0, we set the training goal as either making the mean square error between actual outputs and target outputs converge to a level of 10^{-4} or a total 6000 epochs of training. Both the hidden and output layers use tan-sigmoid transfer functions.

Table I compares the recognition rates by using different groups of 50 informative genes selected by the four criteria with m=3, 4, 5, and 6.

TABLE I
RECOGNITION RATES COMPARISON [%]

Methods	No. of input dimensions			
	3	4	5	6
ED	91.2	94.1	94.1	94.1
SP	97.1	97.1	97.1	97.1
SNR	94.1	94.1	94.1	94.1
ILT	94.1	94.1	94.1	94.1

From Table I, it is clear to see that SP has the highest recognition rate among the four methods. Our proposed ILT has a better performance then ED, and it has a similar recognition rate with SNR but they misclassify different samples on 4 dimensional input. Table II shows the misclassified sample IDs.

It should be noted that all of these four methods have a common misclassified sample #66, and this sample is also predicted incorrectly or weakly predicted by many other approaches reported in the other literature [7], [8], [14], [18]. Another sample #67 is also not properly assigned also using some other classification methods [7], [8], [14], [19]. From Figure 3, it is clear to see that there always exist the AML testing sample (#66) locates inside the ALL class, and there are one or two ALL testing samples are also quite close to the AML class.

To further investigate our proposed ILT, we reduce the number of informative genes selected. Instead of choosing 25 genes from each class, we choose 5, 10, 15 and 20 top ranked genes from each class. As a result, we have 10, 20, 30 and 40

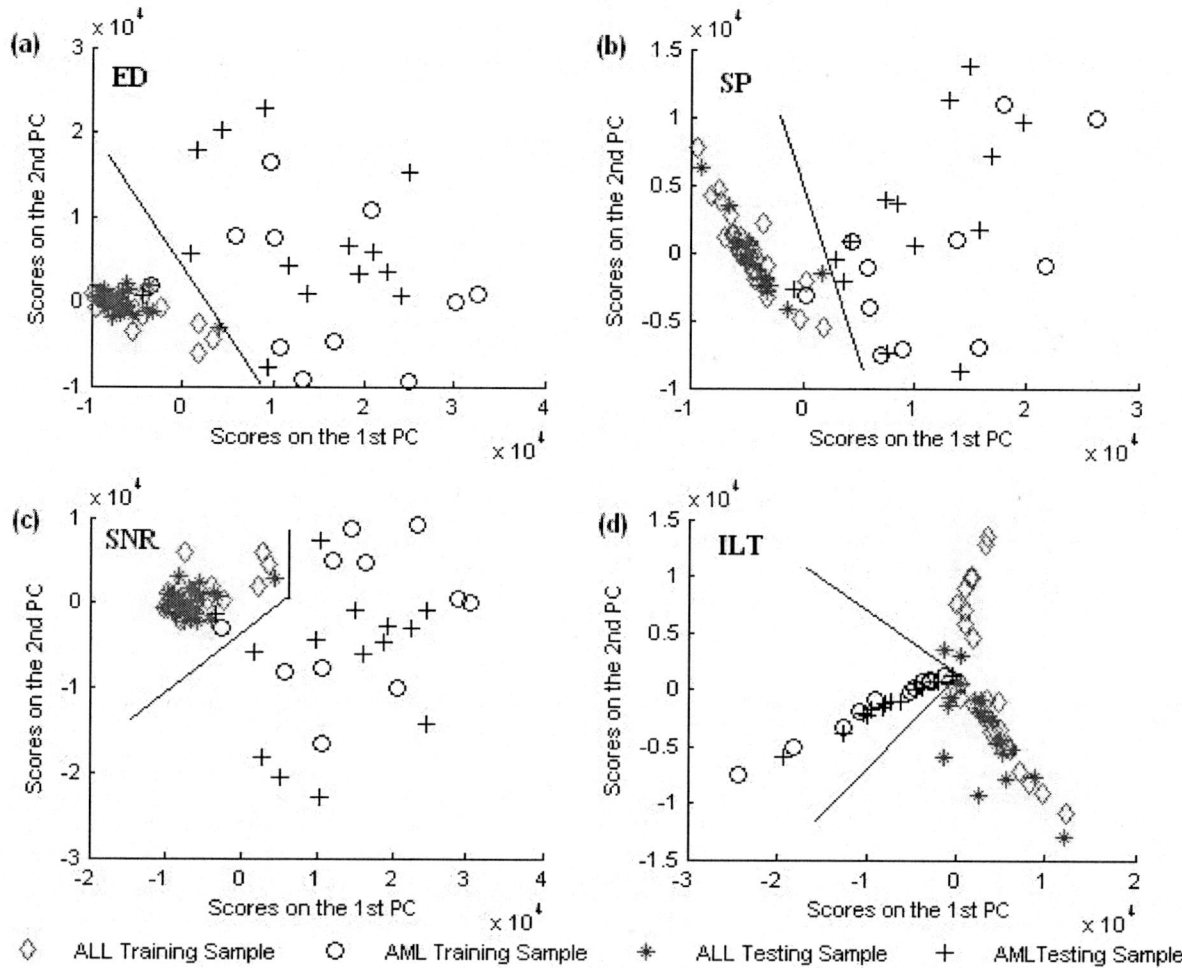

Fig. 3. Visualization of 72 Leukemia samples in reduced dimensional (2D) space using informative genes selected by different techniques. (a) Euclidean Distance; (b) Spearman Correlation; (c) Signal-to-Noise Ratio measure; (d) Information Loss Technique.

TABLE II
MISCLASSIFIED SAMPLES

Methods	No. of input dimensions			
	3	4	5	6
ED	66, 67, 43	66, 43	66, 67	66, 67
SP	66	66	66	66
SNR	66, 67	66, 43	66, 67	66, 67
ILT	66, 67	66, 67	66, 67	66, 67

TABLE III
RECOGNITION RATES [%]

No. of genes	No. of input dimensions			
	3	4	5	6
10	94.1	97.1	94.1	94.1
20	94.1	94.1	94.1	97.1
30	94.1	94.1	91.2	94.1
40	94.1	94.1	94.1	94.1

informative genes, respectively. The following Table III compares the recognition rates when we use different numbers of informative genes as well as different numbers of dimensions of input vectors.

It is clear to see that the best recognition rate 97.1% can be achieved when we use the group of 10 informative genes with 4 dimensional inputs, or we use the group of 20 informative genes with 6 dimensional inputs.

Recently, SVD is also used by many other researchers to select the feature genes, such as the Seeded Region Growing algorithm proposed by Liu et al. [20] and the application of SVD is studied in [21]. Compared with these methods, our proposed ILT requires little computation and is easier to be implemented. The advantage of our MLP-based dimension reduction classifier is that input vector has very low dimensions, so it is much faster to train an MLP network compared to the one has large input dimensions. It requires only about 5 to 15 seconds to train a proper network. Besides, the number of hidden neurons in the MLP can be small.

V. CONCLUSIONS

The Golub et al.'s microarray data set is challenging because the appearance of the two types of acute leukemias is highly similar. There have been many attempts to work out this problem with different gene selection and class prediction methods [7], [12], [18], [19]. In this paper, we have considered Euclidean Distance, Spearman Correlation, Signal-to-Noise Ratio measure and Information Loss Technique. The Information Loss Technique is based on the idea of disjoint models [14]. Since SVD is a technique mostly used for linear data, by its own, it does not work well on data sets with highly similar patterns. We adopt SNR to improve the performance of SVD in gene selection procedure.

Our proposed MLP-based dimension reduction classifier takes little training time and provides us a high prediction rate. This classifier utilizes the significant features of SVD, and the performance of a simple MLP network is greatly improved.

REFERENCES

[1] Y. Moreau et al., "Functional bioinformatics of microarray data: from expression to regulation," *Proceedings of the IEEE*, vol. 90, pp. 1722-1743, Nov. 2002.

[2] V. Roth and T. Lange, "Bayesian class discovery in microarray datasets," *IEEE Trans. Biomed. Eng.*, vol. 51, pp. 707-718, 2004.

[3] H. Yin, "ViSOM-A novel method for multivariate data projection and structure visualization," *IEEE Trans. Neural Networks*, vol. 13, pp. 237-243, 2002.

[4] F. Azuaje, "A computational neural approach to support the discovery of gene function and classes of cancer," *IEEE Trans. Biomed. Eng.*, vol. 48, pp. 332-339, 2001.

[5] O. Alter, P. O. Brown, and D. Botstein, "Singular value decomposition for genome-wide expression data processing and modeling," *PNAS*, vol. 97, no. 18, pp. 10101-10106, 2000.

[6] M. E. Wall, A. Rechtseiner, and L. M. Rocha, "Singular value decomposition and principal component analysis," in D. P. Berrar, W. Dubitzky, and M. Granzow, *A Practical Approach to Microarray Data Analysis*, Kluwer: Norwell, pp. 91-109, MA, 2003.

[7] T. R. Golub et al., "Molecular classification of cancer: Class discovery and class prediction by gene expression monitoring," *Science*, vol. 286, pp. 531-537, 1999.

[8] S. B. Cho and J. Ryu, "Classifying gene expression data of cancer using classifier ensemble with mutually exclusive features," *Proceedings of the IEEE*, vol. 90, pp. 1744-1753, Nov. 2002.

[9] T. Sawa, and L. Ohno-Machado, "A neural network-based similarity index for clustering DNA microarray data," *Computers in Biology and Medicine*, vol. 33, pp. 1-15, 2003.

[10] D. K. Slonim et al., "Class prediction and discovery using gene expression data," *Proceedings of the 4th Annual International Conference on Computational Molecular Biology (RECOMB)*, pp. 263-272, Tokyo, Japan, 2000.

[11] R. Bijlani et al., "Prediction of biologically significant components from microarray data: Independently consistent expression discriminator (ICED)," *Bioinformatics*, vol. 19, pp. 62-70, 2003.

[12] J. Misra et al., "Interactive exploration of microarray gene expression patterns in a reduced dimensional space," *Genome Res.*, vol. 12, pp. 1112–1120, 2002.

[13] J. E. Freund and G. A. Simon, *Modern elementary statistics*, New Jersey: Prentice Hall, Inc. 1997.

[14] S. Bicciato, A. Luchini, and C. Di Bello, "PCA disjoint models for multiclass cancer analysis using gene expression data," *Bioinformatics*, Vol. 19, pp. 571-578, 2003.

[15] Z. Boger, "Artificial neural networks methods for identification of the most relevant genes from gene expression array data," *Proceedings of the International Joint Conference on Neural Networks (IJCNN)*, pp. 3095-3100, 2003.

[16] J. Khan et al., "Classification and diagnostic prediction of cancers using gene expression profiling and artificial neural networks," *Nature Medicine*, vol. 7(6), pp. 673-679, 2001.

[17] S. Haykin, *Neural networks: A comprehensive foundation*. New Jersey: Prentice Hall, Inc. 1999.

[18] L. M. Fu and E. S. Youn, "Improving reliability of gene selection from microarray functional genomics data," *IEEE Trans. Info. Tech. in Biomedicine*, vol. 7, pp. 191-196, 2003.

[19] D. V. Nguyen and D. M. Rocke, "Multi-class cancer classification via partial least squares with gene expression profiles," *Bioinformatics*, Vol. 18, pp. 1216-1226, 2002.

[20] B. Liu, C. Wan and L. Wang, "Unsupervised gene selection via spectral biclustering," *Proceedings of the International Joint Conference on Neural Networks (IJCNN)*, pp. 1681-1686, 2004.

[21] Z. H. Duan et al., "Application of singular value decomposition and functional clustering to analyzing gene expression profiles of renal cell carcinoma," *Proceedings of IEEE Bioinformatics Conference* (CSB'03), pp. 392-393, 2003.

Neural Networks for Gene Expression Analysis and Gene Selection from DNA Microarray

Jagdish Chandra Patra, Qin Zhen, Ee Luang Ang and Amitabha Das
School of Computer Engineering, Nanyang Technological University, Singapore 639798
Email: {aspatra, 148101347, aselang, and asadas}@ntu.edu.sg

Abstract— We propose two approaches for microarray gene expression analysis and gene selection using neural networks. Using these approaches, only those genes which help sample classification are selected from the original set of genes, and the redundant genes expression patterns involved in the huge microarray matrix are eliminated so that dimensionality of the matrix is reduced from a few thousands to a much smaller number. An unsupervised SOM based technique and another supervised single layer perceptron based technique have been utilized for this purpose. Performance of these two approaches is compared in terms of accuracy, implementation and execution time.

I. INTRODUCTION

Nowadays, a generic approach to cancer classification based on gene expression monitoring by DNA microarrays is widely applied. This technology allows screening large number of genes to see whether they are active under various conditions and can assist biologists to understand the behaviors of various tumors based on the gene-expression. Normally, for each sample, several thousand of genes are measured for their mRNA expression levels [1], [2]. The high dimensionality of the data matrix is a big challenge for data analysis and meaningful information extraction. To overcome this problem, we need to identify a "class distinguisher", which is a much smaller group of genes than the original set of genes, and they can, in combination, help to classify cancers and to predict unknown sample. Here, two different neural network-based approaches are used to analyze the Alizadeh et al. dataset [3].

Alizadeh et al. dataset uses microarray to characterize gene expression patterns in three lymphoid malignancies: DLBCL (47 samples), FL (9 samples) and CLL (11 samples), and also 29 non-lymphoma samples. Thus, this dataset consists of in total 96 samples, each with expression values of 4026 genes. Our task is to (1) find a class distinguisher between lymphoma and non-lymphoma; (2) find a class distinguisher between DLBCLs and non-DLBCLs (FLs and CLLs); (3) find a class distinguisher between the two subtypes of DLBCL, which are GC B-like DLBCLs and Activated B-like DLBCLs.

II. APPROACH 1: BASED ON DISCRIMINATION FACTOR AND SELF-ORGANIZING MAPS

Golub et al. [4] have presented a novel method for selecting the genes whose expression pattern is strongly correlated with the class distinction. Each gene's degree of correlation with class distinction is calculated as follows. Each gene is represented by an expression vector $v(g) = (e_{g1}, e_{g2}, \ldots, e_{gn})$, where e_{gi} denotes the expression level of gene g in ith sample in the dataset. A measure of correlation was calculated for each gene. Firstly the means and SDs (standard derivations) of the log of the expression levels of gene g for the samples in class 1 and class 2 need to be calculated. Let $[m1(g), s1(g)]$ and $[m2(g), s2(g)]$ denote these values respectively and computed as

$$m1(g) = (1/c1)(e_{g1} + e_{g2} + \ldots + e_{gn}), \quad (1)$$

$$s1(g) = \sqrt{(1/c1)[(e_{g1} - m1(g))^2 + \ldots + (e_{gn} - m1(g))^2]}, \quad (2)$$

where c1 is number of samples in class 1.

The mean and SD for class 2 are calculated using (1) and (2) as well. Let us define a discrimination factor DF(g) given by

$$DF(g) = [m1(g) - m2(g)]/[s1(g) + s2(g)]. \quad (3)$$

Large values of $|DF(g)|$ indicate a strong correlation between the expression pattern of gene g and the class distinction, while the sign of $DF(g)$ being positive or negative corresponds to g being more highly expressed in class 1 or class 2.

The informative gene selection phase involved all the samples in the dataset. In this experiment, the 96 samples (each with expression values of 4026 genes) in original dataset were first divided into two classes, Lymphoma (cancer) and Non-lymphoma (normal). The samples were labeled as

Lymphoma (C_1) (67 samples):
  (i) FL, (ii) CLL, (iii) DLBCL-g (GC B-like DLBCL), and
  (iv) DLBCL-a (Activated B-like DLBCL), and
Non-lymphoma (C_2) (29 samples):
  (i) Blood-B-r (resting blood B), (ii) Blood-B-a (activated blood B), (iii) Lymph-Node, (iv) Tonsil, (v) Cell Line, and
  (vi) Blood T (Resting/Activated T).
Thereafter, the three tasks, each looks for a class distinguisher, were carried out.

A. Task 1: A Class Distinguisher Between Lymphoma and Non-lymphoma

Let us assign class 1 (C_1) as lymphoma and class 2 (C_2) as non-lymphoma. After calculating $DF(g)$ for all the 4026 genes, 15 genes with largest *DF(g)* are selected to be used to identify lymphoma class, and another 15 genes with smallest *DF(g)*, i.e. negative and with largest absolute values are selected to identify non-lymphoma class. The 30 genes combined together to form the lymphoma and non-lymphoma distinguisher as shown in Fig. 1.

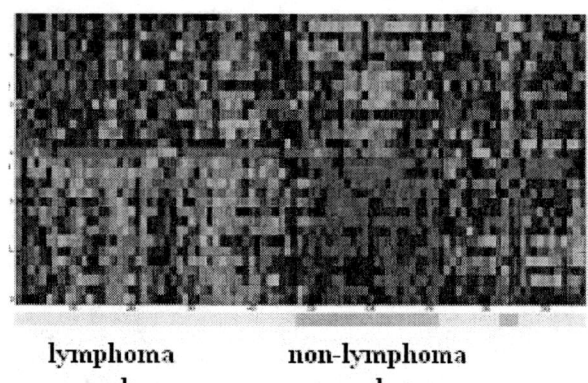

Fig. 1. Selected 30 genes as lymphoma and non-lymphoma distinguisher.

A self-organizing map (SOM) [5], [6] was employed to visualize the distribution of all 96 samples based on their expression patterns of these 30 genes.

The algorithm of SOM works as follows: firstly define a two-dimensional grid of nodes, which can be of hexagonal or rectangular geometry. Initially input samples, each with expression values for 30 genes, are randomly allocated to one of the nodes, and then during the iterative training process, for each input sample, the winning node gets its weight updated and the sample is assigned to this node. Besides, the weights of the nodes neighboring to the winning node are also updated. At the end of the training process, the nodes of the SOM grid have clusters of co-expression samples assigned to them, and the map captures the distribution of the input samples.

The size of the map needs to be chosen according to number of samples involved, too large map may cause too many blank nodes and too small one may make the boundaries of clusters unclear. After a series of experiments with different map sizes, 4x4 is found to be sufficient and appropriate to describe the samples.

An SOM was initialized with a size of 4x4 nodes, with initial radius for neighborhood of 3, and initial learning rate $\alpha(0)$ of 0.1. A Gaussian function was used as neighborhood function. The learning rate $\alpha(t)$ decreases when iteration number, *t* increases according to

$$\alpha(t) = \alpha(0)*(0.005/\alpha(0))^{((t-1)/trainlen)}, \quad (4)$$

where the *trainlen* is the training length in term of epochs. These parameters were used for all experiments using SOM in this manuscript.

CLL(9)	FL(4) DLBCL-a(2)	DLBCL-g(3) FL(3)	DLBCL-g(11) DLBCL-a(4)
CLL(2)	Blood-B-r(1)	DLBCL-g(2) FL(2) DLBCL-a(1)	DLBCL-a(5) DLBCL-g(3)
Blood-B-r(1)	Blood-B-r(1)	DLBCL-g(2)	DLBCL-a(7) DLBCL-g(2) Tonsil(1)
Blood-T(7) Cell-line(5) Blood-B-a(4)	Blood-B-a(4) Blood-B-r(1) Cell-line(1)	Blood-B-a(2) Lym-Node(1)	DLBCL-a(4) DLBCL-g(1)

Fig. 2. Distribution of all 96 samples based on lymphoma and non-lymphoma distinguisher.

Each sample was an input of 30 dimensions corresponding to 30 genes' expression values, and the 96 samples were used to train the SOM (4x4) with training length of 15 epochs. The trained map is shown in Fig. 2. The dark line separates lymphoma samples and non-lymphoma samples. The number within the brackets beside the sample label indicates the number of samples assigned to that node.

B. Task 2: A Class Distinguisher Between DLBCL and Non-DLBCL

Similar scheme was used to find DLBCL (C_{1-1}) and non-DLBCL (C_{1-2}) distinguisher. In this case, only 67 lymphoma samples were involved in the experiment. Again, 30 genes were selected using the DF method to form a class distinguisher and shown in Fig. 3.

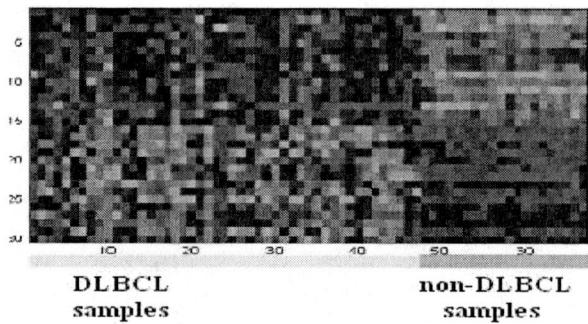

Fig. 3. Selected 30 genes as DLBCL and non-DLBCL distinguisher.

Each Lymphoma sample of dimension 30 can be used as input to an SOM and be visualized in a similar way as task 1. Due to space limitation, the figure of the trained map is not shown here.

C. Task 3: A Class Distinguisher Between Two Subtypes of DLBCLs

This task was to find class distinguisher between GC B-like DLBCL (C_{1-1-1}) and Activated B-like DLBCL (C_{1-1-2}). By using same scheme and 47 DLBCL samples, 30 genes which form the DLBCL subtypes distinguisher were found and shown in Fig. 4.

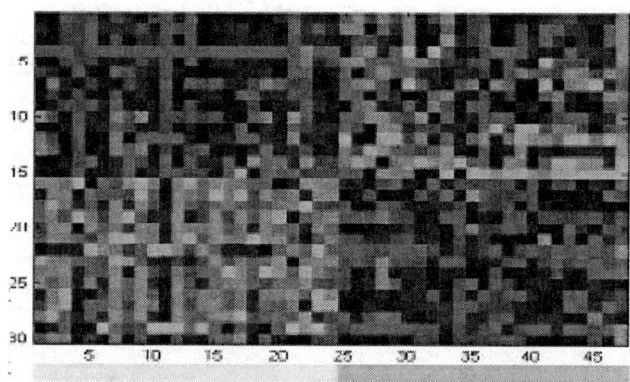

GC B-like DLBCL samples　　**Activated B-like DLBCL samples**

Fig. 4. Selected 30 genes as DLBCL subtype distinguisher.

Besides the original 3 tasks, an extra class distinguisher (a set of 30 genes) which distinguishes between FL and CLL was found and shown in Fig. 5.

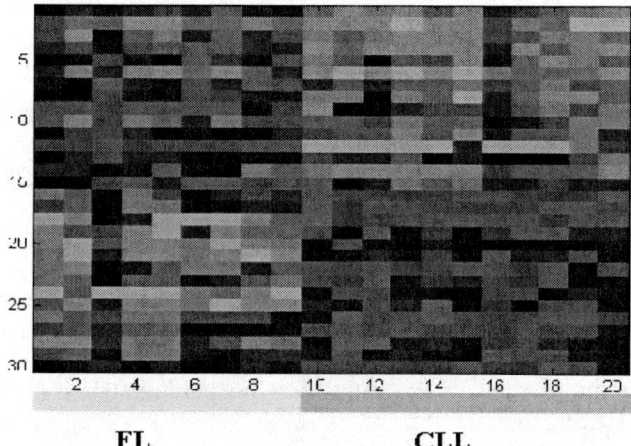

FL　　**CLL**

Fig. 5. Selected 30 genes FL and CLL distinguisher.

So far, four class distinguishers have been found using the DF/SOM approach. The two distinguishers found in task 2 and 3, as well as the distinguisher between FLs and CLLs, which in total consist of 90 genes are applied on lymphoma samples. Now each of the 90-dimensional 67 lymphoma samples was used as an input to an SOM with training length of 15 epochs. They were clearly distributed into 4 groups as shown in Fig. 6.

CLL(11)		DLBCL-a(6)	DLBCL-a(10)
		DLBCL-a(2)	DLBCL-a(5)
FL(1)	DLBCL-g(1)	DLBCL-g(1)	DLBCL-g(3)
FL(8)	DLBCL-g(2)	DLBCL-g(6)	DLBCL-g(11)

Fig. 6. Distribution of 67 lymphoma samples based on three lymphoma distinguishers (set of 90 genes).

D. Testing Phase

In testing phase, the quality of each of the previously discovered class distinguishers, i.e. how well they can classify samples, was examined. First of all, the dataset with 90 selected genes were split into 3 subsets A, B and C, preserving approximately the same ratio of samples of class 1 and class 2 in each subset. Their details are summarized in Table I - III.

TABLE I
THREE SUBSETS OF ALL 96 SAMPLES

Subset	No. of lymphoma	No. of non-lymphoma
A	22	9
B	22	10
C	23	10

TABLE II
THREE SUBSETS OF THE 67 LYMPHOMA SAMPLES

Subset	No. of DLBCL	No. of non-DLBCL
A	15	6
B	16	7
C	16	7

TABLE III
THREE SUBSETS OF THE 47 DLBCL SAMPLES

Subset	No. of GC B-like DLBCL	No. of Activated B-like DLBCL
A	8	7
B	8	8
C	8	8

To test the experimental result of each of the 3 tasks, first, we used the combination of any two of subsets A, B and C as training dataset to obtain a trained SOM, and then used the left out subset for testing. For each sample in testing dataset, its best matching unit of the map (the winning node) indicates to which class it belongs. The number of samples which were correctly classified (classification rate) in testing phase is summarized in Table IV.

TABLE IV

TESTING OF RESULTS FOR DF/SOM APPROACH

Task 1			
Training Data	Testing Data	Classification Rate	
		Lymphoma	Non-Lymphoma
B+C	A	21/22	8/9
A+C	B	21/22	9/10
A+B	C	22/23	10/10
Task 2			
Training Data	Testing Data	Classification Rate	
		DLBCL	Non-DLBCL
B+C	A	14/15	6/6
A+C	B	15/16	7/7
A+B	C	16/16	7/7
Task 3			
Training Data	Testing Data	Classification Rate	
		GC B-like DLBCL	Activated B-like DLBCL
B+C	A	7/8	6/7
A+C	B	7/8	8/8
A+B	C	7/8	8/8

Based on testing results from Table IV, it can be concluded that this DF/SOM approach can generate class distinguishers with reasonably good classification rates.

For future unknown samples, it can be first classified into either lymphoma or non-lymphoma using the trained map shown in Fig. 2. If this sample happens to be a lymphoma sample, it can be further classified into one of the four types of lymphoma using the trained map shown in Fig. 6.

III. APPROACH 2: BASED ON SINGLE LAYER PERCEPTRON

The second approach for discovering class distinguisher is to adopt a single layer neural network [7],[8] as proposed by Narayanan et al. [9]. In this method, the weights linking input gene nodes to output node were examined, thresholds based on standard deviations were calculated to provide a selection criterion for a smaller group of genes. Thereafter, these genes were used in a second round of the gene selection procedure.

We adopt a method to change the DNA microarray data into a three-valued gene expression, in which each expression value was set to 1, 0.5 or 0. Firstly, for every gene g, its expression vector is $v(g) = (e_{g1}, e_{g2}, ..., e_{g96})$, the mean expression value for all the 96 samples was calculated as:

$$mean(g) = (1/96)(e_{g1}+e_{g2}+...+e_{g96}). \quad (4)$$

Two threshold Thr1 and Thr2 were calculated as

$$Thr1 = mean(g)-(1/5)*(mean(g)-min(g)), \quad (5)$$

$$Thr2 = mean(g)+(1/5)*(max(g)-mean(g), \quad (6)$$

where $min(g)$ and $max(g)$ represent the smallest and largest expression values across 96 samples for gene g. All the expression values greater than Thr2 were set to 1, the expression values smaller than Thr1 were set to 0, and the expression values in between the two thresholds were set to 0.5. The purpose of this change is probably to remove the noises existing in the dataset and to reduce the computation complexity.

A. Task 1: A Class Distinguisher Between Lymphoma and Non-lymphoma

Training datasets and testing datasets in Table I - III were also used in this approach. The Backpropagation algorithm [9] with a learning rate of 0.01 was chosen to create and train the single layer neural networks. The weights were randomly initialized. There are 4026 input nodes, each corresponds to one gene. Therefore, the weight vector has 4026 dimensions. To train the neural networks, each sample was used as an input. The activation value of the output node is the sum of weighted inputs as given by:

$$Y(s) = (w_{g1}s_{g1} + w_{g2}s_{g2} + ... +w_{g4026}s_{g4026}) \quad (7)$$

where $Y(s)$ is the activation value to output node for a sample s, and $w_{gi}s_{gi}$ is the weight of the link between each input node i and output node multiplied with expression value of gene gi in s. The transfer function for the output node is a logistic/sigmoid with output values between 0 and 1. The learning rule is the standard perceptron learning rule: $wj(t+1) = wj(t) + \eta(d-y)s$, where connection weight wj at iteration $t+1$ is the sum of its weight at iteration t and the difference between the desired output d and actual output y for an input sample s multiplied with step size η that can vary between 0 and 1.

Three neural networks were created. Firstly, the combination of subset B and C was used to train network1 (100 epochs), secondly, the combination of subset A and C was then used to train network2 (100 epochs) and thirdly, combination of subset A and B was used to train network3. In each training process, the target output for lymphoma sample was 1 and for non-lymphoma sample was 0.

After training of the there neural networks, three sets of weights were obtained, which are expressed as

$$\begin{aligned} W_1 &= [w_{1-1}, w_{1-2}, ... w_{1-4026}], \\ W_2 &= [w_{2-1}, w_{2-2}, ... w_{2-4026}], \\ W_3 &= [w_{3-1}, w_{3-2}, ... w_{3-4026}]. \end{aligned} \quad (8)$$

These weight vectors were then added together to get W_{sum} = [w_{s-1}, w_{s-2}, ... w_{s-4026}]. The mean M and SD were calculated across all the dimensions in the vector W_{sum}, and two thresholds were set as Thr3 = M+2D, Thr4 = M-2D. If the value of the weight w_{s-g} is greater than Thr3 or less than Thr4, gene g survives, otherwise it was eliminated. In this round, 180 genes out of the original 4026 genes satisfied the above criteria. These 180 gene values were then extracted from the full database, and then were again split into three subsets, A, B and C, and now each input has only 180 dimensions.

The above scheme was repeated, and this time, using the above threshold criteria, only 10 genes survived. Since the reduction from 180 genes to 10 appeared too severe, a more relaxed criterion for setting the thresholds, i.e., M± D was used. In this way, 180 genes were reduced to 48 genes. The expression levels of these 48 genes were used for classification in subsequent classification tasks.

To test the results of task 1, we extracted the 48 genes' expression together with 96 samples' class information, and then split them into 3 subsets A, B and C. Firstly, we used B and C to train a neural network with 48 input nodes and learning rate of 0.01, and then used A as testing data. For each sample s in subset A, if the output from the neural network was above 0.9, s was signified as lymphoma, and if the output was below 0.1, s was signified as non-lymphoma. Thereafter, we used another two subsets to train a neural network and the left out subset to test in the similar way. The classification rates are summarized in Table V.

TABLE V

TESTING RESULTS FOR APPROACH 2, TASK 1

Task 1			
Training Data	Testing Data	Classification Rate	
		Lymphoma	Non-Lymphoma
B+C	A	21/22	9/9
A+C	B	20/22	10/10
A+B	C	22/23	10/10

B. Task 2: A Class Distinguisher Between DLBCL and non-DLBCL

We used similar scheme and subsets in Table II to find a DLBCL and Non-DLBCL distinguisher. After first round of reduction, 4026 genes were reduced to 184, and they were further reduced to 56 genes in the second round. Testing was done in the same way as task 1. Table VI summarizes the results.

TABLE VI

TESTING RESULTS FOR APPROACH 2, TASK 2

Task 2			
Training Data	Testing Data	Classification Rate	
		DLBCL	Non-DLBCL
B+C	A	15/15	6/6
A+C	B	16/16	7/7
A+B	C	16/16	7/7

C. Task 3: A Class Distinguisher Between Two Subtypes of DLBCLs

In this task, three subsets shown in Table III were involved. 4026 genes were reduced to 176 in the first round and further reduced to 51 genes in the second round. Testing results are summarized in Table VII.

TABLE VII

TESTING RESULTS FOR APPROACH 2, TASK 3

Task 3			
Training Data	Testing Data	Classification Rate	
		GC B-like DLBCL	Activated B-like DLBCL
B+C	A	8/8	7/7
A+C	B	8/8	8/8
A+B	C	8/8	8/8

From Table V-VII, it is noticed that this approach was able to provide higher classification rates than approach 1. For task 1, only 4 lymphoma samples were misclassified, and for task 2 and 3, all samples were properly classified.

For future unknown cases, they were just needed to be used as inputs to a neural network which is trained with a dataset that consists of the class distinguishers found using this approach. By examining the value of output, the unknown sample can be classified.

IV. MAJOR CONTRIBUTIONS

We improved the methods presented in the two papers [4], [9] and applied them to Alizadeh et al. dataset [3]. The method in paper [4] uses statistical method for unknown sample classification. The Discrimination Factor Approach we proposed chooses to use SOM instead, which is relatively simpler since no complex computation needs to be involved. Besides unknown sample classification, it can capture and visualize the distribution of samples as well.

In the Single Layer Perceptron Neural Network-based approach, we proposed a new mathematical method to change original dataset into discrete-valued one instead of using the commercial software used in [9]. The testing results show that this alternative works well.

Approach 1 is easy to implement and relatively faster to find class distinguisher genes. It can produce accurate results and the number of genes in the class distinguisher can be specified. An SOM in this case is chosen for classification of future unknown samples so the distribution of samples can also be visualized. This approach is suitable for datasets with different class distinctions.

Approach 2 produces even more accurate results and its testing phase and classification for unknown sample is simple and straightforward. It is generally applicable for most datasets. However, it has a disadvantage that the first round of gene reduction is always slow due to high dimensionality of the inputs and weights of the neural networks. Therefore, it takes longer time to train the neural networks for a huge dataset. Moreover, the number of genes in class distinguishers cannot be specified beforehand. The comparison between their timing issues are summarized in Table VIII.

TABLE VIII
COMPARISON BETWEEN THE TIMING ISSUES OF THE TWO APPROACHES

Task	Time for Finding Class Distinguisher	
	Approach 1	Approach 2
1	4 s	770 s
2	3 s	687 s
3	3 s	635 s

In comparison to another neural network-based sample classification approach named SFAM [10], which has also been applied to Alizadeh et al. dataset, the two approaches we proposed have several advantages summarized as follows:

1) The two approaches we proposed have both gene selection and sample classification functionality. In contrast, the SFAM approach in [10] can only classify samples based on the genes selected in Alizadeh et al. experiment [3].

2) The approaches we proposed have higher classification accuracy than SFAM approach. Accuracy [10] is defined as:

$$Accuracy = (TP + TN)/N, \quad (9)$$

where TP (true positive) is the number of class 1 samples correctly identified, TN (true negative) is the number of class 2 samples correctly identified and N is the total number of samples involved. SFAM approach was used to classify 45 DLBCL samples and 18 normal samples, and the highest accuracy obtained was 76%. In contrast, when classifying 67 lymphoma samples and 29 normal samples, the two approaches we proposed gave accuracy of at least 93.5%.

V. CONCLUSION

Nowadays, DNA microarrays are widely applied in the field of cancer classification, the high dimensionality of the data matrix is a big challenge for data analysis and meaningful information extraction. Various approaches based on neural networks can be applied to gene profiling datasets for gene selection and dimensionality reduction. The two approaches we proposed here are based on the methods presented by some other papers [4],[9], but have been modified in some ways so that they are improved in terms of functionality, difficulties of implementation, or cost of implementations /application. These two approaches are also compared in terms of accuracy, implementation and execution time, so different approaches can be selected on a case-by-case basis. Moreover, they were compared with SFAM approach [10] and they offer advantages in terms of functionality and classification accuracy.

REFERENCES

[1] K. Wang et al., "Monitoring gene expression profile changes in ovarian carcinomas using cDNA microarray," *Gene*, vol. 299, pp. 101-108, Mar. 1999.
[2] J. Derisi et al., "Use of cDNA microarray to analyze gene expression patterns in human cancers," *Nature Genet*, vol. 14, pp. 457-460, Dec. 1996.
[3] A. A. Alizadeh et al., "Distinct types of diffuse large B-cell lymphoma identified by gene expression profiling," *Nature*, vol. 43, pp. 503-511, 2000.
[4] T. R. Golub et al., "Molecular classification of cancer: class discovery and class prediction by Gene Expression Monitoring," *Science*, vol. 286, pp 531-537, Oct. 1999.
[5] J. C. Bezdek et al., "A note on self-organizing semantic maps," *IEEE Transaction on Neural Networks*, vol. 6, pp. 1029-1035, Sep. 1995.
[6] J. Vesanto et al. "Clustering of the self-organizing map," *IEEE Transaction on Neural Networks*, vol. 11, pp. 586-600, May 2000.
[7] S. Dennis et al., "*Introduction to Neural Networks*," available online: www2.psy.uq.edu.au/~brainway/Manual/WhatIs.html, 1997.
[8] S. Haykin, "*Neural Networks: A Comprehensive Foundation*," New Jersey: Pretice Hall, Inc. 1999.
[9] A. Narayanan et al., "Single-layer artificial neural networks for gene expression analysis," *Neurocomputing*, vol 61, pp. 217-240, 2004.
[10] F. Azuaje, "A computational neural approach to support the discovery of gene function and classes of cancer," *IEEE Transactions of Biomedical Engineering*, vol.48, pp. 332-338, Mar. 2001.

The Molecules Module of the Brain Architecture Management System

Mihail Bota
The NIBS Neuroscience Program
University of Southern California
Los Angeles, CA, 90089
mbota@usc.edu

Larry W. Swanson
The NIBS Neuroscience Program
University of Southern California
Los Angeles, CA, 90089
lswanson@usc.edu

Abstract

We describe in this paper a new module of the Brain Architecture Management System (BAMS; http://brancusi.usc.edu/bkms). The *Molecules* module of BAMS makes this the first online knowledge management system that handles chemoarchitectonical data of brain regions in multiple species. This module allows insertion of complex reports of molecule presence as collated from the literature. The database structure of the module includes representation of molecule expression in different cell types as revealed by various techniques, coexpression data in different brain regions or cell types, and the physiological state of experimental animals. The module also allows insertion of time dependent experimental data. The web interface of this module allows users to construct lists of brain regions where a molecule is present depending on the physiological state, retrieve further details about inserted records, and compare the time dependent data within or across experiments.

I. Introduction

The large quantity of information that exists in neurosciences makes searching and interpretation a difficult task. Further difficulties with the interpretation and integration of data arise from the different levels of central nervous system (CNS) organization. Any region of the mammalian brain can be described with respect to several levels of organization: from patterns of gene expression under specific experimental conditions, to structural, chemical, and physiological characteristics of neurons and glial cells, to specific roles in functional networks of brain regions in a particular species.

To address these problems we have started to develop an online knowledge management system, the Brain Architecture Management System (BAMS, http://brancusi.usc.edu/bkms) for systematizing, organizing, and processing neuroscience information relevant to different levels of CNS organization.

The structure of BAMS allows insertion of data about brain regions, cell types, neural pathways, and molecules collated from the literature or recorded by researchers. BAMS includes several inference engines that establish general qualitative topological relations between brain regions, reconstruct projection patterns of brain regions of interest, and construct possible networks of brain regions from connectivity data inserted in the system

We describe in this paper the structure of a new module of BAMS, the *Molecules* module, which allows insertion of molecules data pertaining to different brain regions and cell types. We also describe here the user interfaces designed for searching for molecules in BAMS. The database structure and inference engines of BAMS are described in [1].

II. Results

BAMS is hosted on a Dell 8200 desktop computer with a Pentium III processor running under the Windows 2000 operating system, with IIS 6.0. The backend relational database of BAMS was created in MySQl, and PHP was used to construct web interfaces, and inference engines. The architecture of BAMS is constructed on three levels: a set of tables constructed in MySQL that store data collated from the literature (or inserted by neuroanatomists), an intermediate level encoded in PHP that includes queries and algorithms for processing data populating BAMS, and an output level that is mainly in an HTML tabular format and graphics.

A. Molecules module database structure

The general object-relationship schema (OR) schema of BAMS is presented in Figure 1.

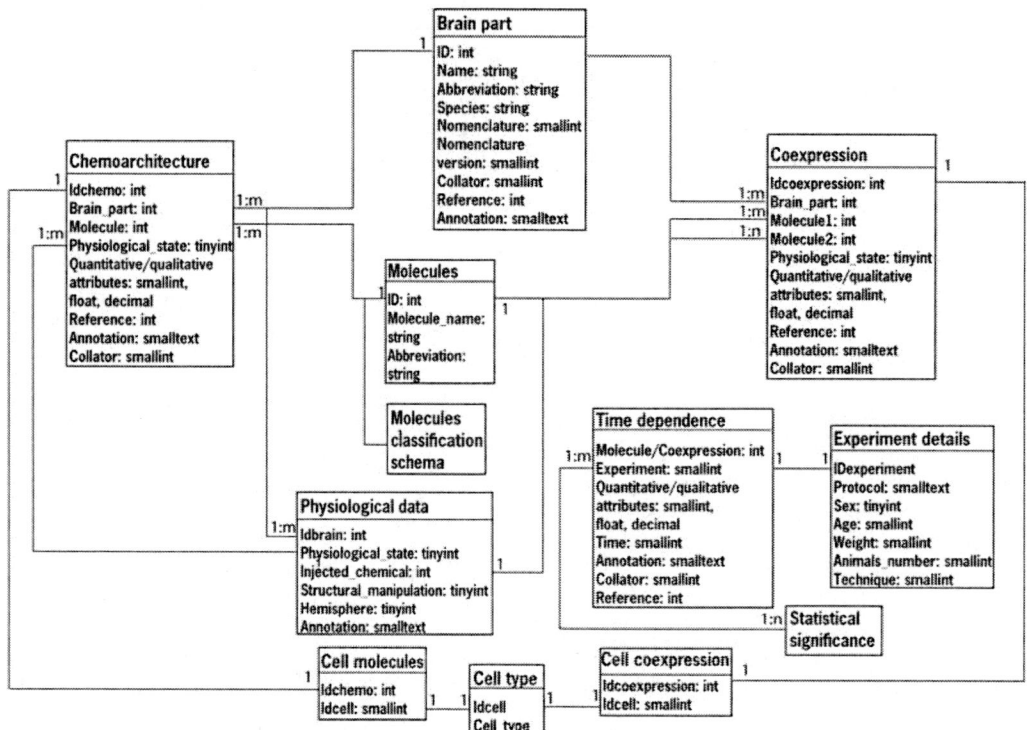

Figure 1. The object-relationship schema of the BAMS' *Molecules* module.

Each of the objects and relations shown in the figure can be captured in more than one table. The backend MySQL relational database of the BAMS' *Molecules* module consists of 17 tables, which are listed in Table 1.

Table 1. The tables included in the *Molecules* module of BAMS.

Table in BAMS	Encodes for
Brain part	unique identification and basic information about brain parts collated from different neuroanatomical atlases or nomenclatures
Molecule	Name and abbreviation of those chemicals inserted in BAMS
Molecule_type	the major classes of molecules allowed in BAMS: cell associated or releasable by neurons
Molecule_releasable	subclasses of molecules that considered in BAMS to be releasable by neurons
Cell_associated	subclasses of molecules that considered in BAMS to be found in cells and are not released by neurons
Enzymes	basic information about the enzymes inserted in BAMS
Receptors	basic information about the receptors inserted in BAMS
Receptors_subunits	basic information about the subunits of receptors inserted in BAMS
Chemoarchitecture	chemoarchitecture reports as collated from the literature
Coexpression	reports of coexpression of molecules identified in different brain regions or cell types, and collated from the literature
Time_dependence-chemoarchitecture	reports of time dependent chemical data
Time_dependence-coexpression	reports of time dependent coexpression data
Experiment	basic information about a set of experimental data grouped by a specific procedure and reported in a collated reference
Experimental_animal	information such as species (strain), sex, age, weight of experimental animals used in tract-tracing experiments
Statistical_significance	information about the statistically relevant data measured across or within experiments
Physiological_state	the allowed values of the physiological state of the experimental animals
Manipulation_type	information about the allowed of the chemical or structural manipulations allowed in BAMS
Manipulation_data	information such as the location, hemisphere, associated annotation about the physical or chemical manipulation performed in the experimental animals

literature, and the database tables in BAMS that hold information about inserted references, are described in [1] and [2].

All data inserted thus far in the *Molecules* module are collated from the literature. Method of handling the

The table *Brain part* contains the unique identification of brain parts (gray matter, fiber tracts, or ventricles) as collated from neuroanatomical nomenclatures, and it was described in

[1]. The table *Chemoarchitecture* allows insertion of a large range of experimental data: from qualitative assessments of presence or absence of molecules in different brain regions to quantitative measurements of those in different parts of the central nervous system (CNS). Qualitative attributes that describe the distribution of a molecule in a brain region include the staining strength, staining pattern, and topographical position of stained cells in the brain region. The assessment of qualitative strengths is similar to that of neuroanatomical projections between brain regions and it has been described in detail in [1]. The table *Chemoarchitecture* allows insertion of data pertaining to cell counts, percentages of cells out of the total or per area, average number of labeled cells and the sample's standard deviation. Quantitative and semi-quantitative data that can be inserted in this table include optical absorption, absorption level relative to background, and standard deviation.

The module *Molecules* also allows insertion of qualitative or quantitative reports of molecule expression in different cell types, as revealed by immunocytochemistry or by mRNA in situ hybridization. BAMS's *Molecules* module includes the table *Coexpression* that contains reports of molecule coexpression in brain regions or cell types under various physiological conditions, as collated from the literature.

The presence or absence of a molecule in a brain region or cell type often depends on the age, sex and/or physiological state of the experimental animals. Therefore, any database that stores data related to presence of molecules in different brain regions should include a representation of the animal's age, sex and physiological state (see Figure 1). The BAMS' *Molecules* module includes a simple representation of the physiological state of the experimental animals, which is encoded in the following tables: *Physiological state*, *Manipulation_type*, and *Manipulation_data*. The table *Physiological_state* encodes for the values allowed in BAMS, which are "normal" and "manipulated". An experimental animal is considered to be in a "normal" physiological state when the authors of the collated reference state that no special procedure was applied. The physiological state "manipulated" refers to either injections of chemicals, or to structural lesions in different brain regions or parts of the experimental animal. Therefore, the physiological state "manipulated" is represented in BAMS by two possible values: "chemical manipulation" and "structural manipulation", which are encoded in the table *Manipulation_type*. The table *Manipulation_data* stores details about the lesioned brain parts, the side of the brain where the procedure was performed, the injected chemicals or the lesioned brain regions, and annotations from the collated references.

The *Molecules* module of BAMS includes several tables that allow insertion of time dependent chemical data. The range of experimental data and of variables that can be inserted in the tables *Time_dependence-chemoarchitecture* and *Times_dependence-coexpression* are identical with those of *Chemoarchitecture* and *Coexpression*, respectively. Records inserted in either of these tables are grouped in experiments, as reported in collated references. This allows us to record the statistical significance of experimental data calculated within or across experiments as reported in the collated references. Summary information about the collated experiments and the animals is stored in the tables *Experiment* and *Experimental_animals*, respectively.

B. Molecules classification schema

The BAMS' *Molecules* module includes a simple classification schema of molecules. As a preliminary starting point, we consider two general classes of molecules, "releasable by neurons" and "cell associated", that are encoded in the table *Molecule_type*. These two classes partition completely the set of molecules that can be inserted in BAMS, because any chemical that can be identified in a brain region is considered here for simplicity to be produced by neurons (glial cells will be incorporated in the future). For simplicity, the present partition of molecules in BAMS is of the disjoint type. That is, any molecule can be classified in either of the general classes, but can not be an instance of both. The design of the *Molecules* module allows each of these two classes to be further divided in subclasses. The class "cell associated" is subdivided at present into two subclasses: "enzymes" and "receptors". The class "receptors" is further subdivided into "receptor subunits". Each of these classes and subclasses is assigned to a table that encodes for relationships between parents and children, and names and abbreviations of the classified molecules. The classification schema included in the *Molecules* module allows insertion of new children of either of the most general classes.

C. Searching for molecules in BAMS

Users can search for related information about molecules identified in brain regions by using a form that displays the molecules inserted in BAMS and arranged according to the classification schema. The result of this search is a list of brain regions where the searched molecule was identified, and the associated experimental conditions. Details about the presence of a molecule in a brain region can be accessed by clicking on the link associated to the experimental condition and shown in Figure 2.

Brain parts where corticotropin-releasing hormone is present	Experimental condition	Data about presence of corticotropin-releasing hormone in: PVHap manipulated state							
		Manipulation	Cell pool in the region	Hemisphere	Qualitative density of CRH in PVHap	Labeled cells count	Percentage labeled cells	Relative to basal	Annotation
Paraventricular nucleus of the hypothalamus, parvicellular division, periventricular part (PVHpv)	manipulated state	Type of manipulation: Chemical Chemical treatment: colchicine	everywhere	bilateral	not assigned	258	13.00	not measured	Collator note: see Figure 2 page 168. The percentage of labeled cells was calculated using the numbers provided in the legend of Figure 2 and represents the ratio between the labeled cells in the associated region and the total number of labeled cells in this experiment.
Paraventricular nucleus of the hypothalamus, parvicellular division, medial parvicellular part, dorsal zone (PVHmpd)	basal state manipulated state								
Paraventricular nucleus of the hypothalamus, parvicellular division, anterior parvicellular part (PVHap)	manipulated state								
Paraventricular nucleus of the hypothalamus, magnocellular division (PVHm)	manipulated state	Type of manipulation: Chemical Chemical treatment: colchicine	unclear	bilateral	exists	0	0.00	not measured	Coexpression data.
Paraventricular nucleus of the hypothalamus, magnocellular division, posterior magnocellular part (PVHpm)	manipulated state	Page 1119: most animals received a single injection of 50 to 100 micrograms of colchicine into the lateral ventricle 48 to 72 h before perfusion to arrest axonal transport and thereby enhance the immunohistochemical staining of neuropeptides in cell bodies							

Figure 2. The result of search of brain regions where corticotropin-releasing hormone (CRH) was identified. Users can view details of the records associated to each of the retrieved brain regions such as qualitative density, cell counts, spatial characteristics of the cells that express the molecule and associated annotations by clicking on the links associated with the experimental conditions. For reports associated to manipulated state, users can further view the type of manipulation, the injected chemicals, and details of the experimental procedure.

Users can also view all the molecules identified in a brain region when they search for brain parts. The result of search for brain parts in BAMS is a page that summarizes the data collated by researchers or inferred by the system and associated with the part of interest. A detailed description of the BAMS web interfaces is provided in [1]. If a brain region is associated in BAMS with several molecules, they are returned in the page that summarizes it, as shown in Figure 3.

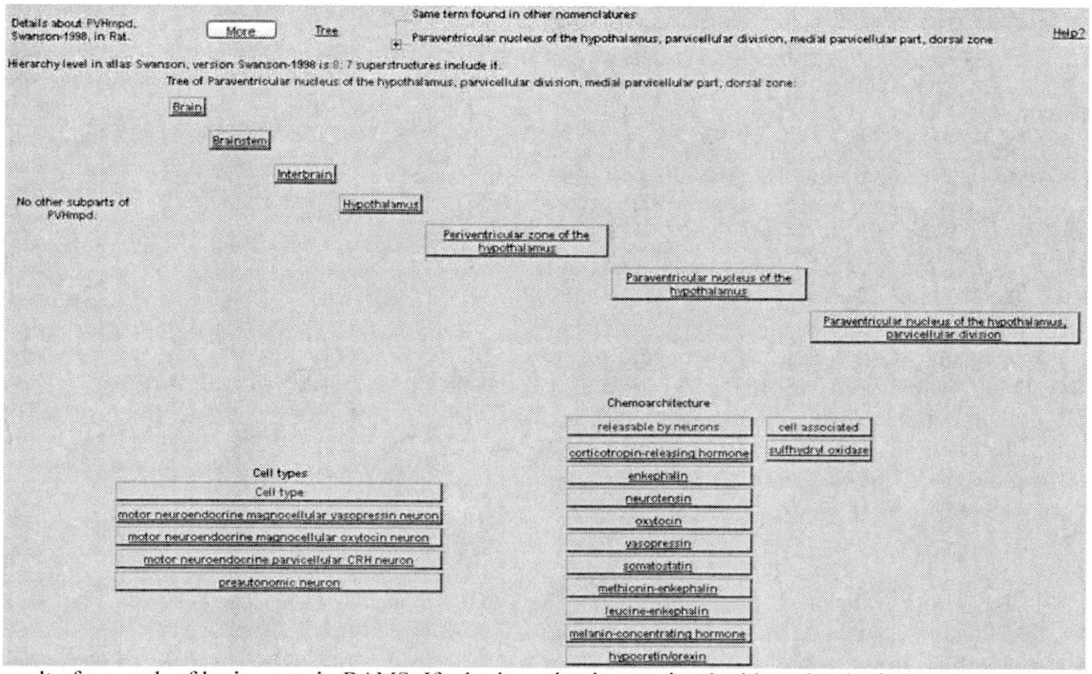

Figure 3. The result of a search of brain parts in BAMS. If a brain region is associated with molecules in BAMS, these will be listed under the category "Chemoarchitecture" and classified according to the *Molecule's* classification schema.

Users can access further information about each of the retrieved molecules by clicking on the associated links. The result of this action is shown in Figure 4. Records associated with the molecule of interest are grouped by experimental condition, by presence of the molecule in the brain region or its expression of it in different cell types, and by the technique that was used: immunohistochemistry or mRNA in situ hybridization.

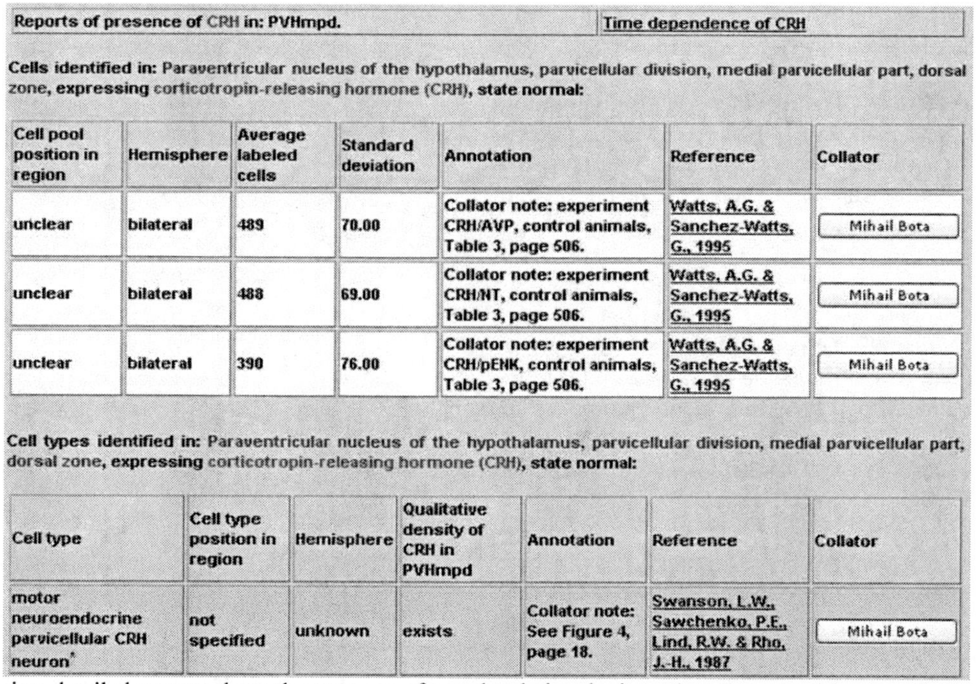

Figure 4. Users can view detailed reports about the presence of a molecule in a brain region. Reports of a molecule that is associated with a brain region are organized according to several criteria: physiological state of the animal, presence of the molecule in the brain region, or its expression in cell types, and the employed technique.

If a molecule identified in a brain region is associated in BAMS with time dependent data, users can access this information by clicking on a link called "Time dependence" as shown in Figure 4.

The time dependent molecular data are grouped by experiment, reference, and experimental state of the animals.

D. Inserted data

The *Molecules* module of BAMS contains more than 3000 reports related to the presence of 18 molecules in the rat CNS. Overall, BAMS contains 11 brain nomenclatures from five species: human, macaque (*Macaca fascicularis*), cat, rat, and mouse, more than 19,000 reports of neuroanatomical projections as collated from the literature since 1962 and related generally to the visual and limbic systems of the rat, and data referring to 24 cell types identified in 37 rat brain regions that are defined in the Swanson-1998 nomenclature [8].

III. Conclusions

In this article we have described the structure and major features of the BAMS' *Molecules* module, which has been designed for the online handling of gene expression data identified in different brain regions or cell types, and collated from the literature.

This is part of an expanding effort in the emerging field of neuroinformatics. Several research groups have developed online knowledge management systems that handle data at different levels of nervous system organization: brain region nomenclatures [2-5, 7], neuroanatomical projections [2, 4, 5, 7], and cytology [2, 6]. Two systems that share similar features with BAMS are NeuroNames (http://braininfo.rprc.washington.edu) [3] and CoCoMac (http://cocomac.org) [5, 7]. However, none of these systems includes a representation of molecules data identified in various brain regions and cell types. BAMS is to our knowledge the first online neuroinformatic system that manipulates neurobiological data across four levels of organization of CNS: molecules, cell types, brain regions, and networks of brain regions.

The present status of BAMS is "in progress" because we continue to add new data and extend its functionality. New features of BAMS will include inference engines for automatic comparison of the molecules data according to the age, sex and other attributes of the experimental animals. This will allow users to run complex queries, such as extracting gene expression patterns in specific cell types or brain regions in certain experimental conditions.

Acknowledgment

This work was supported by NIH/NIMH Grant MH61223 and by NINDS Grant NS-16668, and the NINDS/NIMH/NIBIB/NLM Grant NS050792-01.

References

[1] M. Bota, H-W. Dong, and L.W. Swanson, The Brain Architecture Management System, *Neuroinformatics*, vol. 3, in press, 2005.

[2] M. Bota and M.A. Arbib, "Integrating Databases and Expert Systems for the Analysis of Brain Structures: Connections, Similarities and Homologies", *Neuroinformatics*, vol. 2, pp. 19-58, 2004.

[3] D.M. Bowden and R.F. Martin, A digital Rosetta stone for primate brain terminology. In: Bloom, F.E, Bjorklund, A., Hokfelt, T. (Eds.), *Handbook of Chemical Neuroanatomy vol. 13: The Primate Nervous System, part I*, pp 1-37, Amsterdam: Elsevier, 1997.

[4] G.A.P.C. Burns, Knowledge mechanics and the NeuroScholar project: a new approach to neuroscientific theory. In Arbib M.A., Grethe J. (Eds) *Computing the Brain: A Guide to Neuroinformatics*, pp 319-336, San Diego: Academic Press, 2001.

[5] R. Kötter, Online retrieval, processing, and visualization of primate connectivity data from the CoCoMac Database, *Neuroinformatics*, vol. 2, pp. 127-144, 2004.

[6] L. Marenco, P. Nadkarni, E. Skoufos, G. Shepherd, and P. Miller, Neuronal database integration, the Senselab EAV data model, *Proceedings of AMIA Symposium*, pp. 102–6, 1999.

[7] K.E. Stephan, L. Kamper, A. Bozkurt, G.A.P.C. Burns, M. P. Young, and R. Kötter, Advanced database methodology for the Collation of Connectivity data on the Macaque brain (CoCoMac). *Philosophical Transactions of the Royal Society London B: Biological Sciences*, vol. 356, pp. 1159-1186, 2001.

[8] L.W. Swanson, *Maps: Structure of the Rat Brain*, Amsterdam: Elsevier. 1998.

Protein Flexibility Modeling Using Kernel Based Methods

Xue-wen Chen and Jeremy Chen

Department of Electrical Engineering and Computer Science, The University of Kansas,
1520 West 15th Street, Lawrence, KS 66045

Abstract -- Proteins play an essential role in nearly all cell functions such as composing cellular structure, promoting chemical reactions, carrying messages from one cell to another and acting as antibodies. The multiplicity of functions that proteins execute is attributed to their 3-D conformational structures. Protein flexibility is an important link between protein structure and function. Understanding the conformational changes of a protein molecule is essential in discovering the protein structure and function relationships underlying most biological processes and has underappreciated implications in drug design. However, modeling protein flexibility is a very computationally challenging problem with a large number of degrees of freedom involved. In order to address this important challenge, the paper studies protein dynamics and develop a kernel based computational model to characterize protein conformational changes and to reduce the redundancy in protein conformers.

I. INTRODUCTION

The recent completion of the human genome project has paved the way for new post-genomic research paradigms that exploit genome functions [1]. Research has increasingly focused on the study of proteins, giving rise to the discipline of proteomics. As the products of gene-regulated synthesis, proteins play an essential role in nearly all cell functions such as composing cellular structure, promoting chemical reactions, carrying messages from one cell to another and acting as antibodies. Many proteins actually serve more than one of the above roles. The multiplicity of functions that proteins execute is attributed to both their diversity of chemical composition and to the variety of three-dimensional (3-D) conformations that proteins can adopt. Of the two protein properties, chemical composition is much easier to characterize, but 3-D structure has the most direct relationship with protein function. It is thus critical for us to understand protein 3-D structures in order to better understand questions like how genes work and how our bodies function. With the advanced technologies such as X-ray crystallography [2] and Nuclear Magnetic Resonance (NMR) [3], a large amount of protein structure data at atomic resolutions are currently available. It is now possible, and increasingly imperative, to study protein 3-D structures and intermolecular complexes.

Protein flexibility refers to the capacity of the protein to experience dynamic changes in conformation under biological conditions. It is an important link between protein structure and function [4, 5]. In most cases, proteins undergo conformational changes while executing their functions, especially upon complex formation. This affects their interactions with other molecules, and thus their biological functions. Although analysis of a single protein conformation provides certain information about protein operations, understanding the conformational changes of a protein molecule is essential in discovering the protein structure and function relationships underlying many biological processes and has underappreciated implications in drug design. This is especially true when the conformational changes occur at the same time as (and sometimes play a critical role in) ligand-protein or protein-protein binding processes.

Research interests have increasingly focused on collective mode based protein flexibility modeling. This approach allows for the representation of full protein flexibility. It decomposes the protein flexibility into collective modes of motion. Recent studies demonstrate that a few dominant modes can characterize most of the protein dynamics, i.e., the protein flexibility can be represented in a reduced space. Normal mode analysis methods [6-7] exploiting simple harmonic oscillations about an energy minimum have been used to represent protein flexibility with a few degrees of freedom. Zacharias and Sklenar [8] and Philippopoulos and Lim [9] use harmonic modes derived from the eigen-analyses of a Hessian matrix of the potential energy function to describe DNA flexibility; the number of degrees of freedom characterizing protein flexibility is significantly reduced. The singular value decomposition (SVD) is a commonly used method to analyze MD trajectories of atomic fluctuations in protein flexibility modeling [10-12]. The SVD based approach can characterize the collective motions in MD trajectories that are not revealed in MD simulations [13]. Another frequently used protein flexibility modeling method is principal component analysis (PCA) that reduces the modeling complexity. Garcia [14] applied PCA in molecular dynamic simulations to study protein conformational changes. PCA is applied to model the flexibility of parallel and antiparallel β–sheets [15] and α–helices [16], which reveal the underlying structures and characterize the deformations observed in real structures. While normal mode methods are limited in deficient solvent modeling and the existence of multiple energy minima during a large scale motion [17], PCA is an appropriate model if the protein flexibility is Gaussian or is governed by second-order correlations. Most recently, Teodoro et al. [17] used PCA to reduce the number of degrees of freedom for protein flexibility modeling. The fifty most significant principal components, derived from the thousands of degrees of freedom in protein conformational space, capture more than 80% of the overall conformational variance. In [17], PCA has been applied to HIV-1 protease and Aldose reductase. In both cases, a reduced basis representation of protein flexibility is obtained which retains a large portion of the relevant protein conformers.

All of the aforementioned approaches for full protein flexibility modeling are globally linear methods. As a result, they may not capture the nonlinearity of the original data with a few dominant bases. For example, neither SVD nor PCA is able to extract wave modes. Protein flexibility is inherently nonlinear [14]. This motivates the use of a nonlinear modeling method that can extract higher-order correlations between atoms in the protein structures. Hence, nonlinear dimensional reduction methods are ultimately necessary for protein flexibility modeling. In this paper, we will study the kernel principal component analysis (KPCA) method for protein dynamic modeling. We will employ KPCA to decompose protein dynamics into a few dominant and representative modes, which shed insights into the underlining mechanism of protein flexibility effects. As a nonlinear dimensionality reduction method, KPCA has been successfully applied in various image analysis areas such as image modeling [18] and face recognition [19]. In contrast to the previously mentioned modeling methods, KPCA can capture higher-order statistics that are important in characterizing protein dynamics and reduce the degrees of freedom in the data.

The paper is organized into four sections. Section II describes the kernel based modeling method. In section III, we present the experimental results. Finally, conclusions are drawn in Section IV.

II. KERNEL BASED PROTEIN FLEXIBILITY MODELING

Protein flexibility can be represented by a set of conformational vectors consisting of the time-evolved displacements of each atom. Each structural conformational vector is of the form

$$x = [d_{1x}, d_{1y}, d_{1z}, d_{2x}, d_{2y}, d_{2z}, \cdots, d_{nx}, d_{ny}, d_{nz}]^T \quad (1)$$

where $[d_{jx}, d_{jy}, d_{jz}]^T$ represents Cartesian coordinates for the jth atom, and n is the number of atoms (thus, the degrees of freedom for each conformation is $N = 3n$).

Given a set of m protein conformations $x_k \in R^N$, $k = 1, \ldots, m$, we first nonlinearly map the data $x_1, \ldots, x_m$ into a potentially much higher dimensional feature space F by $\Phi : R^N \to F$. In the higher dimensional feature space, a simple representation of the protein flexibility can be found by solving the eigen problem of the covariance matrix C

$$C = \frac{1}{N} \sum_{i=1}^{N} \Phi(x_j) \Phi(x_j)^T. \quad (2)$$

i.e., finding $\lambda > 0, V \neq 0$ with

$$\lambda V = CV = \frac{1}{N} \sum_{i=1}^{N} (\Phi(x_j)^T \cdot V) \Phi(x_j). \quad (3)$$

The eigenvectors V with nonzero eigenvalues are in the span of the mapped data, i.e., $V \in span\{\Phi(x_1), \cdots, \Phi(x_m)\}$ as seen from Eq. (3), i.e.,

$$V = \sum_{i=1}^{m} \alpha_i \Phi(x_j), \quad (4)$$

where $[\alpha_1, \cdots, \alpha_m]$ are the expansion coefficients. The new degrees of freedom can be formed by projecting nonlinear mapping of the protein structures onto the principal components V. A few of the principal components V are capable of capturing most of the variability of protein dynamics. The contribution of the few dominant components to the overall motion is decided by the corresponding eigenvalues. Thus, we can model the protein flexibility by retaining only these new degrees of freedom that are significantly more representative of protein motions than others. The number of new degrees of freedom is typically much smaller than the original number of degrees of freedom and represents collective motions effectively characterizing the protein flexibility.

As the feature space F may have arbitrarily large dimensionality, it is impractical to carry out the nonlinear mapping Φ explicitly and solve the eigen equation (3) directly. Instead, KPCA uses a highly effective trick, namely Mercer kernels [20-22], for computing inner products. A Mercer kernel is a function $k(x, y)$ giving rise to a positive matrix $K_{ij} = k(x_i, x_j)$ for all data sets $\{x_1, ..., x_m\}$ [22]. Mercer kernels provide an elegant way to deal with nonlinear algorithms without mapping the data explicitly. Define the $n \times n$ matrix K by

$$K_{ij} = k(x_i, x_j) = (\Phi(x_i) \cdot \Phi(x_j)). \quad (5)$$

Instead of solving Eq. (3) for eigenvectors V, we compute the eigen problem for the expansion coefficients α_j, that is now solely dependent on the kernel function [23],

$$\lambda \alpha = K \alpha. \quad (6)$$

where $\alpha = [\alpha_1, \cdots, \alpha_m]^T$. For extracting the degrees of freedom of a new protein conformation x with kernel PCA, we simply project the mapped pattern $\Phi(x)$ onto V^k

$$(V^k \cdot \Phi(x)) = \sum_{i=1}^{m} \alpha_i^k (\Phi(x_i) \cdot \Phi(x)) = \sum_{i=1}^{m} \alpha_i^k k(x_i, x) \quad (7)$$

From Eq. (7), we can see that to model the protein flexibility with new degrees of freedom, only the kernel function k matters. The choice of the kernel function k implicitly determines the mapping Φ and the nonlinear feature space F. Examples of commonly used kernels are polynomial kernels $k(x, y) = (x \cdot y + c)^d$, ($c \geq 0$ and d odd) and the Gaussian kernels $k(x, y) = e^{-(\|x-y\|^2 / 2\sigma^2)}$.

As the solutions V^k of Eq. (3) need to be normalized vectors, we impose the constraints on the solutions (λ_k, α^k) of Eq. (6): $\lambda_k (\alpha^k \cdot \alpha^k) = 1$ in F. Also, as in PCA algorithms, the data needs to be centered in high-dimensional space F. This can be done by simply substituting the kernel matrix K with $\hat{K} = K - 1_m K - K 1_m + 1_m K 1_m$, where $(1_m)_{ij} = 1/m$ [23].

Solving Eqs. (6) and (7) gives rise to the new degrees of freedom to model protein flexibility. The new degrees of freedom are capable of capturing the nonlinearity embedded in protein motions without having to carry out the nonlinear mapping Φ explicitly.

III. EXPERIMENTAL RESULTS

We will consider the HIV-1 protease [24] as our test model. The HIV is formed from long polyprotein chains during viral replication. An HIV protease is an enzyme that cleaves the peptide bond at a specific point of the polyprotein chain, which turns into small pieces of proteins that eventually becomes a mature virus. The enzyme therefore is an attractive target in anti-AIDS drug design, and the effect of binding various inhibitors on the protease structure is currently the focus of intensive research. Because of its dynamic structure variability, there have been many experimental structures discovered for this protein, and they all bind to different ligands depending on their structural view [25]. This represents an important cause of failure to predict the correct binding enzyme-substrate energies. This protein emphasizes the importance of understanding protein flexibility. If the motions of proteins could be accurately and efficiently modeled, it could significantly improve the computational drug design process.

A. SIMULATING CONFORMATIONAL PROTEIN DATA

To generate the coordinates of the protein at different time steps, molecular dynamic software called NAMD is used [26]. Before running the NAMD program, the initial structure (pdb file) of the protein (4HVP) is downloaded from the PDB protein data bank [27]. This structure is determined by X-ray crystallography, which does not contain hydrogen atoms in 4HVP. We use a program called 'psfgen' to generate the PSF (Protein Structure file) file which includes the missing hydrogen atoms by guessing its coordinates using CHARM22 topology file. The topology file defines the atom types used in the force field, the atom names, type, bonds, and partial charges of each residue type. The PSF file contains all of the molecule-specific information needed to apply a particular force field to a molecular system. The complete structure is then solvated in a water box using a molecule visualization program called VMD in preparation for the simulation (see figure 1 for 4HVP in water box). The system is then simulated using NAMD with CHARM22 parameter file, and a configuration file. The parameter file contains all of the numerical constants needed to evaluate forces and energies. The configuration file includes information about the simulation environments such as the boundary coordinates, temperature, and number of steps. The simulation is carried out in a water box as shown in Figure 1 using periodic boundary conditions, particle mesh Ewald full electrostatic integration, and pressure and temperature coupling using the Berendsen algorithm at a temperature of 300 Kelvin. The coordinates is record on a .dcd file each time step of 100 femtoseconds. The .dcd output file is stored in binary code so that the coordinates and velocity information may be kept to high precision.

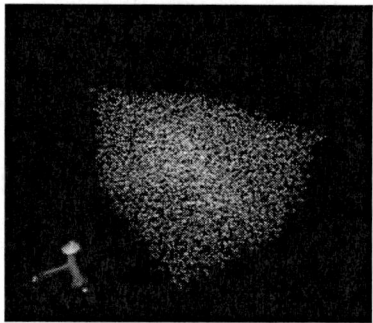

Figure 1. VMD generated images of 4HVP solvated in a water box in angle 1 with y-axis on top.

B. MODELING THE PROTEIN FLEXIBILITY

Two different data sets are used in comparing the effectiveness of different modeling methods. Both of the data sets belong to the conformational changes of the protein 4HVP from the simulation, except that the first data set contains only the coordinates of the active site and the second data set contains the coordinates of the whole system. Both of the datasets have the exact same number of time steps, which is from time step 0 to 290,000. Each time step is 2 fs, meaning the MD program simulate for around .60 ns. The time steps are recorded on the data sets every 50 steps or 100 fs.

The kernels used in our experiments are polynomial and Gaussian kernels. These two kernels are the most frequently used kernels because of their effectiveness in recognizing non-linear data. The original linear PCA method is also tested so comparison can be made in which method can capture the motions of the protein conformations with fewer possible number of principal components (and thus, the lower degrees of freedom).

Active Site Experiment: The KPCA model is first applied to active site data. We apply the polynomial kernel to the data set with different degrees to see the effect it has on the total variance captured by the principal components. As for the RBF kernel, there is minimal performance change when the parameters were configured differently. As a result, only one parameter setting (set to 50) in RBF was sufficient enough to compare its performance with other methods. Figure 2 shows the fraction of total variance captured versus number of principal components. As one can see, every single one of the polynomial kernel used outperforms the linear PCA in terms of using fewer principal components to describe the variance in the system. The RBF kernel's principal components accounts for about the same amount of variance as the linear PCA.

The optimal degree in polynomial kernel found is 19, which accounts for about 83% of the total variance using just the first principal component. This dominant principal component alone can capture most of conformation changes around the active site. One interesting observation was that the amount of variance captured by using degrees higher than 19 begins to deteriorate slowly as it gets higher than degree 19. For example, degree 25 captures 82% of the total variance using the first principal component, which is 1% lower than degree 19. As one can observe, as the number of principal components increases, the fraction of variance for all the methods starts converging to 1.

Figure 3 shows the total number of principal components needed to achieve a certain fraction of total variance in the active site. In order to capture 80% of the total variance around the active site, PCA needs 5 principal components whereas KPCA (polynomial degree of 19 and 20) only needs 1 principal component. To describe 95% of the total motion around the active site, PCA needs 35 principal components. On the other hand, KPCA needs only a total of 11 principal components to describe 95% of the total motion.

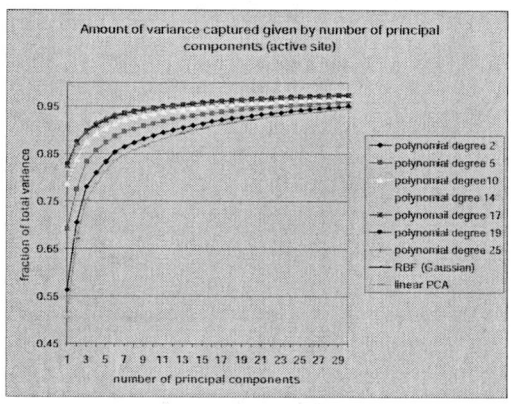

Figure 2. The fraction of total variance captured given number of principal components.

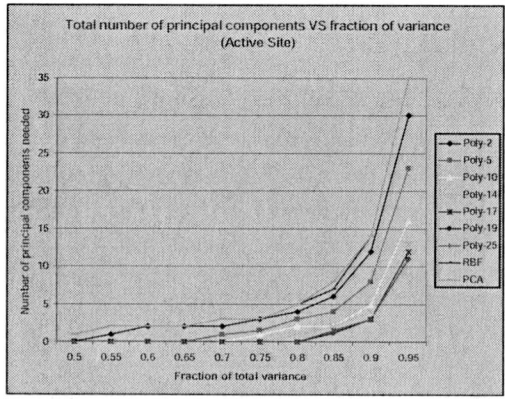

Figure 3. Total number of principal components needed to achieve a certain fraction of total variance in the active site.

Entire System Experiment: We also test the method on entire protein system. The results (Figure 4) are similar to the ones we obtain from active site except that besides having to capture the motion of the active site, other non major conformation changes are also described in the principal components. One interesting result is that the first component of polynomial KPCA with degree 2 accounts for only 52.9% of total variance, while linear PCA's first component accounts for around 53.6%. But by using two principal components, poly KPCA of degree 2 accounts for 68%, while PCA accounts for 66%. For the polynomial KPCA with degree of 25, the first component describes around 64% of the total conformation change for the entire system, over a 10% increase comparing to the first principal component of PCA. These values are smaller than the previous experiment's value because the total number of degrees of freedom considered is much larger. Unlike the previous experiment where adding the second principal components only result in a minor change, the two principal components for polynomial KPCA of degree 25 has a combined total variance of around 80% (See figure 4). Although the total number of degree of freedom is much larger, most of the atom coordinates are redundant in the system except for the area around the active site, and some extra sidechain movements. These sidechain movements can explain the reason why the second principle component combining with the first accounts for around 80% of the total variation in the system. By representing the degrees of freedom using this new basis from KPCA, we are able to capture most of the conformation changes in the entire system.

The results in figure 5 show the amount of variance captured given the number of principal components. As one can clearly observe, the number of principal components needed for KPCA to describe the motion of the entire system is lower than using PCA. One interesting observation is that the number of principal components needed for PCA and KPCA starts to spread out at 90% of the total variance. To capture 90% of the total motion, KPCA (polynomial of 19 and 25) needs only 10 principal components whereas PCA needs 27 principal components. The difference widens as the total variance reaches 95%. For KPCA (polynomial 25), it needs around 41 principal components to describe 95% of total variance. On the other hand, PCA requires 120 principal components, which is three times more than that of KPCA.

IV. CONCLUSIONS

This paper studies protein dynamics and a computational model to characterize protein conformational changes as well as to reduce redundancy within an assembly of protein conformers. The stochastic model is based on kernel principal component analysis (KPCA), which is capable of capturing the nonlinearity of conformational motion and reducing the degrees of freedom in the data. The reduced degrees of freedom retain significantly representative information of protein flexibility, while substantially reducing the system complexity. We employ KPCA to decompose protein dynamics into a few dominant and representative modes, which shed insights into the underlining mechanism of protein flexibility effects. As seen from our experimental results, the first principal component of KPCA accounts for about 83% of the total conformation changes around the active site, while PCA only accounts for 50%. By using just 4 dominant principal components, KPCA is able to account for 90% of the total variance at the active site. On the contrary, PCA needs around 16 principal components to reach 90% of the total variance. This is due to KPCA's ability to capture the nonlinear motions in the datasets. This finding further verifies the paper by [14], which states that nonlinear motions are responsible for most of the atomic fluctuations in protein.

It is interesting to note that different kernels may have different impact on the modeling results, as can be seen from our results. We also test the same methods on other protein conformational data and similar results are obtained. Why polynominal kernels perform better than RBF ones are unclear at this moment. More tests are needed to find answers. Another issue is the reconstruction of the original structures, which is much more complex because the mapped nonlinear space is implicit and unknown. This is an area of research which we will further extend from this paper.

The method described here can also be applied to other protein structures problems, e.g., protein structure comparisons by extracting few dominate eigenvectors. Our future work will address this.

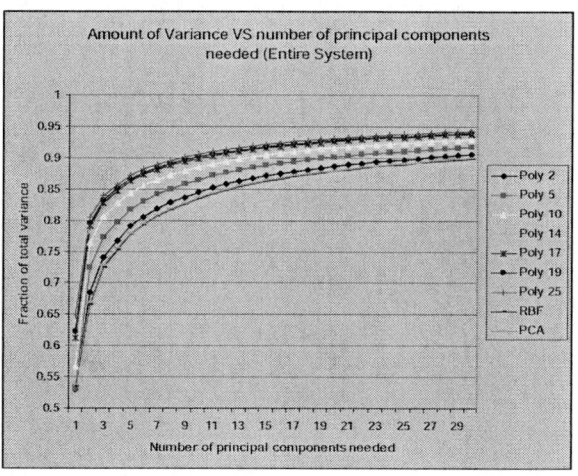

Figure 4. Result of applying several dimensionality reduction methods on all the atoms in the entire system.

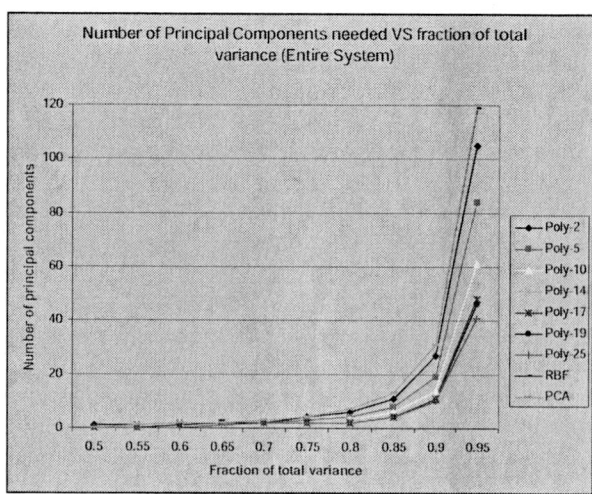

Figure 5. The amount of variance given kernel type and the number of principal components.

ACKNOWLEDGMENT

This publication was made possible by NIH Grant P20 RR17708 from the Institutional Development Award (IDeA) Program of the National Center for Research Resources.

REFERENCES

[1]. F. Collins, E. green, A. Guttmacher, and M. Guyer, "A vision for the future of genomics research," *Nature,* 422, pp. 835-884, 2003.

[2]. G. Rhodes, *Crystallography Mode Crystal Clear.* Academic Press, London, 1993.

[3]. K. Wuthrich, *NMR of Proteins and Nucleic Acids.* John Wiley & Sons, New York, 1986.

[4]. D. Koshland, "Application of a theory of enzyme specificity to protein synthesis," *Proc. Natl. Acad. Sci. U.S.,* 44, pp. 98-104, 1958.

[5]. H. Carlson and J. McCammon, "Accommodating Protein Flexibility in Computational Drug Design," *Molecular Pharmacology,* 57, pp. 213–218, 2000.

[6]. R. Levy, and M. Karplus, "Vibrational approach to the dynamics of an alpha-helix," *Biopolymers,* 18, pp. 2465-2495, 1979.

[7]. A. Mackerell, 'All-atom empirical potential for molecular modeling and dynamic studies of protein,' *J. Phys. Chem.* B 102, pp. 3586-3616, 1998.

[8]. M. Zacharias, and H. Sklenar, "Harmonic modes as variables to approximately account for receptor flexibility in ligand-receptor docking simulation: application to DNA minor groove ligand complex," *Journal of Computational Chemistry* 20, pp. 287-300, 1999.

[9]. M. Philippopoulos and C. Lim, "Exploring the dynamic information content of a protein NMR structure: comparison of a molecular dynamics simulation with the NMR and X-ray structures of Escherichia coli ribonuclease," *Proteins* 36, pp. 87-110, 1999.

[10]. T. Romo, J. Clarage, D. Sorensen, and G. Phillips, Jr. "Automatic identification of discrete substates in proteins: singular value decomposition analysis of time-averaged crystallographic refinements," *Proteins* 22, pp. 311-321, 1995.

[11]. A. Garcia and J. Harman, "Simulations of CRP:(cAMP)(2) in noncrystalline environments show a subunit transition from the open to the closed conformation," *Protein Sci.* 5, pp. 62-71, 1996.

[12]. P. Doriker, A. Atilgan, and i. Bahar, "Dynamics of proteins predicted by molecular dynamics simulations and analytical approaches: Application to alpha-Amylase Inhibitor," *Proteins,* 40, pp. 512-524, 2000.

[13]. P. Doruker, I. Bahar, C. Baysal, and B. Erman, "Collective deformations in proteins determined by a mode analysis of molecular dynamic trajectories," *Polymer* 43, pp. 431-439, 2002.

[14]. A. Garcia, "Large-amplitude nonlinear motion in protein," *Physical Review Letters* 68, pp. 2696-2699, 1992.

[15]. E. Emberly, R. Mukhopadhyay, C. Tang, and N. Wingreen, 'Flexibility of β-sheets: Principal-component analysis of database protein structure,' *Proteins* 55, pp. 91-98, 2004.

[16]. E. Emberly, R. Mukhopadhyay, N. Wingreen, and C. Tang, "Flexibility of alpha-helices: Results of a statistical analysis of database protein structures," *J. Mol. Biol.* 327, pp. 229-237, 2003.

[17]. M. Teodoro, G. Phillips, and L. Kavraki, "A dimensionality reduction approach to modeling protein flexibility," *Proceeding of the Sixth Annual Conference on Computational Molecular Biology (RECOMB)* 2002.

[18]. K. Kim, M. Franz, and B. Scholkopf, "Image modeling based on kernel principal component analysis," submitted to IEEE Trans. on PAMI, available in http://www.kyb.tuebingen.mpg.de/publications/pdfs/pdf2453.pdf.

[19]. K. Kim, K. Jung, and H. Kim, "Face recognition using kernel principal component analysis," *IEEE Signal Processing Letters* 9, pp. 40-42, 2002.

[20]. V. Vapnik, *The Nature of Statistical Learning Theory.* New York; Springer-Verlag, 1995.

[21]. K.-R. Muller, S. Mike, G. Ratsch, K. Tsuda, and B. Scholkopf, "An introduction to kernel-based learning algorithms," *IEEE Trans. on Neural Networks,* 12, pp. 181-201, 2001.

[22]. S. Saitoh. *Theory of Reproducing kernels and Its Applications.* Longman scientific & Technical, Harlow, England, 1988.

[23]. B. Scholkopf, A. Smola, and K. Muller, "Nonlinear component analysis as a kernel eigenvalue problem," *Neural Computation,* 10, pp. 1299-1319, 1998.

[24]. J. Vondrasek, C. van Buskirk, and A. Wlodawer, "Database of three dimensional structures of HIV proteinases," *Nat. Struct. Biol.,* 4, pp. 8-9, 1997.

[25]. Teodoro, M.L., G.N. Phillips, Jr., and L.E. Kavraki. "Understanding Protein Flexibility Through Dimensionality Reduction," *Journal of Computational Biology, 10(3-4),* pp. 617-634, 2003.

[26]. http://www.ks.uiuc.edu/Research/namd/.

[27]. http://www.rcsb.org/pdb/.

An empirical comparison of individual machine learning techniques and ensemble approaches in protein structural class prediction

Valnaide G. Bittencourt*, Marjory C. C. Abreu[†], Marcilio C. P. de Souto[†] and Anne M. de P. Canuto[†]

*Department of Computing and Automation
Federal University of Rio Grande do Norte
Natal, RN, Brazil, 59072-970
E-mail: valnaide@dca.ufrn.br

[†]Department of Informatics and
Applied Mathematics
Federal University of Rio Grande do Norte
Natal, RN, Brazil, 59072-970
E-mail: majo_abreu@yahoo.com.br,marcilio@dimap.ufrn.br,anne@dimap.ufrn

Abstract— Protein fold recognition is an important approach to structure discovery without relying on sequence similarity. In this context, computer-based tools, mainly the techniques from Machine Learning (ML), have became essential considering the large volume of data. We present an empirical comparison of individual machine learning techniques (k-Nearest Neighbor, Naive Bayes, Decision Trees, Support Vector Machines and Neural Networks) and ensemble approaches (Bagging and Boosting) to the task of protein structural class prediction.

I. Introduction

One of the most important goals of bioinformatics is the ability to predict tertiary (three-dimensional - 3-D) structure and thereby function from protein sequence information [1]. The ability to exactly predict structures and functions could revolutionize medicine, pharmacology and chemistry. Two common computational approaches to identify protein function are sequence analysis and structure analysis. Sequence analysis is based on a comparison between unknown sequences with those whose function is already known. However, two proteins can be structurally similar suggesting a common evolutionary origin, but could not have significant sequence similarity [2]. In addition, although two sequences can present a high degree of sequence similarity, they still could not share the same function.

Thus, in this paper, we focus on the approach of determining structure similarity without sequence similarity, using Machine Learning (ML) methods [1], [3], [4], [5], such as support vector machines and ensemble of decision trees. More specifically, we address the problem of recognizing structural class in protein folds. Proteins are said to have a common fold, which is a common 3-D pattern, if they have the same major secondary structure[1] in the same arrangement and with the same topology [6].

[1]Secondary structure refers to local structural elements such as hairpins, helixes, beta-pleated sheets, etc.

In our analysis, like in [3], we presume that the number of folds is restricted. Therefore, the focus is on structural predictions in the context of a particular classification of 3-D folds. There are several famous classification databases such as the Structure Classification of Protein (SCOP) and the Class, Architecture, Topology, and Homologous superfamily (CATH) [7], [8]. These different classification databases of proteins focus on their own characteristics. For example, the SCOP database, which will be used in this work, is a hierarchical classification of known protein structures, organized according to their evolutionary and structural relationship. Such a database is divided into four hierarchical levels: class, fold, superfamily, and family.

II. Material and Methods

We perform an empirical comparison of rule based systems such as Decision Trees and statistical learning systems such as Naive Bayes, k-Nearest Neighbor, Support Vector Machines and Neural Networks, and ensemble methods such as Bagging and Boosting to the task of protein structural class prediction. All the learning methods used in our study were obtained from the WEKA machine learning package [9] (http://www.cs.waikato.ac.nz/~ml/weka/).

A. Dataset

We use the dataset made available by the authors in [5] (http://www.brc.dcs.gla.ac.uk/~actan/eKISS/data.htm). This dataset is a modification of the original dataset created and used in [3], [4]. This original dataset (http://www.nersc.gov/~cding/protein/) is formed by a training set (Ntrain) and a test set (Ntest). The training set was extracted from the (PDB_selects) sets [10] and comprises 313 proteins from 27 most populated SCOP folds (more than seven examples for each fold). For this set, all the pairwise sequence identities are less than 35%. The test set was extracted from the PDB_40D [7]. Such a set contains 386 representatives (excluding the sequences already in the training set) of the same 27 SCOP folds with the pairwise sequence identities less than 35%.

The features used in the learning system were extracted from protein sequences according to the method described in [11]. In that work, they considered several features for predicting protein folds using global description of the chain of amino acids representing proteins. Such descriptors were computed from physical, chemical, and structural properties of the constituent amino acids: hydrophobicity, polarity, polarizability, predicted secondary structure, normalized van der Waals volume and amino acid composition of the protein sequence.

These descriptors essentially represent the frequencies with which such properties change along the sequence and their distribution in the chain. Each of this properties is described by a vector with 21 continuous attributes (with exception of the amino acid composition, for there are only 20 amino acids). In our work, in order to form an input pattern, we use all descriptors with all their features at once and one attribute representing the length of the protein, that is, our input vector has 126 attributes.

It is important to point out that [5] cleaned their dataset in relation to original dataset in [3], [4] by removing errors from both training and testing examples. Also the authors applied the protein fold classification according to SCOP 1.61 [12] and Astral 1.61 [13] with sequence identity less than 40% (November 2002). After performing this stage, the resulting dataset contained 582 examples distributed in 25 SCOP folds or, in a higher hierarchical level, four SCOP structural classes (all-α, all-β, $\alpha + \beta$, and α/β) plus a class for those proteins not in any of the former classes (*small*) - see Table I.

TABLE I
DISTRIBUTION OF PROTEINS AMONG STRUCTURAL CLASSES

Structural Class	Examples
all-α	111
all-β	177
α/β	203
$\alpha + \beta$	46
Small	45
Total	582

Since the 27 protein folds can be grouped into four structural classes, as pointed out in [14], a two-level recognition can be done. At level one a protein to be recognized is assign to one of the four structural class (all-α, all-β, $\alpha+\beta$, and α/β), while at level two, the respective protein is classified in one of the 27 folds. Recognition can include either level of both. In this paper, we will work only at level one. That is, in our work, we will use this dataset with the four SCOP classification (plus the additional class *small*) as the classes to be learned by our ML techniques.

B. Evaluation

The comparison of two supervised learning methods is, often, accomplished by analyzing the statistical significance of the difference between the mean of the classification error rate, on independent test sets, of the methods evaluated. In order to evaluate the mean of the error rate, several (distinct) data sets are needed. However, the number of data sets available is often limited. One way to overcome this problem is to divide the data sets into training and test sets by the use of a k-fold cross validation procedure [15], [16], [9].

This procedure can be used to compare supervised methods, even if only one data set is available. The procedure works as follows. The data set is divided into k disjoint equal size sets. Then, training is performed in k steps, each time using a different fold as the test set and the union of the remaining folds as the training set. Applying the distinct algorithms to the same folds with k at least equal to 10, the statistical significance of the differences between the methods can be measured, based on the mean of the error rate from the test sets [15], [16], [9].

III. RELATED WORK

In terms of protein fold recognition, [3] used three multi-classification methods (one-versus-others, unique one-versus-others, and all-versus-all), implemented with 2-class classifiers (either support vector machines or neural networks) as their building block. In [17], the authors used ensembles of Discretized Interpretable Multi-Layer Perceptrons to learn two datasets realted to protein fold prediction. Different to the work in [3], in [17] each network learns the 27 folds simultaneously. Bagging and arcing combined the outputs of the networks.

In [3], it was observed that classical learning methods perform badly due to the imbalanced proportion of the data, causing a high rate of false positive. Motivated by this problem, in [5] the authors devised a system called ensemble Knowledge for Imbalance Sample Sets (eKISS) and applied it to a version of the dataset in [3]. The aim of the eKISS is to generate one-versus-others classifiers which are capable of learning over multi-class examples under the skewed normal distribution of training examples, as well as providing explanation to the user.

In contrast to the previously reviewed papers, in order to cope with the multi-class protein fold classification problem, [18] propose a hierarchical learning architecture (HLA). At the first level of HLA, neural networks classify the data into the four major SCOP classes. In the second level, the system has another set of networks, which further classifies the data into the 27 folds. The proposed architecture can house a set of either neural networks or support vector machines as building blocks.

The most closely related work to ours is the one in [14]. In such a work, the authors applied the k-Local Hyperplane Distance Neighbor algorithm (HKNN) to, among other things, the problem of protein structural class prediction. For this problem, they obtained an average accuracy of 82%. However, we cannot compare this result directly with the ones obtained in our paper, since the datasets and methodology for developing the experiments were different - for example, in order to measure the performance of the classifiers, they used the holdout method and we applied a 10 replication of 10-fold cross validation.

IV. EXPERIMENTS

Our experiments were accomplished by presenting the dataset to the individual ML methods and to ensembles (bagging and boosting). In fact, each method was run with a 10 replication of stratified 10-fold cross validation (generating 100 classifiers). The values for the parameters of the ML algorithms were chosen as follows.

For example, for an algorithm with only one parameter, an initial value for such a parameter was chosen followed by the run of the algorithm. Then, experiments with a larger and smaller value were also performed. If with the initially chosen value the classifier obtained had the best results (in terms of validation error), then no more experiments were performed. Otherwise, the same process was repeated for the parameter value with the best result so far. Of course, this procedure becomes more time consuming with the increasing in the number of parameters to be investigated.

Using the previous procedure, we arrived to the following values for the parameters of the ML algorithms (WEKA implementation [9]):

- k-Nearest Neighbor (k-NN): k was set to 1 and the distance weighting to 1/distance. All other parameters were set to their default.
- Naive Bayes (NB): the kernel estimator was set to True. All other parameters were set to their default.
- Decision Tree (DT): all parameters were set to their default.
- Support Vector Machine (SVM): C was set to 2^6 and the exponent to 2. All the other parameters were set to their default.
- Neural Networks (NN): the number of hidden nodes was set to 10, the learning rate to 10^{-3}, the momentum term to 0.9, the maximum number of iteration to 1000, and the validation set size to 10%. All the other parameters were set to their default.
- Bagging DT, Bagging SVM, Bagging NN: for the individual (base) classifiers the same parameter settings as defined above were used. For the Bagging process, the number of iteration was set to 100 and all other parameters were set to their default.
- AdaBoosting DT, AdaBoosting SVM, AdaBoosting NN: for the individual (base) classifiers the same parameter settings as defined above were used. For the Boosting process, the number of iteration was set to 100 and all other parameters were set to their default.

Each of the previous ML method, as already mentioned, was trained with a 10 replication of 10-fold cross validation of the dataset, considering the best parameter setting found. Than, for all experiments, the mean of the percentage of incorrectly classified training patterns on independent test sets were measured. Next, these means were compared two by means of paired t-test, as described in [16], [15].

V. RESULTS

Before starting the investigation of the performance of the ensembles, we analyze the performance of the individual classifiers.

A. Individual Classifiers

Table II presents, for each ML algorithm, the mean and standard deviation of the percentage of incorrectly classified examples on independent test sets. According to this table, SVM obtained a lower classification error than the other methods (17.60%). The null hypotheses were rejected in favor of SVM in comparison to DT, k-NN and NB at $\alpha = 0.05$, where $\alpha = 0.05$ stands for the significance level of the equal means hypothesis test. However, no significance difference was detected between SVM and NN ($\alpha = 0.05$).

TABLE II
PERFORMANCE (ERROR RATE) OF THE INDIVIDUAL ML ALGORITHMS

Algorithm	Mean	St. Dev.
DT	25.21%	5.74%
k-NN	24.34%	4.82%
NB	22.04%	5.27%
SVM	17.60%	4.54%
NN	18.79%	2.62%

B. Ensembles

Table III and Table IV present, respectively, the mean and standard deviation of the percentage of incorrectly classified examples on independent test sets for the ensembles techniques of Bagging and Boosting. The ensembles generated with these techniques used as base classifiers all the individual ML learning algorithms previously presented in Table II, with exception of k-NN and NB which in the preliminary experiments did not showed suitable for the task.

TABLE III
PERFORMANCE (ERROR RATE) OF THE BAGGING ENSEMBLES

Algorithm	Mean	St. Dev.
Bagging DT	18.55%	5.17%
Bagging SVM	17.60%	4.54%
Bagging NN	18.91%	2.53%

With respect to the results obtained with the Bagging ensembles (Table III), no significant differences were detected among them ($\alpha = 0.05$). Regarding the results achieved with the Boosting ensembles, according to Table IV, Boosting DT obtained a lower classification error rate than the other methods (15.80%). The null hypotheses were rejected in favor of Boosting DT in comparison to Boosting SVM and Boosting

TABLE IV
PERFORMANCE (ERROR RATE) OF THE BOOSTING ENSEMBLES

Algorithm	Mean	St. Dev.
Boosting DT	15.80%	5.04%
Bagging SVM	19.32%	4.60%
Bagging NN	18.78%	4.24%

NN at $\alpha = 0.05$. However, no significance difference was detected between Boosting SVM and Boosting NN ($\alpha = 0.05$).

VI. FINAL REMARKS

Figure 1 summarizes the results obtained with DT, SVM and NN, as well as their respective ensembles with bagging and boosting.

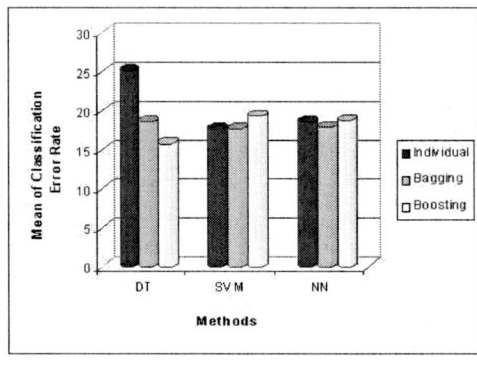

Fig. 1. Summary of the Results

Observing this figure we can see a consistent improvement in the results obtained with ensembles methods that used Decision Trees (DT) as the base classifier. Recall that the original result obtained for DT as individual method was represented by an error rate mean of 25.21%. Then, with the use of Bagging DT this mean dropped to 18.55%. By applying Boosting DT, we achieved an even lower error rate mean (15.80%) than that achieved with Bagging DT, with $\alpha = 0.05$.

In terms of SVM and NN, the results obtained with the ensemble techniques did not show the same improvement as in the case of DT. For example, no significance difference was detected between Bagging SVM and the individual SVM ($\alpha = 0.05$). In the case of Boosting SVM, the ensemble formed showed a significant poorer performance when compared to the individual SVM ($\alpha = 0.05$). For NN, no significance difference was detected with respect to Bagging NN and Boosting NN ($\alpha = 0.05$).

Considering the best results obtained in our experiments (in terms of both lower error rate mean and the size of the classifier generated), we choose the Boosting DT and the individual SVM and NN for a more detailed comparison, as shown in Tables V, VI and VII. We can observe that Boosting DT presents, for each class individually, a better performance than those obtained by the SVM and NN. Even so, although the Boosting method [19], [9] puts extra weight on the training patterns that represents the probability of a pattern to be misclassified, such a method was not able to deal efficiently with the problems in the class $\alpha + \beta$. From these tables we can see that such a class is the hardest one to be correctly predicted. In fact, in a previous experimental study, [20] showed that a significant number of proteins in the class $\alpha + \beta$ were misclassified in all-α and all-β classes.

TABLE V
BOOSTING DT

All-α	All-β	α/β	$\alpha + \beta$	Small
13.51%	14.69%	9.36%	69.56%	0%

TABLE VI
INDIVIDUAL SVM

All-α	All-β	α/β	$\alpha + \beta$	Small
13.51%	19.20%	10.83%	73.91%	2.22%

TABLE VII
INDIVIDUAL NN

All-α	All-β	α/β	$\alpha + \beta$	Small
16.21%	16.38%	11.33%	93.48%	6.67%

ACKNOWLEDGMENT

The authors would like to thank the financial support of CNPq/FAPERN via grants 350200/2004-1 and 552431/2002-8.

REFERENCES

[1] P. Baldi and S. Brunak, *Bioinformatics: the Machine Learning Approach*, second edition ed. MIT Press, 1998.
[2] D. T. Jones, "GenTHREADER: an efficient and reliable protein fold recognition method for genomic sequences," *J. Mol. Biol.*, vol. 287, pp. 797–815, 1999.
[3] C. H. Q. Ding and I. Dubchak, "Multi-class protein fold recognition using support vector machines and neural networks." *Bioinformatics*, vol. 17, no. 4, pp. 349–358, 2001.
[4] I. Dubchak, I. Muchnik, S. R. Holdbrook, and S. H. Kim, "Prediction of protein folding class using global description of amino acid sequence," *Proc. Natl. Acad. Sci.*, vol. 92, pp. 8700–8704, 1995.
[5] A. C. Tan, D. Gilbert, and Y. Deville, "Multi-class protein fold classification using a new ensemble machine learning approach," *Genome Informatics*, vol. 14, pp. 206–217, 2003.
[6] M. W. Craven, R. J. Mural, L. J. Hauser, and E. C. Uberbacher, "Predicting protein folding classes without overly relying on homology," in *Proc. of ISBM*, vol. 3, 1995, pp. 98–106.
[7] L. LoConte, B. Ailey, T. J. P. Hubbard, S. E. Brenner, A. G. Murzin, and C. Chothia, "Scop: a structural classification of proteins database." *Nucleic Acids Research*, vol. 28, no. 1, pp. 257–259, 2000.
[8] F. M. G. Pearl, D. Lee, J. E. Bray, I. Sillitoe, A. E. Todd, A. P. Harrison, J. M. Thornton, and C. A. Orengo, "Assigning genomic sequences to cath." *Nucleic Acids Research*, vol. 28, no. 1, pp. 277–282, 2000.

[9] I. H. Witten and E. Frank, *Data mining: practical machine learning tools and techniques with Java implementation.* USA: Morgan Kaufman Publishers, 2000.

[10] U. Hobohm and C. Sander, "Enlarged representative set of proteins," *Protein Sci.*, vol. 3, pp. 522–524, 1994.

[11] I. Dubchak, I. Muchnik, and S. H. Kim, "Protein folding class predictor for SCOP: approach based on global descriptors," in *Proc. of 5th ISBM*, 1997, pp. 104–107.

[12] L. LoConte, S. E. Brenner, T. J. P. Hubbard, C. Chothia, and A. G. Murzin, "SCOP database in 2002: refinements accommodate structural genomics," *Nucleic Acids Research*, vol. 30, no. 1, pp. 264–267, 2002.

[13] J.-M. Chandonia, N. S. Walker, L. L. Conte, P. Koehl, M. Levitt, and S. E. Brenner, "ASTRAL compendium enhancements," *Nucleic Acids Research*, vol. 30, no. 1, pp. 260–263, 2002.

[14] O. Okun, "Protein fold recognition with k-local hyperplane distance nearest neighbor algorithm," in *Proc. of Second European Workshop on Data Mining and Text Mining for Bioinformatics*, 2004, pp. 51–57.

[15] T. Mitchell, *Machine Learning.* New York: McGraw Hill, 1997.

[16] T. G. Dietterich, "Approximate statistical test for comparing supervised classification learning algorithms," *Neural Computation*, vol. 10, no. 7, pp. 1895–1923, 1998.

[17] G. Bologna and R. D. Appel, "A comparison study on protein fold recognition," in *Proc. of 9th International Conference on Neural Information Processing*, vol. 5, 2002, pp. 2492–2496.

[18] C. D. Huang, C. T. Lin, and N. R. Pal, "Hierarchical learning architecture with automatic feature selection for multiclass protein fold classification," *IEEE Trans. on Nanobioscience*, vol. 2, no. 4, 2003.

[19] T. G. Dietterich, "Ensemble methods in machine learning." in *Multiple Classifier Systems*, ser. Lecture Notes in Computer Science, vol. 1857, 2000, pp. 1–15.

[20] A. Chinnasamy, W.-K. Sung, and A. Mittal, "Protein structure and fold prediction using tree-augmented bayesian classifier," in *Pacific Symposium on Biocomputing*, 2004, pp. 387–398.

Protein Secondary Structure Prediction Using Machine Learning

BaiFang Zhang, Zhihang Chen and Yi Lu Murphey
Intelligent Systems Lab
Department of Electrical and Computer Engineering
The University of Michigan-Dearborn
Dearborn, MI 48128-1491
yilu@umich.edu

Abstract This paper presents an intelligent system for protein secondary structure prediction. The system consists of three pairwisely trained neural networks and a Bayesian inference function applied to the neural network outputs for accurate prediction. We tested our system on two well-known protein data set drawn from PDB, our system showed top performances on both data sets.

I. Introduction

Proteomes contains a cell's total protein expression at a given time. Proteomics is the large-scale analysis of complete genomes. Proteome analysis involves in determining protein-encoding genes' sequence and function, and the precise biochemical state of each protein in its post-translational form. X-ray and NMR (Nuclear Magnetic resonance) are the two traditional methods for determining the structure and function of a protein. However, these methods are too costly and time consuming. Furthermore, protein interactions are complex and their native operating environments are very specific, which are often difficult to replicate in the laboratory. So scientists are turning to computer methods that can rapidly sift through massive amounts of data and help determine the structure and function of all the proteins in a given genome [2].

In this paper we present our research in applying machine learning to proteomic problems. Proteins are polymer chains composed of 20 simpler building blocks, or amino acids that function as the molecular machines of living organisms. Current estimates indicate that different proteins exist in a human body range from 100,000 to several times of this number. Every protein is a sequence of several to tens of thousands amino acids.

Proteins are first characterized by their primary sequences, the amino acid sequence, and then fold into complex tertiary (3D) structure, which decides the corresponding biological functions. It is well-known that proteins fold spontaneously and reproducibly to a unique 3-D structure in aqueous solution [12].

There are two classes of proteins, membrane proteins and globular proteins. Most of the work in the bioinformatics community is focused on globular protein structure, which represents a large fraction of all proteins. The prediction of membrane structure is an important problem that remains largely unsolved.

The goal of secondary structure prediction is to classify a pattern of residues in amino acid sequences as protein secondary structure elements: α-helix, β-strand or coil. A number of methods have been proposed for protein secondary structure prediction. In particular machine learning techniques have been actively investigated including neural networks [2], decision trees [8], Hidden Markov Models [1], Support Vector Machines [7][11] and data mining [10]. Over the years, performance of protein secondary structure prediction has steadily improved, however the performances are still not satisfactory. The current technologies give the predictive accuracies of protein secondary structure in the range of 60% to 75% [1][5][12].

This paper presents a machine learning approach that gives

the performance of protein prediction better than those published in the literature. We use a one-against-one modeling to train three neural networks, each classifies a pair of classes. The output from the three neural networks are sent to a Bayesian Inference function to produce the final prediction.

II. Machine Learning For Protein Analysis

Fig. 1 illustrates the machine learning system we developed for protein prediction. Let a protein sequence be $p=p_1p_2...,p_n$, where p_i is an amino acid whose secondary structure needs to be determined. There are 20 standard amino acids in protein. Typically they are denoted using either one letter code or three letter code [5][10].

The protein secondary structures can be categorized into several states [2][11]. Researchers focused on classifying these states into three consolidated classes: helix(H), strand(E) and coil(C) classes. It has been well accepted that the order of amino acids in an amino acid sequence plays the most important role in determining their secondary structure. A common practice is to use a window size of n such that the secondary structure of amino acid p_i is predicted based on the residue p_{j-n}, ..., p_j, ..., p_{j+n}. However it is *not* known that how many neighbors of an amino acid, namely, what is the best n, should be used to accurately predict the secondary structure of each amino acid. Currently n is determined primarily by trial-and-error. Typically n=5, 7, 9, ..., 15 have been used in experiments.

The pre-process component shown in Figure 1 generates residues of length n from the protein sequence and then encodes them in binary strings. One popular encoding scheme, called orthogonal encoding, uses 20 bits for each amino acid [11]. The 20 standard amino acid are ordered 1 through 20, and the *i*th amino acid has the binary codeword of 20 bits with the *i*th bit set to "1" and all others to "0"s, for i=1, 2, ..., 20. A residue with window size n is encoded in 20x(2n+1) bits with the binary codewords of amino acids concatenated based on their order in the window. The dimension of residue vector increases rapidly as n increases. In general higher dimension of input vector usually leads to more complex neural network architecture. In order to reduce the input dimension, we use 5 bits to encode the 20 standard amino acids in an effort to reduce the complexity of neural networks. In the case of window size 5, a residue vector has 5 * 11 = 55 dimensions, which is a lot shorter than the residue vector using orthogonal encoding, which is 20*11=220 dimensions.

We modeled protein secondary structure prediction problem using three pairwisely trained neural networks, NN_{HE}, NN_{HC} and NN_{CE}. The NN_{HE} was trained using the residue vectors belonging to either the H or E classes, the NN_{HC} was trained with the residue vectors belonging to either the H or C classes, and the NN_{CE} with the C and E classes. For any input vector x, x is sent to all three neural networks, NN_{HE}, NN_{HC} and NN_{CE}. Each of the three neural networks output the confidence values of x being the two classes it is trained to predict.

Most neural network systems trained to predict the protein secondary structures also use three neural networks, however, each of the three is trained using a one-against-all(OAA) scheme [2][11]. In an OAA modeling, the three neural networks, NN_H, NN_E and NN_C are trained as follows. The output function of NN_H, f_H, is trained to output 1 in an input vector belongs to the H class otherwise, $f_H = 0$. The system prediction for an input vector is the class whose corresponding neural network has the highest output value.

Research in multi-class neural network systems showed that a system contains the pairwisely trained neural networks can generalize better than the neural networks trained using one-against-all [6]. In the experiment section we will also show that the system of the pairwisely trained neural networks combined with Bayesian inference function gives more accurate predictions than the OAA systems. One reason for the pairwisely trained neural networks being more successful than the neural networks trained using OAA is that they provide redundancy. In the protein secondary structure prediction case, each input vector receives predictions from two differently trained neural networks. If one neural network makes a mistake, x may still receive a correct prediction if the other neural network does a good job. On the other hand, in OAA, each x receives one confident vote from one neural network. If that neural network makes a mistake, x has little chance to receive a correct prediction.

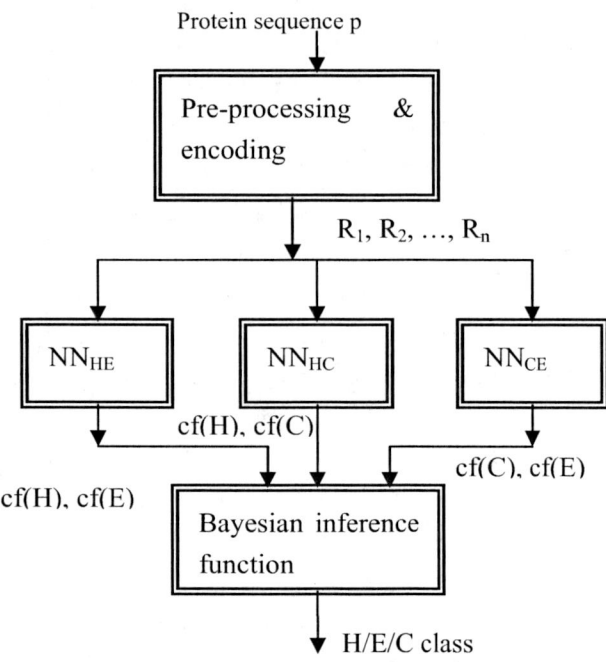

Fig 1: A system with pairwisely trained neural networks and Bayesian decision rule for protein secondary prediction.

III. Bayesian Inference Function

The three pairwisely trained neural networks, NN_{HE}, NN_{HC} and NN_{CE} have output functions $F_{HE}(x, W_{HE})$, $F_{HC}(x, W_{HC})$, and $F_{CE}(x, W_{CE})$, where x is an input vector, and W_{HC}, W_{HC}, and W_{CE} are the trained weights of the respective neural networks. For an input vector x, each neural network output function generates two values to indicate the confidence of x belonging to the two classes the neural network is trained to predict. For example, we have $F_{HC}(x, W_{HC}) = (C_{HC}^H, C_{HC}^C)$, where C_{HC}^H and C_{HC}^C are the confident values of x being class H and C respectively. C_{HC}^H and C_{HC}^C can be the output value of the activation function of the output node in NN_{HC}.

We denote the output of three networks as $O = <F_{HE}, F_{HC}, F_{CE}>$, the final decision function for the input vector x being either class H, E or C is

$$\arg\max_{C,H,E}(P(C|O), P(H|O), P(E|O))$$

where three the posterior probability

$P(C|O), P(H|O), P(E|O)$ can be expressed as follows using the Bayes rule.

$$P(H|O) = \frac{P(O|H)P(H)}{P(O)}$$

$$P(E|O) = \frac{P(O|E)P(E)}{P(O)}$$

$$P(C|O) = \frac{P(O|C)P(C)}{P(O)}$$

The following discusses the implementation of P(H|O). Since F_{CE} does not output any information on class H, we have

$$P(O|H) = P(<F_{HE}, F_{HC}>|H).$$

Furthermore, since NN_{HE} and NN_{HC} are trained independently, here we just assume these two neural networks output F_{HE} and F_{HC} are also independent. So it is reasonable to define

$$P(<F_{HE}, F_{HC}>|H) \equiv C_{HE}^H + C_{HC}^H,$$

where C_{HE}^H and C_{HC}^H are the confident value output from neural network NN_{HE} and NN_{CE} for input vector x being class H. One method to calculate P(H) (P(E) and P(C)) is based on the fraction of residue vectors of class H (E and C) in the entire training data. Specifically, they can be calculated by the following formulas:

$$P(H) = \frac{|\Omega_H|}{|\Omega|}, P(C) = \frac{|\Omega_C|}{|\Omega|}, P(E) = \frac{|\Omega_E|}{|\Omega|},$$

where Ω is the entire training data set, $\Omega_H, \Omega_E, \Omega_C$ are the training examples belonging to class H, E, C respectively. Obviously we have

$$P(C) + P(H) + P(E) = 1.$$

P(E|O) and P(C|O) can be similarly implemented.

IV. Experiments

We have conducted a number of experiments to test the system described in this paper. There are two data collections drawn from two well-known protein banks, PDB [3] and CB513[4]. The PDB data used in our experiments contain 400 proteins, totaling 41917 residues. The CB513 data used in our experiment contain 513 proteins, totaling 55642 residues. Each data collection is decomposed into training and test data: PDB_{TR} contains 300 protein sequences with 110530 residues, and the PDB_{test} contains 100 protein sequences with 31,669 residues. The $CB513_{TR}$ contains 393 sequences with 41452 residues, and the $CB513_{test}$ contains 120 protein sequences with 14190 residues.

The neural network architectures used in NN_{HE}, NN_{HC} and NN_{CE} are the same: feed-forward back-propagation with one hidden layer of 20 neurons (We also try other numbers of neurons, but 20 neurons in the hidden layer gives best performance). A window size of 9 is used to form protein residues and, therefore, the input residue vector has a dimension of 5*19. For the purpose of comparison we also implemented two other neural network architectures, one-against-all in one neural network, and one-against-all in three neural networks combined with a Winner-Take-All (WTA) scheme.

The most widely used accuracy index for secondary structure prediction is the three-state per-residue accuracy (Q_3), which gives the percentage of correctly predicted residues in all of the three states (classes), H, E and C:

$$Q_3 = \frac{P_H + P_E + P_C}{T}$$

where P_H, P_E, P_C are the number of residues predicted correctly by a prediction system in state alpha helix, strand and coil respectively, T is the total number of residues. Table 1 and Table 2 shows the performances of the proposed system, UMD-OAO+Bayesian and two other neural network systems we implemented UMD-OAO+WTA and UMD-OAA. Table 1 also listed some other systems published in recent literatures on data drawn from PDB. Note the performances of our three systems UMD-OAO+Bayesian, UMD-OAO+WTA, and UMD-OAA are all at the top. The UMD-OAO+WTA differs from the UMD-OAO+Bayesian in the decision module that integrates the output from the three pairwisely trained neural networks, NN_{HE}, NN_{HC} and NN_{CE}. The UMD-OAO+WTA system takes the votes from the three networks, and he class that gets the majority vote is the predicted class. The UMD-OAA system is a single neural network with an output layer containing 3 nodes, O_1, O_2, and O_3. Each class in {H, E, C} is encoded in 3 bits, and the codeword for H is 100, E 010 and, C 001. The training process is as follows. For an input x, output function of the neural network at node i, f_i, is set to 1 if and only if the input x belongs to class i, otherwise it is set to 0, for i = 1, 2 and 3.

For the DPB data, the UMD systems performed quite well in comparison with other published results. The OAO+Bayesian system has the best performance over all the published systems. For the CB513 data set, all three systems achieved more than 70% with the UMD-OAO+Bayesian giving the top performance: 74.8%

The results achieved on both data collections show that a neural network system modeled with OAO gives better performance than the neural network system modeled with the OAA. According to our extensive research [4], the OAA modeling scheme suffers from unbalanced data problem. In particular in this application, the E and C classes have much less residues in protein sequences than the H classes, therefore the OAA scheme is not a good one to use to predict protein secondary structures. In our training data from the PDB, the data distribution for the three classes are H: 48%, E: 30%, C:22%, and the CB513 gives the similar distribution over the three classes.

Table 1. The performances of the proposed system, the two systems trained with one-against-one scheme, and the performances of systems published in literature on the PDB data.

	Method	Performance
Yang & Wang, 2003[9]	Bayesian Inference Network	72.6%
Selbig, & et al, 1999[6]	Decision tree	72.9%
Xu & et al, 1999 [8]	Data Mining tool C5	75%
Aydin, and Altunbasak, 2004 [1]	Semi Markov HMM	69.2%
Wang and Zhang (2002)[7]	Naïve Bayes	61.5%
UMD-OAO + Bayesian	OAO+Bayesian inference	75.8%
UMD-OAO+ WTA	Three OAO neural networks with WTA	72.9%
UMD-OAA	One neural network with 3 output nodes	72.7%

Table 2. The performances of the three systems we implement on the CB513 data.

	Method	Performance
UMD-OAO + Bayesian	OAO+Bayesian inference	74.8%
UMD-OAO+ WTA	Three OAO neural networks with WTA	71.5%
UMD-OAA	One neural network with 3 output nodes	71.1%

V. Conclusion

We have presented a neural network system that effectively predicts the protein secondary structures. The proposed system, UMD-OAO+Bayesian, contains three neural networks, each was trained with the modeling scheme of One-Against-One, and a Bayesian inference function that integrates the output from these three neural networks to produce the final class prediction. The most of published neural network systems for protein secondary structure prediction were trained using the One-Against-All modeling scheme, which, in general, suffers from unbalanced data problem. Our experiment results also showed that the Bayesian inference function gives better performance in comparison to the majority vote decision rule. Overall the UMD-OAO+Bayesian system gave very good performances on the two well-known databases, PDB and CB513. However there are a few improvements can be made. All existing protein secondary structure prediction approaches showed the weakest performance on the E class [2]. Although the overall performance of our system is higher than those published, our system performance on the E class of amino acids is also lower than the other two classes. This research problem is currently under our study.

References

[1] Zafer Aydin, Yucel Altunbasak and Mark Borodovsky, "Protein secondary structure prediction with semi-markov HMMs," in *Proc. IEEE Int. Conf. on Acoustics Speech and Signal Processing (ICASSP), Montreal, Canada, May 2004*

[2] Pierre Baldi, Bianluca Pollastri, "A machine Learning Strategy for Protein Analysis" *IEEE Intelligent System* 2002

[3] H.M. Berman, J. Westbrook, Z. Feng, G. Gilliland, T.N. Bhat, H. Weissig, I.N. Shindyalov, P.E. Bourne: The Protein Data Bank. *Nucleic Acids Research*, 28 pp. 235-242 (2000)

[4] J. Cuff and J. G. Barton, "Application of multiple sequence alignment profiles to improve protein secondary structure prediction," *Proteins Structure, Function and Genetics*, vol. 40 pp. 502-511, 2000.

[5] Madhavi K. Ganapathiraju, Judith Klein-Seetharanman, N. Balakrishnan, and Raj Redd, "Characterization of protein secondary structure pp Application of latent semantic analysis using different vocabularies," IEEE Signal

Processing Magazine, May 2004, pp. 78-87.

[6] Guobing Ou, Yi L. Murphey, Lee Feldkamp, "Multiclass Pattern Classification Using Neural Networks," International Conference on Pattern Recognition, Cambridge, UK, 2004.

[7] Nguyen and Raja Pakes, "Combining GOR Techniques with Support Vector Machines for Protein Secondary Structure Prediction", *Seventh International Conference on Control Automation and Vision, 2002.*

[8] Joachim Selbig, Theo Mevissen, and Thomas Lengauer, "Decision tree-based formation of consensus protein secondary structure prediction," *Bioinformatics* 15: 1039-1046. 1999

[9] Peng-Liang Wang and Du Zhang, "Protein Secondary Structure Prediction with Bayesian Learning Method," *Proceedings of the 14th IEEE International Conference on Tools with Artificial Intelligence (ICTAI'02)*

[10] H. Xu, K. Lau, L.Lu, D. Zhang "Protein Secondary Structure Prediction Using Data Mining Tool C5", *the Proceedings of the Eleventh IEEE International Conference on Tools with AI, Chicago, November 1999*, pp.107-110.

[11] Xiaochun Yang, Bin Wang, and Yiu-Kai Ng, "A Protein Secondary Structure Prediction Framework Based on the Support Vector Machine," Proceedings of the Fourth International Conference on Web-Age Information Management (WAIM'03), August 2003, pp. 266-277, LNCS 2762, Springer.

[12] Mohanned J. Zaki, Shan Jin, and Chris Bystroff, "Mining Residue Contacts in Proteins Using Local Structure Predictions," *IEEE Transactions on Systems, Man and Cybernetics – Part B:Cybernetics*, Vol. 33, No. 5, October, 2003

Protein Secondary Structure Prediction with a Hybrid RNN/HMM System

Jinmiao Chen
School of Computer Engineering
Nanyang Technological University
Singapore, 639798
E-mail: pg05205549@ntu.edu.sg

Narendra S. Chaudhari
School of Computer Engineering
Nanyang Technological University
Singapore, 639798
E-mail: asnarendra@ntu.edu.sg

Abstract—In this paper, we propose a hybrid RNN/HMM system for protein secondary structure prediction, where each secondary structure segment is approximated by a second-order recurrent neural network embedded in the state of a segmental hidden Markov model. We evaluate the hybrid system on the RS126 and CB396 sets and obtain promising results.

I. INTRODUCTION

Proteins are polypeptide chains carrying out most of the basic functions of life at the molecular level. The chain can be viewed as a linear sequence over the 20-letter amino acid alphabet that folds into complex 3D structure which is essential to their function. Predicting the 3D structure of protein based on the linear sequence of amino acids is a fundamental open problem in computational molecular biology. As the protein secondary structure is the linear representation of its 3D structure, one of the current approaches is to firstly predict the secondary structure, and then obtain the 3-D structure.

As depicted in Figure 1, the secondary structure of a protein assigns segments of consecutive residues to one of several conformational classes: α-helix(H), β-sheet(E), or coil, the remaining type(C). These classes reflect the participation of each amino acid residue in local conformations of the chain. Protein secondary structure prediction is to classify a pattern of residues in amino acid sequences to a corresponding secondary structure type.

Fig. 1. Protein secondary structure prediction

During the last few decades, much effort has been made toward solving the problem of protein secondary structure prediction with various approaches [5], [6], [7], [8], [4], [3], [13], [17], [14], [15], [16]. Early protein secondary structure predictors, such as GOR techniques [5], PHD method [6], nearest-neighbor methods [7] and support vector machines [8], are based on a fixed-length local window around a particular amino acid of interest. Recently, most improvements in accuracy were achieved by methods considering nonlocal interactions in the sequence which occur outside a fixed-length window, for example Bayesian Segmentation of Protein Secondary Structure [4] and Bidirectional Recurrent Neural Networks [3]. In this paper, we address the problem by developing a hybrid recurrent neural network/segmental hidden Markov model. This model extends segmental HMM by embedding RNNs in each state, in order to simulate intra-segment distribution and exploit multiple sequence alignment profiles.

II. MODEL DESCRIPTION

The sequence/structure relationship in proteins can be represented based on segments of secondary structure and the secondary structure can be fully specified in terms of segment types and segment length. The sequence of segment types and segment length are denoted as $\mathbf{Q} = [Q_1, Q_2, ..., Q_m]$ and $\mathbf{L} = [L_1, L_2, ..., L_m]$ respectively where m is the number of segments. An example is given in Figure 2.

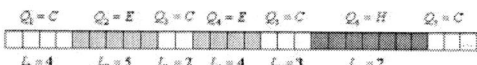

Fig. 2. Representation of the secondary structure of a protein sequence in terms of structural segments.

From the perspective of generative models, we can develop an explicit probabilistic model for the sequence/structure relationship in the form of a segmental hidden Markov model (Figure 3). The segmental HMM is a generalization of HMM in which each state generates a variable-length sequence of observations. The generalized state G_t usually contains the state Q_t and the length of the segment L_t. The segment types of protein secondary structure are considered as the set of discrete states. Each segment type possesses an underlying generator, which generates a variable-length segment of amino acids. In Figure 3, $y_1, ..., y_T$ represents the amino acid sequence and the sequence below is the corresponding secondary structure. A variable-length segment of observations associated with random length L_t is generated by the state Q_t.

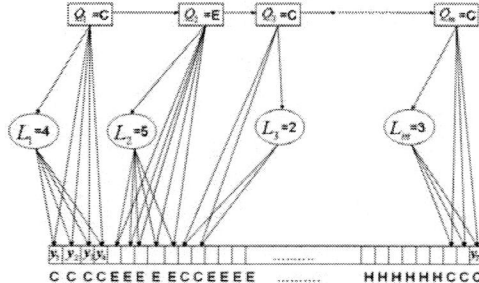

Fig. 3. The segmental hidden Markov model illustrated as generative processes.

A. Algorithms for Inference

In this section, we discuss the task of recovering the unobserved $\mathbf{G} = \{\mathbf{Q}, \mathbf{L}\}$ given an observed sequence $y_{1:T}$, which is inherently a problem of statistical inference.

Normally, there are two important measures of the segmental variables $\{\mathbf{Q}, \mathbf{L}\}$ given a sequence of observation:
- The most probable segmental variables in the posterior distribution(MAP estimate).
- The marginal posterior mode estimate.

We employ the Viterbi and forward-backward algorithms for the MAP and marginal posterior mode estimate respectively.

1) Viterbi algorithm: The Viterbi variable $V_t(q, l)$ denotes the probability of the most probable path ending in state q with duration l after reading the first t observations. The probability $V_t(q, l)$ is computed by:

$$V_t(q, l) = P(y_{t-l+1:t}|q, l) \max_{q', l'} P(q, l|q', l') V_{t-l}(q', l') \tag{1}$$

where $P(y_{t-l+1:t}|q, l)$ represents the likelihood of segment $y_{t-l+1:t}$ given the generalized state $G_t = \{Q_t = q, L_t = l\}$.

2) Forward-backward algorithm: The forward and backward variables are defined as follows:

$$\alpha_t(q, l) = P(Q_t = q, L_t = l, y_{1:t})$$
$$= P(y_{t-l+1:t}|q, l) \sum_{q'} \sum_{l'} P(q, l|q', l') \alpha_{t-l}(q', l') \tag{2}$$

$$\beta_t(q, l) = P(y_{t+1:T}|Q_t = q, L_t = l)$$
$$= \sum_{q'} \sum_{l'} \beta_{t+l'}(q', l') P(y_{t+1:t+l'}|q', l') P(q', l'|q, l) \tag{3}$$

with the standard assumption that

$$P(q, l|q', l') = P(q|q') P(l|q)$$
$$P(q', l'|q, l) = P(q'|q) P(l'|q') \tag{4}$$

where $P(q|q')$ and $P(q'|q)$ are state transition probabilities, $P(l|q)$ and $P(l'|q')$ are the segmental length distribution of the type q and q' respectively.

We may then compute the marginal posteriors required for

$$P(Q_t = q, L_t = l|y_{1:T}) = \frac{P(Q_t = q, L_t = l, y_{1:T})}{P(y_{1:T})} \tag{5}$$

as below

$$P(Q_t = q, L_t = l, y_{1:T})$$
$$= P(Q_t = q, L_t = l, y_{1:t}) P(y_{t+1:T}|Q_t = q, L_t = l, y_{1:t})$$
$$= P(Q_t = q, L_t = l, y_{1:t}) P(y_{t+1:T}|Q_t = q, L_t = l)$$
$$= \alpha_t(q, l) \beta_t(q, l) \tag{6}$$

B. Intra-Segment Model: Recurrent Neural Network

The likelihood of each segment $P(y_{t-l+1:t}|q, l)$ can be an arbitrary distribution. If $P(y_{t-l+1:t}|q, l) = \prod_{i=t-l+1}^{t} P(y_i|q)$, this is an explicit duration HMM [12]. If $P(y_{t-l+1:t}|q, l)$ is modelled by an HMM or state-space model(linear-dynamic system), this is called a segment model [11]. In computational biology, $P(y_{t-l+1:t}|q, l)$ is often modelled by a weight matrix or higher-order Markov chain [10]. All the above methods are unsatisfactory. Some of them, such as weight matrix and HMM, need a large number of training samples to achieve an acceptable generalization performance; some can not accept continuous input data, for example the BSPSS algorithm fails to incorporate multiple sequence alignment profiles. In order to avoid these problems, our system models the intra-segment distribution with recurrent neural networks, which can generalize well and deal with discrete data as well as continuous data.

The likelihood function $P(y_{t-l+1:t}|q, l)$ for segment $y_{t-l+1:t}$ can be written as the product of the conditional probabilities of individual observations

$$P(y_{t-l+1:t}|q, l) = P(y_{t-l+2}|y_{t-l+1}, q)$$
$$P(y_{t-l+3}|y_{t-l+1:t-l+2}, q) \ldots P(y_t|y_{t-l+1:t-1}, q) \tag{7}$$

by applying $P(X, Y) = P(X|Y) P(Y)$ many times. The conditional probabilities are simulated with a second-order recurrent neural network (SORNN), which is an Elman's network with a second-order next-state function (Figure 4). The SORNN predicts the probability of the next symbol given the previous and current symbols, i.e. $P(y_{t+1}|y_{1:t})$. Three SORNNs are used as statistical models for the three types of secondary structure(C,H,E) respectively.

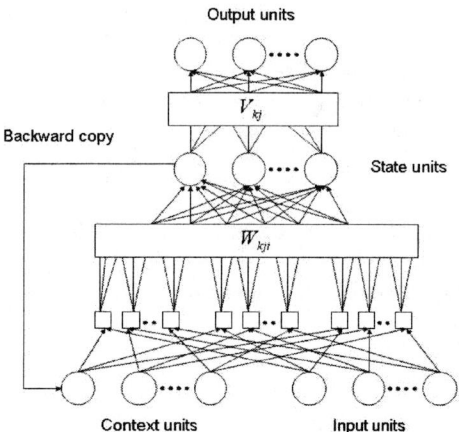

Fig. 4. Second-order recurrent neural network

The SORNN reads one symbol per cycle and the target output is the next symbol. When a_l(the l-th symbol in the amino acid alphabet) is read, the input vector is $I_i = \delta_{il}(\delta_{il}$ is 1 if $i = l$ and 0 else) for single sequence prediction. If multiple alignments of homologous sequences are available, position-specific scoring matrices are fed to the SORNN as inputs. The state and output units are updated as follows

$$S_k^t = g(\sum_j \sum_i W_{kji} S_j^{t-1} I_i^t) \quad (8)$$

$$O_k^t = g(\sum_j V_{kj} S_j^t) \quad (9)$$

The network is trained with the Real Time Recurrent Learning algorithm [9]. The error function is given by

$$E = \sum_t \sum_k \frac{1}{2}(O_k^t - I_k^{t+1})^2 \quad (10)$$

This error function has a minimum when O_k^t is the conditional probability of getting symbol a_k after reading the first t symbols.

C. Parameter Estimation

The model we describe above has two classes of free parameters:

- The parameters that specify discrete distributions, which include the state transition probabilities for $P(Q_t|Q_{t-1})$ and the segmental length distributions for $P(L_t|Q_t)$.
- Connection weights of the three SORNNs, each of which is associated to one state of the segmental HMM, corresponding to one type of secondary structure.

Because the training database contains only amino acid sequences with known secondary structures, no Baum-Welch type iteration is required during estimation of the first class of parameters. They can be directly estimated by their relative frequency of occurrence in the training data set. The second class of parameters are learned with the RTRL algorithm.

III. EXPERIMENTS

In order to evaluate the accuracy of our approach, we choose Schmidler's Bayesian segmentation(BSPSS) algorithm [4] for comparison. For both the hybrid RNN/HMM system and the BSPSS algorithm, we used the RS126 set for training and the CB396 set for testing.

A. Data Preparation

1) The RS126 set: It is a non-homologous dataset according to the definition given by Rost and Sandar [6]. They used percentage identity to measure the homology and defined non-homologous to mean that no two proteins in the dataset share more than 25% sequence identity over a length of more than 80% residues. The protein chains and multiple sequence alignments of the RS126 set are available at http://www.compbio.dundee.ac.uk/~www-jpred/data/pred_res/.

2) The CB396 set: Cuff, J. and Barton, G. have developed a new non-redundant dataset of 396 protein domains for evaluation of PSS prediction algorithms [2]. The protein chains and multiple sequence alignments of the CB396 set are available at http://www.compbio.dundee.ac.uk/~www-jpred/data/pred_res/. The CB396 set does not include any of the 126 proteins in the RS126 set, nor does it contain homologs of those 126 proteins as measured by a stringent test of sequence similarity. Therefore, the RS126 and the CB396 sets are a suitable pair of training and testing sets for evaluation of PSS prediction methods.

3) Multiple Sequence Alignment Profiles: Prediction from a multiple alignment profile of protein sequences rather than a single sequence has long been recognized as a way to improve prediction accuracy. During evolution, residues with similar physico-chemical properties are conserved if they are important to the fold or function of the protein. The sequence alignment of homologous proteins accords with their structural alignment and aligned residues usually have similar secondary structures. The multiple-sequence alignment profiles can be generated from BLAST or PSI-BLAST program. In our experiments, we used PSI-BLAST generated profiles for the RS126 and CB396 sets.

B. Main Results

The hybrid RNN/HMM system uses single sequence as well as multiple sequence alignment profiles. Results are given in Table I and Table II.

TABLE I
THE PERFORMANCE OF THE HYBRID RNN/HMM SYSTEM USING SINGLE SEQUENCE ONLY

	Q3	Q_E	Q_H	Q_C	C_E	C_H	C_C
MAP	62.98	26.09	74.02	73.66	0.27	0.49	0.44
MARG	68.48	47.55	68.93	79.46	0.46	0.56	0.49

TABLE II
THE PERFORMANCE OF THE HYBRID RNN/HMM SYSTEM USING MULTIPLE SEQUENCE ALIGNMENT PROFILES

	Q3	Q_E	Q_H	Q_C	C_E	C_H	C_C
MAP	73.36	63.32	70.64	81.12	0.46	0.63	0.66
MARG	76.30	70.21	71.19	83.93	0.55	0.67	0.67

MAP denotes the most probable posterior estimate, while MARG denotes marginal posterior mode estimate. Q_3 is the overall three-state prediction percentage defined as the ratio of correctly predicted residues to the total number of residues. Q_E, Q_H and Q_C are the percentage of correctly predicted residues observed in class E, H, C respectively. C_H, C_E, C_C are the Matthews' correlation coefficients [1].

For comparison purposes, we also implemented the BSPSS algorithm proposed by Schmidler et al. [4], which can use the single sequence information only. The validation results are recorded in Table III.

TABLE III
THE PERFORMANCE OF THE BSPSS ALGORITHM

	Q3	Q_E	Q_H	Q_C	C_E	C_H	C_C
MAP	61.52	21.03	77.15	70.24	0.22	0.46	0.43
MARG	66.98	40.81	72.57	76.45	0.42	0.54	0.47

We observed that the marginal posterior mode is more accurate than the MAP estimate, which shows that averaging over all the possible segmentations helps. The results obtained from our model show a great improvement over those of the BSPSS algorithm. The current best methods achieve accuracies of about 75% when multiple alignments of homologous sequences are available, and 71% for single sequence predictions. As observed from Table I and Table II, the prediction accuracy of our model is competitive with other contemporary methods.

IV. CONCLUSIONS

This paper describes work on a hybrid RNN/HMM system for protein secondary structure prediction. Thanks to its flexibility and generalization capability, the second-order RNN embedded in the segmental HMM enables the system to learn the intra-segment distribution better than other segmental models and to incorporate multiple sequence alignment profiles easily. The experimental results indicate that the prediction performance of our system is better than that of the BSPSS algorithm and competitive with other contemporary methods.

REFERENCES

[1] B. Matthews, "Comparison of the Predicted and Observed Secondary Structure of t4 Phage Lysozyme", Biochim. Biophys, vol. 405, pp. 442-451, 1975.
[2] J. Cuff and G. Barton, "Evaluation and Improvement of Multiple Sequence Methods for Protein Secondary Structure Prediction", Proteins, vol. 34, pp. 508-519, 1999.
[3] G. Pollastri, D. Przybylski, B. Rost and P. Baldi, "Improving the Prediction of Protein Secondary Structure in Three and Eight Classes Using Recurrent Neural Networks and Profiles", Proteins, vol. 47, pp. 228-235, 2002.
[4] C. S. Schmidler, J. S. Liu and D. L. Brutlag, "Bayesian Segmentation of Protein Secondary Structure", Journal of Computational Biology, vol. 7, pp. 233-248, 2000.
[5] J. Gibrat, J. Garnier and B. Robson, "Further Developments of Protein Secondary Structure Prediction Using Information Theory", J. Mol. Biol., vol. 198, pp. 425-443, 1987.
[6] B. Rost and C. Sander, "Prediction of Protein Secondary Structure at Better than 70% accuracy", J. Mol. Biol. vol. 232, pp. 584-599, 1993.
[7] T. Yi and E. Lander, "Protein Secondary Structure Prediction Using Nearest-Neighbor methods", J. Mol. Biol., vol. 232, pp. 1117-1129, 1993.
[8] S. Hua and Z. Sun, "A Novel Method of Protein Secondary Structure Prediction with High Segment Overlap Measure: Support Vector Machine Approach", J. Mol. Biol. vol. 308, pp. 397-407, 2001.
[9] R. J. Williams and D. Zipser,"A Learning Algorithm for Continually Running fully Recurrent Neural Networks", Neural Computation, vol. 1, pp. 270-280, 1989.
[10] C. Burge and S. Karlin, "Prediction of Complete Gene Structure in Human Genomic DNA", J. Mol. Biol., vol. 268, pp. 78-94, 1997.
[11] M. Ostendorf, V. Digalakis, and O. Kimball, "From HMMs to Segment Models: a Unified View of Stochastic Modeling for Speech Recognition", IEEE Trans. on Speech and Audio Processing, vol. 4(5), pp. 360-378, 1996.
[12] C. D. Mitchell, M. P. Harper, and L. H. Jamieson, "On the Complexity of Explicit Duration HMMs", IEEE Transactions on Speech and Audio Processing, vol. 3(3), May, 1995.
[13] W. Chu and Z. Ghahramani, "A Graphical Model for Protein Secondary Structure Prediction", Prodeedings of the 21st International Conference on Machine Learning, Banff, Canada, July,2004.
[14] V. Robles, et. al. "Bayesian network multi-classifiers for protein secondary structure prediction", Artificial Intelligence in Medicine, vol. 31(2), pp. 117-136, 2004.
[15] K. P. Wu, H. N. Lin, J. M. Chang, T. Y. Sung and W. L. Hsu, "HYPROSP: a Hybrid Protein Secondary Structure Prediction Algorithmła Knowledge-Based Approach", Nucleic Acids Research, vol. 32(17), pp. 5059-5065, 2004.
[16] Z. Aydin, Y. Altunbasak and M. Borodovsky, "Protein Secondary Structure Prediction with Semi-Markov HMMs,", in Proc. IEEE Int. Conf. on Acoustics Speech and Signal Processing (ICASSP), Montreal, Canada, May 2004.
[17] W. Chu, Z. Ghahramani and D. L. Wild, "Protein Secondary Structure Prediction Using Sigmoid Belief Networks to Parameterize Segmental Semi-Markov Models", in Proc. of European Symposium on Artificial Neural Networks(ESANN), 2004.

Entropy Based Disease Classification of Proteomic Mass Spectrometry Data of the Human Serum by a Support Vector Machine

Terje Kristensen and Gaurav Kumar
Department of Computer Engineering,
Bergen University College, Nygårdsgaten 112,
N-5020 Bergen, Norway
E-mail: tkr@hib.no

Abstract—Disease diagnostics using proteomic patterns is a new platform that is developed to detect early-stage cancer. Proteomic pattern analysis uses the overall pattern to diagnose disease states without the need to identify the components within the pattern. The patterns are generated from Mass Spectrometry (MS) data, and an algorithm is developed to decipher the patterns within the mass spectrometry data to discriminate between serum taken from healthy and cancer-affected individuals.

There is need for cancer biomarkers with more accurate diagnostic capability. Use of MS is such a technique. Mass spectrometry data of the human serum consist of intensities of various ions present in the sample. A typical sample can have about 15000 different ions present. A very important question then is which ions are the best classifiers.

We have used an information-theoretical concept, information gain, to measure how well a given attribute separates the training examples according to the target classification. The method measures the drop in the entropy of the system caused by selecting a particular attribute. The lower the drop, the better the attribute. Our algorithm first selects the attributes with highest information gain and then classifies the diseased and healthy data based on these attributes using Support Vector Machines (SVM). The method achieves very strong performance.

IndexTerms- Mass spectrometry, proteomics, entropy, information gain, SVM.

I. INTRODUCTION

Disease diagnostics using proteomic patterns [1] has recently been developed as a diagnostic tool which does not rely on the identification of the proteins detected. The ability to discriminate patterns from serum acquired from healthy individuals, from serum of cancer-affected individuals is the most important aspect of this technique. Proteomic pattern diagnostics is a type of pattern diagnostics based on the analysis of a huge amount of data to find disease patterns in the proteins expressed. Serum proteomic signatures from mass spectrometry data are used as a diagnostic classifier of proteomic signatures from high dimensional MS data.

Such an approach has given very promising results in detection of early stage cancer [10]. The blood proteome is changing constantly as a consequence of the perfusion of organ systems. Small peptide fragments are removed from the actual disease organ and are contained in the blood serum. These fragments contain low molecular weight molecules which exist below the range of detection of conventional techniques. As a result researchers have turned to mass spectrometry that exhibits optimal performance in the low mass range [6], [9].

MS is a powerful analytical tool for determining masses of bio-molecules in a complex sample mixture. Such a technique is used to identify compounds. Detection of compounds can be accomplished with very minute quantities. This means that compounds can be identified at very low concentration in chemically complex mixtures. Experimental conditions that effect the molecular composition of a sample will also affect its mass spectrum. Mass spectrometry is used to test for the presence of different kinds of molecules, and the presence of such molecules may indicate an enzymatic change, a disease state or a certain cell type condition.

Mass spectrometry data consists of a set of m/z values (m is the atomic mass and z is the charge of the ion) and the corresponding relative intensities of all molecules present with that m/z ratio. The mass spectrometry data of a chemical sample thus is an indication of presence or absence of the actual molecules. The data might therefore be used to predict the presence of a disease condition and distinguish it from a sample taken from a healthy individual or any other living organism in general with a circulatory system.

Since the mass spectrometry data consist of intensities of thousands of molecules in a sample, it cannot be analysed manually. Computational methods such as artificial neural networks (ANN) should be suitable to do such an analysis. In two earlier papers we have shown that use of ANN techniques are suitable, for instance, to classify between eukaryotic or prokaryotic cells [4], [5]. However, in this paper we want to study how SVM can be used to perform an analysis to discriminate between different types of cancers.

The database used consists of individuals suffering from either ovarian or prostatic cancer, in addition to healthy persons. A problem when using a MS technique is how to select the most suitable attributes from a database of about 15000 attributes, to train the network. In this paper we have used an information-theoretic measure based on the entropy concept to discriminate between the most important attributes [7].

II. ENTROPY AND INFORMATION GAIN

Given a collection S, containing positive and negative examples of some target concept, the entropy S relative to this boolean classification is defined by

$$\text{Entropy}(S) = -p_+ \log_2 p_+ - p_- \log_2 p_- \qquad (1)$$

where p+ is the proportion of positive examples in S and p⁻ is the proportion of negative examples in S.

In (1) we have defined entropy for boolean classification. For a general case, if the target attribute can take on n different values, the entropy of S relative to a n-wise classification would be

$$\text{Entropy}(S) = -\sum_{i=1}^{n} p_i \log_2 p_i \qquad (2)$$

where pi is the proportion of S belonging to class i. The entropy concept in (2), characterises the impurity of an arbitrary collection of examples, can now be used to define another important concept in information theory, the information gain.

The information gain measures the expected reduction in entropy. Given the entropy as a measure of the impurity in a collection of training examples, we now define a measure of effectiveness of an attribute in classifying the training data. The information gain simply measures the expected reduction in the entropy caused by partitioning the examples according to this attribute. More precisely, the information gain, Gain(S,A) of an attribute A, relative to a collection of examples S, is defined as

$$\text{Gain}(S,A) = \text{Entropy}(S) - \sum_{i=1}^{n} \text{Entropy}(S_{v_i}) \qquad (3)$$

where $v_1, v_2, \ldots v_n$ is the set of all possible values of attribute A, S_{v_r} is the subset of S for which the attribute A has the value v_r i.e., $S_{v_r} = \{s \in S \mid A(s) = v_r\}$.

In the above representation, the first term is just the entropy of the original collection S, and the second term is the expected value of the entropy after S is partitioned using attribute A. The expected entropy described by the second term is simply the sum of the entropies of each subset S_{vr}, weighted by the fraction of examples $|S_{v_r}| / |S|$ that belong to S_{v_r}. Gain(S,A) is therefore the expected reduction in entropy caused by knowing the value of attribute A. An important point to note is that the above representation cannot be used if the attribute A is continuous-valued.

A. Incorporating the Continuous-Valued Attributes

Our initial definition of information gain restricts the attributes to take on a discrete set of values. This restriction can easily be removed so that continuous valued decision attributes can be incorporated. This can be accomplished by dynamically defining new discrete values attributes that partition the continuous attribute value into a discrete set of intervals. In particular, for a attribute A that is continuous-valued, the algorithm can dynamically create a new boolean attribute Ac that is true if A < c and false otherwise. The choice of the threshold c is based on the maximum information gain achieved.

Once the best classifying attributes have been selected the SVM can be used to train the data based on these selected attributes.

III. SVM THEORY

SVM is a computationally efficient learning technique that is now being widely used in pattern recognition and classification problems [2]. This approach has been derived from some of the ideas of statistical learning theory regarding controlling the generalization abilities of a learning machine [11], [12].

In this approach the machine learns an optimum hyper-plane that classifies the given pattern. By use of kernel functions, the input feature space by applications of a non-linear function can be transformed into a higher dimensional space where the optimum hyper-plane can be learnt. This gives a flexibility of using one of many learning models by changing the kernel functions.

A. SVM Classifier

The basic idea of a SVM classifier is illustrated in Fig.1. This figure shows the simplest case in which the data vectors (marked by 'X' s and 'O' s) can be separated by a hyper-plane. In such a case there may exist many separating hyper-planes.

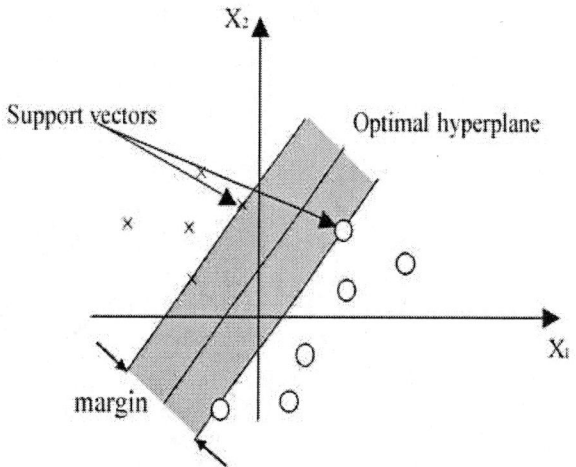

Fig. 1. Support Vector Machines classification defined by a linear hyper-plane that maximizes the separating margins between the classes.

Among them, the SVM classifier seeks the separating hyper-plane that produces the largest separation margins.

In the more general case, in which the data points are not linearly separable in the input space, a non-linear transformation is used to map the data vectors into a high-dimensional space (called feature space) prior to applying the linear maximum margin classifier. To avoid the potential pitfall of over-fitting in this higher dimensional space, a SVM uses a kernel function in which the non-linear mapping is implicitly embedded. A function qualifies as a kernel function if it satisfies the Mercer's condition [11].

With the use of a kernel function, the discriminant function in a SVM classifier has the following form :

$$f(x) = \sum_{i=1}^{N} \alpha_i y_i K(x_i, x) + b \qquad (4)$$

where $K(\cdot,\cdot)$ is the kernel function, x_i are the support vectors determined from the training data, y_i is the class indicator (e.g. +1 and -1 for a two class problem) associated with each x_i, N is the number of supporting vectors determined during training, α is the Lagrange multiplier for each point in the training set and b is a scalar representing the perpendicular distance of the hyper-plane from origin..

Support vectors are elements of the training set that lie either exactly on or inside the decision boundaries of the classifier. In essence, they consist of those training examples that are most difficult to classify. The SVM classifier uses these borderline examples to define its decision boundary between the two classes.

B. The SVM Kernel Functions

The kernel function plays a central role of implicitly mapping the input vectors into a high dimensional feature space, in which better separability is achieved. The most commonly used kernel functions are the polynomial kernel given by :

$$K(x_i, x_j) = (x_i^T x_j + 1)^p, \text{ where } p > 0 \text{ is a constant} \qquad (5)$$

or the Gaussian radial basis function (RBF) kernel given by

$$K(x_i, x_j) = \exp(-\|x_i - x_j\|^2 / 2\sigma^2) \qquad (6)$$

where $\sigma > 0$ is a constant that defines the kernel width. Both of these kernels satisfy the Mercer's condition mentioned above.

IV. SVM TRAINING

In the experiments we have used databases from the NIH and FDA Clinical Proteomics Program Data Bank [8]. The data set consisted of different m/z values and their intensities. Each of the above databases is divided into healthy and diseased sets. The files in each of these datasets are comma delimited. The above algorithm helps us to find the best attributes for classification of diseased and healthy samples.

Since the m/z values are continuous, we need to find a 'c' for each of the entropy calculations. This value is decided based on the maximum information gain achieved. Once this value is found, we can use the same method as we used to handle the entropy calculation for discrete values. A table is then prepared for all the m/z attributes versus the reduction in entropy they bring about. This table relates the usefulness of each attribute.

Once the best attributes are found we use the LIBSVM toolbox [3] to classify the spectrums into diseased and healthy categories, based on only those attributes. We see that using this method we can reduce the number of attributes needed for classification of diseased versus healthy sample. In previous experiments using SVM one selects 7-8 attributes randomly and use these for classification [10]. Our method makes the whole process more organised and also gives better results.

During the training phase the variables in the kernel function and the regularization parameter C have to be determined. The training samples were divided into m equal subsets of equal size and a methodology based on *one-versus one* was used in the classification regime. The experiments were done with various parameters settings. The model with the best generalization, e.g least error, was then selected.

V. EXPERIMENTS AND RESULTS

Once the best attributes have been estimated we used these attributes for SVM classification. We performed the training of SVM using the best 5 attributes followed by the best 4 attributes and so on. Finally, we train the SVM using only the best attribute. The results have been summarized in table 1 given underneath.

Accuracy %	C = 1	C = 100	C = 500
Best 5	99.2	100	100
Best 4	99.2	100	100
Best 3	99.2	100	100
Best 2	98.8	100	100
Best 1	96.8	97.6	98.1

Table 1. SVM performance classification of the 1-5 best attribute values.

From table 1 we see that perfect classification is achieved by using only 3-5 attributes. In [10], 7-8 attributes are selected randomly and used for classification. By use of the method presented in this paper we are able to give priority to the different attributes, based on their information gain, which gives optimal classification.

The columns in table 1 denote the performance of the SVM classifier at various values of the cost parameter C. The larger the value of C, the better the classification. The rows denote the performance in percent, dependent on the number of attributes taken for training of the SVM. We see that a larger number of attributes give a higher accuracy.

VI. Conclusion

Proteomic pattern diagnostics represents a new paradigm for disease detection. This type of analysis requires only a small amount of blood from which MS spectra are generated. The most promising aspects with such an analysis are a very high throughput because the MS spectra can be determined in very short time. In such an analysis the pattern itself, independent of the identity of the proteins, is the discriminator. This may be done before the identity of the proteins is determined.

The MS platform is promising to use for cancer diagnostics. By use of MS one can generate complex proteomic spectra from an extreme small volume of blood in short time. Combined with nano-technology this platform can generate new tools, created at the intersection between proteomics and the nano-technology.

In such a future perspective we might also introduce nano-harvesting agents into the blood serum that are able to diagnose on the fly, based on the MS data taken. Such nano-particles with their diagnostics cargo, can communicate remotely with a computer, and the status of the blood serum may be checked to reveal the signatures of these biomarkers.

In this paper we have developed a new method that predicts the best attributes to be used to classify the most appropriately disease attributes. Once these attributes have been determined, using the concept of information gain, we can train a SVM network for classification of cancer vs. non-cancer samples.

A very high classification accuracy (100%) is obtained in the experiments using the best 5 attributes for training of the SVM. This result is superior to previously applied methods such as ANN and probabilistic classification [10], as far as we know.

Acknowledgements

The authors wish to acknowledge associate professor Alvhild Alette Bjørkum, Faculty of Engineering, Biomedical Laboratory Sciences Program, Bergen University College for letting us know about this new platform of proteomic pattern analysis, based on MS data, and how it can be used to diagnose early-stage cancer. Without her introduction to this field this paper would not have been possible.

References

[1] Aebersold R., Mann,M. Mass spectrometry based on proteomics. Nature 422, 2003.
[2] Burges, C.J.C A Tutorial on Support Vector Machines for Pattern Recognition. *Knowledge Discovery and Data Mining*, 2(2), 1998.
[3] Chih-Chung Chang and Chih-Jen Lin. LIBSVM : a library for Support Vector Machines. available online at http://www.csie.ntu.edu.tw/cjlin/libsvm, 2001.
[4] Kristensen,T., Patel,R. Classification of Eukaryotic and Prokaryotic Cells by a Backpropagtion network. In Proceedings of I.E.E.E International Joint Conference on Neural Computing, IJCNN 2003, Portland, Oregon, USA.
[5] Kristensen, T. Prototypes of ANN Biomedical Pattern Recognition Systems. In Proceedings of IASTED International Conference on Simulation and Modelling (ASM 2002) Crete, Greece, 2002.
[6] Liotta, A.L., Ferrari,M., Petricoin,E. Clinical proteomics written in blood. Nature 2003, 425:905.
[7] Mitchell,T.M. Machine Learning. International Editions 1997. McGraww-Hill Companies, 1997.
[8] NIH and FSA clinical Proteomics Program Databank, 2002. http://www.clinicalproteomics.steem.com
[9] Petricoin,E., Liotta,A.L.. Seldi-tof-based serum proteomic pattern diagnostics for early detection of cancer. Current Opinion in Biotechnology 2004, 15: 24-30.
[10] Lilian,R.H., Farid,H., Donald,B.R. Probabilistic Disease Classification of Expression-Dependent Proteomic Data from Mass Spectrometry of Human Serum, Journal of Computational Biology Volume 10, Number 6, 2003
[11] Vapnik,V.N. Statistical Learning Theory. Wiley, New York, 1998.
[12] Vapnik,V.N. An overview of statistical learning theory. IEEE Transactions on Neural Networks, 10,Sep 1999.

A Comparative Study on Term Weighting Schemes for Text Categorization

Man LAN[†‡], Sam-Yuan SUNG[†], Hwee-Boon LOW[‡], Chew-Lim TAN[†]

[†]Department of Computer Science, School of Computing, National University of Singapore
3 Science Drive 2, Singapore 117543
E-mail: {lanman, ssung, tancl}@comp.nus.edu.sg

[‡]Institute for Infocomm Research
21 Heng Mui Keng Terrace, Singapore 119613
E-mail: {lanman, hweeboon}@i2r.a-star.edu.sg

Abstract— The term weighting scheme, which is used to convert documents into vectors in the term spaces, is a vital step in automatic text categorization. The previous studies showed that term weighting schemes dominate the performance rather than the kernel functions of SVMs for the text categorization task. In this paper, we conducted experiments to compare various term weighting schemes with SVM on two widely-used benchmark data sets. We also presented a new term weighting scheme $tf.rf$ for text categorization. The cross-scheme comparison was performed by using McNemar's Tests. The controlled experimental results showed that the newly proposed $tf.rf$ scheme is significantly better than other term weighting schemes. Compared with schemes related with tf factor alone, the idf factor does not improve or even decrease the term's discriminating power for text categorization. The $binary$ and $tf.chi$ representations significantly underperform the other term weighting schemes.

I. INTRODUCTION

Text categorization, the task of automatically assigning unlabelled documents into predefined categories, has been widely studied in the recent decades. Usually, the content of a textual document is transformed into a vector in the term space by using the bag-of-words approach, $d_j = (w_{1j}, ..., w_{kj})$, where k is the set of terms (sometimes called features). The value of w_{kj} between $(0, 1)$ represents how much the term t_k contributes to the semantics of document d_j. The bag-of-words approach is simple as it ignores semantic and syntactic information, but it performs well in practice.

The promising classifiers applied to text categorization are usually borrowed from the traditional machine learning field. Among them, support vector machines (SVM) are one of the most successful solutions [8], [9]. Many researchers have studied text categorization based on different term weighting schemes and different kernel functions of SVMs [8], [9], [1], [4]. In [1], the authors pointed out that it is the text representation schemes which dominate the performance of text categorization rather than the kernel functions of SVM. That is, choosing an appropriate term weighting scheme is more important than choosing and tuning kernel functions of SVM for text categorization.

However, even given these previous studies, we can not definitely draw a conclusion as to which term weighting scheme is better than others for SVM-based text categorization, "Because we have to bear in mind that comparisons are reliable only when based on experiments performed by the same author under carefully controlled conditions" [16]. In this case, various "background conditions" [16] such as, different data preparation (stemming, stop words removal, feature selection, different term weighting schemes), different benchmark data collections, different classifiers with various parameters, and even different evaluation methods (micro- and macro-averaged precision, recall, accuracy, error, break-even point or ROC) have been adopted by different researchers.

For this purpose, our paper focuses on the comparison of various term weighting schemes only. That is, we only change the term weighting schemes by using the bag-of-words approach, while the remaining background conditions such as, data preparation, classifier and evaluation measures remain unchanged. Specifically, our benchmark adopted the linear SVM algorithm. The reasons why we choose linear kernel function of SVM in our experiments are listed in Section II-E. Consequently, after building such a fixed universal platform, these comparative experiments made on it are reliable. In addition, we used the McNemar's tests [7] to validate if there is significant difference between two term weighting schemes with respect to the micro-averaged break-even point performance analysis.

This paper is structured as follows. Section II reviews related works and analyzes the term's discriminating power for text categorization. Section III describes the comparative experiments, discussions and results. Conclusions are drawn in Section IV.

II. RELATED WORKS

In this section, we adopt a tabular representation similar to [15]. A number of term weighting factors are listed in these tables and each term weighting scheme consists of three factors, term frequency, collection frequency, and length normalization components.

A. Term Frequency Factor

Table I summaries four term frequency components which were used in our experiments, including a binary weight, a normal raw term frequency, a logarithm of term frequency and a inverse term frequency. Among them, binary representation

TABLE I
TERM FREQUENCY COMPONENT

1.0	Binary weight equal to 1 for terms present in a vector (term frequency is ignored)
tf	Raw term frequency (number of times a term occurs in a document)
$1 + log(tf)$	Logarithm of the term frequency to scale the effect of unfavorably high term frequency
$1 - \frac{r}{r+tf}$	Inverse term frequency (ITF), usually $r = 1$

TABLE II
COLLECTION FREQUENCY COMPONENT

1.0	No change in weight; use original term frequency component
$log(\frac{N}{n_i})$	Multiply original tf factor by an inverse collection frequency factor (is the total number of documents in collection, and n_i is the number of documents to which a term is assigned)
$log(\frac{n_i-}{n_i})$	Multiply tf factor by a *term relevance* weight (i.e. probabilistic inverse document frequency)
χ^2	Multiply χ^2 value of each term in each category
$log(1 + \frac{n_i}{n_{i-}})$	Our newly proposed factor (n_i is the same as above, and n_i is the number of documents which contain the term and belong to the negative categories)

is the most simplest scheme and has been used in certain machine learning algorithms such as Naive Bayes, decision tree, where floating number format of term frequency might not be used. The normal raw term frequency has been widely used. The logarithm operation is used to scale the effect of unfavorably high term frequency in one document. Inspired by the inverse document frequency, ITF (inverse term frequency) was presented by [1].

B. Collection Frequency Factor

Five different collection frequency components are defined in Table II, which represent multipliers of 1 that ignores the collection frequency factor, a conventional inverse collection frequency factor (idf), a probabilistic inverse collection frequency ($idf\ pr\ b$), a χ^2 factor (χ^2), and a new relevance frequency (rf) factor proposed by us which considers the relevant document distribution, respectively.

It is clear to note that for multi-label classification problem, the benchmark on each corpus was simplified into multiple binary classification experiments. That is, in each experiment, a chosen category was tagged as the positive category and the other categories in the same corpus were combined as the negative category.

The traditional idf component which was thought to improve the term's discriminating power by pulling out the relevant documents from the irrelevant documents was borrowed from the information retrieval domain. However, in text categorization domain, things might be a bit different. Let's consider the examples in Figure 1.

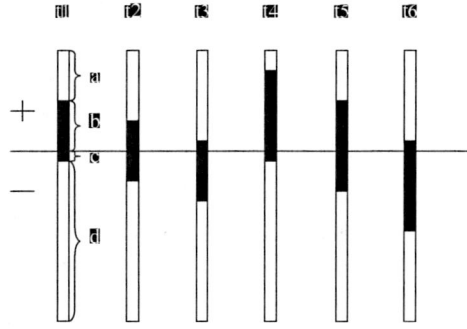

Fig. 1. Comparison of different distribution of documents which contain the six terms in the collection

Figure 1 shows the distribution of documents which contain the six terms, $t1, t2, t3, t4, t5$ and $t6$ in one chosen positive category. The heights of the columns above and below the horizontal line denote the number of documents in the positive and negative categories respectively. The height of the shaded part is the number of documents which contain this term. We assume the six terms have the same term frequency (tf). Then the several collection frequency factors are defined as

$$idf = g(\frac{N}{b+c}) \quad (1)$$
$$idf\ pr\ b = g(\frac{a+d}{b+c}) \quad (2)$$
$$\chi^2 = N * \frac{(a*d\ b*c)^2}{(a+d)(b+c)(a+b)(c+d)} \quad (3)$$
$$rf = g(2 + \frac{b}{c}) \quad (4)$$

where $N = a + b + c + d$. In general, $d \gg a, b, c$.

The first three terms have the same $idf1$ and the last three terms share the same $idf2$. It is clear to find that $idf2$ is less than $idf1$. Thus, the traditional idf factor gives more weighting to the first three terms than the last three terms. But when we look at the first three terms only, we can easily find that these three terms show different discriminating power to text categorization. $t1$ and $t3$ contribute more power to discriminate the documents in the positive and negative categories respectively but $t2$ gives little contribution to this categorization. Therefore, the traditional $tf.idf$ representation scheme might lose its ability to discriminate these positive documents from the negative ones with respect to the first three terms. Things are similar for the last three terms. Based on this analysis, we proposed a new factor *relevance frequency* rf to improve the term's discriminating power. We assigned the constant value 2 in the rf formula because the base of this logarithm operation is 2. Compared with the first three collection frequency factors, the rf factor does not involve the d value. Since the d value is much larger than a, b and c and dominates the results of the first three formulae, it depresses the significant effects of b and c to appropriately express the term's discriminating power for text categorization. That is the reason why we developed the rf factor which omits the d value and appropriately improves the effects of b and c.

Therefore, in the above case, we weight more to $t1$ than $t2$ and $t3$ since $t1$ contributes more to the positive category by using rf factor. Similarly, $t4$ is weighted more than $t5$ and $t6$ by adopting our new factor. The reason why we give more weight to the terms which are assigned more in the positive documents than in the negative ones is that the terms in the negative category are widely dispersed due to the various topics of the negative category while the terms in the positive category are more concentrated on the topic of the positive category. We will validate whether this newly proposed factor rf has more discriminating power than idf factor in the later experiments.

Besides these collection frequency factors, other complicated factors combined with feature selection metrics, such as *Odds Ratio, information gain*, χ^2, *gain ratio* have been presented [6], [5]. In [13], the authors postulated that it is the sophistication of the feature weighting method rather than its apparent compatibility with the learning algorithm that improves classification performance. In [6], the authors asserted that $tf * CHI$ is most effective in their experiments with a SVMs-based text categorization rather than $tf.idf$. Since these schemes have been seldom compared and have not been shown universally encouraging results up to date, we also include one χ^2 factor as a typical representative in our experiments.

C. Normalization Factor

To eliminate the length effect, we use the *cosine* normalization to limit the term weighting range within $(0, 1)$. Specially, the binary feature representation does not use any normalization since the original value is 0 or 1. Assuming that w_{kj} represents the weight of term t_k in document d_j, the final term weight w_{kj} might then be defined as $w_{kj}/\sqrt{\sum_k (w_{kj}^2)}$.

D. Combined Term Weighting Schemes

By variously combining the three components, we compared the following ten term weighting schemes listed in Table III. Most of these term weighting schemes have been widely used in information retrieval and text categorization and/or have shown good performance in practice [15], [2], [8], [9]. For example, ITF representation proposed by [1] is included because the experimental results showed that when combined with linear kernel of SVM it needs the minimum of support vectors (i.e. best generalization).

Actually, the first four term weighting schemes are different variants of tf factor. Then the next four schemes are different variants of the traditional $tf.idf$ scheme. The $tf.chi$ scheme is a typical representation which combines tf factor with one feature selection metric (here is χ^2). The last weighting representation is our newly proposed scheme based on the analysis of term's discriminating power in Section II-B.

Noted that other weighting schemes may exist, but these ten term weighting schemes were chosen due to their reported

TABLE III
SUMMARY OF VARIOUS TERM WEIGHTING SCHEMES

Name	Description
$binary$	binary feature representation
tf	tf only
$logtf$	$log(1 + tf)$
ITF	$1 - 1/(1 + tf)$
idf	idf only
$tf.idf$	traditional $tf.idf$
$logtf.idf$	$log(1 + tf).idf$
$tf.idf$-$prob$	probabilistic idf, actually is the approximate $tf.term\ relevance$
$tf.chi$	$tf.\chi^2$
$tf.rf$	$tf.relevance\ frequency$ is our new weighting scheme

superior classification results or their typical representation when using support vector machines.

E. Support Vector Machines for Text Categorization

The promising approaches to text categorization tasks were usually borrowed from traditional machine learning algorithms, such as kNN, decision tree, Naive Bayes, Neural Network, Linear Regression, Support Vector Machines, and Boosting, etc. Among them, support vector machines (SVM) are one of the most successful solutions [8], [9]. In general, SVMs have been classified into three categories based on three different kernel functions, namely, linear, polynomial and radial based function (RBF).

Specifically, our benchmark adopted the linear SVM rather than non-linear SVM. The reason why we chose linear kernel function of SVM in our experiments are listed as follows. First, linear SVM is simple and fast [8]. Second, our preliminary experimental results showed that the linear SVM performs better than the non-linear models, even at the preliminary optimal tuning level the accuracy achieved with RBF kernel is lower than that of linear (0.8 vs 0.9). This result contradicts our anticipation of better performance by a more sophisticated kernel when dealing with numerous dimensional features but it also corroborates with the findings in [18], [8]. Third, this result might be considered preliminary, but our current focus is on the comparison of term weighting schemes rather than how to tune the parameters of kernel functions. Following the established practice in text categorization, throughout this paper we used an SVM with a linear kernel as the benchmark classifier algorithm. The SVM software we used is LIBSVM-2.6 [3].

III. COMPARATIVE EXPERIMENTS

A. Performance Measures

Classification effectiveness is usually measured by using *precision* and *recall*. *Precision* is the proportion of truly positive examples labelled positive by the system that were truly positive and *recall* is the proportion of truly positive examples that were labelled positive by the system.

Our experiments adopted the *precision/recall break-even point* as a measure of performance, which is defined as

TABLE IV
MCNEMAR'S TEST CONTINGENCY TABLE

$n00$: Number of examples misclassified by both classifiers f and f_B	$n01$: Number of examples misclassified by f but not by f_B
$n10$: Number of examples misclassified by classifiers f_B but not by f	$n11$: Number of examples misclassified by neither f nor f_B

the value where *recall* equals to *precision*. To get a single *break-even point* value over all binary classification tasks, the learning task is repeated for various values of these parameters and yield the hypothetical point at which *precision* and *recall* are equal. When working with linear kernel function of support vector machines, we set one global penalty costs of error on the positive and negative examples in the whole corpus to obtain this break-even point.

B. Significance Tests

To compare the performance between two term weighting schemes, we employed the McNemar's significance tests [7] based on the micro-averaged precision/recall *break-even point*. McNemar's test is a χ 2-based significance test for goodness of fit that compares the distribution of counts expected under the null hypothesis to the observed counts. The McNemar's test can be summarized as follow.

Two classifiers f and f_B based on two different term weighting schemes were performed on the test set. For each example in test set, we recorded how it was classified and constructed the following contingency table (Table IV):

The null hypothesis for the significance test states that on the test set, two classifiers f and f_B will have the same error rate, which means that $n10 = n01$. Then the statistic χ is defined as

$$\chi = \frac{(|n01 - n10| - 1)^2}{n01 + n10} \quad (5)$$

where $n01$ and $n10$ are defined in Table IV.

Dietterich showed that under the null hypothesis, χ is approximately distributed as χ^2 distribution with 1 degree of freedom, where the significance levels 0.01 and 0.001 corresponded to the two thresholds $\chi_0 = 6.64$ and $\chi_1 = 10.83$ respectively. Given a χ score computed based on the performance of a pair of classifiers f and f_B, we compared χ with threshold values χ_0 and χ_1 to determine if f is superior to f_B at significance levels of 0.01 and 0.001 respectively. If the null hypothesis is correct, then the probability that this quantity is greater than 6.64 is less than 0.01. Otherwise we may reject the null hypothesis in favor of the hypothesis that the two term weighting schemes have different performance when trained on the particular training set.

C. Data Sets

1) Reuters News Corpus: The documents from the top ten largest categories of the Reuters-21578 document collection were used in our experiments. We adopted the bag-of-words approach for the documents. According to the ModApte split, the 9,980 news stories have been partitioned into a training set of 7,193 documents and a test set of 2,787 documents. Stop words (292 stop words), punctuation and numbers were removed. The Porter's stemming was performed to reduce words to their base forms [14]. The threshold of the minimal term length is 4. Null vectors (i.e. vectors with all attributes valued 0) were removed from the data set. The resulting vocabulary has 15937 words (terms or features).

By using the χ^2 statistics ranking metric for feature selection, the top p features per category were selected from the training sets. In our experiments, we set $p = \{25, 50, 75, 150, 300, 600, 900, 1200, 1800, 2400\}$ respectively. Since SVM have the capability to deal with high dimensional features, and the previous works showed that feature selection does not improve or even slightly degrades the SVM performance [1], [12], we also conducted experiments by inputting the full words (after remove stop words, stemming and set minimal term length as 4) without feature selection.

One noticeable issue of Reuters corpus is the skewed category distribution problem. Among the top ten categories which have 7193 training documents, the most common category has a training set frequency of 2877 (40%), but 80% of the categories have less than 7.5% instances.

2) 20 Newsgroups Corpus: The 20 Newsgroups corpus is a collection of approximate 20,000 newsgroup documents evenly divided among 20 discussion groups and each document is labelled as one of the 20 categories which correspond to the name of the newsgroup that the document was posted to.

Due to the huge number of documents in this corpus to be dealt with, we randomly selected the first 200 training samples and the first 100 testing samples per category. On a chosen category, 200 positive training samples and 3800 negative training samples evenly distributed in the other 19 categories were used by the classifiers. Our experiments compared the different term weighting schemes' performance based on the fixed number of training/testing sets. Compared with the skewed category distribution in the Reuters corpus, the 20 categories in the 20 Newsgroups corpus are uniform distribution.

The resulting vocabulary, after removing stop words (513 stop words) and these words that occur less than 3 and 6 times in the positive and negative categories respectively, has 50088 words. According to the χ^2 statistics metric, the top p features were selected as feature sets, where p belongs to $\{5, 25, 50, 75, 100, 150, 200, 250, 300, 400, 500\}$.

D. Results

Figure 2 depicts the micro-averaged break-even point performance on the Reuters data set. The performance of different term weighting schemes at a small vocabulary size can not be summarized in one sentence but the trends are distinctive that the break-even points of different term weighting schemes increase as the number of the features grows. All term weighting schemes reached a maximum of break-even point at the full vocabulary. Among these, the best break-even point 0.9272 was reached at the full vocabulary by using our newly proposed scheme $tf.rf$. The $tf.rf$ scheme has always been shown significant better performance than others when the number of features is larger than 5000. The following significance tests results supported this observation.

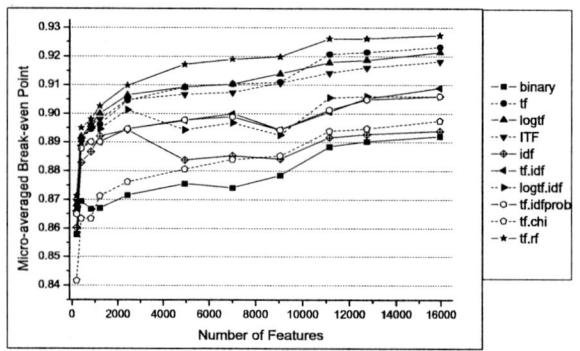

Fig. 2. Micro-averaged break-even points results for the Reuters-21578 top ten categories by using ten term weighting schemes at different numbers of features

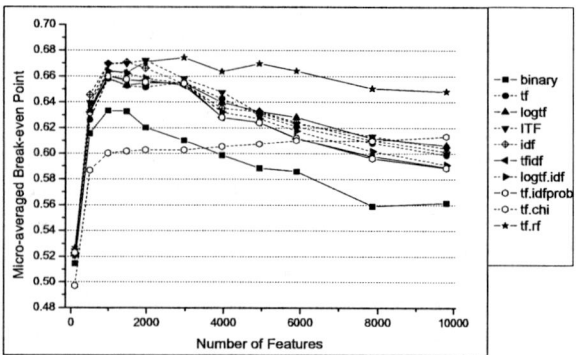

Fig. 3. Micro-averaged break-even points results for the 20 Newsgroups corpus by using ten term weighting schemes at different numbers of features

Table V summarizes the statistical significance tests results on the Reuters data set at different numbers of features, where the term weighting schemes with insignificant performance differences are grouped into one set, "$<$" and "$<<$" denotes worse than at significance level 0.01 and 0.001 respectively.

TABLE V
STATISTICAL SIGNIFICANCE TESTS RESULTS ON REUTERS-21578 AT DIFFERENT NUMBERS OF FEATURES. "$<$" AND "$<<$" DENOTES WORSE THAN AT SIGNIFICANCE LEVEL 0.01 AND 0.001 RESPECTIVELY; "$\{\}$" DENOTES NO SIGNIFICANT DIFFERENCE IN THE SET.

#_Features	McNemar's Test
200	$\{tf.chi\} << \{$all the others$\}$
400 − 1500	$\{binary, tf.chi\} << \{$all the others$\}$
2500	$\{binary, tf.chi\} << \{idf, tf.idf, tf.idf\text{-}prob\} < \{$all the others$\}$
5000-All	$\{binary, idf, tf.chi\} << \{tf.idf, logtf.idf, tf.idf\text{-}prob\} << \{tf, logtf, ITF\} < \{tf.rf\}$

Figure 3 shows the micro-averaged break-even point results on the 20 Newsgroups data set. Unlike the trends on the Reuters data set, the performance curves on the 20 Newsgroups were not monotonically increasing. All term weighting schemes reached their maximum break-even point at a small vocabulary range from 1000 to 3000. The best break-even point 0.6743 was also achieved by using our newly proposed scheme $tf.rf$ at a vocabulary size of 3000.

Table VI summarizes the statistical significance tests results on the 20 Newsgroups data set at different numbers of features, where the term weighting schemes with insignificant performance differences are grouped into one set, "$<$" and "$<<$" denotes worse than at significance level 0.01 and 0.001 respectively.

E. Discussion

To achieve high performance in terms with break-even point, different numbers of vocabularies were required for the two data sets. The categories in the Reuters data set often consist of diverse subject matters which involve overlapping vocabularies. For example, the documents in the same *acquisition* category may involve diverse subjects about acquisition. In this case, large vocabularies are required for adequate classification performance. Hence, for the Reuters data set, the full vocabulary are required to achieve the best break-even point. However, in the 20 Newsgroups data set, all documents in a category are about a single narrow subject with limited vocabulary. Thus, 50 – 100 vocabularies per category are sufficient for best performance for the 20 Newsgroups data set.

TABLE VI
STATISTICAL SIGNIFICANCE TESTS RESULTS ON THE 20 NEWSGROUPS AT DIFFERENT NUMBERS OF FEATURES. "$<$" AND "$<<$" DENOTES WORSE THAN AT SIGNIFICANCE LEVEL 0.01 AND 0.001 RESPECTIVELY; "$\{\}$" DENOTES NO SIGNIFICANT DIFFERENCE IN THE SET.

#_Features	McNemar's Test Result
100 − 500	$\{tf.chi\} << \{$all the others$\}$
1000	$\{tf.chi\} << \{binary\} << \{$all the others$\}$
1500	$\{tf.chi\} << \{binary\} < \{$all the others$\} < \{ITF, idf, tf.rf\}$
2000	$\{binary, tf.chi\} << \{$all the others$\} < \{ITF, tf.rf\}$
3000 − 5000	$\{binary, tf.chi\} << \{$all the others$\} < \{tf.rf\}$
6000 − 10000	$\{binary\} << \{$all the others$\} << \{tf.rf\}$

Even though the best performances were reached at different numbers of vocabularies, these term weighting schemes have been shown consistent performance compared with others on the two different data sets.

Firstly, our newly proposed scheme $tf.rf$ showed significant better performance than the others in the two different data sets based on different category distributions. Both of the best break-even points were achieved by using the newly proposed $tf.rf$ scheme on the two data sets. This result also verifies our analysis in Section II-B that the *relevance frequency* improves the term's discriminating power for text categorization.

Secondly, there was no observation that idf factor adds discriminating power when combined with tf factor together. In the Reuters data set, the three term weighting schemes related with term frequency alone, tf, gtf and ITF achieved higher break-even points than these schemes combined with idf factor, $tf.idf$, $gtf.idf$ and $tf.idf\text{-}pr\ b$. In the 20 Newsgroups data set, the differences between these schemes related with tf alone or with idf or both were not significant. This result shows that the idf factor gives no discriminating power or even decrease discriminating power to the features.

Thirdly, compared with other schemes, the $binary$ and $tf.chi$ scheme showed consistently worse performance even when they achieved the best break-even point performance. The $binary$ weighting scheme ignores the information of term frequency which is crucial to the representation of the content of the document. This might be the reason why these schemes related with term frequency show drastically better performance than $binary$ scheme. The $tf.chi$ scheme, as a representative of term weighting schemes combined with feature selection measure, although taking the collection distribution into consideration, showed even worse performance than $binary$ representation at a small vocabulary size in the two data sets. As we analyzed in Section II-B, the d value dominates the χ^2 value and the resulting term weighting value can not express the term's discriminating power as appropriate as the $tf.rf$. Although $tf.chi$ showed slow increasing trend in the 20 Newsgroups data set and got the higher performance at larger number of vocabularies, its best break-even point performance was still worse than that of the others. Specifically, the $tf.\chi^2$ scheme has been showed no significant different or even worse performance than the $tf.idf$ scheme. This finding contradicts with the previous result in [6].

Generally, the ITF scheme has comparable as good performance in the two data sets as other schemes related with term frequency alone, such as tf and gtf factor, but still worse than the $tf.rf$ scheme.

It is clearly to know that all the observations are supported by the following McNemar's significance tests.

IV. Conclusions

In this paper we reported a comparative study on several widely-used term weighting schemes with SVM-based text categorization and also proposed a newly term weighting scheme $tf.rf$ based on the analysis of discriminating power. With respect to the micro-averaged break-even point performance analysis, our conclusions are:

- Our newly proposed term weighting scheme $tf.rf$ shows significant better performance than other schemes based on two widely-used data sets with different category distributions
- The schemes related with term frequency alone, such as tf, gtf, ITF show rather good performance but still worse than the $tf.rf$ scheme
- The idf and χ^2 factor, taking the collection distribution into consideration, do not improve or even decrease the term's discriminating power for text categorization
- The $binary$ and $tf.chi$ representations significantly underperform the other term weighting schemes

References

[1] E. Leopold and J. Kindermann. Text categorization with support vector machines. how to represent texts in input space?. *Machine Learning*, 46(1-3):423 – 444, January - February - March 2002.
[2] C. Buckley, G. Salton, J. Allan, and A. Singhal. Automatic query expansion using SMART: TREC-3. In *Text REtrieval Conference*, 1994.
[3] C.-C. Chang and C.-J. Lin. *LIBSVM: a library for support vector machines*, 2001. Software available at http://www.csie.ntu.edu.tw/~cjlin/libsvm.
[4] P. Dai, U. Iurgel, and G. Rigoll. A novel feature combination approach for spoken document classification with support vector machines. 2003.
[5] F. Debole and F. Sebastiani. Supervised term weighting for automated text categorization. In *Proceedings of the 2003 ACM symposium on Applied computing*, pages 784–788. ACM Press, 2003.
[6] Z.-H. Deng, S.-W. Tang, D.-Q. Yang, M. Zhang, L.-Y. Li, and K. Q. Xie. A comparative study on feature weight in text categorization, March 2004.
[7] T. G. Dietterich. Approximate statistical tests for comparing supervised classification learning algorithms. *Neural Comput.*, 10(7):1895–1923, 1998.
[8] S. Dumais, J. Platt, D. Heckerman, and M. Sahami. Inductive learning algorithms and representations for text categorization. In *Proceedings of the seventh international conference on Information and knowledge management*, pages 148–155. ACM Press, 1998.
[9] T. Joachims. Text categorization with support vector machines: learning with many relevant features. In C. Nédellec and C. Rouveirol, editors, *Proceedings of ECML-98, 10th European Conference on Machine Learning*, number 1398, pages 137–142, Chemnitz, DE, 1998. Springer Verlag, Heidelberg, DE.
[10] A. Kehagias, V. Petridis, V. Kaburlasos, and P. Fragkou. A comparison of word- and sense-based text categorization using several classification algorithms. *Journal of Intelligent Information Systems*, 21(3):227–247, November 2003.
[11] D. D. Lewis. An evaluation of phrasal and clustered representations on a text categorization task. In N. J. Belkin, P. Ingwersen, and A. M. Pejtersen, editors, *Proceedings of the 15th Annual International ACM SIGIR Conference on Research and Development in Information Retrieval. Copenhagen, Denmark, June 21-24, 1992*, pages 37–50. ACM, 1992.
[12] D. D. Lewis, Y. Yang, T. G. Rose, and F. Li. Rcv1: A new benchmark collection for text categorization research. *J. Mach. Learn. Res.*, 5:361–397, 2004.
[13] D. Mladenic, J. Brank, M. Grobelnik, and N. Milic-Frayling. Feature selection using linear classifier weights: interaction with classification models. In *Proceedings of the 27th annual international conference on Research and development in information retrieval*, pages 234–241. ACM Press, 2004.
[14] M. Porter. An algorithm for suffix stripping. *Program*, pages 130–137, 1980.
[15] G. Salton and C. Buckley. Term-weighting approaches in automatic text retrieval. *Inf. Process. Manage.*, 24(5):513–523, 1988.
[16] F. Sebastiani. Machine learning in automated text categorization. *ACM Comput. Surv.*, 34(1):1–47, 2002.
[17] H. Wu and G. Salton. A comparison of search term weighting: term relevance vs. inverse document frequency. In *Proceedings of the 4th annual international ACM SIGIR conference on Information storage and retrieval*, pages 30–39. ACM Press, 1981.
[18] Y. Yang and X. Liu. A re-examination of text categorization methods. In *Proceedings of the 22nd annual international ACM SIGIR conference on Research and development in information retrieval*, pages 42 – 49. ACM Press, 1999.

One Class Support Vector Machine based Non-Relevance Feedback Document Retrieval

Takashi Onoda
System Engineering Res. Lab.
Central Research Institute of
Electric Power Industry
2-11-1, Iwado Kita, Komae-shi,
Tokyo 201-8511 JAPAN
E-mail: onoda@criepi.denken.or.jp

Hiroshi Murata
System Engineering Res. Lab.
Central Research Institute of
Electric Power Industry
2-11-1 Iwado Kita, Komae-shi,
Tokyo 201-8511 JAPAN
E-mail: murata@criepi.denken.or.jp

Seiji Yamada
National Institute of Informatics
2-1-2 Hitotsubashi, Chiyoda-ku,
Tokyo 101-8430 JAPAN
E-mail: seiji@nii.ac.jp

Abstract—This paper reports a new document retrieval method using non-relevant documents. From a large data set of documents, we need to find documents that relate to human interesting in as few iterations of human testing or checking as possible. In each iteration a comparatively small batch of documents is evaluated for relating to the human interesting. We applied active learning techniques based on Support Vector Machine for evaluating successive batches, which is called *relevance feedback*. Our proposed approach has been very useful for document retrieval with relevance feedback experimentally. The relevance feedback needs a set of relevant and non-relevant documents to work usefully. However, the initial retrieved documents, which are displayed to a user, sometimes don't include relevant documents. In order to solve this problem, we propose a new feedback method using information of non-relevant documents only. We named this method *"non-relevance feedback document retrieval"*. The non-relevance feedback document retrieval is based on One-class Support Vector Machine. Our experimental results show that this method can retrieve relevant documents using information of non-relevant documents only.

I. INTRODUCTION

As the Internet technology progresses, accessible information by end users is explosively increasing. In this situation, we can now easily access a huge document database through the Web. However it is hard for a user to retrieve relevant documents from which he/she can obtain useful information, and a lot of studies have been done in information retrieval, especially document retrieval [1]. Some works for such document retrieval have been reported in TREC (Text Retrieval Conference) [2] for English documents, IREX (Information Retrieval and Extraction Exercise) [3] and NTCIR (NII-NACSIS Test Collection for Information Retrieval System) [4] for Japanese documents.

In most frameworks for information retrieval, a vector space model in which a document is described with a high-dimensional vector is used [5]. An information retrieval system using a vector space model computes the similarity between a query vector and document vectors by the cosine of the two vectors and indicates a user a list of retrieved documents.

In general, since a user hardly describes a precise query in the first trial, interactive approach to modify the query vector using the evaluation of the documents on a list of

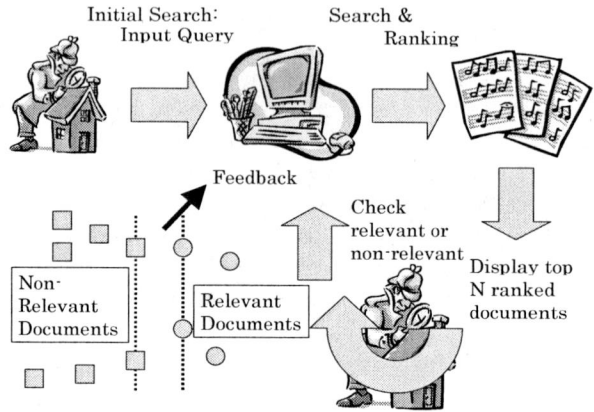

Fig. 1. Outline of the relevance feedback documents retrieval: The gray arrow parts are made iteratively to retrieve useful documents for the user. This iteration is called feedback iteration in the information retrieval research area.

retrieved documents by a user. This method is called *relevance feedback* [6] and used widely in information retrieval systems. In this method, a user directly evaluates whether a document in a list of retrieved documents is relevant or non-relevant, and a system modifies the query vector using the user evaluation. A traditional way to modify a query vector is a simple learning rule to reduce the difference between the query vector and documents evaluated as relevant by a user (see Figure 1).

In another approach, relevant and irrelevant document vectors are considered as positive and negative examples, and relevance feedback is transposed to a binary class classification problem [7]. For the binary class classification problem, Support Vector Machines (which are called SVMs) have shown the excellent ability. And some studies applied SVM to the text classification problems [8] and the information retrieval problems [9]. Recently, we have proposed a relevance feedback framework with SVM as *active learning* and shown the usefulness of our proposed method experimentally [10].

The initial retrieved documents, which are displayed to a user, sometimes don't include relevant documents. In this case,

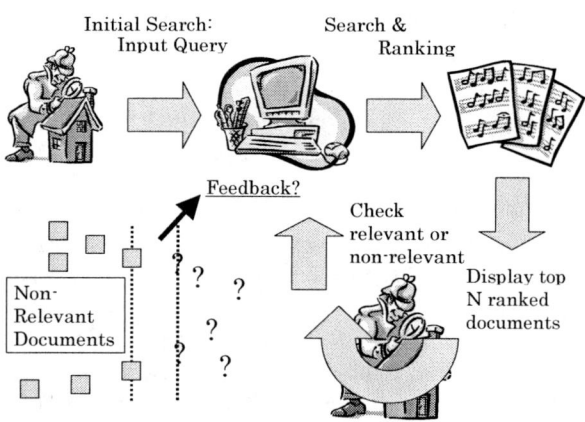

Fig. 2. Outline of a problem in the relevance feedback documents retrieval: The gray arrow parts are made iteratively to retrieve useful documents for the user. This iteration is called feedback iteration in the information retrieval research area. But if the evaluation of the user has only non-relevant documents, ordinary relevace feedback methods can not feed back the information of useful retrieval.

almost all relevance feedback document retrieval systems do not work well, because the systems need relevant and non-relevant documents to construct a binary class classification problem (see Figure 2).

While a machine learning research field has some methods which can deal with one class classification problem. In the above document retrieval case, we can use non-relevant documents information only. Therefore, we consider this retrieval situation is as same as one class classification problems.

In this paper, we propose a framework of an interactive document retrieval using non-relevant documents information only. We call this interactive document retrieval as "*non-relevance feedback document retrieval*", because we can use only non-relevant documents information. Our proposed non-relevance document retrieval is based on One Class Support Vector Machine(One-Class SVM) [11]. One-Class SVM can generate a discriminant hyperplane that can separate the non-relevant documents which are evaluated by a user. Our proposed method can display documents, which may be relevant documents for the user, using the discriminant hyperplane.

In the remaining parts of this paper, we explain the One-Class SVM algorithm in the next section briefly, and propose our document retrieval method based on One-Class SVM in the third section. In the fourth section, in order to evaluate the effectiveness of our approach, we made experiments using a TREC data set of Los Angels Times and discuss the experimental results. Finally we conclude our work and discuss our future work in the fifth section.

II. ONE-CLASS SVM

Schölkopf et al. suggested a method of adapting the SVM methodology to one-class classification problem. Essentially, after transforming the feature via a kernel, they treat the origin as the only member of the second class. The using "relaxation parameters" they separate the image of the one class from

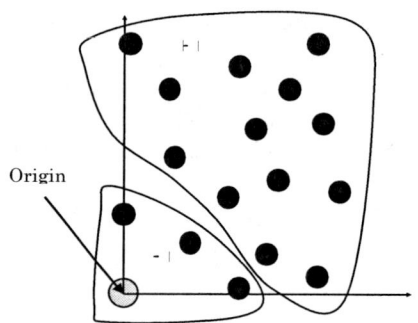

Fig. 3. One-Class SVM Classifier: the origin is the only original member of the second class.

the origin. Then the standard two-class SVM techniques are employed.

One-class SVM [11] returns a function f that takes the value +1 in a "small" region capturing most of the training data points, and -1 elsewhere.

The algorithm can be summarized as mapping the data into a feature space H using an appropriate kernel function, and then trying to separate the mapped vectors from the origin with maximum margin (see Figure 3).

Let the training data be

$$\mathbf{x}_1, \ldots, \mathbf{x}_\ell \tag{1}$$

belonging to one class X, where X is a compact subset of R^N and ℓ is the number of observations. Let $\Phi : X \to H$ be a kernel map which transforms the training examples to feature space. The dot product in the image of Φ can be computed by evaluating some simple kernel

$$k(\mathbf{x}, \mathbf{y}) = (\Phi(\mathbf{x}) \cdot \Phi(\mathbf{y})) \tag{2}$$

such as the linear kernel, which is used in our experiment,

$$k(\mathbf{x}, \mathbf{y}) = \mathbf{x}^\top \mathbf{y}. \tag{3}$$

The strategy is to map the data into the feature space corresponding to the kernel, and to separate them from the origin with maximum margin. Then, to separate the data set from the origin, one needs to solve the following quadratic program:

$$\min_{\mathbf{w} \in H, \xi \in R^\ell, \rho \in R^N} \frac{1}{2}\|\mathbf{w}\|^2 + \frac{1}{\nu\ell}\sum_i \xi_i - \rho$$
$$\text{subject to} \quad (\mathbf{w} \cdot \Phi(\mathbf{x}_i)) \geq \rho - \xi_i, \tag{4}$$
$$\xi_i \geq 0.$$

Here, $\nu \in (0,1)$ is an upper bound on the fraction of outliers, and a lower bound on the fraction of Support Vectors (SVs).

Since nonzero slack variables ξ_i are penalized in the objective function, we can expect that if $\mathbf{w}$ and ρ solve this problem, then the decision function

$$f(\mathbf{x}) = \text{sgn}\left((\mathbf{w} \cdot \Phi(\mathbf{x})) - \rho\right) \tag{5}$$

will be positive for most examples $\mathbf{x}_i$ contained in the training set, while the SV type regularization term $\|w\|$ will still be small. The actual trade-off between these two is controlled by ν. For a new point $\mathbf{x}$, the value $f(\mathbf{x})$ is determined by evaluating which side of the hyperplane it falls on, in feature space.

Using multipliers $\alpha_i, \beta_i \geq 0$, we introduce a Lagrangian

$$L(\mathbf{w}, \boldsymbol{\xi}, \rho, \boldsymbol{\alpha}, \boldsymbol{\beta}) =$$
$$\frac{1}{2}\|\mathbf{w}\|^2 + \frac{1}{\nu\ell}\sum_i \xi_i - \rho$$
$$- \sum_i \alpha_i((\mathbf{w}\cdot\mathbf{x}_i) - \rho + \xi_i) - \sum_i \beta_i \xi_i \quad (6)$$

and set the derivatives with respect to the primal variables $\mathbf{w}, \xi_i, \rho$ equal to zero, yielding

$$\mathbf{w} = \sum_i \alpha_i \mathbf{x}_i, \quad (7)$$
$$\alpha_i = \frac{1}{\nu\ell} - \beta_i \leq \frac{1}{\nu\ell}, \quad \sum_i \alpha_i = 1. \quad (8)$$

In Eqn. (7), all patterns $\{\mathbf{x}_i : i \in [\ell], \alpha_i > 0\}$ are called Support Vectors. Using Eqn. (2), the SV expansion transforms the decision function Eqn. (5)

$$f(\mathbf{x}) = \text{sgn}\left(\sum_i \alpha_i k(\mathbf{x}_i, \mathbf{x}) - \rho\right). \quad (9)$$

Substituting Eqn. (7) and Eqn. (8) into Eqn. (6), we obtain the dual problem:

$$\min_{\boldsymbol{\alpha}} \quad \frac{1}{2}\sum_{i,j} \alpha_i \alpha_j k(\mathbf{x}_i, \mathbf{x}_j) \quad (10)$$
$$\text{subject to} \quad 0 \leq \alpha_i \leq \frac{1}{\nu\ell}, \quad \sum_i \alpha_i = 1. \quad (11)$$

One can show that at the optimum, the two inequality constraints Eqn. (4) become equalities if α_i and β_i are nonzero, i.e. if $0 < \alpha \leq 1/(\nu\ell)$. Therefore, we can recover ρ by exploiting that for any such α_i, the corresponding pattern $\mathbf{x}_i$ satisfies

$$\rho = (\mathbf{w}\cdot\mathbf{x}_i) = \sum_j \alpha_j \mathbf{x}_j \cdot \mathbf{x}_i. \quad (12)$$

Note that if ν approaches to 0, the upper boundaries on the Lagrange multipliers tend to infinity, i.e. the second inequality constraint in Eqn. (11) becomes void. The problem then resembles the corresponding *hard margin* algorithm, since the penalization of errors becomes infinite, as can be seen from the primal objective function Eqn. (4). It is still a feasible problem, since we have placed no restriction on ρ, so ρ can become a large negative number in order to satisfy Eqn. (4). If we had required $\rho \geq 0$ from the start, we would have ended up with the constraint $\sum_i \alpha_i \geq 1$ instead of the corresponding equality constraint in Eqn. (11), and the multipliers α_i could have diverged.

In our research we used the LIBSVM. This is an integrated tool for support vector classification and regression which can handle one-class SVM using the Schölkopf etc algorithms. The LIBSVM is available at http://www.csie.ntu.edu.tw/~cjlin/libsvm.

III. NON-RELEVANCE FEEDBACK DOCUMENT RETRIEVAL

In this section, we describe our proposed method of document retrieval based on Non-relevant documents using One-class SVM.

In relevance feedback document retrieval, the user has the option of labeling some of the top ranked documents according to whether they are relevant or non-relevant. The labeled documents along with the original request are then given to a supervised learning procedure to produce a new classifier. The new classifier is used to produce a new ranking, which retrievals more relevant documents at higher ranks than the original did (see Figure 1) [10].

The initial retrieved documents, which are displayed to a user, sometimes don't include relevant documents. In this case, almost all relevance feedback document retrieval systems do not contribute to efficient document retrieval, because the systems need relevant and non-relevant documents to construct a binary class classification problem (see Figure 2).

The One-Class SVM can generate discriminant hyperplane for the one class using one class training data. Consequently, we propose to apply One-Class SVM in a "non-relevance feedback document retrieval method." The retrieval steps of proposed method perform as follows:

Step 1: **Preparation of documents for the first feedback**
The conventional information retrieval system based on vector space model displays the top N ranked documents along with a request query to the user. In our method, the top N ranked documents are selected by using the cosine distance between the request query vector and each document vectors for the first feedback iteration.

Step 2: **Judgment of documents**
The user then classifiers these N documents into relevant or non-relevant. If the user labels all N documents non-relevant, the documents are labeled "+1" and go to the next step. If the user classifies the N documents into relevant documents and non-relevant documents, the non-relevant documents are labeled "+1" and relevant documents are labeled "-1" and then our previous proposed relevant feedback method is adopted [10].

Step 3: **Determination of non-relevant documents area based on non-relevant documents**
The discriminant hyperplane for classifying non-relevant documents area is generated by using One-Class SVM. In order to generate the hyperplane, the One-Class SVM learns labeled non-relevant documents which are evaluated in the previous step (see Figure 4).

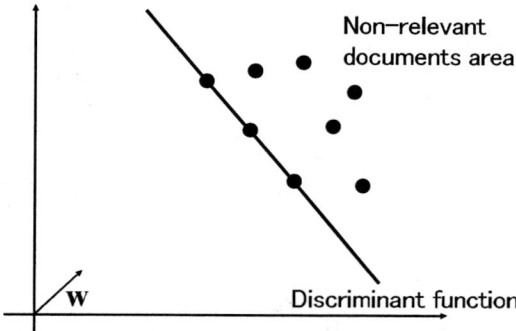

Fig. 4. Generation of a hyperplane to discriminate non-relevant documents area: Circles denote documents which are checked non-relevant by a user. The solid line denotes the discriminant hyperplane.

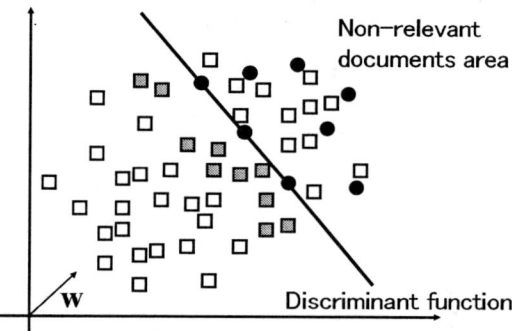

Fig. 5. Mapped non-checked documents into the feature space: Boxes denote non-checked documents which are mapped into the feature space. Circles denotes checked documents which are mapped into the feature space. Gray boxes denotes the displayed documents to a user in the next iteration. These documents are in the "not non-relevant document area" and near the discriminant hyperplane.

Step 4: Classification of all documents and Selection of retrieved documents

The One-class SVM learned by previous step can classifies the whole documents as non-relevant or not non-relevant. The documents which are discriminated in "not non-relevant area" are newly selected. From the selected documents, the top N ranked documents, which are ranked in the order of the distance from the non-relevant documents area, are shown to user as the document retrieval results of the system (see Figure 5). These N documents have high existence probability of initial keywords. Then return to Step 2.

The feature of our One-Class SVM based non-relevant feedback document retrieval is the selection of displayed documents to a user in Step 4. Our proposed method selects the documents which are discriminated as "not non-relevant" and near the discriminant hyperplane between "non-relevant documents and "not non-relevant documents. Generally if the system got the opposite information from a user, the system should select the information, which is far from the opposite information area, for displaying to the user. However, in our case, the classified non-relevant documents by the user includes a request query vector of the user. Therefore, if we select the documents, which are far from the non-relevant documents area, the documents may not include the request query of the user. Our selected documents (see Figure 5) is expected that the probability of the relevant documents for the user is high, because the documents are not non-relevant and may include the query vector of the user.

IV. EXPERIMENTS

A. Experimental setting

We made experiments for evaluating the effectiveness of our interactive document retrieval based on non-relevant documents using One-Class SVM described in section III. The document data set we used is a set of articles in the Los Angels Times which is widely used in the document retrieval conference TREC [2]. The data set has about 130 thousands articles. The average number of words in a article is 526. This data set includes not only queries but also the relevant documents to each query. Thus we used the queries for the experiments. We used three topics for experiments and show these topics in Table I. These topics do not have relevant documents in top 20 ranked documents in the order of the cosine distance between the query vector and document vectors. Our experiments set the size of N of displayed documents presented in Step 1 in the section III to 10 or 20.

We used TFIDF [1], which is one of the most popular methods in information retrieval to generate document feature vectors, and the concrete equation [12] of a weight of a term t in a document d w_t^d are in the following.

$$w_t^d = L \times t \times u \quad (13)$$

$$L = \frac{1 + \log(tf(t,d))}{1 + \log(\text{average of } tf(t,d) \text{ in } d)} \quad \text{(TF)}$$

$$t = \log\left(\frac{n+1}{df(t)}\right) \quad \text{(IDF)}$$

$$u = \frac{1}{0.8 + 0.2 \frac{uniq(d)}{\text{average of } uniq(d)}} \quad \text{(normalization)}$$

The notations in these equation denote as follows:

- w_t^d is a weight of a term t in a document d,
- $tf(t,d)$ is a frequency of a term t in a document d,
- n is the total number of documents in a data set,

TABLE I
TOPICS, QUERY WORDS AND THE NUMBER OF RELEVANT DOCUMENTS IN THE LOS ANGELS TIMES USED FOR EXPERIMENTS

topic	query words	# of relevant doc.
306	Africa, civilian, death	34
343	police, death	88
383	mental, ill, drug	55

- $df(t)$ is the number of documents including a term t,
- $uniq(d)$ is the number of different terms in a document d.

In our experiments, we used the linear kernel for One-class SVM learning, and found a discriminant function for the One-class SVM classifier in the feature space. The vector space model of documents is high dimensional space. Moreover, the number of the documents which are evaluated by a user is small. Therefore, we do not need to use the kernel trick and the parameter ν (see section II) is set adequately small value ($\nu = 0.01$). The small ν means hard margin in the One-Class SVM and it is important to make hard margin in our problem.

For comparison with our approach, two information retrieval methods were used. The first is an information retrieval method that does not use a feedback, namely documents are retrieved using the rank in vector space model (VSM). The second is an information retrieval method using the conventional Rocchio-based relevance feedback [6] which is widely used in information retrieval research.

The Rocchio-based relevance feedback modifies a query vector Q_i by evaluation of a user using the following equation.

$$Q_{i+1} = Q_i + \alpha \sum_{x \in R_r} x - \beta \sum_{x \in R_n} x, \quad (14)$$

where R_r is a set of documents which were evaluated as relevant documents by a user at the ith feedback, and R_n is a set of documents which were evaluated as non-relevant documents at the i feedback. α and β are weights for relevant and non-relevant documents respectively. In this experiment, we set $\alpha = 1.0$, $\beta = 0.5$ which are known adequate experimentally.

B. Experimental results

Here, we describe the relationships between the performances of the proposed method and the number of feedback iterations. Table II shows the number of retrieved relevant documents at each feedback iteration. At each feedback iteration, the system displays ten higher ranked "not non-relevant documents," which are near the discriminant hyperplane, for our proposed method. We also show the retrieved documents of the Rocchio-based method at each feedback iteration for comparing to the proposed method in table II.

We can see from this table that our non-relevance feedback approach gives the higher performance in terms of the number of iteration for retrieving relevant document. On the other hand, the Rocchio-based feedback method cannot search a relevant document in all cases. The vector space model without feedback is better than Rocchio-based feedback. After all, we can believe that the proposed method can make an effective document retrieval using only non-relevant documents, and the Rocchio-based feedback method can not work well when the system can receive the only non-relevant documents information.

Table III gave the number of retrieved relevant documents at each feedback iteration. At each feedback iteration, the system

TABLE II

THE NUMBER OF RETRIEVED RELEVANT DOCUMENTS AT EACH ITERATION: THE NUMBER OF DISPLAYED DOCUMENTS IS 10 AT EACH ITERATION

topic 308	# of retrieved relevant doc.		
# of iterations	Proposed method	VSM	Rocchio
1	1	0	0
2	–	0	0
3	–	1	0
4	–	–	0
5	–	–	0
topic 343	# of retrieved relevant doc.		
# of iterations	Proposed method	VSM	Rocchio
1	0	0	0
2	1	0	0
3	–	0	0
4	–	0	0
5	–	0	0
topic 383	# of retrieved relevant doc.		
# of iterations	Proposed method	VSM	Rocchio
1	0	0	0
2	1	0	0
3	–	0	0
4	–	1	0
5	–	–	0

TABLE III

THE NUMBER OF RETRIEVED RELEVANT DOCUMENTS AT EACH ITERATION: THE NUMBER OF DISPLAYED DOCUMENTS IS 20 AT EACH ITERATION

topic 306	# of retrieved relevant doc.		
# of iterations	Proposed method	VSM	Rocchio
1	1	1	0
2	–	–	0
3	–	–	0
4	–	–	0
5	–	–	0
topic 343	# of retrieved relevant doc.		
# of iterations	Proposed method	VSM	Rocchio
1	1	0	0
2	–	0	0
3	–	0	0
4	–	1	0
5	–	–	0
topic 383	# of retrieved relevant doc.		
# of iterations	Proposed method	VSM	Rocchio
1	1	0	0
2	–	1	0
3	–	–	0
4	–	–	0
5	–	–	0

displays twenty higher ranked "not non-relevant documents," which are near the discriminant hyperplane, for our proposed method. We also show the retrieved documents of the Rocchio-based method at each feedback iteration for comparing to proposed method in table III.

We can observe from this table that our non-relevance feedback approach gives the higher performance in terms of the number of iteration for retrieving relevant documents, and the same experimental results as table II about the Rocchio-based method and VSM.

In table II, a user already have seen twenty documents

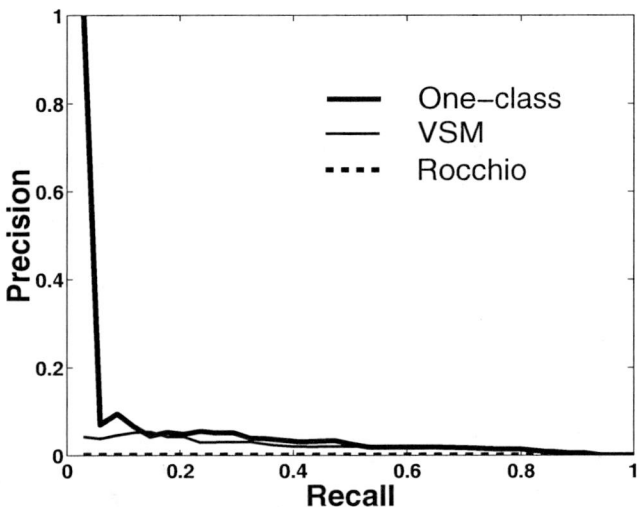

Fig. 6. The precision and recall curve of topic no. 304 at the second iteration.

at the first iteration. Before the fist iteration, the user have to see ten documents, which are retrieved results using the cosine distance between a query vector and document vectors in VSM. In table III, the user also have seen forty documents at the first iteration. Before the fist iteration, the user also have to see ten documents to evaluate the documents, which are retrieved results using the cosine distance between a query vector and document vectors in VSM. When we compare the experimental results of table II with the results of table III, we can observe that the small number of displayed documents makes more effective document retrieval performance than the large number of displayed documents. In table II, the user had to see thirty documents by finding the first relevant document about topic 343 and 383. In table III, the user had to see forty documents by finding the first relevant document about topic 343 and 383. Therefore, we believe that the early non-relevance feedback is useful for an interactive document retrieval.

We also show a precision and recall curve in figure 6. This figure is the precision and recall curve of topic no. 306 at the second iteration. From this figure, we can understand that all precision-recall curves are not good. However, our proposed approach is more efficient than the two other approaches.

V. Conclusion

In this paper, we proposed the non-relevance feedback document retrieval based on One-Class SVM using only non-relevant documents for a user. In our non-relevance feedback document retrieval, the system use only non-relevant documents information. One-Class SVM can generate a discriminant hyperplane of observed one class information, so our proposed method adopted One-Class SVM for non-relevance feedback document retrieval.

This paper compared our method with a conventional relevance feedback method and a vector space model without feedback. Experimental results on a set of articles in the Los Angels Times showed that the proposed method gave a consistently better performance than the compared method. Therefore we believe that our proposed One-Class SVM based approach is very useful for the document retrieval with only non-relevant documents information.

If our proposed non-relevant feedback document retrieval method find and display relevant documents for a user, the system will switch from our non-relevant feedback method to ordinary relevance feedback document retrieval method immediately. When one see this procedure, one may think that there are few chances of using our non-relevant feedback method in an interactive document retrieval. However, we guess that our non-relevant feedback method has a lot of chances in the interactive document retrieval. Because it is very hard for the interactive document retrieval to find relevant documents using a few keywords in a large database. For instance, consider a case where we want to search patent information related our research. In the first, we input a few keywords to find our interesting patent information. And then we can see too many patent documents. Can we find our interesting information in them easily ? We think it is very difficult to find interesting information in the top 100 documents. Therefore, we believe that our proposed non-relevance feedback method is useful for an effective interactive document retrieval.

This paper proposed that the system should display the documents which are in the "not non-relevant" documents area and near the discriminant hyperplane of One-Class SVM at each feedback iteration. However, we do not discuss how the selection of documents influence both the effective learning and the performance of information retrieval theoretically. This point is our future work.

References

[1] R. B. Yates and B. R. Neto, *Modern Information Retrieval*. Addison Wesley, 1999.
[2] TREC Web page, "http://trec.nist.gov/."
[3] IREX, "http://cs.nyu.edu/cs/projects/proteus/irex/."
[4] NTCIR, "http://www.rd.nacsis.ac.jp/~ntcadm/."
[5] G. Salton and J. McGill, *Introduction to modern information retrieval*. McGraw-Hill, 1983.
[6] G. Salton, Ed., *Relevance feedback in information retrieval*. Englewood Cliffs, N.J.: Prentice Hall, 1971, pp. 313–323.
[7] M. Okabe and S. Yamada, "Interactive document retrieval with relational learning," in *Proceedings of the 16th ACM Symposium on Applied Computing*, 2001, pp. 27–31.
[8] S. Tong and D. Koller, "Support vector machine active learning with applications to text classification," in *Journal of Machine Learning Research*, vol. 2, 2001, pp. 45–66.
[9] H. Drucker, B. Shahrary, and D. C. Gibbon, "Relevance feedback using support vector machines," in *Proceedings of the Eighteenth International Conference on Machine Learning*, 2001, pp. 122–129. [Online]. Available: citeseer.nj.nec.com/443262.html
[10] T. Onoda, H. Murata, and S. Yamada, "Relevance feedback with active learning for document retrieval," in *Proc. of IJCNN2003*, 2003, pp. 1757–1762.
[11] B. Schölkopf, J. Platt, J. Shawe-Taylor, A. Smola, and R. Williamson, "Estimating the support for a high-dimensional distribution," Microsoft Research, One Microsoft Way Redmon WA 98052, Tech. Rep. MSR-TR-99-87, 1999.
[12] R. Schapire, Y. Singer, and A. Singhal, "Boosting and rocchio applied to text filtering," in *Proceedings of the Twenty-First Annual International ACM SIGIR*, 1998, pp. 215–223.

Text Clustering with NTSO
(Neural Text Self Organizer)

Taeho Jo and Nathalie Japkowicz
SITE (School of Information Technology and Engineering)
University of Ottawa
Ottawa Ontario Canada, K1N6N5
Email: tjo018@site.uottawa.ca and nat@site.uottawa.ca

Abstract— Text clustering is the process of segmenting a particular collection of texts into subgroups including content-based similar ones. This study proposes a new neural network, called NTSO (Neural Text Self Organizer), which is suitable for text clustering. This neural network uses string vectors instead of numerical vectors as its input vectors and its weight vectors are different from those of other unsupervised neural networks such as Kohonen Networks and ART (Adaptive Resonance Theory), although it is similar to Kohonen Networks at the architecture level and in its learning process. Intuitively, text is better represented by a string vector than by a numerical vector. The representation of texts into numerical vectors leads to two main problems: sparse distribution and huge dimensionality of the feature vectors. This study proposes an unsupervised neural network that uses string vectors for text clustering, to address these problems.

I. INTRODUCTION

There are two ways to organize a collection of texts. One is text categorization and the other is text clustering. The former requires prior knowledge about the collection of texts to predefine categories and labels texts manually to prepare sample texts. If we don't have such knowledge, we must use the latter. Text clustering has higher complexity in its computation than text categorization, but it does not require prior knowledge.
Many studies have proposed machine-learning-based approaches including neural networks for text categorization and text clustering [1][2][3][4][5]. When these kinds of approaches are applied to these problems, each text must be represented into a numerical feature vector. Such representation causes two main problems: the huge dimension and sparse distribution of each feature vector, which means that zero values are very dominant in these vectors. The huge dimensionality leads to very slow computation for text categorization and text clustering and the inefficient allocation of system resources while the sparse distribution reduces the discrimination of feature vectors. Due to these two problems, text categorization and text clustering are currently implemented in a very impractical manner for information systems in the real world.
Although many studies proposed feature selection methods for reducing the dimension of feature vectors, such solutions do not solve our two problems. With regard to the first problem, the huge dimensionality of the feature vectors, they reduced more than 10,000 dimensions to several hundreds dimensions, but we are not satisfied by such reductions which are still too small. They do not consider our second problem, the sparse distribution in feature space. The proposed neural network for text clustering uses string vector instead of numerical vector, so both problems will be addressed.
S. Kaski and his colleagues developed WEBSOM, the system for text clustering with SOM (Self Organizing Map)[1] in 1998 [4]. WEBSOM displays the results of text clustering graphically for browsing collection of documents. In WEBSOM, a word category map is built in a competitive layer; each node in the layer corresponds to a set of similar words [4]. Like for text categorization, each document was represented into a feature vector; its dimension was 315 [4]. This system performs text clustering by modifying the weights between the feature vector and the winner node in the competitive layer. The winner node corresponds to the set of similar words nearest to the feature vector in Euclidean distance.
Bote and his colleagues developed a text clustering system using Kohonen Networks in 2002 [5]. Their proposed system of text clustering is similar to WEBSOM in that Kohonen Networks are used as the algorithm for text clustering. However, their system presents some differences with rWEBSOM. First, WEBSOM builds a word category map in the competitive layer, while their system of text clustering 20*20 unnamed nodes in the layer. Second, WEBSOM targeted unlabeled documents [1][4], while this system requires labeled ones [5]. The goal of their research is not to cluster documents per se, but to map labeled documents into 20 * 20 nodes, topologically. Hence the two previous studies are identical with respect to text clustering using Kohonen Network, but they are different in their goals.
Kohonen and his colleagues implemented a modified version of WEBSOM to apply it more practically to a massive document collection in 2000 [1]. The modified version of WEBSOM is identical to the previous version [4] in the process of text clustering. Its modification is just in the

---

[1] Since it was proposed by Kohonen, it is called Kohonen Networks [6]

definition of the data structure for text clustering whose goal is the fast computation of text clustering. The modified version is compared to the previous version on 6,840,567 patent abstracts with respect to accuracy and speed. The result shows that the modified version reduces the time taken by text clustering by 90% while maintaining its performance [1].

In all the previous research, each text must be represented by a feature vector for text clustering [4][5]. Previous studies on text clustering regarded such representation as a natural process. For example, for WEBSOM, the dimension of the feature vectors is 315 in the original version [10] and 500 in the modified version [1]. In the previous research of Bote and his colleague, the dimension of the feature vector reaches even 1,200 for text clustering in spite of feature selection. This previous research shows that at least several hundreds of dimensions of feature vectors are required for text clustering.

The first contribution of this research is to address the two main problems emanaying from the representation of documents into numerical vectors, by replacing traditional machine learning algorithms by the proposed neural network for text clustering. Previous research applied mainly Naïve Bayes [7][8][9], SVM (Support Vector Machine) [10][11], and Back Propagation [12] to text categorization, and Kohonen Network [1][4], single link [12], complete link [12], and single pass [12] to text clustering. All of these approaches to text categorization and text clustering require the representation of documents into numerical vectors.

NTSO (Neural Text Self Organizer) considers a semantic similarity between two words rather than a lexical one. It uses string vectors as its input vectors and weight vectors, and needs the calculation of their semantic similarity. A similarity matrix in word by word is built from a collection of texts to obtain semantic similarity between input vectors and weight vectors given as string vectors. Each entry in such matrix indicates semantic similarity between two words. Such similarity is based on their collocations within the same text and their weights indicating the degree of their content based importance in each text.

II. TEXT REPRESENTATION

Since texts are unstructured data in natural languages and computers can not process them directly, they should be encoded into structured data. This section describes two ways to do that. One is for traditional neural networks, and the other is for the proposed new approach.

A. Numerical Vectors

This subsection describes the traditional way to encode texts. In this method, texts are represented into numerical vectors. Main machine learning algorithms such as NB (Naïve Bayes), SVM (Support Vector Machine), MLP (Multi-Layer Perceptron), and Kohonen Network use numerical vectors as their input vectors. This method is necessary to apply such machine learning algorithms for text categorization and text clustering. This subsection describes such a way briefly and points out its disadvantages.

Features as attributes of numerical vectors representing texts are words in a collection of texts. If all of words were used as their features, their dimension would be more than 10,000; such a dimension is not feasible for text categorization and text clustering. Previous research suggested several methods of feature selection, such as mutual information, chi-square, frequency based method, and information theory based method [13].

There are three ways to define feature values in numerical vectors representing texts. The first way is to use a binary value for each word indicating its presence or absence in the text. The second way is to use the frequency of each word in each text as its value. In this way, each element is an integer. The third way is to use the weight of each word as a feature value. Such a weight is computed from the equation (1).

$$w_{it} = f_{it}(\log_2 N - \log_2 d_t + 1) \qquad (1)$$

where w_{it} is the weight of the word, t in the text, t, f_{it} is the frequency of the word, t in the text, t, N is the number of texts in the corpus, and d_t is the number of texts including the word t.

This way of representing texts causes two main problems, as discussed previously: a huge dimension and the sparse distribution of the numerical vectors. The former leads to text categorization or text clustering taking too much system resources for their computation and it makes their automation very impractical. The sparse distribution of numerical vectors reduces the discrimination among them, because of the tiny scale of Euclidean distance. Two numerical vectors representing two texts on different topics may have a Euclidean distance very close to zero.

B. String Vectors

Another way to represent texts is to encode them into string vectors. This approach is more appropriate for texts than numerical vectors by intuition, since texts consist of strings, not numerical vectors. This subsection presents a previous successful case of using string vectors for text categorization and describes its definition and the process of encoding texts.

T. Jo suggested a new supervised neural network, called NTC (Neural Text Categorizer), using string vectors, for text categorization in 2000 [14]. He validated its performance by comparing it with other approaches such as Naïve Bayes, SVM (Support Vector Machine), and Back Propagation on Reuter 21578, as a standard test bed for text categorization [15]. His study shows that string vector is more appropriate for text categorization than numerical vector in text categorization.

To encode texts into string vectors, they should be indexed into lists of words and their frequencies, through the process illustrated in figure 1. Through the first step, tokenization, a text is segmented into tokens by white space. For each token, it is converted into a root form through the second step, stemming and exception handling. For example, a plural noun is converted into a singular form and a verb in past tense is changed into its root form. The last step removes stop words, which perform a grammatical function regardless of the content of the text. Stop words include prepositions, conjunctions, particles, auxiliary verbs, and so on. The final result of this process is a list of words and their frequencies in a text. From these lists, as many words as there are dimensions are selected based on their frequencies.

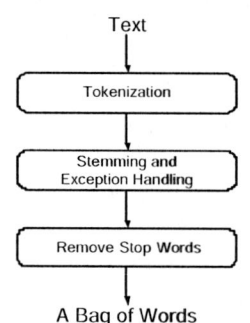

Fig. 1. The Process of Indexing Texts

A string vector is the finite ordered set consisting of words as its elements. The number of elements a string vector contains is called its dimension like in a numerical vector. A string vector should be distinguished from a bag of words, since it is infinite unordered set of words. A d dimensional string vector is expressed as in equation (2),

$$x_i = [t_{i1}, t_{i2}, ..., t_{id}] \quad (2)$$

where t_{ij} is the j th word in the i th string vector.

III. OPERATIONS ON STRING VECTORS

NTSO (Neural Text Self Organizer) needs to compute the similarity between two string vectors and update a weight vector. Weight vectors are updated by substituting its elements by inter-words (see below). So it is necessary to define operations on string vectors. This section will describe two operators necessary for training NTSO (Neural Text Self Organizer).

A similarity matrix should be built from the given collection of texts before defining two operators on string vectors. Each entry in the matrix indicates the semantic similarity between two words based on their collocation and weights in a text. The similarity matrix is defined word by word from the given collection of texts. It is expressed by the symmetry function and square matrix shown in equation (3).

$$S = \begin{bmatrix} S_{11} & S_{12} & \cdots & S_{1N} \\ S_{21} & S_{22} & \cdots & S_{2N} \\ \cdots & \cdots & \cdots & \cdots \\ S_{N1} & S_{N2} & \cdots & S_{NN} \end{bmatrix}$$

$$S_{ij} = S_{ji} = sim(t_i, t_j) \quad (3)$$

An element, S_{ij}, of the similarity matrix, S, indicates the similarity between two words, t_i and t_j. It is computed by equation (4).

$$S_{ij} = \frac{\sum_{d \in D_i \cap D_j}(w_{di} + w_{dj})}{\sum_{d \in D_i} w_{di} + \sum_{d \in D_j} w_{dj}} \quad (4)$$

where D_i is the set of documents including the word, t_i, D_j is the set of documents including the word, t_j, w_{di} is the weight (See section 2.A) of the word, t_i, in document, d, and w_{dj} is the weight of the word, t_j, in document, d. As illustrated in the equation (4), the similarity between two words is based on their collocation in same document.

If a similarity matrix is built from the corpus with equation (3), we can compute the similarity between two string vectors, denoted by $x_i = [t_{i1}, t_{i2}, ..., t_{id}]$ and $x_j = [t_{j1}, t_{j2}, ..., t_{jd}]$. The similarity $sim(t_{ik}, t_{jk})$ between two words, t_{ik} and t_{jk} is indicated by the entry, S_{ij} of the row and column corresponding to such words or its reverse, S_{ji} in the similarity matrix. The similarity between two string vectors x_i and x_j denoted by $sim(x_i, x_j)$ is computed by equation (5).

$$sim(x_i, x_j) = \frac{1}{d}\sum_{k=1}^{d} sim(t_{ik}, t_{jk}) \quad (5)$$

Given two words t_i and t_j. An inter-word tk is a word presenting a higher similarity to both t_i and t_j than the similarity between t_i and t_j. Such similarity is defined by the similarity matrix built from the given corpus. First, we find the similarity between two words from the similarity matrix to find inter-words between them. And we extract words with higher similarity with both of them from the similarity matrix. The set of inter-words between two words denoted by t_i and t_j, denoted by I_{ij} is expressed by equation (6).

$$I_{ij} = I(t_i, t_j) = \{t_k \mid t_k \quad s(t_i, t_k) \geq s(t_i, t_j) \\ \wedge s(t_j, t_k) \geq s(t_j, t_i)\} \quad (6)$$

IV. NTSO

This section will describe an unsupervised symbolic neural network called NTSO (Neural Text Self Organizer), which uses string vectors as its weight vectors and input vectors. Traditional approaches to text clustering, such as SOM (Self Organizing Map), require the representation of texts into numerical vectors. The motivation for this model is to avoid using numerical vectors.

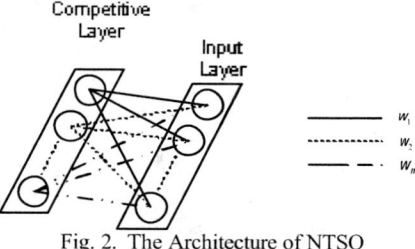

Fig. 2. The Architecture of NTSO

Figure 2 illustrates the architecture of NTSO (Neural Text Self Organizer). Like Kohonen Networks, it consists of two layers, input layer and competitive layer; the proposed neural based model is identical to Kohonen Networks in this respect. The input layer receives an input vector representing a text, and a competitive layer indicating clusters; each node in this layer corresponds to each cluster. The weight vectors between the input layer and the competitive layer indicates the prototypicality of the vectors representing the cluster. Figure 2 represents the relationship between each weight vector and its cluster using different kinds of lines. Nodes in the competitive layer are competitive with each other based on their similarity between their weight vectors and input vectors; the winner node in that layer is the node with highest similarity between its corresponding weight vector and the given input vector. Learning in this model is the process of updating weight vectors corresponding to the winner node for the input node.

This unsupervised model needs the initialization of weights like other neural networks before clustering string vectors representing texts. This proposed unsupervised neural network has weight vectors in string vectors. Weight vectors in this model are prototypical vectors that represent clusters like in the SOM (Self Organization Map) algorithm. Each weight vector corresponds to each node indicating a cluster in the competitive layer. Such weight vectors are initialized with one of the following methods.

- **Corpus based Initialization**: Initializes the weight vectors by selecting words in the corpus as their elements, at random
- **Sample based Initialization**: Initializes weight vectors by selecting some of the given training examples.

Clustering in this unsupervised model is the process of optimizing the weight vectors as prototypical vectors representing the clusters and arranging string vectors representing the documents into their corresponding clusters. At first, the weight vectors are initialized using one of the above methods. Whenever an input vector is assigned, similarities between weight vectors and the input vectors, are computed with equation (5) in section, 3. Only the weight vector corresponding to the maximum similarity with the input vector is updated, following the learning rule of Kohonen Network, by replacing the words in the weight vectors with the inter-words, described in equation (6).. Let's denote a random element of a particular set, S by $\mathrm{rand}(S)$. Therefore, a random element of inter-word set, I_{ij} between two words, t_i and t_j is denoted by $\mathrm{rand}(I_{ij})$. The update of the weight vectors is expressed by equation (7),

$$w_i = [t_{i1}^w, t_{i2}^w, \ldots, t_{id}^w]$$
$$x_j = [t_{j1}^x, t_{j2}^x, \ldots, t_{jd}^x]$$
$$w_i \rightarrow [\mathrm{rand}(I(t_{i1}^w, t_{j1}^x)), \mathrm{rand}(I(t_{i2}^w, t_{j2}^x)), \quad (7)$$
$$\ldots, \mathrm{rand}(I(t_{id}^w, t_{jd}^x))]$$

where w_i is the I th weight vector corresponding to the winner node in the competitive layer, x_j is the j th input vector, and $\mathrm{rand}(I(t_{ik}^w, t_{jk}^x))$ is a random element of the inter-word set between two words, t_{ik}^w and t_{jk}^x belonging to the weight vector, w_i, and the input vector, x_j, respectively. The process of updating the weight vectors is repeated until they converge.

V. EXPERIMENTS AND RESULTS

This section presents the results obtained by NTSO (Neural Text Self Organizer) and Kohonen Network with respect to their performance and their speed. The reason for adopting Kohonen Network to compare with NTSO is that 1) Kohonen Networks are very much used in text clustering research [1][4][5]. Since NTSO is based on Kohonen Networks, the comparison of NTSO with Kohonen Networks amounts to comparing the numerical and string vector representations of text.

Three collections of news articles are used in these experiments. The first collection includes four hundreds news articles labeled with one of four categories in ASCII text files. Predefined categories in such collection are "corporate news", "criminal law enforcement", "economical index", and "Internet". We obtained this collection by copying news articles from the web site, www.newspage.com, and pasting them as ASCII text files, individually. Each category includes one hundred news articles. This collection is used to evaluate clustering performance of NTSO (Neural Text Self Organizer) and Kohonen Network based on the consistence between their target categories and their clusters corresponding to predefined categories. The evaluation measures used for this experiment are accuracy and F-measure. Depending on the result from this experiment, the dimension and the number of training iterations will be determined differently, and the clustering time of two approaches will be evaluated based on these different conditions.

The second collection is another domain of news articles in XML format. It includes 18,708 news articles. Ten thousands of news articles among them are encoded into string vectors and numerical vectors to apply the two neural networks. Since they are unlabeled, this collection will be used to evaluate only clustering time of the two approaches.

The third collection for this experiment is Reuter 21578 used as a standard test bed to evaluate approaches to text categorization [13]. Each news article in this collection has more than one category. It is very complicated to evaluate the performance of text clustering with this collection as with the first collection. Like for the second collection, ten thousands news articles are selected at random among them for the evaluation of clustering time.

Words are extracted as features for numerical vectors for Kohonen Network by indexing texts, except stop words, through the process illustrated in figure 1. These experiments adopt the frequency based method as a feature selection method, since it is most popular and simplest. The feature values are set to frequencies of words in each text. They are normalized by dividing them by the maximum frequency, in preprocessing step.

Phases involved in training the Kohonen Network are the initialization of weight vectors, their update, and the arrangement of input vectors into their corresponding clusters. In the first phase, the weight vectors are initialized by randomizing normalized values in this experiment. Parameters of Kohonen Network, learning rate and the number of repetition of training it are set to 0.3 and 200 respectively, through fine tuning. Texts are arranged into the cluster corresponding to the weight vector with the minimum Euclidean distance from its numerical vector.

The similarity matrix is built in this experiment, collection by collection. In the first collection, all news articles are used to build it, and in the second collection and the third collection, only one thousand news articles among them are used to do that, because of the restriction of execution time and memory. Since it is possible to continue clustering, once a similarity matrix is built, the time for building it, is counted out in the evaluation of clustering time of NTSO (Neural Text Self Organizer).

In NTSO, the weight vectors are initialized with corpus based initialization. They are updated with inter-words between elements in the weight vectors and input vectors. Through tuning, the number of repetition of training NTSO is set to only ten; only ten repetitions is feasible for clustering texts with NTSO. String vectors representing texts are arranged into their corresponding clusters corresponding to the weight vector with its maximum similarity.

Table 1 and table 2 show the results of clustering performance of Kohonen Network and NTSO respectively. Each row of these tables indicates the dimensions of numerical vectors and string vectors and each column shows performance measures. Each cluster is mapped to each category, one to one, based on the majority of categories in it. The accuracy is computed based on the consistence rate between their target categories and their arranged categories corresponding to clusters. The F-measure is computed with the recall and the precision averaged over four categories.

NTSO shows better performance than Kohonen Network as illustrated in table 1 and table 2. It outperforms Kohonen Network 1.5 times in accuracy and even more than three times in F-measure. Furthermore, it clusters news articles with only ten dimensions of string vectors, while Kohonen Networks fail to work better than NTSO despite using 200 dimensions. When experiments on the second and the third collection is performed to evaluate the clustering speed, the dimension is set to ten and two hundreds for NTSO and for Kohonen Network, respectively.

TABLE I
THE CLUSTERING PERFORMANCE IN KOHONEN NETWORK

Dimension	Accuracy	F-Measure
10	0.255	0.110
50	0.255	0.110
100	0.255	0.110
200	0.282	0.123

TABLE II
THE CLUSTERING PERFORMANCE IN NTSO

Dimension	Accuracy	F-Measure
5	0.325	0.248
10	0.475	0.458
20	0.350	0.238
50	0.350	0.238

Although NTSO worked better than Kohonen Network, both approaches do not show feasible performance. Kohonen Networks failed to cluster news articles into four groups: almost all the news articles are grouped into one cluster. The reason is that initialized weight vectors have no sparse distribution, while input vectors have a sparse distribution. One of two problems, the sparse distribution, in representing texts into numerical vectors comes true. NTSO segments the collection of news articles not into four, but into two or three clusters. This comes from the initialization of the weight vectors and shows that corpus based weight initialization is not ideal.

Figures 3 and 4 show the clustering time taken by Kohonen Networks and NTSO on the second and third collections, respectively. The x-axis indicates the amount of time for clustering and the y-axis shows the number of news articles involved in the clustering. The solid line indicates the trend of time in clustering news articles with Kohonen Network, and the dotted line shows the one displayed by NTSO. The two figures show that NTSO costs less time in clustering news articles than Kohonen Network. The reason is that the dimension of string vectors and the number of repetition for NTSO are smaller than for Kohonen Networks.

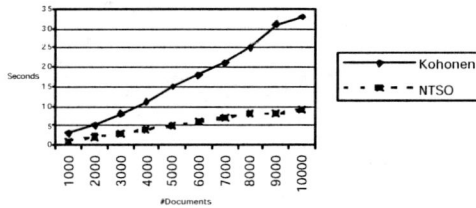

Fig. 3. Clustering Speed in the Second Collection

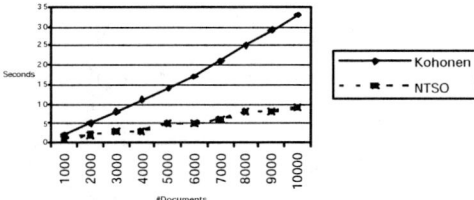

Fig. 4. Clustering Speed in the Third Collection

As mentioned above, NTSO takes less time to cluster news articles than Kohonen Network, because of the smaller dimension of string vectors and number of training repetition is feasible and far less in NTSO (Neural Text Self Organizer) than those in Kohonen Network. The dimension and the number of training repetitions are set differently based on the rows displayed in bold letters in table 1 and table2; the first collection is used as the validation set to the second and the third. If both parameters were set identically in both approaches, NTSO would take much more time than Kohonen Networks in clustering texts. For example, NTSO takes 0.9 seconds per training repetition of 10,000 news articles, while Kohonen Networks take only 0.171 seconds per such repetition, in spite of such different dimensions for both. Note, however, that NTSO requires less effort than Kohonen Network to achieve similar clustering performance.

V. CONCLUSION

Experiments in the previous section showed that NTSO works better than Kohonen Networks, with respect to clustering performance and clustering time. This study implies that the representation of texts into string vectors is more appropriate than the representation into numerical vectors for text clustering. The significance of this study is to address two main problems from the traditional representation of texts, by proposing a new unsupervised neural network using string vectors as its weight vectors and input vectors.

As mentioned in previous sections, NTSO requires the construction of a similarity matrix to perform operations on string vectors. The experiment for the evaluation of clustering time did not count the time for building the similarity matrix. Actually, it took very much time to build it; if we consider the time taken to build it, NTSO is a very expensive algorithm.

To make NTSO more practical, it is necessary to address the high cost of building the similarity matrix from the collection of texts. If all the words are used to build it other than stop words, it costs very much time to do that. We can consider three solutions to this problem for future research. The first solution consists of building a similarity matrix with only keywords from texts. The second solution consists of replacing the construction of the similarity matrix by word sense acquisition. The third solution consists of performing such operations on string vectors directly in the collection of texts. The remaining task for this study is to address the problem problem of similarity matrix building with one of these solutions.

REFERENCES

[1] T. Kohonen, S. Kaski, K. Lagus, J. Salojarvi, V. Paatero, and A. Saarela, "Self Organization of Linguistic Features and Clustering Algorithms for Topic Document Clustering", , The Proceedings of 23rd ACM SIGIR, 2000, pp224-231.
[2] Erik D. Wiener, "A Neural Network Approach to Topic Spotting in Text", The Thesis of Master of University of Colorado, 1995.
[3] Miguel E. Ruiz and Padmini Srinivasan, "Hierarchical Text Categorization Using Neural Networks", Information Retrieval, Vol 5, No 1, pp87-118, 2002.
[4] Samuel Kaski, Timo Honkela, Krista Lagus, and Teuvo Kohonen, "WEBSOM-Self Organizing Maps of Document Collections", Neurocomputing, Vol 21, pp101-117, 1998.
[5] Guerrero Bote, P. Vincent, Moya Anegon Felix de, and Victor H. Solana, "Document Organization using Kohonen's Algorithm", Information Processing and Management, Vol 38, No 1, pp79-89, 2002.
[6] T. Kohonen. "Self Organized Formation of Topologically Correct Feature Maps, Biological Cybernetics, Vol 43, pp59-69, 1982.
[7] Tom M. Mitchell, *Machine Learning*, McGraw-Hill, 1997.
[8] Dunja Mladenic and Marko Grobelink, "Feature Selection for unbalanced class distribution and Naïve Bayes", The Proceedings of International Conference on Machine Learning, 1999, pp256-267.
[9] Ion Androutsopoulos, John Koutsias, Konstantinos V. Chandrinos, and Constantine D. Spyropoulos, "An Experimental Comparison of Naïve Bayes and Keyword-based Anti-spam Filtering with personal email message", The Proceedings of 23rd ACM SIGIR, 2000, pp160-167.
[10] T. Joachims, "Text Categorization with Support Vector Machines: Learning with many Relevant Features", The Proceedings of 10th European Conference on Machine Learning, 1998, pp143-151.
[11] H. Drucker, Donghui Wu, and V. N. Vapnik, "Support Vector Machines for Spam Categorization", IEEE Transaction on Neural Networks, Vol 10, No 5, pp1048-1054, 1999.
[12] Vasileois Hatzivassiloglou, Luis Gravano, and Ankineedu Maganti, "An Investigation of Linguistic Features and Clustering Algorithms for Topic Document Clustering", The Proceedings of 23rd ACM SIGIR, 2000, pp224-231.
[13] Fabrizio Sebastiani, "Machine Learning in Automated Text Categorization", ACM Computing Survey, Vol. 34, pp1-47, 2002.
[14] Taeho Jo, "NeuroTextCategorizer: A New Model of Neural Network for Text Categorization", The Proceedings of International Conference of Neural Information Processing 2000, Taejon South Korea, 2000, pp280-285
[15] Taeho Jo, "Machine Learning based Approach to Text Categorization with Resampling Methods", The Proceedings of the 8th World Multi-Conference on Systemics, Cybernetics and Informatics, Orlando, USA, 2004, pp93-98.

A Neuro-SVM Model for Text Classification using Latent Semantic Indexing

Vikramjit Mitra[1] Chia-Jiu Wang[2] Satarupa Banerjee[3]
Email: vmitra@du.edu, satarupa_b@hotmail.com, cwang@eas.uccs.edu
[1]Worcester Polytechnic Institute, Department of Electrical Engineering, Worcester, MA
[2]University of Colorado, ECE Department, Colorado Springs, CO
[3]Villanova University, CIS Department, Villanova, PA

Abstract — This paper presents a new model integrating a recurrent neural network (RNN) and a least squares support vector machine (LS-SVM) for classification of document titles according to different predetermined categories. The new model proposed in this paper is abbreviated as Neuro-SVM. Based on the Neuro-SVM model, a system is implemented, using latent semantic indexing (LSI) to generate probabilistic coefficients from document titles, which are used as the input to the system. The system's performance is demonstrated with a corpus of 96956 words, from University of Denver's Penrose Library catalogue and the accuracy rate of the proposed system is found to be 99.66%.

This paper aims to organize the materials available in a library, which have both electronic materials as well as physical documents. A library cataloging system stores the entire information of a material in their database that results in higher storage space requirement and increased processing time. This paper presents the results of implementing an LSI based Neuro-SVM parallel architecture for text classification. The proposed hybrid architecture is found to perform with a high accuracy as a text-classifying agent and the results obtain claim the potential of using this technique for next generation semantic text classification.

I. INTRODUCTION

Text classification (TC) is the technique of analyzing electronic text based documents to assign predetermined categories in a supervised learning environment. TC assigns texts to some predefined categories based on their content and internal structure and helps in organizing the documents and text materials. It not only organizes text materials but also assists in classification, filtering, organized searching etc. The key issues in TC are feature coding and classifier design.

Support Vector Machine (SVM) is a kernel-based learning algorithm proposed by Vapnik [1], which maps data items into high-dimensional space and where information about their mutual positions is used for classification, regression or clustering. SVMs have found one of their prominent applications in TC, where standard representation of documents is a very high dimensional vector. The pioneering researches of Joachims [2] and others [3] have proved the suitability of SVM for text classification. Information retrieval (IR) by SVM for TC fails to establish the semantic relation between the different terms. The solution to this problem is Latent Semantic Indexing (LSI) [4], which is a well-known technique for IR that establishes semantic relations between terms and has been found to perform well with SVMs [5] for text classification. Wermter et al. [6] has shown that Recurrent Neural Networks are highly efficient as TC agents. The dynamic short-term memory of the RNN allows the processing of text sequences in a robust manner, which results in high prediction precision rate.

II. LATENT SEMANTIC INDEXING

Latent Semantic Indexing (LSI) [9] is an information retrieval and text classification technique that incorporates semantic information based on similarity between words or documents. It extracts the underlying semantic structure [10] of a word corpus by estimating the most significant statistical factors in the weighted word space. LSI considers documents or titles that have many common words to be semantically close and those with few words in common to be semantically distant. Keyword based search engines fail for synonymous words as there is no exact match, but LSI based agents are successful in such a case as they look for similarity values [8].

At the beginning LSI algorithm purges all the extraneous words from a document or title [8], leaving only content words likely to have semantic meaning and also it gets rid of the common endings by the use of 'Porter Stemming' algorithm. This helps to eliminate the noise generating words and characters that hinders the decision making task. The outcome of LSI processing is a matrix representation of the corpus, with rows representing the words in the vocabulary and columns denoting the documents. This is a large sparse matrix where each value in the matrix is a weighted frequency of the corresponding term in the corresponding document. This large sparse matrix is reduced to a compressed matrix based on Singular Value Decomposition (SVD) technique.

A. Partially Recurrent Neural Networks

Partially Recurrent Neural Networks [11] start with a fully Recurrent Network and add a feed forward connection that bypasses the recurrency, effectively treating the recurrent part as a state memory. These recurrent networks have an infinite memory depth and thus find relationships through time as well as through the instantaneous input space. Most real-world data contains information in its time structure. Recurrent networks are the state-of-the-art in nonlinear time series prediction, classification, system identification, and temporal pattern classification. A fully recurrent network with N processing elements (PEs) has N^2 weights.

B. Support Vector Machines

The concept of SVM was first introduced by Vapnik [13], which is based on the principle of structural risk minimization. SVM algorithm uses the values of the different classes as training vectors and uses those vectors to obtain a hyperplane in order to optimally separate the different classes without error. The goal of this classifier is to find an optimal separating hyperplane that maximizes the distance between the hyperplane and the nearest data point of each class [12]. SVMs learn linear decision rule, given by Equ.(1)

$$h(\hat{u}) = sign\{\hat{w} \cdot \hat{u} + b\} \quad (1)$$

which is described by a weight vector, $\hat{w}$, and a threshold value, b. The input to the system is a vector of n training samples

$$S_n = ((\hat{u}_1, y_1), \ldots, (\hat{u}_n, y_n)), \hat{u}_i \in R^n, y_i \in \{+1, -1\} \quad (2)$$

For a linearly separable sample vector, the SVM finds the hyperplane with the maximum Euclidean distance to the nearest point. In the case where a linear boundary is inappropriate the SVM can map the input vector, into a high dimensional feature space [13]. By selecting the nonlinear mapping as a priori, the SVM constructs an optimal separating hyperplane in this higher dimensional space. This idea exploits the method of Aizerman et al. (*1964*), which enables the curse of dimensionality (Bellman, *1961*) to be addressed.

The idea of kernel function is to enable operations to be performed in the input space rather than the potentially high dimensional feature space. Due to this the inner product does not need to be evaluated in the feature space, which provides a way of addressing the curse of dimensionality. The theory of Reproducing Kernel Hilbert Space (RKHS) (Wahba, *1990*; Aronszajn, *1950*; Girosi, *1997*; Heckman, *1997*), claims that an inner product in feature space has an equivalent Kernel in input space,

$$K(x, x^l) = <\Phi(x), \Phi(x^l)> \quad (3)$$

SVMs can have different kernel functions; this paper implements the Gaussian Radial Basis Function as the SVM kernel. The Gaussian Radial Basis Function (GRBF) has received significant attention and its form is given by

$$K(x, x^l) = exp(-|x - x^l|^2 / 2\sigma^2) \quad (4)$$

Classical techniques utilizing RBFs employ a method of clustering to select a subset of centers [12]. The most attractive feature of SVM is its implicit selection process, with each support vector contributing on local Gaussian functions, centered at that data point. SVMs are the solution to the data over fitting problem posed by Neural Networks. Least Square Support Vector Machine (LS-SVM) is a reformulation to the standard SVM [14,15]. LS-SVMs are closely related to regularization networks [16] and Gaussian processes [17] but additionally emphasize and exploit primal-dual interpretations.

C. Why Neuro-SVM with LSI?

Kernel based learning algorithms such as SVMs are found to work with high accuracy in text categorization. SVM algorithm maps items to a high-dimensional space and uses the information of their inner products for classification, this approach makes SVM suitable for TC, as standard representation of documents and text titles are usually very high dimensional vectors and standard information retrieval techniques are precisely based on the inner product of the vectors [1]. Joachims research [20] have proved the efficiency and appropriateness of SVM for text classification. Wermetr [6] proposed an RNN based text classifier, which performed with a high accuracy. Cristianini [1] and Banerjee et al. [5] has shown that LSI-SVM hybrid models incorporate more information in the kernel as it includes the semantic relation between the data terms. In an SVM or RNN based IR system, titles that have related topics but uses synonymous or different terms are mapped to distant regions in feature space. LSI enables the system to capture the semantic information and hence establishes the similarity between two titles by considering the relation between two terms. The high classification efficiency of SVM and RNNs and the semantic information retrieval capability of LSI have encouraged this research to consider a hybrid Neuro-SVM model based on LSI.

III. TEXT CLASSIFICATION

The corpus of real-world document titles considered in this research is obtained from University of Denver, Penrose library catalogue. The corpus consists of *18966* titles where each of them belongs to one or more of the six categories: Engineering (ENG), Mathematics (MTH), Music (MUS), History (HIS), Economics & Management (ECM) and Literature and Arts (LAR), shown in Table 1. The total number of words in this corpus is *96956*, with *12564* different words. *3000* titles from the corpus, selected equally from each category were used to train the LS-SVM and the Recurrent Neural Networks in supervised learning mode. The remaining *15966* titles were used for the testing. The block diagram of the proposed system is presented in Fig. 1.

The proposed system accepts document titles in the form of text strings. These text strings are separated into corresponding words segments by the word separator module, which feeds the individual words one at a time to the LSI module. LSI purges the words that have no semantic meaning and then processes the remaining by '*Porter Stemmer*' to remove the common endings from them. The resultant words are processed to generate the LSI coefficients, which are fed to the cascaded LS-SVM modules and the RNNs, as shown in Fig 2. The LSI coefficients are presented as semantic significant vectors 'V', which determines the frequency of word occurrences in different semantic categories. The conclusions drawn by the LS-SVMs are then multiplied with the conclusions drawn by the Recurrent Neural Network and the resultant vector, A, is fed to the Decision Logic (DL), which presents the final decision.

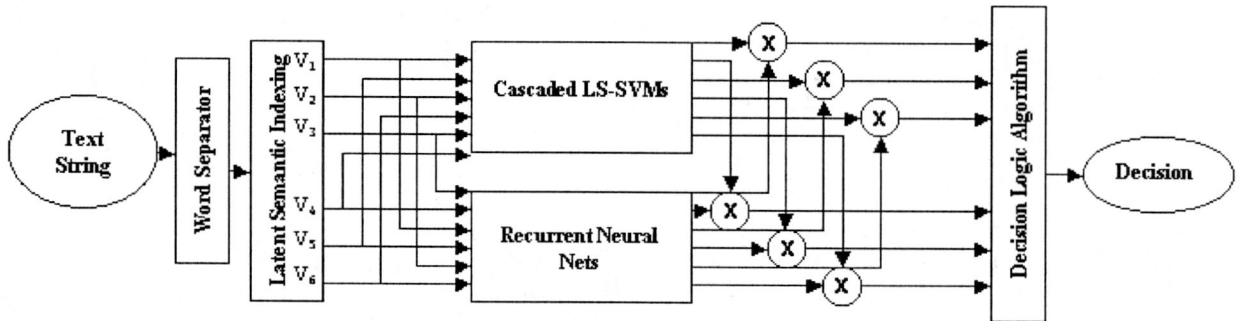

Fig. 1 Block Diagram of the proposed Nero-SVM system.

TABLE 1. TITLE EXAMPLES FROM the CORPUS AND THEIR CATEGORIES

Semantic Category	Title
Engineering (ENG)	Handbook of chemical engineering calculations Software engineering for image processing systems
Mathematics (MTH)	A structural account of mathematics Discrete mathematics with applications
Music (MUS)	Musical lives of young children Polish music since Szymanowski
History (HIS)	From slave to pharaoh The Roman Empire at bay
Economics and Management (ECM)	Economics of standards in information networks Operations, strategy, and technology
Literature and Arts (LAR)	Admired and understood Modern art and the grotesque

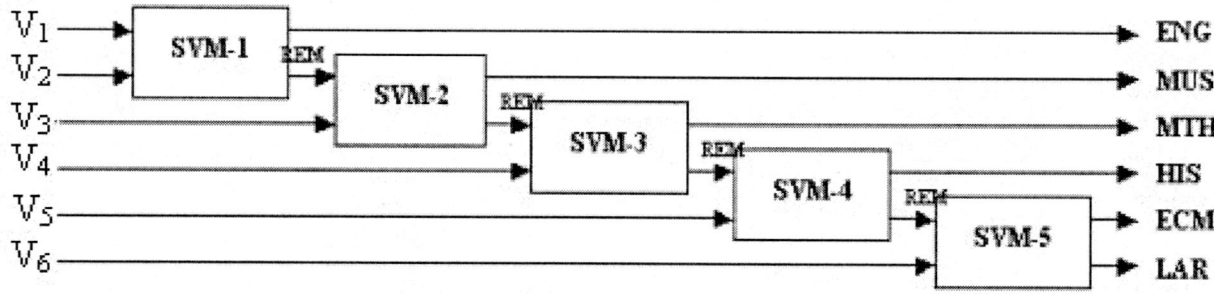

Fig. 2. Block Diagram of the Cascaded LS-SVM

IV. SIMULATION RESULTS

Construction of an LS-SVM module requires two parameters, γ, the regularization parameter and σ^2, the Gaussian bandwidth. The γ determines the trade-off between the fitting error minimization and the smoothness. These parameters are inferred by optimizing the cost at the initial levels of inference and are optimized by the use of Bayesian framework. Before optimizing the parameters, the model was initialized with suitable starting values, and then the system was tuned to obtain the values of γ and σ^2. These values were used as the initial values for a three stage Bayesian optimization, where the Bayesian framework is initialized at the first stage, optimized γ value was obtained in the second stage and the optimized σ^2 value was obtained in the third stage. The parameter values used in this research are presented in Table 2.

The partially Recurrent Neural Network was constructed using Neuro-Solution Version-5 [11], and were trained in a supervised learning environment. The RNN's parameter values are presented in Table 3.

The LS-SVM module is designed as a 6-input 6-output system containing 5 cascaded LS-SVM elements presented in Fig. 1, where the first 4 LS-SVM elements classify between one category and the rest, where as the last one classifies between two categories. The 6 inputs correspond to the 6 LSI coefficients. The test result obtained from the proposed LS-SVM module is presented below in Table 4. The RNN is designed as 6-input and 6-output system, with 4 hidden layers, where the inputs correspond to 6 LSI coefficients. The desired and obtained outputs from the RNNs are presented in Table 5. The dot product of the output vectors obtained from the two branches of the proposed parallel architecture results in vector A, which is fed the Decision Logic (DL) Module, that makes an intelligent guess based on its input. The rule base of the decision logic is presented in Table 6, where it can be observed that the DL makes the final Text Classification based on the input values of vector, A, using a threshold value of 0.5.

The rule base presented in Table 6 gives inferences only for a limited number of cases as it assumes that only a single member of vector A can have value more than the threshold. Certain cases might arise where more than one member of the vector, A, have values greater than the threshold. In such a case, the decision will comprise all the weighted categories, corresponding to which the vectors are ≥ 0.5. This research incorporates all the possible combination of vector A, for which values are greater than the threshold value. Table 7 gives the decision values before and after the DL module. Table 8 presents the accuracy for text classification of the proposed Neuro-SVM based system. The bar diagram presented in Fig. 3 presents the histogram plot of the prediction accuracy for different classes.

TABLE 2. LS- SVM PARAMETER VALUE

Tuning Parameters	Parameter Values
Optimization Routine	*Gridsearch*
Cost function	*crossvalidate*
γ *(LS-SVM-1)*	*1.379*
σ^2 *(LS-SVM-1)*	*12.254*
γ *(LS-SVM-2)*	*0.0677*
σ^2 *(LS-SVM-2)*	*1.212*
γ *(LS-SVM-3)*	*0.786*
σ^2 *(LS-SVM-3)*	*0.421*
γ *(LS-SVM-4)*	*0.533*
σ^2 *(LS-SVM-4)*	*0.198*
γ *(LS-SVM-5)*	*0.028*
σ^2 *(LS-SVM-5)*	*0.137*

TABLE 3. RNN PARAMETER VALUE

RNN Parameters	Parameter Values
Recurrency	*Partial*
Learning Rule	*Momentum*
Transfer Function	*Sigmoid*
Input Layer	*Axon*
Number of Hidden Layer	*4*
Number of PE (Layer-1)	*120*
Number of PE (Layer-2)	*180*
Number of PE (Layer-3)	*120*
Number of PE (Layer-4)	*60*
Number of Epochs	*126756*
Momentum Value	*0.85*

TABLE 4. LS-SVM OUTPUT

Test Category	SVM Output						Desired Output					
ENG	1	0	0	0	0	0	1	0	0	0	0	0
MUS	0	1	0	1	0	0	0	1	0	0	0	0
MTH	0	0	1	0	0	0	0	0	1	0	0	0
HIS	0	0	0	1	0	1	0	0	0	1	0	0
ECM	0	0	0	0	1	0	0	0	0	0	1	0
LAR	0	0	0	0	0	1	0	0	0	0	0	1

TABLE 5 RNN OUTPUT

Category	RNN Output						Desired Output					
ENG	0.89	0.00	0.07	0.04	0.01	0.00	1	0	0	0	0	0
MUS	0.00	0.93	0.04	0.05	0.00	0.03	0	1	0	0	0	0
MTH	0.10	0.05	0.82	0.00	0.10	0.05	0	0	1	0	0	0
HIS	0.04	0.07	0.00	0.90	0.04	0.07	0	0	0	1	0	0
ECM	0.00	0.03	0.05	0.01	0.92	0.00	0	0	0	0	1	0

LAR	0.00	0.01	0.00	0.10	0.03	0.86	0	0	0	0	0	1

TABLE 6. RULE BASE OF THE DECISION LOGIC

Vectors / Categories	A1	A2	A3	A4	A5	A6
ENG	$0.5 \leq A1$	$A2 < 0.5$	$A3 < 0.5$	$A4 < 0.5$	$A5 < 0.5$	$A6 < 0.5$
MTH	$A1 < 0.5$	$0.5 \leq A2$	$A3 < 0.5$	$A4 < 0.5$	$A5 < 0.5$	$A6 < 0.5$
MUS	$A1 < 0.5$	$A2 < 0.5$	$0.5 \leq A3$	$A4 < 0.5$	$A5 < 0.5$	$A6 < 0.5$
HIS	$A1 < 0.5$	$A2 < 0.5$	$A3 < 0.5$	$0.5 \leq A4$	$A5 < 0.5$	$A6 < 0.5$
ECM	$A1 < 0.5$	$A2 < 0.5$	$A3 < 0.5$	$A4 < 0.5$	$0.5 \leq A1$	$A6 < 0.5$
LAR	$A1 < 0.5$	$A2 < 0.5$	$A3 < 0.5$	$A4 < 0.5$	$A5 < 0.5$	$0.5 \leq A1$

TABLE 7 DIFFERENT STAGES OF THE TEXT CLASSIFICATION MODULE

RNN x LS-SVM Output						Decision Logic Output						Inference
ENG	MTH	HIS	MUS	ECM	LAR	ENG	MTH	HIS	MUS	ECM	LAR	
0.91	0.00	0.03	0.00	0.00	0.00	1.0	0.0	0.0	0.0	0.0	0.0	ENG
0.72	0.00	0.00	0.01	0.00	0.00	1.0	0.0	0.0	0.0	0.0	0.0	ENG
0.00	0.61	0.00	0.00	0.00	0.00	0.0	1.0	0.0	0.0	0.0	0.0	MTH
0.00	0.51	0.00	0.29	0.00	0.00	0.0	1.0	0.0	0.0	0.0	0.0	MTH
0.00	0.00	0.91	0.00	0.00	0.00	0.0	0.0	1.0	0.0	0.0	0.0	HIS
0.00	0.01	0.90	0.00	0.00	0.10	0.0	0.0	1.0	0.0	0.0	0.0	HIS
0.00	0.00	0.00	0.63	0.00	0.00	0.0	0.0	0.0	1.0	0.0	0.0	MUS
0.00	0.00	0.13	0.94	0.19	0.00	0.0	0.0	0.0	1.0	0.0	0.0	MUS
0.00	0.00	0.00	0.11	0.92	0.01	0.0	0.0	0.0	0.0	1.0	0.0	ECM
0.00	0.10	0.00	0.15	0.94	0.00	0.0	0.0	0.0	0.0	1.0	0.0	ECM
0.00	0.00	0.00	0.21	0.01	0.86	0.0	0.0	0.0	0.0	0.0	1.0	LAR
0.00	0.01	0.23	0.00	0.00	0.92	0.0	0.0	0.0	0.0	0.0	1.0	LAR

TABLE 8. NEURO-SVM TEXT CLASSIFIER RESULTS

Category	Training Set (%)	Test Set (%)
ENG	100.0	99.9
MTH	100.0	100.0
HIS	99.8	98.7
MUS	99.9	99.8
ECM	100.0	99.9
LAR	99.8	99.7
All Titles	99.92	99.66

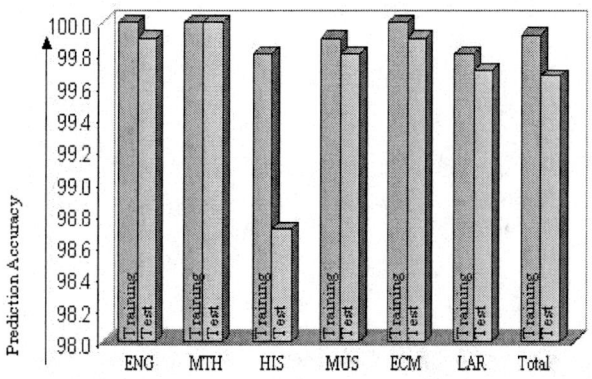

Fig. 3. Histogram plot of the prediction accuracy for different classes.

The DL module based on a rule base makes a wise prediction of the text categories to which a specific string of word belongs. The output of the system is thus the final decision presented by the DL. In case of a multi-class problem, the DL will present the weighted decision of both the classes.

V. CONCLUSIONS

In this paper we have presented and analyzed an LSI based Neuro-SVM hybrid model for text classification. With a corpus of *96956* word corpus the prediction accuracy rate was fairly high, with *99.66%* accuracy in classifying the titles. *500* titles from each category, that is *3000* titles altogether were used to train the LS-SVM and the RNN module in a supervised learning environment. *15966* titles, which is *2661* title/category were used to test the proposed system.

The high accuracy of the proposed system justifiably claims that Neuro-SVMs are highly capable to perform text classification tasks and coupled with LSI module they are robust enough to perform TC efficiently even for noisy text documents. Previous works on text classification have implemented neural networks and linear SVMs, where Recurrent Neural Networks and Linear SVMs showed an accuracy of *93.05%* [2] and *97%* respectively. This paper aims to combine SVM and RNN based approaches for TC. The high precision rate obtained from implementing GRBF kernels in LS-SVM [5] for TC has prompted our research to use the same type of kernel for the cascaded SVM module. The accuracy of the proposed system clearly outperforms the previous methods, which is attributed to the combined performance of LSI and Neuro-SVM.

Neuro-SVM based approach with LSI technique for document/title encoding has never been implemented so far, for a high scale task of text categorization. Due to the limitation of title varieties and computation facilities, the presented research has addressed a classification between 6 categories. Practical application of the proposed text-classifying agent will involve a large number of categories with high volume of document titles, hence future direction should aim to increase the number of experimental categories as well as the size of the experimental corpus to observe the robustness and predictive accuracy of the system.

ACKNOWLEDGEMENT

The authors would like to acknowledge Penrose Library, University of Denver, for providing real world experimental data.

REFERENCES

[1] Vapnik V., 'Statistical Learning Theory', *Wiley & Sons*, Chichester, GB, 1998.
[2] Joachims T., 'Text Categorization with Support Vector Machines', in the proceedings of *European Conference on Machine Learning ECML-98*.
[3] Dumais S.T., Letsche T.A., Littman M.L. and Landauer T.K., 'Automatic cross-language retrieval using latent semantic indexing', in AAAI Spring Symposium on *Cross-Language Text and Speech Retrieval*, 1997.
[4] Deerwester S., Dumais S.T., Furnas G.W., Landauer T.K. and Harshman R.A., 'Indexing by Latent Semantic Analysis', Journal of the *American Society for Information Science*, 41(6), pp 391-407, 1990.
[5] Banerjee S., Wang C.J., Mitra V., 'Text Classification with Least Square Support Vector Machines and Latent Semantic Indexing', In the proceedings of *International Joint Conference of Neural Network*, IEEE & INNS, 2004.
[6] Wermter S., Arevian G. and Panchev C., 'Recurrent Neural Network Learning for Text Routing', In the proceedings of *ICANN'99*.
[7] Foltz P.W., Kintsch W., and Landauer T.K., 'The Measurement of Textual Coherence with Latent Semantic Analysis', *Discourse Processes*, 25, 285-307, (1998).
[8] Foltz P. 'Using Latent Semantic Indexing for Information Filtering', in RB Allen (Ed.) Proceedings of the *Conference on Office Information Systems*, Cambridge, MA, 40-47, (1990).
[9] Bellegarda R., 'A Multi-Span Language Modeling Framework for Large Vocabulary Speech Recognition', *IEEE Transaction Speech and Audio Processing*, pp. 456-467, Sep., 1998.
[10] Landauer T.K. and Dumais S.T., 'Solution to Plato's Problem: The Latent Semantic Analysis Theory of Acquisition, Induction and Representation of Knowledge', *Psychological Review*, 104(2), 211-240 (1977).
[11] Principe, Euliano and Lefebvre, 'Neural and Adaptive Systems: Fundamentals through Simulations', John Wiley & Sons, Inc. 2000.
[12] Gunn S.R., 'Support Vector Machines for Classification and Regression', Technical Report, *Dept of Electronics and Computer Science, University of Southampton*, (1998).
[13] Vapnik V., 'Statistical Learning Theory', *Wiley & Sons*, Chichester, GB, 1998.
[14] Suykens J., Vandewalle J., 'Least square support vector machine classifiers', *Neural Processing Letters*, 9(3), 293-300, (1999).
[15] Van Gestel T., Suykens J., Baesens B., Viaene S., Vanthienen J., Dedene G., De Moor B. and Vandewalle J., 'Benchmarking least square support vector machine classifiers' *Machine Learning*, in press, (2001).
[16] Evgeniou T., Pontil M. and Poggio T., 'Regularization networks and Support Vector Machines,' *Advances in Computational Mathematics*, 13(1), pp 1-50, (2000).
[17] Wahba G., 'Spline Models for observational data', *SIAM-90*, 59, (1990).

Fast Text Categorization with Min-Max Modular Support Vector Machines

Feng-Yao Liu, Ke Wu, Hai Zhao, and Bao-Liang Lu
Department of Computer Science and Engineering, Shanghai Jiao Tong University
1954 Hua Shan Rd., Shanghai 200030, China
Email: blu@cs.sjtu.edu.cn

Abstract— The min-max modular support vector machines (M^3-SVMs) have been proposed for solving large-scale and complex multiclass classification problems. In this paper, we apply the M^3-SVMs to multilabel text categrization and introduce a new task decomposition strategy into M^3-SVMs. A multilabel classification task can be split up into a set of two-class classification tasks. These two-class tasks are to discriminate the $\mathcal{C}$ class from non-$\mathcal{C}$ class. If these two class tasks are still hard to be learned, we can further divide them into a set of two-class tasks as small as needed and fast training of SVMs on massive multilabel texts can be easily implemented in a massively parallel way. Furthermore, we proposed a new task decomposition strategy called hyperplane task decomposition to improve generalization performance. The experimental results on the RCV1-v2 indicate that the new method has better generalization performance than traditional SVMs and previous M^3-SVMs using random task decomposition, and is much faster than traditional SVMs.

I. INTRODUCTION

With the rapid growth of online information, text classification has become one of the key techniques for handling and organization of text data. Various pattern classification methods have been applied to text classification for the need. Due to their powerful learning ability and good generalization performance, Support Vector Machines (SVMs) [1][2] have been successfully applied to various pattern classification problems. Joachims (1997) [3] and Yang (1999) [4] made experiments on the same text data set respectively. Both experimental results showed that SVMs yield lower error rate than many other classification techniques, such as Naive Bayes and K-Nearest Neighbors. However, to train SVMs on large-scale problems is a time-consuming task, since their training time is at least quadratic to the number of training samples. Therefore, it is a hard work to learn a large-scale text data set using traditional SVMs.

On the other hand, Lu and Ito (1999) [5] proposed a min-max modular (M^3) network for solving large-scale and complex multiclass classification problems effortlessly and efficiently. And the network model has been applied to learning large-scale, real world multiclass problems such as part-of-speech tagging and classification of high-dimensional, single-trial electroencephalogram signals. Recently, Lu and his colleagues [6] have proposed a part-versus-part task decomposition method and a new modular SVM, called min-max modular support vector machine (M^3-SVM), which was developed for solving large-scale multiclass problems.

In this paper, we will apply M^3-SVMs to multilabel text classification and adopt several new strategies of dividing a large-scale sample data set into many small sample data sets to try to investigate the influence of different task decomposition methods on the generalization performance and training time.

This paper is structured as follows. In the section II, M^3-SVMs are introduced briefly. In the section III, several different task composition strategies are listed. Then in the section IV, we designed a set of experiments on a large-scale multilabel text classification. And the training time and the performance of text classification using SVMs and different M^3-SVMs will be compared. In Section V, conclusions are outlined.

II. MIN-MAX MODULAR SUPPORT VECTOR MACHINES

The min-max modular support vector machine [6] is a method that divides a complex classification problem into many small independent two-class classification problems and then integrates these small SVMs according to two module combination rules, namely the minimization principle and the maximization principle [5].

For a two-class problem $\mathcal{T}$, let $\mathcal{X}^+$ denote the positive training data set belonging to a particular category $\mathcal{C}$ and $\mathcal{X}^-$ denote the negative training data set not belonging to $\mathcal{C}$.

$$\mathcal{X}^+ = \{(x_i^+, +1)\}_{i=1}^{l^+}, \quad \mathcal{X}^- = \{(x_i^-, -1)\}_{i=1}^{l^-} \quad (1)$$

where $x_i \in \mathbf{R}^n$ is the input vector, and l^+ and l^- are the total number of positive training data and negative training data of the two-class problem, respectively.

According to [6], $\mathcal{X}^+$ and $\mathcal{X}^-$ can be partitioned into N^+ and N^- subsets respectively,

$$\mathcal{X}_j^+ = \{(x_i^{+j}, +1)\}_{i=1}^{l_j^+}, \quad \text{for } j = 1, \ldots, N^+ \quad (2)$$

$$\mathcal{X}_j^- = \{(x_i^{-j}, -1)\}_{i=1}^{l_j^-}, \quad \text{for } j = 1, \ldots, N^- \quad (3)$$

where $\cup_{j=1}^{N^+} \mathcal{X}_j^+ = \mathcal{X}^+$, $1 \leq N^+ \leq l^+$, and $\cup_{j=1}^{N^-} \mathcal{X}_j^- = \mathcal{X}^-$, $1 \leq N^- \leq l^-$.

After decomposing the training data sets $\mathcal{X}^+$ and $\mathcal{X}^-$, the original two-class problem $\mathcal{T}$ is divided into $N^+ \times N^-$ relatively smaller and more balanced two-class subproblems $\mathcal{T}^{(i,j)}$ as follows:

$$(\mathcal{T}^{(i,j)})^+ = \mathcal{X}_i^+, \quad (\mathcal{T}^{(i,j)})^- = \mathcal{X}_j^- \quad (4)$$

TABLE I
RESULTS ON CCAT, WHERE C=0.5

method		# SVMs	CPU time (s.)		Speed up		performance		
			parallel	serial	parallel	serial	P	R	F_1
1		1	898	898	-	-	94.9	91.3	93.0
2		4	290	989	3.10	0.91	94.9	90.7	92.8
		9	125	934	7.2	0.96	94.9	90.2	92.5
		16	56	670	16.0	1.34	94.8	89.9	92.3
		30	32	667	28.1	1.35	93.6	90.9	92.2
3	a	4	373	839	2.41	1.07	94.4	91.6	93.0
		9	178	688	5.04	1.31	94.6	91.7	93.1
		16	84	540	10.7	1.66	94.5	91.7	93.1
		30	47	563	19.1	1.60	93.5	92.7	93.1
	b	4	379	930	2.37	0.97	94.5	91.6	93.1
		9	178	854	5.04	1.05	94.8	91.6	93.2
		16	85	621	10.56	1.45	94.6	91.6	93.1
		30	48	647	18.71	1.39	93.7	92.6	93.2
	c	4	379	978	2.37	0.92	94.6	91.5	93.0
		9	177	929	5.07	0.97	94.8	91.5	93.2
		16	85	677	10.56	1.33	94.7	91.5	93.1
		30	52	707	17.27	1.27	93.8	92.6	93.2
	d	4	374	1023	2.40	0.88	94.7	91.5	93.1
		9	179	1009	5.02	0.89	94.9	91.5	93.2
		16	87	781	10.32	1.15	94.7	91.6	93.1
		30	53	754	16.94	1.19	93.9	92.6	93.2
	e	4	426	1260	2.11	0.71	94.8	91.5	93.1
		9	214	1003	4.20	0.90	95.0	91.3	93.1
		16	110	975	8.16	0.92	94.9	91.5	93.2
		30	60	894	14.97	1.00	94.0	92.6	93.3

TABLE II
RESULTS ON ECAT, WHERE C=0.5

method		# SVMs	CPU time (s.)		Speed up		performance		
			parallel	serial	parallel	serial	P	R	F_1
1		1	607	607	-	-	92.7	64.1	75.8
2		3	186	531	3.26	1.14	84.7	74.7	79.4
		7	53	347	11.45	1.75	73.8	82.5	77.9
		20	21	365	28.90	1.66	78.5	78.3	78.4
		26	16	365	37.94	1.66	74.5	81.1	77.7
3	a	3	234	461	2.59	1.32	87.9	71.0	78.6
		7	66	307	9.20	1.98	80.4	78.9	79.6
		20	34	300	17.85	2.02	82.6	77.5	80.0
		26	26	310	23.35	1.96	79.0	80.6	79.8
	b	3	233	501	2.61	1.21	88.7	70.3	78.4
		7	68	334	8.93	1.82	81.5	78.0	79.7
		20	34	343	17.85	1.77	83.4	77.2	80.2
		26	27	353	22.48	1.72	79.8	80.1	79.9
	c	3	233	519	2.61	1.17	89.1	70.0	78.4
		7	72	350	8.43	1.73	82.0	77.5	79.7
		20	36	363	16.86	1.67	83.8	76.9	80.2
		26	28	373	21.68	1.63	80.2	79.9	80.0
	d	3	254	579	2.39	1.05	89.4	69.6	78.3
		7	79	379	7.68	1.60	82.6	77.1	79.7
		20	38	391	15.97	1.55	83.8	76.9	80.2
		26	30	402	20.23	1.51	80.5	79.8	80.1
	e	3	239	590	2.54	1.03	89.9	68.9	78.0
		7	85	428	7.14	1.42	83.7	76.3	79.8
		20	42	451	14.45	1.35	84.1	76.7	80.3
		26	34	473	17.85	1.28	81.2	79.7	80.4

where $(\mathcal{T}^{(i,j)})^+$ and $(\mathcal{T}^{(i,j)})^-$ denote the positive and negative training data set of subproblem $\mathcal{T}^{(i,j)}$ respectively.

In the learning phase, all the two-class subproblems are independent from each other and can be efficiently learned in a massively parallel way.

After training, the $N^+ \times N^-$ smaller SVMs are integrated into an M^3-SVM with N^+ MIN units and one MAX unit according to two combination principles [5][6] as follows,

$$\mathcal{T}^i(x) = \min_{j=1}^{N^-} \mathcal{T}^{(i,j)}(x) \quad \text{and} \quad \mathcal{T}(x) = \max_{i=1}^{N^+} \mathcal{T}^i(x) \quad (5)$$
$$\text{for} \quad i = 1, ..., N^+$$

where $\mathcal{T}^{(i,j)}(x)$ denotes the transfer function of the trained SVM corresponding to the two-class subproblem $\mathcal{T}^{(i,j)}$, and $\mathcal{T}^i(x)$ denotes the transfer function of a combination of N^- SVMs integrated by the MIN unit.

III. TWO TYPES OF TASK DECOMPOSITION STRATEGIES

Task decomposition is one of the two key problems in the M^3-SVM. In this section, we will introduce two types of task decomposition methods. One is the random task decomposition strategy, and the other is the hyperplane task decomposition strategy [7].

A. Random Task Decomposition Strategy

The random task decomposition method is a simple and straightforward strategy. It means that we randomly pick up samples to form a new smaller and more balanced training data set. We refer to the M^3-SVM using random decomposition as M^3-SVM (R). Though the strategy can be implemented easily, it might lead to partial loss of statistical properties of original training data and thus result in the decrease in the performance of text classification.

B. Hyperplane Task Decomposition Strategy

An ideal decomposition method is the one doing no damage to generalization performance. In order to achieve this goal, we hope to maintain the structural properties of the smaller data sets as those of original data set after task decomposition. Based on the idea, we first introduce a specific hyperplane, and then divide original training set into smaller training set using a series of hyperplanes which are parallel with the hyperplane introduced. We refer to the M^3-SVM using the proposed hyperplane task decomposition strategy as M^3-SVM (H).

Now our problem is whether the hyperplane task decomposition strategy is the most reasonable. In order to get a more balanced training set, we also tentatively let some training samples in the neighborhood of these hyperplanes

TABLE III
RESULTS ON GCAT, WHERE C=0.5

method		# SVMs	CPU time (s.)		Speed up		performance		
			parallel	serial	parallel	serial	P	R	F_1
1		1	785	785	-	-	95.5	89.1	92.2
2		3	309	805	2.54	0.98	90.8	93.9	92.3
		8	126	675	6.23	1.16	92.7	91.9	92.3
		18	44	511	17.84	1.54	92.5	91.7	92.1
		24	35	522	22.43	1.50	90.1	93.3	91.7
3	a	3	374	750	2.10	1.05	92.8	91.7	92.2
		8	141	552	5.57	1.42	93.5	91.0	92.2
		18	55	448	14.27	1.75	93.2	90.9	92.1
		24	45	474	17.44	1.66	91.1	92.4	91.8
	b	3	375	789	2.10	0.99	93.1	91.4	92.3
		8	142	658	5.53	1.19	93.7	90.9	92.3
		18	55	519	14.27	1.51	93.3	91.0	92.1
		24	45	532	17.44	1.48	91.3	92.4	91.9
	c	3	378	807	2.08	0.97	93.3	91.3	92.3
		8	141	719	5.57	1.09	93.7	90.9	92.3
		18	55	552	14.27	1.42	93.3	91.1	92.2
		24	46	572	17.07	1.37	91.3	92.4	91.9
	d	3	387	872	2.03	0.90	93.4	91.1	92.3
		8	151	825	5.20	0.95	93.7	90.9	92.3
		18	58	609	13.53	1.29	93.4	91.1	92.2
		24	47	635	16.70	1.24	91.5	92.4	91.9
	e	3	393	923	2.00	0.85	93.7	90.9	92.3
		8	182	937	4.31	0.84	93.9	90.9	92.4
		18	64	691	12.27	1.14	93.4	91.2	92.3
		24	51	708	15.39	1.11	91.7	92.4	92.0

TABLE IV
RESULTS ON MCAT, WHERE C=0.5

method		# SVMs	CPU time (s.)		Speed up		performance		
			parallel	serial	parallel	serial	P	R	F_1
1		1	636	636	-	-	94.5	87.2	90.7
2		4	184	663	3.46	0.96	87.9	93.7	90.7
		12	49	411	12.98	1.55	89.6	91.7	90.6
		24	25	419	25.44	1.52	90.4	90.8	90.6
		40	15	462	42.40	1.38	90.7	89.8	90.3
3	a	4	179	571	3.55	1.11	89.5	92.1	90.7
		12	53	350	12.00	1.82	90.5	91.4	91.0
		24	31	355	20.52	1.79	91.2	90.8	91.0
		40	22	396	28.91	1.61	91.4	90.2	90.8
	b	4	194.	614	3.28	1.04	90.2	91.6	90.9
		12	58	394	10.97	1.61	90.8	91.4	91.1
		24	32	408	19.88	1.56	91.5	90.8	91.1
		40	23	449	27.65	1.42	91.6	90.4	91.0
	c	4	204	639	3.12	0.99	90.5	91.4	90.9
		12	61	418	10.43	1.52	91.0	91.4	91.2
		24	34	438	18.71	1.45	91.5	90.8	91.2
		40	23	471	27.65	1.35	91.7	90.4	91.0
	d	4	224	694	2.84	0.92	90.8	91.1	91.0
		12	67	477	9.49	1.33	91.0	91.4	91.2
		24	37	479	17.19	1.33	91.6	90.8	91.2
		40	25	537	25.44	1.18	91.8	90.4	91.1
	e	4	239	737	2.66	0.86	91.3	90.7	91.0
		12	73	561	8.71	1.13	91.3	91.1	91.2
		24	39	540	16.31	1.18	91.7	90.8	91.3
		40	28	595	22.71	1.07	91.8	90.3	91.1

simultaneously belong to two smaller and more balanced training set divided by hyperplanes, since massive data set in the real world could be fuzzy. We refer to the part of small training set simultaneously belonging to adjacent training set as overlap of the small training set.

Suppose we divide the training data set of class C_i into N_i subsets. According to the above discussions, the M^3-SVM (H) method can be described as follows.

Step 1 Compute the distance between each training sample x of class C_i and hyperplane $H : Az = 0$ as follows,

$$dist(x, H) = \frac{Ax}{||A||} \quad (6)$$

where $x = [x_1, ..., x_n]$ is sample vector, $A = [a_1, ..., a_n]$ is the normal vector of hyperplanes, and $z = [z_1, ..., z_n]$ is any point in hyperplane H.

Step 2 Sort the training data according to the value of $dist(x, H)$.

Step 3 Divide the ordered sequence of training data to N_i parts equally, and then we can get more balanced subsets whose sizes are almost the same.

Step 4 Construct M^3-SVMs according to section II

From the above decomposition procedure, we can see that the hyperplane task decomposition can be easily implemented.

However, a problem remained is how to determine the normal vector A of hyperplane. Experimentally, we take $A = [1, 1, ..., 1]$. There are two reasons that we choose this value of A. Firstly, in most cases of text categorization, the dimensions of sample vectors are very sparse. Therefore, in order to validly separate those samples mostly in every coordinates axis or planes, hyperplanes we used had better not be parallel with the coordinates axis or planes. The most effective way is to set their normal vector be 45 degree against all coordinates axis or planes, which leads to the results of setting a normal vector in which all elements are 1. Secondly, a hyperplane decomposition is equally a sorting operation of all input data according to all dimensional elements under a specified weight vector, which is just the normal vector A. Since we don't often own much prior knowledge of text data sets, and it is hard to determine which dimensional element is more important, therefore, it is natural to give the same weights on each dimension of all data. An illustration of hyperplane decomposition for sparse vectors in a two-dimension space is given in Fig. 1.

IV. EXPERIMENTS

In this section, we present experimental results for a text classification problem to indicate that the proposed hyperplane task decomposition method for M^3-SVMs is effective. We

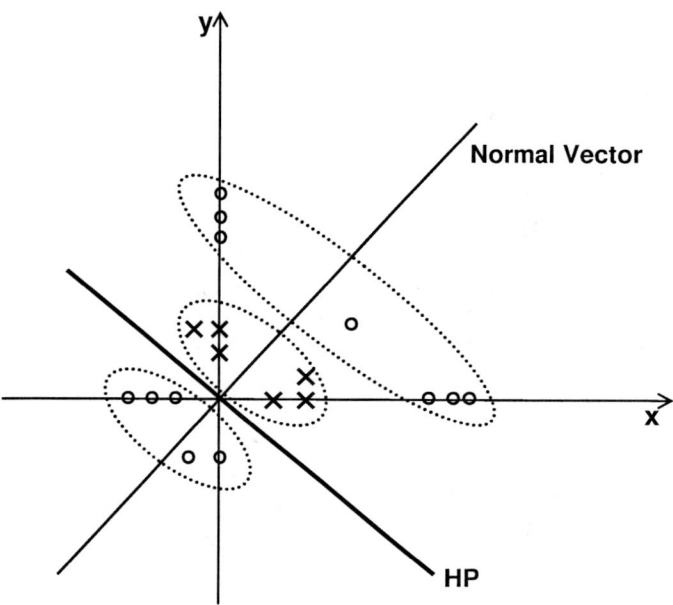

Fig. 1. Hyperplane in a two-dimension space where most sample vectors are sparse vectors. Forks and circles belong to one class. The dashed ellipses denote that the samples in it are clustered into a subproblem data set. HP is the so-called hyperplane, since this is a two-dimension space.

use the revised edition of Reuters Corpus Volume I (RCV1-v2) [8], for this study. There is an archive of over 800,000 manually categorized newswire stories in the full collections. In the simulations, we selected the top four classes, namely CCAT, ECAT, GCAT and MCAT, as given classes. CCAT denotes corporate/Industrial class, ECAT economics class, GCAT government/social class and MCAT markets class. Our training set has a size of 23,149 samples, and our testing set has a size of 199,328 samples from the first of four test data sets . The number of features for representing texts in the simulations is 47,152.

Now, the data set falls into the multilabel setting. Here we adopt the "one-versus-rest" strategy. Namely, a multilabel task [9] can be split up into a set of two-class classification tasks. Each category is treated as a separate two-class classification problem. Such a two-class problem only answers the question of whether or not a document should be assigned to a particular category. Therefore our multilabel classification task can be converted into four two-class classification tasks. Then we adopt the "part-versus-part" strategy, and each two-class classification task is decomposed into a series of two-class subproblems using different decomposition strategies.

After training all individual SVMs employed to solve two-class subproblems, we use min-max combination strategies to integrate the trained individual SVMs into a M^3-SVM. The version of the SVMs package is Libsvm2.4. We reprogram it into the MPI parallel program, namely M^3-SVMs. All the simulations were performed on an IBM p690 machine. It totally has 32 CPUs each of which is Power 4, 1.3GHZ.

To compare the performance of M^3-SVM(H) with traditional SVM and M^3-SVM(R), the text classification problem was learned by traditional SVM, M^3-SVM(R) and M^3-SVM(H) respectively. For the reason that, in many text categorization cases, linear kernel function can get a better generalization performance than other kernel functions such as polynomial and radial basis functions. So in our simulations, we take it as the main kernel function of SVMs. We have also used RBF kernel function to validate the former judgment. According to the discussion in Section III-B, we set the hyperplane $H: Az = 0$ with ones normal vector.

In Tables I through IV, '1', '2', and '3' denote that SVM, M^3-SVM(R), and M^3-SVM(H) are used in the simulation respectively. '#SVMs', 'P' and 'R' refer to the number of SVM classifiers, precision and recall. 'a', 'b', 'c', 'd', and 'e' respectively stand for no overlapping, 10% overlapping, 15% overlapping, 20% overlapping, and 30% overlapping of training data of subproblems for M^3-SVM(H) method.

We have made four groups of experiments according to different parameter C, which controls the tradeoff between complexity of the machine and the number of nonseparable points. In the simulations, we take C as 0.5, 1, 2 and 4 respectively. However, we only list the detailed results of each class with C=0.5, since the results are comparatively more representative than others for almost all methods.

For evaluating the effectiveness of category assignments by classifiers to documents, we use the standard recall, precision and F_1 measure[10]. Recall is defined to be the radio of the total number of correct assignments to correct assignments by the system. Precision is the ratio of the total number of the system's assignments to correct assignments by the system.

$$R = \frac{tp}{tp + fn}, \quad P = \frac{tp}{tp + fp} \quad (7)$$

where tp is the number of documents a system correctly assigns to the category (true positives), fp is the number of documents a system incorrectly assigns to the category (false positives), and fn is the number of documents that belong to the category but which the system does not assign to the category (false negatives).

The F_1 measure corresponds to the harmonic mean of recall and precision in the following form:

$$F_1 = \frac{2tp}{2tp + fp + fn} = \frac{2RP}{R + P} \quad (8)$$

where R is recall, and P is precision.

F_1 has been widely used in cross-method comparisons. Thus it is our main interest in the simulations.

From the experimental results shown in Tables I through IV, we can draw the following conclusions:

a. Even though all of the individual SVMs were trained in serial, M^3-SVMs including M^3-SVMs(R) and M^3-SVMs(H) is also much faster than traditional SVMs for four classes on the whole. And with the increase of classifiers, M^3-SVMs need less and less training time.

b. In most cases, the generalization performance of M^3-SVMs(R) is fluctuant. In some cases, M^3-SVMs(R) has better generalization performance than traditional SVM and in other

TABLE V
COMPARISON OF GENERALIZATION PERFORMANCE AND TRAINING TIME AMONG METHODS, WHERE C=0.5

category	method		# SVMs	CPU time (s.) parallel	CPU time (s.) serial	Speed up parallel	Speed up serial	performance precision	performance recall	performance F_1
CCAT	SVM		1	898	898	-	-	94.9	91.3	93.0
	M^3-SVM(R)		4	290	989	3.10	0.91	94.9	90.7	92.8
	M^3-SVM(H)	no overlap	30	47	563	19.1	1.60	93.5	92.7	93.1
		10% overlap	30	48	647	18.71	1.39	93.7	92.6	93.2
		15% overlap	30	52	707	17.27	1.27	93.8	92.6	93.2
		20% overlap	30	53	754	16.94	1.19	93.9	92.6	93.2
		30% overlap	30	60	894	14.97	1.00	94.0	92.6	**93.3**
ECAT	SVM		1	607	607	-	-	92.7	64.1	75.8
	M^3-SVM (R)		3	186	531	3.26	1.14	84.7	74.7	79.4
	M^3-SVM (H)	no overlap	20	34	300	17.85	2.02	82.6	77.5	80.0
		10% overlap	20	34	343	17.85	1.77	83.4	77.2	80.2
		15% overlap	20	36	363	16.86	1.67	83.8	76.9	80.2
		20% overlap	20	38	391	15.97	1.55	83.8	76.9	80.2
		30% overlap	26	34	473	17.85	1.28	81.2	79.7	**80.4**
GCAT	SVM		1	785	785	-	-	95.5	89.1	92.2
	M^3-SVM (R)		8	126	675	6.23	1.16	92.7	91.9	92.3
	M^3-SVM (H)	no overlap	8	141	552	5.57	1.42	93.5	91.0	92.2
		10% overlap	8	142	658	5.53	1.19	93.7	91.0	92.3
		15% overlap	8	141	719	5.57	1.09	93.7	90.9	92.3
		20% overlap	8	151	825	5.20	0.95	93.7	90.9	92.3
		30% overlap	8	182	937	4.31	0.84	93.9	90.9	**92.4**
MCAT	SVM		1	636	636	-	-	94.5	87.2	90.7
	M^3-SVM (R)		4	184	663	3.46	0.96	87.9	93.7	90.7
	M^3-SVM (H)	no overlap	24	31	355	20.52	1.79	91.2	90.8	91.0
		10% overlap	24	32	408	19.88	1.56	91.5	90.8	91.1
		15% overlap	24	34	438	18.71	1.45	91.5	90.8	91.2
		20% overlap	24	37	479	17.19	1.33	91.6	90.8	91.2
		30% overlap	24	39	540	16.31	1.18	91.7	90.8	**91.3**

cases, the reverse occurs. The experimental results support that in some case, random task decomposition might damage structual properties of original training data. However, when the generalization performance is very bad for some training set, for example for class ECAT, the generalization performance of M^3-SVM(R) can also be raised by 4.6% at the best case and still by 1.9% at the worst case.

c. In most cases, M^3-SVMs(H) shows better generalization performance than traditional SVMs and M^3-SVMs(R). And with the increasing number of classifiers, M^3-SVMs(H) has better and better generalization performance. On the other hand, while the number of the classifiers increases, training time also is on the decrease.

d. In all cases, M^3-SVMs(R) and M^3-SVMs(H) need much less training time than traditional SVMs, and compared with M^3-SVMs(H), M^3-SVMs(R) needs a little less training time. The communication expense in M^3-SVMs in the testing phase focuses on the MIN and MAX procedure, but this time cost is trivial.

For more clear comparison, we organize experimental results of different methods with all best generalization performance for each particular class into Table V. And we also give a detailed comparison on the performance of different methods corresponding to different parameter C in Table VI. The meanings of 'a', 'b', 'c', 'd' and 'e' are the same as Table I. We can see that M^3-SVMs, especially M^3-SVMs(H), is the best choice for text classification problems.

V. Conclusions

We have presented a new hyperplane task decomposition strategy for M^3-SVMs for multilabel text classification. The advantages of the proposed method over traditional SVMs are its parallelism and scalability. Experimental results proved this point. And compared with M^3-SVM (R), M^3-SVMs (H) has better generalization performance. When overlap ratio of training set is appropriate, M^3-SVMs (H) has better generalization performance. With the increase in the number of classifiers, the performance of M^3-SVMs (H) could reach a maximum. A future work is to search for breakpoint between overlapping ratio and the number of classifiers and analyze the effectiveness of the hyperplane decomposition strategy theoretically.

TABLE VI

COMPARISON OF GENERALIZATION PERFORMANCE AMONG DIFFERENT PARAMETER C FOR FOUR CLASSES

category	method		# SVMs	C=0.5			C=1			C=2			C=4		
				P	R	F_1	P	R	F_1	P	R	F_1	P	R	F_1
CCAT	SVM		1	94.9	91.3	93.0	93.4	92.3	92.8	93.2	90.5	91.8	91.4	88.8	90.1
	M^3-SVM(R)		4	94.9	90.7	92.8	94.4	90.9	92.6	93.6	90.3	91.9	92.3	89.2	90.7
	M^3-SVM(H)	a	30	93.5	92.7	93.1	93.5	92.4	93.0	92.9	91.3	92.1	91.8	90.2	91.0
		b	30	93.7	92.6	93.2	93.7	92.3	93.0	93.0	91.2	92.1	91.9	90.0	90.9
		c	30	93.8	92.6	93.2	93.7	92.3	93.0	93.1	91.1	92.1	92.0	90.0	91.0
		d	30	93.9	92.6	93.2	93.7	92.3	93.0	93.0	91.1	92.1	91.9	90.0	90.9
		e	30	94.0	92.6	**93.3**	93.9	92.3	93.1	93.2	91.0	92.1	92.0	89.7	90.8
ECAT	SVM		1	92.7	64.1	75.8	90.0	67.5	77.2	86.1	69.0	76.6	80.4	68.8	74.2
	M^3-SVM (R)		3	84.7	74.7	79.4	83.8	75.4	79.1	91.4	73.7	77.4	78.5	71.0	74.6
	M^3-SVM (H)	a	20	82.6	77.5	80.0	82.0	77.7	79.8	80.8	75.8	78.2	79.6	73.1	76.2
		b	20	83.4	77.2	80.2	82.6	77.4	79.9	81.0	75.6	78.2	79.3	73.1	76.1
		c	20	83.8	76.9	80.2	82.9	77.2	80.0	81.2	75.5	78.3	78.7	73.8	76.2
		d	20	83.8	76.9	80.2	82.9	77.2	80.0	81.2	75.5	78.3	78.7	73.8	76.2
		e	26	81.2	79.7	**80.4**	81.1	78.9	80.0	81.6	75.1	78.2	80.1	72.4	76.1
GCAT	SVM		1	95.5	89.1	92.2	94.9	89.4	92.0	93.4	88.7	91.0	90.9	86.8	88.8
	M^3-SVM (R)		8	92.7	91.9	92.3	92.7	91.6	92.1	91.9	90.6	91.2	90.8	89.0	89.9
	M^3-SVM (H)	a	8	93.5	91.0	92.2	93.2	90.6	91.9	92.1	89.3	90.7	90.5	87.6	89.0
		b	8	93.7	91.0	92.3	93.3	90.5	91.9	92.4	89.2	90.8	90.8	87.5	89.1
		c	8	93.7	90.9	92.3	93.4	90.5	91.9	92.3	89.3	90.8	90.7	87.4	89.0
		d	8	93.7	90.9	92.3	93.4	90.5	91.9	92.4	89.3	90.8	90.8	87.4	89.1
		e	8	93.9	90.9	**92.4**	93.5	90.5	92.0	92.6	89.2	90.9	90.9	87.3	89.0
MCAT	SVM		1	94.5	87.2	90.7	93.7	88.0	90.7	91.9	88.3	90.1	88.5	87.5	88.0
	M^3-SVM (R)		4	87.9	93.7	90.7	88.1	93.1	90.5	87.9	91.7	89.7	87.1	89.2	88.1
	M^3-SVM (H)	a	24	91.2	90.8	91.0	91.1	91.1	91.1	90.3	90.4	90.4	89.4	88.9	89.1
		b	24	91.5	90.8	91.1	91.2	91.1	91.1	90.3	90.4	90.3	89.3	88.8	89.0
		c	24	91.5	90.8	91.2	91.2	91.1	91.2	90.3	90.4	90.3	89.3	88.8	89.1
		d	24	91.6	90.8	91.2	91.2	91.0	91.1	90.4	90.3	90.3	89.4	88.8	89.1
		e	24	91.7	90.8	**91.3**	91.3	91.0	91.2	90.5	90.3	90.4	89.4	88.9	89.2

Acknowledgments

This research was partially supported by the National Natural Science Foundation of China via the grants NSFC 60375022 and NSFC 60473040, as well as Open Fund of Grid Computing Center, Shanghai Jiao Tong University.

References

[1] C. Cortes and V. N. Vapnik, "Support-vector network", Machine Learning, Vol. 20 (1995) 273-297
[2] V. N. Vapnik, Statistical Learning Theory, John Wiley and Sons, New York, 1998
[3] Thorsten Joachims, "Text categorization with support vector machine: Learning with many relevant features", Technical report, University of Dortmund, Computer Science Department, 1997
[4] Yiming Yang and Xin Liu, "A re-examination of text categorization methods", In: Proceedings of the ACM SIGIR Conference on Research and Development in Information Retrieval, 1999
[5] B. L. Lu and M. Ito, "Task Decomposition and Module Combination Based on Class Relations: a Modular Neural Network for Pattern Classification", IEEE Transactions on Neural Networks, 1999, Vol.10, pp.1244-1256.
[6] B. L. Lu, K. A. Wang, M. Utiyama, H. Isahara, "A part-versus-part method for massively parallel training of support vector machines", In: Proceedings of IJCNN'04, Budapast, July25-29 (2004) 735-740.
[7] Kai-An Wang, Hai Zhao and Bao-Liang Lu, "Task Decomposition Using Geometric Relation for Min-Max Modular SVMs", Advances in Neural Networks-ISNN2005, LNCS 3496, pp.887-892, Chongqing, China, May 29-June 2, 2005
[8] David D. Lewis, Yiming Yang, Tony G. Rose, Fan Li, "RCV1: a new benchmark collection for text categorization research", Journal of Machine Learning Research 5 (2004) 361-397
[9] Thorsten Joachims, Learning to classify text using support vector machine:method, theory, and algorithms. Kluwer Academic Publishers, 2002
[10] David D.Lewis, "Evaluating and optimizing autonomous text classification systems". In Proceedings of the 18th Annual International ACM SIGIR Conference on Research and Development in Information Retrieval (SIGIR 95), pages 246-254,1995.

Weight Sharing on Naive Bayes Document Model

Kazumi Saito
NTT Communication Science Laboratories
2-4 Hikaridai, Seika, Kyoto 619–0237 Japan
E-mail: saito@cslab.kecl.ntt.co.jp

Ryohei Nakano
Nagoya Institute of Technology
Gokiso-cho, Showa-ku, Nagoya 466–8555 Japan
E-mail: nakano@ics.nitech.ac.jp

Abstract— In this paper, we study weight sharing on the naive Bayes document model. Firstly we consider splitting words into a relatively small number of groups such that words in each group have the same parameter value. This problem can be regarded as a probabilistic parameter sharing task. In this task, we formalize the problem in terms of maximum likelihood estimation, and then propose an algorithm for this purpose. Secondly we focus on an adaptive hyperparameter estimation problem based on prior distributions constructed by using such word groups. This problem can be regarded as a hyperparameter sharing task. In this task, we describe a framework and algorithm, which enables to derive the unique optimal solution in the context of leave-one-out cross validation. In our experiments using a benchmark document set called webkb, we show a series of simulation results using the proposed algorithms.

I. INTRODUCTION

In knowledge discovery using neural networks, an important and challenging research issue is to automatically find a succinct network structure from data. As a technique for such structuring, we have focused on *weight sharing* (Bishop, 1995; Haykin, 1999; Saito & Nakano, 2002). Weight sharing means constraining the choice of weight values such that weights in a network are divided into clusters, and weights within the same cluster are constrained to have the same value called a *common weight*.

For these type of problems, we have proposed a method called Bidirectional Clustering of Weight (Saito & Nakano, 2002), and applied it to both regression and classification types of tasks for finding multivariate polynomial-type functions (Nakano & Saito, 2002) and m-of-n classification rules (Towell & Shavlik, 1993), respectively. As other types of tasks, we study both a probabilistic parameter sharing task and a hyperparameter sharing task in this paper. More specifically, as an interesting and useful probabilistic model, we focus on the naive Bayes document model because of its simplicity and robustness.

For a given set of document samples, one of the fundamental tasks on text mining is to automatically divide a set of words into a relatively small number of groups according to frequency of words such as very high, high, and so on. Clearly this problem can be regarded as the probabilistic parameter sharing task. On the other hand, it is well recognized that by preparing an adequate prior distribution for the naive Bayes model, we can reasonably improve its generalization performance. This problem can be formalized as the hyperparameter sharing task.

This paper studies weight sharing on the naive Bayes document model. Firstly we consider splitting words into a relatively small number of groups such that words in each group have the same parameter value. In this problem, we formalize the problem in terms of maximum likelihood estimation, and then propose an algorithm for this purpose. Secondly we focus on an adaptive hyperparameter estimation problem based on prior distributions constructed by using such word groups. For this problem, we describe a framework and algorithm, which enables to derive the unique optimal hyperparameters in the context of leave-one-out cross validation. In our experiments using a benchmark document set, we show a series of simulation results using the proposed algorithms.

II. PROBABILISTIC PARAMETER SHARING

In this section, after explaining a text representation, we describe a notion of degree distributions and the naive Bayes model. Then we formalize our words split problem corresponding to the probabilistic parameter sharing task. Finally we propose a learning algorithm used in our experiments.

A. Framework

We firstly explain a text representation used in this paper. Let $\{x^\mu : \mu = 1, \cdots, N\}$ be a set of N samples represented by word-frequency vectors. Let $(w_1, \cdots, w_V)$ be a set of words identified with vocabularies. Here V denotes the number of distinct words appearing in all the documents. Then we can express each word-frequency vector by $x^\mu = (x_1^\mu, \cdots, x_V^\mu)$, i.e., x_i^μ is a frequency of the i-th word occurrence in the document x^μ. Since each document is represented just as a word-frequency vector by ignoring the appearing order of words in it, this representation is called the BOW (bag-of-words) text representation (e.g., Manning & Schütze, 1999).

B. Degree Distribution

Let A_k be a set of words whose word-frequency is k, i.e.,

$$A_k = \left\{ w_i : \sum_{\mu=1}^{N} x_i^\mu = k \right\}. \quad (1)$$

Hereafter k is referred to as *word degree* ($k \geq 0$). Let a_k be the number of elements (words) in A_k, then we can consider the following probability.

$$p(k) = \frac{a_k}{\sum_{k=1}^{K} a_k} = \frac{a_k}{V}. \quad (2)$$

Here K is the maximum degree among all words.

As shown in Figure 1 using the webkb data set described later, we can observe that the degree distribution is very closely approximated by a power law like distribution, i.e.,

$$p(k) \propto k^{-\gamma}. \qquad (3)$$

Here γ is referred to as the degree exponent. It is well known that the link degrees in growing networks such as Web hyperlink networks also show similar distributions (e.g. Barabasi & Oltvai, 2004).

C. Naive Bayes Model

For text mining based on the BOW representation, the naive Bayes model (Duda, Hart, & Stork, 2000) has been widely used because of its simplicity and robustness. In this model, a document is assumed to be generated according to a multinomial distribution. Here let θ_i be a parameter value of the multinomial distribution corresponding to the appearance of the i-th word, then by using the following formula, we can obtain the probability that the document x is generated.

$$P(\boldsymbol{x}) \propto \prod_{i=1}^{V} \theta_i^{x_i}, \quad \theta_i > 0, \quad \sum_{i=1}^{V} \theta_i = 1. \qquad (4)$$

For a given set of training samples $\{\boldsymbol{x}^\mu : \mu = 1, \cdots, N\}$, we can consider the following logarithmic likelihood term for estimating parameter values $\{\theta_i\}$ of multinomial distributions.

$$L(\Theta) = \sum_{\mu=1}^{N} \log P(\boldsymbol{x}^\mu) = \sum_{\mu=1}^{N} \sum_{i=1}^{V} x_i^\mu \log(\theta_i). \qquad (5)$$

Then, by using the method of Lagrange multipliers (Luenberger, 1984), we can analytically calculate the optimal solution as follows.

$$\widehat{\theta}_i = \frac{\sum_{\mu=1}^{N} x_i^\mu}{\sum_{\mu=1}^{N} \sum_{i=1}^{V} x_i^\mu}. \qquad (6)$$

Here we can easily see that for the words whose degree is the same, their parameter value is the same. Namely we can see a natural weight sharing structure in the naive Bayes model. Actually in the case of the webkb data set, the number of distinct words is $V = 22855$, while the number of different parameter values is 570.

D. Words Split Problem

As mentioned earlier, our first goal is to split words into a relatively small number of groups so as to maximize its logarithmic likelihood value. Firstly we consider splitting words into two groups, B_1 and B_2, as follows:

$$B_1(s) = \{A_k : k \le s\}, \quad B_2(s) = \{A_k : k > s\}. \qquad (7)$$

Here s is a split point based on word degree. Note that the total numbers of words in B_1 and B_2 can be calculated by $\sum_{k=1}^{s} a_k$ and $\sum_{k=s+1}^{K} a_k$, respectively. Similarly the total frequencies of words in all the document with respect to B_1 and B_2 can be calculated by $\sum_{k=1}^{s} k a_k$ and $\sum_{k=s+1}^{K} k a_k$, respectively.

Now let ϕ_g be a common parameter for the group B_g, then we can express the logarithmic likelihood term as follows:

$$L(\phi_1, \phi_2) = \sum_{k=1}^{s} k a_k \log \phi_1 + \sum_{k=s+1}^{K} k a_k \log \phi_2. \qquad (8)$$

Here since a sum of parameter values over all the words must be one, we need to consider the following constraints:

$$\phi_1 \sum_{k=1}^{s} a_k + \phi_2 \sum_{k=s+1}^{K} a_k = 1. \qquad (9)$$

Thus by using the method of Lagrange multipliers, we can analytically calculate the optimal parameter values as follows:

$$\phi_1 = \frac{\sum_{k=1}^{s} k a_k}{M \sum_{k=1}^{s} a_k}, \quad \phi_2 = \frac{\sum_{k=s+1}^{K} k a_k}{M \sum_{k=s+1}^{K} a_k}, \qquad (10)$$

where M denotes the total frequencies of words in all the document calculated by $M = \sum_{k=1}^{K} k a_k$. Therefore by ignoring the terms independent to our maximization, we can express our objective function as follows:

$$L(s) = \sum_{k=1}^{s} k a_k \log \frac{\sum_{k=1}^{s} k a_k}{\sum_{k=1}^{s} a_k} + \sum_{k=s+1}^{K} k a_k \log \frac{\sum_{k=s+1}^{K} k a_k}{\sum_{k=s+1}^{K} a_k}. \qquad (11)$$

Next we consider splitting words into G groups. Let s be a (G+1)-dimensional vector consisting of both extreme points s_0 and s_G and a series of $G-1$ split points, defined by:

$$\boldsymbol{s} = (s_0, s_1, \cdots, s_G), \quad s_0 = 0, \quad s_G = K. \qquad (12)$$

Then by considering the following logarithmic likelihood function $L(\phi)$

$$L(\boldsymbol{\phi}) = \sum_{g=0}^{G-1} \sum_{k=s_g}^{s_{g+1}} k a_k \log \phi_{g+1}, \qquad (13)$$

and the following constraints over parameter values ϕ

$$\sum_{g=0}^{G-1} \phi_{g+1} \sum_{k=s_g}^{s_{g+1}} a_k = 1, \qquad (14)$$

we can easily see that the objective function defined in Eq. (11) can be generalized as follows:

$$L(\boldsymbol{s}) = \sum_{g=0}^{G-1} \sum_{k=s_g}^{s_{g+1}} k a_k \log \frac{\sum_{k=s_g}^{s_{g+1}} k a_k}{\sum_{k=s_g}^{s_{g+1}} a_k}. \qquad (15)$$

Here the free parameters in $\boldsymbol{s}$ are $s_1, \cdots, s_{G-1}$.

E. Words Split Algorithm

When the number of split points G is not so large, we can perform exhaustive search in order to find the optimal split vector $\boldsymbol{s}$. However, for a larger number G, it is practically impossible to resort to such strategy. As shown in Figures 2 and 3 described later in our experiments, since the objective function defined in Eq. (15) is expected to be unimodal with respect to split vector s, we adopt the following simple greedy algorithm.

The algorithm is summarized as follows:
step1 Initialize s by $s_1 = 1, \cdots, s_{G-1} = G - 1$.
step2 Set $g = G - 1$ and $F = 0$.
step3 If $g = 0$ and $F = 0$ then terminate; else if $g = 0$ then go to **step2**.
step4 Generate s' by incrementing s only at the g-th position ($s'_g = s_g + 1$). If $s'_g = s_{g+1}$ then $g = g - 1$ and go to **step3**.
step5 If $L(s) < L(s')$ then set $s = s'$, $F = 1$ and go to **step4**; otherwise set $g = g - 1$ and go to **step3**.

Clearly it is possible to improve the above algorithm by modifying some steps such as the initialization method in **step1**. However, since efficiency is not so important in this paper, we straightforwardly applied the above method in our experiments.

III. Hyperparameter Sharing

In this section, after explaining a basic notion of the maximum a posterior estimate, we describe a framework of the adaptive hyperparameter estimation problem that enables to derive the unique optimal solution in the context of leave-one-out cross validation. Then we extend this framework to the case that a prior distribution is constructed by using some word groups. Finally we describe a learning algorithm used in our experiments.

A. MAP Estimation

As mentioned earlier, we can calculate the maximum likelihood estimate of the naive Bayes from Eq. (6). However, results by this estimation are likely to over-fit to the training samples, and its generalization performance for an unseen test sample is usually poor.

To overcome this problem, by assuming the prior distribution of parameter vectors $\{\theta\}$ is a Dirichlet distribution (Blei, Ng & Jordan, 2003), the following learning objective function has been widely adopted for deriving the maximum a posteriori estimate with respect to the parameter distribution.

$$J(\Theta) = L(\Theta) + \lambda \sum_{i=1}^{V} \log(\theta_i), \quad (16)$$

where λ stands for a hyperparameter. Recall that when maximizing $J(\Theta)$, we need to consider constraint functions described in Eq. (4). Thus, by using the method of Lagrange multipliers, we can analytically calculate the optimal solution as follows.

$$\widehat{\theta}_i = \frac{\sum_{\mu=1}^{N} x_i^{\mu} + \lambda}{\sum_{\mu=1}^{N} \sum_{i=1}^{V} x_i^{\mu} + V\lambda}. \quad (17)$$

Here when the hyperparameter value is set to $\lambda = 1$, it corresponds to the Laplace smoothing.

B. Adaptive Estimation

For a given set of data, we must consider a criterion to adequately evaluate the learning results obtained by changing λ. For this purpose, we introduce an objective function for hyperparameters derived from the procedure of *cross-validation*, frequently used for evaluating the generalization performance of learned networks (Bishop, 1995).

First of all we normalize each word frequency vector, i.e., $\sum_{i=1}^{V} x_i^{\mu} = 1$. Let α be a transformed hyperparameter defined by

$$\alpha = \frac{N-1}{N-1+V\lambda}. \quad (18)$$

Note that the transformed hyperparameter α, which is independent to each sample, determines the hyperparameter λ uniquely. Then we can easily see that the LOO (Leave-One-Out) optimally estimated parameter value can be expressed by

$$\widehat{\theta}_i^{(-\nu)} = \alpha x_i^{(-\nu)} + (1-\alpha)\frac{1}{V}, \quad (19)$$

where the LOO sample $x_i^{(-\nu)}$ is defined by

$$x_i^{(-\nu)} = \frac{\sum_{\mu=1}^{N} x_i^{\mu} - x_i^{\nu}}{N-1}. \quad (20)$$

Thus we can obtain the following sum of logarithmic likelihood based on the procedure of LOO cross-validation.

$$L_2(\alpha) = \sum_{\nu=1}^{N} \sum_{i=1}^{V} x_i^{\nu} \log(\alpha x_i^{(-\nu)} + (1-\alpha)\frac{1}{V}). \quad (21)$$

Therefore by regarding $L_2(\alpha)$ as the objective function and maximizing it with respect to α, we can adaptively estimate an adequate value of hyperparameter λ.

C. Extension Using Word Groups

In the above derivation, we assumed that the hyperparameter value is the same for all words. However, we might want to change the values for certain word groups. In this paper, we consider using the word groups obtained by the method in the previous section.

Assume that we have already obtained a set of word groups $\{B_1, \cdots, B_G\}$. Here we denote the number of words in B_g by b_g, i.e., $\sum_{g=1}^{G} b_g = V$. Let $\boldsymbol{\lambda} = (\lambda_1, \cdots, \lambda_G)$ be a vector of hyperparameters corresponding to word groups. By defining a mapping function $f(i) \in \{1, \cdots, G\}$ from a word i to its group g, we can express the MAP objective function as follows:

$$J_2(\Theta) = L(\Theta) + \sum_{i=1}^{V} \lambda_{f(i)} \log(\theta_i), \quad (22)$$

Then we can obtain the estimated parameter value as follows:

$$\widehat{\theta}_i = \frac{\sum_{\mu=1}^{N} x_i^{\mu} + \lambda_{f(i)}}{N + \sum_{i=1}^{V} \lambda_{f(i)}} = \frac{\sum_{\mu=1}^{N} x_i^{\mu} + \lambda_{f(i)}}{N + \sum_{g=1}^{G} b_g \lambda_g}. \quad (23)$$

Here recall that we normalize each word frequency vector.

Now we define a vector of transformed hyperparameters $\boldsymbol{\alpha} = (\alpha_0, \alpha_1, \cdots, \alpha_G)$ as follows:

$$\alpha_g = \begin{cases} (N-1)/(N-1+\sum_{g=1}^{G} b_g \lambda_g) & (g=0), \\ b_g \lambda_g/(N-1+\sum_{g=1}^{G} b_g \lambda_g) & (g \geq 1). \end{cases} \quad (24)$$

Here note that $\sum_{g=0}^{G} \alpha_g = 1$. Then we can obtain the LOO estimated parameter as follows:

$$\widehat{\theta}_i^{(-\nu)} = \alpha_0 x_i^{(-\nu)} + \frac{\alpha_{f(i)}}{b_{f(i)}}. \quad (25)$$

Thus we can obtain the following sum of logarithmic likelihood based on the procedure of LOO cross-validation.

$$L_3(\boldsymbol{\alpha}) = \sum_{\nu=1}^{N} \sum_{i=1}^{V} x_i^\nu \log(\alpha_0 x_i^{(-\nu)} + \frac{\alpha_{f(i)}}{b_{f(i)}}). \quad (26)$$

Again by regarding $L_3(\boldsymbol{\alpha})$ as the objective function and maximizing it with respect to $\boldsymbol{\alpha}$, we can adaptively estimate an adequate vector of hyperparameters $\boldsymbol{\lambda}$. Here we can easily see that $L_3(\boldsymbol{\alpha})$ is a natural extension to $L_2(\boldsymbol{\alpha})$

D. Estimation Algorithm

It is guaranteed that we can obtain the unique optimal vector $\widehat{\boldsymbol{\alpha}}$ because $L_3(\boldsymbol{\alpha})$ is a convex function defined in a convex region, i.e., $\sum_{g=0}^{G} \alpha_g = 1$ (e.g., Fletcher, 1987). In this paper we employ the EM algorithm (Dempster, Laird & Rubin, 1977) in order to estimate hyperparameter vector $\boldsymbol{\alpha}$.

Let $\boldsymbol{\alpha}^{(t)}$ be a vector of transformed hyperparameters at algorithm step t. Then by considering the following posterior probabilities,

$$q_{i,1}^\nu = \frac{\alpha_0^{(t)} x_i^{(-\nu)}}{\alpha_0^{(t)} x_i^{(-\nu)} + \frac{\alpha_{f(i)}^{(t)}}{b_{f(i)}}}, \quad q_{i,2}^\nu = \frac{\frac{\alpha_{f(i)}^{(t)}}{b_{f(i)}}}{\alpha_0^{(t)} x_i^{(-\nu)} + \frac{\alpha_{f(i)}^{(t)}}{b_{f(i)}}}, \quad (27)$$

we can define the following Q function used in the EM algorithm.

$$Q(\boldsymbol{\alpha}; \boldsymbol{\alpha}^{(t)}) = \sum_{\nu=1}^{N} \sum_{i=1}^{V} x_i^\nu (q_{i,1}^\nu \log(\alpha_0 x_i^{(-\nu)}) + q_{i,2}^\nu \log(\frac{\alpha_{f(i)}}{b_{f(i)}})). \quad (28)$$

Thus we can update the hyperparameter values as follows:

$$\alpha_0^{(t+1)} = \frac{1}{N} \sum_{\nu=1}^{N} \sum_{i=1}^{V} x_i^\nu q_{i,1}^\nu, \quad \alpha_g^{(t+1)} = \frac{1}{N} \sum_{\nu=1}^{N} \sum_{f(i)=g} x_i^\nu q_{i,2}^\nu. \quad (29)$$

In virtue of the EM algorithm, by starting from arbitrary initial hyperparameter $\boldsymbol{\alpha}^{(0)}$, we can obtain the optimally estimated hyperparameter vector.

IV. SIMULATION RESULTS

In this section, after explaining our experiment settings, we examine the degree distribution based on word frequencies. Then we report a series of simulation results on probabilistic parameter sharing formalized as the words split problem. Finally we show an initial experimental result on hyperparameter sharing.

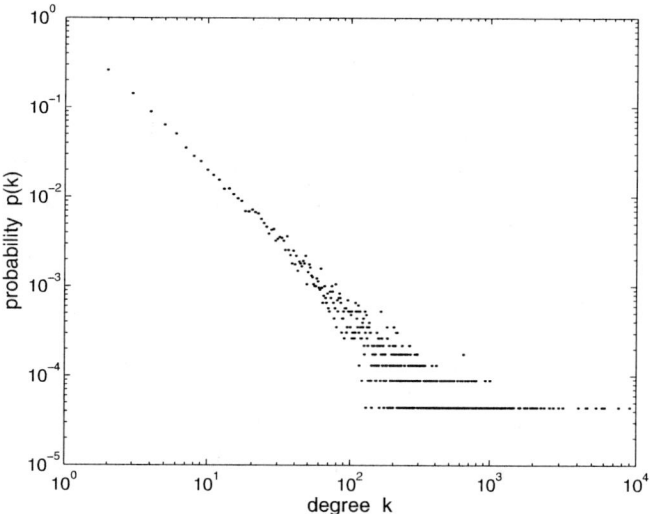

Fig. 1. Degree distribution.

A. Experiment Settings & Degree Distribution

We performed a series of empirical evaluations by using a benchmark document set called webkb (Nigam, Lafferty & McCallum, 1999). In our experiments, the documents were preprocessed as follows: firstly, we stemmed some words for identifying certain vocabularies such as conjugated verbs by using Porter's stemming algorithm (Porter, 1980), and excluded 571 stop-words (Salton, 1988) and vocabularies whose word-frequencies are less than one in all the documents. As a result, the numbers of distinct words and documents were 4191 and 22855, respectively. Here we ignored class information of each document.

First of all, we examined the degree distribution based on word frequencies using the webkb data set. Figure 1 shows the experimental results. Clearly we can observe a distribution just like a power law. As mentioned earlier, it is well known that the link degrees in growing networks such as Web hyperlink networks also show similar distributions (Barabasi & Oltvai, 2004). However, the degree exponent γ obtained from Figure 1 by using the maximum likelihood estimate was around 1.5, i.e., this value was substantially smaller than those obtained from growing networks, which are usually greater than 2. Our conjecture is that this is because the growing rate of total word numbers is very small.

B. Probabilistic Parameter Sharing

Firstly we examined the configuration of our objective function on the words split problem in the case that the number of word groups is 2. Figure 2 shows the objective function values with respect to split point s, i.e., this corresponds to plots of Eq. (11). From this figure, we can observe a unimodal curve that is almost symmetrical in the logarithmic scale with respect to degree. Moreover, we can observe that the curve in some small degree region is quite smooth, while it changes to somehow serrated curves in the large degree region. The latter

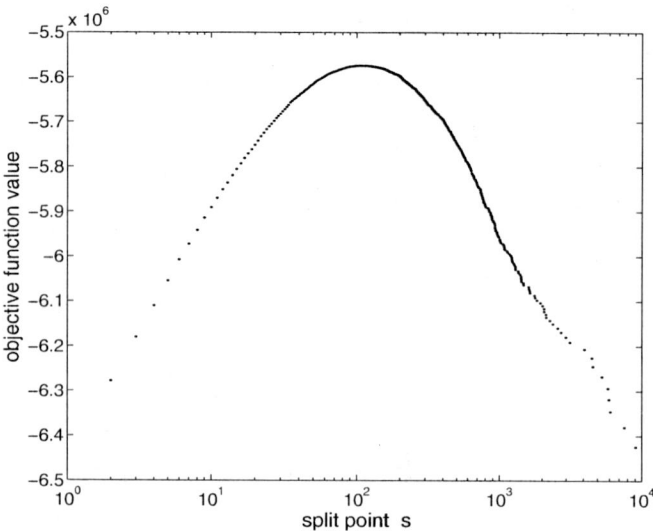

Fig. 2. Objective function of words split problem ($G = 2$).

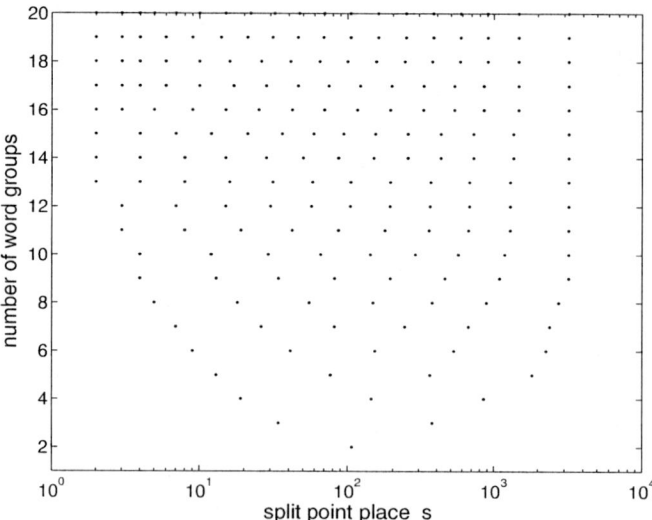

Fig. 4. Distribution of split points.

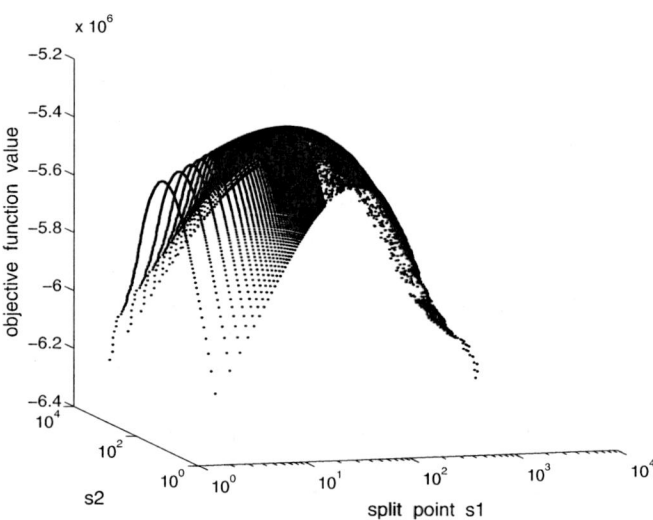

Fig. 3. Objective function of words split problem ($G = 3$).

characteristics reasonably coincides with the plots in Figure 1.

Secondly we performed a further experiment to examine characteristics of our objective function in the case that the number of word groups is 3. Figure 3 shows the experimental result. Note that this corresponds to plots of Eq. (15) with $G = 3$. From this figure, we can observe a naturally extended characteristics in comparison to Figure 2. Thus these experimental results suggest that the objective function with any number of word groups might be unimodal. Moreover we can expect that our words split algorithm works reasonably. However, we need further experiments or theoretical studies in order to judge whether this claim would be true or not.

Thirdly we examined how words split points change by increasing the number of word groups. Figure 4 shows experimental result, where we changed numbers of word groups from 2 to 20. This experimental result shows that the split points diverged uniformly in the logarithmic scale with respect to degree. Clearly the above series of experimental results commonly suggest that the logarithmic degree played an interesting role in order to examine a parameter sharing structure on the naive Bayes document model.

Finally we examined how the objective function values improve by increasing the number of word groups. Figure 5 shows the experimental result, where we also changed numbers of word groups from 2 to 20. Here note that the straight line in this figure stands for the upper bound calculated from the maximum likelihood estimate on the naive Bayes document model. This experimental result shows that the objective function values were improved rapidly and they approached close to the upper bound even if the number of word groups are not so large. This result also supports that our words split algorithm worked reasonably.

C. Hyperparameter Sharing

We examined how generalization performance is improved by introducing the prior distribution constructed by some word groups. To this end, we randomly divided the data set into training and test data sets with the same numbers of documents. Since the evaluation using only one pair of training and test sample sets is not reliable, we constructed ten pairs of such sample sets on the basis of independent random sampling.

Figure 6 shows the average generalization performances over ten trials, where we changed the number of word groups (hyperparameters) from 1 to 5. Here note that since the logarithmic likelihood decreases as the total word frequency in a document set increases, we normalized the generalization performance of each test set according to the total word frequency. This experimental results indicate that by considering an adequate hyperparameter sharing, we can improve the generalization performances.

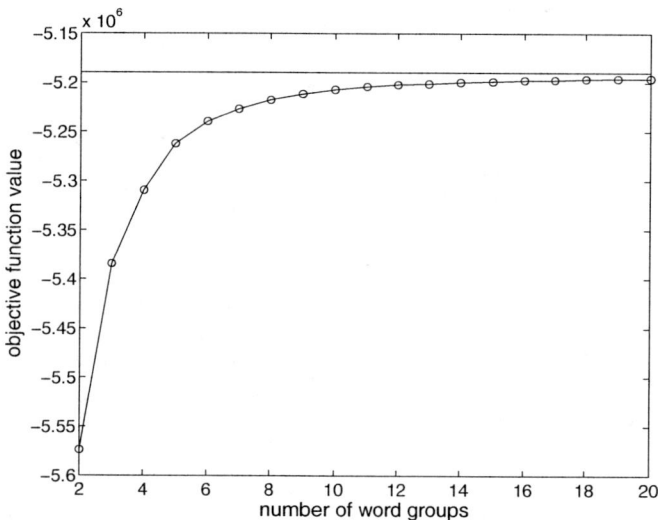

Fig. 5. Convergence property of objective function.

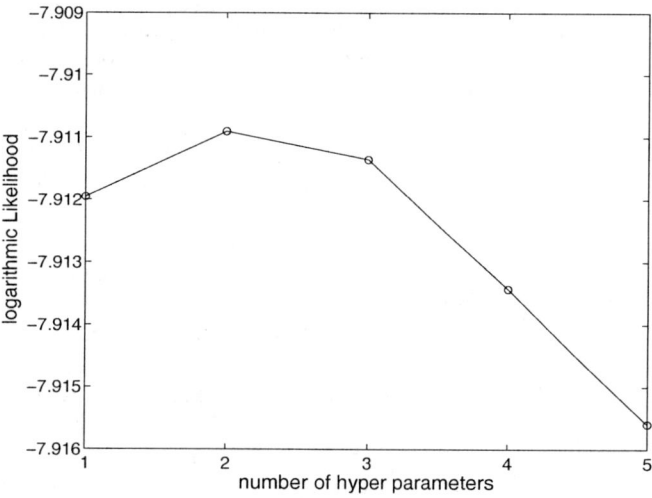

Fig. 6. Influence of the number of hyperparameters on performance.

V. DISCUSSION AND FUTURE WORK

In the neural information processing field, the idea of *weight sharing* in a layered neural network is known to imitate some aspects of mammalian visual processing system. Thereby, the technique of weight sharing was used to build translation invariance into the response of the network for two-dimensional character recognition (Bishop 1995). In such usage, however, which weights should have the same value was determined in the design process of receptive fields in a network.

There exist a number of existing work on weight sharing. Nowlan and Hinton (1992) proposed the idea of *soft weight sharing*, where the distribution of weight values is modelled as a mixture of Gaussians and a learning algorithm automatically decides which weights should be tied together having the same distribution. Towell and Shavlik (1993) also introduced the idea of *weight clustering* in their rule extraction algorithm from a trained neural network. However, such existing work focused only on supervised learning tasks. In this paper, we have proposed new frameworks and algorithms on unsupervised learning tasks.

Although we have been encouraged by our results to date, there remain a number of directions in which we must extend our frameworks and algorithms before they are applied to more practical problems. But we believe that some important steps have been taken along for studying both probabilistic parameter sharing and hyperparameter sharing. In the future, we plan to carry out further experiments to evaluate these methods using a wider variety of problems.

VI. CONCLUSIONS

This paper investigated weight-sharing structures of the naive Bayes document model. Firstly we formalized words split problem and proposed the words split algorithm. Our experimental result on the issue shows that words could be splitted into a very small number of groups with little loss of representational power. Secondly to overcome the over-fitting, we extended the above framework to hyperparameter sharing, and proposed an algorithm to get a solution. Our preliminary experiment shows generalization performance can be improved by the adequate hyperparameter sharing.

ACKNOWLEDGMENT

This work was partly supported by NTT Communication Science Laboratories, Nippon Telegraph and Telephone Corporation.

REFERENCES

[1] Barabasi, A. L. & Oltvar, Z. N. (2004). Network biology: Understanding the cell's functional organization. *Nature Review, 5,* 101–114.
[2] Bishop, C. M. (1995). *Neural networks for pattern recognition.* Clarendon Press.
[3] Blei, D. M., Ng, A. Y., & Jordan, M. I. (2003). Latent Dirichlet allocation. *Journal of Machine Learning Research, 3,* 993–1022.
[4] Dempster, A. P., Laird, N. M., & Rubin, D. B. (1977). Maximum likelihood from incomplete data via EM algorithm. *J. Royal Statist. Soc. Ser. B (methodology), 39,* 1–38.
[5] Duda, R. O., Hart, P. E., & Stork, D. G. (2000). *Pattern classification (2nd Ed.).* John Wiley & Sons.
[6] Fletcher. R. (1987). *Practical methods of optimization.* John Wiley & Sons.
[7] Haykin. S. (1999). *Neural networks - a comprehensive foundation, 2nd edition.* Prentice-Hall.
[8] Luenberger, D. G. (1984). *Linear and nonlinear programming.* Addison-Wesley.
[9] Manning. C. D. & Schütze, H. (1999). *Foundations of statistical natural language processing.* MIT press.
[10] Nakano. R. & Saito, K. (2002). Discovering polynomials to fit multivariate data having numeric and nominal variables. *Progress in Discovery Science, LNAI 2281,* 482–493.
[11] Nigam, k., Lafferty, J., & McCallum, A. (1999) Using maximum entropy for text classification. Presented at the *IJCAI-1999: Workshop on Machine Learning for Information Filtering*
[12] Nowlan S. J., & Hinton G. E. (1992). Simplifying neural networks by soft weight sharing. *Neural Computation, 4,* 473–493.
[13] Porter, M. F. (1980). An algorithm for suffix stripping. *Program, 14,* 130–137.
[14] Saito, K. & Nakano, R. (2002). Structuring Neural Networks through Bidirectional Clustering of Weights. *Proceedings of the International Conference on Discovery Science.* (pp. 206–219).
[15] Salton, G. (1988). *Automatic text processing.* Addison-Wesley.
[16] Towell G. G. & Shavlik J. W. (1993). Extracting refined rules from knowledge-based neural networks. *Machine Learning, 13,* 71–101.

Optimization of Parameters for Effective Web Information Retrieval Using an Evolutionary Algorithm

John Zakos
School of Information Technology
Griffith University
Queensland 4215 Australia
j.zakos@gu.edu.au

Ping Zhang
School of Information Technology
Bond University
Queensland 4215 Australia
pzhang@staff.bond.edu.au

Brijesh Verma
School of Information Technology
Central Queensland University
Queensland 4702 Australia
b.verma@cqu.edu.au

Abstract- In this paper we present an approach based on the application of an evolutionary algorithm to optimally tune the parameters of a novel technique for effective web information retrieval. Context matching is a context-based technique for the ad-hoc retrieval of web documents that relies on a number of inter-related parameters that define the nature of the context it uses. Its aim is to dynamically generate a context-based measure of term significance during retrieval that can be used as an indicator of document relevancy and ultimately contribute to a documents rank score. But the optimal setting of context matching parameters is an important aspect of the technique to ensure effective retrieval. Thus, the goal of this paper is to investigate the use of an evolutionary algorithm for the optimization of context matching parameters and compare its performance to an iterative technique that exhaustively explores combinations of parameters. We show how the most effective settings for parameters are obtained efficiently through the evolutionary algorithm. We also show how context matching, through the use of these optimized parameters, achieves effective retrieval results on benchmark data that are a significant improvement on previously published results.

I. Introduction

Evolutionary algorithms have been previously used for optimization in information retrieval. Trotman [1] presents a technique to optimize document structure weights through genetic algorithms to improve retrieval. In similar work, Kim et al [2] use a genetic algorithm to learn the most important structures in HTML documents. In [3,4,5], evolutionary algorithms are investigated for information retrieval with new mutation and crossover operators being proposed. Gordon [6] proposes a genetic algorithm-based approach to select best indexes for retrieval while Morgan et al [7] use a genetic algorithm to select additional terms from a dictionary.

In addition to evolutionary algorithms, other machine learning approaches to information retrieval have been studied [8]. Neural approaches to web information retrieval include the application of the inference network model for the combination of evidence [9] and the WEBSOM system [10]. Hyperlink-based evidence and content-based evidence can be fused and a belief of relevance can be derived from the inference network model [9]. WEBSOM [10] is a two layered Kohonen SOM approach that caters for the visualization and retrieval of large web document collections. A modified adaptive resonance theory algorithm has been proposed for the categorization of web documents [11].

A technique called *context matching* (CM) is presented in this paper. It is a technique that generates term confidence in a fundamentally different way to traditional *term frequency* (TF) [12,13]. CM does not rely on the number of times a particular term appears in a document to determine whether it is significant or not. With CM, a term appearing infrequently within a document that contains thousands of terms can potentially be given a high confidence. Vice versa, a term appearing frequently within a document can potentially be assigned a low confidence. This is a significant characteristic of CM that makes it fundamentally different to TF.

But to perform context matching, the technique relies on the setting of its parameters to perform effectively. These parameters primarily determine the nature of the context to consider when context matching is performed. Context is the most important aspect of the technique and the setting of parameters ultimately effectiveness the overall effectiveness of the system. The main focus of this paper is to investigate the application of an evolutionary algorithm for the setting of these parameters, while introducing the context matching technique in a web information retrieval setting.

The use of context in information retrieval is not a new idea. Jing et al [14] use context as a basis of measuring the semantic distances between words. Billhardt et al [15] propose a context-based vector space model for information retrieval. The WEBSOM [10] system is an example of another way in which context has been used for information retrieval through the clustering of web documents.

The remainder of paper is organized into 4 further sections. The next section describes the proposed technique. Section 3 describes the technique for parameter optimization. Section 4 presents the experimental setup. Section 5 presents an analysis and discussion of results and in section 6 we conclude and outline the future direction of research.

II. Proposed Technique

The context of both terms in documents and terms in queries is fundamental to CM. The main aim of the technique is, given an inputted query, to use the context of the query to match it against the context of a term in a document to ultimately determine the significance of the term to that potentially relevant document. The result is the generation of a *context matching confidence* (CMC), which is a term significance indicator than can potentially be used as a substitute or co-contributor of TF.

Given a query Q and a document collection DC, the technique can be broadly outlined with the following steps:

Step 1. Generate **Query Context** QC for Q
Step 2. For every document D in DC containing an occurrence of a query term q in Q
   Step 2.1. **Match** QC with the term context TC of term q in D to generate the context matching confidence CMC.
   Step 2.2. **Combine** CMC with TF to give term confidence for q in D.

The technique is described further throughout the following sections.

A. Query Context

The context of a query consists of two sub-contexts, each of which are a set of terms:
1. Set original query terms Q, and
2. Set of related terms QR.

These two sets of terms are sub-contexts and together they form the query context $QC = \{Q, QR\}$. Each term in each set has a relatedness value in the range [0,1] that indicates how related that term is to the original query Q. A value of 1 indicates maximum relatedness where a value of zero indicates that the term not related.

To determine the set of related terms QR for the query Q, the technique relies on the use of query expansion using local feedback [16-18]. Typically, an initial run is executed to obtain an initial list of ranked documents and the terms of the top n documents are assumed to be relevant and then interpreted to selected the best m terms to make up the set QR. We employ the use of

$$TSV_t = w.r \quad (1)$$

to rank candidate terms, where w is a weight (typically IDF) indicating the significance of term t, and r is the number of relevant documents t appears in. This same method to select expanded terms has been used successfully for traditional query expansion [16]. Terms are ranked using TSV and the top m are chosen to form QR.

Once QR has been determined, is used as part of the query context QC that can now be used for matching. Each term in the original query Q and related terms QR is given a default relatedness value of 1, indicating that it is very related to the query.

B. Matching

The aim of matching is to determine the confidence that a term in a document is relevant to that document in the context of the query. If a query term occurs in a document and it occurs in the context of the query, then it is considered to be important and given a high confidence.

Given a term q and a set of terms that constitute a context C (i.e. Q or QR), then the *contextual importance* (CI) of the occurrence of q in document D can be calculated:

$$CI_{q,C,D} = \frac{\sum_{c \in C} \text{Dist}(CD_{q,c,D}) \times R_c}{\sum_{c \in C} R_c} \quad (2)$$

where c is a term in the context C, $CD_{q,c,D}$ is the minimum distance between all of the occurrences of q and c in D. Distance is measured by counting the number of word separating q from c (this is calculated using term position information stored in the index). R_c is the relatedness of c (see Section 2.1), $\text{Dist}(CD_{q,c,D})$ is a membership function of distance importance that returns a value in the range [1,0]. The smaller $CD_{q,c,D}$ is the closer $\text{Dist}(CD_{q,c,D})$ will be to 1. This function can be either of type Gaussian, hard limiter, or linear.

For each query term q, the technique generates contextual importance using both the original query Q and related terms QR as contexts. The final measure is the *context matching confidence* (CMC), which is a combination of the CI from both sub-contexts. Given a query term q in the query Q, its CMC is calculated as follows:

$$CMC_{q,D} = (CI_{q,Q,D} \times wl) + (CI_{q,QR,D} \times (1 - wl)) \quad (3)$$

where wl is a weighting factor that is set to 0.5 by default. The resultant CMC is a value in the range [0,1] where a value close to 1 indicates a high confidence that the term q occurring in document D is an important indicator of relevance for D given Q.

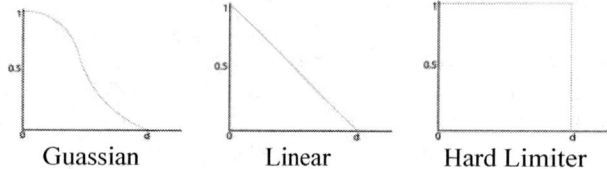

Figure 1. Distance functions for Dist(*CD*).

C. Combining CMC and TF

Given that matching has been performed and we have a CMC value for a term q in a document D, the final step of the technique is to combine CMC with TF to give a final term confidence measure.

TF is calculated as follows:

$$TF_{q,D} = \frac{\log(count_q + 1)}{\log(numWords_D + 1)} \quad (4)$$

where $count_q$ is the number of times q occurred in D, and $numWords_D$ is the number of terms in document D. Having both $TF_{q,D}$ and $CMC_{q,D}$, the term confidence TC of q in D is calculated by

$$TC_{q,D} = (TF_{q,D} \times w2) + (CMC_{q,D} \times (1-w2)) \quad (5)$$

where $w2$ is a weighting factor that is set to 0.5 by default.

III. Parameter Optimization

In a recent study by Billerbeck et al [18], they discovered that the selection of ideal parameters for query expansion is a difficult task. They raise questions as to whether optimal parameters can actually be tuned at all for certain types of queries. Our research, in part, is related to the issues investigated by Billerbeck et al as we explore possibilities for determining ideal parameters for query expansion / context matching through the use of an evolutionary algorithm and manual combinations. The context matching parameters considered for optimization are d, m, n and $Dist(CD)$ as introduced in the previous section.

A. Evolutionary Algorithm

An evolutionary algorithm is used for selecting the ideal parameters. Each individual in the population represents a candidate set of parameters:
- d is an integer value between 1 and 65535,
- m is an integer between 1 and 20,
- $Dist(CD)$ is a value that can be:
    0 (Gaussian), 1 (hard limiter) or 2 (linear),
- n is an integer between 1 to 50.

1-point crossover with the crossover rate 0.9 is used in all the experiments. The mutation for every parameter in the individual is performed separately with mutation rate of 0.02. For mutation of parameter d, a random integer value between 1 and 10 is added or subtracted. Parameter m and $Dist(CD)$ are mutated by adding or subtracting a value 1, Mutation for parameter n is performed by adding or subtracting a value between 1 and 5.

The roulette wheel selection strategy is used in the algorithm for parameter selection. The fitness of the chromosome is calculated according to the average precision produced by the evolved parameter set.

There were 30 individuals in each population. At the very start of the algorithm, 29 of these individuals were initialized randomly and the remaining member was set with the parameters discovered to be most effective through the trial of different combinations (see next section). This was done to give the evolutionary algorithm a better idea as to what is a good combination of parameters, instead of requiring it to start with a full random set of individuals.

The fitness of an individual is determined through calculating the retrieval effectiveness (average precision) for the run using the set of parameters specified by that individual.

The evolutionary algorithm stops processing after no or little change in the average fitness of a population over a number of successive populations.

B. Manual Combinations of Parameters

We wanted to test the effectiveness of the technique by iteratively experimenting with different combinations distance functions $Dist(CD)$ and varying the parameters distance d and number of terms m. For each experiment d was set to 10, 30, 50, 100, 250, 1000 or 65535 and m was set to 3, 5, 10 or 20. We ran experiments with all combinations of these values for d, m and $Dist(CD)$. For all these experiments, $n=20$ to retrieve the top ranked documents of the initial for query expansion/context generation. This resulted in 84 different combinations of parameters settings. If we were to explore for various values of n or finer values of parameters, then the number of combinations of parameters would of unrealistically been in the hundreds or thousands.

IV. Experimental Setup

Ad-hoc retrieval experiments were run on the TREC benchmark web document collection WT2g, which consists of 247,491 web documents along with 50 queries with corresponding relevance judgments. A standard inverted index was used to index the collection and each node in the index stored a document ID, TF and each position of the term in the document.

Given a query Q, the retrieval function used to calculate the score for document D is

$$score_{D,Q} = \sum_{q \in Q} TC_{q,D} \times IDF_q \quad (6)$$

where q is a term in the query, $TC_{q,D}$ is the term confidence of term q in document D and IDF_q is the inverse document frequency of q:

$$IDF_q = \log_2 \frac{N}{n_q} + 1 \quad (7)$$

where N is the number of documents in the collection and n_q is the number of documents in which term q occurs.

To obtain a list of initial documents from which the query expansion technique could extract related terms for QR, standard TFxIDF was used:

$$score_{D,Q} = \sum_{q \in Q} TF_{q,D} \times IDF_q \quad (8)$$

This run also acts as the baseline for comparison against all other runs. The top 1000 documents are used to evaluate retrieval effectiveness by calculating average precision, precision at 20 and number of relevant documents retrieved.

V. Results and Analysis

The main focus of this research was to ascertain the most ideal parameters for m, d, $Dist(CD)$ and n and compare the effectiveness of parameters given by the evolutionary algorithm to that of manual combinations. But we also wanted to make comparisons context matching against the baseline performance and other systems.

Table 1. Result of the baseline run.

Avg. Prec.	Prec. @ 20	#Rel. Docs
0.2987	0.346	1775

Table 1 shows the result of the baseline run, which uses Equation 8 for retrieval. We can see that an average precision of 0.2987 was achieved.

Table 2 shows the best 10 results of CM for combinations of parameters selected manually, which uses Equation 6 for retrieval. The best run which uses $m = 10$, $d = 250$ and a linear distance function, achieves an average precision of 0.4142, 38.68% better than the baseline run. Infact, all CM runs comfortably outperformed the baseline run.

The worse performing CM run was when $m = 3$, $d = 65535$ using a hard limiter distance function. This is not surprising at all as 3 terms do not provide much contextual information and 65535 positions is an extremely large context area to be considering during matching. This run though still achieved an average precision of 0.3428 and outperforms the baseline by 14.75%.

All of the top 10 results shown in Table 2 utilized 5 or more terms for context at a distance of 250 or less. Also, most of them utilized linear or Gaussian functions for distance. This confirms that observation that terms appearing in a close context to each other are a good indicator of significance. The linear and Gaussian functions capture this by rewarding smaller distances with a value closer to 1, where as the hard limiter distance function ignores with its constant return value for all values smaller than d.

Table 3 shows the results of the 10 best performing combination of parameters given by the evolutionary algorithm. Each combination set here represents an individual in the population. When initializing the population, one of the individuals was set with the best set of parameters ($m = 10$, $d = 250$, linear distance function, $n = 20$) observed from the

Table 2. Top 10 manual combinations of parameters for context matching.

m	d	$Dist(CD)$	n	Avg. Prec.	% Δ	Prec. @ 20	#Rel. Docs
10	250	Linear	20	0.4142	+38.68%	0.417	1864
5	100	Linear	20	0.4137	+38.49%	0.420	1864
5	250	Gaussian	20	0.4136	+38.47%	0.433	1853
10	100	Linear	20	0.4135	+38.44%	0.417	1864
10	250	Gaussian	20	0.4130	+38.27%	0.416	1858
5	250	Linear	20	0.4125	+38.10%	0.432	1859
5	100	Gaussian	20	0.4112	+37.66%	0.420	1869
20	250	Linear	20	0.4097	+37.15%	0.417	1861
10	100	Gaussian	20	0.4095	+37.09%	0.415	1867
20	100	Linear	20	0.4092	+37.00%	0.410	1869

Table 3. Optimal 10 combinations of parameters for context matching from evolutionary algorithm.

m	d	$Dist(CD)$	n	Avg. Prec.	% Δ	Prec. @ 20	#Rel. Docs
7	255	Linear	20	0.4190	+40.27%	0.430	1860
7	250	Linear	20	0.4189	+40.25%	0.427	1859
6	255	Linear	20	0.4168	+39.55%	0.432	1859
11	250	Linear	20	0.4163	+39.36%	0.415	1863
10	250	Linear	20	0.4142	+38.67%	0.417	1864
11	260	Linear	20	0.4142	+38.66%	0.416	1865
10	250	Gaussian	16	0.4103	+37.36%	0.412	1858
6	551	Linear	20	0.4101	+37.31%	0.433	1870
6	560	Linear	20	0.4094	+37.07%	0.433	1872
11	551	Linear	20	0.4078	+36.53%	0.421	1862

previous set of experiments with manual combination. The evolutionary algorithm ran for 73 generations, producing a total of 30x73=2190 prospective individuals during the evolutionary process.

The fittest individual achieved an average precision of 0.4190 with $m = 7$, $d = 255$, a linear distance function and $n = 20$. This is approximately 1.6% better than the best performing result obtained through manual selection of parameters that achieved an average precision of 0.4142.

The most significant difference between best sets performing parameters for evolutionary algorithm vs. manual combination is:

1. The evolutionary algorithm found that a value for m of 6 or 7 was most effective.
2. The linear distance dominated the evolutionary algorithm results as the most ideal distance function.
3. A distance of 560 can be an effective distance value. There was no manual combination that explored this range for distance d, but it was found to contribute to effective retrieval by the evolutionary algorithm.
4. This is mostly consistent with the results obtained through the manual setting of parameters as shown in Table 2.

The evolutionary algorithm can optimize the parameter set very efficiently. Looking at Figure 2, we can see that after just 20 generations the overall population fitness had reached a relatively high state. By about 65 generations, the fitness plateaus and an *optimal* state has been achieved. This is in contrast to the potentially thousands of iterations that would be needed to fully exhaust parameter settings with manual combinations.

Figure 2 also shows the variation of the minimum fitness value of an individual in a population across generations. It is interesting to observe how the minimum and average lines roughly correlate and the minimum tends emphasizes lulls in the average line. As is desirable, both lines follow a continuous upward path toward higher precisions across the number of generations that were processed.

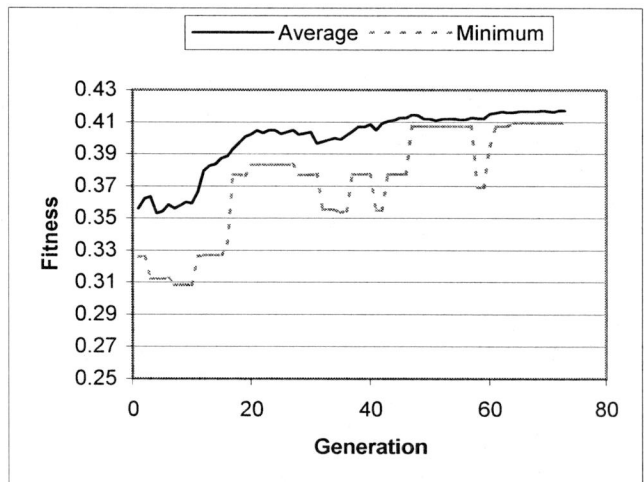

Figure 2. Average and minimum fitness of population across generations.

The first chromosome with a fitness better than the best result obtained by manual combination occurred at generation 29. This is the fourth best evolutionary algorithm result that achieved an average precision of 0.4163 with $m = 11$, $d = 250$, a linear distance function and $n = 20$. The most unfit individual occurred during generation 2 at a fitness of 0.3082 with $m = 2$, $d = 28848$, a hard limiter distance function and $n = 48$.

The previous best performing system on the same benchmark data was that of Microsoft that achieved an average precision of 0.3829 at TREC 8 [19]. It used OKAPI weighting and traditional query expansion in a content-based only retrieval approach. The CM technique outperforms this by 9.42% with its top performing result of 0.4190 given by the evolutionary algorithm. This obviously is a very encouraging result especially since these results are preliminary and with future research still to be performed to advance the technique even more.

VI. Conclusion

We have proposed an evolutionary algorithm based approach to optimally tune the parameters of a context matching technique for effective web information retrieval. We have shown how an evolutionary algorithm can be effectively used to find the most optimal parameters for context matching.

The proposed approach has been implemented and tested on the TREC benchmark web document collection WT2g. The results obtained using the evolutionary approach are much better than a simple exhaustive exploration of manual combinations of parameters.

In future research, we plan to investigate the evolutionary optimization of values for $w1$ and $w2$ to ascertain the ideal parameters for combination and better understand the significance of the CMC vs. TF.

Also, we plan to investigate the use of sentences as a unit of distance, rather than term position. Finally, we will investigate assigning terms weighted relatedness values in the range [0,1] to potentially make CM more effective.

Acknowledgement

This research has been partially funded by Central Queensland University (CQU) under its merit grant scheme. Authors would like to thank CQU for supporting this research.

References

[1] A. Trotman, "Choosing Document Structure Weights," Information Processing and Management, vol. 41, pp. 243-264, 2005.

[2] S. Kim and B. Zhang, "Genetic Mining of HTML Structures for Effective Web-Document Retrieval," Applied Intelligence, vol. 18, no. 3, pp. 243-256, 2003.

[3] M. Boughanem, C. Chrisment and L. Tamine, "On using Genetic Algorithms for Multimodal Relevance Optimization in Information Retrieval," Journal of the American Society for Information Science and Technology, vol. 53, no. 11, pp. 934–942, 2002.

[4] J. Horng, & C. Yeh. "Applying Genetic Algorithms to Query Optimization in Document Retrieval." Information Processing & Management, vol. 36, no. 5, pp. 737–759, 2000.

[5] D. Vrajitoru, "Large Population or Many Generations for Genetic Algorithms? Implications in Information Retrieval," Soft Computing in Information Retrieval. Techniques and Applications, pp. 199–222. Physica-Verlag, 2000.

[6] M. Gordon, "Probabilistic and Genetic Algorithms in Document Retrieval," Communications of the ACM, vol. 31, no. 10, pp. 1208–1218, 1998.

[7] J. Morgan and A. Kilgour, "Personalising On-line Information Retrieval Support with a Genetic Algorithm," Poly-Model 16: Applications of Artificial Intelligence, pp. 142–149, 1996.

[8] H. Chen, "Machine Learning for Information Retrieval: Neural Networks, Symbolic Learning, and Genetic Algorithms," Journal of the American Society for Information Science, vil. 46, no. 3, 194–216, 1995.

[9] T. Tsikrika and M. Lalmas, "Combining Evidence for Web Retrieval Using the Inference Network Model: An Experimental Study," Information Processing and Management, vol. 40, pp. 751–772, 2004.

[10] T. Honkela, S. Kaski, K. Lagus and T. Kohonen, "WEBSOM - Self-Organizing Maps of Document Collections," in Proceedings of WSOM'97 (Workshop on Self-Organizing Maps), Espoo, Finland, pp. 310-315, 1997.

[11] N. Vlajic and H. Card, "Categorizing Web Pages on the Subject of Neural Networks," Elsevier Science Journal of Network and Computer Applications, vol. 21, no. 2, pp. 91-105, 1999.

[12] H. Luhn, "A Statistical Approach to Mechanized Encoding and Searching of Literary In formation," IBM Journal of Research and Development, vol. 1, no. 4, pp. 309-317, 1957.

[13] R. Baeza-Yates and B. Ribeiro-Neto, "Modern Information Retrieval," Addison Wesley, New York, 1999.

[14] H. Jing and E. Tzoukermann, "Information retrieval based on context distance and morphology," in Proceedings of the 22nd Annual International ACM SIGIR Conference on Research and Development in information Retrieval, pp. 90-96, 1999.

[15] H. Billhardt, D. Borrajo and V. Maojo, " A Context Vector Model for Information Retrieval," Journal of the American Society for Information Science and Technology, vol. 53, no. 3, pp. 236 – 249, 2002.

[16] J. Xu and B. Croft, "Query Expansion Using Local and Global Document Analysis," in Proceedings of the Nineteenth Annual International ACM SIGIR Conference on Research and Development in Information Retrieval, pp. 4-11, 1996.

[17] S. Walker, S. Robertson, M. Boughanem, G. Jones and K. Sparck Jones, "Okapi at TREC-6 Automatic ad hoc, VLC, routing, filtering and QSDR," in Proceedings of the Sixth Text Retrieval Conference (TREC-6), Gaithersburg, USA, pp. 125-136, 1997.

[18] B. Billerbeck and J. Zobel, "Questioning Query Expansion: An Examination of Behaviour and Parameters", in Proceedings of the Australasian Database Conference, Dunedin, New Zealand, vol. 27, pp. 69-76, 2004.

[19] S. Robertson and S. Walker, "Okapi/Keenbow at TREC-8," in Proceedings of the Eighth Text Retrieval Conference (TREC-8), Gaithersburg, USA, pp. 151-161, 1999.

Snap-drift learning for Phrase Recognition

Sin Wee Lee
Computational Intelligence Group
School of Computing
Leeds Metropolitan University,
Headingley Campus, Beckett Park,
Leeds LS6 3QS, United Kingdom.
s.w.lee@leedsmet.ac.uk

Dominic Palmer-Brown
School of Computing and Technology
University of East London
Longbridge Road
Barking,
London, UK
d.palmer-brown@uel.ac.uk

Abstract— This paper presents a new application of the *snap-drift* algorithm [1]: phrase recognition using a set of phrases from the *Lancaster Parsed Corpus (LPC)* [2]. The learning algorithm is the *classifier* version of *snap-drift*. In this version, along with the complementary concepts of fast minimalist learning (*snap*) and slow *drift* towards the input pattern, each node of the Snap-Drift Neural Network (SDNN) swaps between snap and drift modes when declining performance is indicated on that particular node. This method enables the SDNN to learn at node level, in the sense that each node has its learning mode toggled independently of the other nodes. Learning on each node is also reinforced by enabling learning with a probability that decreases with increasing performance. The simulations demonstrate that learning is stable, and the results have consistently shown similar classification performance and advantages in terms of speed in comparison with a Multilayer Perceptron (MLP) and back-propagation [3, 4] applied to the same problem.

I. INTRODUCTION

Phrase recognition has long been a well-defined and well known application and a benchmark for testing the performance for neural networks in the field of Natural Language Processing [NLP] [5-7]. The availability of different corpora, such as the Lancaster Parsed Corpus [LPC] has provided valuable data for machine learning.

A. Adaptive Resonance Theory

Adaptive Resonance was introduced by Stephen Grossberg [8, 9]. More recent developments have led to various types of ART networks: ART1 [10] self-organises recognition categories for arbitrary sequences of binary input sequences; ART2, does the same for either binary or analogue inputs [11]. Subsequently, instantiations and developments of the theory, such as ART3 [12] have been used to implement parallel searches of compressed or distributed recognition codes (output categories) in a neural network hierarchy. Following the successful implementation of the theory in real-time applications, further development has seen the creation of ART2-A [13], which is 2 or 3 orders of magnitude faster than ART2. The fuzzy extension of ART, Fuzzy ART [14], incorporated computations from fuzzy set theory into the ART1 architecture. Extensions to ART networks to allow supervised learning were also introduced [15]. ARTMAP [16] and Fuzzy ARTMAP [17] autonomously learn to classify based on predictive success; and there are several other versions of ART network [18-20], including supervised multi-layer, self-growing systems [15], [21].

B. Motivations

The *snap-drift* learning algorithm first emerged as an attempt to overcome the limitations of ART learning in non-stationary environments where self-organisation needs to take account of periodic or occasional performance feedback. Since then, the *snap-drift* algorithm has proved invaluable for continuous learning in several applications. The *reinforcement* versions [22, 23] of *snap-drift* are used in the classification of user requests in an active computer network simulation environment whereby the system is able to discover alternative solutions in response to varying performance requirements. Furthermore, the *unsupervised snap-drift* algorithm, without any form of reinforcement, has been used in the analysis and interpretation of data representing interactions between trainee network managers and a simulated network management system [24]. New patterns of the user behaviour were discovered.

The unsupervised version of *snap-drift* has also been used in feature discovery and clustering of speech waveforms from non-stammering and stammering speakers. Phonetically meaningful properties of non-stammering and stammering speech are discovered, and rapid automatic classification of into stammering and non-stammering speech is possible.

This paper describes the further exploration of *snap-drift*, in the form of a classifier, in attempting to discover and recognize phrases extracted from LPC. Comparisons carried out between *snap-drift* and MLP with back-propagation will be presented, showing that the former is faster and just as effective.

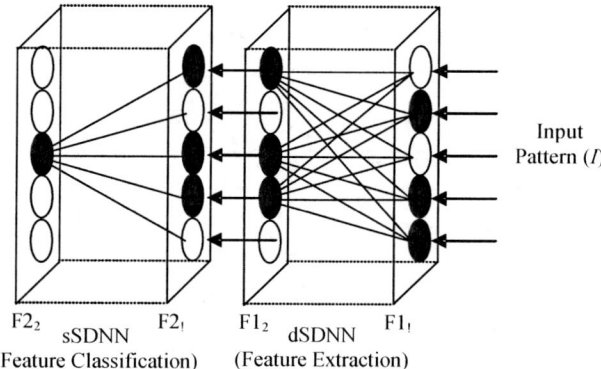

Fig. 1. SDNN Architecture

II. THE SNAP-DRIFT NEURAL NETWORK (SDNN)

The modular neural network, modified from the performance-guided Adaptive Resonance Theory (P-ART) network first introduced by Lee and Palmer-Brown [1], is shown in Fig. 1.

On presentation of an input patterns at the input layer $F0_1$, distributed SDNN (dSDNN) will learn to group them according to their general features using *snap-drift*. In this case, the five $F2_1$ nodes (D=5) whose weight prototypes best match the current input pattern, are used as the input data to the selection SDNN (sSDNN) module for the purposes of feature classification. In both of the SDNN modules, the standard matching and reset mechanism of ART [10, 25] is discarded. Instead, in the dSDNN module, the output nodes with the highest net input are *always* accepted as winners. In the sSDNN module, a quality assurance threshold is introduced. If the net input of a sSDNN node is above the threshold, the output node is accepted as the winner, otherwise a new uncommitted output node will be recruited as the winner and initialised with the current input pattern.

In this *classifier* version of SDNN, the performance is calculated separately for each sSDNN node, and is the proportion of times in which its activation as winner contributes to successful classifications. Together with the probabilistic aspect to enhance reinforcement and stability, introduced in [23], the main purpose of node level performance calculation is to enable the sSDNN to retain the learning of nodes with successful adaptation, by continuing learning with the same learning mode if the node performance has increased since the last performance update. Alternatively, if the performance of a particular node decreased since the last epoch, or since the last epoch it was selected as a winner for learning of an input pattern, the learning mode of that particular sSDNN node will be swapped to the alternative learning node to encourage re-learning to occur in order to improve the performance of the node. This is also applied to the dSDNN nodes where the sSDNN inputs are generated. Thus, the learning mode of each of the sSDNN output nodes varies during each learning epoch. The following is a summary of the steps that occur in SDNN:

Step 1: Initialise parameters for each node: ($\alpha = 1$, $\sigma = 0$), epochs = 500, D=5

Step 2: For each epoch (t)

    Measure or calculate the performance of each sSDNN node over the last epoch, $P_{sSDNN}(t)$

    Set probability of learning on that node, PL = 1 − $P_{sSDNN}(t)$

Step 2.1: Find the D winning nodes at $F1_2$ with the largest net input.

Step 2.2: Process the output patterns of $F1_2$ as input pattern of $F2_1$.

Step 2.3: Find the node at $F2_2$ with the largest net input.

Step 2.4: Test the threshold condition:

    IF (the net input of the node is greater than the threshold)

    THEN

    Test: **Learning Mode Selection** condition

    Weights of the dSDNN and sSDNN output nodes are adapted according to the **Learning Mode Selection.**

    ELSE

    An uncommitted sSDNN is selected and its weights are adapted with ($\alpha = 1$, $\sigma = 0$).

Learning Mode Selection condition:

    IF ($P_{sSDNN}(t) < P_{sSDNN}(t-1)$)

    Weights of dSDNN and sSDNN output nodes are adapted with probability PL using the alternative learning procedure: (α, σ) becomes inverse(α, σ) for the node.

    ELSE

    Weights of dSDNN and sSDNN output nodes are adapted with probability PL, using the same learning procedure for the node as in epoch (t − 1): (α, σ).

III. THE SNAP-DRIFT ALGORITHM

The learning algorithm uses a novel combination of a modified form of Adaptive Resonance Theory (*snap*) [10] and Learning Vector Quantisation *(drift)* [26]. In simple terms, the basis of the snap-drift weight update algorithm can be stated as:

$$Snap\text{-}Drift = \alpha(Fast\_Learning\_ART) + \sigma(LVQ) \quad (1)$$

The top-down learning of both of the modules in the neural system is as follows:

$$w_{Ji}^{(new)} = \alpha(I \cap w_{Ji}^{(old)}) + \sigma(w_{Ji}^{(old)} + \beta(I - w_{Ji}^{(old)})) \quad (2)$$

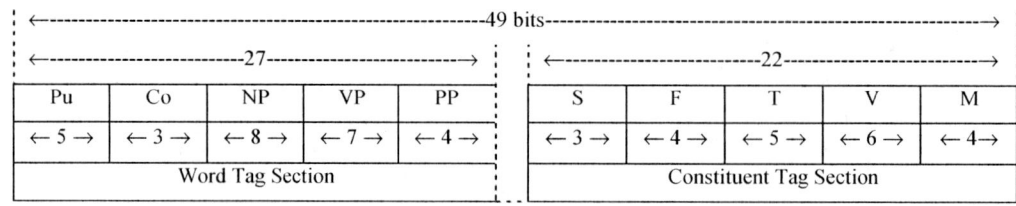

Fig. 2 Input Field Representation

where w_{Ji} = top-down weights vectors; I = binary input vectors, and β = the drift speed constant = 0.5.

When $\alpha = 1$, fast, minimalist (snap) learning is invoked:

$$w_{Ji}^{(new)} = I \cap w_{Ji}^{(old)} \quad (3)$$

In contrast, when $\sigma = 1$, (2) simplifies to:

$$w_{Ji}^{(new)} = w_{Ji}^{(old)} + \beta (I - w_{Ji}^{(old)}) \quad (4)$$

which causes a simple form of clustering at a speed determined by β. The bottom-up learning of the neural system is simply a normalised version of the top-down learning.

$$w_{iJ}^{(new)} = w_{Ji}^{(new)} / |w_{Ji}^{(new)}| \quad (5)$$

where $w_{iJ}^{(new)}$ = top-down weights of the network after learning.

IV. THE SDNN SIMULATION

A. Lancaster Parsed Corpus (LPC)

The LPC is a corpus of English sentences and is a subset of the Lancaster/Oslo-Bergen Corpus (LOB). Each word is tagged with its syntactic category and each sentence in the LPC has undergone syntactic analysis in the form of labeled bracketing. In the simulations, a subset of samples from the LPC used in [3] is adopted for the sake of comparison.

B. Input Representation

The design of the input patterns is according to the structure of the pre-tagged corpus [2]. This is achieved by separating the input space into several regions where each corresponds to a different symbol type. For the input set used in SDNN, there are 9 groups of symbol type, represented by separate fields in the input vector.

A total of 49 bits are used to encode all the symbol types. Fig. 2 shows the 10 input fields of an input vector. The terminal symbol groups are: punctuation (Pu), conjunction (Co), nouns (NP), verbs (VP) and prepositions (PP). The non-terminal symbol groups are Sentences (S), Finite clauses (F), Non-finite clauses (T), major phrase types (V) and minor phrase types (M). Together with 4 *Look Back* symbols and 1 *Look Ahead* symbol [3], this makes the total number of input fields = 15. By using linear binary coding for each symbol type within each input field, the input size of the SDNN is 49 x 15 = 735. With the available Pre-tagged sentences in, we generate 254 input patterns, from all stages of parsing, typically involving mixtures of terminal and non-terminal symbols.

C. Training and Test Inputs

Half of the input set (127) is used to train the SDNN. During each epoch, 10 input patterns out of the 127 training inputs are randomly selected after which the performance of each sSDNN node and overall system performance are calculated. After 500 epochs, the SDNN is tested.

There are 2 types of test input: *Natural* Test inputs, consist of a mixture of training and new input patterns that SDNN never encountered before (154 patterns); and *Pure* test data, which consists only of input patterns that SDNN has never encountered before (89 patterns). Table I shows the number of input patterns for each symbol type.

TABLE I

Symbol Type	Symbol and Description	No. of Input
Minor Phrase	E = Label used for existential 'there'	2
Major Phrase	J = An adjective phrase	4
	N = A noun phrase	83
	Na = A noun phrase marked as subject of the verb	16
	P = A prepositional phrase	14
	Po = A prepositional phrase beginning with preposition 'of'	8
	R = An adverb phrase	12
	Rq = an adverb phrase beginning with a wh-word, e.g. 'How dp you feel?' or 'How long'	1
	V = A finite 'verb phrase' i.e. one that exclude objects, complements	49
	Vi = Non-finite verb phrase	5
Sentence	S = Sentence	50
	S& = Compound sentence	2
	S+ = Subsequent conjoin of compound sentence	2
Non-finite and Verbless Clause	Ti = To-infinitive clause	4

TABLE II

Epoch	Average Performance (%)
1 – 50	70.67
51 – 100	69.89
101 – 150	75.43
151 – 200	83.25
201 – 250	82.34
251 – 300	91.78
301 – 350	93.45
350 – 400	92.98
401 – 450	94.87

TABLE III

Network Type	Total No. of input	No. of patterns per epoch	No. of epochs	Total no. of patterns presentation	No. of hidden layer nodes	No. of corresponding Tags	Correct Classifications	Overall performance (%)
MLP connectionist parser phrase recogniser	2588 (TD)	2588	800	2070400	50	72	-	-
	2765 (ND)	-	-	-	50	72	2461	89.01
	2433 (PD)	-	-	-	50	72	2132	87.63
SDNN	**127 (TD)**	**10**	**~250**	**2500**	**50**	**14**	**119**	**93.47**
	154 (ND)	-	-	-	**50**	**14**	**138**	**89.65**
	89 (PD)	-	-	-	**50**	**14**	**78**	**86.98**
Back propagation	127 (TD)	127	~128	16256	50	14	125	98.76
	154 (ND)	-	-	-	50	14	135	87.80
	89 (PD)	-	-	-	50	14	74	83.05

A. Simulation 1: Results and Discussions

In simulation 1, we looked at the average performance improvement that can be achieved by using the whole set of available input patterns to train the SDNN. Table II shows the results of the simulation, where it is shown that after just 150 epochs, SDNN is able to achieve an average performance of 75%, and after ~300 training epochs, SDNN has achieved an overall performance of average 94%, and has converged.

B. Comparisons between Snap-Drift and MLP with Back-Propagation

Table III shows the comparison between the results from the MLP connectionist parser phrase recognizer [3], the SDNN, and a simple back-propagation network. The results from each of the neural networks can be divided into 3: results during training (TD), results from testing using *Natural* test data (ND) and results from testing using just *Pure* test data (PD).

By comparing the results between SDNN and a simple back-propagation network, with both using the same set of data, we can see that SDNN has obvious advantages in the speed of learning. During training, the SDNN network only required 2500 randomly selected training data to achieve a performance of 93%, whilst back-propagation required 6 times the number of input presentations to achieve performance of 98%. During testing, SDNN correctly classifies 4 more patterns than MLP, This is not a clearly statistically significant difference in performance, but it is, taken over many simulations, clear evidence of comparable performance between the two approaches. Furthermore, the main reason why SDNN and the backpropagation network are unable to achieve maximum performance is mainly to do with the number of input patterns for each of the symbols, which varies greatly and is insufficient in some cases. For example, symbols E, S& and S+ only have 2 input patterns corresponding to them. Chance disctates that all of the input patterns may happen to be used exclusively as either testing or training data. When these inputs are selected for testing, e.g. S+ and S&, unsurprisingly they tend to be recognized as S.

If we compare SDNN results with the MLP connectionist parser phrase recognizer that uses a much larger set of inputs, 20 times larger than the one used by SDNN, that phrase recognizer required 100 times more input presentations which is about 5 times more for each input pattern to be learnt.

C. Conclusions and Future Work

In conclusion, the *snap-drift* algorithm has shown potential in phrase recognition. The results show the learning of the SDNN is fast, stable and reliable in recognizing the input patterns and is able to group them according to their internal structure. This is still the preliminary stage of the research into this application, but comparisons with results achieved by an MLP with back-propagation on the same task have shown that SDNN has the right dynamics and capability to equal if not better the MLP, and at a higher speed. The next stage will be applying SDNN with a larger set of input patterns to see how it scales up in this task

REFERENCES

[1] S. W. Lee, D. Palmer-Brown and C. M. Roadknight, "Performance-guided Neural Network for Rapidly Self-Organising Active Network Management," *Neurocomputing*, Vol. 61C, 2004, pp. 5 – 20.

[2] R. Garside, G. Leech and T. Varadi, *Manual of Information to Accompany the Lancaster Parsed Corpus*: Department of English, University of Oslo, 1987.

[3] J. Tepper, H. M. Powell and D. Palmer-Brown, "A Corpus-based connectionist Architecture for Large-scale Natural Language Parsing," *Connection Science*, Vol. 14, No. 2, 2002, pp. 93 – 114.

[4] D. E. Rumelhart, G. E. Hinton and R. J. William, "Learning Representation by Back-Propagation Error," in *Parallel Distributed Processing, Explorations in the Microstructure of Cognition, Vol. 1: Foundations*, D. E. Rumelhart and J. L. McClelland, eds., MIT Press, 1986, pp. 318 – 362.

[5] Marshall R. Mayberry, III, and Risto Miikkulainen, "SARDSRN: A Neural Network Shift-Reduce Parser," *Proceedings of the 16th IJCAI*, 1999, Stockholm, Sweden, pp. 820-825.

[6] S. Das, C. L. Giles and G. Z. Sun, "Learning Context-Free Grammars: Capabilities and Limitations of a Recurrent Neural Network with an External Stack Memory," *Proceedings of the 4th Annual Conference of the Cognitive Science Society*, 1992, pp. 791-796.

[7] J. N. Rushton, "Natural Language Parsing using Simple Neural Networks," *Proceedings of ICAI*, 2003.

[8] S. Grossberg, "Adaptive Pattern Classification and Universal Recoding. I. Parallel Development and Coding of Neural Feature Detectors," *Biol. Cybern.*, Vol. 23, 1976, pp. 121 - 134.

[9] S. Grossberg, "Adaptive Pattern Classification and Universal Recoding. II. Feedback, Expectation, Olfaction, and Illusions," *Biol. Cybern.*, Vol. 23, 1976, pp. 187 - 202.

[10] G. A. Carpenter and S. Grossberg, "A Massively Parallel Architecture for a Self-Organising Neural Pattern Recognition Machine," *Computer Vision, Graphics and Image Processing*, Vol. 37, 1987, pp. 54-115.

[11] G. A. Carpenter and S. Grossberg, "ART2: Self-Organization of Stable Category Recognition Codes for Analogue Pattern, *Applied Optics*," Vol. 26, 1987, pp. 4919 -4930.

[12] G. A. Carpenter and S. Grossberg, "ART 3: Hierarchical Search Using Chemical Transmitter in Self-Organizing Pattern Recognition Architectures," *Neural Networks*, Vol. 3, No. 4, 1990, pp. 129 - 152.

[13] G. A. Carpenter, S. Grossberg and D.B. Rosen, "ART 2-A: An Adaptive Resonance Algorithm for Rapid Category Learning and Recognition," *Neural Networks*, Vol. 4, 1991, pp. 493 - 504.

[14] G. A. Carpenter, S. Grossberg, and D. B. Rosen, "Fuzzy ART: Fast Stable Learning and Categorization of Analogue Pattern by an Adaptive Resonance System," *Neural Networks*, Vol. 4, 1991, pp. 759 - 771.

[15] D. Palmer-Brown, "High Speed Learning in a Supervised, Self Growing Net," in *1992 Proc. ICANN*, Vol. 2, pp. 1159-1162.

[16] G. A. Carpenter, S. Grossberg, and J. H. Reynold, "ARTMAP: Supervised Real-Time Learning and Classification of Nonstationary Data by a Self-Organizing Neural Networks," *Neural Networks*, Vol. 4, 1991, pp. 565 - 588.

[17] G. A. Carpenter, S. Grossberg, A. Markuzon, J. H. Reynold, and D. B. Rosen, "Fuzzy ARTMAP: A Neural Network Architecture for Incremental Supervised Learning of Analogue Multidimensional Maps," *IEEE Trans. Neural Network*, Vol. 3, No. 5, 1992, pp. 698 - 713.

[18] A-H Tan, "Cascade ARTMAP: Integrating Neural Computation and Symbolic Knowledge Processing," *IEEE Trans. Neural Networks*, Vol. 8, No. 2, 1997, pp. 237 – 250.

[19] G. A. Carpenter, B. Milenova, and B. Noeske, "dARTMAP: A Neural Network for Fast Distributed Supervised Learning," *Neural Networks*, Vol. 11, 1998, pp. 793 – 813.

[20] G. Bartfai, and R. White, "Incremental Learning and Optimization of Hierarchical Clustering with ART-based Modular Networks," in *Innovations in ART Neural Networks*, L. C. Jain, B. Lazzerini, and U. Halici, Eds. Physica-Verlag, 2000, pp. 87 – 132.

[21] S. Barker, H. Powell, and D. Palmer-Brown, "Size Invariant Attention Focusing (with ANNs)", in *1996 Proc. Int. Symp. Multi-Technology Information Processing*.

[22] S. W. Lee, D. Palmer-Brown, J. Tepper, and C. M. Roadknight, "Snap-Drift: Real-time Performance-guided Learning," *Proceedings of IJCNN*, 2003, Portland, Oregon, Vol. 2, pp. 1412 – 1416.

[23] S. W. Lee, D. Palmer-Brown and C. M. Roadknight, "Reinforced Snap-Drift Learning for Proxylet Selection in Active Computer Networks," *Proceedings of IJCNN*, 2004, Budapest, Hungary, Vol. 2, pp. 1545 – 1550.

[24] H. Donelan, C. Pattinson, D. Palmer-Brown and S. W. Lee, "The Analysis of Network Manager's Behaviour using a Self-Organising Neural Networks," *Proceedings of ESM*, Magdeburg, Germany, 2004, pp. 111 – 116..

[25] G. A. Carpenter, and S. Grossberg, "Search Mechanism for Adaptive Resonance Theory (ART) Architecture," *Proceedings of IJCNN*, 1989, Vol. I, pp. 201 – 205.

[26] T. Kohonen, "Improved Versions of Learning Vector Quantization," *Proceedings of IJCNN*, 1990, Vol. 1, pp. 545 – 550.

An Adaptive Function Neural Network(ADFUNN) for Phrase Recognition

Miao Kang
Computational Intelligence Research Group
School of Computing
Leeds Metropolitan University
Leeds LS6 3QS, United Kingdom
E-mail: m.kang@leedsmet.ac.uk

Dominic Palmer-Brown
School of Computing and Technology
University of East London
Longbridge Road Barking
London, United Kindom
E-mail: d.palmer-brown@uel.ac.uk

Abstract—We describe an adaptive function neural network (ADFUNN) [1], and apply it to the natural language processing task of phrase recognition. ADFUNN is based on a linear piecewise neuron activation function that is modified by a novel gradient descent supervised learning algorithm. Linearly inseparable problems can be learned with ADFUNN, rapidly and without hidden neurons. We perform phrase recognition on a set of phrases from the Lancaster Parsed Corpus (LPC) [2]. Generalisation rises to 100% with 150 training patterns (out of a total of 254).

I. Motivation

The artificial neuron derives from a joint biological-computational perspective. Summing weighted inputs is biologically plausible, and adapting a weight is a reasonable model for a modifiable synapse. But the common assumption that the output activation function is fixed is for computational rather than biological reasons. A fixed analytical function facilitates mathematical analysis to a greater degree than an empirical one. Nonetheless, there are some computational benefits to modifiable activation functions, and they may be biologically plausible as well. Neuroscience is beginning to suggest that neuromodulators play a role in learning by modifying the neuron's activation function [10,11]. From a computational point of view, it is surprising if real neurons are essentially fixed entities with no adaptive aspect, except at their synapses, since such a restriction leads to non-linear responses requiring many neurons.

Multi-Layer Perceptrons (MLPs) can be very effective, but if the activation function is not optimal, neither is the number of hiddens which in turn depends on the function. Adapting a slope-related parameter of the activation function may help, but not if the analytic shape of the function is unsuited to the problem domain. In contrast, with an adaptive function approach it should be possible to learn linearly inseparable problems fast, even without hidden nodes.

The simplest test case is the two input exclusive-OR. A single classic artificial neuron is incapable of solving it, yet with an adaptive activation function, the solution is readily learnable with one neuron [1]. Another case is the Iris dataset [4] which consists of 150 four dimensional data. This linearly inseparable problem can be solved by a 4 input x 3 output ADFUNN [1] without a hidden node. The generalisation reaches 100% with 80% of the testing patterns, within 100 epochs. In this paper, we present a general learning algorithm for adaptive function neurons and apply it to phrase recognition.

II. Background

Connectionist parsers are neural network based systems designed to process words or their syntactic types (tags) to produce a correct syntactic interpretation, or parse, of complete sentences [7]. These neural-network-based systems are, for instance, Multi-Layer Perceptrons (MLP), Simple Recurrent Networks (SRN), Recursive Autoassociation Memory (RAAM), or localist networks [7, 8, and 9].

In the early 1990s, the first modular distributed parsers typically consisted of combinations of feedforward multi-layer perceptron (FF-MLP), SRN and RAAM architectures. The purpose of decomposing the parsing task into sub-modules is often to simplify the network's learning task, and to reduce training set size and complexity; or to evaluate the computational and cognitive plausibility of a given composition of modules [7].

Hybrid connectionist parsers combine neural networks with symbolic modules or processes. In hybrid parsers the symbolic modules are assigned to tasks such as: short-term storage of parse states; long-term storage of structured knowledge, such as grammar rules, semantic networks, and tree structures; and symbol manipulation and communication to control the parsing process and coordinate interactions between (connectionist) modules [7].

Connectionist parsers are assessed according to their ability to learn to represent syntactic structures from examples automatically, without being presented with symbolic grammar rules. In particular, phrase recognition has proved to be a good test of neural networks, as both learners and parsers.

III. A Single Layer Adaptive Function Network

We provide a means of solving linearly inseparable problems using a simple adaptive function neural network (ADFUNN), based on a single layer of linear piecewise function neurons. As shown in figure 2, we calculate $\sum aw$, obtain the output error and then adapt the two f points by Δf, using a function modifying version of the delta rule, as outlined in A.

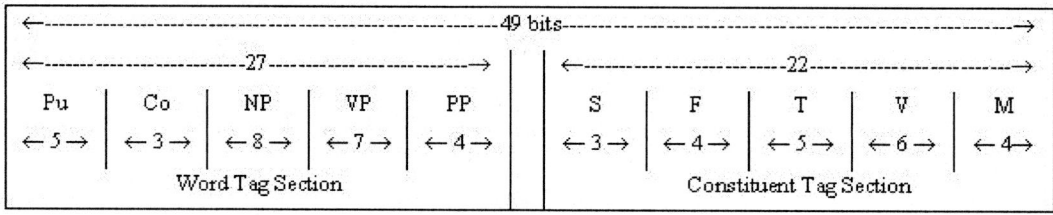

Fig. 1. Input Fields Representation

A. General Learning Rule

The weights and activation functions are adapted in parallel, using the following algorithm:
A = input node activation, E = output node error.
WL, FL: learning rates for weights and functions.
Step1: calculate output error, E, for input, A.
Step2: adapt weights to each output neuron:
$\Delta w = WL \times Fslope \times A \times E$
$w' = w + \Delta w$
weight normalization
Step3: adapt function for each output neuron:
$\Delta f(\sum aw) = FL \times E$
$f' = f + \Delta f$
Step4: $f(\sum aw) = f'(\sum aw); w = w'$.
Step5: randomly select a pattern to train
Step6: repeat step 1 to step 5 until the output error tends to a steady state

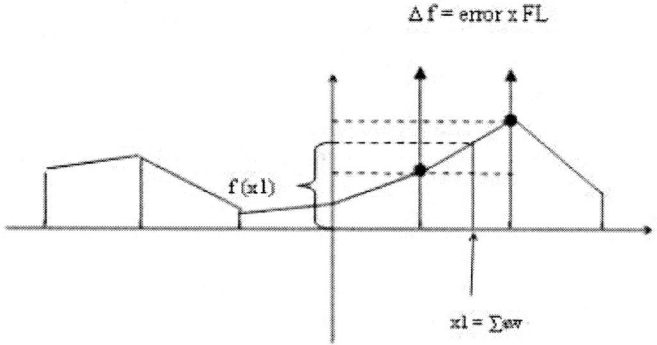

Fig. 2. Adapting a Piecewise Function in ADFUNN

In figure 2, x1 is only approximately equidistant from the two f-points, yet both these points are adapted by Δf. In our future work, the two f-points will be adapted on a proximal-proportional basis, whereby the change to each point is in proportion to its proximity to x1.

B. Phrase Recognition Using ADFUNN

Applying ADFUNN to phrase recognition, we generate the input patterns using the pre-tagged corpus in [2]. Each symbol type corresponds to several regions as a result of separating the input space. A total of 49 bits are used to encode all possible input symbols as shown in figure 1. The terminal symbol groups are: punctuation (Pu), conjunctions (Co), nouns (NP), verbs (VP) and prepositions (PP). The non-terminal symbol groups are sentences (S), finite clauses (F) non-finite clauses (T), major phrase types (V) and minor phrase types (M). There are 4 look-back symbols, 10 phrasal symbols and 1 look-ahead symbol, which makes a total of 15 inputs symbols. Thus, the total number of inputs is 49 bits x 15 symbols = 735. We generated 254 input patterns using the pre-tagged sentences in [3, 5].

According to LPC [2], constituent tags can be sub-divided into five main groups: sentence tags, finite clause tags, non-finite and verbless clause tags, major phrase tags, and minor phrase tags. There are 41 constituent tags altogether [3], and so 41 outputs are needed. The anticipated output value is either 0 or 1 and only one output should ideally be 1 for each input pattern. The format of the output is, for instance: 100. The first output in this case represents sentence, the other 40 outputs are 0. This indicates the input pattern is a sentence. When the output is, for example: 00100, and the 17th output is 1, the input pattern should be a verb phrase.

Thus we have a 735 input and 41 output network to deal with the phrase recognition, using 254 input patterns. Weights are initialized to zero. F-points are initialized randomly in the range (0, 1). Each F point is simply the value of the activation function for a given input sum. F-points are equally spaced, and the function value between points is on the straight line between them. $\sum aw$ has a know range: [-5, 5]. 2001 points are considered sufficient to encode the data precisely, giving a resolution of 0.05 on the function.

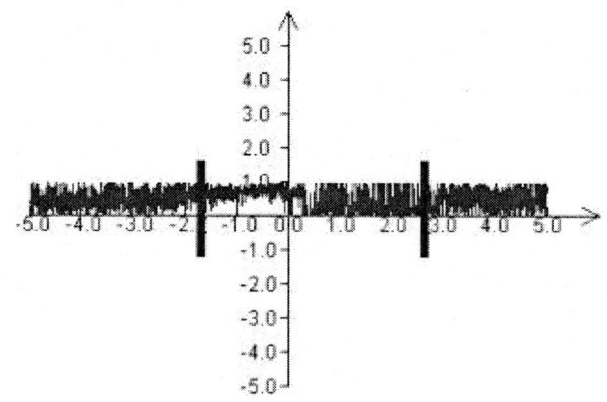

Fig. 3. Sentence

Clearly, every dataset will have its own range, therefore in general we need two learning constants, WL and FL. WL depends on input data range and the F-point interval (0.05 in

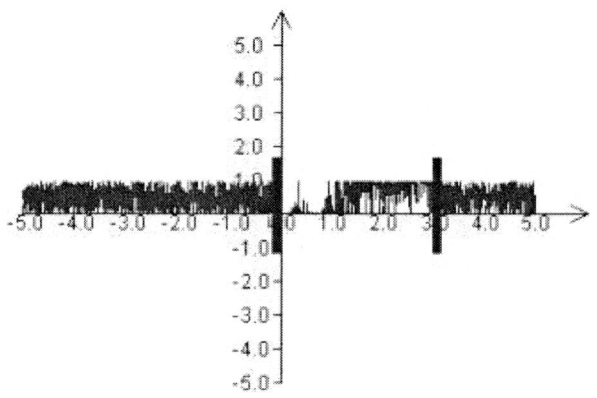

Fig. 4. Noun Phrase

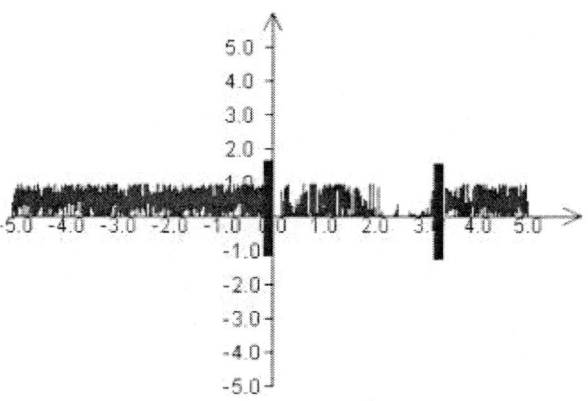

Fig. 5. Verb Phrase

this case), whereas FL depends solely on the required output range. We choose WL = 0.00001, FL = 0.1 to adapt weights and functions respectively. According to the general learning rule we have Δw = WL x Fslope x A x E and $\Delta f(\sum aw)$ = FL x E. Over many simulations, each consuming about 400 epochs, the average error tends to 0, and 100% generalisation can be achieved with 150 training patterns (out of 254). We only list 3 phrase types out of the 41 in figures 3, 4 and 5 because of space limitation. They are for the major types: sentence, noun phrase and verb phrase.

In figures 3, 4 and 5, the functions between the two superimposed borders mark the learned region, within which adaptation has occurred. From this we can conclude that the $\sum aw$ in the range (-2, 0) for the sentence function (first output out of 41) activates a sentence output in all or at least the most cases. Similarly, the $\sum aw$ in the range (1, 3) for the noun phrase (23rd output out of 41) activates a noun phrase output as well in most of the circumstances. The $\sum aw$ between (0.1, 2) for the verb phrase (17th output out of 41) will usually activate a verb phrase output. In the verb phrases case, the chances of being a verb phrase decrease steadily towards the edges of the range (0.1, 2), whereas in the case of noun phrases, the range is more clear cut. This shows the flexibility of an adaptive function since the verb phrase curve is distinctive but quite unlike a standard sigmoid or threshold.

IV. RESULT AND DATA ANALYSIS

A. Simulation Result

This experiment is run 30 times (30 simulations). We can't achieve 100% generalisation using 100 training patterns (out of 254), however we can obtain 100% generalisation with 150 training patterns. The functions are clearly non-linear and non-monotonic, illustrating the value of the adaptive function method which is able to acquire these functions. We can interpret the data by considering weights and functions together.

Generalisation	Best (%)	Average (%)	Worst (%)
200 training 54 testing	100.0	100.0	100.0
150 training 104 testing	100.0	99.04	98.07
100 training 154 testing	95.46	92.21	88.96

Fig. 6. Generalisation Ability Table

B. Data and Weights Analysis

Locating the strongest 100 or so weights for sentence(S), verb phrase (VP) and noun phrase (NP), we are able to see some inputs are most important for that output and only these input tags will activate that output neuron. Therefore by looking at the weights we can tell which input tags are most important for each neuron (See Table I for sentence, Table II for verb phrase and Table III for noun phrase).

For instance, if we take an input pattern as: X X NP VP, ATI NN X X X X X X X, CC and the expected output for this pattern is noun phrase. The values for the 41 outputs should be: 00100, in which the 23rd output is 1, for noun phrase. The Xs are all empty, i.e. no symbol and thus they are zeros. NP = 100111, VP = 100001, ATI = 10001000, NN = 10011100 and CC = 110, using the word tags from the LPC [2]. If we look back at figure 1, we can write this input pattern as a binary number, totaling 735 inputs altogether. Taking those input tags for noun phrase, we get $\sum aw$ = 2.8. Returning to figure 4, the corresponding Y $\approx$ 1. It indicates the noun phrase has been activated. The tags in Table I to III are:

NP: noun phrase
VP: verb phrase
RP: adverbial phrase
JP: adjectival phrase
PP: prepositional phrase
Rq: an adverb phrase beginning with a wh-word, e.g. 'How do you feel' or 'how long'
Ti: to-infinitive clause
E: label used for existential 'there' i.e. 'There' is nothing wrong
CC: conjunction e.g. AND, AND/OR, BUT, OR, YET
Na: a noun phrase marked as subject of verb
Po: a prepositional phrase beginning with the preposition 'of'
N: nouns
V: verbs

TABLE I
INPUT TAGS FOR SENTENCE

1	2	3	4	5	6	7	8	9	10	11	12	13	14	15
				NP	NP	NP	NP							
				VP	VP	VP	JP							
				RP	RP	RP	RP							
				PP	PP	PP	PP							
				Rq		JP	Ti							
				E		Ti								
				CC										

TABLE II
INPUT TAGS FOR VERB PHRASES

1	2	3	4	5	6	7	8	9	10	11	12	13	14	15
NP	VP	NP	NP	V	V	V	V							N
Na		Na	Na	VP	VP	VP	VP							V
		RP	RP											P
		CC	CP											JP
			CC											CC
			Rq											
			E											

TABLE III
INPUT TAGS FOR NOUN PHRASES

1	2	3	4	5	6	7	8	9	10	11	12	13	14	15
NP	NP	NP	VP	N	N	N	N							N
VP	VP	VP	RP	NP	NP	NP	NP							V
RP	RP	Rq	P	V	Po	P	Po							P
P	Na	Na	V			Po								CC
N	N	N	CC											
CC	CC	CC												
		Vi	E											
			Vi											

P: prepositions
ATI: singular or plural article(THE, NO)
NN: singular common noun

V. RELATED WORK

A. Comparisons Between ADFUNN and MLP with Back-Propagation

We compare the performance of ADFUNN, the MLP connectionist parser phrase recognizer from [3, 5] and a simple back-propagation network, in figure 7. TD is the result for the training data, ND is the result for testing using natural test data and PD is the result for testing using just pure test data. Natural test data is where patterns that have already occurred in the training are left in the test dataset, whereas for the pure test data they are remained.

The most obvious advantage of ADFUNN is the lack of hidden neurons, whereas 50 hidden layer nodes are required in the other two networks. Additionally, ADFUNN achieves

Network Type	Total No. of input	No. of patterns per epoch	No. of epochs	Total no. of patterns presentation	No. of hidden layer nodes	No. of corresponding Tags	Correct Classifications	Overall performance (%)
Connectionist parser MLP phrase recogniser	2588 (TD)	2588	800	2070400	50	72	-	-
	2765 (ND)	-	-	-	50	72	2461	89.01
	2433 (PD)	-	-	-	50	72	2132	87.63
Back propagation	127 (TD)	127	~128	16256	50	14	125	98.76
	154 (ND)	-	-	-	50	14	135	87.80
	89 (PD)	-	-	-	50	14	74	83.05
ADFUNN (30 simulations)	127 (TD)	127	~400	50800	0	14	127	100.0
	154 (ND)	-	-	-	0	14	142	92.21
	89 (PD)	-	-	-	0	14	80	89.89

Fig. 7. Comparisons Between ADFUNN and MLP

100% correct classification compared to 98.76% and 89.01% for the best of MLP and back-propagation networks.

B. Related Approaches

Pizza et al. [13] use an adaptive spline approach to function modification, and elsewhere both Fiori and Piazza use [12, 14] a Digital Look-Up Table (LUT) for the activation function. ADFUNN is more general than the digital LUT approach, in the sense that it is an analogue algorithm incorporating linear piecewise interpolation between points. This analogue approach is effective for both sharp edges and smooth functions.

In the cubic analytic spline approach, a cubic level of complexity is assumed and a good suboptimal solution to the cubic spline curve fitting problem is applied. If the required function is linear, or a step, ramp or pulse function, splines are inappropriate; and in ADFUNN, we don't have the same problem of smoothness control that is faced by adaptive splines. Initial high precision allows for any f-shape, and subsequently, the function curve can be simplified by locating stationary points and removing all points that have not been adapted, or where f is constant over a subrange.

In addition, LUT requires a bounded input address and a suitable linear transformation (scaling and offset adding) has to be performed on the output of the linear combiner in order to obtain the best LUT address; a problem not faced in ADFUNN which uses linear interpolation. Our method is essentially analogue and so hardware implementation is non trivial, but feasible using a combination of digital memory for F-points, amplifiers performing linear interpolation, and multiplier circuits.

VI. CONCLUSION AND FUTURE WORK

This paper presented a new application of ADFUNN to phrase recognition. It is highly effective for classification and exhibits impressive generalization with no hidden nodes.

In more complex domains, there will be a need to use hidden nodes in a ML-ADFUNN to represent arbitrary concave decision functions. However, just as the single layer ADFUNN is more powerful than the SLP, we predict that the multi-layer ADFUNN will be more powerful in learning than MLPs, and may well require fewer hidden neurons.

In the meantime, ADFUNN has performed better than expected, so we have yet to establish the limits of the single layer system. The MLP improves with greater training (compare parser with BP in Table IV). It is therefore worthwhile scaling up to the full dataset to see how ADFUNN generalisation fares.

REFERENCES

[1] D.Palmer-Brown and M.Kang, "ADFUNN:An Adaptive Function Neural Network", *to appear in the 7th International Conference on Adaptive and Natural Computing Algorithms*,Coimbra(Portugal), 2005.

[2] R.Garside, G.Leech and T.Varadi, *Manual of Information to Accompany the Lancaster Parsed Corpus*, Department of English, University of Oslo, 1987.

[3] J. Tepper, H. M. Powell and D. Palmer-Brown, "A Corpus-based connectionist Architecture for Large-scale Natural Language Parsing," *Connection Science*, 2002, vol. 14, no. 2, pp. 93 - 114.

[4] R. A. Fisher. *The Use of Multiple Measurements in Taxonomic Problems*, Annals of Eugenics 7, pp. 178-188, 1936.

[5] J. A. Tepper, *Corpus-based Connectionist Parsing* , PhD Thesis, Faculty of Engineering and Computing, The Nottingham Trent University, 2000.

[6] H. T. Siegelmann, E.D. Sontag and C. L. Giles, "Complexity of language recognition by neural networks," *Proceedings of the 12th World Computer Congress on Algorithm, Software and architecture*, Elsevier, Amsterdam, The Netherlands, 1992, vol.1, pp. 329-335.

[7] D. Palmer-Brown, J. Tepper and H. Powell, "Connectionist Natural Language Parsing", Trends in Cognitive Sciences, vol. 6, no.10, 2002.

[8] J. Elman, "Finding Structure in Time", *Trends in Cognitive Sciences*, vol. 14, pp. 179-211, 1990.

[9] J. Pollack, "Recursive distributed representations", *Artificial Intelligent*, vol. 46, pp. 77-105, 1990.

[10] G. Scheler, "Regulation of Neuromodulator Efficacy: Implications for Whole-Neuron and Synaptic Plasticity", *Progress in Neurobiology*, vol.72, no.6, 2004.

[11] G. Scheler, "Memorization in a neural network with adjustable transfer function and conditional gating", *Quantitative Biology*, 2004.

[12] F. Piazza, A. Uncini, and M. Zenobi, "Neural Networks with Digital LUT Activation Function", *Proceedings of International Joint Conference on Neural Networks(IJCNN'93)*, Nagoya(Japan), vol. 2, pp.1401-1404, 1993.

[13] A. Uncini, F. Piazza, L. Vecci, "Learning and Approximation Capabilities of Adaptive Spline Activation Function Neural Networks", *Neural Networks*, vol. 11, no. 2, pp. 259-270, 1998.

[14] S. Fiori, "Hybrid independent component analysis by adaptive LUT activation function neurons", *Neural Networks*, vol. 15, pp.85-94, 2002.

Treatment of Missing Data Using Neural Networks and Genetic Algorithms

Mussa Abdella
School of Electrical and Information Engineering
University of the Witwatersrand
Johannesburg, South Africa
m.abdella@ee.wits.ac.za

Tshilidzi Marwala
School of Electrical and Information Engineering
University of the Witwatersrand
Johannesburg, South Africa
t.marwala@ee.wits.ac.za

Abstract— This paper introduces a method aimed at approximating missing data in a database using a combination of genetic algorithms and neural networks. The proposed method uses genetic algorithm to minimise an error function derived from an auto-associative neural network. An investigation on using the proposed method to accurately approximate missing data as the number of missing cases within a single record increases is conducted. Multi Layer Perceptron (MLP) and Radial Basis Function (RBF) neural networks are employed. Results obtained using RBF are found to be better than those from the MLP. Results from a combination of both MLP and RBF are found to be better than those obtained using either MLP or RBF individually.

I. INTRODUCTION

Inferences made from available data for a certain application depends on the completeness and quality of the data being used in the analysis. Thus, inferences made from a complete data are most likely to be more accurate than those made from incomplete data. Moreover there are time critical applications which require us to estimate or approximate the values of some missing variables that have to be supplied in relation to the values of other corresponding variables. Such situations may arise in a system which uses a number of instruments and in some cases one or more of the sensors used in the system fail. In such situation the value of the missing sensor has to be estimated within a short time and with great precision, and by taking into account the values of the other sensors in the system. Approximation of the missing values in such situations require to estimate the missing value taking into account of the interrelationships that exists between the values of other corresponding variables.

Missing data in a database may arise due to various reasons. It can arise due to data entry errors, respondents non-response to some items on data collection process, failure of instruments and other various reasons. In Table I we have a database consisting five variables, namely x_1, x_2, x_3, x_4, and x_5 where the values for some variables are missing. Assuming we have

TABLE I
TABLE WITH MISSING VALUES

x_1	x_2	x_3	x_4	x_5
25	3.5	?	5000	-3.5
?	6.9	5.6	?	0.5
45	3.6	9.5	1500	46.5
27	9.7	?	3000	?

a database consisting records of the five variables. But some of the observations for some variables in various records are not available. How do we know the values for the missing entries? Are there ways to approximate the missing data depending on the interrelationships that exist between the variables in the database? Thus, the aim of this paper is to use neural networks and genetic algorithms to approximate the missing data in such situations.

II. BACKGROUND

A. Missing Data

Missing data creates various problems in many applications which depend on good access to accurate data. Hence, methods to handle missing data have been an area of research in statistics, mathematics and other various disciplines [1][2][3][21]. The reasonable way to handle missing data depends upon how data points become missing.

According to [4] there are three types of missing data mechanisms. These are Missing Completely at Random (MCAR), Missing at Random (MAR) and non-ignorable. MCAR situation arises if the probability of missing value for variable X is unrelated to the value X itself or to any other variable in the data set. This refers to data where the absence of data does not depend on the variable of interest or any other variable in the data set [3]. MAR arises if the probability of missing data on a particular variable X depends on other variables, but not on X itself and the non-ignorable case arises if the probability of missing data X is related to the value of X itself even if we control the other variables in the analysis [2].

Depending on the mechanism of missing data, currently various methods are being used to treat missing data. For a detailed discussion on the various missing data imputation methods used to handle missing data refer to [2][3][4] and [5].

B. Neural Networks

A neural network is an information processing paradigm that is inspired by the way biological nervous systems, like the brain process information. It is a machine that is designed to model the way in which the brain performs a particular task or function of interest [7].

A neural network consists of four main parts [7]. These are the processing units u_j, where each u_j has a certain activation level $a_j(t)$ at any point in time, weighted interconnections between the various processing units which determine how the activation of one unit leads to input for another unit, an activation rule which acts on the set of input signals at a unit to produce a new output signal, and a learning rule that specifies how to adjust the weights for a given input/output pair [7][20].

Due to their ability to derive meaning from complicated data, neural networks are used to extract patterns and detect trends that are too complex to be noticed by many other computer techniques [8]. A trained neural network can be considered as an expert in the category of information it has been given to analyse [6]. This expert can then be used to provide predictions given new situations. Because of their ability to adapt to a non-linear data neural networks are also being used to model various non-linear applications [7][8].

The arrangement of neural processing units and their interconnections can have a profound impact on the processing capabilities of a neural network [7]. Hence, there are many different connection of how the data flows between the input, hidden and output layers. The following section details the architecture of the two neural networks employed in this paper.

1) Multi-Layer Perceptrons (MLP): MLP neural networks consist of multiple layers of computational units, usually interconnected in a feed-forward way [7][8]. Each neuron in one layer is directly connected to the neurons of the subsequent layer. A fully connected two layered MLP architecture was used in the experiment. A NETLAB toolbox that runs in MATLAB discussed in [9] has been used to implement the MLP neural network. A two-layered MLP architecture was used because of the universal approximation theorem, which states that a two layered architecture is adequate for MLP [9]. The network can be described as follows:

$$Y_k = \sum_{j=1}^{M} W_{kj}^{(2)} tanh\left(\sum_{i=1}^{d} W_{ji}^{(1)} X_i + b_j^{(1)}\right) + b_k^{(2)} \quad (1)$$

Where $W_{ji}^{(1)}$ and $W_{kj}^{(2)}$ are the first and second layer matrices to be minimized, $b^{(1)}$ and $b^{(2)}$ are the bias parameters associated with the hidden units, X_i is the input, d is the number of inputs and M is the number of hidden units.

The linear activation function was used for the output units and the hyperbolic tangent function (tanh) was used in the hidden layers. The Scaled Conjugate Gradient (SCG) method was used as the optimization technique in training the MLP network. SCG method was used because it has been found to solve the optimization problems encountered when training an MLP network more efficiently than the gradient descent and conjugate gradient methods [10]. The MLP network has 14 inputs, 10 hidden neurons and 14 output units.

2) Radial-Basis Function (RBF): RBF networks are feed-forward networks trained using a supervised training algorithm [7]. They are typically configured with a single hidden layer of units whose activation function is selected from a class of functions called basis functions. The activation of hidden units in a RBF network is given by a non-linear function of the distance between the input vector and a prototype vector [10].

While similar to back propagation in many aspects, radial basis function networks have several advantages. They usually train much faster than back propagation networks and less prone to problems with non-stationary inputs due to the behavior of the radial basis function [10]. The RBF network can be described as

$$Y_k(X) = \sum_{j=1}^{M} W_{jk}\phi_j(X) \quad (2)$$

Where W_{ij} are the output weights, each corresponding to the connection between a hidden unit and an output unit, M represents the number of output units, $\phi_j(X)$ is the jth non-linear activation function, X the input vector, and $K = 1, 2, 3, ..., M$ [10].

Like the MLP a NETLAB toolbox that runs in MATLAB discussed in [9] was used to implement the RBF architecture. The network has 14 inputs, 10 hidden neurons and 14 output units.

C. Genetic Algorithms (GAs)

GAs are algorithms used to find approximate solutions to difficult problems through application of the principles of evolutionary biology to computer science [11][12]. They use biologically derived techniques such as inheritance, mutation, natural selection, and recombination to approximate an optimal solution to difficult problems [14]. Genetic algorithms view learning as a competition among a population of evolving candidate problem solutions. A fitness function evaluates each solution to decide whether it will contribute to the next generation of solutions. Through operations analogous to gene transfer in sexual reproduction, the algorithm creates a new population of candidate solutions [14][19].

The three most important aspects of using genetic algorithms are [11][15] definition of the objective function, definition and implementation of the genetic representation, and definition and implementation of the genetic operators. GAs have been proved to be successful in optimization problems such as wire routing, scheduling, adaptive control, game playing, cognitive modeling, transportation problems, traveling salesman problems, optimal control problems, and database query optimization [11][13].

The MATLAB implementation of genetic algorithm described in [15] has been used to implement the genetic algorithm. After executing the program with different genetic operators, optimal operators that gave best results were selected to be used in conducting the experiment.

III. METHOD

The neural network was trained to recall to itself (predict its input vector). Mathematically this neural network can be written as

$$\vec{Y} = f(\vec{X}, \vec{W}) \quad (3)$$

Where $\vec{Y}$ is the output vector, $\vec{X}$ the input vector and $\vec{W}$ the vector of weights. Since the network is trained to predict its own input vector, the input vector $\vec{X}$ will be approximately equal to output vector $\vec{Y}$ ($\vec{X} \approx \vec{Y}$).

In reality the input vector $\vec{X}$ and output vector $\vec{Y}$ will not always be perfectly the same hence, we will have an error function expressed as the difference between the input and output vector. Thus, the error can be formulated as

$$e = \vec{X} - \vec{Y} \quad (4)$$

Substituting the value of $\vec{Y}$ from (3) into (4) we get

$$e = \vec{X} - f(\vec{X}, \vec{W}) \quad (5)$$

We want the error to be minimum and non-negative. Hence, the error function can be rewritten as a square of equation (5)

$$e = (\vec{X} - f(\vec{X}, \vec{W}))^2 \quad (6)$$

In the case of missing data, some of the values for the input vector $\vec{X}$ are not available. Hence, we can categorize the input vector ($\vec{X}$) elements into $\vec{X}$ known represented by ($\vec{X}_k$) and $\vec{X}$ unknown represented by ($\vec{X}_u$). Rewriting equation (6) in terms of $\vec{X}_k$ and $\vec{X}_u$ we have

$$e = \left(\left\{ \begin{array}{c} \vec{X}_k \\ \vec{X}_u \end{array} \right\} - f\left(\left\{ \begin{array}{c} \vec{X}_k \\ \vec{X}_u \end{array} \right\}, \vec{W} \right) \right)^2 \quad (7)$$

To approximate the missing input values, equation (7) is minimized using genetic algorithm. Genetic algorithm was chosen because it has a higher probability of finding the global optimum solution than traditional optimization methods [19][11][17]. Since a genetic algorithm always finds the maximum value, the negative of equation (7) was supplied to the GA as a fitness function. Thus, the final error function minimized using the genetic algorithm is

$$e = -\left(\left\{ \begin{array}{c} \vec{X}_k \\ \vec{X}_u \end{array} \right\} - f\left(\left\{ \begin{array}{c} \vec{X}_k \\ \vec{X}_u \end{array} \right\}, \vec{W} \right) \right)^2 \quad (8)$$

For the individual cases of MLP and RBF, Equation (8) was used as the fitness function, where f in the equation refers to either MLP or RBF accordingly. The fitness function used in the genetic algorithm for the combined case was a simple linear combination of the MLP and RBF networks. The error function used in this case was the negative of Equation (9).

$$e = \left(\left\{ \begin{array}{c} \vec{X}_k \\ \vec{X}_u \end{array} \right\} - f_1\left(\left\{ \begin{array}{c} \vec{X}_k \\ \vec{X}_u \end{array} \right\}, \vec{W} \right) \right)^2 + \\ \left(\left\{ \begin{array}{c} \vec{X}_k \\ \vec{X}_u \end{array} \right\} - f_2\left(\left\{ \begin{array}{c} \vec{X}_k \\ \vec{X}_u \end{array} \right\}, \vec{W} \right) \right)^2 \quad (9)$$

In Equation (9) f_1 refers to the MLP function and f_2 refers to the RBF function.

Figure 1 depicts the graphical representation of proposed model. The error function is derived from the input and output vector obtained from the trained neural network. The error function is then minimized using genetic algorithm to approximate the missing variables in the error function.

IV. RESULT AND DISCUSSION

An MLP and RBF networks with 10 hidden neurons, 14 inputs and 14 outputs were trained on the data obtained from South African Breweries (SAB). A total of 198 training inputs were provided for each network architecture. Each element of the database was removed and approximated using the model.

Cases of 1, 2, 3, 4, and 5 missing values in a single record were examined to investigate the accuracy of the approximated values as the number of missing cases within a single record increases. To asses the accuracy of the values approximated using the model the standard error and correlation coefficient were calculated for each missing case.

We have used the following terms to measure the modeling quality: (i) Standard error (Se) and (ii) Correlation coefficient (r). For a given data $x_1, x_2, ..., x_n$ and corresponding

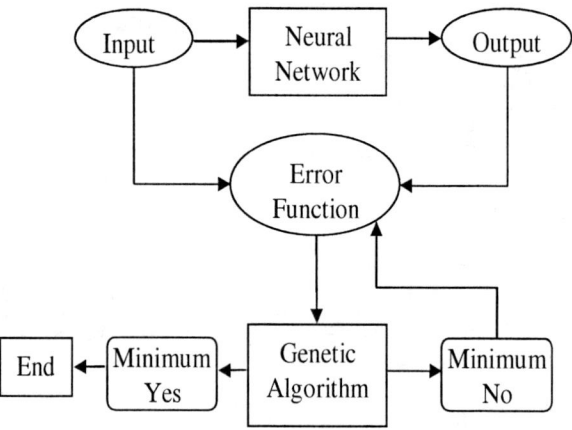

Fig. 1. Schematic representation of proposed model

approximated values $\hat{x}_1, \hat{x}_2, ..., \hat{x}_n$ the Standard error (Se) is computed as [18]

$$Se = \sqrt{\frac{\sum_{i=1}^{n}(x_i - \hat{x}_i)^2}{n}} \quad (10)$$

and the correlation coefficient (r) is computed as [18]

$$r = \frac{\sum_{i=1}^{n}(x_i - \overline{x}_i)(\hat{x}_i - \overline{\hat{x}}_i)}{\left[\sum_{i=1}^{n}(x_i - \overline{x}_i)^2 \sum_{i=1}^{n}(\hat{x}_i - \overline{\hat{x}}_i)^2 \right]^{1/2}} \quad (11)$$

Where $\overline{x}_i$ and $\overline{\hat{x}}$ are the means of actual missing data and approximated values, respectively.

The error "Se" estimates the capability of the model to predict the known data set [16]. The higher the value of "Se" the less reliable the approximations and vice versa. The correlation coefficient measures the linear relationship between two variables. The absolute value of "r" provides an indication of the strength of the relationship. The value of "r" varies between negative 1 and positive 1, with -1 or 1 indicating a perfect linear relationship, and r = 0 indicating no relationship. The sign of the correlation coefficient indicates whether the two variables are positively or negatively related [18]. Here,"r" measures the degree of relationship between the actual missing data and corresponding approximated values using the model. A positive value indicates a direct relationship between the actual missing data and its approximated value using the model. The more closer the value of "r" to 1 the more strong the relationship. As the strength of the relationship between the predicted values and actual values increases so does the correlation coefficient.

The result of the correlation and standard error measures obtained from the experiment are given in Tables II and III, respectively. The results are also depicted in Figures 2 and 3 for easy comparison between the results found by MLP, RBF and their combination (MLP+RBF). The results show that the models approximation to the missing data to be highly accurate. There is no significant difference among the approximations obtained for the different number of missing cases within a single record. Approximations obtained using the combined approach in all the missing cases are better than the corresponding values found using either MLP or RBF individually.

Approximations obtained using RBF in all the missing cases are far better than corresponding values found using MLP. This could be due to the fact that MLP is more complex than RBF in terms of the order of non-linearity. Therefore, MLP has more local optimum points than RBF. Better results found using RBF network also shows that the neural network architecture employed in training the data set have a crucial impact on the results. It also shows that using the combined approach in the error function leads to better results.

A sample of the actual missing data and approximated values using the model for the 14 variables used in the model are presented in Tables IV V, and VI and Figures 4, 5, 6, 7, and 8. The results show that the models approximated value of the missing data to be similar to the actual missing values. It can also be observed that estimates found for 1, 2, 3, 4, and 5 missing cases are not significantly different within each other.

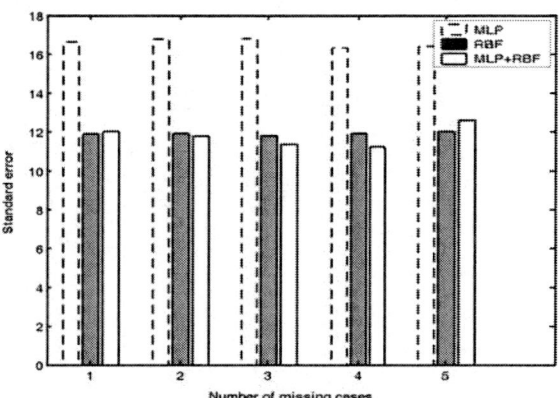

Fig. 3. Standard error MLP, RBF, and MLP+RBF

TABLE II
CORRELATION COEFFICIENT

	Number of Missing Values				
	1	2	3	4	5
MLP	0.94	0.939	0.939	0.933	0.938
RBF	0.968	0.969	0.970	0.970	0.968
MLP+RBF	0.96	0.97	0.97	0.97	0.96

TABLE III
STANDARD ERROR

	Number of Missing Vales				
	1	2	3	4	5
MLP	16.62	16.77	16.8	16.31	16.4
RBF	11.89	11.92	11.80	11.92	12.02
MLP+RBF	12.02	11.78	11.36	11.23	12.60

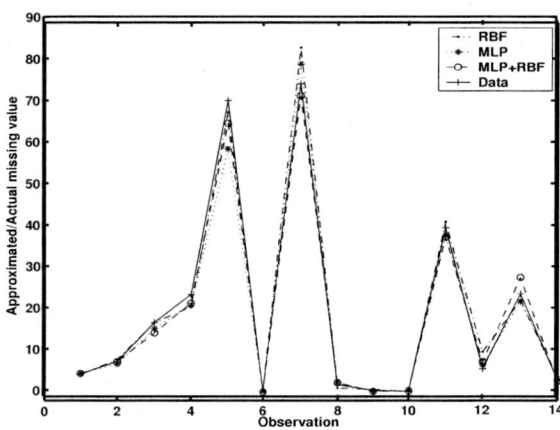

Fig. 4. One missing case: actual vs. approximated values using MLP, RBF, and MLP+RBF

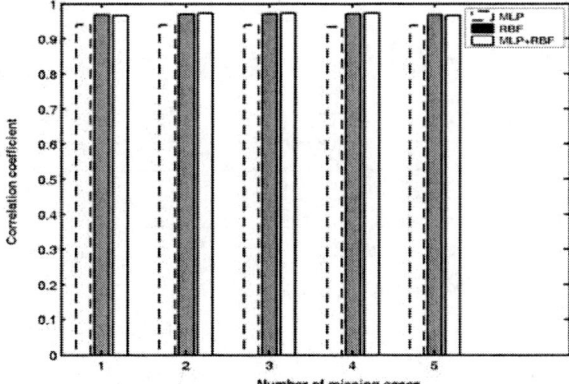

Fig. 2. Correlation coefficient MLP, RBF, and MLP+RBF

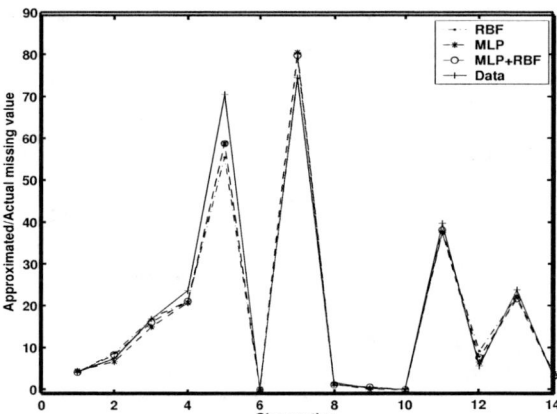

Fig. 5. Two missing case: actual vs. approximated values using MLP, RBF, and MLP+RBF

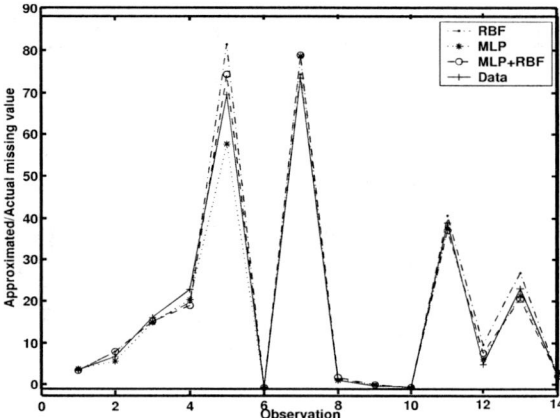

Fig. 6. Three missing case: actual vs. approximated values using MLP, RBF, and MLP+RBF

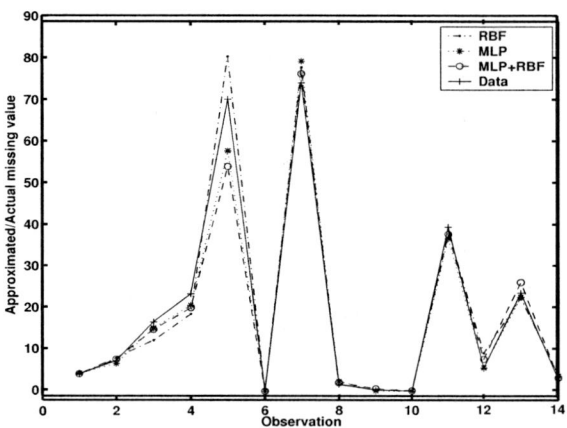

Fig. 7. Four missing case: actual vs. approximated values using MLP, RBF, and MLP+RBF

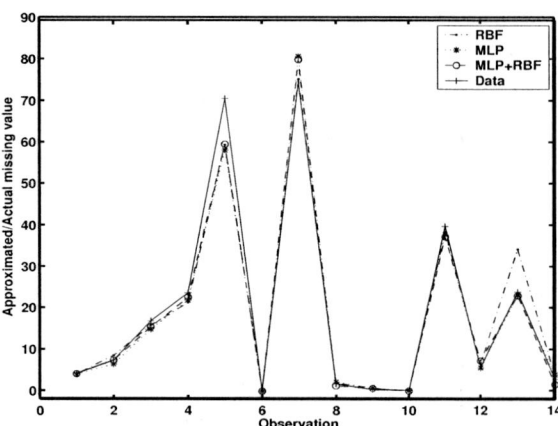

Fig. 8. Five missing case: actual vs. approximated values using MLP, RBF, and MLP+RBF

TABLE IV
ACTUAL AND APPROXIMATED VALUES USING MLP

Data	Number of missing values in a record				
	1	2	3	4	5
4.28	4.54	4.54	4.53	4.47	4.07
7.5	6.86	6.79	6.41	6.80	6.52
17	15.50	15.10	15.8	15.5	15.0
23.8	21.20	20.90	21.3	21.0	22.0
71	59.20	59.20	59.0	58.5	58.4
0.1	0.18	0.17	0.17	0.05	0.02
75	79.90	81.1	80.3	80.3	81.2
1.8	2.48	2.41	1.81	2.54	2.21
0.4	0.10	0.104	0.72	0.22	0.72
0.2	0.58	0.06	0.02	0.11	0.159
40	38.10	37.8	38.4	37.2	38.0
5.7	6.64	6.66	6.96	5.82	5.67
24	22.10	22.4	22.3	23.0	23.2
2.9	3.23	3.86	3.74	3.83	3.97

TABLE V
ACTUAL AND APPROXIMATED VALUES USING RBF

Data	Number of missing values in a record				
	1	2	3	4	5
4.28	4.21	4.20	4.12	4.25	4.13
7.5	7.89	8.79	8.71	8.21	8.65
17	16.96	17.16	16.04	12.48	15.95
23.8	20.74	21.25	20.60	18.88	21.43
71	68.11	55.83	83.21	81.46	59.78
0.1	0.06	0.04	0.05	0.05	0.08
75	83.92	74.84	75.96	78.79	75.70
1.8	1.00	1.14	2.15	1.73	2.01
0.4	0.70	0.71	0.76	0.55	0.71
0.2	0.10	0.10	0.09	0.16	0.11
40	56.45	57.73	61.73	62.16	62.65
5.7	9.79	9.30	10.43	9.33	6.54
24	22.40	22.52	27.81	36.79	34.45
2.9	3.31	3.48	2.87	3.98	3.50

TABLE VI
ACTUAL AND APPROXIMATED VALUES USING MLP+RBF

Data	Number of missing cases in a record				
	1	2	3	4	5
4.28	4.50	4.20	4.12	4.24	4.20
7.5	7.40	8.42	8.71	7.85	7.47
17	14.46	16.17	16.04	15.13	15.53
23.8	21.63	21.24	19.88	20.38	22.67
71	65.38	59.16	75.92	54.66	59.89
0.1	0.01	0.04	0.06	0.07	0.03
75	72.09	80.37	80.56	77.16	80.44
1.8	2.26	1.20	2.50	2.21	1.30
0.4	0.20	0.71	0.75	0.72	0.67
0.2	0.30	0.11	0.11	0.21	0.10
40	37.66	38.36	38.13	38.23	37.43
5.7	7.40	7.78	8.40	7.87	7.34
24	27.91	21.87	21.51	26.55	23.09
2.9	2.56	3.35	2.81	3.33	1.61

V. CONCLUSION

Neural networks and genetic algorithms are proposed to predict missing data in a database. An auto-associative neural network is trained to predict its own input. An error function is derived as the square of the difference of the output vector from the trained neural network and the input vector. Since some of the input vectors are missing, the error function is expressed in terms of the known and unknown components of the input vector. Genetic algorithm is used to approximate the missing values in the input vector that best minimise the error function. RBF and MLP neural networks are used to train the neural network. Moreover a combination of both RBF and MLP trained networks was employed to investigate if it could lead to better results. It is found that the model can approximate missing values with great accuracy. Though there is a slight decrease in correlation coefficient, there was no significant reduction in accuracy of results observed as the number of missing cases within a single record gets larger. Results found using the combination of both RBF and MLP are slightly better than RBF. Results found using RBF are far better than MLP.

REFERENCES

[1] Y. Yuan. "Multiple imputation for missing data: Concepts and new development." In *SUGI Paper 267-25*. 2000.

[2] P. Allison. "Multiple imputation for missing data: A cautionary tale." In *Sociological Methods and Research*, vol. 28, pp. 301–309. 2000.

[3] D. B. Rubin. "Multiple Imputations in Sample Surveys - A Phenomenological Bayesian Approach to Nonresponse." In *The Proceedings of the Survey Research Methods Section of the American Statistical Association*, pp. 20–34. 1978.

[4] R. Little and D. Rubin. *Statistical analysis with missing data*. New York: John Wiley and Sons, first ed., 1987.

[5] M. Hu, S. Savucci, and M. Choen. "Evaluation of Some Popular Imputation Algorithms." In *Proceedings of the Survey Research Methods Section of the American Statistical Association*, pp. 308–313. 1998.

[6] Y. Yoon and L. L. Peterson. "Artificial neural networks: an emerging new technique." In *Proceedings of the 1990 ACM SIGBDP conference on Trends and directions in expert systems*, pp. 417–422. ACM Press, 1990.

[7] S. Haykin. *Neural Networks*. New Jersey: Prentice-Hall, second ed., 1999.

[8] M. H. Hassoun. *Fundamentals of Artificial Neural Networks*. Cambridge, Massachusetts: MIT Press, 1995.

[9] I. T. Nabney. *Netlab: Algorithms for Pattern Recognition*. United Kingdom: Springer-Verlag, 2001.

[10] C. M. Bishop. *Neural Networks for Pattern Recognition*. Oxford: Oxford University Press, 1995.

[11] Z. Michalewicz. *Genetic Algorithms + Data Structures = Evolution Programs*. Berling Heidelberg, New York: Springer-Verlag, third ed., 1996.

[12] S. Forrest. "Genetic algorithms." *ACM Comput. Surv.*, vol. 28, no. 1, pp. 77–80, 1996.

[13] P. C. Pendharkar and J. A. Rodger. "An empirical study of non-binary genetic algorithm-based neural approaches for classification." In *Proceeding of the 20th international conference on Information Systems*, pp. 155–165. Association for Information Systems, 1999.

[14] W. Banzhaf, P. Nordin, R. Keller, and F. Francone. *Genetic Programming-an introduction: on the automatic evolution of computer programs and its applications*. California: Morgan Kaufmann Publishers, fifth ed., 1998.

[15] C. R. Houck, J. A. Joines, and M. G. Kay. "A genetic algorithm for function optimisation: a matlab implementation." Tech. Rep. NCSU-IE TR 95-09, Carolina State University, 1995.

[16] T. Kolarik and G. Rudorfer. "Time series forecasting using neural networks." In *Proceedings of the international conference on APL : the language and its applications*, pp. 86–94. ACM Press, 1994.

[17] M. Jones and A. Konstam. "The use of genetic algorithms and neural networks to investigate the Baldwin effect." In *Proceedings of the 1999 ACM symposium on Applied computing*, pp. 275–279. ACM Press, 1999.

[18] N. Draper and H. Smith. *Applied regression analysis*. New York: J. Wiley, third ed., 1998.

[19] D. Goldberg. *Genetic Algorithms in Search, Optimization, and Machine Learning*. Reading, MA: Addison-Wesley, 1989.

[20] J. Freeman and D. Skapura. *Neural Networks: Algorithms, Applications and Programming Techniques*. Addison-Wesley, 1991.

[21] P. Roth. "Missing data: A conceptual overview for applied psychologists." In *Personnel Psychology*, vol. 47, pp. 537–560. 1994.

An Iterative Relevance Feedback Learning Algorithm For Image Retrieval Systems

S. Srinivasan and M. R. Azimi-Sadjadi

Department of Electrical and Computer Engineering
Colorado State University
Fort Collins CO, 80523, USA
Email: {skumar,azimi}@engr.colostate.edu

Abstract— A new feature adaptation mechanism is proposed in this paper that captures the relevance feedback information provided by the expert users. This relevance information is retained for future usage and subsequently made available to other users. The search and retrieval processes are implemented through a two-layer connectionist network structure and the relevance feedback learning is incorporated by appropriately modifying the network structure. The developed algorithm is tested on an electro-optical imagery database collected from different underwater mine-like and non-mine-like objects.

I. INTRODUCTION

Most of the existing image retrieval systems are designed for general-purpose search and retrieval applications and are ill-suited for scenarios where the domain of applications is limited to specific databases with expert users. In certain applications in industry, education, medical, military, and remote sensing, accuracy of search/retrieval and adaptability to data and environmental changes are of utmost importance. Nonetheless, the difficulty in finding features that are true representative of the images compromises the performance of the retrieval system. Incorporating relevance feedback from expert users is a common way to improve the performance of the retrieval system.

Most retrieval systems that use relevant feedback-based learning, lack full control over the position as well as ranks of the listed images. Moreover, those systems that utilize relevance feedback learning for large databases must face the problems of modifying, in real-time, an overwhelming number of parameters. Retrieval systems [1],[2] mostly apply relevance feedback learning temporarily on a user-basis and only during a particular session. Some of these systems rely on Rocchio's formula [3] for query modification or query expansion. Although, through the learning and by using user's feedback, the system can deliver a refined list of images, the information is not kept for future usage by other expert users. In other words, these systems are not designed to continuously learn from expert users by modifying their internal parameters in response to relevance feedback. The main goal of our work is to develop a flexible, retrieval system that is able to continually learn through expert user feedback and subsequently provide the learnt information to other users as well.

II. RELEVANCE FEEDBACK

The principal idea behind relevance feedback is learning hidden concepts in the images from the expert users. When a query is submitted to the retrieval system, a number of images are listed, among which there is one (or more) most relevant image(s). If this image is not already in the first position in the list, the expert user(s) must evaluate the listed images and identify and vote on the most relevant one(s). The problem of relevance feedback learning can be viewed as a constrained optimization problem [4] where the main goal of the learning is to lift the most relevant image while the constraint involves retaining other relevant images listed by the image retrieval system. A new feature adaptation mechanism that captures the relevance information provided by the expert users is discussed in this section. The proposed feature adaptation mechanism ensures that the position of the relevant image is lifted while those of the other images are not changed. This procedure is described next.

A. Feature Adaptation

Let $\underline{x}_k^{(t)}$ be the feature vector of the kth image $I_k, \forall k \in [1, N]$ where N is the number of images in the database. The superscript (t) represents the index for the times the original feature vector is modified through the relevance feedback and voting from the expert users. The image feature vectors are first mean corrected based upon the mean vector of all samples in the database and normalized such that after mean correction and normalization $\underline{x}_k^{(t)T} \underline{x}_k^{(t)} = 1, \forall k \in [1, N]$. The same is true for the applied query image. Now, if $\underline{q}_i$ is the ith query image ($\underline{q}_i^t \underline{q}_i = 1$), then the rank of the kth image for this query is,

$$r_{ik} = \underline{q}_i^T \underline{x}_k^{(t)} \qquad (1)$$

When the user submits query $\underline{q}_1$, the system searches and ranks the images in the database. The user evaluates the list of retrieved images and if not satisfied with the ranking of the images in the results list, he/she identifies a particular image, evaluates it and elevates or demotes the image based on whether or not it is relevant to the query image. Let us assume that the kth image I_k, as identified by the expert user, is the most relevant image for this query $\underline{q}_1$ but it does not appear as the top ranked image in the results list. Now, the expert user selects the kth image and specifies a new desired rank. This relevance information provided by the expert user is to be captured such that after applying the relevance feedback, the kth image appears as the most relevant image in the results list.

Let r_{1k} be the rank of the kth image for the submitted query $\underline{q}_1$ before any relevance feedback and $\hat{r}_{1k}$ be the desired rank as specified by the expert user. Then, original feature vector of this image I_k should be mapped from $\underline{x}_k^{(t)}$ to $\underline{x}_k^{(t+1)}$ in order to capture the information provided by the user without changing the ranks of the other listed images. The proposed feature vector adaptation is,

$$\underline{x}_k^{(t+1)} = \underline{x}_k^{(t)} + \alpha_1 \underline{\tilde{q}}_1 \qquad (2)$$

where α_1 can be found to satisfy the new rank requirement that $\underline{q}_1^T \underline{x}_k^{(t+1)} = \hat{r}_{1k}$ and $\underline{\tilde{q}}_1$ is the "innovation" or error vector which is orthogonal to the original image feature vector $\underline{x}_k^{(t)}$. It can be seen in (2) that the feature adaptation procedure is similar to the codebook vector update process of Learning Vector Quantization [5].

Now we need to find $\underline{\tilde{q}}_1$ and α_1 in order to guarantee that the image I_k is voted to the desired position. Incorporating new information using orthogonally computed error vectors through Gram-Schmidt orthogonalization procedure is commonly employed in neural networks [6]. Using Gram-Schmidt orthogonalization procedure, the orthogonal vector $\underline{\tilde{q}}_1$ can be constructed from the known set of vectors $\{\underline{x}_k^{(t)}, \underline{q}_1\}$ as,

$$\underline{\tilde{q}}_1 = \underline{q}_1 - (\underline{q}_1^T \underline{x}_k^{(t)}) \underline{x}_k^{(t)} \qquad (3)$$

Since we require that $\underline{q}_1^T \underline{x}_k^{(t+1)} = \hat{r}_{1k}$, from (2) and (3) we have,

$$\alpha_1 = \frac{\hat{r}_{1k} - r_{1k}}{\underline{\tilde{q}}_1^T \underline{\tilde{q}}_1} \qquad (4)$$

The term $\underline{\tilde{q}}_1$ can be seen as an orthogonal innovation or error vector in the original feature vector needed to yield the desired rank. Orthogonality to $\underline{x}_k^{(t)}$ ensures retaining the information learnt during the previous training. It should be noted that before incorporating this feedback information, when image I_k is submitted as a query image, the most relevant image retrieved by the network is I_k with rank 1. The proposed feature adaptation mechanism ensures that this is true even after the adaptation of the original feature vector. This is due to the fact that $\underline{x}_k^{(t)}$ is orthogonal to the innovation vector $\underline{\tilde{q}}_1$. It should also be noted that since the feature vectors of the other listed images are not modified, the rank of those images do not change since the query is not changed. Thus, relevance feedback information provided by the expert user is captured by the system with minimal modification to the system parameters.

Now that the relevance feedback information of query $\underline{q}_1$ on image I_k provided by the expert user is captured and stored in the network. Let us assume that for another query $\underline{q}_2$ also the kth image is the most relevant one, but it does not appear as the top ranked image in the list. The desired rank of the kth image as specified by the expert user is $\hat{r}_{2k}$. This additional new relevance information for query $\underline{q}_2$ should be captured while also retaining the information learnt during the previous iteration for query $\underline{q}_1$. In this case, the proposed feature adaptation process maps the feature vector from $\underline{x}_k^{(t+1)}$ to $\underline{x}_k^{(t+2)}$ to capture the new information i.e.,

$$\underline{x}_k^{(t+2)} = \underline{x}_k^{(t)} + \alpha_1 \underline{\tilde{q}}_1 + \alpha_2 \underline{\tilde{q}}_2 \qquad (5)$$

where α_1 and α_2 can be found to satisfy the new rank requirement and at the same time preserve the already learnt information in the previous learning iteration, ie.,

$$\underline{q}_1^T \underline{x}_k^{(t+2)} = \hat{r}_{1k} \qquad (6)$$
$$\underline{q}_2^T \underline{x}_k^{(t+2)} = \hat{r}_{2k} \qquad (7)$$

The error vectors $\underline{\tilde{q}}_1$ and $\underline{\tilde{q}}_2$ can now be determined from $\{\underline{x}_k^{(t)}, \underline{q}_1, \underline{q}_2\}$ using the Gram-Schmidt orthogonalization procedure. Note that $\underline{\tilde{q}}_1$ is the same as in (3). Thus, $\underline{\tilde{q}}_2$ that is orthogonal to both $\underline{\tilde{q}}_1$ and $\underline{x}_k^{(t)}$ is given by,

$$\underline{\tilde{q}}_2 = \underline{q}_2 - (\underline{q}_2^T \underline{\tilde{q}}_1) \underline{\tilde{q}}_1 - (\underline{q}_2^T \underline{x}_k^{(t)}) \underline{x}_k^{(t)} \qquad (8)$$

Since the feature vector is expanded in terms of orthogonal vectors, the solution for α_1 is the same as that in (4) while the solution for α_2 is obtained using (7) as,

$$\alpha_2 = \frac{\hat{r}_{2k} - r_{2k}}{\underline{\tilde{q}}_2^T \underline{\tilde{q}}_2} \qquad (9)$$

Thus, choosing α_1 and α_2 as in (4) and (9) and choosing $\underline{\tilde{q}}_1$ and $\underline{\tilde{q}}_2$ as in (3) and (8), the feature adaptation in (5) will ensure that the kth image is the most relevant image for queries $\underline{q}_1$ and $\underline{q}_2$ with the user specified desired ranks.

In general, if the kth image is voted for the set of queries $\{\underline{q}_1 \cdots \underline{q}_K\}$, the mapped feature vector is,

$$\underline{x}_k^{(t+K)} = \underline{x}_k^{(t)} + \sum_{i=1}^{K} \alpha_i \underline{\tilde{q}}_i \qquad (10)$$

with

$$\underline{\tilde{q}}_1 = \underline{q}_1 - (\underline{q}_1^T \underline{x}_k^{(t)}) \underline{x}_k^{(t)}, \qquad (11)$$

$$\underline{\tilde{q}}_i = \underline{q}_i - \sum_{j=1}^{i-1} (\underline{q}_i^T \underline{\tilde{q}}_j) \underline{\tilde{q}}_j - (\underline{q}_i^T \underline{x}_k^{(t)}) \underline{x}_k^{(t)}, \forall i \in [2, K] \quad (12)$$

and

$$\alpha_i = \frac{\hat{r}_{ik} - r_{ik}}{\underline{\tilde{q}}_i^T \underline{\tilde{q}}_i} \qquad \forall i \in [1, K] \qquad (13)$$

Remark 1

From (11) and (13) it can be observed that, to incorporate new relevance information while retaining the previous learning, the α's learnt in the previous iteration do not have to be updated. That is, it is only sufficient to find the new α to capture the new information. This is due to the property

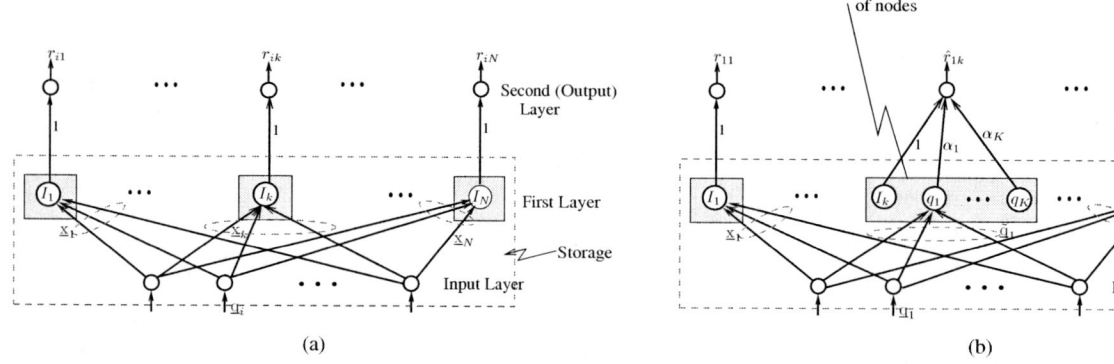

Fig. 1. Network structure (a) with initial setup and (b) after K iterations of relevance feedback on image I_k.

that the error vectors $\{\tilde{\underline{q}}_1 \cdots \tilde{\underline{q}}_K\}$ are all mutually orthogonal. This is highly desirable considering the fact that this leads to an efficient on-line learning scheme.

Remark 2

If an image is elevated for a submitted query, then the corresponding α will be positive in which case the feature vector of the voted image tends to move closer to the query image feature. Similarly, if the image is demoted for a given query, then the corresponding α will be negative in which case the feature vector of the voted image tends to move away from the query image. This can be viewed in the context of Rocchio's formula [7] for query mapping. Given a set of relevant and non-relevant images for a query, the Rocchio's formula for generating the optimal query is,

$$\hat{\underline{q}} = \frac{\sum_{\underline{x}_i \in D_R} \underline{x}_i}{|X_R|} - \frac{\sum_{\underline{x}_i \in X_{NR}} \underline{x}_i}{|X_{NR}|} \quad (14)$$

where X_R and X_{NR} are the sets of relevant and non-relevant documents, respectively, and $|.|$ stands for the cardinality of the set. The optimal query tends to move towards the relevant samples and move away from the non-relevant samples.

III. PROPOSED TWO-LAYER CONNECTIONIST NETWORK

A. Initial network

The search and retrieval processes and relevance feedback learning from the expert user can be implemented using a two-layer connectionist network structure. The initial structure of the proposed two-layer connectionist structure before incorporating any relevance feedback information is shown in Figure 1(a). Each input $j \in [1, n]$ corresponds to one of the image attributes or components in the feature vector. Similarly, each node $k \in [1, N]$ in the first layer represents an image I_k. The connection weight between the input j and node k in the first layer is $x_{kj}^{(t)}$, i.e. the jth component of the feature vector $\underline{x}_k^{(t)}$. The creation of nodes in different layers and setting up the weights is referred as the *initial training*. The image search and retrieval can be achieved in our connectionist system by propagating the query $\underline{q}_i$ at the input nodes of the network shown in Figure 1(a). When query $\underline{q}_i$ is submitted, output of the kth node in the output layer is $r_{ik} = \underline{q}_i^T \underline{x}_k^{(t)}$, which is the rank of the kth image measured against the query $\underline{q}_i$. Clearly, if $\underline{q}_i = \underline{x}_k^{(t)}$, then the rank of the kth image is $r_{ik} = 1$.

B. Network updating for relevance feedback

To incorporate relevance feedback information using the learning mechanism in (10), the network in Figure 1(a) has to be updated. The updating takes place in the feedback pool of the nodes corresponding to the voted image(s) via a node addition mechanism. This is done without updating the weights of the initial network. Figure 1(b) shows the updated network after the kth image is voted for the set of queries $\{\underline{q}_1 \cdots \underline{q}_K\}$. Each image will be represented by a group of nodes in the first layer called *feedback pool*. Every time an image is voted for some query image, a node corresponding to the query image is added to the corresponding feedback pool in the first layer. In this case, when the kth image is voted for the queries $\{\underline{q}_1 \cdots \underline{q}_K\}$, a node representing each of these queries is added in the corresponding pool. The incoming connection weights from the inputs to the newly added nodes are the vectors $\tilde{\underline{q}}_1 \cdots \tilde{\underline{q}}_K$ as shown in Figure 1(b). The connection weights from each of the newly added nodes to the kth output node are the $\alpha's$, found using (13). As mentioned before, the incoming weights to the first node (labelled by I_k) in this pool is $\underline{x}_k^{(t)}$ and not changed.

IV. RELEVANCE FEEDBACK RESULTS

The performance of the retrieval system is evaluated on a relatively large electro-optical (EO) imagery database collected from different underwater mine-like and types of non-mine-like objects. For each object, the EO sensor produces a pair of contrast and range images [8]. In order to provide statistically reliable results, additional synthetic images are generated by the perspective transformation of the original images at various grazing angles, namely $14°$, $27°$, $37°$ and $45°$. The feature vector is a composite vector formed of 18 shape-dependent Zernike moments [9] of order 7 extracted from the binary silhouettes (resulting from the union of range and contrast binary silhouettes), along with 16 texture-dependent features using the gray level co-occurrence matrices (GLCM)

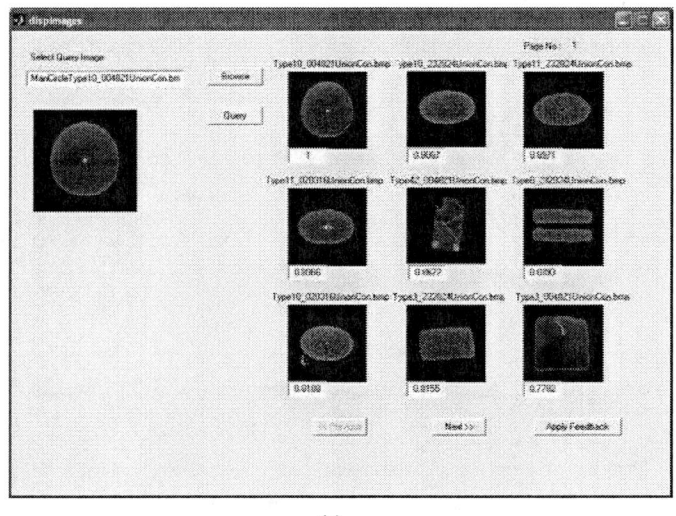 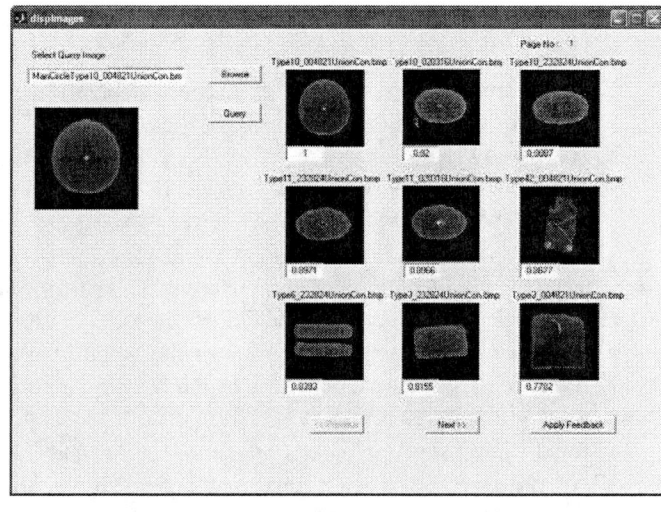

(a)   (b)

Fig. 2. User interface and the retrieved result of the image retrieval system, (a) before and (b) after relevance feedback.

[10]. The images are divided into two subsets, namely the training and testing. The training data set consists of feature vectors of the original mine-like and non mine-like images whereas, the testing data set is composed of feature vectors of the synthetically generated cases. The initial network is setup using the feature vectors in the training data set. The class labels are known for all the objects in the database. Relevance feedback is then applied to promote the most relevant images to the top of the search results list.

A. User Interface of the retrieval system

The developed user interface (UI) of our image retrieval system can be seen in Figure 2. Expert users can browse and select the query image. The selected query image (a circular, small-holed, non mine-like object of type 10) can be seen in the upper left side of the UI. In this case, the chosen query image is part of the images in the training set. The top nine retrieved images and their associated scores for this submitted query can also be seen in this figure. Note that this search result list is obtained using the initially trained network, without any previous relevance feedback. If the user is not satisfied with the search result, he/she can select any retrieved image, assign a new score and apply relevance feedback via the learning through the feature adaptation. The top two images and the seventh image in the retrieved list belongs to the same class as the submitted query image. We choose the seventh ranked image as the second most relevant with the user specified desired rank of 0.92 (rank before relevance feedback was 0.8188). It is desirable that the class of the top retrieved images corresponds to that of the submitted query. Figure 2 (b) shows the retrieved images after applying this relevance feedback learning. As can be seen, the voted image now appears at the desired third position via the relevance feedback learning. While promoting this image, it can also be observed that the rank of other images do not change for this query. Furthermore, this information is retained for subsequent usage by other expert users.

B. Study of convergence of relevance feedback learning

Ideally, while incorporating relevance feedback learning for a submitted query, the ranks and positions of the voted images should not change for other queries either. Note that "other queries" here refer to all queries except the ones for which the image is voted through relevance feedback. However, since the relevance feedback learning involves modifying the feature vector of the image to reach the desired ranking, this requirement may not always happen.

For example, let us assume that the kth image is voted K times and the adapted system is queried with the lth training image, using (10) the rank of the kth image for this query $\underline{x}_l^{(t)}$ is,

$$\underline{x}_l^{(t)^T}\underline{x}_k^{(t+K)} = \underline{x}_l^{(t)^T}\underline{x}_k^{(t)} + \sum_{i=1}^{K} \alpha_i \underline{x}_l^{(t)^T}\tilde{\underline{q}}_i$$
$$= r_{lk} + \sum_{i=1}^{K} \alpha_i \underline{x}_l^{(t)^T}\tilde{\underline{q}}_i \quad (15)$$

where r_{lk} is the rank of the kth image for this query before any relevance feedback learning. The second term in the right hand side represents the deviation in the rank of the voted image. Stabilization of the rank deviations after several rounds of feedback implies convergence of the second term or convergence of the adapted feature vectors. In this subsection, a set of experiments is carried out to test the convergence of the adapted feature vectors by observing the rank deviations after several rounds of feedback.

From (15) we can observe that, there are three factors that can affect the deviations in the rank of the voted images for other queries.

1) How much of new information in queries $\tilde{\underline{q}}_i$'s overlaps with $\underline{x}_l^{(t)}$.
2) The strength of $\alpha_i's$, which in turn depends on the amount of elevation in the rank of the voted image (see equation (13)).
3) Number of times (K) the kth image is voted on during the relevance feedback.

The deviation in the rank of the voted image is studied with respect to the above mentioned three factors. The performance measure used to evaluate the deviation in the rank is the average percentage change in the rank of the voted image for other queries. A good understanding of the learning algorithm can be obtained by studying the performance of the system,

- for different steps of percent elevation in the rank of the voted image with respect to its rank before any feedback. For evaluation purposes, we have chosen the percent elevation to vary from 10% to 90% in steps of 10% (i.e. small to large values of $\alpha_i's$).
- for different number of times the relevance feedback learning is applied (i.e. wrt K). For our evaluation, relevance feedback learning is applied up to $K = 5$ times.

The statistics needed to evaluate the performance of the system in terms of the average percentage change in the rank of the voted image are obtained as detailed below.

1) Select an image of some object type from the training set. This image is chosen to be voted in step (4).
2) From the testing set, choose 10 query images of the same type as the image selected in step (1).
3) Query the system using the images chosen in step(2) and observe the rank of the image selected in step (1). This gives the rank of the selected image before any relevance feedback learning.
4) From the training set, choose a query image of the same type as the selected image in step (1). Query the retrieval system and vote on the image selected in step (1), specifying the new desired rank.
5) Now, repeat step (3) to generate the rank of the selected (or voted) image after relevance feedback learning.
6) Knowing the rank of the voted image before and after relevance feedback, calculate the percent change in the rank of the voted image. Note that this percent change in the rank (of the voted image in step (1)) is observed for the query images (chosen in step (2)) contained in the testing set.
7) Repeat steps (1) to (6) for 30 different object types (hence different voted images) and calculate the average percent change in the ranks of the voted images.

The average percent change is observed for different rounds (1 to 5) of relevance feedback learning. For different rounds of relevance feedback, the query image in step (4) changes but the voted image remains the same.

The questions regarding the stability of the learning process are answered in Figures 3. This figure shows the change in percent deviation in the ranks of the voted image between two consecutive iterations of relevance feedback for the case

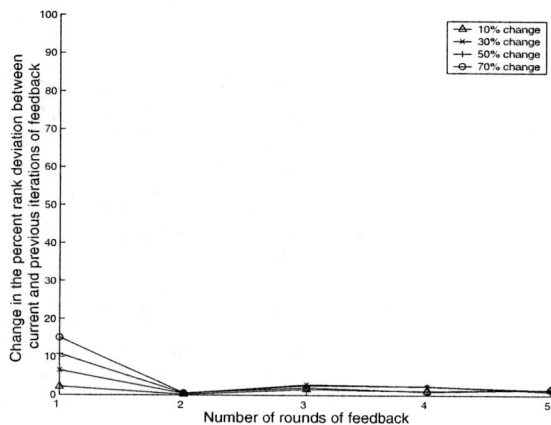

Fig. 3. Convergence of the percent change after several rounds of feedback.

when the object type in the voted image and query images are the same. It can be observed that between iterations 4 and 5, the percent change in the rank of the voted image increased only by 1.5%. Similar results are observed for the case when the object type in the voted image and the query images are different. These results attest to the fact that the rank deviations of the voted image stabilizes after several rounds of relevance feedback. The stabilization of the rank deviations implies that the adapted feature vector also stabilizes after several rounds of feedback. However, this study does not tell us whether convergence of the adapted feature vector implies improvement in the overall performance of the retrieval system. Our next study is aimed at observing this behavior in terms of the percent recall of the retrieval system.

C. Study of generalization ability of the learning algorithm

By voting the most relevant images to the top of the retrieved list, percent recall for queries from the training set can be improved to 100%. Generalization is the ability of the learning algorithm to extend this improvement of recall to queries outside the training set. The following study is performed to evaluate this property in terms of the percent change in the recall after several rounds of relevance feedback.

In the training data set, typically there are only 3 or 4 images corresponding to objects of the same type. Consequently, evaluating the percent recall based on the training set will not provide a reasonably accurate representation. Thus, along with the original mine-like and non mine-like images some of the synthetically generated images are also used in the training data set. As mentioned before, for each image in the training set, four synthetic images are created out of which two are used here in the training set. This allows us to have 9 to 12 images with same object types in the training set, hence producing a statistically richer data set. The estimated recall from this extended image database would give a reasonable insight into the generalization ability of the learning.

The testing procedure for studying the generalization behavior is briefly explained below.

1) From the training set, choose a query image of some

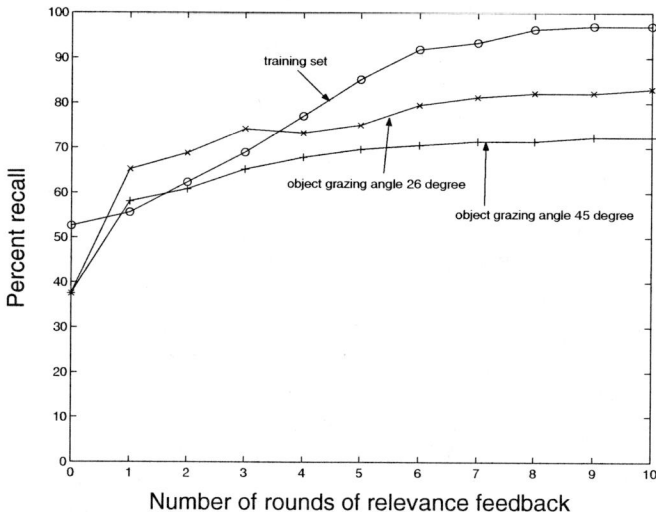

Fig. 4. Percent recall after several rounds of relevance feedback on the training and testing set.

object type.
2) From the testing set, choose two synthetic images (corresponding to two different grazing angles) of the same type as the one chosen in step (1).
3) Query the system using the training image chosen in step (1). Select an image that is relevant to the query image from the search list and vote on it. To find the percent recall for any given query, choose a threshold equal to the total number of images in the database that are relevant to the query image. Now, percent recall after querying is, $100(\frac{number\ of\ relevant\ images\ within\ the\ threshold}{total\ number\ of\ relevant\ images})$
4) Query the system using the images chosen from the testing set in step (2) and observe the percent recall. This gives the percent recall for images that are not seen previously by the system.
5) Repeat steps (1) to (4) for 20 different object types to find the average recall of queries chosen in step(1) and step (2) separately.
6) Repeat steps (1) to (5) for several rounds (1 to 10) of feedback. In each round of feedback, a new image is voted and the query image is kept the same.

Figure 4 shows the improvement in the percent recall after several (1-10) rounds of relevance feedback for the training and testing data sets. It can be observed that before any feedback, the recall is 53% and after 10 rounds of feedback the recall is increased to 97%. This demonstrates the fact that, the proposed feature adaptation algorithm is capable of capturing the information provided by the expert users successfully. The plots marked 'x' and '+' corresponds to the percent recall for the synthetic images generated with grazing angle of 26° and 45°, respectively. From Figure 4, it can readily be observed that for images at grazing angle 26°, the percent recall before any feedback was 37.5% and after 10 rounds of feedback it increased to 83%; while for images at grazing angle 45°, the percent recall increased from 37.5% to 72.3% after 10 rounds of feedback. In cases when the synthetic image is generated at grazing angle of 45°, the distortion in the synthetic image compared to the original image is very high. Therefore, the feature vectors between the original image and this synthetic image vary significantly and hence the improvement in recall is not very high. However, the considerable increase in the recall clearly demonstrates the generalization ability of our relevance feedback learning algorithm.

V. CONCLUSION

In this paper, it has been shown that the relevance feedback information provided by the expert user could be captured through a new feature adaptation mechanism. It is also shown that the search and retrieval processes can be implemented through a two-layer connectionist network structure and that the relevance feedback learning can also be incorporated into this network structure by appropriately adding nodes in the corresponding feedback pools. In our model, ranking of the images for the submitted query is based on the correlation between image and the query, which is a second order property. However, with the use of kernels, higher order statistics can be utilized to improve the retrieval efficiency and the overall effectiveness of the system. Since, the image similarity function is the dot product of the query and image feature vector and also capturing the expert user information involves dot products (between image feature vector and innovation vector), the learning algorithm can easily be extended to kernel domains. This should be studied in future research.

ACKNOWLEDGMENT

The authors would like to thank NSWC Coastal Systems Station (CSS), Panama City, FL for providing the electro-optical imagery database for this study.

REFERENCES

[1] K. Porkaew, M. Ortega, and S. Mehrota, "Query reformulation for content based multimedia retrieval in mars," *IEEE International Conference on Multimedia Computing and Systems*, vol. 2, pp. 747–751, June 1999.
[2] H. M. T. Onoda and S. Yamada, "Relevance feedback with active learning for document retrieval," *Proceedings of the International Joint Conference on Neural Networks*, vol. 3, pp. 1757 – 1762, 2003.
[3] R. Baeza and B. Ribeiro, *Modern Information Retrieval*. New York: Addison-Wesley, 1999.
[4] M. R. Azimi-Sadjadi, J. Salazar, and S. Srinivasan, "An adaptable connectionist text retrieval system with relevance feedback," in *Proceedings of IEEE Intl. Joint Conf. on Neural Networks*, Budapest, July 2004.
[5] S. Haykin, *Neural Networks: A Comprehensive Foundation*. Prentice Hall, 1998.
[6] J. Zhang and A. J. Morris, "A sequential learning approach for single hidden layer neural networks," *Neural Networks*, vol. 11, no. 1, pp. 65–80, 1998.
[7] J.J. Rocchio, Relevance feedback in information retrieval, In: G. Salton(ed), *The Smart retrieval system: Experiments in Automatic Document Processing*. Englewood Cliffs, 1971.
[8] J. S. Taylor and M. C. Hulgan, "Electo-optic identification research program," *Proc. of 2002 MTS/IEEE Oceans Conference, Biloxi*, vol. 2, pp. 994–1002, October 2002.
[9] A. Khotanzad and Y. H. Hong, "Invariant image recognition by zernike moments," *IEEE Trans. on Pattern Analysis and Machine Intelligence*, vol. 12.
[10] R. M. Haralick, K. Shanmugam, and I. Dinstein, "Textural features for image classification," *IEEE Trans. Systems, Man, and Cybernetics*, pp. 610–621, 1973.

Design of an Optical Fixed-Weight Learning Neural Network

A. Steven Younger and Emmett Redd
Department of Physics, Astronomy, and Materials Science
Southwest Missouri State University
Springfield, MO 65804
E-mail: asy313f@smsu.edu or EmmettRedd@smsu.edu

Abstract--This paper deals with the design, analysis, and simulation of a prototype Optical Fixed-Weight Learning Neural Network. This type of network could have learning rates five orders of magnitude faster than networks based on Von-Neumann platforms. This network has an embedded learning algorithm and dynamically learns new mappings by changing recurrent neural signal strengths. This will greatly speed up optical neural network learning since the medium containing the synaptic weights does not change during learning. Software simulations suggest that this design is sound. The physical implementation and evaluation of the prototype will be reported elsewhere.

I. INTRODUCTION

We will present the concept of an Optical Fixed-Weight Learning Neural Network. The constraints on the network due to the physical properties of the optical system will be examined. A design method called analytic construction will be presented, which we used to design an Optical FWL-NN. Scaling issues will be described in some detail. We will discuss how to compute the necessary fixed-synaptic weights. The results were used to create a simple network capable of learning any linearly separable, two argument Boolean function. Finally, we will present the results of software simulations of the Optical FWL-NN. The physical implementation and evaluation of a hardware prototype will be reported elsewhere

Optical Neural Networks are the fastest method available today for performing neural computations. Systems employing laser diodes and high-speed operational amplifiers have estimated synaptic processing rates of 100,000 times a high-end Pentium[1]. Today, Optical DSP processors that can perform up to 8,000 billion synaptic operations per second are commercially available (Lenslet, Inc. EnLight 256).

Given this speed advantage, why are Optical Neural Networks not more commonly used? One reason is that the training of these networks cannot use the full speed of the optical hardware. Learning changes the synaptic weights, which requires changing the medium on which the synaptic information in stored. In some systems, this is a holographic plate or slide. Other systems use a Spatial Light Modulator (SLM). A new slide must be produced or weights must be downloaded to the SLM. Both of these are slow compared to the forward propagation of the optical neural network.

We propose to integrate learning into the network such that the high-speed hardware can be used during learning as well as forward propagation. This will be done by developing an Optical Fixed-Weight Learning Neural Network (FWL-NN).

A. Fixed-Weight Learning Neural Networks

Several researchers have investigated FWL-NNs [2-6]. Most (perhaps all) implementations of FWL-NN up to now have been as software-based entities. FWL-NNs are a type of recurrent neural network. They have two features that distinguish them from other neural networks. First, FWL-NNs store the function mapping information in dynamic, recurrent signal loops instead of synaptic weights. During learning, the network itself dynamically adjusts these internal recurrent neural signals. This approach is similar to biological working memory, where information is thought to be stored in recurrent neural pathways.

The second distinction of FWL-NNs is that the learning algorithm is embedded or encoded in its synaptic weights. The synaptic weights encode the ability to learn any mapping (from a large, possibly infinite set of mappings) instead of just a particular mapping, as in conventional neural networks.

This FWL-NN uses an on-line (always learning) version of Backpropagation. However, any learning algorithm (on-line or off-line) can be implemented as a FWL-NN [2].

B. Optical Neural Networks

A schematic of an optical neural network **stratum** is shown in Figure 1. A stratum is a layer of neurons together with their synaptic computations. Light from a **source** passes through a high-speed **modulator** which encodes the source neuron, n_i, activation level, x_i. Only one of the many source neurons is shown. The light is directed by **presynaptic optics** onto the **synaptic medium**. The interaction of the optical neural signal with the synaptic medium (attenuation) performs the synaptic computation (i.e. $W_{ij} \cdot x_i$). **Postsynaptic**

optics such as a cylindrical lens directs the results from all source neurons onto the **light detector** (target neuron n_j). The detector performs the spatial summation $s_j = \sum_i W_{ij} \cdot x_i$ of the signals from all source neurons. An electronic device such as an **operational amplifier** performs the squashing function (such as $\text{logsig}(s) = 1/(1-e^{-s})$). The final activations are then sent to the next stratum, and/or to the external system.

II. CREATING A FWL-NN

A. Meta-Learning

How are the synaptic weights for the FWL-NN derived? Most researchers have used a method called *meta-learning* or *adaptive behavior* [5-7]. Meta-learning is *learning how to learn* (or learn better). It uses a large set of example function mappings to derive a learning algorithm. An optimization algorithm adjusts the synaptic weights in such a way as to minimize a given error metric (usually total squared error over all meta-training data.)

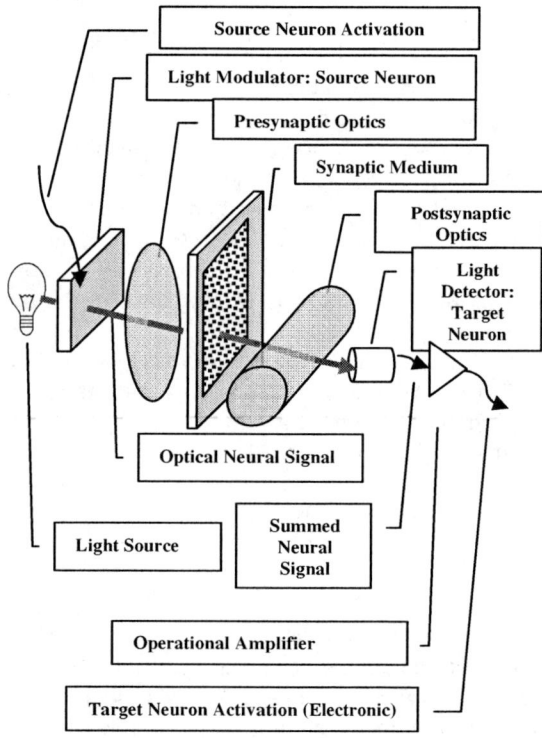

Figure 1. Schematic of a stratum of an optical neural network.

The resulting learning algorithms (synaptic weights) have proven to be very fast and accurate at learning functions from the meta-training set [7]. However, because of concerns about the generalization ability of meta-learning derived learning algorithms [6], we have rejected meta-learning for this FWL-NN project.

B. Analytic Construction

Extending a method [4] that we now call *analytic construction*, we derived a FWL-NN that contains an on-line Backpropagation learning algorithm. This insures that the FWL-NN will generalize as well as any standard (non-fixed-weight learning) on-line Backpropagation.

Previous FWL-NNs containing Backpropagation used higher-order $\Sigma - \Pi$ synapses [8], which are not easy to implement in optical hardware. We used analytic construction to derive a first-order (i.e. standard synapse) FWL-NN that contains Backpropagation, which can be much more easily implemented in optical hardware.

Figure 2 illustrates the construction of a FWL-NN, which is equivalent to a non-fixed-weight single-synapse neural network that learns by Backpropagation. Figure 2(a) shows computer using the Backpropagation algorithm to compute a new synaptic weight during the neural network learning process. It computes the synaptic weight change $\Delta W(t-1)$ using the Backpropagation formula $\Delta W(t-1) = x(t-1) \cdot y(t-1) \cdot (1 - y(t-1)) \cdot (y(t-1) - T(t-1))$.

With learning rate η, a weight decay term ε, and the $\Delta W(t-1)$ value, the computer calculates the new synaptic weight $W(t) = (1-\varepsilon) \cdot W(t-1) - \eta \Delta W(t-1)$. The next time a network input is presented, the new weight is used in the synaptic operation (multiplication of input signal $x(t)$ by new synaptic weight), i.e. $s(t) = W(t-1) \cdot x(t)$.

For a FWL-NN (Figure 2(b)), all of the above computations are done *by neural networks* (called sub-networks), which operate on (and produce as output) *neural signals*. No synaptic weights are changed as the FWL-NN learns a new mapping. Only the neural signals change

C. Universal Approximation

From the Universal Approximation Theorem we know that there exist sub-networks that can perform any learning algorithm including Backpropagation [2]. We created these sub-networks by training them for the appropriate functions. We then assembled them into a complete FWL-NN.

Rather than continue to use "weight signal" or "recurrent neural signal" as a term, we will use the word **potency**. These potencies have also been called "flying weights." [9] We trained a neural network to multiply the source signal and potency together. Since this fixed-weight network performs a function similar to a synapse but is beyond one like a transistor is beyond a resistor, we call it a **tranapse**. Similarly, the potency comes from a Backpropagation formalism which includes an error signal. Since error in Greek is πλανη, the error signal will be produced by a fixed-weight network called a **planapse**.

The outputs of several tranapses can be combined by a single neuron. This works like a neuron that has potencies rather than weights. Since the potencies are the recurrent signals discussed above, the combination of tranapses, planapses, and a neuron will be called a **recurron**. These able-to-learn recurrons can be connected together as a recurrent neural network, i.e. a **recurral** network. Later, we will discuss construction and simulation of a recurron.

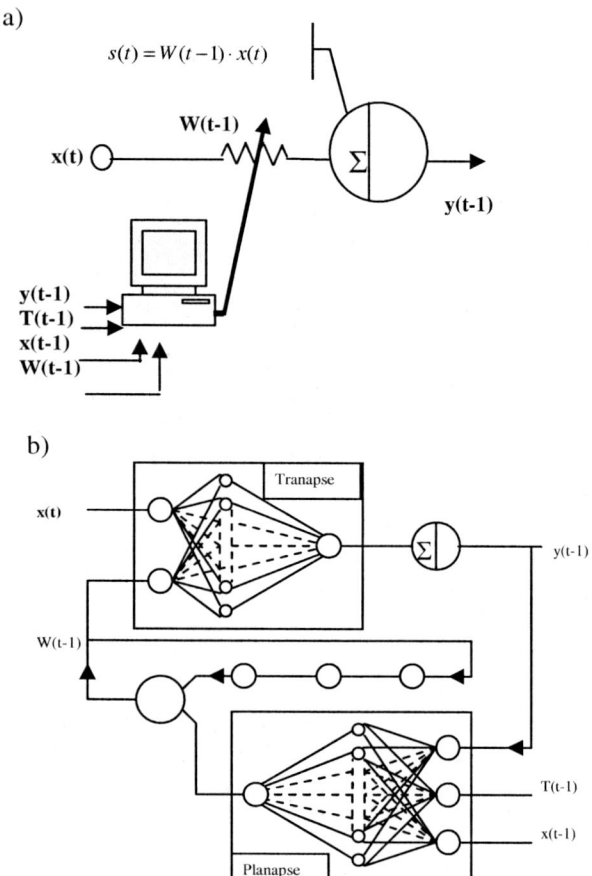

Figure 2. (a) Single-synapse, changing-weight neural network. (b) Equivalent Fixed-Weight Learning Neural Network.

III. CURRENT CONSTRAINTS DUE TO THE OPTICAL HARDWARE

The optical neural signal can be encoded by any of several methods, such as analog intensity level modulation (driven by a D/A converter), pulse-width modulation, or pulse-train modulation. The first scheme operates faster, but achieving reproducible linear response is problematic, especially with larger numbers of significant bits of precision. The other two methods are slower, but allow for easier extensibility to greater number of significant bits.

No matter which scheme is used, the signal has a limited precision (number of significant bits), a minimum value (zero) and a maximum value (full intensity), which we set to unity.

For our prototype, we decided to use a Digital Micromirror Device (DMD) to spatially and temporally modulate the light. The DMD is a rectangular array of 1 Million micromirrors on a one-square-inch integrated circuit. Each mirror can be independently and rapidly switched from an 'on' state to an 'off' state. The DMD can support the pulse-width and pulse-train encoding schemes.

Attenuation in an optical medium ranges from opaque (zero synaptic weight) to transparent (unit synaptic weight). Positive and negative synaptic weights are done separately in different regions of the medium and combined later in the neuron.

The synaptic weight range of $[-1,+1]$ is not sufficient for most neural networks. However, linear scaling can extend the range to $[-\omega,+\omega]$, where $\omega>0$ and is large enough to encompass the (absolute) maximum synaptic weight in the network. An ω of 4 to 10 is usually adequate.

There is also the spatial bandwidth of the medium to consider. How many pixels should be used per synapse, and how many grayscale levels should be used? While many media can support 8 to 12 bits per pixel of gray, these tend to have a nonlinear attenuation per grey level. Also, consistency of the grayscale between individual media is poor.

For our prototype, we decided to use 35mm photographic slides. Slides from commercial slide makers have about 16 Megapixels. Binary area encoding (each pixel either 0 or 1) of the synapses will allow us to use linear grayscale calibration. Our initial FWL-NNs consist of about 250 synapses, allowing 64 Kilopixels per synapse, or 16 bits of precision.

For the prototype array of target neurons, we will use a CCD camera to allow maximum flexibility for detection and integration schemes, albeit at a slower speed than op-amp based detectors.

IV. TRAINING THE BACKPROPAGATION

A. Scaling

1) Neural Network Weight Scaling: This scaling is necessary to keep the optical signals as near unity as possible making the best use of the system's dynamic range. As discussed above, the positive and negative weights have been separated into different regions of the slide. The neuron summation function includes a negative sign when summing the negative region signals. Then, of the weights associated with a single neuron, they are divided by the largest weight (in absolute value). To compensate for the division, this largest weight then multiplies the output of the neuron's summation function. This is easy in optical systems, since the detected optical signals must be amplified (scaled) as part of the summation process anyway.

This scaling has not yet been implemented on individual fixed-weight neurons. Rather, the largest weight in a layer of neurons has scaled all weights and neuron summation function outputs in that layer. Scaling individual neuron weights may be done in the future if the necessary coding results in benefits to justify it.

2) Potency Scaling: As discussed above, scaling of the potencies is necessary because of the limited physical range of optical signals. To properly implement optical FWL-NN, we must correctly convert the unlimited range of the FWL-NN operations into the limited range of the optical system. Formally putting free-range limits as superscripts, the recurrent, free-range gradient descent rule of Backpropagation looks like:

$$\overset{-\omega,+\omega}{P}(t) = (1-\varepsilon)\cdot \overset{-\omega,+\omega}{P}(t-1) - \eta \cdot \overset{-\xi,+\xi}{\Delta P}(t-1)$$

where ε is small enough that most of the previous potency remains and η is of a size so ΔP will have reasonable impact on P without causing oscillation. Since the P's and ΔP's are optical signals in the range [0,1] we actually have an equation that looks like:

$$\overset{0,1}{P}(t) = A \cdot \overset{0,1}{P}(t-1) + B \cdot \overset{0,1}{\Delta P}(t-1) + C$$

where A, B, and C need to be determined in terms of ε, η, ω, and ξ.

A formal way to determine A, B, and C involves an augmented rotation matrix multiplication. In a single matrix multiply, it can do scaling, rotation, and translation. Rotation is not needed here. The full matrix results from multiplying five relatively-simple-to-develop augmented matrices together. The first one to operate on our P and ΔP signals scales $\overset{0,1}{\Delta P}$ to its free range value of $\overset{-\xi,+\xi}{\Delta P}$; $\begin{bmatrix} 1 & 0 & 0 \\ 0 & 2\xi & -\xi \\ 0 & 0 & 1 \end{bmatrix}$. The next one, $\begin{bmatrix} 2\omega & 0 & -\omega \\ 0 & 1 & 0 \\ 0 & 0 & 1 \end{bmatrix}$, scales $\overset{0,1}{P}$ to its free range value of $\overset{-\omega,+\omega}{P}$. The third matrix $\begin{bmatrix} 1-\varepsilon & -\eta & 0 \\ 0 & 1 & 0 \\ 0 & 0 & 1 \end{bmatrix}$ performs the recurrent, free-range Backpropagation mentioned above, combining $\overset{-\omega,+\omega}{P}(t-1)$ and $\overset{-\xi,+\xi}{\Delta P}(t-1)$ in a way consistent with scaling. The fourth matrix $\begin{bmatrix} \frac{1}{\omega} & 0 & 0 \\ 0 & 1 & 0 \\ 0 & 0 & 1 \end{bmatrix}$ scales the $\overset{-\omega,+\omega}{P}(t)$ into a range [-1,1]. The fifth matrix $\begin{bmatrix} \frac{1}{2} & 0 & \frac{1}{2} \\ 0 & 1 & 0 \\ 0 & 0 & 1 \end{bmatrix}$ puts $\overset{-1,+1}{P}(t)$ into a nominal range of [0,1]. This is followed by a clipping function to absolutely make the range [0,1] and the signal, $\overset{0,1}{P}(t)$. Multiplying these five matrices together and using it in the rotation vector-matrix multiplication:

$$\begin{bmatrix} \overset{0,1}{P}(t) \\ \overset{0,1}{\Delta P}(t) \\ 1 \end{bmatrix} = \begin{bmatrix} 1-\varepsilon & -\frac{\eta\xi}{\omega} & \frac{\varepsilon}{2}+\frac{\eta\xi}{2\omega} \\ 0 & 2\xi & -\xi \\ 0 & 0 & 1 \end{bmatrix} \times \begin{bmatrix} \overset{0,1}{P}(t-1) \\ \overset{0,1}{\Delta P}(t-1) \\ 1 \end{bmatrix}$$

causes $A = 1-\varepsilon$, $B = -\frac{\eta\xi}{\omega}$, $C = \frac{\varepsilon}{2} + \frac{\eta\xi}{2\omega}$. Some may think all this matrix multiplication unnecessary, but it really keeps each individual scaling operation simple and separable. In fact, to keep the last section of our MATLAB code consistent, we separated out the last matrix and included its scaling with the clipping function (together calling them "linsig", a linear analog to logsig) and used A', B', and C' resulting from multiplying the first four.

B. Backpropagation via Backpropagation

We used Backpropagation to train our sub-networks to do Backpropagation. That is, to obtain the fixed weights for a tranapse, planapse, or combination, we trained these three-layer neural sub-networks using a version of Backpropagation. Care had to be used because we were training a small network that had to generalize well.

V. BUILDING A RECURRON

A. Recurral Network Topology

We are only at the beginning stages of building a recurral network. Our first attempt was to build a network that can learn all linearly separable two-input Boolean functions. The set includes the AND, OR, NOR, but excludes XOR and its complement. Table I shows this set of mappings with XOR and its complement in red. These functions can be learned by a single neuron with two synaptic weights and one threshold. A single recurron with three potencies should also be able to learn these functions [2].

B. "Pages" Defined

Although neural networks are often visualized as planar, we found this very difficult when trying to duplicate tranapses and planapses. The fixed-weights for the various neurons had to be shifted in the arrays in a way which was not consistent from one tranapse/planapse network size to another. We then decided to use a third dimension in our weight matrices and put each tranapse/planapse combination on a separate "page" as shown in Figure 3. This allowed each tranapse/planapse combination to have weights and connections identical in the first two matrix dimensions, the planar pages. This helped partially automate combining the tranapse/planapse into a recurron. The final output neuron had to have signals coming from multiple pages. And its output has to be fed back to each page.

TABLE I. Boolean Function Truth Table

A,B	0,0	0,1	1,0	1,1	Index
TRUE	1	1	1	1	1.6
NOR	1	1	1	0	1.5
(A→B)	1	1	0	1	1.4
~A	1	1	0	0	1.3
(B→A)	1	0	1	1	1.2
~B	1	0	1	0	1.1
EXOR	1	0	0	1	1.0
NAND	1	0	0	0	0.9
OR	0	1	1	1	0.8
XOR	0	1	1	0	0.7
B	0	1	0	1	0.6
~(B→A)	0	1	0	0	0.5
A	0	0	1	1	0.4
~(A→B)	0	0	1	0	0.3
AND	0	0	0	1	0.2
FALSE	0	0	0	0	0.1

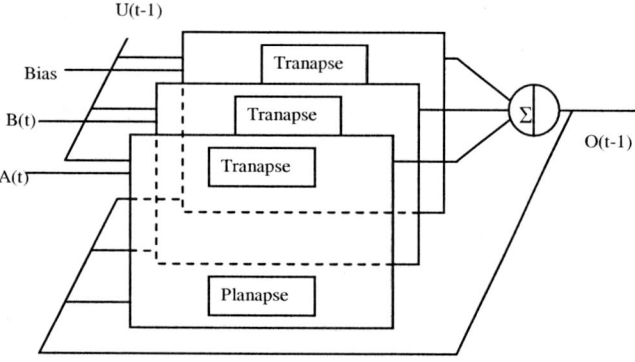

Figure 3. Page representation of the described recurron. The A(t) and B(t) represent the Boolean inputs, U(t-1) is the previous target, and Bias is required; O(t-1) is the previous output.

VI. SIMULATION AND TESTING

This network was tested on a software-based 'medium grain" simulator written in MATLAB. The simulation included the effects of limited range neural signals, synaptic weights, and multi-phase synchronous neurons. The recurron was made up of three tranapses, three planapses, and a single neuron. The three inputs were a bias signal plus the two Boolean inputs. A true output signal was also provided.

A. Generating the Test Data

The test dataset was generated by the algorithm:

repeat M times:
   randomly select a function from Table I (call it Λ)
   repeat N times:
      randomly select $A, B \in \{0,1\}$
      compute $T = \Lambda(A, B)$, where $T \in \{0,1\}$
      output A,B,T, and identifying index for Λ
   next N
next M

B. Simulation Results.

Figures 4 and 5 show simulation results. For example, Figure 4 step 1500, the Boolean function being presented to the recurron was $\Lambda = A \vee B$ as indicated by the function index value (dashed line). As shown by the plot, the squared error of the recurron was initially large, because it had not yet learned the mapping. However, after about 25 steps, the recurron error had fallen to a small value, indicating that learning had taken place.

After step 2000, the function was changed. This time, $\Lambda = \sim(B \rightarrow A)$. The recurron error immediately jumped up and stayed up until the recurron learned the new function (about step 2050).

Note small burst of errors in the Figure 4 around steps 4940 – 4960. We believe this is due to the finite range of the potency signals and the on-line nature of the learning algorithm. This behavior was previously reported in [4].

Figure 5 shows another simulation run. Note that at step 1200, the recurron took longer than average time to learn. This is because the test mapping went from function B→A to its complementary function ~(B→A).

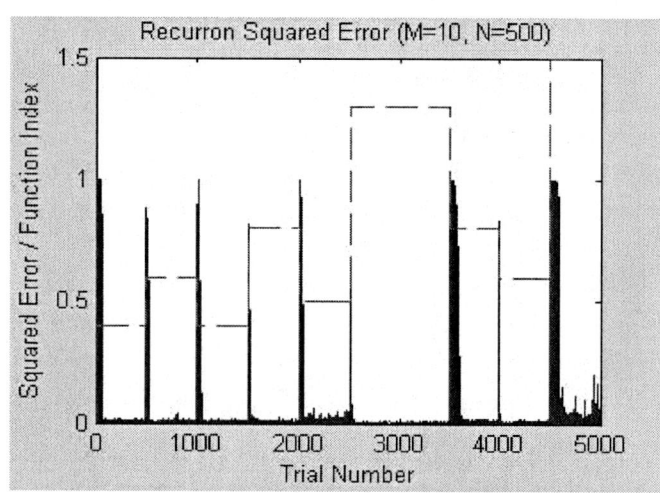

Figure 4. Simulated Recurron Squared Error (M=10, N=500) Dashed line shows the index of the Boolean function being learned (see Table I). Squared error has a maximum value of 1.0 when recurron output = ~(Target). Since recurron's output is not digital, error can range [0,1].

Table II shows the overall mean squared error (MSE), the MSE after learning has occurred (we gave the recurron 100 steps to learn), and the percentage of correct recurron predictions after learning. We defined the networks prediction to be correct if $(T-O)^2 < \frac{1}{4}$, and incorrect otherwise.

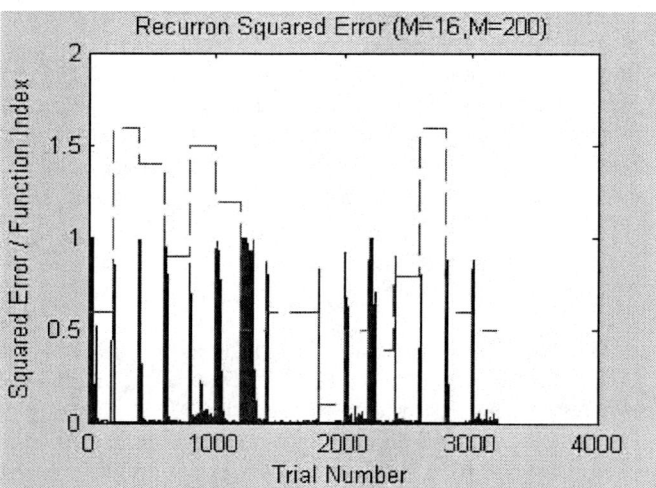

Figure 5. Simulated Recurron Squared Error (M=16,N=200). Same caption as Figure 4.

Table II. Simulation Results

Fig #	M	N	overall MSE	MSE after learning	% correct after learning
4	10	500	0.028	0.0073	100
5	16	200	0.046	0.0085	99.7

VII. CONCLUSION AND FUTURE WORK

The software simulations of our design of an Optical Fixed-Weight Learning Neural Network prototype confirm that such a network is feasible. We can account for the constraints on the network imposed by the physics of the optical neural system. The resulting Optical FWL-NN should be able to learn at a speed substantially faster than networks based on Von-Neumann hardware. It also should be able to generalize as well as Backpropagation does.

Besides construction and evaluation of the physical prototype, future work may involve reducing the learning algorithm overhead costs and incorporation of Holographic and non-linear optical components [10].

ACKNOWLEDGEMENTS

This work was supported in part by Data Fusion Corporation of Northglenn, Colorado through a grant from US Army Space and Missile Defense Command. DASG60-02-P-0192. This material is based upon work supported by the National Science Foundation under Grant No. 0446660.

REFERENCES

[1] Paul E. Keller and Arthur F. Gmitro, "Operational Parameters of an Opto-Electronic Neural Network Employing Fixed-Planar Holographic Interconnects," *World Congress on Neural Networks 1993 (WCNN' 93)*.

[2] N. E. Cotter and P. R. Conwell, "Learning algorithms and fixed dynamics," *Proceedings of the International Conference on Neural Networks 91*, vol. I pp. 799-804 IEEE 1991.

[3] Lee A. Feldkamp, Danil V. Prokhorov, Timothy Feldkamp, "Conditioned Adaptive Behavior from Kalman Filter Trained Recurrent Networks," *IJCNN' 03* IEEE 2003.

[4] A. Steven Younger, P. R. Conwell, and N. E. Cotter, "Fixed-Weight On-Line Learning," *IEEE Transactions on Neural Networks*. Vol.10 No. 2, pp. 272-283 March 1999.

[5] Danil V. Prokhorov, Lee A. Feldkamp and Ivan Yu. Tyukin, "Adaptive Behavior with Fixed Weights in RNN: An Overview," *IJCNN'02* IEEE 2002.

[6] James T. Lo and Devasis Bassu. "Adaptive vs. Accomodative Neural Networks for Adaptive System Identification," *IJCNN'01* IEEE 2001.

[7] Sepp Hochreiter, A. Steven Younger and Peter R. Conwell, "Learning To Learn Using Gradient Descent," *Proceedings of the International Conference on Artificial Neural Networks*. Springer Verlag 2001.

[8] E. Fiesler, "Neural Network Classification and Formalization," *Computer Standards & Interfaces*, vol. 16 no. 3 pp. 231-239 1994.

[9] Paul Werbos, private communication, 2004.

[10] Yaser S. Abu-Mostafa and Demtri Psaltis, "Optical Neural Computers," *Scientific American* March 1987.

Forgetful Logic Circuits for Pulse-Mode Neural Networks[1]

Richard B. Wells, Anindya Bhattacharya, Ben Sharon, Priyank Gupta, Sam Young, Sanjeev Giri, Terseer Ityavyar, and Dave Cox

MRC Institute
University of Idaho
Moscow, ID 83844-1024, USA
wellsrb@ieee.org

Abstract – **We introduce a new class of pulse-mode circuit, called forgetful logic. Forgetful logic circuits can be used to implement more complex waveform signaling in pulse-mode artificial neural network circuits. The basic operation of forgetful logic is first explained. Its application is then illustrated by numerous examples.**

I. INTRODUCTION

There is very strong biological evidence that signal-dependent elastic modulation of synaptic weights and neuronal excitability plays a key role in information processing in the brain. Relatively rapid, short-term variations in synaptic efficacy is now believed to be responsible for a transient and reconfigurable 'functional column' organization in the visual cortex [1]-[2]. Dynamical recruitment of neurons into functional units by various selection processes have been theoretically studied by Edelman [3], Pearson et al. [4], Linsker [5], and Anderson and Van Essen [6]. Transient elastic modulation of synaptic efficacy is a central feature in the dynamic link architecture paradigm of neural computing [7]-[8]. One well-known example of the use of elastic modulation is provided by the vigilance parameter in ARTMAP networks[9]. It has long been accepted that firing rate encoding is one method by which information can be presented in a pulse-mode neural network, and it is likewise known that rate-dependent mechanisms exist in biological neural networks that filter information based on both pulse rate and the duration of a signaling tetanus [10]. Similarly, information may also be encoded through synchrony of firing patterns [10]-[12], and it is obvious that synchrony and rate/duration encoding can be combined in determining elastic modulations of synaptic efficacy. Many biological synapses, for instance, show selectivity to both pulse repetition rate and tetanus duration [10].

In this paper we present simple circuits for implementing these sorts of elastic modulation features in pulse-mode artificial neural networks and illustrate its use with some examples of rate- and tetanus-duration selectivity in networks comprised of previously reported mixed-signal VLSI pulse-mode neurons [13]-[16]. The circuit is selective for ranges of input firing rates and number of pulses received. If the firing rate is below the selection range the circuits do not activate, and within the designed frequency range the circuits require a minimum number of incoming pulses before activation. They are based on a logic circuit consisting of a pass element, one or two inverters, and a biasing element that sets its dynamic characteristics. We call circuits based on this design "forgetful logic" circuits (FLCs).

II. BASIC FORGETFUL LATCH CIRCUIT

The basic logic element is the non-inverting forgetful latch (FL) depicted in Figure 1. M2 – M5 comprise a biasing stick, which can be common to several FLCs in a VLSI implementation. M6 and M7 bias a storage node at the gates of inverter M8-M9. A single high-level input pulse applied to M1 charges the storage node and results in a HIGH level output from inverter M10-M11. When the input pulse goes LOW, M1 opens and current source M7 slowly discharges the gate capacitance at the storage node. The output pulse remains high for a brief time determined by the gate capacitance and the value of the drain current of M7. Thus, the input pulse is briefly 'stretched' at the output, typically for about 2.89 μsec for a 1 μsec input pulse in our designs, beyond the end of the input pulse. The FL then 'forgets' and the output goes LOW again.

Figure 2 illustrates the response of the FL to isolated input pulses and to a high-frequency tetanus. Note that for high-rate input pulse trains the FL maintains a constant HIGH output level. This behavior signals the on-going presence of

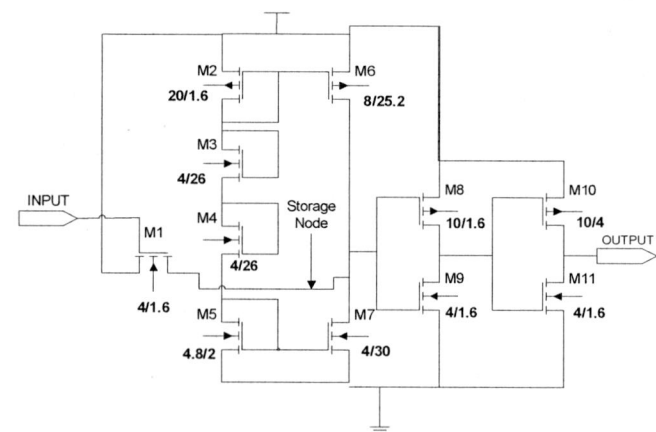

Figure 1: Basic Non-inverting Forgetful Latch Circuit. By eliminating M10 and M11 an inverting forgetful latch is obtained. Typical W/L ratios are shown in the figure.

---

[1] This work is supported by the NSF-Idaho EPSCoR Program and by the National Science Foundation under award number EPS-0132626.

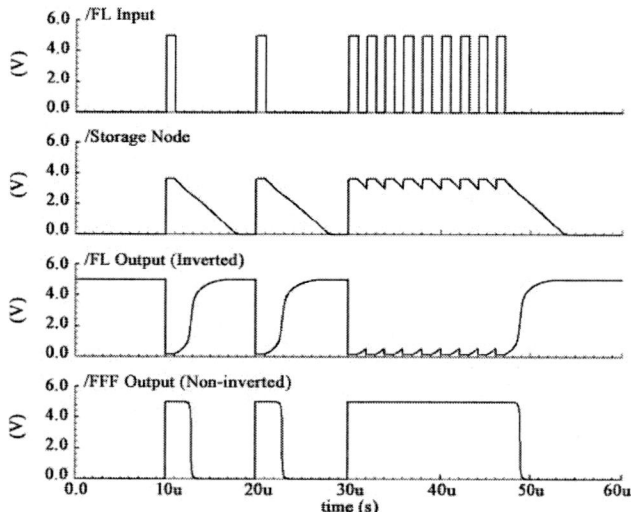

Figure 2: Pulse-rate dependence of the response of the basic forgetful latch.

signaling activity at the FL input and is a characteristic used in constructing the various other signal processing functions implemented using forgetful logic. The FL output pulse width for a single isolated input pulse is given by

$$\tau = \frac{C(V_{DD} - V_{SP} - V_t)}{I} + \tau_{in} \quad (1)$$

where τ is the output pulse width, C is the total gate capacitance at the storage node, V_{DD} is the power supply voltage, V_{SP} is the switching threshold of M8-M9, V_t is the threshold of the n-channel device, I is the drain current of M7, and τ_{in} is the width of the input pulse. At input pulse rates above a threshold given by $1/(\tau + \tau_{in})$ the logic ceases to be "forgetful."

III. THE FORGETFUL FLIPFLOP

The cascade of two inverting forgetful latches, typically with different design values for τ, comprises a forgetful flipflop (FFF). The circuit is shown in Figure 3. M2-M5 comprise the bias stick. M1 and M6-M9 comprise the first FL, while M10-M14 comprise the second FL. Under quiescent conditions the output is LOW and the storage node at the drain of M12 is charged. τ at M12 is set to be larger than that of M7 such that the second FL cannot respond to single input pulses at the gate of M1. Rather, an input tetanus is required before the FFF output will respond.

The number of input pulses in the tetanus and the minimum input pulse rate required to evoke an output response from the FFF depends on the relative values of τ for the two stages. It is possible to achieve a wide range in the length of the tetanus required and in the delay-to-output assert and pulse width of the FFF output pulse. As a matter of terminology, we refer to FFF designs that respond relatively quickly and have output pulses that reset shortly

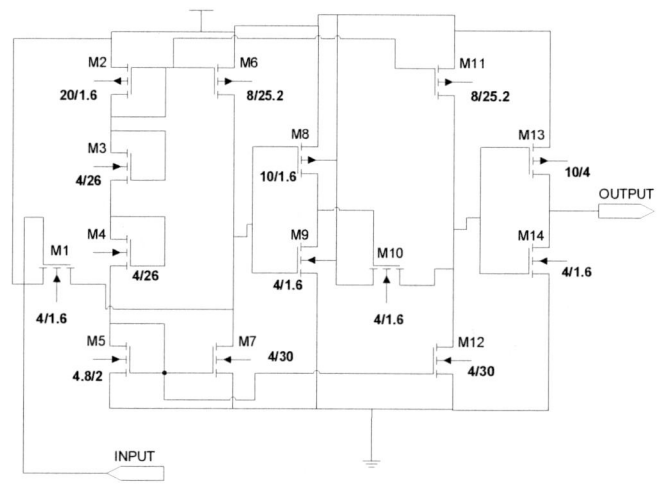

Figure 3: Basic forgetful flipflop (FFF) circuit with typical W/L values.

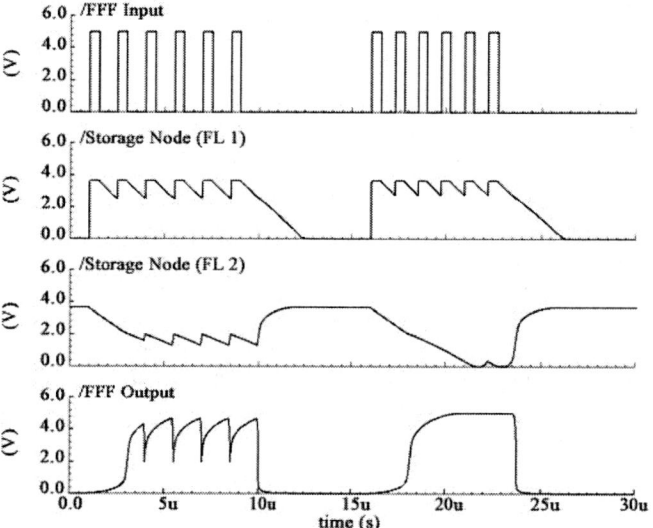

Figure 4: Input/output responses for 333 kpps and 400 kpps input pulse rates for a forgetful flipflop designed to produce a facilitation response. The leftmost output response is called a "twitch" response; the rightmost response is called a "complete" response. The FFF is designed to not respond to input pulse rates below 200 kpps.

after the end of the tetanus as a "facilitation" response; designs that require a longer tetanus or which hold the output pulse HIGH for a longer period of time after the end of the tetanus are called "augmentation" responses.

The basic action of the FFF is illustrated in Figure 4 for a design that implements a facilitation response. The FFF circuit which produces this response ignores input pulse trains that arrive at a pulse rate of less than 200 kpps and has a peak output response of only 1 volt for input pulse rates of 250 kpps when the input pulses are 1 μsec wide. The input pulse rates shown in this figure are 333 kpps and 400 kpps, respectively. Figure 5 graphs the time the FFF output remains above 1 volt as a function of input pulse rate for input pulses of 1 μsec width. (1 volt is the minimum synapse threshold for the artificial neurons used as application examples in sec. IV).

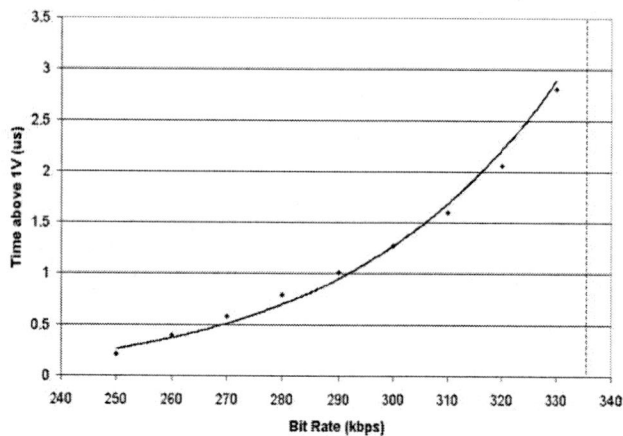

Figure 5: FFF output pulse width (> 1 volt) vs. input pulse rate for a continuous input tetanus of 1 μsec-wide input pulses for the circuit illustrated by figure 4. For input pulse rates above 360 kpps the FFF exhibits a complete (that is, dc-level) output response.

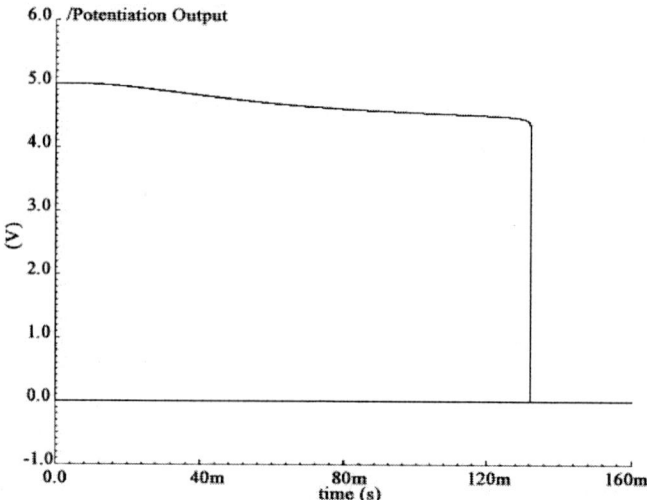

Figure 7: Response of a potentiation FFF.

A simple addition to the basic FFF produces the ability to maintain an active HIGH-level output signal for a sizable fraction of a second. The circuit is shown in Figure 6 below. M1 – M14 comprise a standard FFF. M15 – M18 implement a long-term memory FFF (LT-FFF). Under quiescent conditions, a LOW-level output turns on "keeper" transistor M16 and keeps the storage node at M17-M18 charged to V_{DD}. When a HIGH-level input is applied to M15 the storage node is discharged and the output goes HIGH. After the gate of M15 returns to a LOW value, leakage current through M16 slowly recharges the storage node. The storage time for the LT-FFF is determined by the switching threshold V_{SP} for M18. We call the response of this circuit a "potentiation" response.

Figure 7 illustrates a typical potentiation response. An input tetanus of 1 μsec pulses at 500 kpps was applied to the circuit of figure 6 for 18 μsec. The tetanus was then terminated. The LT-FFF output went high at approximately 10 μsec and maintained this high-level output state for 132 msec. In our work, we typically use LT-FFF designs for potentiation response in the range from about 20 msec up to the response illustrated in figure 7.

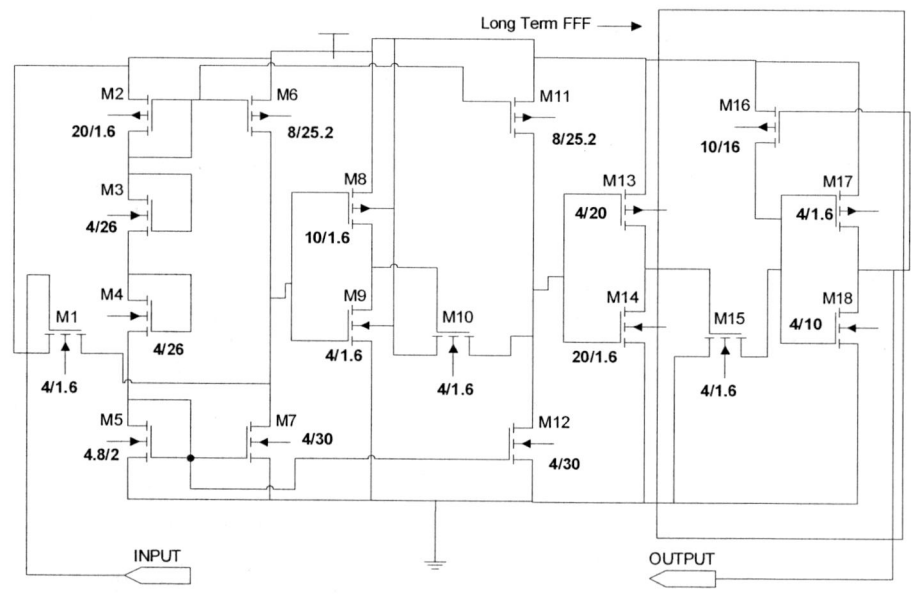

Figure 6: Potentiating forgetful flipflop. M1-M14 comprise two cascaded inverting forgetful latches. M15-M18 comprise a forgetful element with long-term memory. When the output signal is LOW, M16 maintains the gates of inverter M17-M18 at a HIGH level. When the gate of M15 receives a HIGH signal, M15 discharges the gates of M17 and M18 and the output goes HIGH. In this state, leakage current through M16 slowly recharges the gate voltages of M17-M18 after the input to M15 goes LOW. HIGH-level outputs from this FFF can be maintained for more than 100 msec.

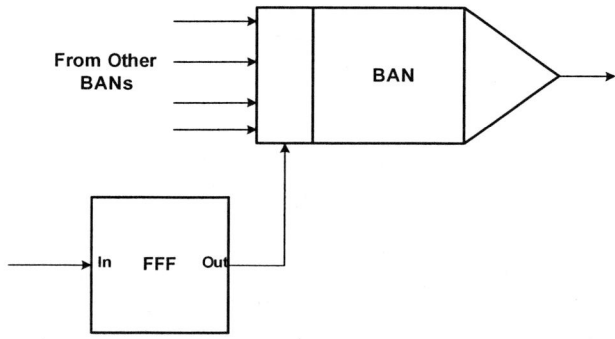

Figure 8: FFF used to increase sensitivity of a BAN neuron. A HIGH output from the FFF adds a DC bias to the input of the leaky integrator (LI) in the BAN. This additional bias decreases the number of synchronous synaptic inputs required to evoke an AP from the BAN.

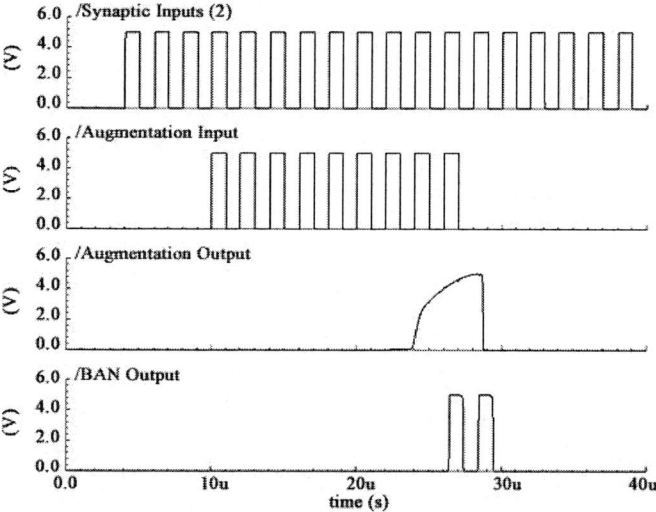

Figure 9: Waveforms for augmentation of firing sensitivity of a BAN for the circuit of figure 8. The top trace shows the two synchronous synaptic inputs to the BAN. The second trace shows the input to the FFF. The third trace is the FFF output. The bottom trace is the BAN output. By replacing the FFF with a LT-FFF, augmentation of firing sensitivity can be maintained for a longer time period after the FFF input ceases.

IV. APPLICATIONS OF FORGETFUL LOGIC

In this section we illustrate some of the applications of forgetful logic in pulse-mode neural networks. The neuron element used is a previously reported design known as a biomimic artificial neuron (BAN) [13], [16]. The first application is the use of a FFF to increase the sensitivity of a neuron to excitatory synaptic inputs. The circuit is illustrated in Figure 8. The BAN was designed such that a minimum of four synchronous synaptic inputs is required to fire an action potential (AP). A FFF output is applied to a synaptic input with the synaptic weight set such that: 1) the FFF cannot by itself stimulate an AP from the BAN, and 2) when the FFF input is HIGH two other synchronous synaptic inputs suffice to produce an AP. Figure 9 shows two synchronous BAN inputs, the input pulse train to the FFF, the FFF output, and the BAN output. In this illustration, the FFF was designed to respond after a 7-pulse tetanus at 500 kpps before

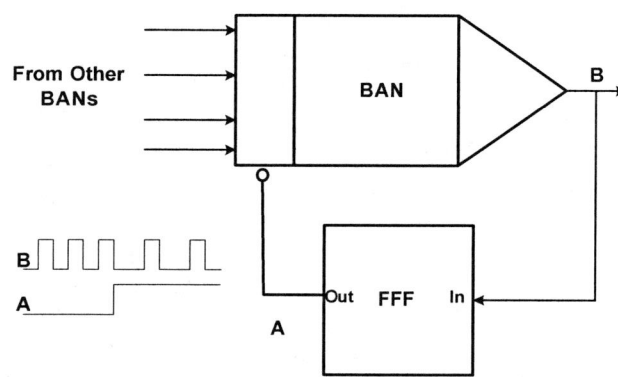

Figure 10: FFF used as feedback to an inhibitory synapse to produce accommodation in the BAN output firing rate. Conceptual waveforms are shown in the figure. A high-rate output at B eventually induces a high output from the FFF, which is fed back to an inhibitory synapse. This feedback lowers the firing rate at B. If firing rate B is slowed sufficiently, the FFF will eventually go inactive, thereby re-enabling the higher firing rate.

augmenting the sensitivity of the BAN. The augmentation input would remain applied so long as the FFF continued to receive the input tetanus. By replacing the FFF with a LT-FFF, augmentation of the BAN inputs can be maintained for a much longer period of time after the FFF input ceases. This technique can be used to enable specific cell groups of BAN neurons to implement re-configurable neurocomputing functional units. Similarly, by applying the FFF output to an inhibitory BAN input [16], the sensitivity of the BAN to synaptic inputs is reduced and, if the inhibitory weight of the BAN is large enough, can even be suppressed entirely (disabling of BAN cell assemblies). It should also be noted that because the FFF acts as a filter to low firing-rates, the augmentation action can be made frequency-selective. This has potential application for rate-dependent binding code specifications in pulse-mode neural networks.

A trivial variation on this scheme can be used to produce an accommodation response from a BAN neuron. This is illustrated in Figure 10. Assume that a firing response is induced in the BAN such that the firing rate at B is high enough to invoke a response in the FFF. When the FFF output goes HIGH, its signal is applied to an inhibitory synaptic input at the BAN, thereby reducing the BAN firing rate [16]. This mode of pulse coding is called an accommodation response by biologists and is frequently observed in numerous biological neurons. If the rate at B is reduced sufficiently (by selection of the inhibitory synaptic weight), the FFF, which acts as a high-pass rate filter, will eventually de-assert its output, thereby re-enabling the higher firing rate.

By combining positive feedback from a FL with negative feedback from a FFF, a BAN can be made to exhibit burst firing patterns. This is illustrated in Figure 11. Here the synaptic weight at A is set high enough that the FL signal invokes an AP from the BAN. Because the FL output pulse is wider than that of the BAN, the BAN re-triggers after its refractory period and re-fires [16].

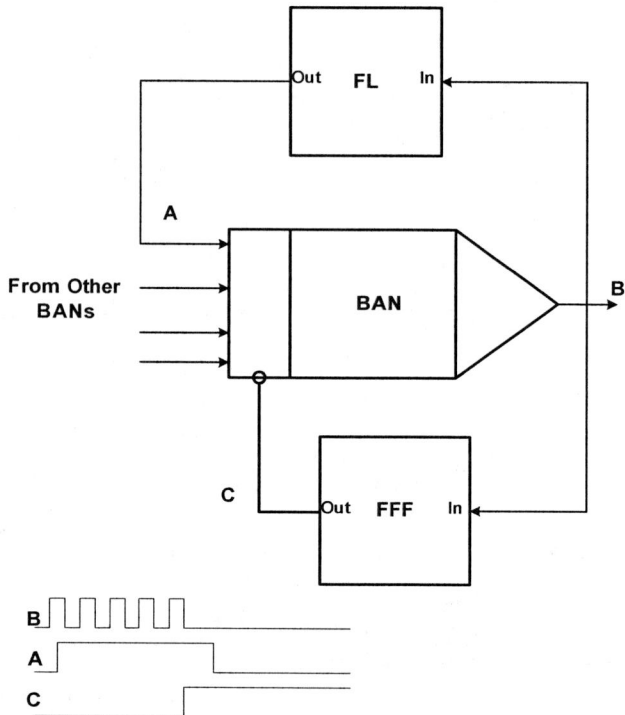

Figure 11: Forgetful logic used to turn a BAN integrate-and-fire cell into a bursting cell. Forgetful latch FL is applied to an excitatory synapse having a synaptic weight high enough to ensure re-firing of the BAN. After a burst length determined by the design of the FFF, FFF signal C is asserted at an inhibitory synapse. The weight of this synapse is set sufficiently high to ensure that C inhibits further firing. Firing at B can resume after the FFF output discharges and returns to the LOW state. Waveform schematics are shown in the figure.

After a number of pulses at B determined by the design of the FFF, the output at C is asserted at an inhibitory synapse. The synaptic weight of this synapse is set high enough to ensure that C completely inhibits further firing. After the FFF discharges, C is de-asserted and the BAN can again respond to its other synaptic inputs.

The BAN design responds to inhibitory synaptic inputs differently than excitatory synapses [16]. In particular, the response time for inhibitory BAN inputs is faster than that of the excitatory synapses because of the method used to discharge the BAN's leaky integrator (LI). This difference can be exploited to obtain the linking field behavior of an Eckhorn neural network [11] using integrate-and-fire BAN devices. The scheme is illustrated in Figure 12. An inverting FL is used as the feedback device from the second layer of the Eckhorn network. Its output is therefore normally HIGH and is applied to inhibitory synapses in the first (and elsewhere in the second, see [11]) layer. The synaptic weight of this input is set so that it is not high enough to prevent the BANs from firing in response to sufficient excitation of their synaptic inputs. When the second-layer BAN fires, the output of the inverting FL is de-asserted, which effectively raises the sensitivity of the BANs to their excitatory inputs. This mimics the linking field effect of a conventional Eckhorn neuron.

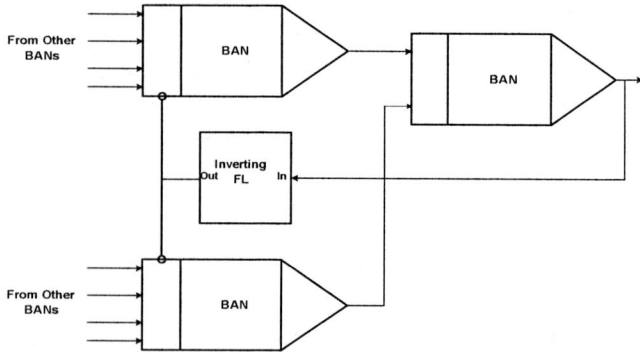

Figure 12: Mimicking the linking field effect of an Eckhorn neural network using an inverting FL and integrate-and-fire BAN neurons. It is to be noted that in most reported Eckhorn network designs, the linking field time constant is short compared to the feeding field time constant. This requirement is satisfied by the relatively short pulse duration of the forgetful latch, as shown in figure 2.

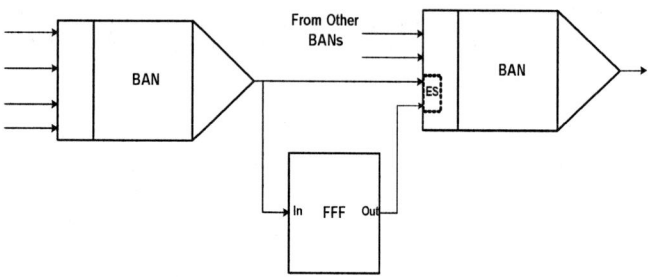

Figure 13: Short-term synaptic weight modulation using a FFF. The standard synaptic input of a BAN is modified by adding an additional control input to which the FFF is connected. When the FFF output goes HIGH, this input switches additional current to the synaptic input, thereby increasing the synaptic weight. The actual application of synaptic current to the BAN's LI is controlled by the direct connection to the source BAN. The FFF output goes high only in response to a tetanus at its input of sufficiently high frequency to invoke an output response from the FFF.

As a final application example, a FFF can be used to obtain short-term modulation of synaptic weights. The scheme is illustrated in Figure 13. To implement weight modulation, a trivial modification must be made to the standard BAN synaptic input discussed in [13], [16]. In the standard BAN design, a HIGH level input at a synapse switches current to an internal summing resistor at which the voltage input to the BAN's LI is obtained. To make an elastic synapse (ES), all that is required is that a second switch, which routes additional current through the main synaptic switch, be added. When the FFF output goes HIGH, this switch is activated, thereby adding to the synaptic current produced by the direct connection between BANs. The synaptic weight of a BAN is determined by the total current switched to the summing resistor. With aperiodic or low-rate input pulses, the FFF output remains LOW. However, the FFF will respond to a high-frequency tetanus by asserting its output as shown in the earlier figures.

V DISCUSSION

Test devices were fabricated using the 5V, 1.5 um MOSIS® process. SPICE simulations were carried out using BSIM3v3 (level 8) modeling. Agreement between simulation predictions and measured device performance was excellent. Actual W/L ratios of the devices are application dependent, but typical values are shown in the circuit figures provided above. Total power dissipation excluding the common bias stick (5 uW) in typical applications averages less than 0.5 uW per FFF at 500 kHz operation. In the worst-case applications we have looked at (not illustrated in this paper) [17] total power dissipation can be as much as 5 uW for some FFFs in the network.

The circuit designs are centered at the process design center. We simulated process variation effects over the process-specified "4-corners" variation range. All devices operated over this range with worst case process-induced pulse width variations in FLs of +43% (slow-slow corner)/ -22 % (fast-slow corner).

In summary, this paper introduced forgetful logic and illustrated its application to pulse-mode neural networks. The well-known integrate-and-fire neuron has for many years been the most popular hardware implementation for artificial neurons owing to its simplicity. However, it has also been long recognized that the I&F neuron is somewhat limited in the types and methods of information encoding it is capable of achieving. Forgetful logic was developed in order to provide a richer repertoire of signal encoding capabilities and to provide a simple means of short-term synaptic weight modulation to support work in dynamic link architectures.

Because forgetful logic is still quite new, it is presently not clear what the full range of its potential as a signal processing element in pulse-mode neural network circuitry will eventually prove to be. We have carried out additional and as yet unpublished or not widely distributed work exploring what can be done using forgetful logic circuits, and our results so far have been encouraging [17]. From our preliminary work, it appears to be possible to implement artificial neurons entirely from forgetful logic. We have early, and so far successful, results with implementing all four major classes of Wilson neuron models [18] using only forgetful logic. The application examples provided in this paper illustrate the ease with which forgetful logic processing elements can augment the basic capabilities of the integrate-and-fire neuron. The hardware implementation of forgetful logic elements is barely more complex than standard logic elements, and so forgetful logic at this time appears to hold significant promise as a cost-effective means for implementing pulse-mode neural networks in VLSI.

VI REFERENCES

[1] Hubel, D.H. and Wiesel, T.N., "Functional architecture of macaque monkey visual cortex," *Proc. Roy. Soc. Ser. B.*, vol. 198, pp. 1-59, 1977.

[2] White, E.L., *Cortical Circuits*, Boston, MA: Birkhauser, 1989.

[3] Edelman, G.M., "Group selection and phasic reentrant signaling: A theory of higher brain function," in *The Mindful Brain* (G.M. Edelman & V.B. Mountcastle, eds.) Cambridge, MA: MIT Press, 1978, pp. 51-100.

[4] Pearson, J.C., Finkel, L.H. and Edelman, G.M., "Plasticity in the organization of adult cerebral cortical maps: A computer simulation based on neuronal group selection," *J. Neurosci.*, vol. 7, pp. 4209-4223, 1987.

[5] Linsker, R., "From basic network principles to neural architecture: Emergence of orientation columns," *Proc. Nat. Acad. Sci. USA*, vol. 83, pp. 8779-8783, 1986.

[6] Anderson, C.H. and Van Essen, D.C., "Shifter circuits: A computational strategy for dynamic aspects of visual processing," *Proc. Nat. Acad. Sci. USA*, vol. 84, pp. 6297-6301, 1987.

[7] C.v.d. Malsburg, "Dynamic link architecture," in *Handbook of Brain Theory and Neural Networks* (M. Arbib, ed.) 2nd ed., Cambridge, MA: MIT Press, 2003, pp. 365-368.

[8] C.v.d. Malsburg, "The correlation theory of brain function," in *Models of Neural Networks II* (E. Domany, J.L. van Hemmen, K. Schulten, eds.), NY: Springer-Verlag, 1994, pp. 95-120.

[9] G.A. Carpenter and S. Grossberg, "ART 3: hierarchical search using chemical transmitters in self-organizing pattern recognition architectures," *Neural Networks*, vol. 3, pp. 129-152, 1990.

[10] R.C. Malenka and S.A. Siegelbaum, "Synaptic plasticity," in *Synapses* (W.M. Cowan, T.C. Südof, C.F. Stevens, eds.), Baltimore, MR, John Hopkins University Press, 2001, pp. 393-454.

[11] R. Eckhorn, H.J. Reitboeck, M. Arndt, & P. Dicke, "Feature linking via synchronization among distributed assemblies: Simulations from cat visual cortex," *Neural Computat.*, vol. 2, pp. 293-307, 1990.

[12] M. Abeles, *Corticonics*, Cambridge, UK: Cambridge University Press, 1991.

[13] B.C. Barnes, R.B. Wells and J.F. Frenzel, "PWM characteristics of a capacitor-free integrate-and-fire neuron," *IEE Electron. Letters*, vol. 39, no. 16, Aug. 2003, pp. 1191-1193.

[14] B. Sharon and R.B. Wells, "VLSI implementation of neuromime pulse generator for Eckhorn neurons," *IEE Electron. Letters*, vol. 40, no. 18, Sept., 2004, pp. 1143-1144.

[15] B. Sharon and R.B. Wells, "An Eckhorn neuron dendrite circuit VLSI implementation," to appear.

[16] B.C. Barnes and R.B. Wells, "A versatile pulse-mode biomimic artificial neuron using a capacitor-free integrate-and-fire technique," *Proc. 29th An. Conf. IEEE Indus. Electron. Soc.* (IECON'03), Nov. 2-6, 2003, pp. 2968-2972.

[17] A. Bhattacharya, *Forgetful Logic and Its Applications in the VLSI Implementation of Pulse-Coded Neural Networks*, M.S. Thesis, the University of Idaho, Moscow, ID, April, 2004.

[18] H.R. Wilson, "Simplified dynamics of human and mammalian neocortical neurons," *J. Theor. Biol.*, vol. 200, pp. 375-388, 1999.

Artificial Neural Network Computation on Graphic Process Unit

Zhongwen Luo, Hongzhi Liu and Xincai Wu

Faculty of Information, China University of Geoscience(Wuhan), Wuhan 430074,China
E-mail : luozw@cug.edu.cn, liuhz87.student@sina.com, xcwu@cug.edu.cn

Abstract

Artificial Neural Network (ANN) is widely used in pattern recognition related area. In some case, the computational load is very heavy, in other case, real time process is required. So there is a need to apply a parallel algorithm on it, and usually the computation for ANN is inherently parallel. In this paper, graphic hardware is used to speed up the computation of ANN. In recent years, graphic processing unit (GPU) grows faster than CPU. Graphic hardware venders provide programmability on GPU. In this paper, application of commodity available GPU for two kinds of ANN models was explored. One is the self-organizing maps (SOM); the other is multi layer perceptron (MLP). The computation result shows that ANN computing on GPU is much faster than on standard CPU when the neural network is large. And some design rules for improve the efficiency on GPU are given.

Keywords: Graphic Process Unit; ANN; SOM; MLP

I. INTRODUCTION

Artificial neural network is widely used in classification and pattern recognition. In this paper, two kinds of ANN, self-organizing maps (SOM) [1] and multi layer perceptron (MLP), are implemented on graphic hardware for speed up the computation.

MLP is a very simple neural network, the process is linear with one input layer, several hidden layer, and an output layer. It is usually trained by back propagation (BP) algorithm. SOM consists of one layer of n-dimensional units (neurons). It is fully connected with the network input. Additionally, there exist lateral connections through which a topological structure is imposed. For the standard model, the topology is a regular two-dimensional map instantiated by connections between each unit and its direct neighbors.

For relative works, Kyoung-Su Oh et al.[2] implement an GPU based MLP for classify the text area in a image, and give an almost 20 time speed up over CPU. Thomas Rolfes[3] gives an artificial neural network implementation using a GPU-based BLAS level 3 style single-precisions general matrix-matrix product. Bohn[4] describes an SOM calculation method based on OpenGL hardware speed-up on SGI workstation, which inspired our work to further deploy the possibility to implement ANN calculation based on PC commodity graphic hardware.

In recent years, the graphic hardware performance is doubled every 12 months which is much faster than CPU's performance increase speed which is doubled every 18 months. And GPU vendors had make programmability on GPU, which make it possible for implement general-purpose computation.

In this paper, two kinds of ANN computation on GPU are given. In section 2, SOM computation model and implementation on graphic hardware is discussed. In section 3, MLP computation model and implementation on GPU is discussed. In section 4, the computation result and comparison are given for both CPU and GPU. In section 5, some of the design details and lessons we learned during implementation are given. In section 6, conclusion and some future works are given.

II. COMPUTATIONAL MODEL AND IMPLEMENT METHOD FOR SOM

A. The SOM Computational Model

The SOM takes a two-step computation: search for the best matching unit (BMU) and modify the map according to a distance function of the lateral connections. Usually, the Euclid distance is chosen as similarity measure method. The calculation formula takes as follow:

$$\| W_b - \xi \| < \| W_i - \xi \| \quad \text{for any i;} \quad [1]$$

Modify the unit value regarding a distance function of the lateral connections as follow.

$$W_i^{new} = W_i^{old} - \varepsilon \Omega(r_b, r_i) * (W_i^{old} - \xi) \quad [2]$$

As Bohn described, three OpenGL[5] extension functions are needed, they are blending, glColorMatrix and glminmax. These functions are fully support by SGI workstation, but only partially supported by PC graphic hardware. So it is difficult to fully implement SOM on OpenGL. Fortunately, current GPU provide more programmability, which makes it possible for implement the SOM calculation on GPU.

B. SOM Implementation on Programmable GPU

As discussed in the previous part, not all OpenGL functions supported by SGI workstation are supported by PC commodity graphic hardware. But recently, graphic hardware vendors provide programmability and some high-level program language[6,7]. This kind of programmability is at a lower level than OpenGL, and is more powerful than fixed OpenGL function. In this implementation, Cg [8] (C for graphic) is chosen as developing environment.

As described in previous part, the calculation contains two steps. The first is finding the best matching unit, and the second is adjusting the value according to the distance from BMU.

For finding the BMU, two steps are needed. In the first step, similarity measurement is calculated; in the second step, the minimum values which represent the BMU are found and located. The similarity computation code for GPU takes as follow:

Half 4 temp= tex2D(texture,coords) -intrain;

c.x = dot(temp,temp);

c.yz= coords.xy;

The first two sentences calculate the square of Euclid distance of two vectors, the third sentence save the unit coordinate, which will be used late for locating the best match unit.

The main difficulty in Cg computation comes from finding the minimum value and determination its location, for there is no global variable in Cg environment. We use a multipass method to calculate it. Our scheme shows as Fig 1. In each pass we find the minimum value of four units show as colored and save the result in a small size texture. After some step, the size decrease to 1, and we can get the minimum value and its location.

After get BMU, we can adjust the self-organize map according to equation [2].

III. MLP FOR REAL TIME BALL RECOGNIZING IN FIRA SOCCER ROBOT

A. Background

Currently, there are two main world soccer-robot competition, one is RoboCup[9], the other is FIRA[10]. In both case, Object are identified by their unique color. But in the near future, these color cues may be removed, so new vision algorithms based on model are needed to cope with the situation. The model based algorithm for finding ball

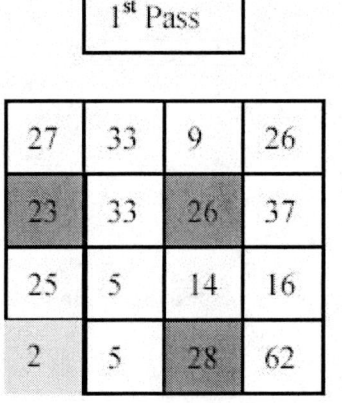
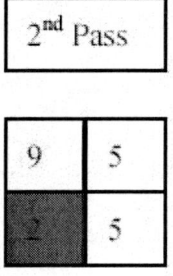

Fig. 1: Scheme for find the minimum value

and non-ball location will discussed below.

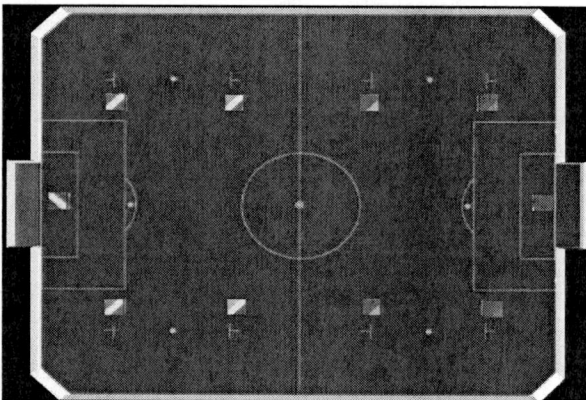

Fig 2. An image from FIRA SimuroSot

Fig2 shows an image taken from FIRA robot soccer 5vs5 simulator. Our task is to develop a model to recognize the ball, and then using this model to recognize the ball in real time.

For each location, the characters are calculated considering the color value at a small area around the location. The area radius takes as 7, which is shown in Fig 3,

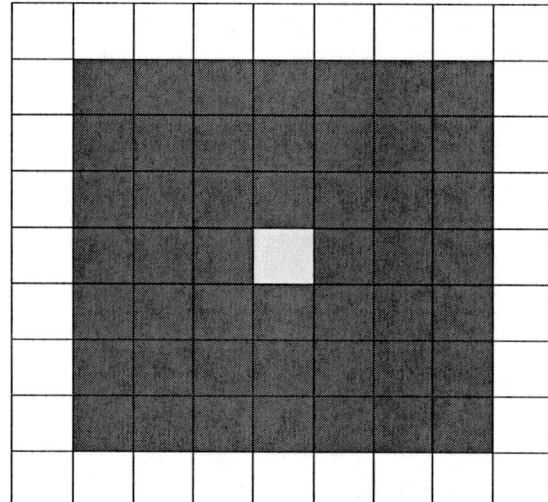

Fig 3. region for character calculation

Seven parameters are selected as characters of the ball. There are 3 average value of the colors red, green and blue around the concerning position:

$$mean_{x,y} = \sum_{i=-3}^{3}\sum_{j=-3}^{3} c_{x+i,y+j} \Big/ 49$$

3 standard deviation of the colors red green and blue:

$$delta_{x,y} = \sqrt{\sum_{i=-3}^{3}\sum_{j=-3}^{3}(c_{x+i,y+j} - mean_{x,y})^2 \Big/ 48}$$

And the luminance:

$$luminance = r + g + b$$

B. Computational Model of MLP

Three layer MLP neural network is selected to recognize the ball. The input layer consists of seven nodes for seven characters. The hidden layer consists of three nodes, and the output layer consists of just one node. Back propagation method was chosen to train the network.

The train set takes as follow. 16 locations are selected from each of 10 robot cars, 4 locations are selected from center of ball, and one location is selected from background field. Totally, 165 locations are selected as the train set. For each selected location, seven characters are calculated and take as an element of the train set.

The trained MLP is used to recognize and trace the ball in real time.

There are two main computation steps for MLP used as the classification machine. The first one is matrix multiplication:

$$net = w \bullet x + b \qquad [3]$$

The second one is sigmoid function calculation:

$$\sigma(net) = \frac{1}{1 + e^{-net}} \qquad [4]$$

As for the determination of ball on robot soccer, the MLP calculation was applied on each point in the play ground. And MLP was used to distinguish between ball and non-ball position.

C. MLP Implementation on Graphic Hardware

Current GPU has a limited instruction length and a limited number of temporary variables for calculation at each location. So multipass is needed for complex problem. For MLP discussed in this section, three passes are performed. In the first pass, average values of three color and luminance are calculated. In the second pass, the standard deviations of the three colors are calculated. In the third pass, classification result is got from MLP calculation on the characteristic.

In this calculation, we use a new Nvidia's GF6000 serious graphic hardware. The reason is that the ATI's GPU supports very few numbers of operations in each pass; so more passes are need for MLP calculation. Old Nvidia's GPU does not support fully float texture, which is crucial for the precision of result.

IV. RESULTS AND DISCUSSION

The environment for CPU computing is INTEL P4 2.4G. Based on this PC, ATI 9550 and Nvidia GF5700 GPU are used for SOM computing, Nvidia GF6200 GPU is used for MLP computing.

A. CPU and GPU Train Time for SOM and Discussion

Usually the train process for self organize map is time consuming when the map is large enough. So there is a need to speed up the training procedure. For our test problem, 80 data are chosen for training the SOM and average time for the computation on CPU and GPU can be reached. The result is shown in Fig 4.

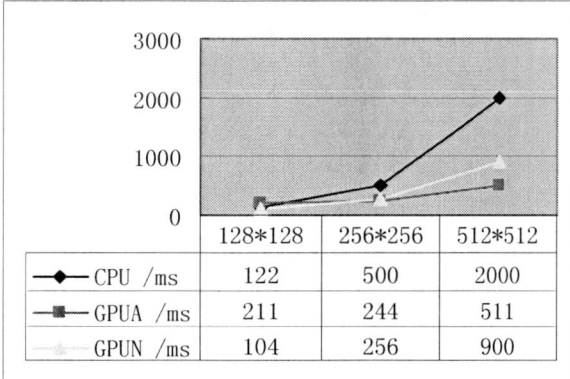

Fig. 4: SOM train computing time on GPU and CPU

The result shows that GPU based implementation is faster than CPU, especially for large self organize map. As map size increase, the computation time on GPU increase slowly than that on CPU. And different GPU had different result, for Nvidia's GPU, it takes the least time for small size SOM like 128*128, but for ATI's GPU it takes the least time for larger size SOM like 256*256. The difference may come from vendor's hardware implementation. The result shows that ATI's graphic card takes more time for the compile of program and the code is better optimized so computation time decrease with more data, but Nvidia's graphic card takes less time for compile and takes more time to computing.

B. MLP Computation Time for CPU and GPU

The application of MLP in this paper is to trace the ball in robot soccer in real time. The result is shown in table 1.

The result shows that GPU based MLP computation is about 200 times faster than that of CPU. And the result also shows that GPU computation is fast enough for the locating of the ball in real time.

TABLE I: MLP COMPUTATION ON CPU AND GPU.

CPU /ms	11328
GPUN /ms	46

V. SOME IMPLEMENTATION DETAILS AND LESSONS

To increase the efficiency, some basic rule should obey. The main rules are given below.

First, create the GPU hardware program only once and enable it when it is needed. The reason is that when a new program is created, it will be compiled by Cg, which is time consuming.

Second, if possible, do one's best to decrease the calculation passes. For computation scheme described in section 2.2, the main bottleneck is at finding minimum procedure. The test shows that the bottleneck comes from multi-pass used in finding minimum procedure. Table 2 shows result for different scheme of finding the minimum. To decrease the pass, we make two changes, the first is to combine the value calculation with one pass of find minimum, and the second is to combine two pass of find minimum computation into one pass. Instead of calculate 4 units, 16 units are calculated. GPUA represent calculation on ATI graphic card and GPUN represent the calculation on NVIDIA graphic card. The performance increase is clear, especially for Nvidia's graphic card.

TABLE II: COMPARISON BETWEEN MORE AND FEW PASS

KFM size	128*128	256*256	512*512
GPUA more pass /ms	366	400	533
GPUA few pass /ms	211	244	511
GPUN more pass /ms	190	640	2889
GPUN few pass /ms	104	256	900

Third, do best to decrease the data exchange between CPU and GPU. Usually OpenGL's PBuffer are used to save the intermediate result in a texture on GPU and reuse it as an input data. Harris[3] had created a class called "Render to Texture" to easy the use of PBuffer. We had used this class in our program.

Fourth, hardware from different venders usually has different property. So if one implementation is not work at one kind of hardware, try another implementation. For example, in the calculation of minimum value, firstly we use the following code:

```
c=tex2D(texture,coords).x<tex2D(texture,coords+half2(0,offset)).x? tex2D(texture,coords) : tex2D(texture,coords+half2(0,offset));
```

Which can give the correct result in ATI card, but can not get correct result in an Nvidia's card, we think that the inner parallel schemes makes the difference. To work around it, the above sentence is changed to the following logical equivalent one:

```
half4 c=tex2D(tex,coords);

if (c.x>tex2D(tex,coords+half2(0,half_side)).x)

    c=tex2D(tex,coords+half2(0,half_side));
```

Then the result is correct for both graphic cards.

VI. CONCLUSION

In this paper, implementation for two ANN models on graphic hardware is given. Inherent parallelism of commodity graphic hardware is used to accelerate the computation of ANN. The result shows that GPU is capable for some of ANN calculation, the graphic hardware make it possible for an increasing performance/cost ratio on the area of large size ANN computation.

Compared to Bohn's initial computation on SGI workstation, our implementation has two benefits. One is our calculation is more precise, for we had use the float point computing. The other is that we only use a commodity available graphic card, which is much more easily available than SGI workstation so can be widely used.

The implementation on graphic hardware introduce in this paper has other implicit benefit too. For the SOM computing, a multi-texture or 3-D texture can be used to store the map and make more general SOM computing without the restriction of the vector length of 4. For the MLP used in robot soccer, some graphic hardware have "video in" function, using this kind of graphic hardware; image information can be retrieved directly from camera and store on graphic memory, and don't need to transfer data between CPU and GPU, which will speed the process.

We can also do other general ANN computation on GPU, because GPU provide almost all arithmetic operation, logic operation and some important mathematic function. And for the application of neural network on images, it is more naive to make such computing on a graphic hardware.

For future works, one is to make other kinds of ANN computation on GPU. The other is to further deploy the MLP on more real situation of robot soccer, which include select better parameter and use faster algorithm on GPU.

REFERENCES

[1] Teuvo Kohonen. Self-organizing maps. Springer Verlag, New York, 1997.

[2] Kyoung-Su Oh, Keechul Jung, GPU implementation of neural networks, Pattern Recognition 37, 6, 1311-1314, 2004

[3] Thomas Rolfes. Artificial Neural Networks on Programmable Graphics Hardware, in Game Programming Gems 4,pp373-378, 2004

[4] Bohn, C.A. Kohonen Feature Mapping Through Graphics Hardware. In Proceedings of 3rd Int. Conference on Computational Intelligence and Neurosciences 1998. 1998.

[5] Woo, M., Neider, J., Davis, T., Shreiner, D. OPENGL Programming Guide,Addison-Wisley,1999

[6] Femando R. and Killgard, M.J. The Cg Tutorial: The Definitive Guide to Programmable Real-Time Graphics Addison-Wisley, 2003

[7] Harris, M. http://www.gpgpu.org/developer/, 2003

[8] Mark, W.R., Glanville, R. S., Akeley, K. and Killgard, M.J. 2003. Cg : A system for programming graphics hardware in a C-like language. ACM Trans. Graph. 22, 3, 896-907

[9] http://www.robocup.com

[10] http://www.fira.net

Circuit Implementation of Multi-Thresholded Neuron (MTN) Using BiCMOS Technology

Xiaolei Zhu[1,2][*], Jizhong Shen[1]

[1] Department of Information Science and
Electronic Engineering
Zhejiang University
Hangzhou, Zhejiang, China 310027

[*] E-mail: xl_zhu@tsinghua.edu.cn

Baoyong Chi[2], Zhihua Wang[2][**]

[2] Institute of Microelectronics
Tsinghua University
Beijing, China 100084

[**] E-mail: zhihua@tsinghua.edu.cn

Abstract—By analysing the principle of multi-thresholded neurons (MTNs), a methodology is developed for designing multi-thresholded neuron circuits (MTNCs). First, two n-channel MOS transistors are employed to design the voltage-mode synapse circuit with high simplicity and linearity. Second, a BiCMOS technique based circuit named Judgement-converting switch (JCS) is proposed. The JCS whose threshold is voltage-controlled current signal, provides an ability of converting the voltage signal to current signal. Based on this possibility, an approach is put forward to design multi-thresholded judgement function circuits (MTJFCs). Finally, single MTNC is designed for implementing XOR operation at switch level. Simulation results with PSPICE show that the designed circuits not only have the correct logic function but also small propagation delay.

I. Introduction

In the proceedings of theoretical foundation and analysis of neural networks published by IEEE in 1992[1], the Artificial Neural Network (ANN) was defined as an arbitrary architecture that consists of a large amount of parallel computational neurons. From this definition, it is clear that the neurons are the most basic elements, which affect the scale, complexity and robust performance of ANN. Multi-thrsholded neurons (MTNs), proposed in recent years[2-4], have many thresholds and activation states and they can also be taken as a lot of Single-thresholded neurons (STNs) in pattern classification. A large number of neurons can be reduced by contrast with applying to implement the same pattern classification using STNs. Based on this possibility, research on MTNs has attracted much attention for recent years[8-10].

The hardware implementation of ANN is a main challenge in ANN research and it can generally be achieved by using VLSI techniques, optical techniques and biology techniques. The VLSI techniques have the advantages in terms of maturity, high precision and high noise resistant ability over the other two techniques. For this reason, the VLIS techniques are considered the most efficient way for neural hardware implementation by neural networks communities[11]. In addition, the VLSI implementation of neurons is the key problem to be solved in ANN hardware realization. Since the later 1980's, many researchers and famous well known multi-national companies have devoted themselves to researching on the ANN VLSI implementation and a lot of utility artificial neural chips (ANCs) have been developed. Yet when compared to the biology neural system, the neurons in ANCs are small in number and the function of these ANCs is limited for application[12]. Thus, it is important to enhance the information processing abilities of single neuron in order to improve the whole ANCs' function under the current integrated circuit technique condition. It seems the demerits of STNs based ANCs can be overcome by using MTNs. The schemes of binary neurons' VLSI implementation can be found in many literatures[8-17]. However, the research on MTNs' VLSI implementation is still lagging.

In this paper, a BiCMOS technique based MTNC is proposed. The synapse circuits employs two n-channel MOS transistors operate in certain region and the multi-thresholded function circuit is formed by using BiCMOS technique based circuit that is called JCS. Further, in accordance with the transfer characteristics of the MTNs, a general methodology is presented to design the multi-thresholded judgement function circuits (MTJFCs) from switch level. Lastly, the MTN circuit which implements XOR operation is designed from switch level All designed circuits are simulated and verified by the Pspcice program.

II. Conception of MTN model

The MTN module shown in Fig.1(a) has several output values and its transfer function has many ascend thresholds and descend thresholds. The numbers of thresholds are related to the complexity of the problem to be solved. Fig.1(b) presents a typical MTN's transfer function curves. The transfer function of the MTN is expressed by the following equation:

$$y = f(\sum_{i=1}^{n} w_i \cdot x_i)$$

$$f(u) = \begin{cases} M-1, u \in (\theta_j, \theta_{j+1}] \cup (\theta_k, \theta_{k+1}] \cup \dots \\ M-2, u \in (\theta_p, \theta_{p+1}] \cup (\theta_q, \theta_{q+1}] \cup \dots \\ \dots, \quad \dots \\ 0, \quad u \in (\theta_s, \theta_{s+1}] \cup (\theta_t, \theta_{t+1}] \cup \dots \end{cases} \quad (1)$$

where w_i is the i th connecting weights between the premise neuron and the conclusion neuron, x_i is the i th premise neuron or its output, symbol $\cup$ represents the combine operation, variable $j, k, p, q, \dots s, t \in \{0, 1, 2, \dots, n\}$, both n and M are arbitrary natural numbers, and meanwhile $j \neq k \neq p \neq q \neq \dots \neq s \neq t$. Variable M stands for the output value that neuron generates in different threshold circumscription and variable θ presents the ascend or descend threshold of MTN. The attracted functions of this MTN lie in the fact that it not only partitions the input R^n space into several hyper planar zones by using many thresholds in neuron's output transfer function, but also marks these different zones with different aviation states as required[4]. An MNT with two different thresholds θ_0, θ_1 and the value of M equals two is nominated dual-thresholded two-valued neuron. Similarly, an MTN with n different thresholds $\theta_0, \theta_1, \dots, \theta_{n-1}$, and the value of M equals n is named n-thresholded m-valued neuron.

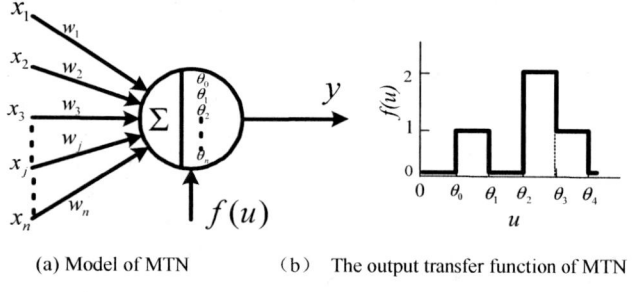

(a) Model of MTN (b) The output transfer function of MTN

Fig. 1. Model and output transfer function of MTN

III. Circuit design of MTN

A. Design of Synapse Circuits

Synapse is the connection between different neurons. In theoretical neural wok models, synapse performs the weighted-sum operation as defined in equation(1). Hence, a large number of multipliers are needed in hardware implementation of neural networks. In order to transplant such a complex and massive neural system on a single die with VLSI technology, we should make each synapse circuit occupy a very small silicon area and provide a relative linear multiplication performance. High accuracy can be achieved with digital technology though, the digital circuits take up large chip areas as a demerit of realizing a magnitude neural system in a single chip. In analog neural hardware implementation, as compared, the high accuracy and linearity found in digital implementation is the traded off for the simplicity, speed and low power consumption. Taking advantage of some self-features of a CMOS transistor, we can easily realize multiplication function using single transistor. As simple as this method is, the simplest structure is at the cost of low accuracy and small dynamic range. How to design a synapse circuit of high simplicity and high precision linearity is our first consideration. Literature [19] proposed a Dual-MosFET equivalent resistor. We do some modifications and improvements on the circuits and find this Dual-MosFET structure suits well for implementing multiplication function required by synapse circuits.

Dual-MosFET synapse circuit consists of two n-channel MOS transistors connected in parallel as presented in Fig.2 (a), where M_1 and M_2 denote two MOS transistors with depletion mode and strengthen mode, respectively. If the gate voltage $V_g > 1V$ and the drain voltage $0V < V_d < 1V$, then transistor M_1 and M_2 will operate in linear region and saturated region, respectively. According to the basic characteristic of a MOS transistor, we derive following relations:

When $V_{ds} < V_{gs} - V_{t1}$, transistor M_1 operates in the linear region, current through M_1 is expressed as:

$$I_{ds} = k[2(V_{gs} - V_{t1})V_{ds} - V_{ds}^2] \quad (2)$$

When $0 < V_{gs} - V_{t2} < V_{ds}$, transistor M_2 operates in the saturated region, current through M_2 is expressed as:

$$I_{ds2} = k(V_{ds} - V_{t2})^2 \quad (3)$$

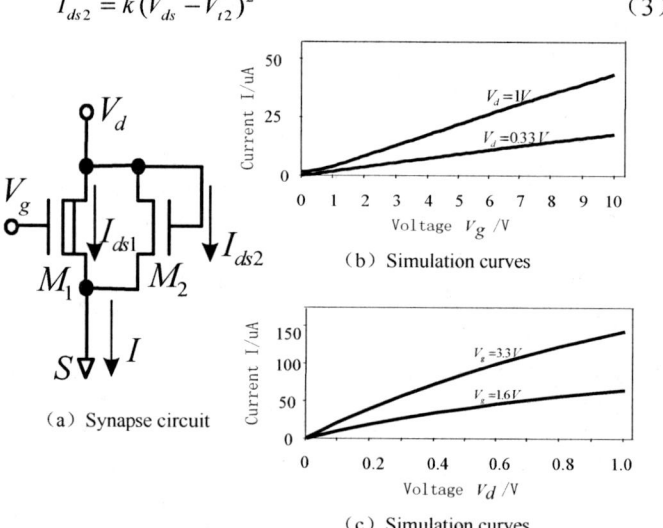

(a) Synapse circuit

(b) Simulation curves

(c) Simulation curves

Fig. 2. Dual-MosFET synapse circuit and its drain current simulation curves

The two in (2) & (3) currents are summed at the source point where two transistors are connected together, and hence we derive the total current:

$$I = I_{ds1} + I_{ds2}$$
$$= k[2(V_{gs} - V_{t1})V_{ds} - V_{ds}^2] + k(V_{ds} - V_{t2})^2 \quad (4)$$
$$= 2kV_{gs}V_{ds} - k[V_{t2}^2 - 2(V_{t1} + V_{t2})V_{ds}]$$

In equations (2) ~ (4), V_{t1} and V_{t2} are the threshold voltages for transistor M_1 and M_2. The variable k in equation (4) is equal to $U_n W C_{ox} / 2L$, where U_n denotes electron velocity, C_{ox} stands for the capacitance per unit area and W/L is the width-length ratio. With 0.8 uM standard BiCMOS technology parameters [18], the value of k is around $14.5 uA/V^2$. Assume that the threshold $V_{t1} = -0.1V$ and $V_{t2} = 0.1V$, the last item of equation (4) can be omitted. Therefore, equation (4) can be simplified as:
$$I \approx 2kV_g \cdot V_d \quad (5)$$
From equation (5), it is clear that the value of total current I is proportional to the product of gate voltage V_g, drain voltage V_d and a constant value k. If we take V_g as an input signal and V_d as a weight signal of a neuron, then the circuit shown in Fig.2 (a) obviously behaves as a multiplier. This circuit has been simulated by Pspice with the same 0.8 uM standard BiCMOS technology parameters as mentioned above. The results are presented in Fig.2 (b) and (c) where Fig.2 (b) plots I versus V_g for two values of V_d: 0.33 V and 1 V; Fig.2 (c) plots I versus V_d for two valueds of V_g: 1.6 V and 3.3 V. The designed circuit, as theoreticaly expected, has good linear performance with relatively large dynamic range when n-channel MOS transistor M_1 and M_2 are set to operate in certain regions.

Since the output of each synapse circuits shown in Fig.2 (a) is a current signal, the currents from different synapses circuits can then be easily summed by connecting their output nets at one point. This results in the following expression for summed current:
$$I_{sum} \approx 2k \sum_{i=1}^{n} V_{gi} \cdot V_{di} \quad (6)$$
where V_{gi} denotes the i th input signal and V_{di} stands for the i th weight signal of synapse in a neural network. Two synapse circuits are applied to perform the weighted-sum function of neurons as presented in Fig.3 (a), where voltage signals w_1 and w_2 denote their weight values while voltage signals x_1 and x_2 stand for their input values. The neuron takes the outputs of these two synapses and sums them with a current signal u. Suppose voltage signals x_1 and x_2 are taken as two ternary digits, ie. $X_1, X_2 \in \{0, 1, 2\}$, voltage signals w_1 and w_2 correspond to two weight values 3^0 and 3^1, respectively, then value of a current signal $u = k(w_1 x_1 + w_2 x_2)$ stands for a value of decimal digit corresponding to the value of ternary digit $X_2 X_1$ where k is a constant value. Such a function can be easily achieved by two synapses connected in parallel as shown in Fig.3 (a). Each synapse multiplies an input (voltage signal) by a stored weight (voltage signal), sums them and then passes them as an output (current signal). In order to make two n-channel MOS transistors in synapse circuits operate separately in saturated and linear region as required, and as well the value w_2 should be set three times the value w_1 in the case of ternary-digit system, we set signal variables $w_1 = 0.33V$, $w_2 = 1V$, $x_1, x_2 \in (0V, 1.6V, 3.3V)$. With the same technology parameters mentioned before, this circuits is simulated by Pspice and results a transient characteristic curves as shown in Fig. 3 (b). The results show that the input signal x_1, x_2 and output signal u match exactly with the converting relation between ternary-digit system and decimal-digit system. Furthermore, it also verifies that the designed synapse circuits have a good ability to perform the weighted-sum function.

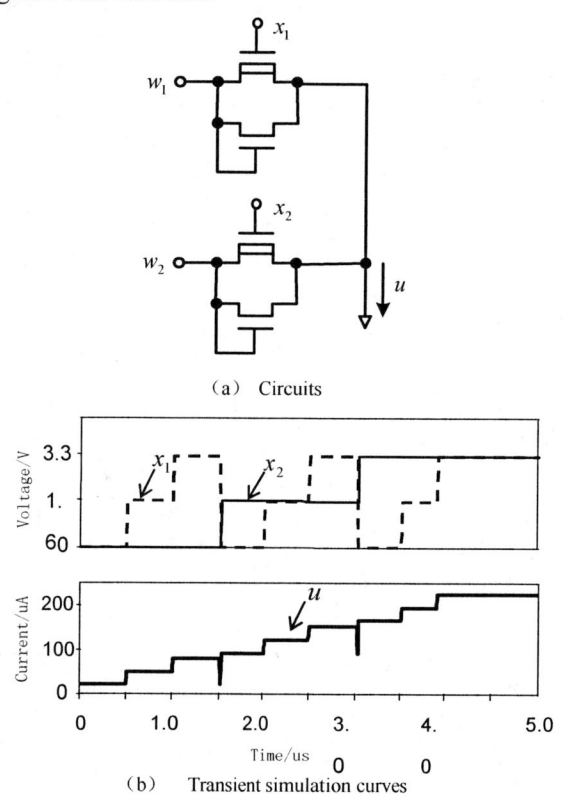

Fig.3. Weighted-summed function by two synapse circuits and its simulation curves

B. Design of Multi-thresholded Judgement Function Circuits (MTJFCs)

The threshold processing unit is somewhat a key part of a neuron since it determines the output transfer function of a neuron. Most neural networks are considered as two states with a single threshold in each neuron. The transfer functions they use are: Linear threshold logic, Hard limiter and Sigmoid function[20]. In these cases, common feature of their functions is that they have a single threshold. In turn, the MTNs have many ascend /descend thresholds and multiple output aviations. The output transfer function of MTNs, as a matter of fact, can be described as a certain kind of multi-thresholded judgement function. For the purpose of implementing the MTNs by VLSI technology, a corresponding appropriate method should be found to design the circuits that fulfill the multi-thresholded judgement function. Inspired by the clipping voltage switching theory[21], we probe to find an appropriate method to design MTJFCs that will be discussed in following subsection.

According to equation (6), each synapse multiplies an input (voltage signal) by a stored weight (voltage signal) and each neuron takes the output (current signal) of several synapses, sums them and then passes them through a multi-thresholded judgement function. In order to pass this weighted-sum signal to the next neuron, the oriented MTJFCs should have the abilities of converting the current signal to voltage signal. For this purpose, a judgement-converting switch (JCS) based on BiCMOS technique is designed as a core unit of the MTJFCs. The circuit diagram is shown in Fig.4, where M_θ, M_R and T denote two n-channel MOS transistors and a bipolar transistor respectively. M_R is chosen as a load transistor. In this circuit, input current I_{in} is distributed at point b. When transistor T is turned on, due to the junction voltage V_{be}, the voltage value at point b is fixed around 0.8V. Assuming M_θ operates in the linear region, the current through M_θ can be expressed as:

$$I_\theta = k[2(V_\theta - V_t)V_{be} - V_{be}^2] \tag{7}$$

where V_t is the threshold and V_θ is the gate voltage of MOS transistor M_θ. From equation (7), it is clear that M_θ behaves as a voltage controlled current source. As far as bipolar transistor T is concerned, it has two cases: when $I_{in} > I_\theta$, T is turned on and the output is set at low level (voltage signal); when $I_{in} < I_\theta$, T is turned off and output is pulled up to high level (voltage signal). That is, the whole circuit shown in Fig.4 can be taken as a JCS that fulfills two functions: judgement and converting. In order to describe the process that switching states control the output signal transmission, we use clipping voltage switches theory to define such an operation as:

$$S\nabla\alpha = \begin{cases} S, & \alpha = T; \\ m-1, & \alpha = F. \end{cases} \tag{8}$$

In equation (8), variable $S \in \{0, 1, K, m-2\}$ is used to denote output of the switch and variable $\alpha \in \{T, F\}$ represents two switching states (on and off) of a bipolar transistor. According to the definitions and related properties of the above operation, we can derive the universal expression of an arbitrary two-valued function:

$$f = 0\nabla\alpha \tag{9}$$

A circuit described as equation (9) has a general structure[21] as presented in Fig. 5 This structure can be explained by two following cases: when switching variable $\alpha = T$, the value of function f is set 0, and when switching $\alpha = T$, the value of function f is set 1. Therefore, designing a two-valued MTJFC turns out to probe the simplest expression of switching variable item α in function f and then implement it with several transistors.

The output transfer function of MTN is realized by a MTJFC that has single input and single output. Based on the above analysis of JCS presented in Fig. 4, we consider the MTJFC should perform the following functions: compare the input (current signal) with threshold (current signal), judge which circumscription the input signal belongs to and then generate a corresponding output (voltage signal). Note that

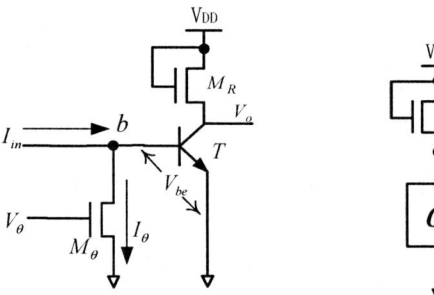

Fig.4. JSC circuit   Fig.5. General structure of two-valued MTJFCs

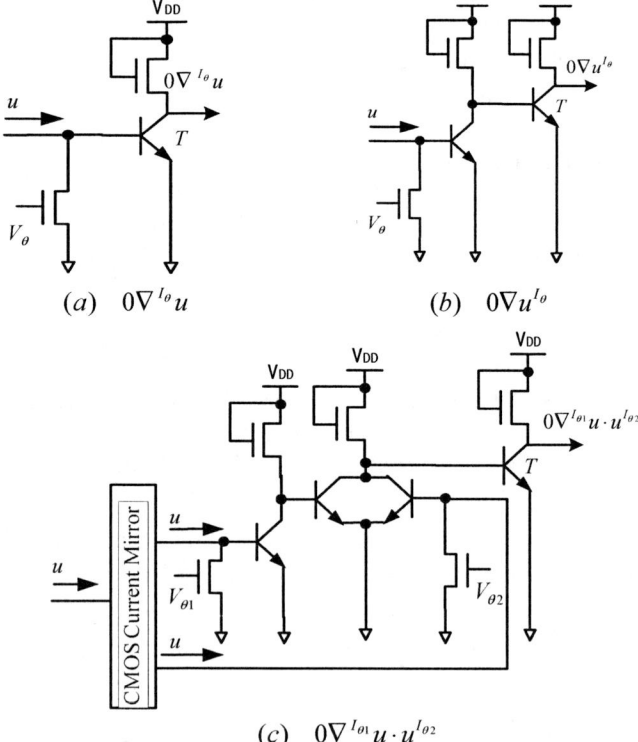

Fig.6. Basic function term circuits

the two-valued MTJFC consists of three types of basic function terms: $0\nabla^{I_\theta}u$、$0\nabla u^{I_\theta}$ and $0\nabla^{I_{\theta1}}u \cdot u^{I_{\theta2}}$, and they can be explained by the following equations:

$$0\nabla^{I_\theta}u = \begin{cases} 0, & u > I_\theta; \\ 1, & u < I_\theta. \end{cases} \quad (10)$$

$$0\nabla u^{I_\theta} = \begin{cases} 0, & u < I_\theta; \\ 1, & u > I_\theta. \end{cases} \quad (11)$$

$$0\nabla^{I_{\theta1}}u \cdot u^{I_{\theta2}} = \begin{cases} 0, & I_{\theta1} < u < I_{\theta2}; \\ 1, & Other. \end{cases} \quad (12)$$

where variable u in above three equations denotes the summed current signal, I_θ is threshold (current signal) defined as equation (7). According to the features of JCS presented in Fig.4, three basic function term circuits, corresponding to equation (10), (11) and (12), respectively, are designed from switch level as presented in Fig.6. A CMOS current circuit in Fig.6 (c) is used for obtaining two currents in exactly the same as the input current and passes them to JCS. Provided with equation (9) and three basic function term circuits shown in Fig.6, any arbitrary MTJFCs can be easily designed from switch level.

IV. Design example

In classical neural networks, it is well known that an XOR operation requires a three-layer network composed of three STNs to achieve as shown in Fig.7(a). Whereas, as an extension of STN, MTN makes it possible for neural networks perform the same function as STNs do using pretty small number of MTNs. We just take XOR operation as an example, according to the features defined in equation (1), single dual-thresholded two-valued neuron presented in Fig. 7(b) is enough for accomplishing such XOR operation achievement. For designing this MTNC for XOR operation, we should write firstly its output transfer function:

$$\left. \begin{array}{l} y = f(1 \cdot x_1 + 1 \cdot x_2); \\ f(u) = \begin{cases} 0 & u \leq 0.5 \text{ or } u \geq 1.5; \\ 1, & 0.5 < u \leq 1.5. \end{cases} \end{array} \right\} \quad (13)$$

Secondly, according to equations (9)~(13), the switch level expression of multi-thresholded judgement function for XOR operation can be written as following:

$$f = 0\nabla\alpha = 0\nabla(u^{I_{0.5}} + {}^{I_{1.5}}u) = 0\nabla u^{I_{0.5}} \cap 0\nabla^{I_{1.5}}u \quad (14)$$

Finally, combined with the general structure of two-valued circuits shown in Fig.5 and three basic function term circuits presented in Fig.6, a dual-thresholded two-valued neuron circuit for XOR operation can be easily designed at switch level. Both circuit diagram and its transient simulation result is presented in Fig. 8. During simulation with Pspice, the input signals $x_1, x_2 \in \{0V, 3.3V\}$, weight signals $w_1 = w_2 = 1V$, thresholds $V_{\theta1}$ and $V_{\theta2}$ are set 2V and 5V according to equation (7), supply voltage $V_{DD} = 3.3V$ and load of this circuits is the same type of MTN circuit. By measuement, its average propagation delay is $18\,ns$. The simulation result of this circuit shows it not only has the correct logic function but also has small propagation delay. Besides, on the condition that the techniques and the structure in form are the same, as for considering the hardware cost, the implementation of XOR operation by MTNC need only 13 MOS transistors, 3 bipolar transistors and 3 connecting wires, while the same operation by STN circuits requires 28 MOS transistors, 6 bipolar transistors and 7 connecting wires. Therefore, large amount of hardware expense is reduced by using MTN circuits compared with its counterparts.

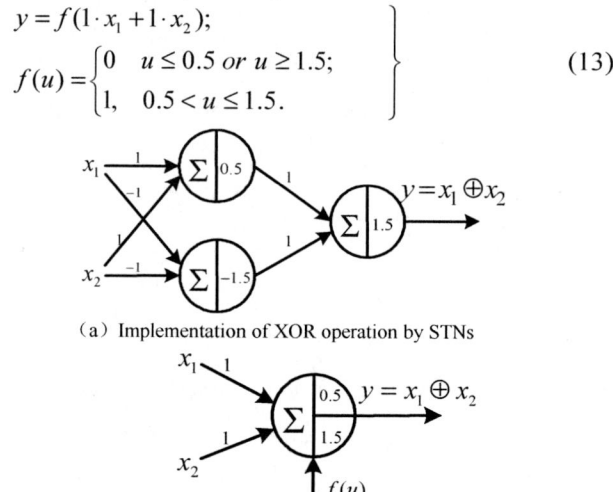

(a) Implementation of XOR operation by STNs

(b) Implementation of XOR operation by MTNs

Fig. 7. Implementation of XOR operation by neurons

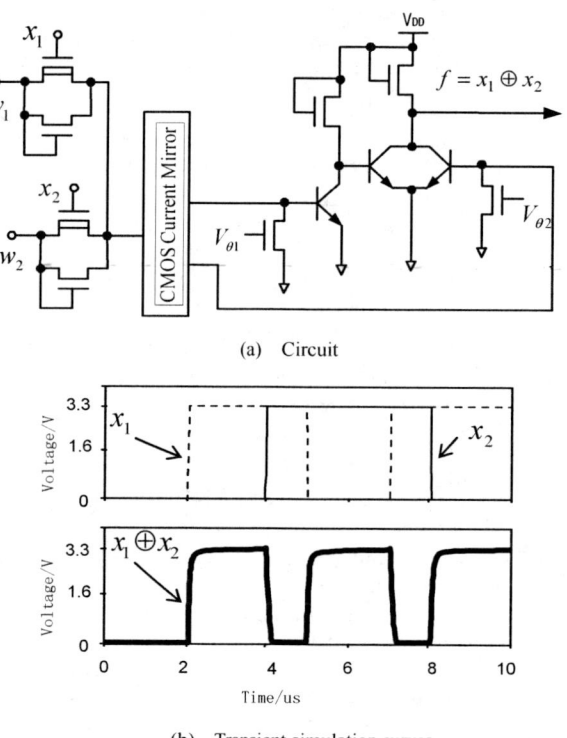

(a) Circuit

(b) Transient simulation curves

Fig. 8. Dual-thresholded two-valued neuron circuit for XOR operation and its transient curves

V. Conclusion

This paper probes a design methodology for implementing an MTN with VLSI technology. Firstly, two n-channel MOS transistors are employed to design a synapse circuit with high simplicity, speed and linearity. Then, a BiCMOS technique based JCS circuit whose threshold is voltage-controlled current is designed to provide the abilities of comparing the current input with threshold, judging which circumscription the input signal belongs to and passing out a corresponding voltage output. Since its simplicity and flexibility, this JCS is chosen as a core unit of threshold function circuits of MTN. Based on it, inspired by the clipping voltage switches theory, we proposed a general methodology to design the MTJFCs that is considered the key part of MTNCs at switch level. Finally, a dual-thresholded two-valued neuron circuit is designed for implementing the XOR operation. The simulation results with PSPICE showed that the designed circuits have not only the correct logic function but work in high speed. Hence, the proposed methodology is verified as a simple, canonical and effective way to design the MTJFCs. Further, the designed MTNCs which is based on BiCMOS technique combines the advantages of speed and high-drive capabilities of bipolar circuits as well as the low-power and high-density of CMOS circuits. In addition, the input stage of this MTN is continuous voltage-mode circuits which are more economized than digital neurons, and the output stage is voltage-mode switching circuits which lead to high precision. Despite of those, it is worth mentioning that the MTN circuits decreased large amount of hardware expense, on the condition of achieving the same logic function, compared with the STN circuits. Generally speaking, the proposed MTN circuits are pretty suitable for implementing the ANNs with VLSI technology and in the meanwhile improve the hardware performance of ANNs.

ACKNOWLEDGMENT

This work was supported in part by the Zhejiang Province Science Foundation under grant no. Y104368 and National Science Foundation of China under grant no. 60475018, etc.

REFERENCE

[1] Clifford Lau edited. Neural networks: Theoretical foundation and analysis[J]. IEEE PRESS, A Selected Peprint Volume, Neural Networks Council, Sponsor. 1992.
[2] Gisutham B, Srikanthan T, Asari K V. A high speed flat CORCIC based neuron with multi-level activ- ation function for robust pattern recognition[A]. Proceedings of Fifth IEEE International Workshop on Computer Architectures for Machine Perception [C]. Padova: IEEE, 2000.87-94.
[3] Moraga C, et al. New lamps for old! (generalized multiple-valued neurons)[A]. Proceedings of the 29th IEEE International Symposium on Multiple-Valued Logic[C]. Freiburg: IEEE, 1999. 36-41.
[4] Wang Shoujue. Multi-valued neuron (MVN) and Multi-thresholded neuron(MTN), their combination and applications[J]. ACTA Electronica Sinica, 1996, 3(3): 1-6.
[5] Yuh J, Newcomb R W. Circuits for multi-level neuron nonlinearities[A]. International Joint Conference on Neural Networks[C], Baltimore: IEEE,1992. vol.2: 27 -32.
[6] Au R., Yamashita T, Shibata T, Ohmi T. Neuron-MOS multiple-valued memory technology for intelligent data processing.[A]. The 41st IEEE International Solid-State Circuits Conference [C].San Francisco: IEEE, 1994. 270-271.
[7] Ngom A, et al. Minimization of multivalued multithreshold perceptrons using genetic algorithms[A]. Proceedings of the 28th IEEE International Symposium on Multiple-Valued Logic [C]. Fukuoka: IEEE, 1998. 209-214.
[8] Torsten L. Hardware learning in analogue VLSI neural networks [D]. Lyngby. University of Denmark, 1994. 1-6.
[9] Chible H. Analog circuit for synapse neural networks VLSI implementation [A]. The 7th IEEE International Conference on Circuits and Systems[C]. Jounieh: IEEE, 2000. vol.2:1004-1007.
[10] Bermak A, et al. VLSI implementation of a neural network classifier based on the saturating linear activation Function [A]. Proceedings of the 9th International Conference on Neural Information Processing [C]. Singapore: IEEE, 2002. 981-985.
[11] Hasler P, Akers L A. VLSI neural systems and circuits[A]. International Conference on Computer and Communications [C], Phoenix: IEEE, 1990. 31- 37.
[12] Choi J, Sheu B J. Neural Information Pressing and VLSI[M]. Boston Kluwer Academic Publishers, 1995.
[13] Tomlinson M S, et al. A digital neural network architecture for VLSI [A]. International Joint Conference on Neural Networks, II [C]. San Diego: IEEE, 1990.545-550.
[14] Cesare A, Meyer E. Hardware requirements for digital VLSI implementation of neural networks [A]. International Joint Conference on Neural Networks [C], Singapore: IEEE, 1991. 1873-1878.
[15] Richard C, marwan J, et al. A hybrid analog and digital VLSI neural network for intracardiac morphology classification[J]. IEEE Journal of Solid State Circuits, 1995, 30(5): 108-111.
[16] Koosh V F, Goodman R. VLSI neural network with digital weights and analog multipliers[A]. The 2001 IEEE International Symposium on Circuits and Systems[C]. Sydney: IEEE, 2001. vol.3: 233-236.
[17] Meed C. Analog VLSI and Neural System[M]. Mass: Addison-Wesley, 1989.
[18] Tadahiro K, Yoshinori S, Kenji M. Analysis and optimization of BiCOMS gate circuits[J]. IEEE Transction on Solid-state Circuits, 1994, 29(6): 671 -678.
[19] Shen Jie, Jin Dongming, Li Zhijian. Dual- MOS FETs equivalent resistor[J]. Journal of Tsinghua University (Sci& Tech), 1999, 39(5): 104- 107.
[20] Lippman Richard P. An introduction to computing with neural nets [J]. IEEE ASSP Magzine, April, 1987. 4-7.
[21] Wu Xunwei, Zhao Xiaojie. Design of ternary nMOS circuits based on theory of clipping voltage switches [J], Int.J. Electronics, 1993, 75(1): 91-102.
[22] Behzad Razavi. Design of analog CMOS integrate circuits[M]. McGraw-Hill. Inc. 2001: 113-116.

FPGA Implementation of Pulse Coupled Oscillator

Yutaka Maeda and Makito Nakatsuka
Department of Electrical Engineering and Computer Science
Faculty of Engineering, Kansai University
3-3-35, Yamate-cho, Suita 564-8680 JAPAN
E-mail: maedayut@kansai-u.ac.jp

Abstract—This paper proposes a learning scheme for pulse coupled oscillators using the simultaneous perturbation optimization method. Moreover, hardware implementation of the pulse coupled oscillator with learning capability using field programmable gate array is described.

It is complicated for ordinary method to find proper parameter values in the pulse coupled oscillator for a proper period, since the pulse coupled oscillator is a kind of recurrent network. The simultaneous perturbation optimization method can give a simple solution to this problem. In addition, this scheme is suitable for hardware realization.

Some simulation results of the learning method for pulse coupled oscillators are shown. At the same time, we fabricated FPGA pulse coupled oscillator system with learning mechanism. Results by the hardware system are also shown.

I. INTRODUCTION

Nowadays, field programmable gate array(FPGA) is very promising device in the industrial field to realize digital electronic circuits. It is important to deduce the time to market. At the same time, FPGA is very useful tool to make neural systems. Hardware neural systems can realize many inherent features such as pararellism, operation speed.

Recently, pulse coupled neural networks are intriguing target in research of neural computation. However, we have many hard tissues like learning capability, hardware implementation and applications in the area.

The pulse coupled oscillator contains some parameters to maintain a series of pulse outputs. Therefore, it is important to find a method which gives proper values of the parameters, that is, learning scheme. Ordinary the gradient type of learning method is proposed for the pulse coupled oscillators[1]. However, the gradient method for the recurrent networks is difficult to implement. Especially, hardware realization of the scheme seems impossible.

In this paper, we propose a learning scheme for pulse coupled oscillators using the simultaneous perturbation optimization method. The proposed learning scheme using the simultaneous perturbation is very simple and easy to implement. Moreover, FPGA implementation of the pulse coupled oscillators with the learning mechanism is described.

II. PULSE COUPLED OSCILLATOR

In this paper, we consider a kind of pulse neuron. Fig.1 shows our model of the neuron.

The pulse coupled oscillator consists of the two pulse neurons. The pulse coupled oscillator is depicted in Fig.2.

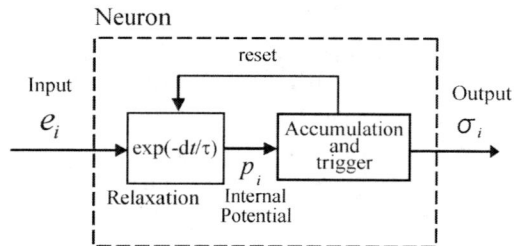

Fig. 1. Neuron model.

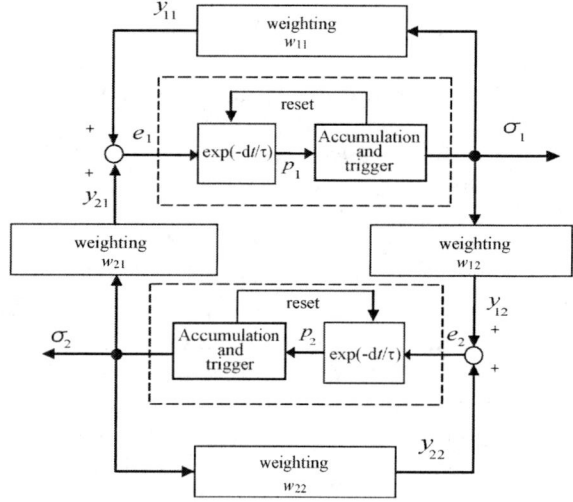

Fig. 2. Pulse coupled oscillator consisted of the two neurons.

Outputs of the neurons are connected to the other neuron and themselves with weighting factor.

Mathematical expression of the pulse coupled oscillator is described below.

$$\sigma_i(t) = \sum_{k_i=1}^{K_i} \delta(t - t_{i,k_i}) \quad (1)$$

$$t_{i,k_i} = \min[t : t > t_{i,k_i-1}, I_i(t) \geq s] \quad (2)$$

$$e_i(t) = \sum_{j=1}^{M} w_{ji}\sigma_i(t) \quad (3)$$

$$p_i(t) = p_i(t - dt)exp(-\frac{dt}{\tau}) + e_i(t) \quad (4)$$

$$p_i(0) = p_i^0, \quad p_i\left(t_{i,k_i}^+\right) = 0, \quad k_i = 1, 2, \cdots, K_i \quad (5)$$

$$I_i(t) = \sum_{t=t_{i,k_i-1}+dt}^{t} p_i(t) \quad (6)$$

$$I_i(0) = 0, \quad I_i\left(t_{i,k_i}^+\right) = 0, \quad k_i = 1, 2, \cdots, K_i \quad (7)$$

σ_i denotes output pulses of the i-th neuron, δ means the Kronecker's delta. e denotes a total input, that is, e is a weighted summation of the two outputs of another neuron and itself. p is an internal parameter of the neuron with relaxation factor, τ is time-constant for relaxation, I is an accumulated potential of the internal potential of p, s is a threshold value. When the accumulated potential I exceeds the threshold s, then we have a pulse and the state of the neuron is reset. This accumulation and trigger can be regard as a time delay factor. t_{i,k_i} is the point when we have the pulse.

In this pulse coupled oscillator, we have some parameters to adjust. The neuron model itself contains one internal parameter, therefore we have to set the two internal parameters. Moreover, there exist four weights. Totally, we have six parameters in the oscillator.

In order to obtain and maintain desired oscillatory outputs, it is essential to find proper values of these six parameters. From this point, the learning mechanism is very important.

Y.Kuroe, K. Selvaratnam and T.Mori discussed the details of a similar pulse coupled oscillator and proposed a method of a synthesis for the oscillator[1], [2] as well.

III. Learning Scheme of the Pulse Coupled Oscillator Using the Simultaneous Perturbation

The pulse coupled oscillator is a recurrent neural network, therefore it is difficult to employ the usual back-propagation learning. For example, Y.Kuroe describes a gradient type of learning for the pulse coupled oscillator[1]. However, this process is complicated and it seems difficult to realize by hardware systems.

On the other hand, the simultaneous perturbation optimization method is very simple stochastic gradient method which does not require the gradient of an objective function but only two values of the function. The simultaneous perturbation was introduced by J.C.Spall[3] in 1987. Convergence of the algorithm was proved in the framework of the stochastic approximation method[4]. Independently, Y. Maeda also have proposed a learning rule of neural networks based on the SP method and reported a comparison between the SP type of learning rule of neural networks, the simple finite difference type of learning rule and the ordinary back-propagation method[5]. J.Alespector et al. and G.Cauwenberghs also proposed a parallel gradient descent method and stochastic error-descent algorithm, respectively, which are identical to the simultaneous perturbation learning rule[8], [9]. Many applications of the SP technique are reported in the fields of neural networks[10] and their hardware implementation[11], [12].

Now, we propose a learning scheme using the simultaneous perturbation optimization method. First of all, we have to define an evaluation or an error. Our goal is to obtain the pulses with proper interval. Thus the difference between positions of actual pulses and ideal positions of corresponding desired pulses gives a clue to evaluate how well the oscillator works(See Fig.3). $\ell(=0, 1, \cdots)$ denotes the block number.

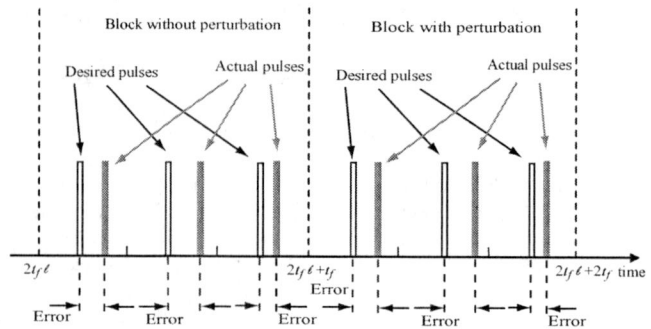

Fig. 3. Evaluating positions of pulses.

We use the following error function J.

$$J(\boldsymbol{w}) = \frac{1}{2}\sum_{i=1}^{M}\sum_{k_i=1}^{K_i}\left(t_{i,k_i}^d - t_{i,k_i}^a\right)^2 \quad (8)$$
$$(i = 1, 2, \cdots, M)$$

Moreover, we need two error values; one without the perturbation and the other with the perturbation. Therefore, we adopt a block interval processing. The first block in Fig. 3 is used to obtain the error without the perturbation. The second period is used for the error with the perturbation. t_f is period of the block.

Based on the error, we use the following recursion to find suitable values in the pulse coupled oscillator:

$$\boldsymbol{w}_{t+1} = \boldsymbol{w}_t - \alpha \boldsymbol{\Delta} w_t \quad (9)$$

$$\Delta w_t^n = \frac{J(\boldsymbol{w}_t + c\boldsymbol{v}_t) - J(\boldsymbol{w}_t)}{cv_t^n} \quad (n = 1, 2, \cdots, 6) \quad (10)$$

where $\boldsymbol{w}_t$ means the parameter vector contained in the oscillator at the t-th iteration. This consists of six parameters. $c(\neq 0)$ is a magnitude of the perturbation. $\boldsymbol{v}$ and v^n represent the sign vector and its n-th component whose value is +1 or -1. $J(\boldsymbol{w} + c\boldsymbol{v})$ and $J(\boldsymbol{w})$ denote the error values with the perturbation and without this, respectively. $\alpha(> 0)$ is an adjustment factor for the modification. The perturbation has to satisfy the following properties:

$$\begin{array}{l} E(\boldsymbol{v}_t) = 0 \\ E\left(v_{t_1}^{n_1} v_{t_2}^{n_2}\right) = \xi^2 \delta_{n_1 n_2} \delta_{t_1 t_2} \end{array} \quad (11)$$

That is, the sign element v_t^n, which is +1 or -1, is generated randomly. This element is independent with iteration t and the other sign elements.

$(J(\boldsymbol{w}_t + c\boldsymbol{v}_t) - J(\boldsymbol{w}_t))/cv_t^n$ of Eq.(10) shows an estimator of the gradient of the error function. This method uses a kind of difference approximation. However, unlike the ordinary difference approximation the simultaneous perturbation does require only two values of the error, even if the number of the parameters is large. We know that the method is a stochastic gradient method.

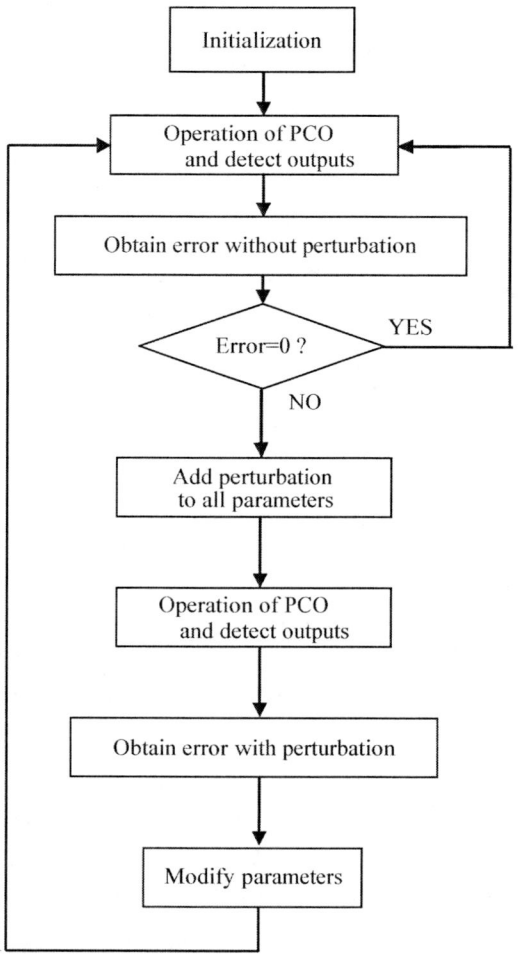

Fig. 4. Flowchart of the learning scheme.

Note that only two values of the error are required to update six parameters. As a result, the flow of the learning is very simple(See Fig. 4). Learning scheme is as follows:

1) Set initial values of the pulse coupled oscillator.
2) Run the pulse coupled oscillator. We obtain a series of pulses.
3) Obtain an evaluation without the perturbation(Obtain $J(\boldsymbol{w}_t)$.). Then the first half of a time block is used. The first three pulses of this period are used to evaluate the accuracy of the position of the pulses based on Eq.(8). If the evaluation is not enough to end, then go to the next step.
4) Add the perturbation to all of the parameters in the oscillator. Then, we obtain pulses in the last half of the time block. We have the error with the perturbation(Obtain $J(\boldsymbol{w}_t + c\boldsymbol{v}_t)$.).
5) Using Eqs.(9) and (10), we update the six parameters of the pulse coupled oscillator.
6) Go to the step 2.

Fig.4 shows the flowchart of the learning scheme. As we can see, the procedure is very simple and only two error values are required to update parameters.

IV. SIMULATION RESULTS

We would like to find a periodic oscillation with one second period(See pulses in Fig.6). Initial values of weights are all 30. Initial values of internal parameters are all 50. The perturbation c and the coefficient α are 1.0 and 5.0, respectively. These parameters are determined through preliminary experiments.

Fig. 5 and Fig. 6 show results of the output pulses σ before learning and after learning, respectively. Moreover, two internal states p and I are described in this figures as well.

Before learning, the period of the output pulses is not one second. It is about 0.5 second and unstable (See Fig. 5). After about 150 learning, the period is just one second and stable. The internal states are also stable and periodic (See Fig. 6).

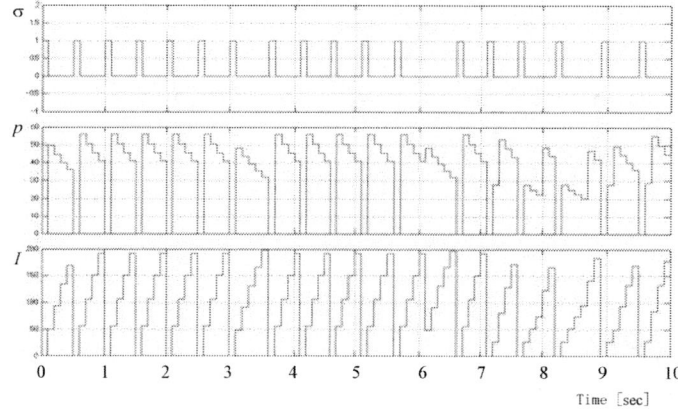

Fig. 5. Output pulses before learning.

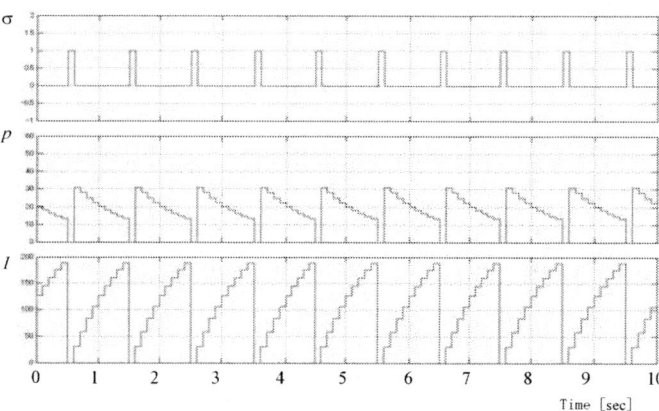

Fig. 6. Output pulses after learning.

Fig. 7 shows change of the error in learning process. As the learning proceeds, the error decreases. About 900 seconds is enough to maintain the period of one second.

We have six parameters. However, weights w_{11} and w_{22}, w_{12} and w_{21}, the internal parameters p_1^0 and p_2^0 have same

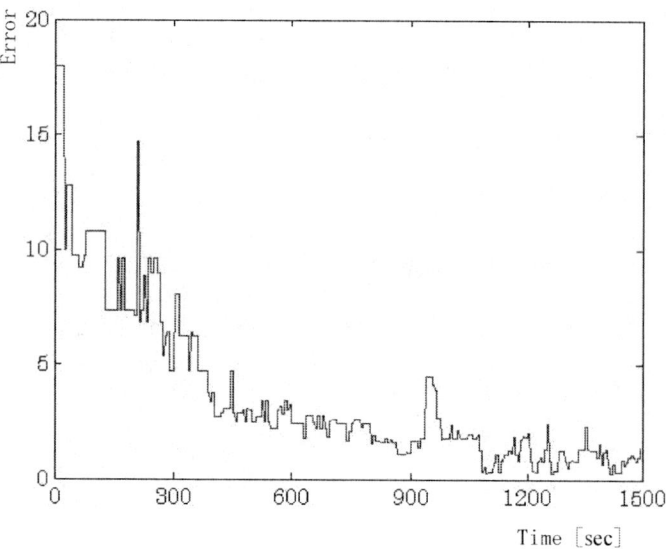

Fig. 7. Change of the error.

property. Therefore, we can adjust these parameters under the following conditions:

$$w_{11} = w_{22},$$
$$w_{12} = w_{21}, \quad (12)$$
$$p_1^0 = p_2^0$$

We expect faster convergence for the conditions. Leaning process is shown in Fig. 8. About 400 learning is enough to obtain the ideal pulses.

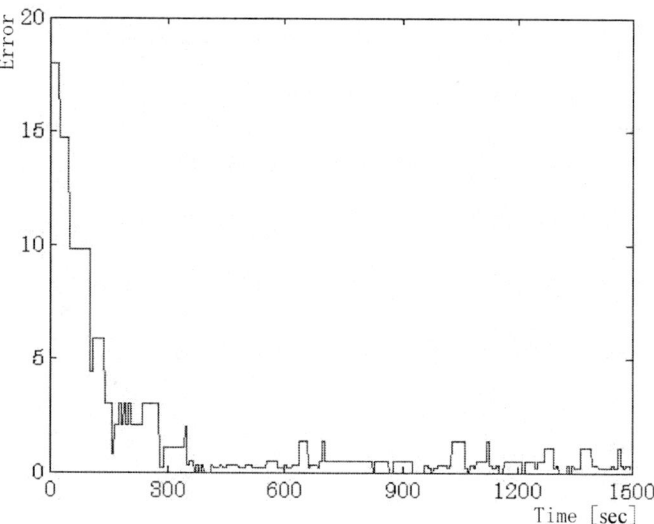

Fig. 8. Change of the error under the condition (12).

Next, we add disturbances in the learning process in order to confirm bounce of the system. Arrows in Fig. 9 show some points when we add disturbances to the system. The period of the pulses changes, that is, the error increases temporarily. However, the learning mechanism compensates the disturbances. Therefore, the error decreases soon. The period of the pulses keeps one second. We can confirm stability of the system and the learning scheme.

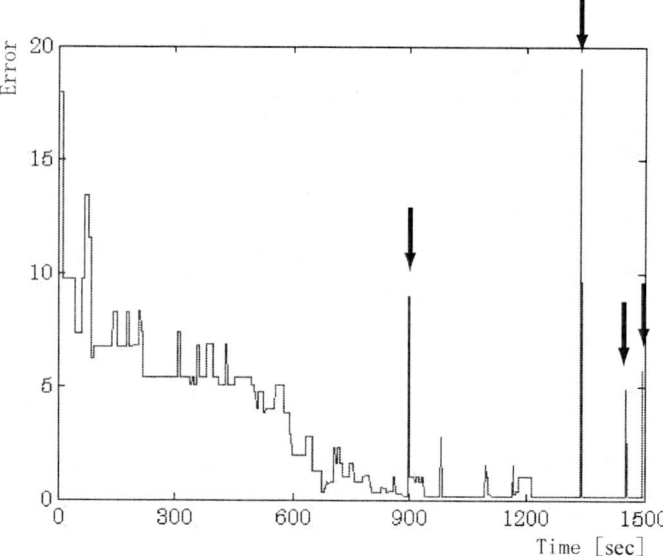

Fig. 9. Change of the error under disturbances.

If we require other pulse pattern or period, we have to construct a proper evaluation function similar to Eq.(3). It is relatively easy for us to make new evaluation function, because we know a situation of the desired pulses. Based on the error function, we repeated the learning procedure so as to reduce the error.

V. FPGA SYSTEM OF PULSE COUPLED OSCILLATOR

VHDL (VHSIC Hardware Description Language) is a very popular HDL for describing or designing digital circuits. In the basic design of this research, VHDL is used. With the simultaneous perturbation learning scheme, we can easily design hardware neural systems with learning capability.

The design result by VHDL is configured on FPGA through Synplify Pro and Quartus II. MU200-SX60 system(Mitsubishi Electric Micro-Computer Application Software Co.,Ltd) with Altera Stratix EP1S60F1020C6, which has 57,120 logic elements and two 4Mbit RAM, is used(See Fig.10.).

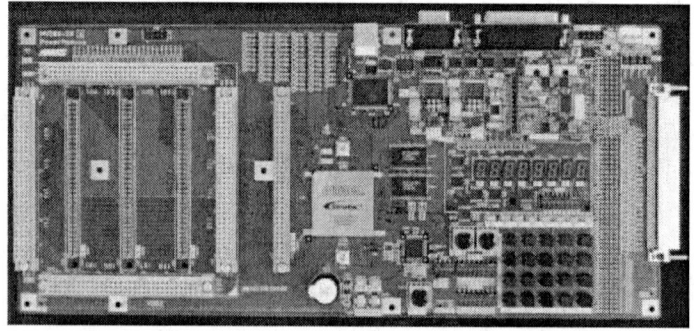

Fig. 10. Picture of FPGA system(MU200-SX60).

we adopt a single precision floating-point representation of the numerical values. 32 bits with 1 sign bit, 8 exponent bits and 23 mantissa bits of IEEE754 standard are used to represent a numerical value. This representation was sufficient to describe the operation. Arithmetic operations used here are standard procedures.

For this design, 5,428 logic elements out of 57,120(about 10%), 16 DSP block 9-bit elements out of 144(about 11%) are used. No memory was used.

The overall configuration of the pulse coupled oscillator is shown in Fig.11. The pulse coupled oscillator system is composed of pulse coupled oscillator unit, learning unit, memory units and control unit.

The pulse coupled oscillator unit realizes practical operation of the pulse coupled oscillator. The unit consists of two neuron models of Fig.1 and weighted coupling. This unit operates with certain parameters and with the perturbed parameters in turn, based on parameters in the parameter memory part. Outputs pulses are sent to the learning unit.

The learning unit observes the outputs of the pulse coupled oscillator unit. The learning unit detects time difference between practical firing timing and the corresponding desired firing timing. The time difference is converted to numerical quantity. Finally, the quantity yields modifying quantities for all parameters based on the simultaneous perturbation method.

The state machine and some counters in the control unit control overall operation of the system.

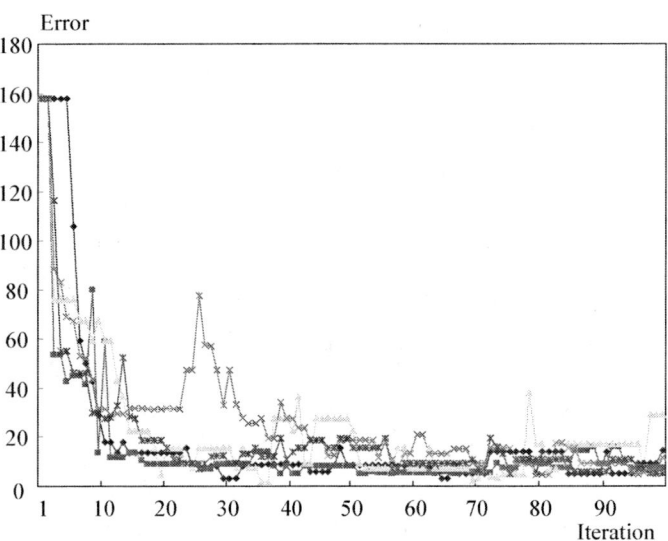

Fig. 12. Operation result by the FPGA system.

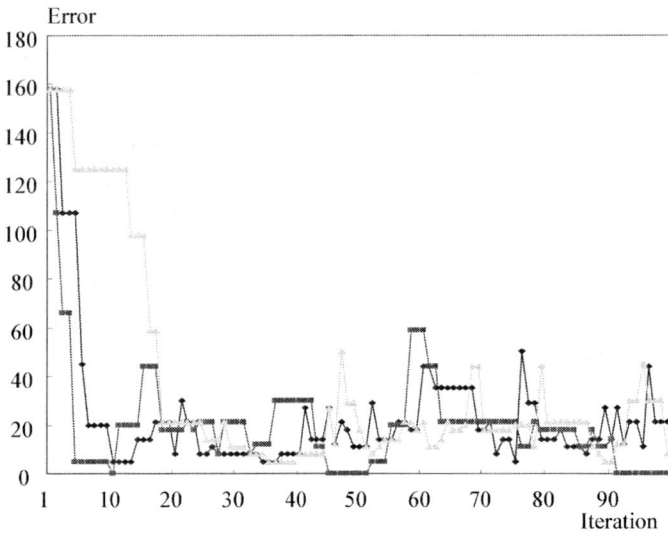

Fig. 13. Operation result by the FPGA system under condition (12).

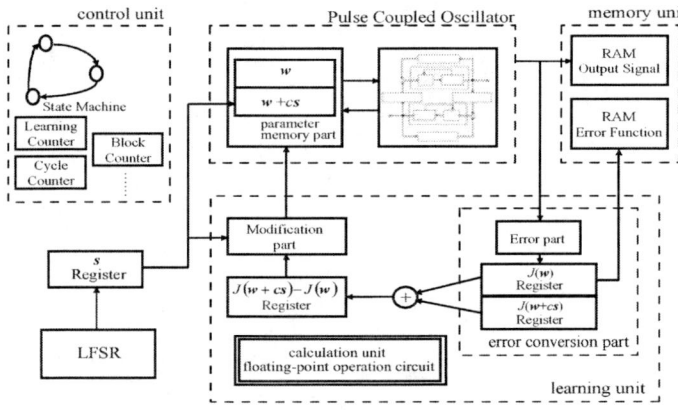

Fig. 11. Configuration of pulse coupled oscillator.

Fig.13 and Fig.12 illustrate some actual operation results of the system. Different sequences of sign give different learning curves. These five results are depicted. Fig.12 shows results under conditions (12).

As iteration proceeds, the error decreases. For both case, about 50 modifications of the parameters gives the desired firing timing.

VI. CONCLUSION

In this paper, we propose a learning scheme for pulse coupled oscillators using the simultaneous perturbation optimization method. The result shows that the learning scheme can find proper values of the oscillator.

Moreover, we implemented the pulse coupled oscillator with learning capability using the simultaneous perturbation method. We verified the operation. At the same time, the learning scheme is also confirmed. We can anticipate application of the hardware system.

ACKNOWLEDGMENT

This work was financially supported by Grant-in-Aid for Scientific Research(No.16500142) of the Ministry of Education, Culture, Sports, Science and Technology of Japan.

REFERENCES

[1] K. Selvaratnam, Y. Kuroe, T. Mori, "Learning methods of Recurrent Spiking Neural Networks – Transient and Oscillatory Spike Trains," *SYSTEMS, CONTROL and INFORMATION*, vol. 13, pp. 95–104, March 2000.
[2] Y. Kuroe, T. Mori, "Spiking neural oscillators," *Proceddings of SICE Annual Conference 2002*, pp. 765–769, 2002.

[3] J. C. Spall : "A stochastic approximation technique for generating maximum likelihood parameter estimation," *Proceedings of the 1987 American Control Conference*, pp. 1161–1167, 1987.

[4] J. C. Spall : "Multivariate stochastic approximation using a simultaneous perturbation gradient approximation," *IEEE trans. on Automatic Control*, vol. 37, pp. 332–341, March 1992.

[5] Y. Maeda, H. Hirano and Y. Kanata : "A learning rule of neural networks via simultaneous perturbation and its hardware implementation," *Neural Networks*, vol. 8, pp. 251–259, 1995.

[6] J. C. Spall and J. A. Cristion : "Nonlinear adaptive control using neural networks : Estimation with a smoothed form of simultaneous perturbation gradient approximation," *Statistica Sinica*, vol. 4, pp. 1-27, 1994.

[7] D. C. Chin : "Comparative study of stochastic algorithms for system optimization based on gradient approximations," *IEEE trans. on Systems, Man, and Cybernetics-Part B:Cybernetics*, vol. 27, pp. 244–249, 1997.

[8] J. Alespector, R. Meir, B. Yuhas, A. Jayakumar, D. Lippe, "A parallel gradient descent method for learning in analog vlsi neural networks," in: S. Hanson, J. Cowan, C. Lee (Eds.), *Advances in neural information processing systems*, vol. 5, Morgan Kaufmann Publisher, Cambridge, MA, pp. 836–844, 1993 .

[9] G. Cauwenberghs, "A fast stochastic error-descent algorithm for supervised learning and optimization," in: S.J.Hanson, J.D.Cowan, C. Lee (Eds.), *Advances in neural information processing systems*, vol. 5, Morgan Kaufmann Publisher, Cambridge, MA, pp. 244–251, 1993.

[10] Y. Maeda and R. J. P. de Figueiredo,: "Learning rules for neurocontroller via simultaneous perturbation," *IEEE Trans. on Neural Networks*, vol. 8, pp. 1119–1130, May 1997.

[11] Y. Maeda, A.Nakazawa and Y.Kanata : "Hardware implementation of a pulse density neural network using simultaneous perturbation learning rule," *Analog Integrated Circuits and Signal Processing*, vol. 18, pp. 153–162, 1999

[12] Y. Maeda, T. Tada, "FPGA implementation of a pulse density neural network with learning ability using simultaneous perturbation," *IEEE Trans. on Neural Networks*, vol. 14, pp. 688–695, May 2003.

Analog Current-Mode CMOS Implementation of Central Pattern Generator for Robot Locomotion

Kazuki Nakada, Tetsuya Asai, Tetsuya Hirose, Yoshihito Amemiya
Department of Electrical and Engineering
Hokkaido University
Sapporo, 060-8628
E-mail: nakada@sapiens-ei.eng.hokudai.ac.jp

Abstract— We propose an analog current-mode central pattern generator (CPG). Our circuit is based on the neural oscillator proposed by Matsuoka, well known as a building block for constructing a robot locomotion controller. We modified the Matsuoka's oscillator to be suitable for analog current-mode implementation, and implemented it as an analog integrated circuit with current-mode low-pass filters. The oscillator circuit operates in the subthreshold region under the low-supply voltages, and thus low power consumption can be expected. We constructed a CPG circuit with four oscillator circuits. Through SPICE simulations, we confirmed that the CPG circuit generates stable phase-locked oscillation corresponding to typical locomotion of patterns of animals, and that the amplitude and frequency of the oscillation can be controlled by tuning bias currents over a wide range.

I. INTRODUCTION

Locomotor behavior of animals, such as walking, running, flying, and swimming, is generated by the central nervous system, called the central pattern generator (CPG) [1]. A CPG consists of sets of neural oscillators, situated in the ganglion or spinal cord. Induced by inputs from higher level, a CPG generates rhythmic neural activity activating muscles in the absence of sensory inputs, resulting in locomotor behavior of animals. While not necessary for generating rhythmic activity, sensory inputs regulate such rhythmic activity over a wide range [1]. As a result, CPG adapts locomotor behavior to unpredictable environments.

During the past decade, many researchers have utilized such adaptability of CPG to locomotion control in robotics [5]-[7]. Taga *et al.* have used a CPG model that consists of the neural oscillator model proposed by Matsuoka [3], in simulating for biped locomotion [5]. Kimura *et al.* developed a CPG-based controller for quadruped robot locomotion on rough terrain [7]. Williamson also developed a CPG-based controller for rhythmic arm movements [6]. Lewis and his colleagues developed and mounted CPG chips on biped walking robots [12]-[13]. In these works, sensory feedback plays a critical role to high adaptability of CPG-based locomotion control.

In previous works, many CPG chips have been developed [8]-[17]. As a CPG chip, it is desirable to control the frequency and amplitude of the oscillation in the CPG chip over a wide range because such controllability is necessary to utilize sensor feedback efficiently in adapting the oscillation generated by the CPG chip to a given environments.

The aim of this work is to implement an analog CPG circuit with high controllability of the amplitude and frequency of the oscillation. We designed an analog current-mode neural oscillator, which operates in the subthreshold region under the low-supply voltages, based on the neural oscillator model proposed by Matsuoka. We also constructed a CPG circuit from the neural oscillator circuits. As a result, the CPG circuit generates stable phase-locked oscillation, and the amplitude and frequency of the oscillation can be controlled by tuning bias currents over a wide range.

II. HALF-CENTER OSCILLATOR CIRCUIT

We proposed an analog current-mode circuit implementing a half-center oscillator oscillator as a building block for constructing a CPG circuit.

A. Half-center Oscillator Model

We here describe a half-center oscillator model for analog current-mode implementation. Brown proposed the concept of the half-center oscillator to account for the alternating rhythmic activity in the flexor and extensor motoneuron during walking in cat [2]. A half-center oscillator consists of two neurons, a flexor half-center and an extensor half-center, with reciprocal inhibition (Fig. 1). The half-centers alternatively activate flexor and extensor muscles in the absence of pacemaker cells. Each half-center has dynamic properties such as self-inhibition, fatigue or adaptation. The flexor half-center activates the flexor muscles and suppresses the extensor half-center via synaptic inhibition in the flexion phase, in turn, due to the self-inhibition and adaptation, transition from the flexion phase to extension phase occurs.

Matsuoka proposed a half-center oscillator model that consists of two-neurons, described by the following system equations [3]:

$$\tau_u \frac{du_i}{dt} = -u_i + s - \beta v_i - w_{ij} f(u_j) \quad (1)$$

$$\tau_v \frac{dv_i}{dt} = -v_i + f(u_i) \quad (2)$$

where the nonlinear function $f(x) = \max(0, x)$, u_i represents the inner state of the i-th neuron, v_i an adaptation variable of the neuron ($i = 1, 2$), s a tonic input, w_{ij} a synaptic strength between the i-th and j-th neuron, β the adaptation

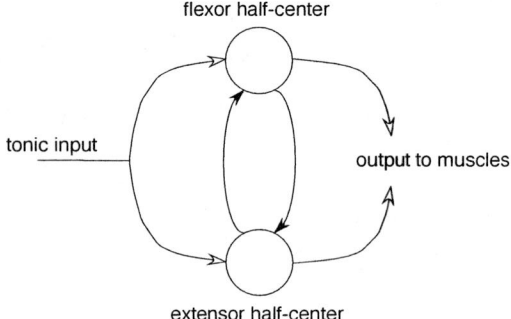

Fig. 1. Schematic of the half-center oscillator. Black and white arrows represent inhibitory and excitatory synapses.

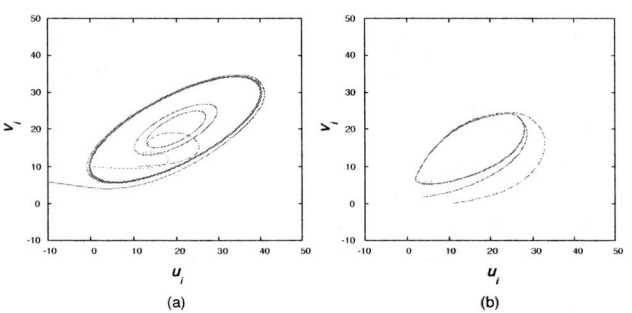

Fig. 2. Phase-plane portraits of (a) the Matsuoka model and (b) the proposed model. There exists multiple steady states for same parameter values in the Matsuoka model.

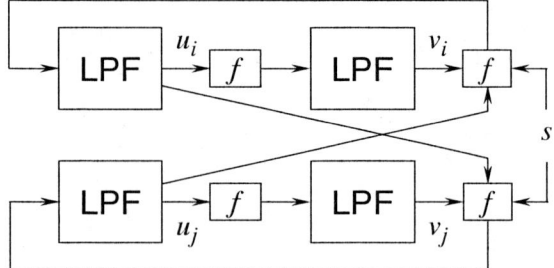

Fig. 3. Block diagram of the proposed model, where LPF represents a low-pass filter and f the nonlinear function.

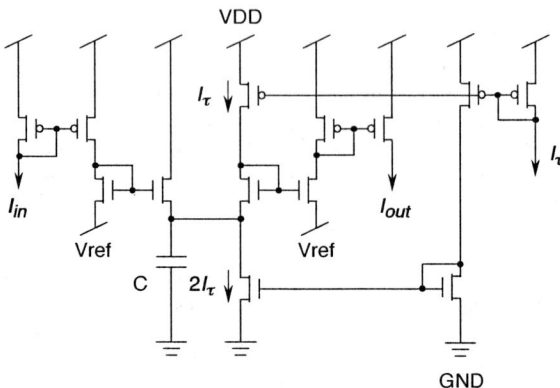

Fig. 4. Schematic of current-mode low-pass filter.

effectiveness, τ_u a time constant of the self-inhibition, and τ_v a time constant of the adaptation effect.

This model generates limit-cycle oscillations depending on these parameters. The stability and properties of this model are analyzed in [3]-[4]. The amplitude of the oscillation is proportional to a tonic input, and the frequency and shape of the oscillation can be controlled by tuning the ratio of time constants. Utilizing such properties, this model has been fluently used in robotics [5]-[7]. Taga et al. have used it in simulating for biped locomotion. Williamson has applied it to control robot arm movements [6]. Kimura et al. applied it to control a quadruped robot on rough terrain [7].

Despite these advantages, a problem is that this model has multiple solutions for a same parameter set, as it is shown in Fig. 2. This occurs when we determine a parameter set to make all variables positive. To avoid this problem, we modified the Matsuoka model as follows:

$$\tau_u \frac{du_i}{dt} = -u_i + f(s - \beta v_i - w_{ij} u_j) \quad (3)$$
$$\tau_v \frac{dv_i}{dt} = -v_i + f(u_i) \quad (4)$$

where all variables and parameters are same as in (1)-(2). As a result, we can obtain a limit-cycle solution such that all variables are positive, and thus this model is suitable to implement as an analog current-mode circuit that uses uni-directional currents.

B. Circuit Architecture

We implemented the half-center oscillator model described in the previous section as an analog current-mode circuit.

The proposed model consists of four low-pass filters and nonlinear functions (Fig. 3). Thus, it can be implemented with current-mode low-pass filters and current mirrors. The current-mode low-pass filter (Fig. 4) operates in log-domain based on the dynamic translinear principle [18]. The circuit dynamics is expressed by the following equation:

$$\tau \frac{dI_{out}}{dt} = -I_{out} + I_{in} \quad (5)$$

where I_{in} is the input current, I_{out} the output current, and τ the time constant expressed by:

$$\tau = \frac{CU_T}{I_\tau} \quad (6)$$

where C the capacitance, U_T the thermal voltage, and I_τ the bias current. The nonlinear function defined by (3) can be easily implemented with current mirrors. We constructed a half-center oscillator circuit from current-mode low-pass filters and current mirrors, as shown in Fig. 5. The circuit dynamics is expressed by the following equations:

$$\tau \frac{dI_{u_i}}{dt} = -I_{u_i} + f(I_s - \beta I_{v_i} - w I_{u_j}) \quad (7)$$
$$\tau \frac{dI_{v_i}}{dt} = -I_{v_i} + f(I_{u_i}) \quad (8)$$

where I_{u_i} are the currents that corresponds to the inner state of the i-th neuron, I_{v_i} the currents that corresponds

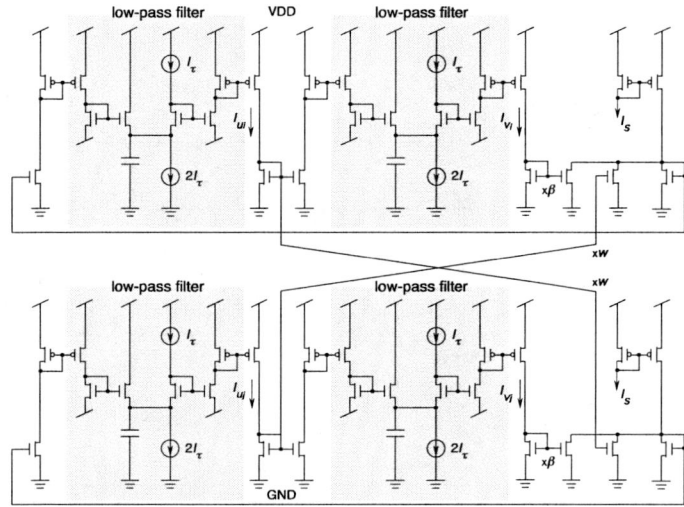

Fig. 5. Schematic of the oscillator circuit.

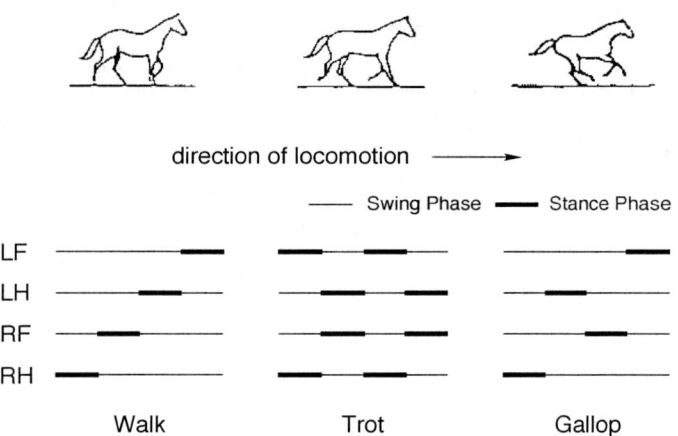

Fig. 6. Phase diagrams of typical locomotion patterns of mammals.

to an adaptation variable of the neuron, I_s the currents that corresponds to a tonic input, w_{ij} a synaptic strength between the i-th and j-th neuron, β the adaptation effectiveness, and τ a time constant. The parameters w_{ij} and β are determined by the aspect ratio of transistors comprising current mirrors. The time constant can be controlled by tuning the bias current I_τ. Depending on these circuit parameters, this circuit generates a stable limit-cycle oscillation.

III. CPG Circuit for Quadruped Locomotion

We here describe a CPG circuit for controlling interlimb coordination in quadruped locomotion.

In nature, animals show a wide variety of locomotion behaviors. For instance, horses show distinct locomotion patterns, such as walk, trot, and gallop. These patterns are characterized by phase relation ship in limb movements. In other words, these locomotion patterns are also considered as phase-locked oscillation of the limbs. Figure 6 shows phase diagrams of typical locomotion patterns of mammals like horses, where LF, LH, RF, and RH represent the left forelimb, left hindlimb, right forelimb, and right forelimb, and bold and thin lines represent stance phases and swing phase during locomotion.

We constructed a CPG circuit from four half-center oscillator circuits. The CPG circuit generates phase-locked oscillation patterns corresponding to typical locomotion patterns of animals according to its network configurations (Fig. 7).

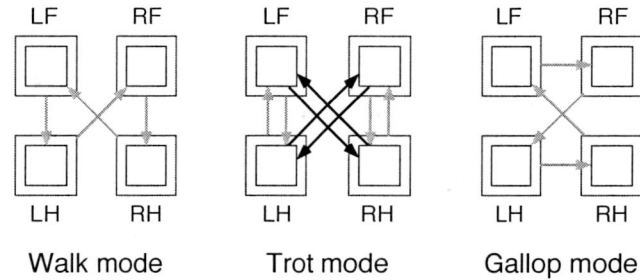

Fig. 7. Network configurations of CPG circuit.

The circuit dynamics of the network circuit in walk mode are represented as follows:

$$\tau \frac{dI_{u_{\{1,2\}}}^{\text{LF}}}{dt} = -I_{u_{\{1,2\}}}^{\text{LF}} + f(I_{s,u_{\{1,2\}}}^{\text{LF}} - \beta I_{v_{\{1,2\}}}^{\text{LF}} - w I_{u_{\{2,1\}}}^{\text{LF}}) \quad (9)$$

$$\tau \frac{dI_{u_{\{1,2\}}}^{\text{LH}}}{dt} = -I_{u_{\{1,2\}}}^{\text{LH}} + f(I_{s,u_{\{1,2\}}}^{\text{LH}} - \beta I_{v_{\{1,2\}}}^{\text{LH}} - w I_{u_{\{2,1\}}}^{\text{LH}}) \quad (10)$$

$$\tau \frac{dI_{u_{\{1,2\}}}^{\text{RF}}}{dt} = -I_{u_{\{1,2\}}}^{\text{RF}} + f(I_{s,u_{\{1,2\}}}^{\text{RF}} - \beta I_{v_{\{1,2\}}}^{\text{RF}} - w I_{u_{\{2,1\}}}^{\text{RF}}) \quad (11)$$

$$\tau \frac{dI_{u_{\{1,2\}}}^{\text{RH}}}{dt} = -I_{u_{\{1,2\}}}^{\text{RH}} + f(I_{s,u_{\{1,2\}}}^{\text{RH}} - \beta I_{v_{\{1,2\}}}^{\text{RH}} - w I_{u_{\{2,1\}}}^{\text{RH}}) \quad (12)$$

$$\tau \frac{dI_{v_{\{1,2\}}}^{\text{LF}}}{dt} = -I_{v_{\{1,2\}}}^{\text{LF}} + f(I_{v_{\{1,2\}}}^{\text{LF}})$$

$$\tau \frac{dI_{v_{\{1,2\}}}^{\text{LH}}}{dt} = -I_{v_{\{1,2\}}}^{\text{LH}} + f(I_{v_{\{1,2\}}}^{\text{LH}}) \quad (13)$$

$$\tau \frac{dI_{v_{\{1,2\}}}^{\text{RF}}}{dt} = -I_{v_{\{1,2\}}}^{\text{RF}} + f(I_{v_{\{1,2\}}}^{\text{RF}}) \quad (14)$$

$$\tau \frac{dI_{v_{\{1,2\}}}^{\text{RH}}}{dt} = -I_{v_{\{1,2\}}}^{\text{RH}} + f(I_{v_{\{1,2\}}}^{\text{RH}}) \quad (15)$$

where $I_{u_i}^{\text{LF,LH,RF,RH}}$ are the currents that correspond to the inner state of the i-th neuron at the joint of LF, LH, RF and RH, and $I_{v_i}^{\text{LF,LH,RF,RH}}$ the currents that correspond to an adaptation variable of the neuron at the joint of LF, LH, RF, and RH. The currents $I_{s,u_i}^{\text{LF}}, I_{s,u_i}^{\text{LH}}, I_{s,u_i}^{\text{RF}}$ and I_{s,u_i}^{RH} ($i=1,2$) are represented as follows:

$$I_{s,u_{\{1,2\}}}^{\text{LF}} = I_s + \gamma I_{u_{\{2,1\}}}^{\text{RH}} \quad (16)$$

$$I_{s,u_{\{1,2\}}}^{\text{LH}} = I_s + \gamma I_{u_{\{2,1\}}}^{\text{LF}} \quad (17)$$

$$I_{s,u_{\{1,2\}}}^{\text{RF}} = I_s + \gamma I_{u_{\{2,1\}}}^{\text{LH}} \quad (18)$$

$$I_{s,u_{\{1,2\}}}^{\text{RH}} = I_s + \gamma I_{u_{\{2,1\}}}^{\text{RF}} \quad (19)$$

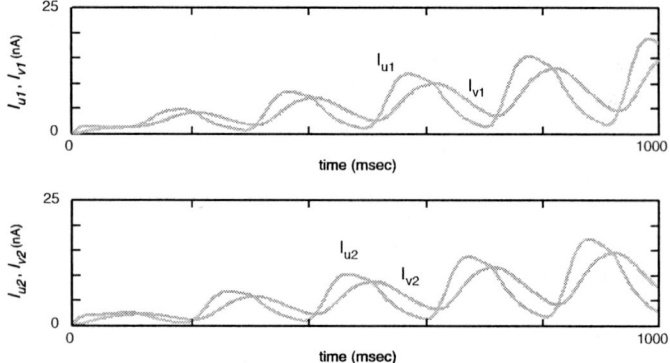

Fig. 8. Waveforms of currents of half-center oscillator circuit.

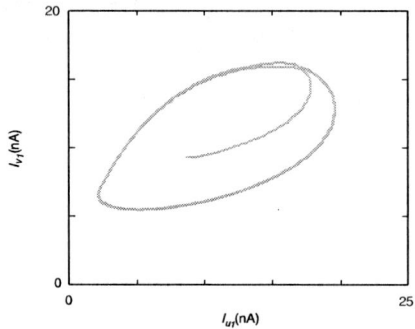

Fig. 9. Phase-plane portrait of currents of half-center oscillator circuit.

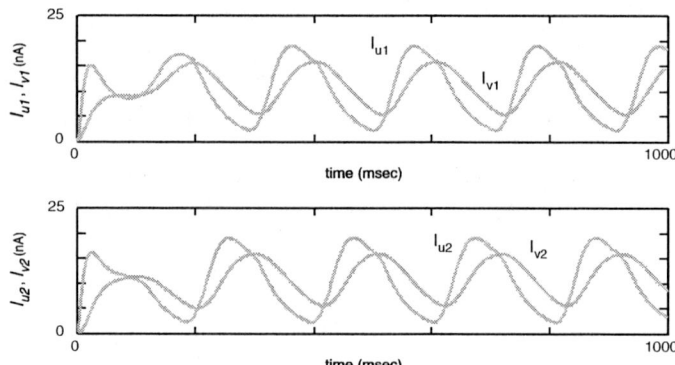

Fig. 10. Amplitude modulation of waveforms of currents of half-center oscillator circuit.

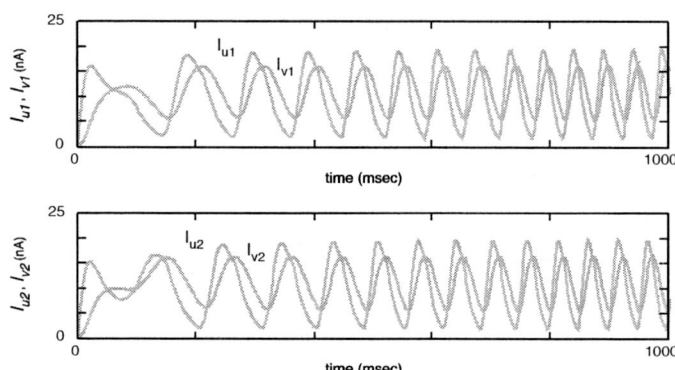

Fig. 11. Frequency modulation of waveforms of currents of half-center oscillator circuit.

where I_s are the current that correspond to a tonic input, and γ a synaptic strength.

The circuit dynamics of the network circuit in trot mode are also represented by (9) - (12), where the currents I_{s,u_i}^{LF}, I_{s,u_i}^{LH}, I_{s,u_i}^{RF} and I_{s,u_i}^{RH} are represented as follows:

$$I_{s,u_{\{1,2\}}}^{\text{LF}} = I_s + \gamma I_{u_{\{1,2\}}}^{\text{RH}} + \gamma I_{u_{\{2,1\}}}^{\text{LH}} \quad (20)$$

$$I_{s,u_{\{1,2\}}}^{\text{LH}} = I_s + \gamma I_{u_{\{1,2\}}}^{\text{RF}} + \gamma I_{u_{\{2,1\}}}^{\text{LF}} \quad (21)$$

$$I_{s,u_{\{1,2\}}}^{\text{RF}} = I_s + \gamma I_{u_{\{1,2\}}}^{\text{LH}} + \gamma I_{u_{\{2,1\}}}^{\text{RH}} \quad (22)$$

$$I_{s,u_{\{1,2\}}}^{\text{RH}} = I_s + \gamma I_{u_{\{1,2\}}}^{\text{LF}} + \gamma I_{u_{\{2,1\}}}^{\text{RF}}, \quad (23)$$

and the circuit dynamics of the network circuit in gallop mode are also represented by (9) - (12), where the currents I_{s,u_i}^{LF}, I_{s,u_i}^{LH}, I_{s,u_i}^{RF} and I_{s,u_i}^{RH} are represented as follows:

$$I_{s,u_{\{1,2\}}}^{\text{LF}} = I_s + \gamma I_{u_{\{2,1\}}}^{\text{RH}} \quad (24)$$

$$I_{s,u_{\{1,2\}}}^{\text{LH}} = I_s + \gamma I_{u_{\{2,1\}}}^{\text{RF}} \quad (25)$$

$$I_{s,u_{\{1,2\}}}^{\text{RF}} = I_s + \gamma I_{u_{\{2,1\}}}^{\text{LF}} \quad (26)$$

$$I_{s,u_{\{1,2\}}}^{\text{RH}} = I_s + \gamma I_{u_{\{2,1\}}}^{\text{LH}}. \quad (27)$$

IV. SIMULATION RESULTS

We verified the operation of the half-center oscillator circuit and the CPG circuit with SPICE simulation. In the following simulations, we used MOSIS AMIS 1.5-μm LEVEL 49 model parameters. The gate length L of the transistor was set at L=9.6 μm, the gate width W of the minimum-size transistor was set at W=9.6 μm, the capacitance C=10 nF, and the supply voltages were set at VDD=1.5 V and Vref=0.35 V.

A. Half-center oscillator circuit

We here show the rhythmic pattern generation in the half-center oscillator circuit. Figure 8 shows the waveforms of the currents I_{u_i} and I_{v_i}, where the parameters β=5 and w_{ij}=4, and the bias currents were set at I_τ=10 nA and I_s=100 nA. The equilibrium currents of the circuit are calculated by solving the following equations:

$$\frac{dI_{u_i}}{dt} = \frac{dI_{v_i}}{dt} = 0, \; (i = 1, 2) \quad (28)$$

that yield:

$$I_{u_o} = I_s - \beta I_{v_o} - w_{ij}I_{u_o}, \; I_{v_o} = I_{u_o} \quad (29)$$

where I_{u_o} and I_{v_o} represent the equilibrium currents. Thus, the equilibrium currents become I_{u_o}=I_{v_o}=$I_s/10$. Figure 9 shows a closed (I_{u_i}, I_{v_i}) phase plane portrait. These results show the stable oscillation of the circuit.

The amplitude of the oscillation is proportional to the bias currents I_s because I_{u_i} and I_{v_i} are scaled by I_s. We changed the amplitude of the oscillation by tuning the bias current I_s

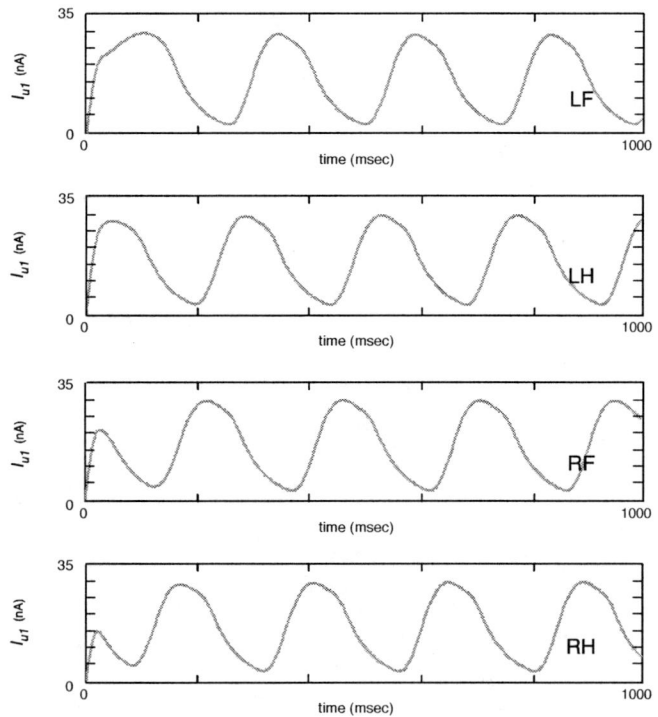

Fig. 12. Waveforms of currents of CPG circuit operating in walk mode.

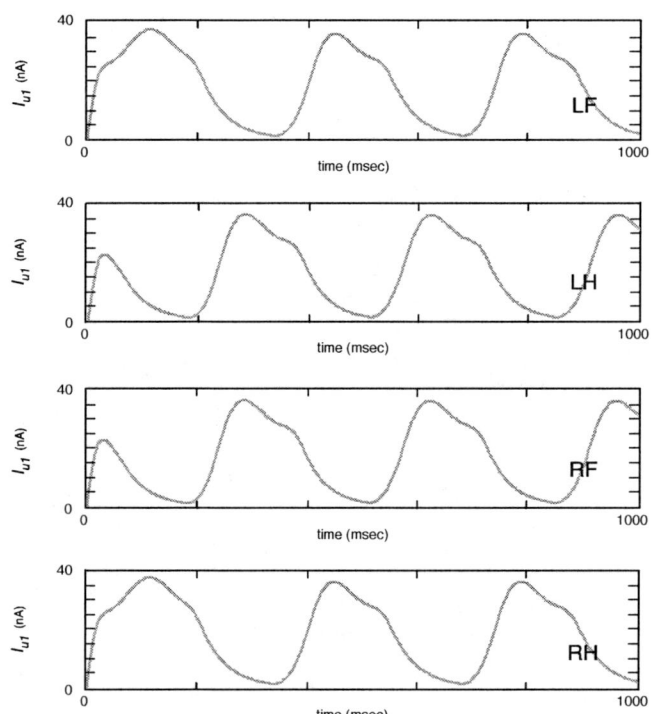

Fig. 13. Waveforms of currents of CPG circuit operating in trot mode.

from 10 nA to 100 nA as shown in Fig. 10. We also changed the frequency of the oscillation by tuning the bias current I_τ from 10 nA to 50 nA as shown in Fig. 11. These controllability of the amplitude and frequency of the oscillation are suitable for a building block for constructing a CPG controller.

B. CPG network circuit

We show the phase-locked oscillation in the CPG circuit. In the following simulations, we set the parameters $\beta=3$, $w_{ij}=3$, and $\gamma=0.33$. The synaptic strength γ are implemented with current mirrors as well as β and w. These parameters are fixed at the design stage. Figure 12 show the waveforms of the currents $I_{u_1}^{\text{LF,LH,RF,RH}}$ of the CPG circuit operating in the walk mode. Figure 13 shows the waveforms of the currents $I_{u_1}^{\text{LF,LH,RF,RH}}$ of the CPG circuit operating in the trot mode.

If we assumed that these curents give target joint angles to LF, RF, LH and RH of a robot, and then these phase-locked oscillation of the currents are considered as the typical locomotion patterns shown in Fig. 6.

We also show the amplitude modulation in the CPG circuit. When we decreased the bias current I_s of the half-center oscillator circuit for the individual joint RF from 100 nA to 75 nA at 2500 msec, the amplitude of the current $I_{u_1}^{\text{RF}}$ was decreased. Figure 14 and 15 show the amplitude of the oscillation in the walk and trot mode, respectively.

These results show that the amplitude of the individual half-center oscillator circuit can be controlled independent of others. Such amplitude modulation is utilized to control quadruped robot locomotion.

V. CONCLUSIONS

We have designed an analog current-mode CMOS circuit for controlling interlimb coordination in quadruped robot locomotion. In previous works, many CPG circuits have been proposed [8]-[17]. As a CPG circuit, it is desirable to control the amplitude and frequency of the oscillation over a wide range. Hence, we have implemented the half-center oscillator model with high controllability of the amplitude and frequency of the oscillation as an analog current-mode circuit to use its controllability efficiently. The half-center oscillator circuit consists of four current-mode low-pass filters and several current mirrors. We have constructed a CPG circuit from four half-center oscillator circuits. The CPG circuit operates in subthreshold region under the low-supply voltages. Thus, low power consumption can be expected as well as previous current-mode neuromorphic chips [21].

Through SPICE simulations, we have shown that the CPG circuit generates stable phase-locked oscillation corresponding to the typical locomotion patterns of animals, and that the amplitude of the individual half-center oscillator circuit can be controlled independent of others. These characteristics of our circuit are suitable for controlling quadruped robot locomotion.

REFERENCES

[1] F. Delcomyn, *Foundations of Neurobiology*, New York: W. H. Freeman and Co., 1997.

[2] G. Brown, "On the nature of the fundamental activity of the nervous centers: together with an analysis of the conditioning of the rhythmic activity in progression, and a theory of the evolution of function in the nervous system," *J. Physiol.*, vol. 48, pp. 18-46, 1914.

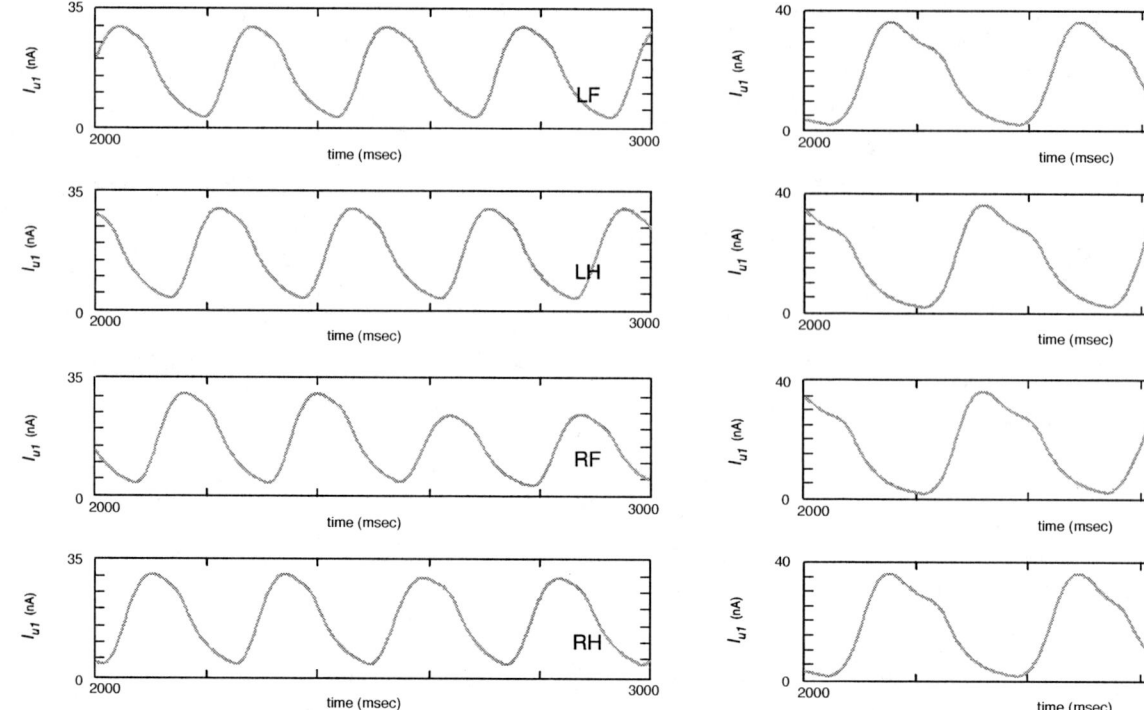

Fig. 14. Amplitude modulation of CPG circuit operating in walk mode.

Fig. 15. Amplitude modulation of CPG circuit operating in trot mode.

[3] K. Matsuoka, "Sustained oscillations generated by mutually inhibiting neurons with adaptation." *Biol. Cybern.*, vol. 52, pp. 367-376, 1983.

[4] K. Matsuoka, "Mechanism of frequency and pattern control in the neural rhythm generators," *Biol. Cybern.*, vol. 56, pp. 345-353, 1987.

[5] G. Taga, Y. Yamaguchi and H. Shimizu, "Self-organaized control of bipedal locomotion by neural oscillators in unpredictable environment," *Biol. Cybern.*, vol. 65, pp.147-159, 1991.

[6] M. Wiiliamson, "Neural Control of Rhythmic Arm Movements" *Neural Networks, special issue on neural control of movement*, 1998.

[7] H. Kimura, Y. Fukuoka, and K. Konaga, "Adaptive dynamic walking of a quadruped robot by using neural system model", *ADVANCED ROBOTICS*, vol. 15, no. 8, pp. 859-876, 2001.

[8] S. Ryckebusch, J. M. Bower, C. A. Mead, "Modeling small oscillating biological networks in analog VLSI," *Adv. Neural Information processing Syst.*, vol. 1, pp. 384-393, 1989.

[9] S. Still. and M. W. Tilden, "Controller for a four legged walking machine," in *Neuromorphic Systems Engineering Silicon from Neurobiology*, Eds: L. S. Smith and A. Hamilton, World Scientific: Singapore, pp. 138-148, 1998.

[10] S. Still, B. Scholkopf, K. Hepp, R. J. Douglas, "Four-legged walking gait control using a neuromorphic chip interfaced to a support vector learning algorithm", *Adv. Neural Information processing Syst.*, vol. 13, pp. 741-747, 2001.

[11] G. Patel, J. Holleman, S. DeWeerth, "Analog VLSI model of intersegmental cordination with nearest-neighbor coupling," *Adv. Neural Information processing Syst.*, vol. 10, pp. 710-725, 1998.

[12] M. A. Lewis, M. J. Harttmann, R. Etienne-Cummings, A. H. Cohen, "Control of a robot leg with an adaptive aVLSI CPG chip," *Neurocomputing*, vol. 38-40, pp. 1409-1421, 2001.

[13] F. Tenore, R. Etienne-Cummings, and M. A. Lewis, "A programmable array of silicon neurons for the control of legged locomotion," presented at *the International Symposium on Circuits and Systems*, Vancouver, 2004

[14] K. Nakada, T. Asai, and Y. Amemiya, "An analog central pattern generator for interlimb coordination in quadruped locomotion," *IEEE Trans. on Neural Networks*, vol. 14, no. 5, pp. 1356-1365, 2003.

[15] K. Nakada, T. Asai, and Y. Amemiya, "Analog CMOS implementation of a CNN-based locomotion controller with floating-gate devices," *IEEE Trans. Circuits and Syst. -I*, in press.

[16] M. Branciforte, G. Di Bernardo, F. Doddo, L. Occhipinti, "Reaction-Diffusion CNN design for a new class of biologically- inspired processors in artificial locomotion applications", in *Seventh International Conference on Microelectronics for Neural, Fuzzy and Bio-Inspired Systems*, pp. 69-77, Granada, Spain, 1999.

[17] P. Arena, S. Castorina, L. Fortuna, M. Frasca, M. Ruta, "A CNN chip for robot locomotion control", in *Proc. IEEE Int. Symp. Circuits Systems*, vol. 3, May 2003, pp. 510-513.

[18] J. Mulder, A. C. van der Woerd, W. A. Serdijn, H. M. van Roermund, "General current-mode analysis method for translinear filters," *IEEE Tran. Circuits and Syst. -I*, vol. 44, pp. 193-197, 1997.

[19] A. McEwan and A. van Schaik "A silicon representation of the meddis inner hair cell model," in *Proc. the ICSC Symposia on Intelligent Systems and Application*, paper 1544-078, 2000.

[20] W. Germanovix, C. Toumazou, "Design of a micropower current-mode log-domain analog cochlear implant", *IEEE Tran. Circuits and Syst. -II*, Vol. 47, No. 10, pp. 1023-1026, 2000.

[21] T. Serrano-Gotarredona and B. Linares-Barranco, "Log-domain implementation of complex dynamics reaction-diffusion neural networks", *IEEE Trans. on Neural Networks*, vol. 14, no. 5, pp. 1337-1355, 2003.

Toward an Analog VLSI Implementation of a Decision Making Model

Yili Quan
Department of Electrical Engineering
University at Buffalo, The State University of New York
Buffalo, NY 14260
Email: yiliquan@acsu.buffalo.edu

Albert H. Titus
Department of Electrical Engineering
University at Buffalo, The State University of New York
Buffalo, NY 14260
Email: ahtitus@eng.buffalo.edu

ABSTRACT- This paper describes an analog circuit implementation of on-chip learning for the Lens Model by using Adaptive Linear Neuron networks (ADALINE). The on-chip learning circuit has been designed using MOS transistors operating in the subthreshold regime. The proposed circuit has been developed and simulated using the CMOS 1.5µm AMI ABN process. The parameters of the correlation coefficient equation are current signals that can be controlled through the voltages to produce the square root behavior. The circuit is biased at 1.5V to lower the power dissipation. Spice simulations are included to illustrate the circuit performance.

I. INTRODUCTION

The Lens Model [1] was developed by Brunswik in 1950's to represent the relationship of the environment and an organism/animal in the environment. This model has been applied to judgment situations where the "organism," most often a human [2], must make decisions based on information it has about the environment; these are termed "cues." The Lens Model provides dual, symmetric models of both the human judge and the environment. The judgments (Y_S) and the environmental criterion to be judged (Y_E) are described as linear combinations of environmental cues (cue_i), or available information in the environment. In this way, both the judgment policy and the environmental structure in terms of cue-criterion relationships are captured. Because the models are based on the same environmental information (the cues), the fit between the model of the human judge and the environmental structure can be formally measured. Essentially, this comparison allows assessment of the extent to which a linear representation modeling an individual's judgment policy reflects, or has adapted to, the structure of the environment. Additionally, the extent to which individuals' judgments are consistent with a linear judgment policy model can be assessed using Lens Model parameters. Thus, a Lens Model approach is useful for identifying characteristics of successful judgment performance. In addition, the model provides an estimate of the actual judgments and environmental criteria; these estimates are $\tilde{Y}_S$ and $\tilde{Y}_E$. The estimates are a linear approximation to the actual value using a weighted sum of the cues, as shown in equation (1).

$$\tilde{Y} = \beta_1 \cdot cue_1 + \beta_2 \cdot cue_2 + \beta_3 \cdot cue_3 + ... \quad (1)$$

where the β_i values are the termed the "beta weights" or the coefficients for the linear fit. The measure of a curve fit, the correlation coefficient (r), can be computed for this fit (see equation (1)). The Lens Model uses five r values, termed R_S, G, C, R_E, and r_a, as parameters descriptive of the task environment and judgment performance. The sum of squares for the fit:

$$S_{xx} = \sum_i (x_i - \bar{x})^2 \quad (2)$$

is used to compute the r's:

$$r = \hat{\beta}_1 \cdot \sqrt{\frac{S_{xx}}{S_{yy}}} \quad (3)$$

Adaptive learning is one of the key elements for pattern recognition, classification, association, or function approximation [3]. In general, during the learning phase, most adaptive neural networks require the adaptation of weights to minimize the error (the difference between the actual output and the desired output of the network). ADALINE (Adaptive Linear Neuron) [3] is one type of adaptive systems advanced by Bernard Widrow and his student, Marcian Hoff in 1960's. The learning rule used is LMS (Least Mean Square) or the Widrow-Hoff learning rule, also known as the delta rule. Since the Lens model is based on linear regression and correlation coefficients, the primary block of the Lenschip is the ADALINE, which implements the regression function.

In this paper, we present novel circuits that allow enable the analog hardware implementation of the Lens Model. The learning rule is implemented in analog circuitry, which uses MOSFETs in weak inversion to realize the LMS learning function. The DC supply voltage of the circuits is 1.5V, which minimizes power dissipation, and the transistor sizes are optimized for very compact implementation on a chip.

II. LENSCHIP OVERVIEW

As stated, the Lens model is based on linear regression and correlation coefficients. For this system, the ADALINE has a single layer and single output. The inputs to the ADALINE are the cues, the weights are the regression coefficients, and the output is the sum of the weighted inputs. This is exactly the form of a multivariate regression equation:

$$\tilde{Y} = \beta_1 \cdot cue_1 + \beta_2 \cdot cue_2 + \beta_3 \cdot cue_3 + ... \quad (4)$$

The ADALINE computes the estimated output, $\tilde{Y}$, but the actual output, either Y_E or Y_S, is used to adjust the weights after each decision is made. Implementation of the ADALINE is accomplished with a standard multiplier (such as a Gilbert multiplier) and a current summing circuit. Each decision and decision estimate must then be stored to compute the correlation coefficients. This is accomplished using capacitors in a simple DRAM configuration. Finally the correlation coefficients must be calculated, which is done in the correlator blocks shown in Figure 1. The correlator block is composed of difference squaring circuits (see [4]), square root circuits and a ratio circuit.

The difference squaring circuit produces a current that is a function of the difference of two voltages squared:

$$I_{out,i} = k(V_1 - V_2)^2 \quad (5)$$

This can be used to compute the sum of squares as shown in equation (2) by summing currents at a node, where V_1 is the x_i and V_2 is the mean, $\overline{x}$. Thus, the parameters R_S, G, C, R_E, and r_a in Lens Model, can be calculated using the ADALINE to find the beta value, and the sum of squares, as shown in equation (3).

Overall, the system design requires many weight circuits (see for example, [4]) and storage elements; this will dictate the specific number of cues and how many judgment sets can be implemented. It is likely that the final Lenschip system will actually require multiple chips, connected together, to achieve full functionality.

In this paper, we discuss the components that make up the learning portion of the system, the correlator, and the ADALINE. We present simulation results for our novel circuitry used in the correlator circuit and show the integrated circuit layout for fabrication in the AMI 1.5μm process.

III. CORRELATOR COMPONENTS

The architecture of the ADALINE adaptation and learning model is based on the system discussed in [3]. To implement the functions in analog hardware, we need three functions: square (x^2), square root ($\sqrt{x}$), and division or ratio ($\frac{x}{y}$).

A. Squaring Circuit

The learning circuit consists of two parts, which implement equations (2) and (3). For the squared residual, we use a standard squaring circuits which has been reported in the literature [5]; the basic circuit is shown in Figure 2.

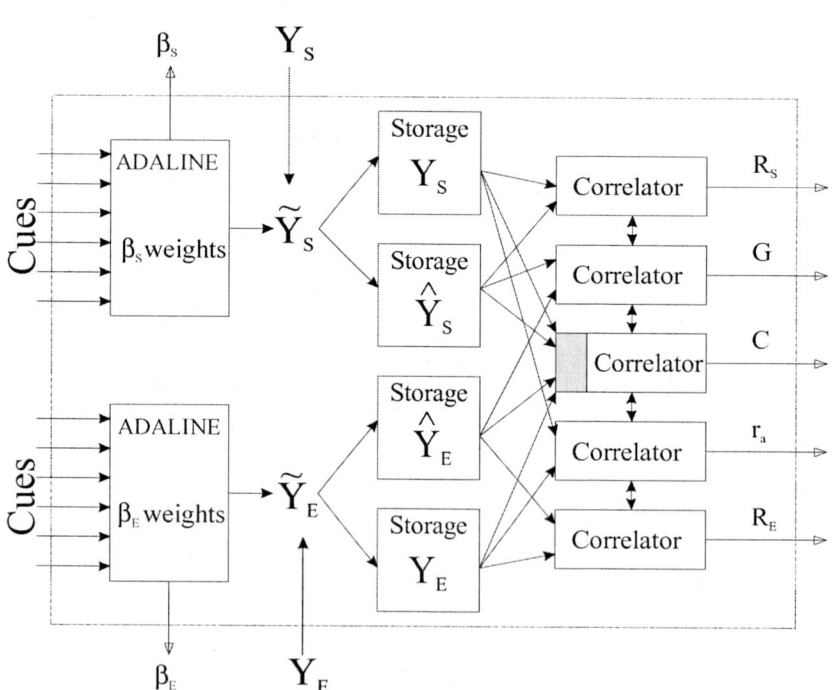

Fig. 1. Block diagram of the Lenschip.

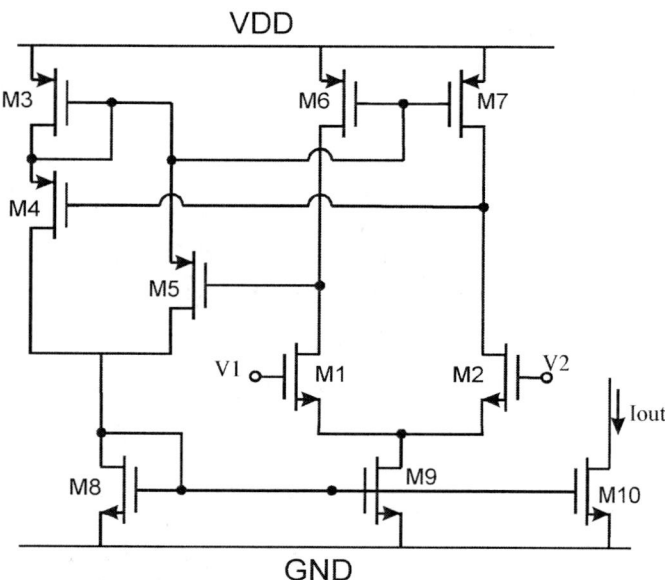

Fig. 2. The squaring circuit.

M1 and M2 are the matched adaptively biased differential pair, using the negative feedback to transform this differential pair into squaring circuit. Under proper conditions, I_c can be expressed as:

$$I_c = \frac{5K_{n1}}{4}(V_1 - V_2)^2 \qquad (6)$$

B. Ratio Circuit

The foundation for the circuits that implement the square root and ratio functions is the stacked MOS Translinear (TL) loop [6], as shown in Figure 3.

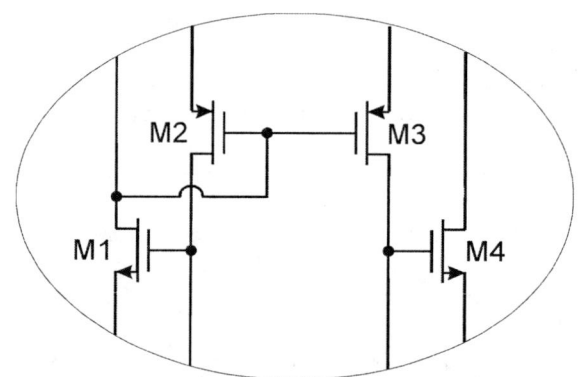

Fig. 3. Stacked MOS Translinear (TL) Loop

If we ignore temperature variations and make all the transistors the same size (so the $\lambda^2 I_0^2$ term can be eliminated from the equation), we can applying the Kirchoff's Voltage Law (KVL) to the loop to obtain the current relationship expressed as: $I_1 I_2 = I_3 I_4$., where I_i is the drain current for MOSFET Mi. This can be rearranged so one current is expressed by the other three as: $I_4 = \dfrac{I_1 I_2}{I_3}$. To obtain the ratio of two terms, one current (I_1 or I_2) is held constant. Figure 4 shows the full implementation of the divider.

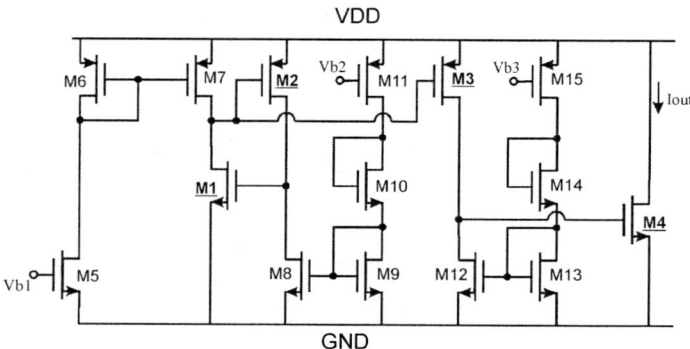

Fig. 4. Full schematic of the ratio (divider) circuit. *Vb1-Vb3* are externally controlled bias voltages.

In Figure 4, MOSFETS M1, M2, M3 and M4 form the main loop of the stacked translinear loop. On the left, M5 – M7 provide the current to M1; M8 to M118 and M12 to M15 are the bias circuits that provide current to M2 and M4, respectively. The drain current of M4 (labeled *Iout*) is the desired output that represents the quotient.

C. Square Root Circuit

Several square root circuits have been previously implemented [6-11]. In these, the MOS transistors are working in strong inversion or linear mode. In our work, we realize the divider circuit and square root circuit using MOSFETs operating in the subthreshold mode. Subthreshold operation is defined by an exponential voltage-current relationship and also uses very little current resulting in low power consumption.

For MOS transistors operating in the subthreshold mode, the relationship of gate-source voltage and the channel current is given by:

$$I = \frac{W}{L} I_o e^{(kv_g - v_s)/U_t} \qquad (7)$$

where W and L define the size of the transistors, I_0 is the subthreshold pre-exponential current factor; U_t is the thermal dynamic voltage. The concept of the square-root circuit is shown in Figure 5a, while Figure 5b is the actual implementation. Similar to the divider circuit analysis, we apply KVL around the loop, and make currents I_3 and I_4 equal, to obtain:

$$I_{out}^2 = I_1 \cdot I_2 \qquad (8)$$

This can be rewritten as:

$$I_{out} = \sqrt{I_1 I_2} \qquad (9)$$

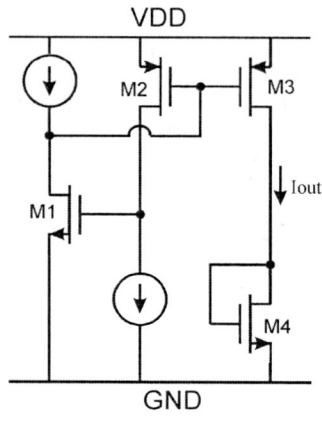

To realize the final correlation coefficient relationship defined in equation 3, the output currents from two square root circuits can be applied as the input to one divider, and then the output current from the divider can be written as:

$$I_{out} = \frac{I_{ref}\sqrt{I_{1A}I_{2A}}}{\sqrt{I_{1B}I_{2B}}} \qquad (10)$$

If I_{1A} and I_{1B} are identical, then equation (10) simplifies to:

$$I_{out} = I_{ref}\sqrt{\frac{I_{2A}}{I_{2B}}} \qquad (11)$$

This current mode equation implements the function that defines the correlation coefficient as shown in equation (3). Figure 6 shows the circuit schematic. The outputs from both square root blocks are the inputs to the ratio circuit. From Figure 6, $I_{outA} = \sqrt{I_{1A}I_{2A}}$ and $I_{outB} = \sqrt{I_{1B}I_{2B}}$, so $I_{out} = \frac{I_{ref} I_{outA}}{I_{outB}}$.

IV. SIMULATION RESULTS

For the two new circuit blocks, we compare the actual SPICE simulation values with the theoretical values computed from the equations. Figure 7 shows the simulation result for the circuit in Figure 5b with I_2 held constant and sweeping the other input, I_1, from 5nA to 100nA. The output current range is from 10nA to 80nA. The SPICE simulation results closely match the desired results predicted by equation (9), which is indicated by the dashed line in Figure 7.

We also compare the simulated responses of the complete correlator circuit (shown in Fig. 6) to the ideal responses. These comparisons are illustrated in Figure 8. I_{1A} and I_{1B} are held constant and equal to I_{ref}; these are set by the bias voltages $V1A$ and $V1B$ (see Fig 6). The input current, I_{2A} is swept from 5nA to 100nA. $I2B$ is set equal to $100nA - I_{2A}$. To determine the proper range of operation with respect to the reference current, the simulation results are plotted for I_{ref}

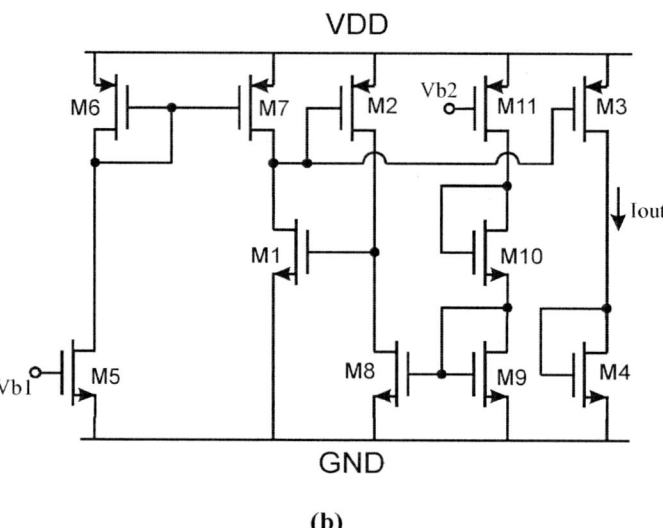

Fig 5. Circuit diagram of square root (a) concept diagram and (b) actual implementation

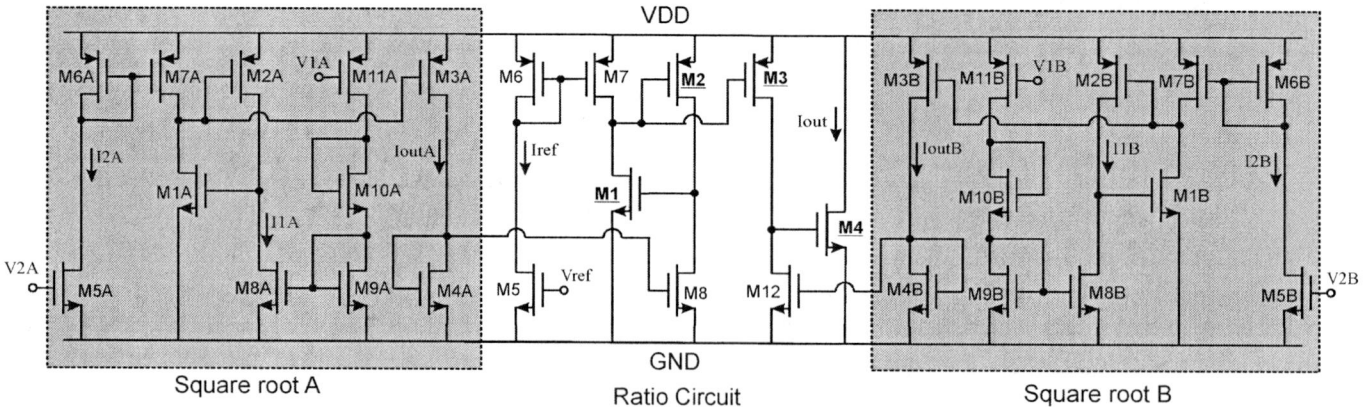

Fig. 6. Complete correlator circuit.

values of 20nA, 30nA and 50nA. In Figure 8, it is clear that the circuit performs quite well over this range of I_{2A} for I_{ref} <30nA. For I_{ref} =50nA, we see that the error (difference between the simulated output and theoretical value) is the largest.

will be fabricated in the AMI 1.5μm process through MOSIS (www.mosis.org).

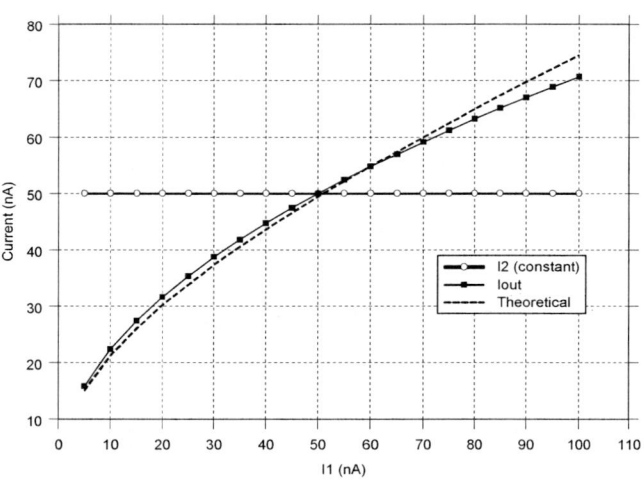

Fig 7. Spice simulation of the square root circuit showing I_{out} compared with the theoretical square root of $I1$.

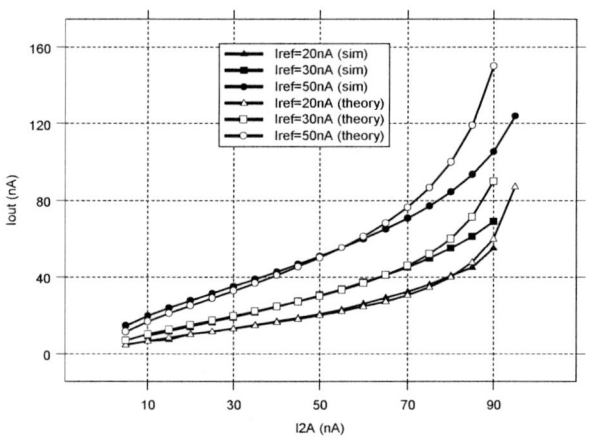

Fig 8. I_{out} as a function of I_{2A} for different values of I_{ref} to show operating range. In this simulation, the value for I_{2B}=100(nA)-I_{2A}, I_{1A}=I_{1B}=I_{ref}. The solid symbols are the SPICE simulation results, the open symbols are theoretical values calculated from equation (11).

The physical layout is shown in Figure 9. The non-optimized layout measures 240μm x 260μm (using a λ=0.8μm fabrication technology); the optimized layout will be closer to 200μm x 220μm. The top block and bottom blocks are the square root circuits. The outputs from these are the inputs to the ratio circuit in the center. The correlator circuit forms the main component of the LensChip, which

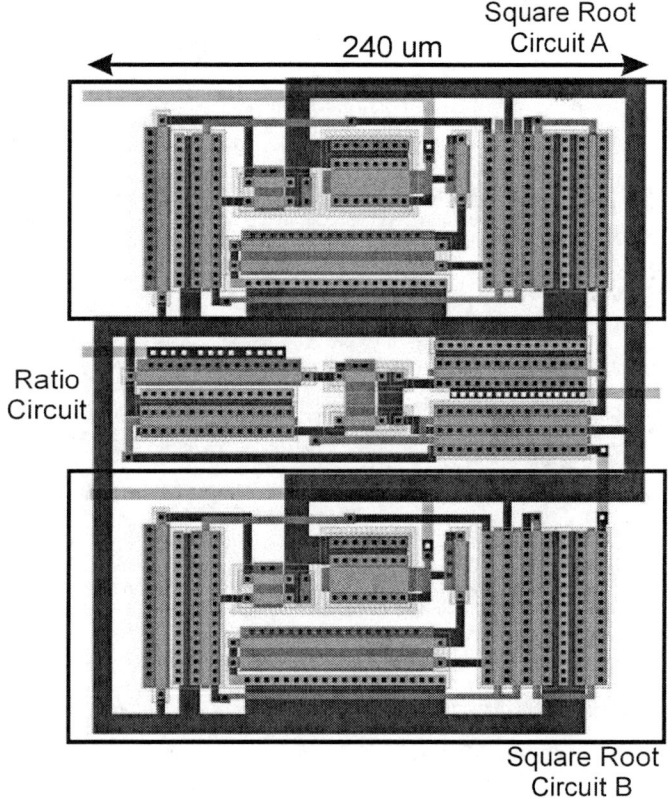

Fig. 9. Layout of the Correlator Circuit. The top and bottom blocks are the square root circuits, and the middle block is the ratio circuit.

V. CONCLUSION

In conclusion, we present novel subthreshold square root and ratio circuits. These form a functional block in analog VLSI that computes the correlation factors for the judgment making model called the Lens Model. The entire system, an IC termed the Lenschip, is designed for fabrication through MOSIS using the AMI 1.5μm process. The chip also uses the ADALINE (Adaptive Linear Neuron) function implemented in analog MOSFETs operating in the subthreshold mode. Results comparing SPICE simulations and theoretical responses have been included. The simulation results verify the function of the correlator and the ADALINE. Because of the use of subthreshold-mode circuits with a voltage supply of 1.5V, the system is very well suited for low-power artificial neural network learning implementations in standard CMOS processes.

Acknowledgements

The authors would like to thank Dr. Ann M. Bisantz for important discussions on the Lens Model. This work was supported in part by the Nation Science Foundation CAREER award 9984386.

References

[1] E. Brunswick, "Representative design and probabilistic theory in a functional psychology.," *Psychological Review*, vol. 62, pp. 193 - 217, 1955.

[2] A. M. Bisantz, A. Kirlik, P. Gay, D. Phipps, N. Walker, and A. D. Fisk, "Modeling and analysis of a dynamic judgment task using a lesn model approach," *IEEE Transactions on Systems, Man, and Cybernetics: Part A: Systems and Humans*, vol. 30, pp. 1 - 12, 2000.

[3] L. Fausett, *Fundamentals of Neural Networks: Architectures, Algorithms, and Applications*. Upper Saddle River, NJ, USA: Prentice-Hall, Inc., 1994.

[4] V. A. Pedroni, "Error-compensated analog cells for vector multiplication and vector quantization," *IEEE Transactions on Circuits & Systems II-Analog & Digital Signal Processing*, vol. 48, pp. 511-519, 2001.

[5] A. M. Ismail and A. M. Soliman, "Novel CMOS Wide-Linear-Range Transconductance Amplifier," *IEEE Transactions on Circuits and Systems I: Fundamental Theory and Applications*, vol. 47, pp. 1248-1253, 2000.

[6] A. G. Andreou, K. A. Boahen, P. O. Pouliquen, A. Pavasovic, R. E. Jenkins, and K. Strohbehn, "Current-mode Subthreshold MOS Circuits for Analog VLSI Neural Systems," *IEEE Transactions on Neural Networks*, vol. 2, pp. 205-213, 1991.

[7] A. J. Lopez-Martin and A. Carlosena, "A tunable CMOS square-root domain oscillator," *Proceedings of the 2000 IEEE International Symposium on Circuits and Systems*, vol. 5, pp. 573-576, 2000.

[8] R. M. Fox, "Design-oriented analysis of log-domain circuits," *IEEE Transactions on Circuits and Systems II: Analog and Digital Signal Processing*, vol. 45, pp. 918-921, 1998.

[9] M. van der Gevel and J. C. Kuenen, "sqrt(x) circuit based on a novel, back-gate-using multiplier," *Electronics Letters*, vol. 30, pp. 183-184, 1994.

[10] S. Vlassis and C. Psychalinos, "A square-root domain differentiator," *IEEE International Symposium on Circuits and Systems (ISCAS) 2002*, vol. 2, pp. II-217-II-220 vol.2, 2002.

[11] G.-J. Yu, B.-D. Liu, Y. C. Hsu, and C.-Y. Huang, "Design of log domain low-pass filters by MOSFET square law," *Proceedings of the Second IEEE Asia Pacific Conference on ASICs 2000*, pp. 9-12, 2000.

On Kolmogorov's Superpositions: Novel Gates and Circuits for Nanoelectronics?

Valeriu Beiu[1] and Artur Zawadzki[2]

[1] School of Electrical Engineering and Computer Science, Washington State University
Pullman, Washington 99164-2752, USA, vbeiu@eecs.wsu.edu

[2] Department of Biological and Agricultural Engineering, University of Idaho
Moscow, ID 83844-0904, USA, zawada734@yahoo.com

Abstract—Based on explicit numerical constructions for Kolmogorov's superpositions (KS) linear size circuits implementing arbitrary Boolean functions (BFs) are possible. Because classical Boolean as well as threshold logic (TL) implementations, require exponential size in the worst case, it follows that, size-optimal solutions for implementing arbitrary BFs should rely (at least partly) on KS-inspired gates (KGs). In this paper, we examine BFs of three inputs in detail and show that even the size given by KS can be reduced when Boolean gates (BGs) could be optimally combined with KGs (low precision analog gates). This shows that there is room for improving on the synthesis of BFs. Finally, we will show that the size obtained when optimally combining BGs and KGs can be reduced even further if we are allowed to also use TL gates. Such systematic size reductions could help alleviate the challenging power consumption problem. They advocate for the design of KGs, as well as for the development of the theory, the algorithms, and the CAD tools that could take advantage of optimal combinations of different logic gates and design styles.

Index Terms—Kolmogorov's superpositions, circuit design, circuit size, Boolean logic, threshold logic, low power.

I. INTRODUCTION

The problem we are going to discuss is that of the *size* of circuits implementing arbitrary Boolean functions (BFs) $f: \mathbb{B}^n \to \mathbb{B}$, $\mathbb{B} = \{0,1\}$. This is a well-studied and important problem as its optimal solution translates into minimum *size* Boolean circuits—achieving minimum *area* and *power* dissipation. An optimal solution depends on the set of gates used to implement the functions. In particular it is well known that implementing arbitrary BFs using classical Boolean gates (BGs, *i.e.*, AND/OR gates), requires $O(2^n)$ size circuits (*e.g.*, for PARITY). By changing the set of gates one can do better. For example, using threshold logic gates (TLGs) the bound is $O(2^{n/2})$ (see [1]–[3]). It is also true that these bounds reveal the existence of an exponential gap, and suggest that TLGs are more powerful than BGs. Even more, the smaller bounds for TLGs have been obtained for small constant *depths*, as TLGs are perceptrons, hence 'approximating' shallow computing neural structures. It is possible to reduce the *size* of TL circuits even more by allowing non-constant *depths*, but results are known only for a few particular classes of BFs

[4]. Two difficult aspects when trying to implementing TLGs in hardware are [5]: the large *fan-ins*, and the precision of the *weights*. The known results relating *fan-in* to precision [3], [6], [7] show that:

$$2^{(\Delta-1)/2} < weight < (\Delta+1)^{(\Delta+1)/2} / 2^{\Delta}, \tag{1}$$

for any *fan-in* $\Delta > 3$, or between Δ and $\Delta\log\Delta$ bits per *weight*, so the precision can be as high as $O(n\log n)$ bits per *weight*.

Stronger results with respect to the *size* of the circuits implementing BFs can be obtained only if the elementary gates are more powerful than TLGs, *e.g.*, multi-threshold TLGs [8], [9], or multiple valued logic gates [10], [11].

In this paper we will advocate for using Kolmogorov's superpositions (KS). This theorem shows that there is a solution requiring only $2n+1$ functions of one variable which can approximate any $f:[0,1]^n \to \mathbb{R}$. Such a linear *size* solution applied to circuit design would clearly be optimal.

The paper will start by presenting Hilbert's thirteenth problem and KS in Section II. Motivations for using KS for BFs will be given in Section III, while the particular case of three input BFs will be analyzed in Section IV. Conclusions and future directions of research are ending the paper.

II. KOLMOGOROV'S SUPERPOSITIONS

In 1900 the German mathematician David Hilbert challenged mathematicians to solve 23 fundamental problems [12]. The 23 problems he presented were considered important for further development of mathematics, and time has proven that they did inspire many groundbreaking investigations. In the thirteenth of these problems he conjectured that *there exist continuous multivariate functions that cannot be decomposed as a finite superposition of continuous functions of fewer variables*. By that time it was known that equations $a_n x^n + a_{n-1} x^{n-1} + \ldots + a_1 x + a_0 = 0$ of degree $n \leq 4$ are solvable by functions that can be represented as substitutions of purely algebraic operations. As a consequence of Galois' theory from 1830, it was also known that in general this is not possible for equations of degree $n \geq 5$. The algebraic operations (addition, subtraction, multiplication, division, and roots) are operations of at most two arguments. These led Hilbert to the conjecture that algebraic equations of higher degree cannot in general be solved by functions that can be represented as substitutions of continuous functions of only two variables.

Hilbert's thirteenth problem was refuted by Kolmogorov in 1956 [13] and by Arnol'd in 1957 [14]). In 1957 Kolmogorov also proved a much stronger results: a general theorem where the functions in the decomposition are one dimensional, known as *Kolmogorov's superpositions (KS) theorem* [15]. Arnol'd also made noteworthy contributions [16], [17].

KS theorem states that any multivariate continuous real-valued function can be represented as a superposition and composition of continuous functions of only one variable. Formally, for each integer $n \geq 2$, there exist $2n + 1$ functions ψ_q, $q = 0, \ldots, 2n$ in $C([0,1]^n)$, $\psi_q(x) = \sum_{p=1}^{n} \psi_{pq}(x_p)$, $x = (x_1, \ldots, x_n) \in [0,1]^n$, $\psi_q \in C([0,1]^n)$, $p = 1, \ldots, n$, such that any f in $C([0,1]^n)$ is representable as $f(x) = \sum_{q=0}^{2n} \phi_q(\psi_q(x))$, $\phi_q \in C(\mathbb{R})$, $q = 0, \ldots, 2n$. The symbol $C(X)$ denotes the space of continuous real-valued functions on the topological space X. This means that for every real-valued continuous function $f: [0,1]^n \to \mathbb{R}$ there are continuous functions ϕ_q such that

$$f(x_1,\ldots,x_n) = \sum_{q=0}^{2n} \phi_q \left[\sum_{p=1}^{n} \psi_{pq}(x_p) \right], \qquad (2)$$

where the functions ψ_{pq} are universal for the given dimension n, *i.e.*, are independent of the function f, while only the functions ϕ_q depend on f (see Fig. 1).

Such results were further refined by Sprecher [18], [19], and by Lorenz [20]. Sprecher ([18], [21], [23]) showed that for a given $\delta > 0$ there is a rational a, $0 < a < \delta$, such as the unknown approximation mapping could be generated by replacing the set of functions ψ_{pq} by $\lambda^p \psi_q$, where λ is an independent constant and ψ_q are monotonic increasing functions:

$$f(x_1,\ldots,x_n) = \sum_{q=0}^{2n} \phi_q \left[\sum_{p=1}^{n} \lambda^p \psi(x_p + aq) + b_q \right]. \qquad (3)$$

Here λ can be any nonzero number which satisfies no equation $\Sigma_p a_p \lambda^p = 0$, with rational coefficients a_p (not all zero). This has been rewritten (equivalently) as:

$$f(x_1,\ldots,x_n) = \sum_{q=0}^{2n} \phi_q \left[\sum_{p=1}^{n} \lambda_p \psi(x_p + qa) \right], \qquad (4)$$

where a is a constant, $\{\lambda_p\}$ is a sequence of positive integrally independent numbers (*i.e.*, if $\Sigma_p t_p \lambda_p \neq 0$ for any finite selection of integers t_p for which $\Sigma_p |t_p| \neq 0$), and $\psi: \mathbb{R}^+ \to \mathbb{R}^+$ is a continuous monotonically increasing function. Both he function ψ and the constants λ_p are independent of the function f and of the dimension n.

Another improvement is due to Lorenz [20], namely that the function ϕ_q could be replaced by only one function ϕ. Lorentz's lemma states that for each continuous function $f: [0,1]^n \to \mathbb{R}$ there exists some continuous function $\phi: [0,1] \to \mathbb{R}$ such that

$$\left\| f - \sum_{q=0}^{2n} \phi \left[\sum_{p=1}^{n} \lambda_p \psi(x_p) \right] \right\| < \theta \|f\| \text{ and } \|\phi\| < \|f\|/n \qquad (5)$$

for $n \geq 2$, $\gamma \geq 2n + 2$, and $\theta = (2n + 1)/(2n + 2)$.

Probably, the first application of KS, and a construction approximating ψ (based on [18], [21], [23]), was presented by de Figueiredo [24]. The construction of ψ was obtained as the uniform limit of a sequence ψ_r, $r \to \infty$, where ψ_r was a continuous nondecreasing piecewise linear function. This has shown that an approximation could be constructed, and provided a procedure for synthesis of (nonlinear) systems. Figueiredo's experience on simulating ψ, also revealed that KS representation "is fragile and sensitive to perturbations."

Hecht-Nielsen in 1987 [25] realized that Sprecher's version of KS could be interpreted as a multiplayer feed forward neural network (NN), therefore showing that NNs are universal approximators.

The functions ψ and ϕ required by the enhanced versions of KS are highly non-smooth (can even have fractal graphs), which might be the reason why Hilbert's intuition failed. This led Girosi and Paggio [26] toward the conclusion that KS was not relevant for NNs, where smooth functions are the norm. Kůrková has also been investigating the topic [27], and showed that it is possible to adapt KS to NNs [28], [30]. She showed that the functions ψ and ϕ can be approximated by *staircase-like functions*, and also that NNs with standard sigmoidal activations functions σ, and only two hidden layers, could approximate any continuous function with arbitrary precision, but the number of units needed for a good approximation is exponential on n.

More recently, many constructive aspects of KS were detailed [31]–[36]. Sprecher proved [34], [35] that there exists a unique continuous function ψ, which is strictly increasing. For given integers $n \geq 2$ and $\gamma \geq 2n+2$, the function ψ is defined such that for each integer k

$$\psi\left(\sum_{r=1}^{k} i_r \gamma^{-r}\right) = \sum_{r=1}^{k} \tilde{i}_r 2^{-m_r} \gamma^{-(n^{r-m_r}-1)/(n-1)} \qquad (6)$$

where $\tilde{i}_r := i_r - (\gamma - 2)\langle i_r \rangle$, $m_r := \langle i_r \rangle (1 + \sum_{s=1}^{r-1}\prod_{t=s}^{r-1}[i_r])$, for all $r = 1, \ldots, k$; $\langle i_1 \rangle = 0$, $[i_1] = 0$; $\langle i_r \rangle = 0$ if $i_r = 0, \ldots, \gamma-2$ and $\langle i_r \rangle = 1$ if $i_r = \gamma-1$; $[i_r] = 0$ if $i_r = 0, \ldots, \gamma-3$ and $[i_r] = 1$ if

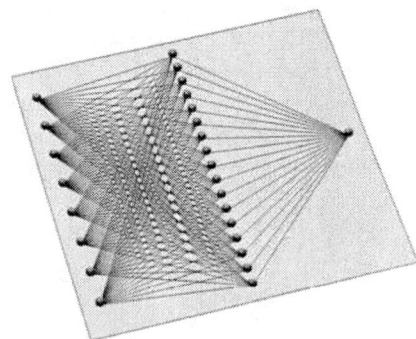

Fig. 1. Direct implementation of $f: [0,1]^n \to \mathbb{R}$ based on Kolmogorov's superpositions (KS): n inputs, $2n+1$ hidden nodes, and one output node.

$i_r = \gamma-2, \gamma-1, r \geq 2$. If $\lambda_1 = 1$, $\lambda_p = \sum_{r=1}^{\infty} \gamma^{-(p-1)(n^r-1)/(n-1)}$ for $p = 2, ..., n$, and $a = 1/\gamma/(\gamma-1)$, eq. (4) is satisfied. Here, γ can be interpreted as a base, while k is the precision in number of digits. The fact that γ depends on n, makes it that the function ψ and the constants λ_p will also depend on n.

Sprecher's constructive solution was detailed by Brattka [37], Neruda *et al.* [38], and Koppen [39]. They rely on (arbitrary precision) staircase-like approximations (see Fig. 2) similar to de Figueiredo's approximation [24], and also advocated by Kůrková [28], [30].

For more insights on KS, the interested reader should consult several recent reviews [40]–[43].

III. BOOLEAN FUNCTIONS AND NANOELECTRONICS

A generalization of KS with respect to the basic space has also been presented [44], but there are few results for the case when the basic space is not compact ([45]–[47]), and there seems to be no generalization to non-Euclidean spaces. Although KS was intended for approximating real functions, it can be used for implementing BFs. The possibility of using KS for the synthesis of BFs was suggested in [48]–[50]. If we limit the functions to $f: \mathbb{B}^n \to \mathbb{B}$, one digit of precision $k = 1$ might be enough (remember that $\gamma \geq 6$). This gives $\psi(0.i_1) = 0.i_1$, *i.e.*, the identity function [49]. Such a solution relies on (very simple analog) comparison with a constant $\psi(x_p + qa) = x_p + qa$. An analog comparison between two inputs would depart from KS (see examples in [48]), but would still be in line with Hilbert's 13th problem. As the precision is limited, an inverter can do the job. Unfortunately, KS leads to large *fan-in* = $2n + 1$, and requires very precise *weights*: λ_p are represented as a double exponential in base γ (see eq. (6)). For BFs the precision is reduced to $(2n + 2)^{-n}$, or $O(n \log n)$ bits per *weight*, *i.e.*, the same precision as the worst-case precision required by TLGs (see eq. (1)). One alternative is the constructions from [51], which are based on $(r!)^{-1}$ instead of λ_p, which might reduce precision, but not significantly. Nanoelectronic implementations are and will be precision limited (noise, variations, etc.), hence an arbitrary BF should be decomposed into simpler BFs (of fewer variables). This is in agreement with previous results showing that VLSI-optimal implementations of BFs using TLGs are obtained for *fan-ins* ≤ 6 [52].

One very important aspect when considering scaled VLSI/nanoelectronics is the challenging power consumption problem [53]–[56]. In this context, the results from [57], [58], which show that hybrid analog/digital implementations appear to be the most energy efficient ones, are of interest. Informally, the fact that analog circuits can do better than digital ones could be understood as the number of devices required to perform a computation is higher in digital than analog circuits, and the switching activity is lower in analog circuits. Additionally, one bit per wire is always present in digital computations. The power and area tradeoffs utilization as a function of the output signal-to-noise ratio, show area and power advantages of analog computation at low values of signal-to-noise ratio (see [57]). Therefore, (very) low precision analog computations might have an edge, and—when optimally combined with digital—could lead to power efficient solutions.

Based on the potential advantages with respect to power, we investigate extending the existing compendium of logic gates by a few analog gates of small *fan-in*, inspired by KS. We shall call these KS-inspired gates (KGs).

IV. ON BOOLEAN FUNCTIONS OF THREE INPUTS

In this section we will analyze the synthesis of BFs of three inputs. We start with the 3D view of the probability of being in one of the four states of a Karnaugh map for two input (x, y) BFs (see Fig. 3). This was generated by considering the four Boolean input combinations: (0,0), (0,1), (1,0), and (1,1). When an input switches, the voltage associated to that input will have to go through (unstable) analog values, hence the probabilities associated to those values should be lower. Obviously, the lowest probability is that of having both inputs at $V_{DD}/2$. We have used Gaussians, and the contour plot in Fig. 3 shows several circular equi-probable lines around the four corners. Between the four maximums (in the corners) and the minimum (in the middle $(V_{DD}/2, V_{DD}/2)$), there is a separating contour that is almost a square. This suggests that the lines forming the square are optimal (from a probabilistic point of view). These are at $\pm 45°$, *i.e.*, $x \pm y = c$, hence depending on both inputs. The extension of this idea to three Boolean inputs (x, y, z) is shown in Fig. 4. The contour map suggests that the same $x \pm y = c$ are optimal. The analog gates implementing $x \pm y = c$ are comparators. *These are KGs in the sense that variables are reduced and the identity function is used.*

We have analyzed all the 256 BFs of three inputs, but shall present here only the 70 BFs corresponding to the cases when there are four "ones" and four "zeros" in the truth table (normally considered the worst-case ones). Fig. 5 presents the optimized results when using only KGs. The same 70 cases,

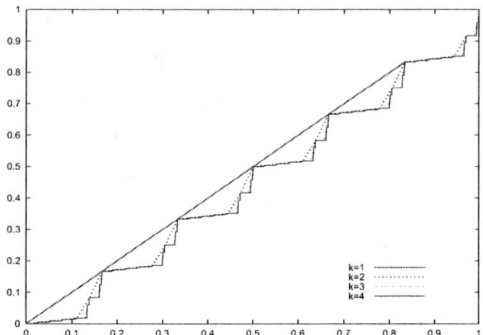

Fig. 2. Sprecher's function ψ for $n = 2$ and $\gamma = 10$ (k is the precision in number of digits in base γ). This is similar to functions detailed in de Figueiredo [24], Brattka [37], Neruda *et al.* [38], and Koppen [39] (see also [59]). It shows that a staircase function (see also [28], [30]) can be an approximation for $k > 1$, while for $k = 1$ the identity function can be used.

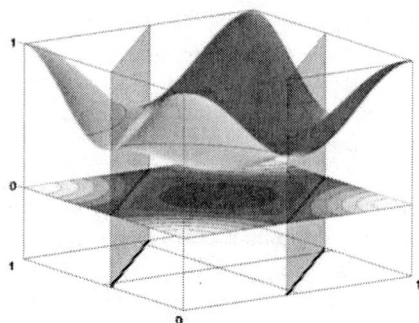

Fig. 3. 3D probability view on top of a generic Karnaugh map for BFs of two inputs.

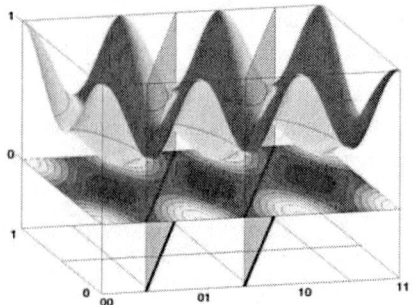

Fig. 4. 3D probability view on top of a generic Karnaugh map for BFs of three inputs.

minimized using BGs, are detailed in Fig. 6. In most cases the BG solution leads to a smaller size, but for a few cases KGs can improve. The results are presented in Fig. 7. It can be seen that the use of KGs lead to a simpler solution in 8 out of the 70 cases (11%), while in 4 cases (6%) a combination of KGs and BGs is minimal.

The final step was to allow majority gates of three inputs (MAJ-3) in these optimizations. The results are presented in Fig. 8. Only 8 BFs require KGs, while MAJ-3 gates improve on 8 other functions.

To get a better understanding, we have plotted in Fig. 9 the number of gates (*size*) in the hidden layer when using the three different types of logic: BGs, KGs, and MAJ (symmetric). Note that we did not properly use KS theorem, so in this sense $2n+1$ is incorrect here. The results presented in Fig. 8 show that *at most three gates are needed in the hidden layer*, which is four gates less than KS ($2*3+1=7$), and one less than worst BF case ($2^3/2=4$). Reductions down to only one gate have been proven in [59], but were obtained with direct connections between the input and the output layer. A hybrid neural architecture using both linear and threshold-like activations for n-input XOR is discussed in [60], where it is shown that it requires the least number of weights.

The results from this optimized first layer can be combined (in subsequent layers) by using:

- KGs, leading to a mostly analog implementation;
- BGs, TLGs, multi-threshold TLGs, or multi-valued logic gates, leading to mixtures of analog and digital gates.

This suggests that KGs should be designed and included in a library of gates. Such an approach will lead to *size*-optimal solutions, while we expect that these will also be *area*-optimal, *significantly reducing power and energy*.

V. Conclusions

The size of circuits implementing BFs can be reduced (theoretically, from $2^n/2$ to $2n + 1$ gates in the first layer) by allowing KGs. These are analog gates that raise implementation and reliability concerns, and limit the applicability of the method to (very) small *fan-in* gates, suggesting that the KGs should be included in advanced libraries of gates.

An interesting aspect we have investigated only for $n = 3$ is

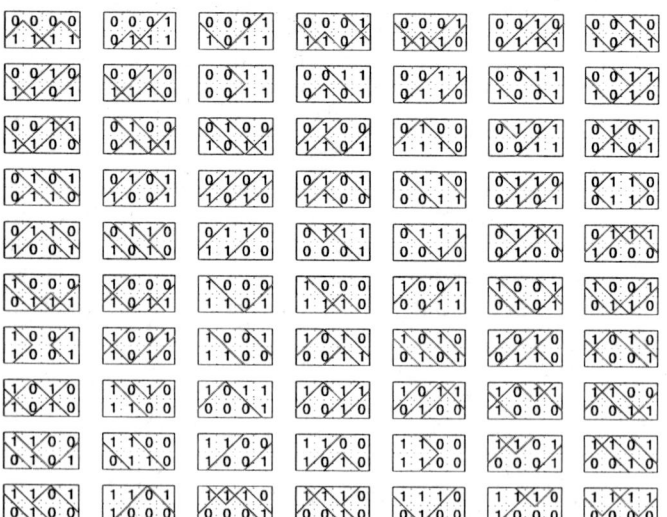

Fig. 5. Using a KGs (with $k = 1$) for implementing BFs of three inputs (for all cases having four "ones" and four "zeros" in their truth table).

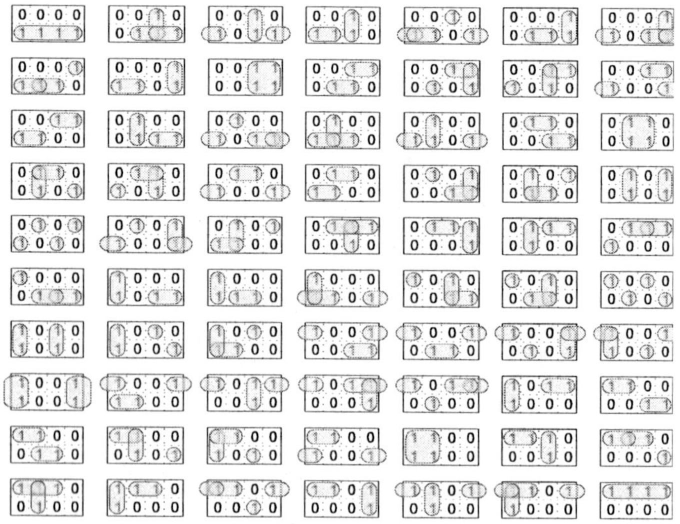

Fig. 6. Classical BGs optimization for all the cases of BFs of three inputs having four "ones" and four "zeros" in their truth table (worst case).

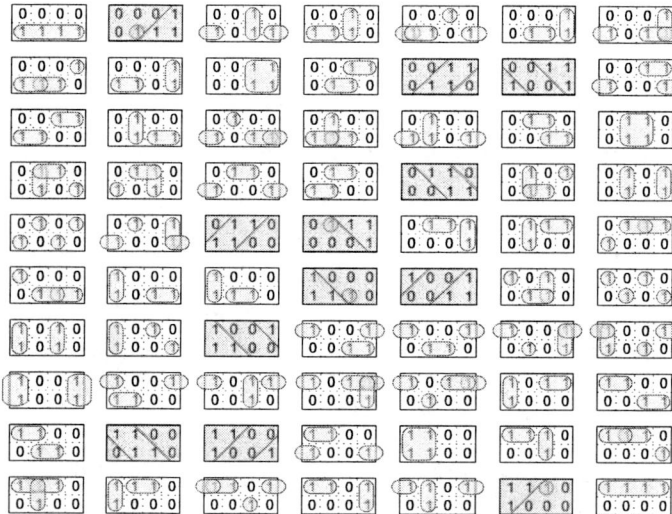

Fig. 7. Optimization using both BGs and KGs for all BFs of three inputs having four "ones" and four "zeros" in their truth table (worst case). KGs are able to improve in 12 out of the 70 cases.

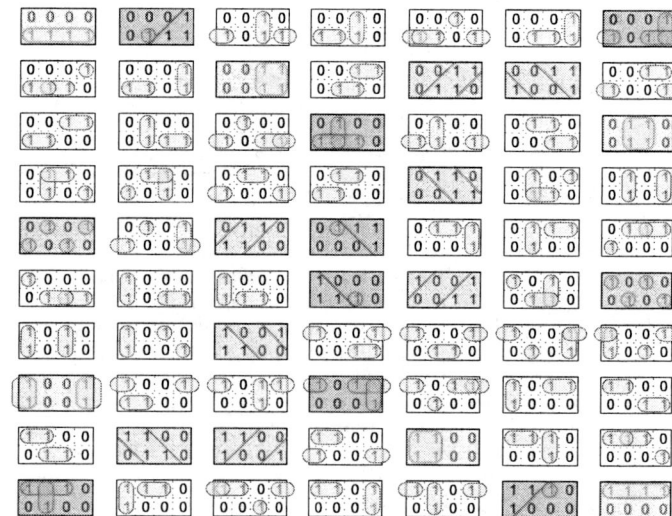

Fig. 8. Combined synthesis for BFs of three inputs for all the cases having four "ones" and four "zeros" in their truth table (worst cases). The six yellow shaded Karnaugh maps are trivial, the eight red shaded Karnaugh maps are variations of MAJ-3, the eight blue shaded Karnaugh maps use KGs, while the two green-shaded Karnaugh maps are the XOR functions.

that of allowing combinations of BGs and KGs for reducing the *size* of circuits. The *size* can be reduced even further by also allowing MAJ gates.

Our expectation is that *power* (and *area*) could be reduced as compared to classical Boolean implementations, due to the smaller *size*, the reduced switching activity, and because low precision analog gates will dissipate less [57], [58].

It seems that the optimal combination of different types of gates has the potential of minimizing circuit *size*. To make this happened, a lot of research/effort is needed on:

- the theory for optimally combining BGs, TLGs and KGs;
- the optimal implementations of KGs;
- the development of CAD tools able to take advantage of the different logic styles.

High-level logic synthesis tool for optimizing arbitrary BFs are clearly needed, considering that emerging nano devices such as resonant tunneling devices (RTD), single electron tunneling (SET), and molecular ones have been used to implement TLGs (see [60], [62]).

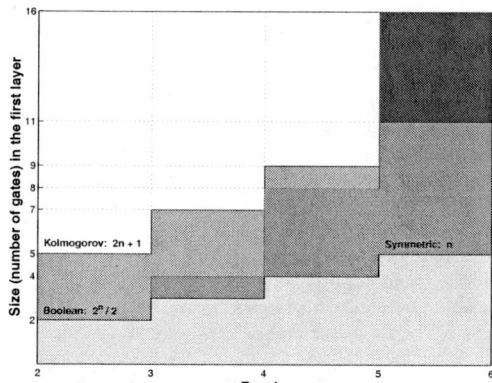

Fig. 9. Size of the first layer when using KS $(2n+1)$, Boolean gates $(2^n/2)$, and threshold logic gates for implementing symmetric functions (n).

REFERENCES

[1] E. I. Nechiporuk, "The synthesis of networks from threshold elements," *Prob. Kiber.*, **11**, pp. 49–62, 1964 [*Autom. Express*, **7**, pp. 27–32 and pp. 35–39, 1964].

[2] O. B. Lupanov, "On circuits of threshold elements," *Dokl. Akad. Nauk SSSR*, **202**, pp. 1288–1291, 1971 [*Sov. Phys. Dokl.*, **17**, pp. 91–93, 1972].

[3] S. Muroga, *Threshold Logic and Its Applications*, John Wiley, New York, 1971.

[4] V. Beiu, "A survey of perceptron circuit complexity results," *Proc. Intl. Joint Conf. Neural Networks IJCNN*, Portland, USA, 2003, pp. 989–994.

[5] V. Beiu, J. M. Quintana, and M. J. Avedillo, "VLSI implementation of threshold logic: A comprehensive survey," *IEEE Trans. Neural Networks*, **14**(5), pp. 1217–1243, 2003.

[6] J. Myhill, and W. H. Kautz, "On the size of weights required for linear-input switching functions," *IRE Trans. Electr. Comp.*, vol. EC-10, pp. 288–290, 1961.

[7] J. Håstad, "On the size of weights for threshold gates," *SIAM J. Discr. Math.*, **7**(3), pp. 484–492, 1994.

[8] D. R. Haring, "Multi-threshold threshold elements," *IEEE Trans. Electr. Comp.*, **EC-15**(1), pp. 45–65, 1966.

[9] T. A. Diep, "Capacity of multilevel threshold devices," *IEEE Trans. Info. Th.*, **44**(1), pp. 241–255, 1998.

[10] S. L. Hurst, "Multiple-valued logic: Its status and its future," *IEEE Trans. Comp.*, **33**(12), pp. 1160–1179, 1984.

[11] K. C. Smith, "Multiple valued logic: A tutorial and appreciation," *IEEE Comp.*, **21**(4), pp. 17–27, 1988.

[12] D. Hilbert, "Mathematische probleme," *Nachr. Akad. Wiss. Göttingen*, pp. 253–297, 1900 [*Bull. Amer. Math. Soc.*, **8**, pp. 437–479, 1902].

[13] A. N. Kolmogorov, "On the representation of continuous functions of several variables by superposition of continuous functions of fewer variables," *Dokl. Akad. Nauk SSSR*, **108**(2), pp. 179–182, 1956 [*Amer. Math. Soc. Transl.*, (2) **17**, pp. 369–373, 1961].

[14] V. I. Arnol'd, "On functions of three variables," *Dokl. Akad. Nauk SSSR*, **114**(4), pp. 679–681, 1957 [*Amer. Math. Soc. Transl.*, (2) **28**, pp. 51–54, 1963].

[15] A. N. Kolmogorov, "On the representation of continuous functions of many variables by superpositions of continuous functions of one variable and addition," *Dokl. Akad. Nauk SSSR*, **114**(5), pp. 953–956, 1957 [*Amer. Math. Soc. Transl.*, (2) **28**, pp. 55–59, 1963].

[16] V. I. Arnol'd, "On the representation of functions of several variables by superposition of functions of fewer variables," *Mat. Prosveshchenie*, **3**, pp. 41–61, 1958.

[17] V. I. Arnol'd, "On the representation of continuous functions of three variables by superpositions of continuous functions of two variables," *Mat. Sb.*, **48**, pp. 3–74, 1959 [*Amer. Math. Soc. Transl.*, (2) **28**, pp. 61–147, 1963].

[18] D. A. Sprecher, "On the structure of continuous function of several variables," *Trans. Amer. Math. Soc.*, **115**(3), pp. 340–355, 1965.

[19] D. A. Sprecher, "A representation theorem for continuous functions of several variables," *Proc. Amer. Math. Soc.*, **16**, pp. 200–203, 1965.

[20] G. G. Lorenz, "Representation of functions of several variables by function of one variable, Chp. 11 in *Approximations of Functions* (Athena Series, Selected Topics on Mathematics), Holt, Rinehart, and Winston, New York, 1966.

[21] D. A. Sprecher, "On the structure of representations of continuous functions of several variables as finite sums of continuous functions of one variable," *Proc. Amer. Math. Soc.*, **17**(1), pp. 98–105, 1966.

[22] D. A. Sprecher, "On best approximations in several variables," *J. für die reine und angewandte Math.*, **229**, pp. 117–130, 1968.

[23] D. A. Sprecher, "An improvement in the superposition theorem of Kolmogorov," *J. Math. Anal. Appl.*, **38**, pp. 208–213, 1972.

[24] R. J. P. de Figueiredo, "Implications and applications of Kolmogorov's superposition theorem," *IEEE Trans. Autom. Control*, **25**(6), pp. 1227–1231, 1980.

[25] R. Hecht-Nielsen, "Kolmogorov's mapping neural network existence theorem," *Proc. Intl. Conf. Neural Networks ICNN'87*, San Diego, USA, vol. 3, 11–14, 1987.

[26] F. Girosi, and T. Poggio, "Representation properties of networks: Kolmogorov's theorem is irrelevant," *Neural Computation*, **1**(4), pp. 465–469, 1989.

[27] V. Kůrková, "13th Hilbert's problem and neural networks," in M. Novák, and E. Pelikán (eds.): *Theoretical Aspects of Neurocomputing* (Proc. NEURONET'90, Prague, Czech Republic), Word Scientific, Singapore, pp. 213–216, 1991.

[28] V. Kůrková, "Kolmogorov's theorem is relevant," *Neural Computation*, **3**(4), pp. 617–622, 1991.

[29] N. E. Cotter, and T. J. Guillerm, "The CMAC and a theorem of Kolmogorov," *Neural Networks*, **5**(2), pp. 221–228, 1992.

[30] V. Kůrková, "Kolmogorov's theorem and multilayer neural networks," *Neural Networks*, **5**(3), pp. 501–506, 1992.

[31] D. A. Sprecher, "A universal mapping for Kolmogorov's superposition theorem," *Neural Networks*, **6**(8), pp. 1089–1094, 1993.

[32] H. Katsuura, and D. A. Sprecher, "Computational aspects of Kolmogorov's superposition theorem," *Neural Networks*, **7**(3), pp. 455–461, 1994.

[33] M. Nees, "Approximative versions of Kolmogorov's superposition theorem, proved constructively," *J. Comp. Appl. Math.*, **54**(2), pp. 239–250, 1994.

[34] D. A. Sprecher, "A numerical implementation of Kolmogorov's superpositions," *Neural Networks*, **9**(5), pp. 765–772, 1996.

[35] D. A. Sprecher, "A numerical construction of a universal function for Kolmogorov's superpositions," *Neural Network World*, **6**(4), pp. 711–718, 1996.

[36] D. A. Sprecher, "A numerical implementation of Kolmogorov's superpositions II," *Neural Networks*, **10**(3), pp. 447–457, 1997.

[37] V. Brattka, "A computable Kolmogorov superposition theorem," in J. Blanck, V. Brattka, P. Hertling, and K. Weihrauch (Eds.): *Computability and Complexity in Analysis*, volume 272 of Informatik Berichte, FernUniversität Hagen, pp. 7–22, 2000.

[38] R. Neruda, A. Štědry, and J. Drkošová, "Towards feasible learning algorithm based on Kolmogorov theorem," *Proc. Intl. Conf. Artif. Intel. AI'00*, Las Vegas, USA, 2000, vol. 2, pp. 915–920.

[39] M. Köppen, "On the training of a Kolmogorov network," *Proc. Intl Conf. Artif. Neural Networks ICANN'02*, Madrid, Spain, Springer LNCS 2415, 2002, pp. 474–479.

[40] D. Tikk, L. T. Kóczy, T. D. Gedeon, "A survey on universal approximation and its limits in soft computing techniques," *Intl. J. Approx. Reasoning*, **33**(2), pp. 185–202, 2003.

[41] A. N. Shiryaev (Ed.), *A. N. Kolmogorov, Anniversary Book*, Fizmatlit, Moscow, 2003.

[42] *Russian Math. Survey*, **59**(1), special issue dedicated to A. N. Kolmogorov, 2004.

[43] A. G. Vituškin, "On Hilbert's thirteenth problem and related questions," *Russian Math. Survey*, **59**(1), pp. 11–25, 2004.

[44] P. A. Ostrand, "Dimension of metric spaces and Hilbert's problem 13," *Bull. Amer. Math. Soc.*, **71**(2), pp. 619–622, 1965.

[45] R. Doss, "A superposition theorem for unbounded continuous functions," *Trans. Amer. Math. Soc.*, **10**, pp. 249–259, 1968.

[46] S. Demko, "A superposition theorem for bounded continuous functions," *Proc. Amer. Math. Soc.*, **66**, pp. 75–78, 1977.

[47] Y. Hattori, "Dimension and superposition of bounded continuous functions on locally compact, separable metric spaces," *Topl. Appl.*, **54**(1), pp. 123–132, 1993.

[48] V. Beiu, "Optimization of circuits using a constructive learning algorithm," in A.B. Bulsari and S. Kallio (Eds.): *Neural Networks in Engineering Systems* (Proc. EANN'97, Stockholm, Sweden), Åbo Akademis Tryckeri, 1997, pp. 291–294.

[49] V. Beiu, "Neural inspired parallel computations require analog processors," *Proc. Intl. Parallel Comp. Electr. Eng. Conf. PARELEC'98*, Bialystok, Poland, 1998, pp. 39–53.

[50] V. Beiu, "On Kolmogorov's superposition and Boolean functions," *Proc. Brazilian Symp. Neural Networks SBRN'98*, Belo Horizonte, Brazil, 1998, pp. 55–60.

[51] B. L. Fridman, "An improvement in the smoothness of the functions in Kolmogorov's superposition theorem," *Dokl. Acad. Nauk SSSR*, **177**(5), pp. 1019–1022, 1967 [*Soviet Math. Dokl.*, **8**(6), pp. 1550–1553, 1967].

[52] V. Beiu, and H. E. Makaruk, "Deeper sparser nets can be optimal," *Neural Proc. Lett.*, **8**(3), pp. 201–210, 1998.

[53] *International Technology Roadmap for Semiconductors* (ITRS), 2004. http://public.itrs.net/

[54] L. Chang, Y.-K. Choi, D. Ha, P. Ranade, S. Xiong, J. Bokor, C. Hu, and T.-J. King, "Extremely scaled silicon nano-CMOS devices," *Proc. IEEE*, **91**(11), pp. 1860–1873, Nov. 2003.

[55] V. Beiu, U. Rückert, S. Roy, and J. Nyathi, "On nanoelectronic architectural challenges and solutions," *Proc. IEEE Conf. Nanotech. IEEE-NANO'04*, Munich, Germany, 2004, pp. 628–631.

[56] C. Piguet, J. Gautier, C. Heer, I. O'Connor, and U. Schlichtmann, "Extremely low-power logic," *Proc. Design, Autom. & Test in Europe Conf. DATE'04*, Paris, France, 2004, vol. 1, pp. 656–661.

[57] R. Sarpeshkar, "Analog versus digital: Extrapolating from electronics to neurobiology," *Neural Computation*, **10**(7), pp. 1601–1638, 1998.

[58] R. Sarpeshkar, and M. O'Halloran, "Scalable hybrid computation with spikes," *Neural Computations*, **14**(9), pp. 2003–2038, 2002.

[59] D. Liu, M. E. Hohil, and S. H. Smith, "N-bit parity neural networks: New solutions based on linear programming," *Neurocomputing*, **48**, pp. 477–488, 2002.

[60] B. M. Wilamowski, D. Hunter, and A. Malinowski, "Solving parity-N problems with feedforward neural networks," *Proc. Intl. Conf. Neural Networks IJCNN'03*, Portland, USA, 2003, pp. 2546–2551.

[61] R. Zhang, P. Gupta, L. Zhong, and N. K. Jha, "Threshold network synthesis and optimization and its application to nanotechnologies," *IEEE Trans. CAD*, **24**(1), pp. 107–118, 2005 [Preliminary version as "Synthesis and optimization of threshold logic networks with application to nanotechnologies," *Proc. Design, Autom. & Test in Europe DATE'04*, Paris, France, 2004, pp. 904–909].

[62] M. J. Avedillo, and J. M Quintana, "A threshold logic synthesis tool for RTD circuits," *Proc. Euromicro Symp. Digital Sys. Design DSD'04*, Rennes, France, 2004, pp. 624–627.

Hardware Implementation of CMAC and B-Spline Neural Networks for Embedded Applications

Qiuye Zhao and Donald S. Reay
School of Engineering and Physical Sciences
Heriot-Watt University
Edinburgh, UK EH14 4AS
E-mail: D.S.Reay@hw.ac.uk

Abstract—The cerebellar model articulation controller (CMAC) is particularly well suited to real-time embedded applications on account of its fast learning, local generalisation, and ease of either software or hardware implementation. Among its drawbacks are a large memory requirement and the inability to model function derivatives. These drawbacks are addressed by the B-spline neural network (BSNN) at the cost of greater computational complexity. This paper describes a simple modification to the CMAC network that yields characteristics equivalent to an order two BSNN, including function derivative modelling, for the same computational complexity as CMAC and is suitable for high speed hardware implementation in embedded applications. Two alternative approaches to its realisation, namely schematic entry and the Handel-C hardware programming language, using a field programmable gate array (FPGA) are described and compared.

I. INTRODUCTION

The cerebellar model articulation controller (CMAC) [1] is particularly well suited to real-time embedded applications on account of its fast learning, local generalisation, and ease of either software or hardware implementation. Its hardware implementation has been described by a number of authors [2], [3], [4], [5]. Among its drawbacks are a large memory requirement, especially for high dimensional inputs, and the inability to model function derivatives. In addition, the original CMAC has a reduced modelling capability in the case of multivariate inputs [6], [7].

One possible solution to the latter problem is to increase the number of basis functions used [8] but this increases both the memory and computational requirements. The use of higher order basis functions in a CMAC [8], [9], [10] is a means of improving its modelling capability and of enabling it to model function derivatives, and the use of B-splines as higher order CMAC basis functions has been proposed [8], [11]. However, this modification increases the computational requirements of the network. The B-spline neural network (BSNN) [6] is closely related to CMAC and can model both a multivariate function and its derivatives but at the cost of greater computational complexity than CMAC. In particular, the BSNN requires multiplication operations and more than one author has commented on the difficulties this presents to a low cost hardware implementation [4], [7]. Horvath [11] attributes better learning capabilities (than conventional CMAC) to higher order CMACs that require multipliers and proposes efficient multiplier hardware.

This paper describes a simple modification to the CMAC network that yields characteristics equivalent to an order two BSNN for the same computational complexity as CMAC and is suitable for high speed hardware implementation in embedded applications. It enables function derivatives to be computed but does not involve multiplication operations. It assumes quantised (integer) inputs but this is not a major limitation in many embedded applications. Two alternative approaches to its realisation, namely schematic entry and the Handel-C hardware programming language, using a field programmable gate array (FPGA) are described and compared.

The motivation for this work was provided by use of a B-spline neural network to model the non-linear flux characteristics of a switched reluctance motor (SRM) in real-time [12]. Previously, a CMAC network, implemented in hardware [3], had been used to learn suitable current demand waveforms for an SRM [13] but was unable to model the required function derivatives.

II. DESCRIPTION OF APPLICATION

The use of a BSNN to model the flux characteristics of an SRM and thus enable instantaneous torque estimation is described in detail by Lin [12]. For the purposes of this paper it is sufficient to note that this application required a network with two inputs, current and position, derived from an analogue to digital converter and an optical encoder respectively. As such the inputs were quantised to integer values. Insofar as the input was low dimensional and quantised it is typical of many other embedded applications. The nature of the application provided the motivation to find a high-speed, inexpensive network implementation.

III. COMMON STRUCTURE OF CMAC AND B-SPLINE NETWORKS

A. B-Spline Network

The B-spline network can be classified as a kind of associative memory network (AMN). The basic network can be decomposed into two mapping systems, a static nonlinear mapping and an adaptive linear mapping as shown in figure 1. The n-dimensional input to the network is denoted by x, and it is the network designer's responsibility to normalise the input vector and define r_i input knots on the ith input axis such that these knots form a lattice of p' cells ($p' = \prod_1^n (r_i + 1)$),

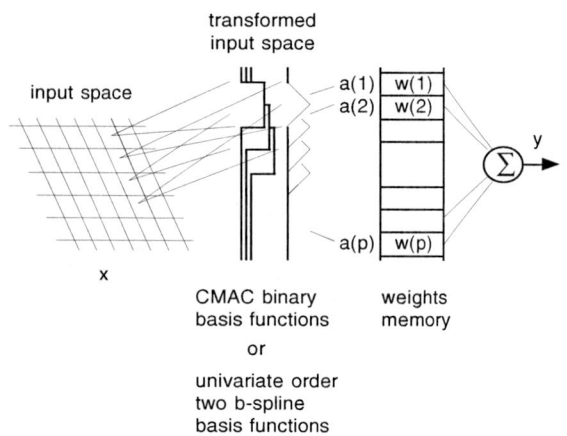

Fig. 1. The common structure of CMAC and B-spline networks.

on which ρ multivariate basis functions are defined. The multivariate basis functions are formed by taking the tensor products of the univariate basis functions defined on each input dimension.

For B-spline networks, the univariate basis functions are piecewise polynomials of order k generated by B-spline recurrence relationships. The width of the support of each univariate basis function, in which region a basis function is non-zero, i.e. activated, is defined by the designer and called the *generalization width*. The output of the ith multivariate basis function is denoted by a_i, and the vector **a** is called the *association vector* or *transformed input vector*.

B. CMAC network

The cerebellar model articulation controller (CMAC) is another AMN and shares the structure of the B-spline network shown in figure 1, except that in the original CMAC network the basis functions are binary and in order to ensure that exactly ρ supports cover each input cell, a set of ρ displaced overlays is formed, where each overlay consists of the union of adjacent non-overlapping supports. Any input lies within the support of only one basis function in each overlay, and so any input lies within the supports of exactly ρ basis functions. Since the CMAC basis functions are binary, the network output is simply the sum of ρ weights corresponding to the ρ active basis functions.

IV. CMAC B-SPLINE NETWORK

A. Background

CMAC is often used in on-line, non-linear, real-time modelling and control applications, due to its fast learning speed, long-term convergence, low computational cost and suitability for hardware implementation. However, there are some drawbacks to the original CMAC network. First, CMAC produces piecewise constant outputs, which are discontinuous at the normalised input vector knots, so CMAC is not a good choice for applications in which continuous outputs or derivatives of outputs are required. Second, the modelling ability of the original multivariate CMAC network is limited. Third, although only ρ basis functions are activated by any one input and only ρ weights need to be summed to form the network output, the total number of weights required is exponentially dependent on input dimension n, so considerable memory space is required.

Regarding the first problem, different types of higher order basis functions have been proposed in order to generate a continuous network output and fully cover the lattice. Among these, B-splines are an important set of candidates [6]. However, one problem with using B-spline basis functions on the predefined supports of CMAC is that the order of the piecewise polynomials, which is directly determined by the width of the support (equal to the generalisation parameter defined by the designer), will be too high for most applications.

The B-spline neural network is an alternative to the higher-order CMAC described in [8]. In the torque estimation application, two particularly useful properties of the BSNN are that derivatives of the network output can be computed, and that less weight memory space is required and high-speed on-chip FPGA RAM can be used for storing weights. Unfortunately, since the BSNN output calculation involves multiplication, greater resources are required of the FPGA and the network output calculation may be slower than that of CMAC.

A new algorithm is proposed in this paper that combines the advantages of both CMAC and B-spline networks and can be implemented in hardware without the need for multiplication operations.

There are two ways to understand the algorithm of the CMAC B-spline network. From the first viewpoint, this algorithm is another version of the CMAC algorithm with a different calculation process for the weight addresses. From the second viewpoint, the continuous basis functions of the B-spline network are quantised and the multiplications involved in the network output calculation can be decomposed into additions. Since the structures of CMAC network and the B-spline network are similar, the modified calculation of the B-spline network is very similar to the process of the calculation of CMAC network, which is more suitable for hardware implementation. As described in the following subsections, the first viewpoint helps in implementing this algorithm in hardware and the second one helps in understanding the modelling ability of the CMAC B-spline network compared with B-spline and CMAC networks.

B. Address Calculation in the CMAC B-spline Network

A practical view of CMAC is that its operation comprises the computation of a number, ρ, of addresses from an input, x, and the summation of the contents of those ρ addresses to form an output. Assuming the input values to be to be integers and ρ to be an integer power of two, a method of calculating the ith weight address from a two-dimensional input is shown diagrammatically in figure 2. Here $ofs[i][j]$ represents the displacement of the ith overlay in the jth input dimension. This method was used in a previous hardware implementation [3].

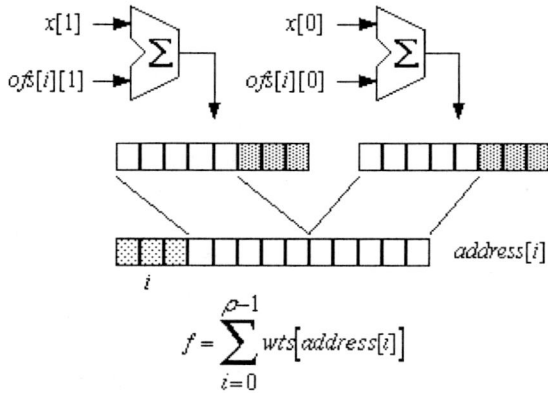

Fig. 2. CMAC and CMAC B-spline address calculation methods.

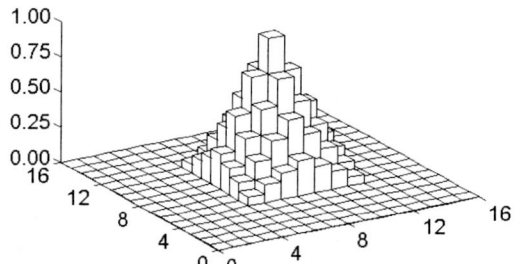

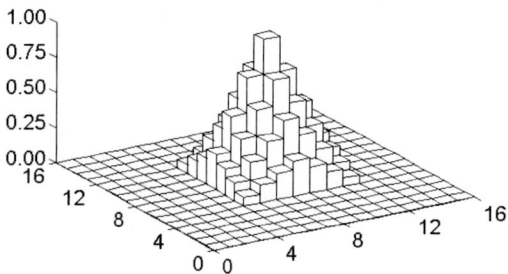

In the original CMAC, the value of ρ is chosen by the designer. In the case of a fully-covered CMAC [7], the value of ρ must equal the full number of possible, resolvable displacements of the overlay and is exponentially dependent on the dimension of the input.

A simple modification to this address calculation scheme is to omit the $\log 2(\rho)$ most significant bits from the address shown in figure 2. In effect, the ρ overlays of basis functions are collapsed into one and the number of weights required is reduced by a factor of ρ. Using this scheme, although ρ address calculations are made, only 2^n different addresses are possible for any one input and the kth of those 2^n different addresses will be calculated $freq_k$ out of ρ times where $\sum_{k=1}^{2^n} freq_k = \rho$. Using

$$f = \sum_{i=0}^{\rho-1} wts[address[i]] \quad (1)$$

to calculate the network output, the frequency of occurrence $freq_k$ of each of the 2^n possible different addresses for an input is not made explicit but in effect the network output is described by

$$f = \sum_{k=1}^{2^n} freq_k * wts[address_k] \quad (2)$$

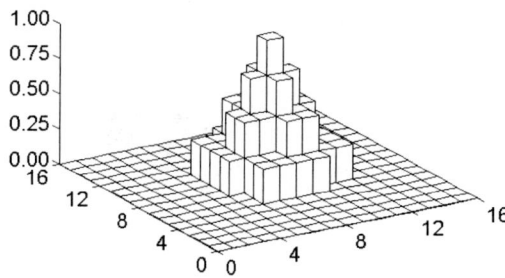

Thus $freq_k$ has a similar role to that of the activation of a basis function in the BSNN. Figure 3(a) shows the output of an order two BSNN with two integer inputs where just one weight value is non-zero. It illustrates one of the (discretised) multivariate basis functions. An input falling within the support of the basis function will contribute to the network output a value equal to the activation of the basis function, represented in figure 3(a) by its height, multiplied by its corresponding weight.

Figures 3(b) and 3(c) show the outputs of two CMAC B-spline networks each with one non-zero weight. In each case, the output is formed by the sum of ρ weights corresponding to overlapping and displaced binary basis functions. In figure 3(b), ρ is equal to 16 which in this example represents the fully covered situation and in 3(c) ρ is equal to 4.

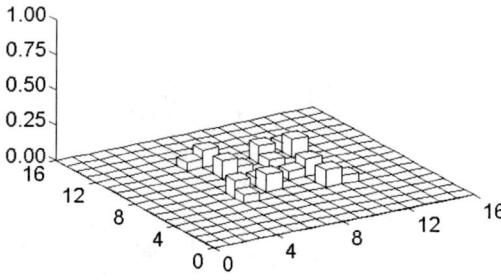

Fig. 3. Basis functions for (a) BSNN (quantised inputs), (b) CMAC B-spline, $\rho = 16$, (c) CMAC B-spline, $\rho = 4$, and (d) error between basis functions (a) and (c).

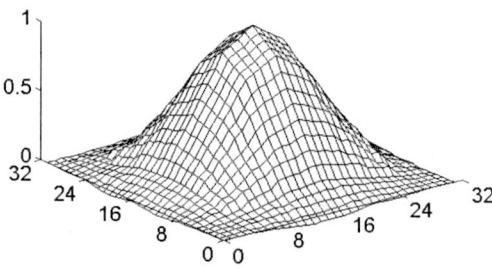

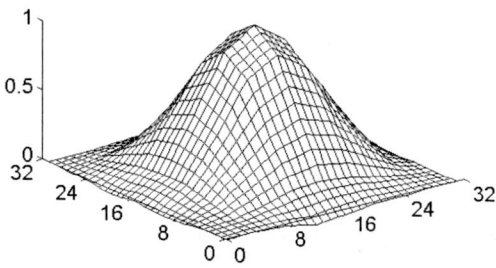

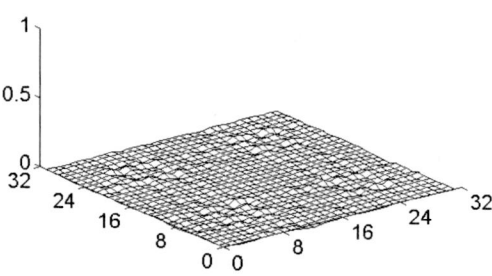

Fig. 4. Network outputs for (a) CMAC B-spline, $\rho = 4$ and (b) BSNN using the basis functions of figures 3(c) and 3(a) respectively, trained on 400 random examples of function $(0.5 - 0.5*\cos(x[0]))*(0.5 - 0.5*\cos(x[1]))$. (c) error between (a) and (b).

The heights of the output functions represent the numbers of times, $freq_k$ (out of ρ), the address of the non-zero weight are calculated for a particular input and hence the number of times that weight will be added to the overall output. The peaks of the network output functions correspond to inputs for which ρ out of ρ addresses calculated are equal to the address of the one non-zero weight.

Allowing for a factor of ρ difference in the values of the single non-zero weights, figures 3(a) and 3(b) are identical and the plot of figure 3(c) is an approximation to that of the other two. Figure 3(d) shows the difference between figures 3(a) and 3(c).

The characteristics, including modelling capability, of the fully-covered CMAC B-spline and the BSNN are equivalent.

As the generalisation parameter, ρ decreases, the degree of accuracy of the representation of B-spline basis functions by the CMAC B-spline algorithm decreases.

However, although the degree of accuracy of representation of the B-spline basis function by the CMAC B-spline algorithm decreases as the generalisation parameter decreases, the modelling ability of the CMAC B-spline decreases far less significantly (see figure 4.)

Figure 5 further demonstrates the modelling capabilities of the CMAC B-spline network. A conventional CMAC, an order two BSNN and a CMAC B-spline network, equivalent in that the CMAC B-spline was based on the conventional CMAC and its basis functions approximated those of the BSNN, were each trained using 200 randomly distributed examples of the function y = (0.5 - 0.5*cos(x[0]))*(0.5 - 0.5*cos(x[1])). Figure 6 shows the corresponding errors during training and confirms the similarity between the modelling characteristics of the CMAC B-spline and BSNN. The CMAC B-spline output calculation does not involve any multiplication operations.

In addition, the CMAC B-spline is capable of computing function derivatives without involving multiplication operations. The calculation method is illustrated in figure 8 and the partial derivatives obtained using this method are shown in figure 7.

In short, while the fully-covered CMAC B-spline is equivalent to an order two BSNN with quantised inputs, the CMAC B-spline using a smaller generalisation parameter approximates the order two BSNN sufficiently well to give useful practical results at very low computational cost.

V. FPGA Implementation of CMAC and B-spline Networks

A block diagram of the hardware design and implementation method for B-spline and CMAC networks is shown in figure 9. Computer 1, which is connected to the Spartan-IIE board, is used for FPGA design and FPGA implementation. Computer 2 is used to program the TMS320F243 and to transfer data to and from the DSP during testing. The FPGA is connected to the i/o bus of the DSP as a memory-mapped peripheral.

The DSP is responsible for generating training patterns and transferring the input and output vectors to and from the FPGA. The FPGA is responsible for implementing the CMAC or B-spline network.

The design flow is shown in figure 10. Three different development packages were used for hardware design and implementation; DK2.0 (Celoxica), ISE 5.1 (Xilinx), and Code Composer Studio (Texas Instruments).

A. The Handel-C hardware programming language

Handel-C was used to design the FPGA implementation of the CMAC B-spline network. Handel-C is a high level language for the implementation of algorithms in hardware. The most distinctive characteristics of Handel-C and DK2.0 are a software-like hardware design environment and the

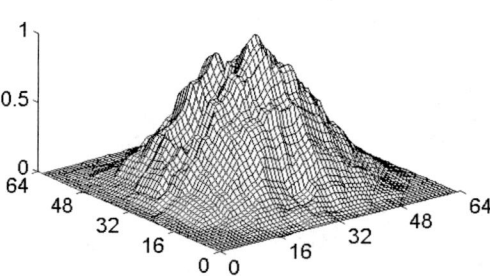
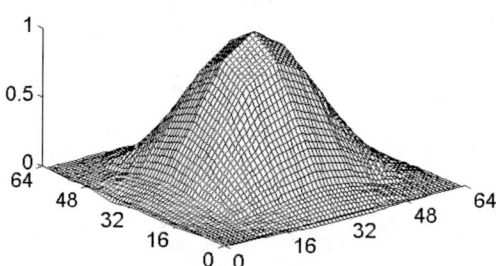
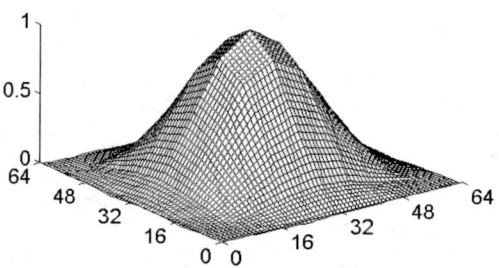

Fig. 5. Network outputs for (a) CMAC, (b) CMAC B-spline and (c) BSNN trained for 200 epochs using 200 random examples of function $(0.5 - 0.5 * \cos(x[0])) * (0.5 - 0.5 * \cos(x[1]))$

convenience afforded hardware co-design with other higher level software programming languages.

B. Hardware Programming vs. Schematic Design

As an alternative to using Handel-C, schematic entry was used to implement the CMAC B-spline on the Spartan-IIE FPGA. Both methods resulted in successful implementation of a functionally equivalent network although, for reasons related to the handling of clock signals in Handel-C, the details of the interface with the DSP and the maximum reliable clock speeds were slightly different. Table I summarises the performance and resource requirements of the two implementations.

The fact that it was a practical proposition to design a

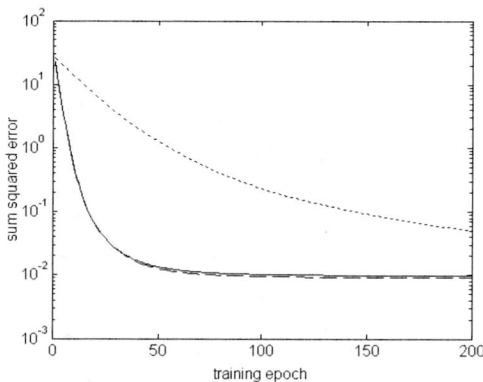

Fig. 6. Sum squared error over training set vs. training epoch for CMAC B-spline, $\rho = 8\ \beta = 0.01$, compared with order two B-spline (quantised inputs), $\beta = 0.08$, (dashed line) and CMAC, $\rho = 8\ \beta = 0.01$ (dotted line).

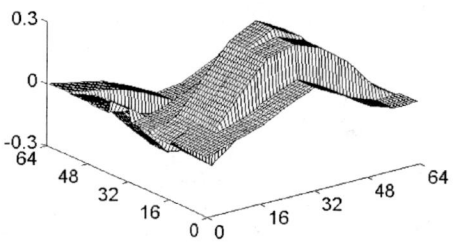

Fig. 7. Partial derivative of function shown in figure 5 learned by CMAC B-spline, computed using method shown in figure 8.

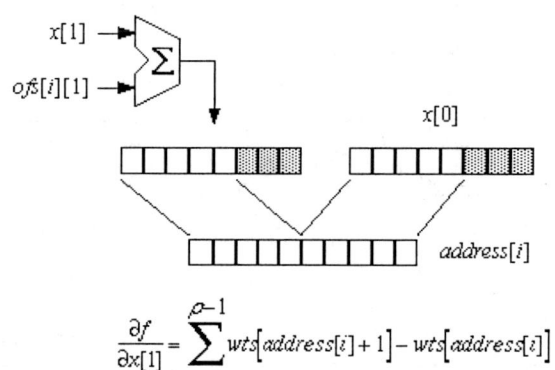

Fig. 8. CMAC B-spline address calculation method for function derivatives.

implementation method	FPGA clock speed	output computation time	FPGA SLICEs used
schematic	150MHz	100ns	70
Handel-C	100MHz	120ns	842

TABLE I

COMPARISON OF PERFORMANCE AND RESOURCE REQUIREMENTS OF SCHEMATIC ENTRY AND HANDEL-C IMPLEMENTATIONS OF CMAC B-SPLINE USING XILINX SPARTAN-IIE.

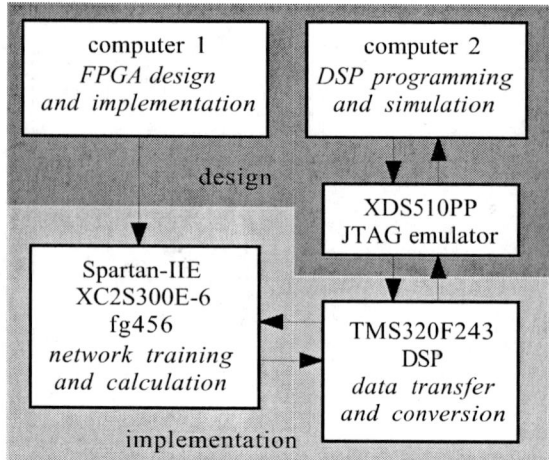

Fig. 9. Hardware design and implementation method.

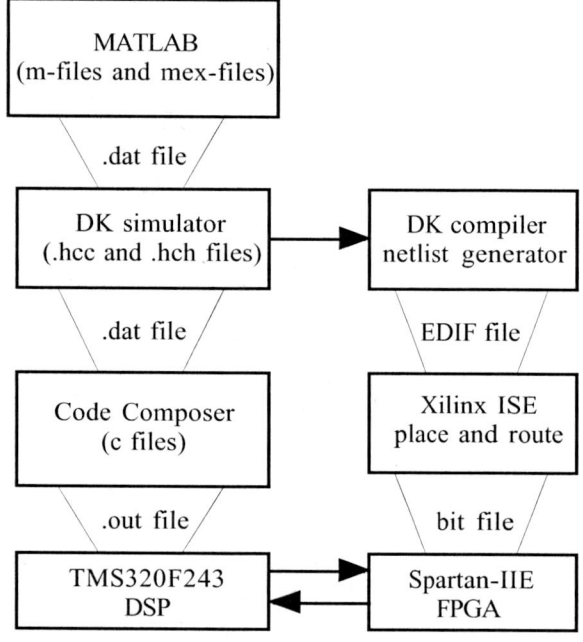

Fig. 10. Handel-C based design flow.

more efficient and better performing implementation using schematic capture highlights the simplicity of the CMAC B-spline architecture. The main advantage of the Handel-C method lies in the relative ease with which parameter values may be changed. In addition, Handel-C has advantages for co-simulation, code extension and re-use of models. The best method of hardware design is to integrate different methods in order to exploit their particular advantages. For example, within the schematic design it was convenient to implement control of the various registers, multiplexers and adders involved using a state machine written in Verilog. Finally it should be noted that Handel-C appears to be a rapidly developing language and while some practical difficulties were encountered in its use, it is anticipated that these may soon be overcome.

VI. CONCLUSIONS

This paper describes a high-speed hardware implementation of a CMAC B-spline neural network based on a simple modification to the original CMAC network.

A CMAC B-spline network using the maximum resolvable number of overlays gives exactly the same results as an order two BSNN with quantised inputs. The approximation error due to reducing the number of overlays used in the CMAC B-spline is very small after training. Function derivatives may be computed from the CMAC B-spline without the need for multiplication.

Compared with CMAC, CMAC B-spline uses fewer weights, learns faster, and still requires no multipliers.

The reduction in memory required and the increased capability of modern FPGA devices, e.g. Spartan-IIE, means that there is no longer a requirement for external SRAM, yielding a practical embedded solution.

REFERENCES

[1] J.S. Albus, "Data Storage in the Cerebellar Model Articulation Controller (CMAC)," Trans. ASME, J. Dyn. Sys., Meas. And Control, vol. 97, no. 3, pp. 228-233, Sept. 1975

[2] W.T. Miller, B.A. Box and E.C. Whitney, "Design and Implementation of a High Speed CMAC Neural Network Using Programmable CMOS Logic Arrays," Advances in Neural Information Processing Systems, ed. R.P. Lippmann, Morgan Kaufmann, San Mateo, CA, 1991, pp. 1022-1027

[3] D.S. Reay, T.C. Green and B.W. Williams, "Hardware Implementation of a Neural Network with Application to the Control of a Switched Reluctance Motor," Proc. Neuro-Nîmes, Paris, 1994

[4] W.S. Mischo, "A CMAC-Type Neural Memory for Control Applications," Proc. 5th Int. Conf. on Microelectronics for Neural Networks, Lausanne, Feb. 1996, pp.161-167

[5] J.S. Ker, Y.H. Kuo, R.C. Wen and B.D. Liu, "Hardware Realization of Higher-order CMAC Model for Color Calibration," IEEE Trans. Neural Networks, vol. 8, no. 6, 1997, pp1545-1556

[6] M. Brown and C.J. Harris, "Neurofuzzy Adaptive Modelling and Control," Prentice Hall, New York, 1994

[7] T. Szabo and G. Horvath, "CMAC and its Extensions for Efficient System Modelling and Diagnosis," Int. Jnl. Applied Maths and Computation, vol. 9, no. 3, 1999, pp.571-598

[8] S.H. Lane, D.A. Handelman and J.J. Gelfand, "Theory and Development of Higher-Order CMAC Neural Networks," IEEE Control Systems Magazine, April 1992, pp.23-30

[9] S. Wang and H. Lu, "Fuzzy System and CMAC Network with B-Spline Membership/Basis Functions Can Approximate a Smooth Function and its Derivatives," Int. J. Computational Intelligence and Applications, vol.3, no. 3, 2003, pp. 265-279

[10] C.T. Chiang and C.S. Lin, "CMAC with General Basis Functions," Neural Networks, vol. 9, no. 7, 1996, pp.1199-1211

[11] G. Horvath, "CMAC: Reconsidering an Old Neural Network," Proc. Intelligent Control Systems and Signal Processing, ICONS 2003, Faro, 2003, pp.173-178

[12] Z. Lin, D.S. Reay, B.W. Williams and X. He, "On-Line Torque Estimation in a Switched Reluctance Motor for Torque Ripple Minimization," Proc. IEEE International Symposium on Industrial Electronics, Ajaccio France, 2004, pp.981-985

[13] D.S. Reay, T.C. Green and B.W. Williams, "Application of Associative Memory Neural Networks to the Control of a Switched Reluctance Motor," Proc. IECON93, November 1993, pp. 200-206

DSP-Based Neural Systems for the Perceptual Assessment of Visual Quality

Paolo Gastaldo, Giovanni Parodi, and Rodolfo Zunino

Department of Biophysical and Electronic Engineering, University of Genoa
Via Opera Pia 11a, 16145 Genova, Italy – E-mail: {gastaldo, giovanni.parodi, zunino} @dibe.unige.it

Abstract – The paper presents an efficient hardware realization of Circular Back Propagation (CBP) networks on Digital Signal Processors (DSP). The resulting neural-system is aimed at enhancing "smart" TV displays and supports the estimation of perceptual quality of visual signals. The DSP-based neuro-platform operates on raw digital signals and yields the associate estimate of perceived quality in real time. Experimental results confirm both evaluation accuracy and timing performance.

I. INTRODUCTION

The evaluation of perceived quality of visual signals is a crucial issue in multimedia technologies. In the area of display manufacturing, advanced algorithms aim at enhancing on-screen pictures [1]; likewise, adaptive video broadcasters measure quality to adjust bandwidth [2]. In either case, one ultimately needs to assess the performances of the applied algorithms, but complex perceptual phenomena make it difficult to predict the perceived quality at the user end.

Previous research showed that neural networks can successfully support objective quality assessment, for both contrast-enhanced imaging [1] and digital video [2,3]. A feature-extraction mechanism works out a numerical description of the processed signal; the obtained features feed the neural network that actually predicts the perceived quality.

"Smart" multimedia technologies aim to embed the neural model in dedicated, inexpensive equipment that monitor user-perceived quality in real time. Therefore, this paper presents the DSP-based support of a perceptual quality estimation system.

From a theoretical perspective, the research analyzes the objective model of quality prediction; from a computational viewpoint, it gives design guidelines for implementing the neuro-system on a Digital Signal Processors (DSPs) platform. Both the eventual cost of machinery and power dissipation are crucial issues in embedded applications, hence the design method assumes fixed-point platforms that typically have simpler architectures and lower costs than their floating-point counterparts.

II. NEURAL NETWORK-BASED QUALITY ASSESSMENT

Objective models of perceived quality decouple the signal-description task (i.e., feature extraction) from the actual quality assessment by neural processing (Fig.1). These approaches apply effectively to both still images [1] and digital video signals [2], as they allow one to avoid an explicit, analytical model of the perceptual phenomenon. This paper presents an efficient hardware implementation of the neural-based system for quality assessment of still images.

A. Feature Extraction

Previous research [1,2] performed a statistical analysis

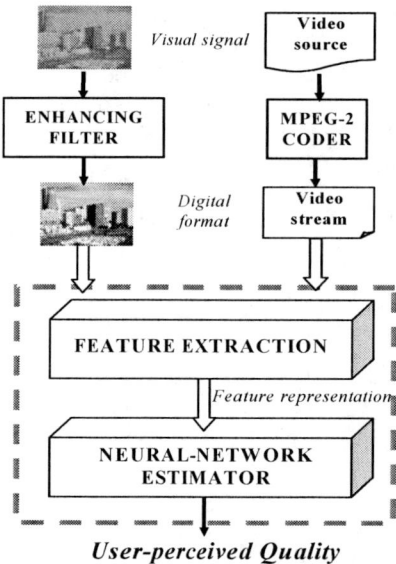

Fig.1 - The objective estimation model (dashed box) for image- and video-quality assessment using unsupervised methods for feature selection. That work singled out the set of relevant features for the quality-assessment task. Thus, an embedded-electronic implementation should perform feature extraction and quality prediction; at run time, the features are continuously evaluated on the current digital signal to provide input stimuli to the neural network.

In the image-enhancement application considered here [1], features describe pixel luminance distribution. A picture is split into non-overlapping blocks and the features are worked out separately for each block; finally, one summarizes the distribution of the evaluated features into global statistical descriptors (e.g., average and median values). In the quality assessment of digital video, the features are extracted from the compressed bitstreams and involve both quantization levels and motion-compensation parameters [2].

The approach described in [1] showed that features extracted from the co-occurrence matrix [4] give the best results in perceived quality estimation. A co-occurrence matrix, C_λ, characterizes textural properties, and describes the spatial dependences among grey tones within an image subregion, λ, that includes $r_\lambda \times c_\lambda$ pixels; the matrix element $C_\lambda(i,j,r,\omega)$ counts the pairs of pixels that: 1) have grey levels i and j, respectively, and 2) are separated by r radial units at an angle ω to the horizontal axis. If one defines Δh, Δv, as the horizontal and vertical displacements in the ω direction, respectively, then one has:

$$\Delta v = r\lceil \sin\omega \rceil \quad \Delta h = \begin{cases} r\lceil \cos\omega \rceil; & 0 < \omega < \pi/2 \\ r\lfloor \cos\omega \rfloor; & \pi/2 < \omega < \pi \end{cases} \quad (1)$$

and the formal expression for the co-occurrence matrix elements can be written as

$$C_\lambda(i,j,r,\omega) = |\{(m,n) \in \lambda \mid \lambda[m,n] = i;\ \lambda[m+\Delta h, n+\Delta v] = j\}| \quad (2)$$

with $i,j = 0,\ldots, N$, where $|\,.\,|$ denotes the cardinality of a set, and N is the highest pixel level (usually grey level).

Several, different features can be extracted from the co-occurrence matrix; the approach described in [1] eventually designed an objective metric including four objective measures:

$$co\_entropy = -\sum_{i,j} C_\lambda(i,j,r,\omega) \log_2 C_\lambda(i,j,r,\omega) \quad (3)$$

$$co\_absv = \sum_z z P_z(r,\omega) \quad (4)$$

$$co\_cont = \sum_z z^2 P_z(r,\omega) \quad (5)$$

$$co\_diffVar = \left[\sum_z (z - co\_absv)^2 P_z(r,\omega)\right]^{1/2} \quad (6)$$

where:

$$P_z(r,\omega) = \sum_{\substack{i,j \\ |i-j|=z}} C_\lambda(i,j,r,\omega);\quad (0 \le z < n_l - 1). \quad (7)$$

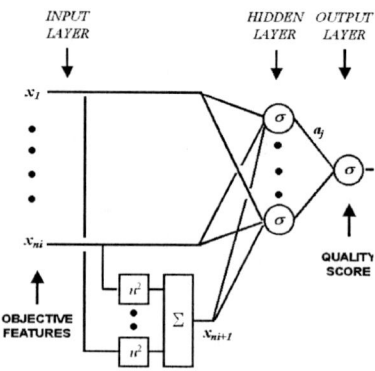

Fig.2 – The CBP neural-network model

B. Neural Quality Estimation

The "Circular Back Propagation" (CBP) model [5] combines two functional layers of neurons including n_h and one units, respectively. The input layer feeds the extracted features, x_i ($i=1,\ldots n_i$), to the j-th neurons in the hidden layer by a set of weights, $w_i^{(j)}$ ($i=0 \ldots n_i+1$). Hidden neurons support a sigmoidal nonlinearity, a_j ($j=1,\ldots, n_h$):

$$a_j = \sigma\left(w_0^{(j)} + \sum_{i=1}^{n_i} w_i^{(j)} x_i + \sum_{i=1}^{n_i} w_{n_i+1}^{(j)} x_i^2\right) \quad (8)$$

where $\sigma(x) = (1 + e^{-x})^{-1}$

The *output* layer prompts the network response, y, as a scalar quantity that codes the overall quality rating; it is worked out as

$$y = \sigma\left(w_0^{(0)} + \sum_{j=1}^{n_h} w_j^{(0)} a_j\right) \quad (9)$$

The specific nature of the CBP model as a feedforward network, mainly based on sum of products operations, fits perfectly the computational characteristics of most DSP devices.

III. HARDWARE SUPPORT OF NEURAL QUALITY ESTIMATION

A. Architectural Issues

Two crucial issues characterize the implementation of a real-time system on a DSP processor: 1) exploiting the limited amount of on-chip memory for highest efficiency, and 2) suitably sizing the computational power of the processor to meet real-time requirements.

Memory occupation mainly relates to the feature-extraction process. Indeed, the co-occurrence matrix requires N^2 cells (N is the number of pixel levels). The

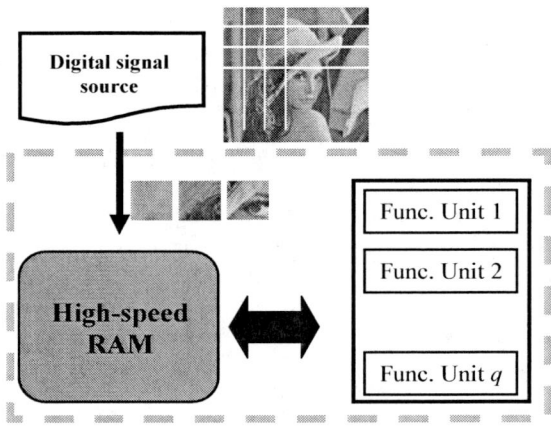

Fig 3 – Memory and computing architecture for DSP implementation

B. Optimizing Throughput in Feature Extraction via DMA

Feature extraction involves the computation of the co-occurrence matrix and the actual feature computation. As discussed in the previous section, the former task conveys a limited execution time as compared with the latter one. Therefore, this section focuses on the bandwidth optimizations for the feature-extraction mechanism.

The DSP-internal RAM operates as a fast caching device, where matrix subsections are copied in turns. That high-speed RAM makes up for the usually limited bandwidth supported by external signal sources. To attain optimal performance, data transfer to/from the cache should proceed in parallel with ongoing computations. The specific internal architectures of DSP devices allow one to attain this goal, as the Harvard schema provides separate, independent memory sections for program and data buses. Moreover, DMA channels allow independent memory loading from external to internal memory.

To speed up feature extraction, the external memory holds the whole co-occurrence matrix, co_occ, and four rows at a time are loaded into the DSP internal memory. A ping-pong schema providing two internal buffers manages the transfer process for optimal efficiency. Image pixels are first stored in buffer b_int_1, then they are copied in buffer b_int_2. The feature-extraction process operates on b_int_2, while another, independent transfer proceeds in parallel from co_occ to b_int_1. Figure 4 outlines the transfer-management algorithm. Dashed boxes represent the code sections that require external memory access. The flowchart points out that

matrix symmetry reduces that figure to $N^2/2$. Quality-assessment systems typically process gray-level images (8 bit-per-pixel images), hence one has $N=256$ and an overall memory requirement of 2 MB. Such a large memory is available only in the memory external to the DSP. Thus, to implement feature extraction efficiently, *bandwidth* becomes a critical aspect in transferring data from external RAM to the on-DSP memory and vice versa. Although the limited resources invariably require some sequential, multiplexing operation to/from external RAM, the simple definitions of quantities do not make that process a major hindrance from a computational viewpoint.

Conversely, when considering the DSP-based support of the feedforward network, the amount of numerical quantities involved in (8) and (9) is much smaller than the number of variables processed in the feature-extraction process. As a result, computational speed becomes paramount in the estimation process, whereas bandwidth is less important. Another important remark is that such systems typically adopt a fixed-point representation of quantities. In final DSP implementations, this imposes a careful evaluation of the word length of the core CPU, because the word length fixes the precision available for the Qn format.

Regardless of both the level of parallelism within the device core and the fabrication technology, a general model for the eventual design strategy follows the architectural approach sketched in Fig.3. The high-speed caching RAM makes up for the usually limited bandwidth supported by external signal sources. Optimal performance requires that data transfer to the cache proceeds in parallel with ongoing computations. This results in two basic design guidelines: first, the internal RAM should be partitioned and accessed in parallel (Harvard architecture); secondly, the device must provide DMA operation for independent memory loading.

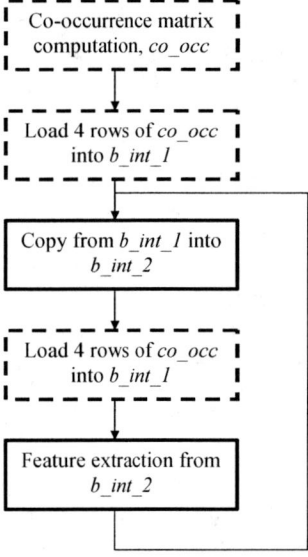

Fig.4 – Feature extraction strategy. The loop iterates over square blocks in the luminance channel

the data transfer between memories and the feature extraction process can execute in parallel. The overhead induced by allocating two internal buffers and the related transfer mechanism is largely compensated by the gain in architectural parallelism.

The DMA capability of most DSPs has a crucial role in the overall mechanism. A general DMA transfer protocol includes three tasks: (A) register set-up to select the data that has to be transferred (B) data transfer between the different memory sections (C) verification of the data-transfer completion.

Denote with T_A, T_B, and T_C the times required to complete the above steps; then the overall time, T_{FE}, to accomplish the feature-extraction process without any wait state must satisfy the constraint:

$$T_A + T_B + T_C \leq T_{FE} \quad (10)$$

Expression (10) ensures that when the feature extraction process over the *i-th* image block is completed, the (*i*+1)–th block is available in the internal cache memory, so that feature processing can proceed without delays.

The architectural assumption about the buffering overhead imposes an additional constraint on the above quantities:

$$T_A + T_C \ll T_B \quad (11)$$

The condition (11) requires that the overhead implied in the initialization and stopping phase of each memory transfer is negligible with respect to the effective data-transfer time.

C. DSP Features for Optimized Neural-Network Support

Real-time quality prediction eventually requires an efficient implementation of CBP on fixed-point DSPs. One can reasonably assume that the training phase of the neural network is accomplished off-line and is not aimed at DSP-based platforms. Indeed, the ultimate research goal is a low-cost implementation of quality predictors for run-time operation.

A crucial issue clearly consists in controlling the accuracy of the implemented system. An important advantage of using a Qn format is that one can exploit (Very Long Instruction Word) VLIW data-level parallelism: packing several values in one memory word enables the DSP core to fetch data simultaneously, thus increasing the effective data-transfer bandwidth. On the other hand, a fixed-point representation brings about some loss in precision, as compared with the performance that could be attained by the higher resolutions provided by floating-point representations.

Several factors contribute to generate approximation noise. As a first source of quantization error, one should consider how DSP-based support nonlinear functions that would require massive computation (as is the case of an exponential function). In expression (8), the ideal sigmoid, $\sigma(x)$, is replaced with a relatively inexpensive implementation based on a fixed-step Look-Up Table (LUT), denoted as $\sigma_q[k\Delta x]$, where Δx is the quantization step in the x axis and k is the actual index entry to the LUT. The second noise source stems from the fact that the CBP weights are quantized using $n+1$ bits according to the Qn standard format (n value bits + sign).

The quantization mechanisms required by the HW implementation clearly affect the effectiveness of the neural estimator. The resulting degradation in accuracy, $QE(n)$, can be measured as

$$QE(n) = E\{[y - y(n)]^2\} \quad (12)$$

where y is the ideal network output obtained from the training process, $y(n)$ is the output of the quantized network in the Qn format, and $E\{\}$ denotes the average over the sample space, x. In principle, expression (12) sets the network HW-design process as an optimization problem, requiring one to minimize (12) over the precision level, n. In fact, architectural features of the target processor also condition the eventual precision setting. Indeed, the basic computational core of a CBP network (8)-(9) mainly involves independent inner products within hidden and output neurons.

Figure 5 outlines the digital implementation of the generic *k*-th neuron, whose algebraic core requires two memory-read cycles, one multiply-and-accumulate (MAC) operation, and one LUT access. These requirements clearly well fit the Harvard structure of DSPs in terms of memory configuration.

In a fixed-point format, however, the precision in summation and multiplication results play a crucial role, since multiplying two Qn numbers requires a careful balance between register length (as large as possible) and hardware circuit complexity (as small as possible). The eventual precision setting, n, must ensure a satisfactory trade-off between performances and precision.

All the above factors may interact in a very intricate fashion depending on the target DSP architecture; in addition, the specific problem setting is quite difficult because the cost function (12) is highly nonlinear and its formulation requires integer-programming techniques.

As a result, the present research pursues a generalization-driven approach to the eventual network design. The best-performing precision setting, n, results

---

for $i=1,...,number\ of\ inputs$
   load   input coordinate x_i, weight coefficient w_i
   multiply_and_accumulate $r = r + x_i \cdot w_i$
   store $a = \sigma_q(r)$

Fig. 5 – The core of the neural quality estimator

from a sample-based procedure, in which a set of CBP networks, implemented at increasing precision levels, n, are trained, and the associated distortions, $QE(n)$, on a test sample, are measured. In such a cross-validation based method, the optimal precision setting, n^*, is the solution of the problem:

$$n^* = \arg\min_n QE_T(n) = \arg\min_n E_T\{[y - y(n)]^2\} \quad (13)$$

where $E_T\{\}$ now estimates generalization performance by averaging the distortion cost empirically over a test set.

IV. EXPERIMENTAL RESULTS

A. Application and Architectural Issues

Real-time constraints related to the target application did not require the quality-prediction cycle to be performed on each frame of the video stream; in fact, an operating speed in the range 2-5 frames per second was rated sufficient to attain a satisfactory estimate of perceived quality.

This section describes the results obtained from the actual implementation of the neural-network quality prediction system on a TMS320C6201 Texas Instruments® DSP (denoted, in the following, as 'C6201' for brevity), running at a clock speed of 167 MHz. This device is a 32-bit fixed-point processor with a VLIW architecture. The internal DSP architecture features a duplicate computational structure arranged into two independent sections (A and B side, respectively). Each side is endowed with one multiplier and two arithmetical/logical units. The CPU core contains 32 registers supporting a 32-bit representation and 8 functional units, including six arithmetic units and two multipliers. Thus, the C6201 can execute up to eight different instructions per clock cycle. This development platform supports DMA data transfer between internal and external data memory, thereby fulfilling the bandwidth condition for optimal data-transfer rates.

The eventual code size of the overall system proved too big for being stored in the internal program memory of the DSP, hence external memory held program instructions and the DSP-internal program memory served as a cache. As the critical segments involved a few loops, temporal and spatial locality in the code made it possible to attain good performances without relevant overhead for code fetching.

B. Bandwidth Control in Feature Extraction

When implemented on the C6201 architecture, the DMA-based approach described in Section III.B yielded the performance results shown in Table I. The Table gives the clock cycles required individual code sections, although those sections actually executed in parallel as anticipated in Fig.5.

TABLE I
Timing performances for the feature-extraction process

FUNCTION	CK CYCLES
Second order features extraction from an image block (T)	830456
Test for DMA memory transfer end (T_C)	69
Co-occurrence matrix computation	63088
Register set-up time (T_A)	40

As a result of minimizing the overhead of the start and the end phase of each DMA transfer, the results confirm that the data transfer through DMA completes before the end-checking routine activates. This allows us to implements a system in which there are not idle loops required to wait for data-transfer epilogue.

The experimental results proposed in TABLE I confirm the equation 10 and 11 introduced in section III.B, assuming that, as pointed out by the simulations accomplished, $T \approx T_B$.

C. Optimization of CBP Network Computations

Section III.C clarified that a suitable setting of the precision, n, in the representation of quantities (especially network weights) can prove critical for the eventual system performance. In general, one expects that multiple instances of byte-wise elements are more suitable to be implemented on a commercial DSP.

Therefore, a massive campaign of experiments addressed the modeling of the prediction performance for increasing values of n. The tests involved first a training phase using a classical back-propagation algorithm with floating-point precision; then a cross-validation approach evaluated the run-time performance on a test set at varying fixed-point approximations.

Empirical evidence (Fig.6) first pointed out that an 8-bit quantization level conveyed an unacceptable degradation for the quality problem at hand. Instead, $QE_T(n)$ asymptotically kept smaller than 0.001 when $n>11$ bits were used to represent both network weights

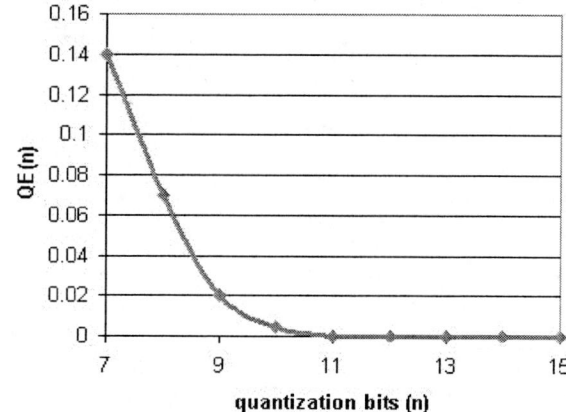

Fig.6 – Performance degradation brought about by fixed-point quantization.

TABLE II
Computational effects of different precision settings in the DSP-based CBP implementation

Fixed-point Format	Complexity (clock cycles)
Q15	4894
Q31	58450

TABLE III
Compiler feedback about the exploitation of functional units in the dot-product critical loop.

Functional Unit	Operations	A-side	B-side
.L	Arithmetic, compare, Logical	3	1
.S	Arithmetic, Logical, Branches	3	3
.D	Address calculation Loads and stores	6	3
.M	Multiply	6	6

and input features. As a result, the Q15 representation met the accuracy requirements and, at the same time, allowed one to exploit the available 16-bit multipliers in parallel within the C6201 DSP core.

The subsequent optimization of the CBP network computational core on the target platform involved different steps. The first action developed a custom inner-product routine, which outperformed the manufacturer's specifications, as provided by the optimized TI library. Interestingly, such a result was achieved by an inline version of the dot product written in C language, which gave better performances that corresponding assembly code at the (minor) cost of a larger code size.

Table II presents the timing performances of the neural network implementation, and clearly indicates the relative advantage of the Q15 format over the classical, larger 32-bit representation. Experimental evidence showed that a 16-bit quantization level resulted in a computational speed-up of one order of magnitude as compared with a Q31 format. Such a notable increase in efficiency is the consequence of 1) the VLIW architecture of the DSP, capable of loading multiple data while fetching one word from the memory, and 2) the parallel use of computational resources (especially, MAC units) within the DSP core. That result can be supported by the feedback provided by the Texas-Instruments compiler. Table III gives the feedback information for the critical loop within the dot-product routine.

The measures prove that the functional units within the DSP core are fully exploited; the multiplication operation is the major bottleneck in the code, hardly unexpected when considering the nature of the operations involved. Moreover, there is a perfect balance in operations between the A and B-side. This means that the proposed

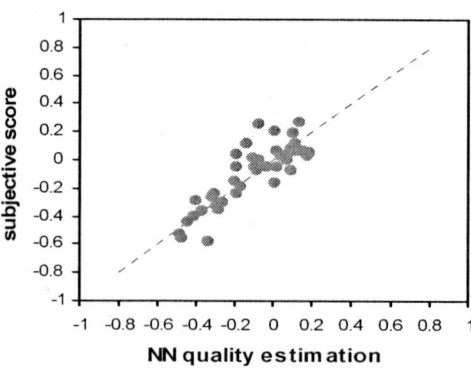

Fig. 7 - Scatter plot of quality values estimated by the NN versus subjective scores.

software architecture exploits as much as possible the computational power of the DSP.

Experimental measurements showed that the complete quality-estimation cycle for an image of size 252x189 pixels took about 450 ms, thus well lying within application specifications. Figure 7 gives the estimated objective quality (x axis) as a function of the subjective scores (on the y axis) on a test set of images. The concentration of data points around the diagonal line of this plot confirms the good generalization performance of the neural-network assessment system.

V. CONCLUSIONS

The paper described the implementation of an embedded neural system on DSP platform, aimed at the real time support of perceived quality estimation in smart video displays. The main result of this research consists in a general methodology, providing guidelines for the efficient implementation of application-driven neural networks on low-cost machinery. The approach effectiveness was proved by a set of test images.

VI. REFERENCES

[1] P. Gastaldo, R. Zunino, E. Vicario, I. Heynderickx, "CBP Neural network for objective assessment of image quality," *Proc. IJCNN 2003*, Portland USA, pp. 194-9.
[2] P. Gastaldo, R. Zunino, S. Rovetta, "Objective assessment of MPEG-2 video quality" *SPIE J.Electronic Imaging*, vol. 11, pp. 365-74, July 2002.
[3] P. Gastaldo, S. Rovetta, R. Zunino, "Objective quality assessment of MPEG-2 video streams by using CBP neural networks," *IEEE TNN*, vol.13, pp. 939-47, July 2002.
[4] R. M. Haralick, "Statistical and Structural Approaches to Texture," *Proc. IEEE*, vol. 67, pp. 786-804, May 1979.
[5] S. Ridella, S. Rovetta, R. Zunino, "Circular back-propagation networks for classification," *IEEE TNN*, vol. 8, pp. 84-97, Jan 1997.

AUTHOR INDEX

Use the bookmarks to navigate to the first letter of the author's last name. Scroll to the author name and select the BLUE paper title links to open that paper.

Hazem M. Abbas
Performance of Neural Classifiers for Fabric Faults Classification 1995

Ashraf M. Abdelbar
An Evolved Seeega Player Capable of Strong Novice-Level Play 332
Experimental Evaluation of a Hybrid Method for Configuring Ensemble Encoding Receptors 989
Fuzzy PSO: A Generalization of Particle Swarm Optimization 1086
Negative Reinforcement and Backtrack-Points for Recurrent Neural Networks for Cost-Based Abduction 827

Mussa Abdella
Treatment of Missing Data Using Neural 598

Suzan Abdelshahid
Fuzzy PSO: A Generalization of Particle Swarm Optimization 1086

Mohamed Abdulhady
Performance of Neural Classifiers for Fabric Faults Classification 1995

Ahmad Abdulkader
Training with Heterogeneous Data 90

Shigeo Abe
Incremental Learning for Online Face Recognition 3174
SVM Ensembles for Selecting the Relevant Feature Subsets 943

Udantha Abeyratne
Tracking the States of a Nonlinear System in the Weight-Space of a Feed-Forward Neural Network 96

Sabeur Abid
Fast Training of Multilayer Perceptrons with a Mixed Norm Algorithm 1018

Robert Abrahart
A Comparative Study of Artificial Neural Network Techniques for River Stage Forecasting 2666
Neural Network Modelling of the 20-Year Flood Event for 850 Catchments Across the UK 2637
Neural Network River Discharge Forecasters: An Empirical Investigation of Hidden Unit Processing Functions Based on Two Different Catchments 2655

Dimitri Abramov
Neurobiological Data Sustaining Opponent Processing Operations on Self Organizing Networks as Tools for the Modeling of Hippocampal Dynamics 2135

Marjory Abreu
An empirical comparison of individual machine learning techniques and ensemble approaches in protein structural class prediction 527

Pamela Abshire
Fisher Information Quantifies Task-Specific Performance in the Blowfly Photoreceptor 274

Giuseppe Acciani
An Automatic Method to Detect Missing Components in Manufactured Products 2324

Ranjan Acharyya
Classification of Infrasound Events Using Using Radial Basis Function Neural Networks 2649

Masaharu Adachi
An Analysis of Associative Chaotic Neurodynamics by Using Surrogate Neurons 758

Andre Adami
Feature Selection by Independent Component Analysis and Mutual Information Maximization in EEG Signal Classification 3011

Rod Adams
Evolving High Capacity Associative Memories with Efficient Wiring 3168
Using real-valued meta classifiers to integrate binding site predictions 481

Mathias Adankon
Optimizing Resources in Model Selection for Support Vectors Machines 925

Indra Adrianto
A Spatiotemporal Approach to Tornado Prediction 1642

Khurshid Ahmad
Are ARIMA Neural Network Hybrids Better than Single Models? 3192

Kazuyuki Aihara
Improved Chaotic Neuro-Computer with Output-Coding for Quadratic Assignment Problems 3312

Cao Aize
Weighted Support Vector Machine for Data Classification 859

Masatake Akutagawa
Tracking the States of a Nonlinear System in the Weight-Space of a Feed-Forward Neural Network 96

Tayeb Al Karim
Modified Time-Based Multilayer Perceptron for Sensor Networks and Image Processing Applications 2201

Shadi Al Shehabi
Multi-Topographic Neural Network Communication and Generalization for Multi-Viewpoint Analysis 1564

Ana Maria Aleksandrowicz
Neural Network Approaches to Personal Change in Psychotherapy 2139

Gilson Alencar
Hybrid Neural-Phenomenological Sub-Models and its Application to Earth-space Path Signal Attenuation Prediction 2372

Polyxeni Alexiou
A Neural Network-based Prediction Model of AR Inhibitory Activity from a Sparse Set of Compounds 2411

Mark Alexiuk
Stochastic Feature Selection for the Discrimination of Biomedical Spectra 3029

Shilton Alistair
A convergence rate estimate for the SVM Decomposition Method 931

Carlos Alzate
Extending Kernel Principal Component Analysis to
  General Underlying Loss Functions 214

Iz Al-Dein Al-Zyoud
Detection of Actuator Faults Using a Dynamic Neural
  Network for the Attitude Control Subsystem of a Satellite 1746

Habiboulaye Amadou Boubacar
Self-Adaptive Kernel Machine: Online Clustering in RKHS 1977

Yoshihito Amemiya
Analog Current-Mode Implementation of Central Pattern
  Generator for Robot Locomotion 639
Noise Performance of Single-Electron Depressing Synapses for
  Neuronal Synchrony Detection 2849

Georgios Anagnostopoulos
An Experimental Comparison of Semi-Supervised ARTMAP
  Architectures, GCS and GNG Classifiers 3121
On the design of an Ellipsoid ARTMAP classifier within the
  Fuzzy Adaptive System ART Framework 469
Parallelizing the Fuzzy ARTMAP Algorithm on a Beowulf Cluster ...475

Charles Anderson
Modeling Reward Functions for Incomplete State
  Representations via Echo State Networks 2995
Optimizing Neural Model Templates using Covariance
  Matrix Adaptation and Fourier Analysis 2162

Razvan Andonie
Feature Ranking using Supervised Neural Gas and Informational Energy 1269

Rauber Andreas
A visualization technique for Self-Organizing Maps with
  vector fields to obtain the cluster structure at desired levels of detail 1558

Emad A.M. Andrews
Negative Reinforcement and Backtrack-Points for Recurrent
  Neural Networks for Cost-Based Abduction 827

Ee Luang Ang
A Fast Neural Network-Based Detection and Tracking of Dim
  Moving Targets in FLIR Imagery 3144
Neural Network-Based Analysis of DNA Microarray Data 503
Neural Networks for Gene Expression Analysis and Gene
  Selection from DNA Microarray 509

Davide Anguita
K-Fold Generalization Capability Assessment for
  Support Vector Classifiers 855
The Effects of Quantization on Support Vector Machines
  with Gaussian Kernel 681

Kazuma Aoki
Feature Subset Selection for Support Vector Machines
  using Confident Margin 907

Hisashi Aomori
Lossless High Dynamic Range Image Coding based on
  Lifting Scheme using Nonlinear Interpolative Effect of
  Discrete-Time Cellular Neural Networks 1681

Ronaldo Aquino
A comparative study of neural network to artificial noses 2081

Juan Carlos Aragon
"Cognitive" Memory 3296

Osamu Araki
Two state transitions mediated by spontaneous and/or intensive
  stimulus on an integrate-and-fire neural network model 2150

Nancy Arana-Daniel
MIMO SVMs for classification and regression using the
  geometric algebra framework 895

Aluizio F. R. Araujo
Ability to Skip Steps Emerging from Chaotic Dynamics 741

Daniel Araujo
Cluster Ensemble for Gene Expression Microarray Data 487

Glaucio Araujo
Neurobiological Data Sustaining Opponent Processing
  Operations on Self Organizing Networks as Tools for
  the Modeling of Hippocampal Dynamics 2135

Jeronimo Arenas-Garcia
Designing RBF classifiers for weighted Boosting 1057

Jorge Armony
Computational Models of Emotion 1598

George Aronoff
Reinforcement Learning Approach to Individualization
  of Chronic Pharmacotherapy 3290

Hideki Asai
An Efficient Learning Algorithm for Finding Multiple
  Solutions Based on Fixed-Point Homotopy Method 978

Tetsuya Asai
Analog Current-Mode Implementation of Central Pattern
  Generator for Robot Locomotion 639
Noise Performance of Single-Electron Depressing Synapses
  for Neuronal Synchrony Detection 2849

Vijayan Asari
On Using an Associative Memory for Improving Digital Color
  Images: Color Characterization, Enhancement, and Color Balancing 1830

Mauro Assis
Hybrid Neural-Phenomenological Sub-Models and its Application
  to Earth-space Path Signal Attenuation Prediction 2372

Adiel Astudillo
Cosmetic Defect Classification Found in Ophthalmic Lenses Using
  Artificial Neural Networks 2330

Snorre Aunet
Low-Voltage Pseudo Floating-Gate Reconfigurable Linear 675
Ultra Low Power Fault Tolerant Neural Inspired CMOS logic 2843

Jim Austin
A Neural Supergraph Matching Architecture 2453

Hanif Azhar
A Chaos Synchronization-Based Dynamic Vision Model
  for Image Segmentation 3075

Mahmood Azimi-Sadjadi
An Iterative Relevance Feedback Learning Algorithm
  For Image Retrieval Systems 604
Relation between Kernel CCA and Kernel FDA 226

Bruno Azzerboni
PCA and ICA for the Extraction of EEG Dominant Components
  in Cerebral Death Assessment 2532

Natasha Bagotskaya
Prediction of time to event for censored data: ridge regression with linear constraints in kernel space 1033

Tatiana Baidyk
Image Recognition Systems with Permutative Coding 1788

Volker Baier
Motion Perception with Recurrent Self-Organizing Maps Based Models 1182

Leemon Baird
One-Step Neural Network Inversion with PDF Learning and Emulation 966

Evan Balaban
Faithful Retinotopic Maps with Local Optimum Rules, Axonal Competition, and Hebbian Learning 2760

Sumitha Balasuriya
A Biologically Inspired Computational Vision Front-end based on a Self-Organised Pseudo-Randomly Tessellated Artificial Retina..........3069

Patrick Baldasare
Predicting Customer Behavior via Calling Links 2555

Shankar Baliga
Optical Flame Detection Using Large-Scale Artificial Neural Networks 1959

Rosangela Ballini
Streamflow forecasting using neural networks and fuzzy clustering techniques 2631

Tao Ban
SVM Ensembles for Selecting the Relevant Feature Subsets 943

Satarupa Banerjee
A Neuro-SVM Model for Text Classification using Latent Semantic Indexing 564

Mahmud Bani-Yaghoub
Application of Polymer Microstructures with Controlled Surface Chemistries as a Platform for Creating and Interfacing with Synthetic Neural Networks 3116

Thanasis Barbounis
Locally Recurrent Neural Networks Optimal Filtering Algorithms: Application to Wind Speed Prediction Using Spatial Correlation 2711

Raluca Barjovanu
Application of Polymer Microstructures with Controlled Surface Chemistries as a Platform for Creating and Interfacing with Synthetic Neural Networks 3116

Senen Barro
A vigilance-free ART network with general geometry internal classes 463

Ana Barros
Environmental Informatics - Long-Lead Flood Forecasting Using Bayesian Neural Networks 3133

Alan J. Barton
Virtual Reality Visual Data Mining with Nonlinear Discriminant Neural Networks: Application to Leukemia and Alzheimer Gene Expression Data 2475

Roohollah Barzamini
Short Term Load Forecasting for Iran National Power System and Its Regions Using Multi Layer Perceptron and Fuzzy Inference systems 2619

Faisal Bashir
A Motion Trajectory Based Video Retrieval System Using Parallel Adaptive Self Organizing Maps.............................1800

Gustavo Bastos
A Simpler Bayesian Network Model for Genetic Regulatory Network Inference 304

Thayne Batty
Building a Cheaper Artificial Brain........................685

Ingo Bax
Face Detection and Identification Using a Hierarchical Feed-forward Recognition Architecture 1675

Eduardo Bayro-Corrochano
MIMO SVMs for classification and regression using the geometric algebra framework 895
Object Recognition Using Neurocomputing and Conformal Computing Geometry 1872

Valeriu Beiu
On Kolmogorov's Superpositions: Novel Gates and Circuits for Nanoelectronics?........................651
Ultra Low Power Fault Tolerant Neural Inspired CMOS logic 2843

Holger Bekel
SOM Based Image Data Structuring in an Augmented Reality Scenario........................3278

Marek Belohlavek
Neural Network and Principal Component Analyses of Highly Variable Myocardial Mechanical Waveforms Derived from Echocardiographic Ultrasound Images 3017

Lotfi Ben Romdhane
Distributed Computation for Neural-Based Abductive Reasoning 833

Habib Benali
Heading For Data-Driven Measures of Effective Connectivity in Functional MRI 1528
Reorganization and Plasticity in the Adult Brain During Learning of Motor Skills 1523

Jennings Benjamin
Evolutionary Training of a Biologically Realistic Spino-neuromuscular System 280

Lubica Benuskova
A Computational Neurogenetic Model of a Spiking Neuron 446

Yngvar Berg
Low-Voltage Pseudo Floating-Gate Reconfigurable Linear 675

Theodore Berger
Replacing Damaged Brain Regions with Biomimetic Microelectronic Neural Prostheses to Restore Cognitive Function 3109

Hugues Bersini
Introduction of an Hebbian unsupervised learning algorithm 1552
Learning cycles brings chaos in continuous Hopfield networks.....................770

Alberto Bertoni
Random projections for assessing gene expression cluster stability...............149

Michael Bevan
Predicting sugar regulation in Arabidopsis thaliana using kernel learning methods 167

Valeria Bezerra
A Comparative Analysis of the Performance of Hybrid and
  Non-Hybrid Multi-classifier Systems 1941

Anindya Bhattacharya
Forgetful Logic Circuits for Pulse-Mode Neural Networks 616

Biswa Bhattacharya
Machine Learning in Soil Classification 2694
Modelling Harbour Sedimentation Using ANN and M5 Model Trees 2643

Ivan Biasi
A Reconfigurable Parallel Architecture for SVM Classification 2867

Luiz Biondi
Further Results on the EKF-CRTRL Equalizer for Fast Fading and
  Frequency Selective Channels 2367

Maheshwari Biradar
Orientated Texture Segmentation for Detecting Defects 2001

Valnaide Bittencourt
An empirical comparison of individual machine learning techniques
  and ensemble approaches in protein structural class prediction 527
Cluster Ensemble for Gene Expression Microarray Data 487

Matthias Boehm
An Algorithm for Automatic Assignment of Artifact-Related Independent
  Components in Biomedical SIgnal Analysis 2463

Zvi Boger
Optical Flame Detection Using Large-Scale Artificial Neural Networks 1959

Graeme Bonham-Carter
Time Dependent Neural Network Models For Detecting Changes
  Of State In Earth and Planetary Processes.................................1710

Andrea Boni
A Reconfigurable Parallel Architecture for SVM Classification 2867

Piero Bonissone
Fuzzy ROC Curves for Unsupervised Nonparametric Ensemble Techniques..3040

Edward Boone
The Effect of Normal Adult Aging on Standard PCA Face
  Recognition Accuracy Rates 2018

Tatjana Bortnik
Chaos and Speech Rhythm 2070

Joy Bose
An Associative Memory for the Online Recognition and
  Prediction of Temporal Sequences 1223

Mihail Bota
The Molecules Module of the Brain Architecture Management System 515

Silvia Botelho
A method to extract Non-Linear Principal Components of
  Large Datasets - An application in Skill Transfer.................................2736

Celso Bottura
Discrete-Time Systems Neuro-Riccati Equation Solution 2261

Martin Bouchard
Recurrent Neural Equalization for Communication Channels
  in Impulsive Noise Environments 3232

Sabri Boughorbel
The Intermediate Matching Kernel for Image Local Features 889

Nozha Boujemaa
The Intermediate Matching Kernel for Image Local Features 889

Mounir Boukadoum
SCRAM: Statistically Converging Recurrent Associative Memory 723

Maria Boulougoura
Neural network-based approach for the classification of
  wireless-capsule endoscopic images.................................2423

Slim Boumaiza
Application of Neural Networks to 3G Power Amplifier Modeling..............2378

Belgacem Bouzaiene-Ayari
Approximate Dynamic Programming for High Dimensional
  Resource Allocation Problems 2989

Nabila Bouzida
ICA And a Gauge of Filter for the Automatic Filtering of an EEG Signal......2508

Chris Bowerman
Spatio-Temporal Neural Data Mining Architecture in Learning Robots 2802

Giovanni Bozza
The Effects of Quantization on Support Vector Machines with
  Gaussian Kernel 681

Julien Brajard
Atmospheric correction and oceanic constituents retrieval
  with a neuro-variational method.................................1621

Almut Branner
Physiological Activation of the Hind Limb Muscles of the
  Anesthetized Cat Using the Utah Slanted Electrode Array.....................3103

Guillaume Brat
Challenges in verification and validation of autonomous
  systems for space exploration 2909

Jean-Jules Brault
Harmonic Envelope Prediction for Realistic Speech Synthesis
  Using Kernel Interpolation 2059
Implementation of an MLP-based DOA System Using a
  Reduced Number of MM-wave Antenna Elements 3220
Simulated Control of a Tracking Mobile Robot by Four
  aVLSI Integrate-and-Fire Neurons Paired into Maps 695

Diana Bravo
Fingerprint Recognition Using Modular Neural Networks
  and Fuzzy Integrals for Response Integration.................................2589

David Brawn
Multi-class Support Vector Machines for Modeling HIV/AIDS Treatment
  Adherence using Patient Data 2417

Michael Brier
Reinforcement Learning Approach to Individualization of Chronic
  Pharmacotherapy.................................3290

Alisson V. de Brito
A novel Approach to reduce Interconnect Complexity in
  ANN Hardware Implementation 2861

Alceu Britto Jr.
Optimizing Class-Related Thresholds with Particle Swarm Optimization 1511

Keith E. Brown
Classification and Verification through the Combination of the Multi-Layer
 Perceptron and Auto-Association Neural Networks 1166

Michael Brueckner
A Soft Bayes Perceptron 2064
The p-Center Machine 1000

Luiz Brunelli
A novel Approach to reduce Interconnect Complexity
 in ANN Hardware Implementation 2861

Gioacchino Brunetti
An Automatic Method to Detect Missing Components in
 Manufactured Products 2324

Luciana P. P. Bueno
Ability to Skip Steps Emerging from Chaotic Dynamics........................741

Daniel Bullock
Modeling Cortico-Subcortical Interactions During Planning,
 Learning, and Voluntary Control of Actions 1653

Baptiste Bullot
Comparison of Linear and Non-linear Data Projection
 Techniques in Recognizing Universal Facial Expressions 3087

Timothy Bumpus
Classification of Plantar Pressure and Heel Acceleration
 Patterns Using Neural Networks 3007

Joel Burdick
Getting Better Signals Out of the Brain: Decoding
 Algorithms and Autonomous Electrodes 3115

Keith Bush
Modeling Reward Functions for Incomplete State
 Representations via Echo State Networks 2995
Optimizing Neural Model Templates using Covariance
 Matrix Adaptation and Fourier Analysis 2162

Sylvain Busson
Individualized HRTFs From Few Measurements: a Statistical
 Learning Approach 2041

Qutang Cai
Learning Probability Density Functions from Marginal Distributions with
 Applications to Gaussian Mixtures 1148

Wenjian Cai
Real-time Control of Variable Air Volume System Using a
 SPSA Based Neural Controller..2255
Supply Air Temperature Control of AHU with a Cascade
 Control Strategy and a SPSA Based Neural Controller 2243

Xindi Cai
Engine Data Classification with Simultaneous Recurrent
 Network Using a Hybrid PSO-EA Algorithm 2319

Lee Calcraft
Evolving High Capacity Associative Memories with Efficient Wiring............3168

Jerome Callut
Fbeta Support Vector Machines 1443

Luiz Caloba
Hybrid Neural-Phenomenological Sub-Models and its
 Application to Earth-space Path Signal Attenuation Prediction 2372

David Calvert
Detection of Disease Outbreaks in Pharmaceutical Sales:
 Neural Networks and Threshold Algorithms 3138

Fatih Camci
Dynamic Bayesian Networks for Machine Diagnostics:
 Hierarchical Hidden Markov Models vs. Competitive Learning 1752

Haroldo Fraga Campos Velho
A multilayer perceptron approach for the retrieval of
 vertical temperature profiles from satellite radiation data 2689

Alex Cannon
Nonlinear Principal Predictor Analysis Using Neural Networks 1630

Anne Canuto
A Comparative Analysis of the Performance of Hybrid
 and Non-Hybrid Multi-classifier Systems 1941
An empirical comparison of individual machine learning
 techniques and ensemble approaches in protein
 structural class prediction 527

Jaime Cardoso
SVMs Applied to Objective Aesthetic Evaluation of
 Conservative Breast Cancer Treatment 2481

Maria Joao Cardoso
SVMs Applied to Objective Aesthetic Evaluation of
 Conservative Breast Cancer Treatment 2481

Gail Carpenter
Brain Categorization: Learning, Attention, and Consciousness....................1609
Self-Organizing Hierarchical Knowledge Discovery
 by an ARTMAP Information Fusion System 452

Otavio Carpinteiro
A hierarchical hybrid neural model with time
 integrators in long-term peak-load forecasting 2960

James Carroll
Task Similarity Measures for Transfer in Reinforcement
 Learning Task Libraries 803

Joao Carlos Carvalho
A multilayer perceptron approach for the retrieval of
 vertical temperature profiles from satellite radiation data 2689

David Casasent
Automatic Target Recognition Using New Support Vector Machine 84
Pruning Support Vectors for Imbalanced Data Classification 1883

Claudio Castellanos-Sanchez
Digital Implementation of a Bio-inspired Neural Model for Motion Estimation....3255

Oscar Castillo
Face Recognition Using Modular Neural Networks and
 Fuzzy Sugeno Integral for Response Integration..........................349
Fingerprint Recognition Using Modular Neural Networks
 and Fuzzy Integrals for Response Integration..............................2589
Optimization of Modular Neural Networks Using
 Hierarchical Genetic Algorithms Applied to Speech Recognition 1400

Bernardino Castillo-Toledo
On Output Regulation for SISO Nonlinear Systems with Dynamic Neural
 Networks 372

Jose Castro
Parallelizing the Fuzzy ARTMAP Algorithm on a Beowulf Cluster 475

Angel Cataron
Feature Ranking using Supervised Neural Gas and Informational Energy 1269

Thomas Caudell
Modification of the ART-1 Architecture Based on Category
  Theoretic Design Principles 457

Gavin Cawley
A Simple Trick for Constructing Bayesian Formulations of
  Sparse Kernel Learning Methods 1425
Predicting sugar regulation in Arabidopsis thaliana using
  kernel learning methods 167
Sparse Bayesian learning and the relevance multi-layer perceptron 1320

Wang Ce
Building a Cheaper Artificial Brain 685

Michal Cernansky
Feed-forward Echo State Networks 1479

Mario Chacon
Cosmetic Defect Classification Found in Ophthalmic
  Lenses Using Artificial Neural Networks 2330

Amit Chadha
Parallelizing the Fuzzy ARTMAP Algorithm on a Beowulf Cluster 475

Des Chambers
Bayesian ANN Classifier for ECG Arrhythmia Diagnostic System:
  A Comparison Study 2383

Pinaki Chanda
Low Order Modeling for Multiple Moving Sound Synthesis using
  Head-related Transfer Functions' Principal Basis Vectors 2036

Darby Tien-Hau Chang
Data Classification with a Relaxed Model of Variable Kernel
  Density Estimation 2831

Jyh-Yeong Chang
A New Scene Analysis Using Genetic Algorithm Based
  Fuzzy ID3 Method 1770

Tzyy-Shuh Chang
Identifying knowledge domain and incremental new
  class learning in SVM 2742

Zhang Changshui
Spectral Feature Analysis 1971

Pornchai Chanyagorn
Collective Behavior Implementation in Powerline
  Surveillance Sensor Network 1735

Arnaud Charil
Connectivity of anatomical and functional MRI data 1534

Sylvain Chartier
SCRAM: Statistically Converging Recurrent Associative Memory 723

Narendra S. Chaudhari
Fast Constructive-Covering Approach for Neural Networks 2167
Neural Network-Based Analysis of DNA Microarray Data 503
Nonlinear Channel Equalization with QAM Signal
  Using Chebyshev Artificial Neural Network 3214
Protein Secondary Structure Prediction with a Hybrid
  RNN/HMM System 538

Chien-Yu Chen
A Novel Radial Basis Function Network Classifier with Centers
  Set by Hierarchical Clustering 1383
Data Classification with a Relaxed Model of Variable
  Kernel Density Estimation 2831

Ching-Han Chen
Low Complexity Iris Recognition Based on Wavelet
  Probabilistic Neural Networks 1930

Jeremy Chen
Protein Flexibility Modeling Using Kernel Based Methods 521

Jinmiao Chen
Protein Secondary Structure Prediction with a
  Hybrid RNN/HMM System 538

Liang Chen
Pattern Classification by Assembling Small Neural Networks 1947

Mingming Chen
A Single-Layer Radial Basis Function Network
  Classifier and Its Applications 1045

Peng Chen
Predicting Protein-Protein Interactions Based on
  Protein-Domain Relationships 316
Prediction of Contact Map Integrated PNN with Conformational Energy 499

Shin-Kuan Chen
Skin Color Segmentation by Histogram-Based
  Neural Fuzzy Network 3058
Temporal Hand Gesture Recognition By Fuzzified
  TSK-Type Recurrent Fuzzy Network 1848

Wei Chen
A Classifier Ensemble Model and Its Applications 1172

Xilin Chen
Learning Informative Features for Spatial
  Histogram-Based Object Detection 1806

Xue-wen Chen
Protein Flexibility Modeling Using Kernel Based Methods 521
Pruning Support Vectors for Imbalanced Data Classification 1883

ZhiHang Chen
Protein secondary structure prediction using machine learning 532

Mohamed Cheriet
Estimating Accurate Multi-class Probabilities with
  Support Vector Machines 1906
Fast Training of Multilayer Perceptrons with a Mixed Norm Algorithm 1018
Optimizing Resources in Model Selection for Support Vectors Machines 925

Vladimir Cherkassky
A Combined SVM and LDA Approach for Classification 1455
Characterization of Data Complexity for SVM Methods 919
Panel discussion: Applications of Learning and Data-Driven
  Methods to Earth Sciences and Climate Modeling 1728

Pak-Ming Cheung
Kernel Relevant Component Analysis for Distance Metric Learning 954

Baoyong Chi
Circuit Implementation of Multi-Thresholded Neuron (MTN)
  Using BiCMOS Technology 627

Tung-Sheng Chiang
Adaptive Tanaka-Sugeno Fuzzy Cerebellar Model Articulation
  Controller for Output Tracking Control 2284
Robust Output Tracking CMAC Control: The T-S Fuzzy
  Model-Based Approach 2290

Ernesto Chiarantoni
An Automatic Method to Detect Missing Components in
  Manufactured Products 2324

Youcef Chibani
Fuzzy integral for a rapid mixture of support vector machines 901

Xiang-Fang Chin
Finding a Succinct Multi-layer Perceptron Having Shared Weights 1418

Ratna Babu Chinnam
Dynamic Bayesian Networks for Machine Diagnostics:
  Hierarchical Hidden Markov Models vs. Competitive Learning 1752

Chian-Song Chiu
Adaptive Tanaka-Sugeno Fuzzy Cerebellar Model Articulation
  Controller for Output Tracking Control 2284
Robust Output Tracking CMAC Control: The T-S Fuzzy
  Model-Based Approach 2290

Chien-Wen Cho
A New Scene Analysis Using Genetic Algorithm
  Based Fuzzy ID3 Method 1770

Yoonsuck Choe
Facilitatory Neural Activity Compensating for Neural
  Delays as a Potential Cause of the Flash-Lag Effect 268

Chong-Ho Choi
Combined Subspace Method Using Global and Local
  Features for Face Recognition 2030

Jinhyuk Choi
The Bifurcating Neuron Network 3 2184

Jongsoo Choi
Recurrent Neural Equalization for Communication
  Channels in Impulsive Noise Environments 3232

Florence Choong
FPGA Realization of Power Quality Disturbance Detection:
  An Approach with Wavelet, ANN and Fuzzy Logic 2613

Vincent Choqueuse
Individualized HRTFs From Few Measurements: a Statistical
  Learning Approach 2041

Ming-Dah Chou
Robustness of the NN Approach to Emulating Atmospheric
  Long Wave Radiation in Complex Climate Models 2661

Eliane Christo
Neurobiological Data Sustaining Opponent Processing
  Operations on Self Organizing Networks as Tools for
  the Modeling of Hippocampal Dynamics 2135

Canine Christopher
Evolutionary Training of a Biologically Realistic
  Spino-neuromuscular System 280

Chia-Chin Chu
Indirect Field-oriented Linear Induction Motor Drive with
  Petri Fuzzy-neural-network Control 378

Chia-Te Chu
Low Complexity Iris Recognition Based on Wavelet
  Probabilistic Neural Networks 1930

Opas Chutatape
A SVM Approach for Detection of Hemorrhages in
  Background Diabetic Retinopathy 2435

Angelo Ciaramella
BSS Toolbox for Delayed and Convolved Mixtures 1245
Data Visualization Methodologies for Data
  Mining Systems in Bioinformatics 143

Paul Cisek
A computational model of reach decisions in the
  primate cerebral cortex 1648

Gregory Clark
Aircraft Cabin Noise Minimization via Neural Network Inverse Model 2341
Physiological Activation of the Hind Limb Muscles of the
  Anesthetized Cat Using the Utah Slanted Electrode Array 3103

Fabrice Clerot
Individualized HRTFs From Few Measurements: a
  Statistical Learning Approach 2041

Pedro Coelho
Further Results on the EKF-CRTRL Equalizer for Fast Fading
  and Frequency Selective Channels 2367

Paul Conilione
Effect of Non-Target Examples on E.coli Promoters Recognition
  Using Neural Networks 310

Michael Corwin
Reliable Determination of Sleep Versus Wake from Heart
  Rate Variability Using Neural Networks 2394

Elaine Costa
Input and Data Selection Applied to Heart Disease Diagnosis 2389

Isabele Costa
Embedded FastICA Algorithm Applied to the Sensor Noise
  Extraction Problem of Foundation Fieldbus Network 2217

Paulin Coulibaly
Streamflow Forecasting with Uncertainty Estimate Using Bayesian
  Learning for ANN 2680
Temporal Neural Networks for Downscaling Climate Variability
  and Extremes 1636

Denis Cousineau
Learning of an XOR Problem in the Presence of Noise and Redundancy 2111

Krzysztof Cpalka
Flexible Takagi-Sugeno Fuzzy Systems 1764

Louis-Philippe Crevier
A framework for the verification of air quality forecasting
  models using self-organizing feature maps 2302

Sven Crone
Evolutionary Neural Classification for Evaluation of
  Retail Stores and Decision Support 1499

Ernesto Cuadros-Vargas
Introduction to the SAM-SOM* and MAM-SOM* Families 2966

Bojan Cukic
An Approach To Predicting Non-Deterministic
   Neural Network Behavior 2921
Validity Index in Dynamic Cell Structures 2931

Yaser H. Dakrowry
Performance of Neural Classifiers for Fabric Faults Classification..........1995

Florence d'Alche-Buc
Time Series Filtering, Smoothing and Learning using the
   Kernel Kalman Filter 1449

James Dankert
An Analysis of Gradient-Based Policy Iteration 2977

Eric Danneville
Implementation of an MLP-based DOA System Using a
   Reduced Number of MM-wave Antenna Elements 3220

Jorge Dantas de Melo
Embedded FastICA Algorithm Applied to the Sensor Noise
   Extraction Problem of Foundation Fieldbus Network...........2217
The k-Server Problem: A Reinforcement Learning Approach..........798

Paolo Dario
New Memory Model for Humanoid Robots -Introduction of Co-Associative
   Memory Using Mutually Coupled Chaotic Neural Networks-........2790

Marjorie Darrah
Rule Extraction as a Formal Method for the Verification and
   Validation of Neural Networks 2915

Amitabha Das
A Fast Neural Network-Based Detection and Tracking of
   Dim Moving Targets in FLIR Imagery...........................3144
Neural Networks for Gene Expression Analysis and Gene
   Selection from DNA Microarray 509
Nonlinear Channel Equalization with QAM Signal Using
   Chebyshev Artificial Neural Network 3214
Post Nonlinear Blind Source Separation by Geometric Linearization 244

Neil Davey
Evolving High Capacity Associative Memories with Efficient Wiring.........3168

Christian Dawson
A Comparative Study of Artificial Neural Network
   Techniques for River Stage Forecasting 2666
Neural Network Modelling of the 20-Year Flood Event for
   850 Catchments Across the UK 2637

Rodrigo de Bem
A method to extract Non-Linear Principal Components of
   Large Datasets - An application in Skill Transfer...............2736

Jos De Brabanter
Maximal Variation and Missing Values for Componentwise
   Support Vector Machines 2814

Rui de Figueiredo
The Role of the RKH Space F in the Analysis and Design of
   Recurrent Neural Networks 1473

Hugo de Garis
Building a Cheaper Artificial Brain................................685

Bart De Moor
Maximal Variation and Missing Values for Componentwise
   Support Vector Machines 2814

Marcilio de Souto
A Comparative Analysis of the Performance of Hybrid and
   Non-Hybrid Multi-classifier Systems 1941
An empirical comparison of individual machine learning
   techniques and ensemble approaches in protein
   structural class prediction 527
Cluster Ensemble for Gene Expression Microarray Data 487

Sam Deadwyler
Replacing Damaged Brain Regions with Biomimetic Microelectronic
   Neural Prostheses to Restore Cognitive Function 3109

Yasuhiro Dejima
Analysis of Signal Separation and Signal Distortion in Feedforward and
   Feedback Blind Source Separation Based on Source Spectra 1257

Oleksiy Dekhtyarenko
Systematic Rewiring in Associative Neural Networks with Small-World
   Architecture..1178

Guido Del Vescovo
A Symbolic Approach to the Solution of F-Classification Problems 1953

Thomas DeMarse
Adaptive Flight Control with Living Neuronal Networks on
   Microelectrode Arrays 1548
Towards the Modeling of Dissociated Cortical Tissue in the
   Liquid State Machine Framework 2179

James Demmel
Second-order backpropagation algorithms for a
   stagewise-partitioned separable Hessian matrix................1027

Reza Derakhshani
GETnet: A General Framework for Evolutionary
   Temporal Neural Networks 3150

Manish Deshmukh
A Novel Fuzzy Clustering Neural Network 1989
Fourier Fuzzy Neural Network for Clustering of
   Objects Based on the Gross Shape and its
   Application to Handwritten Character Recognition..............1918
Modular General Hyperline Segment Neural Network 1912

Guy Desjardins
A Self-Organizing Map for Concept Classification
   in Information Retrieval 1570

Ezequiel Di Paolo
Constraints on Body Movement during Visual Development
   Affect Behavior of Evolutionary Robots 2778

Yonas Dibike
Temporal Neural Networks for Downscaling Climate
   Variability and Extremes 1636

Werner Dilger
A Soft Bayes Perceptron 2064

Nikitas J. Dimopoulos
A Neural Network-based Prediction Model of AR Inhibitory
   Activity from a Sparse Set of Compounds 2411

Ivan Dimov
Could Early Visual Processes be Sufficient to Label Motions?..........1687

Michael Dittenbach
Investigation of Alternative Strategies and Quality Measures
  for Controlling the Growth Process of the Growing
  Hierarchical Self-Organizing Map 2954

Karl Dockendorf
Adaptive Flight Control with Living Neuronal Networks
  on Microelectrode Arrays 1548

Peggy Doerschuk
A Simple Hierarchical Approximation RBF Neural Network 1389

Jianxiong Dong
Algorithms of Fast SVM Evaluation based on Subspace Projection 865

Adriao Doria Duarte Neto
Embedded FastICA Algorithm Applied to the Sensor Noise
  Extraction Problem of Foundation Fieldbus Network 2217
The k-Server Problem: A Reinforcement Learning Approach 798

Rene Doursat
Bridging the Gap Between Vision and Language:
  A Morphodynamical Model of Spatial Categories 2903

Julien Doyon
Heading For Data-Driven Measures of Effective Connectivity
  in Functional MRI 1528
Reorganization and Plasticity in the Adult Brain During
  Learning of Motor Skills 1523

John Drakopoulos
Training with Heterogeneous Data 90

Stuart Dreyfus
Second-order backpropagation algorithms for a stagewise-partitioned
  separable Hessian matrix 1027

Michael Drumheller
Testing Decision Systems with Classification Components 2927

Ji-Xiang Du
Neural Network-based Shape Recognition using Generalized
  Differential Evolution Training Algorithm 2012

Baofu Duan
Iterative Feature Weighting for Identification of Relevant Features
  with Radial Basis Function Networks 1063

Jeffrey Dungen
Simulated Control of a Tracking Mobile Robot by Four aVLSI
  Integrate-and-Fire Neurons Paired into Maps 695

Pierre Dupont
Fbeta Support Vector Machines 1443

Rolf Eckmiller
Optimization of a learning algorithm for tactile pattern generation 2087

Victoria Edge
Detection of Disease Outbreaks in Pharmaceutical Sales:
  Neural Networks and Threshold Algorithms 3138

Hazem EL-Bakry
A Modified Frequency Domain Cross Correlation Implemented
  in MATLAB for Fast Sub-Image Detection Using Neural Networks 1794
Fast Pattern Detection Using Neural Networks and Cross
  Correlation in the Frequency Domain 1900
Normalized Neural Networks for Fast Pattern Detection 1889

Mourad Elhadef
Distributed Computation for Neural-Based Abductive Reasoning 833

Mostafa A. El-Hemaly
Negative Reinforcement and Backtrack-Points for Recurrent
  Neural Networks for Cost-Based Abduction 827

Victor Eliashberg
Ensembles of membrane proteins as statistical mixed-signal computers 2173

Mark Elshaw
Spatio-Temporal Neural Data Mining Architecture in Learning Robots 2802

Amin Elshorbagy
Wavelet Networks: An Alternative to Classical Neural Networks 2674

Mark Embrechts
Fuzzy ROC Curves for Unsupervised Nonparametric
  Ensemble Techniques 3040

Takahiro Emoto
Tracking the States of a Nonlinear System in the Weight-Space
  of a Feed-Forward Neural Network 96

Paulo Cesar Endo Joaquim
Artificial Neural Networks for Temporal Processing Applied to Prediction
  of Electric Energy Generation in Small Hydroelectric Power Stations 2625

Abdellatif Ennaji
Incremental growing neural gas learns topologies 1211

Deniz Erdogmus
Feature Selection by Independent Component Analysis
  and Mutual Information Maximization in EEG Signal Classification 3011
Maximally Discriminative Spectral Feature Projections
  Using Mutual Information 208

Bilgin Ersoy
Brain Categorization: Learning, Attention, and Consciousness 1609

Harry Erwin
A Recurrent Neural Network for Sound-Source Motion Tracking
  and Prediction 2232

Pablo A. Estevez
Color Image Segmentation Using Fuzzy Min-Max Neural Networks 3052
Cross-Entropy Approach to Data Visualization Based on the
  Neural Gas Network 2724
Non-Linear Mappings Based on Particle Swarm Optimization 1487

Steven Estrada
Modeling Emotional Influences on Human Decision Making Under Risk 1657

Paul Evangelista
Fuzzy ROC Curves for Unsupervised Nonparametric Ensemble Techniques 3040

Alan Evans
Connectivity of anatomical and functional MRI data 1534

Karim Faid
Application of Polymer Microstructures with Controlled
  Surface Chemistries as a Platform for Creating and Interfacing
  with Synthetic Neural Networks 3116

Tasos Falas
Symbolic Rule Extraction with a Scaled Conjugate Gradient
  Version of CLARION 845

Michael Fassino
Predicting Customer Behavior via Calling Links 2555

Diego Federici
Fault-tolerance by Regeneration: Using Development to
  Achieve Robust Self-Healing Neural Networks..................................2808

Wang Fei
Spectral Feature Analysis 1971

Christy Fernandez
Independent Component Analysis Applications in Physics......................2213

Manuel Fernandez-Delgado
A vigilance-free ART network with general geometry internal classes 463

Mercedes Fernandez-Redondo
A Comparison of Combination Methods for Ensembles of RBF Networks 1137
A Research on Combination Methods for Ensembles of
  Multilayer Feedforward 1125
New Experiments on Ensembles of Multilayer Feedforward
  for Classification Problems 1120

Aida Ferreira
A comparative study of neural network to artificial noses 2081

Anibal R. Figueiras-Vidal
Designing RBF classifiers for weighted Boosting......................................1057

Mateus Figueiredo
A method to extract Non-Linear Principal Components of
  Large Datasets - An application in Skill Transfer...............................2736

Cristian J. Figueroa
Cross-Entropy Approach to Data Visualization Based on the
  Neural Gas Network 2724
Non-Linear Mappings Based on Particle Swarm Optimization 1487

John Flanagan
Robust Continuous Learning in a WTA Neural Network for
  Clustering Symbol Strings 1217

Alexandru Floares
Feedback Linearization Using Neural Networks Applied to Advanced
  Pharmacodynamic and Pharmacogenomic Systems 173

Dario Floreano
Constraints on Body Movement during Visual Development Affect
  Behavior of Evolutionary Robots 2778

Rodrigo J. Flores
Color Image Segmentation Using Fuzzy Min-Max Neural Networks............3052

Farhat Fnaiech
Fast Training of Multilayer Perceptrons with a Mixed Norm Algorithm 1018

Eric Fock
A new saliency measure for inputs selection and node pruning
  in neural network 960

Anatoly Fonarev
Decorrelating Parametrical Neural Network 1023

Girolamo Fornarelli
An Automatic Method to Detect Missing Components in
  Manufactured Products 2324

Pierre-Alexandre Fournier
Harmonic Envelope Prediction for Realistic Speech Synthesis
  Using Kernel Interpolation 2059

Michael Fox-Rabinovitz
Complex Hybrid Models Combining Deterministic and Machine
  Learning Components as a New Synergetic Paradigm in
  Numerical Climate Modeling and Weather Prediction 1615
Robustness of the NN Approach to Emulating Atmospheric
  Long Wave Radiation in Complex Climate Models 2661

Nickolaos Fragopanagos
Modelling the Interaction of Attention and Emotion 1663

Roseli Francelin
Introduction to the SAM-SOM* and MAM-SOM* Families 2966

Andrew Frank
Application of a CMAC Neural Network to the Control
  of a Parallel Hybrid-Electric Propulsion System for a
  Small Unmanned Aerial Vehicle...355

Walter Freeman
Cinematographic Construction by Brains of Knowledge from Information 120
Temporal Discontinuities in Neocortical Dynamics 3156

Raimundo C. S. Freire
A novel Approach to reduce Interconnect Complexity in
  ANN Hardware Implementation 2861

Roman Fresnedo
Testing Decision Systems with Classification Components 2927

Herve Frezza-Buet
Coherent learning in cortical maps: A generic approach 2885

Holger Froehlich
Assignment Kernels For Chemical Compounds..913
Efficient Parameter Selection for Support Vector Machines in
  Classification and Regression via Model-Based Global Optimization 1431
Functional Grouping of Genes Using Spectral Clustering
  and Gene Ontology...298
Which Features Trigger Action Potentials in Cortical Neurons in Vivo?..........250

Shoichiro Fujisawa
Design and Experimental Evaluation of a 3-Mass Speed Control
  System with a Hybrid Structure of Sliding Mode Controller and CMAC ..2272

Yukari Fujita
Quantum Gauged Neural Networks: Learning and Recalling 1108

Kunihiko Fukushima
Neural Network Model for Analyzing Optic Flow 1669

Edgar Fuller
An Approach To Predicting Non-Deterministic Neural Network Behavior 2921

Steve Furber
An Associative Memory for the Online Recognition and
  Prediction of Temporal Sequences 1223

Tetsuo Furukawa
Modular Network SOM (mnSOM): From Vector Space to Function Space ..1581

Richard Gagne
Creation of Long-term Mental Representations using the
  Dimension of Fractal dendrites...2129

Simon Gagne
Creation of Long-term Mental Representations using the
  Dimension of Fractal dendrites 2129

Aliasgar Gangardiwala
Dynamically Weighted Majority Voting for Incremental
  Learning and Comparison of Three Boosting Based Approaches 1131

Daqi Gao
A Classifier Ensemble Model and Its Applications 1172
A Combinative Function Approximation Model and Its
  Applications to Electronic Noses 2093
A Single-Layer Radial Basis Function Network Classifier
  and Its Applications 1045
An Improved Kernel Fisher Discriminant Classifier and
  Its Applications 1274

Dayong Gao
Bayesian ANN Classifier for ECG Arrhythmia Diagnostic System:
  A Comparison Study 2383

Wen Gao
Learning Informative Features for Spatial Histogram-Based
  Object Detection 1806

Zhi Gao
Continuous On-line Identification of Nonlinear Plants in
  Power Systems with Missing Sensor Measurements 1729

Joao Luis Garcia Rosa
BioAnt - Biologically Plausible Computer Simulation of an
  Environment with Ants 1505

Paolo Gastaldo
DSP-Based Neural Systems for the Perceptual Assessment of Visual Quality .. 663

Stephane Gaudreault
A framework for the verification of air quality forecasting
  models using self-organizing feature maps 2302

Vincent Gautier
Visual Deficiency: Cognitive Performance and Adaptive Image Processing .. 1824

Adam Gaweda
Reinforcement Learning Approach to Individualization of Chronic
  Pharmacotherapy 3290

Martin Geike
Emulation Engine for Spiking Neurons and Adaptive Synaptic Weights 3261

Abraham George
Approximate Dynamic Programming for High Dimensional
  Resource Allocation Problems 2989

Dileep George
A Hierarchical Bayesian Model of Invariant Pattern Recognition
  in the Visual Cortex 1812

Michael Georgiopoulos
An Experimental Comparison of Semi-Supervised ARTMAP
  Architectures, GCS and GNG Classifiers 3121
Parallelizing the Fuzzy ARTMAP Algorithm on a Beowulf Cluster 475

Greg Gerhardt
Replacing Damaged Brain Regions with Biomimetic
  Microelectronic Neural Prostheses to Restore Cognitive Function 3109

Byron Gerlach
Pruning Support Vectors for Imbalanced Data Classification 1883

Mark Gerstein
Inferring Protein-Protein Interactions Using Interaction Network Topologies 161

Fadhel M. Ghannouchi
Application of Neural Networks to 3G Power Amplifier Modeling 2378

Peter Gibbs
Feasibility of multi-layered perceptron network in discriminating
  breast magnetic resonance imaging lesions 2493

Robin Gilbert
Maximum Margin Classifiers with Noisy Data: A Robust Optimization 2826

Domingos Savio Giordani
Artificial neural networks associated to calorimetry to preview
  polymer composition of high solid content emulsion copolymerizations .. 2237

Bernard Girau
Digital Implementation of a Bio-inspired Neural Model for
  Motion Estimation 3255

Ramunas Girdziusas
Gaussian Processes of Nonlinear Diffusion Filtering 1012

Robert Godin
A Self-Organizing Map for Concept Classification in
  Information Retrieval 1570

Carl Gold
Fast Bayesian Support Vector Machine Parameter Tuning
  with the Nystrom Method 2820

Dinani Gomes
A vigilance-free ART network with general geometry internal classes 463

Felipe Gomez-Castaneda
Prototype Robotic Arm Assisted by Smart CMOS Vision Chips 2296

Eduardo Gomez-Sanchez
On the design of an Ellipsoid ARTMAP classifier within the
  Fuzzy Adaptive System ART Framework 469

Vanessa Gomez-Verdejo
Designing RBF classifiers for weighted Boosting 1057

Claudia Gonzalez
Face Recognition Using Modular Neural Networks and Fuzzy
  Sugeno Integral for Response Integration 349

Felma Gonzalez
Face Recognition Using Modular Neural Networks and Fuzzy
  Sugeno Integral for Response Integration 349

Eric Goodman
Effectively Using Recurrently-Connected Spiking Neural Networks 1542

Chandan Gope
Neural Network Classification of EEG Signals using Time-Frequency
  Representation 2502

Anatoli Gorchetchnikov
Spatially and Temporally Local Spike-Timing-Dependent Plasticity Rule 390

Marco Gori
A New Model for Learning in Graph Domains 729

Dmitry Gorodnichy
Associative neural networks as means for low-resolution
  video-based recognition 3093

Dilip Goswami
Towards the Modeling of Dissociated Cortical Tissue in the
    Liquid State Machine Framework 2179

Stanley Gotshall
Evolutionary Training of a Biologically Realistic
    Spino-neuromuscular System 280

John Granacki
Replacing Damaged Brain Regions with Biomimetic
    Microelectronic Neural Prostheses to Restore Cognitive Function 3109

Eric Granger
Factors of Overtraining with Fuzzy ARTMAP Neural Networks 1075

Daniel Graupe
A Motion Trajectory Based Video Retrieval System Using
    Parallel Adaptive Self Organizing Maps 1800

Alex Graves
Framewise Phoneme Classification with Bidirectional LSTM Networks 2047

Patrick Griep
Emulation Engine for Spiking Neurons and Adaptive Synaptic Weights 3261

Stephen Grossberg
Brain Categorization: Learning, Attention, and Consciousness 1609

Ralph Grothmann
Dynamical Consistent Recurrent Neural Networks 1537

Peter Gruber
An Algorithm for Automatic Assignment of Artifact-Related
    Independent Components in Biomedical Signal Analysis 2463
On the Use of Clustering and Local Singular Spectrum Analysis
    to Remove Ocular Artifacts from Electroencephalograms 2514

Xiao Gu
Neural Network-based Shape Recognition using Generalized
    Differential Evolution Training Algorithm 2012

Xiaodong Gu
General Design Approach to Unit-linking PCNN for Image Processing 1836

Ling Guan
Dynamic Feature Fusion in the Self Organising Tree Map -
    applied to the segmentation of Biofilm Images 2441
Using Knowledge of the Region of Interest (ROI) in Automatic
    Image Retrieval Learning 1854

Xavier Guilbeault
A framework for the verification of air quality forecasting
    models using self-organizing feature maps 2302

Katia Guimaraes
A Simpler Bayesian Network Model for Genetic Regulatory
    Network Inference 304

Chengyi Guo
Real-time Control of Variable Air Volume System Using a
    SPSA Based Neural Controller 2255
Supply Air Temperature Control of AHU with a Cascade
    Control Strategy and a SPSA Based Neural Controller 2243

Wei Guo
Predictive Control Based on Feedforward Neural Network
    for Strong Nonlinear System 2266

Priyank Gupta
Forgetful Logic Circuits for Pulse-Mode Neural Networks 616

Srikanth Gururajan
An Approach To Predicting Non-Deterministic Neural Network Behavior 2921
Validity Index in Dynamic Cell Structures 2931

Daniel Gutchess
Identifying knowledge domain and incremental new class
    learning in SVM 2742

Glenn Guthrie
Detection of Disease Outbreaks in Pharmaceutical Sales:
    Neural Networks and Threshold Algorithms 3138

Ricardo Gutierrez-Osuna
Mixture Segmentation and Background Suppression in
    Chemosensor Arrays with a Model of Olfactory Bulb-Cortex interaction 131

Eyasu Habtemariam
Artificial Intelligence for Conflict Management 2583

Shi Haixiang
A Hybrid Neural Network for Optimal TDMA Transmission
    Scheduling in Packet Radio Networks 3210

John Hallam
Increased Swimming Control with Evolved Lamprey CPG Controllers 2195

Fredric Ham
Classification of Infrasound Events Using Using Radial Basis
    Function Neural Networks 2649

Hiroshi Hamanaka
Novel Digital Spiking Neuron and its Pulse-Coupled Network:
    Spike Position Coding and Multiplex Communication 3249

Emily Hamilton
Neural Network Based Detection of Fetal Heart Rate Patterns 2400

Andrew Hamilton-Wright
Comparing "Pattern Discovery" and Back-Propagation Classifiers 1286

Dongho Han
Sparse Channel Estimation With Regularization Method Using
    Convolution Inequality For Entropy 2359

Il Song Han
Biologically plausible VLSI neural network implementation
    with asynchronous neuron and spike-based synapse 3244

Jun-Hua Han
A Novel Image Retrieval System Based on BP Neural Network 2561

Min Han
Analyzing the State Space Property of Echo State Networks for
    Chaotic System Prediction 1412
Predictive Control Based on Feedforward Neural Network for
    Strong Nonlinear System 2266

Thomas Hanselmann
Continuous Adaptive Critic Desigs 3001

Ronald G. Harley
Continuous On-line Identification of Nonlinear Plants in Power
    Systems with Missing Sensor Measurements 1729
System and Method for Determining Harmonic Contributions
    from Non-Linear Loads Using Recurrent Neural Networks 366

Frederick Harmon
Application of a CMAC Neural Network to the Control of a
    Parallel Hybrid-Electric Propulsion System for a Small
    Unmanned Aerial Vehicle 355

Derek Harter
Evolving Neurodynamic Controllers for Autonomous Robots 137

Matthew Hartley
Attention as Sigma-Pi Controlled Ach-Based Feedback 256
Knowing your place: Subfield specific involvement in hippocampal
    spatial processing 2879

Markus Harva
A Variational Bayesian Method for Rectified Factor Analysis 185

Mohammed Hasan
Diagonally Weighted and Shifted Criteria for Minor and Principal
    Component Extraction 1251
Weighted Rayleigh Quotients for Minor and Principal
    Component Extraction 1263

Md. Hasanuzzaman
Blind Separation of Convolved Sources using the Information
    Maximization Approach 1239

Shuji Hashimoto
On the Evaluation of Relevance Learning by a Multi-layer Perceptron 3204

Deena O. Hassan
Experimental Evaluation of a Hybrid Method for Configuring
    Ensemble Encoding Receptors 989

Michael E. Hasselmo
An Integrate and Fire Model of Prefrontal Cortex provides a
    Biological Implementation of Action Selection in
    Reinforcement Learning Theory that Reuses Known Representations 2873
Hebbian Synaptic Modification in Cortical Circuits and
    Memory-Guided Behavior in Spatial Alternation and
    Delayed Non-Match to Position 2754
Spatially and Temporally Local Spike-Timing-Dependent Plasticity Rule 390

Mohamad Hassoun
A Weighted Voting Model of Associative Memory: Theoretical Analysis 1193

Jeff Hawkins
A Hierarchical Bayesian Model of Invariant Pattern
    Recognition in the Visual Cortex 1812

Yoshihiro Hayakawa
Retrieval Property of Associative Memory with Negative Resistance 1187

Hatsuo Hayashi
Synchronized Theta Rhythm Selection in a Dentate Gyrus Network Model 405

Terumine Hayashi
Dynamic construction of fault tolerant multi-layer neural networks} 995

Yongbao He
Learning a Hierarchical Fuzzy System with Autonomous
    Navigation as an Example 3063

Michael Healy
Modification of the ART-1 Architecture Based on Category
    Theoretic Design Principles 457

Gunther Heidemann
Face Detection and Identification Using a Hierarchical
    Feed-forward Recognition Architecture 1675
SOM Based Image Data Structuring in an Augmented Reality Scenario 3278

Sebastien Helie
SCRAM: Statistically Converging Recurrent Associative Memory 723

Heik Heinrich Hellmich
Emulation Engine for Spiking Neurons and Adaptive Synaptic Weights 3261

James Henderson
Deriving Kernels from MLP Probability Estimators for Large
    Categorization Problems 937

Philippe Henniges
Factors of Overtraining with Fuzzy ARTMAP Neural Networks 1075

Emilio del Moral Hernandez
Non-Homogenous Structures in Neural Networks with
    Chaotic Recursive Nodes: Dealing with Diverse Multi-assemblies
    Architectures, Connectivity and Arbitrary Bifurcating Nodes 3306
Using Independent Subspace Analysis to Build Independent
    Spectral Representations of Images 1860

Rodrigo Hernandez
Non-Linear Mappings Based on Particle Swarm Optimization 1487

Alberto Hernandez Avalos
On Output Regulation for SISO Nonlinear Systems with
    Dynamic Neural Networks 372

Carlos Hernandez-Espinosa
A Comparison of Combination Methods for Ensembles of RBF Networks 1137
A Research on Combination Methods for Ensembles of
    Multilayer Feedforward 1125
New Experiments on Ensembles of Multilayer Feedforward
    for Classification Problems 1120

Malcolm Heywood
Evaluation of Cluster Combination Functions for Mixture of Experts 1154
Training the SOFM Efficiently: An Example from Intrusion Detection 1575

Hiroomi Hikawa
A New Pulse Mode Self Organizing Map Hardware with
    Digital Phase Locked Loops 2855

Geoffrey Hinton
Embedding via clustering: Using spectral information to
    guide dimensionality reduction 3198
Learning Nonlinear Constraints with Contrastive Backpropagation 1302

Takashi Hiramatsu
Quantum Gauged Neural Networks: Learning and Recalling 1108

Akihide Hirano
Analysis of Signal Separation and Signal Distortion in Feedforward and
    Feedback Blind Source Separation Based on Source Spectra 1257

Kotaro Hirasawa
Application of Multi-Branch Neural Networks to Stock Market Prediction 2544
Performance Optimization of Function Localization Neural Network
    by Using Reinforcement Learning 1314

Tetsuya Hirose
Analog Current-Mode Implementation of Central Pattern Generator
    for Robot Locomotion 639

Etsumasa Hiura
Dynamical Behavior of a Chaotic Neural Network and its Application
    to Optimization Problems 753

Sepp Hochreiter
Optimal Gradient-Based Learning Using Importance Weights 114
Optimal Kernels for Unsupervised Learning 1895

Mark Holmes
Temporal Discontinuities in Neocortical Dynamics 3156

Lars Holmstrom
On-Line System Identification Using Context Discernment 792

Nakaji Honda
A Comparative Study of the IDS method and Feed
    forward Neural Networks 1776

Yo Horikawa
Modification of Correlation Kernels in SVM, KPCA and
    KCCA in Texture Classification 2006

Yoshihiko Horio
Improved Chaotic Neuro-Computer with Output-Coding for
    Quadratic Assignment Problems 3312

Akihide Horita
Analysis of Signal Separation and Signal Distortion in Feedforward
    and Feedback Blind Source Separation Based on Source Spectra 1257

Tikara Hosino
Stochastic Complexity of Variational Bayesian Hidden Markov Models 1114

Yanfeng Hou
A Fuzzy Approach for Key Variables Identification of EMG
    Evaluation System 2520

William Hsieh
Nonlinear Complex Principal Component Analysis and Its Applications 1626

Chun-Fei Hsu
Wavelet-Neural-Network-Based Backstepping Control for Chaotic Systems 384

Ming-Kai Hsu
Chaotic Associative Memory and Private V-mails 2595

Jinglu Hu
Application of Multi-Branch Neural Networks to Stock Market Prediction 2544
Performance Optimization of Function Localization Neural
    Network by Using Reinforcement Learning 1314

Xiao Hu
Aircraft Cabin Noise Minimization via Neural Network Inverse Model 2341

De-Shuang Huang
A Novel Image Retrieval System Based on BP Neural Network 2561
Blind Inversion of Wiener System for Single Source 1235
Characterizing Human Gene Splice Sites Using
    Evolved Regular Expressions 493
Natural Image Compression Using An Extended Non-Negative
    Sparse Coding Neural Network Technique 1866
Neural Network-based Shape Recognition using Generalized
    Differential Evolution Training Algorithm 2012
Predicting Protein-Protein Interactions Based on
    Protein-Domain Relationships 316
Prediction of Contact Map Integrated PNN with Conformational Energy 499

Guang-Bin Huang
Protein Sequence Classification Using Extreme Learning Machine 1406
Time Series Study of GGAP-RBF Network: Predictions of
    Nasdaq Stock and Nitrate Contamination of Drinking Water 3127

Xiaofei Huang
A New Kind of Hopfield Networks for Finding Global Optimum 764

Brian Huber
Parallelizing the Fuzzy ARTMAP Algorithm on a Beowulf Cluster 475

Mark Humayun
Artificial Vision by Electrical Stimulation of the Retina 3100

Chihli Hung
A Constructive and Hierarchical Self-Organising Model in A
    Non-Stationary Environment 2948

Javid Huseynov
Optical Flame Detection Using Large-Scale Artificial Neural Networks 1959

Thuan Huynh
Effective neural network pruning using cross-validation 972

Shien-Ching Hwang
Data Classification with a Relaxed Model of Variable Kernel
    Density Estimation 2831

Khan Iftekharuddin
A Chaos Synchronization-Based Dynamic Vision Model for
    Image Segmentation 3075

Jukka Iivarinen
The Evolving Tree, a Hierarchical Tool for Unsupervised Data Analysis 1395

Alexander Ilin
Semiblind source separation of climate data detects
    El Nino as the component with the highest interannual variability 1722

Roman Ilin
Stability Conditions of the full KII Model of Excitatory and
    Inhibitory Neural Populations 3162

Shawn Ingkiriwang
One-Step Neural Network Inversion with PDF Learning and Emulation 966

Hirotaka Inoue
Self-Organizing Neural Grove and Its Applications 1205

Francesco Iorio
BSS Toolbox for Delayed and Convolved Mixtures 1245

Maurizio Ipsale
PCA and ICA for the Extraction of EEG Dominant Components
    in Cerebral Death Assessment 2532

Takeshi Iritani
2 Types of Complex-Valued Hopfield Networks and the
    Application to a Traffic Signal Control 782

Satoru Ishizuka
Synchronized Theta Rhythm Selection in a Dentate
    Gyrus Network Model 405

Kazuko Itoh
New Memory Model for Humanoid Robots -Introduction of Co-Associative
    Memory Using Mutually Coupled Chaotic Neural Networks- 2790

Artem Ivanov
Model of Neuron-Like Systems.Examples of Dynamic Processes 1842

Alexander Iversen
Classification and Verification through the Combination of the Multi-Layer
    Perceptron and Auto-Association Neural Networks 1166

Akira Iwata
Feature Subset Selection for Support Vector Machines
    using Confident Margin 907

Alfred Jacobs
Reinforcement Learning Approach to Individualization of Chronic
    Pharmacotherapy 3290

Snehal Jadhav
Orientated Texture Segmentation for Detecting Defects 2001

Herbert Jaeger
Reservoir Riddles: Suggestions for Echo State Network Research 1460

Cedric Jamet
Atmospheric correction and oceanic constituents retrieval
with a neuro-variational method................1621

Seun T. Jan
Efficient Video Object Classifier using Locality-Enhanced
Support Vector Machines 1936

Tony Jan
Vector Quantized Radial Basis Function Neural Network with
Embedded Multiple Local Linear Models for Financial Prediction 2538

Boris Jansen
Neural Networks Following a Binary Approach Applied to the Integer Prime-
Factorization Problem................2577

Nathalie Japkowicz
Text Clustering with NTSO 558

Kyu-Hwa Jeong
An Information Theoretic Approach to Adaptive System Training
Using Unlabeled Data 191

B. W. Jervis
Fast Training of Multilayer Perceptrons with a Mixed Norm Algorithm 1018

HongBin Jia
Identifying knowledge domain and incremental new
class learning in SVM................2742
Speaker Identification Using Speech and Lip Features 2565

Jie Jiang
Learning a Hierarchical Fuzzy System with Autonomous
Navigation as an Example 3063

Wei Jiang
ECG Signal Classification using Block-based Neural Networks 326

Licheng Jiao
A Directional Multi-resolution Ridgelet Network 1331
A Ridgelet Kernel Approach for Regression using Particle
Swarm Optimization Algorithm 2837

Fan Jin
A Model of Document Clustering Using Ant Colony Algorithm
and Validity Index 2730

Xu Jing
Artificial Cognitive BP-CT Ant Routing Algorithm 1098

Wang Jingdong
Spectral Feature Analysis 1971

Li Jing-Jing
Characterizing Human Gene Splice Sites Using Evolved
Regular Expressions 493

Taeho Jo
Text Clustering with NTSO 558

Ari Jonsson
Challenges in verification and validation of autonomous systems
for space exploration 2909

Sanjay Joshi
Application of a CMAC Neural Network to the Control of a Parallel
Hybrid-Electric Propulsion System for a Small Unmanned Aerial Vehicle 355

Chia-Feng Juang
Skin Color Segmentation by Histogram-Based Neural Fuzzy Network 3058
Temporal Hand Gesture Recognition By Fuzzified
TSK-Type Recurrent Fuzzy Network 1848

Cynthia Junqueira
Least-Squares Support Vector Machines for DOA Estimation:
A Step-by-Step Description and Sensitivity Analysis 3226

Ata Kaban
A Variational Bayesian Method for Rectified Factor Analysis................185

Ryo Kagaya
Noise Performance of Single-Electron Depressing Synapses
for Neuronal Synchrony Detection 2849

Yoshitsugu Kakemoto
Nonlinear dynamics on VSF-Network 747

Alex Kalos
Automated Heuristic Growing of Neural Networks for Nonlinear
Time Series Models 320

Prem K. Kalra
Learning with Single Integrate-and-Fire Neuron 2156

Shadi Kamalvand
Short Term Load Forecasting for Iran National Power System and
Its Regions Using Multi Layer Perceptron and Fuzzy Inference systems 2619

Mohamed Kamel
A Model of Document Clustering Using Ant Colony Algorithm and
Validity Index 2730

Ryotaro Kamimura
Information maximization and cost minimization in
information-theoretic competitive learning 202

Daesung Kang
Pattern De-Noising Based on Support Vector Data Description................949

Miao Kang
An Adaptive Function Neural Network (ADFUNN) for
Phrase Recognition................593

Mehdi Karrari
A Neuro-Fuzzy Based Sensor and Actuator Fault Estimation
Scheme for Unknown Nonlinear Systems 2335

Dimitrios Karras
Improved Spam e-Mail Filtering Based on Committee
Machines and Information Theoretic Feature Extraction 179

Waldemar Karwowski
A Fuzzy Approach for Key Variables Identification of
EMG Evaluation System 2520

Nikola Kasabov
A Computational Neurogenetic Model of a Spiking Neuron 446
Incremental Learning for Online Face Recognition 3174
Transductive Modeling with GA Parameter Optimization 839

Naoto Katsumata
Similar-Image Retrieval Systems Using ICA and PCA Bases................1229

Kazuo Kawada
Design and Experimental Evaluation of a 3-Mass Speed
 Control System with a Hybrid Structure of Sliding Mode
 Controller and CMAC 2272

Kohei Kawakami
Lossless High Dynamic Range Image Coding based on Lifting
 Scheme using Nonlinear Interpolative Effect of Discrete-Time
 Cellular Neural Networks 1681

Paul Kaye
Using real-valued meta classifiers to integrate binding site predictions 481

Nasser Kehtarnavaz
Neural Network Classification of EEG Signals using Time-Frequency
 Representation 2502

Mohammad Khan
Streamflow Forecasting with Uncertainty Estimate Using
 Bayesian Learning for ANN 2680

Ashfaq Khokhar
A Motion Trajectory Based Video Retrieval System Using
 Parallel Adaptive Self Organizing Maps 1800

Khashayar Khorasani
Blind Separation of Convolved Sources using the
 Information Maximization Approach 1239
Detection of Actuator Faults Using a Dynamic Neural
 Network for the Attitude Control Subsystem of a Satellite 1746
Dynamic Neural Network-based Estimator for Fault Diagnosis
 in Reaction Wheel Actuator of Satellite Attitude Control System 2347

Foaad Khosmood
Automatic Source Attribution: A Neural Networks Approach 2718

Abbas Khosravi
A Neuro-Fuzzy Based Sensor and Actuator Fault Estimation
 Scheme for Unknown Nonlinear Systems 2335
Short Term Load Forecasting for Iran National Power System
 and Its Regions Using Multi Layer Perceptron and
 Fuzzy Inference systems 2619

Chunghoon Kim
Combined Subspace Method Using Global and Local Features
 for Face Recognition 2030

Jongho Kim
Pattern De-Noising Based on Support Vector Data Description 949

Maria Kim
Vector Quantized Radial Basis Function Neural Network with
 Embedded Multiple Local Linear Models for Financial Prediction 2538

Sung-Phil Kim
Comparison of TDNN Training Algorithms in Brain Machine Interfaces 2459
Sparse Channel Estimation With Regularization Method
 Using Convolution Inequality For Entropy 2359

Masahiro Kimura
Multinomial PCA for Extracting Major Latent Topics
 from Document Streams 238

Sherif Kinawy
An Evolved Seeega Player Capable of Strong Novice-Level Play 332

Mitsunaga Kinjo
Basic Property of a Quantum Neural Network
 Composed of Kane's Qubits 1104

Yohsuke Kinouchi
Tracking the States of a Nonlinear System in the Weight-Space
 of a Feed-Forward Neural Network 96

Hidehiko Kita
Dynamic construction of fault tolerant multi-layer neural networks} 995

Daisuke Kitakoshi
Yet Faster Method to Optimize SVR Hyperparameters based
 on Minimizing Cross-Validation Error 871

Heinrich Klar
Emulation Engine for Spiking Neurons and
 Adaptive Synaptic Weights 3261

Raymond Klein
A Continuous Attractor Neural Network Model of Divided
 Visual Attention 2897
Motivational Modulation of Endogenous Inputs to the
 Superior Colliculus 262

Stefan Klinger
A Neural Supergraph Matching Architecture 2453

Gregory Klotz
ART2 Based Classification of Sparse High Dimensional
 Parameter Sets For A Simulation Parameter Selection Assistant 1081

James Knight
Optimizing Neural Model Templates using Covariance
 Matrix Adaptation and Fourier Analysis 2162

Kenji Kobayashi
Yet Faster Method to Optimize SVR Hyperparameters based
 on Minimizing Cross-Validation Error 871

Vassilis Kodogiannis
Neural network-based approach for the classification of
 wireless-capsule endoscopic images 2423

Randal Koene
An Integrate and Fire Model of Prefrontal Cortex provides a
 Biological Implementation of Action Selection in Reinforcement
 Learning Theory that Reuses Known Representations 2873

Joao Eduardo Kogler, Jr.
Using Independent Subspace Analysis to Build Independent
 Spectral Representations of Images 1860

Hui Kong
Generalized 2D Principal Component Analysis 108

Seong Kong
ECG Signal Classification using Block-based Neural Networks 326
Evolvable Neural Networks based on Developmental Models
 for Mobile Robot Navigation 337

Yoshio Kon'no
Rich phenomena of pulse-coupled spiking neurons with triangular
 waveform input 400

Josef Korinek
Neural Network and Principal Component Analyses of Highly Variable
 Myocardial Mechanical Waveforms Derived from Echocardiographic
 Ultrasound Images 3017

Pierre Kornprobst
Could Early Visual Processes be Sufficient to Label Motions? 1687

Bart Kosko
Noise Benefits in Spiking Retinal and Sensory Neuron Models 410

Satoshi Kosuge
Chaotic Associative Memory using Internal Patterns for
   Image Retrieval by Color and Shape Information..................3318

Robert Kozma
A Chaos Synchronization-Based Dynamic Vision Model for
   Image Segmentation 3075
Analysis of Phase Transitions in KIV with Amygdala during
   Simulated Navigation Control 125
Stability Conditions of the full KII Model of Excitatory and
   Inhibitory Neural Populations 3162

Maria Alvina Krahenbuhl
Artificial neural networks associated to calorimetry to preview
   polymer composition of high solid content emulsion copolymerizations ..2237

Vladimir Krasnopolsky
Complex Hybrid Models Combining Deterministic and
   Machine Learning Components as a New Synergetic
   Paradigm in Numerical Climate Modeling and Weather Prediction 1615
Panel discussion: Applications of Learning and Data-Driven
   Methods to Earth Sciences and Climate Modeling 1728
Robustness of the NN Approach to Emulating Atmospheric
   Long Wave Radiation in Complex Climate Models 2661

Terje Kristensen
Entropy Based Disease Classification of Proteomic Mass Sepectrometry
   Data of the Human Serum by a Support Vector Machine 542

Boris Kryzhanovsky
Decorrelating Parametrical Neural Network 1023

Vladimir Kryzhanovsky
Decorrelating Parametrical Neural Network 1023

Adam Krzyzak
Algorithms of Fast SVM Evaluation based on Subspace Projection 865

Ksuan-Chun Ku
Temporal Hand Gesture Recognition By Fuzzified TSK-Type
   Recurrent Fuzzy Network 1848

Mauricio Kugler
Feature Subset Selection for Support Vector Machines using
   Confident Margin 907

Gaurav Kumar
Entropy Based Disease Classification of Proteomic Mass Sepectrometry
   Data of the Human Serum by a Support Vector Machine 542

Franz Kurfess
Automatic Source Attribution: A Neural Networks Approach 2718

Yasuaki Kuroe
2 Types of Complex-Valued Hopfield Networks and the
   Application to a Traffic Signal Control 782
A Method of Oscillatory Trajectory Generation Using Recurrent
   Hybrid Neural Networks..................706

Susumu Kuroyanagi
Feature Subset Selection for Support Vector Machines using
   Confident Margin 907

Ernst Kussul
Image Recognition Systems with Permutative Coding 1788

James T. Kwok
Data-Dependent Kernels for High-Dimensional Data Classification 102
Kernel Relevant Component Analysis for Distance Metric Learning..................954
Pattern De-Noising Based on Support Vector Data Description..................949

Matthew Kyan
Dynamic Feature Fusion in the Self Organising Tree Map -
   applied to the segmentation of Biofilm Images..................2441

Fabio La Foresta
PCA and ICA for the Extraction of EEG Dominant Components
   in Cerebral Death Assessment 2532

Jorma Laaksonen
Gaussian Processes of Nonlinear Diffusion Filtering 1012

Hao Lac
Feature Subset Selection via Multi-Objective Genetic Algorithm 1349

Monica Lagazio
Artificial Intelligence for Conflict Management..................2583

Daniel Lai
A convergence rate estimate for the SVM Decomposition Method 931

Valliappa Lakshmanan
A Spatiotemporal Approach to Tornado Prediction..................1642

Karl Lalonde
Investigations into the Analysis of Remote Sensing Images
   with a Growing Neural Gas 1698

H.K. Lam
A variable-parameter neural network trained by improved
   genetic algorithm and its application 1343
Design and stabilization of sampled-data neural-network-based
   control systems 2249

Frank Lambert
System and Method for Determining Harmonic Contributions
   from Non-Linear Loads Using Recurrent Neural Networks 366

Jean-Charles Lamirel
Multi-Topographic Neural Network Communication and
   Generalization for Multi-Viewpoint Analysis 1564

Jing Lan
Direct Adaptive Control: An Echo State Network and Genetic Algorithm
   Approach 1483

Man Lan
A Comparative Study on Term Weighting Schemes for Text Categorization....546

Tian Lan
Feature Selection by Independent Component Analysis and
   Mutual Information Maximization in EEG Signal Classification 3011

Hugo Landry
A framework for the verification of air quality forecasting models
   using self-organizing feature maps..................2302

Elmar W. Lang
An Algorithm for Automatic Assignment of Artifact-Related
   Independent Components in Biomedical SIgnal Analysis..................2463
On the Use of Clustering and Local Singular Spectrum Analysis to
   Remove Ocular Artifacts from Electroencephalograms 2514

Kurt Larson
Modification of the ART-1 Architecture Based on Category
   Theoretic Design Principles 457

Joshua Lau
Extraction of event related potentials from EEG signals using
ICA with reference 2526

Philippe Lauret
A new saliency measure for inputs selection and node pruning
in neural network 960

Jean-Jacques Laurin
Implementation of an MLP-based DOA System Using a
Reduced Number of MM-wave Antenna Elements 3220

Willian Lautenschlager
A method to extract Non-Linear Principal Components
of Large Datasets - An application in Skill Transfer 2736

Erik M. Laxdal
A Neural Network-based Prediction Model of AR Inhibitory
Activity from a Sparse Set of Compounds 2411

Quang Le
An Experimental Comparison of Semi-Supervised ARTMAP
Architectures, GCS and GNG Classifiers 3121

Thanh-Nhat Le
A New N-Parallel Updating Method of the Hopfield-Type Neural
Network for N-Queens Problem 788

Manoel Leandro L. Junior
The k-Server Problem: A Reinforcement Learning Approach 798

Stephane Lecoeuche
Self-Adaptive Kernel Machine: Online Clustering in RKHS 1977

Dong-Wook Lee
Evolvable Neural Networks based on Developmental Models for
Mobile Robot Navigation 337

Geehyuk Lee
The Bifurcating Neuron Network 3 2184

Jong-Seok Lee
Discriminative Training of Hidden Markov Models by Multiobjective
Optimization for Visual Speech Recognition 2053

Kee-Khoon Lee
Predicting sugar regulation in Arabidopsis thaliana using kernel
learning methods 167

Kyungsuk David Lee
Extraction of Frame-Difference Features based on PCA and ICA for
Lip-Reading 232

Michelle Jeungeun Lee
Extraction of Frame-Difference Features based on PCA and ICA for
Lip-Reading 232

Sin Wee Lee
Snap-drift Learning for Phrase Recognition 588

Soo-Young Lee
Extraction of Frame-Difference Features based on PCA and ICA for
Lip-Reading 232

Tsu-Tian Lee
Support Vector Regression Performance Analysis and Systematic
Parameter Selection 877
Wavelet-Neural-Network-Based Backstepping Control for Chaotic Systems ... 384

Young-Chan Lee
Classification of Infrasound Events Using Using Radial Basis
Function Neural Networks 2649

Vincent Lemaire
Individualized HRTFs From Few Measurements: a Statistical
Learning Approach 2041

Rafael Leme
A hierarchical hybrid neural model with time integrators in
long-term peak-load forecasting 2960

George Lendaris
On-Line System Identification Using Context Discernment 792
Reinforcement Learning and the Frame Problem 2971

Jason Lerch
Connectivity of anatomical and functional MRI data 1534

F. H. F. Leung
A variable-parameter neural network trained by improved
genetic algorithm and its application 1343
Design and stabilization of sampled-data neural-network-based
control systems 2249
Genetic Algorithm-Based Variable Translation Wavelet Neural
Network and its Application 1365
Real-Coded Genetic Algorithm with Average-Bound Crossover
and Wavelet Mutation for Network Parameters Learning 1325

Shu Hung Leung
Evolution Strategies on Connection Weights into Modified
Gradient Function for Multi-layer Neural Network 1371

Daniel Levine
Modeling Emotional Influences on Human Decision Making Under Risk 1657
Neural Network Approaches to Personal Change in Psychotherapy 2139

Aaron Lewicke
Reliable Determination of Sleep Versus Wake from Heart Rate
Variability Using Neural Networks 2394

Fuxin Li
A Better Scaled Local Tangent Space Alignment Algorithm 1006

Honnge Li
Retrieval Property of Associative Memory with Negative Resistance 1187

Xin Li
Speaker Identification Using Speech and Lip Features 2565

Xuchun Li
A Study of AdaBoost with SVM Based Weak Learners 196
Generalized 2D Principal Component Analysis 108
Sequential Bootstrapped Support Vector Machines - A SVM Accelerator 1437

Yixue Li
Prediction of Contact Map Integrated PNN with Conformational Energy 499

Yongli Li
A Classifier Ensemble Model and Its Applications 1172
A Combinative Function Approximation Model and Its
Applications to Electronic Noses 2093
A Single-Layer Radial Basis Function Network Classifier
and Its Applications 1045
An Improved Kernel Fisher Discriminant Classifier and Its Applications 1274

Hui-Cheng Lian
An Algorithm for Pruning Redundant Modules in
Min-Max Modular Network 1983

Guanglan Liao
Feature Selection and Condition Monitoring of Gearbox Using SOM 2313

Sandra Lien
Lotto-Type Competitive Learning with Particle Swarm Features 1517

Heejin Lim
Facilitatory Neural Activity Compensating for Neural
   Delays as a Potential Cause of the Flash-Lag Effect 268

Clodoaldo A. M. Lima
Least-Squares Support Vector Machines for DOA Estimation:
   A Step-by-Step Description and Sensitivity Analysis 3226
Mixture of Heterogeneous Experts Applied to Time Series:
   A Comparative Study 1160

Chih-Min Lin
Wavelet-Neural-Network-Based Backstepping Control for Chaotic Systems 384

Feng Lin
Multi-class Support Vector Machines for Modeling HIV/AIDS Treatment
   Adherence using Patient Data 2417

Lin Lin
Text Extraction from Name Cards Using Neural Network 1818

Pao-Tsun Lin
Support Vector Regression Performance Analysis and
   Systematic Parameter Selection 877

S. H. Ling
A variable-parameter neural network trained by improved
   genetic algorithm and its application 1343
Genetic Algorithm-Based Variable Translation Wavelet
   Neural Network and its Application 1365
Real-Coded Genetic Algorithm with Average-Bound Crossover
   and Wavelet Mutation for Network Parameters Learning 1325

Wang Lipo
A Hybrid Neural Network for Optimal TDMA Transmission
   Scheduling in Packet Radio Networks 3210

Steven Liss
Dynamic Feature Fusion in the Self Organising Tree Map -
   applied to the segmentation of Biofilm Images.............2441

Chunyu Liu
Artificial Cognitive BP-CT Ant Routing Algorithm 1098

Derong Liu
A Self-Organizing Neural Network Approach for the Identification
   of Motifs with Insertions and Deletions in Protein Sequences 292

Feng Liu
Neural Network Model for Time Series Prediction by
   Reinforcement Learning 809

Feng-Yao Liu
Fast Text Categorization with Min-Max Modular
   Support Vector Machines 570

Hongzhi Liu
Artificial Neural Network Computation on Graphic Process Unit 622

Shubao Liu
A New K-Winners-Take-All Neural Network 712
Bi-Criteria Torque Optimization of Redundant Manipulators
   Based on a Simplified Dual Neural Network.............2796

Taijun Liu
Application of Neural Networks to 3G Power Amplifier Modeling..........2378

Tao Liu
Modeling of Spiral Inductors Using Artificial Neural Network 2353

Xiuwen Liu
Nonlinearity and Optimal Component Analysis 220

Yan Liu
Validity Index in Dynamic Cell Structures 2931

Yi Liu
One-Against-All Multi-Class SVM Classification Using Reliability Measures 849

Yong Liu
How to Find Different Neural Networks by Negative Correlation Learning ..3330

Zihong Liu
A New Hybrid Neural System Interfacing Neurons and Silicon
   Hardware for Fast Signal Recognition 3238

Stephane Loiselle
Exploration of Rank Order Coding with Spiking Neural Networks
   for Speech Recognition........................2076

Tat-Ming Lok
A Novel Image Retrieval System Based on BP Neural Network 2561

Liliane M. F. Lona
Artificial neural networks associated to calorimetry to preview
   polymer composition of high solid content emulsion copolymerizations ..2237

Giuseppe Longo
Data Visualization Methodologies for Data Mining Systems
   in Bioinformatics 143

Carlos Lopez-Franco
Object Recognition Using Neurocomputing and Conformal
   Computing Geometry 1872

Ilia Lossev
Prediction of time to event for censored data: ridge regression
   with linear constraints in kernel space 1033

Ninel Losseva
Prediction of time to event for censored data: ridge regression
   with linear constraints in kernel space 1033

Hwee Boon Low
A Comparative Study on Term Weighting Schemes for Text Categorization....546

Diego G. Loyola R.
Applications of Neural Network Methods to the Processing
   of Earth Observation Satellite Data 1704

Bao-Liang Lu
An Algorithm for Pruning Redundant Modules in
   Min-Max Modular Network......................1983
Fast Text Categorization with Min-Max Modular
   Support Vector Machines 570
On Efficient Selection of Binary Classifiers for Min-Max Modular Classifier 3186

Zhao Lu
Multi-class Support Vector Machines for Modeling HIV/AIDS Treatment
   Adherence using Patient Data 2417

Mark Luborsky
Multi-class Support Vector Machines for Modeling HIV/AIDS Treatment
   Adherence using Patient Data 2417

Dennis Lucarelli
Using Domain Knowledge to Constrain Structure Learning
  in a Bayesian Bioagent Detector 2601

Teresa Ludermir
A comparative study of neural network to artificial noses 2081

Andrew Luk
Evolution Strategies on Connection Weights into Modified
  Gradient Function for Multi-layer Neural Network 1371
Lotto-Type Competitive Learning with Particle Swarm Features 1517

Ivette Luna
Streamflow forecasting using neural networks and fuzzy
  clustering techniques 2631

Xiao Luo
Comparison of a SOM Based Sequence Analysis System
  and Naive Bayesian Classifier for Spam Filtering 2571

Zhongwen Luo
Artificial Neural Network Computation on Graphic Process Unit 622

Gerard Lyons
Bayesian ANN Classifier for ECG Arrhythmia Diagnostic System:
  A Comparison Study 2383

Yunqian Ma
Characterization of Data Complexity for SVM Methods 919

Robert MacCallum
Characterizing Human Gene Splice Sites Using
  Evolved Regular Expressions 493

Macieszczak Maciej
Neural Network Based Detection of Fetal Heart Rate Patterns 2400

Leonardo Macrini
Input and Data Selection Applied to Heart Disease Diagnosis 2389

Michael Madden
Bayesian ANN Classifier for ECG Arrhythmia Diagnostic System:
  A Comparison Study 2383

Yutaka Maeda
FPGA Implementation of Pulse Coupled Oscillator 633

Marina Magalhaes
Streamflow forecasting using neural networks and fuzzy
  clustering techniques 2631

Punamchand Mahajan
A Novel Fuzzy Clustering Neural Network 1989

Prabhakar Mahalingam
Harmonic Detection using Wavelet TRansforms 2228

Philipp Mahr
Emulation Engine for Spiking Neurons and Adaptive Synaptic Weights 3261

Shannon Majowicz
The Use of Clustering to Analyze Symptom-Based
  Case Definitions for Acute Gastrointestinal Illness 2429

Matej Makula
Feed-forward Echo State Networks 1479

Antonin Malik
Information-Theoretic Feature Selection Algorithms for Text Classification 3272

Mary Malliaris
Forecasting Energy Product Prices 3284

Steven Malliaris
Forecasting Energy Product Prices 3284

James Malone
Spatio-Temporal Neural Data Mining Architecture in Learning Robots 2802

Nadia Mammone
Independent Component Analysis and High-Order Statistics
  for Automatic Artifact Rejection 2447

Armando Manduca
Neural Network and Principal Component Analyses of Highly Variable
  Myocardial Mechanical Waveforms Derived from Echocardiographic
  Ultrasound Images 3017

Michail Maniadakis
A Hierarchical Coevolutionary Method to Support brain-Lesion Modelling 434

Salah Maouche
Self-Adaptive Kernel Machine: Online Clustering in RKHS 1977

Thierry Mara
A new saliency measure for inputs selection and node
  pruning in neural network 960

Gary F. Marcus
NeuroGene: Integrated Simulation of Gene Regulation,
  Neural Activity and Neurodevelopment 428

Dragos Margineantu
Testing Decision Systems with Classification Components 2927

Bozena Marianska
Automatic recognition of the blood cells of myelogenous
  leukemia using SVM 2496

Palaniswami Marimuthu
A convergence rate estimate for the SVM Decomposition Method 931

Tomasz Markiewicz
Automatic recognition of the blood cells of myelogenous
  leukemia using SVM 2496
OLS versus SVM approach to learning of RBF network 1051

Momcilo Markus
Issues in Designing Automated Minimal Resource Allocation
  Neural Networks 2671

Vasilis Marmarelis
Replacing Damaged Brain Regions with Biomimetic
  Microelectronic Neural Prostheses to Restore Cognitive Function 3109

Samantha Marocco
Classification of Plantar Pressure and Heel Acceleration
  Patterns Using Neural Networks 3007

Salvatore Marra
Design of Neural Predictors using Tools of Chaos Theory and
  Bayesian Learning 2222

William Marras
A Fuzzy Approach for Key Variables Identification of EMG
  Evaluation System 2520

Guillaume Marrelec
Heading For Data-Driven Measures of Effective Connectivity in
  Functional MRI 1528

Siegfried Martens
Self-Organizing Hierarchical Knowledge Discovery by an
ARTMAP Information Fusion System 452

Joel Martin
A framework for the verification of air quality forecasting
models using self-organizing feature maps 2302

Gabriela Martinez
Optimization of Modular Neural Networks Using Hierarchical
Genetic Algorithms Applied to Speech Recognition 1400

Daves Martins
Neurobiological Data Sustaining Opponent Processing
Operations on Self Organizing Networks as Tools for
the Modeling of Hippocampal Dynamics..................................2135

Antonio Martins da Silva
On the Use of Clustering and Local Singular Spectrum
Analysis to Remove Ocular Artifacts from Electroencephalograms 2514

Tshilidzi Marwala
Artificial Intelligence for Conflict Management..................................2583
Treatment of Missing Data Using Neural..................................598

Louis Massey
Real-World Text Clustering with Adaptive Resonance
Theory Neural Networks..................................2748

Paris Mastorocostas
A Constrained Optimization Algorithm for Training
Locally Recurrent Globally Feedforward Neural Networks 717
A Recurrent Fuzzy-Neural Filter for Real-Time Separation of Lung Sounds 3023

Francesco Masulli
A New Approach to Hierarchical Clustering for
the Analysis of Genomic Data 155

Satoshi Matsuda
A Neural Network Model for the Decision-Making
Process Based on AHP 821

Tetsuo Matsui
Quantum Gauged Neural Networks: Learning and Recalling 1108

Takashi Matsumoto
On-line Bayesian Change Detection Scheme for
Unknown Nonlinear Systems via Sequential Monte Carlo..................2207

Yasuo Matsuyama
Similar-Image Retrieval Systems Using ICA and PCA Bases..................1229

Joy Mazumdar
System and Method for Determining Harmonic Contributions from
Non-Linear Loads Using Recurrent Neural Networks 366

Daniel McDonnall
Physiological Activation of the Hind Limb Muscles of the
Anesthetized Cat Using the Utah Slanted Electrode Array..................3103

Ken McGarry
Spatio-Temporal Neural Data Mining Architecture in Learning Robots 2802

Eileen McMahon
Neural Network and Principal Component Analyses of Highly Variable
Myocardial Mechanical Waveforms Derived from Echocardiographic
Ultrasound Images 3017

Carver Mead
Neuromorphic Engineering: Overview and Potential 3334

Geoffrey Mealing
Application of Polymer Microstructures with Controlled Surface
Chemistries as a Platform for Creating and Interfacing with
Synthetic Neural Networks 3116

Larry Medsker
Independent Component Analysis Applications in Physics..................2213

Tassilo Meindl
Intelligent systems for meteorological events forecast 2686

Elmar U. K. Melcher
A novel Approach to reduce Interconnect Complexity in
ANN Hardware Implementation 2861

Patricia Melin
Face Recognition Using Modular Neural Networks and Fuzzy
Sugeno Integral for Response Integration 349
Fingerprint Recognition Using Modular Neural Networks and
Fuzzy Integrals for Response Integration 2589
Optimization of Modular Neural Networks Using Hierarchical
Genetic Algorithms Applied to Speech Recognition 1400

Roland Memisevic
Embedding via clustering: Using spectral information to guide
dimensionality reduction 3198

Olivier Menard
Coherent learning in cortical maps: A generic approach 2885

Mohammad Bagher Menhaj
Short Term Load Forecasting for Iran National Power System
and Its Regions Using Multi Layer Perceptron and Fuzzy
Inference systems 2619

David Meunier
Evolutionary supervision of a dynamical neural network allows
learning with on-going weights 1493

Anke Meyer-Baese
Exploratory Data Analysis of Dynamic Cerebral Contrast-Enhanced
Perfusion MRI Time-Series..................................2406

Dittenbach Michael
A visualization technique for Self-Organizing Maps with vector
fields to obtain the cluster structure at desired levels of detail 1558

R. Lyu Michael
A Novel Image Retrieval System Based on BP Neural Network 2561

Howard Michel
Processing Landsat TM Data Using Complex-Valued NRBF
Neural Network..................................3081

John Mielke
Application of Polymer Microstructures with Controlled Surface
Chemistries as a Platform for Creating and Interfacing with
Synthetic Neural Networks 3116

Jonathan Milgram
Estimating Accurate Multi-class Probabilities with Support Vector Machines..1906

Britain Mills
Modeling Emotional Influences on Human Decision Making Under Risk 1657

Washington Mio
Nonlinearity and Optimal Component Analysis 220

Sussany Mirelli
A Comparative Analysis of the Performance of Hybrid and
   Non-Hybrid Multi-classifier Systems 1941

Deepak Mishra
Learning with Single Integrate-and-Fire Neuron 2156

Vikramjit Mitra
A Neuro-SVM Model for Text Classification using Latent
   Semantic Indexing 564

Kei Miura
A Method of Oscillatory Trajectory Generation Using
   Recurrent Hybrid Neural Networks 706

Hiroyasu Miwa
New Memory Model for Humanoid Robots -Introduction of Co-Associative
   Memory Using Mutually Coupled Chaotic Neural Networks- 2790

Eiji Mizutani
Second-order backpropagation algorithms for a
   stagewise-partitioned separable Hessian matrix 1027

Andriy Mnih
Learning Nonlinear Constraints with Contrastive Backpropagation 1302

Nisha Mohan
Transductive Modeling with GA Parameter Optimization 839

Faisal Mohd Yasin
FPGA Realization of Power Quality Disturbance Detection:
   An Approach with Wavelet, ANN and Fuzzy Logic 2613

Colin Molter
Introduction of an Hebbian unsupervised learning algorithm 1552
Learning cycles brings chaos in continuous Hopfield networks 770

Oury Monchi
fMRI experiments and computational models of the function
   of the prefrontal cortex and the basal ganglia: a review 1593

Robert Monette
Application of Polymer Microstructures with Controlled Surface
   Chemistries as a Platform for Creating and Interfacing with
   Synthetic Neural Networks 3116

Gabriele Monfardini
A New Model for Learning in Graph Domains 729

Walter Moniaci
Intelligent systems for meteorological events forecast 2686

Md. Monirul Kabir
Convergence of Coherent Components of Neural Networks by Positive
   Correlation Learning 2105

Francesco Carlo Morabito
Design of Neural Predictors using Tools of Chaos Theory and
   Bayesian Learning 2222
Independent Component Analysis and High-Order Statistics
   for Automatic Artifact Rejection 2447
PCA and ICA for the Extraction of EEG Dominant Components
   in Cerebral Death Assessment 2532

Anderson Moreira
Neurobiological Data Sustaining Opponent Processing Operations
   on Self Organizing Networks as Tools for the Modeling
   of Hippocampal Dynamics 2135

Jose Moreno-Cadenas
Prototype Robotic Arm Assisted by Smart CMOS Vision Chips 2296

Koji Mori
Improved Chaotic Neuro-Computer with Output-Coding for
   Quadratic Assignment Problems 3312

Takashi Morie
A Digital LSI Architecture of Elastic Graph Matching and Its
   FPGA Implementation 689

Kenji Morishita
Modular Network SOM (mnSOM): From Vector Space to Function Space .. 1581

Bryan Morse
Edge Inference for Image Interpolation 1782

Oleg Mosalov
A Model of Baldwin Effect in Populations of Self-Learning Agents 1355

Leszek Moszczynski
Automatic recognition of the blood cells of myelogenous
   leukemia using SVM 2496

Cyril Moulin
Atmospheric correction and oceanic constituents retrieval
   with a neuro-variational method 1621

Xiaoyan Mu
A Weighted Voting Model of Associative Memory: Theoretical Analysis 1193

Mehmet Muezzinoglu
A Recurrent RBF Network Model for Nearest Neighbor Classification 343
Reinforcement Learning Approach to Individualization of Chronic
   Pharmacotherapy 3290

Paisarn Muneesawang
Using Knowledge of the Region of Interest (ROI) in Automatic
   Image Retrieval Learning 1854

Masayuki Murakami
A Comparative Study of the IDS method and Feedforward
   Neural Networks 1776

K. Murase
Convergence of Coherent Components of Neural Networks
   by Positive Correlation Learning 2105

Hiroshi Murata
One Class Support Vector Machine based Non-Relevance
   Feedback Document Retrieval 552

Yi Murphey
Identifying knowledge domain and incremental new
   class learning in SVM 2742
Protein secondary structure prediction using machine learning 532
Speaker Identification Using Speech and Lip Features 2565

Alan Murray
Increased Swimming Control with Evolved Lamprey CPG Controllers 2195

John Murray
A Recurrent Neural Network for Sound-Source Motion
   Tracking and Prediction 2232

Sreenivas Muthyala
Feasibility of multi-layered perceptron network in discriminating
   breast magnetic resonance imaging lesions 2493

Mark Myers
Analysis of Phase Transitions in KIV with Amygdala during
  Simulated Navigation Control 125

Shreesh Mysore
Modeling Structural Plasticity in the Barn Owl Auditory
  Localization System with a Spike-Time Dependent
  Hebbian Learning Rule 2766

Oivind Naess
Low-Voltage Pseudo Floating-Gate Reconfigurable Linear 675

Hirofumi Nagashino
Tracking the States of a Nonlinear System in the
  Weight-Space of a Feed-Forward Neural Network............................96

Dinesh Nair
Neural Network Classification of EEG Signals using
  Time-Frequency Representation 2502

Kazuki Nakada
Analog Current-Mode Implementation of Central Pattern
  Generator for Robot Locomotion 639

Yohei Nakada
On-line Bayesian Change Detection Scheme for Unknown
  Nonlinear Systems via Sequential Monte Carlo 2207

Koji Nakajima
Basic Property of a Quantum Neural Network Composed
  of Kane's Qubits 1104
Retrieval Property of Associative Memory with Negative Resistance............1187

Yuuki Nakamiya
Basic Property of a Quantum Neural Network Composed
  of Kane's Qubits 1104

Kiyomi Nakamura,
Face Recognition Method Independent of Rotation and Size Variations 2024

Ryohei Nakano
Finding a Succinct Multi-layer Perceptron Having Shared Weights 1418
Weight Sharing on Naive Bayes Document Model................................576
Yet Faster Method to Optimize SVR Hyperparameters based on
  Minimizing Cross-Validation Error 871

Teppei Nakano
A Digital LSI Architecture of Elastic Graph Matching
  and Its FPGA Implementation...689

Shinichi Nakasuka
Nonlinear dynamics on VSF-Network 747

Makito Nakatsuka
FPGA Implementation of Pulse Coupled Oscillator 633

Kenji Nakayama
Analysis of Signal Separation and Signal Distortion in Feedforward and
  Feedback Blind Source Separation Based on Source Spectra 1257
Neural Networks Following a Binary Approach Applied to the
  Integer Prime-Factorization Problem 2577

Mani Nallasamy
A convergence rate estimate for the SVM Decomposition Method 931

Sridhar Narayan
An Analysis of Overfitting in MLP Networks 984
Experimental Evaluation of a Hybrid Method for Configuring
  Ensemble Encoding Receptors 989

Hiroyuki Narihisa
Self-Organizing Neural Grove and Its Applications 1205

Salwa Nassar
Performance of Neural Classifiers for Fabric Faults Classification................1995

Bjoern Naundorf
Which Features Trigger Action Potentials in Cortical Neurons in Vivo?...........250

Soudabeh Nayeri
Independent Component Analysis Applications in Physics 2213

Ayat Nedjem
Optimizing Resources in Model Selection for Support Vectors Machines........925

Hassiba Nemmour
Fuzzy integral for a rapid mixture of support vector machines.....................901

Stewart Neufeld
Multi-class Support Vector Machines for Modeling HIV/AIDS Treatment
  Adherence using Patient Data 2417

Richard Neville
Third-order generalization and a new approach to
  systematically categorizing higher-order generalization 1924

Geok See Ng
Neural Network Model for Time Series Prediction by
  Reinforcement Learning...809
Ovarian Cancer Diagnosis Using Complementary Learning
  Fuzzy Neural Network...3034
Post Nonlinear Blind Source Separation by Geometric Linearization 244

Sin Chun Ng
Evolution Strategies on Connection Weights into Modified
  Gradient Function for Multi-layer Neural Network 1371

Thang Viet Nguyen
Post Nonlinear Blind Source Separation by Geometric Linearization 244

Jie Ni
Sequential Neuron Pruning Algorithm for RBF Network with
  Guaranteed Stability 1069

Rozenn Nicol
Individualized HRTFs From Few Measurements: a Statistical
  Learning Approach 2041

Giorgos Nikiforidis
Spiking Neural Network Training Using Evolutionary Algorithms 2190

Nikolay Nikolaev
Sequential Relevance Vector Machine Learning from Time Series................1308

Hiroshi Ninomiya
An Efficient Learning Algorithm for Finding Multiple Solutions
  Based on Fixed-Point Homotopy Method.....................................978

Ikuko Nishikawa
2 Types of Complex-Valued Hopfield Networks and the
  Application to a Traffic Signal Control 782

Lyle Noakes
Continuous Adaptive Critic Desigs 3001

Richard Normann
Physiological Activation of the Hind Limb Muscles of the
  Anesthetized Cat Using the Utah Slanted Electrode Array..................3103

Jana Novovicova
  Information-Theoretic Feature Selection Algorithms for Text Classification 3272

Anto Satriyo Nugroho
  Feature Subset Selection for Support Vector Machines using
    Confident Margin 907

Irina Nuidel
  Model of Neuron-Like Systems.Examples of Dynamic Processes 1842

Yuko Nukariya
  New Memory Model for Humanoid Robots -Introduction of Co-Associative
    Memory Using Mutually Coupled Chaotic Neural Networks-..................2790

Klaus Obermayer
  Optimal Gradient-Based Learning Using Importance Weights 114
  Optimal Kernels for Unsupervised Learning 1895

Masanobu Obika
  Design and Experimental Evaluation of a 3-Mass Speed Control
    System with a Hybrid Structure of Sliding Mode Controller and CMAC ..2272

Jiyong Oh
  Combined Subspace Method Using Global and Local Features for Face
    Recognition 2030

Masaya Ohta
  A Neural Phase Rotator for PAPR Reduction of PCC-OFDM Signal 2363

Erkki Oja
  Semiblind source separation of climate data detects El Nino as
    the component with the highest interannual variability 1722
  The Evolving Tree, a Hierarchical Tool for Unsupervised Data Analysis........1395

Richard Olinger
  Modification of the ART-1 Architecture Based on Category Theoretic Design
    Principles 457

Fabrizzio Oliveira
  Neurobiological Data Sustaining Opponent Processing Operations
    on Self Organizing Networks as Tools for the Modeling of
    Hippocampal Dynamics 2135

Jose Oliveira
  Embedded FastICA Algorithm Applied to the Sensor Noise Extraction
    Problem of Foundation Fieldbus Network 2217

Luiz S. Oliveira
  Optimizing Class-Related Thresholds with Particle Swarm Optimization 1511

Takashi Onoda
  One Class Support Vector Machine based Non-Relevance Feedback
    Document Retrieval..552

Manuel Ortega-Moral
  Designing RBF classifiers for weighted Boosting 1057

Yuko Osana
  Chaotic Associative Memory using Internal Patterns for Image
    Retrieval by Color and Shape Information 3318

Stanislaw Osowski
  Automatic recognition of the blood cells of myelogenous
    leukemia using SVM..2496
  OLS versus SVM approach to learning of RBF network 1051

Tsuyoshi Otake
  Lossless High Dynamic Range Image Coding based on
    Lifting Scheme using Nonlinear Interpolative Effect of
    Discrete-Time Cellular Neural Networks 1681

Guobin Ou
  Speaker Identification Using Speech and Lip Features 2565

Yu-Yen Ou
  A Novel Radial Basis Function Network Classifier with Centers
    Set by Hierarchical Clustering 1383
  Data Classification with a Relaxed Model of Variable Kernel
    Density Estimation 2831

Takahide Oya
  Noise Performance of Single-Electron Depressing Synapses for Neuronal
    Synchrony Detection..2849

Yen-Jen Oyang
  A Novel Radial Basis Function Network Classifier with Centers Set by
    Hierarchical Clustering 1383
  Data Classification with a Relaxed Model of Variable
    Kernel Density Estimation 2831

Seiichi Ozawa
  Incremental Learning for Online Face Recognition 3174

Umut Ozertem
  Maximally Discriminative Spectral Feature Projections Using
    Mutual Information 208

Mustafa C. Ozturk
  Computing with Transiently Stable States 1467

Alberto Paccanaro
  Inferring Protein-Protein Interactions Using Interaction Network Topologies 161

Jussi Pakkanen
  The Evolving Tree, a Hierarchical Tool for Unsupervised Data Analysis........1395

Dominic Palmer-Brown
  An Adaptive Function Neural Network (ADFUNN) for Phrase Recognition 593
  Snap-drift Learning for Phrase Recognition 588

Rinku Panchal
  Classification of Breast Abnormalities in Digital Mammograms using
    Image and BI-RADS Features in Conjunction with Neural Network..........2487

Gavyn Pang
  Comparative genomic study of Parkinson's disease candidate genes 422

Shaoning Pang
  Incremental Learning for Online Face Recognition 3174

Yoh-Han Pao
  Iterative Feature Weighting for Identification of Relevant
    Features with Radial Basis Function Networks 1063

Mikhail Parakhin
  Prediction of time to event for censored data: ridge regression
    with linear constraints in kernel space 1033

Kamban Parasuraman
  Wavelet Networks: An Alternative to Classical Neural Networks................2674

Cheol Hoon Park
  Discriminative Training of Hidden Markov Models by
    Multiobjective Optimization for Visual Speech Recognition 2053

Jooyoung Park
  Pattern De-Noising Based on Support Vector Data Description....................949

Sungjin Park
Classification of Infrasound Events Using Using Radial Basis
  Function Neural Networks..2649
Low Order Modeling for Multiple Moving Sound Synthesis
  using Head-related Transfer Functions' Principal Basis Vectors 2036

Giovanni Parodi
DSP-Based Neural Systems for the Perceptual Assessment of
  Visual Quality 663

Rafael Parra-Hernandez
A Neural Network-based Prediction Model of AR
  Inhibitory Activity from a Sparse Set of Compounds..............................2411

Eros Pasero
Intelligent systems for meteorological events forecast 2686

Ashok Patel
Noise Benefits in Spiking Retinal and Sensory Neuron Models 410

Leena Patel
Increased Swimming Control with Evolved Lamprey CPG Controllers 2195

Pradeep Patil
A Novel Fuzzy Clustering Neural Network 1989
Fourier Fuzzy Neural Network for Clustering of Objects Based on the
  Gross Shape and its Application to Handwritten Character Recognition..1918
Modular General Hyperline Segment Neural Network 1912
Orientated Texture Segmentation for Detecting Defects 2001

Jagdish Chandra Patra
A Fast Neural Network-Based Detection and Tracking of Dim
  Moving Targets in FLIR Imagery 3144
Fast Constructive-Covering Approach for Neural Networks 2167
Neural Network-Based Analysis of DNA Microarray Data 503
Neural Networks for Gene Expression Analysis and Gene
  Selection from DNA Microarray 509
Nonlinear Channel Equalization with QAM Signal Using
  Chebyshev Artificial Neural Network 3214
Post Nonlinear Blind Source Separation by Geometric Linearization 244

Helene Paugam-Moisy
A Multiple BAM for Hetero-association and Multisensory
  Integration Modelling 2117
Evolutionary supervision of a dynamical neural network
  allows learning with on-going weights 1493

Anindya Paul
Dual Kalman Filters for Autonomous Terrain Aided Navigation in
  Unknown Environments 2784

Michael Pavel
Feature Selection by Independent Component Analysis and
  Mutual Information Maximization in EEG Signal Classification 3011

Misha Pavel
A Spiking Neuron Representation of Auditory Signals 416

Nicos Pavlidis
Spiking Neural Network Training Using Evolutionary Algorithms 2190

Sainath Pawaskar
A Simple Hierarchical Approximation RBF Neural Network 1389

Carlos Pedreira
Input and Data Selection Applied to Heart Disease Diagnosis 2389

deLima Pedro
An Integrated Fault Tolerant Control Framework Using Adaptive
  Critic Design 2983

Witold Pedrycz
Stochastic Feature Selection for the Discrimination of Biomedical Spectra 3029

Jin-Song Pei
Neural Network Initialization with Prototypes -
  A Case Study in Function Approximation 1377

Kristiaan Pelckmans
Maximal Variation and Missing Values for Componentwise
  Support Vector Machines 2814

Melanie Pelegrini-Issac
Heading For Data-Driven Measures of Effective Connectivity
  in Functional MRI 1528

Parag Pendharkar
A Threshold Varying Bisection Method for Cost Sensitive
  Learning in Neural Networks 1039

Chunyi Peng
Learning Probability Density Functions from Marginal Distributions
  with Applications to Gaussian Mixtures 1148

Ross Peralta
On the design of an Ellipsoid ARTMAP classifier within the
  Fuzzy Adaptive System ART Framework 469

Claudio A. Perez
Color Image Segmentation Using Fuzzy Min-Max Neural Networks...........3052

Leonid Perlovsky
Neural Network with Fuzzy Dynamic Logic 3046

Hwai-Sheng Perng
Skin Color Segmentation by Histogram-Based Neural Fuzzy Network 3058

Gregory Peterson
ECG Signal Classification using Block-based Neural Networks 326

Jean Petitot
Bridging the Gap Between Vision and Language:
  A Morphodynamical Model of Spatial Categories 2903

Vassilios Petridis
The Emergence of Verbs in an Artificial Life Simulation 1337

Laurent Peyrodie
ICA And a Gauge of Filter for the Automatic Filtering
  of an EEG Signal 2508

Ali Pezeshki
Relation between Kernel CCA and Kernel FDA 226

Cong-Kha Pham
A New N-Parallel Updating Method of the Hopfield-Type
  Neural Network for N-Queens Problem 788

Steve Piche
A Disturbance Rejection based Neural Network
  Algorithm for Control of Air Pollution Emissions 2937

Filip Piekniewski
Phase Diagrams for Locally Hopfield Neural Networks in
  Presence of Correlated Patterns 776

Joaquim Pinto da Costa
SVMs Applied to Objective Aesthetic Evaluation of Conservative
  Breast Cancer Treatment 2481

Davide Piombo
Analog Current-Mode Design for Soft-Max Computation 669

Nick Pizzi
Stochastic Feature Selection for the Discrimination of Biomedical Spectra 3029

Vassilis Plagianakos
Computational Intelligence Techniques for Acute Leukemia
  Gene Expression Data Classification 2469
Spiking Neural Network Training Using Evolutionary Algorithms 2190

Georg Poelzlbauer
A visualization technique for Self-Organizing Maps with vector
  fields to obtain the cluster structure at desired levels of detail 1558
Investigation of Alternative Strategies and Quality Measures
  for Controlling the Growth Process of the Growing
  Hierarchical Self-Organizing Map 2954

Wei Beng Poh
Nonlinear Channel Equalization with QAM Signal Using
  Chebyshev Artificial Neural Network 3214

Ryan Poirier
Effect of Curriculum on the Consolidation of Neural Network
  Task Knowledge 2123

Robi Polikar
Dynamically Weighted Majority Voting for Incremental
  Learning and Comparison of Three Boosting Based Approaches 1131

Victor Ponce-Ponce
Prototype Robotic Arm Assisted by Smart CMOS Vision Chips 2296

Ken Ports
An Experimental Comparison of Semi-Supervised ARTMAP
  Architectures, GCS and GNG Classifiers 3121

Warren Powell
Approximate Dynamic Programming for High Dimensional
  Resource Allocation Problems 2989

Daniel Pressnitzer
Exploration of Rank Order Coding with Spiking Neural
  Networks for Speech Recognition 2076

Jose C. Principe
An Information Theoretic Approach to Adaptive System
  Training Using Unlabeled Data 191
Comparison of TDNN Training Algorithms in Brain Machine Interfaces 2459
Computing with Transiently Stable States 1467
Direct Adaptive Control: An Echo State Network and Genetic
  Algorithm Approach 1483
Sparse Channel Estimation With Regularization Method Using
  Convolution Inequality For Entropy 2359
Towards the Modeling of Dissociated Cortical Tissue in the
  Liquid State Machine Framework 2179

Sangeetha Priya
Harmonic Detection using Wavelet TRansforms 2228

Danil Prokhorov
A Model of Baldwin Effect in Populations of Self-Learning Agents 1355
Echo State Networks: Appeal and Challenges............................. 1463

Robert Proulx
A Self-Organizing Map for Concept Classification
  in Information Retrieval 1570
SCRAM: Statistically Converging Recurrent Associative Memory 723

Yann Prudent
Incremental growing neural gas learns topologies 1211

Wilfredo J. Puma-Villanueva
Mixture of Heterogeneous Experts Applied to Time Series:
  A Comparative Study 1160

Carlos Puntonet
An Algorithm for Automatic Assignment of Artifact-Related
  Independent Components in Biomedical Signal Analysis............................. 2463

Christophe Py
Application of Polymer Microstructures with Controlled
  Surface Chemistries as a Platform for Creating and
  Interfacing with Synthetic Neural Networks............................. 3116

Zhao Qiangfu
Normalized Neural Networks for Fast Pattern Detection 1889

Wei Qiao
Continuous On-line Identification of Nonlinear Plants in
  Power Systems with Missing Sensor Measurements 1729

Song Qing
A Robust Deterministic Annealing Algorithm for Data Clustering 1878
Pre-selection of Working Set for SVM Decomposition Algorithm 883
Weighted Support Vector Machine for Data Classification 859

Wei Qu
A Motion Trajectory Based Video Retrieval System Using
  Parallel Adaptive Self Organizing Maps............................. 1800

Long Quan
Data-Dependent Kernels for High-Dimensional Data Classification 102

Yili Quan
Toward an Analog VLSI Implementation of a Decision Making Model 645

Steven Quartz
Modeling Structural Plasticity in the Barn Owl Auditory
  Localization System with a Spike-Time Dependent
  Hebbian Learning Rule 2766

Chai Quek
Neural Network Model for Time Series Prediction by
  Reinforcement Learning............................. 809
Ovarian Cancer Diagnosis Using Complementary Learning
  Fuzzy Neural Network 3034

Paulo Quintanilha Filho
A hierarchical hybrid neural model with time integrators in
  long-term peak-load forecasting 2960

Marco Rafanelli
Emulation Engine for Spiking Neurons and Adaptive Synaptic Weights 3261

Giancarlo Raiconi
Data Visualization Methodologies for Data Mining
  Systems in Bioinformatics 143

Tapani Raiko
Learning Nonlinear State-Space Models for Control 815

Miika Rajala
Transient Dynamics of Non-Linear Models Describing
  Multi-Stable Stochastic Systems 3324

Jagath Rajapakse
Comparative genomic study of Parkinson's disease candidate genes 422
Extraction of event related potentials from EEG signals using
   ICA with reference 2526

Bapi Raju
Role of Presynaptic Reuptake on Dopamine Modulation of
   Cortico-striatal Activity in TD Learning 2145

Liva Ralaivola
Time Series Filtering, Smoothing and Learning using the
   Kernel Kalman Filter 1449

Baranidharan Raman
Mixture Segmentation and Background Suppression in
   Chemosensor Arrays with a Model of Olfactory
   Bulb-Cortex interaction 131

Juan M. Ramirez
Power System Reduced Model by Artificial Neural Networks 2607

Sanjay Rattan
Nonlinear Complex Principal Component Analysis and Its Applications 1626

Andreas Rauber
Investigation of Alternative Strategies and Quality Measures
   for Controlling the Growth Process of the Growing
   Hierarchical Self-Organizing Map 2954

Sudipta Ray
Learning with Single Integrate-and-Fire Neuron 2156

Donald Reay
Hardware Implementation of CMAC and B-Spline Neural
   Networks for Embedded Applications 657

Mamun Bin Ibne Reaz
FPGA Realization of Power Quality Disturbance Detection:
   An Approach with Wavelet, ANN and Fuzzy Logic..........................2613

Emmett Redd
Design of an Optical Fixed-Weight Learning Neural Network 610

Robert Redhead
Evaluation of Cluster Combination Functions for Mixture of Experts 1154

Vladimir Redko
A Model of Baldwin Effect in Populations of Self-Learning Agents 1355

Kamel Rekab
Classification of Infrasound Events Using Using Radial
   Basis Function Neural Networks 2649

Germano Resconi
Genome Space and Structure Genome Invariants 440

Emanuelle Reynaud
A Multiple BAM for Hetero-association and Multisensory
   Integration Modelling 2117

Leonid Reznik
Modified Time-Based Multilayer Perceptron for Sensor
   Networks and Image Processing Applications 2201

Luis J. Ricalde
Inverse Optimal Nonlinear Recurrent High Order Neural Observer 361

Karl Ricanek, Jr.
The Effect of Normal Adult Aging on Standard PCA Face
   Recognition Accuracy Rates 2018

Samuel Richie
On the design of an Ellipsoid ARTMAP classifier within the
   Fuzzy Adaptive System ART Framework 469
Parallelizing the Fuzzy ARTMAP Algorithm on a Beowulf Cluster 475

Michael B. Richman
Determination of optimal batch size in incremental approach
   for tornado detection 2706

Sandro Ridella
K-Fold Generalization Capability Assessment for Support Vector Classifiers ..855

Risto Ritala
Transient Dynamics of Non-Linear Models Describing
   Multi-Stable Stochastic Systems 3324

Helge Ritter
Face Detection and Identification Using a Hierarchical
   Feed-forward Recognition Architecture 1675
SOM Based Image Data Structuring in an Augmented
   Reality Scenario..3278

Jose Rivera
Cosmetic Defect Classification Found in Ophthalmic
   Lenses Using Artificial Neural Networks 2330

Fabio Rivieccio
K-Fold Generalization Capability Assessment for
   Support Vector Classifiers 855

Antonello Rizzi
A Symbolic Approach to the Solution of F-Classification Problems 1953

Mark Robinson
Using real-valued meta classifiers to integrate binding site predictions 481

Dora Rodriguez
Cosmetic Defect Classification Found in Ophthalmic
   Lenses Using Artificial Neural Networks 2330

Joao Marcos T. Romano
Least-Squares Support Vector Machines for DOA Estimation:
   A Step-by-Step Description and Sensitivity Analysis 3226

Enrique Romero
An Experimental Study of Several Decision Issues for Feature
   Selection with Multi-Layer Perceptrons 1965

Venkateswarlu Ronda
Generalized 2D Principal Component Analysis 108

Joao Luis Rosa
Artificial Neural Networks for Temporal Processing Applied to
   Prediction of Electric Energy Generation in Small Hydroelectric
   Power Stations...2625

Jean Rouat
Exploration of Rank Order Coding with Spiking Neural
   Networks for Speech Recognition 2076

Nicolas Rougier
Using Neural Dynamics to Switch Attention..2891

Stefano Rovetta
A New Approach to Hierarchical Clustering for the
   Analysis of Genomic Data 155

Jose de Jesus Rubio
Recurrent Neural Networks Training with Stable Risk-Sensitive
   Kalman Filter Algorithm 700

Gerben Ruessink
Nonlinear Complex Principal Component Analysis and Its Applications 1626

Alistair Rust
Using real-valued meta classifiers to integrate binding site predictions 481

Leszek Rutkowski
Flexible Takagi-Sugeno Fuzzy Systems 1764

Jose A. Ruz-Hernandez
Neural Networks based Scheme for Fault Diagnosis in
    Fossil Electric Power Plants 1740

Leszek Rybicki
Simulating A-Life Using Boltzmann Machines..1092

Kamel Saadi
Predicting sugar regulation in Arabidopsis thaliana using
    kernel learning methods 167

Paul Sabiston
A Disturbance Rejection based Neural Network Algorithm
    for Control of Air Pollution Emissions 2937

Robert Sabourin
Estimating Accurate Multi-class Probabilities with Support
    Vector Machines 1906
Factors of Overtraining with Fuzzy ARTMAP Neural Networks 1075
Optimizing Class-Related Thresholds with Particle Swarm Optimization 1511

Kazumi Saito
Cross-Entropy Approach to Data Visualization Based
    on the Neural Gas Network 2724
Finding a Succinct Multi-layer Perceptron Having Shared Weights 1418
Multinomial PCA for Extracting Major Latent Topics from
    Document Streams 238
Weight Sharing on Naive Bayes Document Model..576

Toshimichi Saito
Novel Digital Spiking Neuron and its Pulse-Coupled Network:
    Spike Position Coding and Multiplex Communication............................3249
Rich phenomena of pulse-coupled spiking neurons with
    triangular waveform input 400
Synthesis of Binary Cellular Automata based on Binary Neural Networks ..1361

Kazutoshi Sakakibara
2 Types of Complex-Valued Hopfield Networks and the
    Application to a Traffic Signal Control 782

Tsukasa Sakamoto
Face Recognition Method Independent of Rotation and Size Variations 2024

Anshu Saksena
Using Domain Knowledge to Constrain Structure Learning
    in a Bayesian Bioagent Detector 2601

Utku Salihoglu
Introduction of an Hebbian unsupervised learning algorithm.......................1552
Learning cycles brings chaos in continuous Hopfield networks.....................770

Edgar N. Sanchez
Inverse Optimal Nonlinear Recurrent High Order Neural Observer 361
Neural Networks based Scheme for Fault Diagnosis in
    Fossil Electric Power Plants 1740

Andrea Sankar
Multi-class Support Vector Machines for Modeling HIV/AIDS
    Treatment Adherence using Patient Data 2417

Roberto Santiago
On-Line System Identification Using Context Discernment 792
Reinforcement Learning and the Frame Problem..2971

Amilton Martins dos Santos
Artificial neural networks associated to calorimetry to preview
    polymer composition of high solid content emulsion copolymerizations ..2237

Araken Santos
A Comparative Analysis of the Performance of Hybrid and
    Non-Hybrid Multi-classifier Systems 1941

Carlos Silva Santos
Using Independent Subspace Analysis to Build Independent Spectral
    Representations of Images..1860

Euripedes P. dos Santos
Mixture of Heterogeneous Experts Applied to Time Series:
    A Comparative Study 1160

P. Saratchandran
Time Series Study of GGAP-RBF Network: Predictions of Nasdaq
    Stock and Nitrate Contamination of Drinking Water 3127

Takafumi Sasakawa
Performance Optimization of Function Localization
    Neural Network by Using Reinforcement Learning 1314

Jason Satel
Motivational Modulation of Endogenous Inputs to the Superior Colliculus 262

Shigeo Sato
Basic Property of a Quantum Neural Network Composed of Kane's Qubits 1104

Yasuji Sawada
A Phase-equation Model for a Large Phase Lead in Manual
    Tracking Caused by Intermittent Visual Information..............................1693

Hisham Sayed
An Evolved Seeega Player Capable of Strong Novice-Level Play 332

Edward Sazonov
Classification of Plantar Pressure and Heel Acceleration Patterns
    Using Neural Networks 3007
Reliable Determination of Sleep Versus Wake from Heart Rate
    Variability Using Neural Networks 2394

Franco Scarselli
A New Model for Learning in Graph Domains 729

Anton Schaefer
Dynamical Consistent Recurrent Neural Networks 1537

Anne-Catherine Scherlen
Visual Deficiency: Cognitive Performance and Adaptive Image Processing ..1824

Juergen Schmidhuber
Framewise Phoneme Classification with Bidirectional LSTM Networks 2047

Marvin Oliver Schneider
BioAnt - Biologically Plausible Computer Simulation of an
    Environment with Ants 1505

Dan Schonfeld
A Motion Trajectory Based Video Retrieval System
    Using Parallel Adaptive Self Organizing Maps 1800

Tomasz Schreiber
Phase Diagrams for Locally Hopfield Neural Networks in
    Presence of Correlated Patterns 776

Klaus Schuch
Towards the Modeling of Dissociated Cortical Tissue in the Liquid
State Machine Framework 2179

Stephanie Schuckers
Reliable Determination of Sleep Versus Wake from Heart Rate
Variability Using Neural Networks 2394

Jimmy Secretan
Parallelizing the Fuzzy ARTMAP Algorithm on a Beowulf Cluster 475

Linda See
A Comparative Study of Artificial Neural Network Techniques for
River Stage Forecasting 2666
Neural Network Modelling of the 20-Year Flood Event for
850 Catchments Across the UK 2637
Neural Network River Discharge Forecasters: An Empirical Investigation of
Hidden Unit Processing Functions Based on Two Different Catchments 2655

Abd-Krim Seghouane
Multivariate Regression Model Selection with KIC for Extrapolation Cases ..1292

Ming-Jung Seow
On Using an Associative Memory for Improving Digital
Color Images: Color Characterization, Enhancement,
and Color Balancing 1830

Kevin Seppi
Task Similarity Measures for Transfer in Reinforcement
Learning Task Libraries 803

Gursel Serpen
Empirical Approximation for Lyapunov Functions with
Artificial Neural Nets 735

Rudy Setiono
Effective neural network pruning using cross-validation 972

Md. Shahjahan
Convergence of Coherent Components of Neural Networks
by Positive Correlation Learning 2105

Asaad Shamseldin
A Comparative Study of Artificial Neural Network Techniques
for River Stage Forecasting 2666
Neural Network Modelling of the 20-Year Flood Event for
850 Catchments Across the UK 2637
Neural Network River Discharge Forecasters: An Empirical
Investigation of Hidden Unit Processing Functions Based
on Two Different Catchments 2655

Li Shang
Blind Inversion of Wiener System for Single Source 1235
Natural Image Compression Using An Extended Non-Negative
Sparse Coding Neural Network Technique 1866

Jon Shapiro
An Associative Memory for the Online Recognition and
Prediction of Temporal Sequences 1223

Ben Sharon
Forgetful Logic Circuits for Pulse-Mode Neural Networks 616

Helen C. Shen
Data-Dependent Kernels for High-Dimensional Data Classification 102

Jizhong Shen
Circuit Implementation of Multi-Thresholded Neuron
(MTN) Using BiCMOS Technology 627

Liu Sheng
A Robust Deterministic Annealing Algorithm for Data Clustering 1878
Pre-selection of Working Set for SVM Decomposition Algorithm............883

Tielin Shi
Feature Selection and Condition Monitoring of Gearbox Using SOM 2313

Zhiwei Shi
Analyzing the State Space Property of Echo State Networks
for Chaotic System Prediction 1412

Motoki Shiga
An Optimal Entropy Estimator for Discrete Random Variables 1280

Elcio Hideiti Shiguemori
A multilayer perceptron approach for the retrieval of vertical
temperature profiles from satellite radiation data 2689

Kazuhiro Shimonomura
An Orientation-Selective Multi-chip aVLSI Applicable to Texture Analysis 3267

D. L. Shrestha
Estimation of Prediction Intervals for the Model Outputs using
Machine Learning 2700

Gary Shubinsky
Optical Flame Detection Using Large-Scale Artificial Neural Networks 1959

Jennie Si
An Analysis of Gradient-Based Policy Iteration 2977

Paul Siebert
A Biologically Inspired Computational Vision Front-end based on a
Self-Organised Pseudo-Randomly Tessellated Artificial Retina 3069

Shirlly Silva
Cluster Ensemble for Gene Expression Microarray Data 487

Daniel L. Silver
Effect of Curriculum on the Consolidation of Neural Network
Task Knowledge..2123

Kwee-Bo Sim
Evolvable Neural Networks based on Developmental Models
for Mobile Robot Navigation..337

Hugo Simao
Approximate Dynamic Programming for High Dimensional
Resource Allocation Problems 2989

Jose Demisio Simoes da Silva
A multilayer perceptron approach for the retrieval of vertical
temperature profiles from satellite radiation data 2689

Sylvain Sirois
Hebbian motor control in a robot-embedded model of habituation..............2772

Oleg Skljarov
Chaos and Speech Rhythm 2070

David Smalenberger
One-Step Neural Network Inversion with PDF Learning and Emulation 966

Travis Smith
A Spatiotemporal Approach to Tornado Prediction....................................1642

Andrew Smyth
Neural Network Initialization with Prototypes - A Case Study in Function
Approximation..1377

Secundino Soares
Streamflow forecasting using neural networks and fuzzy
  clustering techniques 2631

Ehsan Sobhani Tehrani
Dynamic Neural Network-based Estimator for Fault Diagnosis in
  Reaction Wheel Actuator of Satellite Attitude Control System 2347

Ossama Soliman
An Evolved Seeega Player Capable of Strong Novice-Level Play 332

Peter Sollich
Fast Bayesian Support Vector Machine Parameter Tuning with the
  Nystrom Method 2820

Dimitri P. Solomatine
Estimation of Prediction Intervals for the Model Outputs using
  Machine Learning 2700
Local and Hybrid Learning Models in Forecasting Natural Phenomena........1716
Machine Learning in Soil Classification 2694
Modelling Harbour Sedimentation Using ANN and M5 Model Trees 2643
Panel discussion: Applications of Learning and Data-Driven Methods
  to Earth Sciences and Climate Modeling 1728

Hyung-Jin Son
Determination of optimal batch size in incremental
  approach for tornado detection 2706

Qing Song
Real-time Control of Variable Air Volume System Using a
  SPSA Based Neural Controller 2255
Robust Information Clustering 1296
Sequential Neuron Pruning Algorithm for RBF Network
  with Guaranteed Stability 1069
Supply Air Temperature Control of AHU with a Cascade
  Control Strategy and a SPSA Based Neural Controller 2243

Yangqiu Song
New Boosting Methods of Gaussian Processes for Regression 1142

Milan Sonka
Neural Network and Principal Component Analyses of Highly Variable
  Myocardial Mechanical Waveforms Derived from Echocardiographic
  Ultrasound Images 3017

Josep Maria Sopena
An Experimental Study of Several Decision Issues for Feature
  Selection with Multi-Layer Perceptrons 1965

Nora Speer
Functional Grouping of Genes Using Spectral Clustering and
  Gene Ontology 298

Christian Spieth
Functional Grouping of Genes Using Spectral Clustering and
  Gene Ontology 298

SaravanaKumar Srinivasan
An Iterative Relevance Feedback Learning Algorithm For Image
  Retrieval Systems 604

Deborah Stacey
ART2 Based Classification of Sparse High Dimensional Parameter
  Sets For A Simulation Parameter Selection Assistant 1081
Detection of Disease Outbreaks in Pharmaceutical Sales: Neural
  Networks and Threshold Algorithms 3138
Feature Subset Selection via Multi-Objective Genetic Algorithm 1349
The Use of Clustering to Analyze Symptom-Based Case
  Definitions for Acute Gastrointestinal Illness 2429

Kurt Stadlthanner
An Algorithm for Automatic Assignment of Artifact-Related Independent
  Components in Biomedical Signal Analysis 2463

Andreas Stafylopatis
Symbolic Rule Extraction with a Scaled Conjugate Gradient
  Version of CLARION 845

Robert Stahlbock
Evolutionary Neural Classification for Evaluation of Retail
  Stores and Decision Support 1499

Antonino Staiano
Data Visualization Methodologies for Data Mining Systems
  in Bioinformatics 143

Dominic Standage
A Continuous Attractor Neural Network Model of Divided
  Visual Attention 2897
Differences in the subthreshold dynamics of leaky
  integrate-and-fire and Hodgkin-Huxley neuron models 396

Daniel W. Stashuk
Comparing "Pattern Discovery" and Back-Propagation Classifiers 1286

Richard Stein
Physiological Activation of the Hind Limb Muscles of the
  Anesthetized Cat Using the Utah Slanted Electrode Array 3103

Rasmus Storjohann
NeuroGene: Integrated Simulation of Gene Regulation, Neural
  Activity and Neurodevelopment 428

Antonio Strafella
Cortico-Basal Ganglia Functional Connectivity Investigated with
  Transcranial Magnetic Stimulation 1525

Greg Stumpf
A Spatiotemporal Approach to Tornado Prediction 1642

Shun-Feng Su
Support Vector Regression Performance Analysis and Systematic
  Parameter Selection 877

Dionisio A. Suarez
Neural Networks based Scheme for Fault Diagnosis in Fossil
  Electric Power Plants 1740

Ching Y. Suen
Algorithms of Fast SVM Evaluation based on Subspace Projection 865

Mohd Shahiman Sulaiman
FPGA Realization of Power Quality Disturbance Detection:
  An Approach with Wavelet, ANN and Fuzzy Logic 2613

Xiaobo Sun
Artificial Cognitive BP-CT Ant Routing Algorithm 1098

Yi Sun
Using real-valued meta classifiers to integrate binding site predictions 481

Zhan-Li Sun
Blind Inversion of Wiener System for Single Source 1235
Natural Image Compression Using An Extended Non-Negative
  Sparse Coding Neural Network Technique 1866

N. Sundararajan
Time Series Study of GGAP-RBF Network: Predictions of
  Nasdaq Stock and Nitrate Contamination of Drinking Water 3127

Eric Sung
A Study of AdaBoost with SVM Based Weak Learners 196
Sequential Bootstrapped Support Vector Machines - A SVM Accelerator 1437

Sam Yuan Sung
A Comparative Study on Term Weighting Schemes for
  Text Categorization 546

Peter Sussner
New Results on Binary Auto- and Heteroassociative
  Morphological Memories 1199

Ricardo Suyama
Least-Squares Support Vector Machines for DOA Estimation:
  A Step-by-Step Description and Sensitivity Analysis 3226

Johan A. K. Suykens
Extending Kernel Principal Component Analysis to
  General Underlying Loss Functions 214
Maximal Variation and Missing Values for Componentwise
  Support Vector Machines 2814

Kenji Suzuki
On the Evaluation of Relevance Learning by a Multi-layer Perceptron 3204

Mototaka Suzuki
Constraints on Body Movement during Visual Development
  Affect Behavior of Evolutionary Robots 2778

Larry Swanson
The Molecules Module of the Brain Architecture Management System 515

Harold Szu
Chaotic Associative Memory and Private V-mails 2595
Collective Behavior Implementation in Powerline
  Surveillance Sensor Network 1735

Boleslaw Szymanski
Fuzzy ROC Curves for Unsupervised Nonparametric
  Ensemble Techniques 3040

S. Tafazoli
Dynamic Neural Network-based Estimator for Fault Diagnosis
  in Reaction Wheel Actuator of Satellite Attitude Control System 2347

Roberto Tagliaferri
BSS Toolbox for Delayed and Convolved Mixtures 1245
Data Visualization Methodologies for Data Mining
  Systems in Bioinformatics 143

Gene A. Tagliarini
An Analysis of Overfitting in MLP Networks 984
Experimental Evaluation of a Hybrid Method for Configuring
  Ensemble Encoding Receptors 989

Keisuke Taguchi
Synthesis of Binary Cellular Automata based on Binary Neural Networks .. 1361

Yasuhiro Takachi
A Phase-equation Model for a Large Phase Lead in Manual
  Tracking Caused by Intermittent Visual Information 1693

Nobuaki Takahashi
Lossless High Dynamic Range Image Coding based on Lifting
  Scheme using Nonlinear Interpolative Effect of Discrete-Time
  Cellular Neural Networks 1681

Osamu Takahashi
Basic Property of a Quantum Neural Network Composed
  of Kane's Qubits 1104

Atsuo Takanishi
New Memory Model for Humanoid Robots -Introduction of Co-Associative
  Memory Using Mutually Coupled Chaotic Neural Networks- 2790

Hironobu Takano
Face Recognition Method Independent of Rotation and Size Variations 2024

Hideaki Takanobu
New Memory Model for Humanoid Robots -Introduction of Co-Associative
  Memory Using Mutually Coupled Chaotic Neural Networks- 2790

Haruhiko Takase
Dynamic construction of fault tolerant multi-layer neural networks 995

Nicola Talbot
A Simple Trick for Constructing Bayesian Formulations of Sparse
  Kernel Learning Methods 1425
Sparse Bayesian learning and the relevance multi-layer perceptron 1320

Heidar Ali Talebi
A Neuro-Fuzzy Based Sensor and Actuator Fault Estimation
  Scheme for Unknown Nonlinear Systems 2335

Annabell Tamariz
Discrete-Time Systems Neuro-Riccati Equation Solution 2261

Chew Lim Tan
A Comparative Study on Term Weighting Schemes for Text Categorization.... 546
Text Extraction from Name Cards Using Neural Network 1818

Tuan Zea Tan
Ovarian Cancer Diagnosis Using Complementary Learning Fuzzy Neural
  Network 3034

Yusuke Tanahashi
Finding a Succinct Multi-layer Perceptron Having Shared Weights 1418

Mamoru Tanaka
Lossless High Dynamic Range Image Coding based on Lifting
  Scheme using Nonlinear Interpolative Effect of Discrete-Time
  Cellular Neural Networks 1681

Toshijiro Tanaka
Dynamical Behavior of a Chaotic Neural Network and its
  Application to Optimization Problems 753

Armand Tanguay, Jr.
Replacing Damaged Brain Regions with Biomimetic Microelectronic
  Neural Prostheses to Restore Cognitive Function 3109

Centeno Tania
A method to extract Non-Linear Principal Components of Large
  Datasets - An application in Skill Transfer 2736

Xiaoli Tao
Processing Landsat TM Data Using Complex-Valued NRBF Neural Network 3081

Joe Tapia
Parallelizing the Fuzzy ARTMAP Algorithm on a Beowulf Cluster 475

Jean-Philippe Tarel
The Intermediate Matching Kernel for Image Local Features 889

Tugba Taskaya-Temizel
Are ARIMA Neural Network Hybrids Better than Single Models? 3192

Dimitris Tasoulis
Computational Intelligence Techniques for Acute Leukemia
    Gene Expression Data Classification 2469
Spiking Neural Network Training Using Evolutionary Algorithms 2190

Katsumi Tateno
Synchronized Theta Rhythm Selection in a Dentate Gyrus Network Model 405

Leng Phuan Alex Tay
A Novel Hybrid Learning Scheme For Pattern Recognition 2099
Hierarchical Fast Learning Artificial Neural Network 3300

Brian Taylor
Rule Extraction as a Formal Method for the Verification and
    Validation of Neural Networks 2915

John Taylor
Attention as Sigma-Pi Controlled Ach-Based Feedback 256
Knowing your place: Subfield specific involvement in
    hippocampal spatial processing 2879
Modelling the Interaction of Attention and Emotion 1663
Neural Networks of the Brain: Their Analysis and
    Relation to Brain Images 1603

Neill Taylor
Attention as Sigma-Pi Controlled Ach-Based Feedback 256
Knowing your place: Subfield specific involvement in hippocampal
    spatial processing 2879

Nicholas K. Taylor
Classification and Verification through the Combination of the Multi-Layer
    Perceptron and Auto-Association Neural Networks 1166

Ana Rita Teixeira
An Algorithm for Automatic Assignment of Artifact-Related Independent
    Components in Biomedical SIgnal Analysis..2463
On the Use of Clustering and Local Singular Spectrum Analysis to
    Remove Ocular Artifacts from Electroencephalograms 2514

Marcelo Teixeira
Fuzzy Multi-Hidden Markov Predictor in Electric Load Forecasting 1758

Eam Khwang Teoh
Generalized 2D Principal Component Analysis 108

Soule Terence
Evolutionary Training of a Biologically Realistic
    Spino-neuromuscular System 280

Fabian Theis
An Algorithm for Automatic Assignment of Artifact-Related
    Independent Components in Biomedical SIgnal Analysis.......................2463

John Theocharis
A Recurrent Fuzzy-Neural Filter for Real-Time Separation of Lung Sounds 3023
Locally Recurrent Neural Networks Optimal Filtering Algorithms:
    Application to Wind Speed Prediction Using Spatial Correlation............2711

Sylvie Thiria
Atmospheric correction and oceanic constituents retrieval with
    a neuro-variational method 1621

Jean-Philippe Thivierge
Faithful Retinotopic Maps with Local Optimum Rules, Axonal
    Competition, and Hebbian Learning...2760

Simon Thorpe
Exploration of Rank Order Coding with Spiking Neural Networks
    for Speech Recognition 2076

Christoph Tietz
Dynamical Consistent Recurrent Neural Networks 1537

Peter Tino
Sequential Relevance Vector Machine Learning from Time Series................1308

Ivan Titov
Deriving Kernels from MLP Probability Estimators for
    Large Categorization Problems 937

Albert Titus
Toward an Analog VLSI Implementation of a Decision Making Model 645

Soon Toh
Incremental Learning for Online Face Recognition 3174

Kazuya Tohyama
Neural Network Model for Analyzing Optic Flow 1669

Kazuhiro Tokunaga
Modular Network SOM (mnSOM): From Vector Space to Function Space ..1581

Ana Maria Tome
An Algorithm for Automatic Assignment of Artifact-Related Independent
    Components in Biomedical SIgnal Analysis..2463
On the Use of Clustering and Local Singular Spectrum Analysis to
    Remove Ocular Artifacts from Electroencephalograms 2514

Chikahiro Tomita
An Efficient Learning Algorithm for Finding Multiple Solutions
    Based on Fixed-Point Homotopy Method..978

Tong Tong
A Combinative Function Approximation Model and Its Applications
    to Electronic Noses 2093

Hiroyuki Torikai
Novel Digital Spiking Neuron and its Pulse-Coupled Network:
    Spike Position Coding and Multiplex Communication..........................3249
Rich phenomena of pulse-coupled spiking neurons with triangular
    waveform input 400
Synthesis of Binary Cellular Automata based on Binary Neural Networks ..1361

Matti Tornio
Learning Nonlinear State-Space Models for Control 815

Neil Toronto
Edge Inference for Image Interpolation 1782

Cesar Torres-Huitzil
Digital Implementation of a Bio-inspired Neural Model
    for Motion Estimation 3255

Joaquin Torres-Sospedra
A Comparison of Combination Methods for Ensembles of RBF Networks 1137
A Research on Combination Methods for Ensembles of
    Multilayer Feedforward 1125
New Experiments on Ensembles of Multilayer Feedforward
    for Classification Problems 1120

Anastasios-Antonios Toulkeridis
The Emergence of Verbs in an Artificial Life Simulation.............................1337

Theodore B. Trafalis
Determination of optimal batch size in incremental
    approach for tornado detection 2706
Maximum Margin Classifiers with Noisy Data: A Robust Optimization........2826

Panos Trahanias
A Hierarchical Coevolutionary Method to Support brain-Lesion Modelling 434

Thomas Trappenberg
A Continuous Attractor Neural Network Model of Divided Visual Attention..2897
Differences in the subthreshold dynamics of leaky
    integrate-and-fire and Hodgkin-Huxley neuron models 396
Motivational Modulation of Endogenous Inputs to the Superior Colliculus 262

Matt Travis
Aircraft Cabin Noise Minimization via Neural Network Inverse Model 2341

Roger Tremblay
Application of Polymer Microstructures with Controlled Surface
    Chemistries as a Platform for Creating and Interfacing with
    Synthetic Neural Networks 3116

Valery Trifonov
Inferring Protein-Protein Interactions Using Interaction Network Topologies 161

Ivor W. Tsang
Kernel Relevant Component Analysis for Distance Metric Learning................954
Pattern De-Noising Based on Support Vector Data Description....................949

Kazuki Tsutsumi
Two state transitions mediated by spontaneous and/or intensive
    stimulus on an integrate-and-fire neural network model......................2150

Ching-Hsiang Tu
Total Sliding-mode-based Genetic Algorithm Control for Linear
    Piezoelectric Ceramic Motor Drive 2278

Lindsay Turnbull
Feasibility of multi-layered perceptron network in discriminating
    breast magnetic resonance imaging lesions 2493

Naonori Ueda
Multinomial PCA for Extracting Major Latent Topics from Document Streams ..238

Julio Valdes
Panel discussion: Applications of Learning and Data-Driven
    Methods to Earth Sciences and Climate Modeling 1728

Julio J. Valdes
Time Dependent Neural Network Models For Detecting Changes
    Of State In Earth and Planetary Processes...................................1710
Virtual Reality Visual Data Mining with Nonlinear Discriminant
    Neural Networks: Application to Leukemia and Alzheimer
    Gene Expression Data 2475

Giorgio Valentini
Random projections for assessing gene expression cluster stability................149

Harri Valpola
Semiblind source separation of climate data detects El Nino as the
    component with the highest interannual variability 1722

Christian Vasseur
ICA And a Gauge of Filter for the Automatic Filtering of an EEG Signal......2508

Dan Ventura
Edge Inference for Image Interpolation 1782
Effectively Using Recurrently-Connected Spiking Neural Networks 1542

Brijesh Verma
Classification of Breast Abnormalities in Digital Mammograms using
    Image and BI-RADS Features in Conjunction with Neural Network..........2487
Optimization of Context Matching Parameters for Web Information
    Retrieval Using an Evolutionary Algorithm...................................582

Massimiliano Versace
Spatially and Temporally Local Spike-Timing-Dependent Plasticity Rule 390

Mario Versaci
Design of Neural Predictors using Tools of Chaos Theory
    and Bayesian Learning 2222

John Vian
Aircraft Cabin Noise Minimization via Neural Network Inverse Model 2341

Thierry Vieville
Could Early Visual Processes be Sufficient to Label Motions?.....................1687

Julien Vitay
Using Neural Dynamics to Switch Attention...2891

Cristiani Vitral
Neurobiological Data Sustaining Opponent Processing
    Operations on Self Organizing Networks as Tools for
    the Modeling of Hippocampal Dynamics 2135

Renan Vitral
Neurobiological Data Sustaining Opponent Processing
    Operations on Self Organizing Networks as Tools for
    the Modeling of Hippocampal Dynamics 2135

Raluca Voicu
Application of Polymer Microstructures with Controlled
    Surface Chemistries as a Platform for Creating and
    Interfacing with Synthetic Neural Networks...................................3116

Maxim Volgushev
Which Features Trigger Action Potentials in Cortical Neurons in Vivo?..........250

Gregory Von Pless
Modified Time-Based Multilayer Perceptron for Sensor
    Networks and Image Processing Applications 2201

Fernando J. Von Zuben
Least-Squares Support Vector Machines for DOA Estimation:
    A Step-by-Step Description and Sensitivity Analysis 3226
Mixture of Heterogeneous Experts Applied to Time Series:
    A Comparative Study 1160

Michael Vrahatis
Computational Intelligence Techniques for Acute Leukemia
    Gene Expression Data Classification 2469

Michael Vrahatis
Spiking Neural Network Training Using Evolutionary Algorithms 2190

Rong-Jong Wai
Indirect Field-oriented Linear Induction Motor Drive with Petri
    Fuzzy-neural-network Control..378
Total Sliding-mode-based Genetic Algorithm Control for Linear
    Piezoelectric Ceramic Motor Drive 2278

Eric Wan
Dual Kalman Filters for Autonomous Terrain Aided Navigation in
    Unknown Environments..2784

Bing Wang
Predicting Protein-Protein Interactions Based on Protein-Domain
    Relationships 316
Prediction of Contact Map Integrated PNN with Conformational Energy 499

Chia-Jiu Wang
A Neuro-SVM Model for Text Classification using Latent Semantic Indexing ..564

Di Wang
Fast Constructive-Covering Approach for Neural Networks 2167

Dianhui Wang
Effect of Non-Target Examples on E.coli Promoters Recognition
  Using Neural Networks 310
Protein Sequence Classification Using Extreme Learning Machine 1406

Guoping Wang
A Spiking Neuron Representation of Auditory Signals 416

Hongye Wang
Collective Behavior Implementation in Powerline Surveillance
  Sensor Network 1735

I-Jeng Wang
Using Domain Knowledge to Constrain Structure Learning in
  a Bayesian Bioagent Detector 2601

Jian Gang Wang
Generalized 2D Principal Component Analysis 108

Jincheng Wang
Predictive Control Based on Feedforward Neural Network for
  Strong Nonlinear System 2266

Jingdong Wang
Data-Dependent Kernels for High-Dimensional Data Classification 102

Jue Wang
A Better Scaled Local Tangent Space Alignment Algorithm 1006

Jun Wang
A New K-Winners-Take-All Neural Network 712
Bi-Criteria Torque Optimization of Redundant Manipulators
  Based on a Simplified Dual Neural Network..........................2796

Lei Wang
A Study of AdaBoost with SVM Based Weak Learners 196
Generalized 2D Principal Component Analysis 108
Neural Network-Based Analysis of DNA Microarray Data 503

Min Wang
A Directional Multi-resolution Ridgelet Network 1331
A Ridgelet Kernel Approach for Regression using Particle
  Swarm Optimization Algorithm 2837

Xiao-Feng Wang
Neural Network-based Shape Recognition using Generalized
  Differential Evolution Training Algorithm 2012

Ying Wang
Time Series Study of GGAP-RBF Network: Predictions of
  Nasdaq Stock and Nitrate Contamination of Drinking Water 3127

Yiwen Wang
Comparison of TDNN Training Algorithms in Brain Machine Interfaces 2459

Yu-Chiang Wang
Automatic Target Recognition Using New Support Vector Machine 84

Zhen Wang
An Improved Kernel Fisher Discriminant Classifier and Its Applications........1274

Zhihua Wang
A New Hybrid Neural System Interfacing Neurons and
  Silicon Hardware for Fast Signal Recognition 3238
Circuit Implementation of Multi-Thresholded Neuron
  (MTN) Using BiCMOS Technology 627

Shesharao Wanjerkhede
Role of Presynaptic Reuptake on Dopamine Modulation
  of Cortico-striatal Activity in TD Learning............................2145

Philip Warrick
Neural Network Based Detection of Fetal Heart Rate Patterns 2400

Kazuho Watanabe
Stochastic Complexity of Variational Bayesian Hidden Markov Models 1114

Sumio Watanabe
Stochastic Complexity of Variational Bayesian Hidden Markov Models 1114

Paul Watta
A Weighted Voting Model of Associative Memory: Theoretical Analysis......1193

Joerg Wegner
Assignment Kernels For Chemical Compounds.............................913

James Weiland
Artificial Vision by Electrical Stimulation of the Retina......................3100

Richard B. Wells
Forgetful Logic Circuits for Pulse-Mode Neural Networks 616

Stefan Wermter
A Constructive and Hierarchical Self-Organising Model
  in A Non-Stationary Environment......................................2948
A Recurrent Neural Network for Sound-Source
  Motion Tracking and Prediction 2232
Spatio-Temporal Neural Data Mining Architecture in Learning Robots 2802

Leigh Wetmore
Training the SOFM Efficiently: An Example from Intrusion Detection............1575

Ferdinan Widjaja
A Fast Neural Network-Based Detection and Tracking of
  Dim Moving Targets in FLIR Imagery...................................3144

Bernard Widrow
"Cognitive" Memory 3296

Robert Wilby
A Comparative Study of Artificial Neural Network
  Techniques for River Stage Forecasting 2666
Neural Network Modelling of the 20-Year Flood Event for
  850 Catchments Across the UK 2637

Carsten Wilks
Optimization of a learning algorithm for tactile pattern generation 2087

Fred Wolf
Which Features Trigger Action Potentials in Cortical Neurons in Vivo?..........250

Lai Ping Wong
A Novel Hybrid Learning Scheme For Pattern Recognition 2099
Hierarchical Fast Learning Artificial Neural Network 3300

Keith Worsley
Connectivity of anatomical and functional MRI data...................1534

Joseph Wright
Neural Network Initialization with Prototypes -
  A Case Study in Function Approximation 1377

Ke Wu
Fast Text Categorization with Min-Max Modular Support
  Vector Machines 570

Xincai Wu
Artificial Neural Network Computation on Graphic Process Unit 622

Zheng Wu
Ranked Centroid Projection: A Data Visualization Approach
  for Self-organizing Maps 1587

Donald C. Wunsch II
Aircraft Cabin Noise Minimization via Neural Network Inverse Model 2341
Engine Data Classification with Simultaneous Recurrent Network
  Using a Hybrid PSO-EA Algorithm 2319
Fuzzy PSO: A Generalization of Particle Swarm Optimization 1086
Gene Regulatory Networks Inference with Recurrent
  Neural Network Models 286
Image Recognition Systems with Permutative Coding 1788
Negative Reinforcement and Backtrack-Points for Recurrent
  Neural Networks for Cost-Based Abduction 827

Simei Wysoski
A Computational Neurogenetic Model of a Spiking Neuron 446

Jianhui Xi
Analyzing the State Space Property of Echo State Networks
  for Chaotic System Prediction 1412

Li Xiaoou
Recurrent Neural Networks Training with Stable Risk-Sensitive
  Kalman Filter Algorithm 700

Wu Xiao-Run
Characterizing Human Gene Splice Sites Using Evolved
  Regular Expressions 493

Tao Xiong
A Combined SVM and LDA Approach for Classification 1455

Xiaoxu Xiong
A Self-Organizing Neural Network Approach for the Identification
  of Motifs with Insertions and Deletions in Protein Sequences 292

Dongming Xu
Direct Adaptive Control: An Echo State Network and
  Genetic Algorithm Approach 1483

Jian Xu
A Novel Hybrid Learning Scheme For Pattern Recognition 2099
Hierarchical Fast Learning Artificial Neural Network 3300

Jian-Wu Xu
An Information Theoretic Approach to Adaptive System Training
  Using Unlabeled Data 191

Peng Xu
Fisher Information Quantifies Task-Specific Performance in the
  Blowfly Photoreceptor 274

Rui Xu
Gene Regulatory Networks Inference with Recurrent
  Neural Network Models 286

Jianping Xuan
Feature Selection and Condition Monitoring of Gearbox Using SOM 2313

Abhishek Yadav
Learning with Single Integrate-and-Fire Neuron 2156

R. N. Yadav
Learning with Single Integrate-and-Fire Neuron 2156

Tetsuya Yagi
An Orientation-Selective Multi-chip aVLSI Applicable to Texture Analysis 3267

Vladimir Yakhno
Model of Neuron-Like Systems. Examples of Dynamic Processes 1842

Hideyuki Yamada
A Neural Phase Rotator for PAPR Reduction of PCC-OFDM Signal 2363

Makoto Yamada
Relation between Kernel CCA and Kernel FDA 226

Seiji Yamada
One Class Support Vector Machine based Non-Relevance
  Feedback Document Retrieval 552

Takashi Yamamichi
Synthesis of Binary Cellular Automata based on Binary Neural Networks .. 1361

Toru Yamamoto
Design and Experimental Evaluation of a 3-Mass Speed Control
  System with a Hybrid Structure of Sliding Mode Controller and CMAC .. 2272

Katsumi Yamashita
A Neural Phase Rotator for PAPR Reduction of PCC-OFDM Signal 2363
Application of Multi-Branch Neural Networks to Stock Market Prediction 2544

Takashi Yamashita
Application of Multi-Branch Neural Networks to Stock Market Prediction 2544

Masayuki Yamauchi
Lossless High Dynamic Range Image Coding based on
  Lifting Scheme using Nonlinear Interpolative Effect of
  Discrete-Time Cellular Neural Networks 1681

Lian Yan
Predicting Customer Behavior via Calling Links 2555

Jian Yang
A Better Scaled Local Tangent Space Alignment Algorithm 1006

Lei Yang
An Analysis of Gradient-Based Policy Iteration 2977

Shuyuan Yang
A Directional Multi-resolution Ridgelet Network 1331
A Ridgelet Kernel Approach for Regression using Particle
  Swarm Optimization Algorithm 2837

Xulei Yang
A Robust Deterministic Annealing Algorithm for Data Clustering 1878
Pre-selection of Working Set for SVM Decomposition Algorithm 883
Weighted Support Vector Machine for Data Classification 859

Yan Yang
A Model of Document Clustering Using Ant Colony Algorithm
  and Validity Index 2730

Xiaochao Yao
Speaker Identification Using Speech and Lip Features 2565

Syozo Yasui
Modular Network SOM (mnSOM): From Vector Space to Function Space .. 1581

Tet Hin Yeap
Recurrent Neural Equalization for Communication Channels
  in Impulsive Noise Environments 3232

Mohammed Yeasin
Comparison of Linear and Non-linear Data Projection
  Techniques in Recognizing Universal Facial Expressions 3087

Gary Yen
An Integrated Fault Tolerant Control Framework Using
  Adaptive Critic Design 2983
Ranked Centroid Projection: A Data Visualization Approach
  for Self-organizing Maps 1587

Sampath Yerramalla
An Approach To Predicting Non-Deterministic Neural Network Behavior 2921
Validity Index in Dynamic Cell Structures 2931

Hao Ying
Multi-class Support Vector Machines for Modeling HIV/AIDS Treatment
  Adherence using Patient Data 2417

Li Yixue
Predicting Protein-Protein Interactions Based on
  Protein-Domain Relationships 316

Yasunari Yokota
An Optimal Entropy Estimator for Discrete Random Variables 1280

Robert Young
Modification of the ART-1 Architecture Based on Category
  Theoretic Design Principles 457

Sam Young
Forgetful Logic Circuits for Pulse-Mode Neural Networks 616

A. Steven Younger
Design of an Optical Fixed-Weight Learning Neural Network 610

Daoheng Yu
General Design Approach to Unit-linking PCNN for Image Processing 1836

Haiyuan Yu
Inferring Protein-Protein Interactions Using Interaction Network Topologies 161

Wen Yu
Recurrent Neural Networks Training with Stable Risk-Sensitive
  Kalman Filter Algorithm 700

Zhiping Yu
Modeling of Spiral Inductors Using Artificial Neural Network 2353

Zhu Yunping
Predicting Protein-Protein Interactions Based on Protein-Domain
  Relationships 316

Anthony Zaknich
Continuous Adaptive Critic Desigs 3001

John Zakos
Optimization of Context Matching Parameters for Web
  Information Retrieval Using an Evolutionary Algorithm 582

Antonio Zambroni de Souza
A hierarchical hybrid neural model with time integrators in
  long-term peak-load forecasting 2960

Gerson Zaverucha
Fuzzy Multi-Hidden Markov Predictor in Electric Load Forecasting 1758

Artur Zawadzki
On Kolmogorov's Superpositions: Novel Gates and Circuits
  for Nanoelectronics? 651

Massimiliano Zecca
New Memory Model for Humanoid Robots -Introduction of Co-Associative
  Memory Using Mutually Coupled Chaotic Neural Networks-...................2790

Stacey Zeigler
Classification of Plantar Pressure and Heel Acceleration Patterns Using Neural
  Networks 3007

Andreas Zell
Assignment Kernels For Chemical Compounds.................................913
Efficient Parameter Selection for Support Vector Machines
  in Classification and Regression via Model-Based
  Global Optimization 1431
Functional Grouping of Genes Using Spectral Clustering
  and Gene Ontology 298

Shuqing Zeng
A Gradient Descending Solution to the LASSO Criteria 2942
Learning a Hierarchical Fuzzy System with Autonomous
  Navigation as an Example 3063

BaiFang Zhang
Protein secondary structure prediction using machine learning 532

Changshui Zhang
Learning Probability Density Functions from Marginal Distributions with
  Applications to Gaussian Mixtures 1148
New Boosting Methods of Gaussian Processes for Regression 1142

Feng Zhang
Bayesian Neural Networks for Nonlinear Multivariate
  Manufacturing Process Monitoring 2308

Honghai Zhang
Neural Network and Principal Component Analyses of Highly Variable
  Myocardial Mechanical Waveforms Derived from Echocardiographic
  Ultrasound Images 3017

Hongming Zhang
Learning Informative Features for Spatial Histogram-Based
  Object Detection 1806

Huaguang Zhang
A Self-Organizing Neural Network Approach for the
  Identification of Motifs with Insertions and Deletions in
  Protein Sequences 292

Liming Zhang
General Design Approach to Unit-linking PCNN for Image Processing 1836

Nan Zhang
A Gradient Descending Solution to the LASSO Criteria 2942

Ping Zhang
Optimization of Context Matching Parameters for Web
  Information Retrieval Using an Evolutionary Algorithm 582

Qiang Zhang
Nonlinearity and Optimal Component Analysis 220

Wenjun Zhang
Modeling of Spiral Inductors Using Artificial Neural Network 2353

Xiaohui Zhang
A SVM Approach for Detection of Hemorrhages in
  Background Diabetic Retinopathy 2435

Debin Zhao
Learning Informative Features for Spatial Histogram-Based
  Object Detection 1806

Hai Zhao
Fast Text Categorization with Min-Max Modular Support
   Vector Machines 570
On Efficient Selection of Binary Classifiers for Min-Max
   Modular Classifier 3186

Qiangfu Zhao
A Modified Frequency Domain Cross Correlation Implemented
   in MATLAB for Fast Sub-Image Detection Using Neural Networks 1794
Fast Pattern Detection Using Neural Networks and Cross
   Correlation in the Frequency Domain 1900

Qiuye Zhao
Hardware Implementation of CMAC and B-Spline Neural
   Networks for Embedded Applications 657

Qin Zhen
Neural Networks for Gene Expression Analysis and Gene
   Selection from DNA Microarray 509

Chun-Hou Zheng
Blind Inversion of Wiener System for Single Source 1235
Natural Image Compression Using An Extended
   Non-Negative Sparse Coding Neural Network Technique 1866

Yi Zheng
Towards the Modeling of Dissociated Cortical Tissue in the
   Liquid State Machine Framework 2179

Yuan F. Zheng
One-Against-All Multi-Class SVM Classification Using Reliability Measures 849

Shi Zhong
Efficient Online Spherical K-means Clustering 3180

Dmitry Zhora
Data Preprocessing for Stock Market Forecasting using
   Random Subspace Classifier Network 2549

Shangming Zhu
A Classifier Ensemble Model and Its Applications 1172

Xiaolei Zhu
Circuit Implementation of Multi-Thresholded Neuron (MTN)
   Using BiCMOS Technology 627

Yan Zhu
Sequential Bootstrapped Support Vector Machines - A SVM Accelerator 1437

Yunping Zhu
Prediction of Contact Map Integrated PNN with Conformational Energy 499

Eric Zilli
Hebbian Synaptic Modification in Cortical Circuits and
   Memory-Guided Behavior in Spatial Alternation and
   Delayed Non-Match to Position 2754

Hans-Georg Zimmermann
Dynamical Consistent Recurrent Neural Networks 1537

Nur Zincir-Heywood
Comparison of a SOM Based Sequence Analysis System
   and Naive Bayesian Classifier for Spam Filtering 2571
Training the SOFM Efficiently: An Example from Intrusion Detection 1575

Alessandro Zorat
A Reconfigurable Parallel Architecture for SVM Classification 2867

Rodolfo Zunino
Analog Current-Mode Design for Soft-Max Computation 669
DSP-Based Neural Systems for the Perceptual Assessment of
   Visual Quality 663

Jacek Zurada
A Fuzzy Approach for Key Variables Identification of EMG
   Evaluation System 2520
A Recurrent RBF Network Model for Nearest Neighbor Classification 343
Reinforcement Learning Approach to Individualization of Chronic
   Pharmacotherapy 3290